1608 December 9. Born into the family of John Milton Sr. and his wife, Sara, at the family home, "The Spreadeagle," Bread Street, London. The large house is within several blocks of St. Paul's Cathedral, in a well-to-do mercantile neighborhood. John Milton Sr. is a prosperous scrivener–legal aide, real-estate agent, notary, preparer of documents, money-lender. He has also composed liturgical music.

1615 November 24. Brother Christopher born.

1618 Portrait painted by Cornelius Janssen (Leo Miller, *Milton's Portraits* 7–9). Milton is tutored at home by Thomas Young, a Scottish Presbyterian who will come to be identified with the Puritan movement. Young will present Milton with a Hebrew Bible and will trade Latin and Greek verses with him.

1620(?) Enters St. Paul's school, under the high master Alexander Gil. After Milton's death, his brother Christopher would tell John Aubrey, "When he [John] went to Schoole, when he was very young he studied very hard and sate-up very late, commonly till 12 or one a clock at night, & his father ordered the mayde to sitt-up for him, and in those years composed many Copies of Verses: which might well become a riper age" (Darbishire 10). After the age of twelve, the young Milton "rarely retired to bed from my studies until midnight" (Columbia 8: 119). His best friend at St. Paul's is Charles Diodati, son of a prominent Protestant Italian physician. Charles will matriculate at Trinity College, Cambridge, February 7, 1623. Milton is also instituting a long-term friendship with Alexander Gil the younger, an under-usher at St. Paul's, about ten years older than he.
July 4. Milton's father is appointed as one of four trustees of the Blackfriars Playhouse.

1623 November 15. A secret Catholic chapel near the Milton home caves in, killing 90. Alexander Gil composes Latin verses depicting the event as punishment for "Papism."
November 27. Together with his mother, witnesses the marriage settlement of his sister Anne and Edward Phillips. Sara Milton's unique signature proves that she could sign her name.

1625 February 12. Admitted to Christ's College, Cambridge, under tutor William Chappell.

1627 Dispute with Chappell causes him to be sent home or "rusticated" temporarily. While in London, Milton informs Charles Diodati that he is reading classical comedies and tragedies. When he returns to Cambridge, he is assigned a new tutor, Nathaniel Tovey.
June 11. John Milton, Sr., lends his son's future father-in-law, Richard Powell, £500, potentially earning his son £24 yearly in interest.

1628 September 4. Alexander Gil is arrested by order of Archbishop Laud, after drinking a toast to enemies of the King.

1629 Expresses dissatisfaction with the curriculum at Cambridge in his first Prolusion: avows that possibly half his audience of fellow students "bear[s] malice" toward him (French 1: 150). Portrait painted (?). Sees, and will later deride, dramatic performances at Cambridge (French 1: 204).
December 25. Composes "On the Morning of Christ's Nativity" before dawn, and refers to it in Elegy 6, to Charles Diodati.
Receives A.B. degree

1630 Charles Diodati attends the University of Geneva, Switzerland. Edward King, who will become the subject of Milton's "Lycidas," is given a fellowship at Christ's College.

1631 February. Christopher Milton matriculates at Christ's College, under Nathaniel Tovey.

1632 Milton's "On Shakespeare" published in the second folio of Shakespeare's works.
July 3. Takes M.A. cum laude at Cambridge. He has evidently been on much better terms with fellow students, since his poems on the death of Hobson indicate convivial behavior (Parker 1: 94), and his last college exercise, the *Oratio pro Arte* ("oration on behalf of art"), discusses, among other things, the value of worthy and congenial friendship.
Retires to family homes at Hammersmith, near London, and at Horton, in Buckinghamshire, to study for five years, at his father's expense, occasionally visiting London "for the

purposes of learning something new in mathematics or music, in which I then delighted" (Columbia 8: 120).

November. Christopher Milton admitted to Inner Temple, London, to study law.

1634 September 29. *Comus* performed as part of the ceremonies honoring the installation of Thomas Egerton, the Lord President of Wales, at Ludlow Castle, on the border of England and Wales. Sir Henry Wotton, Provost of Eton College, will be given a copy of the masque. Trades Greek and Latin verses with Alexander Gil the younger.

1637 *Comus* is published, anonymously at first. The court composer, Henry Lawes, writes the music and apparently supervises publication.
April 3. Mother Sara dies and is buried at the Horton parish church.
November 2. Writes to Charles Diodati that he is finishing an intense and "great period of my studies" (French 1: 343).
November. Writes "Lycidas" (Edward King, Milton's college mate commemorated in the poem, had drowned August 10).

1638 "Lycidas" is first published at Cambridge in a memorial volume for Edward King, *Justa Eduardo King Naufrago* ("In memory of Edward King, shipwrecked").

April (?) 1638, through early 1639

Tours Western Europe. Meets Hugo Grotius, the famous Dutch legal scholar and poet in Paris May (?) 1638. He then concentrates on Italy—Florence, Siena, Rome, Venice, Milan, and Naples. Returns by way of Geneva.

1638 Well received at meetings of the Academia Svogliati in Florence, where he reads his own Latin poetry. Presumably he goes to Vallombrosa, a monastery near Florence, which he will mention in *Paradise Lost*. Probably visits the astronomer Galileo, under house arrest by the Inquisition in Florence. In Rome he attends an opera at the palace of Cardinal Francesco Barberini, nephew to the Pope. Visits the Vatican Library. In Naples, meets the biographer of Torquato Tasso, Giovanni Battista, Marquis of Manso. The Latin poem "Mansus" will be written in Manso's honor.

Cancels a trip to Greece, apparently because of rumors of impending civil war in England. Learns of Charles Diodati's death (Charles was buried in London on August 27), possibly while visiting Giovanni Diodati, theologian and uncle of Charles, in Geneva.

1639–1640 Settles in London, founding a kind of private secondary school or academy, at first only with his nephews Edward and John Phillips as his pupils but later with aristocratic children as well.
Charles I invades Scotland (1639). The Long Parliament is convened (1640).

1640 June 30. Repossesses his future father-in-law Richard Powell's lands in Wheatley for non-payment of debt.

1641 May. *Of Reformation* published.
June or July. *Of Prelatical Episcopacy* published.
July. *Animadversions* published.

1642 February. *The Reason of Church Government* published.
May (?). *An Apology for Smectymnuus* published (the *ty* in the name represents Milton's teacher at St. Paul's, Thomas Young).
May. Marries Mary Powell. She leaves him about a month later, to return to the Powell family household in Forest Hill near Oxford, and refuses at first to return. The Powell family declare on the side of the Royalists.
August. Civil War begins.
October. Milton's brother Christopher begins service on the side of the Royalists while in residence in the city of Reading (Parker 231). The Royalist army maintains its headquarters in Oxford. Battle of Edgehill October 23.

1643 August 1. *The Doctrine and Discipline of Divorce* first published.

1644 February 2. Second, augmented edition of *The Doctrine and Discipline* published.
June 5. *Of Education* published.
July 2. Battle of Marston Moor (turning point in the War).
August 6. *The Judgment of Martin Bucer Concerning Divorce* published.
November 23. *Areopagitica* published.

The Riverside Milton

Edited by
Roy Flannagan
Ohio University

Houghton Mifflin Company   Boston   New York

For Anne Villers and Elisabeth Flannagan

Senior Sponsoring Editor: Suzanne Phelps Weir
Senior Associate Editor: Janet Edmonds
Editorial Assistant: Terri Teleen
Editorial Production Coordinator: Carla Thompson
Associate Production/Design Coordinator: Jodi O'Rourke
Senior Manufacturing Coordinator: Priscilla J. Abreu
Marketing Manager: Nancy Lyman
Marketing Associate: Jennifer Marsella

Cover Design: Sandra Burch
Cover Image: Andrea Mantegna (1431–1506), *Samson and Delilah*, National Gallery, London. The Bridgeman Art Library.

Printed in the U.S.A.

Library of Congress Catalog Card Number: 97-72469

ISBN: 0-395-80999-1

456789-DW-07 06 05 04 03

CONTENTS

MAJOR POEMS:

PROSE

Preface

After the years I have now spent editing Milton, I know how the editors of Milton fudge, or ride hobbyhorses of our own manufacture. We compensate for our inevitable ignorance of one field or another by emphasizing our learning in another. Merritt Hughes is strong on political history, as is Don Wolfe and many of the editors of the Yale *Prose*. John Carey and Alastair Fowler are both strong classicists. Edward Le Comte loves puns and double entendres. Stephen Orgel and Jonathan Goldberg are up to the minute (1990) in critical theory. Gordon Campbell is always on top of biographical fact. John Shawcross is impeccably memorious when it comes to getting the text and the dates right. John Leonard (his edition of the poetry is forthcoming from Penguin) has unrivaled critical perception. Barbara Lewalski, of course, is the modern master of genre. Though an occasional note of mine might make gentle fun of any of these modern editors, I have nothing but respect for their patience, their fortitude, their martyrdom in what is the most severe test of any editor's skills, the editing of Milton's poetry or prose.

It is especially difficult to edit Milton at this moment, near the millennium—largely because of the explosion of scholarly articles and books since 1968, an explosion admirably recorded in the 4571 entries in Huckabay and Klemp's *Annotated Bibliography* published in 1996. As the editor of *Milton Quarterly* since it began as the *Milton Newsletter* in 1967, I have witnessed and I have been a compliant partner in what has been uncharitably labeled the "Milton Industry." The North American Milton Industry did produce much verbiage in its enthusiasm to publish rather than perish, but it also inspired a spirit of international cooperation and goodwill among scholars devoted to the most difficult of all English poets. We needed each other, in the fight to discover Milton's elusive meaning and obvious significance.

THE ARRANGEMENT OF TEXTS FOR THE POETRY IN THIS EDITION

There is no such thing as a consistent conventional order for Milton's poetry in any edition of his complete poetry and selected prose. The various published versions of his poetry, as with the 1645 *Poems*, can be treated as units and edited as such, as Brooks and Hardy and Orgel and Goldberg have presented them; or the editor can try to establish the chronology of each poem (something of a thankless task, since dates can rarely be proven, even when Milton has assigned a poem a date of composition) and edit the poems in the supposed order of their composition or publication (Hughes, Shawcross, Carey and Fowler). If an editor chooses to arrange the poems by dates, the continuity of the original collections of the poems is lost. If an editor chooses to arrange as Milton and his publishers did, the coherence and security of arranging by date is lost.

If an edition does try to preserve Milton's (or his publisher's) original order of presentation, then the Latin and Italian and Greek poems appear in their original sequence, either presented among the English poems (Italian or Greek or Latin), or set off in a separate book meant to complement an English book (the Latin poetry in the 1645 *Poems*, presented as *Elegiarum* and *Sylvarum*). I believe that preserving Milton's original generic schemes and chronological order is slightly better than trying to force his poems out of the generic or linguistic arrangement in which they were originally published. I could argue for either type of edition, but I have tried to honor the seventeenth-century arrangement of Milton's texts because I believe that he exerted control over how his work was presented on the pages of the 1645 and even the 1673 *Poems*. I might rest my case on the fact that the great majority of Milton scholars now active have little idea what *sylvarum* means, since they have not been exposed to the Latin poetry in its original arrangement.

WHAT IS INCLUDED

The simple answer to this question is that I have included most of the works included by Merritt Hughes, in an edition that has been the standard since 1957, on the grounds that a modern edition should not fix what isn't broken. At the same time, I have included more from the divorce tracts, on the grounds that modern readers might be more interested in the gender wisdom expressed there than, perhaps, the politics of beheading a king. There is a major problem in deciding what to include of the *De Doctrina Christiana*, since the authorship and the provenance of the tract has recently been called into question, but I have (with the help of Tom Corns) selected passages most pertinent to the study of Milton's poetry and those most likely to be his original work.

OLD-SPELLING TEXTS

Milton's texts should be distanced from his modern readers, because they are distanced by time and by the evolution and the fluidity of the English language. The word *grace*, for instance, meant something quite different in 1667 from what it means at present, and the word spelled *sovran* signifies a sound quite different from that of *sovereign*. If one adds together the all-but-invisible elements of spelling, punctuation, capitalization, and italics, Milton's English as he presented it in manuscript and in print has an utterly different texture from that of acceptable modern English style. I believe that it is the modern editor's duty to preserve the texture of Milton's prose and poetry as it appeared in his own time—not for antiquarian purposes but in order to emphasize its difference and its distance from our own usage.

I hesitate to use the definitive term "diplomatic edition" of any of my editions of the various printed texts and manuscripts of Milton printed below, but in most cases my edition does represent a copy of one particular text (as with the 1674 second edition of *Paradise Lost*, for which I used my own copy in concert with the facsimile of Fletcher). If my transcription of that text varies from it, because of what has been discovered by collating the various states or issues of the original printed or manuscript texts, I inform the reader of the change in my annotations.

ANNOTATION

I was asked recently to define my philosophy of annotation (there now exists a philosophy of annotation, but only a very recently developed one), and I was urged by a group of eminent scholars and editors to be sure that my annotations (as opposed to my introductions) were wiped clean of "interpretive notes" or notes that might make a student say "Don't tell me what to think." I have sympathy for such a student, and, in modern colloquial terms, I have tried to stay out of his or her face, in my annotations. My philosophy of annotation generally conforms to the current conservative wisdom among editors: the place for editorial opinions is in introductions, not annotations.

ERRORS

There will be errors in this edition, as there are in all editions. Modern editors must deal with what Speed Hill has cleverly called "the calculus of error," the fact that human fallibility must create or allow error. Error might occur in (1) the text itself (including types of errors peculiar to the modern art of word processing), (2) in the critical apparatus (say, getting the date or the page numbers of an article wrong), or (3) in the interpretation (as with calling Milton a Puritan without defining the term as time changed it). My own role as the person responsible for providing camera-ready copy to the publisher makes me doubly responsible for errors in formatting, in copying, or in presenting scholarship. That is the bad part. The good part about composing a book using a computer and sophisticated software is that the book is perfectible. If you, the reader, write to the editor and compositor, at my e-mail address

flannaga@oak.cats.ohiou.edu
I can turn immediately to the right file and make a correction or add a clarification. I invite you to do so.

MILTON SCHOLARS: THE COMMUNITY

The quality of creative, sensitive, and industrious scholars that Milton has always attracted is phenomenal, from Samuel Johnson to William Empson, from Northrop Frye to Stanley Fish, from Samuel Taylor Coleridge and William Blake to Barbara Lewalski and Diane McColley, from William Riley Parker and Balachandra Rajan to Stephen Orgel and Jonathan Goldberg. In the twentieth century, Milton scholars have regularly been Regius Professors in England and Presidents of the Modern Language Association of America. René-François de Chateaubriand wrote a biography, Thomas Jefferson made notes to himself on Milton's prosody and his ideas concerning freedom of the press, and Teddy Roosevelt included Milton's Sonnet 16 in his monograph on Oliver Cromwell.

ACKNOWLEDGMENTS

The Riverside Milton has been designed, with all respect, to be the most complete and thoroughly annotated one-volume text since Merritt Hughes's 1957 edition. Having met Merritt Hughes while we both were fellows at the Folger Library in the mid-Sixties, I have great respect for his work.

I have also been fortunate while working on this edition to be able to correspond via e-mail with experts all over the world, including Michael Lieb, Alastair Fowler, John King, Diane McColley, Stella Revard, Carol Barton, Edward Jones, Neil Forsyth, Gordon Campbell, Anne Coldiron, Hugh Wilson, Barbara Lewalski, John Hale, Paul Sellin, Diana Benet, and many others with specific knowledge of biography, historical events, or texts. Bill Hunter, Tom Corns, Paul Klemp, John Leonard, and John Shawcross read large chunks of one or another group of works in manuscript, for which I am very grateful—though I am well aware I could have used their skills to review the monstrous manuscript in its entirety (though for me to ask them to do so might have strained our friendships). And I have been fortunate to have the advice and editorial cooperation of graduate and undergraduate students including Jim Orrick, Karen Fatula, Neil Browne, Blake Rodger, Jim Wells, Meredith Erlewine, Joanne Myers, Patrick Smith, Jason Holtman, Natalie Fields, Chris Pealer, and Peggy Cheney, all of whom (and more whom I am failing to remember, for which my apologies) read and commented on parts of the manuscript in different drafts.

For the images from the 1688 *Paradise Lost* I am indebted to my friend Lars Lutton, of the Photographic

Services in Instructional Media at Ohio University; for the scanning of excerpts from the Yale Milton edition, I am indebted to Peggy Sattler and Sam Girton in Instructional Media. I owe special gratitude for help with formatting to my good friend Lori Vandermark, in Publishing Services, SUNY Binghamton.

The edition is unique in that I am providing camera-ready copy for a major publisher (with, of course, advice and consent). My editor at Macmillan for *Paradise Lost* (the incomparable Anthony English, now at Oxford University Press) and my team of editors at Houghton Mifflin—George Kane, Jayne Fargnoli, Suzanne Phelps Weir, Janet Edmonds, Terri Teleen, and my fellow patient martyr Carla Thompson—have all nurtured my efforts, allowed me my excesses up to a point, and nursed the neuroses that inevitably come out of dazed early-morning editing of an impossibly long book.

I owe a special debt of gratitude to John Shawcross, for answering my detailed queries about texts and critical points always in detail, always with kind tolerance for my errors. I have imposed on him to write an extensive note on the texts of Milton's works and on Milton's spelling practices—so that the Riverside reader may share in his encyclopedic knowledge.

I consider the Riverside Milton a contribution to a world-wide community of scholars I have grown to admire and love.

Bibliography of Essential Works

Works listed here will be referred to by the name of the author and a page number throughout this edition.
Editions of Milton's works are indicated with an asterisk.

AGE OF MILTON. *The Age of Milton: Backgrounds to Seventeenth-Century Literature.* Ed. C. A. Patrides and Raymond B. Waddington. New York: Barnes & Noble, 1980.

AV or KING JAMES BIBLE. *The Holy Bible.* Authorized King James Version. Oxford: Oxford UP, n.d.

*BROOKS AND HARDY. Cleanth Brooks and John Edward Hardy, eds. *Poems of Mr. John Milton: The 1645 Edition with essays in Analysis.* London: Dennis Dobson, 1957.

*BUSH, Douglas. *The Complete Poetical Works of John Milton.* Boston: Houghton Mifflin, 1965.

CAMBRIDGE COMPANION. *The Cambridge Companion to Milton.* Ed. Dennis Danielson. Cambridge: Cambridge UP, 1989.

*CAMPBELL, Gordon, ed. *John Milton: Complete English Poems,* Of Education, Areopagitica. 4th ed., updated. London: Dent, 1993. See also CHRONOLOGY.

*CAREY, John, ed. *John Milton: Complete Shorter Poems.* London: Longman, 1968, 1981.

*CAREY (1997), John, ed. *John Milton: Complete Shorter Poems. Second Edition.* London: Longman, 1997.

CHRONOLOGY. *A Milton Chronology.* Ed. Gordon Campbell. London: Methuen, 1997.

COLUMBIA. Frank A. Patterson, gen. ed. *The Works of John Milton.* 18 vols. New York: Columbia UP, 1931–38.

DARBISHIRE, Helen, ed. *The Early Lives of Milton.* New York: Barnes & Noble, 1965.

*DARBISHIRE EDITION. *The Poetical Works of John Milton.* Ed. Helen Darbishire. 2 vols. Oxford: Clarendon P, 1952.

*DAVIES, Tony, ed. *John Milton: Selected Shorter Poems and Prose.* London: Routledge, 1988.

*FLETCHER, Harris F., ed. *John Milton's Complete Poetical Works, Reproduced in Photographic Facsimile.* 4 vols. Urbana: U of Illinois P, 1943–48.

*FOWLER, Alastair, ed. *John Milton: Paradise Lost.* London: Longman, 1968, 1971.

FRENCH, J. Milton. *The Life Records of John Milton.* 5 vols. New York: Gordian P, 1966.

GENEVA BIBLE. *The Geneva Bible: A Facsimile of the 1560 Edition.* Intro. Lloyd E. Berry. Madison: U of Wisconsin P, 1969.

HILL, Christopher. *Milton and the English Revolution.* New York: Viking, 1977.

HUCKABAY, Calvin. *John Milton: An Annotated Bibliography 1929–1968.* Rev. ed. Pittsburgh: Duquesne UP, 1969.

HUCKABAY AND KLEMP. *John Milton: An Annotated Bibliography, 1968–1988.* Comp. Calvin Huckabay and ed. Paul Klemp. Pittsburgh: Duquesne UP, 1996.

*HUGHES, Merritt Y, ed. *John Milton: Complete Poems and Major Prose.* New York: Odyssey, 1957.

INGRAM AND SWAIM. *A Concordance to Milton's English Poetry.* Ed. William Ingram and Kathleen Swaim. Oxford: Clarendon P, 1972.

JONES, Edward. *Milton's Sonnets: An Annotated Bibliography, 1900–1992.* Binghamton, NY: Medieval & Renaissance Texts & Studies, 1994.

KLEMP, Paul J. *The Essential Milton: An Annotated Bibliography of Major Modern Studies.* Boston: G. K. Hall, 1989.

LE COMTE, Edward. *A Milton Dictionary.* New York: Philosophical Library, 1961.

*LE COMTE EDITION. *John Milton:* Paradise Lost *and Other Poems.* Ed. Edward Le Comte. New York: New American Library Mentor, 1961.

*LEONARD, John, ed. *John Milton: The Complete Poems.* London: Penguin, 1998.

MASSON, David. *The Life of John Milton: Narrated in Connection with the Political, Ecclesiastical, and Literary History of His Time.* 6 vols. London: Macmillan, 1875.

MILTON ENCYCLOPEDIA. *A Milton Encyclopedia*. Ed. William B. Hunter, with John Steadman and John Shawcross. Lewisburg: Bucknell UP, 1978–83.

MILTON HANDBOOK. James Holly Hanford. *A Milton Handbook*. 5th ed. New York: Appleton-Century-Crofts, 1970.

*NEWTON, Thomas, ed. [*Paradise Regain'd, Paradise Lost*, minor poetry]. 4 vols. London: Tonson, et. al., 1766.

*ORGEL AND GOLDBERG. Orgel, Stephen, and Jonathan Goldberg, eds. *The Oxford Authors: John Milton*. Oxford: Oxford UP, 1990.

PARKER, William Riley. *Milton: A Biography*. Oxford: Clarendon P, 1968. Rev. ed., ed. Gordon Campbell, 1997.

*PATRIDES, C. A., ed. *John Milton: Selected Prose*. Rev. ed. Columbia: U of Missouri P, 1985.

*PATTERSON, Frank Allen, ed. *The Student's Milton, Being the Complete Poems of John Milton with the Greater Part of his Prose Works, now Printed in One Volume, together with new Translations into English of his Italian, Latin, and Greek Poems*. Rev. ed. New York: F. S. Crofts, 1934.

SANDYS, George. *Ovid's Metamorphosis Englished, Mythologized, and Represented in Figures*. Ed. Karl K. Hulley and Stanley T. Vandersall. Lincoln: U of Nebraska P, 1970.

SHAWCROSS, John. *John Milton: The Self and the World*. Lexington: UP of Kentucky, 1993.

*SHAWCROSS EDITION. *The Complete Poetry of John Milton*. Ed. John T. Shawcross. Rev. ed. New York: Doubleday Anchor, 1971.

STERNE AND KOLLMEIER. *A Concordance to the English Prose of John Milton*. Binghamton, NY: Medieval & Renaissance Texts & Studies, 1985.

VARIORUM. *A Variorum Commentary on the Poems of John Milton*. 7 projected vols., 4 completed. New York: Columbia UP, 1970–.

*VERITY, A. W., ed. *Milton:* Paradise Lost. 2 vols. Cambridge: Cambridge UP, 1936.

YALE. *The Complete Prose Works of John Milton*. Don M. Wolfe, gen. ed. 8 vols. New Haven, CT: Yale UP, 1953–82.

The Texts of Milton's Works

John T. Shawcross
University of Kentucky

The canon and text of John Milton's works pose fewer difficulties than those of many other British Renaissance authors and thus are often assumed to be settled. Since he published his poetry during his lifetime in two editions of shorter poems, two editions of *Paradise Lost (PL)*, and a volume presenting *Paradise Regain'd (PR)* and *Samson Agonistes (SA)*, almost all of the poetic canon is established. The few poetic items not so included are two Latin epigrams found in holograph with his Commonplace Book (CPB), two lines of poetry written on the back of a letter found with the CPB in holograph and apparently composed by him, verses included in the prose tracts, four sonnets recorded in the Trinity Manuscript (TM) and published by his nephew Edward Phillips in 1694, and one poem, usually called "Hobson's Epitaph," which has been argued indecisively as coming from his pen. Yet we might reason that there were a number of psalm translations over the years that he deigned not to include among the shorter works, and other poems have been suggested with little foundation by enthusiasts eager to augment the poetic canon. The prose has likewise been generally established by lifetime publication. "A Postscript" to *An Answer to a Book Entituled, An Humble Remonstrance* (1641) by Smectymnuus and published Latin versions of a Dutch and a Spanish manifesto (1652 and 1655 respectively) have also been advanced as his, although absolute certainty of authorship is missing. The numerous other prose works that have been cited on the basis of someone's guess are without foundation. Posthumous works that seem to be assuredly his—*Literæ Pseudo-Senatûs Anglicani* (1676), *Character of the Long Parliament* (1681), *A Brief History of Moscovia* (1682), *Letter to a Friend* (1698), *The Present Means and Brief Delineation of a Free Commonwealth* (1698)—and manuscript items—a prolusion, material in the TM, the generally holographic CPB, the scribal "Proposalls of certaine expedients for yᵉ pʳventing of a civill war now feard, & yᵉ settling of a firme governmᵗ.," as well as the scribal "De doctrina christiana" (DDC), though the last is questionable as to authorship—would appear to establish the prose canon. Additional state papers may have been produced by Milton, and there have been various tracts, particularly from the politically and religiously turbulent 1640s, that have been advanced at different times as Milton's but with no positive consensus. (See Shawcross [1984] for other printings or transcripts of a few poems and of the state papers.)

Because of lifetime publication and the unfounded belief that he oversaw printings of the works somewhat as we handle proofreading today, scholars have often ignored the uncertainties that single publication, or even ensuing editions based upon an earlier printing, might raise, and have assumed that such matters as spelling, punctuation, capitalization, italics, and paragraphing are, for the most part, as Milton wrote and desired. However, such examples as the notorious error in *PL* VII, 451, of "Fowle" (1667) / "Foul" (1674) for "Soul," pointed out by Richard Bentley in 1732 (an example of foul case or misreading of a long s as an f) and unlikely forms like "*Nectar*" ("Lycidas," 175) and "jeat" ("Lycidas," 144) in 1645 and 1673[1] indicate compositorial readings unchanged in ensuing editions, giving the lie to assumptions about the reliability of the texts.

PARADISE LOST AND ACCIDENTALS

The text of *PL* is found in a manuscript of Book I owned by the J. Pierpont Morgan Library, in the hand of an amanuensis referred to as D by James Holly Hanford (102),[2] with various corrections by at least two other hands, one being that of Edward Phillips, and in the editions of 1667 and 1674. The first edition, a quarto in ten books, was reissued five times in 1667–1669 (with six different title pages); the second reissue of 1668 added two versions of "The Printer to the Reader," a discussion of "The Verse" apparently because of negative reaction to its unrhymed poetry (as well, it seems, as an answer to John Dryden's *Essay on Dramatick Poesie* [1668]), Arguments for each book gathered together, and Errata. The reissues of 1669 omit "The Printer to the Reader"; the list of errata is continued and no changes were made. There are numerous press variants and a resetting of a few signatures was made for the 1669 issue (see Fletcher). Marks on the Book I manuscript indicate that it was the copy-text for 1667, and there is a licensing notation by Richard Royston for Archbishop Gilbert Sheldon, the probable reason for the survival of this single book in manuscript. The differences in spelling and accidentals between the manuscript and the 1667 printing of Book I, despite the use of the manuscript as copy-text, offer stentorian evidence that the compositor (or compositors) altered the text as he set it. The assumption that the remaining books generally reflect Milton's practices is clearly unfounded. The evidence of Book I indicates that the 1667 text sometimes reproduces the text of the manuscript but more often alters it, not only in spellings but in other accidentals as well.

However, the manuscript itself very frequently does not record what would have been Milton's practices: for just a very few examples, see the spelling of "their" in ll. 337, 349, 383, 478, and 530; or of "being," 154; "here," 260; "some," 294. With the exception of "thir" in l. 349, the 1667 printing repeats these spellings. The change from the manuscript's "their" to "thir" in l. 349 is particularly interesting because the manuscript has "thir" in l. 348 but 1667 changes that to "their." In all, the manuscript of the first book gives "thir" sixty-four times and "their" five (as noted above); and the first edition prints "thir" thirty times (only one, as just noted, being an alteration) but "their" thirty-nine times (four of which are found in the manuscript). Fourteen of the examples of "thir" in 1667 occur in the last part of the book, from l. 687 through l. 793, without variation, suggesting that the compositor was more attentive to the manuscript from which he was setting, that he simply gave up "correcting" the text, or that two compositors were involved who differed in their attention to the copy-text. (See Moyles, Shawcross [1958, *PMLA* 1963, *HLQ* 1963, 1967], as well as Treip and Falconer.) I here discuss orthography, but other issues include capitalization, italicization, paragraphing, and punctuation; e.g., "mans," I, 1, MS, but "Mans," 1667, and "Men," I, 16, MS, but "men," 1667; or "like a temple, where pilasters," I, 713, MS, but "like a Temple, where *Pilasters*," 1667 (the capitalization seems unjustified and the italicization of one but not the other noun is not only inconsistent but unwarranted). Note also ll. 242 and 331 which are not indented in the MS; each is preceded by a bracket, added apparently to indicate indentation, possibly by the compositor. Indentations at these points are justified, but in like fashion l. 376 should also have been indented but is not in either the MS or 1667. In the MS a semicolon in l. 15 is replaced by a comma in 1667; a comma is added after "Spirit," l. 17, and "pure," l. 18, in 1667, but deleted in l. 21. While the punctuation of the edition is arguably preferable in the first three cases, the deletion in "satst brooding on the vast Abysse, / And mad'st it pregnant" (21) removes a common usage in compounds for Milton (as in "Of mans first disobedience, & the fruit / Of that forbidd'n tree" [1–2]), and further one might argue that the comma at the end of l. 8 in both texts inaccurately alters a run-on line.

The matter is more complicated and more instructive than these remarks indicate. The compositor(s) of 1667 consistently spelled "their" except in ll. 363, 378, 481 (and the change at l. 349), through l. 483 and then again in ll. 614–668; in ll. 499–612 and 687–793 (as noted) the spelling is that of the manuscript, "thir," except in ll. 530 (twice) and 608. Thus, for the most part the 1667 compositor followed his copy-text in regard to the spelling of the third personal plural pronominal possessive adjective from l. 481 to the end with nine exceptions. This may be evidence of a second compositor, but

it seems unusual that a single book would be divided between compositors; the more likely situation would be division in an approximate middle, at the beginning of Book VII, or individual books. It should also be noted that Amanuensis D wrote "the" (probably because he had begun to write "their"), but changed it to "thir" in the course of writing (ll. 614, 616); at l. 388 he first wrote "there," deleted it, and wrote "thir"; and "the slumber," l. 377, in the manuscript is repeated in both 1667 and 1674, but "thir slumber" is surely the correct reading as Bentley surmised.[3] These manuscript errors would occur in copying, not in putting down what would have been said orally, pointing to some earlier manuscript from which Amanuensis D made his transcription. In this case it should also be remarked that the differences in the manuscript from what would seem to have been Milton's own practices may owe their existence to this scribe.

The printing house for 1667 was that of Mary and Samuel Simmons (identified as "S. Simmons" in the second issue of 1668 and the two issues of 1669); they had two presses and employed an apprentice and five workmen. Who may have been the specific compositor or compositors cannot be determined, but we may have two or three or even four people involved (one perhaps having been given the job of setting the preliminary sheets in 1668 and resetting sigs. Z and Vv, which seem more faithfully reproduced, and apparently another charged with the resetting of the preliminary sheets in 1669).

What is particularly important for Milton's text is the unfounded theory, supported by Darbishire, Fletcher, and Hughes, that he employed two different spellings to show a stressed or an unstressed word, the incomplete and often inconsistent evidence being "their" or "thir" in the editions of *PL*. This theory has been extended to other words (like "onely / only"), where it also is not borne out by holograph spellings, including "be" and the pronominal forms "he," "she," "we," and "ye." It might be remarked that Milton never spelled "hee" in manuscript although the other words have mixed use, and that the first transcription of Sonnet 14 in the Trinity MS reads "Faith shew'd yᵉ way, & shee who saw them best" (9), which was rewritten in the second transcription (soon afterwards) to "Faith shew'd the way, and she who saw them best," giving the lie to any differentiation for stress. (The line was revised further in the second transcription, to delete the pronoun altogether.)

The spellings of "being / beeing," "here / heer," and "some / som" mentioned before, though they are only three examples from a great many, are likewise instructive. *PL* I, 154 and 161, read "being" in the manuscript, 1667, and 1674; in holograph materials Milton spelled "beeing" twenty-seven times and never "being." Perhaps his spelling was purposive to avoid a reading of "ei" as a digraph, although "beeing" is not an uncommon spelling at that time. "Here" is consistent in all three texts (ll. 71, 142, 151, 258, 260, 261, 321, 692), although Milton himself wrote only "heere" before a shift to simplification by omission of final idle "e" from around 1641 ("heere," twenty-nine times; "heer," four times). "Some" occurs in ll. 204, 205, 294, 731, 732, 783 in all three texts, but the word in l. 524 is "some" in manuscript, "som" in 1667, and "some" again in 1674. The very next word "glimpse" ("Obscure some glimpse of joy, to haue found thir cheife" in manuscript) becomes "glimps" in 1667 and in 1674 ("Obscure som glimps of joy, to have found thir chief" and "Obscure some glimps of joy, to have found thir chief" respectively). Milton wrote "some" sixty times before around 1641 and "som" three times thereafter. Evidence of his practices in holograph omitting idle final "e" suggests that he would have omitted the "e" on "glimps" after that date; note it is that spelling that recurs in both editions of the epic at IV, 867; VI, 642; [VII, 793 or] VIII, 156; as well as both editions of "L'Allegro," 107, and in *Of Reformation*, p. 21. However, the word "[mis]cheif / [mis]chief" adds another factor: Milton wrote the digraph "ei" nine times (the latest being in CPB, 53, entry dated 1644–47 by Ruth Mohl in *CPW*, I, 378) and never "ie" in holograph materials; the practice is also seen in words like "breif" and "greif." The two editions consistently give "chief" in Book I (ll. 128, 381, 524, 566, 762), although the manuscript has "ei" in the first three cases. *Of Reformation*, for one prose instance, shows "cheif(e)" and "chief(e)" nine times each and "mischeif" once, but "mischief(e)" five times. Sonnet 16 (in an amanuensis's hand; that is, in Milton's nephew John Phillips's hand; see Shawcross 1959) has "cheif" in l. 1, although Edward Phillips printed it as "Chief" in 1694; and "ie" is erroneously consistent in all printings of all other poems.[4]

Such significant alterations in the 1667 edition of Book I of *PL* from its manuscript copy-text as have been cited above complicate our understanding of the creation of the printed text. "Thir," 349, and "som" and "glimps," 524, may suggest that someone communicated those spellings to the compositor—perhaps a corrector (that is, a proofreader in today's terminology) altered these spellings though he missed most others that might have been changed. Alternatively, they may suggest that the compositor was influenced by the manuscript's "thir" in l. 348 (although he changed that to "their") and by the length of l. 524, which fills out the full line space, avoiding runover, and thus he omitted the final "e" on "som," "glimps," and "cheif" from the manuscript (although he spelled the word "chief") and used the

manuscript's shorter spelling "thir." The printed text may thus exemplify at times other conditions of setting type that have no connection with Milton's specific text. Whatever the answers to these conundrums may be, it is clear that the texts of the manuscript (and presumably of the manuscript of the rest of the poem) and of 1667 cannot be relied upon as presenting the text that Milton himself would have written. Some specifics in the manuscript may be more reliable than their counterparts in 1667, but 1667 yields little trust in a "Miltonic" text.

The manuscript that we have is a transcription, as stated before; it was probably needed because its former copy was not one easily usable by a compositor. The new copy that we have contains some of Milton's odder spellings, carried over probably from the former copy (for example, "deceav'd," 35; "wast," 60; "waight," 227; "sovran," 246; "bestirr," 334; "chuse," 428; "perfet," 550; "signes," 605; "op'n'd," 689; "hunderd," 709; "eeve," 743); but also some of the scribe's (or a former scribe's?) spellings (for example, "darke," 22; "arm's," 94; "designs," 213; "hee," 214; "evening," two syllables, and "ffesole," using the commonplace ff as capital, both 289; the consistent "Egipt[s]," 339, 421, 480, 488, 721 [Milton spelled only "Ægypt," four examples]). Further evidence of these two textual levels in the manuscript (there are more) lies in "reign," given throughout except for "raign," 102, and "raigning," 124; in l. 261 "ra," apparently unfinished, is completed as "reign"; and in l. 637 "raignes" was changed to "reignes."

These matters of transmission thus call into question the text of any work in terms of reflection of a "Miltonic" text.[5] But they also lead to the possibilities 1) that texts produced before his blindness (total blindness came by February 1652), including those works written before his blindness but published afterward (like *Accidence Commenc't Grammar*, 1669), may have been printed from copies in his own hand and thus may reflect more of his own accidentals than otherwise might have occurred, and 2) that texts written after his blindness, when they reflect peculiarities of things like spelling, owe their existence to an amanuensis who knew Milton's practices or, because they were former students, who were taught Milton's practices, or who may have put down dictated forms.[6]

PARADISE LOST, PRELIMINARY SHEETS, 1668–69

There were two printing of these pages, that for 1668₂ and 1669₁ and that for 1669₂, a resetting of type. The Verse, written assuredly in 1668, shows various spellings used by Milton, implying a scribe who was attuned to Milton's practices and a compositor (see before) who was more faithful than the original 1667 compositor(s).

We find, among others, "thir," "exprest," "grac't," "eares," "Ancients," "esteem'd," and "troublesom." Yet commonplace but non-Miltonic spelling also occurs: "Verse," "being," "some," "worse," and "therefore." The 1669 reprinting alters some of the spelling (of those cited, "ears" and "troublesome") and makes the error "Meetet" (for "Meeter," a possible Miltonic spelling; note, e. g., "Peeter," CPB, 179, 185, 220, or "Steevn," CPB, 186, and "Steev'n," *Eikonoklastes*, p. 142, both editions). Gilbert argued that "parts of the Arguments are earlier than the final form of the poem itself" (pp. 27–32), and the spelling may bear that out, for the Arguments show a lot of Miltonic practices, suggesting that their first composition may lie even before 1651 or were put down (or copied) by a scribe who knew Milton's practices better than Amanuensis D. It is not only "thir" that appears without exception (three times each in I and II, once in III, seven times in IV, four times in V, twice in VIII, four times in IX, and twice in X), but also such representative words as "determin," I; "wayes," II; "undergoe," III; "choycest," V; "Machins," VI; "human," VIII; "foretels," IX. The compositor of the second printing retains "thir" but changes the cited words to "determine," "ways," "undergo," "choicest," "humane," "foretells."

The incompetency of the typesetter of the 1669 reprinting of the preliminary sheets is seen in the following (the left-hand reading is that of 1668; the right-hand, that of 1669): I, This / The; II, shall / should; III, his right hand / the right hand; plac't here / plac't there 1669; IV, find him / find him out; V, appearance / appearing; VII, search / seek; IX, Son / Angels; rejects / rejccts; X, but declares / and declares; Cherubim / Cherubims; happ'n / happen. That the 1674 compositor also made errors in reproducing the Arguments (which were distributed before each book and which divided those for VII into two for VII and VIII, and those for X into two for XI and XII) can be seen in X, meet / met State 1, 1674; full assembly / full of assembly 1674; taste / take 1674. Note too that Argument XII in 1674 concludes with a comma!

The *Errata* have been particularly important in textual discussions of Milton's poems and spelling. There are only thirteen items listed, despite all the errors or problems cited above, with the added comment, "Other literal faults the Reader of himself may Correct." (The 1669 resetting even makes an error, giving "Honoraim" as correction for "Heronaim," V, 409, which 1668 had corrected to "Horonaim.") The first three corrections from Book I appear in the manuscript; the fourth does not, and raises a question thereby. Also, the first correction changing "th' Eternal" to "Eternal" in l. 25, is curious, for the manuscript has "th' eternal" which the

compositor set; "th'" then is deleted, which the erratum indicates. What is the time sequence for these actions? and does this give evidence of a "corrector" making both changes? All errata are followed in 1674 (with "Heav'n" rather than "Heaven" in V, [now] 659) except for changing "we" to "wee" in II, 414. The combination of the fourth change in Book I, the Miltonic "hunderds" instead of "hundreds" (the reading of the manuscript) in I, 760, and of "wee" or "we" (not made, however, in 1674) has led to statements of Milton's acting (through Edward Phillips?) to impose his spelling preferences on his text (and that is extrapolated then to include *all* texts) and to the alleged differentiation of stressed and unstressed forms. Fletcher's commitment to the stressing principle (in spite of his numerous notations of its not being in evidence in specific lines of the poem) leads him to say (Vol. III, p. 136n): "The 1668 *Errata* call for 'wee' here, but as this is the only one of those *Errata* not followed by the 1674 compositor, I am inclined to believe that Milton here changed his mind. It seems a little difficult to stress the word." We of course do not know whether the copy-text for Book II read "wee" in this line, thus explaining the erratum, but since the copy-text for Book I did not read "hunderds," the two items imply that someone with a knowledge of Milton's practices acted as a corrector. An intentional proofreading of the text, however, could not have been undertaken, as all the continued errors indicate, and so about all one can conclude is that these two items were caught (along with the eleven other obvious typographical errors) through a rough and rapid perusal by someone aware of at least one, if not two, of Milton's practices.

PARADISE LOST, 1674, AND THE TEXT

The second, octavo edition of Milton's epic underwent a number of changes. Most notable to begin with, of course, is the revision of a ten-book epic with structural, symbolic, and numerological associations into a twelve-book epic nullifying most of those associations. Why Milton did this has been long under discussion. The clearest reason that arises is that epics had taken the form of twenty-four books (*The Iliad* and *The Odyssey*) or twelve books (*The Aeneid* in Virgil's overgoing of Homer by halving the "standard" length). Edmund Spenser projected twelve books of Aristotelian virtues for *The Faerie Queene* and talked in a letter to Sir Walter Ralegh of maybe even extending his work to twenty-four books. Twelve was the length expected by the reading public, and particularly by the "neoclassical" reading public of the Restoration and early eighteenth century, which saw the translation of Virgil by John Dryden and of both Homeric works by Alexander Pope. Did Milton *want* to change his format? did he *want* to change it to conform to the "standard" and thus make comparisons more explicit? or was he, with six issues finally selling out or their sheets being greatly reduced over perhaps seven years, argued into making the alteration so that more sales of a second edition would occur? The preliminary additions in 1668 make similar concessions by providing a kind of trot for this long and involved poem and by providing a defense of its prosodic form. In any case, the two very long Books VII and X were divided into two, each at convenient spots, making new Books VII, VIII, and XII the shortest books of the epic (640, 653, 649 lines respectively; the next shortest is III at 742 lines). Thus, Book VII became VII and VIII; VIII became IX; IX became X; and X became XI and XII. To effect the changes at the beginning of new Books VIII and XII, Milton added ll. 1–3 and 1–5 respectively. But the central symbolic and ideationally meaningful middle line with its significant first word in Ed. 1 was thus offset: "Ascended, at his right hand Victorie" with reference to the Son (VI, 762). To try to maintain that central position other adjustments for the additional eight lines were made, but in error as a result, Hunter has shown, of the mislineation of Book III in 1667. A marginal "600" in Book III was not given and "610" was placed alongside l. 600, throwing off the count by ten lines for the first error. Line "730" was set alongside l. 720, but then "740" was set alongside l. 721 in two states of the text (yielding 761 lines for the full book). Then, in the third state, "740" was deleted from a position alongside l. 721 and placed next to l. 731 (yielding 751 lines for the full book). There are, of course, 742 lines in this book. In toto, fifteen lines are added to the second edition,[7] eight to effect the breaks into additional books and seven supposedly to balance, but since the 1667 lineation was off by nine lines, the central line of the poem in the second edition is meaninglessly shifted.

All of this implies not only a careless printer for 1667 but a not very astute amanuensis for 1674, who nonetheless did cause alterations in the second edition at Milton's direction and, at times, in the direction of his spelling practices. A notable example is the spelling of "thir" in the 1674 edition. "Their" is changed from 1667 thirty-eight times in Book I (twice in second states only); 1674 retains "thir" from 1667 twenty-nine times (once in a second state only), retains "their" three times (twice in first states only), and changes "thir" to "their" in a first state only. One "thir" disappears through textual revision. Therefore the final state of the second edition of Book I gives "thir" throughout except at line 267 (the reading of 1667). The remainder of the poem evidences "thir" except for (fourteen examples) II, 277, 362; III, 59, 118, 400; VI, 690; VII, 453; IX, 725, 948; X, 242, 440,

628; XI, 740; XII, 107, all taken over from their 1667 printing. "Theirs" is consistent: IV, 513 (despite "thir" in the same line); IX, 806; XII, 400, 409, 434; no example of the word appears in Milton's holograph materials. Amongst such corrections and changes made by the "corrector" for the 1674 printing would seem to be: (1) "th'hospitable dore," I, 504, replacing "hospitable Dores." (2) "Expos'd a matron to avoid," I, 505, replacing "Yielded thir Matrons to prevent." (3) "fainting," I, 530, replacing "fainted." (4) "With," III, 594, replacing "Which." (5) "now," V, 627, inserted, being necessary for meter. (6) "sleights, IX, 92, replacing "fleights." (7) "aught," IX, 347, replacing "ought." (8) "made," IX, 632, replacing "make." (9) "Avengers," X, 241, replacing "Avenger" ("their" in l. 242 indicates that it should be plural). (10) insertion of "then," X, 827, needed for meter. (11) "who," XI, 879, replacing "that," not a necessary change. (12) "The," XII, 191, replacing "This."

The second edition was printed by Samuel Simmons; it has been speculated without foundation that Edward Phillips was the person who saw the second edition through the press. The evidence for that thought is his holograph statement written in John Aubrey's "Minutes of the Life of Mr John Milton" alongside the listing of "Paradise [bracket] lost 4to. / regaind 4to." "Ed. Philips his cheif [inserted] Amanuensis." Dating for such scribal work, be it noted, is not given, nor whether both epics or only one was intended.

Nonetheless, not all necessary corrections of a verbal or like nature were made: (1) "ought," I, 159, is retained; it should be "aught" as in the manuscript. (2) "the," I, 377 (noted above), persists from the manuscript in 1667 and 1674; it should be "thir." (3) "Capital," I, 756, continues from the incorrect respelling of "Capitoll" in the manuscript. (4) "Medal," III, 592, is in error for the correct "Mettal" (or "Metal"). (5) V, 361, is inaccurately indented in both editions. (6) IX, 1183, "Women" instead of "Woman" ("her" in l. 1184 indicates that this should be singular and that it refers to the general category, not specific people). (7) "So Death," X, 989–90, printed in l. 990 although it should complete l. 989. Indeed, there are a number of erroneous changes made in 1674: (1) "where," II, 282, changed from "were." (2) "her," II, 483, changed from "thir." (3) "this," II, 527, changed from "his." (4) "of," IV, 451, changed from "on." (5) "shadie," IV, 705, changed from "shadier." (6) "Thy," IV, 928, changed from "The." (7) "and," VIII, 269, changed from "as." (8) VIII, 398, not indented. (9) "bear," IX, 213, changed from "hear." (10) "Likeliest," IX, 394, changed from "Likest." (11) "hath," IX, 922, changed from "hast." (12) "me," IX, 1019, changed from "we." (13) "from," IX, 1092, changed from "for." (14) "for," IX,

1093, changed from "from." (15) "might," X, 58, changed from "may." (16) "these," X, 397, changed from "those." (17) "fair," X, 550, omitted. (18) "to the amplest," XI, 380, altered from "to amplest." (19) "that derive," XI, 427, altered from "that sin derive." (20) "Well," XII, 534, changed from "Will."

Note also three errors made in the second state of some pages in Book VII: (1) "To hoarce or mute, though fall'n on evil dayes," (25) which changed the last word and its punctuation to "tongues;" as a result of the last word on the next line, "tongues;". (2) "But Knowledge is as food, and needs no less" (126) became "But knowledge is a food, and needs no less". (3) "Then staid the fervid Wheeles, and in his hand" (224) became "Then staid his fervid Wheels, and in his hand". "Erroneous" changes in spelling in 1674 are manifest, despite "corrections" like the spelling of "thir."

With these data one cannot be sure which text offers what Milton wrote in the following examples: (1) the manuscript reads "This fiery Surge," I, 173, but both editions give "The fiery Surge." (2) The manuscript has "For these the Race of Israel oft forsook," I, 432, but the editions say, "For those the Race of *Israel* oft forsook." (3) "Of dauntless valour," I, 603, became "Of dauntless courage" in the editions, and one must ask whether this was a studied change on Milton's part, the only one if so in Book I. (4) A crux lies in I, 703, which reads in the manuscript and 1667 "With wondrous [art] Art founded the [massy] massie Ore," or did Milton change this in 1674 to "With wond'rous Art found out the massie Ore"? (5) "Our walks at noon," IV, 647, sounds more accurate than 1674's "Our walk at noon." (6) Should V, 257, be indented as it is in State 3 of 1667, or not, as in States 1 and 2 and 1674, which apparently followed one of those states? (7) Does VII, 366, refer to Lucifer, the Morning Star ("his") or to the planet Venus ("her")? The line reads in 1667 / 1674: "And hence the Morning Planet guilds his / her horns." (8) Beginning the line, "Not nocent yet," IX, 186, in 1667, may occur because l. 185 began with "Not yet in horrid Shade"; 1674 changes it to "Nor nocent yet," a preferable reading. (9) The difference in X, 408, is the difference between the subjunctive and an indicative: "If your joynt power prevaile, th' affaires of Hell / No detriment need feare" (1667) and "If your joynt power prevailes, th' affaires of Hell / No detriment need feare" (1674). (10) Another crux has been XI, 651, "But call in aide, which tacks a bloody Fray" (1667) against "But callin [*sic*] aide, which makes a bloody Fray" (1674). Someone (the compositor perhaps) apparently did not know the word "tacks" (meaning, rapidly diverges into) and so altered it to a bland term. (11) XII, 238, undergoes a major change which only Milton should have made: "he grants them thir desire"

became "he grants what they besaught."

The conclusions that an editor is driven to by the foregoing data are that 1674 must be the copy-text employed for any new edition, but that various and numerous changes of a verbal or like nature are required, some with "authority" from the manuscript, some with "authority" from 1667. The text that will emerge will nonetheless not be the text that we can be assured Milton would have produced himself. Other questions arise: does the editor alter the spellings to Milton's demonstrable practices or not? does the editor create a text consistent in its spellings? The problems of punctuation that Falconer examines compound our uncertainty and some difficulties with indentation have been mentioned in the previous statistics. While italics seem to be handled as one would expect, "Red-Sea Coast," I, 306, and "*Phalanx,*" I, 550, give one pause. The manuscript doesn't even capitalize "red-sea coast" and does not indicate italics; these citations in 1674 are the same in 1667 and thus suggest that attention was *not* paid to the accidental matter of italics in the preparation of the second edition. Likewise the use of capitals at first glance seems appropriate for proper nouns or special designation, but then one sees "Suffering," I, 158, and "Marle," I, 295, and recognizes the hyperbolic use of capitalization throughout. The manuscript capitalized "Marle" but not "suffering."

While *PL* does not offer the textual difficulties that the poetry of John Donne does, or the mare's nest of "bad" and "good" quartos that Shakespeareans must unravel, it is not the simple, definitive text that many scholars seem to assume. The problems evinced make clear the inaccuracy of assuming that works of single text—*SA* for one instance or "Il Penseroso" for another—have no real textual difficulties; they make clear that a text—*Areopagitica* for one instance or Psalms 1–8 for another—may render certain Miltonic forms because he probably wrote the manuscript on which, eventually, printing was based or because his scribe was aware of his practices or was explicitly told what to write, but also that they very frequently present the compositor's practices and errors, as well as those of any intervening scribe. And most emphatically the foregoing data indicate that Milton was often not concerned with total exactness, or at least did nothing to get it, but that at times he was concerned about some specific accidental matters. This will be borne out by close inspection of both the prose and the poetry, and I proceed to other matters concerning the texts of Milton's canon, hoping that the *fact* of unreliability of text is recognized.

POEMS IN PRINTED VERSIONS ONLY

While some of Milton's poems appear in manuscript

versions, most are found only in the collections of 1645 and 1673 along with the 1671 edition of *PR* and *SA*. The poems that are repeated in 1673 from the earlier edition indicate the lack of attention to a "Miltonic" text and the frequent alteration into more "updated" forms, some of which yield "Miltonic" spellings, but which most of the time do not. The inference, thus, for the texts of new poems in the 1673 edition is that they, like *PL*, will show agreement and disagreement with what might have been Milton's composition and preferences, but that agreement may not necessarily require Milton's presence behind the form printed except in oddities like "thir" or "som." The text of "Il Penseroso" in 1673, for one instance, shows the compositor making errors in disagreement with the 1645 printing: "offended," rather than "offended." in l. 21; "mirth." rather than "mirth," in l. 81; "unsphear." rather than "unsphear" in l. 88; "sing." rather than "sing," in l. 143; "pale." rather than "pale," in l. 156; "spell" rather than "spell," in l. 170. It also changes the "Miltonic" spelling of 1645: "some / som" in ll. 5, 86, 139; "therefore / therfore" in l. 15; "deign / daign" in l. 56; "Even-Song / eeven-Song" in l. 64; "comely / comly" in l. 125; "something / somthing" in l. 174. The 1673 text is clearly not a reliable one. Suggested by the appearance of some of these spellings in 1645 ("som," "therfore," "comly") is that its copy-text was a retranscription (made sometime around 1645 or so) of what would have been the text prior to 1641, when the poem was written, for Milton altered his spelling of such words by omission of idle final "e" around that time. Thus, for that reason, 1645 gives "Goddes," ll. 11, 132, and "sweetnes," l. 164, but holograph evidence indicates that Milton altered such spelling to double final "s" sometime after 1646. The 1673 spellings of these words with double final "s," however, while agreeing with what came to be his spelling, are the result of a general updating such as we seem to see also in "musical," l. 62, and "drowsie," l. 83 (rather than "drousie").

But 1645, which furnishes the only valid text that we have of the poem, offers a text with errors or with non-Miltonic forms that persist in 1673, indicating the lack of careful attention or of a "Miltonic" proofreader: "Ore," l. 16 (despite "o'er" in l. 60); "The," l. 91 (although for meter it should be "Th'"); and "dream," l. 147, and "fail," l. 155, and "blow," l. 161, all of which should have no punctuation. Milton often omitted end punctuation in poems transcribed into the TM, particularly commas. The compositor of 1645 has end punctuation, very frequently commas, for most lines and is thus, it seems, in these three cases simply setting end punctuation without recourse to meaning or his copy-text. Other end-line commas, therefore, may also be of his, not Milton's, doing. Being at the mercy of the 1645 text (repeated in 1673), we read l. 162

as "To the full voic'd Quire below." Is "Quire" one or two syllables? "Quire(s)" is one syllable in sixteen other examples in Milton's verse, with only a seventeenth in "A Mask," 112, offering pause. In that example it rhymes with "fire," always a monosyllable in the poetry, the two lines (111–12), a rhymed couplet, apparently being truncated tetrameters. The line in "Il Penseroso" should be a tetrameter, being surrounded by tetrameters (ll. 151 through the end), but it is possible that it is truncated and as Milton wrote it. But with only one valid text can we be sure? If not, what word of one syllable may have been omitted? (In l. 57, 1645 prints "Id," which was corrected by Milton in the presentation copy in the Bodleian Library; no other corrections are made to the poem.)

When we have a holograph transcription of a poem, we may be on surer ground that a printed text may be in error (barring an error in holograph or what appears to be an authorial alteration). In "Arcades," for instance, ll. 48–49 read in the TM: "and all my plants I save from nightlie ill / of noysome winds, or blasting vapours chill", but 1645 (and 1673) print: "And all my Plants I save from nightly ill, / Of noisom winds, and blasting vapours chill." Aside from the respellings (at least one removing a Miltonic form) and the questionable capitalization of "Plants," the difference between "or" and "and" creates a difference in the meaning projected. The "and" implies that the winds and the vapours occur together at night, and this is what is "ill," but the "or" implies two separate possibilities for creating "ill": winds by themselves and vapours by themselves. Did Milton alter his text or did the compositor intervene? Further, the indentations in Song 3 are different in manuscript and print, but it was being worked out in manuscript: l. 96 aligns with 97, 99, 101, 104–105, 109, yet in print ll. 96 and 104–105 are not indented, and the position of l. 109, indented further, may result from the addition of ll. 106–107. That indentation can create problems for later critics is clear from 1673's misreading of 1645 in l. 27 of "Upon the Circumcision." It is indented in 1645 and l. 28 indented further, but it appears at the start of a new page and the compositor of 1673 did not recognize that and placed it on the margin with l. 28 indented. He should have realized the parallelism of indentation of ll. 13–14 with 27–28, but obviously was not sensitive to such matters. Unfortunately, Merritt Y. Hughes unthinkingly followed the 1673 printing and modern scholars, quoting those lines and discussing the poem's structure, have been no more sensitive than the 1673 compositor was. Milton had revised ll. 12–14 and 26–28, indenting only ll. 13 and 27, so that the copy in 1645 is *also* out of agreement with what would seem to be his text. (A more grievous error that a modern scholar made—but was corrected before printing—was to follow

Hughes's last line of "On Time," an indented alexandrine that was broken into two by the printer to fit his line length, yielding a pentameter and a separate single foot. The 1957 printer was apparently misled by the copy in Hughes's 1937 edition which has "O Time" as a further indented runover of the line.)

The poems for which we have only one text, recognizing that the second edition in 1673 of poems printed in 1645 may have no authority, are all the poems except "Epitaph on the Marchioness of Winchester," Sonnets 7–17, 21–23, the three English odes, "Arcades," "A Mask," "Lycidas," and "Ode to Rous," and those with other printings, "On Shakespear," the Hobson poems (which also have a manuscript and separate print tradition), and "Epitaphium Damonis." The problems of the Latin poems in 1645 and in 1673 make clear the lack of reliability that can be extrapolated for all of these one-text works. "Elegia prima," 13, for instance, in 1645 shows three states: "molles, / molles / molle"; 29 in 1673 shows two states for "auditur / auditor", and 40, two states for "Interdum / Intredum". These at least were discovered, and Milton's holograph correction in the Bodleian copy of 1645 of "Elegia septima," 21 ("æterno" instead of "ærerno"), was made in 1673. But "suit," 2, in this same poem, appears in both editions (it should be "fuit"); as well as "fætus," "Elegia quarta," 89 (it should be "fœtus"); "seu," "In quintum Novembris," 20 (it should be "ceu"); "ad sit," "Mansus," 83 (it should be "adsit"). These and others offer little reliance on either printing. Two examples: "Ad eandem" ("Altera Torquatum"), 8, in 1645 has "desipuiiset," which 1673 prints as "desipulisset" and changes in an erratum to the correct "desipuisset"; but 1673 erroneously changes 1645's "cornua" in "In eandem" ("Purgatorem animæ"), 4, to "corona" and inaccurately indents l. 12. It repeats an error in "In quintum Novembris," as noted above, misprints "notat," 45, but changes it to "natat" in an erratum; corrects "casúque," 125, to "casúmque" and changes "semifractaque," 143, to "præruptaque"; yet it errs in "unamimes" (13, "unanimes"); "tantamina possunt." (43, "tentamina possunt,"); indentation of l. 75; "pontum" (108, "Pontum"); "timor" (148, "Timor"); "penius" (159, "penitùs").

The 1645 printing exhibits unreliabilities, as does the 1673 printing even though it is following the first edition. What thus should be the reliance upon new poems in 1673, say "The Fifth Ode" (probably first written down by Milton himself), Sonnet 19 (written down by an amanuensis), or the early "At a Vacation Exercise"? Non-Miltonic spellings in the first poem include "near" and "some" (or is the poem to be dated before around 1641?); still Milton's orthography seems to persist in words like "bedew'd," "enjoyes," "alwayes" (2), "vow'd,"

"untry'd." Sonnet 19 poses cruxes: (1) the strange "ask; But" in l. 8 calls for either a period or a small letter, and indeed it would seem to be the volta of the sonnet (displaced from what a reader might expect in a Petrarchan sonnet; Milton frequently revised its usual position); (2) the string of commas in ll. 10–12 are not rhetorical or grammatical: the first ("gifts, who") might better be "gifts. Who" and the third ("best, his") might better be "best: his". Are the questions we have about the accidentals (these and others) the fault of the scribe who first wrote the sonnet down, or a transcriber who produced a fair copy for the printer, or the compositor? An editor should do something more than merely reproduce. And "At a Vacation Exercise," discovered, it would seem, when Milton looked through his older manuscript materials (a search that apparently also turned up the familiar letters and especially the seven prolusions published the next year in 1674—we suspect that there were more letters and prolusions written though not saved or at least not found), has its own difficulties. First, it should be part of the sixth prolusion published in 1674, but positioning there is uncertain; second, it is printed between "The Fifth Ode" and "On the Forces of Conscience" but repositioned after "The Fair Infant Elegy" by an erratum; third, 1673 has "hollowed" in l. 98 though it should be "hallow'd"; and fourth, despite numerous "early" spellings such as Milton's manuscripts exhibit (like "imperfect," "lipps," "come," "chuse," "dore," "dayes," "Armes"), some unlikely items also appear ("Believe," "toys," "rove," "their" [3], "resign," "befriend," "being," "antient"), all commonplace and "updated" spellings.

The 1671 quarto volume of the brief epic and the dramatic poem fares no better. William Riley Parker's discussion of the text of *SA* can also be applied to the text of *PR*: "Numerous inconsistencies of spelling in the 1671 edition argue the use of several amanuenses for the manuscript sent to the printer, and/or intervention of the compositor. There are three different kinds of spelling inconsistency. Let us notice first the omission from the 1671 text of some of Milton's known or supposed preferences . . . . A second kind of inconsistency of spelling is purely internal: there are about sixty words for which the 1671 text offers two different spellings, ignoring capitalization. . . . A third kind of inconsistency of spelling, also internal, involves capitalization" (81, 82, 86), and he adds, "Despite all the carelessness and confusion suggested by the foregoing observations, it should not be overlooked that the 1671 text contains a number of examples of what students have come to recognize as distinctively 'Miltonic' spellings" (89). Specific examples of each kind are given, and he notes a number of errors in punctuation as well (90). One simply cannot rely upon the text before us for either poem. The errata given for both, the strange "Omissa" for the drama and the unintelligible paragraphing of "It suffices . . ." in "Of that sort of Dramatic Poem which is call'd Tragedy" and lack of sentence break after "fift Act," and nonrecorded errors scream out compositorial unreliability. Among the obvious errors that are not recorded in the errata are: "ought" for "aught" (*PR* I, 333); "rested" for "wrested" (*PR* I, 470); "in sight" for "insight" (*PR* III, 238); "complements" for "compliments" (*PR* IV, 124); "was" for "wast" (*PR* IV, 217); "aught" for "ought" (*PR* IV, 288); and "sent" for "scent" (*SA*, 720).

POEMS IN MANUSCRIPT AND IN PRINT

Reproduction of manuscript copies of poems would seem to be a solution when trying to publish authentic texts. But in Milton's case (and probably all cases) it is not so simple. In the TM in Milton's hand are transcriptions of "Arcades," "A Mask," Sonnets 7–15 (the seventh being included in a prose letter transcribed in the manuscript), "On Time," "Upon the Circumcision," and "Lycidas," and a first working of "At a Solemn Music," which is then revised and recopied in two and a half further drafts. All poems show revisions or development, most of the time by Milton but in some cases by amanuenses; Sonnets 11–14 are also recopied by a scribe in the extant quarto sheets. In the hands of scribes, in the folio sheets, are Sonnets 16–17 and "On the Forcers of Conscience"; in the quire, 21 (missing ll. 1–4) through 23. (Apparently now lost from the quarto gathering were scribal transcriptions of Sonnets 15–21 [ll. 1–4] and "On the Forcers of Conscience.") (There is also a scribal version of "Ad Joannem Rousium" in the Bodleian Library.) We have already seen what occurred textually to Sonnet 11 ("I did but prompt the age") from Milton's autograph to a scribe's transcription and into print (1673); see n. 6 here. Two other examples should suffice to indicate the inadvisability of simply reproducing a manuscript text or relying upon its printed version.

Sonnet 10, the Margaret Ley poem, is in Milton's hand in the TM. Lines 2–4, 6–8, 10, and 13–14 all employ a lowercase letter at the beginning of the line. (Milton generally employed a lowercase letter at the beginning of lines in all the autograph poems recorded in the TM.) The manuscript has a heading, "To ye Lady Margaret Ley," but Milton apparently eschewed all sonnet headings later on despite those on the 1673 Sonnets 11 (given as 12), 13, and 18. Italics are not indicated in the manuscript, but 1645 and 1673 logically italicize three words; Milton's ampersand is replaced; and his capitals are retained except for "Vertues," 12. His spellings "Earle," 1, "daies," 10, and "Honourd," 14, are

changed in both editions, as well as "kill'd," 8, in 1645 ("Kil'd"). His meaningful accent on "Chæronéa," 7, is maintained in 1645 but dropped in 1673. We might accept the addition of commas at the ends of lines 2, 3, 10, 13 (although they are not necessary except for that in 10 according to modern usage), but 1673 changes that in 3 to a period, which is flatly wrong, and 1645 does not give one in 10. Yet both editions print an intrusive and unnecessary comma in 9 ("Though later born, then to have known the dayes"). It is clear that Milton's text is not that of either 1645 or 1673, but the manuscript text does not present what is general printing practice either.

Sonnet 23, in the formal hand of Jeremy Picard, does not totally present Milton's practices: note "soe" and "cleare," 12, and what of "Mee thought" as two words? The only words at the beginning of lines that are capitalized are in ll. 1, 5, 13–14. 1673 capitalizes "Saint," 1; "Son" and "Husband," 3; "Law," 6; "Heaven," 8; "O," 13; and one wonders whether Milton might not have accepted some or all of these. The added final commas in 1673 in 2, 3, 5, 10 seem wise, but the internal comma after "goodness," 11, and its omission at the end of 13 are wrong. What the collation of this sonnet points to as a text is the combining of both manuscript and print versions, and perhaps with further emendation, as in spelling "cleer" and "Heav'n."

That conclusion rises as a general principle for the presentation of the poetry, recognizing that Milton erred himself, that he was not always consistent, that the manuscript poetry was not put down as copy-text for a printed edition, and that intervening hands—scribe and compositor—may have followed copy, made errors, and altered through lack of attention and put down what would have been the scribe's or the compositor's normal forms. This conclusion is borne out by a study of the text of "Lycidas," which appears in Milton's autograph in the TM, with further alterations by him; in the 1638 *Justa Edovardo King Naufrago*, with some corrections in his hand in presentation copies; in the 1645 (and hence 1673) text, based apparently on an altered copy of 1638 probably made by an amanuensis. (For full details see Shawcross, 1962.) We may note here a few specific matters. In the TM, l. 10 is twice given as hypermetric ("who would not sing for Lycidas? he well knew") and in Milton's holograph correction of the Cambridge University Library and British Library (C.21.c.42) copies of 1638. What does a modern editor print? 1638's "lord," l. 51, is corrected in both copies to "lov'd," the reading of TM, 1645, 1673. 1638's "the" instead of "your" in l. 53 was corrected in the Cambridge copy; "your" is the reading of TM, 1645, and 1673. 1638's "Ah," l. 56, is corrected to "Ay" from the TM in 1645,

1673. Milton's "incessant," l. 64, is never otherwise re-corded. 1673 errs in l. 65 by omission of the first letter of "tend," which is in all other texts. 1638's "stridly," l. 66, is corrected to "strictly" from the TM in 1645, 1673. 1638's "do" instead of "use" in l. 67 was corrected in both the CUL and BL copies, and it is the reading of TM, 1645, and 1673. 1638's "where," l. 73, is corrected to "when" from the TM in 1645, 1673. Milton's "in-wraught," l. 105, is never otherwise recorded. The error of "smites," l. 131, in 1638 is corrected to "smite" in 1645, 1673. 1638's "humming," l. 157, is the reading of TM, but the CUL and BL copies record "whelming," the word given in 1645 and 1673. 1638's "oazie," l. 175, is corrected in the CUL copy to "oozie" but the margin also has "oosie"; TM reads "oozie" and 1645 and 1673 give "oozy." Line 176 does not appear in 1638; it is added in the CUL and BL copies (part of the line is torn off in the BL copy), 1645, and 1673. As lines 10, 64, 105 indicate, Milton's text has not been reproduced in these early editions (and thus in almost all editions thereafter). It is also clear that 1638 frequently erred as it did in not indenting ll. 25, 50, 64, 85, and 103. The continuance of forms like *Nectar* and "jeat" in 1645 and 1673 from 1638 also document their textual unreliability, as do such examples as "rhyme," l. 11 (Milton, "rime"); "nurst," l. 23 ("nurs't"); "shears," l. 75 ("sheares"); "mouthes," l. 119 ("mouths").

That 1638 served as basic copy-text for 1645 is established by the textual details above, but it is also clear that the 1638 text was corrected and amplified by someone, apparently not Milton himself. Note that Milton's original "glimmering," l. 26, also in 1638, is replaced in the TM by "opening," the reading of 1645 and 1673. TM and 1638 have "Oft till the ev'n-starre bright" in l. 30, but this was changed in manuscript to "Oft till the starre that rose in Evning bright," picked up by the scribe and given as "Oft till the Star that rose, at Ev'ning, bright" in 1645 and 1673. Not only is Milton's spelling "Evning" not given and unnecessary commas are added, but that little word "in" is altered to "at," creating a slightly different reading for the line. Similarly, "burnisht," l. 31, is altered to "westring," although 1645 and 1673 "misspell" it as "westering." "Hid in," l. 69, became "Or with" in revision and thus in 1645 and 1673. Special problems exist with ll. 129 and 149. Milton wrote "dayly devours apace, and nothing sed," l. 129, then deleted "nothing" and replaced it with "little" in the margin. He apparently remembered that there were protests against Archbishop Laud and his policies, for example, by Henry Burton, William Prynne, and John Bastwick. "Little" is the reading of 1638, but apparently the scribe saw "nothing," somehow missed "little" (or ʾought that the x or * over the crossed-out "nothing"

meant reinstatement) and caused 1645 to read "nothing." The frequent use of x or * indicates replacement of a word, the mark being given in the text proper and usually also with the replacement given in the margin. In l. 149, in a section added to the first transcription of the poem and then rewritten, Milton wrote: "bid Amaranthus all his beautie shed," rewritten as "bid Amaranthus all his beauties shed." The three printed versions all give "beauty" and we must indecisively wonder what it was Milton wanted finally.

One last point is to be considered, as also seen in revisions to *PL*. Milton seems often to polish his texts even after they have been printed, and thus the alteration in the "Nativity Ode," ll. 143–44, from "Th'enameld *Arras* of the Rainbow wearing, / And Mercy set between," to "Orb'd in a Rain-bow; and like glories wearing / Mercy will sit between," we can only accept as authorial. The most interesting such alteration occurs in the last line of "At a Solemn Music." In the TM Milton *four* times wrote, "To live & sing with him in endlesse morne of light," a doctrinally and even logically inaccurate concept: God does not join in the singing of the palmers before his throne! The error was caught and the line in 1645 became "To live with him, and sing in endles morn of light."

PROSE WORKS PUBLISHED DURING MILTON'S LIFETIME
Remarks on Milton's poetry indicate the possible textual approach to editions of the prose: (1) is the text reproduced as published (with obvious errors, like turned letters, corrected and noted)? (2) is the text made consistent unto itself as to spelling or punctuation or italicization? (3) is the text emended to reflect what seems to be known as Milton's practices in such matters as spelling or punctuation? The five antiprelatical tracts, published in 1641–42, all quartos, were printed by various compositors and published by different booksellers: *Of Reformation, Of Prelatical Episcopacy,* and *Animadversions upon the Remonstrants Defence Against Smectymnuus* (all 1641) record Thomas Underhill as publisher. Either Richard Oulton alone or he and Gregory Dexter set the text of the first; "R. O. & G. D.," the second; and apparently the same two printers, the third. *The Reason of Church-Government* (the first tract with Milton's name in full on the title page) and *An Apology Against a Pamphlet Call'd A Modest Confutation* (both 1642), were printed for John Rothwell by E. G. (that is, Edward Griffin). The last two were reissued together with a new title page for the volume listing both (but *Apology* is listed first, though written and printed later than *Reason*) and the same 1641/2 title page for *Reason* accompanies its reissue. (See Shawcross 1984, for bibliographic details of all prose works, and Shawcross 1974,

for discussion of all prose works.) There is a clear division between printers in *Episcopacy* (Oulton, sig. A; Dexter, sigs. B–C) and *Animadversions* (Oulton, sigs. B–G; Dexter, sigs. H–K), but not in *Reformation*. The textual problems of multiple compositors mentioned before in the discussion of *PL* exist for these works, each of which shows variant states; there are errata for *Reformation*, two separate issues for *Episcopacy*, and a cancel of sigs. G3–4, which would have been pp. 45–48, in *Animadversions*. Griffin's work also has variant states and errata. What seem to be Milton's preferred spellings come through often in all five tracts but are also changed very often in all five tracts. The antiprelatical tracts join other "Anglican" (State Church) thinkers to argue against a hierarchy of bishops between the parishioner, the minister, and God; they are not "Puritan."

Related to the religious argument of these works is *An Answer to a Book Entitvled, an Humble Remonstrance* by SMECTYMNUUS (that is, Stephen Marshall, Edward Calamy, Thomas Young, Matthew Newcomen, and William Spurstow), which prints "A Postscript" on sigs. M–N, pp. 85–94, in one issue, and on sigs. N–O, pp. 95–104, in another. There is no notation of publisher or printer for the first issue, but the second says: "Printed for *I. Rothwell* , and are to be sold by *T. N.* at the Bible in Popes-Head-Alley, 1641." "T. N." is not identified. It was reprinted or reissued four times as *Smectymnuus Redivivus* (1654, by T. C. for John Rothwell, and edited with a preface by Thomas Manton; twice in 1660, reissued for John Rothwell, each with new title page; and 1661, for John Rothwell, a new edition). Milton's authorship of "A Postscript" has been argued by Don M. Wolfe (*CPW*, I, 961–65); its spelling seems to corroborate the assignment to Milton despite much that does not (note, among others, "accurs't," 86; "dores," 87; "revenewes," 90; "turnay," 91).

The tracts on divorce number four, but the first was revised to almost double its original length creating what might be considered a fifth tract. The first edition of *The Doctrine and Discipline of Divorce*, printed by Thomas Payne and Matthew Simmons in late July or August 1643, is in forty-eight quarto pages with two pages of errata. The second edition in 1644 does not list the printer(s), who may have been Simmons alone, and is now in eighty-two pages, with errata on the last page. Numerous signatures are in various states, and copies seem to be composites of corrected and uncorrected states with none being completely one or the other (see Thompson). Further, there are significant manuscript corrections in various copies, made by a printing house scribe (who sometimes made errors in entering those corrections) apparently following a list of items. The copy-text would seem to have been an augmented copy

of 1643 because some compositorial errors persist; however, 1644 often changes the Miltonic spelling of 1643 despite its often close reproduction of such spelling in added sections. The work was republished the next year, again without printer(s) recorded, derived from various corrected and uncorrected sheets of Ed. 2 and with errata not made but still cited; there are two states. Another edition, sometimes called the fourth although it is a pirated printing made to appear as if it were the third edition, also is dated 1645. No errata are listed but not all corrections were made; two minor variants have been noticed among copies. Immediate differences from the third edition can be observed on the title page: there is no border; "and" (not "&"); "*J. M.* " (rather than "*I. M.* '); "Imprinted 1n the Year 1645." (rather than "Imprinted in the yeare 1645."). There are other differences on the title page, and pp. 42–47 are incorrectly numbered and pp. 69–72 are repeated in pagination, making the last page appear as 78. A modern editor clearly has an additional problem in offering Milton's text to a contemporary audience that is much concerned with Milton's ideas about divorce and marriage in relation to his treatment of Adam and Eve and of Samson and Dalila. The first edition represents Milton's basic thinking about the question, and the second edition, extrapolations of those arguments largely in reaction to negative comments from various divines, who perhaps had not actually read the work. On the title page of the second edition he added a quotation, Proverbs xviii: 13: "He that answereth a matter before he heareth it, it is folly and shame unto him," suggesting that he suspected that his antagonists had not read his argument. The second edition adds an address "To the Parlament," references to various authorities, and elaborations of concepts of Christian liberty and reason. A contemporary scholar would be wise to examine both editions separately to understand Milton's developing attitudes toward marriage and divorce; a compounded edition (such as that in the *CPW*) is a "nontext." A Dutch translation of Ed. 1 has been recently discovered, published in Middelburgh by Iacob de Laet in 1655; the translator is uncertain, although the work has been assigned to Gisbertus Vaetius.

With antagonism so observable against his argument, he proceeded to publish parts of Chapters 15–47 of Book II of *De Regno Christi ad Edwardo VI* by an important sixteenth-century religious figure: *The Ivdgement of Martin Bucer, Concerning Divorce. Writt'n to Edward the sixt, in his second Book of the Kingdom of Christ. And now English. Wherin a late Book restoring the Doctrine and Discipline of Divorce, is heer confirm'd and justify'd by the authoritie of Martin Bucer* (printed by Matthew Simmons, 1644). It includes testimonies, a preface to the Parliament, and a postscript. But the antagonism did not go away: one rebuttal, *An Answer to a Book, Intituled, The Doctrine and Discipline of Divorce, or, A Plea for Ladies and Gentlewomen, and all other Maried Women against Divorce* (1644), presents a mild argument in disagreement and an appeal to women to dissuade from approval those like the all-male Parliament to whom Milton had appealed. Indeed, the play of contemporary gender forces in this 1640s issue of divorce has been inadequately looked at in recent discussions of the issue. In reaction in March 1645 Milton published two coeval works on the subject, *Tetrachordon* and *Colasterion*, the first envisioned as a major and long statement (110 pages) giving light to the whole matter by examining four scriptural passages on marriage and the "nullities" of marriage, the second a shorter rebuttal (27 pages) of one argument that specifically had taken Milton's first tract to task. Through the examination of Genesis i: 27–28; Deuteronomy xxiv: 1–2; Matthew v: 31–32; and 1 Corinthians vii: 10–16 (the four [tetra] strands [chordon] making up the harmonized statement), *Tetrachordon* was to provide "light" (knowledge, understanding) that divorce was not only justified but approved under certain circumstances even by the Bible. The "scourge" (or cat-o-nine-tails) that the word *Colasterion* means becomes a kind of reflected light (though "cold" in argument) to lead one through the darkness (night) of ignorance such as he thought the unnamed antagonist of *An Answer* exhibited. The relationship between Milton's two coeval works is alluded to in "I did but prompt the age" (with original manuscript title of "On the detraction wch follow'd upon my writing certain treatises") through the image of the twin children of Zeus and Leto (Latona), Apollo, the sun, and Diana, the moon. *Tetrachordon* was printed by Payne and Simmons in a clearly divided text, with (apparently) Simmons's first half showing decidedly more attention to what would have been his copy-text than Payne's, and *Colasterion* was set by Simmons alone, in a text which is closer to Miltonic orthography than most others. Sigs. G1–2 in *Tetrachordon* are mispaged 37–40 (rather than 41–44) and the error is continued; there are errata and two states of text.

Vilification of Milton for his ideas on divorce—as "fornicator," for example, and as "founder" of a "sect"—continued through the eighteenth century, and along with his attack on Charles I in *Eikonoklastes* and his antimonarchical works, they are the base of disregard and rejection of his prose.

The two best-known and most often reprinted prose works were also published in 1644: *Of Education* in June and *Areopagitica* in November. The first has no title page but was registered to Thomas Underhill, the publisher of the first three of Milton's tracts, on 4 June 1644. It is addressed to Samuel Hartlib, who has been suggested as the person who caused it to be printed. We do not know its printer and there are no peculiarities in the text to point to any printing house. It is referred to in letters and books, and was included in the 1673 edition of the *Poems*, a reason for its frequency in the eighteenth century after Jacob Tonson republished all the poems other than *PL* in one volume and then included *Of Education* in the 1713 edition. The title page of 1713 lists the edition, referring actually to *PR*, as the fifth, although it is the sixth.

Areopagitica, which is a formal oration arguing against prepublication censorship, was provoked by a section of the Licensing Order of Parliament in 1643, which continued the decree of the Star Chamber in 1637. (The Star Chamber was abolished in 1641 and control of the press went to Parliament, which was incited by the Presbyterian Westminster Assembly to enforce the order.) The decree provided for searching out and seizing any unlicensed printing presses and books and for apprehending authors or printers of such materials. I have shown, through a study of the types and ornaments, that the printer was Augustine Mathewes, who lost his license in 1637 but continued to print anonymously. He printed Milton's *A Mask* in 1637/8 and perhaps *Epitaphium Damonis* in 1640? while unlicensed. The printing of the tract is poor, showing numerous broken types and having variant states, and its orthography is a mixture of Miltonic and non-Miltonic forms, while its frequent lack of paragraphing (none, for example, from the last line on p. 9 through the middle of p. 19) is questionable. Some copies have a manuscript correction on p. 12 of "wayfaring" to "warfaring."

Milton's antimonarchical and governmental works fall into two groups and extend over some years. The influential *Tenure of Kings and Magistrates* of February 1649 brought him to the attention of the government then being formed under Oliver Cromwell and the Council of State, and he became Secretary for Foreign Tongues ("Latin Secretary") to the Council until the dissolution of the government in 1659. His total blindness from around the beginning of 1652 as well as family problems curtailed his activities, and others were appointed to assist or, in the case of John Thurloe, to take over the Secretary's expanding duties. From this period, in addition to state papers (primarily documents sent to foreign powers for Cromwell or the Council which he composed in Latin, for the most part on the basis of briefer English versions), he produced three important commissioned works and two additional ones related to

Concluded with the Irish Rebels, and Papists (1649), *Eikonoklastes* (1649), *Pro Populo Anglicano Defensio* (1651), *Pro Populo Anglicano Defensio Secunda* (1654), and *Pro Se Defensio* (1655); a further item is *Joannis Philippi Angli Responsio Ad Apologiam Anonymi* (1652). *Articles of Peace* prints documents concerning James Butler, Earl of Ormond, and his actions with the Irish on behalf of Charles I, and Milton's "Observations" upon these documents (pp. 45–65). This governmental work was printed on 16 May 1649 by Matthew Simmons, who had become the official printer to the Council of State. Errors are very numerous and suggest that an apprentice may have been assigned its composing.

The first edition of *Eikonoklastes* in October or November 1649 was not well printed orthographically according to what should have been Milton's text, and it has two states. Though its legend says it was printed by Simmons, its "non-Miltonic" forms suggest that it was set by an apprentice. This text, rather than the second edition, reappears in all other printings of the work until 1756 when Richard Baron published a new edition with a preface and a few notes. In any case, it was reprinted in 1650 by a different printing house. It is somewhat augmented (the title page says "much enlarg'd"), in two issues, "Printed by *T. N.* and are to be sold by *Tho. Brewster* and *G. Moule*" and then "Printed by *Thomas Newcomb*." There are press variants. The text is greatly improved and shows greater accordance with Milton's spelling practices, probably because Newcomb must have followed the augmented manuscript rather than a copy of the first edition. The text, however, is not thoroughly altered in the direction of Milton's practices. It was translated into French by John Dury in 1652, printed by Dugard and published for Nicholas Bourne. This edition has errata and is in two states.

The "First Defense," as it is called, was published in quarto in three different issues (the last in two states) in 1651 from Dugard's press with an official second edition ("Editio emendatior") in folio also in 1651. Thereafter there were numerous pirated editions (and issues) in Europe in 1651 and 1652, some of which include an index of topics, as well as a Dutch translation in 1651 and an English translation by Joseph Washington in 1692 (see Madan for full description of the numerous editions). These continental editions all falsely purport to be from Dugard's press and show great variations among themselves and within a single edition. (The second issue of Madan 4, probably printed shortly before 15 March 1651 at Utrecht by Theodorus ab Ackersdijck and Gisbertus à Zijll, has a cancel title page with a date that looks like "1650," the 0 being partially erased and reflecting Old Style dating. Early scholarly notices,

because of this, erroneously dated the work a year before it was actually published.) In 1658 a revised edition, in duodecimo, with an important postscript, appeared from the press of Thomas Newcomb. Washington's translation was apparently published in London by Nathaniel Rolls, who is listed on the title page of the second reissue of 1695 (both give the 1692 printing with cancel title pages). Included is a preface by Washington and an advertisement listing books in the controversy over the authorship of *Eikon Basilike* while noting that "The Learned Answer to this Book of Mr. *Milton*, being published in *Latin*, is very well worth Translating, for the benefit of *English* Readers" (p. [247]).

The work had been ordered by the Council of State on 8 January 1650 to answer *Defensio Regia pro Carolo I* (1649) by Claude de Saumaise (a French divine and diplomat known by the Latin form of his name, Salmasius). The two books were also published together by the Dutch printer Adrian Vlacq, who reissued different issues of both works with new title pages and sometimes with an introductory preface. The official English order for printing Milton's tract was given on 23 December 1650; it was registered on 31 December 1650; and it appeared on 24 February 1650/1 (the date on the title page is 1651).

To counter personal charges and criticisms, and because he was now blind in late 1651, Milton's nephew John Phillips produced *Joannis Philip Angli Responsio Ad Apologiam Anonymi cujusdam tenebrionis pro Rege & Populo Angicano infantissimam*, dated 1652 but probably printed in December 1651 by Dugard. There were three counterfeit publications of the work in 1652, actually from Jean Jansson in Amsterdam (two) and Ludovic Elzevier in Leyden. It is generally believed that Milton contributed much to this volume and it is thus affiliated with Milton's canon of prose works. Later in continuing diatribe, Milton wrote *Joannis Miltoni Angli Pro Populo Anglicano Defensio Secunda. Contra infamem libellum anonymum cui titulus, Regii sanguinis clamor ad cœlum adversus parricidas Anglicanos*, printed by Newcomb in 1654, thinking the author was Alexander More rather than Peter Du Moulin. It is an octavo with errata and was followed in the same year by two pirated editions by Vlacq, both duodecimo, the first purporting also to be printed by Newcomb in London and the second, based on that text, from The Hague, with "Præfatio ad Lectorem" by Vlacq. Vlacq then reissued this second piracy and added to it a reissue of More's *Fides Publica*, published separately by him in 1654. The volume includes a foreword by Georgius Crantzius and the retitled "Typographus Pro Se-Ipso" by Vlacq. He again reissued these works together in 1655, without changing the date from 1654 on the title page, and now including the date from 1654 on the title page, and now including More's *Supplementum*, which he had added to a reissue of the separate *Fides Publica* in 1655, but again without changing the date. Bibliographically all these editions and issues are more complicated than even these statements indicate. More's work attempts to reverse Milton's attacks upon him, just as Milton's "Second Defense," particularly with its long biographical section, attempts to reverse Du Moulin's invective. In turn Milton produced *Joannis Miltoni Angli pro se Defensio contra Alexandrum Morum Ecclesiasten* in 1655, an octavo in various states, printed by Newcomb, and again immediately pirated by Vlacq from The Hague in duodecimo. Milton, often wittily, plays upon More's reputed scandalous behavior.

These last two defenses, written of course, after his blindness, were put down first by an amanuensis; the "First Defense" may also have had extensive scribal input, and the additions to the 1658 edition would have been scribal. The editions of the Latin texts in the Columbia Edition of Milton's works (CE), Vols. 7–9, make numerous alterations in the texts and record the numerous differences in the first, second, and last edition of the "First Defense." Again we have evidence of unreliable Latin texts in need of various kinds of correction; e. g., "astringam," B₁ in 1651 becomes "perstringam" in 1658; "perfundere," B₁v (1651), "perfunderet" (1658); "negotio nuper," B₂v (1651), "nuper negotio" (1658); "eam in," p. 204 (1651), "eam si in" (1658).

The second group of tracts that may be considered together as attacks on monarchism or governmental matters are *The Tenure* (1649), *A Treatise of Civil Power in Ecclesiastical Causes: Shewing that it is not lawfull for any power on earth to compell in matters of Religion* (1659), *Considerations Touching the likeliest means to remove Hirelings out of the church* (1659), *The Readie and Easie Way to Establish a Free Commonwealth, and the Excellence therof Compar'd with the inconveniences and dangers of readmitting kingship in this nation* (1660), *Brief Notes Upon a Late Sermon* (1660), *Of True Religion, Hæresie, Schism, Toleration* (1673), and a translation, *A declaration, of Letters Patents* (1674). The first tract, as was noted before, brought Milton to the attention of the new government then being formed in February 1649, the next four items involve attempts to influence the nature of the Restoration of the monarchy with Charles II in 1660, clearly unavoidable by that time, and the two items toward the end of his life concern contemporary governmental issues. *Tenure* was printed by Matthew Simmons by 13 February 1649, having been composed between 15 and 29 January, while Charles I's trial was taking place. This edition, showing both a "Miltonic" and an "un-Miltonic" text, is in two slightly different

states, running forty-two pages. The second edition, which is a fully reset publication by Simmons, is in three issues, with two states of text for the first issue and the second state only in the succeeding two issues. Two editions, three issues, and two states of text, all before 15 February 1650 at the latest, suggest that the work was read and in demand. The second edition used a corrected and supplemented copy of the first edition, with accidentals altered both in the direction of what seem to be Milton's practices and oppositely. Neither the first nor the second edition is, thus, a good and satisfactory text to represent what Milton himself wrote. The second edition, sixty pages in length, has only slight additions (about ten), some changes in wording, and supplementary testimonies and scriptural arguments (just over thirteen pages). During the succession controversy someone altered the first edition to argue for William III's election to kingship in *Pro Populo Adversus Tyranno: Or the Sovereign Right and Power of the People Over Tyrants, Clearly Stated, and Plainly Proved. With some Reflections on the Late Posture of Affairs. By a True Protestant English-man, and Well-Wisher to Posterity* (1689). The publisher was Randal Taylor.

Civil Power was printed in February 1659 by Newcomb, in two states; *Hirelings* appeared in August by "T. N. for L. Chapman," in two states; *Ready and Easy Way* was printed by "T. N." for Livewell Chapman in February/March, and in a second revised and augmented edition with only the legend, "Printed for the Author," in early April; and *Brief Notes* was printed in April in two states with no printer or publisher indicated. *Civil Power* is most concerned with religious matters that a government might impose rather than political ideologies per se, and its promised companion piece, *Hirelings,* is also clearly in opposition to tithing and state remuneration of the clergy (an issue that lies also behind Sonnet 16 to Cromwell in 1652). Part of the first was paraphrased by William Denton as "The Summe of Mr. J. M. His Treatise," pp. 1–3, in *Jus Cæsaris* (1681), and the second was reprinted as *A Supplement to Dr. Du Moulin, Treating of the Likeliest Means to Remove Hirelings out of the Church of England* in 1680, with textual variations. *Civil Power* was written between December 1658 and mid-February 1659, but the assumption that *Hirelings* was written shortly thereafter is probably wrong. Hunter has shown that the date is more likely to be 1652/1653 (see Hunter 1967). The first edition of *Readie and Easy Way* was probably rushed to press in an effort to influence the settlement then under consideration (errata are published in *Mercurius Politicus*, No. 610, 1–8 March 1660, p. 1151) and its second edition is a much more developed argument. The first edition is a quarto in only 18 pages whereas the second is a duode-

Of True Religion is an argument against governmental actions that attempted to curtail religious dissent but that also, it was suspected, opened up acceptance of Roman Catholicism; Milton's aim is to inhibit the "Growth of Popery." Many of the ideas are iterated from *Civil Power*. The translation so late in his life of *Diploma Electionis S. R. M. Poloniæ* (1674) has seemed curious to commentators, but its analogous relationship to the Exclusion controversy places it as argument for elective monarchy (see von Maltzahn). The work announces the election of the Crown General Jan Sobieski as successor to the recently deceased King Michael of Poland. There are a few slightly different printings noted in the few copies of Milton's work that have survived.

Other volumes published during Milton's lifetime include *Accedence Commenc't Grammar* (1669, in two issues with errata), *The History of Britain* (1670), *Artis Logicæ Plenior Institutio* (1672 and 1673, two editions), and *Epistolarum Familiarium Liber Unus* (1674, with Prolusions). These works were written earlier and we may owe their existence to Milton's going through his manuscripts after publication of *Paradise Lost* in 1667, thus including revisions and developments of *Paradise Regain'd* and *Samson Agonistes* (1671), if early dating for either or both poems has any validity, and the three early poems included in the 1673 second edition of the *Poems* (that is, "Apologus de Rustico et Hero," "On the Death of a Fair Infant Dying of a Cough," and "At a Vacation Exercise"). The "Familiar Letters" include almost all now known, others that must have been written having disappeared; and the "Prolusions," according to the publisher Brabazon Aylmer's preface, owe their existence to his desire for something more to fill up a slim volume. The "Liber Unus" may imply a second volume that would have included the Letters of State, not published until 1676 in Holland. Because these were state papers from the Cromwellian government, efforts to have them published ran into difficulties. The six books of *History of Britain* have been variously dated from 1648 through around 1650, the orthography of the text suggesting Milton's original autograph, combined with a scribe's completion, additions, or rewriting. Analysis of the spelling suggests that books I and II were written sometime around 1646–48; book III, middle or late 1648; book IV, late 1648–early 1649; book V in 1650 and book VI sometime later. The printer and publisher of the first edition were J[ohn] M[acock] and James Allestry, and the volume includes the first printing of the portrait by William Faithorne that became the basis for many further versions in the seventeenth century and throughout the eighteenth century. A quarto in 368 pages, it provides errata and an index. A new issue was called for in 1671 because of Allestry's death and the acquisition of rights by Spencer Hickman. There are various states of the text. Publishing rights changed hands a few times, but a new edition did not appear until 1677, an octavo in two different issues, one printed by Macock for John Martyn (416 pp. with corrections of the former errata), the other printed by Macock for Mark Pardoe in 1678. Another edition (although in the past called an issue of the preceding) came in 1695 by R. E. for R[obert] Scot[t], R[ichard] Chiswell, R[ichard] Bently, and G[eorge] Sawbridge, sold by A[bel] Swall and T[imothy] Child. This issue, however, had been registered by Scott on 21 August 1683. A second issue of this third edition also appeared in 1695 but this time for Richard Chiswell and sold by Nathaniel Roles [i.e., Rolls]. Perhaps sales did not warrant publishing in 1683, but Milton's literary prominence because of the 1688 fourth folio edition of *Paradise Lost* may have suggested this new edition and second issue in 1695.

There were also several works published posthumously. Removed from *History of Britain* in 1670 was a section on the Long Parliament in book III, published in 1681 as *Mr John Miltons Character of the Long Parliament, and Assembly of Divines. In MDCXLI. Omitted in his other works, and never before Printed. And very seasonable for these times.* Who caused it to be omitted and why have been subjects of debate with no confirmed conclusions, but certainly the text was as "seasonable" in 1670 as it was in 1681. The work is also found in a separate scribal copy owned by Harvard University, called "The Digression to com in Lib. 3 page 110." Its text is somewhat longer than the printed version, with numerous variations; its spelling is a mixture of what could have derived from Milton's writing and what would not. The discussion concerns the confusion within the Long Parliament during the first four months of 1648; the date 1641 on the title page refers to the beginning of the second Long Parliament called by Charles.

A Brief History of Moscovia was printed by Miles Flesher for Brabazon Aylmer in February (?) 1682. Its dating has been quite various. My own suggestion has been 1642–middle 1644 on the basis of orthography that changes in mid-1644 and Milton's three citations from Samuel Purchas in the CPB, dated 1642–44 (*CPW*, I, 368, 382–83), since *Hakluytus Posthumus or Purchas His Pilgrimes* (1625) was the most important source for Milton's history.

Discovered by Robert Lemon in 1823 and published in Latin and an English translation by Charles R. Sumner in 1825, *De doctrina christiana* has been generally accepted as Milton's, despite some doubt soon after its discovery, until William B. Hunter raised the issue of authorship in 1991 (see Hunter, 1992). A review of the investigation of the question by Gordon Campbell, Thomas N. Corns, John K. Hale, David Holmes, and Fiona Tweedie, has appeared on the World Wide Web and will appear in the October 1997 issue of *Milton Quarterly*. Sumner's translation has been reprinted and employed generally, with some revision in John St. John's edition of the prose in 1853 and the Columbia Edition; John Carey's translation is in *CPW* VI. Neither translation is satisfactory for the specific Latin of the treatise and especially for connotations that it evokes; see my remarks and altered translations of two important sections (Shawcross, 1993, pp. 133–34, 136). Various kinds of analyses have recently been undertaken by a group of scholars, noted before, whose findings lead them to affirm Milton's authorship but with questions concerning it, nonetheless, and further examinations by Hunter seem to continue to leave the question open at this time. The Latin is in the hands of two amanuenses, Daniel Skinner and Jeremy Picard, and with additions and emendations by perhaps five to eight others. The manuscript has 745 numbered pages (pp. 625–35 are numbered twice); Skinner wrote through p. 196, apparently copying Picard's earlier writing, and Picard produced the rest. The suggested date of composition, which probably extended over many years, has been based on circumstantial evidence with little true foundation; at least sections postdate 1657 when Brian Walton's Polyglot Bible (used in the work) was published.

Two additional items must be mentioned here, two collected editions of the prose. The first, *The Works of John Milton. Printed in the Year MDCXCVII*, without printer or publisher noted, includes most of the English prose, giving the second edition of *Tenure* and the first editions of *Eikonoklastes* and *Ready and Easy Way*. The second, *A Complete Collection of the Historical, Political, and Miscellaneous Works of John Milton, Both English and Latin. With som Papers never before Publish'd. In Three Volumes, To which is Prefix'd the Life of the Author*, was supposedly printed in Amsterdam but really in London by John Darby; the Life is by John Toland. This edition prints *History of Britain* in a version allegedly revised and augmented by Milton; gives the first editions of *Tenure* and *Eikonoklastes*, the second edition of *Ready and Easy Way*, the translations of *Defensio prima* by Joseph Washington and the *Letters of State* by Edward Phillips, and two new items ("Letter to a Friend" and "Present Means"), as well as John Phillips's *Responsio*. Only *The Character of the Long Parliament* is omitted.

Notes

[1] The full text of "Lycidas" in the 1638 *Justa Edovardo King Naufrago* is in italics, the word "*Nectar*" is capitalized, and the spelling is "jeat." But the holograph text in the TM reads "nectar" and "jet" (twice). Although changes are made from the earlier printing, the 1645 and 1673 texts repeat the 1638 forms of these two words, retaining italics and a capital letter for the first as if it were a proper noun; in the 1645 printing of the poem proper nouns, including "*Satyrs*" and "*Fauns*" (34), are understandably so treated.

[2] This scribe also entered two citations in the CPB, uncertainly dated; see pp. 197 (Dante), 249 (Nicetas Acominatus). These entries in the CPB suggest that the amanuensis was not a professional scribe and that he may have been a student of Milton's at some time. The manuscript of Book I of *Paradise Lost* does not look like the handwriting of a professional scribe such as we see in the Bridgewater MS of "A Mask."

[3] The major point to be observed about the spelling of this word is that in holograph materials Milton spelled only "thire" 102 times before around 1641 and "thir" fifteen times from around 1641 through around 1651 (after which time he was blind). The single occurrence of "their" is found in Sonnet 15, l. 8, although "thir" appears just above in l. 7. But Milton wrote "her" as examination of the TM will show and some later tampering created "their"; the word "her" points to a quite different meaning for the line (and sonnet) which accords with the political circumstances behind it: "the fals North displaies / her brok'n league, to impe her serpent wings." Reference is to Scotland and its breaking of the Solemn League and Covenant with Parliament, not to the "new rebellions [that] raise / Thir Hydra heads" (see Shawcross 1955). Most modern editions present an erroneous text for this line and thus much commentary has gone astray on the issue at hand.

[4] These include "A Mask," 591, in 1637, 1645, 1673, and the Bridgewater MS, even though Milton wrote "mischeife" very clearly in the TM; "Another on the Same," 21, in its 1640, 1645, 1657, and 1673 printings; "Il Penseroso," 51, in 1645 and 1673; "Fair Infant Elegy," 3, "At a Vacation Exercise," 18, Psalm VII, 57, and Psalm LXXXIII, 11, in 1673; *PR* I, 263; II, 464; III, 123; IV, 440; and *SA*, 66, 457, 554, 754, 1039, 1249, 1452. Books II–XII of *PL* also give the same spelling throughout in both editions with the one significant change of "chiefly," XII, 599 (that is, X, 1490, in 1667) from the first printing of the first edition to "cheifly" in the second

printing of sig. Vv (1669). Does this mean that the compositor resetting those pages picked up the copy-text (manuscript) with a "correct" spelling rather than a copy of the first printing? As noted before and in Falconer's work, the compositor of the resetting of sig. Vv was different from the compositor(s) of the 1667 text.

That Milton did not change his spelling of these words (except for the omission of the final idle "e") appears by the frequency of examples of his practices in one of the last tracts he probably originally penned himself, *Eikonoklastes*.

[5]During Milton's time language was undergoing various changes, including orthography, and various educators engaged in attempts to reform it. There was a move toward consistency and toward simplification, primarily built on pronunciation and ridding words of unessential elements (like idle final "e" as in "darke"). Among those whom Milton may have known and whose works he may have studied were Alexander Gil, *Logomia Anglica* (London, 1621), especially "De Syllaba, Chapter VII; Richard Mulcaster, *The First Part of the Elementarie which entreateth of Right Writing of our English Tung* (1582); and John Hewes, *A Perfect Survey of the English Tongue* (1624). The value of preserving Milton's accidentals lies in the significance of spelling for phonetics, metrics, and etymological puns; of italics for emphasis; of capitalization for emphasis and elevated or special importance; in paragraphing for unifying sections and contrast with preceding or following material.

[6]What happens to such a poem as Sonnet 11 ("I did but prompt the age") is particularly instructive. There is a transcription in Milton's hand in the TM (in the original quire sheets), a copy from an unidentified scribe in the TM (in later quarto sheets), and its printing in 1673. Milton wrote (among others) "thir," l. 1; "clogs," l. 1; "known," l. 2; "ancient," l. 2; "Owls," l. 4; "hindes," l. 5; "Rail'd," l. 6; "bawl," l. 9; "thir," l. 9; "farr," l. 13; "roav," l. 13. All these spellings (including the retention of the "e" in plurals of words ending "-ind") represent Milton's practice after around 1641. The scribe alters these to "theire," "knowne," "Owles," "their," "far," "roave," repeating Milton's "clogs," "ancient," "hindes," "Rail'd," and "bawl." The scribe, in other words, repeats some of Milton's forms, changes some of Milton's forms, and gives no evidence (here and elsewhere) of knowing Milton's preferences. What the copy-text for 1673 was we do not know; the heading by Jeremy Picard in the Trinity MS, "these sonnets follow ye 10. in ye printed booke," however, suggests that if the quarto sheets were not the copy-text at least they were the source of the

copy-text for 1673. In print the scribe's "their" (with idle "e" deleted), "Owles," "their," "far," and "roave" are continued, and Milton's and the scribe's other spellings are changed: "cloggs," "antient," "Hinds," "Raild," and "bawle." The compositor (W. R., perhaps William Rawlins; the publisher was Thomas Dring) also differs from the scribal text with "known" as well as other examples, a pattern in 1673 of deletion of final idle "e" despite "bawle." The spelling practice of the compositor, it seems, appears in "cloggs," "Doggs," "Froggs," "Hoggs," and "antient," the last being demonstrable in other poems as well. The scribe was surely not a pupil of Milton's, nor could he have been given any more instruction than to copy the text (and apparently change "buzzards," 4, to "Cuckoes").

[7]The line changes are: V, 636, 638–39, added, with revisions in ll. 637 and 640; VIII, 1–3, added, with change in l. 4; XI, 485–87, added; XI, 551–52, created from single line 548; XII, 1–5, added.

Works Cited

Aubrey, John. "Minutes for Milton's Life." Bodleian Library. Aubrey MS 8, ff. 63–66, 68–68v.

Bentley, Richard, ed. *Paradise Lost*. London, 1732.

Falconer, Rachel. "Punctuation and the Influence of Compositors in *Paradise Lost*." Bibliography essay for the MLitt., Exeter College, Oxford, 1987.

Fletcher, Harris Francis, ed. *John Milton's Complete Poetical Works Reproduced in Photographic Facsimile*. Urbana: University of Illinois Press, 1943–45. Vol. I, printed and manuscript texts of the shorter poems; Vol. II, *Paradise Lost*, 1667(–69), and MS of Book I; Vol. III, *Paradise Lost*, 1674; Vol. IV, *Paradise Regain'd* and *Samson Agonistes*.

Gilbert, Allan H. *On the Composition of* Paradise Lost. Chapel Hill: University of North Carolina Press, 1947.

Hanford, James Holly. "The Chronology of Milton's Private Studies," *John Milton Poet and Humanist: Essays by James Holly Hanford*, ed. John S. Diekhoff. Cleveland, OH: The Press of Western Reserve University, 1966.

Hughes, Merritt Y., ed. *John Milton: Complete Poems and Major Prose*. New York: Odyssey Press, 1957 (frequently reprinted). (See also *John Milton:* Paradise Regained, The Minor Poems, and Samson Agonistes *Complete and Arranged Chronologically*. New York: Odyssey Press, 1937.)

Hunter, William B., ed. "Considerations Touching the Likeliest Means to Remove Hirelings," in *The Prose of John Milton*, ed. J. Max Patrick. (New York: Anchor Books, Doubleday, 1967).

_____. "The Center of *Paradise Lost*." *English Language Notes* 7 (1969): 32–34.

_____. "The Provenance of the *Christian Doctrine*." *Studies in English Literature* 32 (1992): 129–66.

Justa Edovardo King naufrago [etc.]. (Cambridge: Thomas Buck and Roger Daniel, 1638).

Madan, Francis Falconer. "A Revised Bibliography of Salmasius's *Defensio Regia* and Milton's *Pro Populo Anglicano Defensio*," *The Library*, Fifth Series, 9 (1954): 101–21.

Milton, John. Commonplace Book. British Library. Additional MS 36,354.

_____. *Complete Prose Works*. New Haven: Yale University Press, 1953–82. Eight vols., gen. ed. Don M. Wolfe. (*CPW*)

_____. "De doctrina christiana." Public Record Office, London. SP 9/61.

_____. "Mane citus lectum fuge" (prolusion); "Carmina Elegiaca" ("Surge, age, surge," "Ignavus satrapam dedecet"). Harry Ransom Humanities Center, University of Texas. MS 127.

_____. *Paradise Lost*. London, 1667(–1669).

_____. *Paradise Lost*. London, 1674.

_____. *Paradise Regain'd To which is added Samson Agonistes*. London, 1671.

_____. *Poems of Mr. John Milton*. London, 1645.

_____. *Poems, &c. upon Several Occasions*. London, 1673.

_____. "Proposalls of Certain expedients [etc.]." Columbia University Library. MS X823 M64/S52. [Also includes copies of state papers.]

_____. Trinity MS. Trinity College Library, Cambridge. MS R.3.4.

_____. *The Works of John Milton*, gen. ed. Frank Patterson. Eighteen volumes in twenty-one. New York: Columbia University Press, 1931–38. (CE)

Moyles, R. G. *The Text of* Paradise Lost: *A Study in Editorial Practice*. Toronto: University of Toronto Press, 1978.

Parker, William Riley. "Notes on the Text of *Samson Agonistes* ," pp. 80–90, in *Milton Studies in Honor of Harris Francis Fletcher*. Urbana: University of Illinois Press, 1961.

Phillips, Edward. *Letters of State*. London, 1694.

Shawcross, John T. "Milton's *Fairfax* Sonnet." *Notes & Queries* 200 (1955): 195–96.

_____. "Milton's Spelling: Its Biographical and Critical Implications." Dissertation, New York University, 1958.

_____. "Notes on Milton's Amanuenses." *Journal of English and Germanic Philology* 58 (1959): 29–38.

_____. "Establishment of a Text of Milton's Poems through a Study of *Lycidas*." *Papers of the Bibliographical Society of America* 56 (1962): 317–31.

_____. "What We Can Learn from Milton's Spelling." *Huntington Library Quarterly* 26 (1963): 351–62.

_____. "One Aspect of Milton's Spelling: Idle Final E." *PMLA* 78 (1963): 501–10.

_____. "Orthography and the Text of *Paradise Lost*," pp. 120–53, in *Language and Style in Milton; A Symposium in Honor of the Tercentenary of* Paradise Lost, ed. Ronald David Emma and John T. Shawcross. New York: Frederick Ungar, 1967.

_____. "A Survey of Milton's Prose Works," pp. 291–391, in *Achievements of the Left Hand: Essays on the Prose of John Milton*, ed. Michael Lieb and John T. Shawcross. Amherst: University of Massachusetts Press, 1974.

_____. *Milton: A Bibliography for the Years 1624–1700*. Binghamton, N.Y.: Medieval & Renaissance Texts & Studies, 1984.

_____. *John Milton: The Self and the World*. Lexington: University Press of Kentucky, 1993.

Thompson, Claud A. "'Coded' Signatures: A Printer's Clue to the Bibliographical Tangle of *The Doctrine and Discipline of Divorce* (1644)." *Papers of the Bibliographical Society of America* 68 (1974): 297–305.

_____. "*The Doctrine and Discipline of Divorce*, 1643–1645: A Bibliographical Study." *Transactions of the Cambridge Bibliographical Society* 7 (1977): 74–93.

Treip, Mindele. *Milton's Punctuation and Changing English Usage, 1582–1676*. London: Methuen, 1970.

von Maltzahn, Nicholas. "The Whig Milton," pp. 229–53, in *Milton and Republicanism*, ed. David Armitage, Armand Himy, and Quentin Skinner. Cambridge: Cambridge University Press, 1995.

Comments on Milton's Spelling

Milton's spelling practices in holograph indicate the following:

1. He often used various spellings for the same word or for similar words.

2. He developed a simplification of some spellings around 1639–41 onward, some groups showing change at later times.

3. He was, nonetheless, not always consistent.

4. Amanuenses may reflect his spelling, may reflect an apparent misunderstanding of his practices, may reflect their own spelling, and were often inconsistent.

5. Compositors may reproduce the spelling of their copy-texts (perhaps sometimes in Milton's holograph and sometimes in the writing of an amanuensis), may reproduce their own spelling, may make a variety of errors, and were not consistent.

General Remarks

1. Final redundant -e is usually omitted on uncompounded and uninflected words; includes these and like words: "child," "mind," "chast," "tast," "tomb," "don," "gon," "roav," "aw," "ow," "fals," "com," "som."
    a. "Be" and the pronomials ("he," "me," "she," "we," "ye") are mixed but no example of "hee" in manuscript and few of "bee"; no stressing seen in "she" or "shee."
    b. But "sate," "earle," "signe" and other -ign words, "doe" and "goe," "woe," and (?) "heroe."

2. Final redundant -e is usually omitted on words with suffixes beginning with a vowel; includes "linage," "therin" (etc.), "heerin," and note "comming."

3. Final redundant -e is usually omitted on words with suffixals beginning with a consonant; includes "argument," "falshood," "woful(l)," "houshold," "somthing," "only" (never "onely" in holograph; no principle of stress observed).

4. Usually omission of "e" in inflected words; includes "wolvs," "warrs," "confederats."
    a. Retention of "e" when root word (before ca. 1641) used final "e" occurs and may persist later on. Particularly noticeable are words like "appeares," "almes," "dispaires," although spellings without the "e" also occur regularly.

b. Inflected spellings of words ending "-ay": "-aies" and "-ayes" and "-ays."

5. Preterites and participles depend upon the sound of the ending:
    sonant endings are "-ed" ("aged," "winged")
    "-eed" or "-ied" if sound is e and if ending is in "-ee," "-ie," "-y"
    "-'d" if ending in the sound of b, g (-g, -ge), l (spelled -ll, -wl, -le), l (spelled -l, but also "-d" perhaps in error), m (spelled -m, -m(b), -mn, -me), n (spelled -gn, -ne), n (spelled -n, but also "-d" perhaps in error), ng, r (spelled -re, -rr), r (spelled -r, but also "-d" perhaps in error), th, v, z (spelled -se, -ze), ow, sound of a (as in -ey, -aigh, -eigh), aw, oy, sound of o (as in -ow [follow], -o), oo (as in -oo, -ew, -ue), sound of i (spelled -y, as in "deny'd" but also when spelled -ie or -y it becomes "-i'd" as in "crucifi'd")
    "-aid" for "laid," "paid," "said" (but a few "sed") and the sound of a ending in "-ay" (like "betraid")
    "-'t" for words ending in the sound of k (-ke), p (-pe), s (-ce, -se), with the e deleted ("bak't")
    "-t" for words ending in the sound of f (-f, -gh), k (-k), p (-p), s (-s, -se, -ss) as in "repulst" where Milton would have spelled "repuls" as the root word, but also as in "ceast"—perhaps this is another error of omission, and "addrest" or "blest' with one s omitted; x, sh, ch (-ch, tch)
    Nota Bene: the ending with only -d occurs only with the final sound of l, n, and r, but all of these could be omissions of the apostrophe; there are a number of examples for each, though fewer in each case than with -'d as the ending.

6. Until ca. middle 1644 he spelled "-ck" and after that date "-c."

7. There are frequent elisions shown by apostrophe or by compression, as in "evning" or "beckning" or "adventrous," but sometimes the apostrophe is also used.

8. He used the etymologically correct ligature (as in "hæmony" or "dæmon") but for common words he seems to have shifted to just e (as in "æternal" and then "eternal"); this includes "præ-" except that he appears to persist at times in using the ligature.

9. He is careful about accent marks as in "Chæronéa" and "Ligéas"; note that the accent is NOT needed in "Nereus" since it is a two-syllable name (Ner us) just as "Orpheus" is only two syllables; modern pronunciation is wrong (pronunciation should be Orf us).

10. Words made up of two or more separate word elements were usually written as broken word elements ("mean(e) while," "in stead"), including reflexive pronouns ("our selv[e]s," "her self," but always "himself[e]," "themselv[e]s").

11. Possessives: add s to a noun ending in a consonant other than "ch" or "s" and a noun ending in a silent "e," -ey," or "w"; add es to nouns ending in "ch" and to common one- or two-syllable singular nouns ending in s; and add "'s" to nouns ending in a sounded vowel, including "-y" but excluding "-ay," "-ey," "-oy," and "-w" (confusion with these). Others (like plurals) just remain the same.

12. Biblical (Hebraic) names ending in -ah are sometimes spelled -a (as in "Dina," "Debora") but generally they are spelled as in "Jehovah."

A List of Milton's Probable Spelling Preferences

One form is given when there seems to be clear preference; two forms are given when there is divided practice; an asterisk is appended when one of the two forms seems preferable. Questionable entries are indicated by (?).

again
agast
among
ancient
anough
anow
appear
Artur
asswage [etc.]
atcheiv
atturney (?)
autority
avaritious
battel
battlement
begger
beeing
beleef
beleev
bin [for *been*]
blear
blew [for *blue*]
blood
bowr
brest
brethren
Brittish
buisness [through ca. 1639-41, *buisnesse*; ca. 1641-46, *buisnes*; *buisness* thereafter: applies to all other words ending -less or -ness]
burden
caitif (?)
carroll
cattel
chace
chappel
cheif (etc., that is, other -ie- words)
chere

childern
choak
chois
chuse, choos (?), choose
cipress (?)
citty
clear, cleer
clime (for *climb*)
cloak
cloath(s) (that is, *cloth, clothe, clothes*)
cloud
coap (noun; that is, vestment)
colledge (?)
collegue
comming
compleat
concent
consort
cope (verb)
cord (for *chord*)
counseler (etc.)
*counterfet, counterfeit
countnance
country
covnant
Creet
daigne
dammage
dayly
dear, deer
debaush
democraty
dettors
dore
dread, dred
dum, dumm, dumb
Ebrew
eek
eevn, eev'n
eevning
embassador
endeavor
e're (in poetry)
ere (in prose [?])
extasie
*extreme, extream (?)
eye, eie (?)
fadom
fain (that is, *feign*)
faln
fantasm
fantastic

farder
farding
feavor
fellon
fift
fleam (that is, *phlegm*)
floar
flood
flote
flowr
*forfet, forfeit
forrage
*forren, foren, forrein, forrain
forrest
freind (etc.)
frier
furder
gastly
goverment
gracious
greif, greef
greiv, greev
guift
guild (that is, *gild*)
gulph
hacney (etc.)
hainous
heavn, heav'n
heark
hearken
heer
herb
herd
hight
honour (etc.)
hoord
howr
human
hunderd
iland
ile (that is, *isle*)
ile (that is, *I'll*)
jocond
journy, journey
joyn
joynt
kitchin
knaw
learn, lern
least (that is, both *least* and *lest*)
leasure
leven
lewd

licor
lim, limm, limb
linnen
loose (that is, both *loose* and *lose*)
lowr
lushious
maister
malicious
marchand
mariage
mary
massacher
Mathew
mattin
meer
metafor
mould
murder
neece
neer
noysom
num, numm
oak
offendor (etc.)
orfan
ofspring
only
ordnary
o're
pamflet
*paradise, paradice
pardnable
parlament
Peeter
peice, peece
pennance
perfection (?)
perfet
perswade
perswasion
Pharise
Philistims
pitty
politician
powl (that is, *poll*)
powr (that is, *pour*)
poyson, poison
pretious
prisner
profane
profet
pursivant
quire

*raigne, reigne
receav
rejoyce
releif, releef
releiv, releev
remors
*renown, renoun
revennue
rime
roav
robe
rode (that is, *road*)
*rowl, roul (that is, *roll*)
*rowse, rouse
runnagate
sammon
satyr
scars
schism
scholler
scowr
sease
sensualty
shew
shoar
shoo
showr
silvan
sithe
sixt
slope
smoak
soder
sollicit
solliciter (etc.)
souldier
sours
sovran
sowr
spacious, spatious
sphear
*spread, spred
stear
steddy
stedfast
Steevn
stile
stoln
strain
strait
stroak
sudden
*supreme, supream

surfet
suspicion
sute (?) (that is, *suit*)
suttle
swoln
tapstry
terf
term
theam, theme
theef
then (that is, both *than* and *then*)
thir
thred
throughly
throw(e)s (?) (that is, *throes*)
thum, thumm
tizic
*tollerate, tolerate (?)
tongue
towr
travail
trial, tryal
twelf
twentith
two
unquenshable
ventrous
verdit
vertue
vicount
visard
vitious
voiage
voley (?)
voutsafe
waigh
-wealth
wardrope
*western, westren (etc.)
Wicklef (?)
*widdow, widow (?)
wisard
year, yeer
yeeld, yeild
yoke
young
zelot

JOHN AUBREY
MINUTES OF THE LIFE OF MR. JOHN MILTON

John Aubrey the antiquarian (1626–97) was, like many antiquarians and biographers, a packrat for information. His manuscript notes look at first glance chaotic, with their scribbles, blank spaces to be filled in, marginalia written in sideways, drawings, and queries to himself and to others, to be answered later. Darbishire believes, and I agree, that there was a method behind the chaos, and that Aubrey was one of the new breed among biographers, not a worshiper of saints or the writer of funeral orations but a careful seeker after primary witnesses (xi–xiii). Aubrey allows people who knew Milton well—Edward Phillips, Christopher Milton, and Elizabeth Minshull Milton, to write their own answers to his questions in the blank spaces Aubrey provided them. In his busy way, he usually went back to his witnesses to get the answers. His persistence has provided us with immediate and valuable details about the life of Milton.

By modern standards, Aubrey might be considered superstitious for his dabbling in magic and astrology, but judged by his own time he was a virtuoso, a scrupulous scientist. By any standards, he was a master of the significant detail, as well as being a connoisseur of high-grade gossip.

As the author of a treatise on education (Hunter 14), Aubrey was professionally concerned with what Milton had written. He made several pages of notes after reading *Of Education* (Bodleian MS Aubrey A 10, 147f, as cited by Hunter 54). Aubrey had dealings with Milton's friend Samuel Hartlib and with other members of Hartlib's circle of educational visionaries. Aubrey, who moved in many circles, was also a member of the Society of the Rota, together with Milton's amanuensis and biographer Cyriack Skinner and with the early political scientist James Harrington. His life touched Milton's at many intersections. After Milton's death, he played sleuth for Anthony à Wood, seeking Cambridge graduates with Oxford associations, a category into which Milton fit.

All the tidbits of Aubrey's "Minutes" are invaluable to the biographer of Milton, since they are almost all tested against the memory of people who knew the poet. Anthony à Wood commissioned, then depended on Aubrey's notes (Shawcross 146), adding very little to the information his friend had collected. Even Aubrey's marginal or interlinear interpolations are important for what they reveal, as in "his schoolmaster was a puritan" as an explanation for Milton's short hair as a child, and "whip't him" as an explanation of what "unkindness" Milton met with at the hands of his Cambridge tutor, William Chappell. Aubrey himself knew that his subjects came alive in the details, and he told his friends that people in future generations would thank him, some day, for what he had saved that would otherwise have been lost.

The conscientious scholar should not trust my transcriptions or those of the various editors of Aubrey's Lives. Looking at Aubrey's notes is as much a graphic experience as a literary one, especially because Aubrey was an amateur architectural draftsman, astrologer, and genealogist. He provides one page of coats of arms in a Milton family tree (Darbishire 8), for instance, that I could not reproduce without an image of Aubrey's graphics. Probably the best transcription to date of Aubrey's life of Milton, for its scrupulousness, is that of Darbishire (though Parker prefers the excerpts as quoted in French's *Life Records*—see Parker 669), and I have modeled my own transcription on hers, with constant reference to a photographic facsimile of the original. I have followed her practice of underlining extensive quoted material, as when Edward Phillips writes in his own catalogue of Milton's published works. Because there are no printer's characters for them available to me, I have expanded the figures of "p" with a bar through it to "per" and "m" with a line over it to "mm," representing two standard abbreviations. Aubrey's "qu" normally means, in English, "Ask this question."

TEXT

I have used the text of Helen Darbishire, but with reference to a photostatic copy of Aubrey's notes. My text corrects that of Darbishire in a number of small ways. I realize that my text will be difficult to quote from with all its typographical peculiarities, but to preserve Aubrey's notes with some of their peculiarities intact, I think, is better than to try to smooth the text for easy reading.

Works Cited

Aubrey, John. *Aubrey's Brief Lives*. Ed. Oliver Lawson Dick. First publ. Secker and Warburg, 1949. Ann Arbor: U of Michigan P, 1992.

------. *Brief Lives*. Ed. Richard Barber. Totowa, NJ: Barnes & Noble, 1982.

Darbishire, Helen, ed. *The Early Lives of Milton*. New York: Barnes & Noble, 1965.

Hunter, Michael. *John Aubrey and the Realm of Learning*. New York: Science History Publications, 1975.

Shawcross, John T. *John Milton: The Self and the World*. Lexington, KY: UP of Kentucky, 1993.

[Minutes of the Life of Mr John Milton]

His mother was a Bradshaw.   Q.Xpr.Milton
Crest an Arme dexter   [his brother the
holding an Eagles   Inner Temple]
head & Neck erased G.   Bencher.
                       ~~Barrister.~~

Mr John Milton
was of an Oxfordshire familie his Grandfather.......
                        neer Shotover
[a Rom: Cath:] of Holton in Oxfordshire ~~neer Whately.~~
                  at Christchurch
His father was brought-up in ye Univ^ty of Oxon: · and

his gr.father disinherited him because he kept not the
    Q. he found a Bible in English in his chamber
Catholique Religion so ~~that~~ therupon he came to
London, and became a Scrivener [brought up by a
friend of his, was not an Apprentice] and gott a plentiful
estate by it & left it off many yeares before he dyed. He
was an ingeniouse man, delighted in Musiq. composed
many Songs now in print especially that of Oriana. his
son Jo: was borne in Bread street in
        Spread Eagle
London at ye ~~Rose,~~ wch was his house, he had also
in y^t street   the Rose and other houses in other places
~~there~~ another house.

   He was borne A° D^m......the...day of...about.....a clock
in the ......
          old Mr
He went to schoole to ~~Dr~~ Gill at Paules schoole; went
                          at
to Christs College in Cambr: ~~very young~~ [Sc. About
fifteen   at
                       least
~~thirteen was the most~~ where he stayed eight yeares: then
he travelled into Franc & Italie. At Geneva he
contracted a great friendship with ~~Carolo Diodati,~~...
    Had Sr H. Wotton's commendatory lrs
~~son of~~ the learned Dr Diodati of Geneva   [vide his
                      who delighted
Poems.] He was acquainted beyond sea with Sr Henry
in his company
Wotton Ambassador at Venice. He was severall
Q. how many. Resp. Two yeares.   just upon
yeares beyond sea, & returned to England ~~a...little~~
the breaking out of the   stet.
~~before the~~ Civill warres ~~brake out~~. He was ~~Latin~~
     the parliament
Secretary to ~~Oliver Cromwell.~~

      D^m   his schoolmaster was
                 a puritan in

A° ~~aetatis~~ 1619, he was ten yeares old, as by his
                Essex, who cutt his haire short
picture: & was then a Poet.
 ❧she went from him to her Mother at...ye Kings quarters neer Oxford
~~He parted from her~~ A° D^m...and wrote the triple chord, about Divorce
He married his first wife........Powell of ....Fosthill
without her husband's consent
She went · to her mother in the Kings quarters. Shee died A° D^m...
in Oxonshire A° D^m.........by whom he had 4 children:
hath two daughters living: Deborah was his Amanuensis, he taught her Latin, & to read Greeke ~~and~~
     Q
~~Hebrew~~ to him, when he had lost his eiesight, wch was
A° D^m....

☞Resp. of middle stature
    Q. quot feet I am high.   abroun
He was scarce so tall as I am. he had light browne
           exceeding   his eye a dark gray
hayre, his complex^n very faire*.   ovall face. His
           very well & like
widowe has his picture drawne · when a Cambridge
schollar [*he was so faire y^t they called him the Lady
of X^ts coll:]   She has his picture when a Cambridge
schollar, wch ought to be engraven: for the Pictures
before his bookes are not *at all* like him.
         Mris Eliz: Minshull
   He mar^d his 2^d wife A°......ye yeare before the
a gent. Person a peacefull & agreable humour.
Sicknesse.
    After he was blind he wrote these following Bookes
viz.
    Paradise lost
    Paradise regained
    Grammar
    Dictionarie—imperfect Q+
he was a Spare man

~~He married Eliz. 2^d wife A° D^m 16...~~
   different Rell:
 ❧Two opinions doe not well on the same Boulster.
                      the K's
She was a...........Royalist, & went to hr mother near
Quarters
Oxford. I have so much charity for her y^t she might
not wrong his bed but what man (especially contem-
                      & stormd
plative) w^d like to have a young wife environ'd· by the
sons of Mars[1] and those of the enemi partie.

    He lived in several places. e.g. Holbourn neer K's

---

[1] Aubrey, something of an astrologer, used the sign of the planet Mars
here instead of the name.

gate.

He died in Bunhill opposite to the Artillery garden-wall.

did dwell

His harmonicall, and ingeniouse soul dwelt in a beautiful & well proportioned body—In toto nusquam corpore menda fuit. Ovid.[2]

a very good

He had an ~~extraordinary~~ memory: but I believe y[t] his excellent method of thinking & disposing did much to helpe his memorie.

I heard that after he was blind, that he was writing
in the hand of Moyses Pitt
a Latin Dictionary. Vidua Affirmat she gave all his
among w[ch] this Dict. imperfect
papers · to his Nephew, that he brought up, a sister's
son:.......Philips, who lives neer the Maypole in

Q

the Strand. She has a great many letters by her from learned men his acquaintance, both of England & beyond sea.

about

His eiesight was decaying 20 yeares before his death.
starke
Q. when quite Blind. His father read w[th]out spectacles at 84. His mother had very weake eies, & used spectacles presently after she was thirty yeares old.

Of a very cheerfull humour.

Seldome tooke any Physique, only sometimes he tooke Manna

He was very healthy, & free from all diseases, and only towards his later end he was visited wth the Gowte spring & Fall: he would be chearfull even in his Gowte-fitts; & sing.

y[e] gow[t] struck in

He died of ~~a feaver at his house in Juinn street~~
the 9th or 10th of Novemb. 1674 as appeares by his Apothecaryes Booke.
~~about the 64th yeare of his age~~

upper end of

He lies buried in S[t] Giles Cripplegate · chancell at the right hand ~~v. his stone~~. mdm[3] his stone is now removed; ~~for~~ about 2 yeares since [now 1681] the steppes to the communion table were raysed. I ghesse Jo: Speed & He lie together.

Q. his nephew M[r] Edw. Philips for a perfect

Catalogue of his writings. mdm. He wrote a little Tract. of *Education*.

Mdm M[r] Theodore Haak R.S.S. hath translated halfe his Paradise lost into High Dutch in such blank verse, wch is very well liked of by Germanus Fabricius Professor at Heidelberg, who sent to Mr Haak a letter upon this Translation—Incredible est quantum nos omnes effecerit gravitas styli, & copia lectissimorum verborum et........v. the letter.

Sc: at 4 a clock manè

He was an early riser. yea, after he had lost his sight. He had a man read to him: the first thing he read was the Hebrew bible, & y[t] was at 4[h] manè-4/2[h]+. then

contemplated

he ~~thought~~. At 7 his man came to him again & then

and wrote

read to him · till dinner: the writing was as much a

2 Maried in Dublin to one

as the reading. His da: Deborah could read to

sells silke etc

Mr. Clarke [a mercer] very like her father.
him Latin: Ital. & French & Greeke. The other

1

sister is Mary, more like hr mother. After dinner he

at a time

used to walke 3 or 4 houres · he always had a Garden where he lived: went to bed about 9. Temperate ~~man,~~ rarely dranke between meales. Extreme pleasant in his conversation, & at dinner, supper &c: but Satyricall. He pronounced y[e] letter R very hard†[4]

†a certaine signe of a Satyricall Witt fr. Jo: Dreyden[5]

good

He had a delicate tuneable Voice & had ~~great~~ skill: his father instructed him: he had an Organ in his house: he played on that most. His exercise was chiefly walking.

by learned

He was visited much: more then he did desire.

He was mightily importuned to goe into Fr. & Italie [foreigners came much to see him] and much admired him, & offered to him great perferments. to come over to them, & the only inducement of severall foreigners that came over into England, was chiefly to see O. Protector & Mr. J. Milton, & would see the house & chamber wher he was borne: he was much more admired abrode then at home.

---

[2] Edward Le Comte, *Milton Re-Viewed* (New York: Garland, 1991) points to the irony of Aubrey using Ovid's description of Corinna's perfect body to apply to Milton's (52, 65n.8).
[3] The abbreviation stands for "memorandum." In the MS it is written with a line through the stem of the "d."

[4] In the left margin, on a vertical axis, is "Littera canina," describing the letter R as being the "letter of the dog."
[5] Written on the next leaf, with the † sign to guide the reader.

His familiar learned Acquaintance were

Mr. Andrew Marvell, Mr. Skinner, Dr. Padgett M.D.
Mr.........Skinner, who was his disciple.
Jo: Dreyden Esq. Poet Laureate, who very much
admires him, & went to him to have leave to putt
his Paradise-lost into a Drama in Rhyme: Mr.
Milton received him civilly, & told him he would
give him leave to tagge his Verses.

His widowe assures me that Mr. Hobbs was not one
of his acquaintance: yᵗ her husband did not like him at
                                    grant
all: but he would acknowledge him to be a man of
great parts, a learned man. Their Interests & tenets
                        did run counter to each other
were diametrically opposed. v. Mr. Hobbes Behemoth.

Catalogˢ Librorum.
        twice printed. Some writt but at 18.
1. Poems 8º printed at.......
                        Of Reformacõn
2. Ειχονοκλασης printed at........

3. Pro. Pop. Ang. Defensio contra Salmasium.

4. Tetrachrodon: 4ᵗᵒ of Divorce.

5. Paradise lost 4to.   chief
6.   regaind 4to. Edw. Philips his Aman-
uensis⁵
7. Latin Epistles. 8vo. Familiar
              Politique

8. Latin Grammar in English. 8º.

9. The History of Britian from yᵉ first tradiconall
      beginning, continued to the Norman Conquest.
      4ᵗᵒ Lõdon. MDCLXX. FOR James Alestry.
      Rose & Crowne P's ch-yard. Scripsit prout per
      effigiem [sed falsam] 1670. aetate 62.

10. A Letter, of Education to Mʳ S. Hartlib. [wᵗʰ
      his Poëms]
11. A Brief History of Muscovia: and other less
                              Advertisement
      known Countries lyeing Eastward. writt by
      the Author's owne hand before he lost his Sight:
      and intended to have printed it before his death.

12. His Logick. 13.⁶ Idea Theologiae in MS. In yᵉ
      a merchant's sonne
      hands of Mʳ Skinner · in Marke Lane. Mdm,
      there was one Mʳ Skinner of yᵉ Jerkers office
      up a paire of staires at the Custome-house. Q.

From his Bro: Chr. Milton.
      When he went to Schoole, when he was very
young he studied very hard and sate-up very late,
commonly till 12 or one aclock at night, & his father
ordered yᵉ mayde to sitt-up for him, and in those
[10]
yeares composed many Copies of verses, wᶜʰ might well
become a riper age. And was a very hard student in the
University, & performed all his exercises there wᵗʰ very
good applause. His 1ˢᵗ Tutor there was Mʳ Chappell,
                              whip't him
from whom receiving some unkindnesse, he was afterwards (though it seemed opposed to⁷ yᵉ Rules of yᵉ Coll:) transferred to the Tuition of one Mʳ Tovell, who dyed
Parson of Lutterworth.
      I have been told, that the Father composed a Song
of fourscore parts, for the Lantgrave of Hess, for wᶜʰ
      or a noble present   about 1647
Highnesse sent a medall of Gold. He dyed ~~in that
yeare that the Army marched thorough the City~~ buried
in Cripple-gate-ch: from his house in the Barbican.

☞ Q. Mr. Chr. Milton to see the date of his
      Bro: Birth.
qr whither   1. Of Reformation⁸
2 books.   2. The reason of church
                              government.
        3. A defence of Smectymnuus.
All these in   4. The Doctrin & disciplin
of divorce.
prosecution 5. Colasterion.
of yᵉ same   6. The Judgement of
Martin Bucer.
subject   7. Tetrachordon [of
Divorce].
        8. Areopagitica, viz. for yᵉ libertie of ye
          Presse.
          Of Education

---

⁵ Darbishire believes that Edward Phillips wrote in the information
about himself, all that is underlined.

⁶ The entry "14." is in the left margin: "He wrote a Dictionary called
Idioma Linguae Latinae, from Mʳ Packer who was his Scholar."
⁷ Aubrey uses the sign for "opposed to."
⁸ Darbishire believes this list to be in Edward Phillips's hand, with
marginal "All these in prosecution of yᵉ same subject," and the
interlinear "[of Divorce]" and "His Logick" written in Aubrey's hand.

Iconoclastes
Tenure of Kings & Magistrates.
Defensio populi anglicani
                                   His Logick
Defensio 2ᵈ contra Morum
Defensio 3ᵗⁱᵃ
Of yᵉ power of yᵉ civil Magistrate in
Ecclesiastical affairs
Against Hirelings [against Tithes]
Of a Commonwealth
Against Dʳ Griffith
Of Toleration Heresie & Schisme

He went to travell about yᵉ year 1638 & was abroad
about a years space cheifly in Italy   immediately after
his return he took a lodging at Mʳ Russell's a Taylour
in Sᵗ Brides churchyard & took into his tuition his
sisters two sons Edw: & John Philips yᵉ first 10 the
other 9 years of age & in a years time made them capable
of interpreting a Latin authour at sight & within 3
years they went through yᵉ best of Latin & Greec
& wᵗʰ him the use of the Globes*⁹
Poets Lucretius & Manilius of yᵉ Latins; Hesiod,
                                   Apollonii Argonautica
Aratus, Dionysus Afer, Oppian...................................&
Quintus Calaber. Cato, Varro, & Columella de Re
rusticâ were the very first Authors they learn't.

As he was severe on one hand, so he was most familiar
and free in his conversation to those to whome most
severe in his way of education—NB. He made his
Nephews Songsters, and sing from the time they were
with him.

John Milton was born the 9ᵗʰ of December 1608 die
veneris half an howr after 6 in the morning.¹⁰

Why do ye not set downe where Joh. Milton was
borne?¹¹

from Mr E. Philips.
†His Invention was much more free and easie in the
Æquinoxes than at the Solstices; as he more particularly
found in writing his Paradise lost. Mʳ
                                   then
Edw. Philip his, [his Nephew and Amanuensis] hath†¹²
All the time of writing his Paradise lost, his veine began
at the Autumnall Æquinoctiall and ceased at the

Vernall or thereabouts (I believe about May) and this
was 4 or 5 yeares of his doeing it. He began about 2
yeares before the K. came-in, and finished about 3 yeares
after the K's Restauracōn.

Q. Mr J. Playford per Wilby's sett of Oriana's.
             4ᵗʰ
In the 2ᵈ or 3ᵈ . Booke of Paradise lost, there are about
6 verses of Satan's exclamation to the Sun, wᶜʰ Mʳ E. Ph.
Remembers, about 15 or 16 yeares before ever his Poëm
was thought of,   wᶜʰ verses were intended for the
Beginning of a Tragoedie wᶜʰ he had designed, but was
diverted from it by other businesse.

Whatever he wrote against Monarchie was out of no
           or out of any faction, or Interest
animosity to the King's person, but out of a pure zeall
to the Liberty Mankind, wᶜʰ he thought would be
greater under a free state than under a Monarchall
goverment. His being so conversant in Livy and the
Rom: authors and the greatnes he saw donne by the
Rom: commonwealth & the virtue of their great
           Captaines
Commanders induc't him to.
           a Royalist
His first wife (Mrs Powell) was brought up & lived
                                   dancing &c
where there was a great deale of company & merriment,
and when she came to live wᵗʰ her husband at Mʳ
Russells in St. Brides ch: yd, she found it very solitary:
no company came to her, often-times heard his
           2   1
Nephews cry, and beaten. This life was irkesome to her;
& so she went to her Parents at Fosthill: he sent for her
(after some time) and I think his servant was evilly
entreated, but as for matter of wronging his bed, I never
heard the least suspicion: nor had he of that, any
Jealousie.

from Mʳ Abr. Hill.
mdm his sharp writing against Alexander More of
Holland upon a mistake notwithstanding he had given
him by the Ambassador all satisfaction to the contrary,
☙ viz that

☞ Q, the Ambassadors name of Mʳ Hill
           Resp. Newport yᵉ Dutch Ambassador
Q. Mʳ Allan of Edm: hall Oxon. of Mʳ J. Milton's
life writt by himselfe v. pagg.

☙viz. that the booke [called Clamor Cœli] was writt
by Peter du Moulin. well that was all one, when he had
he having writt it, it should goe into the world. one of
them was as bad as the other.

---

⁹ Aubrey's marginal note reads "*and some Rudiments of Arithm: &
Geom:"
¹⁰ Darbishire identifies the writer of this sentence as the widow
Elizabeth Minshull Milton.
¹¹ Darbishire identifies the writer of this sentence as Anthony à Wood.
¹² The section between the two † marks was crossed out.

his sight began to faile him at first, upon his writing against Salmasius, and before 'twas fully compleated one eie absolutely failed; upon the writing of other books after that his other eie decayed.

write his name in red letters on his Pictures, wth his widowe, to preserve.

ANONYMOUS LIFE OF MILTON
CYRIACK SKINNER ?

This account is written later than Aubrey's minutes and, together with Aubrey's notes, is the basis for Wood's biography. As much as Wood the Royalist defames Milton's character for his taking part in supporting regicide, the Anonymous Biographer defends Milton for being altruistic, civic-minded, and generous. One can illustrate Wood's politics by noting how he borrowed the Anonymous Biographer's description of Milton's personality as "affable," but significantly left out the adjective "sweet" (Darbishire xv).

The Anonymous Life is the Bodleian Wood MS. D. 4. I have transcribed it from Darbishire, comparing Parsons's transcription with those of Darbishire and Hughes, and with a copy of the original manuscript. Sadly, neither Darbishire nor Parsons is to be trusted in the attribution of the authorship to John Phillips or Nathaniel Paget, respectively, though John Phillips might still have a few advocates.

Shawcross calls this "a brief, anonymous life (probably by his former student, amanuensis, and friend Cyriack Skinner)" (17). Since it is derived in large part from Milton's autobiographical writings in the Latin defenses, and since it complements what Aubrey and Edward Phillips wrote, it should be compared closely with all the other early lives, in order for the reader to pick out what in it is independent of other sources. Much of it does seem to be based on firsthand observation, as with the descriptions of Milton's physical appearance, his habits of poetic composition, and his death.

Though the author is self-effacing and does not sign his own manuscript, what he wrote has authority. If he was indeed Skinner, we know from Milton's sonnets that he valued Cyriack as a serious and learned young man. This Cyriack Skinner (1627-1700; he should be distinguished from the Daniel Skinner [b. 1651?] who also served Milton as an amanuensis) had been trained as a lawyer in Lincoln's Inn (Parker 312). After May 1654 he lived near Milton in Petty France, Westminster, and he may have brought Milton together with Marvell

(Parker 426, 452, 1044). Skinner was a member of James Harrington's Society of the Rota, a group of serious intellectuals (including John Aubrey) who met in 1659 at Miles's coffee house to discuss such things as the proper division of political power amongst legislative bodies (Parker 537). Milton entrusted Cyriack Skinner with care of his excise bonds, perhaps because Skinner was a lawyer, in the dark days of 1660 (Parker 562).

As compared with the careless and flamboyant writer Edward Phillips, Skinner seems conservative in his handling of facts and cautious in interpreting them. He avoids Phillips's gross errors in dating. His account lacks Phillips's color but seems honest and accurate. Frankly, Skinner seems more subtle, intelligent, and perceptive than Phillips, and he is certainly more scrupulous about getting his facts straight. Samuel Hartlib described Skinner as "a traveller and a most accomplished gentleman and universal scholar for mathematics Greek Latin French etcetera not far dwelling from Mr Milton and mighty studious" (quoted in Campbell, *Chronology*, 1656). Skinner knows much about the circumstances of Milton's pamphlet wars with Salmasius and Alexander More, as if he were a witness of composition and publication. He does not mention that he served Milton as an amanuensis, but he knows much of what happened in the Milton household from about 1642, when Skinner was twelve. Edward Phillips's biography is excellent on Milton's houses; Skinner has a similar aptitude for discussing Milton's finances.

Matching the biography's demonstration of inside knowledge of Milton's financial and legal affairs, especially at the Restoration, with Skinner's known whereabouts and interests might present convincing evidence that Skinner is indeed the author. News of the £200 in excise bonds that Milton lost in 1660 might also help us identify Cyriack as his financial representative.

Skinner's writing is sophisticated, judicious, careful; his sentences are all of measured length, and they possess gravity and substance; he is theologically adept and subtle, though Parker does not think him a theologian (882); and he is as cautious as a lawyer in court about how he defines terms.

Parker very usefully summarizes the possible connections between Milton and Skinner (881–82). Skinner does get some few facts wrong, understandably, in the biography, but he adds details, such as Milton's burial of his father in St. Giles Cripplegate, that show his close personal association with the poet. Parker theorizes that Skinner may well have become Milton's pupil in 1640. If that is true, Skinner knew Milton as a member of his household, then as an intimate friend, from 1640 through the Restoration in 1660.

Works Cited

Benham, Allen R. "The So-Called Anonymous or Earliest Life of Milton." *ELH* 6 (1939): 245–55.

Darbishire, Helen. *The Early Lives of Milton*. London: Constable, 1962. Repr. 1966. Repr. New York: Barnes & Noble, 1965.

Parsons, Edward. "Concerning 'The Earliest Life of Milton.'" *ELH* 9 (1942): 106–15. Reply by Benham in ELH 9 (1942): 116–17.

–––––––. "The Earliest Life of Milton," *The English Historical Review* 17 (1902): 95–110. Repr. *Colorado College Studies*, 1903.

Pask, Kevin. *The Emergence of the English Author: Scripting the Life of the Poet in Early Modern England*. Cambridge: Cambridge UP, 1996.

Shawcross, John T. *John Milton: The Self and the World*. Lexington: UP of Kentucky, 1993.

The Life of Mr John Milton

To write the Lives of Single Persons is then a commendable Undertaking, when by it some Moral benefit is design'd to Mankind. Hee who has that in aim, will not imploy his time or Pen, to record the history of bad men, how successful or great soever they may have bin; unless by relating thir Tragical ends (which, through the just Judgment of the Almighty, most commonly overtakes them) or by discriminating, with a due note of Infamy, whatever is criminal in thir actions, hee warn the Reader to flee thir example.

But to celebrate, whether the Guifts or Graces, the natural Endowments, or acquir'd laudable Habitts of Persons eminent in thir Generations, while it gives glory to God, the bestower of all good things, and (by furnishing a Modell) tends to the edification of our Brethren, is little less than the duty of every Christian: Which seems acknowledg'd by the late Supervisors of our Common Prayer; when they added to the Collect for the Church militant, a Clause commemorating the Saints and Servants of God departed this life in his Fear.

That Hee who is the subject of this discourse, made it his endeavor to bee thought worthy of that high Character, will, I make no doubt, appear to the impartial Reader from the particulars, wch I shall with all sincerity relate of his life and Works.

The learned Mr John Milton, born about the year sixteen hundred and eight, is said to bee descended from an antient Knightly Family in Buckinghamshire, that gave name to the chief place of thir abode. However that bee, his Father was entitled to a true Nobility in the Apostle Pauls Heraldry; having bin disinherited about ye beginning of Queen Elizabeths reign by his Father a Romanist, who had an estate of five hundred pound a yeer at Stainton St. John in Oxfordshire, for

reading the Bible.[1] Upon this occasion he came yong to London, and beeing taken care of by a relation of his a Scrivener, he became free of that profession;[2] and was so prosperous in it, and the Consortship of a prudent virtuous Wife, as to bee able to breed up in a liberal manner, and provide a competency[3] for two Sons, and a Daughter: After which, out of a moderation not usual with such as have tasted the sweets of gain, and perhaps naturally inclin'd rather to a retir'd life by his addiction to Music (for his skill in which hee stands registred among the Composers of his time) he gave over his trade, and went to live in the Country.

Thus his eldest Son had his institution to learning both under public, and private Master; under whom, through the pregnancy of his Parts,[4] & his indefatigable industry (sitting up constantly at his Study till midnight) hee profited exceedingly; and early in that time wrote several grave and religious Poems, and paraphras'd some of Davids Psalms.

At about eighteen yeers of age[5] hee went to Christs College in Cambridge; where for his diligent study, his performance of public exercises, and for choice Verses, written on the occasions usually solemniz'd by the Universities, as well for his virtuous and sober life, hee was in high esteem wth the best of his time.

After taking his degree of Master of Arts hee left the University, and, having no design to take upon him any of the particular learned Professions, apply'd himselfe for five yeers, at his Fathers house in the Country, to the diligent reading of the best Classic Authors, both Divine & Humane;[6] sometimes repairing to London, from wch hee was not farr distant, for learning Music and the Mathematics.

Beeing now become Master of what useful knowledge was to bee had in Books, and competently skill'd amongst others, in the Italian language, hee made choice of that Country to travel into; in order to polish his Conversation, & learn to know Men. And having receiv'd instructions how to demean[7] himselfe with that wise observing Nation, as well as how to shape his Journy, from Sr Henry Wotton, whose esteem of him

---

[1] Compare Aubrey's note "Quaere—he found a Bible in English, in his chamber."
[2] He was freed of his apprenticeship. Aubrey wrote "brought up by a friend of his; was not an apprentice."
[3] An estate competent to live from; an adequate living.
[4] The readiness of his natural abilities.
[5] Actually, Milton matriculated at Christ's College on February 12, 1625, at the age of 16.
[6] Most probably the "divine" authors would be the Christian Church Fathers, and the "humane" authors would be secular authors writing before and after the beginning of the Christian era.
[7] Employ, concern.

appeers in an elegant letter to him upon that Subject, he took his way[8] through France. In this Kingdom,[9] the manners & Genius of which hee had no admiration, hee made small stay, nor contracted any Acquaintance; save that, with the recommendation of Lord Scudamore,[10] our Kings Ambassador at Paris, hee waited on Hugo Grotius, who was there under that Character[11] from the Crown of Sweden.

Hasting to Italy by way of Nice, & passing through Genua Lighorn[12] & Pisa hee arriv'd at Florence. Here hee liv'd[13] two months in familiar & elegant conversation with the choice Witts of that Citty and was admitted by them to their private Academies; an Oeconomy[14] much practis'd among the Virtuosi of those parts, for the communication of Polite literature, as well as for the cementing of friendships. The reputation hee had with them they express'd in several Commendatory Verses, wch are extant in his book of Poems.

From Florence hee went to Rome, where, as in all places, hee spent his time in the choicest company; and amongst others there, in that of Lucas Holstein.[15]

At Naples, which was his next remove, hee became acquainted wth Marquis Manso, a learned Person, and so aged as to have bin Contemporary and intimate wth Torquato Tasso, the famous Italian Heroic.[16] This Nobleman oblig'd him by very particular civilities, accompanying him to see the rarities of the place, and paying him Visitts at his lodging; Also sent him the testimony of a great esteem in this Distich

Ut Mens, forma Decor Tacies, Mos, si Pietas sic,
Non Anglus, verum herclé Angelus ipse fores.[17]

Yet excus'd himselfe at parting for not having bin able to do him more honour, by reason of his resolute owning his Religion:[18] This hee did whensoever by any ones enquiry occasion was offred; not otherwise forward[19] to enter upon discourse of that Nature. Nor did hee decline its defense in the like circumstances even in

Rome it self on his return thether; though hee had bin advis'd by letters from som friends to Naples, that the English Jesuits design'd to do him mischief on that account. Before his leaving Naples hee return'd the Marquis an[20] acknowledgement of his great favors in an elegant Copy of Verses entitl'd Mansus wch is extant amongst his other latin Poems.[21]

From Rome hee revisited Florence for the sake of his charming friends there; and then proceeded to Venice where he shipp'd what books he had bought[22] & through the delicious[23] country of Lombardy, and over the Alps to Geneva, where he liv'd in familiar conversation with the famous Diodati.[24] Thence through France hee returnd home, having, with no ill management of his time, spent about fifteen moneths abroad.

Hee had by this time laid in a large stock of knowlege, which as he design'd not for the purchase of Wealth, so neither intended hee[25] it, as a Misers hoard, to ly useless: Having therefore[26] taken a house, to bee[27] at full ease and quiet, and gotten his books about him, hee sett himselfe upon Compositions, tending either to the public benefit of Mankind, and especially his Countrymen, or to the advancement of the Commonwealth of Learning. And his first labours were very happily dedicated to, what had the chiefest place in his affections, and had bin no small part of his Study, the service of Religion.

It was now the Year 1640: And the Nation was much divided upon the Controversies about Church Government, between the Prelatical party, and the Dissenters, or, as they were commonly then calld, Puritans. He had study'd Religion in the Bible and the best Authors, had strictly liv'd up to it's Rules, and had no temporal concern depending upon any Hierarchy, to render him suspected, either to himselfe, or others, as one that writt for Interest;[28] and therefore[29] with great boldness, & Zeal offer'd his Judgment, first in two *Books of Reformation*[30] by way of address to a friend, And then

---

[8] The word "Journy" was replaced by "way."
[9] The words "wch," and "hee made no stay, having" were crossed out after "Kingdom."
[10] The words "he waited" were deleted here.
[11] Official position (that of ambassador).
[12] Genoa (Genova) and Leghorn (Livorno).
[13] The word "pass'd" was replaced by "liv'd."
[14] Set of rules, procedure.
[15] After the name but deleted is "Library Keeper at the Vatican." A letter above leads to the margin, where "For I am not certain that he was the library keeper." is also crossed out.
[16] Probably "heroic poet."
[17] For a translation, see below, p. 175.
[18] "Acknowledging his Protestantism."
[19] Inclined, disposed.

[20] The words "a large" were replaced by "an."
[21] Skinner had first written "an elegant Poem wch is amongst his other latin Verses."
[22] The phrase "where...bought" was inserted above the line.
[23] The word "pleasant" was replaced by "delicious."
[24] Giovanni or Jean Diodati (1576–1649), uncle of Milton's friend Charles, well-known Protestant theologian, professor, and Bible scholar.
[25] The word "that" after "hee" was deleted.
[26] The phrase "gotten his books about him" was deleted.
[27] The word "full" was deleted.
[28] In other words, the Milton family was well-off and John Jr. did not need to establish himself as part of the church hierarchy; he was not professionally beholden to any establishment and therefore he could think independently.
[29] The word "thence" was deleted and replaced by "therefore."
[30] The phrase "and then" was deleted.

in answer to a Bishop hee writt of *Prelatical Episcopacy* and *The Reason of Church Governm'*. After that [30] *Animadversions upon the Remonstrants defence* (the work of Bishop Hall) *against Smectymnyus* and *Apology for those Animadversions.*

In this while, his manner of Settlement[31] fitting him for the reception of a Wife, hee in a moneths time (according to his practice of not wasting that precious Talent)[32] courted, marryed, and brought home from Forresthall[33] near Oxford a Daughter of Mr Powell. But shee, that was very Young, & had bin bred in a family of plenty and freedom, being not well pleas'd with his reserv'd manner of life, within a few days left him, and went back[34] into the Country with her Mother: Nor though hee sent severall pressing invitations could hee prevayl wth her to return, till about foure yeers after, when Oxford was surrendr'd (the nighness of her Fathers house to that Garrison having for the most part of the meantime hindred any communication between them) shee of her own accord came, & submitted to him; pleading that her Mother had bin the inciter of her to that frowardness. Hee in this Interval,[35] who had entred into that State for the end design'd by God & Nature, and was then in the full vigor of his Manhood, could ill bear the disappointment hee mett with by her obstinate absenting: And therefore thought upon a Divorce, that hee might be free to marry another; concerning which hee also was in treaty. The lawfulness and expedience of this, duly regulat in order to all those purposes, for which Marriage was at first instituted; had upon full consideration& reading good Authors bin formerly his opinion: And the neccessity of justifying himselfe now concurring with the opportunity, acceptable to him, of instructing others in a point of so great concern[36] to the peace and preservation of Families; and so likely to prevent temptations as well as mischiefs,[37] hee first writt *The Doctrine and Discipline of Divorce,* then *Colasterion,* and after *Tetrachordon:* In these[38] hee taught the right use and design of Marriage; then the Original & practise of Divorces amongst the

Jews, and show'd[39] that our Savior, in those foure places of the Evangelists, meant not the abrogating but rectifying the abuses of it;[40] rendring to that purpose another Sense of the word Fornication (and wch is also the Opinion amongst others of Mr Selden in his *Uxor Hebræa*) then what is commonly received. Martin Bucers Judgment in this matter hee likewise translated into English. The Assembly of Divines then sitting at Westminster, though formerly obliged by his learned Pen in the defence of Smectymnyus, and other thir controversies with the Bishops, now impatient of having the Clergies[41] Jurisdiction, as they reckoned[42] it, invaded, instead of answering, or disproving what those books[43] had asserted, caus'd him to be summon'd for them before the Lords. But that house, whether approving[44] the Doctrine, or not favoring his Accusers, soon dismiss'd him.

This was the mending of a decay in the Superstructure, and had for object onely the well beeing of private Persons, or at most of Families; His small treatise *Of Education,* address'd to Mr Hartlib, was the laying a Foundation also of Public Weale: In it hee prescrib'd an easy and delightful method for training up Gentry in such a manner to all sorts of Literature, as that they might at the same time by like degrees advance in Virtue, and Abilities to serve their Country; subjoyning directions for their attayning other necessary, or Ornamental accomplishments: And it seem'd hee design'd in some measure to put this in practise. He had from his first settling taken care of instructing his two Nephews by his Sister Phillips, and, as it happen'd, the Sonn of some friend: Now hee took a large house, where the Earle of Barrimore, sent by his Aunt the Lady Ranalagh, Sr Thomas Gardiner of Essex, and others were under his Tuition: But whether it were that the tempers of our Gentry would not beare the strictness of his Discipline, or for what other reason, hee continud that course but a while.

His next public work, and which seem'd to bee his particular Province, who was so jealous in promoting Knowledge, was *Areopagitica,* written in manner of an Oration, to vindicate the Freedom of the Press from the Tyranny of Licensers; Who either inslav'd to the Dicttes of those that put them into Office, or prejudic'd by thir

---

[30] "After that for a first and second" was crossed out.

[31] In other words, Milton's father had established his settlement or his personal endowment from family funds: he was prosperous enough to marry.

[32] An allusion to the Parable of the Talents (Matthew 25), to which Milton also referred in Sonnet 19 ("When I consider").

[33] Written "Forrest Hill" at first, which is more nearly correct for the name of the Powell estate.

[34] First written as "returned."

[35] Originally "in this mean time." "Interval" replaced "mean time," and "the" became "this."

[36] The words "so necessary" were deleted for "of so great concern."

[37] The phrase "to sin" was substituted for "as well as mischiefs."

[38] Replacing "which."

---

[39] For "show'd," the passage originally read "by expounding after other correct [?] divines the foure passages in the Evangelists."

[40] The phrase "among the Jews" at this point was crossed out.

[41] Originally "the Jurisdiction." The "the" was changed to "their," and finally "the Clergies" substituted.

[42] The word "term'd" was first written, then deleted.

[43] The word "he" instead of "those books" was written originally, then deleted.

[44] Originally "not disliking," then that phrase was deleted.

own Ignorance, are wont to hinder ye comming out of any thing[45] which is not consonant to the common receiv'd Opinions, and by that means deprive the public of the benefit of many usefull labours.

Hitherto all his Writings had for subject the propagation of Religion or[46] Learning, or the bettering some more private concerns of Mankind: In Political matters hee had publish'd nothing. And it was now the time for the King's comming upon his Tryal, when some of the Presbiterian Ministers, out of malignity to the Independent Party, who had supplanted them, more than from any principles of Loyalty, asserted clamorously in thir Sermons and Writings the Privilege of Kings from all accountableness, Or (to speak in the Language of this time) Non resistance & Passive Obedience to bee the Doctrine of all the Reformed Churches. This general Thesis, which incourag'd all manner of Tyranny, hee opposed by good Arguments, and the Authorities of several eminently learned Protestants in a Book titled *The Tenure of Kings*, but without any particular application to the dispute then on foot in this Nation.

Upon the change of Government which succeeded the King's death hee was, without any seeking of his, by the means of a private Acquaintance, who was then a member of the new Council of State, chosen Latin Secretary. In this public Station his abilities & the acuteness of his parts,[47] which had lyen hid in his privacy, were soon taken notice of, and hee was pitch'd upon to elude the Artifice of Εἰκὼν βασιλικὴ. This hee had no sooner perform'd, answerably to the expectation from his Witt & Pen, in Εἰκονοκλάςης, but another Adventure expected[48] him.

Salmasius a Professor in Holland, who had in a large Treatise, not long before, maintain'd the parity of Church Governors against Episcopacy, put out *Defensio Caroli Regis*, and in it, amongst other absurdities, Justify'd (as indeed it was unavoidable in the defense of that cause, which was styl'd Bellum Episcopale) to the contradiction of his former Book, the pretensions of the Bishops. Him Mr. Milton by the order of his Masters answerd in[49] *Defensio pro populo Anglicano*; both in more correct Latin, to the shame of the others Grammarship, and by much better reasoning. For Salmasius beeing a Forrainer, & grossly ignorant of our Laws & Constitution (which in all Nations are the respective distinguishing Principles of Government)

either brought no arguments from thence, or such onely (and by him not seldom mistaken or misapply'd) as were partially suggested to him by those whose cause hee had undertaken; and which, having during the many yeers of our divisions been often ventilated, receiv'd an easy solution. Nor had hee given proof of deeper learning in that which is properly call'd Politics, while hee made use of trite Instance, as that of the Government of Bees, & such like to prove the preeminency of Monarchy: and all along so confounded it with Tyranny (as also hee did the Episcopal with the Papal Government) that hee might better have pass'd for a Defender of the Grand Signor, and the Council of Trent, then of a lawful King and a Reformed Church. For this and reneging his former Principles hee was by Mr. Milton facetiously expos'd: Nor did hee ever reply, though hee liv'd three years after.

But what hee wisely declin'd, the further provoking such an Adversary, or persisting to defend a Cause hee so ill understood, was attempted in *Clamor Regij Sanguinis &c*: in which Salmasius was hugely extoll'd, and Mr Milton as falsly defam'd. The Anonymous Author, Mr. Milton, who had by his last book gain'd great esteem and many friends among the Learned abroad, by whom, and by public Ministers comming hether hee was often visited, soon discover'd to bee Morus, formerly a Professor & Minister at Geneva, then living in Holland. Him in *Secunda Defensio pro populo Anglicano* he render'd ridiculous for his trivial and weak Treatise under so Tragical a title, conteyning little of Argument, which had not before suffr'd with Salmasius. And because it consisted most of Railing & false Reproches, hee, in no unpleasant manner, from very good testimonies retorted upon him the true history of his notorious Impurities, bot at Geneva, and Leyden. Himselfe hee also, by giving a particular ingenuous account of his who life Vindicated from those scurrilous aspersions, with which that Book had indevor'd to blemish him: Adding perhaps thereby also reputation to the cause hee defended, at least, with impartial Readers, when they should reflect upon the different qualifications of the respective Champions. And when Morus afterwards strove to cleer himselfe of beeing the Author, & to represent Mr. Milton as an injurious Defamer in that particular, hee in *Defensio pro se* by very good testimonies, and other circumstantial proofs justify'd his having fixd it there, and made good sport of the others shallow Evasions.

While hee was thus employ'd his Eysight totally faild him; not through any immediat or sudden Judgment, as his Adversaries insultingly affirm'd; but from a weakness which his hard nightly study in his youth had first occasion'd, and which by degrees had for some

---

[45] The phrase "New or" was deleted here.
[46] An "&" was deleted, for "or."
[47] Unique abilities, as in "he was a man of parts."
[48] Awaited.
[49] Replacing a deleted "by."

time before depriv'd him of the use of one Ey: And the Issues and Seatons,[50] made use of to save or retrieve that, were thought by drawing away the Spirits, which should have supply'd the Optic Vessells, to have hasten'd the loss of the other. He was indeed advis'd by his Physitians of the danger, in his condition, attending so great intentness as that work requir'd. But hee, who was resolute in going through with what upon good consideration hee at any time design'd, and to whom the love of Truth and his Country was[51] dearer then all things, would not for any danger decline thir defense.

Nor did his Darkness discourage or disable him from prosecuting, with the help of Amanuenses, the[52] former design of his calmer Studies. And hee had now more leisure, beeing dispens'd with,[53] by having a Substitute allowd him, and sometimes Instructions sent home to him, from attending in his office[54] of Secretary.

It was now that hee began that laborious work of amassing out of all the Classic Authors, both in Prose and Verse, a[55] *Latin Thesaurus* to the emendation of that done by Stephanus; Also the composing *Paradise Lost* And the framing a *Body of Divinity* out of the Bible: All which, notwithstanding the several Calamities befalling him in his fortunes, he finish'd after the Restoration: As also the *British history* down to the Conquest, *Paradise regaind*, *Samson Agonistes*, a Tragedy, *Logica* & *Accedence commenc'd Grammar* & had begun a *Greek Thesaurus*; having scarce left any part of learning unimprov'd by him: As in *Paradise lost & Regain'd* hee more especially taught all Virtue.

In these Works, and the instruction of some Youth of other at the entreaty of his friends, hee in great Serenity spent his time & expir'd no less calmly in the Yeare 1674.

He had a naturally Sharp Witt, and steddy Judgment; which helps toward attaining Learning hee improv'd by an indefatigable attention to his Study; and was supported in that by a Temperance, allways observ'd by him, but in his Youth even with great Nicety. Yet he did not reckon this Talent but as intrusted with him; and therefore dedicated all his labours to the glory of God, & some public Good; Neither binding himselfe to any of the gainfull Professions, nor having any worldly

Interest for aim in what he taught. Hee made no address or Court for the emploiment of Latin Secretary, though his eminent fittness for it appear by his printed Letters of that time. And hee was so farr from beeing concern'd in the corrupt designs of his Masters, that whilst in his first and second *Defension pro populo Anglicano* he was an Advocate for Liberty against Tyranny & Oppression (which to him seem'd the case, as well by the public Declarations on the one side [and hee was a Stranger to thir private Counsels] as by the Arguments on the other side, which run mainly upon the justifying of exorbitant & lawless power) hee took care all along strictly to define, and persuade to true Liberty, and especially in very solemn Perorations at the close of those Books; where hee also, little less than Prophetically, denounc'd the Punishments due to the abusers of that Specious name. And as hee was not link'd to one Party by self Interest,[56] so neither was hee divided from the other by Animosity; but was forward to do any of them good Offices, when their particular Cases afforded him ground to appeer on thir behalf. And especially, if on the score of Witt or Learning, they could lay claim to his peculiar[57] Patronage. Of which were instances, among others, the Grand child of the famous Spencer, a Papist suffering in his concerns in Ireland, and S[r] William Davenant when taken Prisoner, for both of whom hee procur'd relief.

This his Sincerity, and disentanglement of any private ends with his Sentiments relating to the Public, proceeded no doubt from a higher Principle, but was in great part supported,[58] and temptations to the contrary avoided by his constant Frugality; which enabl'd him at first to live within compass of the moderate Patrimony his Father left him, and afterwards to bear with patience, and no discomposure[59] of his way of living, the great losses which befell him in his Fortunes. Yett he was not sparing to buy good Books; of which hee left a fair Collection; and was generous in relieving the wants of his Friends. Of his Gentleness[60] and Humanity hee likewise gave signal proof in receiving home, and living in good accord till her death with his first wife, after shee had so obstinately absented from him: During which time, as neither in any other Scene of his life, was hee blemish'd with the least Unchastity.

From so Christian a Life, so great Learning, and so unbyass'd a search after Truth it is not probable any

---

[50] A seton was "A thread, piece of tape, or the like, drawn through a fold of skin so as to maintain an issue or opening for discharges, or drawn through a sinus or cavity to keep this from healing up" (*OED* 1). Apparently such a thread was drawn through the eyelid, to allow drainage of "Spirits" or liquids thought harmful.
[51] Replacing a deleted "were."
[52] Replacing a deleted "his."
[53] Probably "excused from [his earlier duties]."
[54] The word "office" replaced a deleted "place."
[55] Replacing a deleted "that."

[56] See Darbishire 30n for a first draft of this passage.
[57] Special.
[58] The phrase "by his frugality" was deleted.
[59] The phrase "small alteration" was deleted, for "no discomposure."
[60] This word began as "genero[sity?]," then became "Gentleness," perhaps because "generous" had just been used.

errors in Doctrin should spring. And therefore his Judgment in his Body of Divinity concerning some speculative points, differing perhaps from that commonly receiv'd, (and which is thought to bee the reason that never was printed) neither ought rashly to bee condemnd, and however himselfe not to bee uncharitably censur'd; who by beeing a constant[62] Champion for the liberty of Opining, expressd much Candor towards others. But that this Age is insensible of the great obligations it has to him, is too apparent in that hee has no better a Pen to celebrate his Memory.

Hee was of a moderate Stature, and well proportion'd, of a ruddy Complexion, light brown Hair, & handsom Features; save that his Eyes were none of the quickest. But his blindness, which proceeded from a Gutta Serena, added no further blemish to them. His deportment was sweet and affable; and his Gate erect & Manly, bespeaking Courage and undauntedness (or a Nil conscire).[63] On which account hee wore a Sword while hee had his Sight, and was skilld in using it. Hee had an excellent Ear, and could bear a part both in Vocal & Instrumental Music. His moderate Estate left him by his Father was through his good Oeconomy sufficient to maintain him. Out of his Secretary's Salary hee had sav'd two thousand pounds, which being lodg'd in the Excise, and that Bank failing upon the Restoration, hee utterly lost; Beside which, and the ceasing of his Imploiment hee had no damage by that[64] change of Affairs.[65] For he early sued out his Pardon; and by means of that, when the Serjeant of the house of Commons had officiously seisd him, was quickly set at liberty. He had too at the first return of the Court in good manners[66] left his house in Petty France, which had a door into the Park; and in all other things demeaning himselfe peaceably, was so farr from being reckon'd disaffected, that he was visited at his house on Bun-hill by a Chief Officer of State, and desir'd to imploy his Pen on thir behalf. And when the Subject of Divorce was under consideration with the Lord,s upon the account of the Lord Ross, hee was consulted by an eminent[67] Member of that house. By the great fire in 1660 hee had a house in Bread street burnt: wch was all the Real Estate hee had. Hee rendred his Studies and various Works more easy & pleasant by allotting them thir several portions of the day. Of these the time friendly to the Muses fell to his Poetry; And hee waking

early (as is the use of temperate men) had commonly a good Stock of Verses ready against his Amanuensis came; which if it happend to bee later than ordinary, hee would complain, saying *hee wanted to bee milkd.* The Evenings hee likewise spent in reading some choice Poets, by way of refreshment after the days toyl, and to store his Fancy against Morning. Besides his ordinary lectures out of the Bible and the[68] best Commentators on the week day, That was his sole subject on Sundays. And Davids Psalms were in esteem with him above all Poetry. The Youths that hee instructed from time to time servd him often as Amanuenses, & some elderly persons were glad for the benefit of his learned Conversation, to perform that Office. His first Wife dy'd a while after his blindness seizd him, leaving him three Daughters, that liv'd to bee Women. He marry'd two more, whereof one surviv'd him. He dy'd in a fitt of the Gout, but with so little pain or Emotion, that the time of his expiring was not perceiv'd by those in the room. And though hee had bin long troubl'd with that disease, insomuch that his Knuckles were all callous, yet was hee not ever observ'd to be very impatient. Hee had this Elogy in common with the Patriarchs and Kings of Israel that he was gather'd to his people;[69] for hee happen'd to bee bury'd in Cripplegate where about thirty yeer before hee had by chance also interrd his Father.

Anthony à Wood
From *Fasti Oxonienses* (1691)

Anthony à Wood (1632–1695; Wood was probably also calling attention to his name by writing it in an affected way with the accent mark), historian of Oxford University, was, above all else, loyal to King Charles II and to his beheaded father Charles I. Most of the time Wood faithfully follow his friend's, John Aubrey's, notes on Milton's life. For Wood's *Athenæ Oxonienses* and *Fasti Oxonienses*, published together as one volume, Aubrey sought out biographical information about prominent persons with an connection to Oxford (Shawcross 277). Wood's account depends utterly on Aubrey's research, to the point where Parker believes it to be nearly worthless on its own.

Wood respects his subject as a poet, as a well-educated man, and as a writer of prose as well as poetry, but he is rabidly angry at Milton the regicide. He writes that

---

[62] Replacing "so constant a."
[63] A clear conscience.
[64] Replaces "the."
[65] Replaces the deleted "Government."
[66] Originally "prudently."
[67] The phrase "an eminent" replaced "no mean."
[68] Replaces "its."
[69] The phrase "was gather'd to his people" replaced "slept with his Fathers," perhaps because "Father" was used below.

Eikonoklastes was published "to the horror of all sober men," meaning of course all persons on the side of the martyred King. In summing up Milton's politics, Wood rages:

> . . . he became a great Antimonarchist, a bitter Enemy to K. *Ch.* I. and at length arrived to that monstrous and unparallel'd height of profligate impudence, as in print to justify the most execrable Murder of him the best of Kings . . . .

When Milton left his house in Petty France, Wood the Royalist writes that he "absconded, for fear of being brought to a legal Tryal." And elsewhere in the 1691–92 edition of the *Fasti*, Wood calls Milton "the impudent liar" (col. 582). Wood, in other words, is not to be trusted on the subject of Milton's politics.

Wood organizes Aubrey's notes to make a coherent and readable biography.

TEXT

I have relied on a copy of the of *Fasti Oxonienses* (1691–92), and on Wood's annotated copy, Bodleian Wood 431.a, as reproduced by Darbishire. In comparing the original with Darbishire's copy of it, I have noticed and corrected a number of small errors.

Works Cited

Darbishire, Helen, ed.. *The Early Lives of Milton*. New York: Barnes & Noble, 1965.

Pask, Kevin. *The Emergence of the English Author: Scripting the Life of the Poet in Early Modern England*. Cambridge: Cambridge UP, 1996.

Shawcross, John T. *John Milton: The Self and the World*. Lexington: UP of Kentucky, 1993.

Wood, Anthony à. *Athenae oxonienses. An exact history of all the writers and bishops who have had their education in the most ancient and famous University of Oxford, from the fifteenth year of King Henry the Seventh, Dom. 1500, to the end of the year 1690. . . . To which are added, the fasti, or annals, of the said University, for the same time. By Anthony Wood*. London, 1691–92.

—. *Athenae oxonienses, an exact history of all the writers and bishops who have had their education in the University of Oxford; to which are added the Fasti; or, Annals of the said university*. Ed. Philip Bliss. Four vols. London, 1813–20. Repr. New York: Johnson Reprint Corp., 1967.

FROM *FASTI OXONIENSES* OR *ANNALS* OF THE UNIVERSITY OF OXFORD

ANTHONY À WOOD
1691

This year[1] was incorporated Master of Arts *John Milton*, not that it appears so in the Register, for the reason I have told you in the Incorporations 1629, but from his own mouth to my friend,[2] who was well acquainted with, and had from him, and from his Relations after his death, most of this account of his life and writings following. (1) That he was born in *Breadstreet* within the City of *London*, between 6 and 7 a clock in the morning of the ninth of *Decemb.* an. 1608. (2) That his father *Joh. Milton* who was a Scrivner living at the *Spread Eagle*[1] in the said street, was a Native of *Halton* in *Oxfordshire*, and his mother named *Sarah* was of the antient family of the *Bradshaws*. (3) That his Grandfather *Milton* whose Christian name was *John*, as he thinks, was an Under-Ranger or Keeper of the Forest of *Shotover* near to the said town of *Halton*, but descended from those of his name who had lived beyond all record at *Milton* near *Halton* and *Thame* in *Oxfordshire*. Which Grandfather being a zealous Papist, did put away, or, as some say, disinherit, his Son, because he was a Protestant, which made him retire to *London*, to seek, in a manner, his fortune. (4) That he the said *John Milton* the Author was educated mostly in *Pauls* school under *Alex. Gill* senior, and thence at 15 years of age was sent to *Christs* Coll. in *Cambridge*, where he was put under the tuition of *Will. Chappell*, afterwards Bishop of *Ross* in *Ireland*, and there, as at School for 3 years before, 'twas usual with him to sit up till midnight at his book, which was the first thing that brought his eyes into the danger of blindness. By this his indefatigable study he profited exceedingly, wrot then several Poems, paraphras'd some of *David's Psalms*, performed the collegiate and academic exercise to the admiration of all, and was esteemed to be a vertuous and sober person, yet not to be ignorant of his own parts. (5) That after he had taken the degrees in Arts, he

---

[1] 1635, as noted at the head of Wood's notes on different people who had received degrees from Oxford in that year.
[2] Wood's record is the only one we have that Milton was indeed registered as MA at Oxford.
[1] [This note is Wood's}The arms that *Joh. Milton* did use and seal his letters with, were, *Argent " spread Eagle with two heads gules, legg'd and beak'd sable.* [The heraldic language signifies that the field or background for the coat of arms was silver (argent), the eagle itself was red (gules), and the legs and beak of the eagle were black (sable).]

left the University of his own accord, and was not expelled for misdemeanors, as his Adversaries have said. Whereupon retiring to his Fathers house in the Country, he spent some time in turning over Latin and Greek Authors, and now and then made[2] excursions into the great City to buy books, to the end that he might be instructed in Mathematicks and musick, in which last he became excellent, and by the help of his Mathematicks could compose a Song or Lesson. (6) That after five years being thus spent, and his Mother (who was very charitable to the poor) dead, he did design to travel, so that obtaining the rudiments of the Ital. Tongue, and Instructions how to demean himself from Sir *Hen. Wotton*, who delighted in his company, and gave him Letters of commendation to certain persons living at *Venice*, he travelled into *Italy*, an. 1638. (7) That in his way thither, he touched at *Paris*, where *Joh. Scudamore*, Vicount *Slego*, Embassador from K. *Ch.* I to the French king, received him kindly, and by his means became known to *Hugo Grotius*, then and there Embassador from the Qu. of *Sweden*; but the manners and genius of that place being not agreeable to his mind, he soon left it. (8) That thence by *Geneva* and other places of note, he went into *Italy*, and thro *Legorne, Pisa*, etc. he went to *Florence* where continuing two months, he became acquainted with several learned men, and familiar with the choicest Wits of that great City, who introduced and admitted him into their private Academies, whereby he saw and learn'd their fashions of literature. (9) That from thence he went to *Sena* and *Rome*, in both which places he spent his time among the most learned there, *Lucas Holsteinius* being one; and from thence he journied to *Naples* where he was introduced into the Acquaintance of *Joh. Bapt. Mansus* an Italian Marquess (to whom *Torquatus Tassus* an Italian poet wrot his book *De amicitia*) who shewed great civilities to him, accompanied him to see the rarities of that place, visited him at his Lodgings, and sent to, the testimony of his great esteem for, him, in this Distich,

Ut mens, forma, decor, facies mos, si pietas sic,
  Non Anglus, verum herculè Angelus ipse fores.

And excus'd himself at parting for not having been able to do him more honour, by reason of his resolute owning his (Protestant) religion: which resoluteness he using at *Rome*, many there were that dared not to express their civilities towards him, which otherwise they would have done: And I have heard it confidently

related, that for his said Resolutions, which out of policy, and for his own safety, might have been then spared, the English Priests at *Rome* were highly disgusted, and it was question'd, whether the Jesuits his Countrymen there, did not design to do him mischief. Before he left *Naples* he return'd the Marquess an acknowledgment of his great favours in an elegant copy of Verses entit. *Mansus*, which is among the Latin Poems. (10) That from thence (*Naples*) he thought to have gone into *Sicily* and *Greece*, but upon second thought he continue in *Italy*, and went to *Luca, Bononia, Ferrara*, and at length to *Venice*; where continuing a month, he went and visited *Verona* and *Millan*. (11) That after he had ship'd the books and other goods which he had bought in his travels, he returned thro *Lombardy*, and over the *Alpes* to *Geneva*, where spending some time, he became familiar with the famous *Joh. Deodate* D.D. Thence, going thro *France*, he returned home, well fraught with Knowledge and Manners, after he had been absent one year and three months. (12) That soon after he setled in a house in S. *Bride's* Churchyard, near *Fleetstreet* in *London*, where he instructed in the Lat. Tongue two Youths named *John* and *Edw. Philips*, the Sons of his Sister *Anne* by her Husband *Edward Philips*: both which were afterwards Writers, and the eldest principl'd as his Uncle. But the times soon after changing, and the Rebellion thereupon breaking forth, *Milton* sided with the Faction, and being a man of parts, was therefore more capable than another of doing mischief, especially by his pen, as by those books which I shall anon mention, will appear. (13) That at first we find him a Presbyterian and a most sharp and violent opposer of Prelacy, the established ecclesiastical Discipline and the orthodox Clergy. (14) That shortly after he did set on foot and maintained very odd and novel Positions concerning Divorce, and then taking part with the Independents, he became a great Antimonarchist, a bitter Enemy to K. *Ch.* I. and at length arrived to that monstrous and unparallel'd height of profligate impudence, as in print to justifie the most execrable Murder of him the best of Kings, as I shall anon tell you. Afterwards being made Latin Secretary to the Parliament, we find him a Commonwealths man, a hater of all things that looked towards a single person, a great reproacher of the Universities, scholastical degrees, decency and uniformity in the Church. (15) That when *Oliver* ascended the Throne, he became the Latin Secretary, and proved to him very serviceable when employed in business of weight and moment, and did great matters to obtain a name and wealth. To conclude, he was a person of wonderful parts, of a very sharp, biting and satyrical wit. He was a good Philosopher and Historian, an excellent Poet, Latinist,

---

[2] [Wood's note}See in Joh. Milton's book intit. *Defensio secunda: Edit. Hag. Com.* 1654, p. 61., &c.

Grecian and Hebritian, a good Mathematician and Musitian, and so rarely endowed by nature, that had he been but honestly principled, he might have been highly useful to that party, against which he all along appeared with much malice and bitterness. As for the things which he hath published, are these, (1) *Of Reformation, touching Church Discipline in England, and the causes that hitherto have hindred it, &c.* Lond. 1641. qu.[3] At which time, as before, the Nation was much divided upon the Controversies about Church Government between the prelatical party, and Puritans, and therefore *Milton* did with great boldness and zeal offer his judgment as to those matters in his said book of Reformation. (2) *Animadversions upon the Remonstrants defence against Smectymnus.* Lond. 1641. qu. Which *Rem. Defence* was written (as 'tis said) by Dr. *Jos. Hall*, Bishop of *Exeter*. (3) *Apology against the humble Remonstrant.* This was written in vindication of his *Animadversions.* (4) *Against prelatical Episcopacy.* This I have not yet seen. (5) *The reason of Church Government;* nor this. (6) *The doctrine and discipline of divorce,* &c. in two books. Lond. 1644-45, qu. To which is added in some Copies a translation of *The judgment of Mart. Bucer concerning divorce,* &c. It must be now known, that after his settlement, upon his return from his Travels, he in a months time courted, married, and brought home to his house in *London,* a Wife from *Forsthill* lying between *Halton* and *Oxford,* named *Mary* the daughter of Mr. ___ *Powell* of that place Gent. But she, who was very young, and had been bred in a family of plenty and freedom, being not well pleas'd with her Husbands retired manner of life, did shortly after leave him and went back in the Country with her Mother. Whereupon, tho he sent divers pressing invitations, yet he could not prevail with her to come back, till about 4 years after when the Garrison of *Oxon* was surrendred (the nighness of her Fathers house to which having for the most part of the mean time hindred any communication between them) she of her own accord returned and submitted to him, pleading that her Mother had been the chief promoter of her frowardness. But he being not able to bear this abuse, did therefore upon consideration, after he had consulted many eminent Authors, write the said book of Divorce, with intentions to be separated from her, but by the compromising of her Relations the matter did not take effect: so that she continuing with him ever after till her

death, he had several Children by here, of whom *Deborah* was the third daughter, trained up by the Father in Lat. and Greek, and made by him his Amanuensis. (7) *Tetrachordon: Expositions upon the four chief places in Scripture, which treat on marriage.* On Gen. 1,27, 28, &c. Lond. 1646. qu. (8) *Colasterion: A reply to a nameless answer against the doctrine and discipline of divorce* &c. printed 1645. qu. Upon his publication of the said three books of Marriage and Divorce, the *Assembly of Divines* then sitting at *Westminster* took special notice of them, and thereupon, tho the Author had obliged them by his pen in his defence of *Smectymnus* and other their Controversies had with the Bishops, they impatient of having the Clergies jurisdiction (as they reckon'd it) invaded, did, instead of answering, or disproving what those books had asserted, cause him to be summoned before the House of Lords: but that House, whether approving the Doctrine, or not favouring his Accusers, did soon dismiss him. To these things I must add, that after his Majesties Restauration, when the subject of Divorce was under consideration with the Lords upon the account of *John* Lord *Ros* or *Roos* his separation from his Wife *Anne Pierpont* eldest Daughter to *Henry* Marquess of *Dorchester,* he was consulted by an eminent Member of that House, as he was about that time by a chief Officer of State, as being the prime person that was knowing in that affair. (9) *Of Education,* written or addressed to Mr. *Sam. Hartlib.* In this Treatise he prescrib'd an easie and delightful method for the training up of Gentry to all sorts of Literature, that they might at the same time by like degrees advance in virtue and abilities to serve their Country, subjoyning directions for their obtaining other necessary or ornamental Accomplishments. And to this end that he might put it in practice, he took a larger house, where the Earl of *Barrimore* sent by his Aunt the lady *Rannelagh,* Sir *Thomas Gardiner* of *Essex,* to be there with others (besides his two Nephews) under his Tuition. But whether it were that the tempers of our Gentry would not bear the strictness of his discipline, or for what other reasons I cannot tell, he continued that course but a while. (10) *Areopagetica: A speech for the Liberty of unlicensed printing, to the Parliament of England.* Lond. 1644. qu. written to vindicate the freedom of the Press from the Tyranny of Licensers, who for several Reasons deprive the publick of the benefit of many useful Authors. (11) *Poemata: quorum pleraque intra annum ætatis vigesimum conscripsit author,* &c. Lond. 1645. oct. (12) *A mask.*—printed 1645. oct. (13) *Poems,* &c.—printed the same year. Hitherto we find him only to have published political things, but when he saw, upon the coming of K. *Charles* I. to his Tryal, the Presbyterian Ministers clamorously to assert

---

[3] Wood and his typesetter use abbreviations throughout that a modern student may have problems with. After each book title, for one example, Wood identifies it as "fol." (folio), "qu." (quarto), "oct." (octavo), or "tw" (duodecimo), referring to the various sizes of books, depending on how the original sheet from the printing press was folded.

in their Sermons and Writings the privileges of Kings from all accountableness, or (to speak in the language of that time) Non-resistance and Passive Obedience to be the Doctrine of all the reformed Churches (which he took to be only their malignity against the Independents who had supplanted them, more than for any principles of Loyalty) he therefore to appose that *Thesis* (which as he conceiv'd did encourage all manner of Tyranny) did write and publish from divers Arguments and Authorities, (13) *The tenure of Kings and Magistrates: proving that it is lawful,* &c. *to call to account a Tyrant or King, and after due conviction to depose and put him to death,* &c. *Lond.* 1649–50. qu. Soon after the King being beheaded to the great astonishment of all the World, and the Government thereupon changed, he was, without any seeking of his, by the endeavours of a private acquaintance, who was a member of the new *Council of State,* chosen Latin Secretary, as I have before told you. In this publick station his abilities and acuteness of parts, which had been in a manner kept private, were soon taken notice of, and he was pitch'd upon to elude *the artifice* (so it was then by the Faction called) of *Eikon Basilice.* Whereupon he soon after published (14) *Iconoclastes in answer to a book entit.* Eikon Basilice, the portrature of his sacred Majesty in his solitudes and sufferings. *Lond.* 1649–50. qu. *ib.* 1690, oct. which being published to the horror of all sober men, nay even to the Presbyterians themselves, yet by the then dominant party it was esteemed an excellent piece, and perform'd answerably to the expectation of his Wit and Pen. After the Return of King *Charles* 2, this book was called in by Proclamation, dated 13 *Aug.* 1660, at which time the Author (who a little before had left his house in *Petty France* which had a door going into S. *James's* park) absconded, for fear of being brought to a legal Tryal, and so consequently of receiving condign Punishment. At the same time also, was called in a book of *John Goodwin,* then lately a Minister in *Colemanstreet* in *Lond.* entit. *The Obstructors of Justice;* written in defence of the Sentence against his Majesty *Charles* I.[4] At which time also the said *Goodwin* absconded to prevent Justice. Soon after the publication of *Iconclastes, Salmasius,* a professor in *Holland,* who had in a large Treatise not long before, maintained, as 'tis said, the parity of Church Governors against Episcopacy, did publish *Defensio regia, pro Carolo* I. *Rege Angliæ,* wherein he justified several matters, as *Milton* conceived, to the contradiction of his former book. Whereupon he wrot

---

[4] Darbishire adds "From a MS. note of Wood, the editors of the second edition of the *Fasti,* 1721, insert here: 'Mr. John Milton is also thought to be the author of *The grand Case of Conscience concerning the Engagement stated and resolv'd,* &c. *Lond.* 1650. qu. 3.sh."

and published, (15) *Pro populo Anglicano defensio contra Claudii Anonymi alias Salmasii defensionem regiam.* Lond. 1651. fol. said to be written in more correct Latin than that of *Salmasius.* While *Milton* was writing the said book, his sight began to fail him, and before it was fully compleated, one of his eyes did absolutely perish. In the month of *June* the same year (1651) the said book was burnt at *Tholouse* by an arrest from the Parliament, under the Government of the Duke of *Orleans:* and in *Sept.* following it was the usual practice of *Marchm. Nedham* a great crony of *Milton,* to abuse *Salmasius* in his publick Mercury called *Politicus,* (as *Milton* had done before in his *Defensio*) by saying among other things that *Christina* Qu. of *Sweden* had cashiered him her favour, by understanding that he was *a pernicious parasite, and a promoter of Tyranny.* After his Majesties Restauration, this book also was called in by the same Proclamation before mention'd. But so it was, that in 1652, a certain book entit. *Regii sanguinis clamor,* &c. being published, *Salmasius* was highly extol'd in it, and *Milton* had his just character given therein. The nameless Author of which being for a considerable time sought out, but in vain, by *Milton,* he at length learn'd by certain Ministers of State sent to the Republick of *England,* (who would sometimes visit him as a learned man) that it was written by one *Alex. More,* formerly a Professor and Minister at *Geneva,* then living in *Holland.* Whereupon he published (16) *Pro populo Anglicano defensio secunda, contra infamem libellum Anonymum, cui titulus,* Regii sanguinis clamor ad cœlum adversus patricidas Anglicanos. *Lond.* 1654, and at *Hag. Com.* the same year, in oct. Upon the writing of this book, the Author *Milton* lost the other eye; and tho to his charge he used many means, yet he could never recover either of his eyes. This book entit. *Reg. sang. clam.* &c. tho written by Dr. *Peter du Moulin,* Prebendary of *Canterbury,* as it afterwards well appeared, yet *Milton* upon the reports before mention'd could not be convinced to the contrary, but that it was written by the said *More,* and therefore not only abused him in his Answers, but by his friend *Nedham* in his *Politicus,* whereby the reputation of that learned person was severely touched. (17) *Pro se defensio contra Alex. Morum Ecclesiaste, libelli famosi, cui tit.* Regii sanguinis clamor, &c. *Lond.* 1655, oct. In this book he is exceeding bitter against *Morus,* and pretends to give a true history of his notorious Impurities both at *Geneva* and *Leyden,* and an account of his own particular life to vindicate himself from what, as he thought, was scurrilously said of him by *Morus.* At the end of the said book, the Author *Milton* added *Ad Alex. Mori supplementum responsio.* About the time that he had finished these things, he had more leisure, and time at command, and being dispenced with by having a substitute allowed him, and sometimes Instructions sent home to him from attending his office of Secretary, he began that laborious work of amassing out of all the classick Authors both in prose and verse a Latin *Thesaurus*, to the emendation of that done by *Stephanus*; also the composing of *Paradise lost*, and of the framing a *Body of Divinity* out of the Bible. All which, notwithstanding the several troubles that befell him in his fortunes, he finished after his Majesty's Restauration. But to go on with the Cat. of his Books according to time, take these as they follow; (18) *Treatise of civil power in ecclesiastical causes*, &c. Lond. 1659. in tw. (19) *Considerations touching the likeliest means to remove Hirelings out of the Church.* Lond. 1659. in two sheets and an half in qu. (20) *Ready and easie way to establish a free Commonwealth, and the excellencies thereof compared with*, &c. Lond. 1659, in two sheets and an half in qu. This being published in *Feb.* the same year, was answer'd by *G.S.* in his *Dignity of Kingship*. (21) *Brief notes upon a late Sermon titled*, The fear of God and the King, &c. *Lond.* 1660. qu. See more in *Matthew Griffith* among the Writers, *an.* 1665. (22) *Accedence commenced Grammar*, &c. pr. 1661 in oct. (23) *Paradise lost:* a Poem in 10 books, *Lond.* 1669. qu. pr. in fol. with cuts, *an.* 1688. (24) *Paradise Regain'd:* a Poem in four books. *Lond.* 1670. qu. pr. in fol. with cuts, *an.* 1688. (25) *History of Britany from the first traditional beginning, continued to the Norman Conquest.* Lond. 1670, qu. This History when it first came abroad, had only the reputation of the putting of our old Authors neatly together in a connex'd story, not abstaining from some lashes at the ignorance, or I know not what, of those times. (26) *Artis Logicæ plenior institutio ad Petri Rami methodum concinnata.* Lond. 1672, in tw. (27) *Of true Religion, Heresie, Schism, Toleration, and what best means may be used against the growth and increase of Popery*, Lond. 1673. qu. (28) *Poems*, &c. *on several occasions, both English and Latin*, &c. *composed at several times.* Lond. 1673-4. oct. Among these are mixed some of his Poems before mention'd, made in his youthful years. (29) *Epistolarum familiarium lib.* I. Lond. 1674. oct. (30) *Prolusiones quædam Oratoriæ in Coll. Christi habitæ*, printed with the *familiar Epistles*. (31) *Literæ Pseudo-senatus Anglicani, Cromwellii, reliquorum per duellium nomine ac jussu conscriptæ.* printed in 1676. in tw. (32) *Character of the Long Parliament, and of the Assembly of Divines.* Lond. 1681. in 2 sheets in qu. In which book is a notable account of their Ignorance, Treachery, and Hypocrisie. (33) *Brief History of Muscovia and of other less known Countries, lying eastward of Russia as far as Cathay*, &c. Lond. 1682. oct. (34) *The rights of the People over Tyrants*, printed lately in qu. These, I think, are all the things that he

hath yet extant: those that are not, are *The body of Divinity*, which my friend calls *Idea Theologiæ*, now, or at least lately, in the hands of the Authors Acquaintance called *Cyr. Skinner*,[5] living in *Mark lane, London*, and the *Latin Thesaurus*[6] in those of *Edw. Philipps* his Nephew. At length this great Scholar and frequent Writer dying in his house at *Bunhill* near *London*, in a fit of the Gout, but with so little pain, that the time of his expiring was not perceived by those in the room, on the ninth or tenth day of *Novemb.* 1674, was buried in the grave of his Father, (who died very aged about 1647) in the Chancel of the Church of S. *Giles* near *Cripplegate, London.* See more of him in Sir *Walter Raleigh* among the Writers, numb. 458. He was of a moderate Stature, and well proportion'd, of a ruddy Complexion, light brown hair, and had handsome features, yet his eyes were none of the quickest. When he was a Student in *Cambridge*, he was so fair and clear, that many called him the *Lady of Christ's Coll.* His deportment was affable, and his gate erect and manly, bespeaking courage and undauntedness. On which account he wore a sword while he had his sight, and was skill'd in using it. He had a delicate tuneable voice, an excellent ear, could play on the Organ, and bear a part in vocal and instrumental Musick. The Estate which his Father left him was but indifferent, yet by his frugality he made it serve him and his. Out of his Secretaries Salary he saved 2000 *l.* which being lodg'd in the Excise, and that bank failing upon his Majesties Restauration, he utterly lost that sum. By the great Fire which hapned in *London* in the beginning of *Sept.* 1660, he had a house in *Breadstreet* burnt, which was all the real Estate that he had then left. To conclude, he was more admired abroad, and by Foreigners, than at home; and was much visited by them when he liv'd in *Petty France*, some of whom have out of pure devotion gone to *Breadstreet* to see the house and chamber where he was born, *&c.*

---

[5] Wood mistakes Cyriack Skinner for Daniel Skinner; Aubrey had made the correct identification.

[6] Darbishire points to a note Wood pasted into his annotated copy of *Fasti Oxoniensis*: "Jo. Milton. A Dictionary compleated and improved with great exactness from the several works of Stephens, Gouldman, Holyoke, Dr. Littleton, a manuscript of Mr. Joh. Milton &c for the use of Schooles—printed at Cambridge in qu. At the end of a sheet Almanack 1693."

Edward Phillips, born in 1630, was the elder son of Anne Milton Phillips (Milton's sister) and her husband Edward. As a pupil of John Milton, Edward Jr. must have lived with him for a number of years, and he served as his uncle's amanuensis on many documented occasions. As the biography shows, he remained remarkably loyal to his uncle's memory, though perhaps differing from him in sympathy for royalism, or loyalty to Charles II, after the Restoration.

Phillips's short biography of his uncle was written to preface his edition of Milton's *Letters of State* published in 1694. The title page calls it "An Account of his Life. Together with several of his Poems; and a Catalogue of his Works, never before Printed." Phillips's editions of several of Milton's sonnets are notable if highly inaccurate, as is his catalogue of all of Milton's published works known to him, which parallels that in Aubrey and Wood.

Phillips's life of Milton is undeservedly notorious for getting wrong the dates of Milton's birth (1608 and not 1606, as Phillips has it) and his death (1674 and not 1673). On the other hand, as Dr. Johnson realized, Phillips has an excellent memory for places, and he tells us something about a total of eleven houses that Milton lived in (Darbishire xiii). Without him, we would not know that Milton was supposed to be courting a mysterious Miss Davis after his first wife Mary Powell deserted him. Nor would we know Milton's favorite times of composition during the year (autumn through spring equinoxes), or that *Paradise Lost* had some sort of existence much earlier in Milton's life than its publication date of 1667, as a tragedy with speeches by Satan as a character. Nor would we have the picture of Milton unpuritanically celebrating gaudy days with young men-about-town.

TEXT

This edition reproduces the text of a copy of the 1694 *Letters of State* preserved in the Library of the Union Theological Seminary in New York and made available through University Microfilms. I appreciate the help of Hugh Wilson, whose transcription of the text I have consulted and corrected, as he has corrected mine.

THE

LIFE

OF

Mr. John Milton.

OF all the several parts of History, that which sets forth the Lives, and Commemorates the most remarkable Actions, Sayings, or Writings of Famous and Illustrious Persons, whether in War or Peace; whether many together, or any one in particular, as it is not the least useful in it self, so it is in the highest Vogue and Esteem among the Studious and Reading part of Mankind. The most Eminent in this way of History were among the Ancients, *Plutarch* and *Diogenes Laertius* of the *Greeks*; the first wrote the Lives, for the most part, of the most Renowned Heroes and Warriours of the *Greeks* and *Romans*; the other the Lives of the Ancient *Greek* Philosophers. And *Cornelius Nepos* (or as some will have it *Aemilius Probus*) of the *Latins*, who wrote the Lives of the most Illustrious *Greek* and *Roman* Generals. Among the Moderns, *Machiavel* a Noble *Florentine*, who Elegantly wrote the Life of *Castrucio Castracano*, Lord of *Luca*. And of our Nation, Sir *Fulk Grevil*, who wrote the Life of his most intimate Friend Sir *Philip Sidney*: Mr. *Thomas Stanly* of *Cumberlo-Green*, who made a most Elaborate improvement to the foresaid *Laertius*, by adding to what he found in him, what by diligent search and enquiry he Collected from other Authors of best Authority.

Isaac Walton, who wrote the Lives of Sir *Henry Wotton*, Dr. *Donne*; and for his Divine Poems, the admired Mr. *George Herbert*. Lastly, not to mention several other Biographers of considerable Note, the Great *Gassendus* of *France*, the worthy Celebrator of two no less worthy Subjects of his impartial Pen; *viz.* the Noble Philosopher *Epicurus*, and the most politely Learned Virtuoso of his Age, his Country-man, Monsieur *Periesk*. And pitty it is the Person whose memory we have here undertaken to perpetuate by recounting the most memorable Transactions of his Life, (though his Works sufficiently recommend him to the World) finds not a well-informed Pen able to set him forth, equal with the best of those here mentioned; for doubtless had his Fame been as much spread through

Europe in *Thuanus*'s time as now is, and hath been for several Years, he had justly merited from that Great Historian, an Eulogy not inferiour to the highest, by him given to all the Learned and Ingenious that liv'd within the compass of his History. For we may safely and justly affirm, that take him in all respects, for Acumen of Wit, Quickness of Apprehension, Sagacity of Judgement, Depth of Argument, and Elegancy of Style, as well in *Latin* as *English*, as well in Verse as Prose, he is scarce to be parallel'd by any of the best of Writers our Nation hath in any Age brought forth. He was Born in *London*, in a House in *Breadstreet*, the Lease whereof, as I take it, but for certain it was a House in *Breadstreet*, became in time part of his Estate, in the Year of our Lord, 1606. His Father *John Milton*, an Honest, Worthy, and Substantial Citizen of *London*, by Profession a Scrivener; to which Profession he voluntarily betook himself, by the advice and assistance of an intimate Friend of his, Eminent in that Calling, upon his being cast out by his Father, a bigotted *Roman Catholick*, for embracing, when Young, the Protestant Faith, and abjuring the Popish Tenets; for he is said to have been Descended of an Ancient Family of the *Miltons*, of *Milton*, near *Abington* in *Oxfordshire*; where they had been a long time seated, as appears by the Monuments still to be seen in *Milton*-Church, till one of the Family having taken the wrong side, in the Contests between the Houses of *York* and *Lancaster*, was sequestred of all his Estate, but what he held by his Wife. However, certain it is, that this Vocation he followed for many Years, at his said House in *Breadstreet*, with success suitable to his Industry, and prudent conduct of his Affairs; yet he did not so far quit his own Generous and Ingenious Inclinations, as to make himself wholly a Slave to the World; for he sometimes found vacant hours to the Study (which he made his recreation) of the Noble Science of Musick, in which he advanc'd to that perfection, that as I have been told, and as I take it, by our Author himself, he Composed an *In Nomine* of Forty Parts: for which he was rewarded with a Gold Medal and Chain by a *Polish* Prince, to whom he presented it. However, this is a truth not to be denied, that for several Songs of his Composition, after the way of these times, three or four of which are still to be seen in Old *Wilby*'s set of Ayres, besides some Compositions of his in *Ravenscrofs* Psalms, he gained the Reputation of a considerable Master in this most charming of all the Liberal Sciences: Yet all this while, he managed his Grand Affair of this World with such Prudence and Diligence, that by the assistance of Divine Providence favouring his honest endeavours, he gained a Competent Estate, whereby he was enabled to make a handsom Provision both for the Education and Maintenance of his Children; for three he had, and no more, all by one Wife, *Sarah*, of the Family of the *Castons*, derived originally from *Wales*. A Woman of Incomparable Vertue and Goodness; *John* the Eldest, the Subject of our present Work. *Christopher*, and an onely Daughter *Ann*; *Christopher* being principally designed for the Study of the Common Law of *England*, was Entered Young a Student of the *Inner-Temple*, of which House he lived to be an Ancient Bencher, and keeping close to that Study and Profession all his Life-time, except in the time of the Civil Wars of *England*; when being a great favourer and assertor of the King's Cause, and Obnoxious to the Parliament's side, by acting to his utmost power against them, so long as he kept his Station at *Reading*; and after that Town was taken by the Parliament Forces, being forced to quit his House there, he steer'd his course according to the Motion of the King's Army.

But when the War was ended with Victory and Success to the Parliament Party, by the Valour of General *Fairfax*, and the Craft and Conduct of *Cromwell*; and his composition made by the help of his Brother's Interest, with the then prevailing Power; he betook himself again to his former Study and Profession, following Chamber-Practice every Term, yet came to no Advancement in the World in a long time, except some small Employ in the Town of *Ipswich*, where (and near it) he lived all the latter time of his Life. For he was a person of a modest quiet temper, preferring Justice and Vertue before all Worldly Pleasure or Grandeur: but in the beginning of the Reign of K. *James* the II. for his known Integrity and Ability in the Law, he was by some Persons of Quality recommended to the King, and at a Call of Serjeants received the Coif, and the same day was Sworn one of the Barons of the Exchequer, and soon after made one of the Judges of the Common Pleas; but his Years and Indisposition not well brooking the Fatigue of publick Imployment, he continued not long in either of these Stations, but having his *Quietus est*, retired to a Country Life, his Study and Devotion. *Ann*, the onely Daughter of the said *John Milton* the Elder, had a considerable Dowry given her by her Father, in Marriage with *Edward Philips*, (the Son of *Edward Philips* of *Shrewsbury*,) who coming up Young to Town, was bred up in the Crown-Office in Chancery, and at length came to be Secondary of the Office under Old Mr. *Bembo*; by him she had, besides other Children that dyed Infants, two Sons yet surviving, of whom more hereafter; and by a second Husband, Mr. *Thomas Agar*, (who, upon the Death of his Intimate Friend Mr. *Philips*) worthily Succeeded in the place, which except sometime of Exclusion before and during the *Interregnum*, he held for many Years, and left it to Mr. *Thomas Milton* (the Son of the aforementioned Sir *Christopher*) who at this day executes it with great Reputation and Ability. Two Daughters, *Mary* who died very Young, and *Ann* yet surviving.

But to hasten back to the matter at hand; *John* our Author, who was destin'd to be the Ornament and Glory of his Countrey, was sent, together with his Brother, to *Paul*'s school, whereof Dr. *Gill* the Elder was then Chief Master; where he was enter'd into the first Rudiments of Learning, and advanced therein with that admirable Success, not more by the Discipline of the School and good Instructions of his Masters, (for that he had another Master possibly at his Father's house, appears by the Fourth Elegy of his Latin Poems written in his 18th year, to *Thomas Young* Pastor of the *English* Company of Merchants at *Hamborough*, wherein he owns and stiles him his Master) than by his own happy Genius, prompt Wit and Apprehension, and insuperable Industry; for he generally sate up half the Night, as well in voluntary Improvements of his own choice, as the exact perfecting of his School-Exercises: So that at the Age of 15 he was full ripe for Academick Learning, and accordingly was sent to the University of *Cambridge*; where in *Christ's College*, under the Tuition of a very Eminent Learned man, whose Name I cannot call to mind, he Studied Seven years, and took his Degree of Master of Arts; and for extraordinary Wit and Reading he had shown in his Performances to attain his Degree, (some whereof spoken at a Vacation-Exercise in his 19th. year of Age, are to be yet seen in his Miscellaneous Poems) he was lov'd and admir'd by the whole University, particularly by the Fellows and most Ingenious Persons of his House. Among the rest there was a Young Gentleman, one Mr. *King*, with whom, for his great Learning and Parts, he had contracted a particular Friendship and Intimacy; whose death (for he was drown'd on the *Irish* Seas in his passage from *Chester* to *Ireland*) he bewails in that most excellent Monody in his fore-mentioned Poems) Intituled *Lycidas*. Never was the loss of Friend so Elegantly lamented; and among the rest of his Juvenile Poems, some he wrote at the Age of 15, which contain a Poetical Genius scarce to be parallel'd by any *English* Writer. Soon after he had taken his Master's Degree, he thought fit to leave the University: Not upon any disgust or discontent for want of Preferment, as some Ill-willers have reported; nor upon any cause whatsoever forc'd to flie, as his Detractors maliciously feign; but from which aspersion he sufficiently clears himself in his Second Answer to *Alexander Morus*, the Author of a Book call'd, *Clamor Regii Sanguinis ad Cælum*, the chief of his Calumniators; in which he plainly makes it out, that after his leaving the University, to the no small trouble of his Fellow-Collegiates, who in general regretted his Absence, he for the space of Five years lived for the most part with his Father and Mother at their house at *Horton* near *Colebrook* in *Barkshire*; whither his[1] Father, having got an Estate to his content, and left off all business, was retir'd from the Cares and Fatigues of the world. After the said term of Five years, his Mother then dying, he was willing to add to his acquired Learning the observation of Foreign Customs, Manners, and Institutions; and thereupon took a resolution to Travel, more especially designing for *Italy*; and accordingly, with his Father's Consent and Assistance, he put himself into an Equipage suitable to such a Design; and so intending to go by way of *France*, he set out for *Paris* accompanied onely by one Man, who attended him through all his Travels; for his Prudence was his Guide, and his Learning his Introduction and Presentation to Persons of most Eminent Quality. However, he had also a most Civil and Obliging Letter of Direction and Advice from Sir *Henry Wootton* then Provost of *Eaton*, and formerly Resident Embassador from King *James* the First to the State of *Venice*; which Letter is to be seen in the First Edition of his Miscellaneous Poems. At *Paris*, being Recommended by the said Sir *Henry* and other Persons of Quality, he went first to wait upon my Lord *Scudamore*, then Embassador in *France* from King *Charles* the First. My Lord receiv'd him with wonderful Civility; and understanding he had a desire to make a Visit to the great *Hugo Grotius*, he sent several of his Attendants to wait upon him, and to present him in his Name to that Renowned Doctor and Statesman, who was at that time Embassador from *Christina* Queen of *Sweden*, to the *French* King. *Grotius* took the Visit kindly, and gave him Entertainment suitable to his Worth, and the high Commendations he had heard of him. After a few days, not intending to make the usual Tour of *France*, he took his leave of my Lord, who at his departure from *Paris*, gave him Letters to the *English* Merchants residing in any part through which he was to Travel, in which they were requested to shew him all the Kindness, and do him all the Good Offices that lay in their Power.

From *Paris* he hastened on his Journey to *Nicæa*, where he took Shipping, and in a short space arrived at *Genoa*; from whence he went to *Leghorn*, thence to *Pisa*, and so to *Florence*: In this City he met with many charming Objects,[1] which Invited him to stay longer time than he intended; the pleasant Scituation of the Place, the Nobleness of the Structures, the exact

---

[1] Probably "things to look at."

Humanity and Civility of the Inhabitants, the more Polite and Refined sort of Language there, than elsewhere. During the time of his stay here, which was about Two Months, he Visited all the private Academies of the City, which are Places establish'd for the improvement of Wit and Learning, and maintained a Correspondence and perpetual Friendship among Gentlemen fitly qualified for such an Institution: and such sort of Academies there are in all or most of the most noted Cities in *Italy*.   Visiting these Places, he was soon taken notice of by the most Learned and Ingenious of the Nobility, and the Grand Wits of *Florence*, who caress'd him with all the Honours and Civilities imaginable, particularly *Jacobo Gaddi, Carolo Dati, An-tonio Francini, Frescobaldo, Cultellino, Banmatthei* and *Clementillo:*[2] Whereof *Gaddi* hath a large Elegant *Italian Canzonet* in his Praise: *Dati*, a Latin Epistle; both Printed before his Latin Poems, together with a Latin Distich of the Marquess of *Villa*, and another of *Selvaggi*, and a Latin *Tetrastick* of *Giovanni Salsilli* a *Roman*.   From *Florence* he took his Journey to *Siena*, from thence to *Rome*; where he was detain'd much about the same time he had been at *Florence*; as well as by his desire of seeing all the Rarities and Antiquities of that most Glorious and Renowned City, as by the Conversation of *Lucas Holstenius*, and other Learned and Ingenious men; who highly valued his Acquaintance, and treated him with all possible Respect.

From *Rome* he Travelled to *Naples*, where he was introduced by a certain Hermite, who accompanied him in his Journey from *Rome* thither, into the Knowledge of *Giovanni Baptista Manso*, Marquess of *Villa*, a *Neapolitan* by Birth, a Person of high Nobility, Vertue, and Honour, to Whom the famous *Italian* Poet, *Torquato Tasso*, Wrote his Treatise *de Amicitia*; and moreover mentions him with great Honour in that illustrious Poem of his, Intituled, *Gierusalemme Liberata*.[3] This Noble Marquess received him with extraordinary Respect and Civility, and went with him himself to give him a sight of all that was of Note and Remark in the City, particularly the Viceroys Palace, and was often in Person to Visit him at his Lodging. Moreover, this Noble Marquess honoured him so far, as to make a Latin Distich in his Praise, as hath been already mentioned; which being no less pithy then short, though already in Print, it will not be unworth the while here to repeat.

Ut Mens, Forma, Decor, Facies, si★[4] Pietas, sic,
  Non Anglus, Verum Hercle Angelus ipse foret.[5]

In return of this Honour, and in gratitude for the many Favours and Civilities received of him, he presented him at his departure with a large Latin Eclogue, Intituled, *Mansus*, afterward's Published among his Latin Poems. The Marquess at his taking leave of him, gave him this Complement, That he would have done him many more Offices of Kindness and Civility, but was therefore rendered incapable, in regard he had been over-liberal in his speech against the Religion of the Country.

He had entertain'd some thoughts of passing over into *Sicily* and *Greece*, but was diverted by the News he receiv'd from *England*, that Affairs there were tending towards a Civil War; thinking it a thing unworthy in him to be taking his Pleasure in Foreign Parts, while his Countrymen at home were Fighting for their Liberty: But first resolv'd to see *Rome* once more; and though the Merchants gave him a caution that the Jesuits were hatching designs against him, in case he should return thither, by reason of the freedom he took in all his discourses of Religion; nevertheless he ventured to prosecute his Resolution, and to *Rome* the second time he went, determining with himself not industriously to begin to fall into any Discourse about Religion; but, being ask'd, not to deny or endeavour to conceal his own Sentiments; Two Months he staid at *Rome*; and in all that time never flinch'd, but was ready to defend the Orthodox Faith against all Opposers; and so well he succeeded therein, that Good Providence guarding him, he went safe from *Rome* back to *Florence*, where his return to his Friends of that City was welcomed with as much Joy and Affection, as had it been to his Friends and Relations in his own Countrey, he could not have come a more joyful and welcome Guest. Here, having staid as long as at his first coming, excepting an excursion of a few days to *Luca*, crossing the *Apennine*, and passing through *Bononia*[6] and *Ferrara*, he arriv'd at *Venice*; where when he had spent a Month's time in viewing of that stately City, and shipp'd a Parcel of curious and rare Books which had pick'd up in his Travels; particularly a Chest or two of choice Musick-books of the best Masters flourishing about that time in

[2] The names are usually written Jacopo Gaddi, Carlo Dati, Coltellino, and Benedetto Bonmatthei or Buonmatthei.
[3] Written as "*Gieruemme*" in the 1694 edition. Probably the compositor thought he had put the "*sal*" on the previous line.

[4] The star before "*Pietas*" is a footnote marker, and in the footnote is "This word relates to his being a Protestant not a *Roman*-Catholick."
[5] Probably an unintentional error for "*fores*," as in all other versions of the epigram.
[6] The classical name for the city of Bologna, which Milton seems to have passed through, along with Ferrara, on his way to Venice.

Italy, namely *Luca Marenzo, Monte Verde, Horatio Vecchi, Cifa*, the Prince of *Venosa* and several others, he took his course through *Verona, Milan*, and the *Pœnine Alps*, and so by the Lake *Leman* to *Geneva*, where he staid for some time, and had daily converse with the most Learned *Giovanni Deodati*, Theology-Professor in that City; and so returning through *France*, by the same way he had passed it going to *Italy*, he, after a Peregrination of one compleat Year and about Three Months, arrived safe in *England*, about the time of the Kings making his second Expedition against the *Scots*. Soon after his return, and visits paid to his Father and other Friends, he took him a Lodging in St. *Brides* Church-yard, at the House of one *Russel* a Taylor, where he first undertook the Education and Instruction of his Sister's two Sons, the Younger whereof had been wholly committed to his Charge and Care. And here by the way, I judge it not impertinent to mention the many Authors both of the Latin and Greek, which through his excellent judgment and way of Teaching, far above the Pedantry of common publick Schools (where such Authors are scarce ever heard of) were run over within no greater compass of time, then from Ten to Fifteen or Sixteen Years of Age. Of the Latin the four Grand Authors, *De Re Rustica, Cato, Varro, Columella* and *Palladius; Cornelius Celsus*, an Ancient Physician of the *Romans*; a great part of *Pliny's* Natural History; *Vitruvius* his Architecture, *Frontinus* his Stratagems, with the two Egregious[7] Poets, *Lucretius* and *Manilius*. Of the Greek; *Hesiod*, a Poet equal with *Homer; Aratus* his *Phænomena*, and *Diosemeia, Dionysius Afer de situ Orbis, Oppian's Cynegeticks & Halieuticks. Quintus Calaber* his Poem of the *Trojan* War continued from *Homer; Apollonius, Rhodius* his Argonuticks, and in Prose, *Plutarch's Placita Philosophorum &* Περι Παιδων Αγογιας, *Geminus's* Astronomy; *Xenophon's Cyri Institutio & Anabasis, Aelians Tacticks*, and *Polyænus* his Warlike Stratagems; thus by teaching he in some measure increased his own knowledge, having the reading of all these Authors as it were by Proxy; and all this might possibly have conduced to the preserving of his Eye-sight, had he not, moreover, been perpetually busied in his own Laborious Undertakings of the Book or Pen. Nor did the time thus Studiously imployed in conquering the *Greek* and *Latin* Tongues, hinder the attaining to the chief Oriental Languages, *viz*. The *Hebrew, Caldee* and *Syriac*, so far as to go through the *Pentateuch*, or Five Books of *Moses* in *Hebrew*, to make a good entrance into the *Targum*, or *Chaldee* Paraphrase, and to understand several Chapters of St.

Matthew in the *Syriac* Testament: besides an Introduction into several Arts and Sciences, by reading *Urstisius* his Arithmetick, *Riffs* Geometry, *Petiscus* his Trigonometry, *Johannes de Sacro Bosco de Sphæra*; and into the *Italian* and *French* Tongues, by reading in *Italian, Giovan Villani's* History of the Transactions between several petty States of *Italy*; and in *French* a great part of *Pierre Davity*, the famous Geographer of *France* in his time. The *Sunday's* work was for the most part the Reading each day a Chapter of the *Greek* Testament, and hearing his Learned Exposition upon the same, (and how this savoured of Atheism in him, I leave to the courteous Backbiter to judge). The next work after this, was the writing from his own dictation, some part, from time to time, of a Tractate which he thought fit to collect from the ablest of Divines, who had written of that Subject; *Amesius, Wollebius*, &c. *viz*. A perfect System of Divinity, of which more hereafter. Now persons so far Manuducted[8] into the highest paths of Literature both Divine and Human, had they received his documents with the same Acuteness of Wit and Apprehension, the same Industry, Alacrity, and Thirst after Knowledge, as the Instructer was indued with, what Prodigies of Wit and Learning might they have proved! the Scholars might in some degree have come near to the equalling of the Master, or at least have in some sort made good what he seems to predict in the close of an Elegy he made in the Seventeenth Year of his Age, upon the Death of one of his Sister's Children (a Daughter), who died in her Infancy.

Then thou, the Mother of so sweet a Child,
Her false Imagin'd Loss cease to Lament,
And Wisely Learn to curb thy Sorrows Wild;
This if thou do, he will an Offspring give,
That to the Worlds last end shall make thy
                                          (Name to live.

But to return to the Thread of our Discourse; he made no long stay in his Lodgings in St. *Brides* Church-yard; necessity of having a place to dispose his Books in, and other Goods fit for the furnishing of a good handsome House, hastning him to take one; and accordingly a pretty Garden-House he took in *Aldersgate*-Street, at the end of an Entry,[9] and therefore the fitter for his turn, by the reason of the Privacy, besides that there are few Streets in *London* more free from Noise then that.

---

[7] Probably "remarkably good" (see *OED* 2.b, including Milton's usage).

[8] Led by the hand: in this case personally taught or led to wisdom.
[9] "A passage between houses, whether or not leading to an open space beyond; an alley. Now only dial. Also, an avenue, approach to a house" (*OED* 7.b, citing this instance).

Here first it was that his Academick Erudition was put in practice, and Vigorously proceeded, he himself giving an Example to those under him, (for it was not long after taking this House, e're his Elder Nephew was put to Board with him also) of hard Study, and spare Diet; only this advantage he had, that once in three Weeks or a Month, he would drop into the Society of some Young Sparks[10] of his Acquaintance, the chief whereof were Mr. *Alphry*, and Mr. *Miller*, two Gentlemen of *Gray*'s-Inn, the *Beau*'s of those Times, but nothing near so bad as those now-a-days; with these Gentlemen he would so far make bold with his Body, as now and then to keep a Gawdy day.[11]

In this House he continued several Years, in the one or two first whereof, he set out several Treatises, *viz.* That of *Reformation*; that against *Prelatical Episcopacy*; The *Reason of Church-Government*; The *Defence of Smectimnuus*, at least the greatest part of them, but as I take it, all; and some time after, one Sheet[12] of Education, which he Dedicated to Mr. *Samuel Hartlib*, he that wrote so much of Husbandry; this Sheet is Printed at the end of the Second Edition of his Poems; and lastly, *Areopagitica*. During the time also of his continuance in this House, there fell out several Occasions of the Increasing of his Family. His Father, who till the taking of *Reading* by the Earl of *Essex* his Forces, had lived with his other Son at his House there, was upon that Son's dissettlement necessitated to betake himself to this his Eldest Son, with whom he lived for some Years, even to his Dying Day. In the next place he had an Addition of some Scholars; to which may be added, his entring into Matrimony; but he had his Wife's company so small a time, that he may well be said to have become a single man again soon after. About *Whitsuntide* it was, or a little after, that he took a Journey in the Country; no body about him certainly knowing the Reason, or that it was any more than a Journey of Recreation: after a Month's stay, home he returns a Married-man, that went out a Batchelor; his Wife being *Mary*, the Eldest Daughter of Mr. *Richard Powell*, then a Justice of Peace, of *Forresthil*, near *Shotover* in *Oxfordshire*; some few of her nearest Relations accompanying the Bride to her new Habitation; which by reason the Father nor any body else were yet come, was able to receive them; where the

Feasting held for some days in Celebration of the Nuptials, and for entertainment of the Bride's Friends. At length they took their leave, and returning to *Foresthill*, left the Sister behind; probably not much to her satisfaction, as appeared by the Sequel; by that time she had for a Month or thereabout led a Philosophical Life, (after having been used to a great House, and much Company and Joviality). Her Friends, possibly incited by her own desire, made earnest suit by Letter, to have her Company the remaining part of the Summer, which was granted, on condition of her return at the time appointed, *Michalemas*,[13] or thereabout: In the mean time came his Father, and some of the foremention'd Disciples. And now the Studies went on with so much the more Vigour, as there were more Hands and Heads employ'd; the old Gentleman living wholly retired to his Rest and Devotion, without the least trouble imaginable. Our Author, now as it were a single man again, made it his chief diversion now and then in an Evening to visit the Lady *Margaret Lee*,[14] Daughter to the ——*Lee*, Earl of *Marlborough*, Lord High Treasurer of *England*, and President of the Privy Councel to King *James* the First. This Lady being a Woman of great Wit and Ingenuity, had a particular Honour for him, and took much delight in his Company, as likewise her Husband Captain *Hobson*, a very Accomplish'd Gentleman; and what Esteem he at the same time had for Her, appears by a Sonnet he made in praise of her, to be seen among his other Sonnets in his Extant Poems. *Michalemas* being come, and no news of his Wife's return, he sent for her by Letter, and receiving no answer, sent several other Letters, which were also unanswered; so that at last he dispatch'd down a Foot-Messenger with a Letter, desiring her return; but the Messenger came back not only without an answer, at least a satisfactory one, but to the best of my remembrance, reported that he was dismissed with some sort of Contempt; this proceeding, in all probability, was grounded upon no other Cause but this, namely, That the Family being generally addicted to the Cavalier Party, as they called it, and some of them possibly ingaged in the King's Service, who by this time had his Head Quarters at *Oxford*, and was in some Prospect of Success, they began to repent them of having Matched the Eldest Daughter of the Family to a Person so contrary to them in Opinion; and thought it would be a blot in their Escutcheon, when ever that Court should come to Flourish again; however, it so incensed our

---

[10] Fashionable young men.

[11] One of up to four days per year of celebration or revelry at the universities (Oxford or Cambridge) or at the London Inns of Court.

[12] Probably "In printing and bookbinding, a piece of paper . . . printed and folded so as to form pages of a required size (folio, quarto, etc.). Also, a quantity of printed matter equal to that contained in a sheet" (*OED* 6.a).

---

[13] A variant spelling for Michaelmas, one of the four quarter-days of the English business year, the Feast of St. Michael, September 29.

[14] Usually spelled "Lady Margaret Ley," as in most editions of Milton's poetry, including the 1645 *Poems*.

Author, that he thought it would be dishonourable ever to receive her again, after such a repulse; so that he forthwith prepared to Fortify himself with Arguments for such a Resolution, and accordingly wrote two Treatises, by which he undertook to maintain, That it was against Reason, (and the enjoyment of it not proveable by Scripture), for any Married Couple disagreeable in Humour and Temper, or having an aversion to each, to be forc'd to live yok'd together all their Days. The first was, His Doctrine and Discipline of Divorce; of which there was Printed a Second Edition, with some Additions. The other in prosecution of[15] the first, was styled, *Tetrachordon*. Then the better to confirm his own Opinion, by the attestation of others, he set out a Piece called the Judgement of *Martin Bucer*, a Protestant Minister, being a Translation, out of that Reverend Divine, of some part of his Works, exactly agreeing with him in Sentiment. Lastly, he wrote in answer to a Pragmatical Clerk,[16] who needs must give himself the Honour of Writing against so great a Man, His Colasterion, or Rod of Correction for a Sawcy Impertinent. Not very long after the setting forth of these Treatises, having application made to him by several Gentlemen of his acquaintance, for the Education of their Sons, as understanding haply the Progress he had infixed by his first undertakings of that nature, he laid out for a larger House, and soon found it out; but in the interim before he removed, there fell out a passage, which though it altered not the whole Course he was going to Steer, yet it put a stop or rather end to a grand Affair, which was more than probably thought to be then in agitation: It was indeed a design of Marrying one of Dr. *Davis*'s Daughters, a very Handsome and Witty Gentlewoman, but averse as it is said to this Motion;[17] however, the Intelligence hereof, and the then declining State of the King's Cause, and consequently of the Circumstances of Justice *Powell*'s family, caused them to set all Engines on Work,[18] to restore the late Married Woman to the Station wherein they had a little before had planted her; at last this device was pitch'd upon. There dwelt in the Lane of St. *Martins Le Grand*, which was hard by, a Relation of our Author's, one *Blackborough*, whom it was known he often visited, and upon this occasion the visits were the more narrowly observd, and possibly there might be a Combination between both Parties; the Friends on both

sides concentring in the same action though on different behalfs. One time above the rest, he making his usual visit, the Wife was ready in another Room, and on a sudden he was surprised to see one whom he thought to have never seen more, making Submission and begging Pardon on her Knees before him; he might probably at first make some shew of aversion and rejection; but partly his own generous nature, more inclinable to Reconciliation than to perseverance in Anger and Revenge; and partly the strong intercession of Friends on both sides, soon brought him to an Act of Oblivion, and a firm League of Peace for the future; and it was at length concluded, That she should remain at a Friend's house, till such time as he was settled in his New house at *Barbican*, and all things for her reception in order; the place agreed on for her present abode, was the Widow *Webber*'s house in St. *Clement*'s Church-yard, whose Second Daughter had been Married to the other Brother many years before; the first fruits of her return to her Husband was a brave[19] Girl, born within a year after; though, whether by ill Constitution, or want of Care, she grew more and more decrepit. But it was not only by Children that she increas'd the number of the Family, for in no very long time after her coming, she had a great resort[20] of her Kindred with her in the House, *viz.* her Father and Mother, and several of her Brothers and Sisters, which were in all pretty Numerous; who upon his Father's Sickning and Dying soon after went away. And now the House look'd again like a House of the Muses only, tho the accession of Scholars was not great. Possibly his proceeding thus far in the Education of Youth may have been the occasion of some of his Adversaries calling him Pædagogue and Schoolmaster: Whereas it is well known he never set up for a Publick School to teach all the young Fry of a Parish, but only was willing to impart his Learning and Knowledge to Relations, and the Sons of some Gentlemen that were his intimate Friends; besides, that neither his Converse, nor his Writings, nor his manner of Teaching ever savour'd in the least any thing of Pedantry; and probably he might have some prospect of putting in Practice his Academical Institution, according to the Model laid down in his Sheet of Education. The Progress of which design was afterwards diverted by a Series of Alteration in the Affairs of State; for I am much mistaken, if there were not about this time a design in Agitation of making him Adjutant-General in

---

[15] "Following up."
[16] Something like a busy-body clerk, whom Milton called a "servingman" (Yale 2: 741).
[17] Proposal or suggestion.
[18] Probably "set all contrivances at work." The family was investigating any plot that might help the couple get back together.

---

[19] Handsome, healthy.
[20] Probably "General or habitual repair of persons to some place or person" (*OED* 4); in other words, Mary Powell had relatives around her who offered her support.

Sir *William Waller*'s Army;[21] but the new modelling of the Army soon following, prov'd an obstruction to that design; and Sir *William*, his Commission being laid down, began, as the common saying is, to turn *Cat in Pan*. It was not long after the March of *Fairfax* and *Cromwel* through the City of *London* with the whole Army, to quell the Insurrections *Brown* and *Massy*, now Malcontents also, were endeavouring to raise in the City against the Armies proceedings, ere he left his great House in *Barbican*, and betook himself to a smaller in *High Holborn*, among those that open backward into *Lincolns-Inn*-Fields, here he liv'd a private and quiet Life, still prosecuting his Studies and curious Search into Knowledge, the grand Affair perpetually of his Life; till such time as the War being now at an end, with compleat Victory to the Parliament's side, as the Parliament then stood purg'd of all it's Dissenting Members, and the King after some Treaties with the Army, *re Infecta*, brought to his Tryal; the form of Government being now chang'd into a Free State, he was hereupon oblig'd to Write a Treatise, call'd the *Tenure of Kings and Magistrates*. After which his thoughts were bent upon retiring again to his own private Studies, and falling upon such Subjects as his proper Genius prompted him to Write of, among which was the History of our own Nation from the Beginning till the *Norman* Conquest, wherein he had made some progress. When for this his last Treatise, reviving the fame of other things he had formerly Published, being more and more taken notice of for his excellency of Stile, and depth of Judgement, he was courted into the Service of this new Commonwealth, and at last prevail'd with (for he never hunted after Preferment, nor affected the Tintamar[22] and Hurry of Publick business) to take upon him the Office of *Latin* Secretary to the Counsel of State for all their Letters to Foreign Princes and States; for they stuck to this Noble and Generous Resolution, not to write to any, or receive Answers from them, but in a Language most proper to maintain a Correspondence among the Learned of all Nations in this part of the World; scorning to carry on their Affairs in the Wheedling, Lisping Jargon of the Cringing *French*,[23] especialy having a Minister of State able to cope with the ablest any Prince or State could imploy for the Latin tongue; and so well he acquitted

himself in this station, that he gain'd from abroad both Reputation to himself, and Credit to the State that Employed him; and it was well the business of his Office came not very fast upon him, for he was scarce well warm in his Secretaryship, before other Work flow'd in upon him, which took him up for some considerable time. In the first place there came out a Book said to have been written by the King, and finished a little before his Death, Entituled, Ἐικὼν Βασιλικη, that is, *The Royal Image*; a Book highly cryed up for it's smooth Style, and pathetical Composure; wherefore to obviate the impression it was like to make among the *Many*, he was obliged to Write an Answer, which he Entituled Ἐικονοκλαςης, or *Image-Breaker*; and upon the heels of that, out comes in Publick the great Kill-cow of *Christendom*, with his *Defensio Regis contra Populum Anglicanum*: a Man so Famous and cryed up for his *Plinian Exercitations*, and other Pieces of reputed Learning, that there could no where have been found a Champion that durst lift up the Pen against so formidable an Adversary, had not our little *English David* had the Courage to undertake this great *French Goliah*, to whom he gave such a hit in the Forehead, that he presently staggered, and soon after fell; for immediately upon the coming out of the Answer, Entituled, *Defensio Populi Anglicani, contra Claudium Anonymum*, &c. he that till then had been Chief Minister and Superintendant in the Court of the Learned *Christina* Queen of *Sweden*, dwindled in esteem to that degree, that he at last vouchsafed to speak to the meanest Servant. In short, he was dismiss'd with so cold and slighting an Adieu, that after a faint dying Reply, he was glad to have recourse to Death, the remedy of Evils, and ender of Controversies: And now I presume our Author had some breathing space; but it was not long; for though *Salmasius* was departed, he left some stings behind, new Enemies started up, Barkers, though no great Biters; who the first Assertor of *Salmasius* his Cause was, is not certainly known, but variously conjectur'd at, some supposing it to be one *Janus* a Lawyer of *Grays-Inn*, some Dr. *Bramhal*, made by King *Charles* the Second after his Restauration Archbishop of *Armagh* in *Ireland*; but whoever the Author was, the Book was thought fit to be taken into correction, and our Author not thinking it worth his own undertaking, to the disturbing the progress of whatever more chosen work he had then in hands, committed this task to the youngest of his Nephews, but with such exact Emendations before it went to the Press, that it might have very well have passed for his, but that he was willing the person that took the pains to prepare it for his Examination and Polishment, should have the Name and Credit of being the Author; so that it came forth

---

[21] For further speculations about Milton's potential military career or his interest in military strategy, see various works by James Freeman, Stella Revard, and especially *Captain or Colonel: The Soldier in Milton's Life and Art* (Columbia: U of Missouri P, 1984).

[22] Meaningless noise, hurlyburly.

[23] Phillips's linguistic bias against French might reflect that of Milton as well, though Phillips, as he has written, studied his geography in French, under Milton.

under this Title, *Joannis Philippi Angli Defensio pro Populo Anglicano contra*, &c. during the Writing and Publishing of this Book, he lodg'd at one *Thomson*'s next door to the *Bull-head* tavern at *Charing Cross*, opening into the *Spring-Garden*, which seems to have been only a Lodging taken, till his designed Apartment in *Scotland-Yard* was prepared for him; for hither he soon removed from the foresaid place; and here his third Child, a Son was born, which through the ill usage, or bad Constitution of an ill chosen Nurse, died an Infant; from this Apartment, whether he thought it not healthy, or otherwise convenient for his use, or whatever else was the reason, he soon after took a pretty Garden-house in *Petty-France* in *Westminster*, next door to the Lord *Scudamore*'s and opening into St. *James*'s Park; here he remain'd no less than Eight years, namely, from the year 1652, till within a few weeks of King *Charles* the 2d's. Restoration. In this House his first Wife dying in Childbed, he Married a Second, who after a Year's time died in Childbed also; this his Second Marriage was about Two or Three years after his being wholly depriv'd of Sight, which was just going, about the time of his Answering *Salmasius*; whereupon his Adversaries gladly take occasion of imputing his blindness as a Judgment upon him for his Answering the King's Book, &c. whereas it is most certainly known, that his Sight, what with his continual Study, his being subject to the Head-ake, and his perpetual tampering with Physick[24] to preserve it, had been decaying for above a dozen years before, and the sight of one for a long time clearly lost. Here he wrote, by his *Amanuensis*, his Two Answers to *Alexander More*; who upon the last Answer quitted the field. So that being now quiet from State-Adversaries and publick Contests, he had leisure again for his own Studies and private Designs; which were his foresaid *History of* England, and a New *Thesaurus Linguæ Latinæ*, according to the manner of *Stephanus*; a work he had been long since Collecting from his own Reading, and still went on with it at times, even very near to his dying day; but the Papers after his death were so discomposed and deficient, that it could not be made fit for the Press; However, what there was of it, was made use of for another Dictionary. But the Heighth of his Noble Fancy and Invention began now to be seriously and mainly imployed in a Subject worthy of such a Muse, *viz.* A Heroick Poem, Entituled, *Paradise Lost*; the Noblest in the general Esteem of Learned and Judicious Persons, of any yet written by any either Ancient or Modern: This Subject was first designed a Tragedy, and

in the Fourth Book of the Poem there are Ten Verses, which several Years before the Poem was begun, were shewn to me, and some others, as designed for the very beginning of the said Tragedy. The Verses are these;

O Thou that with surpassing Glory
Crown'd!
Look'st from thy sole Dominion, like the
God
Of this New World; at whose sight
all the Stars
Hide their diminish'd Heads; to thee I
call,
But with no friendly Voice; and add thy
Name,
O Sun! to tell thee how I hate thy Beams
That bring to my remembrance, from what
State
I fell; how Glorious once above
thy Sphere;
Till Pride and worse Ambition threw me
down,
Warring in Heaven, against Heaven's Glo-
rious King.

There is another very remarkable Passage in the Composure of this Poem, which I have a particular occasion to remember; for whereas I had the perusal of it from the very beginning; for some years, as I went from time to time to Visit him, in a Parcel of Ten, Twenty, or Thirty Verses at a Time, which being Written by whatever hand came next, might possibly want Correction as to the Orthography and Pointing;[25] having as the Summer came on, not been shewed any for a considerable while, and desiring the reason thereof, was answered, That his Vein never happily flow'd, but from the *Autumnal Equinoctial* to the *Vernal*,[26] and that whatever he attempted was never to his satisfaction, though he courted his fancy never so much; so that in all the years he was about this Poem, he may be said to have spent but half his time therein. It was but a little before the King's Restoration that he Wrote and Published his Book in *Defence of a Commonwealth*; so undaunted he was in declaring his true Sentiments to the world; and not long before, his Power of the *Civil*

---

[24] Medicine, or in this case the application of herbal remedies.

[25] Spelling and punctuation.

[26] The OED note on "equinox" is helpful: "One of the two periods in the year when the days and nights are equal in length all over the earth, owing to the sun's crossing the equator. Hence, the precise moment at which the sun crosses the equator. The vernal or spring equinox is at present on the 20 March, and the autumnal on the 22 or 23 September. Just before the reformation of the calendar they were 11 days earlier."

Magistrate in Ecclesiastical Affairs; and *his Treatise against Hirelings*, just upon the King's coming over;[27] having a little before been sequestred[28] from his Office of *Latin* Secretary, and the Salary thereunto belonging, he was forc'd to leave his House also, in *Petty France*, where all the time of his abode there, which was eight years, as above-mentioned, he was frequently visited by persons of Quality, particularly my Lady *Ranala*, whose Son for some time he instructed; all Learned Foreigners of Note, who could not part out of this City, without giving a visit to a person so Eminent; and lastly, by particular Friends that had a high esteem for him, *viz.* Mr. *Andrew Marvel*, young *Laurence* (the Son of him that was President of *Oliver's* Council) to whom there is a Sonnet among the rest, in his Printed Poems; Mr. *Marchamont Needham*, the Writer of *Politicus*; but above all, Mr. *Cyriak Skinner* whom he honoured with two Sonnets, one long since publick among his Poems; the other but newly Printed. His next removal[29] was, by the advice of those that wisht him well, and had a concern for his preservation, into a place of retirement and abscondence,[30] till such time as the current of affairs for the future should instruct him what farther course to take; it was a Friend's House in *Bartholomew-Close*, where he liv'd till the Act of Oblivion came forth; which it pleased God, prov'd as favourable to him as could be hop'd or expected, through the intercession of some that stood[31] his Friends both in Council and Parliament; particularly in the House of Commons, Mr. *Andrew Marvel*, a Member for *Hull*, acted vigorously in his behalf, and made considerable party for him; so that, together with *John Goodwin* of *Coleman-Street*, he was only so far excepted as not to bear any Office in the Commonwealth. Soon after appearing again in publick, he took a House in *Holborn* near *Red Lyon Fields*, where he stayed not long before his Pardon having pass'd the Seal, he remov'd to *Jewin Street*; there he liv'd when he married his 3d. Wife, recommended to him by his old Friend Dr. *Paget* in *Coleman-street*; but he stay'd not long after his new Marriage, ere he remov'd to a House in the *Artillery*-walk leading to *Bunhill Fields*. And this was his last Stage in this World, but it was of many years continuance, more perhaps than he had had in any other place besides. Here he finisht his noble Poem, and publisht it in the year 1666. the first Edition was Printed in Quarto by one *Simmons*, a Printer in

Aldersgate-Street, the other in a large Octavo, by *Starky* near *Temple-Bar*, amended, enlarg'd, and differently dispos'd as to the Number of Books, by his own Hand, that is by his own appointment; the last set forth, many years since his death, in a large Folio with Cuts added by *Jacob Tonson*. Here it was also that he finisht and publisht his History of our Nation till the Conquest, all compleat so far as he went, some Passages only excepted, which being thought too sharp against the Clergy, could not pass the Hand of the Licencer, were in the Hands of the late Earl of *Anglesey* while he liv'd; where at present is uncertain. It cannot certainly be concluded when he wrote his excellent Tragedy entitled *Samson Agonistes*, but sure enough it is that it came forth after his publication of *Paradice lost*, together with his other Poem call'd *Paradice regain'd* which doubtless was begun and finisht and Printed after the other was publisht, and that in a wonderful short space considering the sublimeness of it; however it is generally censur'd to be much inferiour to the other, though he could not hear with patience any such thing when related to him; possibly the Subject may not afford such variety of Invention, but it is thought by the most judicious to be little or nothing inferiour to the other, for stile and decorum. The said Earl of *Anglesy* whom he presented with a Copy of the unlicens'd Papers of his History, came often here to visit him, as very much coveting his society and converse; as likewise others of the Nobility, and many persons of eminent quality; nor were the visits of Foreigners ever more frequent than in this place, almost to his dying day. His Treatise of True Religion, Heresy, Schism, and Toleration, &c. was doubtless the last thing of his writing that was publisht before his Death. He had, as I remember, prepared for the Press an answer to some little scribing Quack in *London*, who had written a Scurrilous Libel against him; but whether by the disswasion of Friends, as thinking him a Fellow not worth his notice, or for what other cause I know not, this Answer was never publisht. He died in the year 1673, towards the latter end of the Summer, and had a very decent interment according to his Quality, in the Church of St. *Giles Cripplegate*, being attended from his House to the Church by several Gentlemen then in Town, his principal well-wishers[32] and admirers. He had three Daughters who surviv'd him many years (and a Son) all by his first Wife (of whom sufficient mention hath been made.) *Anne* his Eldest as abovesaid, and *Mary* his Second, who were both born at his House in *Barbican*; and *Debora* the youngest, who is

---

[27] King Charles "came over" from France by way of the island of Jersey for his Restoration.

[28] Deprived of, relieved from.

[29] Move from one residence to another.

[30] Fugitive concealment.

[31] Remained (standing up for him).

---

[32] In *1694* the word was written "wellwi-shers." I presume that the compositor put the hyphen in the wrong place.

yet living, born at his House in *Petty-France*; between whom and his Second Daughter, the Son, named *John* was born as above-mention'd, at his Apartment in *Scotland Yard*. By his Second Wife, *Catharine* the Daughter of Captain *Woodcock* of *Hackney*, he had only one Daughter, of which the Mother the first year after her Marriage died in Child bed, and the Child also within a Month after. By his Third Wife *Elizabeth* the Daughter of one Mr. *Minshal* of *Cheshire*, (and Kins-woman to Dr. *Paget*) surviv'd him, and is said to be yet living, he never had any Child; and those he had by the First he made serviceable to him in that very particular in which he most wanted their Service, and supplied his want of Eye-sight by their Eyes and Tongue; for though he had daily about him one or other to Read to him, some persons of Man's Estate, who of their own accord greedily catch'd at the opportunity of being his Readers, that they might as well reap the benefit of what they Read to him, as oblige him by the benefit of their reading; others of younger years sent by their Parents to the same end; yet excusing only the Eldest Daughter by reason of her bodily Infirmity, and difficult utterance of Speech, (which to say truth I doubt was the Principal cause of excusing her) the other two were Condemn'd to the performance of Reading, and exactly pro-nouncing of all the Languages of what ever Book he should at one time or other think fit to peruse. *Viz.* The *Hebrew* (and I think the *Syriac*) the *Greek*, the *Latin*, the *Italian*, *Spanish* and *French*. All which sorts of Books to be confined to Read, without understanding one word, must needs be a Tryal of Patience, almost beyond endurance; yet it was endured by both for a long time, yet the irksomeness of this imployment could not always be concealed, but broke out more and more into expressions of uneasiness; so that at length they were all (even the Eldest also) sent out to learn some Curious and Ingenious sorts of Manufacture, that are proper for Women to learn, particularly Imbroideries in Gold or Silver. It had been happy indeed if the Daughters of such a Person had been made in some measure Inheritrixes of their Father's Learning; but since Fate otherwise decreed, the greatest Honour that can be ascribed to this now living (and so would have been to the others, had they lived) is to be Daughter to a man of his extraordinary Character.

He is said to have dyed worth 1500 *l.* in Money (a considerable Estate, all things considered) besides Houshold Goods; for he sustained such losses as might well have broke any person less frugal and temperate then himself; no less then 2000 *l.* which he had put for Security and improvement into the Excise Office, but neglecting to recal it in time, could never after get it out, with all the Power and Interest he had in the Great

ones of those Times; besides another great Sum, by mismanagement and for want of good advice.

Thus I have reduced into form and order what ever I have been able to rally up, either from the recollection of my own memory, of things transacted while I was with him, or the Information of others equally conver-sant afterwards, or from his own mouth by frequent visits to the last.

I shall conclude with two material passages, which though they relate not immediately to our Author, or his own particular concerns; yet in regard they hapned during his publick employ, and consequently fell most especially under his cognisance; it will not be amiss here to subjoin them. The first was this,

Before the War broke forth between the States of *England* and the *Dutch*, the *Hollanders* sent over Three Embassadours in order to an accommodation; but they returning *re infecta*, the *Dutch* sent away a *Plenipotentiary*,[33] to offer Peace upon much milder terms, or at least to gain more time.   But this *Pleni-potentiary* could not make such haste, but that the Parliament had procured a Copy of their Instructions in *Holland*, which were delivered by our Author to his Kinsman that was then with him, to Translate for the Council to view, before the said *Plenipotentiary* had taken Shipping for *England*; an Answer to all he had in Charge lay ready for him, before he made his publick entry into *London*.

In the next place there came a person with a very sump-tuous train, pretending himself an Agent from the Prince of *Conde*, then in Arms against Cardinal *Mazarine*: The Parliament mistrusting him, set their Instrument so busily at work, that in Four or Five Days they had procured Intelligence from *Paris*, that he was a Spy from K. *Charles*; whereupon the very next Morning our Author's Kinsman was sent to him, with an Order of Councel commanding him to depart the Kingdom within Three Days, or expect the Punishment of a Spy.

By these two remarkable passages, we may clearly discover the Industry and good Intelligence of those Times.

Here is a catalogue added of every Book of his that was ever publish'd, which to my knowledge is full and compleat.

---

[33] Envoy or messenger of a sovereign ruler.

TO
Oliver Cromwell.

CRomwell our Chief of Men, that through a Croud,
  Not of War only, but distractions rude;
Guided by Faith, and Matchless Fortitude:
To Peace and Truth, thy Glorious way hast Plough'd,
And Fought God's Battels, and his Work pursu'd,
While *Darwent* Streams with Blood of *Scots* imbru'd;
And *Dunbarfield* resound thy Praises loud,
And *Worchester's* Laureat Wreath; yet much remains
To Conquer still; Peace hath her Victories
No less than those of War; new Foes arise
Threatning to bind our Souls in secular Chains,
Help us to save Free Conscience from the paw
Of Hireling Wolves, whose Gospel is their Maw.

To my Lord FAIRFAX.

FAirfax, whose Name in Arms through Europe rings,
  And fills all Mouths with Envy or with Praise,
  And all her Jealous Monarchs with Amaze.
And Rumours loud which daunt remotest Kings,
Thy firm unshaken Valour ever brings
Victory home, while new Rebellions raise
Their Hydra-heads, and the false *North* displays
Her broken League to Imp her Serpent Wings:
O yet! a Nobler task awaits thy Hand,
For what can War, but Acts of War still breed,
Till injur'd Truth from Violence be freed;
And publick Faith be rescu'd from the Brand
Of publick Fraud; in vain doth Valour bleed,
While Avarice and Rapine shares the Land.

To Sir *HENRY VANE.*

VANE, Young in years, but in Sage Councels old,
  Then whom a better Senator ne're held
The Helm of *Rome,* when Gowns, not Arms, repell'd
The fierce *Epirote,* and the *African* bold,
Whether to settle Peace, or to unfold
The Drift of hollow States, hard to be Spell'd;
Then to advise how War may best be upheld,
Mann'd by her Two main Nerves, Iron and Gold,
  In all her Equipage: Besides, to know
Both Spiritual and Civil, what each means,
What serves each, thou hast learn'd, which few have done.
The bounds of either Sword to thee we owe;
Therefore on thy Right hand Religion leans,
And reckons thee in chief her Eldest Son.

To Mr. *CYRIAC SKINNER*
Upon his Blindness.

CYRIAC this Three years day, these Eyes though clear
  To outward view of blemish or Spot,
Bereft of Sight, their Seeing have forgot:
Nor to their idle Orbs doth day appear,
Or Sun, or Moon, or Star, throughout the Year;
Or Man, or Woman; yet I argue not
Against Heaven's Hand, or Will, nor bate one jot
Of Heart or Hope; but still bear up, and steer
Right onward. What supports me, dost thou ask?
The Conscience, Friend, to have lost them over ply'd
In Liberties Defence, my noble task;
Of which all *Europe* rings from side to side.
This thought might lead me through this World's vain mask
Content, though blind, had I no other Guide.

A
CATALOGUE
OF

Mr. *John Milton*'s Works.

ΕΙΚΟΝΟΚΓΑΣΤΗΣ In Answer to a Book,
  Entituled, ΕΙΚΏΝ ΒΑΣΙΛΑΙΚΗ, The Portraiture
of his Sacred Majesty in his Solitudes and Sufferings.

  The Tenure of Kings and Magistrates; proving, That
it is Lawful, and hath been held so through all Ages, for
any who have the Power, to call to Account a Tyrant,
or Wicked King; and after due Conviction to Depose
and put him to Death, if the ordinary Magistrate have
neglected or denied to do it; and that they who of late so
much blame Deposing, are the men that did it
themselves. 4to.

  Observations upon the Articles of Peace with the
Irish Rebels, on the Letter of *Ormond* to Colonel *Jones,*
and the Representation of the Presbytery of *Belfast.* 4to.

  The ready and easie way to establish a Free Commonwealth; and the Excellency thereof compared with the
Inconveniences and Dangers of Readmitting Kingship in
this Nation. 4to.

Areopagitica; A Speech of *John Milton* for the Liberty of Unlicensed Printing, to the Parliament of *England*. 4*to*.

Brief Notes upon the Sermon Enititled, *The Fear of God and the King*, Preach'd and since Publish'd by *Matthew Griffith*, D. D. and Chaplain to the late King; wherein many notorious Wrestings of Scripture, and other Falsities are observed: By *J. M.* 4*to*.

Of Reformation touching Church-Discipline in *England*, and the Causes that hitherto have hindred it. Two Books written to a Friend. 4*to*.

Of Prelatical Episcopacy, and whether it may be deduc'd from the Apostolical times by vertue of those Testimonies which are alledged to that purpose in some late Treatises; one whereof goes under the Name of *James* Archbishop of *Armagh*. 4*to*.

Animadversions upon the Remonstrants defence against *Smectymnuus*, with the Reason of Church-Government. 4*to*.

An Apology for *Smectymnuus*, with theReason of Church-Government. 4*to*.

The Reason of Church-Government urged against Prelacy. In Two Books. 4*to*.

Of True Religion, Heresie, Schism, Toleration, and what best means may be used against the Growth of Popery. 4*to*.

The Doctrine and Discipline of Divorce, restored, to the Good of both Sexes, from the Bondage of Canon Law and other mistakes, to the true meaning of Scripture in the Law and Gospel compared. Wherein also are set down the bad consequences of Abolishing, or Condemning of Sin, that which the Law of God allows, and Christ abolisht not. Now the second time Revised, and much Augmented in Two Books. To the Parliament of *England*, with the Assembly. In 4*to*.

Colasterion. A Reply to a nameless Answer against the Doctrine and Discipline of Divorce. Wherein the Trivial Author of that Answer is discovered, the Licenser conferr'd with, and the Opinion which they traduce defended. 4*to*.

Tetrachordon: Expositions upon the Four chief Places in Scripture, which Treat of Marriage, or Nullities in Marriage, on *Genesis* 1. 27, 28. Compar'd and Explain'd by *Genesis* 2. 18, 23, 24. *Deut.* 24. 1, 2. *Matt.* 5. 31, 32. with *Matt.* 19. from the 3d. to the 11. *verse.* 1 *Cor.* 7. from the 10th. to the 16th. Wherein the Doctrine and Discipline of Divorce, as was lately Published, is confirmed by Explanation of Scripture, by Testimony of Ancient Fathers, of Civil Laws, in the Primitive Church, of Famousest Reformed Divines: And lastly, by an intended act of the Parliament and Church of *England* in the last year of *Edward* the Sixth. 4*to*.

The Judgment of *Martin Bucer* concerning Divorce, written to *Edward* the Sixth, in his second Book of the Kingdom of Christ, and now *Englished*; wherein a late Book restoring the Doctrine and Discipline of Divorce is here Confirmed and Justified by the Authority of *Martin Bucer*. To the Parliament of *England*. 4*to*.

The History of *Brittain*, that part especially now called *England*: From the first Traditional Beginning, continued to the *Norman* Conquest. Collected out of the Ancientest and best Authors thereof, in 4*to*.

Paradice lost, A Poem in Twelve Books in 4*to*.

Paradice regain'd, a Poem in four Books; to which is added *Samson* Agonistes. *Octav*.

Poems upon several Occasions, both *English* and *Latin*, &c. Composed at several times.

A brief History of *Muscovia*, and of other less known Countries, lying *Eastward* of *Prussia*, as far as *Cathay*; gathered from the writings of several Eye-witnesses. *Oct*.

A Treatise of Civil Power in Ecclesiastical Causes, shewing that it is not Lawfull for any Power on Earth, to Compel in Matters of Religion. *Twelves*.

Considerations touching the likeliest means to remove Hirelings out of the Church; wherein is also discours'd, of *Tythes*, *Church-Fees*, and *Church-Revenues*; and whether any maintenance of Ministers can be settled by Law. *Twelves*.

A Declaration, or Letters Patents of the Election of *John* King of *Poland*. A translation.

Opera Latina, *Viz.*

Defensio pro populo Anglicano. *The same lately Translated into English.*

Defensio Secunda.

Defensio Pro se.

Defensio Miltoni per Johannem Phillippum.

Literæ Pseudo-Senatûs Cromwellii Reliquorumque perduellium nomine ac jussu conscriptæ a J. M. *Twelves*.

Johannis Miltoni Angli Epistolarum Familiarium Liber unus: Quibus Accesserunt, jam olim in Collegio Adolescentis, Prolusiones Quædam Oratoriæ. *Octavo*.

Accidence Commenct[34] Grammar.

Johannis Miltoni Angli Artis Logicæ Plenior Institutio ad Petri Rami Methodum Concinnata: Adjecta est Praxis Annalytica & Petri Rami vita libris Duobus. *Twelves*.

---

[34] Printed "Commenet" incorrectly.

POEMS

OF

Mr. *John Milton*,

BOTH

ENGLISH and LATIN,

Compos'd at several times.

Printed by his true Copies.

The SONGS were set in Musick by
Mr. HENRY LAWES Gentleman of
the KINGS Chappel, and one
of His MAIESTIES
Private Musick.

—— *Baccare frontem*
Cingite, ne vati noceat mala lingua futuro,
Virgil, Eclog. 7.

Printed and publish'd according to
ORDER.

LONDON,
Printed by *Ruth Raworth* for *Humphrey Moseley*,
and are to be sold at the signe of the Princes
Arms in *Pauls* Church-yard. 1645.

The 1645 *Poems*

MILTON AND HUMPHREY MOSELEY

The title page of Milton's first slender but rich volume of poetry emphasizes the fact that English and Latin poems are published together (Revard), and it claims that the printer has used "true copies" or copies of the poems provided by the author. It also connects Milton with the court of Charles I through Henry Lawes, one of the king's band of private musicians. It may make Milton appear more of a Cavalier than a Puritan, since his portrait on the facing page has dancing pastoral figures in the background (Spear 192), which may mean that Milton was cultivating a "light and dancing posture" (Martz 5). The 1645 *Poems* has also been passed by the censor ("*according to ORDER*"). It has been printed by the widow Ruth Raworth, for the well-known publisher of poets, Humphrey Moseley, who provides a preface, and it will be sold from one of the shops in St. Paul's Cathedral courtyard. There are typographical hints throughout the 1645 *Poems* that Milton helped design the book (Martz 5), perhaps with the shape of the commemorative volume to Edward King, *Justa Edovardo King Naufrago* (Wittreich 127) in mind.

Humphrey Moseley had published poetry by remarkably good writers. His editions of the poems of Edmund Waller were especially popular in 1645 (Parker 289). Some of Waller's lyric poems were, like Milton's songs in the masque, set to music by Henry Lawes. Humphrey Moseley had a publishing record which reflected his good taste more than his political preferences. He published or sold at least some of the books of Lancelot Andrewes, Francis Bacon, Beaumont and Fletcher, Luis de Camões, George Chapman, Abraham Cowley, William Crashaw, William Davenant, John Denham, René Descartes, John Donne, Hugo Grotius, Giovanni Baptista Guarini, Joseph Hall, Henry Lawes, Giovanni Francesco Loredano, Gervase Markham, Philip Massinger, Francis Quarles, Sir Walter Ralegh, Sir John Suckling, and Edmund Waller. Milton, in other words, was in very good company. But Moseley was a Royalist printer. Lois Potter, citing Louis Martz and Michael Wilding, reiterates the belief that "Moseley's presentation of the [1645] volume was designed to turn his author, against his will, into a crypto-royalist" (162). Various other Milton scholars have attempted to find evidence of Milton's early radicalism in the 1645 volume, but the fact is that many of the poems are dedicated to aristocrats, dead or alive, with some of those honored, as with the Earl of Bridgewater, quite close to the king (see Spear 189). The printer Moseley and the engraver of the notoriously bad portrait of Milton (see Hale), William Marshall, provide a link between John Donne, whom Moseley published; Archbishop Laud, whose portrait Marshall had engraved; and King Charles I, who would also be the subject for Marshall's most famous posthumous engraving of the beheaded king as martyr, in *Eikon Basilike*, published in 1649, which Milton would answer in *Eikonoklastes*.

In Vergil's Seventh Eclogue, sometimes called "The Singing Match," the shepherd Thyrsis (the name Milton appropriated for the Henry Lawes role in his masque) addresses his rival Corydon and other shepherds: "Arcadian shepherds, adorn your nascent poet with ivy leaves, and make Codrus burst himself with envy; or, if he praises me too much, *bind my forehead with foxglove, to stop his evil tongue from hurting your future poet*" (the emphasized words translate those on the title page; Rieu's translation 82). A budding genius must protect himself against envy and slander, Milton's stance in poems like "I did but prompt the age."

Before 1645, Milton had published only "Lycidas," the Hobson poems, the poem to the memory of Shakespeare in the Second Folio, and the anonymous version of *A Mask*. We might conjecture that Moseley is inflating the young Milton's reputation in order to sell his book. But Milton had gained notoriety for the divorce pamphlets published between 1642 and 1645, and for the 1644 *Areopagitica*, which defied the very licensing order that was necessary to the licensing of the 1645 *Poems*.

Moseley's introduction shows that he studied the poetry in the volume with care: he knew that Milton admired Spenser, for instance, and he seems to quote indirectly from "Lycidas." As Wittreich has shown, Moseley and Milton may have combined to emphasize the importance of "Lycidas" even in the table of contents (127–29).

Works Cited

Moseley, C. W. D. *The Poetic Birth: Milton's Poems of 1645.* Aldershot, Eng.: Scolar, 1991.

Hale, John K. "Milton's Greek Epigram." *Milton Quarterly* 16 (1982): 8–9.

Martz, Louis L. "The Rising Poet." *The Lyric and Dramatic Milton: Selected Papers from the English Institute.* Ed. Joseph H. Summers. New York: Columbia UP, 1965. 3–33.

Potter, Lois. *Secret Rites and Secret Writing: Royalist Literature, 1641–1660.* Cambridge: Cambridge UP, 1989.

Revard, Stella P. *Milton and the Tangles of Neaera's Hair.* Columbia: U of Missouri P, 1997.

Spear, Gary. "Reading Before the Lines: Typography, Iconography, and the Author in Milton's 1645 Frontispiece." *New Ways of Looking at Old Texts: Papers of the Renaissance English Text Society 1985-1991.* Ed. W. Speed Hill. Binghamton, NY: Medieval & Renaissance Texts & Studies, 1993. 187-94.

Vergil. *Virgil: The Pastoral Poems,* trans. E.V. Rieu. Baltimore: Penguin, 1949.

Wittreich, Joseph Anthony, Jr. *Visionary Poetics: Milton's Tradition and His Legacy.* San Marino, CA: Huntington Library, 1979.

THE
STATIONER
TO THE
READER.

IT is not any private respect of gain, *Gentle* Reader, *for the slightest Pamphlet is nowadayes more vendible then the Works of learnedest men; but it is the love I have to our own Language that hath made me diligent to collect, and set forth such* Peeces *both in Prose and Vers, as may renew the wonted honour and esteem of our English tongue; and it's the worth of these both English and Latin* Poems, *not the flourish of any prefixed* encomions[1] *that can invite thee to buy them, though these are not without the highest Commentations and Applause of the learnedst* Academicks, *both domestick and forrein: And amongst those of our own Countrey, the unparallel'd attestation of that renowned Provost of* Eaton, *Sir* Henry Wootton: *I know not thy palat how it relishes such dainties, nor how harmonious thy soul is; perhaps more trivial* Airs[2] *may please thee better. But howsoever thy opinion is spent upon these, that incouragement I have already received from the most ingenious men in their clear and courteous entertainment of Mr.* Wallers *late choice Peeces, hath once more made me adventure into the World, presenting it with these ever-green, and not to be blasted Laurels. The Authors more peculiar excellency in these studies, was too well known to conceal his Papers, or to keep me from attempting to sollicit them from him. Let the event guide it self which way it will, I shall deserve of the age, by bringing into the Light as true a Birth, as the Muses have brought forth since our famous* Spencer *wrote; whose Poems in these English ones are as rarely imitated, as sweetly excell'd. Reader if thou art Eagle-eied to censure their worth, I am not fearful to expose them to thy exactest perusal.*

Thine to command

HUMPH. MOSELEY.

The Nativity Ode

What is often called the Nativity Ode without quotation marks or italics in the title is a joyful, spirited Christmas poem sent in 1629 to Milton's friend Charles Diodati, accompanied by a Latin verse letter, Elegy 6. The Nativity Ode is the first poem the reader sees in Milton's *Poems Both English and Latin*, his first book of poetry, published in 1645. The twenty-one-year-old Milton as he pictures himself in the poem seems to be proudly self-conscious. He is inspired, as he says, by the heavenly muse. If indeed the poem was written before dawn on that Christmas morning, it is the tour-de-force of a youthful poet, showing great virtuosity in the varying stanza forms of its proem, the four introductory stanzas, and of the hymn proper. Though Milton would later reject the "jingling sounds of like endings" and the "modern bondage of rhyming" when called upon to defend the blank verse of *Paradise Lost*, in the Nativity Ode he displays a mastery of rhyme and a youthful excitement in using it.

Milton wrote to Charles Diodati that he had composed the Nativity Ode as a birthday present for Christ, implying that the poem had been written very quickly, in the first light of Christmas morning, 1629.

I am singing about the King, bringer of peace via his divinity, and the holy times promised by the sacred books, and about the infant cries of our Lord, and his being stabled under a lowly roof, he who with his Father governs the realms above. I am singing the stars and the heavenly hosts who sang in mid-air, and the gods suddenly destroyed in their own shrines. I give these gifts for the birthday of Christ—gifts the first light of dawn brought me. For you also these modest thoughts have been piped out in my native tongue, and you will be, when I recite them, the judge of them.

The freshness of the nativity poem complements its early-morning composition and its birthday message, although what Milton describes as a quickly written poem need not be unpremeditated (and some critics argue that

---

[1]Encomia, poems of praise.
[2]Inconsequential popular songs.

it was not composed in haste). Like most of Milton's great poems written in traditional genres, the Nativity Ode summarizes the content of every classical ode or nativity hymn he had read, while reinterpreting and adding fresh touches in theme, imagery, rhetoric—even in sound. Milton's picturing the poem as a birthday present to Christ the King may be misleading, since the poem itself is in no way like a modern Christmas card. It is more like a Christmas carol (Martz 53).

The poet appears in his own poem only as part of a first-person plural "we" who present the poem as if the author and reader were one of the Wise Men bringing gifts to the infant Christ. Milton's self-presentation in the poem is both humble and arrogant: it may be presumptuous of the young poet to present himself as one of the Magi, but he disarms that sort of criticism when he calls the poem his "humble ode" (24) or "tedious Song" (239).

Milton often includes an apology for his poetry or a disclaimer within his early poems in English. At the beginning of "Lycidas," for instance, he talks about his premature attempt to write poetry in terms of "fingers rude" shattering leaves and at the end of the same poem he pictures himself in the role of poet as an "uncouth Swain." The pose of humility in each poem does offset the potential arrogance of daring to write yet another elegy or yet another Nativity poem. See MacCallum for a discussion of Milton's suppression of the first-person pronoun and of his own individuality in the poem.

Milton's words would allow us to call the poem both a hymn and an ode, twin genres that Philip Rollinson has ably discussed. It is a hymn, in both the Christian and the Hellenistic senses of the term. Callimachus is perhaps the best-known Greek composer of hymns, the subjects addressed being members of the Greek pantheon such as Zeus and Artemis. Milton's nativity poem is an ode in that it is like the extended lyric poems of Pindar, usually written to celebrate a heroic person or achievement. Instead of glorifying an athlete in the ancient Olympian games, as Pindar did, Milton celebrates the infant Christ, more powerful in his cradle than was Hercules. Hercules, wrote Pindar in his first Nemean Ode, strangled snakes in his infancy. Just as he undercut pagan heroism, Milton reduced the pagan gods to Christian devils (Moloch in Stanza 23 is "the grisly king, / In dismall dance about the furnace blue"). Those "gods" worshiped by pagans are exorcized or banished at the birth of Christ.

THE GENRE OF THE NATIVITY POEM

In the late sixteenth and early seventeenth century, Edmund Spenser, John Donne, Thomas Traherne, and Robert Southwell all wrote poems celebrating the Na-

tivity. Southwell's "The Burning Babe" is perhaps the most often anthologized. For a collection of such nativity poems accompanied by reproductions of pictorial art, see Sledge, who calls the Nativity Ode "the finest Nativity poem in English literature" and "Milton's first great poem" (98). Elaine Safer traces poetic precedents of Milton's poem to Vergil's fourth "Messianic" eclogue; Prudentius's fourth-century *Apotheosis*, which describes the cessation of the oracles, and his nativity hymn "Kalends Januarius"; as well as Tasso's "Canzone sopra la Cappella del Presepio" (canzone on the Presepio Chapel) and other early sixteenth-century works by the Latin poet Mantuan and the Italian pastoral poet Jacopo Sannazaro. Carey points out parallels with Torquato Tasso's "Nel giorno della Natività" (98). Seeking English sources, Maren-Sofie Røstvig believes Milton derived stanza patterns from Giles Fletcher's *Christ's Victory and Triumph* (1610). Certainly, Milton's use of such exuberant, vociferous language in compounds like "pale-ey'd Priest" in "No nightly trance, or breathed spell, / Inspire's the pale-ey'd Priest from the prophetic cell" (179–80) echoes the poetic style of Josuah Sylvester, translating DuBartas's *Divine Weekes and Works*. In her edition of Sylvester's translation, Susan Snyder identifies one defining characteristic of his style as "thumping liveliness" (1: 59); Milton's style, to his credit, is more subtle, and its subtlety owes more to Spenser than to Sylvester (Clanton).

POETIC LANGUAGE AND IMAGERY

Milton describes ideal poetry as "simple, sensuous, and passionate" (*Of Education*; Yale 2: 403), adjectives that fit the poetic style of the Nativity Ode. The images within the poem derive from the natural world and are therefore simple or basic, as with clouds or snow. The imagery of the poem is also sensuous, sometimes physically appealing, sometimes repulsive, describing moral states of good or evil. The poem also represents the intellectual engagement and the passion of the author for his subject, yet it is intellectually stimulating, not just the kind of mindless "air" that Humphrey Moseley had criticized in his preface to the 1645 *Poems*.

The image of the old dragon Satan who "Swindges the scaly Horrour of his foulded tail" in Stanza 18, matching the onomatopoetic verb "Swindges" with the almost-allegorical "Horrour," shocks the reader as much as does Macbeth's "I have supp'd full with horrors" (5.5.13). Milton's image is an arresting catachresis, an implied metaphor, or mixture of the real and the metaphysical; yet we are brought back to pictorial reality with the image of the "foulded tail." Milton in one image can appeal to the senses (even the tactile, as in "scaly"), demonstrate moral indignation and revulsion at a picture of evil, allude to the Bible, perhaps borrow an effective image partly from Shakespeare, and, while doing all that, make his reader's mind leap from a sensuous image of a dragon's tail to a vision of cosmic horror.

The language and imagery of the Nativity Ode are both obviously and subtly biblical, being derived not only from the accounts of the Nativity at the beginnings of all four gospels, but from less well-remembered passages such as Revelation 12 (Swanson and Mulryan). The poem is also recognizably Protestant, deemphasizing the role of the Virgin Mary in the Nativity and emphasizing the sinfulness of nature even as Christ is born to cleanse it.

Milton fills the Nativity Ode with images of music, appropriate for the son of a composer. The younger John Milton was an active musician and would become a lyricist for the composer Henry Lawes (Brennecke 128). Musical terms in the Nativity Ode include "close," "symphony," "hymn," "strain" (the noun), "choir," "trumpet," and the word "music" itself. Milton would also have associated singing with worship, formal or private. Anyone who has heard or has sung the Anglican service of Morning Prayer might be familiar with one of the most joyful Psalms, "O all ye Works of the Lord, bless ye the Lord: praise him, and magnify him for ever," which Milton might have heard at St. Paul's school or in any parish church service. At St. Paul's Milton would also have been taught to translate (and most probably to sing) the psalms. His role in writing the Nativity Ode combines that of David as joyful psalmist in the Old Testament with that of a Magus or Wise Man singing a hymn of praise to the infant Christ. As Mary Ann Radzinowicz cleverly puts it, the Nativity Ode is "a poem not only based on Luke's New Testament psalms but composed of numerous topoi from the Psalms set by the Book of Common Prayer to be read at Christmastime" (ix). Both odes and hymns are meant to be sung, in their original form, and Milton, perhaps in honor of his father, may have thought of himself as part composer, part poet, part prophet, and part psalmist. The question of the prophetic identity of the poet in the Nativity Ode is discussed by Kerrigan (192–99).

The Nativity Ode follows a simple A-B-A or slow-fast-slow structure like that of the sonata. A first quiet section announces the subject and pictures the Nativity. Beginning at the end of Stanza 16, a second, more boisterous or raucous section, which might be compared to a musical scherzo, recreates the banishment of the pagan gods vividly, with their "hideous humm," "hollow shreik," "voice of weeping," and "sighing." The last section, beginning pianissimo at Stanza 27, returns quietly to the Virgin and Child. In a well-respected article, Arthur Barker discusses the three-part structure of the poem, with an emphasis somewhat different from my own.

The poem would fit a conventional definition of baroque art in music, visual art, or architecture, because of the raw energy barely contained within the limits of its frames. When he wrote the poem, Milton had not yet been directly exposed to the great baroque art of Italy, though he might have seen reflections of it in the costuming of Italianate masques and public spectacles designed by Inigo Jones and performed in London in the first quarter of the seventeenth century (Peacock; Demaray 31–40). Milton's image of Peace descending through the sphere in Stanza III, or the "yellow-skirted *Fayes*" of Stanza 26, may owe something to masque staging and costuming. The painter Peter Paul Rubens, incidentally, was to come to London in the early 1630s to decorate rooms of Buckingham Palace (as with the "Landscape with St. George") and to plan the panels for the ceiling of Charles I's Banqueting House at Whitehall Palace (finished 1634; see Spencer 124n) in a sublimely baroque style, with swirling events occurring in mid-air, as they do in masques and in the Nativity Ode.

Martz, however, sees the decorum of the poem as more plain than baroque: "This decorum of an ancient and traditional simplicity pervades every aspect of the poem, versification, language, scene painting, imagery, and theme" (55).

POLITICAL SUBTEXTS

There may be a political undercurrent in the Nativity Ode. Stella Revard has recently examined the image of Apollo in a historical context to determine that the Greek sun god was closely associated with the Barbarini family, some of whom Milton would meet in Italy in 1638. Maffeo Barbarini was Pope at the time when the Nativity Ode was being written (1629). Charles I was also associated with the sun and with Apollo. Milton's banishment of Apollo—the god and the symbol—may be a symptom of his future antimonarchical stance.

Certainly Milton meant to criticize the Greek and Roman and the Egyptian pantheons of gods that he believed were banished when Christianity was born. The cessation of the old oracles, in his estimation, is of more significance than the Pax Romana—the famous period of peace during which time Christ was born.

NUMERICAL PATTERN

The four seven-line iambic stanzas of the Proem each end with an Alexandrine, a six-beat iambic line, and the twenty-seven eight-line iambic stanzas of the Hymn each end with an Alexandrine. Milton may be playing with a finely knit numerical structure (the musical and mathematical theories of Pythagoras could be important for interpreting the poem's structure) that would have had significance to some readers in the Renaissance.

Readers might have looked at the numbers for their poetic or musical value or for their mystical or Christian significance. Modern scholars, however, have not yet agreed on what stanza pattern or syllable count might have numerological significance. Neville Davies believes that "[t]he poem is bound together by an articulating pattern of matching threads appearing and reappearing symmetrically around its centre," which "sets up a web of tensions that prevents the accreted units from disintegrating" (104–05). The proem stanzas rhyme AB AB B CC, and the Hymn stanzas rhyme AA B CC B DD. Maren-Sofie Røstvig points out that "[t]he structural numbers of the introduction—4, 7, and 28—enact the weekly and seasonal cycles of Time . . ." (62–63). Two "paragraphs" also exist typographically within each stanza of the Hymn, and each indented line within the stanza rhymes with the other, but Milton often breaks the customary end-stopped pattern of stanzas by running a verse paragraph from one stanza to another, as between stanzas 17 and 23, or 23 and 24, at least once with a comma and not a period between stanzas. He seems quite conscious that rhymed stanzas with heavily accented syllables may quickly become monotonous.

PROSODY AND SCANSION

The poet Gerard Manley Hopkins, who admired Milton's sounds and poetic rhythms, would have found in the poem cleverly elided or slurred-over syllables that elude a strict iambic pattern—what Hopkins called "sprung" or "counterpointed" rhythm. "Swindges the scaly Horrour of his foulded tail," for instance, can be read as an iambic hexameter line with a trochaic opening foot. Milton thus varies the sound without interrupting the meter. Hopkins wrote that ". . . Milton is the great standard in the use of counterpoint. . . . [T]hat is, each line (or nearly so) has two different coexisting scansions" (185). Hopkins might also have admired "the compression of the syntax" in Milton's lines (Ricks 91), as in "And bid the weltring waves their oozy channel keep" (124), which is not only effective in its imagery and syntax—as with the rare adjective "oozy"—but in its variety of consonant and vowel sounds. The modern Welsh poet Dylan Thomas, also struck by the compression of images and syntax and by the sounds of the poem, memorized the Nativity Ode and could recite it; he must have admired the extraordinary poetic energy of the young Milton.

As Martz points out, Milton's prosody reflects the practice of his most-respected poetic ancestors:

The four prefatory stanzas, written in a variety of rhyme royal, suggest the use of this ancient stanza-form by Chaucer and the Chaucerians, by Spenser, in *The Ruines of Time* and the *Fowre Hymnes*, and by Shakespeare, in *Lucrece*; while the modification into hexameter in the final line declares a further allegiance to Spenser and the Spenserians. (53–54)

TEXT

The text here reproduced is that of the *Poems of Mr. John Milton* of 1645, with Stanza 15 rewritten as in the revised version in *Poems, &c. upon Several Occasions* of 1673. The stanza as it appeared in 1645 is reconstructed in the notes for cross-reference. The premier position of the poem both in Milton's 1645 and 1673 collections may indicate that he thought highly of it. "Lycidas" was carefully placed last by the editor in the memorial volume to Edward King, and Milton's masque has the same position of honor in the 1645 *Poems*.

Milton made only one significant change in the text of the Nativity Ode between editions, but his care in revising Stanza 15 shows that he did not lose interest in the poem. Miltonic spellings such as "sovran" seem to indicate that he had influence over the typesetting, as do the shapes of the poems on the pages. Any theory of spelling preferences, however, should be approached cautiously (consult Shawcross, "Spelling"). The copy text chosen is *1645* because *1673* does not improve on the accidentals (details of spelling and punctuation) of the earlier edition. In some instances, however, as with the change from "wrath" to "wroth" at line 171, the reading of the later edition seems to correct the earlier, and the punctuation of *1673* may improve at times on the inconsistency of *1645*. In cases in which the later edition obviously corrects the earlier, I have made changes and included notes to that effect.

Works Cited
Editions are marked with an asterisk.

Barker, Arthur E. "The Pattern of Milton's Nativity Ode." *University of Toronto Quarterly* 10 (1941): 167–81.

Brennecke, Ernest, Jr. *John Milton the Elder and His Music*. New York: Octagon, 1973.

Clanton, Jann Aldredge. "Love Descending: A Study of Spenser's *Fowre Hymnes* and Milton's *Nativity Ode*." Diss. Texas Christian U, 1978.

Davies, Neville. "*Laid artfully together*: Stanzaic Design in Milton's 'On the Morning of Christ's Nativity.' " Røstvig, *Fair Forms*, 85–118.

Demaray, John G. *Milton and the Masque Tradition: The Early Poems, "Arcades," and "Comus."* Cambridge, MA: Harvard UP, 1968.

Hopkins, Gerard Manley. *Poems and Prose of Gerard Manley Hopkins*. Ed. W. H. Gardner. Baltimore, MD: Penguin, 1961.

Kerrigan, William. *The Prophetic Milton*. Charlottesville: UP of Virginia, 1974. 192–99.

MacCallum, Hugh. "The Narrator of Milton's *On the Morning of Christ's Nativity*." *Familiar Colloquy: Essays Presented to Arthur Edward Barker*. Ed. Patricia Brückman. Toronto: Oberon, 1978. 179–95.

Martz, Louis L. *Milton: Poet of Exile*. Second ed. New Haven, CT: Yale UP, 1986.

*Milton, John. *Complete Shorter Poems*. Ed. John Carey. London: Longman, 1981.

*——. Paradise Regain'd. *A Poem, in Four Books. To Which is Added* Samson Agonistes: *and Poems upon Several Occasions*. Ed. Thomas Newton. London: Tonson, 1766.

Patterson, Annabel. *Pastoral and Ideology: Virgil to Valéry*. Berkeley: U of California P, 1987.

Peacock, John. *The Stage Designs of Inigo Jones: The European Context*. Cambridge: Cambridge UP, 1995.

Radzinowicz, Mary Ann. *Milton's Epics and the Book of Psalms*. Princeton, NJ: Princeton UP, 1989.

Revard, Stella P. "Apollo and Christ in the Seventeenth-Century Religious Lyric." *New Perspectives on the Seventeenth-Century English Religious Lyric*. Ed. John Roberts. Columbia: U of Missouri P, 1994. 143–67.

Ricks, Christopher. *Milton's Grand Style*. Oxford: Clarendon, 1963.

Rollinson, Philip B. "Milton's Nativity Ode and the Decorum of Genre." *Milton Studies* 7 (1975): 165–88.

Røstvig, Maren-Sofie. "Elaborate Song: Conceptual Structure in Milton's 'On the Morning of Christ's Nativity.' " *Fair Forms: Essays in English Literature from Spenser to Jane Austen*. Ed. Røstvig. Cambridge: Brewer, 1975. 54–84.

Safer, Elaine. "On the Morning of Christ's Nativity." *A Milton Encyclopedia*. Gen. ed. William B. Hunter. Lewisburg, PA: Bucknell UP, 1986.

Shawcross, John. "Spelling." *A Milton Encyclopedia*. Gen. ed. William B. Hunter. Lewisburg, PA: Bucknell UP, 1986.

Sledge, Linda. *Shivering Babe, Victorious Lord*. Grand Rapids, MI: Eerdmans, 1981.

Snyder, Susan, ed. *The Divine Weeks and Works of Guillaume de Saluste, Sieur du Bartas Translated by Josuah Sylvester*. 2 vols. Oxford: Clarendon, 1979.

Spencer, Jeffry B. *Heroic Nature*. Evanston, IL: Northwestern UP, 1973.

Swanson, Donald, and John Mulryan. "Milton's *On the Morning of Christ's Nativity*: The Virgilian and Biblical Matrices." *Milton Quarterly* 23 (1989): 59–66.

Tasso, Torquato. "Nel giorno della Natività." *Rime*. Venice, 1621.

On the morning of CHRISTS
Nativity. Compos'd 1629.[1]

I.

THis is the Month, and this the happy morn
    Wherin the Son of Heav'ns eternal King,
    Of wedded Maid, and Virgin Mother born,[2]
Our great redemption from above did bring;
For so the holy sages° once did sing,   OLD TESTAMENT PROPHETS   5
    That he our deadly forfeit[3] should release,
And with his Father work us a perpetual peace.

II.

That glorious Form,[4] that Light unsufferable,°   UNENDURABLE
And that far-beaming blaze of Majesty,
Wherwith he wont at Heav'ns high Councel-Table,   10
To sit the midst of Trinal Unity,[5]
He laid aside; and here with us to be,
    Forsook the Courts of everlasting Day,
And chose with us a darksom° House of mortal Clay.[6]   GLOOMY

III.

Say Heav'nly Muse, shall not thy sacred vein[7]   15
Afford a present to the Infant God?
Hast thou no vers, no hymn, or solemn strein,
To welcom him to this his new abode,
Now while the Heav'n by the Suns team untrod,[8]
    Hath took no print of the approching light,   20
And[9] all the spangled host keep watch in squadrons bright?

IV.

See how from far upon the Eastern rode°   ROAD
The Star-led Wisards° haste with odours sweet:[10]   THE THREE WISE MEN
O run, prevent° them with thy humble ode,   ANTICIPATE

---

[1]"Compos'd 1629" was omitted in *1673.*

[2]Shawcross (63n) notes the chiasmus, or symbolic criss crossing of figures, in "wedded Maid" and "Virgin Mother" (3), though making the sign of the cross, even metaphorically, might be an act that Milton would not endorse.

[3]"Something to which the right is lost by the commission of a crime or fault [in this case Original Sin]; hence, a penal fine, a penalty for breach of contract or neglect of duty" (*OED* 2).

[4]"In the Scholastic philosophy: 'The essential determinant principle of a thing; that which makes anything (matter) a determinate species or kind of being; the essential creative quality'" (*OED* 4.a). Milton would define the term in 1644, but not very helpfully: "The *Form* by which the thing is what it is" (*Tetrachordon*; Yale 2: 608).

[5]The unity represented by the mystery of the Holy Trinity, three in one.

[6]Christ, as a "form" or perfect picture of God's glory, came down from his position as part of the Trinity in heaven to become incarnate. His body, like that of Adam, is made of "mortal Clay." His majesty is manifested in blazing and unendurable light, as with the burning bush which appears to Moses in Exodus 3. Compare "Bright effluence of bright essence increate" in *Paradise Lost* 3.6.

[7]Probably in the sense of *OED* 11: "A natural tendency towards, a special aptitude or capacity for, the production of literary or artistic work; a particular strain of talent or genius."

[8]The pre-dawn heaven, before the entrance of the sun god Apollo's chariot.

[9]The "and" is repeated incorrectly in *1673.*

[10]The three Wise Men of Matthew 2 were associated with Persia and Chaldea and called Magi, which signified "Philosophers, Priests, or astronomers" (Geneva Bible marginalia, Matthew 2.1). Spenser associates them with "Ægyptian wisards" who had insight into reading prophecies in the stars (*Faerie Queene* 5.8).

And lay it lowly at his blessed feet; 25
Have thou the honour first, thy Lord to greet,
  And joyn thy voice unto the Angel Quire,° CHOIR
From out his secret Altar toucht with hallow'd fire.[11]

The Hymn.

I.

IT was the Winter wilde,
While the Heav'n-born-childe 30
  All meanly wrapt in the rude manger lies;
Nature in aw to him
Had doff't° her gawdy trim, TAKEN OFF
  With her great Master so to sympathize:
It was no season then for her 35
To wanton with the Sun her lusty Paramour.

II.

Onely with speeches fair
She woo's the gentle Air
  To hide her guilty front° with innocent Snow, FOREHEAD, FACE
And on her naked shame, 40
Pollute° with sinfull blame, POLLUTED
  The Saintly Vail of Maiden white to throw,
Confounded, that her Makers eyes
Should look so neer upon her foul deformities.[12]

III.

But he her fears to cease, 45
Sent down the meek-eyd Peace,
  She crown'd with Olive green,[13] came softly sliding
Down through the turning sphear
His ready Harbinger,° FORERUNNER
  With Turtle wing[14] the amorous clouds dividing, 50
And waving wide her mirtle wand,[15]
She strikes a universall Peace through Sea and Land.[16]

---

[11]When Isaiah complains that he is a "man of unclean lips," he adds "Then flew one of the seraphims unto me, having a live coal in his hands, which he had taken with the tongs from off the altar: And he laid it upon my mouth, and said, Lo, this hath touched thy lips; and thine iniquity is taken away, and thy sin purged" (Isaiah 6.5–7). In *Reason of Church Government* Milton refers to God sending "out his Seraphim with the hallow'd fire of his Altar to touch and purify the lips of whom he pleases" (Yale 1: 821). Here "secret," as Gordon Campbell points out (28n), may mean "set apart." I would add "Kept from the knowledge of the uninitiated" (*OED* 2.e).

[12]Nature is polluted by Original Sin. For the infection of nature, see *Paradise Lost* 10.613–719.

[13]The wreath of olive leaves still associated with peace.

[14]With the wings of a turtle dove, an emblem not only of human love as with Dante's Paolo and Francesca (*Inferno*, Canto 5) but of the Spirit of God as light, descending on Jesus in Matthew 4.16.

[15]As Carey points out (51), the myrtle is associated with Venus in Vergil, *Eclogues* 7.62; "amorous" clouds also suggest Zeus's coming in the form of a cloud to seduce Io (Ovid, *Metamorphoses* 1.5). The point may be that peace brings fertility to earth.

[16]Peace is pictured conventionally as being crowned with an olive wreath and flying down toward earth through one of the nine revolving spheres of the clustered planets; she ushers in the period usually called the "pax Romana" but which Milton here associates with the coming of Christianity.

IV.

No War, or Battails sound
Was heard the World around: *(cosmic sphere / whole world)*
  The idle spear and shield were high up hung; *(word order)*
The hooked° Chariot stood   ARMED WITH SCYTHES   55
Unstain'd with hostile blood,[17]
  The Trumpet spake not to the armed throng,
And Kings sate still with awfull° eye,   AWE-INSPIRING
As if they surely knew their sovran Lord was by.[18]   60

V.

But peacefull was the night
Wherin the Prince of light
  His raign of peace upon the earth began:
The Windes with wonder whist,°   SILENCED
Smoothly the waters kist,   65
  Whispering new joyes to the milde Ocean,[19]
Who now hath quite forgot to rave,
While Birds of Calm[20] sit brooding on the charmed wave.

VI.

The Stars with deep amaze°   AMAZEMENT
Stand fixt in stedfast gaze,   70
  Bending one way their pretious influence,[21]
And will not take their flight,
For all the morning light,
(morning star)   Or *Lucifer* [22] that often warn'd them thence;
But in their glimmering Orbs[23] did glow,   75
Untill their Lord himself bespake, and bid them go.

VII.

And though the shady gloom
Had given day her room,
  The Sun himself with-held his wonted speed,
And hid his head for shame,   80
As his inferiour flame,

---

[17]Milton seems to have pronounced "blood" to rhyme with "stood." For contemporary usage, see E. J. Dobson, *English Pronunciation 1500–1700* (2 vols.; Oxford: Clarendon, 1968): 1:160. Chariots "with hooks" are spoken of in 2 Maccabees 13.2.

[18]In the last two lines, the spelling of both "sate" and "sovran" may indicate that Milton may be exerting some pressure on the printing house manager or compositor to spell words as he did in his own manuscripts.

[19]Pronounced with three distinct syllables. Spenser (or his printer) sometimes spelled the word "Occæan," as in the *Ruines of Time* 541 (*Spenser's Minor Poems*, ed. Ernest de Sélincourt [Oxford: Clarendon, 1910]: 144).

[20]The halcyon birds or kingfishers, whose nesting was supposed to keep the sea calm (see Pliny the Elder, *Natural History* 10.47), were also associated with the coming of Christ as peacemaker. Here they are part of a good spell cast by the coming of Christ, since they are "brooding"—or creating life; compare the image in *Paradise Lost* 1.20–21—on a "charmed wave."

[21]The power and influence exerted by heavenly bodies on humankind; Carey (71n) points to "the sweet influences of Pleiades" in Job 38.31.

[22]Milton pictures the stars as being astrologically focused on Christ, temporarily locked in time, and therefore fixing their influence on the Nativity, refusing to be banished by daylight. "*Lucifer*" here is not the fallen angel but the morning star, actually Venus, called in Latin the "light-bearer." Pliny the Elder outlines the ancient world's beliefs about Lucifer as it relates to Venus and Vesper: "Below the sun revolves a large planet called Venus, with alternate orbits, and indeed its alternative names confirm its rivalry with the sun and moon. When it comes in advance and rises before dawn, it is called Lucifer, as being another sun and bringing the dawn. When, on the other hand, it shines after sunset, it is called Vesper, as prolonging the daylight or performing the function of the moon" (*Natural History: A Selection*, ed. John F. Healy [New York: Penguin, 1991]: 15). Milton would hold to Pliny's definitions whenever he mentions Venus, Lucifer, or Vesper in all of his poetry, which will make "Morning Star," "Venus," and "Lucifer" synonymous with each other, and "Vesper" synonymous with "Evening Star." In Isaiah 14.12, Lucifer is called "son of the morning."

[23]The planet Venus is pictured in "her glimmering sphere" in *Midsummer Night's Dream* 3.2.61.

The new-enlighten'd world no more should need;[24]
He saw a greater Sun appear *[play on word]*
Then° his bright Throne,[25] or burning Axletree could bear.   THAN

VIII.

The Shepherds on the Lawn,   85
Or ere° the point of dawn,   BEFORE
  Sate simply chatting in a rustick row;
Full little thought they than,
That the mighty *Pan*[26] *(all)*
  Was kindly[27] com to live with them below;   90
Perhaps their loves, or els their sheep,[28]
Was all that did their silly° thoughts so busie keep.   INNOCENT

IX.

When such musick sweet
Their hearts and ears did greet,
  As never was by mortall finger strook,°   STRUCK   95
Divinely-warbled voice
Answering the stringed noise,[29]
  As all their souls in blisfull rapture took:°   SEIZED, ENCHANTED
The Air such pleasure loth to lose,
With thousand echo's still prolongs each heav'nly close.[30]   100

X.

Nature that heard such sound
Beneath the hollow round[31]
  Of *Cynthia*'s seat, the Airy region thrilling,°   PIERCING
Now was almost won
To think her part was don,   105
  And that her raign had here its last fulfilling;
She knew such harmony alone
Could hold all Heav'n and Earth in happier union.

---

[24]When God shows John a vision of "the holy city, new Jerusalem" (Revelation 21.2), "the city had no need of the sun, neither of the moon, to shine in it: for the glory of God did lighten it, and the Lamb is the light thereof" (21.23).

[25]Phoebus Apollo as sun god has a bright emerald throne in Ovid, *Metamorphoses* 2.24. The burning axletree is literally the spoke in the wheel of the sun god's chariot, but poetically it may be extended to mean "The pole of the heaven; the heaven, the sky" (*OED* 2.b), as in George Sandys's translation of the *Metamorphoses* 1.7: "And burne heauens Axeltree." All of Milton's other poetic references to "Axle" point specifically to this axis of the heavens, as with "the Suns Axle" pushed off course after the Fall (*Paradise Lost* 10.670).

[26]Pan may seem an unusual god to pair with the infant Christ. But one of the meanings of "pan" in classical Greek is "all," and since he was a shepherd or goatherd god and hence identifiable with Christ as good shepherd, "pantheism" could readily be taken over into Christianity as a pagan shadowy type of Christian truth. Milton most likely took his characterization from Spenser's "mighty *Pan*" in the July Eclogue of Spenser's *Shepheardes Calender* (144), since in *Areopagitica* (Yale 1: 723) he quoted a long passage from the May Eclogue picturing Pan as "The Shepheards God" (113; Milton quoted lines 103–31). For an examination of the image of Pan in the poem, see Kathleen M. Swaim, "'Mighty Pan': Tradition and an Image in Milton's Nativity *Hymn*," *Studies in Philology* 68 (1971): 484–95.

[27]Both kindliness and kinship are suggested in "kindly" here.

[28]The juxtaposition of the shepherds' "loves," their lovers or paramours, and their sheep, shows Milton making gentle fun of the cloddishness of simple shepherds. As Annabel Patterson puts it, "The poem fully demotes its own pastoral content" at this point (157).

[29]The word could mean "An agreeable or melodious sound" (*OED* 4.a).

[30]"Close" is a musical term indicating a cadence or a resolving chord. The term "warble" had a positive connotation in the contexts of song or poem for Milton, as did "noise" in a musical sense (*OED* sb. 5), as with "make a joyful noise unto God" (Psalm 66.1). The picture is of musicians singing and playing stringed instruments with such skill that the performance causes rapture in the audience. That image is common in Milton's poetry, as in "Il Penseroso" 161–66.

[31]The sphere of the Moon, who is here named Cynthia (rather than Diana) from her birthplace, Mt. Cynthus, on the island of Delos. Her "seat" would be her dwelling place within the Moon's hollow sphere, which is thought to enclose the Earth.

XI.

At last surrounds their sight
A Globe[32] of circular light,   110
   That with long beams the shame-fac't night array'd,[33]
The helmed Cherubim
And sworded Seraphim,
   Are seen in glittering ranks with wings displaid,
Harping in loud and solemn quire,   115
With unexpressive° notes to Heav'ns new-born Heir.   INEXPRESSIBLE

XII.

Such Musick (as 'tis said)
Before was never made,
   But° when of old the sons of morning[34] sung,   EXCEPT
While the Creator Great   120
His constellations set,
   And the well-ballanc't world on hinges[35] hung,
And cast the dark foundations deep,
And bid the weltring[36] waves their oozy channel keep.

XIII.

Ring out ye Chrystall sphears,[37]   125
Once bless our human ears,
   (If ye have power to touch our senses so)
And let your silver chime
Move in melodious time,[38]
   And let the Base[39] of Heav'ns deep Organ blow,   130
And with your ninefold harmony
Make up full consort to th' Angelike symphony.[40]

XIV.

For if such holy Song
Enwrap our fancy long,

---

[32]Though Carey (110) finds a parallel meaning for "globe" as a military formation in *Paradise Lost* 2.512, I see no reason not to read it here as "sphere [of light]."

[33]The night is shamefaced because of the dark actions it might hide; it arrays or dresses the Moon with moonbeams.

[34]Compare Job 38.4, 7–8: "Where wast thou when I laid the foundations of the earth?" and "When the morning stars sang together, and all the sons of God shouted for joy? Or who shut up the sea with doors, when it brake forth, as if it had issued out of the womb?"

[35]One transferred (not literal) sense of hinge was "[t]he axis of the earth; the two poles about which the earth revolves, and, by extension, the four cardinal points" (*OED* 3, citing this instance).

[36]The word suggests "aimlessly surging," or "raging," as if the waves were moving at random or in fury before being brought under control at creation.

[37]According to the Pythagorean conception of a musical universe, each of the spheres surrounding the Earth produced a note, ringing out in the course of its revolution. Milton's *Arcades* discusses the tradition of the music of the spheres (63–72); his second Prolusion also asserts that only Pythagoras among all humans could hear the music (Yale 1: 234–39). The Lady in Milton's *Comus* will also be able to hear sounds that other mortals cannot hear (458).

[38]The punctuation mark here is broken in *1645*, and, as Fletcher points out, is undecipherable: it may be a semicolon or it may be a comma. I have chosen the comma, even though *1673* elects to use a semicolon, because the lighter punctuation seems more appropriate preceding the "And" clauses that follow, as with the comma followed by an "And" clause at 137 below.

[39]Most likely the lowest (bass) notes of the organ. "In Baroque music, the existence of the basso continuo or thoroughbass showed the importance of the bass part in governing the harmony" (*Norton/Grove Concise Encyclopedia of Music* [New York: Norton, 1988], "Bass"). A modern-spelling editor should render it as "bass" rather than "base," though the two words have always been related, and a pun may exist, as Orgel conjectures (130n), between "base of the universe (earth)" and "bass" as in "bass voice." I agree with the *OED* in assigning the word as Milton uses it here a musical sense (see "base" n .4).

[40]Milton pictures the whole created universe as singing one great anthem or hymn, with nine harmonizing choirs of angels in the nine enfolded planetary spheres (Newton 24n) singing as in a cathedral, the chime of their voices—the music of the spheres—matched to the bass notes of a heavenly organ. By "symphony" Milton seems to mean one of the "choral symphonies" of *Paradise Lost* 11.595. Normal mortals after the Fall were thought not to be able to hear the music of the spheres, but Pythagoras or a divinely inspired poet might have the capacity. The entire poem "At a Solemn Musick" is devoted to the theme of recapturing "the fair musick that all creatures made / . . . whilst they stood / In first obedience, and their state of good" (21–24).

Time will run back, and fetch the age of gold,[41]   135
And speckl'd[42] vanity
Will sicken soon and die,
  And leprous sin will melt from earthly mould,[43]
And Hell it self will pass away,
And leave her dolorous mansions to the peering[44] day.   140

      XV.
Yea Truth, and Justice[45] then
Will down return to men,
  Orb'd in° a Rain-bow; and like glories wearing   ENCIRCLED BY
Mercy will sit between,[46]
Thron'd in Celestial sheen,   145
  With radiant feet the tissued[47] clouds down stearing,
And Heav'n as at som festivall,
Will open wide the Gates of her high Palace Hall.

      XVI.
But wisest Fate[48] sayes no,
This must not yet be so,
  The Babe lies yet in smiling Infancy,   150
That on the bitter cross
Must redeem our loss;
  So both himself and us to glorifie:
Yet first to those ychain'd[49] in sleep,
The wakefull trump of doom[50] must thunder through the deep,[51]   155

---

[41]Ovid, among others, defined the Golden Age: "The *Golden Age* was first; which uncompeld, / And without rule, in faith and Truth exceld" (*Metamorphoses* 1.89–90; trans. George Sandys; *Ovid's Metamorphosis Englished, Mythologized, and Represented in Figures,* ed. Karl K. Hulley and Stanley T. Vandersall [Lincoln: U of Nebraska P, 1970]: 27–28). During the Age of Gold as pictured by Ovid, there was no corruption of the body or soul, and neither human vanity nor the body was disfigured by what Christians would label as sin. Christians would be obliged to see the Age of Gold as a "shadowy type" of Eden before the Fall. See Davis P. Harding, *Milton and the Renaissance Ovid* (Urbana: U of Illinois P, 1946) for the Renaissance Christian reading of Ovid's *Metamorphoses.* See also Richard J. DuRocher, *Milton and Ovid* (Ithaca, NY: Cornell UP, 1985): Chapter 1.

[42]"Of sin, vice, etc.: Characterized by, full of, moral blemishes or defects" (*OED* 1.c, citing this instance).

[43]The picture seems to be one of disfigured flesh melting away as the body works its way toward perfection at Judgment Day. Carey points out that Sylvester's translation of DuBartas uses the phrase "leprosie of Sin" (Carey 138n).

[44]The *OED* defines "peering" in its only citation for the past participle as "looking narrowly and curiously" or "peeping," citing this instance.

[45]The goddess Astraea, who is pictured departing from the earth in Milton's Elegy 4, line 81. Psalm 85.10 gives the context for the scene: "Mercy and truth are met together, righteousness and peace have kissed each other."

[46]The *1645* text reads "Th' enameld *Arras* of the Rainbow wearing. / And Mercy set between . . . ." Milton seems to have changed the lines to draw attention from the rainbow and focus it on the allegorical Daughters of God—Truth, Justice, and Mercy—who also represent aspects of God usually pictured in the Trinity. The word "*Arras*" may have been set in italics only because it looked foreign to a compositor, since it is not a place name or a proper name. The same sort of error of italics seems to occur with "*Fayes*" at 235 below, except that the name might have been stretched to become a proper noun, as in a phrase like "Queen of Faery."

[47]"Woven; especially woven with gold or silver thread" (*OED* 1).

[48]Fate is equated with the will of God in *Paradise Lost* 7.173.

[49]Past participles beginning with "y-" were archaic by the 1640s and here represent a return to an earlier poetic diction, specifically that of Spenser, who was also archaically imitating Chaucer. Milton dropped the usage after "star-ypointing pyramid" in "On Shakespeare," and "yclept *Euphrosyne*" in "L'Allegro." Campbell (155n) points out how wittily that Milton here has created a prosthetic archaism, since the "y-" prefix should attach only to a past participle derived from Anglo-Saxon, whereas "ychained" would have had to have been derived from Old French.

[50]The trumpet supposed to echo from the four corners of the earth at Judgment Day (Matthew 24.31; 1 Corinthians 15.52). It is compared in the next stanza with "the trumpet exceeding loud" (Exodus 19.16), which sounds before and during the time when Moses receives instruction from God on Mt. Sinai.

[51]Notice the comma at the end of the stanza, which allows for the sentence to continue into the next. It is the "wakeful trump" that makes the "horrid clang." Though Campbell reproduces the comma, many modern editors, including Shawcross, Carey, and Orgel, do not. The comma is clear in *1645,* but it can be mistaken for a period in *1673* (Fletcher, I believe, misread it in his note in the facsimile).

XVII.

With such a horrid clang[52]
As on mount *Sinai* rang
  While the red fire, and smouldring clouds out brake:
The aged Earth[53] agast   160
With terrour of that blast,
  Shall from the surface to the center shake;
When at the worlds last session,[54]
The dreadfull Judge in middle Air[55] shall spread his throne.

XVIII.

And then at last our bliss   165
Full and perfect is,
  But now begins; for from this happy day
Th' old Dragon[56] under ground
In straiter° limits bound,   NARROWER
  Not half so far casts his usurped sway,   170
And wroth°[57] to see his Kingdom fail,   ANGRY
Swindges[58] the scaly Horrour of his foulded tail.

XIX.

The Oracles are dumm,[59]
No voice or hideous humm
  Runs through the arched roof in words deceiving.°   DECEITFUL WORDS   175
Apollo from his shrine
Can no more divine,°   PREDICT THE FUTURE
  With hollow shreik the steep of *Delphos* leaving.
No nightly trance, or breathed spell,
Inspire's the pale-ey'd[60] Priest from the prophetic cell.   180

[handwritten margin note: Silencing of all competing religions]

XX.

The lonely mountains o're,
And the resounding shore,

---

[52]Carey points out (158–59n) that Milton may be taking "clang" from the Vulgate "clangorque buccinae," which the Authorized Version translates as "voice of the trumpet" (Exodus 19.16).

[53]Milton's "Naturam non pati senium" ("Nature does not allow decay") is devoted to proving that Nature does not grow old in a way analogous to the aging process in humans.

[54]Pronounced with three syllables, the word "session" retains one of the Latin meanings of "sessio," "a seated decision-making body."

[55]Compare the image of Christ passing judgment in Michelangelo's famous end-panel in the Sistine Chapel. Judgment of all souls was often pictured as it is in Michelangelo's panel, in the middle of the air, the region where angels took residence when they were not in Heaven or on Earth. Milton again draws a comparison between the manifestations of God during the transmission of the Ten Commandments (Exodus 19.18–19) and at Judgment Day, when "The heavens being on fire shall be dissolved, and the elements shall melt with fervent heat" (2 Peter 3.12).

[56]Satan, "the dragon, that old serpent, which is the Devil" (Revelation 20.2) and the "dragon . . . [whose] tail drew the third part of the stars of heaven" (Revelation 12.3–4).

[57]The line in *1645* has "wrath," which is not correct as an adjective form; I have corrected the line according to the *1673* reading.

[58]Josuah Sylvester, in his translation of DuBartas's *Weeks and Works*, pictures a lion in the arena in Rome "often swindging with his sinnewie traine" (1.6.399; Snyder 1: 273). To "swinge" is "to whip about, lash out."

[59]As Carey points out, Milton almost surely borrowed the imagery of the passage on the cessation of the oracles from Prudentius's *Apotheosis* 438–43, which "mentions the silence of the caves at Delphi (Milton's 'Delphos', where Apollo had an oracle on the steep slope of Parnassus), the fanatic priest panting and foaming at the mouth, and the silencing of Hammon in Libya (203). In the same poem Apollo is tormented with pain by the words of exorcism, and shrieks (*heiulat*) (402–3, 412–13); at the heathen sacrifice (460–502) the priest breaks off because he senses that a Christian is present, and he sees Persephone fleeing in dread; his spells (*carmina*) are of no effect; the flames go out and the laurel falls from the flamen's head" (173–80n).

[60]Probably analogous to being "pale with fear." The word "Priest" is not used in a Christian context, and Milton often uses the word in a negative context, because of its association with Roman Catholic priests or Anglican prelates.

A voice of weeping heard, and loud lament;
From haunted spring, and dale
  Edg'd with poplar pale,[61]
The parting Genius° is with sighing sent,   THE SPIRIT OF THE PLACE   185
With flowre-inwov'n tresses torn
The Nimphs in twilight shade of tangled thickets mourn.

XXI.

In consecrated Earth,
And on the holy Hearth,
  The *Lars*, and *Lemures*[62] moan with midnight plaint,   190
In Urns, and Altars round,
A drear, and dying sound
  Affrights the *Flamins* at their service quaint;[63]
And the chill Marble seems to sweat,[64]   195
While each peculiar power[65] forgoes his wonted seat.

XXII.

Peor, and *Baalim*,[66]
Forsake their Temples dim,
  With that twise-batter'd god of *Palestine*,
And mooned *Ashtaroth*,[67]   200
Heav'ns Queen and Mother both,
  Now sits not girt° with Tapers holy shine,[68]   SURROUNDED
The Libyc *Hammon*[69] shrinks his horn,
In vain the *Tyrian* Maids their wounded *Thamuz* mourn.[70]

---

[61]The comma follows that of *1673* rather than the period of *1645*. As Carey (185n) and others have pointed out "poplar pale" may echo the "albaque poplus" of Horace, *Odes* 2.3.9, alluding to the silvery leaves of the poplar tree.

[62]The Lares and the Lemures were Roman gods of the hearth and household, associated with the spirits of dead ancestors, benign or evil. Milton pictures them as being the subjects of superstitious and mistaken worship. The Roman Flamens (194 below), like the other "pale-ey'd Priest[s]," are pictured as being ineffective at invoking any true god.

[63]"Strange, unusual, unfamiliar, odd, curious" (*OED* A.7, citing this instance). Milton may or may not be using the adjective respectfully.

[64]An omen of evil, as with Caesar's death in Vergil, *Georgics* 1.480, and Ovid, *Metamorphoses* 15.792.

[65]"A celestial or spiritual being having control or influence; a deity, a divinity. Chiefly in plural, originating in its application to the pagan divinities; often in asseveration or exclamation, as *by (all) the powers! merciful powers!*" (*OED* 7).

[66]Baal-peor is a Phoenician deity associated with the mountain Peor (Numbers 23.28, Psalm 106.28). The Baalim (Hebrew plural of Baal) are Phoenician deities connected with shepherding; Milton seems to be constructing a generic plural to signify various heathen gods (Judges 2.11). Dagon, cast down twice and hence "twise-batter'd" in 1 Samuel 5.4, will figure again as the chief idol enemy of Samson's god in *Samson Agonistes* and as the "sea monster, upward man / And downward fish" of *Paradise Lost* 1.462–63.

[67]The goddess Ashtaroth would have been accompanied by the moon and hence she is "mooned," with the implication that she should be pictured with crescent-shaped horns. Ashtaroth is a Phoenician goddess associated with the Egyptian Astarte and the Greek Aphrodite or the Roman Venus. She is discussed again in *Paradise Lost* 1.437–46, where her worship becomes the subject of Solomon's idolatry. As goddess of the moon, she would hold claim to be the mother of heaven (Carey [200n] cites Selden, *De Dis Syris*, 1617, 2.2, following Newton). Milton uses the generic plural of "Ashtoreth," the principal goddess in the Phoenician pantheon. Again he emphasizes that the pagan gods were so common as to have generic names and that they were associated with bestial forms.

[68]Ashtaroth is pictured as a forerunner of the Virgin Mary, girded (surrounded) by tapers (thin votive candles). Milton may be mocking what he considered to be idolatrous practices on the part of Roman Catholics of his time.

[69]Normally both "Libyc" (i.e., "Libyan") and "Hammon" would be in italics, since "Libyc" is an adjective derived from a place name, as with "*Memphian*" below (214); the compositor seems to have made a mistake. "*Hammon*" is Jupiter Ammon, worshiped in the form of a ram in Libya; hence he also has horns.

[70]Thammuz is the Phoenician Adonis, mourned by maidens in Tyre (*Paradise Lost* 1.446–52), and he therefore can be associated with regeneration. Isis is Egyptian and pictured with the head of a "brutish" cow; Horus, also Egyptian, is hawk-headed; Anubis guides the dead and has the head of a jackal; and Osiris, like the Greek Hades or Roman Pluto, is judge of the dead. Apis, the sacred bull, was supposed to be buried in the temple of Sarapis at Memphis. Typhon, associated with Satan and sea storms, killed Osiris, scattering the seeds of truth in the process. Zeus in turn killed Typhon with a thunder-bolt. In *Paradise Lost* 1.437–521, Milton reiterates this catalogue of "bestial gods" that the Israelites and Greeks were tempted to worship. Ezekiel 8.14 describes "women weeping for Tammuz."

XXIII.

And sullen *Moloch*[71] fled,   205
Had left in shadows dred,
  His burning Idol all of blackest hue;[72]
In vain with Cymbals ring,
They call the grisly° king,   GHASTLY, HORRIBLE
  In dismall° dance about the furnace blue;   DREADFUL, EVIL   210
The brutish gods of *Nile* as fast,
Isis[73] and *Orus*, and the Dog *Anubis* hast.°   HASTEN

XXIV.

Nor is *Osiris*[74] seen
In *Memphian* Grove, or Green,
  Trampling the unshowr'd° Grasse with lowings loud: DRY   215
Nor can he be at rest
Within his sacred chest,
  Naught but profoundest Hell can be his shroud,
In vain with Timbrel'd Anthems[75] dark
The sable-stoled Sorcerers bear his worship Ark.[76]   220

XXV.

He feels from *Juda*'s Land[77]
The dredded Infants hand,
  The rayes of *Bethlehem* blind his dusky eyn;°   EYES
Nor all the gods beside,
Longer dare abide,   225
  Not *Typhon*[78] huge ending in snaky twine:
Our Babe to shew his Godhead true,
Can in his swadling bands controul the damned crew.[79]

---

[71]Moloch will figure prominently in *Paradise Lost* as a militant Semitic god, worshiped in the form of a bronze statue which was also an oven, a "furnace blue" into which frenzied followers threw babies as sacrificial victims. Carey quotes George Sandys, *A Relation of a Journey* (1615): "the *Hebrews* sacrificed their children to *Molech*, an Idoll of brasse, having the head of a calfe, the rest of a kingly figure, with armes extended to receive the miserable sacrifice, seared to death with his burning embracements. For the Idoll was hollow within, and filled with fire. And lest their lamentable shrieks should sad the hearts of their parents, the Priests of *Molech* did deafe their eares with the continual clang of trumpets and timbrels." "Molech" is mentioned in 2 Kings 23.10: "that no man might make his son or his daughter pass through the fire to Molech."
[72]The heavier semicolon of *1673* may correct the lighter comma of *1645*. The same correction is made in 210 below. The idol would be black in hue, I should think, because it is a furnace and thus covered with soot.
[73]Egyptian earth goddess, said by Herodotus to be horned like a cow, "as the Greeks represent Io" (*History* 2.41; trans. Grene 148). Orus is the Egyptian sun god and son of Isis. His son, Anubis, is pictured with a jackal's or dog's head.
[74]Principal Egyptian god, called Apis as well, worshiped in the form of a black bull with a white triangle on its forehead (Herodotus, *History* 3.27–29).
[75]Sung anthems accompanied by rhythmic beating on a percussion instrument resembling the tabor or tamborine.
[76]Herodotus describes the Egyptian festival devoted to Ares in Pampremis, in which the image of the god is carried about "in a small wooden gilt shrine" or ark (*History* 2.63; trans. Grene 158).
[77]Matthew 2.6 identifies Bethlehem in the land of Judah (in Judea) as Christ's birthplace.
[78]In Greek mythology Typhon or Typhoeus, a hundred-headed, fire-breathing giant with a body that was serpentine below the waist, makes war successfully for a time against the Olympian gods. Zeus was supposed to have buried Typhon beneath Mt. Aetna. Typhon, in some accounts father of the winds, has also given his name to typhoons. In Egyptian mythology Typhon is an alternative name for the wicked Set who kills Osiris. Milton conflates the earlier mythologies to find a type for Satan. To begin studying Typhon, see Hesiod, *Theogony* 820, where he is pictured with a hundred snaky heads.
[79]Christ in his swaddling clothes in the cradle here is pictured as being able to control the entire rout of pagan monsters. The image of Hercules strangling serpents in his cradle was supposed to be a "shadowy type" prefiguring the Christian truth, for which see F. Michael Krouse, *Milton's Samson and the Christian Tradition* (Princeton, NJ: Princeton UP, 1949): 44–45.

XXVI.

So when the Sun in bed,
Curtain'd with cloudy red,
  Pillows his chin upon an Orient° wave,   EASTERN   230
The flocking shadows° pale,   GHOSTS
Troop to th' infernall jail,
  Each fetter'd[80] Ghost slips to his severall° grave,   SEPARATE
And the yellow-skirted *Fayes*,   235
Fly after the Night-steeds, leaving their Moon-lov'd maze.[81]

XXVII.

But see the Virgin blest,
Hath laid her Babe to rest.[82]
  Time is our tedious Song should here have ending:[83]
Heav'ns youngest teemed° Star,   MOST RECENTLY BORN 240
Hath fixt her polisht Car,[84]
  Her sleeping Lord with Handmaid Lamp attending:[85]
And all about the Courtly Stable,
Bright-harnest° Angels sit in order serviceable.[86]   DRESSED IN SHINING ARMOR

---

[80]"Chained [to the human body]."

[81]Night fairies, or fays, are pictured leaving a customary gathering place, a maze. (Compare *Midsummer Night's Dream* 2.1.99, which pictures "the quaint mazes in the wanton green," where the fairies dance their "moonlight revels," in order to fly off with a night-mare—a witch thought to ride humans like a succubus or cause feelings of suffocation in those who were attacked while asleep). Milton's fays, like Shakespeare's, are here demonic, not friendly or "pert" as they are in "L'Allegro," and their maze and frantic night-flight both show the error of their ways. They are "yellow-skirted" presumably because they are lit by moonlight. Carey (235n) reminds us that in the seventeenth-century "fays" were associated with Roman and Greek goddesses of childbirth; thus Carey finds their position at the end of the poem, where Christ's birth occurs, significant.

[82]The simple picture of the Virgin and Child in the manger allays fear of all the demons forced to flee by Christ's presence on earth. The tone of the poem at this point is that of a pure-hearted song after a witches' sabbath.

[83]The colon of *1673* seems preferable to the comma of *1645*, since a full stop is called for, as with "attending" at 242 below.

[84]The comma of *1673* has been selected, rather than the period of *1645*.

[85]As with the Columbia edition, but not that of Shawcross, I have chosen to reproduce the colon of *1673* rather than what appears to be a period in *1645*.

[86]An echo of the Proem, Stanza 3, where the "spangled host" is "keep[ing] watch." Angels are pictured as in medieval and Renaissance iconography, dressed in shining armor (in military harness), but also sitting in strict military order, which would be serviceable to a militant God seeking to lead an army against evil, as in the War in Heaven of *Paradise Lost*. Heaven's youngest or most recently born star (compare the usage in *Paradise Lost* 6.154: "The Earth obey'd, and . . . teem'd at a Birth Innumerous living Creatures") is the Star of Bethlehem, pictured, like the sun, in a chariot ("Car"). The image seems close to that of people who embody Christian patience in Sonnet 16: "They also serve who only stand and wait," another image of Christian patience used like this one as a coda to a poem.

A Paraphrase on *Psalm* 114.

This and the following *Psalm* were don
by the Author at fifteen yeers old.[1]

WHen the blest seed of *Terah*'s faithfull Son,[2]
  After long toil their liberty had won,
And past from *Pharian*[3] fields to *Canaan* Land,
Led by the strength of the Almighties hand,
Jehovah's wonders were in *Israel* shown,   5
His praise and glory was in *Israel* known.
That saw the troubl'd Sea, and shivering fled,
And sought to hide his froth-becurled head[4]
Low in the earth, *Jordans* clear streams recoil,
As a faint host that hath receiv'd the foil.[5]   10
The high, huge-bellied Mountains skip like Rams
Amongst their Ews, the little Hills like Lambs.
Why fled the Ocean?[6] And why skipt the Mountains?
Why turned *Jordan* toward his Crystall Fountains?
Shake earth, and at the presence be agast   15
Of him that ever was, and ay° shall last,   FOREVER
That glassy flouds from rugged rocks can crush,
And make soft rills from fiery flint-stones gush.

---

[1]Milton's headnote would date the two Psalm paraphrases in 1623 or 1624, "near the end of his attendance at St Paul's School" (*Variorum* 2.1: 111). As James Holly Hanford points out, the "stylistic inspiration" of the two translations is "Sylvester, whose rich and elaborate though somewhat undignified language apparently satisfied Milton's youthful sense of verbal beauty" (quoted in *Variorum* 2.1: 113).

[2]Abraham, as in Genesis 11:27, "Terah begat Abram, ..." Abraham is described as "faithful" in contrast to his father Terah, who was idolatrous.

[3]Egyptian. The island of Pharos, in the bay of the city of Alexandria, was the location of a famous lighthouse, one of the Seven Wonders of the ancient world, and "pharos" in Greek came to mean "lighthouse." Here Milton is simply using the adjective form but choosing the less-familiar name, as in Sylvester's DuBartas 1.1.500.

[4]Compound adjectives are typical of Sylvester's translation of DuBartas. As Sylvester's editor, Susan Snyder, puts it, "Sylvester's influence [in this poem] is unmistakable in the compound epithets ('froth-becurled,' 'huge-bellied') and in whole lines like the two concluding ones" (Snyder 1: 83). By the time Milton wrote *Paradise Lost*, however, the influence of Sylvester's translation had all but vanished from his style.

[5]The "faint host" is a cowardly army, and what they receive is defeat ("foil").

[6]Probably trisyllabic.

Psalm 136

Let us with a gladsom mind
Praise the Lord, for he is kind,
  For his mercies ay endure,
  Ever faithfull, ever sure.

Let us blaze his Name abroad,   5
For of gods he is the God;
  For, &c.

O let us his praises tell,
That[1] doth the wrathfull tyrants quell,   10
  For, &c.

That with his miracles doth make
Amazed Heav'n and Earth to shake.
  For, &c.   15

That by his wisdom did create
The painted Heav'ns so full of state.°   DIGNITY
  For his, &c.   20

That did the solid Earth ordain
To rise above the watry plain.
  For his, &c.

That by his all-commanding might,   25
Did fill the new-made world with light.
  For his, &c.

And caus'd the Golden-tressed Sun,
All the day long his cours to run.   30
  For his, &c.

The horned Moon to shine by night,
Amongst her spangled sisters bright.
  For his, &c.   35

He with his thunder-clasping hand,[2]
Smote[3] the first-born of *Egypt* Land.
  For his, &c.   40

And in despight of *Pharao* fell,°   DEADLY
He brought from thence his *Israel*.
  For, &c.[4]

The ruddy waves he cleft in twain,   45
Of the *Erythræan* main.[5]
  For, &c.

The floods stood still like Walls of Glass,[6]
While the Hebrew Bands did pass.   50
  For, &c.

But full soon they did devour
The Tawny King[7] with all his power.
  For, &c.   55

His chosen people he did bless
In the wastfull Wildernes.
  For, &c.   60

In bloody battail he brought down
Kings of prowess and renown.
  For, &c.

He foild bold *Seon*[8] and his host,   65
That rul'd the *Amorrean*[9] coast.
  For, &c.

And large-lim'd *Og*[10] he did subdue,
With all his over-hardy crew.   70
  For, &c.

And to his servant *Israel*,°   JACOB
He gave their Land therin to dwell.
  For, &c.   75

He hath with a piteous eye
Beheld us in our misery.
  For, &c.   80

---

[1]For "That" in lines 10, 13, 17, 21, and 25, *1673* substitutes "Who," which has the effect of personalizing the identity of God.
[2]His hand grasping a lightning bolt. There is no lightning bolt either in Exodus or in the King James Psalm 136.
[3]*1645* has "mote," for which the "S" was carelessly not set; *1673* corrects the error.
[4]The compositor who set *1645* alternated between "For his, &c" and "For, &c," which *1673* regularizes to "For his, &c" throughout, but he was consistent in "For, &c" after he began setting type on his p. 15.

[5]The Red Sea. Sylvester, in *Bethulians Rescue* 2.232, uses the phrase "the Erythraean ruddy Billowes rose."
[6]Compare *Paradise Lost* 12.197, "As on drie land between two christal walls." Exodus 14.22 describes the walls of water through which the Israelites pass.
[7]Pharaoh, tawny because he is Egyptian and dark of skin.
[8]Sihon, king of the Amorites in Numbers 21.21.
[9]Sylvester used "th'*Ammorrean Hare*, / Foyl'd" (*Divine Weeks* 2.2.4.556–57).
[10]King of Bashan, identified as doomed by God to lose in battle to Moses, in Numbers 21.33–34. A bed belonging to Og captured in that battle was said to measure about thirteen by sixteen feet: hence "large-lim[b]'d."

And freed us from the slavery
Of the invading enimy.
   For, *&c.*

All living creatures he doth feed,   85
And with full hand supplies their need.
   For, *&c.*

Let us therfore warble[11] forth
His mighty Majesty and worth.   90
   For, *&c.*

That his mansion hath on high
Above the reach of mortall ey.
  For his mercies ay endure,   95
  Ever faithfull, ever sure.

The Passion
(1630?)

The poem must have been intended to be a companion to the Nativity Ode, the "joyous news of heav'nly Infants birth," and was quite likely written on the occasion of Easter, 1630. Perhaps "The Circumcision" should be counted as part of a trio of poems examining the birth, initiation, and death of Jesus. The nagging question remains for critics and biographers: if Milton disliked the poem and thought it beyond his abilities at the time he wrote it, according to his postscript, why should he have included it in his printed poetry in 1645 and 1673? Perhaps the easiest answer would be that he wished to preserve all his work, including his revised manuscripts and his mistakes, for posterity (Hunter).

"The Passion" is generally rated as Milton's worst English poem, perhaps because the death of Christ on the cross was a distasteful subject to Protestants of Milton's era, who would have associated the Crucifixion with Roman Catholic iconography; John Donne, of Roman Catholic upbringing, might often dwell on the subject, but Milton's heart is not in this poem, and the imagery seems forced or contrived.

Shawcross calls the poem "inept and overreaching" (*John Milton* 49). Philip Gallagher emphasizes the probability that what Milton preserved is just a proem or prologue, one which proves only "the futility of attempting to write a divine poem in the absence of divine inspiration" (44).

TEXT
   There are no manuscript versions of the poem, and but one textual variant between *1645* and *1673*, at line 22: the "latter" of *1645* becomes "latest" in *1673*.

Works Cited

Gallagher, Phillip. "Milton's 'The Passion': Inspired Mediocrity." *Milton Quarterly* 11 (1977): 44–50.

Hunter, William B. "John Milton, Autobiographer." *Milton Quarterly* 8 (1974): 100–04.

Shawcross, John T. *John Milton: The Self and the World*. Lexington: UP of Kentucky, 1993.

---

[11]Milton uses the word always in a positive sense, for spontaneous artistic creativity, especially in the writing of poetry, as when he describes Shakespeare as a poet who can "Warble his native Wood-notes wild" ("L'Allegro" 134). Sylvester uses "warble forth" in *Divine Weeks*, 1.2.1036.

The Passion

I.

E Re-while° of Musick, and Ethereal mirth,[1]　　　　　　FORMERLY
Wherwith the stage of Ayr and Earth did ring,[2]
And joyous news of heav'nly Infants birth,
My muse with Angels did divide[3] to sing;
But headlong joy is ever on the wing,　　　　　　　　　　　　　5
　　In Wintry solstice like the shortn'd light
Soon swallow'd up in dark and long out-living night.

II.

For now to sorrow must I tune my song,
And set my Harpe to notes of saddest wo,
Which on our dearest Lord did sease° er'e long,　　　SEIZE　　　10
Dangers, and snares, and wrongs, and worse then so,
Which he for us did freely undergo.
　　Most perfect *Heroe*,[4] try'd in heaviest plight
Of labours huge and hard, too hard for human wight.°　　HUMAN BEING

III.

He sov'ran Priest stooping his regall head　　　　　　　　　　15
That dropt with odorous oil down his fair eyes,
Poor fleshly Tabernacle entered,[5]
His starry front° low-rooft beneath the skies;　　　FOREHEAD
O what a Mask was there, what a disguise!
　　Yet more; the stroke of death he must abide,　　　　　20
Then lies him meekly down fast by his Brethrens side.

IV.

These latter[6] scenes confine my roving vers,
To this Horizon is my *Phœbus*[7] bound,[8]
His Godlike acts; and his temptations fierce,
And former sufferings other where are found;　　　　　　　25
Loud o're the rest *Cremona*'s Trump doth sound;[9]
　　Me softer airs befit, and softer strings
Of Lute, or Viol[10] still, more apt for mournful things.

---

[1]"Ethereal" in this case would be equivalent to "heavenly," and the music would be the music of the spheres.

[2]The punctuation mark at the end of the line is not clear, and it may be a semicolon, but I agree with Shawcross that a comma is preferred.

[3]A musical term suggesting the division into choral units, "To perform with 'divisions'; . . . to descant" (*OED* 11.b), as illustrated by Spenser's "Most heauenly melody / About the bed sweet musicke did diuide" (*Faerie Queene* 1.5.17). Milton's muse will sing antiphonally with angels.

[4]Jesus is defined here as if competitive with Hercules, performing gigantic labors beyond the capability of ordinary humans. The comparison is based on the assumption that classical myths were shadowy types of Christian truth. The baby Jesus is also compared with Hercules in the Nativity Ode 224–28.

[5]Jesus, as the reigning priest of Christianity anointed with oil in Matthew 26.7–13 and Hebrews 1.9, stoops to assume the fleshly "Tabernacle" of the human body; his forehead, or "front," is still heavenly, spangled with stars, as he descends to earth.

[6]Carey accepts the reading of *1673*, "latest," as does Campbell, but with Shawcross I prefer "latter," the reading of *1645*. Compare "latter task" in "Vacation Exercise" 8. Orgel and Goldberg, as if to exemplify the confusion, print "later" in the text but "latter" in their note.

[7]Phoebus Apollo, often associated with Christ as well as being the god of poetic inspiration and father of the Muses.

[8]Shawcross substitutes a semicolon here, though there is a clear comma in *1645* and in *1673*. I believe "His Godlike acts" refers to the acts of *Phœbus* (Christ). Also, there is a clear semicolon after "Godlike acts" in *1645*, though Shawcross replaces it with a comma. I read "temptations" and "sufferings" both as the subjects of the verb "are found."

[9]Probably an allusion to Girolamo Vida's short epic poem, the *Christiad*, composed in Vida's home city, Cremona. Milton contrasts his shorter, "softer" lyric mode with the rougher epic mode. If Milton's lyric might be accompanied by the softer, melancholy tones of the viol or lute, Vida's epic poetry might best be accompanied by brass instruments.

[10]Milton did indeed play the viol, an ancestor of the violincello held between the legs like the cello but with the bow held with the hand below it; with composers for the bass viol like Marin Marais (1656–1728), the bass viol, at least, does produce a melancholy sound. We do not know if Milton played the lute.

V.

Befriend me night best Patroness of grief,
Over the Pole thy thickest mantle throw,   30
And work my flatter'd fancy to belief,[11]
That Heav'n and Earth are colour'd with my wo;
My sorrows are too dark for day to know:
  The leaves should all be black wheron I write,
And letters where my tears have washt a wannish white.[12]   35

VI.

See see the Chariot, and those rushing wheels,
That whirl'd the Prophet up at *Chebar* flood,[13]
My spirit som transporting *Cherub* feels,
To bear me where the Towers of *Salem*[14] stood,
Once glorious Towers, now sunk in guiltles blood;   40
  There doth my soul in holy vision sit
In pensive trance, and anguish, and ecstatick fit.[15]

VII.

Mine eye hath found that sad Sepulchral rock[16]
That was the Casket° of Heav'ns richest store,   TREASURE BOX
And here though grief my feeble hands up-lock,[17]   45
Yet on the softned Quarry would I score°   ENGRAVE
My plaining° vers as lively as before;   MOURNFUL
  For sure so well instructed are my tears,
That they would fitly fall in order'd Characters.

VIII.

Or should I thence hurried on viewles° wing,   INVISIBLE   50
Take up a weeping[18] on the Mountains wilde,
The gentle neighbourhood of grove and spring
Would soon unboosom all thir Echoes milde,
And I (for grief is easily beguild)
  Might think th' infection of my sorrows loud,   55
Had got° a race of mourners on som pregnant cloud.[19]   BEGOTTEN, CONCEIVED

> *This subject the Author finding to be above the yeers he had,
>   when he wrote it, and nothing satisfi'd with what was
>   begun, left it unfinisht.*

---

[11]"And make it so that my inflated imagination will present a true image."
[12]Funeral notices might at least have a black border, or be printed with white lettering on a black background.
[13]The prophet is Ezekiel, whose vision of a divine chariot is described in Ezekiel 1. The image was obviously important to Milton, as shown in M. J. Doherty, "Ezekiel's Voice: Milton's Prophetic Exile and the *Merkavah* in *Lycidas*," *Milton Quarterly* 23 (1989): 89–121.
[14]Jerusalem, which, Shawcross reminds us (79n10), was consecrated as a site for divine poetry because the psalmist David had lived there.
[15]A thorough definition of poetic inspiration. For an examination of the passage in relation to Milton in his role as poet-prophet, see Kerrigan, *Prophetic* 199–201.
[16]Christ's sepulcher (Mark 15.46; Matthew 27.60) was supposed to have been hewn out of a single rock. It is presumed that the "softned Quarry" is "the mass of rock from which the sepulchre was hewn," following *OED* 2.2: "A large mass of stone or rock in its natural state, capable of being quarried" (see Variorum 2.1: 160n46).
[17] The hands are locked in the gesture of praying.
[18] The idiom "a weeping," as in "he lay a-weeping," is recorded in *OED* 1.b, citing this instance.
[19] The image of an infection begetting tears as being like a race of mourners born in a rain cloud is far-fetched but not hard to follow, but this bit of metaphysical excess seems, to me at least, to be tasteless or awkward. For an image of a similar process, successfully borrowed from the *Iliad*, see *Paradise Lost* 4.500.

On Time

In this conventional address to time, designed to be "set on a clock case," Milton's youthful poetic style is still very much beholden to Sylvester, emphasizing compound adjectives such as "leaden-stepping," "happy-making," and "heavn'ly-guided." The metrics and line-division are reminiscent of "Lycidas." The imagery complements that of the Nativity Ode. For one example, compare the last image in this poem with the images of angels sitting in "order serviceable" at 244.

Dating the poem is difficult. Parker ties it to *Arcades* and suggests Christmas 1630 or early 1631 (761n49), but Shawcross would put it in 1637. Fletcher had assigned it even earlier, 1626–27, when Milton was still at Cambridge (2.417–23).

TEXT

The poem appears in Milton's handwriting in the Trinity Manuscript, on a page with "Upon the Circumcision." The words "To be set on a clock case" were written in, then scratched out, just after the title. Parker believes that "it is transcribed, not composed,

there" (761n49). There are no significant variants between the manuscript and the two printed copies. Characteristic of Milton's manuscript poems, "On Time" in the Trinity Manuscript contains almost no capital letters at the beginnings of lines and very little punctuation before the one period at the end. In this manuscript, Milton capitalizes "Time," "Æternity," "Joy," "Truth," "Peace," "Love," "Death," "Chance," and "Time" (again). Such capitalization, erratically augmented in the printed versions, emphasizes the allegorical entities in the poem, and makes clear the parallel between Truth, Peace, and Love, and Death, Chance, and Time. Carey's edition capitalizes the last series of three but not the first, which is misleading.

Works Cited

Fletcher, Harris F. *The Intellectual Development of John Milton.* 2 vols. Urbana: U of Illinois P, 1956–61.

Shawcross, John T. "Speculations on the Dating of the Trinity MS of Milton's Poems." *Modern Language Notes* 75 (1960): 11–17.

On Time

FLy envious *Time*, till thou run out thy race,
Call on the lazy leaden-stepping[1] hours,
Whose speed is but the heavy Plummets pace;
And glut thy self with what thy womb devours,[2]
Which is no more then what is false and vain, 5
And meerly mortal dross;[3]
So little is our loss,
So little is thy gain.
For when as each thing bad thou hast entomb'd,
And last of all, thy greedy self consum'd, 10
Then long Eternity shall greet our bliss
With an individual kiss;[4]
And Joy shall overtake us as a flood,[5]
When every thing that is sincerely good
And perfectly divine, 15

---

[1]Aside from the metaphorical implications in picturing heavy lead moving slowly, the consistent image is of a lead plummet, in this case a clock weight, pulling down gradually but activating the mechanism that ticks off seconds and hours. Time is pictured as envious, as Shawcross points out (155n1), because the god Chronos, as pictured by Hesiod in *Theogony* 453–67, is jealous of his children and devours them as each is born.
[2]The word "womb" could mean "stomach" and therefore represent a male or female organ. See *OED* 1.b.
[3]Dregs, worthless material left over after something good (in this case the soul) is removed.
[4]Probably a kiss for each individual.
[5]Pronounced to rhyme with modern "good."

With Truth, and Peace, and Love shall ever shine
About the supreme[6] Throne
Of him, t' whose happy-making sight alone,
When once our heav'nly-guided soul shall clime,
Then all this Earthy grosnes quit,   20
Attir'd with Stars, we shall for ever sit,
   Triumphing over Death, and Chance, and thee O Time.

Upon the Circumcision.

The poem was written in Milton's handwriting just below "On Time" on one leaf of the Trinity Manuscript. Unlike "On Time," it appears to be a draft and includes revisions near the right margin. It reads

ye flaming Powers, & winged Warriours bright
that erst with musick, & triumphant song
first heard by happie watchfull shepheards eare
so sweetly sung yor joy the clouds along
through the soft silence of the listening night
now ~~mourne~~ mourne & if sad share wth us to beare
yor fiery essence can distill no teare
burne in yor sighs, & borrow
Seas wept from our deepe sorrow
he who wth all heav'ns heraldry whileare
~~entred~~ enter'd the world, now bleeds to give us ease

alas how soone our sin   Alas how soon our sin
sore doth begin his infancie to sease   sore doth begin
Oh more exceeding love or law more just His infancy to sease
just law indeed but more exceeding love
for wee by rightfull doome remedilesse
were lost in death till he that dwelt above
high-thron'd in secret blisse for us fraile dust
emptied his glory even to nakednesse
and y^t great cov'nant wch wee still transgresse
intirely satisfi'd
and the full ~~wrauth~~ wrath beside
of vengefull Justice bore for our excesse
and seals obedience first wth wounding smart
this day, but ~~Oh~~ ere long   This day, but O ere long
huge pangs & strong will peirce more neere his hart
                 Huge pangs & strong
            ~~Shall~~ will peirce more neere his heart.

Upon the Circumcision.

YE flaming Powers, and winged Warriours bright,[1]
  That erst with Musick, and triumphant song
First heard by happy watchful Shepherds ear,
So sweetly sung your Joy the Clouds along[2]
Through the soft silence of the list'ning night;   5
Now mourn, and if sad share with us to bear
Your fiery essence[3] can distill no tear,
Burn in your sighs, and borrow

---

[6]Accented on the first syllable.
[1]"Powers" represented one of the traditional seven orders of angels, the equivalent of the Latin "Potentas," sometimes translated as Potentates, in charge of order in celestial pathways (Gustav Davidson, *A Dictionary of Angels* [New York: The Free Press, 1967]: "Powers"). Angels are often pictured in warrior dress.
[2] The clouds are pictured as being the "Joy" of the angels, probably because the angels were thought to be in charge of heavenly motion.
[3] Some orders of angels were supposed to live within the element of fire; that element naturally would dry tears. The speaker pictures those people weeping for the pain of the infant Jesus as crying huge bodies of water (what Donne calls the "tear floods" and "sigh tempests" of Petrarchan poetry); those bodies of water can then be used to express grief by the flaming angels as well.

Seas wept from our deep sorrow,
He who with all Heav'ns heraldry whileare°   EREWHILE, ONCE   10
Enter'd the world, now bleeds to give us ease;
Alas, how soon our sin
    Sore doth begin
       His Infancy to sease!°   SEIZE
O more exceeding love or law more just?   15
Just law indeed, but more exceeding love!
For we by rightfull doom remediles
Were lost in death, till he that dwelt above[4]
High thron'd in secret bliss, for us frail dust
Emptied his glory, ev'n to nakednes;   20
And that great Cov'nant[5] which we still transgress
Intirely satisfi'd,
And the full wrath beside
Of vengeful Justice bore° for our excess,   BORNE, ENDURED
And seals obedience first with wounding smart   25
This day, but O ere long
Huge pangs and strong
    Will pierce more neer his heart.

At a Solemn Musick.

Like the sonnets to Lawes, "At a Solemn Musick" is concerned with the deep relationship between poetry and the music that complements it. Human music and verse echo celestial music, the angelic music of the spheres (for the trope of echo, see Hollander, *Figure*). Though original sin has created discord, the union of music and poetry always attempts to recreate original harmony and life without sin. Here blessed Sirens, unlike the temptresses who seduce men into shipwreck in the *Odyssey*, are idealized Voice and Verse working together, a beautiful voice singing beautiful poetry. Music becomes a pathway back into the good graces of God; writing poetry and singing it are a means of rejoining the celestial consort.

The verse form is close to that of the Italian canzone, a form that would give Milton the freedom "to develop the long and elaborate sentence which is to be a structural element in all his mature poetry" (Prince 85, discussing ll.18–25 of "At a Solemn Musick").

---

[4] A paraphrase may help. "Although he had been living as a holy mystery in heaven, for us frail humans Christ gives over his glory freely (the process of making himself worthless or 'emptying,' in theological terms 'kenosis,' is first set out in Philippians 2.6–11) and even allows himself to be presented as a naked human babe. The 'great covenant' is the law of the Old Testament, which we still cannot satisfy, but that Christ's purpose is to fulfill entirely. Christ will also bear fully the responsibility we humans have for incurring divine wrath and the just vengeance of God for our sins. On the day of the circumcision, Christ gives a sign ('seal') to humankind when his obedience answers for the disobedience of Adam and Eve. His 'wounding smart' at the circumcision will be followed, sadly, by his crucifixion, when his side will be pierced and when he will die for the sins of humankind." Milton's imagery, his allusions to the Bible, and his syntax are all extraordinarily concise, involuted, and difficult to unravel. The poem does cover Christ's initiation into adulthood, just as the Nativity Ode covered his birth, *Paradise Regain'd* will cover his trial, and "The Passion" covered his death.

[5] "Covenant" (always pronounced and usually spelled "cov'nant") came to have very rich associations for Milton, specifically in his prose when it is concerned with various covenants made between God and human beings beginning with the covenant of the rainbow with Noah. This is a covenant usually taken as a sign of peace between God and humanity after the fall of Adam and Eve and after God forgives humankind for the sins that led to the flood that drowned all but the family of Noah. From the original covenant with God, Milton expanded the meaning into what should be the positive covenant of marriage (Yale 2: 254) or a covenant between a king and his people (Yale 3: 600).

TEXT

Taking up two folio leaves of the Trinity Manuscript, versions of what became "At a Solemn Musick" show it to be one of the most heavily revised of Milton's shorter poems. As Carey (1997) neatly summarizes, "The Trinity MS has two heavily corrected preliminary drafts, followed by a fair copy of the whole" (167). For comparison with the version printed in *1645*, I will include here my transcription of the last version of the manuscript poem.

Blest paire of Sirens, pledges of heavens joy,
Spheare borne, harmonious sisters Voice, & Verse
Wed yor divine sounds, & mixt power employ
dead things wth inbreath'd sense able to peirce
and to our high-rays'd phantasie præsent
that undisturbed song of pure concent
ay sung before the sapphire-colour'd throne
to him that sitts theron
with saintly shout, & sollemne jubilie
where the bright Seraphim in burning row
thire loud up-lifted angell trumpetts blow
and the Cherubick hoast in thousand quires
touch thire immortall harps of golden wires
wth those just spirits that weare victorious palmes
hymns devout & holy psalmes
singing everlastingly.
That wee on earth wth undiscording voice
may rightly answere that melodious noise
                  did
as once we ˄could till disproportion'd sin
jarr'd against natures chime, & wth harsh din
broke the faire musick that all creatures made
to thire great Lord whose love thire motion ~~sw~~sway'd
in p̱fect diapason whilst they stood
in first obedience, & thire state of good
oh may wee soone againe renew that song
& keepe in tune wth heav'n, till God e're long
to his celestiall consort us unite
To live & sing wth him in endlesse morne of light

The compositor of *1645* regularizes Milton's initial words in each line so that each line begins with a capital letter; he (or she—we don't know) regularizes spellings of words like "their" or "pierce," when Milton's practice varies from the norm; the compositor imposes punctuation for pauses within lines and at the ends, where the manuscript has none; and he imposes a system of spelling on words that Milton does not capitalize—a system that Milton might well not have endorsed, since it sacralizes nouns like "Heav'ns" (as compared with "heavens"), "Angel," and "Spirits." Even "Hymns" and "Psalms" are capitalized, in addition to "Saintly" and "Celestial."

The compositor of *1645* botched one word: he substituted the more-familiar "content" for "concent" in line 6. As Carey points out, in a copy of *1645* in the Bodleian Library (8° M168 Art), a contemporary hand, possibly Milton's, has crossed out "content" and substituted "concent" in the margin; the correction was also made in *1673*. The very last line of the poem was often rewritten in the earlier manuscript versions, but never does it appear as it does in print: the last three manuscript versions all read "To live & sing wth him in endlesse morne of light." Milton, in any case, preferred to end the poem with a Spenserian Alexandrine, a line with six stresses.

Works Cited

Harper, John. " 'One equal music': the Music of Milton's Youth." *Milton Quarterly* 31 (1997): 1–10.

Hollander, John. *The Figure of Echo: A Mode of Allusion in Milton and After.* Berkeley: U of California P, 1981.

———. *The Untuning of the Sky: Ideas of Music in English Poetry, 1500–1700.* New York: Norton, 1970.

Le Huray, Peter. "The fair musick that all creatures made." *The Age of Milton.* Ed. C. A. Patrides and Raymond B. Waddington. Manchester, Eng.: Manchester UP, 1980. 241–72.

Prince, F. T. *The Italian Element in Milton's Verse.* Oxford: Clarendon UP, 1954.

At a Solemn Musick

Blest pair of *Sirens*, pledges of Heav'ns joy,
Sphear-born harmonious Sisters, Voice, and Vers,
Wed your divine sounds, and mixt power employ

Dead things with inbreath'd sense able to pierce,[1]
And to our high-rais'd phantasie° present,   IMAGINATION   5
That undisturbed Song[2] of pure concent,°   HARMONIOUS AGREEMENT
Ay° sung before the saphire-colour'd throne   FOREVER
To him that sits theron
With Saintly shout, and solemn Jubily,°   JUBILEE, FORMAL CELEBRATION
Where the bright Seraphim in burning row[3]   10
Their loud up-lifted Angel trumpets blow,
And the Cherubick host in thousand quires
Touch their immortal Harps of golden wires,
With those just Spirits that wear victorious Palms,[4]
Hymns devout and holy Psalms   15
Singing everlastingly;
That we on Earth with undiscording voice
May rightly answer that melodious noise;°   MUSIC
As once we did, till disproportion'd sin
Jarr'd against natures chime, and with harsh din   20
Broke the fair musick that all creatures made[5]
To their great Lord, whose love their motion sway'd
In perfect Diapason,[6] whilst they stood
In first obedience, and their state of good.
O may we soon again renew that Song,
And keep in tune with Heav'n, till God ere long   25
To his celestial consort[7] us unite,
To live with him, and sing in endles morn of light.

An Epitaph on the Marchioness of *Winchester.*

The Marchioness, Jane Savage, wife of Lord John St. John Paulet, the Marquis of Winchester, died with her infant son on April 15, 1631, probably because of infection following the lancing of an abscess. She was twenty-three (Milton was only a year younger, as Parker points out [95]). Her father was Thomas, Viscount Savage, and, through her mother's line, she was heir to Thomas, who also held at one time or another the titles of Lord Darcy, Viscount Colchester, and Earl Rivers.

Milton was undoubtedly in Cambridge (the river Cam is referred to in line 59) when he composed the poem. The occasion might not have been unlike that which provoked "Lycidas"—a proposed collection of memorial poems, including one by Ben Jonson. Politically, it is

---

[1] Just as Orpheus was said to have been able by his music to inspire human emotions in stones or bodies of water. See Patricia Vicari, "The Triumph of Death: Orpheus in Spenser and Milton," *Orpheus: The Metamorphoses of a Myth*, ed. John Warden (Toronto: U of Toronto P, 1982): 207–30.

[2] Unlike any song created for human beings, poetry sung to the glory of God has no spiritual or temporal limitations. It is undisturbed in the sense that it cannot be interrupted by human distractions.

[3] The next four lines have been set to music in what has become a vocal-showplace for lyric sopranos, George Frideric Handel's "Let the Bright Seraphim," planted incongruously in the oratorio that Handel composed based on Milton's *Samson Agonistes, Samson.* In 1991, Kathleen Battle recorded the aria on the compact disk *Baroque Duet* (Sony Classical SK 46672).

[4] Revelation 7.9 mentions a multitude of people from the tribes of Israel and "of all nations," being given seals indicating their salvation; the multitude "stood before the throne, and before the Lamb, clothed with white robes, and palms in their hands." For Milton's use of that chapter in Revelation to support theological doctrine concerning angels, see *On Christian Doctrine* (Yale 6: 345).

[5] Apparently a reference to the innocence of the Garden of Eden, where all creatures participated in and could hear the "music of the spheres," before the entrance of jarring sin.

[6] Probably "Complete concord, harmony, or agreement," the sense cited for this usage in *OED* 2, but the musical sense of the term, often vaguely defined, had to do with harmony among eight regular intervals of notes played together. Hollander calls it "the great octave into which all creatures were cast by the moving power of divine love" (*Untuning* 329).

[7] A group of musicians, presumably an angelic orchestra and choir such as those pictured in Heaven in *Paradise Lost*, where angels sing "Unfained Halleluiahs" to God (6.744). For the context of musical consorts in the early 1700s, see Le Huray.

worth noting that the Paulet family was Roman Catholic, and that in the poem Milton assumes an aristocratic stance (with honorific references to viscounts and earls), as if he might have been expecting patronage (Parker 96).

TEXT

British Museum MS Sloane 1446, ff. 37ᵛ–38, records a variant from the published text, possibly an earlier draft version allowed to circulate by Milton:

> Seven times had the yeerlie starre
> in everie signe sett upp his carr

> Since for her they did request
> the god that sitts at marriage feast
> (when first the earlie Matrons runne
> to greete her of her lovelie sonne. (15–20)

The title of the manuscript version of the poem, "On the Marchionesse of Winchester whoe died in Child bedd. Ap: 15. 1631," confirms a date of death endorsed by other historical records (Parker 767). It had been seven years since the birth of Jane Paulet's first son.

An Epitaph on the Marchioness of *Winchester*.

THis rich Marble doth enterr°   INTER, ENCLOSE THE BODY OF
 The honour'd Wife of *Winchester*,
A Vicounts daughter, an Earls heir,
Besides what her vertues fair
Added to her noble birth,   5
More then she could own from Earth.
Summers three times eight save one
She had told,° alas too soon,   COUNTED
After so short time of breath,
To house with darknes, and with death.   10
Yet had the number of her days
Bin as compleat as was her praise,
Nature and fate had had no strife
In giving limit to her life.
Her high birth, and her graces sweet,   15
Quickly found a lover meet;°   FITTING, PROPER
The Virgin quire for her request
The God° that sits at marriage feast;   THE GOD OF MARRIAGE, HYMEN
He at their invoking came
But with a scarce-wel-lighted flame;   20
And in his Garland as he stood,
Ye might discern a Cipress bud.[1]
Once had the early Matrons run
To greet her of a lovely son,[2]
And now with second hope she goes,   25
And calls *Lucina* to her throws;°   LABORS IN CHILDBIRTH
But whether[3] by mischance° or blame   EXTREME BAD FORTUNE
Atropos for *Lucina* came;
And with remorsles cruelty,

---

[1] The cypress bud would indicate the coming of death, cypress being a tree associated with mourning, and the scarcely lit torch would indicate the brevity of the marriage. Jane Paulet was married at sixteen and died at twenty-three.

[2] The matrons had, on the birth of Jane Paulet's first son, run to tell her the news, just as Roman matrons had done during the ancient festival of the Matralia (Shawcross 104n3). The manuscript has "her lovely son."

[3] The manuscript has "whither," which might make some sense, since movement to a place is implied; though the logical distinction implied in "whether" seems more plausible.

Spoil'd at once both fruit and tree:
The haples Babe before his birth
Had burial, yet not laid in earth, 30
And the languisht Mothers Womb
Was not long a living Tomb.
So have I seen som tender slip° CUT FLOWER
Sav'd with care from Winters nip, 35
The pride of her carnation train,
Pluck't up by som unheedy swain,
Who onely thought to crop the flowr
New shot up from vernall[4] showr; 40
But the fair blossom hangs the head
Side-ways as on[5] a dying bed,
And those Pearls of dew she[6] wears,
Prove to be presaging tears
Which the sad morn had let fall 45
On her hast'ning[7] funerall.
Gentle Lady may thy grave
Peace and quiet ever have;
After this thy travail sore
Sweet rest sease° thee evermore, SEIZE 50
That to give the world encrease,
Shortned hast thy own lives° lease, LIFE'S
Here besides the sorrowing[8]
That thy noble House doth bring,
Here be tears of perfect moan° LAMENT 55
Wept for thee in *Helicon*,
And som Flowers, and som Bays,
For thy Hears°to strew the ways, HEARSE
Sent thee from the banks of *Came*,[9]
Devoted to thy vertuous name; 60
Whilst[10] thou bright Saint high sit'st in glory,
Next her much like to thee in story,
That fair *Syrian* Shepherdess,[11]
Who[12] after yeers of barrennes,
The highly favour'd *Joseph* bore 65
To him that serv'd for her before,
And at her next birth much like thee,
Through pangs fled to felicity,
Far within the boosom bright
Of blazing Majesty and Light,[13] 70

---

[4]The manuscript has "a vernall." "Vernal" means "springlike," after the vernal equinox.
[5]The manuscript has "one."
[6]The manuscript has "it," apparently referring to the bed rather than to the woman.
[7]The manuscript has "hastinge."
[8]The manuscript indents this line.
[9]The Cam River, from which Cambridge takes its name.
[10]The manuscript has "While."
[11]Rachel, the wife of Jacob, bore a son, Benjamin, after years of barrenness, but died in childbirth (Genesis 35.17–19). The comparison between the two wives is not otherwise apt.
[12]The manuscript has "w[ch.]."
[13]The manuscript has "might."

There with thee, new welcom Saint,[14]
Like fortunes may her soul acquaint,
With thee there clad in radiant sheen,
No Marchioness, but now a Queen.

SONG
On *May* morning.

The poem seems to be closely allied with Milton's Latin Elegy 5, *In adventum veris (Anno aetatis 20)*, which also celebrates the coming of spring and is dated in his twentieth year. Hanford identifies the poetic style as being "in the classic Jonsonian rather than in the Fletcherian tradition" (*Handbook* [1970]: 115); there are no intricate metaphysical comparisons ("conceits").

We are in the mirthful world of "L'Allegro" rather than the somber world of "The Passion." It is a light and somewhat pagan world, and the fun and frolic in it are innocent, not dark like the mirth in Milton's *Comus*.

TEXT

There is no manuscript version of the poem, and *1673* copies *1645* without substantial variants.

NOw the bright morning Star,[1] Dayes harbinger,°
Comes dancing from the East, and leads with her
The Flowry *May*, who from her green lap[2] throws
The yellow Cowslip, and the pale Primrose.[3]
  Hail bounteous *May* that dost inspire
  Mirth and youth,[4] and warm desire,[5]
  Woods and Groves, are of thy dressing,
  Hill and Dale, doth boast thy blessing.[6]
Thus we salute thee with our early Song,
And welcome thee, and wish thee long.

                                 FORERUNNER

                                              5

                                            10

On *Shakespear.* 1630.

Because it provides one of the only explicit links between two great English poets, this poem has perhaps been praised more than its due. Milton's biographer, William Riley Parker, thought it an inferior poem, "one of his poorest, stiffly conventional and singularly uninformative" (*Milton* 90). Though it is conventional as an epitaph and is unoriginal in that it perhaps copies epitaphs attributed to Shakespeare himself (*Variorum* 2.1:

208), it contains a valuable early critical evaluation of the native genius that allowed Shakespeare's "easie numbers" (his verse) to "flow." The rumor perpetuated by Ben Jonson and the editors of the First Folio was that Shakespeare never blotted a line (". . .would he had blotted a thousand," lamented Jonson [quoted in Schoenbaum 259]) and that his native genius flowed in verse—a rumor that Milton here endorses. The image is

---

[14]The word "Saint" has religious resonance in the context of this poem alone, since the Paulet family was Roman Catholic, but Milton came to use it in the sense of "good men" (*Reason of Church Government*; Yale 1: 805).
[1]Venus, as in *Paradise Lost* 5.708, "Morning Starr."
[2]Compare "Earths freshest softest lap" in *Paradise Lost* 9.1041.
[3]Carey compares "pale primroses" in Shakespeare's *Winter's Tale* 4.4.122 (91n4). The primrose or cowslip does bear pale yellowish flowers in early spring.
[4]Although *1673* has no comma here, it does have a superfluous space which a comma might have occupied. It was Milton's manuscript practice often to put a comma before an "and" or ampersand in the middle of a line.
[5]A positive use of the word "mirth," as in "heart-easing Mirth" in "L'Allegro" 13, but not like the "tumult of loud Mirth" of *Comus* 202. In a Christian context, however, "warm desire" might be offensive, close to the "Savage heat" of *Comus* 358.
[6]The broken piece of punctuation in *1673* at this point could be a semicolon or a colon.

of Shakespeare's being able to "Warble his native Wood-notes wilde" in "L'Allegro" 134.

TEXT

This memorial poem was printed for the first time in the 1632 Second Folio of Shakespeare's works, in three identifiable states, with the title "An Epitaph on the admirable Dramaticke Poet W. SHAKESPEARE." Between the first and second state, "*starre-ypointed*" became "*starre-ypointing.*" Also, between the Second Folio and the *Poems* (1640) "live-long" became "lasting." The reflexive pronoun "it self" (13) had been "her selfe" in 1632 and "our selfe" in 1640. In Shakespeare's *Poems* of 1640, Milton's poem was printed with "*I. M.*" (standing for "John Milton") following the poem; in the 1632 Folio there had been no attempt to identify an author. There are no significant variants between *1645* and *1673*.

Work Cited

Schoenbaum, Samuel. *William Shakespere: A Compact Documentary Life.* Rev. ed. Oxford: Oxford UP, 1987.

On *Shakespear*. 1630.

WHat needs my *Shakespear* for his honour'd Bones,
The labour of an age in piled Stones,[1]
Or that his hallow'd reliques[2] should be hid
Under a Star-ypointing[3] *Pyramid?*
Dear son of memory, great heir of Fame,   5
What need'st thou such weak witnes of thy name?
Thou in our wonder and astonishment
Hast built thy self a live-long[4] Monument.
For whilst to th' shame of slow-endeavouring art,
Thy easie numbers flow, and that each heart[5]   10
Hath from the leaves of thy unvalu'd° Book,   INVALUABLE

[handwritten annotations: "milton posing shakespea as a muse." / "keeper of history"; "meter" beside lines 9–10]

---

[1] Milton's imagery and rhymes seem to be taken from "An Epitaph on S[r] Edward Standly. Ingraven on his Tombe in Tong Church":
  Not monumentall stones preserves our Fame;
  Nor sky-aspiring Piramides our name;
  The memory of him for whom this standes
  Shall out live marble and defacers hands
    When all to times consumption shall bee given,
    Standly for whom this stands shall stand in Heaven.
This epitaph, and the one that accompanies it, "On S[r] Thomas Standly," were supposed to have been written by Shakespeare:
  Ask who lies heere but doe not wheepe;
  Hee is not deade; Hee doth but sleepe;
  This stony Register is for his bones,
  His Fame is more perpetuall, then these stones,
    And his owne goodnesse wth him selfe being gone,
    Shall live when Earthly monument is nonne.
I quote from the transcription made by E. K. Chambers in *William Shakespeare: A Study of Facts and Problems* (Oxford: Clarendon, 1988): 1: 551. Since Chambers records no version of the two epitaphs to the Stanleys printed before 1664, the question remains how Milton might have seen the poems. Tong is a small town in Shropshire, not far from Birmingham, and not very far from Ludlow, the setting of Milton's *Comus*. Gordon Campbell reminds me that the church at Tong actually contains tombs shaped like pyramids (e-mail correspondence January 1996).
[2] An odd thing for a Protestant to say, since, as Milton well knew, Roman Catholics valued relics, usually the bones of saints or articles of their clothing kept in churches to help sanctify the site, much more than Protestants were supposed to. Is there a hint here that Milton knew rumors of Shakespeare's Catholic inclinations, that prompted one Oxford chaplain to say of him, fifty years after his death, "He died a papist" (quoted in Samuel Schoenbaum, *William Shakespeare: A Compact Documentary Life* [New York: Oxford UP, 1987]: 55).
[3] One state of the 1632 Folio has "*starre-ypointed.*" Either form would be grammatically correct, though archaic in usage. The present participle "pointing," however, indicates immediacy. The archaic form could be imitative of Spenser's general practice, though Carey points out that Spenser never used the prefix "y-" before a present participle (123n4).
[4] The word had been "*lasting*" in the 1632 Folio, but "*live-long*" again in 1640.
[5] The rhyme word was "*part*" in the 1632 Folio. H.W. Garrod preferred "*part*" to "*heart*" ("Milton's Lines on Shakespeare," *Essays and Studies* 12 [1926]: 204).

Those Delphick[6] lines with deep impression took,
Then thou our fancy of it self[7] bereaving,
Dost make us Marble with too much conceaving;[8]
And so Sepulcher'd in such pomp dost[9] lie,
That Kings for such a Tomb would wish to die.   15

*A monument
that will live
forever!*

On the University Carrier (1631)

The poems that Milton wrote on the occasion of the death, in January 1631, of the eighty-two-year-old Thomas Hobson, were jokes—jokes about death and about a Cambridge tradesman. Hobson plied his trade of carrier between Cambridge and his base in London, the Bull Tavern. He also provided horses for Cambridge University students. He was such a colorful character that many of the students memorialized him in poetry. Hobson was most notorious as the inventor of "Hobson's choice." The choice was no choice at all: you could rent any horse you like just so long as it was the one next to the door.

Milton and the other epitaph writers tried to duplicate Hobson's patterns of speech, and perhaps even his jog-trot gait, in their poetry. Cambridge students often wrote serious elegies about important people: the elegies for Hobson were comic relief from such heavy poetic chores. "It is plain," the *Variorum* editors write, "that [Milton's] feelings are largely disengaged . . ." (2.1: 214–15), though his poems show some affection for the character.

The rules for such a student-oriented poem would be that it should be written in English, it should be slangy or colloquial, and the idioms should be those of carters or carriers—not of gentlemen. If such poetry were published at all, it would be published in collections of jests or jokes.

TEXT

There are no significant variants between *1645* and *1673*, though the obvious mistake—"A" for "And" in line two—was corrected. Shawcross believes that the correction of "A" to "And" in the Bodleian Library copy of *1645* is in Milton's hand (*Complete* 627). The poem is printed in *Wit Restor'd* (1658) with the title "*Another*." It exists as well in Folger MS 1.21, 79ᵛ–80ʳ, with the title "On Hobson who dyed in the vacancy of his Carrage by reason of the Sicknes att Cambridge. 1630." I have included variants in the notes under "1658" and "Folger."

---

[6]Ordinarily the adjective made from a proper noun would be in italics but this does not occur in any of the editions of the poem that appeared in Milton's lifetime, which suggests that the various texts had a common origin, or that all were copied from one original. "Delphic" would refer to the oracle of Apollo at Delphi and mean "prophetic," fitting with the possible allusion to Niobe below.

[7]In the 1632 Folio, the pronoun became "*her self*"; in the 1640 *Poems* it became "*our selfe*." The Variorum editors prefer "*our selfe*" (2.1: 211).

[8] "Too much thinking makes us turn to stone." Milton is playing on the same idea he developed in the phrase "Forget thy self to Marble" in "Il Penseroso" 42. Behind the image may be the myth of Niobe, who was turned to stone, along with her children, for her arrogant behavior toward Latona—bragging that her children were greater than Latona's children, Apollo and Diana (Ovid, *Metamorphoses* 5). Like Niobe, the mourner for Shakespeare becomes, by the process of grieving, a monument to his memory.

[9]In Shakespeare's *Poems* of 1640, the word printed was "doth."

On the University Carrier who sickn'd in the time of his vacancy,[1] being forbid to go to *London*, by reason of the Plague.

HEre lies old *Hobson*, Death hath broke his girt,[2]
And[3] here alas, hath laid him in the dirt,[4]
Or els the ways° being foul, twenty to one,   ROADS
He's here stuck in a slough,° and overthrown.   MUD HOLE
'Twas such a shifter, that if truth were known,   5
Death was half glad when he had got him down;
For he had any time this ten yeers full,
Dodg'd[5] with him, betwixt *Cambridge* and the Bull.[6]
And surely, Death could never have prevail'd,
Had not his weekly cours of carriage[7] fail'd;   10
But lately finding him so long at home,
And thinking now his journeys end was come,
And that he had tane° up his latest Inne,   TAKEN
In the kind office of a Chamberlin[8]
Shew'd him his room where he must lodge that night,   15
Pull'd off his Boots, and took away the light:
If any ask for him, it shall be sed,
Hobson has supt, and's newly gon to bed.

Another on the Same.

Not even beer could revive poor dead Hobson! Although he was close to immortal by virtue of his age and the regularity of his appointed rounds, nevertheless he died. The poem, like the plague-ridden city of London, may suffer from the contagion of puns that infest it, but it is clever: Milton may have allowed both Hobson poems in the 1645 and 1673 collections to show that he did have a light side and that he could, like Homer and Vergil before him, play with inconsequential subjects (see Yale 2: 510–11 for his opinion about the instructional use of humorous poetry).

---

[1]The time when he could not be occupied in his normal trade, because of the plague—an empty spot in his busy schedule.

[2]There are puns or allusions to Hobson's colorful language in almost every line: the idiom "broke his girth" would refer to a horse having broken its belly-band or girth, something similar to "bust a gut." I am presuming that Milton is making fun of Hobson's girth, or his being overweight. Later, "twenty to one" seems to refer to a Hobson habit of betting on anything.

[3] In 1645, only the "A" of "And" printed. Though Fletcher (170n2) makes a case that "here" was also a noun meaning "army," it is obvious that the reading "And" of *1673* should be preferred, especially if Milton himself corrected the word in the Bodleian copy.

[4]In the collection of jokes and jests, *Wit Restor'd* (London, 1568), the first two lines of this poem appeared as "HEre lies old *Hobson!* Death hath his desire, / And here (alasse) hath left him in the mire. . . ."

[5]The words "drifter," "shifter," and "Dodge" all suggest something slightly criminal about Hobson's activities; apparently he was a successful confidence man as well as carrier. A dodge, for instance, was a criminal evasion: to give someone the dodge was equivalent to giving them the slip or escaping from justice. Since Death is pictured as dodging with Hobson, Hobson might be pictured as giving Death the slip as well, especially since his career had lasted almost sixty years.

[6]The Bull Inn, Bishopsgate Street, London, the street being one of the main avenues through the city wall, at Bishop's Gate, from the north. The 1658 version reads "Dogg'd him 'twixt Cambridge and the London-Bull."

[7]A "course of carriage" is a route for someone providing hauling services, a carrier's regular route, but the carrier in the seventeenth century would be hauling things in a horse-drawn wagon. See *OED* "carriage," 1.a: "Carrying or bearing from one place to another; conveyance."

[8]A chamberlain, in this sense, is the attendant in charge of bedchambers at an inn (see *OED* 3). The 1658 reading is "Death in the likenesse of a Chamberlin," and the Folger MS "In craftie likenes of a Chamberlin" (*Variorum* 216n14). Here the chamberlain Death is kindly, and helps Hobson off with his boots before turning off the final light.

Text

There are no significant variants between *1645* and *1673*. Other printed versions occur in jest books such as *A Banquet of Jests* (1640), where the poem was called "*Upon old Hobson the Carrier of Cambridge*," and *Wit Restor'd* (1658). There are manuscript versions in Bodleian Malone MS 21; in the Huntington Library MS, H. M. 116, pp. 100–01; and in the St. John's Library, Cambridge, MS S, 32, ff. 18ᵛ–19ʳ.

Notes will refer to "Malone," to "Huntington," and to "St. John's." The title in Malone is "*On Hobson yᵉ Cambridge carrier who died 1630 in yᵉ vacancy of his carriage by reason of yᵉ sicknesse then hott at Cambridge*." As the *Variorum* editors point out, "Lines 15–20 and 25–6 are lacking in 1640, Malone, Huntington, [and St. John's . . .] and lines 13–26 in 1658" (2.1: 217). In other words, the other printed and manuscript versions are incomplete.

Another on the Same

HEre lieth one who did most truly prove,
   That he could never die while he could move,
So hung his destiny never to rot
While he might still jogg on, and keep his trot,[1]
Made of sphear-metal, never to decay[2]   5
Untill his revolution was at stay.
Time numbers motion, yet (without a crime
'Gainst old truth) motion number'd out his time;[3]
And like an Engin mov'd with wheel and waight,
His principles being ceast, he ended strait,[4]   10
Rest that gives all men life, gave him his death,
And too much breathing° put him out of breath;   EXERCISE
Nor were it contradiction to affirm
Too long vacation hastned on his term.°   THE END OF HIS LIFE
Meerly to drive the time away he sickn'd,   15
Fainted, and died, nor would with Ale be quickn'd;°   BROUGHT TO LIFE
Nay, quoth he, on his swooning bed outstretch'd,
If I may not carry, sure Ile ne're be fetch'd,[5]
But vow though the cross Doctors all stood hearers,
For one Carrier put down to make six bearers.[6]   20
Ease was his chief disease, and to judge right,
He di'd for heavines that his Cart went light,[7]
His leasure told him that his time was com,
And lack of load, made his life burdensom,
That even to his last breath (ther be that say't)   25

---

[1]Though the *OED* does not include any use of the noun "jog-trot" earlier than 1698, I believe Milton is describing Hobson's gait in terms of a kind of shambling horse-gait: "A jogging trot; a slow regular jerky pace (usually of a horse, or on horseback)" (*OED* A.1).

[2]The spheres in which heavenly bodies were supposed to orbit were made of a "metal" like quartz, or crystal, which would ring true and never decay. Hobson's mettle seems to decay when he is taken out of his sphere.

[3]According to Aristotle, time measures motion (*Physics* 4.11–12). For Milton's use of the concept as part of his own theological system, see *On Christian Doctrine* 1.7.

[4]Apparently, because he no longer had a "first principle" moving his sphere, he died and thus went rigid in rigor mortis. He is "strait" possibly because he is strapped for cash (as in "in dire straits"), he is thin (as in "straight as an arrow") because he has lost weight, and he is stiff (as in "straight as a board"). Milton seems to pun on as many senses of "strait" and "straight" as are listed in the *OED*.

[5]As with "jog" and "trot," the pun is on the common colloquial phrase "fetch and carry." If Hobson can't carry, he seems to say petulantly, then he will refuse to be fetched.

[6]Possibly the doctors are the dons of Cambridge, crossing or opposing the journeys of Hobson (Carey 125n19), but I think medical doctors just as likely: they are "cross" or peevish because it is going to take six pallbearers to carry out one dead carrier.

[7]He died, in other words, because his enforced leisure made him heavy of heart; as his cart grew lighter, his heart grew heavier.

As he were prest to death, he cry'd more waight;[8]
But had his doings lasted as they were,
He had bin an immortall Carrier.[9]
Obedient to the Moon he spent his date
In cours reciprocal,[10] and had his fate
Linkt to the mutual flowing of the Seas,
Yet (strange to think) his wain was his increase:[11]
His Letters are deliver'd all and gon,
Onely remains this superscription.[12]

30

L'Allegro and *Il Penseroso*.

The twin poems "L'Allegro" and "Il Penseroso" are almost certainly meant to be taken as representing two equally valuable attitudes toward living life. In Italian, the word "allegro" as an adjective has a specific musical association with a lively tempo, but as a noun it meant something like "The Happy Person." "Il Penseroso" (usually spelled "il pensieroso") translates easily into "The Thoughtful Person."

Perhaps it is not an exercise in the "biographical fallacy" to see Milton's close friend Charles Diodati as the festive and lighthearted happy man and Milton himself as the more studious, melancholy, and thoughtful one; certainly Milton's Latin epistles to Diodati suggest two such contrasting personalities.

Writing in his native English rather than the universal language Latin, Milton is aware of his debt to the poetry of Shakespeare and Ben Jonson, the only two English poets ever mentioned in his own poetry. He also borrows phrasing from Christopher Marlowe, Michael Drayton, Josuah Sylvester, and his beloved Spenser. Because his own twin poems are pastoral in content, he can look to plays like *Midsummer Night's Dream* or the pastoral masque tradition of the Jacobean or Caroline court, as well as to the pastoral poetry of Spenser, for how to address such subjects as fairy queens or hobgoblins.

Both the poems should both be read aloud, because it is obvious that the sounds of words such as "busy" (perhaps "beesy," to suggest the restless activities of bees) or "crank" or even "Laughter [ho-ho-] holding" both his sides may be musical puns, as the composer Handel was to exploit in his oratorio "*L'Allegro, Il Penseroso, ed Il Moderato*" (1740). Milton's language is rich, many-layered, and delightful.

TEXT

Undoubtedly the text of *1673* was set directly from *1645*, since there are no substantive corrections and very few changes in accidentals like capitalization. It is almost as if the compositor had been instructed to pay attention to every spelling of every word. Spellings such as "Boosom'd," "watch-towre," "y-cleap'd," "Lantskip" (for "landscape"), or "Lanthorn" may indicate something about pronunciation, as do all the compound words indicated by hyphens, though I see no system in the capitalization (the noun "Hounds" is capitalized in one line, but the noun "horn" is not). The compositor of *1673* followed his copy with great faithfulness. Since no major corrections were made between the two editions, I have followed *1645*.

Works Cited

Herman, Peter. "'Advent'rous Song': Milton's Early Poetry and the Muse-haters." *Squitter-wits and Muse-haters: Sidney, Spenser, Milton and Renaissance Antipoetic Sentiment*. Detroit, MI: Wayne State UP, 1996. 173–259.

Revard, Stella. "'L'Allegro' and 'Il Penseroso': Classical Tradition and Renaissance Mythography." *PMLA* 101 (1986): 338–50.

---

[8]"As if he were being pressed to death [a common form of torture], he cried 'More weight [in order to die faster].'" When he was performing as a carrier, or in filling his wagon, Hobson might have in life cried out for more weight (which would mean more money).
[9]If he had lived any longer, he probably would have been taken up into the heavens as a constellation.
[10]As with the moon, his course between Cambridge and London was regular and cyclical. It would also be governed by the tide, since his wagon would be carrying the letters mentioned in 33, destined for boats heading for continental Europe. The puns are on "wain,"as "wagon," and "wane," as "decrease in influence or good fortune."
[11]His wagon, in other words, made his fortune.
[12] Milton can't stop punning. Just as letters have to have superscriptions, or inside addresses, so Hobson's tomb needs an epitaph or something written over his head.

L'Allegro

Hence loathed Melancholy[1]
   Of *Cerberus*, and blackest midnight born,
In *Stygian* Cave forlorn[2]
   'Mongst horrid shapes, and shreiks, and sights unholy,
Find out som uncouth° cell,   UNKNOWN   5
   Wher brooding darknes spreads his jealous wings,
And the night-Raven sings;[3]
   There under *Ebon*° shades, and low-brow'd Rocks,   BLACK
As ragged as thy Locks,
   In dark *Cimmerian*[4] desert ever dwell.[5]   10

But com thou Goddes fair and free,
In Heav'n ycleap'd° *Euphrosyne*,[6]   CALLED, NAMED
And by men, heart-easing Mirth,[7]
Whom lovely *Venus* at a birth
With two sister Graces more   15
To Ivy-crowned *Bacchus* bore;
Or whether (as som Sager sing)[8]
The frolick Wind that breathes the Spring,[9]

---

[1]The playwright John Marston, in *Scourge of Villainie* 3.1, had described Melancholy in remarkably similar images:
   Sleep grim Reproofe, my jocond Muse dooth sing
   In other keys, to nimbler fingering.
   Dull sprighted Melancholy, leave my braine
   To hell Cimerian night, in lively vaine
   I strive to paint, then hence all darke intent
   And sullen frownes, come sporting merriment,
   Cheeke dimpling laughter, crowne my very soule
   With jouisance. . . . (quoted in *Variorum* 2.1: 270)
Marston had written a masque for Lady Alice, Countess Dowager of Derby, subject of Milton's *Arcades*, in 1607 (Parker 758). Milton's twin poems also seem to owe a great deal to the prefatory poem to Robert Burton's *Anatomy of Melancholy*, "The Authors Abstract of Melancholy," which begins
   WHen I goe musing all alone,
   Thinking of divers things fore-knowne,
   When I build Castles in the aire,
   Void of sorrow and voide of feare,
   Pleasing my selfe with phantasmes sweet,
   Me thinkes the time runnes very fleet.
         All my joyes to this are folly,
         Naught so sweet as melancholy. (ed. Thomas C. Faulkner, et al. [Oxford: Clarendon, 1989]: 1: lxix)
[2]The three-headed dog Cerberus guarded the gate of the classical Hell, Hades; "Stygian" is the adjective derived from the name of the River Styx, one of the rivers traditionally thought to lead to Hades. As Carey points out (132n), the shrieks might be the wailing of dead children heard outside the cave of Cerberus by Aeneas in the *Aeneid* 6.426–27.
[3]"A nocturnal bird, variously identified as a night-owl, night-heron, or nightjar, or imagined as a distinct species" (*OED* 1).
[4]In the *Odyssey* 11.13–19, Odysseus visits the land of the Cimmerians, who live so near the edge of the world that they are in perpetual darkness. "Cimmerian darkness" was proverbial, as in "*In Quintum Novembris*" 60.
[5]The rhyme scheme of the little proem that introduces "L'Allegro" is not consistent with an expected stanza pattern: it is ABBA CDDEEC, not treated as a quatrain and a couplet but as a six-line unit, with two couplets enclosed within the C rhyme—where one might expect CDDC EE. It is a mirror of the ten lines that begin "Il Penseroso."
[6]The classical three Graces—lovers of dance and love songs—were Aglaia, Euphrosyne, and Thalia, the daughters of Zeus and Eurynome and companions to the nine Muses (Hesiod, *Theogony* 907–11; 63–64). The word "heaven" here is classical, rather than Christian, and stands for the Olympian seat of the gods. Just as he will make Comus the son of Bacchus and Circe, Milton here makes Mirth the daughter of Venus, though as the *Variorum* editors point out, Horace had linked the Graces with Venus and Bacchus (*Carminum* 3.21.21–24).
[7]As Neville Davies has noticed, Milton may be punning on the sound of "heart-easing" and "heart-teasing," illustrating the practice of "cranking," or demonstrating wit and good humor by twisting the sound and sense of words: see "Milton and the Art of Cranking," *Milton Quarterly* 23 (1989): 1–7.
[8]Milton gives us an alternative ancestry for Mirth; thus he might be the "sager" ("wiser") for the suggestion. What is implied is that where Mirth came from doesn't matter: getting there is all the fun, in the sense that the begetting of Mirth must be joyful and guilt-free. Ben Jonson had also linked Zephyr (the west wind) and Aurora. See Allen H. Gilbert, *Symbolic Persons in the Masques of Ben Jonson* (Durham, NC: Duke UP, 1948): 159.
[9]"The joyous wind exhales the sweet odors of spring" (see *Variorum* 2.1: 275).

Zephir with *Aurora* playing,
As he met her once a Maying,
There on Beds of Violets blew,
And fresh-blown Roses washt in dew,
Fill'd her° with thee a daughter fair,   °BEGOT
So bucksom, blith, and debonair.[10]
Haste thee nymph, and bring with thee
Jest and youthful Jollity,
Quips and Cranks,[11] and wanton Wiles,
Nods, and Becks, and Wreathed Smiles,[12]
Such as hang on *Hebe*'s[13] cheek,
And love to live in dimple sleek;[14]
Sport[15] that wrincled Care derides,
And Laughter holding both his sides.
Com, and trip it as you go
On the light fantastick toe,[16]
And in thy right hand lead with thee,
The Mountain Nymph, sweet Liberty;[17]
And if I give thee honour due,
Mirth, admit me of thy crue[18]
To live with her, and live with thee,
In unreproved pleasures free;[19]
To hear the Lark[20] begin his flight,
And singing startle the dull night,
From his watch-towre in the skies,
Till the dappled dawn doth rise;

20

25

30

35

40

---

[10]A possible echo of Shakespeare, *Pericles* 1 (Prologue) 22–23: "a female heir, / So buxom, blithe, and full of face." "Buxom" did not mean "bosomy," but rather "easy-going, pliable, unresisting." Likewise, "debonair" might be close to "affable, courteous, sweet, friendly" (see *Variorum* 2.1: 276).

[11]"Quips" were witty sayings; a "crank" was a word or phrase twisted from its normal meaning to become something funny: "A twist or fanciful turn of speech; a humorous turn, a verbal trick or conceit" (*OED* 3).

[12]Milton may be making a distinction between a nod, with the head moving forward, and a beck, an upward-moving head gesture. Smiles are wreathed because, to make them, the face becomes a kind of wreath.

[13]Hebe is the cup-bearer of the Olympic gods; her name in Greek means "youth." "For Milton she is a type of youthful bloom and beauty (cf. *Comus* 289)" (*Variorum* 2.1: 278).

[14]Smiles do live in dimples, and dimples live in smooth (youthful) or sleek and plump faces. Also, a personified Smile lives in a dimple the way that a fairy in *Midsummer Night's Dream* might live in a flower. Compare the Fairy's reference to ". . . rubies, fairy favors, / [where] In those freckles live their savors" (2.1.12–13).

[15]"Sport," "Care," and "Laughter" are all personifications, as if in dialogue with one another. Usually the word "sport" has a negative connotation in Milton's usage: here Sport is ridiculing the old Care, as if youth were insulting aged dignity.

[16]Newton is the first editor to point out the resemblance to Ariel's fairy tetrameter lines in Shakespeare's *The Tempest*:

> Before you can say "come" and "go,"
> And breathe twice, and cry "so, so,"
> Each one, tripping on his toe,
> Will be here with mop and mow. (4.1.44–47)

In Milton's usage here, "trip" means to step lively, as in a dance, and "fantastic" means something like "imagined" or even "imaginative." The setting in *The Tempest* is that of an introduction to the fantastic world of a masque, not unlike the dances in Milton's masque.

[17]Liberty and truth may traditionally be associated with high places, as when John Donne pictures the quest for truth as the climbing of a tortuous trail to the top of a high hill in Satire 3, but Marjorie Nicolson has shown that there was a shift in the seventeenth century between thinking of mountains in terms of "wens" or "blisters" and thinking of them as evidence of the glory of God. See *Mountain Gloom and Mountain Glory: The Development of the Aesthetics of the Infinite* (New York: Norton, 1959): 152–53.

[18]"Crew," usually a word with negative connotations in Milton and in Shakespeare.

[19]An echo of Marlowe's very famous "Passionate Shepherd to His Love":

> Come live with me and be my love,
> And we will all the pleasures prove,
> That valleys, groves, hills, and fields,
> Woods, or steepy mountain yields.

[20]The lark's song is a "sudden shrill burst of song" which may come before dawn (Warton). Phyllis MacKenzie, in "Milton's Visual Imagination: An Answer to T. S. Eliot," *University of Toronto Quarterly* 16 (1946), comments on the "robust realism" of an adjective like "startle" (19).

Then to com in spight of sorrow,[21]   45
And at my window bid good morrow,
Through the Sweet-Briar, or the Vine,
Or the twisted Eglantine.[22]
While the Cock with lively din,
Scatters the rear of darknes thin,[23]   50
And to the stack,° or the Barn dore,   HAYSTACK
Stoutly struts his Dames before,[24]
Oft list'ning how the Hounds and horn,
Chearly° rouse the slumbring morn,   CHEERFULLY
From the side of som Hoar Hill,[25]   55
Through[26] the high wood echoing shrill.
Som time walking not unseen[27]
By Hedge-row Elms, on Hillocks green,
Right against the Eastern gate,
Wher the great Sun begins his state,[28]   60
Rob'd in flames, and Amber light,
The clouds in thousand Liveries dight,[29]
While the Plowman neer at hand,
Whistles ore the Furrow'd Land,
And the Milkmaid singeth blithe,   65
And the Mower whets his sithe,°   SCYTHE, MOWING BLADE
And every Shepherd tells his tale[30]
Under the Hawthorn in the dale.
Streit mine eye hath caught new pleasures
Whilst the Lantskip° round it measures,°   LANDSCAPE   MOVES   70
Russet° Lawns, and Fallows Gray,[31]   REDDISH BROWN
Where the nibling flocks do stray,
Mountains on whose barren brest
The labouring clouds do often rest:[32]
Meadows trim with Daisies pide,°   PIED, VARIEGATED   75
Shallow Brooks, and Rivers wide.
Towers, and Battlements it sees
Boosom'd high in tufted Trees,

---

[21]There is a question here of exactly who it is who comes to the window—the lark or a personage that critics identify as L'Allegro himself or as the poet. The majority of critical opinion supports L'Allegro rather than the lark (*Variorum* 2.1: 281–84), though a strong case has also been made for the dawn coming to the window.

[22]Milton's botanical information may be imprecise, since, even in Warton's time (1740s), sweet briar and eglantine were the same bush; Warton concluded that "twisted Eglantine" must mean "Honeysuckle" (quoted in *Variorum* 2.1: 284). Honeysuckle, or woodbine, twists itself around bushes.

[23]Unexpectedly, this is a military image: the rooster, with his noise, causes the thinned-out rear guard of darkness to scatter.

[24]Milton may well be remembering Chaucer's image of the petty-proud rooster Chaunticleer, in the beast fable recounted in *The Nun's Priest's Tale* (Chaunticleer is first mentioned at 2849): the happy singing, stoutness, and strutting fit the image of the average rooster, but of course human characteristics like pride are easily attached to the animal. For another image of the rooster, see *Prolusion* 1, 136.

[25]Presumably the hill is gray with what looks like frost, as when hillsides are "grey from absence of foliage" (*OED* 4).

[26]Possibly pronounced with two syllables (the word was often spelled "thorough" as in Marvell's "Thorough the iron gates of life").

[27]Many commentators have pointed out L'Allegro's fondness for society. Here he is seen, whereas in "Il Penseroso" 65, the title character is "unseen."

[28]The sun is pictured as a great monarch, clothed in flames and attended by servants dressed ("dight") in the livery of their master.

[29]I am assuming that the faint mark that looks like a period in copies of *1645* should be the comma of *1673*.

[30]Two meanings of "tells his tale" are possible: (1) "tells his story"; or (2) "counts his herd of sheep." I would be inclined toward (1). In Thomas Browne's *Brittania's Pastorals* 1.3.355–56, "Full many a shepherd with his lovely lass / Sit telling tales upon the clover grass" (quoted in *Variorum* 2.1: 288).

[31]The contrast is between grazing lands (lawns) and cultivated or plowed fields (fallows).

[32]Clouds may be depicted as feminine because they grow round and give birth to life-giving rain. Milton was later to associate clouds with Ixion's trick to give Jupiter a cloud to make love to instead of Juno (Yale 2: 597; *Tetrachordon*).

Wher perhaps som beauty lies,[33]
The Cynosure of neighbouring eyes.   80
Hard by, a Cottage chimney smokes,
From betwixt two aged Okes,
Where *Corydon* and *Thyrsis* met,[34]
Are at their savory dinner set
Of Hearbs, and other Country Messes,[35]   85
Which the neat-handed *Phillis* dresses;
And then in haste her Bowre° she leaves,   COTTAGE
With *Thestylis* to bind the Sheaves;[36]
Or if the earlier season lead
To the tann'd Haycock in the Mead,°   MEADOW   90
Som times with secure° delight   CAREFREE
The up-land Hamlets° will invite,   SMALL VILLAGES
When the merry Bells ring round,
And the jocond rebecks[37] sound
To many a youth, and many a maid,   95
Dancing in the Chequer'd shade;
And young and old com forth to play
On a Sunshine Holyday,
Till the live-long day-light fail,
Then to the Spicy Nut-brown Ale,[38]   100
With stories told of many a feat,
How *Faery Mab*[39] the junkets[40] eat,
She was pincht, and pull'd she sed,
And he by Friars Lanthorn led[41]

[33]We are now firmly in the world of romantic epic and courtly love, with the castles, battlements, towers, and the Beauty, who is equated with the cynosure, literally the constellation of Ursa Minor, the North Star, a "guiding light" for mariners steering ships at night. Figuratively, a cynosure is "Something that attracts attention by its brilliancy or beauty; a centre of attraction, interest, or admiration" (*OED* 2.b, citing this instance).

[34]At this point the English shepherds, in a cottage distinguished for having oak trees in the front, have been given the names of Greek pastoral figures, Corydon and Thyrsis, with other Vergilian shepherds, Phillis and Thestylis, to follow (see the Eclogues 2, 3, 5, 7). Milton may have had personalized meanings for Thyrsis (at least he assigns the name to the Henry Lawes's role in his masque).

[35]A usage still preserved in rural speech in the United States, as in "a mess of fresh fish," or "a mess of greens." More commonly known is the phrase "mess hall," meaning the place where a variety of food is served. The word "herb" was used of any low-growing plant, so that we can assume that Phillis is preparing a salad, perhaps composed of what might be known today as weeds, such as dandelion, chicory, or comfrey.

[36]Binding up the sheaves of grain would be an occupation for the fall, whereas building a haystack of cured or tanned hay would be a summer activity.

[37]A smaller and more primitive ancestor of the violin or fiddle, usually with three strings, played on the shoulder or on the lap. Milton, being a player of the viols, might look upon the rebec as a countrified or less-sophisticated instrument: he does associate rebecs with bagpipes and fiddles played in rural villages, but not in a condescending way (Yale 2: 525; *Areopagitica*).

[38]The color of the shells of hazelnuts might best describe "nut-brown." What is now called "real ale" in England is apt to be dark, brownish, and opaque. Ale also can be spiced, as it is still in Belgian beers.

[39]In *Romeo and Juliet*, the queen of the fairies is Mab, but "queen" might be used lightly (a "quean" was a prostitute), since Mercutio calls Mab not queen but "the fairies' midwife" (1.4.54), and he makes her into the equivalent of a female malicious Puck. Milton may be adopting Mercutio's invention of "Queen Mab" and associating her with fairy mischief without asking whether she was just the product of Shakespeare's imagination, but, as the *Variorum* editors point out, Milton's source for her character is more apt to have been Ben Jonson's *Entertainment at Althorpe*:

>Not so nimbly as your feet,
>When about the creame-bowles sweet,
>You, and all your Elves doe meet.
>This is Mab the mistris-Faerie,
>That doth nightly rob the dayrie,. . .
>Shee, that pinches countrey wenches,
>If they rub not cleane their benches. (quoted in *Variorum* 2.1: 294)

[40]Probably sweet cheese dishes or confections in general, as with the generic "sweets."

[41]The Friar's lantern, possibly an apparition based on a combination of the images of a ghostly monk in a cowl and what is called "fool's fire," the "ignis fatuus" supposed to be used by demons to attract humans to a death in the midst of sin and without salvation. Speculations about a real friar are surveyed in the *Variorum* 2.1: 296).

Tells how the drudging *Goblin*[42] swet,   105
To ern his Cream-bowle duly set,[43]
When in one night, ere glimps of morn,
His shadowy Flale hath thresh'd the Corn°   GRAIN
That ten day-labourers could not end,
Then lies him down the Lubbar[44] Fend.°   FIEND   110
And stretch'd out all the Chimney's length,[45]
Basks at the fire his hairy strength;
And Crop-full[46] out of dores he flings,
Ere the first Cock his Mattin rings.[47]
Thus don the Tales, to bed they creep,[48]   115
By whispering Winds soon lull'd asleep.
Towred Cities please us then,[49]
And the busie humm of men,
Where throngs of Knights and Barons bold,
In weeds° of Peace high triumphs hold,   GARMENTS   120
With store of Ladies, whose bright eies
Rain influence, and judge the prise
Of Wit, or Arms, while both contend
To win her Grace, whom all commend.
There let *Hymen*[50] oft appear   125
In Saffron robe, with Taper clear,
And pomp, and feast, and revelry,
With mask, and antique Pageantry,[51]
Such sights as youthfull Poets dream
On Summer eeves by haunted stream.[52]   130
Then to the well-trod stage anon,
If *Jonsons* learned Sock[53] be on,
Or sweetest *Shakespear*[54] fancies childe,

---

[42]Puck, or the Hobgoblin, here treated as a kind of Santa Claus figure, in that the homeowner is supposed to placate a potentially malicious or michievous being with gifts of food. This goblin is not so threatening, but he is also not close to Shakespeare's character in *Midsummer Night's Dream*. He can accomplish in one night what it takes ten laborers to do in a full day's work—if he is fed.

[43]Again the faintly inked mark of *1645* became a correct comma in *1673*.

[44]A big, clumsy, stupid fellow, like a servant who is too stupid to do anything except fetch and carry.

[45]Presumably this loutish goblin is rather tall: the hearth before most kitchen fireplaces (as with the "chimney" here) would have been over six feet wide.

[46]"Filled to the brim." If a chicken's crop is full, its neck is puffed out, making what it has just eaten visible. In this case the hobgoblin has just eaten cream and perhaps the white bread traditionally set out for him (see *Variorum* 2.1: 297).

[47]The first cock to sing in the early hours of the morning would perform the same service as would the church officials who would ring matins, announcing the first hour of public morning prayer—waking townspeople up.

[48]This is the end of a narrative within a narrative, by which device Milton frees himself of the accusation of holding superstitious beliefs about fairies; lines 102–14 are attributed to country folk inspired by ale.

[49]The setting remains romantic and medieval but changes from the upland hamlet to the city. Aristocrats meet there to determine the fate of nations and, incidentally, to compete for the attention of courtly ladies using their jousting ability or their wits.

[50]God of marriage, usually pictured in a purple robe and carrying a torch, rather than in Milton's saffron-yellow robe and carrying a taper or thin candle. At wedding feasts, classically educated guests were supposed to invoke him, calling his name frantically, because not to have him at the feast would be to invite bad luck for the marriage. Shakespeare uses him as a character in *As You Like It*, and Spenser invokes him in his *Epithalamion*, his own wedding song.

[51]"With masques and old-fashioned pageantry." The motif of the good old days (in this case, the good old days of marriage feasts) fits the pattern of imagery derived from chivalry.

[52]An image of a young and melancholy—and slightly silly—poet not unlike the image of a lovesick Romeo that his father Montague and Benvolio paint in *Romeo and Juliet* 1.1.118–55.

[53]Ben Jonson is pictured wearing the slipper worn by the Greek comic actor. In the seventeenth century, the word "sock" usually meant "a slipper with a low heel." For Milton's contrast between comic "sock" and tragic "buskin," see Yale 1: 879; *An Apology*.

[54]The words to describe Shakespeare are rich and revealing. Milton seems to have preferred Shakespeare the romance or comedy writer to the tragedian, judging by his allusions to *Midsummer Night's Dream*, *As You Like It*, and *The Tempest* in his earlier poetry, though *Romeo and Juliet* also seems to have been a favorite. Jonson had used the adjective "sweet" of Shakespeare in the famous phrase "Sweet Swan of Avon." A child of fancy would be an imaginative child or a child with a fantastic imagination. The native wood-notes seem to refer to the bucolic settings of his comedies and perhaps also to

Warble his native Wood-notes wilde,
And ever against eating Cares, 135
Lap me in soft *Lydian* Aires,[55]
Married to immortal verse
Such as the meeting soul may pierce[56]
In notes, with many a winding bout
Of lincked sweetnes long drawn out,[57] 140
With wanton heed, and giddy cunning,
The melting voice through mazes running;[58]
Untwisting all the chains that ty
The hidden soul of harmony.
That *Orpheus*[59] self may heave his head 145
From golden slumber on a bed
Of heapt *Elysian*[60] flowres, and hear
Such streins as would have won the ear
Of *Pluto*, to have quite set free
His half regain'd *Eurydice.* 150
These delights, if thou canst give,
Mirth with thee, I mean to live.

noit at conclusion of Il penseroso [handwritten marginal note]

Il Penseroso.

Hence vain deluding joyes,[1]
    The brood of folly[2] without father bred,
How little you bested,[3]
    Or fill the fixed mind with all your toyes; °   USELESS FANCIES
Dwell in som idle brain, 5
    And fancies fond° with gaudy shapes possess,   FOOLISH

Stratford in Warwickshire; "warbling" was always a positive term for Milton, standing for the inspired singing of a bird like the nightingale.

[55]"Airs" has its Italian meaning "arias," or "beautiful melodies." The Lydian mode, one of the ancient Greek musical modes, was thought to be soft, perhaps melancholy at times, and suitable to love poetry. Scholars discussing this passage argue whether Milton meant his "*Lydian*" to be a pejorative term, since the other modes, the ceremonial and solemn Dorian or the warlike and mournful Phrygian, would have been considered more serious in purpose (*Variorum* 2.1: 304–305).

[56]"Such as the willing soul allows to penetrate it or be inspired by it."

[57]Milton is using musical terminology to suggest an extended sweet melody analogous, perhaps, to the verse paragraph in a "canzone." The linking of notes in a sequence creates coherent smoothness, and the length of the melodic line might help cause a breathtaking ecstasy in singer and audience.

[58]The adjectives "wanton" and "giddy" and the noun "cunning" all suggest the potentially deceptive, magical qualities of art.

[59]Read as "*Orpheus's* self." Orpheus is the master musician of Greek tradition, who lost his wife, Eurydice, to a snakebite and went to Hades to reclaim her, making Cerberus and later Pluto, the god of the underworld, weep with the power of his music. Eurydice is only "half regain'd" because Pluto set the rule that, when leaving Hades, Orpheus was not allowed to look back at her, and Orpheus breaks the rule. Orpheus's music creates sympathy in all living things and has power even over death; Renaissance poets looked to the myth of Orpheus to explain the semidivine nature of the poet. Patricia Vicari, in "The Triumph of Art, the Triumph of Death: Orpheus in Spenser and Milton" (in *Orpheus: The Metamorphoses of a Myth*, ed. John Warden [Toronto: U of Toronto P, 1982]: 207–30), discusses Milton's near-obsession with the myth, which provides a key to understanding "Lycidas" and *Comus*.

[60]The Elysian Fields (or Elysium) represented the place, sometimes pictured as an island in Hades, where dead heroes like Achilles lived. See the *Aeneid* 6.637–65.

[1]As Stella Revard reminds me, "To complicate things there is a goddess Vesta who is Saturn's mother. And Zephyr who plays with Aurora is Aurora's son and Mirth's alternate father. Mirth is the third of the Graces and the parentage Venus/Bacchus is allowed, but is not the first classical choice. The Graces are usually the daughters of Jove and Eurynome" (e-mail message of 31 March 1997). Mirth is born of a union between the god Bacchus and the goddess Venus (see "L'Allegro" 14–24). Melancholy is born of Saturn and his mother Vesta, according to Milton. The ten-line incantation at the beginning of the song banishes Mirth as if removing her spell.

[2]The phrase "brood of folly" had been used by Ben Jonson in *Love Freed from Ignorance* (Jonson 7: 367). As with Mirth, Milton is setting up a genealogy for the joys of Mirth, but they are bred somehow without a father.

[3]Probably should be read as "How little you bestead," or "How little you helped."

As thick and numberless
    As the gay motes° that people the Sun Beams,   MINUTE DUST PARTICLES
Or likest hovering dreams
    The fickle Pensioners of *Morpheus* train.[4]   10

But hail thou Goddes, sage and holy,
Hail divinest Melancholy,[5]
Whose Saintly visage is too bright
To hit the Sense of human sight;[6]
And therfore to our weaker view,   15
Ore laid with black staid Wisdoms hue.
Black,[7] but such as in esteem,
Prince *Memnons* sister[8] might beseem,°   APPEAR TO BE
Or that Starr'd *Ethiope* Queen[9] that strove
To set her beauties praise above   20
The Sea Nymphs, and their powers offended.
Yet thou art higher far descended,
Thee bright-hair'd *Vesta*[10] long of yore,
To solitary *Saturn*[11] bore;
His daughter she (in *Saturns* raign,   25
Such mixture was not held a stain)
Oft in glimmering Bowres,[12] and glades
He met her, and in secret shades
Of woody *Ida*'s inmost grove,[13]
While yet there was no fear of *Jove*.[14]   30
Com pensive Nun,[15] devout and pure,
Sober, stedfast, and demure,[16]
All in a robe of darkest grain,

---

[4]Dreams are pictured as lesser and inconsistent ("fickle") attendants to Morpheus, the son of the god of sleep, Somnus. A pensioner could be an employee given a small allowance for doing nothing. Dreams would hover above the head of the sleeping person, as if part of a train (group of attendants).

[5]The rhyme holy / Melancholy gives us the hint to pronounce "Melancholy" more like the French word than the modern "collie," in this instance, but see the rhyme at 61–62.

[6]Milton makes Melancholy into a saint and a nun, something rather curious for a Protestant Englishman in the 1630s. Here Melancholy has the semidivine ability to hear the music of the spheres, a characteristic shared by the Lady in *Comus* (for her capability to hear sounds other mortals cannot, see 458).

[7]The color of Melancholy, associated with the bodily humor, black bile.

[8]A very esoteric reference, possibly to Dictys Cretensis, *Ephemeris Belli Troiani* 6, who identifies the Ethiopian King Memnon's sister as Himera (Carey 140n). Memnon was supposed to have brought 10,000 men to the Trojan War, to aid his uncle, Priam.

[9]Cassiopæia, a queen of Ethiopia who claimed to be more beautiful than the sea nymphs, the Nereids, and thereby incurred the wrath of Neptune. Her daughter Andromeda was chained to a rock as a sacrificial meal for a sea monster but was rescued by Perseus. Cassiopæia herself was changed into the constellation; hence she is "starred."

[10]The Roman goddess of the hearth and home, served in her Roman shrine by the Vestal Virgins, who kept an eternal flame burning there. Milton apparently invented the detail of Saturn's fatherhood of Vesta, since Hesiod makes her the daughter of Chronos (Saturn) and Rhea (*Theogony* 454). Saturn's reign was rumored to be a time of sexual licence, and the god would have been associated with melancholy, as in the adjective "saturnine," which meant "sluggish, cold, and gloomy in temperament" (*OED* A.1.b).

[11]Saturn, or Chronos, ruled during the Age of Gold (Hesiod, *Works and Days* 111–29; and Ovid, *Metamorphoses* 1.89–115). More importantly, his planet governed the behavior of "saturnine" people, whose personality or temperament was naturally melancholy.

[12]Probably wooded retreats shaded by trees that let in glimmers of sunlight.

[13]Possibly the Cretan Mt. Ida, where Zeus lived as he plotted the overthrow of his father, Chronos (*Diodorus Siculus* 5.66). Saturn and Jove, Milton believed, were "first in *Creet* / And *Ida* known" (*Paradise Lost* 1.514–15).

[14]It may be worth noting that Jove is being set up here as a tyrannical monarch, ruling by fear rather than by the consent of the governed. Given the political climate even in the 1630s, and Milton's later position as orator on the side of civil and domestic liberty, "fear of *Jove*" may anticipate an anti-monarchical position.

[15]The *Variorum* editors remind us (2.1: 315) that "nun" need not have implied the Roman Catholic office, since it might mean "A priestess or votaress of some pagan deity," (*OED* 1.b). Marlowe's phrase for Hero, "Venus's nun" (*Hero and Leander* 1.45), seems similar to Milton's usage, though his nun does seem to have Christian surroundings.

[16]When used "Of persons (and their bearing, speech, etc.)," demure meant "Sober, grave, serious; reserved or composed in demeanour" (*OED* 2, citing this instance).

Flowing with majestick train,
And sable stole of *Cipres* Lawn,[17]   35
Over thy decent° shoulders drawn.   PROPERLY COVERED
Com, but keep thy wonted° state,   CUSTOMARY
With eev'n step, and musing gate,°   THOUGHTFUL GAIT
And looks commercing° with the skies,   COMMUNICATING
Thy rapt soul sitting in thine eyes:[18]   40
There held in holy passion still,
Forget thy self to Marble,[19] till
With a sad° Leaden[20] downward cast,   SERIOUS
Thou fix them on the earth as fast.°   FIRMLY
And joyn with thee calm Peace, and Quiet,[21]   45
Spare Fast, that oft with gods doth diet,
And hears the Muses in a ring,[22]
Ay° round about *Joves* Altar sing.   ALWAYS
And adde to these retired leasure,
That in trim Gardens takes his pleasure;   50
But first, and chiefest, with thee bring,
Him that yon soars on golden wing,
Guiding the fiery-wheeled throne,[23]
The Cherub Contemplation,[24]
And the mute Silence hist along,[25]   55
'Less° *Philomel* will daign a Song,[26]   UNLESS
In[27] her sweetest, saddest plight,°   SITUATION
Smoothing the rugged brow of night,[28]
While *Cynthia*[29] checks° her Dragon yoke,   REINS IN

[17]Lawn was a fine linen fabric resembling cambric, imported originally from the island of Cyprus. Though the fabric lawn was usually white, Cypress lawn was black and hence could be associated with melancholy or with mourning. The adjective "sable" reinforces the blackness of lawn, and a stole might be a veil or a robe or mantle. Albrecht Dürer's famous etching of Melancholy shows her with a veil that partly cloaks her face.

[18]Apparently the image is of the goddess Melancholy in a religious trance while receiving inspiration from Heaven. As William Kerrigan acknowledges, a melancholy poet could request the "vatic possession of the Apollonian Muses" (*The Prophetic Milton* [Charlottesville: UP of Virginia, 1974]: 47).

[19]"Lose yourself in the trance until your body becomes marble." Compare "On *Shakespear*" 13–14, where Shakespeare becomes his own monument.

[20]The metal lead is associated with the god Saturn in the Renaissance system of astrological correspondences. Shakespeare associates lead with contemplation in *Love's Labor's Lost* 4.3.321.

[21]The capitalization might confirm that we are in the presence of allegorical figures, as with "Spare Fast," pictured as dining with the gods. Peace, Quiet, and Temperance as expressed in fasting (not eating to excess) would represent as natural a combination as Faith, Hope, and Chastity (*Mask* 971–72) or "Faith, Love, Vertue" (*Paradise Lost* 3.335).

[22]The customary image of Muses or Graces, dancing in a ring.

[23]The chariot that the prophet Ezekiel pictures in his vision (Ezekiel 10.1–2, 9–22), made of sapphire and with wheels within wheels. Cherubim faces are pictured in the wheels, and cherubim carry the chariot by means of their wings toward Heaven. For extensive examination of the image and its value to Milton, see Lieb and Doherty.

[24]Probably the "-tion" of "Contemplation" should be pronounced as a disyllable, with its last syllable rhymed with "throne." The *Variorum* editors find a source for identifying the angelic order, Cherubim, with the contemplation of God, in Pico della Mirandola's *Oration on the Dignity of Man* (2.2: 318). Seraphim, Cherubim, and Thrones were the three highest orders of angels, according to Pseudo-Dionysius, *Of the Celestial Hierarchy*. For a recent translation, see Pseudo-Dionysius, *The Complete Works*, trans. Colm Luibheid (New York: Paulist, 1987): 143–92.

[25]Curious syntax, since "hist" seems to be a verb. One recorded (*OED* v. 1) sense of "hist" as verb is equivalent to the modern "shush," "be silent," with this line cited as its first instance. I read the meaning of the clause as "And the quiet Silence [accompanying Peace and Quiet] moves along without noise," but that does seem redundant, at best.

[26]"Unless Philomel [the nightingale] will agree to sing a song." The story of Philomela, Procne, and Tereus is told in Book 6 of Ovid's *Metamorphoses*. Sandys notes the meaning of Philomela's name, "lover of musicke," and remarks that "no bird hath so sweet a voice among all the silvan musitians: singing fifteene dayes and nights together, when the leaves begin to afford her a shelter, with little or no intermission. . . . shee alone in her songs expressing the exact art of Musicke in infinite variety" (*Ovid's Metamorphosis, Englished, Mythologized, and Represented in Figures*, by George Sandys, ed. Karl K. Hulley and Stanley T. Vandersall [Lincoln: U of Nebraska P]: 300).

[27]*1645* has "Id" here, an obvious typographical error for "In," and corrected by *1673*.

[28]Probably "frowning," as in *Paradise Regain'd* 2.164 or *OED* adj. 1, 3.b.

[29]The goddess of the Moon, here associated with Medea by mode of transportation, since it is Medea who invokes a dragon-drawn chariot from the goddess Hecate. Hecate, Luna, Diana, and Proserpina were all associated with a moon-chariot that might be drawn by a team of dragons. See Davis B. Harding, *Milton and the Renaissance Ovid* (Urbana: U of Illinois P, 1947): 50.

Gently o're th' accustom'd Oke;   60
Sweet Bird[30] that shunn'st the noise of folly,
Most musicall, most melancholy!
Thee Chauntress° oft the Woods among,   SINGER
I woo to hear thy eeven Song;[31]
And missing thee, I walk unseen   65
On the dry smooth-shaven Green,[32]
To behold the wandring Moon,
Riding neer her highest noon,[33]
Like one that had bin led astray
Through the Heav'ns wide pathles way;   70
And oft, as if her head she bow'd,
Stooping through a fleecy cloud.
Oft on a Plat° of rising ground,   SMALL PATCH, PLOT
I hear the far-off *Curfeu*[34] sound,
Over som wide-water'd shoar,   75
Swinging slow with sullen roar;[35]
Or if the Ayr° will not permit,   WEATHER
Som still removed[36] place will fit,
Where glowing Embers through the room
Teach light to counterfeit a gloom,   80
Far from all resort of mirth,
Save the Cricket on the hearth,
Or the Belmans drousie charm,
To bless the dores from nightly harm:[37]
Or let my Lamp at midnight hour,   85
Be seen in som high lonely Towr,
Where I may oft out-watch the *Bear*,[38]
With thrice great *Hermes*,[39] or unsphear
The spirit of *Plato*[40] to unfold

---

[30]The nightingale, a migratory bird that appears in England in June. Its habits of shyness and of singing at dusk in a long and lovely melodic line made it the equivalent in nature of the melancholy poet, for whom Milton often used it as a symbol, as in Sonnet 1.1–2 or *A Mask* 234, 566.

[31]Possibly with the overtones of "even-song," or evening hymn, corresponding to "Mattin" in "L'Allegro" 113. Both terms associate music with church liturgy, both Roman Catholic and Anglican.

[32]A green might be a grassy area where sheep would crop the vegetation close to the ground, giving it the appearance of just having been shaved. As Carey points out (142n), the hyphenated phrase is also close to similar phrases in Sylvester's DuBartas.

[33]Presumably the noon of night would be midnight, when the moon might be at its highest point, though Milton is deliberately imprecise about time when he uses "neer" rather than "at" (*Variorum* 2.1: 321).

[34]The italics are unusual on a word that should have been familiar, and not at all foreign, to the printer or typesetter, since it had been used in England for hundreds of years. The compositor of *1673* followed in the use of italics, as if imitating his copy-text without thinking about it. The curfew would be sounded or rung out at dusk, when people in villages were advised to extinguish fires (the French version of the word is *couvre-feu*).

[35]A precise description of the slow and solemn (one possible meaning of "sullen") movement of a curfew bell, which produces a loud sound, a roar (*OED* n. 1.2.a)

[36]Probably the place is quiet and remote.

[37]A bellman or watchman would toll the night hour on his bell and even knock on doors to inform inhabitants that no intruders were about, using a formula like "Two o'clock and all's well."

[38]The constellation of Ursa Major, which never sets and thus is up until dawn. A watch is a vigil throughout the night, for purposes of guard duty or religious observation.

[39]Hermes Trismegistus, or the "thrice great *Hermes*" was thought to be a mystical philosopher supposedly writing in the second or third centuries CE. The cryptic writings were ascribed to the Egyptian god Thoth, who was in turn identified by Greeks living in Alexandria as Hermes and later by the Romans as Mercurius. Marsilio Ficino translated the *Corpus Hermeticum*, the known body of work by Hermes Trismegistus, into Latin at the command of Cosimo de Medici in 1463. Francis Bacon, Ben Jonson, Henry Vaughan, Thomas Browne, and Henry More were all influenced by what came to be known as Hermeticism. For a modern edition, see Walter Scott, trans., *Hermetica* (Lower Lake, CA: Atrium Publishers Group, 1993). For the authoritative account of the growth of Hermeticism, see Frances Yates, *Giordano Bruno and the Hermetic Tradition* (Chicago, IL: U of Chicago P, 1964),

[40]Since the Hermetic writings were part Platonism and part mystical religion, the shift to Plato, who is pictured as living within a planetary sphere, would have seemed logical. According to Plato's *Timaeus* (41–42), the souls of great men ascended after their deaths up into the spheres of stars. The image may also evoke the idea of the music of the spheres or harmony of the universe.

What Worlds, or what vast Regions hold   90
The immortal mind that hath forsook
Her mansion in this fleshly nook:[41]
And of those *Dæmons* that are found
In fire, air, flood, or under ground,[42]
Whose power hath a true consent   95
With Planet, or with Element.
Som time let Gorgeous Tragedy[43]
In Scepter'd Pall[44] com sweeping by,
Presenting *Thebs*, or *Pelops* line,[45]
Or the tale of *Troy* divine.   100
Or what (though rare) of later age,
Ennobled hath the Buskind stage.[46]
But, O sad Virgin, that thy power   FOREMOST OF ALL NERDS & POETS
Might raise *Musæus*[47] from his bower,
Or bid the soul of *Orpheus* sing   105
Such notes as warbled to the string,
Drew Iron tears down *Pluto*'s cheek,[48]
And made Hell grant what Love did seek.[49]
Or call up him that left half told
The story of *Cambuscan* bold,[50]   110
Of *Camball*, and of *Algarsife*,
And who had *Canace*[51] to wife,
That own'd the vertuous Ring and Glass,
And of the wondrous Hors of Brass,
On which the *Tartar* King[52] did ride;   115
And if ought els, great *Bards*[53] beside,
In sage and solemn tunes have sung,
Of Turneys° and of Trophies° hung;   TOURNAMENTS   SPOILS

[41]Plato in the *Phaedo* and elsewhere developed the idea of the human soul as being trapped during our lives within our bodies (our "fleshly nook"), only to escape after death to become a part of a heavenly body.

[42]The idea of daemons or spirits inhabiting earth, air, fire, and water may have been derived from Platonism or Hermeticism. According to Frances Yates, Milton may be trying to "suggest the atmosphere of the Hermetic trance, when the immortal mind forsakes the body, and religiously consorts with demons, that is to say, gains the experience which gives it miraculous or magical powers" (*Giordano Bruno* 280).

[43]Apparently Milton is representing Greek tragedy as it was originally performed, not the productions of the Elizabethan theater.

[44]Milton may be representing a king or queen's staff of office, a scepter, as wrapped in pall, a rich purple cloth (*OED* 1.1) associated with royalty. Royalty, of course, would be the subject of tragedy. In Latin, the *palla* is the mantle or long robe worn by the tragic actor.

[45]The royal house of Thebes is associated with Oedipus and his family; Pelops was the patriarch of the family of Agamemnon, Orestes, Electra, and Iphigenia; the city of Troy, supposed to be divine in origin, supplied tragic subjects from the Homeric epics, such as Euripides' *Trojan Women* or Sophocles' *Ajax*.

[46]The Elizabethan or Shakespearean theater is slighted by comparison with Greek tragedy, in the phrase "though rare." A tragic actor in Greece (but not in the Elizabethan theater) would have worn a buskin, or high boot, as compared with the "Sock" of comedy alluded to in "L'Allegro" 132.

[47]We have turned from what was often considered to be the highest form of poetry in the Renaissance, the tragic, to the lyric, with Musaeus, mythical son of Orpheus, and Orpheus himself, whose music was capable of making stones weep, or Pluto, the king of the underworld. In the *Aeneid* 6.639–68, Orpheus is pictured singing and Musaeus leads a group of the dead in Elysium, chanting from within a grove fragrant with laurel.

[48]The tears that Orpheus's music was supposed to have extracted from the eyes of Pluto might well have been rust-colored, coming from the iron heart of the king of the dead.

[49]Orpheus's love, in other words, sought its object, Eurydice, and his music forced Hell (or its ruler Pluto) to give him back his wife. See "L'Allegro" 145.

[50]The list of writers now seems to have shifted away from classical tragedy to Milton's favorite English poets, since Chaucer is the poet whose *Squire's Tale* is incomplete, and Spenser attempted to complete the story in *Faerie Queene* 4.2.30–3.52. Milton may have found spellings approximating "*Camball*" and "*Cambuscan*" in Speght's edition of Chaucer, which he owned (*Variorum* 2.1: 328–29).

[51]Pronounced with three syllables. "Canacee" is the way it is ordinarily spelled in modern old-spelling editions of Chaucer.

[52]See Chaucer's *Squire's Tale*, which identifies "*Cambuscan*" or Cambyuskan (probably Genghis Khan, which was written "Camius Khan" in Latin) as a king of Tartary. He is visited by "a knyght upon a steede of bras" (*The Riverside Chaucer*, gen. ed. Larry D. Benson [third ed.; Boston: Houghton Mifflin, 1987]: 170).

[53]It is hard to determine how many bards or ritualistic poets Milton might be including in the category, since he will use the term "*Bards*" as synonymous with "*Druids*" in "Lycidas" 53.

Of Forests, and inchantments drear,[54]
Where more is meant then meets the ear.[55]
Thus night oft see me in thy pale career,[56]   120
Till civil-suited° Morn appeer,   DECENTLY DRESSED
Not trickt and frounc't° as she was wont,   WITH CURLED HAIR
With the Attick Boy[57] to hunt,
But Cherchef't[58] in a comly Cloud,   125
While rocking Winds are Piping loud,
Or usher'd with a shower still,[59]
When the gust hath blown his fill,
Ending on the russling Leaves,
With minute° drops from off the Eaves.   SMALL   130
And when the Sun begins to fling
His flaring beams, me Goddes° bring   THE GODDESS MELANCHOLY
To arched walks of twilight groves,
And shadows brown that *Sylvan*[60] loves
Of Pine, or monumental Oake,   135
Where the rude Ax with heaved stroke,
Was never heard the Nymphs to daunt,
Or fright them from their hallow'd haunt.
There in close covert by som Brook,
Where no profaner eye may look,   140
Hide me from Day's garish° eie,   ESPECIALLY BRIGHT
While the Bee with Honied thie,[61]
That at her flowry work doth sing,
And the Waters murmuring
With such consort as they keep,   145
Entice the dewy-feather'd Sleep;[62]
And let som strange mysterious dream,
Wave at his Wings in Airy stream,
Of lively portrature display'd,[63]
Softly on my eye-lids laid.[64]   150
And as I wake, sweet musick breath°   BREATHE
Above, about, or underneath,
Sent by som spirit to mortals good,

---

[54]Milton was apparently the first to use the poetically shortened version of "dreary," in the Nativity Ode 193.

[55]An allusion to the allegorical method of Spenser, who retold the story of Canace from Chaucer, but who added the element of allegory. Milton may echo Spenser's "allegories which depend for some of their effect on an air of mystery" (Elizabeth Heale, The Faerie Queene: *A Reader's Guide* [Cambridge: Cambridge UP, 1987]: 12).

[56]"See me often thus, Night, when you are in your pale course across the sky."

[57]A glancing allusion to Cephalus, an Athenian ("Attick") prince and a hunter who is made to cause the death of his wife Procris because he is loved by the jealous Aurora, goddess of the dawn. Milton seems to emphasize the fickle nature of Aurora in adulterously courting Cephalus since both "trickt" and "frounc't" suggest wanton flirtation. See Elegy 5.51, where Cephalus is called Aeolides.

[58]"Kerchiefed," with head covered by a kerchief. The spelling is unusual and may indicate an Italian hard "ch" pronunciation imposed on English ("Cherchef't" is not listed as a variant spelling in the *OED*).

[59]Dawn is ushered in by a quiet ("still") shower.

[60]Sylvanus, Roman god of forests, sometimes associated with Pan, as in Elegy 5.121–22.

[61]Bees are actually carrying pollen rather than honey in the sacs on their thighs, but there were literary precedents in Vergil's *Eclogues* 1.54–55 and in Michael Drayton's phrase "Each bee with Honey on her laden thye" (*The Owle* 121, quoted from *The Works*, eds. J. W. Hebel, Kathleen Tillotson, and B. H. Newdigate [London: Shakespeare Head, 1931–41]: 2.483).

[62]A winged figure, as in 148; the dews of evening would accompany his visitation.

[63]One of Milton's rare references to visual art, in this case lifelike portraiture, the image of a dream as depicted by a painter.

[64]Apparently the dream is borne to the sleeper on the wings of Sleep and laid on his eyelids.

Or th' unseen Genius of the Wood.[65]
But let my due feet never fail,   155
To walk the studious Cloysters pale,[66]
And love the high embowed Roof,
With antick Pillars massy proof,[67]
And storied Windows richly dight,°   ORNAMENTED
Casting a dimm religious light.   160
There let the pealing Organ blow,
To the full voic'd Quire below,
In Service high, and Anthems cleer,
As may with sweetnes, through mine ear,
Dissolve me into extasies,[68]   165
And bring all Heav'n before mine eyes.
And may at last my weary age
Find out the peacefull hermitage,
The Hairy Gown and Mossy Cell,[69]
Where I may sit and rightly spell,[70]   170
Of every Star that Heav'n doth shew,
And every Herb that sips the dew;
Till old experience do attain
To somthing like Prophetic strain.
These pleasures *Melancholy*[71] give,   175
And I with thee will choose to live.

SONNETS.

Milton's twenty-four sonnets begin with imitations of Italian models, specifically sonnets by Francesco Petrarch, Giovanni Della Casa (whose *Rime* of 1563 Milton owned in a copy annotated by him in Italian and preserved in the New York Public Library), Pietro Bembo, Benedetto Varchi, and Torquato Tasso. By proceeding immediately from an English sonnet, no. 1, into an Italian sonnet, no. 2 in the 1645 *Poems*, Milton is declaring that in his eyes the two languages are equally the languages of the sonnet. But Milton does not emulate Shakespeare or Sidney in style or content, though he certainly knew their sonnets. As Carey points out, "Della Casa, like Bembo, from whose experiments he profited, gave his sonnets a complex and artificial word-order by devices such as inversion, interpolation and suspension of grammar, in order to create the impression of an intricate syntax akin to Latin" (89n). F. T. Prince declares, "The Sonnet to the Nightingale is indeed Italian in its form and manner. It recalls Bembo in its slightly solemn trifling, its very literary tone, and

---

[65]Presumably like the Genius of the Wood in *Arcades* 62–78, who can hear and imitate the Music of the Spheres; but any local wood might be supposed to be protected or overseen by tutelary spirits, good demons, or geniuses.

[66]Probably not the cloister of a Roman Catholic monastery but the cloister of a university college, as at Cambridge, where chapels usually are present in each older college, defined as "A covered walk or arcade connected with a monastery, college, or large church, serving as a way of communication between different parts of the group of buildings, and sometimes as a place of exercise or study . . ." (*OED* 3). A "pale" in this case is an enclosure and has nothing to do with complexion.

[67]Though editors hesitate to assign a specific meaning to the syntax, the image seems to indicate that the columns are massive enough and strong enough to bear the weight of the roof. The pillar probably is antique in the sense "of a venerable age," rather than "covered with grotesque figures."

[68]The soul is separated ("dissolved" in the sense of *OED* "dissolve" 1). For a comprehensive account of what religious ecstasy had to do with poetic inspiration, see Kerrigan, *The Prophetic Milton*, especially Chapter 1.

[69]In view of Milton's later career as antiprelatical and anti-Roman Catholic pamphleteer and as the author of Sonnet 18, "Avenge O Lord," the image in "Il Penseroso" of the author in his projected old age as a hermit wearing a hair shirt and living in a mossy monastic cell seems regressive, as does the author's reverence for nuns, cloisters, stained glass, dark chapels, and anthems, all of which he would later condemn as a member of Cromwell's Interregnum government, which advocated the systematic destruction of church ornaments and deemphasized church ritual and ceremony.

[70]In the sense of *OED* v. 2.2.b. "To make out, understand, decipher, or comprehend, by study."

[71]For the first time, the proper noun is italicized, which might indicate some special status for Melancholy as a saintly allegorical entity.

even in the epigrammatic turn of its conclusion" (*The Italian Element in Milton's Verse* [Oxford: Clarendon, 1969]: 96).

The sonnets in Italian, numbered 2, 3, and 4, plus the canzone, are abstract and distant love poems to a woman named Emilia, whose name is buried in Sonnet 2. Edward Le Comte believes that her last name may be Varco, but speculations about her identity range from Emilia Lanyer, the poet, to some anonymous member of the circle of friends of Charles Diodati's family. She is not exactly Milton's "dark lady," though she is described as being foreign and having dark eyes and eyelashes. She could represent the young poet's wish-fulfillment as he imagines that it is about time that he write love poetry, even if it is to a fictitious woman, if he is to be practicing in the sonnet mode.

The young man seems to be falling in love with love—and with the idea of being a poet. Curiously, Milton felt the need to tell his best male friend about his new love in Sonnet 4, in the language—Italian—of the Diodati family.

Like Milton's Latin poems that deal with love, his Italian poems are highly derivative from his models in that language. To look at Baldi's Italian edition of Milton's sonnets, with its heavy annotations referring to phrases and images borrowed from the earlier Italian sonneteers, is to realize how much Milton depended on his models for his imagery and speech patterns. I should point out, as Campbell does, that Milton's Italian poems were written almost ten years before he visited that country: thus he was writing in a language not his own, and writing to an audience (the Diodati family) of native speakers, a feat requiring colossal nerve. Having created a fantasy Italy containing the arts of poetry and music in his early Italian poetry, he was to visit and fall in love with the country itself in 1638.

Work Cited

Baldi, Sergio. "Poesie Italiane di Milton." *Studi Miltoniani*. Università degli Studi Di Firenze Istituto de Lingue e Letterature Germaniche, Slave e Ugrofinniche Facoltà di Lettere e Filosofia. Firenze: Eurografica Spa, 1985. 7–32.

I.

O Nightingale, that on yon bloomy Spray[1]
    Warbl'st at eeve, when all the Woods are still,
Thou with fresh hope the Lovers heart dost fill,
    While the jolly hours[2] lead on propitious *May*,
Thy liquid notes that close the eye of Day,[3]
    First heard before the shallow Cuccoo's bill[4]
    Portend success in love; O if *Jove*'s will
Have linkt that amorous power to thy soft lay,
Now timely sing, ere the rude Bird of Hate[5]
    Foretell my hopeles doom in som Grove ny:
    As thou from yeer to yeer hast sung too late
For my relief; yet hadst no reason why,
    Whether the Muse, or Love call thee his mate,
    Both them I serve, and of their train am I.

[1]As Carey and others have pointed out, the entire first line echoes Bembo, *Rime* (Venice, 1564), no. 45: "O rosignuol, che'n queste verdi fronde" (90). What Milton adds to the tradition of nightingale poetry is his lifelong identification of himself with the bird that sings so beautifully at twilight. See John L. Lievsay, "Milton among the Nightingales," *Renaissance Papers 1958, 1959, 1960* (1961): 36–45.

[2]Seen in terms of classical mythology as the Horae, the Hours, three goddesses who presided over spring, summer, and winter, often represented as dancing or opening the gates of heaven.

[3]The adjective "liquid" is especially appropriate for the song of the nightingale, which is an elaborate trill and a melodic cascade. Milton succeeds in describing the nightingale's song as accurately as a naturalist while retaining its value as an image inspirational to poets. The cuckoo's song, on the other hand, is a two-note song (very like that reproduced in a good cuckoo clock), repetitious, and, because of the associations between cuckoos and cuckolds— the cuckoo lays its eggs in other birds' nests— a sinister activity. In contrasting the cuckoo and the nightingale, Milton follows a literary tradition going back at least to a poem thought in Renaissance England to be by Chaucer, *The Cuckoo and the Nightingale*, which exploits the popular tradition that it was better to hear the nightingale's song in spring before hearing the cuckoo's song, since the first would lead to love and the second to cuckoldry.

[4]Presumably the cuckoo's song is issuing from its bill, and the song is unpleasant—"shallow" may mean "lacking in resonance" (*OED* 4), but "shallow" may also mean "lacking in depth of feeling" (*OED* 6.c).

[5]The cuckoo, whose call may prophesy jealousy or revenge as a result of adultery or sexual betrayal.

II.[1]

Donna leggiadra il cui bel nome honora
　L'herbosa val di Rheno, e il nobil varco,
　Ben è colui d'ogni valore scarco
　Qual tuo spirto gentil non innamora,
Che dolcemente mostra si di fuora   5
　De suoi[2] atti soavi giamai parco,
　E i don', che son d'amor saette ed arco,
　Là[3] onde l'alta tua virtù s'infiora.
Quando tu vaga parli, o lieta canti
　Che mover possa duro alpestre legno,   10
　Guardi ciascun a gli occhi, ed a gli orecchi
L'entrata, chi di te si truova indegno;
　Gratia sola di su gli vaglia, inanti
　Che'l disio amoroso al cuor s'invecchi.

II.

Handsome woman, whose lovely name honors the green valley of the Reno and the famous ford,[4] any man is worthless who does not fall in love with your noble spirit—that spirit which expresses itself sweetly, never neglectful of giving those soft looks and graces which are Cupid's bow and arrows, there where your virtue is rewarded. When you speak or sing, fortunate lady (your singing would invoke love in rough trees and bring them off the mountains),[5] every unworthy man should guard his eyes and ears. Heavenly grace alone is what would prevent love's desire from fixing itself in his heart permanently.

no virtue [handwritten marginal note]

Divine love. [handwritten note]

---

[1]Since Milton numbers this first Italian sonnet as "II" and since its love theme and its imagery are so close to that of Sonnet 1, editors assume that it should be dated close to 1630 (Milton had purchased the Della Casa volume in December of 1629). There is a name for the lady honored in the poem buried in the imagery, as J. S. Smart first proved in "The Italian Singer in Milton's Sonnet," *Musical Antiquary* 4 (1913): 91–97; see also *The Sonnets of Milton* (Oxford: Clarendon, 1966). The name is Emilia, as Milton's identification of the region through which the river Reno runs—Emilia Romagna—indicates. Edward Le Comte suggests that her last name, Varco, may also be hidden in the sonnet ("Shakespeare's Emilia and Milton's: The Parameters of Research," *Milton Quarterly* 18 [1984]: 81–84), but the word "varco" was translated as "ford," a shallow passage across a river, in Florio's Italian Dictionary, *New World of Words* (1611).
[2]Printed as "sui" in *1673*.
[3]"Là" (with the accent mark) represents "there" (as opposed to "here") in English, whereas "La" is the definite article "The." Virtually all editors assume that the compositors made a mistake here when they used "La" in place of "Là," both in *1645* and in *1673*, though Carey translates "there" but leaves the accent off.

[4]The river Reno borders the Italian region of the Emilia-Romagna; the famous ford is that on the Rubicon River, in the same region, which Caesar crossed in order to assume his dictatorship in Rome. E.A.J. Honigmann's *Milton's Sonnets* (New York: St. Martin's, 1966) provides a full context.
[5]The beloved lady becomes Orpheus in her ability to move inanimate nature to human emotions through song. Neither Cupid's bow and arrows, represented in her looks or bearing, nor the potential Siren song of her beautiful voice threaten a virtuous man.

III.

Qual in colle aspro, al imbrunir di sera
  L'avezza giovinetta pastorella
  Va bagnando l'herbetta strana e bella
Che mal si spande a disusata spera
Fuor di sua natía alma primavera,
  Cosi[1] Amor meco insù la lingua snella[2]
  Desta il fior novo de strania favella,
  Mentre io di te, vezzosamente altera,
Canto, dal mio buon popol non inteso
E'l bel Tamigi cangio col bel Arno.
  Amor lo volse, ed io a l'altrui peso
Seppi ch' Amor cosa mai volse indarno.
  Deh! foss' il mio cuor lento e'l duro seno
  A chi pianta dal ciel si buon terreno.

5

River→

10

III.

As on a rough hill, at the darkening of evening, the young native shepherdess goes about watering the exotic, beautiful little plant that can hardly spread its leaves, so far from its native and nourishing spring climate,[3] so Love awakens my ready tongue to flower in a foreign language as I sing to you, graceful and proud lady, my language not understood by good men of my country, as I exchange my Thames for your beautiful Arno.[4] Love wished it so, and Love wishes for nothing in vain, as I know by the pains of others. O that my slow heart and hard breast were more fertile soil for the gardener of heaven to plant in.

Is he not worthy of love?

---

[1]Shawcross corrects this to "Così," but the accent mark is not there in *1645*.
[2]The "*suella*" of 1645 incorrectly turns the letter "n."

---

[3]Compare the medicinal plant mentioned by the Attendant Spirit in *Comus* that flowers "in another Countrey, as he said, . . . but not in this soyl" (632-33).
[4]Presumably the Tuscan dialect associated with the city of Florence and its river, the Arno.

Canzone.[1]

*R*idonsi donne e giovani amorosi
M'accostandosi attorno, e perche scrivi,
Perche tu scrivi in lingua ignota e strana
Verseggiando d'amor, e come t'osi?
Dinne, se la tua speme sia mai vana, 5
E de pensieri lo miglior t'arrivi;
Cosi mi van burlando, altri rivi
Altri lidi t'aspettan, & altre onde
Nelle cui verdi sponde
Spuntati ad hor, ad hor a la tua chioma 10
L'immortal guiderdon d'eterne frondi
Perche alle spalle tue soverchia soma?
  Canzon dirotti, e tu per me rispondi
Dice mia Donna, e'l suo dir, è il mio cuore
Questa è lingua di cui si vanta Amore. 15

Canzone.

Laughing ladies and young lovers bother me. "Why do you write, why do you write in an unknown foreign language, scribbling verses of love; how do you dare to? Tell us, so that your hopes won't ever be vain, and your better thoughts will come." Just so, they make fun of me: "Other shores, other streams are waiting for you, where sprout immortal garlands[2] made of eternal leaves for your hair; why add such a burden to your shoulders?"

Canzone, I will tell you, and then you will answer for me as well, "This is the language that Love brags in."

Living outside life
Inside words.

---

[1] A canzone, in Italian poetry issuing originally from Petrarch and Dante, was a musical poem with lines of varying length and an irregular or inconsistent rhyme-scheme. The usual canzone had more than one stanza and a "commiato" (valediction); Milton's canzone is truncated to one stanza, but it does contain a commiato. The influence of the irregular lines and rhyme scheme of the canzone can be seen in "Lycidas," "At a Solemn Musick," and even in *Samson Agonistes.*

---

[2] Compare the famous passage from *Areopagitica*: "I cannot praise a fugitive and cloister'd vertue, unexercis'd & unbreath'd, that never sallies out and sees her adversary, but slinks out of the race, where that immortall garland is to be run for, not without dust and heat" (Yale 2: 515).

IV.

Diodati, e te'l dirò con maraviglia,
   Quel ritroso io ch' amor spreggiar soléa
   E de suoi lacci spesso mi redéa
   Gia caddi, ov' huom dabben talhor s'impiglia.
Ne treccie d'oro, ne guancia vermiglia   5
   M'abbaglian sì, ma sotto novia idea
   Pellegrina[1] bellezza che'l cuor bea,
   Portamenti alti honesti, e nelle ciglia
Quel sereno fulgor d'amabil nero,
   Parole adorne di lingua piu d'una,   10
   E'l cantar che di mezzo l'hemispero
Traviar ben può la faticosa Luna,
   E degli occhi suoi auventa si gran fuoco
   Che l'incerar gli orecchi mi fia poco.

IV.

Diodati, and I say it to you with amazement, that I, the stubborn one who used to scorn love and often laughed at his snares, have now fallen into his net, where a good man might sometimes be entangled. No golden ringlets or tinted cheeks[2] deceive me, but that foreign beauty based on an ideal new to me makes my heart warm, she carrying herself virtuously, her eyes darkly blazing, her speech adorned with more than one language, and singing that would take the laboring moon off course in the middle of its hemisphere;[3] there is such fire in her eyes that there's no use for me to plug my ears with wax.[4]

temptation

---

[1] "Pellegrina" carries the idea of "exotic pilgrim from a foreign land."

[2] Compare Comus 752-53, "What need a vemeil-tinctur'd lip for that / Love-darting eyes, or tresses like the Morn?"
[3] Carey points to Vergil, *Eclogues* 8.69, where Alphesiboeus grants songs the power to draw the moon down from heaven (2nd ed. 97n).
[4] Odysseus instructs his sailors to plug their ears with wax so they cannot hear the Sirens' song (*Odyssey* 12.177).

V.

Per certo i bei vostr'occhi,[1] Donna mia[2]
Esser non può[3] che non sian lo mio sole
Sì mi percuoton forte, come ei suole
Per l' arene di Libia chi s' invia,
Mentre un caldo vapor (nè senti pria)
Da quel lato si spinge ove mi duole,
Che forse amanti nelle lor parole
Chiaman sospir; io non so che si sia:
Parte rinchiusa, e turbida si cela
Scosso mi il petto, e poi n'uscendo poco
Quivi d'attorno o s'agghiaccia, o s'ingiela;
Ma quanto a gli occhi giunge a trovar[4] loco
Tutte le notti a me suol far piovose
Finche mia Alba rivien colma di rose.

V.

For sure, my Lady, your beautiful eyes could be nothing less than my sun; they hit me as the sun hits a man who makes his way across the sands of Lybia; meanwhile a hot vapor (not felt before) rises from that side of me where I am hurting,[5] something that lovers in their language call a sigh; part of that, pent up and shaken, hides, a little is shaken out, and chills or freezes everything around it; but that part of it that reaches my eyes makes all nights tearful for me alone, until my Dawn returns, full of roses.[6]

[handwritten margin note: desire]

[handwritten margin note: Is he talking about blind love? or how love blinds us because it takes the space from regimen, study + focus?]

---

[1]The comma does not appear in *1645*; it is added in *1673*.
[2]Even though Shakespeare made fun of awe-inspiring or radiant eyes in "My mistress's eyes are nothing like the sun," the image of the loved-one's eyes as being like a sun drying the lover's moist desire, or causing him to cry buckets or rivers at night, was a consistent part of European love poetry from Dante and Petrarch onward (see Petrarch, *Rime* 3.4 and 9.10–11) through Ronsard and Tasso (*Rime* 75.3). For other parallel images, see the notes in Smart and Baldi. Nardo finds in this sonnet "the desire to transcend the self in love and service" (*Milton's Sonnets and the Ideal Community* [Lincoln: U of Nebraska P, 1979]: 33).
[3]I have added the accents here and with "nè" in line 5.
[4]Written as "*e trovar*" in *1673*.

[5]Something like a love melancholy pictured as a dangerous vapor rising from the vicinity of the poet's heart.
[6]The last several lines of Milton's Sonnet 23, "Mee though I saw my late espoused saint," may echo the last two lines of the Italian sonnet: "But O as to imbrace me she enclin'd, / I wak'd, she fled, and day brought back my night."

VI.

Giovane piano, e semplicetto amante
  Poi che fuggir me stesso in dubbio sono,
  Madonna a voi del mio cuor l'humil dono
  Farò divoto; io certo a prove tante
L'hebbi fedele, intrepido, costante,   5
  De pensieri leggiadro, accorto, e buono;
  Quando rugge il gran mondo, e scocca il tuono,
  S'arma di se, e d'intero diamante,[1]
Tanto del forse, e d'invidia sicuro,
  Di timori, e speranze al popol use   10
  Quanto d'ingegno, e d'alto valor vago,
E di cetra sonora, e delle muse:
  Sol troverete in tal parte men duro
  Ove amor mise l'insanabil ago.

VI.

Being a young, quiet, and artless lover,[2] because I am confused how I might run away from myself, I give you the humble gift of my heart, lady, with devotion; I have tested it often and found it to be faithful, fearless, constant, pure in thought, gracious, circumspect, good; when the whole earth shakes and lightning strikes, my heart arms itself with internal adamant, safe from bad luck and envy, the fears and aspirations of ordinary men, through its reserve of so much talent and courage, on behalf of the resonant lyre and the Muses: you will find my heart less yielding only where Love has hit it with his incurable dart.

---

[1]"Diamond" and "adamant" (meaning the hardest imaginable substance) were apparently synonymous for Milton. Compare "arming in compleat diamond" (*An Apology*, Yale 1: 900) with "armd in Adamant and Gold" in *Paradise Lost* 6.110. I am thankful to Baldi 30n. for pointing this out.

[2]The sonnet says much more about the lover than the beloved, characterizing the poet as quiet, naive in love, humble, devoted, faithful, courageous, constant, pure, gracious, thoughtful, and good. Compare the "special virtues, connected with a man's duty towards himself" in *On Christian Doctrine* 2, Chapters 9 and 19.

Sonnet 7 (1632?)

Parker dates this sonnet in December 1632, given Milton's use of the Latin phrase "Anno aetatis" to mean "at the age of" rather than "in the year of age." The sonnet is closely allied with the "Letter to an Unknown Friend," which it accompanied. The friend (possibly Thomas Young) had warned Milton "that the howres of the night passe on (for so I call my life as yet obscure, & unserviceable to mankind) & that the day wth me is at hand wherin Christ commands all to labour while there is light" (Yale 1: 319). This very revealing letter was not published during Milton's lifetime but exists in the Trinity College Manuscript, in two states; it should be seen in a facsimile because Milton revised it carefully, canceling certain passages and adding others.

Like the letter, Milton's sonnet, which he describes as "made up in a Petrarchian stanza" (Yale 1: 320), concerns itself with ambition, study, and productivity. It expresses the fear that the leisured course of study Milton had been pursuing at the family homes at Horton and Hammersmith was not leading toward his goals of personal fame and a life of public service (Shawcross). The "terrible seasing of him that hid the talent" in Matthew 25.14–30 was Milton's example of unfulfilled promise, and God is the frightening, but in the end kindly, taskmaster. Haskin provides an ample context for the place of the parable of the talents in Milton's spiritual autobiography (Chapter 2), and he instructs us how to read Sonnet 7 in terms of his own accountability and his obedience to God (111).

The sonnet adapts the Elizabethan English sonnet form to the Italian: the diction is simple and colloquial at times, but amplified (Partridge) and dignified. The rhyme scheme is ABBA ABBA, then CDE set off cleverly against a partly reversed DCE.

TEXT

The 1645 *Poems* makes few changes in the version preserved in the Trinity College Manuscript, though the spelling "twentith" (it might be "twenti'th") in the manuscript might indicate how Milton wanted the word to be pronounced. There are but two marks of punctuation in the manuscript, the commas that appear in the middle of lines 9 and 12. In the manuscript, Milton capitalizes "Time" (twice) and "Youth," but not "truth," "heaven," or "task-maisters." The compositor of *1645* made Milton's "heaven" into the monosyllabic, capitalized "Heav'n," most likely to fit the metrics. The 1673 edition makes no substantial corrections, and it adds errors ("Soln" for "Stoln").

Works Cited

Haskin, Dayton. *Milton's Burden of Interpretation*. Philadelphia: U of Pennsylvania P, 1994.

Parker, William Riley. "Some Problems in the Chronology of Milton's Early Poems." *Review of English Studies* 11 (1935): 276–83.

Partridge, A. C. "Milton." *The Language of Renaissance Poetry: Spenser, Shakespeare, Donne, Milton*. London: Deutsch, 1971. 268–70.

Shawcross, John T. "Milton's Decision to Become a Poet." *Modern Language Quarterly* 24 (1963): 21–30.

Svendsen, Kester. "Milton's 'On His Having Arrived at the Age of Twenty-Three.'" *Explicator* 7 (1949): Item 53.

VII.

How soon hath Time the suttle theef of youth,
  Stoln on his wing my three and twentieth yeer!
  My hasting dayes flie on with full career,
  But my late spring no bud or blossom shew'th.
Perhaps my semblance might deceive the truth,   5
  That I to manhood am arriv'd so near,
  And inward ripenes doth much less appear,
  That som more timely-happy spirits indu'th.[1]
Yet be it less or more, or soon or slow,
  It shall be still in strictest measure eev'n,   10
  To that same lot, however mean, or high,
Toward which Time leads me, and the will of Heav'n;
  All is, if I have grace to use it so,
  As ever in my great task Masters eye.[2]

---

[1] It may well be idle speculation to try to determine which poets (if he is talking about poets) were productive or "timely-happy" earlier in their lives than Milton was, but Abraham Cowley and Edmund Spenser, the first contemporary and the second from an earlier generation, have been suggested.

[2] Kester Svendsen suggests that we should read the lines as "All that matters is whether I have grace to use my ripeness in accordance with the will of God as one ever in His sight."

Sonnet 8 (1642)

Sonnet 8.
On his dore when yᵉ Citty expected an assault
When the assault was intended to yᵉ Citty

The title in the first line after "Sonnet 8" above is that of an amanuensis in the Trinity Manuscript; it was struck through, and Milton wrote the second title below it. The second title removes a literal door from the fiction of the poem, though biographers and critics have speculated whether Milton might have wanted to protect his property during potential skirmishes in London in 1642 (Parker [232] notes that the feared battles never occurred).

The sonnet represents a kind of serious joke: the poet supposedly pins a copy of a poem to his door during time of war, in order to protect himself and his property against desecration and destruction. Pindar, Euripides, and Plutarch are his classical role models for the poet, and Alexander the Great his example of a military leader civilized by the effects of poetry. The Captain or Colonel arriving at the poet's door, in Milton's fiction, is granted immortality through the artistry of the poem.

Parker notes the sardonic humor: "Only a few words in this sonnet betray the humorous and ironic tone: the 'knight in arms' was practically as obsolete in English warfare as the 'spear' by 1642. One should also notice that both Pindar and Euripides (unlike Milton) were dead and famous when their houses were spared by conquering armies" (232).

Text

1645 applies consistent punctuation and capitalization, as well as italics, to the scribal version preserved in the Trinity Manuscript, though it follows the spellings of "sease" (seize), "dores," "bowre," and "towre." There are no significant corrections or variants in *1673*, which scrupulously echoes *1645*.

Works Cited

Fallon, Robert T. "Milton's 'defenseless doors': The Limits of Irony." *Milton Quarterly* 13 (1979): 146–51.

Hanford, James Holly. "Milton and the Art of War." *Studies in Philology* 18 (1921): 232–66.

Parker, William Riley. *Milton: A Biography*. Ed. Gordon Campbell. 2nd ed. Oxford: Clarendon, 1996.

VIII.

Captain or Colonel, or Knight in Arms,
  Whose chance on these defenceless dores may sease,°   SEIZE
  If ever deed of honour did thee please,
  Guard them, and him within protect from harms,
He can requite thee, for he knows the charms   5
  That call Fame on such gentle acts as these,
  And he can spred thy Name o're Lands and Seas,
  What ever clime the Suns bright circle warms.
Lift not thy spear against the Muses Bowre,
  The great *Emathian* Conqueror[3] bid spare   10
  The house of *Pindarus*, when Temple and Towre
Went to the ground: And the repeated air
  Of sad° *Electra*'s Poet[4] had the power   SERIOUS, SOLEMN
  To save th' *Athenian* Walls from ruine bare.°   COMPLETE RUIN

---

[3]Alexander the Great. Emathia was a province of Macedonia, where his father Philip was king. According to Plutarch, Alexander spared the house of Pindar while his army was in the process of destroying Thebes (*Alexander* 11).
[4]Euripides, Milton's favorite Greek playwright. The opening chorus of *Electra* was supposed to have been designed to dissuade Sparta from sacking Athens in 404 BCE.

Sonnet 9 (1642?)

Sonnet 9.
Lady that in the prime

No one knows for sure when this sonnet was written or to whom it was addressed. Suggestions for the Lady range from Mary Powell Milton (Miller) to the opposite extreme, the mysterious Miss Davis, whom Milton was courting, supposedly, after Mary Powell deserted him (Masson 3: 436).

The poem is certainly about a very young woman about to be married, who seems to be holding her own against people jealous of her and unreasonably severe about her behavior. She answers their "spleen" with "pity and ruth."

Haskin sees the figure of Ruth as "a model for relating creativity with political engagement" (156n). Mary, on the other hand, was associated by scriptural tradition with Mary Magdalene, so that Milton "was alluding to a figure whose past may have been . . . badly tainted: a figure whose past qualified her to be the sort of sinner to whom grace abounds" (159). Interpreting the scriptures, in this case, "seemed unsettling and even threatening" (169).

TEXT

Here is my transcription of the poem as it appears in the Trinity College Manuscript:

Ladie, that in yᵉ prime of earliest youth
    wisely hast shun'd yᵉ broad way ɇ yᵉ green
    and with those few art eminently seen
    that labour up yᵉ hill of heavnly Truth
The better part with Mary ɇ with Ruth
    chosen thou hast; ɇ they yᵗ overween
    and at thy ~~blooming~~ vertues fret their spleen
            ˣprospering ˣgrowing vertues
    no anger find in thee, but pitty ɇ ruth.
Thy care is fixt, ɇ zealously attends
    to fill thy odorous lamp with deeds of light
Thou when the Bridegroom with his feastfull freinds
    ~~opens the dore of Bliss, that howre of night,~~
                (night
                howr
    Passes to bliss at yᵉ midd ~~watch~~
    hast gain'd thy entrance, virgin wise ɇ pure.

For this edition, *1645* is followed, with reference to the manuscript version in Milton's hand.

Works Cited

Haskin, Dayton. "Choosing the Better Part with Mary and with Ruth." *Of Poetry and Politics: New Essays on Milton and His World*. Ed. Paul G. Stanwood. Binghamton, NY: Medieval & Renaissance Texts & Studies, 1995. 153–69.

Masson, David. *The Life of John Milton, and the History of His Time*. 6 vols. London: Macmillan, 1873.

Miller, Leo. "John Milton's 'Lost' Sonnet to Mary Powell." *Milton Quarterly* 25 (1991): 102–07.

IX.

Lady that in the prime of earliest youth,
    Wisely hast shun'd the broad way and the green,
    And with those few art eminently seen,
    That labour up the Hill of heav'nly Truth,[1]
The better part with *Mary* and with *Ruth*,[2]
    Chosen thou hast, and they that overween,°
    And at thy growing vertues fret their spleen,°
    No anger find in thee, but pity and ruth.°
Thy care is fixt, and zealously attends
    To fill thy odorous Lamp with deeds of light,
    And Hope that reaps not shame. Therefore be sure
Thou, when the Bridegroom with his feastfull friends
    Passes to bliss at the mid hour of night,
    Hast gain'd thy entrance, Virgin wise and pure.[3]

5

PRESUME

VENT THEIR EXTREME ANGER

COMPASSION

10

---

[1] A common image: the hill of Truth is difficult to ascend, as in Donne's Satire 3.79; compare *Paradise Regain'd* 2.217.

[2] Hughes's note is helpful and concise: "Mary, whom Jesus praised for choosing 'that good part, which shall not be taken from her' (Luke x, 42), and Ruth, who gave up her home in Moab to live with her Hebrew mother-in-law, Naomi (Ruth i, 14) traditionally exemplified Christian womanhood." *1645* has the line as "The better part with *Mary*, and the *Ruth*," which is corrected by *1673*'s "The better part with *Mary*, and with *Ruth*." For a full exposition of the meaning of the two figures in seventeenth-century biblical exegesis, see Haskin.

[3] The parable of the wise and foolish virgins (Matthew 25.1–13) provides the replenished lamps, the bridegroom, and the gaining of the entrance (*Variorum* 2.2: 382).

Sonnet 10.

Sonnet X.
To the Lady Margaret Ley

Milton gave this sonnet the title "To ye Lady Margaret Ley," but only in the Trinity Manuscript in his own handwriting. The reader of the 1645 *Poems* was supposed to decipher the identities of the "Daughter" and the "Earle, once President" mentioned in the sonnet. Lady Margaret Ley was daughter to James Ley, who became Lord Chief Justice of England in 1621, best known for presiding over the trial of Lord Chancellor Francis Bacon in the House of Lords. Charles I created James Ley Earl of Marlborough, and Ley became Lord High Treasurer, then Lord President of the Council (*Variorum* 2.2: 383). Lady Margaret lived unmarried with her father until his death in 1629, but she married John Hobson in 1641, and Milton apparently knew the couple as neighbors in Aldersgate Street.

Lady Margaret is addressed by her maiden name, making it hard to determine the date of the poem, though it seems likely that the familiar tone results from Milton's being acquainted with the family. Edward Phillips reports, "This Lady being a Woman of great Wit and Ingenuity, had a particular Honour for him, and took much delight in his Company, as likewise her husband Captain Hobson, a very Accomplish'd Gentleman" (Darbishire 64).

X.
Daughter to that good Earl, once President
  Of *Englands* Counsel, and her Treasury,
  Who liv'd in both, unstain'd with gold or fee,
  And left them both, more in himself content,
Till the sad breaking of that Parlament
  Broke him,[4] as that dishonest victory
  At *Chæronéa*,[5] fatal to liberty
  Kil'd with report that Old man eloquent,[6]
Though later born, then to have known the dayes
  Wherin your Father flourisht, yet by you
  Madam, me thinks I see him living yet;
So well your words his noble vertues praise,
  That all both judge you to relate them true,
  And to possess them, Honour'd *Margaret*.

Rudrum points to the technical and rhetorical achievement of the poem in complimenting the Earl, but not at the expense of complimenting his daughter: "All of the energy of the poem up to this point is compressed into that eleventh line: it is because of this that one is not driven to protest that the sonnet is really a compliment to the Earl rather than to his daughter" (88).

The sonnet is a tribute to an uncorrupted public official, a tribute to friendship with a woman (Nardo 49–53), and an endorsement of civil duteousness in the person of Isocrates, Milton's alter ego in *Areopagitica*, who starved himself to death as a protest against Athens's and Thebes's loss of independence in the battle of Chaeronea. The poem is also playful in that, like the sonnets of Tasso and others, it puns on the name of its subject, "margheríta," meaning "pearl" in Italian, as well as the woman's name (Nardo 52).

Works Cited

Nardo, Anna K. *Milton's Sonnets and the Ideal Community*. Lincoln: U of Nebraska P, 1979.

Rudrum, Alan. *A Critical Commentary on Milton's "Comus" & Shorter Poems*. London: Macmillan, 1967.

---

[4]When Parliament was dissolved forcibly, on March 10, 1629, after the House of Commons passed a resolution against King Charles's policies, the news apparently broke the spirit of Lady Margaret's father, the Earl, who died on March 14. As the *Variorum* editors point out, "No doubt Milton had Lady Margaret's authority for the belief that the news hastened his end" (2.2: 385).

[5]A case where the accented letter "á" and the digraph "æ" in the spelling of the word in *1645* help us to determine the pronunciation, as John Shawcross reminds me in an e-mail message of 5 July 1997.

[6]Traditionally, the aged orator Isocrates had starved himself to death in protest when Philip of Macedon deprived the Athenian and Theban city-states of their liberty by winning the battle of Chaeronea in 338 BCE.

Arcades (1632?)

OCCASION

This small-scale aristocratic entertainment was most probably part of an evening celebration (see line 39), which was thought by Demaray to be held outside (note the elm trees; Demaray 49, 53). But Brown has persuasively argued that "*Arcades* was surely played indoors, in whatever great chamber Harefield offered, in the evening after supper, perhaps making some use of carefully placed lights" (51). The entertainment honored Alice Spencer Egerton, Countess Dowager of Derby, mother-in-law and stepmother of John Egerton, Earl of Bridgewater. The Earl would later become a patron of Milton for the commissioning of Milton's *Comus*.

The Dowager Countess had been the patron of her kinsman Edmund Spenser: she was something of a phenomenon as patron to a number of talented poets. Her large estate, which gives its name to the small village of Harefield in Buckinghamshire and was within a day's ride of London in Milton's time, was the site of the entertainment. At twenty-one and as a student at Cambridge, Milton was invited, perhaps through business connections of his father, to contribute this bit of entertainment to the general festivities. More likely it was the court musician Henry Lawes, who wrote the music for the entertainment (the music has not survived), who suggested Milton for the job (Parker, *Milton* 80–81). Both Lawes and Milton may have known that Queen Elizabeth had been similarly celebrated at Harefield by Sir John Davies on July 31, 1602 (Demaray 53).

NAME AND GENRE

The name means "the Arcadians," and the association is classical and pastoral, Arcady being a mountain region of the Greek Peloponnesus famous for its shepherds, nymphs, and pastoral poetry. We should pronounce the word "Ar'-ca-dees," to distinguish it from "arcade." Critics now call Milton's work part of an aristocratic entertainment (Brown has canonized the term), a miniature "pageant" (Parker 81), or a masque-like, flattering celebration of the Countess Dowager. The title *Arcades*, added to the printed version but not present in the Trinity Manuscript, presumes a pastoral setting in a new Arcadia presided over by the Countess, with gentle swains and a less aristocratic Genius of the Wood, all of whom are assembled to honor the rural queen.

Milton was well versed in the tradition of presenting Arcadia. He knew Sir Philip Sidney's *Arcadia* (1590), which he was to defame in 1650 as a "vain amatorious Poem" (*Eikonoklastes*; Yale 3: 362). *Arcades* honors the pastoral poetry of Spenser, Shakespeare, Jonson, Michael Drayton, William Browne, and George Wither, among other English poets who had used pastoral and Arcadian settings (Demaray 50–51). The pastoral tradition was also alive and well in Italy, with Tasso, Minturno, Sannazaro, and Guarini as chief practitioners.

THEMES AND IMAGERY

The movement of the masquers to the chair or throne of state provides what Brown calls "an obviously expressive device" (41). Such a movement will be echoed by the quest of the children for their father in *Comus*. The Countess' children and grandchildren likewise approach and honor her. She is enthroned, seemingly a source of light, a sun-queen or Latona (Hunt 47), mother of the Sun (Apollo) and the Moon (Diana). The power of the Genius to hear the music of the spheres and to protect the estate against evil charms indicates the magical and moral power of the artist (Milton would not use the term in its modern sense) who freely serves the god-given rights of aristocrats like the Countess and her descendants.

TEXT

The copy-text is *1645*, with constant reference to the manuscript version in Milton's hand present in the Trinity College Manuscript. At several points on the pages of the original manuscript of *Arcades*, there are tears in the manuscript that obliterate the text, but the original stage directions, and the changes in the text, do tell the reader how Milton's ideas evolved as he wrote.

Works Cited

Brown, Cedric C. *John Milton's Aristocratic Entertainments*. Cambridge: Cambridge UP, 1985.

Demaray, John G. *Milton and the Masque Tradition: The Early Poems, "Arcades," & Comus*. Cambridge, MA: Harvard UP, 1968.

Hunt, Caroline. "Milton's Latona and the Roman Tone of *Arcades*." *Seventeenth-Century News* 52 (1994): 46-50.

Arcades.

Part of an entertainment presented to
the Countess Dowager of *Darby* at *Harefield*,
by som Noble persons of her Family, who
appear on the Scene in pastoral habit, moving
toward the seat of State, with this Song.[1]

1. *SONG.*

Ook Nymphs, and Shepherds look,
   What sudden blaze of majesty
Is that which we from hence descry°   GET SIGHT OF
Too divine to be mistook:
   This this is she   5
To whom our vows° and wishes bend,   FAITHFUL ATTACHMENTS
Heer our solemn search hath end.

Fame that her high worth to raise,
Seem'd erst so lavish and profuse,
We may justly now accuse   10
Of detraction from her praise,[2]
   Less then half we find exprest,
   Envy bid conceal the rest.[3]

Mark what radiant state she spreds,
In circle round her shining throne,[4]   15
Shooting her beams like silver threds,
This this is she alone,
   Sitting[5] like a Goddes bright,
   In the center of her light.

Might she the wise *Latona*[6] be,   20
Or the towred *Cybele*,[7]
Mother of a hunderd[8] gods;

---

[1]Which end of the entertainment was Arcades meant to fit? Most critics believe that it began the festivities, but John Shawcross sees it as the ending piece ("The Manuscript of 'Arcades,'" *Notes & Queries* 204 [1959]: 3). We are told that some members of her quite large and extended family present the entertainment, and that, dressed as shepherds and nymphs, they move toward her "seat of State," presumably a throne. In the Trinity Manuscript, before the title, there is written "Part of a maske," then, beneath that, crossed out, "Looke nymphs & shepherds looke heere ends our quest / since at last o' eyes are blest." The "maske" becomes "Entertainment," and the first two lines of the entertainment no longer speak of ending a quest, not, at least, until "here our sollemne search hath end" closes the entertainment. The fact that the search is ended may indicate that Milton's part of the entertainment was indeed last on the list of festivities.

[2]The first state of these three lines in the Trinity Manuscript is "now seems guiltie of abuse / and detraction from her praise / lesse then halfe she hath express't." For changes between the manuscript and the printed text of *1645*, the reader should consult a facsimile.

[3]The line first read "Envie bid her hide the rest." Then "her hide" was struck through and "conceale" written above.

[4]The light imagery suggests that the throne of state in which the Countess is sitting is heavily illuminated and that the "Noble persons" are proceeding toward that source of light and power.

[5]The Trinity Manuscript had "seated" first, then that was crossed out, with "sitting" inserted above the line replacing it.

[6]The goddess Latona, mother of Apollo and Artemis, with Jove as father. Where her wisdom comes from, in classical tradition, is uncertain, but certainly the Countess is complimented on being the mother of children as successful as Apollo and Artemis.

[7]Cybele was identified with Rhea and Ops, wife of Saturn, and mother of Juno and Jove. She is described as "*turrita*" or crowned with turrets like a castle, in Vergil, *Aeneid* 6.784–87. Again, motherhood and power are emphasized.

[8]Milton's usual spelling of "hundred," but ironically, Trinity Manuscript reads "hundred."

Juno[9] dare's not give her odds;
  Who had thought this clime had held
  A deity so unparalel'd?   25

  As they com forward, the Genius of the Wood
    appears, and turning toward them, speaks.[10]

G*En.* Stay gentle° Swains, for though in this disguise,   ARISTOCRATIC

I see bright honour[11] sparkle through your eyes,
Of famous *Arcady* ye are, and sprung
Of that renowned flood, so often sung,
Divine *Alpheus*,[12] who by secret sluse,°   HIDDEN CHANNEL   30
Stole under Seas to meet his *Arethuse*;
And ye the breathing Roses[13] of the Wood,
Fair silver-buskind[14] Nymphs as great and good,
I know this quest of yours, and free intent
Was all in honour and devotion ment   35
To the great Mistres of yon princely shrine,
Whom with low reverence I adore as mine,
And with all helpful service will comply
To further this nights glad solemnity;
And lead ye where ye may more neer behold   40
What shallow-searching *Fame*[15] had left untold;
Which I full oft amidst these shades alone
Have sate to wonder at, and gaze upon:
For know by lot from *Jove* I am the powr[16]
Of this fair Wood, and live in Oak'n bowr,°   LODGE, WOODLAND RETREAT   45
To nurse the Saplings tall, and curl the grove
With Ringlets quaint,° and wanton windings wove.   ARTFULLY PLACED
And all my Plants I save from nightly ill,[17]
Of noisom winds, and blasting° vapours chill.   INFECTIOUS, HARMFUL

---

[9]Milton first wrote "*Juno*," drew a line through it, substituted "*Ceres*" above; but he also underlined "*Juno*," perhaps indicating that the name should be reinstated. Obviously, he wavered as to which goddess to use to stand for the Countess here, possibly because the relationships among Jove, Latona (his mistress), Cybele (possibly his mother), and Juno (his wife, often deceived), were becoming too complicated. The choice of Ceres, goddess of grain and fecundity, might have suggested the bounteous generosity of the Countess (*Variorum* 2.2: 534).

[10]The stage directions in the Trinity Manuscript tell a slightly different story of the action: "The Genius of yᵉ wood rises ['rises' is cancelled and 'appeares' is written above it] & turning towards them speakes," with "As they ~~offer to~~ come forward" written in to the right of "appeares." Picturing the "Noble persons" offering to come forward is different from picturing them coming forward, and the Genius of the Wood "appeares," rather than rising, in the earlier stage direction. The Genius may have been sitting, or he may have been on some rising piece of stage machinery, like that of the Attendant Spirit in the Ludlow masque.

[11]Probably a reference to their aristocratic demeanor, represented in their eyes shining through their vizards or masks.

[12]Milton makes the river Alpheus, mentioned by Homer in *Iliad* 11.725–28, into an immortal god. The river was supposed to descend from Arcadia under the sea and reemerge at Ortygia, near Sicily. The symbolic flow of water, together with the myth of Alpheus (the god) pursuing the nymph Arethusa to Ortygia, signified the connections between Greek pastoral poetry and its descendant, Sicilian pastoral poetry (see "Lycidas" 132).

[13]The nymphs are described as human flowers, beautiful and sweet-smelling.

[14]Possibly a reference to an actual costume detail—silvery soft knee-boots—but with classical precedents and associations with contemporary poets; compare Marlowe's Hero, wearing "Buskins of shels al silvered" (*Variorum* 2.2: 536).

[15]The goddess standing for rumor, or distorted or superficial report. The manuscript has "those ve[r]tues wᶜʰ dull" before "Fame," corrected in the margin to "what shallow." Fame is either dull or shallow.

[16]Genius, or spirit protecting the place; "power" also associates Genius with an angelic order (*OED* 1.7, 8). At the beginning of the next line, "& charge" was written and then canceled. There was also a line on the following leaf of the Trinity Manuscript on which "live a thousand yeares" was written and canceled, to be followed with "to nurse the saplings tall, and curle the grove / wᵗʰin ringlets quaint, & wanton windings wove. . .," with the "in" canceled in "wᵗʰin."

[17]The Genius is casting a counterspell against various evil omens—noisome winds, blasting vapors, evil dew, thwarting lightning, evilly disposed planet, or canker worm. Sabrina in Milton's masque does something similar to dispel the magic of Comus (910–18).

And from the Boughs[18] brush off the evil dew,   50
And heal the harms of thwarting thunder° blew,   LIGHTNING CUTTING ACROSS THE SKY
Or what the cross dire-looking Planet smites,
Or hurtfull Worm with canker'd venom bites.
When Eev'ning gray° doth rise, I fetch my round[19]   TWILIGHT
Over the mount, and all this hallow'd ground,   55
And early ere the odorous° breath of morn   FRAGRANT, SWEET-SMELLING
Awakes the slumbring leaves,[20] or tasseld horn[21]
Shakes the high thicket, haste I all about,
Number my ranks,[22] and visit every sprout
With puissant words, and murmurs made to bless,[23]   60
But els in deep of night when drowsines
Hath lockt up mortal sense,[24] then listen I
To the celestial *Sirens* harmony,
That sit upon the nine enfolded Sphears,[25]
And sing to those that hold the vital shears,   65
And turn[26] the Adamantine spindle round,
On which the fate of gods and men is wound.
Such sweet compulsion doth in musick ly,
To lull the daughters of *Necessity*,
And keep unsteddy Nature to her law,   70
And the low world in measur'd motion draw
After the heavenly tune, which none can hear[27]
Of human mould with grosse unpurged ear;[28]
And yet such musick worthiest were to blaze
The peerles height of her immortal praise,   75
Whose lustre leads us, and for her most fit,
If my inferior hand or voice could hit
Inimitable sounds, yet as we go,
What ere the skill of lesser gods can show,
I will assay, her worth to celebrate,   80
And so attend ye toward her glittering state;°   THRONE OF STATE
Where ye may all that are of noble stemm[29]
Approach, and kiss her sacred vestures hemm.

---

[18]Instead of "Boughs," "leaves" was in the manuscript. It was canceled, and "bowes" written above.

[19]"I make my rounds," as would a watchman or security guard.

[20]The phrase read "awakes the leaves" in the manuscript, then "leaves" was canceled, and the phrase became "slumbring leaves."

[21]Probably the same sort of hunting horn heard in "L'Allegro" 53, here with a tasseled strap to make it easier to control when one is blowing it while riding (see Spenser, *Faerie Queene* 1.8.3).

[22]Probably he is counting the rows of his herbs. The manuscript reads "& number all my rancks, & every sprout," with "visit" written above, between "&" and "every."

[23]As a good magician, he empowers the plants with his words and murmuring spells that bless them.

[24]In the manuscript the lines originally read "when drousiness / hath chain'd mortalitie then listen I," but "hath chain'd mortalitie" was crossed through and "hath lockt up" added to replace it in the left margin. Above "hath chain'd mortalitie" is written "mortall eyes sense."

[25]According to the design of three-dimensional armillary spheres (working models of the universe) that Milton might have been familiar with, the concentric rings of the planets would be enfolded in the sense of folding around one another (see Plato, *Republic* 10.616–17). Milton's system uses nine spheres, each controlled, according to Plato, by a benevolent Siren singing one note. The whole ensemble sang in harmony—the Music of the Spheres. The Sirens are connected with the Fates—daughters of Necessity—Clotho, Lachesis, and Atropos, who collectively have control of the thread of life for each human being.

[26]Originally "turning" in the manuscript, with "ing" crossed through.

[27]In the manuscript, "heare" was repeated at the beginning of the next line, then canceled.

[28]As the *Variorum* editors point out (2.2: 540), Milton had been concerned with the few mortals who might be able to hear the music of the spheres in Prolusion 2, Nativity Ode 138, and *Comus* 17, 243.

[29]Families can have "branches," or, in this case, "stems."

2. SONG.

O'Re the smooth enameld green
 Where no print of step hath been,[30]   85
Follow me as I sing,
And touch the warbled[31] string.

Under the shady roof[32]
Of branching Elm Star-proof,[33]
 Follow me,   90
I will bring you where she sits,
Clad in splendor as befits
 Her deity.
Such a rural Queen
All *Arcadia* hath not seen.   95

  3. SONG.

NYmphs and Shepherds dance no more
 By sandy *Ladons*[34] Lillied banks.
On old *Lycæus* or *Cyllene* hoar,[35]
 Trip no more in twilight ranks,
Though *Erymanth*[36] your loss deplore,   100
 A better soyl shall give ye thanks.
From the stony *Mænalus*,[37]
Bring your Flocks, and live with us,
Here ye shall have greater grace,
To serve the Lady of this place.   105
 Though *Syrinx* your *Pans* Mistres were,[38]
 Yet *Syrinx* well might wait on her.
  Such a rural Queen[39]
 All *Arcadia* hath not seen.

---

[30]Compare "printless feet" in *Comus* 897. The image unites the nymph Sabrina and the Noble Persons as being light on their feet, but fairies also were supposed to leave no footprint behind.

[31]Possibly "plucked," but this usage is recorded as unique to Milton in the *OED*, under the participial adjective 2.

[32]The line may have read "of the shadie   branching elme" (check the manuscript closely for this), then "of branching elme" was canceled on that line and moved to begin the next line.

[33]The cover of the elms protects those under them against the malignant influence, or the light, of any star.

[34]A reference to removal from Arcadia, where the river Ladon flows to the Alpheus. Milton seems to have been reading Sandys's translation of Ovid, where he got the adjective "sandy" for Ladon (*Metamorphoses* 1.702). Sir Philip Sidney and William Browne had used the image before Milton (*Variorum* 2.2: 542).

[35]Two mountains of Arcadia. Lycaeus was the home of Pan. When pursued by the god, Syrinx fled there (*Metamorphoses* 1.698–99). The adjective "hoar" (white or frosty) might be there for the rhyme or for a pictorial description of a snow-capped mountain. Like the lilies, it seems to be a detail created to add color to the story.

[36]Either the tall mountain in Arcadia, with mostly negative connotations, since Heracles kills the savage Erymanthian boar there (*Metamorphoses* 2.5.499), or another of Arcadia's rivers which also flows into the Alpheus.

[37]Yet another Arcadian mountain, also sacred to Pan (*Metamorphoses* 1.5.216).

[38]Warton was the first to point out that Ben Jonson had used very similar language in his *Entertainment at Althrope*. See *Ben Jonson*, ed. C. H. Herford and P. and E. Simpson (11 vols.; Oxford: Clarendon: 1925–52): 7: 121: "And the Dame hath Syrinx grace! / O that Pan were now in place." Lines that have been reconstructed as "though [Syr]inx yoʳ Pans mistresse were / yet we[ll m]ight Syrinx wait on her" were written to the right of the Song "O're the smooth enameld green."

[39]Milton was still playing with Syrinx in the margin: he wrote a line from "Queene" in the manuscript to "though ~~yet~~ w Syrinx," with "Syrinx" enclosed in a circle.

Lycidas (1637)

Milton calls Edward King's death the "sad occasion dear" that caused the poem to be written. On August 10, 1637, Milton's classmate at Christ's College was drowned off the coast of North Wales, quite near the island of Anglesey and the port of Holyhead, in the Irish Sea. Not long after embarking from the port city Chester, within sight of the coast, his ship hit a rock and sank quickly. He was supposed to have died heroically, kneeling in prayer on the deck of his ship while others were scrambling to save their lives (for the context, see Franson). King may have intended to visit relatives in Ireland. We know that he made a will before he undertook what was then a short but perilous voyage, generously leaving books from his library and money to Christ's College. King was a promising young scholar of Irish descent who had in 1637 won a royal fellowship at Cambridge, was studying for the ministry, wrote poetry in Latin, and was apparently very popular within the college. His poems in Latin, recently collected by Norman Postlethwaite and Gordon Campbell in a special issue of *Milton Quarterly*, "pale, almost, into insignificance in comparison to the Latin poems of his friend Milton" (82).

Meanwhile Milton, in studious postgraduate retirement at his father's rural home in Hammersmith, volunteered or was asked to write a poem for the volume that fellows of Christ's put together in King's memory—perhaps as an answer to the memorial volume for Ben Jonson planned at Oxford (Le Comte i). Milton dated his composition November 1637, in his own manuscript.

The small quarto volume of thirty-six poems in Latin, Greek, and English that Milton's associates put together at Cambridge was subdivided into an ancient-language section and an English section, each provided with identical names in Latin or English. The Latin title is "Justa Edovardo King naufrago . . ." and the English "Obsequys for Edward King, Ship-wrecked . . . ." "Lycidas" was probably placed last in the English section of the volume for a reason: a modern reader who ploughs through the other affected and pretentious poems in the volume would be tempted to say it was placed there because it is obviously the best of the lot. Edward Le Comte calls it "the only poem of quality" in the volume (v). The style of the other poetry is fashionably metaphysical—in the school of John Donne but not as technically or philosophically proficient as his poetry. The poems are often built on extravagant conceits in which tears shed for the death of King become waterfalls or floods covering the face of the earth. "Lycidas" is, by the current standards displayed in *Justa*, old-fashioned and Spenserian in style: it looks back to the language, imagery, and syntax of native English pastoral, most specifically to Spenser's *Shepheardes Calender* (in *Animadversions*, Milton writes that "our admired Spenser" in that work "personates our Prelates, whose whole life is a recantation of their pastorall vow. . ." [Yale 1: 722]). In the 1645 edition of his poetry Milton would add an extra sentence to his headnote, beyond what he had written in his manuscript or in the 1637 *Justa* volume, to the effect that the poem "by occasion foretels the ruine of our corrupted Clergy then in their height."

THEME AND VARIATIONS; STYLE

The theme of "Lycidas" is the death of a young man in his prime. The "uncouth Swain" pictured singing the poem while accompanying himself on a shepherd's panpipes or syrinx is another young man contemplating the death of his friend, and his own death. As Northrop Frye perhaps uncharitably put it, Milton was so fond of elegiac poetry in his youth that he "had been practising since adolescence on every fresh corpse in sight, from the university beadle to the fair infant dying of a cough" (210). Since Milton believed that inward ripeness was necessary for great poetic achievements, and composing a work of art "doctrinal and exemplary to a nation" (*Reason of Church Government*; Yale 1: 815) might require a full lifetime of preparation, the prospect of the death of a promising young poet was especially upsetting to him, so much so that he made what was often an impersonal genre, the pastoral, into a form of poetry that is almost confessional. It is probably worth noting that Ben Jonson, certainly known to Milton by his reputation, if not in person, died in the same month as King did in 1637, and, more importantly, that Milton's mother died in April of that year.

We do not know how well Milton knew Edward King. In a college with just over 250 men in residence, Milton must have met King, but Milton had been out of college and in self-educative retirement for five years when he was apparently asked to write one of a number of memorial poems, in his choice of Latin, Greek, or English. Edward Phillips wrote that Milton had "a particular Friendship and Intimacy" (Darbishire, *Early Lives* 54) with King, but Phillips's biography was published in 1694, and he is not always a reliable witness, especially for events that occurred when his uncle was young.

Negative critics since Dr. Samuel Johnson have questioned Milton's sincerity in expressing his sorrow in such an artificial genre as pastoral, but Milton chose the pastoral mode quite carefully. Johnson's savage critique of "Lycidas" in his *Life of Milton* expresses Johnson's personal bias against pastoral. The form of "Lycidas," he writes, is "that of a pastoral, easy, vulgar, and therefore disgusting" (426), but Johnson's criticism does not take account of the bias in favor of pastoral in the seventeenth century. The image of shepherds, especially in England, where in Parliament the economic welfare of the country is still symbolized by sacks of wool, works on several levels simultaneously. Christ is of course the Good Shepherd, and the Twenty-third Psalm, beginning "The Lord is my shepherd . . . ," summarizes humankind's intimate relationship with God in pastoral terms. Christ's College, Cambridge, was in Milton's era still in a pastoral setting, with its own lawns and sheep grazing to help keep the grass short. Milton and King together were studying for the pastorate, since they both would have been expected to be ordained in the Church of England upon graduation. There was also in traditional pastoral poetry a subtradition of satire and invective. The May, July, and September Eclogues of Edmund Spenser's *Shepheardes Calender* celebrate righteous indignation against corruption within the English Church, and Petrarch, Boccaccio, and the very popular Italian poet called Mantuan (Johannes Baptista Spagnolo, 1448–1516), who wrote eclogues in Latin, had all used the genre to instruct and criticize as well as to embody a golden and ideal age of innocent nymphs and swains.

Milton's compassion, especially for the effect of death on the living, is perhaps more powerful in the English of "Lycidas" than it will be in the Latin poem he wrote to the memory of his best childhood friend. *Epitaphium Damonis*, written to the memory of Charles Diodati, who died when Milton was in Italy in 1639, is very close to "Lycidas" in spirit, but, as Rajan puts it, "the greater grief provoked the lesser poem" ("Lycidas," in *Milton Encyclopedia* 42). In both poems death inspires sincere sorrow—both for the dead, who are removed from mortal time, and the living, who feel just how limited may be their time to achieve fame.

Even a reader who cannot enjoy images of shepherds either in a realistic rural landscape or in a Christian metaphor can still sympathize with the problems of a young man faced with the death of an exact contemporary. Both Milton and King must have been considered to be full of promise, and both competed for the same laurels. King died, leaving Milton with what might in modern terms be called survivor guilt. According to J. B. Leishman, however, the major

purpose of classical elegy is not to mourn but to memorialize the dead (273). The very poem Milton writes is a bid for the immortality that Edward King was denied. "Lycidas" is not just a monologue but a series of soul-searching conversations with Jove and the Muses and Apollo (all of them used metaphorically to represent aspects of the Christian God) about the artist's immortality. Hence the poem can be viewed dramatically, as a small tragedy with several speaking parts, and it can also be seen as prefiguring heroic or epic poetry. The term "eclogue" in the seventeenth century had come to mean a dramatic dialogue with several voices engaged in conversation, as in some of the months in Spenser's *Shepheardes Calender* (1579) or Tasso's popular little pastoral drama *Aminta* (1573). Though "Lycidas" is a pastoral and therefore necessarily in a low style, the "Phoebus" section contains glimpses of heroic style. Milton calls attention to the changes both by introducing the dignified Phoebus Apollo (Revard 17–21) and by mentioning the "dread voice" of St. Peter at line 132. Low and Knott have discussed the pastoral, georgic, and epic modes, which "correspond to three social ranks or occupations: shepherd, farmer, and soldier," and "take place in three locales: pasture, field, and castle"; "pastoral celebrates play and leisure, georgic celebrates work, and epic celebrates fighting" (Low 4). Knott believes that the Milton of *Paradise Lost*, even within the epic genre, continued to maintain a "pastoral vision."

GENRE AND SOURCES

Milton's two chief literary models for pastoral elegy are most likely to have been the Sicilian Greek Theocritus (especially his first Idyll) and the Roman Vergil (especially his fifth Eclogue). Milton's poetic style, choice of imagery, and format all reflect the entire pastoral tradition behind him. For excerpts from the classical eclogues that might have influenced "Lycidas," see Elledge. Milton's apostrophes to various important personages, refrains, exclamations of grief, use of personification and the pathetic fallacy in the response of nature to the death of King—all reflect most pastoral elegies, dirges, laments, epicedia, epitaphia, threnodies, eclogues, bucolics (terms familiar to Renaissance poetic theory; see Julius Caesar Scaliger *Poetics*, as translated in Elledge 107–11) ever written. The name "Lycidas" is a generic shepherd's name, and it will be used again by Milton in *Epitaphium Damonis*. It carries no weight of specific allusion except to the tradition of pastoral poetry. J. M. Evans brilliantly summarizes the transmission of the pastoral tradition from its earliest Greek roots through the Italian Renaissance to Milton. But Milton as always is emulative within a genre, trying to better his predecessors at the same time that he imitates them. Many pastoral poems include catalogues of flowers, but Milton's catalogue (142–51) is probably the most exquisite and thoughtful, and the "flower passage"—we know from the Trinity Manuscript—was carefully revised (see Rajan, "Lycidas," in *Milton Encyclopedia* 40). Milton took a genre which, as Dr. Johnson rightly pointed out, was usually tired and dull, and revivified it with real emotion, fresh imagery, and a new musical beauty of expression in English.

After Vergil had set the example of a sophisticated poet reflecting on the pastoral life in his eclogues, as J. H. Hanford established in a classic article on the backgrounds of "Lycidas" (Patrides 41–43), the poet did not need to be a real shepherd to write good pastoral poetry. The poetic contest between Sicilian shepherds could quickly become an image of the pursuit of excellence among urban poets. Death is death, whether it comes in the country, at sea, or at court.

Milton may ask a Sicilian muse for help with the genre, but he still writes about English people in an English setting, using an unaffected English vocabulary which is not notably Latinate in its word derivation. Thus he owes a debt not only to Vergil and Theocritus for inspiration but to Edmund Spenser, Sir Philip Sidney, and Michael Drayton. What Milton took from the pastoral Shakespeare of *Midsummer Night's Dream* or *Venus and Adonis*, or even from more somber works such as *The Winter's Tale* (Sims) as well as from the best of the other English pastoral or topographical poets, was an exuberance for the freshness of English scenes, English words, English images. It is as if the excellence of the previous English pastoral writers extending back to Chaucer gave Milton the license to enjoy writing poetry in his own language. Even while he was emulating Spenser's tone, subject matter, and style, Milton modernized and simplified his own poetic vocabulary, choosing not to use the archaisms typical of Spenser, such as "rathe," "quills," "daffadillies," and "guerdon," very often. Even Spenser's contemporary editor "E. K." had been aware that Spenser's vocabulary was antiquarian. E. K. labeled the archaic past participle "y-blent" a "poeticall addition" (Spenser 45).

"Lycidas" is not only a thoroughly English poem but a Puritan English poem as well. It rails against the impurity of the corrupt English clergy in 1637 and predicts the downfall of the followers of Archbishop Laud. The headnote about the downfall of the clergy added in 1645 makes clear the political implications of the poem. The poet of "Lycidas" also claims a Puritan inner light and prophetic power. Edward King is apotheosized, sainted, at the end of the poem in a distinctively Puritan way: he dies but is translated to Heaven to join the "Saints above" (those are not Roman Catholic saints, since there are no miracles attached to their deaths, but rather heroic examples of Protestant piety) to participate in a celestial wedding feast. The language and imagery are not so much classical as biblical. The governing images of the poem, the images of greatest importance, are all biblical. Phrasing from "Yet once more" (see Lieb's article on the biblical imagery in the first few lines) to "pilot of the *Galilean* lake" to "him that walked the waves" is biblical, and the most important single image in the poem is that of the Good Shepherd, Christ.

"Lycidas" is usually called a pastoral elegy, but Milton himself calls it a "monody," a term from seventeenth-century technical descriptions both of pastoral poetry and of vocal music. In the pastoral tradition a monody was what might be loosely called an interior monologue, or soliloquy, spoken by a single shepherd, usually lamenting the loss of someone who has died or of a lover who has left him. Musically, monody is a form of operatic solo—usually a lament sung for a lost or dead lover or friend, as with Claudio Monteverdi's aria "Lament of Arianna," from *Orfeo*, an opera first performed in 1608, perhaps the single most famous and influential piece of vocal music of the seventeenth century. Clay Hunt concluded that the structure and the genre of the poem are musical and Italianate, that its form is that of the "canzone" and that it has "a beginning *mezzoforte* in the pastoral style (middle and 'lyric') working to a *forte*; then a change of key and a double *forte* in the second style (lofty, and heroic-tragic); and a concluding modulation back toward the lower dynamics and more lyrical movement of the verse in the opening key" (135). In the first quarter of the seventeenth century, both opera—musical drama—and the idea of monophonic song were being born together in Italy. Through the circle of composers in which his father moved, Milton heard of and witnessed performances of monophonic music. The strong presence of Orpheus in the poem might be partly explained by the association of monody with early opera, since the subject of the first two known operas, those of Jacopo Peri and Claudio Monteverdi, inevitably was Orpheus, whose myth embodied the power of combining words and music in song.

Even though "Lycidas" is a monody, it does contain a variety of voices, as quoted by the main speaker, whom Milton identifies at the end as an overheard "uncouth Swain." The swain, however uncouth, is capable of playing a sensitive wind instrument, and he sings his song with "eager thought," which I take to be inspired ideas. The "lay" he sings is "*Dorick*." Some editors think the word ties the poem to Sicily, but it is more likely that "Lycidas" was composed in the "stern gravity of the Greek Dorian mode" (Hunt 149), a classical and medieval musical mode associated with funeral music.

Milton's use of the pastoral genre is not at all restricted to "Lycidas" or to pastoral elegy. As Rajan points out (*Milton Encyclopedia* 41), Milton's *Arcades* is placed immediately before "Lycidas" in *1645* and *1673*, and the imagery of the later pastoral "entertainment" is very close to that of "Lycidas"; so for that matter is the imagery of *Comus*, "L'Allegro," and "Il Penseroso." The pastoral mode (in the musical as well as the poetic sense—see Hunt 187) was quite properly associated with a young poet, who might in later years graduate to the tragic and heroic. Pastoral was associated with the "low" erotic and amatory verse Milton was to reject in the verses appended to Elegy 7, but as Low and Knott have observed, Milton could reject some of what he considered to be trivial aspects of pastoral in his more heroic mature poetry while conscientiously preserving others.

All that said, "Lycidas" is not limited to the ancient classical pastoral tradition, or even to the Christian English one. Probably the French writers of eclogues, Ronsard and Marot, influenced Milton, at least through Spenser's imitation of both. Italian writers like Petrarch, Boccaccio, Castiglione, and Sannazaro wrote pastoral or piscatory (fisherman's) eclogues imitative of Vergil's. Sannazaro's first piscatory eclogue contains the name "Lycidas" (as well as the more arcane pastoral name "Panope," used by Vergil in *Aeneid* 5.240) and is devoted to the memory of a drowned shepherdess. Hanford believes that Sannazaro may have given Milton the notion of the dead person's becoming the genius and protector of the shore near where he or she was drowned. The very verse form of "Lycidas" is Italianate, with its irregular short lines and deliberately inconsistent rhyme scheme, as in a canzone. Clay Hunt was not the first to note the resemblance in metrics and line arrangement between "Lycidas" and the choruses in Guarini's famous pastoral drama *Il Pastor Fido* (1589; see Prince 71–81). Tasso's prosody in the Italian of his *Aminta* is another likely influence. *Aminta* uses verse paragraphs and alternating line-lengths; it mixes rhyming and non-rhyming lines; and it contains similar rhythms and pacing of words within the lines. The last eight lines of "Lycidas" are a perfect *ottava rima* stanza, as in Boiardo's *Orlando Innamorato* or Ariosto's *Orlando Furioso*, and Boiardo and Ariosto in turn were imitating a stanza pattern Dante used.

UNITY OF CRAFTSMANSHIP, COHERENCE IN IMAGERY

As with musical themes and motifs in an opera or a symphony, the imagery of "Lycidas" seems to hold the poem together, though critics since Dr. Johnson have worried about its discordant combination of sorrow for the death of the fellow poet with indignation against church corruption. Johnson objected to the juxtaposition of pastoral commonplaces and highest Christian truths. Some critics such as E. M. W. Tillyard have suggested that King is not the subject of the poem: Milton is (Patrides 64). Hence the poem is supposed to have a schizophrenic split between its stated and its real subject, a hidden agenda of self-pity under its outward show of grief. But the pastoral tradition established in Vergil's fifth eclogue had always mixed important subject matter, important and instructive to an entire nation, with homely pastoral images. Renaissance English pastoral, especially since Spenser, had had no problem satirizing national corruption in an apparently innocuous pastoral setting. Tillyard may be correct to observe that Milton is worrying more about his own death than King's: after all, King is already dead, and life belongs to the living; but to say something like that causes a split in the reader. The poem is falsely accused of incoherence, since in grieving for a dead friend we almost inevitably feel self-pity.

Modern critics, especially those such as Rosemond Tuve (73–111), who have examined Milton's imagery closely, tend to think of "Lycidas" as being given a tight coherence by its imagery. The image of the good shepherd, the image of water as death-dealing but purifying element controlled by the figure of Christ walking on water, the image of flowers strewn on the hearse of Lycidas, thereby covering death with beautiful life: all these give coherence to the poem. The more one studies "Lycidas," the more cohesive it becomes, because Milton's political and theological stance in 1637 was part of his poetry: the discordant satire against the corrupt clergy is expressed in that ugliest-sounding description of what they do as anti-musicians: "Grate on their scrannel Pipes of wretched straw." The ugliness of the sound and of the image is intentional discord and is part of Milton's larger unifying plan.

TEXT

What looks like a working draft (as opposed to a "fair copy") of "Lycidas" is preserved in Milton's handwriting as part of the Trinity Manuscript, so-named because it was left under somewhat mysterious circumstances to the Trinity College Library at Cambridge, where it remains today. "Lycidas" was first published in *Justa Edovardo King Naufrago* (1638), but the best copy-text (text to use as a base model for a modern edition) is *1645*, which represents a cleaner text than *Justa*, which itself was apparently a not-very-carefully-prepared printing of what might have been a fair copy of the text in Milton's Trinity Manuscript. The *Justa* volume prints "Lord" instead of "Lov'd" at line 51 and the nonsense word "stridley" for "strictly" at line 66; it leaves out line 177 entirely. The mistakes indicate that the compositor who set the poem set it from a manuscript and misread the author's handwriting, and that the printed text was probably not corrected in any proof stage. Milton did apparently make corrections in presentation copies of the *Justa* volume, some of which can be seen in the Scolar Press facsimile. The 1645 text may have been corrected in its trip through the press: line 173 has a semicolon at its end in some of the copies of the volume, indicating that corrections might have been made while the book was in the process of being printed. *1645* certainly presents a more accurate version of the text than does the *Justa* volume of 1638—which does not mean that an editor should not consult it when the 1645 text or punctuation seems muddled.

The 1673 text seems to be based on *1645*, but it introduces new errors, so it has no independent authority. In some few cases the Trinity Manuscript represents what seems to be an improvement over any printed text. Milton added "well" to line 10 in his own hand in some presentation copies of *1638*, and "well" is in the Trinity Manuscript. Also, in two presentation copies of *1638*, he changed "humming" to "whelming" in line 157, a change not in the manuscript. Milton also made one diplomatic or politically significant change in his text: in line 129, in the manuscript, Milton canceled "nothing" and wrote "little" instead. In the *Justa* volume, the word is "little," which in context is more diplomatic and more cautious about corruption in the church; in *1645* the word is restored to "nothing," a much less cautious noun. The conclusion I think we can draw from the changes back and forth is that Milton in the year 1638 was more apprehensive of censorship or persecution; in the year 1645 he could risk the more dogmatic and less diplomatic "nothing." I have chosen to print "nothing," since it seems to represent Milton's later wishes.

We can compare the Trinity Manuscript with *1645* and come up with a portrait of the compositor working for the printer Ruth Raworth. He apparently imposed his house style on what Milton wrote, especially in punctuation, spelling, and capitalization. Milton's manuscript is notably light in its punctuation, often omitting commas on the way to an end-of-sentence mark such as the colon, semicolon, or period. Milton also rarely uses an exclamation mark. He capitalizes only important nouns, such as "Muse" or "Dolphins," and he does not capitalize adjectives. His spelling of past participles seems to lean away from the use of the apostrophe for elided medial syllables, as with "battning," or elided ending syllables, such as "-ed" or "-t," as in ". . . hayrd" or "nurst." The compositor has some un-Miltonic spelling habits, as when he spells Milton's less common "thir" as the preferred "their"; he capitalizes less important nouns and adjectives much more often; and he generally prefers to use the apostrophe for elided syllables. He is very liberal in adding punctuation, placing some mark—not always an appropriate or accurate one—after almost every line. Shawcross takes the various forms of the text of "Lycidas" as providing a strong suggestion as to what an editor should do with the texts of the rest of Milton's poetry: I agree in part with his conclusions, but I feel uneasy about imposing a spelling system and punctuation system derived mainly from the manuscript of "Lycidas" on all the rest of Milton's printed poetry. It may well have been that Milton expected his printer, within reason, to regularize or standardize his light punctuation and inconsistent spelling.

The draft of the Trinity Manuscript, whether or not it is an early draft, does not represent Milton's last wishes about what form the poem should take in print: its punctuation, for instance, is too light for any printed version, and it does not capitalize the first word in each line. Nor can we trust *Justa* for the best reading, because it was not carefully proofread; Milton himself corrected some but not all misprints in presentation copies. And *1673* adds nothing new. Our best text, then, is *1645*. The text here reproduced is that of the 1645 *Poems*, with some additions made by Milton himself to the printed text; and variants from other printed versions or manuscripts will be recorded in the notes. Changes from *1645* are noted.

Works Cited

Elledge, Scott, ed. *Milton's "Lycidas."* New York: Harper & Row, 1966.

Evans, J. Martin. *The Road from Horton: Looking Backwards in "Lycidas."* ELS Monograph Ser. No. 28. Victoria, British Columbia: Department of English, U of Victoria, 1983.

Fleissner, Robert. "Milton's *Lycidas*, Lines 130-31." *Explicator* 41 (1983): 23–25.

Franson, J. Karl. "The Fatal Voyage of Edward King." *Milton Studies* 25 (1989): 43–67.

Frye, Northrop. "Literature as Context: Milton's *Lycidas*." Patrides, *Milton's "Lycidas."* 204–15.

Hunt, Clay. *"Lycidas" and the Italian Critics.* New Haven, CT: Yale UP, 1979.

Johnson, Samuel. "John Milton: 1608–1674." *Lives of the Poets. Samuel Johnson: Selected Poetry and Prose.* Ed. Frank Brady and W. K. Wimsatt. Berkeley: U of California P, 1977. 385–444.

Knott, John R. *Milton's Pastoral Vision: An Approach to* Paradise Lost. Chicago, IL: U of Chicago P, 1971.

Le Comte, Edward, ed. and trans. *"Justa Edovardo King": A Facsimile Edition of the Memorial Volume in which Milton's "Lycidas" First Appeared.* Norwood, PA: Norwood Editions, 1978.

Leishman, J. B. *Milton's Minor Poems.* Ed. Geoffrey Tillotson. Pittsburgh, PA: U of Pittsburgh P, 1969.

Lieb, Michael. "'Yet Once More': The Formulaic Opening of 'Lycidas'." *Milton Quarterly* 12 (1978): 23–28.

Low, Anthony. *The Georgic Revolution.* Princeton, NJ: Princeton UP, 1985.

Milton, John. *Poems.* Trinity College Manuscript. Menston: Scolar P, 1970.

Patrides, C. A., ed. *Milton's "Lycidas": The Tradition and the Poem.* Rev. ed. Columbia: U of Missouri P, 1983.

Postlethwaite, Norman, and Gordon Campbell. "Edward King, Milton's 'Lycidas': Poems and Documents." *Milton Quarterly* 28 (1994): 77–111.

Prince, F. T. *The Italian Element in Milton's Verse.* Oxford: Clarendon, 1954.

Rajan, Balachandra. "*Lycidas*: The Shattering of the Leaves." *The Lofty Rhyme: A Study of Milton's Major Poetry.* Coral Gables, FL: U of Miami P, 1970.

Revard, Stella P. *Milton and the Tangles of Neaera's Hair: The Making of the 1645 Poems.* Columbia: U of Missouri P, 1997.

Shawcross, John T. "Establishment of the Text of Milton's Poems through a Study of 'Lycidas.'" *Papers of the Bibliographical Society of America* 56 (1962): 317–31.

Sims, James H. "Perdita's Flowers o' th' Spring and Vernal Flowers in *Lycidas*." *Shakespeare Quarterly* 22 (1971): 87–90.

Spenser, Edmund. *Spenser's Minor Poems.* Ed. Ernest de Sélincourt. Oxford: Clarendon, 1910.

Tuve, Rosemond. *Images and Themes in Five Poems by Milton.* Cambridge, MA: Harvard UP, 1957.

Lycidas.

In this Monody the Author bewails a
learned Friend, unfortunately drown'd in his Passage
from *Chester* on the *Irish* Seas, 1637. And by
occasion foretels the ruine of our corrupted
Clergy then in their height.[1]

Yet once more, O ye Laurels, and once more
  Ye Myrtles brown, with Ivy never-sear,°   NEVER WITHERED
I com to pluck your Berries harsh and crude,°   UNRIPE
And with forc'd fingers rude,
Shatter your leaves[2] before the mellowing year.[3]   5
Bitter constraint, and sad occasion° dear,   UPSETTING EVENT
Compels me to disturb your season due:
For *Lycidas*[4] is dead, dead ere his prime
Young *Lycidas*, and hath not left his peer:
Who would not sing for *Lycidas?* he well[5] knew   10
Himself[6] to sing, and build the lofty rhyme.
He must not flote upon his watry bear   BIER, BURIAL PLATFORM
Unwept, and welter° to the parching wind,   TOSS ABOUT
Without the meed° of som melodious tear.[7]   AID
  Begin then, Sisters of the sacred well,[8]   15
That from beneath the seat of *Jove* doth spring,
Begin, and somwhat loudly sweep the string.
Hence with denial vain, and coy excuse,[9]
So may som gentle Muse[10]

---

[1]A "monody" is a musical lament usually sung by one member of a chorus. Milton's friend Edward King (1612–37) had the extreme bad fortune to be drowned in his passage across the Irish Sea. In the Latin paragraph that prefaces *Justa Edovardo King* he is said to have "fallen forward on his knees, and breathing a life which was immortal, in the act of prayer going down with the vessel, rendered up his soul to God, Aug. 10, 1637, aged 25" (translated in Masson 1: 514). The ship sank within sight of the land; recently scholars have been trying to persuade underwater archeological teams to explore off the coast near Holyhead for the location of the wreck. The poem is "occasional" in another sense as well, since it uses King's death as the occasion, in 1637, to predict (prophetically, as it turned out) the overthrow of the Church of England hierarchy under Archbishop Laud. At the time the poem was written, the Laudian clergy was in full power; the word "height" suggests arrogance. Milton did not include the sentence about the clergy in the 1638 *Justa*, possibly because it would have been too inflammatory.
[2]The evergreen leaves are of the laurel, sacred to Apollo; the myrtle, sacred to Venus; and the ivy, sacred to Bacchus. Laurel might crown all poets; myrtle, love poets; and ivy, ecstatic poets inspired by the wine drunk sacramentally by worshipers of Bacchus.
[3]Milton pictures himself as an immature or at least unready poet, forced by the death of King to write poetry before he had reached "inward ripenes" (see Sonnet 7). He pictures the act of his writing poetry as a violent shattering or seizure of the laurels before he was ready to write mature poetry. The verb "shatter" seems to be used in the transferred sense of "To scatter, disperse, throw about in all directions; to cause (seed, leaves, etc.) to fall or be shed" (*OED* 1, citing this instance). For the possible violation of genre, see Rajan, "Shattering." See also Michael Lieb, "'Yet Once More': The Formulaic Opening of *Lycidas*," *Milton Quarterly* 12 (1978): 23–28.
[4]Milton may have remembered the violent death at sea of a warrior named Lycidas described by Lucan. Lucan's Lycidas is caught by a grapnel hook hurled from an opposing ship. His comrades grab his legs, but the force of the hook pulls his body in two (*Civil Wars* 3.657–68). Such a gory death might have associated the name of Lycidas with the violent death at sea of Edward King, and with the dismemberment and sea transport of Orpheus.
[5]Milton added the "well" to several extant copies of the 1638 *Justa Edovardo King* volume. It is extrametrical but was left uncanceled in the Trinity Manuscript. Shawcross includes it; other modern editors, such as Campbell, Carey, and Orgel, do not.
[6]Supply "how" before "to sing" and "to build."
[7]Probably used in the transferred sense of "elegy," as Orgel suggests (14n).
[8]The nine Muses, daughters of Zeus and Mnemosyne (Memory), whose sacred well, Aganippe, is said to be on Mt. Helicon in Greece, on a lower level than the "seat of *Jove*." The Muses are invoked formally here to "somwhat loudly sweep the string," perhaps in a minor key, or perhaps mezzo forte, as Hunt suggests, in memory of Edward King.
[9]"Down with any vain excuse or denial."
[10]In a transferred sense, "One under the guidance of a Muse, a poet" (*OED* 1.c, citing this instance).

With lucky[11] words favour my destin'd Urn,   *HIS OWN POETRY*   20
And as he passes turn,
And bid fair peace be to my sable shrowd.[12]
For we were nurst upon the self-same hill,   *PASTORAL*
Fed the same flock, by fountain, shade, and rill.°

   Together both, ere the high Lawns[13] appear'd   25
Under the opening[14] eye-lids of the morn,
We drove afield,[15] and both together heard
What time the Gray-fly[16] winds her sultry horn,
Batt'ning our flocks[17] with the fresh dews of night,
Oft till the Star that rose, at Ev'ning, bright[18]   30
Toward Heav'ns descent had slop'd his westering wheel.[19]
Mean while the Rural ditties[20] were not mute,
Temper'd to th' Oaten Flute,[21]
Rough *Satyrs* danc'd;[22] and *Fauns* with clov'n heel,
From the glad sound would not be absent long,   35
And old *Damœtas* lov'd to hear our song.[23]

   But O the heavy change, now thou art gon,
Now thou art gon, and never must return!
Thee Shepherd, thee the Woods, and desert Caves,
With wilde Thyme and the gadding° Vine o'regrown,   WANDERING   40
And all their echoes mourn.
The Willows, and the Hazle Copses green,
Shall now no more be seen,
Fanning their joyous Leaves to thy soft layes.[24]
As killing as the Canker° to the Rose,   CANKER WORM   45
Or Taint-worm[25] to the weanling Herds that graze,

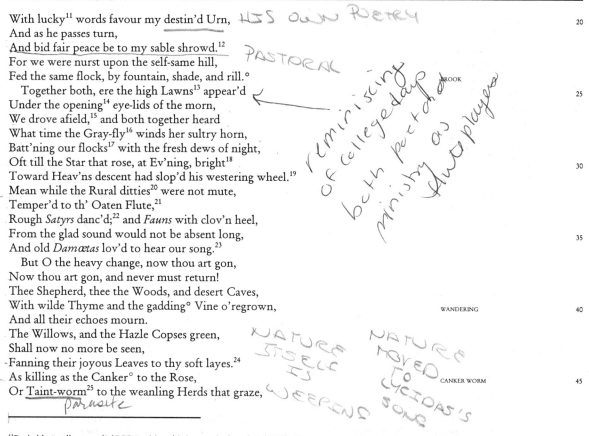

reminiscing of college days both poet and minister as two players   BROOK

NATURE ITSELF IS WEEPING   *NATURE MOVED TO LYCIDAS'S SONG*

parasite

---

[11]Probably "well-omened" (*OED* 3, citing this instance), though 1.d, "Of a literary composition: Having an unstudied or unsought felicity," might also be appropriate.

[12]"Black burial sheet," used in a transferred sense and quite possibly meaning "grave."

[13]A lawn was "An open space between woods; a glade" (*OED* 2.a, citing this instance); here the glade would also be on a higher elevation, the area that first caught the rays of the rising sun.

[14]Milton canceled the word "glimmering" here in the Trinity Manuscript and replaced it with "opening."

[15]*1645* has "a field," and the manuscript "afeild."

[16]As a possible meaning for "gray-fly," the *OED* speculates "perhaps a dor-beetle." Thyer's note in Newton's 1752 edition labels it "A brownish kind of beetle powdered with a little white, commonly known by the name of cockchaffer or dorrfly." Milton helps define "dorrs" as annoying summer flies in *Colasterion*: "Infested, somtimes at his face, with dorrs and horsflies" (Yale 2: 757). The gray-fly "winds" or blows its horn (*OED* 2.c) in the sense that it emits a humming sound as it flies.

[17]Probably "fattening" or "watering."

[18]The line reads "Oft till the ev'n-starre bright" in *1638* and in the Trinity Manuscript.

[19]The adjective "burnisht," present in the manuscript and in *1638*, probably referring to the coppery glow in the sky at nightfall, was emended to "westring," meaning "inclining toward the west." The evening star is Hesperus or Venus. The sphere or wheel in which the planet is resident is pictured on the downward slope of the heavens.

[20]A ditty was a "short simple song; often used of the songs of birds, or applied depreciatively" (*OED* 2, citing this instance).

[21]A flute like the panpipe, made out of a hollow reed and suitable to accompany a pastoral ditty.

[22]The Trinity Manuscript has "danc't; and": the punctuation seems to divide the independent clauses more clearly; the lighter comma of *1645* is preferable.

[23]The entire pastoral scene—two shepherds pictured singing "Rural ditties" together under various seasonal conditions—works as a literal picture of Milton and King together on the "Lawns" at Cambridge (there is still a lawn behind Christ's College), as a metaphor of two university students who thought themselves bucolic poets, and of two potential "good shepherds." In John 10.11 Christ pictures himself as the good shepherd; here Milton contrasts the good shepherd with "he that is an hireling, and not the shepherd, whose own the sheep are not, [who] seeth the wolf coming, and leaveth the sheep, and fleeth: and the wolf catcheth them and scattereth the sheep" (John 10.12). No one has identified "old *Damœtas*," though he is assumed to be someone like either Nathaniel Tovey or Joseph Mead, tutors who would have had contact with both Milton and King at Cambridge. Sidney's *Arcadia* 2.103 pictures a "Dametas . . . teching [another shepherd] how with his sheephooke to catch a wanton Lambe." Milton seems to picture most of his classmates "satirically" as "Rough *Satyrs*," since satyrs were usually pictured as lecherous, hairy beasts.

[24]A lay is "A short lyric or narrative poem intended to be sung" (*OED* 4.1). The adjective "soft" indicates that Milton may have considered lays to be a lower form of poetry, as when he describes the poetry of the school of Ovid as "smooth Elegiack poetry" (*An Apology*; Yale 1: 889). The opposite of "soft" as it is used here might be "rigorous" or "disciplined."

[25]An intestinal parasite fatal to young calves.

Or Frost to Flowers, that their gay wardrop²⁶ wear,   DEATH | DECAY
When first the White thorn blows;°   BLOSSOMS
Such, *Lycidas*, thy loss to Shepherds ear.
   Where were ye Nymphs when the remorseless deep — OCEAN   50
Clos'd o're the head of your lov'd²⁷ *Lycidas*?
For neither were ye playing on the steep,°   PRECIPITOUS SLOPE
Where your old *Bards*,²⁸ the famous *Druids* ly,
Nor on the shaggy top of *Mona* high,
Nor yet where *Deva* spreads her wisard° stream: MAGICALLY POTENT   55
Ay me, I fondly° dream!   FOOLISHLY
Had ye bin there—for what could that have don?
What could the Muse²⁹ her self that *Orpheus* bore,³⁰
The Muse her self, for her inchanting son
Whom Universal nature did lament,   60
When by the rout that made the hideous roar,
His goary visage down the stream was sent,
Down the swift *Hebrus* to the *Lesbian* shore.³¹
   Alas! What boots it° with uncessant care   WHAT DOES IT MATTER

---

²⁶Personifies flowers as wearing brightly colored wardrobes (Nicholas Breton had used the image in 1592: "Came Flora forth. . . . Laying abroad the wardrope of her wealth, Her fairest flowers" [cited in *OED* "wardrobe," 2.b]). In the Trinity Manuscript Milton had written "gay buttons beare" and then canceled it for the better image.

²⁷Milton had written what appears to be "youn[g]" in the Trinity Manuscript (unless, as Paul Klemp reminds me, he wrote after "yoʳ" "your" and then canceled it), then canceled it for "lov'd." The *Justa* compositor misread the word as "lord."

²⁸"An ancient Celtic order of minstrel-poets, whose primary function appears to have been to compose and sing (usually to the harp) verses celebrating the achievements of chiefs and warriors, and who committed to verse historical and traditional facts, religious precepts, laws, genealogies, etc." (*OED* 1). Milton uses his syntax to identify the nymphs as worshipers of the druids; both are located properly on Celtic islands such as Anglesey ("*Mona*") or on rivers such as the Dee ("*Deva*") in Chester, said to have been called "divine" by "Britons long ygone" in Spenser, *Faerie Queene* 4.11.39.

²⁹Calliope, the Muse who was supposed to be the daughter of Jupiter and Mnemosyne (see "L'Allegro" 12), is mother to Orpheus. Orpheus by Ovid's account in *Metamorphoses* 11 is torn apart by Thracian women, Maenads or ecstatic worshipers of Bacchus, jealous of his love for young boys after the death of Eurydice. Even though the birds and beasts and even rocks weep for him, the Maenads tear him apart. The Hebrus River carries his head and lyre, still singing together in harmony, across the sea to the island of Lesbos, and the spirit of Orpheus is reunited with that of Eurydice in the underworld.

³⁰The theme of the death and dismemberment of Orpheus is introduced. In the Trinity Manuscript, Milton wrote the following lines with an asterisk at their head to indicate that they should be inserted:

               whome universal nature ~~might~~ᵈⁱᵈ lament
               when by the rout that made the hideous roare
*goarie   his ~~divine~~ ^ᵍᵒʳⁱᵉ visage downe the streame was sent
               downe the swift Hebrus to yᵉ Lesbian shoare.

In the text of the poem proper in the Trinity Manuscript, Milton's revisions show further trouble with the Orpheus passage. This was added on the right margin:

               whome universal nature
               might lament
               ~~and heaven and hel deplore~~
               ~~when his divine head downe~~
               the streame was sent
               downe the swift Hebrus to the
               Lesbian shore.

And these lines were canceled:

~~when shee beheld (the gods farre sighted bee)~~
~~his goarie scalpe rowle downe the Thracian lee~~

Apparently Milton had problems with the decorum of "goarie scalp" which became "divine head," "divine visage," and "gorie visage," before it settled down to become "goary visage" in *1645*.

³¹Milton pictures English nymphs serving bards or Druids, and living, like Vergil's nymphs, in mountain caves ("playing on the steep"). "Mona" is identified as home to the Druids by Michael Drayton in *Polyolbion* 9.415–29; Anglesey is appropriate because it is in the Irish Sea. The Druids were supposed to have made blood sacrifices at the feet of certain oak trees and to have used the mistletoe, which grew in the oaks, in their ritual.

To tend the homely slighted Shepherds trade,   65
And strictly meditate the thankles Muse,[32]
Were it not better don as others use,
To sport with *Amaryllis* in the shade,
Or with[33] the tangles of *Neæra*'s hair?
Fame[34] is the spur that the clear spirit[35] doth raise   70
(That last infirmity of Noble mind)[36]
To scorn delights, and live laborious days;
But the fair Guerdon° when we hope to find,
And think to burst out into sudden blaze,
Comes the blind *Fury*[37] with th' abhorred shears,   75
And slits the thin-spun life. But not the praise,
Phœbus° repli'd, and touch'd my trembling ears;[38]   APOLLO
Fame is no plant that grows on mortal soil,
Nor in the glistering foil[39]
Set off to th' world, nor in broad rumour[40] lies,   80
But lives and spreds aloft by those pure eyes,
And perfet witness of all judging *Jove*;
As he pronounces lastly on each deed,
Of so much fame in Heav'n expect thy meed.°   JUST REWARD
    O fountain *Arethuse*,[41] and thou honour'd floud,   85
Smooth-sliding *Mincius*, crown'd with vocall reeds,
That strain I heard was of a higher mood:
But now my Oate proceeds,[42]

---

[32]Milton recreates the shepherd not only in the role of pastor or minister to a flock in church but as a solitary poet contemplating the writing of great poetry—his own projected role, in fact.

[33]The Trinity Manuscript omits "Or" and has "Hid in the tangles," which is more sensuous but does not differentiate sport with Neæra from sport with Amaryllis, and thus makes playing with the nymphs appear to be an orgy. The names of the nymphs are conventional, Amaryllis being found in Vergil, *Eclogues* 1.4–5 and 2.14–15, and Naæra in *Eclogues* 3.3. Both names were often used in Renaissance love poetry.

[34]The goddess Fama who in Vergil, *Aeneid* 4, appears as "A terrible, grotesque monster, each feather upon whose body— / Incredible though it sounds—has a sleepless eye beneath it, / And for every eye she has also a tongue, a voice and a pricked ear" (C. Day Lewis trans. 181–83). Milton's allegorical figure is much more benign and might be read as "God-given reputation."

[35]Almost surely pronounced as a monosyllable.

[36]Vergil had pictured Fame in the *Aeneid* flying over the rooftops of Carthage with the news of the affair of Dido and Aeneas, but Milton's image is more enigmatic in that Fame is an infirmity of mind but one that indicates nobility of spirit. Though Milton sometimes used the phrase "ill fame" in his prose (Yale 2: 292; 5: 81), the word "fame" has a positive context almost always in his poetry and prose, and fame is not treated as an infirmity of mind. The poet's search for fame and immortality may be debilitating or enervating, but it is also noble. Milton seems to have seen the race for fame as a search for immortality and thus linked with God's judgment. Perhaps the quest for fame is the same as "the race, where that immortall garland is to be run for, not without dust and heat" mentioned in *Areopagitica* (Yale 2: 515).

[37]Warton's note avoids the confusion between Fates and Furies: "Milton, however, does not here confound the Fates and the Furies. He only calls Destiny a Fury" (quoted in Todd 75n). The phrase "blinde Furie" appears in Spenser, *Ruins of Rome* 24. Destiny carries shears in Shakespeare, *King John* 4.2, though more often the shears were associated with the Fates—Clotho, Lachesis, and Atropos—who were assigned respectively the duties of spinning the thread of life, measuring it, and then cutting it off. Since the Furies (Eumenides) were worshiped alongside the Fates (Parcae or Moerae), the two sets of sisters were often conflated or confused. Hesiod pictures the Fates as "ruthless [and] avenging" (*Theogony* 217; Loeb trans.), and Lucan pictures both Furies and Fates presiding over the fate of warriors in battle in *Civil Wars* 4.12–20.

[38]The ears are presumably trembling because of the power of the god; the image echoes similar classical references to the gods' "getting the ear" of mortals. Compare Vergil, *Eclogues* 6.3–4. But John Leonard has investigated the fact that religious dissenters in 1637 might have literally feared for their ears, in "'Trembling ears': The Historical Moment of *Lycidas*," *The Journal of Medieval and Renaissance Studies* 21 (1991): 59–81. William Prynne, among others, had had his ears cut off in 1637 for writing antiprelatical pamphlets (pamphlets that criticized Archbishop Laud's distribution of power among the English clergy).

[39]The thin foil of beaten silver or gold used to set off a precious stone by reflecting light on it, the sense of *OED* n. 1.a.

[40]Milton takes "fame" beyond the Latin sense of "rumor" and into the realms of what the Christian God deems worthy of recognition. The sense "broad rumour" seems to be lower than his estimation of what "fame" should mean.

[41]The fountain Arethusa in Sicily, associated with inspiration for pastoral poets (see *Arcades* 30–31); Mincius is the river most often associated with Vergil's home city Mantua, through which it runs. The terms reeds, oat, quill, and pipes all have to do with musical instruments such as syrinxes or flutes (the Latin *aveva* signified an oaten panpipe) fashioned out of hollow plants. In *Comus* 345 Milton describes a "pastoral reed with oaten stops . . . ." Because Apollo has been speaking or singing in a strain higher than that of pastoral poetry, the poet must change back into a pastoral mode, or mood.

[42]"Moves on, after interruption" (*OED* 1).

And listens to the Herald of the Sea[43]
That came in *Neptune*'s plea,
He ask'd the Waves, and ask'd the Fellon° winds,   MURDEROUS   90
What hard mishap hath doom'd this gentle swain?
And question'd every gust of rugged wings[44]
That blows from off each beaked Promontory,
They knew not of his story,   95
And sage *Hippotades*[45] their answer brings,
That not a blast was from his dungeon stray'd,
The Ayr was calm, and on the level brine,
Sleek *Panope*[46] with all her sisters play'd.
It was that fatall and perfidious Bark°   SMALL SHIP   100
Built in th' eclipse, and rigg'd with curses dark,[47]
That sunk so low that sacred head of thine.

    Next *Camus*,[48] reverend Sire, went footing slow,
His Mantle hairy, and his Bonnet sedge,°   RUSHES, UNDERWATER GRASS
Inwrought with figures dim, and on the edge   105
Like to that sanguine flower inscrib'd with woe.
Ah! Who hath reft (quoth he) my dearest pledge?   BEST-LOVED CHILD
Last came, and last did go,
The Pilot of the *Galilean* lake,[49]
Two massy Keyes he bore of metals twain,   110
(The Golden opes, the Iron shuts amain)°   WITH FULL FORCE
He shook his Miter'd locks, and stern bespake,
How well could I have spar'd for thee young swain,
Anow° of such as for their bellies sake,   ENOUGH
Creep and intrude, and climb into the fold?   115
Of other care they little reck'ning make,
Then how to scramble at the shearers feast,
And shove away the worthy bidden guest.
Blind mouthes![50] that scarce themselves know how to hold
A Sheep-hook,° or have learn'd ought els the least   SHEPHERD'S CROOK   120
That to the faithfull Herdmans art belongs!
What recks it them? What need they? They are sped;[51]

---

[43]Triton, the sea deity usually pictured as blowing a trumpet, whom Hesiod describes as "great, wide-ruling Triton, [who] owns the depths of the sea, . . . an awful god" (*Theogony* 930–33; Loeb trans.). He was supposed to have the ability to settle the seas or quell storms. Here he comes to apologize for the actions of his father Neptune for seeming to cause King's death.
[44]Triton questions each gust of wind, each represented as a birdlike force, roosting in turn on the beaks of promontories facing the sea.
[45]The less-familiar Homeric name for Aeolus (*Odyssey* 10.3, 36), the keeper of the winds in classical mythology. Vergil in *Aeneid* 1.62 pictures Aeolus as Hippotades exercising discretion in selecting winds. Hippotades had a reputation for wisdom perhaps based on Diodorus Siculus's speculation that he invented sails and taught mariners how to predict storms (Starnes and Talbert 231); thus he could be described as wise or "sage."
[46]Panope was one of the Nereids or fifty sea nymphs, daughters of Nereus and Doris.
[47]The ship that carried Edward King is described as being accursed because it was built (according to the poet's vengeful imagination) during an eclipse and hexed by some unknown malevolent spirit before it left port.
[48]The river Cam, which winds slowly through the city of Cambridge, is personified as an old and revered man, but retains its riverish characteristics of moving slowly and being filled with sedge, which indeed looks "hairy." The sight of the personified river is melancholy: its very appearance suggests the mystical learning of a wizard, whose coat would be "Inwrought with figures dim"; the flower is the hyacinth, often blood red in color, named for the dead shepherd Hyacinthus, beloved of other shepherds, and supposedly inscribed with a Greek word transliterated as "AI," meaning "Alas." Ovid tells the story in *Metamorphoses* 10.164–219. Milton's exclamations of "alas" and "ay me" imitate the sounds of Greek and Italian distress words.
[49]St. Peter, a fisherman on the Sea of Galilee, who is pictured here wearing the miter of the founder of the Christian Church. His two keys open and shut the gates of Heaven. His diatribe against hirelings in the English Church is very much Milton's opinion about the state of affairs in 1637, that the young men going into the ministry often sought benefices or church livings out of greed, neglecting their "flocks" to the point of spiritual hunger or illness. The pastoral image remains consistent throughout the passage. St. Peter as pilot is matched later with Christ as "him who walk'd the waves" on the Sea of Galilee.
[50]An arresting image, not far from the metaphysical juxtapositions of John Donne's poetry, as in the "spider love" of "Twicknam Garden."
[51]"What does it matter to them? What do they need? Their career has been advanced."

And when they list,° their lean and flashy songs   when it pleases them
Grate on their scrannel Pipes of wretched straw,[52]
The hungry Sheep look up, and are not fed,   125
But swoln with wind, and the rank mist they draw,
Rot inwardly, and foul contagion spread:[53]
Besides what the grim Woolf[54] with privy[55] paw
Daily devours apace, and little[56] sed,
But that two-handed engine at the door,   130
Stands ready to smite once, and smite no more.[57]

    Return *Alpheus*,[58] the dread voice[59] is past,
That shrunk thy streams; Return *Sicilian* Muse,[60]
And call the Vales, and bid them hither cast
Their Bels, and Flourets of a thousand hues.   135
Ye valleys low where the milde whispers use,
Of shades and wanton winds, and gushing brooks,
On whose fresh lap the swart Star[61] sparely[62] looks,
Throw[63] hither all your quaint enameld eyes,
That on the green terf suck the honied showers,   140
And purple all the ground with vernal flowres.[64]

---

[52]As many critics have pointed out (see Corns 73, for one), the ugliness of the sounds of the words as in the unique provincial word "scrannel" ("shriveled"; see *OED* 1) reflects the moral ugliness of what the false ministers within the church are doing.

[53]Milton compares what is happening within the structure of the English Church with diseases or eating disorders of sheep that cause bloat. Instead of being well-fed, these ecclesiastical sheep eat toxic air and spread their disease from one to the other.

[54]Presumably the agents of the Roman Catholic Church, seeking converts. Compare Spenser, *Shepheardes Calender*, "Maye" 27–29: ". . .There crept in Wolves, ful of fraude and guile, / That oft devoured their own sheepe, / And often the shepheards, that did hem keep" (de Sélincourt 50). The Jesuits, whose coat of arms included two wolves, were especially liable to be accused of such secret proselytizing. All three of Milton's Latin poems on the Gunpowder Plot emphasize the importance of a real or imagined Catholic threat to English political and religious stability.

[55]"Secret," with perhaps a pun based on the phrase "Privy Council," signifying a council of church and state officials convened secretly by a monarch.

[56]A textual crux, since in the manuscript Milton crossed out "nothing" and substituted "little" in the margin, but *1645* prints "nothing." Shawcross emends to "little," Carey and most other modern editors allow "nothing" to stand.

[57]No scholar has been able to determine exactly what the "two-handed engine" is. The image has become perhaps the most famous crux in English literature. The best-informed guesses are that the engine may be some sort of weapon, such as the "huge two-handed sway" of Michael's sword in *Paradise Lost* 6.251. It may well be based on the two-edged sword issuing out of God's mouth in Revelation 1.16, but the "two-edged sword" or Psalm 146.6 has also been advanced as a source. Milton uses "engine" normally in a mechanical sense, as in the phrase "engines of war." In *Reason of Church-government* he uses it of instruments of torture: "such engines of terror [which] God hath given into the hand of his minister as to search the tenderest angles of the heart" (Yale 1: 847). Scales of divine judgment, a sheep hook, shears of destiny, and the keys of St. Peter have been suggested by Franson, Carter Revard, and Fleissner, among others.

[58]Alpheus is a river on the Peloponnesian peninsula in Greece and also the god of the river. Alpheus the god fell in love with the nymph Arethusa and pursued her until the goddess Diana, to whom Arethusa was devoted, changed her into a fountain. Since the fountain Arethusa is on Ortygia, a small island near Syracuse in Sicily, the river Alphaeus was thought to burrow under the Mediterranean and come up unsalted in the fountain of Arethusa. When Ovid retells the story in *Metamorphoses* 5.570–642, he connects Arethusa with Proserpina and Ceres, since in her voyage underground Arethusa witnesses Hades.

[59]The voice of St. Peter is presumably as frighteningly prophetic as the voice of God speaking in the whirlwind in Job 38.1, and just as devastating as a whirlwind might be in nature, as in shrinking streams by sucking their water into the vortex.

[60]Exactly who the Sicilian Muse is cannot be determined, though Loh thinks the reference is to Arethusa (133n), as a fountain or source of pastoral poetic inspiration.

[61]The "dog star" Sirius has its ascendancy in the night sky during the hottest days of the year; its blackness might be connected with its drying or searing effect.

[62]"Faintly" in the manuscript, though Milton first wrote "sparely" in the body of the text, then crossed it out and wrote "faintly" in the margin, crossing that out to return to "sparely." For "sparely," the *OED* suggests "In a sparing, frugal, or stinted manner; not fully, amply, or copiously," citing this instance.

[63]The manuscript has "bring" crossed out and "thrown" substituted in the margin.

[64]The catalogue of flowers that follows exists in two versions on the first page of Milton's drafts of the poem. The first version reads:

    Bring the rathe primrose that unwedded dies
    ~~colla~~ colouring the pale cheeke of uninjoyd love
    and that sad floure that strove
    to write his owne woes on the vermeil graine
    next adde Narcissus y[t] still weeps in vaine
    the woodbine and y[e] pancie freakt wth jet
    the glowing violet
    the cowslip wan that hangs his pensive head

Bring the rathe° Primrose that forsaken dies.
The tufted Crow-toe, and pale Gessamine,
The white Pink, and the Pansie freakt with jeat,
The glowing Violet,[65]   145
The Musk-rose, and the well attir'd Woodbine,
With Cowslips wan that hang the pensive hed,
And every flower that sad embroidery wears:
Bid *Amaranthus* all his beauty shed,
And Daffadillies fill their cups with tears,   150
To strew the Laureat Herse where *Lycid* lies.
For so to interpose a little ease,
Let our frail[66] thoughts dally with false surmise.
Ay me! Whilst thee the shores,[67] and sounding Seas
Wash far away, where ere thy bones are hurld,   155
Whether beyond the stormy *Hebrides*,[68]
Where thou perhaps under the whelming[69] tide
Visit'st the bottom of the monstrous world;[70]
Or whether thou to our moist vows deny'd,
Sleep'st by the fable of *Bellerus*[71] old,   160
Where the great vision of the guarded Mount[72]
Looks toward *Namancos* and *Bayona*'s hold;
Look homeward Angel now, and melt with ruth.
And, O ye *Dolphins*, waft the haples youth.
    Weep no more, woful Shepherds weep no more,   165
For *Lycidas* your sorrow is not dead,
Sunk though he be beneath the watry floar,
So sinks the day-star in the Ocean bed,
And yet anon repairs his drooping head,
And tricks° his beams, and with new spangled Ore,[73]   170
Flames in the forehead of the morning sky:

Handwritten marginal notes: "flowers processione in his honour" · READY TO BLOOM · "NATURE BEDECKS FUNERAL BEAR" · "where Lycidas went?" · WATER HAS WAFTED US AWAY · "St. michael angel of judgement" · DECKS OUT · RISES IN HEAVEN

---

and every bud that sorrows liverie weares
let Daffadillies fill thire cups. ᵂⁱᵗʰ teares
bid Amaranthus all his beautie shed
to strew the laureat herse &c.

Notice that "unwedded" became "forsaken," that the "pale cheeke of uninjoyd love" became "pale Gessamin," that "the garish columbine" of the corrected version in the manuscript (not shown here) became "the well-attir'd Woodbine." Narcissus, the flower and the mythological figure, has been removed, perhaps significantly.

[65]*1645* and *1673* both have a period here; since we are in the midst of a catalogue of parallel items, the comma of *1638* might be less misleading.

[66]Substituted for "sad," which is crossed out in the manuscript.

[67]The word "shoars" is substituted for the canceled "floods" in the manuscript.

[68]The islands off the coast of Scotland.

[69]Both the manuscript and *Justa* read "humming," which must have been corrected for the 1645 edition.

[70]Compare similar scenes of what must have been, in a time without diving equipment, a very mysterious ocean floor, as in Shakespeare, *Richard III*: "Methought I saw a thousand fearful wracks; / A thousand men that fishes gnawed upon . . ." (1.4.24–25).

[71]The name Bellerus is substituted for "Corineus" crossed through in the manuscript. Corineus was one of the legendary heroes who were supposed to have come to Britain with Brutus, Aeneas's great-grandson, to rule over Cornwall, to which he was supposed to have given his name (see Milton, *History of Britain*, Yale 5: 16); "Bellerus" may be derived from "Bellerium," the Latin name for Land's End in Cornwall (Carey 160n). "Bellerus" fits the meter of the line; "Corineus" does not.

[72]Mount St. Michael's, not far from Land's End on the Cornish coast of England, looks across the English Channel to Mont St. Michel in France, and, beyond that, to the northwestern province of Nemancos in Spain and the fortress of Bayona near Cap Finisterre. Both "Namancos" and "Bayona" appear in several atlases, such as that of Ortelius published in 1606, to which Milton had access. St. Michael is the patron saint of England; he was present at St. Michael's Mount in the person of a real or imagined ("vision") statue in a niche carved into the side of the mount, looking out presumably as the guardian of English Protestantism against the threat represented by Catholic Spain. Milton petitions the saint to look back at England in a show of pity ("ruth") for the death of Edward King. Todd (1852 ed., 3.339–42) was the first editor of Milton to discover the allusion to St. Michael's Mount. Dolphins were supposed in classical tradition to have offered aid to poets in distress at sea, starting with Arion, in Hyginus's Fable 194.

[73]Probably the ore of some shiny metal like gold or brass, since here the sense seems to be that the morning is decked out by sparkling, fiery spangles (small bits of beaten metal sewn into costumes).

So *Lycidas* sunk low, but mounted high,[74]
Through the dear might of him that walk'd the waves:[75]
Where other groves, and other streams along,
With *Nectar* pure his oozy Lock's he laves,   175
And hears the unexpressive° nuptiall Song,[76]   INEXPRESSIBLE
In the blest Kingdoms meek of joy and love.
There entertain him all the Saints above,
In solemn troops, and sweet Societies
That sing, and singing in their glory move,   180
And wipe the tears for ever from his eyes.
Now *Lycidas* the Shepherds weep no more,
Hence forth thou art the Genius of the shore,[77]
In thy large recompense, and shalt be good
To all that wander in that perilous[78] flood.   185
    Thus sang the uncouth Swain to th' Okes and rills,
While the still morn went out with Sandals gray;[79]
He touch'd the tender stops of various Quills,
With eager thought warbling his *Dorick* lay:[80]
And now the Sun had stretch'd out[81] all the hills,   190
And now was dropt into the Western bay;
At last he rose, and twitch'd his Mantle blew:[82]
To morrow to fresh Woods, and Pastures new.

---

[74]The same sort of analogy was often made for the descent of Christ into Hell and the ascension into Heaven as described in the Apostle's Creed.

[75]The manuscript includes a colon at this point; some copies of *1645* have a semicolon while others have a colon; the change may have been made while the book was in press.

[76]Milton seems to be conflating two biblical passages, Revelation 19.7, "the marriage of the Lamb is come," and Revelation 14.4, "These are they which were not defiled with women; for they are virgins. These are they which follow the Lamb whithersoever he goeth. These were redeemed from among men, being the first-fruits unto God and to the Lamb." From the two passages, he put together a picture of virgins who died young celebrating in a compensatory celestial marriage feast; compare the ending of "Epitaphium Damonis." At the heavenly festival, Lycidas would be able to wash and purify the locks of his hair soiled by the ooze of the sea.

[77]The spirit who protects the shore. A "genius loci" is the spirit who guards a particular locale, just as there is a "Genius of the Wood" in "Il Penseroso" 154 and a similar Genius in *Arcades*.

[78]The line scans iambically if the word is pronounced as a disyllable, though it is not written that way in any of the editions. Compare the phonetic spelling reproduced in *Animadversions*: "with this parlous criticism" (Yale 1: 666).

[79]The morning is pictured as the old man Tithonus, who was rendered immortal but not ageless by his lover, the goddess Aurora; thus he is "still" and wears sandals. I follow *1638* in using the semicolon, as compared with the comma of *1645* and *1673*, at the end of this line, on the grounds that "He" in the next sentence would seem to refer to the personified "morn" without it. The word "uncouth" usually meant "unknown" rather than "ill-mannered" in seventeenth-century usage (compare *Paradise Lost* 10.475), but Milton might also have been suggesting "foreign," "uncultured," or "strange." Compare *OED* 6: "Of an unfamiliar or strange appearance or form; spec., having an odd, uncomely, awkward, or clumsy shape or bearing."

[80]The image seems to be more musical than poetic or geographical; Milton used the adjective "Dorick" only one time in his English prose, to mean a "grave" piece of music (*Areopagitica*; Yale 2: 523). Sir Henry Wotton, in his letter prefaced to *Comus*, uses the term musically as well: he speaks of "a certain Dorique delicacy in [Milton's] Songs and Odes." The reference to "eager thought" seems analogous to "unpremeditated verse." The music, in other words, is spontaneous and inspired. The word "warbling," as always in Milton's usage, has the positive connotation of spontaneous creation, as with "warble his native wood-notes wild" as applied to Shakespeare in "L'Allegro" 134. The syrinx (panpipe) has a number of reeds or quills, hollow of course, with stops or finger-holes to be used in controlling sound.

[81]"Prolonged [by extending their shadows]."

[82]Perhaps the swain's mantle is blue because he associates himself with early Britons, who painted themselves with woad, a blue dye. "In Spenser, *F.Q.* I x 14, Speranza wears blue" (Carey 192n).

Comus (1634)

NAMING

Milton called his masque by a generic title—*A Mask Presented At Ludlow-Castle, 1634* (*1645, 1673*) or simply "A maske 1634" (Trinity Manuscript) or "A Maske" (Bridgewater Manuscript, or BMS). For any succeeding generation to name Milton's generic masque *Comus* is a little like calling *Paradise Lost* "Satan," but the name *Comus* "was used by Toland in his biography, 1698, and by Elijah Fenton, 1725" (Le Comte, *Milton Dictionary* 71).

By the time the masque was rewritten by John Dalton with music by Thomas Arne (the composer of "Hail, Brittania") in 1738, the title had stuck, and it is very hard to dislodge. Carey and Shawcross in their editions attempted to restore the name *A Maske*; Orgel and Goldberg followed suit; and Campbell split the issue, writing both his title and his running head as "*A Masque (Comus).*"

Comus's name is, nevertheless, a very evocative one, coming out of the same Greek root that produced the Latin noun *comedo*, meaning "glutton," the Latin noun *comes*, from which "companion" is derived, and the adjective *comestibilis*, "edible," as in the English word "comestibles," or "edible things." The Greek κόμος indicates a banquet or a revel, and the god of such a feast might be a god of mirth or undisciplined revelry. The name Comus was used generically for gods or demigods presiding over feasts or riots, from Ericius Puteanus's dream-vision *Comus* (1608, published 1634; see Mish; see also Brown 65) to Ben Jonson's *Pleasure Reconciled to Virtue* (in manuscript until 1640; see Brown 58).

The generic name "The Lady" is no less evocative, especially if one recalls that Milton's nickname at Christ's College, and one that he apparently did not relish, was "the Lady of Christ's College" (see Campbell, "Milton" 235 for the context). Of course, Lady Alice Egerton was a lady, but to transform her into The Lady elevates her to something like allegorical status, representing in one person all female aristocrats, or all women who possess nobility of mind.

The Attendant Spirit, with another generic name, is called a dæmon in the various manuscripts. The word in Greek implies "spirit" more than it does "evil spirit." Milton seems to use the word *dæmon* in the Platonic sense of a divine spirit who may have a presence on earth and who may exert a good influence on human beings. In Milton's terms he is also a *genius loci*, a spirit who inhabits and protects a certain region. He is Thyrsis (a name derived from classical Greek pastoral poetry), and a swain—a shepherd or worker in the fields

of a great lord. As if those weren't enough different roles, he is a shepherd-musician, since he can sing, and he is Henry Lawes, thinly disguised—the music master to the Bridgewater children.

Likewise, Sabrina is the tutelary spirit (protector or guardian) who inhabits and stands for the river Severn, one of the chief rivers of England and Wales, and Milton extracts her character from English history and legend. She is "the daughter of *Locrine,*" a victim of domestic violence who survives the ordeal and becomes divine to aid others in similar danger.

THE HISTORICAL CONTEXT OF MASQUES: METAMORPHOSES

The Roman poet Ovid's long and fascinating collection of stories of changes from one life form into another in the *Metamorphoses* influenced Milton as it did Spenser and Shakespeare before him. The masque was the perfect medium for depicting such colorful transformations. Comus has the power through his sorcerer's potions and necromantic spells to turn men and women into beasts. From Hesiod, Homer, Ovid, and Apuleius, Milton could have taken the general idea of the power of herbal medicine or of the classical gods to change humans into other life forms. What is more important to the moral structure of Milton's masque is the idea that by having bestial thoughts humans can of their own free will transform themselves into subhuman life forms. Thinking nasty thoughts can make one a beast.

As a modern reader can see by glancing through George Sandys's moralized translation of the *Metamorphosis* (1632), seventeenth-century English readers understood Ovid's stories as allegories. There had indeed been a tradition of moralizing Ovid that extended as far back as the time of Chaucer (Harding 90–91). Every choice to become a beast was a moral choice. The story of Bacchus and the Tyrhennian pirates turned into dolphins (see *Comus* 47–48), for instance, was

> by the *Greekes* devised; and withall to deterre from rapine and perjury, which seldome escapes the divine vengeance. The fantasticall resemblances of Lynxes, Tygres, and Panthers, are the terrors of conscience, which drive the guilty to dispaire and ruine.
> (Sandys 167)

Mindele Treip can therefore speak of *Comus* as "Milton's success in the highly allegorical masque form" (*Allegorical* 140).

The theme of transformation or metamorphosis lent itself readily to different manifestations of civic allegory: a splendid triumphal procession of a national hero; a lord mayor's procession that might celebrate the prominence of a city like London; or the "progress" of a noble lord from one city or aristocratic estate to another (Treip, "*Comus*"). Putting on splendid costumes and parading through the streets or on the stage produced what Milton was to call "mask and antique pageantry" ("L'Allegro" 128).

The process of masquing, as in masked balls, also fit quite well into the self-fashioning of Renaissance aristocrats. A masque celebrating a godlike or heroic figure—or even a stock character from the *commedia dell'arte*—would allow an aristocrat to masquerade as his or her favorite Greek god or goddess, or favorite character type. A fitting image of Queen Elizabeth, who was known as the Virgin Queen, for instance, was that of Diana, the goddess of chastity and the moon (Berry). The Lady in *Comus* will be another devotee of Diana, "a deity who guides young women through all the stages of their life from maidenhood to marriage to motherhood" (Revard 135).

Playwrights like Ben Jonson in combination with costume and set designers like Inigo Jones might be called into collaboration to present spectacles that glorified aristocrats (Saslow, Peacock). Since aristocrats would in their own person symbolize the stability of their rule, the masque might represent a ruler temporarily and ineffectually threatened by some representative of disorder or chaos—a figure like Pluto, god of the underworld, or Bacchus, god of uncontrolled drinking. That same ruler or his agents would then defeat the forces of disorder and darkness. The ruler commissioning Milton's masque is the Earl of Bridgewater, the aristocrats are three of his children, and the threat to their power and their person is Comus.

ARISTOCRATIC ENTERTAINMENTS

Cedric Brown prefers the term "aristocratic entertainment" over "masque" to describe the genre of Milton's "Arcades" and *Comus*. In discovering that there was another masque performed for the Earl of Bridgewater on his progress toward Ludlow, the Chirk Castle Entertainment, Brown ("Chirk") establishes that the aristocracy could be very well celebrated in any place. Another aristocrat could pay the bill for costumes, musician, actors, and dancers, for a production within the walls of his castle. The politics of such aristocratic entertainments would be the politics of flattery, as Orgel shows, but Norbrook, Marcus, McGuire, and Wilding all demonstrate how there might be a hidden political agenda even in an aristocratic entertainment that might subvert the flattery. Thus *Comus* has been seen as a "Puritan masque," a "radical masque," or a masque that offers instructions to the masses—not just aristocratic flattery of an important and powerful family.

OCCASION

In 1968 William Riley Parker could write "*Comus* was a children's entertainment, requested by children and acted by children, with admiring elders more as spectators than participants" (132). Parker reiterates that "The masque was essentially a children's party" (142). He also deemphasizes its part in the masque tradition, writing "*Comus* is more like a play than are the other masques of its time" (130), and it is his opinion that the masque was "written, by necessity, without benefit of spectacle" (129). This is not quite accurate.

We have come to realize that the masque now called *Comus* was not a children's party but part of a state occasion. It was written to honor one of the most trusted members of Charles I's Privy Council, the Earl of Bridgewater, upon his installation in an important civic and legal position, that of Lord President of Wales and the Marches. We also know, through the research of Cedric Brown, that before the Earl of Bridgewater had come to assume his post in the Welsh Marches (the word means "border areas" or "marks" and in this case included all of Herefordshire, Worcestershire, Shropshire, and Gloucestershire), he had made a stately progress, similar to a king or queen's progress, from London, accompanied by his entourage, visiting the grand homes and castles along the way. The family of the Earl was entertained as it made its progress with other dramatic performances, such as the "Chirk Castle Entertainment." When the family did arrive in Ludlow, local officials and townspeople were invited to participate in a festive presentation of Milton's masque at the Castle, in a production directed by Henry Lawes, an eminent composer who was a member of the King's Music and the musical tutor to the Bridgewater family.

The family, possessors of one of the best libraries in England, was cultivated and erudite. The Earl was urbane and well educated, and his wife, who may have been the prime mover of the masque, was knowledgeable enough to have recently purchased George Herbert's *The Temple*. At least four of their fifteen children had sung, acted, or danced in some of the best Caroline masques before they saw or participated in *Comus*. Thanks to the recent research of Cedric Brown, Mary Anne McGuire, Christopher Hill, John Creaser, William B. Hunter, Michael Wilding, and Leah Marcus, we know a great deal more about the social and political contexts of England in the 1630s, and about the Bridgewater family—and its ties with the sponsor of "Arcades," the Countess Dowager of Derby. We also know more about the duties and responsibilities of the Lord President of Wales, and about the town of Ludlow in 1634.

Though three of the performers in the masque were children under sixteen, those children were grand and important—they had all been painted as splendid little adults before they were ten—and they all were given difficult lines to say and musically sophisticated songs to sing. Though young by modern standards, Lady Alice was at fifteen a marriageable adult. Milton's masque might be thought of as a presentation of Lady Alice, as a pageant glorifying the Lord President of Wales, and as a civic ceremony in the border town of Ludlow, but it is not just a children's party.

SCANDALS IN THE FAMILY AND WITCHCRAFT

Despite the national importance of the Earl, there was more than a hint of scandal in the Bridgewater family. In 1631, Mervyn Touchet, the Second Earl of Castlehaven and brother-in-law to the Earl of Bridgewater's wife, was executed for sexual offenses. Touchet had raped maidservants in his household, sodomized male servants, and forced his wife to participate in his orgies. The Castlehaven scandal was of national proportions, the seventeenth-century equivalent of a modern front-page story in a tabloid specializing in the intimate lives of the rich and famous. But the question remains of how the scandal might have affected the composition or the reception of a masque written to be performed three years after the scandalous events had occurred.

Neither Creaser nor Brown believes that the Castlehaven scandal had much effect on Milton's masque, but Breasted and Mundhenk did establish the possible relevance of the scandal to the masque and to various cuts made in the Bridgewater Manuscript, cuts that seem to indicate a censor worried about the family reputation. Hunter still can believe that the scandal is "of major importance for an understanding of *Comus*" (*Milton's* 25).

Another juicy bit of family gossip was unearthed by Barbara Breasted, this time in a letter from one of the Bridgewater family physicians, and a relative by marriage, Sir Robert Napier. Lady Alice Egerton, shortly before Comus was written, was reported to have been ill because she may have been bewitched. The line between mental illness, physical ailments, and witchcraft was a thin one in the 1630s. If Comus is a "damned wizard" and a "damned Magician," capable of "blear illusion," the story of Lady Alice's bewitchment may bear listening to.

There is certainly witchcraft in Comus. The critical question for readers is whether to believe in it or to dismiss it. The witchcraft may be a part of Welsh folklore, as Violet O'Valle tried to establish in 1983, but it also may be English superstition, encouraged by King James's fascination with demonology (Demaray, "The Temple" 64–65). Whatever witchcraft there is in the masque may be Homeric, patterned after the witchery of Circe, or it may be Ovidian, after the magical transformations and insanity associated with Bacchus in the story of Pentheus, or the potent witchcraft of Medea. Less well known today is the witchcraft of transformation in Apuleius's *Metamorphosis* (the title is sometimes translated as *The Golden Ass*), a Roman protonovel in which a man is turned into a donkey, as victim of a witch's revenge for his lack of faith in witchcraft. Comus's beast-headed rout is derived from Circe's beastly victims and Apuleius's bewitched donkey. His parade of beast-headed masquers can be seen not only in Milton's masque but in an illustration from the 1632 French *Ballet du Château de Bicêtre* (Peacock 145); similar stage figures existed in Italy. DiSalvo notes the resemblance between Comus's band and other "night-travelers" (118) or Italian bands of witches and sorcerers (Ginzburg).

There is other tabloid material associated with the Bridgewater family and possibly with Milton's masque. Leah Marcus, working with the Egerton papers in the Huntington Library ("Milton's"), has discovered that the Earl of Bridgewater, formerly rumored to have had Puritan leanings, was at least a consistent opponent of Archbishop Laud, especially over questions of court jurisdiction. Marcus believes that *Comus* displays an "elemental radicalism" which complements the politics of its patron ("Milieu"). It may be significant that the word *king* is never used in the masque.

As Lord President of Wales and the Marches, Bridgewater seems to have been a fair and impartial judge, learned and humane. Marcus sketched out one locally well-known and protracted case of sexual abuse in which the Earl had been immersed just prior to the time Comus was produced. The Earl's jurisdiction overlapped that apportioned to the English Church (hence that of Archbishop William Laud) in such cases. The illiterate and defenseless Margery Evans, who might well be called a "haples virgin" (350), was raped in the Severn Valley, by a gentleman with some local power. Instead of capitulating to her rapist and his servant, she raised hue and cry after them, and was herself unjustly imprisoned. With the help of an aunt who could write, she eventually appealed to the King and his representative, the Earl of Bridgewater. The Earl's careful unraveling of the case demonstrates administrative intelligence, patience, the ability to detect fraud even in high officials, and a remarkable sympathy with the downtrodden and oppressed.

The Margery Evans case might make as valid a claim for being a topical inspiration of a masque about the potential despoiling of innocence by brutality (Milton's Lady is in danger of being raped) as does the better-known Castlehaven scandal. As Michael Lieb points out, the theme of "the danger that beset those votaries of chastity [Milton] held in such high esteem" remained on his mind after he had written the masque (108; see Yale 1: 370).

THE LITURGY FOR MICHAELMAS

The date of the masque, according to Hunter ("Liturgical"), may be significantly attached to the celebration of Michaelmas within the Anglican Church calendar, the feast of the Archangel St. Michael celebrated on September 29, "one of the four quarter-days of the English business year" (*OED*). Michaelmas was a time of potential misrule or of what was called the "lawless hour," not unlike Halloween; thus it was an appropriate time to unleash a figure like Comus, a god of misrule. Taaffe and Berkowitz discuss the probable references to Michaelmas revels in the Lady's first speech (170–79).

MUSIC

Milton's masque is informed by music, by which I mean not only that it contains singing and dancing, but that it is controlled by the metaphor of the music of the spheres—that celestial music supposed by Christians to be generated by the spirits of angels moving harmoniously through the spheres in planets and stars that were supposed to circle Earth. A pure spirit on Earth, like Milton's Lady, might be able to hear the music of the spheres and distinguish well-ordered and heavenly music from wild and unruly measures such as those danced by Comus and his riotous crew. Such a wild dance breaks off at 145, when the holy presence of the Lady dispels it.

The music in *Comus* makes it operatic (Martz), though on a lower scale than grand opera. I should immediately add that opera as we know it today was only just being invented in the first quarter of the seventeenth century (Harper 6–7). What is generally acclaimed to be the finest early opera, Claudio Monteverdi's *Orfeo*, was first performed in Mantua, Italy, in 1607. The musical genre quickly traveled to England, where the musical circle that included Milton's composer-father came to emulate its unique combination of solo airs or arias with dance and pageantry. Though Milton's masque was written to be performed in a provincial castle, the work is infected with the spirit of opera just as was Henry Lawes, its composer. Lawes once set a list of Italian nonsense words to his own music, satirizing the British affectation for Italian opera,

but he also emulated the great Italian arias, such as Monteverdi's "Lament for Ariadne," in his own music (Willetts 7–9). His forte, one that endeared him to Milton, was for word setting, what Lawes himself called the ability "to shape *Notes* to the *Words* and *Sense*" (Willetts 3; see Basile).

POETIC STYLE

Stevie Davies calls attention to "Sleek couplets, dancing Spenserian measures, classicist urbanity and a harmonically subtle blank verse inherited from Renaissance dramatic poets, especially Shakespeare"; all those elements are kept under "superb rhetorical control" (71). A. C. Partridge summarizes the blank verse of the masque: "The style of Shakespeare is to be seen everywhere; but Milton has more sonorous flights, greater volubility of argument, bookishness of phrase, and wealth of allusions" (272). The plays of Shakespeare most often cited as sources for Milton's masque are, quite naturally, the most masque-like: *A Midsummer Night's Dream*, *As You Like It*, and *The Tempest*. The freshness and richness of Milton's poetic style may be due in part to his newly minted words, of which Corns notes more than sixty in the masque, a sharp contrast to the practice in the much longer *Samson Agonistes*, in which there are only twenty or so (50–51). The famous "hæmony" is Milton's word, as are "dew-besprent," "cedar'n," "swink't," "smooth-hair'd," "rushy-fringed," "rosy-bosom'd," and "Root-bound." The participial forms are Spenserian; the compounds sound more like Josuah Sylvester's translation of DuBartas's *Divine Weeks and Works*, an extraordinarily popular work in the early seventeenth century (Snyder in Sylvester 72–95). Some of the groups of related words, the collocations, sound like the language of the King James Bible or of Shakespeare: compare "pillar'd firmament," with "bow'd welkin" or the sentence "There I suck the liquid ayr" (Corns 57). Milton may have borrowed his unusual phrase "printless feet" (897) from *The Tempest*'s "printless foot" (5.1.34), and he may owe his reference to the fierceness of mountaineers (426) to *The Tempest* 3.3.44.

THEMES AND IMAGERY

How much of an allegory is Milton's masque? The Lady may be considered to be Chastity, or something closer to the meaning of the Latin *castitas*, "purity of morals, morality" (Lewis and Short, *A Latin Dictionary*), and, if there is an allegorical structure, it is what Milton outlined in an autobiographical aside written in defense of his own moral choice in *An Apology*:

Thus from the Laureat fraternity of Poets, riper

yeares, and the ceaseless round of study and reading led me to the shady spaces of philosophy, but chiefly to the divine volumes of *Plato*, and his equal *Xenophon*. Where if I should tell ye what I learnt, of chastity and love, I meane that which is truly so, whose charming cup is only vertue which she bears in her hand to those who are worth. The rest are cheated with a thick intoxicating potion which a certaine Sorceresse the abuser of loves name carries about; and how the first and chiefest office of love, begins and ends in the soule, producing those happy twins of her divine generation knowledge and vertue, with such abstracted sublimities as these, it might be worth your listning, Readers. . . .

(*An Apology against a Pamphlet* [1642]; Yale 1: 891–92)

The "certaine Sorceresse" can be related to Comus's mother Circe, and the "thick intoxicating potion" seems identical to that carried by Comus. Comus does indeed abuse "loves name," and in the masque virtue protects both chastity and love. Love begins and ends in the soul, but it is fertile, producing Knowledge and Virtue. The moral structure that Milton here outlines seems to fit the masque perfectly. Plato and Xenophon are the philosophers whose ideas underlie the masque (Samuel ch. 7), and the twins Knowledge and Virtue are those mentioned in Plato's *Symposium* 209A; they find their counterparts in "Youth and Joy," in *Comus* 1011.

If the Lady is "Chastity" (the modern term may be misleading, since Milton considered it possible to be "chaste" within the institution of marriage and after begetting children), then Comus is something like Licentiousness, Gluttony, or Excess (the opposites of Temperance). Comus's rout are those who give in to any of those vices (see Wentersdorf for the meaning of the various beasts in classical lore). The Attendant Spirit is a Dæmon in the Platonic sense of "emissary of the gods"; hence he can represent the high moral position of a Christianized "Jove" on Earth. The two brothers conduct a philosophical dialogue, in the manner of a Platonic symposium. Sabrina is a tutelary spirit, a river goddess imbued with moral power because she herself has successfully escaped the violence engendered by jealousy and rage. As an example of "the fury of *Guendolen*," that jealous stepmother of British history and legend throws "her Daughter *Sabra* . . . into a river: and to leave a Monument of revenge, proclaims, that the stream be thenceforth call'd after the Damsels name; which by length of time is chang'd now to *Sabrina*, or *Severn*" (Milton, *History of Britain*; Yale 5: 18).

NEOPLATONISM AND FICINO: WHERE DOES CHRISTIANITY FIT IN?

In his loosely allegorical structure (Swaim), Milton glorifies Plato and Neoplatonic philosophers such as Ficino (Jayne), he amplifies not only Ovidian but English mythology with figures like Sabrina, and he works out of his own personal philosophical and religious convictions by allowing the Lady and Comus or the two brothers to debate questions of the use of nature's bounty or the purpose of purity of mind and body in exceptional human beings.

The masque also is and is not a Christian document. At times Comus is identified closely with Hell, as when he practices "hellish charms" (613). His union with Cotytto or Hecate would have been taken as links with demonic or hellish figures. Circe's charms are "witcheries" (523), and Comus himself is a "necromancer" (649) in one place and a "Sorcerer" in others (521, 940). The Attendant Spirit is identified with what appears to be a Christian Heaven, where a thinly disguised Christian God rules as Jove. And the Lady addresses one angel (214); her chastity may be supported by "a thousand liveried Angels" who "lacky her" (455); and her singing provides "Divine inchanting ravishment" (245)—at least when Comus hears it. But there are a few signs in Milton's revisions of the Trinity Manuscript that he would like the reader to deemphasize the Christian elements of the masque: for instance, he excises the phrases "paradise" and "heaven gates" from the Lady's apostrophe to Faith, Hope, and Chastity, and he also cuts the phrases "good heaven" (Trinity Manuscript 21.32) and "hel brewd" (cut from 696) from other lines in the manuscript. Any deemphasis on Christian elements would highlight the kinds of classical or mythological elements that Revard stresses.

The imagery in the masque follows its moral and psychological structures. There is much to do with light as representing the power of God, much to do with the cleansing power of water, much to do with foods of various sorts (mostly tempting ones). There is much to do with sex—enough to frighten a Freudian. Just the one image, "the Dragon woom / Of Stygian darknes spets her thickest gloom, / And makes one blot of all the ayr" (131–33) takes us deeply into the perverse sexual reversal of decent values that Milton thought always present in evil. Kerrigan fixes on the image of the "root-bound Lady," to interpret her "No" to Comus as meaning "Yes," but Leonard takes issue with that opinion. From a different psychological perspective, Stevie Davies sees the Lady as carrying "the full weight and value of Milton's eremitical repression and sublimation of his sexual desires" (71).

THE SICK DEMIGOD

Morally, Comus is sick, and the Lady is healthy and therefore able to resist his evil. Trying to reverse her values, he accuses her of being ill with the sickness melancholy and producing "meer moral babble" in her melancholia, but she in turn attacks his "gay rhetoric" ("frivolous argumentation") without hesitation and quite forcefully. Comus admits she is right, in an aside: "She fables not" (800).

The amoral Comus sees the institution of marriage only in terms of power, a ploy to make the Lady his "Queen," and he sees his followers as slaves to his will. She looks at marriage as the Attendant Spirit does, as in the marriage of Cupid and Psyche, of the beautiful body in union with the beautiful soul or spirit. The image of marriage we are left with at the end of the masque is healthy, if idealistic, not unlike that of Adam and Eve before the Fall.

FROM COMUS TO SATAN

As one of my graduate students wrote on an exam, Comus is like "an adolescent Satan" (see Calhoun for the idea that the masque focuses on adolescence). If he has "clustring locks" (55) like his father or if he can be dragged "by the curls" (608), he would seem to be young. Morally, Comus is like a Satan in the making, except that we see much less of him: we do not see him, for instance, corrupting the men and women in his rout, nor do we see him conducting the "abhorred rites" to Cotytto or Hecate. Both Comus and Satan try at length to corrupt a young woman; Comus fails and Satan succeeds.

Rather than being like Satan himself, Comus is a follower of Satan (Blondel), through his sponsorship of heathen gods, his perverse and excessive quest for pleasure or abundance, and his attempt to pollute innocence in the form of the chaste Lady. He is a hypocritical shape-shifter, like Milton's Satan in the Serpent, and he is a powerful orator, whose speeches on the theme of *carpe diem* or on the use of "Beauty" as "natures coyn," which "must not be hoorded, / But must be currant" (739–40), are seductive and persuasive. But the Lady is not Eve: she is an intellectual and moral warrior, a kind of empowered Christian soldier descended from figures like Spenser's Britomart or Una. She quickly sees through Comus's disguise, she is not taken in by his hollow rhetoric, and she dismisses his attempts to seduce or corrupt her as easily as Milton's Jesus answers Satan in *Paradise Regain'd*. In the masque, a strong woman defeats a male made weak by his wickedness. In classical terms, "the Lady, in resisting a powerful god figure, also reverses this mythic pattern, acting the part of a female Odysseus outwitting a male

Circe" (Revard 136–37). The Lady's chastity, backed by her moral conviction and accompanied by the celestial harmony represented by the Attendant Spirit and the white magic represented by Sabrina, overcomes temptation in the form of what Comus represents, "carnal sensuality" (474), or "sensuall Folly, and Intemperance" (975). As Shawcross points out, "the masque is an elaboration of the temptation in the wilderness (see Matthew 4:1–11 and Luke 4:1–13) in mortal terms" (*John Milton* 50–51).

STAGING AND COSTUMING

In putting Milton's masque on stage today, questions have to be asked and answered about the age and appearance of Comus himself. If he has those "clustring locks," he would seem to be young, yet he may also be as ageless as the god Bacchus. I have seen the part of Comus acted either as a "Greek god" (muscular physique, athletic grace, curly black hair) or as a "dirty old man" (elegant thinness, cynical sneer, unctuous movement). Both character types worked equally well on stage. A third type, perhaps less likely, would be the fat, Bacchus-like Comus of "Comus and his train," pictured in Kogan 96, one of Inigo Jones's illustrations for Ben Jonson's *Pleasure Reconciled to Virtue* (see also Orgel and Strong 283).

Stage properties must have included the ugly heads for the various beast figures and possibly a mechanism for helping the Attendant Spirit to descend to stage or to help Sabrina to rise to stage level. Lawes might well have borrowed costumes from court masques he had been involved in earlier; his costume designs might well have derived from those of the Florentine Bernardo Buontalenti (for Arion, see Saslow, Plate 14, and for a sea nymph Plate 13) or from those of Inigo Jones (for a watery spirit, see Peacock Plate 77, or for a Naiad Plate 59).

There is even an illustration from a French ballet of 1632 with a dance of sorcerers and monsters (Peacock, Plate 78), together with Inigo Jones's drawings of antimasque characters (Peacock, Plate 86) and a number of architectural or pastoral stage settings, such as a sketch of what appears to be an arbor, for a theatrical performed at Chatsworth House (Peacock, Plate 129). A modern set designer and costume manager could work easily from seventeenth-century records.

TEXT

The copy-text for this edition is the printed version of the 1645 *Poems*. The text of *Comus* is the most complicated to edit of all Milton's texts (Flannagan, "Editing"), because the masque exists in the Trinity College Manuscript, the Bridgewater Manuscript, the

1637 edition published presumably by Henry Lawes and with the permission of the Bridgewater family, the 1645 *Poems*, and the 1673 *Poems, &c. upon Several Occasions.* Each of the manuscripts and each of the printed texts may have integrity and value of its own, and editors argue which of the four versions is the most worthy of preservation. S. E. Sprott has helped editors and scholars by collecting three of the texts in one parallel-text volume, but an editor must still choose among the various texts for the cleanest, the best integrated, and the most representative of the author's wishes—if and when such wishes might be guessed at. Also, five songs from the masque, with the lyrics written in between the musical clefs, exist in two different versions, one of them most often called the Lawes Manuscript because it is in the handwriting of Henry Lawes (British Library Additional Manuscript 53723) and the other a scribal copy of the same songs preserved as British Library Additional Manuscript 11,518. The music manuscripts are valuable mostly because they preserve the only bits of music we have for the performance; hence they are still used as the source of music played and sung for any performance, though "there are a number of musical differences between the two manuscripts" (Shawcross, *John Milton* 631), and there are several verbal variants that might be used in discussing the relations between words and music (Willetts).

THE TRINITY COLLEGE MANUSCRIPT

The Trinity College Manuscript, called that because it was given to Trinity College, Cambridge, after Milton's death, contains a late draft of Milton's manuscript of what is there called *A Maske 1634*. It is only a working draft, mostly in Milton's hand, but it might have been consulted when the 1645 text was set (Sprott 13). To Sprott, the inconclusive readings of the manuscript suggest "that it was not long, if ever, intended as a fair copy"; instead, it "served Milton early and late as a working copy for private reference" (4). Sprott traces the uses of pens with different nibs through about fifteen stages of revision, at least one in a hand probably not Milton's and perhaps that of an amanuensis working on the manuscript in connection with the edition of Milton's poems published in 1673 (Sprott 13). The Trinity Manuscript version of the masque should be studied in detail because it shows Milton in the process of composition and because it demonstrates his sometimes inconsistent practices of spelling, punctuation, capitalization, and emphasis. Some of the spelling preferences from the Trinity Manuscript, such as "vertue" as opposed to "virtue," may come through in one or another of the printed texts. The manuscript also shows in its cancelations words or phrases that Milton deleted

or reworked. Thus it reveals changes based on poetic taste and judgment.

Evidently Milton thought the Younger Brother had gone too far when he at first described his sister as being like "forsaken Proserpine / when the big ["rowling" was at one point substituted for "wallowing"] wallowing flakes of pitchie clowds / & darknesse wound her in" (lines originally following 373 in printed versions). And the Elder Brother was about to have an encounter with "the shaggiest ruffian / that lurks by hedge or lane of this dead circuit" (lines originally to follow 428 in printed versions), but that shaggy ruffian was cut before the text reached print. Comus was meant to say "this is your morall stuff the very tilted lees / & setlings of a melancholy blood" in one canceled phrase in the Trinity Manuscript, when, in the printed version, he says, much more gracefully, "This is meere morall babble, and direct / Against the canon laws of our foundation" (1637, 841–42). The curious canceled phrase "tilted lees" has already been the subject of one article which discusses it in terms of bodily fluids (Sokol).

Agari speculates on the meaning of some of Milton's orthographical practices, and C. S. Lewis, Diekhoff, Shawcross, Brown, and Creaser have all addressed the issues of the changes between manuscript versions or between manuscripts and printed texts. I have taken an unusual liberty for an editor in reproducing passages from the Trinity Manuscript or Bridgewater Manuscript in my notes, when there are significant variations or omissions from the printed texts.

Cedric Brown has discussed the implications of the Bridgewater Manuscript, concluding that "what disappeared in Bridgewater were passages construed by some careful censor as *uncomplimentary* or indecorous" (*John Milton's* 175). If he is correct, the text of that manuscript is not authoritative and "Neither [its] cuts nor variants should . . . be assumed to carry the weight of Milton's decision" (175). Brown sees the additions to the 1637 text as part of "a decision to exploit the new functions of the text as 'poem' from author to reader" (177).

William B. Hunter has attempted to reconstruct a performance version, or what he calls "A Tentative Promptbook for *Comus*," as an appendix to his *Milton's Comus: Family Piece* (61–94). He argues that the Bridgewater Manuscript is closer to performance than any other text and that the 1645 text is furthest from the performance version. The 1645 text, Hunter believes, was "offered . . . as poetry to its readers rather than as drama; and so it has for the most part remained" (61). Hunter would presumably not agree with Brown that a censor has intervened in the Bridgewater Manuscript. Neither would Shawcross. Shawcross summarizes his "general conclusion" after years of

[margin note, handwritten:] Some differences in wording + printed draft

studying the text: "the problem is that the TM is a text that keeps getting changed. [It] was transcribed before or from a text before the BMS was written down; . . . the TM was then altered and the BMS was then written down; and . . . the TM continued to be altered." Also, "there were changes made in the BMS which are not reflected in the TM (largely in the beginning/ending, and in the [stage] directions)" (letter of August 23, 1992). I agree with that conclusion.

1637

The text of *1637* may be closest to the author's intentions as of that date, though the Latin epigraph on the title page and the anonymity of the volume (Milton's name was not on the title page) might be interpreted as a silent disclaimer. The arrangement of information on the title page and Lawes's letter also indicate a closer attachment between the masque and the Bridgewater family than Milton might have wanted to emphasize in 1645, when Wotton's praise seems to be displayed as prominently as the patronage of the Earl of Bridgewater. There is much less flattery of the Earl's family in the front matter of the masque in *1645* than there was in *1637*. The movement from the two manuscript versions through the first two printed versions, in other words, is from "aristocratic entertainment" to intellectual achievement, the masque as an occasional dramatic piece and the masque as a poetic achievement on its own.

Brown, McGuire, Wilding, and Marcus may all be correct in assuming that a reformist or radical spirit active in the masque becomes more visible in the printed versions than in the manuscripts. The printed page also yields clues in its presentation of Milton himself (Hale) or in its encoded typography and orthography (see Lennard 52–83), as to what Milton meant.

1645

Like Shawcross, I have chosen to use *1645* as my copy-text, with a close eye to the Trinity Manuscript for significant variants or more extensive stage directions, and to the 1637 text for accidentals, specifically spelling and punctuation. I am assuming throughout that Milton took more care and responsibility for the printing of the masque in the year 1645 than he did when Lawes had it printed in 1637. Though *1645* was set from *1637*, Diekhoff concludes that "whoever did it must have made his corrections by means of constant reference back to the Trinity manuscript" (*A Maske* 274). My assumptions about the text of the masque are largely in agreement with those of Philip Gaskell; as Gaskell suggests, "The best answer [to the problem of presenting the textual apparatus to a non-specialist reader] may be

to record the isolated Trinity Manuscript variants and the variants in the other printed texts in footnotes—they do not add up to very many altogether—but to give transcripts in an appendix of those passages in Trinity Manuscript where the variation is great" (60). I part company with Gaskell in his choice of 1637 as copy-text because I believe along with John Hale that the 1645 *Poems* is a self-conscious volume in which Milton took pains to preserve his work, and arrange it, in a coherent and carefully supervised form.

As the reader of this introduction can see, there is no consensus of opinion on how to arrive at the best text of the masque. Sprott does not reproduce the 1645 text, perhaps because it would not fit even his wide pages, and he reconstructs what he calls "a hypothetical fair copy" of the masque, one which has not been used as the model for any edition that I know of. Shawcross chooses *1645* but Gaskell selects *1637*; Hunter prefers a composite acting version; and Diekhoff transcribes the Bridgewater Manuscript in order to help scholars compare the manuscript text throughout, by means of his notes, to *1645*. John Creaser prefers *1673* as representing Milton's last wishes for the text, but Creaser, unlike Shawcross or myself, prefers a modernized text. John Carey imposes modern spelling, most of the time, on Milton's words, but he retains most of the punctuation of *1673*. Shawcross imposes what he believes to be Miltonic spellings current in 1645 on the text of *1645*. To this jumble I will add what I hope will be a faithful copy of the text of the 1645 *Poems*, disturbed only by changes referred to in the notes. Having become wary of the different spelling systems imposed over the years by Darbishire, Hughes, and Shawcross, I have come to the conclusion that *1645*, checked against all other manuscripts and early printed versions, should be followed closely in all details of orthography and punctuation.

For the sake of convenience, in the notes I will call the Trinity Manuscript by its full name, or just "the manuscript," but I will call the Bridgewater Manuscript "BMS."

Works Cited

(Editions or books containing editions or line-by-line commentary on *Comus* are identified with an asterisk.)

Adams, Robert M. "Reading *Comus*." *Milton & the Modern Critics.* Ithaca, NY: Cornell UP, 1955. 1–34.

Agari, Mashahiko. "A Note on Milton's Trinity MS." *Modern Language Notes* 22 (1984): 23–26.

Arthos, John. "Milton, Ficino, and the *Charmides*." *Studies in the Renaissance* 6 (1959): 261–74.

------. *"On* A Mask Presented at Ludlow-Castle*" by John Milton.* University of Michigan Contributions in Modern Philology, No. 20. Ann Arbor: U of Michigan P, 1954.

Baker, Stewart A. "Eros and the Three Shepherds of *Comus*." *Rice University Studies* 61 (1975): 13–26.

Banks, Theodore Howard. *Milton's Imagery.* New York: Columbia UP, 1950.

Barber. C. L. *"A Mask Presented at Ludlow Castle*: The Masque as a Masque." *The Lyric and Dramatic Milton.* Ed. Joseph H. Summers. Selected Papers from the English Institute. New York: Columbia UP, 1965. 35–63.

Basile, Mary Elizabeth. "The Music of *A Maske.*" *Milton Quarterly* 27 (1993): 85–98.

Bergeron, David M. *Twentieth-Century Criticism of English Masques, Pageants, and Entertainments, 1558–1642.* Checklists in the Humanities and Education. San Antonio, TX: Trinity UP, 1972.

Berkowitz, M. S. "An Earl's Michaelmas in Wales: Some Thoughts on the Original Presentation of *Comus.*" *Milton Quarterly* 13 (1979): 122–25.

Berry, Philippa. *Of Chastity and Power: Elizabethan Literature and the Unmarried Queen.* New York: Routledge, 1989.

*Blondel, Jacques. *Le Comus de John Milton: Masque Neptunien.* Seconde édition revue et complétée. Paris: Presses Universitaires de France, 1964.

Breasted, Barbara. "Another Bewitching of Lady Alice Egerton, the Lady of *Comus.*" *N&Q* 17 (1970): 411–12.

------. "*Comus* and the Castlehaven Scandal." *Milton Studies* 3 (1971): 201–24.

Bredbeck, Gregory W. *Sodomy and Interpretation: Marlowe to Milton.* Ithaca, NY: Cornell UP, 1991.

Brown, Cedric C. "The Chirk Castle Entertainment of 1634." *Milton Quarterly* 11 (1977): 76–86.

----. *John Milton's Aristocratic Entertainments.* Cambridge: Cambridge UP, 1985.

Burnett, Archie. *Milton's Style: The Shorter Poems,* Paradise Regained, *and* Samson Agonistes. London: Longman, 1981.

Calhoun, Thomas O. "On John Milton's *A Mask at Ludlow.*" *Milton Studies* 6 (1974): 165–79.

*Campbell, Gordon, ed. *John Milton. Complete English Poems, Of Education, Areopagitica.* 4th ed. London: Dent, 1990.

------. "Milton and the Lives of the Ancients." *Journal of the Warburg and Courtauld Institutes* 47 (1984): 234–38.

*Carey, John, ed. *John Milton. Complete Shorter Poems.* New York: Longman, 1981. 2nd ed., 1997.

Chatfield, Hale. "An Additional Look at the Meaning of *Comus.*" *Milton Quarterly* 11 (1977): 86–89.

Coiro, Ann Baynes. "Milton and Class Identity: The Publication of

Areopagitica and the 1645 *Poems.*" *Journal of Medieval and Renaissance Studies* 22 (1992): 261–89.

Corns, Thomas. *Milton's Language.* London: Blackwell, 1990.

Creaser, John. "Milton's *Comus*: The Irrelevance of the Castlehaven Scandal." *Notes and Queries* 31 (1984): 307–17.

------. "'The present aid of this occasion': The Setting of *Comus.*" *The Court Masque.* Ed. David Lindley. Manchester: Manchester UP, 1984. 111–34.

Davies, Stevie. *Milton.* New York: St. Martin's, 1991.

Demaray, John G. *Milton and the Masque Tradition: The Early Poems,* Arcades, *and* Comus. Cambridge, MA: Harvard UP, 1968.

------. "The Temple of the Mind: Cosmic Iconography in Milton's *A Mask.*" Comus: *Contexts.* Ed. Flannagan. 59–76.

*Diekhoff, John S., ed. A Maske at Ludlow: *Essays on Milton's* Comus. Cleveland, OH: P of Case Western Reserve U, 1968. 251–75.

DiSalvo, Jacqueline. "Fear of Flying: Milton on the Boundaries between Witchcraft and Inspiration." *English Literary Renaissance* 18 (1988): 114–37.

------. "The Text of *Comus,* 1634 to 1645." *PMLA* 52 (1937): 705–27.

Donker, Marjorie, and George M. Muldrow. *Dictionary of Literary-Rhetorical Conventions of the English Renaissance.* Westport, CT: Greenwood, 1982.

Drayton, Michael. *The Poly-Olbion: A Chorographicall Description of Great Britain.* London, 1622. Facsimile ed. New York: Burt Franklin, 1970.

*Egerton, Lady Alix, ed. *Milton's* Comus, *Being the Bridgewater Manuscript with Notes and a Short Family Memory.* London: Dent, 1910.

Evans, Willa McClung. *Henry Lawes, Musician and Friend of Poets.* New York: MLA, 1941.

Fish, Stanley E. "Problem Solving in *Comus.*" *Illustrious Evidence.* Ed. Earl Miner. Berkeley: U of California P, 1975.

Flannagan, Roy "*Comus.*" *The Cambridge Companion to Milton.* Ed. Dennis Danielson. Cambridge: Cambridge UP, 1989. 21–34.

Flannagan, Roy, ed. Comus: *Contexts.* Special issue of *Milton Quarterly* 21 (1987).

------. "Editing Milton's Masque." *TEXT* 9 (1996): 234–59.

Flosdorf, James W. "'Gums of Glutinous Heat': A Query." *Milton Quarterly* 7 (1973): 4–5.

*Foss, Hubert J., ed. *The Mask of Comus: The Poem, Originally Called* A Mask Presented at Ludlow Castle, 1634, &c., *Edited by E. H. Visiak. The Airs of the Five Songs Reprinted from the Composer's Autograph Manuscript.* New York: Nonesuch, 1937.

Gaskell, Phillip. *From Writer to Reader: Studies in Editorial Method.* Oxford: Clarendon, 1978.

Ginzburg, Carlo. *The Night Battles: Witchcraft and Agrarian Cults in the*

Sixteenth and Seventeenth Centuries. Trans. John and Anne Tedeschi. Baltimore, MD: Johns Hopkins UP, 1992.

Hale, John K. "Milton's Self-Presentation in *Poems . . . 1645.*" *Milton Quarterly* 25 (1991): 37–48.

Halpern, Richard. "Puritanism and Maenadism in *A Masque.*" *Rewriting the Renaissance: The Discourses of Sexual Difference in Early Modern Europe.* Ed. Margaret W. Ferguson, Maureen Quilligan, and Nancy J. Vickers. Chicago, IL: U of Chicago P, 1986. 88–105.

Harding, Davis P. *The Club of Hercules: Studies in the Classical Background of* Paradise Lost. Urbana: U of Illinois P, 1962.

Harper, John. "'One equal music': The Music of Milton's Youth." *Milton Quarterly* 31 (1997): 1–10.

Hesiod. *The Homeric Hymns and Homerica.* Trans. Hugh G. Evelyn-White. Cambridge, MA: Harvard UP, 1970.

Hill, Christopher. *Milton and the English Revolution.* New York: Viking, 1978.

Himy, Armand. "De Comus à Satan." *John Milton: Pensée, Mythe et Structure dan le* Paradis Perdu. Villeneuve d'Ascq, Fr.: Publications de l'Université de Lille III, 1977. 67–85.

Hunter, William B. "The Liturgical Context of *Comus.*" *English Language Notes* 10 (1972): 11–15.

——. *Milton's* Comus: *Family Piece.* Troy, NY: Whitston, 1983.

Jayne, Sears. "The Subject of Milton's Ludlow Mask." *PMLA* 74 (1959): 533–43. Revised version in *Milton: Modern Essays in Criticism.* Ed. Arthur E. Barker. Oxford: Oxford UP, 1965. 88–111.

Kerrigan, William. *The Sacred Complex: On the Psychogenesis of* Paradise Lost. Cambridge, MA: Harvard UP, 1983.

Kirkconnell, G. Watson. *Awake the Courteous Echo: The Themes and Prosody of* Comus, Lycidas *and* Paradise Regained *in World Literature with Translations of the Major Analogues.* Toronto: U of Toronto P, 1973.

Kogan, Stephen. *The Hieroglyphic King: Wisdom and Idolatry in Seventeenth-Century Masque.* Cranbury, NJ: Associated University Presses, 1986.

Le Comte, Edward. *Milton and Sex.* New York: Columbia UP, 1978.

——. *A Milton Dictionary.* New York: Philosophical Library, 1961.

Leishman, J. B. *Milton's Minor Poems.* Pittsburgh, PA: Duquesne UP, 1989.

Lennard, John. *But I Digress: The Exploitation of Parentheses in English Printed Verse.* Oxford: Clarendon, 1991.

Leonard, John. "Saying 'No' to Freud: Milton's *A Mask* and Sexual Assault." *Milton Quarterly* 25 (1991): 129–40.

Lewis, C. S. *Rehabilitations and Other Essays.* New York: Oxford UP, 1939.

Lieb, Michael. *Milton and the Culture of Violence.* Ithaca, NY: Cornell UP, 1994.

*Loh, Beiyei, ed. *A Student's Edition of Milton.* 2 vols. Beijing: Commercial Press, 1990.

MacDonald, Michael. *Mystical Bedlam: Madness, Anxiety, and Healing in Seventeenth-Century England.* New York: Cambridge UP, 1981.

McGuire, Maryann Cale. *Milton's Puritan Masque.* Athens: U of Georgia P, 1983.

McHenry, James Patrick. *A Milton Herbal.* Special issue of *Milton Quarterly* 25 (1991).

Marcus, Leah Sinanoglou. "The Milieu of Milton's *Comus*: Judicial Reform at Ludlow and the Problem of Sexual Assault." *Criticism* 25 (1983): 293–327.

——. "Milton's Anti-Laudian Masque." *The Politics of Mirth: Jonson, Herrick, Milton, Marvell, and the Defense of Old Holiday Pastimes.* Chicago, IL: U of Chicago P, 1986. 169–212.

Martz, Louis L. "The Music of *Comus.*" *Illustrious Evidence: Approaches to English Literature of the Early Seventeenth Century.* Ed. Earl Miner. Berkeley: U of California P, 1975. 93–113.

Miller, William S. *The Mythology of Milton's* Comus. New York: Garland, 1988.

Mish, Charles C. "*Comus* and Bryce Blair's *Vision of Theodorus Verax.*" *Milton Newsletter* 1 (1967): 39–40.

Mortimer, Anthony. "*Comus* and Michaelmas." *English Studies* 65 (1984): 111–19.

Moseley, C. W. R. D. *The Poetic Birth: Milton's* Poems *of 1645.* Aldershot, Eng.: Scolar, 1991.

Mundhenk, Rosemary Karmelich. "Dark Scandal and the Sun-Clad Power of Chastity: The Historical Milieu of Milton's *Comus.*" *Studies in English Literature, 1500–1900* 15 (1975): 141–52.

Norbrook, David. "The Politics of Milton's Early Poetry." *Poetry and Politics in the English Renaissance.* Boston, MA: Routledge, 1984. 235–85; 327–35.

Orgel, Stephen. *The Jonsonian Masque.* Cambridge, MA: Harvard UP, 1965.

*——, and Jonathan Goldberg, eds. *John Milton.* Oxford: Oxford UP, 1990.

——, and Roy Strong. *Inigo Jones: The Theatre of the Stuart Court.* 2 vols. Berkeley: U of California P, 1973.

Otten, Charlotte. "Milton's Haemony." *English Literary Renaissance (ELR)* 5 (1975): 81–95.

O'Valle, Violet. "Milton's *Comus* and Welsh Oral Tradition." *Milton Studies* 18 (1983): 25–44.

Parker, William Riley. *Milton: A Biography.* Oxford: Clarendon, 1968. Rev. ed., Gordon Campbell, ed. Oxford: Clarendon, 1997.

Partridge, A. C. *The Language of Renaissance Poetry: Spenser, Shakespeare, Donne, Milton.* London: Deutsch, 1971.

Patterson, Annabel. "'L'Allegro,' 'Il Penseroso' and *Comus*: The Logic of Recombination." *Milton Quarterly* 9 (1975): 75–79.

Peacock, John. *The Stage Designs of Inigo Jones: The European Context.* Cambridge: Cambridge UP, 1996.

Revard, Stella P. *Milton and the Tangles of Neaera's Hair.* Columbia: U of Missouri P, 1997.

Samuel, Irene. *Plato and Milton.* Ithaca, NY: Cornell UP, 1947.

Sandys, George. *Ovid's* Metamorphosis *Englished, Mythologized, and Represented in Figures by George Sandys.* Ed. Karl K. Hulley and Stanley T. Vandersall. Lincoln: U of Nebraska P, 1970.

Saslow, James M. *The Medici Wedding of 1589: Florentine Festival as Theatrum Mundi.* New Haven, CT: Yale UP, 1996.

Shawcross, John T. "Certain Relationships of the Manuscripts of 'Comus.'" *Papers of the Bibliographical Society of America* 54 (1960): 38–56.

——. "Henry Lawes's Setting of Songs for Milton's 'Comus.'" *Journal of the Rutgers University Library* 28 (1964): 22–28.

——. *John Milton: The Self and the World.* Lexington: UP of Kentucky, 1993.

——. "Two Comments." *Milton Quarterly* 7 (1973): 97–98.

Sokol, B. J. "'Tilted Lees,' Dragons, *Haemony*, Menarche, Spirit, and Matter in *Comus.*" *Review of English Studies* 41 (1990): 309–24.

*Sprott, S. E., ed. *John Milton: "A Maske," the Earlier Versions.* Toronto: U of Toronto P, 1973.

Stevens, David H. "The Bridgewater Manuscript of *Comus.*" *Milton Papers.* Chicago, IL: U of Chicago P, 1927. 14–20.

Stow, John. *The Survey of London.* Ed. H. B. Wheatley. London: Dent, 1987.

Swaim, Kathleen M. "Allegorical Poetry in Milton's Ludlow Mask." *Milton Studies* 16 (1982): 167–99.

Sylvester, Josuah, trans. *The Divine Weeks and Works of Guillaume de Saluste, Sieur du Bartas.* Ed. Susan Snyder. 2 vols. Oxford: Clarendon, 1979.

Taaffe, James G. "Michaelmas, the 'Lawless Hour,' and the Occasion of Milton's *Comus.*" *English Language Notes* 6 (1969): 257–62.

*Todd, Henry John. See *Paradise Lost* bibliography.

Treip, Mindele Anne. *Allegorical Poetics and the Epic: The Renaissance Tradition to* Paradise Lost. Lexington: U of Kentucky P, 1994.

——. *Comus* as Progress." *Milton Quarterly* 20 (1986): 1–13.

Turner, James Grantham. *One Flesh: Paradisal Marriage and Sexual Relations in the Age of Milton.* Oxford: Clarendon, 1987.

Tuve, Rosemond. *Images and Themes in Five Poems by Milton.* Cambridge, MA: Harvard UP, 1957.

*Warton, Joseph. See *Paradise Lost* bibliography.

Wentersdorf, Karl P. "The 'Rout of Monsters' in *Comus.*" *Milton Quarterly* 12 (1978): 119–25.

Wilding, Michael. "Milton's 'A Masque Presented at Ludlow Castle, 1634': Theater and Politics on the Border." Comus: *Contexts.* Ed. Flannagan. 35–51.

Wilkenfeld, Roger B. "A Mask." In *A Milton Encyclopedia.* Ed. William B. Hunter. Lewisburg, PA: Bucknell UP, 1978–83.

Willetts, Pamela J. *The Henry Lawes Manuscript.* London: British Museum, 1969.

Woodhouse, A. S. P. "The Argument of Milton's *Comus.*" *University of Toronto Quarterly* 11 (1941): 46–71. Rpt. *The Heavenly Muse: A Preface to Milton.* Ed. Hugh MacCallum. Toronto: U of Toronto P, 1972. 55–98.

*Woodhouse, A. S. P., and Douglas Bush, eds. *A Variorum Commentary on The Poems of John Milton. Volume Two (Part Three). The Minor English Poems.* New York: Columbia UP, 1972.

A
MASK
Of the same
AUTHOR
PRESENTED
At *LUDLOW*-Castle,
1634.
Before
The Earl of BRIDGEWATER
Then President of WALES.

Anno Dom. 1645.[1]

To the Right Honourable,
JOHN Lord Vicount BRACLY,[2]
Son and Heir apparent to the Earl
of *Bridgewater, &c.*

MY LORD,

This Poem, *which receiv'd its first occasion of Birth from your Self, and others of your Noble Family, and much honour from your own Person in the performance, now returns again to make a finall Dedication of it self to you. Although not openly acknowledg'd by the Author, yet it is a legitimate off-spring, so lovely, and so much desired, that the often Copying of it hath tir'd my Pen to give my severall friends satisfaction,[3] and brought me to a necessity of producing it to the publike view; and now to offer it up in all rightfull devotion to those fair Hopes, and rare Endowments of your much-promising Youth, which give a full assurance, to all that know you, of a future excellence. Live sweet Lord to be the honour of your Name, and receive this as your own, from the hands of him, who hath by many favours been long oblig'd to your most honour'd Parents, and as in this representation your attendant* Thyrsis, *so now in all reall expression*

Your faithfull, and most

humble Servant

H. LAWES.[4]

---

[1] The title page of the 1637 edition had read, after "1634," *On Michaelmasse night, before the* RIGHT HONOURABLE, JOHN *Earle of Bridgewater, Vicount* BRACKLY, *Lord Præsident of* WALES, And one of His MAIESTIES most honorable Privie Counsell." To that was added the Latin epigraph, taken from Vergil's Second Eclogue 58–59, "*Eheu quid volui misero mihi! floribus austrum / Perditus,*" which can be translated "Alas, what I have wished of my miserable self! I have allowed the south wind to ruin my flowers." The image is one of the desecration of art when it is exposed to the attention of the masses. There may be a subtext in the use of the quotation from the eclogue, since Le Comte correctly identifies the subject of that eclogue as "homosexual" (*Milton and Sex* 9), and Bredbeck adds to that "the vernacular eroticisms associated with Virgil's second eclogue interface provocatively with the actual social occasion of the mask" and with the responsibilities of the Earl in the rape trial of Margery Evans's attackers and the scandal surrounding his family name (212). Milton's name had not appeared on the title page of the 1637 edition.

[2] The second Earl of Bridgewater, Vicount Brackley and the Elder Brother in 1634, according to John Diekhoff, wrote in to the Bridgewater Manuscript "author Jo. Milton" (Diekhoff, *A Maske* 5). The same Earl, fifteen years after the performance, wrote his later opinion of Milton on the title page of his copy of Milton's *Defensio pro Populo Anglicano*: "Liber igne, Author furca, dignissimi," which might be translated, "A book most worthy to be burned, its author hanged" (Diekhoff 5n; Brown 170, 204n).

[3] Lawes may or may not have copied the manuscript more than once, but no copy exists in his hand.

[4] This "Epistle Dedicatorie," as it is called in the 1637 edition, is flattery written by a family retainer directed toward the heir-apparent of the Duke of Bridgewater. Parker calls it "a graceful dedication by Lawes to John Egerton" (1: 156).

The Copy of a Letter Writt'n

By Sir HENRY WOOTTON,[5]
To the Author, upon the
following Poem.

From the Colledge, this 13. of April, 1638.

SIR,

IT was a special favour, when you lately bestowed upon me here, the first taste of your acquaintance, though no longer then to make me know that I wanted more time to value it, and to enjoy it rightly; and in truth, if I could then have imagined your farther stay in these parts, which I understood afterwards by Mr. *H.*,[6] I would have been bold in our vulgar phrase to mend my draught[7] (for you left me with an extreme thirst) and to have begged your conversation again, joyntly with your said learned Friend, at a poor[8] meal or two, that we might have banded together som good Authors of the antient time: Among which, I observed you to have been familiar.

Since your going, you have charg'd me with new Obligations, both for a very kinde Letter from you dated the sixth of this Month, and for a dainty peece of entertainment which came therwith. Wherin I should much commend the Tragical part,[9] if the Lyrical did not ravish me with a certain Dorique delicacy[10] in your Songs and Odes, wherunto I must plainly confess to have seen yet nothing parallel in our Language: *Ipsa mollities.*[11] But I must not omit to tell you, that I now onely owe you thanks for intimating unto me (how modestly soever) the true Artificer.[12] For the work it self, I had view'd som good while before, with singular delight, having receiv'd it from our common Friend Mr. *R.*[13] in the very close of the late *R*'s Poems,[14] Printed at *Oxford*, wherunto it was added (as I now suppose) that the Accessory might help out the Principal, according to the Art of *Stationers*,[15] and to leave the Reader *Con la bocca dolce.*[16]

Now Sir, concerning your travels, wherin I may chalenge a little more priviledge of Discours with you; I suppose you will not blanch[17] *Paris* in your way; therfore I have been bold to trouble you with a few lines to Mr. *M. B.*[18] whom you shall easily find attending the young Lord *S.*[19] as his Governour, and you may surely receive from him good directions for the shaping of your farther journey into *Italy*, where he did reside by my choice som time for the King, after my own recess[20] from *Venice*.

---

[5]Sir Henry Wotton (1568–1639) was ambassador to various continental European countries or cities, most notably Venice, over a career of public service spanning twenty years. In 1624 he returned to England to become Provost of Eton College, which was about five miles from the Milton home at Horton in Buckinghamshire. On April 6, 1638, Milton wrote to Wotton, enclosing a copy of *Comus* and mentioning his planned trip to the Continent. Wotton had read the work, but anonymously; thus he expresses delight to learn the identity of the author. The letter that Milton perhaps presumptuously published is Wotton's generous reply to Milton. It is valuable as the very first, and one of the most perceptive, criticisms of the masque.
[6]Usually identified as John Hales, a fellow of Eton College described by Wotton as his "walking library" (Parker 147; Yale 1: 340).
[7]I.e., "Amend my draft," or "quench my thirst with a draft of something liquid." Wotton pictures himself as thirsting after Milton's conversation.
[8]A modest or unpretentious meal among friends.
[9]Wotton seems to be speaking of a tragic style (not subject matter) in Milton's masque. The term "tragical" as it was used as early as 1548 could mean "having the elevated or dignified style of tragedy" (*OED* 2); the adjective was used of masque as well as tragic style.
[10]The word Doric seems to mean "rustic" or "pastoral" here, as it does in "Lycidas" 189, when the "uncouth Swain" is pictured as "With eager thought warbling his *Dorick* lay." Wotton's critical terms seem to be precise rather than gratuitous. The word could mean "martial" or "severe," as Milton uses it in the phrase "grave and *Dorick*" in *Areopagitica* (Yale 2: 523). The poetic term is derived from the Dorian dialect of ancient Greece, from the region of Doris in central Greece near Mt. Parnassus, and associated with the pastoral poetry of Theocritus, Bion, and Moschus.
[11]"A thing uniquely gentle [or delicate] in itself."
[12]"The actual author." Apparently Wotton had read the masque, either in manuscript or in a copy of the 1637 edition given him earlier by Mr. R., without realizing that Milton was the author.
[13]Someone not yet identified. The use of initials would indicate that Wotton's letter is private correspondence, and that, when it was to be published in the 1645 *Poems*, the letter should remove the names of anyone mentioned by name in it, to protect their privacy.
[14]Thomas Randolph's *Poems*, published posthumously in Oxford in 1638. Randolph (1605–35) had been at Trinity College, Cambridge, and had been a boisterous friend of Ben Jonson, and a fellow playwright.
[15]Wotton is alluding to the practice of printers or stationers (paper- or booksellers) of binding a work of less value with one of more value in order to sell more copies of the former.
[16]"With a sweet taste in his mouth."
[17]To "pass without notice, miss, omit" (*OED* 2, citing this passage).
[18]Michael Branthwaite, who had served under Wotton when he was English Ambassador to Venice.
[19]James Scudamore (1624–68), son of the present English ambassador to Paris, Viscount John Scudamore (1601–71).
[20]Departure from the ambassadorship.

I should think that your best Line will be thorow the whole length of *France* to *Marseilles*, and thence by Sea to *Genoa*, whence the passage into *Tuscany* is as Diurnal as a *Gravesend* Barge:[21] I hasten as you do to *Florence*, or *Siena*, the rather to tell you a short story from the interest you have given me in your safety.

At *Siena* I was tabled in the House of one *Alberto Scipioni* an old *Roman* Courtier in dangerous times, having bin Steward to the *Duca di Pagliano*, who with all his Family were strangled, save this onely man that escap'd by foresight of the Tempest: With him I had often much chat of those affairs; Into which he took pleasure to look back from his Native Harbour; and at my departure toward *Rome* (which had been the center of his experience) I had wonn confidence enough to beg his advice, how I might carry my self securely there, without offence of others, or of mine own conscience. *Signor Arrigo mio* (sayes he) *I pensieri stretti, & il viso sciolto*[22] will go safely over the whole World: Of which *Delphian* Oracle (for so I have found it) your judgement doth need no commentary; and therfore (Sir) I will commit you with it to the best of all securities, Gods dear love, remaining

> Your Friend as much at command
> as any of longer date
> *Henry Wootton.*

Postscript.

S IR, *I have expresly sent this my Foot-boy to prevent your departure without som acknowledgement from me of the receipt of your obliging Letter, having my self through som busines, I know not how, neglected the ordinary conveyance. In any part where I shall understand you fixed, I shall be glad, and diligent to entertain you with Home-Novelties;[23] even for som fomentation of our friendship, too soon interrupted in the Cradle.*

The Persons.[24]

The attendant Spirit afterwards in
  the habit° of *Thyrsis*.   DRESS
Comus with his crew.
The Lady.
I. Brother.
2. Brother.
Sabrina the Nymph.

The cheif persons which presented,[25]
  were

The Lord *Bracly*,
Mr. *Thomas Egerton* his Brother,
The Lady *Alice Egerton*.

---

[21]Gravesend barges made regular trips from Gravesend in Kent to London (Stow 195). Thus the trip that Wotton is discussing, from Genoa to Livorno, is scheduled daily and is as regular as clockwork.

[22]Translated by Wotton as "My Signior Harry, your thoughts close, and your countenance loose" (Logan Pearsall Smith, *The Life and Letters of Sir Henry Wotton* [Oxford: Oxford UP, 1907]: 364).

[23]Presumably letters with the news of events at home.

[24]Proper names in the text are usually in italics, as are stage directions. Speech attributes vary slightly, as with *Comus* and *Com.* The indenting of the text in *1645* is followed as closely as possible.

[25]They "presented" in the sense that they came before an aristocratic audience, as in *OED* 1.a: "To bring or place (a person) before, into the presence of, or under the notice of, another; to introduce, esp. formally or ceremoniously; spec. to introduce at court, or before a sovereign or other superior." The persons who played Sabrina and Comus, apparently common citizens of Ludlow or professional actors, are not thought worthy enough to name in this list. Neither is the author or Henry Lawes, despite his prominence as a composer.

A
MASK

Presented
At Ludlow-Castle,
1634. *&c.*

The first Scene discovers[26] a wilde Wood.

The attendant Spirit descends or enters.[27]

Before the starry threshold of *Joves* Court[28]
My mansion° is, where those immortal shapes   DWELLING
Of bright aereal Spirits live insphear'd[29]
In Regions milde of calm and serene° Ayr,   CLEAR

---

[26]"either "shows" or "is uncovered to reveal." The *OED* gives as one definition "To afford a view of, to show," citing *Paradise Lost* 1.64: "From those flames / No light, but rather darkness visible / Serv'd only to discover sights of woe." The question of staging at this point is whether there should be or was a curtain that was pulled aside to reveal the first set.

[27]The stage direction at least indicates the possibility of stage machinery that would allow Henry Lawes, playing the Attendant Spirit or Thyrsis, to be lowered from above to stage level (see Demaray 105). If the character had descended from the clouds, the entrance would have indicated his semidivine nature. Stage directions in the Trinity Manuscript read "the first scene discovers a wild wood." and "A Guardian spirit, or Dæmon."

[28] "*Jove*" can be safely taken here to mean the Christian God, since the Spirit lives most probably in the eighth sphere, which is "starry" because it is the sphere of the fixed stars in the Ptolemaic arrangement of the universe. Since the Attendant Spirit is "aereal," he is beneath the rank of angels, who would be composed of ether and therefore be "ethereal" (as in *Paradise Lost* 1.45).

[29]In "Il Penseroso" 88, the spirit of Plato was said to "unsphear," or bring itself down to Earth from its fixed heavenly position, for the poet's benefit.

Above[30] the smoak and stirr of this dim[31] spot,   5
Which men call Earth, and with low-thoughted care
Confin'd, and pester'd° in this pin-fold° here,   CROWDED   ANIMAL PEN
Strive to keep up a frail, and Feaverish being[32]
Unmindfull of the crown that Vertue[33] gives
After this mortal change, to her true Servants   10
Amongst the enthron'd gods on Sainted seats.[34]
Yet som there be that by due steps aspire
To lay their just hands on that Golden Key
That ope's the Palace of Eternity:
To such my errand° is, and but for such,   MISSION   15
I would not soil these pure Ambrosial weeds,°   ROBES
With the rank vapours of this Sin-worn mould.[35]
    But to my task.[36] *Neptune* besides[37] the sway°   GOVERNANCE
Of every salt Flood, and each ebbing Stream,
Took in by lot twixt high, and neather *Jove,*   20
Imperial rule of all the Sea-girt Iles[38]

---

[30]At this point the following passage has had a large X drawn through it, and it contains these revisions:

                                                          where the banks
        amidst the ~~gardens~~ Hesp[er]ian gardens, ~~on whose bancks~~
                        2   1
        ~~aeternall roses grow & hyacinth~~
        bedew'd wth nectar, & celestiall songs
                  *yeeld
        æternal roses grow, & hyacinth   ~~blow~~ *grow *~~blosme~~
        & fruits of golden rind, on whoſe faire tree
                                ever
        the scalie-harnest ~~waetchfull~~ dragons · keeps
           uninchanted
        his ~~never charmed~~ eye, & round the verge
        & sacred limits of this *~~happie~~ Isle ~~blissfull~~ *blisfull
        the jealous ocean that old river winds
        his farre-extended armes till wth steepe fall
        halfe his wast flood ye wide Atlantique fills
        & halfe the slow unfadom'd ~~poole of styx~~ Stygian poole   (wonder
        ~~I doubt me gentle mortalls these may seeme~~ but soft I was not sent to court yor
        ~~strange distances to heare & unknowne climes~~ wth distant worlds, & strange removed clim
        yet thence I come and oft frō thence behold

I have tried to represent the arrangement of the manuscript on the page as closely as possible, but the reader is encouraged to see the facsimile edition published by Scolar Press, *John Milton. Poems. Reproduced in Facsimile from the Manuscript in Trinity College, Cambridge. With a Transcript* (1972). In the 1972 edition of this facsimile, some errors in B. A. Wright's original transcription have been corrected. Sprott made a separate transcription in his edition, and his arrangement on the page allows comparison with his transcription of the Bridgewater Manuscript (BMS) and *1637.*
[31]In this line Milton in the Trinity Manuscript added an "a" by means of a caret to the word "smoke," to make it "smoake," and he struck through the word "narrow," removing it before "dim."
[32]Lines 7 and 8 were transposed in the manuscript, with a "2" and a "1" in the left margin to show what their order should be, and the line "beyond the written date of mortall change" was in between the two, and crossed through. Milton picked up the phrase "mortall change" two lines down.
[33]*OED* 1.a gives "virtue" as a "quality of persons": "The power or operative influence inherent in a supernatural or divine being." The word also has overtones of "manliness" (from the Latin *vir,* "man"), "fortitude," "magical efficacy," and "chastity," and, when it was emphasized by capitalization or italics, "Virtue" could signify an order of angels (West 51). Milton believed that "The heathen Philosophers thought that vertue was for its owne sake inestimable, and the greatest gaine of a teacher to make a soule vertuous," and he asked, "Was morall vertue so lovely, and so alluring, and heathen men so enamour'd of her, as to teach and study her with greatest neglect and contempt of worldly profit and advancement," comparing the pagan idea of moral virtue with Christian piety (*Areopagitica*; Yale 1: 719). The Yale editors note a reference to Xenophon, *Memorabilia* 21.2.6–8.
[34]Not the Olympian gods (though the analogy works well) but "saints" in the sense of "good human beings who have died and gone to heaven."
[35]The primal clay, or, less heroically, the earth out of which Earth was constructed. It would be "Sin-worn" after the Fall of humankind.
[36]Milton first wrote "but to my buisnesse now," then struck through "buisnesse now" and inserted "taske" by means of a caret.
[37]Milton first wrote "whose sway," and then substituted "besids the sway" in the manuscript.
[38]The line was first written "impial ~~the~~ rule ~~& title~~ of ~~each~~ sea-girt Isles," with "impial" outside the left margin and with a line under "p" to indicate it should be expanded, in this case, to "imperial."

That like to rich, and various gemms inlay[39]
The unadorned boosom of the Deep,
Which he to grace his tributary gods
By course commits to severall goverment,[40]   25
And gives them leave to wear their Saphire crowns,
And weild their little tridents, but this Ile
The greatest, and the best of all the main[41]
He quarters° to his blu-hair'd deities,[42]   DIVIDES INTO FOUR PARTS
And all this tract that fronts the falling Sun[43]   30
A noble Peer of mickle trust, and power
Has in his charge, with temper'd awe[44] to guide
An old, and haughty Nation proud in Arms:[45] — welch
Where his fair off-spring nurs't in Princely lore,[46]
Are coming to attend their Fathers state,[47]   35
And new-entrusted Scepter, but their way
Lies through the perplex't paths of this drear° Wood,   DREARY, FRIGHTENING
The nodding horror[48] of whose shady brows
Threats the forlorn and wandring Passinger.
But that by quick command from Soveran *Jove*   40
I was dispatcht for their defence, and guard;
And listen why, for I will tell ye now
What never yet was heard in Tale or Song[49]
From[50] old, or modern Bard in Hall, or Bowr.   45

    Bacchus[51] that first from out° the purple Grape,   OUT OF
Crush't the sweet poyson of mis-used Wine[52]

knows it can be healthy but abuse contradicts

---

[39]The phrase was first written "gemms inlay," then that phrase was replaced with "& various gems inlay" in the manuscript.

[40]Neptune, in other words, has, in order to confer status on the gods associated with rivers or tributaries feeding into the ocean, given the government of different islands to them.

[41]Milton wrote "his empire" first in the manuscript, then substituted "the maine." The word can be read as "mainland" or the entire territory of the island of England, Scotland, and Wales.

[42]Presumably they have blue hair because they are spirits of the water. In Jonson's *Masque of Blackness*, as Carey points out (29n), six Tritons are introduced with "their upper parts humane, save that their haires were blue, as partaking of the sea-colour." Jonson himself in a marginal note cites Ovid, *Metamorphoses* 1.333: "*caeruleum Tritona.*"

[43]That is, Wales and the Marches (English counties bordering Wales). The peer is the Earl of Bridgewater, and he has "mickle trust" in that he has great power invested in him. The word "*mickle*" is an archaism often used by Spenser.

[44]Power tempered by justice.

[45]The nation of the Welsh people, whose reputation for ferocity in war might be typified by Shakespeare's characterization of Owen Glendower (*1 Henry IV*} as a fierce, lawless, superstitious, overbearing warlord. That characterization owes much to seventeenth-century English popular prejudgement of the Welsh.

[46]The Bridgewater children, in other words, have been educated to be princes and princesses. Thus they are trained in the arts of singing, dancing, and reciting poetry.

[47]Probably "a sound, healthy, flourishing, prosperous condition" (*OED* 6a)—that of the Earl, her father—or "Costly and imposing display, such as befits persons of rank and wealth; splendour, magnificence (in manner of life, clothing, furniture, buildings, retinue, etc.)" (*OED* 17a).

[48]Probably intended to suggest that the wood is enchanted and symbolic, as in Tasso, *Jerusalem Delivered* 13.2: "From Godfrey's camp a grove a little way, / Amid the valleys deep, grows out of sight, / Thick with old trees, whose horrid arms display / An ugly shade, like everlasting night" (trans. Edward Fairfax, ed. John Charles Nelson [NY: Capricorn, n.d. [1968?]).

[49]A verbal formula common in Renaissance epic poetry, as in Harington's translation of Ariosto, *Orlando Furioso* 1.2: "I will no less Orlando's act declare, / A tale in prose ne verse yet sung or said, / Who fell bestraught with love, a hap most rare / To one that erst was counted wise and staid" (*Ariosto's Orlando Furioso. Selections from the Translation of Sir John Harington*, ed. Rudolf Gottfried [Bloomington: Indiana UP, 1963]). Milton will re-employ the formula, following Ariosto and Harington more closely, in *Paradise Lost* 1.16.

[50]"By" was struck through and replaced by "from" in the left margin of the manuscript.

[51]Milton creates his own version of Comus's parentage, making him the son of Bacchus and Circe. The *Homeric Hymn to Dionysus* 7 and Ovid, in the *Metamorphoses* 3.521–691, tell the story of Dionysus or Bacchus as a young man (in the Homeric hymn, at least) who is captured by Tyrrhenian (taken to mean "Etruscan" or "Tuscan") pirates. The mariners are transformed into dolphins by the god. Milton sets the story in the Tyrrhenian Sea, west of Italy.

[52]Lest Milton be taken for the kind of Puritan who would condemn drinking wine in a knee-jerk reaction, notice the word "mis-used." In the rest of his poetry and prose, Milton never condemned moderate drinking and eating. See, for example, Sonnet 20, "*Lawrence* of vertuous Father vertuous Son."

After the *Tuscan* Mariners transform'd
Coasting the *Tyrrhene* shore, as the winds listed,
On *Circes* Iland fell (who knows not *Circe*   50
The daughter of the Sun? Whose charmed Cup
Whoever tasted, lost his upright shape,
And downward fell into a groveling Swine)
This Nymph that gaz'd upon his clustring locks,
With Ivy berries wreath'd, and his blithe youth,   55
Had by him, ere he parted thence, a Son
Much like his Father, but his Mother more,[53]
Whom therfore she brought up and *Comus* nam'd,[54]
Who ripe, and frolick of his full grown age,[55]
Roaving the *Celtick*,[56] and *Iberian* fields,   60
At last betakes him to this ominous Wood,
And in thick shelter[57] of black shades imbowr'd,
Excells his Mother at her mighty[58] Art,
Offring to every weary Travailer,
His orient liquor[59] in a Crystal Glasse, —   65
To quench the drouth of *Phœbus*, which as they taste
(For most do taste through fond[60] intemperate thirst)
Soon as the Potion works, their human count'nance,
Th' express resemblance of the gods, is chang'd
Into som brutish form of Woolf, or Bear,   70
Or Ounce, or Tiger, Hog, or bearded Goat,[61]
All other parts remaining as[62] they were,
And they, so perfect° is their misery,
Not once perceive their foul disfigurement,
But boast themselves more comely then before   75
And all their friends, and native home forget

---

[53]The fact that Comus resembles his mother Circe more than his father Bacchus may indicate only that he follows his mother's practice of transforming humans into beasts, or it may indicate that Comus should be taken as of ambivalent sexuality (for a full discussion of the treatment of sexuality in the masque, see Kerrigan, *Sacred* 22–72).

[54]The phrase was "and nam'd him Comus," then "nam'd him" was partly struck through and "nam'd" and "whome" added to the right in the manuscript; "whome" replaces "w^ch" at the beginning of the line.

[55]How old is Comus? All we know for sure is that he is "full grown." He may be as ageless as a god, since he is the son of Venus and Bacchus, but the character on stage has been played convincingly both as sturdy adolescent (State University College of New York at Buffalo, 1984) and as "dirty old man" (Christ College, Cambridge, 1985). We know about Comus's appearance only that he has curly hair.

[56]Milton identified "Celtica" with "Gaul" or France (*Observations upon the Articles of Peace*, Yale 3: 325). "Iberia" is Spain.

[57]Milton first wrote "covert," then crossed it out and replaced it with a marginal "shelter." The covert or blanket of trees in the woods thus offers shelter but it also can hide the misdeeds of Comus and his rout.

[58]Written "potent" at first, then that was struck through and "mightie" inserted above the line.

[59]"Glistening or gleaming liquid." Presumably this is an intoxicating potion akin to wine viewed as "sweet poyson." In the Trinity Manuscript, Milton has the Lady call what is in the cup "hel bru'd liquor," and Comus call it a "cordiall julep," which includes "spirits of balme & fragrant syrops mixed" (24).

[60]Milton first wrote "weake," in the manuscript, then replaced it with "fond"; we can assume that he considered the two words nearly synonymous.

[61]George Sandys's translation of and commentary on Ovid's *Metamorphoses* sums up the moral and psychological transformation of humankind into beasts: Circe is " . . . daughter to the *Sun* and *Persis*, . . . lustfully by nature," who transforms Scylla by means of poison into a "monstrous deformity; her loynes invironed with howling Wolves and barking dogs, not a part of her body. . . . *Scylla* represents a Virgin; who as long as chast in thought, and in body unspotted, appears of an excellent beauthy, attracting all eyes upon her, and wounding the Gods themselves with affection . . . . That the upper part of her body, is feigned to retaine a humane figure, and the lower to be bestial; intimates how man, a divine creature, endued with wisdome and intelligence, in whose superiour parts, as in a high tower, that immortall spirit resideth, who only of all that hath life erects his lookes unto heaven, can never so degenerate into a beast, as when he giveth himselfe over to the lowe delights of those baser parts of the body, Dogs and Wolfes, the blind & salvage fury of concupiscence" (quoted from Sandys's notes on *Metamorphoses* 14 in *Ovid's Metamorphosis Englished, Mythologized, and Represented in Figures* by George Sandys, ed. Karl K. Hulley and Stanley T. Vandersall [Lincoln: U of Nebraska P, 1970]: 645). When Circe gains dominion over humans, she "deformes our soules with all bestial vices; alluring some to inordinate *Venus*; others to anger, cruelty, and ever excess of passion: the Swines, the Lyons, and the Wolves produced by her sensuall charms; which are not to bee resisted, but by the divine assistance, Moly, the guift of *Mercury*, which signifies temperance" (654).

[62]Milton first wrote "as before they were," then struck through "before," probably because it was redundant.

To roule with pleasure in a sensual stie.
Therfore when any favour'd of high *Jove*,
Chances to passe through this adventrous[63] glade,
Swift as the Sparkle of a glancing Star,
I shoot from Heav'n to give him safe convoy,°   ESCORT   80
As now I do: But first I must put off
These my skie robes spun out of *Iris* Wooff,[64]
And take the Weeds° and likenes of a Swain,   CLOTHES
That to the service of this house belongs,[65]   85
Who with his soft Pipe, and smooth-dittied[66] Song,
Well knows to still the wilde winds when they roar,
And hush the waving Woods, nor of lesse faith,
And in this office of his Mountain watch,
Likeliest,[67] and neerest to the present ayd   90
Of this occasion. But I hear the tread
Of hatefull steps, I must be viewles[68] now.

> Comus *enters with a Charming Rod*[69] *in one hand,*
> *his* Glass° *in the other, with him a rout of Mon-*   GOBLET
> *sters headed like sundry sorts of wilde Beasts,*
> *but otherwise like Men and Women,*[70] *their Ap-*
> *parel glistring,° they com in making a riotous*   GLIMMERING, GLITTERING
> *and unruly noise, with Torches in their hands.*

---

[63]"Full of risk or peril; hazardous, perilous" (*OED* 2, citing this instance).

[64]The Attendant Spirit is wearing a rainbow-colored costume, which must be similar to the "purfl'd scarf" mentioned in 995 below, since he is associated with Iris, the goddess of the rainbow. Iris's "woof" would be part of the fabric, woven both in the warp (threads in a vertical direction) and the woof (threads in a horizontal direction).

[65]The swain or shepherd is in service to the houschold of the Egerton family. Like Lycidas, he "well knows" (compare l. 10, as in the Trinity Manuscript) how to play his pipe so effectively that, like Orpheus, he can calm winds.

[66]This may be a technical term from composing, signifying that the melodies or words of the light songs the swain sang were smooth and therefore pleasing to the ear. Compare the use of "dittied" cited in the *OED*: "1597 [Thomas] Morley [the composer] *Introd. Mus.* 172: You must have an especiall care of causing your parts [of a ditty] give place one to another . . . nor can you cause them rest till they haue expressed that part of the dittying which they haue begun.'"

[67]Milton first wrote the next few lines thus:

            the
        neerest & likliest to ~~give~~ præsent ~~aide chance~~ aide
[o]f ye occasion ~~of this occasion;~~ but I heare the tread
 hatefull
 of ~~virgin~~ steps I must be veiwle∫se now ~~Exit~~ goes out
 occasion ~~of the occasion,~~ but I heare the tread
 ~~hateful~~
 of ~~virgin~~ steps I must be veiwle∫se now.

The word order of "neerest & likliest" has been reversed by BMS and remains so in printed versions. Milton had some difficulty deciding between "aide" and "chance," apparently choosing "aide" because "chance" might suggest the intervention of fate. The occasion is made more specific with "this." The most interesting change is from "virgin steps" to "hateful steps," because the "virgin" suggests that the Lady was intended to enter next, not Comus.

[68]"Invisible."

[69]A magician's wand, used to cast charms, hence "charming." The Trinity Manuscript reads:
            wth a charming rod & ~~glasse~~ of liquor
    Comus enters· with his rout all headed like some wild beasts thire
                                come on in
        garments some like mens & some like womens they ~~begin~~ a wild &
        ~~humorous~~ antick fashion
    intrant κωμάζοντες

The details of the glass being filled with some sort of "liquor," and the people engaging in the humorous antic (in its noun form, often a wild dance) all add meaning to the masque as it is performed, and the definition of the rout as κωμάζοντες identifies the followers of Comus as dissolute "sons [and daughters] of Belial." I am obliged to Mark Womack for pointing out that the meaning of "glasse" is close to "goblet" (e-mail 31 March 1998).

[70]The fact that the rout is made up of both males and females may suggest either that Comus has corrupted both sexes and included both in his "abhorred rites" (535) or that the dancers will, as is customary in masques, incorporate pairs of men and women, both in Comus's rout and in the country dancers employed in the final dance.

Comus.[71] The Star that bids the Shepherd fold,[72]
Now the top of Heav'n doth hold,
And the gilded Car of Day,   95
His glowing Axle[73] doth allay°   COOL DOWN
In the steep[74] *Atlantick*[75] stream,
And the slope° Sun his upward beam   DESCENDING
Shoots against the dusky Pole,[76]
Pacing toward the other gole[77]   100
Of his Chamber in the East.
Mean while welcom Joy, and Feast,
Midnight shout, and revelry,
Tipsie dance, and Jollity.
Braid your Locks with rosie Twine[78]   105
Dropping odours, dropping Wine.
Rigor[79] now is gon to bed,
And Advice with scrupulous head,[80]
Strict Age, and sowre Severity,
With their grave Saws° in slumber ly.   VERY SERIOUS SAYINGS   110
We that are of purer fire[81]
Imitate the Starry Quire,°   CHOIR
Who in their nightly watchfull Sphears,
Lead in[82] swift round the Months and Years.
The Sounds, and Seas[83] with all their finny drove[84]   115
Now to the Moon in wavering Morrice° move,[85]   MORRIS DANCE
And on the Tawny[86] Sands and Shelves,[87]
Trip the pert Fairies and the dapper Elves;[88]

---

[71]Comus speaks in iambic tetrameter, more appropriate by conventions of the Elizabethan theater for supernatural beings.

[72]In the sense of *OED* verb 2: "To shut up (sheep, etc.) in a fold, to pen; occas. with up; also absol. Of hurdles: To serve for penning." The star is Hesperus, the evening star, as referred to as leading shepherds in for the night in Vergil, *Eclogues* 6.85–86: " . . . till the lads were warned to drive home and to count their sheep, by Vesper, as he trod unwelcome into the listening sky" (trans. Rieu).

[73]The shining axletree (axle plus wheel with radiating spokes) of Apollo's sun-chariot, the "burning axletree" of the Nativity Ode 84. Ovid (*Metamorphoses* 2.107–11) describes the chariot as "the work of Vulcan, / Axle and pole of gold, and tires of gold, / And spokes of silver, and along the yoke / Crysolites shone, and every kind of jewel / Gave back the bright reflection" (trans. Humphries).

[74]"Of water: Having a headlong course, flowing precipitously" (*OED* adj. 2.e).

[75]In the manuscript, Milton first wrote "Tartessian," from the ancient town of Tartessus, supposed to be the place where the Sun unharnessed his horses at the end of the day, but he struck out the less familiar name and replaced it with "Atlantick."

[76]Probably "the heavens," the secondary meaning of Latin *polus*. Milton first wrote "northren" in the line, replaced it with "dusky" in the margin, then underlined "northren" to reinstate it. How "dusky" was allowed to remain can only be guessed, since BMS has "Northerne" and *1637* has "duskie."

[77]Evidently the chariot is being paced as if it were in a Roman chariot race, which would also aim toward a goal which was—excuse the rhyme and the pun—a pole.

[78]"Entwine your hair with chains of roses."

[79]The word suggests not only rigidity but the maintenance of a straight course or moral direction, as in "his morals were rigorous." Milton speaks of "the rigor of Christs answer," for instance, in the *Doctrine and Discipline of Divorce* (Yale 2: 311). Rigor is also being pictured as an allegorical entity, accompanied by Advice, Strict Age, and Severity.

[80]This line is damaged in the manuscript. Sprott reconstructs it as "[A]dvice & ~~nice~~ [~~w~~] w^th ~~her~~ scrupulous head." At least we can tell for sure that "Advice," the allegorical figure, was meant to be feminine, but the "her" was excised because it was not needed for the scansion of the line.

[81]Presumably, being spirits, Comus and the other gods would be made of the flamelike fifth element ether, hence the "purer fire." But notice that what they do is "imitate" because, being classical gods, they are only pale imitations of, or demonic representations of, angels.

[82]The phrase "lead w^th" in the original line in the Trinity Manuscript was changed to "lead in."

[83]Milton uses the phrase "Sounds, and Seas" apparently to mean the sea and its tributaries; compare "Forthwith the Sounds and Seas, each Creek and Bay / With Frie innumerable swarme" (*Paradise Lost* 7.399–400).

[84]A famous instance of poetic diction, much imitated in eighteenth-century verse. The phrase was lifted verbatim from Spenser, *Faerie Queene* 3.8.29: "*Proteus* . . . did rove / Along the fomy waves driving his finny drove." A "finny drove" is apparently a school of finned fish.

[85]The seas with all their fish move like a wavering or waving line of morris (originally Moorish) dancers.

[86]Milton first wrote "yellow" in the manuscript, then crossed it out and replaced it with "tawnie." The choice may have been on behalf of the sound of the word rather than the color it describes.

[87]Sands would be above water level, shelves below it.

[88]The adjective "dapper" was "Applied to a little person who is trim or smart in his ways and movement" (*OED* 2.b), citing this instance.

By dimpled Brook, and Fountain brim,
The Wood-Nymphs deckt with Daisies trim,
Their merry wakes and pastimes[89] keep: 120
What hath night to do with sleep?
Night hath better sweets to prove,
Venus now wakes, and wak'ns Love.
Come let us our rights° begin,   RITES   125
Tis onely day-light that makes Sin[90]
Which these dun° shades will ne're report.   DARK
Hail Goddesse of Nocturnal sport[91]
Dark-vaild *Cotytto*,[92] t' whom the secret flame
Of mid-night Torches burns; mysterious Dame[93]   130
That ne're art call'd, but when the Dragon woom[94]
Of Stygian darknes spets° her thickest gloom,   SPITS
And makes one blot of all the ayr,
Stay° thy cloudy Ebon chair,°   DON'T MOVE   CHARIOT
Wherin thou rid'st with *Hecat'*,[95] and befriend   135

---

[89]For an explanation of the political implications for "merry wakes and pastimes," see Leah Sinanoglou Marcus, *The Politics of Mirth: Jonson, Herrick, Milton, Marvell, and the Defense of Old Holiday Pastimes* (Chicago, IL: U Chicago P, 1986).

[90]Comus's facile reasoning appeals to anyone who might want to hide sinful actions under cover of darkness. If sin can only occur in daylight, then one can get away with murder after dark. By the same logic, "What hath night to do with sleep?" can easily be answered (by the normal nocturnal sleeper) with "Everything."

[91]Almost always a negative word in Milton's usage, sport seems always to suggest sexual dalliance rather than innocent play.

[92]The Thracian fertility goddess Cotytto presided over secret orgiastic rites. She was supposed by some to be the same as Proserpina, or Ceres. The sexual debaucheries of her rites are attacked by Juvenal in *Satires* 2.91–92: " . . . the orgies blaze, like the torches, in secret. / Here's a lad making his eyebrows long, with damp soot on a needle, / Here's one taking a swig from a goblet shaped like a phallus, / Another one fixing his eyes, with a golden net on his long hair" (trans. Humphries). I have restored the hyphen in "Dark-vaild" as it is in the Trinity Manuscript, BMS, and *1637*, but I should add that Milton in his manuscript might be in error when he writes "to whome" in the same line; BMS has a space before "whome" which might indicate a query on the part of the scribe, and *1637* has the correct "t'whom."

[93]Cotytto is mysterious because she was worshiped in what were considered to be holy mysteries. She is a venerable "Dame" from Comus's point of view.

[94]The passage concerning the chair of Cotytto was heavily revised. Here is how it appears in the Trinity Manuscript:

                                                          when the dragon womb
                    of Stygian darkneſse spits her thickest glo·°m ˚and makes one blot
            *and makes a blot of nature and throws a blot · of all yᵉ aire
                        clowdie
            stay thy polisht ebon chaire   (& befreind
                                        none   ⊕wherin thou ridst ridst wᵗʰ Hecate·
        of still all thy dues bee don & nought· left out & favour our close revelrie jocondrie
        ere the blabbing eastreane scout   us thy vow'd preists till utmost end

Compare Shakespeare's "foul womb of night" (*Henry V* 5.4.4). The association between dragon and womb may indicate the association between night and Satan as perverse dragon, giving birth to evil. The association between Stygian darkness (i.e., from the river Styx in Hades, read as the Christian Hell) and the dragon suggests that the dragon issues from Hell and thus is related to the "dragon, that old serpent" of Revelation 20.2, usually taken to mean Satan. A team of dragons was supposed to pull the chariot of Diana, the moon, across the sky, as in "Night's swift dragons cut the clouds full fast" (Shakespeare, *Midsummer Night's Dream* 3.2.379). Sokol finds a hidden reference in the excised "Tilted lees" of the manuscript to menstruation and the melancholy supposedly produced by it. The dragon womb is also supposed to darken the air with "dragon menses" (316). Though the image of a womb (read often as "vagina" in the seventeenth century) spitting gloom is disquieting, even coming from Comus, "spitting" would be a peculiar image of menstruation, and menstruation would not be something for the masque to discuss openly before the Bridgewater family and its guests. The excised phrase "throws a blot" suggests a perverse birth rather than menstruation: night is a perverse and evil reflection of day, and the triform goddess made up of Proserpina, Diana, and Hecate suggests to seventeenth-century Christians an unholy and unnatural blending of madness, chastity, and evil sexuality—all opposed to the light of Christian truth. The image of the dragon chariot, however, is not always negative: Ceres, the mother of Proserpina, also rides in a "chariot drawne by winged Dragons, all over the World, to teach the use of husbandry unto mortals" (Sandys 262).

[95]The apostrophe is not a typographical error: it indicates that a syllable has been left off "Hecate." In the manuscript Milton first wrote "Hecate," then struck through the "e" and wrote in an apostrophe above it, with a caret beneath to indicate that it should be inserted. Contrast *Hecate*, with three syllables, at 534. Diana, Proserpina, and Hecate, thought to be three faces of the same deity, together drove the moon chariot. Worship of Diana promoted a late medieval cult of women who believed that they could "ride with Diana the pagan goddess and a huge throng of women on chosen beasts in the hours of night" (Regino of Prüm, *De Ecclesiasticus Disciplinis* in J. P. Migne, *Patrologia Latina* [Paris, 1878–90]: 132, 152, translated in Valerie I. J. Flint, *The Rise of Magic in Early Medieval Europe* [Princeton: Princeton UP, 1991]: 122). For a colorful recreation of some of these cults in Italy, see Carlo Ginzburg, *The Night Battles: Witchcraft and Agrarian Cults in the Sixteenth and Seventeenth Centuries*, trans. John and Anne Tedeschi (Baltimore, MD: Johns Hopkins

Us thy vow'd Priests, till utmost end
Of all thy dues[96] be done, and none left out,
Ere the blabbing Eastern scout,[97]
The nice° Morn on th' *Indian* steep[98]   EXACT, PRECISELY ON TIME
From her cabin'd loop hole peep,[99]   140
And to the tel-tale Sun discry
Our conceal'd Solemnity.
Com, knit hands, and beat the ground,[100]
In[101] a light fantastick round.

    The Measure.[102]

Break off, break off, I feel[103] the different pace,   145
Of som chast footing neer about this ground,
Run to your shrouds,° within these Brakes and Trees,[104]   HIDING PLACES
Our number may affright: Som Virgin sure
(For so I can distinguish by mine Art)
Benighted in these Woods.[105] Now to my charms,[106]   150
And to my wily trains,[107] I shall e're long
Be well stock't with as fair a herd as graz'd
About my Mother *Circe*. Thus I hurl   *Comus' mother*
My dazling[108] Spells into the spungy ayr,[109]
Of power to cheat the eye with blear[110] illusion,   155
And give it false presentments,° lest[111] the place   PRESENTIMENTS, FOREBODINGS
And my quaint habits° breed astonishment,   EXOTIC CLOTHES
And put the Damsel to suspicious flight,
Which must not be, for that's against my course;

[handwritten marginalia: Imposing his will, his test]

UP, 1992).

[96]"A payment legally due or obligatory" (*OED* 4.a); in other words, his followers owe dues to Comus or to the night.

[97]The morning, probably the goddess Aurora, pictured by his enemy Comus as a spy who might report back to an army, like a scout.

[98]Apparently on the steep slope of an Indian mountain. The sunrise is pictured as occurring here, the sunset near the Straits of Gibralter.

[99]The dawn is pictured as a witness to forbidden rites (those of Cotytto). Michael Wilding has investigated the possible political implications of such spying ("Milton's" 40).

[100]The revelers join hands in a round, forming the kind of knot popular in seventeenth-century dance figures. Compare the wavering Morris dancers mentioned earlier. Having their hands joined or knit in air, the dancers might bend as a unit to beat the ground.

[101]In the Trinity Manuscript Milton again replaced "w^th" with "in," and he first wrote "& frolick," only to strike it through and replace it with "fantastick." The latter adjective adds the element of the supernatural.

[102]In the manuscript, the measure is said to be "in a wild rude & wanton antick," which suggests that the music for the dance of Comus's rite mirrored the moral disorder of the "comazontes."

[103]Milton first wrote "heare" in the manuscript, then deleted it and replaced it with "feele," thereby endowing Comus with something like extrasensory perception.

[104]To the right of this line, the manuscript adds the stage direction "they all scatter." Milton first added, after "ground," these two lines: "some virgin sure benighted in these woods / for so I can distinguish by myne art," then decided to redistribute the lines as they are below, with "for . . . art" entered in parentheses, as an aside. See John Lennard, *But I Digress: The Exploitation of Parentheses in English Printed Verse* (Oxford: Clarendon P, 1991), for many useful suggestions about how a poet, together with a printer, might indicate various shades of meaning using parentheses for emphasis.

[105]One would expect an "is" before "Benighted," but the verb "benight" meant "To be overtaken by the darkness of night (before reaching a place of shelter)" (*OED* 1), and it could be used intransitively.

[106]Milton first wrote "traines," then struck it out and replaced it with "charmes" to the right in the line, perhaps because he went on to write "wilie trains" in the next line.

[107]The manuscript had "mothers charmes," which was replaced by "wilie trains." The word "train" could suggest a deceit, a snare, or a charm (as with an amulet, to ward off evil).

[108]Milton first wrote "powder'd," then replaced it with "dazling" in the manuscript. "Thus I hurl" seems to be a stage direction as well: Comus at this point tosses something that glitters, perhaps a type of stage powder or "Magick dust" (165), into the air, and it catches the light and distracts the eye.

[109]The air apparently absorbs the powder as a sponge absorbs water, though the word "spongy" could just signify "insubstantial."

[110]As in "bleary-eyed," that is, not distinct or clearly seen. Milton first wrote "power to cheat the eye wth sleight," then struck through "sleight," inserted a caret and wrote "blind" above the line, struck through that, and put in "bleare" instead.

[111]Milton first wrote "else," then struck it for "lest."

I under fair pretence of friendly ends,　　　　　　　　　　　　　　160
And well plac't words of glozing courtesie°　　　　　FLATTERING, INSINCERE POLITENESS
Baited with reasons not unplausible
Wind me into the easie-hearted° man,　　　　　　　　GULLIBLE, TRUSTING
And hugg° him into snares.[112] When once her eye　　CARESS
Hath met the vertue° of this Magick dust,　　　　　　POWER　　　　　165
I shall appear som harmles Villager
Whom thrift[113] keeps up about his Country gear,[114]
But here she comes, I fairly[115] step aside
And hearken,[116] if I may, her busines[117] here.

　　The Lady enters.

This way the noise was, if mine ear be true,　　　　　　　　　　　　170
My best[118] guide now, me thought° it was the sound　　IT SEEMED TO ME
Of Riot, and ill manag'd Merriment,
Such as the jocond Flute, or gamesom Pipe
Stirs up amoungst[119] the loose unleter'd Hinds,°　　IGNORANT HOUSEHOLD SERVANTS
When for their teeming Flocks, and granges full[120]　　　　　　　　175
In wanton dance they praise[121] the bounteous *Pan,*
And thank the gods amiss.[122] I should be loath
To meet the rudenesse, and swill'd[123] insolence
Of such late Wassailers;[124] yet O where els
Shall I inform° my unacquainted° feet　　　　DIRECT　　INEXPERIENC'D　　180
In the blind mazes of this tangl'd Wood?[125]
My Brothers when they saw me wearied out
With this long way,° resolving here to lodge　　　　COURSE OF TRAVEL
Under the spreading favour° of these Pines,　　　　GOOD WILL
Stept as they se'd to the next Thicket side　　　　　　　　　　185

[Handwritten marginal annotations: "Comus' mask sets a Trap Deception Thyrsis- Family Shepherd." and "hearing was her best guide:"]

---

[112]Comus describes the general methodology of Satan: after winding his way into the heart of unwitting persons, he snares or nets them, like a hunter, but with a "mortal snare" (*Paradise Lost* 4.8). Compare 567 below, when the Lady is in danger: "How sweet thou sing'st, how neer the deadly snare!" Milton first wrote "hugge him into nets," then struck through "nets" and inserted "snares" above the line with a caret.

[113]A hand not recognizable as Milton's has underlined the word "thrift," with a different pen and a lighter ink, and written "thirst," also underlined, in the right margin (see Sprott 13 for tentative identification of the hand of this "intruder"). The emendation "thirst" was not accepted for any printed edition, and indeed it does not make much sense as a substitution.

[114]Apparently the word here means "goods, movable property" (*OED* 3.9, citing this example), though it can also mean "clothes." The thriftiness of the country-man makes him take care to maintain his property. The magic dust that Comus has thrown seems to cause the Lady not to see him as he is but as the villager; she sees him for what he is beginning at 658.

[115]The word suggests "speciously," or "deceptively," as well as "cleverly."

[116]He steps aside in order to harken to what she is saying privately, or overhear her.

[117]The spelling of the manuscript, "buisnesse," indicates that the word should be pronounced as a disyllable.

[118]The word "best" was inserted in the line by means of a caret.

[119]I have restored the word as in the manuscript, rather than accepting the reading of "amonge" or "among" in BMS, *1637*, *1645*, or *1673*.

[120]The "loose unleter'd Hinds" are celebrating the seasons of spring, when, in a good year, the livestock bear young prolifically, or are "teeming," and fall, when granaries or granges are full. Milton first wrote "garners," then replaced it with "granges."

[121]Milton first wrote "they praise," then crossed that out and put "adore" above the line, then underlined "they praise" to restore it. He did the same sort of cancelation and restoration between "when" and "that."

[122]Her description of revelry and misrules seems to Mortimer and Taaffe to indicate the celebration of Michaelmas eve. See Introduction, "Liturgy." If such a celebration gets out of hand, even though it may be intended reverently, the revelers are misdirected in their celebration: getting drunk is not a good way to worship. Here Pan is the Greek god associated with revelry and panic, rather than the "mighty *Pan*" of the Nativity Ode 89, who is to be identified with Christ.

[123]The insolence is caused by drinking too much too fast: Milton's is the only recorded instance of the word "swilled" used as a participial adjective according to the *OED*.

[124]Carousers or rioters, drinking "wassails," or drinking healths to each other in rounds. Milton's use of the noun meaning something like "rioters" is the first recorded in the *OED*.

[125]Milton first wrote "in the blind ~~alleys~~ of ~~these~~ this ~~arched~~ wood," then made the substitutions as in the line printed in *1645*. The quotation mark after "wood" was not in the Trinity Manuscript or BMS (BMS had a comma, Trinity nothing), but first appeared in *1637*.

To bring me Berries, or such cooling fruit
As the kind hospitable Woods provide.
They left me then, when the gray-hooded Eev'n
Like a sad Votarist in Palmers weed[126]
Rose from the hindmost wheels of *Phœbus* wain.[127]   190
But where they are, and why they came not back,
Is now the labour of my thoughts,[128] 'tis likeliest
They had ingag'd their wandring[129] steps too far,
And envious darknes,[130] e're they could return,
Had stole them from me,[131] els O theevish Night   195
Why shouldst thou, but for som fellonious end,
In thy dark lantern[132] thus close up the Stars,
That nature hung in Heav'n, and fill'd their Lamps
With everlasting oil, to give due[133] light
To the misled and lonely Travailer?   200
This is[134] the place, as well as I may guess,
Whence eev'n now the tumult of loud Mirth
Was rife, and perfet[135] in my list'ning ear,
Yet nought but single darknes[136] do I find.
What might this be? A thousand fantasies   205
Begin to throng into my memory
Of calling° shapes, and beckning shadows dire,   *BECKONING*
And airy tongues, that syllable mens names[137]
On Sands, and Shoars, and desert Wildernesses.
These thoughts may startle well, but not astound   210
The vertuous mind, that ever walks attended
By a strong siding[138] champion Conscience.------[139]
O welcom pure ey'd Faith, white-handed Hope,

---

[126]The evening is a monastic figure. A votarist is someone bound by a vow to perform a religious duty. A palmer is "A pilgrim who had returned from the Holy Land, in sign of which he carried a palm-branch or palm-leaf" (*OED* 1). Franciscan friars, in England at least, were called "Grey Friars," but of course the dawn might itself be gray. The *Variorum* editors assume that Evening is feminine; votarists were often female, but palmers were more apt to be male. Lines 203–05 are not in BMS.

[127]The chariot of the sun-god Phoebus Apollo. Milton first wrote "chaire," then struck it through and wrote "waine" to the right of it.

[128]A modern style of punctuation would probably use a colon or semicolon at this point. Most editors who modernize do just that.

[129]Milton first wrote "youthly," then struck it through and wrote "wandring" above the line.

[130]The line at first read "to the soone parting light and envious darknesse," then "to the soone parting light" was struck through and "ere they could returne" added.

[131]From this point through "tufted grove" (225 below) has been omitted in BMS, perhaps to save time in performance.

[132]If the night carries a lantern, it is a lantern of darkness, one that would correspond to the moral state of being "benighted." Compare Frances Quarles's phrase cited under "lantern" in the *OED*: "Alas, what serves our reason, / But, like dark lanthornes, to accomplish Treason / With greater closenesse" (*Emblems* [1635] 5.12.289). Thieves would also hide booty under a cover of darkness; thus the night is by transferred sense a thief, especially when it seems to hide away the stars in a "lantern of darkness."

[133]The phrase was first written "give thire light," then "thire" was struck through and "due" was added in the margin.

[134]Milton put a caret between "is" and "place" but did not add a "the" above the line; subsequent printed editions added it.

[135]"Duly completed." In other words, she heard it all, in all its rifeness or abundance. The spelling "perfet" follows Milton's preferred usage, though the manuscript has "perfect."

[136]Perhaps a singular or uniquely bad darkness, since it is also spoken of as "envious" and "theevish."

[137]The line was first written as "and ayrie toungs *that lure night wanderers*" with what looks like "wandring" scratched through to form "wanderers." Then Milton added "that syllable mens nams" in the margin to insert at the point of the asterisk. It is there in the manuscript. The Lady rightfully fears the babble of night voices, any one of which might lead to damnation, since, like a will-o'-the-wisp or *ignis fatuus*, they beckon her in different dangerous directions.

[138]Taking the side of (Milton's is the first use of the word recorded in the *OED*).

[139]The long line at this point in the manuscript and in the early printed editions may indicate another stage direction (compare what happens at 332), perhaps even a tableau consisting of the figures of Conscience, Faith, Hope, and Chastity. Either that or Milton wants the audience to imagine what the Lady sees. Hunter adds an interpolated stage direction "*Tableaux appear of the three Virtues illuminated*" (Comus: *Family Piece* 70), but he does not represent the dash.

Thou hov'ring[140] Angel girt with° golden wings,   GIRDED, DRESSED IN

And thou unblemish't[141] form[142] of Chastity,   215

I see ye visibly,[143] and now beleeve

That he,[144] the Supreme[145] good, t'whom all things ill°   ALL EVIL THINGS

Are but as slavish officers of vengeance,[146]

Would send a glistring Guardian[147] if need were

To keep my life and honour unassail'd.   220

Was I deceiv'd, or did a sable cloud

Turn forth her silver lining on the night?[148]

I did not err, there does a sable cloud

Turn forth her silver lining on the night,

And casts a gleam over this tufted[149] Grove.   225

I cannot hallow to my Brothers, but

Such noise[150] as I can make to be heard farthest

Ile venter,[151] for my new enliv'nd spirits[152]

Prompt me; and they perhaps are not far off.

      SONG.[153]

   Sweet Echo, sweetest Nymph that liv'st unseen   230

     Within thy airy shell [154]

   By slow Meander's *margent green,*[155]

---

[140]Milton first wrote "flittering," then the scribe who made various insertions in the manuscript, with or without Milton's authority, wisely replaced it with "hov'ring" in the margin. Shawcross prefers "flittering," on the grounds that "hov'ring" "debilitates the effect of 'flittering'" ("Certain Relationships" 42n). I am instead bothered by the image of a flittering angel. Even as originally used, the word suggested aimless, trembling, or compulsive movement. I have restored the "hov'ring" of the manuscript, rather than the trisyllable of "hovering" of *1645.*

[141]Milton first wrote "unspotted," then replaced it with "unblemish't."

[142]The word *form* here and elsewhere in the masque seems to signify an ideal or the Platonic sense of the divine essence of a thing, what Milton called "The *Form* by which the thing is what it is" (*Tetrachordon;* Yale 2: 608). Milton associated the word with the artist's conception of the ideal.

[143]At this point, Milton first wrote "& while I see yee / this dusky hollow is a paradice / & heaven gates ore my head," then struck through those lines and began again with "& now I beleeve." Perhaps the removal of the lines and the images is part of his running attempt not to use obviously Christian references, as with "paradice" and "heaven gates."

[144]The "he" was added to the line in the manuscript by means of a caret.

[145]Accented on the first syllable.

[146]A clear reference to the Christian God, who is the "supreme good," and who regards all evil doers as agents or "officers" in the larger scheme of providence.

[147]The Attendant Spirit is called "A Guardian spirit, or Dæmon" at the beginning of the manuscript: thus God has indeed sent a glistering (i.e., dressed in sky robes) guardian to help protect the Lady's honor. Milton first wrote "cherub," then replaced it with "guardian," perhaps another attempt to avoid Christian imagery.

[148]The Lady's rhetorical question, followed by an answer that mimics the question, which seems funny out of context, may have been intended as a performance cue for a stagehand to shine a light simulating the moon. A black ("sable") cloud would have a silver lining if it were outlined by the moon's light behind it.

[149]Sylvester's translation of DuBartas uses the same idiom: "The Tufted Tops of sacred *Libanon*" (Snyder ed., 2.4.2.1096).

[150]The word did not suggest, necessarily, a very loud or rude sound. In other words, she wants to make enough of a sound so that her brothers may hear it, but she cannot hail them as loudly as they can hail her: that would be unLadylike.

[151]The spelling here may indeed indicate Milton's phonetic preference, since he does spell the word "venter" in the manuscript.

[152]Her spirits have been lifted or enlivened by the possibility that her brothers are not far off.

[153]In Henry Lawes's manuscript, the song reads: "sweet Echo, sweetest Nymph that liv'st unseen, within thy Airy shell by slow Meanders margent green & in thy violet imbroiderd Vale where the Love lorn Nightingale nightly to thee her sad song mourneth well Canst thou not tell me of a gentle Pair that likest thy Narcissus are? O if thou have hid them in some flowry Cave tell me but where sweet Queen of Pity Daughter of the Sphere so may'st thou be Transplanted to the Skyes & hold a Counterpoint to all Heav'ns Harmonies" (line divisions cannot be indicated easily, because of the musical clefs). Significant variants are with "Queen of Pity" vs. "Queen of Parly," "thy violet" vs. "the violet," "Transplanted" vs. *translated,* and "& hold a Counterpoint to all Heav'ns Harmonies" vs. "*And give resounding grace to all Heav'ns Harmonies.*" In every case, Lawes is modifying the text insensitively, though "hold a Counterpoint" appears as a canceled phrase in the Trinity Manuscript and a reinstated one in BMS.

[154]Milton was undecided about this word—he first wrote "cell" before replacing it with "shell." Carey finds "shell" as meaning "the vault of the sky" (230n) and cites Starnes and Talbert 249, but at 873 the shell seems to be a conch shell. Perhaps Echo is being pictured as Venus is by Botticelli, as inhabiting a shell. "Cell" would suggest monastic isolation appropriate for the nymph Echo, who pined away for Narcissus in a cave.

[155]By the banks ("margins") of the classical Greek river Meander's slowly moving stream. Milton inserted "slow" by means of a caret in the manuscript and also added the same word in the right margin.

And in the violet-imbroider'd vale
  Where the love-lorn[156] *Nightingale*
Nightly to thee her sad Song mourneth well.   235
Canst thou not tell me of a gentle Pair
  That likest thy Narcissus *are?*
   O if thou have
  Hid them in som flowry Cave,
   Tell me but where   240
Sweet Queen of Parly,[157] *Daughter of the Sphear,*
So maist thou be translated° to the skies,   CARRIED UP
And give resounding grace to all Heav'ns Harmonies.[158]

  Com. Can any mortal mixture of Earths mould[159]
Breath such Divine inchanting ravishment?[160]   245
Sure° somthing holy lodges in that brest,   SURELY
And with these raptures moves the vocal air
To testifie his hidd'n residence;[161]
How sweetly did they float upon the wings
Of silence, through the empty-vaulted night   250
At every fall smoothing the Raven doune[162]
Of darknes till it smil'd:[163] I have oft heard
My Mother *Circe* with the Sirens three,[164]

---

[156]Milton is the first to use this by-now-familiar phrase, but here it might mean "lost through love," since Philomela, the nightingale, is raped by her brother-in-law Tereus in the myth and has her tongue ripped out, for which she compensates by singing. The story is told by Ovid in *Metamorphoses* 6.
[157]An appropriate title for Echo, who answers all remarks aimed at her with an echo. In Humphries's translation, for instance, Narcissus asks, "Is anybody here?" and Echo replies, "Here." The word *parley* does suggest debate, however, since it is closely related to French *parler* and Italian *parlare*, both meaning "to speak."
[158]Milton first wrote "~~And hold a counterpoint~~ to all heavns harmonies," then, after striking through the first phrase, wrote "and give resounding grace" in the margin. Presumably, "hold a counterpoint" would be more pleasing to Lawes because of its musical term "counterpoint," "the art of combining two simultaneous musical lines" (*Norton/Grove Concise Encyclopedia of Music*), but "give resounding grace" adds more biblical or theological force to the line. Henry Lawes's manuscript version of the song presents the last two lines as "So maist thou be transplanted to the Skyes / And hold a Counterpoint to All Heavn's Harmonies" (see Diekhoff, *A Maske* 246). Apparently Lawes added the nonsensical "transplanted" and kept the musical term.
[159]As with Adam's creation out of clay, all earthly beings are assumed to be made out of Earth's "mould."
[160]A curious word here, "ravishment" suggests that the potential rapist is himself "seized" or put in raptures by the Lady's song. Something similar happens to Milton's Satan when he is rendered "stupidly good" by the vision of Eve's beauty in Book 9 of *Paradise Lost*:

                her every Aire
     Of gesture or lest action overawd
     His Malice, and with rapine sweet bereav'd
     His fierceness of the fierce intent it brought. (459–62)

Notice the use of the word "rapine."
[161]The Lady's spirit, evidence of her divine nature, creates what might be thought of as holy or inspired sounds, something similar to a Muse's response to an invocation. The possessive "his" (which would be neuter "its" today) refers to the "something holy." The opposite of this kind of inspired song would be Satan's movement of the Serpent's tongue, through demonic possession, to create a voice.
[162]The softer feathers (down) of the raven.
[163]According to which critic one reads, the images are either a lovely mixture appealing to various senses or a jumble of mixed metaphors. "The music floats upon the silence as if borne on wings through the empty vault of night; then, with a change of image, dark night is likened to a bird, a raven, whose ruffled plumes are smoothed by the caressing cadence [see *OED* "fall" 10] till the very darkness seems to smile" (*Variorum* 2.3: 895).
[164]Milton associates the Sirens with Circe with no classical precedent, though Horace had mentioned them both in the same line (*Epodes* 1.2.23). Milton first wrote

                                          ~~sitting~~
     my mother Circe wth the Sirens three   ·amidst the flowrie-kirtl'd Naiade^s
                                           potent
                           culling thire ~~potent~~ hearbes & balefull druggs
                             (~~powerfull~~)

                  ~~mighty~~ X

Amidst the flowry-kirtl'd *Naiades*[165]
Culling their Potent hearbs, and balefull drugs,[166]   255
Who as they sung, would take the prison'd soul,[167]
And lap° it in *Elysium*, *Scylla* wept,[168]   ENFOLD, WRAP
And chid her barking waves into attention,
And fell° *Charybdis* murmur'd soft applause:[169]   DEADLY
Yet they in pleasing slumber lull'd the sense,
And in sweet madnes rob'd it of it self,[170]   260
But such a sacred, and home-felt[171] delight,
Such sober certainty of waking bliss
I never heard till now. Ile speak to her
And she shall be my Queen.[172] Hail forren wonder[173]
Whom certain these rough shades[174] did never breed   265
Unlesse the Goddes that in rurall shrine
Dwell'st[175] here with *Pan*, or *Silvan*,[176] by blest Song
Forbidding every bleak unkindly Fog
To touch the prosperous[177] growth of this tall Wood.[178]   270
    La. Nay gentle Shepherd[179] ill is lost[180] that praise
That is addrest to unattending Ears,

The passage to the right was inserted by means of a line drawn to it from "three."

[165]In Ovid the nymphs attending Circe are Nereids, or sea nymphs (*Metamorphoses* 14: 261–67), which Milton appropriately changes to Naiades, nymphs of freshwater springs and rivers, here given garlands or kirtles of flowers.

[166]The word could refer to any innocent spice, or to a harmful or toxic medication. See *OED* n. 1.

[167]The soul as it is imprisoned in the body. The word "take" might mean "capture," "seize magically," or "captivate" (compare Nativity Ode 98).

[168]Milton canceled the "would weepe" in "Scylla would weepe" and substituted the much more effective simple past tense "Scylla wept."

[169]The song of the Sirens had the power to make the most ferocious monster calm and humane. Scylla was the barking monster supposed to be on one side of the Straits of Messina, between Sicily and Italy, and Charybdis the whirlpool on the other. The idiom "between Scylla and Charybdis" would be equivalent to the modern "between a rock and a hard place."

[170]False ecstasy, as opposed to true divine inspiration.

[171]Since Milton's is the first recorded usage of this compound, we must derive a meaning from this instance. "Felt *at home*, intimately, or in one's heart" is the definition the *OED* derives from the way the word is used here, but Milton may also have been working with the virtues issuing naturally from the good upbringing of the Egerton home, the "family values" with which the Lady is imbued, including the sobriety and piety alluded to here. The contrast is between the sophisticated, exotic, and degenerate song of the Sirens and the song of the Lady, produced in homely but holy surroundings and engendering bliss. Compare Comus's scorn for "homely features" at 748: Comus's position toward the family is, of course, hostile.

[172]Comus's presumptuousness in taking the Lady as a potential bride must have shocked the original audience of the masque, since any marriage he proposes would be a horrible misalliance between a noble Lady and a bestial necromancer. Before he has heard the Lady sing, he has only been talking about adding to his "herd" (152). The word "breed" in the next line may provide a hidden subtext, though it does not apply to Comus's projected marriage with the Lady.

[173]Satan similarly begins his flattery of Eve:
    Wonder not, sovran Mistress, if perhaps
    Thou canst, who art sole Wonder, much less arm
    Thy looks, the Heav'n of mildness, with disdain,
    Displeas'd that I approach thee thus, and gaze
    Insatiate, I thus single, nor have feard
    Thy awful brow, more awful thus retir'd. (9.532–37)
Comus's address to the Lady as "forren wonder" suggests that he is treating her as a bit of exotica to be wondered at, and both Comus and Satan appear to be Petrarchan lovers facing the potential disdain of a proud lady.

[174]That is, the rough woods near Ludlow, where only humble rural gods, like Pan or Sylvan, might live. Comus suggests that the Lady is from some exotic foreign capital rather than the woods of Herefordshire. He is only half right, and his flattery is exaggerated to the point of outrageous hyperbole.

[175]In the manuscript Milton first wrote a word that appears to be "liv'st," then struck it through and wrote "dwell'st" in the right margin.

[176]Milton may be giving the reader a choice between two names for deities sometimes assumed to be the same, Pan being the better known. Sylvanus, whose name implies his association with "sylvae," or woods, is a woodland deity, like Pan half man and half goat. Vergil pictures Pan and Sylvanus together, Sylvanus with "flowering fennel and tall lilies nodding from his head," and Pan "stained with vermilion and with blood-red elderberry juice" (*Eclogues* 10. 25, 27, trans. Rieu).

[177]Milton canceled "prospering" and substituted "prosperous" in the right margin, by means of an asterisk.

[178]To the Lady's song is ascribed the power to dispel fogs, themselves associated with pestilence or evil. Satan hides himself in mist in *Paradise Lost* 9.75, 158, 180.

[179]We are led to believe, though there has been no costume change, that the Lady is genuinely deceived into thinking that Comus is a shepherd or gentle villager; thus his magic dust has indeed bleared her eyes, though she immediately sees through his pretentious rhetoric.

[180]Not the same as "all is lost," the phrase probably means that such a scheme is bound to go astray, or is bound for a bad end.

Not any boast of skill, but extreme[181] shift
How to regain my sever'd company[182]
Compell'd me to awake the courteous Echo   275
To give me answer from her mossie Couch.[183]
  Co. What chance good Lady hath bereft you thus?[184]
  La. Dim darknes, and this leavy Labyrinth.°   LEAFY MAZE
  Co. Could that divide you from neer-ushering[185] guides?
  La. They left me weary[186] on a grassie terf.[187]   280
  Co. By falshood, or discourtesie, or why?[188]
  La. To seek i'th vally som cool[189] friendly Spring.
  Co. And left your fair side all unguarded Lady?
  La. They were but twain, and purpos'd quick return.
  Co. Perhaps fore-stalling night prevented them.[190]   285
  La. How easie my misfortune is to hit!°
  Co. Imports their loss, beside the present need?[191]   DISCOVER
  La. No less then[192] if I should my brothers loose.
  Co. Were they of manly prime, or youthful bloom?[193]
  La. As smooth as *Hebe*'s their unrazor'd° lips.   NOT YET SHAVEN   290
  Co. Two such I saw, what time° the labour'd Oxe   WHEN
In his loose traces from the furrow came,[194]
And the swink't hedger at his Supper sate;[195]
I saw them under a green mantling vine
That crawls along the side of yon small hill,   295
Plucking ripe clusters from the tender shoots,
Their port° was more then human, as they stood;   DEPORTMENT
I took it for a faëry vision
Of som gay creatures of the element[196]

---

[181]Accented on the first syllable.

[182]"How to regain the company [of my two brothers] cut off from me."

[183]The nymph Echo might be pictured on a mossy couch because she lived in caves and woods, where she pined away for love of Narcissus. See Ovid, *Metamorphoses* 3.346–400, for the story of Echo and Narcissus. After "to give me answere" in the manuscript, Milton repeated "to give me," then struck through it, and he added a "t" to "couch" by means of a caret, making it "coutch"; the correction might indicate a phonetic preference.

[184]What follows is a staccato dialogue in the form of Greek tragic stichomythia, literally a series of one-liners between two characters. As Hughes points out, the device "gave curious excitement to encounters between strangers, as . . . in Sophocles' *Oedipus at Colonus*" (quoted from Hughes's edition of 1937, in *Variorum* 2.3: 898). Milton's use of the Greek form of dialogue, though it may seem strained on the page, can be performed as rapid exchange of repartee between two potential enemies.

[185]An usher was a male attendant on a lady (*OED* 2.b). The manuscript at first read "thire ushering hands."

[186]The word was first written as the past tense, "wearied," then the final "d" was struck through.

[187]It seems to have been customary to put grassy sod on stone benches in the woods, to make them more comfortable (see *OED* "turf" 1: "Vpon a benche coueryd wyth grene torues, we satte downe," quoted from Robinson's 1551 translation of Thomas More's *Utopia*, Chapter 1).

[188]Comus imputes the worst of motives to the brothers, in a kind of smear campaign to denigrate them and thereby replace them with himself in the Lady's affection.

[189]The word was written above the line in the manuscript and added by means of a caret.

[190]"Perhaps night fell too rapidly, keeping them from finding you."

[191]"Does losing them mean anything to you, outside of your present need for them?"

[192]"Then" was repeated in the line, then the second crossed through.

[193]"Were they in the prime of manhood, or in adolescence?" This might be a leading question, since Comus needs to know who might be defending the Lady against his assaults.

[194]Comus is talking in pastoral terms, rather precisely: he is dating the coming of the evening by the time when the hard-worked ("labour'd") ox, with his harness loosened, returns from the day's work spent in the furrows he has just plowed.

[195]Another English pastoral scene: the hard-worked ("swink't") hedger (maintainer of hedgerow fences) sits down to his dinner. Milton's is the first instance of the adjective "swinked" recorded in the *OED*, and all other recorded usage of the word is derived from this instance.

[196]The *OED*, citing this instance, is probably correct: "The sky; ? also, the atmosphere. Obs.[This sense is app. due to med.L. *elementum ignis* as a name of the starry sphere; but there may be a mixture of the sense *air*]" (10.a).

That in the colours of the Rainbow live[197]　　　　　　　　　　　　　　　　300
And play i'th plighted° clouds. I was aw-strook,　　　PLEATED, FOLDED
And as I past, I worshipt; if those you seek
It were a journey like the path to Heav'n,
To help you find them.[198] *La.* Gentle villager
What readiest way would bring me to that place?　　　　　　　　　　　　　　　305
　　Co. Due west it rises from this shrubby° point.　　　THICKLY WOODED
　　La. To find out that, good Shepherd, I suppose,
In such a scant allowance of Star-light,
Would overtask the best Land-Pilots art,
Without the sure guess[199] of well-practiz'd feet.　　　　　　　　　　　　　　310
　　Co. I know each lane, and every alley green[200]
Dingle,[201] or bushy dell of this wide[202] Wood,
And every bosky bourn[203] from side to side
My daily walks and ancient neighbourhood,[204]
And if your stray attendance° be yet lodg'd,　　　STRAYED ATTENDANTS　　315
Or shroud° within these limits, I shall know[205]　　　TAKE SHELTER
Ere morrow wake, or the low roosted lark[206]
From her thach't pallat rowse, if otherwise
I can conduct you Lady to a low
But loyal cottage,[207] where you may be safe　　　　　　　　　　　　　　　320
Till further quest.[208] *La.* Shepherd I take thy word,
And trust thy honest offer'd courtesie,[209]

---

[197]If they do resemble the rainbow, at least in Comus's imagination, the imagery allies them with the Attendant Spirit, who wears the rainbow coat, but as usual Comus's picture of them is distorted, flattering hyperbole, and his response to two mortals—worshiping them—is improper and idolatrous, even if they are noble children.

[198]The phrase in the manuscript was originally "find them out," but the "out" was struck through.

[199]The line originally was written "w^thout sure steerage of," then "the" was added after "w^thout" and "steerage of" was struck through. "Steerage" is a nautical term meaning "skilled guidance."

[200]"Flat patch of grass, fit for easy travel."

[201]Another rural word, perhaps even with a Welsh flavor in honor of the locale. Michael Drayton, a Welshman, had used the noun before Milton; the sense was "A deep dell or hollow; now usually applied (app. after Milton) to one that is closely wooded or shaded with trees; but, according to Ray and in mod. Yorkshire dialect, the name of a deep narrow cleft between hills" (*OED* 1, citing Milton's usage here as the second recorded instance after Drayton's).

[202]The word was originally "wide," then that word was underlined and "wild" added in the right margin by the scribe who made corrections on the manuscript. I agree with Shawcross's restoration of "wide," though the printed versions have "wild" or "wilde." BMS also prints "wide," indicating that the correction made on the manuscript was not seen by the scribe who wrote out BMS.

[203]"Every stream lined with trees," though "bourn" could have the meaning "boundary" or, in this case, "hedgerow boundary." Milton was repeating himself again as he wrote the line, since he wrote "bosky" three times in a row (spelling it the same way each time), striking through the adjective twice before settling on it.

[204]Milton first wrote the incorrect "nieghbour," then struck through that and wrote "neighbourhood."

[205]The line was apparently first written as "w^thin these limits I shall know," adding "shroudie" before "limits" by means of an "x" mark referring to the word in the right margin. Thus "shroudie" was first an adjective, meaning "dark" or "concealing" and then it became an active verb meaning something like "seek shelter" or "conceal oneself." Loh points to Spenser's usage in *Shepheardes Calender* "February" 122: "And in his small bushes used to shrowde."

[206]Skylarks, traditionally associated with the dawn, do indeed roost near the ground and build a thatched pallet of a nest. The scribe who made additions to the manuscript corrected Milton's "palate" to "pallat" in the margin, underlining it as he had done with "wide." I have left that correction in place, since "palate," in the 1630s as well as now, might have been confused with the word meaning "the roof of the mouth" or "the seat of taste." In the manuscript, the two lines originally were written as:

~~ere the lark rowse rowſe~~ ere morrow wake or the low-roosted Larke
　　　　　　　　from her thetch't ~~rowse~~ palate rowse, if otherwise pallat

Again, Milton was having problems deciding on whether or not to use "rowse" and thus he repeated it.

[207]The cottage is lowly but loyal presumably to the Lady's father, the legal magistrate of the countryside; thus she would be safe there.

[208]The manuscript adds "be made" after "quest," then strikes it out. Milton apparently removed the redundant verb construction as he decided to begin the Lady's next speech on this line.

[209]With a certain amount of irony, because she is wrong about Comus, the Lady says, truthfully, that courtesy is often more readily found in the houses of the lowly than in courts, though it was named from the latter. One question mulled over by critics is whether the Lady is speaking what Milton might consider to be the truth, a path that might lead her to renounce her aristocratic position. See Wilding, "Milton's" 48–50.

Which oft is sooner found in lowly sheds[210]
With smoaky rafters, then in tapstry Halls[211]
And Courts of Princes, where[212] it first was nam'd,   325
And yet is most pretended:[213] In a place
Less warranted° then this,[214] or less secure   APPROVED, SANCTIONED
I cannot be, that I should fear to change it,
Eie me[215] blest Providence, and square my triall —→ *trusting her faith*
To my proportion'd strength.[216] Shepherd lead on.----[217]   330

prayer to GOD

                    The two Brothers.

    Eld. Bro. Unmuffle[218] ye faint stars, and thou fair Moon[219]
That wontst[220] to love the travailers benizon,°   BLESSING
Stoop° thy pale visage through an amber cloud,   BOW DOWN
And disinherit *Chaos*, that raigns here
In double night of darknes,° and of shades;   INTENSE DARKNESS   335
Or if your influence[221] be quite damm'd up
With black usurping mists, som gentle taper
Though a rush Candle[222] from the wicker hole
Of som clay habitation[223] visit us
With thy[224] long levell'd rule° of streaming light,   SHAFT   340
And thou shalt be our star of *Arcady*,
Or *Tyrian* Cynosure.[225] *2 Bro.* Or if our eyes
Be barr'd that happines,° might we but hear   GOOD FORTUNE
The folded flocks pen'd in their watled cotes,[226]

---

[210]Probably outbuildings, or only temporary living places, as compared with cottages.

[211]Grand halls hung with tapestries.

[212]Milton first wrote "were" incorrectly, added an "h" above the word, then struck through that word and wrote "where" next to it.

[213]The beginning of the line at first read "& is prætended yet," but then Milton struck out the last three words and rewrote "yet is most prætended."

[214]The manuscript added "I cannot be" after "this," and then struck it out.

[215]Milton was apparently uncertain at first about "eye me," since he crossed out "eye," then he wrote it again in the left margin. He also wrote "square this tryall" at first, struck through "this" and added "my" above the line by means of a caret.

[216]The Lady addresses Providence (controlled, of course, by a Christian God) and asks that her abilities be proportional to her trial. Milton describes England, in *Animadversions* (1641), as "this Iland under the speciall indulgent eye of his [i.e., God's] providence" (Yale 1: 704). For a full explanation of Milton's beliefs concerning the effects of divine providence on history, see "Of God's Providence, or His Universal Government of Things," Chapter 8 in his *On Christian Doctrine*.

[217]The long dash again (see also 212) indicates that something happens—in this case the exit of the Lady and of Comus disguised as the villager. The stage directions in the manuscript are "Exeunt" (after "Shepheard lead on"), followed on the next line by "the tow brothers enter."

[218]"Unveil." The *OED*, though it does not cite this passage, does cite Thomas Benlowes (1652), possibly echoing Milton: "Benlowes *Theoph.* xi. lxxii, Unmuffle, ye dim clouds, and disinherit From black usurping mists his spirit."

[219]In an unusual move, Milton first wrote a capital "M," then wrote the uncapitalized "moone" beside it.

[220]"Is accustomed to." Milton first wrote "wond'st," then thought better of what he probably considered a misspelling and wrote "wont'st."

[221]In the astrological sense, of the influence that a heavenly body exerts on the lives of human beings or terrestrial events. Thus the influence of a planet or star might be dammed up or prevented from entering Earth's atmosphere by a fog or mist.

[222]Candles were sometimes made from rush or reed material, to retain the wax and prevent the candle from burning too quickly. Within the candle proper would have been the taper, or thin cylinder of wax.

[223]"Through the crude window of a clay hut," probably the wicker transom of a window cut in a wattle-and-daub structure like the temporary shelter of a shepherd. The Elder Brother is asking, quite elaborately, for light either from the moon or from a candle in a hut, to guide them.

[224]Milton first wrote "a long," then crossed out "a" and substituted "thy" by means of a caret.

[225]In the myth of Callisto (see Ovid, *Metamorphoses* 2.409–531), this princess of Arcadia and follower of Diana is raped by Jupiter and gives birth to a son Arcas; in revenge Juno transforms her into a bear and, to compensate, Jupiter makes her into the constellation Ursa Minor, called Cynosura, or "the dog's tail" (see "L'Allegro" 80). Phoenician ("*Tyrian*") sailors were supposed to steer by the "Lesser Bear" constellation. The myth may be pertinent to Comus's behavior. Sandys comments that Jupiter "now turnes himselfe into the figure of chastitie; *Diana Calisto's* Goddesse. Vice is ashamed of vice: and so ugly, that it cannot deceave but under the pretext of Virtue; as the Divell in the shape of an Angell of light" (112).

[226]The flock of sheep would be "folded" or penned up in a sheepfold constructed of wattles or hurdles, that is, "stakes interlaced with branches" (*OED wattle* sb. 1.1). Compare "Shepherds pen thir Flocks at eeve / In hurdl'd Cotes" (*Paradise Lost* 4.185–86). In the line in the manuscript, Milton added "thire" by means of a caret before "watled," and he corrected a word which Sprott nonsensically transcribes as "c[osat]."

Or sound of pastoral reed with oaten stops,[227]   345
Or whistle from the Lodge,[228] or village cock
Count the night watches to his feathery Dames,[229]
T'would be som solace yet, som little chearing
In this close[230] dungeon of innumerous° bowes.   INNUMERABLE
But O that haples virgin our lost sister   350
Where may she wander now, whether[231] betake her
From the chill dew,[232] amongst rude burrs and thistles?
Perhaps som cold bank is her boulster° now   PILLOW, BOLSTER
Or 'gainst the rugged bark of som broad Elm
Leans her unpillow'd head fraught with sad fears.   355
What if in wild amazement, and affright,°   TERRIFIED
Or while we speak within the direfull grasp
Of Savage hunger, or of Savage heat?[233]
   Eld. Bro. Peace brother, be not over-exquisite[234]
To cast the fashion° of uncertain evils;   PREDICT   360
For grant they be so, while they rest° unknown,   REMAIN
What need a man forestall his date of grief,
And run to meet what he would most avoid?
Or if they be but false alarms of Fear,
How bitter is such[235] self-delusion?   365
I do not think my sister so to seek,°   SO MUCH AT FAULT
Or so unprincipl'd[236] in vertues book,
And the sweet peace that goodnes boosoms° ever,   HARBORS
As that the single want° of light and noise[237]   MERE LACK
(Not being in danger, as I trust she is not)   370
Could stir° the constant mood[238] of her calm thoughts,   TROUBLE

---

[227]The sound of something like a syrinx, or panpipe, constructed of hollow reeds ("oats") of differing lengths and with holes ("stops") cut in each, tied together and used by shepherds to make music.

[228]The shepherd, or some forest-dweller, might be heard inside his bower or lodge, whistling. Milton at first spelled the word "wistle," then struck it out and wrote "whistle" to the right.

[229]The village rooster would serve as a kind of watchman during the night, marking the various watches of the night (traditional divisions of the hours) by his crowing. His "feathery Dames," as with Chaucer's Dame Pertelot in "The Nun's Priest's Tale," would be his flock of hens.

[230]In the sense of "confining" or "smothering," as in the modern idiom "the air is close in here." Milton first wrote the line "in lone dungeon of innumerous bowes," then struck through "lone" and added "this" by means of a caret, and "sad" (deleted) and then "close" after "lone" by means of a caret.

[231]Though "wither" (echoing "Where") would seem to be the better choice of words in context, all extant versions, including the Trinity Manuscript, have "whether." Hughes, Carey, Orgel and Goldberg, and Campbell, among others, make the change silently, but Shawcross does not

[232]Milton revised what are in the printed versions 366–76 heavily, using an attached leaf to add new text. He canceled "p[er]happs some cold hard banke" to replace it with "amongst rude burrs & thistles"; he canceled "in this dead solitude surrounding wilde"; he replaced "p[er]happs some cold banck is" but then reinstated it; and he first wrote "she leans her thoughtfull head musing at our unkindnesse," but canceled the "she" and from "her" through "unkindnesse." This last cancelation indicates that Milton did not want the brothers to be thought "unkind." Milton first wrote

    so fares as did forsaken Proserpine
    when the big ["rowling" added above the line] wallowing flakes of pitchie clowds
    & darknesse wond ["u" above the line] her in.

Evidently, he thought the image extreme: though the image of the forsaken Proserpine made it into the BMS, it did not appear in print. The possibly offensive image of "Savage hunger, or of Savage heat" was, however, allowed to stand in *1637* and in *1645*. The lines after the Elder Brother's "peace, brother, peace" (BMS 360) up to "I doe not thinke my sister soe to seeke" (BMS 361) were cut from BMS, again perhaps because of performance economy.

[233]This sentence has no verb, though a reader might be expected to supply "she is" after "What if" or "we speak." The absence of the verb may be due to the revisions in the manuscript, which has no punctuation after "fears." Another possibility is that the Elder Brother cuts his brother off in midsentence with "Peace brother."

[234]The *OED* cites one instance from 1565 of "over-exquisite" as synonymous with "curious," which might be understood as "fastidious." The Elder Brother, voice of common sense, is cautioning his brother not to be hysterically precise about unknown evils.

[235]Milton first wrote "this," then canceled it for "such."

[236]The first instance of the word in the *OED*.

[237]This line was originally written "as that the single ["want" added above by means of a caret] of light & noise (not beeing in danger, as I trust she is not)."

[238]Probably "steady courage" (see *OED* 2.a). Milton first wrote either "steadie" (Scolar facsimile transcription) or "stable" (Sprott), then replaced it with "constant."

And put them into mis-becoming plight.[239]
Vertue could[240] see to do what vertue would
By her own radiant light,[241] though Sun and Moon
Were in the flat Sea[242] sunk. And Wisdoms self[243]   375
Oft seeks to° sweet retired Solitude,[244]   RESORTS TO
Where with her best nurse Contemplation
She plumes her feathers, and lets grow her wings ⏤
That in the various bustle of resort[245]
Were all to ruffl'd,[246] and somtimes impair'd.[247]   380
He that has light within his own cleer[248] brest
May sit i'th center,[249] and enjoy bright day,
But he that hides a dark soul, and foul thoughts[250]
Benighted walks under the mid-day Sun;
Himself is his own dungeon.[251]   385
   2. *Bro.* Tis most true
That musing meditation most affects
The Pensive[252] secrecy of desert cell,[253]
Far from the cheerfull haunt of men, and[254] herds,°   MULTITUDES
And sits as safe as in a Senat house,
For who would rob a Hermit of his Weeds,[255]   390
His few Books, or his Beads,[256] or Maple Dish,[257]
Or do his gray hairs any violence?
But beauty like the fair Hesperian Tree[258]

---

[239]"Put them into 'amazement' (above 355 . . .)" (*Variorum* 2.3: 906).

[240]The manuscript adds "ad all her" at this point, then strikes it out.

[241]Virtue, in other words, provides its own illumination. Compare "Vertue gives her selfe light" (Spenser, *Faerie Queene* 1.1.12).

[242]Compare the "levell brine" of "Lycidas" 97.

[243]The masque is now in an allegorical mode, with Virtue, Wisdom, Solitude, and Contemplation interacting. Wisdom seeks out sweet Solitude, where, accompanied also by her nourisher Contemplation, she allows the wings of her soul to grow. For the image of the winged soul emerging, see Plato, *Phaedrus* 246C.

[244]Milton wrote "oft seeks to solitarie sweet retire" first in the manuscript, then corrected it as it is in the printed texts.

[245]Milton uses the noun *bustle* for the first time it has been recorded in English. The phrase seems to mean "in the hustle and bustle of society." "Resort" here seems to mean an aggregation of people (*OED* 5.a, citing this instance).

[246]I.e., "All-to-ruffled," or completely ruffled, tousled.

[247]Milton may be contemplating his own retirement in 374–79, if Pattison (cited in *Variorum* 2.3: 906) is correct. Milton repeated the image of flying in his letter to Diodati "*Quid agam vero?*" (*Epistola* 7) written three years later.

[248]Probably close to the Latin *clarus*, meaning, among other things, "Brilliant, celebrated, renowned" (Lewis and Short II.B). Compare "Lycidas" 70. Again, Milton seems to be thinking in terms of the retirement from society necessary to nourish a great spirit to produce a work of art. In the manuscript, he inserted "owne" by means of a caret before "cleere."

[249]Probably in the center of the earth, as far from a light source as could be imagined.

[250]The next two lines in the manuscript read "walks in black vapours, though the noontyde brand / blaze in the summer soltice," but those lines were replaced with "benighted . . . dungeon."

[251]Compare the image of "the Dungeon of our Tyrant" in *Paradise Lost* 10.466, where Satan's usage is ironic, since he is also his own dungeon, carrying Hell around within himself (4.20–21). Compare also *Samson Agonistes* "Thou art become (O worst imprisonment!) / The Dungeon of thy self" (155–56). The Younger Brother's answer completes the line of poetry. At this point I begin counting two lines separated on the page in *1645* (but not written so in the manuscript) as one line.

[252]The compositor of *1645* here blindly follows the capitalization of the adjective in *1637*, even though neither of the manuscripts has a capital, and it was unorthodox to capitalize an adjective in current printing practice.

[253]Hermitage, or place of solitary retreat for a faithful person.

[254]Milton first wrote "or," but he canceled it and inserted "and" by means of a caret.

[255]His garments. Milton seems to have been trying to create an internal rhyme here, since he first wrote "beads," crossed that out, wrote "gowne," crossed that out and inserted "weeds" above it, then put "beads" again in the margin. Apparently he was juggling "hairie gowne" and "beads" in the next line at the same time, inserting "few" and "or" to try to justify the metrics of the line while retaining "weeds" and "beads."

[256]The manuscript had, at first, "his hairie gowne" (i.e., the hair shirt of the monk), then Milton substituted "beads."

[257]The trencher or single wooden plate or bowl a hermit might possess.

[258]The tree with apples of gold guarded by the Hesperides, daughters of Hesperus, on command of Juno, is a recurring image in Milton's poetry. Because she feared that her husband Jupiter was about to have the golden fruit stolen, Hera also set a dragon to guard the fruit (in some accounts Hesperus installs the dragon). Ben Jonson, in *Every Man in His Humor* (1601 ed.) had employed the same image:
   Who will not judge him worthy to be robd,

Laden with blooming gold, had need the guard
Of dragon watch with uninchanted eye,[259]　　　　　　　　　395
To save her blossoms, and defend her fruit[260]
From the rash hand of bold Incontinence.[261]
You may as well spred out the unsun'd[262] heaps
Of Misers treasure by an out-laws den,
And tell me it is safe, as bid me hope[263]　　　　　　　　　400
Danger[264] will wink on° Opportunity,　　　　　　　BE BLIND TO
And let a single helpless maiden pass
Uninjur'd in this wilde surrounding wast.°[265]　　　　　WASTE AREA, WILDERNESS
Of night, or lonelines it recks me not,°　　　　　　　IT DOESN'T MATTER TO ME
I fear the dred events that dog them both,[266]　　　　　　　　405
Lest som ill greeting° touch attempt the person[267]　　　UNWELCOME
Of our unowned[268] sister.
　Eld. Bro. I do not, brother,[269]
Inferr, as if I thought[270] my sisters state
Secure without all doubt, or controversie:[271]
Yet where an equall poise° of hope and fear　　　　　BALANCE　　　　410
Does arbitrate th' event, my nature is
That I encline to hope, rather then fear,

That sets his doores wide open to a theefe,
And shewes the felon, where his treasure lyes?
Againe, what earthy spirit but will attempt
To taste the fruite of beauties golden tree,
When leaden sleepe seales up the dragons eyes?
O beauty is a Project of some power,
Chiefely when oportunitie attends her. (3.1.16–23)
For an astute analysis of the passages in Jonson and Milton, see C. S. Lewis, *Rehabilitations and Other Essays* (New York: Oxford UP, 1939): 167, and *Variorum* 2.3: 908.
[259]In order to deceive a monstrous guardian of some sort, whether it be Argus or the dragon of the Hesperides, one had to practice magic, either by singing it to sleep or by giving it a sleeping potion or a poison. Compare "uninchanted eye" in the manuscript, which replaced the canceled "never charmed."
[260]The word was first misspelled "frite," a "u" was added by means of a caret, and then the incorrect word was scratched through and the correct "fruite" added.
[261]The use of the allegorical figure Incontinence helps to identify Comus with that vice: he is incontinent in the sense that he believes in the overuse of natural abundance, as in drinking not for pleasure but for drunkenness.
[262]"Unsunned," not left outside for everyone to covet. Normally the treasure would be hoarded away in darkness.
[263]The manuscript first had "thinke," then Milton deleted it for "hope."
[264]Probably "power to do injury" (*OED* 1.b), as the *Variorum* editors suggest (2.3: 909).
[265]The manuscript first read "vast, & hideous wild," which was deleted and "wide surrounding wast" added.
[266]"I fear the kinds of things that dog a woman both when she goes out in darkness or when she is alone."
[267]The wording suggests "tempt" and "threaten violence to the person of" by "touch."
[268]"Unacknowledged," in the sense that she has been temporarily and unwillingly disowned by her brothers. The word also implies that a sister or daughter was considered the property of her brothers or father under normal circumstances, since "unowned" is also used of, say, a lost domestic animal. Cotgrave defined "unowned" property as "things which bee left, abandoned, escheated, or vnowned" (quoted to support *OED* "unowned" 1).
[269]This line metrically completes the line above it, and it was written as part of that line in the manuscript: "of our unowned sister. I Bro: I doe not brother . . . ." Notice that "unowned" has three syllables.
[270]He does not "argue or conclude that" (*Variorum* 2.3: 909). The context is that of rhetorical debate, almost as if the two brothers were conducting disputations in college. After the word "no" the manuscript inserts these lines:
　　　　　r
~~besh..ew me but I would~~ I could be willing though now i'th darke to trie
　　encounter
a tough· ~~passado~~ wth the shaggiest ruffian
that lurks by hedge or lane of this dead circuit
to have her by by side, though I were sure
she might be free from perill where she is
The lines were allowed to stand in BMS but excised from all printed versions. BMS gives what is essentially the corrected version of these lines, beginning "I could be willinge though now i'th darke to trie . . . ." See the Introduction, "Text." The *Variorum* editors add "The phrase *dead circuit* is unusual: *circuit* evidently means a given area or region; *dead* has perhaps a now obsolete meaning, 'causing death, deadly, mortal' (*OED* 9)" (2.3: 909–10).
[271]In the manuscript the line reads "secure, w^thout all doubt or question, no." The word "controversie" was added for the first time in *1637*.

And banish gladly[272] squint suspicion.[273]
My sister is not so defenceless left
As you imagine, she has a hidden strength   415
Which you remember not.
  2. Bro. What hidden strength,
Unless the strength of Heav'n, if you mean that?
  Eld. Bro. I mean that too, but yet a hidden strength[274]   *Chastity*
Which if Heav'n gave it, may be term'd her own:[275]
'Tis chastity, my brother, chastity: *Reason + Logic*   420
She that has that, is clad in compleat steel,[276]
And like a quiver'd[277] Nymph with Arrows keen
May trace° huge Forests, and unharbour'd Heaths,[278]   EXPLORE
Infamous[279] Hills, and sandy perilous[280] wildes,
Where through[281] the sacred rayes[282] of Chastity,   425
No savage fierce, Bandite,[283] or mountaneer[284]
Will[285] dare to soyl her Virgin purity,
Yea there, where very° desolation dwels   TRUE
By grots,° and caverns shag'd[286] with horrid[287] shades,[288]   GROTTOES
She may pass on with unblench't[289] majesty,   430
Be it not don in pride, or in presumption.

---

[272]In the manuscript Milton included a superscript "1" under "banish" and a "2" under "gladly," indicating that he wanted the word order to be "banish gladly," but no further manuscript or printed version followed that order. Shawcross restores "banish gladly" and I agree with the emendation. Milton also reworked the spelling of "suspition" to "suspicion."

[273]Suspicion is personified, as a person who squints suspiciously.

[274]Milton had some problems with spelling the word in the four present occurrences, writing it first "strength," then "strenth," then "strength" again and finally "strenth" with a "g" inserted by means of a caret. "Strength" was the more common form in the seventeenth century, but both "strenth" and "strynth" also are recorded in the *OED*.

[275]One is born chaste or pure, but with the liability to lose the virtue. Thus the Lady possesses Chastity, and it is hers to maintain.

[276]The phrase "complete steel" suggests "in full armor," but here the armor is that of the good Christian soldier, protected by virtue. "Complete" is accented on the first syllable. The two lines beginning after "steele" in the manuscript were heavily revised:

>   up   (keene
> & may (. poi̇n any needfull acciden   and like a quiverd nymph wth arrows
>   don   in
> may be it not ____ in pride or wilfull tempting) præsumption)
>   trace
> may . walke through huge forrests, & unharbour'd heaths
>   infamous hills, & þe sandie perilous wilds

The passage may be critically important because it mentions "pride" or "wilfull tempting"—the only instance of any word connected with "tempt" among the various texts of the masque.

[277]Milton's is the first recorded use of "quivered": "Provided or equipped with a quiver" (*OED* 1).

[278]A tract of waste land, not normally a location for a harbor. *OED* gives "affording no shelter" as its definition for "unharboured," citing only Milton's usage, but the definition is questionable.

[279]Presumably accented on the second syllable, though *OED* notes what the editors considered to be a preference in Milton for "in´famous."

[280]The spelling does not help here, and the manuscript has "perilous" as well, but the metrics would dictate that the noun be represented as a disyllable, and it would probably have been pronounced "par´-lous."

[281]"Through the agency of."

[282]Milton originally wrote "aw," struck through the word, added "rays" above the line and also in the right margin. He is using "ray" metaphorically, to mean an emanation from "mental and moral influences, etc., compárable to light" (*OED* noun 1.c, citing this passage).

[283]Apparently accented on the second syllable as with the Italian plural *banditti* (but not a trisyllable as in *bandito*).

[284]"Mountain man," in the negative sense of the phrase: a rough and crude hill-person.

[285]Milton first wrote "shall," struck through it, and wrote "will" in the left margin.

[286]"Made shaggy with; covered with shaggy growth."

[287]"Menacing, bristling." The Latin *horridus*, "standing on end, bristling," is usually not far from Milton's meaning for the word "horrid" in English.

[288]The line after this one was "& yawning dens where glaring monsters house" in the manuscript, but Milton struck through the line, perhaps because its images were becoming indecorous.

[289]Milton's is the first use of the adjective recorded in the *OED*: "Not blenched or turned aside; undismayed, unflinching" (1). Milton wrote the word once, as "majestie," scratched it out, but then rewrote it as the same word to the right.

Som say no evil thing that walks by night²⁹⁰
In fog, or fire, by lake, or moorish fen,²⁹¹
Blew meager° Hag, or stubborn unlaid ghost,²⁹²   EMACIATED, WITHERED
That breaks his magick chains²⁹³ at *curfeu*²⁹⁴ time,   435
No goblin, or swart Faëry of the mine,²⁹⁵
Hath hurtfull²⁹⁶ power o're true virginity.
Do you beleeve me yet, or shall I call
Antiquity from the old Schools of Greece²⁹⁷
To testifie the arms²⁹⁸ of Chastity?   440
Hence had the huntress *Dian* her dred bow
Fair silver-shafted Queen for ever chaste,²⁹⁹
Wherwith she tam'd the brinded³⁰⁰ lioness
And spotted mountain pard,° but set at nought   PANTHER OR LEOPARD
The frivolous bolt° of *Cupid*, gods and men   ARROW   445
Fear'd her stern frown, and she was queen oth' Woods.
What was that snaky-headed *Gorgon* sheild
That wise *Minerva* wore, unconquer'd³⁰¹ Virgin,
Wherwith she freez'd her foes to congeal'd³⁰² stone?
But rigid looks of Chast austerity,   450
And noble grace that dash't brute violence

---

²⁹⁰The rhythm, tone (awe-inspired), mood, and content of this description of ghosts is very close to that of Marcellus in *Hamlet* after Hamlet's father's ghost has appeared:

> Some say that ever 'gainst that season comes
> Wherein our Saviour's birth is celebrated,
> This bird of dawning singeth all night long,
> And then they say no spirit dare stir abroad,
> The nights are wholesome, then no planets strike,
> No fairy takes, nor witch hath power to charm,
> So hallowed, and so gracious, is that time. (1.1.158–64)

In the manuscript, Milton began the line "Some say," then struck through that and wrote "Nay more" above the line, struck through that and wrote "Some say" again to its right. Perhaps he was deciding whether or not to use the Shakespearean formula.
²⁹¹Bog or swamp, located on a desolate moor.
²⁹²The ghost issues forth from its grave at night because it is stubbornly restless, probably due to guilt or to some unavenged crime it knows about. In the manuscript Milton originally wrote "wrinckled hagge," crossed it out, wrote "wrincl'd" in the margin, crossed that out, then inserted "meager" above the line, apparently thinking of "meager" and "wrinckled" as being close to synonymous. Shakespeare associates the adjective "meager" with "ghost," as in *2 Henry VI* 3.2.161–62 and *King John* 3.4.84–85.
²⁹³The tradition of ghosts in chains, as with Dickens's ghost of Jacob Marley, goes back many years, though there are no ghosts in chains in Shakespeare's plays: the idea was that the encumbrances of sin and worldly possessions weigh down the spirits of the unquiet dead, a literal interpretation of the "bonds of hell." Here Milton qualifies the chains with the adjective "magic," and thereby undercuts the moral effect of portraying ghosts as members of the legion of the damned. If ghosts are stubborn and wear magic chains, they may seem more comic than horrible. The attitude here toward ghosts seems to be like Hamlet's: fearful, a bit superstitious; reverent, but at the same time comic.
²⁹⁴The italicized form of the word is probably due to the compositor's taking it as foreign, in this case French, though the word was common enough in English (originally it had been constructed of two French words indicating that the fire should be covered at that time of day). It is also italicized as "*Curfeu*" in "Il Penseroso" 74.
²⁹⁵A fairy who lived in a mine (one supposed habitation of fairies) might well be black from dust, hence "swart."
²⁹⁶This word was added to the line in the manuscript by means of a caret.
²⁹⁷One might expect this place name "Greece" to be italicized, and Shawcross does italicize it, but it is not so in *1645*, nor is it in *1637*; it is in *1673*. The debate between the two brothers resembles the kinds of public discussions that college students at Cambridge or Oxford in Milton's day would have conducted; as various critics have pointed out, the debate "proceeds from the classical to the Christian" (*Variorum* 2.3: 913).
²⁹⁸In the military sense of "protective or aggressive armor or arms."
²⁹⁹Milton added this line after "bow" and before "wherwith" in the manuscript.
³⁰⁰Literally "burnt," but often brindled or mottled flame color, as a tawny lion.
³⁰¹The word at this point in the original line in the manuscript was "æternall," while "unvanquish't" was added by means of an asterisk to the right of the line, then that was canceled for "unconquer'd" written in above it. The immortality of the gods was taken for granted, but the state of a virgin goddess as being unconquered or unvanquished would be more remarkable. The Gorgon's head on Minerva's shield did indeed freeze a viewer to "congeal'd stone." Milton first wrote what appears to be the participle "freezing" at the beginning of the next line, but misspelled it "freezind."
³⁰²Accented on the first syllable. "Congealed" here would be the same as "frozen," or "calcified," or "turned to stone."

With sudden adoration,[303] and blank aw.[304]
So dear to Heav'n is Saintly chastity,
That when a soul is found[305] sincerely so,
A thousand liveried Angels lacky her,[306]   455
Driving far off each thing of sin and guilt,[307]
And in cleer dream, and solemn vision[308]
Tell her of things that[309] no gross ear[310] can hear,
Till oft convers° with heav'nly habitants   FREQUENT CONVERSATIONS
Begin to cast a beam on th' outward shape,   460
The unpolluted temple of the mind,[311]
And turns it[312] by degrees to the souls essence,
Till all be made immortal:[313] but when lust
By unchaste looks, loose gestures, and foul talk,
But most by leud and lavish act of sin,[314]   465
Lets in defilement to the inward parts,
The soul grows clotted by contagion,
Imbodies, and imbrutes, till she[315] quite loose°[316]   LOSE
The divine[317] property of her first being.
Such are those thick and gloomy shadows damp[318]   470
Oft seen in Charnell vaults,[319] and Sepulchers[320]
Lingering, and sitting by a new made grave,
As loath to leave the body that it lov'd,[321]

---

[303]Milton first wrote the line as "wth suddaine adoration of her purenesse of bright rays," then "of . . . rays" was expunged and, either before or after that occurred, "and blank aw" was added after "purenesse."

[304]"Stupefied awe," or "suspended evil." The word "blank" here suggests not having any moral coloration. The goddesses Artemis (Diana) and Athene (Minerva) were supposed to be brought up together (Diodorus Siculus 5.3.4), and Eros (Cupid), when asked why he spared them from the affliction of love, was said to be frightened of Athene's severe look and the Gorgon head on her shield, and to have overlooked Artemis because she was always hunting.

[305]Milton changed the active construction "when it finds" to the passive "when a soule is found sincerely so," by canceling "it finds" and adding "is found" above the line by means of a caret.

[306]Milton mixes Christian imagery with that of aristocratic heraldry. Chastity is pictured as a heavenly aristocrat, with thousands of angels in her service (serving as her lackeys) and therefore wearing her livery. He altered the spelling from the nonsensical "lakey" to "lackey" by inserting the "c" above the line in the manuscript.

[307]Driving off ghosts, goblins, or any type of evil spirits, in other words.

[308]Pronounced with three distinct syllables.

[309]Milton inserted the "that" above the line in the manuscript.

[310]An ear whose sensitivity has been dulled by sin and worldliness; hence its perception is gross.

[311]John 2.21 quotes Jesus indirectly: "He spake of the temple of his body." The idea of the body of the Christian individual being the outward temple of the inward mind is a pervasive one in Christian thinking. Milton alludes to the belief that the "flesh" is "the temple of the body, as in John ii.21" (*On Christian Doctrine* 1.5; Yale 6: 233).

[312]Milton first wrote "turnes by," then struck through the second word.

[313]The idea of the soul working its way up to spirituality despite the encumbrances of the body is Platonic (*Phaedo* 81B–D); it is explained most completely in *Paradise Lost* 5.469–503.

[314]Presumably by fornication, or illicit sexual intercourse. What Milton expunged from the line is instructive: he struck through "the lacivious" before "act of sin," and softened the adjectives just slightly to read "lewd & lavish."

[315]The English word "Soul" may be feminine so far as Milton is concerned because it is associated with Cupid's bride Psyche. The Latin word that is usually translated "soul" is *anima*, a noun that can be converted to the masculine *animus* if the word searched for is "wind" or "breath." The Latin *animus / anima* is connected philosophically and theologically with the Greek Ψύχη, from which "Psyche" is derived. I was reminded by a reader that "soul" is often considered to be feminine in contemporary English usage, as in *Hamlet* 3.2. 63, "Since my dear soul was mistress of her choice . . . ."

[316]The manuscript first has the phrase "loose quite," but then Milton changes the word order by putting a "1" under "quite" and a "2" under "loose."

[317]Apparently accented on the first syllable.

[318]"Of the nature of, or belonging to, a *damp* or noxious exhalation" (*OED* 1, citing Milton's use of the word as the first recorded). In its noun form, a damp would be an unhealthy atmosphere thought to be arising out of excess humidity, to bring or help cause disease.

[319]Usually mass gravesites or burial houses, as compared to single-family sepulchers.

[320]The word was at first "monume[nts]," which Milton struck through and changed to the more forcible "sepulchers."

[321]The image is common, but it may have its origin in Plato, *Phaedo*, in which a corporeal soul, "flits about the monuments and the tombs, where shadowy shapes of souls have been seen, figures of those souls which were not set free in purity but retain something of the visible" (81D; Loeb trans.).

And link't it self° by carnal sensualty[322]   LINKED TO ITSELF

To a degenerate and degraded state.   475

  2. Bro. How charming is divine Philosophy![323] —

Not harsh, and crabbed as dull fools suppose,

But musical as is *Apollo*'s lute,[324]

And a perpetual feast of nectar'd[325] sweets,

Where no crude surfet raigns. *Eld. Bro.* List,° list, I hear[326]   LISTEN   480

Som far off hallow break the silent Air.[327]

  2. Bro. Me thought so too;[328] what should it be?

  Eld. Bro. For certain

Either[329] som one like us night-founder'd[330] here,

Or els som neighbour Wood-man, or at worst,

Som roaving Robber calling to his fellows.[331]   485

  2. Bro. Heav'n keep my sister, agen agen and neer,[332]

Best draw, and stand upon our guard.[333]

  Eld. Bro. Ile hallow,

If he be friendly he comes well, if not,[334]

Defence is a good cause, and Heav'n be for us.[335]

The attendant Spirit habited like a Shepherd.[336]

---

[322]The spelling of the word is important for its phonetic and metric values. It has three, not five, syllables. Here *1645* agrees with the manuscript "sensualtie" but not with BMS, *1637*, or *1673*. Among recent editors, Carey keeps "sensuality" but tells the reader about the manuscript "sensualty" (spelling it wrong) in a note. Orgel and Goldberg modernize to "sensuality." Campbell recognizes the metrics and, even in a modernized text, uses "sensualty."

[323]This line is apt to bring a laugh in performance, because of the leap from charnel houses to divine philosophy. In the manuscript there is a stage direction to the right of "philosophy," "Hallow within," which was deleted, and "hallow farre off" was added in the margin to the right of "silent aire" below, which may help to excuse the dramatic inappropriateness of the Younger Brother's response. Milton must have added the stage direction before he finished the line, since when he wrote from the left, he had to wrap the "phy" of "philosophy" above the line.

[324]Since Apollo was god of all the fine arts and patron of the nine Muses, he would be connected with both philosophy and sacred song (hence the mention of his lute).

[325]Nectar and ambrosia were the traditional foods of the Greek gods, supposed to help confer immortality. Both were thought to be sweet tasting or sweet smelling.

[326]Milton wrote "list, me thought I heard," to the right of the line, but then he deleted "me thought" and the "d" at the end of "heard" while adding an "e" to make it present tense.

[327]The stage direction "hallow farre off" was written to the right of the line in the manuscript. The stage direction appears in no other early edition, but it can be inferred by what the Elder Brother says.

[328]"It seemed so to me as well."

[329]The word was written once, then struck through, then reinstated in the manuscript.

[330]"Stranded or abandoned because of the night's darkness."

[331]The line in the Trinity Manuscript first read:

                        hedge

some roaving   some ~~curl'd. man of yᵉ swoord~~ calling to his fellows

robber

Milton put an X through the phrase "some roaving robber." The "roaving robber" was at first, apparently, a "curl'd hedge man of yᵉ swoord," apparently similar to the previously mentioned "swinck't hedger" or disreputable "mountain man." Why he is "curl'd" I would only guess: perhaps his unkempt hair is like that of Comus.

[332]He hears the shout; or hallow, again, and nearer to them. Milton first wrote the redundant "yet agen, agen & nèere," then struck through the "yet."

[333]"We had best draw our swords and be on guard."

[334]The manuscript, following "if not," has

                              ~~a just Defence is a~~

     scratch

     ~~he may chaⁿnce. had best looke to his forehead. heere be brambles~~

     defence is a good cause & heav'n be for us

Apparently Milton first wrote "he may chance scratch" perhaps to be followed by "his forehead" (underlined), then he altered that to "he had best looke to his forehead. heere be brambles." What the Elder Brother is offering is certainly a threat, but instead of the "iron stakes" offering violence to begin with, he first thought of Comus as doing damage to himself, then of the brothers somehow damaging Comus's scalp (with brambles?), then he arrived at the "pointed stakes," and from thence to "iron stakes." As something of an idle bit of detective work, it might be offered that between the first and last revisions, Milton came to understand that the Bridgewater brothers would be wearing the children's equivalent of swords.

[335]"May Heaven be on our side [in whatever fight might ensue]."

[336]The stage direction in the Trinity Manuscript is "he hallows ~~hallo~~ the guardian Dæmon hallows agen & enters in the habit of shepheard."

That hallow I should know, what are you?[337] speak;   490
Com not too neer, you fall on iron stakes[338] else.
   Spir. What voice is that?[339] my young Lord? speak agen.
   2. Bro. O brother, 'tis my fathers[340] Shepherd sure.
   Eld. Bro. Thyrsis?[341] Whose artful strains have oft delaid

Reliable tutor

The huddling brook to hear his madrigal,[342]   495
And sweeten'd every muskrose[343] of the dale,[344]
How cam'st thou here good Swain?[345] Hath any ram
Slip't from the fold,[346] or young Kid lost his dam,°   MOTHER
Or straggling weather[347] the pen't° stock forsook?   PENNED, PENT UP
How couldst thou find this dark sequester'd nook?   500
   Spir. O my lov'd masters heir, and his next joy,[348]
I came not here on such a trivial toy
As a stray'd Ewe,[349] or to pursue the stealth
Of pilfering Woolf, not all the fleecy wealth[350]
That doth enrich these Downs, is worth a thought   505
To this my errand, and the care[351] it brought.
But O my Virgin Lady, where is she?
How chance she is not in your company?
   Eld. Bro. To tell thee sadly Shepherd, without blame,
Or our neglect, we lost her as we came.   510
   Spir.[352] Ay me unhappy![353] then my fears are true.
   El. Bro. What fears good *Thyrsis?*[354] Prethee° briefly shew.[355]   I PRAY YOU
   Spir.[356] Ile tell ye, 'tis not vain, or fabulous,
(Though so esteem'd by shallow ignorance)

---

[337]In the manuscript the word "you" is written above the line after "are," but there is no question mark. Commas were added in *1637*, and the question mark in *1645*.

[338]In effect, their swords, though why those swords are said to be "iron" I cannot determine. The manuscript first had "pointed stakes," which makes more sense metaphorically; "pointed" was deleted for "iron." The phrase "too neere" was at first deleted but then reinstated by underlining.

[339]I have restored the punctuation of the manuscript, in which the line reads "Dæ. what voice is that? my yong lord? speake agen." Modern punctuation usage might put a colon after "that." He answers his own question with another, more pointed, one: "Whose voice is that? My young lord's?"

[340]The word is "father" in *1637* and *1645*, but not in the Trinity or Bridgewater manuscript. I have restored the manuscript reading.

[341]Milton changed the spelling from "Thirsis" to "Thyrsis," perhaps to emphasize the name's Greek origin.

[342]Probably not the many-voiced madrigal, but the solo madrigal first composed in the early seventeenth century (see "Madrigal" in *The Norton/Grove Concise Encyclopedia of Music* [New York: Norton, 1988]). If Thyrsis has the power to still the water of a brook, his musical ability must be close to that of Orpheus.

[343]A specific type of roses, growing wild ("of the dale"), which give off a musky odor when the stems are rubbed.

[344]Milton first wrote "valley," then struck it out for "dale."

[345]Both Trinity Manuscript and BMS have "shepheard," but *1637* and *1645* have "Swaine" and "Swain." So far as we can determine, the change in the printed editions was authorial. There is certainly a problem in deciding whether to call the Attendant Spirit "Dæmon" or "Shepherd." The speech prefix "Shep." was crossed out at 513 below and "Dæ." drawn in in the left margin, just as "shep." was changed to "Thyrsis" in 512.

[346]In the manuscript Milton first wrote "leapt ore the penne," canceled it, but added "slip't" in the left margin and restored the "penne" by underlining it. He also began to write "ki," possibly blotted it with his pen, then scratched it out and wrote "kid" to the right.

[347]Castrated male sheep, perhaps more apt to roam or straggle and get lost than the ewes (who would keep watch over their lambs), or the rams (jealous of the ewes). The manuscript has the line "or straggling weather ~~hath~~ the pen't flock ~~flock~~ forsook?"

[348]Because the Elder Brother would be the heir apparent to the earldom, he would be his father's nearest or next joy.

[349]"I did not come here on such a trivial errand as a search for a lost sheep."

[350]Flocks of sheep, their wool, their meat, and their fleece would indeed constitute the wealth of the countryside near Ludlow.

[351]In the Latin sense of "responsibility," as in the line from the old ballad, "Greensleeves was all my care."

[352]The speech prefix in the manuscript is "Sheph." In BMS it is "Dæ:," making the abbreviation for "Daemon." In *1637*, "Spir." begins to occur.

[353]There is no punctuation at this point in *1645*. I have restored the exclamation point of the Trinity Manuscript, as does Shawcross.

[354]Changed by means of an asterisk from "shep." in the line to "Thyrsis" in the right margin.

[355]"I pray you tell me, as concisely as you can."

[356]"Shep." is struck through in the manuscript, and "Dæ." added in the left margin.

What the sage Poets taught by th' heav'nly Muse,[357]   515
Storied of old in high immortal vers
Of dire *Chimera*'s[358] and inchanted Iles,[359]
And rifted Rocks[360] whose entrance leads to hell,
For such there be, but unbelief is blind.[361]
   Within the navil[362] of this hideous Wood,   520
Immur'd in cypress shades[363] a Sorcerer dwels
Of *Bacchus*, and of *Circe* born, great *Comus*,
Deep skill'd[364] in all his mothers witcheries,
And here to every thirsty wanderer,
By sly enticement gives his banefull cup,   525
With many murmurs mixt,[365] whose pleasing poison
The visage quite transforms of him that drinks,
And the[366] inglorious likenes of a beast
Fixes instead,[367] unmoulding reasons mintage[368]
Character'd[369] in the face; this have I learn't   530
Tending my flocks hard by° i'th hilly crofts,[370]   NEARBY
That brow this bottom glade,[371] whence night by night
He and his monstrous rout are heard to howl
Like stabl'd wolves,[372] or tigers at their prey,
Doing abhorred rites to *Hecate*   535
In their obscured haunts of inmost bowres.
Yet have they[373] many baits, and guilefull spells
To inveigle and invite th' unwary sense[374]
Of them that pass unweeting[375] by the way.

---

[357]The Attendant Spirit at this point seems to be speaking pure Milton on the subject of heroic poetry. Milton discusses his own youthful reading in heroic romances in *An Apology against a Pamphlet* (1642): " . . . I betook me among those lofty Fables and Romances, which recount in solemne canto's the deeds of Knighthood founded by our victorious Kings; & from thence had in renowne over all Christendome" (Yale 1: 890–91).

[358]The deadly ("dire") monster who breathes fire from a lion's head but has a goat's body and a dragon's tail (Homer, *Iliad* 6.179–82; and Vergil, *Aeneid* 6.288). Compare *Paradise Lost* 2.628, where chimeras are grouped with hydras and gorgons.

[359]Islands such as those of Circe or Calypso in the *Odyssey*, or that of Alcina in Ariosto's *Orlando Furioso* 6.34–38.

[360]"Rocks split to form an entrance-way."

[361]Milton added this line—apparently as an afterthought—in the right margin in the manuscript.

[362]The absolute center of the woods (*OED* 2.a). The paragraph beginning here is unusual: it is not indicated in the manuscript, but there is an indentation in BMS and that indentation made it into the printed editions. It seems fitting that the Attendant Spirit's narrative begin a new paragraph.

[363]"Walled up in the deep shade provided by cypress trees." The cypress tree was often associated with death or mourning, and its shades would hide the "abhorred rites" of Cotytto.

[364]Milton may have first tried to write "deepe learnt," then "deepe enur'd," settling on "deepe skill'd."

[365]The murmurs would be incantatory formulas recited by the sorcerer Comus.

[366]An asterisk before "the" is answered in the right margin by the word "makes," to form "makes the inglorious likenesse of a beast," but "makes" has been struck through, probably for metrical reasons.

[367]Milton added "fixes instead," in the left margin, to a line that that consisted only of "unmoulding reasons mintage."

[368]The image is from coining: by altering the mold into which the molten metal was poured, a coin-maker could change the mintage or image on the coin. Reason was the minter who made the human image originally in its upright and noble shape; Comus remakes the image, by means of his potion, into that of a "grov'ling swine."

[369]Having an image on it (as when letters on a printed page are spoken of as "characters"), but also "being imbued with human character." Patrick McHenry has demonstrated the seventeenth-century belief in "signatures" in plants due in part to the influence of Paracelsus (1493–1541): such a theory might use a walnut, shaped like a brain, as brain medicine (McHenry 3–5).

[370]The manuscript reads "i'th pastur'd lawn's" at first, then "pastur'd" and "lawn's" have been struck through and "hillie" and "crofts" added above the line. Milton also changed the number of the verb, making "brows" in the next line "brow." A hilly croft would be equivalent to a pastured lawn, in the sense that both would represent fenced pasture in the hills.

[371]"The small hill-farms that sit in the brow or head of this opening in the forest."

[372]Confined or stabled wolves might be expected to howl to get out.

[373]Milton wrote the word once, scratched it out, then wrote it again. He also slipped, apparently, with the spelling of "guileful," beginning it "gil," then scratching that out to replace it with "guilefull."

[374]Milton wrote the nonsensical "spell," carrying it absent-mindedly from the line above, then canceled it for "sense."

[375]Milton seems to prefer this adjective to describe the unwariness of potential sinners. Compare Eve's being described as "unweeting" in *Paradise Lost* 10.335, 916.

This evening late by then the chewing flocks   540
Had ta'n their supper on the savoury Herb
Of Knot-grass dew-besprent,[376] and were in fold,
I sate me down to watch upon a bank
With Ivy canopied,° and interwove   OVERHUNG
With flaunting° Hony-suckle,[377] and began   WAVING PROUDLY   545
Wrapt° in a pleasing fit of melancholy[378]   ENRAPTURED
To meditate my rural minstrelsie,
Till fancy° had her fill, but ere a close[379]   IMAGINATION
The wonted° roar was up amidst the Woods,   CUSTOMARY
And fill'd the Air with barbarous dissonance,   550
At which I ceas't,[380] and listen'd them° a while,   LISTENED TO THEM
Till an unusuall stop[381] of sudden silence
Gave respit to the drowsie flighted[382] steeds
That draw the litter of close-curtain'd sleep.[383]
At last a soft and solemn breathing sound[384]   555
Rose like a steam of rich distill'd Perfumes,
And stole upon the Air, that even Silence
Was took e're she was ware,[385] and wish't she might
Deny her nature, and be never more
Still to be so[386] displac't. I was all eare,°   ALL EARS   560

---

[376]Knot-grass was a kind of spreading weed that might cover waste ground and on which sheep or goats might feed. It is wet with dew because of the time of day.

[377]In the manuscript Milton first wrote "wth suckling honiesuckle," then canceled "suckling" and wrote "blowing" above the line; then in the margin he wrote "flaunting," canceled that for "blowing" (i.e., "blooming") above the line, then reinstated "flaunting" to the right. "Suckling honeysuckle" would have been redundant (the noun "suckling" meant not only a nursing infant but "honeysuckle" as well), "blowing" (i.e., blooming) as applying to plants was conventional; "flaunting," with its hint of personification, may give the image movement and vitality.

[378]Here something like "pleasant introspection, leading to creativity." From a seventeenth-century physician's point of view, melancholy could be a dangerous mental disease, akin to depression, or a creative state of mind, leading to the production of songs or sonnets. For two perspectives on melancholy, see "L'Allegro" and "Il Penseroso," the first of which treats it as "loathed" and the second in the more positive sense described here. This line and the next were in reversed order in the manuscript, but Milton corrected that by putting a number 2 and 1 to the left of them.

[379]The phrase was "the close," then "the" was canceled and "a" added above the line by means of a caret. A "close" is a musical ending, "The conclusion of a musical phrase, theme, or movement; a cadence" (*OED* n. 2).

[380]Apparently Milton wanted at first to write this in present tense, "at wch I cease, & listen them awhile." He apparently changed "cease" to "ceas'd," and "listen" to "listend," inserting the second "d" by means of a caret.

[381]Perhaps used in the musical sense, in which a silence would indicate the end of a passage, in the "barbarous dissonance."

[382]A textual crux, since the manuscript reads "flighted," but, starting with BMS, all other early versions have "frighted." How the horses can be drowsy and frighted at the same time is hard to say, whereas they are certainly "flighted" or "winged." The *OED* reads the construction as "drousie-flighted steeds" (where the editors took the phrase, assigned to "*Comus* 1634," is unclear) and defines "flighted" as "Having a certain flight or speed," basing its definition primarily on this excised version. Milton invented the word, according to the *OED*. Shawcross prefers "frighted," as do most modern editors, though Campbell (following the *OED*'s invented citation) modernizes to "drowsy-flighted." Since Milton in the next line hyphenated "close-curtain'd," it is obvious that he did not want the construction hyphenated, though the horses might better be described as drowsy and also flighted, rather than drowsy and affrighted.

[383]The horses of the moon-chariot traditionally driven by Diana, Hecate, or Persephone are spoken of as being both drowsy and winged (if "flighted" is correct), and the chariot itself as being curtained like a Renaissance aristocrat's sedan chair ("litter") or bed. I have replaced the comma of *1645* with a period, on the grounds that Milton provided no punctuation at all in the Trinity Manuscript, but he did begin the next line with an unusual capital letter, indicating that a new sentence was beginning.

[384]Again an image possibly from grammar, in which aspiration may be indicated by "breathings," or music, in which a breathing time or breath-pause might be indicated by a comma. The music here seems to be "breathy." Milton first wrote the two and a half lines as:

```
                                *still soft*
        At last a soft · & sollemne breathing sound *sweet soft
                a                           *slow
            rose, like · the softe steame of· distill'd p[er]fumes *slow *rich
            and stole upon the aire,
```
The breathing sound may be soft, still, or sweet.

[385]This appears to be another allegorical image implying rape, or of being seized unaware. Silence is carried off before she (though Latin *silentium* is neuter) can take stock of what is happening.

[386]The word was added above the line, by means of a caret.

And took in strains that might create a soul[387]
Under the ribs of Death, but O ere long
Too well I did perceive it was the voice
Of my most honour'd Lady, your dear sister.
Amaz'd I stood, harrow'd with grief and fear,   565
And O poor hapless Nightingale thought I,
How sweet thou sing'st, how neer the deadly snare![388]
Then down the Lawns° I ran with headlong hast   GLADES
Through paths, and turnings oft'n trod by day,
Till guided by mine ear I found the place   570
Where that damn'd wisard hid in sly disguise
(For so by certain signes I knew) had met
Already, ere my best speed could prævent,°   COME BEFORE
The aidless[389] innocent Lady his wish't prey,[390]
Who gently° ask't if he had seen such two,   POLITELY 575
Supposing him som neighbour villager;
Longer I durst not stay,[391] but soon I guess't
Ye were the two she mean't, with that I sprung
Into swift flight,[392] till I had found you here,
But furder[393] know I not. *2. Bro.* O night and shades, 580
How are ye joyn'd with hell in triple knot
Against th' unarmed weakness of one Virgin
Alone, and helpless! Is this the confidence
You gave me Brother? *Eld. Bro.* Yes, and keep it still,
Lean on it safely, not a period°   SENTENCE 585
Shall be unsaid for me: against the threats
Of malice or of sorcery, or that power
Which erring men call Chance,[394] this I hold firm,
Vertue may be assail'd, but never hurt,
Surpriz'd by unjust force, but not enthrall'd,°[395] ENSLAVED 590
Yea even that which mischief[396] meant most harm,
Shall in the happy trial prove most glory.[397]

---

[387]"I listened to musical strains or melodies that would make Death himself human." The understood analogy is with Orpheus, who made the king of the underworld, Pluto, weep because his music was so beautiful. "While thus he sung, and struck the quavering strings, / The bloodlesse Shadowes wept" (Sandys 454).

[388]A recurring and evocative image in Milton's poetry (see, for instance, *Paradise Lost* 7.435–36), the nightingale who sings as if inspired at dusk is associated in mythology with Philomela, an innocent virgin who is raped and mutilated by her brother-in-law Tereus in Book 6 of Ovid's *Metamorphoses*; Philomela and her sister Procne are avenged on Tereus and changed into a nightingale and a swallow, respectively. In his commentary on Book 6, Sandys comes very close to Milton's interpretation of the character and the symbol: "The Nightingall chanting in the solitary woods; deservedly called *Philomela*, or a lover of musicke, in that no bird hath so sweet a voice among all the silvan musitians: singing fifteene days and nights together, when the leaves begin to afford her a shelter, with little or no intermission . . . , she alone in her songs expressing the exact art of Musicke in infinite variety. Neither have all the same tunes and divisions, which shewes their skill to be more then naturall" (300).

[389]The word replaced the canceled "helplesse," perhaps because Milton had already used "haplesse" to modify "nightingale" (566 above).

[390]Milton first wrote "who tooke him" to the right of this line and "who gen" at the beginning of the next line. Where he might have been headed with "who tooke him" is hard to ascertain, but it has a line drawn to it, an indication that the phrase was to begin an inserted line.

[391]In other words, the Attendant Spirit did overhear some of the dialogue between Comus and the Lady but did not intervene; instead he went looking for her two brothers.

[392]He did not run away: he flew straight to the brothers.

[393]"Further," a common spelling variant in the seventeenth century. This line began with "and this," and then the phrase was canceled.

[394]In a providential theology, there is no such thing as fate independent of God's will. Thus pagan "destiny" or "fate" or "chance" should have no meaning to a Christian.

[395]The manuscript adds the word "and" at the end of this line, then cancels it, probably to replace it with the similar "Yea" at the beginning of the next line.

[396]A stronger word than it is now, mischief meant genuinely evil doings, or wrongs against which a legal grievance might be filed (*OED* 3.a).

[397]Even such a serious mischief as that of Comus might, by God's providence, produce fortunate results.

But evil on it self shall back recoyl,[398]
And mix[399] no more with goodness,[400] when at last
Gather'd like scum,[401] and setl'd to it self   595
It shall be in eternal restless change
Self-fed, and self-consum'd,[402] if this fail,
The pillar'd firmament[403] is rott'nness,
And earths base built on stubble.[404] But com let's on.°   LET'S GO ON
Against th' opposing will and arm of Heav'n   600
May never this just sword be lifted up,
But for that damn'd magician,[405] let him be girt°   SURROUNDED
With all the greisly legions that troop
Under the sooty flag of *Acheron*,[406]
Harpyies[407] and *Hydra*'s, or all the monstrous forms[408]   605
'Twixt *Africa*, and *Inde*, Ile find him out,
And force him to restore his purchase° back,[409]   PLUNDER
Or drag him by the curls,[410] to a foul death,
Curs'd as his life.
  Spir. Alas good ventrous° youth,   COURAGEOUS, VENTURESOME
I love thy courage yet, and bold Emprise,[411]   610
But here thy sword can do thee little stead,[412]
Farr other arms, and other weapons must
Be those that quell the might of hellish charms,°   SPELLS

— They need the Spiritual to help.

---

[398]A pervasive image of evil in Milton's poetry, "backfiring" or recoiling, turning on itself, as in *Paradise Lost* 4.17–18.

[399]The line began with what appear to be two false starts, "till all to place."

[400]The image shifts here to make evil and good naturally repellant to each other, like oil and water.

[401]Sediment, or lees: what is left, say, in wine, after the liquid has been allowed to sit—but with all the moral force of the modern word "scum" when it is used of people.

[402]Like a chaos, on the one hand, or like Hell, where evil recoils on itself endlessly.

[403]An image based on the biblical notion that the firmament of the universe was supported on pillars, derived from 1 Samuel 2.8: " . . . for the pillars of the earth are the Lord's, and he hath set the world upon them."

[404]Probably another biblically derived image, that of building a house on a solid foundation such as rock, as compared with an unstable foundation of sand (Christ's famous image, Matthew 7.26), or, worse, stubble, which would have been the remnants of grain stalks after the valuable seeds and stalks had been harvested.

[405]This reference to Comus as being damned and, in the next line, his alliance with the troops of Hell, both associate him closely with Satan. See Merritt Y. Hughes, "'Devils to Adore for Deities,'" *Studies in Honor of DeWitt T. Starnes.*, ed. Thomas P. Harrison, et al. (Austin: U of Texas P, 1967): 241–58.

[406]Thought to be one of the rivers of Hell and thus a possible division of the military forces of Hell, according to division by boundary. Thus the regions of Acheron or Styx or Phlegethon all might carry their own ensign or flag. Any hellish flag would be sooty because of the conception of classical Hades or Christian Hell as a place of fire.

[407]The unusual spelling might indicate the derivation of the English name from Latin *Harpyiae*, which is counted as a quadrasyllable in Latin poetry. Here, according to iambic scansion, the name might be pronounced as a trisyllable, or at least accented on the second syllable.

[408]The manuscript read "harpyes & Hydra's or ·["all" inserted above the line] the monstrous buggs," and both BMS and *1637* have "buggs" and "bugs" respectively. I am assuming that Milton made the change to "forms" while in the process of preparing a manuscript for *1645*, though Shawcross retains "buggs," possibly following the argument of C. S. Lewis, who, in *Review of English Studies* 8 (1932), regrets that Milton rejects the "more forcible, native word . . . in favour of the comparatively colourless loan word" (174). It may well be, however, that "bugs" was removed because it was ambiguous in context, since the word's meaning in the seventeenth century included both "insects" (*OED* 2) and "bugbears" (*OED* 1).

[409]The line originally read "and force him to release his new got prey," then "release . . . prey" was struck through and "restore his purchase back" added to the right. Restoring stolen booty may not represent as much of a personal threat as releasing prey. Decorum must have been a problem in this speech, since the brothers need to be threatening Comus's evil, yet if they themselves appear too violent or abusive, their speeches may be taken as too extreme, or, worse, ridiculous.

[410]Perhaps the only indication in the masque of what Comus looks like: he must have had curly hair. Milton altered the spelling "curles" to "curls." After "curls," the manuscript added "& cleave his scalpe / downe to the ~~hipps lowest~~ hips." BMS and *1637* agree essentially on the reading of *1637*:

  And force him to restore his purchase backe
  Or drag him by the curles, and cleave his scalpe
  Downe to the hipps.

[411]A variant spelling and pronunciation of "enterprise." The Elder Brother is both adventurous and enterprising.

[412]"Here your sword is of little use to you." Milton had problems with using "sword" instead of "steele" in the line: he wrote "swo," scratched that, wrote "sword" above the line and inserted the same word by means of an asterisk in the left margin. Finally he restored "steele" by underlining it. The end of the line originally read "can doe thee little stead," then "little stead" was struck through and "small availe" written to its right. Finally, "little stead" was restored by being underlined.

He with his bare wand[413] can unthred thy joynts,[414]
And crumble all thy sinews.[415]   615
   Eld. Bro. Why prethee Shepherd
How durst thou then thy self approach so neer
As to make this relation?°   TELL THIS STORY
   Spir. Care and utmost shifts[416]
How to secure the Lady from surprisal,
Brought to my mind a certain Shepherd Lad[417]
Of small regard to see to,[418] yet well skill'd   620
In every vertuous° plant and healing herb   POWERFUL
That spreds her verdant° leaf to th' morning ray.   GREEN
He lov'd me well, and oft would beg me sing,
Which when I did, he on the tender grass
Would sit, and hearken even to extasie,[419]   625
And in requitall ope his leather'n[420] scrip,°   SHEPHERD'S BAG
And shew me simples[421] of a thousand names[422]
Telling their strange and vigorous faculties;°   STRONG PROPERTIES
Amongst the rest a small unsightly root,
But of divine effect,[423] he cull'd me out;   630
The leaf was darkish, and had prickles on it,[424]
But in another Countrey, as he said,
Bore a bright golden flowre, but not in this soyl:
Unknown, and like esteem'd, and the dull swayn
Treads on it daily with his clouted[425] shoon,   635
And yet more med'cinal is it then that *Moly*[426]
That *Hermes* once to wise *Ulysses* gave;[427]

---

[413]His charming "rod" or magician's wand, used to cast spells. The problem the brothers will face will be to turn the wand upside down, in order to reverse Comus's power. Something similar happened to the torches carried by the god of marriage, Hymen, and his followers during the marriage ceremony.

[414]"Pull you apart limb by limb." The phrase "unthread thy joints" was first written "unquilt thy joynts" in the manuscript, then "unquilt" was canceled and "unthred" written in the margin. "Unquilt" (the *OED* records only two uses of the word, one of which is this one) seems to mean "uncover," or "take the quilt off [someone]," or possibly "unthread a quilt."

[415]Literally, "pulverize your tendons," though "sinew" might also mean "muscle." There may be a logical progression between what is described in "unthread" to what is described in "crumble," since the second is worse qualitatively and quantitatively than the first. The *Variorum* interprets: "the magician can as it were draw out the sinews (threads) that control the joints and scatter them in fragments" (2.3: 928–29), but Milton apparently first wrote "unquilt thy joynts / & crumble every sinew" (altering "every sinew" to "all thy sinews.") I see images of pulling apart and smashing rather than drawing out and scattering, but the point is arguable.

[416]"Contingency plans," as in the modern idiom "shifts for himself or herself."

[417]Who is the Shepherd Lad? He may be Milton's friend Charles Diodati (Newton began that bit of literary gossip), or he may be Milton himself (James Holly Hanford made that identification in the *Times Literary Supplement* 3 November 1932: 815). If Milton is the Shepherd Lad, then the ability of Lawes's song to put him into ecstasy would seem to make sense. Other critics have suggested obscure poets that Milton may have known, or St. Paul, or even Christ (see the *Variorum* 2.3: 929).

[418]"Of insignificant appearance," as in the idiom "He wasn't much to look at."

[419]"Even reach the verge of a trance or enraptured state."

[420]Milton added an "a" to "letherne," to make it "leatherne."

[421]"A medicine or medicament composed or concocted of only one constituent, esp. of one herb or plant (obs.); hence, a plant or herb employed for medical purposes" (*OED* 6).

[422]Milton first wrote "hews," then canceled it for "names" in the manuscript.

[423]"Effect given its power by God." The plant is sacred, in other words, and contains God's healing power.

[424]The passage included in lines 631–37 was omitted from BMS, but not from any printed version. Other than economy, I can see no reason for the cut.

[425]Either "patched up" (*OED* 1) or "studded with clout-nails" (*OED* 2), the latter of which might better fit the context of crushing the plant.

[426]The manuscript had "ancient Moly that Mercury to wise Ulysses gave," but Milton canceled "ancient," and canceled "that Mercury" in order to replace it with "wch Hermes once." The word "ancient" might indicate only that Moly should be associated with the ancient poet Homer; Mercury's name—the name of the Roman god—would be interchangeable for Hermes, the name of his Greek equivalent.

[427]Odysseus mentions Hermes's gift of moly, to protect him against the spells of Circe, in *Odyssey* 10.302–06. Charlotte F. Otten has almost surely pinned the meaning of Milton's "haemony" to St. John's wort, also called "androsaemon" (signifying the color of human blood, in Greek), "hypericon," and "daemonifugium" (a purgative for demons). In "Milton's Haemony," *ELR* 5 (1975): 81–95, she establishes that Milton's every piece of description of the properties of the plant and its medicinal effects, as they were outlined in botanical manuals such as Henry Lyte's *A Niewe Herball* (1578), fits what was written of St. John's wort. The antiquarian and sometime biographer of Milton, John Aubrey, recorded Henry Lawes's use of "*Hypericon* put under his

He call'd it *Hæmony*, and gave it me,
And bad me keep it as of sovran[428] use
'Gainst all inchantments, mildew blast,[429] or damp[430]   640
Or gastly furies apparition;[431]
I purs't it up, but little reck'ning made,[432]
Till now that this extremity compell'd,[433]
But now I find it true; for by this means
I knew the foul inchanter though disguis'd,   645
Enter'd the very lime-twigs of his spells,[434]
And yet came off: if you have this about you
(As I will give you when we go)[435] you may
Boldly assault the necromancers[436] hall;
Where if he be, with dauntless hardihood,[437]   650
And brandish't blade[438] rush on him, break his glass,
And shed the lushious liquor[439] on the ground,
But° sease his wand, though he and his curst crew   ONLY
Feirce[440] signe of battail make, and menace high,
Or like the sons of *Vulcan*[441] vomit smoak,   655
Yet will they soon retire, if he but shrink.[442]
    Eld. Bro. Thyrsis lead on apace, Ile follow thee,
And som good angel bear a sheild before us.[443]

Pillow" (quoted in Otten 90) to ward off ghosts at night. St. John's wort might also be used by young girls to ward off demon lovers, because the demons "could not consummate their love . . . because they could not tolerate the smell of this herb: a devil finds the smell of hypericon-androsaemon putrid" (paraphrased from the *Magna Vita S. Hugonis Episcopi Lincolniensi*, ed. James F. Dimock [London: 1864]: v. viii, 269–73, in Otten 93). It may be relevant to this question that St. John's wort has been recently discovered to be an anti-depressant and prescribed as such in twentieth-century medicine..

[428]Milton's spelling of the word, to be distinguished from the modern "sovereign." Probably the spelling indicates a preference for or memory of the Italian *sovràno*.

[429]See *OED* 3, "attrib. and Comb., as mildew-blast, -drop, -plant; mildew-gangrene, -mortification, gangrene produced by diseased grain, such as gangrenous ergotism (Syd. Soc. Lex. 1890); mildew-grass, grass tainted with mildew," citing this passage. If sheep eat mildewed hay, they poison themselves. In the seventeenth century, the "blasting" of such hay might have been thought the work of an evil spirit.

[430]"An exhalation, a vapour or gas, of a noxious kind" (*OED* 1.a). Either an offensive smelling, infectious, poisonous, or explosive exhalation, as with methane rising from a swamp. Some of the original senses of the word—having to do with both poison or mood change—may survive in the idiom "dampened enthusiasm." As late as the nineteenth century, moody people were described as having an attack of the vapors.

[431]A ghost resembling one of the classical Furies, represented with snakes instead of hair, carrying torches and whips of scorpions, and dressed in bloody black rags.

[432]"I put it in my scrip and thought little of it."

[433]"Until this present desperate situation compelled me to remember it."

[434]By means of the haemony root, he has been able to detect the hypocritical disguise assumed by Comus and enter into the very snares that he has erected for the Lady. Lime-twig snares were coated with "bird-lime," a sticky, glutinous substance made from the bark of the holm-oak that caused fleeing birds to run into and adhere to the sticks so that they might be collected by hunters. The fowler used bird-lime in conjunction with other types of mechanical snares and nets.

[435]Milton first wrote "(as I will give you as wee goe)," then canceled "as wee goe" and first inserted "when on the way" above the line, then crossed that out and wrote "when we goe." in the right margin.

[436]A magician or wizard who summons up the spirits of the dead in order to accomplish evil ends. Milton first wrote "his necromantik hall," then, by crossing out "his" for "yᵉ" and crossing out "ik," reconstructed "necromantik" as "necromancers" by inserting the "cers" above the line.

[437]"Boldness, hardiness; audacity" (*OED* 1); Milton apparently coined the word. He first wrote "wᵗʰ suddaine violence," then canceled that for "dauntless hardihood," which then was altered slightly to "dauntless hardyhood." Of course, "suddaine violence" is less complimentary of the two brothers than "dauntless hardyhood."

[438]The word was first written as plural "blades," then the "s" was struck through.

[439]Milton first wrote "and powre the lushious potion," then canceled "powre" and "potion" for "shed" and "liquor."

[440]Milton's spelling preference might have come through here, since the manuscript spells "feirce," BMS alters to the more acceptable "fierce," then *1637* and *1645* revert to "Feirce."

[441]The forge of Vulcan (the Greek Hephaistos; Milton uses the less common name "Mulciber" for him in *Paradise Lost* 1.740) was supposed to be under Mt. Aetna, on the island of Sicily. Various giants or Titans were also thought to have been buried in the earth during combats with the Olympian gods, and thus to be the cause of volcanoes or other types of harmful eruptions.

[442]"Cower, shrink with fear."

[443]One of the few references to Christian angels allowed to slip into the masque. The line first read "& good heaven cast his best regard upon us," but that was canceled in its entirety and the line as it appears in print added to the right of the line above.

The Scene changes[444] to a stately Palace, set out with
all manner of deliciousness: soft Musick, Tables
spred with all dainties. Comus appears with his
rabble,[445] and the Lady set in an inchanted Chair, to
whom he offers his Glass, which she puts by, and
goes about to rise.

  Comus. Nay Lady sit; if I but wave this wand
Your nervs° are all chain'd up in Alablaster,[446]   SINEWS, MUSCLES   660
And you a statue;[447] or as *Daphne* was
Root-bound,[448] that fled *Apollo.*[449]
  La. Fool do not boast,[450]
Thou canst not touch the freedom of my minde
With all thy charms, although this corporal rinde[451]
Thou haste immanacl'd, while Heav'n sees good.[452]   665
  Co. Why are you vext Lady? why do you frown?
Here[453] dwel no frowns, nor anger, from these gates
Sorrow flies farr: See here be all the pleasures
That fancy can beget on youthfull thoughts,[454]

---

[444]In the manuscript, Milton wrote:

> the scene ~~cha~~ changes to a stately pallace set out wth all manner
>   tables spred wth all dainties
> of deliciousnesse.· Comus is discover'd wth his rabble. & the Ladie set in
> an inchanted chaire. She offers to rise

BMS alters the stage directions to read:

> The *Sceane* changes to a stately pallace set out wth all mann^r
> manner of delitiousness, tables spred with all dainties
> Comus ap~~pe~~es wth his rabble, and the lady set in an
> inchaunted chayre, to whgome he offers his vlasse
> wch she puts by, and goes about to rise.

The first printed text, *1637*, eliminates Milton's redundancy in "all dainties / of deliciousnesse" to make it simply "all dainties," and then interestingly adds "soft musicke" after "deliciousnesse." Both BMS and *1637* alter "Comus is discovered" to "Comus appears," and both of those also add "to whome he offers his glasse, which she puts by" to what Milton had written in the manuscript. Both BMS and *1637* also alter "She offers to rise" to "goes about to rise." The changes indicate the addition of music and perhaps a change in staging between having Comus "appear" (in a puff of smoke?) to having him "discovered" (possibly having a curtain or scrim removed to uncover a scene within). Certainly BMS adds the details about Comus's offering the Lady the glass and her refusing. I read "She offers to rise" as meaning something very close to "makes a motion as if to rise."
[445]This word and "rout" clearly establish that Comus's followers are a dissolute and unruly bunch; in addition, they have the heads of beasts. Modern staging might make them gesticulate grotesquely and make ugly or animalistic noises.
[446]Carbonate of lime, used by the ancient Egyptians for statuary. The word was spelled "alablaster" more commonly than it was "alabaster" in seventeenth-century English usage.
[447]The manuscript added "fixt" at this point, with commas around it, but then Milton struck it out.
[448]Daphne is "rootbound" in the sense that, as she is being pursued by the god Apollo, who wants to rape her, her prayer for deliverance is answered and she becomes a tree: her "Haire into leaves, her Armes to branches grow: / And late swift feet, now rootes, are lesse then slow" (*Metamorphoses* 1.549–50, trans. Sandys). Like the Lady, Daphne "affects *Diana*, which is chastity" (Sandys's commentary, 73). For a psychological examination of the image of the Lady as rootbound, see Kerrigan's chapter on the rootbound Lady (*The Sacred Complex* 22–72).
[449]I have corrected the comma of *1645*. The comma remains, possibly because in the Trinity Manuscript Milton had written the line as "root-bound that fled Apollo." followed by "why doe ye frowne, ..."
[450]The next four lines, the Lady's immediate retort, were inserted in the right margin in the manuscript. They first began "La: foole thou art over proud," with "thou art over proud" then struck through. At the end of the four lines, Milton changed "why doe ye frowne" to "Co. why are you vext Ladie, why doe yo.· frow[ne]," to make a new full line, as compared with the half-line he had constructed before.
[451]The body, pictured as the nearly worthless "rind" whose principal purpose is to enclose the precious immortal soul.
[452]"You cannot touch my mind, even though you have put my body in manacles or fetters, so long as Heaven can discern well what is happening."
[453]Milton first wrote "heere fro" at the beginning of the line, then canceled it for "heere dwell no frownes." He also changed "or" to "nor," by means of a caret and an "n" above the line.
[454]Another image of immoral fecundity and birth, with fancy begetting groups of illicit and extravagant pleasures. The next several lines in the manuscript were written as

>   ~~invent~~
> that ~~youth & fancie~~ fancie can ~~beget~~ on youthfull thoughts
>   *fresh
> when the ~~brifke~~ blood ~~returns~~ grows lively & returnes   *fresh

When the fresh blood[455] grows lively, and returns   670
Brisk as the *April* buds in Primrose-season.[456]
And first behold this cordial Julep[457] here
That flames, and dances in his crystal bounds[458]
With spirits of balm,[459] and fragrant Syrops mixt.
Not that *Nepenthes*[460] which the wife of *Thone*,   675
In *Egypt* gave to *Jove*-born *Helena*
Is of such power to stir up joy as this,
To life so friendly,[461] or so cool to thirst.
Why should you be so cruel to your self,
And to those dainty limms which nature lent   680
For gentle usage, and soft delicacy?°   VOLUPTUOUSNESS
But you invert the cov'nants of her trust,[462]   *HE'S BLAMING HER*
And harshly deal like an ill borrower
With that which you receiv'd on other terms,
Scorning the unexempt[463] condition[464]   685
By which all mortal frailty must subsist,
Refreshment after toil, ease after pain,
That have been tir'd all day without repast,
And timely rest have wanted, but fair Virgin
This will restore[465] all soon.   690
  La. 'Twill not false traitor,
'Twill not restore the truth and honesty
That thou hast banish't from thy tongue with lies,
Was this the cottage, and the safe abode
Thou told'st me of? What grim aspects[466] are these,

<hr>

bri∫k as the Aprills budds in primrose season
Milton tried to substitute "invent" for "beget" but evidently did not find it strong enough and reinstated "beget."
[455]Presumably the blood of a young and "briske" being in spring, though "fresh blood" can mean a new and vital strain entered into a breeding line of animals.
[456]The lines from "and first behold" through "O foolishnesse of men" were added in what Milton referred to as "the pasted leafe," a leaf of the manuscript that was inserted between leaves numbered 22 and 23 in the manuscript.
[457]Originally a medicinal drink sweetened and sometimes chilled to make the medicine more palatable. Here Comus describes his julep as being "cordial," or good for the heart.
[458]The glass or cup that Comus carries, then, should be crystal.
[459]"Distilled spirits of healing herbs." A balm was usually an ointment associated with the balsam tree, as in the famous biblical "balm of Gilead" (Jeremiah 8.22), but it could be any healing potion.
[460]An Egyptian potion supposed to induce forgetfulness and relieve the taker of pain, given to Helen of Troy (daughter of Zeus) by "Polydamia, the wife of Thon, . . . a woman of Egypt," where the "earth . . . bears greatest store of drugs, many that are healing . . . and many that are baneful" (Homer, *Odyssey* 4.219–32; trans. Loeb).
[461]George Sandys's translation of Homer's phrase about nepenthes as "a friend to life" (*Relation* [1615]: 126; see *Variorum* 2.3: 941–42) may be Milton's source. What Comus offers, however, is a dangerous potion designed to make the victim susceptible to all types of human voluptuousness.
[462]Comus is legalistic, discussing "A particular clause of agreement contained in a deed; e.g. the ordinary covenants to pay rent, etc. in a lease" (*OED* 3b) that the Lady has supposedly made with nature.
[463]Milton's use of this negative form of "exempt" is unique as recorded in the *OED*. It seems to follow from the contract mentioned just above. One should not forget that Milton's father was a scrivener and moneylender, his brother Christopher a lawyer, and Milton himself a sometime collector of debts owed with interest accruing to him or to his father.
[464]Probably pronounced as four syllables, with a stress on the second and fourth syllables.
[465]A restorative was "A food, cordial, or medicine, which has the effect of restoring health or strength (*OED* B 1.a). Comus advertises his potion to be a restorative or cordial.
[466]Accented on the second syllable. The word might mean "faces" or "looks," but the Latin **aspectus** also has the sense of "sight," so the Lady may be saying "What grim sights are these?"

These ougly-headed° Monsters?[467] Mercy guard me![468]   UGLY-HEADED   695
Hence with thy brew'd inchantments, foul deceiver,
Hast thou betrai'd my credulous innocence[469]
With visor'd[470] falshood, and base° forgery,   LOWER-CLASS
And wouldst thou seek again to trap me here
With lickerish baits° fit to ensnare a brute?   SENSUAL LURES   700
Were it a draft for *Juno* when she banquets,
I would not taste thy treasonous offer; none
But such as are good men can give good things,[471]
And that which is not good, is not delicious
To a wel-govern'd and wise appetite.   705
     Co. O foolishnes of men! that lend their ears
To those budge[472] doctors of the *Stoick* Furr,[473]
And fetch their precepts from the *Cynick* Tub,[474]
Praising the lean and sallow Abstinence.
Wherefore did Nature powre° her bounties forth,   POUR   710
With such a full and unwithdrawing[475] hand,
Covering the earth with odours, fruits,[476] and flocks,
Thronging[477] the Seas with spawn innumerable,[478]
But all to please, and sate the curious taste?[479]

---

[467]"Oughly" (the spelling of *1645*) and "ougly" (the spelling of the manuscript in two instances) were variant spellings of "ugly." In this case, I have restored the spelling of The manuscript and *1638*. Milton first wrote "musl'd monsters" in The manuscript, then canceled it.

[468]Milton worked over the passage carefully in the manuscript:

~~(m[erc]ie gua[r]d me~~
           ~~me of?~~   ougly   what ~~grim aspects are these?~~
~~[t]hou toldst amou.ngst these [h] musl'd monsters.~~   ~~mercie guard me~~
                    ~~bow have I bin betrai'd~~
           ~~O my simplicity what sights are these?~~ w^th ~~darke disguises   bruage~~
~~whether deluded   & soothing flatteries~~
           ~~and soothing lies . soothing flatteries, hence~~ w^th ~~thy trecherous kindness~~
                    ~~falshood~~   ~~bru'd sorcerie~~
           ~~thou ma[n of lies & falshood fraud; if thou give me it~~
           ~~I throw~~ it ~~on the ground, were it a draft for Juno~~
                    ~~should reject~~
           ~~I hate it from thy hands treasonous offer, none~~
           ~~but such as are good men can give good things~~

Notice that Milton first put "how have I bin betrai'd" and "O my simplicity" in the Lady's response, but he decided to allow her less "simplicity" and more strength in later states of what he wrote. The phrase "soothing flatteries" serves as a comment on Comus's rhetorical strategies, as does "treacherous kindnesse"; the use of "fraud" associates Comus with Satan (see *Paradise Lost* 1.646, 4.121).

[469]Only because she was innocent, in other words, did she believe him.

[470]The word might create a subtext for the masque, since a synonym for "visored" would be "masked." In a sense, the masque presents the unmasking of Comus, as the deceitful hypocrit he is.

[471]Newton was the first to trace the idea (inverted) back to Euripides, *Medea* 618: "No profit is there in a villain's gifts" (trans. Loeb), but certainly for Milton the belief that only people with a good conscience can deliver good things was a Christian one.

[472]Milton is the first to use the phrase "budge doctor," which may mean only that the learned men Comus mocks wore fur as part of their academic costume (see *OED* "budge" [adj.] 1). The noun "budge" meant a lambskin with fur attached: hence the Stoic fur mentioned at the end of this line. Milton crossed out "gowne" in the manuscript and substituted "furre."

[473]In the manuscript Milton first wrote "gowne," then canceled it and wrote "furre" to the right.

[474]Comus is reducing two philosophical schools to ridiculous emblems, as if Stoics (followers of Marcus Aurelius, Seneca, or Marcus Aurelius) could be identified by their academic costume, or Cynics by the tub that Diogenes carried with him and used for shelter. For various speculations about "budge" and academic gowns, see the *Variorum* 2.3: 944-45.

[475]The first instance of this participial adjective recorded in the *OED*.

[476]Milton first wrote "odours, & wth fruits," then canceled "& w^th" and, apparently, added "& flocks."

[477]Milton first wrote "cramming," then struck it through and substituted "thronging" in the left margin.

[478]The line originally read "the feilds wth cattell & the aire wth fowle," then Milton crossed that out and added "but all to please & sate the curious taste" to the right of the line.

[479]Critics have seen Milton's respect and even love for the abundance and the sensual appeal of nature in Comus's lines. It is true that there is nothing wrong with the abundance and fecundity of nature: what is wrong is the perverse or excessive, incontinent use of nature, everything implied in the phrase "sate the curious taste." Here "curious" would suggest not only "fastidious" but "over-exquisite."

And set to work millions of spinning Worms,   715
That in their green shops[480] weave the smooth-hair'd silk
To deck[481] her Sons, and that no corner might
Be vacant of her plenty, in her own loyns
She hutch't[482] th' all-worship ore, and precious gems
To store her children with; if all the world   720
Should in a pet° of temperance feed on Pulse,[483]   FIT
Drink the clear stream, and nothing wear but Freize,[484]
Th' all-giver would be unthank't, would be unprais'd,
Not half his riches known, and yet despis'd,
And we should serve him as a grudging master,   725
As a penurious niggard° of his wealth,   MISER
And live like Natures bastards, not her sons,
Who would be quite surcharg'd° with her own weight,   SURFEITED, OVERLOADED
And strangl'd with her waste fertility;[485]
Th' earth cumber'd, and the wing'd air dark't with plumes,[486]   730
The herds would over-multitude[487] their Lords,
The Sea o'refraught would swell, & th' unsought diamonds
Would so emblaze the forhead of the Deep,[488]
And so bestudd with Stars, that they below
Would grow inur'd to light, and com at last   735
To gaze upon the Sun with shameless brows.
List Lady be not coy, and be not cosen'd°   TRICKED, HOODWINKED
With that same vaunted name Virginity,[489]
Beauty is natures coyn, must not be hoorded,
But must be currant,[490] and the good thereof   740
Consists in mutual and partak'n bliss,
Unsavoury in th' injoyment of it self[491]
If you let slip time, like a neglected rose
It withers on the stalk with languish't head.
Beauty is natures brag and must be shown°   DISPLAYED   745
In courts, at feasts, and high solemnities°   IMPORTANT CEREMONIES
Where most may wonder at the workmanship;
It is for homely features to keep home,

---

[480]Probably the mulberry trees seen as workshops in which silkworms manufactured the nests from which the "smooth-hair'd" silk was extracted and then woven.

[481]Milton first wrote "to deck," replaced that with "to adorne" above the line, then wrote "deck" again to the right of "to adorne."

[482]"Stored in a hutch or chest," perhaps with the implication here of being impregnated with the ore and hoarding it until it can be "born."

[483]In the manuscript, Milton wrote "pulse," crossed it out, replaced it with "fetches," and then wrote "pulse" again. Fetches or vetches were "The bean-like fruit[s] of various species of the leguminous plant Vicia" (*OED* vetch 1), and vetch was thought to be a kind of pulse (any leguminous bean used as food). Comus is scorning the practice of eating and drinking simply, a practice that Milton himself endorsed.

[484]Frieze was a coarse woolen cloth with a frizzled nap inside and out, worn by poorer people.

[485]The image is one of an unchecked jungle in which the fertility of all living things strangles life; thus, by Comus's logic, the fertility is wasted.

[486]The weight of overproducing animals will encumber the earth, and the wings of birds darken the air. *OED* records Milton's usage of "wing'd" meaning "filled with wings" (1.c) as unique.

[487]Milton is using a noun as if it were a verb, stretching the meaning of "multitude" in a way analogous to Shakespeare's "multitudinous seas" (*Macbeth* 2.2.59). The usage is unique, so far as what is recorded for "over-multitude" in the *OED*.

[488]Not the ocean but the center of the earth, made to be teeming with precious stones, the Deep being personified as a kind of Eastern potentate with a precious stone ornamenting his forehead.

[489]Again, Comus uses the external and meaningless name to stand for a virtue or a way of life, just as he has identified Cynics with tubs. The thrust of his argument is materialistic and immoral.

[490]The Lady is like Nature's coinage, which, according to Comus, should be spent as soon as possible, rather than hoarded. There may be word-play on "current," which in its Latin root would contain the root "running." Comus also implies that it is fashionable to be promiscuous.

[491]Most modern editors add a period here, but none of the manuscripts or early editions have one at this point.

They had their name thence; course complexions[492]
And cheeks of sorry grain will serve to ply   750
The sampler, and to teize the huswifes wooll.[493]
What need a vermeil-tinctur'd° lip for that   DYED SCARLET
Love-darting eyes, or tresses like the Morn?[494]
There was another meaning in these gifts,
Think what, and be adviz'd, you are but young yet.[495]   755
   La. I had not thought to have unlockt[496] my lips
In this unhallow'd air, but that this Jugler[497]
Would think to charm my judgement, as mine eyes
Obtruding false rules pranckt° in reasons garb.°   DECKED OUT   CLOTHING
I hate when vice can bolt[498] her arguments   760
And vertue has no tongue to check her pride:
Impostor do not[499] charge most innocent nature,
As if she would[500] her children should be riotous

---

[492]"Coarse complexions." Milton wrote "coarse" and then "beetle brows" in the the manuscript and then advisedly changed the latter to "complexions." "Beetle-browed" would indicate overhanging or shaggy forehead (see *OED*) and "coarse complexions" might indicate rural ugliness—a face rendered old-looking through the action of wind or sun. The phrase "sorry grain" would indicate unhealthy or unattractive coloring, as in "paleface."

[493]Two homely images, plying or busily working on a sampler or picture constructed using needlework techniques, or comb ("teize") the housewife's raw wool so that it can be more easily woven.

[494]Phrases borrowed from extravagant or bombastic poetry, as with "her sweet, love-darting Eyne" (Sylvester's DuBartas 2.3.4.838; ed. Snyder). The "tresses" are apparently as golden as the dawn.

[495]Hints at sexual innuendo, as in "Guess what I meant, Lady?" The following passage was excised from the manuscript. I have removed the lines through the excised passages, in order to make them easier to read:

         & looke upon this cord[ia]ll julep [—]
      that flames & dances in his ch crystall bounds
      wth spirits of balme & fragrant syrops mixt
      not that nepenthes wch the wife of Thôn
      in Ægypt gave to Jove borne Helena
      is of such power to stirre up joy as this
      to life freintly so, or so coole to thirst
           2   1
      poore ladie thou hast need of some refreshing
      that hast bin tir'd all day w^thout repast
      and timely rest haast wanted heeere sweet Ladie faire[-]virgin
      this will restore all soone La stand back false traitor
      thou can'st not touch the freedome of my mynd
      wth all thy charmes although this corporall rind
      thou haſt immanacl'd, while heaven sees good
      was this the cottage, & the safe abode   (m[erc]ie gua[r]d me
      me of?   ougly   rim aſpects are these?
[t]hou toldst amou·ngst these [h] musl'd monsters·   mercie guard me
           bow have I bin betrai'd
      O my simplicity what sights are these? wth darke disguises   bruage
     whether deluded   & soothing flatteries
      and soothing lies · soothing flatteries, hence wth thy trecherous kindness
           falshood   bru'd sorcerie
      thou ma<u>n of</u> lies & <u>falshood</u> fraud, if thou give me it
      I throw ^it on the ground, were it a draft for Juno
           should reject
      I hate it from thy hands treasonous offer, none
           but such as are good men can give good things

[496]The manuscript reads "unlock."

[497]Suggests not only someone who juggles for a living but someone who, like a magician, conjurer, or juggler, fools the eye or creates illusions to deceive an audience.

[498]"To examine by sifting; to search and try. *to bolt out*: to find out, or separate by sifting" (*OED* v. 2). Milton altered the spelling "boult" to "bolt" in the manuscript, but "boult" is the less-ambiguous spelling recommended (at least for modern usage) in the *OED.*.

[499]The "not" was added above the line in the manuscript.

[500]Milton first wrote "ment" in the manuscript, then struck it through and wrote "would" above the line. The sense of the revised passage is "if she willed that her children should be unruly in using her abundance."

With her abundance, she good cateress[501]
Means[502] her provision onely to the good   765
That live according to her sober laws,
And holy dictate of spare Temperance:
If every just man that now pines with want
Had but a moderate and beseeming share
Of that which lewdly pamper'd Luxury   770
Now heaps upon som few with vast excess,[503]
Natures full blessings would be well dispenc't
In unsuperfluous eeven proportion,[504]
And she no whit encomber'd with her store,°   BOUNTY, ABUNDANCE
And then the giver would be better thank't,   775
His praise due paid, for swinish gluttony
Ne're looks to Heav'n amidst his gorgeous feast,[505]
But with besotted° base ingratitude   MUDDY-HEADED, SOTTISH
Cramms, and blasphemes his feeder. Shall I go on?[506]
Or have I said anough? To him that dares   780
Arm his profane tongue with contemptuous words
Against the Sun-clad power of Chastity,
Fain would I somthing say, yet to what end?
Thou has nor Eare, nor Soul to apprehend
The sublime[507] notion, and high mystery[508]   785
That must be utter'd to unfold the sage
And serious doctrine of Virginity,[509]
And thou art worthy that thou shouldst not know
More happines then this thy present lot.
Enjoy your deer Wit, and gay Rhetorick°   DECORATIVE ARGUMENTATION   790
That hath so well been taught her dazling fence,[510]
Thou are not fit to hear thy self convinc't;°   CONFUTED
Yet should I try, the uncontrouled° worth   UNDISPUTED
Of this pure cause would kindle my rap't° spirits   ENRAPTURED
To such a flame of sacred vehemence,[511]   795
That dumb things would be mov'd to sympathize,
And the brute Earth would lend her nerves and shake,

---

[501]Milton's is the first recorded instance in the *OED* of the use of "cateress," meaning "female supplier of goods, usually to a household."

[502]Milton first write "intends," then struck it through and wrote "means" after it, carrying the sense of the "ment" excised two lines above.

[503]What Milton puts in the Lady's mouth does seem to be a leveling sentiment, a kind of "power to the people" idea, that would undercut her aristocratic status. If wealth and status produce people who are pampered to the point of obscenity, and if that wealth should be taken away from the rich and fairly distributed among the poor, where would the Earl of Bridgewater, one of the richest men in England, be?

[504]The word has mathematical and musical dimensions, as well as moral one. Proportional music would have been balanced and evenly harmonic, numbers in proper proportions would set up harmony, say, in architecture, or in any art that demands mathematical balance.

[505]The phrase sounds proverbial, but Tilley's *Dictionary of the Proverbs in England in the Sixteenth and Seventeenth Centuries* (Ann Arbor: U of Michigan P, 1950) does not record a similar proverb. A possible source recorded by Carey is Plato, *Republic* 586A: "those who have no experience of wisdom and virtue . . . but with eyes ever bent upon the earth and heads bowed down over their tables they feast like cattle, grazing and copulating . . . ." (Loeb trans., 2: 391). BMS makes "feast" plural.

[506]From this line through "Com, no more" (806) was not in the manuscript or BMS.

[507]Accented on the first syllable.

[508]As compared with Comus's profane and "abhorred rites" to a pagan god, the Lady's doctrine of holy virginity is a religious mystery. The clear implication is that it is a mystery and a doctrine of the Christian Church, though Milton is clearly not discussing the celibacy of monastic orders within the Roman Catholic Church.

[509]"CHASTITY," Milton wrote in *On Christian Doctrine*, means "forbearance from the unlawful lusts of the flesh; it is also called purity" (2.9; Yale 6: 726). He seems to have associated chastity (which may be simple virginity or purity in general), temperance, sanctity, and sobriety as being among the "Special Virtues" described in 2.9.

[510]Literally a fencing maneuver, but here transferred in sense to mean something like "dodge."

[511]The usual meaning for this word in Milton's usage is "impetuosity" (see *OED* 2) or "mindlessness" (see the Argument for Book 9 in *Paradise Lost*), but here it seems to mean "sacred ecstasy."

Till all thy magick structures rear'd so high,
Were shatter'd into heaps o're thy false head.[512]
  Co. She fables not,[513] I feel that I do fear   800
Her words set off by som superior power;
And though not mortal, yet a cold shuddring[514] dew
Dips me all o're, as when the wrath of *Jove*
Speaks thunder, and the chains of *Erebus*
To some of *Saturns* crew.[515] I must dissemble,   805
And try° her yet more strongly. Com, no more,   TEST, ATTEMPT
This is meer moral babble, and direct
Against the canon laws of our foundation;[516]
I must not suffer this, yet 'tis but the lees°   DREGS
And setlings of a melancholy blood;[517]   810
But this will cure all[518] streight, one sip of this
Will bathe the drooping spirits in delight
Beyond the bliss[519] of dreams. Be wise, and taste.----[520]

The Brothers rush in with Swords drawn, wrest his
  Glass[521] out of his hand, and break it against the
  ground; his rout make signe of resistance, but
  are all driven in; The attendant Spirit comes
  in.

  Spir. What, have you let the false enchanter scape?   *Comus escapes*
O ye mistook, ye should have snatcht his wand   815

---

[512]The power of the Lady's inspired state would rival or better that of Orpheus, who could move stones to tears, or the god Neptune, who could cause earthquakes. Even from her passive position, she has the power to pulverize his castle or his rhetoric. Comus's answer as Milton first wrote it was as follows:

       Co. Come ~~y'are too morall~~
       ~~your moral stuffe   tilted~~
    this is meere morall stuffe the very · ~~lees~~ this meere moral bable, & direct
                        against the canon laws of our foundation
   ~~& settlings of a melancholy blood~~

The excised phrase "tilted lees" has suggested to Sokol that Milton was about to have Comus accuse the Lady of having a disruption of her bodily humors caused by menstruation ("tilted lees" and "the settlings of a melancholy blood" mean the same in seventeenth-century medical terminology).

[513]This is an aside, spoken directly to the audience, and it is used like the soliloquys of Shakespeare's Richard III, to engage the audience in the villain's plot. Comus returns to direct discourse with "Com, no more," at 806 below.

[514]In a transferred image, the cold dew that normally causes people to shudder is described itself as shuddering, and then it "dips" Comus or drenches him, the way that a sheep is said to be "dipped." See *OED* 2.b.

[515]Some of Saturn's or Chronos's "crew," the Titans, revolted against Zeus and the Olympian gods and were cast down in chains into the infernal region of Erebus—an obvious parallel with the rebellion of the fallen angels. See Hesiod, *Theogony* 617–721. God speaks through thunder and lightning, as in the Bible (1 Samuel 7.10, among other instances).

[516]The nagging question here is "Which canon laws is Comus addressing?" Normally "canon law" would be law which governs the Church. Comus is likely "posing as a sort of priest of misrule" (*Variorum* 2.3: 955).

[517]Comus is treating melancholy as a disease that left settling dregs in the blood itself, the result of which might be the vapors that cause lunacy or insanity.

[518]Though so far as I know the phrase "cure-all" had not yet been invented, Comus is offering his potion as a cure-all and a panacea; it also resembles an opiate like nepenthes.

[519]Milton first wrote "beyond of dreames," then added "ye blisse" above the line, with a caret between "beyond" and "of."

[520]Another series of dashes indicating dramatic action, though the dashes were not present in the manuscript. The stage directions in the manuscript are
        the brothers rush in strike his glasse downe the ~~monsters~~ shapes make
        as though they would resist but are all driven in. Dæmon enters wth them.

[521]BMS adds "of liquor" to "glasse." Also, the last clause of the stage direction is written "the *Demon* is to come in with [to?] the brothers," which makes it clear that the three of them appear together, though the BMS stage direction is ambiguous: if the brothers were already present, who would be in the process of "coming in"?

And bound him fast; without his rod[522] revers't,
And backward mutters of dissevering power,[523]
We cannot free the Lady that sits here[524]
In stony fetters fixt, and motionless;
Yet stay, be not disturb'd, now I bethink me,   820
Som other means I have which may be us'd,
Which once of *Melibæus* old I learnt
The soothest Shepherd that ere pip't on plains.[525]
   There is a gentle[526] Nymph not farr from hence,
That with moist curb° sways the smooth Severn stream,   RESTRAINT   825
Sabrina is her name, a Virgin pure,
Whilom° she was the daughter of *Locrine*,   AT ONE TIME
That had the Scepter from his father *Brute*.
She guiltless damsell flying the mad pursuit
Of her enraged stepdame *Guendolen*,[527]   830
Commended her fair innocence to the flood
That stay'd her flight with his cross-flowing course,
The water Nymphs that in the bottom plaid,
Held up their pearled wrists[528] and took her in,
Bearing her straight to aged *Nereus* Hall,   835
Who piteous of° her woes, rear'd her lank° head,   SYMPATHETIC WITH   DROOPING
And gave her to his daughters to imbathe
In nectar'd lavers strew'd with Asphodil,[529]
And through the porch[530] and inlet of each sense
Dropt in Ambrosial Oils[531] till she reviv'd,   840
And underwent a quick immortal change
Made Goddess of the River; still she retains
Her maid'n gentlenes,[532] and oft at Eeve

---

[522]The manuscript first had "art," then that was struck through and "rod" added by means of a caret, above the line. Reversing a magician's rod, turning it upside down, would obviate his power, as in Sandys's translation of Ovid *Metamorphoses* 14.300, wherein Ulysses forces Circe to transform the beasts who were his men back into their human shapes and disperses her charms using a more powerful magic, during which struggle "her wand [is] reverst." Homeopathic medicine reverses spells: "As there are remedies in nature against naturall evills; so are there charms against the malice of charmes: one witch undoing what another hath done . . . as here *Circe* her selfe disinchants the Mates of *Ulysses*" (Sandys 652–53).

[523]I take this to mean something like "parting shots," or Comus's last attempts at incantations as he runs away.

[524]The manuscript has "wee cannot free the La. that ~~remaines~~ heere sits," but BMS and *1637* have the word-order as "sits here."

[525]In honoring Spenser by referring to him as Melibæus, Milton also imitates his language with "pip'd on plains," since the first line of *The Faerie Queene* was "A Gentle Knight was pricking on the plaine."

[526]The adjective would indicate not only that her nature is gentle but that she is of noble or aristocratic descent, like the Bridgewater family. This line was not indented in the manuscript, but it was indented (and "*Nimphe*" put in italics) in BMS and *1637*.

[527]The name is spelled so in the manuscript and *1637*, but it is "Gwendolen" in BMS. Because the spelling "stepdame" is Milton's in the manuscript, I have restored it in preference to "stepdam" in *1637* and *1645*; both forms of the word mean "stepmother." Milton seems to have changed and ornamented the myth of the origin of the river Severn from that first recorded by Geoffrey of Monmouth in his *Historia Regum Britanniae* 2.6 (see Yale 1: 369n2). The story is complicated, genealogically. Corineus, the king who according to some accounts gave Cornwall its name, is father of Estrildis. Locrine (son of Brutus, the mythical Trojan founder of Britain) contracts marriage on his own initiative with Estrildis but is forced by Corineus to marry Guendolen. Estrildis in rebellion against her father sneaks out to rendezvous with Locrine. When Corineus dies, Locrine marries Estrildis, divorcing Guendolen. Guendolen goes to Wales, vengefully recruits her and Locrine's son, Medan (brought up by Corineus). With her son Guendolen fights Locrine, who dies of an arrow wound, after which Guendolen, after crowning Medan king of Britain, throws Estrildis and Sabra, her daughter, into the river subsequently called Sabrina or Severn. Their corpses were "dissolv.d into that crystall streame, / [their] curles to curled waves, which plainlie still appeare / The same in water now, that once in locks they were" (Drayton 91).

[528]Wrists wet with water drops that look like pearls. Milton first wrote "white wrists to receave her in," then canceled "white" for "pearled" above the line and canceled "receave" for "& ~~carie take~~ took" above the line.

[529]In basins filled with nectar and strewn with the flower asphodel (according to *OED* 1.b "By the poets made an immortal flower, and said to cover the Elysian meads. (Cf. Homer *Odyss*. XI. 539)."

[530]Close to the sense of *Hamlet* 1.5.63, "porches of my ears." The porch is apparently the vestibule of each sense receptor and the inlet its entry into the body.

[531]After her bath amid the petals of the immortal asphodel, she will be anointed with the oil of godly ambrosia.

[532]Probably in both senses of "aristocratic bearing" and "gentle and kindly disposition."

Visits the herds along the twilight meadows,
Helping all urchin blasts,[533] and ill luck signes　　　　　　　　845
That the shrewd medling Elfe[534] delights to make,
Which she with pretious viold liquors[535] heals.
For which the Shepherds at thire[536] festivals
Carrol° her goodnes lowd in rustick layes,[537]　　　　SING JOYFULLY ABOUT
And throw sweet garland wreaths into her stream　　　　　　　　850
Of pancies, pinks, and gaudy Daffadils.[538]
And, as the old Swain said,[539] she can unlock
The clasping charm,[540] and thaw the numming spell,[541]
If she be right° invok't in warbled Song,　　　　　RIGHTLY, PROPERLY
For maid'nhood she loves, and will be swift　　　　　　　　　855
To aid a Virgin, such as was her self
In hard besetting need,[542] this will I try
And adde the power of som adjuring verse.

　　SONG.

Sabrina fair —
　Listen where thou art sitting[543]
Under the glassie, cool, translucent wave,　　　　　　　　860
　In twisted braids of Lillies knitting°　　　　　KNOTTING
The loose train[544] *of thy amber-dropping*[545] *hair,*
　Listen for dear honours° sake,　　　　　CHASTITY'S

---

[533]Blasts of bad luck issuing from evil or mischievous elves or fairies, who were supposed at times to take the form of hedgehogs, or urchins. Sokol believes that Sabrina's "connection with mothering is shown particularly in how she visits [the herds]. This refers to her charitable practice of curing wounded udders, relieving and promoting maternal nurture" (321). Sabrina here is certainly visiting the herds and undoing the spells of evil spirits; whether she is "mothering" in unlocking such charms is a question difficult to answer.

[534]Elves were thought to be more malevolent and demonic than they might be thought of today, as "elf" is first defined in *OED* 1.a: "The name of a class of supernatural beings, in early Teutonic belief supposed to possess formidable magical powers, exercised variously for the benefit or the injury of mankind."

[535]Liquids in vials or glass containers, in which would be stored medicines or potions.

[536]I have restored the spelling of the manuscript, as compared with "their" in BMS, *1637*, and *1645*.

[537]Here possibly the more primitive form of a long narrative poem, as in the *Nibelungenlied* or *Beowulf*.

[538]The line read as follows in the manuscript:

　　　　　　　　　　pinks * *
　　　　　　of pancies. &̶ ̶o̶f̶ ̶b̶o̶n̶n̶i̶e̶ daffadils　　*gawdie

The varieties of flowers are increased to three, and the less colorful "bonnie" (i.e. "beautiful") changed to "gawdie."

[539]Apparently still referring to Spenser, though what is reported here is information that might have been gleaned from Geoffrey of Monmouth or Michael Drayton (see *Variorum* 2.3: 961–62), but not from Spenser.

[540]Apparently the kind of charm that might render one immobile, as the Lady has been.

[541]The kind of soporific or opiate potion, numbing to the senses, that Comus has been offering the Lady, as with nepenthes. The line in the manuscript read:

　　　　　　　　　　　　　　　　　　　　　　　　　　thaw the
　　　　the　　　　　e̶a̶c̶h̶ claſping chaʳme &̶ ̶s̶e̶c̶r̶e̶t̶ ̶h̶o̶l̶d̶i̶n̶g̶ ̶s̶p̶e̶l̶l̶.̶ m̶e̶l̶t̶ ̶e̶a̶c̶h̶ num[m]ing spell

Apparently "secret holding spell" is equivalent to "num[m]ing spell."

[542]Instead of "In hard besetting need," the manuscript read "in honord vertues cause," and the next line read :

　　　　　　　　　　power　　　　*
　　　　　and adde the p̶o̶w̶e̶r̶ ̶c̶a̶l̶l̶ of some s̶t̶r̶o̶n̶g̶ verse adjuring

The word "adjuring" (i.e., "swearing," "testifying") is meant to replace "strong," "power" is at first deleted but then reinstated by means of the underlining and by its being written in again above the line.

[543]The line in the manuscript reads "Listen v̶i̶r̶g̶i̶n̶ where thou s̶i̶t̶'̶s̶t̶ art sitting."

[544]Milton first miswrote this word as "thine" or something like it, tried to correct it by writing an "r" above the line, then scratched out his original word and rewrote it as "traine" to the right.

[545]Probably "shedding perfumes," since ambergris, called "amber" in the seventeenth century (see *OED* 1), was one major source of perfume, though various editors have read the word as suggesting that the color of the river resembles that of the semiprecious stone amber.

Goddess of the silver lake,[546]   865
   Listen and save.[547]

Listen[548] and appear to us[549]
In name of great *Oceanus*,[550]
By th' earth-shaking[551] *Neptune*'s mace,[552]
And *Tethys*[553] grave majestick pace,   870
By hoary *Nereus*[554] wrincled look,
And the *Carpathian*[555] wisards hook,
By scaly *Tritons* winding shell,[556]
And old sooth-saying *Glaucus* spell,[557]
By *Leucothea*'s[558] lovely hands,   875
And her son[559] that rules the strands,
By *Thetis* tinsel-slipper'd feet,[560]
And the Songs of *Sirens* sweet,[561]

---

[546]A lake could be "A small stream of running water; also, a channel for water" (*OED* 3). The Severn River was called "silver *Severn*" by Michael Drayton in *Poly-Olbion* 2.283.

[547]Immediately after the song, BMS adds the significant stage direction, "The verse to singe or not." The song, as conceived of by the scribe who wrote down the BMS and whoever was instructing that person to prepare the copy, was designed to be sung or spoken by the Attendant Spirit. Lawes, in other words, might have been allowed either to recite the song as a poem, or sing it.

[548]The meter becomes, through 889, iambic tetrameter in couplets, used, as in Shakespeare, for incantations or the summoning or controlling of spirits. See, for instance, the First Fairy's song in *Midsummer Night's Dream* 2.2.9–12.

[549]The manuscript adds the stage direction "to be said" after this line, indicating that the song is now ended.

[550]Pronounced with emphasis on the second and last syllables. Oceanus, son of Heaven (Coelus) and Earth (Terra), was a sea deity, said to be a powerful god whose influence wrapped the earth as the oceans do, like a snake. He is sometimes reckoned to be father of all the gods. He and his wife Tethys were parents to all the most prominent rivers in the world and to the 3000 Oceanides, his daughters the sea nymphs, who included Amphitrite and Urania. See Homer, *Odyssey* 3, and Hesiod, *Theogony* 349.

[551]I have restored the elision present in "th'earth" as in the manuscript, BMS and *1637*. The lines "by th'earthshaking neptunes mace . . . by leucotheas" were a marginal insertion in The manuscript. In The manuscript the "el br" has the lines "by hoarie . . . hooke," the "2 bro" has "by scalie Tritons . . . strands," then the Elder Brother has "by Lewcotheas lovely hands . . . strands," then the Younger Brother has "by Thetis tinsel-slipperd feet . . . sweet," and finally the Elder brother finishes off the last two couplets, "by dead Parthenopes deare tombe . . . locks." The Attendant Spirit, who never stops speaking in The manuscript or *1637*, enters back in with "By all the Nimphes" and continues through "Listen & save." Brown believes that "The decision to change the verses to something . . . more typical of masques [dialogue in couplets] may connect with the decision to make the boys join the Spirit in summoning Sabrina" (118).

[552]Often confused with Oceanus, at least in visual art, Neptune is also god of the sea, but the Olympian god and thus one of the possible offspring of Oceanus. He is an earth-shaker because he not only causes tides and storm at sea but also earthquakes. Neptune is usually pictured looking like Oceanus, that is, with a full beard, but he is often not placed in the ocean in Renaissance paintings but in a chariot shaped like a shell.

[553]Tethys is the wife of Oceanus, daughter of Uranus and Terra, and the mother of the chief rivers. She was sometimes confused with her granddaughter Thetis, the wife of Peleus and the mother of Achilles. See Homer, *Iliad* 14.5.302.

[554]Son of Oceanus and Terra. His daughters are the Nereids, he is also pictured as a sea deity with a long (blue) beard, and he is also known as prophet and shape-shifter. Here he is pictured as old, wrinkled, and gray ("hoary").

[555]Proteus is the wizard (translating the Latin *vates*) from the island of Carpathia, in the Mediterranean between Rhodes and Crete. In Vergil, *Georgics* 4.387, he is pictured as the shepherd of Neptune's herds of sea creatures and therefore carrying a shepherd's crook.

[556]Triton, Neptune's herald, is pictured either with a winding or curled horn, or winding (blowing) his shell horn like a herald to attract attention to his master. Like any sea deity, he might be pictured as having the scales of a fish. Sandys's commentary on the *Metamorphoses* gives him "a body covered with small and hard scales. . . ." He is also pictured "winding a shell" (1632, 32; Hulley ed. 69).

[557]Glaucus was a fisherman from Euboea who ate a magic herb and was thereby transformed into an immortal sea god and given prophetic power (Ovid, *Metamorphoses* 13.904–68). Spenser mentions him in *Faerie Queene* 4.11.13 as someone to whom soothsayers paid attention.

[558]A sea goddess called, at first, Ino. Pursued by the wrath of Juno for being the foster-mother of Bacchus and proclaiming his power, she is transformed by Neptune into a marine deity with the Greek name Leucothea, which literally means "the white goddess" (see the *Variorum* 2.3: 964–65). She is also identified with the Roman Matuta, goddess of the dawn, and for that reason Milton may have given her the epithet resembling Homer's "rosy-fingered dawn."

[559]The roman god of harbors is called by the various names "Melicertes," "Palaemon," or "Portunus." See Vergil, *Georgics* 1.436–37, where sailors, having arrived safely in port, invoke him in thanks.

[560]Thetis is one of the Nereids who is identified by the epithet "silver-footed" in Homer's *Iliad* 18.124. Her tinsel-covered slippers may not have been thought of as gaudy, since the word "tinsel" meant "Made to sparkle or glitter by the interweaving of gold or silver thread, by brocading with such thread, or by overlaying with a thin coating of gold or silver" (*OED* n. 3a).

[561]The songs of the Sirens may have been "sweet" but they were traditionally dangerous or fatal to human beings who heard their song on the sea and, entranced, drove their ships on rocks, or left their bones in a heap before the Sirens, as in the *Odyssey* 12.39–54 and 165–200. As Revard points out, Milton may have two sets of Sirens in mind—those who cause sailors to wreck and those who, according to Plato, guide the heavenly spheres, the "Blest pair of *Sirens*" of "At a Solemn Musick" (*Milton* 142–43).

By dead *Parthenope*'s dear tomb,[562]
And fair *Ligea's*[563] golden comb,   880
Wherwith she sits on diamond rocks[564]
Sleeking her soft alluring locks,[565]
By all the *Nymphs* that nightly dance
Upon thy streams with wily glance,
Rise, rise, and heave° thy rosie head   LIFT   885
From thy coral-pav'n[566] bed,
And bridle in thy headlong wave,[567]
Till thou our summons answer'd have.

      Listen and save.

Sabrina rises, attended by water-Nymphs, and sings.[568]

  By the rushy-fringed bank,   890
Where grows the Willow and the Osier dank,[569]
    My sliding° Chariot stayes,°   GLIDING   STOPS MOVING
Thick set with Agat,[570] *and the azurn*[571] *sheen*
Of Turkis° blew, and Emrauld green   TURQUOISE
    That in the channell strayes,[572]   895
    Whilst from off the waters fleet
    Thus I set my printles feet[573]

---

[562]Parthenope, one of the Sirens, was used by Milton as a prototype of the enchanting singer when he compared the Roman soprano, Leonora Baroni, in "*Ad eandem*" 1–2. She was "dear" enough to have a celebrated tomb near Naples, and to have the city renamed in her honor (Vergil, *Georgics* 4.564).
[563]Pronounced with emphasis on the second syllable (Milton added an acute accent over the "e" in the manuscript). Another of the Sirens, Ligea is mentioned by Vergil in *Georgics* 4.336. Drayton makes her into a benign river nymph who "maintaines the Birds harmonious layes, / Which sing on Rivers banks amongst the slender sprayes" in *Poly-Olbion* 20.127–28.
[564]Probably "rocks shining like diamonds because of the reflections cast by the sea water washing over them."
[565]Ligea is pictured as sweet but seductive, using a golden comb to dress her hair, a fetish analogous to the "tangles of *Neæra*'s hair" in "Lycidas" 69. The hair is "alluring," while the nightly dance of the nymphs is, like the dances of Comus and his followers, accompanied by what appear to be lascivious "wily glance[s]." The *Variorum* editors conjecture, "Might the word [wily] mean 'seductive' in an innocent sense?" (2.3: 966), but it need not be innocent: with the arrival of the Sirens, we are in morally dangerous territory.
[566]Milton changed the spelling from "paved" to "paven" by deleting the "d" and adding the "n" in the manuscript.
[567]The image is from horseback riding: the nymphs are asked to rein in, curb, or use the bridle to control the waves, as if they were hard-to-control horses. Compare 824–25 above.
[568]The manuscript and BMS have "attended wth the water nymphs," making the nymphs particular by the use of the definite article. No music exists for Sabrina's song, nor can we discern for sure who played the part. Brown notes "The matter is of some interpretative importance, for there was reason for Sabrina to be distinct from the family: the pretence is that she is a resource from the region itself" (35). Sabrina rises, presumably from the riverbed, by means of stage machinery.
[569]Both the willow and the osier grow near to and depend upon water and therefore could be described as "dank" or soaked with water.
[570]A series of colors defined in terms of precious or semiprecious stones. The *Variorum* editors paraphrase, "the chariot is set with agate and blue turquoise and green emerald, of which the lustre seems to take on a wayward motion when reflected in the flowing water" (2.3: 968). "Turkish blue" refers to the turquoise or "Turkey stone," which Masson reports to have been imported through Turkey, though originating in Persia (see *Variorum* 2.3: 968). "Azurn" is a form of the word "azure" that Milton apparently made up; it means the color of lapis lazuli, or blue-green.
[571]Milton invented this form of the adjective "azure" (i.e., clear blue or the shade of lapis lazuli), perhaps on the model of the Italian *azzurrino*, which means "clear blue." BMS, perhaps in resistance to the neologism, corrected to a nonsensical "azur'd."
[572]The line in the manuscript reads:

thick set wth Agat, and the azurne sheene

    of ~~turquis~~ turkis blew, & ~~emrald~~ emrauld greene

      ~~that my rich wheeles inlayes~~ that in the channell straies

Notice that the original complex of images had to do with the colors inlaid in the wheels, but that it was changed to indicate colors that might be associated with the river itself. Changes in spelling from "turquis" to "turkis" and from "emrald" to "emrauld" might indicate something about pronunciation; certainly "emrauld" should be pronounced as a disyllable and not spelled with three syllables, and the sound of the modern "turquoise" is quite different from "Turkis."
[573]The feet of fairies were not supposed to leave a footprint or bend a grass stem. Shakespeare uses the same image in "on the sands with printless foot" (*Tempest* 5.1.34) as Prospero discusses the motions of elves or fairies. Weightlessness or speed are being emphasized in the sliding chariot, the straying channel, the fleet waters, the unbending cowslips, and the feet that leave no prints.

O're the Cowslips Velvet head,[574]
That bends not as I tread,
Gentle swain at thy request[575]   900
I am here.

Spir.[576] Goddess dear
We implore thy powerful hand
To undoe the charmed[577] band°   BOND OR SPELL
Of true Virgin here distrest,   905
Through the force, and through the wile
Of unblest inchanter vile.
    Sab. Shepherd 'tis my office best[578]
To help insnared chastity;
Brightest[579] Lady look on me,   910
Thus I sprinkle on thy brest[580]
Drops that from my fountain pure,
I have kept of pretious cure,°   SPIRITUAL CHARGE, POTENCY
Thrice upon thy fingers tip,
Thrice upon thy rubied[581] lip,   915
Next this marble venom'd seat
Smear'd with gumms of glutenous heat[582]
I touch with chaste palms moist and cold,[583]
Now the spell hath lost his hold;
And I must haste ere morning hour   920
To wait in *Amphitrite's* bowr.[584]

---

[574]Cowslips or primroses might indeed have a flower with a velvety texture like that of the pansy.

[575]Milton wrote what was apparently the beginning of "behest," "behe," then crossed it out and wrote in "request."

[576]The speech prefix throughout is "Dæ" for "Daemon." It is "De" in BMS. Notice that the half line "*I am here*" (900) is echoed in the rhyme "Goddess dear." The rhyme scheme continues to be iambic tetrameter couplets, with the intervention of songs, to the end of the masque, a pattern which fits with the various incantations, such as that which runs from 910 to 921 and that of 922–37, the end of which is signaled by a line space.

[577]Milton seems to have begun the word "magic" in the manuscript, gotten as far as "mag" and then scratched it out to write "charmed" instead. In saying the lines aloud, one might expect to elide "t' undo" to make the line scan iambically, but Milton did not write it that way in , and compositors avoided that particular elision.

[578]"It is my best duty and accomplishment."

[579]Milton wrote "virtuous," then struck through it to write "Brightest" in the manuscript; "virtuousest" makes an awkward superlative, but Milton did use it once, in *Paradise Lost* 8.550.

[580]Milton corrected the misspelled "best" to "brest" by inserting an "r" in ; BMS altered the phrase to the lest decorous "this brest." Reading the passage in a Freudian context, Kerrigan notes: "Her [Sabrina's] first gesture purifies the breast, earliest source of food" (47).

[581]Shakespeare used this adjective, meaning "Coloured like a ruby; ruby-tinged" (*OED*), first, in *Pericles* 5.Prol. 8, to refer to the color of a cherry, but the proverbial expression was "ruby lipped," even in the 1640s, when Herrick used it in his "Short Hymn to Venus."

[582]A phrase worrisome or titillating to modern scholars, who read it as everything from "sperm" (Shawcross; Kerrigan 47) to "sticky menses" (Sokol 323n). Kerrigan writes that "the dominant iconography of paralysis on a throne is anal" (47). To me the use of "envenom'd" suggests something toxic or maleficent concocted by Comus. However, "glutinous" suggests "buttocks" to some critics (from "gluteus maximus"; see Le Comte 1–2) and ropey birdlime to others. "Heat" suggests, to some critics, sexual excitement either on the part of the Lady (Turner 177n, but see Leonard) or on the part of Comus. Since Flosdorf's query, and the replies to it in *Milton Quarterly* and at the beginning of Le Comte's book, the image has become a center of interpretive interest, what critics love, a new crux.

[583]In other words, she opposes her cool and most humors to the dry and gummy heat of the envenomed seat. Her hands and the touch of them are curative, and they can remove the evil power of the hot venom. One virgin helps another, creatively, curing her of the evil spell cast on her.

[584]The line may have first been written "waite in [for?] Amphitrite ~~in her~~ bowre" in the manuscript, then Milton wrote in "To" in the left margin. Sabrina says she must go before morning to attend at the bedchamber when Amphitrite awakens. Sabrina is pictured as a lady-in-waiting to the queen of the sea, Neptune's wife. I disagree with the *Variorum* editors that "Her *bowr* stands for Neptune's court" (2.3: 969), since Milton almost always uses the word for a small and intimate, rather than a large and public, place. It may be worth noting that Amphitrite, daughter of Oceanus and Thetys, married Neptune despite a vow of perpetual celebacy and then gave birth to Triton. She has the power to calm the seas (Hesiod 254).

*Sabrina descends, and the Lady rises out
    of her seat.*[585]

Spir. Virgin, daughter of *Locrine*[586]
Sprung of old *Anchises* line,
May thy brimmed[587] waves for this
Their full tribute[588] never miss   925
From a thousand petty rills,°   RIVULETS, SMALL STREAMS
That tumble down the[589] snowy hills:
Summer drouth,° or singed° air   DROUGHT   PARCHED DRY
Never scorch thy tresses fair,
Nor wet *Octobers* torrent flood   930
Thy molten crystal fill with mudd,[590]
May thy billows rowl ashoar
The beryl and the golden ore,[591]
May thy lofty head be crown'd
With many a tower and terrass round,[592]   935
And here and there thy banks upon
With Groves of myrrhe, and cinnamon.[593]
Com Lady[594] while Heaven lends us grace,[595]
Let us fly this cursed place,
Lest the Sorcerer us intice   940
With som other new device.°   CLEVER TRICK
Not a waste, or needless sound[596]
Till we com to holier ground,
I shall be your faithfull guide
Through this gloomy covert° wide,   THICKET   945
And not many furlongs[597] thence
Is your Fathers residence,
Where this night are met[598] in state[599]

---

[585]The stage directions are marginal in the manuscript, and strategically placed. After "heate" "Sa brina descends" is written to the right of that line. After "lost his hold" Milton writes a long dash in the right margin and then "the Ladie riſes out of her seate." The effect on the stage would have been dramatic visually, since Sabrina is disappearing below as the Lady is rising out of her seat.

[586]The *Variorum* editors summarize: " . . . Brutus, who led the Trojan settlement of Britain and was the father of Locrine and grandfather of Sabrina, was himself the son of Silvius, son of Ascanius, son of Aeneas, whose father Anchises died on the voyage to Italy (Virgil, *A.* 3.708-11)" (2.3: 969-70).

[587]Milton first wrote "crystall," then struck through it and wrote "brimmed" above the line, calling attention to it with a caret.

[588]Probably a pun on tribute as meaning both "thing of value given to a person in authority" and "tributary stream." Milton uses the word again similarly in *Paradise Regain'd* 3.257-58: "rivers . . . meeting joyn'd thir tribute to the Sea."

[589]Milton first wrote "down from," then replace the preposition "from" with the article "the."

[590]The "silver" Severn, being a tidal river and rather shallow, would indeed become muddy with a heavy influx of rain.

[591]Perhaps the Severn was expected to produce, in its sediment washed up on shore, gold and semiprecious stones, as in the class of stones grouped under the term "beryl."

[592]The landscape might invoke that of the castle at Ludlow, which is perched on a cliff and is indeed towered, though Ludlow is not on the Severn but on one of its tributaries. See David Lloyd, "Ludlow Castle," *Milton Quarterly* 21 (1987): 52-58.

[593]These cannot be local references; editors have found them to be biblical (as in Proverbs 7.17), but not Welsh. With the end of this line, another little prayer has been said, a polite valediction to Sabrina, and the Lady and Spirit are free to move on. The stage direction at this point in is "Song ends" and BMS follows that, but *1637* and *1645* do not.

[594]BMS gives the "Com Lady" line, which BMS alters to "Come sister while heav'n lends us grace," to move through "holier ground" (943), to the Elder Brother, again involving the Bridgewater family more in performance. has no speech prefixes, because the entire speech is spoken (or the first part sung, the second spoken) by the Attendant Spirit, whom Milton identifies as "Dæ."

[595]Heaven would only lend them grace because, within the Christian system, sinful humans do not deserve it: it must be loaned to them by God.

[596]"Don't waste words until we get to safer, holier ground."

[597]The length of a furrow in what was about a ten-acre tract of common agricultural land in England, now reckoned as 220 yards or 1/8 mile; used as a measurement in the U.S. only in horse racing.

[598]The manuscript first had "come," then that was crossed through and replaced by "met" above the line.

[599]"In full ceremonial dress, as their estate or rank would dictate."

Many a friend[600] to gratulate
His wish't presence,[601] and beside
All the Swains that there[602] abide,
With Jiggs,[603] and rural dance resort,
We shall catch them at their[604] sport,
And our sudden coming there
Will double all their mirth and chere;
Com let us haste, the Stars grow[605] high,
But night sits[606] monarch yet in the mid sky.[607]

950

955

The Scene changes presenting Ludlow *Town and
the Presidents Castle, then com in Countrey-
Dancers, after them the attendant Spirit, with
the two Brothers and the Lady.*[608]

---

[600]Brown has noted that "we must imagine the presence of a fair number of people connected with the president and court" and that "We know, too, that some townspeople were invited" (36).

[601]The implication, which follows what we know of historical fact, is that the Earl has been absent and is returning to Ludlow (Brown 32–34).

[602]The Trinity Manuscript and BMS both have "neere," though *1637* and *1645* have "there."

[603]Defined as "A lively, rapid, springy kind of dance" (*OED* 1.a), but Milton seems to be making a contrast between jigs and country dances. The stage direction in the Trinity Manuscript after "mid skie" is:

> the scene changes and then is præsented Ludlow towne
> & the præsidents castle then enter countrie dances & such
> like gambols &c.

Perhaps gambols should be thought of as jigs as contrasted with country dances, though the gambol or frisk generally involved much leaping (see *OED* "gambol"). The presence of "nimbler" and "speedier" "toeing" in the excised words suggests that the dances were indeed fast and athletic.

[604]BMS has "this."

[605]Milton first wrote "are," then put an asterisk above the line and "grow" in the right margin.

[606]Milton first wrote "night reignes," then added "But" in the left margin and then crossed through "reignes" and replaced it with "sitts monarch" to its right.

[607]In the manuscript the stage direction "Exeunt" is to the right of this line.

[608]In the manuscript the stage direction reads:

> the Scene changes and then is præsented Ludlow towne
> & the præsidents castle then enter countrie dances & such
> like gambols &c.

>   at
> ~~After~~ those sports the Dæmon wth ye 2 bro. & the Ladie enter
>   the Dæmon sings

BMS changes the wording in to some extent, removing "such like gambols" and adding "towards the end of those sports the demon with the 2 brothers and the ladye come in." Timing may be important here since "After those sports" in is not the same as "towards the end of those sports" in BMS. In "the Dæmon sings," in BMS "the spiritt singes" and in *1637* "Song" begins and then "Spir." is added as a speech prefix.

SONG.[609]

Spir. *Back Shepherds, back, anough your play,*
Till next Sun-shine holiday,
Here be without duck or nod   960
Other trippings to be trod
Of lighter toes, and such Court guise
As Mercury *did first devise*
With the mincing Dryades
On the Lawns and on the Leas.   965

This second Song presents them to their
    father and mother.

Noble Lord, and Lady bright,
I have brought ye new delight,
Here behold so goodly grown
Three fair branches of your own,
Heav'n hath timely tri'd° their youth,   TESTED   970
Their faith, their patience,[610] and their truth.
And sent them here through hard assays
With[611] a crown of deathless Praise,[612]
To triumph in victorious dance
O're sensual Folly, and Intemperance.[613]   975

---

[609]Milton made a number of changes in this two-part song, perhaps in conjunction with Henry Lawes, who was setting his words to music. Here is Milton's version of the first song in :

        Back shepheards back enough yo ͬ play
        till next sunshine Holyday
        heere be wth out duck or nod
        other trippings to be trod
        ~~nimbler~~   such neate
                                      of lighter toes, & such court guise
of lighter of ~~speedier~~ toeing, & ~~courtly~~ guise
                                     *first
        ~~such~~ as ~~Hermes~~ did   devise   Mercury *first
        wth the mincing Dryades
        on the lawns, & on the leas

Lawes's version of the song, with his musical notation included, is preserved in British Museum Additional Manuscript 53723:
        Back Shepherds Back enough your Play till the next ſunshine   Holiday Here be without Duck or Nod
other trippings to be trod of   lighter Toes & ſuch Court Guiſe as Mercury did first devise w ^{th} y^{u}
    [possibly "y^{e}"] mincing Dryades o're the Lawns & o're the Leas.
Lawes has smoothed out rough edges on the phrasing, adding the "the" between "till" and "next" and making "on the lawns, & and on the leas" into "o're the Lawns & o're the Leas."

[610]The manuscript has "patience" crossed through, "temperance" added in the margin, then that same "temperance" has been crossed through and "patience" added above, with the "patience" within the line reinstated by an underline. Considering the importance of the virtue patience in the later writing of Milton, the change is significant here. Patience does seem to be the broader of the two virtues. Also, since intemperance will be mentioned shortly, including temperance at this point would seem redundant.

[611]The manuscript originally had "to a crowne," but Milton crossed through "to" and wrote "w^{th}" in the left margin.

[612]In searching for a rhyme, Milton first wrote "bays" (i.e., laurels), then, perhaps thinking a poet's crown inappropriate for the children, he crossed it out and substituted "praise."

[613]Lawes's version of the second song reads:
    Noble Lord & Lady bright I have brought you new delight Here behold ſo goodly
    growne Three fair Branches of your own Heav'n hath timely try'd their Youth their
    Faith their Patience & their Truth and ſent them here thro' hard aſsays with a
    Crown of Deathleſs Praise to triumph in victorious Dance o're ſenſual Folly and
    Intemperance.

The dances ended, the Spirit Epiloguizes.[614]

Spir. To the Ocean now I fly,[615]
And those happy climes that ly
Where day never shuts his eye,
Up in the broad fields of the sky:
There I suck the liquid° ayr   TRANSPARENT, CLEAR   980
All amidst the Gardens fair

---

[614]Milton had written a messy draft of this speech, the epilogue of the play.

                    they dance.   the dances all ended
          the Dæmon sings. or sayes

          To the Ocean now I fly
          and those happie climes that lie
          where day never shuts his eye
          up in the *~~plaine~~ feilds of the skie *broad
          farr beyond ye earths end
                      low
          where the welkin ~~cleere~~ doth bend
          ther I suck the liquid aire
          all amidst the gardens faire
          Hesperus ~~neeces~~
          of ~~Atlas~~ & his ~~daughters~~ three

< note: beginning with the next line, the passage that leads through the word "Exit" has an ex drawn through it >

          that sing about the golden tree
          there æternall summer dwells
          and west winds wth muſky wing
          about the ~~myrtle~~* alleys fling   *cedar'ne
    nard   balmy
  ~~balme~~   ~~balme~~, and casia's ~~fragrant~~ smells
                    *
          Iris there w^th ~~garnish't~~ bow   *~~garish~~ humid
          waters the odorous banks y^t blow
          flowers of more mingled hew
                purfl'd
          then her ~~watchet~~ · scarfe can shew
          yellow, watched, greene, & blew
          and drenches oft wth manna dew
          beds of Hyachinth, & roses
          where many a cherub soft reposes
                taske   smoothly
          now my *~~message well~~ is done   *buiſneſse
                2 1
          I can fly, or I can run
                      earths
          quickly to the ~~earths~~ greene · end
                2 1
          where the bow'd welkin slow doth bend
          and from thence can soare as soone
          to the corners of ye moone
          mortalls that would follow me
          love vertue she alone is free
          she can teach yee how to clime
          higher then the sphærie chime
          or if vertue feeble were
                      stoope
          heaven it selfe would bo· w to her. Exit

He canceled that draft, signalled by "The Dæmon sings or says" in , then he re-wrote it in a very fair hand, making very few final changes.
[615]Carey notes, citing Plutarch's *Moralia* 590 C–D, "this ocean is the celestial sphere; the islands, stars and planets" (974–5n).

Of *Hesperus*,[616] and his daughters three
That sing about the golden tree:
Along the crisped[617] shades and bowres
Revels the spruce° and jocond Spring,   LIVELY   985
The Graces, and the rosie-boosom'd Howres,[618]
Thither all their bounties bring,
That there eternal Summer dwells,
And West winds, with musky° wing   PERFUMED
About the cedar'n alleys[619] fling   990
Nard,[620] and *Cassia*'s balmy smels.
Iris[621] there with humid bow,
Waters the odorous banks that blow
Flowers of more mingled hew
Then her purfl'd scarf[622] can shew,   995
And drenches with *Elysian*[623] dew
(List mortals, if your ears be true)
Beds of *Hyacinth*,[624] and roses
Where young *Adonis*[625] oft reposes,
Waxing well° of his deep wound   BECOMING WELL, RECOVERING   1000
In slumber soft, and on the ground

---

[616]In the manuscript, Milton wrote:
        all amidst the gardens faire
      Hesperus   ~~neeces~~
     of ~~Atlas~~ & his ~~daughters~~ three
The changes indicate that Milton was trying to decide between the name of Atlas or Hesperus, sometimes taken as the same demi-god. The daughters of Hesperus, the Hesperides, were the guardians of the sacred apples, the capture of which was one of the labors of Hercules. Diodorus Siculus (4) was the first to confuse the Hesperides with the Atlantides, or daughters of Atlas, but there were supposed to be three or four Hesperides (Apollodorus mentions Aegle, Erythia, Vesta, and Arethusa—see 3, ch. 5) and seven Atlantides (Maia, Electra, Taygeta, Asterope, Merope, Alcyone, and Celaeno). To confuse things even more, the Atlantides were often called Hesperides because their mother was Hesperis: their constellation is the Pleiades. The placement of the gardens of the Hesperides was likewise confused between an island supposedly located near where the sun set and the western mountains of Africa, where Mt. Atlas was supposed to have been located.
[617]The word meant "crinkly" or "tightly curled" when applied to hair, but when it is "Applied to trees: [its] sense [is] uncertain" (*OED* 4), citing this instance.
[618] Presumably the Hours as they usher in spring are wearing roses on their bosom, as with the image of spring in Botticelli's famous painting "Primavera." As the *Variorum* editors point out, the bringing of dawn might suggest the adjective "rosy" (2.3: 980).
[619]Lanes overhung with cedar trees. Milton first had written "myrtle" in , and he may have made the change to emphasize the more aromatic cedar. Milton made up the adjectival form "cedarn," according to the *OED*.
[620]The biblical "spikenard" (as in the Song of Songs 1.12, 4.14), an aromatic root. Cassia is likewise a biblical aromatic oil produced from the cassia tree and having an odor resembling cinnamon (see Exodus 30.24). Milton uses the combination again in *Paradise Lost*: "flouring Odours, Cassia, Nard, and Balme" (5.293).
[621]The goddess who controls the rainbow, one of the Oceanides, usually pictured with multicolored wings.
[622]Milton wrote "flowers of more mingled hew
               purfl'd
      then her ~~watchet~~ · scarfe can shew"
in the manuscript. The adjective "watchet" probably indicates the color blue, though it is of an indeterminate origin and can on occasion mean "yellow." The adjective "purfled" may be easier to trace as "Bordered; esp. having a decorative or ornamental border; bordered with embroidery, gold lace, fur, etc.; fringed; in vaguer use, embroidered, decorated. Also fig." (*OED* 1). The scarf seems to represent the variegated colors that Iris, the rainbow, is wearing.
[623]Milton first wrote "*Sabæan* dew," then replaced "*Sabæan*" with "*Elyssian*." Sabæa or Saba was a town of Arabia made famous by Vergil (*Aeneid* 1.5.420) for its aromatic frankincense and myrrh. The Elysian fields, home of the classical Greek virtuous dead, were located in various places, the Fortunate Isles off the coast of Africa in the Atlantic, in Italy, in the center of the earth, or on the moon.
[624]"*Hyacinth*" is italicized presumably because it is the name of the classical deity Hyacinthus as well as of the flower. Hyacinthus was beloved of Apollo, who killed him by accident but transformed him into the flower, thereby immortalizing his memory.
[625]In the first state of this passage in the Trinity Manuscript, Milton had only "where many a cherub soft reposes": thus he replaces generic cherubs with a specific Adonis. As the *Variorum* editors note, lines 995–1010 "were evidently written (as Hurd, reported by Warton and Todd, seems to have been the first to notice) with Spenser's Garden of Adonis in mind (*F.Q.* 3.6.43–50)" (2.3.982–83), but there is also Shakespeare's "Venus and Adonis" as a potential source.

Sadly sits th' *Assyrian* Queen;[626]
But farr above in spangled sheen
Celestial *Cupid*[627] her fam'd Son advanc't,°   RAISED ON HIGH
Holds his dear *Psyche*[628] sweet intranc't[629]   1005
After her wandring labours long,
Till free consent the gods among
Make her his eternal Bride,
And from her fair unspotted side
Two blissful twins are to be born,   1010
Youth and Joy; so *Jove* hath sworn.[630]
  But now my task is smoothly don,[631]
I can fly, or I can run[632]
Quickly to the green earths end,
Where the bow'd welkin° slow doth bend,   VAULTED SKY   1015
And from thence can soar as soon
To the corners of the Moon.[633]
  Mortals that would follow me,   } *Diff good <-> Evil*
Love vertue,[634] she alone is free,
She can teach ye how to clime   1020

Accommodation - Heaven will save you.

---

[626]Venus, goddess of love, who wooed and then maintained Adonis as her favorite, and was grief-stricken when he received a mortal wound while hunting wild boar. Milton's associating her with the Phoenician Astarte (Pausanias 1.14.6) may be intended to connect her with pagan and wanton rites, though there is no hint in *Comus* that physical love, as practiced within marriage, is in any way degraded (see *Variorum* 2.3: 984–85). There does seem to be implied a contrast between the love of Venus as profane and outside marriage and the love of Cupid and Psyche, within a marriage sanctified by the gods.
[627]Milton is forcing a connection not made in classical literature between Venus, her son Cupid, and his wife Psyche, in order to contrast the profane love of Venus for Adonis with the pure or sacred love of Cupid (Eros or love itself) with Psyche (the mind). Venus was jealous of Psyche, according to Apuleius, removed her from Cupid, and forced her to do impossible tasks, driving her to death with the work (*The Golden Ass* 4.28–6.24). Milton was interested in the myth of Psyche's labors as a symbolic representation of the way that grains of truth or goodness can be extracted from masses of evil knowledge: " . . . the knowledge of good is so involv'd and interwoven with the knowledge of 'evill, and in so many cunning resemblances hardly to be discern'd, that those confused seeds which were impos'd on *Psyche* as an incessant labour to cull out, and sort asunder, were not more intermixt" (*Areopagitica*; Yale 2: 514). Venus had given Psyche a large amount of various seeds and asked her to separate them according to their varieties. The fact that Cupid is here "Celestial" indicates that Milton wants the reader to take the love of Cupid for Psyche as heavenly, and the marriage of Cupid and Psyche as being an ideal marriage.
[628]The story of Psyche's (her name can mean "Human Spirit" or "Mind") marriage with Cupid or Eros, the god of love, is told in what is now called Apuleius's *Metamorphoses* (it has been known in the past as *The Golden Ass* because it is concerned with the transformation of a man into a donkey, and is told mostly from the perspective of the ass) 5 and 6. After an almost impossibly difficult series of ordeals brought on her by Cupid's jealous mother, Venus, Psyche is enabled to marry Cupid by Jupiter himself: "Thus in proper form Psyche was given in marriage to Cupid. And when her time was come, a daughter was born to them, whom we call by the name Pleasure" (Loeb trans., 6.24).
[629]"To throw into a state of mind resembling a trance; to put 'out of oneself'; to overpower with strong feeling, as delight, fear, etc." (*OED* 1.b, citing this instance).
[630]Though the passage may be built on slightly skewed mythology (Psyche was supposed according to classical versions to have given birth to Voluptas, or Pleasure), Milton seems to be implying that the Lady Alice will soon be married and that her marriage is sure to be like the marriage of Cupid and Psyche, blessed in heaven, and produce the best of offspring, Youth and Joy. The image of the cups (see Columbia 3: 305; Yale 1:891), as the *Variorum* editors point out, "indicates that Milton is recalling Circe and hence Comus" (2.3: 987).
[631]The manuscript contains many changes in the first draft of the following lines:

                          taske   smoothly
            now my *~~message well~~ is done   *buiſneſse
                                2 1
            I can fly, or I can run
                                              earths
            quickly to the ~~earths~~ greene · end

[632]The Attendant Spirit is speaking in patterns like those of Shakespeare's Puck or Ariel. He does have the capacity to cover huge distances over land or in the air. Compare *Midsummer Night's Dream* "We the globe can compass soon, / Swifter than the wand'ring moon" (4.1.100–1).
[633]The Moon also has corners in *Macbeth* 3.5.23: "the corners of the moon." The idea here is that of travel to the end of the imaginable universe.
[634]The *Variorum* editors comment, "There is precedent in Jonson's masques for ending thus on a didactic note in praise of virtue" (2.3:988), but other editors have added that Milton is ending on a Platonic note (see *Phaedrus* 246–56) and, beyond that, a Christian one.

Higher then the Spheary chime;[635]
Or if Vertue feeble were,
Heav'n it self would stoop to her.[636] ACCHOORTION

    The End.

---

[635] Presumably higher than the universe as it was classically conceived, outside of the Ptolemaic spheres, designed "to parallel on this lower level the song of the angels (cf. *PL* 5.618–27)" (*Variorum* 2.3: 989). Milton's is the second usage of the adjective recorded in the *OED*, after Shakespeare's: "What wicked and dissembling glass of mine, / Made me compare with Hermia's sphery eyne" (*Midsummer Night's Dream* 2.2.99).

[636] According to the theological distinction, humankind does not deserve grace, but God freely condescends (not in the negative sense) or "stoops" to extend it to us. In his earlier draft of the epilogue, Milton wrote the lines as

               or if vertue feeble were

                      stoope

           heaven it selfe would bo·w to her

The verb "bow" was apparently too strong to represent God's extension of grace. In what may have been an act of egotism designed for future generations, Milton wrote the last two lines of his masque in the guest book of Count Camillo Cerdogni while he was in Geneva in 1639 (Parker, *Milton* 181).

Joannis   Miltoni

LONDINENSIS

POEMATA.

Quorum peraque intra
Annum ætatis Vigesimum
Conscripsit.

Nunc primum Edita.

LONDINI,

Typis *R. R.* Prostant ad Insignia Principis,
in Cœmeterio D. *Pauli,* apud *Humphredum
Moseley.* 1645.

Elegiarum and *Sylvarum*

Milton's Latin poetry is a separate book within a book, in the 1645 and again in the 1673 *Poems*. Just as the poems in memory of Edward King in which "Lycidas" first appeared (Le Comte) were divided into an English section and a Latin and Greek section, Milton separated out his Latin poetry (but not the modern Italian poetry or translations such as that of the ode by Horace) into a volume with its own title page. Further subdivisions of the Latin poetry were into *Elegiarum*, poems in the elegiac distich (couplet alternating hexameter and pentameter lines), and *Sylvarum*, by which Milton probably meant lyric poems in forms other than elegiac. As Masson points out, "he thought it permissible to call anything an Elegy that was written in the ordinary elegiac verse of alternate Hexameter and Pentameter" (3: 452).

Milton knew that his century associated elegies with pastoral poetry—most of his elegies are pastoral—and with the great themes of love and death. Most elegiac poetry, like that of Ovid, deals with the subject of erotic love, a subject that Donne and Milton both considered trivial when compared with a subject as great as "Mans First Disobedience" (*Paradise Lost* 1.1). Ovid himself joked that he had attempted to write heroic or epic poetry in straight hexameter, but that Cupid stole a foot from his second line; Milton would eventually disavow his own attempts at what he called "vain amatorious" poetry of the kind written by Sir Philip Sidney in his pastoral romance *Arcadia* (*Eikonoklastes*; Yale 3: 362).

The audience for Milton's Latin poetry was different from that for his English poetry. It was at once more international and better educated. When he went to Italy and appeared at some of the academies in Florence in 1638, he apparently read his Latin poetry, not the Italian poetry he had earlier composed. In later years, he would write to his Italian friends in the universal language, the *lingua franca* of his time, Latin. But as he compared himself with Dante and Petrarch, Ariosto and Tasso—all of whom wrote in Latin as well as their native Italian—Milton realized that his best bid for immortality was with his English poetry, because it would be more original and less derivative than his Latin poetry, with its phrases borrowed from the masters such as Vergil and Ovid, might be.

Milton realized that his own Latin erotic poetry (hesitant ever to describe a real woman) was restricted in emotional range. An epic like *Paradise Lost* might contain a few love lyrics, but love lyrics could never contain epic scope or richness. Similarly, poetry in an elegiac mode, though it dealt with the important theme of coping with death, was in itself a dead end. Milton knew, however, that there was something to be learned by emulating the great elegists such as Ovid, Catullus, Tibullus, or Propertius, even if that meant slavish imitation of their imagery and a wholesale borrowing of their pure Roman vocabulary. Milton's Latin poetry can be more intimate than his English poetry (Rand), perhaps because the Latin audience, though broader than an exclusively English one, was better educated. Milton writes not only personal verse letters in Latin, but he writes about the death of his best friend, Charles Diodati, in the *Epitaphium Damonis*; he writes to define his relationship with his father in *Ad Patrem*; and he defines his vocation as a poet for the first time in *Mansus*, written to the Italian poet Manso.

Miller has shown that Milton's style in his Latin prose was severely classical, especially after he became Cromwell's Secretary for Foreign Tongues: Milton was, after all, a Latin lexicographer, and his thesaurus of Latin words was appropriated as the source of the Latin dictionary published in 1697 by Adam Littleton (his dates are 1627–1694; see Parker 1167). Milton made himself expert in the use of his second language, the international language of his time, and his ambition seems to have included excellence in Latin poetry and prose.

TRANSLATIONS

The translations are modeled on those of the Columbia Milton. They have been updated, simplified, and sometimes changed utterly from the quaint Victorian English of the Columbia translators, in order to be better understood by the audience of this volume. Responsibility for any errors or mistranslations that might have inadvertently occurred is mine.

TEXT

The copy-text is *1645*, but with occasional corrections based on *1673*. Testimonials to Milton have been included, but I have kept my annotations for them brief.

Works Cited

Campbell, Gordon. "Imitation in *Epitaphium Damonis*." *Milton Studies* 19 (1984): 165–77.

Le Comte, Edward, ed. *Justa Edovardo King: A Facsimile Edition of the Memorial Volume in which Milton's "Lycidas" First Appeared, with Introduction, Translations, and Notes by Edward Le Comte*. N.p.: Norwood Editions, 1978.

Miller, Leo. "Lexicographer Milton Leads Us to Rediscover His Unknown Works." *Milton Quarterly* 25 (1991): 58–63.

Rand, E. K. "Milton in Rustication." *Studies in Philology* 19 (1922): 109–35.

Revard, Stella P. *Milton and the Tangles of Neaera's Hair: The Making of the 1645 Poems*. Columbia: U of Missouri P, 1997.

HÆc quæ sequuntur de Authore testimonia, tametsi ipse intelligebat non tam de se quàm supra se esse dicta, eò quòd preclaro ingenio viri, nec non amici ita fere solent laudare, ut omnia suis potius virtutibus, quàm veratati congruentia nimis cupidè assingant, noluit tamen horum egregiam in se voluntatem non esse notam; Cum alii præfertim ut id faceret magnopere suaderent. Dum enim nimiæ laudis invidiam totis ab se viribus amolitur, sibique quod plus æquo est non attributum esse mavult, judicium interim hominum cordatorum atque illustrium quin summo sibi honori ducat, negare non potest.[1]

Here follow testimonials with respect to the author. He was perfectly well aware that they were uttered not so much about him as over him, because men of preeminent ability who are one's friends as well have a habit of phrasing their eulogies in such a way that they conjure up, eagerly, what, from beginning to end, befits their own merits rather than the truth. Yet the author was unwilling that the kindly feeling entertained for him by the writers of these testimonials should not be known, especially since others were very earnestly urging him to make them generally known. For, while he is seeking earnestly to ward off the distaste that excessive praise occasions, and prefers that he should not be credited with more than is his due, he cannot, in the meantime, deny that he sees a signal honor to himself in the favorable judgment of distinguished men of intellect.

---

[1] The tributes to Milton, from Manso in Naples, from Salsilli and "Selvaggi" of Rome, and especially that of the Florentine Francini, are worth reading for what they tell us about Milton's valued Italian friendships and about Milton's desire for poetic fame. For Francini, Milton is in love with fame, a "*Fabro quasi divino,*" a "nearly divine maker [of poetry]," and a student of international culture. For Salsilli and Selvaggi, Milton will be counted with Homer, Vergil, and Tasso for poetic greatness. After Milton's death, in the 1688 folio edition of *Paradise Lost*, John Dryden would recognize the prophetic power of Selvaggi's comparison by echoing it in the epigram that appears with Milton's portrait.

Joannes Baptista Mansus, Marchio
Villensis Neapolitanus ad Joannem
Miltonium Anglum.

UT mens, forma, decor, facies, mos, si pietas sic,
Non Anglus,[2] verùm herclè Angelus ipse fores.

Giovanni Battista Manso, Marquis
of Villa, of Naples, to John
Milton, Englishman.

IF your piety matched your intellect, your figure,
your grace and charm, your bearing, your manners,
you would be, not an Angle, but a true Angel.

Ad Joannem Miltonem Anglum triplici
poeseos laureâ coronandum Græcâ nimirum,
Latinâ, atque Hetruscâ, Epigramma
Joannis Salsilli Romani.

CEde Meles, cedat depressa Mincius urna;
Sebetus Tassum desinat usque loqui;
At Thamesis victor cunctis ferat altior undas
Nam per te, Milto, par tribus unus erit.

An Epigram by Giovanni Salsilli, a Roman,
on John Milton, Englishman, who deserves a
coronal fashioned of the triple laurel of
poesy—Greek, Latin, and Italian.

YIeld, Meles, yield; let Mincius, too, lowering his
urn, yield; let Sebetus cease to have Tasso forever
on his tongue. But let the victor Thames flow on with
waves greater than those of every other stream, for,
thanks to you, Milton, he will be the best of the three.

Ad Joannem Miltonum.

GRæcia Mæonidem, jactet sibi Roma Maronem,
Anglia Miltonum jactat utrique parem.
Selvaggi.

Selvaggi to John Milton.

LEt Greece boast, if she will, of Mæonia's son, let
Rome boast to herself of Maro! England boasts of
Milton, in his one self a full match for the other two
combined.
Selvaggi

---

[2] Punning on "Englishman" and "angel" in Latin.

Al Signor Gio. Miltoni Nobile
Inglese.
ODE.

ERgimi all' Etra ò Clio
    Perche di stelle intreccierò corona
    Non più del Biondo Dio
La Fronde eterna in Pindo, e in Elicona,
Diensi a merto maggior, maggiori i fregi,   5
A'celeste virtù celesti pregi.

Non puo del tempo edace
Rimaner preda, eterno alto valore
Non può l'oblio rapace
Furar dalle memorie eccelso onore,   10
Su l'arco di mia cetra un dardo forte
Virtù m'adatti, e ferirò la morte.

Del Ocean profondo
Cinta dagli ampi gorghi Anglia risiede
Separata dal mondo,   15
Però che il suo valor l'umano eccede:
Questa feconda sà produrre Eroi,
Ch' hanno a ragion del sovruman tra noi.

Alla virtù sbandica
Danno ne i petti lor fido ricetto,   20
Quella gli é sol gradita,
Perche in lei san trovar gioia, e diletto;
Ridillo tu Giovanni e mostra in tanto
Con tua vera virtù, vero il mio Canto.

Lungi dal Patrio lido   25
Spense Zeusi l'industre ardente bramà;
Ch' udio d'Helena il grido
Con aurea tromba rimnombar la fama,
E per poterla effigiare al paro
Dalle più belle Idee trasse i priù raro.   30

Cosi l'Ape Ingegnosa
Trae con industria il suo liquor pregiato
Dal giglio e dalla rosa,
E quanti vaghi fiori ornano il prato;
Formano un dolce suo a diverse Chorde,   35
Fan varie voci melodia concorde.

Di bella gloria amante
Milton dal Ciel natío per varie parti
Le peregrine piante
Volgesti a recercar scienze, ed arti;   40
Del Gallo regnator vedesti i Regni,
E dell' Italia ancor gl' Eroi pin degni.

To Mr. John Milton, Gentleman
of England.
ODE.

Lift me to Heaven, Clio, so that I can make a crown out of stars. Not here exists the foliage, eternal on Pindus and on Helicon, of the fair-haired Apollo. For greatest merit be greatest prize due, for godlike virtue, rewards from the gods.

Time cannot kill eternal worth. Rapacious oblivion cannot rob memory of forever youthful glory. May virtue fit a worthy arrow to the bow of my lyre, and I will strike Death to death.

Belted by the vast eddies of the deep Ocean sits England, cut off from the world, because her qualities excel the qualities of all the rest: it is the power of her fertile womb that brings forth heroes whom we justly name as more than men.

In their hearts Virtue, in other places banished, finds secure rest, of them alone beloved because in her alone can they find joy and pleasure. This will you make known again, O Milton. With your true virtue goes my true song.

Zeuxis carried his burning zeal far from the shores of his native land; for he heard the golden horn of Fame heralding Helen's glory; and worthily to make her likeness he sought the rarest among the most beautiful of Ideas.

From rose, from lily, from all the comely flowers that adorn the meadow, the clever bee laboriously extracts his priceless sweet. So does tuneful music flow from varied strings, concordant melody from many voices.

So, enamored of beautiful Fame, you turned your wandering feet, O Milton, from your native country, in quest of the sciences and arts. You saw the realms of the conquering Gaul, and you met the most worthy heroes of Italy.

Fabro quasi divino
Sol virtù rintracciando il tuo pensiero
Vide in ogni confino   45
Chi di nobil valor calca il sentiero;
L' ottimo dal miglior dopo scegliea
Per fabbricar d'ogni virtu l' Idea.

Quanti nacquero in Flora
O in lei del parlar Tosco appreser l'arte,   50
La cui memoria onora
Il mondo fatta eterna in dotte carte,
Volesti ricercar per tuo tesoro,
E parlasti con lor nell' opre loro.

Nell' altera Babelle   55
Per te il parlar confuse Giove in vano,
Che per varie favelle
Di se stessa trofeo cadde su'l piano:
Ch' Ode oltr' all Anglia il suo piu degno Idioma
Spagna, Francia, Toscana, e Grecia e Roma.   60

I piu profondi arcani
Ch' occulta la natura e in cielo e in terra
Ch' à Ingegni sovrumani
Troppo avara tal' hor gli chiude, e serra,
Chiaramente conosci, e giungi al fine   65
Della moral virtude al gran confine.

Non batta il Tempo l'ale,
Fermisi immoto, e in un fermin si gl'anni,
Che di virtù immortale
Scorron di troppo ingiuriosi a i danni;   70
Che s'opre degne di Poema o storia
Furon gia, l' hai presenti alla memoria.

Dammi tuo dolce Cetra
Se vuoi ch' io dica del tuo dolce canto,
Ch' inalzandoti all' Etra   75
Di farti huomo celeste ottiene il vanto,
Il Tamigi il dirà che gl' è concesso
Per te suo cigno pareggiar Permesso.

Io che in riva del Arno
Tento spiegar tuo merto alto, e preclaro   80
So che fatico indarno,
E ad ammirar, non a lodarlo imparo;
Freno dunque la lingua, e ascolto il core
Che ti prende a lodar con lo stupore.
      Del sig. Antonio Francini gentilhuomo
                        Fiorentino.

Half-divine writer, your thought, emulating virtue in itself, sought out in your travels the truly noble beings. Among the best of the better sort, you chose to construct an Idea that included all the virtues.

All those poets of Florence—whether her own sons or masters though their heritage of the Tuscan dialect—whose memory, immortalized in learned pages, gives honor to humankind, you treasure up in yourself, communing with them in their works.

Jupiter vainly confused the languages as he transformed the proud Tower of Babel, when, self-defeated, it fell to level ground. For from your lips not only England, but Spain, France, Tuscany, Greece, Rome, hear each her noblest speech.

You have mastered the deepest secrets which Nature hides, jealously concealing them to superior minds in Heaven or on Earth, too often covetously concealing them to superhuman minds, to reach at last the great boundaries of moral wisdom.

Let Time stop beating his wings, may he arrest his flight. Those years that do wrong discourteously to immortal virtue would stop proceeding. You have within your memory every meritorious poem or history ever made.

But if I must sing of your sweet song, which exalts you to the skies and demonstrates your divine prophetic power, give me your lyre. Through you, its swan, may Thames proclaim equality with Permessus.

Vainly do I, on the bank of the Arno, try to describe your shining excellence; for I admire you more than I have power to praise you. I must control my tongue and listen to my heart which, inspired, sings your praise.

By Antonio Francini, Esquire, Gentleman of Florence.

JOANNI MILTONI LONDINIENSI.

Juveni Patria, virtutibus eximio,

Viro qui multa peregrinatione, studio cuncta orbis terrararum loca perspexit, ut novus Ulysses omnia ubique ab omnibus apprehenderet.

Polyglotto, in cujus ore linguæ jam deperditæ sic reviviscunt, ut idiomata omnia sint in ejus laudibus infacunda; Et jure ea percallet ut admirationes & plausus populorum ab propria sapientia excitatos, intelligat.

Illi, cujus animi dotes corporisque, sensus ad admirationem commovent, & per ipsam motum cuique auferunt; cujus opera ad plausus hortantur, sed venustate[1] vocem laudatoribus adimunt.

Cui in Memoria totus Orbis: In intellectu Sapientia. in voluntate ardor gloriæ. in ore Eloquentia: Harmonicos cœlestium[2] Sphærarum sonitus Astronomia Duce audienti,[3] Characteres mirabilium naturæ per quos Dei magnitudo describitur magistra Philosophia legenti; Antiquitatum latebras, vetustatis excidia, eruditionis ambages comite assidua autorum Lectione.

         Exquirenti, restauranti, percurrenti.
         At cur nitor in arduum?

Illi in cujus vertutibus evulgandis ora Famæ non sufficiant, nec hominum stupor in laudandis satis est. Reverentiæ & amoris ergo hoc ejus meritis debitum admirationis tributum offert Carolus Datus Patricius Florentinus.
         Tanto homini servus, tantæ virtutis amator.

TO JOHN MILTON OF LONDON.[4]

A young man distinguished by the land of his birth and by his personal merits,

TO a man who, through his journeys to foreign lands, has viewed every place in the wide world, so that, like a modern Ulysses, he may understand from every people, everywhere, all that each has to offer;

to a polyglot, master of many tongues, on whose lips languages already wholly dead live again with such vigor and might that every speech, when it is employed to praise him, loses its power of utterance—he is, himself, thorough master of them all, so that he understands the expressions of admiration and approval called forth from the peoples by his singular intelligence;

to a man whose endowments of mind and body move the senses to admiration, and yet through that very admiration rob every man of power to move, whose masterpieces urge all men to applause, yet by their grace, their charm rob of voice all them who would be happy to applaud;

to a man in whose memory the whole wide world is lodged, in whose intellect wisdom, in whose affections an ardent passion for glory, in whose mouth eloquence, who, with astronomy as his guide, hears the harmonies of the heavenly spheres, with philosophy as his teacher reads and interprets the true meaning of those marvels of nature by which the greatness of God is portrayed, who, with constant reading of these authors as his comrade, probes the hidden mysteries of bygone days, restores whatever the distance of time has obscured, and covers all the intricacies of learning

         Seeking out, restoring, running through
         For what purpose this work of duty?

to him, in the promotion of whom the tongues of Rumor herself would prove too few, whose merits are not eulogized as they deserve even by the dumbfounded admiration of the world, to him, by way of reverence and affection, this tribute of admiration, the just praise of his merits, is offered by Charles Dati, a nobleman of Florence, offered to this great man by his humble servant, passionate admirer of such outstanding merit.

---

[1]Corrected from "*vaststate*" in *1673*.
[2]Emended in *1673* from "*celestium*" in *1645*.
[3]Emended from "*audieuti*" (inverted "n") in *1673*.

---

[4]Dati's tribute is very perceptive in what it points out in Milton's character and abilities. Dati's Milton is handsome and brilliant; he has an incredible memory; he is dedicated to fame; he is knowledgeable in astronomy to the point where, by metaphoric extension, he can hear the music of the spheres; he is historian, philosopher, and theologian; and he is especially well read in the esoteric details of history.

Elegy 1
To Charles Diodati
(Spring 1626?)

Girl watching and theater going are two of the subjects of Milton's first Latin elegy. His confidant in this verse-letter is his best friend from St. Paul's School, Charles Diodati. It is spring. He is away from Cambridge and staying in London. And he is enjoying his vacation, whether or not it has been occasioned by his temporarily being "sent down," or "rusticated" (both contemporary terms for being temporarily expelled) from Christ's College. Milton has discovered that he does not like his tutor, William Chappell (Miller), the man Aubrey said "whipt him" and someone who might have remained his enemy throughout his life (Campbell, *Chronology* May 4, 1654).

He speaks about plays as if he had seen them in London, but those plays he describes seem to be Roman comedy and tragedy rather than Elizabethan English plays, and they seem to have been seen or read at Cambridge, not watched in London—unless the "rounded theater" is the Globe. As Howard-Hill has shown, Milton may never have gone near a theater in London: "Not a phrase [in Elegy 1] suggests actual experience of the public stage" (113). Even Milton's intimacy with the poetry of his "sweetest *Shakespeare*" ("L'Allegro" 133) or "my *Shakespeare*" ("On Shakespeare" 1) or with Ben Jonson ("L'Allegro" 132) might have been through books such as the folio editions of both dramatists. It may be only a pleasant fantasy to picture the young John Milton wandering down Bread Street to the Mermaid Tavern, to listen to Jonson and Shakespeare, or crossing the river to see their plays. Milton somehow did learn enough about dramaturgy to produce a masque, in 1634, that shows the influence of Jonson and Shakespeare.

Milton admits that he borrows his life from books he reads. He does enter the real world sufficiently to declare that English girls—from a safe distance—are the most beautiful in all the world. Though the shy poet in this elegy would like to be in love, "[t]he virgins [in it] could almost be the maidens on antique vases, except that the flames—'blandas flammas'—that they shoot forth from their eyes suggest the seductive fires from the eyes of a Cynthia" (Revard 15). In other words, female beauty as manifested in the eyes or the hair is dangerous or debilitating to the young male poet, but, at this point in Milton's career, it is dangerous only in the abstract. He can look but he must not touch.

Milton identifies with the great Roman poet of elegiac love poetry, Ovid, after Ovid had been exiled to Tomis, a remote port on the Black Sea, but he also implies that, had Ovid not been exiled, or if his exile was to a city as stimulating as London, then the Roman elegist would have been as great an epic poet as Homer or Vergil. The poet should learn his trade at elegiac poetry and then mature to become an epic writer. The more stimulating his environment, as with Rome or London, the better his poetry may be.

TEXT

1673, in the case of this and others of the Latin poems, corrects a number of errors in *1645*. Though *1645* will remain the copy-text, each correction will be noted.

Works Cited

Howard-Hill, T. H. "Milton and 'the rounded theatre's pomp.'" *Of Poetry and Politics: New Essays on Milton and His World*. Ed. P. G. Stanwood. Binghamton, NY: Medieval & Renaissance Texts & Studies, 1995. 95–120.

Miller, Leo. "Milton's Clash with Chappell: A Suggested Reconstruction." *Milton Quarterly* 14 (1980): 77–87.

Revard, Stella P. *Milton and the Tangles of Neaera's Hair: The Making of the 1645* Poems. Columbia: U of Missouri P, 1997.

ELEGIARUM
Liber primus.

Elegia prima ad *Carolum Diodatum.*

TAndem, chare, tuæ mihi pervenere tabellæ,
    Pertulit & voces nuntia charta tuas,
    Pertulit occiduâ Devæ Cestrensis ab orâ
Vergivium prono qua petit amne salum.
Multùm crede juvat terras aluisse remotas   5
    Pectus amans nostri, tamque fidele caput,
Quòdque mihi lepidum tellus longinqua sodalem
    Debet, at unde brevi reddere jussa velit.
Me tenet urbs refluâ quam Thamesis alluit undâ,
    Meque nec invitum patria dulcis habet.   10
Jam nec arundiferum mihi cura revisere Camum,
    Nec dudum vetiti melaris angit amor.
Nuda nec arva placent, umbrasque negantia molles,
    Quàm male Phœbicolis convenit ille locus!
Nec duri libet usque minas perferre magistri   15
    Cæteraque ingenio non subeunda meo.
Si sit hoc exilium patrios adiisse penates,
    Et vacuum curis otia grata sequi,
Non ego vel profugi nomen, sortemve recuso,
    Lætus & exilii conditione fruor.   20
O utinam vates nunquam graviora tulisset
    Ille Tomitano flebilis exul agro;
Non tunc Jonio quicquam cessisset Homero
    Neve foret victo laus tibi prima Maro.
Tempora nam licet hic placidis dare libera Musis,   25
    Et totum rapiunt me mea vita libri.
Excipit hinc fessum sinuosi pompa theatri,
    Et vocat ad plausus garrula scena suos.
Seu catus auditur senior, seu prodigus hæres,
    Seu procus, aut positá casside miles adest,   30
Sive decennali fœcundus lite patronus
    Detonat inculto barbara verba foro,
Sæpe vafer gnato succurrit servus amanti,
    Et nasum rigidi fallit ubique Patris;

ELEGIES
Book 1.

Elegy 1, to *Charles Diodati*

AT last, dear friend, your letter has come to my hand, and its sheets, serving as messenger, have brought your voice to my ears, yes, brought it from afar, from the western bank of the Dee, by Chester, where the Dee with down-rushing waters makes for the Irish sea. Much, believe me, does it please me that distant lands have nurtured a heart so full of love for me, a soul so loyal, and that a distant place owes me a charming comrade, a distant place, yes, but ready to deliver him soon to me at my command.

I am still in the city that the Thames washes with its tide; I am, though not against my will, in the charming city of my birth. Now I am in no rush to see the reedy Cam again, nor am I pining for love of my hearth gods there, this long time denied me. I find no pleasure in barren fields that offer no gentle shade; how ill-adapted is such a place to the worshipers of Phœbus! I am not of a mind to bear the constant threats of an unbending tutor, and all the other trials that are not to be met by a nature such as mine. If it be exile for a man to visit his home, his father's house, and, free of all anxieties, to pursue the delights of leisure, then I refuse not the name of exile, nor, if you will, exile itself; happily, I enjoy the terms imposed by "exile." If only the poet had never had to put up with more—that famous bard who was a weeping exile in Tomis: he had then been a match for Ionia's son Homer, and you, Vergil, outdone, and the first prize of praise would not now be yours![1] I am privileged here to have hours free of all else but the gentle Muses, and my books—my true life—carry me away with them, mastering me utterly. Presently, when I am weary, the splendor of the rounded theater welcomes me, and summons me to praise it, whether I am listening to some stereotyped wise old geezer, or to a wasteful heir, or a suitor is on stage, or a soldier, with his helmet laid aside. Sometimes a lawyer, grown rich through a suit ten years old, thunders out his jargon in a court full of ignorance. Often a roguish slave rescues a lovesick son, and at every turn tricks the son's inflexible father.

---

[1]If Ovid had not been exiled to Tomis by the emperor Augustus, Milton implies, he might have written a great Latin epic.

Sæpe novos illic virgo mirata calores　　　35
　　Quid sit amor nescit, dum quoque nescit, amat.
Sive cruentatum furiosa Tragœdia sceptrum
　　Quassat, & effusis crinibus ora rotat,
Et dolet, & specto, juvat & spectasse dolendo,
　　Interdum & lacrymis dulcis amaror inest:　　　40
Seu puer infelix indelibata reliquit
　　Gaudia, & abrupto flendus amore cadit,
Seu ferus é[2] tenebris iterat Styga criminis ultor
　　Conscia funereo pectora torre movens,
Seu mæret Pelopeia domus, seu nobilis Ili,　　　45
　　Aut luit incestos aula Creontis avos.
Sed neque sub tecto semper nec in urbe latemus,
　　Irrita nec nobis tempora veris eunt.
Nos quoque lucus habet vicinâ consitus ulmo
　　Atque suburbani nobilis umbra loci.　　　50
Sæpius hic blandas spirantia sydera flammas
　　Virgineos videas præteriisse choros.
Ah quoties dignæ stupui miracula formæ
　　Quæ possit[3] senium vel reparare Jovis;
Ah quoties vidi superantia lumina gemmas,　　　55
　　Atque faces quotquot volvit uterque polus;
Collaque bis vivi Pelopis quæ brachia vincant,
　　Quæque fluit puro nectare tincta via,
Et decus eximium frontis, tremulosque capillos,
　　Aurea quæ fallax retia tendit Amor.　　　60
Pellacesque genas, ad quas hyacinthina sordet
　　Purpura, & ipse tui floris, Adoni, rubor.
Cedite laudatæ toties Heroides olim,
　　Et quæcunque vagum cepit amica Jovem.
Cedite Achæmeniæ turritâ fronte puellæ,　　　65
　　Et quot Susa colunt, Memnoniamque Ninon.
Vos etiam Danaæ fasces submittite Nymphæ,
　　Et vos Iliacæ, Romuleæque nurus.
Nec Pompeianas Tarpëia Musa columnas
　　Jactet, & Ausoniis plena theatra stolis.　　　70
Gloria Virginibus debetur prima Britannis,
　　Extera sat tibi sit fœmina posse sequi.
Tuque urbs Dardaniis Londinum structa colonis
　　Turrigerum laté conspicienda caput,
Tu nimium felix intra tua mœnia claudis　　　75
　　Quicquid formosi pendulus orbis habet.

Often there is a virgin, who doesn't know what love is, who still falls in love. Sometimes Tragedy, with flowing hair and rolling eyes, shakes her bloody scepter. It hurts to watch, and yet I look, and find pleasure in looking. Sometimes there is a sweet bitterness in the tears I shed, if some lad leaves life with joys untasted, his love extinguished, fit subject for tears. Or if a merciless avenger of a crime, out of hell, re-crosses the Styx, and with his funeral brand frightens conscience-stricken souls, or if sorrow overwhelms the house of Pelops or the lordly house of Ilium, or if Creon's court makes atonement for incestuous ancestors.

　Yet I don't hide always indoors or within the city itself, nor does springtime slip by me. A grove dense with elms, near the city, and a shady spot, are where I stay. There you can see constant troops of young girls, stars exhaling erotic fires. How often have I stared in rapture at some marvelous body, with the power to rejuvenate old Jove himself. How often have I seen eyes brighter than jewels, brighter than the stars that circle the poles, and necks whiter than the arms of twice-resurrected Pelops,[4] and that streaming Milky Way bathed in pure nectar. How often have I seen a perfect forehead, and hair dancing, the golden net that Cupid, prince of tricksters, spreads, and seductive cheeks. Matched against such cheeks, the hyacinth's crimson beauty, even the blushing hues of your own flower, Adonis,[5] seem dull and tarnished. Yield to her, heroic maidens so often praised; yield, too, every maid that ever caught the roving eye of Jove. Give up, maids of Achæmenia[6] in castellated headdresses. And all the maids of Susa or in Memnon's Nineveh.[7] Surrender, nymphs of Greece, Troy, and Rome. Let not now the Tarpeian Muse boast of Pompey's Colonnades, or of the theaters crowded with Roman matrons. British maidens deserve first prize. Take second, women of other lands. You, London, built by Trojan settlers, whose towers can be seen from far away, you are all too blessed to enclose within your walls whatever beauty can be found anywhere in this pendent earth.

---

[2]The accent was added in *1673*.
[3]*1673* replaces *1645* "posset" with "possit."

[4]Son of Tantalus, murdered by his father in an attempt to fool the gods into eating human flesh. Only Ceres, mourning the loss of her daughter Eurydice, eats part of his shoulder, which Jupiter magically replaces with an ivory joint (Ovid, *Metamorphoses* 6.503–11).
[5]The anemone sprung from the blood of the dying Adonis (*Metamorphoses* 10.731–39).
[6]Royal household of Persia (Herodotus 1.125).
[7]Tithonus, father of Memnon, was supposed to have founded Susa; Memnon was buried in Syria (Strabo 15.3.2 and 2.1.31).

Non tibi tot cælo scintillant astra sereno
   Endymioneæ turba ministra deæ,
Quot tibi conspicuæ formáque auróque puellæ
   Per medias radiant turba videnda vias.   80
Creditur huc geminis venisse invecta columbis
   Alma pharetrigero milite cincta Venus,
Huic Cnidon, & riguas Simoentis flumine valles,
   Huic Paphon, & roseam posthabitura Cypron.
 Ast ego, dum pueri sinit indulgentia cæci,   85
   Mœnia quàm subitò linquere fausta paro;
Et vitare procul malefidæ infamia Circes
   Atria, divini Molyos usus ope.
Stat quoque juncosas Cami remeare paludes,
   Atque iterum raucæ murmur adire Scholæ.   90
Interea fidi parvum cape munus amici,
   Paucaque in alternos verba coacta modos.

The stars that sparkle for you in the unclouded skies—the multitude that serves Endymion's goddess[8]—don't add up to the number of beautiful, golden maids who shine into all eyes throughout your streets. Men believe the story that kind Venus came to this city, riding in a chariot drawn by twin doves, guarded by her archers, because she intended to put Cnidus[9] below it, together with the vales wet with the dew of the river Simois, and Paphos, and Cyprus,[10] land of roses. Yet, while blind Cupid permits, I am getting ready to leave these city walls quickly, and with the aid of the divine plant moly[11] to run away from the ill-famed halls of deceptive Circe. I am resolved to return to the reedy marshes of the Cam, and again to face the uproar of the noisy University. Meanwhile, take this humble gift, sent by a loyal friend, a word or two forced into elegiac meter.

Elegy 2
On the Death of the Beadle
of the University of Cambridge

Richard Ridding was appointed Esquire Beadle of Cambridge University in 1596. His most notable duties in that position, as Milton describes them, were to rouse students (perhaps from their beds) to attend official University ceremonies and to carry the University mace, the symbol of its power and authority, in procession before the Vice-Chancellor. The Beadle served, then, as did Mercury (Cyllenius), messenger of Apollo until his death on September 26, 1626. Milton may have been asked to contribute a poem for a projected memorial volume or for reading at a public ceremony of mourning. As an undergraduate often called upon to write memorial poems to University figures, he may even have begun the poem with one subject, John Gostlin, who would be remembered in *In Obitum Procancellarii*, and ended with Ridding (Miller).

The presence of the witch doctor Medea and of Coronides (Aesculapius, the legendary Greek physician) might lead the reader to think that the original subject was Dr. Gostlin. Thessaly, home of Medea, was famous for its sorcery and magic potions. Medea was supposed to have restored Jason's father, Aeson, to life by draining his body of blood and replacing it with an herbal concoction (Ovid *Metamorphoses* 7.162–296).

TEXT

1645, followed here, has a comma after "tuo" in 12 which *1673* omits. There are no significant variants.

Work Cited

Miller, Leo. "Dating Milton's 1626 Obituaries." *Notes & Queries* 27 (1980): 323–24.

---

[8]Diana, goddess who drove the chariot of the moon.
[9]A town associated with the worship of Venus (Horace *Odes* 1.30).
[10]All places sacred to Venus. The river Simois is on Mt. Ida, where Paris awarded the apple to Venus, as the most beautiful of three goddesses.
[11]Important to Milton as the herb used as a charm to ward off the spells of Circe (*Odyssey* 10.305). Compare *Comus* 636.

Elegia secunda, Anno ætatis 17.
In obitum Præconis Academici Cantabrigiensis.

TE, qui conspicuus baculo fulgente solebas
　Palladium toties ore ciere gregem,
Ultima præconum præconem te quoque sæva
　Mors rapit, officio nec favet ipsa suo.
Candidiora licet fuerint tibi tempora plumis　　　5
　Sub quibus accipimus delituisse Jovem,
O dignus tamen Hæmonio juvenescere succo,
　Dignus in Æsonios vivere posse dies,
Dignus quem Stygiis medicâ revocaret ab undis
　Arte Coronides, sæpe rogante dea.　　　10
Tu si jussus eras acies accire togatas,
　Et celer à¹² Phœbo nuntius ire tuo,
Talis in Iliacâ stabat Cyllenius aula
　Alipes, æthereâ missus ab arce Patris.
Talis & Eurybates ante ora furentis Achillei　　　15
　Rettulit Atridæ jussa severa ducis.
Magna sepulchrorum regina, satelles Averni
　Sæva nimis Musis, Palladi sæva nimis,
Quin illos rapias qui pondus inutile terræ,
　Turba quidem est telis ista petenda tuis.　　　20
Vestibus hunc igitur pullis Academia luge,
　Et madeant lachrymis nigra feretra tuis.
Fundat & ipsa modos querebunda Elegéia tristes,
　Personet & totis nænia mœsta scholis.

Elegy 2, written when he was seventeen.
On the Death of the Beadle of the University of Cambridge.

ONce, notable for carrying your shining mace, you called, over and over, to rouse the flock of Palladian students with your loud beadle's voice: but now Death, the last beadle, who knows no mercy, summons you, showing no respect for the office. Though your temples were whiter than the down of the swan that hid Jupiter, yet you were worthy to have had your youth restored by Thessalian potions, worthy to have power to live on till you reached the years of Æson, worthy to be recalled from the waves of Styx itself by Coronides, through his medical skill, through the repeated prayers of the goddess. Whenever you were bidden to summon the lines of students in their academic gowns, and to go like Cyllenius, swift messenger from his father Apollo, you looked as the wing-footed god looked when he stood in the Trojan court, sent thither from his father's citadel high in the skies, or as Eurybates looked when, standing before the face of enraged Achilles, he brought to him the austere commands of Atrides. O Death, queen of tombs, servant of Avernus, too cruel to the Muses, too cruel to Pallas, why should you not rather discard a useless burden to humankind? There are plenty of them for you to target. Grieve then, Cambridge, for this man, and wear black. May his hearse be wet with your tears. May sad Elegy herself pour out harmonious laments, and may the colleges echo with a song of lament.

---

¹²The accent mark was added in *1673*.

Elegy 3.
On the Death of the Bishop of Winchester (1626).

Lancelot Andrewes, Bishop of Winchester (and Ely, earlier), famous as one of the most eloquent preachers of his time, died September 25, 1626. Church of England bishops like Andrewes were soon to be criticized by Milton and others in the antiprelatical tracts of the 1640s. Carey points to Milton in 1641 attacking Andrewes's "shallow reasoning" in defense of the Anglican hierarchy (see Yale 1: 768–74). The very bishop's robes that Milton describes as splendid in this poem will become symbolic of the decadent power of the prelates in his pamphlets of the early 1640s. But when Milton writes of Andrewes's death in 1626, perhaps under pressure from his university mates to produce a poetic obituary, he seems in awe of the Bishop's authority as theologian, as translator of the King James Bible, and as an orator mesmerizing in the pulpit.

The mixture of classical and Christian imagery, especially in the last line, might strike the modern reader oddly, as an example of Christian syncretism, or blending of the pagan and sacred. Milton seems to have seen the death of holy men (such as Charles Diodati and Edward King, as well as Bishop Andrewes) as a combi-nation of pagan and Christian marriage rites, since he pictures each man in a marriage ceremony apparently based on the "marriage of the lamb" described symbolically in Revelation 19.7.

Milton's last line echoes the last line of Ovid's *Amores* 1.5, "proveniant medii sic mihi saepe dies," translated in the Loeb volume as "May my lot bring many a midday like this." In Ovid, this summary appears after a scene of the poet-lover's gently stripping his mistress's clothes away in order to make love with her. The echo is outrageous, but it has a similar effect as the celestial marriage (described in terms of orgies) arranged for Charles Diodati at the end of the *Epitaphium Damonis*. As John Shawcross suggests in an e-mail note (2 July 1997), the poem may be something of a spoof, with the bishop's death as its obvious subject and late teenage eroticism as its subtext.

TEXT

There are no significant variants between the two editions; *1645* is followed here.

Elegia tertia, Anno ætatis 17.
In obitum Præsulis Wintoniensis.

Mœstus eram, & tacitus nullo comitante sedebam,
    Hærebantque animo tristia plura meo,
Protinus en subiit funestæ cladis imago
    Fecit in Angliaco quam Libitina solo;
Dum procerum ingressa est splendentes marmore turres   5
    Dira sepulchrali mors metuenda face;
Pulsavitque auro gravidos & jaspide muros,
    Nec metuit satrapum sternere falce greges.
Tunc memini clarique ducis, fratrisque verendi
    Intempestivis ossa cremata rogis.   10
Et memini Heroum quos vidit ad æthera raptos,
    Flevit & amissos Belgia tota duces.
At te præcipuè luxi dignissime præsul,
    Wintoniæque olim gloria magna tuæ;

Elegy 3, written when he was seventeen.
On the Death of the Bishop of Winchester.

I was sorrowful, sitting with no comrade, silent. Many reasons for grief were troubling my soul. All at once a picture came into my mind of the depressing slaughter visited on the English by Libitina,[1] when cursed Death, dreaded by all men for her fearsome torch, walked inside the towered palaces of the great, palaces shining with marble, beat down walls heavy with jasper and with gold, and had no qualms in cutting down hosts of mighty princes with her scythe. Then I thought of a glorious Prince, and of his brother in arms, a man deserving of all reverence, their bodies burned by funeral pyres built before they should be. I thought as well about the heroes whom Belgia saw caught up swiftly to the high skies, Belgia who wept throughout her land for lost captains. But I grieved more for you, most worthy Bishop, crowning glory of your beloved Winchester;

---

[1] Roman goddess presiding over the care of corpses and regulating of funerals.

Delicui fletu, & tristi sic ore querebar,   15
  Mors fera Tartareo diva secunda Jovi,
Nonne satis quod sylva tuas persentiat iras,
  Et quod in herbosos jus tibi detur agros,
Quodque afflata tuo marcescant lilia tabo,
  Et crocus, & pulchræ Cypridi sacra rosa,   20
Nec sinis ut semper fluvio contermina quercus
  Miretur lapsus prætereuntis aquæ?
Et tibi succumbit liquido quæ plurima cælo
  Evehitur pennis quamlibet augur avis,
Et quæ mille nigris errant animalia sylvis,   25
  Et quod alunt mutum Proteos antra pecus.
Invida, tanta tibi cum sit concessa potestas;
  Quid juvat humanâ tingere cæde manus?
Nobileque in pectus certas acuisse sagittas,
  Semideamque animam sede fugâsse suâ?   30
Talia dum lacrymans alto sub pectore volvo,
  Roscidus occiduis Hesperus exit aquis,
Et Tartessiaco submerserat æquore currum
  Phœbus, ab eöo littore mensus iter.
Nec mora, membra cavo posui refovenda cubili,   35
  Condiderant oculos noxque soporque meos.
Cum mihi visus eram lato spatiarier agro,
  Heu nequit ingenium visa referre meum.
Illic puniceâ radiabant omnia luce,
  Ut matutino cum juga sole rubent.   40
Ac veluti cum pandit opes Thaumantia proles,
  Vestitu nituit multicolore solum.
Non dea tam variis ornavit floribus hortos
  Alcinoi, Zephyro Chloris amata levi.
Flumina vernantes lambunt argentea campos,   45
  Ditior Hesperio flavet arena Tago.
Serpit odoriferas per opes levis aura Favoni,
  Aura sub innumeris humida nata rosis.

I dissolved in tears, and overcome with grief I said, "Merciless Death, goddess second in power only to Tartarean Jove, isn't it enough that the woods feel your rage, and you are given power over the green fields, and that the lilies die from your rotten breath, and the crocus, and the rose sacred to the lovely Cypris,[2] and that you don't allow the oak to look forever on the stream, marveling at the flowing water? The countless birds that fly through the sky give in to you, even though they are prophets foretelling the future. Also the thousands of beasts that wander dark forests, and the silent herds nurtured in the grottoes of Proteus. Since such great power has been granted you, why, envious Death, do you dye your hands with the blood of dead human beings, sharpening your accurate darts aimed at a noble breast, to drive out a godlike soul?"

As I wept and turned over such thoughts deep within me, Hesperus, damp with dew, arose from the Western sea, and Phoebus sinks his chariot beneath Tartessus.[3] Without delay, on my hollow bed I stretched out my body, hoping for it to be restored; buried in sleep, I felt as if I were strolling in a spacious field. Oh, I haven't inspiration enough to tell of the things I saw. There everything glowed with red light, like mountain ranges reddened with the early morning sun, and the earth shone with a thousand colors, as when Thaumas's daughter[4] spreads out her riches. Not so varied were the flowers with which the goddess, Chloris, beloved of gentle Zephyrus, decked out the Gardens of Alcinous.[5] Silver streams washed green bottom lands; their yellow sand gleams, richer than the sands of Hesperian Tagus.[6] The light gales of Favonius[7] blow through scented leaves, the dewy breath of numberless roses.

---

[2]Venus, for whom the rose was sacred.
[3]The Sun goes down, in other words, and the Evening Star, Hesperus, associated with the planet Venus, rises. When the planet preceded the sun, it was called Lucifer.
[4]Iris, goddess of the rainbow. Chloris is the Greek name for the goddess of flowers (Flora in Latin), who is married to the west wind, Zephyrus (Ovid, *Fasti* 5.197–206).
[5]The famous gardens of Alcinous, king of the Phaeacians, blooming through all seasons (Homer, *Odyssey* 7.112–32).
[6]The Tagus River, in Spain and Portugal, known for its golden sand.
[7]The West Wind.

Talis in extremis terra Gangetidis oris
    Luciferi[8] regis fingitur esse domus.   50
Ipse racemiteris dum densas vitibus umbras
    Et pellucentes miror ubique locos,
Ecce mihi subito Præsul[9] Wintonius astat,
    Sydereum nitido fulsit in ore jubar;
Vestis ad auratos defluxit candida talos,   55
    Infula divinum cinxerat alba caput.
Dumque senex tali incedit venerandus amictu,
    Intremuit læto florea terra sono.
Agmina gemmatis plaudunt cælestia pennis,
    Pura triumphali personat æthra tubâ.   60
Quisque novum amplexu comitem cantuque salutat,
    Hosque aliquis placido misit ab ore sonos;
Nate veni, & patrii felix cape gaudia regni,
    Semper ab hinc duro, nate, labore vaca.
Dixit, & aligeræ tetigerunt nablia turmæ,   65
    At mihi cum tenebris aurea pulsa quies.
Flebam turbatos Cephaleiâ pellice somnos,
    Talia contingant somnia sæpe mihi.

Such a place, imagined by men, is the palace of the royal star of dawn, in a far-distant land, the land of the Ganges. While I marvel at the close-set shadows cast by clustering vines, and at the radiant spaces all about me, all of a sudden near me stood the Bishop of Winchester. A radiance as of the stars shone in his face. His white robe flowed down to his golden ankles, and a white crown wreathed his godlike head. While the aged bishop moved on—a reverend figure, so gloriously robed— the flowery earth vibrated with a joyous sound; heaven's hosts clapped their jeweled wings; and the air, pure and undefiled, rang with notes of a triumphal trumpet. Each angel greeted his new comrade with embraces and with songs, and one issued these words from calm and peaceful lips: "Come here, my son; in gladness gather the joys of your Father's kingdom; henceforth always, my son, be free from cruel labor." This said, the winged squadrons touched their harps.[10] But with the passing of the darkness, my golden dream was ended; I wept at the disturbance of my sleep by the mistress of Cephalus.[11]

May I often be lucky enough to have such dreams.

Elegy 4. To Thomas Young

The Scottish Presbyterian Thomas Young (1587?-1655) may have led the youthful Milton toward Puritanism. At some time between 1618 and 1620, when Young was apparently exiled to the German city of Hamburg, he was Milton's tutor, possibly the person whom Aubrey describes as "a puritan in Essex, who cutt his haire short." Scottish by birth, Young may have tutored the young Milton in his own home in Essex. Tutor and pupil remained good friends and in political sympathy with each other for many years.

In response to Bishop Hall's *A Humble Remonstrance* (1640), which attempted to demonstrate the divine right of bishops, Young helped to write an *Answer*, signing his initials as part of the acronym name "Smectymnuus" (Parker 12–13), built out of "TY" plus the initials of Stephen Marshall, Edmund Calamy, Matthew Newcomen, and William (beginning with a double u) Spurstowe.

TEXT
1673 offers no significant variants for *1645*, the text followed here.

---

[8]The star Milton associates with dawn, a light-bearer as the name implies, which has nothing in this case to do with Lucifer, the Christian angel supposed to be like a star, a "son of the morning" fallen from Heaven (Isaiah 14.12).
[9]Capitalization is added in *1673*.

[10]Echoing the "voice of the harpers harping with their harps" in Revelation 14.13).
[11]The goddess of the dawn, Aurora, who is the lover of Cephalus (Ovid, *Metamorphoses* 7.700–13).

Elegia quarta. Anno ætatis 18.

Ad Thomam Junium præceptorem
suum apud mercatores Anglicos Hamburgæ
agentes Pastoris munere fungentem.[1]

CUrre per immensum subitò mea littera pontum,
    I, pete Teutonicos læve per æquor agros,
Segnes rumpe moras, & nil, precor, obstet eunti,
    Et festinantis nil remoretur iter.
Ipse ego Sicanio frænantem carcere ventos   5
    Æolon, & virides sollicitabo Deos;
Cæruleamque suis comitatam Dorida Nymphis,
    Ut tibi dent placidam per sua regna viam.
At tu, si poteris, celeres tibi sume jugales,
    Vecta quibus Colchis fugit ab ore viri.   10
Aut queis Triptolemus Scythicas devenit in oras
    Gratus Eleusinâ missus ab urbe puer.
Atque ubi Germanas flavere videbis arenas
    Ditis ad Hamburgæ mœnia flecte gradum,
Dicitur occiso quæ ducere nomen ab Hamâ,   15
    Cimbrica quem fertur clava dedisse neci.
Vivit ibi antiquæ clarus pietatis honore
    Præsul Christicolas pascere doctus oves;
Ille quidem est animæ plusquam pars altera nostræ,
    Dimidio vitæ vivere cogor ego.   20
Hei mihi quot pelagi, quot montes interjecti
    Me faciunt aliâ parte carere mei!
Charior ille mihi quam tu doctissime Graium
    Cliniadi, pronepos qui Telamonis erat.
Quámque Stagirites generoso magnus alumno,   25
    Quem peperit Libyco Chaonis alma Jovi.
Qualis Amyntorides, qualis Philyrëius[2] Heros
    Myrmidonum regi, talis & ille mihi.
Primus ego Aonios illo præeunte recessus
    Lustrabam, & bifidi sacra vireta jugi,   30
Pieriosque hausi latices, Clioque favente,
    Castalio sparsi læta ter ora mero.

Elegy 4. Written when he was eighteen.

To Thomas Young, His Teacher,
Serving Now as Chaplain among the English
Merchants Resident in Hamburg.

SPeed with all haste, my letter, across the unbounded ocean. Go! Seek out Germany over the sea's smooth paths. No idle delays. Let nothing block your way. I myself will petition Æolus, who curbs the winds in their Sicanian den, and the green gods of the sea, and Doris,[3] too, blue as the sky, attended by her nymphs, to grant you quiet passage through their kingdoms. If you can, use that swift team that drew Medea's car as it fled from her husband, or those charming Triptolemus[4] used to make his way to Scythia from the city of Eleusis. When you shall see the yellow sands of Germany, turn toward the walls of rich Hamburg, the city which, according to legend, gets its name from Hama, who is supposed to have been killed by a Danish club.[5] A famous pastor lives there, honored for years for his piety, well trained to feed the sheep that follow Christ. He is truly more than half of me. I am forced to lead only half a life. Oh, how many distant seas, how many mountains between us force me to forego the very half of my self! He is dearer than were you, most learned of the Greeks, to Clinias's son, who was of Telamon's line, and dearer than the mighty Stagirite to his noble pupil,[6] whom the gracious young woman of Chaonia bore as son to Lybian Jove. What Amyntor's son, what Philyra's hero-son were to the king of the Myrmidons,[7] that was this minister to me. He led the way for me, when I first crossed Aonia's retreats and the holy lawns of the forked mountain, when I drank from the Pierian spring, and, favored by Clio, I sprinkled my happy lips three times with Castalian wine.

---

[3]Wife of the sea god Nereus and mother of the Nereids, the sea nymphs.
[4]Son of Oceanus and Terra, allowed by the goddess Ceres to drive her dragon chariot and spread knowledge of agriculture throughout the earth (Ovid, *Metamorphoses* 5.646).
[5]Milton borrows the legend, according to Carey, from Stephanus, but he substituted a club for a sword (1997 ed. of Carey, 57n).
[6]A very roundabout way of identifying Socrates, friend of Alcibiades, son of Clinias and supposed descendent of the Homeric Telamon (Plato, *Alcibiades* 121A), and Aristotle—called the Stagirite because he was born at Stageira—the famous tutor to Alexander the Great. Milton flatters Young as tutor and himself as pupil.
[7]References to two of the tutors of Achilles, who was king of the Myrmidons—Chiron and Phoenix, son of Amyntor (see Ovid, *Metamorphoses* 2.676).

---

[1]There are commas after "*suum*" and "*agentes*" in *1673*.
[2]*1673* has what appears to be "Philyrêius," incorrectly.

Flammeus at signum ter viderat arietis Æthon,
    Induxitque auro lanea terga novo,
Bisque novo terram sparsisti Chlori senilem   35
    Gramine, bisque tuas abstulit Auster opes:
Necdum ejus licuit mihi lumina pascere vultu,
    Aut linguæ dulces aure bibisse sonos.
Vade igitur, cursuque Eurum præverte sonorum,
    Quàm sit opus monitis res docet, ipsa vides.   40
Invenies dulci cum conjuge forte sedentem,
    Mulcentem gremio pignora chara suo,
Forsitan aut veterum prælarga volumina patrum
    Versantem, aut veri biblia sacra Dei.
Cælestive animas saturantem rore tenellas,   45
    Grande salutiferæ religionis opus.
Utque solet, multam, sit dicere cura salutem,
    Dicere quam decuit, si modo adesset, herum.
Hæc quoque paulum oculos in humum defixa modestos,
    Verba verecundo sis memor ore loqui: 50
Hæc tibi, si teneris vacat inter prælia Musis
    Mittit ab Angliaco littore fida manus.
Accipe sinceram, quamvis sit sera, salutem;
    Fiat & hoc ipso gratior illa tibi.
Sera quidem, sed vera fuit, quam casta recepit   55
    Icaris a lento Penelopeia viro.
Ast ego quid volui manifestum tollere crimen,
    Ipse quod ex omni parte levare nequit.
Arguitur tardus meritò, noxamque fatetur,
    Et pudet officium deseruisse suum.   60
To modò da veniam fasso, veniamque roganti,
    Crimina diminui, quæ patuere, solent.
Non ferus in pavidos rictus diducit hiantes,
    Vulnifico pronos nec rapit ungue leo.
Sæpe sarissiferi crudelia pectora Thracis   65
    Supplicis ad mœstas deliçuere preces.
Extensæque manus avertunt fulminis ictus,
    Placat & iratos hostia parva Deos.
Jamque diu scripsisse tibi fuit impetus illi,
    Neve moras ultra ducere passus Amor.   70
Nam vaga Fama refert, heu nuntia vera malorum!
    In tibi finitimis bella tumere locis,
Teque tuàmque urbem truculento milite cingi,
    Et jam Saxonicos arma parasse duces.

But flaming Æthon[8] saw the sign of the Ram three times, and three times spread new gold on the fleece of the Ram, and twice you, Chloris,[9] sprinkled the age-old earth with spring greenery, and twice Auster stole away your riches: yet it was not my privilege to feast mine eyes on his face, or to hear with my ears the sweet strains of his voice.

Go on, then, and outrun the thundering East Wind. You will see how much you will need my warnings. Perhaps you will find him sitting with his charming wife, as he holds the dear pledges of their love, or as he perhaps turns the leaves of the books of the Church Fathers, or the Holy Bible of the one true God, or as he feeds with the dew of heaven delicate souls, the great mission of redemption. Give him the customary hearty greetings, as if it were your master's greeting, if only he were there himself. Fixing modest eyes for a moment on the ground, give this message to him as well: "A loyal hand sends these words—if there is leisure, amid battles, for the Muses—to you from England. Accept a greeting heartfelt, if delayed; let it, by its very lateness, be to you all the more welcome. The greeting that chaste Penelope, daughter of Icarius, received from her delayed husband was late, but sincere. But stop: why should I be purging my guilt, clear to all men, which he himself is utterly unable to extenuate? He is convicted laggard, rightly convicted, too, and he himself admits his guilt, and is ashamed that he was traitor to his friendly office, his duty. Grant forgiveness to him, now that he has confessed, and is begging for forgiveness: sins ever are made less when they lie open to view. A wild beast doesn't offer his wide-open jaws to panic-stricken victims, nor does a lion drag his wounding claws over those who lie prone. The cruel hearts of the spear-bearing Thracians have many a time melted at the pitiful prayer of suppliants: outstretched hands divert lightning bolts, and angry gods are soothed by a tiny victim offered in sacrifice.

"He has felt the need for a long time to write you, and Love would not allow him to delay longer, for wide-ranging Rumor tells a story—Rumor, messenger all too truthful about bad things—a story that in neighboring towns wars are brewing, that you and your city are surrounded by grim soldiers, and that the Saxon captains are in military readiness.

---

[8]One of the horses of the sun: the reference adds up to describe a three-year period.

[9]The Greek version of the goddess of flowers, Flora. Carey identifies her festival at the end of April as evidence that "There had been three vernal equinoxes since M. saw Young, but Chloris had only twice 'spread fresh turf.' The date of composition must therefore be late March or early April" (1996 ed., 58n).

Te circum latè campos populatur Enyo,   75
   Et sata carne virûm[10] jam cruor arva rigat.
Germanisque suum concessit Thracia Martem,
   Illuc Odrysios Mars pater egit equos.
Perpetuóque comans jam deflorescit oliva,
   Fugit & ærisonam Diva perosa tubam,   80
Fugit io terris, & jam non ultima virgo
   Creditur ad superas justa volasse domos.
Te tamen intereà belli circumsonat horror,
   Vivis & ignoto solus inópsque solo;
Et, tibi quam patrii non exhibuere penates   85
   Sede peregrinâ quæris egenus opem.
Patria dura parens, & saxis sævior albis
   Spumea quæ pulsat littoris unda tui,
Siccine te decet innocuos exponere fœtus;[11]
   Siccine in externam ferrea cogis humum,   90
Et sinis ut terris quærant alimenta remotis
   Quos tibi prospiciens miserat ipse Deus,
Et qui læta ferunt de cælo nuntia, quique
   Quæ via post cineres ducat ad astra, docent?
Digna quidem Stygiis quæ viva clausa tenebris,   95
   Æternâque animæ digna perire fame!
Haud aliter vates terræ Thesbitidis olim
   Pressit inassueto devia tesqua pede,
Desertasque Arabum salebras, dum regis Achabi
   Effugit atque tuas, Sidoni dira, manus.   100
Talis & horrisono laceratus membra flagello,
   Paulus ab Æmathiâ pellitur urbe Cilix.
Piscosæque ipsum Gergessæ civis Jesum
   Finibus ingratus jussit abire suis.
At tu sume animos, nec spes cadat anxia curis   105
   Nec tua concutiat decolor ossa metus.
Sis etenim quamvis fulgentibus obsitus armis,
   Intententque tibi millia tela necem,
At nullis vel inerme latus violabitur armis,
   Deque tuo cuspis nulla cruore bibet.   110

Surrounding you, Enyo[12] is ravaging far and wide, and already blood is watering the arable soil fertilized with the flesh of men. Thrace has surrendered Mars to the Germans; father Mars has driven his Odrysian[13] horses into Germany. The fully-leaved olive is withering; the goddess that loathed the battle trumpet with its brazen clangor is gone. See the righteous maiden Astraea,[14] the last to leave earth, has flown, men believe, to a heavenly home. Around you resounds horrid noise of war: you live alone, poor, in an unfamiliar land, and in your need are seeking in a foreign home the sustenance which the Penates of your homeland denied you. Hard, unyielding mother England, more savage than its chalk cliffs battered by the foaming sea, is it seemly for you to expose your children who have done no harm. Do you, with a heart of iron, force them into a foreign land, and allow those whom God himself, taking thought for you, sent, who bring you good news from Heaven, who teach you what way, when men are dust, leads them to the stars—do you allow them, I ask, to seek their food in lands so remote? You should, then, be living in Stygian darkness, worthy to perish by the never-ending hunger of the soul. Even so the Tishbite prophet[15] once walked with unaccustomed feet wild wastes, where there were no paths, trod, too, rough stretches of Araby's deserts, as he fled King Ahab, and from your hands, too, accursed woman of Sidon.

   In such a way, too, Paul of Cilicia was driven from Emathia,[16] his back torn by the whistling scourge, and Jesus himself was bidden by the ungrateful citizens of Gergessa, land of fishermen, to remove himself from their borders.[17] But take heart: don't let your hopes perish, overcome by anxiety, and don't let fear, which makes your face pale, destroy your body. For, though you are surrounded by weapons, and though a thousand swords threaten you with a violent death, yet no weapon will harm your undefended person and no spear point will drink your blood.

---

[10]*1673* adds the accent.
[11]Printed as "fætus" in both *1645* and *1673*; I have made the emendation, as do Hughes and Goldberg and Orgel.

---

[12]Goddess of war, similar to Bellona in Roman mythology (Homer, *Iliad* 5.333).
[13]Thracian, as in Ovid, *Metamorphoses* 6.490.
[14]The goddess identified with justice, whose exit as the last of the gods leaving the earth indicated the end of the Iron Age in war and injustice, as described in Ovid, *Metamorphoses* 1.149–54.
[15]The prophet Elijah, who flees the wicked Ahab and Jezebel (daughter of Ethbaal, King of Sidon) in 1 Kings 19.1–18.
[16]In Acts 16.9–40, Paul and his companion Silas are beaten and urged to leave Philippi in Macedonia.
[17]Matthew 8.28–34 describes Jesus, having cast out devils in the land of the Gergesenes, being asked by the people to leave.

Namque eris ipse Dei radiante sub ægide tutus,
    Ille tibi custos, & pugil ille tibi;
Ille Sionææ qui tot sub mœnibus arcis
    Assyrios fudit nocte silente viros;
Inque fugam vertit quos in Samaritidas oras   115
    Misit ab antiquis prisca Damascus agris,
Terruit & densas pavido cum rege cohortes,
    Aere dum vacuo buccina clara sonat,
Cornea pulvereum dum verberat ungula campum,
    Currus arenosam dum quatit actus humum,   120
Auditurque hinnitus equorum ad bella ruentûm,
    Et strepitus ferri, murmuraque alta virûm.
Et tu (quod superest miseris) sperare memento,
    Et tua magnanimo pectore vince mala.
Nec dubites quandoque frui melioribus annis,   125
    Atque iterum patrios posse videre lares.

For you yourself will be kept safe under the gleaming shield of God; He will preserve you and be your champion—He, who, under the walls of Zion in one quiet night slaughtered so many Assyrians, and routed the men that ancient Damascus had sent from her fertile land against Samaria, who filled with fright the cramped battalions and their cowering king, while through the empty air the clanging trumpet sounded, while sharp hooves battered the plain to dust, while the chariots driven at full speed shook the sandy ground, and you could hear the horses neighing as they sped off to war and the clank of iron and the deep-throated war-cries of men. Remember to hope (so much the unfortunate can do) and by the high spirit of your heart master your worries; don't doubt that you will enjoy brighter years, and that you will have it in your power once again to see the hearth gods of your fathers.

Elegy 5.
On the Coming of Spring.

Latin poetry about the advent of spring was certainly common throughout Europe in the Renaissance, as Carey's list of preceding Italian, French, and Scottish neo-Latin poems, including those of Sannazaro and George Buchanan, on the subject illustrates (1997 ed., 83), but it may still be best to measure the poem against the famous paintings of Botticelli and Poussin as Hughes and Mario Praz suggest (Hughes 37), and to see it as Milton's enthusiastic reception of spring as the season of his own poetic inspiration as well as the return of life.

This poem should certainly be compared with Milton's English "Song: On May Morning," with which it is often paired (as it is in Hughes), though the dating of the English poem cannot be determined with certainty. The enthusiastic and joyful treatment with which it treats its subject also makes it comparable to the Nativity Ode and "L'Allegro" and "Il Penseroso."

TEXT
    Copy-text is *1645*, with notes provided for each variant.

Elegia quinta, Anno ætatis 20.

In adventum veris.

IN se perpetuo Tempus revolubile gyro
  Jam revocat Zephyros vere tepente novos.
Induiturque brevem Tellus reparata juventam,
  Jamque soluta gelu dulce virescit humus.
Fallor? an & nobis redeunt in carmina vires,   5
  Ingeniumque mihi munere veris adest?
Munere veris adest, iterumque vigescit ab illo
  (Quis putet) atque aliquod jam sibi poscit opus.
Castalis ante oculos, bifidumque cacumen oberrat,
  Et mihi Pyrenen somnia nocte ferunt.   10
Concitaque arcano fervent mihi pectora motu,
  Et furor, & sonitus me sacer intùs agit.
Delius ipse venit, video Penëide lauro
  Implicitos crines, Delius ipse venit.
Jam mihi mens liquidi raptatur in ardua cœli,   15
  Perque vagas nubes corpore liber eo.
Perque umbras, perque antra feror penetralia vatum,
  Et mihi fana patent interiora Deûm.
Intuiturque animus toto quid agatur Olympo,
  Nec fugiunt oculos Tartara cæca meos.   20
Quid tam grande sonat distento spiritus ore?
  Quid parit hæc rabies, quid sacer iste furor?
Ver mihi, quod dedit ingenium, cantabitur illo;
  Profuerint isto reddita dona modo.
Jam Philomela tuos foliis adoperta novellis   25
  Instituis modulos, dum silet omne nemus.
Urbe ego, tu sylvâ simul incipiamus utrique,
  Et simul adventum veris uterque canat.
Veris io rediere vices, celebremus honores
  Veris, & hoc subeat Musa perennis[1] opus.   30
Jam sol Æthiopas fugiens Tithoniaque arva,
  Flectit ad Arctöas aurea lora plagas.
Est breve noctis iter, brevis est mora noctis opacæ
  Horrida cum tenebris exulat illa suis.

Elegy 5, written when he was 20.

On the coming of spring.

Time that circles itself forever is now calling the fresh zephyrs, since the spring is becoming warm. Refreshed Earth is clothing herself with a temporary youth, and now the ground free of frost and ice is growing pleasantly green. Am I fooling myself or is strength returning to my songs as well, and have I, thanks to spring, inspiration on call? Is inspiration here as a gift of spring, and is it again taking life from the spring? Is it? Is it demanding now for itself some achievement, some creation? The waters of the Castalian spring dance before me, and the forked peak, and at night dreams bring Pirene to me.[2] My soul is deeply stirred, glows with mysterious impulses; the madness of inspiration and holy sounds stir me to my depths. The god of Delos himself is coming—I see his braided hair twined with Penean laurel—Apollo himself is coming. Now my mind whirls up to the heights of the sky and, free of my body, I move among the roving clouds. I am led through shades and grottoes, the secret places of the bards; the inmost shrines of the gods are open to me; my mind's eye can see whatever is done in all Olympus, or in the dark depths of Tartarus. What song is my spirit singing so loudly, mouth agape? What will come of this frenzy, this sacred insanity? The spring, source of my inspiration, will be the theme; her gifts to me will be repaid.

Now Philomela,[3] hidden in new leaves, you are beginning your song while the grove is otherwise silent: let the two of us begin together, in the city I, you in the woodland; let us two, each in his own part, sing the coming of the spring. The springtime (sing it) has returned; let us honor her and sound her praises; let this be the job of the ever-living Muse. Already the Sun, as he flees from the Æthiopians and from Tithonus's cultivated lands, guides his golden reins toward the northern regions. The night's journey is short; shuddering night and her darkness are going into exile.

---

[1] In *1645*, "quotannis." This is almost certainly a correction ordered by Milton.

---

[2] Three classical sources of inspiration: the Castalian spring of Milton's Elegy 4.30; the fountain of Pirene in Corinth, where the horse that came to represent poetic frenzy, Pegasus, was tamed; and the twin peaks of Mt. Parnassus, home of the Muses. Milton would use each of these images often, in Latin and in English.

[3] Nightingale, source of inspiration and poetic counterpart to Milton.

Jamque Lycaonius plaustrum cæleste Boötes   35
　　Non longâ sequitur fessus ut ante viâ,
Nunc etiam solitas circum Jovis atria toto
　　Excubias agitant sydera rara polo.
Nam dolus, & cædes, & vis cum nocte recessit,
　　Neve Giganteum Dii timuere scelus.   40
Forte aliquis scopuli recubans in vertice pastor,
　　Roscida cum primo sole rubescit humus,
Hac, ait, hac certè caruisti nocte puellâ
　　Phœbe tuâ, celeres quæ retineret equos.
Læta suas repetit sylvas, pharetramque resumit   45
　　Cynthia, Luciferas ut videt alta rotas,
Et tenues ponens radios gaudere videtur
　　Officium fieri tam breve fratris ope.
Desere, Phœbus ait, thalamos Aurora seniles,
　　Quid juvat effœto procubuisse toro?   50
Te manet Æolides viridi venator in herba,
　　Surge, tuos ignes altus Hymettus habet.
Flava verecundo dea crimen in ore fatetur,
　　Et matutinos ocyus urget equos.
Exuit invisam Tellus rediviva senectam,   55
　　Et cupit amplexus Phœbe subire tuos;
Et cupit, & digna est, quid enim formosius illâ,
　　Pandit ut omniferos luxuriosa sinus,
Atque Arabum spirat messes, & ab ore venusto
　　Mitia cum Paphiis fundit amoma rosis.   60
Ecce coronatur sacro frons ardua luco,
　　Cingit ut Idæam pinea turris Opim;
Et vario madidos intexit flore capillos,
　　Floribus & visa est posse placere suis.
Floribus effusos ut erat redimita capillos   65
　　Tænario[4] placuit diva Sicana Deo.
Aspice Phœbe tibi faciles hortantur amores,
　　Mellitasque movent flamina verna preces.
Cinnameâ Zephyrus leve plaudit odorifer alâ,
　　Blanditiasque tibi ferre videntur aves.   70
Nec sine dote tuos temeraria quærit amores
　　Terra, nec optatos poscit egena toros,
Alma salutiferum medicos tibi gramen in usus
　　Præbet, & hinc titulos adjuvat ipsa tuos.

Lycaonian Boötes now no longer follows the Wain through the skies, in a long, tiresome journey; wide apart now, too, are the stars that throughout the skies guard the halls of Jove.[5] For, with the passing of the night, Guile, and Carnage, and Violence have withdrawn, and the gods have ceased to fear the crimes of the Giants. It may be that some shepherd, as he reclines on top of a crag, when the first ray makes the dewy ground red, cries, "Last night at least, Phoebus, you didn't have a girl you selected to rein in your horses." When Cynthia sees the wheels that bring daylight, she joyfully takes up her quiver and seeks her beloved forests. Removing her rays, now dimmed, she is obviously glad that her job is shortened by the aid of her brother.

"Get out of that bed," cries Phoebus, "out of old man Tithonus's bed. Why lie in bed with someone who's impotent? The hunter Aeolides is waiting. Get up: your boyfriend is on lofty Hymettus." The golden-haired goddess admits her guilt, blushing, and spurs the horses of early morning. Earth, full of life, puts off detested age, and longs, Phoebus, to enter your arms. She longs for them, and deserves them too, for what is more gloriously lovely than Earth, when, in full luxuriance, she bares her breast, mother of all things, and breathes out the perfumes of Araby, and from her lovely lips pours forth balmy balsam and the roses of Paphos? Look: her high forehead is flowered like the holy grove of pines that encircles Ops, goddess of Ida; she weaves multicolored flowers into her dewy hair, knowing that by her own flowers she could charm, even as the Sicanian goddess, when her flowing hair was plaited with flowers, pleased the god of Taenarum. Look, Apollo, look! Love easily won calls on you, and spring breezes carry honeyed love messages. Fragrant Zephyrus beats lightly with his cinnamon-scented wings, and the birds can be seen bringing love-tokens to you. Earth is not so rash as to be without a dowry when she seeks your love, nor poverty-burdened does she demand the marriage bed. She craves; no, as giver of life, she offers you health-giving herbs for healing uses, and thus adds to your distinctions, your fair titles.

---

[4]In *1673*, "Tenario."

---

[5]The coming of dawn as charted by the movement of constellations toward different parts of the earth. The Ethiopians live on the equator; Tithonus, lover of Aurora, the dawn, has his fields in the east. As Carey points out, "After the vernal equinox the sun rises north of east," and "*Arctos* is the constellation of the Bear, hence the adjective *arctous*, northern" (1997 ed., 85n).

Quòd si te pretium, si te fulgentia tangunt   75
    Munera, (muneribus sæpe coemptus Amor)
Illa tibi ostentat quascunque sub æquore vasto,
    Et superinjectis montibus abdit opes.
An quoties cum tu clivoso fessus Olympo
    In vespertinas præcipitaris aquas,   80
Cur te, inquit, cursu languentem Phœbe diurno
    Hesperiis recipit Cærula mater aquis?
Quid tibi cum Tethy? Quid cum Tartesside lymphâ,
    Dia quid immundo perluis ora salo?
Frigora Phœbe meâ melius captabis in umbrâ,   85
    Huc ades, ardentes imbue rore comas.
Mollior egelidâ veniet tibi somnus in herbâ,
    Huc ades, & gremio lumina pone meo.
Quáque jaces circum mulcebit lene susurrans
    Aura per humentes corpora fusa rosas.   90
Nec me (crede mihi) terrent Semelëia fata,
    Nec Phäetontéo fumidus axis equo;
Cum tu Phœbe tuo sapientius uteris igni,
    Huc ades & gremio lumina pone meo.
Sic Tellus lasciva suos suspirat amores;   95
    Matris in exemplum cætera turba ruunt.
Nunc etenim toto currit vagus orbe Cupido,
    Languentesque fovet solis ab igne faces.
Insonuere novis lethalia cornua nervis,
    Triste micant ferro tela corusca novo.   100

But if rich offerings, if gleaming gifts touch your heart (love is often purchased with gifts), she parades before your eyes whatsoever treasures she hides away in the deeps, and under the piled-up mountains. Oh, how often, when utterly wearied by the steep path up Olympus you jump into twilight waters, does Earth cry out, "Why, when you are utterly exhausted by your day-long course, why is it the sea-green mother who welcomes you with the Western waters? What have you to do with Tethys?[6] Or the waters of Tartessus?[7] Why do you wash your holy face with profane sea-water? You will enjoy the cool shade I offer: come here to me; soak your fiery hair in the dew. Sweeter sleep will come to you on the cool grass: come to me, and lay your shining head on my breast. Where you lie, the breezes, whispering softly round about us, will soothe our bodies as we recline at ease on dewy rose petals. For me—believe my words—fate has no terrors, nor the car set smoking by Phaethon's horses.[8] Using your fires more wisely now, come to me, and lay your bright rays on my bosom."

Thus the wanton Earth breathes out her passion, and all the other creatures everywhere rush to follow her example. In spring Cupid speeds where he wants to, through all the length and breadth of the world, and rekindles his dying torch in the fire of the sun. His deadly bow twangs with new strings, his arrows shine ominously with new steel tips.

---

[6]Compare "*Tethys*" in *Comus* 870 as a sea goddess and mother to rivers.
[7]Tartessus is a town in Spain near the Pillars of Hercules, where the Romans believed that Apollo unharnessed his tired horses at the end of the day (Ovid, *Metamorphoses* 14.416)
[8]The famous story of the fall of Apollo's son Phaeton as he attempted to drive his father's sun chariot is told in Ovid, *Metamorphoses* 2.19–328.

Jamque vel invictam tentat superasse Dianam,
    Quæque sedet sacro Vesta pudica foco.
Ipsa senescentem reparat Venus annua formam,
    Atque iterum tepido creditur orta mari.
Marmoreas juvenes clamant Hymenæe per urbes,   105
    Littus⁹ io Hymen, & cava saxa sonant.
Cultior ille venit tunicâque decentior aptâ,
    Puniceum redolet vestis odora crocum.
Egrediturque frequens ad amœni gaudia veris
    Virgineos¹⁰ auro cincta puella sinus.   110
Votum est cuique suum, votum est tamen omnibus unum,
    Ut sibi quem cupiat, det Cytherea virum.
Nunc quoque septenâ modulatur arundine pastor,
    Et sua quæ jungat carmina Phyllis habet.
Navita nocturno placat sua sydera cantu,   115
    Delphinasque leves ad vada summa vocat.
Jupiter ipse alto cum conjuge ludit Olympo,
    Convocat & famulos ad sua festa Deos.
Nunc etiam Satyri cum sera crepuscula surgunt,
    Pervolitant celeri florea rura choro,   120
Sylvanusque suâ Cyparissi fronde revinctus,
    Semicaperque Deus, semideusque caper.
Quæque sub arboribus Dryades latuere vetustis
    Per juga, per solos expatiantur agros.
Per sata luxuriat fruticetaque Mænalius Pan,   125
    Vix Cybele mater, vix sibi tuta Ceres,
Atque aliquam cupidus prædatur Oreada Faunus,
    Consulit in trepidos dum sibi Nympha pedes,
Jamque latet, latitansque cupit male tecta videri,
    Et fugit, & fugiens pervelit ipsa capi.   130
Dii quoque non dubitant cælo præponere sylvas,
    Et sua quisque sibi numina lucus habet.
Et sua quisque diu sibi numina lucus habeto,
    Nec vos arboreâ dii precor ite domo.
Te referant miseris te Jupiter aurea terris   135
    Sæcla, quid ad nimbos aspera tela redis?
Tu saltem lentè rapidos age Phœbe jugales
    Quà potes, & sensim tempora veris eant.
Brumaque productas tardè ferat hispida noctes,
    Ingruat & nostro serior umbra polo.   140

And now he is straining with all his might to conquer the unconquered Diana, yes, and chaste Vesta who sits by the holy hearth. Venus herself renews, year by year, her aging body, and, so men believe, rises from the warm sea. Through marble cities young men cry, loudly, Hymenaeus![11] The seashore and the hollow crags sound forth Io Hymen! Hymen comes, richly dressed, handsomeness itself in his form-fitting tunic; his fragrant vestments smell like the crimson crocus. In hosts the maids, their virgin breasts bound in by gold, go out to reap the joys of lovely spring. Each has her own unique vow, her own prayer, yet they all have the same prayer: each asks that Cytherea give her the mate she desires. Now too the shepherd plays his syrinx, and Phyllis has songs of her own to add to his. At night the sailor sings to placate his stars, and calls the agile dolphins to the surface of the sea. Jupiter himself frolics with his wife on high Olympus, and he summons his attendant gods to the feast. Now the satyrs, too, when the late twilight rises, fly in swift bands across the flowering countryside, and Sylvanus, crowned with his favorite cypress leaves—Sylvanus, a god half goat and a goat half god. The Dryads who earlier hid in the aged trees now wander the mountain ridges and lonely fields. Pan scampers through grain field and through coverts, mother Cybele, and Ceres, too, can just find safety for themselves. Lusty Faunus catches one of the Oreads, but the nymph saves herself by trusting to her trembling feet; now she hides, but not effectively; even as she hides, she is eager to be seen; she runs, but as she runs, she would be run down. The gods, too, choose these woods rather than their mountain: every grove has for itself its own special deities.

Long may every grove have for itself its own unique deities: don't leave your leafy homes, please, gods! May other ages of gold bring you back again, Jupiter, to this wretched planet. Why do you return to the clouds you use as weapons? Drive your swift team slowly, Phoebus, as slowly as you can, and help the spring pass slowly. May rough winter be slow as well to bring his long nights, and may it be late in each day before the shadows dim the sky.

---

⁹*1673* has "Litus."
¹⁰*1645* has "Virgineas." I have corrected as in *1673*.

[11]The cry to the god of marriage, Hymen, as practiced in Spenser's "Epithalamion," and exemplified by Shakespeare's use of the god as a character in *As You Like It*, and by Milton's in "L'Allegro" 125.

Elegy 6.
To Charles Diodati, Lingering in the Country.

The mood is festive and warm in this verse-letter to Milton's friend Charles Diodati, written in December of 1629, when Milton was twenty-one. Both young men are enjoying the holiday season. But Milton declares that in order to be the kind of serious epic poet that he aspires to be, he must give up the festive, elegiac, drunken inspiration of ode-writers like Pindar or elegists like Ovid in favor of the austere, temperate, rigorous, dedicated, disciplined life demanded of an epic poet. The argument between the two ways of life exemplified in "L'Allegro" and "Il Penseroso" is extended into a discussion of the two basic types of poets, the lyric, loose-living Ovid and the drinker Pindar, or the deeply serious, scrupulous, scholarly epic poet like Homer or Vergil (for the context of the Latin elegies within Milton's poetic career, see Shawcross).

From Edward Phillips we know that Milton in later life was personally "of hard Study, and spare Diet," but that he kept an occasional "gawdy day," imitating college festivities by having friends over for wine and conversation. The Horatian sonnet to Milton's young friend Henry Laurence celebrates such an occasion.

The overriding critical question is how seriously to take the debate within the poem. To see the young John Milton dedicating himself to a life of drinking pure water from a beech bowl seems a little ridiculous (Graves's picture of the prissy Milton through his first wife's eyes is misguided but amusing). On the other hand, *Paradise Lost* will be the product of such an exemplary personal life, the life of the serious scholar poet. Milton probably never deviated from living a life of moderate eating and exercise: his healthy lifestyle might, for all we know, have contributed to his alertness into what was then a very ripe old age. The Nativity Ode, almost surely the poem referred to at the end of this elegy (Low), represents a turning away from the subjects of love or festive good times and toward a subject as serious as the birth of Christ.

Works Cited

Graves, Robert. *Wife to Mr. Milton: The Story of Marie Powell*. Chicago, IL: Academy Chicago, 1979.

Low, Anthony. "The Unity of Milton's *Elegia Sexta*." *English Literary Renaissance* 11 (1981): 213–23.

Shawcross, John T. "Form and Content in Milton's Latin Elegies." *Huntington Library Quarterly* 33 (1970): 331–50.

Elegia sexta.
Ad Carolum Diodatum ruri commorantem.

Qui cum idibus Decemb. scripsisset, & sua carmina excu-
sari postulasset si solito minus essent bona, quòd inter
lautitias quibus erat ab amicis exceptus, haud satis
felicem operam Musis dare se posse affirmabat, hunc
habuit responsum.

Mitto tibi sanam non pleno ventre salutem,
    Quâ tu distento forte carere potes.
At tua quid nostram prolectat Musa camœnam,
    Nec sinit optatas posse sequi tenebras?
Carmine scire velis quàm te redamémque colámque,   5
    Crede mihi vix hoc carmine scire queas.
Nam neque noster amor modulis includitur arctis,
    Nec venit ad claudos integer ipse pedes.
Quàm bene solennes epulas, hilaremque Decembrim
    Festaque cœlifugam quæ coluere Deum,   10
Deliciasque refers, hyberni gaudia ruris,
    Haustaque per lepidos Gallica musta focos.
Quid quereris refugam vino dapibusque poesin?
    Carmen amat Bacchum, Carmina Bacchus amat.
Nec puduit Phœbum virides gestasse corymbos,   15
    Atque hederam lauro præposuisse suæ.
Sæpius Aoniis clamavit collibus Euœ
    Mista Thyonêo turba novena choro.
Naso Corallæis mala carmina misit ab agris:
    Non illic epulæ non sata vitis erat.   20
Quid nisi vina, rosasque racemiferumque Lyæum
    Cantavit brevibus Teia Musa modis?
Pindaricosque inflat numeros Teumesius Euan,
    Et redolet sumptum pagina quæque merum.
Dum gravis everso currus crepat axe supinus,   25
    Et volat Eléo pulvere fuscus eques.
Quadrimoque madens Lyricen Romanus Jaccho
    Dulce canit Glyceran, flavicomamque Chloen.
Jam quoque lauta tibi generoso mensa paratu,
    Mentis alit vires, ingeniumque fovet.   30
Massica fœcundam despumant pocula venam,
    Fundis & ex ipso condita metra cado.
Addimus his artes, fusumque per intima Phœbum
    Corda, favent uni Bacchus, Apollo, Ceres.

Elegy 6.
To Charles Diodati, Lingering in the Country.

When Diodati had written December 13, saying that, if his
verses should be less good than usual, they should be
forgiven, because, entertained so splendidly by his
friends, he neglected the Muses, he had this answer.

With a stomach anything but full, I send you a prayer for sound health, which you, perhaps, with
your stomach stuffed, may need badly. But why does
your Muse seek to lure mine to come out? Why does
your Muse not allow mine to court the obscurity she
craves? If you do want to learn through my verses how
warmly I love you, how dearly I cherish you, that,
believe me, you won't learn through this song, for my
love cannot be bound in tight-fitting metrics, and, being
healthy, does not come to you limping on elegiac feet.[1]
How well you describe the solemn feasts, and December merry-making, the feast days that honor the God
who came down from Heaven, the delights and the joys
of the countryside in winter, and the French wine
drunk down beside the warm hearth! Why do you complain that poetry is banished by wine and feast? Song
loves Bacchus, Bacchus loves songs. Apollo wasn't shy
to wear the green ivy berries, or to set the ivy wreath
above his own laurel. The nine Muses on the Aonian
hillside, mingling with the Bacchic troop, have cried
aloud, Euoe! The songs that Ovid sent from the lands of
the Coralli were poor songs, no rich feasts were there,
the vine had not been planted. Of what but wines, and
roses, and cluster-bearing Lyæus did the Teian Anacre-
on sing in his neat short verses? Teumesian Bacchus inspired Pindar's odes; Pindar's every page reeks with the
wine he drank—as the heavy chariot, its axle crushed,
crashes overturned, and the horseman flies by, black
with the dust of Elis. The lyricist of Rome was drunk
with four-year-old wine as he sang sweetly of Glycera
and of the golden blonde Chloe. In your case, too, the
fat table stimulates your mind and inspires you. Massic
wine foams over with a rich flood of song, and you
pour out poetry from the wine bottle. You have artistry
as well, and Phoebus in your soul: Bacchus, Apollo,
Ceres favor you as they favor no one else.

---

[1]Limping because of the uneven hexameter and pentameter lines of
elegiac couplets in Latin.

Scilicet haud mirum tam dulcia carmina per te   35
    Numine composito tres peperisse Deos.
Nunc quoque Thressa tibi cælato barbitos auro
    Insonat argutâ molliter icta manu;
Auditurque chelys suspensa tapetia circum,
    Virgineos tremulâ quæ regat arte pedes.   40
Illa tuas saltem teneant spectacula Musas,
    Et revocent, quantum crapula pellit iners.
Crede mihi dum psallit ebur, comitataque plectrum
    Implet odoratos festa chorea tholos,
Percipies tacitum per pectora serpere Phœbum,   45
    Quale repentinus permeat ossa calor,
Perque puellares oculos digitumque sonantem
    Irruet in totos lapsa Thalia sinus.
Namque Elegía levis multorum cura deorum est,
    Et vocat ad numeros quemlibet illa suos;   50
Liber adest elegis, Eratoque, Ceresque, Venusque,
    Et cum purpureâ matre tenellus Amor.
Talibus inde licent convivia larga poetis,
    Sæpius & veteri commaduisse mero.
At qui bella refert, & adulto sub Jove cælum,   55
    Heroasque pios, semideosque duces,
Et nunc sancta canit superum consulta deorum,
    Nunc latrata fero regna profunda cane,
Ille quidem parcè Samii pro more magistri
    Vivat, & innocuos præbeat herba cibos;   60
Stet prope fagineo pellucida lympha catillo,
    Sobriaque è puro pocula fonte bibat.
Additur huic scelerisque vacans, & casta juventus,
    Et rigidi mores, & sine labe manus.
Qualis veste nitens sacrâ, & lustralibus undis   65
    Surgis ad infensos augur iture Deos.
Hoc ritu vixisse ferunt post rapta sagacem
    Lumina Tiresian, Ogygiumque Linon,
Et lare devoto profugum Calchanta, senemque
    Orpheon edomitis sola per antra feris;   70
Sic dapis exiguus, sic rivi potor Homerus
    Dulichium vexit per freta longa virum,
Et per Monstrificam[2] Perseiæ Phœbados aulam,
    Et vada fœmineis insidiosa sonis,
Perque tuas rex ime domos, ubi sanguine nigro   75
    Dicitur umbrarum detinuisse greges.

It is no wonder, then, that through you three gods, their divine powers conjoined, gave birth to songs so sweet. Now the Thracian lyre, too, with its fretted gold, sounds for you, touched softly by an artist hand. Amid the hanging tapestries is heard the lyre that with its skillful dancing measures guides the feet of the maidens. Let sights so glorious detain your Muse at least, and let them call back whatever inspiration enervating indulgence in wine drives away. Believe me, while the ivory sends forth its strains, and the holiday throng of dancers, keeping time to the plectrum, fill the vaulted, perfumed chambers, you will know that Phoebus is making his way voicelessly through your heart, even as some glow of warmth makes it way through your marrow; and through the maidens' eyes, and through their fingers as they play their music, Thalia will posses your heart and master it. For light-footed Elegy is the concern of many gods: she numbers whatever god she can persuade. Bacchus cultivates elegies: so, too, Erato, and Ceres, and Venus, and dainty Cupid, by his rosy mother's side. For elegiac poets, feasts are their privilege, and again and again to soak themselves in aged wine.

But if a poet sings of wars, of Heaven ruled by a Jove no longer a boy, of dutiful heroes, of commanders who are demigods, if he sings on the one hand about the holy counsels of the gods above, then of the depths where the savage hound howls, he should live a simple, frugal life, after the fashion of the teacher who came from Samos; let herbs offer him food that doesn't upset his system, let the purest of water stand near him, in a beech bowl, and let him drink soberly from a pure spring. Such a poet should be required to have a youth chaste and free of crime, and an austere character, together with a good name; such a person as a prophet-priest, dressed in holy vestments and bathed in holy waters, prepared to face the angry gods. In this way wise Tiresias lived, after the onset of his blindness, and Theban Linus, and Calchas, exiled from his hearth, a hearth doomed to destruction, and aged Orpheus, in the lonely grottoes, after he had tamed the wild beasts. So Homer, sparing of food, and a drinker of water, ferried Ulysses across the long straits, through the monster-making court of Circe and the shallows made treacherous by the Sirens' songs, yes, even through the underworld, when, so men say, with black blood he fixed in their tracks the ghosts.

---

[2]Not capitalized in *1645*.

Diis etenim sacer est vates, divûmque sacerdos,
  Spirat & occultum pectus, & ora Jovem.
At tu siquid agam, scitabere (si modò saltem
  Esse putas tanti noscere siquid agam)   80
Paciferum canimus cælesti semine regem,
  Faustaque sacratis sæcula pacta libris,
Vagitumque Dei, & stabulantem paupere tecto
  Qui suprema suo cum patre regna colit.
Stelliparumque polum, modulantesque æthere turmas, 85
  Et subitò elisos ad sua fana Deos.
Dona quidem dedimus Christi natalibus illa,
  Illa sub auroram lux mihi prima tulit.
Te quoque pressa manent patriis meditata cicutis,
  Tu mihi, cui recitem, judicis instar eris.   90

For the poet is sacred to the gods, he is priest of the gods; the depths of his soul, and his very lips live and breathe Jove. If you seek to learn what I am doing (if you think it worth your while to know what I am doing), I am writing a hymn to the King born of heavenly seed, the bringer of peace, and the blessed generations covenanted by the holy books, and the infant cry of God, and the stabling under a poor roof of him who shares Heaven with his Father, and about the skies giving birth to a new star, about the hosts of heaven who sang, and about the pagan gods suddenly demolished in their shrines. Some little poems also await you, for which you may serve as judge as I read them to you.

Elegia septima, Anno ætatis undevigesimo.[1]

NOndum blanda tuas leges Amathusia norâm,[2]
  Et Paphio vacuum pectus ab igne fuit.
Sæpe cupidineas, puerilia tela, sagittas,
  Atque tuum sprevi maxime, numen, Amor.
Tu puer imbelles dixi transfige columbas,   5
  Conveniunt tenero mollia bella duci.
Aut de passeribus tumidos age, parve, triumphos,
  Hæc sunt militiæ digna trophæa tuæ:[3]
In genus humanum quid inania dirigis arma?
  Non valet in fortes ista pharetra viros.   10
Non tulit hoc Cyprius, (neque enim Deus ullus ad iras
  Promptior) & duplici jam ferus igne calet.
Ver erat, & summæ radians per culmina villæ
  Attulerat primam lux tibi Maie diem:
At mihi adhuc refugam quærebant lumina noctem   15
  Nec matutinum sustinuere jubar.
Astat Amor lecto, pictis Amor impiger alis,
  Prodidit astantem mota pharetra Deum:
Prodidit & facies, & dulce minantis ocelli,
  Et quicquid puero, dignum & Amore fuit.   20
Talis in æterno juvenis Sigeius Olympo
  Miscet amatori pocula plena Jovi;
Aut qui formosas pellexit ad oscula nymphas
  Thiodamantæus Naiade raptus Hylas;

Elegy 7, written when he was nineteen.

I Did not yet know your rules, seductive Amathusia,[4] and my breast was still free of Venus's fire. Again and again I turned aside Cupid's arrows, as little boy's darts. I spurned your godhead, mighty Cupid. "Go, boy," I said, "shoot doves that don't understand fighting, since only unmanly wars are fitting to a tiny captain, or else, you little baby, triumph over sparrows, worthy of your warfare. Why aim your idle darts against humankind? Your arrows can't beat sturdy heroes." The boy from Cyprus could not endure what I said (no other god becomes angry faster), and he became doubly angry.

It was spring, and the light, shining over the roof of the tall farmhouse had ushered in the first of May. But my eyes still longed for the fading night and could not tolerate the brightness of morning. Love stood by my bed, quick Love, with sparkling wings. The rattling of his quiver betrayed the god as he stood beside me; his face, too, betrayed him, and his lovely eyes with their sweet threats, and whatever else was worthy of a lad, worthy even of Love. This is what the Trojan boy[5] who mixes brimming goblets on Olympus for the infatuated Jove looks like, or the lad who lured the lovely nymphs to his kisses, Theodamas's son, Hylas, stolen by a Naiad.[6]

---

[1]Editors and biographers have pointed out that Milton uses the ordinal number "*undevigesimo*" instead of the simpler form "*Anno aetatis* 17," say, as he does at the head of Elegy 3. What this might mean (if it signifies anything) Carey adduces as "When he was nineteen" (1997 ed., 72).
[2]The circumflex is incorrectly over the "o" in *1673*.
[3]The colon from *1673* replaces the period of *1645*.

[4]Venus, esoterically named for a temple at Amathus on Cyprus, first, then for her more familiar connection with Paphos on the same island.
[5]Ganymede, stolen away from earth by Jove in the form of an eagle; the area of Troy is represented here as Sigeum, a promontory in Troas. For the story, see Ovid, *Metamorphoses* 10.155–61.
[6]Theodamas was king of the Dryopes. His son Hylas was dragged down to the depths of a fountain by nymphs infatuated with his beauty. Carey points to Propertius 1.20.6 as Milton's source (1997 ed., 73n).

Addideratque iras, sed & has decuisse putares,   25
  Addideratque truces, nec sine felle minas.
Et miser exemplo sapuisses tutiùs, inquit,
  Nunc mea quid possit dextera testis eris.
Inter & expertos vires numerabere nostras,
  Et faciam vero per tua damna fidem.   30
Ipse ego si nescis strato Pythone superbum
  Edomui Phœbum, cessit & ille mihi;
Et quoties meminit Peneidos, ipse fatetur
  Certiùs & graviùs tela nocere mea.
Me nequit adductum curvare peritiùs arcum,   35
  Qui post terga solet vincere Parthus eques.
Cydoniusque mihi cedit venator, & ille
  Inscius uxori qui necis author erat.
Est etiam nobis ingens quoque victus Orion,
  Herculeæque manus, Herculeusque comes.   40
Jupiter ipse licet sua fulmina torqueat in me,
  Hærebunt lateri spicula nostra Jovis.
Cetera quæ dubitas meliùs mea tela docebunt,
  Et tua non leviter corda petenda mihi.
Nec te stulte tuæ poterunt defendere Musæ,   45
  Nec tibi Phœbæus porriget anguis opem.
Dixit, & aurato quatiens mucrone sagittam,
  Evolat in tepidos Cypridos ille sinus.
At mihi risuro tonuit ferus ore minaci,
  Et mihi de puero non metus ullus erat.   50
Et modò quà nostri spatiantur in urbe Quirites[7]
  Et modò villarum proxima rura placent.
Turba frequens, faciéque simillima turba dearum
  Splendida per medias itque reditque vias.
Auctaque luce dies gemino fulgore coruscat,   55
  Fallor? an & radios hinc quoque Phœbus habet.
Hæc ego non fugi spectacula grata severus,
  Impetus & quò me fert juvenilis, agor.
Lumina luminibus malè providus obvia misi,
  Neve oculos potui continuisse meos.   60

Cupid had grown angry (this made him even more beautiful), and he added wild and bitter threats. Then he said, "Wretch, you had grown wise through reading of the experience of others; now you will testify yourself to the power of my right arm. You will be numbered among men who have pushed me; with the example by your sufferings I will build credibility. It was I myself who completely tamed Phoebus, even when he was exulting in defeating Python, to me even that glorious god yielded; as often as he recalls Daphne, he confesses that my arrows are more accurate and deadly than his. The Parthian horseman cannot draw and bend his bow as fast as I can—the horseman whose habit it is to win his fight by shooting backwards.

The Cydonian[8] hunter concedes to me as well; so, too, did he who unwillingly caused his wife's violent death. I overcame mighty Orion[9] as well, and the hands of Hercules and his comrade.[10] Even if Jove tried to hurl his lightning bolts at me, my darts would hit his side first. Whatever else you doubt, my shafts will teach you more than words that I can hurt you deeply. Fool, the Muses you love don't have the power to defend you, nor will Phoebus's serpent cure you."

Thus he spoke. Then he shook a gold-tipped arrow[11] at me and flew to the warm breasts of Venus. But I was inclined to ignore the threats the boy thundered at me, and I did not fear him. Sometimes I found delight in the parts of the city where our citizens promenade, sometimes in the nearby country-side near rural houses. Hosts of girls, with faces like goddesses moved to and fro through the walkways, shiningly beautiful. Thus the day had a double brightness. Do I deceive myself, or do the sun's rays emanate from them? I did not run like a prude away from such sights. No, I let myself be driven wherever youthful impulse took me. Lacking any foreknowledge, I sent my stares to meet their eyes; I couldn't stop myself.

---

[7]The word connects citizens of London with citizens of imperial Rome, which may be the reason for its capitalization in both editions.

[8]The Cydonians, from the island of Crete, had legendary skill as archers, as did the Parthians (Vergil, *Aeneid* 12.859).
[9]The hunter Orion, whose pursuit of the daughters of Atlas, the Pleiades, resulted in the constellation bearing his name. For the love-sick Orion, see Ovid, *Ars Amatoria* 1.731.
[10]Hercules was famous as a promiscuous lover as well as strongman. Hughes identifies the companion tentatively as Jason, since Hercules and Jason were both together as Argonauts.
[11]Traditionally, the gold-tipped arrows of Cupid caused love to occur, and the lead-tipped arrows drove love away, as in Ovid, *Metamorphoses* 1.468–72, in which Cupid uses arrows from both sets on Apollo and Daphne.

Unam forte aliis supereminuisse notabam,
    Principium nostri lux erat illa mali.
Sic Venus optaret mortalibus ipsa videri,
    Sic regina Deûm conspicienda fuit.
Hanc memor objecit nobis malus ille Cupido,   65
    Solus & hos nobis texuit antè dolos.
Nec procul ipse vafer latuit, multæque sagittæ,
    Et facis a tergo grande pependit onus.
Nec mora, nunc ciliis hæsit, nunc virginis ori,
    Insilit hinc labiis, insidet inde genis: 70
Et quascunque agilis partes jaculator oberrat,
    Hei mihi, mille locis pectus inerme ferit.
Protinus insoliti subierunt corda furores,
    Uror amans intùs, flammaque totus eram.
Interea misero quæ jam mihi sola placebat,   75
    Ablata est oculis non reditura meis.
Ast ego progredior tacitè querebundus, & excors,
    Et dubius volui sæpe referre pedem.
Findor, & hæc remanet, sequitur pars altera votum,
    Raptaque tàm subitò gaudia flere juvat.   80
Sic dolet amissum proles Junonia cœlum,
    Inter Lemniacos præcipitata focos.
Talis & abreptum solem respexit, ad Orcum
    Vectus ab attonitis Amphiaraus equis.
Quid faciam infelix, & luctu victus, amores   85
    Nec licet inceptos ponere, neve sequi.
O utinam spectare semel mihi detur amatos
    Vultus, & coràm tristia verba loqui;
Forsitan & duro non est adamante creata,
    Forte nec ad nostras surdeat illa preces.   90
Crede mihi nullus sic infeliciter arsit,
    Ponar in exemplo primus & unus ego.
Parce precor teneri cum sis Deus ales amoris,
    Pugnent officio nec tua facta tuo.
Jam tuus O certè est mihi formidabilis arcus,   95
    Nate deâ, jaculis nec minus igne potens:

Then by chance I saw one more beautiful than any of the others: her radiance was the beginning of all my downfall.[12] So might Venus have wished herself to look; this is what the queen of the gods must have looked like. Sly Cupid, remembering, threw this young woman at me; he alone had woven the nets for me. Nearby the clever boy hid himself; many arrows and a huge load of torches hung from his back. Without pausing, he clung first to her eyelids, then to her face, then settled on her lips, then was seated on her cheeks: wherever he landed the little bowman wounded me (o me) in a thousand places, in my defenseless heart. Immediately I became frenzied: I burned; all my being was on fire with love. Meanwhile, the one woman who could now possess my tortured soul left my sight, never to be seen again. But I went on, silently in pain, empty of wit, and distractedly I told myself to retrace my steps. I am ripped in half: half of me waits, the other half follows my heart's desire; I find pleasure in weeping for the joys so suddenly wrested from me. So Juno's son[13] wept for his lost heaven, after he was flung down among the houses of Lemnos. So Amphiaraus,[14] when he was carried to Orcus by his panicked horses, looked back at the sun that had been snatched from his sight. What am I to do, a poor wretch overcome by grief and out of luck? I can't lay aside the love I have welcomed or pursue it. May I see her beloved face one more time, and tell my sad story in her presence. Perhaps she is not as hard as adamant,[15] perhaps she would not be deaf to my prayers. Believe me, no other man has ever fallen so unluckily in love: I will become a pattern of love's wretchedness, me and me alone. Spare me, Cupid, I pray, since you are the winged god of soft love. Let not your deeds be at odds with your gracious office. Now, now at least, your bow is full of terrors for me, O child of a goddess, child not less potent by your fires than by your darts.

---

[12]Milton's fictional susceptibility to female beauty (*Variorum* 1: 19) certainly appeared to have brought about a real-life hasty romance and marriage with Mary Powell, which Edward Phillips describes in these humorous terms: "after a Month's stay [with the Powell family at Forest Hill], home he returns a Married-man, that went out a Batchelor."

[13]Vulcan, or Hephaestus, called Mulciber in *Paradise Lost* 1.740, son of Juno, thrown off Olympus as Satan is thrown out of Heaven, to fall a number of days and to land on the island of Lemnos (Homer, *Iliad* 1.590–93).

[14]One of the famous seven heroes who besieged Thebes, whose chariot was swallowed up by the earth. After looking back plaintively, he descends into Orcus, the underworld of the dead in Roman mythology. Carey traces this scene to Statius, *Thebaid* 7.690–823.

[15]The hardest substance imaginable, sometimes identified with steel, sometimes with diamond. Compare Theocritus 3.39, in which a woman who resists a man is described in terms of adamant.

Et tua fumabunt nostris altaria donis,
    Solus & in superis tu mihi summus eris.
Deme meos tandem, verùm nec deme furores,
    Nescio cur, miser est suaviter omnis amans: 100
Tu modo da facilis, posthæc mea siqua futura est,
    Cuspis amaturos figat ut una duos.

Your altars will smoke with my sacrifice, you will be my true god, supreme among the celestial powers. Take my madness from me. No, don't take it away. I don't know why, but all lovers are wretched in a way that delights them. But in the future please make it happen that, if I fall in love, the same arrow that pierces me will pierce her heart as well.

"Haec Ego Mente."[16]

Hæc ego mente olim lævâ, studioque supino
    Nequitiæ posui vana trophæa meæ.
Scilicet abreptum sic me malus impulit error,
    Indocilisque ætas prava magistra fuit.
Donec Socraticos umbrosa Academia rivos   5
    Præbuit, admissum dedocuitque jugum.
Protinus extinctis ex illo tempore flammis,
    Cincta rigent multo pectora nostra gelu.
Unde suis frigus metuit puer ipse Sagittis,
    Et Diomedéam vim timet ipsa Venus.   10

"Haec Ego Mente."

These lines are the worthless reminders of my lightheadedness, which I once cultivated with a warped and low spirit. Error seduced me and led me to it, until the Academy offered me its shady banks and taught me how to release myself of the yoke. From that time, the flames were put out. My heart is frozen, surrounded by layers of ice, so that even the boy Cupid himself is afraid that his arrows may be frozen, and Venus fears the strength of a Diomedes.

The Gunpowder Plot Poems

Milton wrote a series of poems on the subject of the outrageous plot, scheduled for November 5, 1605, to blow up King James and the Houses of Parliament. Of course the event occurred before Milton was born; but the King died in 1625, sermons were preached regularly on or near the anniversary date (Revard), and Guy Fawkes Day, a time for bonfires and celebrations of deliverance from the potential tyranny of the Roman Catholic conspirators, was instituted by an official act soon after the event. A prayer of thanksgiving was even added to the Book of Common Prayer, to remind churchgoers of the event and to help make sure nothing like it could happen again.

According to David Cressy, the celebrations began almost immediately after the plot was foiled in 1605. In early 1606 Parliament passed "An act for a public thanksgiving to Almighty God every year on the fifth day of November . . . to the end this unfained thankfulness may never be forgotten, but be had in perpetual remembrance."

Because of their differing verse forms, presumably, the three short poems on the Gunpowder Plot and the four lines on the invention of gunpowder were separated in *1645* and *1673* from *In Quintum Novembris*, which was included not with the *Elegiarum* but with the *Sylvarum*. The longer poem is nevertheless the more ambitious work toward which the epigrammatic shorter poems are leading. All of the poems on what was called "the Powder-Plot" might have been planned for a public memorial celebration.

Works Cited

Cressy, David. "The Fifth of November Remembered." *The Myths of the English.* Ed. Roy Porter. Cambridge: Polity, 1993.

Revard, Stella P. "Milton's Gunpowder Poems and Satan's Conspiracy." *Milton Studies* 4 (1972): 63–77.

---

[16]These ten lines, usually referred to just as "Haec ego mente," were placed strategically in the 1645 and 1673 volumes to follow an elegy devoted to erotic love. The lines renounce the kind of poetry Milton had been writing and suggest that he had issued himself an urgent call to follow his destiny to his inspired vocation, that of a Christian epic poet. The swaggering imagery in the lines, however, as Diomedes/Milton defeats Venus (Homer *Iliad* 5.330–51) invites the reader not to take the lines too seriously.

In proditionem Bombardicam.

Cum simul in regem nuper satrapasque Britannos
　　Ausus es infandum perfide Fauxe nefas,
Fallor? An & mitis voluisti ex parte videri,
　　Et pensare malâ cum pietate scelus;
Scilicet hos alti missurus ad atria cæli,   5
　　Sulphureo curru flammivolisque rotis.
Qualiter ille feris caput inviolabile Parcis
　　Liquis Jördanios turbine raptus agros.

In eandem.

Siccine tentasti cælo donásse Jäcobum
　　Quæ septemgemino Belua monte lates?
Ni meliora tuum poterit dare munera numen,
　　Parce precor donis insidiosa tuis.
Ille quidem sine te consortia serus adivit   5
　　Astra, nec inferni pulveris usus ope.
Sic potiùs fœdos in cælum pelle cucullos,
　　Et quot habet brutos Roma profana Deos,
Namque hac aut aliá nisi quemque adjuveris arte,
　　Crede mihi cæli vix bene scandet iter.   10

In eandem.

PUrgatorem animæ derisit Jacobus ignem,
　　Et sine quo superûm non adeunda domus.
Frenduit hoc trinâ monstrum Latiale coronâ
　　Movit & horrificùm cornua[1] dena minax.
Et nec inultus ait temnes mea sacra Britanne,   5
　　Supplicium spretá relligione dabis.
Et si stelligeras unquam penetraveris arces,
　　Non nisi per flammas triste patebit iter.
O quâm funesto cecinisti proxima vero,
　　Verbaque ponderibus vix caritura suis!   10
Nam prope Tartareo sublime rotatus ab igni
　　Ibat ad æthereas umbra perusta plagas.

[1]*1673* misprints "corona."

On the Gunpowder Plot.

WHen, traitor Fawkes,[2] you sinned your unmentionable sin at once against the King and the English nobility, did you, or am I wrong, think to be considered meek and gentle, and to cover your crime with an evil piety? No doubt you thought to send them to high heaven, in a sulphur chariot, with wheels of twisting flame, just like the man whom the Fates could not harm was swept from the fields of Jordan to Heaven in the whirlwind.[3]

On the same.

WAs it in this way you tried to send King James to heaven, you beast, skulking on the seven hills? Traitor, keep such gifts to yourself, unless your imitation godhead can give better gifts. He indeed, without your aid, took his way to the celestial brotherhood, in the fullness of age, without the aid of your hellish powder. So use it to blow up to the skies loathsome monks and as many brutish gods as pagan Rome possesses, for, unless you give each of them such a boost, he will hardly (believe me) climb easily up the road to heaven.

On the Same.

JAmes scorned the fires of Purgatory,[4] without whose aid Heaven cannot be approached. This made the Latin beast, with its triple crown, gnash its teeth, and caused its ten horns to shake with horrific threats.[5] And it cried, "You won't go unpunished for cheapening my sacred rites, son of Britain; you will pay for spurning religion, and, if you ever get to the starry heights, it will only be through the sorrowful road of flame." How close to deadly truth was your prophecy, words scarcely lacking in due weight, for he almost did make his way to Heaven thrown high by Tartarean fire, a ghost utterly consumed by flames.

[2]Guy Fawkes was caught in the act of trying to ignite more than 300 pounds of dynamite planted under the houses of Parliament.
[3]The prophet Elijah, swept up by a whirlwind to Heaven in a chariot of fire, with horses of fire, without having to die, in 2 Kings 2.1–11.
[4]James I ridiculed the notion of Purgatory, as Walter MacKellar established in *Modern Language Review* 18 (1923): 472–73.
[5]The Roman Catholic Church viewed from a Protestant perspective as the beast with ten horns of Revelation 13.1. Latium was the region of Italy in which Rome was located.

In eandem.

QUem modò Roma suis devoverat impia diris,
  Et Styge damnarât Tænarioque sinu,
Hunc vice mutatâ jam tollere gestit ad astra,
  Et cupit ad superos evehere usque Deos.

On the Same.

THat man godless Rome had just recently cursed,
  and had condemned to the Styx and the Taenarian
gulf; now Rome, changing her tune completely, is eager
to raise him to the skies, even to the gods on high.

In inventorem Bombardæ.

JApetionidem laudavit cæca vetustas,
  Qui tulit ætheream solis ab axe facem;
At mihi major erit, qui lurida creditur arma,
  Et trifidum fulmen surripuisse Jovi.

On the Inventor of Gunpowder.

JApetus's son[6] was praised by the ancient blind seers
  because he brought heavenly fire from the sun god's
chariot: but to me he will be the greater man who, as
the world believes, stole from Jove his ghastly trident
and his thunderbolt.[7]

Ad Leonoram Romæ canentem.

ANgelus unicuique suus (sic credite gentes)
  Obtigit æthereis ales ab ordinibus.
Quid mirum? Leonora tibi si gloria major,
  Nam tua præsentem vox sonat ipsa Deum.
Aut Deus, aut vacui certè mens tertia cœli   5
  Per tua secretò guttura serpit agens;
Serpit agens, facilisque docet mortalia corda
  Sensim immortali assuescere posse sono.
Quòd si cuncta quidem Deus est, per cunctaque fusus,
  In te unâ loquitur, cætera mutus habet.   10

To Leonora Singing in Rome.

EAch man (so they say) is destined to have a winged
  angel from the host of Heaven. Why is it strange,
then, Leonora, if you have even a greater glory, since
your voice echoes a present god? God, or at least the
third intelligence having left Heaven, makes his way
through your throat unseen, and teaches mortals to become intuitively accustomed to immortal sounds. If all
things are God, and God comes through everything, it
is still through you alone that He speaks: to everything
else He possesses He gives no such voice.

Ad eandem.

ALtera Torquatum cepit Leonora Poëtam,
  Cujus ab insano cessit amore furens.
Ah miser ille tuo quantò feliciùs ævo
  Perditus, & propter te Leonora foret!
Et te Pieriâ sensisset voce canentem   5
  Aurea maternæ fila movere lyræ,
Quamvis Dircæo torsisset lumina Pentheo
  Sævior, aut totus desipuisset iners,
Tu tamen errantes cæcâ vertigine sensus
  Voce eadem poteras composuisse tuâ;   10
Et poteras ægro spirans sub corde quietem
  Flexanimo cantu restituisse sibi.

To the Same.

THe other Leonora captured Torquato, the poet; his
  mad love of her drove him insane. Poor man, how
much more blessedly had he been destroyed now, Leonora, and because of you, if he had been aware that, as
you sang with Pierian voice, you set in motion the golden
strings of your mother's harp.[8] Though he had rolled his
eyes more savagely than Dircæan Pentheus,[9] or though he
had utterly lost his wit and strength, yet you, likewise, by
your voice could have calmed his wandering senses, and
you, breathing peace into his lovesick heart, could, by
your soul-swaying strains, have restored him.

---

[6]Prometheus, supposed to have stolen from the gods and then preserved for humankind the gift of fire (Hesiod, *Theogony* 562–69).

[7]In *Paradise Lost*, Milton assigns the invention of gunpowder not to a human being but to Satan's legions. In 6.485, cannonry is first discharged. Satan is also often associated with fire as a destructive element, and something like gunpowder at 4.815.

[8]Leonora Baroni sings with the inspiration of the Muses, associated with the spring that flowed on Mt. Pierus. Her mother did, in fact, accompany her on a harp during their concerts.

[9]Hero of Euripides' *The Bacchae*, the victim at least of the insanity of his mother and daughter, who, inspired by Bacchus to a murderous frenzy, tear him apart for daring to defy the god.

Ad eandem.

CRedula quid liquidam Sirena Neapoli jactas,
    Claraque Parthenopes fana Achelöiados,
Littoreamque tuâ defunctam Naiada ripâ
    Corpora Chalcidico sacra dedisse rogo?
Illa quidem vivitque, & amœnâ Tibridis undâ   5
    Mutavit rauci murmura Pausilipi.
Illic Romulidûm studiis ornata secundis,
    Atque homines cantu detinet atque Deos.

To the Same.

WHy, gullible Naples, do you boast of the liquid-voiced Siren, and of the glorious shrine of Parthenope, daughter of Achelous? Why do you boast that you consigned to a Chalcidian funeral-pyre a Naiad of the seashore like Parthenope, who died on your shore? She lives, now: she has exchanged the sea-roar of booming Posilipo for the gentle waves of the Tiber. There, basking in the adoration of Rome's sons, she with her singing captures mortals and gods alike.

Apologus de Rustico & Hero.
[Added at this point in *1673*]

RUsticus ex Malo sapidissima poma quotannis
    Legit, & urbano lecta dedit Domino:
Hic incredibili fructûs dulcedine Captus
    Malum ipsam in proprias transtulit areolas.
Hactenus illa ferax, sed longo debilis ævo,   5
    Mota solo assueto, protinùs aret iners.
Quod tandem ut patuit Domino, spe lusus inani,
    Damnavit celeres in sua damna manus.
Atque ait, Heu quantò satius fuit illa Coloni
    (Parva licet) grato dona tulisse animo!   10
Possem Ego avaritiam frœnare, gulamque voracem:
    Nunc periere mihi & fœtus & ipsa parens.

The Fable of the Peasant and the Landlord.

A Peasant gathered the tastiest apples each year from a tree and gave them to his landlord in the city. Enthralled by the incredible sweetness of the fruit, the landlord transplanted the same tree to his own gardens. The tree, though it had always borne fruit, was really old and weak. When it was moved from its accustomed soil, it withered and became barren. When this was clear at last to the landlord, that he was deluded by a false hope, he cursed himself for being so quick to bring about his own loss. And he said, "Alas, how much better had it been to accept those gifts of my tenant graciously, small though they were? If only I could have kept my greed and hunger under control. Now I have lost both the fruit and the tree."

Elegiarum Finis.

Sylvarum Liber.[1]

Anno ætatis 16. In obitum Procancellarii medici.

PArére fati discite legibus,
   Manusque Parcæ jam date supplices,
     Qui pendulum telluris orbem
      Iäpeti[2] colitis nepotes.
Vos si relicto mors vaga Tænaro   5
Semel vocârit flebilis, heu moræ
     Tentantur incassùm dolique;
      Per tenebras Stygis ire certum est.
Si destinatam pellere dextera
Mortem valeret, non ferus Hercules   10
     Nessi venenatus cruore
      Æmathiâ jacuisset Oetâ.
Nec fraude turpi Palladis invidæ
Vidisset occisum Ilion Hectora, aut
     Quem larva Pelidis peremit   15
      Ense Locro, Jove lacrymante.
Si triste fatum verba Hecatëia
Fugare possint, Telegoni parens
     Vixisset infamis, potentique
      Ægiali soror usa virgâ.   20
Numenque trinum fallere si queant
Artes medentûm, ignotaque gramina,
     Non gnarus herbarum Machaon
      Eurypyli cecidisset hastâ.
Læsisset & nec te Philyreie   25
Sagitta echidnæ perlita sanguine,
     Nec tela te fulmenque avitum
      Case puer genitricis alvo.

Poems in Various Meters.

Written when he was 16. On the death of the Vice-Chancellor, a Physician.[3]

LEarn to obey the laws of fate, and raise, at last, your hands in suppliance to the Parcae,[4] you that dwell on the suspended globe of the earth, you grandchildren of Iapetus.[5] If Death, who goes where she wants, in leaving Tartarus calls you once with her tearful voice, it is sure, despite your delays, your guile, your tricks, that you must cross the dark Styx. If arm-strength had the power to drive away destined death, then Hercules the invincible would not have fallen to death on Emathian Oeta, poisoned by the blood of Nessus, nor would Troy have seen Hector slain through the shameful guile of spiteful Pallas, or Sarpedon whom the ghost of Patroclus killed with his Locrian sword, while Jove himself wept. If Hecate's magic words had power to put doleful Fate to flight, Circe would have lived on in infamy; so too Medea, sister of Absyrtus, would have lived on by the use of her all-powerful wand. And if the arts of the healers and herbs unknown had power to beguile the three goddesses, Machaon would not have been killed by the spear of Eurypylus. Nor would you, son of Philyra, have been wounded by the arrow that was smeared with the Hydra's blood, nor would your grandsire's missiles and his lightning bolt have slain you, Æsculapius, child cut from your mother's womb.

---

[1] A new chronology begins with this section in the 1645 and 1673 *Poems*. The announcement "*Elegiarum Finis*" at the end of the previous section leads us to a new, miniaturized title page announcing the *Silvarum Liber*, another little book of poems not in elegiac meter but on various subjects. The first poem in this little collection is that on the death of the vice-chancellor, written when Milton was sixteen (it is likely, though, that he was seventeen), then we move on to the more extensive *In Quintum Novembris*, written when Milton was a little older.
[2] I have kept the spelling of *1673*, as does Columbia. *1645* appears to be "Jápeti."

---

[3] Dr. John Gostlin, Regius Professor of Medicine and Vice-Chancellor of Cambridge University since 1623. He died October 21, 1626.
[4] The three Fates, usually pictured as spinning out, extending, then cutting the thread of human life.
[5] Mankind was supposed to have been created by Prometheus, not his brother Epimetheus, who was the "unwiser Son / Of *Japhet*" (*Paradise Lost* 4.716–17).

Tuque O alumno major Apolline,
Gentis togatæ cui regimen datum,　　　　　　　30
　　Frondosa quem nunc Cirrha luget,
　　　　Et mediis Helicon in undis,
Jam præfuisses Palladio gregi
Lætus, superstes, nec sine gloria,
　　Nec puppe lustrasses Charontis　　　　　　35
　　　　Horribiles barathri recessus.
　At fila rupit Persephone tua
Irata, cum te viderit artibus
　　Succoque pollenti tot atris
　　　　Faucibus eripuisse mortis.　　　　　　40
Colende præses, membra precor tua
Molli quiescant cespite, & ex tuo
　　Crescant rosæ, calthæque busto,
　　　　Purpureoque hyacinthus ore.
Sit mite de te judicium Æaci,　　　　　　　45
Subrideatque Ætnæa Proserpina,
　　Interque felices perennis
　　　　Elysio spatiere campo.

You, too, Vice-Chancellor, yes, you, greater than your foster child Apollo, to whom was assigned control over the gown-clad bunch, for whom now leafy Cirrha[6] is mourning, and Helicon, too, in the midst of his waters, you would be yet alive, happy, presiding, not without joy, over Pallas's flock, and you would not, in Charon's boat, have visited the grim deeps of Tartarus's pit. But Persephone snapped your thread of life, angered because she saw that by your arts and by your all-powerful potions you had snatched so many from the black jaws of Death. Master, worthy to be cherished, may your limbs, I pray, rest quiet below the soft turf, and from the place of your burial may roses grow, and marigolds, and the crimson-faced hyacinth. Mild be Lacus's judgment on you, and may Ætnæan Proserpina[7] smile upon you; may you stroll in endless life amid the blessed in the Elysian plains.

---

[6]Town sacred to Apollo (god of physicians) near Delphi.
[7]Proserpina or Persephone would be associated with Aetna and Sicily because she was abducted while on the field of Enna in Sicily (see *Paradise Lost* 4.269).

In Quintum Novembris (1626)

Milton's miniature Latin epic on the subject of the Gunpowder Plot is an exuberant full-dress rehearsal for *Paradise Lost.* By the age of seventeen, Milton had undoubtedly worked with Vergil's *Aeneid* in the schoolboy exercise of translating passages into English and then back into Latin, with artful variants, perhaps concentrating on a set piece in the *Aeneid* like the description of the goddess Fama or Rumor in Book 4.173–97. Since it was indeed rumor that disclosed the existence of the Gunpowder Plot in November of 1605, the classical image worked very well for Jacobean England.

The young poet could also interpret the Gunpowder Plot in terms of a Satanic Roman Catholic conspiracy to counter the Reformation, since English kings and queens since Henry VIII, with the one exception of Mary Tudor (mentioned in line 127), had officially supported Protestantism. The conclusion of the poem "celebrates the triumph of an English Protestantism over the schemes of papal Rome" (Revard 86; see Cressy, "Protestant").

In Quintum Novembris attaches itself to classical epic by the reference to Troy in the first line. The poem also descends into hell, a trip taken by Homer and Vergil, and a trip made sacred by Christ's descent into hell for three days after his death, as described in the Apostles' Creed. Milton's poem appropriated the classical underworld, a place full of local color in the sense that it had wailing ghosts, souls in torment, barking dogs, rolling flames, and "darkness visible" (*Paradise Lost* 1.63). Thus Milton was allowed to present a glorious dramatic scene of Satan in disguise (as St. Francis!) tempting the degenerate pope. In its vivid, baroque extravagance, the poem has elements of Senecan tragedy and of Jacobean and Caroline masque (Demaray).

With his highly developed satirical wit, Milton pictured the triple-crowned pope and his mistresses, a procession of worshipers honoring gods made of bread (mocking transubstantiation in Holy Communion), and priests looking suspiciously like drunken revelers celebrating Bacchus.

Of course Milton's position is that of royalist party-line propaganda, reinforcing the popular image of a good King James. As Christopher Hill puts it, Milton throughout his career "assumed that God had a special interest in the English people" (282). The moral structure of the poem is as simple as that of a comic book or a science fiction movie—good defeats evil in one round—and it is just as entertaining for an enthusiastic audience. *In Quintum Novembris* is meant to celebrate the national feast on November 5, Guy Fawkes Day, raucously observed with bonfires and church bells (Cressy, *Bonfires*). English schoolchildren are to this day taught to sing about it:

> Remember, remember, the fifth of November,
> Gunpowder, treason and plot.
> We see no reason why
> Gunpowder treason
> Should ever be forgot!

Guy Fawkes Day is celebrated by Milton in epigrams and then again in the miniature epic, all poems that can be viewed as part of English popular culture. Like "L'Allegro," *In Quintum Novembris* celebrates youthful festivity, but, as in "Il Penseroso," the poem achieves high seriousness when it rejects mirth and concentrates on evil.

Works Cited

Cressy, David. *Bonfires and Bells.* Berkeley: U of California P, 1989.

------. "The Protestant Calendar and the Vocabulary of Celebration in Early Modern England." *Journal of British Studies* 29 (1990): 31–52.

Demaray, John G. "Gunpowder and the Problem of Theatrical Heroic Form: *In Quintum Novembris.*" *Milton Studies* 19 (1984): 3–19.

Hill, Christopher. *Milton and the English Revolution.* New York: Viking, 1977.

Revard, Stella P. *Milton and the Tangles of Neaera's Hair: The Making of the 1645* Poems. Columbia: U of Missouri P, 1997.

In quintum Novembris, Anno ætatis 17.

JAm pius extremâ veniens Jäcobus ab arcto
Teucrigenas populos, latéque patentia regna
Albionum tenuit, jamque inviolabile fœdus
Sceptra Caledoniis conjunxerat Anglica Scotis:
Pacificusque novo felix divesque sedebat   5
In solio, occultique doli securus & hostis:
Cum ferus ignifluo regnans Acheronte tyrannus,
Eumenidum pater, æthereo vagus exul Olympo,
Forte per immensum terrarum erraverat orbem,
Dinumerans sceleris socios, vernasque fideles,   10
Participes regni post funera mœsta futuros;
Hic tempestates medio ciet aëre diras,
Illic unanimes odium struit inter amicos,
Armat & invictas in mutua viscera gentes;
Regnaque olivifera vertit florentia pace,   15
Et quoscunque videt puræ virtutis amantes,
Hos cupit adjicere imperio, fraudumque magister
Tentat inaccessum sceleri corrumpere pectus,
Insidiasque locat tacitas, cassesque latentes
Tendit, ut incautos rapiat, seu Caspia Tigris   20
Insequitur trepidam deserta per avia prædam
Nocte sub illuni, & somno nictantibus astris.
Talibus infestat populos Summanus & urbes
Cinctus cæruleæ fumanti turbine flammæ.
Jamque fluentisonis albentia rupibus arva   25
Apparent, & terra Deo dilecta marino,
Cui nomen dederat quondam Neptunia proles
Amphitryoniaden qui non dubitavit atrocem
Æquore tranato furiali poscere bello,
Ante expugnatæ crudelia sæcula Troiæ.   30
    At simul hanc opibusque & festâ pace beatam
Aspicit, & pingues donis Cerealibus agros,
Quodque magis doluit, venerantem numina veri
Sancta Dei populum, tandem suspiria rupit
Tartareos ignes & luridum olentia sulphur.   35

On the Fifth of November, Written when he was 17.

NOw good James was come from the far north and ruled the people descended from the Trojans, over the wide domain of Albion. At last a firm treaty had united England to the Scots of Caledonia, and James, bearer of peace, blessed, rich, was seated on his new throne, now worrying about secret plots or a terrorist. At the same time the merciless tyrant[8] who is king of fiery Acheron, the father of the Eumenides, homeless exile from the skies of Olympus, had idly wandered throughout the land, hunting up his allies in crime, his faithful slaves, those born to slavery, destined to share his fate in Hell after death. Here he makes tornadoes in mid-air,[9] there makes enemies of former good friends; he arms invincible peoples against each other and he destroys the peace of kingdoms. Whichever person he sees who loves pure virtue, he wants to corrupt, and, master of multifaceted guile, he seeks out innocent souls to make them sin; he lays quiet plots, sets out concealed nets to capture the unwary, as the Caspian tigress follows her panic-stricken prey through the trackless wastes, on moonless nights when the stars wink sleepily.[10] In the same way, the god Summanus attacks peoples and cities, cloaked in a smoky whirlwind of dark blue fire.

Presently, the white cliffs echoing with the surf appear, the land loved by the god of the sea, which once upon a time Neptune's son Albion[11] had named, that same Neptune's son who did not hesitate to cross the sea to challenge Amphitryon's fierce son to enraged battle, before the later cruel age of the siege of Troy. As soon as he sees this land, blessed with riches and with holiday peace, its fields abundant with the gifts of Ceres—and a sight that upset him more, a people who worshiped the divine power of the true God—he gives out sighs that stink of Tartarean fires and of gleaming sulphur.

[8]Satan, here pictured as resembling Pluto, classical king of the underworld, where the rivers of Acheron and Phlegethon (74 below) flow, and as one possible choice as the father of the Eumenides, the Furies, who exacted the vengeance of the gods on criminals. As Hughes points out, Milton may be thinking of Satan as the father of Sin and Death, as in *Paradise Lost* (15n).

[9]Demons and fallen angels were supposed to live in the middle region of the air (compare *Paradise Lost* 1.516 and *Paradise Regain'd* 4.409–16).

[10]Perhaps Milton's first epic simile, created with a nod to Statius, *Thebaid* 10.288–89, and Vergil, *Aeneid* 9.59–66.

[11]Albion was, according to British folklore, the giant son of Neptune who ruled and gave his name to the island. See Milton, *History of Britain* (Yale 5: 6–7).

Qualia Trinacriâ trux ab Jove clausus in Ætna
Efflat tabifico monstrosus ab ore Tiphœus.
Ignescunt oculi, stridetque adamantinus[12] ordo
Dentis, ut armorum fragor, ictaque cuspide cuspis.
Atque pererrato solum hoc lacrymabile mundo   40
Inveni, dixit, gens hæc mihi sola rebellis,
Contemtrixque jugi, nostrâque potentior arte.
Illa tamen, mea si quicquam tentamina possunt,
Non feret hoc impune diu, non ibit inulta,
Hactenus; & piceis liquido natat aëre pennis;   45
Quâ volat, adversi præcursant agmine venti,
Densantur nubes, & crebra tonitrua fulgent.

   Jamque pruinosas velox superaverat alpes,
Et tenet Ausoniæ fines, à parte sinistrâ
Nimbifer Appenninus erat, priscique Sabini,   50
Dextra veneficiis infamis Hetruria, nec non
Te furtiva Tibris Thetidi videt oscula dantem;
Hinc Mavortigenæ consistit in arce Quirini.
Reddiderant dubiam jam sera crepuscula lucem,
Cum circumgreditur totam Tricoronifer urbem,   55
Panificosque Deos portat, scapulisque virorum
Evehitur, præseunt summisso[13] poplite reges,
Et mendicantum series longissima fratrum;
Cereaque in manibus gestant funalia cæci,
Cimmeriis nati in tenebris, vitamque trahentes.   60
Templa dein multis subeunt lucentia tædis
(Vesper erat sacer iste Petro) fremitúsque canentum
Sæpe tholos implet vacuos, & inane locorum.
Qualiter exululat Bromius, Bromiique caterva,
Orgia cantantes in Echionio Aracyntho,   65
Dum tremit attonitus vitreis Asopus in undis,
Et procul ipse cavâ responsat rupe Cithæron.

The sighs are such as the grim creature, penned in by Jove within Trinacrian Ætna,[14] monstrous Typhæus, breathes forth from his corrupting mouth. His eyes are on fire, and his adamantine teeth grind loudly, like weapons—spears clanging on spears. Then he says, "Though I have been over the whole world, this is the one and only race that fights against me, that rebukes my rulership, that is stronger than my cleverness. But if I have any power left, they won't hold out against me, and they will not remain unpunished." Done with his speech, he takes flight, his wings black as pitch. Wherever he flies, the winds resist him, clouds become dense, and lightning flashes quickly.

And now he had flown swiftly beyond the frozen Alps, reaching the edges of Ausonia.[15] On his left were the cloud-touching Apennines, the ancient Sabines; on his right Etruria, infamous for sorcery.[16] He sees you, Tiber, as you kiss the sea. Then he alighted on the hill of Quirinus,[17] son of Mars. By this time the late twilight had made the light doubtful, at the hour when the Bearer of the Triple Crown makes the rounds of the City, carried on the shoulders of men, bearing with him his gods, made out of bread. Princes genuflecting go before, and a long line of beggars, carrying tapers—all of them born in Cimmerian darkness, dragging out their lives in it. Then they enter churches lighted by torches (it was St. Peter's Eve), and the roar of the chanting monks filled the vaulted chambers, with Bromian howls, and those of Bromius's rout as they chant their orgiastic hymns on Echionian Aracynthus,[18] while Æsopus quivers, underneath his glassy waves, and Cithaeron itself, far away, answers from hollow cliffs.

---

[12]In *1673* "*adamantius*" was corrected by the *Errata*.
[13]Probably incorrectly emended to "submisso" in *1673*.

---

[14]Trinacria is the island of Sicily. Jove was supposed to have trapped the Titan Typhoeus beneath Sicily, but the giant's mouth was presumably Mt. Etna, the active volcano, which will appear again in *Paradise Lost* 1.233.
[15]Milton is creating an aerial view of Italy (Ausonia), something that Vergil does often in the *Aeneid* (see the *Variorum* 1.168 for examples).
[16]Etruria is Tuscany. Etrurian shady places, not sorceries, will figure in a more favorable light in *Paradise Lost* 1.303. As the *Variorum* points out, Etruria was not normally associated with witchcraft (1: 178n).
[17]The Quirinal Hill, in Rome.
[18]Followers of the Bromius ("the noisy one") or Bacchus, celebrating in Boeotia, where the river Asopus and the Cithaeron range of hills were located. Echion was one of the men sprung from the dragon's teeth that Cadmus sowed and one of the builders of the city of Thebes (Ovid, *Metamorphoses* 3.311).

His igitur tandem solenni more peractis,
Nox senis amplexus Erebi taciturna reliquit,
Præcipitesque impellit equos stimulante flagello,   70
Captum oculis Typhlonta, Melanchætemque ferocem,
Atque Acherontæo prognatam patre Siopen
Torpidam, & hirsutis horrentem Phrica capillis.
Interea regum domitor, Phlegetontius hæres
Ingreditur thalamost (neque enim secretus adulter   75
Producit steriles molli sine pellice noctes)
At vix compositos somnus claudebat ocellos,
Cum niger umbrarum dominus, rectorque silentum,
Prædatorque hominum falsâ sub imagine tectus
Astitit, assumptis micuerunt tempora canis,   80
Barba sinus promissa tegit, cineracea longe
Syrmate verrit humum vestis, pendetque cucullus
Vertice de raso, & ne quicquam desit ad artes,
Cannabeo lumbos constrinxit fune salaces,
Tarda fenestratis figens vestigia calceis.   85
Talis, uti fama est, vastâ Franciscus eremo
Tetra vagabatur solus per lustra ferarum,
Sylvestrique tulit genti pia verba salutis
Impius, atque lupos domuit, Lybicosque leones.

　　Subdolus at tali Serpens velatus amictu   90 .
Solvit in has fallax ora execrantia voces;
Dormis nate? Etiamne tuos sopor opprimit artus
Immemor O fidei, pecorumque oblite tuorum,[19]
Dum cathedram venerande tuam, diademaque triplex
Ridet Hyperboreo gens barbara nata sub axe,   95

When these rites had at length been carried out, Night quietly extracted herself from the embraces of aged Erebus,[20] and with her sharp whip drove her horses—blind Typhlon; savage Melanchætes; Siope, filly of an Acherontean sire; and Phrix, a shuddering figure with her shaggy mane—at headlong speed.[21] Meanwhile, the King Tamer Pope, Phlegethon's heir,[22] entered his bridal chambers (for this nightcrawling adulterer spends no night without a wanton mistress). But scarcely were his eyes fixed and closing in sleep when the black lord of the ghosts, ruler of the silent folk, who preys on humankind, in a deceptive disguise, appeared at his side. His temples gleamed with the white locks he had assumed; a long beard covered his chest; ash-colored vestments swept the ground with a long train; a monk's hood hung from beneath his tonsure; and, so that nothing might be missing in his disguise, he bound his lustful loins with a hemp rope and fit out his feet in sandals with crossed thongs. Such a figure, so it is said, was Francis,[23] as he wandered alone in the vast desert, in the hideous habitats of wild beasts, bearing godly words of salvation to poor peasants, a godless creature himself, who tamed the wolves and the lions of Libya.

Disguised in this way, that sly serpent opens his lips to utter words like these: "Are you asleep, my son?[24] Does deep slumber still weigh down your body? O negligent of faith and flock—and that while your throne, you who should be venerated, and your triple diadem are laughed to scorn by the barbarous northerners from Hyperborea,[25] your rights spurned by the British archers.

---

[19]The punctuation in *1645* is a comma, which seems less appropriate to the exclamation.

[20]Incestuous mates, Night and Erebus were the children of Chaos and parents of Aether and Day (Hesiod, *Theogony* 123–25). As the *Variorum* reminds us, Erebus might be the place Hades or the god of darkness (1: 181n).

[21]The horses of the Night, or their names, at least, are partly a Miltonic concoction, derived from Apollo's horses in Ovid (*Metamorphoses* 2. 153–54) with some of them identified by Spenser as Pluto's horses (*Faerie Queene* 1.5.20, 28). The Moon's chariot is usually driven by dragons in Milton's mythology, as in "Il Penseroso" 59.

[22]Heir to the fiery stream of hell.

[23]Milton makes merciless fun of St. Francis, known best in Protestant circles for preaching to birds, walking barefoot, and taming the wolf of Gubbio (a town near St. Francis's home, Assisi).

[24]Echoed, perversely, in *Paradise Lost* 5.673–74, Satan speaking to Beelzebub: "Sleepst thou Companion dear, what sleep can close /Thy eyelids?"

[25]Read as "remote islanders from the north," with a reference added to the English archers, who were famous for using the longbow with great accuracy in battle.

Dumque pharetrati spernunt tua jura Britanni:[26]
Surge, age, surge piger, Latius quem Cæsar adorat,
Cui reserata patet convexi janua cæli,
Turgentes animos, & fastus frange procaces,
Sacrilegique sciant, tua quid maledictio possit,   100
Et quid Apostolicæ possit custodia clavis;
Et memor Hesperiæ disjectam ulciscere classem,
Mersaque Iberorum lato vexilla profundo,
Sanctorumque cruci tot corpora fixa probrosæ,
Thermodoontéa nuper regnante puella.   105
At tu si tenero mavis torpescere lecto
Crescentesque negas hosti contundere vires,
Tyrrhenum implebit numeroso milite Pontum,
Signaque Aventino ponet fulgentia colle:
Relliquias veterum franget, flammisque cremabit,   110
Sacraque calcabit pedibus tua colla profanis,
Cujus gaudebant soleïs dare basia reges.
Nec tamen hunc bellis & aperto Marte lacesses,
Irritus ille labor, tu callidus utere fraude,
Quælibet hæreticis disponere retia fas est;   115
Jamque ad consilium extremis rex magnus ab oris
Patricios vocat, & procerum de stirpe creatos,
Grandævosque patres trabeâ, canisque verendos;
Hos tu membratim poteris conspergere in auras,
Atque dare in cineres, nitrati pulveris igne   120
Ædibus injecto, quà convenere, sub imis.
Protinus ipse igitur quoscumque habet Anglia fidos
Propositi, factique mone, quisquámne tuorum
Audebit summi non jussa facessere Papæ.
Perculsosque metu subito, casúmque[27] stupentes   125
Invadat vel Gallus atrox, vel sævus Iberus.
Sæcula sic illic tandem Mariana redibunt,
Tuque in belligeros iterum dominaberis Anglos.
Et nequid timeas, divos divasque secundas
Accipe, quotque tuis celebrantur numina fastis.   130
Dixit & adscitos ponens malefidus amictus
Fugit ad infandam, regnum illætabile, Lethen.
    Jam rosea Eoas pandens Tithonia portas
Vestit inauratas redeunti lumine terras;
Mæstaque adhuc nigri deplorans funera nati   135
Irrigat ambrosiis montana cacumina guttis;
Cum somnos pepulit stellatæ janitor aulæ
Nocturnos visus, & somnia grata revolvens.

You are the one honored by the emperor of Germany,[28] you the one the unlocked gates of Heaven are opened for. Break their arrogant spirits, and break their insolence. Let these sacrilegious sinners know what power there is in your excommunicative curse, or in the apostolic key. Remembering all slights, avenge the scattered Spanish Armada, and the Iberian flags under the sea, and the many bodies of your saints pinned on the shameful cross, while the Amazonian Queen reigned.[29] But, if you prefer to lie back on your soft, luxurious couch, and refuse to beat down the growing might of your foe, he will fill the Tyrrhenian Sea with his many soldiers and fix his battle flags on the Aventine Hill; he will break to pieces what is left of things that are old, and burn them with flames, and trample you with godless feet, though kings were happy to kiss your sandals.[30] And yet do not confront him in open warfare: such would be vain, since a master of guile makes use of trickery; it is right for you to set whatever nets you will to snare heretics. At this moment their mighty king is summoning to council his border lords and is summoning men born of the blood of princes, and aged counselors, to be reverenced for their cloaks and their gray hair; all of these, all of them, you will have the power to scatter from limb to limb in the air, by setting off gunpowder under the foundation of their meeting house. Tell any of the faithful in England right away about this plan: will any one of your sons risk not carrying out the orders of the sovereign Pope? Afterwards, when they are utterly confused and amazed by the catastrophe, let the French and the Spanish invade them. Thus the Marian rule will be reestablished at last in England, and you will be lord of the warlike English. Don't have one fear: just be aware that the gods and goddesses are all in favor, all those worshiped on your holy days." So said the traitor, and then, abandoning his disguise, he fled to Lethe, his unspeakable, joyless realm.

    By this time, rosy Dawn is opening the eastern gates to clothe the golden earth with returning light and lamenting still the mournful death of her dark son Memnon.[31] She is sprinkling the mountain tops with ambrosial drops. The doorkeeper of the stars shakes off his sleep and emerges from sweet dreams.

---

[26]The punctuation in *1645* was a semicolon.
[27]Misprinted "casúque" in *1645*.

[28]Various Holy Roman Empire rulers who submitted to papal authority.
[29]Elizabeth I of England, who of course did not persecute those considered heretics as vociferously as had Mary Tudor.
[30]Kissing the pope's foot (or that of the statue of St. Peter in the Roman basilica) is a ritual that Milton deprecates, but it is based on scriptural authority (Luke 7.37–38).
[31]The son of Aurora (the dawn) and Tithonus, Memnon was the Ethiopian king killed by Achilles during the Trojan War (Hesiod, *Theogony* 984–85). His complexion is dark because Ethiopians were traditionally considered to be black (compare "Il Penseroso" 18).

Est locus æternâ septus caligine noctis
Vasta ruinosi quondam fundamina tecti,   140
Nunc torvi spelunca Phoni, Prodotæque bilinguis
Effera quos uno peperit Discordia partu.
Hic inter cæmenta jacent præruptaque[32] saxa,
Ossa inhumata virûm, & trajecta cadavera ferro;
Hic Dolus intortis semper sedet ater ocellis,   145
Jurgiaque, & stimulis armata Calumnia fauces,
Et Furor, atque viæ moriendi mille videntur
Et Timor, exanguisque locum circumvolat Horror,
Perpetuoque leves per muta silentia Manes
Exululant tellus & sanguine conscia stagnat.   150
Ipsi etiam pavidi latitant penetralibus antri
Et Phonos, & Prodotes, nulloque sequente per antrum
Antrum horrens, scopulosum, atrum feralibus umbris
Diffugiunt sontes, & retrò lumina vortunt,
Hos pugiles Romæ per sæcula longa fideles   155
Evocat antistes Babylonius, atque ita fatur.
Finibus occiduis circumfusum incolit æquor
Gens exosa mihi, prudens natura negavit
Indignam penitùs nostro conjungere mundo;
Illuc, sic jubeo, celeri contendite gressu,   160
Tartareoque leves difflentur pulvere in auras
Et rex & pariter satrapæ, scelerata propago
Et quotquot fidei caluere cupidine veræ
Consilii socios adhibete, operisque ministros.
Finierat, rigidi cupidè paruere gemelli.   165

There is a place, pinned in with the eternal darkness of night, once the giant foundations of a building now in ruins, now the refuge of grim Murder and double-tongued Treachery, two children born at once to savage Discord. Here amid heaps of rubble and jagged boulders lie unburied bones of men and corpses run through with steel; here sits Guile, black and cross-eyed, forever, and Strife and Calumny, armed with fangs; one sees Frenzy here, a thousand ways to go to death, and Panic; bloodless Horror flits about, and restless ghosts howl relentlessly in the silence. The conscious earth shrieks at the rottenness and the blood. In the depths of the cave skulk Murder himself and Treachery, and, though no one follows them through the horrendous cavern, craggy, black with deathly shadows, they fly this way and that, these guilty creatures, looking behind them. These were the champions of Rome, loyal many years, that the Babylonian priest calls out, and thus he speaks: "By the sea that flows to the horizon in the west lives a nation that I loathe. Because it is unworthy, prophetic Nature refused to join it closely to our world. Go there quickly (I am bid to tell you) and let the king and all his nobles be blown up by hellish dust into the winds, that wicked brood; and take with you as co-conspirators as many as have burned with zeal for the true faith." So he ended. Eagerly the merciless twins obeyed.

---

[32]Replaces "semifractaque" in *1645*.

Interea longo flectens curvamine cælos
Despicit æthereâ dominus qui fulgurat arce,
Vanaque perversæ ridet conamina turbæ,
Atque sui causam populi volet ipse tueri.
    Esse ferunt spatium, quà distat ab Aside terra   170
Fertilis Europe, & spectat Mareotidas undas;
Hic turris posita est Titanidos ardua Famæ
Ærea, lata, sonans, rutilis vicinior astris
Quàm superimpositum vel Athos vel Pelion Ossæ
Mille fores aditusque patent, totidemque fenestræ,   175
Amplaque per tenues translucent atria muros;
Excitat hic varios plebs agglomerata susurros;
Qualiter instrepitant circum mulctralia bombis
Agmina muscarum, aut texto per ovilia junco,
Dum Canis æstivum cœli petit ardua culmen   180
Ipsa quidem summâ sedet ultrix matris in arce,
Auribus innumeris cinctum caput eminet olli,
Queis sonitum exiguum trahit, atque levissima captat
Murmura, ab extremis patuli confinibus orbis.
Nec tot Aristoride servator inique juvencæ   185
Isidos, immiti volvebas lumina vultu,
Lumina non unquam tacito nutantia somno,
Lumina subjectas late spectantia terras.
Istis illa solet loca luce carentia sæpe
Perlustrare, etiam radianti impervia soli.   190

Meantime, the Lord who bends the Heavens in their wide arc and hurls his lightning from the stronghold of the skies looks down and laughs at the vain attempts of the perverse crew.

There is an expanse, men say, where fertile Europe is separated from Asia, fronting Lake Mareotis. Here is set up the high tower of Rumor, daughter of the Earth, a tower made of bronze, spacious, loud-echoing, nearer to the ruddy stars than Athos or Pelion is when piled on Ossa. It has a thousand doorways, a thousand approaches that stand wide open, and as many windows, and through the thin walls gleam the spacious halls within. A rabble rout, gathered here, buzzes with varied whisperings, like the noises made by the swarms of flies when they buzz about the milking-pails, or in the sheepcotes of rushes interwoven, when the Dog-Star is seeking the heights of heaven, the peak of the skies in the summer days. Rumor herself is seated at the very top of her fortress, Rumor, avenger of her mother Earth. Her head stands out, with its innumerable ears, which hear every sound from the furthest reaches of the wide earth. You, Arestor's son Argus, guardian of the heifer known later as Isis, did not have as many eyes as she has, eyes that never nodded out, eyes that kept watch over all the lands. With these eyes Rumor can travel frequently to dark places, impenetrable even to the glittering sun.

Millenisque loquax auditaque visaque linguis
Cuilibet effundit temeraria, veráque mendax
Nunc minuit, modò confictis sermonibus auget.
Sed tamen a nostro meruisti carmine laudes
Fama, bonum quo non aliud veracius ullum,   195
Nobis digna cani, nec te memorasse pigebit
Carmine tam longo, servati scilicet Angli
Officiis vaga diva tuis, tibi reddimus æqua.
Te Deus æternos motu qui temperat ignes,
Fulmine præmisso alloquitur, terráque tremente: 200
Fama siles? an te latet impia Papistarum
Conjurata cohors in meque meosque Britannos,
Et nova sceptrigero cædes meditata Jäcobo:
Nec plura, illa statim sensit mandata Tonantis,
Et satis antè fugax stridentes induit alas,   205
Induit & variis exilia corpora plumis;
Dextra tubam gestat Temesæo ex ære sonoram.
Nec mora jam pennis cedentes remigat auras,
Atque parum est cursu celeres prævertere nubes,
Jam ventos, jam solis equos post terga reliquit: 210
Et primò Angliacas solito de more per urbes
Ambiguas voces, incertaque murmura spargit,
Mox arguta dolos, & detestabile vulgat
Proditionis opus, nec non facta horrida dictu,
Authoresque addit sceleris, nec garrula cæcis   215
Insidiis loca structa silet; stupuere relatis,
Et pariter juvenes, pariter tremuere puellæ,
Effætique senes pariter, tantæque ruinæ
Sensus ad ætatem subitò penetraverat omnem
Attamen interea populi miserescit ab alto   220
Æthereus pater, & crudelibus obstitit ausis
Papicolûm; capti pœnas raptantur ad acres;
At pia thura Deo, & grati solvuntur honores;
Compita læta focis genialibus omnia fumant;
Turba choros juvenilis agit: Quintoque Novembris   225
Nulla Dies toto occurrit celebratior anno.

Speaking constantly with a thousand tongues, this reckless creature babbles to anyone listening what she has seen or heard; skilled in lies, she diminishes or magnifies fictions of her own imagining.

But you have earned praises from my song, Rumor, for one good deed never surpassed for truth. You deserve to be celebrated by me, and I won't regret that I went on about you; for it was by your doing, wide-roaming goddess, that we English were saved, and we owe you for that. To you that God who moves the stars and the lightning-bolt spoke, while the earth trembled, "Rumor, are you silent? can't you see that godless bunch of Papists, that rout conspiring against me and my Britons, and can you see nothing of the unprecedented murder planned against King James?"

So much He said: no more. But she immediately understood the injunctions of the Lord of the Thunder, and, though she was swift before, she puts on even speedier wings, and clothes her light body with many plumes: her right hand carries a trumpet of Temesaean bronze. Without delay, she flies through the yielding breezes. Not content just to outstrip swift clouds, she leaves behind her the winds, the horses of the sun. First, as she usually does, she flits about England scattering miscellaneous ambiguous bits of stories, then more loudly she tells all—the trickery and the cursed work of betrayal, full of horror in the telling; she reveals the authors of the crime; she doesn't hold her peace about the places equipped with hidden treachery. Everyone who heard was dumbfounded hearing her tales; young men, young maidens, weak old men alike shuddered. People of all ages were struck by such a great disaster.

But our Heavenly Father was looking down on His people with pity, and stopped the Papists' cruel enterprise. The perpetrators are arrested and punished sharply. Incense is burned and honors given to God. There is merrymaking at every crossroad; young people dance; in the whole year no day is celebrated more than the Fifth of November.

On the Death of the Bishop of Ely
(1626)

Nicholas Felton (born about 1556) succeeded Lance-lot Andrewes as Bishop of Ely, and remained in the post from 1619 until his death in 1626. Though Andrewes was much more famous both as preacher and as author, Felton was his friend and fellow translator of the Authorized Version of the Bible. Both men were Master of Pembroke College, Cambridge. Milton appropriately honored both bishops in poems that closely echo each other; the memorial to Felton, though it is in "iambic verse of alternate trimeters and dimeters" (*Variorum* 1: 201) and not elegiac meter, is modeled on Elegy 3.

Dating the various obituary poems is difficult, and there is disagreement over whether this poem is later than the elegy (Miller; *Variorum* 1: 67; Carey, 1997 ed., 27, 51).

Work Cited

Miller, Leo. "Dating Milton's 1626 Obituaries." *Notes & Queries* 27 (1980): 323–24.

Anno ætatis 17. In obitum Præsulis Eliensis. (1626)

Adhuc madentes rore squalebant genæ,
   Et sicca nondum lumina
Adhuc liquentis imbre turgebant salis,
   Quem nuper effudi pius,
Dum mæsta charo justa persolvi rogo   5
   Wintoniensis præsulis.
Cum centilinguis Fama (proh semper mali
   Cladisque vera nuntia)
Spargit per urbes divitis Britanniæ,
   Populosque Neptuno satos,   10
Cessisse morti, & ferreis sororibus
   Te generis humani decus,
Qui rex sacrorum illâ fuisti in insulâ
   Quæ nomen Anguillæ tenet.
Tunc inquietum pectus irâ protinus   15
   Ebulliebat fervidâ,
Tumulis potentem sæpe devovens deam:
   Nec vota Naso in Ibida
Concepit alto diriora pectore,
   Graiusque vates parciùs   20
Turpem Lycambis execratus est dolum,
   Sponsamque[1] Neobolen suam.
At ecce diras ipse dum fundo graves,
   Et imprecor neci necem,
Audisse tales videor attonitus sonos   25
   Leni, sub aurâ, flamine:
Cæcos furores pone, pone vitream
   Bilemque & irritas minas,
Quid temerè violas non nocenda numina,
   Subitoque ad iras percita.   30
Non est, ut arbitraris elusus miser,
   Mors atra Noctis filia,
Erebóve patre creta, sive Erinnye,
   Vastóve nata sub Chao:
Ast illa cælo missa stellato, Dei   35
   Messes ubique colligit;
Animasque mole carneâ reconditas
   In lucem & auras evocat:
Ut cum fugaces excitant Horæ diem
   Themidos Jovisque filiæ;   40

---

[1]There was an inverted letter "u" in *1645*, corrected in *1673*.

On the Death of the Bishop of Ely. Written when he was 17.

MY cheeks were still wet, still stained with the dew, and my eyes were not yet dry. They were swollen with the rain of melting salt tears that I poured forth, while to the mournful funeral pyre of the Bishop of Winchester I paid in full the rites that were his due, when Rumor, she of the hundred tongues, always the messenger too truthful about disaster, buzzed through the cities of rich Britain, among the peoples descended from Neptune, with the news that you had yielded to Death and to the iron-hearted Fates, you the glory of the human race and king of holy men in that island of eels, Anguilla.[2] Then my troubled heart boiled over with anger, cursing the mighty goddess Death to death. The curses that Ovid conceived in the depths of his soul against Ibis[3] weren't any worse; no worse did the Grecian poet Archilochus[4] curse the low trickery of Lycambes, and of Neobule, his promised bride. But look: while I was spouting out heavy curses and praying death would come on the head of Death, it seemed that I heard, absolutely amazed, these words, carried by a gentle voice[5] in the gale: "Throw aside your blind frenzies, your melancholy, and your vain threats. Why do you try so stupidly to overcome powers that are insuperable, powers easily stirred into rage? Death is not what you think it is, you poor deluded mortal. She is not the dark daughter of Night, nor of Erebus, nor of the Fury Erinys, nor was she born of unbounded Chaos. Sent from heaven, she gathers from all places the harvests of God. She calls souls wrapped in masses of flesh into the light and air, just as the Hours, daughters of Themis and Jove, awake the day.

---

[2]The city of Ely's name is made to refer to eels, since in Latin *"Anguillæ"* may refer to eels or snakes. Ely was also considered an island because it was in a swampy region reclaimed from the sea by Roman diking and draining.

[3]Ovid (Publius Ovidius Naso) wrote the poem *Ibis* as invective against an unidentified enemy.

[4]Archilochus—when refused the hand of Neobole by her father, Lycambes—attacked him so vociferously in a poem that Lycambes hanged himself. Among many references to the story are those in Ovid, *Ibis* 53–54; 521–22.

[5]The voice of the bishop himself, which continues to the end of the poem. Modernized texts usually add quotation marks to the beginning and end of the speech.

Et sempiterni ducit ad vultus patris;
  At justa raptat impios
Sub regna furvi luctuosa Tartari,
  Sedesque subterraneas
Hanc ut vocantem lætus audivi, citò   45
  Fœdum reliqui carcerem,
Volatilesque faustus inter milites
  Ad astra sublimis feror:
Vates ut olim raptus ad cœlum senex
  Auriga currus ignei,   50
Non me Boötis terruere lucidi
  Sarraca tarda frigore, aut
Formidolosi Scorpionis brachia,
  Non ensis Orion tuus.
Prætervolavi fulgidi solis globum,   55
  Longéque sub pedibus deam
Vidi triformem, dum coercebat suos
  Frænis dracones aureis.
Erraticorum syderum per ordines,
  Per lacteas vehor plagas,   60
Velocitatem sæpe miratus novam,
  Donec nitentes ad fores
Ventum est Olympi, & regiam Crystallinam, &
  Stratum smaragdis Atrium.
Sed hic tacebo, nam quis effari queat   65
  Oriundus humano patre
Amœnitates illius loci, mihi
  Sat est in æternum frui.

Death leads such souls to the face of the Everlasting Father. But Death is also the one who quite rightly consigns the wicked to the sorrowful kingdoms of dusky Tartarus, beneath the earth. When to my joy I heard Death calling, swiftly I left my loathsome prison,[6] and amid winged soldiers I was carried in blessedness high up to the stars, just as Elijah was translated to the heavens as the driver of a chariot of fire.[7] I wasn't frightened by the Wain of gleaming Boötes,[8] a wagon slowed by the cold of the north, or by the claws of the fearsome Scorpion,[9] or even by your sword, Orion. I flew past the ball of the gleaming sun, and I saw far below my feet the glowing goddess, tri-form Diana,[10] as she controlled her team of dragons with golden reins. I was carried by assorted wandering planets, and through the expanses of the Milky Way, marveling at my new-found swiftness, until we came to the shining gates of Olympus, and to the palace of crystal, and the halls paved with emeralds. But here I will hold my peace, for what mortal would have the strength to tell the whole story of the loveliness of that place? I think it is enough to enjoy Heaven forever."

---

[6]The body, from the perspective of being "Confin'd, and pester'd in this pin-fold here" on earth (Comus 7).

[7]Elijah's translation to heaven is also described in *Paradise Regain'd* 2.16–17.

[8]The constellation of the Bear, which sets late and is found in the northern region of the sky, hence is associated with cold.

[9]The constellation Scorpio, which frightens Phaethon when he drives the chariot of the sun near it (Ovid, *Metamorphoses* 2.195–200).

[10]The goddess, who drives her moon-chariot through the skies and is tri-form because she is associated with Apollo's sister Diana, Hecate (goddess of witches), and Proserpina (Ovid, *Metamorphoses* 6.94). Her chariot, in this case, is drawn by dragons. The metaphoric associations of the moon are deeply ambiguous and include lunacy, witchcraft, chastity, hellishness, and demonic (or just nightly) inspiration.

That Nature Does not Grow Old (1628?)

Though the subject of this poem seems likely to have been that of an academic exercise—perhaps that mentioned in the letter of July 2, 1628, to Alexander Gil (Yale 1: 313–15)—there is no way to know for sure when Milton wrote it. According to Parker, "There can be little doubt . . . that [the poem] was an academic exercise, composed for a student audience at Cambridge. The problem is to find the occasion which prompted it" (773). The tone of the *Naturam* is serious, though a few of the kinds of puns expected of such an exercise can be found toward the beginning.

Scholars have discovered that a contemporary debate existed about the decay of nature discussed in George Hakewill's *An Apologie or Declaration of the Power and Providence of God* (London, 1627), to which Milton may be contributing, since Hakewill had connections with the Diodati family (Parker 773).

Milton's poem is in the form of a classical oration arguing that nature has not decayed (Sessions), and it uses an appropriately calm dactylic hexameter, as do half of the poems in the *Sylvarum* (Oberhelman), to accomplish that goal.

Works Cited

Oberhelman, Steven M., and John Mulryan. "Milton's Use of Classical Meters in the *Sylvarum Liber*." *Modern Philology* 81 (1983): 131–45.

Sessions, William A. "Milton's *Naturam*." *Milton Studies* 19 (1984): 53–72.

Naturam non pati senium.

HEu quàm perpetuis erroribus acta fatiscit
Avia mens hominum, tenebrisque immersa profundis
Oedipodioniam volvit sub pectore noctem!
Quæ vesana suis metiri facta deorum
Audet, & incisas leges adamante perenni   5
Assimilare suis, nulloque solubile sæclo
Consilium fati perituris alligat horis.
   Ergóne marcescet sulcantibus obsita rugis
Naturæ facies, & rerum publica mater
Omniparum contracta uterum sterilescet ab ævo?   10
Et se fassa senem malè certis passibus ibit
Sidereum tremebunda caput? num tetra vetustas
Annorumque æterna fames, squalorque situsque
Sidera vexabunt? an & insatiabile Tempus
Esuriet Cælum, rapietque in viscera patrem?   15
Heu, potuitne suas imprudens Jupiter arces
Hoc contra munîsse[11] nefas, & Temporis isto
Exemisse malo, gyrosque dedisse perennes?
Ergo erit ut quandoque sono dilapsa tremendo
Convexi tabulata ruant, atque obvius ictu   20
Stridat uterque polus, superâque ut Olympius aulâ
Decidat, horribilisque retectâ Gorgone Pallas.
Qualis in Ægæam proles Junonia Lemnon
Deturbata sacro cecidit de limine cæli.

That Nature does not grow old.

OH, how persistent are the errors that drive man's wandering mind to exhaustion! How deep the darkness is which eats him, when he carries the blind night of Oedipus within his soul. Insane, man dares in his mind to measure his own acts against those of God, to measure the laws of gods cut in immortal adamant by his own laws; he links what the Fates have decreed immortally with his own temporary life.

Will the face of Nature, overlaid with furrows of wrinkles, wither, and will the common mother of all things, her all-producing womb shrunk, become barren in old age? Will she, admitting she is decrepit, walk unsteadily, her starry head quaking? Will loathsome time and the incessant corrosion of the years, will squalor and rust, bother the stars? And will insatiable Chronos eat the skies, and stuff his own father into his maw?[12] Alas, Jove was so improvident. Couldn't he have fortified his own citadels against this evil, exempted them from Time's evil? Or set them spinning forever? It will happen, there will be a day when the firmament of heaven collapses, and each of the four poles will cry out when they feel the shock. Olympian Jove will fall from on high,[13] and Pallas Athene, a frightening figure with the Gorgon's head on her shield, will fall just as Juno's son, routed from the sacred threshold of the skies, fell on Lemnos in the Aegean.

---

[11]The circumflex was added in *1673*.

---

[12]The god Chronos (Saturn or *Tempus*) did indeed devour his children as soon as they were born.
[13]Various Olympian gods are described in the act of falling, resembling closely the various Egyptian and Greek gods in the Nativity Ode when they are first confronted by the existence of Christ.

Tu quoque Phœbe tui casus imitabere nati   25
Præcipiti curru, subitáque ferere ruinâ
Pronus, & extinctâ fumabit lampade Nereus,
Et dabit attonito feralia sibila ponto.
Tunc etiam aërei divulsis sedibus Hæmi
Dissultabit apex, imoque allisa barathro   30
Terrebunt Stygium dejecta Ceraunia Ditem
In superos quibus usus erat, fraternaque bella.
     At Pater omnipotens fundatis fortius astris
Consuluit rerum summæ, certoque peregit
Pondere fatorum lances, atque ordine summo   35
Singula perpetuum jussit servare tenorem.
Volvitur hinc lapsu mundi rota prima diurno;
Raptat, & ambitos sociâ vertigine cælos.
Tardior haud solito Saturnus, & acer ut olim
Fulmineùm rutilat cristatâ casside Mavors.   40
Floridus æternùm Phœbus juvenile coruscat,
Nec fovet effœtas loca per declivia terras
Devexo temone Deus; sed semper amicá
Luce potens eadem currit per signa rotarum,
Surgit odoratis pariter formosus ab Indis   45
Æthereum pecus albenti qui cogit Olympo
Mane vocans, & serus agens in pascua cæli,
Temporis & gemino dispertit regna colore.
Fulget, obitque vices alterno Delia cornu,
Cæruleumque ignem paribus complectitur ulnis.   50
Nec variant elementa fidem, solitóque fragore
Lurida perculsas jaculantur fulmina rupes.
Nec per inane furit leviori murmure Corus,
Stringit & armiferos æquali horrore Gelonos
Trux Aquilo, spiratque hyemem, nimbosque volutat.   55
Utque solet, Siculi diverberat ima Pelori
Rex maris, & raucâ circumstrepit æquora conchâ
Oceani Tubicen, nec vastâ mole minorem
Ægæona ferunt dorso Balearica cete.
Sed neque Terra tibi sæcli vigor ille vetusti   60
Priscus abest, servatque suum Narcissus odorem,

You too, Phoebus, with your sun chariot rushing headlong, will imitate the fall of your own son Phaethon, down in a quick crash, and Nereus[14] will belch steam as he puts out the sun, and the sea will hiss terrifyingly. Then will the highest peak of Haemus[15] split, and its foundations be ripped apart, and the Ceraunian mountains, as they were when Dis threw them at the Titans, will be dumped into the deepest pit of hell as brother fights brother.

No. The Almighty Father as he set the stars balanced the weights of destiny precisely and commanded each thing to keep an ordered course for all eternity. This is why the Primum Mobile[16] spins in appointed daily movement, and takes with it the circling skies.

Saturn is no slower than he usually is, and Mars, as fiery as he used to be, with his crested helmet, still glows like a lightning bolt. Phoebus looks forever youthful; he doesn't bother to aim his sun-chariot downward toward a worn-out earth, but with his customary friendly light he keeps to the same path left by his chariot wheels. The morning star Lucifer, who gathers the flock of Heaven together as the sky becomes white and calls them together as morning begins, driving them out as well in the evening into the pastures, dividing the two kingdoms of time with varied colors, rises beautiful as always from the spice-filled Indies. Delia shines as well, and with waxing and waning phases fulfills her various roles, with her arms as ever embracing the fire of heaven. The elements do not break faith: lightning crashes as usual and shatters cliffs. Corus[17] continues to rage furiously through the empty air; wild Aquilo touches the armed Scythians with frost and rolling clouds. The King of the Deep beats at the foundation of Sicilian Mount Pelorus;[18] the Oceanic trumpeter sounds his shell all through the depths; the Balearic whales bear Aegaeon on their backs[19] no smaller than the giant he always was. Neither do you, Earth, lack your old-time vigor. Narcissus[20] still preserves his fragrance.

---

[14]Usually described as the Old Man of the Sea, father of the Nereids (Hesiod, *Theogony* 233–36).

[15]A mountain on the border between Thrace and Thessaly.

[16]The First Mover (for Christians, God), who sets the spheres in which heavenly bodies are contained in motion.

[17]Various winds are named: Corus is the northwest wind, Aquilo the northeast. Geographical charts that Milton was familiar with might picture winds blowing from various quarters of the compass (see Gordon Campbell, "Milton's Catalogue of the Winds," *Milton Quarterly* 18 (1984): 125–28.

[18]See *Paradise Lost* 1.232, for a reference to the same event.

[19]The hundred-armed giant Aegaeon (called Briareus, according to Homer, by men [*Iliad* 1.403–04]) rides the backs of whales in Ovid, *Metamorphoses* 2.9–10. Sandys translates "the tall / Big-brawned *Aegaeon* mounted on a Whale" (ed. Hulley).

[20]The flower and the mythological self-worshiper.

Et puer ille suum tenet & puer ille decorem
Phœbe tuusque & Cypri tuus, nec ditior olim
Terra datum sceleri celavit montibus aurum
Conscia, vel sub aquis gemmas. Sic denique in ævum 65
Ibit cunctarum series justissima rerum,
Donec flamma orbem populabitur ultima, latè
Circumplexa polos, & vasti culmina cæli;
Ingentique rogo flagrabit machina mundi.

That boy of yours, Phoebus, maintains his beauty, and, Venus, so does that Adonis of yours. The Earth wasn't richer back when guilty thieves buried gold in her mountains or hid jewels under her waters.

So, then, the rightful order of things will rightfully proceed to infinity, until the last fire will lay waste all the land from pole to pole, from mountain top to mountain top, and the frame of the world burns on one giant funeral pyre.[21]

---

[21]The question under consideration is how the world will end. In *On Christian Doctrine*, Milton discussed "the death of this foul and polluted world itself, that is, its end and conflagration," using 2 Peter 3.7, "they are kept for the fire until the day of judgment when wicked men will be destroyed" as support for the idea (Yale 6: 627–28).

On the Platonic Idea
(1628?)

These are probably the verses mentioned by Milton in his letter to Alexander Gil of July 2, 1628, as the "*leviculas . . . nugas*" ("inconsequential jokes") that were part of a response to a formal disputation held at the Cambridge University commencement on July 1. If that is true, Milton lost very little time before sending what was a customary printed copy ("*typis donata*") of the verses to his friend and former tutor. What may have been the equivalent of a commencement program has not survived, but the poem is printed, without explanation of where it came from, in both *1645* and *1673*.

This would not be the only time Milton made fun of Aristotle and obscure commentary on his work: he would also do so in Prolusion 3, perhaps as an insult to his Aristotelian tutor William Chappell (Miller).

Milton continued his debate between Aristotelianism and Platonism throughout his career (Lieb). His loyalty to Plato and his attraction to the cryptic writings of the neoplatonist called Hermes Trismegistus (Brooks-Davies) are demonstrated most obviously whenever Milton mentions Hermes, as in "Il Penseroso" 88, or when the Lady in *Comus* mentions the word "Form" or "Idea." For an investigation of the influence of Plato's philosophy on Milton, see Samuel's book.

Works Cited

Brooks-Davies, Douglas. "The Early Milton and the Hermetics of Revolution: *L'Allegro* and *Il Penseroso* and *Comus*." *The Mercurial Monarch: Magical Politics from Spenser to Pope*. Manchester, Eng.: Manchester UP, 1983. 124–49.

Lieb, Michael. "Milton and the Metaphysics of Form." *Studies in Philology* 71 (1974): 206–24.

Miller, Leo. "Milton's Clash with Chappell: A Suggested Reconstruction." *Milton Quarterly* 14 (1980): 77–87.

Samuel, Irene. *Plato and Milton*. Ithaca, NY: Cornell UP, 1947.

De Idea Platonica quemadmodum
Aristoteles intellexit.

Dicite sacrorum præsides nemorum deæ,
  Tuque O noveni perbeata numinis
Memoria mater, quæque in immenso procul
Antro recumbis otiosa Æternitas,
Monumenta servans, & ratas leges Jovis,   5
Cælique fastos atque ephemeridas Deûm,
Quis ille primus cujus ex imagine
Natura solers[1] finxit humanum genus,
Æternus, incorruptus, æquævus polo,
Unusque & universus, exemplar Dei?   10
Haud ille Palladis gemellus innubæ
Interna proles insidet menti Jovis;
Sed quamlibet natura sit communior,
Tamen seorsùs extat ad morem unius,
Et, mira, certo stringitur spatio loci;   15
Seu sempiternus ille syderum comes
Cæli pererrat ordines decemplicis,
Citimúmve terris incolit Lunæ globum:
Sive inter animas corpus adituras sedens
Obliviosas torpet ad Lethes aquas: 20

On the Platonic Idea, as Aristotle
Understood It.

TEll me, goddesses[2] who watch over the sacred woods; tell me, Memory, most blessed mother of the nine goddesses; tell me, Eternity, who lies down at leisure in your distant cave, preserving antiquities, the immutable ordinances of Jove, the calendars of Heaven, and the diaries of the gods; tell me please who was the first being that clever nature made into the model for humans—that first, eternal, incorruptible, single yet universal person, as old as heaven, the pattern for God to use. He doesn't live concealed in the brain of Jove like a twin brother of Athena, the virgin never married.[3] Though his nature is shared by all, it exists as a unique being, and (strange to tell) is confined to a specific bit of space. It may be that as an immortal comrade of the stars, he wanders through the ten circles of the spheres, or lives like a man in the moon—that nearest heavenly body—or perhaps he is seated on the banks of the Lethe,[4] among souls about to enter bodies, without sense, void of life.

---

[1] Printed as "sollers" in *1645*.

[2] Unidentified; perhaps the Muses, though ordinarily Milton is quite specific about the gods or demigods he is invoking.
[3] Athena, the goddess sprung in full armor from the forehead of Jove.
[4] In the *Aeneid*, Anchises explains, as Aeneas looks at the spirits, that a dead soul may drink the water of the underworld river Lethe to forget a previous existence, in order to return to earth in another body (6.713–51). For the theory of metempsychosis, see Plato, *Republic* 10. 617–18.

Sive in remotâ forte terrarum plagâ
Incedit ingens hominis archetypus gigas,
Et diis tremendus erigit celsum caput
Atlante major portitore syderum.
Non cui profundum cæcitas lumen dedit   25
Dircæus augur vidit hunc alto sinu;
Non hunc silenti nocte Plëiones nepos
Vatum sagaci præpes ostendit choro;
Non hunc sacerdos novit Assyrius, licet
Longos vetusti commemoret atavos Nini,   30
Priscumque Belon, inclytumque Osiridem.
Non ille trino gloriosus nomine
Ter magnus Hermes (ut sit arcani sciens)
Talem reliquit Isidis cultoribus.
At tu perenne ruris Academi decus   35
(Hæc monstra si tu primus induxti scholis)
Jam jam pöetas urbis exules tuæ
Revocabis, ipse fabulator maximus,
Aut institutor ipse migrabis foras.

Perhaps in some distant place he walks about as a mighty giant, this archetype, and raises high his towering head, a figure to be dreaded by gods, taller than Atlas himself, who carries the stars.[5] The Dircaean prophet Tiresias, whose very blindness gave him deep insight,[6] never in his deepest soul could perceive that man; Pleione's winged grandson[7] never in the silent night showed him to the bright assortment of the seers. The Assyrian priest had never heard of him, though he could recite the long history of Ninus's[8] forefathers, and primitive Belus,[9] and famous Osiris. Nor did Hermes,[10] the thrice great, the glorious seer with the triple name, skilled though he was in secret lore, ever tell the name of that man to the worshipers of Isis.

But you, Plato, everlasting glory of the groves of Academe, if you were pioneer in bringing such monsters into the schools, you should recall the poets, exiled from your Republic, since you yourself are greatest of all storytellers, or else banish yourself.[11]

---

[5]The famous image of the Titan Atlas carrying the world balanced on his head and shoulders may be found in Hesiod, *Theogony* 507–20.

[6]Even at this early stage of his career, Milton contrasts spiritual insight in blind prophets like Tiresias with moral blindness in ordinary mortals; Tiresias is Dircean (Theban) because Dirce was a fountain near Thebes.

[7]The god Mercury, son of Maia, one of the Pleiades. This Mercury should be distinguished from "thrice great *Hermes*" of "Il Penseroso" 88, shortly to appear in the poem.

[8]Milton seems to be drawing on a work he admired, John Selden's *De Dis Syris* (1617), for details about the history of Assyria and its Queen Semiramis and King Ninus (Carey, 1997 ed., 70n).

[9]Bel (Assyrian), or Baal and Beelzebub (Hebrew) were all associated with one another. For Osiris as Milton conceived of him, see the Nativity Ode 213.

[10]Hermes Trismegistus, semimythical wise man identified with the Egyptian deity Thoth and associated through a collection of cryptic writings with various neoplatonic ideas such as that of the philosopher-poet (Brooks-Davies).

[11]Plato was notorious for banishing poets (while of course providing them with imagery and being something of a poet himself) in the *Republic* 10.595–607.

To my Father
(1631–32?)

Milton's poem thanks his father, John Milton Sr., for the extraordinary support he gave to the education of his eldest son. The poem also argues with his father, gently, about the son's choice to become a poet. Trying to date "*Ad Patrem*" may be a futile exercise, since it could have been written at various points of Milton's career. It has been dated from 1630 to 1640 (Carey, 1997 ed. 153–54), with no convincing evidence to support any of the various dates.

John Milton Sr. (who lived, in his later years, with both his sons) seems to have recognized early that his son John was an exceptional child. The early biographers note that the elder Milton supported his son's scholarly proclivities by hiring servants to stay up with the child as he read late at night; that after Milton finished his formal study at Cambridge, his father provided a rural retreat and perhaps city lodgings for his son to read and study in; and that his father sent him abroad on what must have been an expensive grand tour, with a manservant and enough money to travel extensively and to purchase music books that would accommodate his own tastes as well as those of his father.

What hasn't been noted in the poem, that I know of, is an underlying theme of sons rebelling against fathers. John Milton Sr. rebelled against his own father, a Roman Catholic who, according to Aubrey, disowned him for possessing an English Bible. The poet's rebellion was much less momentous or traumatic to his family: he chose to be an artist, in the modern sense of the word.

He chose to be like his father in his role of composer, but not like his brother or his father in their role of lawyer or businessman (Brennecke, Chapter 7). He knew his adopted role as prophetic, inspired, semidivine poet would someday allow him to take a seat among the immortals (102).

The father continued to nurture the son well into his thirties, and the son continued to help manage his father's various real estate and legal affairs. The scrivener John Milton gave his son control of various interest-bearing accounts and mortgages from which the poet could profit (for legal details, see French). One of the mortgages that the son administered was that of the Powell family, and it was the collection of arrears on this debt that led to Milton's initially unhappy marriage with Mary Powell.

John Milton Sr. would live quietly with his eldest son from 1643 until his death in 1647. Edward Phillips tells us that the father caused little or no bother in his son's household. The father and the son were united after death as artists: with some historical irony, the work of both men still appears together in the *Hymnal of the Protestant Episcopal Church in the United States of America 1940*, in a hymn based on the son's translations of Psalms 82, 85, and 86, with a melody harmonized by the father (General Hymn no. 312; see Spaeth 12–16, and Harper for discussions of music in the Milton household).

Works Cited

Brennecke, Ernest, Jr. *John Milton the Elder and His Music*. New York: Octagon Books, 1973.

French, J. Milton. *Milton in Chancery: New Chapters in the Lives of the Poet and His Father*. New York: Modern Language Association, 1939.

Harper, John. "'One equal music': the Music of Milton's Youth." *Milton Quarterly* 31 (1997): 1–10.

Spaeth, Sigmund. *Milton's Knowledge of Music*. Ann Arbor: U of Michigan P, 1963.

Ad Patrem.

NUnc mea Pierios cupiam per pectora fontes
Irriguas torquere vias, totumque per ora
Volvere laxatum gemino de vertice rivum;
Ut tenues oblita sonos audacibus alis
Surgat in officium venerandi Musa parentis.   5
Hoc utcunque tibi gratum pater optime carmen
Exiguum meditatur opus, nec novimus ipsi
Aptiùs à nobis quæ possint munera donis
Respondere tuis, quamvis nec maxima possint
Respondere tuis, nedum ut par gratia donis   10
Esse queat, vacuis quæ redditur arida verbis.
Sed tamen hæc nostros ostendit pagina census,
Et quod habemus opum chartâ numeravimus istâ[1]
Quæ mihi sunt nullæ, nisi quas dedit aurea Clio
Quas mihi semoto somni peperere sub antro,   15
Et nemoris laureta sacri Parnassides umbræ.
    Nec tu vatis opus divinum despice carmen,
Quo nihil æthereos ortus, & semina cæli,
Nil magis humanam commendat origine mentem,
Sancta Promethéæ retinens vestigia flammæ.   20
Carmen amant superi, tremebundaque Tartara
carmen
Ima ciere valet, divosque ligare profundos,
Et triplici duros Manes adamante coercet.
Carmine sepositi retegunt arcana futuri
Phœbades, & tremulæ pallantes ora Sibyllæ;   25
Carmina sacrificus sollennes pangit ad aras
Aurea seu sternit motantem cornua taurum;
Seu cùm fata sagax fumantibus abdita fibris
Consulit, & tepidis Parcam scrutatur in extis.

To my Father.

IWould this instant gladly have the Pierian springs
divert their waters through my heart; I would love to
have the stream trickling from the twin peaks[2] pour
over my lips, to the point where my Muse will forget
lower forms of poetry and rise on bold wings to pay due
homage to my father. Whether or not it is welcome, it
is for you, my worthy father, that my Muse is working
at this small offering. I don't know what gifts from me
can repay your gifts properly, though not even the
greatest gifts can answer yours: far less can the gratitude
that is rendered through empty words be a match for
gifts so large. Yet, after all, this page is all the wealth I
have, I have counted it out on this sheet of paper, and
that wealth is nothing but what golden Clio[3] has given
me, whatever sleep has brought me as I lay in some
secret cave in a sacred laurel grove, in the shady valleys
of Parnassus.

    Do not despise divine poetry, creation of the pro-
phetic bard: nothing better shows our heavenly origins,
our divine seed, our human intellect, those holy traces
of Promethean fire.[4] The gods love poetry, and song has
power to stir the depths of quaking Tartarus, to seize
the gods of the underworld; song binds unfeeling ghosts
with triple bands of steel. In poetry the secrets of the
far-distant future are revealed by the daughters of Apollo, and by ecstatic, pale-lipped Sibyl.[5] The priest composes songs at the holy altars, either while he sacrifices
the bull as it tosses its gilded horns, or while he
examines the prophecies hidden in the steaming entrails,
searching for fate in the beast's guts.

---

[2]The Pierian springs issue from the two peaks of Parnassus mentioned
so often in Milton's Latin poetry.

[3]The Muse of history, Clio, is traditionally allied with Calliope, the
Muse of epic poetry. The *Iliad* is part of the history of Troy and of
Athens; and the *Aeneid* is an account of what happened between the fall
of Troy and the founding of Rome.

[4]Prometheus, as the etymology of his name indicates, represented
"forethought," or decision-making based on careful consideration. His
theft of fire from the gods has often been taken as the gift of civilization
(Hesiod, *Theogony* 565).

[5]The Muses and the Sibyls, sources of divine inspiration from Apollo.
Both might tremble and speak with distorted voice while inspired.

Nos etiam patrium tunc cum repetemus Olympum, 30
Æternæque moræ stabunt immobilis ævi,
Ibimus auratis per cæli templa coronis,
Dulcia suaviloquo sociantes carmina plectro,
Astra quibus, geminique poli convexa sonabunt.
Spiritus & rapidos qui circinat igneus orbes, 35
Nunc quoque sydereis intercinit ipse choreis
Immortale melos, & inenarrabile carmen;
Torrida dum rutilus compescit sibila serpens,
Demissoque ferox gladio mansuescit Orion;
Stellarum nec sentit onus Maurusius Atlas. 40
Carmina regales epulas ornare solebant,
Cum nondum luxus, vastæque immensa vorago
Nota gulæ, & modico spumabat cœna Lyæo.
Tum de more sedens festa ad convivia vates
Æsculeâ intonsos redimitus ab arbore crines, 45
Heroumque actus, imitandaque gesta canebat,
Et chaos, & positi latè fundamina mundi,
Reptantesque Deos, & alentes numina glandes,
Et nondum Ætnæo⁶ quæsitum fulmen ab antro.
Denique quid vocis modulamen inane juvabit, 50
Verborum sensusque vacans, numerique loquacis?
Silvestres decet iste choros, non Orphea cantus,
Qui tenuit fluvios & quercubus addidit aures
Carmine, non citharâ, simulachraque functa canendo
Compulit in lacrymas; habet has à carmine laudes. 55

So I too, when I revisit my native Olympus, and time stands immovable, endlessly delayed, I will go through the heavens wearing a golden crown, marrying my sweet words to the soft music of the lute:[7] those songs will ring through the stars, from pole to pole. At the same time, the fiery spirit flying around among the swiftly turning spheres, in the middle of the choir of stars, sings an immortal melody, beyond description, while the glittering Serpent stops hissing, and savage Orion lowers his sword and turns gentle;[8] Mauretanian Atlas no longer feels the weight on his shoulders.[9]

Songs used to adorn noble feasts of kings back when luxury and the huge mouth of gluttony were as yet unknown, and banquet tables ran over only with modest wines. In those days, the bard,[10] seated as custom directed at the holiday feast, his flowing hair wreathed with oak leaves, sang of the achievements of heroes worthy of emulation, and sang of chaos and the broad foundations of the world, and of gods who crawled about eating acorns,[11] and the lightning-bolt not yet extracted from its cave underneath Mount Aetna. What pleasure after all will there be in music well attuned if it is empty of the human voice, or empty of words and their meanings, or of rhythms of speech?[12] Such strains befit woodland choirboys, not Orpheus, who by his singing and not his lute captivated streams, and caused oak trees to grow ears to listen to his songs, and by his singing made lifeless ghosts weep: it is from his song that he has these praises.

---

⁶*1673* incorrectly emends to "Ætneo."

[7]Milton elevates himself to the position of the elders before the throne of God in Revelation 4.4, who "had on their heads crowns of gold" and played on the harps mentioned at 4.8

[8]The constellations of the Serpent and Orion will be suspended in their motion. For Orion, see also the elegy on the death of the Bishop of Ely, 54.

[9]Atlas is pictured as holding up the heavens in what is now the region around Morocco.

[10]A possible combination of British bard and prophetic poet, as with the Druids, associated with oak trees, and a generic classical figure like Orpheus, who could command pity from an oak, or make a spirit in the underworld weep (Ovid, *Metamorphoses* 10.14; 10.41).

[11]In the Golden Age, according to Ovid, humankind could live on a vegetarian diet including acorns (*Metamorphoses* 1.106).

[12]It may not be necessary here to choose between words and music, as to which has the greater effect on the human spirit, but in his poems to the musician Henry Lawes, Milton addresses the problem of choice.

Nec tu perge precor sacras contemnere Musas,
Nec vanas inopesque puta, quarum ipse peritus
Munere, mille sonos numeros componis ad aptos,
Millibus & vocem modulis variare canoram
Doctus, Arionii meritò sis nominis hæres.   60
Nunc tibi quid mirum, si me genuisse poëtam
Contigerit, charo si tam propè sanguine juncti
Cognatas artes, studiumque affine sequamur:
Ipse volens Phœbus se dispertire duobus,
Altera dona mihi, dedit altera dona parenti,   65
Dividuumque Deum genitorque puerque tenemus.

Tu tamen ut simules teneras odisse camœnas,
Non odisse reor, neque enim, pater, ire jubebas
Quà via lata patet, quà pronior area lucri,
Certaque condendi fulget spes aurea nummi: 70
Nec rapis ad leges, malè custoditaque gentis
Jura, nec insulsis damnas clamoribus aures.
Sed magis excultam cupiens ditescere mentem,
Me procul urbano strepitu, secessibus altis
Abductum Aoniæ jucunda per otia ripæ   75
Phœbæo lateri comitem sinis ire beatum.
Officium chari taceo commune parentis,
Me poscunt majora, tuo pater optime sumptu
Cùm mihi Romuleæ patuit facundia linguæ,
Et Latii veneres, & quæ Jovis ora decebant   80
Grandia magniloquis elata vocabula Graiis,
Addere suasisti quos jactat Gallia flores,
Et quam degeneri novus Italus ore loquelam
Fundit, Barbaricos testatus voce tumultus,
Quæque Palæstinus loquitur mysteria vates.   85

Please, do not scorn the holy Muses; don't think that they are idle or unprofitable, since you yourself compose a thousand melodies through their generosity, fitted skillfully to your voice. May you inherit the fame of Arion.[13] How is it strange then for you to have fathered me, a poet, if you and I so closely tied by blood should pursue like-minded arts and kindred studies? Apollo, wanting to divide himself between us, gave half his gifts to me and the other half to my father, so we both have shares of the god. Though you pretend to hate the delicate Muses, I don't think you really do hate them, since you haven't made me go where the highway is wide and open, where the money is, where the fortune-hunters are. You do not force me to enter the legal profession, to study the poorly-guarded statutes of our country, nor do you force me to listen to its clamors. Instead, eager to enrich my mind, you allowed me to draw away from the noise of the city into deep seclusion, and you allowed me the pleasant leisure of the Aonian spring, walking by my blessed comrade Apollo's side.

I will not mention the favors that fathers usually allow their cherished sons: there are more important things for me to talk about. When, at your expense, best of fathers, the eloquence of the Latin tongue was made accessible to me, with all its beauties, and those exalted words of the Greeks, masters of a noble language, words that grace the mouth of powerful Jove himself, you urged me to add the language bragged of by the French, and the talk that the modern Italian pours out of his degenerate lips (proof that barbarians invaded);[14] you also urged me to learn the mysteries that the seers and the prophets of Palestine speak of.

---

[13] Legendary Greek lyric poet who became famous and wealthy through his art, most noted for having been saved from drowning by the sympathy of dolphins, who carried him to shore (alluded to in Propertius, *Elegies* 2.26).

[14] The contrast seems to be between the barbarism of modern Italian speech and the noble language of Dante and Petrarch. Milton expressed interest in the pronunciation of Italian when he referred to the work of the linguist Benedetto Buonmattei (1581–1647; see Parker 824).

Denique quicquid habet cœlum, subjectaque cœlo
Terra parens, terræque & cœlo interfluus aer,
Quicquid & unda tegit, pontique agitabile marmor,
Per te nosse licet, per te, si nosse libebit.
Dimotàque venit spectanda scientia nube,   90
Nudaque conspicuos inclinat ad oscula vultus,
Ni fugisse velim, ni sit libâsse molestum.

   I nunc, confer opes quisquis malesanus avitas
Austriaci gazas, Perüanaque regna præoptas.
Quæ potuit majora pater tribuisse, vel ipse   95
Jupiter, excepto, donâsset ut omnia, cœlo?
Non potiora dedit, quamvis & tuta fuissent,
Publica qui juveni commisit lumina nato
Atque Hyperionios currus, & fræna diei,
Et circum undantem radiatù â luce tiaram.   100
Ergo ego jam doctæ pars quamlibet ima catervæ
Victrices hederas inter, laurosque sedebo,
Jamque nec obscurus populo miscebor inerti,
Vitabuntque oculos vestigia nostra profanos.
Este procul vigiles curæ, procul este querelæ,   105
Invidiæque acies transverso tortilis hirquo,
Sæva nec anguiferos extende Calumnia rictus;
In me triste nihil fædissima turba potestis,
Nec vestri sum juris ego; securaque tutus
Pectora, vipereo gradiar sublimis ab ictu.   110

   At tibi, chare pater, postquam non æqua merenti
Posse referre datur, nec dona rependere factis,
Sit memorâsse satis, repetitaque munera grato
Percensere animo, fidæque reponere menti.

   Et vos, O nostri, juvenilia carmina, lusus,   115
Si modo perpetuos sperare audebitis annos,
Et domini superesse rogo, lucemque tueri,
Nec spisso rapient oblivia nigra sub Orco,
Forsitan has laudes, decantatumque parentis
Nomen, ad exemplum, sero servabitis ævo.   120

If I should want, it would be my privilege to learn about whatever is in the sky, on earth, beneath the sky, whatever is covered by water and the turbulent marbled sea, all thanks to you. Parting the clouds, naked science[15] comes to be seen: she gives me her bright face to kiss, unless I would run from her, unless I thought it a burden to taste her kisses.

Go on, then—match your wealth with mine: all of you who unwholesomely prefer the royal treasures of Austria or those of Peru.[16] What greater wealth could have been given by a father, or by Jove himself, though he had given all the world, unless he had thrown in the sky as well? Those weren't any better gifts that the father gave who allowed his youthful son the sun, the property of all humankind, and Hyperion's chariot, and the reins to control the day, and the tiara shimmering with rays of light? Since I am already a part, though only a low part, of the troop of learned people, I will sit someday among those who wear crowns of ivy and of laurel; I will not mix any longer with the witless populace; I will keep out of the sight of common people. Keep away from me, insomniac worries, complaints, and the crooked squint of Envy. Don't open your snake-like jaws at me, Slander. You can't touch me, you nasty crew; I am not in your power. I will walk safe, with a clear conscience, my head held above your vipers' stings.

But, dear father, since I cannot repay you, or balance your gifts with my achievements, let it suffice that I have at least mentioned them, and I am storing them in my loyal memory.

And you, my youthful verses, my sportive exercises,[17] I wish that you are just bold enough to hope for immortality, to survive your master's funeral pyre and keep your eyes on the light. If black loss of memory doesn't spin you down below to the underworld, you can guard this eulogy and my father's name, an example for future ages.

---

[15]Perhaps a picture of an allegorical entity, something like "Knowledge," or "Universal Knowledge." The Latin word could signify "experience" or "knowledge." The picture of an erotic relationship with a naked goddess probably demonstrates Milton's passion for learning in general.
[16]Peruvian gold was an object of Spanish conquest; presumably the reference to Austria suggests the wealth of the Holy Roman Empire.
[17]Presumably the poems published in 1645, some of which are "sportive exercises" (Carey's translation is "pastimes"), in the sense that they are light-hearted or trivial, and some of which Milton pictures as worth preserving for all eternity.

Psalm 114.
(1634)

Ἰσραὴλ ὅτε πα' ἴδες, ὅτ' ἀγλαὰ φῦλ' Ἰακώβου
Αἰγύπτιον λίπε δῆμον, ἀπεχθέα, Βαρβαρόφωνον,
Δὴ τότε μοῦνον ἔην ὅσιον γένος υἷες Ἰούδα.
Ἐν δὲ θεὸς λαοῖσι μέγα κρείων βασίλευεν.
Εἶδε καὶ ἐντροπάδην φύγαδ' ἐρρώησε θάλασσα
Κύματι εἰλυμένη ῥοθίῳ, ὁδ' ἄρ' ἐστυφελίχθη
Ἰρὸς Ἰορδάνης ποτὶ ἀργυροειδέα πηγὴν.
Ἐκ δ' ὄρεα σκαρθμοῖσιν ἀπειρέσια κλονέοντο,
Ὡς κριοὶ σφριγόωντες ἐϋτραφερῷ ἐν ἀλωῇ.
Βαιότεραι δ' ἄμα πᾶσαι ἀνασκίρτησαν ἐρίπναι,
Οἷα παραὶ σύριγγι φίλῃ ὑπὸ μητέρι ἄρνες.
Τίπτε σύγ' αἰνὰ θάλασσα πέλωρ φύγαδ' ἐρρώησας;
Κύματι εἰλυμένη ῥοθίῳ; τί δ' ἄρ' ἐστυψελίχθης
Ἰρὸς Ἰορδάνη ποτὶ ἀργυροειδέα πηγὴν;
Τίπτ' ὄρεα σκαρθμοῖν ἀπειρέσια κλονέεσθε
Ὡς κριοὶ σφριγόωντες ἐϋτραφερῷ ἐν ἀλωῇ;
Βαιοτέραι τί δ' ἂρ ὕμμες ἀνασκίρτησατ' ἐρίπναι,
Οἷα παραὶ σύριγγι φίλῃ ὑπὸ μητέρι ἄρνες,
Σείεο γαῖα τρέουσα θεὸν μεγάλ' ἐκτυπέοτα
Γαῖα θεὸν τρείους' ὕπατον σέβας Ἰσσακίδαο
Ὅς τε καὶ ἐκ σπιλάδων ποταμοὺς χέε μορμύροντας,
Κρήνηντ' ἀέναον πέτρης ἀπὸ δακρυοέσσης.

*Philosophus ad regem quendam qui
eum ingnotum & insontem inter reos forte captum inscius damnaverat, τὴν ἐπὶ θανάτῳ
πορευόμενος hæc subito misit.*

Ὦ ἄνα εἰ ὀλέσῃς με τὸν ἔννομον, οὐδέ τιν' ἀνδρῶν
Δεινὸν ὅλως δράσαντα, σοφώτατον ἴσθι κάρηνον
Ῥηϊδίως ἀφέλοιο, τὸ δ' ὕστερον αὖθι νοήσεις,
Μαφιδίως δ' ἂρ ἔπειτα τεὸν πρὸς θυμὸν ὀδυρῇ,
Τοιόν δ' ἐκ πόλιος περιώνυμον ἄλκαρ ὀλέσσας.

Psalm 114.

When the children of Israel, when the glorious tribes of Jacob left the land of Egypt, a land hateful, of barbarous speech, in that day the sons of Judah were the one holy race, and among its peoples God was king, a king of great might. The sea saw it, and humbly, coiled up in its roaring waters, gave strength to the fugitive, and the holy Jordan was flung violently back toward its silvery fountains. The giant mountains tossed themselves about, and leaped this way and that, even as rams, full of vigor, in a nourishing vineyard. Why, you smaller crags, did you skip, even as lambs do at the sound of the syrinx, beneath their loving mothers? Shake yourself, Earth, tremble in fear before the Lord as he makes a mighty noise, shake, Earth, fearing the Lord, the loftiest majesty of the son of Isaac, of God who, even from the crags by the sea, poured forth the roaring rivers, and from the dripping rock an everflowing fountain.

A king, finding by chance, among men deeply guilty, a philosopher, whom he did not know at all, and who was wholly innocent, condemned the philosopher to death. As the philosopher was going along the road to death, he suddenly sent these verses to the king.

King, if you will kill me, a man who abides by the law, who has done nothing harmful to anyone, so easily, be aware that you would destroy a life, but afterwards you would realize what you had done, and then, all in vain, you would lament in your own soul, because you destroyed such a famous bulwark of your city.

To Salzilli
(1638?)

We know little of Milton's contact with Giovanni Salzilli (Latin "Salsilli") of Rome other than the four lines of Latin verse Milton quoted at the beginning of his own Latin poetry in the 1645 *Poems*. Salzilli was apparently a member of the Roman Academy of the Fantastics ("*Fantastici*") and contributed to a collection of verse the academicians published in 1637. Salzilli's comparison between Milton and Homer, Vergil, and Tasso was flattery that the young Milton was happy to receive; after Milton's death, John Dryden echoed it in his verses attached to the portrait of Milton published in the 1688 Folio of *Paradise Lost*.

Milton may have exchanged poetry with Salzilli (Haan, Freeman). If he knew that Salzilli was ill, and sent him "*Ad Salsilli*" as a kind of get-well card, their acquaintance might have been close, but Salzilli is not among Milton's known Italian correspondents.

TEXT

There are no significant variants between *1645* and *1673*.

Works Cited

Freeman, James A. "Milton's Roman Connection: Giovanni Salzilli." *Milton Studies* 19 (1984): 87–104.

Haan, Estelle. "'Written encomiums': Milton's Latin Poetry in Its Italian Context." *Milton in Italy: Contexts, Images, Contradictions.* Ed. Mario A. DiCesare. Binghamton, NY: Medieval & Renaissance Texts and Studies, 1991. 521–47.

Ad Salsillum Poetam Romanum ægrotantem.

SCAZONTES.

O Musa gressum quæ volens trahis claudum,
  Vulcanioque tarda gaudes incessu,
Nec sentis illud in loco minus gratum,
Quàm cùm decentes flava Dëiope suras
Alternat aureum ante Junonis lectum.[1]   5
Adesdum & hæc s'is verba pauca Salsillo
Refer, cam na nostra cui tantum est cordi,
Quamque ille magnis prætulit immeritò divis.
Hæc ergo alumnus ille Londini Milto,[2]
Diebus hisce qui suum linquens nidum   10
Polique tractum, (pessimus ubi ventorum,
Insanientis impotensque pulmonis
Pernix anhela sub Jove exercet flabra)
Venit feraces Itali soli ad glebas,
Visum superbâ cognitas urbes famâ   15
Virosque doctæque indolem juventutis,
Tibi optat idem hic fausta multa Salsille,
Habitumque fesso corpori penitùs sanum;
Cui nunc profunda bilis infestat renes,
Præcordiisque fixa damnosùm spirat.   20

To Salzilli, a Roman Poet as He Lay Ill.

SCAZONS.[3]

O Muse who on your own trails a limping foot, and slow of step takes pleasure in limping like Vulcan,[4] thinking the limp no less attractive than when golden-haired Deiope[5] flashes her handsome calves, one at a time, next to the golden couch of Juno, stand by me, please, and, if you will, carry these few words to Salzilli, who takes my poetry so warmly to his heart, preferring it, undeservedly, to that of truly powerful poets.

These verses that foster-son of yours in London, Milton, sends to him—that same Milton who not long ago left his proper nest and his own portion of Heaven, where the worst of the winds, powerless to control its crazy breath, pants in cold blasts. He came to fruitful Italy, to see its highly reputed cities, its regal men, and to experience the fine sensibilities of its learned youth. He begs you for blessings, Salzilli, and prays that your recuperating body will become whole again. At the moment you are bilious and your kidneys ache.

---

[3]Scazons were verses in "limping" iambic meter, a form also called choliambus. Although the form was usually "mimetic, a deformed meter for the subject of depravity" (*New Princeton Encyclopedia of Poetry and Poetics*, "Choliambus"), Milton seems to be using it here to mimic or sympathize with physical disability, the illness of Salzilli.
[4]Vulcan, or Mulciber, was made lame by being thrown from Heaven by Jove (*Paradise Lost* 1.740; Elegy 7, 81–82).
[5]Known as one of the most beautiful of nymphs (Vergil, *Aeneid* 1.71–75).

---

[1]The comma of *1645* was corrected to a period in *1673*.
[2]The punctuation is a semicolon in *1645*.

Nec id pepercit impia quòd tu Romano
Tam cultus ore Lesbium condis melos.
O dulce divúm munus, O salus Hebes
Germana! Tuque Phœbe morborum terror
Pythone cæso, sive tu magis Pæan   25
Libenter audis, hic tuus sacerdos est.
Querceta Fauni, vosque rore vinoso
Colles benigni, mitis Evandri[6] sedes,
Siquid salubre vallibus frondet vestris,
Levamen ægro ferte certatim vati.   30
Sic ille charis redditus rursùm Musis
Vicina dulci prata mulcebit cantu.
Ipse inter atros emirabitur lucos
Numa, ubi beatum degit otium æternum,
Suam reclivis semper Ægeriam spectans.   35
Tumidusque & ipse Tibris hinc delinitus
Spei favebit annuæ colonorum:
Nec in sepulchris ibit obsessum reges
Nimiùm sinistro laxus irruens loro:
Sed fræna melius temperabit undarum,   40
Adusque curvi salsa regna Portumni.

That irreverent bile wouldn't spare you, though you are so cultured as to be able to create Greek poetry despite your Roman tongue. O sweet gift of the gods, Good Health, sister of Hebe; and Apollo, avenger of disease ever since you killed the Python,[7] you, Paean,[8] hear this in good humor. This man is a true priest of Faunus,[9] of the oak groves and hills of Rome, generous with wine, Evander's[10] home. If anything among your herbs can bring health, take it in the spirit of healthy competition to heal your sick poet. This being done, he, restored to the dear Muses, will once again sing his sweet song to the neighboring meadows. Numa himself will be amazed, in dark groves, where that immortal god lives his life of leisure, blessed, gazing forever, with his head inclined toward his beloved Egeria.[11] The Tiber, too, even though its flooding is calmed, will favor the farmers year by year: there will be no more rushing to attack kings in their tombs, unrestrained, with his left rein too slack, but rather he will govern more skillfully the reins of his waves, through all his course to Portumnus.[12]

---

[6]Printed as "Euandri" in *1645*.

[7]A monstrous serpent who had threatened Apollo's mother, Latona, before she gave birth to Diana and Apollo; as soon as he was born, Apollo killed Python with his arrows, then commemorated the event with the institution of the Pythian games.
[8]Apollo's name in his function as healer.
[9]The woodland god Faunus was the father of Latinus, who gave his name to the tribe of Latini, who were in turn supposed to have produced the language Latin (*Aeneid* 7.45–48).
[10]A native of Arcadia in Greece who was supposed to have founded a colony on the site of Rome (Vergil, *Aeneid* 8.100).
[11]Numa, second of the legendary kings of Rome, was supposed to have been civilized by conversations with the water nymph Egeria (Plutarch, "Numa" 4).
[12]In this case the sea is represented by the god Portumnus, usually associated with harbors. The Tiber River connected Rome with the sea and its port, Ostia; the river also occasionally flooded its left bank (Horace, *Odes* 1.2.13–20).

Mansus.

Milton wrote in the *Second Defense* that, while he was in Naples in November and December of 1638,

> . . . I was introduced by a certain Eremite Friar, with whom I had made the journey from Rome, to Giovanni Baptista Manso, Marquis of Villa, a man of high rank and influence, to whom the famous Italian poet, Torquato Tasso, dedicated his work on friendship. As long as I was there I found him a very true friend. He personally conducted me through the various quarters of the city and the Viceregal Court, and more than once came to my lodgings to call. When I was leaving he gravely apologized because even though he had especially wished to show me many more attentions, he could not do so in that city, since I was unwilling to be circumspect in regard to religion.   (Yale 4: 618)

The seventy-eight-year-old Manso was indeed a cultured gentleman, patron of the epic poet Torquato Tasso and the lyric poet Giambattista Marino. Tasso had composed poetry in Manso's house in the 1580s and 1590s, finishing the *Gerusalemme Conquistata* there in 1594. And Milton thought enough of the poetry of Marino to quote him in the prefatory material to the 1645 *Poems*. Marino's most famous poem, *L'Adone* (1623), a pastoral celebrating the love of Venus and Adonis, is alluded to in Milton's line 11 in *Mansus*.

When Milton visited the city, Naples still evoked memories of ancient Roman and modern poets, since it was associated with Vergil and Cicero among the ancients, and Sannazaro as well as Tasso and Marino among the moderns. Cumae, where the famous Sibyl was supposed to prophesy, was nearby, as was Pozzuoli (classical Puteoli), with bubbling hot springs that reminded visitors what Hell might look like.

Milton refers to such Neapolitan place names and mythological characters as Typhoeus, Parthenope, Arethusa, Pompeii, Setebo, and Capri (see Arthos 101–03) throughout his poetry and prose. His visit with Manso and his excursions in Naples put him in touch with the entire tradition of Latin and modern Italian epic poetry and set him thinking about writing a worthy national epic on the subject of England's great hero, King Arthur. Such an epic might be modeled on the various versions of *Jerusalem Delivered* that Tasso had written.

On the other hand, even Manso may have thought that Milton's fair complexion made him resemble an angel, his Protestantism and his English nationality made him a somewhat objectionable "Angle" (Haan 535). In the midst of complimenting his generous host, Milton's poem may also be a subtle assertion of the supremacy of English religion and poetry over that represented by Manso's patronage. At the end of the poem (535–36), an angelic Milton in an English heaven sings his own Protestant hymns of praise.

Works Cited

Arthos, John. *Milton and the Italian Cities*. London: Bowes, 1968.

Haan, Estelle. "'Written encomiums': Milton's Latin Poetry in Its Italian Context." *Milton in Italy: Context, Images, Contradictions*. Ed. Mario A. DiCesare. Binghamton: Medieval & Renaissance Texts & Studies, 1991. 521–47.

Revard, Stella P. *The Tangles of Neaera's Hair: The Making of the 1645 Poems*. Columbia: U of Missouri P, 1997.

Mansus.

Joannes Baptista Mansus Marchio Villensis vir ingenii laude, tum literarum studio, nec non & bellicâ virtute apud Italos clarus in primis est. Ad quem Torquati Tassi dialogus extat de Amicitiâ[1] scriptus; erat enim Tassi amicissimus; ab quo etiam inter Campaniæ principes celebratur, in illo poemate cui titulus Gerusalemme conquistata, *lib. 20.*

Fra cavalier magnanimi, è cortesi
Risplende il Manso——

Manso.

Giovanni Baptista Manso, Marquis of Villa, is a man preeminently famous among the Italians, for intellectual merit, devotion to literature, and warlike prowess. It was to him that Torquato Tasso addressed his Dialogue on Friendship, a dialogue still extant, for he was a close friend of Tasso. Tasso mentions him with high praise among the princes of Italy, in the poem entitled Gerusalemme Conquistata, *Book 20.*

Among knights magnanimous and courteous
Manso shines———

---

[1]The circumflex accent, indicating the ablative, was dropped in *1673*.

Is authorem Neapoli commorantem summâ benevolentiâ
prosecutus est, multaque ei detulit humanitatis officia.
Ad hunc itaque hospes ille antequam ab eâ urbe discede-
ret, ut ne ingratum se ostenderet, hoc carmen misit.

Hæc quoque Manse tuæ meditantur carmina laudi
Pierides, tibi Manse choro notissime Phœbi,
Quandoquidem ille alium haud æquo est dignatus honore
Post Galii cineres, & Mecænatis Hetrusci.
Tu quoque si nostræ tantùm valet aura Camœnæ,   5
Victrices hederas inter, laurosque sedebis.
Te pridem magno felix concordia Tasso
Junxit, & æternis inscripsit nomina chartis.
Mox tibi dulciloquum non inscia Musa Marinum
Tradidit, ille tuum dici se gaudet alumnum,   10
Dum canit Assyrios divûm prolixus amores;
Mollis & Ausonias stupefecit carmine nymphas.
Ille itidem moriens tibi soli debita vates
Ossa tibi soli, supremaque vota reliquit.
Nec manes pietas tua chara fefellit amici,   15
Vidimus arridentem operoso exære poetam.
Nec satis hoc visum est in utrumque, & nec pia cessant
Officia in tumulo, cupis integros rapere Orco,
Quà potes, atque avidas Parcarum eludere leges:
Amborum genus, & variâ sub sorte peractam   20
Describis vitam, moresque, & dona Minervæ;
Æmulus illius Mycalen qui natus ad altam
Rettulit Æolii vitam facundus Homeri.
Ergo ego te Cliûs & magni nomine Phœbi
Manse pater, jubeo longum salvere per ævum   25
Missus Hyperboreo juvenis peregrinus ab axe.

When the author visited Naples, Manso gave him un-
bounded good will, and did him many kindnesses,
born of his true humaneness. Therefore before he left
the city, the visitor sent this poem, that he might show
himself not ungrateful.

With these songs, the daughters of Pieria[2] are preparing carefully to praise you, Manso, well known to the choir of Phoebus; he has thought no one worthy of an equal honor, since the time when Gallus and Etruscan Maecenas[3] became dust. You, too—if my song has power great enough—will have a seat among the victors crowned with ivy and laurel. You joined hearts with mighty Tasso, and by doing so inscribed your names on everlasting scrolls. More recently the wise Muse gave you sweettongued Marini; he loved being called your fosterchild while he sang about the Assyrian loves of Venus and Adonis, and, noble poet that he was, he captivated the young women of Italy. As he lay dying, he left his body to you alone, entrusting his final wishes to you. Your loving devotion did not abuse his spirit: I have seen his eyes smiling from the beautiful bronze bust. That wasn't enough for both friends: your duties to them did not stop with their burial. You snatch them from the very doors of the underworld and cheat the fates by writing about their lineage, their personal highs and lows, their personalities, and their gifted intelligence. You are rival to Herodotus of lofty Mycale[4] as biographer of Aolian Homer. Therefore I wish you health in a long life, in the names of Clio and of mighty Phoebus. I speak as a young man from a foreign land, sent from the Hyperborean[5] quarter of the world.

---

[2]The Muses, associated as ever with the Pierian Spring in Thessaly.
[3]Maecenas (d. 8 BCE), the best-known Roman patron of the arts, benefactor to Vergil among others. Cornelius Gallus, friend of Vergil, commemorated him in his *Eclogue* 6.64–73.
[4]Herodotus, associated with the promontory Mycale, near Halicarnassus, in Ionia, where the historian was born.
[5]Northern. Geographically vague, although as Carey points out, Diodorus Siculus places the island of the Hyperboreans beyond the land of the Celts (1997 ed., 265n).

Nec tu longinquam bonus aspernabere Musam,[6]
Quæ nuper gelidá vix enutrita sub Arcto
Imprudens Italas ausa est volitare per urbes.
Nos etiam in nostro modulantes flumine cygnos   30
Credimus obscuras noctis sensisse per umbras,
Quà Thamesis latè[7] puris argenteus urnis
Oceani glaucos perfundit gurgite crines.
Quin & in has quondam pervenit Tityrus oras.
Sed neque nos genus incultum, nec inutile Phœbo,   35
Quà plaga septeno mundi sulcata Trione
Brumalem patitur longâ sub nocte Boöten.
Nos etiam colimus Phœbum, nos munera Phœbo
Flaventes spicas, & lutea mala canistris,
Halantemque crocum (perhibet nisi vana vetustas)   40
Misimus, & lectas Druidum de gente choreas.
(Gens Druides antiqua sacris operata deorum
Heroum laudes imitandaque gesta canebant)
Hinc quoties festo cingunt altaria cantu
Delo in herbosâ Graiæ de more puellæ   45
Carminibus lætis memorant Corineida Loxo,
Fatidicamque Upin, cum flavicomá Hecaërge
Nuda Caledonio variatas pectora fuco.
Fortunate senex, ergo quacunque per orbem
Torquati decus, & nomen celebrabitur ingens,   50
Claraque perpetui succrescet fama Marini,
Tu quoque in ora frequens venies plausumque virorum,
Et parili carpes iter immortale volatu.
Dicetur tum sponte tuos habitâsse[8] penates
Cynthius, & famulas venisse ad limina Musas: 55

Since you are so gracious, you will not scorn a Muse who comes from so far, and, though not well-nurtured under the frozen Bear,[9] has recently ventured a flight through the cities of Italy. I too believe I have heard swans through the dark shadows of night—swans singing on my own river, where the silvery Thames with its pure urns bathes its gray hair with the turbulent currents of the ocean. Our Tityrus, Chaucer, once visited your land.

But we English are not an uncultured people, or useless to Phoebus, in that region of the world which gives in to wintry Boötes during long nights and is furrowed by the Wagon with its seven-fold team.[10] We worship Phoebus too: we have sent him gifts, yellow ears of grain, and flame-colored apples in baskets, and fragrant crocus (unless that ancient story is inaccurate);[11] we sent too choirs chosen from the Druids. The Druids, a time-honored race, busy with the holy rites of the gods, used to sing the praises of heroes, the achievements worthy of imitation. This is why, whenever the maidens of Greece, after their custom, circle the altar on Delos, they sing joyful songs that mention Loxo, daughter of Corineus, and fatal prophet Upis, and Hecaerge, gods whose bare breasts were dyed with woad.[12]

Fortunate old gentleman! Wherever in the world the reputation and the name of Torquato is honored, and the fame of immortal Marini grows with new brightness, your name will come again and again to men's lips and you will fly to immortality with them. It will be said that in your day Apollo lived in your house and that the Muses were servants at your door.

---

[9]The constellation, to which Milton often attaches the northern climate of England (as compared with Italy).

[10]The constellation of Ursa Major, the Great Bear, was also supposed to look like a wagon with seven oxen yoked to it.

[11]Apollo's mother, Leto, was supposed to have been born on the island of the Hyperboreans (see Diodorus Siculus 2.47.2–3); hence Milton could make the association between followers of Apollo and Druid followers of Belin, also a god of healing (Carey, 1997 ed., 265n).

[12]Milton borrows scenes from Herodotus, *History* 4.33–35, and Callimachus *Hymns* 4.283–99 to establish a connection between Greek worship of Apollo at Delos and Hyperborean worship of Opis and Arge. Callimachus mentions the maidens Upis, Loxo, and Hecaerge, picturing them together in the process of worshiping on Delos. The woad is the blue stain, perhaps a kind of war paint, which distinguished the Britons according to Caesar, *Gallic Wars* 5.14. Corineus is the giant who was given the land of Cornwall, named for him, for defeating Gogmagog (Milton, *History of Britain*; Yale 5.16).

---

[6]Not capitalized in *1673*. Ben Jonson had famously described Shakespeare as "sweet Swan of *Avon*" (*Works*, ed. Herford and Simpson, 8: 392). Milton's allusion to Tityrus and to English poets as swans associated with the Thames links him with Chaucer, Shakespeare, and Jonson.

[7]*1673* does not preserve the accent mark.

[8]The circumflex was added in *1673*.

At non sponte domum tamen idem, & regis adivit
Rura Pheretiadæ cælo fugitivus Apollo;
Ille licet magnum Alciden susceperat hospes;
Tantùm ubi clamosos placuit vitare bubulcos,
Nobile mansueti cessit Chironis in antrum,   60
Irriguos inter saltus frondosaque tecta
Peneium prope rivum: ibi sæpe sub ilice nigrâ
Ad citharæ strepitum blandâ prece victus amici
Exilii duros lenibat voce labores.
Tum neque ripa suo, barathro nec fixa sub imo,   65
Saxa stetere loco, nutat Trachinia rupes,
Nec sentit solitas, immania pondera, silvas,
Emotæque suis properant de collibus orni,
Mulcenturque novo maculosi carmine lynces.
Diis dilecte senex, te Jupiter æquus oportet   70
Nascentem, & miti lustrarit lumine Phœbus,
Atlantisque nepos; neque enim nisi charus ab ortu
Diis superis poterit magno favisse poetæ.
Hinc longæva tibi lento sub flore senectus
Vernat, & Æsonios lucratur vivida fusos,   75
Nondum deciduos servans tibi frontis honores,
Ingeniumque vigens, & adultum mentis acumen.
O mihi si mea sors talem concedat amicum
Phœbæos decorâsse viros qui tam bene nôrit,[13]
Si quando indigenas revocabo in carmina reges,   80
Arturumque etiam sub terris bella moventem;
Aut dicam invictæ sociali fœdere mensæ,
Magnanimos Heroas, & (O modo spiritus adsit)
Frangam Saxonicas Britonum sub Marte phalanges.

Yet that same Apollo, running from Heaven, came without knowing where he was to the farm of King Admetus,[14] though Admetus had entertained the guest Hercules.

Whenever Apollo wanted relief from a noisy plowman, he retreated to the famous cave of the gentle Chiron,[15] amid the humid woodland pastures and wooded shades of the river Peneus. At his friend's asking, he would often sing music issuing from his anger to relieve the hardships of exile. Then the banks could not remain where they were supposed to be, and neither could the boulders fixed in the pit of Tartarus; the Trachinian cliff nodded to the music, no longer feeling the giant burden of its forests; the mountain ashes, dislodged, hurried down from their hills, and spotted lynxes were calmed by music never heard before.

Old man beloved by gods, Jupiter must have been on your side when you were born, and Phoebus and the good grandson of Atlas[16] both looked kindly on your birth, for, unless he is dear to the gods, a man will never have the chance to have the friendship of a mighty poet. This is why your old age remains as green as spring, and by its vigor it keeps its thread as long as Aeson's,[17] preserving your handsome face, your alert intellect, and your sharp, mature wit. May my fate give me a friend so fine, one who knows so well how to honor the true-hearted followers of Apollo, if I ever recall in my poetry the kings of my native land, and Arthur,[18] who caused wars even beneath the earth, or the noble-hearted heroes of the Round Table, made invincible by their fellowship. O may the spirit help me, as mighty Britons break Saxon battle formations.

---

[13]The circumflex was added in *1673*.

[14]Apollo was banished from Olympus for killing the Cyclopes. He served a sentence as herdsman to King Admetus of Pherae in Thessaly, son of Pheres. After his first wife died, Admetus married Alcestis and was granted immortality by Apollo, if he could find someone to die for him. Alcestis volunteered. Hence Milton connected the singing of Apollo at the court of Admetus with the death and resurrection of Alcestis, who figures so prominently in "Methought I saw my late espoused saint." Hercules, Admetus's guest, delivered Alcestis from the grave.

[15]The most civilized of the Centaurs, half men and half horses (Homer, *Iliad* 11.832). Milton attempts to locate the cave of Chiron on Mt. Pelion, not far from Pherae; he apparently invented the conversations between Apollo and Chiron (see Carey, 1997 ed., 266n); and he makes Apollo's music parallel that of Orpheus in its ability to arouse sympathy even in the underworld (Tartarus).

[16]Mercury, god of eloquence and son of Maia (*Paradise Lost* 5.285).

[17]Father of Jason, who was in turn famous as an Argonaut (as were Admetus and Hercules) and was the husband of Medea. When Aeson was old and infirm, Medea restored his youth by replacing his blood supply with an herbal infusion.

[18]Milton contemplates what seems to be an epic poem on the subject of King Arthur, though he did not list any subject having directly to do with Arthur in the lists of possible tragedies or heroic poems in the Trinity Manuscript (Columbia 18: 241–44).

Tandem ubi non tacitæ permensus tempora vitæ,   85
Annorumque satur cineri sua jura relinquam,
Ille mihi lecto madidis astaret ocellis,
Astanti sat erit si dicam sim tibi curæ;
Ille meos artus liventi morte solutos
Curaret parvâ componi molliter urnâ.   90
Forsitan & nostros ducat de marmore vultus,
Nectens aut Paphiâ myrti aut Parnasside lauri
Fronde comas, at ego securâ pace quiescam.
Tum quoque, si qua fides, si præmia certa bonorum,
Ipse ego cælicolûm semotus in æthera divûm,   95
Quò labor & mens pura vehunt, atque ignea virtus
Secreti hæc aliquâ mundi de parte videbo
(Quantum fata sinunt) & totâ mente serenùm
Ridens purpureo suffundar lumine vultus
Et simul æthereo plaudam mihi lætus Olympo.   100

At last when, having fully measured out my life, not without poetry, at a ripe old age, when I have given honor to the grave, then that friend would stand by me weeping, and it would be sufficient for me to say to him, "See to my memory."[19] He would be sure to have my remains saved nobly in a little urn. Perhaps he would have my features carved in marble, hair encircled by a wreath of myrtle from Paphos or laurel from Parnassus; and I will die safe and at peace. Then, if I can be sure of anything, and if the righteous really are rewarded, I will live in the home of the heavenly gods, the place where duty and a pure mind and burning virtue take a man, and watch the earth and its activity, if the Fates permit, from some corner of that distant world. With a smile from my soul and a bright flush in my face, I will joyfully celebrate myself in ethereal Olympus.

---

[19]The passage anticipates the stance of the surviving poet in both "Lycidas" and *Epitaphium Damonis*. Whether Milton knew of Charles Diodati's death when he wrote *Mansus* is a matter of continuing debate among biographers of Milton.

Epitaphium Damonis.

The *Epitaphium Damonis* is Milton's tribute to the memory of his friend Charles Diodati. Diodati, whose surname means "gift of God," was buried on August 28, 1638, in London, while Milton was traveling abroad in Italy. When Diodati died, Milton was quite possibly in Tuscany, his friend's ancestral homeland. As Cedric Brown has written, Milton's epitaph is "a poem in which the memory of his dead friend and a sense of Italy are entwined" ("Horatian" 335). Because it is a pastoral poem, the *Epitaphium Damonis* can easily be compared with the English pastoral elegy "Lycidas," except that Diodati was a much closer friend to the poet than was Edward King. Perhaps Milton chose to write in Latin in honor of the fact that he had often written to Diodati in Latin verse-letters: the two young men exchanged a witty, sometimes bashful, sometimes innocently intimate correspondence. *Epitaphium Damonis* is Milton's last letter to Diodati.

Milton had a number of debts to the Diodati family. Charles Diodati's father, the medical doctor Theodore Diodati, may have introduced the young Milton to the world of Italian language, literature, and music. Father and son probably introduced the young Milton to the world of medicine.

Milton would have found relatives of the English Diodatis not only in the Tuscan city of Lucca (Dorian 5) but throughout western Europe. In passing through Paris on his way to Italy, Milton could have met with Elie Diodati, friend to Galileo (Dorian 172–73), and when he stopped in Geneva on his way back to England, he visited with the eminent Protestant theologian and biblical commentator, Giovanni Diodati (Parker 714–15), with whom Charles Diodati had studied.

RENAISSANCE PASTORAL ELEGY

Latin pastoral and elegiac poetry by the famous author of *The Courtier*, Baldassare Castiglione, may have influenced Milton's poem. Castiglione's "Alcon" focuses on a friend whose moment of death is not witnessed by the poet, and there are a number of other parallels between the two elegies (Haan 524–25). Classical precedents include pastoral elegies by Theocritus (his lament for Daphnis), Moschus (lament for Bion), and Vergil (final eclogue). The collections of texts and critical essays on "Lycidas" by Elledge and Patrides both either print or allude to many of Milton's possible source materials in Latin pastoral elegy. Patrides reproduces the edition of H. W. Garrod and the excellent translation of Helen Waddell.

Though the poem is indeed a pastoral elegy in proper

Augustan Latin, Milton sends a Christian message to his reader in the final image of Diodati's celebration of the wedding feast described in Revelation 14.4: "These are they which were not defiled with women; for they are virgins." According to Renaissance commentaries on the passage, good Christian men who died before marrying were guaranteed an easy entrance to Heaven. The heavenly marriage pictured as the reward for living a virginal life was sometimes linked with the "marriage of the Lamb" described in Revelation 19.7. As John Leonard points out, "However unseasonable to modern ears, Milton's exaltation of Diodati's premarital chastity accords with the decorum of his age" ("Milton's Vow" 195). Leonard believes that Milton took no such vow of chastity himself, although he might praise the innocent Edward King or Charles Diodati. He certainly did not rule out marriage for himself or for other young men.

The poem has no easily defined structure, though the repetition of the refrain divides it according to a discrete pattern: some critics have seen the poem as divided into three or more parts. Woodhouse, for example, divided it into "movements" arranged in this order:

1. (18–34),   to introduce the subject;
2. (35–56),   to describe the poet's loneliness;
3. (57–123), to describe the procession of mourners and the poet's self-reproach for his absence;
4. (124–78), to introduce a "bold digression" on the effects of Milton's Italian journey on his plans for future poetry;
5. (179–97), to explain the relationship between the poetic plans, the visit to Italy, and the treasures the poet was planning to give to Diodati, had he lived; and
6. (198–219), a sudden return to Damon, in the process of becoming immortal in heavenly ecstasy (see *Variorum* 1: 291–93).

The refrain is used intermittently: it "develops quite different meanings at different points in the poem, and these progressive changes of meaning are among the most important structural elements of the poem" (Condee 107).

DEATH AND SINCERITY

Critics have questioned Milton's sincerity in mourning Diodati, just as they have, since Dr. Johnson, questioned the sincerity of his grief for Edward King in "Lycidas." Douglas Bush did not rate the elegy highly:

> . . . the elegy as a whole, though commonly placed at the head of his Latin poems, may be thought an

imperfect success. Unlike most pastoral elegies, it is wholly concerned with the feelings of a single mourner, the poet; and yet, in spite of or because of his very real grief, Milton is unwontedly diffuse and seems to pad the poem with pastoral artifice which is seldom re-created with anything like the power and intensity of *Lycidas*. (162)

But I see the grief Milton expressed in this Latin poem as not only "very real," but successful, and the imagery as not "padded." Memories of Florence and Lucca remind Milton of Diodati; memories of Manso remind him of plans for the future he had shared with Diodati; living flowers remind him of herbs with which the young physician could not heal himself; the loss of Diodati's future reminds him to make plans for his own immortality through poetry. I have no doubt that Milton loved his friend dearly and felt his death acutely. The comparison implied in Milton's naming his friend Damon (to his Pythias) unites the two as eternal symbols of friendship.

TEXT

There is a unique copy of an anonymous and undated edition in the British Library (C. 57.d.48) that contains only two significant verbal variants ("Londini" added at the end, and "onundus" for "oriundus" in the argument) but is much more lightly punctuated than *1645* or *1673*

(see Carey 268 for punctuation variants). Shawcross dates the edition "1640 (?)" or possibly "1639 (?)" ("The Date" 265). The text I follow is that of *1645*, which introduces what might be allegorical capitalization on the phrases "Ore Sacro" (207) and "Orgia Thyrso" (219), but avoids other forms of emphasis.

Works Cited

Condee, Ralph W. *Structure in Milton's Poetry: From the Foundations to the Pinnacles*. University Park: Pennsylvania SUP, 1974.

Dorian, Donald C. *The English Diodatis. A History of Charles Diodati's Family and His Friendship with Milton*. New Brunswick, NY: Rutgers UP, 1950.

Elledge, Scott. *Milton's "Lycidas" Edited to Serve as an Introduction to Criticism*. New York: Harper & Row, 1966.

Haan, Estelle. "'Written encomiums': Milton's Latin Poetry in Its Italian Context." *Milton in Italy: Contexts, Images, Contradictions*. Ed. Mario A. Di Cesare. Binghamton, NY: Medieval & Renaissance Texts & Studies, 1991. 521–47.

Leonard, John. "Milton's Vow of Celibacy: A Reconsideration of the Evidence." *Of Poetry and Politics: New Essays on Milton and His World*. Ed. P. G. Stanwood. Binghamton, NY: Medieval & Renaissance Texts & Studies, 1995. 187–201.

Patrides, C. A. *Milton's* Lycidas: *The Tradition and the Poem*. Columbia: U Missouri P, 1983.

Shawcross, John T. "The Date of the Separate Edition of Milton's 'Epitaphium Damonis.'" *Studies in Bibliography* 18 (1965): 262–65.

EPITAPHIUM

D A M O N I S.

ARGUMENTUM.[20]

THyrsis & Damon ejusdem viciniæ Pastores, eadem studia sequuti a pueritiâ amici erant, ut qui plurimùm. Thyrsis animi causâ profectus peregrè de obitu Damonis nuncium accepit. Domum postea reversus, & rem ita esse comperto, se, suamque solitudinem hoc carmine deplorat. Damonis autem sub personâ hîc intelligitur Carolus Deodatus ex urbe Hetruriæ Luca paterno genere oriundus, cætera Anglus; ingenio, doctrina, clarissimisque cæteris virtutibus, dum viveret, juvenis egregius.

EPITAPH FOR

D A M O N.

SUBJECT.

THyrsis and Damon, shepherds of the same neighborhood, friends since childhood, followed almost the same course of study. Thyrsis heard of Damon's death while abroad for self-improvement. When he had returned home and found that the news was true, he lamented his own loneliness in this song. Charles Diodati, seen here as Damon, was descended by his father's side from the Tuscan city of Lucca but in all other ways was English; endowed with virtues, he was, while he lived, a promising young man.

---

[20]As with the books of *Paradise Lost*, an "Argumentum," or a statement of the subject of the poem, is provided in prose. Both the Greek pastoral names of Thyrsis, used for the Attendant Spirit in the masque and again in "L'Allegro" 83, and Damon, one of a proverbial pair of male friends, Damon and Pythias, seem especially rich for Milton.

EPITAPHIUM

DAMONIS.

Himerides nymphæ (nam vos & Daphnin & Hylan,
Et plorata diu meministis fata Bionis)
Dicite Sicelicum Thamesina per oppida carmen:
Quas miser effudit voces, quæ murmura Thyrsis,
Et quibus assiduis exercuit antra querelis,   5
Fluminaque, fontesque vagos, nemorumque recessus,
Dum sibi præreptum queritur Damona, neque altam
Luctibus exemit noctem loca sola pererrans.
Et jam bis viridi surgebat culmus arista,
Et totidem flavas numerabant horrea messes,   10
Ex quo summa dies tulerat Damona sub umbras,
Nec dum aderat Thyrsis; pastorem scilicet illum
Dulcis amor Musæ Thusca retinebat in urbe.
Ast ubi mens expleta domum, pecorisque relicti
Cura vocat, simul assuetâ seditque sub ulmo,   15
Tum vero amissum tum denique sentit amicum,
Cœpit & immensum sic exonerare dolorem.

  Ite domum impasti, domino jam non vacat, agni.
Hei mihi! quæ terris, quæ dicam numina cœlo,
Postquam te immiti rapuerunt funere Damon;   20
Siccine nos linquis, tua sic sine nomine virtus
Ibit, & obscuris numero sociabitur umbris?
At non ille, animas virgâ quit dividit aureâ,
Ista velit, dignumque tui te ducat in agmen,
Ignavumque procul pecus arceat omne silentum.   25

EPITAPH FOR

DAMON.

NYmphs of Himera[1] (you who remember both Daphnis and Hylas and Bion's[2] sad destiny, long mourned for) sing your Sicilian song through towns along the Thames: What cries, what murmurs wretched Thyrsis[3] poured out, and with what constant questions he bothered the caves, rivers, wandering streams, and wooded recesses, lamenting Damon to himself—Damon prematurely taken. Nor could he banish deep night with grieving, now the stalk had risen twice with its green beard of grain,[4] and twice the yellow harvests were counted in granaries, since Damon's last day had taken him down among the shadows, yet still Thyrsis wasn't there; the love of a sweet Muse was surely detaining that shepherd in a Tuscan city. But when he had seen enough while abroad, and his anxiety for the flock he had left behind called him home, he sat beneath a familiar elm tree and at last felt the loss of his friend, and he began to express the immense loss thus.

  Go home unfed, lambs, your master has no time for you. Oh me! What earthly, what heavenly spirits can I address, since they have seized you with unremitting death; thus are you leaving us, thus your virtue will become anonymous and will become familiar with the number of obscure ghosts? But he who divides the souls with a golden wand[5] would not want this—he would lead you to those worthy of you, and keep away the silent, worthless, lazy herd.

---

[1]Water nymphs from the river Himera, in Sicily, one of the islands famous for pastoral poetry in the classical era. Compare "*Sicilian* Muse" in "Lycidas" 133.

[2]The Greek and Sicilian pastoral poet of the second century AD, credited in the Renaissance with writing the "Lament for Adonis," which was parallel in content to Milton's epitaph.

[3]Milton calls himself "Thyrsis" just as he takes the role of the "uncouth swain" in "Lycidas."

[4]Scholars have argued over what the two harvests might mean: John Shawcross, in "*Epitaphium Damonis* Lines 9–13 and the Date of Composition," *Modern Language Notes* 71 (1956): 322–24, writes that, since there were two wheat harvests in Tuscany in one summer, Milton must be referring to October–November 1639. Sergio Baldi, from the vantage point of living in Tuscany, denies Shawcross's assumption and suggests that autumn or winter 1640 is more likely ("The Date of Composition of *Epitaphium Damonis*," *N&Q* 25 [1978]: 508–09). Bush (*Variorum* 1: 298–99) believes that the passage has nothing to do with Italian harvests.

[5]In Greek and Latin mythology, the god Hermes or Mercury, who used a wand (*virga*) to divide the spirits (Vergil, *Aeneid* 4.242–43).

Ite domum impasti, domino jam non vacat, agni.
Quicquid erit, certè nisi me lupus antè videbit,
Indeplorato non comminuere sepulcro,
Constabitque tuus tibi honos, longúmque vigebit
Inter pastores: Illi tibi vota secundo　　　30
Solvere post Daphnin, post Daphnin dicere laudes
Gaudebunt, dum rura Pales, dum Faunus amabit:
Si quid id est, priscamque fidem coluisse, piúmque,
Palladiásque artes, sociúmque habuisse canorum.

　　Ite domum impasti, domino jam non vacat, agni.　35
Hæc tibi certa manent, tibi erunt hæc præmia Damon,
At mihi quid tandem fiet modò? quis mihi fidus
Hærebit lateri comes, ut tu sæpe solebas
Frigoribus duris, & per loca fœta pruinis,
Aut rapido sub sole, siti morientibus herbis?　　40
Sive opus in magnos fuit eminùs ire leones
Aut avidos terrere lupos præsepibus altis;
Quis fando sopire diem, cantuque solebit?

　　Ite domum impasti, domino jam non vacat, agni.
Pectora cui credam? Quis me lenire docebit　　45
Mordaces curas, quis longam fallere noctem
Dulcibus alloquiis, grato cùm sibilat igni
Molle pyrum, & nucibus strepitat focus, at malus auster
Miscet cuncta foris, & desuper intonat ulmo.

　　Ite domum impasti, domino jam non vacat, agni.　50
Aut æstate, dies medio dum vertitur axe,
Cum Pan æsculeâ somnum capit abditus umbrâ,
Et repetunt sub aquis sibi nota sedilia nymphæ.
Pastoresque latent, stertit sub sæpe[6] colonus,
Quis mihi blanditiásque tuas, quis tum mihi risus,　55
Cecropiosque sales referet, cultosque lepores?

　　Ite domum impasti, domino jam non vacat, agni.
At jam solus agros, jam pascua solus oberro,
Sicubi ramosæ densantur vallibus umbræ,
Hic serum expecto, supra caput imber & Eurus　60
Triste sonant, fractæque agitata crepuscula silvæ.

Go home unfed, lambs, your master has no time for you now. Whatever will be, this is sure: unless a wolf takes me first,[7] you will not crumble to dust in the grave without being mourned. Your reputation will outlive you, in the words of shepherds, for many years to come. They will be pleased to make their vows to you, second only to those to Daphnis, and to praise you, second only to Daphnis, as long as Pales[8] or Faunus loves the country; unless it is worthless to cherish old-fashioned faith, a pious man, the intelligence of an Athene, or a poet as comrade.

Go home unfed, lambs, your master has no time for you. These rewards surely remain, they are with you, Damon, but what will become of me? What faithful friend will stand by me, as you did, in the cold of winter and through regions full of snow, or under the searing sun, with plants dying of thirst? whether the task was to challenge full-grown lions, to frighten the greedy wolves away from the tall sheepfolds; who will be in the habit of soothing the day by speaking and singing?

Go home unfed, lambs, your master has no time for you. To whom should I open my heart? Who will teach me to calm eating cares,[9] or how to beguile a long night with talking? Your body will not become dust in the tomb unmourned. The sweet conversation in your honor, while the soft pear exhales steam while on the fire, will be constant among shepherds, as the hearth crackles with roasting nuts, and as the wicked south wind disorients people and thunders through the elms.

Go home unfed, lambs, your master has no time for you. Or in summer, when days are all noon, and Pan sleeps secreted in the shade of an oak tree, and nymphs return to their customary places beneath the waters, and shepherds bed down, and the farmer snores under the hedge, who will remind me of your charms, your laughter, your salty Athenian wit,[10] your cultured jokes?

Go home unfed, lambs, your master has no time for you. But now I wander alone in the fields, alone in pastures, wherever creeping shadows deepen in valleys, I wait for evening, the rain and the southeast wind whistling over my head sadly, together with the trees distorted by twilight.

---

[7]Referring to the superstition that if a man were seen by a wolf before he himself saw the wolf, he would become mute. As Carey points out, Vergil's *Eclogue* 9.53–54, illustrates the belief (1997 ed., 273n).
[8]Minor goddess associated with rural places, mentioned also in *Paradise Lost* 9.393. Her festival in April marked the "birthday" of Rome.
[9]Compare "L'Allegro" 135, from which I borrow the English phrase.
[10]"Athenian" seems less obscure than "Cecropian," but Cecrops was the first king of Attica and a mythological founder of Athens. Athenian or Attic wit is proverbial.

---

[6]Corrected from "sepe" in *1645* and *1673*.

Ite domum impasti, domino jam non vacat, agni.
Heu quàm culta mihi priùs arva procacibus herbis
Involvuntur, & ipsa situ seges alta fatiscit!
Innuba neglecto marcescit & uva racemo,   65
Nec myrteta juvant; ovium quoque tædet, at illæ
Mœrent, inque suum convertunt ora magistrum.

Ite domum impasti, domino jam non vacat, agni.
Tityrus ad corylos vocat, Alphesibœus ad ornos,
Ad salices Aegon, ad flumina pulcher Amyntas,   70
Hîc gelidi fontes, hîc illita gramina musco,
Hîc Zephyri, hîc placidas interstrepit arbutus undas;
Ista canunt surdo, frutices ego nactus abibam.

Ite domum impasti, domino jam not vacat, agni.
Mopsus ad hæc, nam me redeuntem forte notârat   75
(Et callebat avium linguas, & sydera Mopsus)
Thyrsi quid hoc? dixit, quæ te coquit improba bilis?
Aut te perdit amor, aut te malè fascinat astrum,
Saturni grave sæpe fuit pastoribus astrum,
Intimaque obliquo figit præcordia plumbo.   80

Ite domum impasti, domino jam non vacat, agni.
Mirantur nymphæ, & quid te Thyrsi futurum est?
Quid tibi vis? ajunt, non hæc solet esse juventæ
Nubila frons, oculique truces, vultusque severi,
Illa choros, lususque leves, & semper amorem   85
Jure petit, bis ille miser qui serus amavit.

Ite domum impasti, domino jam non vacat, agni.
Venit Hyas, Dryopéque, & filia Baucidis Aegle
Docta modos, citharæque sciens, sed perdita fastu,
Venit Idumanii Chloris vicina fluenti;   90
Nil me blanditiæ, nil me solantia verba,
Nil me, si quid adest, movet, aut spes ulla futuri.

Go home unfed, lambs, your master has no time for you. Alas, how my once cared-for fields are overgrown with weeds, and full-grown grain is weighed down, neglected. The unmarried grape withers on its untended vine, nor can the myrtle flourish; my sheep also upset me, they grieve and turn their faces from their master.

Go home unfed, lambs, your master has no time for you. Tityrus[11] calls the hazel tree; Alphesiboeus[12] the mountain ash; to the willows Aegon; handsome Amyntas to the rivers; here are the icy fountains, here the mossy turf, here the spring breezes, here arbutus mixes its whispers with those of quiet waves; they sing to the deaf; I vanish among the plant life.

Go home unfed, lambs, your master has no time for you. Mopsus added to these words, having by chance seen me returning (he once understood the language of birds and stars): "Thyrsis, what's this?" he said, "what is eating you? Either love damns you, or a malign planet bewitches you. The planet Saturn[13] often has caused trouble for shepherds, and its leaden rays of influence have pierced the inmost heart."

Go home unfed, lambs, your master has no time for you. The nymphs are filled with awe; they exclaim, "Thyrsis, what will become of you, what do you want for yourself? Young brows are not usually furrowed, eyes gloomy, face severe; youth should look for dance, light entertainment, and love. Twice wretched is the old man who falls in love."

Go home unfed, lambs, your master has no time for you. Hyas[14] came, Dryope,[15] and the daughter of Baucis,[16] Aegle, schooled in music modes and skilled at the harp, but ruined by pride; Chloris came, from near the Idumanean river; neither flattery nor words of comfort move me—nothing does—nor do I have hopes for the future.

---

[11]Not a reference to Chaucer here (as in *Mansus* 34), but more likely a generic name for any Greek shepherd.
[12]The three shepherds here all appear in Vergilian eclogues; Amyntas is handsome presumably because he is loved by Menalcas in Eclogue 3. Possibly this Amyntas makes Milton think of Tasso's *Aminta*, which is alluded to below with Mopsus, a character noted for his understanding of the language of birds in *Aminta* 11.2.459.
[13]Those born under the sign of Saturn were thought to possess a melancholy temperament and be saturnine. The metal associated with the god was lead: it mirrored a heavy and dense personality.
[14]A handsome young hunter killed by a lioness in Ovid, *Fasti* 5.169–82.
[15]Oechalian maiden noted for her beauty, changed into a lotus tree after having been deflowered by Apollo to produce the child Amphissos. She inadvertently plucked berries from a lotus that was in turn inhabited by another nymph (Ovid, *Metamorphoses* 9.325–93).
[16]Baucis and Philemon were the couple famous for their piety and generosity in Ovid, *Metamorphoses* 8.631–724, but no daughter is mentioned there. Aegle is a Naiad in Vergil, *Eclogues* 6.21; Chloris and the Idumanean river, as well as the musician Aegle, may represent real people known to Milton and Diodati.

Ite domum impasti, domino jam non vacat, agni.
Hei mihi quam similes ludunt per prata juvenci,
Omnes unanimi secum sibi lege sodales,　　　　95
Nec magis hunc alio quisquam secernit amicum
De grege, sic densi veniunt ad pabula thoes,
Inque vicem hirsuti paribus junguntur onagri;
Lex eadem pelagi, deserto in littore Proteus
Agmina Phocarum[17] numerat, vilisque volucrum　　　100
Passer habet semper quicum sit, & omnia circum
Farra libens volitet, serò sua tecta revisens,
Quem si fors letho objecit, seu milvus adunco
Fata tulit rostro, seu stravit arundine fossor,
Protinus ille alium socio petit inde volatu.　　　105
Nos durum genus, & diris exercita fatis
Gens homines aliena animis, & pectore discors,
Vix sibi quisque parem de millibus invenit unum,
Aut si sors dederit tandem non aspera votis,
Illum inopina dies quâ non speraveris horâ　　　110
Surripit, æternum linquens in sæcula damnum.

　　Ite domum impasti, domino jam non vacat, agni.
Heu quis me ignotas traxit vagus error in oras
Ire per aëreas rupes, Alpemque nivosam!
Ecquid erat tanti Romam vidisse sepultam?　　　115
Quamvis illa foret, qualem dum viseret olim,
Tityrus ipse suas & oves & rura reliquit;
Ut te tam dulci possem caruisse sodale,
Possem tot maria alta, tot interponere montes,
Tot sylvas, tot saxa tibi, fluviosque sonantes.　　　120
Ah certè extremùm licuisset tangere dextram,
Et bene compositos placidè morientis ocellos,
Et dixisse vale, nostri memor ibis ad astra.

　　Ite domum impasti, domino jam non vacat, agni.
Quamquam etiam vestri nunquam meminisse pigebit
Pastores Thusci, Musis operata juventus,
Hic Charis, atque Lepos; & Thuscus tu quoque Damon,
Antiquâ genus unde petis Lucumonis ab urbe.
O ego quantus eram, gelidi cum stratus ad Arni
Murmura, populeumque nemus, quà mollior herba,　130
Carpere nunc violas, nunc summas carpere myrtos,
Et potui Lycidæ certantem audire Menalcam.
Ipse etiam tentare ausus sum, nec puto multùm
Displicui, nam sunt & apud me munera vestra
Fiscellæ, calathique & cerea vincla cicutæ,　　　135
Quin & nostra suas docuerunt nomina fagos
Et Datis, & Francinus, erant & vocibus ambo
Et studiis noti, Lydorum sanguinis ambo.

Go home unfed, lambs, your master has no time for you. Ah me, how predictably the young bulls play together, all as one, a law unto themselves. Neither does one seek out one friend from the herd; in the same way, the wolves come to their food in packs, the hairy wild donkeys pair up like that; the law of the sea is the same, Proteus[18] counts his herd of seals on his deserted shore; and the least important bird, the sparrow, always has a mate, and flies freely to the grains, returning to his nest, and if he is killed by chance or a bird of prey hooks him with its beak, or a peasant gets him with an arrow, he soon seeks to fly with another. We humans are a hard lot, driven by wretched fates, alien in spirit, unbalanced in heart. In a thousand people, scarcely can we find one soul mate. If at last, not hardened to ignore our prayers, fate grants us one, then comes an unexpected hour, if one trusts time, and steals him away, leaving a permanent loss.

Go home unfed, lambs, your master has no time for you. Ah, what wandering fantasy led me to unknown lands to pass stone precipices and snowy Alps! Was it so valuable to see the tombs of Rome? Even if it was as when Tityrus[19] himself once saw it, who left his sheep and his countryside, just as I was able to be away from you, dear companion, that I could put between us deep seas, mountains, so many forests, so many rocks, so many resounding rivers. Oh, surely I should have been able to touch his right hand at the end, close his lids during his peaceful death, and to have said goodbye to him proceeding to heaven, remembering me.

Go home unfed, lambs, your master has no time for you. I will never regret remembering you, though, shepherds of Tuscany, young men devoted to the Muses; here was Charity, with Conviviality. You also were Tuscan, Damon, of ancient Luccan heritage. O how grand I was, when, stretched out by the murmuring cold Arno, and the poplar grove, the soft grass, I could gather violets, or the tips of myrtles, and I could hear Lycidas debating with Menalcas. I even dared to compete, nor do I think I displeased, for your poetic gifts are still with me, baskets of twigs, or wicker, and panpipes cemented together with wax. Dati and Francini[20] made native beeches resound with my name—both of them known for their poetry, both of them from good Lydian stock.

---

[17]"Seal." Shawcross has removed the capitalization from the Latin word, which possibly a compositor has imposed on it, thinking it is a proper name.

[18]The shape-shifting sea deity who tended various sea-creatures for Neptune (*Odyssey* 4.360).
[19]Following the *Variorum*, Carey (1997 ed., 276n) sees this Tityrus as an allusion to Vergil, *Eclogues* 1.26, but if that is true, "Tityrus" means at least three different persons in this poem and in *Mansus* 34. Yet the information given seems equally true of Chaucer.
[20]Carlo Dati and Antonio Francini both wrote encomia to Milton, and Milton remained in touch by mail with Dati after the visit to Italy.

Ite domum impasti, domino jam non vacat, agni.
Hæc mihi tum læto dictabat roscida luna,   140
Dum solus teneros claudebam cratibus hœdos.
Ah quoties dixi, cùm te cinis ater habebat,
Nunc canit, aut lepori nunc tendit retia Damon,
Vimina nunc texit, varios sibi quod sit in usus;
Et quæ tum facili sperabam mente futura   145
Arripui voto levis, & præsentia finxi,
Heus bone numquid agis? nisi te quid forte retardat,
Imus? & argutâ paulùm recubamus in umbra,
Aut ad aquas Colni, aut ubi jugera Cassibelauni?
Tu mihi percurres medicos, tua gramina, succos,   150
Helleborúmque, humilésque crocos, foliûmque hyacinthi,
Quasque habet ista palus herbas, artesque medentûm,
Ah pereant herbæ, pereant artesque medentûm
Gramina, postquam ipsi nil profecere magistro.
Ipse etiam, nam nescio quid mihi grande sonabat   155
Fistula, ab undecimâ jam lux est altera nocte,
Et tum forte novis admôram labra cicutis,
Dissiluere tamen rupta compage, nec ultra
Ferre graves potuere sonos, dubito quoque ne sim
Turgidulus, tamen & referam, vos cedite silvæ.   160
      Ite domum impasti, domino jam non vacat, agni.
Ipse ego Dardanias Rutupina per æquora puppes
Dicam, & Pandrasidos regnum vetus Inogeniæ,
Brennúmque Arviragúmque duces, priscúmque Belinum,
Et tandem Armoricos Britonum sub lege colonos;   165
Tum gravidam Arturo fatali fraude Jögernen
Mendaces vultus, assumptáque Gorlöis arma,
Merlini dolus. O mihi tum si vita supersit,
Tu procul annosa pendebis fistula pinu
Multùm oblita mihi, aut patriis mutata camœnis   170
Brittonicum strides, quid enim? Omnia non licet uni
Non sperasse uni licet omnia, mi satis ampla
Merces, & mihi grande decus (sim ignotus in ævum
Tum licet, externo penitúsque inglorius orbi)

Go home unfed, lambs, your master has no time for you. These things were spoken to me by the dewy moon while, happy, I enclosed the young lambs in wicker. Oh, how often did I say (even after you became ashes) now Damon is singing, or setting his nets for a hare, now he weaves willow twigs for various tasks. Forgetting your death, I dwelt on scenes from the future I tenderly hoped for, and imagined were realities. Oh, good friend, what are you doing? If you are not busy, let us go stretch out in the complete or mottled shade, either by the waters of the Colne,[21] or where the lands of Cassibelaunus lay. You will run through your medical remedies for me, your herbs—your hellebore, your humble crocus, sprig of hyacinth, what plants the marsh holds, and the physician's pharmacy. Oh, let the plants perish, and medic arts and herbs; they have done nothing for their master. And I—for my pipe was playing some lofty piece, I don't know, some eleven nights ago—I had by chance set my lips to a new set of panpipes; nevertheless, when their binding broke, they could not carry a serious tune. I fear as well that I am being pretentious, yet I will sing in that mode. Let me pass on, woods.[22]

Go home unfed, lambs, your master has no time for you. I myself will sing the ships of Troy through the Rutupian Sea, the old kingdom of Inogene,[23] daughter of Pandrasus, the chieftains Brennus and Arviragus, and old Belinus, and finally the Amorican settlers, under the law of the Britons, next Igraine pregnant with Arthur by fatal fraud—Gorlois's counterfeit face and false arms, the fakery of Merlin.[24] Oh if life remains, you my pipe will hang at some distance on an ancient pine tree forgotten by me, or, transformed, you will shriek out harshly a tale of Britain in English.[25] What then? One man can't do everything, nor can one hope to. I will have enough of a reward, a great glory (even if I remain forever unknown, inglorious to the outside world),

---

[21]A tributary of the Thames River that flows near the village of Horton, where Milton's father maintained a home. The British war-lord Cassivellaunus, mentioned by Julius Caesar in the *Gallic Wars* 5.11, ruled over a territory that included what is now Buckinghamshire, which is where Horton is located. For the territory of "Cassibilan," see Milton's *History of Britain*, Yale 5.53.

[22]Apparently this rejection of the woods represents a break with the pastoral mode and a transition into the heroic subject matter and high tone of heroic poetry discussed in the next section of the poem.

[23]A list of potential subjects for noble poems on British themes derived from the history of Geoffrey of Monmouth, as with Imogen, the Trojan Brutus's wife, a link between England and Troy (1.9–11).

[24]Geoffrey of Monmouth tells the story of how Uther Pendragon beget his son, who will become King Arthur, through a disguise created by Merlin. Deceiving Igraine, Uther appears to her as her former husband, Gorlois, King of Cornwall (8.19).

[25]He will hang up his shepherd's pipe in order to tell nobler stories.

Si me flava comas legat Usa, & potor Alauni,   175
Vorticibúsque frequens Abra, & nemus omne Treantæ,
Et Thamesis meus ante omnes, & fusca metallis
Tamara, & extremis me discant Orcades undis.

    Ite domum impasti, domino jam non vacat, agni.
Hæc tibi servabam lentâ sub cortice lauri,   180
Hæc, & plura simul, tum quæ mihi pocula Mansus,
Mansus Chalcidicæ non ultima gloria ripæ
Bina dedit, mirum artis opus, mirandus & ipse,
Et circùm gemino cælaverat argumento:
In medio rubri maris unda, & odoriferum ver   185
Littora longa Arabum, & sudantes balsama silvæ,
Has inter Phœnix divina avis, unica terris
Cæruleùm fulgens diversicoloribus alis
Auroram vitreis surgentem respicit undis.
Parte alia polus omnipatens, & magnus Olympus,   190
Quis putet? hic quoque Amor, pictæque in nube pharetræ,
Arma corusca faces, et spicula tincta pyropo;
Nec tenues animas, pectúsque ignobile vulgi
Hinc ferit, at circùm flammantia lumina torquens
Semper in erectum spargit sua tela per orbes   195
Impiger, & pronos nunquam collimat ad ictus,
Hinc mentes ardere sacræ, formæque deorum.

if yellow-haired Ouse[26] reads my poetry, and he who drinks from the Alaun, the Humber full of whirlpools, and all the woods of Trent, but before all of them my Thames, and the Orkneys in the distant seas hear me.

Go home unfed, lambs, your master has no time for you. I was saving these things under the soft bark of a laurel, these and more, at the same time those two cups that Manso[27] gave me—not the least glory of the Neapolitan shore, a wonderful work of art, himself a wonder, he had them engraved with a two-fold theme, in the middle the waves of the Red Sea, and the spice-smelling spring, the long coastline of Arabia, the woods sweating balsam, in which the Phoenix, eternal bird, unique on earth, gleaming sky-blue with varicolored wings, watches Aurora riding glassy waves. In another part of the design are the wide-reaching sky and great Olympus. Here—who would have thought it?—is Eros, his quiver encircled by a cloud, his armor gleaming, his torches and arrows gleaming golden bronze; for this reason he does not strike the inconsequential people or the uncultured herd, but, whirling his fiery eyes, he fires constant arrows upward through the spheres;[28] they inflame the minds of the holy, and kindle even the gods.

---

[26]A series of English rivers derived in part from Camden's *Brittania* and perhaps from Drayton's *Poly-Olbion*, all of which add up to the celebration of Milton's native land. The Ouse was known for yellow sand; the Humber would swirl because it is tidal; the Tamar, being in Cornwall, might contain tin from the mines located there.

[27]Scholars have been trying to determine if the cups supposedly given to Milton were really cups or whether they were in reality two books. Theocritus 1.29–56 provided a description of a cup (perhaps itself an imitation of the epic description of a shield containing a narrative picture). Michele De Filippis, in "Milton and Manso: Cups or Books?" (*PMLA* 51 [1936]: 745–56, argues that the "cups" are two of Manso's books, given as a token to Milton upon his leaving Naples.

[28]For the process of translation to the skies (an apotheosis, in Christian terms) or of a metamorphosis of a human being into a constellation, see Alastair Fowler, *Time's Purpled Masquers: Stars in the Afterlife in Renaissance English Literature* (Oxford: Clarendon, 1996).

Tu quoque in his, nec me fallit spes lubrica Damon,
Tu quoque in his certè es, nam quò tua dulcis abiret
Sanctáque simplicitas, nam quò tua candida virtus? 200
Nec te Lethæo fas quæsivisse sub orco,
Nec tibi conveniunt lacrymæ, nec flebimus ultrà,
Ite procul lacrymæ, purum colit æthera Damon,
Æthera purus habet, pluvium pede reppulit arcum;
Heroúmque animas inter, divósque perennes, 205
Æthereos haurit latices & gaudia potat
Ore Sacro. Quin tu cœli post jura recepta
Dexter ades, placidúsque fave quicúnque vocaris,
Seu tu noster eris Damon, sive æquior audis
Diodotus, quo te divino nomine cuncti 210
Cœlicolæ norint, sylvísque vocabere Damon.
Quòd tibi purpureus pudor, & sine labe juventus
Grata fuit, quòd nulla tori libata voluptas,
En etiam tibi virginei servantur honores;
Ipse caput nitidum cinctus rutilante corona, 215
Lætáque[29] frondentis gestans umbracula palmæ
Æternùm perages immortales hymenæos;
Cantus ubi, choreisque furit lyra mista beatis,
Festa Sionæo bacchantur & Orgia Thyrso.

FINIS.

You are also among these—nor am I deceived, Damon—you also are among these, surely, for where else might your sweet and holy simplicity have gone, where else your shining virtue? Neither would it be proper to seek you in Lethe's Orcus:[30] there's nothing here for tears, nor shall I shed them any more. Away tears, Damon lives in pure ether,[31] he stands above the rainbow; among the spirits of heroes and immortal gods, he drinks the nectar of heaven, and drinks in their joy with his sacred mouth. But you, Damon, be present after the rites of Heaven are received; please favor me, whether you will be known as our Damon, or more fairly Diodati, by which divine name all in Heaven will know you, and in the woods you will still be called Damon. Because the blush of modesty was all you knew, and because your youth was without blame, because you never married, likewise the honors of virginity are retained for you; you yourself, with head encircled with a shining crown and carrying the happy palm-fronds, will forever take part in the marriage celebration; where song joined with the harp rage in blessed dance, and orgies like those of Bacchus under the Thyrsus of Sion.[32]

END.

---

[29]Corrected from "Letáque" in *1645* and *1673*.

[30]Orcus is the classical underground world, equivalent to the Christian Hell, and Lethe one of its rivers.

[31]Diodati is not in the underworld but in the ethereal kingdom of the Christian Heaven. The movement from pagan to Christian may indicate a turn toward the high seriousness of dealing with death in universal Christian terms, rather than (Milton thought) the limited understanding of classical pastoral or epic.

[32]The passage in Revelation 14.1–5 being interpreted here is as follows: "And I looked, and, lo, a Lamb stood on the mount Sion, and with him an hundred forty and four thousand, having his Father's name written in their foreheads. And I heard a voice from heaven, as the voice of many waters, and as the voice of a great thunder: and I heard the voice of harpers harping with their harps: And they sung as it were a new song before the throne, and before the four beasts, and the elders: and no man could learn that song but the hundred and forty and four thousand, which were redeemed from the earth. These are they which were not defiled with women; for they are virgins. These are they which follow the Lamb whithersoever he goeth. These were redeemed from among men, being the firstfruits unto God and to the Lamb. And in their mouth was found no guile: for they are without fault before the throne of God." For such an apotheosis as planned for Edward King, see the ending of "Lycidas."

On The Engraver of His Portrait. (1645)

Milton played a rather cruel joke on William Marshall, the engraver of the portrait which appears facing the title page of the 1645 *Poems*. The engraver was forced to engrave an insulting poem in Greek, presumably a language he could not understand, beneath his ugly attempt at a likeness of the poet (Hale).

Parker's severe judgment may be justified: "the face is that of a sour old fellow with a double chin and pockets under his eyes, looking exceedingly silly and trying to hide what might be a withered arm" (289).

Work Cited

Hale, John K. "Milton's Greek Epigram." *Milton Quarterly* 16 (1982): 8–9.

In Effigiei eius Sculptor

Ἀμαθεῖ γεγράφθαι χειρὶ τνήδε μὲν εἰκόνα
Φαίης τάχ ἄν, πρὸς εἶδος αὐτοφυὲς βλέπων
Τὸν δ᾽ἐκτυπωτὸν οὐκ ἐπιγνόντες φίλοι
Γελᾶτε φαύλου δυσμίμημα ζωγράφου.

On the Engraver of his Portrait.

This likeness you would, perhaps, say had been graven by an unskillful hand, were you to look at the shape that nature made. But since, good friends, you know not him whose face is modeled here, you laugh at this poor image by a worthless artist.

POEMS, &c.

UPON

Several Occasions.

BY

Mr. *JOHN MILTON:*

Both ENGLISH and LATIN, &c.
Composed at several times.

With a small Tractate of

EDUCATION
To Mr. HARTLIB.

LONDON,
Printed for *Tho. Dring* at the *Blew Anchor*
next *Mitre Court* over against *Fetter
Lane* in *Fleet-street.*   1673.[1]

---

[1]I have reconstructed the title page of the "*Blew Anchor*" second issue of Milton's 1673 *Poems* (John Shawcross, *Milton: A Bibliography for the Years 1624–1700* [Binghamton, NY: Medieval & Renaissance Texts & Studies, 1984]: item 314, p. 85). The "&c." in the title implies the addition of the prose tract *Of Education.* The title page also seems to stress the importance of the Latin as well as the English poetry, and the fact that many of the poems are dated ("Composed at several times"). Unlike the description on the title page of *1645,* where the Poems are just poems, here they are Poems "upon Several Occasions." In both title pages, Milton is "Mr.," writing as an ordinary citizen, without an "Esq." to emphasize his gentlemanly status.

"On the Death of a Fair Infant"
(1628)

Though Milton's "Anno ætatis 17," meaning "in the year I was seventeen," would place the composition of the poem from December 1625 to December 1626, Parker discovered that Anne Phillips, the subject of the poem, was buried on January 22, 1628. Though Carey is in favor of an earlier date, Parker's evidence would indicate that the poem is close to the Nativity Ode and the Latin *Naturam non pati senium* in date of composition. This seems to be substantiated by the poem's themes and versification. John Shawcross's supposition may be correct, that the compositor of *1673* probably confused "17" and "19" in what we presume to be the handwritten copy he was following.

In poetic style and stanza pattern, Milton is more indebted to Spenser, to Josuah Sylvester, and possibly to Phineas Fletcher than to the schools of Ben Jonson or John Donne, though the imagery is at times close to metaphysical (as with "thy beauties lie in wormie bed" in 31). The imagery is also erotic, something of a curiosity in a poem on the death of a child. The poem is also academic in the sense that at least one critic has found elements in it of classical oration (Wilson). The rhyme royal stanzas (AB AB BCC) end in a Spenserian flourish, with an Alexandrine, six-beat line; the form of the poem may also represent Milton's earliest attempt at a Pindaric ode (Revard 56, 59).

Critics debate what the death of his sister's infant daughter might have meant to the young Milton, but obviously grief and mortality provided subject matter for many of Milton's youthful poems. The grief is temporary, however, since it leads to the consolation of a new pregnancy and a child to come—emotional relief for the mother, at least. The imagery of the poem is artificial and ornamental, but most critics would agree that it is energetic and successful within the restrictions of its stanza form. Many of its idioms and some of its images will be polished and refined to appear again, reconditioned, in Milton's mature poetry.

TEXT

The only text available is that of *1673*. Though there are a few careless typographical errors in that text (such as "cown'd" for "crown'd"), and a few un-Miltonic spelling forms (as with "poast"), elisions are handled skillfully, as are hyphenated compounds ("heav'n-lov'd innocence"), and the text seems faithful to Milton's known orthographical habits.

Works Cited

Revard, Stella P. *Milton and the Tangles of Neaera's Hair: The Making of the 1645* Poems. Columbia: U of Missouri P, 1997.

Wilson, Gayle Edward. "Milton's Praise of 'A Fair Infant.'" *Milton Quarterly* 22 (1988): 307.

Anno ætatis 17.
On the Death of a fair Infant dying of a Cough.

I.

O Fairest flower no sooner blown° but blasted,
   Soft silken Primrose fading timelesslie,
Summers chief honour if thou hadst out-lasted,
Bleak winters force that made thy blossome drie;
For he being amorous on° that lovely die°
   That did thy cheek envermeil,° thought to kiss
But kill'd alas, and then bewayl'd his fatal bliss.

IN BLOOM

IN LOVE WITH   DYE   5
MAKE VERMILLION

II.

For since grim *Aquilo*[1] his charioter
By boistrous rape th' *Athenian* damsel got,
He thought it toucht his Deitie full neer,   10

---

[1]Milton makes Aquilo, the north wind usually called Boreas, into the charioteer of Winter. Boreas was a rejected suitor of Orithyia, daughter to Erechtheus, king of the city-state of Athens. Scorned because he was from Thrace, Boreas carried Orithyia off to his mountainous region by force (Ovid, *Metamorphoses* 6.682–713). One would normally expect the proper name to be in italics, but it was not printed so in *1673*; as also with "Athenian," just below. I have converted both to italics.

If likewise he some fair one wedded not,
Thereby to wipe away th' infamous blot,
   Of long-uncoupled bed, and childless eld,°   OLD AGE
Which 'mongst the wanton gods a foul reproach was held.

III.

So mounting up in ycie-pearled carr,[2]   15
Through middle empire of the freezing aire[3]
He wandered long, till thee he spy'd from farr,
There ended was his quest, there ceast his care.
Down he descended from his Snow-soft chaire,°   CHARIOT
   But all unwares with his cold-kind embrace   20
Unhous'd thy Virgin Soul from her fair biding place.

IV.

Yet art thou not inglorious in thy fate;
For so *Apollo*, with unweeting hand
Whilome° did slay his dearly-loved mate   ONCE IN THE PAST
Young *Hyacinth* born on *Eurotas* strand[4]   25
Young *Hyacinth* the pride of *Spartan* land;
   But then transform'd him to a purple flower[5]
Alack that so to change thee winter had no power.

V.

Yet can I not perswade me thou art dead
Or that thy coarse° corrupts in earths dark wombe.   CORPSE   30
Or that thy beauties lie in wormie bed,
Hid from the world in a low delved[6] tombe;
Could Heav'n for pittie thee so strictly doom?
   Oh no? for something in thy face did shine
Above mortalitie that shew'd thou wast divine.   35

VI.

Resolve me then oh Soul most surely blest
(If so it be that thou these plaints° dost hear)   CRIES OF SORROW
Tell me bright Spirit where e're thou hoverest
Whether above that high first-moving Spheare[7]
Or in the Elisian fields (if such there were.)   40
   Oh say me true if thou wert mortal wight
And why from us so quickly thou didst take thy flight.

VII.

Wert thou some Starr which from the ruin'd roofe

---

[2]Chariot covered with pearls of ice. "Ycie-pearled" might echo Sylvester's *Divine Weekes* 2.3.1.293, "Ice-pearl."

[3]The heavens were divided into three regions, the middle one sometimes reserved for demonic activities or Christ's judgment at the end of time (*Paradise Regain'd* 2.117; Nativity Ode 164).

[4]Probably "*Eurota's*" in *1673* was an error for "*Eurotas*," as noted first by Newton.

[5]The hyacinth flower is pictured, red as blood, in Lycidas 106, supposedly inscribed with a sign of Apollo's grief. The allusion is to a homosexual passion between god and mortal. The west wind, Zephyr, was jealous because he was in love with Hyacinthus as well and caused a quoit that Apollo had thrown to fly at Hyacinthus and kill him, upon which Apollo generated the flower from his blood and transformed him into a constellation. Adam, in *Paradise Lost*, has "Hyacinthin Locks" (4.301).

[6]Presumably a tomb below ground, "delved," or dug.

[7]The Primum Mobile, or most-distant sphere, thought to provide motions to the other spheres within an earth-centered universe.

Of shak't Olympus by mischance didst fall;
Which carefull *Jove* in natures true behoofe
Took up, and in fit place did reinstall?
Or did of late earths Sonnes besiege the wall
   Of sheenie[8] Heav'n, and thou some goddess fled
Amongst us here below to hide thy nectar'd[9] head.

VIII.

Or wert thou that just Maid who once before
Forsook the hated earth, O tell me sooth
And cam'st again to visit us once more?
Or wert thou[10] that sweet smiling Youth!
Or that crown'd[11] Matron sage white-robed truth?
   Or any other of that heav'nly brood
Let down in clowdie throne[12] to do the world some good.

IX.

Or wert thou of the golden-winged hoast,
Who having clad thy self in humane weed,°
To earth from thy præfixed seat didst poast,°
And after short abode flie back with speed,
As if to shew what creatures Heav'n doth breed,
   Thereby to set the hearts of men on fire
To scorn the sordid world, and unto Heav'n aspire.

X.

But oh why didst thou not stay here below
To bless us with thy heav'n-lov'd innocence,
To slake his wrath whom sin hath made our foe
To turn Swift-rushing black perdition hence,
Or drive away the slaughtering pestilence,[13]
   To stand 'twixt us and our deserved smart°
But thou canst best perform that office where thou art.

XI.

Then thou the mother of so sweet a child
Her false imagin'd loss cease to lament,
And wisely learn to curb thy sorrows wild;
Think what a present thou to God hast sent,
And render him with patience what he lent;[14]
   This if thou do he will an off-spring give,

45

50

55

60

65

70

75

CLOTHING

POST, TRAVEL QUICKLY

PAIN CAUSED BY A WOUND

---

[8]Milton invented the word, according to the *OED*. It seems to mean "having a high gloss or sheen."

[9]Lycidas also has a head washed with nectar (175), which suggests a kind of anointing with fluid that helps to confer immortality (nectar and ambrosia are the traditional drink and food of the Olympian gods). Milton associates nectar with angels in *Paradise Lost* 5.633. John Shawcross, in "Milton's Nectar: Symbol of Immortality," *English Miscellany* 16 (1965): 131–41, discusses the image recurring in Milton's early poetry, in terms of classical and Christian significance.

[10]The eighteenth-century editor Thomas Warton noted that the line is imperfect metrically, lacking a disyllable, and Shawcross among others has inserted "Mercy" at this point. But the *Variorum* editors point out that Peace might work better, if not Virtue, although one has one syllable and the other two, and both are gendered as female in Christian iconography (2.1: 132–33). Lacking evidence, I have left the line as it is in *1673*, as does Carey, but Campbell inserts "[Mercy.]"

[11]*1673* has "cown'd." Editors emend to "crown'd."

[12]Like a figure in a masque (the Attendant Spirit in the Ludlow masque "descends or enters," in one version of the text) or a figure in a baroque painting, say by Rubens or Tiepolo.

[13]The plague, which often decimated the population of London throughout Milton's career.

[14]God loaned the child to her mother; the return of the child due to death, then, is not so painful.

Sonnet XI.
"A Book was writ"
(1647?)

The sonnets numbered XI and XII in *1673* were both numbered 12, apparently, in the Trinity Manuscript. On the leaf of the Trinity Manuscript on which the two versions of the poems appear together, Milton wrote, "these sonnets follow ye 10. in ye printed booke," followed by "On the detraccon which followed upon my writeng certaine treatises." On the earlier version of "I did but prompt," Milton had written "on the ~~detraction~~ wch follow'd .^{up}on my writing certain treatises."

Milton had also written an earlier version of "A book was writ," in which a number of corrections were entered. For instance, that version began "I writt a book of late call'd Tetrachordon, / and weav'd it close both matter, form, & stile, / It went off well about ye town a while, / numbring good wits; but now is seldom por'd on." Milton changed active voice to passive in the first sentence, and he changed the colloquial "It went off well about ye town" to "the subject new; it walk'd ye town." And he changed "wits" to "intellects."

Though the sonnet is in a conventional Petrarchan rhyme scheme, hence associated with love poetry, it is topical and satirical, making gentle fun of Scottish names hard to pronounce, of readers lined up at bookstalls in London who say "Bless us!" when they can't pronounce a name. He even enjoys tricks like splitting the London place name "Mile- /end" between two lines. Rhymes like "por'd on" and "word on" or "Gallasp" and "gasp" and "Asp" are meant to be funny. Though he may not be violating the genre of the Petrarchan sonnet, Milton certainly helps to expand its boundaries.

The poet Milton is reacting with good humor to the almost universally negative reception of his prose divorce treatises, *The Doctrine and Discipline of Divorce*, *Tetrachordon*, *The Judgement of Martin Bucer*, and *Colasterion*. Those who attacked Milton were an ecumenical mixture of Puritans and Anglicans. Sonnet 11 "complains with wry humour, not of the opposition to [*Tetrachordon*], but of neglect, and of the ignorance which cannot be brought to understand even the title" (*Variorum* 2.2: 389).

TEXT

The *1673* version is not carefully printed, with two corrections listed in the *Errata*. I have used the later version found in the Trinity Manuscript as the primary source of my text, with constant reference to the earlier manuscript version and to the printed text of *1673*.

XI.

A Book was[1] writ of late call'd *Tetrachordon*;
  And wov'n close,[2] both matter, form and stile;
  The Subject new: it walk'd the Town° a while,
  Numbring good intellects; now seldom por'd on.
Cries the stall-reader, bless us! what a word on
  A title page is this! and some in file
  Stand spelling fals,[3] while one might walk to Mile-
End Green. Why is it[4] harder Sirs then Gordon,
Colkitto,[5] or Macdonnel, or Galasp?[6]
  Those rugged names to our like mouths grow sleek[7]
  That would have made *Quintilian*[8] stare and gasp.

LONDON

5

10

---

[1]Written as "was was" in *1673* and not corrected in the Errata.
[2]The image of weaving applies to the four cords of the title *Tetrachordon*, which in turn referred to the four places in Scripture which "treat of Mariage, or nullities in Mariage" (title page of *Tetrachordon*).
[3]Spelling out each letter one by one (semiliterate form of finger-reading, touching letter by letter).
[4]The "it" is supplied from the Errata.
[5]Corrected from "Coliktto" to "Colkitto" by the Errata.
[6]All these Scottish names or nicknames may refer to the same person (*Variorum* 2.2: 391); the point is that all the names seem barbarous and ugly to an Englishman. Quintilian, *Institutes* 1.5.8, may be noted because he was in favor of euphony in making names (8.3), a practice that Milton would follow with respect to names like "Dalila."
[7]The line in the first Trinity Manuscript version of the poem read "those barbarous names to our like mouths grow sleek," with "barbarous" struck through and "rough-hewn" added above, then, in the right margin, "rough hewn" struck out, with "rugged" replacing it. The imagery in "like mouths grow sleek" is puzzling, since the mouths presumably do not resemble the barbarous names they pronounce.
[8]The Roman rhetorician Quintilian (d. AD 95) was well known for writing about the corruption of elegance in the Latin language. His *Institutiones Oratoricae* discuss oratory and rhetoric in greater detail than that of any treatise since Aristotle's *On Rhetoric*.

Thy age, like ours, O Soul of Sir *John Cheek*,[9]
  Hated not Learning wors then Toad or Asp;
  When thou taught'st *Cambridge*, and King *Edward* Greek.[10]

Sonnet 12.
"I did but prompt the age."
"On the same."
(1646)

The title "*On the same*" refers not just to *Tetrachordon* as the subject, but to all the divorce tracts. As a package, the divorce tracts were part of a Miltonic plan to restore or install domestic, civil, and religious liberty in England as he would set it forth in the *Second Defense of the English People*. The sonnet makes a distinction familiar to all readers of Milton's prose, that between liberty (exercise of free will) and licence (the abuse of choice in an act of licentiousness). It also contains another familiar idea: that none but a good man or woman can understand how to appreciate liberty. According to Maresca, the poem unites the myth of Latona's children with the mysteries of the Gospels.

As various critics have pointed out, the tone of the sonnet is angry (Parker 896–97) or satirical (Du Rocher), whereas the tone of "A book was writ" is bemused and tranquil. Milton seems to be smarting from the hurt of reading a number of pamphlets berating him and suggesting that his books be burned.

He is in attack mode, as suggested by the image of casting pearls before swine (Matthew 7.6). The gentle laughter at the stall readers and the unpronounceable names in "A book was writ" has been replaced with invective.

Text

The poem exists in three states, two in manuscript in Trinity Manuscript, and one in the printed text of *1673*. The copy-text is *1673*, with constant reference to the manuscript versions.

Works Cited

Du Rocher, Richard. "The Wealth and Blood of Milton's Sonnet XI." *Milton Quarterly* 17 (1983): 15–17.

Maresca, Thomas. "The Latona Myth in Milton's Sonnet XII." *Modern Language Notes* 76 (1961): 491–94.

XII. *On the same.*

I did but prompt the age to quit their cloggs[1]
  By the known rules of antient libertie,
  When strait° a barbarous noise environs° me   RIGHT AWAY   SURROUNDS
Of Owles and Cuckoes,[2] Asses, Apes and Doggs.
As when those Hinds° that were transform'd to Froggs   PEASANTS   5
  Raild at *Latona's* twin-born progenie[3]
  Which after held the Sun and Moon in fee.°   AS A RIGHTFUL POSSESSION
  But this is got by casting Pearl to Hoggs;[4]
That bawle for freedom in their senceless mood,
  And still° revolt when truth would set them free.[5]   CONSTANTLY   10

[9] Milton is lamenting the loss of the understanding of Greek in what he seems to have considered to be a golden age of kingship in England, that of Edward VI. Such understanding is embodied in Sir John Cheke (1514–57), famous for inspiring students to read the Greek classics in the original (*Variorum* 2.2: 391–92). Milton wrote that "Sir *John Cheeke* the Kings Tutor, [was] a man at that time counted the learnedest of Englishmen, & for piety not inferior . . . " (*Tetrachordon;* Yale 2: 716).

[10] The word "Greek" was wrapped upward above the line in *1673*, with an open parenthesis to show that it was from the line below. According to usual practice, the adjective should have been italicized.

[1] Probably, that is, "release themselves from their shackles," since a clog could be a yoke put on a prisoner to impede movement. It could also mean the wooden shoes worn by peasants (as in "clog-dancing").

[2] The first manuscript version of the poem had "buzzards" rather than "Cuckoes."

[3] The twins engendered by Jupiter and Latona are Apollo, the sun god, and Diana, goddess of the moon (Ovid, *Metamorphoses* 6.331–82). Shawcross, following Parker, compares Milton's twin pamphlets, *Tetrachordon* and *Colasterion*, to the god and goddess (200n). Peasants from Lycia who refused to give Latona anything to drink were turned into frogs by Jupiter.

[4] There may be a pun buried in "Hoggs," since a "Mr. Justice *Bacon*" was ordered to examine Milton, for ignoring the regulations about book licensing, in December 1644 (Honigmann 117).

[5] The line in Trinity Manuscript 1 read "hate the truth wherby they should be free," corrected to appear as "still revolt when Truth would set them free."

Licence they mean when they cry libertie;
For who loves that, must first be wise and good;
    But from that mark how far they roave[6] we see
    For all this wast° of wealth, and loss of blood.[7]

WASTE

Sonnet 13
To Mr. H. Lawes, on his Aires.
"Harry whose tunefull and well
measur'd Song" (1646)

Henry Lawes (1596–1662) wrote the music for Milton's masque and probably for "Arcades" as well. Lawes
was a member from 1630 of the King's Private Music
and he was music master to the Egerton family, spon-
sors of Milton's Ludlow masque, for which he wrote the
music. This sonnet introduced Lawes's Musick For Three
Voices (1648), indicating that Lawes not only acknowledged his collaboration with poets like Milton (as well
as Jonson, Donne, Herrick, Katherine Phillips, William
Cartwright, Thomas Carew, and others), but that he
was proud of his ability to write music that complemented lyric poetry. Milton commends Lawes for his
ability to allow the poetry to be understood through the
melodic line, honoring not only voice but verse.

Lawes is still lauded in the work of musicologists for
his sympathetic settings of lyrical poetry (le Huray), but
his songs are most apt to be recorded or heard in concert
today only as a result of his association with Milton.

TEXT

There are five authoritative versions of this poem:
Milton's two original drafts, the scribal revision also
present in the Trinity Manuscript, the version published
in 1648, and the version of 1673. Each has something to

XIII.
To Mr. H. Lawes, on his Aires.

Harry whose tunefull and well measur'd Song
    First taught our English Musick how to span
    Words with just note and accent, not to scan

add to our understanding of the context of the poem
(Emslie). Milton's first draft, for instance, was titled "To
my freind Mr Hen. Laws Feb. 9. 1645." That title gives
us a date and the word "freind," which suggests intimacy
rather than just casual acquaintance. The second draft,
also in Milton's hand, gives us "To M^r. Hen: Laws on
the publishing of his Aires," a more formal title, perhaps
intended for publication. The third draft repeats the
second title, but adds an e to "Laws" and removes "the
publishing of," which again suggests correction of the
spelling of the name and a still further shortening of the
title for the economy of publication. In 1673, the title is
reduced to its essentials, "To Mr. H. Lawes, on his Aires."

The text of the poem as it was published in the Lawes
collection in 1648 adds a significant note on line ten.
There is an asterisk before the word "story," and a marginal note explaining, "The story of Ariadne set by him
in Music," indicating Lawes's famous setting of Cartwright's Lament of Ariadne. Without Lawes's note, we
would not know of the connection with Cartwright.

The copy-text for this edition is that of 1673, with
constant reference to the other printed version and to
the manuscript versions in the Trinity Manuscript.

Works Cited

Emslie, Macdonald. "Milton on Lawes: The Trinity MS Revisions."
    Music in English Renaissance Drama. Lexington: UP of Kentucky,
    1968. 96–102.

le Huray, Peter. "'The fair musick that all creatures made." Ed. C. A.
    Patrides and Raymond Waddington. Manchester, Eng.: Manchester
    UP, 1980. 241–55.

---

[6]The image of roving from the mark was probably derived from archery, in which "rovers" were arrows that missed their mark, and "to rove" meant to
shoot at a mark that was constantly shifting, or to shoot at random.
[7]A serious reference to the emerging civil war in England, in which wealth would be wasted as well as human blood.

With *Midas* Ears, committing[1] short and long;
Thy worth[2] and skill exempts thee from the throng,
    With praise enough for Envy to look wan;[3]
    To after age thou shalt be writ the man,
    That with smooth aire° could'st humor best our tongue.[4]   MELODY   5
Thou honour'st Verse, and Verse must lend[5] her wing
    To honour thee, the Priest of *Phœbus* Quire°   APOLLO'S CHOIR   10
    That tun'st their happiest lines in Hymn, or Story.[6]
Dante shall give Fame leave to set thee higher
    Then his *Casella*, whom he woo'd to sing
    Met in the milder shades of Purgatory.[7]

Sonnet 14.
"When Faith and Love"
(1646?)

We would not know that this sonnet was written in memory of Ms. Catharine Thomason, wife of Milton's friend the bookseller George Thomason, except for a few accidents of preservation. For the first of three versions of the poem preserved in the Trinity Manuscript, Milton uses the title "On ye religious memorie of Mrs Catharine Thomason my christian freind deceas'd Decem. 1646," but, as was his custom, he scratched through that title, making parts of it very hard to read. For years, editors misread the name as "Thomson," until J. S. Smart discovered that the subject of the poem really was Catherine Thomason, wife of the bookseller who collected the more than 22,000 books and pamphlets from the period of the Civil War (1640–60) now preserved in the British Museum as the Thomason Tracts (Honigmann 134–35).

Ms. Thomason was erudite, extremely well read, the daughter as well as the wife of a bookseller, with a substantial library of her own (Honigmann 135). Catherine Thomason was buried on December 12, 1646, leaving at least eight children. Milton's sonnet might have been written on December 16, since he began to write "16" before "Decem. 1646" in his title, but he crossed through the number 16 (*Variorum* 2.2: 407).

As Shawcross points out, "The poem is a tissue of biblical allusions, such as the Christian armor of Faith and Love (Eph. Vi. 13–24), the just who shall live by faith (Gal. iii. 11), the meek who inherit the earth (Matt. V.5), the alms to God (Acts x. 4), the river of immortality (Rev. xxii. 1)" (*John Milton* 202).

TEXT

There are three versions of this sonnet in the Trinity Manuscript: a rough draft in Milton's hand, his fair copy, and a scribal copy. My copy-text is *1673*, compared closely against all three manuscript versions.

XIV.

When Faith and Love which parted from thee never,
    Had ripen'd thy just soul to dwell with God,

---

[1]The first manuscript state has "misjoyning" temporarily replacing "committing." In their eighteenth-century edition, the Richardsons reported the meaning of "commiting" as "offending against quantity and harmony" (*Variorum* 2.2: 403). Midas's donkey-ears, presumably, would lie up or lie down, creating the look of random inequality, and a jackass like Midas would hardly be able to judge musical art sensitively (Ovid, *Metamorphoses* 11.153–93). Perhaps the unmusical "hee-haw" of the donkey's voice is also part of Milton's humor.
[2]The first manuscript version gives "worth" replaced by "wit," with "worth" reinstated.
[3]The first version reads "and gives thee praise above the pipe of Pan."
[4]Printed without the "e" in all copies examined by Fletcher. The line in the first manuscript version reads "that didst reform thy art, the chief among."
[5]Printed "send" in *1673*. This is a case where *1648* and the three states of the Trinity Manuscript have more authority than does *1673*.
[6]The 1648 printing has this marginal note: "The story of Ariadne set by him in Music." This is Cartwright's *Ariadne Deserted*, for which Lawes's music was not printed until publication of his *Ayres and Dialogues* (1653). The lament of Ariadne or Arianne had also been set more famously in Italy by Claudio Monteverdi.
[7]Dante met his music teacher Casella in *Purgatorio* 2.76–117, and Casella, asked to sing, sings one of Dante's songs. The milder shades imply a contrast with the more severe extremes of the *Inferno*, or a contrast between the degree of darkness in different levels of Purgatory. The word "milder" had been "mildest" in the first manuscript version.

Meekly thou didst resign this earthy load[1]
  Of Death, call'd Life; which us from life doth sever.[2]
Thy Works and Alms and all thy good Endeavour[3]   5
  Staid not behind, nor in the grave were trod;°   BURIED UNDERFOOT
  But as Faith pointed with her golden rod,
  Follow'd thee up to joy and bliss for ever.
Love led them on, and Faith who knew them best
  Thy hand-maids, clad them o're with purple beams   10
  And azure wings, that up they flew so drest,
And speak the truth of thee on glorious Theams[4]
  Before the Judge, who thenceforth bid thee rest
  And drink thy fill of pure immortal streams.[5]

Sonnet 18.
"On the late Massacher in Piemont"
(1655)

We have only the text of *1673* for this sonnet (no manuscript exists; and the number assigned to the poem in 1673 is "XV."), and that presents a vivid picture of an atrocity against an obscure Protestant sect centered in the Piedmont region of Italy, near the Swiss border. The Waldensians or Vaudois were originally followers of a French merchant named Pierre Valdes, who had broken with the Roman Catholic Church around 1179. Milton may have been misled by current history to think the sect more ancient than it really was.

On April 24, 1655, a rag-tag army of French and Irish troops under the command of the Duke of Savoy began a cruel persecution of the Waldensians, apparently including scenes very like those recreated by Milton in the sonnet. Oliver Cromwell issued an official protest directed at the Duke of *Savoy* and drafted by Milton on May 15 (*Variorum* 2.2: 431). Cromwell showed his own commitment to the cause by contributing £2000 to the relief of the survivors (Honigmann 164). Milton's sonnet is frank propaganda, but it is an effective series of images of religious persecution reinforced by biblical language and imagery, and there is no reason to think it at all insincere. Protestant resistance to Roman Catholicism needed the sort of martyrs that the early Christian Church had had, and the persecution of the Cathars in France or the Waldensians in Italy, or the atrocities of the St. Bartholemew's Day Massacre in Paris in the late sixteenth century, provided Protestantism with its martyrs. Milton borrows the idea that the blood of martyrs is the seed of the church from the Church Father Tertullian (*Apologeticus* 59).

Milton apparently used a professional reader to provide him with contemporary accounts that described the massacre vividly, with images like "Others being naked were tyed neck and heels together, and rowled down from the tops of great Mountains" (quoted in Honigmann 165; see also Shawcross).

The sonnet is also a virtuoso poet's scream of anger, breathless and intense. It must have been dictated by the blind poet to an amanuensis. The written form preserves the voice of the poet in colloquial, unpretentious words and strong rhythmical biblical formulas such as "Avenge O Lord" or "Forget not" (Revelation 6.10). In form the sonnet is Petrarchan, but the mode, of course, is that of invective (it is accusatory) rather than erotic. In structure, it may be more subtle and complicated than it first appears (Svendsen).

TEXT

There are no manuscript versions of the poem, thus the only text available is that of *1673*, itself corrected once in line 10 by the *Errata* ("so" to "sow").

---

[1]In the first manuscript version Milton apparently wrote "earthy clod," scratched through "clod" and wrote "load" at the end of the line.
[2]This line was first written "Of Flesh & sin, wch man from heav'n doth sever." In his first draft, Milton corrected it to read "Of death call'd life, wch us from life doth sever."
[3]Readers should consult the first manuscript version to see all insertions and deletions in place, but after "Endeavor" in the first version came "Strait follow'd thee the path that Saints have trod / Still as they journey'd from this dark abode / Up to ye Realm of peace & Joy for ever, / Faith who led on ye way, & knew them best / thy handmaids . . . ."
[4]Possibly "Theames" are musical strains (one sense of theme being "plainsong") sung by Love and Faith on behalf of the dead Ms. Thomason (Honigmann 137). But the verb "spake" seems to work against a musical interpretation.
[5]Editors since Warton have noted the allusion to the waters of life in Psalm 36.8,9: "Thou shalt make them drink of the river of thy pleasures. Fow with thee is the fountain of life." Compare Revelation 22.1,17.

Works Cited

Shawcross, John T. A Note on the Piedmont Massacre. *Milton Quarterly*
6 (1972): 36.

Svendsen, Kester. "Milton's Sonnet on the Massacre in Piedmont."
Shakespeare Association Bulletin 20 (1945): 147–55

XVIII.[1]
On the late Massacher in Piemont.[2]

Avenge O Lord thy slaughter'd Saints,[3] whose bones
  Lie scatter'd on the Alpine mountains cold,
  Ev'n them who kept thy truth so pure of old
  When all our Fathers worship't Stocks and Stones,[4]
Forget not: in thy book record their groanes   5
  Who were thy Sheep and in their antient Fold
  Slayn by the bloody *Piemontese* that roll'd
  Mother with Infant down the Rocks. Their moans
The Vales redoubl'd to the Hills, and they
  To Heav'n. Their martyr'd blood and ashes sow[5]   10
  O're all th' *Italian* fields where still doth sway
The triple Tyrant:° that from these may grow   THE POPE
  A hunder'd-fold, who having learnt thy way
  Early may fly the *Babylonian* wo.

Sonnet 19.
"When I consider how my light is spent"
(1652?)

Considering that the order of presentation of the sonnets in *1673*, "When I consider" could have been written after the Piedmontese sonnet, at some point after 1655. It has also been related by means of its positive tone to the sociable sonnets inviting the company of Skinner and Lawrence. Dating it has been complicated to no end by the phrase "E're half my days," which has set critics and biographers off on various chases (Parker). Milton is also known to have become blind late in 1651 or early in 1652, when he was 42; hence Sonnet 19 is related to Sonnet 22, which may commemorate the third anniversary of his becoming blind (*Variorum* 2.2: 443). Honigmann would have liked to have placed the composition in the year 1644, because that date would place Milton at the age of 35, a more plausible "half [his] days" by the biblical computation of the life of man as the proverbial "three score years and ten" (derived from Psalm 90.10), but Honigmann's dating would make Milton's blindness anticipated, not realized. Dating the poem 1652(?), as does Carey, seems a better guess.

The poem casts the poet as an afflicted Job. It addresses the issue of blindness as a punishment supposedly visited on Milton by God for his political stance with respect to king-killing. But it concentrates mostly on the Parable of the Talents (Matthew 25.14–30), illustrating "that command in the gospel set out by the terrible seasing of him that hid the talent" (Milton's "Letter to a friend"). The parable creates an "uneasy place" for Milton (Haskin, Chapter 2) in that it lays down a terrible penalty for hiding one's ability or not realizing

---

[1]The number assigned the sonnet in *1673* is "XV."
[2]The title is uncharacteristically included in *1673*, and the spelling of "*Massacher*" and "Piemont" seem to be the author's.
[3]For Puritans, the word "saint" was stretched to mean "good people," with a potential degradation of the process of canonization intended. In other words, "saint" is a title that common people like the slaughtered Waldensians can deserve.
[4]Probably effigies of gods carved out of wood-stock and stones, but the phrase "stocks and stones," meaning primitive effigies, was proverbial.
[5]The Errata change "so" to "sow." The blood and ashes of the slain martyrs will sow figurative dragon's teeth, an army of martyrs who will avoid the Whore of Babylon, the "*Babylonian* wo," represented by the Roman Catholic Church.

one's potential, but it is reassuring in that it carries with that penalty a high reward for those who, like Milton, overcome affliction in the process of realizing their talents. In weakness and infirmity lies the poet's strength.

TEXT

The text exists only in the printed version of *1673*. Line 12 in *1673* is not indented, which I presume is a compositor's error.

Works Cited

Haskin, Dayton. *Milton's Burden of Interpretation*. Philadelphia: U of Pennsylvania P, 1994.

Parker, William Riley. "The Dates of Milton's Sonnets on Blindness." *PMLA* 73 (1958): 196–200.

XIX.[1]

When I consider how my light is spent,°
    E're half my days, in this dark world and wide,
    And that one Talent which is death to hide,
    Lodg'd with me useless, though my Soul more bent
To serve therewith my Maker, and present   5
    My true account, least he returning chide,
    Doth God exact day labour, light deny'd, *(Sight)*
    I fondly ask; But patience[2] to prevent *foolishly*
That murmur, soon replies, God doth not need
    Either man's work or his own gifts, who best   10
    Bear his milde yoak, they serve him best, his State
Is Kingly.[3] Thousands at his bidding speed
    And post o're Land and Ocean without rest:
    They also serve who only stand and waite.[4]

[handwritten: On milton's Blindness]   COMPLETELY EXTINGUISHED

Sonnet 20.
"*Lawrence* of vertuous Father."
(1655?)

"Relax, Lawrence," this sonnet seems to day, "and enjoy yourself with me, with food and drink and music." The food is spare but choice, the wine good, the music Florentine (Marjara)—all designed to dispel the melancholy of winter by pleasant companionship and pleasant pastimes. Also, the sonnet comes out strongly in favor of the "delights" of life, the pleasant interludes of food

and music necessary for a healthy balance between work and play. Readers of this sonnet can throw aside any notion that Milton was in person a dour or unpleasantly dutiful Puritan. Like the ode to Rouse, this poem is Horatian (Brown 333–34; Finley), urbane, comfortable, pleasant, relaxed.

Edward Lawrence is called by his last name, to identify him with his father (Cyriack Skinner will be addressed more familiarly by his first name). Henry Lawrence had been Lord President of Oliver Cromwell's Council of State from 1653–59. His son Edward (1633–57) was also a Member of Parliament.

---

[1]Numbered "XVI" in *1673*.
[2]Patience might be read as an allegorical presence, as in *Samson Agonistes* 1296.
[3]The line is indented in *1673*.
[4]One of Milton's most famous lines and images, often misapplied or applied humorously. The word "waite" here most likely implies "stay in expectation" (Honigmann 176). The line may echo Ephesians 6.13–14: "Wherefore take unto you the whole armour of God, that ye may be able to withstand in the evil day, and having done all, to stand. Stand therefore, having your loins girt about with truth, and having on the breastplate of righteousness." See James L. Jackson and Walter E. Weese. "'. . . Who Only Stand and Wait': Milton's Sonnet 'On His Blindness'" (*Modern Language Notes* 72 [1957]: 91–93, for supporting evidence.

Young Edward was apparently a frequent visitor to Milton's house in Petty France, in Westminister, not far from the Houses of Parliament. Milton lived in Petty France from 1652–60. Honigmann speculates that the two men might have discovered the mire (mud) and the dank fields while walking in St. James's Park, adjacent to Milton's house (177).

Since XIX, "When I consider" had been dated XVI in *1673*, this sonnet, which immediately followed it, was numbered XVII. Editors normally assign the number XX to "Lawrence *of vertuous Father*" and allow "Vane, *young in yeares*" to have the number XVII.

TEXT

1673 provides the only version of the text available. There are no detectable errors in the text.

Works Cited

Brown, Cedric. "Horatian Signatures: Milton and Civilized Community." *Milton and Italy: Contexts, Images, Contradictions.* Ed. Mario A. Di Cesare. Binghamton, NY: Medieval & Renaissance Texts & Studies, 1991. 329–44.

Finley, John H. "Milton and Horace: A Study of Milton's Sonnets." *Harvard Studies in Classical Philology* 48 (1937): 29–73.

Marjara, Harinder S. "Milton's 'Chromatick jarres' and 'Tuscan Aire.'" *Milton Quarterly* 19 (1985):11–13.

XX.[1]

Lawrence of vertuous Father <u>vertuous</u> Son,[2]
   Now that the Fields are dank,° and ways are mire,°   WET   MUDDY
   Where shall we sometimes meet, and by the fire
   Help wast a sullen° day; what may be won   MELANCHOLY
From the hard Season gaining: time will run   5
   On smoother, till *Favonius*[3] re-inspire°   BREATHE ON AGAIN
   The frozen earth; and cloth in fresh attire
   The Lillie and Rose, that neither sow'd nor spun.[4]
What neat repast° shall feast us, light and choice,[5]   CAREFULLY PREPARED MEAL
   Of Attick tast, with Wine, whence we may rise   10
   To hear the Lute well toucht, or artfull voice
Warble immortal Notes and *Tuskan* Ayre?[6]
   He who of those delights can judge, and spare[7]
   To interpose them oft, is not unwise.

Sonnet 21.
"*Cyriack*, whose Grandsire"
(1655?)

Cyriack Skinner (1627–1700), Milton's pupil, his probable amanuensis, and his likely biographer as well, was familiar enough to Milton to be addressed here by his first name. He inherited his grandfather's, Sir Edward Coke's (1552–1634), love for the law and was a student at Lincoln's Inn. Sir Edward had been Chief Justice of the King's Bench. His *Institutes of the Law of England* is still a monument in legal history.

Sonnets 20 and 21 are linked by the idea that leisure complements a life of hard study. Milton reminds young Lawrence and young Skinner that they should have an occasional "gaudy day," or time out from official duties. At the same time, both are reminded of their heritage of important public service through their father's or grandfather's reputation (Vance).

The poems show a Milton who is certainly not a Puritan with the motto "Thou shalt not," but a warm

[1]Numbered "XVII" in *1673*.
[2]An echo of Horace *Odes* 1.16: "O matre pulchra filia pulchrior." Horace, Finley notes (*Variorum* 2.2: 473), was fond of beginning his poems addressed to individuals with references to their ancestors, as is Milton here and in Sonnets 10 and 21.
[3]The West Wind (usually Zephyr), named Favonius in Horace *Odes* 1.4. Milton's allusion to Horace's name indicates that we should take the tone of the sonnet as being like that of Horace's various odes dedicated to good living and friendship, as with Ode 1.11.
[4]"Consider the lilies of the field, how they grow; they toil not, neither do they spin" (Matthew 6.28).
[5]By all accounts, Milton ate sparingly but well, a kind of Renaissance health-food diet. Here his diet emulates ancient Greek (Attic) simplicity.
[6]Perhaps alluding to the sheet music Milton had brought back from Italy (Darbishire 59).
[7]Either "afford, spare time for," or "forbear," depending on which editor or critic one believes. *Variorum* 2.2.474–76 summarizes the debate.

friend to his pupils, a man with a gentle sense of humor, and a man who enjoys the good things of life; he is relaxed to the point of being able to pun about his own afflicted eyes.

TEXT

The text exists in a scribal draft in the Trinity Manuscript, but there the poem is missing its first four lines. Copy-text for this edition is *1673*, with close attention to what is available of the poem in the Trinity Manuscript.

Works Cited

Parker, William Riley. "The 'Anonymous Life' of Milton." *Times Literary Supplement* 13 September 1957. 547.

Vance, John A. "God's Advocate and His Pupils: Milton's Sonnets to Lawrence and Skinner." *South Atlantic Bulletin* 42 (1977): 31–40.

XXI.[1]

Cyriack, whose Grandsire on the Royal Bench
  Of Brittish *Themis*,[2] with[3] no mean applause
  Pronounc't and in his volumes taught our Lawes,
  Which others at their Barr so often wrench;[4]
To day deep thoughts resolve with me to drench°   DROWN   5
  In mirth, that after no repenting drawes;
  Let *Euclid* rest and *Archimedes* pause,[5]
  And what the *Swede* intend,[6] and what the *French*.
To measure life, learn thou betimes,° and know   EARLY
  Toward solid good what leads the nearest way;   10
  For other things mild Heav'n a time ordains,
And disapproves that care, though wise in show,
  That with superfluous burden loads the day,
  And when God sends a cheerful hour, refrains.

Sonnet 23.
"Methought I saw"
(1658?)

This sonnet is perhaps the most intensely personal of all the sonnets, based on an actual dream of wish fulfillment, the reunion of Milton and a wife who died as a result of childbirth. From the first verb, "saw," the poem is a poignant reminder that the husband quite possibly had never seen the wife that he describes so lovingly, but that he will at last have "sight of her in heaven, without restraint."

The problem for biographers and critics alike is to identify which wife Milton was describing, since both Katherine Woodcock and Mary Powell Milton had died as a result of childbirth. Katherine Woodcock, whom Milton had married on November 12, 1656, bore him a daughter, Katherine, on October 19, 1657, and died on February 3, 1658. Mary Powell had died in May of 1652, shortly after bearing a daughter, Deborah (born May 2). Shawcross and others identify the hand of the amanuensis who copied the poem in the Trinity Manuscript as that of Jeremy Picard, who began work for Milton in 1658 and apparently entered the deaths of Katherine and her daughter in the Milton family Bible. Milton's nuncupative (dictated) will, as Shawcross points out, con-

---

[1]Numbered "XVIII" in *1673*.
[2]Justice, the Roman goddess. The "bench" is the King's Bench, where Sir Edward Coke became Chief Justice is 1613. His volumes were the *Institutes* and the *Reports*.
[3]The "with with" of *1673* has been corrected.
[4]The verb suggests a twisting of Coke's principles in the modern courtroom—a hint of what Milton might have thought about lawyers.
[5]"Suspend your study of mathematics and physics."
[6]The manuscript has "intends and," with no comma. Discussing what the contemporary Swedes (under Milton's correspondent, Queen Christina) or the French (under Cardinal Mazarin) intend would be the equivalent of modern diplomatic history, or at least news of current events—worthy topics of conversation between the Secretary for Foreign Tongues and a young man like Cyriack Skinner, thinking of a career of public service or diplomacy.

tains "unsentimental references" to Mary Powell Milton (246). But Parker insists that she is the only wife who died in childbirth, and that lines 5 and 6 point to Mary.

Arguments for the poem's dedication to Katherine or Mary depend on etymology (see Le Comte: the Greek "katharos" means "pure," and there is an emphasis on purity in the poem), or on the "veiled" face (suggesting that Milton must have been blind as he married her). Arguments in favor of Mary as the subject associate her with Mary the mother of Christ, or they try to establish her death as having come before the end of the period of purification mandated in Leviticus 12.5 (Carey 413). Anthony Low, however, returns to Katherine as the subject, as he refutes the idea that Milton would honor an Anglican ritual such as "churching," ritual purification after childbirth.

Whichever wife the poem addresses, it is moving and beautiful, a dream-vision that is poignant and immediate.

The dating of the poem must be based on which wife is referred to. I incline toward 1658, because I believe that the poem is more apt to refer to Milton's relationship with Katherine. I would add the evidence of the poem's being placed last in the Trinity Manuscript and its connection with Picard, though, as Carey sensibly points out, the fact that the poem was copied in 1658 does not mean it was written then (413).

TEXT

There are two authoritative versions of the sonnet, the text published in *1673* and a scribal copy preserved as the very last entry in the Trinity Manuscript. The manuscript version is more lightly punctuated, and it contains no italics or capitalization other than on proper names. *1673* adds a number of commas and capitalizes nouns randomly.

Neither text has any obvious error, and it is hard to determine if one text or the other is closer to the author's projected wishes, since both preserve the same elisions with past participles. It is impossible to say for sure that Milton generally preferred that the words that begin lines should be capitalized, since initial words aren't usually capitalized in his holograph poems, but they always are in print. I have left the text as it appears in *1673*.

Works Cited

Le Comte, Edward. "The Veiled Face of Milton's Wife." *Notes and Queries* 199 (1954): 245–46.

Low, Anthony. "Milton's Last Sonnet." *Milton Quarterly* 9 (1975): 80–82.

Parker, William Riley. "Milton's Last Sonnet Again." *Review of English Studies* 2 (1951): 147–52.

XXIII.

Methought I saw my late espoused Saint
   Brought to me like *Alcestis*[1] from the grave,
   Whom *Joves* great Son to her glad Husband gave,
   Rescu'd from death by force though pale and faint.
Mine as whom washt from spot of child-bed taint,   5
   Purification in the old Law did save,
   And such, as yet once more I trust to have
   Full sight of her in Heaven[2] without restraint,
Came vested° all in white, pure as her mind: DRESSED
   Her face was vail'd, yet to my fancied sight,   10
   Love, sweetness, goodness in her person shin'd
So clear, as in no face with more delight.
   But O as to embrace me she enclin'd,°   LEANED
   I wak'd, she fled, and day brought back my night.[3]

---

[1] In Euripides's *Alcestis*, the heroine, Admetus's wife, sacrifices her life for her husband's sake. Heracles ("*Joves* great son"), who has been hospitably treated in Admetus's house even though Alcestis dies while he is there, wrestles with Death in order to force him to release her, then brings her back to her husband, veiled but alive. Admetus, when he sees her disguised in the veil, says "as I look on her, I think I see / my wife. It churns my heart to tumult, and the tears / break streaming from my eyes" (Lattimore trans., 1065–68).

[2] The words "saint," "son," "husband," "law," and "heaven" are not capitalized in the Trinity Manuscript, which might indicate a Miltonic preference imposed on the scribe; on the other hand, the word "heaven" is not written as a monosyllable either in the Trinity Manuscript or in *1673*. Shawcross makes the text of the poem conform to what he believes to be Milton's spelling, capitalization, and elision, altering "heaven" to "heav'n" and "the old" to "th' old" in order to make it appear a monosyllable.

[3] The line may imply that during his dream he recovered his eyesight but lost it with waking.

The Fifth Ode of Horace, Book 1 (1646–48?)

It is important to see the original Latin poem side by side with Milton's translation, as the two appear in *1673*. Probably the two as a unit constitute the most carefully printed two pages in the volume. As Shawcross puts it, "Milton aimed at reproducing Horace's quantitative meters, and so subjoined the Latin text to allow the reader to evaluate his rendition" (209). For anyone who has struggled to translate the sophisticated and intricate poetry of Horace into English, Milton's translation is a marvel: it is concise, precise, definitive; it is faithful to the original; and it creates its own integrity as an English poem. The English is not in Milton's poetic style, because its style deeply honors Horace's in Latin; it is an exercise in how to write poetry in either language. As the *Variorum* puts it, "If the style does not much resemble that of the early Milton, it does not much resemble that of the later poet either; in fact it is unique" (2.2: 504).

TEXT

The only extant text is that of *1673*. The publication date of Milton's Latin source-text may help date the English translation, since the text, Shawcross believes, is from *Quinti Horatii Flacci poëmata scholiis siva annotationibus a I. Bond illustrata* (Amsterdam: G. J. Blaeuw, 1636). Shawcross therefore dates the translation 1646–48(?); Carey, on the other hand, puts the translation in late 1629(?). Though his dating of the translation is disputed in the *Variorum* 505, I agree with Shawcross's reasoning that it is a mature poem and perhaps coincides with similar prosodic experiments in *Samson Agonistes*.

Works Cited

Leishman, J.B. *Translating Horace*. Oxford: Oxford UP, 1956.

Shawcross, John T. "Of Chronology and the Dates of Milton's Translation from Horace and the *New Forcers of Conscience*." *Studies in English Literature* (*SEL*) 3 (1963): 77–84.

The fifth Ode of Horace. *Lib.* I.

Quis multa gracilis te puer in Rosa, *Rendred almost word for word without Rhyme according to to the Latin Measure, as near as the Language will permit.*

WHat slender Youth bedew'd with liquid odours[1]
    Courts thee on Roses in some pleasant Cave,
        Pyrrha for whom bindst thou
        In wreaths thy golden Hair,
Plain in thy neatness; O how oft shall he   5
On Faith and changed Gods complain: and Seas
        Rough with black winds and storms
        Unwonted shall admire:
Who now enjoyes thee credulous, all Gold,
Who always vacant always amiable   10
        Hopes thee; of flattering gales
        Unmindfull. Hapless they
To whom thou untry'd seem'st fair. Me in my vow'd
Picture the sacred walls declares t' have hung
        My dank and dropping weeds   15
        To the stern God of sea.

AD PYRRHAM Ode *V.*

Horatius ex Pyrrhæ illecebris tanquam è naufragio enataverat, cujus amore irretitos, affirmat esse miseros.

QUis multa gracilis te puer in rosa
   Perfusus liquidis urget ororibus,
      Grato, Pyrrha, *sub antro?*
      Cui flavam religas comam
Simplex unditie? Heu quoties fidem
Mutatosque deos flebit, & aspera
      Nigris æquora ventis
      Emirabitur insolens,
Qui nunc te fruitur credulus aurea:
Qui semper vacuam, semper amabilem
      Sperat, nescius auræ
      Fallacis. miseri quibus
Intentata nites. Me tabula sacer
Votiva paries indicat uvida
      Suspendisse potenti
      Vestimenta maris Deo.

---

[1]Perfumes, as in Nativity Ode 23.

"At a Vacation Exercise"
(1628)

In *1673*, this poem is out of sequence with the translation of Horace placed before it. As the Errata point out, the poem "should have come in" between "Fair Infant" and "The Passion," which would have helped give it a chronological context. The Latin headnote identifies it as written when Milton was nineteen, and as a part of a vacation exercise, at Christ's College, Cambridge, held in English and Latin. This particular vacation exercise, a display of talent and learning (and sometimes obscene wit), was held during summer vacation in 1628, a vacation which Carey reminds us extended from July until early October (76). The poem in English followed a Latin "Oratio" and a "Prolusio," the first designed to illustrate the point that entertainment should be interposed with serious studies and the second designed to insult various members of the audience, gently and with wit, playing on names with double meanings such as "Rivers" (Radzinowicz). The students were supposed to show themselves equally adept either at debating or cracking jokes, either in Latin or English.

Milton's part in the festivities shows him as an early rebel against intellectual fashions, attacking Aristotelian logic even at the moment he was arguing like an Aristotelian orator (Campbell). The poem also shows his allegiance to his native language and his pride in English poetry, especially that of Spenser, Shakespeare, Sylvester, and Jonson, while he seems to react against the preciosity and dense wit of metaphysical poetry produced by those he calls "our late fantasticks."

TEXT

The only text we have is that of *1673*, augmented by the *Errata*.

Works Cited

Campbell, Gordon. "The Satire on Aristotelian Logic in Milton's Vacation Exercise." *English Language Notes* 15 (1977): 106–10.

Radzinowicz, Mary Ann. "'To play in the Socratic Manner': Oxymoron in Milton's *At a Vacation Exercise in the Colledge*." *University of Hartford Studies in Literature* 17 (1985): 1–11.

Anno Ætatis 19. *At a Vacation Exercise in the*
    Colledge, part Latin, *part* English. *The* Latin
    speeches ended, the English *thus began.*

Hail native Language, that by sinews weak
  Didst move my first endeavouring tongue to speak,
And mad'st imperfect words with childish tripps,
Half unpronounc't, slide through my infant-lipps,
Driving dum silence from the portal dore,   5
Where he had mutely sate two years before:
Here I salute thee and thy pardon ask,
That now I use thee in my latter task:
Small loss it is that thence can come unto thee,
I know my tongue but little Grace can do thee: 10
Thou needst not be ambitious to be first,
Believe me I have thither packt the worst:[2]
And, if it happen as I did forecast,
The daintest[3] dishes shall be serv'd up last.
I pray thee then deny me not thy aide   15
For this same small neglect that I have made:
But haste thee strait° to do me once a Pleasure,   IMMEDIATELY
And from thy wardrope bring thy chiefest treasure;
Not those new fangled toys, and triming slight°   INCONSEQUENTIAL TRIMMINGS
Which takes our late fantasticks with delight,   20

---

[2]Probably a reference to the lame jokes in Milton's Prolusion 6. English should not be anxious to come first, because the speaker has put the worst things first, in the prolusion.
[3]Though the *OED* does not record "daintest," it does record "dainteth," so the word as preserved in *1673* may have been an acceptable variant for "daintiest."

But cull those richest Robes, and gay'st° attire   MOST FESTIVE, BRIGHTEST
Which deepest Spirits, and choicest Wits° desire: INTELLECTUALS
I have some naked thoughts that rove about
And loudly knock to have their passage out;[4]
And wearie of their place do only stay   25
Till thou hast deck't them in thy best aray;°   ARRAY, SET OF CLOTHES
That so they may without suspect or fears
Fly swiftly to this fair Assembly's ears;
Yet I had rather, if I were to chuse,
Thy service in some graver subject use,   30
Such as may make thee search thy coffers[5] round,
Before thou cloath my fancy in fit sound:
Such where the deep transported mind may soare
Above the wheeling poles, and at Heav'ns dore
Look in, and see each blissful Deitie   35
How he before the thunderous throne doth lie,
Listening to what unshorn[6] *Apollo* sings
To th' touch of golden wires, while *Hebe*[7] brings
Immortal Nectar to her Kingly Sire:
Then passing through the Spheres[8] of watchful fire,   40
And mistie Regions of wide air next under,
And hills of Snow and lofts of piled Thunder,[9]
May tell at length how green-ey'd *Neptune* raves,[10]
In Heav'ns defiance mustering all his waves;
Then sing of secret things that came to pass   45
When Beldam° Nature in her cradle was;   ·OLD MOTHER NATURE·
And last of Kings and Queens and Hero's[11] old,
Such as the wise *Demodocus*[12] once told
In solemn Songs at King *Alcinous* feast,
While sad *Ulisses* soul and all the rest   50
Are held with his melodious harmonie
In willing chains and sweet captivitie.
But fie my wandring Muse how thou dost stray!
Expectance calls thee now another way,
Thou know'st it must be now thy only bent   55
To keep in compass of thy Predicament:[13]
Then quick about thy purpos'd business come,
That to the next I may resign my Roome.

---

[4]Perhaps this couplet comes as close as Milton ever got to presenting an image of which Donne would have been proud.

[5]Presumably boxes or chests in which their metaphorical clothing of wit is stored.

[6]Emulating the classical epithet for Apollo in Homer, *Iliad* 20.39, as Carey points out (77).

[7]Cup-bearer to the gods and daughter of Zeus and Hera.

[8]Written "Spherse," an obvious typographical error, in *1673*. The Spheres are the solid rings that represent the orbits of heavenly bodies. To a Christian they might be watchful in the sense that they are under the control of God, who sets them in motion. Ovid describes them as "vigiles flammas" ("fiery watchmen") in the *Art of Love* 3.463.

[9]Apparently a mound of thunderbolts kept ready for Zeus's use.

[10]The sea god is pictured as in angry rebellion against the rest of the Olympian gods for the blinding of his son, Cyclops. He may be "green-ey'd" as Shakespeare's characterization of jealousy is in *Othello* 3.3.166.

[11]The word is not a proper name but a plural generic noun, modern "heroes," thus the italics of *1673* are not appropriate.

[12]While enjoying the hospitality of King Alcinous in Phaecia, Ulysses weeps to hear the epic singer Demodocus sing of the Trojan War (*Odyssey* 8.499–522). Using hindsight, we might picture the young Milton looking forward to singing of "some graver subject" in his own epic.

[13]The word is used technically here, to mean "the ten categories or classes of predications formed by Aristotle" (*OED* 1). When Milton appears as Ens, the Absolute Being, he will be assuming the role of the father of the ten categories.

Then Ens *is represented as Father of the Præ-*
 dicaments his ten Sons, whereof the Eldest
 stood for Substance *with his Canons, which*
 Ens *thus speaking, explains.*[14]

GOod luck befriend thee Son; for at thy birth
 The Faiery Ladies daunc't upon the hearth;   60
Thy drowsie Nurse[15] hath sworn she did them spie
Come tripping to the Room where thou didst lie;
And sweetly singing round about thy Bed
Strew all their blessings on thy sleeping Head.
She heard them give thee this, that thou should'st still   65
From eyes of mortals walk invisible,
Yet there is something that doth force my fear,
For once it was my dismal hap° to hear   HORRIBLY BAD FORTUNE
A *Sibyl* old, bow-bent with crooked age,
That far events full wisely could presage,   70
And in times long and dark Prospective Glass[16]
Fore-saw what future dayes should bring to pass,
Your Son, said she, (nor can you it prevent)
Shall subject be to many an Accident.[17]
O're all his Brethren he shall Reign as King,   75
Yet every one shall make him underling,
And those that cannot live from him asunder
Ungratefully shall strive to keep him under,
In worth and excellence he shall out-go them,
Yet being above them, he shall be below them;   80
From others he shall stand in need of nothing,
Yet on his Brothers shall depend for Cloathing.
To find a Foe it shall not be his hap,
And peace shall lull him in her flowry lap;[18]
Yet shall he live in strife, and at his dore   85
Devouring war shall never cease to roare:
Yea it shall be his natural property
To harbour those that are at enmity.
What power, what force, what mighty spell, if not
Your learned hands, can loose this Gordian knot?[19]   90

The next Quantity *and* Quality, *spake in Prose,*
 then Relation *was call'd by his Name.*

---

[14]As father, Milton will introduce his sons, the ten Categories: Substance together with its nine Accidents, Quantity, Quality, Relation, Place, Time, Position, Action, and Passion. The Accidents were also called Predicaments—"the classes into which fell whatever could be 'predicated' of any particulary entity" (*Variorum* 2.1: 147)—in the scholastic logic still taught at Milton's Cambridge. The "*Canons*" are the general rules of the system of logic. Though Milton parodies scholastic logic, he participates in it while he makes fun of it.

[15]An English nurse who might be compared with the Nurse of *Romeo and Juliet* (introduced in 1.3), she and her image tie this poem to the "Bellmans drowsie charm" of "Il Penseroso" 83.

[16]Like the witches of *Macbeth* 4.1, this hag-like Sibyl can show the future by means of mirrors or crystal ball.

[17]Punning on accident/accidental in the logical system, as well as the common meaning of "unpredictable event."

[18]The phrase will be repeated in *Paradise Lost* 4.254.

[19]An emblem of difficulty, the Gordian knot binding the chariot of the Phrygian king Gordius could not be untied until Alexander the Great was supposed to have cut it with his sword.

R Ivers arise;[20] whether thou be the Son,
Of utmost *Tweed*, or *Oose*, or gulphie *Dun*,[21]
Or *Trent*,[22] who like some earth-born Giant spreads
His thirty Armes along the indented Meads,[23]
Or sullen *Mole*[24] that runneth underneath,   95
Or *Severn* swift, guilty of Maidens death,[25]
Or Rockie *Avon*,[26] or of Sedgie *Lee*,
Or Coaly *Tine*, or antient hallowed[27] *Dee*,
Or *Humber* loud[28] that keep'st[29] the *Scythians* Name,
Or *Medway* smooth, or Royal Towred *Thame*.[30]   100

   The rest was Prose.

"On the New Forcers of Conscience" (1646)

   This is a caudal sonnet, fourteen lines plus a tail—a "cauda" in Latin. It is strictly topical, having to do with events that occurred toward the end of 1646. The old forcers of conscience would have been the prelate lords, the old church hierarchy outlawed by the Presbyterian majority in Parliament; what Milton is complaining about is that an evil new hierarchy seemed to have replaced the evil old hierarchy.

   Episcopacy had been abolished in January 1643; legal preaching had been restricted to ministers ordained Presbyterian; the *Book of Common Prayer* was banned (not for the first time) on August 26, 1645; and bishops and archbishops were abolished on October 9, 1646. The new Presbyterian hierarchy that replaced the old Episcopal hierarchy seemed to indulge itself in the same sort of pluralities (multiple church livings allowed to one ordained minister). It also seemed to be corrupt in its name-calling and in its own brand of censorship. Its Presbyters, in other words, were just Laudian Bishops, under another name.

TEXT

   The sonnet was supposed to be inserted after Sonnet 11 (numbered 12 in the Trinity Manuscript) by the directive: "on ye forcers of Conscience to come immediately in heer turn over the leafe." In other words, it

---

[20]Masson discovered through the researches of W. G. Clark that George and Nizell Rivers, sons of Sir John Rivers, were admitted to Christ's College as freshmen on May 10, 1628. Milton makes good use of the pun on their name. His catalogue of rivers serves the purpose of parodying the current fashion for "patriotic topography" (David Daiches, quoted in the *Variorum* 2.1: 148) embodied in Michael Drayton's *Poly-Olbion*. See A. H. Gilbert, *A Geographical Dictionary of Milton* (New Haven: Yale UP, 1919), for a description of the rivers Milton mentions.
[21]The description of the rivers is based on Milton's reading in Spenser and Drayton. The Tweed River is "utmost" because it is on the border of England and Scotland; the "Ouze" is defined as the Isis in *Faerie Queene* 4.11.24; the "*Dun*" is the Don in Yorkshire, which is "gulphie" because it is filled with eddies (*OED* 1); according to Drayton, the Don was "lively" (*Poly-Olbion* 28.47; see *Variorum* 2.1: 148).
[22]The etymology of Trent ("thirty" as in French "trente") seemed to be descriptive of its tributaries, what Drayton called the "thirtie Floods, that wayt the Trent upon" (*Poly-Olbion* 26.171). In this and other descriptions of rivers, Drayton and Spenser echo each other, and Milton, either seriously or parodically, imitates them, perhaps without having seen any of the rivers involved.
[23]The striking image of the water indenting land can be found in Sylvester: "silver Torrents rush; / Indenting Meads" (*Little Bartas* 480–81; quoted in *Variorum* 2.1: 149).
[24]The proper name "Mole" was not italicized in *1673*, perhaps because the compositor took it to be a generic underground sluice of some sort, but I have followed Shawcross in restoring the italics. The Mole is indeed supposed to be a female river and the lover of the male Thames, according to Drayton, and to have run underground in order to escape her parents and join him (*Poly-Olbion* 17.49–64).
[25]This is the same Severn River that is supposedly guarded by and named for Sabrina, the nymph who helps save the Lady in Milton's *Comus*. Milton retells the myth in the *History of Britain*, where "the fury of *Guendolen*" causes her to throw "*Estrildis* and her Daughter *Sabra* . . . into a river: and to leave a Monument of revenge, proclaims, that the stream be thenceforth call'd after the Damsels name; which by length of time is chang'd now to *Sabrina*, or *Severn*" (Yale 5: 18).
[26]Each of the rivers is defined in terms of its characteristic sedge (marsh grass growing in water), its rocks, or its coal (the Tyne runs by Newcastle, proverbially famous for its coal. Again, Spenser and Drayton refer to the Avon, the Tyne, and the Lee using similar characteristics (*Variorum* 2.1: 149).
[27]The "hollowed" of *1673* is an error. The Dee would have been hallowed because it was a river with ancient religious associations for the Druids, among others. Milton may have lifted the phrase (again) from Michael Drayton, who uses it in *Poly-Olbion* 10.215.
[28]The Humber was supposed to have taken its name from a Scythian chief who drowned there (*Poly-Olbion* 8.45–46). Milton records him as "*Humber* King of the *Hunns* . . . in a River drown'd, which to this day retains his name" (*History of Britain*; Yale 5: 18).
[29]The "keeps'" of *1673* seems to be an error.
[30]The mouth of the Medway and the mouth of the Thames both issue into the sea in Kent. Warton found a reference to a Medway "wont so still to slide" in Ludovic Bryskett, "Mourning Muse of Thestylis" 159. The Thames would be towered especially as it ran by Windsor Castle and Hampton Court.

was supposed to be among the sonnets, but in *1673* it is placed between "At a Vacation Exercise" and "*Arcades*." Its tone is very similar to that of the sonnets that begin "A Book was Writ" and "I Did but Prompt the Age," though Mueller believes this sonnet to be more refined. Milton's sardonic humor comes through most clearly in a canceled phrase: "shallow *Edwards*" was at first "hare braind Edwards."

The copy of the sonnet in the Trinity Manuscript is by a scribe, with corrections by a second scribe. The printed version of *1673* contains several errors corrected by the Errata, "of" for "off" in the first line, and "bank" for the less-familiar "bauk" in 17. *1673* provides the copy-text for this edition, with its longer title; corrections and revisions are noted.

Works Cited

Mueller, Janel. "The Mastery of Decorum: Politics as Poetry in Milton's Sonnets." *Critical Inquiry* 13 (1987): 475–508.

Shawcross, John. "Of Chronology and the Dates of Milton's Translations from Horace and the *New Forcers of Conscience*." *Studies in English Literature, 1500–1900*. 3 (1963): 77–84.

On the new forcers of Conscience under the Long PARLIAMENT.

Because you have thrown off[1] your Prelate Lord[2]
   And with stiff Vowes renounc'd his Liturgie
To seise the widdow'd whore Pluralitie[3]
From them whose sin ye envi'd, not abhor'd,[4]
Dare ye for this adjure° the Civill Sword   SWEAR AN OATH TO   5
   To force our Consciences that Christ set free,
   And ride us with a classic Hierarchy[5]
Taught by meer *A.S.* and *Rotherford?*[6]
Men whose Life, Learning, Faith and pure intent
   Would have been held in high esteem with *Paul*   10
   Must now be nam'd and printed Hereticks
By shallow *Edwards*[7] and Scotch what d' ye call;
   But we do hope to find out all your tricks,
   Your plots and packings[8] wors then those of *Trent*,[9]
                That so the Parliament   15
May with their wholsome and preventive Shears

---

[1] The "of" in *1673* is corrected by the "off" in the Trinity Manuscript.

[2] Since Archbishop William Laud was chief prelate, Milton may be burying a pun in "Laud"/"Lord."

[3] The Trinity Manuscript had "the vacant whore," corrected to "the widow'd whore," giving the image more of an emotional than a spatial dimension.

[4] There is probably a play on "whore"/ "abhor" (compare *Othello* 4.2.161–62).

[5] The phrase "classic hierarchy" is a technical one, since the Presbyterian hierarchy had its own judicial system, with "an ascending order of courts: parochial eldership, presbytery (or *classis*), provincial synod, national assembly; of these the chief disciplinary bodies were the first and second, the eldership referring cases to the presbytery or *classis*" (*Variorum* 2.1: 514).

[6] "A.S.", who may be "mere" in the sense that Milton may have known him only by his initials, was Adam Stewart, a Scottish divine and author of anti-Independent pamphlets. Samuel Rutherford had written *Lex, Rex* (1644), advocating the king's responsibility to the people for having been given authority over them, anticipating Milton's *Tenure of Kings and Magistrates* (*Variorum* 2.1: 514).

[7] Milton had first dictated "hare braind Edwards," then corrected the "hare braind" to "shallow" in the margin. Thomas Edwards wrote the monumental *Gangraena* (editions in 1645, 1646), in which he made what Milton might have called a shallow or hare-brained attack on *The Doctrine and Discipline of Divorce*. The Scotch "what'd ye call" might be Robert Baillie, who had also attacked Milton in print.

[8] The Trinity Manuscript establishes the plural, whereas *1673* has "packing."

[9] The Council of Trent (1545–63). Milton compares the repressive Westminster Assembly to the disorganized and intermittent Council of Trent, whose ultimate purpose, according to Paolo Sarpi, had been to stifle Protestant dissent and establish Inquisitorial repression. Bush points out that *A Vindication of the Answer* (1641), possibly written in part by Milton, uses the phrase "such packing . . . as perhaps worse was not at the Councell of Trent" (82; quoted in *Variorum* 2.2: 516).

Clip your Phylacteries,[10] though bauk[11] your Ears

And succour our just Fears
When they[12] shall read this clearly in your charge
New Presbyter is but *Old Priest* writ Large.[13]

20

Translations of Psalms 1–8

Psalms 1–8, translated and dated in various months of 1653, and Psalms 80–88, translated in 1648, were arranged in *1673* not in the order of translation but in the order in which they appear in the Bible. Hence we see Milton's earlier prosodic work second and his later work first. The important question for biographers is why each group of Psalms was translated when it was. In dating each translated Psalm so carefully, Milton signals the reader that the dating is important to him.

Though the reader of this edition can easily compare these translations with those of the King James Bible or of a modern translation, Milton's work might be studied on its own for its metrical variety, its use of rhyme, or its phrasing and imagery, as Hunter suggests. In Psalm 2, for instance, Milton informs his reader that he will be working in tercets, as did Dante in *The Divine Comedy*. Often the way the line should be read aloud will be signaled by its elisions, as with "The bloodi' and guileful man," or "sinners in th' assembly of just men."

Radzinowicz makes it clear how Milton studied the various types of lyric poetry presented in the Psalms in order to incorporate their forms and structures, their decorum and rhetoric, their individual voices and narrative positions into *Paradise Lost* (4).

The best way for any poet to study the Psalms closely, of course, is to translate them. Milton was using the translations, apparently, to practice his prosody, in various meters, syllabic arrangements, and stanza patterns, as he did with his translation of the Horatian ode "Ad Pyrrham." Jacobus adds that he might have been practicing his logical and rhetorical skills as well.

TEXT

The Psalms are very lightly punctuated in *1673*, indicating that the compositor may well have been following a holograph manuscript, since Milton's punctuation in poetry was always light from line to line. Perhaps following the author's manuscript affected capitalization and spelling as well.

Works Cited

Hunter, William B. "Milton Translates the Psalms." *Philological Quarterly* 40 (1961): 485–94.

Jacobus, Lee A. "Milton Metaphrast: Logic and Rhetoric in Psalm 1." *Milton Studies* 23 (1987): 119–32.

Radzinowicz, Mary Ann. *Milton's Epics and the Book of Psalms.* Princeton, NJ: Princeton UP, 1989.

PSAL. I. *Done into Verse*, 1653.

Bless'd is the man who hath not walk'd astray
In counsel of the wicked, and ith' way
Of sinners hath not stood, and in the seat
Of scorners hath not sate. But in the great

---

[10]Phylacteries were small leather boxes containing four passages from scripture; they were tied on the wrists or foreheads of orthodox Jews to remind them to honor the passages on days other than the Sabbath. Milton compares the practice of wearing phylacteries with any other of what he considers ostentatious displays of piety, his coined usage in *Tetrachordon* (Yale 4: 68) cited as *OED* 1.b. To clip the phylacteries would be to trim the fringes of any such religious ornament.

[11]Printed as "bank" in *1673* but corrected by the Errata to "bauk," which means (among other things) "to seize" (see *OED* 2.2.e), referring to the process of cutting off the ears of dissenters like William Prynne (in 1633). The first version of the line in TM was "Cropp yee as close as marginall P___s eares," an obvious allusion to William Prynne, whose ears were clipped twice, for reasserting his Presbyterian opinions, the second time in 1637. For the context, see John Leonard, "'Trembling ears': the historical moment of *Lycidas*," *The Journal of Medieval and Renaissance Studies (JMRS)* 21 (1991): 59–81. Calling him "marginal Prynne" refers to Prynne's (to Milton) annoying habit of covering the margins of his books with citations, something that Milton did only sparingly.

[12]Written first as "you" in the Trinity Manuscript, then canceled and replaced by "they."

[13]First written as "at large," then the "at" was canceled. What Milton implies with "writ Large" is that the English people got more of the same thing from the Presbyterians as they did from the Laudian Church, only more so: a "priest" became a "PRESBYTER."

Jehovahs Law is ever his delight,   5
And in his Law he studies day and night.
He shall be as a tree which planted grows
By watry streams, and in his season knows
To yield his fruit, and his leaf shall not fall,
And what he takes in hand shall prosper all.   10
Not so the wicked, but as chaff which fann'd
The wind drives, so the wicked shall not stand
In judgment,[1] or abide their tryal then,
Nor sinners in th' assembly of just men.
For the Lord knows th' upright way of the just,   15
And the way of bad men to ruine must.

    PSAL. II. *Done* Aug. 8. 1653. *Terzetti.*[1]

WHy do the Gentiles tumult, and the Nations
    Muse[2] a vain thing, the Kings of th' earth
    With power, and Princes in their Congregations
Lay deep their plots together through each Land,
    Against the Lord and his Messiah dear   5
    Let us break off, say they, by strength of hand
Their bonds, and cast from us, no more to wear,
    Their twisted cords: he who in Heaven doth dwell
    Shall laugh, the Lord shall scoff them, then severe
Speak to them in his wrath, and in his fell   10
    And fierce ire trouble them; but I saith hee
    Anointed[3] have my King (though ye rebell)
On Sion my holi'hill. A firm decree
    I will declare; the Lord to me hath say'd
    Thou art my Son[4] I have begotten thee   15
This day; ask of me, and the grant is made;
    As thy possession I on thee bestow
    Th' Heathen, and as thy conquest to be sway'd
Earths utmost bounds: them shalt thou bring full low
    With Iron Scepter bruis'd, and them disperse   20
    Like to a potters vessel shiver'd so.
And now be wise at length ye Kings averse
    Be taught ye Judges of the earth; with fear
    Jehovah[5] serve, and let your joy converse
With trembling; kiss the Son least he appear   25
    In anger and ye perish in the way
    If once his wrath take fire like fuel sere.°   DRY
Happy all those who have in him their stay.°   MAINSTAY, MORAL CENTER

---

[1]The "jugdment" of *1673* is an obvious misprint.
[1]In terza rima, the metrical and rhyme scheme of Dante's *Divine Comedy*, in which three-line units are linked with each other by rhyming ABA BCB, and so on, in an interlocking pattern.
[2]Not capitalized in *1673*, probably by oversight.
[3]Another lower-case letter began this line in *1673*.
[4]Some editors add a semicolon here.
[5]The name might have been in italics, as in Psalm I, but "Messiah" is not in italics in Psalm 2, and neither is "Jehovah" in Psalm 4, or from that point on in the 1673 volume.

PSAL. 3. Aug. 9. 1653.[1]

When he fled from Absalom.

Lord how many are my foes
 How many those
  That in arms against me rise
   Many are they
  That of my life distrustfully doth say,   5
No help for him in God there lies.
But thou Lord art my shield my glory,
   Thee through my story
  Th' exalter of my head I count
   Aloud I cry'd   10
  Unto Jehovah, he full soon reply'd
And heard me from his holy mount.
I lay and slept, I wak'd again,
  For my sustain
  Was the Lord. Of many millions   15
   The populous rout
  I fear not though incamping round about
They pitch against me their Pavillions.
Rise Lord, save me my God for thou
  Hast smote ere now   20
  On the cheek-bone all my foes,
   Of men abhor'd
  Hast broke the teeth. This help was from the Lord
Thy blessing on thy people flows.

PSAL. IV. *Aug.* 10. 1653.

Answer me when I call
 God of my rightousness
In straights and in distress
Thou didst me disinthrall
And set at large; now spare,   5
 Now pity me, and hear my earnest prai'r.
Great ones how long will ye
My glory have in scorn
How long be thus forborn
Still to love vanity,   10
To love, to seek, to prize
 Things false and vain and nothing else but lies?
Yet know the Lord hath chose
Chose to himself a part
The good and meek of heart   15
(For whom to chuse he knows)
Jehovah from on high

---

[1]Irregularities continue to appear in the printing of the Psalms. Numbering will vary between Roman and Arabic, as will italic usage ("PSAL. 3" vs. "*PSAL.* IV."). Also, punctuation is so light as to be incorrect by seventeenth-century standards as well as twentieth-century standards, as with the lack of a period or semicolon after "rise" in l.4.

Will hear my voyce what time to him I crie.
Be aw'd, and do not sin,
Speak to your hearts alone,   20
Upon your beds, each one,
And be at peace within.
Offer the offerings just
    Of righteousness and in Jehovah trust.
Many there be that say   25
Who yet will shew us good?
Talking like this worlds brood;
But Lord, thus let me pray,
On us lift up the light
    Lift up the favour of thy count'nance bright.   30
Into my heart more joy
And gladness thou has put
Then when a year of glut
Their stores doth over-cloy
And from their plenteous grounds   35
    With vast increase their corn and wine abounds
In peace at once will I
Both lay me down and sleep
For thou alone dost keep
Me safe where ere I lie
As in a rocky Cell   40
    Thou Lord alone in safety mak'st me dwell.

PSAL. V. *Aug.* 12. 1653.

JEhovah to my words give ear
    My meditation waigh
The voyce of my complaining hear
My King and God for unto thee I pray.
    Jehovah thou my early voyce   5
        Shalt in the morning hear
    Ith' morning I to thee with choyce
Will rank my Prayers, and watch till thou appear.
    For thou are not a God that takes
        In wickedness delight   10
    Evil with thee no biding makes
Fools or mad men stand not within thy sight.
    All workers of iniquity
        Thou hat'st; and them unblest
    Thou wilt destroy that speak a ly   15
The bloodi' and guileful man God doth detest.
    But I will in thy mercies dear
        Thy numerous mercies go
    Into thy house; I in thy fear
Will towards thy holy temple worship low   20
    Lord lead me in thy righteousness
        Lead me because of those
    That do observe If I transgress
Set thy wayes right before, where my step goes.

For in his faltring mouth unstable   25
   No word is firm or sooth
Their inside, troubles miserable;
An open grave their throat, their tongue they smooth.
   God, find them guilty, let them fall
     By their own counsels quell'd;   30
   Push them in their rebellions all
Still on; for against thee they have rebell'd;
   Then all who trust in thee shall bring
     Their joy, while thou from blame
   Defend'st them, they shall ever sing   35
And shall triumph in thee, who love thy name.
   For thou Jehovah wilt be found
     To bless the just man still,
   As with a shield thou wilt surround
Him with thy lasting favour and good will.   40

PSAL. VI. *Aug.* 13. 1653.

L Ord in thine anger do not reprehend me
   Nor in thy hot displeasure me correct;
Pity me Lord for I am much deject°   DEJECTED
   Am very weak and faint; heal and amend me,
For all my bones, that even with anguish ake,   5
   Are troubled, yea my soul is troubled sore°   SORELY TROUBLED
And thou O Lord how long? turn Lord, restore
   My soul, O save me for thy goodness sake
For in death no remembrance is of thee;
   Who in the grave can celebrate thy praise?   10
Wearied I am with sighing out my dayes,
   Nightly my Couch I make a kind of Sea;
My Bed I water with my tears; mine Eie
   Through grief consumes, is waxen° old and dark   HAS BECOME
Ith' mid'st of all mine enemies that mark.°   OBSERVE   15
   Depart all ye that work iniquitie,
Depart from me, for the voice of my weeping
   The Lord hath heard, the Lord hath heard my prai'r
My supplication with acceptance fair
   The Lord will own, and have me in his keeping.   20
Mine enemies shall all be blank and dash't
   With much confusion; then grow red with shame,
They shall return in hast the way they came
   And in a moment shall be quite abash't.

PSAL. VII. Aug. 14. 1653.

Upon the words of Chush *the* Benjamite *against*
  him.

L Ord my God to thee I flie
  Save me and secure me under

Thy protection while I crie,
Least as a Lion (and no wonder)
He hast to tear my Soul asunder   5
Tearing and no rescue nigh.

Lord my God if I have thought
Or done this, if wickedness
Be in my hands, if I have wrought
Ill to him that meant me peace,   10
Or to him have render'd less,
And not fre'd° my foe for naught;   FREED

Let th' enemy pursue my soul
And overtake it, let him tread
My life down to the earth and roul   15
In the dust my glory dead,
In the dust and there out spread
Lodge it with dishonour foul.

Rise Jehovah in thine ire
Rouze thy self amidst the rage   20
Of my foes that urge like fire;
And wake for me their furi' asswage;
Judgment here thou didst ingage
And command which I desire.

So th' assemblies of each Nation   25
Will surround thee, seeking right,
Thence to thy glorious habitation
Return on high and in their sight.
Jehovah judgeth most upright
All people from the worlds foundation.   30

Judge me Lord, be judge in this
According to my righteousness
And the innocence which is
Upon me: cause at length to cease
Of evil men the wickedness   35
And their power that do amiss.

But the just establish fast,
Since thou art the just God that tries
Hearts and reins. On God is cast
My defence, and in him lies   40
In him who both just and wise
Saves th' upright of Heart at last.

God is a just Judge and severe,
And God is every day offended;
If th' unjust will not forbear,   45
His Sword he whets, his Bow hath bended
Already, and for him intended
The tools of death, that waits him near.

(His arrows purposely made he
For them that persecute.) Behold
He travels big with vanitie,   50
Trouble he hath conceav'd of old
As in a womb, and from that mould
Hath at length brought forth a Lie.

He dig'd a pit, and delv'd it deep,
And fell into the pit he made,   55
His mischief that due course doth keep,
Turns on his head, and his ill trade
Of violence will undelay'd
Fall on his crown with ruine steep.   60

Then will I Jehovah's praise
According to his justice raise
And sing the Name and Deitie
Of Jehovah the most high.

PSAL. VIII. *Aug.* 14. 1653.

O Jehovah our Lord how wondrous great
       And glorious is thy name through all the earth?
So as above the Heavens thy praise to set
    Out of the tender mouths of latest bearth,°   BIRTH

Out of the mouths of babes and suckling thou   5
    Hast founded strength because of all thy foes
To stint th' enemy, and slack th' avengers brow
    That bends his rage thy providence to oppose.[1]

When I behold thy Heavens, thy Fingers art,
    The Moon and Starrs which thou so bright hast set,   10
In the pure firmament, then saith my heart,
    O what is man that thou remembrest yet,
And think'st upon him; or of man begot
    That him thou visit'st and of him art found;
Scarce to be less then Gods, thou mad'st his lot,   15
    With honour and with state thou hast him crown'd.

O're the works of thy hand thou mad'st him Lord,
    Thou has put all under his lordly feet,
All Flocks, and Herds, by thy commanding word,
    All beasts that in the field or forrest meet,   20

Fowl of the Heavens, and Fish that through the wet
    Sea-paths in shoals do slide. And know no dearth.

---

[1]I have supplied the comma not present in 1673, as do most editors.

O Jehovah our Lord how wondrous great
   And glorious is thy name through all the earth.

Psalms 80–88
(1648)

Psalms 80–88, translated four years earlier than his 1653 translations of Psalms 1–8, are presented on the page with more of Milton's editorial apparatus intact. Hebrew words are glossed to the right of the lines in which they occur. Milton's additions to the original are printed in italics. His versions should be compared with those of the King James Bible and the Geneva Bible. Milton's work is not notably original: Hunter found that about fifty percent of the lines in Milton's translations exist in earlier published psalters.

Shawcross emphasizes the fact that the nine Psalms were translated "in the midst of the Civil Wars," and that they "reflect [Milton's] dejection caused by his pusillanimous fellow countrymen and the . . . hope for enlightened leadership" (164).

TEXT

These and the other psalm translations exist only in the 1673 text.

Works Cited

Hunter, William B. "Milton Translates the Psalms." *Philological Quarterly* 28 (1949): 125–44.

Shawcross, John T. *John Milton: The Self & the World*. Lexington: UP of Kentucky, 1993.

April. 1648. J.M.

Nine of the Psalms done into Metre, wherein all but what is in a different Character, are the very words of the Text, translated from the Original.

PSAL. LXXX.

1

T Hou Shepherd that dost Israel *keep*
   Give ear *in time of need*,
Who leadest like a flock of sheep
   Thy loved Josephs seed,
That sitt'st between the Cherubs *bright*   5
   Between their wings out-spread
Shine forth, *and from thy cloud give light,*
   And on our foes thy dread
2 In Ephraims view and Benjamins,
   And in Manasse's sight   10
Awake* thy strength, come, and *be seen*   *Gnorera.
   To save us *by thy might.*
3 Turn us again, *thy grace divine*
   To us O God *vouchsafe*;
Cause thou thy face on us to shine   15
   And then we shall be safe.
4 Lord God of Hosts, how long wilt thou,
   How long wilt thou declare
Thy* smoaking wrath, *and angry brow*   *Gnashanta.
   Against thy peoples praier.[1]   20

---

[1]Misprinted as "praire" in *1673*.

5 Thou feed'st them with the bread of tears,
  Their bread with tears they eat,
And mak'st them* largely drink the tears   *Shalish.
  Wherwith their cheeks are wet.
6 A strife thou mak'st us and a prey   25
  To every neighbour foe,
Among themselves they* laugh, they* play,
  And* flouts at us they throw   *Jilnagu
7 Return us, and thy grace divine,
  O God of Hosts vouchsafe   30
Cause thou thy face on us to shine,
  And then we shall be safe.
8 A Vine from Ægypt thou has brought,
  Thy free love made it thine,
And drov'st out Nations proud and haut   35
  To plant this lovely Vine.
9 Thou did'st prepare for it a place
  And root it deep and fast
That it began to grow apace,
  And fill'd the land at last.   40
10 With her green shade that cover'd all,
  The Hills were over-spread
Her Bows as high as Cedars tall
  Advanc'd their lofty head.
11 Her branches on the western side   45
  Down to the Sea she sent,
And upward to that river wide
  Her other branches went.
12 Why has thou laid her Hedges low
  And brok'n down her Fence,   50
That all may pluck her, as they go,
  With rudest violence?
3 The tusked Boar out of the wood
  Up turns it by the roots,
Wild Beasts there brouze, and make their food   55
  Her grapes and tender Shoots.
14 Return now, God of Hosts, look down
  From Heav'n, thy Seat divine,
Behold us, but without a frown,
  And visit this thy Vine.   60
15 Visit this Vine, which thy right hand
  Hath set, and planted long,
And the young branch, that for thy self
  Thou has made firm and strong.
16 But now it is consum'd with fire,   65
  And cut with Axes down,
They perish at thy dreadfull ire,
  At thy rebuke and frown.
17 Upon the man of thy right hand
  Let thy good hand be laid,   70
Upon the Son of Man, whom thou
  Strong for thy self hast made.
18 So shall we not go back from thee

To wayes of sin and shame,
Quick'n us thou, then *gladly* wee
　　Shall call upon thy Name.
Return us, *and thy grace divine*
　　Lord God of Hosts *voutsafe,*[2]
Cause thou thy face on us to shine,
　　And then we shall be safe.

75

PSAL. LXXXI.

1

TO God our strength sing loud, *and clear*
　　Sing loud to God *our King,*
To Jacobs God, *that all may hear*
　　Loud acclamations ring.
2 Prepare a Hymn, prepare a Song
　　The Timbrel hither bring
The *cheerfull* Psaltry bring along
　　And Harp *with* pleasant *string,*
3 Blow, *as is wont,* in the new Moon
　　With Trumpets *lofty sound,*
Th' appointed time, the day wheron
　　Our solemn Feast *comes round.*
4 This was a Statute *giv'n of old*
　　For Israel *to observe*
A Law of Jacobs God, *to hold*
　　From whence they might not swerve.
5 This he a Testimony ordain'd
　　In Joseph, *not to change,*
When as he pass'd through Ægypt land;
　　The Tongue I heard, was strange.
6 From burden, *and from slavish toyle*
　　I set his shoulder free;
His hands from pots, *and*[1] *mirie° soyle*　　　　　　　MUDDY
　　Deliver'd were by me.
7 When trouble did thee sore assaile,
　　On me then didst thou call,
And I to free thee *did not* faile,
　　And led thee out of thrall.°　　　　　　THRALLDOM, SERVANTHOOD
I answer'd thee* in thunder deep　　　**Be Sether ragnam.*
　　With clouds encompass'd round;
I tri'd thee at the water steep
　　Of Meriba *renown'd.*
8 Hear O my people, *heark'n well,*
　　I testifie to thee
Thou antient stock of Israel,
　　If thou wilt list to mee,

5

10

15

20

25

30

35

---

[2]A Miltonic spelling, unusual in the Psalm translations, comes through. Compare "*vouchsafe*" at l. 14 above.
[1]*1673* has an inverted letter on "aud," which I have corrected.

9 Through out the land of thy abode
    No alien God shall be
Nor shalt thou to a forein God
    In honour bend thy knee.   40
10 I am the Lord thy God which brought
    Thee out of Ægypt land
Ask large enough, and I, *besought*,
    Will grant thy full demand.
11 And yet my people would not hear,   45
    Nor hearken to my voice;
And Israel *whom I lov'd so dear*
    Mislik'd° me for his choice.   OFFENDED
12 Then did I leave them to their will
    And to their wandring mind;   50
Their own conceits° they follow'd still   CONCEPTIONS, NOTIONS
    Their own devises blind.
13 O that my people would *be wise*
    To serve me *all their daies*,
And O that Israel would *advise*   55
    To walk my *righteous* waies.
14 Then would I soon bring down their foes
    That now so proudly rise,
And turn my hand against *all those*
    That are their enemies.   60
15 Who hate the Lord should *then be fain*
    To bow to him and bend,
But *they, his People, should remain*,
    Their time should have no end.
16 And we would feed them *from the shock*,   65
    With flowr of finest wheat,
And satisfie them from the rock
    With Honey *for their Meat*.

PSAL. LXXXII.

1

G Od in the *great *assembly stands
    Of Kings and lordly States,   * *Bagnadath-el*.
†Among the gods† on both his hands   +*Bekerev*.
    He judges and debates.
2 How long will ye *pervert the right   *Tishphetu*   5
    With *judgment false and wrong   *gnavel*.
Favouring the wicked *by your might*.
    Who thence grow bold and strong
3 *Regard the *weak and fatherless   *Shiphtu-dal*.
    *Dispatch the *poor mans cause,   10
And †raise the man in deep distress
    By †just and equal Lawes.   †*Hatzdiku*.
4 Defend the poor and desolate,
    And rescue from the hands
Of wicked men the low estate   15

Of him *that help demands*.
5 They know not nor will understand,
   In darkness they walk on
The Earths foundations all are *mov'd
   And *out of order gon.   *Jimmotu.   20
6 I said that ye were Gods, yea all
   The Sons of God most high
7 But ye shall die like men, and fall
   As other Princes *die*.
8 Rise God, * judge thou the earth *in might*,   25
   This *wicked* earth *redress,   *Shiphta.
For thou art he who shalt by right
   The Nations all possess.

PSAL. LXXXIII.

1
B E not thou silent *now at length*
   O God hold not thy peace,
Sit not thou still O God of *strength*
   We cry and do not cease.
2 For lo thy *furious* foes now *swell   5
   And *storm outrageously,   *Jehemajun.
And they that hate thee *proud and fell*
   Exalt their heads full hie.
3 Against thy people they †contrive   †*Jagnarimu*
†Their Plots and Counsels deep,   †*Sod*.   10
*Them to ensnare they chiefly strive   **Jithjagnatsu gnal*.
   *Whom thou dost hide and keep.   *Tsephuneca
4 Come let us cut them off say they,
   Till they no Nation be
That Israels name for ever may   15
   Be lost in memory.
5 For they consult †with all their might,   †*Lev jachdau*.
   And all as one in mind
Themselves against thee they unite
   And in firm union bind.   20
6 The tents of Edom, and the brood
   Of *scornful* Ishmael,
Moab, with them of Hagars blood
   That in the Desart dwell,
7 Gebal and Ammon *there conspire*,   25
   And *hateful* Amalec,
The Philistims, and they of Tyre
   Whose bounds the Sea doth check.
8 With them great Asshur also bands
   And doth confirm the knot,   30
All these have lent their armed hands
   To aid the Sons of Lot.
9 Do to them as to Midian *bold*

That wasted all the Coast
To Sisera, and as *is told*   35
   Thou didst to Jabins *hoast,*
When at the brook of Kishon *old*
   They were repulst and slain,
10 At Endor quite cut off, and rowl'd   40
   As dung upon the plain.
11 As Zeb and Oreb evil sped
   So let their Princes speed
As Zeba, and Zalmunna *bled*
   So let their Princes *bleed.*
12 *For they amidst their pride* have said   45
   By right now shall we seize
Gods houses, and *will now invade*
   †Their stately Palaces.   †*Neoth Elohim*
13 My God, oh make them as a wheel   *bears both.*
   No quiet let them find,
Giddy and *restless* let *them reel*   50
   Like stubble from the wind.
14 As when an *aged* wood takes fire
   Which on a sudden straies,
The *greedy* flame runs hier and hier
   Till all the mountains blaze,   55
15 So with thy whirlwind them pursue,
   And with thy tempest chase;
16 *And till they *yield thee honour due;   **They seek*
   Lord fill with shame their face.   *thy Name,* Heb.   60
17 Asham'd and troubl'd let them be,
   Troubl'd and sham'd for ever,
Ever confounded, and so die
   With shame, *and scape it never.*
18 Then shall they know that thou whose name
   Jehova is alone,   65
Art the most high, and *thou the same*
   O're all the earth *art one.*

PSAL. LXXXIV.

1 How[1] lovely are thy dwellings fair!
   O Lord of Hoasts, how dear
The *pleasant* Tabernacles are!
   Where thou do'st dwell so near.
2 My Soul doth long and almost die   5
   Thy Courts O Lord to see,
My heart and flesh aloud do crie,
   O living God, for thee.
3 There ev'n the Sparrow *freed from wrong*

---

[1]Normally the psalm would begin with a dropped capital letter, but here the compositor forgets, as he forgot from time to time to put "PSAL." in italics.

Hath found a house of *rest*,   10
The Swallow there, to lay her young
  Hath built her *brooding* nest,
Ev'n by thy Altars Lord of Hoasts
  They find their safe abode,
And home they fly from round the Coasts   15
  Toward thee, My King, my God.
4 Happy, who in thy house reside
  Where thee they ever praise,
5 Happy, whose strength in thee doth bide,
  And in their hearts thy waies.   20
6 They pass through Baca's *thirstie* Vale,
  That dry and barren ground
As through a fruitfull watry Dale
  Where Springs and Showrs abound.
7 They journey on from strength to strength   25
  With joy and gladsom cheer
Till all before *our* God *at length*
  In Sion do appear.
8 Lord God of Hoasts hear *now* my praier
  O Jacobs God give ear,   30
9 Thou God our shield look on the face
  Of thy anointed *dear*.
10 For one day in thy Courts to be
  Is better, *and more blest*
Then *in the joyes of Vanity*,   35
  A thousand daies *at best*.
I in the temple of my God
  Had rather keep a dore,°   BE A DOORKEEPER
Then dwell in Tents, *and rich abode*
  With Sin *for evermore*.   40
11 For God the Lord both Sun and Shield
  Gives grace and glory *bright*,
No good from them shall be with-held
  Whose waies are just and right.
12 Lord *God* of Hoasts *that raign'st on high*,   45
  That man is *truly* blest,
Who *only* on thee doth relie,
  And in thee only rest.

PSAL. LXXXV.

1
THy Land to favour graciously
  Thou hast not Lord been slack,°   SLOW
Thou hast from *hard* Captivity
  Returned Jacob back.
2 Th' inquity thou didst forgive   5
  That wrought thy people woe,
And all their Sin, *that did thee grieve*
  Hast hid *where none shall know*.

3 Thine anger all thou hadst remov'd,
  And calmly didst return   10
From thy †fierce wrath which we had prov'd   †*Heb.*
  Far worse then fire to burn.   *The burning heat*
4 God of our saving health and peace,   *of thy wrath.*
  Turn us, and us restore,
Thine indignation cause to cease   15
  Toward us, and *chide no more.*
5 Wilt thou be angry without end,
  For ever angry thus
Wilt thou thy frowning ire extend
  From age to age on us?   20
6 Wilt thou not *turn, and hear our voice   **Heb. Turn*
  And us again *revive,   *to quicken us*
That so thy people may rejoyce
  By thee preserv'd alive.
7 Cause us to see thy goodness Lord,   25
  To us thy mercy shew
Thy saving health to us afford
  And life in us renew.
8 And now what God the Lord will speak
  I will *go strait and* hear,   30
For to his people he speaks peace
  And to his Saints *full dear,*
To his dear Saints he will speak peace,
  But let them never more
Return to folly, but *surcease*   35
  To trespass as before.
9 Surely to such as do him fear
  Salvation is at hand
And glory shall *ere long appear*
  To dwell within our Land.   40
10 Mercy and Truth *that long were miss'd*
  Now *joyfully* are met
Sweet Peace and Righteousness have kiss'd
  And hand in hand are set.
11 Truth from the earth *like to a flowr*   45
  Shall bud and blossom *then,*
And Justice from her heavenly bowr
  Look down *on mortal men.*
12 The Lord will also then bestow
  Whatever thing is good[1]   50
Our Land shall forth in plenty throw
  Her fruits to be our food.
13 Before him Righteousness shall go
  His Royal Harbinger,
Then *will he come, and not be slow   55
  His footsteps cannot err.
      Heb. *He will set his steps to the way.*[2]

---

[1]Most editors add a period, but of course a semicolon would do, as Shawcross's edition supplies.
[2]This marginal gloss, for some reason, is set below the last line, instead of to the right of l. 85.

PSAL. LXXXVI.

1
THy gracious ear, O Lord, encline,
   O hear me *I thee pray*,
For I am poor, and almost pine
   with need, *and sad decay*.
2 Preserve my soul, for †I have trod
   Thy waies, and love the just,
Save thou thy servant O my God
   Who *still* in thee doth trust.
3 Pitty me Lord for daily thee
   I call; 4. O make rejoyce
Thy Servants Soul; for Lord to thee
   I lift my soul *and voice*,
5 For thou art good, thou Lord art prone
   To pardon, thou to all
Art full of mercy, thou *alone*
   To them that on thee call.
6 Unto my supplication Lord
  give ear, and to the crie
Of my *incessant* praiers afford
   Thy hearing graciously.
7 I in the day of my distress
   Will call on thee *for aid*;
For thou wilt *grant* me *free access*
   And answer, what I pray'd.
8 Like thee among the gods is none
   O *Lord*,[1] nor any works
Of all that other gods have done
   Like to thy *glorious* works.
9 The Nations all whom thou hast made
   Shall come, and *all shall frame*
To bow them low before thee Lord,
   And glorifie thy name.
10 For great thou art, and wonders great
   By thy strong hand are done,
Thou *in thy everlasting Seat*
   Remainest God alone.
11 Teach me O Lord thy way *most right*,
   I in thy truth will bide,
To fear thy name my heart unite
   So shall it never slide.
12 Thee will I praise O Lord my God
   Thee honour, and adore
With my whole heart, and blaze abroad
   Thy name for ever more.
13 For great thy mercy is toward me,
   And thou hast free'd my Soul

†Heb. *I am good,
loving, a doer of
good and holy
things.*

5

10

15

20

25

30

35

40

45

---

[1]The word "Lord" begins with an italic letter in *1673.*

Eev'n from the lowest Hell set free
   From deepest darkness foul.
14 O God the proud against me rise
   And violent men are met   50
To seek my life, and in their eyes
   No fear of thee have set.
15 But thou Lord art the God most mild
   Readiest thy grace to shew,
Slow to be angry, and *art stil'd*   55
   Most mercifull, most true.
16 O turn to me *thy face at length*,
   And me have mercy on,
Unto thy servant give thy strength,
   And save thy hand-maids Son.   60
17 Some sign of good to me afford,
   And let my foes *then* see
And be asham'd, because thou Lord
   Do'st help and comfort me.

PSAL. LXXXVII.

1

A Mong the holy Mountains *high*
   Is his foundation fast,
There Seated in his Sanctuary,
   His Temple there is plac't.
2 Sions *fair* Gates the Lord loves more   5
   Then all the dwellings *faire*
Of Jacobs Land, *though there be store*,°   ABUNDANCE
   And all within his care.
3 City of God, most glorious things
   Of thee *abroad* are spoke;   10
4 I mention Egypt, *where proud Kings*
   Did our forefathers yoke,
I mention Babel to my friends,
   Philistia *full of scorn*,
And Tyre with Ethiops *utmost ends*,   15
   Lo this man there was born:
5 But *twise that praise shall in our ear*
   Be said of Sion *last*
This and this man was born in her,
   High God shall fix her fast.   20
6 The Lord shall write it in a Scrowle
   That ne're shall be out-worn
When he the Nations doth enrowle
   That this man there was born.
7 Both they who sing, and they who dance   25
   With sacred Songs are there,
In thee *fresh brooks, and soft streams glance*
   And all my fountains *clear.*

PSAL. LXXXVIII.

1
L Ord God that dost me save and keep,
      All day to thee I cry;
And all night long, before thee *weep*
    Before thee *prostrate* lie.
2 Into thy presence let my praier   5
    With sighs devout ascend
And to my cries, that *ceaseless are*,
    Thine ear with favour bend.
3 For cloy'd with woes and trouble store
    Surcharg'd my Soul doth lie,   10
My life at *deaths uncherful dore*
    Unto the grave draws nigh.
4 Reck'n'd I am with them that pass
    Down to the *dismal* pit
I am a *man, but weak alas   *Heb. *A man without*   15
    And for that name unfit.   *manly strength*,
5 From life discharg'd and parted quite
    Among the dead *to sleep*,
And like the slain *in bloody fight*
    That in the grave lie *deep*.   20
Whom thou rememberest no more,
    Dost never more regard,
Them from thy hand deliver'd o're
    Deaths hideous house hath barr'd.
6 Thou in the lowest pit *profound*   25
    Hast set me *all forlorn*,
Where thickest darkness *hovers round*,
    In horrid deeps *to mourn*.
7 Thy wrath *from which no shelter saves*
    Full sore doth press on me;   30
*Thou break'st upon me all thy waves,   *The* Hebr.
    *And all thy waves break me.   *bears both.*
8 Thou dost my friends from me estrange,
    And mak'st me odious,
Me to them odious, *for they change*,   35
    And I here pent up thus.
9 Through sorrow, and affliction great
    Mine eye grows dim and dead,
Lord all the day I thee entreat,
    My hands to thee I spread.   40
10 Wilt thou do wonders on the dead,
    Shall the deceas'd arise
And praise thee *from their loathsom bed*
    With pale and hollow eyes?
11 Shall they thy loving kindness tell   45
    On whom the grave *hath hold*,
Or they *who* in perdition *dwell*
    Thy faithfulness *unfold?*
12 In darkness can thy mighty *hand*

Or wondrous acts be known,   50
Thy justice in the *gloomy* land
  Of *dark* oblivion?
13 But I to thee O Lord do cry
  E're yet my life be spent,   55
And *up to thee* my praier *doth hie*
  Each morn, and thee prevent.
14 Why wilt thou Lord my soul forsake,
  And hide thy face from me,
15 That am already bruis'd, and †shake   †*Heb. Præ*   60
  With terror sent from thee;   *Concussione.*
Bruz'd, and afflicted and *so low*
  As ready to expire,
While I thy terrors undergo
  Astonish'd with thine ire.   65
16 Thy fierce wrath over me doth flow
  Thy threatnings cut me through.
17 All day they round about me go,
  Like waves they me persue.
18 Lover and friend thou hast remov'd   70
  And sever'd from me far.
They *fly me now* whom I have lov'd,
  And as in darkness are.

    F I N I S.

Ode to John Rouse, Librarian of the Bodleian
(Jan. 23. 1646.)

Dated "Jan. 23. 1646" when it first appeared in print, in the 1673 *Poems*, the ode to Rouse is the last poem in the Latin half of the volume. It is also preserved in a manuscript leaf pasted onto the verso of the title page of the Latin poetry in a copy of the 1645 *Poems* (Bodleian MS. Latin Miscellany d.77), images of which appear in Sotheby's *Ramblings* and in Fletcher's facsimiles. Shawcross identifies the scribe of this manuscript as John Phillips.

John Rouse or Rous (1574–1652) became librarian of the Bodley in 1620. In 1622, Lucas Holsten or Holstenius, who would be librarian of the Vatican when Milton visited Rome in 1638, signed in as Rouse's guest at the Bodleian (Philip 42). It is just possible that Milton knew of the association between the two librarians.

Milton's gift to Rouse of his 1645 *Poems* was accompanied by bound-together copies of a number of Milton's prose works, including *Areopagitica*, the divorce tracts, and *Of Education*. The whole package was inscribed to Rouse in Latin with Milton's list of the included works (Bodleian Arch. B. e.44). Milton knew quite well that depositing his books in the Bodleian would be likely to preserve them for immortality, keep them out of the hands of the rabble, and be likely to preserve them even in a time of civil war.

Milton's gift of the eleven prose tracts and the book of poems to the Bodleian might indicate that the two men shared some political sympathy, antiroyalist or antiprelatical, since Rouse had apparently requested that Milton send the volumes to be deposited at the Bodleian, and Rouse was known to refuse even King Charles's request for books on loan (the Bodleian is not a lending library). The first copy of the 1645 *Poems* that Milton sent was lost, as one can see by the headnote to the poem; Milton takes the loss of that book as his excuse to address its replacement volume as if it had a personality of its own.

Parker pointed out that the versification of the ode is close to that of *Samson Agonistes* in English; the versification is also described in many of the same terms as those used of *Samson*'s prosody in Milton's preface to the tragedy. This "bold experiment, a Latin imitation of a Greek tragic chorus" (*Milton* 306), is also Milton's last poem in Latin, or at least the last we know of.

TEXT

I have followed the only printed text, that of *1673*, though I have referred constantly to the manuscript, especially for accented letters.

Works Cited

Philip, Ian. *The Bodleian Library in the Seventeenth & Eighteenth Centuries*. Oxford: Clarendon, 1983.

Shawcross, John T. "Notes on Milton's Amanuenses." *JEGP: Journal of English and Germanic Philology* 58 (1959): 29–38.

Ad *Joannem Roüsium*, Oxoniensis Academiæ Bibliothecarium.

De libro poëmatum amisso, quem ille sibi denuò
mitti postulabat, ut cum aliis nostris in
Bibliotheca publica reponeret, Ode.
Strophe 1.

Gemelle cultu simplici gaudens liber,
Fronde licet geminâ,
Munditiéque nitens non operosâ,
Quam manus attulit
Juvenilis olim,   5
Sedula tamen haud nimii poetæ;
Dum vagus Ausonias nunc per umbras
Nunc Britannica per vireta lusit
Insons populi, barbitóque devius
Indulsit patrio, mox itidem pectine Daunio   10
Longinquum intonuit melos
Vicinis, & humum vix tetigit pede;
Antistrophe.

Quis te, parve liber, quis te fratribus
Subduxit reliquis dolo?
Cum tu missus ab urbe,   15
Docto jugiter obsecrante amico,
Illustre tendebas iter
Thamesis ad incunabula
Cærulei patris,
Fontes ubi limpidi   20
Aonidum, thyasusque sacer
Orbi notus per immensos
Temporum lapsus redeunte cœlo,
Celeberque futurus in ævum;
Strophe 2.

Modò quis deus, aut editus deo   25
Pristinam gentis miseratus indolem
(Si satis noxas luimus priores
Mollique luxu degener otium)
Tollat nefandos civium tumultus,
Almaque revocet studia sanctus   30
Et relegatas sine sede Musas
Jam penè totis finibus Angligenûm;
Immundasque volucres
Unguibus imminentes
Figat Apollineâ pharetrâ,   35
Phinéamque abigat pestem procul amne Pegaséo.

To *John Rouse*, Librarian of Oxford University.

*On a lost book of poems, for which he requested a
replacement, so that he could place it in the public
library with my other books, this Ode.*
Strophe 1.

A twin book,[1] rejoicing in one binding, with a double
title page, bright and neat with the unstudied neatness
of a boyish hand, but not yet that of an assured poet,
written while that poet, wandering at will, enjoyed
himself in green places, places not spoiled by a croud of
people, and gave free rein to the music of his native lute,
or presently strumming with a Daunian[2] quill gave out
with a foreign song, with his feet hardly touching the
ground.

Antistrophe 1.

Who stole you, little book, who filched you by some
trick from your brother books, when you were sent
from the city immediately because a learned friend had
requested them, on the trip on the Thames tow-path,
toward the source of Father Thames's dark stream,
where the clear springs of the Aonides[3] are found, and
the holy Bacchic dance: Oxford, known to all the world
as long as the sky turns through the immeasurable cycles of time, destined for fame throughout all ages?

Strophe 2.

May some god, or some man born of the gods, be
moved by sympathy for the native talent our country
has displayed for centuries, only if we have atoned sufficiently for our earlier sins and our effeminate luxury,
and might stop this damned civil war and its skirmishes
and restore with holy power our vital pursuits, recall
the vagrant Muses, banished now from almost every
corner of England, and pierce with Apollo's arrows the
detestable harpies that hover over us with their claws,
driving Phineus's rout away from the river of Pegasus.[4]

---

[1]The 1645 *Poems* of Milton is a twin book because it had two separate
divisions and systems of pagination, the first in English, the second in
Latin. The laurel leaves are convenient images for separate title pages.
[2]Probably "Italian," referring to the Italian poems. Daunius was the
Roman name for a part of what is now the region of Apulia.
[3]Mount Parnassus, where the Muses were supposed to have lived, is in
Aonia; hence the Muses are "Aonides."
[4]The poet invokes a god like Apollo, a poet and a slayer of monsters, to
kill the harpies of civil war now hovering over England. In Apollonius's
Argonautica 2.187–93, the harpies punish Phineus by defiling and
stealing his food. The winged horse Pegasus, associated with inspiration

Antistrophe.

Quin tu, libelle, nuntii licet malâ
Fide, vel oscitantiâ
Semel erraveris agmine fratrum,
Seu quis te teneat specus,   40
Seu qua te latebra, forsan unde vili
Callo teréris institoris insulsi,
Lætare felix, en iterum tibi
Spes nova fulget posse profundam
Fugere Lethen, vehique Superam   45
In Jovis aulam remige pennâ;

Strophe 3.

Nam te Roüsius sui
Optat peculî, numeróque justo
Sibi pollicitum queritur abesse,
Rogatque venias ille cujus inclyta   50
Sunt data virûm monumenta curæ:
Téque adytis etiam sacris
Voluit reponi quibus & ipse præsidet
Æternorum operum custos fidelis,
Quæstorque gazæ nobilioris,   55
Quàm cui præfuit Iön
Clarus Erechtheides
Opulenta dei per templa parentis
Fulvosque tripodas, donaque Delphica
Iön Actæâ genitus Creüsâ.

Antistrophe 2.

Little book, though by the bad faith of the messenger, or if you like by his drowsy negligence, you have strayed, from the company of your brothers, it may be that you are in some cave or hidden shelf, being rubbed by the calloused hand of some tasteless bookseller, you should rejoice. A new hope shines on you, a hope that you can escape from the depths of Lethe[5] and, beating your wings, fly up to the high courts of Jove.

Strophe 3.

Now Rouse wants you to be part of his collection, and he complains that, though you were promised to him, you are missing from the list, and he asks that you come to him, to that same Rouse to whose care the glorious memorials of humankind have been given. He wants you to have a place in those sanctuaries he rules over, faithful keeper of immortal works, custodian of a treasure more glorious than that which Ion[6] guarded, Ion the famous child of Erechtheus's daughter, Actaean Creusa, in the sumptuously decorated temple of his father Apollo, with its golden tripods and the treasures of Delphi.

---

and the Muses, struck his hoof on Mount Helicon to cause the spring of Hippocrene to begin to flow. The river of Pegasus here is by extension the Thames, on a branch of which Oxford sits.

[5]The river of the underworld known for inducing forgetfulness.
[6]In Euripides' play *Ion*, Hermes begins the action by describing how Apollo compelled the daughter of Erechtheus, Creusa, to take him as her lover. Ashamed of the child the union produced, Creusa exposed him to die, but Apollo had the child brought to Delphi, where he is raised in service to the god and where he protects such treasures as the golden tripod captured from Plataea.

Antistrophe.

Ergo tu visere lucos
Musarum ibis amœnos,
Diamque Phœbi rursùs ibis in domum
Oxoniâ quam valle colit
Delo posthabitâ,   65
Bifidóque Parnassi jugo:
Ibis honestus,
Postquam egregiam tu quoque sortem
Nactus abis, dextri prece sollicitatus amici.
Illic legéris inter alta nomina   70
Authorum, Graiæ simul & Latinæ
Antiqua gentis lumina, & verum decus.

Epodos.

Vos tandem haud vacui mei labores,
Quicquid hoc sterile fudit ingenium,
Jam serò placidam sperare jubeo   75
Perfunctam invidiâ requiem, sedesque beatas
Quas bonus Hermes
Et tutela dabit solers Roüsi,
Quò neque lingua procax vulgi penetrabit, atque longè
Turba legentum prava facesset;   80
At ultimi nepotes,
Et cordatior ætas
Judicia rebus æquiora forsitan
Adhibebit integro sinu.
Tum livore sepulto,   85
Si quid meremur sana posteritas sciet
Roüsio favente.

Ode tribus constat Strophis, totidémque Antistrophis
unâ demùm epodo clausis, quàs, tametsi omnes nec ver-
suum numero, nec certis ubique colis exactè respon-
deant, ita tamen secuimus, commodè legendi potius,
quàm ad antiquos concinendi modos rationem spec-
tantes. Alioquin hoc genus rectiùs fortasse dici mono-
strophicum debuerat. Metra partim'sunt κατὰ σχέσιν,
partim ἀπολελυμένα. Phaleucia quæ sunt, spondæum
tertio loco bis admittunt, quod idem in secundo loco
Catullus ad libitum fecit.

Antistrophe 3.

Therefore you shall go to view the lovely groves of the Muses; you shall go again to the divine structure where Apollo lives in the Vale of Oxford, which he prefers to Delos or the twin peaks of Parnassus. You will go in honor, after you have left me, for you have been remarkably fortunate: you have received an urgent invitation from a friend who wants the best for you. There you will be read among authors who were the ancient guides and now are the best glories of Greek and Latin civilization.

Epode.

So, my hard work, you haven't been in vain, so it appears, and my barren intellect hasn't dribbled out worthless drivel. Now I can tell you at last to look forward to a calm and quiet rest, relieved of all envy, and I ask you to hope for the blessed home that kindly Hermes and Rouse the careful guardian will provide, places where the insolent babble of the ignorant will never enter, away from the mass of worthless readers. But perhaps the children of future generations, in a wiser distant age, will see all things more justly. Then, when envy and malice are dead, if we deserve anything, the bright minds of the future will know, thanks to Rouse, what, if anything, I deserve.

The ode consists of three strophes, the same number of antistrophes, and finally, one concluding epode. Though the strophes and the antistrophes do not exactly correspond either in the number of lines or distribution of their metrical unites, I have nevertheless divided them in order to make the poem easier to read, being concerned that they may be read conveniently rather than that they may be chanted after the fashion of the ancient method. Otherwise, it had been more proper, perhaps, to call this sort of writing "monostrophic." The meters are determined partly by correlation, and they are partly free. In the Phaleucian lines[7] I admit two spondees in the third foot: Catullus admits a spondee at will in the second foot.

---

[7]Carey points out that in the regular Phaleucian line there is a spondee, a dactyl, and three trochees (1997 ed., 306n). Milton displays his knowledge of the metrics of Catullus and contrasts his practice, perhaps competitively, with that of the Roman poet.

Uncollected Poems from the Trinity College Manuscript

Sonnet 15
"On the Lord General Fairfax"
July (?), 1648

Thomas Fairfax (1612–71) became commander in chief of the New Model Army in January 1645. His most famous victory was the defeat of King Charles I's forces at Naseby on June 14 of that year. The hopes Milton pins on him in this sonnet, to become a leader in peace as well as war, were not realized, since he would resign his position in 1650, in protest against the execution of the King. Andrew Marvell's "Upon Appleton House" addresses Lord Fairfax in 1650 or thereabouts, and possibly criticizes him for his retirement from civic duty (Kermode 301).

Milton's deleted title in the Trinity Manuscript, restored below, helps date the poem to the time immediately before the news of the capture of Colchester reached London, August 27, 1648 (Shawcross edition 638). This poem and the sonnet to Cromwell were not printed in *1673*, probably because they could have gotten Milton into further trouble as a regicide. Milton's models for writing political sonnets, including those to Cromwell and Vane, might have included the Pindaric sonnets of the Italian Gabriello Chiabrera (Revard 515–16).

TEXT

The poem exists in Milton's handwriting in the Trinity Manuscript, but Edward Phillips published another version in his edition of Milton's *Letters of State* (1694). Newton's assessment of Phillips's editorial work is still valid: " . . . the printed copies, probably being taken at first from memory, are wonderfully incorrect; whole verses are omitted, and the beauty of these sonnets is in great measure defac'd and destroy'd" (1766 ed.; 235). No lines are omitted in Phillips's text of the Fairfax sonnet, but the replacement of the phrase "that daunt remotest kings" with "that daunt remotest things" gives some idea of the sloppiness of Phillips's transcription.

The fair copy of the poem in the Trinity Manuscript, then, is the copy-text for this edition. Shawcross has questioned the readings in the Trinity Manuscript of "her" instead of "their" in line 8 and "warrs" instead of "warr" in line 10. The reader might take note of the capitalization in the last four lines: Milton seems to be elevating abstract terms to allegorical status by his unusual emphasis.

Works Cited

Kermode, Frank, and Keith Walker, eds. *Andrew Marvell*. Oxford: Oxford UP, 1990.

Revard, Stella. "Milton and Chiabrera." *Milton in Italy: Contexts, Images, Contradictions*. Ed. Mario A. DiCesare. Binghamton, NY: Medieval & Renaissance Texts and Studies, 1991. 505–20.

Shawcross, John T. "Milton's Fairfax Sonnet." *Notes & Queries* 200 (1955): 195–96.

15
On yᵉ Lord Gen. Fairfax at yᵉ seige of Colchester[1]

Fairfax, whose name in armes through Europe rings
    Filling each mouth with envy, or with praise,
    And all her jealous monarchs with amaze,
    And rumors loud,[2] that daunt remotest kings,
Thy firm unshak'n vertue ever brings   5
    Victory home, though new rebellions raise
    Thir Hydra heads, & the fals North[3] displaies

---

[1]This title was crossed out in the Trinity Manuscript. Between "A book was writ," numbered 12 in the Trinity Manuscript, and this sonnet, numbered 15, was a note "on yᵉ forcers of Conscience to come in heer," in Milton's hand with one ink, then "turn over the leafe" below that, in another ink. Number 16 in TM is the sonnet to Cromwell (in a scribal hand), which immediately follows the Fairfax sonnet, but numbers 13 and 14 in TM are the sonnets to Lawes and to Mrs. Thomason.

[2]The word "loudd" was written in and then crossed through, with the corrected version of the word to the right.

[3]Scotland, invading England in violation of the Solemn League and Covenant.

her brok'n league, to impe her serpent wings,[4]
O yet a nobler task awaites thy hand;
      For what can Warrs but endless War still breed,
      Till Truth, & Right from Violence be freed,   10
And[5] Public Faith cleard from the shamefull brand
      Of Public Fraud. In vain doth Valour bleed
      While Avarice, & Rapine share the land.

Sonnet 16.
To the Lord Generall Cromwell
(May 1652)

By 1652, Oliver Cromwell had taken Fairfax's place as Commander of the New Model Army, three years after the King had been executed. Cromwell defeated the Scots at Darwen in August of 1648; at Dunbar in Scotland in 1651; and at Worcester in 1651. As in the poem to Fairfax, Milton attempts to define the statesman's role in peacetime England. The quotable phrase of the poem, "peace hath her victories / No less renow'd then warr," echoes "For what can Warrs but endless warr still breed" in the Fairfax sonnet and "Warr wearied hath perform'd what Warr can do" in *Paradise Lost* 6.695. If he had ever been enthusiastic about war, Milton was almost certainly tired of it by 1652 (see Fallon for a corrective to that opinion).

Cromwell was a member of the Committee for Propagation of the Gospel, appointed on February 10, 1652. Certain of its members had proposed limiting dissent, which Cromwell opposed, and paying the clergy through collection of tithes.

In Milton's mind, stifling dissent would bond church and state, creating "secular chains," and paying the clergy from tithes would make "hireling wolves" of the clergymen.

TEXT

Like the sonnets to Fairfax and Vane, this sonnet was not printed in Milton's lifetime, most probably because of its political stance. It exists only in a scribal copy, with revisions by a second scribe, in the Trinity Manuscript. The only printed version is in Phillips's *Letters of State* (1694), somewhat garbled, with the absurd "Croud" instead of "cloud" in line 1, and with line 5 omitted altogether.

Works Cited

Fallon, Robert Thomas. *Captain or Colonel: The Soldier in Milton's Life and Art.* Columbia: U of Missouri P, 1984.

Herz, Judith Scherer. "Milton and Marvell: The Poet as Fit Reader." *Modern Language Quarterly* 39 (1978): 240–41.

Woolrych, Austin. "Milton and Cromwell: 'A Short but Scandalous Night of Interruption?'" *Achievements of the Left Hand: Essays on the Prose of John Milton.* Ed. Michael Lieb and John T. Shawcross. Amherst: U of Massachusetts P, 1974. 185–218.

16
To The Lord Generall Cromwell May 1652[1]
On the proposalls of certaine ministers at y[e] Commtee
for Propagation of the Gospell

Cromwell, our cheif of men, who through a cloud[2]
      Not of warr onely, but detractions[3] rude,

---

[4]Here Phillips's edition might be helpful, since it uses "her" instead of "their." As Shawcross points out in the note cited above, Milton never spelled the word "their." The serpent wings on the Hydra have caused editors problems, but the problem is solved for Shawcross if Scotland is to be pictured as a winged serpent or dragon. The Hydra with its eight heads that sprouted other heads as soon as each was cut off (Apollodorus 2.5.2) was a proverbial symbol for problems that seemed to multiply.

[5]To the right of "And" was a repeated "An" crossed through.

[1]The two-line title of the sonnet was crossed through in TM, so that the number 16 was all that was left to identify it. The sonnet is written in the neat hand of an amanuensis or scribe, with corrections inserted by a second scribe, but the spelling might have been imposed by Milton with respect to the words "chief" and "feild."

[2]*1694* has "Croud."

[3]*1694* has "distractions."

Guided by faith & matchless Fortitude[4]
To peace & truth thy glorious way hast plough'd,
And on the neck[5] of crowned Fortune proud   5
  Hast reard Gods Trophies & his work pursu'd,[6]
  While Darwen stream[7]with[8] blood of Scotts imbru'd,°   REDDENED
  And Dunbarr feild[9] resounds[10] thy praises loud,
And Worcesters laureat wreath; yet much remaines
  To conquer still; peace hath her victories   10
  No less renownd then warr,[11] new foes aries°   ARISE
Threatning to bind our souls with[12] secular chaines:
  Helpe us to save free Conscience from the paw
  Of hireling wolves[13] whose Gospell is their maw.

Sonnet 17
To Sir Henry Vane the Younger

Sir Henry Vane the Elder died in 1655; his son, Sir Henry Vane the Younger (1613–1662), advocated an extreme form of Puritanism that set him in opposition at times to Oliver Cromwell, especially with regard to the division of church and state (Willcock). Milton was supposed to have sent this sonnet to him on July 3, 1652, according to Vane's first biographer George Sikes, in *The Life and Death of Sir Henry Vane* (1662; see the *Variorum* 2.2.426), where the poem first appeared in print. Edward Phillips published a version of it in his edition of Milton's *Letters of State* (1694), as part of his biography of his uncle. In the Trinity Manuscript, the poem to Vane is much-corrected and in the hand of a scribe. The title was written "To Sr Henry Vane the younger," then that title was crossed through and apparently the sonnet number "17" was added.

The sonnet is a companion to Sonnets 15 and 16. It comments on Vane's negotiations for an English union with Scotland, and on his peacemaking efforts with the Dutch, which sadly broke down as the Anglo-Dutch War began. Vane would prepare the English navy for that war. As with his petition to Cromwell in Sonnet 16, Milton praises Vane's policies concerning religious tolerance and the separation of church and state; he may have favored the more extreme position of Vane over the less extreme position of Cromwell (Kelley).

Text

The Trinity Manuscript transcription is the copy-text for this edition. Neither Sikes nor Phillips's transcriptions add substantially to our knowledge of the text, but variants from Phillips are noted.

Works Cited

Kelley, Maurice. "Milton's Later Sonnets and the Cambridge Manuscript." *Modern Philology* 54 (1956): 20–25.

Willcock, John. *Life of Sir Henry Vane the Younger: Statesman and Mystic (1613–1662)*. London: St. Catherine's P, 1913.

[4]*1694* adds a colon here.
[5]Most probably the neck of the beheaded king, Charles I. A trophy would be "A structure erected (originally on the field of battle, later in any public place) as a memorial of a victory in war, consisting of arms or other spoils taken from the enemy, hung upon a tree, pillar, etc. and dedicated to some divinity" (*OED* 1).
[6]The two lines in *1694* read "To Peace and Truth, thy Glorious way hast Plough'd, / And fought God's Battels, and his Work pursu'd . . . ."
[7]*1694* has "*Darwent* Streams."
[8]I have expanded "w^th."
[9]The first version of the phrase here in Trinity Manuscript was "Dunbar feild," then that was struck through and "Worsters laureat wreath" written above the line. The phrases, in other words, were transposed, then arranged as they had been originally.
[10]*1694* has "resound."
[11]*1694* has "No less than those of War."
[12]I have expanded "w^th."
[13]*1694* inserts a comma here.

17
To Sir Henry Vane the Younger

Vane, young in yeares, but in sage counsell old,
    Then whom a better Senatour nere held
    The helme of Rome, when gowns not armes repelld
    The feirce Epeirot & the African bold,[1]
Whether to settle peace or to unfold   5
    The drift of hollow states[2] hard to be spelld,
    Then to advise how warr may best,[3] upheld,
    Move by[4] her two maine nerves, Iron & Gold[5]
In all her equipage; besides to know
    Both spirituall powre[6] & civill, what each meanes,[7]   10
    What severs[8] each thou 'hast learnt, which[9] few have don[10]
The bounds of either sword to thee we ow.
    Therfore on thy firme[11] hand religion leanes
    In peace, and reck'ns thee her eldest son.[12]

---

[1]Pyrrhus, King of Epirus, and Hannibal, of the African capital of Carthage, both invaded Rome in the third century BCE. Roman senators distinguished themselves in their resistance to the invasions. Their gowns, the Roman togas ornamented according to senatorial rank, would be emblems of their power.
[2]A satirical jibe at the "hollowness" of Holland and at the difficulty of pronouncing outlandish Dutch names (compare the Scottish names in "A book was writ" 8–9). Milton invariably uses the word "hollow" to indicate dangerous moral vacuity, whether for demonic logic (*Paradise Lost* 2.112) or for evil-appearing eyes (Psalm 88.44).
[3]The phrase read "best be [no comma]" in *1694*.
[4]Trinity Manuscript has "on" instead of "by" written in in two places but canceled both times. *1694* has "Mann'd" instead of "Move."
[5]Machiavelli (*Discourses* Book 2, Chapter 10) wrote that "riches are not the nerves of war as is generally believed" (Milton, Commonplace Book, as translated in Yale 1: 415). The handwriting in the Commonplace Book might help to date the entry in 1651 or 1652, according to Maurice Kelley, "Milton and Machiavelli's Discorsi," *Studies in Bibliography* 4 (1951–52): 123–27.
[6]The word "powre" is omitted in *1694*.
[7]Originally written "what it meanes," with "it meanes" canceled and "each meanes" added to the right. The entire line as originally written was "What powre the Church & what the civill meanes."
[8]*1694* has "serves."
[9]I have expanded "w^{ch}."
[10]Trinity Manuscript should be consulted at this point, but the line originally read "Thou teachest best, which few have ever don."
[11]Originally written as "right hand" with "right" canceled and "firme" written above. In *1694* "firm" was replaced by "Right."
[12]The line in *1694* reads "And reckons thee in chief her Eldest Son."

Sonnet 22
"Cyriack, this three years day"

Milton's less-famous poem about his blindness is, like the sonnet numbered 21, addressed to his friend and amanuensis, Cyriack Skinner. It is found in the Trinity Manuscript, probably in Skinner's hand, with no title but the number 22 centered above it. Dating the sonnet depends on when Milton might have considered himself completely blind. Biographers continue to argue over when that might be; but perhaps the best guess is three years after Herman Mylius reported him to be completely blind (March 5, 1652; *Chronology* 135), or 1655. Milton's letter to Philaris, dated September 28, 1655, shows his understandable concern with the causes and symptoms of his affliction.

Milton's formal "I" in the poem claims that his sight was lost in a good cause, the defense of liberty, with God or Heaven guiding him in his "noble task." His position is very close to that pictured in the *Defensio Secunda* (1651), in which he defends himself against the charge that his blindness was divine punishment for his having defended the execution of Charles I.

TEXT

I follow the Trinity Manuscript version. The 1694 *Letters of State* does supply the title "To Mr. *Cyriac Skinner Upon his Blindness*" but its text is corrupt in each word it alters from the TMS.

22
"Cyriack, this three years day"

Cyriack, this three years day these eys, though clear
   To outward view, of blemish or of spot;[1]
   Bereft of light thir seeing have forgot,
   Nor to thir[2] idle orbs doth sight appear
Of Sun or Moon or Starre throughout the year,[3]   5
   Or man or woman. Yet I argue not
   Against heavns[4] hand or will, nor bate a jot
   Of heart or hope; but still bear up[5] and steer
Right onward.[6] What supports me dost thou ask?
   The conscience, Friend, to have lost them overply'd   10
   In libertyes defence, my noble task,
Of which all *Europe* talks from side to side.
   This thought might lead me through the worlds vain mask°   MASQUE
   Content though blind, had I no better guide.

[1]Milton seems to have been proud of the fact that his eyes, despite their affliction, showed no outward sign of damage (*Defensio Secunda*; Yale 4:1, 583).

[2]The word was first written "their," then the "e" was deleted by means of a line drawn through it—perhaps evidence of Milton's imposing a spelling scheme on his amanuensis.

[3]The line is, as John Ulreich reminds me (e-mail of September 8, 1998), reminiscent of Ecclesiastes 12.2, "while the sun, or the light, or the moon, or the stars, be not darkened, nor the clouds return after the rain." Compare *Paradise Lost* 3.40–45.

[4]First written "Gods," then that was scratched out and "heavns" was written above the line and added as well in the margin.

[5]First written "attend to steer," then "attend to" was deleted by lines drawn through it, and "bear up and" added above the line and in the margin as well.

[6]First written "Uphillward," then that was scratched through and "Right onward" written above and also added in the left margin.

Latin Verses Found with the Commonplace Book.
Carmina Elegiaca ("Elegiac Verses")
(1624?)

Alfred Horwood discovered a loose manuscript leaf, badly damaged, of Latin poetry in the same box as Milton's Commonplace Book, then in the possession of Sir Frederick Graham (Horwood [3]). The manuscript leaf is now in the Humanities Research Center at the University of Texas, Austin (Pre-1700 MS 127). The leaf contains what appear to be grammar school exercises on the theme of early rising, in Milton's handwriting; on the reverse of the leaf is a prose theme on the same subject. The light punctuation of the poetry, which Shawcross's edition modernizes and Carey's retains may be indicative of a lifelong habit on Milton's part.

Only the first poem is in elegiac meter; the "Ignavus satrapam" is, as Carey points out, in the Lesser Asclepiad meter (two or three choriambs—made up of condensed trochees and iambs in one foot of four syllables—preceded by a spondee and followed by an iamb).

The young Milton not only echoes the customary stock phrases from the Latin poetry he would have been translating in school (see the *Variorum* 1.2: 333–36); he also celebrates a theme he would take to heart, since he remained a dutiful early-riser throughout his life.

TEXT

The manuscript version is unique and must be followed.

Work Cited

Horwood, A. J. *A Common-place Book of John Milton.* London: Chiswick P, 1876. Revised ed. 1877.

Carmina Elegiaca.

Surge, age surge, leves, iam convenit, excute[6] somnos,
    Lux oritur, tepidi fulcra relinque tori
Iam canit excubitor gallus prænuncius ales
    Solis et invigilans ad sua quemque vocat
Flammiger Eois Titan caput exerit undis   5
    Et spargit nitidum læta per arva iubar
Daulias argutum modulatur ab ilice carmen
    Edit et excultos mitis alauda modos
Iam rosa fragrantes spirat siluestris odores
    Iam redolent violæ luxuriatque seges   10
Ecce novo campos Zephyritis gramine vestit
    Fertilis, et vitreo rore madescit humus
Segnes invenias molli vix talia lecto
    Cum premat imbellis lumina fessa sopor
Illic languentes abrumpunt somnia somnos[7]   15
    Et turbant animum tristia multa tuum
Illic tabifici generantur semina morbi
    Qui pote torpentem posse valere virum
Surge age surge, leves, iam convenit, excute[8] somnos
    Lux oritur, tepidi fulcra relinque tori.   20

Elegiac Verses.

Get up, go on, get up; now it is time, stop your lazy sleeping. It's becoming light. Come from the four posts of your warm bed. Now the sentinel rooster crows, announcer of the sun, and calls everyone to work. The fiery Titan[9] puts his head above the waves of the East, and throws his bright sunlight over the happy fields. The Daulian bird[10] trills her clear song from the oak tree, and the gentle lark pours out her exquisite harmonies. Now the wild rose breathes out perfumes, now violets smell sweet, and the standing grain dances joyfully. Look: the fruit-bearing Flora clothes the fields with new grass, and the ground grows wet with sparkling dew. Lazybones, you are not likely to find such things on a downy bed while unwarlike slumber closes tired eyes. There, your idle sleep is disturbed with dreams, and many sorrows bother you. There are bred the seeds of wasting disease. How can an inactive person be strong! Get up, come on, get up! It's time. Stop those worthless slumbers. It's getting light. Come out from among the posts of that warm bed.

---

[6]The word "*arcere*" was replaced by "*excute*" written above it (though "*arcere*" was never deleted).
[7]As Carey points out (1997 ed., 11n), Milton first wrote "*somnum*" in error.
[8]Repeating what he had done in the first line, Milton wrote "*arcere*," deleted it, and inserted "*excute.*"

---

[9]The sun, here identified as the Titan Hyperion.
[10]The nightingale, as in the story of Philomela and Tereus (Ovid, *Metamorphoses* 6.668–74). Philomela becomes a nightingale, her sister a swallow.

Ignavus satrapam[11]

Ignavus satrapam dedecet inclytum
Somnus qui populo multifido præst.
Dum Dauni veteris filius[12] armiger
Stratus purpureo p[rocu]buit st[rato][13]
Audax Eurialus, Nisus et impiger
Invasere cati nocte sub horrida
Torpentes Rutilos castraque Volscia
Hinc codes oritur clamor et absonus.[14]

"Kings Should Not Oversleep"

Idle sleep doesn't become a famous ruler who rules many and varied people. While the armed Turnus, son of old Daunus, lay stretched on a luxurious couch, bold Eurialus and opportunistic Nisus, crafty in the grim night, attacked the sleeping Rutilans and the Volscian camp. Hence slaughter rises and discordant clamor.

Verses from *Pro Populo Anglicano defensio*[1]
(1650)

Quis expedivit Salmasio *suam* Hundredam,[2]
Picámque docuit nostra verba conari?
Magister artis venter, et Jacobæi
Centum, exulantis viscera marsupii regis.
Quòd si dolosi spes refulserit nummi,   5
Ipse Antichristi qui modò primatum Papæ
Minatus uno est dissipare sufflatu,
Cantabit ultrò Cardinalitium *melos.*

Who prompted Salmasius with his "hundreda" and taught the magpie to try out our words? He the Master of Arts of his belly was led by 100 Jacobuses[5] (the offal of the exiled king's purse). Because if a hope for a dishonest bit of coin flashed, this person, who recently threatened to wreck the supremacy of the Pope, the Antichrist, with one puff,[6] would happily sing the song of Cardinals.

Verses from *Defensio Secunda*[3]
(1653)

Gaudete Scombri, & quicquid est piscium salo,
Qui frigidâ hyeme incolitis algentes freta,
Vestrûm misertus ille Salmasius eques[4]
Bonus amicire nuditatem cogitat;
Chartæque largus apparat papyrinos   5
Vobis cucullos præferentes Claudii
Insignia nomenque decus Salmasii,
Gestetis ut per omne cetarium forum
Equitis clientes, scriniis mungentium
Cubito virorum, et capsulis gratissimos.   10

Rejoice, mackerel and all salt-sea fish that spend winters in freezing cold seas, that good knight Salmasius in pity thinks about clothing your nakedness; generous with his abundant paper, he furnishes cones[7] that display his name and insignia, so that throughout the fishmarket you may exult yourselves as the knight's followers in the chests and boxes of men who wipe their noses on their sleeves.[8]

---

[11]I have borrowed Carey's clever title.
[12]Turnus is the son of Daunus (for the attack, see the *Aeneid* 9.176–449).
[13]The reconstruction is that of the Columbia editors. Carey's reconstruction is "procubuit thoro," perhaps following Shawcross.
[14]There was more after this point, but the leaf is too much damaged for anything more to be read.
[1]The Yale editors of what is translated as "A Defence of the People of England" comment that Milton's model is "apparently the prologue to the *Choliambi* of Persius (Yale 4.1: 487n), and John Leonard notices that quoted passages from Persius are indicated by italics (*John Milton: The Complete Poems* [London: Penguin, 1998]: 974n).
[2]Claude Saumaise (1588–1653) or Salmasius had condemned the act of regicide in *Defensio regia pro Carolo I ad Serenissimum Magnæ Britanniæ regem Carolum II*, published in 1649. Milton was commissioned to respond in *Pro Populo Anglicano defensio* in 1650. He made fun of Salmasius's bad Latin in belaboring the English legal term for a division of land, "hundred," while trying to turn it into the Latin "*hundreda.*"
[3]The poem was supposed to have been written to celebrate yet another publication of Salmasius, whom Milton characterizes as a whale who has so much compassion for fish that he "has destined so many volumes to wrap them properly" (Yale 4.1: 580).
[4]Milton may be playing on Salmasius=Salmon; and, though Salmasius had been created a Knight of the Order of St. Michael by Louis XIII, Milton disparages his title, as not held in high respect (Yale 4.1: 581n).

[5]The Jacobus, a gold coin worth a little more than a pound, had been named for James I. Salmasius was supposed to have been paid 100 Jacobuses for having written *Defensio Regia*, which he later denied.
[6]Salmasius, as a Protestant, had attacked the papal supremacy in *De primatu papæ* (1645; Shawcross 228n.). The joke is extended with the puff of smoke, since the election of a new Pope, by vote of an assembly of cardinals, is signaled by a puff of smoke from the Vatican.
[7]Paper cones were used to wrap fish or other foods in the market, providing them with "cowls" at the same time. Salmasius's monogrammed stationary, including his coat of arms, wraps fish.
[8]It was an ancient joke that fishmongers, with their hands on smelly fish, had to wipe their noses with their sleeves.

Three Poets, *in three distant* Ages *born,*
Greece, Italy, *and* England *did adorn.*
The First *in loftiness of thought Surpaſs'd,*
The Next *in* Majesty; *in both the* Last.
The force of Nature *coud no farther goe:*
To make a Third *she joynd the former two.*

Paradise Lost: Introduction

I. A SHORT HISTORY OF THE EPIC GENRE

A modern student may be familiar with the word *epic* only in a debased meaning, as in "epic experience" (an advertisement for white-water rafting), or "epic adventure" (a tired movie about pirates). For Milton the word would have meant the noblest works of Homer, Vergil, Dante, Boiardo, Tasso, Spenser—the most high-minded writers he could think of—writing in their most expansive genre. To Milton epic was the highest type of poetry, the best art a civilization might create to ensure its immortality. The best of epics in turn epitomized entire civilizations by summarizing their most noble accomplishments and aspirations in one emblem of national pride. Epics should be long, full, rich, wise, inventive, and beautiful. Epics should be the most difficult of all poems to write, and they should demand intelligence, wit, and patience of their readers.

A poet, like any conscientious craftsperson, had to spend his youth learning his trade as an apprentice and working his way up through the lesser genres of sonnet or other form of love lyric, eclogue (usually a short pastoral poem imitative of Vergil's *Eclogues*, also called *Bucolics*), pastoral elegy, georgic (pastoral poem imitating Vergil's *Georgics* and celebrating farm husbandry or work), epithalamion (marriage hymn), masque, even tragedy, all in order to prepare him to write epic. Throughout Milton's early poetic career, in which he wrote in most of these genres, Milton feared "shattering the leaves"—violating the laurels or myrtles of poetic achievement, or writing before his style was matured—and even in *Paradise Lost* he feared writing in "an age too late" (9.44). Timeliness, in the sense of "good timing," and personal readiness for each poetic mode, from love lyric to elegy to epic, were of greatest importance to him. So was decorum, what Milton called "the grand master peece to observe" (*Of Education*, Yale 2: 405; see Kranidas). The decorum of any special genre might be a kind of style sheet for everything from a "choice of musical forms complementary to the subject" (Hardison 38) to the choice of rhyme scheme, of plot line, or of the subject itself. The proper decorum for each genre might be found in examples drawn from conventional songs, sonnets, elegies, or epics, but it might also be found in the genres incorporated into the most important book of all, the Bible. Milton would have seen decorum—fitting the proper style and proper poetic format to the proper genre—in terms of universal laws. For the late Middle Ages and early Renaissance, the decorum of the various genres can be reduced to a simple formula:

> . . . pastoral, georgic, and epic are written in three styles: low, middle, and high. They correspond to three social ranks or occupations: shepherd, farmer, and soldier. They may take place in three locales: pasture, field, and castle; and they may be symbolized by three kinds of tree: the beech, the fruit-tree, and the laurel . . . . [P]astoral celebrates play and leisure, georgic celebrates work, and epic celebrates fighting. (Low 4)

Though he certainly would have disagreed with the idea that epic should celebrate war and nothing but war, or even love and nothing but love, Milton just as surely believes that there were laws governing the composition of epic poems: in *The Reason of Church Government* (1642) he discusses his own ambitions to write in the genre "of highest hope, and hardest attempting, whether that Epick form whereof the two poems of *Homer*, and those other two of *Virgil* and *Tasso* are a diffuse, and the book of *Job* a brief model" (Yale 1: 813). He goes on to disagree with some of the rules of Aristotle's *Poetics*, such as the notion that tragedy is a higher genre than epic. He prefers some of the rules of near-contemporary Italian critics of the epic, whom he would choose to follow also in matters of epic style. Among those modern critics, Milton mentions Ludovico Castelvetro and Antonio Minturno; he might also use Julius Caesar Scaliger, who published an encyclopedic *Poetics* in 1561, and he certainly uses Tasso's *Discourses on the Heroic Poem* (1587). Milton also discusses the importance of the choice of a hero, which in 1642 he could see only in terms of a national figure such as Arthur in England, Godfrey of Bouillon (one of Tasso's heroes) in Italy or Charlemagne in France. In his catalogue of noble genres in *The Reason of Church Government*, Milton places epic first and tragedy a close second, a ranking which follows Tasso's theory of the epic as opposed to Aristotle's. To simplify, then, Milton follows contemporary Italian critical theory rather than that derived only from Aristotle, and he values the genres and poetic examples of the Bible as much as or more than those from any other single literary work.

1. EPIC AS A COMPENDIUM
OF POETIC STYLES AND GENRES

As far as modern critics have been able to discern (see Lewalski's *Paradise Lost* and "Genres"), Milton seems to have believed that all noble genres merged in epic. Roger Rollin wittily turns Polonius's phrase to bear on *Paradise Lost*: he finds the epic "Tragical-Comical-Historical-Pastoral" (using Polonius's phrase from *Hamlet*) with all of the genres converging. For instance, Milton's epic includes:

an *epithalamion* for the marriage of Adam and Eve; a complete *tragedy* in Book 9 (Shaw, "Milton's Choice"); *morning and evening hymns; odes*, according to the varied definitions of Pindar, Callimachus, and Horace; *extended historical narratives* as in Lucan's *Civil War* (W. R. Johnson); *masques* (Demaray, *Milton's*); *topographical poetry* as in Michael Drayton's *Poly-Olbion; romance* (in several different generic senses of the word); and even *satire* and comic or grotesque scenes or images, as with the gruesome farce of misidentification featuring Satan, Sin and Death.

Milton's practice in "lower" genres, such as lyric or erotic poetry (the sonnets in English and Italian and some of the Latin elegies), elegiac poetry ("Lycidas" and other memorial poems in English and Latin), epigram (miscellaneous short poems devoted to small subjects), pastoral and georgic ("Lycidas" and other early Latin poems), is valuable in itself, but each limited genre will become a part of the all-inclusive epic. Milton seems to subsume many modes and genres under the inclusive name *epic*, without losing the unity of the all-inclusive "diffuse" type of long epic. The Italian epic poet Torquato Tasso had sought such a goal of unity-in-diversity in his massive romantic epic *Jerusalem Delivered* (first complete edition, 1581) and Tasso might have been Milton's model at least for designing and devising the style of an epic.

In western European literature, the epic genre begins with Homer's *Iliad* and *Odyssey* (850–750 BC). The most ancient of Mediterranean cultures other than that of Greece seem to have produced similar bodies of oral epic poetry, some few of which, like the Babylonian *Gilgamesh* (c. 1000 BC), were written down. Like most of ancient memorized poetry composed for largely illiterate societies, the Homeric poems were sung or at least chanted, an essential fact for Milton, who compares himself to Homer as a blind, singing poet. Homer's epics defined the epic genre for western Europe and set the subject matter for subsequent epic either as heroic warfare, with the siege of Troy as prime example, or as the heroic quest, with the voyage of Odysseus towards his homeland in Ithaca. Milton's reading of Homeric

materials, however, did not end with Homer: pupils tutored by Milton were asked to read the continuation of the *Iliad* attributed to Quintus of Smyrna (fourth century AD), which Milton's nephew Edward Phillips calls "*Quintus Calaber* his poem of the *Trojan* War continued from *Homer*" (Darbishire, *Early Lives* 60). By the time Milton wrote *Paradise Lost* he may have been more interested in bettering the classical epics than he was in imitating them, but, since he remembered everything he read, there are echoes not only of Homer but of Quintus of Smyrna in Milton's epic.

2. JASON AND AENEAS

Apollonius of Rhodes, a Hellenistic poet who flourished in the third century BCE, added elements to the epic tradition in his *Argonautica*, another story of a quest, that of Jason and the crew of heroes named after their ship the *Argo*, for the Golden Fleece. The *Argonautica* is a brief epic which includes a version of the romance of Jason and Medea and a varied assortment of supernatural monsters such as the Gorgon Medusa with her snaky hair, the grotesque bird-footed Harpies, and magicians or sorceresses like Medea. The *Argonautica* made the subjects of dangerous love and the sinister supernatural a part of the epic. Milton taught the work of Apollonius to his nephews (Phillips, *Life*, in Darbishire *Early Lives* 60), as well as Homer and Vergil.

Vergil's *Aeneid* (late first century BC) takes the Homeric hero Aeneas from Troy through Carthage and on to the founding of Rome. The Roman epic contains an unforgettable love affair, that of Dido and Aeneas. Milton knew his Vergil and his Homer by heart and perhaps felt sympathy with the life and career of Vergil (Campbell, "Milton"). Vergil's epic provided him with an elegant and somewhat artificial or "literary" model for epic style; it provided him with a subtle analysis of love psychology; and it gave him an expanded sense of the classical underworld, what in Christian lore would become Hell. Vergil's Aeneas also provided an example of a hero with a high sense of mission and a characteristic reverence for the gods: Vergil's epithet for Aeneas is "pious." It makes an easy transition, for a Christian epic writer, to move from the pious Aeneas to the pious Christ or the pious Abdiel.

3. METAMORPHOSES AND HEROIC WARFARE

Ovid's *Metamorphoses* (first century AD), which Milton also admired especially in his youth and taught to his pupils (DuRocher, Harding), has the bulk of an epic and has sometimes been defined as one. It is, nevertheless, a collection of many short stories told in poetry and held together loosely by the great mythological theme of metamorphosis, or the change from one life form into another. Perhaps because he so often wrote about love and lust, Ovid was looked upon as an "amorous" poet by Milton and his schoolfellows, too trivial a writer to be compared with the highly serious Homer or Vergil. The tradition of "Ovid moralized," or the Christianizing of Ovid's love psychology, especially as practiced by George Sandys, the Elizabethan translator and commentator, represented an attempt to make Ovid serious enough to be acceptable to theologians or philosophers (Harding).

Statius, a contemporary of Vergil and Ovid, attempted an epic in his *Thebais* or *Thebaid* (AD 90 or 91), which is concerned with the "Seven against Thebes," or the heroic siege of that city by seven generals, and the quarrel between Oedipus's sons Eteocles and Polyneices. The *Thebaid* contains extended catalogues of warriors and descriptions of funeral games—too large a volume of both for the tastes of most modern readers. Neither Statius's story nor his elaborate and hyperbolic style was ever to catch the English imagination, but Dante had honored Statius as a proto-Christian in the *Divine Comedy*, *Purgatorio*, Cantos 21 and 22, and Statius's emphasis on macabre magic, enchanted woods, lovers and dragons made his epic one of the ancestors of romance. Statius's elevated, bookish style and his allusiveness may have appealed to Milton.

4. CIVIL WAR AND ATOMIC THEORY

Lucan's *Civil War* (published about AD 62 or 63; also known as the *Pharsalia* for the chief battle described in it) concerns itself primarily with a partisan view of historical Roman leaders such as Julius Caesar and Pompey. It traces their campaigns and strategies carefully; it characterizes the tyranny of Caesar as a pattern of evil civic behavior; and it offers the ideal of the ascetic life of the Stoic philosopher Cato. With Lucan's *Civil War*, epic expanded its subject matter to include recent history, and, since Lucan was well-trained in rhetoric and oratory, it developed the art of the heroic declamatory speech, which had earlier been heard in Greek historians such as Herodotus but had not before Lucan become such a fixed part of epic. From Lucan, Milton might have taken the idea that evil statesmen, as with Satan, Beelzebub, Belial, Moloch, and Mammon, might nevertheless be great and charismatic orators (W. R. Johnson, 104n and passim).

Though Lucretius's six-book *De Rerum Natura*, usually translated as *On the Nature of Things* (finished before 55 BC), is more an Epicurean treatise on the atomic structure of the universe than an epic, it is often compared with *Paradise Lost* for its seriousness of philosophical purpose and the gravity of its style. From Lucretius's example, Milton could have deduced that an epic might be a compendium of philosophical or religious belief as well as an heroic story. Lucretius's depiction of chaos might also have interested Milton (Curry), as would his inclusion of science as a suitable subject for an epic-length poem (Rogers). The theme of acquisition of knowledge is strong in both Lucretius and Milton, as is the correction of delusion or error (Hardie).

5. MEDIEVAL TO RENAISSANCE EPIC: DANTE, VIDA, AND THE ARTHURIAN CYCLE

As early as his trip to Italy in 1638 Milton wrote in his short Latin poem to Giovanni Battista Manso, *Mansus*, that his ambition was to compose a national heroic poem, in vernacular English as opposed to Latin, on the subject of King Arthur, whom he saw in the late 1630s and early 1640s as a model English king. By the 1650s and 1660s, perhaps because the Civil Wars had pushed him beyond believing in the perfectible Britain he had pictured in *Areopagitica*, he rejected King Arthur, a personage whom he had also come to suspect as being wholly legendary. The very institution of kingship was suspect for Milton, who had written pamphlets in defense of the judicious execution of Charles I. So was mindless patriotism, to a man who sadly came to believe that "One's country is wherever it is well with one" (letter to Peter Heimbach; trans. Columbia 12: 115).

Milton had also come to believe that the theme of disobedience of the first man and woman, who included in their genes the entire human race, was more important in the sight of God than the deeds of any single legendary military hero. Arthur and his kind distinguish themselves chiefly by pulling mythical swords out of lakes, slaying dragons, establishing confederacies of warlords, constantly seeking out brutal combat or occasionally winning as a prize a fickle or unfaithful damsel—all of which added up to what Milton labeled the "long and tedious havoc [of] fabl'd Knights / In Battels feign'd" and "tinsel Trappings" (*Paradise Lost* 9.30–31, 36) of romantic epic. The legends surrounding King Arthur were not serious enough subject matter for the epic that Milton wanted to write: neither romantic love nor quest for legendary icon nor constant hand-to-hand combat interested him.

The subject matter of Dante, though it did include romantic love, did interest Milton. Dante, whose *Divine Comedy* (finished c. 1315) the young Milton read attentively and reverently (he cites it often in his *Commonplace Book*), had as his subject no single hero or quest but salvation for Everyman or for all Christians. Dante's character within the epic, a persona often referred to by critics as "Dante the pilgrim," humbly led by the almost divine poet Vergil, replaces any traditional hero in his poem. Dante as pilgrim becomes the focal point of the epic, in the sense that he witnesses every-thing that happens, but he is not a bold or brutal hero. Instead he reacts sensitively to everything he sees, sometimes weeping or fainting in sympathy with a sinner. The author, in other words, could replace the hero as the central personage in the epic poem. Milton will choose to do much the same thing in his own relationship with the epic: the poet will be a speaking character and will have a close relationship with his reader (Samuel, *Dante and Milton*).

Unlike Milton's epic, which moves from Hell to Heaven to Paradise to the Fall to the "Paradise within," Dante's epic moves in symmetrical pilgrimages from contemporary Earth through Hell and then through Purgatory to Heaven. Dante's epic, divided into three sections of thirty-three cantos (Hell has thirty-four, so that the total may equal 100), each shorter than any of Milton's books, was mathematically well-measured. Its poetic style is just as symmetrical. Dante's *terza rima*, a pattern of rhyme built on interlocking three-line seg-ments, is so well-balanced and precise that T. S. Eliot found it nearly impossible to duplicate in English.

Dante's symbolic recreation of the universe, despite being arranged as beautifully as a rose window in a medieval cathedral, was Roman Catholic and therefore repugnant to the Protestant Milton who saw Catholi-cism mainly in terms of religious oppression. He was to label the religion "papist" more than forty times in his prose works.

Another Roman Catholic epic, Marco Girolamo Vida's six-book *Christiad* (1535), took as its subject epi-sodes in the life of Christ, more an example for Milton in *Paradise Regain'd* than in *Paradise Lost*. Dante and Vida wrote for the religious and high-minded, and they did not often try to please the irreverent secular audi-ence that might be more interested in Boccaccio's baw-dy tales in the *Decameron*. Like most medieval and early Renaissance Christian writers, Dante and Vida dwelt on the creation of humankind in Adam and Eve, on Origi-nal Sin, and on salvation through good works and faith. Again, however, Milton would have rejected certain Roman Catholic perspectives on the life of Christ, such as an emphasis on the character of the Virgin Mary, cele-brated by both Vida and Dante but generally neglected by Milton because of her association with what a Pro-testant might have called "Mariolatry."

6. PROTESTANT RELIGIOUS EPIC

Protestants as well as Catholics could write about cre-ation, about the innocent Adam and Eve, and about the Fall. The French Huguenot Guillaume de Salluste, Seigneur DuBartas, wrote the epic *La Semaine* (1578), which is generically labeled as an *hexameron*: that is, it

focuses on the six days of creation. Josuah Sylvester translated DuBartas's work into English in the very popular *Divine Weekes and Workes* (1592), a translation that profoundly influenced English poetic style (Snyder 1.72–95; Steadman, *Moral*). Tasso's *Il Mondo Creato* (c. 1592) is the Roman Catholic poetic hexameron, but it never gained the popularity of DuBartas's work or Syl-vester's translation.

The Dutch jurist and statesman Hugo Grotius's Latin play *Adamus Exul* (1601) is a Protestant hexameral dra-ma that perhaps influenced the younger Milton to de-sign his own "Adam Unparadiz'd" as a play rather than an epic. The Dutch Vondel's plays *Lucifer* (1654) and *Adam* (1664; see Gérard) are among the hundreds of stories, plays, and even operas based on the stories of the Creation and Fall that might have influenced Milton. Milton met Grotius in Paris in 1638, and he was surely aware of the importance of Vondel in the European intellectual community. The subjects of creation, the Fall of Satan, and the Fall of Humankind were popular enough in western Europe in Milton's era to be called fashionable, among Protestants and Catholics alike.

Probably the three most important subjects for all works of art, especially visual art, in the seventeenth century were Adam and Eve, the Virgin Mary, and the Crucifixion. Because of his protestantism, Milton was not especially interested in the latter two. The matter of the Fall of Adam and Eve, he could see, was the most nearly universal of any widely-depicted narrative in the Renaissance.

7. ROMANTIC EPIC

The romance or romantic epic, from the *Romance of the Rose* (1237–1277) to Matteo Boiardo's *Orlando Inna-morato* ("Orlando in Love," 1487), mixed the ideals of courtly love and chivalric behavior with the goriest of martial arts in a long series of episodes dealing with knightly quests either for love of a worthy or unworthy damsel or for honor in combat. Romances often embo-died varieties of heroism in different characters, from Thomas Malory's churlish Sir Kay and slightly more gentle Lancelot to the sweet Tristan of French legend, who is the fatal lover of Isolde and hence a spiritual an-cestor of Romeo, and the Sir Gawain of *Sir Gawain and the Green Knight* (fourteenth century), the skeptical and suave high-minded knight who successfully resists witchy seduction. The very popular medieval *Romance of the Rose*, translated by Chaucer, and the even better-known *Chanson de Roland* were the two most famous French romances. *Tiran lo Blanc* ("Tiran the White"; Martorell), the Catalan medieval romantic novel, also concerns itself with high-minded Christian chivalry (as well as erotic adventures). The best-respected romances in the English tradition are *Sir Gawain and the Green Knight*, which Milton could not have known (the manuscript had not been discovered yet: see Mulryan, *Milton*), and Spenser's *Faerie Queene*, which he knew and admired greatly (Logan and Teskey).

8. COMIC VARIATIONS

Satirical reactions to the ridiculous situations romantic heroes sometimes got themselves into are a part of romance as early as Chaucer's comic knight Sir Thopas. Comedy exists even in the sometimes ironic *Sir Gawain* and certainly in Cervantes's picaresque *Don Quixote* (completed 1615), which questions the value of physical heroism in the famous scene of Don Quixote tilting at windmills. Ariosto's *Orlando Furioso* (first complete edition 1532), in its very title of "the insane Orlando" or "Orlando mad for love," treats melancholy love as insanity (Ferrand). It also treats most of the ideals of courtly behavior with irony. For instance, one of Ariosto's heroines, Bradamante, tries to commit suicide for love, but she succeeds only in stabbing herself unsuccessfully because of her armor-plating.

As a genre, romance often mixes well with comedy in a pastoral setting, as it would in Ariosto's pastoral scenes and later in Shakespeare's *Midsummer Night's Dream* and *As You Like It*, as well as in the island romance *The Tempest*. Milton parodies romance, rather savagely, in the excessively polite dialogue and romantic compliments exchanged among the dismal and unholy trio, Satan, Sin, and Death. At the same time, the love between Adam and Eve in the Garden of Eden is the prototype of all ideal country romances.

The genre of romance is mainly secular and not necessarily high-minded—by its nature more Ovidian than Vergilian. Milton rejected it, for *Paradise Lost* at least, as a genre unworthy of epic, except in the beautiful but decorous and restrained love scenes between Adam and Eve. The experience of Eden transforms romance into what it should be, or creates it as idyllic love. Boiardo, Ariosto, and Tasso had been important to Milton in his younger career, at least when he was writing "L'Allegro" and "Il Penseroso," but the Italian romances were much more distant and perhaps even alien to him in the 1650s and 1660s when he was composing *Paradise Lost*.

9. SPENSERIAN EPIC

Apparently Milton in his later career rejected even the noble English romance of Spenser's *Faerie Queene*. The *Faerie Queene* is a romance more of epic length and heft—as Fowler points out, its cantos signal romance, but its books indicate epic (*Kind* 95)—and it celebrates English nationalism more than *Sir Gawain*, especially since its fairy queen is closely allied with Queen Elizabeth. Milton did acknowledge to John Dryden that

Spenser was his "original," or his source among the English poets. Milton also called Spenser "a better teacher then . . . *Aquinas*" (*Areopagitica*, Yale 2: 516), but ultimately he must reject Spenser's subject matter and much of his poetic style. Spenser remains a heavy influence on the rich diction and sensuous imagery of *Paradise Lost*, but he is publicly dismissed by Milton when the subjects of all romantic epics are dismissed in the invocation to Book 9 (Greenlaw, Guillory).

The Italian romance writers are also best known, in *Paradise Lost* at least, for being rejected. Milton seems to lump them all under the "tedious havoc" and "tinsel Trappings" labels. Romance and chivalric epic were of course not an Italian monopoly. In Portugal, Camoëns's Vergilian *Lusiads* (1572) made the voyages of Vasco Da Gama seem exemplary and heroic (the *Lusiads* were translated into English by the man who would become Charles II's Latin Secretary, Richard Fanshawe, in 1655; see Bowra). The Spanish Jorge de Montemayor's extensive Neoplatonic prose romance *Diana* (1559) had been remarkably popular in continental Europe. The *Diana* made its way across the English Channel and was translated for the Countess of Pembroke—to whom her brother Sir Philip Sidney dedicated *Arcadia*—and was popular with King James I and John Donne (Montemayor 7). When Milton repeats the verbal formula used often in Renaissance epic and romance and says that he intends to do something that had not been done "in *Prose* or *Rhime*" (1.16, my emphasis), he evidently had works like the *Diana* in mind. Columbus and Galileo had both been made into the subjects of forgettable Columbiads or Galileids (Harris), and some of the Italian poets wrote memorable mock-epics, as with Alessandro Tassoni's *La Secchia Rapita* ("The Stolen Bucket," first authorized edition 1624).

There is a serious political question here about the epic of colonial conquest: is Satan on the side of the Conquistadores? In other words, is colonialism evil? Or is the Christian conquest of pagan lands legitimate and heroic? Do Adam and Eve help civilize the animals in Eden, or do they exploit them? Martin Evans has attempted to answer some of these questions in *Milton's Imperial Epic*.

Kirkconnell made a mighty effort to collect all of the analogues of *Paradise Lost* in *The Celestial Cycle*, but even he missed some of the epic and romantic literature that was so popular all over western Europe, especially that of the generation of Spenserian poets that just preceded Milton's (William B. Hunter, *English Spenserians*).

10. EPIC WARFARE, MAGIC, AND LOVE: BLOODY AND INCREDIBLE PLOTS

One problem with romantic and chivalric epic had always been the repetition of battle scenes. Milton satirizes such scenes as the "havoc" (9.30). Description of warfare or even of jousting cannot be varied much. Even when the modern reader takes into account the leisured aristocratic reading audience of the 1530s, which presumably had long and idle winters indoors to read through romances, by sunlight or candlelight, the battle scenes still may have been deemed monotonous. The Italian aristocratic war-lords or *condottieri*, when they had time to read at all, may have enjoyed the countless battles and indiscriminate killing in a Boiardo epic (Murrin, *History* 199–201), but they eventually found the wit and grace of Ariosto's varied narrative, or the religious fervor of Tasso, more interesting.

Magic—derived from Apollonius, Ovid, Vergil, or Apuleius—was also adapted to Christianity in the romantic epics of Italy, France, and England, perhaps to help take the focus off love and war. Italian or English magicians and sorcerers were probably descended from the Greek Medea or Latin Hecate, the underworld equivalent of Diana, also an attendant on Proserpina, depicted by Vergil and Ovid as a witch. The witchy woman of classical Greece and Rome had in turn evolved into figures like Arthurian magic-makers Merlin and Morgan Le Fay. White magic, as in the good magic of Shakespeare's Prospero, makes its appearance through the front door of *Paradise Lost* when Ithuriel touches Satan with his spear and effects a transformation. Black magic enters through the back door when Satan, Sin, and Death practice tricks of mutual intimidation (see Mebane and Thorndike for backgrounds of magic in English literature). I shouldn't need to stress that magic, fairies, necromancy, astrology, curses, amulets, and love potions were all taken quite seriously throughout the seventeenth century.

The kind of love embodied in the often re-told stories of Tristan and Isolde, Lancelot and Guinevere, or Orlando and Angelica (descended from the romantic heroes and heroines of works like Ovid's *Heroides*; see my articles "Ovid" and "Ariosto" in *A Milton Encyclopedia*, ed. William B. Hunter) could become in the Italian romantic epics more of a motivating power than martial prowess or magic. Ariosto, who wrote for a largely female courtly audience, seems less interested in combat than in his heroine Angelica's constant teasing of men. Angelica causes each of the mighty heroes who pursues her to become her weak love-slave. The sorceress Alcina in *Orlando Furioso* is even worse at the same game because she uses love-magic to reduce heroes to effeminate and useless fops.

Tasso, on the other hand, is obsessively religious and zealously militaristic in his religious war against infidels or pagans. He is also superstitious and neurotically romantic—he juggles bloody battles, sorcerers' conjurations, and the guiltiest of love scenes almost equally in *Jerusalem Delivered*.

Milton replaces Ariosto's flirtatious Angelica with the married Eve, he avoids religiosity, and he puts conjuration and other forms of black magic clearly on the side of Satan.

Milton also largely rejects extended description of epic battles. His one series of battle scenes, the War in Heaven, is a sardonic comedy of gigantic proportions, as Arnold Stein first showed in *Answerable Style*. Milton also rejected heroism when it was expressed only in trial by combat, preferring the Christian virtue of patience and the act of heroic martyrdom. He rejected the epic quest for a false icon, such as the chase after a faithless woman like Angelica. He rejected warrior heroines such as Vergil's Camilla, first mentioned at the end of *Aeneid* 7, Spenser's Britomart, or Ariosto's Bradamante. Milton makes Satan into his own version of the classical soldier or knight of romance, undercutting all of the pagan values embodied in the fierce Achilles or the wily Odysseus (Lord 173–84; Newman 380–81). Satan and Moloch are more like Tasso's Christian or infidel warriors than are Michael or Abdiel. The higher quest for eternal life replaces the quest for a talisman like the Holy Grail. For Milton, chivalry was dead, and good riddance to it.

11. SPENSERIAN ALLEGORY AND ENGLISH NATIONALISM

Spenser had avoided some of the tedium of describing battle by making the warriors allegorical. Allegory, though it is currently unfashionable, had the value in the Renaissance of legitimizing scenes of combat. The tedious battles of romantic epic, in Spenser's hands, were not only reduced in number (as compared with the many in Boiardo) but rendered morally purposeful. If Truth is fighting Hypocrisy, the battle seems more important than if, say, Sir Kay is fighting Mordred. If moral titans are fighting, combat should have a cosmic dimension, as in the fight for Everyman's immortal soul, with characters like Knowledge or Good Deeds. Joseph Beaumont's little-known but worthy epic *Psyche* (1648) translated allegorical epic into Church of England (as opposed to Puritan) theology by telling a story of the voyage of the soul, as if Beaumont were writing a Spenserian version of *Pilgrim's Progress*. But neither Beaumont's epic nor John Donne's much shorter voyage or progress of the soul, also named after the demigoddess associated with the mind, "Psyche," seems to have had as much influence on Milton (if either had any at all) as did Spenser's allegorical *Faerie Queene*.

Nationalistic or chauvinistic epics such as the *Faerie Queene* could also glorify one's homeland. Michael Drayton, capitalizing on a new interest in the antiquities of England due to the Tudor and Stuart monarchies, had managed to find enough excitement in stories about various places in England to write his epic-sized topographical poem *Poly-Olbion* (first complete edition 1622). Using the *topos* or specific geographical location as his taking-off point, Drayton assigned many local English rivers a nymph with a story to tell, in the manner of Ovid, a manner imitated by Milton with Sabrina, the nymph of the Severn River, in *Comus*. Topographical poetry glorified English places, a tradition that Milton had to reject in an epic on the fall of humankind. Drayton's poetic language, however, was derived from Spenser, as Milton's would be. If one wants to pursue topographical and nationalistic poetry of the late English Renaissance, William B. Hunter has provided an anthology of the writings of Drayton and some others of his general school in *The English Spenserians*.

Abraham Cowley was also to carry on the nationalistic tradition of Spenser, Drayton, and Lucan before them, but Cowley in his short biblical epic *Davideis* (first published 1656) used the biblical subject of King David as a thinly-disguised political allegory. In his *The Civil War* (Books 2 and 3 were only recently discovered; Book 1 was first published posthumously in 1679), Cowley would update Lucan's type of epic to include gruesome descriptions of the English Civil Wars. Phineas Fletcher, another of the Spenserian school of English poets, at least dabbled in the extended Lucretian philosophical narrative in his *The Purple Island* (1633), an epic-length work that allegorizes and categorizes different types of evil, as Milton was to do in creating such fallen angels as Mammon or Belial, who stand for acquisitiveness or perversion of the intellect. But Milton rejected the external trappings of Spenser's allegory and Cowley's bellicose or Drayton's nationalistic subject matter, together with Joseph Beaumont's Anglican allegory. The one sustained allegory of *Paradise Lost*, that of Satan, Sin, and Death, parodies the Christian Trinity in infernal terms. Just how much residual or buried allegory may remain in *Paradise Lost* is the subject of a recent monography by Mindele Treip.

Many Milton scholars have tried to find the political allegory they feel must be buried in *Paradise Lost*, but, other than a general comparison between Satan and Charles I, or between the parliament of Pandemonium and the English Parliament, not much can be said, even though Milton was more closely involved in national or international politics and diplomacy than was any other English or Continental epic author. Recent research by Robert Fallon, Knoppers, Loewenstein, and Achinstein, sometimes in the name of "historicizing Milton" (as in Achinstein's title), has turned up more evidence to show that the epic is indeed a political statement—though

obviously Milton had to be cautious about what he said about kingship or republicanism, or he might quite literally have been hanged, in 1667, for being a regicide.

12. EPIC REMNANTS IN LITERARY DEVICES USED IN *PARADISE LOST*: THE TRANSFORMATION OF CLASSICAL EPIC

Milton in *Paradise Lost* uses all the obvious epic devices, but he significantly rejects epic themes and devices he feels are beneath Christian epic:

o he begins in the middle of the action (the Latin epic formula of *in medias res*);

o he catalogues proper names of people or of exotic places;

o he uses extended epic similes that are exhaustive comparisons between the unfamiliar (fallen angels, Satan) and the familiar (fallen leaves, vulture);

o he emulates various methods of oral composition, such as organization in books or *cantos* (*cantare* meaning "to sing" in Italian). Milton in his "song" makes much of his being blind but at the same time prophetic or oracular like Homer or Tiresias.

Milton writes against the grain of classical epic (Spencer) in the sense that he rejects the Homeric and Vergilian theme of the wrath of the gods and their irrational and bitter pursuit of heroes; he also rejects the theme of Achilles's choice between a long dull life and a short and glorious one; and he rejects the narrative of heroic quest—Odysseus's for his home in Ithaca or Aeneas's for Rome. Milton parodies the belligerent epic hero in the false but convincingly defiant heroism of Satan, and he parodies the epic quest in Satan's long and dangerous, but un-heroic, flights across the boundaries of the universe. Milton contrasts the less-important piety of the epic hero such as Aeneas, who is merely founding a city, with that of Adam and Eve, in whose repentance and atonement lies the whole fate of the human race. Milton also makes more of the epic descent into hell than did Homer or Vergil. Hell meant damnation to a Christian—more horrifying than the shadowy kingdoms of Hades, Dis, or Orcus in Greek or Roman myth. Milton makes more of the characterization of the types of evil in Hell in his demonic council than Homer or Vergil made of their versions of the underworld, which might seem only to be the place the poet visited while calling on dead human friends or enemies. Each of the demonic orators in Milton's Pandemonium is a grand representative of a complex of evils, capable of debating on the level of the Roman Cicero. Instead of being exemplars, say, of one Deadly Sin, as in Dante's *Inferno*, they represent networks of evil, or evil personality types. No voices quite so grand are heard from the classical hells, though Dante's condemned sinners can represent powerful characterizations of complex sins such as arrogance combined with heresy (Farinata) or defiance of God (Vanni Fucci).

13. THE THEME OF TEMPTATION

In his earlier poems, Milton had run variations on the theme of temptation—the theme central to *Paradise Lost*—as if he were practicing for his masterwork. Milton's Gunpowder Plot poems, written in his youth and in Latin—especially *In Quintum Novembris*—describe Satanic plots against the King. The Nativity Ode, which concentrates on the banishing of demonic pagan idols at the birth of Christ, prefigures the treatment of the fallen angels in the two epics. The character Comus is precursor both to Belial and Satan (Flannagan, "Belial"). Hanford's seminal article, "The Temptation Motive in Milton," explains the pervasiveness of the theme in Milton's prose and poetry.

There are two sets of successful temptations in *Paradise Lost*, Satan's temptation of the angels and Satan's temptation of Eve (and, through her, of Adam). The angels fall "Self-tempted, self-deprav'd," whereas "Man falls deceiv'd / By the other first" (3.130–31). In his role as the author of evil, Satan is also father of lies, and his method of tempting is always "By mixing somewhat true to vent more lyes" (*Paradise Regain'd* 1.433). He uses any weaknesses of character he can perceive to flatter, cajole, and seduce humankind to disobey the commandment not to eat of the fruit of the Tree of Knowledge of Good and Evil: as God had predicted, "Man should be seduc't / And flatter'd out of all, believing lies / Against his maker" (10.41–43).

God sees providentially that the Seed, who is also the Son, or Jesus Christ, will resist temptation. Milton's *Paradise Regain'd* answers the accusation that Thomas Ellwood's question implied, when he supposedly said to Milton "Thou hast said much here on paradise lost, but what hast thou to say of paradise found?" (quoted in Parker, *Milton* 1: 597). The first work concentrates on temptation, the second concentrates on resisting temptation; Jesus's finding the Paradise within complements Adam's loss of Eden.

14. EPIC ONE-UPMANSHIP

Milton is combative and competitive even with those predecessor epic poets he admires most (Blessington, DiCesare, Martindale). At one time or another in *Paradise Lost*, he disparagingly alludes to the Homeric shield of Achilles, the Vergilian wrath of Juno, the unseemly anger of Turnus, and Aeneas's faithless rejection of Dido. The grotesque red and black devils that populate Dante's *Inferno* (they even appear in Michelangelo's *Last Judgment*) seem to have been to Milton ridiculous monstrosities. The twisted physical convolutions of earlier underworlds, even Dante's symmetrical spirals or terraces, became the evasive convolutions of Satan's evil mind. Evil in *Paradise Lost* is internalized and psychological: it is not limited to any identifiable physical locale other than the battleground of the soul.

Even the Renaissance epic hero's conquest of space through flight became in Milton's hands a ridiculous image of the tatterdemalion and shoddy Satan struggling to keep his shredded wings in flight-worthy condition on his way toward Eden.

That is not to say that Milton threw out all of what he had valued in classic and Renaissance epic: he did retain a sense of important celebration or ritual, he kept the political subtexts (in the modern sense of "hidden agendas" or in Milton's words places or situations "where more is meant than meets the ear" ["Il Penseroso" 20]) of Tasso and Spenser and he included more personal subtexts than any earlier epic poet. He even gave what was perhaps grudging honor to his native land by writing in an elevated form of its language: he answered the English people who made him a political outcast in 1660 by raising the usage standards of the English language. But he converted the struggles that had almost always in earlier epics been expressed as human battle into moral warfare for the possession of potentially immortal souls, as John Steadman points out (*Epic and Tragic Structure*; see also Martindale).

15. RENAISSANCE EPIC THEORY

Milton gave special favor to the Italian critics whenever he discussed or taught epic, as he advocated teaching it in *Of Education* (1644). Despite his fierce rejection of Roman Catholicism, which he labeled "monkish and miserable sophistry" (*Reason of Church Government*, Yale 1: 854), Milton knew and respected the greatest Italian epic, the *Divine Comedy*, as a work of art: Milton's epic takes on a high religious seriousness that is a respectful emulation of Dante's stance in his epic, and both poets are equally involved in and distanced from their subjects. Milton also often referred respectfully to Dante, Ariosto, and the other Italian epic writers who chose to write in the vernacular, because by doing so they ennobled their native speech. What they did for Tuscan or Florentine Italian, he would do for English, ennobling, heightening, and enriching his native tongue.

Girolamo Vida chose to write his epic and criticism not in his native Italian but in Latin. His short Vergilian epic *The Christiad* (1535) may have provided Milton with the form and part of the content for *Paradise Regain'd*. Vida also loosely codified the rules for writing epic poetry in his *De Arte Poetica* (1527). He included instructions on such subjects as how to make the verse form echo the sense of any passage, as when the rough struggle of plowing a field is echoed by the roughness and laboriousness of the verse: "each figure [image] has its own characteristic visage suited to its excellences, its own peculiar garb, and its own sound" (3.381–82, trans. Ralph G. Williams).

By the time Tasso wrote his *Discourses on the Heroic Poem* (1567–70), the genre of epic had taken on many rules for choice of subject matter, format or design and choice of fitting words and poetic style or decorum, some of them based on the practices of Homer and Vergil and some on those of Dante. Tasso believed that epic should be true to life and imitate the actions of human beings, but it should also be marvelous and emphasize wondrous events. It should also teach the reader how to live and thus it should be instructive or didactic.

Epic style should be heroic, its language the vernacular idiom of the poet elevated by such devices as inversion, long periodic sentences, and enjambment ("run-on lines," drawing out sense from line to line). It should deal with a Christian subject, preferably of national interest, far enough removed from the present to allow for poetic license with the plot. It should celebrate the wonders or marvels of angels or devils, rather than the "false" wonders of pagan monsters. The epic hero or heroes should embody Christian magnanimity. The poet should have as his chief purpose not sensual delight in pretty pictures but usefulness in moral instruction. The poet ought to know everything and overlook nothing, and "no one can be a good poet who is not a good man" (Tasso, as summarized by Cavalchini and Samuel 12). The tone of an epic should be uniformly serious, and any humor admitted ought to be heavy and sardonic (see my "Tasso," in *A Milton Encyclopedia*, ed. William B. Hunter).

Milton rejects Renaissance epic plot clichés, such as the pursuit of beautiful but often faithless women. He has no problem with a holy quest such as that of Spenser's Red Cross Knight pursuing Una as Truth, but he clearly rejects the institution of chivalry, as represented in jousts, in the pursuit of monsters, in romance—expressed in the conflict between love and honor—as a theme. He takes the quest for holiness more seriously, though he would reject the pursuit of any idol or icon. He also takes very seriously the pursuit of holiness within the individual. Christian knights may be tempted in a constant trial of goodness or fight a Christian moral warfare, but they would not fight in random combat.

Milton makes clear the contrast between fantasy and illusion and between sordid reality (perhaps best represented in the *Orlando Furioso* of Ariosto) and ideal reality (best represented in Spenser). He takes from romantic epic the mode of allegory, the device of portraying real

or imagined humans as flying from place to place, and what might be called the optics of epic—changes in perspective from God's-eye-view to devil's-eye-view. Milton self-consciously emulates many of the devices of the romantic epic, but he also competitively parodies most of them at the same time.

16. EPIC AS ANATOMY OR COMPENDIUM OF ALL KNOWLEDGE

The epic, and especially *Paradise Lost*, also can be viewed as an anatomy, a compendium of all knowledge on one subject (see Northrop Frye, *Anatomy*, and Colie). Milton tries to replace all human knowledge as it was perceived by Homer or Tasso with his own system of history, natural science, and theology. He seems to want to teach his reader how to be civilized, but in a Christian and humanistic setting. He actively competes with the "feigning" subject matter of classical and romantic epics, replacing what he considers the blind superstition of classical darkness or Counter-Reformation Catholicism with the true inner light of his own Protestant Christianity. Milton's epic, in its scope and in its display of knowledge and the wisdom of the ages, is not unlike Robert Burton's enormous *Anatomy of Melancholy* (published in many revisions throughout the seventeenth century); it is an exhaustive treatise on the subject of the Fall of Humankind.

The epic genre evolves in Milton's hands. Even within the broader confines of the Bible, he narrows his epic subjects to the most important sacred themes: the innocence and sin of Adam and Eve in *Paradise Lost*, and the redemption of humankind in the Son's resistance to temptation and rejection of Satan in *Paradise Regain'd*. Milton's "grand theme," in both epics as in his other longer forms, "is the attainment of freedom through a single-handed combat with temptation" (Lord, "Epic," in *A Milton Encyclopedia*).

17. SUMMARY: EPIC AS A LIFELONG TASK

Paradise Lost was the chief end of Milton's poetic ambition, which seems always to have been to write the great epic in English. His entire plan of education in St. Paul's School and Cambridge, with private tutors and on his own, his travels focusing on the land of Dante and Tasso, even his life as political controversialist, had prepared him to write the definitive English epic, or in this case the unique epic in English on a universal theme, the loss of Paradise by all humankind.

Milton's epic is an international and universal poem which is at the same time an extremely personal document referring to lifelong interests and passions. Milton, according to George de Forest Lord, "Far from concealing traces of personality . . . emphasizes the emotional, psychological, and spiritual circumstances in which he was composing his poem" ("Epic," *A Milton Encyclopedia*). *Paradise Lost* expresses strong personal opinions on such varied subjects as angelic digestion (West 114–16), tyranny, divorce, and the varied destinations of the soul and body after death. In one sense the epic is an egocentric statement, but in another *Paradise Lost* is truly humble—the Epic Voice admits it is nothing without the aid of the Christian muse. In the memorable phrase of Richard Helgerson, Milton is a "self-crowned laureate," and, if Helgerson is correct, ". . . sometime in the late 1650s he began to forge a new role for the laureate based exclusively on the functions of poet and prophet" (280). One should not forget that the generation of Puritan writers to which Milton belonged was characterized by the habit of writing autobiographies (see Diekhoff, *Milton on Himself*, and William B. Hunter, "John Milton, Autobiographer"). The poem is proud, intellectually engaging, combative, and competitive, but it is also profoundly humble when Milton puts himself in the hands of his Christian muse.

II. MILTON'S THEOLOGY AND *PARADISE LOST*

Perhaps what made Milton's epic definitive was a system of religious definitions written by Milton himself. *On Christian Doctrine* is Milton's codification of his own personal religious beliefs. It may have been intended for a larger audience (Hunter, "Audience"), and much of it may have been borrowed from an unidentified treatise in Milton's possession (Hunter, "Provenance"), but it is also a very meaningful private document. If it were written today, its title might be "Doing It My Way" or "What I Believe," because it defines Milton's theological position rather arrogantly, with frequent contemptuous references to "some people" who disagree with him (Yale 6: 218). It also seems to provide structural underpinning for *Paradise Lost*. Milton's title, in Latin *De Doctrina Christiana*, was probably borrowed from the treatise with the same name and a similar purpose written by St. Augustine (354–430 AD), and Milton's treatise and his epic are very close in interpretation of Original Sin to Augustine's more famous *City of God* (Fiore, *Milton*; Patrides, *Milton and the Christian Tradition*). *On Christian Doctrine*, though it seems to be unfinished (Gordon Campbell, "*De Doctrina*"), also provides Milton's clearest definitions for the motives and characterization of all the major figures, good and evil, whose actions or thoughts move his epics, from the Son of God to Moloch to Abdiel. Modern theologians and historians of the Puritan movement have closely examined Milton's treatise or *medulla* (the "mar-

row" of divinity, or one's innermost feeling about the sacred) and found that it often borders on beliefs considered heretical by the established English church of Milton's era, which is not surprising, considering Milton's politics (Kelley, *Argument*; Adamson, Hunter and Patrides, *Bright Essence*).

Christopher Hill's *Milton and the English Revolution* establishes Milton's connection with various radical theological sects and political movements of his own era, from Anabaptists and Seekers to Muggletonians and Quakers. Milton's Quaker friends Thomas Ellwood and Isaac Penington, Jr. were often jailed for their beliefs, especially after the Restoration (Parker *Milton* 1: 597; Achinstein). Though he perhaps makes Milton into even more of a radical theologian than he was, Hill is the most distinguished historian of the period to have written extensively about Milton in an historical context (but see also Wedgwood, Woolrych).

Paradise Lost is a theological epic built on a theme of international importance. Modern students should take the theology of the epic seriously, but one need not be Christian to appreciate the struggle between good and evil or the human misunderstandings between husband and wife so vividly depicted in the epic. As the product of strong Puritan individualism (William B. Hunter, "John Milton: Autobiographer"; Helgerson; Stein, *Art*), *Paradise Lost* certainly has its theological foundation in Milton's personal statement of faith. Milton's theological definitions help give the epic clarity and force. Nothing like a great theological epic would ever be written after Milton, though there are similar works written during Milton's era, unknown now except to scholars, such as Beaumont's *Psyche*.

The work of another of Milton's contemporaries, Abraham Cowley's Royalist biblical story, the *Davideis*, is based on the life of King David. Derived from a different poetic and political lineage, it is closer to Sylvester's translation of DuBartas in its fervid tone and extravagant style than to *Paradise Lost*. Cowley's work is not likely to have been known to Milton, though Milton had considered writing dramas on many Old Testament subjects. Religious and biblical epic was in the air in Milton's England, with the great example of Spenser still looming from the Elizabethan era, but *Paradise Lost* was its only great manifestation.

Each of the Italian romantic epics had expressed the theology of its author. Ariosto had given lip-service to the Christianity of his time, but his overriding irony makes the *Orlando Furioso* difficult to call a Christian document. Tasso's Counter-Reformation zeal and his morbid and even insane (his contemporaries thought him crazy) emphasis on the horrors more than the pleasures of religion separate the tone of his epic from

Milton's more cleanly-defined and positive Protestantism (Lewalski, *Protestant Poetics*; Gregerson).

1. DISCOVERY OF *ON CHRISTIAN DOCTRINE*: ONGOING ARGUMENTS ABOUT HERESY

On Christian Doctrine was discovered by Robert Lemon, Deputy Keeper of His Majesty's State Papers, while Lemon was cataloguing some seventeenth-century British state papers at Whitehall in 1823. When it was translated by Charles Sumner in 1825, it shocked Anglican theologians with its unorthodox opinions about polygamy (Leo Miller, *John Milton*) and about the subordination of the Son of God to the Father. The general heterodoxy of the work shocked nineteenth-century churchmen because conventional Christianity normally treats the Trinity as made up of coequal entities and considers polygamy as much a sin as fornication. Debate over Milton's theology, however, has caused literary critics ever since *On Christian Doctrine* was discovered to examine the theology of *Paradise Lost* alongside the often heretical beliefs Milton expressed in the treatise, including radical subordinationism (MacCallum, *Sons of God*), Arminianism, the belief that the soul goes to sleep at death, and other major and minor heresies. Though the provenance of the treatise has recently been disputed by William B. Hunter ("The Provenance"), the theology of the treatise seems to match that of the epic closely. A forthcoming article on the provenance of *On Christian Doctrine* might help to clarify the issues (*Milton Quarterly* monograph, scheduled for October, 1997).

There is some evidence, however, that Milton softened the harder edges of his heresies in the epic, perhaps to help get *Paradise Lost* past the Restoration censor. The Church of England examiner, Thomas Tomkyns, who we know read at least Book 1, reportedly had objections to some passages he found to be politically, if not theologically, rebellious and hence dangerous to the young government of Charles II in the Restoration (Parker, *Milton* 1100).

2. *ON CHRISTIAN DOCTRINE* AS THE FOUNDATION FOR *PARADISE LOST*

On Christian Doctrine discusses in detail all the theological subjects important to *Paradise Lost*: the nature of God as father, judge, and avenger of evil; the creation; the origin of evil, which cannot be blamed on God merely because He had foreknowledge of it; free will and predestination; the Fall; the prevenient grace issued by God to undeserving human beings, like a line of godly credit; confession, atonement and eventual salvation. The angels who fall are self-tempted, self-depraved. Humankind on the other hand is tempted by Satan first and is therefore capable of atonement and the receipt of grace. Satan embodies the process of hardening of the

heart, like the Egyptian Pharaoh in Exodus. Most of human history (Milton's Books 11 and 12) unfortunately mirrors that process. Behind Milton's theological system, though, he seems to avoid the term "providence." Providence in *Paradise Lost* after it is first mentioned (1.25) is God's carefully guided plan of history. Milton uses the terms "divine providence" (*Reason of Church-Government*, Yale 1: 751) and "eternall providence" (Yale 1: 835), assuming that their meaning is commonplace, and it is "divin Providence" he finds responsible "for suffering *Adam* to transgresse" (*Areopagitica*, Yale 2: 527).

Another theological concept not in the foreground of *Paradise Lost* but certainly present in phrases like "A paradise within thee, happier farr" (12.587) is the idea that the Fall was a good thing in the long run. Critics have argued through much of the twentieth century over whether Milton believed in the "fortunate fall" (Lovejoy, "Milton"; Shumaker; Bell; Mollenkott, "Milton's Rejection"). The recent consensus, as represented by Mollenkott, rejects the notion that the process of the first sin was in any way "happy" in the modern sense, though the paradise within might be happier as a mental state than it could be as a pleasant physical location.

3. FREEDOM

Milton's theology has political, social, and deeply personal implications. Milton discussed the freedom of the will in terms political and domestic: freedom from a tyrannical marriage was as important to him as freedom of the press and freedom from a dictator. Milton pictured himself in his prose as the constant advocate of liberty, as opposed to license or licentious behavior: phrases like "Christian liberty," "liberty of conscience," "civil liberty," and "native liberty," echo throughout his works. He defined liberty as "the nurse of all great wits" (*Areopagitica*, Yale 2: 559). The opposite of liberty was servility, especially servile behavior toward a tyrant. A tyrant of any form was "something utterly base," and tyrants in general were "the meanest of slaves; they are slaves even to their own slaves" (*Second Defence*, Yale 4: 562, 563).

Idolatry also enslaved the individual. Idolatrous worship of false gods was analogous to irrational respect paid to a false king. In the home as well, any man's worship of the "outside" of a woman was equally reprehensible. All idols should be broken, and the righteous individual must be an iconoclast whenever he is faced with a false god.

Milton's God was not only judge and avenger but father and creator. When, in his youth at St. Paul's School, Milton went every morning to what was called "Matins" or the morning service at the cathedral, he would have heard God called the being "in whose service is perfect freedom" (Second Collect for Peace, Morning Prayer, *Book of Common Prayer*). All wickedness and rebellion against the nature of things (and for Milton God made all things out of His own substance) is weakness. God is righteously angry at sinners; cruel and destructive sin deserves equally cruel and destructive punishment.

Milton's youth and middle age were spent in an increasingly chaotic religious and political era. The Cambridge colleges when he was in attendance there were sharply divided into "high church," "low church," and "Puritan." Bowing to the cross, wearing certain vestments, or using incense in a college chapel—these were all acts with political significance. Milton's theology must have been influenced by the liturgy he was forced to hear weekly in church, since attendance was legally required, and by what he would have heard daily when he attended St. Paul's School (Stroup, D. L. Clark). The mature theology of his *On Christian Doctrine* can be related to that of other Puritan divines who constructed similar systems, such household names of the early seventeenth century as William Perkins, William Ames, Richard Baxter, and Johan Wolleb (Kelley, "Milton's Debt"). Though the Puritan movement in which Milton participated was widely distributed in countless sects, his theology together with his politics easily fit its tradition (Bennett, *Reviving*; Fink; Geisst; Hill; Wedgwood; Wolfe).

To try to summarize Milton's theology in this short a space is impossible; interested students should read the entire *On Christian Doctrine* in Carey's translation in the Yale *Prose*. They should also consult Patrides's *Milton and the Christian Tradition*, Evans's Paradise Lost *and the Genesis Tradition*, and various books and articles by Patrides, William B. Hunter, Kelley, and Bauman.

4. THE BIBLE AS THE ONE ESSENTIAL BOOK

Milton came to believe that the Bible contained everything necessary for the salvation of humankind (Sims 8–9). Some parts of the Bible—certainly Genesis, the Psalms, the stories of Samson and some of the other judges in Judges, the Book of Isaiah, the Book of Ezekiel, the Book of Job, some of the epistles assigned to St. Paul and Revelation—seem to have influenced him or attracted him more than others (see Rogal for a tabulation), though Milton had the entire canonical Bible and the Apocrypha within easy recall in his memory. A quick look through Bauman's scriptural index to *On Christian Doctrine* will establish how comprehensively Milton studied the Bible. He knew the book as well as any preacher or commentator of his time—so well that he would often substitute his own translation of a word

or passage into Latin or English in preference to those of St. Jerome's Vulgate Latin translation or the Latin translation that Protestants preferred, that of Junius and Tremelius, or the contemporary English King James or Authorized Version. Milton's nephew and former pupil Edward Phillips reported that Milton preferred that his students read in the original: "The *Sunday's* work was for the most part the Reading each day a Chapter of the *Greek* Testament, and hearing his Learned Exposition upon the same . . ." (*Life*, in Darbishire, *Early Lives* 61).

The Bible (to paraphrase *On Christian Doctrine*) was the only book the Christian had to read; it was unified and coherent; it contained within itself the best examples of all important literary genres. The entire book had a kind of mystical significance: the word *Holy* in Holy Bible was taken very seriously. The Psalms were the best examples of lyric poetry (Radzinowicz, *Milton's Epics*), and they were to be translated partly for practice in different verse forms, as Milton paraphrased or translated various of them at different times in his life. The Book of Job was in itself the model of a brief epic. The choruses of Revelation were examples of high tragedy. Man's first disobedience and temptation as described in Genesis might be the noblest subject either for tragedy or for heroic poetry.

Milton's ideas about the essential value of the Bible to every aspect of life, including the providing of literary models, were not unique to his era or limited to those whose political or theological alliances would label them Puritans. Poets as diverse as Tasso and DuBartas, John Donne and George Herbert, all would have agreed with Milton on the importance of the Bible to every decision one made in life.

Milton's is the unique Puritan epic, though the novelistic allegory *Pilgrim's Progress* (part 1 published 1678, part 2 1684) of John Bunyan is related to *Paradise Lost*, but on a much simpler and more popular level. Beyond the historical movement of Puritanism, and beyond Milton's youthful patriotism, *Paradise Lost* represents an attempt to rise above nationalism or secularism into universal biblical archetype.

Typology is the matching of Old Testament with New Testament figures as types or echoes of each other. It makes of the Bible a coherent and seamless document in which there are no contradictions. Christian progress could be seen in the historical march "from shadowie Types to Truth" (12.303), from Joshua of the Old Testament to Jesus in the New (Madsen; MacCallum, *Sons*; Tayler). The Bible was always Milton's most important source, a fact that can sometimes be neglected by a modern audience. In editing *Paradise Lost* using computerized cross-referencing of words or phrases, I have discovered that Milton's vocabulary is pervaded by networked biblical phrasing, so that an image undeveloped in an Old Testament passage might be expanded and completed by cross-references to a similar image in the New Testament. The influence of the Bible on his poetic style and imagery, in other words, is even more pervasive than that imagined by Sims.

Milton's allusions to the Bible are networked the way that the cross-references in the Geneva Bible are interconnected: a reference to "Ye shalbe as gods" in Genesis 3.5, for instance, is connected in the Geneva Bible to Ecclesiasticus (the apocryphal book) 25, a chapter dealing with betraying and malicious wives, and Ecclesiasticus 33, a chapter dealing with the image of God as potter, molding the clay of human nature. A second cross-reference points to 1 Timothy 2.14, which the Geneva Bible translates as "And Adam was not deceived, but the woman was deceived, & was in the transgression." When one turns to that passage in 1 Timothy, further marginalia tell us "The woman was first deceived, & so became the instrument of Satan to deceive the man: and thogh therefore God punisheth them with subjection and pain in their travel [i.e. *travail*, or the labor of giving birth], yet if they be faithful and godlie in their vocation, they shal be saved." The phrase "in the transgression" is glossed "That is, giltie of the transgression." The Geneva Bible interpreted itself as the reader progressed from text to margin to parallel text.

The theological concept of accommodation—that God's mysteries must be explained in the Bible and elsewhere in terms that human beings can understand—is also important to our understanding of the events of *Paradise Lost* (Patrides, "The Godhead"). For instance, it is useful for Raphael, in retelling the events of the War in Heaven, to picture the angels in bodily shapes and to imagine them hurling the equivalent of mountains at one another, because such pictures are accommodated to what human beings can understand through the five senses. Milton assumes that angelic sense and understanding can deal with stimuli that we cannot perceive

(we cannot perceive the angelic fifth element, ether, or life as it exists in the empyrean or the highest heavenly sphere), or with something as esoteric as the angelic digestive system, or with the way the entire cosmos functions. The theory of accommodation (Lieb, *Dialectics*) works well for a poet who must look constantly for correspondences in order to enliven his style.

III. THE FABLE

1. EARLY OUTLINES FOR DRAMAS ON THE FALL

The word *fable*, at least for the earliest English critics such as Joseph Addison, who made the first systematic study of *Paradise Lost*, meant "plot." Milton was characteristically scrupulous in plotting first his dramatic versions and then his epic. He made four drafts, two with full plots, for a morality play or five-act Christian tragedy based on Adam's Fall or his banishment or his loss of Paradise. The manuscript was eventually donated to Trinity College, Cambridge, where it remains. How it got to Trinity College is a mystery. It may have been through the agency of Milton's unscrupulous amanuensis Daniel Skinner, the manuscript offered as a kind of bribe for an academic appointment. The Trinity Manuscript's lists of dramatic and epic subjects are usually dated 1640–42. The four outlines printed below were never intended for publication: they are drafts employing sparse punctuation and inconsistent capitalization and spelling. Words are canceled, replaced, crossed out again, and each of the first two lists is crossed out. I have added punctuation and decipherment of uncertain words in brackets, and I have inserted matter from the margin or from another sheet that Milton showed he wanted inserted by means of several types of insertion symbols. The first draft is the first entry in a list of biblical subjects for tragedies. Milton first wrote the two lists of "the Persons" (shown on the next page), then put a large X through both and went on with what is written after "Paradise Lost."

the Persons	the Persons
Michael	Moses
Heavenly Love	
	or Divine (Wisedome
	~~Michael.~~Justice. Mercie
Chorus of Angels	Heavenly Love
Lucifer	The Evening Starre Hesperus
Adam	Chorus of Angels
with the serpent	Lucifer
Eve	Adam
Conscience	Eve
Death	Conscience
	~~Death~~
Labour \	Labour \
Sicknesse		Sicknesse	
Discontent	Mutes	Discontent	Mutes
Ignorance		Ignorance	
with others /	Feare	
Faith	Death /
Hope	Faith
Charity.	Hope
	Charity

Paradise lost   The Persons

Moses [προλογίζει] recounting how he assum'd his true bodie,
   that it corrupts not because of his with god in the mount
   declares the like of Enoch and Eliah, besides the purity of yᵉ
   pl[ace] that certaine pure winds, dues, and clouds praeserve it
   from corruption whence [ex]horts to the sight of god, tells they
   cannot se Adam in the state of innocence by reason of thire
   sin

Justice
Mercie   debating what should become of man if he fall
Wisdome
Chorus of Angels sing a hymne of yᵉ creation
   Act 2.
Heavenly Love
Evening starre
chorus sing the mariage song and describe Paradice
   Act 3.
Lucifer contriving Adams ruine
  Chorus feares for Adam and relates Lucifers rebellion and fall
   Act 4.
Adam
Eve   fallen
Conscience cites them to Gods Examination
  chorus bewails and tells the good Ada[m] hath lost
   Act 5.

Adam and Eve, driven out of Paradice
praesented by an angel with
Labour greife hatred Envie warre famine Pestilence

sicknesse	\	mutes to whom he gives
discontent	|	thire names
[Igno]rance	|	likewise winter, heat Tempest &c.
Feare	|	enterd into y^e world
Death	/	
Faith	\	
Hope	|	comfort him and instruct him
Charity	/	

　chorus breifly concludes

[Several pages later in the Trinity Manuscript, under the heading "Adams Banishment," which was crossed out and replaced by "Adam unparadiz'd," Milton again outlined his plot:]

The angel Gabriel, either descending or entring, shewing since this globe was created, his frequency as much on earth, as in heavn, describes Paradise. next [Milton wrote "first," then crossed it out and replaced it in the margin with "next"] the chorus shewing the reason of his comming to keep his watch in Paradise after Lucifers rebellion by command from god, & withall expressing his desire to see, & know more concerning this excellent new creature man. the angel Gabriel as by his name signifying a prince of power tracing paradise with a more free office passes [Milton crossed out "comes"] by the station of ye chorus & desired by them relates what he knew of man[,] as the creation of Eve with thire love, & mariage. after this Lucifer appeares after his overthrow, bemoans himself, seeks revenge on man[.] the chorus prepare resistance at his first approach[.] at last after discourse of enmity on either side he departs[,] wherat the chorus sings of the battell, & victorie in heavn against him & his accomplices, as before after the first act was sung a hymn of the creation. [insertion from opposite leaf, in quotation marks] "heer again may appear Lucifer relating, & insulting in what he had don to the destruction of man." man next & Eve having by this time bin seduc't by the serpent appeares confusedly cover'd with leaves[.] conscience in a shape accuses him, Justice cites him to the place whither Jehova call'd for him[.] in the mean while the chorus entertains the stage, & his [is?] inform'd by some angel the manner of his fall [Milton inserted "heer the chorus bewailes Adams fall." by means of a symbol] Adam then & Eve returne[,] accuse one another but especially Adam layes the blame to his wife, is stubborn in his offence[.] Justice appeares[,] reason with him[,] convinces him [Milton inserted "the chorus

admonisheth Adam, & bids him beware by Lucifers example of impenitence" by means of a footnote symbol][.] the Angel is sent to banish them out of paradice but before causes to passe before his eyes in shapes a mask of all the evills of this life & world[.] he is humbl'd[,] relents, dispaires. at last appeares Mercy[,] comforts him[,]&~~brings~~in~~faith[,]~~hope~~&~~ ~~charity~~ promises the Messiah, then calls in faith, hope, & charity, instructs him[,] he repents[,] gives god the glory, submitts to his penalty[.] the chorus breifly concludes. compare this with the former draught.

There must have been intermediate stages of later outlines before Milton changed the tragedy "Adam unparadiz'd" into the epic *Paradise Lost*. Edward Phillips, Milton's nephew, remembered "This Subject was first designed a Tragedy, and in the Fourth Book of the Poem there are Ten Verses [Phillips quotes ten lines, 32–41], which several Years before the Poem was begun, were shewn to me, and some others, as designed for the very beginning of the said Tragedy" (Darbishire, *Early Lives* 72).

What can we make of the transition from a five-act biblical tragedy that looks as if it were descended from morality plays like *Everyman* and from Milton's highly serious masque (substitute "Attendant Spirit" for "angel Gabriel" above) to a neoclassical or baroque epic that was first published in ten books? According to whichever analyst one reads, from Gilbert to Hanford to Barker to Shawcross, Milton either retained the hidden five-act structure, or he rearranged it or dropped it completely. The tragedy may, like *Samson Agonistes*, have never been intended for the stage. If Phillips is right about Satan's apostrophe to the sun at 4.32–113—that it began the tragedy—then the Grand Consult of Books 1 and 2 of *Paradise Lost* probably was not part of "Adam unparadiz'd," and the tragedy focused on the Fall more tightly than the epic. Events such as the War in Heaven were apparently to be described by messengers as off-stage action in the tragedy, in what must have been less extensive than the long narratives of Raphael or Michael in the epic. It may well be that these long narratives, especially those of the Creation, the War in Heaven, and the "masques" of subsequent history, outgrew the dimensions of classical tragedy, or the Aristotelian unities of time, place, and action. Milton did retain the vital elements of tragedy, from the soliloquy (Satan's address to the sun is an example) to the catharsis of pity and fear caused in the reader by the sad eventuality of the Fall.

2. MOVEMENT AWAY FROM ALLEGORICAL DRAMA

The change from allegorical drama into much-less-allegorical epic left only the remnants of allegory in the epic, such as the characters Satan, Sin, and Death (Murrin, *Allegorical*), but one can identify most of the allegorical abstractions mentioned in the outlines, such as Heavenly Love or Famine, in the actions of characters in *Paradise Lost*. The Son obviously represents Heavenly Love. Death, with his gaunt or skeletal shape, looks like an emblem of Famine ending in death. One can see from the first outline that "Michael" is crossed out and "Justice" substituted. Allegory traditionally had "included such features as personification, abstraction, metaphorically doubled chains of discourse and of narrative, generated subcharacters, deletion of nonsignificant description and several topics (journey, battle, monster, disease)" (Fowler, *Kinds* 192). Milton includes vestiges of such allegorical features, but *Paradise Lost* should probably not be called an allegory. As Murrin points out, Milton deliberately chose not to allegorize such events as the War in Heaven, "and this choice signals the end of a tradition" (*Allegorical* 153). But Murrin may be overstating the case, since vestiges of allegory appear consistently throughout *Paradise Lost* (see Treip).

Angels, who themselves can be characterized either allegorically or according to the etymology of their names, have speaking parts both in the tragedy and in the epic. Milton is illustrating the pleasant idea that before the Fall the interchange among God, angels, and humankind was much easier. In the epic Raphael and Michael sometimes speak as the Chorus would have spoken in the planned tragedy, telling of events that only the angels would have known about. An allegorical character like Justice could become part of the Son's character, when the Son is acting as judge or mediator, or Michael's, when he too pronounces judgment on the fallen Adam and Eve. Likewise Heavenly Love can be an attribute either of the Father or the Son, or of the Godhead in general. The Son's character can include the allegorical Mercy, as when He offers forgiveness to Adam and Eve.

Finally, the Epic Voice or narrator took over most of the functions of the dramatic Chorus and allowed Milton to become a character in his own epic.

3. THE TRAGEDY WITHIN THE EPIC

The tragedy of Adam and Eve still exists intact within the larger structure of the epic. Adam's tragic conflict comes between his duty—obedience to God—and his loyalty to his flesh and blood, Eve. Eve herself is a tragic heroine deceived by Satan into becoming a cause for her own death, that of her husband, and that of all humankind. Book 9 is a small, self-contained tragedy, which Milton as Epic Voice signals when he writes that he will "change / Those Notes to Tragic" in the invocation to that book. The tragedy of Adam and Eve as a unit is inevitable, it arises out of flaws in both their characters, and it is occasioned by understandable but reprehensible disobedience of a command easy to obey.

The outline's masque (the generic term is used as with *Comus*) of all evils brought into the world by disobedience remains in the epic's long episodic historical narrative of the last two books, a series of scenes in *tableaux vivants*, or even more like a series of movie montages.

4. TEN BOOKS INTO TWELVE: THE QUESTION OF STRUCTURE

Beyond the question of the epic's having five acts, there still remains the question of ten books vs. twelve, over which scholars still debate hotly. What do the numbers signify? Milton had a traditional choice of epic format between ten books (or multiples of ten) or twelve. The ten-book division in which the epic first appears in 1667 neatly divides into five two-book sections dealing with Hell and Eden before the Fall, as William B. Hunter reminds me in a letter. Numerological critics such as Fowler (see the introduction to his edition of *Paradise Lost*), Røstvig, or Shawcross (*With Mortal Voice*) still make much of how the center of the epic shifts when the numbers of books or lines change. Though Homer and Vergil used twelve and multiples of twelve, Lucan's *Civil War* was in ten books, Ovid's *Metamorphoses* in fifteen. Milton may have been asked or even coerced to change ten to twelve by his publisher, just as he was asked to provide arguments and a justification for "why the Poem Rimes not" (Samuel Simmons's note "The Printer to the Reader," 1668 title page).

Milton renumbered his books for the 1674 edition. The critical apparatus consisting of his note on "The Verse," the Arguments for each book and critical support from Andrew Marvell and Samuel Barrow were added in the 1668 issue of the text. In what he added, Milton seems to become defensive and aggressive at the same time. He belligerently accedes to the request of his publisher to provide a reason why the poem did not rhyme, providing a series of book-summaries so that the readers would have things explained for them. He also was asked, perhaps, to change the arrangement of books to accommodate current taste for twelve-book epics. Milton, judging by his acrimonious note on "The Verse," was dragged by his publisher or by his first readers' responses into concessions to popular taste. On his own, he asked only for a "fit audience, though few" (7.31). He did, however, dutifully divide Book 7 into Books 7 and 8, and Book 10 into Books 11 and 12, adding just enough new lines to provide transitions at the beginnings of newly-formed books.

5. CLOSURE: THE LAST TWO BOOKS AS "UNTRANSMUTED LUMP OF FUTURITY"

They were called that by C. S. Lewis, and "inartistic" as well (*Preface* 125). The pejorative phrases have stuck, since a modern audience is not especially interested in the process of providence working its mysterious way on human history, or in the seventeenth-century version of the Bible as history. So what is there to say for the last two books? One should read the eloquent defense of them by Summers in *The Muse's Method*, or Patrides's in *The Phoenix and the Ladder*, to discover that though Milton did not take the easy way out, his solutions to the narrative problems were graceful, according to Summers: "Surely the poet might have provided [Adam and Eve] a brief vision or narration of the promised Seed, the possibility of the inward paradise and the final paradise and sent them forth rejoicing" (189), but he did not. Instead, "The final books complete the education of Adam and the reader" (190). "Virtue as well as sin is developed by trial. The final books provide for both Adam and the reader the final temptations. If each sustains the vision of providence, he will have earned it" (191).

One should think of the last two books as the inevitably tragic cycle of human folly, the sadder parts of history repeating themselves, with only a few good people to redeem events or show a godlike pattern behind all the sad wars and idolatries. Though it may seem so to the modern reader who has never read the Bible from end to end, Milton the poet does not go to sleep in the last two books. Milton's "fit reader" may be expected to have read the Bible with fascination, as history.

Christian typology, the belief that events of the Old Testament foreshadow those of the New, governs the structure of Milton's biblical history, but that same typology may put off a modern audience reading the Old and New Testaments as two separate series of historical documents more than as unified Christian doctrine. Many, many critics have argued with Lewis's premature conclusions (and Lewis had himself followed Addison and others who had expressed a general dislike for the last two books), including Rosenblatt and Waddington.

Whatever the effect of the "lump" of biblical history, and of Michael's catechizing Adam in the last few pages of *Paradise Lost*, the ending, with its picture of Adam and Eve once again hand in hand, sadder but wiser, is deeply moving. They are somehow together and alone, both are isolated or "solitary," yet they are also one in that they are united again. When the reader remembers their holding hands before the Fall and their separation just before it, their being reunited is even more poignant.

6. QUESTIONS OF THE NARRATION: INVOCATIONS AND NUMEROLOGICAL PATTERNS

Despite the changes in the structure of the poem, the invocations—direct personal appeals from the poet to the muse—were always placed strategically. In the 1674 edition they appear at the beginnings of Books 1, 3, 7 and 9 (in 1667 they would have been at 1, 3, 7, and 8). Again, numerological critics argue over the significance of the placement of each invocation. The sequence 1, 3, 7, 9 seems to represent an ordered arrangement which can be made into either a numerological or musical metaphor according to principles associated with the Greek Neoplatonist Pythagoras (Røstvig, Qvarnström), the sixteenth-century mystic Jacob Boehme (Hughes, "'Myself'"), or the Italian Renaissance philosophers Pico della Mirandola and Marsilio Ficino (Jayne). Fixler ("Plato's Four Furors") along with others has identified the invocation at Book 1 as a Platonic vision of the poet united with God, that in Book 3 as illumination, that of Book 7 as purification, and that of Book 9 as the soul's awakening. And Lee Johnson finds a significant pattern in the invocation of Book 1, whose "asymmetrical form . . . expresses the symbolic value of what is known as the 'divine proportion,' which is based not on numbers but on pure geometry" ("Milton's" 71). To frustrate efforts at interpretation even further, William B. Hunter and Stevie Davies argue that there are only three proper invocations, at 1, 3, and 7, and that the three invocations they identify are addressed to persons of the Trinity.

7. THE INSPIRED NARRATOR AS EPIC VOICE: MILTON AND HIS MUSE

There is also the problem of what to call the narrator: Is he Milton? Should he be called the Epic Voice—somehow larger than Milton and part of timeless epic formula—in the epithet popularized by Ferry? Is that fictive narrator, as Fish believes, playing a cat-and-mouse game to entrap the reader "surprised by sin"? I have no easy answers for these two intriguing questions. Though I have adopted the accepted term "Epic Voice" for Milton's narrator, I am acutely aware that at times the narrator is a public personage—a spokesperson for his nation and his faith—and at times he is no one else but John Milton, blind and alienated after the Restoration of the very king whose father's execution Milton had defended. I do not believe, but I cannot support my position using the intentional fallacy, that Milton would stoop so low as to practice entrapment on his reader, though I do believe that he would willingly have divided his readers into those "fit though few" and those unfit, just as with the sheep who are divided from the goats at the Last Judgment.

No doubt Milton believed in the inspiration and divine ecstasy, the Neoplatonic "furor" and the apocalyptic vision, of the inspired Christian poet (Kerrigan, *Prophetic Milton*). He asks specifically in his invocations that he as poet be inspired by the same Spirit that inspired Moses and impregnated chaos with meaning. He also associates inspiration with the quest for wisdom, or Wisdom, the sister of Urania, and with what seems to be a divinely-inspired natural song, that of the nightingale (Clark and McMunn, *Beasts* 88–95). The inspiration of the Epic Voice is associated with light—the light flowing from God, his effluence, or the "inner light" of the Puritan movement. Feminist or psychological critics such as Mollenkott ("Some Implications"), Hunter and Davies, or Kerrigan find significance in Milton's psychological subordination of himself in his feminine muse Urania, in a symbolic sexual unity or androgyny; it is as if Milton had to become godlike, subsuming both sexes in one being, in order to embody godlike creativity. "The quality of the emotion surrounding Urania is intense and personal: her communication of light and insight takes the form of a haunting and humane love relationship, as of mother to son (by analogy with Calliope and Orpheus)" (Hunter and Davies 31).

Neoplatonic theories of poetics, such as that embraced by Marsilio Ficino, held that poets, second only to philosophers, were capable of communing directly with God, through what was called the *furor poeticus*. As Vickers points out, "The problem that this concept poses is its contradiction between a theory of divine inspiration and one of rhetorical invention, with all its stress on planning and craftsmanship" (738). The poet's power and divinity might also enable him or her to put the soul of the reader in tune with divine harmony. In their flirtation with alchemy and numerology, the Florentine Neoplatonists also asserted that poetry was in harmony with the meaning hidden in the mo-

tions of all nature, from the motion of the planets on down to what we might call the motion of the atoms in chemistry. Milton in turn seems to have flirted with the theories of the Florentine Neoplatonists in arriving at his relationship between himself and his muse.

Urania had been invoked by DuBartas both as the Muse of Astronomy and as the Christian Muse. The association between a muse who controls the heavenly bodies and the Prime Mover who does the same thing would have been inevitable, given Christian typology. Urania is not only invoked by DuBartas in the *Divine Weekes* (Steadman, *Moral* 14–19), she is the subject of Lady Mary Wroth's prose epic *The Countess of Montgomeries Urania* (1621; see Lily B. Campbell). For a complete examination of theories of the Christian Muse and Urania, see Riggs, Gregory, and Schindler.

IV. RHETORICAL STRATEGIES: POETRY AS ARGUMENT AND POETRY AS MUSICAL COMPOSITION

1. THIS GREAT ARGUMENT

The phrase "this great Argument" (1.24) can be taken in at least two senses: "this great subject matter" (the Fall of humankind) and "this great series of debates over the nature of humankind and the causes of evil." Both senses of the word were current in Milton's era. As John Shawcross reminds me in a letter, "argument" is a rhetorical term that "means roughly what we would call 'thesis.'" Milton was a logician and a rhetorician: he had been made quite conscious by his training at St. Paul's School and Cambridge of the devices of argumentation and debate (Donald L. Clark). His education would also have made him aware that eloquence, like decorum, could be a masterpiece of human expression. His plan for the rhetorical strategies of *Paradise Lost* is well in place beneath the obvious structure of books and verse paragraphs. Milton's rhetoric is perhaps aimed at a fit audience capable of understanding or appreciating the hundreds of different types of arguments, the variants in true or fallacious logic, the subtle and sometimes almost subliminal shifts in tone or imagery that signify arrival at wisdom or descent into error in his characters, right reason on the one hand or the perverse and Satanic patterns of thought on the other. For the Renaissance philosopher, rhetoric was not separated from poetics: Aristotle's *Rhetoric* would be seen as complementary to his *Poetics* in that poetry written by a "perfect" man "skilled in praise and blame" (Vickers 735) should imitate life at its best, giving a good moral example of how to live. Rhetoric should be the art of convincing an audience of the truth of an issue by any means possible (Vickers, Weinberg). Sir Philip Sidney, whose *Arcadia*

Milton had cited with admiration and whose *Apology for Poesy* he surely knew, believed that the poet should be a good man (not like the poets that Plato might have banished from the Republic), and that poetry has the power to move readers to virtue and well-doing (Vickers 737). Even the Reformation leader Martin Luther had written "The Holy Spirit is the best rhetorician and logician, and therefore He speaks most clearly" (quoted in Christopher 15). Milton did, however, come to distrust the empty flourishes that Satanic rhetoric might employ (Broadbent, "Milton's Rhetoric").

Milton's unit of rhetorical or logical meaning is the verse paragraph, but so much happens within any verse paragraph of *Paradise Lost* that books have been written illustrating Miltonic phrases (as when the novelist Mary Webb used *Precious Bane* for a title). Though he can develop what amounts to a large orchestral suite within a long verse paragraph, Milton may also see numerological structures in varieties of caesural pauses or in single words within a line; he talks of poetry in terms of "numbers" and he seems to mean more by the term than just "counted groupings of accented syllables."

In Milton's poetry there are single images, such as the similes dissected by Whaler ("Miltonic Simile") or classified by Widmer, and image clusters, such as those identified by Banks or Tuve. The editors of the 1688 folio of *Paradise Lost* separated each verse paragraph from the one before and the one after by spacing, an indication that early readers could see the importance of the units.

As is appropriate for a blind and musical poet, there are sounds and sound clusters within the verse paragraphs that signify strongly, such as those surrounding the words "woe" or "sole" or its homonym "soul." A word may signify musically or semiotically. Milton certainly puns most seriously, as when the sexually-ravaged Sin is described as "dismaid" (or "dismaided") and Adam after the Fall is described as "not deceav'd" (or "dis-Eved"; see Shoaf's and Patricia Parker's discussions of such wordplay). Even the innocent prefix "dis-" can become important if Milton wants us to connect it with one of the proper names for hell, Dis (Forsyth, "Of Man's First Dis").

2. WORD MUSIC: *PARADISE LOST* AS OPERA

Though it is hard to discuss poetry as music unless it is lyric poetry that has been given a musical setting, Milton as an active musician and son of a composer, and as the lyricist for Henry Lawes's music with the songs in *Comus*, is certainly as musical as a poet can be. He seems to have planned verse paragraphs as structures with both musical arrangement and logical and rhetorical structure. His musical terminology is so precise it

seems written by a musicologist, speaking in an educated way about musical genres or modes, as with "Lydian airs" or the Doric mode. A verse paragraph can be composed in a form approximating that of a sonata, a small symphony, or a fugue, using musical crescendos and diminuendos, arias, hymns, or love songs.

Among nineteenth-century critics, it was fashionable to speak of Milton's "organ voice." The analogy is still valid. Milton controlled one instrument, his verse, but that instrument could be programmed as with the many voices of the organ and it could be operated quietly or with all stops out. Baroque music and poetry are full of devices such as overtones and echoes, as the modern poet John Hollander has eloquently demonstrated. Milton can produce the effect in poetry of operatic arias either with very little or no accompaniment (as in the basso continuo accompaniment of early opera arias; see Satan's apostrophe to the sun at 4.32–113) or hymns sung by voices in unison (as when Adam and Eve pray singing in the duet at 5.153–208). Heavenly choirs sing a hymn to marriage mentioned at 4.710, and Adam and Eve join "thir vocal Worship to the Quire / Of Creatures wanting voice," which one can take to mean that they sing a hymn with orchestral accompaniment, at 9.198–99. *Paradise Lost* is operatic on the scale of Mozart's *Magic Flute*, which extends infinitely into the worlds of magic and freemasonry, or Verdi's *Aida*, which can contain heroic choruses and tender arias, or, for that matter, pyramids and elephants.

The operas of Monteverdi, such as the *Orfeo*, provide a contemporary musical analogue to Milton's poetry. *Orfeo*, like the epics of Milton, is a comparatively static work of art, since it contains much oration and little action, but the beauty of the arias and the choruses carries the entire work of art. For one standard recording of that work, an interested reader might listen to *L'Orfeo*, conducted by Nikolaus Harnancourt, Vienna Concentus Musicus, Teldec 8.35020 (in compact disc). In the eighteenth century, both Handel and Haydn set Milton's words to music, in Haydn's oratorio *The Creation* (1798), which translates parts of Book 6 into German, and Handel's *Samson* (1743), which sets *Samson Agonistes* also as an oratorio. *Samson* has been recorded by Raymond Leppard and the English Chamber Orchestra on four vinyl discs by Erato (71240), and *The Creation* on two compact discs by Leonard Bernstein with the Bavarian Radio Symphony and Chorus for Deutche Grammophon (419765-2).

3. MUSIC AND WORD-CHOICE: ECHOES OF ETYMOLOGIES

The music of Milton's poetry should probably be addressed in conjunction with his word-choice and his prosody, both of which are linguistically very complex. Milton is a polyglot poet, incorporating the understanding of many languages into his amplified English (Hale, "Milton's Self-Presentation"). Sometimes he writes an inflected language, or a language with more clearly defined declensions, something like Latin-in-English, but it is too simple-minded to say his poetic diction is merely Latinate; Corns, in *Milton's Language*, takes pains to correct the common misapprehension and assert that his diction is often not Latinate. The very first sentence of the epic, however, waits until the sixth line to give us its verb, just as the first sentence of Vergil's *Aeneid* waits to give us the same verb, *cano*, which means "I sing."

Milton is also the most etymological of poets: he may use a word in two English senses, several Latin senses, and a Greek sense, all at the same time, as with the words "essence" and "effluence." There is deep, never trivial, wit in the choice of words, wit in the placement of words within each phrase, innovative wrenching of word-meanings, clever changes in tense, inversions or intentional rearrangement of normal syntax, and alteration of parts of speech. Milton's language is always in restless flux, but always under strict control: that is why it is often called "baroque."

A number of the words Milton coined are in negative form, as with "disespouse" or "undelighted": he seems to enjoy defining words by their opposites, according to the *via negativa* practice of the logicians (defining by oppositional comparisons) who followed Peter Ramus (see Ong's various books and articles). Milton is especially fond of making up negative compound words, such as "unbesought," "undelighted," "disespouse," or "inabstinence" (Gray 71). William B. Hunter has counted more than one thousand coinages attributed to Milton in the *Oxford English Dictionary*, including such common words today as "baffled," "beaming," "bickering," "blandished," and "brewed," and those are just for the letter B ("New Words" 226).

Milton never stops playing with grammar or syntax. His playfulness is part of the way he defines creativity, with reference to God the creator or with the poet acting as God's inspired voice. Corns makes the point that what might distinguish Milton's poetry from most contemporary verse is "lexical playfulness" (65), which can show itself in outright puns or the more subtle "plays on homonymic ambiguity" (65), as with "sole" and "soul." Are these musical effects or rhetorical ones? Traditional categories break down when one discusses the relationship between language and music in Milton (but see Hollander's noble attempts to do just that).

4. PROSODY AND POETIC STYLE

Milton cleverly does away with rhyme in *Paradise Lost*. I say cleverly because rhyme is cleverly replaced by assonance and consonance, or it is subtly buried within rather than at the ends of lines. As he says in "The Verse," he considers the jingling of like endings to be monotonous. But rhyme reappears in a more subtle manifestation within the iambic line, providing part of the connective tissue inside and between lines. Coherence and integrity are augmented by alliteration and the most subtle assonance and consonance, as in the dramatic poetry of the Shakespeare of *The Tempest* and *King Lear*, written long after Shakespeare had given up the couplets of *Romeo and Juliet* and *Richard II*. Milton demonstrates some control over sound and rhythm through his own loose system of punctuation and phonetic spelling (the reader may judge how loose both systems are by looking at holograph materials such as the outlines to "Adam unparadiz'd" above), or at some of the hand-written sonnets in which the single mark of punctuation is the period at the end.

Milton also uses the pauses within lines very carefully, never distributing them at random, to produce what Gerard Manley Hopkins was to call "counterpoint" and "sprung rhythm" (Hopkins, "Introduction" liv–lviii), rhythmic units that can reverse or turn each other inside out. Milton writes lines of poetry that appear to be iambic pentameter if you count the feet regularly but really contain hidden reversed feet or elongated or truncated sounds that echo meaning and substance rather than a regular, and hence monotonous, beat. He builds his poetry on syllable-count and on stress; William B. Hunter, following the analysis of Milton's prosody devised by the poet Robert Bridges in 1921, counts lines that vary in the number of stresses from three all the way up to eight, but with the syllabic count remaining fixed almost always at ten ("The Sources" 198). Milton heavily favors ending his line on a masculine, accented syllable, with frequent enjambment or continuous rhythm from one line to the next, as with "the Fruit / Of that Forbidden Tree . . . " (1.1–2). He avoids feminine feet or feet with final unstressed syllables at the ends of lines. He varies the caesura, or the definitive pause within the line, placing it more freely than any other dramatist or non-dramatic writer Hunter could locate (199). He controls elisions or the elided syllables in words most carefully, allowing the reader to choose between pronouncing a word like "spirit" as a monosyllable (and perhaps pronounced "sprite") or disyllable, or "Israel" as a disyllable or trisyllable. Always, Milton was searching for the "fit quantity of Syllables" he mentions in "The Verse."

Milton's syllabic prosody is always in flux, just as are his grammar and word usage; a reader senses a constantly shifting and reinvented language, as if Milton were never content to leave the words or phrases in the patterns in which he found them. According to Hardison, "Milton not only rejected rhyme, but he created a form that is unrivaled, even today, for the rich complexity of its syntax, its epic similes and its metaphors based on the *via negativa*, and the polysyllabic and ornamental nature of its vocabulary" (*Prosody* 266).

Although he did not altogether reject Aristotle's *Poetics* (see Prince or Steadman, *The Wall*, on Milton's poetics), Milton chose Tasso as his guide to what poetic style should be, rejecting (by the time he wrote *Paradise Lost*) much of the pastoral apparatus—the allusions to nymphs and swains, sheep and goats—of Spenser and Sidney, and rejecting the colloquialism and linguistic extravagance of Sylvester's translation of DuBartas. Sylvester's exuberance certainly influenced the young Milton, as shown by the echoes of DuBartas that appear in Milton's youthful poetry, but Milton's sense of decorum in epic poetry (and in most of the genres he used) made him reject most contemporary references, along with any phrases that were commonplace or slangy. Here are some words and images chosen completely at random from a page in Sylvester, together with reasons why Milton might have rejected them by the time he wrote *Paradise Lost*:

maister of misse-order	obvious alliteration
dabbled heeles	undignified picture of part of the anatomy
Leach-man [doctor]	too colloquial, dated
Pure goldie-lockes *Sol*	demeaning reference to the sun, slang
Faire daintie *Venus*	"daintie" is colloquial; it demeans the goddess
fine Prince-humour-pleaser	unnecessarily complex compound word

("Fourth Day of the First Weeke" 1: 217)

Sylvester's poetic style is exuberant and lively, inherently theatrical, but his is the kind of poetry—vivid, strained, ornamented, highly artificial—one might imitate in youth and reject in old age. John Dryden did just that with Sylvester's translation of DuBartas's epic: he confesses to having enjoyed it in his youth but then having rejected its imagery in his maturity as "abominable fustian, that is, thoughts and words ill sorted, and without the least relation to each other" (quoted from the dedication to *The Spanish Fryar* [1681], by Winn 338; see also Winn 29–35). The influence of Sylvester's trans-

lation of DuBartas can still be seen in *Paradise Lost*, especially in Milton's prosody, but it has diminished considerably from what it was in Milton's earlier pastoral poetry.

Milton kept what he might use of Sylvester's style within his own sense of decorum, what he thought proper poetic style in an epic. When Satan treks over "Rocks, Caves, Lakes, Fens, Bogs, Dens, and shades of death" (2.621), the extravagant list in monosyllables is not only musical: it sounds like what Snyder calls the "thumping liveliness" of Sylvester's DuBartas (1: 59). But Milton's use of compounds, his use of alliteration, his rhythms in general, became more subtle and complex after he had outgrown his Sylvester period (Ricks, *Milton's Grand Style*).

V. THE EPIC POEM AND THE SISTER ARTS—ARCHITECTURE AND PAINTING

There is also an architecture in the entire poem and in the separate books. The Christian God for Milton was what Sylvester and DuBartas called "*great Architect of Wonders*" (*Divine Weekes* 1.1.13), a *deus artifex* whose creative work should be echoed by the poet as maker or architect. Milton does for poetry what Michelangelo did for painting. The powerful cycle of creation, human history, and the Last Judgment in the Sistine Chapel corresponds closely with what Milton created in *Paradise Lost*. Milton's search for the muse has also been compared by Treip with the search for inspiration of the painter Raphael, who also depicted Urania as the most important of muses (*Descend*). Milton's deep and sometimes dark characterization and his use of darkness and bright light remind one of the depth and breadth of the portraits of Rembrandt, with their use of the deep-shading technique of chiaroscuro to delineate human character. Caravaggio is the great Italian master of chiaroscuro, especially good at picturing the evil and the perverse, in searing light or oppressive darkness.

From the best of the baroque pictorial artists, Milton may have learned the use of curved or undulating rather than straight lines, the use of constant motion (as in the swirling, panoramic paintings of Rubens), and the interruption of normal linear time sequences. The word "cartoon" is aptly used both for the outline of a sequence of scenes in a Renaissance fresco and for the modern popular art form, in which linear events are often replaced by panels depicting simultaneous events. From the Old Masters Milton may have learned how to create the illusion of depth and perspective that sometimes fools the eye. Like a Rubens or a Veronese working in oils, Milton can create in words the synaesthesia of smells, sights, and sounds one can see in a scene of opulence and voluptuous color, as with Rubens's *Rape of the Sabines*. Milton employed the variety of visual and temporal impressions, real and reflected, that one can detect in the great manipulation of perspective with the visual artists, as with Velázquez's *Las Meninas*. Milton seems to have associated rapid and futile motion with the demonic powers, but God is expressed in grand majestic sweeps, as when the chariot of paternal deity sweeps the front in the War of Heaven—a subject that baroque artists were thrilled to paint. Roland Frye (*Milton's Imagery*), Roston, Daniells (*Milton*), Lieb (*Poetics*), McColley (*A Gust*), and Treip ("Descend") have all explored the relationship between Milton's poetry and its sister arts (the subject of the essays edited by Labriola and Sichi). All of them are right in debunking the notion of T. S. Eliot expressed in "Milton I" that visual elements were weak in *Paradise Lost* or that Milton lacked visual imagination.

VI. THE MAN AND THE POEM

1. MILTON'S SENSE OF HUMOR

A modern university wit might say that this section should be left blank. It comes as a great surprise to anyone who has accepted the stereotype of Milton as the frowning Puritan to discover that he did indeed have a subtle, sensitive, sardonic, witty sense of humor. Most of his early biographers made it a point to comment on his wry wit. Even Milton's God has a sense of humor, and evil (from God's perspective, at least) is amusingly impotent, the way that Charlie Chaplin portrays Hitler in *The Great Dictator*. If Milton consciously embedded the pun "dismaid" in his characterization of Sin (who has lost her maidenhead to Satan), or if he even pokes gentle fun at what the Bible means by God's "back parts" and if he does have God joke with Adam about his unfixated lust, all those instances demonstrate a human voice and a sense of humor behind a somber theological epic. Christopher Hill concludes that "Milton had a far greater sense of humour, of fun, than he has been given credit for. He liked teasing" (472). Perhaps the great Russian critic Mikhail Bakhtin has best identified the Renaissance conception of laughter to which Milton would have subscribed:

> Laughter has a deep philosophical meaning, it is one of the essential forms of the truth concerning the world as a whole, concerning history and man; it is a peculiar point of view relative to the world; the world is seen anew, no less (and perhaps more) profoundly than when seen from the serious standpoint. Therefore, laughter is just as admissible in great

literature, posing universal problems, as seriousness. Certain essential aspects of the world are accessible only to laughter. (66)

Milton was by all accounts personally neither dour nor especially puritanical. Milton's nephew Edward Phillips reports that he could enjoy a "Gawdy-day" or holiday from studies with fashionable young men-about-town (Darbishire 612), he was a play-goer and at least an imagined romantic lover (like Romeo) in his youth, and he wrote sonnets praising companionship celebrated over good wine and food. He also was not a Puritan in the negative sense of that term when it came to describing prelapsarian sexuality: "Thou shalt not" does not apply to Adam and Eve's sexuality before the Fall. Milton could not have written the passages about unfallen desire in *Paradise Lost* 4 without believing in the value of desire in procreation (Turner).

His humor, though, is sometimes bitter or caustic. Whenever he speaks of politics or the abuses of religion, as in the Limbo of Vanity scene toward the end of Book 3, Milton's characteristic tone in *Paradise Lost* is sardonic, an infection he may have caught from the bitterness and paranoia of Tasso, or from the savage and scornful opinionatedness of Lucan, who calls Alexander the Great "a plague on the world, an all-destructive / Thunderbolt, a comet that boded ruin for mankind!" (250) and who characterizes Julius Caesar as ruthless, ambitious, cynical, irreverent, and hypocritical (Lucan, Books 9 and 10). Milton's humor in *Paradise Lost* is not destructive, though it can be satirical when it deals with abuses within the structure of the Christian church. The Catholic emphasis on beads and indulgences amused him, and he was angered at the cynicism and opportunism within the Anglican church hierarchy, which Milton saw metaphorically as the open-jawed wolf in sheep's clothing.

The political and religious satire which is a subtext of *Paradise Lost* must have struck the first illustrators of the epic, in 1688, as humorous: why else would Satan have been pictured in Roman armor (background of the illustration to Book 1), and why else would figures in the distant background in Pandemonium be wearing papal mitres? In the pamphlet wars of the 1640s, Milton had learned well how to use sardonic humor as a weapon.

Milton had a very serious sense of humor, especially acute in his use of irony. He believed that "parables, hyperboles, fables and the various uses of irony are not falsehoods since they are calculated not to deceive but instruct . . . " (*On Christian Doctrine* 2.13, Yale 6: 761). His language is sometimes a sea of irony, with an undertow of sardonic allusions, and (if you will excuse the extended metaphor) a riptide of puns that carries away a naive or unsuspecting reader.

2. SCHOOLMASTER MILTON AND THE DIDACTIC EPIC

Difficulties planned carefully by Milton make *Paradise Lost*, in the modern college cliché, a "learning experience." Allusions are carefully buried at times; esoteric names are chosen instead of more common ones (the "unwiser son of Japhet," for instance, is Milton's name for Prometheus's brother Epimetheus). But Milton's policy with his own pupils was to bring them out, "opening" the secrets of texts for them, and his personal teaching method applies to the relationship between writer and reader in *Paradise Lost*. Hence the Arguments, whether or not they were coerced from Milton by his publisher, both tease and instruct the careful reader. Often Milton will define a difficult poetic phrase like "darkness visible" hundreds of lines after it first appears, perhaps to see whether the reader is really fit. Almost never does a sentence mean only one thing in *Paradise Lost*: the reader always feels like a pupil facing a steep learning curve. Truth is represented by the scattered seeds of Psyche as in the myth retold by Apuleius, or it is at the top of a steep and winding path.

A less obvious problem with Milton the schoolmaster is what might be called his intellectual arrogance. The immensity of the man's achievements in prose and poetry hangs over the reader of any single piece Milton has written. We readers must come to terms with his phenomenal memory, creativity, and definitiveness. Milton's near total recall or eidetic memory of everything he ever read is intimidating. Not only that: Milton has a strong opinion about everything he has seen, heard, or read, and he always has scripture and personal reminiscence and literary precedent to back him up. Even after he went blind, Milton could recall what he had read so accurately that specific editions can be located from passages he dictated to amanuenses (Boswell ix–x). His memory, intelligence, and breadth of knowledge are indeed amazing and awe-inspiring.

And Milton could be formidable when he demonstrated righteous anger or God's wrath. Though Milton valued the Christian duty of charity toward one's neighbor, he could also believe that "There is some hatred . . . which is a religious duty, as when we hate the enemies of God or of the church" (*On Christian Doctrine* 2.11, Yale 6: 743). And though he believed in the virtue of humility, he believed that "HUMILITY gives a man a modest opinion of himself and prevents him from blowing his own trumpet, *except when it is really called for*" (*On Christian Doctrine* 2.9, Yale 6: 733; my italics). Love is something that should "be controlled so that we love most the things which are most worthy of love,

and hate most the things which are most hateful" (*On Christian Doctrine* 2.8, Yale 6: 720). The reader who would like to see Milton's righteous anger and scorn in action should read random passages in Milton's adversarial and combative prose tracts such as his *Apology against a Pamphlet* (1642), which one of his editors characterized as "sharp sarcasm, bitter wrangling, unreasoning and even indecent vituperation, pettiness" (Yale 1: 866).

Nevertheless, it is a grave error to see Milton the man as an inhumane monster, or even as a domestic tyrant forcing his daughters to take dictation, as in the famous Hungarian painting of him now located on a staircase in the New York Public Library. Though there is evidence that Milton asked two of his three daughters to read to him in languages they may or may not have understood, and that several of his daughters rebelled against him, selling some of his books to get spending money, there is no evidence that he forced his daughters to take endless dictation. "No one, of course, today," wrote John Shawcross in 1967, "seriously considers that any one of the girls was his amanuensis for *Paradise Lost*, though the legend persists in the popular mind" ("Orthography" 121), but as late as 1991 I have heard a famous bibliographer begin a sentence, "As Milton was dictating to his daughters, ..." There are at least five different handwritings detectable in the manuscript to Book 1, and a similar number in the manuscript of *On Christian Doctrine*, which leads one to believe that Milton distributed the work in both cases among many different capable scribes. One of his daughters, Deborah, remembered her father as "Delightful Company, the Life of the Conversation," and a man of "Unaffected Chearfulness and Civility" (see Parker 1: 638), and she spontaneously exclaimed "'Tis My Father, 'tis my Dear Father!" (Richardsons, in Darbishire, *Early Lives* 229) when she saw her father's portrait many years after his death. Milton had educated Deborah well enough for her to become a schoolmistress, teaching Latin. If she had been traumatized by any tyranny on her father's part, his youngest daughter's behavior in later years certainly does not reflect it. In 1665, when *Paradise Lost* was probably being completed, Anne, Milton's eldest daughter, who seems to have been mentally defective, was about nineteen, Mary about seventeen, and Deborah about thirteen, as noted by Shawcross ("Orthography" 121); the question then becomes "Who was capable of taking dictation?" rather than "Who was forced to take dictation?"

3. THE ENGLISH REVOLUTIONARY AND THE POEM

Of course Milton's experience as apologist and diplomatic correspondent for the Interregnum government of Oliver Cromwell must have influenced *Paradise Lost*, but the subtle question to answer is how. Earlier annotators and biographers have been quick to point out that the debate in Pandemonium parallels parliamentary debates that Milton witnessed, but they also testify to Milton's reading in classical debate literature, such as in the first-century BCE Roman orator Cicero's *Against Catiline*. Though his experience in the Parliamentary government must have affected Milton, he seems to have gone to great lengths to keep contemporary politics and English history out of the epic—perhaps to avoid the censorship he might have expected, or to avoid the tediousness of recounting political events (Abraham Cowley fell into that trap in his *Civil War*).

Milton's stance as narrator seems to be like that of one of his singular just men: alone, isolated, out-of-fashion, in danger, he must speak to a small but fit audience of people who can see beyond the current "evil days" toward the kind of freedom he had envisioned for his country in *Areopagitica*, where England is pictured as young, strong, and far-sighted. *Paradise Lost* is deliberately *not* topical, perhaps because of Milton's disillusionment with his homeland, to the point where he could write, at least to his friends, "One's country is wherever it is well with one" (letter to Heimbach; Columbia 12: 115). That is no wonder. According to the Richardsons, Milton's early biographers and annotators, Milton "was in Perpetual Terror of being Assassinated, though he had Escap'd the Talons of the Law, he knew he had Made Himself Enemies in Abundance. he was so Dejected he would lie Awake whole Nights. He then kept Himself as Private as he could" (French, *Life Records* 4: 358). According to Rosenblatt, Milton replaced bitter memories of nationalism and England itself with an interior geography beyond mere location, though "we sense in *Paradise Lost* the pure longing for the Eden, Jerusalem, and England of his dreams" (62).

Christopher Hill sees Milton as a radical in the midst of his poetry. Milton, Hill believes, "triumphantly wrote *Paradise Lost*, and got it accepted as a great orthodox poem, whilst secretly holding very subversive views about theology and marriage, which, we can now see, are hinted at in the epic" (472). The views of Berry, Bennett, and Davies should be read alongside Hill's, some of them as corrective. Donald McKenzie, while in the process of writing his history of the English book, has come to the conclusion that censorship did not play as important a part in book publication in the 1660s as Hill and others have supposed (letter 22 August 1989). Geisst concludes that Milton's theology elevated his poetic themes to a degree that they converged above the level of politics: "Politics and poetry met in his thought on the level of theology which, in retrospect, made all

human endeavour and institutions subservient and ministerial to its eschatology" (104). Geisst, perhaps too hastily, finds Milton's greatest contribution to political theory to be very close to the spirit of Thoreau's "that government is best which governs least" (104). For further reading about Milton's role as revolutionary prophet and priest, consult Kerrigan's *Prophetic Milton*, Richmond, John Spencer Hill, and Helgerson. For censorship, see Annabel Patterson, *Censorship and Interpretation*.

VII. CRITICAL QUESTIONS

1. THE QUESTION OF GOD
(IS HE A TYRANNICAL SCHOOLMASTER?)

If I may borrow a phrase from Northrop Frye, every time Milton's God opens His "ambrosial mouth," "the sensitive reader cringes" (*Return* 99), perhaps in fear that He is going to put His foot in it. Instead of being a model of a philosopher king, Milton's God (perhaps that should be the Christian or Hebrew God in general) can seem to be a tyrant, whining about sinful man being an ingrate. The modern American novelist, poet, and critic John Updike has a slightly more charitable opinion than Frye's: "The God of Milton derives from the believer's tortured strenuousness" and "Milton's God may be a tedious old bluffer, but he fascinated Milton, and aligned the poet's inspirations in one magnetic field" (244, 245–46). Another formidable modern critic, William Empson, dislikes Milton's God (and the generic Hebrew and Christian God) personally and intensely; Empson declares his own atheism with vigor in *Milton's God*. A. J. A. Waldock's clever criticism is based on the ideas that Milton's God must be what Northrop Frye calls a "smug and wily old hypocrite" (*Selected Poetry* xviii), that goodness is "featureless" and that Satan by contrast is magnificent—again he becomes the real hero of the poem. Most of those who would like, for one reason or another, to have Milton dislodged from any poetic pantheon, including Robert Graves, F. R. Leavis, and John Peter, all find his God priggish and unattractive. Admittedly, Book 3 of *Paradise Lost* may be the hardest for the modern reader to stomach, mainly because it seems at times to be theology and biblical citation thinly disguised as poetry and because Milton's God, like Milton himself, often sounds as if he is on the defensive, which God of course should not be, being omnipotent, omniscient, and omnipresent.

The problem may be in the "Introducing of God, and the Son of God, as actors in [Milton's] Poem," which John Clarke, in 1731, considered "an unpardonable Boldness" (quoted in Shawcross, *Critical* 263). Even the defender of the poet Milton at the time, the critic Joseph Addison, had to admit "If *Milton*'s Majesty forsakes him any where, it is in those Parts of his Poem, where the Divine Persons are introduced as Speakers" (quoted in Shawcross, *Critical* 178). God had not been a character in Milton's projected drama on the Fall. Deciding to include Him in a speaking role in the epic must have been difficult, but God had appeared as a speaking character in Renaissance epic or drama (see Andreini's *Adamo*, excerpted in Kirkconnell, among others). Milton, "in defiance of all poetic tact" (Frye, *Return* 102), put Him in. He is "Omnipotent, / Immutable, Immortal, Infinite, / Eternal" (3.372–74), all qualities especially hard to characterize, since all of them are nonhuman. His omniscience makes the concept of free will difficult to understand. The logic of first-time readers of *Paradise Lost* often is, "If He knows they are going to do it, why doesn't He stop them?" Milton tries to establish logically and dramatically, both in *On Christian Doctrine* and the epic, what was to his generation a theological commonplace: though God created Adam and Eve, and created them with the liability to fall, He in no way predestined or caused their fall. Roland Frye, in his article on "The Father" in *A Milton Encyclopedia*, makes the cogent point that "Milton's God is the only character in Western literature who is entirely responsible for his own environment, so that the environment He establishes is an important part of His characterization." What this might mean for the reader of *Paradise Lost* is that if the cornucopia of Eden or the loving communion of all of Milton's creation is attractive, then the God responsible for all the goodness should at least be likable.

Part of the problem with Milton's God may be in the way He speaks, in His rhetoric. Even Alexander Pope, writing about Milton in the early eighteenth century, thought that Milton's God talked like a "school divine" (for the context, see Cowper's notes on Book 3, as quoted in Shawcross, *Critical* 371). God's language, purporting to be pure reason, is flat, uncolored, unmetaphorical. The logic at work according to Samuel ("Milton on Learning") is that God represents pure reason and needs to make no metaphors. Being the opposite of the hypocritical Satan, God needs none of Satan's protective coloration or metaphorical masking in His language. So the argument goes.

Milton's God is not fixed in one role, even though He is immutable. He is the Father, and He has a Son with whom He can have dramatic discussions. The Son can also talk with Adam, playfully and warmly, and the Godhead can also manifest Himself as mercy, forgiveness, and grace through the actions of the Son. To students who despise Milton's God as a pettifogging old

blowhard, it might be good to answer, "Look at his creativity, look at his fatherhood, look at his tenderness when he brings Eve out of Adam's side." Of course Milton's God is not a father in the sense that He will die and His estate pass on, but He is a father in His care for His children and His sorrow for their disobedience and sin.

Milton's God is also seen in at least two roles, God the Father and God the Son, with the Son being clearly subordinate to the Father. That makes a problem with nomenclature, when to name God as Father, God as Son, or to use the somewhat cowardly generic "Godhead." Because the Son has not been named Jesus Christ during most of the events described in the epic, Milton's Son of God should not be called Christ, or Jesus; He should be referred to as the Son. To confuse matters even further, there are godly quotations in *Paradise Lost* that cannot with certainty be ascribed either to the Father or to the Son, and they should, in the case of a genuine toss-up, be given to the Godhead. Milton calculatedly mentions Jesus only twice in *Paradise Lost*, both times with reference to the incarnate, historical character (10.183; 12.310).

2. THE QUESTION OF SATAN

Is he the sub-textual hero of *Paradise Lost*, as the poet William Blake believed? Is he the central character or focal point of the epic? What does it mean when the Epic Voice calls him "no Leader but a lyar" (4.949) or "Artificer of fraud" (4.121)? Is the audience "surprised by sin" (Fish) in the sense that readers are meant to believe Satan's lies and participate again in the Original Sin? John Carey believes that the ambiguity in the character of Satan, the descendant of Manichaean dualism, is healthy for criticism, since the argument over Satan helps keep Milton alive for each group of readers who argue whether Milton's Satan is much more interesting, or dynamic, than Milton's God ("Milton's Satan," in Danielson, *Cambridge Companion* 32).

Probably most modern Milton scholars are on the side of the anti-Satanists, in that they do not find his character delightful in any way. Fascinating, but hardly delightful, Satan's universe is one of death, and it is described as perverse. *Perversity* is not meant in a narrowly sexual sense but in all its permutations: anything and everything against nature. Satan is eminent because he is a former angel of high rank, but his is a bad eminence. His glory is unnatural, the reflected glory of a distorting mirror. Even though he is bragging or vaunting aloud, he is inwardly racked with the pain which his evil causes him. His motives are elemental but also the most childish: pride, envy, and revenge. He is self-tempted, self-deceived, so that he cannot fairly blame God for his condition of constant hatred and anguish. He cannot accept that he was created by a good God, but his denial of the fact of his creation is, in the end, stupid. Satan is also weak, comparatively speaking. He is not weaker than Adam and Eve when they are susceptible to sin, but he is weaker than Abdiel—who is an angel of lower rank than Lucifer had been—simply because "All wickedness is weakness" (*Samson Agonistes* 834). Modern psychiatry might see Satan in terms of an inferiority complex, or, in Milton's terms, his "sence of injur'd merit" (*Paradise Lost* 1.98); like a child-abuser, he takes out his own frustrations on the innocent and newly-created—not on a baby in this case but on the newly-born Adam and Eve.

Milton probably understood the traps for the unsuspecting reader he implanted in the characterization of Satan. I do not believe, with William Blake, that Milton was of the devil's party without his knowing it (see *The Marriage of Heaven and Hell*, 1793 edition). The danger of Satan's being characterized as a mirror of goodness in evil, or a thread of evil entwined with good, is that naive readers will be taken in by the ironic power of evil in Satan exactly because it is entwined with good, as in the phrase "that bad eminence." Milton believed that evil was always intermingled, sometimes indivisibly, with good, even in Eden, which made it all the more insidious. Satan should be compared with Milton's Comus, another potentially attractive figure who perverts the abundance of nature for his own seductive purposes and uses human weakness to make men and women his beastly slaves—though Comus is more of a juggler, necromancer, or obvious charlatan than is Satan.

Milton provides various other faces of evil, some of them quite attractive, at least superficially. Beelzebub is the original yes-man who is also the able second-in-command; Belial is the unctuous intellectual, sensuous aesthete, and do-nothing; Mammon is the worshiper of things, a materialistic entrepreneur (a cousin of Thomas Hobbes, whose principles Milton disliked?); and Moloch is the direct and forthright, rabid nihilist, a maniacal general who worships only power.

The historical figure of Satan is that of the "old enemy," the universal enemy of all forms of life. The problem of how to read or interpret Satan has existed certainly since the Gnostic gospels which at times identified him with the Yahweh of Genesis and thereby made him heroic. The sect of the Manichees, against whose heresies St. Augustine wrote, placed Satan's darkness in equal opposition to God's light. The very origin of the idea of Satan as tempter and tyrant was compounded with irony when Satan was identified either as a godlike being himself or as an extraordinarily cunning adversary of God. Forsyth's *The Old Enemy* makes clear

the difficulty from the beginning in interpreting the nature or character of evil, especially in its origins in Lucifer, whose very name means "light-bearer." Milton is quite conscious of the associations between Satan and the morning and evening star, or, for that matter, between Satan and the sun, whose beams he claims to hate.

Each new reader of *Paradise Lost* must make up his or her mind on the issue of whether or not to like Satan, though no one should make a decision about the character based on second-hand or hearsay evidence. If Satan is sympathetic, one might be forced to agree with Blake that Milton was indeed allied with the devil without being aware of it; in other words, Milton did not know what he was doing. But when Milton's Epic Voice tells us that Satan was wracked with pain, or that Satan's hypocrisy is so subtle that it can be detected only by God, the Epic Voice should probably be believed. The reader should also keep in mind that Milton is on record as saying that Satan cannot be stronger than God: "it is intolerable and incredible that evil should be stronger than good and should prove the true supreme power. Therefore God exists" (*On Christian Doctrine*, Yale 6: 131).

3. THE QUESTION OF THE HERO: WHO IS IT?

For those who believe that Adam and Eve are equally bound in their mutual tragedy, there is no problem with this question: the two are the heroes (in the sense of "central personages") of the epic. But they are not epic heroes in the sense that Achilles or Jason or Odysseus or Orlando or Godfrey were heroes. Since Satan is more like Achilles than Adam is, it is tempting to call him the hero of the poem, even though he is not human. He has even been called an heroic figure left over from Elizabethan tragedy, like Macbeth, by no less a critic than Helen Gardner. Other critics looking for a representative of goodness to stand for the heroic have singled out Abdiel. But while all the traditional epic heroes were at least half human, Abdiel is all angel, and his role in the epic comparatively small.

What about the Son? The Son is God, until He is made incarnate as Jesus, but He does do things that epic heroes do, as when He volunteers for the most dangerous of duties (confronting Satan and, later, sacrificing Himself for the sin of humankind). Nevertheless, the Son of God, though He may be a pattern for Christian heroes to follow, cannot be the ultimate human role model, because He is at least half divine.

George de Forest Lord has recently suggested that Milton himself is the "heroic creator" of his own poem, which "allows his epic to assume the form of an extended meditation in which the divine story and his own experiences interact, a form where his own feelings and experiences are mingled with, illustrate, and become a vital part of the story he is telling" (59). So, according to Lord, Milton is the hero of his own epic.

4. NEW EPIC VIRTUES:
PATIENCE AND HEROIC MARTYRDOM

Whether or not he is the hero of his own poem, Milton took care to define the heroic virtues he thought essential to salvation in *On Christian Doctrine*. "PATIENCE is the virtue which shows itself when we peacefully accept God's promises, supported by confidence in the divine providence, power and goodness: also when we bear any evils that we have to bear calmly . . . " (2.3, Yale 6: 662). Also, patience is "the endurance of evils and injuries" (2.10, Yale 6: 739). Accompanying patience is fortitude, "apparent when we repel evils or stand against them unafraid" (6: 738). Zeal is "An eager desire to sanctify the divine name, together with a feeling of indignation against things which tend to the violation or contempt of religion . . . " (2.6; Yale 6: 697). Milton emphasizes the virtues that can exist in the individual mind or soul: charity, righteousness, temperance, sobriety, chastity (forbearance of all desires of the flesh), modesty, decency, contentment, frugality, industry, elegance (discriminating enjoyment of the "finer things"), humility, high-mindedness (I paraphrase Milton's list). In an age which emphasized individual salvation and inner light, Milton seems to have made it a point to add the virtues most admired by Puritan writers to the virtues traditionally associated with epic heroism (Anselment).

Patient fortitude is quite unlike the chest-thumping heroism to be found in pagan role-models like Ajax or Hercules. For what Milton thought of pagan heroics, one should look at his portrait of Harapha in *Samson Agonistes*: Harapha is a muscle-bound, ignorant, boastful giant who also happens to be a coward. Since he worships Baal, he is fair game for Samson's and Milton's scorn.

5. THE ONE JUST MAN:
HOW MANY FACES DOES HE HAVE?

The very few just men whom Milton usually pictures in a lonely battle against evil reflect God's image on earth, since Milton's God is unthinkable apart from his justice and sometimes lonely righteousness. Milton from the beginning of *Paradise Lost* offers a series of independently obedient good and free servants of God. Those individuals bear the "just yoke" (10.1045) of God. They vary, from the "one greater Man," the incarnate Son, to Abdiel, the one just angel who must endure the scorn of the multitude in his rejection of Satan, to Abel, Enoch, and Noah and other figures from biblical history who

provide the kind of "just Men" (7.570) that angels would willingly visit. The "Just Man" (11.681) who endures obloquy for "daring single to be just" (11.703), the "one Man found so perfect and so just" (11.876), is always heroic in *Paradise Lost*, whether he be Job or the "Just Abraham" (12.273). The struggles of the just men in *Paradise Lost* echo the lonely struggle of the Lady in *Comus* and look forward to those lonely battles between the isolated Samson and his adversaries and the Son one-on-one with his adversary, Satan.

6. THE BUGBEAR OF HIERARCHY

Modern students who believe that all humans are equal may have problems with the hierarchy of nature from the inanimate up to God, a hierarchy implied in all of Milton's works. Milton believed that "nothing is more natural, nothing more just, nothing more useful or more advantageous to the human race than that the lesser obey the greater, not the lesser number the greater number, but the lesser virtue the greater virtue, the lesser wisdom the greater wisdom" (*Second Defence*, Yale 4: 636).

Angels are above humankind in their intuitive reasoning and in their proximity to God. God's will sets the necessity for order in the hierarchy among the angels, who are divided into ranks such as dominions, dominations, principalities, thrones, powers, cherubim, and seraphim (West, *Milton*, and his article "Angels" in *A Milton Encyclopedia*). Animals are below humankind, their appetites teaching us what to reject in ourselves as base motives. Below the animals are the "stocks and stones" of inanimate nature—capable of emotion as when Adam's garland withers as a result of sin, but still beneath even the animals.

The entrance of sin into the world increases the distance between hierarchies. It also increases the distance between humans and God, making communication more difficult. Sin creates enmity between humans and animals, and it makes the naturally subordinate into inferiors.

The "two great sexes" which animate the world are male and female, throughout the various species: Milton sees the balance of gender as healthy, though the power between the sexes is not equally distributed (Summers, "The Two Great Sexes," in *The Muse's Method*). Eve does not lose dignity when she follows Adam's direction: she is described as possessing "obsequious [i.e., subordinate] Majestie" (8.509). Her duties as vegetarian cook and chief gardener of Eden are not demeaning: they are part of her domestic honor and glory. Even when she is innocent, Eve is "not equal" to Adam. Modern critics have at times seen Milton as the feminist's "bogey" (Sandra M. Gilbert), but he has been ably defended against the charge of antifeminism by critics such as Lewalski ("Milton"), Webber ("The Politics"), Mollenkott ("Some Implications"), Diane McColley, Shullenberger, Gallagher, and Wittreich, who calls him "feminist Milton." McColley shows clearly how Milton broke from the tradition of antifeminism associated with medieval monks but still being argued in tracts such as John Knox's *The First Blast of the Trumpet against the Monstrous Regiment* [i.e., rule] *of Women* (1558) or Joseph Swetnam's *The Arraignement of Lewd, Idle, Froward and Unconstant Women* (1615). One might remember that Milton gave his youngest daughter the name of Deborah, a prophetess as well as a judge in Judges 4–5, a model of strong and admirable feminine behavior. His own friendships with cultured women such as (perhaps) the Countess Dowager of Derby, sponsor of *Arcades*; the Lady Ranelegh; Lady Margaret Ley; and Catherine Thomason, well-read wife of the bookseller: all of these associations with women show Milton looking for intelligent and capable female friendship.

Milton's Adam and Eve embody innocent and heartfelt sexuality. What Milton might mean in the phrase "Hee for God only, shee for God in him" (4.299) is that the couple recapitulates or mirrors godliness, a process by which God's image is imparted to humankind first through Adam and then through Adam's image Eve (Haller). When Adam worships Eve's image, however, he worships something removed from God's image, an "outside" or a "rind" (as in the skin of an orange), and he thereby becomes an idolater. In terms of Renaissance medicine, Adam is diseased with erotic melancholy in his overvaluing of Eve's image: "love, being caused by a visible form (*species*) that reaches the intellect, is subject to reason, yet being ultimately a motion of the sensible appetite can, through the pneuma and the body's innate heat, *darken man's reason and cause him to seek a particular good in lieu of the true, universal good*" (Ferrand 47; emphasis mine). In worshiping Eve's beauty, Adam loses the higher faculty of his reason and seeks a particular good in Eve rather than the true and universal good of God's image. Though he is not transformed in any vulgar way, Adam becomes insane, or at least unhealthy, in his attraction to Eve's "outside," and he allows her temporarily to become his god. He is something like Ariosto's hero Ruggiero in the clutches of the apparently beautiful witch Alcina, in that he allows the beauty of a woman to weaken him, at least temporarily. Eve's beauty is innocent, even though it is certainly used by Satan to help bring about Adam's downfall.

It is obviously important for Milton to establish that unfallen sexuality and procreation are positive and crea-tive, but the Fall puts a taint on the desire for procreation, as on all other human emotional states. Milton's conception of what was called "domestic economy," marriage and the wife's duties toward the husband, can generally be identified with the Puritan movement (Haller; Roland Frye, "Teachings"). Wives should submit themselves to the rule of their husbands, and be obedient, especially after and because of the Fall (1 Corinthians 14.34; Titus 2.5; see Kelso for the tradition within marriage). Milton's logic is that "It is wrong for one single part of the body—and not one of the important parts—to disobey the rest of the body, and even the head" (*On Christian Doctrine* 2.15, Yale 6: 782). The man, according to 1 Peter 3.7, should pay "honor to the woman as the weaker vessel," however much that phrase "weaker vessel" may irritate modern women and men.

Yet Milton was exceptionally sensitive to women's needs and sensibilities in creating the character Eve, so that a modern critic can dare to call a book on women's attitudes toward Milton *Feminist Milton* (Wittreich). Diane McColley's *Milton's Eve* gives what is probably the most balanced modern view of the character in Milton as measured against the historical tradition, but see also my article "Eve" in *A Milton Encyclopedia* and Gallagher, who perhaps makes too strong a case that Milton is a prototypical feminist.

Judging by sheer numbers of articles, Eve is the character in *Paradise Lost* who currently provokes more critical interest than anyone else except Satan, because her problem is eternal—how best to move within an hierarchical structure that rigidly defines her role as the upholder of "domestic honor" and the bearer of children, or in Eve's case, the seed of all future generations.

Because of monkish medieval antifeminism, it had become traditional to associate Eve with the "crooked rib" (Utley) and to dismiss members of her sex as ignorant but guileful troublemakers. Milton carefully broke with that tradition and constructed the plot of the Fall so that though Eve falls first, Adam's responsibility is no less than hers (perhaps it is more), and, though Eve is the first to consort with the Serpent, she is also the first to repent, at a time when Adam is still "stubborn in his offence" (see the outlines for tragedies above).

7. THE QUESTION OF COSMOLOGY: THE SUN OR THE EARTH AT THE CENTER?

What was called the "new philosophy," the discovery that the earth revolved around the sun, was in the process of replacing the geocentric theory of the universe during Milton's lifetime, though Milton himself took little public notice of it. While in Florence, Milton had made it a point to visit Galileo, who, with the newly-invented telescope (Nicolson, "Milton and the Telescope") had discovered imperfections on what had been considered the perfect heavenly sphere of the moon and had noticed sun spots, another indication that the universe was mutable or imperfect. Far more important, Galileo, following Copernicus, had asserted that the earth was not a stationary body but instead moved around the sun, a very disturbing notion for anyone still holding the comfortable belief that the earth was the center of all creation.

In discussing the phases of the planet Venus or the existence of the moons of Jupiter, Galileo had skated on thin ice with the Inquisitors. For his discoveries Galileo had been branded a heretic and put under house arrest. Though Milton deplored Galileo's persecution at the hands of the Inquisitors, he nevertheless makes the universe of *Paradise Lost* that of Galileo's Ptolemaic forebears, and Milton's cosmology is generally geocentric (Rattansi).

All heavenly bodies are pictured as being in rotation about the earth, and the universe in Northrop Frye's image looks like an onion. Indeed, most three-dimensional cosmic models or armillary spheres of Milton's era do make it look like a translucent onion. Angelic intelligences were thought to propel the heavenly bodies, singing or playing the music of the spheres, creating the universal harmony that the innocent Adam and Eve were capable of hearing but which has been lost to most mortals ever since the Fall.

When Adam asks the embarrassing question amounting to "Who is right, Copernicus or Ptolemy?" Raphael does not give a straight answer (7.66–178). He hedges, in the sense that he says the equivalent of "That's not for you to know, and it doesn't really matter, so long as you believe in God's control over the cosmos. Therefore be 'lowlie wise' (173) and do not question things on a higher plane than you can understand." Raphael's explanation leaves Adam "cleerd of doubt" (179), but it may create doubt in the modern reader.

8. CONSERVATIVE SCIENCE AND SUPERSTITIOUS PRACTICES

The science of *Paradise Lost* is not innovative. According to Svendsen, Milton uses "widely known conventional material in its conventional associations" (4), most of which could have been derived from various Renaissance dictionaries or encyclopedias of natural history, such as that compiled by Peter de la Primaudaye in *The French Academie* (first complete edition 1618). The encyclopedists and the mythographers like Natale Conti (Mulryan "Through" 229–86) were not bound by modern divisions of science; they might write on manners and ethics, diseases and the qualities of metals and stones, the institution of marriage, and the duties of husband toward wife or wife toward husband, and they might lump the study of the human soul with a study of the human body. A summary of world history would have included discussions of the order of angels and the order and number of the celestial spheres (Svendsen 21). Scientific encyclopedists and mythographers were historians and moralists as well. Their science—really, it is better described as *knowledge*—derived from classical sources in Aristotle, Plato, Pythagoras, Empedocles, or Pliny, but pagan sources were always measured against what might be called Christian holism, or the Christian attempt to synthesize all learning under a scheme controlled by providence or God's will.

Milton's knowledge of the science of his time was not that of an "amateur" or scientific dabbler. Milton, so far as we know, performed no scientific experiments, as did his biographer Aubrey or Samuel Pepys. He was in that respect unlike the virtuosi of the Royal Society after the 1660 Restoration. His mind, however, retained bits of what the modern mind might label pseudoscientific misinformation, such as the alchemical description of "Potable gold" (3.608; see Svendsen 29–30) or the myth of sailors anchoring on a whale's back (1.200–208; see Svendsen 33–34).

Svendsen downplays Milton's knowledge of astronomy. He contends that, despite meeting Galileo, Milton constructed something that "is not even a proper system."

> Aside from Raphael's discourse, nearly all astronomy in Milton refers to a geocentric universe: a world composed of a hard outside shell, a Primum Mobile, a crystalline sphere to allow for "trepidation" or retrogradation, a sphere of fixed stars, separate spheres for the seven planets, a sphere of fire, a sphere of air divided into three regions, and the earth. Below and to the left of this world is Hell. (48)

The fall of Adam and Eve knocks the earth off center in Milton's scheme (10.668–78), causing the earth's axis to shift out of its balance with the axis of the sun and causing the natural world to begin the process of decay (Svendsen 71–72).

With their endorsement of witchcraft, Milton's pseudo-scientific beliefs will cause further jars with the modern sensibility. The Bible itself encourages belief in witchcraft since it pictures Saul working in conjunction with the Witch of Endor, who calls up the ghost of Samuel (1 Samuel 28.7–25). The Bible uses terms like "bewitched" (Acts 8.9: "Simon bewitched the people . . ."), and the Bible also makes the pronouncement that the seventeenth century took so seriously: "Thou shalt not suffer a witch to live" (Exodus 22.18). Though the persecution of witches had been endorsed and supported during the reign of James I, witch-hunts were dying down by the time Milton wrote *Paradise Lost* (see Thomas, whose general point of view I am reproducing). Among contemporaries who still took magic seriously were Sir Thomas Browne and Milton's friends Samuel Hartlib and Henry Oldenburg (Thomas 292). Milton's Night-Hag and her attendants the Lapland witches (2.662, 665) probably should be taken seriously as representatives of witchcraft, and Satan himself can be considered witch-like (Hunter, *Descent of Urania* 46–47).

The fairy lore of *Comus* may be almost gone from *Paradise Lost*, but it is not forgotten. Toward the end of Book 1, in a simile, Milton mentions a "belated Peasant" who either "sees, / Or dreams he sees" a "Pigmean Race / Beyond the *Indian* Mount" (780–84): the pygmy-sized race supposedly from faraway India sounds like Shakespearean fairies, as in *Midsummer Night's Dream*, but the peasant is pictured skeptically, as someone too stupid to know the difference between seeing reality and imagining phantasms.

Milton's earth and his cosmic system all subscribe to the pathetic fallacy. His cosmos has feelings, because it is created out of God's essence: when Adam and Eve fall, "Earth felt the wound" (9.782). When Eve falls, the garland Adam is weaving wilts, having felt the effect of death that sin brought into the world. The perfect universe into which they are born is degraded by their sin. The bodies of Adam and Eve respond to the rest of creation, so that before the Fall they pray standing upright (as the Jews did in Jesus's time), in touch with the celestial bodies such as the sun and stars but not worshiping them. The word "upright" does not appear after the Fall occurs in *Paradise Lost*, and the sinful Adam and Eve may indeed be pictured as stooped over with the weight of sin, just as Masaccio and Michelangelo had painted them in their respective Expulsions. Satan's visage is wrecked by his sin to the point where he is barely recognized by his closest cohort, and Adam and Eve are both made conscious of their nakedness, made to feel shame for the first time, by the Fall. The fact of Genesis, that Adam and Eve first became aware that they were naked after they ate the fruit, is expanded to explain the existence of shame thereafter; all nature is ashamed for them.

9. SCIENCE AND KNOWLEDGE OF THE OCCULT

Milton in his youth had subscribed to parts of the "science" or "philosophy" (both terms mean something close to "knowledge") of his day, including what we would call the superstition of hermeticism—a belief in a system of ancient wisdom derived from pseudo-historical beliefs of Chaldeans, Egyptians, ancient Magi (Zoro-astrians), worshipers of Orpheus, and followers of Pythagoras. We know now (and indeed Milton would have known) that such theories were derived from the writings of "Hermes Trismegistus," a mythical entity. Milton had translated his name as "thrice great *Hermes*" in "Il Penseroso" 88. "Hermes" was actually a committee of authors who composed the body of hermetic books about the first century AD (William B. Hunter, "Origin and Destiny" 126). No less an authority than Marsilio Ficino had endorsed and translated the books into Latin in 1471.

The sixteenth-century mystic and hermetic writer Cornelius Agrippa had also pictured the new magus or magician as capable of making a real but spiritual voyage through the spheres and various levels of heaven to commune with a being who at least resembled the Christian God: "no one has such powers but he who has cohabited with the elements, vanquished nature, mounted higher than the heavens, elevating himself above the angels to the archetype itself, with whom he then becomes co-operator and can do all things" (Agrippa's *De occulta philosophia*, translated in Yates 240). The notion of flying up to hear the music of the spheres obviously had appealed to the young Milton, though Sarkar has recently argued that Satan in *Paradise Lost* should be considered both as magus and as astronomer, both, of course, gone wrong.

Milton seems also to have dabbled at least in alchemy, the pseudo-science devoted in part to turning a base metal like lead into gold. According to Babb, Milton "seems to accept the alchemical theory of transmutation; that is, he apparently believes in the theoretical possibility of turning lead or iron into gold (of rendering perfect an imperfect metallic combination)" (31). Alchemy was even more a system of beliefs in an animistic universe, one inhabited by millions of spiritual beings, located in chemicals, plants, or heavenly bodies (Edgar H. Duncan). Abraham's recent book on Milton's friend Andrew Marvell and alchemy confirms the practice within Milton's circle of friends.

Milton certainly believed in the correspondences between heavenly bodies and human activity, what we call astrology, and he apparently had his own horoscope taken in his later life (Rusche). In *Arcades* he mentioned "what the cross dire-looking Planet smites" (52) with the apparent seriousness of a believer in planetary effects on human fortune. Milton's musical friend Henry Lawes believed in wearing amulets to guard against demons and disease (Otten 154), and Milton's friend and co-worker John Dryden "remained an astrological devotee throughout his life" (Thomas 292). So did Milton's biographer John Aubrey. For Milton's belief in the malign influence of the planets after the Fall, we can listen to the Epic Voice indirectly quoting God's instructions concerning the alignment of the heavenly bodies:

> To the blanc Moone
> Her office [the angels] prescrib'd, to th' other five
> Thir planetarie motions and aspects
> In *Sextile*, *Square*, and *Trine*, and *Opposite*,
> Of noxious efficacie, and when to joyne
> In Synod unbenigne, and taught the fixt
> Thir influence malignant when to showre,
> Which of them rising with the Sun, or falling,
> Should prove tempestuous. (10.656–64)

One should qualify the opinion that Milton subscribed to hermeticism or alchemy by saying that he would have seen no conflict, at least when he attended Cambridge or was in his reclusive Horton and Hammersmith period, between hermeticism and alchemy and his own youthful Christianity.

Together with astronomical, astrological, alchemical, and hermetic lore, and potential belief in witchcraft and fairies, Milton includes a wide variety of terraculture or gardening information in *Paradise Lost* (Otten, Hannah Demaray, McHenry). There was a tradition among gardeners in the seventeenth century to emulate God as the supreme gardener of Eden, as with John Parkinson's *Paradisi in Sole* (1629), which shows in its frontispiece Adam and Eve in the process of gardening (reprinted in Rohde, facing p. 144). The amaranth was considered one plant so pure in its nature that it could grow only in Paradise. Milton's Eve is a kind of apothecary or homeopathic physician in her choice of greens and herbs, and in her preparation of fresh fruit drinks. But she should be differentiated from the potentially sinister Friar in *Romeo and Juliet*, since she does not seek out poisonous or narcotic plants. To do so, she would have to be associated with the necromancy of Comus, rather than the white magic of the Attendant Spirit and Sabrina.

Milton was more than a quaint scientist. Both his astronomy and his geography are expert, if not always on the cutting edge of discovery. Hermeticism was respectable in his time, a philosophical system that was believed to be both ancient and Christian yet still helped explain natural phenomena such as the power of the sun or of some plants and minerals. William B. Hunter finds the source of Milton's and Spenser's conception of the soul from the "*Corpus Hermetica*" and illustrates how Milton may have derived from hermetic lore the notion of an earth formed "without life but capable of producing it" with the help of the spirit of God ("Origin and Destiny" 127; for hermeticism, see 126–32). The earth is the female element and water the male, as in *Paradise Lost* 7.278–82, and "[t]he remaining creative energy is placed in the sun [the Demiurge], which thus becomes the source for replenishment of the life principle throughout the entire universe" (Hunter 129). Thus all the universe is derived from God, and neither matter nor the soul can be intrinsically evil.

VIII. THE TEXT OF *PARADISE LOST*

1. ESTABLISHING A TEXT FOR A MODERN AUDIENCE: WHY 1674?

I have chosen the 1674 edition of *Paradise Lost* as my copy-text, by which I mean the text on which this edition is based. Whenever I have deviated from the 1674 edition, a footnote informs the reader. The 1668 and 1669 reissues of the first edition added the apparatus of the arguments, the discussion of the verse, and the errata list. The 1674 "second edition" of *Paradise Lost* is the first complete edition in that it is the first edition in twelve books, also containing the apparatus. It adds a little more than fifteen lines to the text and it makes small but substantive changes throughout, many of which seem to indicate authorial preferences. Though Milton was blind, he seems to have exercised some control over all the printings of his epic, conceivably through Quaker friends, since Quakers, because their published writing was often repressed or found to be subversive, had developed the practice of communal proofreading of their tracts as they went through the press (McKenzie, "Simmons").

In the 1667 first edition of *Paradise Lost*, one can trace in the habits of the compositors who set the text the author's control—or that of whoever might have been acting for him. For instance, the word that is always spelled "their" in modern usage was spelled in the modern way in all instances from the first time it appears until it was changed to "thir" in 1.349, when for the first time that form of the word appears; thereafter, "thir" becomes increasingly frequent until it takes over as the dominant form from line 500 or so to the end of the book, and indeed to the end of the epic. The compositor's will was bent, in other words, until he spelled a common word the way that Milton customarily spelled it. In the 1674 edition, however, the compositor who began the setting of the work had apparently been told from the beginning to spell the word "thir," and generally he and those compositors who worked with him obeyed the order. Moyles concludes "it seems that the 1674 compositor resigned himself to following the less conventional spelling *thir* throughout" (94).

One can see in the example of "their"/"thir" that corrections were being made in the process of printing

1667 and that *1674* attempted to make more extensive corrections of *1667* as its copy-text. Partly for that reason, most editors operating at least in the last ten years have built their texts, whether or not their texts are modernized, on that of *1674* rather than that of *1667*, and all editors have followed *1674* in arranging the epic in twelve books, so that the lineation of the second edition is now standard.

There exists a manuscript—not in Milton's hand (being blind, he rarely did more than sign his name after 1651) but in that of a professional scribe or an amanuensis. The manuscript—we have only Book 1 from it—was apparently used for at least two purposes, to show a fair copy to Charles II's official censor, the cleric Thomas Tomkyns, and to become copy-text for the 1667 edition (the numbers of the sequential gatherings for the printed text are written in on the leaves of the manuscript). The manuscript, coming from a scribe probably paid for the legibility of his handwriting, and his regularity or precision in making what was called a "fair copy," is neither regular nor precise in copying Milton's usage, though it is neat and completely legible.

There is little evidence that Milton imposed a system of spelling on the manuscript of Book 1, though there are a few corrections written in, by what Fletcher and Darbishire identified as at least five different scribes (Moyles 18). There is evidence that the principal amanuensis was copying at least some of Milton's spelling habits, perhaps taking them from a rougher manuscript in the hand of someone who had taken Milton's dictation directly.

Many changes, however, were made by the compositors working for the printers Samuel and Mary Simmons, especially with respect to punctuation, capitalization, and italics (there are no italicized words, for instance, in the manuscript, and many initial letters in lines were corrected in the manuscript from lowercase to uppercase, apparently to conform with printing practices). We have some clue to Milton's habits of composition after he went blind from a letter written in Latin and dated August 15, 1666: " . . . if you should find here anything badly written or not punctuated, blame it on the boy who wrote this down while utterly ignorant of Latin, for I was forced while dictating—and not without some difficulty—to completely spell out every single letter" (Yale 8: 4; there is evidence in this letter to Peter Heimbach that Milton's tone is playful).

We have then the manuscript of Book 1 and the two printed texts, *1667* and *1674*, the first being perhaps closer to the original manuscript in "accidentals" (what bibliographers identify as the brainless acts of typesetting, as with the choice between capitalizing or not capitalizing any given noun). The second printed version, *1674*, incorporates some substantive changes—almost all of them representing improvements—into the text.

The manuscript was most likely copied out under Milton's supervision. Someone instructed the scribe, for instance, to perform the painstaking labor of changing the initial letters of the lines more than 100 times, writing over lowercase letters with capitals. Still, when one compares the manuscript with Milton's earlier holograph materials (those written in his own handwriting), not many of his spelling, punctuation, or capitalization habits show through. Helen Darbishire wrote, "The printed page of the first edition is nearer than the manuscript to what Milton would have written if he could. Yet the printer had his lapses, and in some places the manuscript gives us the authority and is the sole authority" (*Manuscript* xxiii). I disagree at least mildly with Darbishire's first statement but agree with her second. John Shawcross, the prime authority on Milton's spelling habits, cautions me in a letter that the manuscript is not a good source of the text, since the scribe has only a very few habits of capitalization, punctuation, or spelling that can be said with certainty to be Miltonic. Though the manuscript of Book 1 is not a very good text (it uses no italics, for instance), I along with all other editors wish that the manuscript existed for the entire epic, since if it had it would have become the copy-text for any modern edition. I do not believe that the practices observed in one book copied with dubious authority add up to enough evidence from which to deduce a style that should be imposed on the other eleven books.

What, then, is a modern editor to do about the manuscript of Book 1? One has two basic choices: to say the manuscript is not a very good fair copy and disregard most of its readings, or to use the manuscript for all it is worth in editing Book 1 and allow its consistent choices to govern editorial choices (the spelling "Egipt"? "Ezechiel"?) for the rest of the edition. Among the "old-spelling" editors, Darbishire went too far in the second direction and Shawcross may have gone too far in the first, though he does use the manuscript and *1667*. I have used the manuscript to make various editorial choices in Book 1, noting all deviations from the printed text of *1674* in footnotes rather than a separate list of emendations (see Gaskell), but I have in all cases considered the manuscript as not a very reliable transcription. I have used the manuscript only peripherally in helping me determine how to make editorial decisions in later books. I use the manuscript as a corrective only for the Book 1 printed text, though the manuscript can be dead wrong at times, as with "Wither" for "Whether" (133).

2. WHY AN ECLECTIC, OLD-SPELLING TEXT?

Modern spelling may be easier for the modern reader to grasp, a kind of verbal baby food (see my "Editing Milton's Masque" 254–57). But an old-spelling eclectic text of Milton (that is, a text synthesized from the authoritative readings in manuscripts and printed editions) gives the texture, feel, and look of the original (for an opposing view, see Creaser). It also sets a proper historical distance between the modern reader and, in this case, the seventeenth-century author. I agree with Marcus Walsh, that "to ignore the difference of the past, to privilege the critic's quest for significance to himself over the interpreter's quest for the author's meaning, is to run some risk of comparison of author's achievement with critic's achievement, not always to the advantage of the latter; . . . " (182). In Milton's case, the difference between the original and a modernized version may also indicate the preferences of the author, or, if not the author, the accepted publishing practice of his time, most of which the author seems to have endorsed or at least permitted. The practice of the printing house, say in 1674, is almost as instructive in establishing "the difference of the past" as is the practice of the author.

What emerges from an old-spelling text is an artifact with meaning. The artifact is not just "quaint." When he was finishing the onerous job of helping to edit this text, Paul Klemp wrote me, "what a treat to see some puns that disappear with modernized spelling, or some prosody that changes and some pronunciation patterns that are very significant but inaudible in others' editions" (letter of 26 August 1991). Any intelligent reader who compares a modernized text with a reliable old-spelling text should come to the same kinds of conclusions.

To a great extent, the arrangement of text on a page establishes meaning, sometimes in very subtle ways, as with an ornamented frontispiece or filigreed capital letter. More obviously, typography determines meaning in an italicized proper noun or important quotation (in *1674 Eden* is italicized, but Paradise is not; *Satan* is italicized—except for its first few instances in Book 1, but Sin is not—except occasionally in Book 10; and *Death* is italicized three times, when it is cited as a name in Book 2.787, 789, and 804). There is one interesting sequence of italics in Book 10 when *Sin, Death,* and *Grave* are all italicized (10.635), as if they were all being treated as allegorical entities. Quotations from the mouth of God are sometimes italicized, as in "*Wo to the inhabitants on Earth!*" (4.5; actually St. John the Divine is quoting God in Revelation 12.12). Sadly, even many modern editions pay no attention whatsoever to italicized words in the original printed texts, and some few have added italics where none were before. The use of italics in the texts of Milton's translations of the Psalms in the 1645 and 1673 editions of his poetry, to indicate the addition of words not in the original, a conventional practice, shows that he and his printers were quite conscious of creating emphasis with italics. Not since Capel Lofft's edition of the first two books of *Paradise Lost*, in 1793 (Oras 297–303), has an editor paid much attention to such matters as italics.

A modern printer would not, of course, enjoy reproducing broken or crooked letters, and a crude printer's device such as an ornamented initial capital letter from *1674* does not fit in well with perfectly aligned modern type, but modern printing can successfully imitate the look and feel of a seventeenth-century book without admitting into the modern text seventeenth-century errors or imprecise usage of type. In attempting to set this entire Riverside edition for camera-ready copy, I have kept foremost the intention to retain as much of the look and feel of the original texts, from books or manuscripts, as possible, while not sacrificing the convenience of the critical apparatus surrounding the text or the wider margins that are helpful for students to make notes in. Trying not to bore the reader with tedious details, I may have corrected an inverted letter or corrected "foul case" silently on some occasions, but I have noted almost every deviation from the copy-text.

The modern student confronting an old-spelling text has only a few small hurdles to jump. The spelling may look quaint (it really isn't; it is functional, and typical of late seventeenth-century usage), italics may not be where one expects them to be, and colons, semicolons, and question marks may shift in signification toward or away from modern usage. According to one late seventeenth-century manual of orthography, for instance, a semicolon "differs not much from a *Colon* in its *Use,* but requires somewhat a shorter *Pause*" (Care 60).

Milton formed past participles according to a rough system of sound matched with consonants, as with "call'd" on the one hand, but "overarcht" on the other. A spelling like "quire" for the modern "choir" might give some problems, as with "lest" for "least." There are similar problems with "flour" for "flower," "tour'd" for "towered," "loose" for "lose," "rase" for "raze" or "heards" for "herds." The word "farthest" may have been pronounced "fardest" despite the spelling, as with Shakespeare's "murther." Milton seems to have preferred the archaic spelling "Soldan" to the modern "Sultan," and he seems to have preferred "anough" to "enough," "baum" to "balm," "ile" to "isle" and "sovran" to "sovereign."

For anyone who would like to investigate Milton's spelling as part of his sonics or his linguistics, here are a few preferences that I have noted, based on my own research and that of John Shawcross in "Milton's Spelling": Milton favors -ei- forms, as in "cheif," greatly over -ie- forms; he favors doubling some consonants at the ends of words, as with "warr" or "warre," and he always doubles the consonant in "citty"; he shows a clear preference for "battel" or "battell" over any other form of the word; he has some quirky or etymological spellings of biblical names like "Isack" or English phonetic spellings, as with the common "Austine" substituted for "Augustine," or what seem to be phonetic spellings of Greek names, as with "Ganymed"; he prefers the spelling "shew" to "show"; he often splits words, rather than combining them, as with "my self(e)" and even "an other"; he also likes hyphenated compounds; he has the habit of writing words beginning with "ther-" or "wher-" without the following "e" (Shawcross points out in a letter that he changes from "there" to "ther" around 1641); he always writes "thir" or "thire" in preference to "their" and he writes "tow" in preference to "two."

William B. Hunter has used what was the somewhat arbitrary seventeenth-century choice between the adjective form of "my" vs. "mine" and "thy" vs. "thine" to aid in dating *Samson Agonistes*, a choice that may indicate changing practice either in Milton or in his amanuenses and printers. Hunter finds a movement toward "my" and "thy" and away from "mine" and "thine," from early poetry to late. In *Paradise Lost*, he finds, the percentage of choice of "mine" and "thine" over "my" and "thy" is 29%, whereas in the earlier poems it is 73% and in *Samson Agonistes* it has slipped to 9% (*Descent* 221).

Contrary to popular belief perpetuated by Darbishire, Fletcher, and Hughes, Milton did not show any inclination in his holograph manuscripts to write "mee" or "yee" or "onely" for the words when they are poetically accented rather than unaccented syllables (but see Christopher Ricks on the use of doubled vowels in the preface to his New American Library edition of Milton's poetry). The generations of students who have used Hughes's edition and quoted from its text are thus quoting from a text that is, in this peculiarity, misleading, just as Hughes himself may have been misled by the Errata list in early editions that substituted one "wee" for a "we" (Fletcher 2.192).

Despite having his spelling regularized (or sometimes irregularized, as with B. A. Wright's text), Milton is almost alarmingly without any system in spelling, other than the preferences noted above. He seems to use -our- forms about the same number of times he uses -or- forms, as in "honour" vs. "honor," and he is equally arbitrary in writing "marriing" vs. "marrying," or "raigne" vs. "reigne." Milton often uses a silent final "e" arbitrarily: "slaine" is written ten times, "slain" five in

holograph material. Perhaps a computerized study of Milton's spelling practices and preferences, attempting to date each instance, will show shifts in both, but there will always be the possibility of his reverting to an earlier practice or preference.

Milton has an unsystematic preference for curt forms of some words, as with "bin" (for "been"), "cours," "els," "faln," "hous," "sixt," "thir," and "yong," but he also will use the long forms as well as the short forms of the "esse" suffix, as with "sicknesse" or "mistresse." And in his holographical manuscripts he writes "wisdome" or "musick" or "theese" or "passe," all in preference to the shorter form. As much as we would like to see his spelling as consistently economical, economy does not seem to be a strong issue in Milton's choice of one spelling over another. Milton would have learned a consistent system of phonetic spelling from the senior master at St. Paul's School, Alexander Gil the Elder, who had set it forth in his *Logonomia Anglica*, published in 1621, but there is no evidence that Milton took the older Gil's work deeply to heart.

Capitalization seems more arbitrary in Milton's holograph materials than it does in the scribal manuscript of Book 1 (a scribe would have had the professional obligation to regularize or normalize whatever unsystematic mess he had to work from, in his own fair copy). In the haste of composing poetry he himself was writing down, Milton generally does not capitalize first letters in lines of poetry, and he randomly capitalizes proper names, including the names of deities and the Christian God. He often begins the word "god" (meaning the Christian deity) with a lowercase "g." There is also no consistency in his capitalization or spelling of "Heaven" vs. (for example) "heavn" or "Heav'n," though Shawcross finds that he employed different versions of the word at one or another time during his writing career.

The printed texts of *Paradise Lost* generally capitalize nouns, and those rather indiscriminately ("Justice" may be capitalized and a few lines later "judge" may not). One cannot say with safety that all important nouns are capitalized, although "Saviour" and "Angel" are always capitalized (except in the compound "Arch-Angel," which sometimes uses a lowercase "a" in its "angel"). Verbs or adjectives are very rarely capitalized in the printed texts.

Milton thought enough about punctuation to comment on comma usage in the Bible (*On Christian Doctrine* 1.13; Yale 6: 411), but he never used the word "pointing," which was the popular term for "punctuating," and he never used the word "punctuation" in English. Nor did he ever mention commas, semicolons, or apostrophes, and he used the word "period" most often just to mean "sentence." Despite the existence of a book on the subject, Treip's *Milton's Punctuation and Changing English Usage*, there is little evidence that Milton was himself interested in the punctuation of his work. Instead he seems to have counted on amanuenses, editors, and compositors to prepare a manuscript for publication partly by adding punctuation to very lightly punctuated poetry, a practice common enough in periods of "great flexibility, fluidity and change" in patterns of orthography (Partridge 106). A sonnet in Milton's hand, for instance, might have no internal punctuation and only a period at the end, but a printer or compositor might impose five or six marks of punctuation on the poem, presumably with the poet's permission. From what I and others can reconstruct of Milton's habits of printing his poetry, before the onset of blindness, he seems to have allowed printers to provide punctuation, but he took some care to make sure that that punctuation was correct, perhaps when he read proof sheets, even in his Italian poetry (Hale, "Milton's Self-Presentation").

Following the practice of Homer and Vergil as well as standard style for seventeenth-century printing, Milton and his publisher avoided the use of quotation marks to identify direct quotations. Instead, the Epic Voice always introduces a speaker, often with an identifying epithet, as with "Is this the Region, this the Soil, the Clime, / Said then *the lost Arch-Angel* . . . " (1.241–42; emphasis added). The indentation for the beginning of the verse paragraph in this case signals that a quotation is beginning, and the Epic Voice's evaluative epithet, "the lost Arch-Angel," further identifies the speaker; meanwhile the verb "said" assures the reader that someone's direct speech is being reported. Instead of using a comma to introduce a direct quotation in *Paradise Lost*, Milton's rhetorical quotation marks introduce the fact that a speaker is beginning—then he or she speaks—then a period ends one verse paragraph and an indentation signals the beginning of a new quotation.

IX. EDITIONS

1. 1667

The first edition of *Paradise Lost* in Milton's lifetime appeared in 1667, the year after the Great Fire of London. The printing house of Mary and Samuel Simmons, printers of the first and second editions, was flourishing, having been one of the few printing establishments to have escaped the ravages of the fire. The Simmonses had two presses, one apprentice and five workmen, all of whom we know by name: Anthony Wildgoose, aged about 56 in 1668, William Hall and John Walker, both in their mid-forties, and John Warner and Thomas

Westrey, both younger men (McKenzie, "Simmons" 14). Milton sold initial rights for £5, with a further payment of £5 after 1300 copies of three editions "had been sold and retaild off to particular reading Customers" (quoted in McKenzie, "Simmons"). The contract was not a bad one, considering the fact that gentlemen authors like Milton did not expect to be paid high royalties, especially on books of poetry. Milton's widow collected larger sums on subsequent rights, and the contract with Milton had been unusually firm. It may be the first such contract between author and printer on record (Lindenbaum, "Authors" 250). The printers Mary and Samuel Simmons changed the title page in various states of the first edition, possibly to make a book that wasn't selling well look new. Masson suggested that Milton's name was taken off the newly-printed title page in the 1668 issue because the name "JOHN MILTON" was not good advertising after the Restoration (Masson 6: 623), but the name was taken off only in that one issue, and it was replaced by the recognizable initials "J. M." Milton took pride in signing anything of his that appeared in print. Donald McKenzie, after studying the politics and economics of the book trade in the 1660s, concludes "first, the book was fully licensed and entered; second, the use of an author's initials was common practice and hardly made the work anonymous; third, most printers omitted their names, and both Mary and Samuel Simmons must have done so as a matter of course in most of the books they printed; fourth, Peter Parker (the bookseller) was just as much at risk as Simmons or Milton—if either was—and yet his name isn't suppressed from the imprint" ("Simmons" 10).

2. THE REISSUE OF 1668 AND THE 1674 EDITION

The Simmonses must also have heard questions from readers about why the poem was not "properly" organized in twelve books, composed in heroic couplets, or its difficult contents explained in proper epic arguments. "This seems," writes McKenzie, "a clear case of the market making its point, but it also suggests a good and mutually beneficial understanding between Simmons and Milton" ("Simmons" 11). Starting with the reissue (not a new edition) of the second title page of 1668, Samuel Simmons added a publisher's note of his own, and an errata sheet. Milton voluntarily added "The Verse" plus the arguments (composed probably at a somewhat earlier date than the final texts), and he extended the books from ten to twelve for the 1674 edition, with a few additions that some scholars, notably Hunter (his "Belial" argues that the intrusive Belial material antedated 1667), have found significant. In 1674, prefatory matter which is both defensive and aggressive, poems written by Andrew Marvell and Dr. Samuel Barrow respectively, was added. One effect of the additions to the text was, apparently, to cause sales to increase substantially (Lindenbaum, "The Poet").

A different compositor from those who set the poem set the added arguments and the prefatory matter, and the lineation was changed from one issue to the next. Almost surely teams of at least two compositors set both the first and the second editions (part of the work in composing the epic could have been farmed out to another printing shop, but there is no internal evidence that that happened). *1674* made a number of significant small corrections to *1667*, one reason why the great majority of recent editors have chosen it as the better text on which to base a modern edition, even though bibliographical wisdom might be in favor of retaining the accidentals of the earliest edition (Fredson Bowers, letter of 7 May 1989). My conclusions about a team of compositors are based on my own study of the orthography of both editions. The arbitrary choice between colon and semicolon, for instance, from printer's gathering A to printer's gathering B or from book to book shows that clear choices were made to the degree that some books show as much as a 3:1 ratio of one mark of punctuation over the other. My findings have been corroborated by correspondence with Donald McKenzie and by unpublished research conducted by Rachel Falconer while at Exeter College, Oxford University, which she has been kind enough to let me see in manuscript ("Punctuation"). Falconer concluded from a study of gatherings A and Z (Books 1.1–238 and 7.1–238 respectively), that the compositors who set the two gatherings were quite different, finding that "the punctuation of Signature Z is slightly more grammatical, slightly clumsier rhythmically, and considerably heavier than the punctuation of Signature A" (10). McKenzie concluded independently of me, and from his own knowledge and from Falconer's research, "the likelihood is that at least two, possibly three, compositors worked on it [i.e., setting the Milton texts]" ("Simmons," "Addendum"). Apart from the corrections, the second edition copies closely—almost slavishly—from the first, even reproducing some obvious errors.

3. THE 1688 FOLIO AND AFTER

The text of Milton's poetry became a publisher's gold mine starting in 1688 (Geduld, Ch. 5). The 1688 Folio edition of *Paradise Lost*, a handsome volume sold by subscription, the first illustrated edition, helped Jacob Tonson and his heirs make a fortune selling Milton's poetry, though he shared publishing interests in the volume with Richard Bently. Throughout the eighteenth century, the works of Milton remained popular in annotated editions, many of them controlled by Tonson. Tonson published the most eccentric edition of *Paradise Lost* ever done, that of the famous classical scholar Richard Bentley (not the publisher without the "e") published in 1732. Bentley assumed that someone had corrected the blind Milton's text, adding things that Milton would never have allowed. The presence of this fabricated editor allowed Bentley to correct the "corrections." Bentley's emendations uncover genuine errors in one or two cases, but most of the time they were ludicrous, though inventive.

The two most notable fully-annotated editions are the mid-eighteenth-century edition of Thomas Newton and the variorum edition (it is a variorum edition in that it attempted to collect all significant annotations) of Henry John Todd, first published just after the turn of the nineteenth century. Below is a list of all significant editions or collections of annotations I have been able to consult. I have drawn most heavily on Newton, Todd, and Fowler for checking my own annotations, but I have also consulted the editions of Verity, Hughes, Shawcross, Campbell, Elledge, and Loh. Each editor should be cited by name in my notes, with a citation to the line number of his note. "Columbia" in the notes refers to the Columbia edition, edited by F. A. Patterson, and "Yale" to the Yale Prose Edition, edited by Don M. Wolfe. "Fletcher" is the four-volume annotated series of facsimiles assembled by Harris Fletcher. The standard biography of Milton, that of William R. Parker, is often cited, as are the *Life Records* collected by John Milton French (see the list of essential works, in the Preface).

4. EDITIONS CONSULTED, LISTED IN CHRONOLOGICAL ORDER

Patrick Hume (?). *Annotations on Milton's* Paradise Lost. London: Jacob Tonson, 1695.

Richard Bentley, ed. *Milton's* Paradise Lost. *A New Edition.* London: Jacob Tonson, 1732.

Zachary Pearce. *A Review of the Text of Milton's* Paradise Lost. London: John Shuckburgh, 1732.

Jonathan Richardson, father and son. *Explanatory Notes and Remarks on Milton's* Paradise Lost. London: Knapton, 1734.

Francis Peck. *New Memoirs of the Life and Poetical Works of Mr. John Milton.* London, 1740.

James Paterson. *A Complete Commentary, with Etymological, Explanatory, Critical and Classical Notes on Milton's* Paradise Lost. London: R. Walker, 1744.

Thomas Newton, ed. Paradise Lost: *A Poem in Twelve Books.* 2 of 4 vols. "The Sixth Edition." London: Jacob Tonson, 1763. Incorporates the notes of the Richardsons, Peck, Pearce, Addison, John Heylin, John

Jortin, Robert Thyer, William Warburton, and others.

Henry John Todd, ed. *The Poetical Works of John Milton.* 4 vols. "Fifth Edition." London: Longman, 1852.

A. W. Verity, ed. *The Cambridge Milton for Schools.* 10 vols. Pitt Press Series. Cambridge: Cambridge UP, 1891–96. Revised edition of *Comus* added in 1909. Revised edition of *Paradise Lost* added in 1910.

David Masson, ed. *The Poetical Works of John Milton.* 3 vols. London: Macmillan, 1893.

H.C. Beeching, ed. *The Poetical Works of John Milton.* London: Oxford UP, 1928.

Frank A. Patterson, gen. ed. *The Works of John Milton.* 18 vols. New York: Columbia UP, 1931–38.

Frank A. Patterson, ed. *The Student's Milton.* Rev. ed. New York: F. S. Crofts, 1934.

Harris F. Fletcher, ed. *John Milton's Complete Poetical Works, Reproduced in Photographic Facsimile.* 4 vols. Urbana: U of Illinois P, 1943–48.

Northrop Frye, ed. Paradise Lost *and Selected Poetry and Prose.* New York: Rinehart, 1951.

Helen Darbishire, ed. *The Poetical Works of John Milton.* 2 vols. Oxford: Clarendon, 1952–55.

Don M. Wolfe, gen. ed. *Complete Prose Works of John Milton.* 8 vols. in 10. New Haven, CT: Yale UP, 1953–82.

B. A. Wright, ed. *Milton: Poems.* Everyman's Library. London: Dent; New York: Dutton, 1956.

Merritt Y. Hughes, ed. *John Milton: Complete Poems and Major Prose.* New York: Odyssey, 1957.

John T. Shawcross, ed. *The Complete English Poetry of John Milton.* 1963. Rev. ed. [*The Complete Poetry of John Milton*]. Garden City, NY: Anchor-Doubleday, 1971.

Douglas Bush, ed. *The Complete Poetical Works of John Milton.* Boston, MA: Houghton Mifflin, 1965.

John Milton: Paradise Lost, *1667.* Facsimile of the 1667 edition. Menston, Eng.: Scolar, 1968.

Christopher Ricks, ed. *John Milton:* Paradise Lost *and* Paradise Regained. New York: NAL, 1968.

Alastair Fowler, ed. *John Milton:* Paradise Lost. London: Longmans, 1968; revised 1971. Issued as part of John Carey and Alastair Fowler, eds., *Poems of John Milton* (London: Longmans, 1968; revised 1980).

John Broadbent, gen. ed. *The Cambridge Milton for Schools and Colleges.* Cambridge: Cambridge UP, 1972–74.

Scott Elledge, ed. *John Milton:* Paradise Lost. New York: Norton, 1975. "Second Edition" 1993.

Gordon Campbell, ed. *John Milton: The Complete Poems.* London: Dent, 1980. A modernized text edited by Campbell (not that of B. A. Wright, as in the 1980 ed.). "Updated and reissued 1993" as *Complete English Poems,* Of Education, Areopagitica.

Bei-Yei Loh, ed. *A Student's Edition of Milton.* 2 vols. Beijing: The Commercial Press, 1990.

Tony Davies, ed. *John Milton: Selected Longer Poems and Prose.* New York: Routledge, 1992.

Roy Flannagan, ed. *John Milton*: Paradise Lost. New York: Macmillan, 1993.

Robert Ellrodt, ed. *John Milton:* Le Paradie perdu. *Traduction de Chateaubriand.* Édition présentée et annotée par Robert Ellrodt. Paris: Gallimard, 1995.

X. THE 1688 ILLUSTRATIONS

The illustrations for the 1688 folio edition of *Paradise Lost* included a handsome portrait of Milton engraved by Robert White, based on the William Faithorne drawing which had also been the basis for the engraving that provided the frontispiece for Milton's *History of Britain* (1670). Dryden's six-line poem included with the portrait establishes Milton's legitimacy, in the line of Homer and Vergil, as the principal writer of English epic. Dryden's poem, incidentally, looks back to the tribute to Milton by "Selvaggi" published with Milton's 1645 *Poems.*

Illustrators for each of the twelve books of the epic included an Oxford-based team connected with Francis Atterbury and centered on Henry Aldrich, Dean of Christ Church, a college known as a hotbed of Anglicanism. Aldrich, himself an artist, may be responsible for the illustrations for Books 1, 2, and 12. Two of the "inventors," or artists, were Bernard Lens (4, with Peter Paul Bouche as engraver), and John Baptista de Medina (3, 5–11), whose original drawings for the engravings are in the Dyce collection of the Victoria and Albert Museum in London (Shawcross 44; reproduced in Boorsch). Michael Burghers or Burgesse engraved all the plates except that for Book 4.

Taken together, the illustrations represent the first critical commentary on the plot of Milton's epic, a visual outline of events. Most of the illustrations tell the story of the book they represent. They represent the story, but through the perspective of the illustrator as he was in turn influenced by other earlier visual artists (Ravenhall; Frye 68n). The iconography of some of the illustrations, as with that to Book 3, with Satan looking up at an Italianate Christ with a large cross, might not have appealed to the iconoclastic Milton. The Expulsion Scene as reproduced in Book 12 would be familiar from Masaccio's famous Expulsion in the Brancacci Chapel in Florence. For the iconography of the Fall, see Frye and McColley.

Shawcross explicates the illustrations, touching on the fact that most of them "partially depict the substance of the book being illustrated but also indicate the significance of the events of the book beyond its specific lines" (45). Sullivan sees the illustrations for Books 1, 2, 9, and 12 as "a consistent, traditional, seventeenth-century, pessimistic interpretation of *Paradise Lost*: an unheroic Satan personifying rebellion and a monstrous Sin prefigure Adam and Eve's sinful and erroneous rebellion and unfortunate fall into woe and punishment by banishment from Paradise" (74–75).

Schoenberg was the first to point out the possible political satire in the illustration to Book 2, which might make a comparison between Satan and royal statuary ("The Face" 56–57). Also, the first time we see Satan, in the illustration to Book 2, he is significantly dressed in Roman armor, a neoclassical kingly warrior resembling statues of James II, who was forced to abdicate in 1688.

The illustrations serve as a further series of "arguments" or plot-summaries of each book. They complement Milton's arguments. Like the illustrations to Ariosto's *Orlando Furioso*, copied in the Harington translation that Milton knew, they help the reader understand a complex plot (Hulse 68). The narrative of the illustrations sometimes proceeds in whorls of time, as with that for Book 9, in which the earliest sequence described may proceed from right foreground (Adam and Eve talking before the Fall) to the center (Satan confronting the Serpent, before he possesses it), and then on back into the distance, where the viewer can see the separation scene, Eve with the Serpent, then Eve giving the fruit to Adam, and finally Adam and Eve's shamefully having covered their sexual parts with leaves. Nature has become stormy overhead. The effect of such a series of images resembles medieval play cycles, on the one hand, or the modern comic book, on the other.

Works Cited

Boorsch, Suzanne. "The 1688 *Paradise Lost* and Dr. Aldrich." *Metropolitan Museum Journal* 6 (1972): 133–50.

Frye, Roland. *Milton's Imagery and the Visual Arts*. Princeton, NJ: Princeton UP, 1978.

Gardner, Helen. "Milton's First Illustrator." *Essays and Studies* 9 (1956): 27–38. Repr. Gardner, *A Reading of Paradise Lost* (Oxford: Clarendon, 1965): 120–131.

Hughes, Merritt Y. "Some Illustrators of Milton: the Expulsion from Paradise. *Journal of English and Germanic Philology (JEGP)* 60 (1961): 670–79, Repr. *Milton: Modern Essays in Criticism*. Ed. Arthur E. Barker. New York: Oxford UP, 1965. 357–67.

Hulse, Clark. *The Rule of Art: Literature and Painting in the Renaissance*. Chicago: U of Chicago P, 1990.

McColley, Diane Kelsey. *A Gust for Paradise: Milton's Eden and the Visual Arts*. Rutgers, NJ: Rutgers UP, 1993.

Pointon, Marcia R. *Milton and English Art*. Toronto: U of Toronto P, 1970.

Ravenhall, Mary D. "Francis Atterbury and the First Illustrated Edition of *Paradise Lost*." *Milton Quarterly* 16 (1982): 29–36.

――――. "Sources and Meaning in Dr. Aldrich's 1688 Illustrations of *Paradise Lost*." *English Language Notes*. 19 (1982): 208–218.

Schoenberg, Estella. "The Face of Satan." *Ringing the Bell Backward: The Proceedings of the First International Milton Symposium*. Indiana: Indiana U of P Imprint Series, 1982. 46–59.

――――. "Picturing Satan for the 1688 *Paradise Lost*." *Milton's Legacy in the Arts*. Ed. Albert C. Labriola and Edward Sichi. University Park: Pennsylvania SUP, 1988. 1–20.

Shawcross, John T. "The First Illustrations for *Paradise Lost*." *Milton Quarterly* 9 (1975): 43–46.

Sullivan, Ernest, II. "Illustration as Interpretation: *Paradise Lost* from 1688 to 1807." *Milton's Legacy in the Arts*. Ed. Albert C. Labriola and Edward Sichi. University Park: Pennsylvania SUP, 1988. 59–92.

XI. BIBLIOGRAPHY

Abraham, Lyndy. *Marvell and Alchemy*. Aldershot, Eng.: Scolar Press, n.d. [c1990].

Achinstein, Sharon. *Milton and the Revolutionary Reader*. Princeton, NJ: Princeton UP, 1994.

Adams, Robert M. *Ikon: John Milton & the Modern Critics*. Ithaca, NY: Cornell UP, 1955.

Adamson, J. H. "The War in Heaven: The Merkabah." *Bright Essence: Studies in Milton's Theology*, ed. William B. Hunter, C. A. Patrides, and J. H. Adamson. Salt Lake City: U of Utah P, 1973. 103–14.

Addison, Joseph. *Critical Essays from the* Spectator. Ed. Donald F. Bond. Oxford: Oxford UP, 1970.

Anselment, Raymond A. *Loyalist Resolve: Patient Fortitude in the English Civil War*. Newark: U of Delaware P, 1988.

Apollonius of Rhodes. *Argonautica*. Trans. R. C. Seaton. Cambridge, MA: Harvard UP, 1967.

Apuleius. *Metamorphoses*. Ed. and trans. J. Arthur Hanson. 2 vols. Cambridge, MA: Harvard UP, 1989.

Ariosto, Ludovico. *Orlando Furioso*. Trans. Sir John Harington. Ed. Robert McNulty. Oxford: Clarendon, 1972.

Arthos, John. *Milton and the Italian Cities*. London: Bowes, 1968.

Aubrey, John. *Aubrey's Brief Lives*. Ed. Oliver Lawson Dick. Ann Arbor: U of Michigan P, 1962.

Augustine. *The City of God*. Trans. Marcus Dods. New York: Random, 1950.

Austern, Linda Phyllis. "'Sing Againe Syren': The Female Musician and Sexual Enchantment in Elizabethan Life and Literature." *Renaissance Quarterly* 42 (1989): 420–48.

Babb, Lawrence. *The Moral Cosmos of* Paradise Lost. East Lansing: Michigan State UP, 1970.

Bacon, Francis. *The Wisedome of the Ancients*. Trans. Sir Arthur Gorges. London, 1619. Facsimile ed. New York: Garland, 1976.

Baker, Herschel. *The Race of Time: Three Lectures on Renaissance Historiography*. Toronto: U of Toronto P, [1967].

——. *The Wars of Truth: Studies in the Decay of Humanism in the Earlier Seventeenth Century*. Cambridge, MA: Harvard UP, 1952.

Bakhtin, Mikhail. *Rabelais and His World*. Trans. Helene Iswolsky. Bloomington: Indiana UP, 1984.

Banks, Theodore. *Milton's Imagery*. New York: Columbia UP, 1950. New York: AMS, 1969.

Barker, Arthur E. *Milton and the Puritan Dilemma, 1641–1660*. Toronto, Can.: U of Toronto P, 1942.

——, ed. *Milton: Modern Essays in Criticism*. Oxford: Oxford UP, 1965.

Bauman, Michael. *Milton's Arianism*. Sprache und Literatur Band 26. New York: Lang, 1987.

——. *A Scripture Index to John Milton's* De Doctrina Christiana. Binghamton, NY: Medieval & Renaissance Texts & Studies, 1989.

Beaumont, Joseph. *The Complete Poems of Dr. Joseph Beaumont*. Ed. Alexander B. Grosart. 1880. New York: AMS, 1967.

Bell, Millicent. "The Fallacy of the Fall in *Paradise Lost*." *PMLA* 68 (1953): 863–83.

Benet, Diana Treviño. "Abdiel and the Son in the Separation Scene." *Milton Studies* 18 (1983): 129–43.

——, and Michael Lieb, eds. *Literary Milton: Text, Pretext, Context*. Pittsburgh, PA: Duquesne UP, 1994.

Bennett, Joan. *Reviving Liberty: Radical Christian Humanism in Milton's Great Poems*. Cambridge, MA: Harvard UP, 1989.

Berger, Harry, Jr. *Second World and Green World: Studies in Renaissance Fiction-Making*. Berkeley: U of California P, 1988.

Berry, Boyd M. *Process of Speech: Puritan Religious Writing and* Paradise Lost. Baltimore, MD: Johns Hopkins UP, 1976.

Blau, J. L. *The Christian Interpretation of the Cabala in the Renaissance*. New York: Columbia UP, 1944.

Blessington, Francis C. Paradise Lost *and the Classical Epic*. London: Routledge & Kegan Paul, 1979.

——. Paradise Lost: *Ideal and Tragic Epic*. Boston, MA: Hall, 1988.

Blondel, Jacques, ed. *Le Paradis Perdu, 1667–1967*. Études de J. Blondel, P. Brunel, R. Couffignal, H. Gardner, J. Gillet, R. Lejosne, M. Milner, M. Praz, P. Rozenberg, J. Seebacher, R Tschumi. Paris: Minar, 1967.

Bloom, Harold. *The Anxiety of Influence: A Theory of Poetry*. New York: Oxford UP, 1973.

Bodkin, Maud. *Archetypal Patterns in Poetry: Psychological Studies of Imagination*. London: Oxford UP, 1934.

Boiardo, Matteo Maria. *Orlando Innamorato*. Trans. Charles S. Ross. Berkeley: U of California P, 1989.

Boswell, Jackson C. *Milton's Library: A Catalogue of the Remains of John Milton's Library and an Annotated Reconstruction of Milton's Library and Ancillary Readings*. New York: Garland, 1975.

Boulger, James D. *The Calvinist Temper in English Poetry*. The Hague, Neth.: Mouton, 1980.

Bowers, Fredson T. "Adam, Eve, and the Fall in *Paradise Lost*." *PMLA* 84 (1969): 264–73.

Bowra, C. M. *From Virgil to Milton*. London: Macmillan, 1945.

Boyette, Purvis E. "Milton and the Sacred Fire: Sex Symbolism in *Paradise Lost*." *Literary Monographs* 5 (1973): 63–138.

Braden, Gordon. "Epic Anger." *Milton Quarterly* 23 (1989): 28–34.

Bridges, Robert. *Milton's Prosody, with a Chapter on Accentual Verse*. Oxford: Oxford UP, 1921.

Broadbent, J. B. "Milton's Rhetoric." *Modern Philology* 56 (1959): 224–42.

———. *Some Graver Subject: An Essay on* Paradise Lost. London: Chatto, 1960.

Brodwin, Leonora Leet. "Milton and the Renaissance Circe." *Milton Studies* 6 (1974): 21–83.

Browning, Judith E. "Sin, Eve, and Circe: *Paradise Lost* and the Ovidian Circe Tradition." *Milton Studies* 26 (1990): 135–57.

Budick, Sanford. *The Dividing Muse: Images of Sacred Disjunction in Milton's Poetry.* New Haven, CT: Yale UP, 1985.

Burden, Dennis H. *The Logical Epic: A Study of the Argument of* Paradise Lost. Cambridge, MA: Harvard UP, 1967.

Burns, Norman T. *Christian Mortalism from Tyndale to Milton.* Cambridge, MA: Harvard UP, 1972.

Burton, Robert. *The Anatomy of Melancholy.* Ed. Thomas C. Faulkner, Nicholas K. Kiessling, and Rhonda Blair. 2 vols. Oxford: Clarendon, 1989–90.

Bush, Douglas. Paradise Lost *in Our Time: Some Comments.* Ithaca, NY: Cornell UP, 1945.

———. *Science and English Poetry: A Historical Sketch, 1590–1950.* New York: Oxford UP, 1950.

Cable, Lana. *Carnal Rhetoric: Milton's Iconoclasm and the Poetics of Desire.* Durham, NC: Duke UP, 1995.

Camõens, Luis de. *The Lusiads. In Sir Richard Fanshawe's Translation.* Ed. Geoffrey Bullough. Carbondale: Southern Illinois UP, [1964].

Campbell, Gordon. "*De Doctrina Christiana*: Its Structural Principles and Its Unfinished State." *Milton Studies* 9 (1976): 243–60.

———. "Milton and the Lives of the Ancients." *Journal of the Warburg and Courtauld Institutes* 47 (1984): 234–38.

Campbell, Lily B. "The Christian Muse." *Huntington Library Bulletin* 8 (1935): 29–70.

Care, Henry. *The Tutor to True English.* London, 1687.

Carey, John. *Milton.* London: Evans, 1969. New York: Arco, 1970.

———. "Milton's Satan." *The Cambridge Companion to Milton*, ed. Dennis Danielson. Cambridge: Cambridge UP, 1989. 131–45.

Cassedy, Steven. *Flight from Eden: The Origins of Modern Literary Criticism and Theory.* Berkeley: U of California P, 1990.

Cawley, Robert Ralson. *Milton and the Literature of Travel.* Princeton, NJ: Princeton UP, 1951.

Charles, R. H., ed. *The Apocrypha and Pseudepigrapha of the Old Testament.* Oxford: Clarendon, 1913.

Charlesworth, James H. *The Old Testament Pseudepigrapha.* Garden City, NY: Doubleday, 1983.

Chaucer, Geoffrey. *The Riverside Chaucer.* Gen. ed. Larry D. Benson. Boston, MA: Houghton Mifflin, 1987.

Christopher, Georgia B. *Milton and the Science of the Saints.* Princeton, NJ: Princeton UP, 1982.

Cirillo, Albert R. "Noon-Midnight and the Temporal Structure of *Paradise Lost.*" *ELH* 29 (1962): 372–95.

Clark, Donald L. *John Milton at St. Paul's School: A Study of Ancient Rhetoric in English Renaissance Education.* New York: Columbia UP, 1948.

Clark, Willene B., and Meredith T. McMunn, eds. *Beasts and Birds of the Middle Ages: The Bestiary and Its Legacy.* Philadelphia: U of Pennsylvania P, 1989.

Coleridge, Katherine A. *A Descriptive Catalogue of the Milton Collection in the Alexander Turnbull Library, Wellington, New Zealand: Describing Works Printed Before 1801 Held in the Library at December 1975.* New York: Oxford UP, 1980.

Colie, Rosalie. *The Resources of Kind: Genre-Theory in the Renaissance.* Berkeley: U of California P, [1973].

Cope, Jackson I. *The Metaphoric Structure of* Paradise Lost. Baltimore, MD: Johns Hopkins P, 1962.

Corns, Thomas M. *Milton's Language.* London: Basil Blackwell, 1990.

———. *Regaining* Paradise Lost. New York: Longman, 1994.

Creaser, John M. "Editorial Problems in Milton." *Review of English Studies* 34 (1983): 279–303; and 35 (1984): 45–60.

Croll, Morris W. *Style, Rhetoric, and Rhythm.* 1966. Repr. Woodbridge, CT: Oxbow, 1989.

Crump, Galbraith M., ed. *Approaches to Teaching Milton's* Paradise Lost. New York: MLA, 1986.

———. *The Mystical Design of* Paradise Lost. Lewisburg, PA: Bucknell UP, 1975.

Cullen, Patrick. *The Infernal Triad: The Flesh, the World, and the Devil in Spenser and Milton.* Princeton, NJ: Princeton UP, 1974. 97–250.

Curry, Walter C. *Milton's Ontology, Cosmogony and Physics.* Lexington: U of Kentucky P, 1957.

Daiches, David. *Milton.* London: Hutchinson's University Library, 1957. New York: Norton, 1966.

Damrosch, Leopold. *God's Plot and Man's Stories.* Chicago, IL: U of Chicago P, 1985.

Daniells, Roy. "A Happy Rural Seat of Various View." Paradise Lost: *A Tercentenary Tribute.* Ed. Balachandra Rajan. Toronto: U of Toronto P, 1969. 3–17.

———. *Milton, Mannerism and Baroque.* Toronto: U of Toronto P, 1963.

Danielson, Dennis, ed. *The Cambridge Companion to Milton.* Cambridge: Cambridge UP, 1989.

———. "The Fall of Man and Milton's Theodicy." *The Cambridge Companion to Milton.* 113–29.

———. *Milton's Good God: A Study in Literary Theodicy.* Cambridge: Cambridge UP, 1982.

Darbishire, Helen, ed. *The Early Lives of Milton*. London: Constable, 1932.

————. *The Manuscript of Milton's* Paradise Lost, *Book I*. Oxford: Clarendon, 1931.

Davies, Stevie. *Images of Kingship in* Paradise Lost: *Milton's Politics and Christian Liberty*. Columbia: U of Missouri P, 1983.

————. "Milton." *The Feminine Reclaimed: The Idea of Woman in Spenser, Shakespeare and Milton*. Lexington: UP of Kentucky, 1986. 175–247.

Demaray, Hannah Disinger. "Milton's 'Perfect' Paradise and the Landscapes of Italy." *Milton Quarterly* 8 (1974): 33–41.

Demaray, John G. *Milton's Theatrical Epic: The Invention and Design of* Paradise Lost. Cambridge, MA: Harvard UP, 1980.

DiCesare, Mario. "Interrupted Symmetries: *Terza Rima*, Heroic Verse, First Lines, and the Styles of Epic." *Medievalia* 12 (1989): 271–303.

————. *Milton in Italy: Contexts, Images, Contradictions*. Binghamton, NY: Medieval & Renaissance Texts & Studies, 1991.

————. "*Paradise Lost* and the Epic Tradition." *Milton Studies* 1 (1969): 31–50.

Diekhoff, John S. *Milton on Himself: Milton's Utterances upon Himself and His Works*. New York: Oxford UP, 1939. Repr. New York: Humanities, 1965.

————. *Milton's* Paradise Lost: *A Commentary on the Argument*. New York: Columbia UP, 1946. Repr. New York: Humanities, 1958, 1963.

DiSalvo, Jackie. *War of Titans: Blake's Critique of Milton and the Politics of Religion*. Pittsburgh, PA: Pittsburgh UP, 1983.

Dobbins, Austin C. *Milton and the Book of Revelation: The Heavenly Cycle*. University, AL: U of Alabama P, 1975.

Dobson, E. J. *English Pronunciation 1500–1700*. 2 vols. Oxford: Clarendon, 1968.

————. "Milton's Pronunciation." *Language and Style in Milton: A Symposium in Honor of the Tercentenary of* Paradise Lost, ed. Ronald David Emma and John T. Shawcross. New York: Ungar, 1967.

Donne, John. *The Complete Poetry of John Donne*. Ed. John T. Shawcross. Garden City, NY: Doubleday, 1967.

DuBartas. See Sylvester.

Duggan, Margaret M. *English Literature and Backgrounds, 1660–1700: A Selective Critical Guide*. 2 vols. New York: Garland, 1990.

Duncan, Edgar H. "The Natural History of Metals and Minerals in the Universe of Milton's *Paradise Lost*." *Osiris* 11 (1954): 386–421.

Duncan, Joseph E. *Milton's Earthly Paradise: A Historical Study of Eden*. Minneapolis: U of Minnesota P, 1972.

Durham, Charles W., and Kristin Pruitt McColgan, eds. *Spokesperson Milton: Voices in Contemporary Criticism*. Selinsgrove, PA: Susquehanna UP [Associated U Presses], 1994.

Durling, Robert M. *The Figure of the Poet in Renaissance Epic*. Cambridge, MA: Harvard UP, 1965.

DuRocher, Richard J. *Milton and Ovid*. Ithaca, NY: Cornell UP, 1981.

Dyson, A. E., and Julian Lovelock, eds. *Milton*: Paradise Lost, *a Casebook*. London: Macmillan, 1973.

Edmundson, Mark. *Toward Reading Freud: Self-Creation in Milton, Wordsworth, Emerson, and Sigmund Freud*. Princeton, NJ: Princeton UP, 1990.

Eliot, T. S. "Milton I." *On Poetry and Poets*. London: Faber & Faber, 1957. 138–45.

Emma, Ronald D. *Milton's Grammar*. Studies in English Literature, 2. The Hague, Neth.: Mouton, 1964.

————, and John T. Shawcross, eds. *Language and Style in Milton: A Symposium in Honor of the Tercentenary of* Paradise Lost. New York: Ungar, 1967.

Empson, William. *Milton's God*. Rev. ed. London: Chatto & Windus, 1965.

Entzminger, Robert. *Divine Word: Milton and the Redemption of Language*. Pittsburgh, PA: Duquesne UP, 1985.

Esterhammer, Angela. *Creating States: Studies of the Performative Language of John Milton and William Blake*. Toronto: U of Toronto P, 1994.

Ettin, Andrew V. *Literature and the Pastoral*. New Haven, CT: Yale UP, 1984.

Evans, J. Martin. *Milton's Imperial Epic*: Paradise Lost *and the Discourse of Colonialism*. Ithaca, NY: Cornell UP, 1996.

————. Paradise Lost *and the Genesis Tradition*. Oxford: Clarendon, 1968.

Evans, Robert O. *Milton's Elisions*. University of Florida Monographs. Humanities No. 21. Gainesville: U of Florida P, 1966.

Falconer, Rachel. *Orpheus Dis(re)membered: Milton and the Myth of the Poet-Hero*. Sheffield, Eng: Sheffield UP, 1996.

————. "Punctuation and the Influence of Compositors in *Paradise Lost*." Unpublished Bibliography Essay for the MLitt. Qualifying Exam, Exeter College, Oxford U, 16 March 1987.

Fallon, Robert Thomas. *Captain or Colonel: The Soldier in Milton's Life and Art*. Columbia: U of Missouri P, 1984.

————. *Divided Empire: Milton's Political Imagery*. University Park: Pennsylvania SUP, 1995.

Fallon, Stephen M. "Intention and Its Limits in *Paradise Lost*." *Literary Milton*, ed. Benet and Lieb. 161–79.

————. *Milton among the Philosophers: Poetry and Materialism in Seventeenth-Century England*. Ithaca, NY: Cornell UP, 1991.

————. "Milton's Sin and Death: The Ontology of Allegory in *Paradise Lost*." *English Literary Renaissance* 17 (1987): 329–50.

————. "'To Act or Not':Milton's Conception of Divine Freedom," *Journal of the History of Ideas* 49 (1988): 425–49.

Farwell, Marilyn R. "Eve, the Separation Scene, and the Renaissance Idea of Androgyny." *Milton Studies* 14 (1981): 3–20.

Ferrand, Jacques. *A Treatise on Lovesickness*. Trans. and ed. Donald A. Beecher and Massimo Ciavolella. Syracuse, NY: Syracuse UP, 1990.

Ferry, Anne Davidson. *Milton's Epic Voice: The Narrator in* Paradise Lost. Cambridge, MA: Harvard UP, 1963.

Fichter, Andrew. *Poets Historical: Dynastic Epic in the Renaissance*. New Haven, CT: Yale UP, 1982.

Fink, Zera S. "The Theory of the Mixed State and the Development of Milton's Political Thought." *PMLA* 57 (1942): 705–36.

Fiore, Peter A. *Milton and Augustine: Patterns of Augustinian Thought in Milton's* Paradise Lost. University Park: Pennsylvania State UP, 1981.

----, ed. *"Th' Upright Heart and Pure": Essays on John Milton Commemorating the Tercentenary of the Publication of* Paradise Lost. Pittsburgh, PA: Duquesne UP, 1967.

Fish, Stanley Eugene. *Surprised by Sin: The Reader in* Paradise Lost. New York: St. Martin's P, 1967. Repr. Berkeley: U of California P, 1971.

Fixler, Michael. *Milton and the Kingdoms of God*. Evanston, IL: Northwestern UP, 1964.

------. "Plato's Four Furors and the Real Structure of *Paradise Lost*." *PMLA* 92 (1977): 952–62.

Flannagan, Roy C. "Ariosto." *A Milton Encyclopedia*. Ed. William B. Hunter.

---------. "Art, Artists, Galileo and Concordances." *Milton Quarterly* 20 (1986): 103–105.

---------. "Belial and 'Effeminate Slackness' in *Paradise Lost* and *Paradise Regain'd*." *Milton Quarterly* 19 (1985): 9–11.

--------. "Editing Milton's Masque." *TEXT* 9 (1996): 234–59.

-------. "Eve." *A Milton Encyclopedia*. Ed. William B. Hunter.

-------. "Horace." *A Milton Encyclopedia*. Ed. William B. Hunter.

-------. "Tasso." *A Milton Encyclopedia*. Ed. William B. Hunter.

Fletcher, Harris F. *Contributions to a Milton Bibliography, 1800–1930, Being a List of Addenda to Stevens's* Reference Guide to Milton. University of Illinois Studies in Language and Literature, 16. Urbana: U of Illinois P, 1931. New York: Russell, 1967.

—. *The Intellectual Development of John Milton*. 2 vols. Urbana: U of Illinois P, 1956–1962.

Forde, William. *The True Spirit of Milton's Versification Developed in a New and Systematic Arrangement for the First Book of* Paradise Lost, *with an Introductory Essay on Blank Verse*. London, 1831.

Forsyth, Neil. "The Devil in Milton." *Études de Lettres. Revue de la Faculté des Lettres, Université de Lausanne* (1989): 79–96.

-------. "Of Man's First Dis." *Milton in Italy*. Ed. Mario DiCesare. Binghamton, NY: Medieval & Renaissance Texts & Studies, 1991. 345–69.

—. *The Old Enemy: Satan and the Combat Myth*. Princeton, NJ: Princeton UP, 1987.

Fowler, Alastair. *Kinds of Literature: An Introduction to the Theory of Genres and Modes*. Cambridge, MA: Harvard UP, 1982.

Freeman, James A. *Milton and the Martial Muse: "Paradise Lost" and European Traditions of War*. Princeton, NJ: Princeton UP, 1980.

French, J. Milton. *The Life Records of John Milton*. 5 vols. New Brunswick, NJ: Rutgers UP, 1949–58. Repr. New York: Gordian P, 1966.

Froula, Christine. "When Eve Reads Milton: Undoing the Canonical Economy." *Critical Enquiry* 10 (1983): 321–47. Repr. Patterson, *John Milton*.

Frye, Northrop. *Anatomy of Criticism: Four Essays*. Princeton, NJ: Princeton UP, 1957.

—. "The Revelation to Eve." Paradise Lost: *A Tercentenary Tribute*. Ed. Rajan. 18–47.

----. *The Return of Eden: Five Essays on Milton's Epics*. Toronto: U of Toronto P, 1965.

Frye, Roland Mushat. *Milton's Imagery and the Visual Arts: Iconographic Tradition in the Epic Poems*. Princeton, NJ: Princeton UP, 1978.

—. "The Teachings of Classical Puritanism on Conjugal Love." *Studies in the Renaissance* 2 (1955): 148–59.

Gallagher, Phillip. *Milton, the Bible, and Misogyny*. Ed. Eugene R. Cunnar and Gail Mortimer. Columbia: U of Missouri P, 1990.

Gardiner, Eileen, ed. *Visions of Heaven and Hell before Dante*. New York: Italica P, 1989.

Gardner, Helen. *A Reading of* Paradise Lost. Oxford: Clarendon, 1965.

Gaskell, Philip. *From Writer to Reader: Studies in Editorial Method*. Oxford: Clarendon P, 1978.

Geduld, Harry M. *Prince of Publishers: A Study of the Work and Career of Jacob Tonson*. Bloomington: Indiana UP, 1969.

Geisst, Charles R. *The Political Thought of John Milton*. London: Macmillan, 1984.

Gérard, Albert S. "Sex in Eden: Milton, Vondel and Their Unorthodox View of Original Sin." *Comparative Literature and Foreign Languages in Africa Today: Collection of Essays in Honour of Willfried F. Feuser*. Ed. Tunde Okanlawon. Port Harcourt, Nigeria: Pam Unique/Transcontinental Publishers, 1988.

Giamatti, A. Bartlett. "Milton." *The Earthly Paradise and the Renaissance Epic*. Princeton, NJ: Princeton UP, 1966. 295–355.

Gil, Alexander. *Logonomia Anglica*. London: Johannes Beale, 1621. Facsimile ed. Menston, Eng.: Scolar, 1968.

Gilbert, Allan H. *A Geographical Dictionary of Milton*. New Haven, CT: Yale UP, 1919.

-------. "Milton and Galileo." *Studies in Philology* 19 (1922): 152–85.

——. *On the Composition of* Paradise Lost: *A Study of the Ordering and Insertion of Material*. Chapel Hill: U of North Carolina P, 1947.

Gilbert, Sandra M. "Patriarchal Poetry and Women Readers: Reflections on Milton's Bogey." *PMLA* 93 (1978): 368–82. Rpt. *The Madwoman in the Attic: The Woman Writer and the Nineteenth-Century Literary Imagination*. Sandra M. Gilbert and Susan Gubar. New Haven, CT: Yale UP, 1979. 187–212.

Gillet, Jean. *Le Paradis Perdu dans la littérature française de Voltaire à Chateaubriand*. Paris: Librarie Klincksieck, 1975.

Graves, Robert. *On English Poetry; Being an Irregular Approach to the Psychology of This Art, from Evidence Mainly Subjective*. London: Heinemann, 1922.

Gray, J. C. "Milton and the *OED* as Electronic Database." *Milton Quarterly* 23 (1989): 66–73.

Greene, Thomas. *The Descent from Heaven: A Study in Epic Continuity*. New Haven, CT: Yale UP, 1963. 363–418.

Greenlaw, Edwin. "'A Better Teacher than Aquinas.'" *Studies in Philology* 14 (1917): 196–217.

Gregerson, Linda. *The Reformation of the Subject: Spenser, Milton and the English Protestant Epic*. Cambridge: Cambridge UP, 1995.

Gregory, E. R. "Three Muses and a Poet: A Perspective on Milton's Epic Thought." *Milton Studies* 10 (1977): 35–64.

Grose, Christopher. *Milton and the Sense of Tradition*. New Haven, CT: Yale UP, 1988.

—. *Milton's Epic Process: Paradise Lost and Its Miltonic Background*. New Haven, CT: Yale UP, 1973.

Grossman, Marshall. *"Authors to Themselves": Milton and the Revelation of History*. Cambridge: Cambridge UP, 1987.

——. "Milton's Dialectical Visions." *Modern Philology* 82 (1984): 23–39.

Guillory, John. *Poetic Authority: Spenser, Milton, and Literary History*. New York: Columbia UP, 1983.

Hale, John K. "Milton's Self-Presentation in *Poems . . . 1645*." *Milton Quarterly* 25 (1991): 37–48.

—. "The Significance of the Early Translations of *Paradise Lost*." *Philological Quarterly* 63 (1984): 31–53.

Halkett, John. *Milton and the Idea of Matrimony: A Study of the Divorce Tracts and Paradise Lost*. New Haven, CT: Yale UP, 1970.

Haller, William. "'Hail Wedded Love.'" *English Literary History* 13 (1946): 79–97.

—. "The Tragedy of God's Englishman." *Reason and the Imagination: Studies in the History of Ideas, 1600–1800*. Ed. J. A. Mazzeo. New York: Columbia UP, 1962. 201–11.

——, and Malleville Haller. "The Puritan Art of Love." *Huntington Library Quarterly* 5 (1942): 235–72.

Hamlet, Desmond M. *One Greater Man: Justice and Damnation in Paradise Lost*. Lewisburg, PA: Bucknell UP, 1976.

Hanford, James Holly. "The Dramatic Element in *Paradise Lost*." *Studies in Philology* 14 (1917): 178–95. Repr. *John Milton, Poet and Humanist:*

Essays by James Holly Hanford. Cleveland, OH: P of Western Reserve U, 1966. 224–43.

———. "Milton and the Return to Humanism." *Studies in Philology* 16 (1919): 126–47. Rpt. *John Milton, Poet and Humanist: Essays by James Holly Hanford*. Cleveland, OH: P of Western Reserve U, 1966. 161–84.

———. "The Temptation Motive in Milton." *John Milton: Poet and Humanist: Essays by James Holly Hanford*. Cleveland, OH: P of Western Reserve U, 1966.

———, and James G. Taaffe. *A Milton Handbook*. 5th ed. New York: Appleton-Century-Crofts, 1970.

Hardie, Philip. "The Presence of Lucretius in *Paradise Lost*." *Milton Quarterly* 29 (1995): 13–24.

Harding, Davis P. *Milton and the Renaissance Ovid*. Urbana: U of Illinois P, 1946.

Haskin, Dayton. *Milton's Burden of Interpretation*. Philadelphia: U of Pennsylvania P, 1994.

Hardison, O. B., Jr. "In Medias Res in *Paradise Lost*." *Milton Studies* 17 (1983): 27–41.

———. *Prosody and Purpose in the English Renaissance*. Baltimore, MD: Johns Hopkins UP, 1989.

Harris, Neil. "Galileo as Symbol: The 'Tuscan Artist' in *Paradise Lost*." *Estratto da Annali dell Istituto e Museo di Storia della Scienza di Firenze* 10 (1985): 3–29.

Haüblein, Ernst. "Milton's Paraphrase of Genesis: A Stylistic Reading of *Paradise Lost*, Book VII." *Milton Studies* 7 (1975): 101–25.

Helgerson, Richard. *Self-Crowned Laureates: Spenser, Jonson, Milton, and the Literary System*. Berkeley: U of California P, 1983.

Heninger, S. K. *The Cosmological Glass: Renaissance Diagrams of the Universe*. San Marino, CA: Huntington, 1974.

Herman, Peter. *Squiggle-Wits and Muse-haters: Sidney, Spenser, Milton and Renaissance Antipoetic Sentiment*. Detroit, MI: Wayne State UP, 1996.

Herodotus. *The History*. Trans. David Grene. Chicago, IL: U of Chicago P, 1987.

Hesiod. *The Homeric Hymns and Homerica*. Trans. Hugh G. Evelyn-White. Cambridge, MA: Harvard UP, 1970.

Heylyn, Peter. *Cosmographie In Four Bookes*. London, 1652.

Hill, Christopher. *Milton and the English Revolution*. London: Faber, 1977; New York: Viking, 1978.

—. *The Experience of Defeat: Milton and Some Contemporaries*. New York: Viking, 1984.

Hill, John Spencer. *John Milton: Poet, Priest and Prophet*. London: Macmillan, 1979.

Himy, Armand. *John Milton: Pensée, mythe e structure dans le paradis perdu*. Publications de l'Université de Lille III, [n.d.].

—. "*Paradise Lost* as a republican 'tractatus theologicopoliticus.'" *Milton and Republicanism*, ed. David Armitage, Armand Himy, and Quentin Skinner. Cambridge: Cambridge UP, 1995.

Hollander, John. *The Figure of Echo: A Mode of Allusion in Milton and After*. Berkeley: U of California P, 1981.

———. *Melodious Guile*. New Haven, CT: Yale UP, 1988.

———. *The Untuning of the Sky: Ideas of Music in English Poetry, 1500–1700*. Princeton, NJ: Princeton UP, 1961.

Homer. *The* Iliad *Of Homer*. Trans. Richmond Lattimore. Chicago: U of Chicago P, 1961.

——. *The* Odyssey *Of Homer*. Trans. Richmond Lattimore. New York: Harper & Row, 1967.

Hopkins, Gerard Manley. *The Poetical Works of Gerard Manley Hopkins*. Ed. Norman H. Mackenzie. Oxford: Clarendon, 1990.

Huckabay, Calvin. *John Milton: An Annotated Bibliography, 1929–1968*. Rev. ed. Pittsburgh, PA: Duquesne UP, 1970.

——. *John Milton: An Annotated Bibliography, 1968–1988*. Compiled by Calvin Huckabay, edited by Paul J. Klemp. Pittsburgh: Duquesne UP, 1996.

Hughes, Merritt Y. "Devils to Adore for Deities." *Studies in Honor of DeWitt T. Starnes*. Ed. Thomas P. Harrison, et al. Austin: U of Texas P, 1967. 241–58.

——. "Milton's *Eikon Basilike*." *Calm of Mind: Tercentenary Essays on* Paradise Regained *and* Samson Agonistes *in Honor of John S. Diekhoff*. Ed. Joseph Anthony Wittreich, Jr. Cleveland, OH: P of Case Western Reserve U, 1971.

——. "'Myself am Hell.'" *Modern Philology* 54 (1956): 80–94. Repr. Hughes, *Ten Perspectives*. 136–64.

——. "Spenser's Acrasia and the Circe of the Renaissance." *Journal of the History of Ideas* 4 (1943): 381–99.

——. *Ten Perspectives on Milton*. New Haven, CT: Yale UP, 1965.

Hunter, G. K. *Paradise Lost*. London: George Allen, 1980.

Hunter, William B. Jr., Gen. Ed. *A Milton Encyclopedia*. Lewisburg, PA: Bucknell UP, 1978–83.

——. *The Descent of Urania: Studies in Milton, 1946–1988*. Lewisburg, PA: Bucknell UP, 1989.

——, ed. *The English Spenserians*. Salt Lake City: U of Utah P, 1977.

——. "The Heresies of Satan." *The Descent of Urania: Studies in Milton, 1946–1988*. 67–62.

——. "John Milton: Autobiographer." *Milton Quarterly* 8 (1974): 100–104.

——. "Milton's Arianism Reconsidered." *Bright Essence: Studies in Milton's Theology*. Ed. William B. Hunter, C. A. Patrides, and J. H. Adamson. Salt Lake City: U of Utah P, 1971.

——. *Milton's* Comus: *Family Piece*. Troy, New York: Whitston, 1983.

——. "New Words in Milton's English Poems." *The Descent of Urania*. 224–42.

——. "The Origin and Destiny of the Soul." *The Descent of Urania*. 114–36.

——. "The Provenance of the *Christian Doctrine*: Addenda from the Bishop of Salisbury." Studies in English Literature 33 (1993): 191–207.

——. "The Sources of Milton's Prosody." *The Descent of Urania*. 198–212.

——, and Stevie Davies. "Milton's Urania: 'The Meaning, Not the Name I Call.'" *The Descent of Urania*. 31–45.

Huttar, Charles A. "Vallombrosa Revisted." *Milton in Italy*. Ed. Mario DiCesare. Binghamton, NY: Medieval & Renaissance Texts & Studies, 1991. 95-111.

Ingram, William, and Kathleen Swaim. *A Concordance to Milton's English Poetry*. London: Oxford UP, 1972.

Jacobus, Lee A. *Sudden Apprehension: Aspects of Knowledge in* Paradise Lost. The Hague, Neth.: Mouton, 1976.

Jayne, Sears. "Ficino and the Platonism of the English Renaissance." *Comparative Literature* 4 (1952): 214–38.

Johnson, Lee M. "Milton's epic style: the invocations in *Paradise Lost*." *The Cambridge Companion to Milton*. Ed. Dennis Danielson. Cambridge: Cambridge UP, 1989. 65–78.

Johnson, Samuel. "Milton." *Lives of the English Poets*. Ed. George Birkbeck-Hill. Oxford: Clarendon, 1905. 1:84–200.

Johnson, W. R. *Momentary Monsters: Lucan and His Heroes*. Ithaca, NY: Cornell UP, 1987.

Jordan, Richard Douglas. *The Quiet Hero*. Washington, DC: Catholic UP, 1989.

Josephus, Flavius. *History of the Jewish Wars*. Trans. H. St. J. Thackeray. New York: G. P. Putnam's, 1928.

Keeble, N. H. *The Literary Culture of Nonconformity in Later Seventeenth-Century England*. Athens: U of Georgia P, 1987.

Kelley, Maurice. "Milton's Debt to Wolleb's *Compendium Theologiae Christianae*." *PMLA* 50 (1935): 156–65.

——. *This Great Argument: A Study of Milton's* De Doctrina Christiana *as a Gloss upon* Paradise Lost. Princeton, NJ: Princeton UP, 1941.

Kelso, Ruth. *Doctrine for the Lady in the Renaissance*. Urbana, IL: U Illinois P, 1956.

Kermode, Frank, ed. *The Living Milton: Essays by Various Hands*. London: Routledge, 1960.

Kerrigan, William. *The Prophetic Milton*. Charlottesville: UP of Virginia, 1974.

——. *The Sacred Complex: On the Psychogenesis of* Paradise Lost. Cambridge, MA: Harvard UP, 1983.

Kirkconnell, G. Watson. *The Celestial Cycle: The Theme of* Paradise Lost *in World Literature with Translations of the Major Analogues.* Toronto: U of Toronto P, 1952. Repr. New York: Gordian, 1967.

Klemp, Paul J. *The Essential Milton: An Annotated Bibliography of Major Modern Studies.* Boston, MA: G. K. Hall, 1989.

----. Paradise Lost: *An Annotated Bibliography.* Englewood Cliffs, NJ: Scarecrow, 1996.

Knapp, Steven. *Personification and the Sublime, Milton to Coleridge.* Cambridge, MA: Harvard UP, 1985.

Knoppers, Laura Lunger. *Historicizing Milton: Spectacle, Power, and Poetry in Restoration England.* Athens: U of Georgia P, 1994.

Knight, G. Wilson. *Chariot of Wrath: The Message of John Milton to Democracy at War.* London: Faber & Faber, 1942.

Knott, John R., Jr. *Milton's Pastoral Vision: An Approach to* Paradise Lost. Chicago, IL: U of Chicago P, 1971.

----. "*Paradise Lost* and the Fit Reader." *Modern Language Quarterly* 45 (1984): 123–43.

Kranidas, Thomas. *The Fierce Equation: A Study of Milton's Decorum.* The Hague: Mouton, 1965.

------, ed. *New Essays on* Paradise Lost. Berkeley: U of California P, 1969.

Kurth, Burton O. *Milton and Christian Heroism: Biblical Epic Themes and Forms in Seventeenth-Century England.* Berkeley: U of California P, 1959. Rept. Hamden, CT: Shoe String, 1966.

Labriola, Albert C. "The Aesthetics of Self-Diminution: Christian Iconography and *Paradise Lost.*" *Milton Studies* 7 (1975): 267–311.

------. "*Christus Patiens*: The Virtue Patience and *Paradise Lost*, I-II." *The Triumph of Patience. Medieval and Renaissance Studies.* Ed. Gerald J. Schiffhorst. Orlando: U Presses of Florida, 1978.

------. "The Medieval View of Christian History in *Paradise Lost.*" *Milton and the Middle Ages.* Ed. John Mulryan. Lewisburg, PA: Bucknell UP, 1982. 115–32.

------, and Edward Sichi, eds. *Milton's Legacy in the Arts.* University Park: Pennsylvania State UP, 1988.

Landy, Marcia. "Kinship and the Role of Women in *Paradise Lost.*" *Milton Studies* 4 (1972): 3–18.

Lawry, Jon S. *The Shadow of Heaven: Matter and Stance in Milton's Poetry.* Ithaca, NY: Cornell UP, 1968.

Leavis, F. R. *Revaluation; Tradition & Development in English Poetry.* London: Chatto, 1936.

LeComte, Edward S. *A Dictionary of Puns in Milton.* New York: Columbia UP, 1978.

------. *Milton and Sex.* New York: Columbia UP, 1978.

------. *A Milton Dictionary.* New York: Philosophical Library, 1961.

------. *Yet Once More: Verbal and Psychological Pattern in Milton.* New York: Liberal Arts, 1954.

Leonard, John. *Naming in Paradise: Milton and the Language of Adam and Eve.* Oxford: Clarendon, 1990.

-------. "Saying 'No' to Freud: Milton's *A Mask* and Sexual Assault." *Milton Quarterly* 25 (1991): 129–39.

Lewalski, Barbara K. "The Genres of *Paradise Lost.*" *The Cambridge Companion to Milton.* Ed. Dennis Danielson. Cambridge: Cambridge UP, 1989. 79–95.

------. "Milton on Women—Yet Again." *Problems for Feminist Criticism.* Ed. Sally Minogue. London: Routledge, 1990. 46–69.

--------. "Milton on Women—Yet Once More." *Milton Studies* 6 (1974): 3–20.

--------. Paradise Lost *and the Rhetoric of Literary Forms.* Princeton, NJ: Princeton UP, 1985.

--------. *Protestant Poetics and the Seventeenth-Century Religious Lyric.* Princeton, NJ: Princeton UP, 1979.

Lewis, C. S. *A Preface to* Paradise Lost. Oxford: Oxford UP, 1942. Repr. 1960.

Lieb, Michael. *The Dialectics of Creation: Patterns of Birth and Regeneration in* Paradise Lost. Amherst: U of Massachusetts P, 1970.

—. "*Paradise Lost* and the Twentieth-Century Reader." *Cithara* 9 (1969): 27–42.

----. *Poetics of the Holy: A Reading of* Paradise Lost. Chapel Hill: U of North Carolina P, 1981.

----. "S. B.'s 'In Paradisum Amissam': Sublime Commentary." *Milton Quarterly* 19 (1985): 71–78.

Lindenbaum, Peter. "Authors and Publishers in the Late Seventeenth Century: New Evidence on their Relations." *The Library* 17 (1995): 250–69.

--------. *Changing Landscapes.* Athens: U of Georgia P, 1987.

------. "John Milton and the Republican Mode of Literary Production." *The Yearbook of English Studies* 21 (1991): 121–36.

---------. "The Poet in the Marketplace: Milton and Samuel Simmons." Paper delivered at the Fourth International Milton Symposium, University of British Columbia, Vancouver, 4–10 August, 1991.

Loewenstein, David. *Milton and the Drama of History: Historical Vision, Iconoclasm, and the Literary Imagination.* Cambridge: Cambridge UP, 1990.

---------. *Milton:* Paradise Lost. Cambridge: Cambridge UP, 1993.

Logan, George M. and Gordon Teskey, eds. *Unfolded Tales: Essays on Renaissance Romance.* Ithaca, NY: Cornell UP, 1989.

Lord, George de Forest. *Classical Presences in Seventeenth-Century English Poetry.* New Haven, CT: Yale UP, 1987.

----. "Epic." *A Milton Encyclopedia.* Ed. William B. Hunter.

Lovejoy, Arthur O. *The Great Chain of Being: A Study of the History of an Idea.* Cambridge, MA: Harvard UP, 1936.

-------. "Milton and the Paradox of the Fortunate Fall." *Essays in the History of Ideas*. Baltimore, MD: Johns Hopkins UP, 1948. 277–95.

Lovell, Robert. *Panzoologicomineralogia. Or, a Compleat History of Animals and Minerals*. Oxford, 1661.

Low, Anthony. *The Georgic Revolution*. Princeton, NJ: Princeton UP, 1985.

Lucan. *Lucan's* Civil War. Trans. P. F. Widdows. Bloomington: Indiana UP, 1988.

Lucretius. *The Nature of the Universe*. Trans. R. E. Latham. Harmondsworth, Eng.: Penguin, 1951.

Luxon, Thomas H. *Literal Figures: Puritan Allegory and the Reformation Crisis in Representation*. Chicago, IL: U of Chicago P, 1995.

Lyons, Bridget Gellert. *Voices of Melancholy: Studies in Literary Treatments of Melancholy in Renaissance England*. New York: Norton, 1975.

MacCaffrey, Isabel Gamble. Paradise Lost *as "Myth."* Cambridge, MA: Harvard UP, 1959.

MacCallum, Hugh R. "Milton and Figurative Interpretation of the Bible." *University of Toronto Quarterly* 21 (1962): 397–415.

——. "Milton and Sacred History: Books XI and XII of *Paradise Lost*." *Essays in English Literature from the Renaissance to the Victorian Age Presented to A. S. P. Woodhouse*. Ed. Miller Maclure and F. W. Watt. Toronto: U of Toronto P, 1964.

-------. *Milton and the Sons of God: The Divine Image in Milton's Epic Poetry*. Toronto: U of Toronto P, 1986.

Madsen, William G. *From Shadowy Types to Truth: Studies in Milton's Symbolism*. New Haven, CT: Yale UP, 1968.

Manavalan, A. A. *Epic Heroism in Milton and Kamban*. Coimbator, India: Kamban Trust, 1984.

Maresca, Thomas E. "Milton: *Paradise Lost*." *Three English Epics: Studies of* Troilus and Criseyde, The Faerie Queene, *and* Paradise Lost. Lincoln: U of Nebraska P, 1979. 75–142.

Marilla, E. L. *Milton and Modern Man: Selected Essays*. University, AL: U of Alabama P, 1968.

Martindale, Charles. *John Milton and the Transformation of Ancient Epic*. Totowa, NJ: Barnes & Noble, 1986.

Martorell, Jeanot, and Martí Joan de Galba. *Tiran lo Blanc*. Trans.Ray La Fontaine. New York: Peter Lang, 1993.

Martz, Louis L., ed. Paradise Lost: *A Collection of Critical Essays*. Englewood Cliffs, NJ: Prentice Hall, 1966.

——. *The Paradise Within: Studies in Vaughan, Traherne, and Milton*. New Haven, CT: Yale UP, 1964.

——. *Poet of Exile: A Study of Milton's Poetry*. New Haven, CT: Yale UP, 1980.

Marvell, Andrew. *The Poems and Letters of Andrew Marvell*. Ed. H. M. Margoliouth. 3rd ed. Oxford: Clarendon, 1972.

Masson, David. *The Life of John Milton: Narrated in Connexion with the Political, Ecclesiastical, and Literary History of His Time*. 7 vols. Edinburgh, 1881–94. Reprinted New York: Smith, 1946.

McCanles, Michael. "Paradise Lost and the Dialectic of Providence." *Dialectical Criticism and Renaissance Literature*. Ed. McCanles. Berkeley: U of California P, 1975. 120–55.

McColgan, Kristin Pruitt, and Charles W. Durham. *Arenas of Conflict: Milton and the Unfettered Mind*. Selingsgrove, PA: Susquehanna UP [Associated U Presses], 1997.

McColley, Diane. *A Gust for Paradise: Milton's Eden and the Visual Arts*. Urbana: U of Illinois P, 1993.

-------. *Milton's Eve*. Urbana: U of Illinois P, 1983.

McColley, Grant. "*Paradise Lost*." *Harvard Theological Review* 32 (1939): 181–235.

-------. Paradise Lost: *An Account of Its Growth and Major Origins, with a Discussion of Milton's Use of Sources and Literary Patterns*. 1940. Chicago, IL: Packard & Co., 1940. Repr. New York: Russell & Russell, 1963.

McHenry, Patrick. *A Milton Herbal. Milton Quarterly* 30 (1996): 45–115.

McKenzie, Donald F. "Milton's Printers: Matthew, Mary and Samuel Simmons." *Milton Quarterly* 14 (1980): 87–91.

——. "Simmons." Unpublished lecture delivered as one of the Lyell Lectures, University of Oxford, May-June 1988. The "Addendum" was two pages of text omitted from the lecture.

McQueen, William A. "Point of View in *Paradise Lost*: Books I–IV." *Renaissance Papers* (1967): 85–92.

Mebane, John S. *Renaissance Magic & the Return of the Golden Age: The Occult Tradition and Marlowe, Jonson, and Shakespeare*. Lincoln: U of Nebraska P, 1989.

Miller, Leo. *John Milton among the Polygamophiles*. New York: Loewenthal, 1974.

——. *Milton's Portraits*. Special issue of *Milton Quarterly* (1976).

Milner, Andrew. *John Milton and the English Revolution: A Study in the Sociology of Literature*. Totowa, NJ: Barnes & Noble, 1981.

Miner, Earl. "Milton's Laws Divine and Human." *The Restoration Mode from Milton to Dryden*. Princeton, NJ: Princeton UP, 1974.

——. "The Reign of Narrative in *Paradise Lost*." *Milton Studies* 17 (1983): 3–25.

Mirollo, James V. *Mannerism and Renaissance Poetry*. New Haven, CT: Yale UP, 1985.

Mollenkott, Virginia R. "Milton's Rejection of the Fortunate Fall." *Milton Quarterly* 6 (1972): 1–5.

----------. "Milton's Technique of Multiple Choice." *Milton Studies* 6 (1974): 101–11.

----------. "Some Implications of Milton's Androgynous Muse." *Bucknell Review* 24 (1978): 27–36.

Montemayor, Jorge de. *The Diana*. Trans. RoseAnna M. Mueller. Lewiston, NY: Mellen, 1989.

Moore, Leslie E. *Beautiful Sublime: The Making of* Paradise Lost, *1701-1734*. Palo Alto, CA: Stanford UP, 1990.

Moseley, C. W. R. D. *The Poetic Birth: Milton's Poems of 1645*. Brookfield, VT: Gower, 1991.

Moyles, R. G. *The Text of* Paradise Lost: *A Study in Editorial Procedure*. Toronto: U of Toronto P, 1985.

Mulryan, John, ed. *Milton and the Middle Ages*. Lewisburg, PA: Bucknell UP, 1982.

------. *'Through a Glass Darkly': Milton's Reinvention of the Mythological Tradition*. Pittsburgh: Duquesne Studies. Language and Literature Series, Vol. 21 (1996).

Murrin, Michael. *The Allegorical Epic: Essays in Its Rise and Fall*. Chicago, IL: U of Chicago P, 1980.

------. *History and Warfare in Renaissance Epic*. Chicago, IL: U of Chicago P, 1994.

Musacchio, George. *Milton's Adam and Eve: Fallible Perfection*. New York: Lang, 1991.

Myers, Robert Manson. *Handel, Dryden, and Milton: Being a Series of Observations on the Poems of Dryden and Milton, as Alter'd and Adapted by Various Hands, and Set to Music by Mr. Handel, to Which are Added Authetick Texts of Several of Mr. Handel's Oratorios*. Cambridge: Bowes, 1956.

Nabokov, Vladimir. *Notes on Prosody*. Princeton, NJ: Princeton UP, 1964.

Newman, John Kevin. *The Classical Epic Tradition*. Madison: U of Wisconsin P, 1986.

Nicolson, Marjorie Hope. *John Milton: A Reader's Guide to His Poetry*. New York: Farrar, 1963.

------. "Milton and Hobbes." *Studies in Philology* 23 (1926): 405-33.

------. "Milton and the Telescope." *English Literary History* 2 (1935): 1-32.

Norford, Don Parry. "'My Other Half': The Coincidence of Opposites in *Paradise Lost*." *Modern Language Quarterly* 36 (1975): 21-53.

Nyquist, Mary. "The Father's Word/Satan's Wrath." *PMLA* 100 (1985): 187-202.

Ong, Walter J., S. J. "Logic and the Epic Muse." *Achievements of the Left Hand: Essays on the Prose of John Milton*. Ed. Michael Lieb and John T. Shawcross. Amherst: U of Massachusetts P, 1974.

------."Milton's Logical Epic and Evolving Consciousness." *Proceedings of the American Philosophical Society* 120 (1976): 295-305.

------. *Ramus, Method, and Decay of Dialogue*. Cambridge, MA: Harvard UP, 1958.

Oras, Ants. *Milton's Editors and Commentators from Patrick Hume to Henry John Todd (1695-1801): A Study in Critical Views and Methods*. London: Oxford UP, 1931. Repr. New York: Haskell, 1964.

Osgood, Charles Grosvenor. *The Classical Mythology of Milton's English Poems*. New Haven, CT: Yale Studies in English, 1909. Repr. New York: Haskell, 1964.

Otten, Charlotte. *"Environ'd with Eternity": God, Poems, and Plants in Sixteenth- and Seventeenth-Century England*. Lawrence, KS: Coronado, 1985.

Ovid. *Metamorphoses*. Trans. Rolfe Humphries. Bloomington: Indiana UP, 1955.

Parker, Patricia A. "Milton." *Inescapable Romance: Studies in the Poetics of a Mode*. Princeton, NJ: Princeton UP, 1979.

Parker, William Riley. *Milton: A Biography*. 2 vols. Oxford: Clarendon, 1968.

------. *Milton's Debt to Greek Tragedy in* Samson Agonistes. Baltimore, MD: Johns Hopkins UP, 1937.

Parry, Graham. *The Seventeenth Century: The Intellectual and Cultural Context of English Literature*. London: Longman, 1989.

Partridge, A. C. *Orthography in Shakespeare and Elizabethan Drama: A Study of Colloquial Contractions, Elision, Prosody and Punctuation*. Lincoln: U of Nebraska P, 1964.

Patterson, Annabel. *Censorship and Interpretation: The Conditions of Writing and Reading in Early Modern Europe*. Madison: U of Wisconsin P, 1984.

------, ed. *John Milton*. Longman Critical Readers. New York: Longman, 1992.

Patrides, C. A., ed. *An Annotated Critical Bibliography of John Milton*. New York: St. Martin's, 1987.

------, ed. *Approaches to* Paradise Lost: *The York Tercentenary Lectures*. London: Arnold, 1968.

------. "The Godhead in *Paradise Lost*: Dogma or Drama." *Bright Essence: Studies in Milton's Theology*. By Hunter, C. A. Patrides, and J. H. Adamson. Salt Lake City: U of Utah P, 1971: 71-77.

------. *Milton and the Christian Tradition*. Oxford: Clarendon, 1966.

------. *The Phoenix and the Ladder: The Rise and Decline of the Christian View of History*. Berkeley and Los Angeles: U of California P, 1964.

------, ed. *Milton's Epic Poetry: Essays on* Paradise Lost *and* Paradise Regained. Harmondsworth, Eng.: Penguin, 1967.

------, and Joseph A. Wittreich, eds. *The Apocalypse in English Renaissance Thought and Literature: Patterns, Antecedents and Repercussions*. Ithaca, NY: Cornell UP, 1984.

------, and Raymond Waddington, eds. *The Age of Milton*. New York: Barnes & Noble, 1980.

Pecheux, Mother Mary Christopher. "Abraham, Adam, and the Theme of Exile in *Paradise Lost*." *PMLA* 80 (1965): 365-71.

------. "The Concept of the Second Eve in *Paradise Lost*." *PMLA* 75 (1960): 359-66.

——. "The Council Scenes in *Paradise Lost*." *Milton and Scriptural Tradition: The Bible into Poetry*. Ed. James H. Sims and Leland Ryken. Columbia: U of Missouri P, 1984. 82–103.

——. "The Second Adam and the Church in *Paradise Lost*." *ELH* 34 (1967): 173–87.

Peter, John. *A Critique of* Paradise Lost. New York: Columbia UP, 1960.

Plato. *The Collected Dialogues, Including the Letters*. Ed. Edith Hamilton and Huntington Cairns. Princeton, NJ: Princeton UP, 1963.

Pointon, Marcia R. *Milton and English Art*. Toronto: U of Toronto P, 1970.

Porter, William Malin. "A View from 'th' Aonian Mount': Hesiod and Milton's Critique of the Classics." *Classical and Modern Literature* 3 (1982): 5–23.

Potter, Lois. *A Preface to Milton*. Rev. Ed. London: Longman, 1986.

Praz, Mario. "Milton and Poussin." *Seventeenth-Century Studies Presented to Sir Herbert Grierson*. Oxford: Oxford UP, 1938. 192–210.

Prince, F. T. *The Italian Element in Milton's Verse*. Oxford: Clarendon, 1954. Rpt. with corrections 1962, 1969.

Quilligan, Maureen. *Milton's Spenser: The Politics of Reading*. Ithaca, NY: Cornell UP, 1983.

Quint, David. "Epilogue: From Origin to Originality." *Origin and Originality in Renaissance Literature: Versions of the Source*. New Haven, CT: Yale UP, 1983. 207–20.

Qvarnström, Gunnar. *The Enchanted Palace: Some Structural Aspects of* Paradise Lost. Stockholm: Almqvist, 1967.

Radzinowicz, Mary Ann Nevins. *Milton's Epics and the Book of Psalms*. Princeton, NJ: Princeton UP, 1989.

Rajan, Balachandra. *The Lofty Rhyme: A Study of Milton's Major Poetry*. Coral Gables, FL: U of Miami P, 1970.

——. Paradise Lost *and the Seventeenth Century Reader*. London: Chatto & Windus, 1947. Repr. 1962.

——. "*Paradise Lost*: The Uncertain Epic." *Milton Studies* 17 (1983): 105-19. Rev. version in *The Form of the Unfinished: English Poetics from Spenser to Pound*. Princeton, NJ: Princeton UP, 1985. 104–27.

——. "*Paradise Lost*: The Web of Responsibility." Paradise Lost: *A Tercentenary Tribute*. Ed. Rajan. Toronto: U of Toronto P, 1969. 106–40.

Ransom, John Crowe. *God Without Thunder: An Unorthodox Defense of Orthodoxy*. New York: Harcourt Brace, 1930. Repr. Hamden, CT: Archon, 1965.

Rapaport, Herman. *Milton and the Postmodern*. Lincoln: U of Nebraska P, 1983.

Rattansi, P. M. "The Scientific Background." *The Age of Milton*. Ed. C. A. Patrides and Raymond B. Waddington. Totowa, NJ: Barnes, 1980. 197–240.

Reid, David. *The Humanism of Milton's* Paradise Lost. Edinburgh: Edinburgh UP, 1993.

Revard, Stella Purce. "Milton's Dalila and Eve: Filling in the Spaces in the Biblical Text." *Arenas of Conflict: Milton and the Unfettered Mind*. Ed. Kristin Pruitt McColgan and Charles W. Durham. Selingsgrove, PA: Susquehanna UP [Associated U Presses], 1997.

——. *The War in Heaven: 'Paradise Lost' and the Tradition of Satan's Rebellion*. Ithaca, NY: Cornell UP, 1980.

Richmond, Hugh M. *The Christian Revolutionary: John Milton*. Berkeley: U of California P, 1974.

Ricks, Christopher. *Milton's Grand Style*. Oxford: Clarendon, 1963.

Riggs, William G. *The Christian Poet in* Paradise Lost. Berkeley: U of California P, 1974.

Robson, W. W. "*Paradise Lost*: Changing Interpretations and Controversy." *From Donne to Marvell*. Ed. Boris Ford. Rev. ed. Vol. 3 of the *New Pelican Guide to English Literature*. Harmondsworth, Eng.: Penguin, 1982. 239–59.

Rogal, Samuel J. *An Index to the Biblical References, Parallels, and Allusions in the Poetry and Prose of John Milton*. Lewiston, NY: Mellen, 1994.

Rogers, John. *The Matter of Revolution: Science, Poetry, and Politics in the Age of Milton*. Ithaca, NY: Cornell UP, 1996.

Rohde, Eleanour Sinclair. *The Old English Herbals*. London: Longmans, 1922. Repr. Mineola, NY: Dover, 1971.

Rollin, Roger B. "*Paradise Lost*: 'Tragical-Comical-Historical-Pastoral.'" *Milton Studies* 5 (1973): 3–37.

Rosenblatt, Jason P. "Adam's Pisgah Vision: *Paradise Lost*, Books XI and XII." *ELH* 39 (1972): 66–86.

Roston, Murray. *Milton and the Baroque*. London: Macmillan, 1980.

Røstvig, Maren-Sofie. "The Hidden Sense: Milton and the Neoplatonic Method of Numerical Composition." *The Hidden Sense and Other Essays*, by Maren-Sofie Røstvig, Arvid Løsnes, Otto Reinert, and Diderik Røll-Hansen. New York: Humanities, 1963. 1–112.

Rudrum, Alan, ed. *Milton: Modern Judgements*. London: Macmillan, 1968.

Rumrich, John Peter. *Matter of Glory: A New Preface to* Paradise Lost. Pittsburgh, PA: U of Pittsburgh P, 1987.

—— and Stephen Dobranski, eds. *Milton and Heresy*. Cambridge: Cambridge UP, 1997.

——. *Milton Unbound: Controversy and Reinterpretation*. Cambridge: Cambridge UP, 1996.

Rusche, Harry. "A Reading of John Milton's Horoscope." *Milton Quarterly* 13 (1979): 6–11.

Rushdy, Ashraf H. A. *The Empty Garden: The Subject of Late Milton*. Pittsburgh, PA: U of Pittsburgh P, 1992.

Russell, Conrad. *The Causes of the English Civil War*. Oxford: Clarendon P, 1990.

Ryken, Leland. *The Apocalyptic Vision in* Paradise Lost. Ithaca, NY: Cornell UP, 1970.

Samuel, Irene. *Dante and Milton: The* Commedia *and* Paradise Lost. Ithaca, NY: Cornell UP, 1966.

——. "Milton on Learning and Wisdom." *PMLA* 64 (1949): 708–23.

——. *"Paradise Lost." Critical Approaches to Six Major English Works: Beowulf through* Paradise Lost. Ed. R. M. Lumiansky and Herschel Baker. Philadelphia: U of Pennsylvania P, 1968. 209–53.

——. *Plato and Milton.* Cornell Studies in English 35. Ithaca, NY: Cornell UP, 1947.

Sarkar, Malabika. "Milton's Satan and the Renaissance Magus-Astronomer." Paper delivered at the Fourth International Milton Symposium, University of British Columbia, August 4–10, 1991.

Saurat, Denis. *Milton: Man and Thinker.* Rev. ed. Hamden, CT: Archon, 1964.

Schifforst, Gerald J. *John Milton.* Literature and Life: British Writers Series. New York: Continuum, 1990.

Schindler, Walter. *Voice and Crisis: Invocation in Milton's Poetry.* Hamden, CT: Shoe String, 1984.

Schmitt, Charles B., and Quentin Skinner, eds. *The Cambridge History of Renaissance Philosophy.* Cambridge: Cambridge UP, 1988.

Schultz, Howard. *Milton and Forbidden Knowledge.* New York: MLA, 1955.

Schwartz, Regina. *Remembering and Repeating: Biblical Creation in* Paradise Lost. Cambridge: Cambridge UP, 1988.

Sensabaugh, G. F. "Milton on Learning." *Studies in Philology* 43 (1946): 258–72.

Seznec, Jean. *The Survival of the Pagan Gods: The Mythological Tradition and Its Place in Renaissance Humanism and Art.* Princeton, NJ: Princeton UP, 1972.

Shaw, William P. "The Euripidean Influence on Milton's 'Tragedy of Adam.'" *Milton Quarterly* 19 (1985): 29–34.

——. "Milton's Choice of the Epic for *Paradise Lost.*" *English Language Notes* 12 (1974): 15–20.

Shawcross, John T. "The First Illustrations for *Paradise Lost.*" *Milton Quarterly* 9 (1975): 43–46.

——. *John Milton: The Self and the World.* Lexington: UP of Kentucky, 1993.

——. "Milton's Spelling: Its Biographical and Critical Implications." Dissertation, New York U, 1958.

——, ed. *Milton: The Critical Heritage.* New York: Barnes & Noble, 1970.

——, ed. *Milton, 1732–1801: The Critical Heritage.* Boston, MA: Routledge, 1972.

——. "Orthography and the Text of *Paradise Lost.*" *Language and Style in Milton: A Symposium in Honor of the Tercentenary of* Paradise Lost.

Ed. Ronald David Emma and John T. Shawcross. New York: Ungar, 1967. 120–53.

——. *With Mortal Voice: The Creation of* Paradise Lost. Lexington: UP of Kentucky, 1982.

Shoaf, R. A. *Milton, Poet of Duality: A Study of Semiosis in the Poetry and the Prose.* New Haven, CT: Yale UP, 1985.

Shullenberger, William. "Wrestling with the Angel: *Paradise Lost* and Feminist Criticism." *Milton Quarterly* 20 (1986): 69–85.

Shumaker, Wayne. *Unpremeditated Verse: Feeling and Perception in* Paradise Lost. Princeton, NJ: Princeton UP, 1967.

Siegel, Paul N. "Milton and the Humanistic Attitude toward Women." *Journal of the History of Ideas* 11 (1950): 42–53.

Simons, Louise. "'An Immortality Rather than a Life': Milton and the Concubine of Judges 19–21." *Old Testament Women in Western Literature.* Ed. Raymond-Jean Frontain and Jan Wojcik. Conway, AR: UCA P, 1991. 145–173.

Sims, James H. *The Bible in Milton's Epics.* Gainesville: U of Florida P, 1962.

Sloane, Thomas O. *Donne, Milton, and the End of Humanist Rhetoric.* Berkeley: U of California P, 1985.

Snare, Gerald R. "Milton's Siloa's Brook Again." *Milton Quarterly* 4 (1970): 55–57.

Spencer, T. J. B. *"Paradise Lost*: The Anti-Epic." *Approaches to* Paradise Lost: *The York Tercentenary Lectures.* Ed. C. A. Patrides. London: Arnold, 1967.

Spenser, Edmund. *The Faerie Queene.* Ed. A. C. Hamilton. London: Longman, 1977.

Sprott, S. Ernest. *Milton's Art of Prosody.* Oxford: Blackwell, 1953.

Stanwood, P. G. *Of Poetry and Politics: New Essays on Milton and His World.* Binghamton, NY: Medieval & Renaissance Texts & Studies, 1995.

Stapleton, Laurence. "Perspectives of Time in *Paradise Lost.*" *Philological Quarterly* 45 (1966): 734–48.

Starnes, DeWitt T., and Ernest William Talbert. *Classical Myth and Legend in Renaissance Dictionaries.* Chapel Hill: U of North Carolina P, 1955.

Stavely, Keith W. F. *The Politics of Milton's Prose Style.* New Haven, CT: Yale UP, 1975.

——. *Puritan Legacies*: Paradise Lost *and the New England Tradition, 1630–1890.* Ithaca, NY: Cornell UP, 1987.

Steadman, John M. *Epic and Tragic Structure in* Paradise Lost. Chicago, IL: U of Chicago P, 1976.

——. *Milton and the Renaissance Hero.* Oxford: Clarendon, 1967.

——. *Milton's Epic Characters: Image and Idol.* Chapel Hill: U of North Carolina P, 1968.

——. *Moral Fiction in Milton and Spenser.* Columbia: U of Missouri P,

1995.

——. *The Wall of Paradise: Essays on Milton's Poetics.* Baton Rouge: Louisiana State UP, 1985.

Stein, Arnold. *Answerable Style: Essays on* Paradise Lost. Minneapolis: U of Minnesota P, 1953. Seattle: U of Washington P, 1967.

——. *The Art of Presence: The Poet and* Paradise Lost. Berkeley: U of California P, 1977.

——, ed. *On Milton's Poetry.* Greenwich, CT: Fawcett, 1970.

Stevens, David H. *Reference Guide to Milton from 1800 to the Present Day.* Chicago, IL: U of Chicago P, 1930. Repr. New York: Russell & Russell, 1967.

Stevens, Paul. *Imagination and the Presence of Shakespeare in* Paradise Lost. Madison: U of Wisconsin P, 1985.

Stewart, Stanley. *The Enclosed Garden: The Tradition and the Image in Seventeenth-Century Poetry.* Madison: U of Wisconsin P, 1966.

Stoll, Elmer Edgar. "Milton, Classical and Romantic." *Philological Quarterly* 23 (1944): 222–47.

——. "Milton, Puritan of the Seventeenth Century." *Poets and Playwrights: Shakespeare, Jonson, Spenser, Milton.* Minneapolis: U of Minnesota P, 1930. 241–95.

Stow, John. *The Survey of London.* Ed. H. B. Wheatley. London: Dent, 1987.

Stroup, Thomas B. *Religious Rite & Ceremony in Milton's Poetry.* Lexington: U of Kentucky P, 1968.

Summers, Joseph H. *The Muse's Method: An Introduction to* Paradise Lost. Cambridge, MA: Harvard UP, 1962. Repr. Binghamton, NY: Medieval & Early Renaissance Texts & Studies, 1981.

Svendsen, Kester. *Milton and Science.* Cambridge, MA: Harvard UP, 1956. Repr. Westport, CT: Greenwood, 1969.

Swaim, Kathleen M. *Before and After the Fall: Contrasting Modes in* Paradise Lost. Amherst: U of Massachusetts P, 1986.

——. "'Mighty Pan': Tradition and an Image in Milton's Nativity *Hymn.*" *Studies in Philology* 68 (1971): 484–95.

Swan, John. *Speculum Mundi; or, a Glasse Representing the Face of the World.* London, 1635. Expanded ed. 1643.

Sylvester, Josuah, trans. *The Divine Weeks and Works of Guillaume De Saluste Sieur DuBartas Translated by Josuah Sylvester.* Ed. Susan Snyder. 2 vols. Oxford: Clarendon, 1979.

Tanner, John S. *Anxiety in Eden: A Kierkegaardian Reading of* Paradise Lost. Oxford: Oxford UP, 1992.

Tasso, Torquato. *Discourses on the Heroic Poem.* Trans. Mariella Cavalchini and Irene Samuel. Oxford: Clarendon, 1973.

——. *Il Mondo Creato.* Trans. as *Creation of the World* by Joseph Tusiani. Binghamton, NY: Medieval & Renaissance Texts & Studies, 1982.

Tayler, Edward. *Milton's Poetry: Its Development in Time.* Pittsburgh, PA: Duquesne UP, 1979.

Teskey, Gordon. "From Allegory to Dialectic: Imagining Error in Spenser and Milton." *PMLA* 101 (1986): 9–23.

Thomas, Keith. *Religion and the Decline of Magic.* New York: Scribners, 1971.

Thompson, Elbert N. S. "The Theme of *Paradise Lost.*" *PMLA* 28 (1913): 106–20.

Thorndike, Lynn. *A History of Magic and Experimental Science.* 8 vols. New York: Columbia UP, 1923–58.

Thorpe, James. *John Milton: The Inner Life.* San Marino, CA: Huntington, 1983.

——, ed. *Milton Criticism: Selections from Four Centuries.* New York: Rinehart, 1950.

Tilley, Morris P. *A Dictionary of the Proverbs of England in the Sixteenth and Seventeenth Centuries.* Ann Arbor: U of Michigan P, 1950.

Tillyard, E. M. W. *Milton.* Rev. ed. London: Chatto & Windus, 1966.

——. "Milton." *The English Epic and Its Background.* Oxford: Oxford UP, 1954. 430–47.

——. *The Miltonic Setting: Past and Present.* Cambridge: Cambridge UP, 1938.

——. *Studies in Milton.* London: Chatto & Windus, 1951.

Toliver, Harold. *Transported Styles in Shakespeare and Milton.* University Park: Pennsylvania State UP, 1989.

Topsell, Edward. *The Historie of Serpents.* London, 1608.

——. *The History of Four-footed Beasts and Serpents and Insects.* London, 1658. Facsimile ed. New York: Da Capo, 1967.

Travers, Michael Ernest. *The Devotional Experience in the Poetry of John Milton.* Studies in Art and Religious Interpretation 10. Lewiston, NY: Mellen, 1988.

Treip, Mindele. *Allegorical Poetics & the Epic: The Renaissance Tradition to* Paradise Lost. Lexington: UP of Kentucky, 1994.

——. *"Descend from Heav'n Urania": Milton's* Paradise Lost *and Raphael's Cycle in the* Stanza della Segnatura. Victoria, BC: U of Victoria English Department, 1985.

——. *Milton's Punctuation and Changing English Usage, 1582–1676.* London: Methuen, 1970.

Trevelyan, George M. *England under the Stuarts.* 19th ed. London: Methuen, 1947.

Tsuji, Hiroko. *Rhetoric and Truth in Milton: A Conflict between Classical Rhetoric and Biblical Eloquence.* Kyoto, Japan: Yamaguchi, 1991.

Turner, James Grantham. *One Flesh: Paradisal Marriage and Sexual Relations in the Age of Milton.* Oxford: Clarendon, 1987.

Tuve, Rosamond. *Images and Themes in Five Poems by Milton.* Cambridge, MA: Harvard UP, 1957.

Ulreich, John C., Jr. "Milton on the Eucharist: Some Second Thoughts about Sacramentalism." *Milton and the Middle Ages.* Ed. John Mulryan. Lewisburg, PA: Bucknell UP, 1982. 32–56.

Updike, John. *Picked Up Pieces*. New York: Ballantine, 1986.

Utley, Francis Lee. *The Crooked Rib*. Columbus: Ohio State UP, 1944.

Vergil. *The Aeneid*. Trans. C. Day Lewis. Garden City, NY: Doubleday, 1952.

——. *The Pastoral Poems*. Trans. E. V. Rieu. Harmondsworth, Eng.: Penguin, 1949.

Vickers, Brian. "Rhetoric and Poetics." *The Cambridge History of Renaissance Philosophy*. Gen. ed. Charles B. Schmitt. Cambridge: Cambridge UP, 1988. 715–45.

Waddington, Raymond B. "The Death of Adam: Vision and Voice in Books XI and XII of *Paradise Lost*." *Journal of the History of Ideas* 32 (1971): 351–66.

Waldock, A. J. A. Paradise Lost *and Its Critics*. Cambridge: Cambridge UP, 1947.

Walker, Julia M., ed. *Milton and the Idea of Woman*. Urbana: U of Illinois P, 1988.

Walsh, Marcus. "Bentley our Contemporary; or, Editors, Ancient and Modern." *The Theory and Practice of Text-Editing*. Ed. Ian Small and Walsh. Cambridge: Cambridge UP, 1991.

Warden, John, ed. *Orpheus: The Metamorphoses of a Myth*. Toronto: U Toronto P, 1985.

Watkins, Walter B. C. *An Anatomy of Milton's Verse*. Baton Rouge: Louisiana SUP, 1955. Repr. Hamden, CT: Shoe String, 1965.

Webber, Joan Malory. "Jumping the Gap: The Epic Poetry of Milton—and After." *Milton Quarterly* 13 (1979): 107–11.

——. *Milton and His Epic Tradition*. Seattle: U of Washington P, 1979.

——. "The Politics of Poetry: Feminism and *Paradise Lost*." *Milton Studies* 14 (1980): 3–24.

Wedgwood, C. V. *Milton and His World*. New York: Walck, 1969.

Weidhorn, Manfred. *Dreams in Seventeenth-Century English Literature*. The Hague, Neth.: Mouton, 1970.

Weinberg, Bernard. *A History of Literary Criticism in the Italian Renaissance*. Chicago, IL: U of Chicago P, 1961.

——. "Scaliger versus Aristotle on Poetics." *Modern Philology* 39 (1952): 337–60.

Werblowsky, R. J. Zwi. *Lucifer and Prometheus: A Study of Milton's Satan*. London: Routledge, 1952.

West, Robert H. *Milton and the Angels*. Athens: U of Georgia P, 1955.

Whaler, James. *Counterpoint and Symbol: An Inquiry into the Rhythm of Milton's Epic Style*. Copenhagen, Den.: Rosenkilde, 1956.

——. "The Miltonic Simile." *PMLA* 46 (1931): 1034–74.

Whiting, George Wesley. *Milton and This Pendant World*. Austin: U of Texas P, 1958.

Widmer, Kingsley. "The Iconography of Renunciation: The Miltonic Simile." *ELH* 25 (1958): 258–69.

Wilding, Michael. *Milton's* Paradise Lost. Sydney, Austral.: Sydney UP, 1969.

Wilkenfeld, Roger B. "Theoretics or Polemics? Milton Criticism and the 'Dramatic Axiom.'" *PMLA* 82 (1967): 505–15.

Wilkes, G. A. *The Thesis of* Paradise Lost. Parkville, Austral.: Melbourne UP; Cambridge: Cambridge UP, 1961.

Wilkins, Ernest Hatch. *A History of Italian Literature*. Revised by Thomas G. Bergin. Cambridge, MA: Harvard UP, 1974.

Willet, Andrew. *Hexapla in Genesin*. London, 1608.

Willey, Basil. *The Seventeenth-Century Background: Studies in the Thought of the Age in Relation to Poetry and Religion*. New York: Columbia UP, 1952.

Williams, Arnold. *The Common Expositor: An Account of the Commentaries on Genesis, 1527–1633*. Chapel Hill: U of North Carolina P, 1948.

Wilson, A. N. *The Life of John Milton*. New York: Oxford UP, 1983.

Wind, Edgar. *Pagan Mysteries in the Renaissance*. New York: Barnes, 1968.

Winn, James A. *John Dryden and His World*. New Haven, CT: Yale UP, 1987.

Wittreich, Joseph. *Feminist Milton*. Ithaca, NY: Cornell UP, 1987.

————, ed. *Milton and the Line of Vision*. Madison: U of Wisconsin P, 1975.

Wolfe, Don M. *Milton and His England*. Princeton, NJ: Princeton UP, 1971.

——. *Milton in the Puritan Revolution*. New York: Nelson, 1941. New York: Humanities, 1963.

Woodcock, Thomas, and John Martin Robinson. *The Oxford Guide to Heraldry*. New York: Oxford UP, 1990.

Woodhouse, A. S. P. "Pattern in *Paradise Lost*." *University of Toronto Quarterly* 22 (1953): 109–27. Alternative version printed in *The Heavenly Muse: A Preface to Milton*. Ed. Hugh MacCallum. Toronto: U of Toronto P, 1972. 176–207.

Woods, Susanne. *Natural Emphasis: English Versification from Chaucer to Dryden*. San Marino, CA: Huntington, 1984.

Wright, B. A. *Milton's* Paradise Lost: *A Reassessment of the Poem*. London: University Paperbacks, 1968.

Yates, Frances. *Giordano Bruno and the Hermetic Tradition*. Chicago, IL: U of Chicago P, 1964.

Zagorin, Perez. *Milton Aristocrat & Rebel*. Rochester, NY: D. S. Brewer, 1992.

IN
Paradisum Amissam
Summi Poetæ
JOHANNIS MILTONI.[1]

Qui legis Amissam Paradisum, grandia magni
    Carmina Miltoni, quid nisi cuncta legis?
Res cunctas, & cunctarum primordia rerum,
    Et fata, & fines continet iste liber.
Intima panduntur magni penetralia mundi,   5
    Scribitur & toto quicquid in Orbe latet.
Terræque, tractusque maris, cœlumque profundum
    Sulphureumque Erebi, flammivomumque specus.
Quæque colunt terras, Portumque & Tartara cæca,
    Quæque colunt summi lucida regna Poli.   10
Et quodcunque ullis conclusum est finibus usquam,
    Et sine fine Chaos, & sine fine Deus:
Et sine fine magis, si quid magis est sine fine,
    In Christo erga homines conciliatus amor.
Hæc qui speraret quis crederet esse futurum?   15
    Et tamen hæc hodie terra Britanna legit.
O quantos in bella Duces! quæ protulit arma!
    Quæ canit, & quanta prælia dira tuba.
Cœlestes acies! atque in certamine Cœlum!
    Et quæ Cœlestes pugna deceret agros!   20
Quantus in ætheriis tollit se Lucifer armis!
    Atque ipso graditur vix Michaele minor!
Quantis, & quam funestis concurritur iris
    Dum ferus hic stellas protegit, ille rapit!
Dum vulsos Montes ceu Tela reciproca torquent,   25
    Et non mortali desuper igne pluunt:
Stat dubius cui se parti concedat Olympus,
    Et metuit pugnae non superesse suæ.
At simul in cœlis Messiae insignia fulgent,
    Et currus animes, armaque digna Deo,   30
Horrendumque rotæ strident, & sæva rotarum
    Erumpunt torvis fulgura luminibus,
Et flammæ vibrant, & vera tonitrua rauco
    Admistis flammis insonuere Polo:
Excidit attonitis mens omnis, & impetus omnis   35
    Et cassis dextris irrita Tela cadunt.
Ad pœnas fugiunt, & ceu foret Orcus asylum
    Infernis certant condere se tenebris.
Cedite Romani Scriptores, cedite Graii
    Et quos fama recens vel celebravit anus.   40
Hæc quicunque leget tantum cecinesse putabit
    Mæonidem ranas, Virgilium culices.

S.B. M.D.

You who read *Paradise Lost*, sublime poem of the great Milton, what do you read but the story of all things? This poem contains all things, the beginnings of all things, fate, the ends of all things. All the inner workings of the great world are opened, and whatever is hidden in the great Orb revealed. And Earth, and the paths of the seas, and the depths of Heaven, and the sulphureous, flame-vomiting cave of Erebus; all those who live on earth, in the sea, in dark Tartarus, and in the brightest kingdom of Heaven. And anything at all bound by limits, and the limitless chaos or limitless God, and more that is limitless, if anything else is without limit, like the love among men united by Christ. Whoever is there who had hoped for such a work who could believe that it might be written, yet Britain can read this poem today. How great in war are these warriors? What arms do they bear! These things he sings and with such great sounds of his war-trumpet! Celestial arms! And in Heaven, war! And what fighting proper for the fields of Heaven! How much ethereal armor Lucifer carried! Only slightly less than Michael himself bore! With what angelic and deadly anger do they face each other while the one defends the stars, the other attacks! While they toss uprooted mountains, as if they were spears, at each other, rain falls from above with never-dying fire. Olympus stands doubtful as to which force will win and fears it will not survive the battle. But as soon as the ensigns of Messiah shine in the sky with living chariots and arms worthy of God, wheels creak horribly and fierce fires erupt from angry eyes and flames shimmer, and the thunder mixed with flame sounds throughout all Heaven. All the boldness and fury of the stricken enemy fails them, and useless spears fall from weakened hands. They try to hide themselves in eternal darkness. They run to their punishments as if Orcus were a refuge. Give way poets of Rome, give way Greeks, and those celebrated by more recent fame. He who reads this poem will think Homer sang only of frogs, Vergil of gnats.

---

[1]The poem was probably written by Milton's friend, Dr. Samuel Barrow (for Barrow, see A. L. Wyman, "Samuel Barrow, M.D., Physician to Charles II and Admirer of John Milton," *Medical History* 18 (1974): 335-47). Like Andrew Marvell's poem, it concentrates on the immensity of *Paradise Lost*, but it also focuses on the War in Heaven and the Son's triumph on the Chariot of Paternal Deity, as Michael Lieb points out ("S.B."). Erebus (originally the deity who married Nox, or Night) and Orcus (one of the names of Pluto or Hades, god of the underworld) were two classical proper names often used to stand for the region of Hell. Salzilli and "Selvaggi" had both made the comparison between Milton and Homer in their tributary poems to Milton. John Dryden did so also in his three-line poem that prefaced the 1688 folio of Milton's poetry. S.B.'s poem makes a comparison with Homer and Vergil favorable to Milton. S.B. disparages Homer because he supposes him to be the author of a mock epic, *Batrachomyomachia*, or The *Battle of the Frogs and Mice* (Milton actually praises Homer in *Areopagitica* for having the poetic range to write mock epic, in the fragment that had been preserved of the invective poem *Margites* [Yale 2: 510–11]), and he praises Vergil as author of *Culex*, or *The Gnat*.

ON

Paradise Lost.

When I beheld the Poet blind, yet bold,
In slender Book his vast Design unfold,[2]
Messiah Crown'd, Gods Reconcil'd Decree,
Rebelling Angels, the Forbidden Tree,
Heav'n, Hell, Earth, Chaos, All; the Argument   5
Held me a while misdoubting his Intent,[3]
That he would ruine (for I saw him strong)
The sacred Truths to Fable and old Song
(So *Sampson* groap'd the Temples Posts in spight)[4]
The World o'rewhelming to revenge his sight.   10
    Yet as I read, soon growing less severe,
I lik'd his Project,[5] the success did fear;
Through that wide Field how he his way should find
O're which lame Faith leads Understanding blind;
Lest he perplex'd the things he would explain,   15
And what was easie he should render vain.
    Or if a Work so infinite he spann'd,
Jealous I was that some less skilful hand
(Such as disquiet always what is well,
And by ill imitating would excell)   20
Might hence presume the whole Creations day

---

[2] **Andrew Marvell**, author of this encomium (in this case, a poem of praise), probably first read *Paradise Lost* in the first edition of **1667**, a small-quarto volume measuring about five by seven inches, less than an inch thick and therefore "slender."
[3] "Fearing his intentions" or "fearing that he had attempted too much."
[4] *Samson Agonistes* was first published in 1671; thus Marvell might be poking fun gently, either belittling a biblical hero not generally supposed to have acted out of spite or alluding to the climax of Milton's tragedy. Marvell then favorably compares Milton to Samson, implying that Milton did not spite the world out of vengeance for being blind.
[5] "Design or pattern" (*OED* 1) or "plan, proposal" (*OED* 3). The word "success" would signify the completion or outcome of the plan or proposal.

To change in Scenes, and show it in a Play.[6]
    Pardon me, Mighty Poet, nor despise
My causeless, yet not impious, surmise.
But I am now convinc'd, and none will dare   25
Within thy Labours to pretend a share.
Thou hast not miss'd one thought that could be fit,
And all that was improper dost omit:
So that no room is here for Writers left,
But to detect their Ignorance or Theft.[7]
    That Majesty which through thy Work doth Reign   30
Draws the Devout, deterring the Profane.
And things divine thou treatst of in such state
As them preserves, and thee, inviolate.
At once delight and horrour on us seise,   35
Thou singst with so much gravity and ease;
And above humane flight dost soar aloft
With Plume so strong, so equal,[8] and so soft.
The Bird nam'd from that Paradise you sing
So never flaggs, but always keeps on Wing.[9]   40
    Where couldst thou words of such a compass° find?   RANGE
Whence furnish such a vast expence[10] of mind?
Just Heav'n thee like *Tiresias* to requite
Rewards with Prophesie thy loss of sight.[11]
    Well mightst thou scorn thy Readers to allure   45
With tinkling Rhime, of thy own sense secure;
While the *Town-Bayes* writes all the while and spells,[12]
And like a Pack-horse tires without his Bells:

---

[6]An obvious reference to the poet John Dryden, who had worked both with Milton and Marvell in the office of the Secretary for Foreign Tongues under Oliver Cromwell. Though John Aubrey credits Milton with the image of Dryden "tagging" his verses in the process of writing *The State of Innocence* (first published in 1674) in heroic couplets, it is Marvell who exaggerates the image and carries the attack on Dryden much further here, implying that Dryden wanted to profit by the success of *Paradise Lost* by reducing it to a play. Dryden did reduce the epic to his short play, perhaps intended to be a puppet opera. *The State of Innocence* was written, most of it in rhymed couplets, in the very year *Paradise Lost* was first published in its complete form, 1674, though it was not published until 1677 (see Winn, 262). Marvell implies that Dryden's attempt in "tinkling Rhime" only proved to illustrate his "Ignorance" and the "Theft" of Milton's artistry. Rather than being a skillful poet like Milton, Dryden is like a tired pack-horse persuaded to go forward only by the jingling rhythm of his bells. Since Dryden, being Poet Laureate, was satirized as "Mr. Bayes" (*bay* meaning "laurel"), the reference to the "Town-Bayes" ("laureate from London") below is another dig at him, especially since Dryden had been satirized as "John Bayes" in the Duke of Buckingham's parody *The Rehearsal* (1671). Milton was said by his widow Elizabeth Minshull to have pronounced Dryden "no poet, but a good rimist" (see Parker 1: 584, where the phrase is misquoted).
[7]Marvell astutely points out what has become a truism in modern criticism of *Paradise Lost*: faced with the enormity of range and the technical wizardry of the epic, most poets reading it since have been awed or cowed by Milton's mastery, forced to suffer what Harold Bloom has labeled "the anxiety of influence."
[8]"So fitted to the subject," in this case. Marvell might have in mind what Milton called his "answerable style" (9.20, and see Stein, *Answerable Style*, for what Milton may have meant by the term).
[9]The Bird of Paradise, was supposed to have remained in flight throughout its entire lifetime, taking nutrients from the air. The word "Plume" works equally well to mean "pen of the poet" and "wing of the Bird of Paradise." Marvell's poem points out that Milton's great poetic strength is the combination of "gravity," the utmost in seriousness in his subject matter, with apparent "ease" in his style; his "plume" is at the same time strong, equal to its task and soft in its execution of that task.
[10]"Expenditure (of substance, strength, labour, time, etc.)" (*OED* 1.b).
[11]Perhaps following Milton's suggestion (3.36), Marvell compares him to Tiresias, who was punished by Juno with blindness but rewarded by Jove with the gift of prophecy.
[12]In his edition of Marvell's *Poems and Letters*, Margoliouth speculates that "spells" means "does things by spells or stages," each rhymed unit being a spell; but [Margoliouth] cannot support it" (1: 337). More probably, as John Shawcross reminds me, "it means working laboriously, letter by letter, as it were" (letter, September 1991).

Their Fancies like our Bushy-points appear,[13]
The Poets tag them, we for fashion wear.
I too transported by the Mode offend,
And while I meant to Praise thee must Commend.
Thy Verse created like thy Theme sublime,
In Number, Weight, and Measure,[14] needs not Rhime.

RHYME IS FASHION THAT OTHER POETS FOLLOW

50

A. M.

THE

VERSE.

THE *Measure is* English *Heroic Verse without Rime, as that of* Homer *in* Greek, *and of* Virgil *in* Latin; *Rime being no necessary Adjunct or true Ornament of Poem or good Verse, in longer Works especially, but the Invention of a barbarous Age,*[1] *to set off wretched matter and lame Meeter; grac't indeed since by the use of some famous*[2] *modern Poets, carried away by Custom, but much to thir own vexation, hindrance, and constraint to express many things otherwise, and for the most part worse then else they would have exprest them. Not without cause therefore some both* Italian *and* Spanish *Poets of prime note have rejected Rime both in longer and shorter Works,*[3] *as have also long since our best* English *Tragedies,*[4] *as a thing of it self, to all judicious ears, triveal and of no true musical delight; which consists onely in apt Numbers, fit quantity of Syllables, and the sense variously drawn out from one Verse into another,*[5] *not in the jingling sound of like endings, a fault avoyded by the learned Ancients both in Poetry and all good Oratory. This neglect then of Rime so little is to be taken for a defect, though it may seem so perhaps to vulgar Readers, that it rather is to be esteem'd an example set, the first in* English, *of ancient liberty recover'd to Heroic Poem from the troublesom and modern bondage of Rimeing.*[6]

---

[13]Rhyme is compared to the fashionable ties that kept stockings up, what Newton called "the fashion then of wearing tags of metal at the end of their ribbons" (1.lvii). Points "were tasselled ('bushy') or tagged (like modern shoelaces). The 'bushy' fancies [the fancy tassels] are crushed into the tag and lose their quality and character" (Margoliouth 1: 337). Marvell ironically admits to being "transported by the Mode" ("carried away by the fashion"). Marvell also uses the same word, "tag," that Milton was supposed to have used in his conversation with Dryden (as reported by the antiquarian John Aubrey in his notes on Milton's biography) about making the epic into a play: "Mr. Milton recieved him civilly, and told him he would give him leave to tagge his Verses" (Darbishire 7).
[14]Marvell includes all the biblical formulas for measurement (see Ezra 8.34; Matthew 7.2), to suggest that Milton has thought of everything in composing *Paradise Lost.*

[1]The Restoration of Charles II, in 1660, which Milton seems to characterize here as the beginning of a barbarous age, did indeed set off about fifty years of poetic fashion, which Dryden certainly helped to establish, of writing almost exclusively in heroic rhyming couplets, though the form has its precedents in poems such as Marlowe's *Hero and Leander* and Sylvester's translation of DuBartas's *Divine Weeks and Works.* Because of the dominating rhyme scheme—AA, BB, CC—writing in heroic couplets seemed to Milton a kind of poetic bondage.
[2]The "u" in "famous" was printed as an inverted letter, as with the "u" in "*flammivomumque*" in line 8 of "*In Paradisum Amissam*," above. Those kinds of careless errors would normally have been caught in proofreading.
[3]Several Spanish epic translators are noted by Carl W. Cobb in *Philological Quarterly* 42 (1963): 264–67. Among the Italian epic or mock epic poets, Torquato Tasso, author of *Jerusalem Delivered* (first published in 1580), and Alessandro Tassoni, author of *The Stolen Bucket* (*La Secchia Rapita*), first published in 1622, both wrote their epics in rhymed stanzas; but Tasso defended the use of the Italian equivalent of blank verse in the introduction to his *Aminta*, written in 1573 in hendecasyllabic, or eleven-syllable, verse. Tasso's short epic on the Creation, *Il Mondo Creato* (begun c. 1592, completed in 1594), was written in blank verse and may have served as Milton's model for epic prosody. See Tasso, *Creation of the World*, and Prince, *Italian Element.*
[4]Probably the tragedies of Shakespeare or Marlowe, both of whom perfected the early forms of blank verse, or ten-syllable, unrhymed lines.
[5]Milton rejects current fashion and belligerently outlines the way he thinks poetry should be written: in a counted rhythm proper for the subject matter ("apt Numbers"), in a quantity of syllables per line which fits the decorum of the poem (see the irregular lines of "Lycidas" and of *Samson Agonistes*), and in verse paragraphs in which the rhetorical unit of meaning is not stopped at the ends of lines but drawn out by means of enjambment from one line to the end of the verse paragraph. A form like the heroic couplet with its fixed rhyme at the end of every other line would cause the "jingling sound of like endings." See Introduction, "Prosody."
[6]Readers requested of the publisher a "reason of that which stumbled many others, why the Poem Rimes not" (from the publisher Samuel Simmons's note, first published in the second and revised 1668 state), though publisher and readers both probably got more than they had bargained for in the fierceness of Milton's defense of his own practice. Milton answers the ignorance of such "vulgar Readers" with scorn for the fashionable custom of rhyming, though in doing so he was quite self-consciously violating the dominant fashion of the era.

Paradise Lost.

BOOK I.

THE ARGUMENT.[1]

This first Book proposes, first in brief, the whole Subject, *Mans disobedience, and the loss thereupon of Paradise wherein he was plac't:* Then touches *the prime cause of his fall, the Serpent, or rather* Satan *in the Serpent,*[2] *who revolting from God, and drawing to his side many Legions of Angels, was by the command of God driven out of Heaven with all his Crew into the great Deep.*[3] Which action past over, the Poem hasts into the midst of things,[4] presenting *Satan with his Angels now fallen into Hell,* describ'd here, *not in the Center* (for Heaven and Earth may be suppos'd as yet not made, certainly not yet accurst) *but in a place of utter darkness, fitliest call'd Chaos:*[5] *Here* Satan *with his Angels lying on the burning Lake, thunder-struck*[6] *and astonish,*[7] *after a certain space recovers, as from confusion,*[8] *calls up him who next in Order and Dignity lay by him; they confer of thir miserable fall.* Satan *awakens all his Legions, who lay till then in the same manner confounded; They rise, thir Numbers, array of Battel, thir chief Leaders nam'd, according to the Idols known afterwards in* Canaan *and the Countries adjoyning.*[9] *To these* Satan *directs his Speech, comforts them with hope yet of regaining Heaven, but tells them lastly of a new World and new kind of Creature to be created, according to an ancient Prophesie*

[1]The Arguments first for the ten-book and then for the twelve-book *Paradise Lost*, like the note on "The Verse," began to be added in the 1668 state of the poem. It had been fashionable, with epics in Renaissance Italy, England, and France, for the author or translator to provide verse or prose "arguments" (from the Latin *argumentum*, meaning "That which makes clear," or, more neutrally, "subject matter"). What Milton provides is a series of clear and precise summaries for the action in each book. Milton uses the Arguments to interpret and sometimes to explain or justify what he writes in verse in the epic, as when he justifies his not locating Hell in the midst of the earth in the Argument to Book 1 above. There are a few discrepancies between what Milton reports as the narrative of the books and the narrative itself, as in Eve's being awakened by Adam in the Argument to Book 12. Perhaps the discrepancies argue that Milton was taking the arguments from earlier outlines for the epic, outlines later than those preserved in the Trinity Manuscript.

[2]The distinction between (1) Satan in his own shape and (2) the Serpent's body as inhabited by Satan will be theologically important, because Satan when he enters the body of the Serpent in Book 9 will be "possessing" that body and using it for evil purposes; therefore, the Serpent is not the prime cause of Adam and Eve's fall, but Satan in the Serpent. See Steadman, *Epic and Tragic Structure*, for a reconstruction of the causal structure of the Fall.

[3]Milton interprets the events described in Revelation 12.7, 9: "And there was war in heaven: Michael and his angels fought against the dragon; and the dragon fought and his angels, . . . And the great dragon was cast out, that old serpent, called the Devil, and Satan, which deceiveth the whole world: he was cast out into the earth, and his angels were cast out with him."

[4]Milton reminds his readers that he is following the epic formula of beginning "*in medias res,*" in the middle of the events to be described. For background material, see DiCesare, Blessington, and Bowra.

[5]Milton's Hell is not placed in the center of the earth, as was Dante's, because earth was supposed to have been created after, and partly as a result of, the revolt of the angels, since the population of Earth would eventually help repopulate Heaven. Milton felt it "highly improbable that hell should have been prepared within this world, that is, in the bowels of the earth, when the earth had not yet been cursed" (*On Christian Doctrine* 1.33, Yale 6:630). The fall of the angels "took place before even the first beginnings of this world" (*On Christian Doctrine* 1.7, Yale 6:313). It is appropriate that Chaos, the part of "Heaven" from which God withheld His creative power, be the seat of Hell, and it is also appropriate that Hell be as far as possible from Heaven and from light, since "God is light" (1 John 1.5), in the spiritual as well as the physical sense. The phrases "utter darkness" and "outer darkness" are often interchangeable: see Matthew 8.12.

[6]Though Milton distinguished between thunder and lightning, "thunder-struck" included the concept of being hit by lightning, and God's "thunder-bolts" are bolts of lightning.

[7]The word was stronger in meaning, suggesting "completely vanquished" and "filled with fear and awe." After Eve's fall, Adam "amaz'd, / Astonied stood and Blank, while horror chill / Ran through his veins . . . " (9.889–91).

[8]The English word "confusion" had overtones of its theological meaning in later Latin usage, "damnation." The word "confounded" used several sentences later reinforces the meaning. The fallen angels were not only confused, they were damned. Chaucer uses the theological Latin punningly when he has Chaunticleer tell Pertelote "In principio, Mulier est humanis confusio," which he ironically translates as "Womman is mannes joye and al his blis," but which meant something closer to "In the beginning [that is, shortly after creation, with Eve's eating of the fruit], Woman is man's damnation." See the "Nun's Priest's Tale" 257.

[9]For a discussion of how the gods which the Israelites regarded as idols were interpreted by Christian biblical scholars of the Renaissance, see Hughes, "'Devils to Adore.'"

or report in Heaven; for that Angels were long before this visible Creation, was the opinion of many ancient Fathers.[10]
*To find out the truth of this Prophesie, and what to determin thereon he refers to a full Councel. What his Associates thence
attempt.* Pandemonium *the Palace of* Satan *rises, suddenly built out of the Deep:*[11] *The infernal Peers there sit in Councel.*

O F Mans First Disobedience,[12] and the Fruit
Of that Forbidden Tree, whose mortal tast
Brought Death into the World, and all our woe,[13]
With loss of *Eden*,[14] till one greater Man[15]
Restore us, and regain the blissful Seat,[16]   5
Sing Heav'nly Muse,[17] that on the secret top[18]
Of *Oreb*, or of *Sinai*, didst inspire
That Shepherd, who first taught the chosen Seed,
In the Beginning[19] how the Heav'ns and Earth
Rose out of *Chaos*: Or if *Sion* Hill[20]   10
Delight thee more, and *Siloa*'s Brook[21] that flow'd
Fast by the Oracle of God; I thence
Invoke thy aid to my adventrous Song,[22]
That with no middle flight intends to soar
Above th' *Aonian* Mount, while it pursues   15
Things unattempted yet in Prose or Rhime.[23]

[Handwritten annotations: "THE FALL — THERE WILL BE MANY MORE"; "JESUS"; "CHRISTIAN MUSE"; "MOSES AND THE TRIBES OF ISREAL"; "HIS DARLING EPIC"; "HIS WILL SOAR HIGHER THAN OTHER EPICS"]

---

[10]The "ancient Fathers" are the early apologists for the Christian church, men like Justin Martyr, Origen, Tertullian, and Sts. Jerome and Augustine, who wrote often of the origins of sin both among the angels and with Adam and Eve. C. A. Patrides, in *Milton and the Christian Tradition*, examines Milton's treatment of the Church Fathers thoroughly.

[11]Actually it rises "like an Exhalation" out of the earth of Hell's floor (1.710-30).

[12]"Disobedience" will be the subject of the epic; the word "first" implies that there will be many more; the word "Fruit" means "outcome" as well as the fruit that Adam and Eve eat; and the phrase "mortal tast" suggests that the eating of the fruit induces mortality as well as being a "mortal sin." Gregory Machacek has speculated that, since the name Eve in one of its Hebrew variants meant "Of man," Milton is even punning seriously in the first two words of the epic ("Of Man's First Disobedience," *Milton Quarterly* 24 [1990]: 111); another possible serious pun is "Of man's first **Dis**," Dis being one of the Latin names for Hades (Neil Forsyth, "Of Man's First Dis.").

[13]The word "woe" has a sound and meaning that Milton will echo often in *Paradise Lost*, starting at 1.64.

[14]Given the syntax of the sentence, "With loss of *Eden*" is subordinated, indicating that the loss of the place is less important than the disobedience that lost Eden. Eden is a mere place and not the "paradise within thee, happier farr" that Adam and Eve will be told to seek in 12.587.

[15]Jesus Christ, called "the Son" by Milton before his Incarnation, "the Christ" after the Crucifixion. The implication here is that Adam is the lesser man at the beginning of time and that Christ in becoming man, being incarnated, will redeem the sins of Adam. See Romans 5.12,19.

[16]Supply "for us" after "regain." Milton leaves the "blissful Seat" undefined, probably on purpose to suggest the "paradise within" (12.587) which Adam and Eve will regain if they continue a repentant and good life after they leave Eden.

[17]The Heavenly Muse, like the "Fruit" above, is intentionally not named here. Hunter and Davies conjecture that the Heavenly Muse here is the Godhead, including Father, Son, and Holy Ghost (*Descent*). Milton clearly wants his readers at this point to associate the muse whom he will later call "*Urania*" (7.1) with the spirit that inspired Moses, "That Shepherd," to write down the Ten Commandments.

[18]The top of Mount Oreb, also referred to in the Bible as Sinai, where Moses received the Commandments, is hidden at the time by a cloud cover, but it is also secret because only Moses was admitted to it. As William B. Hunter reminds me, "Sinai in Exodus is the same as Horeb in Deuteronomy: the Bible gives both names and Milton follows it" (letter, July 1991).

[19]Echoes the first three words of the King James Bible, which are in turn echoed at the beginning of the Gospel of John. Milton will supply much more detail in his evocation of the Creation scenes of Genesis in Book 7. "That Shepherd" is Moses, thought to be the author of the first five books of the Bible, the Pentateuch; and the "chosen seed" are first the tribes of Israel of the Old Testament and later the Christians. "The seed" also refers to the Son as a descendant of Adam and Eve and of David (see 12.324-30).

[20]The site of the Temple in Jerusalem.

[21]The brook or the pool of Siloa or Siloam may have special significance for Milton as a blind man because it is associated with Christ, who healed a man of blindness near the pool of Siloam (John 9.7). For the academic debate over the meaning of the allusion, see Gerald Snare, "Milton's Siloa's Brook Again," *Milton Quarterly* 4 (1970): 55-57.

[22]The adjective "adventrous" is written as a trisyllable in a spelling that Milton seems to have preferred. The word suggests the daring of his being "Taught by the heav'nly Muse to venture down / The dark descent, and up to reascend" (3.19-20), from Hell to Heaven, in writing the epic, his "Song."

[23]The last two images represent Milton's challenge to classical Greek and Roman epic and to Renaissance epic, since the Aonian Mount is Helicon, the legendary home of the Muses in Boeotia, which was also known as Aonia. The phrase "no middle flight" suggests that Milton's Christian poetry will soar above the subject matter or the capacity of the Greek poets relying on their information from Mount Helicon. The verbal formula "Things unattempted yet in Prose or Rhime" challenges Renaissance epic, since it parodies a phrase used by Ariosto at the beginning of his romantic epic, *Orlando Furioso*, and by other writers of Renaissance romantic epics. In his translation of Ariosto's epic, which Milton was almost surely familiar with, Sir John Harington

And chiefly Thou O Spirit,[24] that dost prefer
Before all Temples th' upright heart and pure,[25]
Instruct me, for Thou know'st; Thou from the first[26]
Wast present, and with mighty wings outspread   20
Dove-like satst brooding on the vast Abyss
And mad'st it pregnant:[27] What in me is dark
Illumin, what is low raise and support;
That to the highth of this great Argument[28]
I may assert° Eternal Providence,   VINDICATE, CHAMPION   25
And justifie the wayes of God to men.
    Say first, for Heav'n hides nothing from thy view
Nor the deep Tract of Hell, say first what cause
Mov'd our Grand Parents in that happy State,
Favour'd of Heav'n so highly, to fall off   30
From thir Creator, and transgress his Will
For one restraint,[29] Lords of the World besides?
Who first seduc'd them to that foul revolt?
Th' infernal Serpent; he it was, whose guile
Stird up with Envy and Revenge, deceiv'd   35
The Mother of Mankind, what time° his Pride   WHEN
Had cast him out from Heav'n,[30] with all his Host°   ARMY
Of Rebel Angels, by whose aid aspiring
To set himself in Glory above his Peers,
He trusted to have equal'd the most High,   40
If he oppos'd; and with ambitious aim
Against the Throne and Monarchy of God
Rais'd impious War in Heav'n and Battel proud
With vain attempt. Him the Almighty Power
Hurld headlong flaming from th' Ethereal Skie   45
With hideous ruine and combustion down
To bottomless perdition, there to dwell

---

translated the phrase as "A tale in prose ne verse yet song or sayd" (*Ludovico Ariosto's Orlando Furioso* 19). The verbal formula represents a common brag of uniqueness for each epic writer.

[24]The word "Spirit" must have been pronounced as a monosyllable here, according to the scansion of the line, though it cannot be spelled that way conveniently without being turned into "sprite," or, less likely, "sprit" or "spirt." The line in the Manuscript reads "And cheifly thou O Spirit that dost prefer," indicating that the compositor began, at least, to put commas around "O Spirit," but managed to include only one of the normal pair.

[25]"Do good, O Lord, unto those that be good, and to them that are upright in their hearts" (Psalm 125.4). "Before all Temples" suggests the general Puritan position that the physical temple or church was less important than the "temple of the mind" (*Comus* 460) or heart. Milton had translated Psalm 7 to describe God as "him who both just and wise / Saves th' upright of Heart at last" (41–42). Of perhaps more importance here is 1 Corinthians 6.19, "What? know ye not that your body is the temple of the Holy Ghost which is in you, which ye have of God, and ye are not your own?"

[26]"And the Spirit of God moved upon the face of the waters" (Genesis 1.2).

[27]Milton does not give an image of the conventional Christian Holy Ghost, because he was not a believer in the traditional Trinity. Here the Spirit of Genesis 1.2 is a world-mother, a manifestation of the creative power of God pictured as a dove brooding on the abyss of Chaos and infusing it with meaning and coherence, to transform it into the universe as we know it. Various critics have pointed out the androgyny or bipolar sexuality of the Spirit here, which may be derived from Hermetic lore (Hunter and Davies; Mollenkott, "Some Implications").

[28]Not an argument in the conventional modern meaning of "debate in which disagreement is expressed." The Latin word *argumentum* meant "subject matter," when the writer was discussing the subject of a play or work of fiction. The phrase "this great Argument" suggests a rhetorical structure, but it also suggests a great subject most worthy of the epic genre which should build "the lofty rhyme" ("Lycidas" 11) on a subject "more doctrinal and exemplary to a nation" (*Reason of Church Government*, Yale 1:815). Compare Milton's use of the word with his arguments to each book of the poem.

[29]"Despite [only] one restraint." The one restraint is the one prohibition given humankind in Eden: not to eat the fruit of the Tree of Knowledge of Good and Evil.

[30]Every word in this little outline of the Fall is very carefully chosen. Satan is the unique "infernal Serpent"; his most characteristic sin is pride. He "seduces" both Adam and Eve ("them") in the sense that he leads them aside (Latin *seducere*) from God, but he deceives Eve by disguising himself and lying convincingly. He uses guile rather than force on Eve, but it is guile agitated by the base motives of envy for the perfect state of humankind and revenge for his having been cast out of Heaven by God. Satan in the Serpent deceived Eve, who in her body as the mother of humankind incorporates the whole future human race. This passage anticipates the expanded story told in Books 5, 6, and 9.

In Adamantine[31] Chains and penal Fire,
Who durst defie th' Omnipotent to Arms.[32]
Nine times the Space that measures Day and Night   50
To mortal men, he with his horrid crew
Lay vanquisht, rowling in the fiery Gulfe
Confounded though immortal: But his doom
Reserv'd him to more wrath; for now the thought
Both of lost happiness and lasting pain   55
Torments him; round he throws his baleful eyes
That witness'd[33] huge affliction and dismay
Mixt with obdurate pride and stedfast hate:
At once as far as Angels kenn[34] he views
The dismal Situation waste and wilde,   60
A Dungeon horrible, on all sides round
As one great Furnace flam'd, yet from those flames
No light, but rather darkness visible[35]
Serv'd onely to discover° sights of woe,   UNCOVER
Regions of sorrow, doleful shades, where peace   65
And rest can never dwell, hope never comes
That comes to all;[36] but torture without end
Still urges,° and a fiery Deluge, fed   PRESSES ON
With ever-burning Sulphur unconsum'd:
Such place Eternal Justice had prepar'd   70
For those rebellious, here thir[37] Prison ordain'd
In utter darkness, and thir portion set
As far remov'd from God and light of Heav'n
As from the Center thrice to th' utmost Pole.[38]
O how unlike the place from whence they fell!   75
There the companions of his fall, o'rewhelm'd
With Floods and Whirlwinds of tempestuous fire,
He soon discerns, and weltring[39] by his side
One next himself in power, and next in crime,
Long after known in *Palestine*, and nam'd   80
Beelzebub. To whom th' Arch-Enemy,
And thence in Heav'n call'd Satan,[40] with bold words
Breaking the horrid silence thus began.

---

[31]The mythical Greek and Roman **adamant** was thought to be the hardest substance in existence; the word was used to define both steel and diamond.
[32]Those looking for musical devices in *Paradise Lost* (see Introduction, "Prosody") might look at the last sentence as a breathtaking decrescendo or diminuendo, building downward from "Him" to "Arms." Details of the fall of the angels conclude Book 6.
[33]Satan's baleful (that is, "Full of malign, deadly, or noxious influence" [*OED* 1]) eyes are witness to his own affliction and dismay, and that of his comrades.
[34]Probably this means "as far as angels have the power to see," but both Campbell (*John Milton* 59n) and Fowler (59n) point out that "kenn" may either be a noun or a verb, depending on whether "Angels" is read as plural or singular possessive.
[35]Famous as an example of **oxymoron**, a phrase, usually made up of two words, which seems to contradict itself but builds meaning out of the paradox, as with "precious bane" at 692. The "impossible" combination expands meaning by a method more common in metaphysical wit, as with an image like John Donne's "spider love" ("Twick'n'am Garden"). See lines 181–83 below for an explanation of how "darkness visible" might be perceived by the senses.
[36]Recalls the famous inscription over Dante's Hell usually translated as "Abandon hope all ye who enter here," **Lasciate ogni speranza, voi ch'entrate** (*Inferno* 3.10).
[37]In the second state of the 1674 edition, someone in the printing house has changed the "their" of the first state to "thir," indicating perhaps that the author may have given orders to revise the spelling of the word throughout. "Thir" (and sometimes its variant "thire") was Milton's preferred spelling of the word whenever he wrote it in his own hand, and in this case "thir" was in the Manuscript as well.
[38]Milton takes pains to exceed the limits set by the classical world for the distance between Hades and the heavens. Homer places Hades as far below Earth as Heaven is above (*Iliad* 8.16), and Vergil places Tartarus twice as far below Heaven (*Aeneid* 6.577).
[39]Compare "Lycidas" 13, where the body of Lycidas is said to "welter"—toss about—on the sea.
[40]The Hebrew word transliterated as "Satan" means "adversary" or, as Milton seems to translate, "Arch-Enemy." Milton will often play on the etymology.

If thou beest he;[41] But O how fall'n! how chang'd
From him, who in the happy Realms of Light   85
Cloth'd with transcendent brightness didst out-shine
Myriads though bright:[42] If he whom mutual league,
United thoughts and counsels, equal hope
And hazard in the Glorious Enterprize,
Joynd with me once, now misery hath joynd   90
In equal ruin: into what Pit thou seest
From what highth fall'n, so much the stronger prov'd
He with his Thunder: and till then who knew
The force of those dire Arms? yet not for those,
Nor what the Potent Victor in his rage[43]   95
Can else inflict, do I repent or change,
Though chang'd in outward lustre;[44] that fixt mind
And high disdain, from sence of injur'd merit,
That with the mightiest rais'd me to contend,
And to the fierce contention brought along   100
Innumerable force of Spirits arm'd
That durst dislike his reign, and me preferring,
His utmost power with adverse power oppos'd
In dubious Battel on the Plains of Heav'n,
And shook his throne. What though the field be lost?   105
All is not lost; the unconquerable Will,
And study of revenge, immortal hate,
And courage never to submit or yield:
And what is else not to be overcome?[45]
That Glory never shall his wrath or might   110
Extort from me. To bow and sue° for grace   ENTREAT, PETITION
With suppliant knee, and deifie his power,
Who from the terrour of this Arm so late
Doubted° his Empire, that were low indeed,   FEARED FOR
That were an ignominy[46] and shame beneath   115
This downfall; since by Fate[47] the strength of Gods
And this Empyreal substance cannot fail,
Since through experience of this great event
In Arms not worse, in foresight much advanc't,
We may with more successful hope resolve   120
To wage by force or guile eternal Warr
Irreconcileable, to our grand Foe,

---

[41]Satan's beginning in mid-sentence, his anacoluthon in leaving out a main clause, may indicate his moral confusion.

[42]Although Satan in this speech is addressing Beelzebub, he may also address his own problem in having been Lucifer, "light-bearer" according to the Latin adjective *lucifer*. Satan as an angel was associated with light and the morning star (the planet Venus). Milton uses "Lucifer" simply to mean the brightest star in the early morning in Nativity Ode 75. Isaiah 14.12, "How art thou fallen from heaven, O Lucifer, son of the morning," was interpreted as referring to Satan through its reference to Nebuchadnezzar as an Old Testament "shadowy type" to be clarified by reference to the New Testament "truth." I am grateful to Richard McMurrin for help identifying Beelzebub as audience for Satan's speech.

[43]Satan imputes "rage" to God, but God's anger is not irrational; God is incapable of rage, since His anger is just and reasonable. See Gordon Braden, "Epic Anger," *Milton Quarterly* 23 (1989): 28–34.

[44]The semicolon of both the early editions seems preferable to the comma of the Manuscript.

[45]The syntax here is very compressed, but the meaning seems to be "What else is there for us to live for except not to be defeated?"

[46]May possibly have been pronounced "ignomy" (a spelling variant of the word, according to the *OED*) in order to make the scansion of the line regular, but, as Fowler points out (115n), the word has four syllables at 6.383, and there is a possibility that the syllables between "y" and the "a" of "and" were elided.

[47]Satan is speaking what might have been truth for the classical authors but would have represented heresy to all Christians. Christian predestination is not fatalism. See William B. Hunter, "Heresies," in *Descent* and Ben Gray Lumpkin, "Fate in *Paradise Lost*," *Studies in Philology* 44 (1947): 56–68.

Who now triumphs, and in th' excess of joy
Sole reigning holds the Tyranny of Heav'n.[48]
  So spake th' Apostate° Angel, though in pain,   DEFECTOR   125
Vaunting aloud, but rackt with deep despare:
And him thus answer'd soon his bold Compeer.[49]
  O Prince, O Chief of many Throned Powers,
That led th' imbattelld Seraphim[50] to Warr
Under thy conduct,[51] and in dreadful deeds   130
Fearless, endanger'd Heav'ns perpetual King;
And put to proof his high Supremacy,
Whether upheld by strength, or Chance, or Fate,[52]
Too well I see and rue the dire event,[53]
That with sad overthrow and foul defeat   135
Hath lost us Heav'n, and all this mighty Host
In horrible destruction laid thus low,
As far as Gods[54] and Heav'nly Essences°   BEINGS
Can perish: for the mind and spirit remains
Invincible, and vigour soon returns,   140
Though all our Glory extinct,[55] and happy state
Here swallow'd up in endless misery.
But what if he our Conquerour, (whom I now
Of force[56] believe Almighty, since no less
Then such could hav orepow'rd such force as ours)   145
Have left us this our spirit and strength intire[57]
Strongly to suffer and support our pains,
That we may so suffice° his vengeful ire,   SATISFY
Or do him mightier service as his thralls
By right of Warr, what e're his business be   150
Here in the heart of Hell to work in Fire,
Or do his Errands in the gloomy Deep;[58]
What can it then avail though yet we feel
Strength undiminisht, or eternal being
To undergo eternal punishment?   155
Whereto with speedy words th' Arch-fiend reply'd.

---

[48]For a corrective to everything Satan says here, see his soliloquy at the beginning of Book 4, especially 37–61, in which he admits (to himself, at least) that God's service was easy and admits that he was only "boasting I could subdue / Th' Omnipotent" (85–86).

[49]One of equal rank or standing, but also comrade or fellow (see *OED* 1,2).

[50]There is hierarchy and rank in Heaven exemplified by the many orders of angels, including Seraphim, Cherubim, Thrones, Dominions, Dominations, and Powers, but since the Seraphim were the highest of the nine angelic orders, Milton often uses "Seraphim" to mean "angels of the better sort," and "Cherubim" to mean "lesser angels." The singular form of the Hebrew noun Seraphim is Seraph, of Cherubim, Cherub. Satan's "Fall'n Cherube" (below, 157), seems to be an insult. Milton may not take the ranking of the angels seriously. See West, *Milton and the Angels*, for discussions of the hierarchies of fallen and unfallen angels.

[51]"Under your leadership." *Conduct* has legal, military, and diplomatic meanings, suggesting "protection" and "superior responsibility." Satan is here supposed to be the mastermind of all plans of war on the part of the fallen angels.

[52]Beelzebub equates the three entities strength, chance, and fate, but nothing happens by chance in Milton's universe; see the note at line 116 above.

[53]"Regret the catastrophic outcome."

[54]Milton, along with many other interpreters, took Genesis 3.5 ("Ye shall be as gods") very literally: pagan idols (and their prototypes, the fallen angels) can be described as "gods," since they will someday be worshiped by idolaters. For the context, see Hughes, "'Devils to Adore.'"

[55]Milton seems to be omitting the normal English "be" between "Glory" and "extinct" and using verbs as if English were an inflected language. The image is of a flame being put out.

[56]The same as "perforce," meaning "of necessity."

[57]There may be no significance in the fact, but lines 146, 148, and 151 rhyme. See notes 20 and 21 above.

[58]God does treat the fallen angels as types of errandboys or drudges, since they have given up the freedom of acting on their own by their violation of their place in the world order. The unfallen angels, on the other hand, act of their free will in serving God. God is the "author of peace, . . . whose service is perfect freedom" ("The Second Collect, for Peace," *Book of Common Prayer*, 1559 ed.). Satan and his legions are self-willed slaves.

> Fall'n Cherube, to be weak is miserable
> Doing or Suffering:[59] but of this be sure,
> To do ought good never will be our task,
> But ever to do ill our sole delight,   160
> As being the contrary to his high will
> Whom we resist. If then his Providence
> Out of our evil seek to bring forth good,
> Our labour must be to pervert[60] that end,
> And out of good still° to find means of evil;   ALWAYS   165
> Which oft times may succeed, so as perhaps
> Shall grieve him, if I fail not,[61] and disturb[62]
> His inmost counsels from thir destind aim.
> But see the angry Victor hath recall'd
> His Ministers[63] of vengeance and pursuit   170
> Back to the Gates of Heav'n: the Sulphurous Hail
> Shot after us in storm, oreblown hath laid[64]
> The fiery[65] Surge, that from the Precipice
> Of Heav'n receiv'd us falling, and the Thunder,
> Wing'd with red Lightning and impetuous rage,   175
> Perhaps hath spent his shafts, and ceases now
> To bellow[66] through the vast and boundless Deep.
> Let us not slip th' occasion,[67] whether scorn,
> Or satiate fury yield it from our Foe.
> Seest thou yon dreary Plain, forlorn and wilde,[68]   180
> The seat of desolation, voyd of light,
> Save what the glimmering of these livid flames
> Casts pale and dreadful?[69] Thither let us tend°   MAKE OUR WAY
> From off the tossing of these fiery waves,
> There rest, if any rest can harbour there,   185
> And reassembling our afflicted Powers,[70]
> Consult how we may henceforth most offend°   ANNOY, CAUSE DIFFICULTY FOR
> Our Enemy, our own loss how repair,
> How overcome this dire Calamity,[71]
> What reinforcement we may gain from Hope,   190

---

[59]Leading an active or passive life, either accomplishing or enduring. If "All wickedness is weakness" (*Samson Agonistes* 834), however, the fallen angels are already both weak and miserable. Satan is insulting an angel of lower rank by calling him "Fall'n Cherube," but he himself is only the "Arch-fiend," or the highest-ranked demon.

[60]The words "pervert" and "perversion," with the literal meaning "someone who has turned away irrevocably (from God)," or "the act of turning away," echo throughout *Paradise Lost*, always used to describe a Satanic or demonic action. After Eve has turned aside from God in the Fall, Adam describes her act as "event perverse!" (9.405).

[61]The four qualifying words or phrases, "If then," "may," "perhaps," and "if I fail not," betray the fact that Satan is again expressing only self-doubt, not conviction.

[62]"To put out of its course" (*OED* 3).

[63]God's ministers (agents of good, human or divine) may perform unpleasant tasks in order to bring about providential results.

[64]The sense of "laid" as in "laid to rest": "caused to subside or abate."

[65]The MS has "This fiery . . . ."

[66]It is Moloch, not God, who has bellowed in his flight during the War in Heaven (6.362). Satan, in other words, is transferring the lack of dignity in his own forces, attributing it to God, who is diminished by being pictured only as "angry Victor."

[67]"Let us not lose the opportunity . . . ." The MS has a colon after "occasion." For those interested in finding acrostics in Milton, the initial letters in the four lines that begin here spell "LOST."

[68]Line 183 rhymes with 187 and 185 with 188 and 191.

[69]The MS of Book 1 has an exclamation point here, clearly an error.

[70]"Downcast armies," but the word *power* also signifies one of the angelic ranks.

[71]"This fateful disaster." The implication is that fate or some natural disaster is to blame for their situation, rather than their own free will. In Latin, **dirus** implies "evil-omened."

If not what resolution from despare.
   Thus Satan talking to his neerest Mate[72]
With Head up-lift above the wave, and Eyes
That sparkling blaz'd, his other Parts besides
Prone on the Flood, extended long and large   195
Lay floating many a rood,[73] in bulk as huge
As whom the Fables name of monstrous size,
Titanian, or *Earth-born*, that warr'd on *Jove*,
Briareos or *Typhon*,[74] who the Den
By ancient *Tarsus*[75] held, or that Sea-beast   200
Leviathan,[76] which God of all his works
Created hugest that swim th' Ocean stream:
Him haply slumbring on the *Norway* foam[77]
The Pilot of some small night-founder'd[78] Skiff,
Deeming some Island, oft, as Sea-men tell,   205
With fixed Anchor in his skaly rind
Moors by his side under the Lee,[79] while Night
Invests° the Sea, and wished Morn delayes:[80]
So stretcht out huge in length the Arch-fiend lay
Chain'd on the burning Lake, nor ever thence   210
Had ris'n or heav'd his head,[81] but that the will
And high permission of all-ruling Heaven
Left him at large to his own dark designs,[82]
That with reiterated crimes he might
Heap on himself damnation, while he sought   215
Evil to others, and enrag'd might see
How all his malice serv'd but to bring forth
Infinite goodness, grace and mercy shewn

---

[72]The choice of the word "Mate" here and elsewhere (see 238 below) suggests a perversion of the normal marriage relationship (as in "help-mate" or "helpmeet") between man and woman, as with the incestuous relationships among Satan, Sin, and Death. Compare Milton's youthful description of Hyacinth as Apollo's "dearly-loved mate" in "On the Death of a Fair Infant" 24.The word that Beelzebub uses of Satan, "Compeer," was also capable of being read ironically, meaning something like "fellow" or "buddy." Satan is a sea-serpent here, modeled after the sea-serpents in the *Aeneid* swimming toward Laocoon: "Rampant they were among the waves, their blood-red crests / Reared up over the water; the rest of them slithered along / The surface, coil after coil sinuously trailing behind them" (2.16–18).

[73]Not the synonym for "cross" but the unit of measurement, the fourth part of an acre.

[74]Briareos, who had serpent legs, and Typhon or Typhoeus, who had a serpent head, were either of the Giant or Titan races, but, since both races fought against Jove and both were punished by being buried beneath Mount Aetna in Sicily, they were often confused or conflated. The implication is that the rebel angels are monstrous and distorted beings and that they live in a fiery, chaotic, disruptive place like a volcano.

[75]The biblical city of Tarsus was in Cilicia, north of the island of Cyprus on the coast of Asia Minor; Pindar, amongst others, located Typhon's den in Cilicia (*Pythian Odes* 1.17).

[76]For the primary source for Leviathan as sea-monster, see Job 41.1, "Canst thou draw out leviathan with an hook? or his tongue with a cord which thou lettest down?"

[77]Milton's editor Newton recounted stories of fish off the coast of Norway being taken as islands, as reported by the cartographers and historians Olaus Magnus and Erik Pontoppidan (205n).

[78]The skiff has been foundered, in this case probably overtaken, by the night; compare *Comus* 207.

[79]On the leeward side, out of the wind.

[80]In this extended epic simile, Milton names a number of the sea beasts alluded to in classical Greek and Roman mythology. The Titans were giants who revolted against Jupiter or Jove, so that anything born of them would be of monstrous size; Briareos or Briareus was a giant with 100 hands and 50 heads who, like Satan, set himself up as equal to the Olympian gods (Hesiod, *Theogony* 820–68). Typhon or Typhoeus was also gigantic, a 100-headed brother of the Titans who revolted against Jupiter and the Olympian gods (Ovid, *Metamorphoses* 5.347–61); he was, along with Briareus, buried under Mount Etna. The huge sea beast Leviathan appears in many bodily forms in biblical commentary (he appears to be a crocodile in Job 41). Thomas Hobbes made him the metaphor for the modern state in *Leviathan* (1651). As the type of a deceptive monster, "Leviathan" became synonymous with Satan, and the story of mariners anchoring on his back only to be swept under to their death was as popular as the similar Will-o'-the-Wisp or *ignis fatuus* story. Ariosto pictures a similar beast in the *Orlando Furioso* 6.37, a whale so large its back seems to be an island.

[81]As in "heaved a sigh," but in this case raised his head with difficulty.

[82]God permits evil to exist (because free will cannot exist without the choice between good and evil) without in any way encouraging it. Here the image is very close to the proverbial "Give him [Satan, in this case] enough rope and he will hang himself."

ADAM & EVE

On Man by him seduc't,[83] but on himself
Treble confusion, wrath and vengeance pour'd.
Forthwith upright he rears from off the Pool   *SATAN GETS OUT OF THE LAKE*   220
His mighty Stature; on each hand the flames
Drivn backward slope thir pointing spires, and rowld
In billows, leave i'th'midst a horrid[84] Vale.
Then with expanded wings he stears his flight   *FLYS OFF*   225
Aloft, incumbent[85] on the dusky Air
That felt unusual weight,[86] till on dry Land
He lights, if it were Land that ever burn'd
With solid, as the Lake with liquid fire;[87]
And such appear'd in hue,° as when the force   FORM. APPEARANCE   230
Of subterranean wind transports a Hill
Torn from *Pelorus*,[88] or the shatter'd side   *VOLCANO*
Of thundring *Ætna*, whose combustible
And fewel'd entrals thence conceiving Fire,
Sublim'd with Mineral fury, aid the Winds,   235
And leave a singed bottom all involv'd[89]
With stench and smoak:[90] Such resting found the sole
Of unblest feet. Him followd[91] his next Mate,
Both glorying to have scap't the *Stygian*[92] flood
As Gods, and by thir own recover'd strength,   240
Not by the sufferance of supernal° Power.   HEAVENLY
    Is this the Region, this the Soil, the Clime,   *SATAN*
Said then the lost Arch-Angel, this the seat
That we must change for Heav'n, this mournful gloom   *LET'S GET USED TO IT*
For that celestial light? Be it so, since he   245
Who now is Sovran[93] can dispose and bid

---

[83]The word "seduc't" is important here because it differentiates the sin of humankind from that of Satan and the fallen angels: Satan and his crew are self-tempted and self-deceived; Adam and Eve are seduced (literally led aside from God) by Satan first. Therefore, Adam and Eve will be capable of regenerating goodness in themselves, and they will be able to ask grace and mercy of God (see 3.129–32). Satan is permitted or allowed by God to heap damnation on himself by an endless round of crimes and sins; the images used elsewhere are those of the cannon recoiling on itself, or the wave rolling back in something like an undertow.

[84]The word retains some of its Latin value of "spiked," since the flames are pointed.

[85]An adjective meaning "That lies . . . with its weight upon something else" (*OED* 1, citing this passage).

[86]The image of the air feeling unusual weight may be borrowed, as Thyer was the first to point out, from the *Fairie Queene* 1.11.18, which also describes a Satanic dragon, flying: " . . . The yielding aire, which nigh too feeble found / Her flitting parts, and element unsound, / To beare so great a weight." See Newton, 226n.

[87]The MS has a comma after "fire," and a semicolon after "hue." Both readings make sense, and choosing between them is difficult. I agree with Shawcross on this reading, but Hunter (in a letter to me) prefers the MS.

[88]One of the largest promontories of Sicily. Aetna, in turn, is the live volcano on Sicily, supposed by various ancient writers (possibly by Hesiod, *Theogony* 860) to be the burial place chosen by Jupiter for the defeated Titans (analogous to the fallen angels), and the forge of Vulcan (Milton's Mulciber, who also was ejected from Heaven). Earthquakes were supposed by some classical naturalists to be the result of underground winds; since the Aeolian island, between Sicily and Italy, were thought to be the home of the winds, it might be appropriate for a subterranean wind to blow a hill out of Pelorus.

[89]"Curved spirally," "Enfolded, enwrapped" (*OED* 1.a,b), with moral implications (if applied to people): "Not straightforward and open; underhand, covert, crooked" (*OED* 2).

[90]Lieb has noted the scatological humor, appropriate in satirizing Satanic eruptions from the earth or perversions of natural processes (*Dialectics* 28–34): an infernal "conceiving" produces the obscene "birth" of a fart, and the burning earth is a fit place to burn the feet of wandering fallen angels, as the feet of devils and sinners are perpetually burned in Dante's *Inferno*. "Sublim'd" is a technical term from alchemy meaning "converted from a solid substance by means of heat into vapor" (adapted from the *OED* definition of "sublimation"). The process of "conceiving" fire within an alchemist's retort (glass vessel) was supposed to make a solid substance into a vapor. See Frances Yates, *Giordano Bruno*, for general information about alchemy and hermeticism, in which Milton must have done some dabbling, to be aware of "thrice great *Hermes*" in "Il Penseroso." See also Edgar H. Duncan, "The Natural," and Wayne Shumaker, *The Occult Sciences*, 160–259, for a discussion of alchemy in the context of the followers of Giordano Bruno.

[91]I have emended the "followed" of *1674* to conform to the Manuscript, because the "followd" of the Manuscript represents a metrically accurate disyllable.

[92]The adjective formed from the name of the river Styx.

[93]The spelling of the early editions seems to indicate Milton's phonetic preference for a version of the English word with two syllables, "Sovran" instead of "sovereign," perhaps following the Italian form of the word, *sovrano*.

What shall be right: fardest° from him is best   FARTHEST
Whom reason hath equald, force hath made supream
Above his equals. Farewel happy Fields
Where Joy for ever dwells: Hail horrours, hail   250
Infernal world, and thou profoundest° Hell   DEEPEST
Receive thy new Possessor: One who brings
A mind not to be chang'd by Place or Time.
The mind is its own place, and in it self
Can make a Heav'n of Hell, a Hell of Heav'n.[94]   255
What matter where, if I be still the same,
And what I should be, all but less then he[95]
Whom Thunder hath made greater? Here at least
We shall be free; th' Almighty hath not built
Here for his envy,[96] will not drive us hence: 260
Here we may reign secure, and in my choyce
To reign is worth ambition though in Hell:
Better to reign in Hell, then serve in Heav'n.[97]
But wherefore let we then our faithful friends,
Th' associates and copartners of our loss   265
Lye thus astonisht on th' oblivious Pool,[98]
And call them not to share with us their part
In this unhappy Mansion,[99] or once more
With rallied Arms to try what may be yet
Regaind in Heav'n, or what more lost in Hell?   270
     So *Satan* spake, and him *Beelzebub*
Thus answer'd. Leader of those Armies bright,
Which but th' Omnipotent none could have foyld,°   DEFEATED
If once they hear that voyce, thir liveliest pledge
Of hope in fears and dangers, heard so oft   275
In worst extreams, and on the perilous edge[100]
Of battel when it rag'd, in all assaults
Thir surest signal, they will soon resume
New courage and revive, though now they lye
Groveling[101] and prostrate on yon Lake of Fire,   280

---

[94]Satan's thinking at this point is heretical and logically fallacious in that the mind may indeed be its own place, but the damned mind cannot make a Heaven of Hell, though the reverse may be true (the Epic Voice, for instance, does "venture down / The dark descent" to witness Hell but returns "safe" [3.19–21] to celestial and to earthly realms, untainted by the experience). Satan contradicts his present sentiments flatly later, when he says "Which way I flie is Hell; my self am Hell" (4.75).

[95]The confused syntax may indicate Satan's confusion of mind, but he seems to be saying that he is as great as anyone except for God, who is made greater than he only by the possession of the lightning bolt. Newton suggests, however, that "all but" might be read "albeit," though he prefers the former reading (257n).

[96]Envy is Satan's motive (see 35, above), which he here imputes to God.

[97]Again, Satan's sentiment makes him look like a kind of Sisyphus, noble in his damnation, yet he admits at the beginning of Book 4 that the "service" in Heaven was light and pleasurable and not "hard" (4.45).

[98]"Lie thus completely thunder-struck on the pool that induces forgetfulness." The river Lethe in the classical hell Tartarus had the power of inducing forgetfulness, but, as Fowler points out (266n), Milton's pool does not wash out the memory and woe of the fallen angels: they are said to long to drink of Lethe in 2.606–14.

[99]Not the modern sense of "grand house," but in the sense of the biblical "stopping place" (compare John 14.2: "In my father's house are many mansions"). See *OED* 2.a,c, and Nativity Ode 140, for reference to the "dolorous mansions" into which Hell is supposedly subdivided. The MS has a semicolon after "mansion."

[100]According to the metrics of the line, "perilous" should be a disyllable, and it might have been pronounced "parlous." The rule that the poet Robert Bridges proposed for understanding Milton's prosody here, however, is, "When unstressed vowels are separated by *l*, they may suffer 'elision' . . . " (30). Newton first pointed out that "edge" may refer to the Latin *acies*, which meant both the edge of a sharp knife and the edge of battle.

[101]Since Milton refers to a man turned into a "groveling Swine" in *Comus* 53, the image of groveling seems to devalue the "courage" mentioned in the previous line.

As we erewhile, astounded and amaz'd,
No wonder, fall'n such a pernicious highth.
   He scarce had ceas't when the superiour Fiend
Was moving toward the shoar; his ponderous shield
Ethereal temper,[102] massy,[103] large and round,   285
Behind him cast; the broad circumference
Hung on his shoulders like the Moon,[104] whose Orb
Through Optic Glass the *Tuscan* Artist views
At Ev'ning from the top of *Fesole*,
Or in *Valdarno*, to descry new Lands,   290
Rivers or Mountains in her spotty Globe.[105]
His Spear, to equal which the tallest Pine
Hewn on *Norwegian* hills, to be the Mast
Of some great Ammiral,[106] were but a wand,
He walkt with[107] to support uneasie steps   295
Over the burning Marle,° not like those steps   CLAY SOIL
On Heavens Azure,[108] and the torrid Clime
Smote on him sore[109] besides, vaulted with Fire;
Nathless[110] he so endur'd, till on the Beach
Of that inflamed Sea, he stood and call'd   300
His Legions, Angel Forms, who lay intrans't°   ENTRANCED, IN A TRANCE
Thick as Autumnal Leaves that strow the Brooks
In *Vallombrosa*, where th' *Etrurian* shades
High overarch't imbowr;[111] or scatterd sedge

---

[102]Presumably the metal of the shield has been tempered or hardened off in ether, thought to be a subtle element that existed only above the earthly sphere. A synonym for "ethereal" would be "heavenly."

[103]Not only massive, but, when applied to precious metals, "Occurring in mass; wrought in solid pieces, without hollow or alloy" (*OED* 1.a). Satan's shield, unlike Satan himself, is not hollow.

[104]Epic similes at least dating back to *Iliad* 19.373 compared the hero's shield to the moon, as did Spenser with Radigund's shield in *Faerie Queene* 5.5.3. Spenser also compares the round shield to the full moon.

[105]Galileo is the "*Tuscan* Artist," that is, the artisan/scientist who made the telescope and lived in Tuscany. Since Milton met Galileo in Florence most probably in 1638, his reference to Galileo in "*Fesole*" or "Fiesole" ("Faesulae" was the Roman spelling) and "*Valdarno*" (no specific place, but the region of the valley of the Arno) may be biographically significant. Galileo was famous for, among other things, his descriptions of the mountains of the moon in *Sidereus Nuncius* ("Heavenly Messenger"), first published in 1610. Milton's simile, along with that of the fallen leaves in Vallombrosa, has caused critics some confusion, since neither Vallombrosa nor Galileo may be pictured in a flattering way. The phrase "spotty Globe" implies that Galileo's moon is somehow imperfect, and the phrase "Tuscan Artist," which seems positive to a modern reader, may have meant "Tuscan artisan" or "Tuscan laborer" to Milton. See Harris, "Galileo as Symbol," and my "Art, Artists, Galileo and Concordances."

[106]The straight Norwegian fir was the tree of choice for ship masts. Here "Ammiral," in a spelling preferred by Milton and preserved in both editions and the *Paradise Lost* MS, means "flagship." According to the simile, the tallest straight piece of wood known to man would be only a small twig or walking stick ("wand" could mean either) when measured alongside the magnitude of Satan. He has an overly heavy or ponderous shield, but is supporting himself with a walking stick.

[107]The Manuscript has a comma at this point, which might make more grammatical sense in conjunction with the comma after "wand," making "He walkt with" into something like a non-restrictive clause. I have followed the practice of most editors, leaving the comma after "wand" but not restoring the comma after "with."

[108]"Azure" is used as a noun meaning "The unclouded vault of heaven" (*OED* 5.a, citing this passage), as well as the color of the heavens. The "vault" would be clear blue (the color azure) and would be a sphere solid enough to walk on (see Introduction, Cosmology). The MS has a semicolon after "Azure."

[109]"The torrid climate afflicted him grievously." Fire arcs above him (outside the sphere of Earth would be a sphere of fire, its heat more oppressive in a torrid zone).

[110]Milton's preferred spelling of "nevertheless," a form not uncommon in the seventeenth century. The disyllable fits the iambic pattern; a trisyllable would not.

[111]Critics argue over whether the simile of the Tuscan ("*Etrurian*," which is the same as "Etruscan") Vallombrosa, a monastery south of Florence that has brooks and, in autumn, fallen leaves in those brooks, is a positive or negative comparison, but all would agree that the simile has a rich and intentional ambiguity. The Italian word "Vallombrosa" suggests the ominous phrase from Psalm 23, "the valley of the shadow of death." Satan's legions are compared with numberless leaves, as the legions of the damned are in Dante's *Inferno* 3.112–15, where the image is of all leaves that fall in autumn. The verb "strow" implies negative confusion; but the image of shade-trees forming a high bower suggests more comforting surroundings, as with the bower of Adam and Eve. See the various discussions of what was originally a Vergilian simile in *Milton and Italy*, ed. DiCesare, especially those of Huttar and Harris.

Afloat, when with fierce Winds *Orion* arm'd[112]   305
Hath vext the Red-Sea Coast, whose waves orethrew
Busirus and his *Memphian* Chivalry,[113]
While with perfidious° hatred they pursu'd   TREACHEROUS
The Sojourners of *Goshen*,[114] who beheld
From the safe shore thir floating Carkases[115]   310
And broken Chariot Wheels, so thick bestrown
Abject and lost lay these, covering the Flood,
Under amazement of thir hideous change.   *THEY ARE IN A TRANCE*
He call'd so loud, that all the hollow Deep[116]
Of Hell resounded. Princes, Potentates,   315
Warriers, the Flowr of Heav'n, once yours, now lost,
If such astonishment[117] as this can sieze   *CALLING*
Eternal spirits; or have ye chos'n this place
After the toyl of Battel to repose
Your wearied vertue,° for the ease you find   STRENGTH   320
To slumber here, as in the Vales of Heav'n?
Or in this abject posture have ye sworn
To adore the Conquerour? who now beholds
Cherube and Seraph[118] rowling in the Flood
With scatter'd Arms and Ensigns,° till anon°   FLAGS   IMMEDIATELY   325
His swift pursuers from Heav'n Gates discern
Th' advantage, and descending tread us down
Thus drooping, or with linked Thunderbolts[119]
Transfix us to the bottom of this Gulfe.
Awake, arise, or be for ever fall'n.   330
     They heard, and were abasht,° and up they sprung   *THEY GET UP*   ASHAMED
Upon the wing, as when men wont to watch
On duty, sleeping found by whom they dread,
Rouse and bestir themselves ere well awake.
Nor did they not perceave the evil plight   335
In which they were, or the fierce pains not feel;
Yet to thir Generals Voyce they soon obeyd
Innumerable. As when the potent Rod   *Comparing to deed in Past*
                                      For Reference.

---

[112]Orion, whose sign in the zodiac, Orion's belt, was supposed to rise during a season of storms, is pictured stirring up the sedge of the Red Sea, to scatter it in numberless particles.

[113]The Pharaoh of the first fourteen chapters of Exodus had become by Milton's era the prototype of evil hard-heartedness, analogous to Satan when he hardens his heart toward God. "God wishes Pharaoh to let the people go, because he orders it: he does not wish it, because he hardens Pharaoh's heart .... He postponed the accomplishment of his will, which was the opposite of Pharaoh's, so that he might punish the latter all the more severely for his prolonged unwillingness" (*On Christian Doctrine* 1.4, Yale 6:177). The name Milton uses for Pharaoh, Busirus, is not in the English Bible, but as Fowler points out, George Sandys, commenting on Ovid, noted that "Busirus . . . is held to be that king of Aegipt who so grievously oppressed the Israelites . . . " (*Ovid's Metamorphosis. Englished Mythologiz'd and Represented in Figures* [1632]). Both "Pharaoh" and "Busirus" were generic names, and Milton may be conflating different pharaohs. What is important in the comparison, however, is the utter defeat of the hard-hearted tyrant Pharaoh, and the numberlessness of his drowned troops, the "floating Carkases."

[114]Goshen was the area in which the Israelites lived during the Egyptian captivity; it was protected by God from the various plagues visited on Egypt and the Egyptians. Thus the Israelites after the Exodus are the "Sojourners" (wanderers) who came from Goshen. The word *sojourners* is often used in the Bible for the Israelites in transit toward the Promised Land.

[115]The Israelites look back on the troops of Pharaoh, who have been hideously changed from living to dead as they drowned when the Red Sea returned to cover them. Moses and the children of Israel sing praise to the Lord triumphantly, "Pharaoh's chariots and his host hath he cast into the sea: his chosen captains also are drowned in the Red sea" (Exodus 15.4).

[116]The Manuscript reads "deeps," a plural which might be answered by the "Vales of Heav'n" in 321.

[117]Complete amazement, as if struck with a thunderclap (the word contains the Latin *tonare*, "to thunder").

[118]According to the *OED*, Milton apparently coined the singular form of this word (the plural is normally "seraphim") in English, deriving the singular from Hebrew usage, as with "cherub" and "cherubim." The King James Bible uses "seraphims" as the plural form.

[119]Probably a comparison with cannon-balls chained together, used in seventeenth-century artillery, which would indeed pin down or "transfix" an enemy.

Of *Amrams* Son in *Egypts* evill day
Wav'd round the Coast, up call'd a pitchy cloud   340
Of *Locusts*, warping on the Eastern Wind,
That ore the Realm of impious *Pharaoh* hung
Like Night, and darken'd all the Land of *Nile*:[120]
So numberless were those bad Angels seen
Hovering on wing under the Cope of Hell[121]   345
'Twixt upper, nether, and surrounding Fires;[122]
Till, as a signal giv'n, th' uplifted Spear
Of thir great Sultan[123] waving to direct
Thir course, in even ballance down they light
On the firm brimstone, and fill all the Plain;   350
A multitude, like which the populous North
Pour'd never from her frozen loyns, to pass
Rhene or the *Danaw*,[124] when her barbarous Sons
Came like a Deluge on the South, and spread
Beneath *Gibraltar*[125] to the *Lybian* sands.   355
Forthwith from every Squadron and each Band
The Heads and Leaders thither hast° where stood   HASTE
Thir great Commander; Godlike shapes and forms
Excelling human, Princely Dignities,
And Powers that earst in Heaven sat on Thrones;   360
Though of thir Names in heav'nly Records now
Be no memorial,[126] blotted out and ras'd
By thir Rebellion, from the Books of Life.[127]
Nor had they yet among the Sons of *Eve*
Got them new Names,[128] till wandring ore the Earth,   365
Through Gods high sufferance for the tryal of man,
By falsities and lyes the greatest part
Of Mankind they corrupted to forsake
God thir Creator, and th' invisible
Glory of him that made them, to transform   370
Oft to the Image of a Brute, adorn'd
With gay° Religions full of Pomp and Gold,   OSTENTATIOUS

---

[120]Amram's Son is Moses, who with his rod (endowed with magical powers by God) brought down the plague of locusts on Pharaoh and his people, followed by the plague of darkness; see Exodus 10.12–15. Compare the image of numberless troops under Pharaoh perishing in the closing of the Red Sea 306–13. The marginal notes to the Geneva Bible explain the process of God's hardening the heart of Pharaoh: "God hardeneth the heartes of the reprobat, that his [God's] glorie thereby might be the more set fourthe, Rom 9.17" (marginal gloss for Exodus 11.9–10 in the 1560 ed.).

[121]Since "cope (i.e., "vault") of heaven" was a proverbial phrase used by Chaucer and by Spenser, Milton's logic must be that Hell also has "over-arching canopy or vault" (*OED* 1) as well.

[122]Hell, vaulted with a cope like Heaven, is (unlike Heaven) enclosed by fire on all sides.

[123]Both "Sultan" and "General" (337) suggest tyranny, as do "Emperor" (378) and "barbarous" (353). Compare "*Barbaric*" at 2.4.

[124]The Rhine or the Danube; the allusion is to the invasions of the Vikings and Goths, moving southward through continental Europe into Libya. The phrase "frozen loyns" is consistent with the perversity embodied in Satan's relationship with Sin, his daughter whom his son Death rapes, and Death, his son who may be seen as his rival for Sin's affection.

[125]Possibly because of a foul-case error (the compositor's case contained an "e" where there should have been an "a"), the word is misspelled "*Gibralter*" in *1674*; I have corrected it according to Fletcher's surmise in his note (3:101). The word is "Gibraltar" in the Manuscript.

[126]I have restored the comma of *1667* and the Manuscript, missing from *1674*.

[127]The bodies of the fallen angels still resemble the princely and even godlike forms they possessed when they sat on lesser thrones surrounding the throne of God in Heaven, but in fact their forms now represent "God-like imitated State" (2.511) and their names have been blotted out of the "book of life" of Revelation 3.5, as if they had never existed; so they are doomed never to be remembered in Heaven. See Leonard, *Naming*, 67–85.

[128]Though "Sons of *Eve*" may only mean "humankind," there was an extra-biblical legend that the "Sons of God" (Genesis 6.1–4) cohabited with the "Daughters of Men" and begot a race of demonic giants. Christian commentators associated the "Sons of God" with the fallen angels, some of whom they thought had become the deities worshipped by tribes warred on by the tribes of Israel. See Evans, Paradise Lost *and the Genesis Tradition*, 55. See also Arnold Williams, *The Common Expositor* and "Renaissance Commentaries on 'Genesis' and Some Elements of the Theology of *Paradise Lost*," *PMLA* 56 [1941]: 151–64. Milton will employ the legend again, and expand on it at length in 11.607–27.

And Devils to adore for Deities:
Then were they known to men by various Names,
And various Idols through the Heathen World.[129]   375
Say, Muse, thir Names then known, who first, who last,
Rous'd from the slumber, on that fiery Couch,
At thir great Emperors call, as next in worth *SATAN IS THE EMPEROR*
Came singly where he stood on the bare strand,
While the promiscuous° croud stood yet aloof?   DISORDERED   380
The chief were those who from the Pit of Hell
Roaming to seek thir prey on earth, durst fix
Thir Seats[130] long after next the Seat of God,
Thir Altars by his Altar,[131] Gods ador'd
Among the Nations round, and durst abide   385
Jehovah thundring out of *Sion*, thron'd
Between the Cherubim;[132] yea, often plac'd
Within his Sanctuary it self thir Shrines,
Abominations; and with cursed things
His holy Rites, and solemn Feasts profan'd,   390
And with thir darkness durst affront his light.
First *Moloch,* horrid King besmear'd with blood
Of human sacrifice, and parents tears,
Though for the noyse of Drums and Timbrels loud
Thir childrens cries unheard, that past through fire   395
To his grim Idol. Him the *Ammonite*
Worshipt in *Rabba* and her watry Plain,
In *Argob* and in *Basan*, to the stream
Of utmost *Arnon*. Nor content with such
Audacious neighbourhood, the wisest heart   400
Of *Solomon*[133] he led by fraud to build   *LIST OF THE FALLEN ANGELS*
His Temple right against the Temple of God
On that opprobrious[134] Hill, and made his Grove
The pleasant Vally of *Hinnom, Tophet* thence
And black *Gehenna* call'd, the Type[135] of Hell.   405

---

[129]The passage 364–375 clearly explains how the fallen angels became idols. See Milton on idolatry—a subject very important to him—at 381–91 and in *On Christian Doctrine* 2.5, Yale 6:690–96.

[130]Local or regional habitations, as in "county seat" or "family seat."

[131]Alludes to contamination of various Old Testament holy places when they were replaced by pagan shrines, as in Solomon's practice, below 402.

[132]God instructed the Israelites to construct gold images of cherubim flanking the Ark of the Covenant (Exodus 25.18–21). In *On Christian Doctrine*, Milton distinguishes between veneration for those images and idolatry: "The images of cherubim ought not to be called idols because they were placed over the ark as representations not of gods but of God's ministers, so no one worshipped them, and they were manufactured at God's express command" (2.5, Yale 6: 693).

[133]Even the wisest of kings, Solomon, could be led (like Eve) by demonic fraud to become idolatrous. Milton notes "Salomon Gynaecocratumenus or Idolomargus aut Thysiazusae. Reg. I. II" ("Solomon woman-governed or idol-mad or [like the] women sacrificers—see 1 Kings 11"; quoted from Yale 8: 556) as a potential subject to dramatize in his notes in the Trinity MS. Belial characterizes Solomon as a victim of beguiling women in *Paradise Regain'd*:

> Women, when nothing else, beguil'd the heart
> Of wisest *Solomon*, and made him build,
> And made him bow to the Gods of his Wives. (2.169-71)

Solomon, because he built temples for the worship of the gods of his many wives, including one to "Chemosh, the abomination of Moab" (1 Kings 11.7; see line 406), was a type of uxoriousness, literally "wife-following," as Adam will be in *Paradise Lost*. Solomon, according to Milton in *On Christian Doctrine*, "is not blamed . . . for marrying many wives but for marrying foreign ones" (1.10; Yale 6: 367). Building an idolatrous temple was a profanation and a pollution of holy land, causing the once pleasant valley of Hinnom (2 Kings 23.10) to become Tophet, for the Christians a type of Hell. The old Solomon in 1 Kings 11 is said to have erected temples to the false gods of his many wives, including Ashtoreth and Chemosh, for which God rebuked him, taking the kingdom away from his lineage.

[134]"On that hill of shame" or "Hill of scandal," in 416.

[135]One of the few times outside of Books 11 and 12 Milton refers to the practice of typology, by which Old Testament images were taken to foreshadow those of the New, or pagan images were taken to be a prophetic shadow of Christian ones. See Madsen, *From Shadowy Types.*

Next *Chemos*, th' obscene dread of *Moabs* Sons,
From *Aroer*[136] to *Nebo*,[137] and the wild
Of Southmost *Abarim*; in *Hesebon*
And *Heronaim*, *Seons* Realm,[138] beyond
The flowry Dale of *Sibma* clad with Vines,   410
And *Eleale* to th' *Asphaltick* Pool.[139]
Peor his other Name, when he entic'd
Israel in *Sittim* on thir march from *Nile*
To do him wanton rites, which cost them woe.[140]
Yet thence his lustful Orgies he enlarg'd   415
Even to that Hill of scandal,[141] by the Grove
Of *Moloch* homicide, lust hard by hate;
Till good *Josiah* drove them thence to Hell.[142]
With these came they, who from the bordring flood
Of old *Euphrates* to the Brook that parts   420
Egypt from *Syrian* ground,[143] had general Names
Of *Baalim* and *Ashtaroth*,[144] those male,
These Feminine. For Spirits when they please
Can either Sex assume, or both; so soft
And uncompounded is thir Essence[145] pure,   425
Not ti'd or manacl'd with joynt or limb,
Nor founded on the brittle strength of bones,
Like cumbrous flesh; but in what shape they choose
Dilated or condens't,[146] bright or obscure,°   DARK
Can execute thir aerie purposes,   430
And works of love or enmity fulfill.[147]

---

[136]For Aroer, see Deuteronomy 3.12. *1674* reads "*Aroar*," which, as Fletcher points out, probably indicates foul case (picking up an *a* from the case supposed to hold the letter *e*). The Manuscript and *1667* read "*Aroer*."

[137]See Isaiah 15.2: " . . . Moab shall howl over Nebo . . . ." Nebo is a mountain mentioned in Deuteronomy 32.49. The context is the defeat of the idolatrous people of Moab, causing the "fields of Heshbon [to] languish, and the vine of Sibmah" (Isaiah 16.8). Horonaim is mentioned in Isaiah 15.5, Hesebon is Heshbon in the Authorized Version; Abarim is connected with Nebo in Numbers 33.47.

[138]Sihon ("Seon") was king of the Amorites (Numbers 21.26), who took the cities Heshbon and Heronaim from the Moabites. Eleale was another Moabite city.

[139]The "*Asphaltick* Pool" is the Dead Sea, called "*lacus Asphaltites*" because of its "bituminous scum" (Fowler 407–11n). The river Jordan flowed into the Dead Sea, and the river and the sea formed the borders of Moab on its southwest side. There is no good reason for "*Asphaltick*" to be in italics, since asphalt is a material, not a place name; but see Thomas N. Corns, *Notes and Queries* n.s. 29 (1982): 22–24, for the conjecture that compositors in various seventeenth-century printing houses may have set unfamiliar or foreign words in italics.

[140]After their release from the Egyptian captivity, the Israelites were led to worship Baal-peor, god of Moab, and to perform other acts of irreverence in Sittim or Shittim. "And Israel abode in Shittim, and the people began to commit whoredom with the daughters of Moab" (Numbers 25.1).

[141]The Mount of Olives, at this point in the history of Israel associated with idolatry, the worship of Baal-peor and Moloch.

[142]King Josiah ordered the removal of the artifacts, burned the groves and broke the idols of Baal and Moloch, Ashtoreth, and Chemosh (2 Kings 23.4, 10, 13–14). The marginal commentary of the Geneva Bible gives the gruesome detail that the worshipers of Moloch "smote on the tabret [a small drum] while their children were burning, that their crye shulde not be heard . . . " (2 Kings 23.10), a good reason for Milton to identify him as "*Moloch* homicide." Milton would have had an interest in Josiah as an iconoclast and as a type of Christ (the names Joshua and Josiah both were similar in Hebrew root to the name Jesus) in his role of cleansing the temple.

[143]The river Euphrates was considered old presumably because it was one of the first mentioned in the Bible (Genesis 2.14). The "brook" has been identified as the river Besor (Fowler 419–21n).

[144]The generic plural forms of groups of gods, the singular forms being Baal and Ashtoreth.

[145]As might be expected, the substance of angels, what they were made of, was hotly debated among theologians. As a definition of Milton's usage here, "Constituent substance" was the best that Samuel Johnson could provide (*OED* 2.c): the angels' essence is whatever constituted their substance.

[146]We will see evidence of Satan's (a fallen angel's) ability to dilate at 4.986–87, when he "Collecting all his might dilated stood, / Like *Teneriff* or *Atlas* unremov'd". In Satan's case the process of dilation is similar to the puffery or physical inflation associated with male animals during courtship rituals.

[147]The androgyny (they can assume either sex) and sexuality (they can make love or at least mingle essences) of angels will provide an important contrast with the separate "two great Sexes" (8.151) of Adam and Eve, as will the angelic ability to dilate or expand, which Satan will make use of in transforming himself into various shapes (as with cherub, seraph, toad, cormorant) which can be a deceitful disguise or the symbolic equivalent of his present moral condition. Satan, as the Bible instructs, can even change himself into an angel of light (2 Corinthians 11.14).

For these[148] the Race of *Israel* oft forsook
Thir living strength, and unfrequented left
His righteous Altar, bowing lowly down
To bestial Gods; for which thir heads as low   435
Bow'd down in Battel, sunk before the Spear
Of despicable foes. With these in troop
Came *Astoreth*,[149] whom the *Phœnicians* call'd
Astarte, Queen of Heav'n, with crescent Horns;
To whose bright Image nightly by the Moon   440
Sidonian Virgins paid thir Vows and Songs,
In *Sion* also not unsung, where stood
Her Temple on th' offensive Mountain, built
By that uxorious King, whose heart though large,
Beguil'd by fair Idolatresses, fell   445
To Idols foul. *Thammuz* came next behind,
Whose annual wound in *Lebanon* allur'd
The *Syrian* Damsels to lament his fate
In amorous dittyes all a Summers day,[150]
While smooth *Adonis* from his native Rock   450
Ran purple to the Sea, suppos'd with blood
Of *Thammuz* yearly wounded: the Love-tale
Infected *Sions* daughters with like heat,
Whose wanton passions in the sacred Porch
Ezekiel[151] saw, when by the Vision led   455
His eye survay'd the dark Idolatries
Of alienated *Judah*. Next came one
Who mourn'd in earnest, when the Captive Ark
Maim'd his brute Image, head and hands lopt off
In his own Temple, on the grunsel° edge,   THRESHOLD   460
Where he fell flat, and sham'd his Worshipers:[152]
Dagon his Name, Sea Monster, upward Man
And downward Fish: yet had his Temple high
Rear'd in *Azotus*, dreaded through the Coast
Of *Palestine*, in *Gath* and *Ascalon*   465
And *Accaron* and *Gaza's*[153] frontier bounds.

---

[148]The text of *1667* reads "these," but whether "these" or the "those" of *1674* is correct seems impossible to determine here, though the Manuscript reads "these." The Columbia editors do not note the variant. Most modern editors, including Fowler, Campbell, and Orgel and Goldberg, choose "those," but Shawcross chooses "these." Notice "these" at 437 below.

[149]Astoreth, Ashtoreth, or Astarte was the *Sidonian* (from Sidon in Phoenicia, hence Phoenician) combination of Diana and Venus, a goddess with the head of a bull whose horns resembled a crescent moon. Milton calls her "mooned *Ashtaroth*" in the Nativity Ode 200. In Jeremiah 44.17–20, the wives of Israelites in Egypt were disowned by God for "burn[ing] incense to the queen of heaven" in idolatry.

[150]A religion summarized in four lines. Thammuz or Tammuz, the lover of Astarte, appears in Ezekiel 8.14, where the prophet is being shown idolatrous "abominations": "at the gate of the Lord's house . . . behold, there sat women weeping for Tammuz." The story of Thammuz was familiar to Milton's readers through accounts in Thomas Fuller's *A Pisgah Sight of Palestine* (4.7.43) and George Sandys's *A Relation of a Journey*, 1615 (Fowler 446n). His worship was connected with fertility cycles, and his festival was held after the summer solstice. Pictured as a youthful god, Thammuz, like Adonis, was slain by a wild boar. The **river** Adonis, when it was stirred up by rain so that its red mud was revealed, was supposed to flow with the blood of Thammuz. See the Nativity Ode 204: "In vain the *Tyrian* Maids their wounded *Thammuz* mourn."

[151]Milton's preferred spelling for this name may have been "Ezechiel" (the Manuscript uses that form) rather than the conventional "Ezekiel."

[152]The image of the god Dagon, when confronted with the power of the ark of God, fell flat on its face, the statue beheaded and dismembered (1 Samuel 5.4). Milton chose with Fuller (2.10.32) to picture Dagon as a fish-god. Dagon will become important as the chief Philistine deity at Gaza in *Samson Agonistes* and Samson's adversary, whose temple he destroys at the end of the tragedy.

[153]Milton uses the Latin Vulgate and Junius/Tremellius forms of each name, as opposed to the Authorized Version's "Ashdod," "Askelon" and "Ekron." See 1 Samuel 5. Note the apostrophe with possessive forms: the usual practice in *1674* is **not** to use the apostrophe with possessives, but this apostrophe might reflect the compositor's use of *1667*, which includes an apostrophe atypical for that volume. See also "*Ely's*" at 495 with the apostrophe, "*Javans*" without it at 508, and then "*Rhea's*" at 513. To make the matter more confusing to a modern reader, seventeenth-century orthography sometimes used

Him follow'd *Rimmon*, whose delightful Seat
Was fair *Damascus*, on the fertil Banks
Of *Abbana* and *Pharphar*, lucid streams.[154]
He also against the house of God was bold: 470
A Leper once he lost and gain'd a King,
Ahaz his sottish° Conquerour, whom he drew   FOOLISH
Gods Altar to disparage and displace
For one of *Syrian* mode, whereon to burn
His odious offrings, and adore the Gods   475
Whom he had vanquisht. After these appear'd
A crew who under Names of old Renown,
Osiris, *Isis*, *Orus* and thir[155] Train
With monstrous shapes and sorceries abus'd
Fanatic *Egypt* and her Priests, to seek   480
Thir wandring Gods disguis'd in brutish forms
Rather then human. Nor did *Israel* scape
Th' infection when thir borrow'd Gold compos'd
The Calf in *Oreb:* and the Rebel King
Doubl'd that sin in *Bethel* and in *Dan*,   485
Lik'ning his Maker to the Grazed Ox,[156]
Jehovah, who in one Night when he pass'd
From *Egypt* marching, equal'd with one stroke
Both her first born and all her bleating Gods.[157]
Belial[158] came last, then whom a Spirit more lewd   490
Fell not from Heaven, or more gross to love
Vice for it self: To him no Temple stood
Or Altar smoak'd; yet who more oft then hee
In Temples and at Altars, when the Priest
Turns Atheist, as did *Ely's* Sons, who fill'd   495
With lust and violence the house of God.
In Courts and Palaces he also Reigns
And in luxurious Cities, where the noyse
Of riot ascends above thir loftiest Towrs,
And injury and outrage: And when Night   500
Darkens the Streets, then wander forth the Sons
Of *Belial*, flown° with insolence and wine.   INFLATED
Witness the Streets of *Sodom*, and that night

---

apostrophes with simple plurals, as with "seat's" at line 796.

[154]Rimmon was a god of the Syrians who had a temple at Damascus located at the juncture of the two rivers (2 Kings 5.12–18). Naaman, a Syrian cured of leprosy by Elisha, turned from worshiping Rimmon (presumably) to worship the god of Israel (2 Kings 5.17), and King Ahaz did the opposite.

[155]One of several spellings altered in different proof-stages of *1674*; "their" becomes "thir." The same happens at 499.

[156]See Psalm 106.19–20: "They made a calf in Horeb, and worshipped the molten image. Thus they changed their glory into the similitude of an ox that eateth grass." King Jeroboam doubled the sin by making two golden calves (1 Kings 12.28–30).

[157]Jupiter Ammon was worshiped as a ram (Newton citing Pearce 482n). In Exodus 12.29, God destroys all the first-born in Egypt, man and beast, and executes judgment on all the Egyptian gods as well.

[158]The portraits of Moloch and Belial, at the beginning and the end of this catalogue of false Old Testament gods, prepare the reader for their part in the debate in Book 2. Belial was associated by Milton with lewdness and lasciviousness, perverse sexuality, excessive sensuality, urban riot, drunkenness, sloth, and sophisticated aristocratic luxury. He is the epitome of everything a good Puritan should despise. Lewd or profligate men were known generically in the Old Testament as "the children of Belial" (Deuteronomy 13.13) or "sons of Belial" (1 Samuel 2.12, referring to the sons of Eli; Judges 19.22). William B. Hunter, in "Belial's Presence," argues that he is intrusive here, added to an earlier version of the text because of the unusual number of lines given him and the wrong position of those lines (he belongs with the Palestinian gods, not between the Egyptian and Greek ones), and my "Belial and 'Effeminate Slackness'" argues that Milton had a fascination with the character of Belial.

In *Gibeah*, when the hospitable[159] door
Expos'd a Matron to avoid worse rape.[160]   505
These were the prime in order and in might;
The rest were long to tell, though far renown'd,
Th' *Ionian* Gods, of *Javans*[161] Issue held
Gods, yet confest later then Heav'n and Earth
Thir boasted Parents; *Titan*[162] Heav'ns first born   510
With his enormous brood, and birthright seis'd
By younger *Saturn*, he from mightier *Jove*
His own and *Rhea's* Son like measure found;
So *Jove* usurping reign'd: these first in *Creet*
And *Ida* known, thence on the Snowy top   515
Of cold *Olympus* rul'd the middle Air[163]
Thir highest Heav'n; or on the *Delphian* Cliff,
Or in *Dodona*, and through all the bounds
Of *Doric* Land; or who with *Saturn* old
Fled over *Adria* to th' *Hesperian* Fields,
And ore the *Celtic* roam'd the utmost Isles.[164]   520
All these and more came flocking; but with looks
Down cast and damp,° yet such wherein appear'd   DEJECTED, DEPRESSED
Obscure some glimps of joy, to have found thir chief
Not in despair, to have found themselves not lost
In loss itself; which on his count'nance cast   525
Like doubtful hue: but he his wonted pride
Soon recollecting, with high words, that bore
Semblance of worth, not substance, gently rais'd

---

[159]In this case a word that normally means "affording welcome" (*OED* 1) seems to be used ironically, to mean "looking as if it were welcoming, when really it will provide death instead."

[160]The text of *1667* reads: "In *Gibeah*, when hospitable Dores / Yielded thir Matrons to prevent worse rape . . . ." The Manuscript, like *1667*, substitutes "avoid" for "prevent." Milton caught his error in the plural "Matrons," since only one maidservant is mentioned in Judges 19, and only one door. "Yielded" is the wrong verb, since the one maidservant is indeed "Expos'd" or set outside defenseless. The "worse rape" is homosexual sodomy; nevertheless, the maidservant is raped to death in the account in Judges. Milton seems to have been especially interested in the story as an example of misdirected brutality with tragic implications (the rape led to tribal retribution). For evidence that Milton did indeed dwell on the passage, see the stage directions in *Comus* following line 22, where Comus's rout is described in terms of the rioters of Judges 19.

[161]Javan was one of the sons of Japheth, who in turn was one of the three sons of Noah (Genesis 10.2). The sons of Javan were " . . . Elishah, and Tarshish, Kittim, and Dodanim. / By these were the isles of the Gentiles divided in their lands; every one after his tongue, after their families, in their nations" (10.4–5). The names of descendants of Noah were used to explain the genealogies of nations and the distribution of languages. The marginalia of the Geneva Bible note "Of Madai, & Javan came the Medes and Grekes" (10.4n); thus the Ionian (Greek) gods came from Javan's issue (his descendants).

[162]Milton explains the origins and genealogy of the Greek and Roman gods. Titan, identified by Vergil with the sun, was the eldest son of Earth and Sky, and his brothers were the Titans, giants ruling over natural forces. Titan gave his brother Saturn the rule, as long as he had no male offspring. Rhea, daughter of Sky and Earth, married Saturn and gave birth to Vesta, Ceres, Juno, Pluto, and Neptune, but Saturn devoured his children as soon as they were born. Rhea then concealed the birth of her son Jupiter. Titan and his brothers made war on Saturn and imprisoned him. Jupiter overcame the Titans, driving them literally underground, freeing his father Saturn only to have to drive him from his kingdom when Saturn conspired to have Jupiter killed. Jupiter subsequently freed his brothers and sisters, who became the gods and goddesses first associated with Crete and Mount Ida, then with Mount Olympus. Milton concentrates on the instability of the Greek hierarchy of gods, and makes them all descendants of the biblical Javan.

[163]The middle air, as compared with the "highest Heav'n" (1.517) where the Christian God lived, was traditionally the realm of demons, since Satan was supposed to control tempests engendered there (Svendsen 99). Compare *Paradise Regain'd* 4.409–16.

[164]Milton disparages the Greek and Roman gods by allowing them only to rule the middle air, traditionally the region of demons, and by concentrating on their confused history of war and usurpation, ignoble flight, and homeless wandering. Milton makes Jupiter appear in Delphi (more often associated with the shrine of Apollo located there), Dodona (the home of the ancient oracle of Jupiter), and "*Doric* Land" (Greece); Saturn flees over the Adriatic Sea to Italy ("*Hesperian* Fields," since the Greeks associated Italy with the place where the western sun set), France ("the *Celtic*," France being known in classical tradition as the home of the Celtic peoples), all the way to the British Isles ("*ultima Thule*," or "the utmost Isles"). Compare the associations noted by Hunter (*Milton's* 40–44) in *Comus* 39–40 between Saturn's island, guarded by Briareus and home to Calypso, and the islands of Anglesey and Man.

Thir fainted[165] courage, and dispel'd thir fears.   530
Then strait° commands that at the warlike sound   IMMEDIATELY
Of Trumpets loud and Clarions[166] be upreard
His mighty Standard; that proud honour claim'd
Azazel[167] as his right, a Cherube tall:
Who forthwith from the glittering Staff unfurld   535
Th' Imperial Ensign, which full high advanc't
Shon like a Meteor streaming to the Wind
With Gemms and Golden lustre rich imblaz'd,
Seraphic arms and Trophies:[168] all the while
Sonorous mettal blowing Martial sounds: 540
At which the universal Host upsent
A shout that tore Hells Concave, and beyond
Frighted the Reign° of *Chaos* and old Night.   REALM, KINGDOM
All in a moment through the gloom were seen
Ten thousand Banners rise into the Air   545
With Orient° Colours waving: with them rose   BRILLIANT, EXOTIC
A Forrest huge of Spears: and thronging Helms
Appear'd, and serried[169] Shields in thick array
Of depth immeasurable: Anon they move
In perfect *Phalanx* to the *Dorian* mood°   MODE   550
Of Flutes and soft Recorders; such as rais'd
To hight of noblest temper Hero's° old   HEROES
Arming to Battel,[170] and in stead of rage
Deliberate valour breath'd, firm and unmov'd
With dread of death to flight or foul retreat,   555
Nor wanting power to mitigate and swage
With solemn touches, troubl'd thoughts, and chase
Anguish and doubt and fear and sorrow and pain
From mortal or immortal minds. Thus they
Breathing united force with fixed[171] thought   560
Mov'd on in silence to soft Pipes that charm'd
Thir painful steps o're the burnt soyle; and now
Advanc't in view, they stand, a horrid° Front   BRISTLING
Of dreadful length and dazling Arms, in guise

---

[165]An editor must make a choice here among the reading of *1674*, "fanting," which makes no sense, "fainted" of *1667* and the Manuscript, or "fainting," the emendation first made in the 1678 third edition. I believe "fainted" is the best choice of the three, because Milton did use it as an adjective (as well as "fainting") in his prose, specifically in *Areopagitica* (Yale 1: 119). Darbishire is with me in this case: most of the other modern editors, including Shawcross, Campbell, and Orgel and Goldberg, are not.

[166]Shrill war trumpets, as distinguished from the peaceful musical instrument (see *OED* 1, which cites this passage).

[167]Cornelius Agrippa names Azazel as one of the four evil angels corresponding to Michael, Raphael, Gabriel, and Uriel, each of whom ruled one compass point in the cosmos (West, *Angels* 68). Thus Azazel would be one of the standard-bearers in battle and would control pestilence or disease supposed to be coming on the wind from his direction. Both in the Bible proper and in the Apocrypha, the name Azazel is the Hebrew equivalent of English "scapegoat" (Enoch 10.4–8; Leviticus 16.8; see West 156). The use of Azazel indicates that Milton knew of various cabbalistic, or supra-biblical traditions, as popularized by Robert Fludd and Johann Reuchlin.

[168]Meteors were traditional emblems of catastrophe and therefore associated by Christians with demonic influence on global environment; the ensign, or banner, displays a variety of seraphic coats of arms and symbolic trophies, as did Roman officials in triumphal processions. Such processions were echoed in Renaissance public ceremony. See Edmund A. Bowles, *Musical Ensembles in Festival Books 1500–1800: An Iconographical & Documentary Survey* (Ann Arbor: UMI Research P, 1989) for many illustrations of musical pageantry over all of western Europe.

[169]"Of files or ranks of armed men: Pressed close together, shoulder to shoulder, in close order." (*OED* ppl.a. 1, citing this instance).

[170]The Dorian was one of the eight classical musical modes, supposed in seventeenth-century music theory to be ideal for the music of war. Milton associated the Dorian mode with "grave" or serious music (*Areopagitica*; Yale 2: 523). The use of the square phalanx (sixteen ranks of men armed with pikes in an impenetrable formation) in war would have been appropriate both in the classical era, since Alexander the Great employed it, and in the Renaissance, when square formations of men and machinery were deployed in battle. See Freeman, *Martial*.

[171]Note that the spelling here and in "armed" below, 567, indicates that the words are disyllables.

Of Warriers old[172] with order'd Spear and Shield,   565
Awaiting what command thir mighty Chief
Had to impose: He through the armed Files
Darts his experienc't eye, and soon traverse[173]
The whole Battalion views, thir order due,
Thir visages and stature as of Gods,   570
Thir number last he summs. And now his heart
Distends with pride, and hardning in his strength
Glories:[174] For never since created man,[175]
Met such imbodied force,[176] as nam'd with these
Could merit more then that small infantry[177]   575
Warr'd on by Cranes: though all the Giant brood
Of *Phlegra*[178] with th' Heroic Race were joyn'd
That fought at *Theb's* and *Ilium*, on each side
Mixt with auxiliar Gods; and what resounds
In Fable or *Romance* of *Uthers* Son   580
Begirt with *British* and *Armoric* Knights;[179]
And all who since, Baptiz'd or Infidel[180]
Jousted in *Aspramont*[181] or *Montalban*,[182]
Damasco,[183] or *Marocco*, or *Trebisond*
Or whom *Biserta* sent from *Afric* shore[184]   585
When *Charlemain* with all his peerage fell
By *Fontarabbia*. Thus far these beyond
Compare of mortal prowess, yet observ'd
Thir dread commander: he above the rest
In shape and gesture proudly eminent   590
Stood like a Towr; his form had yet not lost

---

[172]Milton uses the phrase "Warriers old" or "Hero's old" (552) as formulas from romantic epic, "warriors of old" or "heroes of olden times." The effect is one of antiquing, for satirical purposes.

[173]Soon he "views traverse(ly) (i.e., crosswise; in rank, not in file) the whole battalion" (Loh 568–69n; see *OED* C). Compare 3.488, or *Samson Agonistes* 209, for the use of the similar *transverse* as adverb.

[174]Compare the references to Pharaoh's hardening his heart in note 120 above.

[175]"For never since man was created." The past participle "created" is used as if it were part of a Latin ablative absolute construction.

[176]"Met such a force in one body."

[177]Joseph Addison thought the word "infantry" a pun on "infant" (*Spectator* 297; 9 February 1712, as noted by Fowler 575n). If Satan's forces are to be viewed from God's perspective as childlike, battles with them will be as ridiculous as the classically famous war between cranes and pygmies. Though Satan's pride in his united troops is justified, Milton undercuts the force of the fallen angels, weakened morally by despair, by comparing them to the pygmies (see 780 below).

[178]The combat between the Giants and the Greek gods was supposed to have begun in Phlegra in Macedonia and ended in Phlegra in Italy. See Ovid, *Metamorphoses* 10.151. Often the Titans and Giants were confused in literary usage, though the Giants are said to have been buried under volcanoes in various parts of Greece and Italy.

[179]Milton is lumping the "Matter of Greece" with the "Matter of England" and the "Matter of France": Homer's heroic warfare in the *Iliad* and *Odyssey*; the legends of King Arthur and his knights; and the similar set of legends surrounding Charlemagne. Those three bodies of legend are contrasted with his own "greater" argument. Milton had seriously considered writing an epic based on Arthurian legends, probably in the allegorical mode of Spenser's *Faerie Queene*, in "*Ad Mansus*." Uther's son is Arthur. "Armoric Knights" are knights from Brittany, so called from Armorica, Caesar's name for the region encompassing Brittany and Normandy in northern France.

[180]The names are those of regions popularized by the famous Renaissance epics of Boiardo, *Orlando Innamorato* ("Orlando in Love"), of Ariosto, *Orlando Furioso* ("Orlando Insane"), and of Tasso, *Gerusalemme Liberata* (translated as *Jerusalem Delivered*). Most of the Renaissance epics dealt with the conflict between Moor ("Infidel") and Christian ("Baptiz'd").

[181]A castle near Nice where Charlemagne had fought. See Ariosto, *Orlando Furioso* 17.14, where it is "Aspromont."

[182]The castle of the Renaissance Italian hero Rinaldo, who plays a major part in Luigi Pulci's comic epic, *Morgante Maggiore* (literally "Morgante the Greater"), and in the epics of Boiardo and Ariosto.

[183]Damascus, where Christians and Saracens joust in *Orlando Furioso* in Canto 17.

[184]Bizerta, Tunisia, is the seat of King Agramont in *Orlando Furioso* 18.158. Trebisond and Morocco (the city more than the country at large) were also famed in Renaissance epics as the sites of tournaments.

All her[185] Original brightness, nor appear'd
Less then Arch Angel ruind, and th' excess
Of Glory obscur'd: As when the Sun new ris'n   595
Looks through the Horizontal misty Air
Shorn of his Beams, or from behind the Moon
In dim Eclips disastrous twilight sheds
On half the Nations, and with fear of change
Perplexes Monarchs. Dark'n'd so, yet shon
Above them all th' Arch Angel: but his face   600
Deep scars of Thunder had intrencht, and care
Sat on his faded cheek, but under Browes
Of dauntless courage,[186] and considerate° Pride,   PREMEDITATED
Waiting revenge: cruel his eye, but cast
Signs of remorse and passion to behold   605
The fellows of his crime, the followers rather[187]
(Far other once beheld in bliss) condemn'd
For ever now to have thir lot in pain,
Millions of Spirits for his fault amerc't°   DEPRIVED, PUNISHED
Of Heav'n, and from Eternal Splendors flung   610
For his revolt, yet faithfull how they stood,
Thir Glory witherd. As when Heavens Fire
Hath scath'd° the Forrest Oaks, or Mountain Pines,   SCORCHED
With singed top thir stately growth though bare
Stands on the blasted Heath. He now prepar'd   615
To speak; whereat thir doubl'd Ranks they bend
From wing to wing, and half enclose him round
With all his Peers: attention held them mute.
Thrice he assayd, and thrice in spight of scorn,
Tears such as Angels weep, burst forth:[188] at last   620
Words interwove with sighs found out thir way.
    O Myriads of immortal Spirits, O Powers
Matchless, but with th' Almighty, and that strife
Was not inglorious, though th' event was dire,[189]
As this place testifies, and this dire change   625
Hateful to utter: but what power of mind
Foreseeing or presaging, from the Depth
Of knowledge past or present, could have fear'd,
How such united force of Gods, how such
As stood like these, could ever know repulse?
For who can yet beleeve, though after loss,   630
That all these puissant° Legions, whose exile
Hath emptied Heav'n, shall fail to re-ascend   POWERFUL

---

[185]Milton may be thinking of the Latin and Italian gender of the word "*forma*," which causes him to choose a feminine possessive pronoun, as with "she" used for Latin "*navis*," ship.

[186]The Manuscript here has "valour." The change from "valour" to "courage" is substantive and seems to be an authorial change rather than a typographical error; therefore I have left the word as in both printed versions.

[187]An important distinction, since it makes Satan the "prime cause" of the fall in the angels as well as in man. Followers are not the same as fellows, though the fact that the evil angels were followers does not exempt them from responsibility for their individual choice for evil: they are "self-tempted, self-deprav'd" (3.130). William B. Hunter believes "Milton evidently hears a pun of sorts in the two words" (letter, July 1991).

[188]Theologians had argued over whether angels could weep, but Milton cleverly accommodates the image by hedging: if Satan did weep, it would be with tears such as angels weep, beyond human comprehension.

[189]"The outcome was catastrophic."

Self-rais'd,[190] and repossess thir native seat?
For mee be witness all the Host of Heav'n,   635
If counsels different, or danger shun'd
By mee, have lost our hopes. But he who reigns
Monarch in Heav'n, till then as one secure
Sat on his Throne, upheld by old repute,
Consent or custome,[191] and his Regal State   640
Put forth at full, but still his strength conceal'd,
Which tempted our attempt,[192] and wrought our fall.
Henceforth his might we know, and know our own
So as not either to provoke, or dread
New warr, provok't; our better part remains   645
To work in close° design, by fraud or guile   SECRET
What force effected not: that he no less
At length from us may find, who overcomes
By force, hath overcome but half his foe.
Space may produce new Worlds; whereof so rife   650
There went a fame° in Heav'n that he ere long   RUMOR
Intended to create, and therein plant
A generation, whom his choice regard
Should favour equal to the Sons of Heaven:
Thither, if but to pry, shall be perhaps   655
Our first eruption,[193] thither or elsewhere:
For this Infernal Pit shall never hold
Cælestial Spirits in Bondage, nor th' Abyss
Long under darkness cover. But these thoughts
Full Counsel must mature: Peace is despaird,   660
For who can think Submission? Warr then, Warr
Open or understood must be resolv'd.

   He spake: and to confirm his words, out-flew
Millions of flaming swords, drawn from the thighs[194]
Of mighty Cherubim; the sudden blaze   665
Far round illumin'd hell: highly they rag'd
Against the Highest, and fierce with grasped Arms
Clash'd on thir sounding Shields the din of war,
Hurling defiance toward the Vault of Heav'n.

      There stood a Hill not far whose griesly top   670
Belch'd fire and rowling smoak; the rest entire
Shon with a glossie scurff,[195] undoubted sign
That in his womb was hid metallic Ore,[196]

---

[190]An obvious lie, since, though the evil angels can deceive and deprave themselves, they cannot raise themselves. It is only with God's permission that Satan can rise from the floor of Hell (see 210–20).

[191]Milton ironically allows Satan to use some of his own arguments against stale custom (Milton almost always used the word "custom" negatively) and "old repute," as in the use of "custom" in *Areopagitica* (Yale 2:565). Satan argues like a revolutionary and a regicide, wanting to dethrone the monarch of Heaven whom he imagines as "upheld by old repute."

[192]This kind of empty punning or double meaning, though sometimes practiced by good characters such as Ithuriel or even the Son, is more characteristic of demonic, and especially Satanic, rhetoric. Bad puns seem to be demonic perversions of language, with puns coming from good characters demonstrating healthy wit.

[193]The fallen angels, like the classical Giants, are allied with volcanoes, causing havoc above the earth derived from the heat and pressure issuing from Hell beneath it. Carrying the imagery of various bodies further, they are like pustules, indications of disease within.

[194]The scabbards for the swords, in other words, are on the thighs of the Cherubim.

[195]Scurf is a crust created by hardening of sulphur in combination with other components of volcanic flow, a "sulphurous deposit" (*OED* 3, citing this instance); it may or may not be glossy.

[196]"Womb" could be understood as "a place or medium of conception" (*OED* 2).

The work of Sulphur. Thither wing'd with speed
A numerous Brigad[197] hasten'd. As when Bands   675
Of Pioners with Spade and Pickax arm'd
Forerun the Royal Camp, to trench a Field,
Or cast a Rampart. *Mammon* led them on,
Mammon, the least erected Spirit that fell
From heav'n, for ev'n in heav'n his looks and thoughts   680
Were always downward bent, admiring more
The riches of Heav'ns pavement, trod'n Gold,[198]
Then aught divine or holy else enjoy'd
In vision beatific; by him first
Men also, and by his suggestion taught,   685
Ransack'd the Center, and with impious hands
Rifl'd the bowels of thir mother Earth
For Treasures better hid. Soon had his crew
Op'nd into the Hill a spacious wound
And dig'd out ribs° of Gold. Let none admire   VEINS   690
That riches grow in Hell; that soyle may best
Deserve the precious bane.°[199] And here let those   POISON
Who boast in mortal things, and wond'ring tell
Of *Babel*, and the works of *Memphian* Kings[200]
Learn how thir greatest Monuments of Fame,   695
And Strength and Art are easily out-done
By Spirits reprobate, and in an hour
What in an age they with incessant toyle
And hands innumerable scarce perform.
Nigh on the Plain in many cells prepar'd,   700
That underneath had veins of liquid fire
Sluc'd[201] from the Lake, a second multitude
With wond'rous Art found out[202] the massie[203] Ore,
Severing each kind, and scum'd[204] the Bullion dross:
A third as soon had form'd within the ground   705
A various mould, and from the boyling cells
By strange conveyance fill'd each hollow nook,
As in an Organ from one blast of wind
To many a row of Pipes the sound-board breathes.[205]
Anon out of the earth a Fabrick° huge   BUILDING   710

[VIOLENT LANGUAGE COLOURFUL CULTURE — handwritten annotation]

---

[197]Accented on the first syllable. The line is difficult to scan as iambic, until one makes the elision "num'rous."

[198]The streets of the City of God were supposed to be of "pure gold," as in Revelation 21.21, but Milton makes them resemble a "Sea of Jasper" in 3.363.

[199]A famous oxymoron, as with "darkness visible" (63). If, as many theologians argued, the root of all evil is *cupiditas*, or evil desire for earthly things, the search for gold in the bowels of the earth is a Christian evil as well as a classical one. See Ovid, *Metamorphoses* 1.125–42, for the idea that digging in the earth for wealth associated with Hades was evil. The Golden Age had already declined into the Silver, then the Bronze, and then the Iron Age, during which "The rich earth . . . Was asked for more; [men] dug into her vitals, Pried out the wealth a kinder lord had hidden / In Stygian shadow, all that precious metal, / The root of evil. They found the guilt of iron, / And gold, more guilty still" (trans. Humphries 7).

[200]Milton uses two proverbial examples of pride connected with material things: the Tower of Babel erected by the mighty and proud hunter Nimrod and his followers (see Hardin 38–44 and Genesis 10.8–10), and the pyramids and other monuments erected by Egyptian pharaohs at Memphis and elsewhere. The point of the comparison is that the fallen angels build more magnificently, in the twinkling of an eye, what it takes man ages to construct.

[201]Removed by sluices or drains beneath the lake.

[202]An often-debated textual crux, since *1667* and Manuscript both read "founded"; Fletcher conjectures that Milton meant to write "founded out" but the Third Edition of *1678* accepted "found out" and so do I.

[203]Solid, heavy, and of one piece, specifically used with metals (*OED* 1a).

[204]"Since the bullion is scum which is skimmed as dross from the molten mixture. Milton is perhaps building on the image of "glossie scurff" (672).

[205]I agree with Fletcher (3:115n) that "breaths" of *1667* and *1674* should be expanded, as noted for 5.193, in the *1668 Errata*. The compositor of *1667* apparently ran out of space at the end of the long line and shortened the last word to make it fit.

Rose like an Exhalation, with the sound
Of Dulcet Symphonies[206] and voices sweet,[207]
Built like a Temple, where Pilasters[208] round
Were set, and Doric pillars overlaid
With Golden Architrave; nor did there want   715
Cornice or Freeze, with bossy Sculptures[209] grav'n,
The Roof was fretted[210] Gold. Not *Babilon*,[211]
Nor great *Alcairo*° such magnificence   CAIRO
Equal'd in all thir glories, to inshrine
Belus or *Serapis*[212] thir Gods, or seat   720
Thir Kings, when *Ægypt* with *Assyria* strove
In wealth and luxurie. Th' ascending pile[213]
Stood fixt her stately highth, and strait the dores
Op'ning thir brazen foulds discover wide
Within, her ample spaces, o're the smooth   725
And level pavement: from the arched roof
Pendant by suttle Magic many a row
Of Starry Lamps and blazing Cressets° fed   BASKETS OF FIRE, FOR LIGHT
With *Naphtha* and *Asphaltus* yeilded[214] light
As from a sky. The hasty multitude   730
Admiring enter'd, and the work some praise
And some the Architect: his hand was known
In Heav'n by many a Towred structure high,
Where Scepter'd Angels held thir residence,
And sat as Princes, whom the supreme King   735
Exalted to such power, and gave to rule,
Each in his Hierarchie, the Orders bright.
Nor was his name unheard or unador'd
In ancient *Greece*; and in *Ausonian* land[215]

---

[206]"In the 17th century the term was used . . . for concerted motets, for introductory movements to operas etc., for instrumental introductions and sections within arias and ensembles, and for ensemble pieces which might be classified as sonatas or concertos" (*The Norton/Grove Concise Encyclopedia of Music*, ed. Stanley Sadie [New York: Norton, 1988]).

[207]Probably the key word for interpretive purposes here is "sweet," since the adjective usually has negative overtones in *Paradise Lost*; here it echoes "Dulcet," which means much the same thing. Music is not bad in itself, but demonic music is seductive and enervating, demoralizing those who hear it. Pouring the molten metal becomes the upside-down equivalent of what happens in an organ when "the sound-board breathes," whereby air is compressed and sent upward through brass pipes of varied size and length.

[208]Various critics have pointed out that Pan-demonium (Milton coined the word for what might be called the city hall of Hell) resembles the Pan-theon in Rome. There is no reason I can see for "*Pilasters*" to be italicized as it is in *1674*, other than that a sleepy compositor found it so in *1667*; the Manuscript reads "pilasters," with neither capitalization nor italics.

[209]Sculptures embossed or carved in relief. The modern meaning of "bossy," "demanding," was not current in 1667. An architrave is the "lowest division of the entablature, consisting of the main beam that rests immediately upon the abacus on the capital of a column" (*OED* 1, citing this passage). The frieze is the part of the column above the architrave, and the cornice is the part above the frieze. A golden architrave would be gaudy and overstated.

[210]Ornamented with and perhaps supported by frets ("carved ornaments, **esp** in ceilings, consisting of intersecting lines in relief"—*OED* 3.a]) of gold.

[211]Babylon, because of the Babylonian captivity of the Israelites and the opulence of the famous hanging gardens, became a symbol of demonic luxury, within the Bible itself and certainly within the Protestant tradition of Milton's era, as when papal Rome was called "the whore of Babylon."

[212]*Belus* is the Latinized version of Bel, the Babylonian Baal; see Jeremiah 51.44 "And I will punish Bel in Babylon, and . . . the wall of Babylon shall fall." Serapis is extra-biblical, an Egyptian god identified with the deified king Apis of Apia or Pelasgia (see Augustine, *City of God* 18:5).

[213]The word "pile" was used of a small castle or any large edifice, as with *OED* 3.4: "A lofty mass of buildings; a large building or edifice." Milton uses the word metaphorically in *Samson Agonistes* 1069, in which Harapha's demeanor or "look" is described as "his pile high-built and proud."

[214]Margaret Byard has pointed out the use of torches or cressets to illuminate the interior of St. Peter's in Rome (*Milton Quarterly* 9 [1975]: 65–66), but the same would be true of any large public or private building. See also William A. McClung, "The Architecture of Pandaemonium," *Milton Quarterly* 15 (1981): 109–12. The word "yeilded" looks like a Miltonic spelling, but in this case the spelling appears to be accidental: *1674* is merely following *1667* and both are ignoring the Manuscript, which has "yielded." I have left the spelling intact on the faint grounds that Milton may have intervened somehow in the selection.

[215]The ancient Greeks and Vergil (*Aeneid* 3.171) used "Ausonia" (derived from the name of Odysseus's son Auson) as the name for Italy.

Men call'd him *Mulciber*;[216] and how he fell   740
From Heav'n, they fabl'd, thrown by angry *Jove*
Sheer o're the Chrystal Battlements; from Morn
To Noon he fell, from Noon to dewy Eve,
A Summers day; and with the setting Sun
Dropt from the Zenith like a falling Star,   745
On *Lemnos* th' *Ægæan* Ile: thus they relate,
Erring; for he with this rebellious rout
Fell long before; nor aught avail'd him now
To have built in Heav'n high Towrs; nor did he scape
By all his Engins, but was headlong sent   750
With his industrous crew to build in hell.
Mean while the winged Haralds by command
Of Sovran power, with awful° Ceremony   AWE-INSPIRING
And Trumpets sound throughout the Host proclaim
A solemn Councel forthwith to be held   755
At *Pandæmonium*, the high Capital[217]
Of *Satan* and his Peers: thir summons call'd
From every Band and squared Regiment[218]
By place or choice the worthiest; they anon
With hunderds[219] and with thousands trooping came   760
Attended: all access was throng'd, the Gates
And Porches wide, but chief the spacious Hall
(Though like a cover'd field, where Champions bold
Wont ride in arm'd, and at the Soldans° chair   SULTAN'S
Defi'd the best of *Paynim*[220] chivalry   765
To mortal combat or carreer with Lance)[221]
Thick swarm'd, both on the ground and in the air,
Brusht with the hiss of russling wings. As Bees
In spring time, when the Sun with *Taurus*[222] rides,
Pour forth thir populous youth about the Hive   770
In clusters; they among fresh dews and flowers
Flie to and fro, or on the smoothed Plank,
The suburb of thir Straw-built Cittadel,

---

[216]Mulciber, the Greek Hephaestus, is more commonly known by his Roman name Vulcan. The god, patron of artisans working in metal by means of fire, was cast out of the Olympian heaven by Jupiter. He fell **nine** days (Milton may have wanted to shorten the distance as compared to the fall of the angels) before landing on the island of Lemnos, crippling himself as a result of the fall. Like the biblical Tubal-cain, Mulciber was associated with the art of metal working. Milton sees him as one of the fallen angels whom the ancients mistakenly took for a god and then makes him into an architect and maker of "Engins" (the word has military associations) more than a metal worker and sculptor.

[217]Darbishire thought that the cancelled Manuscript reading "Capitoll" should be restored on the grounds that the reference is to a building (see Robert Adams, *Ikon* 88 for her position and his cogent answer); but then one has to ask why the first spelling was crossed out and why "Capital" was allowed to remain in both printed versions.

[218]*1667* (but not the Manuscript) had reversed "Band and"; *1674* follows the *1668 Errata* and corrects the transposition. The "Regiment" is "squared" because seventeenth-century military strategy suggested that regiments enter battle in rectangles (as in 553). Here "squared" is a dissyllable, as indicated by the spelling out of "-ed."

[219]Again, the *1668 Errata* called for this change, and *1674* effected it. *1678* switches back to the more common "hundreds," and the Manuscript oddly has that as well, even though Milton apparently preferred the form "hunderd."

[220]"Pagan." The Manuscript spells this word "Paynim" (the "y" has been inserted by means of a caret) with no italics; *1674* seems to be slavishly following *1667* (and the MS before the "y" was inserted) in printing "*Panim*." Since the word was spelled "*Paynim*" in *Paradise Regain'd* 3.343, I have restored what I think is the intended spelling and left the italics in place. The compositor may have failed to recognize the word as one alternative form of a common adjective, supposed the word a foreign term, and therefore italicized it; but compare "*Barbaric*" in 2.4. One rationale for the use of italics, as Tom Corns reminds me, is that "*Paynim*" "is the name of a religious group (i.e., non-Christians)" (letter, October 1991).

[221]Milton wryly puts a scene of chivalric jousting in Hell, as before the "Sultan," mimicking jousts like those described in Boiardo's *Orlando Innamorato* or Tasso's *Jerusalem Delivered* and other romantic epics.

[222]The Sun would have been in the constellation of the bull, or Taurus, in mid-April.

New rub'd with Baum,[223] expatiate and confer
Thir State affairs. So thick the aerie crowd   775
Swarm'd and were straitn'd;[224] till the Signal giv'n,
Behold a wonder! they but now who seemd
In bigness to surpass Earths Giant Sons
Now less then smallest Dwarfs, in narrow room
Throng numberless, like that Pigmean Race   780
Beyond the *Indian* Mount, or Faerie Elves,
Whose midnight Revels, by a Forrest side
Or Fountain some belated Peasant sees,
Or dreams he sees, while over-head the Moon
Sits Arbitress,[225] and neerer to the Earth   785
Wheels her pale course, they on thir mirth and dance
Intent, with jocond Music charm[226] his ear;
At once with joy and fear his heart rebounds.
Thus incorporeal Spirits to smallest forms
Reduc'd thir shapes immense,[227] and were at large,[228] ON THE LOOSE   790
Though without number still amidst the Hall
Of that infernal Court. But far within
And in thir own dimensions like themselves
The great Seraphic Lords and Cherubim
In close° recess and secret conclave sat   HIDDEN   795
A thousand Demy-Gods on golden seat's,
Frequent° and full. After short silence then   CROWDED
And summons read, the great consult began.

The End of the First Book.

---

[223]As Robert Adams points out, "If Milton had read proof on his great poem letter by letter, he might have caught himself spelling as 'Baume' in I, 774, a word which he spelled 'balme' in II, 402 . . . " (75). Milton seems to have dictated no consistent spelling of "balm" (see 2.402, 5.293 or 9.629). Adams may be asking too much of a blind poet or a seventeenth-century printing house.

[224]The image is one of dilation and contraction, a process which implies a comparison between bees and fallen angels: swarming, bees are an expanded group, but they must be straightened, or contracted into a thin line, in order to enter the hive.

[225]The Roman Diana, goddess of the moon, was associated in the Renaissance with the witch Hecate and other queens of fairy kingdoms (see *Midsummer Night's Dream* 5.1.384). The moon as arbitress or judge would be frightening, since the moon would govern floods (*Midsummer Night's Dream* 2.1.103) or tearful moods (*Richard II* 3.2.69).

[226]The word "charm" here suggests the apparently harmless but potentially evil use of music, as in the modern idiom "the music was enchanting." Despite the fact that the music is "jocund" (after the Fall, Eve is "jocond and boon" [9.793]), it is deceitful and may charm the peasant's ear so that he cannot recognize the evil behind it.

[227]An example of the angels' ability to dilate, or expand and contract their incorporeal shapes, or, for that matter, to change shapes at will. Again, the optics suggest a God-like perspective.

[228]"Though numberless, they had so contracted their dimensions, as to have room enough to be *au large*, French; *a largo*, Italian; and yet be in the hall" (Richardson, quoted in Todd 1.790n). I take it that they have expanded their shapes, individually, so that the whole assembly can fit in the hall.

Paradise Lost.

BOOK II.

THE ARGUMENT.

The Consultation begun, Satan *debates whether another Battel be to be hazarded for the recovery of Heaven: some advise it, others dissuade: A third proposal is prefer'd, mentioned before by* Satan,[1] *to search the truth of that Prophesie or Tradition in Heaven concerning another world, and another kind of creature equal or not much inferiour to themselves, about this time to be created: Thir doubt who shall be sent on this difficult search:* Satan *thir chief undertakes alone the voyage, is honourd and applauded.[2] The Councel thus ended, the rest betake them several wayes and to several imployments, as thir inclinations lead them, to entertain the time till* Satan *return. He passes on his Journey to Hell Gates, finds them shut, and who sat there to guard them, by whom at length they are op'nd, and discover to him the great Gulf between Hell and Heaven; with what difficulty he passes through, directed by* Chaos,[3] *the Power of that place, to the sight of this new World which he sought.*

H igh on a Throne of Royal State, which far
   Outshon the wealth of *Ormus* and of *Ind,*[4]
   Or where the gorgeous East with richest hand
Showrs on her Kings *Barbaric*[5] Pearl and Gold,
Satan exalted sat, by merit rais'd   5
To that bad eminence; and from despair
Thus high uplifted beyond hope, aspires
Beyond thus high, insatiate to pursue
Vain Warr with Heav'n, and by success° untaught
His proud imaginations thus displaid.   OUTCOME   10
   Powers and Dominions, Deities of Heav'n,
For since no deep within her gulf can hold
Immortal vigor, though opprest and fall'n,
I give not Heav'n for lost. From this descent
Celestial vertues rising, will appear   15

---

[1] Satan, in other words, has rigged the debate to be carried to a conclusion he has planned. Later in this book the Epic Voice summarizes what happens: "Thus Beelzebub / Pleaded his devilish Counsel, first devis'd / By *Satan*" (378–80).

[2] Milton summarizes the plot of the book in this argument, as in the others, and he does not pass judgment on the action. The honor and applause of the fallen angels, are, of course, misdirected. As Gabriel points out, Satan in leaving Hell is merely the first "to fly from pain . . . and to scape his punishment" (4.910–11).

[3] Chaos is an allegorical entity as well as a common noun describing a vast unformed mass from which God withholds creative force (compare "uncreated night," 150 below). The matter out of which God created the universe was not evil: "It was in a confused and disordered state at first, but afterwards God made it ordered and beautiful" (*On Christian Doctrine* 1.7, Yale 6: 308). Hesiod defined Chaos as a shapeless mass of matter which gave birth to Erebus and Night (*Theogony* 118–25), Ovid gave it the status of a minor god (*Metamorphoses* 1.1), and Vergil associated the god with other gods of the underworld (*Aeneid* 4.510); thus Milton was acting within a solid classical tradition as well as a Christian one. For a running commentary on the meaning of Chaos, see John Rumrich, *Matter of Glory: A New Preface to* Paradise Lost (Pittsburgh, PA: U of Pittsburgh P, 1987).

[4] The modern Ormuz and India, famous in Milton's era for ostentatious, pagan wealth and mercantilism. Since Satan was traditionally supposed to have come from either the east or the "frozen loyns" of the north (1.352), he was associated by the English with over-opulent eastern civilizations. Also, since Vandals, Goths, and Mongols had in the past come from the general direction of the east, and since various Islamic and Turkish armies continued to come from the east during the seventeenth century, it became metaphorical to picture the invasion of demonic or pagan forces from that direction.

[5] An intriguing use of italics, since very few other adjectives in *Paradise Lost*, except those derived from proper nouns (as with "*Tartarean*"), are italicized. Fowler notes that the adjective might have been thought to be derived from the place name "Barbary." In the later state of *1667*, however, the non-italicized form was changed to the italicized form, indicating some sort of editorial intervention. Joseph Summers, from the perspective of a literary rather than a textual critic, discusses the way that the adjective "*Barbaric,*" buried in the middle of the line, "exploded the magnificence of Satan's Kingdom" (53). Milton often deflates grandiose images of Satan, undercutting them with a negative modifier, as with "bad eminence" just below. Satan has not lost all former glory: he is still eminent, but his eminence is perverted by evil and thus is bad. He is a negative mirror image of the "good eminence" he used to enjoy. Satan's bad eminence should also be contrasted with the exaltation of the Son to be described later.

More glorious and more dread then from no fall,
And trust themselves to fear no second fate:
Mee though just right, and the fixt Laws of Heav'n
Did first create your Leader, next free choice,
With what besides, in Counsel or in Fight,   20
Hath bin achievd of merit, yet this loss
Thus farr at least recover'd, hath much more
Establisht in a safe unenvied[6] Throne
Yielded with full consent. The happier state
In Heav'n, which follows dignity,[7] might draw   25
Envy from each inferior; but who here
Will envy whom the highest place exposes
Formost to stand against the Thunderers aim
Your bulwark, and condemns to greatest share
Of endless pain? where there is then no good   30
For which to strive, no strife can grow up there
From Faction;[8] for none sure will claim in Hell
Precedence, none, whose portion is so small
Of present pain, that with ambitious mind
Will covet more. With this advantage then   35
To union, and firm Faith, and firm accord,
More then can be in Heav'n, we now return
To claim our just inheritance of old,
Surer to prosper then prosperity
Could have assur'd us;[9] and by what best way,   40
Whether of open Warr or covert guile,
We now debate; who can advise, may speak.

      He ceas'd, and next him *Moloc*,[10] Scepter'd King
Stood up, the strongest and the fiercest Spirit
That fought in Heav'n; now fiercer by despair: 45
His trust was with th' Eternal to be deem'd
Equal in strength, and rather then be less
Car'd not to be at all; with that care lost
Went all his fear: of God, or Hell, or worse
He reck'd° not, and these words thereafter spake.   CARED   50
      My sentence° is for open Warr: Of Wiles,   VOTE
More unexpert, I boast not: them let those
Contrive who need, or when they need, not now.[11]

---

[6]Certainly this should be pronounced as it is today, as a trisyllable; the elided form, "unenvi'd," might cause a confusing mispronunciation and hence all states of the text avoid it. Satan cannot conceive of power without envy, yet such exists in Heaven. Satan has quietly seized the throne in Hell and he is justifying his action, as if he had been voted into office. He argues for the reverse of the "fortunate fall": the fallen angels will somehow improve their lot if they rise out of the horrible depths to which they have fallen. Neither their counsel nor their fight has reflected any glory on them.
[7]"The more fortunate position in Heaven, which is arranged according to true worth."
[8]There is no reason for political factions to grow up in Hell, since there is no reason for any fallen angel to ask for more prominence (or pain in separation from God) than he already has. Satan is lying to the angels while he is in the act of claiming precedence in Hell. He speaks, after all, from a throne.
[9]Hollow word-play (but exquisite mixing of sounds) exposes Satan as the kind of politician who gives the word a bad name. His rhetorical method is "By mixing somewhat true to vent more lyes" (*Paradise Regain'd* 1.433). Satan never tells the entire truth after his fall, but he mixes enough of the truth into any argument to convince any gullible listener.
[10]In this instance the name is spelled without the "h," but in the manuscript of Book 1 it is consistently spelled with the "h," perhaps indicating Milton's preference. Because Moloch is treated in the Old Testament (Amos 5.26) not only as a god but as a king, and because that is what his name means, he is pictured with a scepter. The Geneva Bible uses the name Siccuth for Moloch and names the deity as "Siccuth your king"; the marginal note adds "That idole which you estemed as your King, & caryed about . . . " (1560 ed.).
[11]"Let those who need to think up evasive tactics ('Wiles') construct them now or when they need to in the future." English syntax would not normally expect "them" to be the first word in the clause.

For while they sit contriving, shall the rest,
Millions that stand in Arms, and longing wait
The Signal to ascend, sit lingring here   55
Heav'ns fugitives, and for thir dwelling place
Accept this dark opprobrious[12] Den of shame,
The Prison of his Tyranny who Reigns
By our delay? no, let us rather choose   60
Arm'd with Hell flames and fury all at once
O're Heav'ns high Towrs to force resistless way,
Turning our Tortures into horrid Arms
Against the Torturer; when to meet the noise
Of his Almighty Engin[13] he shall hear   65
Infernal Thunder, and for Lightning see
Black fire and horror shot with equal rage
Among his Angels; and his Throne it self
Mixt with *Tartarean*[14] Sulphur, and strange fire,
His own invented Torments. But perhaps   70
The way seems difficult and steep to scale
With upright wing against a higher foe.
Let such bethink them, if the sleepy drench[15]
Of that forgetful Lake benumm not still,
That in our proper motion we ascend   75
Up to our native seat:[16] descent and fall
To us is adverse. Who but felt of late
When the fierce Foe hung on our brok'n Rear[17]
Insulting, and pursu'd us through the Deep,
With what compulsion and laborious flight   80
We sunk thus low? Th' ascent is easie then;
Th' event° is fear'd; should we again provoke   OUTCOME
Our stronger, some worse way his wrath may find
To our destruction: if there be in Hell
Fear to be worse destroy'd: what can be worse   85
Then to dwell here, driv'n out from bliss, condemn'd
In this abhorred deep to utter woe;
Where pain of unextinguishable fire
Must exercise us without hope of end
The Vassals of his anger, when the Scourge   90
Inexorably, and the torturing hour
Calls us to Penance?[18] More destroy'd then thus

---

[12]In Latin the word *opprobrium* carries a sense of deepest shame, so that all the words surrounding "Den," itself a word associated perhaps with lower forms of animals, form a network of negative connotations.

[13]Apparently the chariot of paternal deity on which the Son rides to victory in the War in Heaven. The word "engine" in Milton's prose and poetry usually implies a mechanical, and specifically a military function.

[14]Tartarus was the deepest region of Homer's and Vergil's Hades, in which the guiltiest and most impious were punished. Dante puts traitors and fraudulent ministers there. See Homer, *Odyssey* 11, and Vergil, *Aeneid* 6.268–90.

[15]A sleeping potion, something like an opiate, as when one drinks of the waters of "that forgetful Lake" or river in Tartarus, Lethe, which cause forgetfulness.

[16]If the fallen angels were still pure, which they obviously are not, the quality of their spirit would lend them buoyancy to rise again to Heaven, in a "proper motion."

[17]Milton often returns to the image of the fallen angels unheroically fleeing from battle, and the ridiculousness of their flight is emphasized here by the sardonic pun in "brok'n Rear." Cowardly flight is a characteristic motion of the fallen angels, from Satan himself to Moloch.

[18]Milton puts the torture of the damned in the context of Roman Catholic mortification of the flesh, as when various monastic orders practiced self-flagellation as a way of denigrating the influence of the flesh, using scourges to whip themselves at appointed hours of penance. The number of the verb "Calls" may be askew, since the plural subjects might ask for "Call," but both *1667* and *1674* use "Calls."

We should be quite abolisht and expire.

What fear we then? what doubt we to incense

His utmost ire?[19] which to the highth enrag'd,   95

Will either quite consume us, and reduce

To nothing this essential,[20] happier farr

Then miserable to have eternal being:

Or if our substance be indeed Divine,[21]

And cannot cease to be, we are at worst   100

On this side nothing; and by proof we feel

Our power sufficient to disturb his Heav'n,

And with perpetual inrodes to Allarme,

Though inaccessible, his fatal Throne:[22]

Which if not Victory is yet Revenge.   105

    He ended frowning, and his look denounc'd°   ANNOUNCED

Desperate revenge, and Battel dangerous

To less then Gods. On th' other side up rose[23]

Belial,[24] in act more graceful and humane;   110

A fairer person lost not Heav'n;[25] he seemd

For dignity compos'd and high exploit:

But all was false and hollow;[26] though his Tongue

Dropt Manna,[27] and could make the worse appear

The better reason, to perplex and dash   115

Maturest Counsels: for his thoughts were low;

To vice industrious, but to Nobler deeds

Timorous and slothful:[28] yet he pleas'd the ear,

And with perswasive accent thus began.

    I should be much for open Warr, O Peers,   120

As not behind in hate; if what was urg'd

Main reason to perswade immediate Warr,

Did not disswade me most, and seem to cast

Ominous conjecture on the whole success:

---

[19]"In what way do we hesitate to stir up his utmost anger?"

[20]Moloch considers complete annihilation of their "essential [being]" preferable to their present condition. His fierce and frowning stance should be measured by what he did in the War in Heaven: run away. The unheroic image of Moloch in Book 6 is deliberately funny: "but anon / Down clov'n to the waste, with shatterd Armes / And uncouth paine [Moloch] fled bellowing" (6.360–62).

[21]The fallen angels still retain some of their substance as "gods," i.e., angels. "Their knowledge is great, but it is a torment to them rather than a consolation; so that they utterly despair of their salvation . . . " (*On Christian Doctrine* 1.9, Yale 6: 349).

[22]Moloch pictures the fallen angels constantly pecking away at Heaven in military forays: "perpetual inrodes" to "Allarme" the throne of God. He knows that the throne is inaccessible, but he suggests that the fallen angels attempt to disturb or alarm it nonetheless. The throne is "fatal" because in Moloch's opinion God's will (i.e., fate) set it where it is.

[23]As opposed to Moloch's position, which might be thought of as on the "right wing," Belial speaks from "th' other side," as if Pandemonium had a two-party house of representatives. The frequent use of the word "peer" referring to the fallen angels (who are not *peers* or *equals* at all, because they exist in a tyrannical state and are all underlings of Satan) reinforces the irony and the political imagery. For characterization of Belial, see my "Belial." Milton has constructed a character type (a "character" in the sense of Theophrastus's *Characters*) with Belial, Moloch, and Mammon. For general information about the influence of Theophrastus, see J. W. Smead, *The Theophrastian "Character": The History of a Literary Genre* (Oxford: Clarendon P, 1985).

[24]The position of the name in the line may indicate that the name was pronounced "Bee-lile," with the accent on the second syllable.

[25]The tradition about Belial current in biblical commentary in Milton's era made him out to be handsome and well-spoken. See Hunter "Belial" and Flannagan "Belial," for other details about him issuing from extensive biblical commentary. Hunter believes that Belial's presence in the epic here and elsewhere is intrusive, the passages dealing with him representing a later addition to the text.

[26]The adjective "hollow" is often used of what Satan says and what various of the fallen angels do; it gathers resonance each time it is used in the poem, and at times leads into an image of hollowness or empty echoes, which allies it with a lethal chaos: what Satan says is hollow, Hell is hollow, Chaos exists in a hollow abyss, the falling angels fight in a "hollow cube" (6.552) and cannons, invented by the Satanic forces, are "hollow Engins long and round" (6.484). Belial looks and sounds good but is hollow at his moral core.

[27]A comparison that suggests blasphemous imitation, since God drops manna into the desert to help feed the Israelites (Numbers 11.9). In other words, Belial's tongue dropped apparent sweetness that sounded almost divine.

[28]Belial is both slothful and lewd, industrious only in the pursuit of vice.

When he who most excels in fact° of Arms,   DEED
In what he counsels and in what excels   125
Mistrustful, grounds his courage on despair
And utter dissolution, as the scope
Of all his aim, after some dire revenge.
First, what Revenge? the Towrs of Heav'n are fill'd   130
With Armed watch, that render all access
Impregnable; oft on the bordering[29] Deep
Encamp thir Legions, or with obscure[30] wing
Scout farr and wide into the Realm of night,
Scorning surprize. Or could we break our way
By force, and at our heels all Hell should rise   135
With blackest Insurrection,[31] to confound
Heav'ns purest Light, yet our great Enemy
All incorruptible would on his Throne
Sit unpolluted, and th' Ethereal mould[32]
Incapable of stain would soon expel   140
Her mischief,[33] and purge off the baser fire
Victorious. Thus repuls'd, our final hope
Is flat despair: we must exasperate[34]
Th' Almighty Victor to spend all his rage,
And that must end us, that must be our cure,   145
To be no more; sad cure; for who would loose,°   LOSE
Though full of pain, this intellectual being,[35]
Those thoughts that wander through Eternity,
To perish rather, swallowd up and lost
In the wide womb° of uncreated night,   VACUITY   150
Devoid of sense[36] and motion? and who knows,
Let this be good, whether our angry Foe
Can give it, or will ever? how he can
Is doubtful; that he never will is sure.
Will he, so wise, let loose at once his ire,   155
Belike° through impotence, or unaware,   PROBABLY
To give his Enemies thir wish, and end
Them in his anger, whom his anger saves
To punish endless? wherefore cease we then?
Say they who counsel Warr, we are decreed,   160
Reserv'd and destin'd to Eternal woe;
Whatever doing, what can we suffer more,
What can we suffer worse? is this then worst,
Thus sitting, thus consulting, thus in Arms?

---

[29]A disyllable, according to the metrics, though not spelled "bord'ring" in any of the texts.

[30]"Dark," as in Italian "*oscuro*." Accented on the first syllable.

[31]The first "n" in "Insurrection" was inverted in all states of *1674*. Like all other editors, I correct it.

[32]The essential building material of which angels would be made, ether, is metaphorically "mould," in the sense that "clay" is the essential building material when God makes Adam. Here "mould" is in no way a negative word.

[33]A stronger word than in the modern usage, and imbued with a strong sense of evil. Witches or demons would have been said to "do mischief."

[34]"To irritate (a person); to provoke to anger; to enrage, incense" (*OED* v. 4).

[35]Perhaps this is the most powerful and seductive thing Belial says, since it suggests (to a modern audience brought up on Albert Camus's myth of Sisyphus) that intellectual sensitivity causes a pain which makes us aware we are alive. Belial's type of intellectual self-awareness may appeal to various audiences, but what he says, as the Epic Voice suggests, is hollow and therefore ultimately meaningless.

[36]"The senses viewed as forming a single faculty; . . . sensation" (*OED* 3). Night, in other words, despite having a womb, should not be considered human because she hasn't the five senses and cannot move.

What when we fled amain, pursu'd and strook[37]   165
With Heav'ns afflicting Thunder, and besought
The Deep to shelter us? this Hell then seem'd
A refuge from those wounds: or when we lay
Chain'd on the burning Lake? that sure was worse.
What if the breath that kindl'd those grim fires   170
Awak'd should blow them into sevenfold rage
And plunge us in the flames? or from above
Should intermitted vengeance arm again
His red right hand to plague us?[38] what if all
Her stores were open'd, and this Firmament   175
Of Hell should spout her Cataracts of Fire,[39]
Impendent horrors,[40] threatning hideous fall
One day upon our heads; while we perhaps
Designing or exhorting glorious warr,
Caught in a fierie Tempest shall be hurl'd   180
Each on his rock transfixt,[41] the sport and prey
Of racking whirlwinds, or for ever sunk
Under yon boyling Ocean, wrapt in Chains;
There to converse with everlasting groans,
Unrespited, unpitied, unrepreevd,[42]   185
Ages of hopeless end; this would be worse.
Warr therefore, open or conceal'd, alike
My voice disswades; for what can force or guile
With him, or who deceive his mind, whose eye
Views all things at one view? he from heav'ns highth[43]   190
All these our motions vain, sees and derides;[44]
Not more Almighty to resist our might
Then wise to frustrate all our plots and wiles.
Shall we then live thus vile, the Race of Heav'n
Thus trampl'd, thus expell'd to suffer here   195
Chains and these Torments? better these then worse
By my advice; since fate inevitable
Subdues us, and Omnipotent Decree,

[handwritten margin note: THINKS ABOUT ALL THE WAYS IT CAN GO WRONG]

---

[37]"What of the time when we fled in every direction, pursued and stricken by God's lightning . . . ?"

[38]A famous classical image of Jupiter with a "red right hand full of lightning bolts" from Horace, *Odes* 1.2.1–4, is here transferred to the Christian God.

[39]Reminiscent of King Lear's mad speech to the elements, which mentions cataracts in the context of waterspouts (*King Lear*, 3.2.2), although here the "Cataracts of Fire" seem to be perverse reflection of the healing rain which might issue from the "cataracts of Heaven" (see Genesis 7.11 and 8.2, and *OED* "cataract" 1).

[40]The horrors are pictured almost allegorically, as hanging like swords of Damocles, ready at any moment to fall on the heads of the fallen angels. Compare Milton's plan for a tragedy based on the Fall: "Adam and Eve, driven out of Paradice praesented by an angel with Labour griefe hatred Envie warre famine Pestilence sicknesse, discontent Ignorance Feare Death" (see "Early Outlines" in the Introduction, III.1). The allegorical figures originally planned for Milton's drama on the subject of the Fall were pictured as "mutes to whome he [Adam] gives thire names."

[41]The implicit comparison is to Prometheus, chained to a rock on a mountain top, exposed to the cruelties of the weather. Compare Aeschylus, *Prometheus Bound* 1.10, where "Might" describes the rock on which Prometheus is exposed. Prometheus, bound in chains of adamant, resembles or foreshadows Satan in that he also rebelled against the chief god in the Olympian heaven, and he stole fire (like Lucifer, he is a light-bearer). Adam later will be compared with "the unwiser Son / Of *Japhet*" (4.716–17), or Epimetheus, Prometheus's brother.

[42]"For Milton, however, the collocations of terms with the same prefix—particularly 'un'—becomes a sort of stylistic motif" with three or four elements (Corns, *Milton's Language* 84).

[43]On this particular page, which begins the D gathering of *1674*, in most copies, someone probably within the printing house has taken pains to ink in letters that did not print properly. The corrections were done with such skill that the naked eye cannot detect most of them. In some modern editions of *Paradise Lost*, such as the Columbia edition, "highth" is printed "hight" because an editor has used a copy in which the corrections had not been made. See Fletcher, 3:126–27. The modern word is "height."

[44]One of the several instances of God's laughter at and derision of evil. Though we humans may take Satan's actions as deadly and terrifying, from the perspective of God (as with the bee and pygmy images at the end of Book 1), the actions of Satan and his legions are a kind of cosmic joke, funnier to God than to fallen humankind.

The Victors will. To suffer, as to doe,
Our strength is equal, nor the Law unjust   200
That so ordains: this was at first resolv'd,
If we were wise, against so great a foe
Contending, and so doubtful what might fall.
I laugh, when those who at the Spear are bold
And vent'rous, if that fail them, shrink and fear   205
What yet they know must follow, to endure
Exile, or ignominy,[45] or bonds, or pain,
The sentence of thir Conquerour: This is now
Our doom; which if we can sustain and bear,
Our Supream[46] Foe in time may much remit   210
His anger, and perhaps thus farr remov'd
Not mind us not offending,[47] satisfi'd
With what is punish't; whence these raging fires
Will slack'n, if his breath stir not thir flames.
Our purer essence then will overcome   215
Thir noxious vapour, or° enur'd not feel,   EITHER
Or chang'd at length, and to the place conformd
In temper and in nature, will receive
Familiar the fierce heat, and void of pain;
This horror will grow milde, this darkness light,   220
Besides what hope the never-ending flight
Of future dayes may bring, what chance, what change
Worth waiting, since our present lot appeers
For happy though but ill, for ill not worst,
If we procure not to our selves more woe.[48]   225
      Thus *Belial* with words cloath'd in reasons garb[49]
Counsel'd ignoble ease, and peaceful sloath,[50]
Not peace: and after him thus *Mammon* spake.[51]
      Either to disinthrone the King of Heav'n
We warr, if warr be best, or to regain   230
Our own right lost: him to unthrone we then
May hope when everlasting Fate shall yeild
To fickle Chance, and *Chaos* judge the strife:
The former vain to hope argues as vain
The latter: for what place can be for us   235
Within Heav'ns bound, unless Heav'ns Lord supream
We overpower? Suppose he should relent
And publish Grace to all, on promise made

---

[45]A trisyllable, according to the iambic pattern of the line. May have been pronounced "ig'nomy," just as the disyllabic "spirit" can sometimes be read as a monosyllable, or, as Bridges suggests (23), the y of "ignominy" may be elided into the vowel o of "or." In every other poetic line in which Milton uses "ignominy," it scans as a trisyllable.

[46]Accented on the first syllable (but Moyles does not agree [100]).

[47]"Perhaps he won't remember we are here as long as we are not acting offensively." The conjecture is nonsense, given the omniscience and eternal memory of God, and the fixity of His decrees. I have found no reference in Milton's theological writings to the possibility of forgiveness for the fallen angels.

[48]Belial's rhetorical style is much closer to Satan's than to Moloch's, in that it is subtle rather than obvious, and indirect rather than direct.

[49]The clear implication is that though his words wear the clothes of reason, they are neither logical nor reasonable. Their dress, in other words, is a hypocritical disguise.

[50]I take these to be the exact opposite of "Patience and Heroic Martyrdom" (9.32) advocated by the narrator as "better" than the virtues usually extolled in classical epics. The spelling "sloath" for the modern "sloth" may give a hint as to its pronunciation, though "slawth" and "slough" were also spelling variants.

[51]Note that Mammon is answering Moloch, not Belial. Hunter ("Belial") observes that line 228 fits perfectly after line 107, indicating that Belial's speech was added.

Of new Subjection; with what eyes could we
Stand in his presence humble, and receive   240
Strict Laws impos'd, to celebrate his Throne
With warbl'd Hymns, and to his Godhead sing
Forc't Halleluiah's; while he Lordly sits
Our envied Sovran, and his Altar breathes
Ambrosial Odours and Ambrosial Flowers,[52]   245
Our servile offerings. This must be our task
In Heav'n,[53] this our delight; how wearisom
Eternity so spent in worship paid
To whom we hate. Let us not then pursue
By force impossible, by leave obtain'd   250
Unacceptable, though in Heav'n, our state
Of splendid vassalage, but rather seek
Our own good from our selves, and from our own
Live to our selves, though in this vast recess,
Free, and to none accountable, preferring   255
Hard liberty before the easie yoke
Of servile Pomp. Our greatness will appeer
Then most conspicuous, when great things of small,
Useful of hurtful, prosperous of adverse
We can create, and in what place so e're   260
Thrive under evil, and work ease out of pain
Through labour and indurance. This deep world
Of darkness do we dread? How oft amidst
Thick clouds and dark doth Heav'ns all-ruling Sire
Choose to reside, his Glory unobscur'd,   265
And with the Majesty of darkness round
Covers his Throne; from whence deep thunders roar
Must'ring thir rage, and Heav'n resembles Hell?[54]
As he our darkness, cannot we his Light
Imitate when we please?[55] This Desart soile   270
Wants not her hidden lustre, Gemms and Gold;[56]
Nor want we skill or art, from whence to raise
Magnificence; and what can Heav'n shew more?
Our torments also may in length of time
Become our Elements, these piercing Fires   275
As soft as now severe, our temper chang'd
Into their temper; which must needs remove
The sensible[57] of pain. All things invite
To peaceful Counsels, and the settl'd State
Of order, how in safety best we may   280
Compose our present evils, with regard

[52]Mammon associates heavenly ("Ambrosial" suggests the Olympian gods' nectar and ambrosia) plants and odors with "servile offerings" to the Christian God.
[53]I have reinstated the comma from *1667*, which *1674* omits.
[54]The image is a perverted one, since the Old Testament God uses darkness or clouds to set off his brilliance, as in the giving of the Ten Commandments, not to make Heaven resemble Hell.
[55]The answer to his question, in a word, is "No," though "darkness visible" (1.63) may be present in Hell.
[56]"This desert soil does not lack a hidden source of light, the gems and gold beneath its surface."
[57]"Whatever there is in the fallen angels that can perceive pain." Here "sensible" is an adjective used as a noun. See *OED* adj. B.3: "The element (in a spiritual being) that is capable of feeling," citing only this example.

Of what we are and were,[58] dismissing quite
All thoughts of warr:[59] ye have what I advise.
   He scarce had finisht, when such murmur filld
Th' Assembly, as when hollow Rocks retain   285
The sound of blustring winds, which all night long
Had rous'd the Sea, now with hoarse cadence lull
Sea-faring men orewatcht,[60] whose Bark by chance
Or Pinnace anchors in a craggy Bay
After the Tempest: Such applause was heard   290
As *Mammon* ended, and his Sentence pleas'd,
Advising peace: for such another Field°   BATTLEFIELD
They dreaded worse then Hell: so much the fear
Of Thunder and the Sword of *Michael*[61]
Wrought still within them; and no less desire   295
To found this nether Empire, which might rise
By pollicy, and long process of time,
In emulation opposite to Heav'n.
Which when *Beelzebub* perceiv'd, then whom,   BEELZEBUB
Satan except, none higher sat,[62] with grave   300
Aspect he rose, and in his rising seem'd
A Pillar of State; deep on his Front° engraven   FOREHEAD
Deliberation sat and public care;
And Princely counsel in his face yet shon,
Majestic though in ruin: sage he stood   305
With *Atlantean* shoulders[63] fit to bear
The weight of mightiest Monarchies; his look
Drew audience and attention still as Night
Or Summers Noon-tide air, while thus he spake.
   Thrones and Imperial Powers, off-spring of heav'n,[64]   310
Ethereal Vertues;[65] or these Titles now
Must we renounce, and changing stile[66] be call'd
Princes of Hell? for so the popular vote
Inclines, here to continue,[67] and build up here
A growing Empire; doubtless; while we dream,   315

---

[58]A genuine textual crux, since *1667* uses "where," and both words make sense. Because of other plays on the verb "to be," I have come to believe that "were" is the better reading. It would also seem that "were" corrects "where," since the one follows the other, but the two words are easy to confuse, in typesetting.

[59]Mammon's argument will counter Satan's plan for war against God's new creation, humankind, and it therefore must be quickly contradicted by Beelzebub—especially because Mammon's argument for peace meets with spontaneous applause and approval.

[60]The image is of tired ("overwatcht" or "too long at their vigil") sailors in port, lulled perhaps to inattention or to sleep by the rhythmic noise of the rough sea. Both "barks" and "pinnaces" were types of small fighting ships.

[61]The Archangel Michael is most often associated with Christian warfare, and he is often pictured with sword in hand, leading the angelic troops in the War in Heaven, or purging Hell at Judgment Day. Michael is named as leader of the heavenly troops in the War in Heaven in Revelation 12.7.

[62]The Protestant biblical scholar was free to interpret "Beelzebub" to mean either "another name for Satan" or "Satan's closest companion." In *On Christian Doctrine*, Milton chose the first interpretation; in the epic, the latter (see West, *Angels* 125). The dramatic or fictional implication is that Beelzebub is so close in character to Satan that one cannot tell their opinions apart, another reason why they are "mates."

[63]A reference to the Titan Atlas, who in the form of a giant or of the African mountain that bears his name carried the heavens on his shoulders.

[64]The text of *1667* has a comma here, which I have restored rather than reproducing the lack of punctuation of *1674*. The syntax calls for the comma, since we are in a series of vocatives. The punctuation style of both *1667* and *1674* is, however, far from consistent.

[65]Each of the "Vertues," as with "Thrones" and "Powers," represents one of the orders of angels. John Salkeld, among others, traced the naming of the hierarchy of angels at least to St. Augustine, in *A Treatise of Angels* (London, 1613); see West, *Angels* 51. Like Satan's speeches in Book 1, Beelzebub's here is marked by anacoluthon, incomplete or abbreviated sentence structure.

[66]To "turn one's style" was "to speak on the other side" (*OED* I.1.d): the fallen angels give up their titles reluctantly and do not want to re-style themselves as princes of Hell.

[67]Although *1674* has a semicolon here, I reproduce the lighter comma of *1667*. Both editions include the unusual semicolons in the next line.

And know not that the King of Heav'n hath doom'd
This place our dungeon, not our safe retreat
Beyond his Potent arm, to live exempt
From Heav'ns high jurisdiction, in new League
Banded against his Throne, but to remaine   320
In strictest bondage, though thus far remov'd,
Under th' inevitable curb, reserv'd
His captive multitude: For he, be sure
In heighth or depth, still first and last will Reign
Sole King, and of his Kingdom loose no part   325
By our revolt, but over Hell extend
His Empire, and with Iron Scepter[68] rule
Us here, as with his Golden those in Heav'n.
What° sit we then projecting peace and Warr?   WHY
Warr hath determin'd us,[69] and foild with loss   330
Irreparable; tearms of peace yet none
Voutsaf't[70] or sought; for what peace will be giv'n
To us enslav'd, but custody severe,
And stripes, and arbitrary punishment
Inflicted? and what peace can we return,   335
But to our power hostility and hate,
Untam'd reluctance, and revenge though slow,
Yet ever plotting how the Conqueror least
May reap his conquest, and may least rejoyce
In doing what we most in suffering feel?[71]   340
Nor will occasion want, nor shall we need
With dangerous expedition to invade
Heav'n, whose high walls fear no assault or Siege,
Or ambush from the Deep. What if we find
Some easier enterprize? There is a place   345
(If ancient and prophetic fame in Heav'n
Err not),[72] another World, the happy seat
Of some new Race call'd *Man*, about this time
To be created like to us, though less
In power and excellence, but favour'd[73] more   350
Of him who rules above; so was his will
Pronounc'd among the Gods, and by an Oath,
That shook Heav'ns whol circumference,[74] confirm'd.
Thither let us bend all our thoughts, to learn
What creatures there inhabit, of what mould,   355
Or substance, how endu'd,° and what thir Power,   ENDOWED, SUPPLIED

[handwritten marginal note: There is no way out. War doesn't work. either way we lose. alternative is to go to new world + undermine God there.]

---

[68]God rules with a gold scepter in Heaven (see Esther 5.2); the iron scepter of Satan (Psalms 2.9) suggests images of both "heavy" tyranny and debased metal, gold being more valuable and higher in the Renaissance scale of being.

[69]The decision to go to war, in other words, has sealed their fate in the past.

[70]The spelling of the word normally spelled "vouchsafed" may indicate Milton's preferred phonetic spelling, as with "lantskip." Thomas Newton, writing in the mid-1700s, reports that "voutsafe" "is rather of a softer sound" (*Paradise Lost* [London: Tonson, et al., 1758; the "Sixth Edition"]).

[71]Milton usually places "doing" and "suffering" as acronyms, meaning something like "actively participating in life" vs. "having things done to you," or "doing" vs. "enduring." As with the characters of L'Allegro and Il Penseroso, the two terms suggest two ways of living or perceiving human life.

[72]I have inserted a comma here, against the evidence of both printed texts, because "another world" is in apposition with "place." The compositors may have had problems with consistent punctuation at the beginnings and ends of parentheses. I have also emended the lowercase "i" in "if" to a capital, which was the correct form of *1667*, and which Columbia, Hughes, and Fowler also silently emend.

[73]Resembling his father more, as in the idiom "He favored his father." Adam is specifically said to have been created in his Father's image, the angels not.

[74]Fowler points to Hebrews 12.16: "Whose voice then shook the earth: but now he hath promised, saying, Yet once more I shake not the earth only, but also heaven," though the Homeric and Roman gods do the same, as in the *Iliad* 1.530 and the *Aeneid* 9.106.

And where thir weakness, how attempted best,
By force or suttlety:[75] Though Heav'n be shut,
And Heav'ns high Arbitrator sit secure
In his own strength, this place may lye expos'd   360
The utmost border of his Kingdom, left
To their[76] defence who hold it: here perhaps
Som advantagious act may be achiev'd
By sudden onset, either with Hell fire
To waste his whole Creation, or possess   365
All as our own, and drive as we were driven,
The punie[77] habitants, or if not drive,°
Seduce them to our Party, that thir God
May prove thir foe, and with repenting hand
Abolish his own works.[78] This would surpass   370
Common revenge, and interrupt his joy
In our Confusion, and our Joy upraise
In his disturbance; when his darling Sons[79]
Hurl'd headlong to partake with us, shall curse
Thir frail Original,[80] and faded bliss,   375
Faded so soon. Advise if this be worth
Attempting,[81] or to sit in darkness here
Hatching vain Empires. Thus *Beelzebub*[82]
Pleaded his devilish Counsel, first devis'd
By *Satan*,[83] and in part propos'd· for whence,   380
But from the Author of all ill could Spring
So deep a malice, to confound the race
Of mankind in one root,[84] and Earth with Hell
To mingle and involve,[85] done all to spite
The great Creatour? But thir spite still serves   385
His glory to augment. The bold design

A WEAKNESS (margin annotation at line 360)

PUT TO ROUT, DRIVE AWAY (gloss at line 367)

---

[75]Presumably "suttlety" is a synonym for "guile" (see 1.34, 121, 646; 2.41, 188, for the repeated pairings of "force" and "guile").

[76]At least one other spelling of "their" (as opposed to "thir") has slipped through in the compositor's work on Book 2. Certainly any compositor setting *Paradise Lost* was instructed to use "thir" consistently throughout.

[77]As editors since Hume have noted, there may be a pun on the etymology of "puny" from the French "*puis né*," "born since us." Adam and Eve before the Fall are not in fact as weak in human terms as the fallen angels are in angelic terms; the fallen angels are rendered weak by their sin, a fact that they are not often willing to admit but one that emerges when Abdiel overcomes Satan in battle (6.327).

[78]God does repent having made Adam and Eve at Genesis 6.7: "And the Lord said, I will destroy man whom I have created from the face of the earth; both man, and beast . . . ; for it repenteth me that I have made them." This, however, was before Noah did indeed find grace "in the eyes of the Lord" (8).

[79]With the adjective "darling," Beelzebub, delivering a speech said to be devised by Satan, exhibits the envy assigned to Satan at 1.35. Envy, in other words, infects Satan and his peers equally.

[80]*1667* "Originals." Either reading is acceptable grammatically, since the word in its singular form may be a collective noun signifying "parentage," but I am assuming that *1674* corrects the earlier edition.

[81]I choose the lighter comma of *1667* rather than the semicolon of *1674*.

[82]Judging by the MS of Book 1, Milton's preferred spelling would have been with the equivalent of an umlaut over the first "e," which many modern editors reproduce, to show that the name should be pronounced "Be-él-ze-bub," rather than "Beel-ze-bub." Apparently the compositors of both the early editions either did not have the umlaut in their font case or decided to avoid the accented letter.

[83]David Daiches may have been the first critic to point out that Satan has rigged the debate and that Beelzebub is here acting as his shill or mouthpiece. "The appearance of free discussion in the debate turns out to be illusory. The assembly are persuaded by Belial and Mammon to vote for peace instead of war, but this goes against Satan's plan, so his second-in-command Beelzebub is put up to propound as though it were his own the scheme already determined on by his master" (*Milton* 172).

[84]Adam and Eve were often pictured in the sixteenth and seventeenth centuries, as in the frontispieces of various Bibles, as the root of an inverted tree of the generations of humankind.

[85]The two verbs "mingle" and "involve" suggest the complexity of the interweaving of evil with good, as with the parallel passage in *Areopagitica*: "Good and evill we know in the field of this World grow up together almost inseparably; and the knowledge of good is . . . involv'd and interwoven with the knowledge of evill" (Yale 2:514).

Pleas'd highly those infernal States,[86] and joy
Sparkl'd in all thir eyes; with full assent
They vote:[87] whereat his speech he thus renews.
    Well have ye judg'd, well ended long debate,   390
Synod of Gods,[88] and like to what ye are,
Great things resolv'd,[89] which from the lowest deep
Will once more lift us up, in spight of Fate,
Neerer our ancient Seat; perhaps in view
Of those bright confines, whence with neighbouring Arms   395
And opportune excursion we may chance
Re-enter Heav'n; or else in some milde Zone
Dwell not unvisited of Heav'ns fair Light
Secure, and at the brightning Orient beam
Purge off this gloom; the soft delicious Air,   400
To heal the scarr of these corrosive Fires
Shall breathe[90] her balme. But first whom shall we send
In search of this new world, whom shall we find
Sufficient?[91] who shall tempt[92] with wandring feet
The dark unbottom'd infinite Abyss   405
And through the palpable obscure[93] find out
His uncouth[94] way, or spread his aerie flight
Upborn° with indefatigable wings   BORNE UP
Over the vast abrupt,[95] ere he arrive
The happy Ile;[96] what strength, what art can then   410
Suffice, or what evasion bear him safe
Through the strict Senteries° and Stations thick   SENTRIES, GUARDS
Of Angels watching round? Here he had need
All circumspection, and we[97] now no less

---

[86]Here Milton uses the word to designate ranks of fallen angels.

[87]The vote shows the vacillation of an easily-swayed assembly of fallen angels, since they had voted for Mammon by their applause and with their approval just before Beelzebub's speech began.

[88]In using the phrase "Synod of Gods," Beelzebub is of course flattering his cohorts, but he is also comparing them to a church council. Milton usually uses the word "Synod" in his combative and controversial prose in a pejorative sense.

[89]Despite the fact that some copies of *1674* show a mark above the comma that might indicate a semicolon, most do not; the lighter comma of *1678* seems preferable.

[90]*1667* "breath," obviously incorrect. It would be possible to breathe balm either in the sense that the fire might emit balm or in the sense that healing balm can be breathed in vapor.

[91]This seems to be a rhetorical question, to be answered immediately by the appearance of Satan. The reader is probably supposed to remember, later, that God in a similar situation asks for a volunteer, and the Son becomes that volunteer of His own will.

[92]The *OED* defines the usage here as "venture upon" (I.2.C), with this as the first instance, but perhaps "attempt" would more simply define the word. There may also be a foreshadowing pun on "tempt" / "attempt."

[93]A Miltonic coinage of phrase, using "obscure" as a noun, meaning "darkness," and modifying it with a sensual or synesthetic adjective, "palpable," meaning "touchable." The result is something like an allegorical entity, "the Darkness which can be perceived feelingly." Corns explains: " . . . as Satan evokes for his infernal audience the prospective horror of traversing chaos, readers too are left groping for some familiar substantive to fix upon: we find instead the shaky premise of a new noun, either the 'obscure', which is palpable, or, if the usual order is inverted, as well it may be, the 'palpable', which is obscure!" (88).

[94]"Unchartered" or "unknown" or "unfamiliar" (see *OED* adj. A 2 a, citing this instance) with just a hint that Satan may be traveling through disreputable areas (compare *Samson Agonistes* 333).

[95]Another wrenching of syntax and normal meaning in a noun phrase, using the Latin etymology of "*ab+ruptus,*" suggesting an enormous gulf and expanding on "vast." "Abrupt" is normally an adjective in English, but Milton's usage here is the first recorded for "abrupt" as a noun standing for the gap between Heaven and Hell (*OED* noun B).

[96]Probably the island of the Hesperides, though there were many paradisal islands to be found in classical and Renaissance epic literature, as with Camoëns's "Island of Love" where Venus and Tethys have an idyll; see the *Lusiads* 9.21–95, and 10. See the other references to the Hesperides below, 3.568–70.

[97]For some reason that has caused all subsequent editors confusion, the *1668 Errata* call for "wee" here, but the word is not stressed in the line (stress should fall on "now"), nor does the compositor of *1674* make the change, though he does make changes for all other corrections listed. I have assumed, with Fletcher (3:136n), that "we" is correct.

Choice in our suffrage;° for on whom we send,   VOTE   415
The weight of all and our last hope relies.
        This said, he sat; and expectation held
His look suspence,[98] awaiting who appeer'd
To second, or oppose, or undertake
The perilous attempt: but all sat mute,   420
Pondering the danger with deep thoughts; and each
In others count'nance read his own dismay
Astonisht: none among the choice and prime
Of those Heav'n-warring Champions could be found[99]
So hardie as to proffer or accept   425
Alone the dreadful voyage; till at last
Satan, whom now transcendent glory rais'd
Above his fellows, with Monarchal pride
Conscious of highest worth, unmov'd thus spake.[100]
        O Progeny of Heav'n, Empyreal Thrones,   430
With reason hath deep silence and demurr°   HESITATION
Seis'd us, though undismaid: long is the way
And hard,[101] that out of Hell leads up to light;
Our prison strong, this huge convex[102] of Fire,
Outrageous[103] to devour, immures us round°   WALLS US IN   435
Ninefold, and gates of burning Adamant
Barr'd over us prohibit all egress.°   MEANS OF EXIT
These past, if any pass, the void profound
Of unessential Night[104] receives him next
Wide gaping, and with utter loss of being[105]   440
Threatens him, plung'd in that abortive[106] gulf.
If thence he scape into what ever world,
Or unknown Region, what remains him less
Then unknown dangers and as hard escape.
But I should ill become this Throne, O Peers,   445
And this Imperial Sov'ranty, adorn'd
With splendor, arm'd with power, if aught propos'd

---

[98]"His attentive look fixed his [facial] expression." *OED* defines "suspense" as "attentive" (adj. 2), citing this instance.

[99]Again, Milton uses heavy irony to suggest that the fallen angels embody the physical military glory of medieval or Renaissance epic heroes, who were always either warring or proceeding on quests.

[100]Satan is playing a part here, so far as I can tell, since he has engineered the proceedings to allow himself to shine forth in all his "transcendent glory." As Fowler points out, a contrast between his behavior and Messiah's at 3.227–29, must be intended, since both volunteer to go alone on a perilous quest.

[101]As contrasted with the "ready and easy way" of Milton's pamphlet beginning with the same phrase, or the Serpent's promise to Eve of "the way" that "is readie, and not long" to the forbidden fruit (9.626). The phrase is Milton's equivalent of Ophelia's "primrose path of dalliance" (*Hamlet* 1.3.50). The way to Heaven, or the way to Truth, by contrast, is always steep and difficult, as in Donne's Satire 3.79–110, where truth is pictured "On a huge hill, / Cragged and steep, . . ." (A. L. Clements ed., *John Donne's Poetry* [NY: Norton, 1966]).

[102]The same vault structure or cope (1.345) mentioned earlier, for Hell as well as the obverse for Heaven (1.669).

[103]The very fires in Hell are pictured as having emotions, in "raging" (213), "piercing" (275), and being "corrosive" (401) to torture and eat away at the fallen angels. Here they are voraciously hungry to eat them.

[104]The same as "uncreated night" in 150, suggesting that God withheld his creation and his essence from night and chaos, but not that night or chaos were inherently evil. For Milton, the universe was made out of matter (Yale 6:307) which was "not an evil thing, nor to be thought of as worthless" (308). Milton used the proof text Exodus 33.23 concerning "the back parts" of God, to illustrate his belief that some parts God used in creation were lower than others (312). "Unessential" could also mean "unimportant"; hence Corns writes, "Milton, with considerable precision, uses it as an epithet for eternal formlessness of night as Satan enters [it] . . . God has given no essential form to night" (94).

[105]More extreme than mere death, which robs one of immortality, this loss of being is perhaps what Belial was referring to as the loss of "intellectual being" (147). Faculty psychology located the intellectual being as separate from and above the physical faculties. Renaissance theories of the organic soul excluded the intellect and the will from functions tied to the body, and thus they were capable of surviving mortal death. See *The Cambridge History of Renaissance Philosophy*, ed. Charles B. Schmitt, et al. (Cambridge: Cambridge UP, 1988): 464–67. Part of the punishment of the fallen angels is having their names and all memory of them in Heaven utterly erased from the Books of Life (see 1.361–63).

[106]See *OED* adj. A.1.b, "rendering fruitless," citing this passage.

And judg'd of public moment, in the shape
Of difficulty or danger could deterr
Mee[107] from attempting. Wherefore do I assume   450
These Royalties,° and not refuse to Reign,   ROYAL TITLES
Refusing to accept as great a share
Of hazard[108] as of honour, due alike
To him who Reigns, and so much to him due
Of hazard more, as he above the rest   455
High honourd sits? Go therfore mighty Powers,
Terror of Heav'n, though fall'n; intend[109] at home,
While here shall be our home, what best may ease
The present misery, and render Hell
More tollerable; if there be cure or charm[110]   460
To respite or deceive, or slack the pain
Of this ill Mansion: intermit no watch
Against a wakeful Foe, while I abroad
Through all the Coasts of dark destruction seek
Deliverance for us all: this enterprize   465
None shall partake with me.[111] Thus saying rose
The Monarch, and prevented all reply,[112]
Prudent, least° from his resolution rais'd   LEST
Others among the chief might offer now
(Certain to be refus'd) what erst they feard;   470
And so refus'd might in opinion stand
His Rivals, winning cheap the high repute
Which he through hazard huge must earn. But they
Dreaded[113] not more th' adventure then his voice
Forbidding; and at once with him they rose;   475
Thir rising all at once was as the sound
Of Thunder heard remote. Towards him they bend
With awful° reverence prone; and as a God   AWE-INSPIRED
Extoll him equal to the highest in Heav'n:
Nor fail'd they to express how much they prais'd,   480
That for the general safety he despis'd
His own: for neither do the Spirits damn'd
Loose all her virtue; least bad men should boast
Thir specious deeds on earth, which glory excites,

---

[107]The earlier of the two states of *1674* had "Me," and here the word seems to be stressed, though in a trochaic, rather than iambic, foot.

[108]For the political implications of this passage, one might compare Milton's image of Charles I "hazarding the welfare of a whole Nation" in *The Tenure of Kings and Magistrates* (Yale 3: 193). Since hazard is also a game of chance (*OED* 1), the repeated image (473 below) suggests how chancy Satan's playing for such high stakes might be.

[109]A sense of the verb unfamiliar to the modern reader, perhaps derived closely from the Latin *intendere*, "stretch out" or "stretch in the direction of." See *OED* v.III.12, "to occupy oneself with," citing this passage.

[110]It is appropriate that fallen angels used devilish charms to deceive themselves into believing they feel better than they do. In Milton's era amulets and other charms were used either to ward off demons or cure diseases. See Michael MacDonald, *Mystical Bedlam* (Madison: U Wisconsin P, 1981), passim, for the use of amulets in seventeenth-century "medicine." See also Otten, *Environ'd*.

[111]The speech may imitate that of Sarpedon to Glaucus (*Iliad* 12.310–28). Newton (450n) thought Milton might be expressing an iconoclastic dislike of kings in the passage.

[112]Satan's announcement tolerates no dissent and preempts or anticipates (the contemporary meaning of "prevent") all reply. The word "alone" buried in the "mon-" root of "Monarch"—and Satan had called God "monarch"—reinforced by Satan's "none," helps announce that Satan's "heroic" choice is an egocentric and predetermined act. In the act of "preventing all reply," he stifles all dissent by anticipating it; any dissent is "Certain to be refus'd." Hell is ruthlessly competitive, and Satan fears for the possibility of "Rivals." In fact, the rest of the fallen angels are too cowardly to compete with him.

[113]The verb implies fear of a tyrant, here and elsewhere in this book.

Or close[114] ambition varnisht o're with zeal.[115]   485
Thus they thir doubtful consultations dark
Ended rejoycing in thir matchless Chief:
As when from mountain tops the dusky clouds
Ascending, while the North wind sleeps, o'respread
Heav'ns chearful face, the lowring Element   490
Scowls ore the dark'nd lantskip Snow, or showre;[116]
If chance the radiant Sun with farewell sweet
Extend his ev'ning beam, the fields revive,
The birds thir notes renew, and bleating herds
Attest thir joy, that hill and valley rings.   495
O shame to men! Devil with Devil damn'd
Firm concord holds, men onely disagree
Of Creatures rational, though under hope
Of heavenly Grace: and God proclaiming peace,
Yet live in hatred, enmity, and strife   500
Among themselves, and levie cruel warres,
Wasting the Earth, each other to destroy:
As if (which might induce us to accord)
Man had not hellish foes anow[117] besides,
That day and night for his destruction waite.   505
   The *Stygian* Counsel thus dissolv'd; and forth
In order came the grand infernal Peers,
Midst came thir mighty Paramount,[118] and seemd
Alone th' Antagonist of Heav'n, nor less
Than Hells dread Emperour with pomp Supream,   510
And God-like imitated State;[119] him round
A Globe of fierie Seraphim inclos'd
With bright imblazonrie,[120] and horrent[121] Arms.
Then of thir Session ended they bid cry°   ANNOUNCE
With Trumpets regal sound the great result: 515
Toward the four winds four speedy Cherubim
Put to thir mouths the sounding Alchymie[122]
By Haralds voice explain'd: the hollow Abyss
Heard farr and wide, and all the host of Hell
With deafning shout, return'd them loud acclaim.   520
Thence more at ease thir minds and somwhat rais'd

---

[114]Here I follow *1667*, in preference to *1674* "clos." "Close" means "secretive" or clandestine.

[115]Compare Milton's sentiments about those martyred for false causes, in *Of Reformation*: the false martyr "is not therfore above all possibility of erring, because hee burnes for some Points of Truth" (Yale 1: 533).

[116]A curious line for the spelling and the usage it exemplifies, since "ore" had been "o're" in 485 and "o'respread" in 489, and "lantskip" probably represents a Milton's phonetic spelling for *landscape*. The verb "Scowls" is also applied to the weather personified—an unusual, if not unique, usage (see *OED* v. 3).

[117]A Miltonic phonetic spelling, probably pronounced "ah-now," for the modern "enough," as in "Lycidas" 114. The concord of the devils here contrasts with the discord of men, perpetually at war with one another: a bitterly ironic narrative statement.

[118]"The grand infernal peers came in order, in the midst of them their grand ruler ['Paramount'] . . . ." Some editors emend the comma after "Peers" to a colon (Elledge does, and Fowler, though he does not make the change, thinks that stronger punctuation is in order); I see no reason to make any change.

[119]The key word in the phrase is "imitated," which functions in a way similar to "*Barbaric*" in 4, to undercut with irony the effect of "God-like . . . State."

[120]Various heraldic devices (see *OED* sb.1.b, "emblazonry," citing this passage), appropriate for a force that prefigures the hundreds of armies that appear in classical and Renaissance epic. Again, the embellishment suggests false style rather than true courage.

[121]A Miltonic coinage, the first recorded use of the word (*OED* a.1). Milton uses a neologism here apparently to make clear that he means "horrible," derived from the Latin participle "*horrens*," though the root of *horrens*, *horreo*, "to stand erect, to bristle," may also help give the image of bristling spears in a spherical formation (compare Vergil, *Aeneid* 10.178, and see Corns 89). Because the angels can move in all dimensions of space, they can form that emblem of perfection, the globe or sphere, even in battle formation, emitting light like an angelic sun.

[122]The trumpets are made of imitation gold, "alchemy gold" (see *OED* 3). The whole scene is a cheap imitation of what the "bright Seraphim" perform in "At a Solemn Music."

By false presumptuous hope, the ranged powers[123]
Disband, and wandring, each his several way
Pursues, as inclination or sad choice
Leads him perplext, where he may likeliest find   525
Truce to his restless thoughts, and entertain
The irksom hours, till his[124] great Chief return.
Part on the Plain, or° in the Air sublime[125]   EITHER
Upon the wing, or in swift Race contend,
As at th' Olympian Games or *Pythian*[126] fields;   530
Part curb thir fierie Steeds, or shun[127] the Goal
With rapid wheels, or fronted° Brigads form.   FACING
As when to warn proud Cities warr appears
Wag'd in the troubl'd Skie, and Armies rush
To Battel in the Clouds,[128] before each Van°   VANGUARD 535
Prick forth the Aerie Knights,[129] and couch thir Spears
Till thickest Legions close; with feats of Arms
From either end of Heav'n the welkin° burns.   SKY
Others with vast *Typhœan*[130] rage more fell
Rend up both Rocks and Hills, and ride the Air   540
In whirlwind;[131] Hell scarce holds the wilde uproar.
As when *Alcides* from *Oechalia*[132] Crown'd
With conquest, felt th' envenom'd robe, and tore
Through pain up by the roots *Thessalian* Pines,
And *Lichas* from the top of *Oeta* threw   545
Into th' *Euboic* Sea. Others more milde,
Retreated in° a silent valley, sing   HAVING RETIRED TO
With notes Angelical to many a Harp
Thir own Heroic deeds and hapless fall
By doom of Battel; and complain that Fate   550

[123]"The armies arranged in ranks."

[124]*1674* has "this," which makes less sense than "thir" or *1667* "his." Since three forms of the masculine singular pronoun have just appeared, the best choice seems to be "his."

[125]Probably "in the upper air" (see *OED* a.1), or at least "aloft," as opposed to being on the ground.

[126]Pythia, a seat of ancient Greek games second only to Olympia, held games devoted to Pythian Apollo near the god's temple at Delphi. Since Apollo had instituted the games to celebrate his victory over the serpent Python, Milton's version might be intended to foreshadow Christ's victory over Satan as serpent. The choice between **not** italicizing "Olympian" and italicizing "*Pythian*" may be significant, if it is intended to devalue what comes from Olympia; more likely it represents carelessness on the part of the compositor.

[127]Probably "to avoid hitting the goal with their chariots." Horace *Odes*, 1.1.4–5, pictures a charioteer taking a corner rapidly, narrowly avoiding the **meta**, or turning point.

[128]Describes what is possibly a mirage or a prophetic image showing the inhabitants of the city a distant army approaching. See Josephus, *The Jewish War* 6.5.3, which describes multiple mirages of chariots and armed battalions in the sky. See also Vergil, *Aeneid* 8.528–29, where Venus gives Aeneas a vision of armies in a thunderstorm.

[129]Again, Milton makes fun of physical heroism in terms of Greek Olympic or Pythian games, or the jousting of "brigades" of knights in Renaissance romantic epics, even those of Spenser, where knights would "Prick forth . . . and couch thir Spears." The verb "prick" here refers to spurring on a horse. See the first line of Book 1 of *The Faerie Queene*. The verb "couch" refers to placing the spear in a ready position for battle (*OED* "couch" 1.7).

[130]With deadly ("fell") rage like that of Typhon or Typhoeus, a hundred-headed giant, son of Tartarus and Terra, who as soon as he was born waged war on behalf of his brother giants against Jove. Eventually the gods were supposed to have buried Typhoeus beneath Mount Aetna in Sicily, though other legends place him elsewhere. See Hesiod, *Theogony* 820, and compare this passage with 1.199.

[131]Witches in Milton's era were generally supposed to "ride the whirlwind." Being tossed in swirling winds, one of the traditional punishments of the damned, as with Paolo and Francesca in Dante, *Inferno* 5.82–142. There may be a reference to *Typhoean* as well, since English "typhon," or more familiarly "typhoon," was a whirlwind. The frustrated evil angels also threw rocks and hills during the War in Heaven (6.639–66).

[132]Corrects the misprint *Oealia* of *1667*. Alcides is Heracles or Hercules, driven insane by the "shirt of Nessus," a tunic poisoned with the blood of the Centaur Nessus, sent him by his wife Dejanira while he is being unfaithful to her with Iole, daughter of the King of Oechalia. In the insane fury caused by the poisoning, Hercules throws his servant Lichas, who had brought the robe, into the sea. Seneca's *Hercules Furens*, popular as a model of revenge tragedy in Milton's youth, deals with the story of Hercules' insanity, but Fowler notes the reliance on Ovid, *Metamorphoses* 9.136, rather than Seneca or Sophocles (*Trachiniae*) in this passage. See also Braden. Milton is again defaming the Greek and Roman myths by revealing only their emphasis on violence, as with the "rage / Of *Turnus*" (9.16–17).

Free Vertue should enthrall to Force or Chance.[133]
Thir Song was partial,[134] but the harmony
(What could it less when Spirits immortal sing?)
Suspended Hell, and took with ravishment
The thronging audience. In discourse more sweet   555
(For Eloquence the Soul, Song charms the Sense,)[135]
Others apart sat on a Hill retir'd,
In thoughts more elevate, and reason'd high
Of Providence, Foreknowledge, Will and Fate,
Fixt Fate, free will, foreknowledg absolute,[136]   560
And found no end, in wandring mazes lost.[137]
Of good and evil much they argu'd then,
Of happiness and final misery,
Passion and Apathie,[138] and glory and shame,
Vain wisdom all, and false Philosophie: 565
Yet with a pleasing sorcerie could charm[139]
Pain for a while or anguish, and excite
Fallacious hope, or arm th' obdured° brest   HARDENED
With stubborn patience as with triple steel.[140]
Another part in Squadrons and gross[141] Bands,   570
On bold adventure to discover wide
That dismal world, if any Clime perhaps
Might yield them easier habitation, bend
Four ways thir flying March, along the Banks
Of four infernal Rivers[142] that disgorge°   VOMIT   575
Into the burning Lake thir baleful streams;[143]
Abhorred *Styx* the flood of deadly hate,
Sad *Acheron* of sorrow, black and deep;

---

[133]A deeply ironic passage, since the fallen angels are attempting to celebrate what is philosophically impossible for them: the freedom of the will. Their heroic complaints focus on the thwarting of free virtue by force or chance, which might have been a valid subject for unenlightened pagan poets but would be ridiculous to a Christian who believes that God's will is fate (7.173) and that neither virtue nor free will could ever be made captive (5.527). The poetic fallen angels are compared implicitly with pre-Christian poets like Homer and Vergil.

[134]Polyphonic or divided into musical parts. The song was also one-sided, according to demonic perspective. Milton allows the fallen angels who are poets and singers beauty of expression, but cautions the attentive reader that their compositions would be sentimental (the word "hapless" signals self-pity) and even trendy or overly fashionable (the word "complain" suggests the familiar lover's "plaint," and may be used as satirically as Marvell uses it in "To His Coy Mistress": "I by the Tide / Of *Humber* would complain" (1.27).

[135]The senses, as compared to higher faculties of the mind or spirit.

[136]The subjects argued over constantly by Christian theologians, including Milton himself, in *On Christian Doctrine*, as in Chapter 4, "Of Predestination," and Chapter 8, "Of God's Providence, or His Universal Government of Things." Again, the irony of having the discussion, among fallen angels self-tempted and condemned, is obvious.

[137]The sardonic humor in the picture of philosophical fallen angels, whose decision to rebel has ordained their fate, debating providence and free will, is similar to that reserved for other misguided heretics, as with the Limbo of Vanity passage (3.445–459). William B. Hunter points out (letter, September 1991) that Chaucer achieves a similar comic effect in "The Nun's Priest's Tale," by discussing the effects of fate in a chicken yard. The corrective parallel for the image of the maze of error would be the intricate formations of the good angels or the complex music they make, but the word "maze," especially as connected with "error," is almost always negative in Milton's poetry. Intricacy is not evil in itself, but confusing mazes that lead us into error are.

[138]"Freedom from, or insensitivity to, suffering; . . . passionless existence" (*OED* 1), the ideal of Stoicism, which Jesus in *Paradise Regain'd* must confront in 4.300–21.

[139]As the inspirers of black magic, the fallen angels practice "charming" rhetoric or philosophy which "ravishes" its audience with an unnatural "sweetness." In fact even their music causes its hearer to become lost in wandering mazes, as will sight of the Serpent's "mazie foulds" (9.161) cause Eve confusion.

[140]An allusion to Horace's well-known "*Aes triplex*," or "triple bronze," referring to the layers of a shield at Ode 1.3.9–10. Milton competitively substitutes the harder metal, steel, for Horace's bronze.

[141]"'Solid' in the geometrical sense; having three dimensions" (*OED* adj. 4, A III 10, which cites this passage).

[142]Note the parallel with the four rivers of Paradise.

[143]Since "baleful" is a word associated with Satan (1.56), it is more strongly negative, and less good-humored, than the modern word. One of the fallen angels' vain pursuits is exploration. Milton did not disparage exploration within his own world and in his own time (he was a collector of maps and atlases and taught his own pupils geography), but the exploration conducted by the fallen angels is escapism and meaningless diversion, to take their minds off pain.

Cocytus, nam'd of lamentation loud
Heard on the ruful stream; fierce *Phlegeton*   580
Whose waves of torrent° fire inflame with rage.[144]   FAST-FLOWING
Farr off from these a slow and silent stream,
Lethe the River of Oblivion roules
Her watrie Labyrinth, whereof who drinks,
Forthwith his former state and being forgets,   585
Forgets both joy and grief, pleasure and pain.[145]
Beyond this flood a frozen Continent[146]
Lies dark and wilde, beat with perpetual storms
Of Whirlwind and dire Hail, which on firm land
Thaws not, but gathers heap,[147] and ruin seems   590
Of ancient pile;[148] all else deep snow and ice,
A gulf profound as that *Serbonian* Bog
Betwixt *Damiata* and mount *Casius* old,[149]
Where Armies whole have sunk: the parching Air
Burns frore,[150] and cold performs th' effect of Fire.   595
Thither by harpy-footed Furies[151] hail'd,[152]
At certain revolutions[153] all the damn'd
Are brought: and feel by turns the bitter change
Of fierce extreams, extreams by change more fierce,
From Beds of raging Fire to starve° in Ice   DESTROY   600
Thir soft Ethereal warmth, and there to pine
Immovable, infixt, and frozen round,
Periods of time, thence hurried back to fire.
They ferry over this *Lethean* Sound°   STRAIT, NARROW CHANNEL
Both to and fro, thir sorrow to augment,   605
And wish and struggle, as they pass, to reach
The tempting stream, with one small drop to loose°   LOSE
In sweet forgetfulness all pain and woe,
All in one moment, and so neer the brink;
But Fate withstands, and to oppose th' attempt   610
Medusa with *Gorgonian* terror guards[154]

---

[144]Compare Alexander Ross, *Mystagogus Poeticus, or the Muses Interpreter*, ed. John R. Glenn (New York: Garland, 1987): "Acheron signifieth joylesse; Styx hatred, from stugeros hatefull; Cocytus complaint or lamentation; . . . Some add the fourth river, called Phlegeton, from burning, by which may be meant the wrath of God which burneth like a river of brimstone" (532–33). Milton also translates each name into a pejorative form, as with "Abhorred *Styx*."
[145]The River Lethe's aimless labyrinth (a hopeless maze) is the pictorial equivalent of "error," or aimless and immoral wandering. The fallen angels not only wander aimlessly but they drink to forget, from the "River of Oblivion."
[146]The classical "house of Hades" had no frozen region; Dante's Satan, however, is enclosed in ice in the region of the Inferno called Dis (*Inferno* 34.28–31). The Christian tradition of fire as well as ice in Hell may take it roots, as Fowler points out, in some of the uncanonical apocryphal books of the Bible, as with a passage in 2 Enoch 10.2–3 (see Charles 2.435).
[147]Gathers mass. An unusual usage for the noun form, probably suggesting a disorderly gathering or chaotic jumble.
[148]Similar in usage to "heap," though "ancient pile" also means "ancient architectural structure."
[149]Serbonis, a lake on the coast of Egypt bordered by quicksand. The giant Typhon was supposed by some accounts to be buried beneath the lake (in other accounts, he was beneath Mt. Aetna, as at 539), and the quicksand was supposed to have the capacity to bury whole armies. Fowler finds frequent mention of Damiata and Mount Casius (here scanned as a disyllable) in Renaissance Italian epics.
[150]"Intensely cold" (*OED* ppl. 2). Extreme heat or cold gives the opposite impression to the senses, so that intensely cold air burns. Corns believes the usage to be archaic (111).
[151]In seventeenth-century emblem books the Furies (also called the Eumenides or Erinyes) were sometimes pictured with the bird-like feet given to Harpies, the disgusting bird-like creatures that plague the Argonauts and Aeneas and make an appearance in Shakespeare's *The Tempest*, as Ariel in disguise (3.2.52, stage direction).
[152]Probably should be read as "haled," meaning "dragged," as in the idiom "haled into court."
[153]Apparently the damned in Milton's Hell serve their punishments in a perpetual round, not as in Vergil's underworld, where the penitent, after completion of "*certain revolutions or periods of time*, have become purified (*Aen.* VI, 745–51)" (Fowler 603–10n).
[154]Medusa, with her head of writhing serpents, is one of the three Gorgons. Because her head has the power to turn men to stone, and the drops of her blood to be transformed into Libyan serpents (see Lucan, *Pharsalia* 9.619–99), Milton associates her with Hell and Satan.

The Ford, and of it self the water flies
All taste of living wight,° as once it fled   HUMAN BEING
The lip of *Tantalus*.[155] Thus roving on
In confus'd march forlorn, th' adventrous[156] Bands   615
With shuddring horror pale, and eyes agast
View'd first thir lamentable lot, and found
No rest: through many a dark and drearie Vaile
They pass'd, and many a Region dolorous,
O're many a Frozen, many a fierie Alpe,[157]   620
Rocks, Caves, Lakes, Fens, Bogs, Dens, and shades of death,[158]
A Universe of death, which God by curse
Created evil, for evil only good,[159]
Where all life dies, death lives, and Nature breeds,
Perverse,[160] all monstrous, all prodigious things,   625
Abominable, inutterable, and worse
Than[161] Fables yet have feign'd, or fear conceiv'd,
Gorgons and *Hydra's*, and *Chimera's*[162] dire.
 Mean while the Adversary of God and Man,
Satan with thoughts inflam'd of highest design[163]   630
Puts on swift wings, and towards the Gates of Hell
Explores his solitary flight; som times
He scours the right hand coast, som times the left,
Now shaves with level wing the Deep, then soares
Up to the fiery Concave touring° high.   TOWERING 635
As when farr off at Sea a Fleet descri'd[164]
Hangs in the Clouds, by *Æquinoctial* Winds

---

[155]Tantalus, a son of Jupiter and king of Lydia supposed to have eaten his own child, Pelops, is usually pictured being punished in the classical hell with water up to the level of his mouth: what is tantalizing about his position is that every time he bends to drink, the water recedes out of his reach (see Homer, *Odyssey* 11.582–92).

[156]Milton can use the word "adventrous" positively, as with his own "adventrous Song" (1.13); here perhaps he is showing that there is at least the vestige of heroism in what the fallen angels do. But adventuring by its very nature is dangerous.

[157]"Alpe" is used generically for any mountain (compare *Samson Agonistes* 628); needless to say, Milton knew of the real mountain range, having crossed the Alps on his way from Italy into Switzerland in 1639.

[158]A metrical tour-de-force of monosyllabic words in an iambic line, memorable for its sound and its experimental quality. Compare 948 and 950.

[159]God creates Hell as evil by cursing the region, even though the creation of evil, by the scheme of divine providence, is designed to promote only good in the end: " . . . God always produces something good and just out of [evil or injustice] and creates, as it were, light out of darkness" (*On Christian Doctrine* 1.8; Yale 6: 333). Line 623, despite looking as if it is "short," actually contains eleven syllables and as such might be unique in the epic. An elision across "for evil" may be intended in order to make the stresses in the line regular.

[160]The words "perverse" and "pervert" (the verb) will often echo within descriptions of what fallen angels do. The word does not indicate sexual preference for Milton; rather it suggests an opposition to any natural process, as in "monstrous" or "prodigious." God creates Hell to be an evil universe of death, but for an ultimately good purpose; if He had created evil without allowing in more powerful opposition, he would be the author of evil (see *On Christian Doctrine* 1.3, Yale 6: 166). The marginalia of the Geneva Bible (James 1.17n) cautions "Seing all good things come of God, we oght not to make him the autor of evil." Milton found it "intolerable and incredible that evil should be stronger than good and should prove the true supreme power" (*On Christian Doctrine* 1.2, Yale 6: 131). Thus evil is always perverse, monstrous, unnatural, or prodigious, and God is always free of the charge of having initiated it.

[161]The more customary "then" is used in *1667*. Likewise, "toward" at 631 in *1667* is corrected in *1674* to "towards."

[162]A small catalogue of the most fearful of classical monsters. The Gorgon Medusa's snaky-haired face can turn people to stone, even after she is beheaded by Perseus; the Hydra is a many-headed monster overcome by Hercules as one of his labors; and the Chimera, offspring of Echidna and Typhon, is a triple-headed or triple-bodied beast supposedly conquered by Bellerophon. "*Chimera's*" should be accented on the second syllable.

[163]Satan is inflamed (appropriate for someone in Hell) with his plan or purpose ("design") to seduce humankind.

[164]Another mirage, as with the army in 535. Satan flying is compared to the fleet seen in mirage by merchants sailing with the trade winds of the vernal equinox in the Indian Ocean ("Ethiopian [Sea]") toward the Cape of Good Hope. The "Trading Flood" is "the part of the world's waters used for trade" (see *OED* sb. 3 for the meaning "waters"). The context is that of colonial conquest (Evans, *Milton's Imperial Epic* 71). Ternate and Tidore are two of the Moluccas or "Spice Islands," both of which were ports of call for the Dutch East India Company. Milton may be drawing on his diplomatic experience as a civil servant in dealing with various merchants of the Low Countries. The entire simile is a living picture of East Indian trade in Milton's era, with some suggestion of evil in the dangerous conquest of expensive and exotic spices and in the choice of the word "Drugs" (though "drugs" in the seventeenth century would have included tea, chocolate, and spices—see *OED* sb. 1). It is again appropriate that Satan be perceived in an illusion, as the word "seem'd" in 642 would indicate.

Close sailing from *Bengala*, or the Iles
Of *Ternate* and *Tidore*, whence Merchants bring
Thir spicie Drugs: they on the Trading Flood[165]   640
Through the wide *Ethiopian* to the Cape
Ply stemming nightly toward the Pole. So seem'd
Farr off the flying Fiend:[166] at last appeer
Hell bounds high reaching to the horrid Roof,
And thrice threefold the Gates; three folds were Brass,   645
Three Iron, three of Adamantine Rock,
Impenetrable,[167] impal'd with circling fire,
Yet unconsum'd. Before the Gates there sat
On either side a formidable shape;[168]
The one seem'd Woman to the waste,° and fair,   WAIST   650
But ended foul[169] in many a scaly fould
Voluminous and vast, a Serpent arm'd
With mortal sting: about her middle round
A cry of Hell Hounds never ceasing bark'd
With wide *Cerberian*[170] mouths full loud, and rung   655
A hideous Peal:[171] yet, when they list, would creep,
If aught disturb'd thir noyse, into her woomb,
And kennel there, yet there still bark'd and howl'd,
Within unseen.[172] Farr less abhorrd than these
Vex'd *Scylla* bathing in the Sea that parts   660
Calabria from the hoarce *Trinacrian* shore:[173]
Nor uglier follow the Night-Hag, when call'd
In secret, riding through the Air she comes
Lur'd with the smell of infant blood, to dance

---

[165]"On the sea given over to trade."

[166]The first time any "fiend" is mentioned. While discussing beings in Hell, Milton has still emphasized the remnants of the angelic in the fallen angels. In Hell it is more convenient for the reader to think in terms of "fallen angels," whereas Satan on the road toward corrupting humankind becomes more fiendlike. The use of words like "fiend," "goblin," and even "pest" (with its French sense of "plague") indicates the real or perceived declension of demonic heroism.

[167]The gates are three-fold, as with the "triple steel" of 151, perhaps to make the comparison with classical armor implicit. The adjective "impal'd" suggests that the flames are like palings or encircling fences.

[168]The whole of the following narrative takes its foundation from the Epistle of James, 1.15: "When lust hath conceived, it bringeth forth sin: and sin, when it is finished, bringeth forth death." The parallel between Father, Son, and Holy Spirit and its degraded image of Satan, Sin, and Death is enforced throughout.

[169]Sin begins at her upper body as "fair," or beautiful, but, as one's line of sight moves down she is revealed as "foul" or loathsome in appearance. She embodies many classical and Christian pictures and metaphors. Her upper parts are tempting for their apparent fair beauty, but her lower parts are foul and serpentine, and she has a stinger in her tail, like a scorpion, or like the Chorus's image of Dalila in *Samson Agonistes* 997. Milton's image, as many critics have pointed out, resembles Homer's Scylla, Ovid's Echidna, and Spenser's Duessa. Sin is a combination of seductive mermaid and serpent with mortal sting, attended by hounds of hell that gnaw on her vitals. Like Tasso's Alcina and Morgana, Sin is born of incest and therefore "is their life ungodly and defamed" (*Jerusalem Delivered* 6.44, Harington trans.). Even to a modern reader, the image of Sin is nightmarish, embodying dreamlike fears of forbidden sexuality (Kerrigan, *Sacred* 187).

[170]The line in *1667* has "Cerberean," which is the more common spelling. Cerberus was the three-headed dog who guarded the entrance of the classical Hades, hence the original Hell hound. Here the Hell hounds are a multitude, as in 10.630.

[171]The voices of normal hounds were said to match each other like the peals of bells: compare the famous passage in *Midsummer Night's Dream*, when Theseus describes the music of his pack of hounds "match'd in mouth like bells" (4.1.123), singing in harmony. This peal, however, is hideous noise.

[172]The "Hell hounds" (offspring of Death, not Satan) are grossly realistic but nightmarish at the same time. Their crawling in and out of Sin's womb is an image Freudian critics think may embody fear of the feminine principle: "The objects Satan recoils from—his obedience, his source, the Son who is his source—are symbolized by the tormented womb of the woman once a part of him" (Kerrigan 187).

[173]Scylla will appear in 1019–20 as a threat to Ulysses. Milton makes her weep in *Comus* 257. Scylla was daughter of Typhon, courted by Glaucus. She rejected him and was punished by Circe, who poisoned the water in which she was bathing, "vexing" Scylla and causing the metamorphosis into the half-woman, half-barking-dogs shape (*Metamorphoses* 14.59). When she committed suicide by jumping into the sea between Calabria in southern Italy and the island of Sicily (the Trinacrian shore because Trinacria—meaning "triangular in shape"—was one of the ancient names of Sicily), she became clashing rocks, which, together with the whirlpools of Charybdis, threatened mariners like Ulysses when they passed through the straits of Messina. The shore is hoarse (I presume) because of the noise of the sea, or the proximity of Mount Aetna, which might roar when active.

With *Lapland* Witches, while the labouring Moon   665
Eclipses at thir charms.[174] The other shape,[175]
If shape it might be call'd that shape had none
Distinguishable in member, joynt, or limb,
Or substance might be call'd that shadow seem'd,
For each seem'd either;[176] black it stood as Night,   670
Fierce as ten Furies, terrible as Hell,
And shook a dreadful Dart; what seem'd his head
The likeness of a Kingly Crown had on.
Satan was now at hand, and from his seat
The Monster moving onward came as fast   675
With horrid strides, Hell trembled as he strode.
Th' undaunted Fiend what this might be admir'd,°   WONDERED AT
Admir'd, not fear'd; God and his Son except,
Created thing[177] naught valu'd he nor shun'd;
And with disdainful look thus first began.   680
    Whence and what art thou, execrable shape,
That dar'st, though grim and terrible, advance
Thy miscreated Front[178] athwart my way
To yonder Gates? through them I mean to pass,
That be assur'd, without leave askt of thee: 685
Retire, or taste thy folly, and learn by proof,°   EXPERIENCE
Hell-born, not to contend with Spirits of Heav'n.
    To whom the Goblin full of wrauth reply'd.[179]
Art thou that Traitor Angel, art thou hee,
Who first broke peace in Heav'n and Faith, till then   690
Unbrok'n, and in proud rebellious Arms
Drew after him the third part of Heav'ns Sons[180]
Conjur'd[181] against the highest, for which both Thou

---

[174]Here Milton mentions witches with no hint of skepticism, though by 1667 the European fervor to hunt down witches had all but died out (it took longer to die out in America; witness the Salem witch trials in 1692). See Keith Thomas, *Religion and the Decline of Magic* (New York: Scribners, 1971): 570–83, which reports that witchcraft was generally disbelieved in England by 1668. The Night Hag, sometimes identified with or associated with the Roman goddess of the crossroads, Hecate, wished to use babies or their blood in her Satanic rituals, and could smell the blood the way a vulture smells death. The Night Hag would ride the whirlwind in the dark of the moon in order to assemble with a coven of other witches, in this case from the northern and hence Satanic region of Lapland, in an orgiastic dance. For the association between sorcery and Lapland, see *Comedy of Errors* 4.3.11. The phrase "laboring Moon" is a Latinism for "*labores lunae*," meaning "the moon in eclipse" (Richardson, quoted in Newton). Apollonius of Rhodes' description of Hecate approximates Milton's Sin: "round her horrible serpents twined themselves among the oak boughs; . . . and sharply howled around her the hounds of hell" (*Argonautica* 277).
[175]The figure of Death is introduced at line 666, a number associated with the Satanic beast described in Revelation 13: "the number of the beast . . . . is Six hundred threescore and six."
[176]The image of Death is especially frightening because it has no shape but that of a shadow. The first illustrators of *Paradise Lost* (illustrations for Books 2 and 10) drew Death as an emaciated human form or skinless skeleton holding a short spear or dart, the familiar image from the medieval Dance of Death. Spenser, however, gave the image of Death the same indistinct outline as in Milton's image: "Unbodied, unsoul'd, unheard, unseene" (*Faerie Queene* 7.7.46). Later Milton will call Death a "vast unhide-bound Corps" (10.601), which suggests a flayed cadaver. Death of course has the ability to destroy the shape of the body. Like Satan and the other fallen angels, Death can shift his shape to become, in his case, a "Maw" or hell-mouth. Death wears a crown possibly because of his association with Hades or Pluto, king of the underworld.
[177]Satan fears nothing in God's creation except for God the Father and the Son.
[178]The word may carry the Latin sense of "face" or "forehead," as well as the front of Death, an emblem of military aggression. As a product of incest, Death's visage is miscreated. The word *athwart* is astrological and suggests that Death, like Satan, is like a comet or misaligned planet whose action thwarts humankind. Just as Satan is compared with the comet in Ophiucus (see Hunter, "Kepler's Star," in *Descend*), Death's front has the power to thwart even Satan.
[179]The regular "house style" punctuation before a direct quotation in both editions is a period; hence the comma present in both editions is probably in error, and I correct it. "Goblin" should be defined as "evil spirit," rather than "mischievous elf."
[180]Though we have been told that the fallen angels number "millions" (1.609), this is the first time we learn they represent a full third of the host of Heaven (see Revelation 12.4). Satan himself has exaggerated that he seduced nearly half the angels (1.633).
[181]"United in conspiracy," with overtones of "having sworn oaths against God," as in one meaning current for "conjuration." When one conjured up evil spirits, one had to forswear God.

And they outcast from God, are here condemn'd
To waste Eternal dayes in woe and pain?   695
And reck'n'st thou thy self with Spirits of Heav'n,
Hell-doom'd, and breath'st defiance here and scorn
Where I reign King, and to enrage thee more,
Thy King and Lord?[182] Back to thy punishment,
False fugitive, and to thy speed add wings,   700
Least with a whip of Scorpions[183] I pursue
Thy lingring, or with one stroke of this Dart
Strange horror seise thee, and pangs unfelt before.
     So spake the grieslie terrour, and in shape,
So speaking and so threatning, grew tenfold   705
More dreadful and deform:[184] on th' other side
Incenst with indignation *Satan* stood
Unterrifi'd, and like a Comet burn'd,
That fires the length of *Ophiucus* huge
In th' Artick Sky, and from his horrid hair   710
Shakes Pestilence and Warr.[185] Each at the Head
Level'd his deadly aime; thir fatall hands
No second stroke intend, and such a frown
Each cast at th' other, as when two black Clouds
With Heav'ns Artillery fraught, come rattling on   715
Over the *Caspian*, then stand front to front
Hov'ring a space, till Winds the signal blow
To joyn thir dark Encounter in mid air:[186]
So frownd the mighty Combatants, that Hell
Grew darker at thir frown, so matcht they stood;   720
For never but once more[187] was either like
To meet so great a foe: and now great deeds
Had been achiev'd, whereof all Hell had rung,
Had not the Snakie Sorceress that sat
Fast by Hell Gate, and kept the fatal Key,   725
Ris'n, and with hideous outcry rush'd between.
     O Father, what intends thy hand, she cry'd,
Against thy only Son?[188] What fury O Son,
Possesses thee to bend that mortal Dart
Against thy Fathers head? and know'st for whom;   730

[handwritten annotations: "① ② ③ Satan/Sin/Evil Sorceress-Sin Father/Son/Holy Ghost (good) Refers to 3 parts of Evil"]

---

[182]A commentary on the potential abuse of kingship. In the spirit of "It takes one to know one," Death identifies Satan as a fellow tyrant, proclaims himself king over Satan while they are both in his (Death's) territory. For the "royal family" of Satan, Sin, and Death, see Davies, *Images* 41–42, and for Satan and King Charles I as tyrant, see Bennett, *Reviving* Chapter 2.

[183]An allusion to 1 Kings 12.11, "my father hath chastised you with whips, but I will chastise you with scorpions," together, perhaps, with the classical image of the Furies tormenting the guilty with whips of scorpions.

[184]Like an angel, Death has the ability to dilate or contract; here his threatning seems more like the boasting stance of a classical warrior, puffing himself up against his opponent Satan.

[185]For the image of Ophiucus as "huge both because it lies in the southern and northern hemispheres and because it ranges a good distance in both," see John T. Shawcross, "The Simile of Satan as a Comet, *Paradise Lost* II, 706–11," *Milton Quarterly* 6 (1972): 5. Both Vergil (*Aeneid* 10.272) and Tasso (*Jerusalem Delivered* 7.52–53) had compared heroes to comets. The hair or tail of the comet (the word *comet* is derived from "κομήτης," Greek for "long-haired") was thought to shed deadly influence on the world, causing war, famine, or plague. The Greek root of Ophiucus, "ὄφις," means "serpent." Thus the comparison is especially apt for Satan, who, like the Roman "Ophiuchus" (Ovid, *Metamorphoses* 2.173), is associated with both the serpent and with the cold north (see 5.689).

[186]Boiardo, *Orlando Innamorato* 1.16.10, compares Orlando and Agricane in combat to two thunderclouds. The Caspian Sea was proverbially stormy. Tasso in *Jerusalem Delivered* 6.38 describes Argantes facing Otho in combat: "as when clouds, together crush'd and bruised, / Pour down a tempest by the Caspian shore" (Fairfax trans.).

[187]That is, at the Last Judgment foretold in Revelation 22.

[188]Parodies "only begotten son" of the Apostles' Creed and John 1.18 and 3.16.

For him who sits above and laughs the while
At thee ordain'd his drudge, to execute
What e're his wrath, which he calls Justice, bids,
His wrath which one day will destroy ye both.
   She spake, and at her words the hellish Pest[189]   735
Forbore, then these to her *Satan* return'd:
   So strange thy outcry, and thy words so strange
Thou interposest, that my sudden hand
Prevented[190] spares to tell thee yet by deeds
What it intends; till first I know of thee,   740
What thing thou art, thus double-form'd,[191] and why
In this infernal Vaile° first met thou call'st   VALE, VALLEY
Me Father, and that Fantasm call'st my Son?
I know thee not, nor ever saw till now
Sight more detestable then him and thee.   745
   T' whom thus the Portress of Hell Gate[192] reply'd;
Hast thou forgot me then, and do I seem
Now in thine eye so foul, once deemd so fair
In Heav'n, when at th' Assembly, and in sight
Of all the Seraphim with thee combin'd   750
In bold conspiracy against Heav'ns King,
All on a sudden miserable pain
Surpris'd thee, dim thine eyes, and dizzie swumm
In darkness, while thy head flames thick and fast
Threw forth, till on the left side op'ning wide,[193]   755
Likest to thee in shape and count'nance bright,
Then shining heav'nly fair, a Goddess arm'd
Out of thy head I sprung:[194] amazement seis'd
All th' Host of Heav'n; back they recoild affraid
At first, and call'd me *Sin*, and for a Sign[195]   760
Portentous[196] held me; but familiar grown,
I pleas'd, and with attractive graces[197] won
The most averse, thee chiefly, who full oft
Thy self in me thy perfect image viewing
Becam'st enamour'd,[198] and such joy thou took'st   765
With me in secret,[199] that my womb conceiv'd
A growing burden.[200] Mean while Warr arose,

[Handwritten marginal note:] When sin was born from death left side associated with cynicism right hand signifies good side left – bad side.

---

[189]The English word was in the 1600s still connected closely with its French sense of "plague" or, metaphorically, a "curse" or "bane" (*OED* 2).

[190]The sense here is that her intervention with strange words has stopped him from attacking her son physically.

[191]Half woman, half serpentine beast.

[192]"Female keeper of the Gate of Hell." Compare the traditional image of St. Peter as keeper of "Heav'ns Wicket" in 3.484.

[193]Sin issues from the left side of Satan's brain, the "sinister" side. Critics writing about Eve have pointed out that she also comes from a rib taken from Adam's left side (8.465). See my article "Eve."

[194]Follows very closely and parodies or ridicules the birth of the warrior-goddess Pallas Athene (Roman Minerva) from the head of Zeus, as in Hesiod, *Theogony* 925–29. There are deep ironies and criticisms of Greek civilization implicit in the comparison, because Athene was a chaste and wise—although warlike—goddess, a bringer of civilization to the Greeks, who out of respect named their principal city after her.

[195]Semiotics, the study of signs or sign-systems, finds Milton's word-play here on "sign" and "sin" very significant, as embodying signals not only in stems of words derived from the same root but in words that resemble each other in spelling or in sound. See Shoaf 23–45.

[196]Literally "carrying heavy weight" but more importantly "carrying auguries [portents] of the future."

[197]Compare "sweet attractive Grace" as applied more innocently to Eve in 4.298.

[198]Not only incestuous love but narcissism, or love for one's clone ("perfect image") in this case, since Sin is not a product of natural birth. In becoming enamored of her, or lusting after her, Satan loves himself.

[199]The idiom "took [his] joy" in this case resembles the idiom "took his pleasure," or "took" her sexually. The secretness of the act in this case makes it more perversely exciting.

[200]The child is not a pleasure to carry but a hellish burden, as if the pregnant Sin were carrying a rock in her uterus.

And fields° were fought in Heav'n; wherein remain   BATTLEFIELDS, BATTLES
(For what could else) to our Almighty Foe
Cleer Victory, to our part loss and rout   770
Through all the Empyrean: down they fell
Driv'n headlong from the Pitch[201] of Heaven, down
Into this Deep, and in the general fall
I also; at which time this powerful Key
Into my hand was giv'n, with charge to keep   775
These Gates for ever shut, which none can pass
Without my op'ning. Pensive here I sat
Alone, but long I sat not, till my womb
Pregnant by thee, and now excessive grown
Prodigious motion felt and rueful throes.   780
At last this odious offspring whom thou seest
Thine own begotten, breaking violent way
Tore through my entrails, that with fear and pain
Distorted, all my nether shape thus grew
Transform'd:[202] but he my inbred enemie   785
Forth issu'd, brandishing his fatal Dart
Made to destroy: I fled, and cry'd out *Death*;[203]
Hell trembl'd at the hideous Name, and sigh'd
From all her Caves, and back resounded *Death*.
I fled, but he pursu'd (though more, it seems,   790
Inflam'd with lust then rage) and swifter far,
Mee overtook his mother all dismaid,[204]
And in embraces forcible and foule
Ingendring with me, of that rape begot
These yelling Monsters that with ceasless cry   795
Surround me, as thou sawst, hourly conceiv'd
And hourly born, with sorrow infinite
To me, for when they list into the womb
That bred them they return, and howle and gnaw
My Bowels,[205] thir repast; then bursting forth   800
Afresh[206] with conscious terrours vex me round,
That rest or intermission none I find.
Before mine eyes in opposition sits
Grim *Death* my Son and foe, who sets them on,
And me his Parent would full soon devour   805
For want of other prey,[207] but that he knows
His end with mine involvd; and knows that I
Should prove a bitter Morsel, and his bane,
When ever that shall be; so Fate pronounc'd.
But thou O Father, I forewarn thee, shun   810

---

[201]Topmost point. The Empyrean is the outermost sphere of the universe, the dwelling place of God.

[202]The metamorphosis of Sin is caused by her unnatural process in giving birth, when Death ripped through her entrails in a kind of horrid Caesarian section, in order to get out.

[203]The first occasion of his being named by another living being. The naming ritual transforms nature, in a way similar to what happens when Eve eats the fruit and "Earth felt the wound" (9.782).

[204]Milton cannot resist the dubious pun "dis-maid," which read as a past participle would mean "deflowered." The entire scene is a hideous parody of the immaculate begetting and virgin birth of Christ, "Of wedded Maid, and Virgin Mother born" (Nativity Ode 3).

[205]Milton may be intentionally confusing womb, bowels, and entrails, to increase the horror.

[206]Written "A fresh" in *1674*, but I have printed the *1667* reading, which is the more common form of the word.

[207]Not only will Death rape his mother but he will, in the sense of his being the giant "maw" that eats all things that die, eat her as well.

His deadly arrow; neither vainly hope
To be invulnerable in those bright Arms,
Though temper'd heav'nly, for that mortal dint,°   STROKE, BLOW
Save he who reigns above, none can resist.
    She finish'd, and the suttle Fiend his lore[208]   815
Soon learnd, now milder, and thus answerd smooth.
Dear Daughter, since thou claim'st me for thy Sire,
And my fair Son here showst me, the dear pledge
Of dalliance had with thee in Heav'n, and joys
Then sweet,[209] now sad to mention, through dire change   820
Befalln us unforeseen, unthought of, know
I come no enemie, but to set free
From out[210] this dark and dismal house of pain,
Both him and thee, and all the heav'nly Host
Of Spirits that in our just pretenses arm'd   825
Fell with us from on high: from them I go
This uncouth errand sole,[211] and one for all
My self expose, with lonely steps to tread
Th' unfounded° deep, and through the void immense   BOTTOMLESS
To search with wandring quest a place foretold   830
Should be, and, by concurring signs, ere now
Created vast and round, a place of bliss
In the Pourlieues[212] of Heav'n, and therein plac't
A race of upstart Creatures, to supply
Perhaps our vacant room, though more remov'd,   835
Least Heav'n surcharg'd° with potent multitude   FILLED TO OVERFLOWING
Might hap to move new broiles:° Be this or aught   BATTLES
Then this more secret now design'd, I haste
To know, and this once known, shall soon return,
And bring ye to the place where Thou and Death   840
Shall dwell at ease, and up and down unseen
Wing silently the buxom Air, imbalm'd
With odours;[213] there ye shall be fed and fill'd
Immeasurably, all things shall be your prey.
He ceas'd, for both seemd highly pleasd, and Death   845
Grinnd horrible a gastly smile, to hear
His famine° should be fill'd, and blest his mawe°   HUNGER   MOUTH
Destin'd to that good hour: no less rejoyc'd
His mother bad, and thus bespake her Sire.
    The key of this infernal Pit by due,   850
And by command of Heav'ns all-powerful King

---

[208]His "lore" is his lesson, here, with the suggestion of superstitious tradition, as in "fairy lore." Satan has learned his lesson, in this case from his daughter who is also his wife, has become milder and will begin talking the way he usually does, smoothly. He has reversed and contradicted himself; his earlier opinion of the hideousness of Death was more nearly accurate.

[209]Milton implicitly satirizes the type of love poetry he must have hated, poetry which used words and phrases like "divine fair," "pledge of dalliance," or "sweet joys," which, together with "Sire," echoes some of the vocabulary of romantic epic and Petrarchan sonnets. Whenever any of these words appear in *Paradise Lost* they are almost automatically suspect, especially "fair," "sweet," and "dalliance."

[210]Supply "of," as "From out of this dark and dismal house."

[211]"I am going this wandering way alone, to places unknown." Here Satan's volunteering for the dangerous trip parodies the Son's volunteering to go to Earth and become subject to incarnation in order to save humankind ("one for all / My self expose" defines the Son's sacrifice precisely).

[212]A rare instance of a French-derived word in Milton's poetry or prose—though the word had been used in English since the fifteenth century—meaning "boundaries."

[213]"Buxom" air is air that offers no resistance; "imbalm'd" means both "balmy," "warm and curative," and "preserved by herbal means after death," so there seems to be an unwitting, self-fulfilling prophecy in what Satan says, since he is talking about the future career of Death.

I keep, by him forbidden to unlock
These Adamantine Gates; against all force
Death ready stands to interpose his dart,
Fearless to be o'rmatcht by living might.   855
But what ow I to his commands above
Who hates me, and hath hither thrust me down
Into this gloom of *Tartarus* profound,
To sit in hateful Office here confin'd,
Inhabitant of Heav'n, and heav'nlie-born,   860
Here in perpetual agonie and pain,
With terrors and with clamors compasst round
Of mine own brood, that on my bowels feed:
Thou art my Father, thou my Author,[214] thou
My being gav'st me; whom should I obey   865
But thee, whom follow? thou wilt bring me soon
To that new world of light and bliss, among
The Gods who live at ease, where I shall Reign
At thy right hand voluptuous,[215] as beseems
Thy daughter and thy darling, without end.   870
     Thus saying, from her side the fatal Key,
Sad instrument of all our woe,[216] she took;
And towards the Gate rouling her bestial train,[217]
Forthwith the huge Porcullis[218] high up drew,
Which but her self not all the *Stygian* powers[219]   875
Could once have mov'd; then in the key-hole turns
Th' intricate wards,[220] and every Bolt and Bar
Of massie Iron or sollid Rock with ease
Unfast'ns: on a sudden° op'n flie   SUDDENLY
With impetuous recoile and jarring sound   880
Th' infernal dores, and on thir hinges grate[221]
Harsh Thunder, that the lowest bottom shook
Of *Erebus*.[222] She op'nd, but to shut
Excel'd her power;[223] the Gates wide op'n stood,
That with extended wings a Bannerd Host   885

---

[214]Eve calls Adam her "Author and Disposer" (4.635) and Adam calls God "Author of this universe" (8.360). Critics debate (see McColley, *Milton's Eve*) whether the similarity has negative significance for the character of Eve or is just part of the parody of Heaven and Earth in the entire scene. Of course Adam is a passive "author" of Eve, and Eve is joyously created by God out of Adam's flesh, quite a different process from the birth of Sin from Satan's imaginings. If the logic is used to suggest that Eve is to Adam as Sin is to Satan, however, then Adam must be to God as Sin is to Satan.

[215]Obviously a parody of Christ sitting at the right hand of God, specifically the imagery of the Nicene Creed: "And [Christ] sitteth on the right hand of the Father: And he shall come again, with glory, to judge both the quick and the dead; Whose kingdom shall have no end" (*The Book of Common Prayer*, 1592 ed.). Milton undercuts the parodic mirror image with the words "voluptuous" and "darling," which lower the tone of the passage to that of a parody of love and reverence.

[216]The fruit of the Tree of the Knowledge of Good and Evil is another such "instrument" of "woe."

[217]Sin is trailed by her serpentine train, as if in a hideous parody of a wedding dress: her snaky lower parts roll along behind her, along with the Hell hounds. By the time he wrote *Paradise Lost*, Milton was generally suspicious of aristocratic trappings such as trains.

[218]Usually "portcullis," from the French "*port*" (gate) plus "*coleice*" (sliding). Neither edition has the more common spelling. The portcullis, most familiar as the latticed castle gate that slid down quickly from above, is an heraldic device which might be used for someone whose office was gatekeeper (porter). Here the gate which will become the gate of hell is designed as a portcullis so that it can be raised and lowered quickly, as it entraps sinners.

[219]Armies associated with the river Styx and hence Hell.

[220]The cuttings made into the key, to define it so that it fits the lock exactly. What is being described metaphorically is the intricacy of sin combined with the ease of opening oneself to it.

[221]Corrected from *1667* "great" in *1674*. No pun seems to be intended between "great" and "grate," and the correction of the *Errata* list seems to be a correction of an ambiguous spelling.

[222]Originally a deity, son of Chaos and Darkness, but here used for the entire region of Hell. Compare *Comus* 804, "the chains of *Erebus*."

[223]Only Christ will have the power to shut the gates, at the Last Judgment (Revelation 11.6; 21.25).

Under spread Ensigns marching might pass through
With Horse and Chariots rankt in loose array;
So wide they stood, and like a Furnace mouth[224]
Cast forth redounding smoak and ruddy flame.
Before thir eyes in sudden view appear   890
The secrets of the hoarie deep, a dark
Illimitable Ocean without bound,
Without dimension, where length, breadth, & highth,
And time and place are lost; where eldest Night
And *Chaos*, Ancestors of Nature,[225] hold   895
Eternal *Anarchie*, amidst the noise
Of endless Warrs, and by confusion stand.
For hot, cold, moist, and dry, four Champions fierce
Strive here for Maistrie, and to Battel bring
Thir embryon Atoms;[226] they around the flag   900
Of each his Faction, in thir several Clanns,
Light-arm'd or heavy, sharp, smooth, swift or slow,
Swarm populous, unnumber'd as the Sands
Of *Barca* or *Cyrene's*[227] torrid soil,
Levied to side with warring Winds, and poise   905
Thir lighter wings.[228] To whom these most adhere,
Hee rules a moment; *Chaos* Umpire[229] sits,
And by decision more imbroiles the fray
By which he Reigns: next him high Arbiter°   JUDGE
Chance governs all. Into this wilde Abyss,[230]   910
The Womb of nature and perhaps her Grave,[231]
Of neither Sea, nor Shore, nor Air, nor Fire,
But all these in thir pregnant causes mixt
Confus'dly, and which thus must ever fight,
Unless th' Almighty Maker them ordain   915
His dark materials to create more Worlds,
Into this wild Abyss the warie fiend
Stood on the brink of Hell and look'd a while,
Pondering his Voyage; for no narrow frith°   FIRTH, NARROW STRIP OF LAND

---

[224]In medieval popular drama, which still existed in performance in Milton's era, the "mouth" of Hell, or its "maw," which Milton also considered to be the mouth of Death, was often presented as a furnace door into which sinners were thrown. See Glynne Wickham, *The Medieval Stage* (Cambridge: Cambridge UP, 1987), specifically the illustration on 90–91, where the hell-mouth resembles the mouth of a sea-beast or leviathan more than a furnace.
[225]Hesiod makes Chaos the eldest of living things, with Night and Erebus his children (*Theogony* 123). For a full discussion of the following passage, see Curry, *Milton's*.
[226]The four elements are fighting for mastery over an uncreated universe. The picture of warring elements is similar to that of Ovid in *Metamorphoses* 1.5–20. Each element has qualities of hot or cold, and moist or dry. The concept of atoms (undivisible units of matter) derives from Lucretius, as do the various shapes described in line 902.
[227]Barca is the desert on the border of Egypt and Tunisia. Cyrene was a city in the arid regions near the site of the modern Tripoli. The name is pronounced as a trisyllable, with emphasis falling on the second syllable.
[228]The sands of the desert are enlisted to the side of warring factions of winds.
[229]Compare the description of conscience as "God's umpire" (3.195), the only other use of the word umpire in Milton's poetry. Here the tone is ironic, because Chaos is not a good umpire and Chance is not a good judge or governor. Any decision Chaos makes causes the elements at war to become more embroiled (more chaotic). Chaos, derived in its details most probably from Lucretius, is "the Deep" of Genesis.
[230]Repeated, to no apparent purpose, in 917 (Milton nodding?).
[231]Translates Lucretius, *On the Nature of Things* 5.259. Lucretius has been arguing that earth and fire are mortal; to prove that earth is mortal, he has it exhaling vapor and dust that mingle with the air on the one hand, and dissolved soil is washed away by floods or just the action of rivers on banks, so that whatever earth contributes to feed others is returned to it by the constant cycling of materials. Thus, as R. E. Latham translates, "it is an observed fact that the universal mother is also the common grave" (Lucretius, *The Nature of the Universe* [Harmondsworth, Eng.: Penguin, 1959]: 178). For seventeenth-century expansion of this theory, see Babb 105–10.

He had to cross. Nor was his eare less peal'd[232]   920
With noises loud and ruinous (to compare
Great things with small) then when *Bellona*[233] storms,
With all her battering Engines bent to rase°   RAZE, DESTROY
Som Capital City; or less then if this frame
Of Heav'n were falling, and these Elements   925
In mutinie had from her Axle[234] torn
The stedfast Earth. At last his Sail-broad Vannes[235]
He spreads for flight, and in the surging smoak
Uplifted spurns the ground, thence many a League
As in a cloudy Chair ascending[236] rides   930
Audacious, but that seat soon failing, meets
A vast vacuitie:° all unawares   EMPTY REGION
Fluttring his pennons vain plumb down he drops[237]
Ten thousand fadom° deep, and to this hour   FATHOMS
Down had been falling, had not by ill chance   935
The strong rebuff of som tumultuous cloud
Instinct° with Fire and Nitre hurried him   CHARGED
As many miles aloft:[238] that furie stay'd,
Quencht in a Boggie *Syrtis*,[239] neither Sea,
Nor good dry Land: nigh founderd[240] on he fares,   940
Treading the crude consistence, half on foot,
Half flying; behoves him now both Oare and Saile.[241]
As when a Gryfon[242] through the Wilderness
With winged course ore Hill or moarie Dale,[243]
Pursues the *Arimaspian*, who by stelth   945
Had from his wakeful custody purloind
The guarded Gold: So eagerly the fiend
Ore bog or steep, through strait, rough, dense, or rare,
With head, hands, wings or feet pursues his way,
And swims or sinks, or wades, or creeps, or flyes:[244]   950
At length a universal hubbub wilde
Of stunning sounds and voices all confus'd

---

[232]"Nor was his ear less violated by the noise." A peal is an extremely sharp sound, as in the peal of a loud bell, or a peal of thunder.

[233]Roman goddess of war, seen in terms of seventeenth-century "battering engines" of war used to level ("rase") a besieged capital city. When Bellona "storms," the storm of war produces peals of thunderous noise.

[234]The earth is perceived as center or axis or axletree of the whole universe, as with the "burning axletree" in the Nativity Ode 84 (though that can be read as the axle of the sun's chariot, as does Shawcross, *Complete Poetry* 66n. 16).

[235]Satan's bulk requires sail-like wings ("Vannes" or fans; compare *Paradise Regain'd* 4.583) to support it in flight.

[236]As at the beginning of Book 2, Satan is pictured in pompous and theatrical exaltation. See Demaray, *Milton's*, for the fallen angels acting out a "masquelike ritual of idolatry" (64).

[237]"Fluttering his wings (Latin '*pennae*,' 'feathers' or 'wings') vainly, he drops straight down (like a plumb line)."

[238]In other words, God's providence allows this explosive updraft, a natural instance of the effect of gunpowder (nitre and sulphur are constituents of gunpowder), to propel Satan back on his shaky course. God can permit evil to proceed without abetting it.

[239]The Syrtes was a stretch of treacherous sandbanks ("bogs") which extended about 500 miles off the coast of North Africa between Carthage in the west and Berenice in the east. Lucan describes them in the *Pharsalia* 9.303-18. "Quencht" suggests not only "extinguished by wetting" but "killed" as well. Milton used the verb for the extinguishing of his eyesight (3.25).

[240]I.e., "nearly bogged down," the verb "founder" still being applied to animals made lame by excess body fluid caused by fever.

[241]"It would make it easier on him now to use both oar and sail to propel himself."

[242]Herodotus (*The History* 3.116) had told the story of Scythian griffins (half-eagle, half-lion) guarding gold against the one-eyed tribe of the Arimaspi. The griffin was subdued by Apollo as Satan will be by Christ (Fowler 943-47n, citing Piero Valeriano, *Hieroglyphica* [Frankfurt, 1613]: 279). The gold of Scythia became associated by Christian commentators with the gold of Ophir, that of King David (11.396-407).

[243]A "moory dale" would presumably be a valley not under cultivation but allowed to be waste land.

[244]The effect is comic, especially with the word "creep" applied to the activity of the formerly magnificent Satan. At the end of this voyage he will be quite bedraggled. The prosodic device is kin to asyndeton (see 7.504 and note), the rapid repetition of curt words or phrases, as in Caesar's "*Veni, vidi, vici*." Fowler (948-50n) notes the appropriateness of the device for rapid sense-impressions of Chaos as Satan flies through.

Born through the hollow dark assaults his eare
With loudest vehemence:[245] thither he plyes,
Undaunted to meet there what ever power   955
Or Spirit of the nethermost Abyss
Might in that noise reside, of whom to ask
Which way the neerest coast of darkness lyes
Bordering on light; when strait° behold the Throne   IMMEDIATELY
Of *Chaos*, and his dark Pavilion° spread   WAR TENT   960
Wide on the wasteful Deep; with him Enthron'd
Sat Sable-vested *Night*, eldest of things,
The Consort of his Reign; and by them stood
Orcus and *Ades*,[246] and the dreaded name
Of *Demogorgon*;[247] *Rumor* next and *Chance*,   965
And *Tumult* and *Confusion* all imbroild,
And *Discord*[248] with a thousand various mouths.
    T' whom *Satan* turning boldly, thus. Ye Powers
And Spirits of this nethermost Abyss
Chaos and *ancient Night*, I come no Spy,   970
With purpose to explore or to disturb
The secrets of your Realm, but by constraint[249]
Wandring this darksome Desart, as my way[250]
Lies through your spacious Empire up to light,
Alone, and without guide, half lost, I seek   975
What readiest path leads where your gloomie bounds
Confine with Heav'n; or if som other place
From your Dominion won, th' Ethereal King
Possesses lately, thither to arrive
I travel this profound,° direct my course;   DEPTH   980
Directed no mean recompence it brings
To your behoof,[251] if I that Region lost,
All usurpation thence expell'd, reduce
To her original darkness and your sway
(Which is my present journey)[252] and once more   985
Erect the Standard there of *ancient Night*;
Yours be th' advantage all, mine the revenge.

---

[245]The word has positive and negative valences in Milton. Adam falls through "vehemence of love" (Argument to Book 9), and here the word seems to refer to mindless (*vehe* + *mens*) and chaotic noise; but Turner (275–76) finds positive values associated with the word in Milton's prose, as if it could mean "zeal" or "inspiration," as well as "mindlessness."

[246]The two names for the place or for the ruler of the underworld were interchangeable.

[247]Milton associated Demogorgon (see Boccaccio, *Genealogia Deorum* 1.6) with Chaos, as in Prolusion 1, in which Milton calls Demogorgon the ancestor of all the gods and identifies him with Chaos. Compare Spenser: "Downe in the bottome of the deepe *Abysse*, / Where *Demogorgon* in dull darkenesse pent / Farre from the view of Gods and heavens blis, / The hideous *Chaos* keepes" (*Faerie Queene* 4.2.47). The naming of the god out loud aroused fear.

[248]The catalogue of allegorical figures seems to be carried over from Milton's earlier plans for a drama on "Adam unparadiz'd," in which he named allegorical persons such as Justice, Mercy, and Wisdom, plus Sickness, Discontent, and Ignorance as part of his dramatis personae (see the Introduction, "Early Outlines"). The "thousand various mouths" may refer to "*Rumor*," proverbially seen in terms of many mouths or tongues.

[249]Quite possibly yet another indication that Satan, having fallen, is under constraint of God, on a mission which God permits. The word "constraint" suggests that he is limited in what he can do, but it may also imply that there is no other path but the one he takes.

[250]In *1674* there is an unnecessary comma here. The whole page of text seems corrupt in *1674*, with nouns and adjectives that are not italicized in *1667* italicized for no good reason, as with "*ancient Night*," which is again italicized in 987. I have not tampered with the italics, on the grounds that "*ancient Night*" may represent a complete Homeric epithet. Allegorical states, as in the early drafts of "Adam unparadiz'd," gain typographical stature through being capitalized or placed in italics.

[251]"If you direct me, your instructions will be worth no paltry repayment on your behalf." Perhaps the convoluted syntax indicates that Satan is attempting to deceive Chaos and Night in order to get past them (Empson 67). Satan is trying to make his way and find his direction in a hostile environment.

[252]Certainly Satan is explaining his voyage in terms flattering to Chaos; his explanation of his purpose of travel to the fallen angels has been utterly different. His whole purpose, he implies here, is to restore Chaos to its original state of darkness and disorder.

   Thus *Satan*; and him thus the Anarch[253] old
With faultring speech and visage incompos'd
Answer'd. I know thee, stranger, who thou art,   990
That mighty leading Angel, who of late
Made head° against Heav'ns King, though overthrown.   RAISED AN ARMY
I saw and heard, for such a numerous Host
Fled not in silence through the frighted deep
With ruin upon ruin, rout on rout,   995
Confusion worse confounded; and Heav'n Gates
Pour'd out by millions her victorious Bands
Pursuing. I upon my Frontieres here
Keep residence; if all I can will serve,
That little which is left so to defend,   1000
Encroacht on still through our[254] intestine broiles°   CIVIL WARS
Weakning the Scepter of old *Night*: first Hell
Your dungeon stretching far and wide beneath;
Now lately Heaven and Earth, another World
Hung ore my Realm, link'd in a golden Chain[255]   1005
To that side Heav'n from whence your Legions fell:
If that way be your walk, you have not farr;
So much the neerer danger; go and speed;[256]
Havock and spoil and ruin are my gain.
   He ceas'd; and *Satan* staid not to reply,   1010
But glad that now his Sea should find a shore,
With fresh alacritie and force renew'd
Springs upward like a Pyramid of fire[257]
Into the wilde expanse, and through the shock
Of fighting Elements, on all sides round   1015
Environ'd wins his way; harder beset
And more endanger'd, then when *Argo* pass'd
Through *Bosporus* betwixt the justling° Rocks:[258]   JOSTLING, CLASHING
Or when *Ulysses* on the Larbord[259] shunnd
Charybdis, and by th' other whirlpool steard.[260]   1020
So he with difficulty and labour hard
Mov'd on, with difficulty and labour hee;
But hee once past, soon after when man fell,
Strange alteration! Sin and Death amain
Following his track, such was the will of Heav'n,   1025
Pav'd after him a broad and beat'n way[261]

---

[253]As "Anarch," Chaos represents no rule at all, or anarchy personified. Milton's is the first usage preserved in the *OED*.

[254]Fletcher contends that "your" is intended here (Fletcher follows Zachary Pearce's suggestion, corroborated by Adams, *Ikon* 98–99) though neither *1667* nor *1674* has it. Shawcross retains "our."

[255]See below, note to line 1053.

[256]Normally the idiom would be "Go and God-speed," but here it is shortened appropriately.

[257]Milton interpreted the upward triangle of the pyramid as symbolic of ambition (see 5.758–59); the first syllable of pyramid is derived from the Greek word for fire (as in pyromaniac).

[258]A reference to the ship *Argo*, named after its builder or the city in the Peloponnesus, sailed in by Jason and his crew and described in the *Argonautica* of Apollonius of Rhodes. Passing through the Bosporus, the Argo was nearly capsized by clashing rocks (*Argonautica* 1). Jason saved the ship by releasing a dove: the Argonauts followed the timing of the dove's flight to take the ship through the rocks safely.

[259]On the left-hand or port side of the ship, as contrasted with starboard, the righthand side.

[260]Ulysses and his crew had to sail between Scylla, a six-headed monster, and Charybdis, a personified whirlpool (*Odyssey* 12), traditionally sited in the Straits of Messina between Sicily and Italy. Scylla (see 659–661) had been a maiden transformed to a shape not unlike Milton's Sin.

[261]Compare Milton's often-repeated phrase "ready and easy way," which resembles the proverbial "primrose path" to some evil deed. Death constructs the bridge in 10.293–305.

Over the dark Abyss, whose boiling Gulf
Tamely endur'd a Bridge of wondrous length
From Hell continu'd reaching th' utmost Orbe[262]
Of this frail World; by which the Spirits[263] perverse   1030
With easie intercourse° pass to and fro   PASSAGE
To tempt or punish mortals, except whom
God and good Angels guard by special grace.[264]
But now at last the sacred influence°   POWER
Of light appears, and from the walls of Heav'n   1035
Shoots farr into the bosom of dim Night
A glimmering dawn; here Nature first begins[265]
Her fardest verge,° and *Chaos* to retire   FARTHEST BOUNDARY
As from her outmost works a brok'n[266] foe
With tumult less and with less hostile din,   1040
That *Satan* with less toil, and now with ease
Wafts on the calmer wave by dubious light
And like a weather-beaten Vessel holds
Gladly the Port, though Shrouds and Tackle[267] torn;
Or in the emptier waste, resembling Air,   1045
Weighs his spread wings,[268] at leasure to behold
Farr off th' Empyreal Heav'n, extended wide
In circuit, undetermind square or round,[269]
With Opal Towrs and Battlements adorn'd
Of living Saphire,[270] once his native Seat;

---

[262]"The outermost sphere containing the orb of the planet Earth."

[263]Apparently a monosyllable here.

[264]Another indication that some beings are considered to be elect. Compare the Father's statement, "Some I have chosen of peculiar grace" (3.183), and see Kelley, *Argument* 82–83.

[265]Here is the first demonstration of creative organization, the result of the creative power of light, as the openings of Book 3 and Book 7 will show.

[266]Printed "brok'd" in most copies of *1674*, but someone, probably in the printer's shop, has inked in the obviously correct "brok'n" in several extant copies. *1667* reads "brok'n," and *1678* also corrects the error.

[267]"Main shrouds [shrouds are ropes issuing from the main mast] and rigging." Satan as ship is nearly derelict, beaten by the weather and with his means of locomotion shredded, "holding for" ("hugging to") port desperately.

[268]The entire image of the epic simile of Satan as ship is hardly heroic: Satan is pictured as a vessel so weather-beaten he is lucky to be afloat, hugging to safe harbor. Satan "weighs" his wings the same way a ship would weigh anchor: he pulls them in and by doing so puts them to rest. Thomas Corns points out to me that this passage may resemble the hard realities of sea-voyages illustrated in Camoëns's *Lusiads* (letter, November 1991).

[269]For "circuit of heaven," see Job 22.14. As with the curvature of the Earth, it is difficult visually to tell whether the edges of the Empyrean are square or round.

[270]The sapphire is native and uncut, hence "living" or naturally in place without having to have been put there by any angelic artisan. Revelation 21.19 establishes that sapphire was used as a foundation stone in the wall of the heavenly city.

1050

And fast by hanging in a golden Chain
This pendant world,[271] in bigness as a Starr
Of smallest Magnitude close by the Moon.[272]
Thither full fraught with mischievous revenge,
Accurst, and in a cursed hour he hies.

1055

The End of the Second Book.

[271]The image of the pendant world takes its origin probably from Homer's description of Zeus bragging that he has the strength to draw up all the other gods if they were suspended from Olympus by a golden chain (*Iliad* 8.18–27), but the image had been allegorized to embrace the idea of a chain of love binding all creation (see Milton's second *Prolusion*). The image here is of the "firm opacous Globe" (3.418) of the Universe hanging by a golden chain (thus "pendant"); its sphere is tiny as compared with the rest of space.
[272]In Renaissance cosmology, the Earth was often pictured, at least in metaphor, as hanging by a golden chain which graphically illustrated its relationship with Heaven and with God. Compare the same image at 1005. S. K. Heninger, Jr., *The Cosmographical Glass* (San Marino, CA: The Huntington Library, 1977) was not able to find a visual representation of the chain (160), though many illustrations exist that show ladders of hierarchy of being and harmony of being (the universe as a musical instrument). See Introduction, Cosmology.

Paradise Lost.

BOOK III.

THE ARGUMENT.

God sitting on his Throne sees Satan *flying towards this world, then newly created;*[1] *shews him to the Son who sat at his right hand; foretells the success of* Satan *in perverting mankind; clears his own Justice and Wisdom from all imputation, having created Man free and able enough to have withstood his Tempter;*[2] *yet declares his purpose of grace towards him, in regard he fell not of his own malice, as did* Satan, *but by him seduc't. The Son of God renders praises to his Father for the manifestation of his gracious purpose towards Man; but God again declares, that Grace cannot be extended towards Man without the satisfaction of divine Justice; Man hath offended the majesty of God by aspiring to God-head, and therefore with all his Progeny devoted*[3] *to death must dye, unless some one can be found sufficient to answer for his offence, and undergo his Punishment. The Son of God freely offers himself a Ransome for Man: the Father accepts him, ordains his incarnation, pronounces his exaltation above all Names in Heaven and Earth; commands all the Angels to adore him; they obey, and hymning to thir Harps in full Quire, celebrate the Father and the Son. Mean while* Satan *alights upon the bare Convex of this Worlds outermost Orb; where wandring he first finds a place since call'd The Lymbo of Vanity; what persons and things fly up thither; thence comes to the Gate of Heaven, describ'd ascending by stairs, and the waters above the Firmament that flow about it: His passage thence to the Orb of the Sun; he finds there* Uriel *the Regent*[4] *of that Orb, but first changes himself into the shape of a meaner Angel,*[5] *and pretending a zealous desire to behold the new Creation and Man whom God had plac't here, inquires of him the place of his habitation, and is directed; alights first on Mount* Niphates.

Hail holy Light, ofspring of Heav'n first-born,
Or of th' Eternal Coeternal beam
May I express thee unblam'd?[6] since God is light,
And never but in unapproached light
Dwelt from Eternitie, dwelt then in thee,
Bright effluence of bright essence increate.[7]

---

[1]Milton writes " . . . it seems likely that that apostasy, as a result of which so many myriads [of the angels] fled, beaten, to the lowest part of heaven, took place before even the first beginnings of this world" (*On Christian Doctrine* 1.7, Yale 6: 313).

[2]God's foreknowledge of the fall of Adam and Eve does not predestine or predetermine their fall, but "his own Justice" still needs to be "cleared." God, "who is supremely good, cannot be the source of wickedness or the evil of crime: on the contrary, he created good out of man's wickedness" (*On Christian Doctrine* 1.8, Yale 6: 331).

[3]"Attached, as a faithful follower [of death]."

[4]Printed as "Regient" in *1674*. In earlier states of this Argument, before *1674*, "Regient" appears in its more common form "Regent." I have restored the earlier state.

[5]Satan will cunningly assume the disguise of an angel of lower rank (in order to deceive Uriel).

[6]An extraordinarily concise apostrophe to God in the form of light based on the supposition that "God is light" (John 1.5); also an invocation from a blind poet to a source of inner light, the "best light which God hath planted in [humankind]" (*Readie and Easie Way*, Yale 7: 456). God is "the Father of light, and fountaine of heavenly grace" (*Animadversions*, Yale 1: 704). Thus Milton pictured God the Father—the "bright essence"—as the father of light, the "Bright effluence" that may be eternal and coeternal at the same time. Light is "first-born" because the first utterance of God in the act of creating the universe is "Let there be light" (Genesis 1.3). Milton humbly invokes light ("May I express thee unblam'd?") because it is an effluence of God and because he personally needs inward radiance to compensate for outward blindness. Hunter and Adamson argue in *Bright Essence* that Milton hails physical light, in contrast with the darkness of the two preceding books. The light is first-born in that it is created on the first day (as in Book 7). It is "increate" in the sense that it is uncreated, its existence preceding that of the created universe. And, it is creative energy (see 2.1037). The Son of God is depicted by early Church Fathers as a beam of light emanating from God the Father, the illumination the light provides being the Spirit. Both physical light and the Son may be coeternal with the Father, or, as a derivative from Him, they may be His "first-born." The "stream" mentioned in line 7 derives from a second image used by the Church Fathers for the Son of God. Its "Fountain" is the spring, its source. One cannot "tell" or discuss this latter, because the Father is completely transcendent and uncreated, approachable only through the Son. This invocation, in other words, is addressed to the light who is the Son.

[7] In Milton's theological system as it is expressed in *On Christian Doctrine*, God in his essence is also "Dark with excessive bright" (below, 380), His brightness expressed in a manner that can be understood by the senses, though God's light is unbearably bright to humans. Subordinationism, the unequal relationship between Milton's Father and Son, has been the subject of much critical debate; see MacCallum, *Milton*, which thoroughly investigates the roles of the Son in *Paradise Lost* and *Paradise Regain'd*, including those of extender or extension of God's power, as model of behavior for Adam and Eve, and as a kind of priest hearing their repentant prayers. The standard work for the relationship between *Paradise Lost* and Milton's *On Christian Doctrine*

Or hear'st thou rather[8] pure Ethereal stream,
Whose Fountain who shall tell? before the Sun,
Before the Heavens thou wert, and at the voice
Of God, as with a Mantle[9] didst invest   10
The rising world of waters dark and deep,
Won from the void and formless infinite.[10]
Thee I re-visit now with bolder wing,[11]
Escap't the *Stygian* Pool, though long detain'd
In that obscure sojourn,[12] while in my flight   15
Through utter and through middle darkness[13] borne
With other notes then to th' *Orphean* Lyre[14]
I sung of *Chaos* and *Eternal Night*,
Taught by the heav'nly Muse[15] to venture down
The dark descent, and up to reascend,   20
Though hard and rare:[16] thee I revisit safe,
And feel thy sovran vital Lamp;[17] but thou
Revisit'st not these eyes, that rowle in vain
To find thy piercing ray, and find no dawn;
So thick a drop serene hath quencht thir Orbs,   25
Or dim suffusion veild.[18] Yet not the more
Cease I to wander where the Muses haunt
Cleer Spring, or shadie Grove, or Sunnie Hill,
Smit with the love of sacred Song;[19] but chief
Thee *Sion* and the flowrie Brooks beneath   30

---

remains Maurice Kelley, *This Great Argument*. See also Bauman, *Milton's Arianism*. Milton's authorship or his part in dictating *On Christian Doctrine* has been hotly debated recently, with a report on the provenance of the theological treatise in the October 1997 issue of *Milton Quarterly*.

[8]"Or would you prefer to hear of." First usage of the Latinate idiom recorded in the *OED* ("hear" 12.b).

[9]Continues to use the images of creation of Genesis 1.1–5, though the word "mantle" (meaning "robe") is not in Genesis in the Authorized Version. The verb "invest" carries both the meaning of "to dress," as with a garment, and "to assign responsibility to."

[10]The creation of the heavens predated the creation of the Sun and the Earth, which were formed out of Chaos by the Voice (analogous to the Word or the Logos) of God. The Geneva Bible glosses "the Spirit of God moved upon the waters" to mean "He mainteined this confused heape by his secret power" and cites Hebrews 11.3, "Through faith we understand that the worlde was ordeined by the worde of God . . . " (Genesis 1.1n; 1560 ed.). The dark and deep "waters" are created by God from the infinite formless chaos, the "void."

[11]The Epic Voice has regained confidence after posing the doubtful question "May I express thee unblam'd?" (3), perhaps because he has more scriptural and classical authority for his description of Heaven and of Eden than he did for his description of Hell.

[12]"That dark voyage." The "Stygian Pool" is a metonymy for Hell; the river Styx or any pool formed from it stands for the whole place.

[13]The middle darkness is associated with Chaos, the utter or outer with Hell. Compare the descent of the Epic Voice described in 7.12–16, and 21–25.

[14]A rejection of the classical sources of inspiration, especially of the Muse who failed to save Orpheus and his wife Eurydice. Milton had asked in vain for the help of the Muses in "Lycidas," since they did not have the power to save Orpheus himself; in his epic he is distancing himself from classical precedents, as when he prefers the brooks of *Sion* (30 below) to any Helicon or any other classical source of cleansing water. The Muses failed Orpheus; Milton, by contrast, has been "Taught by the *heav'nly* Muse" (emphasis supplied). Orpheus also used his lyre to regain his lost wife Eurydice from Hades, but Milton is separating his own song from anything less important than "Mans First Disobedience" (1.1). For Milton's use of the Orpheus myth, see Vicari.

[15]Milton deliberately does not name the heavenly Muse at this point because he emphasizes the meaning, not the name. The Heavenly Muse was popularly known as Urania, because Urania was muse of astronomy. Josuah Sylvester, translator of Du Bartas, in *The Divine Weekes and Works*, ed. Snyder, mentions Helicon as "the lofty mounte / Where sweet Urania sitteth to endite" (1.2.2.6–7; Snyder 1.403). For the popular conception of Urania, see Hunter and Davies, "Milton's Urania." Urania is the narrator of Lady Mary Wroth's prose romance in *The Countesse of Montgomery's Urania* (1621).

[16]Probably should be read "though to reascend is difficult and must proceed through rarefied [as opposed to dense] atmosphere." See "rare" 1 in *OED*.

[17]One presumes that Milton is still invoking holy light in its double meaning and that at this point he is speaking personally of the physical perception of the light and heat of the sun, God's "sovran vital Lamp," though he cannot see (but only feel) that light. The spelling "sovran" seems to indicate Milton's preference for the phonetic form derived not from French *souverein* but from Italian *sovrano*.

[18]Milton refers to his blindness by its contemporary medical name, "*gutta serena*," or "clear drop," or, in Milton's very literal translation, "drop serene." Modern physicians would diagnose the affliction to both eyes as glaucoma, because, as Milton indicates here, it proceeded from the rims of the irises inward, causing the sensation, over time, of a veil being drawn over the eye, a suffusion (thought to be a spreading of one of the bodily humors) causing dimness. The affliction causes no outward change of appearance of the eyes (they are open and clear-looking in the William Faithorne engraving of Milton prefixed to his *History of Britain*). Milton seems to be instructing his readers in medical terminology while at the same time telling future biographers or critics exactly what the sources of his blindness are. See Eleanor Gertrude Brown, *Milton's Blindness* (Columbia U Studies in English and Comparative Literature [New York: Columbia UP, 1934]; repr. New York: Octagon, 1968) for medical interpretation of the biographical evidence.

[19]Alludes to Vergil's prayer in the *Georgics* 2.475, that he be "*percussus amore*," "struck with love of sacred song," by the Muses.

That wash thy hallowd feet, and warbling flow,
Nightly I visit: nor somtimes forget
Those other two equal'd with me in Fate,
So were I equal'd with them in renown,
Blind *Thamyris* and blind *Mæonides*
And *Tiresias* and *Phineus* Prophets old.[20]   35
Then feed on thoughts, that voluntarie move
Harmonious numbers;[21] as the wakeful Bird
Sings darkling, and in shadiest Covert hid
Tunes her nocturnal Note. Thus with the Year   40
Seasons return, but not to me returns
Day, or the sweet approach of Ev'n or Morn,
Or sight of vernal bloom,[22] or Summers Rose,
Or flocks, or heards,° or human face divine;   HERDS
But cloud in stead, and ever-during° dark   EVERLASTING   45
Surrounds me, from the chearful wayes of men
Cut off, and for the Book of knowledg fair
Presented with a Universal blanc°[23]   BLANK, VACUITY
Of Natures works to mee expung'd and ras'd,°   ERASED, OBLITERATED
And wisdome at one entrance quite shut out.   50
So much the rather thou Celestial light
Shine inward, and the mind through all her powers
Irradiate, there plant eyes,[24] all mist from thence
Purge and disperse, that I may see and tell
Of things invisible to mortal sight.   55
   Now had the Almighty Father from above,
From the pure Empyrean where he sits
High Thron'd above all highth, bent down his eye,

---

[20]Homer's surname was Mæonides. Thamyris was a celebrated poet from Thrace mentioned by Homer, *Iliad* 2.594–600, who fell in love with the Muses collectively and challenged them to a singing contest, winner take all. Thamyris lost his eyes, his lute, and his memory in punishment for his presumptuousness. Phineus, a king of Thrace who was also blinded because of his gift of prophecy, was rewarded, as was Tiresias, by insight. Milton described Tiresias as the prophet "whose very blindness gave him boundless light" in "*De Idea Platonica*." Defending his own loss of sight against the accusation that it was the result of his immorality, Milton compared himself to Phineus and Tiresias, recalling in the *Second Defence* "those ancient bards and wise men of the most distant past, whose misfortune the gods, it is said, recompensed with far more potent gifts, and whom men treated with such respect that they preferred to blame the very gods than to impute their blindness to them as a crime" (Yale 4: 584). Milton describes the blind prophets and poets of classical tradition less critically than he did the Muse who failed Orpheus in "Lycidas," but he still distinguishes himself from Thamyris, Homer, Tiresias, and Phineus by his pursuit of "sacred Song" and his visitation of the brooks of Sion rather than any classical brook or fountain. Sion's brooks flow and heal and baptize. Just as Christ washed the feet of his disciples (John 13.5), the brooks wash the feet of Sion. Milton sees himself as a prophet in the Old Testament sense, since prophets such as Isaiah were inspired and also spoke in poetic forms.
[21]Milton discusses the process of inspiration, which he associates with a movement of the will which, in poets, produces "Harmonious numbers," or regular lines of verse that are inspired with harmony. It is probably relevant to mention here that Milton especially liked to compose and dictate his poetry early in the morning, "Saying *hee wanted to bee milkd*" ("John Phillips," Darbishire, *Early* 33). For a close analysis of the process of inspiration, see William Kerrigan, *Prophetic*, passim, and especially the passage dealing with this invocation, 265-66. The process is analogous to the natural inspiration of the nightingale, who trills or warbles a breathtakingly beautiful song at dusk. Milton is accurate in naturalistic detail (the nightingale is a shy bird that hides in "shadiest Covert" and "Sings darkling" in the sense that it remains "wakeful" after nightfall and then sings). Milton strongly identified with the nightingale as inspired singer, both before and after his blindness. The mythological nightingale was identified with Philomela, who sang a melancholy but beautiful song issuing out of horrible adversity (rape and mutilation). Both comparisons work with Milton personally if one considers the affliction of his blindness and his remark that he has "fall'n on evil dayes" in the invocation of Book 7 (7.25).
[22]"The sight of a [flower in] bloom during the vernal equinox, or spring of the year."
[23]Milton dislikes the word "blank" and invests it with a moral significance. For him it has the French sense of whiteness, or lack of color. If virtue, for instance, has no real substance, he considers it "a blank vertue, not a pure; her whitenesse is but an excrementall whitenesse" (*Areopagitica*, Yale 2: 515–16).
[24]An especially effective, almost metaphysical, image, as if written in imitation of Donne or Andrew Marvell, since it yokes things not usually associated, suggests that God's light has the power to sow seeds of vision in the spiritual ground of His worshipers' souls. In his various prose defenses of his stance as a controversialist, Milton often alludes to his own inward light, in modern terms insight, as a replacement for his eyesight. Compare "the light of grace, a better guide then Nature" (*Animadversions*, Yale 1: 702).

His own works and their works at once to view:[25]
About him all the Sanctities of Heaven[26]   60
Stood thick as Starrs, and from his sight receiv'd
Beatitude past utterance;[27] on his right
The radiant image of his Glory sat,
His onely Son;[28] On Earth he first beheld
Our two first Parents, yet the onely two   65
Of mankind, in the happie Garden plac't,
Reaping immortal fruits of joy and love,
Uninterrupted joy, unrivald love
In blissful solitude;[29] he then survey'd
Hell and the Gulf between, and *Satan* there   70
Coasting the wall of Heav'n on this side Night
In the dun° Air sublime, and ready now   DARK
To stoop° with wearied wings, and willing feet   SWOOP DOWN
On the bare outside of this World, that seem'd
Firm land imbosom'd° without Firmament,[30]   ENCLOSED   75
Uncertain which, in Ocean or in Air.
Him God beholding from his prospect high,
Wherein past, present, future he beholds,
Thus to his onely Son foreseeing spake.[31]

     Onely begotten Son, seest thou what rage   80
Transports our adversarie, whom no bounds
Prescrib'd, no barrs of Hell, nor all the chains
Heapt on him there, nor yet the main Abyss
Wide interrupt[32] can hold; so bent he seems
On desparate reveng, that shall redound   85
Upon his own rebellious head. And now
Through all restraint broke loose[33] he wings his way
Not farr off Heav'n, in the Precincts° of light,   REGIONS
Directly towards the new created World,
And Man there plac't, with purpose to assay°   TEST   90
If him by force he can destroy, or worse,
By some false guile pervert; and shall pervert
For man will hark'n to his glozing[34] lyes,

---

[25]Being omniscient and omnipresent, God can see and understand everything in creation in one view. He also comprehends past, present, and future at the same instant; see line 78 below. His throne is in the Empyrean sphere of the heavens.

[26]All of the angelic host, pictured not as "dignitaries," but as "holinesses" or "Sanctities." The comparison "thick as Starrs" is apt because of the numerousness of the angels, but also because Satan is understood to be the "great star" who fell from Heaven in Revelation 8.10.

[27]The vision of God confers beatitude on those who are within sight of Him. Being amongst "all th' Angelic Host that stand / In sight of God enthron'd . . ." (5.535-36) is one of the glories of Heaven that the fallen angels remember and miss.

[28]On the "right hand" of God the Father, the traditional position for the heir to the throne, the Son sits, the effluence or the "radiant image" of His glory.

[29]For Milton solitude is not a state of being alone, even though the word contains the Latin "*solus*," "alone," within it. Being formed of one flesh, Adam and Eve are blissfully "one."

[30]"Curved and firm, but without any obvious underpinning (as a body floating in space). "World" is "universe," as in 2.1052-53. Satan cannot see inside the shell of the universe to the firmament beneath it. Fowler points out that "In chaos the usual categories are confused; cp. ii 939f" (3.76n).

[31]God's tone in the following speech is sardonic in its perspective on Satan, a Satan who is literally carried away ("Transported") by his rage, and "out of bounds," again morally "bent" ("perverted," as in line 92 below) on his revenge. The series of epithets demonstrates how God holds Satan and his other enemies "in derision" and "Laugh'st at thir vain designes and tumults vain" (5.736-37).

[32]The participial noun suggests that the Abyss was violently ripped open, with the Latin sense of "*interruptus*," "torn apart." Fowler's judgment (3.83-84n) is that "interrupt" is "not a Latinism." Fowler reads "interrupt" as "breached," and "wide" as an adverb. But "Wide interrupt" can be read as in apposition with "the main Abyss."

[33]Compare with the proverbial "all Hell broke loose" (4.918).

[34]The word "glozing" was the same as "glossing," or "interpreting." Here it suggests the primary and secondary adjectival meanings listed in the *OED*, "speciously adorned," and "flattering."

And easily transgress the sole Command,[35]
Sole pledge of his obedience: So will fall,
Hee and his faithless Progenie:[36] whose fault?
Whose but his own? ingrate,[37] he had of mee
All he could have; I made him just and right,   95
Sufficient to have stood, though free to fall.[38]
Such I created all th' Ethereal Powers
And Spirits, both them who stood and them who faild;
Freely they stood who stood, and fell who fell.
Not free, what proof could they have givn sincere   100
Of true allegiance, constant Faith or Love,
Where onely what they needs must do, appeard,
Not what they would? what praise could they receive?
What pleasure I from such obedience paid,
When Will and Reason (Reason also is choice)[39]   105
Useless and vain, of freedom both despoild,
Made passive both, had servd necessitie,
Not mee.[40] They therefore as to right belongd,
So were created, nor can justly accuse
Thir maker, or thir making, or thir Fate,   110
As if predestination over-rul'd
Thir will, dispos'd by absolute Decree
Or high foreknowledge; they themselves decreed
Thir own revolt, not I: if I foreknew,
Foreknowledge had no influence on their fault,   115
Which had no less prov'd certain unforeknown.
So without least impulse or shadow of Fate,[41]
Or aught by me immutablie foreseen,
They trespass, Authors[42] to themselves in all
Both what they judge and what they choose; for so   120

---

[35]The command is expressed in Genesis 3.3: "But of the fruit of the tree which is in the midst of the garden, God hath said, Ye shall not eat of it, neither shall ye touch it, lest ye die." Milton did not see the fruit or the tree as having any inherent importance, except as a token of obedience: "The tree of the knowledge of good and evil was not a sacrament, as is commonly thought, for sacraments are meant to be used, not abstained from; but it was a kind of pledge or memorial of obedience" (*On Christian Doctrine* 1.10, Yale 6: 352). See John M. Steadman, "The 'Tree of Life' Symbolism in *Paradise Regained*," *Review of English Studies* NS 11 (1960): 384–91. Just as with the name of Urania, Milton is more interested in the meaning than the name of the fruit. The fruit here is just an indifferent object; the act of disobeying God's one slight command is more important than the token fruit.

[36]Adam's sin is reiterated by his descendants, "his faithless Progenie," as proven by the pageant of human evils narrated by Michael in Book 11, and Adam and Eve stand for the entire human race, as its "root."

[37]Critics interpreting the nature of Milton's God negatively, as does Empson, in *Milton's God*, see this passage as demonstrating God's petulance, especially because the word "ingrate" has such an emotional charge. Georgia Christopher points out that God's relationship with sinners was meant to be especially adversarial: " . . . from the perspective of Hell, God is an unspeakable menace" (*Milton* 116). If one reads the passage as a statement of simple truth—Adam is ungrateful in his disobedience and therefore has brought his punishment upon himself—the problem with God is removed. See Irene Samuel, "Milton on the Province of Rhetoric," *Milton Studies* 10 (1977): 177–93, for Milton's respect for rhetoric, "an art in which he himself was thoroughly grounded and which he expected his readers also to know" (191). God is the good, indeed the perfect, rhetorician, righteously expressing His anger at sinners.

[38]The doctrine of Sufficient Grace held that God created humankind with the grace to resist evil, but with a will that was free, though mutable (5.23637); the doctrine supported the idea of "the liability to fall with which man was created" (Kelley, *This Great Argument* 144).

[39]According to Milton in *Areopagitica*. God "gave [Adam] freedom to choose, for reason is but choosing" (Yale 2: 527).

[40]A short explanation of the doctrine of free will, which Milton espoused throughout *On Christian Doctrine*: " . . . everyone is provided with a sufficient degree of innate reason for him to be able to resist evil desires by his own effort . . . " (1.4, Yale 6: 186). Both the angels and humankind as originally created are provided with enough innate knowledge and reasoning capacity so that they can resist evil; they stand or fall freely. Thus God cannot be held responsible for their fall. God's foreknowledge in no way predestined their fate: " . . . when God gave [Adam] reason, he gave him freedom to choose, for reason is but choosing; he had bin else a meer artificiall *Adam*, such an *Adam* as he is in the motions [puppet-shows]" (*Areopagitica*, Yale 2: 527).

[41]Here as elsewhere, Milton takes pains not to allow Fate any power independent of God, who says "what I will is Fate" (7.173). Milton believed that " . . . God's prescience seems to have nothing to do with the principle or essence of predestination . . . . It is hard to see what purpose is served by introducing God's prescience or foreknowledge about particular individuals into the doctrine of predestination, except that of raising useless and utterly unanswerable questions" (*On Christian Doctrine* 1.4, Yale 6: 183).

[42]A significant word here as elsewhere, suggesting the force of Latin *auctor*, "father" or "progenitor."

I formd them free, and free they must remain,
Till they enthrall° themselves: I else must change   ENSLAVE   125
Thir nature, and revoke the high Decree
Unchangeable, Eternal, which ordain'd
Thir freedom, they themselves ordain'd thir fall.
The first sort by thir own suggestion fell,
Self-tempted, self-deprav'd: Man falls deceiv'd   130
By the other first: Man therefore shall find grace,
The other none:[43] in Mercy and Justice both,
Through Heav'n and Earth, so shall my glorie excel,
But Mercy first and last shall brightest shine.[44]

    Thus while God spake, ambrosial fragrance fill'd[45]   135
All Heav'n, and in the blessed Spirits elect[46]
Sense of new joy ineffable diffus'd:
Beyond compare the Son of God was seen
Most glorious, in him all his Father shon
Substantially express'd,[47] and in his face   140
Divine compassion visibly appeerd,
Love without end, and without measure Grace,
Which uttering thus he to his Father spake.

    O Father, gracious was that word which clos'd
Thy sovran sentence,° that Man should find grace;   JUDGMENT   145
For which both Heav'n and Earth shall high extoll
Thy praises, with th' innumerable sound
Of Hymns and sacred Songs, wherewith thy Throne
Encompass'd shall resound[48] thee ever blest.
For should Man finally be lost, should Man   150
Thy creature late so lov'd, thy youngest Son
Fall circumvented thus by fraud, though joynd
With his own folly?[49] that be from thee farr,
That farr be from thee, Father, who art Judg
Of all things made, and judgest onely right.   155
Or shall the Adversarie thus obtain
His end, and frustrate thine, shall he fulfill

---

[43]An important passage for interpreting the meaning and sequence of sin both in the angels and in humankind. Humankind will be able to find grace, which the fallen angels could not, because the angels tempted and deceived themselves through what I presume to be an instantaneous decision to side with Satan, whereas humankind was first deceived by Satan in the Serpent. The difference in degree of sin makes the difference in the possibility for achieving grace. For a contextual analysis of what Renaissance theologians and Milton thought happened in the Fall, see Steadman, "'Man's First Disobedience.'"

[44]God's Glory (in an allegorical sense) is most obvious, but Mercy will shine brightest to sinners in need of it. Justice is what the crimes and sins of humankind deserve, but Mercy and Grace intervene, in the person of the Son, who offers himself as mediator for the sins of Adam and Eve and their descendants. For the allegorical figures Mercy and Justice, see Milton's outlines for "Adam unparadiz'd" reproduced in the Introduction.

[45]Perhaps following some of the hermetic or Platonic interpretations of the nature of God, Milton allows him to exude an ambrosial (that is godly, since ambrosia was associated with the Greek pantheon) fragrance, just as Milton allows God's "nostrils" to inhale the offerings of the earth. Compare the association of evil with bad odors in 4.166–71 and compare the passage below for the effect of prayers as a kind of incense (9.192–97). See Francelia Butler, "The Holy Spirit and Odors in Paradise Lost," *Milton Newsletter* 3 (1969): 65-69.

[46]Apparently the "elect angels" of 1 Timothy 5.21. "It seems . . . reasonable, however, to suppose that the good angels stand by their own strength, no less than man did before his fall, and that they are called 'elect' only in the sense that they are beloved or choice . . . " (*On Christian Doctrine* 1.9, Yale 6: 344–45).

[47]God's glory, too bright for our senses to take in, is made perceptible in the substance of the Son, who shares that of the Father. Milton explains in *On Christian Doctrine* that there is an hypostatic union of substances between the Father and Son: " . . . the union of two natures in Christ was the mutual hypostatic union of two essences" (1.14, Yale 6: 423). Kelley summarizes: "There is then in Christ a mutual hypostatic union of two natures, that is to say, of two essences, of two substances, and consequently of two persons; . . . " (*This Great Argument* 159).

[48]One of many mimetic echoes in *Paradise Lost*—here "sound" and "resound" or "gracious" and "grace"—in which sound and meaning echo incrementally, gaining meaning in the variations of meaning, in the verbal equivalent of a musical chord.

[49]"Should mankind . . . fall through the agency of Satan, even if Satan's fraud was accompanied by humankind's folly?"

His malice, and thy goodness bring to naught,
Or proud return though to his heavier doom,
Yet with revenge accomplish't and to Hell   160
Draw after him the whole Race of mankind,
By him corrupted? or wilt thou thy self
Abolish thy Creation, and unmake,
For him, what for thy glorie thou hast made?
So should thy goodness and thy greatness both   165
Be questiond and blaspheam'd without defence.[50]
    To whom the great Creatour thus reply'd.
O Son, in whom my Soul hath chief delight,
Son of my bosom, Son who art alone
My word, my wisdom, and effectual might,[51]   170
All hast thou spok'n as my thoughts are, all
As my Eternal purpose hath decreed:
Man shall not quite be lost, but sav'd who will,
Yet not of will in him, but grace in me
Freely voutsaft;[52] once more I will renew   175
His lapsed powers, though forfeit and enthrall'd
By sin to foul exorbitant desires;
Upheld by me, yet once more he shall stand
On even ground against his mortal foe,
By me upheld, that he may know how frail   180
His fall'n condition is, and to me ow
All his deliv'rance, and to none but me.
Some I have chosen of peculiar grace
Elect above the rest;[53] so is my will:
The rest shall hear me call, and oft be warnd   185
Thir sinful state, and to appease betimes°
Th' incensed Deitie, while offerd grace
Invites; for I will cleer thir senses dark,
What may suffice, and soft'n stonie hearts
To pray, repent, and bring obedience due.[54]   190
To Prayer, repentance, and obedience due,
Though but endevord with sincere intent,
Mine ear shall not be slow, mine eye not shut.

---

[50]In this dialogue the Son takes the part of Mercy more than Justice (the Father is addressed as "Judg"), in that he appeals to his father's sense of compassion towards his "youngest Son." The prospect of annihilating his latest creation would make God as destructive as Moloch makes him out to be (2.95-97).
[51]The three synonyms for the Son show how the Son is manifested as subordinate to the Father in Milton's theology: He is God's word, the *logos* (see John 1); He is God's wisdom, expressed in His function of judge (not without mercy) on Judgment Day; and He is the demonstration of God's purposeful might, as when He drives the Chariot of Divine Wrath in the War in Heaven. "Son of my bosom" is a biblical idiom suggesting intimacy, as with "into Abraham's bosom" (Luke 16.22) or "the only begotten Son, which is in the bosom of the Father" (John 1.18). In modern typographical practice, "Word" would probably be capitalized, though it is not in *1667* or *1674*.
[52]"Vouchsafed," here in Milton's preferred spelling of a word which means "entrusted."
[53]"Election" is not so stridently stated in Milton's theology as in conventional Calvinism. "It seems . . . that predestination and election are not particular but only general: that is, they belong to all who believe in their hearts and persist in their belief . . . . Thus the general decree of election is individually applicable to each believer, and is firmly established for those who persevere" (*On Christian Doctrine* 1.4, Yale 6: 176). For the context of Milton's place among the Reformation theologians, see Christopher, *Milton*.
[54]Calvinism holds a more inflexible point of view in which humankind is "totally incapable in any way of contributing toward his own salvation (Calvin, *Institutes* III xxii 1-3)" (see Fowler 173-202n). Because Milton admits prayer, repentance, and obedience as the inroads of humankind toward atonement, together with the "Umpire Conscience" (important enough to warrant italics as a separate entity), Milton's God seems kinder and less relentless in the pursuit of justice, and more inclined toward mercy and the free distribution of grace. Instead of hardening the hearts of Adam and Eve as sinners, Milton's God is inclined to soften them. "To order us to do right but decree that we shall do wrong!—this is not the way God dealt with our forefather, Adam, nor is it the way he deals with those he calls and invites to grace" (*On Christian Doctrine* 1.4, Yale 6: 177). Historically, this position has been called Arminianism.

And I will place within them as a guide
My Umpire *Conscience*,[55] whom if they will hear,
Light after light well us'd they shall attain,   195
And to the end persisting, safe arrive.
This my long sufferance and my day of grace
They who neglect and scorn, shall never taste;
But hard be hard'nd, blind be blinded more,   200
That they may stumble on, and deeper fall;
And none but such from mercy I exclude.[56]
But yet all is not don; Man disobeying,
Disloyal breaks his fealtie, and sinns
Against the high Supremacie of Heav'n,   205
Affecting° God-head,[57] and so loosing all,   ASSUMING, PRETENDING
To expiate his Treason hath naught left,
But to destruction sacred and devote,[58]
He with his whole posteritie must dye,
Dye hee or Justice must; unless for him   210
Som other able, and as willing, pay
The rigid satisfaction,[59] death for death.
Say Heav'nly powers,[60] where shall we find such love,
Which of ye will be mortal to redeem
Mans mortal crime, and just th' unjust to save,   215
Dwels in all Heaven charitie so deare?
    He ask'd, but all the Heav'nly Quire stood mute,[61]
And silence was in Heav'n: on mans behalf
Patron[62] or Intercessor none appeerd,
Much less that durst upon his own head draw   220
The deadly forfeiture, and ransom set.[63]
And now without redemption all mankind
Must have bin lost, adjudg'd to Death and Hell
By doom° severe, had not the Son of God,   DESTINY
In whom the fulness dwels of love divine,[64]   225
His dearest mediation thus renewd.
    Father, thy word is past,[65] man shall find grace;

---

[55]Human conscience, in other words, is a sign of God's natural goodness helping humankind make choices for good instead of evil. The italics on the word throw an emphasis on it as an allegorical entity or as a manifestation of God.

[56]"Although [at times in both Testaments] . . . God openly confesses that it is he who incites the sinner, hardens his heart, blinds him and drives him into error, it must not be concluded that he is the originator even of the very smallest sin, for he is supremely holy" (*On Christian Doctrine* 1.8, Yale 6: 332).

[57]Eve, just after her Fall, also affects Godhead, that is, she attempts to assume God's nature: " . . . nor was God-head from her thought" (9.790).

[58]"But dedicated [as if a priest] and devoted to destruction." The word "sacred" here has the force of "dedicated" used in a negative sense (see *OED* adj. A.2.b, citing this instance). The modern equivalent of the usage might be seen in the formula "dedicated to a life of crime."

[59]The word "satisfaction" is carefully chosen for its theological sense, not of punishment, but of legal satisfaction, as in "He sought satisfaction for his losses." Milton associated satisfaction with the mediatorial function of Christ: "The effect and end of the whole mediatorial administration is the satisfaction of divine justice on behalf of all men, and the shaping of the faithful in the image of Christ[, who] . . . FULLY SATISFIED DIVINE JUSTICE BY FULFILLING THE LAW AND PAYING THE JUST PRICE ON BEHALF OF ALL MEN" (*On Christian Doctrine* 1.16, Yale 6: 443).

[60]The intentional parallel is with Beelzebub's questioning the fallen angels about making the voyage to corrupt Adam and Eve: "But first whom shall we send / In search of this new world, whom shall we find / Sufficient?" (2.402–04).

[61]At this point Milton means to echo the rigged debate in Hell: ". . . but all sat mute, / Pondering the danger with deep thoughts . . ." (2.420–21). Satan's entrance, unlike the Son's, has been carefully staged: it has nothing to do with free will. The Son, without a shred of hypocrisy, volunteers to take on incarnation for the sake of humankind. As Fowler points out (217–26n), the passage inspired John Dryden's imitation in *The Hind and the Panther* 2.499–514.

[62]Probably "an advocate, a pleader" in the legal, Latin-derived sense (see *OED* subs. 2.c, citing this passage).

[63]"The deadly forfeit and prearranged ransom."

[64]Colossians 2:9: "For in him dwelleth all the fulness of the Godhead bodily," another manifestation of the difference between the Father and the Son. The Geneva Bible glosses "in him" as meaning "two distincte natures, and by this worde *dwelleth* he proveth that it is there for ever" (2.9n; 1560 ed).

[65]Includes the senses "Thy will is done" and "Thy judgment is passed."

And shall grace not find means, that finds her way,
The speediest of thy winged messengers,
To visit all thy creatures, and to all   230
Comes unprevented,[66] unimplor'd, unsought,
Happie for man, so coming; he her aide
Can never seek, once dead in sins and lost;
Attonement[67] for himself or offering meet,
Indebted and undon, hath none to bring: 235
Behold mee then, mee for him, life for life
I offer, on mee let thine anger fall;[68]
Account mee man;[69] I for his sake will leave
Thy bosom, and this glorie next to thee
Freely put off,[70] and for him lastly dye   240
Well pleas'd, on me let Death wreck all his rage;
Under his gloomie power I shall not long
Lie vanquisht; thou hast givn me to possess
Life in my self for ever, by thee I live,
Though now to Death I yield, and am his due   245
All that of me can die,[71] yet that debt paid,
Thou wilt not leave me in the loathsom grave
His prey, nor suffer my unspotted Soule
For ever with corruption there to dwell;[72]
But I shall rise Victorious, and subdue   250
My vanquisher, spoild of his vanted° spoile;   VAUNTED, BOASTED ABOUT
Death his deaths wound shall then receive,[73] and stoop
Inglorious, of his mortall sting disarm'd.
I through the ample° Air in Triumph high   SPACIOUS
Shall lead Hell Captive[74] maugre° Hell, and show   IN SPITE OF   255
The powers of darkness bound. Thou at the sight
Pleas'd, out of Heaven shalt look down and smile,[75]
While by thee rais'd I ruin all my Foes,
Death last, and with his Carcass glut the Grave:[76]

---

[66]Alludes to the doctrine of "prevenient grace," or unanticipated (and undeserved) grace that nevertheless comes quickly to humankind even without being sought. God loves humankind and freely offers grace even before it is needed. After the Fall, when Adam and Eve are praying, "Prevenient Grace descending had remov'd / The stonie from thir hearts, & made new flesh / Regenerate grow instead . . . " (11.3–5). Again, this is an Arminian position.
[67]Atonement is "at-one-ness" with God or reconciliation, in this case for sinful humankind.
[68]The rhythmic and repeated "on mees" will also occur when Eve offers to take on the whole burden of the sin of humankind, at 10.935-36, in a context similar to that of the Son's offer.
[69]"Count me as one of humankind," as with the modern idiom "count me in" (see *OED* I.2.b). The Son's imagery may include the sense of His own accountability for the sins of humankind.
[70]The theological doctrine of kenosis, self-limitation of the deity by incarnation, whereby the Son of God "laid aside" his divinity to be remade "in the likeness of men" (see Phillipians 2.6–7).
[71]The human nature of the Son can die, the divine cannot.
[72]In Psalm 16.10, the Old Testament type of Christ, David, says to God: "For thou wilt not leave my soul in hell; neither wilt thou suffer thine Holy One to see corruption." The marginalia of the Geneva Bible makes the comparison between Christ and David explicit: "This is chiefly ment of Christ, by whose resurrection all his members have immortalitie" (16.10n; 1560 ed.).
[73]Fowler (3.251-53n) points out that the wordplay is not gratuitous, since "death is fatally wounded at this stage, but not 'killed' until the second coming of Christ (l. 259)." This passage alludes to the often-quoted passage from 1 Corinthians 15.55–56: "O death, where is thy sting? O grave, where is thy victory? The sting of death is sin; and the strength of sin is in the law."
[74]"The Son when He arose from the Dead, according to Ephesians 4.8, "led captivity captive." Presumably, at the Last Judgment the Son will lead a triumphal procession in which He will exhibit all of Hell's captives.
[75]Another instance of God's sardonic sense of humor, backed by scriptural authority: "And having spoiled principalities and powers, he made a shew of them openly, triumphing over them in it" (Colossians 2.15).
[76]Gruesome, but colored by Milton's sense of righteous anger and hatred for evil "as when we hate the enemies of God or of the church" (*On Christian Doctrine* 2.11, Yale 6: 743). The image is of overflowing graves at Judgment Day, with the mouth of Hell perhaps becoming the grave into which Death's carcass will be the last to be thrown, as Christ inevitably conquers death.

Then with the multitude of my redeemd   260
Shall enter Heaven long absent,[77] and returne,
Father, to see thy face, wherein no cloud
Of anger shall remain, but peace assur'd,
And reconcilement; wrauth shall be no more
Thenceforth, but in thy presence Joy entire.   265
    His words here ended, but his meek aspect
Silent yet spake, and breath'd immortal love
To mortal men, above which only shon
Filial obedience: as a sacrifice
Glad to be offer'd, he attends the will   270
Of his great Father.[78] Admiration seis'd
All Heav'n, what this might mean, and whither tend
Wondring; but soon th' Almighty thus reply'd.[79]
    O thou in Heav'n and Earth the only peace
Found out for mankind under wrauth,[80] O thou   275
My sole complacence!° well thou know'st how dear[81]   SATISFACTION
To me are all my works, nor Man the least
Though last created,[82] that for him I spare
Thee from my bosom and right hand, to save,
By loosing° thee a while, the whole Race lost.   LOSING   280
Thou therefore whom thou only canst redeem,
Thir Nature also to thy Nature joyn;[83]
And be thy self Man among men on Earth,
Made flesh, when time shall be,[84] of Virgin seed,
By wondrous birth: Be thou in *Adams* room°   PLACE, POSITION   285
The Head of all mankind,[85] though *Adams* Son.
As in him perish all men, so in thee
As from a second root shall be restor'd,[86]
As many as are restor'd, without thee none.
His crime makes guiltie all his Sons, thy merit   290

---

[77]Just how long the Son has been away from Heaven before returning has provoked critical discussion of Milton's sense of chronology, as recorded by Fowler (3.261n), but one should keep in mind that the biblical God operates on what might be called a geological scale of time ("For a thousand years in thy sight are but as yesterday when it is past, and as a watch in the night" [Psalm 90.4]), but at the same time perceives all time as the same instant, in a divine foreshortening, part of omniscience and omnipresence.

[78]The Son is clearly subordinate to the will of the Father, and obedient, especially as projected in his incarnation as Christ. See MacCallum, *Milton*, for a consensus of recent opinions about the subordinate relationship between God the Father and His Son.

[79]I have replaced the colon of both early editions with a period on the grounds that periods almost invariably were used to introduce a quotation. Probably the compositor of *1674* was following *1667* without thinking at this point.

[80]"You who are the only solace for fallen mankind under the sentence of wrath for disobedience."

[81]There is a comma at this point in both editions, indicating that the compositor of *1674* was again blindly following an error. Although most editors going back at least to Newton remove the comma, probably because they think no pause is due between "dear" and "To me." Shawcross and Fowler leave it in place, though Fowler notes that it is almost certainly an error. It would seem more logical for there to be a comma after "least," the last word on the next line; perhaps the eye of the *1667* compositor skipped upward to the wrong line.

[82]Perhaps uses the proverbial formula "last but not least," but the reverse argument was often used to support theories that because Eve was created last, she was necessarily inferior to Adam. See Diane McColley, *Milton's Eve*, and Utley, *Crooked Rib*.

[83]This will be the Incarnation, union of God and humankind. Only Jesus will be able to answer for the sins of all humankind, and to do so He must join his nature to that of humankind.

[84]That is, when time as humans know it has come into existence. The marker seems to point out the contrast between godly time and human time.

[85]As in "head of household": "The head of every man is Christ" (1 Corinthians 11.3), who was regarded as the second Adam.

[86]Quoted directly from 1 Corinthians 15.22: "For as in Adam all die, even so in Christ shall all be made alive." Adam and Eve provided the first sinful root of the genealogy of humankind; Christ cleanses the line and begins a "second root." Milton uses the word "Seed" as synonym for all of Adam and Eve's progeny and for Christ.

Imputed[87] shall absolve them who renounce
Thir own both righteous and unrighteous deeds,
And live in thee transplanted,[88] and from thee
Receive new life. So Man, as is most just,
Shall satisfie for Man, be judg'd and die,   295
And dying rise, and rising with him raise
His Brethren, ransomd with his own dear life.
So Heav'nly love shall outdoo Hellish hate
Giving to death,[89] and dying to redeeme,
So dearly to redeem what Hellish hate   300
So easily destroy'd, and still° destroyes   ALWAYS
In those who, when they may, accept not grace.
Nor shalt thou by descending to assume
Mans Nature, less'n or degrade thine owne.
Because thou hast, though Thron'd in highest bliss   305
Equal to God, and equally enjoying
God-like fruition, quitted all to save
A World from utter loss, and hast been found
By Merit[90] more then Birthright Son of God,
Found worthiest to be so by being Good,   310
Farr more then Great or High; because in thee
Love hath abounded more then Glory abounds,
Therefore thy Humiliation shall exalt
With thee thy Manhood also to this Throne;[91]
Here shalt thou sit incarnate, here shalt Reign   315
Both God and Man, Son both of God and Man,
Anointed universal King;[92] all Power
I give thee, reign for ever, and assume
Thy Merits; under thee as Head Supream
Thrones, Princedoms, Powers, Dominions[93] I reduce: 320
All knees to thee shall bow, of them that bide
In Heaven, or Earth, or under Earth in Hell;
When thou attended gloriously from Heav'n
Shalt in the Sky appeer, and from thee send
The summoning Arch-Angels to proclaime   325
Thy dread Tribunal: forthwith from all Windes
The living, and forthwith the cited° dead   SUMMONED
Of all past Ages to the general Doom
Shall hast'n, such a peal shall rouse thir sleep.

---

[87]Adam's sin is transferred to later generations in the taint of "Original Sin" (a term Milton generally avoids), considered a kind of infection causing all human beings to be born disposed toward doing evil. "Imputed" is a theological term for the process of cleansing (the primary sense of Latin **putare** is "to cleanse"). "Just as our sins, then, are imputed to Christ, so Christ's righteousness or merits are imputed to us, through faith" (*On Christian Doctrine* 1.22, Yale 6: 486). The taint of Original Sin is cleansed by the merit of Christ, who can absolve any person who renounces sin and "lives in" him. See Romans 5.17–21.

[88]The horticultural image perpetuates Christ as seed and root. The process is not just one of grafting but transplanting: Adam's root is transplanted in Christ.

[89]Probably "giving in to death," or "consigning himself willingly to death," since Christ will die voluntarily. Loh paraphrases "i.e., yielding to death, and by dying redeem life." Compare Romans 5.10: "For if, when we were enemies, we were reconciled to God by the death of his Son, much more, being reconciled, we shall be saved by his life."

[90]Echoes "by merit rais'd" as applied to Satan's "bad eminence" (2.5–6).

[91]In most copies the semicolon is so faint that it looks like a comma; some editors have therefore transcribed it as a comma.

[92]Although the punctuation mark appears to be a comma in *1674*, Fletcher notes that it is probably a worn semicolon that is printing its dot faintly, and *1667* corroborates the choice of punctuation.

[93]All orders in the angelic hierarchy. See West, *Milton* 133–36.

Then all thy Saints assembl'd, thou shalt judge   330
Bad men and Angels, they arraignd shall sink
Beneath thy Sentence; Hell her numbers full,
Thenceforth shall be for ever shut.[94] Mean while
The World shall burn,[95] and from her ashes spring
New Heav'n and Earth, wherein the just shall dwell,   ARMAGEDDON?   335
And after all thir tribulations long
See golden days, fruitful of golden deeds,
With Joy and Love triumphing,[96] and fair Truth.
Then thou thy regal Scepter shalt lay by,
For regal Scepter then no more shall need,   340
God shall be All in All.[97] But all ye Gods,°   °ANGELS
Adore him, who to compass all this dies,
Adore the Son, and honour him as mee.
    No sooner had th' Almighty ceas't, but all
The multitude of Angels with a shout   345
Loud as from numbers without number, sweet
As from blest voices, uttering joy, Heav'n rung
With Jubilee,[98] and loud Hosanna's filld
Th' eternal Regions: lowly reverent[99]
Towards either Throne they bow, and to the ground   350
With solemn adoration down they cast
Thir Crowns inwove with Amarant and Gold,
Immortal Amarant, a Flour which once
In Paradise, fast by the Tree of Life
Began to bloom, but soon for mans offence   355
To Heav'n remov'd where first it grew, there grows,
And flours aloft shading the Fount of Life,[100]
And where the river of Bliss through midst of Heavn
Rowls o're *Elysian* Flours her Amber stream;[101]
With these that never fade the Spirits elect   360

---

[94]"This will be the first time the gates of Hell are shut since Sin opened them (2.883).

[95]"For a fire is kindled in mine anger, and shall burn unto the lowest hell, and shall consume the earth with her increase, and set on fire the foundations of the mountains" (Deuteronomy 32.22). The Old Testament passage could be used as a prophecy of what would happen on Judgment Day.

[96]1 Peter 1.5–8 discusses the "last time" or Judgment Day "Wherein [the Christians who have not seen Christ] greatly rejoice . . . That the trial of [their] faith, being much more precious than of gold that perisheth, though it be tried with fire, might be found unto praise and honour and glory at the appearing of Jesus Christ: Whom having not seen, [they] love; in whom, though now [they] see him not, yet believing, [they] rejoice with joy unspeakable and full of glory." For the "sceptre of righteousness," see Hebrews 1.8.

[97]The phrase "All in All" as an epithet for the risen Christ is from 1 Corinthians 15.28. Milton subscribed to the theory that at the end of time as humankind perceives it the Earth will be purged by burning. He discusses "the end of the world and the conflagration" in *On Christian Doctrine*, basing his image on the scriptural authority, in part, of 2 Peter 3.7: *the heavens which are now . . . are kept for the fire until the day of judgment when wicked men will be destroyed . . .* " (*On Christian Doctrine* 1.33, Yale 6: 628).

[98]An important celebration as well as a call to rejoice (Psalm 100, which was sung in the Church of England prayer service, begins "*Jubilate deo*"). In Jewish history, the Jubilee was a celebration of freedom held every fifty years (*OED* 1). "Hosanna" would be a cry of praise for God during a Jubilee, as in "Hosanna to the son of David . . . Hosanna in the highest" (Matthew 21.9).

[99]After this word, there is a faint apostrophe in all known copies of *1674*, which, as Fletcher explains, was probably inserted in the line by a compositor who thought it was a space (normally, the space to the right of the line of poetry would be filled out by dummy spaces).

[100]See the opening of this book for reference to the Godhead as fountain of light and hence fountain of life. See also 375 below.

[101]The flower amaranth, like the unicorn, was thought too good to be allowed to remain on Earth after sin had entered Eden, and was thus removed to Heaven, where it had grown originally. The Greek word transliterated as "amaranth," Fowler points out (353–57n), means "unwithering," and its Greek form was used in 1 Peter 5.4: "Ye shall receive a crown of glory that fadeth not away." Probably Milton translates the image from Peter in his own "immortal garland," as used in *Areopagitica* (Yale 2: 515). Since the garland for a victor was a pagan image, Milton Christianizes the garland to avoid associating a specific pagan plant with a Christian reward. The "river of Bliss" waters the amaranth and other Elysian (the adjective from the classical Elysium, the place in the underworld where the virtuous live after death) flowers, and it flows amber because of its purity (on amber as a symbol of purity and clarity, Fowler cites Callimachus, *Hymns* 6.29, and Vergil, *Georgics* 3.522). The whole scene of the celebration of the just needs to be compared with similar celestial celebrations at the end of both "Lycidas" and the "*Epitaphium Damonis*."

Bind thir resplendent locks inwreath'd with beams,
Now in loose Garlands thick thrown off, the bright
Pavement that like a Sea of Jasper shon[102]
Impurpl'd with Celestial Roses smil'd.[103]
Then Crown'd again thir gold'n Harps they took,   365
Harps ever tun'd,[104] that glittering by thir side
Like Quivers hung, and with Præamble sweet
Of charming symphonie they introduce
Thir sacred Song, and waken raptures high;
No voice exempt, no voice but well could joine   370
Melodious part, such concord is in Heav'n.[105]
    Thee Father first they sung[106] Omnipotent,
Immutable, Immortal, Infinite,
Eternal King; thee Author of all being,
Fountain of Light, thy self invisible   375
Amidst the glorious brightness where thou sit'st
Thron'd inaccessible, but when thou shad'st
The full blaze of thy beams, and through a cloud
Drawn round about thee like a radiant Shrine,
Dark with excessive bright thy Skirts[107] appeer,   380
Yet dazle Heav'n, that brightest Seraphim
Approach not, but with both wings veil thir eyes.[108]
Thee next they sang of all Creation first,
Begotten Son, Divine Similitude,
In whose conspicuous count'nance, without cloud[109]   385
Made visible, th' Almighty Father shines,
Whom else° no Creature can behold; on thee   OTHERWISE
Impresst the effulgence[110] of his Glorie abides,
Transfus'd on thee his ample Spirit rests.[111]
Hee Heav'n of Heavens and all the Powers therein   390
By thee created, and by thee threw down
Th' aspiring Dominations:[112] thou that day

[102]For the semiprecious stone jasper, see Revelation 21.11. Mammon has worshiped the pavement of Paradise from quite a different, materialistic perspective (1.679–84).

[103]Spenser also identifies colors with emotions, in *The Faerie Queene* 3.7.17: "Oft from the forrest wildings he did bring, / Whose sides empurpled were with smiling red . . . ." How the pavement can be said to be smiling stretches the imagination of the reader; the syntax might allow the elect to smile, though Loh (364n) assumes that "pavement" is the subject of "smil'd." If the dawn can smile or be cheerful (3.545) or if the ocean can smile (4.165), the logic might run, then a pavement may smile as well.

[104]Perhaps from his own musical training Milton would have known that a harp is one of the most difficult instruments to keep in tune; a heavenly harp would by contrast never need tuning.

[105]Celestial music is perfect: the harps are genuine, not alchemical gold and they stay in tune, so they cannot contribute to a discord. Singing a sacred song is natural to angels, a spontaneous activity in which all take an expert part; the song and harmony ("symphonie") can be genuinely "charming" and produce "rapture." Compare the music of the fallen angels, or the raucous or discordant music and dance of the followers of Comus.

[106]The angels' lyrics are quoted indirectly here, so that the reader has a sense of the Epic Voice reporting the song while at the same time hearing the words of the angels beginning with "Omnipotent." As Tom Corns points out (letter, September 1991), the device allows the poet to share the song with the angelic chorus.

[107]Lest the reader presume that God is wearing a dress or a kilt, He is referred to in Ezekiel 5.3 as having skirts and in Ezekiel 16.8 as having spread His protective skirt over the Son of Man. Here the skirts of His brightness appear to be a kind of penumbra or glow surrounding His form.

[108]The vision of the "Lord [who] sitteth upon a throne" in Isaiah 6 includes "the seraphims: each one had six wings; with twain he covered his face, and with twain he covered his feet, and with twain he did fly."

[109]God often appears to the Israelites in the form of a cloud, presumably because (according to a Christian reading of the Old Testament) sinful humankind cannot perceive truth unveiled. Compare the phrase in *Animadversions*, "thy descending cloud that now covers thy Tabernacle" (Yale 1: 705).

[110]From Latin *effulgens*, "shining forth." In this case, the Son is the "Effulgence of [God the Father's] Glorie, Son belov'd" (6.680).

[111]The roles of Father, Son, and Holy Spirit are again cleverly fused, as source of light, effulgence, and "ample ['widely distributed'] Spirit."

[112]The name of an order of angels (see West 77), used here with a clever turn on "domination" to suggest that the falling angels did indeed aspire to domination.

Thy Fathers dreadful Thunder didst not spare,
Nor stop thy flaming Chariot wheels, that shook
Heav'ns everlasting Frame, while o're the necks   395
Thou drov'st of warring Angels disarraid.[113]
Back from pursuit thy Powers[114] with loud acclaime
Thee only extoll'd, Son of thy Fathers might,
To execute fierce vengeance on his foes,
Not so on Man; him through thir malice fall'n,   400
Father of Mercie and Grace, thou didst not doome
So strictly, but much more to pitie encline,
No sooner did thy dear and onely Son
Perceive thee purpos'd° not to doom frail Man   DETERMINED
So strictly, but much more to pitie enclin'd,   405
He to appease thy wrauth, and end the strife
Of Mercy and Justice in thy face discern'd,
Regardless of the Bliss wherein hee sat
Second to thee, offerd himself to die
For mans offence. O unexampl'd love,[115]   410
Love no where to be found less then Divine!
Hail Son of God, Saviour of Men, thy Name
Shall be the copious matter of my Song
Henceforth, and never shall my Harp thy praise
Forget, nor from thy Fathers praise disjoine.   415
    Thus they in Heav'n, above the starry Sphear,
Thir happie hours in joy and hymning spent.
Mean while upon the firm opacous Globe
Of this round World, whose first convex divides
The luminous inferior Orbs, enclos'd   420
From *Chaos* and th' inroad of Darkness old,
Satan alighted walks: a Globe farr off
It seem'd, now seems a boundless Continent
Dark, waste, and wild, under the frown of Night
Starless expos'd, and ever-threatning storms   425
Of *Chaos* blustring round, inclement skie;
Save on that side which from the wall of Heav'n
Though distant farr som small reflection gaines
Of glimmering air less vext with tempest loud:
Here walk'd the Fiend at large in spacious field.   430
As when a Vultur on *Imaus*[116] bred,
Whose snowie ridge the roving *Tartar* bounds,
Dislodging from a Region scarce of prey
To gorge the flesh of Lambs or yeanling° Kids   NEWBORN
On Hills where Flocks are fed, flies toward the Springs°   SOURCES   435
Of *Ganges* or *Hydaspes*, *Indian* streams;
But in his way lights on the barren Plaines

---

[113]As Lieb has pointed out, war is a "sacral event" in *Paradise Lost* (*Poetics* 247), but the image of the chariot of paternal wrath is balanced by creative use of the vehicle: "The same chariot in which the Son goes out to overwhelm the rebel angels is later used in the Son's mission to create the world (7.197–209)" (297). The event described takes place at the close of Book 6.

[114]Both an order of angels and a synonym for "armies."

[115]An apostrophe put in the form of an authorial aside. The author joins the chorus of angels in praising the Son. The authorial insertion is very similar in purpose to the "Devil with Devil damn'd" aside of 2.496–505.

[116]A mountain in the Himalayas. Both "Himalaya" and "*Imaus*" contain in their etymology the idea of being snowcapped. The "roving *Tartar*" is Genghis Khan, who cannot be contained in his conquests, even by the physical barrier of the Himalayas.

Of *Sericana*, where *Chineses* drive
With Sails and Wind thir canie Waggons light:[117]
So on this windie Sea of Land, the Fiend   440
Walk'd up and down alone bent on his prey,
Alone, for other Creature in this place
Living or liveless° to be found was none,   LIFELESS
None yet, but store° hereafter from the earth   THINGS
Up hither like Aereal vapours flew   445
Of all things transitorie and vain,[118] when Sin
With vanity had filld the works of men:[119]
Both all things vain, and all who in vain things
Built thir fond hopes of Glorie or lasting fame,
Or happiness in this or th' other life;   450
All who have thir reward on Earth, the fruits
Of painful Superstition and blind Zeal,
Naught seeking but the praise of men, here find
Fit retribution, emptie as thir deeds;
All th' unaccomplisht works of Natures hand,   455
Abortive, monstrous, or unkindly° mixt,   UNNATURALLY
Dissolvd on Earth, fleet hither, and in vain,
Till final dissolution, wander here,
Not in the neighbouring Moon, as some have dreamd;[120]
Those argent° Fields more likely habitants,   SILVERY   460
Translated Saints, or middle Spirits hold
Betwixt th' Angelical and Human kinde:
Hither of ill-joynd Sons and Daughters born
First from the ancient World those Giants came
With many a vain exploit, though then renownd:[121]   465
The builders next of *Babel* on the Plain
Of *Sennaar*, and still with vain designe
New *Babels*, had they wherewithall, would build:
Others came single;[122] he who to be deemd
A God, leap'd fondly into *Ætna*[123] flames,   470
Empedocles, and hee who to enjoy

---

[117]Lucan mentions "the people beside the Scythian sea of Maeotis, / Where the ice is so thick that they drive their wagons across it" (*Civil War* 2.720–21; trans. P.F. Widdows (Bloomington: Indiana UP, 1988): 44. Fowler (3.438–39n) unearths the interest in Chinese wind-wagons aroused by Mendoza's *Historie of the Great and Mightie Kingdome of China* (trans. Parke, 1588); Milton's acquaintance Hugo Grotius rode in a Dutch reconstruction of one of the machines. They are "canie" because they are supposed to be constructed out of light bamboo or cane.

[118]See Robert Kantra's book on religious satire, *All Things*, which arose out of an examination of this passage.

[119]The paradox of Sin filling the works of humankind with vanity is worth noting. An example of an immense construction based on vain imaginings is the Tower of Babel.

[120]This limbo of philosophical fools or Limbo of Vanity is constituted similar to Hell, where everything is also monstrous, distorted, and unnatural. Ariosto, in the *Orlando Furioso* 34.70ff, describes a similar place of lost illusions on the Moon, where all lost wits are located, to which Milton seems to be alluding to scornfully as "dreamd." Ariosto's Moon is less seriously satirical than Milton's Limbo of Vanity, which directs scorn at the abuses, as Milton imagined them, in monastic behavior within the Catholic Church. Alexander Pope reused the idea in his *Rape of the Lock*, Canto 5.

[121]The Sons of God and the Daughters of Men, according to a conflation of Old Testament (Genesis 6.4) and various apocryphal books of the Bible, mated to produce "Giants in the Earth." The descendants of Seth, called "Sons of God" and thus allied in legend with the angels before and after their fall, were thought to have intermarried with the idolatrous descendants of Cain. The story was important to Milton to illustrate the use of art or artifice in temptation; miscegenation between fallen angels and women; and a form of idolatry in which foolish men worship women because they use arts which polish life. Milton emphasizes the biblical story by dwelling on it at length in 11.573–636. See Williams, *Common Expositor*, passim, for references to the "sons of God and the daughters of men" or the "sons of Seth." The miscegenation of the Sons of God and Daughters of Men is followed immediately by another story of human folly, the building of the Tower of Babel. See Hardin, "Milton's."

[122]"Singly," or one by one. The follies described can be the result of a mass hysteria, Milton implies, or the delusion of an individual.

[123]The choice between "*Ætna*" as possessive or "*Ætna's*" was arbitrary. Notice "*Plato's Elyssium*," possessive, and "*Embryo's*," plural, even though "Idiots, Eremits and Friers" are all formed in the plural according to what is now accepted usage.

Plato's *Elysium*, leap'd into the Sea,
Cleombrotus,[124] and many more too long,
Embryo's and Idiots, Eremits° and Friers   HERMITS
White, Black and Grey,[125] with all thir trumperie.   475
Here Pilgrims roam, that stray'd so farr to seek
In *Golgotha* him dead, who lives in Heav'n;[126]
And they who to be sure of Paradise
Dying put on the weeds of *Dominic*,[127]   480
Or in *Franciscan* think to pass disguis'd;
They pass the Planets seven, and pass the fixt,
And that Crystalline Sphear whose ballance weighs
The Trepidation talkt, and that first mov'd;[128]
And now Saint *Peter* at Heav'ns Wicket[129] seems
To wait them with his Keys, and now at foot   485
Of Heav'ns ascent they lift thir Feet, when loe
A violent cross wind from either Coast
Blows them transverse ten thousand Leagues awry
Into the devious[130] Air; then might ye see
Cowles, Hoods and Habits with thir wearers tost   490
And flutterd into Raggs, then Reliques, Beads,
Indulgences, Dispenses, Pardons, Bulls,[131]
The sport of Winds: all these upwhirld aloft
Fly o're the backside[132] of the World farr off

---

[124]Horace tells the story of the philosopher-poet Empedocles in his *Art of Poetry* 464–66. In order to be thought a god, Empedocles threw himself into the active core of Mt. Aetna, but the volcano threw out enough of the remains of Empedocles that it was discovered that he was not immortal. Since Dante gives Empedocles a more dignified position in the *Inferno* (4.138), Milton might want his readers to make the association between what he considered to be pointless pagan suicide or Roman Catholic superstition. Cleombrotus's folly, according to the Church Father Lactantius (*Divine Institutes*, Migne ed. 6.408), was to drown himself after misreading Plato's *Phaedo*. Both foolish acts of "pagan" suicide are viewed from Milton's Christian perspective. Callimachus (*Epigrams* 25), Cicero (*Tusculan Disputations* 1.34), and Ovid (*Ibis* 493) all alluded to one or the other suicide.

[125]Those who are immature or born witless, embryos and idiots, are paired with those who become witless (according to Milton) by occupation, hermits (the Austin friars), and the other three orders of friars, wearing the white, black, or gray robes of the various orders of white friars or Carmelites, black friars or Dominicans, or gray friars or Franciscans. Milton also alludes to the superstition that if a dying person put on the robes ("weeds") of a Dominican or Franciscan, even if he had not entered the order, he would be more likely to get to Heaven. Milton's usage with "embryo," which seems to indicate an imperfect or immature human being or miscarried fetus, is not recorded in the *OED*.

[126]As Newton points out, the passage not only ridicules the pilgrimages of palmers to the Holy Land but seems to allude to what was said by the angels who appeared to the Disciples after Christ's resurrection in Luke 24.5–6: " . . . Why seek ye the living among the dead? He is not here, but is risen . . . ."

[127]"Dominican." In the next line, supply "weeds" or "habit" after "*Franciscan*." Milton is playing with adjective vs. noun forms in order to make the lines regular metrically.

[128]The universe described is Ptolemaic, not Copernican. Newton explains it well: "*They pass the planets fix'd*, our planetary or solar system, *and* beyond this *that crystallin sphere*, the chrystallin Heaven, clear as crystal, to which the Ptolemaics attributed a sort of libration or shaking (the *trepidation* so much talk'd of) to account for certain irregularities in the motion of the stars, and beyond this that first mov'd, the primum mobile, the sphere which was both the first mov'd and the first mover, communicating its motions to all the lower spheres; and beyond this was the empyrean Heaven, the seat of God and the Angels" (3.482n). The shaking of the Crystalline Sphere, the ninth sphere in the Ptolemaic system, was thought to be held in balance by the sign Libra as "the equinoctial point, the point of reference for the measurement" (Fowler 481–83n); hence the image of weighing the trepidation. Milton's word "talkt" indicates skepticism about the existence of trepidation.

[129]Milton remains satirical and sardonic: since St. Peter was paramount among the Catholic saints, belief in the saint as icon is here ridiculed when Peter is demeaned as wicket-keeper. A wicket was usually a small door next to a larger one, to be used when the large door was shut (*OED* 1.a), and it was generally associated with gardens. But compare the more respectful image in "Lycidas," 109–31, and note Milton's use of the skeptical "seems": St. Peter seems to be a keeper of Heaven's wicket, but only from the mistaken perspective of "Papists."

[130]Including the sense of "off the main road"; see *OED* adj. 1, citing this instance. The practice of the friars, in this case, is "awry," "devious," or, in modern terms, "off-base."

[131]Milton neatly summarizes all of what he considers to be the iconographical abuses of medieval and Renaissance Catholicism: elaborate vestments, rags, or relics said to be part of the body or costume of Christ, of an Apostle, or of a saint; the beads of the rosary; and papal bulls, dispensations, indulgences, or pardons (absolutions from sin). All are here light things whirled about sportively by the winds of change or fashion. The catalogue of abuses resembles that designed to satirize romantic epics in 9.27–41, but the catalogue also might remind a wary Protestant reader in the 1660s that the Restoration government of Charles II was closely allied with French Roman Catholic interests.

[132]Though Fowler notes that one hemisphere is dark and hence might be associated with the backside of the universe, readers of Milton's controversial prose will also know that he does not hesitate to use a double entendre word like "backside" in religious satire.

Into a *Limbo*[133] large and broad, since calld　　　　　　　　　　　　495
The Paradise of Fools, to few unknown
Long after, now unpeopl'd, and untrod;[134]
All this dark Globe the Fiend found as he pass'd,
And long he wanderd, till at last a gleame
Of dawning light turnd thither-ward in haste　　　　　　　　　　　　500
His travell'd[135] steps; farr distant he descries°　　　　SEES, DISCERNS
Ascending by degrees magnificent
Up to the wall of Heaven a Structure high,[136]
At top whereof, but farr more rich appeerd
The work as of a Kingly Palace Gate　　　　　　　　　　　　505
With Frontispice[137] of Diamond and Gold
Imbellisht, thick with sparkling orient Gemmes
The Portal shon, inimitable on Earth
By Model, or by shading Pencil drawn.[138]
The Stairs were such as whereon *Jacob* saw　　　　　　　　　　　　510
Angels ascending and descending, bands
Of Guardians bright, when he from *Esau* fled
To *Padan-Aram*,[139] in the field of *Luz*
Dreaming by night under the open Skie,
And waking cri'd, *This is the Gate of Heav'n.*[140]　　　　　　　　　　　　515
Each Stair mysteriously was meant,[141] nor stood
There alwayes, but drawn up to Heav'n somtimes
Viewless,° and underneath a bright Sea flow'd　　　　INVISIBLE
Of Jasper, or of liquid Pearle,[142] whereon
Who after came from Earth, sayling arriv'd,　　　　　　　　　　　　520
Wafted by Angels, or flew o're the Lake
Rapt° in a Chariot drawn by fiery Steeds.[143]　　　　SEIZED, TAKEN AWAY

---

[133]The word usually has the Roman Catholic sense of a region adjacent to Hell in which are stored the souls of the just who died before Christ came or the souls of unbaptized infants. Here Milton extends its meaning satirically (*OED* 1.b) to that of a Limbo of Vanity (Addison used that phrase in 1712, speaking about this passage), in which are stored what he believes are the souls of misguided fanatics. Milton's image of the Limbo of Vanity or the Paradise of Fools runs parallel to that of the Moon of Lost Wits in Ariosto's *Orlando Furioso*, Canto 34.

[134]Possibly the Paradise of Fools is uninhabited now because the Reformation has eradicated some of what Milton believes have been abuses.

[135]Richardson (quoted in Todd 501n) first pointed out the possible Italian sense of *travagliato*, "tired," as well as "well-traveled" in the modern sense.

[136]Satan perceives something very like the ladder Jacob sees after he has cheated his brother Esau out of his birthright (Genesis 28.12–13). The comparison between Jacob in his sinful condition and Satan is apt, except that Jacob will repent and Satan cannot.

[137]The image of a frontispiece may suggest the first page or first illustration in a book to a modern reader, but its primary sense in 1667 would have been architectural. An entrance gate or a portico (see *OED* 1, 2) seems intended, though the reference to a "shading Pencil" and "Model" suggests that Milton might have been thinking metaphorically as well as literally.

[138]One of the very few references to the techniques of creating visual art in all of Milton's work. Here, however, the gate of Heaven is described as "inimitable," "unable to be imitated," so it cannot be drawn or modeled.

[139]Since Jacob first went to Padan-Aram and then later dreamt in the field of Luz (Genesis 28.1–7, 19), the comma of both the early editions, absent after "*Padan-Aram*" but present after "*Luz*," seems to have been transposed, as first noticed by Newton.

[140]One of the few instances of italics being used for a direct quotation in the composition of the poem. If the rule of house style dictated that direct quotations of God's voice (as in 4.5) should alone be put in italics, this quotation from the mortal Jacob would not fit the rule. The italics are not there in *1667*; it is hard to determine if they were added by authorial instruction or by accident. There is no period at the end of this sentence in *1674* (though there was one in *1667*), perhaps because the compositor was confused by having to add italics; I have supplied the period, as most editors do.

[141]Because of what various commentaries, biblical or even alchemical, had to say about Jacob's ladder, Milton designates its appearance as a holy mystery and thereby assigns it importance as a symbol. The marginalia of the Geneva Bible give a standard Protestant interpretation: "Christ is the ladder whereby God and man are joyned together, and by whom the Angels ministre unto us: all graces by him are given unto us, & we by him ascende into heaven" (Genesis 28.12n). The ladder was also a powerful image of ascent to God through love of one particular human body (as with Ficino's interpretation of Diotima's ladder; see *The Cambridge History*, ed. Schmidt, 354).

[142]Identified in the Argument to this book as "the waters above the Firmament that flow about it." For the sea of Jasper, see the note on 363–64 above.

[143]Elijah is translated to Heaven (as opposed to dying) in a "chariot of fire" driven by "horses of fire" and propelled by a whirlwind (2 Kings 2.11). Milton gives the reader a choice of images of translation, since the beggar Lazarus was wafted upwards by angels after his death: Lazarus (not the leper whom Christ raised from the dead) "was carried by the angels into Abraham's bosom" (Luke 16.22). Fowler (3.521–22n) points also to an image in Dante's *Purgatorio* 2.25–50, of angels carrying souls to Heaven in a sailing craft.

The Stairs were then let down, whether° to dare   EITHER
The Fiend by easie ascent, or aggravate
His sad exclusion from the dores of Bliss.   525
Direct against which op'nd from beneath,
Just o're the blissful seat of Paradise,
A passage down to th' Earth, a passage wide,
Wider by farr then that of after-times
Over Mount *Sion*, and, though that were large,   530
Over the *Promis'd Land* to God so dear,
By which, to visit oft those happy Tribes,
On high behests his Angels to and fro
Pass'd frequent, and his eye with choice° regard   CAREFUL
From *Paneas* the fount of *Jordans* flood[144]   535
To *Beersaba*, where the *Holy Land*
Borders on *Ægypt* and the *Arabian* shoare;
So wide the op'ning seemd, where bounds were set
To darkness, such as bound the Ocean wave.
Satan from hence now on the lower stair   540
That scal'd by steps of Gold to Heav'n Gate
Looks down with wonder at the sudden view
Of all this World at once. As when a Scout[145]
Through dark and desart wayes with peril gone°   WALKED
All night; at last by break of chearful dawne   545
Obtains the brow of some high-climbing Hill,
Which to his eye discovers unaware
The goodly prospect of some forein land
First-seen, or some renown'd Metropolis
With glistering Spires and Pinnacles adornd,   550
Which now the Rising Sun guilds with his beams.
Such wonder seis'd, though after Heaven seen,
The Spirit maligne, but much more envy seis'd
At sight of all this World beheld so faire.
Round he surveys, and well might, where he stood   555
So high above the circling Canopie
Of Nights extended shade; from Eastern Point
Of *Libra* to the fleecie Starr that bears
Andromeda farr off *Atlantic* Seas
Beyond th' *Horizon*;[146] then from Pole to Pole   560
He views in bredth, and without longer pause
Down right into the Worlds first Region throws
His flight precipitant,° and windes with ease   HEADLONG
Through the pure marble[147] Air his oblique way

---

[144]Paneas is the Greek name for the spring of Dan, supposedly the source of the river ("flood") of Jordan. The phrase "from Dan to Beersheba" was proverbial (see Judges 20.1) for defining the extent of Israel from the headwaters of the Jordan in the north to the Egyptian border in the south or to the Arabian shore of the Dead Sea in the east. "*Beersaba*" is the less familiar Vulgate and Junius–Tremelius spelling of the King James Bible's "Beersheba."
[145]Scout is used in the military sense, meaning "spy sent in advance of an army," as it seems to be in *Comus* 138. The epic simile makes explicit the image of Satan as spy or voyeur, looking down at the Promised Land but bringing with him the envious desire to conquer or subdue what was innocent and good before.
[146]Satan views the extent of the constellations in the heavens from celestial pole to pole, from Libra, the scales, to the Andromeda nebula, which is a "fleecie Starr." It seems to have been a compositor's decision to italicize "*Horizon*," perhaps because he did not recognize the word as a common, not a place name. In *Areopagitica*, Milton italicizes "*horizon*," but only because the word is being treated as a word (Yale 1: 935); otherwise, the word is never emphasized in the prose. But compare "*Æquator*," 617 below, and the even more unusual "*Promis'd Land*" of 531 above.
[147]Possibly "smooth [as marble]" or "variegated," "marbled."

Amongst innumerable Starrs, that shon   565
Stars distant, but nigh hand seemd other Worlds,[148]
Or other Worlds they seemd, or happy Iles,
Like those *Hesperian* Gardens[149] fam'd of old,
Fortunate Fields, and Groves and flourie Vales,
Thrice happy Iles, but who dwelt happy there   570
He stayd not to enquire: above them all
The golden Sun in splendor likest Heaven
Allur'd his eye: Thither his course he bends
Through the calm Firmament; but up or downe
By center, or eccentric, hard to tell,[150]   575
Or Longitude, where the great Luminarie
Alooff the vulgar Constellations thick,[151]
That from his Lordly eye keep distance due,
Dispenses Light from farr; they as they move
Thir Starry[152] dance in numbers that compute   580
Days, months, and years,[153] towards his all-chearing Lamp[154]
Turn swift thir various motions, or are turnd
By his Magnetic beam,[155] that gently warms
The Univers, and to each inward part
With gentle penetration, though unseen,   585
Shoots invisible vertue even to the deep:[156]
So wondrously was set his Station bright.
There lands the Fiend, a spot like which perhaps
Astronomer in the Sun's lucent° Orbe   *LIGHT-PRODUCING*
Through his glaz'd Optic Tube yet never saw.[157]   590
The place he found beyond expression bright,
Compar'd with aught on Earth, Metal[158] or Stone;
Not all parts like, but all alike informd
With radiant light, as glowing Iron with fire;
If mettal, part seemd Gold, part Silver cleer;   595
If stone, Carbuncle most or Chrysolite,
Rubie or Topaz, to the Twelve that shon

---

[148]Speculation about the plurality of worlds, as in the modern debate about other forms of life in the universe, suggested that there might be life on other planets or even happy isles on this planet where paradisal life might exist. Since Satan does not stay to observe, the question is left academic.

[149]The Garden of the Hesperides, daughters of Hesperus, who was in turn associated with the planet Venus or the Evening Star. The Hesperides were appointed to tend the golden apples that Juno gave to Jupiter as a marriage gift. Supposedly near Mt. Atlas in Africa, the garden abounded with all the most delicious fruit. One of the labors of Hercules was to steal some of the golden apples, despite the sleepless dragon supposed to be guarding them. For one version of the story, see Hesiod, *Theogony* 517–20.

[150]Milton hesitates between choosing the Copernican ("center") position and the Ptolemaic ("eccentric").

[151]The constellations are so thick with stars that they appear as a mob, keeping a respectful distance from the Sun as a lord aloof above them. The image recalls that of God as an all-seeing eye, signifying omniscience and omnipresence, while "lordly" suggests omnipotence.

[152]Corrects "Sarry" in *1667*.

[153]The main purpose of the motion of stars was thought to be to keep time for humankind.

[154]A very long line for the *1674* compositor to fit in, hence an ampersand replaced and; in *1667* the compositor used "and," but the last word in the line had to be wrapped below the line. I have restored the "and."

[155]A reference to Johannes Kepler's theory, expressed in his *Astronomia* (Prague, 1609), that the sun exerted magnetic force on other planets—an anticipation of the theory of gravitational pull.

[156]A sexual interpretation of the spread of a seminal lifeforce, "vertue," in the form of light and heat radiating even into the depths of the oceans.

[157]This seems to be a derogatory image of Galileo, who did discover spots on the moon's surface (not the sun's—they were already known), through his optic tube, the telescope, which was "glaz'd" in the sense that it contained glass elements. Compare "spotty Globe" (1.291) for a potentially negative image of what the astronomer saw. It appears that Satan is causing an imaginary sun spot, one which would confuse an astronomer.

[158]This would seem to need emending from the "Medal" of *1667* and *1674* to "Metal," since metal would normally be contrasted with stone, except that 595 mentions and perhaps contrasts "mettal" with "Medal." The construction "If mettal" and "If stone" suggests that those are the two earthly substances being contrasted. Newton's edition was the first to argue for the emendation, on the grounds that both metal and stone appear later (592n).

In *Aarons* Brest-plate,[159] and a stone besides
Imagind rather oft then elsewhere seen,
That stone, or like to that which here below
Philosophers in vain so long have sought,
In vain, though by thir powerful Art they binde
Volatil *Hermes*,[160] and call up unbound
In various shapes old *Proteus* from the Sea,
Draind through a Limbec to his Native forme.
What wonder then if fields and regions here
Breathe forth *Elixir* pure, and Rivers run
Potable Gold,[161] when with one vertuous touch
Th' Arch-chimic Sun[162] so farr from us remote
Produces with Terrestrial Humor mixt
Here in the dark so many precious things
Of colour glorious and effect so rare?[163]
Here matter new to gaze the Devil met
Undazl'd, farr and wide his eye commands,
For sight no obstacle found here, nor shade,
But all Sun-shine, as when his Beams at Noon
Culminate[164] from th' *Æquator*, as they now
Shot upward still direct, whence no way round
Shadow from body opaque can fall, and the Aire,
No where so cleer, sharp'nd his visual ray
To objects distant farr, whereby he soon
Saw within kenn° a glorious Angel stand,
The same whom *John* saw also in the Sun:[165]
His back was turnd, but not his brightness hid;
Of beaming sunnie Raies, a golden tiar°
Circl'd his Head, nor less his Locks behind
Illustrious on his Shoulders fledge[166] with wings
Lay waving round; on som great charge° imploy'd
He seemd, or fixt in cogitation deep.
Glad was the Spirit impure as now in hope
To find who might direct his wandring flight

600

605

610

615

620

OBSERVABLE DISTANCE

TIARA, CROWN   625

COMMISSION

630

---

[159]Exodus 25.7 describes the precious stones the Lord commanded to be set in the ceremonial breastplate lodged in His tabernacle and worn for ritual purposes by Aaron (see Exodus 28.30, 29.5).
[160]Milton spoke of "thrice-great Hermes," Hermes Trismegistus, more respectfully in his youthful "Il Penseroso." "Hermes," William B. Hunter reminds me (letter, September 1991), also stood for the liquid metal mercury, which alchemists attempted to fix or harden into silver. For the search for alchemical lore in hermetic sources, see Frances Yates, *Giordano Bruno.* Here Milton calls Hermes "Volatil" because alchemists tried to capture "explosive" spirits like that represented by Hermes, they also might try to "drain" a constantly changing classical demigod like Proteus by heating his essence and forcing it through the glass of a retort or limbec in order to "capture" his original form. "Volatil" should be accented on the second syllable.
[161]Alchemists would be seeking an elixir which would cure all diseases or mental aberrations, and they might expect special power from drinkable ("Potable") gold, since precious gems and metals such as pearls and gold were supposed to have magical or curative powers. The image here is of the sun as an arch-alchemist or arch-chemist spreading "vertue" with touches of light. Milton's tone throughout his examination of what were to his generation modern scientific discoveries and speculations seems to be consistently skeptical. Svendsen speaks of Milton's general "condemnation of astronomers who attempt to chart the orbits of the planets and speculate beyond due limits" (77), but he admits that "In *Paradise Lost*, Milton certainly girded the sphere with most of the commonly accepted circles . . . " (79).
[162]"The archetypal and elemental chemist, causer of all chemical reactions, the sun."
[163]The sun's heat, even beneath the surface of the Earth, was supposed to engender precious stones. See Svendsen, 29–30, for the relationship between the generative power of the sun and various metals, including "potable gold."
[164]"A heavenly body is said to *culminate* when it reaches the highest, meridian point of its apparent orbit" (Fowler 616–17n). A distinction is being made between the sun's supposed path before the Fall, when it was perpendicular to the equator, and after the Fall, when it had an elliptical path.
[165]Revelation 19.17, supposedly dictated by John the Divine, describes the vision of "an angel standing in the sun." The angel's proclamation to John, according to the Geneva Bible, "signifieth that the day of judgement shalbe cleare and evident; so that none shal be hid: for the trumpet shall blowe a lowde & all shall understand it" (Revelation 19.17, marginal note).
[166]The arch-angel's shoulders are sprouting wings, as in a fledgling bird.

To Paradise the happie seat of Man,
His journies end and our beginning woe.
But first he casts to change his proper shape,
Which else might work° him danger or delay: CAUSE   635
And now a stripling Cherube he appeers,
Not of the prime,[167] yet such as in his face
Youth smil'd Celestial, and to every Limb
Sutable grace diffus'd, so well he feignd;
Under a Coronet his flowing haire   640
In curles on either cheek plaid, wings he wore
Of many a coulourd plume sprinkl'd with Gold,
His habit fit for speed succinct,[168] and held
Before his decent° steps a Silver wand.   CONSIDERATE, THOUGHTFUL
He drew not nigh unheard, the Angel bright,   645
Ere he drew nigh, his radiant visage turnd,
Admonisht by his ear, and strait was known
Th' Arch-Angel *Uriel*, one of the seav'n
Who in Gods presence, neerest to his Throne
Stand ready at command,[169] and are his Eyes[170]   650
That run through all the Heav'ns, or down to th' Earth
Bear his swift errands[171] over moist and dry,
O're Sea and Land: him *Satan* thus accostes.[172]
    Uriel, for thou of those seav'n Spirits that stand
In sight of God's high Throne, gloriously bright,   655
The first art wont his great authentic° will
Interpreter through highest Heav'n to bring,   AUTHORITATIVE
Where all his Sons thy Embassie attend;[173]
And here art likeliest by supream decree
Like honour to obtain, and as his Eye   660
To visit oft this new Creation round;
Unspeakable desire to see, and know
All these his wondrous works, but chiefly Man,
His chief delight and favour, him for whom
All these his works so wondrous he ordaind,   665
Hath brought me from the Quires° of Cherubim   CHOIRS
Alone thus wandring. Brightest Seraph tell
In which of all these shining Orbes hath Man
His fixed seat, or fixed seat hath none,

---

[167]Not of the first rank of angels. Compare the phrase "meaner Angel" in the Argument to this book. Presumably Satan's disguise here is not unlike his appearance when he comes to Eve in her dream, 5.35–94: there "his dewie locks distill'd / *Ambrosia*" (56–57), whereas here the true angel's locks are "Illustrious" and shoulder-length, whereas Satan's hair in his disguise is flowing and curls on his cheeks.

[168]His habit is succinct, Latin *succinctus*, "girded up," hence prepared for action.

[169]For the context of Uriel's being met by Satan, see West 104–105. Satan's guise as a young stripling cherub is "not angelology" (104) in the sense that those who speculated on the nature of angels concluded that angels were ageless; also, Uriel's connection with the sun may represent highly-questionable speculation, rather than accepted opinion, about angelic occupations. For Milton's conservative opinions on the nature of angels, we have only the spare chapter 1.9 of *On Christian Doctrine*, "Of the Special Government of Angels."

[170]Revelation 4.6 describes four "beasts" taken to be cherubim (see Geneva Bible 4.6n) angels, "full of eyes before and behind." Uriel's name, Shawcross reminds us (648n), means "the fire of God."

[171]These angelic errands seem not to be demeaning, though Satan describes them contemptuously in 1.152; Satan's corruption of humankind is described as a "bad Errand" at 10.41.

[172]Though *1674* prints a semicolon here, the usual punctuation as a verse paragraph ends is a period, as in the second state of *1667* (the compositor working at this point in *1674* was apparently setting from the first state).

[173]Loh reconstructs the difficult syntax as "for, of those seven spirits . . . , thou are the first interpreter, wont (i.e., accustomed) to bring his great authentic will through highest heaven where all his sons (i.e., the angels) attend thy embassy (i.e., function of a sovereign's deputy)" (654–58n).

But all these shining Orbes his choice to dwell;[174]   670
That I may find him, and with secret gaze,
Or open admiration him behold
On whom the great Creator hath bestowd
Worlds, and on whom hath all these graces powrd;
That both in him and all things, as is meet,   675
The Universal Maker we may praise;
Who justly hath drivn out his Rebell Foes
To deepest Hell, and to repair that loss
Created this new happie Race of Men
To serve him better: wise are all his wayes.[175]   680
    So spake the false dissembler unperceivd;
For neither Man nor Angel can discern
Hypocrisie, the onely evil that walks
Invisible, except to God alone,[176]
By his permissive will,[177] through Heav'n and Earth: 685
And oft though wisdom wake, suspicion sleeps
At wisdoms Gate, and to simplicitie
Resigns her charge, while goodness thinks no ill
Where no ill seems: Which now for once beguil'd
Uriel, though Regent of the Sun, and held   690
The sharpest sighted Spirit of all in Heav'n;
Who to the fraudulent Impostor foule
In his uprightness answer thus returnd.[178]
    Fair Angel, thy desire which tends to know
The works of God, thereby to glorifie   695
The great Work-Maister,[179] leads to no excess
That reaches blame, but rather merits praise
The more it seems excess, that led thee hither
From thy Empyreal Mansion[180] thus alone,
To witness with thine eyes what some perhaps   700
Contented with report hear onely in heav'n:
For wonderful indeed are all his works,
Pleasant to know, and worthiest to be all
Had in remembrance alwayes with delight;
But what created mind can comprehend   705
Thir number, or the wisdom infinite
That brought them forth, but hid thir causes deep.
I saw when at his Word the formless Mass,[181]

---

[174]Leaves open the possibility of a plurality of worlds: Adam and Eve might be living on various heavenly bodies.

[175]Though Satan's praise takes the form of a kind of ritual politeness, it is accurate and ironically true. He has just accurately recounted exactly why he and the other fallen angels were damned and why Adam and Eve were created.

[176]This fine theological and psychological insight into the nature of evil suggests Spenser's arch-hypocrite Archimago, in *The Faerie Queene* 1. Here Satan by mimicry and by clever feigning of righteous indignation at least temporarily fools the angel of the sun, who ought to be the most clear-sighted of all the angels.

[177]God can permit evil to continue its course without endorsing it, as when ill chance allows Satan to continue on his course toward the Earth 2.927–38, despite his being thrown off by hitting a "vast vacuitie." In the same way, God allows hypocrisy to exist without condoning it.

[178]I have assumed that, because a direct quotation begins on the next line, a new verse paragraph should begin as well, following an almost unvarying house style.

[179]Compare "my great task-maisters eye" in Milton's Sonnet 7.

[180]"Your dwelling place in the Empyrean sphere."

[181]"And the earth was without form, and void; and darkness was upon the face of the deep. And the Spirit of God moved upon the face of the waters" (Genesis 1.2).

This worlds material mould, came to a heap:[182]
Confusion[183] heard his voice, and wilde uproar   710
Stood rul'd, stood vast infinitude confin'd;
Till at his second bidding darkness fled,
Light shon, and order from disorder sprung:
Swift to thir several Quarters hasted then
The cumbrous Elements, Earth, Flood, Aire, Fire,   715
And this Ethereal quintessence of Heav'n[184]
Flew upward, spirited with various forms,
That rowld orbicular, and turnd to Starrs
Numberless, as thou seest, and how they move;
Each had his place appointed, each his course,   720
The rest in circuit walles this Universe.[185]
Look downward on that Globe whose hither side
With light from hence, though but reflected, shines;
That place is Earth the seat of Man, that light
His day, which else as th' other Hemisphere   725
Night would invade, but there the neighbouring Moon
(So call that opposite fair Starr) her aide
Timely interposes, and her monthly round
Still ending, still renewing, through mid Heav'n,[186]
With borrowd light her countenance triform[187]   730
Hence fills and empties to enlighten th' Earth,
And in her pale dominion checks the night.
That spot to which I point is *Paradise*,
Adams abode, those loftie shades[188] his Bowre.
Thy way thou canst not miss, me mine requires.   735

---

[182]The word suggests order rather than disorder—and it has a positive connotation, as opposed to its modern connotation in a phrase like "the car was an old heap."

[183]Another vestige of the allegorical epic, emphasized by the italics placed on the word (the italics are not present in *1667* and hence were added, perhaps as a correction). Confusion, the entity, hears the Word, or Logos of John 1, and is brought under control and under limits. For the full account, see 7.163–242, where "*Chaos* heard [God's] voice." Notice the italics on "*Chaos*," which seems to be parallel with those placed on "*Confusion.*"

[184]The fifth element, from which all the Ptolemaic universe from the Moon on up was supposed to be made. The four other elements remain sublunary.

[185]The reason for the singular verb "walles" seems to be that "The rest" is a collective noun referring to the fixed stars.

[186]Probably the semicolon that is printed here in *1674* is mistaken. The compositor took it from the earlier state of *1667*. The comma after "renewing" also represents the earlier state of *1667*; whether it is the best reading is hard to judge, but I have left it in. The elided form "th' Earth" of 731 and the unelided form "Heaven" of 737 may both represent a mindless duplication of the earlier, uncorrected state of *1667*, but Fletcher points out that the compositor of *1674* corrected "with" to "in" at 741, following the *1668* Errata.

[187]The moon was supposed according to classical mythology to be ruled by a triform deity called Luna in heaven, Diana on Earth, and Hecate or Proserpina in Hades. See Vergil, *Aeneid*, 4.510–17.

[188]Probably "the shelter from the sun afforded by trees" (*OED* III.8), as with 1.303.

   Thus said, he turnd, and *Satan* bowing low,
As to superior Spirits is wont in Heaven,
Where honour due and reverence none neglects,
Took leave, and toward the coast of Earth beneath,
Down from th' Ecliptic, sped with hop'd success,   740
Throws his steep flight in many an Aerie wheele,
Nor staid, till on *Niphates*[189] top he lights.

The End of the Third Book.

---

[189]An appropriate mountain, since it borders on Mesopotamia (or Armenia and Assyria—it is the "*Assyrian* mount" in 4.126) and is the source of the river Tigris.

Paradise Lost.

BOOK IV.

THE ARGUMENT.

Satan *now in prospect of* Eden, *and nigh the place*[1] *where he must now attempt the bold enterprize which he undertook alone against God and Man, falls into many doubts with himself, and many passions, fear, envy, and despare; but at length confirms himself in evil, journeys on to Paradise, whose outward prospect and scituation is discribed, overleaps the bounds, sits in the shape of a Cormorant*[2] *on the Tree of life, as highest in the Garden to look about him. The Garden describ'd; Satans first sight of Adam and Eve; his wonder at thir excellent form and happy state, but with resolution to work thir fall; overhears thir discourse, thence gathers that the Tree of knowledge was forbidden them to eat of, under penalty of death; and thereon intends to found his Temptation, by seducing them to transgress: then leaves them a while, to know further of thir state by some other means. Mean while* Uriel[3] *descending on a Sun-beam warns* Gabriel, *who had in charge the Gate of Paradise, that some evil spirit had escap'd the Deep, and past at Noon by his Sphere in the shape of a good Angel down to Paradise, discovered after by his furious gestures in the Mount.*[4] Gabriel *promises to find him*[5] *ere morning. Night coming on,* Adam *and* Eve[6] *discourse of going to thir rest: thir Bower describ'd; thir Evening worship.* Gabriel *drawing forth his Bands of Night-watch to walk the round of Paradise, appoints two strong Angels to* Adams *Bower, least the evill spirit should be there doing some harm to* Adam *or* Eve *sleeping; there they find him at the ear of* Eve, *tempting her in a dream, and bring him, though unwilling, to* Gabriel; *by whom question'd, he scornfully answers, prepares resistance, but hinder'd by a Sign from Heaven, flies out of Paradise.*

O   For that warning voice, which he who saw
    Th' *Apocalyps*, heard cry in Heaven aloud,
    Then when the Dragon, put to second rout,
    Came furious down to be reveng'd on men,
Wo to the inhabitants on Earth![7] that now,   5
While time was,[8] our first Parents[9] had bin warnd
The coming of thir secret foe, and scap'd
Haply so scap'd his mortal snare; for now
Satan, now first inflam'd with rage, came down,
The Tempter ere th' Accuser of man-kind,[10]   10

---

[1]"Within sight of the place." The words "prospect" and "scituation" (an acceptable variant of "situation" in 1674) meant roughly the same thing.

[2]Its name taken from Latin *corvus marinus*, or "sea-crow," the cormorant is a sea-bird observable from the British coasts and known for its voracious hunting and gluttony in catching fish. "The Old [cormorants] are often Fished with, having a string tyed about their necks, to hinder them from swallowing" (Lovell 146). Fowler (4.196n) points out that Milton may well have been familiar with cormorants owned by King Charles I and kept on public display near Milton's house in Petty France. The cormorant was associated with human gluttony and greed, as embodied in usury or "money-hunger."

[3]Uriel is regent of the sun and one of the four archangels, according to Cornelius Agrippa, and thus of the same rank as Raphael, Michael, and Gabriel. The fact that the keenest-sighted angel has been deceived by Satan's appearance attests to the power of the fallen angel (West 68), but by 129 Uriel is completely aware of Satan's hypocritical disguise.

[4]Satan's anger, expressed in his furious gestures, betrays the fact that he cannot be the angel he is pretending to be. His being "bold" is in no way admirable.

[5]The 1668 state of the Argument reads "find him out."

[6]1674 adds a comma here to earlier versions of the Argument, I think unnecessarily, between subjects and verb.

[7]The "he who saw" is the author of Revelation, and the "warning voice" is the "loud voice" from Heaven mentioned in Revelation 12.10. The Dragon of Revelation 12.3 was identified in 12.9 as Satan. The Dragon corrupts "the third part of the stars of heaven," is warred on and defeated by "Michael and his angels," and is then cast out of Heaven. He seeks vengeance on the "woman clothed with the sun" who, like Eve, bears a seed of "a man child, who was to rule all nations with a rod of iron." The italicized sentence "Wo to the inhabitants on Earth" is a paraphrase of Rev. 12.12. For Milton's use of Revelation, see Dobbins, *Milton*, and Patrides and Wittreich, *The Apocalypse*. The italicized quotation is one of the very rare occurrences in *1674* of a quoted statement appearing in italics, presumably because the cry issues from Heaven.

[8]"While time remained to them before their fall."

[9]The reading of 1667, "first Parents," seems superior to the *1674* "first-Parents."

[10]Satan will first be the tempter of humankind, then the accuser after the Fall. He will take out his own frustration on humankind for having lost the War in Heaven and for having been driven down to Hell.

To wreck° on innocent frail man his loss
Of that first Battel, and his flight to Hell:
Yet not rejoycing in his speed, though bold,
Far off and fearless, nor with cause to boast,
Begins his dire attempt, which nigh the birth   15
Now rowling,[11] boiles in his tumultuous brest,
And like a devillish Engine back recoiles[12]
Upon himself; horror and doubt distract
His troubl'd thoughts, and from the bottom stirr
The Hell within him, for within him Hell   20
He brings, and round about him, nor from Hell
One step no more then from himself can fly
By change of place:[13] Now conscience wakes despair
That slumberd, wakes the bitter memorie
Of what he was, what is, and what must be   25
Worse; of worse deeds worse sufferings must ensue.
Sometimes towards *Eden* which now in his view
Lay pleasant,[14] his grievd looks he fixes sad,
Sometimes towards Heav'n and the full-blazing Sun,
Which now sat high in his Meridian Towre:[15]   30
Then much revolving, thus in sighs began.
   O thou that with surpassing Glory crownd,
Look'st from thy sole Dominion like the God
Of this new World; at whose sight all the Starrs
Hide thir diminisht heads; to thee I call,   35
But with no friendly voice, and add thy name
O Sun, to tell thee how I hate thy beams
That bring to my remembrance from what state
I fell, how glorious once above thy Spheare;
Till Pride and worse Ambition threw me down   40
Warring in Heav'n against Heav'ns matchless King:[16]
Ah wherefore! he deservd no such return
From me, whom he created what I was
In that bright eminence,[17] and with his good

---

[11] The attempt is now "turning in his mind." Compare "revolving" in 31 below and 1.52, in which the fallen angels are physically rolling, and spiritually confused as well. The images of turning, boiling, and recoiling all suggest confused and violent, self-defeating action.

[12] Satan's backfiring mind is like the cannonry the fallen angels invent during the War in Heaven; his plots also recoil on him.

[13] Fowler aptly quotes Sir Thomas Browne, *Religio Medici*: "The heart of man is the place the devill dwels in; I feele sometimes a hell within my selfe" (1.51); and Marlowe's Mephistopheles: "Hell hath no limits, nor is circumscrib'd, / In one selfe place: but where we are is hell, / And where hell is there must we ever be" (*Doctor Faustus*, 1616, ed. Greg, ll. 513–15).

[14] Probably an allusion to the etymology of "Eden" as "pleasure." Compare "pleasant Garden" describing Eden at 215.

[15] The time is noon, when the sun is on the meridian or at its highest point during the day—in this case foreshadowing the time when Eve will decide to eat the fruit. The sun sits in the position of judgment just as Satan is invoking the sun hatefully and making his decision to corrupt mankind. See Cirillo for the importance of events happening at either turning point of the day or night.

[16] According to Edward Phillips, lines 32–41 were shown to him "several Years before the Poem was begun," and were intended as the beginning of a tragedy on the Fall (Darbishire, *Early Lives* 72). Though a speech by Satan does not begin either of the outlines of tragedies on the subject in the Trinity MS, Phillips may be discussing a sketched-in dramatic version. As a soliloquy, the speech resembles the inner thoughts of an evil character much as Claudius's soliloquy in *Hamlet* 3.3.36–72, when he tries to repent but cannot, and Macbeth's more famous "Tomorrow and tomorrow and tomorrow" soliloquy, 5.5.17–28. Both Shakespearean soliloquies express the bitterness of the damned who are unable to repent, and Milton may associate the need to talk to oneself with the state of being fallen. Satan's "revolving" and recoiling and his cursing of the sun cannot resolve the problem of his self-inflicted damnation.

[17] Satan admits here that God created him, a fact that he denies in public at 5.860–61. The phrase "bright eminence" should be contrasted with the "bad eminence" of Satan after his fall (2.6) and perhaps the "Bright effluence" (3.6) assigned to the Son, Satan's foil in the epic. Satan admits honestly that his malice toward God was undeserved and that service to a deserving God was easy. His admission that the God he is still in the process of attacking does not deserve the attack ironically makes Satan likable or admirable, to some readers. Joseph Addison, for instance, writing in 1712, found the speech "bold and noble" and "the finest that is ascribed to Satan in the whole poem" (110, 111).

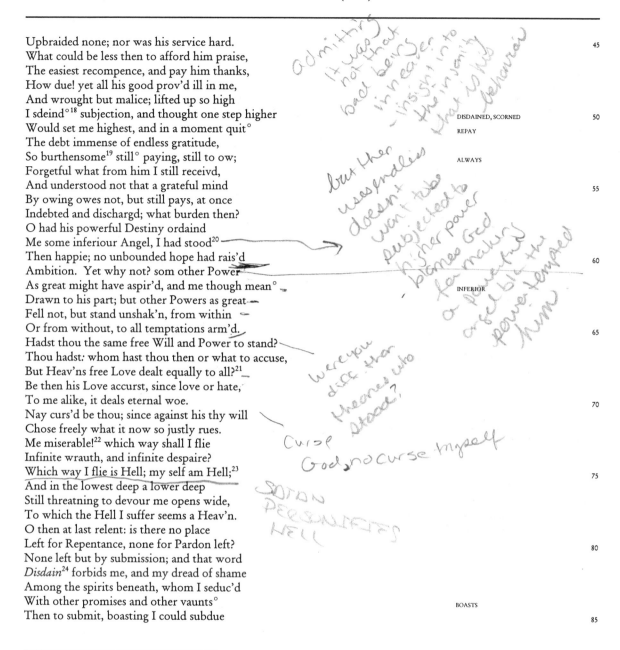

Upbraided none; nor was his service hard.
What could be less then to afford him praise,
The easiest recompence, and pay him thanks,   45
How due! yet all his good prov'd ill in me,
And wrought but malice; lifted up so high
I sdeind°[18] subjection, and thought one step higher   DISDAINED, SCORNED
Would set me highest, and in a moment quit°   50   REPAY
The debt immense of endless gratitude,
So burthensome[19] still° paying, still to ow;   ALWAYS
Forgetful what from him I still receivd,
And understood not that a grateful mind
By owing owes not, but still pays, at once   55
Indebted and dischargd; what burden then?
O had his powerful Destiny ordaind
Me some inferiour Angel, I had stood[20]
Then happie; no unbounded hope had rais'd
Ambition. Yet why not? som other Power   60
As great might have aspir'd, and me though mean°   INFERIOR
Drawn to his part; but other Powers as great
Fell not, but stand unshak'n, from within
Or from without, to all temptations arm'd.
Hadst thou the same free Will and Power to stand?   65
Thou hadst: whom hast thou then or what to accuse,
But Heav'ns free Love dealt equally to all?[21]
Be then his Love accurst, since love or hate,
To me alike, it deals eternal woe.
Nay curs'd be thou; since against his thy will   70
Chose freely what it now so justly rues.
Me miserable![22] which way shall I flie
Infinite wrauth, and infinite despaire?
Which way I flie is Hell; my self am Hell;[23]   75
And in the lowest deep a lower deep
Still threatning to devour me opens wide,
To which the Hell I suffer seems a Heav'n.
O then at last relent: is there no place
Left for Repentance, none for Pardon left?   80
None left but by submission; and that word
Disdain[24] forbids me, and my dread of shame
Among the spirits beneath, whom I seduc'd
With other promises and other vaunts°   BOASTS
Then to submit, boasting I could subdue   85

[18]The form of the word here possibly echoes the Italian *sdegnare*, "to disdain or to scorn," with overtones of aristocratic pride looking down on a lower station, but "sdeign" was used commonly in literary English (see *OED* "sdeign"). Notice that Satan uses "Disdain" at 82.

[19]Pronounced "burdensome" (the spelling, as in "burden" below, seems arbitrary). *1667* inserts a comma here.

[20]Fowler points out the double meaning of "remained" and "stood firm."

[21]The gate of Hell in Dante's *Inferno* has as part of its inscription "DIVINE POWER MADE ME AND SUPREME WISDOM AND PRIMAL LOVE" (3.5); if divine love can create Hell, it can, in a sense, define Satan's behavior.

[22]An exclamation of grief, roughly akin to the Elizabethan and Miltonic "Ay me" (86) or the Italian "Ahimé."

[23]In his descent into his own motivation, Satan merely uncovers more layers of deception, more hellish convolutions. He cannot run away from Hell because it is a part of him. Like the demons in medieval drama, Satan always faces Hell in terms of a devouring mouth. He admits that he has lied to the fallen angels about his reasons for rebellion, but the admission only causes him more pain in realizing the hopelessness of his own position. For a liar to admit he has lied to others may not free him from perpetual or habitual self-deceit.

[24]The italics may stress the importance of the word, as if Disdain—even the word itself—were an allegorical figure standing in Satan's way.

Th' Omnipotent. Ay me, they little know
How dearly I abide that boast so vaine,
Under what torments inwardly I groane;[25]
While they adore me on the Throne of Hell,
With Diadem and Scepter high advanc'd   90
The lower still I fall, onely Supream
In miserie; such joy Ambition findes.[26]
But say I could repent and could obtaine
By Act of Grace[27] my former state; how soon
Would highth[28] recal high thoughts, how soon unsay   95
What feign'd submission swore: ease would recant
Vows made in pain, as violent and void.
For never can true reconcilement grow
Where wounds of deadly hate have peirc'd so deep:
Which would but lead me to a worse relapse[29]   100
And heavier fall: so should I purchase deare
Short intermission bought with double smart.
This knows my punisher; therefore as farr
From granting hee, as I from begging peace:
All hope excluded thus, behold in stead   105
Of us out-cast, exil'd, his new delight,
Mankind created, and for him this World.
So farwel Hope, and with Hope farwel Fear,
Farwel Remorse: all Good to me is lost;
Evil be thou my Good; by thee at least   110
Divided Empire with Heav'ns King I hold
By thee, and more then half perhaps will reigne;[30]
As Man ere long, and this new World shall know.
    Thus while he spake, each passion dimm'd his face
Thrice chang'd with pale, ire, envie and despair,[31]   115
Which marrd his borrow'd visage, and betraid
Him counterfet, if any eye beheld.
For heav'nly mindes from such distempers foule
Are ever cleer. Whereof hee soon aware,
Each perturbation smooth'd with outward calme,   120
Artificer of fraud;[32] and was the first
That practisd falshood under saintly shew,°   SHOW

---

[25]The second state of *1667* has a colon here, but *1674* follows the first state. The choice between the two may well have been arbitrary.

[26]At this point Satan shares many of the characteristics of Shakespeare's Claudius and Macbeth, since both rose to great heights (or sank to great depths) by their ambition. The irony in ambition is that as the body rises higher in worldly positions, the soul falls closer to despair, so that the joy that ambition finds is really misery.

[27]The meaning of the phrase may be legal as well as theological; *OED* 15.b defines "Act of grace" as "a formal pardon, spec. a free and general pardon, granted by an Act of Parliament."

[28] *1674* is clearly in error, with "higth," so I have restored the reading of *1667*.

[29]The later state of *1667* has a comma here, one which I have chosen not to reinstate.

[30]The qualifying "perhaps" again betrays Satan's self-doubt. If indeed he held divided empire with God, the universe would have a Manichaean split between an equally forceful good and evil—a heresy to which Milton never subscribed. "Evil be thou my Good" is a ringing and quotable phrase nevertheless. The extensive speech shows how Satan is psychologically incapable of repenting.

[31]The passions of anger, envy, and despair were all assumed to cause the face to grow pale, as in the proverbial "pale with envy." Satan's face (he is in the guise of a cherub, and cherubim were traditionally said to be red in hue) is dimmed by each passion he feels, so that his anguish is detectable in the various hues. The Argument has also reminded us that his "furious gestures" give his disguise away to observing angels and that he is supposed to be feeling "fear, envy, and despare." Since he is the supreme hypocrite, Satan becomes quickly aware of his own distemper (his disordered humors) and attempts to smooth his own appearance to that of "outward calme." Being quick-sighted, Uriel has already noted the perturbations, because they would be unlikely in a loyal or sinless angel. Since hypocrisy can be detected by God only, Uriel can be forgiven for being deceived by Satan to begin with.

[32]Compare ". . . for he is a liar, and the father of it" (John 8.44), in the words of Jesus describing the Devil.

Deep malice to conceale, couch't with revenge:[33]
Yet not anough had practisd to deceive
Uriel once warnd; whose eye pursu'd him down   125
The way he went, and on th' *Assyrian* mount[34]
Saw him disfigur'd, more then could befall
Spirit of happie sort: his gestures fierce
He markd and mad demeanour, then alone,
As he suppos'd, all unobserv'd, unseen.   130
So on he fares, and to the border comes,
Of *Eden*, where delicious Paradise,
Now nearer, Crowns with her enclosure green,
As with a rural mound the champain head[35]
Of a steep wilderness, whose hairie sides   135
With thicket overgrown, grottesque[36] and wilde,
Access deni'd; and over head up grew
Insuperable highth of loftiest shade,
Cedar, and Pine, and Firr, and branching Palm,
A Silvan Scene,[37] and as the ranks ascend   140
Shade above shade, a woodie Theatre
Of stateliest view.[38] Yet higher then thir tops
The verdurous wall[39] of paradise[40] up sprung:
Which to our general Sire gave prospect large
Into his neather Empire neighbouring round.   145
And higher then that Wall a circling row
Of goodliest Trees loaden with fairest Fruit,
Blossoms and Fruits at once of golden hue
Appeerd,[41] with gay enameld colours mixt:
On which the Sun more glad impress'd his beams   150
Then in fair Evening Cloud, or humid Bow,
When God hath showrd the earth;[42] so lovely seemd
That Lantskip:° And of pure now purer aire   LANDSCAPE
Meets his approach, and to the heart inspires
Vernal° delight and joy, able to drive   SPRING-LIKE   155

---

[33]As Fowler points out, the word "couch't" means not only "hidden" but "quelled, suppressed," and "couch't with" means "inlaid with, set with." One might add "bedded with." Compare "well couch't fraud" in *Paradise Regain'd* 1.97.

[34]Mt. Niphates, in Assyria, northwest of Mesopotamia. Presumably the mountain's height gave Satan a vantage point from which to see Eden. See 3.742.

[35]"The flat, cleared plain on top of a mountainous wilderness." The word "champain" retains the sense of Latin *campus*, an even, flat plain, though, as Tom Corns reminds me, "it is an English word used in an English sense, native since 1400" (letter, September 1991). Dante among others had located Paradise on a mountain with steep sides (*Purgatory* 28.91–102). Lewis 49 pointed out that picturing Paradise in terms of a human body, with a head and hairy sides, would not have upset Milton or his audience. The *hortus conclusus* or enclosed garden is discussed as an important medieval and Renaissance literary theme by Stanley Stewart. Theologians and biblical commentators debated the location of Paradise. The map included in the Geneva Bible shows it as a mound in southern Mesopotamia at the confluence of the Tigris and Euphrates rivers, just as they split to flow into the Persian Gulf. The Tigris and Euphrates split and came together at several points—the different branches were given different names—hence the mention of four rivers in Eden. The southeastern area was Chaldea in the time of Abraham.

[36]In *1674* the correct word of *1667* was corrupted into "gottesque," Fletcher believes, because the compositor did not know the Italianate "grotesque," derived from "grotto."

[37]"Silvan" in the sense of "forested" (from the Latin *silva*, "wood" or "forest") but also a "scene" in the dramatic sense of a stage in which a tragedy will unfold in a "woodie Theatre." The phrase "shade above shade" not only suggests the levels of a stage set, it hints at the coming of death into the world.

[38]From the outside looking in from Satan's point of view, the prospect of Paradise, the garden within the region of Eden, is stately and formidable; from the inside looking out, from Adam and Eve's point of view, it is "A happy rural seat of various view" (247).

[39]The wall made of greenery ("verdure") or vegetation, as in a tall hedgerow.

[40]Though *Eden* is normally italicized as a place name, Paradise is not, though it is at 3.733. The consistent lack of emphasis (in *Paradise Regain'd* as well) might argue that Milton considered Paradise to be a state of mind rather than just the name of a place.

[41]Because of the perfect mix of seasons in Paradise, blossom and fruit could appear simultaneously ("at once"). Though the word "enameld" may suggest the artifice of painting on enamel, it probably meant simply "Beautified with various colors" (*OED* 3).

[42]The image of the rainbow looks forward to God's covenant with Noah after the Flood (described in 11.865–67).

All sadness but despair: now gentle gales[43]
Fanning thir odoriferous wings dispense
Native perfumes, and whisper whence they stole
Those balmie spoiles. As when to them who saile
Beyond the *Cape of Hope*, and now are past   160
Mozambic,[44] off at Sea North-East windes blow
Sabean Odours from the spicie shoare
Of *Arabie* the blest,[45] with such delay
Well pleas'd they slack thir course, and many a League
Chear'd with the grateful smell old Ocean smiles.   165
So entertaind those odorous sweets the Fiend
Who came thir bane, though with them better pleas'd
Then *Asmodeus* with the fishie fume,
That drove him, though enamourd, from the Spouse
Of *Tobits* Son, and with a vengeance sent   170
From *Media* post to *Ægypt*, there fast bound.[46]
    Now to th' ascent of that steep savage° Hill   UNCULTIVATED
Satan had journied on, pensive and slow;
But further way found none, so thick entwin'd,
As one continu'd brake,° the undergrowth   THICKET   175
Of shrubs and tangling bushes had perplext
All path of Man or Beast that past that way:
One Gate there only was, and that look'd East
On th' other side: which when th' arch-fellon saw
Due entrance he disdaind, and in contempt,   180
At one slight bound high over leap'd all bound
Of Hill or highest Wall, and sheer within
Lights on his feet. As when a prowling Wolfe,
Whom hunger drives to seek new haunt for prey,
Watching where Shepherds pen thir Flocks at eeve   185
In hurdl'd Cotes° amid the field secure,   PENS
Leaps o're the fence with ease into the Fould:
Or as a Thief bent to unhoord the cash
Of some rich Burgher,[47] whose substantial dores,

---

[43]The word was not so strong in definition as it is in common usage today, since a gale could be "a wind not tempestuous but stronger than a breeze" (*OED* 1.a).

[44]Accented on the second syllable.

[45]The passage describes the routes of the spice trade in Milton's era, which proceeded from the Portuguese province Mozambique on the east coast of Africa to the island Madagascar. *Sabean* derives from Saba or Sheba, now Yemen. The description of "Arabia felix" or "*Arabie* the blest" and the pleasant odors, as Fowler points out, derive from Diodorus Siculus, 3.46.4: "When the wind is blowing off shore, one finds that the sweet odours exhaled by the myrrh-bearing and other aromatic trees penetrate to the near-by parts of the sea" (155–66n).

[46]The apocryphal book of the Bible, Tobit, still included with the canonical books in various editions in the seventeenth century, tells the story of the good and righteous man Tobit and his son Tobias. Tobias journeys to Media and marries Sarah after she is purified from the stain of having seven previous husbands killed in the marriage chamber by the evil spirit Asmodeus. Tobit had earlier been rendered blind, and the angel Raphael in disguise was sent by God both to cure Tobit's blindness and to "bind" Asmodeus (who has been in love with Sarah) to keep him from doing further mischief. While accompanying Tobias on a journey that Tobit has commanded, Raphael instructs him to burn the heart and liver of a fish to exorcise Asmodeus and use the gall from the same fish to cure his father's blindness. Tobias follows Raphael's formula and successfully drives the demon away to Egypt, where he is bound by Raphael. On his wedding night he offers a prayer that alludes to Adam's marriage: "Thou madest Adam, and gavest him Eva his wife for an helpe, and stay: of them came mankind: thou has said, It is not good, that a man shulde be alone: let us make unto him an aide like unto him self" (Geneva Bible; 1560 ed.). The story would have much appeal to Milton, since it involves the curing of a blind man, it depicts the angel Raphael in easy congress with humans, it shows the behavior of evil spirits toward humans, and it incidentally comments on the nature of marriage. Asmodeus is mentioned in the War in Heaven (6.365), and in *Paradise Regain'd* he is linked to Belial, "The fleshliest Incubus" (2.152). Since he makes Asmodeus second only to Belial in his dissolution, Milton must have remembered Asmodeus's lust and jealousy for Sarah.

[47]Since Milton's father fit the definition of a wealthy burgher living in a large house in a prominent neighborhood (the Spread Eagle, on Bread Street), one wonders if this simile is based on first-hand observation.

Cross-barrd and bolted fast, fear no assault,   190
In at the window climbs, or o're the tiles;
So clomb this first grand Thief into Gods Fould:
So since into his Church lewd° Hirelings climbe.[48]   IGNORANT
Thence up he flew, and on the Tree of Life,[49]
The middle Tree and highest there that grew,   195
Sat like a Cormorant;[50] yet not true Life
Thereby regaind, but sat devising Death
To them who liv'd; nor on the vertue[51] thought
Of that life-giving Plant, but only us'd
For prospect,[52] what well us'd had bin the pledge   200
Of immortality. So little knows
Any, but God alone, to value right
The good before him, but perverts best things
To worst abuse, or to thir meanest use.
Beneath him with new wonder now he views   205
To all delight of human[53] sense expos'd
In narrow room Natures whole wealth, yea more,
A Heav'n on Earth, for blissful Paradise
Of God the Garden was, by him in the East
Of *Eden* planted;[54] *Eden* stretchd her Line   210
From *Auran* Eastward to the Royal Towrs
Of great *Seleucia*, built by *Grecian* Kings,
Or where the Sons of *Eden* long before
Dwelt in *Telassar:*[55] in this pleasant soile
His farr more pleasant Garden God ordaind;[56]   215
Out of the fertil ground he caus'd to grow
All Trees of noblest kind for sight, smell, taste;

---

[48]"But he that is an hireling, and not the shepherd, whose own the sheep are not, seeth the wolf coming, and leaveth the sheep, and fleeth: and the wolf catcheth them and scattereth the sheep" (John 10.12). Milton seems to be consciously referring the reader to his own "Lycidas" and to his prose pamphlet of 1659 dealing with the problems of "hirelings" or corrupt clergy within the English Church (*Considerations Touching the Likeliest Means to Remove Hirelings out of the Church*). Here he is alluding to the abuse, common in the early seventeenth century, of hiring out livings within the Church of England to unqualified and sometimes illiterate "wolves" who would then devour the "flock" of their congregations, one of the many causes of the English Civil Wars. Milton believed that churchmen should earn their livings by other employment, outside the church. The simile combines a rural with an urban image and combines wolves with thieves, implying that Satan, easily leaping the wall of Eden, can outwit man's security as easily as a wolf can steal sheep from what looks like a secure fold or a burglar circumvent a mere doorlock on a rich burger's house.

[49]*1674* omits this comma, which existed in *1667* and which Fletcher thinks represents the earlier compositor's eye skipping ahead (in the manuscript he is setting from) to line 196 as he set 194. Satan, like a cormorant, sits triumphantly in the Tree of Life (not the Tree of the Knowledge of Good and Evil). The irony is that he is death in the midst of virtue and vitality, and the Epic Voice points to the ironic image, rather obviously, just below. Milton regarded the Tree of Knowledge of Good and Evil as "a kind of pledge or memorial of obedience" (*On Christian Doctrine* 1.10; Yale 6: 352), and he thought the Tree of Life "a symbol of eternal life and even perhaps the food of eternal life" (Yale 6: 353).

[50]For popular conceptions about the cormorant, see above, note 2, on the Argument.

[51]"Medicinal strength."

[52]A high place from which to view the surroundings, but what is emphasized here is that Satan uses the very Tree of Life as a mere perch.

[53]Since "human" is used before a noun, "sense," it would seem to be accented on the first syllable and be pronounced like the modern "human," rather than "humane." See *A Treatise of Stops, Points, or Pauses* ... (London, 1680; rept. Menston, Eng.: Scolar P, 1968): 11. By contrast, when the word follows a substantive, it should be spelled with an "e" and pronounced like the modern "humane," even though the meaning remains the same. Contrast "Goddess humane" in 9.732.

[54]"And the Lord God planted a garden eastward in Eden; and there he put the man whom he had formed" (Genesis 2.8). The Garden of Paradise was supposed, first, to emulate Heaven, and, second, to incorporate in itself the seed of all future creation, "Natures whole wealth." The Greek Seleucia was built by Alexander the Great's general Seleucus Nicator, near the site of Babylon. Haran, Milton's *Auran*, would have been about 600 kilometers northeast of Babylon.

[55]As Fowler points out, the name Telassar foreshadows war in the region (see 2 Kings 19.11–12 and Isaiah 37.11–12)—evidence of the Fall in utter destruction of a people: "Have the gods of the nations delivered them which my fathers have destroyed, as Gozan, and Haran, and Rezeph, and the children of Eden which were in Telassar" (Isaiah 37.12).

[56]Compare the caption under a map of the Garden of Eden in the Geneva Bible: " ... this was called Paradise that is, a garden of pleasure, because of the frutefulnes and abundance thereof" (p. 2, 1560 ed.).

And all amid them stood the Tree of Life,
High eminent, blooming Ambrosial Fruit
Of vegetable Gold;[57] and next to Life   220
Our Death the Tree of knowledge grew fast° by,   NEAR
Knowledge of Good bought dear by knowing ill.[58]
Southward through *Eden* went a River large,
Nor chang'd his course, but through the shaggie hill[59]
Pass'd underneath ingulft, for God had thrown   225
That Mountain as his Garden mould[60] high rais'd
Upon the rapid current, which through veins
Of porous Earth with kindly thirst up drawn,
Rose a fresh Fountain, and with many a rill
Waterd the Garden;[61] thence united fell   230
Down the steep glade, and met the neather Flood,
Which from his darksom passage now appeers,
And now divided into four main Streams,[62]
Runs divers,[63] wandring many a famous Realme
And Country whereof here needs no account,   235
But rather to tell how, if Art could tell,
How from that Saphire Fount the crisped[64] Brooks,
Rowling on Orient° Pearl and sands of Gold,[65]   SHINING
With mazie error[66] under pendant shades
Ran Nectar,[67] visiting each plant, and fed   240
Flours worthy of Paradise which not nice Art[68]

---

[57]The fruit of the Tree of Life is naturally gold and resembles the fruit eaten by the Greek gods (ambrosia). The fruit of "vegetable Gold," as Fowler points out, may also have alchemical value in helping to preserve health, since "potable gold" or gold in solution was a variety of the philosopher's stone.

[58]Since the fruit of the Tree of the Knowledge of Good and Evil has no intrinsic value except as a sign of obedience, in Milton's scheme there is no reason to describe it.

[59]The hill is shaggy, like an animal's coat, because it is heavily forested.

[60]Probably "The upper soil of cultivated land: garden-soil" (*OED* sub. 1.3). God has taken care to give Adam and Eve good tillable soil, but one should keep in mind that Adam was also made out of mould, or workable soil, and that God constructs according to a mold or preconceived shape. Here He has "thrown" the mound as if He were a potter (*OED* v. B.6).

[61]According to Genesis 2.6, the Garden of Eden is watered by a mist from the ground, not rain, before the Fall.

[62]Compare Genesis 2.10: "And a river went out of Eden to water the garden; and from thence it was parted, and became into four heads." Paradise, therefore, has no thunderstorms, and its garden has a perpetual source of gentle watering. Fowler finds the chief model for Milton's description in Philo Judaeus, *Questions on Genesis* 2.10–14.

[63]"Runs in diverse directions."

[64]"Indented with wavelets," or "Having a surface curled into minute waves, folds or puckers" (*OED* 2).

[65]Though Genesis describes the rivers of Eden leading into lands where gold might be found (2.11–12), Milton also seems to be indicating the natural and even moral wealth to be found in pure nature, in that the fountain is sapphire, the floor of the brooks is the proverbial "orient pearl" (see *Richard III* 4.4.322), and the banks are gold; the water itself is the true (not the mythological Greek and Roman) nectar. Giamatti has found at least a latent threat in the "mazie error" of the streams: " . . . and as that word, 'mazy,' itself wanders throughout the poem, the latent implications in Nature are activated and we are led to the scene of the Fall" (303). Daniells, however, finds no threat in the picture of Eden as a "happy rural seat," but rather a glorious baroque profusion of rich images.

[66]Both mazes and error are, of course, associated with Satan elsewhere. Here we are to presume that the brooks must be running their natural courses without the imputation of a guilty or sinful universe. Even error can be innocent.

[67]In Ovid's age of Saturn, described in the *Metamorphoses*, " . . . there were rivers / Of milk, and rivers of honey, and golden nectar / Dripped from the dark-green oak-trees" (1.99–101).

[68]Surprisingly, the word "Art" generally has a negative connotation for Milton, as in "if Art could tell" above. See my "Art." The garden here has not been controlled by human artisans, who did, in Milton's time, create formal gardens arranged "In beds and curious knots." See James Grantham Turner, *The Politics*, for discussions of landscaping as political statement, and see Hannah Demaray, "Milton's 'Perfect' Paradise" and John Dixon Hunt, "Milton," for discussions on the context of gardens in *Paradise Lost*. Here Milton contrasts contrived and regulated human gardens with profuse natural gardens such as that of Paradise which God had planted: "And out of the ground made the Lord God to grow every tree that is pleasant to the sight, and good for food; the tree of life also in the midst of the garden, and the tree of knowledge of good and evil" (Genesis 2.9).

In Beds and curious Knots,[69] but Nature boon
Powrd forth profuse on Hill and Dale and Plaine,
Both where the morning Sun first warmly smote
The open field, and where the unpierc't shade   245
Imbround[70] the noontide Bowrs: Thus was this place,
A happy rural seat of various view;
Groves whose rich Trees wept odorous Gumms and Balme,
Others whose fruit burnisht with Golden Rinde
Hung amiable,[71] *Hesperian* Fables true,   250
If true, here only, and of delicious taste:[72]
Betwixt them Lawns, or level Downs,[73] and Flocks
Grasing the tender herb,° were interpos'd,   *EDIBLE GREENS*
Or palmie hilloc,[74] or the flourie lap
Of som irriguous° Valley spred her store,   *IRRIGATED*   255
Flours of all hue, and without Thorn the Rose:[75]
Another side, umbrageous Grots° and Caves   *SHADY GROTTOES*
Of coole recess,[76] o're which the mantling vine[77]
Layes forth her purple Grape, and gently creeps
Luxuriant; mean while murmuring waters fall   260
Down the slope hills, disperst, or in a Lake,[78]
That to the fringed Bank with Myrtle crownd,
Her chrystal mirror holds,[79] unite thir streams.
The Birds thir quire° apply; aires, vernal aires,   *CHOIR*
Breathing the smell of field and grove, attune   265
The trembling leaves,[80] while Universal *Pan*
Knit° with the *Graces* and the *Hours* in dance   *HAND IN HAND*

[handwritten marginalia: "epic like" and "epic amplification"]

---

[69]Flower beds and herb gardens, in Renaissance Europe, were often designed in the form of intricate knots or ciphers, "curious" because they took the viewer great care to untie or undecipher. Eden, Milton implies, needed no such mystery in its design. The frontispiece of Thomas Parkinson's *Paradisi in Sole* (1629), as with Milton's description, shows Adam and Eve tending a profuse and abundant, as opposed to a well-organized or controlled, garden of Eden.

[70]Probably closely allied with the Italian *imbruníre*, poetically used by Ariosto and Tasso for "darkened" (Newton). Compare "umbrage broad / And brown as Evening" (9.1087–88).

[71]"Of a friendly disposition toward humankind." The adjective was used of things as well as people (*OED* 2.b).

[72]The apples of the Hesperides (the nymphs Aegle, Erythia, Vesta, and Arethusa, daughters of Hesperus), supposedly to be found in a grove near Mt. Atlas in Africa and guarded by a dragon, were gathered by Hercules as one of his labors. The name Hesperus was also applied to the planet Venus, called Lucifer when it preceded the sun (605 below). Ovid describes the apples as golden in *Metamorphoses* 4.635–38. Milton is once again comparing the truth of the Christian account with pagan "Fables."

[73]Though downs are usually undulating uplands in English usage, Milton suggests that the grazing grounds of Paradise are "level" and thus easier on the grazing animal or the person who tends it.

[74]Milton allows the tropical palm tree in Paradise just as he allows the plants to be in blossom and fruit at the same time or the animals to be gathered there from all corners of the Earth. The climate is so nearly perfect and the universe in such perfect balance that all vegetation or all animal life can exist happily in the same place. Notice that the valley is personified as a loving mother-figure with a comforting lap filled with flowers.

[75]According to various legends, nature was not threatening or aggressive in Paradise, and life forms such as thornless roses, unicorns (Milton does not mention them), or amaranths (3.352–56), lived there but could not be transported to a fallen natural world. In Eden trees weep healthful balms, valleys have laps, lakes hold mirrors up to banks, vines provide mantles, and birds sing in harmony—all for the sake of humankind.

[76]"Caves which recede into cool depths, or into which one can retire from work." Probably as in *OED recess* 8: "A retired or inner place or part: one of the innermost or remotest parts or corners of anything."

[77]A vine which acts as a mantle, providing shade. Compare *Comus* 294, "green mantling vine."

[78]Milton deliberately gives the reader a choice here: either the waters collect in a lake or they are dispersed. He follows a technique practiced in biblical commentary when the source passage was ambiguous. See Mollenkott, "Milton's Technique."

[79]Fowler believes that the mirror and the myrtle makes implicit a comparison between the Garden of Eden and gardens associated with Venus, whose tree was the myrtle and whose symbol was the mirror.

[80]Like the Heavens when they produce the music of the spheres, the birds and leaves of Paradise are attuned to one another and sing springlike "airs" in "choirs."

Led on th' Eternal Spring.[81] Not that faire field
Of *Enna*, where *Proserpin*[82] gathering flours
Her self a fairer Floure by gloomie *Dis*   270
Was gatherd, which cost *Ceres* all that pain
To seek her through the world; nor that sweet Grove
Of *Daphne* by *Orontes*, and th' inspir'd
Castalian Spring,[83] might with this Paradise
Of *Eden* strive; nor that *Nyseian* Ile   275
Girt with the River *Triton*, where old *Cham*,
Whom Gentiles *Ammon* call and *Lybian Jove*,
Hid *Amalthea* and her Florid° Son   FLUSHED, RED-FACED
Young *Bacchus* from his Stepdame *Rhea's* eye;[84]
Nor where *Abassin*° Kings thir issue Guard,   ABYSSINIAN   280
Mount *Amara*,[85] though this by som suppos'd
True Paradise under the *Ethiop* Line
By *Nilus* head, enclosd with shining Rock,
A whole days journy high, but wide remote
From this *Assyrian* Garden, where the Fiend   285
Saw undelighted all delight, all kind
Of living Creatures new to sight and strange:
Two of far nobler shape erect and tall,
Godlike erect, with native Honour clad[86]
In naked Majestie seemd Lords of all,   290
And worthie seemd, for in thir looks Divine
The image of thir glorious Maker shon,
Truth, wisdome, Sanctitude severe and pure,

---

[81]Since *pan* as a prefix in Greek means "all," "Universal" is an appropriate adjective. This unthreatening Pan may have been associated by Milton with Christ, as in the Nativity Ode 89. See Swaim, "'Mighty Pan.'" Pan is pictured holding hands and dancing with the Graces (Euphrosyne, Aglaia, and Thalia) and the Hours (the *Horae*, or seasons). He is not the sinister goat-god who causes panic; instead his dance, like the harmonious airs, is a picture of Edenic harmony and concord. It is always spring in Eden, because the site, according to Milton, is on the equator and the sun is in perfect perpendicular balance with the equator.

[82]The form and pronunciation of the three-syllable "*Proserpin*" (as in "pro-serpent") is carefully chosen here, since Milton had the choice of "Persephone" or the less familiar "Proserpine" or "Proserpina," which links the mythological innocent victim of an underworld god with serpents. Ovid tells the story of the seizing of Proserpina in the field of Enna by the god of the underworld known as Pluto, Hades, or Dis in the *Metamorphoses* 5.384–678. Proserpina's mother, the vegetation goddess Ceres, was caused pain by the loss; her periodic visits to her daughter beneath the earth brought about winter. The phrase "Her self a fairer Floure" links Proserpina with Eve, "Her self, though fairest unsupported Flour" (9.432).

[83]Daphne, like Eve and Proserpina, was also pursued by gods with evil intent—either by Apollo, during whose pursuit she is changed into a laurel, as in Ovid's *Metamorphoses* 1.450–68, or by one of the Sons of Belial, as in *Paradise Regain'd* 2.187. The grove of Daphne, beside the Syrian river Orontes, near Antioch, had an oracle dedicated to Apollo (the resident priestess, then, would have been "inspired") and a stream named after the Castalian spring of Mt. Parnassus (Diodorus Siculus 4). Milton might have seen Bernini's now-famous statue of Apollo pursuing Daphne in Rome when he visited there in 1638 and 1639. The comma here was added in *1674*; Fletcher believes it to be an authorial correction.

[84]Again, Milton recalls Diodorus Siculus, who writes extensively on the Libyan king Ammon. Diodorus tells the story of Ammon's affair with Amalthea, a maiden who gave birth to Dionysus. To protect mother and son against the jealousy of his wife Rhea, Ammon hid them on the island Nysa, near the site of the modern Mediterranean port Tunis. Ammon was identified with Jupiter as worshiped in Libya and with Noah's son Ham, called Cham in the Vulgate spelling. The river or swamp Triton (also Tritoma in Diodorus 3.53.2) flows around the island as Milton pictures it, now in the Mediterranean south of Tunis.

[85]Milton is dealing with classical place names as they are related to biblical or Christian names. Mt. Amara in Abyssinia, a mountain-top fortress where princes were secluded to avoid outside sedition (see Heylyn, *Cosmographie* 4.64), was situated in a province so pleasant that it was compared with Paradise. The phrase "under the *Ethiop* Line" suggests that Milton thought Amara like Paradise in that both were equatorial and hence temperate in climate. "*Nilus* head" would be the head-waters of the Nile, and Mt. Amara was supposed by Heylyn to be enclosed with shining rock and to be so high as to take a whole day's journey to reach the summit.

[86]The stature of Adam and Eve is heroic; they are the closest earthly echo of the appearance of God because God had made them "in his image" (Genesis 1.27). Their "native Honour" suggests what Puritan marriage writers called "domestic honor," the ennobling of both male and female in the united state of marriage. All of the high ideals of Puritan marriage are built into their relationship—"Truth, wisdome, Sanctitude severe and pure, / Severe but in true filial freedom plac't." See Roland M. Frye, "The Teachings."

Severe[87] but in true filial freedom plac't;
Whence true autoritie in men; though both
Not equal, as thir sex not equal seemd;
For contemplation hee and valour formd,
For softness shee and sweet attractive Grace,
Hee for God only, shee for God in him:[88]
His fair large Front[89] and Eye sublime declar'd
Absolute rule; and Hyacinthin Locks[90]   300
Round from his parted forelock manly hung
Clustring, but not beneath his shoulders broad:
Shee as a vail down to the slender waste
Her unadorned golden tresses wore
Dissheveld, but in wanton ringlets wav'd   305
As the Vine curles her tendrils,[91] which impli'd
Subjection, but requir'd with gentle sway,
And by her yielded, by him best receivd,
Yielded with coy submission,[92] modest pride,
And sweet reluctant amorous delay.[93]   310

---

[87]The adjective "severe" applied to "Sanctitude" or "holiness," suggests the highly serious nature of the resemblance between God as father and Adam and Eve as children: they possess filial freedom, which of course allows the possibility of disobedience. There is a comma here in *1667*, which Fletcher believes necessary. I have left it out, following *1674*.

[88]These two lines have caused much discussion among readers of the last twenty years, because of the phrase "Not equal." According to the two most comprehensive studies of the characterization of Eve and of the sexual relations of Adam and Eve, McColley's *Milton's Eve* and Turner's *One Flesh*, Milton was a moderate, if not a liberal, on the subject of the subordination of women in marriage, though he was bound by St. Paul's various pronouncements about the subordination of women, as in 1 Timothy 2.11: "Let the woman learn in silence with all subjection." See also my article "Eve." Adam's inclinations are toward "contemplation" and "valour," perhaps because he is physically stronger, in a state of military preparedness, and (only perhaps) more thoughtful; but Eve's "softness" and "sweet attractive Grace" are unequivocally positive attributes—"Grace" even suggesting a divine gift. Why Adam is "for God only" and Eve "for God in him" may be explained by Adam's having been created first, and "in God's image," but Milton does seem to imply that Adam is more capable of discourse with God, whereas Eve, by preference, receives God's instruction through Adam because she knows he will "intermix / Grateful digressions, and solve high dispute / With conjugal Caresses" (8.54–56).

[89]A large forehead ("Front") was supposed to indicate intelligence, as in the modern "egghead." An "Eye sublime" would also presumably be looking upward (compare the Latin adverb *sublime*, "aloft"), at least aiming toward Heaven and God.

[90]Perhaps "curled tightly as are the petals in a hyacinth flower," but also with reference to the myth of Hyacinthus, the youth beloved by Apollo and with whose blood the flower was supposedly created by the god (Ovid, *Metamorphoses* 10.163–219). When Athena sheds her favor on Ulysses in the *Odyssey*, she arranges "on his head . . . the curling locks that hung down like hyacinthine petals" (6.231; see Corns 97). Adam's shoulder-length and tightly-curled hair contrasts with Eve's waist-length "wanton ringlets," since her longer hair, according to a biblical tradition, both glorified her and "impli'd / Subjection." See 1 Corinthians 11.15: "But if a woman have long hair, it is a glory to her: for her hair is given to her for a covering." As Fowler points out (4.301–08), Adam's beardless state may be the result of iconographical traditions surrounding the depiction of Apollo. Milton wore his own hair, in his maturity, at shoulder length.

[91]The Genius of the Wood in *Arcades* has as his duty "To nurse the Saplings tall, and curl the grove / With Ringlets quaint, and wanton windings wove" (46–47); thus Milton has earlier associated the words *wanton* and *ringlets* in an innocent context. The curls of women's hair, however, may suggest a tender trap, as in the temptation in Lycidas to dally "with the tangles of *Neæra's* hair" (69). Milton would not have been unaware of what today might be called hair fetishism.

[92]Since Milton used the phrase "coy flurting stile" (*Apology against a Pamphlet*; Yale 1: 873), he might well have been aware of the sexual context of the word "coy," as in Andrew Marvell's title "To His Coy Mistress," but "coy" could also mean "quiet" (*OED* 1) or "shyly reserved," "displaying modest backwardness or shyness" (*OED* 2, 2a, 2b—which cites this instance). The two pairs of adjectives and nouns, "coy submission" and "modest pride," seem to be oxymorons, or self-contradictory phrases: coyness might be aggressive and not submissive flirtation, and modesty is close to the opposite of pride. Both phrases suggest the complexity of Eve's character.

[93]The physical description of 300–11 is rich, carrying everything that Milton had written in the divorce tracts and elsewhere about the ideal and fallen relationships between the sexes in marriage. The oxymoron of Eve's "Yield[ing] . . . with . . . modest pride" (emphasis mine) expresses the ambiguity throughout, as does "impli'd" modifying "Subjection." Eve before the Fall is not subordinate to Adam in a tyrannical society: she can maintain rightful "pride" while retaining innocent "modesty." In Paradise, there is nothing wrong with "sweet reluctant amorous delay," which after the Fall could be Satanically perverted into flirtatiousness. Each attribute of Adam and Eve here described has both an innocent value and a fallen value: Adam's "valour," for instance, is quickly perverted to deadly aggressiveness. Milton believed that Eve was subordinate before the Fall, but gently so, whereas the Fall, by perverting the relationships between men and women, caused the balance of power between the genders to broaden. "Marriage also, if it was not commanded [in Eden], was at any rate instituted, and consisted in the mutual love, delight, help and society of husband and wife, though with the husband having greater authority: . . . ," but "The husband's authority became still greater after the fall" (*On Christian Doctrine* 1.10, Yale 6: 355). Compare 4.637: ". . . God is thy Law, thou mine," before the Fall, with 10.195–96, ". . . to thy Husbands will / Thine shall submit, hee over thee shall rule," after the Fall. Eve's "wanton ringlets" do not imply that she is inherently wayward.

Nor those mysterious parts[94] were then conceald,
Then was not guiltie shame, dishonest shame
Of natures works, honor dishonorable,
Sin-bred, how have ye troubl'd all mankind   315
With shews instead, meer shews of seeming pure,
And banisht from mans life his happiest life,
Simplicitie and spotless innocence.[95]
So passd they naked on, nor shund the sight
Of God or Angel, for they thought no ill: 320
So hand in hand[96] they passd, the lovliest pair
That ever since in loves imbraces met,
Adam the goodliest man of men since borne
His Sons, the fairest of her Daughters *Eve*.[97]
Under a tuft of shade that on a green   325
Stood whispering soft, by a fresh Fountain side
They sat them down, and after no more toil
Of thir sweet Gardning labour[98] then suffic'd
To recommend coole *Zephyr*,[99] and made ease
More easie, wholsom thirst and appetite   330
More grateful, to thir Supper Fruits they fell,
Nectarine[100] Fruits which the compliant boughes
Yielded them, side-long as they sat recline°   RECUMBENT, STRETCHED OUT
On the soft downie Bank damaskt with flours:[101]
The savourie pulp they chew, and in the rinde   335
Still as they thirsted scoop the brimming stream;[102]
Nor gentle purpose,[103] nor endearing smiles
Wanted, nor youthful dalliance as beseems
Fair couple, linkt in happie nuptial League,[104]
Alone as they. About them frisking playd   340

---

[94]The word *mysterious* suggests not only "puzzling because not often seen," but "having a religious significance." What fallen Christians would call the pudendum ("shameful area") was before the Fall innocent and part of what might be called the mystique of sexuality. For Milton, the rites of marriage were also "Mysterious" (743 below).

[95]Milton takes the innocent nudity of Adam as being incapable of shame and he takes shame as a product of the Fall, as he would have been instructed to do by Genesis 3. The word *shews* was powerfully negative, suggesting here that after the Fall the act of dressing or dressing up was a process of elaborate deception, one that gave outward indications of purity but that concealed inner corruption. Like the modern Amish, the English Puritan sects such as the Quakers de-emphasized gaudy or ostentatious apparel, preferring clothes of simple design, muted brown or black in color for men, white or pale blue for women. One Puritan sect, the Adamites, sought Edenic innocence in nudism (Turner 84).

[96]The image of Adam and Eve holding hands, withdrawing hands from each other, and then rejoining hands, will echo through the poem, perhaps the greatest emblem or visual sign of their deep love, to the point where critics sometimes talk about their "handedness." See 4.689, 739; 9.244, 385, 1037; and finally 12.648.

[97]The syntax is confusing: Loh unravels it as "Adam was the goodliest man of men since to be born as his sons, and Eve the fairest of all women to be born as her daughters." The adjective "goodliest" suggests the greatest in beauty or handsomeness, grace, and elegance (*OED* "goodly" 1, 2, 3).

[98]Critics have found different significance in the gardening work of Adam and Eve. It obviously is dignified, perhaps even aristocratic labor (Fowler calls it "a fashionable high-brow activity" in Milton's time—4.328n), but it is also productive work, a result of what would now be called the Protestant work ethic. Anthony Low would have the work as part of the Georgic tradition of rural labor as preparation for urban civic duty (*Georgic Tradition*).

[99]The west wind, a male entity said to produce flowers and fruits by his sweet breath, as in "L'Allegro" 18: "The frolick Wind that breathes the Spring."

[100]Probably "nectarous," filled with nectar, although the fruit nectarine was available in London in the seventeenth century. Since nectarines do not have rinds to speak of, we must assume that the fruits included something like oranges, whose rinds would make disposable drinking cups. Nature provides utensils as well as food.

[101]The bank is as soft as a down comforter and in-woven, or damasked ("Woven with richly-designed figures," *OED* 1), with flowers.

[102]Adam and Eve eat like Romans, or like any picnickers for that matter, half-reclining. They chew on the pulp of the fruit, which is flavorful and delectable ("savoury"), and use the rind as a disposable cup for the pure water.

[103]"Polite conversation," which will be interspersed with the nonverbal "youthful dalliance." Adam and Eve's prelapsarian conversation will be mixed with kisses and other expressions of tender affection.

[104]Like most Protestant theologians, Milton believed God had given Eve to Adam in marriage shortly after their creation (*On Christian Doctrine* 1.10; Yale 6: 355). Adam is created with the understanding of marriage rites even before he meets his wife-to-be (8.486–87).

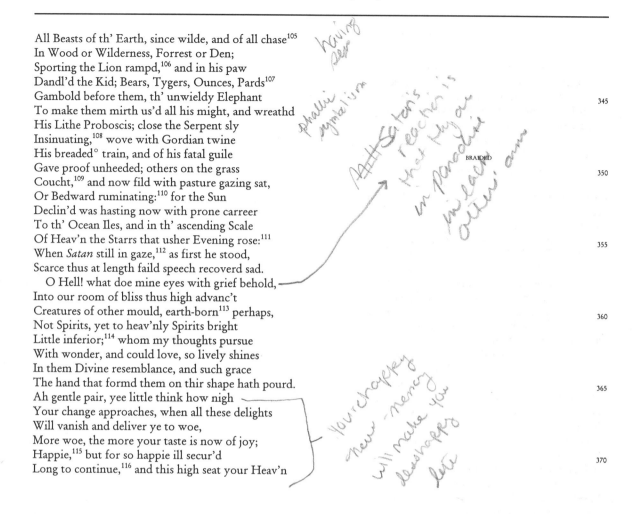

All Beasts of th' Earth, since wilde, and of all chase[105]
In Wood or Wilderness, Forrest or Den;
Sporting the Lion rampd,[106] and in his paw
Dandl'd the Kid; Bears, Tygers, Ounces, Pards[107]
Gambold before them, th' unwieldy Elephant   345
To make them mirth us'd all his might, and wreathd
His Lithe Proboscis; close the Serpent sly
Insinuating,[108] wove with Gordian twine
His breaded° train, and of his fatal guile
Gave proof unheeded; others on the grass   350
Coucht,[109] and now fild with pasture gazing sat,
Or Bedward ruminating:[110] for the Sun
Declin'd was hasting now with prone carreer
To th' Ocean Iles, and in th' ascending Scale
Of Heav'n the Starrs that usher Evening rose:[111]   355
When *Satan* still in gaze,[112] as first he stood,
Scarce thus at length faild speech recoverd sad.
    O Hell! what doe mine eyes with grief behold,
Into our room of bliss thus high advanc't
Creatures of other mould, earth-born[113] perhaps,   360
Not Spirits, yet to heav'nly Spirits bright
Little inferior;[114] whom my thoughts pursue
With wonder, and could love, so lively shines
In them Divine resemblance, and such grace
The hand that formd them on thir shape hath pourd.   365
Ah gentle pair, yee little think how nigh
Your change approaches, when all these delights
Will vanish and deliver ye to woe,
More woe, the more your taste is now of joy;
Happie,[115] but for so happie ill secur'd   370
Long to continue,[116] and this high seat your Heav'n

BRAIDED

---

[105]The word in Milton's era maintains its French meaning (*la chasse* = *hunt*) of "all beasts who would be hunted thereafter."

[106]The heraldic present participle, "rampant," here is converted into a past participle (one not listed in the *OED*). Compare "The Tawnie Lion, pawing to get free / His hinder parts, then springs as broke from Bonds, / And Rampant shakes his Brinded main" (7.464–66). What would be an aggressive gesture after the Fall, the rearing up of the lion, here is a gentle gesture of fatherly affection toward all youthful creatures.

[107]"Ounces" are lynxes or other similar cats, and "Pards" are leopards. There is no comma after "Pards" in *1667*; again, Fletcher thinks it "seems unwanted"; I agree.

[108]The word describes the physical motion of the snake—moving sinuously inward—but it has the moral sense of "working deviously into the imagination." At this point, however, the Serpent is not yet "nocent" (9.186)—the opposite of innocent—since his body has not been possessed by the evil Satan. His woven body is as complicated as the legendary Gordian knot, which no one was able to untie until Alexander the Great cut it at Gordium in Phrygia with his sword, fulfilling a prophecy that whoever untied or broke the knot would conquer Asia.

[109]Probably heraldic, like "rampant," in this case made from "couchant," the French-derived heraldic term meaning " . . . lying with the body resting on the legs and (according to most authors) the head lifted up . . . " (*OED* 2).

[110]Cattle or sheep, as they walk back to their shelter in the evenings, will literally be "ruminating," chewing their cud or rumen, while they appear to be ruminating in the sense of "thinking deeply." The animals are "filled" from eating grass on pasture.

[111]When the sun, having risen in Aries (3.555–61), sets when Libra, or the Scales, rises in the east, as in the autumn equinox, days and nights are in equipoise, as if light and darkness were being weighed on the scale. The sun is said to be setting in the Azores (see 592 below). The scales of Libra will also weigh Satan with cosmic justice at the end of this book.

[112]"Constantly gazing."

[113]Satan senses correctly that Adam and Eve are made out of earth's mould, or clay.

[114]Compare Psalm 8.5: "For thou has made him a little lower than the angels, and hast crowned him with glory and honour." Hebrews 2.7 echoes this verse.

[115]*1667* has a semicolon here, but only in the catchword that appears at the bottom of the previous page.

[116]"Despite being so fortunate, not protected well enough to continue long at it."

Ill fenc't for Heav'n[117] to keep out such a foe
As now is enterd; yet no purpos'd foe
To you whom I could pittie thus forlorne
Though I unpittied: League° with you I seek,   ALLIANCE   375
And mutual amitie so streight,[118] so close,
That I with you must dwell, or you with me
Henceforth; my dwelling haply° may not please   PERHAPS
Like this fair Paradise, your sense,[119] yet such
Accept your Makers work; he gave it me,   380
Which I as freely give; Hell shall unfold,
To entertain you two, her widest Gates,
And send forth all her Kings; there will be room,
Not like these narrow limits, to receive
Your numerous ofspring; if no better place,   385
Thank him who puts me loath to this revenge
On you who wrong me not for him who wrongd.
And should I at your harmless innocence
Melt, as I doe, yet public reason just,
Honour and Empire with revenge enlarg'd,   390
By conquering this new World, compels me now
To do what else though damnd I should abhorre.[120]
So spake the Fiend, and with necessitie,
The Tyrants plea, excus'd his devilish deeds.[121]
Then from his loftie stand on that high Tree   395
Down he alights[122] among the sportful Herd
Of those fourfooted kindes, himself now one,
Now other, as thir shape servd best his end
Neerer to view his prey, and unespi'd°
To mark what of thir state° he more might learn   UNSEEN / CONDITION   400
By word or action markt: about them round
A Lion now he stalkes with fierie glare,
Then as a Tyger, who by chance hath spi'd
In some Purlieu[123] two gentle Fawnes at play,
Strait couches close, then rising changes oft   405

[117]Given that it is Heaven, it is not well enough fenced in to keep out Satan. It might be easier for the modern reader to understand if he or she inserts imaginary commas around "Ill fenc't for Heav'n."

[118]The word is nearly synonymous with "close," but it suggests being bound together in a very narrow circuit. The image is of Adam and Eve being bound together as if locked in the same room (Hell) with Satan as a result of their coming sin. The word "amitie," normally meaning "friendship and mutual love," is of course ironic: what Satan is proposing perversely replaces a "happie nuptial League" (339 above). Also, while he seems to be offering them more room, he is really replacing the happy openness of Paradise with the claustrophobia of Hell.

[119]Object of "may not please" in 378. I read the syntax, with difficulty, as "My dwelling (Hell) may perhaps not please your sense as much as this fair Paradise, yet you should accept such (a place) as your Maker's creation." Satan's syntax, especially in soliloquy, reflects his inner confusion.

[120]Even in soliloquy, Satan lies utterly about his own motives, in this imaginary discussion with Adam and Eve, since he claims he is corrupting them out of "public reason" (a sense of civic responsibility toward the citizens of his country Hell, causing him to attempt to conquer a new world for the sake of Hell's citizens). Satan justifies his own actions on the grounds of responsible colonialism, which only covers his base motives of envy and revenge. Satan's being "compelled" out of necessity indicates his nature as a tyrant: he in effect says "I did it because I had to," which is nonsense.

[121]The Epic Voice, by indirect attribution, firmly establishes Satan as the type of the human tyrant. In his prose, Milton generally associates the term tyrant with evil human rulers, including Roman emperors like Nero or (Milton thought) Constantine and various Popes. For a reader sensitive to political overtones, the term tyrant would unite Satan with a king that Milton thought had abused his power, as with Charles I.

[122]Satan "alights" like a bird (apparently he is still in the shape of the cormorant), but soon demonstrates his ability to change color or shape (the chameleon's ability, associated with dissembling by Shakespeare's Richard III [*3 Henry VI*, 3.2.191]) by assuming the shapes of various animals on the ground. All of the animals whose shape he assumes become more fierce than they had been in this "peaceable kingdom." Each becomes a hunter: instead of dandling a kid, the lion "stalkes with fierie glare."

[123]Originally in English the word meant a tract of land wrongly added to a royal forest, then returned to a rightful owner after further surveying (*OED* 1). Here it seems to mean "outlying region" as "Pourlieues" means "outskirts" in 2.833.

His couchant[124] watch, as one who chose his ground
Whence rushing he might surest seize them both
Grip't in each paw: When *Adam* first of men
To first of women *Eve* thus moving speech,
Turnd him all eare[125] to hear new utterance flow.   410
   Sole partner and sole part of all these joyes,[126]
Dearer thy self then all; needs must the power
That made us, and for us this ample World
Be infinitly good, and of his good
As liberal and free as infinite,[127]   415
That rais'd us from the dust[128] and plac't us here
In all this happiness, who at his hand
Have nothing merited, nor can performe
Aught whereof hee hath need, hee who requires
From us no other service then to keep   420
This one, this easie charge, of all the Trees
In Paradise that bear delicious fruit
So various, not to taste that onely Tree
Of knowledge, planted by the Tree of Life,
So neer grows Death to Life, what ere Death is,   425
Som dreadful thing no doubt;[129] for well thou knowst
God hath pronounc't it death to taste that Tree,
The only sign of our obedience[130] left
Among so many signes of power and rule
Conferrd upon us, and Dominion giv'n   430
Over all other Creatures that possess
Earth, Aire, and Sea. Then let us not think hard
One easie prohibition,[131] who enjoy
Free leave so large to all things else, and choice
Unlimited of manifold delights: 435
But let us ever praise him, and extoll
His bountie, following our delightful task
To prune these growing Plants, and tend these Flours,
Which were it toilsom, yet with thee were sweet.

---

[124]Defined in heraldry as the position of "A beast lying on all fours with its head erect like the sphinx" (*Oxford Guide to Heraldry*, eds. Thomas Woodcock and John Martin Robinson [New York: Oxford UP, 1990]: 199).

[125]Apparently the "him" here is Satan as eavesdropper, but the syntax and the idiom are both difficult to decipher, since Satan hasn't been referred to directly since the "he" in 396, and "him" seems to refer to Adam. Adam is not listening to Eve, however; she, and Satan, are listening to him.

[126]Milton will often play on the various meanings of the word "sole," most of them derived from the Latin adjective "*solus*." Eve is Adam's unique partner, and together they are one. Newton's reading is worth considering, though it asks for a comma after "part": "Thou alone art my partner, and (what is more) Thou alone art part of me, as in ver. 487." I do not see the pun on soul/sole that Newton sees here, though the phrase "United as one individual Soule" (5.610) might make the connection later.

[127]God is infinite or boundless in His liberality or generosity in distributing good things.

[128]After Adam and Eve eat the fruit in Genesis, God reminds Adam that he was taken out of the ground: " . . . for dust thou art, and unto dust thou shalt return" (3.19).

[129]Perhaps Milton nods at this point, since Adam is supposed to have been created knowledgeable about life and death and all things necessary to his salvation: "Man was made in the image of God, and the whole law of nature was so implanted and innate in him that he was in need of no command" (*On Christian Doctrine* 1.10, Yale 6: 353). If Adam's statement is one of implied truth, then he is acknowledging that death (which they need not fear until they sin and it becomes a reality for them) really will be dreadful. William B. Hunter cautions me at this point "Adam has not witnessed death. It is from this speech that Satan learns how to attack Adam and Eve" (marginal note of August 1991), and Thomas Corns cautions "Knowing the nature of death is not critical to Adam's freedom to stand or fall. He *does* know it is dreadful" (marginal note of August 1991). I would stubbornly stand on the opinion that Adam's statement at least **sounds** naive or ingenuous.

[130]Though its fruit is sacred (9.904), the tree has no force in itself but represents either "Sole pledge of [Adam and Eve's] obedience" (3.95) or, here, the "only sign" of that obedience.

[131]"One prohibition easy to obey."

    To whom thus *Eve* repli'd. O thou for whom   440
And from whom I was formd flesh of thy flesh,
And without whom am to no end, my Guide
And Head,[132] what thou has said is just and right.
For wee to him indeed all praises owe,
And daily thanks, I chiefly who enjoy   445
So farr the happier Lot, enjoying thee
Præeminent by so much odds,[133] while thou
Like consort to thy self canst no where find.
That day[134] I oft remember, when from sleep
I first awak't, and found my self repos'd   450
Under a shade of[135] flours, much wondring where
And what I was, whence thither brought, and how.
Nor distant far from thence a murmuring sound
Of waters issu'd from a Cave and spread
Into a liquid Plain, then stood unmov'd   455
Pure as th' expanse of Heav'n; I thither went
With unexperienc't thought,[136] and laid me downe
On the green bank, to look into the cleer
Smooth Lake, that to me seemd another Skie.
As I bent down to look, just opposite,   460
A Shape within the watry gleam appeerd
Bending to look on me, I started back,
It started back, but pleas'd I soon returnd,
Pleas'd it returnd as soon with answering looks
Of sympathie and love;[137] there I had fixt   465
Mine eyes till now, and pin'd with vain desire,
Had not a voice thus warnd me,[138] What thou seest,
What there thou seest fair Creature is thy self,
With thee it came and goes: but follow me,
And I will bring thee where no shadow[139] staies° AWAITS   470
Thy coming, and thy soft imbraces, hee
Whose image thou art, him thou shall enjoy[140]
Inseparablie thine, to him shalt beare

---

[132]St. Paul lays the foundation for the subjugation of women in marriage, "But I would have you know, that the head of every man is Christ; and the head of the woman is the man; and the head of Christ is God" (1 Corinthians 11.3), using the logic later "For the man is not of the woman; but the woman of the man" (8), and "Neither was the man created for the woman; but the woman for the man" (9). Adam's role with respect to Eve is as guide, head and "Author and Disposer" (635 below); he is "Author" in the sense that he gave her being out of his body).

[133]"Superior by so much of a percentage."

[134]Fowler points out that differentiating "That day" from an implied "this day" shows that Adam and Eve have been in Eden more than one day (compare 610-20 below, among other passages that indicate the duration of their stay in Eden).

[135]*1667* has "on," *1674* "of," and the choice between the two is difficult. Newton opted for "on," but most modern editors choose "of." Since flowers are spoken of elsewhere as providing shade, the "of" seems to be a correction.

[136]In other words, she was born with thoughts or ideas, but they had not yet been tested against experience. For the purposes of Milton's narrative, the lake provides a mirror in which Eve can recognize herself, though there will be some danger in the mirror image it provides, if she is led to admire it more than she admires Adam's image (a closer reflection of God's image than is her own). For a Freudian interpretation of what might be narcissistic "sexual overevaluation," see Kerrigan, *Sacred* 70-71.

[137]Though Milton makes no direct connection, there is no way for a reader to avoid the implied comparison with Ovid's Narcissus, who also looked into still water and "saw / An image in the pool, and fell in love / With that unbodied hope, and found a substance / In what was only shadow" (*Metamorphoses* 3.419-22). Narcissus in Ovid's telling of the story, however, has been placed under a curse to love himself; Eve is sinless and, without knowing what a reflection is, falls in love with her own beauty. Though she would have pined away just like Narcissus without intervention, Eve is quickly taught by the divine voice what she sees in the mirror: God is a gentle schoolmaster with her just as He is with Adam before the creation of Eve. In the process of corrupting Eve, in Book 9, Satan will encourage her vanity and help to cause her to worship her own image more than that of Adam or God.

[138]The divine voice that warns Eve is a purely Miltonic invention, and is apparently kin to the "warning voice."

[139]"Ghostly mirror image."

[140]At this point before the Fall, the word "enjoy" carries no evil connotations, but it certainly does after the Fall (9.1032).

Multitudes like thy self, and thence be call'd
Mother of human Race:[141] what could I doe,   475
But follow strait,° invisibly thus led?   IMMEDIATELY
Till I espi'd thee, fair indeed and tall,
Under a Platan,[142] yet methought less faire,
Less winning soft, less amiablie milde,
Then that smooth watry image;[143] back I turnd,   480
Thou following cryd'st aloud, Return faire *Eve*;
Whom fli'st thou? whom thou fli'st, of him thou art,
His flesh, his bone; to give thee being I lent
Out of my side to thee, neerest my heart
Substantial Life,[144] to have thee by my side   485
Henceforth an individual solace[145] dear;
Part of my Soul I seek thee, and thee claim
My other half: with that thy gentle hand
Seisd mine, I yielded, and from that time see
How beauty is excelld by manly grace   490
And wisdom, which alone is truly fair.[146]
    So spake our general Mother,[147] and with eyes
Of conjugal attraction unreprov'd,
And meek surrender,[148] half imbracing leand
On our first Father, half her swelling Breast   495
Naked met his under the flowing Gold
Of her loose tresses hid: he in delight
Both of her Beauty and submissive Charms
Smil'd with superior Love, as *Jupiter*
On *Juno* smiles, when he impregns the Clouds   500
That shed *May* Flowers;[149] and press'd her Matron lip
With kisses pure: aside the Devil[150] turnd

---

[141]"And Adam called his wife's name Eve; because she was the mother of all living" (Genesis 3.20; but the naming occurs after the Fall, so the voice refers to it in the future tense).

[142]Fowler (4.478n) notes that the Platan, or plane tree (related to the North American sycamore), was a symbol of Christ, based on the commentary on the apocryphal Ecclesiasticus 24.16.

[143]Eve's lack of self-awareness, even in her unfallen state, foreshadows Adam's propensity for loving Eve's image "overmuch" (8.565—part of Raphael's warning to Adam not to to be subjected to Eve's "outside"). Here not the voice but Adam himself must persuade her not to love her own image more than she will love Adam.

[144]She represents part of Adam's substance, having been formed from a rib taken from Adam's left side, the side nearer his heart. She really is "flesh of his flesh."

[145]Another pun on *sole*, playing on the idea that though she is an individual and designed to be his meet help or his solace or comfort, she is also part of his being, part of his *soul* (see the next line) and his "other half."

[146]Sexually differentiated pronouns may be important here: "beauty" need not be only feminine, "grace" here is temporarily masculine (but the noun often signifies an attribute of Eve in *Paradise Lost*), and "wisdom" is not necessarily governed by the adjective "manly." Within the ambiguity of the passage, Milton may be implying that wisdom is above sexuality. Latin *sapientia* is a feminine noun.

[147]She is our general mother in the modern genetic sense, because she carries the seed of future generations (Latin *gens*, "that which is begotten"). The "Seed" (capitalized in 10.180 to indicate Jesus) that she will bear will eventually lead to or become Jesus, through the line of King David. Of course Eve is also the mother of all of us and therefore a general or generic mother.

[148]Again, in an innocent context, neither "meek" nor "surrender" seems to be negative in connotation, and the Epic Voice underscores the innocence with the word "unreprov'd."

[149]The image of classical fecundity is appropriate, though it still may jar some readers, since Jupiter is the one who impregnates clouds (not Juno), which then in turn give birth to flowers. In *Georgics* 2.325, Vergil pictures Jupiter descending through the air, pouring fruitful showers (he is a sky god) into his wife Juno. Eve has a "Matron lip" because she is mother (Latin *mater*) of all human beings and, more importantly, because she is a married woman of social rank (*OED* 1).

[150]The reader may have almost forgotten that Satan is watching, but Milton underscores his voyeurism by calling him "the Devil" for the first time here. Though Fowler (4.509–10n) points out that C.S. Lewis's characterization of Satan as a peeping Tom may be wrong if one considers with Empson that Satan's jealousy is open, Schwartz has pointed to the psychological problem of Satan as voyeur—a disturbed viewer who demeans the person being viewed—in *Remembering and Repeating* 54–59. Rajan points out the decline in the epithets for Satan, "how the 'Archfiend' of the first book becomes 'the Fiend' or the 'arch-felon' and how for the first time he begins to be 'the Devil'" (*Paradise Lost* 99).

For envie, yet with jealous leer[151] maligne
Ey'd them askance, and to himself thus plaind.[152]
    Sight hateful, sight tormenting! thus these two   505
Imparadis't in one anothers arms
The happier *Eden*, shall enjoy thir fill
Of bliss on bliss, while I to Hell am thrust,
Where neither joy nor love, but fierce desire,
Among our other torments not the least,   510
Still unfulfill'd with pain of longing pines;
Yet let me not forget what I have gain'd
From thir own mouths; all is not theirs it seems:
One fatal Tree there stands of Knowledge call'd,
Forbidden them to taste: Knowledge forbidd'n?[153]   515
Suspicious, reasonless. Why should thir Lord
Envie them that? can it be sin to know,
Can it be death? and do they onely stand
By Ignorance, is that thir happie state,
The proof of thir obedience and thir faith?   520
O fair foundation laid whereon to build
Thir ruine! Hence I will excite thir minds
With more desire to know, and to reject
Envious commands, invented with designe
To keep them low whom knowledge might exalt   525
Equal with Gods;[154] aspiring to be such,
They taste and die: what likelier can ensue?
But first with narrow[155] search I must walk round
This Garden, and no corner leave unspi'd;
A chance but chance[156] may lead where I may meet   530
Some wandring Spirit of Heav'n, by Fountain side,
Or in thick shade retir'd, from him to draw
What further would be learnt. Live while ye may,
Yet happie pair; enjoy, till I return,
Short pleasures, for long woes are to succeed.   535
    So saying, his proud step he scornful turn'd,
But with sly circumspection,° and began   GLANCES IN ALL DIRECTIONS
Through wood, through waste, o're hill, o're dale his roam.[157]
Mean while in utmost Longitude, where Heav'n
With Earth and Ocean meets, the setting Sun   540

---

[151]As when he appears as the animals with fallen aggressiveness, Satan brings the hellish characteristic of jealousy (the "injur'd Lovers Hell" of 5.450) and the evil gesture of the malignant leer into Eden.

[152]The word "plaind" contains within itself the overtones of "plaint" or "complaint," both associated by Milton with the pleas of a lover toward the object of his affection, and "complained," which suggests more of a whining reaction. Both associated senses of "plaind" seem to be in operation here, because Satan is complaining about something he cannot have—innocent love—and his soliloquy is the plaint of a rejected and envious suitor of Eve. Satan will admit below to his "fierce" and "unfulfill'd" "desire" which "pines" (509–11).

[153]It is not knowledge itself that is forbidden but the knowledge of good and evil as brought into the world by eating the fruit, thereby disobeying God.

[154]Satan is of course imputing his own motive, envy, to God, who certainly has no need or reason to be envious of his creations. Satan's soliloquy looks forward to his temptation of Eve, both in her dream, which Satan will inspire, and in the process of the temptation itself, when she will reason similarly.

[155]"Strict, close, precise, careful" (*OED* 5).

[156]"It is chancy, but chance may lead me to learn something further [or, in this case, to encounter the Serpent and then, in the Serpent, to encounter Eve]."

[157]Satan's actions are described in terms similar to those used for the devious actions of Elizabethan hobgoblins or fairies such as Shakespeare's Puck, whose fairies also travel "over hill, over dale" (*Midsummer Night's Dream* 2.1.2).

Slowly descended,[158] and with right aspect[159]
Against the eastern Gate of Paradise
Leveld his eevning Rayes:[160] it was a Rock
Of Alablaster,[161] pil'd up to the Clouds,
Conspicuous farr,[162] winding with one ascent   545
Accessible from Earth,[163] one entrance high;
The rest was craggie cliff, that overhung
Still as it rose, impossible to climbe.[164]
Betwixt these rockie Pillars *Gabriel* sat
Chief of th' Angelic Guards, awaiting night;   550
About him exercis'd Heroic Games
Th' unarmed Youth of Heav'n, but nigh at hand
Celestial Armourie, Shields, Helmes, and Speares,
Hung high with Diamond flaming, and with Gold.[165]
Thither came *Uriel*, gliding through the Eeven   555
On a Sun beam, swift as a shooting Starr
In *Autumn* thwarts the night, when vapors fir'd
Impress the Air, and shews the Mariner
From what point of his Compass to beware
Impetuous winds:[166] he thus began in haste.   560
   Gabriel, to thee thy course by Lot[167] hath giv'n
Charge and strict watch that to this happie Place
No evil thing approach or enter in;
This day at highth of Noon came to my Spheare[168]
A Spirit, zealous, as he seem'd, to know   565
More of th' Almighties works, and chiefly Man
Gods latest Image: I describ'd° his way   DESCRIED, NOTICED
Bent all on speed, and markt his Aerie Gate;°[169]   AIRY GAIT, SPEED THROUGH THE AIR
But in the Mount° that lies from *Eden* North,   MT. NIPHATES
Where he first lighted, soon discernd his looks   570

---

[158]As Fowler points out (4.541n), Milton may be describing the apparent slowing down of the sun's descent when its image is refracted through the earth's atmosphere. He had, however, described the sun earlier as "hasting" (353).

[159]The "right aspect" is the direct "face" of the sun. The word "aspect" is accented on the second syllable.

[160]"The sun leveled his evening rays to the inner side of the eastern gate of Paradise."

[161]An acceptable alternate spelling of "alabaster."

[162]"Capable of being seen from a great distance."

[163]That is, from the plain east of Paradise.

[164]The description of Paradise poised on an unscalable rock made of alabaster (see Matthew 26.7), with Gabriel on guard at its eastern gate between two pillars, may be symbolic, in the sense that the way to Paradise (or to Heaven) is difficult of access and in that the direction the gate faces, the East (as in "eastward in Eden" of Genesis 3.8; compare 3.24) may be significant, though Milton attaches no special importance to the point of the compass in any of his prose. Gabriel is one of the four archangels. His name, as Hume reminds us, signifies "the man of God, or the strength and power of God," in Hebrew (Newton 549n). He appears in the Old Testament in peaceful roles (Daniel 8.15–27), but he is, as Fowler points out (4.549–50n), associated with Mars, the god of war, and he is linked by apocryphal tradition with the guarding of Paradise.

[165]In contrast with the warlike and sadistic games of the fallen angels (2.528–38), the uncorrupted angels practice unarmed, but with their armor nearby for quick access.

[166]In contrast with the behavior of the fallen angels, who manifest themselves in threatening natural phenomena like whirlwinds (2.541), Uriel comes like a shooting star, an omen that told the seaman from which direction heavy winds might be coming. Shooting stars were thought to be exhalations of earth's vapors, ignited as they came into contact with different elements on their course outward from the earth. Thus the vapors are "fir'd," that is, set on fire, and they "Impress" the air, that is, they engrave themselves on the night air. They were also seen as omens of changing weather. Compare Homer's description of Minerva descending in the form of a shooting star that is also a portent to mariners (*Iliad* 4.75–82).

[167]Compare 1 Chronicles 26.13, where members of the various houses of Israel cast lots in order to determine which gate of the Temple they should guard.

[168]Uriel is pictured as governing the sphere of the Sun, one of the crystalline spheres or bright circles mentioned below, thought to be surrounding the Earth in the Ptolemaic system.

[169]Satan's airy gait indicates that he is ethereal or angelic, not made of earthly substance. Thus his deceitful appearance is at least temporarily convincing. The direction from which he comes, the north, might help to give away his identity.

Alien from Heav'n,[170] with passions foul obscur'd:
Mine eye pursu'd him still, but under shade[171]
Lost sight of him; one of the banisht crew
I fear, hath ventur'd from the deep, to raise
New troubles; him thy care must be to find. 575
    To whom the winged Warriour thus returnd:
Uriel, no wonder if thy perfet sight,[172]
Amid the Suns bright circle where thou sitst,
See farr and wide: in at this Gate none pass
The vigilance[173] here plac't, but such as come 580
Well known from Heav'n; and since Meridian hour°   NOON
No Creature thence: if Spirit of other sort,
So minded, have oreleapt these earthie bounds
On purpose, hard thou knowst it to exclude
Spiritual substance with corporeal barr. 585
But if within the circuit of these walks,[174]
In whatsoever shape he lurk, of whom
Thou tellst, by morrow dawning I shall know.
    So promis'd hee, and *Uriel* to his charge[175]
Returnd on that bright beam, whose point now raisd 590
Bore him slope downward to the Sun now fall'n
Beneath th' *Azores*;[176] whither the prime Orb,[177]
Incredible how swift,[178] had thither rowl'd
Diurnal,[179] or this less volubil[180] Earth
By shorter flight to th' East, had left him there 595
Arraying with reflected Purple and Gold
The Clouds that on his Western Throne attend:
Now came still Eevning on, and Twilight gray
Had in her sober Liverie all things clad;
Silence accompanied, for Beast and Bird, 600
They to thir grassie Couch, these to thir Nests
Were slunk, all but the wakeful Nightingale;
She all night long her amorous descant sung;[181]
Silence was pleas'd: now glow'd the Firmament

---

[170]"Of a being strange to Heaven." Satan's looks now identify him as alien to Heaven.

[171]Probably "under trees." Satan disappeared into the shadows.

[172]Uriel's name means "Light of God"; as one of God's "eyes" and messengers (3.650), he is best characterized by his farsightedness and speed.

[173]A noun constructed from the Latin *vigilans*, a participle meaning "wakefully." Corns writes about this passage: " . . . Milton puts the most pertinent attribute of the guard (Gabriel and Uriel are discussing whether Satan may have entered Paradise unseen) for the guard itself" (92; compare Fowler in 4.580n). Compare the American English usage of "vigilante."

[174]*1667* omits this comma.

[175]Uriel returns to his appointed station, his "charge" in the military sense of "place where he was ordered to stand guard." Probably "charge" is meant in the sense of "A precept, injunction, mandate, order" (*OED* 2.15).

[176]The Azores are the group of islands in the mid-Atlantic due west of Portugal.

[177]The sun, which is the prime orb in the sense that it is the most important "planet."

[178]Note the force of the phrase: at any great distance if the Sun rotated about the earth, its speed must approach incredibility, whereas if the Earth rotates about the Sun, the circuit becomes more credible.

[179]"On a daily basis."

[180]Later, Satan's movement will be said to be "voluble" (9.436) or "rapidly undulating from side to side." In using the conjunction "or" in 594, Milton allows the reader a choice between two systems of arranging the universe, the geocentric Ptolemaic and the heliocentric post-Copernican.

[181]Milton returns to the image of the nightingale, again describing the bird with naturalistic accuracy both as wakeful at dusk and through the night and as singing a descant, or melodious extended warbling song. Technically, in music a descant is a "high, florid part added above the melody of a hymn" (*Norton/Grove Concise Encyclopedia of Music*, ed. Stanley Sadie [New York: Norton, 1988]).

With living Saphirs: *Hesperus*[182] that led   605
The starrie Host, rode brightest, till the Moon
Rising in clouded Majestie,[183] at length
Apparent Queen unvaild her peerless light,
And o're the dark her Silver Mantle threw.

    When *Adam* thus to *Eve*: Fair Consort, th' hour   610
Of night, and all things now retir'd to rest
Mind° us of like repose, since God hath set   REMIND
Labour and rest, as day and night to men
Successive, and the timely dew of sleep
Now falling with soft slumbrous weight inclines   615
Our eye-lids;[184] other Creatures all day long
Rove idle unimploid, and less need rest;
Man hath his daily work of body or mind
Appointed, which declares his Dignitie,
And the regard of Heav'n on all his waies;[185]   620
While other Animals unactive range,
And of thir doings God takes no account.
To morrow ere fresh Morning streak the East
With first approach of light, we must be ris'n,
And at our pleasant labour, to reform   625
Yon flourie Arbors, yonder Allies° green,   ALLEYS
Our walk[186] at noon, with branches overgrown,
That mock our scant manuring,° and require   HAND-FERTILIZING
More hands then ours[187] to lop thir wanton° growth: UNCHECKED
Those Blossoms also, and those dropping Gumms,   630
That lie bestrowne° unsightly and unsmooth,   STREWN ABOUT
Ask riddance,° if we mean to tread with ease;   NEED TO BE THROWN OUT
Mean while, as Nature wills, Night bids us rest.

    To whom thus *Eve* with perfet beauty adornd.[188]
My Author and Disposer, what thou bidst   635
Unargu'd I obey; so God ordains,
God is thy Law, thou mine: to know no more

---

[182]Not only the most visible star of early evening (causing the firmament to glow: see 605 below) but associated both with Venus ("th' Eevning Star / Loves Harbinger" [11.588–89]) and with Lucifer. Misery is "Deaths Harbinger" in 9.13.

[183]Some astronomers considered the markings on the face of the moon to be clouds. Milton describes a full moon here, feminine like Diana, with the clouds in place. Since the moon is the brightest heavenly body at night, she is peerless and an apparent ("visible, plainly seen"—*OED* A.1) queen. She is pictured clothing the darkness with her silver mantle.

[184]Thyer first pointed out a possible borrowing from Spenser's *The Faerie Queene* 1.1.36:

> The drouping Night thus creepeth on them fast
> And the sad humour loading their eye liddes,
> As messenger of *Morpheus* on them cast
> Sweet slombring deaw, the which to slepe them biddes.

(*The Poetical Works of Edmund Spenser*, ed. J. C. Smith and E. De Selincourt [London: Oxford UP, 1912]). Milton also pictures the dawn with opening eyelids in "Lycidas" 26.

[185]"And the care of God regarding everything He does." Adam and Eve lead an active and productive (not merely contemplative life) in Paradise. God is pleased that they are dignified by the process of pleasant work, since He commanded them to "till and keep" the Garden (Genesis 2.15). They get up at dawn enthusiastically just to perform such pleasant duties. Milton's model Protestant theologian John Wolleb (or Wollebius) summarizes what is now known as the "Protestant work ethic": "Industry or love of labour, or the care of getting means honestly, is a Vertue whereby one gets an estate by honest labours, that he may be the better enabled to live comfortably to himselfe, and to others. This was enjoyned in Paradise, Gen. 3.19" (*The Abridgment of Christian Divinity* [London, 1650]: 325–26).

[186]Printed "walks" in *1667*, but "walk" in *1674* seems to be a correction.

[187]One of a number of references to the possibility of children; Adam, in other words, is completely aware of where babies come from.

[188]Here Eve's adornment with what is indeed perfect feminine beauty should not be taken as a threat, and her epithet for Adam, "Author and Disposer," suggests only that he gave her life from his body and hence is author to her the way God is author to them both. Adam is her disposer in the sense that God has given Adam authority over her, to be her guide.

Is womans happiest knowledge and her praise.
With thee conversing I forget all time,
All seasons and thir change, all please alike.   640
Sweet is the breath of morn, her rising sweet,
With charm[189] of earliest Birds; pleasant the Sun
When first on this delightful Land he spreads
His orient° Beams, on herb,[190] tree, fruit, and flour,   °BRIGHT
Glistring with dew; fragrant the fertil earth   645
After soft showers; and sweet the coming on
Of grateful Eevning milde, then silent Night
With this her solemn Bird and this fair Moon,
And these the Gemms of Heav'n, her starrie train:[191]
But neither breath of Morn when she ascends   650
With charm of earliest Birds, nor rising Sun
On this delightful land, nor herb, fruit, floure,
Glistring with dew, nor fragrance after showers,
Nor grateful Eevning mild, nor silent Night
With this her solemn Bird, nor walk by Moon,   655
Or glittering Starr-light without thee is sweet.
But wherfore all night long shine these, for whom
This glorious sight, when sleep hath shut all eyes?
   To whom our general Ancestor repli'd.
Daughter of God and Man, accomplisht *Eve*,[192]   660
Those have thir course to finish, round the Earth,
By morrow Eevning, and from Land to Land
In order, though to Nations yet unborn,
Ministring light prepar'd, they set and rise;
Least total darkness should by Night regaine   665
Her old possession, and extinguish life
In Nature and all things, which these soft fires
Not only enlighten, but with kindly heate
Of various influence foment and warme,
Temper or nourish, or in part shed down   670
Thir stellar vertue[193] on all kinds[194] that grow
On Earth, made hereby apter to receive
Perfection from the Suns more potent Ray.
These then, though unbeheld in deep of night,
Shine not in vain, nor think, though men were none,   675

---

[189]"The blended singing or noise of many birds" (*OED* sub², citing this instance).

[190]A class of green plants that lie close to the earth, as distinguished from the tree, fruit, and flower above it.

[191]Contrast Eve's innocent appreciation of the evening with Satan's perverse description of the same group of natural phenomena—night, moon, stars, nightingale—during Eve's dream (5.37–47).

[192]Adam's epithets for Eve at this point are accurate—she is daughter both of God and man, and she is accomplished not only in that she is "finished" or perfectly constructed by God but in the sense that she is skillful when laboring within the duties usually assigned to women in the seventeenth century, as with preparation of food and gardening. But the word "accomplisht" might look forward to historical temptations described for Adam after the Fall and suggest that women who practice the "Arts that polish Life" (11.610) are potentially dangerous. Eve's accomplishment or giftedness might also parallel that of Pandora, whose name means "All-gifted." Adam will be Eve's instructor from this point on: he receives instruction primarily from God, and she receives it primarily from Adam. All parties are in accord here: she would rather learn from Adam: "hee, she knew would intermix / Grateful digressions, and solve high dispute / With conjugal Caresses, from his Lip / Not Words alone pleas'd her" (8.54–57).

[193]All celestial bodies shed light, the sustaining principle of life, the formative virtue as seen near the end of Book 2 and early in Book 3, on the earth. The image is astrological, suggesting favorable and mild influence over human character and events in human history, but it is also climatic, suggesting the temperate watering and fertilization of earth.

[194]"A race, or a natural group of animals or plants having a common origin" (*OED* 11.a), citing this instance.

That heav'n would want spectators,[195] God want praise;
Millions of spiritual Creatures walk the Earth
Unseen, both when we wake, and when we sleep:[196]
All these with ceaseless praise his works behold
Both day and night: how often[197] from the steep   680
Of echoing Hill or Thicket have we heard
Celestial voices to the midnight air,
Sole, or responsive each to others note
Singing thir great Creator: oft in bands
While they keep watch, or nightly rounding walk   685
With Heav'nly touch of instrumental sounds
In full harmonic number joind, thir songs
Divide the night, and lift our thoughts to Heaven.[198]
    Thus talking hand in hand alone[199] they pass'd
On to thir blissful Bower; it was a place   690
Chos'n by the sovran Planter,[200] when he fram'd
All things to mans delightful use; the roofe
Of thickest covert was inwoven shade
Laurel and Mirtle, and what higher grew
Of firm and fragrant leaf; on either side   695
Acanthus,[201] and each odorous bushie shrub
Fenc'd up the verdant wall; each beauteous flour,
Iris all hues, Roses, and Gessamin°   JASMINE
Rear'd high thir flourisht heads° between, and wrought   FLOWER HEADS IN BLOOM
Mosaic; underfoot the Violet,   700
Crocus, and Hyacinth with rich inlay
Broiderd° the ground, more colour'd then with stone   EMBROIDERED
Of costliest Emblem:[202] other Creature here
Beast, Bird, Insect, or Worm[203] durst enter none;
Such was thir awe of Man. In shadier[204] Bower   705
More sacred and sequesterd, though but feignd,
Pan or *Silvanus* never slept, nor Nymph,

---

[195]Metrical stress should fall on the second syllable of the word, as in modern English (but not American) usage.

[196]A testimony to the animation of the universe and to the presence of "guardian angels" and other invisible spirits—all of whom, Adam argues here, glorify God. Before the Fall, Adam and Eve hear angels sing hymns in harmony and dedicated to God. That angels sang in "responsive hymns" (according to Ignatius, third Bishop of Antioch) was attested by Socrates Scholasticus, in a passage Milton cited in his *Commonplace Book* (Yale 1: 383).

[197]The "often" again suggests that they have been in Eden for more than several days.

[198]Their songs divide the night in the sense of separating the different angelic watches, but the word "division" also had a musical sense, suggesting either that they used florid melodies or that they sang antiphonally or in divided choirs. On this page in *1674*, the compositor has spelled the word "Heav'n," "heav'n," and "Heaven," without any consistency or attention to metrics or capitalization.

[199]Milton apparently takes the unity and oneness of Adam and Eve so seriously as to imply that when they are together they are "alone" or "sole."

[200]God, in His capacity as creator of the Garden of Eden, is analogous to the director of a plantation, or planter, but He also "planted a garden" in Genesis 2.8. Milton uses the word *bower* as a synonym for "Lodge" elsewhere (720 below): the general picture is of a rustic house constructed of laurel and myrtle. The trees may be symbolic, standing for Apollo and Venus, male and female, mind and spirit, according to Fowler (4.694n). Milton had also used both at the beginning of "Lycidas," standing for different types of poetic inspiration.

[201]A compositor may have mistaken an unfamiliar name of a shrub, Acanthus, and later the name of the flower, Iris, to be proper names, since he put them both in italics. Acanthus may be planted on a support wall of the bower because it is associated with architectural pillars or interior decoration. Most of the flowering shrubs and perennials of Eden produce pleasant smells—they are "fragrant" or "odorous." Paradise in general smells very good.

[202]Throughout the description, Milton implies that God's architecture in Eden both anticipates human architecture and supersedes it: the inwoven roof anticipates thatch, the acanthus on either side suggests classical columns or pilasters, the wall is fenced with espaliered flowers which also represent a mosaic, and the arrangement of violets, crocuses, and hyacinth prefigure, but are morally preferable to, a marble floor. The first rural architecture, unfallen, was better than any urban, fallen architecture.

[203]The word was applied not only to what we would call worms but to serpents and to dragons. The implication is that Satan cannot intrude into the bower.

[204]The word "shadie" in *1674* is probably an error, since *1667* has "shadier" and someone has skillfully inked in the "r" in the University of Illinois copy noted by Fletcher.

Nor *Faunus* haunted.[205] Here in close recess
With Flowers, Garlands, and sweet-smelling Herbs
Espoused[206] *Eve* deckt first her nuptial Bed,
And heav'nly Quires the Hymenæan° sung,   *MARRIAGE HYMN*   710
What day the genial Angel[207] to our Sire
Brought her in naked beauty more adorn'd,[208]
More lovely then *Pandora*, whom the Gods
Endowd with all thir gifts,[209] and O too like
In sad event,° when to the unwiser Son   *OUTCOME*   715
Of *Japhet* brought by *Hermes*, she ensnar'd
Mankind with her faire looks, to be aveng'd[210]
On him who had stole *Joves* authentic fire.[211]
    Thus at thir shadie Lodge arriv'd, both stood,[212]
Both turnd, and under op'n Skie ador'd   720
The God that made both Skie, Air, Earth and Heav'n
Which they beheld, the Moons resplendent Globe
And starrie Pole: Thou also mad'st the Night,
Maker Omnipotent, and thou the Day,   725
Which we in our appointed work imployd
Have finisht happie in our mutual help
And mutual love, the Crown of all our bliss
Ordaind by thee, and this delicious place
For us too large, where thy abundance wants°   *LACKS*   730
Partakers, and uncropt falls to the ground.
But thou hast promis'd from us two a Race
To fill the Earth, who shall with us extoll
Thy goodness infinite, both when we wake,
And when we seek, as now, thy gift of sleep.   735

---

[205]Pan, Sylvanus, and Faunus were Greek and Roman satyr gods often identified with one another because all had goat bodies from the waist down. Pan, Christianized as a god of all nature (266–68 above, and Nativity Ode 89), was known in the ancient world as a god of shepherds and hunters. He was also a god of fecundity whose favorite habit, celebrated in thousands of Greek vases, was to chase nymphs. Faunus, whose name in the feminine, **fauna**, has come to mean all the animal kingdom, was a god of vegetation and agriculture whose worship was gradually replaced by that of Pan. Sylvanus, whose kinship with forests is indicated by the *sylva* in his name, presided over gardens and property boundaries. Because Milton associates the various goat gods with superstition, he denigrates them by using the verb *haunted*. But Pan is linked etymologically with *Pan*dora, mentioned just below in comparison to Eve.
[206]She is espoused (married) for the same reason she has a "Matron lip"—she and Adam have been married by God.
[207]The "genial" adjective suggests that the angel who delivered Eve to Adam was Raphael, but we know that Raphael was away on the day of Eve's creation, on a mission that took him to the gates of Hell (8.229). In 8.484–87, Eve is said to be guided by her maker, so there does seem to be a discrepancy in accounts, as is noticed by Allan Gilbert, who thought "Doubtless a 'genial angel,' a sort of Hymen adapted to a Biblical setting, played a part [in an earlier dramatic draft of *Paradise Lost*], now indicated only by a single reference that has survived his having been replaced by the Maker himself" (45–46).
[208]Compare "accomplisht," as applied to Eve (660 above).
[209]Milton provides a contextual etymology for the name Pandora, which means "all-gifted." The gods endow Pandora with her beauty and other "gifts," however, in order to deceive Epimetheus, "the unwiser Son / Of *Japhet*." The wiser son is Prometheus, who steals fire from the gods. Epimetheus is not unwise in an absolute sense, he is just less wise than Prometheus, legendary for his wisdom.
[210]Though the word in *1674* at first appears not to have an apostrophe, on closer looking at the word in copies and facsimiles of the edition, one can detect the faint outline of the apostrophe in the gap between "g" and "d."
[211]Milton is careful to compare the two created women only "In sad event"—that is, in the outcome of both their histories, the bringing of evil into the world. If Eve is being compared with Pandora, then Adam is being compared with Epimetheus, the less intelligent son of Japhet. Jove's fire is "authentic" in that it is "Original, first-hand, prototypical; as opposed to *copied*" (*OED* 4, citing this instance).
[212]It may be worth observing that the pair stand rather than kneel at prayer. This is an evening prayer, atypical for Puritans generally but expected of Anglicans (the *Book of Common Prayer* includes an evening service). Unlike the evening service indicated in the Prayer Book, the prayer of Adam and Eve is spontaneous. Needing nothing, they pray in adoration, not supplication. The political implications of the method of prayer have to do with the fact that their ritual is private and between husband and wife; it is not instituted or commanded of them. The comma of *1667* after "stood" seems preferable to the omitted punctuation of *1674*, since it pairs with the comma after "turnd."

This said unanimous,[213] and other Rites
Observing none, but adoration pure
Which God likes best, into thir inmost bowre
Handed° they went; and eas'd the putting off   HAND IN HAND
These troublesom disguises which wee wear,   740
Strait side by side were laid, nor turnd I weene[214]
Adam from his fair Spouse, nor *Eve* the Rites
Mysterious of connubial Love refus'd:
Whatever Hypocrites austerely talk
Of puritie and place and innocence,   745
Defaming as impure what God declares
Pure, and commands to som, leaves free to all.
Our Maker bids increase, who bids abstain
But our destroyer,[215] foe to God and Man?
Haile wedded Love, mysterious Law, true source   750
Of human ofspring,[216] sole proprietie,[217]
In Paradise of all things common else.
By thee adulterous lust was driv'n from men
Among the bestial herds to raunge, by thee
Founded in Reason, Loyal, Just, and Pure,   755
Relations dear, and all the Charities
Of Father, Son, and Brother first were known.
Farr be it, that I should write thee sin or blame,
Or think thee unbefitting holiest place,
Perpetual Fountain of Domestic sweets,   760
Whose bed is undefil'd and chaste pronounc't,
Present, or past, as Saints and Patriarchs us'd.
Here Love his golden shafts[218] imploies, here lights
His constant Lamp, and waves his purple wings,
Reigns here and revels; not in the bought smile   765
Of Harlots, loveless, joyless, unindeard,
Casual fruition, nor in Court Amours

---

[213]Apparently the prayer is meant to be said in unison, as if Adam and Eve truly speak as one. Whether they improvise and still speak the prayer in unison is a question impossible to answer. The choruses of angels singing God's praise apparently do something quite similar (683–84 above), singing in unison and then antiphonally.

[214]Strictly speaking, Milton does not assert that Adam and Eve made love, since "I weene" means "I assume" or "I guess," but readers from very early on have assumed that Milton's Adam and Eve did have intercourse, since Milton is so careful to mention the "Rites / Mysterious of connubial Love." Coitus before the Fall gave problems to the early Church Fathers, because it suggested that the first-born of Adam and Eve, the murderer Cain, might have been conceived when Adam and Eve were sinless. St. Augustine thought it impossible for instance, for Adam and Eve to make love in Paradise without conception occurring. Augustine concluded " . . . it was after they were expelled from [Paradise] that they came together to beget children, and begot them" (*The City of God* 14.21). For the concept of "one flesh" (see Ephesians 5) in seventeenth-century domestic philosophy, see Turner, *One Flesh*. Milton's authorial aside at this point, a kind of sermon on conjugal love with a hymn, "Haile wedded Love," built into it, is a summary of all he had written on the ideal state of marriage in his divorce tracts. The relationship between husband and wife, he found, is the basis for all other domestic relations and the basis for all domestic law and for charity toward others. Fowler points to other Protestant hexameral poems, as with Du Bartas's *Divine Weekes* (1.6.1055–78), in which Adam sings the marriage hymn. In Sylvester's translation, God commands Adam and Eve "With chaste Embraces to replenish faire / Th'unpeopled World" (*Divine Weekes* 1.292), just as Genesis 1.28 directs. Fowler (4.750–65n) also points out that the three ends of marriage in seventeenth-century life were to provide for society, to procreate, and to provide a remedy for lust.

[215]Milton puts the institution of sacerdotal celibacy, the celibacy of the Roman Catholic clergy, under the control of Satan, "our destroyer." A life in which marriage is not possible is anathema to him.

[216]Probably the compositor misread one elongated "f" as a doubled "s," to produce "ofsspring" in *1674*. *1667* prints "ofspring." I have restored the earlier reading.

[217]The institution of wedded love is the only propriety, as legally defined, in Paradise. Adam and Eve do not own property but they share the proprietarial (ownership) rights in their marriage. This is the "propriety," which was "at first in common" mentioned in *Tetrachordon* (Yale 2: 625). Milton is mixing in legal language he found useful in his divorce tracts to prove that Adam and Eve had joint title to their marriage, though they held all other property in Paradise in "common."

[218]The golden arrows of Cupid, designed to attract love (Cupid's leaden arrows would repel it).

Mixt Dance, or wanton Mask,[219] or Midnight Bal,
Or Serenate, which the starv'd Lover sings
To his proud fair, best quitted with disdain.[220]   770
These lulld by Nightingales imbraceing slept,
And on thir naked limbs the flourie roof
Showrd Roses, which the Morn repair'd.[221] Sleep on
Blest pair; and O yet happiest if ye seek   775
No happier state, and know to know no more.
    Now had night measur'd with her shaddowie Cone[222]
Half way up Hill this vast Sublunar Vault,
And from thir Ivorie Port the Cherubim
Forth issuing at th' accustomd hour stood armd
To thir night watches in warlike Parade,   780
When *Gabriel* to his next in power thus spake.
    Uzziel,[223] half these draw off, and coast the South
With strictest watch; these other wheel° the North,   CIRCLE
Our circuit meets full West. As flame they part
Half wheeling to the Shield, half to the Spear.[224]   785
From these, two strong and suttle[225] Spirits he calld
That neer him stood, and gave them thus in charge.
    Ithuriel and *Zephon*, with wingd speed
Search through this Garden, leave unsearcht no nook,
But chiefly where those two fair Creatures Lodge,   790
Now laid perhaps asleep secure° of harme.   WITHOUT FEAR
This Eevning from the Sun's decline arriv'd
Who[226] tells of som infernal Spirit seen
Hitherward bent (who could have thought?) escap'd
The barrs of Hell, on errand bad no doubt: 795
Such where ye find, seise fast, and hither bring.
    So saying, on he led his radiant Files,°
Daz'ling the Moon; these to the Bower direct   ROWS OF SOLDIERS

---

[219]Presumably Milton has nothing to be ashamed of in having written a masque, since *Comus* is certainly not "wanton." The word also meant "masked ball," a contrast between "Mask" and "Bal" is set up by the conjunction "or." Milton seems to be denigrating the kind of aristocratic entertainment practiced in the reign of James I, during which a dramatic performance led to drunken, all-night dancing. For a description of the Puritan reactions to court excesses, see David Norbrook, "The Reformation of the Masque," in *The Court Masque*, ed. David Lindley (Manchester, Eng.: U of Manchester P, 1984): 94–110. Of course, the Restoration court of Charles II was even better known for its debaucheries. The phrase "Casual fruition," in no way restricted to time or place, is surely one of the most telling phrases ever written to describe loveless copulation.

[220]Milton mocks most of the conventions of Petrarchan love poetry, with its anorexic, cold (*in sereno* in Italian means "on clear and cold nights"), and metaphorically "starved for love" (*starve* also has a secondary meaning of *die*) lover, who sings his serenade to a woman he calls his "proud fair," while she perversely quits or requites him with disdain. The Italianate spelling of the word "Serenate" might lead the reader toward the Petrarchan context. The contrast is between insincere and unnatural art, and natural, heart-felt love. See William Kerrigan and Gordon Braden, "Milton's Coy Eve: *Paradise Lost* and Renaissance Love Poetry," *ELH* 53 (1986): 27–51.

[221]Probably new roses were growing, repairing the damage of the falling buds and petals.

[222]The cone is the shadow of the earth. When the shadow reaches half-way up the hill, it is nine o'clock, since when the shadow is at its greatest height the time is midnight. To produce such a cone, the sun must be substantially larger than the earth. The "port" is the eastern gate of Paradise.

[223]The name *Uzziel* means "Strength of God" (Hume, quoted in Newton 782n). It appears in the Bible only as the name of a human being, in Exodus 6.18; the name *Zephon* ("Searcher of Secrets") is also found in the canonical Bible only as a proper human name (Numbers 26.15). Uzziel's position as next in power to Gabriel may be based on a tradition of rabbinical commentary. The name *Ithuriel* (Discovery of God) is extra-biblical but may come, as Fowler states (4.782–88n), from "the disreputable" apocryphal book *Key of Solomon*. For the names, consult Robert West, "The Names of Milton's Angels," *Studies in Philology* 47 (1950): 211–23, and see various articles on the angels collectively and by individual names in *A Milton Encyclopedia*.

[224]As Newton points out, the directions of the shield, on the left arm, or the spear, held in the right, would indicate right or left turns. It is appropriate that the angels act like flaming heavenly bodies, since traditionally the spheres they moved in were those of the light-emitting stars and planets.

[225]"Intelligent." Here Milton applies a word that Genesis uses to define the serpent to angels, indicating that the Fall corrupts not only people or angels but words as well. Even Milton's subtle serpent before the Fall is not yet "nocent" (9.186).

[226]"One who tells" (Uriel). Uriel tells of the unidentified infernal spirit observed aiming in this direction ("Hitherward bent")—a being who has escaped the bars of Hell.

In search of whom they sought: him there they found
Squat like a Toad,[227] close at the eare of *Eve*;   800
Assaying by his Devilish art to reach
The Organs of her Fancie, and with them forge
Illusions as he list, Phantasms and Dreams,
Or if, inspiring venom, he might taint
Th' animal Spirits that from pure blood arise[228]   805
Like gentle breaths from Rivers pure, thence raise
At least distemperd, discontented thoughts,
Vaine hopes, vaine aimes, inordinate desires
Blown up with high conceits ingendring pride.
Him thus intent *Ithuriel* with his Spear   810
Touch'd lightly; for no falshood can endure
Touch of Celestial temper,[229] but returns
Of force to its own likeness: up he starts
Discoverd and surpriz'd. As when a spark
Lights on a heap of nitrous Powder,[230] laid   815
Fit for the Tun som Magazin to store
Against a rumord Warr, the Smuttie[231] graine
With sudden blaze diffus'd, inflames the Aire:
So started up in his own shape the Fiend.[232]
Back stept those two faire Angels half amaz'd   820
So sudden to behold the grieslie King;
Yet thus, unmovd with fear, accost him soon.
    Which of those rebell Spirits adjudg'd to Hell
Com'st thou, escap'd thy prison, and transform'd,
Why satst thou like an enemie in waite   825
Here watching at the head of these that sleep?
    Know ye not then said *Satan*, fill'd with scorn,
Know ye not mee? ye knew me once no mate[233]
For you, there sitting where ye durst not soare;

---

[227]It should be pointed out that, though Satan is "like a Toad," he is not necessarily in the shape of a toad. Toads were, however, associated with images of Hell and thus with evil, since they often appeared in late-medieval representations of Hell. Satan is pictured infecting Eve's imagination through her ear. The Devil is trying by means of his art to reach the disordered images of her sleeping imagination, and with them to construct a coherent evil dream that will represent an illusion, a fantasm, of her future. "Imagination stored these data [sense impressions gathered during the day] before passing them on to fantasy, which acted to combine and divide them, yielding new images, called *phantasmata*, with no counterparts in external reality" (Katherine Park, "The Organic Soul," in *The Cambridge History of Renaissance Philosophy*, eds. Charles B. Schmitt and Quentin Skinner [Cambridge: Cambridge UP, 1988]: 471). See Hunter, "Eve's Demonic Dream," in *Descent*.

[228]Animal spirits were supposed to be transmitted through the blood. According to what is usually called faculty psychology, the most important organs of the body, liver and heart, manufactured vapors or spirits that traveled either through veins or arteries upward to the brain. Such animal spirits gave direction from the brain to move the body, or to produce apparitions. Satan, breathing (inspiring) venom into Eve's ear, taints the animal spirits in the pure blood, infecting the brain with apparitions. Milton is as exact as the science of his time would permit him to be. See Weidhorn, *Dreams* 130–51. See also William A. McCarthy's article "Dreams" in *A Milton Encyclopedia*.

[229]Presumably Satan cannot endure the touch of a spear whose metal has been tempered (in the metallurgical sense of "hardened off") in celestial ether; the reader is meant to contrast the heavenly metal of the spear with Satan's "distemperd" thoughts.

[230]Gunpowder, composed partly of potassium nitrate or saltpeter. The epic simile is very carefully worked out, since Satan and his legions will invent gunpowder during the War in Heaven (6.470–81), since the gunpowder is carelessly left in a heap (it is ready to be put in its tun, or barrel), since it is being prepared only for the rumor of war, and since it is described in terms of its smuttiness or dirty appearance. Use of this gunpowder is not only dangerous, it is fraudulent and wrong-headed. The pile is also set off completely by chance; the explosion has no reasoning behind it—only carelessness and neglect. The implication is that Satan's kind of fire is no longer like that of the heavenly angels and should be contrasted with "*Joves* authentic fire" (719 above).

[231]A rare capitalized adjective, and capitalized for no discernible reason.

[232]The touch of the celestial spear, like that of a magic wand, apparently changes Satan from whatever shape he was in at the ear of Eve back into his form as degenerate fallen angel, "his own shape." Accompanying his metamorphosis seems to be the puff of smoke still used on stage or in cartoons to indicate the transformation of an evil being back into its own ugly shape. Here what the good angels see is what Beelzebub has seen in Book 1: instead of an angel of light, Satan is an unrecognizable grisly king of the underworld. For this kind of tricky transformation, see Guillory, *Poetic Authority*, 146–71.

[233]"A suitable associate [or adversary]; an equal in eminence of dignity" (*OED* 2.2, citing this instance).

Not to know mee argues your selves unknown,   830
The lowest of your throng; or if ye know,
Why ask ye, and superfluous begin
Your message, like to end as much in vain?[234]
To whom thus *Zephon*, answering scorn with scorn.[235]
    Think not, revolted Spirit, thy shape the same,   835
Or undiminisht brightness, to be known
As when thou stoodst in Heav'n upright and pure;
That Glorie then, when thou no more wast good,
Departed from thee, and thou resembl'st now
Thy sin and place of doom obscure° and foule.   DARK   840
But come, for thou, be sure, shalt give account
To him who sent us, whose charge is to keep
This place inviolable, and these from harm.
    So spake the Cherube, and his grave rebuke
Severe in youthful beautie, added grace   845
Invincible.[236] abasht the Devil stood,
And felt how awful° goodness is, and saw   AWE-INSPIRING
Vertue in her shape how lovly, saw, and pin'd°   PINED
His loss; but chiefly to find here observd
His lustre visibly impar'd; yet seemd   850
Undaunted. If I must contend, said he,
Best with the best, the Sender not the sent,
Or all at once; more glorie will be wonn,
Or less be lost. Thy fear, said *Zephon* bold,
Will save us trial what the least can doe   855
Single against thee wicked, and thence weak.[237]
    The Fiend repli'd not, overcome with rage;
But like a proud Steed reind, went hautie on,
Chaumping his iron curb.[238] to strive or flie
He held it vain; awe from above had quelld   860
His heart, not else dismai'd. Now drew they nigh
The western Point, where those half-rounding guards
Just met, and closing stood in squadron joind
Awaiting next command.[239] To whom thir Chief
Gabriel from the Front thus calld aloud.   865

---

[234]Satan's answer sounds magnificent ("Not to know mee argues your selves unknown" is one of his most memorable lines, and now appears on sweatshirts designed by Miltonists), but he is still deformed beyond recognition by his sin: angels who once knew and honored him can no longer tell who he is. He emphasizes his former superiority in rank, talking down to mere cherubim, but Zephon, like Abdiel during the War in Heaven, can talk back scornfully (835–40 below), proving that Satan's answer is "vain, self-elevating, status-bullying, rather than magnificent" (Roland Swardson, letter of 11 March 1995).
[235]Though Zephon's next quoted speech does not begin a verse paragraph in either of the early editions, it should, in order to maintain consistent house style and in order not to create confusion in the modern reader.
[236]The cherubim enjoy something like perpetual youth: in Renaissance art they were often pictured either as handsome young men or as babies, despite being described by theologians as ageless. Here Zephon embodies grace, his virtue dictating the beauty of his appearance, whereas Satan's sin has scarred his face and diminished his brightness. The effect of character on external appearance was one of the conventions of Renaissance love poetry. To show the existence of that idea in Milton, Fowler quotes from *Reason of Church-Government*, in which angelic military discipline is said to demonstrate itself in physical beauty: " . . . the very visible shape and image of vertue, whereby she is not only seene in the regular gestures and motions of her heavenly paces as she walkes, but also makes the harmony of her voice audible to mortall eares" (Yale 1: 751–52). Eve's beauty before the Fall, of course, is a prime example of goodness so powerful that it "overawd / [Satan's] Malice" in Book 9 (see 9.457–65).
[237]The logic here, very important for understanding the impotence of evil in Milton's work, is "All wickedness is weakness" (*Samson Agonistes* 834).
[238]The various comparisons with animals or inanimate life, from cormorants and toads to horses and even gunpowder, show the physical and moral degradation of Satan. Here he may be proud and haughty but he is also pictured as stupid and as stubborn as a horse, even while controlled by reins and curb bit.
[239]The two divided sections of the squadron of angel guards have reunited (Gabriel had commanded them to disperse in semicircular formations in 782–84 above).

O friends, I hear the tread of nimble feet[240]
Hasting this way, and now by glimps discerne
Ithuriel and *Zephon* through the shade,°   GROVE OF TREES
And with them comes a third of Regal port,°   DEMEANOR
But faded splendor wan; who by his gate°   GAIT   870
And fierce demeanour seems the Prince of Hell,
Not likely to part hence without contest;[241]
Stand firm, for in his look defiance lours.
     He scarce had ended, when those two approachd
And brief related whom they brought, where found,   875
How busied, in what form and posture coucht.°   HIDDEN
     To whom with stern regard thus *Gabriel* spake.
Why hast thou,[242] *Satan*, broke the bounds prescrib'd
To thy transgressions,[243] and disturbd the charge
Of others, who approve not to transgress   880
By thy example,[244] but have power and right
To question thy bold entrance on this place;
Imploi'd it seems to violate sleep, and those
Whose dwelling God hath planted here in bliss?
     To whom thus *Satan*, with contemptuous brow.   885
Gabriel, thou hadst in Heav'n th' esteem of wise,[245]
And such I held thee; but this question askt
Puts me in doubt. Lives ther[246] who loves his pain?
Who would not, finding way, break loose from Hell,
Though thither doomd? Thou wouldst thy self, no doubt,   890
And boldly venture to whatever place
Farthest from pain,[247] where thou mightst hope to change°   EXCHANGE
Torment with ease, and soonest recompence
Dole[248] with delight, which in this place I sought;
To thee no reason; who knowst only good,   895
But evil hast not tri'd: and wilt object
His will who bound us? let him surer barr
His Iron Gates, if he intends our stay
In that dark durance:° thus much what was askt.[249]   PRISON
The rest is true, they found me where they say;   900
But that implies not violence or harme.
     Thus he in scorn. The warlike Angel mov'd,°   ANNOYED
Disdainfully half smiling thus repli'd.
O loss of one in Heav'n to judge of wise,
Since *Satan* fell, whom follie overthrew,   905

---

[240]Perhaps this implied stage direction was written into an earlier dramatic scene. It sounds like *Comus* 91–92: "I hear the tread / Of hatefull steps . . . ."
[241]Accented on the second syllable.
[242]A contest of rank may be going on, since both Satan and Gabriel address each other using the derogatory second person pronoun "thou."
[243]Satan has stepped out of bounds etymologically, since the word *transgression* suggests stepping (Latin *gradus*, step, pace, position) combined with "across" (Latin *trans*). But transgressions can also be sins; the Fall itself is called a transgression.
[244]"Others who do not follow your example to choose to sin."
[245]"You had the reputation in Heaven of being wise."
[246]Supply "anyone who."
[247]Satan admits that he has broken loose from Hell in order to run away from its pain—exactly opposite of what he told the other fallen angels. Gabriel analyzes Satan's equivocation more precisely: he is the first to fly from pain and to try to escape his just punishment, thus he is the biggest coward in Hell.
[248]Probably used in a sense derived from Latin *dolor*, sadness, but with the possible meaning of Latin *dolus*, guile, fraud. The word had been in use in English, however, since 1290 (*OED* sub²).
[249]"I answer thus much for what was asked" (Loh's paraphrase, 899n).

And now returns him[250] from his prison scap't,
Gravely in doubt whether to hold them wise
Or not, who ask what boldness brought him hither
Unlicenc't from his bounds in Hell prescrib'd;
So wise he judges it to fly from pain   910
However,[251] and to scape his punishment.
So judge thou still, presumptuous, till the wrauth,
Which thou incurr'st by flying, meet thy flight
Seavenfold, and scourge[252] that wisdom back to Hell,
Which taught thee yet no better, that no pain   915
Can equal anger infinite provok't.
But wherefore thou alone? wherefore with thee
Came not all Hell broke loose?[253] is pain to them
Less pain, less to be fled, or thou then they
Less hardie to endure? courageous Chief,   920
The first in flight from pain, had'st thou alledg'd
To thy deserted host this cause of flight,
Thou surely hadst not come sole fugitive.
    To which the Fiend thus answerd frowning stern.
Not that I less endure, or shrink from pain,   925
Insulting Angel, well thou knowst I stood°   WITHSTOOD
Thy fiercest, when in Battel to thy aide
The[254] blasting volied Thunder made all speed
And seconded thy else not dreaded Spear.[255]
But still thy words at random, as before,   930
Argue thy inexperience what behooves
From hard assaies and ill successes past
A faithful Leader, not to hazard all
Through wayes of danger by himself untri'd,
I therefore, I alone first undertook   935
To wing the desolate Abyss, and spie
This new created World, whereof in Hell
Fame is not silent, here in hope to find
Better abode, and my afflicted Powers
To settle here on Earth, or in mid Aire;   940
Though for possession put to try once more
What thou and thy gay Legions[256] dare against;
Whose easier business were to serve thir Lord
High up in Heav'n, with songs to hymne his Throne,
And practis'd distances to cringe, not fight.[257]   945
    To whom the warriour Angel[258] soon repli'd.

---

[250]Modern grammar would omit the reflexive "him," although "follie" could be the subject of "returns" and "him" its object.

[251]"In any way he can devise."

[252]Literally "whip that opinion all the way back to Hell." For "Seavenfold," compare "vengeance shall be taken on him sevenfold" (Genesis 4.15).

[253]"Hell is broke loose" is recorded as a proverbial saying as early as 1573 (Tilley H403), but Milton seems to be reinvesting the phrase with dignity.

[254]Probably the "The" of *1667* and not the "Thy" of *1674* is correct, as Fowler points out: "Thy" occurred "probably due to the proximity of other instances of the word" (4.928n).

[255]"And fought back against your otherwise unfrightening spear."

[256]Satan transforms "bright Legions" (6.64) of the War in Heaven into the more diminutive "gay Legions," suggesting that the faithful angels' bright armor is just window-dressing. He is still lying either to himself or to all present, as Gabriel will point out.

[257]"And practiced the proper steps for bowing and scraping, not fighting."

[258]The comma after "Angel" in *1674*, which is not present in *1667*, is not needed. Gabriel's military might (and the courage that lies behind it) is underlined by the epithets applied to him. Here the name "warriour" shows that Satan has been lying when he used the word "cringe."

To say and strait unsay, pretending first
Wise to flie pain, protesting next the Spie,
Argues no Leader but a lyar trac't,
Satan, and couldst thou faithful add?[259] O name,   950
O sacred name of faithfulness profan'd!
Faithful to whom? to thy rebellious crew?
Armie of Fiends, fit body to fit head;
Was this your discipline and faith ingag'd,
Your military obedience, to dissolve   955
Allegeance to th' acknowledg'd[260] Power supream?
And thou sly hypocrite, who now wouldst seem
Patron of liberty, who more then thou
Once fawn'd, and cring'd, and servilly ador'd
Heav'ns awful° Monarch? wherefore but in hope   FEAR-INSPIRING   960
To dispossess him, and thy self to reigne?
But mark what I arreede° thee now, avant;°   ADVISE   BE GONE
Flie thither whence thou fledst: if from this houre
Within these hallowd limits thou appeer,
Back to th' infernal pit I drag thee chaind,   965
And Seale thee so, as henceforth not to scorne
The facil[261] gates of hell too slightly barrd.
     So threatn'd hee, but *Satan* to no threats
Gave heed, but waxing more in rage° repli'd.   GROWING MORE ENRAGED
     Then when I am thy captive talk of chaines,   970
Proud limitarie[262] Cherube, but ere then
Farr heavier load thy self expect to feel
From my prevailing arme, though Heavens King
Ride on thy wings, and thou with thy Compeers,
Us'd to the yoak, draw'st his triumphant wheels   975
In progress through the rode of Heav'n Star-pav'd.[263]
     While thus he spake, th' Angelic Squadron bright[264]
Turnd fierie red, sharpning in mooned hornes
Thir Phalanx, and began to hemm him round
With ported Spears,[265] as thick as when a field   980
Of *Ceres*[266] ripe for harvest waving bends
Her bearded Grove of ears, which way the wind
Swayes them; the careful Plowman doubting stands
Least° on the threshing floor his hopeful sheaves   LEST

---

[259]Gabriel finally discovers who Satan is by recognizing one of his chief traits, lying.

[260]The spelling "acknowldg'd" in *1674* is obviously a misprint for the correct reading of *1667*.

[261]Probably "easily moved." Satan uses the same word of Eve in *Paradise Regain'd* 1.51.

[262]"Bounded." In Latin, *milites limitanei* are soldiers with duty in frontier garrisons; thus Satan is insulting the angels by referring to the fact that they are guarding frontiers. He, however, is the being who is severely limited, morally and physically.

[263]Satan refers to the Chariot of Paternal Deity in which Messiah rides as He conquers the rebellious angels in the War in Heaven (6.749–59), perhaps, as Fowler notes (4.973–76n), the central image of the entire poem. The "rode of Heav'n" is the Milky Way. As usual, Satan lies about the cherubim being yoked to the chariot, since the chariot is propelled by God's will. The lie apparently makes the present squadron of cherubim angry: their native color, red, is intensified, and they proceed to form a crescent battle formation, their phalanx.

[264]Milton seems to be describing a battle formation still used in warfare of his time, while at the same time one that looks like crescent moons—the moon being associated with the goddess Ceres, who appears in the upcoming epic simile. The horns of the crescent moon and of the military formation are sharp and threatening.

[265]The word "ported" is a military term (as in the old command "Port arms") meaning "held diagonally across and close to the body" (see *OED* v.2.1). The spears have been lifted into readiness for battle.

[266]By extension or metonymy, the goddess Ceres becomes the grain she is goddess of.

Prove chaff.[267] On th' other side *Satan* allarm'd   985
Collecting all his might dilated[268] stood,
Like *Teneriff* or *Atlas* unremov'd:[269]
His stature reacht the Skie, and on his Crest
Sat horror Plum'd;[270] nor wanted in his graspe
What seemd both Spear and Shield: now dreadful deeds   990
Might have ensu'd, nor onely Paradise
In this commotion, but the Starrie Cope[271]
Of Heav'n perhaps, or all the Elements
At least had gon to rack,[272] disturbd and torne
With violence of this conflict, had not soon   995
Th' Eternal to prevent such horrid fray°
Hung forth in Heav'n his golden Scales,[273] yet seen
Betwixt *Astrea* and the *Scorpion* signe,
Wherein all things created first he weighd,
The pendulous round Earth with ballanc't Aire   1000
In counterpoise, now ponders[274] all events,
Battels and Realms: in these he put two weights
The sequel° each of parting and of fight;
The latter quick up flew, and kickt the beam;[275]
Which *Gabriel* spying,° thus bespake the Fiend.   1005
     Satan, I know thy strength, and thou knowst mine,
Neither our own but giv'n;[276] what follie then
To boast what Arms can doe, since thine no more
Then Heav'n permits, nor mine, though doubld now
To trample thee as mire:[277] for proof look up,   1010

---

[267]The simile seems to have its roots in John the Baptist's image of wheat and chaff (Matthew 3.12; but compare Psalm 1.4), and Homer, *Iliad* 2.147–50, though Milton simplifies the Homeric comparison between an expectant or apprehensive army, perhaps expecting defeat, and grain waving in a heavy wind. The plowman, more English apparently than Greek, may be an extraneous detail. To compare him to God, as Empson does (172), may be to stretch his importance and distort the passage. If the "bearded Grove of ears" is just an accurate description of the heads of wheat, then the plowman need not be symbolic, or representative either of God or Satan. Empson does believe that the simile "makes the good angels look weak" (172).

[268]Both the unfallen and fallen angels have the ability to expand or contract almost beyond human imagination, though with the fallen angels the shrinking and expanding often can be perceived, from God's perspective, as comic puffery or dwarfism. Here Satan is dilated ("Widened, expanded, extended, diffused" [*OED* ppl.a, citing this instance]) to the size of famous mountains—either Teneriffe, on the Canary island of that name off the coast of Africa, or Atlas, in Mauritania in West Africa, where the Titan Atlas was supposed to be holding up the sky.

[269]Probably, as Fowler notes, "unremovable." *OED* uses the passage to define the word as "Fixed in place; firmly stationed."

[270]Allegory survives in a vivid image: on Satan's head, at its heraldic crest, Horror sits like a helmet, plumed. According to heraldic decoration, a crest was "A figure or device (originally borne by a knight on his helmet) placed on a wreath, coronet or chapeau, and borne above the shield or helmet in a coat of arms" (*OED* 3). Thus Horror is Satan's heraldic device, the figure at the top of his coat of arms. The compositor at this point does no honor to the entity Horror, since the word is not capitalized; instead, "Plum'd" is, for no good reason.

[271]The stars are pictured as a canopy or cope or vault covering the earth.

[272]"Gone to pieces," as in "rack and ruin." The four elements made up everything beneath the moon.

[273]Milton's God, like Homer's Zeus in *Iliad* 8.66–77, balances the fate of beings using a cosmic scale. The constellation is Libra, the Scales, but it is also a sign of divine justice. Here God's will stops a pointless battle in order to demonstrate providence at work—not controlling the free will of Adam and Eve or showing the angelic guard to be useless, but allowing Satan to move on in God's mission to allow him to test Adam and Eve. The image allows us to see how God has balanced the forces of the universe in equipoise from the beginning. The earth is pictured hanging ("pendulous") in balance with the atmosphere around it, as it is pictured in the Homeric epics. The judgment of Milton's God, to differentiate it from that of the Homeric Zeus, is providential, not capricious.

[274]"Weighs" as well as "thinks about," since the etymology of "ponder" includes the meaning of Latin *ponderare*, "to weigh."

[275]In God's providential scheme, fighting at this point would unbalance the coming fate of Adam and Eve and cause the scales of justice to tilt, one side kicking up and hitting the balance beam. When Satan sees the Scales in the sky, he is reminded of the writing on the wall in the biblical tale of Belshazzar: "Thou art weighed in the balances, and art found wanting" (Daniel 5.27). Fowler points out (4.997–1004n) that the constellation of the Serpent associated with Satan, or Anguis (see 3.555–60), would at midnight be directly below that of Libra or the Scales.

[276]Since God has created both, and apportioned their strength according to a scale of goodness (even the lesser of the good angels, as with Abdiel, are stronger than the fallen Satan), it is useless for Satan to put on a show of strength. Satan's strength has been reduced hugely as a result of his fall.

[277]The "mire" was the mud generated in muddy roads as a result of traffic, so Satan here is both "mire" and "trampled in mire," with another biblical passage, Isaiah 10.6, echoing in the background: "I will send him against an hypocritical nation . . . to tread them down like the mire of the streets."

And read thy Lot° in yon celestial Sign   FORTUNE
Where thou are weigh'd, and shown how light, how weak,
If thou resist. The Fiend lookt up and knew
His mounted scale aloft: nor more; but fled
Murmuring, and with him fled the shades of night.   1015

The End of the Fourth Book.

Paradise Lost.

BOOK V.

THE ARGUMENT.

Morning approach't, Eve relates to Adam her troublesome dream; he likes it not, yet comforts her: They come forth to thir day labours: Thir Morning Hymn at the Door of thir Bower. God to render Man inexcusable[1] sends Raphael to admonish him of his obedience, of his free estate, of his enemy near at hand; who he is, and why his enemy, and whatever else may avail Adam to know. Raphael comes down to Paradise, his appearance describ'd, his coming discern'd by Adam afar off sitting at the door of his Bower; he goes out to meet him, brings him to his lodge,[2] entertains him with the choycest fruits of Paradise got together by Eve; thir discourse at Table: Raphael performs his message, minds Adam[3] of his state and of his enemy; relates at Adams request who that enemy is, and how he came to be so, beginning from his first revolt in Heaven, and the occasion thereof; how he drew his Legions after him to the parts of the North, and there incited them to rebel with him, perswading all but only Abdiel a Seraph, who in Argument diswades and opposes him, then forsakes him.

Now Morn her rosie steps in th' Eastern Clime
Advancing, sow'd the earth with Orient Pearle,[4]
When *Adam* wak't, so customd, for his sleep
Was Aerie light[5] from pure digestion bred,
And temperat vapors bland, which th' only sound   5
Of leaves and fuming rills, *Aurora*'s fan,
Lightly dispers'd,[6] and the shrill Matin Song
Of Birds on every bough; so much the more
His wonder was to find unwak'nd *Eve*
With Tresses discompos'd, and glowing Cheek,   10
As through unquiet rest: he on his side
Leaning half-rais'd, with looks of cordial[7] Love
Hung over her enamour'd, and beheld
Beautie, which whether waking or asleep,
Shot forth peculiar Graces;[8] then with voice   15
Milde, as when *Zephyrus* on *Flora* breathes,[9]

---

[1] If Adam knows what his obedience entails, he will act of his own free will, and God's foreknowledge of Adam's disobedience will in no way cause it. God sends Raphael, as the Epic Voice will say below, out of "pittie" (220) for Adam and Eve.

[2] Milton uses the words lodge and bower interchangeably.

[3] "Raphael delivers his message and reminds, [warns, and admonishes] Adam . . . ."

[4] In Homer, Dawn is often "rosy-fingered," but here Morning uses her progress from eastern regions to west to sow the earth either with dew or eastern ("Orient," but the word also means "brilliant") light, depending how one reads "Pearle." The image of Morn suggests that like the rest of the natural world inside and outside of Eden, she is fertile and productive.

[5] Adam's sleep is light because his body is unfallen and his digestion of foods eaten in moderation in Eden is not disturbed and hence can remain "pure." The only gas rising from Adam's stomach is temperate and inoffensive ("bland"). The process of eating will link human and divine in this book. *1667* adds a comma after "light."

[6] The leaves of trees act as the fan of the goddess of morning, Aurora, lightly dispersing the sounds of water rushing in brooks or rills and that of the leaves themselves. Even the shrillness of the morning bird-song is just high-pitched as with the soprano voice and not necessarily harsh.

[7] When Eve is created from Adam's left side, according to Milton's account, "cordial spirits" (8.466) flow forth from near his heart (French *coeur*), hence his cordial looks are quite "heartfelt." The word also had medicinal overtones, since a cordial was a drink supposed to be good for the heart.

[8] Playing on the unfallen and fallen connotations of phrases like "darts of love" or "darting glances." Eve's beauty has the power in itself to shoot out peculiar Graces (the word "peculiar" meant something close to "unique" and may have just a tinge of the modern meaning "odd"). Eve's beauty has the power to make Satan "Stupidly good" (9.465), but its power seems potentially dangerous or volatile. Since Eve's beauty is only her "outside," she is not really responsible, especially in her unfallen state, for the strong effect it may have on Satan or Adam.

[9] Zephyr is the breeze of spring who breathes life in flowers, perhaps through the fecundity of his wife Flora, since between them they have a son, Carpos (see Ovid, *Fasti* 5.5.195). Both Eve and Eden are associated with fecundity as represented in gardens, grain, fruit, flowers, and vines. In all cases, the greenery or fruit is pictured in one marriage or another: Jupiter and Hera, Hades and Proserpina, Vertumnus and Pomona.

Her hand soft touching, whisperd thus. Awake
My fairest, my espous'd, my latest found,[10]
Heav'ns last best gift, my ever new delight,
Awake, the morning shines, and the fresh field   20
Calls us, we lose the prime,[11] to mark how spring
Our tended Plants, how blows° the Citron Grove,   BLOOMS
What drops the Myrrhe, and what the balmie Reed,[12]
How Nature paints her colours, how the Bee
Sits on the Bloom extracting liquid sweet.   25
    Such whispering wak'd her, but with startl'd eye
On *Adam*, whom imbracing, thus she spake.
    O Sole[13] in whom my thoughts find all repose,
My Glorie, my Perfection, glad I see
Thy face, and Morn return'd, for I this Night,   30
Such night till this I never pass'd, have dream'd,
If dream'd, not as I oft am wont, of thee,
Works of day pass't, or morrows next designe,
But of offence and trouble, which my mind
Knew never till this irksom night; methought   35
Close at mine ear one call'd me forth to walk
With gentle voice, I thought it thine;[14] it said,
Why sleepst thou *Eve*? now is the pleasant time,
The cool, the silent, save where silence yields
To the night-warbling Bird, that now awake   40
Tunes sweetest his love-labor'd song;[15] now reignes
Full Orb'd the Moon, and with more pleasing light
Shadowie sets off the face of things;[16] in vain,
If none regard; Heav'n wakes with all his eyes,[17]
Whom to behold but thee, Natures desire,   45

[10]The passage is obviously intended to remind the reader of the Song of Songs: "My beloved spake, and said unto me, Rise up, my love, my fair one, and come away . . . . The flowers appear on the earth; the time of the singing of birds is come, and the voice of the turtle is heard in the land . . . . Arise, my love, my fair one, and come away" (2.10, 12–13). In seventeenth-century biblical commentary, the Song of Songs (sometimes called the Song of Solomon or Canticles) is taken as a prolepsis or prototype of Christ's marriage to the Church: as the Geneva Bible's "Argument" puts it, "In this Song, Salomón by moste swete and comfortable allegories and parables describeth the perfite love of Jesus Christ, the true Salomón and King of peace, and the faithful soule or his Church, which he hathe sanctified and appointed to be his spouse, holy, chast, and without reprehension" (280ʳ, 1560 ed.).

[11]The first hour of the day or the first hour after sunrise or 6 a.m., whichever comes first. Since the sun always rises at the same six o'clock hour in Paradise, as Fowler reminds us (5.18 –25n), prime is always that hour (see 10.651–706).

[12]Two sources of balm, or healing ointment, as in the famous biblical "Balm of Gilead" (Jeremiah 8.22; see Genesis 37.25 for myrrh being associated with balm). The balm and the myrrh were both in the balsam family, producing aromatic gums or resins said to heal wounds or prevent infection. Since the balm would be an exudate of myrrh, it "drops" or forms a ball; the "balmie Reed" seems to be poetic diction as in "cornie [horn-shaped] Reed" (7.321), although Milton is usually very precise about describing plants.

[13]The word seems to be a noun meaning "unique one." But the *OED* a. 5.b cites this instance as illustrating the adjective in the sense of the absolute meaning of "one and only." The word also seems to have a special sense in Milton's vocabulary for the more than close relationship of Adam and Eve: each is one and unique yet they are the same and both are one in the sense that Eve is a part of Adam and in the sense that God makes them one in marriage. Perhaps they are as God the Father and Son, "United as one individual Soule" (610 below); certainly they are "one Flesh, one Heart, one Soule" (8.499), punning on the homonyms "soul" and "sole."

[14]Satan's deception of Eve is quite fiendishly clever: in his hypocrisy (in taking on his series of fraudulent roles), he even assumes Adam's voice. The dream also foreshadows the actual process of the Fall in Book 9, though at many points a kind of subliminal suggestion is present. Here Satan is a seraph, though in Book 9 he will be the Serpent; here Satan is pictured eating the fruit, though in Book 9 he will tell Eve that he has already eaten the fruit.

[15]Milton allows the image he incorporated for himself as poet, that of the nightingale, also to be used as part of Satan's dream scenery, but this nightingale sings a "love-labor'd song," a phrase which suggests lechery or illicit conception ("love-labor"). Newton was the first to point out the problem with the sex of the nightingale (41n): in 4.602 the nightingale is a "she," yet here the bird is masculine, which is accurate in the sense that the male nightingale is the singer, yet perhaps more important is the fact that Satan sings suggestive songs through the voice of the bird.

[16]The beginning of a series of obvious lies, since the light of the moon, being a reflection of the light of the sun, cannot be more pleasant. Moonlight is to Satan what sunlight is to God. Its deceptive shadows are his hiding place and his natural medium.

[17]The eyes are stars and other heavenly bodies, but the image was a common one, as in Spenser, *The Faerie Queene* 3.11.45: " . . . with how many eyes / High heaven beholds sad lovers nightly theeveryes [i.e., "thieveries"]").

In whose sight all things joy, with ravishment
Attracted by thy beauty still to gaze.[18]
I rose as at thy call, but found thee not;
To find thee I directed then my walk;
And on, methought, alone I pass'd through ways   50
That brought me on a sudden to the Tree
Of interdicted° Knowledge: fair[19] it seem'd,   FORBIDDEN
Much fairer to my Fancie° then by day: IMAGINATION
And as I wondring lookt, beside it stood
One shap'd[20] and wing'd like one of those from Heav'n   55
By us oft seen; his dewie locks distill'd
Ambrosia;[21] on that Tree he also gaz'd;
And O fair Plant, said he, with fruit surcharg'd,[22]
Deigns none to ease thy load and taste thy sweet,
Nor° God,[23] nor Man; is Knowledge so despis'd?   NEITHER   60
Or envie, or what reserve forbids to taste?[24]
Forbid who will, none shall from me withhold
Longer thy offerd good, why else set here?
This said he paus'd not, but with ventrous Arme
He pluckt, he tasted;[25] mee damp horror chil'd   65
At such bold words voucht° with a deed so bold: ACCOMPLISHED
But he thus overjoy'd, O Fruit Divine,
Sweet of thy self, but much more sweet thus cropt,
Forbidd'n here, it seems, as onely fit
For God's,[26] yet able to make Gods of Men: 70
And why not Gods of Men, since good, the more
Communicated, more abundant growes,
The Author not impair'd, but honourd more?
Here, happie Creature, fair Angelic *Eve*,[27]
Partake thou also; happie though thou art,   75
Happier thou mayst be, worthier canst not be:

---

[18]That the voice is Satan's is clear by its rhetoric: night is better than day, the moon's light more pleasing than the sun's, all Heaven worships Eve, and Eve's beauty ravishes all nature. Satan is appealing to Eve's unpremeditated vanity. A word like "ravishment" gives away the violent sexuality that Satan is suggesting to Eve in the dream. Satan, having eavesdropped on Eve's questioning the reason for the stars, here explains night to her as a time for worshiping her beauty. Compare the specious reasoning used by Comus in "What hath night to do with sleep?" (*Comus* 122).
[19]The word "fair" often signals a dangerous attractive force in *Paradise Lost,* suggesting that humans are easily seduced by a fair appearance. We know that neither the fruit nor the Tree of Knowledge of Good and Evil is provocative in appearance: it just seems so, in this case to Eve's fancy.
[20]Though no apostrophe is visible in this word in copies of *1674,* the gap between the letters indicates that one was present but dropped below register in the printing process; the apostrophe is clearly printed in *1667.*
[21]The italicized form of the noun was changed from the roman form of *1667,* possibly because the word was thought a proper noun. The word here means a healing oil used by the Greek gods--not the food (*OED* 3). The description of the angel's hair probably derives from Vergil's description of Venus as she leaves Aeneas outside the city of Carthage: "her crown of ambrosial hair breathed out / A heavenly fragrance" (*Aeneid,* trans. C. Day Lewis, 1.403–04).
[22]The tree is overly full of fruit, as if suffering from earth's overabundance. As with Comus in his attempt to seduce the Lady in Milton's masque, Satan makes use of the idea of copiousness (compare the identical use of "surcharg'd" in *Comus* 728) to suggest that Eve should overindulge, or eat herself sick.
[23]"God" should be read as lowercase "god," and it should be understood as meaning "angel" (in Milton's usage of that term), rather than a rival to the one God of Christianity. Satan is hinting that Eve will become "as gods" (Genesis 3.5), which is interpreted as meaning "like the fallen angels."
[24]Satan has told us in soliloquy (4.516–27) that he will be using the prohibition against eating the fruit as the beginning of his temptation. His temptation here generally follows the procedure he will try to duplicate in Book 9, except that here Eve will eat and get away with it, in dream wish-fulfillment as engineered by Satan. Milton is very specific in telling the reader that the dream does not cause her to sin. It may infect her fancy, but as long as her reason does not accept this fancy, she is sinless.
[25]Echoes what happens to Eve in the actual fall: ". . . she pluck'd, she eat" (9.781).
[26]"Gods," the reading of all states of *1667,* seems preferable, although plurals were often formed with an apostrophe (especially plurals in italicized words), a practice reserved only for possessives and contractions today.
[27]One needs to be reminded that Eve is not an angel at this point; to be so would be to jump above Adam in the scale of nature, as when she begins to think in Book 9 that she could be "somtime / Superior" (824–25) to Adam.

Taste this, and be henceforth among the Gods[28]
Thy self a Goddess, not to Earth confind,
But somtimes in the Air, as wee, somtimes
Ascend to Heav'n, by merit thine,[29] and see   80
What life the Gods live there, and such live thou.
So saying, he drew nigh, and to me held,
Even to my mouth of that same fruit held part
Which he had pluckt;[30] the pleasant savourie smell
So quick'nd appetite, that I, methought,   85
Could not but taste. Forthwith up to the Clouds
With him I flew, and underneath beheld
The Earth outstretcht immense, a prospect wide
And various: wondring[31] at my flight and change
To this high exaltation; suddenly   90
My Guide was gon, and I, me thought, sunk down,
And fell asleep; but O how glad I wak'd
To find this but a dream! Thus *Eve* her Night
Related,[32] and thus *Adam* answerd sad.[33]

    Best image of my self and dearer half,   95
The trouble of thy thoughts this night in sleep
Affects me equally; nor can I like
This uncouth[34] dream, of evil sprung I fear;
Yet evil whence? in thee can harbour none,
Created pure. But know that in the Soule   100
Are many lesser Faculties that serve
Reason as chief; among these Fansie[35] next
Her office holds; of all external things,
Which the five watchful Senses represent,
She forms Imaginations, Aerie shapes,   105
Which Reason joyning or disjoyning, frames
All what we affirm or what deny, and call
Our knowledge or opinion; then retires
Into her private Cell[36] when Nature rests.
Oft in her absence mimic Fansie wakes   110

[Handwritten margin notes: "Satan imitating Eve"; "dream"; "SHE IS ADAM'S DEARER HALF"]

---

[28]The word "gods" is ironic throughout the temptation in the dream, since for Satan the word in the plural means "fallen angels." Compare *Paradise Regain'd* 2.178–81, and see Williams, *The Common Expositor* for commentary on the Sons of God and the Daughters of Men and the "Sons of Seth" or "Sethites."

[29]Neither Adam nor Eve yet deserves to ascend to Heaven, though according to Raphael they would be able to earn the privilege (see the use of the word "merit" in 7.157).

[30]The dream temptation differs from the conscious temptation in Book 9 in that Satan in the Serpent will not hold the fruit up to Eve's mouth; she will instead approach the tree, pluck the fruit, and eat it, all of her own volition. In the dream version the imitation cherub remains with her even into the flight described below, but in the real deed Satan deserts her after planting ideas.

[31]Eve is the one who is "wondring," though the syntax seems to leave the participle dangling.

[32]"Thus Eve related the events of the night to Adam."

[33]The word should not suggest that Adam is observing the effects of sin, because Eve has not committed any; instead he answers her with great seriousness and solemnity. Compare Milton's usage in describing the "Sad task" of describing the Fall in Book 9 (13).

[34]The word meant both "strange" (*OED* 3) and "unpleasant, distasteful, unseemly" (*OED* 4).

[35]Roughly equivalent to the modern "fantasy" or "unconscious imagination." Milton describes the process of conscious knowledge or sense impressions being used at night by a "mimic Fansie" to produce disjointed and sometimes upsetting dreams. Milton follows the standard "faculty psychology" of his day. It postulated several mental activities: reason, which should rule; fancy or imagination, the image-making faculty; memory; will; and the common sense, which unites into a single experience data provided by the five senses. Fancy is always active, sleeping or waking. During the sleep of the reason, it produces dreams, which are thus irrational. Dreams may be inspired by God or Satan, and they are the medium by which God chooses to instruct Eve in Books 11 and 12.

[36]May indicate a compartment of the brain, though the image also may show Reason as a kind of pensive nun (it is *her* private cell, and the word *ratio*—reason—is feminine in Latin) as in "Il Penseroso" 169.

To imitate her; but misjoyning shapes,
Wilde work produces oft, and most in dreams,
Ill matching words and deeds long past or late.[37]
Som such resemblances methinks I find
Of our last Eevnings talk, in this thy dream,   115
But with addition strange;[38] yet be not sad.
Evil into the mind of God[39] or Man
May come and go, so unapprov'd, and leave
No spot or blame behind:[40] Which gives me hope
That what in sleep thou didst abhorr to dream,   120
Waking thou never wilt consent to do.[41]
Be not disheart'nd then, nor cloud those looks
That wont to be more chearful and serene
Then° when fair Morning first smiles on the World,   THAN
And let us to our fresh imployments rise   125
Among the Groves, the Fountains, and the Flours
That open now thir choicest bosom'd[42] smells
Reservd from night, and kept for thee in store.[43]
    So cheard he his fair Spouse, and she was cheard,
But silently a gentle tear let fall   130
From either eye, and wip'd them with her haire;[44]
Two other precious drops that ready stood,
Each in thir chrystal[45] sluce, hee ere they fell
Kiss'd as the gracious signs of sweet remorse
And pious awe, that feard to have offended.   135
    So all was cleard,[46] and to the Field they haste.
But first from under shadie arborous roof,[47]
Soon as they forth were come to open sight
Of day-spring,° and the Sun, who scarce up risen   DAWN
With wheels yet hov'ring o're the Ocean brim,[48]   140
Shot paralel to the earth his dewie[49] ray,

---

[37]Adam's eloquent speech is one more indication that he was born intelligent, clearly as he is said to be in *On Christian Doctrine*: "Man was made in the image of God, and the whole law of nature was so implanted and innate in him that he was in need of no command" (1.10; Yale 6: 353).

[38]Perhaps Adam is unable to account for the details that begin with the eating of the fruit in the dream, which have no precedent in the last evening's conversation.

[39]Substitute the meaning "angel" for "God" here, though speculation whether God can think evil thoughts is tantalizing.

[40]Adam acknowledges what Milton seems to want us to believe: that the dream in no way corrupts Eve at this point, because her reason does not approve of what her dream showed her. Milton believed, with St. Augustine (*The City of God* 14.13), that there were two parts to sin, "evil desire, or the will to do evil, and the evil deed itself" (*On Christian Doctrine* 1.11; Yale 6. 388); so far, Eve is not guilty of evil desire.

[41]Some copies of *1667* have a colon here instead of a period.

[42]Some flowers give forth their scents at certain times during the day, morning, afternoon, or evening. Here the scents are imagined as being confined in the flowers' bosoms until they are released in morning.

[43]"Kept in reserve just for you." Fowler (5.128n) sees a "grim dramatic irony" in the phrase, since after the Fall "the heavens and the earth, which are now, . . . are kept in store, reserved unto fire against the day of judgment and perdition of ungodly men" (2 Peter 3.7).

[44]The image of the repentant sinner Mary Magdalene, who also used her hair to wipe away tears (Luke 7.38), is brought to mind, but Eve is remorseful, not repentant; she is pious, not impious; and she fears to offend, rather than being repentant for having offended, because, of course, she hasn't. Milton's picture of Adam kissing away the tears is as moving, however, as any depiction of Mary Magdalene in Renaissance art.

[45]The lowercase "chrystal" of all states of *1667* may be the preferable reading, since adjectives are very rarely capitalized in either early edition: I have restored it.

[46]The word "cleard" could imply that clouds have been lifted (*OED* I.1.c), as in the modern idiom "clear the air," but "to clear from the imputation of guilt, to free from accusation" (*OED* III.9) was also current in 1660.

[47]"The roof provided by trees."

[48]Milton often pictures the Sun in something like the chariot of Apollo, which has a "burning Axletree" (Nativity Ode 84) and wheels; here the chariot is hovering just above the surface of the sea at daybreak.

[49]Both the morning and evening are times in which dew is heavy, thus the sun has a dewy ray in the morning and Mulciber falls "from Noon to dewy Eve" (1.743).

Discovering in wide Lantskip° all the East   LANDSCAPE
Of Paradise[50] and *Edens* happie Plains,
Lowly they bow'd adoring, and began
Thir Orisons,° each Morning duly paid   PRAYERS   145
In various style, for neither various style
Nor holy rapture wanted they to praise
Thir Maker, in fit strains pronounc't or sung
Unmeditated, such prompt eloquence
Flowd from thir lips, in Prose or numerous Verse,[51]   150
More tuneable then needed Lute or Harp[52]
To add more sweetness, and they thus began.

    These are thy glorious works,[53] Parent of good,
Almightie, thine this universal Frame,
Thus wondrous fair; thy self how wondrous then!   155
Unspeakable,[54] who first above these Heavens
To us invisible or dimly seen
In these thy lowest works, yet these declare
Thy goodness beyond thought, and Power Divine:
Speak yee who best can tell, ye Sons of light,   160
Angels, for yee behold him, and with songs
And choral symphonies, Day without Night,[55]
Circle his Throne rejoycing,[56] yee in Heav'n,
On Earth joyn all ye Creatures to extoll
Him first, him last, him midst, and without end.   165
Fairest of Starrs,[57] last in the train of Night,
If better thou belong not to the dawn,
Sure pledge of day, that crownst the smiling Morn
With thy bright Circlet, praise him in thy Spheare[58]
While day arises, that sweet hour of Prime.   170
Thou Sun, of this great World both Eye and Soule,[59]
Acknowledge him thy Greater, sound his praise
In thy eternal course, both when thou climb'st,
And when high Noon hast gaind, and when thou fallst.

---

[50]"Revealing the wide landscape of Eden, lying east of Paradise." Notice that the place name "*Eden*" is in italics, whereas the generic "Paradise" is not; the logic follows that of not italicizing "Heaven."

[51]Milton associates Adam and Eve's method of spontaneous prayer with his own method of composing poetry in the epic, by the use of the echoed words style, praise, strains, sung, prompt, and by his mentioning both prose and *numerous* verse. Milton generally believed that prayer should not be rigidly controlled by a church ceremony or even contained within a church setting. Nevertheless, the morning prayer of Adam and Eve, like the evening prayer that preceded it, echoes some of the liturgy of the Church of England, specifically the Canticle "O all ye works of the Lord, praise thee the Lord," which is often used for a morning service and may be said or sung, and is in turn derived from (among others) Psalms 148 and 150. See Thomas Stroup, *Religious Rite & Ceremony* for Milton's use of various parts of the Church of England service. Also, the fact that their morning hymn needs no accompaniment by lute or harp should not be taken to mean that Milton did not like church music (as with the angels' songs and "choral symphonies" mentioned below).

[52]Some copies of *1667* have a comma after "Harp."

[53]Some states of *1667* omit the comma after "works."

[54]Compare 2 Corinthians 9.15: "Thanks be unto God for his unspeakable gift."

[55]Fowler (5.162n) points out that Milton's Heaven has no time darker than earthly twilight (see 642–46 below).

[56]In medieval and Renaissance iconography, the angels circling the throne of God closely resemble heavenly bodies such as stars and planets circling either the Earth or the Sun.

[57]Fowler notes that the planet Venus "in western elongation rises in the east just before sunrise, and is known as the morning star (Lucifer, Phosphorus)." At the same time, "On every occasion when Venus passes from eastern to western elongation during the hours of darkness, it will be the evening star on the evening immediately preceding the conjunction, and the morning star on the morning immediately following" (5.166–70n). As in the Nativity Ode 74, Lucifer the star is not considered to be inherently evil, despite the association with the angel who fell.

[58]The crystalline sphere in which the planet was said to move.

[59]The iconography of the Sun included picturing it as an eye (the image still persists in the Masonic design on the U.S. dollar bill). If the Sun is an eye and male as compared to the female moon (see 8.150), it can also be an entrance to the soul of the universe. Christ is often pictured in Renaissance iconography as radiating light as if the Son were the Sun.

Moon, that now meetst the orient[60] Sun, now fli'st   175
With the fixt Starrs, fixt in thir Orb that flies,[61]
And yee five other wandring Fires[62] that move
In mystic Dance not without Song,[63] resound
His praise, who out of Darkness call'd up Light.
Aire, and ye Elements the eldest birth   180
Of Natures Womb,[64] that in quaternion° run   A GROUP OF FOUR
Perpetual Circle, multiform; and mix
And nourish all things, let your ceaseless change
Varie to our great Maker still new praise.
Ye Mists and Exhalations that now rise,   185
From Hill or steaming Lake, duskie or grey,[65]
Till the Sun paint your fleecie skirts° with Gold,   OUTSKIRTS, BORDERS
In honour to the Worlds great Author rise,
Whether to deck with Clouds the uncolourd skie,
Or wet the thirstie Earth with falling showers,   190
Rising or falling still advance his praise.
His praise ye Winds, that from four Quarters blow,
Breathe[66] soft or loud; and wave your tops, ye Pines,
With every Plant, in sign of Worship wave.
Fountains and yee, that warble, as ye flow,   195
Melodious murmurs, warbling tune his praise.
Joyn voices all ye living Souls, ye Birds,
That singing up to Heaven Gate ascend,
Bear on your wings and in your notes his praise;
Yee that in Waters glide, and yee that walk   200
The Earth, and stately tread, or lowly creep;
Witness if I[67] be silent, Morn or Eeven,
To Hill, or Valley, Fountain, or fresh shade
Made vocal by my Song, and taught his praise.
Hail universal Lord, be bounteous still   205
To give us onely good; and if the night
Have gathered aught of evil or conceald,
Disperse it, as now light dispels the dark.[68]

---

[60]Both the Sun in the east and the shining Sun.

[61]Like each planet, all the stars were "fixed" in a single sphere that turned in twenty-four hours.

[62]Venus, already mentioned, plus Mars, Saturn, Jupiter, and Mercury. They are "wandring" as opposed to fixed stars because their orbits are elliptical and irregular.

[63]The dance and song of the heavenly bodies are mystic perhaps because time is based on the motion and celestial harmony of the spheres. For the large picture of cosmic biblical iconography that underlies images like these, see Demaray, *Cosmos*.

[64]The four sublunary elements—earth, air, fire, and water—are pictured as being the first-born of nature; thus they are connected with the bringing of order out of chaos in Book 7. The four of them move in a circle composed of the four (the number may have mystical significance), which is a perpetual motion machine embodying the "Grateful vicissitude" of 6.8. The ceaseless change of the elements in combination keeps the universe productive.

[65]Since "dusky" has as its primary meaning in the *OED* "Somewhat black or dark in colour," Milton seems to be differentiating between mists that are black and those that are gray. He may also be trying to establish the prelapsarian (unfallen) goodness of mists and exhalations, as opposed to those mists and fogs thought in the seventeenth century to bring disease and evil spirits by night.

[66]The word was spelled "Breath" in *1667*, then corrected in the 1668 *Errata*.

[67]As in the angelic song in Book 3.372–415, Milton himself or the Epic Voice has joined in the prayer.

[68]The ending of the song should indicate to the reader that Adam and Eve, even before learning of the War in Heaven, are innately aware of what evil is or how it might be concealed in an apparent good (as with evening darkness and mist). As Fowler points out (205–19n), it may also allude to the Collect for the Eighth Sunday after Trinity, which begins (in the 1559 text) "O God, whose providence is never deceived: We humbly beseech thee, that thou wilt put away from us all hurtful things, and give us those things which are profitable for us; through Christ our Lord." If Milton is remembering the ritual of the *Book of Common Prayer*, he is honoring the ceremony of the church against which the many sects and political factions of Puritans had revolted. One should not ignore the fact that Milton was buried with Church of England ceremonies.

So pray'd they innocent,[69] and to thir thoughts
Firm peace recoverd soon and wonted calm.   210
On to thir mornings rural work they haste
Among sweet dewes and flours; where any row
Of Fruit-trees overwoodie reachd too farr
Thir pamperd boughes,[70] and needed hands to check
Fruitless imbraces: or they led the Vine   215
To wed her Elm; she spous'd about him twines
Her mariageable arms, and with her brings
Her dowr th' adopted Clusters, to adorn
His barren leaves.[71] Them thus imploid beheld
With pittie Heav'ns high King, and to him call'd   220
Raphael, the sociable Spirit, that deign'd
To travel with *Tobias*, and secur'd
His marriage with the seaventimes-wedded Maid.[72]
    Raphael, said hee, thou hear'st what stir on Earth
Satan from Hell scap't° through the darksom Gulf   ESCAPED   225
Hath raisd in Paradise, and how disturbd
This night the human pair, how he designes
In them at once to ruin all mankind.
Go therefore, half this day as friend with friend
Converse with *Adam*, in what Bowre or shade   230
Thou find'st him from the heat of Noon retir'd,
To respit° his day-labour with repast,   REPAY
Or with repose; and such discourse bring on,
As may advise him of his happie state,
Happiness in his power left free to will,   235
Left to his own free Will, his Will though free,
Yet mutable; whence warne him to beware
He swerve not too secure:[73] tell him withall°   IN ADDITION
His danger, and from whom, what enemie
Late falln himself from Heav'n, is plotting now   240
The fall of others from like state of bliss;
By violence, no, for that shall be withstood,
But by deceit and lies; this let him know,
Least wilfully transgressing he pretend

---

[69]As if the knowledge of evil taints those who have it, Milton causes the Epic Voice to comment that the prayer of Adam and Eve is innocent, just as he will remind us that Eve, after having had the argument with Adam in Book 9, leaves him "yet sinless" (659). Similarly, when Adam asks Raphael for information about the composition of the universe not given him at birth, he is described as "yet sinless" (7.61).

[70]The fruit trees apparently have too many branches to bear fruit easily and hence are overly woody and need pruning; probably the boughs are pampered in the sense of being leafy or vine-like (compare the French *pampre*, vine branch or shoot, and Latin *pampinus*, tendril or young shoot of a vine).

[71]The topos or image of the vine marrying the elm, still present in the proverbial "clinging vine," is so popular in Milton's era that examples could be quoted infinitely. See Todd H. Sammons, "'As the Vine Curls Her Tendrils': Marriage Topos and Erotic Countertopos in *Paradise Lost*," *Milton Quarterly* 20 (1986): 117–27. Milton uses the image again in *Of Reformation* (Yale 1: 554) to exemplify the marriage between worldly goods and the medieval church. The image once again reinforces the concept of fruitful sexuality in the natural world: marriage is a natural state for trees, animals, and humankind. The image of the married Adam and Eve helping to domesticate and marry vine and elm (even including their dowry, the clusters of fruit) is touching to God, and evokes uncondescending pity.

[72]Milton remembers one of the few stories dealing with easy congress between angel and man, that of Raphael and Tobias in the apocryphal book of Tobit. See the note at 4.171, which discusses the seven disastrous previous marriages of Tobias's bride-to-be, Sarah. The name Raphael means "Health of God" in Hebrew, and Milton's notion of the friendly nature of the archangel seems derived from the account in Tobit.

[73]Compare the phrase "Proudly secure, yet liable to fall" in *Samson Agonistes* 55. Since humankind was created sufficient to have stood, "It follows, then, that if he received any additional commands, whether about the tree of knowledge or about marriage, these had nothing to do with the law of nature, which is itself sufficient to teach whatever is in accord with right reason (i.e., whatever is intrinsically good)" (*On Christian Doctrine* 1.10; Yale 6: 353). Adam, in other words, already has the power within himself to resist evil; thus Raphael's visit is merely an additional warning. Compare 3.96–125 above.

Surprisal, unadmonisht, unforewarnd.[74]   245
    So spake th' Eternal Father, and fulfilld
All Justice: nor delaid the winged Saint[75]
After his charge° receivd; but from among   ORDER, MISSION
Thousand Celestial Ardors,[76] where he stood
Vaild with his gorgeous wings, up springing light   250
Flew through the midst of Heav'n; th' angelic Quires
On each hand parting, to his speed gave way
Through all th' Empyreal[77] road; till at the Gate
Of Heav'n arriv'd, the gate self-opend wide
On golden Hinges turning, as by work   255
Divine the sov'ran Architect had fram'd.[78]
From hence, no cloud, or, to obstruct his sight,
Starr interpos'd, however small he sees,
Not unconform to the other shining Globes,
Earth and the Gard'n of God, with Cedars crownd   260
Above all Hills. As when by night the Glass
Of *Galileo*, less assur'd, observes
Imagind Lands and Regions in the Moon:[79]
Or Pilot from amidst the *Cyclades*
Delos or *Samos*[80] first appeering kenns°   DISCERNS   265
A cloudy spot. Down thither prone in flight[81]
He speeds, and through the vast Ethereal Skie[82]
Sailes between worlds and worlds, with steddie wing
Now on the polar windes, then with quick Fann
Winnows the buxom Air;[83] till within soare[84]   270
Of Towring Eagles, to all the Fowles he seems
A *Phœnix*, gaz'd by all, as that sole Bird
When to enshrine his reliques in the Sun's

[74]Raphael will have "render[ed] Man inexcusable" (Argument) by informing him of the present danger.

[75]The word "saint" in Milton's usage can mean "angel," as in Deuteronomy 33.2, "ten thousands of saints," or "the elect," meaning anyone chosen by God for eternal salvation.

[76]"After having received his order, Raphael, from among the thousands of angels burning with zeal, bounded forward." "Ardors" here may stand for Raphael's "flames" (compare the Latin adjective *ardens*, "burning"), or they may, as Thyer suggested (Todd, 249n), stand for the angels surrounding Raphael, since "Ardors" is also an acceptable translation of "Seraphim." Angels were thought to be equipped with up to six pairs of multicolored wings, as in Ezekiel 25.20 or 1 Kings 6.27, and especially Isaiah 6.2.

[77]The same as "Empyrean," the adjective form of the noun meaning "the highest heaven, that composed of pure fire." Since the word was derived from a Greek adjective meaning "fiery," it carries on the imagery of "Ardors" above. Accented on the second syllable and presumably pronounced differently from "imperial."

[78]One role of God frequently discussed by humanists in the Renaissance was as *deus artifex*, or "God the skilled artisan." As Prime Mover, God is responsible for setting the universe in motion. We have already seen God in the role of gardener (see also 260 below), but here He is responsible for making an ingenious, self-opening gate (as if part of the nature of God were imitated by the cleverest of craftspeople such as Leonardo Da Vinci or Michelangelo). In earlier states of *1667* the next line is indented and the comma after "cloud" omitted; what was apparently an error in starting a new paragraph was rectified in later states and not repeated in *1674*, which was set from the later state of *1667*.

[79]This second image of Galileo is not at all positive, since his telescope is pictured as "less assur'd" and observes only "Imagind Lands and Regions." It is as if the efforts of man at astronomy will never measure up to those of God, just as the eyesight of God will always be more assured.

[80]A "pilot" is a naval navigator, in this case sailing among the circular group of Aegean islands known as the Cyclades (derived from the Greek word for circle), to the island of Delos, birthplace of Apollo and Diana and thought to be floating (10.296), or to Samos, which is not in the same cluster of islands but off the coast of Asia Minor. The pilot is pictured as first recognizing one or another of the islands by interpretation of the clouds above them. It might make the syntax easier if a modern reader imagines commas after "Cyclades" and "appeering." Fowler (5.264–66n) points out that Raphael is compared with a navigator, whereas Satan is compared with a trader, though the god Mercury, to whom Raphael is later compared, is the god of merchants.

[81]"Flying in a downward incline."

[82]The ethereal sky would be out of what we would call Earth's atmosphere, in the region of ether, not air. The worlds he is sailing between could be planets or moons.

[83]"With a quick motion of his wing ('fann') he sifts through the yielding air."

[84]Within the "altitude attained in soaring" (*OED* "soar" as noun, 1).

Bright Temple, to *Ægyptian Theb's* he flies.[85]
At once on th' Eastern cliff of Paradise   275
He lights, and to his proper shape returns
A Seraph wingd;[86] six wings he wore, to shade
His lineaments Divine; the pair that clad
Each shoulder broad, came mantling o're his brest
With regal Ornament;[87] the middle pair   280
Girt like a Starrie Zone° his waste, and round   BELT
Skirted his loines and thighes with downie Gold
And colours dipt in Heav'n; the third his feet
Shaddowd from either heele with featherd maile
Skie-tinctur'd grain. Like *Maia's* son he stood,[88]   285
And shook his Plumes, that Heav'nly fragrance filld
The circuit wide. Strait knew him all the Bands
Of Angels under watch; and to his state,
And to his message° high in honour rise;   ERRAND, MISSION
For on som message high they guessd him bound.   290
Thir glittering Tents he passd, and now is come
Into the blissful field, through Groves of Myrrhe,
And flouring Odours, Cassia, Nard, and Balme;[89]
A Wilderness of sweets; for Nature here
Wantond[90] as in her prime, and plaid at will   295

---

[85]Both editions spell the name "*Phœnix*," a variant listed in the *OED*. The phoenix was the legendary bird that made its own funeral pyre out of various aromatic spices and then rose as a fledgling out of the ashes every 500 years, an emblem of self-contained and regenerated life or of the Resurrection. The fledgling phoenix was supposed, according to Ovid, to fly to Heliopolis, the city of the sun, to deposit its relics at the temple of Apollo (*Metamorphoses* 15.391-407). Herodotus adds the detail about Thebes (*History* 2.73). The bird was supposed to resemble an eagle but to contain both sexes within itself: thus it is androgynous (or hermaphroditic) like Milton's angels. The motto "Life to me is death" was applied to the emblem of the phoenix as illustrated by Cesare Ripa. Compare other uses of the phoenix in "*Epitaphium Damonis*" 187 and in *Samson Agonistes* 1699-1707, where Samson in his self-immolation is compared to the phoenix, a "she" whose "fame survives, / A secular bird ages of lives" (1706-07). Milton seems to be comparing Raphael, as he appears to birds flying alongside him, to a phoenix, but the implied comparison may be to the eternal life of the angels, to their wingedness, or to their androgyny.

[86]If Raphael returns to his own normal shape (his "proper shape") after he alights, then the angelic wings described are symbolic. The seraphim described in Isaiah 6.2 have three pairs of wings, two of which are used to cover their face, two to cover their feet, and two to fly. Apparently Milton is conflating Pliny's or Herodotus's description of the phoenix with Isaiah's description of angels, since the wings' coloration and their downy texture seem to be derived from the *Natural History* 10.2, or from Herodotus 2.73: "he [the phoenix is masculine in his account] has gold on his wings, which are otherwise mostly red, and the outline and size of him are likest to an eagle" (trans. David Grene [Chicago: U of Chicago P, 1987]: 162).

[87]Since purple is the color associated with royalty, the pair of wings that mantle and ornament Raphael's chest seem to be of that color; like the night sky at times, the pair at his midsection are like a golden belt; and the pair that cover his feet with what appears to be a feathery chainmail is the color of the sky in daytime. The wings of full-sized angels (as compared to the miniaturized cherubim or *putti* usually seen) in Renaissance paintings were often variegated in rainbow colors, like a Joseph's coat (see Genesis 37.3); Milton seems to have something like that in mind, since each wing has "colours" (283).

[88]Maia was one of the daughters of Atlas, and as such she was not only a member of the Atlantides but one of the Hesperides, the keepers of Atlas's famous garden where the golden apples sought by Hercules were kept. After death she and her sisters became the Pleiades, the bright constellation, and, because Maia was mated to Jupiter and the union produced Mercury, she was the brightest of the stars in the group. Her son Mercury foreshadows the angel Raphael because he has a winged cap and winged feet. Other angels such as Gabriel in Fairfax's translation of *Jerusalem Delivered* (1.14) shook the dew off their their wings upon landing, but editors have not yet located a source for wings imbued with heavenly fragrance (but see Francelia Butler, "The Holy Spirit and Odors in *Paradise Lost*," *Milton Newsletter* 3 [1969]: 65-69). The fragrance here may have something to do with the other angels' recognition of Raphael: they know him by his heavenly smell. The angelic fragrance also compares with the pleasant odors Raphael in turn experiences in Eden.

[89]Raphael passes the tents of the angels and comes into the Christian equivalent of the Greek Elysian fields, the fields where the souls of the virtuous dead went for a life of eternal pleasure. The vegetation all along his path is biblical. Cassia is a cinnamon-like spice used in preparation for the holy oil used to anoint the Tabernacle in Exodus 30.24; cassia and nard (or spikenard), the precious ointment used to anoint Christ's head in preparation for death in Mark 14.3, were often associated, as in *Comus* 991. Balm we have seen before, but in association with Satan (23 above, and 4.159, 248). What seems most important here is the sweet odor that all the plants put forth.

[90]The sign or signal buried in the word "Wantond" seems to be that Nature can wanton while still having "Virgin Fancies," without becoming guilty or promiscuous, and the adjective form seems again to be innocent in Eve's "wanton ringlets" (4.306). Wantoning here seems to lead to fecundity, which also is innocent. There seems to be a connection between Nature pouring forth sweets and the "mounted Sun" shooting "fervid Raies to warme / Earths inmost womb." Nature before the Fall is innocently but perpetually sexual and fecund. See Joseph Summers, "The Two Great Sexes," in *The Muse's Method* 87-111. The phrase "Wilde above Rule or Art" seems also to represent good nature before it was controlled by man's suspect art or imposed rule, and not nature out of control. Nature is playing out her fantasies here: the implication is that man's art will never come close to the sweetness of the art of

Her Virgin Fancies,[91] pouring forth more sweet,
Wilde above Rule or Art;[92] enormous bliss.
Him through the spicie Forrest onward com
Adam discernd, as in the dore he sat
Of his coole Bowre,[93] while now the mounted Sun   300
Shot down direct his fervid Raies[94] to warme
Earths inmost womb, more warmth then *Adam* needs;[95]
And *Eve* within, due at her hour prepar'd
For dinner savourie fruits,[96] of taste to please
True appetite, and not disrelish thirst   305
Of nectarous draughts between, from milkie stream,[97]
Berrie or Grape: to whom thus *Adam* call'd.
     Haste hither *Eve*, and worth thy sight behold
Eastward among those Trees, what glorious shape
Comes this way moving; seems another Morn[98]   310
Ris'n on mid-noon; som great behest from Heav'n
To us perhaps he brings, and will voutsafe
This day to be our Guest. But goe with speed,
And what thy stores contain, bring forth and poure
Abundance, fit to honour and receive   315
Our Heav'nly stranger; well we may afford
Our givers thir own gifts, and large bestow
From large bestowd, where Nature multiplies
Her fertil growth, and by disburd'ning grows
More fruitful, which instructs us not to spare.[99]   320
     To whom thus *Eve*. *Adam*, earths hallowd mould,[100]
Of God inspir'd, small store[101] will serve, where store,
All seasons, ripe for use hangs on the stalk;
Save what by frugal storing firmness gains

---

nature or the bliss ("enormous" in the sense that it is beyond normal fallen experience) it brings about in the viewer.

[91]Probably more powerful than "matron" fantasies, since magical potency was more closely associated with female virginity (compare Sabrina's role with respect to the Lady's virginity in *Comus*).

[92]"More wild than human calculations or design could make them." The word "enormous" carries on the image, since it suggests "above the norm," or "irregularly large."

[93]As Fowler points out (5.299–300n), the narrative here is based on the Lord's manifestation of "three men" (the Geneva Bible marginalia read "That is, thre Angels in mans shape") to Abraham in Genesis, as "he sat in the tent door in the heat of the day" (18.1). The angels eat heartily of human food (18.8), which seems to be the source of Milton's description of Raphael's "real hunger" (437 below).

[94]The rays of the sun shine down perpendicular to Eden because it is on the equator. The adjective "fervid" suggests the heat of boiling water (Latin *fervidus*, "boiling" or "raging hot"). Some copies of *1667* have a comma after "Raies."

[95]Some copies of *1667* have "need" and omit the semicolon; the problem comes with the long line, the pressure of which seems to have squeezed the letter "s" out of "needs."

[96]Fruits (in the broader sense of "fruits of the earth") that smell and taste good.

[97]The liquids ("draughts" pronounced "drafts" as in "draught beer") that Adam and Eve drink are like nectar; "milkie" was applied to unclarified fruit juices as well as cow's milk, and "stream" again suggests the abundance of food and drink.

[98]"It [the shape] appears to be another morning."

[99]As long as Adam and Eve honor the abundance of nature and do not distort its use to include self-indulgence, as Comus does when he suggests that the abundance of nature should be used to excess (720–29), they are not in danger of sinning. Here Eve argues in favor of using "small store," or being properly frugal with household food stocks.

[100]Scholars have recently argued whether this phrase is in apposition with Adam, or instead is complement to "will serve," so that the sentence would be correctly read "small store or earths hallowd mould inspired of God will serve . . ." (see Philip J. Gallagher, "*Summa contra Pastorem et Lectorem*," *Milton Quarterly* 19 [1985]: 55), but I think it more likely that "earths hallowd mould, / Of God inspir'd" is an epithet for Adam, whose name means clay or earth ("mould") into which God breathed life (and thus is "Of God inspir'd"). The meaning still exists in popular phrases, as in the song that begins "Some people say a man is made out of mud." Since Adam is made of clay, it is appropriate he be called "mould," but respectfully.

[101]In other words, a small amount of stored food ("small store") will suffice, in a place where ample supply ("store") is available in all seasons of the year—except in the case of foods that can be improved by storage. Eve knows that some fruits and vegetables are improved for storage by drying—either to concentrate flavor, as with raisins, or to remove moisture that might cause spoilage. As Fowler wittily points out (5.324–25n), "Eve was in no position to leave such things to the servants."

To nourish, and superfluous moist consumes: 325
But I will haste and from each bough and break,[102]
Each Plant and juciest Gourd will pluck such choice
To entertain our Angel guest,[103] as hee
Beholding shall confess that here on Earth
God hath dispenst his bounties as in Heav'n.   330
   So saying, with dispatchful° looks in haste   QUICK
She turns, on hospitable thoughts intent
What choice to chuse for delicacie best,
What order, so contriv'd as not to mix
Tastes, not well joynd, inelegant, but bring   335
Taste after taste upheld with kindliest change,[104]
Bestirs her then, and from each tender stalk[105]
Whatever Earth all-bearing Mother yields[106]
In *India* East or West, or middle shoare
In *Pontus* or the *Punic* Coast, or where   340
Alcinous reign'd, fruit of all kindes, in coate,
Rough, or smooth rin'd, or bearded husk, or shell[107]
She gathers, Tribute large, and on the board
Heaps with unsparing hand; for drink the Grape
She crushes, inoffensive moust,[108] and meathes[109]   345
From many a berrie, and from sweet kernels prest
She tempers dulcet creams,[110] nor these to hold
Wants her fit vessels pure, then strews the ground
With Rose and Odours from the shrub unfum'd.[111]
Mean while our Primitive° great Sire, to meet   ORIGINAL   350
His god-like Guest, walks forth, without more train
Accompani'd then with his own compleat
Perfections, in himself was all his state,[112]
More solemn then the tedious pomp that waits

---

[102]"Each bough and each brake [copse or thicket in which fruit or vegetables might be found]."

[103]Eve gathers fruits and nuts from trees, fruit such as raspberries or hazelnuts from bushes found in "brakes" (see 4.175), and fruits growing on vines, such as melons.

[104]Compare Sonnet 20, in which Milton enumerates the pleasures of such a "neat repast" (9).

[105]She would be plucking from tender stalks in order to have the ripest fruits. The fruit is prepared so that flavor follows flavor elegantly in a pleasing succession of flavors that mirrors the "grateful vicissitude" of the natural world. Milton seems to be redefining elegant dining according to the clever use of simple foods, "*cuisine minceur.*"

[106]Again the fecundity of Mother Earth is emphasized, perhaps in order to stress the closeness between Eve and Eden. Eden's equatorial climate produces fruit like that famous throughout the known ancient or modern world. In Milton's time both east and west India, or India and the West Indies as we know them today, were famous for providing exotic spices, fruit, or vegetables in all seasons of the year. Pontus was the south shore of the Black Sea, famous for rhubarb and hazelnuts; the Punic coast would have been the coast surrounding Carthage, famous for figs; and the Homeric island of the Phæacian King Alcinous, now Corfu, alluded to again at 9.440-41, was a paradise of perennial fruit somewhere in the Mediterranean (*Odyssey* 7.113-32).

[107]An almost Linnaean classification of fruit according to covering, rough in texture as with nuts or pineapple, smooth as with apricots, bearded as with wheat, or shelled, as with most nuts.

[108]Must, or crushed grapes before the juice has fermented "offensively" into alcoholic wine. The scene associating Eve with the making of nonalcoholic beverages is ironic foreshadowing since the Fall will cause both her and Adam to become "As with new Wine intoxicated both" (9.1008).

[109]The same as "meads," though mead is a sweet wine made from honey; hence the *OED* cites this usage as transferred and poetic, meaning any one of "several made beverages" (1.b).

[110]"She delicately blends digestible sweet creams," with "digestible" implied in the word "tempers," since a perfect temperament might be achieved through a perfect balance of foods, which would in turn match a perfect balance of humors.

[111]Since no fire exists with which to "fume" or smoke herbs or aromatic leaves from shrubs, the spicy leaves ("Odours") and rose petals Eve strews on the ground are "Guiltless of fire" (9.392).

[112]The absence of a train may indicate a sexual distinction between Adam and Eve. Adam needs no "train" of attendants, whereas Eve seems normally to be "Not unattended," but waited on by a train of "Graces" (8.60-61). Adam here contains all his dignified or aristocratic appearance ("state" would be something like "dignity," derived from "estate" or "family holdings" or "position in society") in his own person: he does not need the amplification of attendance. Note, however, that the politics of not having a train would be republican, not monarchical.

On Princes, when thir rich Retinue[113] long   355
Of Horses led, and Grooms besmeard with Gold[114]
Dazles the croud, and sets them all agape.°   OPEN-MOUTHED
Neerer his presence *Adam* though not awd,
Yet with submiss° approach and reverence meek,[115]   SUBMISSIVE
As to a superior Nature, bowing low,   360
   Thus said.[116] Native of Heav'n, for other place
None can then Heav'n such glorious shape contain;
Since by descending from the Thrones above,
Those happie places thou hast deignd a while
To want,° and honour these, voutsafe with us   BE WITHOUT   365
Two onely, who yet by sov'ran gift possess
This spacious ground, in yonder shadie Bowre
To rest, and what the Garden choicest bears
To sit and taste, till this meridian° heat   NOONDAY
Be over, and the Sun more coole decline.   370
   Whom thus the Angelic Vertue[117] answerd milde.
Adam, I therefore came, nor art thou such
Created, or such place hast here to dwell,
As may not oft invite,[118] though Spirits of Heav'n
To visit thee; lead on then where thy Bowre   375
Oreshades; for these mid-hours, till Eevning rise
I have at will. So to the Silvan Lodge
They came, that like *Pomona*'s Arbour smil'd
With flourets deck't and fragrant smells; but *Eve*
Undeckt, save with her self more lovely fair   380
Then Wood-Nymph,[119] or the fairest Goddess feign'd
Of three that in Mount *Ida* naked strove,
Stood to entertain her guest from Heav'n; no vaile
Shee needed, Vertue-proof, no thought infirme
Alterd her cheek. On whom the Angel *Haile*   385
Bestowd, the holy salutation us'd
Long after to blest *Marie*, second *Eve*.[120]

---

[113]Apparently accented on the second syllable, "The usual stressing in the 16th–18th centuries" (*OED*).

[114]Presumably it is their costume that is embroidered garishly and thus "besmeard" with gold ornamentation. The usage of "besmear" is negative in *Reason of Church-government*: " . . . how they dare thus oyle over and besmear so holy an unction . . . " (Yale 1: 860).

[115]Just as Eve is submissive to Adam but not awed by him, Adam treats his superior Raphael with unawed reverence.

[116]An unusual way to begin a paragraph. "Thus said" normally would have been part of the preceding sentence and thus would have been followed, as it is on this new line, by a period.

[117]Might be meant in the generic sense of "powerful angelic being," but "Vertue" (like "Dominion" or "Power," and even "Wheel") was one of the "magnific Titles" (773 below) of angels. Since "Aquinas . . . claims that no angels above Virtues are sent to man" (West 51), perhaps Milton is giving Raphael this rank in order to permit him to visit Adam and Eve.

[118]The syntax is compressed, but the sense seems to be that Eden is naturally hospitable and inviting, even to angels.

[119]The arbor (or lodge or bower) is apparently to be thought of as Eve's domain, and much is said about her character in this passage. The arbor is decked or ornamented but she is not; she is more beautiful than a wood nymph like Pomona, indeed she is more beautiful than Venus, the most beautiful mythical ("feign'd") goddess of the three—Juno, Minerva, and Venus—all judged in the nude by Paris on Mt. Ida (see Ovid, *Heroides* 5, 16, 17). She needs no veil to enhance her nudity, since she is "Vertue-proof" in the sense that her virtue (as with that of the Lady in *Comus*) is all that is needed to protect her against evil. Her cheek is unblushing because she has no evil thoughts to cause it to be flushed, since a flush would indicate a disorder or distemper in her personality. After the Fall, "in her [Eve's] Cheek distemper flushing glowd" (9.887). Milton is also foreshadowing the comparison of Eve to Pomona in flight from Vertumnus at 9.394–95.

[120]Milton, the avowed anti-Roman Catholic, here has Raphael bestow a prelapsarian "Hail, Mary" on Eve; the title is even emphasized by the italicized "*Haile*." At the Annunciation of the second Eve, the Virgin Mary, mother of Christ, the angel Gabriel will address her with the apostrophe "Hail, thou that art hightly favoured, the Lord is with thee: blessed art thou among women" (Luke 1.28). It was a traditional typological comparison that Christ was the second or "last Adam" (1 Corinthians 15.45) and that Mary was the second Eve. Eve is mother of humankind; Mary will be mother of God. Eve is called "mother of all living" in Genesis 3.20. Before the Fall in *Paradise Lost*, she is named Eve only by Raphael and by the Epic Voice (see Leonard 36). Most commentators on Genesis noted that Eve was named only after the Fall, so that her name was often taken negatively, but "mother of all living" was

Haile Mother of Mankind, whose fruitful Womb
Shall fill the World more numerous with thy Sons
Then with these various fruits the Trees of God   390
Have heap'd this Table. Rais'd of grassie terf
Thir Table was, and mossie seats had round,[121]
And on her ample Square[122] from side to side
All *Autumn* pil'd,[123] though *Spring* and *Autumn* here
Danc'd hand in hand. A while discourse they hold;   395
No fear lest Dinner coole;[124] when thus began
Our Authour. Heav'nly stranger, please to taste
These bounties which our Nourisher,[125] from whom
All perfet good unmeasur'd out, descends,
To us for food and for delight hath caus'd   400
The Earth to yield;[126] unsavourie food perhaps
To spiritual Natures;[127] only this I know,
That one Celestial Father gives to all.
    To whom the Angel. Therefore what he gives
(Whose praise be ever sung) to man in part   405
Spiritual, may of purest Spirits be found
No ingrateful food: and food alike those pure
Intelligential° substances require   INTELLECTUAL, ANGELIC
As doth your Rational;[128] and both contain
Within them every lower facultie   410
Of sense, whereby they hear, see, smell, touch, taste,
Tasting concoct, digest, assimilate,

---

certainly not a negative title for Milton (see 4.469–75). After the Fall, the second angel who greets her, Michael, will name her in his salutation: "Haile to thee, / Eve rightly call'd, Mother of all Mankind, / Mother of all things living, since by thee / Man is to live, and all things live for Man" (11.158–61). Eve's motherhood will be one of the things that helps redeem her, since she will bear the seed that will eventually produce the Seed, or Christ. It is no metaphoric accident that her "fruitful Womb" (388) will help overcome the negative effects of eating the Fruit. Unlike many of the commentators, Milton does not distinguish between the Latin "*Ave*," "Hail," and the Hebrew "*Hevah*," or Eve. There is also a pun in Hebrew between the aspirated form of the name and the word for serpent, one which Adam will play on only after the Fall.

[121]Roy Daniells points out "While the table is of turf, the seats are covered with moss, a nice tactile differentiation, in view of what is not being worn" ("A Happy Rural Seat of Various View" 6). Since woodworking had not been invented, the table represents an earlier stage of technology.

[122]Fowler points to the square as "A shape emblematic of virtue and particularly of temperance" (5.393n), perhaps as reflected in the U.S. idiom "square deal" or, more appropriately here, "square meal." The use of the sexual pronoun "her" might indicate the Latin root of table in the feminine noun "*mensa*," but the fecundity of the table, as a metaphor, would also parallel the fecundity of female Nature.

[123]Autumn would be harvest season in the normal fallen world, but in Eden the privilege of harvest is year-round. For comparisons among the dance of the Seasons and that of the Hours or of the Graces, see Demaray, *Cosmos*.

[124]The phrase has been recited by generations of graduate students as an indication of Milton's naïveté, but it does point to the fact that the meal is vegetarian and that cooking has not yet been invented. It might also suggest that Milton's wry sense of humor surfaces here and that he should be laughed with rather than laughed at. The use of fire is also suspect as producing fallen arts; again the phrase "Guiltless of fire" (9.392) might reinforce the innocence of eating uncooked foods.

[125]The roles of God and Adam and Eve shift and intermingle: the Epic Voice calls Adam "Our Authour," meaning that he is the "general Sire" (4.144) or the "general Ancestor" (4.659) or the progenitor of humankind, yet Eve (whose father is Adam, in a sense) calls Adam her "Author and Disposer" (4.635). Here the epithet for God is "Nourisher," yet Eve is nourishing her husband, Raphael, and herself by preparing food in Paradise. Milton may be making further parallels between God and humankind in the next few lines. The Christ of Hebrews 5.8–9 is characterized as Son, author, and emblem of perfection: "Though he were a Son, yet learned he obedience by the things which he suffered; And being made perfect, he became the author of eternal salvation unto all them that obey him" (emphasis supplied).

[126]The spelling "yeild" of *1667* may or may not represent, here and elsewhere, the author's preferred spelling, regularized to the more common "yield" by the compositors of *1674*.

[127]Adam guesses that what smells good and appeals to the appetite of a human might not do so to the refined sensibilities of an angel, but Raphael will correct him.

[128]Raphael illustrates one of the most important differences between angelic and human nature: humans must use their reason to arrive at the truth, whereas angels, as pure spirits or intelligences ("Intelligential substances"), arrive at the truth intuitively or at least "They know by revelation only those things which God sees fit to show them, and they know other things by virtue of their very high intelligence . . . " (*On Christian Doctrine* 1.9; Yale 6: 347–48). Raphael speaks in terms of a ladder of creation or great chain of being in which all lower orders graduate up to or feed into higher ones.

And corporeal to incorporeal[129] turn.
For know, whatever was created, needs
To be sustaind and fed; of Elements   415
The grosser feeds the purer, Earth the Sea,
Earth and the Sea feed Air, the Air those Fires
Ethereal, and as lowest first the Moon;[130]
Whence in her visage round those spots, unpurg'd
Vapours not yet into her substance turnd.[131]   420
Nor doth the Moon no nourishment exhale
From her moist Continent to higher Orbes.
The Sun that light imparts to all, receives
From all his alimental° recompence   NUTRITIONAL
In humid exhalations, and at Even   425
Sups with the Ocean: though in Heav'n the Trees
Of life ambrosial frutage bear, and vines
Yield Nectar, though from off the boughs each Morn
We brush mellifluous Dewes, and find the ground
Cover'd with pearly grain:[132] yet God hath here   430
Varied his bounty so with new delights,
As may compare with Heaven;[133] and to taste
Think not I shall be nice.[134] So down they sat,
And to thir viands[135] fell, nor seemingly
The Angel, nor in mist, the common gloss   435
Of Theologians, but with keen dispatch
Of real hunger, and concoctive heate
To transubstantiate;[136] what redounds, transpires
Through Spirits with ease;[137] nor wonder; if by fire

---

[129]Angelic digestion can turn what had a body on earth into what does not, strictly speaking, have a body in Heaven—from corporeality to incorporeality, from flesh into spirit.

[130]The four sublunary elements are ranked as higher or lower; the lower "feed" the higher and so on up to the level of the fifth element or quintessence (see 3.716). In simple terms, earth feeds sea through erosion, sea feeds air through evaporation, air feeds fire in helping combustion, air seems to feed "exhalations" (comets) or the moon, and the sun drinks the sea. This last phenomenon is visible in the late afternoon when the sun seems to draw up water vapor. The great chain of being (see Lovejoy) is an alimentary as well as a spiritual connection.

[131]Galileo had discussed the "spots" on the moon in *Sidereus Nuncius* (Venice, 1610) as features of the lunar landscape (mountains, really) rather than as planetary exhalations, but here Raphael espouses the older theory. The subject was still a debatable, and politicized, issue. For a perceptive account of Galileo's trial for heresy (principally for beliefs about atomism and its effects on the Host during Communion), see Pietro Redondi, *Galileo Heretic* (Princeton: Princeton UP, 1987).

[132]Raphael describes the biblical phenomenon of manna, what seemed to be a nourishing form of sweet ("mellifluous" means "as sweet as honey") congealed dew that fed the Israelites in the desert, as occurring in Heaven as well. Exodus 16.14 describes manna (as well as quails) as the God-sent food: "And when the dew that lay was gone up, behold, upon the face of the wilderness there lay a small round thing, as small as the hoar frost upon the ground." The Book of John develops the idea of heavenly manna in 6.31 and 58; see also Revelation 2.17. Nectar and ambrosia, traditionally the food of the Greek and Roman gods, has been mentioned before at 2.245 as food available in Heaven, again following the theory that the Greek and Roman myths offered "shadowy types" of the truth of Christianity. See Madsen, *From Shadowy Types.*

[133]The spelling "Heaven," with no elided "e," indicates that the second syllable should be pronounced and the word read as a disyllable.

[134]The word nice could mean "over-fastidious" or "over-scrupulous," as well as "discerning." See *OED* 4.c and d for some of the negative overtones, as with "delicate" or "over-refined."

[135]"Viands" mean any kind of food, though manna was sometimes taken as a kind of meat. See Jack Goldman, "Perspectives of Raphael's Meal In *Paradise Lost*, Book V," *Milton Quarterly* 11 (1977): 31-37, for the argument that the meal the angel ate might have included a variety of foods, including meat.

[136]Angels possess the power in digestion ("concoction" as in *OED* 1) further to heat and transubstantiate or transmute their food from its original form into nourishment. The word transubstantiate had theological overtones by virtue of being associated with what was supposed to be the communion wafer as it was being eaten by the faithful. The communion wafer, according to Roman Catholic commentary and general belief, was supposed to change into the literal body of Christ during the communion service, the process known as "transubstantiation." What is unusual about Milton's angelology is that angels really do eat and do not merely appear to eat. See West, *Milton* 164-69.

[137]"Whatever is excessive or superfluous in the system of angels is excreted through transpiration."

Of sooty coal the Empiric Alchimist[138]   440
Can turn, or holds it possible to turn
Metals of drossiest Ore to perfet Gold
As from the Mine. Mean while at Table *Eve*
Ministerd naked, and thir flowing cups
With pleasant liquors crown'd:° O innocence   TOPPED OFF   445
Deserving Paradise! if ever, then,
Then had the Sons of God excuse to have bin
Enamour'd at that sight;[139] but in those hearts
Love unlibidinous reign'd, nor jealousie
Was understood, the injur'd Lovers Hell.   450
    Thus when with meaths[140] and drinks they had suffic'd,
Not burd'nd Nature,[141] sudden mind arose
In *Adam*, not to let th' occasion pass
Given him by this great Conference to know
Of things above his World, and of thir being   455
Who dwell in Heav'n, whose excellence he saw
Transcend his own so farr, whose radiant forms
Divine effulgence,[142] whose high Power so far
Exceeded human, and his wary speech[143]
Thus to th' Empyreal Minister[144] he fram'd.   460
    Inhabitant with God,[145] now know I well
Thy favour, in this honour done to man,
Under whose lowly roof thou hast voutsaf't
To enter, and these earthly fruits to taste,
Food not of Angels, yet accepted so,   465
As that more willingly thou couldst not seem
At Heav'ns high feasts to have fed: yet what compare?
    To whom the winged Hierarch repli'd.[146]
O *Adam*, one Almightie is, from whom
All things proceed, and up to him return,   470
If not deprav'd from good, created all

---

[138]Empiric alchemists were lower-order alchemists, "hacks" at their trade, as opposed to adept or grand alchemists. See Thomas, *Religion*. Milton expresses some skepticism about all alchemy in the phrase "holds it possible to turn." Nevertheless, the goal of all alchemists was to turn a "base metal" such as lead into gold so pure it might have just come from the mine.

[139]A curious foreshadowing of the story of the Sons of God and Daughters of Men that is shown to Adam by Michael after the Fall (11.621-22), since Raphael would certainly have been "unlibidinous," or "unlustful." Lurking in the background in Eden, however, is Satan, whose desire for the bodily happiness of Adam and Eve, and jealousy of the sensual happiness of Adam, is palpable. Thus Satan will be pictured as a kind of "injured lover," in that he will never win Eve.

[140]The word is printed "meats" in *1674*. John Shawcross writes, via e-mail, "I would now suggest that the printer (or the copyist of the copy used) made an error and what was meant was 'meaths.' See V.345. I think it is a reprise of lines 341-47. Of course, 'meats' could refer to the 'sweet kernels' or the 'fruit . . . in coate . . . or bearded husk, or shell.' It seems most curious that Milton would have used 'meats' here" (11 June 1997). I accept his reading.

[141]The rule of "nothing to excess" is in effect in Paradise, so that when Adam and Eve and Raphael eat, they do not tax nature either by taking too much from it or overburdening their bodies by taking in too much.

[142]"Radiation," but with the theological overtones of the Son as effulgence of the Father, who is light (see 6.680).

[143]Adam's question is not "wary" in the sense of "cunning"; instead, it might be described as "respectful" or "cautious," because Adam in his questioning seeks knowledge which might be unnecessary for human beings to know (since knowledge of some natural phenomena is unnecessary for humans to understand).

[144]"Ministering or caretaking angel from the Empyrean or Empyreal sphere."

[145]"You who live with God."

[146]Raphael, described with the dignified epithet "winged Hierarch" (the orders of angels were formally classified in Milton's era as a "hierarchy"), turns from the subject of angelic digestion to the more important interrelationships between created beings and God. In the incessant flow pictured as issuing to and from God, all creatures will return to God if they are not alienated by choosing evil and thereby depriving themselves of returning to his presence. Since Milton believed that all matter was created out of God's substance ("first matter"), the return of created matter to its origin (but not to unformed chaos) seems natural and inevitable, if sin does not intervene. This is perhaps the fullest statement in English literature of the chain of being, or, as Milton calls it in 509 below, the "scale of Nature." See Curry for a full treatment of the subject, and Hunter, "Milton's Power of Matter," in *Descent*.

Such to perfection, one first matter all,
Indu'd with various forms various degrees
Of substance, and in things that live, of life;
But more refin'd, more spiritous, and pure,
As neerer to him plac't or neerer tending   475
Each in thir several active Sphears assignd,
Till body up to spirit work, in bounds
Proportiond to each kind. So from the root
Springs lighter the green stalk, from thence the leaves   480
More aerie, last the bright consummate° floure   COMPLETE, PERFECT
Spirits odorous breathes: flours and thir fruit
Mans nourishment, by gradual scale sublim'd[147]
To vital Spirits aspire, to animal,
To intellectual, give both life and sense,   485
Fansie and understanding, whence the Soule
Reason receives, and reason is her being,[148]
Discursive, or Intuitive; discourse
Is oftest yours, the latter most is ours,
Differing but in degree, of kind the same.[149]   490
Wonder not then, what God for you saw good
If I refuse not, but convert, as you,
To proper substance; time may come when men
With Angels may participate, and find
No inconvenient Diet, nor too light Fare: 495
And from these corporal nutriments perhaps
Your bodies may at last turn all to Spirit,
Improv'd by tract of time, and wingd ascend
Ethereal, as wee, or may at choice
Here or in Heav'nly Paradises dwell;   500
If ye be found obedient, and retain
Unalterably firm his love entire
Whose progenie you are.[150] Mean while enjoy
Your fill what happiness this happie state
Can comprehend, incapable of more.   505
     To whom the Patriarch of mankind repli'd.[151]
O favourable spirit, propitious° guest,   GRACIOUS
Well hast thou taught the way that might direct
Our knowledge, and the scale of Nature[152] set
From center to circumference, whereon   510

---

[147]An alchemical term, meaning roughly "transmuted into a higher life form by burning"; "sublimation" is defined as "converting a solid substance by means of heat into vapour" (*OED* 1). The image of nature is one of a living tree, an organism, fully cooperating with the good earth beneath and the good air above, epitomized in the pleasant odors that characterize plant life in Paradise. The word "aerie" is positive, and a "consummate floure" is a perfect one.

[148]"Reason is the distinguishing characteristic of the soul."

[149]Angels are supposed to reason intuitively, and therefore much more quickly, than are human beings. "For natural knowledge, at least, the angel does not require discourse: he knows perfectly what is in the sphere of his understanding, without composition or division of things or inferring one of another" (West 47, summarizing Aquinas). Milton, however, by using "oftest" and "most" here, allows both angel and humankind at least occasional discursive and intuitive thinking: angels sometimes are discursive, humans sometimes intuitive.

[150]Raphael has explained that the process of angels' eating human food is analogous to humans' participating, eventually, in spiritual nature. If humankind were to remain obedient, they could have easy discourse with angels as equals. Humans might eventually assume enough of angelic nature even to grow wings and with them ascend to the ethereal regions of Heaven.

[151]Fletcher is undoubtedly correct: the comma printed here in *1674* is "foul case" (a comma got into the case where periods were supposed to be) and should be replaced by the period almost always used before a direct quotation.

[152]Milton pictures nature as a ladder (as in Italian *scala*) stretching from the center of the cosmos (God) and extending outward throughout creation to a place where human beings, by contemplation, might climb toward God.

In contemplation of created things
By steps we may ascend to God. But say,
What meant that caution joind, *if ye be found*
Obedient?[153] can we want° obedience then   LACK
To him, or possibly his love desert   515
Who formd us from the dust,[154] and plac'd us here
Full to the utmost measure of what bliss
Human desires can seek or apprehend?
　　To whom the Angel. Son of Heav'n and Earth,
Attend:° That thou art happie, owe to God;   LISTEN, PAY ATTENTION   520
That thou continu'st such, owe to thy self,
That is, to thy obedience; therein stand.
This was that caution giv'n thee; be advis'd.
God made thee perfet, not immutable;
And good he made thee, but to persevere   525
He left it in thy power, ordaind thy will
By nature free, not over-rul'd by Fate
Inextricable, or strict necessity;[155]
Our voluntarie service he requires,
Not our necessitated, such with him   530
Findes no acceptance, nor can find, for how
Can hearts, not free, be tri'd whether they serve
Willing or no, who will but what they must
By Destinie, and can no other choose?
My self and all th' Angelic Host that stand   535
In sight of God enthron'd, our happie state
Hold, as you yours, while our obedience holds;
On other surety none; freely we serve,[156]
Because wee freely love, as in our will
To love or not; in this we stand or fall: 540
And som are fall'n, to disobedience fall'n,
And so from Heav'n to deepest Hell; O fall
From what high state of bliss into what woe![157]
　　To whom our great Progenitor. Thy words
Attentive, and with more delighted eare,   545
Divine instructer,[158] I have heard, then when
Cherubic Songs by night from neighbouring Hills
Aereal Music[159] send: nor knew I not

---

[153]The extremely important quotation is emphasized by italics in both the 1667 and 1674 editions, as with "*Wo to the inhabitants on Earth*" (4.5).

[154]The "clay" out of which Adam was formed often was extended metaphorically to become the "dust" to which all humankind were supposed to return in death. Compare Milton's "Upon the Circumcision": "For we by rightful doom remediless / Were lost in death, till he that dwelt above / High-thron'd in secret bliss, for us frail dust / Emptied his glory, ev'n to nakedness" (17–20). Raphael will quickly remind Adam that he is the son both of Heaven and Earth in his epithet below.

[155]Raphael outlines Milton's beliefs about the freedom of human will. Though Adam and Eve are created good and perfect in themselves and not at all deficient in understanding, they are nevertheless mutable or changeable, and as such liable to fall, if they disobey God. They love God and obey Him freely. Otherwise, they would be puppet-like and the universe ruled by fate and necessity (as in what Milton considered pagan beliefs) rather than by a providential God. For the state of Adam and Eve before the Fall, see *On Christian Doctrine* 1.10, Yale 6: 351–53. Before the creation of Adam and Eve, the angels have given them an example of freely choosing good voluntary service to God or evil disobedience.

[156]*1667* has a period here, obviously corrected to the comma in *1674*.

[157]A rare apostrophe, for the theory of which see Michael R. G. Spiller, "'Per Chiamare e Per Destare': Apostrophe in Milton's Sonnets," in *Milton in Italy: Contexts, Images, Contradictions*, ed. Mario DiCesare (Binghamton, NY: MRTS, 1991): 477–88.

[158]Adam realizes that Raphael is a kind of schoolmaster sent by God and that what he has been hearing about freedom and disobedience is the best kind of instruction on human behavior. He does not need to be told, however, that he is free to fall, since he knows that innately.

[159]Adam has described hearing the angelic guards singing at 4.680–88.

To be both will and deed created free;
Yet that we never shall forget to love   550
Our maker, and obey him whose command
Single,[160] is yet so just, my constant thoughts
Assur'd me, and still assure: though what thou tellst
Hath past in Heav'n, som doubt within me move,
But more desire to hear, if thou consent,   555
The full relation,° which must needs be strange,   NARRATION, STORY
Worthy of Sacred silence[161] to be heard;
And we have yet large day,[162] for scarce the Sun
Hath finisht half his journey, and scarce begins
His other half in the great Zone of Heav'n.   560
          Thus *Adam* made request, and *Raphael*
After short pause assenting, thus began.
          High matter thou injoinst me, O prime of men,
Sad task[163] and hard, for how shall I relate
To human sense th' invisible exploits   565
Of warring Spirits; how without remorse
The ruin of so many glorious once
And perfet while they stood; how last unfould°
The secrets of another world, perhaps   REVEAL
Not lawful to reveal?[164] yet for thy good   570
This is dispenc't, and what surmounts the reach
Of human sense, I shall delineate so,
By lik'ning spiritual to corporal forms,
As may express them best, though what if Earth
Be but the shadow of Heav'n, and things therein   575
Each to other like, more then on earth is thought?[165]

[Handwritten marginal note: Tell me about the War. Signals the knowledge of the Forbidden Tree. Is it better not to know.]

---

[160]The single commandment to unfallen man mentioned in Genesis 3.3 is not to eat of the fruit of the Tree of Knowledge of Good and Evil. Milton here and elsewhere expresses the ease of obeying just one command; perhaps a contrast is implied between the one simple and easy command and the Ten Commandments, which were designed for fallen humankind and thus took the form of a much more complicated contract. As Fowler comments, having the one command "simplifies the issue before man into a direct choice between eating obediently and eating disobediently," even though eating itself is only a "neutral act" (5.496–500n).

[161]The word "strange" implies that what Adam asks Raphael to relate will be wonderful. Commentators since Richardson have pointed out an allusion to Horace, *Odes* 2.13, in which Horace, thinking of death, contemplates the singing in Hades of Sappho and Alcaeus, heard reverently. Perhaps, as Fowler notes (5.557n), Milton's fit audience would remember that the next few verses described the vulgar shades in Hades asking for stories of tyranny and war.

[162]That is, "we have the greatest part of the day [really rather more than a day, according to *OED large* A.II.5b] remaining to us." Adam is constantly in the process of stretching time to get as much out of Raphael's visit as he can; one gets the impression that he is discovering all he can of what Raphael knows, and treasuring every tidbit. Raphael's "short pause" may indicate that he has noticed Adam's exaggeration, or it may indicate that Adam has asked him to tell a story difficult to narrate.

[163]Raphael as narrator speaks in the same phrase that Milton uses to describe his "Sad task" in 9.13, of telling of the Fall. Raphael here becomes an epic narrator, telling a story within the epic poet's narrative. It was an epic convention for important characters to relate stories of earlier events, what today would be called a "flashback," as when Odysseus tells of his exploits while he is in the Phaeacian court in *Odyssey* 10, or when Aeneas tells of his past history to Dido in *Aeneid* 2. Milton significantly allows two angels, Raphael and Michael, to present long narratives, and he allows both Adam and Eve separately to tell the stories of their creation. As a narrative device, secondary narrators help relieve the potential monotony of having only one epic voice and they help lend credibility to the whole story by adding other dimensions and points of view.

[164]Raphael must be cautious in telling the story of the War in Heaven, because Adam may not be able to understand events that happened in what might be called another dimension of time and space and because what he describes may encroach on knowledge forbidden to Adam and Eve. Milton is perhaps also echoing Aeneas's fear of disclosing secrets of the underworld in *Aeneid* 6.266.

[165]Raphael will accommodate his narrative of the War in Heaven to Adam's understanding, by translating spiritual into corporeal forms. We have entered the world of typology, in which earthly "shadows," as with the allegory of Plato's cave, represent pale reflections of heavenly types. As Milton writes in *On Christian Doctrine*, "God, as he really is, is far beyond man's imagination" (1.2; Yale 6: 133). In his search for truth, man "at first would most easily discern the shadows and, after that, the likenesses or reflections in water of men and other things, and later, the things themselves, and from these he would go on to contemplate the appearances in the heavens and heaven itself, more easily by night, looking at the light of the stars and the moon, than by day the sun and the sun's light. . . . so finally, . . . he would be able to look upon the sun itself and see its true nature, not by reflections in water or phantasms of it in an alien setting, but in and by itself in its own place" (*Republic* 7.516 in *Plato*, ed. Edith Hamilton: 748).

As yet this world was not,[166] and *Chaos* wilde
Reignd where these Heav'ns now rowl, where Earth now rests
Upon her Center pois'd, when on a day
(For Time, though in Eternitie, appli'd
To motion, measures all things durable   580
By present, past, and future) on such day
As Heav'ns great Year[167] brings forth, th' Empyreal Host
Of Angels by Imperial[168] summons call'd,
Innumerable before th' Almighties Throne   585
Forthwith from all the ends of Heav'n appeerd
Under thir Hierarchs in orders bright[169]
Ten thousand thousand Ensignes high advanc'd,
Standards, and Gonfalons[170] twixt Van and Reare
Streame in the Aire, and for distinction serve   590
Of Hierarchies, of Orders, and Degrees;
Or in thir glittering Tissues° bear imblaz'd   FLAGS
Holy Memorials, acts of Zeale and Love
Recorded eminent.[171] Thus when in Orbes
Of circuit inexpressible[172] they stood,   595
Orb within Orb, the Father infinite,
By whom in bliss imbosom'd[173] sat the Son,
Amidst as from a flaming Mount, whose top[174]
Brightness had made invisible,[175] thus spake.
 Hear all ye Angels, Progenie of Light,   600
Thrones, Dominations, Princedoms, Vertues, Powers,[176]
Hear my Decree,[177] which unrevok't shall stand.

---

[166]The earliest point of time described in *Paradise Lost*. According to Milton's chronology, the Earth is not created until after the Fall of the Angels, because it is created as home to the beings who will eventually take the place of the fallen angels in Heaven. "There is certainly no reason why we should conform to the popular belief that motion and time, which is the measure of motion, could not, according to our concepts of 'before' and 'after,' have existed before this world was made. For Aristotle, who taught that motion and time are inherent only in this world, asserted, nevertheless, that this world was eternal" (*On Christian Doctrine* 1.7; Yale 6: 313–14).

[167]The "Great Year" or "Platonic Great Year" was thought to be the beginning of a cycle during which all heavenly bodies would return to the position they were in during creation. The day of the elevation of the Son, therefore, is the day on which all time begins.

[168]Milton associates the Empyreal angels, those who live in the Empyrean, or the highest of heavens, with the imperial summons by God acting as commander of the celestial regions.

[169]Fowler recommends a period at this point (5.587n), but I see no need for one, since the verb "appeerd" seems to govern the "Ten thousand thousand Ensignes." For the enumeration of angels by tens, see Daniel 7.10, a vision in which God as the Ancient of Days is seen attended by "thousand thousands" and "ten thousand times ten thousand." The vision seemed to seventeenth-century Protestant commentators to show the progress of the Greek and Roman empires from justice toward tyranny: the thrones around the Ancient of Days were supposed to be "the places where God and his Angels shulde come to judge these monarchies, which judgement should beginne at the first comming of Christ" (marginal note, Daniel 7.9 in the Geneva Bible, 1560 ed.).

[170]The angelic ensigns are carrying standards anchored at vertical points or gonfalons, on a horizontal beam. "Van" is the vanguard or section of troops stationed at the front of the army formation.

[171]At the fall of the angels, heraldry apparently declined, and the acts of divine zeal and love became the devices of "Seraphic arms and Trophies" on brilliantly colored banners displayed at 1.539.

[172]The circuits of angels in the three-dimensional forms of orbs are so complex and their forms so full of mystery that they cannot be described.

[173]The idiom of the Authorized Version, "in his bosom" or "of his bosom," suggests particular trust or intimacy. Compare 3.169, "Son of my bosom."

[174]*1674* corrects the "whoseop" of *1667*, which had been in turn corrected in the *Errata* of that edition.

[175]Contrast invisible brightness here with "darkness visible" (1.63) in Hell. God's "Skirts" are also "Dark with excessive bright" at 3.380.

[176]A list of the principal orders of angels, following the "thrones, or dominions, or principalities, or powers" of Colossians 1.16, a text used not only to prove the existence of angels but to establish their having been created by Christ. Milton "uses the terms of rank so fluidly that no one has been able to organize his use into a consistent pattern" (West 134); thus "Dominions" might be interchangeable with "Dominations."

[177]An entire chapter of *On Christian Doctrine* is devoted to God's decrees, general or special. "God's first and most excellent SPECIAL DECREE of all concerns HIS SON: primarily by virtue of this he is called FATHER" (1.3; Yale 6: 166), and Psalm 2.7 is cited: "I shall declare the decree: Jehova said to me, You are my son I have begotten you today." From various biblical passages, Milton concludes "it appears that the Son of God was begotten by a decree of the Father" (167). "Begot" has here a special double meaning. "Production of the Son" is the first and literal definition. But second, the phrase of Psalm 2, "This day I have begotten thee," on which this passage is based, is interpreted metaphorically in Acts 13.33, Hebrews 1.5 and 5.5, and 2 Peter 1.17 as the exaltation of the Son. This in turn can be adduced to reveal the superiority of the Son to the angels, as Milton employs it here, or it may be interpreted at the resurrection. Hunter, in "The War in Heaven," has used the latter meanings to interpret the War in Heaven as the Son's victory over

This day I have begot whom I declare
My onely Son, and on this holy Hill
Him have anointed, whom ye now behold   605
At my right hand; your Head I him appoint;
And by my Self have sworn to him shall bow
All knees in Heav'n, and shall confess him Lord:
Under his great Vice-gerent Reign abide
United as one individual Soule   610
For ever happie: him who disobeyes
Mee disobeyes, breaks union, and that day
Cast out from God and blessed vision, falls
Into utter darkness, deep ingulft, his place
Ordain'd without redemption, without end.   615
    So spake th' Omnipotent, and with his words
All seemd well pleas'd, all seem'd, but were not all.[178]
That day, as other solemn dayes, they spent
In song and dance about the sacred Hill,
Mystical dance,[179] which yonder starrie Spheare   620
Of Planets and of fixt in all her Wheeles
Resembles nearest, mazes intricate,
Eccentric, intervolv'd, yet regular
Then most, when most irregular they seem,
And in thir motions harmonie Divine   625
So smooths her charming tones, that Gods own ear
Listens delighted. Eevning now approach'd
(For wee[180] have also our Eevning and our Morn,
Wee ours for change delectable, not need)
Forthwith from dance to sweet repast they turn   630
Desirous;[181] all in Circles as they stood,
Tables are set, and on a sudden pil'd
With Angels Food, and rubied Nectar flows[182]
In Pearl, in Diamond, and massie Gold[183]
Fruit of delicious Vines, the growth of Heav'n.   635
On flours repos'd, and with fresh flourets crownd,[184]

Satan at Easter. The War will last three days, as does the Passion period, and Jesus (in the grave from Friday to Sunday morning) as Son does not participate until the third (Easter morning). The narration of events begins here before Good Friday evening.

[178]The period here is restored from *1667*, though it does not appear in *1674*.

[179]A mystical dance would be one whose meaning could not be completely comprehended by Adam. Both the angelic song and the angelic dance are mystical and magical in the good sense (as in white magic) implied by "charming" (626 below). The mazes of planetary motion are also good mazes, as opposed to the evil mazes of the demons' perverted reasoning (2.561) or of Satan's serpentine body (9.499). Neoplatonic philosophers in the Renaissance such as Ficino built on the Platonic idea of soul as vehicle to form a theory of "the astral body of the soul, an aetheric or spiritual garment accreted by the soul as it descends through the stars and planets into an earthly body. Thus, Ficino … employed the magical consonance between cosmic and human spirits to show how music of proper astrological proportions acting through the medium of *spiritus* could awaken a beneficent resonance between a man and a planet, which always emits a music of its own" (Brian Copenhaver, summarizing Ficino in *The Cambridge History of Renaissance Philosophy*, gen. ed. Charles B. Schmidt [Cambridge: Cambridge UP, 1988]: 284–85).

[180]The word "now" was added in *1674*. Fletcher conjectured that Milton insisted on the doubled e's in "wee," a change from *1667*, and much of Hughes's usage in his edition is predicated from Fletcher's theory, but the pattern of doubled vowels on words accented according to stress in the iambic line is far from consistent. For further information, see Shawcross, "Orthography" 123.

[181]Changed from a comma in *1667*. As Fletcher pointed out, the change seems for the better.

[182]*1667* has a colon at the end of the line, which is apparently superfluous, since no pause is called for before the preposition "In."

[183]The suggestion is that the rarest of earthly riches are common in Heaven, on the grounds that diamond, pearl, or gold represent the best and rarest of earthly substances. The precious drinking vessels are in no way remarkable in Heaven.

[184]This line, apparently left out in *1667*, was added in *1674*, and other substantive changes made at the same time. The result was to throw the lineation of the rest of the book off one line between the two editions until the end of Book 5. The text of *1667*, beginning at 635, reads:

    Fruit of delicious Vines, the growth of Heav'n.
    They eat, they drink, and with refection sweet

They eate, they drink, and in communion sweet
Quaff immortalitie and joy, secure
Of surfet where full measure onely bounds
Excess, before th' all-bounteous[185] King, who showrd   640
With copious hand, rejoycing in thir joy.
Now when ambrosial Night with Clouds exhal'd[186]
From that high mount of God, whence light & shade
Spring both, the face of brightest Heav'n had changd
To grateful Twilight (for Night comes not there   645
In darker veile)[187] and roseat[188] Dews dispos'd
All but the unsleeping eyes of God[189] to rest,
Wide over all the Plain, and wider farr
Then all this globous Earth in Plain out spred,[190]
(Such are the Courts of God) Th' Angelic throng   650
Disperst in Bands and Files thir Camp extend
By living Streams among the Trees of Life,[191]
Pavilions numberless, and sudden reard,
Celestial Tabernacles,[192] where they slept
Fannd with coole Winds, save those who in thir course   655
Melodious Hymns about the sovran Throne
Alternate all night long: but not so wak'd
Satan, so call him now, his former name   (*Lucifer*)
Is heard no more in Heav'n;[193] he of the first,
If not the first Arch-Angel, great in Power,   660
In favour and in præeminence, yet fraught
With envie against the Son of God, that day
Honourd by his great Father, and proclaimd

     Are fill'd, before th' all-bounteous King, who showrd
     With copious hand, rejoycing in thir joy.
Milton apparently decided to replace the more literal "with refection sweet" ("with sweet eating") with the more universal "in communion sweet," which gives the meal Eucharistic overtones, since in the Communion service one would hope to eat and drink immortality. The meal also becomes more noticeably temperate, since Adam and Eve and Raphael are said to be "secure / Of surfet."

[185]The hyphenated reading of *1667* seems preferable to the unhyphenated compound of *1674*. The hyphen was printed lightly in *1667* and the *1674* compositor may not have seen it.

[186]The night is fragrant, since it is perfumed with clouds exhaled from the Mount of God.

[187]Around the throne of God, total darkness never comes: the variety of light, like the "vicissitude" of Paradise, is "grateful" (compare 6.4–8), and see Joseph Summers, "'Grateful Vicissitude,'" in *The Muse's Method* 71–86. The gratefulness of nature itself—grateful for being created—might be compared with Adam after the Fall as "ingrate" (3.97).

[188]Apparently purplish in hue (see 3.364) as with twilight or with some varieties of roses.

[189]Milton takes pains to give his God eyes, ears (3.193), lips (675 below), and even nostrils (9.196), perhaps to establish a kinship of the senses with humankind. Just as the angels eat human food, God perceives through the five senses.

[190]The words "out spred" were printed as one word in *1667*. The Mercator Projection of the Earth, the mapping system devised by Gerhard Kremer (1512–94), whose Latin name was Gerhardus Mercator, did indeed spread out the map of the earth as if it were a plain. Milton as a teacher of (among other things) geography had more than a passing interest in atlases and mapping systems (see Svendsen, Cawley).

[191]Milton seems to be emphasizing the diversity of a prolific Heaven; Revelation 22.1–2 mentions a "pure river of water of life, clear as crystal, proceeding out of the throne of God and the Lamb." In the midst of the "street of it, and on either side of the river, was there the tree of life . . . ." The commentary in the Geneva Bible interpreted the allusion as "to the visible paradise[,] to set forthe more sensibly the spiritual" (1560 ed.). Milton is constructing the scenery of Heaven, including the throne of God, a river that corresponds to those in Eden, and more than one Tree of Life. The nocturnal twilight in Milton's Heaven is set by the phrase "And there shall be no night there" at 22.5 and the perennial spring is signaled by the tree of life bearing twelve varieties of fruit "every month" (22.2).

[192]Biblical commentary associated the picture of the landscape surrounding the throne of God with the "vision of the waters that came out of the Temple" (Geneva Bible headnote; 1560 ed.) described in Ezekiel's vision (Ezekiel 42.1).

[193]For the subtlety employed in not calling Satan "Lucifer" after the Fall, see John Leonard, *Naming* 98–104. The word *in* in this line was omitted in *1667* but corrected in the 1668 *Errata*.

Messiah[194] King anointed, could not beare
Through pride that sight, &[195] thought himself impaird.   665
Deep malice thence conceiving and disdain,
Soon as midnight brought on the duskie houre
Friendliest to sleep and silence, he resolv'd
With all his Legions to dislodge,[196] and leave
Unworshipt, unobey'd the Throne supream[197]   670
Contemptuous, and his next subordinate
Awak'ning, thus to him in secret spake.

    Sleepst thou Companion dear,[198] what sleep can close
Thy eye-lids? and remembrest what Decree
Of yesterday, so late hath past the lips   675
Of Heav'ns Almightie. Thou to me thy thoughts
Wast wont,° I mine to thee was wont to impart;   GLAD, STRONGLY INCLINED
Both waking we were one; how then can now
Thy sleep dissent?° new Laws thou seest impos'd;   NOT CONSENT
New Laws from him who reigns, new minds may raise   680
In us who serve, new Counsels, to debate
What doubtful may ensue, more in this place
To utter is not safe.[199] Assemble thou
Of all those Myriads° which we lead the chief;   MULTITUDES
Tell them that by command, ere yet dim Night   685
Her shadowie Cloud withdraws, I am to haste,
And all who under me thir Banners wave,
Homeward with flying march where we possess
The Quarters of the North,[200] there to prepare
Fit entertainment to receive our King   690
The great *Messiah*, and his new commands,
Who speedily through all the Hierarchies°   ORDERS (OF ANGELS)
Intends to pass triumphant, and give Laws.[201]

    So spake the false Arch-Angel, and infus'd°   INSTILLED
Bad influence into th' unwarie brest   695
Of his Associate; hee together calls,

---

[194]Lucifer's exact rank in Heaven is left open to question here, but he and the Archangel Michael are described as "Equal in thir Creation" at 6.690. Just as Milton does not name Satan "Lucifer," he does not name Christ "Jesus" before the Incarnation; he identifies Christ with the Hebrew word "Messiah" (which means "the Anointed") or the phrases "Son of God" or "King anointed" (see Leonard 103–04). Leonard calls "Christ" "the central hidden name in the poem" (104).

[195]Printed as "and" in *1667*.

[196]As Fowler points out (5.669n), the term is military and means "leave a place of encampment" (*OED* 2b), though there may be a double meaning based on the possible transitive construction "dislodge . . . the Throne supream."

[197]By metonymy, God is identified with His throne; disobeying the throne is disobeying the entity upon it.

[198]The adjective "dear" adds a perverse dimension to the relationship between Satan and his companions, since the word usually suggests the normal affection between members of a family or husband and wife. Compare "Companions deare" at 6.419 and "Dear Daughter" as Satan applies it to Sin at 2.817 (compare also 1.192). The sarcasm is near to that used in calling bad children "little dears." The conversation here is also part of a secret conspiracy between Satan and Beelzebub (we can assume that the "Companion dear" is the same as "his neerest Mate" in 1.192), since Satan and Beelzebub (not named until after the Fall) "were one."

[199]Satan's secretiveness and paranoia are the whisperings of insecure rebellion. Shakespeare's Richard III expresses a similar sentiment, ironically, when he is talking with the brother he is about to have executed: "We are not safe, Clarence; we are not safe" (1.1.70).

[200]Satan's headquarters and his throne were said traditionally to be in the north, from which direction would also come death-dealing cold. The hordes of barbarian invaders of the simile in 1.351 come from the "populous North." As Cawley points out, "Witches, sorcerers, the devil himself hailed from the north" (45). Compare 10.654, 695, for further low opinions of the region.

[201]Satan's mode of address is perverse and evil, especially because his "Companion dear" has not yet been seduced into evil and is still "unwarie." He talks conspiratorially, the way Shakespeare's Richard III talks; he distorts and repeats what his opponent is doing, in verbal patterns that remind one of Iago's "Put money in thy purse" speech (*Othello* 2.1.339–81) in the repetition of "new Laws . . . new minds . . . new Counsels . . . new commands . . . Laws." As in Book 1, Satan will use Beelzebub as his shill or mouthpiece, to help put his plans into action by lying to his troops. Beelzebub in the scene that follows is acting very much the way Buckingham acts in order to establish the legitimacy of Richard III's claims to kingship in *Richard III*.

Or several one by one, the Regent Powers,
Under him Regent, tells, as he was taught,
That the most High commanding, now ere Night,
Now ere dim Night had disincumberd° Heav'n,   RELIEVED   700
The great Hierarchal Standard was to move;
Tells the suggested[202] cause, and casts between
Ambiguous words and jealousies,° to sound   SUSPICIONS, ZEALOUS FEELINGS
Or taint integritie; but all obey'd
The wonted° signal, and superior voice   CUSTOMARY   705
Of thir great Potentate;[203] for great indeed
His name, and high was his degree in Heav'n;
His count'nance, as the Morning Starr[204] that guides
The starrie flock, allur'd them, and with lyes
Drew after him the third part of Heav'ns Host: 710
Mean while th' Eternal eye,[205] whose sight discernes
Abstrusest thoughts, from forth his holy Mount
And from within the golden Lamps that burne
Nightly before him, saw without thir light
Rebellion rising, saw in whom, how spred   715
Among the sons of Morn,[206] what multitudes
Were banded to oppose his high Decree;
And smiling[207] to his onely Son thus said.
    Son, thou in whom my glory I behold
In full resplendence, Heir of all my might,   720
Neerly it now concernes us[208] to be sure
Of our Omnipotence, and with what Arms
We mean to hold what anciently we claim
Of Deitie or Empire, such a foe
Is rising, who intends to erect his Throne   725
Equal to ours, throughout the spacious North;[209]
Nor so content, hath in his thought to try°   PUT TO TEST
In battel, what our Power is, or our right.
Let us advise, and to this hazard[210] draw
With speed what force is left, and all imploy   730
In our defence, lest unawares we lose

---

[202]As Fowler points out (5.702n), the word has negative overtones, as in "insinuating or prompting to evil" (*OED* I.a). Similarly, "casts" suggests plotting or machination.

[203]Compare God's narrative of the fall of the angels in 3.129–32. It seems as if the angels in falling are acquiescing to the power or charisma implied in the name "Potentate." They appear to be military sheep, blindly following a leader, even though they have been described as self-tempted and self-deceived (3.130).

[204]Satan is demonstrating the residual glow of having been the Morning Star or Lucifer, but in this case he has used his brilliance to mislead the angels into the choice for evil. The analogy works well on many levels, since Lucifer is a kind of "Bad Shepherd" misleading heavenly beings, whereas Christ, also associated with the Morning Star in Revelation 22.16, will be the "Good Shepherd" and the guiding light for humankind. Isaiah 14.12 provides the link between the two interpretations of the Morning Star: "How art thou fallen from heaven, O Lucifer, son of the morning!"

[205]It might be useful to compare God as Eye once again with the Masonic eye pictured at the top of the pyramid on the U.S. dollar bill. Both images suggest unsleeping vigilance and omniscience.

[206]Seventeenth-century commentary on Job 38.7 identified the "morning stars" and "sons of God" of that passage as angels, which would link both the good and the evil angels with the Morning Star.

[207]Milton's God is capable of humor both gentle and sardonic. Here he "Justly hast [his foes] in derision" (736 below). As Belial admits, God "All these our motions vain, sees and derides" (2.191). God will see the testing of his omnipotence as ultimately ridiculous. Psalm 2.4 provides the authority for perceiving the humor in the actions of God: "He that sitteth in the heavens shall laugh: the Lord shall have them in derision."

[208]The royal "we," expressing the Father and Son acting as one and with omnipotence. Milton's occasional ambiguity in assigning a speaker to a godly utterance (see "Sovran voice" at 6.56) may indicate his own ambivalence toward the roles of Father and Son.

[209]Another allusion to the coming of evil from the north, as in 689 above and 755 below.

[210]The word here seems to mean only "danger" or "peril," without the element of chance implied when it is used by Satan.

This our high place, our Sanctuarie, our Hill.[211]
    To whom the Son with calm aspect[212] and cleer
Light'ning Divine,[213] ineffable, serene,
Made answer. Mightie Father, thou thy foes   735
Justly hast in derision, and secure
Laugh'st at thir vain designes and tumults vain,
Matter to mee of Glory, whom thir hate
Illustrates,[214] when they see all Regal Power
Giv'n me to quell thir pride, and in event   740
Know whether I be dextrous[215] to subdue
Thy Rebels, or be found the worst in Heav'n.
    So spake the Son, but *Satan* with his Powers° POWERS
Far was advanc't on winged speed, an Host
Innumerable as the Starrs of Night,   745
Or Starrs of Morning, Dew-drops, which the Sun
Impearls on every leaf and every flouer.[216]
Regions they pass'd, the mightie Regencies° DOMINIONS, KINGDOMS
Of Seraphim and Potentates and Thrones
In thir triple Degrees,[217] Regions to which   750
All thy Dominion, *Adam*, is no more
Then what this Garden is to all the Earth,
And all the Sea, from one entire globose[218]
Stretcht into Longitude;[219] which having pass'd
At length into the limits of the North   755
They came, and *Satan* to his Royal seat
High on a Hill,[220] far blazing, as a Mount
Rais'd on a Mount, with Pyramids[221] and Towrs
From Diamond Quarries hew'n, and Rocks of Gold,

[handwritten marginal note: aspire – to loom over. Satan asserts his highness.]

---

[211]God's smile may indicate that this impossibility will not be taken seriously. In no way could an omniscient God be "unawares." The holy hill alludes to Psalm 2.6: "Yet have I set my king upon my holy hill of Zion."

[212]Accented on the second syllable.

[213]Compare the angel described in Matthew 28.3 after the Resurrection, rolling the stone away from Christ's tomb: "His countenance was like lightning, and his raiment white as snow." The passage in Matthew also alludes to the Old Testament angel sent to give the prophet Daniel a vision of the future: "His body also was like the beryl, and his face as the appearance of lightning, and his eyes as lamps of fire . . . " (Daniel 10.6). Perhaps Milton also has in mind the image of the Son as "effluence," in the sense that lightning would be a demonstration of God's wrath, though the wrath here is calm, clear, ineffable (indescribable), and serene.

[214]Literally, "gives luster to," or illuminates, as if the fallen angels will be a foil to the Son. Accented on the second syllable.

[215]A pun on the Son as God the Father's "right hand" (Latin *dextera*).

[216]An unusual spelling, perhaps unique in *Paradise Lost*, and most likely a misreading of the more common "flour," a definite monosyllable.

[217]The nine orders of angels were divided into three groups of hierarchies, according to "Dionysius the Areopagite," called Pseudo-Dionysius. The nine orders Milton names are Cherubim, Seraphim, Thrones, Princedoms, Powers, Vertues, Dominions, Potentates, and (oddly enough) Angels. As West points out, "The Dionysian system, Protestants generally agreed, was overly detailed and a pious fraud," but "This did not mean, however, that Protestants denied either angels or their ranks" (13). Such confusion might help explain Milton's "fluid" (West's term on 134) use of rank. For mention of Potentates among the orders of angels, compare 7.197–98.

[218]Globe. The *OED* identifies this usage as that of an adjective (the noun normally would be "globosity"), but an adjective used as a "quasi-substantive." Milton uses the word more clearly as an adjective in 7.357.

[219]Stretched lengthwise in a flat plane. Again, the image of the world is like that of the Mercator Projection.

[220]A prolepsis or foreshadowing of the scene at the beginning of Book 2. Satan's seat is an imitation or a perverse reflection of God's mount and throne, as in "God-like imitated State" (2.511) or evil emulation of good.

[221]Milton had used the image of sharp-pointed pyramids negatively: "Prelaty's . . . pyramid aspires and sharpens ambition, not to perfection, or unity. . . . [The pyramidal shape itself] is the most dividing, and schismaticall forme that Geometricians know of" (*Reason of Church-government*; Yale 1: 790). Satan himself is pictured as a "Pyramid of fire" at 2.1013. The "Towrs" in the corresponding image is the literal version of Satan's "proud Towers to swift destruction doom'd" of 907 below, but Satan is also described as standing like a tower in 1.591. Milton may well be associating Satan with the Tower of Babel (12.44).

The Palace of great *Lucifer*,[222] (so call   760
That Structure in the Dialect° of men   LANGUAGE
Interpreted) which not long after, he
Affecting° all equality with God,   PRETENDING
In imitation of that Mount whereon
Messiah was declar'd in sight of Heav'n,   765
The Mountain of the Congregation call'd;
For thither he assembl'd all his Train,[223]
Pretending so commanded to consult
About the great reception of thir King,
Thither to come, and with calumnious° Art   FRAUDULENT, LYING   770
Of counterfeted truth thus held thir ears.[224]
    Thrones, Dominations, Princedomes, Vertues, Powers,
If these magnific Titles yet remain
Not meerly titular,[225] since by Decree
Another now hath to himself ingross't   775
All Power,[226] and us eclipst[227] under the name
Of King anointed, for whom all this haste
Of midnight march, and hurried meeting here,
This onely to consult how we may best
With what may be devis'd of honours new   780
Receive him coming to receive from us
Knee-tribute yet unpaid, prostration vile,[228]
Too much to one, but double how endur'd,
To one and to his image now proclaim'd?
But what if better counsels might erect   785
Our minds and teach us to cast off this Yoke?
Will ye submit your necks, and chuse to bend
The supple knee? ye will not, if I trust
To know ye right, or if ye know your selves
Natives and Sons of Heav'n possest before   790
By none, and if not equal all, yet free,
Equally free; for Orders and Degrees
Jarr not with liberty, but well consist.°[229]   COEXIST WITH
Who can in reason then or right assume
Monarchie over such as live by right   795

---

[222]Satan is properly called "Lucifer" only before the Fall, so that when later generations call him that, they misuse the name. Milton himself always applied the name to the angel before the Fall or to the star accordingly named. In 10.425–26, the fallen angel is "Lucifer, so by allusion calld / Of that bright Starr to Satan paragond": thus the star is more entitled to the name than is Satan.

[223]The word implies that Satan needs a train of attendants as an outward sign of his vanity and self-aggrandizement, an implication supported by "knee-tribute" and "prostration vile" of 782 below.

[224]"This council, like all others directed by Satan, is called on a false premise and conducted with a hidden agenda.

[225]Satan's speech is characterized by orotundity and repetition, as with "Titles" and "titular." He is more interested in titles than in substance or achievement. The word "magnific," which means "great-making" as compared with "great," shows how Satan is flattering his audience. Instead of naming the enemy Messiah, he must identify him as "King anointed" and the Father and Son as "one and . . . his image" (784 below). Satan flatters his cohorts by giving them back the angelic titles to which they will soon be no longer entitled, and he avoids naming his enemies directly, perhaps out of fear of their real names (see Leonard 199–200).

[226]The Son has been given omnipotence as an inheritance earned by merit: he has not seized huge power, as "ingross't" suggests.

[227]Ironic, since Satan is spoken of metaphorically as having been eclipsed by the Son/sun, and he consequently hates light and its source.

[228]Compare Satan's threat never "To bow and sue for grace / With suppliant knee, and deifie his power . . ." (1.111–12). As if one mention of bending the knee to God is not enough, he will repeat it in 787. Compare his vision of servility to Gabriel's description of Satan as being servile himself in Heaven: " . . . who more then thou / Once fawn'd, and cring'd, and servilly ador'd / Heav'ns awful Monarch" (4.958–60).

[229]Satan is mixing truth with lies. Orders and degrees, as with the hierarchy of Heaven, do not jar with true liberty; the problem is that as soon as the angels under his command revolt from God they will have elected to live in slavery under Satan. Satan will soon answer his own rhetorical question, "Who can . . . assume / Monarchie . . . ?" by an implicit "I can."

His equals, if in power and splendor less,
In freedome equal? or can introduce
Law and Edict on us, who without law
Erre not,[230] much less for this to be our Lord,
And look for adoration to th' abuse
Of those Imperial Titles which assert
Our being ordain'd to govern, not to serve?[231]   800

    Thus farr his bold discourse without controule
Had audience, when among the Seraphim
Abdiel, then whom none with more zeale[232] ador'd
The Deitie, and divine commands obei'd,   805
Stood up, and in a flame of zeale severe
The current of his fury thus oppos'd.

    O argument blasphemous,[233] false and proud!
Words which no eare ever to hear in Heav'n   810
Expected, least of all from thee, ingrate[234]
In place thy self so high above thy Peeres.
Canst thou with impious obloquie° condemne   ABUSE
The just Decree of God, pronounc't and sworn,
That to his only Son by right endu'd   815
With Regal Scepter, every Soule in Heav'n
Shall bend the knee, and in that honour due
Confess him rightful King?[235] unjust thou saist
Flatly unjust, to binde with Laws the free,
And equal over equals to let Reigne,   820
One over all with unsucceeded power.
Shalt thou give Law to God,[236] shalt thou dispute
With him the points of libertie, who made
Thee what thou art, and formd the Pow'rs of Heav'n
Such as he pleasd, and circumscrib'd thir being?   825
Yet by experience taught we know how good,

---

[230]Satan suggests that angels under his command will be able to live without any rule of law, whereas in a tyranny laws will be enforced without the consent of the governed. Milton believed very much in a rule of law in which a head of state (not necessarily a king) would be responsible to the people first, before his own personal or even political interests. A king like Charles I, not responsive to his people's desires expressed through parliamentary legislation, deserved in Milton's thinking to be deposed or even beheaded. Law should rule above any individual. Satan's speech here should be read alongside Milton's political tracts such as *The Reason of Church-government, The Tenure of Kings and Magistrates, Eikonoklastes,* and *Defence of the English People,* in which he establishes a theory of government by the consent of the governed not unlike that embodied in the United States Constitution.

[231]The irony here is that the angels are permitted to govern only through God's providence; as soon as created beings rebel against their creator, the contract is canceled and the rebels enslave themselves in the attempt to overturn world order.

[232]The word zeal was not negative to Puritans at large, though it was to their enemies (as with Shakespeare in his portrait of Malvolio in *Twelfth Night* or Ben Jonson in his of Zeal-of-the-Land Busy in *Bartholemew Fair*). Though the word comes from a Greek verb meaning "to boil," Milton identifies the emotion with flame (807 below). Abdiel is the embodiment of zeal, in this case righteous indignation. He is one of singular "just men" who embody true faith even before Christ, comparable to Abel, Enoch, and Noah (see *On Christian Doctrine* 1.20; Yale 6: 475). Milton devotes an entire chapter of *On Christian Doctrine* to zeal, which he defines as "An eager desire to sanctify the divine name, together with a feeling of indignation against things which tend to the violation or contempt of religion" (2.6; Yale 6: 697). The name Abdiel was not applied to an angel in the Bible: Milton made up the character and gave him a name that means "Servant of God" (6.29) and is found in the Bible only as one of a catalogue of genealogical names, in 1 Chronicles 5.15. Paul, the most zealous of Christian converts, names himself "Servant of God" in Titus 1.1.

[233]Accented on the second syllable.

[234]The word yokes Satan with the disobedient Adam, described by God as "ingrate . . . [who] had of mee / All he could have" (3.97–98). Abdiel points out that Satan in appointing himself leader among his peers is hardly being democratic.

[235]Abdiel is quoting Scripture, as he does throughout his rebuttal: "Wherefore God also hath highly exalted him . . . That at the name of Jesus every knee should bow, of things in heaven, and things in earth, and things under the earth; And that every tongue should confess that Jesus Christ is Lord, to the glory of God the Father" (Philippians 2.9–1.111).

[236]"Nay but, O man, who are thou that repliest against God? shall the thing formed say to him that formed it, Why hast thout made me thus? Hath not the potter power over the clay, of the same lump to make one vessel unto honour, and another unto dishonour" (Romans 9.20–21)? As part of his blasphemy, Satan is denying that God created him and gave laws (as in "laws of nature") to creation.

And of our good, and of our dignitie
How provident he is, how farr from thought
To make us less, bent rather to exalt
Our happie state under one[237] Head more neer   830
United. But to grant it thee unjust,
That equal over equals Monarch Reigne:
Thy self though great and glorious dost thou count,
Or all Angelic Nature joind in one,
Equal to him begotten Son, by whom   835
As by his Word the mighty Father made
All things,[238] ev'n thee, and all the Spirits of Heav'n
By him created in thir bright degrees,
Crownd them with Glory,[239] and to thir Glory nam'd
Thrones, Dominations, Princedoms, Vertues, Powers,   840
Essential Powers, nor by his Reign obscur'd,[240]
But more illustrious made, since he the Head
One of our number thus reduc't becomes,
His Laws our Laws, all honour to him done
Returns our own. Cease then this impious rage,   845
And tempt not these; but hast'n to appease
Th' incensed Father, and th' incensed Son,
While Pardon may be found in time besought.
    So spake the fervent Angel, but his zeale
None seconded, as out of season judg'd,[241]   850
Or singular and rash, whereat rejoic'd
Th' Apostat,[242] and more haughty thus repli'd.
That we were formd then saist thou? and the work
Of secondarie hands, by task transferd
From Father to his Son? strange point and new!   855
Doctrin which we would know whence learnt: who saw
When this creation was? rememberst thou
Thy making, while the Maker gave thee being?
We know no time when we were not as now;
Know none before us, self-begot, self-rais'd   860
By our own quick'ning power,[243] when fatal course
Had circl'd his full Orbe, the birth mature
Of this our native Heav'n, Ethereal Sons.[244]

---

[237]Some copies of *1667* have "our" here, erroneously echoing the word at the beginning of the line.

[238]"For by him [the Son] were all things created, that are in heaven, and that are in earth, visible and invisible, whether they be thrones, or dominions, or principalities, or powers: all things were created by him, and for him. And he is before all things, and by him all things consist" (Colossians 1.16–17). Milton used the passage to establish the Son as the agency of creation. The "bright degrees" mentioned below are the angelic hierarchies.

[239]"Just as God crowned the angels with glory in creation, so also with humankind, and with Christ when incarnated as man: "For thou has made [man] a little lower than the angels, and has crowned him with glory and honour" (Psalm 8.5).

[240]Abdiel reinstates the value of the orders of angels, which Satan had debased as "magnific Titles" (773 above).

[241]Abdiel's resistance, the Epic Voice notes, is "out of season" or unfashionable, and Abdiel is in danger of becoming a martyr because of his timing alone. The rest of the angels in the process of falling seem to be acting on mass hysteria, like lemmings on a suicidal march to the sea, and Satan will rejoice, increase in haughtiness, and address them almost hysterically after he notices that no one stands behind Abdiel.

[242]Satan as Apostate (the word suggests "standing away from" or separating oneself from God) argues a question that theologians often debated: who actually created the universe? Satan, however, knows very well who created him (see 4.42–44); thus he is lying here.

[243]Actually the fallen angels are only "Self-tempted, self-deprav'd" (3.130). They will succeed in destroying themselves but have taken no part in their own creation. It may help Satan here to argue that the angels were products of spontaneous generation, but Milton's audience would have recognized his lie. Satan himself has to reinstate a godless universe with a "fatal course" as contrasted with a providence governed by a good God.

[244]In denying creation, Satan is making the angels who elect to follow him not "Sons of God" but his own "Ethereal Sons," replacing God's essence with ether. Instead of being created out of God, he avers, the angels were created out of preexistent matter.

Our puissance° is our own, our own right hand   POWER
Shall teach us highest deeds,[245] by proof to try   865
Who is our equal: then thou shalt behold
Whether by supplication we intend
Address, and to begirt th' Almighty Throne
Beseeching or besieging.[246] This report,
These tidings carrie to th' anointed King;   870
And fly, ere evil intercept thy flight.
    He said, and as the sound of waters deep
Hoarce murmur echo'd to his words applause
Through the infinite Host, nor less for that
The flaming Seraph fearless, though alone   875
Encompass'd round with foes, thus answerd bold.[247]
    O alienate from God, O spirit accurst,
Forsak'n of all good; I see thy fall
Determind,[248] and thy hapless crew involv'd
In this perfidious fraud, contagion spred   880
Both of thy crime and punishment: henceforth
No more be troubl'd how to quit the yoke
Of Gods *Messiah*; those indulgent Laws
Will not be now voutsaf't, other Decrees
Against thee are gon forth without recall;   885
That Golden Scepter which thou didst reject
Is now an Iron Rod[249] to bruise[250] and breake
Thy disobedience. Well thou didst advise,
Yet not for thy advise or threats I fly
These wicked Tents devoted,[251] least° the wrauth   LEST   890
Impendent,° raging into sudden flame   SUSPENDED
Distinguish not:[252] for soon expect to feel
His Thunder° on thy head, devouring fire.   LIGHTNING
Then who created thee lamenting learne,
When who can uncreate thee thou shalt know.   895
    So spake the Seraph *Abdiel* faithful found,
Among the faithless, faithful only hee;
Among innumerable false, unmov'd,

---

[245]Satan replaces the right hand of God mentioned in 2.174 with his own right hand, or the collective might of the angels who follow him, fulfilling the prophecy of Psalm 45.4: " . . . and thy right hand shall teach thee terrible things." Satan is predicting the War in Heaven. His use of the courtly words and phrases "puissance" and "highest deeds" show that he is pretending to be a knight at arms, whereas he is more like the type of the cowardly braggart soldier.

[246]Rajan finds the entire speech of Satan full of these kinds of "irrelevant puns" (Paradise Lost *and the Seventeenth-Century Reader* 102).

[247]Milton pictured himself in his invocations in the same stance—alone and surrounded by enemies—as he pictures Abdiel and the other examples of the "one just Man" (11.818).

[248]Compare the summary of the War in Heaven, "Warr hath determin'd us," in 2.330, in which Beelzebub correctly evaluates the result of the War as having fixed the fate of the fallen angels. Satan's decision to go to war against God renders him a creature of fate or determinism: he determines his own fall and those who follow him become a "hapless crew" or one without "hap" or fate on their side. Satan's fraud is built on lies (perfidy), it is a crime against nature, and it is a sickness spread by contagion.

[249]The image of the enforcement of God's law before the falls of angels or humankind as by means of a golden scepter and after the Fall as being by means of an iron rod will be repeated both for angels and for humankind. See 2.327 and Psalm 2.

[250]Echoing the prophecy that Eve's seed will "bruise" the "heel" of the Serpent (Genesis 3.15).

[251]"Tents of wickedness" (as in Psalm 84.10) was a biblical formula, but here Abdiel is leaving an actual encampment. The image of tents may be an allusion to Moses's warning to the Israelites in Numbers 16.25: "Depart, I pray you, from the tents of these wicked men, and touch nothing of theirs, lest ye be consumed in all their sins." The word "devoted" suggests what is in this case illicit worship as in Michael's narrative of the Sons of God and the Daughters of Men, in which the blasphemous sons of Cain live in "Tents / Of wickedness" (11.607–08).

[252]"Lest the wrath [of God], temporarily in abeyance, suddenly burst into flame and devour everything in its path," not distinguishing the good (Abdiel) from the rest.

Unshak'n, unseduc'd, unterrifi'd
His Loyaltie he kept, his Love, his Zeale;   900
Nor number, nor example with him wrought
To swerve from truth, or change his constant mind
Though single.[253] From amidst them forth he pass'd,
Long way[254] through hostile scorn, which he susteind
Superior, nor of violence fear'd aught;   905
And with retorted scorn[255] his back he turn'd
On those proud Towrs[256] to swift destruction doom'd.

The End of the Fifth Book.

---

[253]Again Milton through narrative comment emphasizes the power of the one just and in this case zealous individual.
[254]"Through a long path." The image is one of Abdiel running a gauntlet through the hostile fallen angels.
[255]"Scorn for scorn," or "answered scorn." As Fowler points out (5.906n), there is also a pun on the Latin meaning of *retortus*, which can mean "having turned one's back on."
[256]Perhaps the literal towers erected by Satan, or the proud towers of his imagination, as in "proud imaginations" at 2.10.

Paradise Lost.

BOOK VI.

THE ARGUMENT.

The War in heaven: (handwritten)

Raphael *continues to relate how* Michael *and* Gabriel *were sent forth to battel against* Satan *and his Angels. The first Fight describ'd:* Satan *and his Powers retire under Night:*[1] *He calls a Councel, invents devilish Engines, which in the second dayes Fight put* Michael *and his Angels to some disorder; but they at length pulling up Mountains overwhelm'd both the force and Machins of* Satan: *Yet the Tumult not so ending, God on the third day sends* Messiah *his Son, for whom he had reserv'd the glory of that Victory: Hee in the Power of his Father coming to the place, and causing all his Legions to stand still on either side, with his Chariot and Thunder*[2] *driving into the midst of his Enemies, pursues them unable to resist towards the wall of Heaven; which opening, they leap down with horrour and confusion*[3] *into the place of punishment prepar'd for them in the Deep:* Messiah *returns with triumph to his Father.*

A LL night the dreadless Angel° unpursu'd   THE FEARLESS ABDIEL
    Through Heav'ns wide Champain° held his way, till Morn,   PLAIN
    Wak't by the circling Hours,[4] with rosie hand
    Unbarr'd the gates of Light.   There is a Cave
Within the Mount of God, fast by° his Throne,   VERY NEAR   5
Where light and darkness in perpetual round
Lodge and dislodge by turns, which makes through Heav'n
Grateful vicissitude,[5] like Day and Night;
Light issues forth, and at the other dore
Obsequious° darkness enters, till her houre   FOLLOWING   10
To veile the Heav'n, though darkness there might well
Seem twilight here;[6] and now went forth the Morn
Such as in highest Heav'n, arrayd in Gold
Empyreal,[7] from before her vanisht Night,
Shot through with orient° Beams: when all the Plain   BRIGHT, EASTERN   15
Coverd with thick embatteld Squadrons bright,
Chariots and flaming Armes,[8] and fierie Steeds[9]
Reflecting blaze on blaze, first met his view:

---

[1] "Satan and his armies leave the battle under cover of darkness," suggesting their cowardly retreat.

[2] The Messiah is often pictured in seventeenth-century visual art like Jupiter, with a cluster of thunderbolts in his right hand. For the identification of Jupiter with the Christian God, see Wind, 252–53.

[3] Perhaps this Argument was the source for the opening scene in John Dryden's *The State of Innocence* (written by 1674), the operatic play borrowed with Milton's permission from *Paradise Lost* (Parker, *Milton* 1.635), in which the angels under Satan are pictured as literally falling from above the set and through something like a trap door.

[4] Dawn is pictured as the Christian version of the goddess Aurora, who in turn was pictured often in a rose-colored chariot, opening with "rosy fingers" the gates of the east and sprinkling dew in the path of the light. The Hours circling the throne of God awaken Dawn, pictured leaving her bed just as Vergil's Aurora leaves the bed of Tithonus in the *Aeneid* 4.585. Milton's Hours circle in the same way that heavenly bodies seem to circle the Earth, marking our time.

[5] A phrase very important for the understanding of how both Heaven and Eden function (see Summers's "'Grateful Vicissitude,'" in *The Muse's Method* 71–86), because it indicates that the variety or ceaseless change present in the fluctuations of the seasons is good. Grateful vicissitude is nature's response to God's creation.

[6] As explained above in 5.646n, there is no total darkness in Milton's Heaven.

[7] The nearer to the highest Heaven—the Empyrea— the nearer to God, thus the more precious the metal; hence the Morn is dressed in Empyreal gold.

[8] Seraphim, among the angelic orders, were especially noted for appearing as flames, just as Abdiel appeared "in a flame of zeale severe" at 5.807. Compare "And of the angels he saith, Who maketh his angels spirits, and his ministers a flame of fire" (Hebrews 1.7).

[9] The cliché about war-horses from romantic epic is mixed in skillfully with images of angels burning with zeal.

Warr he perceav'd, warr in procinct,[10] and found
Already known what he for news had thought   20
To have reported: gladly then he mixt
Among those friendly Powers who him receav'd
With joy and acclamations loud, that one
That of so many Myriads[11] fall'n, yet one
Returnd not lost: On to the sacred hill   25
They led him high applauded, and present[12]
Before the seat supream; from whence a voice
From midst a Golden Cloud thus milde was heard.

    Servant of God, well done,[13] well hast thou fought
The better fight, who single[14] hast maintaind   30
Against revolted multitudes the Cause
Of Truth, in word mightier then they in Armes;
And for the testimonie of Truth hast born°   BORNE
Universal reproach, far worse to beare
Then violence: for this was all thy care[15]   35
To stand approv'd in sight of God, though Worlds
Judg'd thee perverse:[16] the easier conquest now
Remains thee, aided by this host of friends,
Back on thy foes more glorious to return
Then scornd thou didst depart, and to subdue   40
By force,[17] who reason for thir Law refuse,
Right reason for thir Law, and for thir King
Messiah, who by right of merit Reigns.   *ORDERLY use of mind*
Go *Michael*[18] of Celestial Armies Prince,
And thou in Military prowess next   45
Gabriel, lead forth to Battel these my Sons
Invincible, lead forth my armed Saints

---

[10]For "in procinct," see *OED* procinct 2 "readiness for action," citing this passage. The Latin phrase *in procinctu* is military usage and means "on the battlefield."

[11]Multitudes or numberless groups (a "myriad" in its Greek root is ten thousand).

[12]Milton seems to be mixing tenses again to give a narrative sense of past and present at the same time: the angels led Abdiel to the sacred hill amidst applause, but then they present him (the him is understood) before the seat and throne of God.

[13]The voice is that of God—whether Father or Son we are not told, though the mildness described may be a trait associated with the Son. God speaks from a cloud to Moses in Exodus 24.16, among other places. Lines 29–37 are a tissue of biblical quotations which establish the meaning of Abdiel's name, since the phrase "Servant of God" defines the Hebrew word "Abdiel." The phrase is common enough in the Old and New Testaments to warrant a separate section in most concordances. To "fight the good fight" is proverbial, but is taken from 1 Timothy 6.12. Psalm 69.7 establishes that "for thy sake I have borne reproach." And Christ uses the phrase "Well done, thou good and faithful servant" in the parable of the talents in Matthew 25.21.

[14]Again, Abdiel's being the "one just" among all the "revolted multitudes" is stressed, in addition to what might be called his individual "Patience and Heroic Martyrdom" (9.32) in opposing only his word against the weapons of the revolting angels. Here the word is indeed mightier than the sword.

[15]A stronger word than in modern usage, perhaps because it might have had associations (by a false etymology) with the Latin *caritas*, which itself was variously defined as "charity," "love," or "devotional responsibility." Perhaps Milton's meaning is closest to *OED* 3, "Serious or grave mental attention." Compare "Greensleeves was all my care" in the traditional English song.

[16]The irony here is that Abdiel's behavior is judged perverse because of what might be called peer pressure among the revolting angels, whereas the entire behavior pattern of Satan's legions is in fact perverse, because it represents a complete "turning aside from" (compare the Latin adjective *perversus*, "turned the wrong way") God.

[17]"To conquer by force those who elect not to have right reason for their law." "Right reason," the Latin *recta ratio*, was a term associated with Stoic and scholastic philosophies. It meant something like "self-evident reasonableness in judging all practical matters." Right reason might be associated by a Christian with "conscience," though Milton uses that word to mean "God's umpire" in humankind. Right reason might be contrasted with the lawlessness of Satan and the fallen angels who accompany him, refusing to acknowledge the rule of law, here associated with accepting Messiah as king (which is the same as accepting the laws of the universe).

[18]In Revelation 12, on which the War in Heaven is based, Michael leads the heavenly angels in battle against the great dragon Satan.

By Thousands and by Millions rang'd for fight;[19]
Equal in number to that Godless crew
Rebellious,[20] them with Fire and hostile Arms   50
Fearless assault, and to the brow[21] of Heav'n
Pursuing drive them out from God and bliss,
Into thir place of punishment, the Gulf
Of *Tartarus*,[22] which ready opens wide
His fiery *Chaos* to receave thir fall.   55
    So spake the Sovran voice, and Clouds began
To darken all the Hill, and smoak to rowl
In duskie wreathes, reluctant flames, the signe
Of wrauth awak't:[23] nor with less dread the loud
Ethereal Trumpet[24] from on high gan° blow: BEGAN TO   60
At which command the Powers Militant,
That stood for Heav'n,[25] in mighty Quadrate[26] joyn'd
Of Union irresistible, mov'd on
In silence thir bright Legions,[27] to the sound
Of instrumental Harmonie that breath'd   65
Heroic Ardor to advent'rous deeds
Under thir God-like Leaders, in the Cause
Of God and his *Messiah*. On they move
Indissolubly[28] firm; nor obvious[29] Hill,
Nor streit'ning Vale,[30] nor Wood, nor Stream divides   70
Thir perfet ranks; for high above the ground
Thir march was, and the passive Air upbore   *accommodation*
Thir nimble tread, as when the total kind°   ALL THE SPECIES

---

[19]In the chapter on angels in *On Christian Doctrine*, Milton notes "There seems to be a leader among the good angels, and he is often called Michael" (1.9; Yale 6: 347). Milton differentiates Michael from Christ as leader of the angels (they were sometimes confused): "whereas Christ alone vanquished Satan and trod him underfoot, Michael is introduced as leader of the angels and Ἀντίπαλος (antagonist) of the prince of the devils: their respective forces were drawn up in battle array and separated after a fairly even fight . . . " (1.9; Yale 6: 347). Gabriel is properly associated with war by his name, which means "Strength of God."

[20]The number of rebel angels was supposed to be one-third of the host of Heaven, but Milton is at pains to make the battle appear a fairly even fight.

[21]Probably "The projecting edge of a cliff or hill" (*OED* 6).

[22]One of the lower regions of classical Hades, where the Titans who warred against Jupiter and where the worst criminals are punished (see Hesiod, *Theogony* 720 and especially Vergil, *Aeneid* 6.577–81). Milton associates Tartarus with Chaos, which he makes into an allegorical place ruled in turn by a being named Chaos. In Milton's theological system, Chaos was the region out of which God created the ordered universe, imposing divine order on chaos. Hell, on the other hand, came into existence specifically for the purpose of housing the fallen angels. Traditionally, Hell was pictured as a fiery maw or mouth; here Chaos is associated with that opening. Even though Chaos is not inherently evil by Milton's reckoning (for the complexity involved in judging whether Chaos is evil, see Schwartz 8–39), it is a place that may be "deprav'd from good" (5.471; see Schwartz 9) and on which good has to be imposed; hence it is a fitting place for the location of Hell.

[23]Milton's God speaks out of a cloud of smoke. The image seems closest to the manifestation of God to the Israelites when the tablets of the Ten Commandments are delivered: "These words the Lord spake unto all your assembly in the mount out of the midst of the fire, of the cloud, and of the thick darkness, with a great voice: and he added no more" (Deuteronomy 5.22). The flames are reluctant because they, as they are personified, hesitate to proclaim the terror of God's wrath. See also Exodus 19.16, 18, for Mt. Sinai's covering of smoke.

[24]It is ethereal because all things in that region of the sky are made out of the element ether. Trumpet calls issuing from Heaven are associated by Milton with Seraphim, and Heaven is "Where the bright Seraphim in burning row / Their loud uplifted angel trumpets blow" ("At a Solemn Musick" 10–11).

[25]"The military forces that represented Heaven."

[26]Some of the battle formations of Milton's era would have been four-sided. More importantly, the thousands of angels are acting as one.

[27]Fowler points out (6.71–72n) that Milton's angels, like the ancient Greek and Roman gods, are supposed to walk above the surface of the ground. They are therefore marching silently, but they are accompanied by harmonic martial music; presumably they march in something like the "perfect Phalanx to the *Dorian* mood / Of Flutes and soft Recorders" (1.550–51). Ironically, the battle formation and the marching habits of the good angels are parodied by those of Satan's legions: "Thus they / Breathing united force with fixed thought / Mov'd on in silence to soft Pipes that charm'd / Thir painful steps o're the burnt soyle" (1.559–62)—except that the good angels are not "charmed" by the pipes, nor are their steps "painful," nor are their thoughts "fixed" in the sense of being "determined," since they act of their own free will.

[28]Apparently stressed on the second syllable.

[29]The hill is obstructive or in the way; compare the Latin adverb *obviam*, "in the way."

[30]"Nor valley, which by its sides might restrict the forward movement of the armies."

Of Birds in orderly array on wing
Came summond over *Eden* to receive 75
Thir names of thee;[31] so over many a tract
Of Heav'n they march'd, and many a Province wide
Tenfold the length of this terrene: at last
Farr in th' Horizon to the North appeer'd
From skirt° to skirt a fierie Region,[32] stretcht   BOUNDARY 80
In battailous aspect,[33] and neerer view
Bristl'd with upright beams[34] innumerable
Of rigid Spears, and Helmets throng'd, and Shields
Various, with boastful Argument portraid,[35]
The banded Powers of *Satan* hasting on 85
With furious expedition;[36] for they weend°   IMAGINED, THOUGHT
That self same day by fight, or by surprize
To win the Mount of God, and on his Throne
To set the envier[37] of his State, the proud
Aspirer, but thir thoughts prov'd fond° and vain   FOOLISH 90
In the mid way: though strange to us it seemd
At first, that Angel should with Angel warr,
And in fierce hosting[38] meet, who wont to meet
So oft in Festivals of joy and love
Unanimous, as sons of one great Sire 95
Hymning th' Eternal Father: but the shout
Of Battel now began, and rushing sound
Of onset ended soon each milder thought.
High in the midst exalted as a God
Th' Apostat in his Sun-bright Chariot sate 100
Idol of Majestie Divine,[39] enclos'd

[handwritten marginal note: Hates Idol but becoming everything Idol.]

---

[31]Raphael reminds Adam that he has had the responsibility of naming the animals (as in Genesis 2.20), including "the fowl of the air." As Fowler points out (6.73–76n), Milton may consciously be competing with Homer and Vergil in comparisons between gathering armies and birds in the *Iliad* 2.459–63 and in the *Aeneid* 7.699–705, since Raphael's simile involves numerical superiority ("total kind") and a more exact matching of tenor and vehicle, since the angels are a multitude arranged in a neat hierarchical pattern just as the birds that come to Adam are arranged by species. The comparison also presumably helps Adam understand the comparative size of the angelic force and of the "Provinces" of Heaven, each of which is ten times as wide as is the entire earth ("terrene," derived from Latin *terra*, earth; the first recorded use of the adjective in its absolute form as noun in the *OED*).

[32]The Russian filmmaker Sergei Eisenstein saw the following series of images, among others (he quotes the passage from 77–86), as examples of "montage" and imitated them in the famous "Battle on Ice" scene in *Alexander Nevsky*. "Studying the pages of [Milton's] poem, and in each individual case analyzing the determining qualities and expressive effects of each example, we become extraordinarily enriched in experience of the audio-visual distribution of images in his sound montage" (*The Film Sense*, trans. and ed. Jay Leyda [New York: Harcourt Brace, 1947]: 58).

[33]"Stretched out in battle line." As is most often true in Milton's poetry, the word "aspect" is accented on the second syllable. The battle line is personified as if it had a unified warlike face ("battailous aspect").

[34]Not "beam" in the sense of "sunbeam": more analogous to the usage in "roof beam," in the sense that the angels carry massive wooden spears, like the masts of ships (compare Satan's spear in 1.292–94). The spears are, as Tom Corns points out to me, "massive wooden spars" (letter, October 1991).

[35]The shields are decorated with heraldic devices depicting boastful stories of the heroic deeds (legitimate questions might be "Who did those deeds, or are they made up," and "When were they in combat before?") of the rebel angels. Unlike some of the angelic warriors depicted in dramatizations of the War in Heaven (Fowler [6.83n] cites Thomas Heywood's *The Hierarchie of the Blessed Angels* [1635]), Milton's angels on both sides carry what appears to be real armor. One should not forget that Raphael is telling this story and accommodating it to images that Adam can understand. Adam may understand the motives for war and even armor as we know it, but he is not born with the power to imagine angelic warfare.

[36]The armies of Satan do not march in order: they hasten on; they are not a unified army: they are more of a "band" as in "band of thieves" (though the word *band* was not necessarily pejorative); and they move not reasonably but "With furious expedition [haste]."

[37]Satan, one of whose chief sins, next to pride, is envy. Satan is envious not of God's virtue but of His estate. Satan's military objective is to capture the throne of God.

[38]The word here suggests the meeting of armed hosts, a meaning not usually associated with hospitality. See *OED* vbl. sb., "The raising of a host or armed multitude," citing this usage. There may be some irony implied, however, between "host" and "hosting," since before this meeting the two factions would have shared God's hospitality. If one force is the host of the other, the hospitality is ironic as well.

[39]Satan is compared implicitly with the pagan Apollo, but we know from 4.37 that he hates the beams of the sun, and the Epic Voice reminds us that he is an apostate, that he is only acting "as a god," and that he is only an "Idol of Majestie Divine," not a true divinity. His chariot is a parody of the "Chariot of Paternal Deitie" (750 below); to worship this image, Milton implies, would be idolatry.

With Flaming Cherubim, and golden Shields;
Then lighted from his gorgeous Throne, for now
'Twixt Host and Host but narrow space was left,
A dreadful intervall, and Front to Front   105
Presented stood in terrible array
Of hideous length: before the cloudie Van,[40]
On the rough edge of battel ere it joyn'd,
Satan with vast and haughtie strides advanc't,
Came towring, armd in Adamant and Gold;   110
Abdiel that sight endur'd not, where he stood
Among the mightiest, bent on highest deeds,
And thus his own undaunted heart explores.[41]
    O Heav'n! that such resemblance of the Highest
Should yet remain, where faith and realtie[42]   115
Remain not; wherfore should not strength and might
There fail where Vertue fails, or weakest prove
Where boldest; though to sight unconquerable?
His puissance,[43] trusting in th' Almightie's aide,
I mean to try, whose Reason I have tri'd   120
Unsound and false; nor is it aught but just,
That he who in debate of Truth hath won,
Should win in Arms, in both disputes alike
Victor; though brutish that contest[44] and foule,
When Reason hath to deal with force, yet so   125
Most reason is that Reason overcome.[45]
    So pondering, and from his armed Peers
Forth stepping opposite, half way he met
His daring foe, at this prevention[46] more
Incens't, and thus securely him defi'd.[47]   130
    Proud, art thou met?[48] thy hope was to have reacht
The highth of thy aspiring unoppos'd,
The Throne of God unguarded, and his side
Abandond at the terror of thy Power
Or potent tongue; fool, not to think how vain   135

---

[40]The two front lines of battle are drawn up, vanguard against vanguard, and Satan is pictured marching up and down in front of his "Van," which is cloudy because of the dust the troops have kicked up.

[41]What follows from Abdiel is recognizable as akin to a soliloquy, its introduction echoing Homer's introduction to Hector's soliloquy (*Iliad* 22.98) just as he is going out to face Achilles in single combat (though Hector is killed). Since Hector, unlike Abdiel, is full of doubts and fears, Milton may be counting on the "fit reader" to contrast, once again, the values of pagan epic with those of Christian. Like Shakespeare, Milton gives good characters such as Jesus in *Paradise Regain'd* and evil characters, such as Satan, soliloquies, speeches that represent their unvoiced thoughts. Broadbent's often cited opinion that soliloquies occur only in fallen beings, therefore, is not accurate. See David Robertson, "Soliloquy and Self-Creation in *Paradise Lost*," paper delivered to the Fourth International Milton Symposium, University of British Columbia, August 1991.

[42]Probably "sincerity," as in *OED* 2.2, citing this passage and calling the usage "rare." As Hughes points out, however, the word may be a shortened form of "reality" or a misprint for "fealtie" or "lealtie," though the conjecture is doubtful.

[43]One of the few nouns of French derivation that Milton preserves in English, the word means "power" or "authority."

[44]Accented on the second syllable.

[45]"It is brutish for reason to have to deal with force, but it is only reasonable that reason should overcome force." By a kind of poetic justice, Abdiel, who has fought only with words against arms before, has the chance here to answer words with heroic force.

[46]Probably "action of forestalling," as in *OED* 4, though the Latin root of *prævenire*, "to come out in front of," or "precede," may enter into the meaning of the word as Milton uses it.

[47]Abdiel is incensed that Satan is standing in his way; he defies the apparently more powerful Satan, depending on the power of his own zeal and faith.

[48]"Proud one, are you confronted?" Satan as embodiment of pride is "met" in the sense that armies "meet" on the battlefield.

Against th' Omnipotent to rise in Arms;[49]
Who out of smallest things could without end
Have rais'd incessant Armies to defeat
Thy folly; or with solitarie hand
Reaching beyond all limit at one blow   140
Unaided could have finisht thee, and whelmd°   OVERWHELMED
Thy Legions under darkness; but thou seest
All are not of thy Train; there be who[50] Faith
Prefer, and Pietie to God, though then
To thee not visible, when I alone   145
Seemd in thy World erroneous to dissent
From all: my Sect[51] thou seest, now learn too late
How few somtimes may know, when thousands err.
    Whom the grand foe with scornful eye askance[52]
Thus answer'd. Ill for thee, but in wisht houre   150
Of my revenge, first sought for thou returnst
From flight, seditious Angel, to receave   *(traitor)*
Thy merited reward, the first assay°   TEST
Of this right hand provok't, since first that tongue
Inspir'd with contradiction durst oppose   155
A third part of the Gods,[53] in Synod[54] met
Thir Deities to assert, who while they feel
Vigour Divine within them, can allow
Omnipotence to none. But well thou comst
Before thy fellows, ambitious to win   160
From me som Plume,[55] that thy success may show
Destruction to the rest: this pause between
(Unanswerd least thou boast) to let thee know;[56]
At first I thought that Libertie and Heav'n
To heav'nly Soules had bin all one; but now   165
I see that most through sloth had rather serve,
Ministring Spirits,[57] traind up in Feast and Song;
Such hast thou arm'd, the Minstrelsie of Heav'n,
Servilitie with freedom to contend,
As both thir deeds compar'd this day shall prove.   170
    To whom in brief thus *Abdiel* stern repli'd.

---

[49]The most concise statement of the ridiculousness of Satan's war with God. God could, if need be, raise an army of any of the "smallest things" to defeat Satan's forces. The point of the combat between Abdiel, a Seraph, and Satan, a former archangel, is that Satan by his sin has weakened himself to the point that an "inferior" angel can easily defeat his folly.

[50]"There are those who." The omission of "those" was common in an idiom in use during Milton's lifetime. The word "Train," here meaning something like "coterie" or "hangers-on," is used contemptuously, as it usually is.

[51]There may indeed be a political reference to all those who opposed the policy of Archbishop William Laud to label any who refused to endorse the official Church of England in the 1630s as "sectaries." Fowler (6.147n) aptly cites *Eikonoklastes*: "I never knew that time in *England*, when men of truest Religion were not counted Sectaries . . ." (Yale 3: 348).

[52]Satan's sidelong glance is analogous to the "squint suspicion" of *Comus* 413.

[53]Roughly synonymous with "angels," but with sinister or ironic overtones, as in "ye shall be as gods" in Genesis 3.5.

[54]Ordinarily a meeting of representatives of the church to determine official dogma, as in the Synod of Dort (1618–19), though Corns points out that "it usually referred quite specifically to a formal assembly of the Church of England or to a tier of church government within a presbyterian organization" (*Milton's* 107). Again, Milton has Satan use the ecclesiastical term with heavy irony.

[55]Conquerors in battle might literally put a feather in their cap gathered from the plumed crest of their defeated opponents.

[56]Satan is crediting Abdiel with his own evil motives, implying that he has come into battle only to win a plume and insinuating that Abdiel will interpret his pauses as indications (as they are) of weakness or indecisiveness.

[57]Ministering spirits would be taken from lower orders of angels—as Satan perceives them, a kind of servant class—whose title in this case forms a bad pun with their office, "Minstrelsie," though there is a biblical precedent for "ministering spirits" in Hebrews 1.14, and, of course, for angels singing songs in Heaven.

[handwritten margin note: abdiel]

Apostat, still thou errst, nor end wilt find
Of erring, from the path of truth remote:
Unjustly thou deprav'st it with the name
Of *Servitude*[58] to serve whom God ordains,
Or Nature; God and Nature bid the same,   175
When he who rules is worthiest, and excells
Them whom he governs.[59] This is servitude,
To serve th' unwise, or him who hath rebelld
Against his worthier, as thine now serve thee,
Thy self not free, but to thy self enthrall'd;[60]   180
Yet leudly[61] dar'st our ministring upbraid.

[handwritten margin note: Satan]

Reign thou in Hell thy Kingdom,[62] let mee serve
In Heav'n God ever blest, and his Divine
Behests obey, worthiest to be obey'd,
Yet Chains in Hell, not Realms expect: mean while   185
From mee returnd, as erst thou saidst, from flight,
This greeting on thy impious Crest[63] receive.
   So saying, a noble stroke he lifted high,
Which hung not, but so swift with tempest fell
On the proud Crest of *Satan*, that no sight,   190
Nor motion of swift thought, less could his Shield
Such ruin intercept: ten paces huge
He back recoild;[64] the tenth on bended knee
His massie Spear upstaid; as if on Earth   195

[handwritten margin note: serpent lice]

Winds under ground or waters forcing way
Sidelong, had push't a Mountain from his seat
Half sunk with all his Pines.[65] Amazement seis'd
The Rebel Thrones,[66] but greater rage to see
Thus foil'd thir mightiest, ours joy filld, and shout,   200
Presage of Victorie[67] and fierce desire
Of Battel: whereat *Michael* bid sound
Th' Arch-Angel trumpet; through the vast of Heaven[68]
It sounded, and the faithful Armies rung
Hosanna[69] to the Highest: nor stood at gaze°   GAZING   205
The adverse Legions, nor less hideous joyn'd

[handwritten margin notes: "Plagiarism in Satan"; "Bondage — what those who follow Satan do."; "Satan vowed he never bend on knee but here he is."; "The Battle Starts"]

---

[58]An unusual use of italics to emphasize a word as word, almost certainly derived from the manuscript, since compositors would normally italicize only proper names.

[59]Again, a very concise statement of the relationship between God and nature—one which explains why the Son's elevation by merit is a natural one, and one for which Satan should have felt no envy.

[60]Satan's decision to commit himself to evil, in other words, enslaves him and anyone who listens to him. The liberty he vaguely brags of is licentiousness, which leads only to a state of slavery to one's desires. The word *self* and especially the prefix *self-* often have negative connotations in Milton's poetry and prose, as in "self-love" (*Samson Agonistes* 1031) or "Self-deprav'd" (3.130).

[61]Probably "ignorantly" or "foolishly," with no connotations of sexual misbehavior.

[62]Satan remembers Abdiel's taunt and turns it into "Better to reign in Hell, then serve in Heav'n" (1.263).

[63]A kind of rejoinder to Satan's plume, which would be part of his "crest," the heraldic device mounted on his helmet.

[64]Whaler (*Counterpoint* 100) finds symbolism here on the logic that if God's creativity can be measured in tens, then Satan's destructiveness can represent a reversal, a kind of negative ten.

[65]The simile again accommodates what happened in a realm Adam cannot imagine with what he could perceive happening—subterranean wind or water causing earthquakes—on earth. That Milton has not lost sight of Raphael as narrator is shown again by the pronoun "ours" used below, 200.

[66]"Thrones" seems to stand (as does "Powers" at times) for all the rebel forces. "Throne" was one of the orders of angels (see West 50–51).

[67]The shout is prediction of the final victory over Satan at the Apocalypse, when " . . . the Lord himself shall descend from heaven, with a shout, with the voice of the archangel, and with the trump of God . . . " (1 Thessalonians 4.16). "Presage," derived from the Latin *præsāgium*, "forboding," is accented on the second syllable.

[68]As Fletcher points out, the second syllable is surely unstressed and the word should have been printed as a monosyllabic "Heav'n."

[69]Another rare use of italics, though perhaps "Hosanna" has been taken by the compositor as a significant quoted word, or a "foreign" (Hebrew) word.

The horrid shock: now storming furie rose,
And clamour such as heard in Heav'n till now
Was never, Arms on Armour clashing bray'd[70]
Horrible discord, and the madding[71] Wheeles　　　　　　　　　210
Of brazen Chariots rag'd; dire was the noise
Of conflict; over head the dismal hiss
Of fiery Darts in flaming volies flew,
And flying vaulted either Host with fire.
So under fierie Cope[72] together rush'd　　　　　　　　　　　215
Both Battels maine,[73] with ruinous assault
And inextinguishable rage; all Heav'n
Resounded, and had Earth bin then, all Earth
Had to her Center shook. What wonder? when
Millions of fierce encountring Angels fought　　　　　　　　220
On either side, the least of whom could weild
These Elements, and arm him with the force
Of all thir Regions: how much more of Power
Armie against Armie numberless to raise
Dreadful combustion[74] warring, and disturb,　　　　　　　225
Though not destroy, thir happie Native seat;
Had not th' Eternal King Omnipotent
From his strong hold of Heav'n high over-rul'd
And limited thir might; though numberd such
As each divided Legion might have seemd　　　　　　　　230
A numerous Host, in strength each armed hand
A Legion;[75] led in fight, yet Leader seemd
Each Warriour single as in Chief, expert
When to advance, or stand, or turn the sway
Of Battel, open when, and when to close　　　　　　　　235
The ridges of grim Warr;[76] no thought of flight,
None of retreat, no unbecoming deed
That argu'd fear; each on himself reli'd,
As onely in his arm the moment lay
Of victorie; deeds of eternal fame　　　　　　　　　　240
Were don, but infinite: for wide was spred
That Warr and various; somtimes on firm ground
A standing fight, then soaring on main° wing　　　　　MIGHTY
Tormented° all the Air; all Air seemd then　　　　　　AGITATED
Conflicting Fire: long time in eeven scale　　　　　　　245
The Battel hung; till *Satan*, who that day
Prodigious power had shewn, and met in Armes
No equal, raunging through the dire attack
Of fighting Seraphim confus'd, at length

---

[70]Apparently the word could describe any grating sound, since a donkey's bray is comparable to the sound of an off-note trumpet, whose sound is in turn comparable to the brassy clash of armor against armor.

[71]Running at an insane pace, "frenzied" (*OED* ppl.a, citing this instance), as in Thomas Hardy's title *Far from the Madding Crowd*.

[72]Here the word seems to mean what *OED* sb. 1, 7d, assigns to it, "A vault or canopy like that of the sky."

[73]The main bodies of both armies, as compared to vanguards or wings; see *OED* "Battle" II, 9.

[74]See *OED* 5.b, "Violent excitement or commotion," citing this passage. Milton is perhaps foreshadowing the invention of gunpowder.

[75]Stresses the individual responsibility of each fighting angel, illustrating their use of free will. Each of them is an "armed hand" as strong in his convictions as an entire legion and each is a leader because each embodies the righteousness of the collective cause.

[76]Probably the image is of opening and closing battle ranks, though no military usage is recorded in the *OED*. A ridge, as is customary usage in English agricultural terms, is "A raised or rounded strip of arable land" (*OED* 5, citing this passage).

Saw where the Sword of *Michael* smote, and fell'd   250
Squadrons at once, with huge two-handed[77] sway
Brandisht aloft the horrid° edge came down   SHARP
Wide wasting; such destruction to withstand
He hasted, and oppos'd the rockie Orb
Of tenfold Adamant,[78] his ample Shield   255
A vast circumference: At his approach
The great Arch-Angel from his warlike toile
Surceas'd,[79] and glad as hoping here to end
Intestine War° in Heav'n, the arch foe subdu'd   CIVIL WAR
Or Captive drag'd in Chains, with hostile frown   260
And visage all enflam'd[80] first thus began.
    Author of evil,[81] unknown till thy revolt,
Unnam'd in Heav'n, now plenteous, as thou seest
These Acts of hateful strife, hateful to all,
Though heaviest by just measure on thy self   265
And thy adherents: how hast thou disturb'd
Heav'ns blessed peace, and into Nature brought
Miserie, uncreated till the crime
Of thy Rebellion?[82] how hast thou instill'd
Thy malice into thousands, once upright   270
And faithful, now prov'd false. But think not here
To trouble Holy Rest;[83] Heav'n casts thee out
From all her Confines. Heav'n the seat of bliss
Brooks° not the works of violence and Warr.   ALLOWS
Hence then, and evil go with thee along   275
Thy ofspring,[84] to the place of evil, Hell,
Thou and thy wicked crew; there mingle broiles,°   BATTLES, RIOTS
Ere this avenging Sword begin thy doome,
Or som more sudden vengeance wing'd from God
Precipitate thee with augmented paine.[85]   280
    So spake the Prince of Angels; to whom thus
The Adversarie.[86] Nor think thou with wind
Of airie threats to aw whom yet with deeds
Thou canst not. Hast thou turnd the least of these

[handwritten margin notes: "Abdiel", "look at what has been created", "Go create stratedgems", "flex for power"]

---

[77]The image of Michael's sword that requires two hands to wield is often used to define the famous crux, the "two-handed engine," in "Lycidas" 130–31. The word "sway" suggests insuperable might.

[78]The hardest substance imaginable, as in "Adamantine Chains" (1.48). Instead of having in mind diamond, a gem often associated with adamant, Milton is more likely to be picturing a unique metal, since a strong metal would be capable of being laminated or heated to red-hot and doubled back on itself, as in samurai swordmaking, and thus be capable of being folded ten times.

[79]Michael stops fighting at least for the time being. *OED* "surcease" 1 reminds us that the word was the older form of "cease," and that it meant "To leave off, desist, stop, cease from some action (finally or temporarily)," citing this passage.

[80]Michael's countenance, like Abdiel's, is enflamed or glowing with zeal.

[81]The word "Author" puts Satan in a special category of creator in *Paradise Lost*, one reserved for God the Father, the Son, and Adam. After the Fall, with Satan, Sin, and Death, and with Adam and Eve, the title "author" suggests only a perverse creator, as when Adam and Eve are described in Book 3 as "Authors to themselves in all / Both what they judge and what they choose . . . " (122–23).

[82]Satan is the unholy inventor of sin and its consequent misery, and he brings them into the natural world.

[83]Milton associated a period of "holy . . . rest" with the Sabbath (*Doctrine and Discipline of Divorce*, Yale 2: 339); here it seems to mean the tranquility of Heaven.

[84]A reminder that Satan has consorted with Sin, as described at 2.764–67.

[85]"In Hell you can continue your quarrels among your own factions, until at Judgment Day you will be conquered once and for all with my sword of vengeance. Or God might send even more sudden vengeance to throw you down rapidly and with more pain." The verb "Precipitate" emphasizes Satan's passivity once he has fallen (Milton apparently invented the noun "precipitance" at 7.291 to express the much happier gathering of waters at Creation).

[86]As compared with "Enemy," a more precise one-word definition of "Satan," who now has not just one name but many generic titles, all standing for the being who defines himself as alien to God.

To flight, or if to fall, but that they rise   285
Unvanquisht, easier to transact° with mee   NEGOTIATE
That thou shouldst hope, imperious, and with threats
To chase me hence? erre not that so shall end
The strife which thou call'st evil, but wee style
The strife of Glorie: which we mean to win,   290
Or turn this Heav'n it self into the Hell
Thou fablest,[87] here however to dwell free,
If not to reign: mean while thy utmost force,
And join him nam'd *Almighty* to thy aid,
I flie not, but have sought thee farr and nigh.   295
    They ended parle,[88] and both addrest° for fight   PREPARED
Unspeakable; for who, though with the tongue
Of Angels,[89] can relate, or to what things
Liken on Earth conspicuous,[90] that may lift
Human imagination to such highth   300
Of Godlike Power:[91] for likest Gods they seemd,
Stood they or mov'd, in stature, motion, arms[92]
Fit to decide the Empire of great Heav'n.
Now wav'd thir fierie Swords, and in the Aire
Made horrid Circles; two broad Suns thir Shields   305
Blaz'd opposite, while expectation stood
In horror;[93] from each hand with speed retir'd
Where erst was thickest fight, th' Angelic throng,
And left large field, unsafe within the wind
Of such commotion, such as to set forth   310
Great things by small.[94] If Natures concord broke,
Among the Constellations warr were sprung,
Two Planets rushing from aspect maligne
Of fiercest opposition in mid Skie,
Should combat, and thir jarring Sphears confound.   315
Together both with next to Almightie Arme[95]
Uplifted imminent, one stroke they aim'd
That might determine,[96] and not need repeate,
As not of power, at once; nor odds appeerd
In might or swift prevention;° but the sword   ANTICIPATION   320
Of *Michael* from the Armorie of God[97]

---

[87]Hell has already come into existence, to house the fallen angels, as soon as they elect to fall (see 53–55 above), so it is Satan who is lying—fabling—about its not existing.

[88]A diplomatic discussion between two enemies on the battlefield (a verb derived from *OED* "parley" 2).

[89]Adapted from the phrase in the famous beginning of 1 Corinthians 13.1, "Though I speak with the tongues of men and of angels, and have not charity, I am become as sounding brass, or a tinkling cymbal."

[90]"Clearly visible, . . . striking to the eye" (*OED* 1, citing this instance).

[91]A reference to the necessity on Raphael's part of accommodating his narrative to Adam's understanding.

[92]Compare the capitalization in line 70; the completely different strategy of assigning capital letters might indicate the presence of a different compositor at this point in the book, one who uses fewer capital letters in lists of ordinary nouns.

[93]Expectation is personified as standing by watching the battle. Compare " . . . on his Crest / Sat horror Plum'd" (4.988–89).

[94]The comma here in both early editions may well have been set incorrectly for a period; *1674* merely copies exactly what *1667* has for the punctuation and capitalization in the line.

[95]The comma was struck out in ink in one of the copies of *1674* that Fletcher examined, and a comma was inserted in the next line after "imminent," an early emendation that I have accepted. Many early editors dropped the comma after "Arme," though its presence in the first and second editions might argue for its authenticity.

[96]"That might settle the outcome."

[97]"The Lord hath opened his armoury, and hath brought forth the weapons of his indignation . . ." (Jeremiah 50.25).

Was giv'n him temperd so, that neither keen
Nor solid might resist that edge:[98] it met
The sword of *Satan* with steep force to smite
Descending, and in half cut sheere, nor staid,   325
But with swift wheele reverse, deep entring shar'd°[99]
All his right side; then *Satan* first knew pain,
And writh'd him to and fro convolv'd;[100] so sore
The griding sword with discontinuous wound[101]
Pass'd through him, but th' Ethereal substance clos'd   330
Not long divisible, and from the gash
A stream of Nectarous humor[102] issuing flow'd
Sanguin, such as Celestial Spirits may bleed,
And all his Armour staind ere while so bright.
Forthwith on all sides to his aide was run[103]   335
By Angels many and strong, who interpos'd
Defence, while others bore him on thir Shields
Back to his Chariot; where it stood retir'd
From off the files[104] of warr; there they him laid
Gnashing for anguish and despite and shame   340
To find himself not matchless, and his pride
Humbl'd by such rebuke, so farr beneath
His confidence to equal God in power.
Yet soon he heal'd; for Spirits that live throughout
Vital in every part, not as frail man   345
In Entrailes, Heart or Head, Liver or Reines,° KIDNEYS
Cannot but by annihilating die;[105]
Nor in thir liquid texture mortal wound
Receive, no more then can the fluid Aire:[106]
All Heart they live, all Head, all Eye, all Eare,   350
All Intellect, all Sense, and as they please,
They Limb themselves, and colour, shape or size

SHEARED, CUT OFF

---

[98]The sword of Michael possesses the two best attributes of a good sword—strength and keenness; thus it cuts in half the sword of Satan, which represents only "solid might." As soon as Michael has cut through the sword of Satan, as a good swordsman he immediately wheels the sword in air, "with swift . . . reverse," to cut Satan himself. As Fowler points out (6.320–23n), Milton outdoes Vergil, who pictures Turnus's sword merely shattering on Aeneas's armor (*Aeneid* 12.741).

[99]"To cut into parts, to cut off" (*OED* v.1 a, citing this passage).

[100]Perhaps this is a motion—convoluted, recoiling, or writhing—that prepares him for adopting the shape of the serpent? Writhing will be the last motion associated with the fallen angels in *Paradise Lost* (10.569).

[101]The word "griding" is Spenserian. Its sound seems to echo its sense of "cutting keenly and painfully through" (see *OED* 1, which cites this passage). A discontinuous wound is, medically speaking, one which has rough edges. This wound, which is horribly serious, is nevertheless capable of healing quickly because it occurs in angelic substance, ether.

[102]The *OED* defines the adjective "nectarous" only as "Resembling nectar." Milton assumes that angels bleed nectar, which I presume is similar to what they drink and to the ether of which they are made. Milton invented the adjective form; it appears in 5.306 as well. Whatever flowed from Satan's side, it served the same function as human blood and hence was "Sanguin."

[103]The Latin idiom *cursum est*, as in "His race was run." The syntax is still confusing in English, but the meaning seems to be "angels quickly ran to his aid from all sides."

[104]The chariot stands in back of the arranged armies, as in "rank and file." It is "retir'd" in the sense that it is for the time being not in active service.

[105]Since the angels have no internal organs, being of one substance or "uncompounded" (1.425, in a passage of similar description of angelic nature and physical attributes), they cannot die in the way that fallen man is accustomed to: they must be uncreated by God or annihilated. Raphael is explaining all this to Adam (and to the reader) as he tells the story. In punctuating the two previous lines, I have replaced the incorrect semicolon after "Reines" of *1674* with the correct comma of *1667*.

[106]Alexander Pope realized that the quick healing of Satan brought something of the farce into the battle, and when a sylph is cut in two in *The Rape of the Lock*, his "airy substance soon unites again" (152).

Assume, as likes them best, condense or rare.[107]
   Mean while in other parts like deeds deservd
Memorial, where the might of *Gabriel*[108] fought,   355
And with fierce Ensignes[109] pierc'd the deep array[110]
Of *Moloc* furious King, who him defi'd,
And at his Chariots wheeles to drag him bound
Threatn'd,[111] nor from the Holie One of Heav'n
Refrein'd his tongue blasphemous;[112] but anon   360
Down clov'n to the waste,° with shatterd Armes   WAIST
And uncouth paine fled bellowing.[113] On each wing
Uriel and *Raphael* his vaunting foe,[114]
Though huge, and in a Rock of Diamond Armd,[115]
Vanquish'd *Adramelec*,[116] and *Asmadai*,[117]   365
Two potent Thrones, that to be less then Gods
Disdain'd, but meaner thoughts learnd in thir flight,
Mangl'd with gastly wounds through Plate and Maile,
Nor stood unmindful *Abdiel* to annoy
The Atheist crew, but with redoubl'd blow   370
Ariel and *Arioc*,[118] and the violence
Of *Ramiel* scorcht and blasted overthrew.
I might relate of thousands, and thir names

Handwritten annotation: Gabriel takes on Moloch

---

[107]As Milton's most complete poetic pronouncement about the nature of angels, lines 344–53 should be compared with Book 1, Chapter 9 of *On Christian Doctrine*, "Of the Special Government of Angels." The sense perception, the intellectual capacity, and the ability to dilate (as Satan does when he is angry at 4.986) or contract (as when Satan takes the forms of such beasts as the cormorant [4.196] or lion or tiger [4.402–03]) and take on various "limbs" are all noteworthy. The idiom "as likes them best" means "as it best pleases them," and "condense or rare" has to do with the contraction or expansion of what would today be called atomic structure.

[108]The characterizing phrase resembles an Homeric epithet such as "Achilles of the swift feet," but "the might of *Gabriel*" also sets off Gabriel's characteristic as if it were an allegorical entity or a synecdoche (a part representing the whole) for him.

[109]Probably "A body of men serving under one banner" (*OED* 6). The word was used during the seventeenth century to define the Latin generic word for "troops," *cohors*.

[110]The arrangement of military ranks in battle (as with *OED* 1, which cites the usage at 2.887).

[111]A parody, perhaps, of Achilles's dragging the body of his victim Hector behind his chariot around the walls of Troy (*Iliad* 22.396–404). As Fowler points out, the War in Heaven begins by looking like the combats of Renaissance epic such as those in Boiardo's *Orlando Innamorato*, but Milton's narrative is "more impressionistic and economical and functional," hence avoiding the "long and tedious havoc" (9.30) of the romantic epics (Fowler 6.357–62n).

[112]Moloch is characterized by his fierceness, his brutality, and, ultimately, his cowardice. In describing him Raphael alludes to 2 Kings 19.22: "Whom has thou reproached and blasphemed? . . . even against the Holy One of Israel." The word blasphemous was accented on the second syllable.

[113]This most undignified portrait of Moloch, cut in half, without the use of his arms, and bellowing in pain, needs to be compared with what he **says** he wants to do in battle in 2.51–105. He pretends to be to Gabriel what Achilles was to Hector, then he blasphemes, is cut to the waist by Gabriel and runs off bellowing—typical of a bull-god. Mars in Book 5 of the *Iliad* does much the same thing when he is wounded by Diomedes: "Then Ares the brazen bellowed with a sound as great as nine thousand men make, or ten thousand, when they cry as they carry into the fighting the fury of the war god" (Lattimore trans., 859–61).

[114]Raphael identifies Uriel first, on one wing of the army, and then himself, described in the third person as the justly triumphing ("vaunting") foe of Moloch and using the name that Adam will eventually know him as. As for the names of fallen angels, "To invent names for the rebel angels would be an unwarranted intrusion upon God's mysteries," but "There is a possible solution. Raphael may be speaking names he knows the rebels will later acquire" (Leonard 80–81). Compare what Michael says at 12.140: "(Things by thir names I call, though yet unnam'd)."

[115]Apparently not the same as adamant, since adamant is material for Satan's shield and diamond here is the material for the angels' armor. Compare 110 above and 542 below.

[116]Though we do not know precisely which angel is fighting which, it would be appropriate, as Fowler points out (3.363–68n), if Uriel fought Adramelec, since Adramelec is an Assyrian sun-god mentioned in 2 Kings 17.31 (see West 152).

[117]Asmadai or Asmodeus would be more familiar as an opponent of Raphael, since they confront one another in the apocryphal Book of Tobit, where Asmodeus is banished by the "fishie fume" mentioned in 4.168 and consequently "fled into the utmost parts of Egypt" (Tobit 8.3; Geneva Bible, 1560 ed.). The "Thrones" comprise one of the angelic orders.

[118]Though his name is more often identified with Shakespeare's spirit in *The Tempest*, "Ariel" means "Lion of God" and is identified with "a city where David dwelt" and specifically with an altar there (Isaiah 29.1–2). The Geneva Bible marginalia inteprets: "The Ebrewe worde Ariel signifieth the lyon of God, & signifieth the altar, because the altar seemed to devoure the sacrifice and was offred to God, as Ezek. 41.16." But West traces a separate history of the name and identity to a pagan god named Ariel who is an earth spirit (152–54). For Arioc, see the "Arioch king of Ellasar" mentioned in Genesis 14.1; West identifies Arioc as "known to demonologists as the spirit of revenge" (154). Ramiel is one of the Sons of God who fall by association with the Daughters of Men in the apocryphal 1 Enoch 6.7.

Eternize here on Earth;[119] but those elect[120]
Angels contented with thir fame in Heav'n   375
Seek not the praise of men: the other sort
In might though wondrous and in Acts of Warr,
Nor of Renown less eager, yet by doome
Canceld from Heav'n and sacred memorie,[121]
Nameless in dark oblivion let them dwell.   380
For strength from Truth divided and from Just,°   JUSTICE
Illaudable,° naught merits but dispraise   UNPRAISEWORTHY
And ignominie, yet to glorie aspires
Vain glorious, and through infamie seeks fame:
Therfore Eternal silence be thir doome.   385
    And now thir Mightiest quelld, the battel swerv'd,
With many an inrode gor'd;[122] deformed rout
Enter'd, and foul disorder; all the ground
With shiverd armour strow'n,° and on a heap   STREWED
Chariot and Charioter lay overturnd   390
And fierie foaming Steeds;[123] what stood, recoyld
Orewearied, through the faint Satanic Host
Defensive scarse,[124] or with pale fear surpris'd,
Then first with fear surpris'd and sense of paine
Fled ignominious, to such evil brought   395
By sin of disobedience, till that hour
Not liable to fear or flight or paine.
Far otherwise th' inviolable Saints
In Cubic Phalanx[125] firm advanc't entire,
Invulnerable, impenitrably arm'd: 400
Such high advantages thir innocence
Gave them above thir foes, not to have sinnd,
Not to have disobei'd; in sight they stood
Unwearied, unobnoxious[126] to be pain'd
By wound, though from thir place by violence mov'd.   405
    Now Night her course began, and over Heav'n
Inducing° darkness,[127] grateful truce impos'd,   LEADING IN

---

[119]Raphael stops the catalogue at this point so as not to immortalize any more fallen angels on earth by naming them in the presence of Adam.

[120]Milton is probably using the word in the general biblical sense of "special" or "distinguished," as "I charge thee before God, and the Lord Jesus Christ, and the elect angels . . ." (1 Timothy 5.21). Since Raphael has just recounted one of his own exploits, the little moral tag that follows this narrative is pedagogical: it teaches Adam one of the lessons of "Lycidas" 78–82.

[121]Because of their free decision to fall, they have doomed themselves and caused to be cancelled from the book of Heaven their names and memory. Compare 1.361–62: "Though of thir Names in heav'nly Records now / Be no memorial, blotted out and ras'd."

[122]Since an inroad was defined figuratively as "A powerful or sudden incursion" (*OED* 2) and since the word was also used for the entrance of mining tunnels, "gor'd" thus is a proper attending verb. Even in a war in Heaven, Milton seems to imply, battle is ugly, deformed, foul, and chaotic: he will have Raphael sum it up as "odious dinn" (408 below). But see Revard, Freeman, and Fallon on Milton and militarism for a complete picture of the nature of rightful Christian warfare from Milton's perspective.

[123]Again, the horses from romantic epic, here not only fiery but covered with foaming perspiration.

[124]Scarcely capable of defending itself.

[125]Perhaps the image has a symbolic value as well as a literal one, since the cube was one emblem of stability and stalwart unity. At any rate, the battle formations of the angels on either side are rectangular. Such a phalanx should offer all but impenetrable sides to any opposition; thus the formation of the good angels maintains its integrity just as they retain their inviolability. Sinning causes physical weakness in the evil angels.

[126]The meaning of the word is quite unlike the modern meaning. Rather than being "inoffensive," the true angels are "not capable of being wounded." If one conflates the two definitions for obnoxious and unobnoxious from the *OED* entries, one gets the meaning "Not exposed or liable to real or imagined harm." In its definition of unobnoxious, *OED* 1 cites this passage.

[127]Fowler calls this "the evening of Day 3 of the poem's action," but time in Heaven is difficult to accommodate to human understanding, since "a thousand years in thy sight [in the sight of God] are but as yesterday when it is past, and as a watch in the night" (Psalm 90.4). Raphael describes another morning at 524 below.

And silence on the odious dinn of Warr:
Under her Cloudie covert both retir'd,
Victor and Vanquisht: on the foughten field[128]   410
Michael and his Angels prevalent[129]
Encamping, plac'd in Guard thir Watches round,
Cherubic waving fires:[130] on th' other part
Satan with his rebellious disappeerd,
Far in the dark dislodg'd,[131] and void of rest,   415
His Potentates to Councel call'd by night;[132]
And in the midst thus undismai'd began.

  O now in danger tri'd, now known in Armes
Not to be overpowerd, Companions deare,
Found worthy not of Libertie alone,   420
Too mean pretense,[133] but what we more affect,
Honour, Dominion, Glorie, and renowne,
Who have sustaind one day in doubtful fight[134]
(And if one day, why not Eternal dayes?)
What Heavens Lord had powerfullest to send   425
Against us from about his Throne, and judg'd
Sufficient to subdue us to his will,
But proves not so: then fallible, it seems,
Of future° we may deem him, though till now   IN THE FUTURE
Omniscient thought.[135] True is,[136] less firmly arm'd,   430
Some disadvantage we endur'd and paine,
Till now not known, but known as soon contemnd,
Since now we find this our Empyreal form
Incapable of mortal injurie
Imperishable, and though peirc'd with wound,   435
Soon closing, and by native vigour heal'd.[137]
Of evil then so small as easie think
The remedie; perhaps more valid° Armes,   POWERFUL
Weapons more violent, when next we meet,
May serve to better us, and worse° our foes,   MAKE WORSE   440
Or equal what between us made the odds,
In Nature none: if other hidden cause

[128]A "foughten field" was idiomatic for a field on which there had been a battle.

[129]"Michael and his angels, as the victorious army."

[130]Since they are known for being fiery, and for being exponents of "divinity full of ideas" (West 150, quoting Agrippa), the cherubim are quite naturally given watch, as they will also be asked to stand guard as Michael guides Adam and Eve out of Paradise (12.628).

[131]In military terminology, when Satan "dislodg'd," he moved his encampment, in this case disappearing with it into darkness.

[132]Editors from Newton (415n) on find the precedent for this nighttime council held by defeated forces in the council called by Agamemnon in *Iliad* 9 after the defeat by Hector, when the Achaians are gripped with panic and terror and Agamemnon himself begins the council in despair, weeping.

[133]Liberty, which Satan here seems to reduce to a "mean ['lower-class'?] pretense," is of much greater moral value than the affectation of honor, dominion, glory, and renown. The fallen angels cannot have all of those good attributes, so they affect them.

[134]Satan is accurate here, in that the outcome of the day's battle has been in doubt, but there is no doubt about the final outcome in any fight against omnipotence, so his parenthetical rhetorical question is idle speculation.

[135]Satan is arguing by means of convoluted and fallacious logic: he says, first, that God has sent His most powerful force against them (He hasn't), and, second, that God has judged the good angels sufficient to stand up to his forces (but God, being omniscient, knows exactly how powerful each force is), and that therefore God is fallible and not omniscient. In fact Satan and his forces have been defeated, though not by a wide margin, and the Father is waiting to give the Son alone the glory of defeating the fallen angels. It is true that so far Satan's army has not suffered mortal injury, but they have fought only fellow angels: God has the power to annihilate them, as Moloch will acknowledge after the battle (2.95–97). Compare Raphael's summary of angelic being, which "Cannot but by annihilating die" (347 above).

[136]"It is true that . . . ."

[137]Is it possible that the former archangel Lucifer would not know the characteristics of angelic being before being wounded? It seems more likely that he is lying here as he does consistently throughout the passage.

Left them Superiour, while we can preserve
Unhurt our mindes, and understanding sound,
Due search and consultation will disclose.[138]　　　　　　　　　　445
　　He sat; and in th' assembly next upstood
Nisroc, of Principalities the prime;[139]
As one he stood escap't from cruel fight,
Sore toild, his riv'n Armes° to havoc hewn,　　　　　　MANGLED ARMOR
And cloudie in aspect[140] thus answering spake.　　　　　　　　　450
Deliverer from new Lords, leader to free
Enjoyment of our right as Gods; yet hard
For Gods, and too unequal work we find
Against unequal armes[141] to fight in paine,
Against unpaind, impassive; from which evil　　　　　　　　　455
Ruin must needs ensue; for what availes
Valour or strength, though matchless, quelld with pain
Which all subdues, and makes remiss the hands
Of Mightiest.　Sense of pleasure we may well
Spare out of life perhaps, and not repine,　　　　　　　　　460
But live content, which is the calmest life:
But pain is perfet miserie, the worst
Of evils, and excessive, overturnes
All patience.[142]　He who therefore can invent
With what more forcible° we may offend　　　　　　FORCIBLY　　465
Our yet unwounded Enemies, or arme
Our selves with like defence, to me deserves
No less then for deliverance what we owe.[143]
　　Whereto with look compos'd *Satan* repli'd.
Not uninvented that, which thou aright　　　　　　　　　470
Believst so main° to our success, I bring;　　　　　　IMPORTANT
Which of us who beholds the bright surface[144]
Of this Ethereous mould[145] whereon we stand,
This continent of spacious Heav'n, adornd
With Plant, Fruit, Flour Ambrosial, Gemms & Gold,　　　　　　475
Whose Eye so superficially surveyes
These things, as not to mind from whence they grow
Deep under ground, materials dark and crude,

---

[138]Satan is "hatching" plots which involve the use of cannonry and gunpowder, the "Weapons more violent." He must think in terms of material, rather than spiritual, power.

[139]According to one of the Renaissance dictionaries that Milton consulted, that of C. Stephanus, the Hebrew name Nisroch (more customarily spelled with the "h") meant "Flight" or "Delicate Temptation" (*vexillum delicatum*: Starnes and Talbert 268), two phrases that might give a clue to his timid character. Nisroch is named in 2 Kings 19.37 (repeated almost verbatim in Isaiah 37.38) as the Assyrian idol in whose temple Sennacherib is worshiping when his sons murder him. In other words, he is another false god who betrays or fails his worshiper.

[140]His armor is cut to pieces and his face is clouded; thus he is frowning, possibly in pain, anguish, or despair. "Aspect" is accented on the second syllable.

[141]Nisroch admits what Satan cannot, that the fight has not really been equal, because the Satanic forces can feel pain, which "quells" them, or quite defeats their morale.

[142]According to Nisroch's better-balanced values, the fallen angels could live without pleasure but they could not live in perpetual pain. It is impossible, in other words, to become accustomed to pain. Patience, as Milton defined it, "is the endurance of evils and injuries" (*On Christian Doctrine* 2.10; Yale 6: 739).

[143]Nisroch eventually persuades himself, apparently, to endorse Satan's plan to invent machines more forcible than the weapons they have been fighting with. Fowler believes that Nisroch veils a threat to try to replace Satan with any leader who can invent some new fighting machine (464–68n), but Satan's "look compos'd" argues that Nisroch plays into another of Satan's gimmicky plans. Nisroch seems more to represent the "drooping chere" and "languisht hope" mentioned in 496–97 below.

[144]Accented on the second syllable.

[145]Like Earth, Heaven has a layer of topsoil, but it is golden mould and made of ether.

Of spiritous and fierie spume,[146] till toucht
With Heav'ns ray, and temperd they shoot forth   480
So beauteous, op'ning to the ambient° light.   SURROUNDING
These in thir dark Nativitie the Deep
Shall yield us pregnant with infernal flame,[147]
Which into hallow° Engins long and round   HOLLOW
Thick-rammd, at th' other bore with touch of fire   485
Dilated and infuriate° shall send forth   ENRAGED
From far with thundring noise among our foes
Such implements of mischief as shall dash
To pieces, and orewhelm whatever stands
Adverse, that they shall fear we have disarmd   490
The Thunderer of his only dreaded bolt.
Nor long shall be our labour, yet ere dawne,
Effect shall end our wish. <u>Mean while revive;</u>
Abandon fear; to strength and counsel[148] joind
<u>Think nothing hard, much less to be despaird.</u>   495
<u>He ended, and his words thir drooping</u> chere°   SPIRIT
Enlightn'd, and thir languisht hope reviv'd.
Th' invention all admir'd,° and each, how hee   WONDERED AT
To be th' inventer miss'd, so easie it seemd
Once found, which yet unfound most would have thought   500
Impossible: yet haply of thy Race[149]
In future dayes, if Malice should abound,
Some one intent on mischief, or inspir'd
With dev'lish machination might devise
Like instrument to plague the Sons of men   505
For sin, on warr and mutual slaughter bent.
Forthwith from Councel to the work they flew,
None arguing stood, innumerable hands
Were ready, in a moment up they turnd
Wide the Celestial soile, and saw beneath   510
Th' originals of Nature in thir crude
Conception; Sulphurous and Nitrous Foame[150]

---

[146]Compare John Phillips (Milton's nephew), in *Poems in the Style of Milton*: " . . . Sulphur, and nitrous spume, enkindling fierce" (quoted in *OED* 1). The process being described is the power of astral bodies to generate minerals or metals or of "higher" metals to engender lesser. One contemporary metallurgical manual, for instance, describes "litharge" as "a spumous excrement of silver" (Robert Lovell, *Panoptiktologia . . . or An Universal History of Mineralls* [Oxford, 1661]: 38). Both Heaven and Hell have a metallic underlayment.
[147]Another perverse system of marriage and begetting, since the flames from the chaotic deep somehow impregnate the fallen angels. The hollow cannons oppose fecundity, since they kill. As Fowler points out (6.472–81n), the image of the cannons is brilliantly witty, applying equally well to breechloading and muzzleloading firearms. The cannons are also phallic in shape but impotent: like the fallen angels they are hollow ("hallow" was an obsolete or dialectic form, but it was preserved by *1667* and *1674*), they dilate, and they are furious. In the cannonry of Milton's era, the artillery in the form of iron balls, chains, or other metal bits and pieces would be loaded from the muzzle end, after the charge had been packed in ("Thick-rammd"). Then fire would be applied to a separate charge of finer gunpowder at the "touchhole," which Milton describes as the "other bore." Ever materialistic, Satan can only think of God in terms of his weaponry, the thunderbolts; the scheme of the cannons is a means of getting one up in firepower.
[148]Good advice. Satan implies that his own battle plans, together with angelic strength, will cause his troops to prevail in battle.
[149]Raphael in his own person and in a kind of authorial aside argues that it would have been fortunate for future humankind (Adam's "Race") if no one had reinvented gunpowder and cannonry. Raphael looks back to the invention, he talks in the present, but he also looks forward to a future Adam has not yet seen. In Raphael's vision of the future, gunpowder punishes the Sons of Men for their sins. The invention of gunpowder was assigned to Satan by Ariosto in the *Orlando Furioso* 9.28–29, followed in turn by Spenser in *The Faerie Queene* 1.7.13, but the notion was a Renaissance commonplace.
[150]The same as the "spume" mentioned earlier—a product of something like volcanic chemistry. Sulphur, charcoal, and potassium nitrate (in modern chemistry) would be scorched or dried by fire (rendered "adust" in the alchemical term) and combined to form gunpowder.

They found, they mingl'd, and with suttle Art,[151]
Concocted and adusted they reduc'd
To blackest grain, and into store convey'd:[152]   515
Part hidd'n veins diggd up (nor hath this Earth
Entrails unlike)[153] of Mineral and Stone,
Whereof to found[154] thir Engins and thir Balls
Of missive ruin; part incentive reed[155]
Provide, pernicious[156] with one touch to fire.   520
So all ere day-spring,° under conscious Night[157]   DAWN
Secret they finish'd, and in order set,
With silent circumspection unespi'd.
Now when fair Morn Orient in Heav'n appeerd[158]
Up rose the Victor Angels, and to Arms   525
The matin Trumpet Sung: in Arms they stood
Of Golden Panoplie,[159] refulgent° Host,   SHINING
Soon banded; others from the dawning Hills
Lookd round, and Scouts each Coast light-armed scoure,[160]
Each quarter, to descrie the distant foe,   530
Where lodg'd, or whither fled, or if for fight,
In motion or in alt:[161] him soon they met
Under spred Ensignes moving nigh, in slow
But firm Battalion; back with speediest Sail
Zophiel,[162] of Cherubim the swiftest wing,   535
Came flying, and in mid Aire aloud thus cri'd.
    Arme, Warriours, Arme for fight, the foe at hand,
Whom fled we thought,[163] will save us long pursuit
This day, fear not his flight; so thick a Cloud[164]
He comes, and settl'd in his face I see   540

---

[151]The word "Art" is not often used positively by Milton; here it is combined with a Satanic or Serpentine adjective "suttle." See my "Art, Artists, Galileo and Concordances." The art is subtle because it involves the skill of an alchemist or chemist who would concoct (mix or brew up together) or adust (dry out) the base minerals in order to construct what we would call a chemical compound.

[152]They conveyed the gunpowder into storage, as in powder kegs, to save it for future use.

[153]As Svendsen points out, the existence of minerals dangerous in the hands of evil beings below the surface stratum in Heaven does not taint the metals themselves: "Existence of gunpowder and gold in Heaven . . . is a proclamation of the neutrality of matter" (121).

[154]The verb "found" is used in its metallurgical sense of "to melt down and reconstitute" (my definition, but see *OED* 3.2, citing this instance).

[155]The balls are missiles, from which the adjective and noun "missive" was formed. Missives would have been military ordnance sent through the air. For "incentive," see *OED* 2, "Having the property of kindling or setting on fire," i.e., incendiary. The "incentive reed" would be a dried stalk lighted in order to fire the touchhole of a cannon.

[156]"Rapid, swift" (*OED* a.2, a meaning listed as "rare," citing this instance), probably following Latin *pernix*, "nimble, swift." The primary sense of the English word was derived from the Latin *perniciosus*, "very destructive," "full of death," itself derived from *perneco*, "kill outright." Milton seems to be using the complete etymology of the word.

[157]Night is defined as "conscious" apparently in order to show that nature (and omniscient God) is always aware of what evil is occurring. I disagree with Fowler (6.521n) that the primary meaning is "guilty" (*OED* 4b) and with Campbell's note on 521, "possessing a guilty knowledge." Hughes sees only "night personified and interested in watching the work" (521n).

[158]A second day of battle in Heaven.

[159]The complete armor of a soldier (*OED* 1, citing this instance), synonymous with "furniture" as used in a military sense.

[160]Scouts, not in full panoply but lightly armed, study the coasts for military activity.

[161]Though it is easiest just to read "halt" for this variant, the idiom "in alt" means "in an excited frame of mind" in the seventeenth century (*OED* s.v. "Alt" 2.b).

[162]The name means "Spy of God," but it is not in the Bible or apocryphal books. Gustav Davidson identifies "Zaphiel" as "a ruler of the order of cherubim, and prince of the planet Saturn," as well as "the preceptor angel of Noah" (*A Dictionary of Angels, Including the Fallen Angels* [New York: Macmillan, 1967]: 325). Zophiel is more a scout, strictly speaking, than a spy.

[163]"Whom we thought to have fled."

[164]Satan throughout *Paradise Lost* is associated with shadows and clouds that obscure rather than reveal truth, but here the allusion may be to 2 Peter 2.17–18: false prophets are compared with "clouds that are carried with a tempest; to whom the mist of darkness is reserved for ever." The same false prophets "speak great swelling words of vanity . . . ."

Sad resolution and secure:[165] let each
His Adamantine coat gird well, and each
Fit well his Helme, gripe° fast his orbed Shield,   GRIP
Born° eevn or high, for this day will pour down,[166]   BORNE, CARRIED   545
If I conjecture aught, no drizling showr,
But ratling storm of Arrows barbd with fire.
So warnd he them aware themselves, and soon
In order, quit° of all impediment;   RELIEVED
Instant without disturb they took Allarm,[167]
And onward move Embattelld; when behold   550
Not distant far with heavie pace the Foe[168]
Approaching gross and huge; in hollow Cube
Training° his devilish Enginrie, impal'd[169]   HAULING BEHIND
On every side with shaddowing Squadrons Deep,[170]
To hide the fraud. At interview[171] both stood   555
A while, but suddenly at head appeerd
Satan: And thus was heard Commanding loud.
   Vanguard, to Right and Left the Front unfould;[172]
That all may see who hate us, how we seek
Peace and composure,[173] and with open brest   560
Stand readie to receive them, if they like
Our overture, and turn not back perverse;[174]
But that I doubt, however witness Heav'n,[175]
Heav'n witness thou anon,[176] while we discharge[177]
Freely our part; yee who appointed stand   565
Do as you have in charge, and briefly touch
What we propound, and loud that all may hear.

---

[165]Satan's face apparently reflects the resolution of the damned, which may be pictured as genuinely solemn or "sad." The faces of the damned in Michelangelo's famous panel of the Last Judgment in the Sistine Chapel might help the reader form an image of what the damned might look like. "Secure" can mean "fixed" or, ironically, "without care."

[166]Zophiel describes how the shields may be held at breast height or higher, to protect against unknown types of missiles coming from on high.

[167]"Instantly, without becoming upset, they took up battle stations, in formation ('Embattelld')." The word alarm, as in Shakespeare's "alarum," signifies a loud call to emergency duty. The point here is that the angels move quietly and with utter confidence in their own righteousness.

[168]The word is used collectively, for Satan with his entire force behind him, stressing the grossness and perhaps the absurdity of the army attempting to hide the artillery.

[169]The "devilish Enginrie" of course is the cannon. The word "impal'd" contains the sense of being fenced about with palings (Milton used it elsewhere to signify the use of hedges), but it is a military term which suggests one type of legion or ordnance surrounded by another, as when pikemen surround and protect infantry.

[170]The squadrons provide a kind of curtain over the cannon; they are deep in the sense that their formation is tight and dense.

[171]That is, they were both staring each other in the eye. See *OED* "interview" 2, "Mutual view of each other," which cites this passage.

[172]The image is of wings unfolding; Milton is picturing elements of military strategy common in infantry movements in the seventeenth century. Milton recommended teaching "the instrumentall science of *Trigonometry*, and from thence to Fortification, *Architecture*, Enginry [i.e., the art of military engineering], or navigation" to young pupils (*Of Education*, Yale 2: 392). They should also learn "the rudiments of their Souldiership in all the skill of embattailing, marching, encamping, fortifying, beseiging and battering . . ." (411). Military tactics to be mastered were taken from historians of strategy such as Frontinus, Aelian, and Polyaenus (Darbishire *Early Lives* 60).

[173]Like most warlike tyrants, Satan declares his mission to be for peace and treaty (a "composure" was a settlement of a dispute, as with *OED* 4). Satan will be "scoffing in ambiguous words" for the duration of his ten-line speech. Everything he says has a double meaning, and everything he says is an insult to the good angels. The phrase "open brest," for instance, ironically suggests open-heartedness, as in "make a clean breast of it," but it also suggests a band of people marching, as in "four-abreast."

[174]"If they like our overture for peace (with the hidden meaning 'the aperture' or bore of our cannon)." The word "perverse" describes not only the act of turning abruptly to run away (Latin *pervertere*, "to turn abruptly"), but it is a word Milton constantly associates with evil action; hence Satan is imputing his own evil actions to the good angels.

[175]1674 has "Heaven," where the metrics call for a monosyllable—mistakenly written out for "Heav'n."

[176]Satan calls Heaven ironically as his witness; an omnipresent and omniscient God has no trouble, of course, witnessing what Satan is doing.

[177]With another pun between "discharge our duty" and "discharge our weapon," and then "touch on" and "touch off the charge," causing a report that will certainly be loud enough to hear. Fowler quotes Walter Savage Landor, "the first overt crime of the refractory angels was *punning*" (Works, ed. T. E. Welby [London: 1927–36]: 5.258). There may even be a pun on the "pound" (as in "pound on") in "propound."

So scoffing in ambiguous words, he scarce[178]
Had ended; when to Right and Left the Front
Divided, and to either Flank retir'd.   570
Which to our eyes discoverd new and strange,
A triple mounted row of Pillars laid
On Wheels[179] (for like to Pillars most they seem'd
Or hollow'd bodies made of Oak or Firr
With branches lopt, in Wood or Mountain fell'd)   575
Brass, Iron, Stonie mould,[180] had not thir mouthes[181]
With hideous orifice gap't on us wide,
Portending hollow[182] truce; at each behind
A Seraph stood, and in his hand a Reed
Stood waving tipt with fire; while we suspense,[183]   580
Collected stood within our thoughts amus'd,
Not long, for sudden all at once thir Reeds
Put forth, and to a narrow vent appli'd
With nicest touch. Immediate in a flame,
But soon obscur'd with smoak, all Heav'n appeerd,   585
From those deep-throated[184] Engins belcht, whose roar   *Cannons*
Emboweld with outragious noise the Air,
And all her entrails tore, disgorging foule
Thir devilish glut, chaind Thunderbolts and Hail
Of Iron Globes, which on the Victor Host   590
Level'd,°[185] with such impetuous furie smote,   AIMED
That whom they hit, none on thir feet might stand,
Though standing else as Rocks, but down they fell
By thousands, Angel on Arch-Angel rowl'd;
The sooner for thir Arms, unarm'd they might   595
Have easily as Spirits evaded swift
By quick contraction or remove;[186] but now
Foule dissipation[187] follow'd and forc't rout;
Nor serv'd it to relax thir serried[188] files.
What should they do? if on they rusht, repulse   600

---

[178]So far as I can tell, the comma belongs after "words," as in *1667*, instead of here, where it appears in *1674*. The compositor accidentally allowed his eye to skip as he moved the comma down the line.

[179]Milton seems to have a very specific type of ordnance in mind, a kind of machine gun passing out of use in combat in the seventeenth century, looking like an organ (hence the name given it, "organ" or *orgue* in French) laid on its side. Organs were capable of firing many rounds in rapid sequence; here the organ has three tiers (to match Messiah's "three-bolted Thunder" in 764 below) composed of many pipes. Fowler cites the *Encyclopaedia Britannica*, 11th ed. (1911): 17.238.

[180]"Made out of brass, iron, or stone."

[181]Beginning with the mouth at this point, the succession leads through a series of images of eating, belching, farting, vomiting, and defecation, from "behind" to "vent" ("anus"), "deep-throated," "belcht," "Emboweld," and "all her entrails tore, disgorging [vomiting] foule / Thir devilish glut."

[182]Their shape has a moral dimension—the hollowness of the cannon's barrel being analogous to the hollowness of Satan's "overture."

[183]"While we, suspending our action, stood puzzled ['amus'd'], collecting our thoughts—but not for long." The scene in front of the unfallen angels has its comic dimensions that even Raphael himself seems to acknowledge, as in the picture of the opposing seraphim putting the reeds to the cannon vents "With nicest ['most scrupulous' or 'most careful'] touch."

[184]The "deep throated" of *1674* is probably wrong, so I have restored the hyphen of *1667*.

[185]The aimed cannon will level the "Victor Host" (the army of victorious good angels). The "devilish glut" being spewed out of the cannon's mouth is also recognizable ordnance, single iron balls together with chain shot, or balls linked with chains, so that, when projected, the spinning combination will cause more damage among the enemy. The guns being leveled (as opposed to fired vertically, as with a mortar) would also decimate personnel.

[186]Had they not been armed, the angels might have been able to dodge the artillery shells, either by contracting their shapes or by making a quick sideways movement ("remove").

[187]"Dispersement." In other words, they ran away in all directions.

[188]"Pressed close together, shoulder to shoulder" (*OED* a, citing this instance). The word should be pronounced as a disyllable (since "seri'd" looks awkward on the page because of the double dots of the eye and the apostrophe, compositors generally avoided the "i'd" elision).

Repeated, and indecent[189] overthrow
Doubl'd, would render them yet more despis'd,
And to thir foes a laughter; for in view
Stood rankt of Seraphim another row
In posture[190] to displode thir second tire   605
Of Thunder: back defeated to return
They worse abhorr'd. *Satan* beheld thir plight,
And to his Mates thus in derision call'd.
    O Friends, why come not on these Victors proud?
Ere while they fierce were coming, and when wee,   610
To entertain them fair with open Front[191]
And Brest, (what could we more?) propounded terms
Of composition,[192] strait° they chang'd thir minds,   IMMEDIATELY
Flew off, and into strange vagaries fell,
As they would dance,[193] yet for a dance they seemd   615
Somwhat extravagant and wilde, perhaps
For joy of offerd peace: but I suppose
If our proposals once again were heard
We should compel them to a quick result.
    To whom thus *Belial*[194] in like gamesom mood.[195]   620
Leader, the terms we sent were terms of weight,
Of hard contents, and full of force urg'd home,
Such as we might perceive amus'd them all,
And stumbl'd many,[196] who receives them right,
Had need from head to foot well understand;[197]   625
Not understood, this gift they have besides,
They shew us when our foes walk not upright.
    So they among themselves in pleasant veine
Stood scoffing, highthn'd in thir thoughts beyond
All doubt of Victorie, eternal might   630
To match with thir inventions they presum'd
So easie, and of his Thunder made a scorn,
And all his Host derided, while they stood
A while in trouble; but they stood not long,
Rage prompted them[198] at length, and found them arms   635
Against such hellish mischief fit to oppose.

---

[189]"Not proper" or "not dignified."

[190]A military term denoting a strictly defined position of artillery men; the "second tire" is the second volley from their weapon, since a "tire" is a volley or broadside. Volleys were often compared to peals of thunder.

[191]Satan cannot stop punning even in triumph, since "open Front" suggests both "honest face" and "front line." The word "fair" is often used ironically in *Paradise Lost*.

[192]"Put forth terms to settle our dispute," perhaps using composition in the sense of "The composing or settling of differences" (*OED* 11).

[193]The good angels fell into strange patterns of behavior, as if they wanted to dance. Aeneas in the *Iliad* 16.617 refers to his opponent in battle, Meriones, as a dancer, but still not capable of dancing away from his spear.

[194]Belial's speech, like Satan's is full of obvious puns. One gets the strong impression that Belial would rather talk than fight, since he is by nature "Timorous and slothful" (2.117). The "terms of weight" they sent were of course cannon shot.

[195]I have substituted the period of *1667* for the comma of *1674*, on the grounds that a period normally announces a direct quotation. Belial may have been infected by Satan's "gamesom mood," as Corns suggests (108), or he may be "imitating Satan, pandering to him," as Paul Klemp suggests (letter, October 1991). The effect of the punning is generally unpleasant, suggesting by its decorum the unattractiveness of its perpetrators (Corns 108).

[196]"Caused many to stumble" as well as "Baffled." Newton substituted a semicolon for the comma here, which might clear up the problem in syntax caused by the change in tense. There is a related problem with "receives," since "who receives them right" must be read as subject to the verb "Had need [to] understand."

[197]There is a pun on understand meaning either "comprehend" or "prop up" (see *OED* I.9). If there is no prop under the good angels (they are not "understood"), then their stumbling will show the fallen angels when they cannot walk upright.

[198]The idiom "Rage ... found them arms" is probably derived from Vergil, *Aeneid* 1.150, *furor arma ministrat*, "in their fury any object serves as a missile."

Forthwith (behold the excellence, the power
Which God hath in his mighty Angels plac'd)
Thir Arms away they threw, and to the Hills
(For Earth hath this variety from Heav'n
Of pleasure situate° in Hill and Dale)[199]   LOCATED   640
Light as the Lightning glimps they ran, they flew,
From thir foundations loosning to and fro
They pluckt the seated Hills with all thir load,
Rocks, Waters, Woods, and by the shaggie tops   645
Up lifting bore them in thir hands:[200] Amaze,°   AMAZEMENT
Be sure, and terrour seis'd the rebel Host,
When coming towards them so dread° they saw   FEARFUL, DREADFUL
The bottom of the Mountains upward turn'd,
Till on those cursed Engins triple-row   650
They saw them whelm'd,[201] and all thir confidence
Under the weight of Mountains buried deep,
Themselves invaded° next, and on thir heads   ATTACKED
Main° Promontories flung, which in the Air   ENTIRE
Came shadowing,[202] and opprest whole Legions arm'd,   655
Thir armor help'd thir harm,[203] crush't in and bruis'd
Into thir substance pent,[204] which wrought them pain
Implacable,[205] and many a dolorous° groan,   SORROWFUL
Long strugling underneath, ere they could wind[206]
Out of such prison, though Spirits of purest light,   660
Purest at first, now gross by sinning grown.[207]
The rest in imitation to like Armes
Betook them, and the neighbouring Hills uptore;
So Hills amid the Air encounterd Hills
Hurl'd to and fro with jaculation dire,[208]   665
That under ground[209] they fought in dismal shade;
Infernal noise; Warr seem'd a civil Game[210]
To this uproar; horrid confusion[211] heapt
Upon confusion rose: and now all Heav'n

[Handwritten marginal notes: "Angels moved Mountains into their way." and "Day 2 / Unfallen angels / Win"]

---

[199]"Earth has inherited its variety of landscape from the hills and dales of Heaven."

[200]Milton had many precedents for describing battles among giants during which hills or mountains were pulled up and thrown as military projectiles, especially the Roman poet Claudian's *Gigantomachia* (c. AD 400). The giants, among whom were Briareus, Typhon, Tityus, and Antaeus, were supposed to have rebelled against the Olympian gods and to have been defeated by Jupiter with the aid of Hercules. Since some of the giants were buried under volcanic mountains that were thrown over them in battle, their story formed an easy classical parallel with that of the fallen angels and a subterranean Hell.

[201]What has happened is hard to envisage, but it turns on the exact meaning of "whelm'd." The evil angels probably see their guns (over-)whelmed by burial under the hills: "whelm'd" carries the sense of being turned over randomly, as Lycidas's body is tossed by the "whelming tide" (157).

[202]"Casting a shadow," with the possible associations of "foreshadowing," which in this case would be predicting present and ultimate defeat for the fallen angels.

[203]Newton notes a similarity in phrasing with *The Faerie Queene* 1.11.27: " . . . That erst him goodly arm'd, now most of all him harm'd."

[204]"Confined painfully ["pent up'] within their own bodies."

[205]Their pain cannot be assuaged or mitigated (see *OED* 2).

[206]"Take a sinuous course" (see *OED* 7.c, d) and compare 3.563–64, "windes . . . his oblique way. . . ."

[207]By sinning, the fallen angels have put on weight, in the sense that their substance has become less fully composed of ethereal light.

[208]A wonderful joint venture in sounds and etymologies, since *jactare* is the Latin verb for "throw" or "hurl" and "dire" is associated with the Furies, Latin *Diræ* or "Dire Sisters" (see *OED* A.b). The act of throwing helps damn the fallen angels.

[209]Like most editors since Newton, I have followed *1667* and removed the comma present at this point in *1674*, since it seems to be an error rather than a correction.

[210]By comparison, war as human beings know it is like a polite game.

[211]The word has the force of its Latin counterpart *confusio*, "chaotic disorder," which in later Latin had the theological meaning "damned."

Had gon to wrack, with ruin overspred,[212]   670
Had not th' Almightie Father where he sits
Shrin'd in his Sanctuarie of Heav'n secure,
Consulting on the sum of things,[213] foreseen
This tumult, and permitted all, advis'd:
That his great purpose he might so fulfill,   675
To honour his Anointed Son aveng'd
Upon his enemies, and to declare
All power on him transferr'd: whence to his Son
Th' Assessor[214] of his Throne he thus began.
    Effulgence[215] of my Glorie, Son belov'd,   680
Son in whose face invisible is beheld
Visibly,[216] what by Deitie I am,
And in whose hand what by Decree I doe,
Second Omnipotence,[217] two dayes are past,
Two dayes, as we compute the dayes of Heav'n,   685
Since *Michael* and his Powers went forth to tame
These disobedient; sore[218] hath been thir fight,
As likeliest was, when two such Foes met arm'd;
For to themselves I left them, and thou knowst,[219]
Equal in their Creation they were form'd,   690
Save what sin hath impaird, which yet hath wrought
Insensibly,[220] for I suspend thir doom;
Whence in perpetual fight they needs must last
Endless, and no solution will be found:
Warr wearied hath perform'd what Warr can do,   695
And to disorder'd rage let loose the reines,[221]
With Mountains as with Weapons arm'd, which makes
Wild work in Heav'n, and dangerous to the maine.[222]
Two dayes are therefore past, the third is thine;
For thee I have ordain'd it, and thus farr   700
Have sufferd,° that the Glorie may be thine   °ALLOWED

---

[212]Milton gives new force to the colloquial phrase "gone to wrack and ruin" (see *OED* "wrack" 2, which cites this instance), as he does to "all Hell broke loose" (4.918) and other normally tame proverbial formulas.

[213]As Fowler points out (6.673n), the phrasing seems to be taken from the Latin idiom *summa rerum* (as in Ovid, "*rerum consule summae*," *Metamorphoses* 2.300), meaning "highest public interest." Milton's "sum" seems to indicate "goal of things" (*OED* 13) as well. The Father conceptualizes Providence, His "great purpose."

[214]The word specifies someone who sits beside and shares (*OED* 1, citing this instance). In this case the Son sits next to the Father's throne and shares in His glory.

[215]Carrying on the image of light flowing outward, "Bright effluence of bright essence increate" (3.6), the Father calls the Son an "Effulgence," from Latin *effulgio*, "shining forth."

[216]The radiance of the Father is so intense that it cannot be beheld by human beings; thus the invisible is revealed in the visible face of the Son (who will assume a human body in the Incarnation). Likewise, Thomas Fuller, following the mystic Robert Fludd, instructed the Protestant minister or divine that he should in sermons be "clouding his high matter with dark language lest otherwise the lustre thereof should dazzle the understanding of the Reader" (*The Worthies of England* [London, 1662]: 78; my thanks to Polly Mander for this reference).

[217]Like "invisible . . . Visibly," an oxymoron expressing the mysterious oneness of God, or sharing, in this case of omnipotence, between the Father and Son.

[218]As in the biblical phrase "sore afflicted," the adjective *sore* means "in terrible pain."

[219]The construction should be read as in the modern idiom "You know it [is true]."

[220]The impairment in the fallen angels, so far, cannot be perceived by the senses.

[221]Despite all the righteous zeal embodied in the action of the good angels, God admits that, despite its being monumental in scale, the War in Heaven provoked only rage and disorder, especially in its "wearied" stage. The "Wild work" has been pictured in terms of burlesque action, which critics since Arnold Stein (*Answerable*) have been inclined to believe is ludicrous, on purpose.

[222]"Dangerous to the entire universe."

Of ending this great Warr, since none but Thou[223]
Can end it. Into thee such Vertue and Grace
Immense I have transfus'd, that all may know
In Heav'n and Hell thy Power above compare,   705
And this perverse Commotion governd thus,
To manifest thee worthiest to be Heir
Of all things, to be Heir and to be King
By Sacred Unction, thy deserved right.[224]
Go then thou Mightiest in thy Fathers might,   710
Ascend my Chariot, guide the rapid Wheeles
That shake Heav'ns basis,° bring forth all my Warr,[225]   FOUNDATION
My Bow and Thunder, my Almightie Arms
Gird on, and Sword upon thy puissant Thigh;
Pursue these sons of Darkness,[226] drive them out   715
From all Heav'ns bounds into the utter° Deep: OUTER
There let them learn, as likes them,[227] to despise
God and *Messiah* his anointed King.
    He said, and on his Son with Rayes direct
Shon full, he all his Father full exprest   720
Ineffably into his face receiv'd,[228]
And thus the filial Godhead answering spake.
    O Father, O Supream of heav'nly Thrones,
First, Highest, Holiest, Best, thou alwayes seekst
To glorifie thy Son, I alwayes thee,   725
As is most just; this I my Glorie account,
My exaltation, and my whole delight,
That thou in me well pleas'd,[229] declarst thy will
Fulfill'd, which to fulfil is all my bliss.
Scepter and Power, thy giving, I assume,   730
And gladlier shall resign, when in the end
Thou shalt be All in All, and I in thee

---

[223]The capitalization is one of the few instances in the typesetting of *Paradise Lost* of a pronoun being capitalized apparently because it is associated with the deity. In his own holograph materials, Milton rarely capitalized Heaven (meaning the abode of God) or even the names of the deity.

[224]The Father, in other words, has transfused virtue and grace into the Son so that the Son's omniscience will be declared and so that the war, a "perverse Commotion," can be governed. Compare Hebrews 1.2: " . . . his Son, whom he hath appointed heir of all things, by whom also he made the worlds." The unction or anointing of the Son (compare 5.603–06) is the Father's outward sign that the Son is the Messiah, but it is the Son's earned right achieved by merit and not a meaningless legacy bestowed by father on son.

[225]The "Warr," as Fowler points out (6.712n), is a synecdoche for all the weapons at God's commands, and the same figure can be found in Dryden's translation of the *Aeneid* 8.572, "His broken Axeltrees, and blunted War," and in Addison's *Cato* 1.4, "th' embattled Elephant, / Loaden with war." Milton may be interpreting the phrase "The Lord is a man of war" in Exodus 15.3, but the image of the Chariot of Paternal Deity is that of Ezekiel, a mystical image of a chariot with wheels within wheels, each controlled by "the spirit of the living creature . . . in the wheels" (1.21). The Chariot is surmounted by a throne in which Milton will picture Messiah riding in triumph.

[226]Compare the description of all the unfallen angels as the "sons of Morn" (5.716).

[227]"As it pleases them" (said ironically).

[228]Compare 2 Corinthians 4.6: "For God, who commanded the light to shine out of darkness, hath shined in our hearts, to give the light of the knowledge of the glory of God in the face of Jesus Christ." The expression of the Father in the Son is ineffable or unutterable because the light is too bright to be recorded by human sense. Compare 681–82 above.

[229]The story of the Baptism of Jesus, recorded in all the gospels, reports either the "Holy Ghost" or the "Spirit of God" descending like a dove on Jesus and a "voice from heaven" saying "Thou art my beloved Son; in thee I am well pleased" (Luke 3.22; compare Matthew 3.17). The passages were taken as evidence for or against the existence of a third member of the Trinity, and Milton scholars have used Milton's recreation of the events of the Baptism to argue that Milton's position was Arian (derived from the heretical doctrine of Arius of Alexandria) in that it eliminated the third member of the Trinity and subordinated the Son to the Father. For various arguments, see Kelley, *This Great Argument*; Patrides, *Milton*; and Hunter and Adamson, *Bright Essence*.

For ever, and in mee all whom thou lov'st:[230]
But whom thou hat'st, I hate, and can put on
Thy terrors,[231] as I put thy mildness on,   735
Image of thee in all things; and shall soon,
Armd with thy might, rid heav'n of these rebell'd,
To thir prepar'd ill Mansion[232] driven down
To chains of darkness, and th' undying Worm,[233]
That from thy just obedience could revolt,   740
Whom to obey is happiness entire.
Then shall thy Saints unmixt, and from th' impure
Farr separate, circling thy holy Mount
Unfained *Halleluiahs*[234] to thee sing,
Hymns of high praise, and I among them chief.   745
So said, he o're his Scepter bowing, rose
From the right hand of Glorie where he sate,
And the third sacred Morn[235] began to shine
Dawning through Heav'n: forth rush'd with whirlwind sound
The Chariot of Paternal Deitie,[236]   750
Flashing thick flames, Wheele within Wheele undrawn,
It self instinct with Spirit, but convoyd
By four Cherubic shapes, four Faces each
Had wondrous, as with Starrs thir bodies all
And Wings were set with Eyes, with Eyes the wheels   755
Of Beril, and careering Fires between;
Over thir heads a chrystal Firmament,
Whereon a Saphir Throne, inlaid with pure
Amber, and colours of the showrie Arch.[237]
Hee in Celestial Panoplie all armd   760

---

[230]A paraphrase of 1 Corinthians 15.24–28: "Then cometh the end, when he shall have delivered up the kingdom to God, even the Father; when he shall have put down all rule and all authority and power. For he must reign, till he hath put all enemies under his feet. The last enemy that shall be destroyed is death. For he hath put all things under his feet. But when he saith all things are put under him, it is manifest that he is excepted, which did put all things under him. And when all things shall be subdued unto him, then shall the Son also himself be subject unto him that put all things under him, that God may be all in all." For the context of the Son's subordination, see MacCallum, *Milton.*

[231]Psalm 139.21: "Do not I hate them, O Lord, that hate thee? And am not I grieved with those that rise up against thee?" The Son's description of Himself indicates that He can assume the wrathful aspects of God as well as the meekness or mildness.

[232]The poor dwelling-place of Hell is the opposite of what Jesus promises his good disciples upon death: "In my Father's house are many mansions . . ." (John 14.2).

[233]Though earthworms, canker-worms, maggots, and snakes were differentiated by those who tried to classify them in seventeenth-century scientific treatises, the term worm was popularly applied to serpents (see *OED* 1), as when Cleopatra's witty servant wishes her "joy of the worm" (*Antony and Cleopatra* 5.2.260), meaning quick suicidal relief from the bite of the asp. Here the "undying Worm" in the sense of "eternally punished Serpent" may be "one of the pains of Hell" (*OED* worm 6.b, citing this instance) or Satan as Serpent, undying until he will be annihilated at the end of time. Jesus in Mark 9.48 defines "hell fire" as a place "where their worm dieth not, and the fire is not quenched."

[234]Contrasts with Mammon's "Forc't Hallelujah's" (without the typographical emphasis of italics; but compare "*Haile*" in 5.385) at 2.243.

[235]The third morning as computed in heavenly time. Since Christ will arise from the dead on the third day after death, typological symmetry is enforced.

[236]An image of God's triumph central to *Paradise Lost.* The image is taken from Ezekiel's extremely complex vision (Ezekiel 1–10), but it is also seen in the context of a seventeenth-century triumphal kingly pageant (see Edmund A. Bowles, *Musical Ensembles in Festival Books, 1500–1800* [Ann Arbor, MI: U.M.I Research P, 1989]). Ezekiel's vision emerges from a whirlwind and cloud and fire. The four cherubim who motivate the chariot are living wheels and wheels within wheels, "their work . . . like unto the colour of a beryl" (1.16). The four cherubim have one likeness. "As for their rings, they were so high that they were dreadful; and their rings were full of eyes round about them four" (1.18). The wheels of the chariot are lifted in the sky, "for the spirit of the living creature was in the wheels" (1.20). "And above the firmament that was over their heads was the likeness of a throne, as the appearance of a sapphire stone: and upon the likeness of the throne was the likeness as the appearance of a man above upon it" (1.26). For the part of the throne-chariot (the Hebrew word for which is transliterated "Merkabah" or "Merkavah") in Renaissance mysticism and Protestant commentary, see Michael Lieb, *Poetics,* 33–45; J. H. Adamson in *Bright Essence,* ed. Hunter; and the exhaustive article "Ezekiel's Voice: Milton's Prophetic Exile and the Merkavah in 'Lycidas,'" by M. J. Doherty in *Milton Quarterly* 23 (1989): 89–121.

[237]Poetic diction for the rainbow.

Of radiant *Urim*,[238] work divinely wrought,
Ascended,[239] at his right hand Victorie
Sate Eagle-wing'd,[240] beside him hung his Bow
And Quiver with three-bolted Thunder stor'd,
And from about him fierce Effusion[241] rowld   765
Of smoak and bickering[242] flame, and sparkles dire;[243]
Attended with ten thousand thousand Saints,[244]
He onward came, farr off his coming shon,
And twentie thousand (I thir number heard)[245]
Chariots of God, half on each hand were seen: 770
Hee on the wings of Cherub rode sublime[246]
On the Chrystallin Skie,[247] in Saphir Thron'd.
Illustrious farr and wide, but by his own
First seen,[248] them unexpected joy surpriz'd,
When the great Ensign of *Messiah* blaz'd   775
Aloft by Angels born, his Sign in Heav'n.[249]
Under whose conduct *Michael* soon reduc'd°   LED BACK
His Armie, circumfus'd° on either Wing,   SPREAD OUT
Under thir Head imbodied all in one.
Before him Power Divine his way prepar'd;   780
At his command the uprooted Hills retir'd
Each to his place, they heard his voice and went
Obsequious,[250] Heav'n his wonted face renewd,[251]
And with fresh Flourets Hill and Valley smil'd.

---

[238]Milton has incorporated into the armor of the cherubim the spiritual armor of Aaron in Exodus 28.30: "And thou shalt put in the breastplace of judgment the Urim and the Thummim; and they shall be upon Aaron's heart, when he goeth in before the Lord . . . ." Fowler (6.749–59n), following Qvarnström, sees numerical and alchemical significance in the placing of the symbolic throne at what he considers to be the numerical center of the ten-book version of *Paradise Lost*. Fowler (6.761n, again following Qvarnström) identifies the Urim with the philosopher's stone, but see Michael Lieb on Protestant commentary about the Urim and Thummim, *Poetics* 55–57.

[239]As Shawcross has pointed out, "Ascended" begins the second half (by his count) of *1667*: "it was the central word of the 1667 edition since 5275 lines precede it and follow it" (6.561n). The Son ascends from the grave at dawn on Easter morning.

[240]The images of Victory (usually a goddess attending Jupiter pictured as in the statue of the winged Victory of Samothrace in the Louvre) and of Jupiter's bird, the eagle, seem to be conflated here.

[241]An effluvium or "copious emission of smoke" (*OED* 1.c, citing this instance). Psalm 18.8 makes it clear what Milton is referring to: a God angry at the psalmist's enemies shakes the earth "because he was wroth. There went up a smoke out of his nostrils, and fire out of his mouth devoured: coals were kindled by it." The thunderbolts mentioned just above may have been inspired by the same passage: "Yea, he sent out his arrows and scattered them [i.e., the 'ungodly men' of 18.4]; and he shot out lightnings and discomforted them" (18.14).

[242]"Corruscating, flashing, quivering" (*OED* 3, citing this as primary instance).

[243]Compare "jaculation dire" in 665 above.

[244]See Revelation 5:11: "And I beheld, and I heard the voice of many angels round about the throne and the beasts and the elders; and the number of them was ten thousand times ten thousand, and thousands of thousands . . . ."

[245]The numbering in multiples of ten may signify order or perfection; see Fowler 769n.

[246]In Psalm 18.10, in the same passage cited above, God "rode upon a cherub, and did fly: yea, he did fly upon the wings of the wind." *Sublime* carries its Latin meaning of "aloft."

[247]"Then I looked, and, behold, in the firmament that was above the head of the cherubims there appeared over them as it were a sapphire stone, as the appearance of the likeness of a throne" (Ezekiel 10.1). In the Ptolemaic system, the crystalline was "a sphere supposed to exist between the primum mobile and the firmament, by means of which the precession of the equinox and the motion of libration [vibration caused by balancing] were accounted for" (*OED* 5). "Chrystallin," as its spelling suggests, should be accented on the second syllable.

[248]Though his presence shines far and wide, Messiah is first seen by or he first reveals himself to his own troops.

[249]"And then shall appear the sign of the Son of man in heaven . . . " (Matthew 24.30).

[250]The uprooted hills respectfully returned to their natural position at the command of Messiah's voice, fulfilling the prophecy of Isaiah 40.4: " . . . the crooked shall be made straight, and the rough places plain."

[251]Milton seems to personify Heaven as male, though the Latin *coelum* is neuter; the pronoun *his*, however, could mean "its" in seventeenth-century English usage.

This saw his hapless Foes but stood obdur'd,[252]   785
And to rebellious fight rallied thir Powers
Insensate,[253] hope conceiving from despair.
In heav'nly Spirits could such perverseness dwell?[254]
But to convince the proud what Signs availe,
Or Wonders move th' obdurate to relent?   790
They hard'nd more by what might most reclame,
Grieving to see his Glorie, at the sight
Took envie, and aspiring to his highth,
Stood reimbattell'd fierce, by force or fraud
Weening to prosper, and at length prevaile   795
Against God and *Messiah*, or to fall
In universal ruin last, and now
To final Battel drew, disdaining flight,
Or faint retreat; when the great Son of God
To all his Host on either hand thus spake.   800

    Stand still in bright array ye Saints,[255] here stand
Ye Angels arm'd, this day from Battel rest;
Faithful hath been your warfare, and of God
Accepted, fearless in his righteous Cause,
And as ye have receivd, so have ye don   805
Invincibly; but of this cursed crew
The punishment to other hand belongs,
Vengeance is his,[256] or whose he sole appoints;
Number to this dayes work is not ordain'd
Nor multitude,[257] stand onely and behold   810
Gods indignation on these Godless pourd
By mee, not you but mee they have despis'd,
Yet envied; against mee is all thir rage,
Because the Father, t' whom in Heav'n supream
Kingdom and Power and Glorie appertains,[258]   815
Hath honourd me according to his will.
Therefore to mee thir doom he hath assig'n'd;[259]
That they may have thir wish, to trie° with mee   MAKE TRIAL
In Battel which the stronger proves, they all,

---

[252]"Hardened," but the term suggests the theologically-defined process of the hardening of the heart—a process associated with that particular Pharaoh of Exodus 14 who detains Moses and the tribes of Israel despite the series of horrible plagues on the Egyptian people. The hearts of the fallen angels are now hardened against repentance: having made the irrevocable decision to sin, they are no longer capable of being reconciled with God. The process of reiterated hardening of the heart can best be seen in Satan's soliloquy at 4.73–113. "Hardening of the heart, then, is usually the last punishment inflicted on inveterate wickedness and unbelief in this life.... God often hardens the hearts of powerful and arrogant world leaders to a remarkable degree so that through their pride and arrogance his glory may be more clearly seen by the nations.... Thus Pharaoh is said to harden his own heart..." (*On Christian Doctrine* 1.8; Yale 6: 336–37).

[253]*OED* 3 defines the term as "Lacking sense or understanding; unintelligent, stupid, senseless, foolish," citing this instance, but the fallen angels are not stupid: they have become "gross" with sinning and have consequently lost the complete use of their senses.

[254]Echoes a famous apostrophe to Juno in the invocation of the *Aeneid* 1.11, *tantæne animis cælestibus iræ*, translated by C. Day Lewis as "Can a divine being be so persevering in anger?" The allusion to Vergil puts the pagan gods squarely in the place of the fallen angels.

[255]Milton returns to focus on Moses in the act of opposing Pharaoh, since Moses asks the Israelites to observe the destruction of the Egyptians with the words "Fear ye not, stand still . . . " (Exodus 14.13).

[256]Paraphrases the famous phrase from Romans 12.19: " . . . Vengeance is mine; I will repay, saith the Lord." Compare Deuteronomy 32.35.

[257]*Messiah* alone will be the appointed agent of God's vengeance.

[258]The singular form of the verb may be a misprint, since the verb has three subjects. The phrase reiterates the Lord's Prayer: "For thine is the kingdom, and the power, and the glory, for ever" (Matthew 6.13).

[259]A very unusual series of elisions and a compositorial mistake, since no letter is elided between "g" and "n."

Or I alone against them,[260] since by strength   820
They measure all, of other excellence
Not emulous, nor care who them excells;
Nor other strife with them do I voutsafe.
　　So spake the Son, and into terrour chang'd
His count'nance too severe to be beheld   825
And full of wrauth bent on his Enemies.
At once the Four spred out thir Starrie wings[261]
With dreadful shade contiguous,[262] and the Orbes[263]
Of his fierce Chariot rowld, as with the sound
Of torrent Floods,[264] or of a numerous Host.°   ARMY   830
Hee on his impious Foes right onward drove,
Gloomie as Night;[265] under his burning Wheeles[266]
The stedfast Empyrean shook throughout,
All but the Throne it self of God.[267] Full soon
Among them he arriv'd; in his right hand   835
Grasping ten thousand Thunders, which he sent
Before him, such as in thir Soules infix'd
Plagues;[268] they astonisht[269] all resistance lost,
All courage; down thir idle weapons drop'd;
O're Shields and Helmes, and helmed heads he rode   840
Of Thrones and mighty Seraphim prostrate,
That wisht the Mountains now might be again
Thrown on them as a shelter from his ire.[270]
Nor less on either side tempestuous fell
His arrows, from the fourfold-visag'd Foure,   845
Distinct[271] with eyes, and from the living Wheels
Distinct alike with multitude of eyes,
One Spirit in them rul'd, and every eye

---

[260]The implication is that Messiah is using force only because the materialistic values of Satan's troops demand a show of force. Messiah's power echoes that of Zeus to oppose that of all the other Olympian gods combined, as when Hephaistos acknowledges "For if the Olympian who handles the lightning should be minded to hurl us [the rest of the gods] out of our places, he is far too strong for any" (*Iliad* 1.580–81; trans. Lattimore).

[261]The four cherubim escorting Messiah spread out the wings decorated with eyes as described in Ezekiel 10.12. Milton is apparently glossing "eyes" as "stars," since stars were idiomatically described as "God's eyes" (compare 3.650–51). The vision in Ezekiel may also be taken as a system of organizing heavenly bodies, or a cosmology, since the wheels within wheels described sounded like (and were often illustrated as) the motion of heavenly bodies, as with Milton's use of the word "Orbes" below. See the illustration of the vision at the beginning of the book of Ezekiel in the Geneva Bible and the many illustrations collected by Michael Lieb in "'The Chariot of Paternal Deitie': Some Visual Renderings," in Labriola and Sichi 21–58.

[262]The shadows of the wings are joined together at their tops (Ezekiel 1.9).

[263]The meaning "circular disk or wheel" (*OED* I.1) may be intended, although the word *orb* suggests that the wheels are analogous to heavenly bodies in their spheres (compare "Suns Orb," 7.361). The wheels as pictured in the illustration of the vision of Ezekiel printed at the beginning of the book in the Geneva Bible clearly appear as astronomical orbs; they are labeled as "Wheles having everie one foure faces" (1560 ed.).

[264]"Not redundant, since a torrent is a fast mountain stream, normally noisy but even more so in a flood state.

[265]Compare the similar idiom used of Death: "Fierce as ten Furies, terrible as Hell" (2.671).

[266]The whole vision of Ezekiel is enclosed in flames, but again Milton may be visualizing a cosmos with a sun-chariot in its midst, as with the "burning Axletree" of the Nativity Ode 84.

[267]It is important that the seat of power of God, his throne, is never shaken. Satan's lie at 1.105 is thereby made more egregious.

[268]Probably yet another reference to the punishment of Pharaoh and the Egyptians, though the plagues under consideration are spiritual. Fowler (6.838n) reminds us that the Latin sense of *plaga* is "a blow, stroke, wound" (as in *OED* 1), but see Corns 99, arguing that "afflicting visitation of divine anger" is the better reading.

[269]A very strong word indicating stupefaction or utter defeat.

[270]In the apocalyptic vision of Revelation 6.16 the kings of the earth and other figures of earthly power "said to the mountains and rocks, Fall on us, and hide us from the face of him that sitteth on the throne, and from the wrath of the Lamb." The "stars of heaven" in 6.13 were generally glossed as fallen angels, so that the first rebellion is thus punished at the end of recorded time, according to Christian chronology. See Patrides, "'Something,'" in Patrides and Wittreich, *Apocalypse* 207–37, and Dobbins, *Milton*, for general information about how Renaissance commentators glossed Revelation.

[271]"Ornamented," a poetic usage derived from one meaning of the Latin adjective *distinctus*. The "fourfold-visag'd Foure" are appropriately ornamented with eyes.

Glar'd lightning, and shot forth pernicious fire[272]   850
Among th' accurst, that witherd all thir strength,
And of thir wonted vigour left them draind,
Exhausted, spiritless, afflicted, fall'n.
Yet half his strength he put not forth, but check'd
His Thunder in mid Volie, for he meant   855
Not to destroy, but root them out of Heav'n:
The overthrown he rais'd, and as a Heard
Of Goats or timerous flock together[273] throngd
Drove them before him Thunder-struck,[274] pursu'd
With terrors and with furies[275] to the bounds
And Chrystal wall of Heav'n, which op'ning wide,   860
Rowld inward, and a spacious Gap disclos'd
Into the wastful[276] Deep; the monstrous sight
Strook them with horror backward, but far worse
Urg'd them behind; headlong themselves they threw
Down from the verge of Heav'n, Eternal wrauth   865
Burnt after them to the bottomless pit.
    Hell heard th' unsufferable noise, Hell saw[277]
Heav'n ruining° from Heav'n and would have fled   FALLING HEADLONG
Affrighted; but strict Fate had cast too deep
Her dark foundations, and too fast had bound.   870
Nine dayes they fell;[278] confounded *Chaos* roard,
And felt tenfold confusion in thir fall
Through his wilde Anarchie, so huge a rout
Incumberd[279] him with ruin: Hell at last
Yawning receavd them whole, and on them clos'd,[280]   875
Hell thir fit habitation fraught with fire
Unquenchable, the house of woe and paine.
Disburd'nd Heav'n rejoic'd, and soon repaird
Her mural breach,[281] returning whence it rowld.
Sole Victor from th' expulsion of his Foes   880

---

[272]Echoed by the effects of Eve's beauty, which, even innocent and asleep, "Shot forth peculiar Graces" (5.15).

[273]Reminiscent of Christ casting out devils who were possessing the insane into the herd of Gaddarine swine (Mark 5.13); the passage also reminds one of the division of all humankind into sheep and goats at the Last Judgment (Matthew 25.32–33). Like the bee simile of 1.768–76, the image is diminutive and scornful. It offended the delicate sensibilities of some eighteenth-century critics because it was such a "low . . . comparison" (Newton 856n).

[274]Milton again seems to be using common idioms as ironic reinforcement of real terrors: when someone is "mad as hell" in Hell, the idiom receives a new force; here "Thunder-struck" is remade as a fresh image.

[275]Throughout this book, "terror" or "terrors," and here "furies," seem to be remnants from the allegory of "mutes" such as "Labour greife hatred Envie warre famine Pestilence sicknesse discontent Ignorance Feare Death" (Trinity MS 33) in Milton's earlier dramatic draft of the epic. "Terror of God" is a phrase used in Genesis 35.5; compare also Job 6.4.

[276]Like a "waste," or a desolate and uninhabited region.

[277]Again, we are temporarily in a morality play in which burning Wrath, Terror, and the Furies pursue the fallen angels, and Hell itself sees them coming and would have fled, except that Fate, having cast the foundations of Hell too deep and too securely, would not allow it to move.

[278]The number may have mystical significance, but it is the same amount of days Mulciber (the less-familiar name for the Greek Hephaistos or the Roman Vulcan) is generally supposed to have fallen when Jupiter cast him out. See 1.740–46, where Milton has the pagan god fall only *one* day. For the nine-days' fall, see also 1.44–53.

[279]Burdened or blocked him up with destruction ("ruin"). Like Moloch bellowing while fleeing battle, Chaos roars. The fall of the angels confuses even Chaos, confounding him in the sense of "confusing utterly" and "damning."

[280]Again, Hell seems to be the Hell-mouth of the morality plays. Hell has a biblical mouth as well, in Isaiah 5.14: "Therefore hell hath enlarged herself, and opened her mouth without measure: and their glory, and their multitude, and their pomp, and he that rejoiceth, shall descend into it."

[281]"The break in Heaven's wall." Heaven's wounds heal as easily as those in angelic substance; and—just as the hills are replaced easily by God's power—the wall is repaired.

Messiah his triumphal Chariot[282] turnd:
To meet him all his Saints, who silent stood
Eye witnesses of his Almightie Acts,
With Jubilie advanc'd; and as they went,
Shaded with branching Palme,[283] each order bright,   885
Sung Triumph, and him sung Victorious King,
Son, Heir, and Lord, to him Dominion giv'n,
Worthiest to Reign: he celebrated rode
Triumphant through mid Heav'n, into the Courts
And Temple of his mightie Father Thron'd   890
On high: who into Glorie him receav'd,
Where now he sits at the right hand of bliss.
    Thus measuring things in Heav'n by things on Earth
At thy request, and that thou maist beware
By what is past, to thee I have reveal'd   895
What might have else to human Race bin hid;
The discord which befel, and Warr in Heav'n
Among th' Angelic Powers, and the deep fall
Of those too high aspiring, who rebelld
With *Satan*, hee who envies now thy state,[284]   900
Who now is plotting how he may seduce°
Thee also from obedience, that with him
Bereavd of happiness thou maist partake
His punishment, Eternal miserie;
Which would be all his solace and revenge,   905
As a despite don against the most High,
Thee once to gaine Companion of his woe.
But list'n not to his Temptations, warne
Thy weaker;[285] let it profit thee to have heard
By terrible Example the reward   910
Of disobedience; firm they might have stood,
Yet fell; remember, and fear to transgress.

LEAD AWAY

The End of the Sixth Book.

---

[282]It is now a triumphal chariot because Messiah is marching in a formal triumph, or celebration of victory (modeled after similar Roman celebrations that included the construction of triumphal arches). When the angels "Sung Triumph," they imitated the Roman soldiers singing *Io triumphe* as they entered the Capitol (Fowler 6.882-92n). The word jubilee also has connotations of the celebration of royalty or conquering heroes at appointed years, though the *OED* 5.b definition, citing 3.348, might restrict it to "joyful shouting."

[283]The scene foreshadows Palm Sunday and the apocalyptic vision of Revelation 7.9.

[284]Raphael clearly draws a moral from the War in Heaven, warning Adam specifically that Satan will act out of pride ("high aspiring") and envy of his estate and will try to tempt Adam and Eve into disobedience in order to gain yet other companions in his despair and misery.

[285]The generic phrase for the wife used in 1 Peter 3.7 is "weaker vessel." Milton may be counting on the allusive force of the passage, which is concerned with the duties of husbands toward wives. Adam's duty toward his wife as the weaker is to protect her and warn her against temptation, a duty in which he will at least be partly derelict in Book 9.

Paradise Lost.

BOOK VII.

THE ARGUMENT.

Raphael *at the request of* Adam *relates how and wherefore this world was first created; that God, after the expelling of Satan and his Angels out of Heaven, declar'd his pleasure to create another World and other Creatures to dwell therein; sends his Son with Glory and attendance of Angels to perform the work of Creation in six dayes: the Angels celebrate with Hymns the performance thereof, and his reascention into Heaven.*

Escend from Heav'n *Urania*, by that name
If rightly thou art call'd,[1] whose Voice divine
Following, above th' *Olympian* Hill I soare,
Above the flight of *Pegasean* wing.[2]
The meaning, not the Name I call: for thou   5
Nor of the Muses nine, nor on the top
Of old *Olympus* dwell'st, but Heav'nlie borne,°   BORN
Before the Hills appeerd, or Fountain flow'd,[3]
Thou with Eternal wisdom didst converse,[4]
Wisdom thy Sister,[5] and with her didst play   10
In presence of th' Almightie Father, pleas'd
With thy Celestial Song. Up led by thee
Into the Heav'n of Heav'ns I have presum'd,
An Earthlie Guest, and drawn Empyreal Aire,
Thy tempring;[6] with like safetie guided down   15
Return me to my Native Element:

[handwritten annotation: A CHRISTIAN MUSE]

---

[1]Milton first gives his muse a name in this, the third of his four invocations, and he stresses that it is the meaning of his Christian muse, not the name, which is important. For the psychological complexities of Milton assuming the identity of the muse, see Davies and Hunter, "Milton's Urania," and Kerrigan, *Prophetic Milton*. A Christian muse, Milton implies, should remain nameless, since the poet will be calling on the same unnamed source that inspired Moses to receive the Ten Commandments or write the books of the Old Testament generally ascribed to him in the seventeenth century.

[2]Outstripping the sources of pagan inspiration, limited to the top of Mt. Olympus, home of the Olympian gods, or Mts. Helicon or Pierus, supposed homes of the nine classical Muses and the Pierian spring, the Epic Voice will soar higher than the winged horse Pegasus could fly. It was a cliché of poetry in Milton's era to claim that the poet could mount the horse of inspiration, Pegasus, and fly like the hero of classical myth, Bellerophon; in a clear attempt to be superior, Milton will overtop the flight of Pegasus or Mt. Olympus and will drink at fountains purer than those of Mt. Helicon. Milton's derogatory tone can be caught by his use of "Hill" with "*Olympian*" and perhaps by his use of "old" paired with "*Olympus* ": Mt. Olympus is a mere hill and can be contemptuously called "old *Olympus*," as if it were worn out.

[3]Christian history begins before the Earth was created, according to Milton's time scheme, so that it predates any conceivable Mt. Olympus or spring or fountain sacred to the Greek or Roman gods.

[4]The words converse and conversation were especially evocative to Milton, suggesting much more than mere chat between human beings. In the divorce tracts, for instance, "conversation is the chiefest and the noblest end of mariage" (*Doctrine and Discipline of Divorce*, Yale 2: 246). Thus he would have defined conversation as an exchange of deeply meaningful ideas. Here it suggests a dialogue as meaningful as that between Adam and Raphael.

[5]Milton conflates traditions about the Hebrew Wisdom and about the Greek Urania. Their relationship with God is the relationship between two sisters innocently playing music in the presence of their father. Milton's source is Proverbs 8, a hymn to wisdom in which Wisdom, personified as feminine, describes her origins: "The Lord possessed me in the beginning of his way, before his works of old. I was set up from everlasting, from the beginning, or ever the earth was. When there were no depths, I was brought forth; when there were no fountains abounding with water. Before the mountains were settled, before the hills was I brought forth: While as yet he had not made the earth, nor the fields, nor the highest part of the dust of the world. When he prepared the heavens, I was there: when he set a compass upon the face of the depth . . . . Then I was by him, as one brought up with him: and I was daily his delight, rejoicing always before him . . . " (22–30). The apocryphal Wisdom of Solomon pictures the "Spirit of wisdome," a very similar source of inspiration to Solomon. She teaches the nature of things, because "she is the breth of the power of God, and a pure influence that floweth from the glorie of the Almightie: therefore can no defiled thing come unto her" (7.25, Geneva Bible, 1560 ed.). Thus Milton makes Urania and Wisdom inspirational sisters and pictures them both playing music as daughters of God before the time of creation. Some sort of personal myth is at work here as well, since Milton is picturing himself as a disciple of wisdom from his earliest age, like Solomon, and then as being led up to the Empyrean Sphere by Urania to emulate (or overhear and record?) her celestial song.

[6]Normally a mortal could not breathe the air of heavenly regions, since heavenly air is presumed to be, like mountain air, thin or scarce. Milton pictures Urania tempering the air of the Empyrean so that he can breathe it, or tempering or modifying his abilities by inspiration so he can exist in it.

Least° from this flying Steed unrein'd, (as once   LEST
Bellerophon, though from a lower Clime)
Dismounted, on th' *Aleian*[7] Field I fall
Erroneous[8] there to wander and forlorne.   20
Half yet remaines unsung, but narrower bound
Within the visible Diurnal Sphere;[9]
Standing on Earth, not rapt above the Pole,[10]
More safe I Sing with mortal voice, unchang'd
To hoarce or mute, though fall'n on evil dayes,   25
On evil dayes though fall'n, and evil tongues;[11]
In darkness, and with dangers compast round,
And solitude; yet not alone, while thou
Visit'st my slumbers Nightly,[12] or when Morn
Purples the East: still govern thou my Song,   30
Urania, and fit audience find, though few.[13]
But drive farr off the barbarous dissonance
Of *Bacchus*[14] and his revellers, the Race
Of that wilde Rout that tore the Thracian Bard
In *Rhodope*,[15] where Woods and Rocks had Eares   35
To rapture, till the savage clamor dround
Both Harp and Voice; nor could the Muse defend
Her Son.[16] So fail not thou, who thee implores:
For thou art Heav'nlie, shee an empty dreame.

---

[7]According to Homer's brief allusion to the myth of Bellerophon (*Iliad* 6.200-202), the young man attempted to fly to heaven on Pegasus but Jupiter stopped him by sending an insect to sting the winged horse. Pegasus thereupon threw Bellerophon, who fell to earth on the Aleian plain in Lycia, and wandered there (Latin *errare* meaning "to wander") until his death.

[8]*1667* has a comma here, probably unnecessarily. The syntax of the clause in modern English would be " . . . lest I fall on the Aleian plain, to wander there erroneous and forlorn."

[9]The Epic Voice (still speaking from Milton's perspective rather than Raphael's) divides the epic at what was in *1674* the juncture between Books 6 and 7 and he restricts the action to the diurnal sphere (the sphere which includes Earth and appears to revolve around us diurnally, or in about a day's time; from Latin *dies*, a day). In the first half of the epic, the Epic Voice has sung of "things invisible to mortal sight" (3.55).

[10]The "Pole" is probably, as Fowler suggests, a synecdoche for the sky, poetic usage as in *OED* 4. The narrator may also be pictured as having formerly looked down on the earth from above the North Pole but now being firmly placed on the planet. The word "rapt" probably represents poetic seizure and prophetic inspiration; see Kerrigan, *Prophetic Milton* 159, 184-85, for the narrator of *Paradise Lost* as prophet.

[11]There is little doubt that Milton is speaking in his own person here, from the perspective of a man whose life was in danger after the Restoration of Charles II, the son of the monarch whose execution Milton had defended in several pamphlets. As a regicide, Milton feared for his life, was at least briefly imprisoned, and from time to time had to go into hiding, especially because he was a vulnerable blind old man. He may even have feared assassination (see Parker 1: 577). The picture of the poet is one of a man encompassed by dangers living in solitude, a state for which he reserves a special veneration in *Paradise Lost*, one embodied in such figures as Abdiel or Noah.

[12]We also know from Milton's early biographers that he composed poetry or at least arose in the extreme early hours of the morning. Cyriack Skinner, Milton's amanuensis (see Parker, 1: 1011, for the "Anonymous Biographer" as Skinner), records Milton saying "hee wanted to bee milkd" of his poetry in the early morning (Darbishire, *Early Lives* 33), and John Toland wrote that "In Summer he would be stirring at four in the Morning, and in Winter at five . . . " (Darbishire 194). Milton's phrasing is biblical, as in Psalm 17.3, addressing God: "thou has proved mine heart; thou hast visited me in the night. . . ."

[13]A famous definition of Milton's ideal audience. Since it had been unfashionable to write epics at least since the time of Spenser, since blank verse was out of fashion, and since Milton's audience would also have been limited by the political and moral climate of the Restoration, he had good reason to believe that his readership at first would have been limited and small.

[14]Returning to the story of Orpheus as celebrated in "Lycidas" 58-63, a story which seemed to represent to Milton the temporary triumph of barbarism over art, since Orpheus, the best of all poets in the legendary ancient world, was ripped apart by Bacchantes, drunken followers of Dionysus or Bacchus. According to some versions of the story Orpheus was torn apart by female Bacchantes jealous of his love for Eurydice, but Milton associates the story with the destructive power of other male and female revelers, whether they be the mixed *comozontes* of *Comus*, the male Sons of Belial and riotous Sodomites (1.500-05), or the female Bacchantes who may be alluded to here. From all indications, Milton had a lifelong phobia of meeting such an end: his sonnet "Captain or Colonel" asks even British soldiers in late 1642 to "Lift not [their] spear against the Muses' Bowre."

[15]The prophetic poet or bard (translating the Latin word *vates* used by Ovid) Orpheus was supposed to have lived in Thrace and to have been torn apart on the Thracian mountain range of Rhodope, sacred to Dionysus. According to many versions of the myth of Orpheus, his singing, accompanied by his playing on lyre or harp, had the power to evoke emotions in inanimate nature and make stones weep and trees throw down their leaves in sympathy. See Ovid, *Metamorphoses* 11.1-60.

[16]Not even Orpheus's mother, the Muse Calliope, had the power to save her son from death; compare "Lycidas" 58-63. In "Lycidas," nothing is said to give the impression that Calliope is "an empty dreame."

Say Goddess,[17] what ensu'd when *Raphael*,   40
The affable Arch-Angel, had forewarn'd
Adam by dire example to beware
Apostasie,° by what befell in Heaven   REBELLION AGAINST GOD
To those Apostates, least the like befall
In Paradise to *Adam* or his Race,   45
Charg'd not to touch the interdicted° Tree,   FORBIDDEN
If they transgress, and slight° that sole command,   IGNORE
So easily obeyd amid the choice
Of all tastes else to please thir appetite,
Though wandring.[18] He with his consorted *Eve*[19]   50
The storie heard attentive,[20] and was fill'd
With admiration, and deep Muse[21] to heare
Of things so high and strange, things to thir thought
So unimaginable as hate in Heav'n,
And Warr so neer the Peace of God in bliss   55
With such confusion: but the evil soon
Driv'n back redounded as a flood on those
From whom it sprung, impossible to mix
With Blessedness. Whence *Adam* soon repeal'd°   ABANDONED
The doubts that in his heart arose: and now   60
Led on, yet sinless,[22] with desire to know
What neerer might concern him, how this World
Of Heav'n and Earth conspicious[23] first began,
When, and whereof created, for what cause,
What within *Eden* or without was done   65
Before his memorie, as one whose drouth°   THIRST
Yet scarce allay'd still eyes the current° streame,   RUNNING
Whose liquid murmur heard new thirst excites,[24]
Proceeded thus to ask his Heav'nly Guest.

   Great things, and full of wonder in our eares,   70
Farr differing from this World, thou has reveal'd
Divine interpreter,[25] by favour sent
Down from the Empyrean to forewarne
Us timely of what might else have bin our loss,
Unknown, which human knowledg could not reach: 75
For which to the infinitly Good we owe
Immortal thanks, and his admonishment
Receave with solemne purpose to observe
Immutably his sovran will, the end

---

[17]Traditional formula for invoking a muse in classical literature, as in *Musa, mihi causas memora*, in the *Aeneid* 1.8, which can be translated "O Muse, tell me the causes . . . ." With "Goddess," Milton consciously moves one step above "Muse."

[18]Probably " . . . not directed by reason or fixed purpose" (*OED* 2.b). Like Eve's "*wanton* ringlets" (4.306, emphasis mine), the word "wandring" seems to be used without moral baggage. Milton does use "wandring" to describe Adam and Eve's unsteady steps as they head out of Eden (12.648): thus it has an unfallen and a fallen meaning.

[19]Eve is Adam's "consort," his wife.

[20]Some slight confusion may be caused by Raphael's advice at the end of Book 6, " . . . warne / Thy weaker" (908–909), which implies that Eve is absent when the warning is given. Here they are said to hear the story together; notice "thir thought" at 53 below.

[21]"Serious thought" or "profound meditation" (*OED* sb. 2.a) complementing the meaning "extreme wonder" for "admiration."

[22]Here as at 9.659 Milton is at pains to stress that neither Adam's scientific inquiry nor Eve's debate with the Serpent is sinful.

[23]A variant spelling of "conspicuous." The word here means "visible," in this case to humankind (as opposed to residents of the Empyrean, who may choose to be visible or invisible in the presence of humans).

[24]Adam is like a man who has drunk from a stream but who is so thirsty still that he eyes the running water with renewed desire.

[25]Echoes Vergil's epithet for Mercury, the messenger of Jove, as *interpres divum* (*Aeneid* 4.378).

Of what we are. But since thou hast voutsaf't   80
Gently for our instruction to impart
Things above Earthly thought, which yet concernd
Our knowing, as to highest wisdom seemd,[26]
Deign to descend now lower, and relate
What may no less perhaps availe us known,   85
How first began this Heav'n which we behold
Distant so high, with moving Fires[27] adornd
Innumerable, and this which yeelds or fills
All space,[28] the ambient Aire wide interfus'd
Imbracing round this florid[29] Earth, what cause[30]   90
Mov'd the Creator in his holy Rest[31]
Through all Eternitie so late to build
In Chaos, and the work begun, how soon
Absolv'd,° if unforbid thou maist unfould
What wee, not to explore the secrets aske   95
Of his Eternal Empire, but the more
To magnifie his works,[32] the more we know.
And the great Light of Day yet wants to run
Much of his Race though steep,[33] suspens[34] in Heav'n
Held by thy voice, thy potent voice he heares,   100
And longer will delay to heare thee tell
His Generation,[35] and the rising Birth
Of Nature from the unapparent° Deep:
Or if the Starr of Eevning and the Moon
Haste to thy audience,[36] Night with her will bring   105
Silence, and Sleep listning to thee will watch,[37]
Or we can bid his absence, till thy Song
End, and dismiss thee[38] ere the Morning shine.
      Thus *Adam* his illustrious[39] Guest besought:
      And thus the Godlike Angel answerd milde.   110
This also thy request with caution askt[40]

---

[26]Possibly "seemed good" (*OED* 2.7.e).

[27]Stars and comets, which seem "adornd" or ornamented from Adam's perspective.

[28]Air can be perceived as filling space or yielding to more substantial matter.

[29]Flower-covered, thus fertile enough to produce abundant growth.

[30]An idiomatic variation of the epic question, as in "say first what cause / Mov'd our Grand Parents" (1.28–29).

[31]Perhaps "Place of resting or residing" (*OED* 5.a).

[32]Adam takes pains to say that his question is not asked in order to uncover God's secrets but to give honor. To "magnifie his works" is a biblical idiom meaning "to glorify his works by praising them." Compare what Mary says at the Annunciation in Luke 1.46: "My soul doth magnify the Lord."

[33]The sun still has much time to run the race of time through the heavens, though the race is on a steep incline. Milton may be echoing a similar request in the *Odyssey*, 11.372–76, when Alcinous asks that Odysseus continue his narrative. Newton replaces the comma after "steep" with a semicolon, to emphasize the strong pause there, and he adds a comma after what he takes to be an appositive phrase, "thy potent voice."

[34]Perhaps "attentive" (*OED* I) and "hanging" (*OED* 4); the word appears to be used like a Latin present participle and it may include the meaning "undecided," since Milton may be offering the reader a choice between the Sun's entering or not entering a new cycle, in this case one of decay (see Fowler 98–100n).

[35]"To hear you tell the story of his creation."

[36]"Or if the evening star and the moon speed up time in order to hasten to hear you."

[37]"Stay awake," as if on vigil or military watch. Night, Silence, and Sleep are all personified, as if part of an allegory.

[38]Supply "[we] dismiss thee," in a polite formula that suggests "we reluctantly let you go." The whole request to Raphael is extremely polite, even flattering (but of course respectfully and honestly). Adam's responses to Raphael illustrate his strong and sincere desire to keep the pleasure of the angel's company, stretching the time out to as great an extent as possible.

[39]Raphael is not only famous but "shining," from Latin *illustrare*—"to light up"—so that the etymological sense of the word seems to be operating as well as its more common meaning.

[40]Raphael immediately responds to Adam's courtesy and to his theologically sound caution or "fear of God" (as in "The fear of the Lord is the beginning of wisdom" [Psalm 111.10] or Job 28.28).

Obtaine: though to recount Almightie works
What words or tongue[41] of Seraph can suffice,
Or heart of man suffice to comprehend?
Yet what thou canst attain, which best may serve   115
To glorifie the Maker, and inferr[42]
Thee also happier, shall not be withheld
Thy hearing, such Commission from above
I have receav'd,[43] to answer thy desire
Of knowledge within bounds;[44] beyond abstain   120
To ask, nor let thine own inventions[45] hope°   HOPE FOR
Things not reveal'd, which th' invisible King,[46]
Onely Omniscient, hath supprest in Night,
To none communicable in Earth or Heaven:
Anough° is left besides to search and know.   ENOUGH   125
But Knowledge is as food, and needs no less
Her Temperance over Appetite, to know
In measure what the mind may well contain,
Oppresses else with Surfet, and soon turns
Wisdom to Folly, as Nourishment to Winde.[47]   130
    Know then, that after *Lucifer* from Heav'n
(So call him,[48] brighter once amidst the Host
Of Angels, then that Starr the Starrs among)
Fell with his flaming Legions through the Deep
Into his place,[49] and the great Son returnd   135
Victorious with his Saints,[50] th' Omnipotent
Eternal Father from his Throne beheld
Thir multitude, and to his Son thus spake.
    At least[51] our envious Foe hath fail'd, who thought
All like himself rebellious, by whose aid   140
This inaccessible high strength, the seat

---

[41]The editor Richard Bentley thought the phrase "words or tongue" redundant and wanted to emend it to "words from tongue," but there is a meaningful distinction between mere words and what might issue from the tongue of a seraph. Also, the heart of humankind can comprehend words issuing from another human but might not be able to comprehend the mysterious speech or imagery of an angel.

[42]"To bring on, bring about, induce, occasion, cause, procure" (*OED* 1). A simple modern paraphrase would be "to make you happier."

[43]Raphael is under orders from God to give Adam such knowledge as is within bounds; he is also on a mission to "render [Adam and Eve] inexcusable" (Book 5, Argument) if they disobey the one commandment.

[44]An important phrase, because it does suggest that forbidden knowledge exists, or at least that knowledge unnecessary for humankind's salvation exists. The analogy that Raphael makes is between satisfying hunger for knowledge and satisfying hunger for food: eating oneself sick is possible for both. Temperance, as always, is the best strategy. Becoming intemperate, Adam and Eve will succumb to the temptation of eating from the Tree of the Knowledge of Good and Evil, so that the real act of eating will run parallel to the symbolic act of disobedience. The one will make them physically sick, the other sick at heart. Milton's anatomical microcosm of the universe makes the result of sin "Winde" or gas; excess knowledge makes for the folly or nonsense of hot air. For the context of "forbidden knowledge," see Schultz, *Milton*.

[45]"Conclusions based on reason," perhaps with a foreboding allusion to Ecclesiastes 7.29: " . . . God hath made man upright; but they have sought out many inventions."

[46]1 Timothy 1.17 describes God as " . . . the King eternal, immortal, invisible, the only wise God. . . ."

[47]Just as eating excess food makes gas in the stomach, gaining useless knowledge helps create the hot air of folly. **Folly** here suggests "damned foolish [not taking the words lightly]."

[48]Raphael allows Satan the name Lucifer, "light-bearer," which associates him with the morning star, in order to coax Adam to contrast what he was, an angel with a dignified name, with what he will become, the generic "enemy," Satan.

[49]Echoes the punishment of Judas Iscariot described in Acts 1.25: "That he may take part of this ministry and apostleship, from which Judas by transgression fell, that he might go to his own place."

[50]Here the word means "angels," since human beings would not be created until after the War in Heaven—though in Puritan literature "saints" often meant "holy ones," or, by extrapolation, "all good Christian people."

[51]Thyer thought that this phrase might be emended to "At last," and Robert Adams endorses the change (94), but to have the Son discuss the War in Heaven in terms of a lengthy struggle would be to undermine the speed with which he has just acted. For the idiom, compare 1.258–59: "Here at least / We shall be free" (and see 2.22 and 8.537, among other places, since Milton was fond of the phrase).

Of Deitie supream, us dispossest,[52]
He trusted to have seis'd, and into fraud[53]
Drew many, whom thir place knows here no more;[54]
Yet farr the greater part have kept, I see,   145
Thir station,° Heav'n yet populous retaines   POSITION IN THE HIERARCHY
Number sufficient to possess her Realmes
Though wide, and this high Temple to frequent
With Ministeries° due and solemn Rites: MINISTRATIONS
But least his heart exalt him in the harme   150
Already done, to have dispeopl'd Heav'n
My damage fondly° deem'd, I can repaire   FOOLISHLY
That detriment, if such it be to lose
Self-lost, and in a moment will create
Another World,[55] out of one man a Race   155
Of men innumerable, there to dwell,
Not here, till by degrees of merit rais'd
They open to themselves at length the way
Up hither, under long obedience tri'd,
And Earth be chang'd to Heav'n, & Heav'n to Earth,   160
One Kingdom, Joy and Union without end.[56]
Mean while inhabit laxe,[57] ye Powers of Heav'n,
And thou my Word, begotten Son, by thee
This I perform, speak thou, and be it don:[58]
My overshadowing Spirit[59] and might with thee   165
I send along, ride forth, and bid the Deep
Within appointed bounds be Heav'n and Earth,
Boundless the Deep, because I am[60] who fill
Infinitude, nor vacuous the space.[61]
Though I uncircumscrib'd my self retire,   170
And put not forth my goodness, which is free

[handwritten annotations: "ASCENT MAN IS NOT STATIC"; "DECREES THE CREATION OF THE NEW WORLD"]

---

[52]"We having been dispossessed." An archaic English usage.

[53]"State of being defrauded or deluded" (*OED* 5, citing Milton's special passive usage, perhaps based on Latin *fraus*). Compare 9.643–44: "So glister'd the dire snake, and into fraud / Led *Eve. . . .*"

[54]Probably the phrasing alludes to Job 7.9–10: " . . . he that goeth down to the grave shall come up no more. He shall return no more to his house, neither shall his place know him any more."

[55]Free will among all beings is again confirmed, since the fallen angels are "Self-lost" (154) and God could instantly or "in a moment" create another world, or any plurality of worlds, to contain humankind. Thus the argument that God creates humankind just to spite the evil angels is defused. Nevertheless, orthodox Christians were supposed to believe with Augustine that God will "by His grace collect, as now He does, a people so numerous, that He thus fills up and repairs the blank made by the fallen angels, and that thus that beloved and heavenly city is not defrauded of the full number of its citizens, but perhaps may even rejoice in a still more overflowing population" (*City of God* 22.1).

[56]The ultimate optimism of humankind's potential to work its way back up to Heaven. Before (or even after) the Fall, humankind will be able to raise itself by degrees of merit, proving its obedience over a long period of time, to the point where the distinction between Heaven and Earth will no longer be necessary. Note that the Father says that humankind will exist, but "Not here."

[57]"Meanwhile, enjoy the extra space that was occupied by the angels who fell." The word "laxe" has some of the meaning of the Latin adverb **laxe**, "loosely, freely, widely, roomily."

[58]God the Father is appointing the Son in His capacity of Logos, the "Word [who] was with God, and the Word [that] was God" (John 1.1); thus when the Son speaks, the will of God to create will be done. The Son, therefore, according to Milton's system, will do the actual work of creation, though whether the Son at that point is called "God" or "Spirit" is a moot point.

[59]The Spirit that "Dove-like satst brooding on the vast Abyss" in 1.21, but not the same as the conventional member of the Holy Trinity, the Holy Spirit or Holy Ghost. According to *On Christian Doctrine*, the Spirit of God mentioned in Genesis 1.2 is "God's divine power, not any particular person" (1.7; Yale 6: 304).

[60]"I am" is the shortened version of one of the names of God (compare "I am that I am," Exodus 3.14, and Milton's commentary on the name in *On Christian Doctrine* 1.2 [Yale 6: 138–39]). The complete syntax of the clause in modern English would be "I am he who fills infinitude."

[61]Milton's God creates the universe out of matter or substance, an extension of Himself (*ex deo*), not out of a vacuum or out of nothing (*ex nihilo*), and that matter is inherently good: "It was in a confused and disordered state at first, but afterwards God made it ordered and beautiful" (*On Christian Doctrine* 1.7; Yale 6: 308). Milton admits in that same chapter that the opinion had been challenged by various theologians, but he nevertheless sticks tenaciously to it. Chaos is not inherently evil: it is just the place from which God has withheld his goodness.

To act or not, Necessitie and Chance
Approach not mee, and what I will is Fate.[62]
   So spake th' Almightie, and to what he spake
His Word, the filial Godhead, gave effect.   175
Immediate are the Acts of God, more swift
Then time or motion, but to human ears
Cannot without process[63] of speech be told,[64]
So told as earthly notion° can receave.   UNDERSTANDING
Great triumph and rejoycing was in Heav'n   180
When such was heard declar'd the Almightie's will;
Glorie they sung to the most High, good will
To future men,[65] and in thir dwellings peace:
Glorie to him whose just avenging ire
Had driven out th' ungodly from his sight   185
And th' habitations of the just;[66] to him
Glorie and praise, whose wisdom had ordain'd
Good out of evil to create,[67] in stead
Of Spirits maligne° a better Race to bring   EVIL
Into thir vacant room, and thence diffuse   190
His good to Worlds and Ages infinite.
So sang the Hierarchies: Mean while the Son
On his great Expedition now appeer'd,
Girt with Omnipotence,[68] with Radiance crown'd
Of Majestie Divine, Sapience and Love   195
Immense, and all his Father in him shon.
About his Chariot numberless were pour'd
Cherub and Seraph, Potentates and Thrones,
And Vertues, winged Spirits, and Chariots wing'd,
From the Armoury of God,[69] where stand of old   200
Myriads between two brazen Mountains lodg'd[70]
Against a solemn day, harnest at hand,
Celestial Equipage;[71] and now came forth
Spontaneous, for within them Spirit livd,
Attendant on thir Lord: Heav'n op'nd wide   205

---

[62]The most concise statement in the epic of Milton's belief that there can be no fate or chance outside the will of God. In *On Christian Doctrine*, Milton contemptuously dismisses those philosophers like the Stoics who "prattle about nature or fate, as if they were to be identified with this supreme being. But nature or *natura* implies by its very name that it was *natam*, born. . . . Surely, too, fate or *fatum* is only what is *fatum*, spoken, by some almighty power" (1.2; Yale 6: 130–31).

[63]Accented on the second syllable by Milton and in general in the seventeenth century (see *OED* note on the pronunciation of the noun).

[64]"When we talk about knowing God, it must be understood in terms of man's limited powers of comprehension. God, as he really is, is far beyond man's imagination, let alone his understanding" (*On Christian Doctrine* 1.2; Yale 6: 133). Boyd Berry interprets what Raphael says to mean that "God's acts are immediate but . . . human 'process of speech' is bound by 'time and motion' and cannot adequately represent them" (*Process* 3).

[65]The familiar formula of the angels celebrating Christ's birth, "Glory to God in the highest, and on earth peace, good will toward men" (Luke 2.14). "Glorie" begins a short prophetic hymn of praise that ends at 191.

[66]Proverbs 3.33: "The curse of the Lord is in the house of the wicked: but he blesseth the habitation of the just."

[67]Compare 12.470–71: "That all this good of evil shall produce, / And evil turn to good. . . ."

[68]The Son is dressed in allegorical or symbolic clothing representing the omnipotence given Him by the Father: He is given the crown of light by the Father because He is the "Fountain of Light" (3.375). He is also accompanied by Sapience as an entity, in the sense of Wisdom as used in the Old Testament (see Radzinowicz, *Milton's* 49–61), and Love expressed perhaps through creation and through both fatherly and brotherly love toward Adam and Eve. Ezekiel's vision with its living chariots again provides much of the imagery.

[69]"The Lord hath opened his armoury" (Jeremiah 50.25).

[70]Images taken from Zechariah's vision in Zechariah 6.1: "And I turned, and lifted up mine eyes, and looked, and behold, there came four chariots out from between two mountains; and the mountains were mountains of brass."

[71]Equipment designed and kept in preparation for the solemn day of the Last Judgment, but the word "Equipage," accented on the first syllable, also meant "military equipment."

Her ever during° Gates, Harmonious sound   ENDURING, DURABLE
On golden Hinges moving,[72] to let forth
The King of Glorie in his powerful Word
And Spirit coming to create new Worlds.
On heav'nly ground they stood, and from the shore   210
They view'd the vast immeasurable Abyss[73]
Outrageous° as a Sea, dark, wasteful, wilde,   UNLIMITED
Up from the bottom turn'd by furious windes
And surging waves, as Mountains to assault
Heav'ns highth, and with the Center mix the Pole.[74]   215
    Silence, ye troubl'd waves, and thou Deep, peace,
Said then th' Omnific[75] Word, your discord end:
    Nor staid, but on the Wings of Cherubim
Uplifted, in Paternal Glorie rode[76]
Farr into *Chaos*, and the World unborn;   220
For *Chaos* heard his voice: him all his Traine
Follow'd in bright procession to behold
Creation, and the wonders of his might.
Then staid the fervid Wheeles, and in his hand
He took the golden Compasses,[77] prepar'd   225
In Gods Eternal store,[78] to circumscribe
This Universe, and all created things:
One foot he center'd, and the other turn'd
Round through the vast profunditie obscure,[79]
And said, thus farr extend, thus farr thy bounds,   230
This be thy just[80] Circumference, O World.
Thus God the Heav'n created, thus the Earth,
Matter unform'd and void: Darkness profound

---

[72]The gates of Heaven, informed or literally moved by "Spirit" (Milton is cautious not to say "Holy Spirit"), open easily and open wide, but they also endure forever, keeping unrepentant sinners out. They open musically on golden hinges with a harmonious sound, as contrasted with the "jarring sound" (2.880) of the opening of the gates of Hell. Also, once the gates of Hell are opened, with "impetuous recoile" (2.880), Sin has no power to close them again; thus free will has more to do with Heaven than Hell.

[73]Chaos, or the Deep, a vast body of uncontrolled and tempestuous (but not evil) matter. It is "wasteful" in the sense that it is full of desolate patches or wastelands. As Schwartz shows, Milton can imply that Chaos is evil and still declare it theologically neutral (8–39).

[74]Just as mountains reach the sky and thus combine the center of the earth with its topmost point, the ocean-like mass is churned up from its depths by the winds, so that sediment appears on the surface. Compare the description of the storm stirred up by the wind-god Aeolus in the *Aeneid* 1.81–91, who strikes the mountains to bring forth all of the winds which then proceed over land as tornadoes and turn up the ocean from its deepest foundation. The skies or poles resound (*Intonueare poli*) with the noise of thunder. The picture is one of life-threatening disorder.

[75]"All-making," the first instance of the word recorded in the *OED*. Milton has put together two common Latin words to make a compound analogous to "omnipotent" in English or *pontifex* in Latin. For a detailed analysis of Milton's use of Genesis here and elsewhere in Book 7, see Haüblein.

[76]The vehicle is the same chariot propelled by cherubim, apparently, that Messiah rode into battle at 6.846, with the burning or "fervid" wheels described at 6.832.

[77]The concept of God as architect or engineer of the universe probably stems from Proverbs 8.27, spoken by "wisdom" and discussing the creation: "When he prepared the heavens, I was there: when he set a compass upon the face of the depth . . . ." The Geneva Bible commentary reads "wisdom" as "the Sonne of God, who was before all time and ever present with the Father" (1560 ed.). The image of creation by compasses was accepted by Dante, who quotes "Divine Thought" describing God at creation as "He that turned His compass about the bounds of the world and within it devised so variously things hidden and manifest. . ." (*Paradiso* 19.40–41). For Milton, God was "uncircumscrib'd" (170 above), so that the act of circumscribing the universe is controlled by a God who cannot be circumscribed.

[78]It may be a legitimate, if mischievous, question to ask who prepared the compasses and from what "place where stores are kept" or warehouse (see *OED* 11, citing this instance) in Heaven they came. At any rate, the storage is eternal and it is maintained by God. The compass itself has one fixed foot, the other being turned to circumscribe or give order to the vast deep of Chaos. The circle that God draws here is presumably not the first He has drawn.

[79]One of a number of startling juxtapositions between abstract and concrete, since "vast" measures space and "obscure" measures degree of darkness, but "profunditie" remains in the realm of ideas. The power of the phrase also owes something to its mixture of sounds, since "vast" is curt but the more orotund "profundity" and "obscure" emphasize long vowels. The sound effects, the synesthesia (translation of one sense impression into another), and the catachresis (apparent misuse of disparate parts of speech or images) are similar to what exists in "palpable obscure" (2.406), "wide interrupt" (3.84), and "vast abrupt" (2.409).

[80]Probably "exact, accurate" (*OED* 6.b), with overtones of "proportional" and "fair and equitable."

Cover'd th' Abyss: but on the watrie calme

His brooding wings the Spirit of God outspred,[81]   235

And vital vertue° infus'd, and vital warmth   POWER, ESSENCE OF LIFE

Throughout the fluid Mass, but downward purg'd

The black tartareous cold Infernal dregs

Adverse to life:[82] then founded, then conglob'd°   BROUGHT TOGETHER

Like things to like, the rest to several place   240

Disparted,° and between spun out the Air,   DIVIDED

And Earth self-ballanc't[83] on her Center hung.

    Let ther be Light,[84] said God, and forthwith Light

Ethereal, first of things, quintessence[85] pure

Sprung from the Deep, and from her Native East   245

To journie through the airie gloom began,

Sphear'd in a radiant Cloud, for yet the Sun

Was not; shee in a cloudie Tabernacle

Sojourn'd the while.[86] God saw the Light was good;

And light from darkness by the Hemisphere   250

Divided: Light the Day, and Darkness Night

He nam'd. Thus was the first Day Eev'n and Morn:[87]

Nor past° uncelebrated, nor unsung   PASSED

By the Celestial Quires, when Orient Light

Exhaling[88] first from Darkness they beheld;   255

Birth-day of Heav'n and Earth; with joy and shout

The hollow Universal Orb they fill'd,

And touch't thir Golden Harps, and hymning prais'd

God and his works, Creatour him they sung,[89]

---

[81]The Spirit of God is here a masculine entity. The Spirit whom Milton invokes at 1.17 also informs the "vast Abyss" and impregnates it, but of course Urania is pictured as feminine.

[82]Whether or not the reader recoils from the scatological image, the Spirit of God seems to embody the universe in the act of creation, infusing virtue and warmth to the upper regions but excreting or purging below "black [melancholic] tartareous [obtaining to Tartarus, the region of classical Hell—*OED* a.2—but also pertaining to an earthy deposit, as in *OED* a.1] cold Infernal [reinforcing 'tartareous'] dregs." The Spirit seems to excrete the regions of Hell. Fowler believes the series of images has "psychological overtones" (236–42n); less politely, they are indeed scatological. Kerrigan writes that "the creator purges away the fecal 'dregs / Adverse to life'" (*Sacred Complex* 69).

[83]The Earth is well-balanced because it is in equilibrium on its north and south poles. In 5.578–79, it is described as "now rest[ing] / Upon her Center pois'd." The hyphenated "self-ballanc't" of *1667* seems preferable to the separate words of *1674*.

[84]Genesis 1.3: "And God said, Let there be light: and there was light." Light was not one of the four elements said to be in perpetual war with one another, so that it could be identified with the quintessence. See Babb, *Moral Cosmos* 28–30, for a general explanation of the relations between the elements and 106 for the quintessence.

[85]Milton identifies the fifth element or quintessence with ether and with the light emanating from God, but it had been called by the alchemists "potable gold," the "elixir," and the essence of the soul (see *OED* citations). Milton apparently stressed the word both on the first (compare 3.716) and the second syllables, as it is accented here. The Latin word for light, *lux*, is feminine, though the sun, *sol*, and the god associated with the sun, Apollo, were both masculine. Milton apparently wants the reader to differentiate this pre-solar light from the sun, identified with what was probably a masculine pronoun, "his," in 370 and 373 below. Since the sun is born in the east each morning, east is "Native" (from *natus*, "born") to light. The sun correspondingly will provide "Orient Light," or light from the east, in the morning.

[86]In the company of many theologians, Milton cleverly avoids the problem of the presence of light without sun by allowing the sun to remain hidden—like an idea in God's mind but in a "cloudie Tabernacle"—as if the Sun were the forerunner of the Ark of the Covenant, kept with mystical reverence within the Tabernacle. "We cannot imagine light without some source of light, but we do not therefore think that a source of light is the same thing as light, or equal in excellence" (*On Christian Doctrine* 1.7; Yale 6: 312). More specifically, Milton's source is Psalm 19, in which "The Heavens declare the glory of God" (1) and in which day and night set out lines (defined in the Geneva Bible marginalia as lines "of great capital letters to shewe unto us Gods glorie" [1560 ed.]). "In them [i.e., the lines] hath he set a tabernacle for the sun . . ." (4). The sun has not yet been created; thus "shee" seems to refer to the light, not the sun.

[87]The account follows that in the first chapter of Genesis verbatim, adding only the scientific detail of the divided hemispheres. Milton follows the Hebrew custom of reckoning a day as beginning in the evening. Fowler (7.249–52n) cites Andrew Willet, *Hexapla in Genesin* (1608): " . . . to account the naturall day from evening to evening" (4).

[88]"Evaporating," but also "emanating from." Probably referring to the phenomenon of sunlight appearing to dissipate mist or fog. *OED* 2.b. sees Milton's usage as the figurative interpretation "To draw up or drive off in the form of a vapour."

[89]According to the voice of God speaking out of the whirlwind in Job 38, when He "laid the foundations of the earth" was also "When the morning stars sang together, and all the sons of God shouted for joy" (4.7).

Both when first Eevning was, and when first Morn.   260
    Again, God said, let ther be Firmament
Amid the Waters, and let it divide
The Waters from the Waters:[90] and God made
The Firmament,[91] expanse of liquid, pure,
Transparent, Elemental Air, diffus'd   265
In circuit to the uttermost convex
Of this great Round: partition firm and sure,
The Waters underneath from those above
Dividing: for as Earth, so he the World[92]
Built on circumfluous[93] Waters calme, in wide   270
Crystallin Ocean,[94] and the loud misrule[95]
Of *Chaos* farr remov'd, least fierce extreames
Contiguous might distemper[96] the whole frame:
And Heav'n he nam'd the Firmament: So Eev'n
And Morning *Chorus*[97] sung the second Day.   275
    The Earth was form'd, but in the Womb as yet
Of Waters, Embryon immature involv'd,[98]
Appeer'd not: over all the face of Earth
Main Ocean[99] flow'd, not idle, but with warme
Prolific°[100] humour soft'ning all her Globe,   LIFE-GIVING   280
Fermented the great Mother to conceave,
Satiate with genial° moisture, when God said   GENERATIVE
Be gather'd now ye Waters under Heav'n
Into one place,[101] and let dry Land appeer.
Immediately[102] the Mountains huge appeer   285
Emergent, and thir broad bare backs upheave
Into the Clouds, thir tops ascend the Skie:
So high as heav'd the tumid° Hills, so low   SWOLLEN
Down sunk a hollow bottom broad and deep,

---

[90]Genesis 1: "And God said, Let there be a firmament in the midst of the waters, and let it divide the waters from the waters. And God made the firmament, and divided the waters which were under the firmament from the waters which were above the firmament: and it was so. And God called the firmament Heaven. And the evening and the morning were the second day" (6–8). It may also be worth noting that "God saw that it was good" after each day's creation.

[91]Milton seems to be attempting to be as scientifically precise as possible, since the nature of a firmament built on liquid and then designed in opaque, soft spheres that could be penetrated (compare 3.574) is difficult to explain. "Expanse," as derived from Latin *expandere*, means "something spread out" and is more precise than the King James's "firmament."

[92]That is, the universe, or the system of spheres within spheres—the same as "this great Round" above.

[93]Waters flowing all around the earth.

[94]If the spheres are liquid and crystalline, they must be enclosed in oceans, as the Earth appears to be. "Crystallin," as the spelling suggests, is accented on the second syllable, and the *OED* (adjective 1) seems to be in error, according to the invariable metrical arrangement throughout Milton's poetry.

[95]Within the realm of Chaos, pictured both as a king and a place, the elements are at war: thus the noisy misrule.

[96]The verb "distemper" had many connotations in the seventeenth century, from "to disturb or derange the due proportion of [elements, humours, etc.]" (*OED* 1) to "intoxicate" (*OED* 4.d). According to the editors of the *OED*, Milton's definition of the word, in 11.56 at least, was "To distemper or mar the condition of; to derange, confuse, put out of joint" (5).

[97]Apparently this is the chorus of morning stars in Job 7 alluded to in 259 above. The use of italics seems unusual, though *"Chorus"* is italicized in *Paradise Regain'd* 4.262.

[98]The Earth is formed only as an embryo enfolded in the womb of the waters, since the face of the Earth is covered with the waters.

[99]One uninterrupted ocean, perceived as a belt around the earth, instead of the divided seas present after land masses are formed.

[100]The warm moisture of the oceans surrounding Mother Earth ferment with the creation of life. Among some of the Renaissance Italian philosophers, celestial warmth acting on the waters of the ocean was thought to be a generative agent out of which other life was born. Girolamo Cardano, for instance, writing in 1554, proposed a theory of life generated from "warmth and moisture" and stressed "the determinant importance of celestial warmth as the agent in every process of generation . . . " (summarized by Alfonso Ingegno in *The Cambridge History of Renaissance Philosophy*, ed. Schmitt, 250).

[101]"And God said, Let the waters under the heaven be gathered together unto one place, and let the dry land appear: and it was so. And God called the dry land Earth; and the gathering together of the waters called he Seas . . . " (Genesis 1.9–10).

[102]The instantaneous speed of God's creation is emphasized, with the repetition of "Hasted," "For haste," and "swift" below.

Capacious bed of Waters: thither they   290
Hasted with glad precipitance, uprowld
As drops on dust conglobing from the drie;[103]
Part rise in crystal Wall, or ridge direct,[104]
For haste; such flight the great command impress'd
On the swift flouds: as Armies at the call   295
Of Trumpet (for of Armies[105] thou hast heard)
Troop to thir Standard, so the watrie throng,
Wave rowling after Wave, where way they found,
If steep, with torrent rapture,[106] if through Plaine,
Soft-ebbing; nor withstood them Rock or Hill,   300
But they, or under ground, or circuit wide
With Serpent errour wandring,[107] found thir way,
And on the washie Oose[108] deep Channels wore;
Easie, e're God had bid the ground be drie,
All but within those banks, where Rivers now   305
Stream, and perpetual draw thir humid traine.[109]
The dry Land, Earth, and the great receptacle
Of congregated Waters he call'd Seas:[110]
And saw that it was good, and said, Let th' Earth
Put forth the verdant Grass, Herb yielding Seed,   310
And Fruit Tree yielding Fruit after her kind;
Whose Seed is in her self upon the Earth.[111]
He scarce had said, when the bare Earth, till then
Desert and bare, unsightly, unadorn'd,
Brought forth the tender Grass, whose verdure clad   315
Her Universal Face with pleasant green,
Then Herbs of every leaf, that sudden flour'd
Op'ning thir various colours, and made gay
Her bosom smelling sweet: and these scarce blown,°   IN BLOOM
Forth flourish't thick the clustring Vine, forth crept   320

---

[103]A homely image of drops of water forming into balls as they land in dust. Forms of the verb "conglobe" are rare, but Milton uses "conglob'd" at 239 above.

[104]The waters rise like the Red Sea parting for Moses as described in 12.197, but perhaps with an allusion to the "sea of glass like unto crystal" before the throne of God in Revelation 4.6.

[105]Adam and Eve have heard of armies, of course, during the narrative of the War in Heaven.

[106]With a "force of movement" ("rapture," as in *OED* 2, citing this instance) like that of a precipitous mountain stream ("torrent").

[107]It cannot be coincidental that Raphael uses a prophetic image, though again even the Serpent (or snakes in general) must be thought of at this point as innocent and "error" as "meandering," when it is used of the movement of streams. With the references to armies and serpents, Raphael's narrative is proleptic: it uses words or images not literally applicable until a later time.

[108]A "soft slimy Ground, where a Ship cannot conveniently cast Anchor" (citation from Milton's nephew, Edward Phillips's *New World of English Words* [1709] as quoted in *OED* 2). It is easy, because the ground is soft, for the floods to cut channels in it.

[109]The rivers are personified as monarchs carrying behind them the wet "traine" (trailing part of their garment) of their waters.

[110]"And God called the dry land Earth; and the gathering together of the waters called he Seas: and God saw that it was good" (Genesis 1.10). In the phrase "congregated Waters," Milton is providing his own translation of the Vulgate *congregationesque aquarum*, as Fowler points out (7.307–12n).

[111]"And God said, Let the earth bring forth grass, the herb yielding seed, and the fruit tree yielding fruit after his kind, whose seed is in itself, upon the earth.... And the earth brought forth grass, and herb yielding seed after his kind, and the tree yielding fruit, whose seed was in itself, after his kind . . ." (Genesis 1.11–12). Notice that Milton changes the sex of the fruit tree, perhaps following the gender of the Latin word for tree, *arbor*, or perhaps indicating feminine nature because the tree is pictured like Eve as a maternal source of a "Seed."

The swelling Gourd,[112] up stood the cornie[113] Reed
Embattell'd in her field: and[114] the humble° Shrub,   LOW-LYING
And Bush with frizl'd hair implicit:° last   ENTWINED
Rose as in Dance the stately Trees, and spred
Thir branches hung with copious Fruit; or gemm'd   325
Thir blossoms:[115] with high woods the hills were crownd,
With tufts the vallies and each fountain side,
With borders long the Rivers. That Earth now
Seemd like to Heav'n, a seat where Gods might dwell,
Or wander with delight, and love to haunt   330
Her sacred shades: though God had yet not rain'd
Upon the Earth, and man to till the ground
None was, but from the Earth a dewie Mist
Went up and waterd all the ground,[116] and each
Plant of the field, which e're it was in the Earth   335
God made, and every Herb,[117] before it grew
On the green stemm; God saw that it was good.
So Eev'n and Morn recorded the Third Day.
     Again th' Almightie spake: Let there be Lights[118]
High in th' expanse[119] of Heaven to divide   340
The Day from Night; and let them be for Signes,
For Seasons, and for Dayes, and circling Years,
And let them be for Lights as I ordaine
Thir Office in the Firmament of Heav'n
To give Light on the Earth; and it was so.   345
And God made two great Lights,[120] great for thir use
To Man, the greater to have rule by Day,
The less by Night alterne:° and made the Starrs,   ALTERNATELY
And set them in the Firmament of Heav'n

---

[112]Since gourds normally have no odor, most editors, following one of Bentley's most cogent emendations, have changed the adjective-noun combination "smelling gourd," found in both *1667* and *1674*, to "swelling gourd." The compositor may have carried the "smelling" down from two lines above. The sweet-smelling bosom of the Earth is probably derived from the " . . . odours of a moste wonderful smel" described on the third day of creation in the apocryphal 2 Esdras 6.44 (Geneva Bible, 1560 ed.).

[113]Possibly the reed was shaped like a horn (following Latin *corneus*, "horn-like"), though a simpler explanation might be that it is shaped like corn (English usage for American "wheat"). *OED* 1 defines "corny" as "of or pertaining to corn," citing this instance. The reed is pictured as part of a defensive military formation (compare 4.980–81), the shrub and bush as having frizzled hair, the trees as if dancing. All of the vegetation is personified to emphasize its liveliness and its fecundity.

[114]*1667* has "add," which provides an acceptable reading, though Shawcross, Campbell, and Fowler do not adopt it (Beeching did, following *1667*). Adams, 107–08, argues for "add" on the grounds that it is preceded by the strong punctuation of the colon, but he may be basing his reading on the printing house usage rather than Milton's, since the compositors were arbitrary in their use of colons and semicolons.

[115]The trees are covered with abundant fruit or with blossoms that look like gems or are in bud (the rare usage is documented in *OED* 1, from the Latin *gemmare*, "to bud"). "Gemmation" is a synonym for "budding." As Fowler points out (7.323n), the image of the bush with frizzled hair resembles the elaborate and sometimes unintentionally comic personifications in Josuah Sylvester's translation of DuBartas.

[116]In Genesis 2, vegetation is said to grow in Eden not because it rains "But there went up a mist from the earth, and watered the whole face of the ground" (6). "Soft showers" do fall at 4.646, but they may issue from fountains rather than from the sky.

[117]The "Lord God made . . . every plant of the field before it was in the earth, and every herb of the field before it grew . . ." (Genesis 2.4–5). The early Church Fathers took God's prefabrication of the plants to signify that the idea or form of the plants existed in God's mind before their creation in Eden. The arguments concerning when the angels were created are similar, since the "event" is not mentioned in Genesis; Augustine got over that problem by saying that God must have included the angels in the command "Let there be light" (*City of God* 11.9).

[118]"And God said, Let there be lights in the firmament of the heaven to divide the day from the night; and let them be for signs, and for seasons, and for days, and years; And let them be for lights in the firmament of the heaven to give light upon the earth: and it was so" (Genesis 1.14–15).

[119]Again, as in 264 above, Milton is using a word he may have thought more precise than the Authorized Version's "firmament"—though, since he repeats "Firmament" at 349 below, he may just have been using a synonym for variety's sake.

[120]"And God made two great lights; the greater light to rule the day, and the lesser light to rule the night: he made the stars also. And God set them in the firmament of the heaven to give light upon the earth. And to rule over the day and over the night, and to divide the light from the darkness: and God saw that it was good" (Genesis 1.16–18). Notice Milton's addition of "vicissitude," which relates what is happening here with the "Grateful vicissitude" of 6.8.

To illuminate the Earth, and rule the Day   350
In thir vicissitude, and rule the Night,
And Light from Darkness to divide. God saw,
Surveying his great Work, that it was good:
For of Celestial Bodies first the Sun
A mightie Spheare he fram'd, unlightsom first,   355
Though of Ethereal Mould:[121] then form'd the Moon
Globose,° and every magnitude of Starrs,   ROUND
And sowd with Starrs the Heav'n thick as a field:
Of Light by farr the greater part he took,
Transplanted from her cloudie Shrine, and plac'd   360
In the Suns Orb, made porous to receive
And drink the liquid Light,[122] firm to retaine
Her gather'd beams, great Palace now of Light.
Hither as to thir Fountain other Starrs[123]
Repairing, in thir gold'n Urns draw Light,   365
And hence the Morning Planet[124] guilds her horns;
By tincture or reflection they augment
Thir small peculiar,[125] though from human sight
So farr remote, with diminution° seen.   DIMINISHED BRIGHTNESS
First in the East his[126] glorious Lamp was seen,   370
Regent of Day, and all th' Horizon round
Invested with bright Rayes, jocond to run[127]
His Longitude through Heav'ns high rode:° the gray   ROAD
Dawn, and the *Pleiades* before him danc'd
Shedding sweet influence:[128] less bright the Moon,   375
But opposite in leveld West was set
His mirror, with full face borrowing her Light
From him,[129] for other light she needed none
In that aspect, and still that distance keepes

---

[121]Before God says "Let there be light," there is only potential light; thus the sun is framed but "unlightsom" at first, even though it is made out of the building material ("Mould") of ether. Earthly mould appears in the Nativity Ode 138, and is the stuff of which Adam is made. William B. Hunter reminds me that "the sun here is only in potentiality; on Day 4 it becomes actual, invested with the extra light from Day 1. Note how from Book 4 light supports life (thus it was created to support all creation on Day 1)" (letter, October 1991).

[122]Having no notion that the sun was composed of hydrogen, scientists of the seventeenth century argued that it might be porous, hollow, and filled with liquid light. Hence the sun could be a palace of light, within its own orb or sphere. See Babb 30–31 for notes on the nature of Milton's sun.

[123]Including planets. The sun is the fountain of light for other heavenly bodies, personified here as attendants, who come like water-gatherers to a central fountain in golden urns.

[124]The same as the "Morning Starr" of 5.708, the planet Venus, which is associated with Lucifer. It appears as a shining crescent in some of the phases that Galileo had discovered; hence the "horns." The phrase in *1667* was "his horns," suggesting that the "Morning Planet" or "Morning Starr" is to be identified with Lucifer or the Son (compare *Paradise Regain'd* 1.294), but the editorial change from "his" to "her" must be intentional and may well be authorial.

[125]The reader is given a choice of light sources for planets and stars. The word "peculiar" here seems to mean "inherent" or "self-generated" as applied to the light of the star or planet. The word "tincture" has overtones of the alchemical elixir, which would generate its own light, as differentiated from light reflected from the sun, though, as Elledge points out (367), the image may be one of dyeing: the Morning Planet may guild her horns either by dyeing them or by using reflected sunlight.

[126]What I consider to be the impossible reading of both 1667 and 1674, "First in his East the . . . ," almost surely transposes "his" and "the," as Fletcher suggests. Most modern editors leave the phrasing intact, but the question would then remain: Who owns "the East"? The "glorious Lamp," on the other hand, is owned by the sun, the "Regent of Day" of the next line.

[127]In Psalm 19.5 the sun at creation is pictured first as an eager bridegroom and then "as a strong man [who 'rejoiceth'] to run a race."

[128]The "sweet influences" of the Pleiades is a phrase taken from Job 38.31. As the marginal note in the Geneva Bible recognizes, groups of stars known as the Pleiades "arise when the sunne is in Taurus, which is the spring time, & bring floures" (1560 ed.). As Fowler points out, "while *Dawn* goes before the sun in his diurnal motion, the *Pleiades* do not. For they are situated in the constellation Taurus, which before the Fall was also the sign Taurus; and the sun is here still in Aries, the preceding sign" (374–75n). Milton, in other words, is quite precise about his astronomy and his placement of astrological signs before the Fall.

[129]A female full moon borrows her light from a male sun, needing no more light than the sun's reflection when she is in that "aspect," or astrological relationship, to the sun. She is "leveld" in that she is exactly opposite the rising sun.

Till night, then in the East her turn she shines,   380
Revolvd on Heav'ns great Axle,[130] and her Reign
With thousand lesser Lights dividual° holds,   SEPARATE
With thousand thousand Starres, that then appeer'd
Spangling the Hemisphere: then first adornd
With thir bright Luminaries that Set and Rose,[131]   385
Glad Eevning and glad Morn crownd the fourth day.
    And God said, let the Waters generate
Reptil with Spawn abundant,[132] living Soule:
And let Fowle flie above the Earth, with wings
Displayd on the op'n Firmament of Heav'n.   390
And God created the great Whales, and each
Soul living,[133] each that crept, which plenteously
The waters generated by thir kindes,
And every Bird of wing after his kinde;
And saw that it was good, and bless'd them, saying,   395
Be fruitful, multiply, and in the Seas
And Lakes and running Streams the waters fill;
And let the Fowle be multiply'd on the Earth.
Forthwith the Sounds and Seas, each Creek and Bay
With Frie[134] innumerable swarme, and Shoales   400
Of Fish that with thir Finns and shining Scales
Glide under the green Wave, in Sculles[135] that oft
Bank the mid Sea:[136] part single or with mate
Graze the Sea weed thir pasture,[137] and through Groves
Of Coral stray, or sporting with quick glance   405
Show to the Sun thir wav'd coats dropt with Gold,[138]
Or in thir Pearlie shells at ease, attend
Moist nutriment, or under Rocks thir food

---

[130]Like Earth, Heaven is pictured as turning on a pole or axle, including stars and planets revolving around it. For the turning of the poles after the Fall, see 10.668-71.

[131]The order is important in that the days will be reckoned as beginning in the evening, but Genesis 1.19 uses the formula "And the evening and the morning were the fourth day."

[132]"And God said, Let the waters bring forth abundantly the moving creature that hath life, and fowl that may fly above the earth in the open firmament of heaven. And God created great whales, and every living creature that moveth, which the waters brought forth abundantly, after their kind, and every winged fowl after his kind: and God saw that it was good. And God blessed them, saying, Be fruitful, and multiply, and fill the waters in the seas, and let fowl multiply in the earth" (Genesis 1.20-22). Newton was the first to notice that "By *reptil* is meant *creeping thing*; and according to [Newton's copy of the Authorized Version] *creeping things* are said to have been created on the fifth day" (388n). The Geneva Bible glossed "creping thing" as "fish and wormes [i.e., snakes] which slide, swimme or crepe" (1560 ed.). Creeping things, in other words, can include various sea animals, as in Psalm 104.25: " . . . this great and wide sea, wherein are things creeping innumerable, both small and great beasts." Water was thought to have generative force, hence it could help to produce both the reptiles and their spawn.

[133]Each living soul, in the sense of "each animate being." In *On Christian Doctrine* 1.7, Milton uses Paul's definition of "soul": "Hence the word **soul** is interpreted by the apostle, I Cor. xv. 45, as meaning *animal*" (Yale 6: 318). 1 Corinthians 15.45, as translated in the Authorized Version, reads "And so it is written, The first man Adam was made a living soul; the last Adam was made a quickening spirit." See Barker, *Milton* 318-19.

[134]As in "small fry," or little offspring.

[135]The editor Patrick Hume defines the term "Sculles" as "Shoals of fish so vast, that they appear like mighty banks in the midst of the sea. *Sculls* and *shoals* are vast multitudes of fish, of the Saxon *sceole*, an assembly" (qtd. in Newton 402n). The modernizing spelling emendation to "schools" (as in Fowler or Orgel and Goldberg, but not in Campbell or Hughes) is misleading.

[136]"That often make up what appears to be a bank in mid-ocean."

[137]At this innocent point, fish, as with land animals, graze on the local vegetation—seaweed; after the Fall they will war with each other and murder for food (compare 10.710-14), though fish seem to be eyeing crustaceans as food in 409 below. Notice, also, that both marriage and a single state exist even among ocean beings.

[138]As Fowler points out (7.406-10n), the context may be allegorical and certainly is heraldic, since the terms "wav'd," "coats," "dropt [spotted] with Gold," and "bended" were all used to describe devices used on coats of arms. The fish are pictured naturalistically and heraldically at the same time, as if they share in the inherent nobility of nature.

In jointed Armour[139] watch: on smooth[140] the Seale,
And bended Dolphins[141] play: part huge of bulk   410
Wallowing unweildie, enormous in thir Gate°   GAIT
Tempest[142] the Ocean: there Leviathan[143]
Hugest of living Creatures, on the Deep
Stretcht like a Promontorie sleeps or swimmes,
And seems a moving Land, and at his Gilles   415
Draws in, and at his Trunck spouts out a Sea.[144]
Mean while the tepid Caves,[145] and Fens and shoares
Thir Brood as numerous hatch, from the Egg that soon
Bursting with kindly rupture forth disclos'd[146]
Thir callow° young, but featherd soon and fledge   UNFEATHERED   420
They summ'd thir Penns,[147] and soaring th' air sublime[148]
With clang[149] despis'd the ground, under a cloud
In prospect;[150] there the Eagle and the Stork
On Cliffs and Cedar tops thir Eyries build:
Part loosly° wing the Region, part more wise   SEPARATELY   425
In common, rang'd in figure wedge[151] thir way,
Intelligent of seasons,[152] and set forth
Thir Aierie Caravan high over Sea's
Flying, and over Lands with mutual wing
Easing thir flight;[153] so stears the prudent Crane   430
Her annual Voiage, born° on Windes; the Aire   BORNE, SUPPORTED

---

[139]Probably the casing of lobsters or other crustaceans that looks like chainmail or armor linked in segments. Heavily-armed troops in the Roundhead army were nick-named "lobsters" because of the way their plate-armor was jointed, as in a lobster's tail (*OED* 3).

[140]Apparently this is a noun meaning "a stretch of comparatively smooth or calm water in a rough sea" (*OED* s.v. *smooth*, sb.1.c), though the first instance of the usage is dated 1840.

[141]The *curvus delphinus* of Latin poetry, which was applied by Ovid to the constellation of the Dolphin as well as to the mammal.

[142]Used as a verb meaning "stir up the waves as a storm would." Also, "to throw into violent commotion, to agitate violently" (*OED* 1).

[143]One would expect the name to be italicized, but the lack of italics might argue that the word is being used to represent the generic sea beast. Again it should be stressed that animal life is not yet "beastly."

[144]Leviathan, the beast described in Job 41 as a fire-spouting monster who stirs up the waters with his tail, and as one of the great sea beasts comparable to Satan in Milton's catalogue in 1.200–208. Here the Leviathan appears to be a cross between a whale (which of course has no gills) and an elephant, but his body, looking like dry land, was a proverbial threat to sailors who landed there. Ariosto, among others, tells the story of unsuspecting mariners landing on a whale's back, thinking it is an island (*Orlando Furioso* Canto 6.37).

[145]The caves would have to be at least "tepid," or lukewarm, in order to support breeding. But literalists may be in trouble here and elsewhere, since in Genesis beasts are created "out of the ground" (2.19) and from water (1.20). Perhaps "Fens" is an attempt to combine the two.

[146]What might otherwise be a violent process, "rupture," is, with the emergence of a fledgling from its shell, a natural ("kindly") birth in which the bird is freed ("disclos'd"). Here "fledge" is "fit to fly" (*OED* adj. 1).

[147]In falconry, when a young hawk was ready to fly, the feathers used for flight ("pens" are the "flight-feathers [*remiges*] or pinions of birds regarded as the organs of flight" [*OED* sb. 2.b, citing this instance]). Hence when the pens were summed or in full complement, the bird could fly. For the use of "summ'd" in this sense, see *Paradise Regain'd* 1.14.

[148]Flying up into the higher regions of the sky.

[149]The harsh sound that seabirds emit in flight, as in "Sea-mews clang" at 11.835. The word *clang* may be a Latinism derived from *clangor*, the sound of a trumpet (Corns 96).

[150]From the perspective at ground level, the groups of high-flying birds appear to be a cloud. As Fowler points out (6.23–46n), all of the birds named were associated emblematically with different virtues.

[151]As in the flying wedge or v-shaped formation of geese, ducks, or storks. The "more wise" flocks of birds who travel in common also form an aerial *caravan*, a group traveling together for mutual security (*OED* 1, though the definition "company in motion," *OED* 3, also fits and is supported by this passage).

[152]We might substitute "aware of circadian rhythms," or "knowledgeable about the changes in the seasons."

[153]Birds gliding in formation were supposed—according to Pliny (*Natural History* 50.10.32) and Elizabethan writers following him—to help support each other in flight, with each bird resting his head on the one in front of him, while the guides in front would shift to the rear when tired. See Svendsen, *Milton* 275-76. Raphael's narration must be proleptic, predicting seasonal conditions after the Fall. The crane was an emblem of military preparedness (as in 1.576) and household thrift. Like the storks, cranes were supposed to "follow the most robust and ancient **leader**, and when weary, substitute the next, the hindmost alwayes makes a *noise* for the rest . . . " (Robert Lovell, *Panzoologicomineralogia. Or a Compleat History of Animals and Minerals* [Oxford, 1661]: 147).

Floats,[154] as they pass, fann'd with unnumber'd plumes:°   FEATHERS
From Branch to Branch the smaller Birds with song
Solac'd the Woods, and spred thir painted wings[155]
Till Ev'n, nor then the solemn Nightingal[156]   435
Ceas'd warbling, but all night tun'd her soft layes:
Others on Silver Lakes and Rivers Bath'd
Thir downie Brest; the Swan with Arched neck
Between her white wings mantling proudly,[157] Rowes
Her state with Oarie feet: yet oft they quit   440
The Dank, and rising on stiff Pennons, towre
The mid Aereal Skie:[158] Others on ground
Walk'd firm; the crested Cock whose clarion sounds
The silent hours, and th' other whose gay Traine
Adorns him,[159] colour'd with the Florid hue   445
Of Rainbows and Starrie Eyes. The Waters thus
With Fish replenisht,° and the Aire with Fowle,   FULLY-STOCKED
Ev'ning and Morn solemniz'd the Fift day.
    The Sixt, and of Creation last arose
With Eevning Harps and Mattin, when God said,   450
Let th' Earth bring forth Soul[160] living in her kinde,
Cattel and Creeping things, and Beast of the Earth,
Each in their kinde. The Earth obey'd, and strait
Op'ning her fertil Woomb teem'd at a Birth[161]
Innumerous living Creatures, perfet formes,[162]   455
Limb'd and full grown: out of the ground up rose
As from his Laire the wilde Beast where he wonns°   LIVES
In Forrest wilde, in Thicket, Brake,[163] or Den;
Among the Trees in Pairs they rose, they walk'd:

---

[154]Undulates, as if it were water.

[155]Fowler (7.434n) finds the phrasing parallel with that of Vergil in *Aeneid* 4.525, *pictae volucres.*

[156]In the fallen world, the nightingale sings only at dusk; here it sings all through the night. The nightingale is a rich personal symbol for Milton, a bird to which he appropriately compares himself, as a singer in the isolated darkness (since he is blind) and as a singer at night (since he composes poetry at night). Compare "Il Penseroso" 56–64, where the nightingale is "most musical, most melancholy"; Milton's sonnet to the nightingale; and, within *Paradise Lost*, 3.38–40, 4.602–04 and 648, 5.40, and 8.518–20.

[157]When the swan arches her neck and spreads her wings, her white wings form a mantle about her. The swan is pictured as regal, as having innate purity of soul; thus she rows in "state," as if she were in a royal barge providing its own motive power. To that, add Corns's evaluation of "mantling": "Milton's swan, like the citizen-rowers of classical Greek galleys, may conduct herself 'proudly', unlike the slaves of Roman or renaissance galleys, whose shoulders are naked to their masters' whips" (93).

[158]The lake and river birds often leave the pool (a "Dank" is a "wet place, pool, marsh, mere" in *OED* sb 2, citing this instance), rise on stiffened feathers ("Pennons"), and soar upward ("towre") into the middle air. The adjective "Aereal," usually written "Aæreal," would be pronounced "Ā-ēr'-yal."

[159]The rooster with his crest, crowing at dawn, is contrasted with the peacock, whose starry eyes in his colorful plumage signify alertness at night (as with the guardian Argus, whose eyes were supposedly incorporated into the peacock's display).

[160]A difficult textual crux, since most editors agree (for once) with Richard Bentley that the word should be "Soul" rather than the "Fowl" of the first three editions because of the phrasing of the King James Bible, "Let the earth bring forth the living creature after his kind, cattle, and creeping thing, and beast of the earth after his kind: and God saw that it was good" (Genesis 1.25). "Soul" seems closer to translating "living creature" than "Fowl" does, and the fowl were created on the fifth day, not the sixth. But see Adams, *Ikon* 94–95, for an argument in favor of "fowl" as a variant spelling of "foal." The phrase "living Souls" appears in 5.197, in apposition with "Birds"!

[161]All the significant words in this line have to do with the process of giving birth: the earth opens her fertile womb (as in a cornucopia) straightway, and the womb is in the process of teeming or bearing offspring with extraordinary fecundity. Masculine entities can have wombs in *Paradise Lost*, as in 1.673, where a volcanic hill is said to have metallic ore hidden in "his womb." According to the *OED*, *his* in its neutral sense "was gradually superseded by **its** from c. 1600 onwards, though the historical *his* lingered in some writers till late in the 17th c."

[162]Usually the word "form" signifies an ideal or unfallen state in *Paradise Lost*, as in "Native forme" (3.605) or "her Heav'nly forme" (9.457). Here the creatures being made are fully formed; enough of them are in an adult stage that the group can generate offspring. The fertilized ocean (282 above) had put the seeds of everything into the earth below it. Now the "Omnific Word" (217 above) calls them into being.

[163]Defined as an "undergrowth / Of shrubs and tangling bushes" at 4.175–76.

The Cattel[164] in the Fields and Meddowes green: 460
Those rare and solitarie, these in flocks
Pasturing at once,[165] and in broad Herds upsprung.
The grassie Clods now Calv'd, now half appeer'd
The Tawnie Lion, pawing to get free
His hinder parts, then springs as broke from Bonds,   465
And Rampant[166] shakes his Brinded[167] main;° the Ounce,[168]   MANE
The Libbard,° and the Tyger, as the Moale   LEOPARD
Rising, the crumbl'd Earth above them threw
In Hillocks;[169] the swift Stag from under ground
Bore up his branching head: scarse from his mould[170]   470
Behemoth[171] biggest born of Earth upheav'd
His vastness: Fleec't the Flocks and bleating rose,
As Plants: ambiguous between Sea and Land[172]
The River Horse and scalie Crocodile.
At once came forth whatever creeps[173] the ground,   475
Insect or Worme; those wav'd thir limber fans
For wings, and smallest Lineaments exact
In all the Liveries dect of Summers pride
With spots of Gold and Purple, azure and green:
These as a line thir long dimension drew,   480
Streaking the ground with sinuous trace; not all
Minims[174] of Nature; some of Serpent kinde
Wondrous in length and corpulence involv'd
Thir Snakie foulds, and added wings.[175] First crept
The Parsimonious Emmet,[176] provident   485

---

[164]Domesticated animals, such as sheep or cows, who would gather in flocks or herds, as opposed to the wild animals ("Those"), which are "rare ['stationed at wide intervals,' *OED* 3.a, citing this instance] and solitarie."

[165]Eating pasture all at the same time, as with sheep. The epithet "broad Herds" may echo the *Iliad* 11.678, as noted first by Newton (7.462n); Lattimore translates "wide-ranging goat-flocks."

[166]The lion is naturalistic and heraldic at the same time, since rampant signifies "Rearing or standing with the fore-paws in the air" (*OED* A.1, citing this instance) and, in heraldic terminology, "Standing on the Sinister hindleg, with both forelegs elevated, the Dexter above the Sinister, and the head in profile" (Cussans, qtd. in *OED* A.1.b.).

[167]Brownish, brindled, streaked with different colors.

[168]A medium-sized wild cat variously identified in the seventeenth century, but most probably the lynx (see *OED* 1 and 2).

[169]So the Italian Renaissance painter Raphael paints Creation in the *Stanza della Segnatura* in the Vatican, with animals struggling upward to be free of the ground. See Treip, *Descend*, for general information about Milton's possible use of the cycle of paintings.

[170]The essential material out of which he is created, which Milton generally prefers to "clay."

[171]Notice the italics, which suggest that either Milton's amanuensis or the compositor, at least, was treating the name as exotic, as with "*Leviathan*" at 1.201 (but not in the Manuscript of Book 1, or at 7.412). The Behemoth, according to the Geneva marginalia for Job 40.10, "is thoght to be the elephant, or some other, which is unknown" (1560 ed., contractions expanded). Milton did not mean it to be the hippopotamus (some of his contemporaries did), or he would not have named the "River Horse" at 474 below. What Leviathan is to the sea, Behemoth is to the land, the largest of all species.

[172]Resembling an amphibian, living both in water and on land.

[173]"Creeping thing" is common enough especially in the Old Testament to be called a biblical epithet which describes all animal life that seems to travel on its belly. Here "Worms" is generic, meaning anything from maggots and snails ("Streaking the ground with sinuous trace") on up to large serpents and dragons. The word "Liveries" is reminiscent of the assigning of fairy rank to the insects like Moth in *Midsummer Night's Dream*.

[174]The smallest forms of life in nature, important perhaps because of Jesus's phrase "Inasmuch as ye have done it unto one of the least of these my brethren, ye have done it unto me" (Matthew 25.40).

[175]"Some of the family of serpents, wonderfully large and bulky, coiled their snakelike folds and added wings" to become like the "fiery flying serpent" of Isaiah 30.6, which at least seems to be a dragon. As Fowler points out (7.483n), Hughes's note assigning "corpulence" to "involved" is incorrect.

[176]The ant, known for its thrift and frequently held as an example of good household economy, as in "Go to the ant, thou sluggard; consider her ways and be wise" (Proverbs 6.6; see also 6.8 for "Provideth her meat [i.e., food] in the summer, and gathereth her food in the harvest"). "Parsimonious" is complimentary, not pejorative, here: the ant is thrifty, not cheap. Also, Milton is praising the model society of the ant for its commonality, good fellowship, and mutual help. Notice that the models for domestic behavior, ant and bee, are both female: the parsimonious female ant manages the household and the female queen bee and workers feed the male "Husband Drone." Drone bees are in fact male, and worker bees are underdeveloped (not queenlike) females; a queen bee would lead a swarm when hives split in the spring. Milton's model for family life is, at this point, certainly not patriarchal. It is also republican, uniting "popular Tribes."

Of future, in small room large heart enclos'd,
Pattern of just equalitie perhaps
Hereafter, join'd in her popular Tribes
Of Commonaltie: swarming next appeer'd
The Female Bee that feeds her Husband Drone 490
Deliciously, and builds her waxen Cells
With Honey stor'd: the rest are numberless,
And thou thir Natures know'st, & gav'st them Names,[177]
Needless[178] to thee repeated; nor unknown
The Serpent suttl'st Beast of all the field,[179] 495
Of huge extent somtimes, with brazen Eyes
And hairie Main terrific,°[180] though to thee TERRIFYING
Not noxious, but obedient at thy call.
Now Heav'n in all her Glorie shon, and rowld
Her motions,[181] as the great first-Movers hand 500
First wheeld thir course; Earth in her rich attire
Consummate° lovly smil'd; Aire, Water, Earth, PERFECT
By Fowl, Fish, Beast, was flown, was swum, was walkt
Frequent;°[182] and of the Sixt day yet remain'd; ABUNDANTLY
There wanted yet the Master work, the end 505
Of all yet don;[183] a Creature who not prone
And Brute as other Creatures, but endu'd
With Sanctitie of Reason, might erect
His Stature, and upright with Front serene[184]
Govern the rest, self-knowing, and from thence 510
Magnanimous[185] to correspond with Heav'n,
But grateful to acknowledge whence his good
Descends, thither with heart and voice and eyes
Directed in Devotion, to adore
And worship God Supream, who made him chief 515
Of all his works: therefore the Omnipotent
Eternal Father (For where is not hee

---

[177]Compare 6.73–76 and 8.342–54, for Adam's naming the animals.

[178]The spelling "Needlest" of both *1667* and *1674* is most probably wrong. Not even Beeching preserves it.

[179]At this point "suttl'st" follows Genesis 3.1: "Now the serpent was more subtil than any beast of the field which the Lord God had made." The emphasis on the serpent is proleptic, but his subtlety is not threatening, "Not noxious, but obedient," at this point.

[180]In Book 9, the serpent will have carbuncular eyes, a crested head, and a "burnisht Neck of verdant Gold" (501).

[181]The motions of heavenly bodies now set in active orbits. God is pictured as setting the wheels in motion.

[182]Fowler (7.502–03n) cites for comparison Hamlet's "The courtier's, soldier's, scholar's eye, tongue, sword" (3.1.160). The rhetorical figure is asyndeton, or a list of nouns without conjunctions, which has the effect of filling a poetic line copiously—just the right figure for signifying abundance. But notice also that there is a pattern (ABC,ABC) in the arrangement of nouns; compare "Rocks, Caves, Lakes, Fens, Bogs, Dens, and shades of death" (2.621) for the same sound effects in Hell.

[183]Humankind is God's last and best creation, a masterwork, defined by erect stature and the ability to reason. So in Ovid, *Metamorphoses* 1.74–82 (trans. Humphries):

> But something else was needed, a finer being,
> More capable of mind, a sage, a ruler,
> So Man was born, it may be, in God's image, . . .
> All other animals look downward; Man,
> Alone, erect, can raise his face toward Heaven.

[184]"Front" strictly speaking means "forehead," but combined with "serene" it also suggests "composed or untroubled face." *OED* 3.b., "Bearing or demeanour in confronting anything," may be close to the right sense here.

[185]A very rich adjective, suggesting the ideal of Aristotelian greatness of mind for humankind—magnanimity being the chief characteristic of heroic personages out of mythology, tragic literature, or history (see Aristotle, *Nichomachean Ethics*, Chapter 6). But magnanimity also included the ambitious quest for great honors on earth; hence Renaissance humanists such as Vives disputed its worth as the chief among virtues (Schmitt, *Renaissance Philosophy* 344).

Present) thus to his Son audibly spake.[186]

    Let us make now Man in our image, Man
In our similitude, and let them[187] rule
Over the Fish and Fowle of Sea and Aire,   *520*
Beast of the Field, and over all the Earth,
And every creeping thing that creeps the ground.
This said, he formd thee, *Adam*, thee O Man
Dust of the ground, and in thy nostrils breath'd   *525*
The breath of Life;[188] in his own Image hee
Created thee, in the Image of God
Express,[189] and thou becam'st a living Soul.
Male he created thee, but thy consort[190]
Female for Race; then bless'd Mankinde, and said,   *530*
Be fruitful, multiplie, and fill the Earth,
Subdue it, and throughout Dominion hold
Over Fish of the Sea, and Fowle of the Aire,
And every living thing that moves on the Earth.[191]
Wherever thus created, for no place   *535*
Is yet distinct by name, thence, as thou know'st
He brought thee into this delicious Grove,[192]
This Garden, planted with the Trees of God,
Delectable both to behold and taste;[193]
And freely all thir pleasant fruit for food
Gave thee, all sorts are here that all th' Earth yields,   *540*
Varietie without end; but of the Tree
Which tasted works° knowledge of Good and Evil,
Thou mai'st not; in the day thou eat'st, thou di'st;[194]
Death is the penaltie impos'd, beware,   *545*
And govern well thy appetite, least sin[195]
Surprise thee, and her black attendant Death.

---

[186]Milton very cleverly avoids the problem of seeming to make God speak to other gods, as in Genesis 1.26: "Let us make man in *our* image" (emphasis supplied), by having the omnipotent and omniscient Father address the Son. When he discusses this bit of God's dialogue in *On Christian Doctrine*, Milton does not ascribe it to a conversation with the Son. "But when God is about to make man he speaks like a person giving careful consideration to something, as if to imply that this is a still greater work; Gen. i. 26: after this God said, let us make man in our image, after our own likeness" (1.7; Yale 6: 316).

[187]As in Genesis 1.26, "let them have dominion," Milton decides to use a plural pronoun, implying "humankind." The dominion is "over the fish of the sea, and over the fowl of the air, and over the cattle, and over all the earth, and over every creeping thing that creepeth on the earth," rendered iambic by Milton below.

[188]"And the Lord God formed man of the dust of the ground, and breathed into his nostrils the breath of life; and man became a living soul" (Genesis 2.7).

[189]"In the express image" is still colloquial usage, but it is biblical here, borrowed very deliberately from a passage in Hebrews describing the Son, "Who being the brightness of his glory, and the express image of his person, and upholding all things by the word of his power, when he had by himself purged our sins, sat down on the right hand of the Majesty on high . . . " (1.3).

[190]Accented on the second syllable. Compare "consorted *Eve*" in 50 above. Eve is created specifically to be Adam's helpmate and helpmeet (fitting partner to her husband) and to perpetuate the "Seed," in which is included not only the rest of the human race but "David's Seed," or Christ.

[191]"And God blessed them, and God said unto them, Be fruitful, and multiply, and replenish the earth, and subdue it: and have dominion over the fish of the sea, and over the fowl of the air, and over every living thing that moveth upon the earth" (Genesis 1.28).

[192]As Fowler points out (7.535–38n), Milton follows the literal interpretation of Josephus (*Antiquities* 1.1.3) that Adam was created outside of Eden and then transported into it. Such an interpretation stresses God's omnipotence and fatherly kindness in bringing Adam to the Garden. "And the Lord God planted a garden eastward in Eden; and there he put the man whom he had formed. . . . And the Lord God took the man, and put him into the garden of Eden to dress it and to keep it" (Genesis 2.8, 15).

[193]In Eden God plants " . . . every tree that is pleasant to the sight and good for food . . . " (Genesis 2.9).

[194]"And the Lord God commanded the man, saying, Of every tree of the garden thou mayest freely eat: But of the tree of the knowledge of good and evil, thou shalt not eat of it: for in the day that thou eatest thereof thou shalt surely die" (Genesis 2.16–17). The Son as judge softens the penalty at 10.209–11 (and thereby avoids the charge of inconsistency between commandment and enforcement).

[195]One of the few cases where modernizing the text (substituting "lest" for "least") might clear up an ambiguity, since Sin (the personified being) here is Death's attendant. Fowler asks "Does this imply that Raphael is not privy to the guilty secret of Death's true relation with Sin?" (6.547n), but I think the question is too precise, because Death can be lover and attendant at the same time.

Here finish'd hee, and all that he had made
View'd, and behold all was entirely good;
So Ev'n and Morn accomplish'd the Sixt day: 550
Yet not till the Creator from his work
Desisting, though unwearied,[196] up returnd
Up to the Heav'n of Heav'ns[197] his high abode,
Thence to behold this new created World
Th' addition of his Empire, how it shew'd° SHOWED 555
In prospect from his Throne, how good, how faire,
Answering his great Idea.[198] Up he rode
Followd with acclamation and the sound
Symphonious[199] of ten thousand Harpes that tun'd° PLAYED
Angelic harmonies: the Earth, the Aire 560
Resounded, (thou remember'st, for thou heardst)
The Heav'ns and all the Constellations rung,[200]
The Planets in thir stations[201] list'ning stood,
While the bright Pomp ascended jubilant.[202]
Open, ye everlasting Gates, they sung,[203] 565
Open, ye Heav'ns, your living dores; let in
The great Creator from his work returnd
Magnificent, his Six days work, a World;
Open, and henceforth oft;[204] for God will deigne
To visit oft the dwellings of just Men 570
Delighted, and with frequent intercourse
Thither will send his winged Messengers
On errands of supernal Grace.[205] So sung
The glorious Train ascending: He through Heav'n,
That open'd wide her blazing Portals, led 575
To Gods Eternal house direct the way,
A broad and ample rode, whose dust is Gold
And pavement Starrs, as Starrs to thee appeer,
Seen in the Galaxie, that Milkie way[206]

God will count worthy to count the dwellings of men.

---

[196]"God's resting on the Seventh Day of Creation [see Genesis 2.2] cannot mean that he was tired" (Burden 9).

[197]The highest of heavens is the Empyrean.

[198]The word "Idea" is Platonic, suggesting that God has a paradigm, "the created image of the eternal gods," in mind before beginning "to make the copy still more like the original" in the process of creation (see *Timaeus* 37c–d, trans. Jowett). In Renaissance Neoplatonism, especially the Christianized Platonism of Marsilio Ficino, "God has created the world not by necessity of nature, but in accordance with a certain purpose of his will" (paraphrased in Schmitt 572).

[199]Like that of large-scale, symphonic harmony. The ten thousand harps represent a biblical generic number. The process of tuning can be pictured in terms of an orchestra being tuned to the pitch of one instrument, in this case the harps.

[200]The heavenly bodies in their crystal spheres are said to have been rung like a peal of bells in a church tower.

[201]As Fletcher notes, the singular form in *1674* should be replaced by the plural of *1667*. The word station is astronomical, signifying the planet's position at its apogee or highest point. The planets at Creation would have been in their perfect alignment, an alignment knocked off balance at the Fall.

[202]Both the words "Pomp" and "jubilant" suggest a triumphant royal procession, almost allegorical in level of abstraction. So Pomp as an entity attending God has a jubilee or timely celebration of the monarchy of God.

[203] "Lift up your heads, O ye gates; even lift them up, ye everlasting doors; and the King of glory shall come in" (Psalm 24.9). The doors of Heaven and of Hell both seem to have independent life, opening and shutting of their own motive power—controlled, of course, by God's will and providence.

[204] "Open now, and, from now on, often." Milton again stresses the easy and frequent visitation between God and man and angel and man before the Fall.

[205]Divine grace issuing from God and hence coming from "on high" (supernal pertains "to a higher world or state of existence" in *OED* A.2, citing this instance).

[206]Fowler identifies the "blazing Portals" as "the tropical signs Capricorn and Cancer that mark the limits of the solar path" (7.575–91n), citing Macrobius's *On the Dream of Scipio*: "The Milky Way girdles the zodiac, its great circle meeting it obliquely so that it crosses it at the two tropical signs, Capricorn and Cancer. Natural philosophers named these the 'portals of the sun' because the solstices lie athwart the sun's path on either side, checking farther progress and causing it to retrace its course across the belt beyond whose limits it never trespasses. Souls are believed to pass through these portals when going from the sky to the earth and returning from the earth to the sky" (1.12.1–2). Ovid describes the Milky Way as "this road [by which] / The gods move toward the palace of the Thunderer, / His royal halls, and, right and left, the dwellings / Of other gods are open, and guests come thronging"

Which nightly as a circling Zone thou seest   580
Pouderd° with Starrs.[207] And now on Earth the Seventh   POWDERED
Eev'ning arose in Eden, for the Sun
Was set, and twilight from the East came on,
Forerunning Night;[208] when at the holy mount
Of Heav'ns high-seated top, th' Impereal Throne   585
Of Godhead, fixt for ever firm and sure,
The Filial Power arriv'd, and sate him down
With his great Father (for he also went
Invisible, yet staid,[209] such priviledge
Hath Omnipresence) and the work ordain'd,   590
Author and end of all things,[210] and from work
Now resting, bless'd and hallowd the Seav'nth day,[211]
As resting on that day from all his work,
But not in silence holy kept; the Harp
Had work and rested not, the solemn Pipe,   595
And Dulcimer, all Organs of sweet stop,
All sounds on Fret by String or Golden Wire
Temper'd soft Tunings, intermixt with Voice
Choral or Unison:[212] of incense Clouds[213]
Fuming from Golden Censers hid the Mount.   600
Creation and the Six dayes acts they sung,[214]
Great are thy works, *Jehovah*, infinite
Thy power; what thought can measure thee or tongue
Relate thee; greater now in thy return
Then from the Giant Angels;[215] thee that day   605
Thy Thunders magnifi'd; but to create

(*Metamorphoses* 1.170–73, trans. Humphries). Only the superior gods are allowed to use the road of the Milky Way in Ovid, as if it were a kind of private highway. The galaxy is the Milky Way here: the "Zone" is the Milky Way as it was traditionally seen as a belt around the night sky. Perhaps, however, the constellations should not be emphasized until after the Fall, when the Earth's plane is skewed.

[207]Only observable after Galileo's use of the telescope.

[208]The evening begins (and time in Eden is reckoned) from sunset to sunset, as observed before; otherwise, "Forerunning" would not make sense.

[209]The text of *1667* has "Invisible, yet staid (such priviledge . . . ," including an extra open parenthesis, which *1674* follows slavishly; both are obviously wrong (see Fletcher). Fowler adds a colon after "staid," but I see no reason to make the addition, since the colon would only strengthen the pause.

[210]The "Author and end" is probably the Son, who is called "author and finisher of our faith" in Hebrews 12.2.

[211]"And on the seventh day God ended his work which he had made; and he rested on the seventh day from all his work which he had made. And God blessed the seventh day, and sanctified it: because that in it he had rested from all his work which God created and made" (Genesis 2.2-3). The seventh day is hallowed in that God "Appointed it to be kept holy, that man might therein consider the excellencie of his workes and Gods goodnes towards him" (Geneva Bible marginalia, 1560 ed.).

[212]Being an accomplished musician who could sing, play the organ and the bass viols, and perhaps even (like his father) compose music, Milton allows the Sabbath in Heaven to be broken only by the pleasant "work" of making music—in a humane ritual that he himself had recommended for pupils in *Of Education* (Yale 2: 409–101). The words "stop," "Fret," "Golden Wire" (as opposed to "String" made of gut), "Temper'd," and "soft Tunings" are all used in musical senses. Stops are "the registers of an organ or harpsichord or the knob drawn to control them," and a fret is "A strip of gut, bone, ivory, wood or metal across the fingerboard of certain string instruments" like the lute and viol. The angelic voices are either singing in unison (all singing one melody) or choral (singing in harmony), in turn. Temperament is "A tuning of a scale in which most or all of the concords are made slightly impure in order that none or few are distastefully so" (*Norton/Grove Concise Encyclopedia of Music* [NY: Macmillan, 1988]). Fowler believes that Milton may intend the dulcimer here not to be the stringed instrument but a kind of bagpipe (*OED* 1.b); I see no reason to substitute the much less common for the more familiar stringed instrument (*OED* 1.a, citing Milton's usage here).

[213]"And another angel came and stood at the altar, having a golden censer; and there was given unto him much incense, that he should offer it with the prayers of all saints upon the golden altar which was before the throne" (Revelation 8.3). The fact that there is incense in Heaven does not mean necessarily that Milton would have approved of the Roman Catholic practice of using incense in church.

[214]Mode of discourse switches from indirect quotation to direct quotation between this line and the next, as the angels launch into the "hymn of the Creation" mentioned in Act I of the third draft of Milton's outline for a tragedy on the theme of Adam unparadised (see Introduction, "The Fable"). The angels are addressing God directly until the end of line 632 below, and Raphael is quoting them; because their warning about Adam and Eve's potential fall is overheard, it is even more forceful.

[215]Here as in descriptions of war in Books 1 and 6, Milton implies that the gigantomachia, or war between the Olympian gods (especially Jupiter) and the Titans or Giants, foreshadows the War in Heaven.

Is greater then created to destroy.[216]
Who can impair thee, mighty King, or bound
Thy Empire? easily the proud attempt
Of Spirits apostat[217] and thir Counsels vaine   610
Thou hast repeld, while impiously they thought
Thee to diminish, and from thee withdraw
The number of thy worshippers. Who seekes
To lessen thee, against his purpose serves
To manifest the more thy might: his evil   615
Thou usest, and from thence creat'st more good.
Witness this new-made World, another Heav'n
From Heaven Gate not farr, founded in view
On the cleer *Hyaline*,[218] the Glassie Sea;
Of amplitude almost immense,° with Starr's[219]   MEASURELESS   620
Numerous, and every Starr perhaps a World[220]
Of destind habitation; but thou know'st
Thir seasons: among these the seat of men,
Earth with her nether Ocean[221] circumfus'd,
Thir pleasant dwelling place. Thrice happie men,   625
And sons of men, whom God hath thus advanc't,
Created in his Image, there to dwell
And worship him, and in reward to rule
Over his Works, on Earth, in Sea, or Air,[222]
And multiply a Race of Worshippers   630
Holy and just: thrice happie if they know
Thir happiness, and persevere upright.[223]
    So sung they, and the Empyrean rung,
With *Halleluiahs:* Thus was Sabbath kept.[224]
And thy request think now fulfill'd, that ask'd   635

---

[216]One of the great *sententiae* of the epic, this truism celebrates the genuine and spontaneous creativity of God, contrasted with the ironic perversity of Satan and the fallen angels, themselves God's creations. Satan, who acknowledges himself created by God, can, after his revolt, express himself only in acts of destruction: he is "our destroyer, foe to God and Man" (4.749). God, however, eventually brings good out of all of Satan's evil.

[217]Rebellious or enemy spirits or fallen angels, apostate here as elsewhere, in noun or adjectival form (as at 5.852 or 1.125), suggesting confirmed rebellion against God.

[218]I agree with Fowler (7.619) that "*Hyaline*" is not a proper name and thus should not have been emphasized by italics and capitalization in the first two editions. Note, however, that Corns regards the word as foreign, difficult, and therefore properly italicized (90). One can sympathize with the compositors' problems: the compositor of *1667* evidently did not recognize the allusion to the "sea of glass like unto crystal" of Revelation 4.6, nor did he recognize the unfamiliar adjective-turned-noun, hyaline (*OED* B.1.), translated directly from the Greek ὑαλίνη of the New Testament. Milton's usage is the first recorded, and all others seem to be derived from this instance. This sea is composed of the waters above the firmament reported in Genesis 1.7.

[219]The word is a simple plural, which was sometimes indicated with an apostrophe preceding the plural "s."

[220]The theory of the plurality of worlds—that God may at any time create other inhabited worlds—which fits the context of the angels' hymn praising God's creativity. Note that the worlds are only potentially inhabited: they may or may not be "destind" to be inhabited, since Milton qualifies the opinion with "perhaps."

[221]The ocean beneath the firmament mentioned in Genesis 1.7.

[222]"Thou madest him to have dominion over the works of thy hands; thou hast put all things under his feet" (Psalm 8.6). The psalmist is speaking of God's relation to humankind throughout all time.

[223]Adam and Eve would be three times happy if they would understand how well off they are in Paradise, and if they would "persevere," or remain without sin. For Raphael to acknowledge that innocence is better than fallen knowledge is to deny that the Fall is in any way "fortunate." See Mollenkott, "Milton's Rejection."

[224]The Sabbath, the day of the completion of creation, was at first kept "holy and inviolable . . . as a memorial of God's completion of creation on the seventh day" (*On Christian Doctrine* 2.7; Yale 6: 705). But Milton believed that Christ's practice of teaching on the Sabbath (John 9.14–16) and Paul's weighing of all days of the week alike (Romans 14.5) meant that "The Sabbath has been done away with, and . . . God has not instituted, in its place, any particular day for his worship" (*On Christian Doctrine* 2.7; Yale 6: 708). Therefore Sunday (as appointed by the church) or any other day of the week should be "a day of voluntary observance" (2.7, Yale 6: 714) and spontaneous worship. Milton allows the angels hymns of spontaneous celebration, but no formal liturgy or ritual for the day. The italics on "*Halleluiahs*" may suggest heavy emphasis; since the word "halleluiah" is usually glossed as "Praise ye the Lord," the emphasis would seem to be proper.

How first this World and face[225] of things began,
And what before thy memorie was don
From the beginning, that posteritie
Informd by thee might know;[226] if else thou seekst
Aught, not surpassing human measure, say.   640

The End of the Seventh Book.

---

[225]"Outward form, appearance" (*OED* II). Compare the Latin noun *facies*, "make, form, figure, shape."
[226]What Raphael has told Adam, he can pass on to his posterity; thus the knowledge imparted by God through Raphael is freely given and freely transmitted.

Paradise Lost.

BOOK VIII.

THE ARGUMENT.

Adam *inquires*[1] *concerning celestial Motions, is doubtfully answer'd, and exhorted to search rather things more worthy of knowledg:* Adam *assents, and still desirous to detain* Raphael, *relates to him what he remember'd since his own Creation, his placing in Paradise, his talk with God concerning solitude and fit society, his first meeting and Nuptials with* Eve, *his discourse with the Angel thereupon; who after admonitions repeated departs.*

THE Angel ended, and in *Adams* Eare
So Charming° left his voice, that he a while ⁣   ENCHANTING
Thought him still speaking, still stood fixt to hear;[2]
Then as new wak't thus gratefully repli'd.
What thanks sufficient, or what recompence   5
Equal have I to render thee, Divine
Hystorian, who thus largely hast allayd[3]
The thirst I had of knowledge, and voutsaf't
This friendly condescention to relate
Things else by me unsearchable, now heard   10
With wonder, but delight, and, as is due,
With glorie attributed[4] to the high
Creator; something yet of doubt remaines,
Which onely thy solution[5] can resolve.
When I behold this goodly Frame,[6] this World   15
Of Heav'n and Earth consisting, and compute[7]
Thir magnitudes, this Earth a spot, a graine,
An Atom, with the Firmament compar'd
And all her numberd[8] Starrs, that seem to rowle
Spaces incomprehensible (for such   20
Thir distance argues and thir swift return
Diurnal)° meerly to officiate[9] light   DAILY

---

[1]The arguments were first printed in the 1668 state of the first edition, before the original Book 7 became Books 7 and 8. In *1668* the first line of the Argument reads "Adam *then inquires,*" and the second line uses the verb "seek" rather than "search." The changes seem to be authorial, since Milton would have had to supervise the dividing of books and arguments. The word "doubtfully" here means "cautiously," as if Raphael were guarding the line between useful and forbidden knowledge. Raphael will be trying to explain the difference between the Copernican and the Ptolemaic theories of the motions of heavenly bodies.

[2]The first three lines of the new Book 8 were added in 1674, and line 4 was modified from "To whom thus *Adam* gratefully repli'd" to read as below. The rapt fixation of Adam on Raphael's last word has classical precedents in the *Odyssey* 13.1, where those who have listened to the story of Odysseus's escape from Scylla and Charybdis "stayed stricken to silence, / held in thrall by the story" (trans. Lattimore), and in the *Argonautica* of Apollonius of Rhodes (1.12), where Orpheus has just completed the story of creation—his audience, as might be expected, falls into rapt silence.

[3]The unusual substitution of "y" for "i" in "Hystorian," "allayd" and "joyn'd" (58 below) might suggest that the stint of a new compositor began with this book. In the arbitrary choices between medial colon and semicolon, the compositor who set Book 7 elected to use 55 medial semicolons and only 20 medial colons, whereas the compositor who set this book chose only 30 semicolons over 40 colons, all but reversing the pattern of the earlier book.

[4]Accented on the first and third syllables.

[5] "A particular instance of solving or settling; an explanation, answer, or decision" (*OED* I.1.b).

[6]As in 5.154, the universe. The phrase "goodly Frame" may echo *Hamlet* 2.2.317: "It goes so heavily with my disposition that this goodly frame, the earth, seems to me a sterile promontory," though "goodly frame" was a common phrase (see *OED* 8).

[7]Probably the comma at this point in both *1667* and *1674* is an error, so I have removed it.

[8]Probably the same sentiment as that expressed in "the very hairs of your head are numbered" (Matthew 10.30), or, more precisely, "He telleth the number of the stars; he calleth them all by their names" (Psalm 147.4). God, in his providence, has all things accounted for and counted.

[9]"To minister, supply" (*OED* 4.a, citing this instance), with the idea of being subservient in the process.

Round this opacous° Earth, this punctual spot,[10]   OPAQUE
One day and night; in all thir vast survey
Useless besides, reasoning I oft admire,   25
How Nature wise and frugal could commit
Such disproportions, with superfluous hand
So many nobler Bodies to create,
Greater so manifold to this one use,[11]
For aught appeers, and on thir Orbs impose   30
Such restless revolution day by day
Repeated, while the sedentarie Earth,
That better might with farr less compass move,
Serv'd by more noble then her self, attaines
Her end without least motion, and receaves,   35
As Tribute such a sumless° journey brought   INCALCULABLE
Of incorporeal speed, her warmth and light;
Speed, to describe whose swiftness Number failes.[12]
    So spake our Sire, and by his count'nance seemd
Entring on studious thoughts abstruse, which *Eve*   40
Perceaving where she sat retir'd in sight,
With lowliness Majestic from her seat,
And Grace that won who saw to wish her stay,[13]
Rose, and went forth among her Fruits and Flours,[14]
To visit how they prosper'd, bud and bloom,   45
Her Nurserie;[15] they at her coming sprung
And toucht by her fair tendance gladlier grew.
Yet went she not, as not with such discourse
Delighted, or not capable her eare
Of what was high: such pleasure she reserv'd,   50
Adam relating, she sole Auditress;[16]
Her Husband the Relater she preferr'd
Before the Angel, and of him to ask
Chose rather; hee, she knew would intermix
Grateful digressions, and solve high dispute   55

---

[10]Seemingly as small as a dot, very small, minute.

[11]"So much greater than this one use would dictate."

[12]Adam, like an innocent but curious amateur astronomer, asks Raphael how and why Nature apparently wastes the extremely rapid motions of "more noble" heavenly bodies, all for the sake of sedentary or immobile earth (earth being, according to the Ptolemaic system, the center of the universe, with all other heavenly bodies revolving around it). If Nature is indeed "wise and frugal," how could she waste so much motion on a planet which, when viewed from the sun, would be tiny? The question is apt in an age which was discovering through the use of the telescope the immensity of the universe. Milton had asked it himself in "Prolusion" 7, and Eve had asked the same question of Adam at 4.657. For scientific background, see Svendsen 43–85, and Rattansi, "The Scientific."

[13]"Grace that won those who saw her to wish her to remain."

[14]Eve's departure might be taken as insulting to her intelligence, but the Pauline injunction commanded women to learn directly from their husbands and at home: "And if they [women] will learn any thing, let them ask their husbands at home: for it is a shame for women to speak in the church" (1 Corinthians 14.35). Likewise, the Epic Voice depicts Eve's desire to learn of more difficult or abstruse matters from Adam himself rather than from the angel. To a modern sensibility, the secondhand learning of women may seem condescending, but Milton anticipates the reader's problem when he has the Epic Voice affirm that Eve was capable of being delighted with such discourse and capable of understanding it: she just wants to hear it more pleasantly from Adam's lips.

[15]Throughout *Paradise Lost* Eve is associated with the garden and with its fecundity. Fowler believes that the associations with the garden link Eve with Venus (8.45–47n), but I would broaden the association, as does Northrop Frye, to include all "feminine" things in nature: "The specifically female part of nature is the earth, and the imagery of caves, labyrinths, and waters issuing from underground recall the process of birth from a womb. Trees and shady spots generally, and more particularly flowers, are also feminine, and so is the moon, the lowest heavenly body" ("The Revelation to Eve" 23). The word "Nurserie" suggests Eve's potential fecundity as well as the garden's, since nurseries would be provided both for germinating plants and for babies (compare *OED* 2 and 4).

[16]Eve as "Auditress" prefers to listen to Adam exclusively rather than to hear Raphael talking in the presence of Adam. The word is a Miltonic coinage illustrating "Milton's commitment to brevity of expression" (Corns 86).

With conjugal Caresses, from his Lip
Not Words alone pleas'd her.[17] O when meet now
Such pairs, in Love and mutual Honour joyn'd?
With Goddess-like demeanour forth she went;
Not unattended, for on her as Queen   60
A pomp of winning Graces waited still,
And from about her shot Darts of desire
Into all Eyes to wish her still in sight.[18]
And *Raphael* now to *Adam*'s doubt propos'd
Benevolent and facil[19] thus repli'd.   65
    To ask or search I blame thee not, for Heav'n
Is as the Book of God[20] before thee set,
Wherein to read his wondrous Works, and learne
His Seasons, Hours, or Dayes, or Months, or Yeares:[21]
This to attain, whether Heav'n move or Earth,   70
Imports not,[22] if thou reck'n right, the rest
From Man or Angel the great Architect
Did wisely to conceal, and not divulge
His secrets to be scann'd° by them who ought   EXAMINED CLOSELY
Rather admire; or if they list to try   75
Conjecture, he his Fabric of the Heav'ns
Hath left to thir disputes, perhaps to move
His laughter at thir quaint Opinions wide
Hereafter, when they come to model Heav'n
And calculate the Starrs, how they will weild   80
The mightie frame, how build, unbuild, contrive
To save appearances, how gird° the Sphear   ENCIRCLE, DRESS, CONFINE
With Centric and Eccentric scribl'd o're,
Cycle and Epicycle, Orb in Orb:[23]
Alreadie by thy reasoning this I guess,   85

---

[17]The phrase "lowliness Majestic," which I take to mean dignity within a position below Adam's but in no way demeaned by lower rank, helps to exalt what might seem to be the retreating position of Eve, and the apostrophe to the couple just below reiterates the Epic Voice's respect. The word "Honour" as applied to the state of marriage would evoke the memory in Milton's readers of the many Puritan tracts on the nature of domestic honor and "economy." See Roland Frye, "Teachings"; Haller, "Hail"; Turner, *One Flesh*; Staveley, *Puritan Legacies*.

[18]The "pomp of winning Graces" waiting on Eve and the "Darts of desire" radiating outward from her might seem part of a fallen world of human nature, but the evil, in this case, must be in the eye of the fallen beholder. Eve is like a goddess and she is queen of Paradise; she also is attended by grace (one should not forget the theological meaning of the word) and she does emanate the proverbial darts of desire—all of which is proleptic, since Eve's "pomp" or in fact any "train" will become suspect after the Fall (10.80). Satan will flatter her by calling her "Queen of this Universe" (9.684), inflating her rightful title, and Adam will be affected by those darts of desire to worship her body idolatrously.

[19]"And Raphael now in answer to Adam's anticipated (as in *OED* "propose" 2.b) doubt, answered gracefully and kindly." The sentence may be closer to inflected Latin than to English. The word "facil" is closer to its Latin root, the adverb *facile*, meaning "easily" or "gracefully"; in this case "facil" implies "easy or graceful of speech," rather than the modern "simplistic."

[20]The proverbial "Book of Nature," which was supposed to demonstrate God at work in ordering the universe. Here the image may be mystical (or "mysterious" in Milton's terminology).

[21]"And God said, Let there be lights in the firmament of heaven to divide the day from the night; and let them be for signs, and for seasons, and for days, and years" (Genesis 1.14).

[22]Milton has Raphael dismiss the distinction between Ptolemaic and Copernican astronomy. Svendsen summarizes: "Raphael gives Adam a technically shallow sketch of the heliocentric system and the doctrine of the plurality of worlds and then dismisses the controversy as insignificant and impertinent to man's duty to God and to himself.... Only the general features of the Ptolemaic system are used, but they are used most cunningly for their focus upon man" (44).

[23]Many models of the conjectured universe made of brass or wood—armillary spheres—still survive from the sixteenth and seventeenth centuries. There is a large collection kept in the Museum of Science and Technology in Florence: their variety and uncertainty in depicting the orbits of planets or stars in a geocentric or heliocentric universe indicate the kind of uncertainty that Raphael has God laughing at in this passage. The angel's contempt is built into the phrases "To save appearances" and "scribl'd o're," the latter of which suggests that all conjectural world systems were constantly being erased and written again. The "Centric and Eccentric" orbits, and the cycles and epicycles used to try to explain the motions of stars and planets do quickly become ridiculous; as Fowler points out, "Copernicus still required as many as thirty-four auxiliary circles, to account for the varying velocities of the planets" (8.83n, citing John Louis Emil Dreyer, *A History of Astronomy from Thales to Kepler* [New York: Dover, 1953]: 331, 343).

Who art to lead thy ofspring,[24] and supposest
That bodies bright and greater should not serve
The less not bright, nor Heav'n such journies run,
Earth sitting still, when she alone receaves
The benefit: consider first, that Great   90
Or Bright inferrs not Excellence: the Earth
Though, in comparison of Heav'n, so small,
Nor glistering,° may of solid good containe   GLITTERING
More plenty then the Sun that barren[25] shines,
Whose vertue on it self workes no effect,   95
But in the fruitful Earth; there first receavd
His beams, unactive else, thir vigour find.
Yet not to Earth are those bright Luminaries
Officious,° but to thee Earths habitant.   OBEDIENT
And for the Heav'ns wide Circuit, let it speak   100
The Makers high magnificence, who built
So spacious, and his Line stretcht out so farr;[26]
That Man may know he dwells not in his own;[27]
An Edifice too large for him to fill,
Lodg'd in a small partition, and the rest   105
Ordain'd for uses to his Lord best known.
The swiftness of those Circles° attribute,[28]   ORBITING HEAVENLY BODIES
Though numberless, to his Omnipotence,
That to corporeal substances could adde
Speed almost Spiritual;[29] mee thou thinkst not slow,   110
Who since the Morning hour set out from Heav'n
Where God resides, and ere mid-day arriv'd
In *Eden*, distance inexpressible
By Numbers that have name. But this I urge,
Admitting Motion in the Heav'ns, to shew   115
Invalid that which thee to doubt it mov'd;
Not that I so affirm, though so it seem
To thee who hast thy dwelling here on Earth.
God to remove his wayes from human sense,
Plac'd Heav'n from Earth so farr, that earthly sight,   120
If it presume, might erre in things too high,
And no advantage gaine. What if the Sun
Be Center to the World, and other Starrs
By his attractive vertue and thir own
Incited, dance about him various rounds?   125
Thir wandring course[30] now high, now low, then hid,

---

[24]Raphael can tell by listening to Adam that he is a born leader and proper "Sire" (father; see 39 above) of the generations to follow because of his questioning mind. Adam, in other words, is an excellent pupil and will be an excellent teacher.

[25]Though the sun generates life elsewhere through its innate power or "vertue," it was thought to contain no life. See William B. Hunter, "Two Notes on Milton," *Modern Language Review* 44 (1949): 89.

[26]In Job 38.5, God asks rhetorically, about the creation of the Earth: "Who hath laid the measures thereof, if thou knowest? or who hath stretched the line upon it?" The image is of measuring boundaries or foundations.

[27]The enormity of the universe makes man conscious that he dwells in God's edifice, not his own.

[28]Accented on the first and third syllables.

[29]The speed of the orbiting bodies cannot be calculated in numbers and hence must be attributed to God's omnipotence. Since each of the heavenly bodies was thought, according to Neoplatonic theory, to be controlled by an angelic spirit, the speed of planetary motion can be conceived of as the speed of thought. See Ficino's commentary on Plotinus's *Enneads* 2.1–3. Raphael uses his own motion as an example, in a homely fashion.

[30]Since the Greek word from which planet is derived means "wandering," Milton's word choice is, as usual, precise.

Progressive, retrograde,[31] or standing still,
In six thou seest,[32] and what if sev'nth to these
The Planet Earth, so stedfast though she seem,
Insensibly three different Motions[33] move?   130
Which else to several Sphears thou must ascribe,
Mov'd contrarie with thwart obliquities,[34]
Or save the Sun his labour, and that swift
Nocturnal and Diurnal rhomb suppos'd,[35]
Invisible else above all Starrs, the Wheele   135
Of Day and Night; which needs not thy beleefe,
If Earth industrious of her self[36] fetch Day
Travelling East, and with her part averse
From the Suns beam meet Night, her other part
Still luminous by his ray. What if that light   140
Sent from her through the wide transpicuous° aire,   TRANSPARENT
To the terrestrial Moon[37] be as a Starr
Enlightning her by Day, as she by Night
This Earth? reciprocal, if Land be there,
Feilds and Inhabitants: Her spots thou seest[38]   145
As Clouds, and Clouds may rain, and Rain produce
Fruits in her soft'nd Soile, for some to eate[39]
Allotted there; and other Suns perhaps
With thir attendant Moons thou wilt descrie
Communicating Male and Femal Light,   150
Which two great Sexes animate the World,[40]
Stor'd in each Orb perhaps with some that live.
For such vast room in Nature unpossest
By living Soule, desert[41] and desolate,

---

[31]Planets move at times in retrograde motion against that of the fixed stars.

[32]The list of planets visible to man: Saturn, Jupiter, Mars, Venus, Mercury, and the Moon. There was a debate over whether or not Earth constituted the seventh planet. Bishop John Wilkins's *Discourse That the Earth May be a Planet* (1640) testifies to current interest.

[33]Fowler summarizes the three motions attributed to Earth by Copernicus: "diurnal rotation, annual orbital revolution about the sun and a 'third motion' or 'motion in declination'" (8.130n). The third "motion of libration" is that "whereby the earth so proceeds in her orbit, as that her axis is constantly parallel to the axis of the world" (Newton 128n).

[34]The Zodiac was defined as the "thwart circle" (*OED* C.1), thwart being used to describe transverse or oblique motion. Milton seems to be describing elliptical orbits of various heavenly bodies.

[35]The "Nocturnal and Diurnal rhomb" is the primum mobile or the invisible or "suppos'd" outer sphere that was the cause of motion in all the other spheres. In Milton's usage "rhomb" is not an equilateral parallelogram but anything that whirls or wheels in space in a lozenge-shaped pattern. Babb points out that "Raphael seems quite ready to give up the intricate Ptolemaic machinery. In fact, his phrase 'rhomb suppos'd' suggests disbelief in the *primum mobile*" (81); but "suppos'd" need not express disbelief. Fowler explains Milton's precise usage in "rhomb": "In diagrams illustrating the Ptolemaic system, the triangle of the sun's rays, together with the triangle of the umbra or darkest central part of the earth's shadow, formed an elongated rhombus (well described as *Nocturnal and diurnal*), which was to be thought of as rotating about its own centroid or the earth's centre, like a pair of spokes of a particoloured wheel" (8.134n).

[36]The "industrious" (i.e., rotating) Earth of the Copernican system is contrasted with the "sedentarie Earth" at line 32 above.

[37]Either made out of earthly mould or "sublunary," "beneath the celestial." Hughes comments that the moon is to be understood "to be inhabitable like the earth" (142n), but Milton here seems to be drawing a distinction between the "terrestrial Moon" and the stars: the moon, being like the earth, receives light, the others radiate it.

[38]The nature of the spots that could be perceived with telescopes of about the power of Galileo (about 30X) was much debated, so that the theory here that they are clouds (rather than seas or craters) would have been plausible. See Rattansi, "Scientific," 231, for the effects of Galileo's discoveries about the surface of the moon and their meaning in terms of contemporary astronomy. Compare the description of Galileo's telescope, which can "descry new Lands, / Rivers or Mountains in her [the moon's] spotty Globe" (1.290–91), and compare Raphael's description of the moon as "moist" at 5.422.

[39]The more the planets resemble Earth, the argument goes, the more likely they also are inhabited. Thus clouds would produce rain that would nurture fruits for the inhabitants to eat.

[40]"Male and Femal Light" here designates either original or reflected light, male suns and female moons. Joseph Summers was the first critic to use this passage to show how Milton constructs a sexually vibrant universe in which the microcosm of the marriage of Adam and Eve mirrors the reciprocal sexuality of the suns and moons that make up the "World." See *The Muse's Method* 87–111.

[41]Accented on the second syllable.

Onely to shine, yet scarce to contribute[42]   155
Each Orb a glimps of Light, conveyd so farr
Down to this habitable,[43] which returnes
Light back to them, is obvious to dispute.[44]
But whether thus these things, or whether not,
Whether the Sun predominant in Heav'n   160
Rise on the Earth, or Earth rise on the Sun,
Hee from the East his flaming rode begin,
Or she from West her silent course advance[45]
With inoffensive pace that spinning sleeps
On her soft Axle, while she paces Eev'n,   165
And beares thee soft with the smooth Air along,
Sollicit not thy thoughts[46] with matters hid,
Leave them to God above, him serve and feare;
Of other Creatures, as him pleases best,
Wherever plac't, let him dispose: joy thou   170
In what he gives to thee, this Paradise
And thy faire *Eve*; Heav'n is for thee too high
To know what passes there; be lowlie wise:[47]
Think onely what concernes thee and thy being;
Dream not of other Worlds, what Creatures there   175
Live, in what state, condition or degree,
Contented that thus farr hath been reveal'd
Not of Earth onely but of highest Heav'n.
     To whom thus *Adam* cleerd of doubt,[48] repli'd.
How fully hast thou satisfi'd mee, pure   180
Intelligence[49] of Heav'n, Angel serene,
And freed from intricacies, taught to live,
The easiest way, nor with perplexing thoughts
To interrupt the sweet of Life, from which
God hath bid dwell farr off all anxious cares,   185
And not molest° us, unless we our selves
Seek them with wandring thoughts, and notions vain.
But apt the Mind or Fancie is to roave
Uncheckt, and of her roaving is no end;[50]

---

[42]Accented on the first and third syllables.

[43]The idiom seems to be "this habitable [earth]" and may be derived from the Greek idiom ἡ οἰκουμένη, "the habitable globe" (see *OED* 1).

[44]"Is open to dispute." As Fowler points out (8.15–38n), Milton disputed the point himself in "Prolusion" 7.

[45]Again, the sun and Earth are sexually differentiated, creating a resonance between the macrocosm of the planets and the microcosm of Adam and Eve. Here, for instance, the sun is more aggressive in motion, whereas the moon is "silent" and "inoffensive" (harmless, but also unobstructed or unimpeded, as in the Latin *inoffensus*).

[46]"Don't disturb your thoughts," following the sense of *OED* solicit I.1, "to make anxious."

[47]The most concise statement of the belief that Adam need not know more than what is necessary for his preservation on earth and his salvation in the eyes of God. The threat of too much knowledge will be realized when Adam and Eve eat of the Tree of Knowledge of Good and Evil: the Fall itself will be "Bad Fruit of Knowledge" (9.1073). It is obvious, however, that Milton's position is not anti-intellectual; instead it limits idle or dangerous speculation about the nature of things beyond the understanding of humankind. In *Of Education*, he proposes a curriculum that strongly emphasizes the practical, from marching in military maneuvers to singing and playing music.

[48]Milton's readers have never felt so clear of doubt as Adam is after hearing two conflicting views of the motions of heavenly bodies.

[49]Spirit, with the overtone that angels as "intelligences" were thought to control the motions of heavenly bodies, as in John Donne's contrast between lovers' bodies and their spirits: " . . . Wee are / Th'intelligences, they the spheare" ("The Ecstasy" 51–52, ed. Helen Gardner).

[50]The contrast is between imagination or fancy on one side and mind or intellect on the other. Unbridled or unchecked fancy may be a source for evil imaginings, as in 5.102–19. Douglas Bush cites a speech by Milton's acquaintance Ralph Cudworth in the House of Commons on 31 March 1647: "We think it is a gallant thing to be fluttering up to heaven with our wings of knowledge and speculation: whereas the highest mystery of a divine life here, and of perfect happiness hereafter, consisteth in nothing but mere obedience to the divine will" (8.159–78n). Raphael's image of descending from "this high pitch" to a lower level of flight (198–99) would illustrate the meaning as well. One should also notice that "Fancie" is feminine, but "Wisdom" is not

Till warn'd, or by experience taught, she learne,   190
That not to know at large of things remote
From use, obscure and suttle, but to know
That which before us lies in daily life,
Is the prime Wisdom,[51] what is more, is fume,[52]   195
Or emptiness, or fond impertinence,
And renders us in things that most concerne
Unpractis'd, unprepar'd, and still to seek.[53]
Therefore from this high pitch let us descend°   DESCEND TO
A lower flight, and speak of things at hand
Useful, whence haply mention may arise   200
Of somthing not unseasonable to ask
By sufferance,° and thy wonted favour deign'd.   PERMISSION
Thee I have heard relating what was don
Ere my remembrance: now hear mee relate
My Storie,[54] which perhaps thou hast not heard;   205
And Day is yet not spent; till then thou seest
How suttly to detaine thee I devise,
Inviting thee to hear while I relate,
Fond,° were it not in hope of thy reply: FOOLISH
For while I sit with thee, I seem in Heav'n,   210
And sweeter thy discourse is to my eare
Then Fruits of Palm-tree pleasantest to thirst[55]
And hunger both, from labour,[56] at the houre
Of sweet repast; they satiate, and soon fill,
Though pleasant, but thy words with Grace Divine   215
Imbu'd, bring to thir sweetness no satietie.[57]
    To whom thus *Raphael* answer'd heav'nly meek.
Nor are thy lips ungraceful,[58] Sire of men,
Nor tongue ineloquent; for God on thee
Abundantly his gifts hath also pour'd   220
Inward and outward both, his image faire:[59]
Speaking or mute all comliness and grace

[Handwritten annotation: RAPHAEL IS COMPLIMENTED BY ADAM'S DISCOURSE / Adam admires Raphael]

---

here assigned a sex; compare 4.490–91.

[51]Some copies of *1667* have a semicolon here.

[52]The word suggests smoke or obscuring haze (as in Latin *fumus* or Italian *fumo*). The sense of "something which when inhaled dulls or confuses the brain" (compare *OED* II.6) may be applicable as well.

[53]"Always to be sought after," which implies "never to be found."

[54]Adam's "account of the events of his life or of some portion of it" (*OED* 4.d, citing this instance). As Adam admits, his telling of his history is a subtle device to detain Raphael in Eden because conversation with the angel is so pleasurable to him. See Robert Bell, "'Blushing like the morn': Milton's Human Comedy," *Milton Quarterly* 15 (1981): 47–55.

[55]"How sweet are thy words unto my taste! yea, sweeter than honey to my mouth" (Psalm 119.103). The fruits of the palm are apparently coconuts, since they provide food and drink.

[56]Having come from work or once being away from it, we find that food and drink are an especially "sweet repast."

[57]Contrast 9.248, where Adam implies that too much of his conversation might "satiate" Eve.

[58]"Thou art fairer than the children of men: grace is poured into thy lips: therefore God hath blessed thee for ever" (Psalm 45.2).

[59]Though the adjective "fair" sometimes has negative or ironic meanings in *Paradise Lost*, as in "fair Idolatresses" in 1.445, as it is applied to Adam as human representative of God's image here it seems to be wholly positive. Adam and Eve are both said by the angel Gabriel to be fair (4.790), but the adjective as applied to women's physical beauty or the Fruit of the Tree of Knowledge often has negative overtones, as in "her faire looks" (4.718) or "fair enticing Fruit" (9.996). There may be an implied contrast between Adam's outward and inward image, the two being reconciled, and Eve's outward image or "outside," which will come to exert too great an effect on Adam. Soon Raphael will warn Adam about Eve's "outside" which is "fair no doubt, and worthy well / Thy cherishing, thy honouring, and thy love, / Not thy subjection" (568–70 below). Throughout this book and in Book 9, there is a subtle interplay between inward and outward and inside and outside. Eve's outside becomes ornamental in the eyes of Adam (that is the negative component of her beauty, which also has the power to make Satan stupidly good), whereas Adam's outside can come to represent only his physical, "outward strength" (9.312).

Attends thee, and each word, each motion formes.[60]
Nor less think wee in Heav'n of thee on Earth
Then of our fellow servant,[61] and inquire   225
Gladly into the wayes of God with Man:[62]
For God we see hath honour'd thee, and set
On Man his Equal Love: say therefore on;
For I that Day was absent, as befell,° *HAPPENED*
Bound on a voyage uncouth and obscure,[63]   230
Farr on excursion toward the Gates of Hell;
Squar'd in full Legion[64] (such command we had)
To see that none thence issu'd forth a spie,
Or enemie, while God was in his work,
Least hee incenst at such eruption bold,   235
Destruction with Creation might have mixt.
Not that they durst without his leave attempt,
But us he sends upon his high behests
For state, as Sovran King, and to enure
Our prompt obedience.[65] Fast we found, fast shut   240
The dismal Gates, and barricado'd strong;
But long ere our approaching heard within
Noise, other then the sound of Dance or Song,
Torment, and loud lament, and furious rage.[66]
Glad we return'd up to the coasts of Light   245
Ere Sabbath Eev'ning:[67] so we had in charge.
But thy relation now; for I attend,[68]
Pleas'd with thy words no less then thou with mine.
    So spake the Godlike Power,[69] and thus our Sire.
For Man to tell how human Life began   250
Is hard; for who himself beginning knew?[70]
Desire with thee still longer to converse

---

[60]The text of *1674* has a comma here, which is so clearly wrong, according to Fletcher, that it represents the compositor's mistakenly taking a broken period as a comma. The Columbia text prints the comma, in error.

[61]Probably echoes the sentiment of the angel in Revelation, who, when the speaker of the book begins worshiping him, says "I am thy fellow-servant, and of thy brethren the prophets" (22.9).

[62]Milton may intend the reader to make a contrast between this happy task and the more difficult task of justifying the ways of God to man after the Fall. Compare 1.26.

[63]"Destined to go on an uncertain and gloomy voyage."

[64]The angels were set in square battle formation, but they were also well-organized, as in the modern idiom "squared away."

[65]William Empson called attention to what he perceived as God's trick on the good angels: "Raphael . . . assumes God gave him a job at the time merely to disappoint him" (110); but the angels' tasks do not just make work. They help establish God's "state" (his public position in the eyes of his followers), and they help "enure" (or harden or discipline) the troups of militant angels. Also, the angels find the gates of Hell barricaded (they are later to be unbarred by Sin [2.883–84]) and hear the laments of the damned angels, gaining firsthand the experience of damnation. What has annoyed critics is the fact that if God is omnipotent, and if He had not given permission for the fallen angels to leave Hell, He would not need to send the good angels to barricade the gates. Even if the commands make unnecessary work, God is justified in making them, as in King Lear's response to the questioning of his authority: "O reason not the need!" (2.4.264). Of course, Raphael's absence also gives Milton an excuse as narrator to allow Adam to tell Raphael of his creation; otherwise, the story would be repeated.

[66]Echoing the image of the frightened Aeneas outside the gate of Tartarus, which is itself surrounded by a river of fire: "From within can be heard the sounds of groaning and brutal lashing, / Sounds of clanking iron, of chains being dragged along" (6.557–58, trans. Lewis). Astolpho, in Ariosto's *Orlando Furioso*, also visited "That fearfull cave that was the mouth of hell, / . . . And heard most woful mourning plaints and cries / Such as from hell were likely to arise" (34.4, trans. Harington [ed. McNulty]). Through the contrast with the "sound of Dance or Song," we are made aware that these distant angelic troops would rather have attended the celebration of the creation of humankind.

[67]The evening which began the Sabbath, the seventh day after creation, during which God "rested."

[68]"But to your story now, because I am waiting."

[69]Though the word "Power" indicates the sixth order of angels (*OED* 8), here it also suggests Raphael's military function in containing the fallen angels, since "power" is also synonymous with "army" (*OED* 9).

[70]Satan asks a similar question at 5.856–61; he does, however, remember his own creation, alluding to it at 4.43.

Induc'd me. As new wak't from soundest sleep
Soft on the flourie herb[71] I found me laid
In Balmie Sweat, which with his Beames the Sun   255
Soon dri'd, and on the reaking[72] moisture fed.
Strait toward Heav'n my wondring Eyes I turnd,
And gaz'd a while the ample Skie, till rais'd
By quick instinctive motion up I sprung,[73]
As thitherward endevoring, and upright   260
Stood on my feet;[74] about me round I saw
Hill, Dale, and shadie Woods, and sunnie Plaines,
And liquid Lapse[75] of murmuring Streams; by these,
Creatures that livd, and movd, and walk'd, or flew,
Birds on the branches warbling;[76] all things smil'd,   265
With fragrance and with joy my heart oreflow'd.
My self I then perus'd, and Limb by Limb
Survey'd, and sometimes went,° and sometimes ran   WALKED
With supple joints, and lively vigour led:[77]
But who I was, or where, or from what cause,   270
Knew not; to speak I tri'd, and forthwith spake,
My Tongue obey'd and readily could name
What e're I saw.[78] Thou Sun, said I, faire Light,
And thou enlight'nd Earth, so fresh and gay,°   BRIGHTLY DRESSED
Ye Hills and Dales, ye Rivers, Woods, and Plaines,   275
And ye that live and move,[79] fair Creatures, tell,
Tell, if ye saw, how came I thus, how here?
Not of my self; by some great Maker then,[80]
In goodness and in power præeminent;
Tell me, how may I know him, how adore,   280
From whom I have that thus I move and live,
And feel that I am happier[81] then I know,
While thus I call'd, and stray'd I knew not whither,
From where I first drew Aire, and first beheld

---

[71]The "flourie herb" would be the green growth near the ground, including grass and flowers but not shrubbery. "Herb" would include everything next to the ground that does not have a woody stem; hence the softness.

[72]Steaming or indicating evaporation. The image of "Balmie Sweat" is not at all negative, since balm in biblical usage is a healing ointment (as in "balm of Gilead"), and the image of the sun feeding on moisture is an indication of microcosmic creativity: the sun helps creation by drying Adam. Compare 5.423–26, where the sun seems to drink the sea.

[73]Contrast the motion of Satan "Instinct with Fire and Nitre" (2.937); Adam's quickness is graceful rather than explosive.

[74]Adam's upright posture immediately differentiates him from the other animals. The uprightness of humankind was thought to be an immediate and recognizable sign of nobility.

[75]The word *lapsus* in Latin, when used of horizontal motion, means a gliding along with gentle or easy motion, but it also means a falling off, or an error, as in lapse. The image here of water is beautiful, but it may be proleptic of the Fall (see Ricks, *Milton's* 111). Milton's usage of lapse is the first recorded in *OED* 6.a for the sense of "gliding" or "flow" used of water.

[76]Singing beautifully or with inspiration. Milton uses the verb warble always in a positive context to define the spontaneous composition of human song or poetry as well, as when Shakespeare "Warble[s] his native Wood-notes wild" ("L'Allegro" 134).

[77]*1667* reads "as lively vigour led: . . . " which Fletcher believes Milton himself may have ordered to be corrected to the reading of *1674*.

[78]Adam's ability to name expands on Genesis: " . . . and whatsoever [he] called every living creature, that was the name thereof" (2.20). Leonard understands that "Milton's God [endows] Adam and Eve with the reason to form an accurate language for themselves" and that "Milton's God endows Adam with knowledge in *Paradise Lost,* but Adam's intellect moves with a life of its own" (12). The naming process is spontaneous in Adam and issues from his "sudden apprehension" (354 below). The first thing Adam names is the sun, a symbol of creativity and divinity.

[79]"For in him we live, and move, and have our being; as certain also of your own poets have said, For we are also his offspring" (Acts 17.28). St. Paul is the speaker, discussing the temple of the unknown god. Compare 281 below.

[80]Adam demonstrates the ability to argue deductively, moving from "if ye saw" to "Not of my self," and concluding "by some great Maker then." He is created, in other words, capable of arguing logically or debating with an angel.

[81]"More fortunate." The word *happier* is often used in *Paradise Lost*, and often used ironically, as when Satan offers Eve a "happier life, [through] knowledge of Good and Evil" (9.697).

This happie Light, when answer none return'd,   285
On a green shadie Bank profuse of Flours
Pensive I sate me down; there gentle sleep
First found me, and with soft oppression seis'd
My droused sense,[82] untroubl'd, though I thought
I then was passing to my former state   290
Insensible, and forthwith to dissolve:
When suddenly stood at my Head a dream,[83]
Whose inward apparition gently mov'd
My fancy to believe I yet had being,
And livd: One came, methought, of shape Divine,   295
And said, thy Mansion wants thee, *Adam*, rise,
First Man, of Men innumerable ordain'd
First Father, call'd by thee I come thy Guide
To the Garden of bliss,[84] thy seat prepar'd.
So saying, by the hand he took me rais'd,   300
And over Fields and Waters, as in Aire
Smooth sliding without step, last led me up
A woodie Mountain;[85] whose high top was plaine,
A Circuit° wide, enclos'd, with goodliest Trees   TRACT
Planted, with Walks, and Bowers, that what I saw   305
Of Earth before scarce pleasant seemd. Each Tree
Load'n with fairest Fruit that hung to the Eye
Tempting,[86] stirr'd in me sudden appetite
To pluck and eate;[87] whereat I wak'd, and found
Before mine Eyes all real, as the dream   310
Had lively shadowd:° Here had new begun   PREDICTED
My wandring, had not hee who was my Guide
Up hither, from among the Trees appeer'd
Presence Divine.[88] Rejoycing, but with aw
In adoration at his feet I fell   315
Submiss:[89] he rear'd me, and Whom thou soughtst I am,
Said mildely, Author of all this thou seest
Above, or round about thee or beneath.
This Paradise I give thee, count it thine

---

[82]The choice of words may again be proleptic or darkly prophetic. Though "oppression" may just indicate heaviness or fatigue and is meliorated by "soft," it is also used of Adam and Eve's slaked lust after the Fall (9.1045); "seis'd" will be echoed when Adam grabs Eve after the Fall (9.1037). The phrase "droused sense" suggests being lulled to sleep, which is what Mercury does to the guardian Argus, described as "more wakeful then to drouze" in 11.131.

[83]The dream is presented allegorically and according to the conventions of classical epic: it is standing at the head of Adam, as when "Dream [an evil dream personified and sent by Zeus] stood then beside [Agamemnon's] head in the likeness of Nestor" (*Iliad* 2.20). Adam's dream is, of course, not evil; but Eve's dream, because it is inspired by Satan, is. Both dreams are inward apparitions which move the imagination or fancy of the dreamer to believe in the reality of what he or she sees. As many critics have pointed out, Adam's dream is one of obedience to God, Eve's of disobedience. See, for example, William B. Hunter, "Eve's Demonic Dream," *ELH* 13 (1946): 255–65.

[84]Following Genesis 2.8 and 15, Adam is assumed to have been created outside of Paradise and then placed in it. Compare the account at 7.535–38.

[85]The Garden of Eden is a walled-in plateau on a mountain top, laid out like a formal gentleman's garden in the seventeenth century. For the influence of traditional Italian garden design on Milton's garden, see Hannah Disinger Demaray, "Milton's 'Perfect' Paradise and the Landscapes of Italy," *Milton Quarterly* 8 (1974): 33–41. The topos or venue of the enclosed garden had long been associated with Eden; see Stanley Stewart, *Enclosed*.

[86]The fruit is tempting to the eye (beautiful?), and it is probably also conveniently placed at eye-level.

[87]The word "Tempting" and the phrase "To pluck and eate" both foreshadow the dream-temptation of Eve, when the Seraph "pluckt" and "tasted" (5.65), and the real temptation of 9.781: "she pluck'd, she eat"; but here Adam is obviously not sinfully inclined to eat forbidden fruit, because the fruit is not yet under prohibition.

[88]The *1674* compositor erroneously substituted a comma here, for the period of *1667*, and I have corrected it. Perhaps, as Thyer thought (see Newton 314n), the comma belongs after "aw."

[89]"Submissive," and probably not with the Latin sense of "cast down," since Adam has fallen on his knees of his own free will. God, in fact, props him up or "rears" him.

To Till[90] and keep, and of the Fruit to eate: 320
Of every Tree that in the Garden growes
Eate freely with glad heart; fear here no dearth:
But of the Tree whose operation brings
Knowledg of good and ill, which I have set
The Pledge of thy Obedience and thy Faith,   325
Amid the Garden by the Tree of Life,
Remember what I warne thee, shun to taste,
And shun the bitter consequence: for know,
The day thou eat'st thereof, my sole command
Transgrest, inevitably thou shalt dye;   330
From that day mortal,[91] and this happie State
Shalt loose,[92] expell'd from hence into a World
Of woe and sorrow. Sternly he pronounc'd
The rigid interdiction,° which resounds   PROHIBITION
Yet dreadful in mine eare, though in my choice   335
Not to incur;[93] but soon his cleer aspect[94]
Return'd and gracious purpose thus renew'd.
Not onely these fair bounds,[95] but all the Earth
To thee and to thy Race I give; as Lords
Possess it, and all things that therein live,   340
Or live in Sea, or Aire, Beast, Fish, and Fowle.[96]
In signe whereof each Bird and Beast behold
After thir kindes;[97] I bring them to receave
From thee thir Names, and pay thee fealtie
With low subjection;[98] understand the same   345
Of Fish within thir watry residence,
Not hither summond, since they cannot change
Thir Element to draw the thinner Aire.[99]
As thus he spake, each Bird and Beast behold
Approaching two and two,[100] These cowring low   350

[handwritten note in margin: Adams Dream Continued]

---

[90]As Fowler points out (8.320–22n), the Authorized Version uses the word "dress" instead of "till" at Genesis 2.15. The verse in the Authorized Version reads "And the Lord God took the man, and put him into the garden of Eden to dress it and to keep it." Milton's choice of the translation "till" may indicate that he does not want honest labor to be considered a punishment for the Fall.

[91]Adam and Eve and their descendants were mortal (capable of dying) from the day on which they ate the fruit. Milton wrote in *On Christian Doctrine*: " . . . it is clear that God, at any rate after the fall of man, laid down a certain limit for human life" (1.8; Yale 6: 339). The theological problem is caused by the ambiguity of God's role in punishing Adam and Eve after the Fall. They are promised what appears to be instantaneous death ("in the day that thou eatest thereof thou shalt surely die" [Genesis 2.17]) if they eat, yet they do not die. Thus Christian theologians, Milton among them, had to argue that Adam and Eve only begin the process of dying when they eat the fruit. Eating the fruit does not kill directly: it induces mortality.

[92]Probably "lose," though Fowler (8.332n) reads the word according to *OED* 7 as "loose," meaning to break up or do away with. The 1688 Folio edition began the trend to read the word only as "lose," since the spelling both in *1667* and *1674* was the ambiguous "loose."

[93]It is within Adam's free will not to choose to eat the fruit. Here the verb *incur* seems to be intransitive, meaning "to render oneself liable to" (*OED* I.2), but the reader might be expected to supply "incur [His wrath]," as in 9.992-93: "to incurr / Divine displeasure."

[94]Accented, as usual, on the second syllable.

[95]"Not only these fair lands within the boundaries of Paradise." Here "bounds" are delimited plots of land.

[96]Following Genesis 1.28–29.

[97]"According to their various natures."

[98]"And out of the ground the Lord God formed every beast of the field, and every fowl of the air; and brought them unto Adam to see what he would call them: and whatsoever Adam called every living creature, that was the name thereof" (Genesis 2.19).

[99]Milton provides logically for the fish, which are not mentioned in Genesis, by saying that they could not be summoned before Adam since they could not breathe "thinner Aire."

[100]The comma here before a capital letter in both early texts poses a unique problem for editors, most of whom take the course of silently emending the capital "T" to a lowercase letter, though Campbell inserts a dash—creatively—to replace the comma and Hughes, who generally modernizes punctuation, leaves the comma and the capital in place. The punctuation does cause confusion, since "These" seems to refer to all beasts, yet might refer only to the birds. In a clear admission of confusion, I leave the text as I find it in *1674* and *1667*.

With blandishment, each Bird stoop'd on his wing.[101]
I nam'd them, as they pass'd, and understood
Thir Nature, with such knowledg God endu'd
My sudden apprehension:[102] but in these
I found not what me thought I wanted still;[103]   355
And to the Heav'nly vision thus presum'd.°   TOOK THE LIBERTY
    O by what Name, for thou above all these,
Above mankinde, or aught then mankinde higher,[104]
Surpassest farr my naming,[105] how may I   360
Adore thee, Author of this Universe,
And all this good to man, for whose well being
So amply, and with hands so liberal
Thou hast provided all things: but with mee
I see not who partakes. In solitude   365
What happiness, who can enjoy alone,
Or all enjoying, what contentment find?
Thus I presumptuous; and the vision bright,
As with a smile more bright'nd, thus repli'd.[106]
    What call'st thou solitude, is not the Earth   370
With various living creatures, and the Aire
Replenisht,[107] and all these at thy command
To come and play before thee, know'st thou not
Thir language[108] and thir wayes, they also know,
And reason not contemptibly; with these   375
Find pastime, and beare rule; thy Realm is large.
So spake the Universal Lord, and seem'd
So ordering. I with leave of speech implor'd,[109]
And humble deprecation[110] thus repli'd.
    Let not my words offend thee, Heav'nly Power,   380
My Maker, be propitious while I speak.
Hast thou not made me here thy substitute,°   DEPUTY
And these inferiour farr beneath me set?
Among unequals what societie

---

[101]A respectful "bow to superior power or authority" (*OED* 2.a).

[102]Adam is "endowed with natural wisdom, holiness and righteousness. . . . Moreover he could not have given names to the animals in that extempore way, without very great intelligence . . . " (*On Christian Doctrine* 1.7; Yale 6: 324).

[103]"It seemed to me I still lacked." In other words, Adam feels something like an innate need for a helpmeet. For God's response to Adam's need, see Genesis 2.20–24.

[104]"Or any that are higher than humankind."

[105]Naming God (whose name is in the Old Testament tradition not pronounceable) is not so easy for Adam as naming the animals. Adam respectfully saves the naming of God for last, since God rules all created nature.

[106]Milton's God does have a sense of humor. His smiles (and His laughter) are not reserved for mocking the ridiculous behavior of evil beings (as in the "derision" of 5.736). The smile here is described obliquely ("As with . . . "), since to describe God's face would be presumptuous. God smiles at evil, sardonically, at 3.257.

[107]"Kept filled with life."

[108]Whatever language the animals speak (and the Serpent will speak to Eve in English, apparently), Adam and Eve understand it. Josephus, *Antiquities* 1.1.4, postulates that all creatures before the Fall spoke the same language. The animals also do not know dissension or predatory behavior; instead they "know" or have understanding (Fowler 8.373n), and they can reason. Thus Eve's discourse with the Serpent will not be surprising to her. Generally accepted opinion in biblical commentary of the seventeenth century was that the world spoke Hebrew before the Fall, though other languages such as Aramaic were suggested.

[109]"Given leave to speak, I implored."

[110]"Prayer for the averting or removal (of evil, disaster, etc.)" (*OED* 2).

Can sort,[111] what harmonie or true delight?
Which must be mutual, in proportion due   385
Giv'n and receiv'd; but in disparitie
The one intense, the other still remiss
Cannot well suite with either, but soon prove
Tedious alike: Of fellowship I speak
Such as I seek, fit to participate   390
All rational delight, wherein the brute
Cannot be human consort; they rejoyce
Each with thir kinde, Lion with Lioness;
So fitly them in pairs thou hast combin'd;
Much less can Bird with Beast, or Fish with Fowle   395
So well converse,[112] nor with the Ox the Ape;
Wors then can Man with Beast, and least of all.
     Whereto th' Almighty answer'd, not displeas'd.[113]
A nice and suttle[114] happiness I see
Thou to thy self proposest, in the choice   400
Of thy Associates, *Adam*, and wilt taste
No pleasure, though in pleasure,[115] solitarie.
What thinkst thou then of mee, and this my State,°
Seem I to thee sufficiently possest
Of happiness, or not? who am alone[116]   405
From all Eternitie, for none I know
Second to me or like, equal much less.
How have I then with whom to hold converse
Save with the Creatures which I made, and those
To me inferiour, infinite descents[117]   410
Beneath what other Creatures are to thee?[118]
     He ceas'd, I lowly answer'd. To attaine
The highth and depth of thy Eternal wayes
All human thoughts come short, Supream of things;
Thou in thy self art perfet, and in thee   415
Is no deficience found; not so is Man,
But in degree, the cause of his desire
By conversation with his like to help,

---

[111]"To suit, fit or agree" or "be in harmony" (*OED* III.18). The order of the universe is made to agree again in musical terms, including "harmonie" and mathematical consonance or "proportion due." But though there should be harmony and resonance between what is low-pitched ("remiss") and what is high-pitched or strung too tightly ("intense"), Adam still feels the differences between his own high order and that of the animals. For perfect harmony he needs one of his own kind, a fitting help for him—or helpmeet.

[112]Not just "to talk with" but "to associate with intimately" (a secondary meaning was "to have sexual intercourse with," which of course is impossible between different animal species). But see Turner 156 for the tradition that "the serpent had coupled with Eve to engender Cain."

[113]God is not displeased because Adam is in the midst of passing a gentle schoolmaster's test of his reasoning powers, discovering on his own that "It is not good that the man should be alone . . . " (as God says in Genesis 2.18). This line is indented in *1667*, which is normal practice at the beginning of a new speaker's dialogue; I have restored the indentation.

[114]Both "nice" and "suttle" suggest refined judgment on the part of Adam. Before the Fall, when the word *subtle* took on evil associations because it was applied in Genesis 3.1 to the serpent, it seems to have only positive connotations. Milton uses the word *nice* to mean, at various times, "fastidious," "ceremonial," or "precise" (see 4.241 or 5.433).

[115]God seems to be punning on the meaning of the name "Paradise" as "pleasure" or "pleasure garden."

[116]Though originating in Genesis 2, these sentiments have been used to support the idea that Milton was an Arian, a heretic denying the Christian Trinity. See 420 below and the note.

[117]"Infinitely lower [than I am] on the ladder of creation."

[118]God's question is that of a schoolmaster, since He knows the answer, but it is also the fatherly trial or test of Adam (see 437 below) and thus can be excused of the accusation that it is cruel.

Or solace his defects.[119] No need that thou
Shouldst propagat,[120] already infinite;   420
And through all numbers absolute, though One;[121]
But Man by number is to manifest
His single imperfection,[122] and beget
Like of his like, his Image multipli'd,
In unitie defective,[123] which requires   425
Collateral love,[124] and deerest amitie.
Thou in thy secresie,° although alone,   RETIREMENT, SECLUSION
Best with thy self accompanied, seek'st not
Social communication, yet so pleas'd,
Canst raise thy Creature to what highth thou wilt   430
Of Union or Communion, deifi'd;[125]
I by conversing cannot these erect
From prone,[126] nor in thir wayes complacence[127] find.
Thus I embold'nd spake, and freedom us'd
Permissive,[128] and acceptance found, which gain'd   435
This answer from the gratious voice Divine.
    Thus farr to try thee, *Adam*, I was pleas'd,
And finde thee knowing not of Beasts alone,
Which thou hast rightly nam'd, but of thy self,
Expressing well the spirit within thee free,   440
My Image, not imparted to the Brute,
Whose fellowship therefore unmeet for thee
Good reason was thou freely shouldst dislike,
And be so minded still; I, ere thou spak'st,
Knew it not good for Man to be alone,[129]   445
And no such companie as then thou saw'st
Intended thee, for trial onely brought,
To see how thou could'st judge of fit and meet:

---

[119]Loh glosses the difficult syntax: "(this is) the reason why he desires to help (i.e., remedy) or solace (i.e., compensate for) his defects by companionship (i.e., 'conversation') with his like" (417–19n). I would add that "conversation" represents a deep and abiding companionship—that of ideal marriage.

[120]It is probably beside the point here to find evidence of Milton's "Arian dogma" in the begetting of the Son by God the Father (Kelley, *This Great Argument* 121), though *On Christian Doctrine* does state that "God could certainly have refrained from the act of generation and yet remained true to his own essence, for he stands in no need of propagation" (1.5; Yale 6: 209).

[121]"Two distinct things cannot be of the same essence. God is one being, not two" *On Christian Doctrine* 1.5; Yale 6: 212).

[122]"His imperfection while he is single." If man were to remain single, he would be defective because incomplete; he is incomplete if left unmarried, even in Paradise. Milton's view opposes that expressed in his friend Andrew Marvell's poem "The Garden":

> Such was that happy Garden-state,
> While Man there walk'd without a Mate:
> After a Place so pure, and sweet,
> What other Help could yet be meet!
> But 'twas beyond a Mortal's share
> To wander solitary there:
> Two Paradises 'twere in one
> To live in Paradise alone. (Margoliouth ed., 1.53)

[123]If man were to remain single, in other words, he would be defective because incomplete.

[124]Parallel or coequal love, side by side, between the sexes in marriage. See *On Christian Doctrine* 1.10.

[125]Either a mystical union with God outside of the miracle thought to occur in Holy Communion, or that union itself. That sort of legitimate union with God should be contrasted with Eve's attempt in the Fall to take on godhead (9.790).

[126]"If the beasts of the earth are prone, I cannot raise them to higher posture or higher undestanding by talking to them."

[127]"Object of joy." Adam takes no delight in discovering or imitating the behavior of animals. As Fowler points out (8.433), God's "sole complacence" is Messiah (3.276).

[128]Adam's freedom is permitted by God. "The matter or object of the divine plan was that angels and men alike should be endowed with free will, so that they could either fall or not fall" (*On Christian Doctrine* 1.3; Yale 6: 163).

[129]"And the Lord God said, It is not good that the man should be alone; I will make him an help meet for him" (Genesis 2.18). Commentators on Genesis inferred from this passage that it was good for God to be alone.

What next I bring shall please thee, be assur'd,
Thy likeness, thy fit help, thy other self,
Thy wish exactly to thy hearts desire.[130]   450

    Hee ended, or I heard no more, for now
My earthly[131] by his Heav'nly overpowerd,
Which it had long stood under, streind to the highth
In that celestial Colloquie° sublime,   CONVERSATION   455
As with an object that excels the sense,
Dazl'd and spent, sunk down, and sought repair
Of sleep,[132] which instantly fell on me, call'd
By Nature as in aide, and clos'd mine eyes.[133]
Mine eyes he clos'd, but op'n left the Cell   460
Of Fancie[134] my internal sight, by which
Abstract as in a transe[135] methought I saw,
Though sleeping, where I lay, and saw the shape
Still glorious before whom awake I stood;
Who stooping op'nd my left side,[136] and took   465
From thence a Rib, with cordial spirits warme,[137]
And Life-blood streaming fresh; wide was the wound,
But suddenly with flesh fill'd up and heal'd:
The Rib he formd and fashond[138] with his hands;
Under his forming hands a Creature grew,   470
Manlike, but different Sex, so lovly faire,
That what seemd fair in all the World, seemed now
Mean, or in her summd up, in her containd
And in her looks,[139] which from that time infus'd

---

[130]Aside from being created in Adam's likeness (just as Adam is created in God's likeness), she is a fitting help, or helpmeet, for him; she will be his other self, since her substance will be taken from his side. She is also his heart's desire because, as Milton has it, she is God's answer for Adam's loneliness. See F. Peczenik, "Fit Help: The Egalitarian Marriage in *Paradise Lost*," *Mosaic* 17 (1984): 29–48.

[131]Supply "nature" here.

[132]Adam is mentally and physically exhausted from the effort of debating his need for a mate with God; when God anesthetizes him for the operation, Adam is not even sure of the exact moment when God ceased speaking. Adam's experience is presented in terms of what appears to be a hypnotic trance (though of course hypnotism was unknown to Milton).

[133]"And the Lord God caused a deep sleep to fall upon Adam, and he slept; and he took one of his ribs, and closed up the flesh instead thereof; And the rib, which the Lord God had taken from man, made he a woman, and brought her unto the man" (Genesis 2.21-22).

[134]"Cell / Of Fancie" is a precise term describing what was thought to be a storage space in the brain for images gathered by the senses during waking time and then recombined by the fancy in sleep. "Imagination stored these data before passing them on to fantasy, which acted to combine and divide them, yielding new images, called phantasmata, with no counterparts in external reality" (Katherine Park, summarizing Aristotelian notions of the soul, in "The Organic Soul," *The Cambridge History of Renaissance Philosophy*, ed. Schmitt: 471). For a demonic use of the same cell of fancy, see 5.112-13.

[135]As in a state of religious ecstasy, when the soul was thought to be abstracted, or pulled out of, the body. Though the word is translated in the King James Genesis 2.21 as "deep sleep," in the Septuagint it is ἔκστασιν. See John Donne's poem "The Ecstasy" for application of the psychology involved in the "out of body" experience of two lovers.

[136]Though there is no biblical authority for it, the rib from which Eve was created was said to have been taken from Adam's left side. Pro-feminist commentators wrote that the left side was "neerest [Adam's] heart" ([4.484], hence the "cordial spirits" or fluids surrounding the heart), but antifeminist commentators concluded that Eve's nature was crooked because of the bent shape of the rib (see Utley, *The Crooked Rib*). Sin is born from the left side of Satan's forehead (2.755), which has led some critics to draw an association between Eve and Sin.

[137]The punctuation mark here in *1674* in copies I have examined is faint and blurred, but it is a semicolon; the comma of *1667* is preferable.

[138]Genesis 2.21 describes the operation: God "... took one of the ribs, and closed up the flesh instead thereof." The rib is "formd" and "fashond" in that its shape is changed from that of a rib to that of a woman. Fowler (8.469n), following Newton (8.469n), points out that this spelling, perhaps based on the French *façonner*, was introduced and then abandoned in the seventeenth century.

[139]Perhaps, as Thyer noted (qtd. in Newton 8.471n), derived from Giambattista Marino's description of the creation of Helen of Troy, which Fowler translates as "So well does beauty's aggregate / In that fair face summed up unite, / Whatever is fair in all the world / Flowers in her" (*Adone*, qtd. in Fowler 8.471-74n). If the allusion exists, the comparison it implies between Eve and Helen of Troy prefigures the danger inherent in Eve's beauty.

And into all things from her Aire inspir'd[141]
The spirit of love and amorous delight.
Shee[142] disappeerd, and left me dark, I wak'd
To find her,[143] or for ever to deplore
Her loss, and other pleasures all abjure: 480
When out of hope,° behold her, not farr off,   BEYOND ALL EXPECTATIONS
Such as I saw her in my dream, adornd
With what all Earth or Heaven could bestow
To make her amiable:° On she came,   WORTHY OF LOVE
Led by her Heav'nly Maker, though unseen,   485
And guided by his voice, nor uninformd
Of nuptial Sanctitie and marriage Rites:
Grace was in all her steps, Heav'n in her Eye,
In every gesture dignitie and love.
I overjoyd could not forbear aloud.[144]   490
    This turn hath made amends; thou has fulfill'd
Thy words, Creator bounteous and benigne,
Giver of all things faire, but fairest this
Of all thy gifts, nor enviest.[145] I now see
Bone of my Bone, Flesh of my Flesh, my Self[146]   495
Before me; Woman is her Name, of Man[147]
Extracted; for this cause he shall forgoe
Father and Mother, and to his Wife adhere;
And they shall be one Flesh, one Heart, one Soule.[148]
She heard me thus, and though divinely brought,   500
Yet Innocence and Virgin Modestie,[149]
Her vertue and the conscience° of her worth,   CONSCIOUSNESS
That would be woo'd, and not unsought be won,
Not obvious, not obtrusive, but retir'd,
The more desirable, or to say all,   505
Nature her self, though pure of sinful thought,
Wrought in her so, that seeing me, she turn'd;[150]

[handwritten margin notes: "Adam's joy at Eve's arrival"; "CONSTRUCTING"]

---

[141]The word "Aire" could be read as "breath" or "demeanor," as in the idiom "She had an air about her." But Eve also inspires or breathes into Adam the spirit (synonymous with "breath") of love and delight.

[142]One of a number of cases when *1674* doubles the single vowel of *1667* on a metrically stressed syllable. Fletcher believed that "the change is almost certainly intentional" (478n), but I would be cautious about making that assumption.

[143]Perhaps an echo of the rhythms of Sonnet 23: "I wak'd, she fled, and day brought back my night."

[144]"Overjoyed, I could not stop myself from saying aloud."

[145]"Nor [is Eve] given to me grudgingly or reluctantly." Richard Bentley wanted to emend the construction from "nor enviest" to "and dearest," but Zachary Pearce argued that "nor enviest" was "join'd in construction to thou hast fulfill'd" and that the sense was "Nor thinkest this gift too good for me" (qtd. Newton 494n). The transitive sense of envy as "grudge, give reluctantly" is cited in *OED* 3.

[146]As with "thy other self" in 450 above.

[147]See the note to 1.1 for an expanded meaning of "of Man."

[148]"And Adam said, This is now bone of my bones, and flesh of my flesh: she shall be called Woman, because she was taken out of man. Therefore shall a man leave his father and his mother, and shall cleave unto his wife: and they shall be one flesh" (Genesis 2.23–24). The Geneva Bible glosses "woman" as "Or, Mannes, because she commeth of man: for in Ebr[ew] Ish, is man, and Ishah the woman" and the Geneva Bible interprets the man's leaving his mother and father as signifying that "mariage requireth a greater duetie of us towarde our wives, then otherwise we are bounde to shewe to our parents" (marginal notes, 1560 ed.).

[149]Eve has a kind of innate, innocent coyness and modesty, which Fowler takes as evidence of the seventeenth-century "taste for disdain or denial on the lady's part" (511n), but I take Eve's "blushing like the Morn" (511 below) not as disdain but as unconscious admission of pleasure. Likewise, "Virgin Modestie" need not have any guilt attached, as Fowler admits. Even "obsequious Majestie" suggests only the act of following in a queenly way (i.e., with dignity).

[150]Eve's account of the same event varies from Adam's in some significant details. She says she turns from him to return to the fair image in the pool, which she thought "less faire, / Less winning soft, less amiablie milde, / Then that smooth watry image" of her own (4.478–80), until Adam finally convinces her "How beauty is excelld by manly grace / And wisdom, which alone is truly fair" (4.490–91). In both narratives, Adam appeals to her sense of domestic honor (in the Puritan marriage manual sense of the word—see Haller, "Hail" and Roland Frye, "Teachings") and submissive duty toward her

Wrought in her so, that seeing me, she turn'd;[150]
I follow'd her, she what was Honour knew,
And with obsequious Majestie approv'd
My pleaded reason. To the Nuptial Bowre   510
I led her blushing like the Morn:[151] all Heav'n,
And happie Constellations on that houre
Shed thir selectest influence;[152] the Earth
Gave sign of gratulation,°and each Hill;   JOY
Joyous the Birds; fresh Gales° and gentle Aires   BREEZES   515
Whisper'd it to the Woods, and from thir wings[153]
Flung Rose, flung Odours from the spicie Shrub,
Disporting, till the amorous Bird of Night[154]
Sung Spousal, and bid haste the Eevning Starr[155]
On his Hill top, to light the bridal Lamp.   520
Thus I have told thee all my State,° and brought   EVERYTHING ABOUT MY CIRCUMSTANCES
My Storie to the sum of earthly bliss
Which I enjoy, and must confess to find
In all things else delight indeed, but such
As us'd or not, works in the mind no change,   525
Nor vehement desire,[156] these delicacies
I mean of Taste, Sight, Smell,[157] Herbs, Fruits, and Flours,
Walks, and the melodie of Birds; but here
Farr otherwise, transported[158] I behold,
Transported touch; here passion first I felt,   530
Commotion° strange, in all enjoyments else   DISTURBANCE, PERTURBATION
Superiour and unmov'd, here onely weake

---

[150]Eve's account of the same event varies from Adam's in some significant details. She says she turns from him to return to the fair image in the pool, which she thought "less faire, / Less winning soft, less amiablie milde, / Then that smooth watry image" of her own (4.478–80), until Adam finally convinces her "How beauty is excelld by manly grace / And wisdom, which alone is truly fair" (4.490–91). In both narratives, Adam appeals to her sense of domestic honor (in the Puritan marriage manual sense of the word—see Haller, "Hail" and Roland Frye, "Teachings") and submissive duty toward her husband. "Marriage is intrinsically honorable," Milton wrote in *On Christian Doctrine*: "and it is not forbidden to any order of men" (1.10; Yale 6: 370). Perhaps the source of the Puritan veneration of domestic honor was Hebrews 13.4: "Marriage is honourable in all, and the bed undefiled: but whoremongerers and adulterers God will judge."
[151]Here blushing is certainly not a sign of guilt—it is connected here and at 11.184 with the dawn. As with Raphael's blush (619 below), it may be a sign of high but innocent pleasure.
[152]Astrological good fortune (the constellations are "happie" as portents of good fortune) is shed on Adam and Eve's nuptials by the position of the constellations, just as the "sweet influence" of the dancing Pleiades is shed on earth at the creation (7.375). After the Fall, the macrocosm will be knocked out of alignment and the stars and planets will begin to shed evil influence on human events (10.651–64). Even the Earth will be jolted out of polar alignment (10.668–71). As one microcosm, the pair Adam and Eve will also become "unhappy" in their alignment, and there will even be talk of divorce.
[153]The "Aires" have wings as they do in *Comus* 989; they whisper, they dispense roses and spicy odors, and they have the power to sing (playing on "airs" as melodies). All nature is celebrating the marriage and potential fecundity of Adam and Eve.
[154]The nightingale, amorous because it is associated with love or is itself loving. If Milton finds an alter-ego in the nightingale (see 3.38 and the note at that point; 5.40), then he is not far from singing the epithalamion of Adam and Eve in his own person. Compare the authorial aria "Haile wedded love" at 4.750–73, and the mention of Adam and Eve asleep, having been "lulld by Nightingales" (4.771). The sex of the nightingale was, however, ambivalent for Milton.
[155]In classical marriage hymns or epithalamia, the planet Venus, Hesperus or the evening star, lights the bridal lamp or a torch to the god of marriage, Hymen. As Fowler points out, "Evening Star" is a character in the second draft of Milton's projected drama on the Fall (519n). See Vergil, *Eclogues* 8.30, and Catullus, *Carminae* 42.1-4. For the various types of hymns in *Paradise Lost*, see Lewalski, *"Paradise Lost"* and Francis R. Blessington, "'That Undisturbed Song of Pure Concent': *Paradise Lost* and the Epic-Hymn," in *Renaissance Genres: Essays on Theory, History, and Interpretation*, ed. Barbara K. Lewalski (Harvard English Studies 14; Cambridge, MA: Harvard UP, 1986): 468–95.
[156]The potentially negative aspect of love, called "passion" in line 530 below, which Adam will endorse in the act of the Fall. See the argument to Book 9, "*vehemence of love*."
[157]The sense of touch may have been omitted because it is too closely associated with carnal desire, as at 579 below, where it is associated with copulation among the beasts.
[158]Being transported is a potentially dangerous experience, since it suggests not only being rendered ecstatic but being put in exile. The chain of associated words, "transported" (repeated for emphasis), "touch," "passion," "Commotion," "strange," and "passion," is also ominous.

Or from my side subducting,° took perhaps   EXTRACTING
More then enough; at least on her bestow'd
Too much of Ornament, in outward shew
Elaborate, of inward less exact.[161]
For well I understand in the prime end   540
Of Nature her th' inferiour, in the mind
And inward Faculties, which most excell,[162]
In outward also her resembling less
His Image who made both, and less expressing
The character of that Dominion giv'n   545
O're other Creatures; yet when I approach
Her loveliness, so absolute she seems
And in her self compleat,[163] so well to know
Her own, that what she wills to do or say,
Seems wisest, vertuousest, discreetest, best;   550
All higher knowledge in her presence falls
Degraded, Wisdom in discourse with her
Looses discount'nanc't, and like folly shewes;[164]
Authority and Reason on her waite,
As one intended first, not after made   555
Occasionally;[165] and to consummate° all,   MAKE PERFECT
Greatness of mind and nobleness thir seat
Build in her loveliest, and create an awe
About her, as a guard Angelic plac't.
To whom the Angel with contracted brow.   560
    Accuse not Nature,[166] she hath don her part;
Do thou but thine, and be not diffident
Of Wisdom, she deserts thee not, if thou
Dismiss not her, when most thou needst her nigh,
By attributing[167] overmuch to things   565
Less excellent, as thou thy self perceav'st.
For what admir'st thou, what transports thee so,
An outside? fair no doubt, and worthy well
Thy cherishing, thy honouring, and thy love,
Not thy subjection: weigh her with thy self;   570

---

[161]Adam's irrational accusation of Eve after the Fall (10.867–908) also builds on the idea that Eve's outward appearance is by nature corrupting, and the idea also figures into the accusation of the entire female sex by the antifeminist Chorus in *Samson Agonistes* (1025–30)—that women are somehow made defective in that their outward shell is elaborate or ornamental, whereas their inward being is less perfect or refined ("exact"). Adam seems to be accusing nature, or God, of creating an imperfect being in Paradise, which rightfully brings the rebuff from Raphael: "Accuse not Nature" (561 below).

[162]Adam acknowledges that his mind and inward faculties, "manly grace / And wisdom" (4.490–91) have been created superior to Eve's. Eve's "outside" also resembles the Maker's image less than Adam's and therefore should not be worshipped for itself; when her image is worshiped, her outside becomes an icon or idol and her worshiper becomes an idolater. Adam's image also better expresses authority or "Dominion"—power over the lower animals.

[163]The only being in creation complete in Himself is God.

[164]Adam skirts idolatry when he admits that knowledge or wisdom loses face (is "dis-countenanced") or appears to be folly when he is in Eve's company.

[165]Eve is made on the occasion of Adam's expressing his need for a helpmeet. The argument built on Eve's creation was that she was made because it was not good for man to be alone. Because she was created after and for Adam, marriage was instituted "with the husband having greater authority" (*On Christian Doctrine* 1.10; Yale 6: 355). Milton seems to accept the argument from 1 Corinthians 11.8–9: "For the man is not of the woman; but the woman of the man. Neither was the man created for the woman; but the woman for the man." Adam at this point is dangerously close to expressing the "vehemence of love" he is guilty of in the Fall, since his overly bright image of her is creating "awe" and shading out rightful images of wisdom, authority, and reason. Thus Raphael's frown should come as no surprise to the reader.

[166]If "God and Nature bid the same" (6.176), then Nature is an extension of God, expressed as feminine because "Mother Nature" (Milton does not use the phrase) is a spirit of fecundity. Raphael makes the connection between Nature and Wisdom, both of whom seem to be treated allegorically here. Though "Nature" is not a character in Milton's outlines for *Paradise Lost*, "Wisedom" is (compare 7.9, where the Muse is pictured in conversation with "Eternal wisdom").

[167]Apparently accented on the first and third syllables.

Then value:[168] Oft times nothing profits more
Then self esteem, grounded on just and right
Well manag'd; of that skill the more thou know'st,
The more she will acknowledge thee her Head,
And to realities yield all her shows;[169]   575
Made so adorn[170] for thy delight the more,
So awful,° that with honour thou maist love   AWE-INSPRING
Thy mate, who sees when thou art seen least wise.
But if the sense of touch whereby mankind
Is propagated seem such dear delight   580
Beyond all other, think the same voutsaf't
To Cattel and each Beast;[171] which would not be
To them made common and divulg'd,° if aught   DISTRIBUTED
Therein enjoy'd were worthy to subdue
The Soule[172] of Man, or passion in him move.   585
What higher in her societie thou findst
Attractive, human,[173] rational, love still;
In loving thou dost well, in passion not,
Wherein true Love consists not; love refines
The thoughts, and heart enlarges, hath his seat   590
In Reason, and is judicious, is the scale[174]
By which to heav'nly Love thou maist ascend,
Not sunk in carnal pleasure, for which cause
Among the Beasts no Mate for thee was found.[175]
To whom thus half abash't[176] *Adam* repli'd.   595
Neither her out-side formd so fair, nor aught
In procreation common to all kindes
(Though higher of the genial° Bed by far,   MARITAL
And with mysterious reverence I deem)[177]
So much delights me[178] as those graceful acts,   600

---

[168]Foreshadows the Son's judgment in Book 10.146–51.

[169]The word *shows* may mean "The external aspect[s] of a person or thing" (*OED* 2), but few senses of the word are positive. Raphael's remark seems to foreshadow Eve's behavior after the Fall, since she certainly has not yet "put on a show" or "acted" in front of Adam; nor does she, until after she is influenced by Satan. After the Fall, Eve's behavior does become theatrical: " . . . in her face excuse / Came Prologue, and Apologie to prompt" (9.853-54).

[170]Milton coined this adjectival form of what is usually a noun (*OED*, only instance). The Italian *adorno*, from which he may have derived his usage, means "naturally beautiful."

[171]To domesticated animals (the biblical "cattle") and to any wild animal.

[172]The *OED* defines "soul" (1.a) as "The principle of thought and action in man, commonly regarded as an entity distinct from the body; the spiritual part of man in contrast to the purely physical. Also occas., the corresponding or analogous principle in animals. Freq. in connexion with, or in contrast to, *body*."

[173]Before 1700 spelled with or without the final "e" could mean either "human" in the modern sense, or "humane," again in the modern sense.

[174]Taken from Neoplatonic theory of the ladder of love. According to Pietro Bembo as he is represented by Castiglione in *The Courtier*, "By the ladder whose lowest rung bears the image of sensual beauty, let us ascend to the sublime abode where heavenly, gracious and true beauty dwells, hidden in the secret recesses of God so that profane eyes may not see it" (translated from *Il libro del cortegiano*, ed. V. Cian [Florence, 1947], by Jill Kraye, in *The Cambridge History of Renaissance Philosophy*, ed. Schmitt: 356).

[175]The "proper fruit" of marriage, according to Milton in *On Christian Doctrine*, is the procreation of children. Since the fall of Adam, the relief of sexual desire has become "a kind of secondary end" (1.10; Yale 6: 370). Thus sexual desire in the unfallen world should have been less important than the desire to procreate.

[176]Note that Adam is only "half abash't": this would indicate that whatever his other half is might be inclined to overvalue Eve's beauty. Turner believes "Adam is only 'half-abasht' because Raphael's model of Love is only half true" (281), but the point is disputable.

[177]There seems to be nothing wrong, in Milton's moral scheme for the epic, in Adam's treating marriage as a holy mystery, and revering it as such, though Milton did attempt to demystify the legal institution of marriage throughout his divorce tracts. As he summarized, carefully, in *On Christian Doctrine*, "Marriage is, by definition, a union of the most intimate kind, but it is not indissoluble or indivisible" (1.10; Yale 6: 371). Also, Milton did not believe that marriage was a sacrament; in the *Doctrine and Discipline of Divorce*, souls in Hell ironically do "not affirm that mariage is either a Sacrament, or a mystery . . . " (Yale 2: 277). Was marriage a mystery to Milton, then? The editors of the Yale volume conclude that his treatment of marriage as a mystery (2: 258) "is not without an element of ambiguity" (277n).

[178]The text of *1667* includes a comma at this point.

Those thousand decencies that daily flow
From all her words and actions mixt with Love
And sweet compliance, which declare unfeign'd
Union of Mind, or in us both one Soule;[179]
Harmonie to behold in wedded pair   605
More grateful then harmonious sound to the eare.
Yet these subject not; I to thee disclose
What inward thence I feel, not therefore foild,[180]
Who meet with various objects, from the sense
Variously representing; yet still free   610
Approve the best, and follow what I approve.
To love thou blam'st me not, for love thou saist
Leads up to Heav'n, is both the way and guide;
Bear with me then, if lawful if what I ask;
Love not the heav'nly Spirits, and how thir Love   615
Express they,[181] by looks onely, or do they mix
Irradiance, virtual or immediate touch?[182]
    To whom the Angel with a smile that glow'd
Celestial rosie red, Loves proper hue,
Answer'd.[183] Let it suffice thee that thou know'st   620
Us happie, and without Love no happiness.
Whatever pure thou in the body enjoy'st
(And pure thou wert created) we enjoy
In eminence, and obstacle find none
Of membrane, joynt, or limb, exclusive barrs: 625
Easier then Air with Air, if Spirits embrace,
Total they mix, Union of Pure with Pure
Desiring; nor restrain'd conveyance need
As Flesh to mix with Flesh, or Soul with Soul.[184]
But I can now no more;[185] the parting Sun   630
Beyond the Earths green Cape and verdant Isles[186]
Hesperean sets, my Signal to depart.
Be strong, live happie, and love, but first of all
Him whom to love is to obey, and keep
His great command; take heed least Passion sway   635
Thy Judgement to do aught, which else free Will
Would not admit; thine and of all thy Sons

---

[179]Perhaps the clearest definition of Adam and Eve's indissoluable union in marriage: they are truly "one soul," and the adjective to be applied to them together is "sole."

[180]As long as Adam does not consent to his inward feelings he may remain sinless, according to Augustine's theory of concupiscence (sinful desire) preceding the act of sin: " . . . the evil act had never been done had not an evil will preceded it" (*City of God*, trans. Dodds: 460).

[181]"And how do they express their love?"

[182]Adam asks definitively how the angels make love, through mutual irradiation (exchange of light emanations), or through "virtual" touch ("virtual as in "[p]ossessed of certain physical virtues or capacities; effective in respect of inherent natural qualities or powers; capable of exerting influence by means of such qualities" [OED 1.b]), or by immediate touch, which I take to be similar to human lovemaking.

[183]It looks very much as if Adam is changing the subject, because he finds his near worship of Eve embarrassing to discuss with Raphael. Raphael's unexpected blush, "Celestial rosie red," is a delightful light touch which expresses the angel's humaneness, and the smile, issuing as all smiles do from the reason (see 9.239), expresses his tolerance and good humor. Fowler believes the angel's blush issues from his zeal or celestial ardor (618–20n), but I see no reason why an angel might not be allowed to blush in answer to an embarrassing question. Raphael's "Let it suffice thee . . . ," a schoolmasterish phrase, suggests good-humored embarrassment.

[184]Angels were supposed to make love by mingling essences somehow, and without friction (see West 169–73).

[185]"I can say no more at this time [because approaching sundown calls me back to Heaven]." Again, Raphael seems to be making excuses for not talking more about angelic sexuality.

[186]The "green Cape" is Cape Verde (where the modern city of Dakar is located, in Senegal) and the "verdant Isles" are the Cape Verde islands, a stopping place for Portuguese and English spice-traders in the seventeenth century, off the coast of Cape Verde and "Beneath th' *Azores*" (4.592).

The weal° or woe in thee is plac't; beware.   WELL-BEING
I in thy persevering shall rejoyce,
And all the Blest: stand fast;[187] to stand or fall   640
Free in thine own Arbitrement° it lies.   ABSOLUTE CHOICE
Perfet within, no outward aid require;[188]
And all temptation to transgress repel.
    So saying, he arose; whom *Adam* thus
Follow'd with benediction.[189] Since to part,   645
Go heavenly Guest, Ethereal Messenger,
Sent from[190] whose sovran goodness I adore.
Gentle to me and affable hath been
Thy condescension,[191] and shall be honour'd ever
With grateful Memorie: thou to mankind   650
Be good and friendly still, and oft return.
    So parted they, the Angel up to Heav'n
From the thick shade, and *Adam* to his Bowre.

The End of the Eighth Book.

---

[187]The punctuation in this line may give us some idea about how Milton or the compositor differentiated between the colon and semicolon. The colon seems to represent a full stop, but what comes after the colon seems to be the message coming from "all the Blest"; the elements before and after the semicolon are more closely related through the verb "stand." Hence it does not represent as strong a stop as the colon.

[188]"Since you are [created] perfect of yourself, you should ask for no outside aid."

[189]Benediction is used in the sense of *OED* 1.d: "as an expression of thanks; spec. as *grace* before or after meals." Milton is demystifying a word associated with Roman Catholic or Protestant church services. See *Paradise Regain'd* 3.127.

[190]Supply "Him."

[191]"Voluntary abnegation for the nonce of the privileges of a superior; affability to one's inferiors, with courteous disregard of difference of rank or position; condescendingness" (*OED* 1). Since Raphael is the "affable Arch-Angel" (7.41), the mutual courtesy and affability seems to fit the relationship between him and Adam and Eve.

Paradise Lost.

BOOK IX.

THE ARGUMENT.

Satan having compast the Earth, with meditated guile[1] returns as a mist[2] by Night into Paradise, enters into the Serpent sleeping. Adam and Eve in the Morning go forth to thir labours, which Eve proposes to divide in several places, each labouring apart: Adam consents not, alledging the danger, lest that Enemy, of whom they were forewarn'd, should attempt her found alone: Eve loath to be thought not circumspect or firm enough, urges her going apart, the rather desirous to make tryal of her strength;[3] Adam at last yields: The Serpent finds her alone; his subtle approach, first gazing, then speaking, with much flattery extolling Eve above all other Creatures. Eve wondring to hear the Serpent speak, asks how he attain'd to human speech and such understanding not till now; the Serpent answers, that by tasting of a certain Tree in the Garden he attain'd both to Speech and Reason, till then void of both: Eve requires him to bring her to that Tree, and finds it to be the Tree of Knowledge forbidden: The Serpent now grown bolder, with many wiles and arguments induces her at length to eat; she pleas'd with the taste deliberates a while whether to impart thereof to Adam or not, at last brings him of the Fruit, relates what perswaded her to eat thereof: Adam at first amaz'd, but perceiving her lost, resolves through vehemence of love[4] to perish with her; and extenuating the trespass,[5] eats also of the Fruit: The Effects thereof in them both; they seek to cover thir nakedness; then fall to variance and accusation of one another.

N O more of talk where God or Angel Guest
With Man, as with his Friend, familiar us'd
To sit indulgent, and with him partake
Rural repast,[6] permitting him the while
Venial discourse unblam'd:[7] I now must change
Those Notes to Tragic;[8] foul distrust, and breach
Disloyal[9] on the part of Man, revolt,
And disobedience: On the part of Heav'n

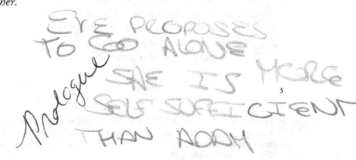

5

---

[1] To tempt Eve and Adam, Satan has devised a plan, with "meditated guile" or malice aforethought, which might be contrasted with the Epic Voice's "unpremeditated Verse" (24). Because Satan bears conscious malice toward Adam and Eve, and because he deceives Eve, he will not be forgiven—whereas humankind, "by fraud . . . seduc'd" (10.485) or "deceiv'd / By the other first," will "therefore . . . find grace" (3.130–31).

[2] Night mists and fogs were associated with evil and pestilence, since moist night air was supposed to have carried contagion; thus it is appropriate for Satan to disguise himself temporarily "wrapt in mist / Of midnight vapor" (158–59), as it is appropriate for the Elder Brother to report of the "Blew meager Hag or stubborn unlaid ghost" that each "walks by night / In fog, or fire, by lake or moorish fen . . . " (*Comus* 432–34). Like night, mists or fogs obscure vision or cause dimness of sight.

[3] Eve's motive for leaving Adam's side is that she does not want to be considered unthoughtful ("not circumspect" or "firm enough"). Thoughtfulness or "higher intellectual" (483) had been and would be more closely associated with Adam, as had firmness; in urging her separation, Eve may be competing with Adam as well as offering a trial of her own strength.

[4] An important phrase, because it contains Adam's motive to fall. "Love" of course is positive, but, as Fowler points out (note to Book 9 *Argument*), the root of vehemence is the Latin *vehemens*, with *ve* acting as a negative prefix offsetting *mens*, mind. Adam's mindless adoration of Eve corresponds to her careless venturing out, "mindless the while" (431 below). Mindlessness in love is a serious offence, since it implies that Adam has allowed passion or "vehement desire" (8.526) to rule over his reason: he thinks that he has specifically disobeyed the Archangel's injunction not to overvalue Eve's outside (8.568), or her beauty. If Eve is mindless when propping flowers, Adam is vehement in resolving to die with her. Despite the word *love*, Adam's mindlessness matches Eve's in recklessness.

[5] Adam will be "compleating . . . the mortal Sin / Original" (1003–04).

[6] "Eat a meal with him in the country." The image is of civilized and familiar discourse between humankind and angel within the peaceful and idyllic rural setting of Eden. Milton makes much of the familiar discourse between humans and divinities before the Fall, as in God's command to Raphael to talk with Adam "as friend with friend" (5.229). It would have been possible, Milton implies, for God himself, or one of the angelic "gods," to sit down with man fondly (Latin *indulgens*, "fond of"), even at a meal together.

[7] Both "Venial" ("forgivable") and "unblam'd" emphasize the sinlessness of the encounter between Raphael and Adam and Eve.

[8] The verb "change" suggests that the Epic Voice is beginning the process of narrating a tragedy. Shaw, "Euripidean," points out that Book 9 is roughly the size of a Euripidean tragedy—1100 lines—and that it is a complete play in itself.

[9] The "breach" is the gap between humankind and God caused by Adam and Eve's contemptible or "foul" distrust of God's command not to eat the fruit and by their disloyal disobedience.

Now alienated, distance and distaste,[10]
Anger and just rebuke, and judgement[11] giv'n,   10
That brought into this World a world of woe,
Sinne and her shadow Death,[12] and Miserie
Deaths Harbinger: Sad task, yet argument
Not less but more Heroic then the wrauth
Of stern *Achilles* on his Foe pursu'd   15
Thrice Fugitive[13] about Troy Wall; or rage
Of *Turnus* for *Lavinia* disespous'd,[14]
Or *Neptun's* ire or *Juno's*,[15] that so long
Perplex'd the Greek and *Cytherea's* Son;
If answerable style[16] I can obtaine   20
Of my Celestial Patroness,[17] who deignes
Her nightly visitation unimplor'd,
And dictates to me slumbring, or inspires
Easie my unpremeditated Verse:[18]
Since first this Subject for Heroic Song   25
Pleas'd me long choosing, and beginning late;
Not sedulous° by Nature to indite°   INDUSTRIOUS   WRITE ABOUT
Warrs, hitherto the onely Argument
Heroic deem'd, chief maistrie to dissect[19]
With long and tedious havoc° fabl'd Knights   UTTER DEVASTATION   30
In Battels feign'd;[20] the better fortitude
Of Patience and Heroic Martyrdom[21]

---

[10]In Milton's serious word-play, "distrust" and "disobedience" as well as "Disloyal[ty]" on man's part is matched by "distance" and "distaste" on God's part and man's "taste" in eating the fruit is matched by God's "distaste" for Adam and Eve's rebellion. For this type of echoing, cumulative, crescendoing word-play built on "dis-" words, see Ricks 66–75, which is complemented by Neil Forsyth, "Of Man's First Dis" and Corns, *Milton's Language* 83–91.

[11]Printed as two words in *1674*.

[12]The description of Death as a shadow of Sin might help the reader form some picture of that being, described before only in terms of shapelessness.

[13]The phrase pictures Achilles "three times running," since Achilles pursued Hector around the walls of Troy three times (*Iliad* 22) before killing him. Reducing the great warrior Hector to an image of a mere fleeing runner, Milton begins a reductive catalogue of chief events of classical epics, all of which his epic, being on a higher subject, will outreach or improve upon. The subject matter of classical epic is reduced to varieties of anger, whereas the Christian God's wrath will be answered by atonement which is then met with forgiveness and mercy.

[14]In the *Aeneid 7*, the hotheaded Turnus, who is, like Aeneas, a suitor of Lavinia, daughter of King Latinus, is protected by Juno but nevertheless eventually is killed in single combat by Aeneas. He is "disespous'd" because he never gets the chance to marry (espouse) Lavinia. Aeneas, on the other hand, does marry her and afterwards founds the city of Lavinium in her honor.

[15]Neptune in his anger begins to pursue "the Greek" Odysseus in *Odyssey* 19 after Odysseus has engineered the death of Neptune's son, the one-eyed giant Polyphemus. Juno's anger follows "*Cytherea's* [Venus's] Son" Aeneas from the onset of the *Aeneid*, partly because of Aeneas's foreshadowed conquering of Carthage, a city sacred to Juno and built by Dido.

[16]Poetic style which matches the quality of the subject matter. The phrase carries within it the idea of the responsibility of the poet directly to God. See Stein, *Answerable*.

[17]Urania is deliberately not named at this point (she was named in the invocation to Book 7, but her name was immediately brought into question [7.1–2]), probably because Milton is more interested in the meaning than the name, but Urania is celestial, being the Muse of Astronomy. Milton does not invoke divine aid as he did in Books 1, 3, and 7; it now is a constant presence to him (see Hunter and Davies, "Milton's Urania").

[18]There is no reason to doubt that Milton did feel himself inspired, visited nightly by a muse or holy spirit who dictated his "unpremeditated" verses to him as he in turn would dictate them to an amanuensis. For the tradition of the prophetic poet, see Kerrigan, *Prophetic Milton* 125–63.

[19]"The chief virtue or skill of which is to picture knights and reconstruct battles."

[20]Turning from classical epic, Milton now rejects the principal subject matter of Renaissance romantic epic writers like Boiardo and Tasso and even his own favorite Spenser. The romantic epics described battles at length; some of the romantic epics were allegorical and all involved "fabl'd Knights" in "Battels feign'd," in *Orlando Innamorato*, *Jerusalem Delivered*, or *The Faerie Queene*. But Homer, Apollonius, Vergil, and Lucan had all emphasized combat in their respective epics. See the Introduction, "A Short History of the Epic Genre."

[21]The phrase focuses meaning on passive heroism and quiet martyrdom, rather than the outward proof of physical ability demonstrated in chivalric epics from *The Song of Roland* to Spenser's *The Faerie Queene*, most of which are concerned primarily with describing real or allegorical combat. Milton's personal position as a blind man obliged by his condition to be passive—a regicide surrounded by the dangers of the Restoration—makes the image especially poignant. Perhaps the greatest embodiment of patience and heroic martyrdom (involving scorn but not death) in *Paradise Lost* is Abdiel, who in his passive resistance to the command of Satan to rebel against God, saying in effect "I will not fight," is the antithesis of the romantic warrior. For the theme, see Richard Jordan, *The Quiet Hero*.

Unsung; or to describe Races and Games,[22]
Or tilting Furniture,[23] emblazon'd Shields,
Impreses quaint, Caparisons and Steeds;[24]　　　　　　　　　　　　　　　　　　35
Bases and tinsel Trappings, gorgious Knights
At Joust and Torneament; then marshal'd Feast
Serv'd up in Hall with Sewers,° and Seneshals;　　　　　　ATTENDANTS AT ROYAL MEALS
The skill of Artifice or Office mean,[25]
Not that which justly gives Heroic name　　　　　　　　　　　　　　　　　　40
To Person or to Poem. Mee of these
Nor skilld nor studious, higher Argument
Remaines,[26] sufficient of it self to raise　　　　　　　　　　THE NAME OF EPIC
That name,° unless an age too late, or cold　　　　　　　　　　　　　　　　45
Climat,[27] or Years damp[28] my intended wing[29]
Deprest, and much they may, if all be mine,
Not Hers who brings it nightly to my Ear.[30]

　　The Sun was sunk, and after him the Starr
Of *Hesperus*,[31] whose Office is to bring
Twilight upon the Earth, short Arbiter°　　　　　　　　　　JUDGE　　　　50
Twixt Day and Night, and now from end to end
Nights hemisphere had veild the Horizon round:
When *Satan* who late° fled before the threats　　　　　　RECENTLY
Of *Gabriel* out of *Eden*, now improv'd°　　　　　　　　MADE EVEN WORSE
In meditated fraud and malice, bent[32]　　　　　　　　　　　　　　　　55

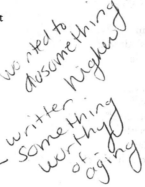

---

[22]The races and games Milton does describe are those of the fallen angels in Hell (2.528-32), parodies of the heroic Olympian or Pythian games of ancient Greece, and, by contrast, the "Heroic Games [of] / Th' unarm'd Youth of Heav'n" (4.551-54), but both descriptions are so short as to emphasize the unimportance of games except as exercises in military preparedness.

[23]"Furnishings or appointments [such as armor or heraldic banners] used in tilts or jousts." Furniture might include "military engines and defensive works" (*OED* 5.a, citing this instance). Milton seems to be using the word scornfully or sardonically.

[24]All the trappings of romantic epics, including jousts and banquets, where a seneschal would oversee the feast and sewers would serve food and drink. Milton uses the characteristic language of romantic epic, in which horses would be "steeds," horse-trappings would be "Caparisons," shields would be "emblazon'd" with heraldic devices, and knights would be "gorgious." "Impreses" are heraldic devices or emblems by which knights would identify themselves (Richard III's impress would be the wild boar, for instance). Most or all of these chivalric terms are characteristic of Spenser's *The Faerie Queene*.

[25]Considering that Milton told Dryden that Spenser was his "original" (see Parker 1: 635 and Patterson, *Milton* 17) and considering that Milton read widely in the Italian epic literature, his rejection of the subject matter of both the Italian romantic epic poets and Spenser seems a denial of his poetic roots. It is as forceful as is Jesus's rejection of classical learning in *Paradise Regain'd*, "But these are false, or little else but dreams, / Conjectures, fancies, built on nothing firm" (4.291-92). Certainly by the time he wrote *Paradise Regain'd* Milton felt that the "majestic unaffected style" of the Old Testament prophets, judges, and psalmists was superior to all other poetry written since. See Mary Ann Radzinowicz, *Milton's Epics* 202, for comments on Milton's use of psalmic style as a model for all poetic utterance. Milton makes the distinction between artisanship in writing poetry ("The skill of Artifice or Office mean") and inspired utterance. Low subject matter would seem to dictate lower quality of poetic composition. For an excellent essay on the effects of the romance tradition on Milton, see Annabel Patterson, "*Paradise Regain'd*: a Last Chance at True Romance," *Milton Studies* 17 (1983): 187-208.

[26]"Given that I am neither skilled in describing these lower subjects, nor studious of how to do so, my higher subject matter is what is left for me to expound."

[27]Milton gives evidence in *The Reason of Church-Government* that he feared that England's climate might be too cold and that the age of the world might be too late for epic to be successful: he felt " . . . that [only if] there be nothing advers in our climat, or the fate of this age" (Yale 1: 814) would it be possible to write an epic like that of Tasso, only on an English subject. As the Yale editor, Ralph Haug, wrote, "The theory that a cold climate would dull intelligence troubled Milton, who was very sensitive to English weather" (1: 814n93).

[28]A verb meaning "dampen" or "stifle, choke, extinguish" (*OED* 1). The adjective usage carried the the meaning of "noxious exhalation" (*OED* adj. 1), as in *Samson Agonistes*: " . . . I a Prisoner chain'd, scarce freely draw / The air imprison'd also, close and damp, / Unwholesome draught . . . " (7-9).

[29]Very rich and personal imagery. Milton pictures himself as an aged, bird-like figure (like the nightingale or like the Holy Spirit as a dove), living in the hostile climate of his native country (literally cold and at least figuratively dangerous to him), aware that the poetry he writes may be anachronistic in its values—but singing and flying despite being oppressed and even physically threatened.

[30]The end of the verse paragraph marks the end of Milton's speaking in his own voice in the epic, in this fourth and last invocation, the others being perhaps significantly placed at the beginnings of Books 1, 3, and 7.

[31]Venus, the evening star, which would rise in the general direction of the Hesperian Isles, off the coast of Africa. The Greek word transliterated "Hesperos" is the same as *vesper* in Latin, adopted by Christians to be the name of the last of the canonical hours. The Hesperian Isles would be due west of Mesopotamia, where Eden was supposed to be located.

[32]The moral dimensions in being "bent," especially if one is disguised as a serpent, are limitless.

On mans destruction, maugre what might hap[33]
Of heavier on himself, fearless return'd.
By Night he fled,[34] and at Midnight return'd
From compassing the Earth, cautious° of day,   WARY
Since *Uriel* Regent of the Sun descri'd°   OBSERVED   60
His entrance, and forewarnd the Cherubim
That kept thir watch; thence full of anguish driv'n,
The space of seven continu'd Nights he rode
With darkness, thrice the Equinoctial Line
He circl'd, four times cross'd the Carr of Night   65
From Pole to Pole, traversing each Colure;[35]
On the eighth return'd, and on the Coast averse[36]
From entrance or Cherubic Watch, by stealth
Found unsuspected way.[37] There was a place,
Now not,[38] though Sin, not Time, first wraught the change,   70
Where *Tigris* at the foot of Paradise
Into a Gulf shot under ground, till part
Rose up a Fountain by the Tree of Life;
In with the River sunk, and with it rose
Satan[39] involv'd in rising Mist, then sought   75
Where to lie hid; Sea he had searcht and Land
From Eden over *Pontus*, and the Poole
Mæotis, up beyond the River *Ob*;[40]
Downward as farr Antartic; and in length
West from *Orontes* to the Ocean barr'd   80
At *Darien*, thence to the Land where flowes
Ganges and *Indus*: thus the Orb° he roam'd   EARTH'S SPHERE
With narrow° search; and with inspection deep   PRECISE
Consider'd every Creature, which of all
Most opportune might serve his Wiles, and found   85
The Serpent suttlest Beast of all the Field.[41]
Him after long debate, irresolute
Of thoughts revolv'd, his final sentence chose

---

[33]"In spite of what might happen." The word *maugre*, "in spite of," is Spenserian usage and an archaism during Milton's lifetime.
[34]The cowardly "fled" negates the effect of "fearless" in the previous line.
[35]Samuel Johnson's definition of **colures** might best be quoted in full: "Two great circles supposed to pass through the poles of the world: one through the equinoctial points Aries and Libra; the other through the solstitial points, Cancer and Capricorn. They are called the equinoctial and solstitial *colures*, and divide the ecliptick into four equal parts" (*Dictionary*, 1765 ed.). The "Carr of Night" I take to be the chariot of the moon. As Fowler points out (9.63n), Satan's week is a travesty of the divine week of creation.
[36]The side opposite from the entrance to Eden, where cherubim are on guard.
[37]Newton summarizes Satan's journey: " . . . Satan was three days compassing the earth from east to west, and four days from north to south, but still kept always in the shade of night; and after a whole week's peregrination in this manner on the eighth night return'd by stealth into Paradise" (63n).
[38]Eden does not exist "now," at the time the reader is reading the poem, after the Fall. Milton in describing Satan's journeys around the Earth shifts temporal perspective, projecting images of the universe both before and after the poles were tilted as a result of the Fall (10.668-71).
[39]The name would normally be italicized. The compositor of *1674* slavishly follows his copy text, *1667*, against the house style of either book. Satan enters Eden via the Tigris, pictured as a river that goes underground after issuing appropriately from the north, the direction identified with Satan or his legions (1.351, 5.689) and appropriately rises in a mist, which would have had the potential to become, in the fallen world, a source of pestilence.
[40]In searching for a hiding place, Satan has flown over the Earth from Eden to Pontus, the Black Sea, and from Palus Maeotis, the Sea of Azov adjacent to the Black Sea, beyond the river Ob, in Siberia, which empties into the Arctic Ocean. He will continue down into Antarctica, crossing the river Orontes in Syria, then the Pacific Ocean which is barred by the isthmus of Darien (now Panama). The usage "barr'd" may be based on Job 38.10, where the Lord describes the laying of the foundations of the earth and breaking up the sea, " . . . set[ting] bars and doors" on it. The Ganges, though far from Mesopotamia, was identified with Pison (Genesis 2.10-11), one of the rivers of Eden; the Ganges and Indus are the principal rivers of India.
[41]Following Genesis 3.1: "Now the serpent was more subtil than any beast of the field which the Lord God had made."

Fit Vessel, fittest Imp[42] of fraud, in whom
To enter, and his dark suggestions hide   90
From sharpest sight: for in the wilie Snake,
Whatever sleights[43] none would suspicious mark,
As from his wit and native suttletie
Proceeding, which in other Beasts observ'd
Doubt might beget of Diabolic pow'r   95
Active within beyond the sense of brute.[44]
Thus he resolv'd, but first from inward griefe
His bursting passion into plaints thus pour'd:[45]

    O Earth, how like to Heav'n, if not preferr'd
More justly, Seat worthier of Gods, as built   100
With second thoughts,[46] reforming what was old!
For what God after better worse would build?[47]
Terrestrial Heav'n, danc't round by other Heav'ns
That shine, yet bear thir bright officious° Lamps,   OBLIGING, KIND
Light above Light, for thee alone, as seems,   105
In thee concentring all thir precious beams
Of sacred influence:[48] As God in Heav'n
Is Center, yet extends to all, so thou
Centring receav'st from all those Orbs; in thee,
Not in themselves, all thir known vertue appeers   110
Productive in Herb, Plant, and nobler birth
Of Creatures animate with gradual[49] life
Of Growth, Sense, Reason, all summ'd up in Man.
With what delight could I have walkt thee round,
If I could joy in aught, sweet interchange   115
Of Hill, and Vallie, Rivers, Woods and Plaines,
Now Land, now Sea, and Shores with Forrest crownd,
Rocks, Dens, and Caves; but I in none of these
Find place or[50] refuge; and the more I see
Pleasures about me, so much more I feel   120
Torment within me, as from the hateful siege

Satan's Soliloquy

many places can hide on Earth

---

[42]The word here does not represent the modern sense of "mischievous little devil" but the seventeenth-century gardening usage of "slip to be grafted on a tree." Here Satan grafts himself on the Serpent, or possesses his body, "imping" the Serpent; the notion of demonic possession may be at work. Satan is pictured here debating with himself, the involutions and contradictions of his own mind echoing the coiling of the serpent's body. Unlike his other appearances as lion, toad, cormorant, or whatever beast he chooses, here he joins with another being in a parody of the Incarnation.

[43]This was written "fleights" in *1667*, which Fletcher believes was due to foul case: the compositor of *1667* pulled the ligature "fl" from his box rather than "sl," but the compositor of *1674* was perhaps instructed to correct the error in his copy-text.

[44]Theologians had often debated the problem with the Serpent's body—the body of an apparently innocent animal—being used by Satan as an instrument of evil, but Genesis had remarked that the Serpent was already "subtle" (3.1) and serpent lore held that the animal was naturally wise. The Geneva Bible editors comment "As Satan can change him selfe into an Angel of light, so did he abuse the wisdome of the serpent to deceave man" and "God suffered Satan to make the serpent his instrument and to speak in him" (1560 ed.). In *Paradise Lost*, the Serpent is used symbolically as an instrument by Satan and punished symbolically by God after the Fall, "in mysterious terms, judg'd as then best" (10.173).

[45]The forced alliteration may indicate the falsity of Satan's passion. Satan's behavior here is very much like what Raphael warned Adam against: an outburst of passion expressed in a "plaint," like a lamentative poem or "complaint" (*OED* 2.b). Satan's apostrophe to the earth and soliloquy here correspond closely with his apostrophe to the sun and soliloquy at 4.32–113, before which he is also pictured as "much revolving" (31), since he is suffering from "revolved thoughts."

[46]That is, profiting from the earlier creation of Heaven (as if God could have second thoughts).

[47]Illogical theology, since an omniscient God would not need to learn from earlier mistakes.

[48]Satan pictures the universe as geocentric, but in terms which suggest that humankind should feel egocentric as well.

[49]"Of or pertaining to degree" (*OED* 1). The very life of the creatures is in accord with their rank in the scale of nature, with the whole scale "summ'd up in Man." Ranking would be determined on the basis of size, variety of senses, and ability to reason. Vegetable life can only grow; animal life other than man can grow and is capable of sense impressions; but only humankind can reason.

[50]Bentley argued that "or" should be "of" here, but Newton paraphrased the sense of the passage as "*but I in none of these find place* to dwell in *or refuge* from divine vengeance" (9.119n).

Of contraries; all good to me becomes
Bane,[51] and in Heav'n much worse would be my state.
But neither here seek I, no nor in Heav'n
To dwell, unless by maistring Heav'ns Supreame;[52]   *— if he can be in charge*   125
Nor hope to be my self[53] less miserable
By what I seek, but others to make such
As I, though thereby worse to me redound:
For onely in destroying I find ease
To my relentless thoughts; and him destroyd,   *Revenge*   130
Or won to what may work his utter loss,
For whom all this was made, all this will soon
Follow, as to him linkt in weal or woe,[54]
In wo then; that destruction wide may range:
To mee shall be the glorie sole among   135
The infernal Powers, in one day to have marr'd
What he *Almightie*[55] styl'd, six Nights and Days[56]
Continu'd making, and who knows how long
Before had bin contriving, though perhaps[57]   *exaggeration —*
Not longer then since I in one Night freed   *really a third*   140
From servitude inglorious welnigh half[58]
Th' Angelic Name, and thinner left the throng
Of his adorers: hee to be aveng'd,
And to repair his numbers thus impair'd,
Whether such vertue spent of old now faild   *— at the very least*   145
More Angels to Create, if they at least   *if they're his*
Are his Created, or to spite us more,
Determin'd to advance into our room[59]
A Creature form'd of Earth, and him endow,
Exalted from so base original,   150
With Heav'nly spoils, our spoils: What he decreed
He effected; Man he made, and for him built
Magnificent this World, and Earth his seat,
Him Lord pronounc'd, and, O indignitie!
Subjected to his service Angel wings,   155
And flaming Ministers[60] to watch and tend

---

[51]"That which causes death or destroys life" (*OED* 2), with overtones of "poison" (*OED* 2.b) and "fatal mischief" (*OED* 5). Satan's statement here reverses what might have seemed an heroically negative contention in the earlier soliloquy that begins "Evil be thou my Good" (4.110).

[52]A noun here, meaning "A supreme authority" (*OED* B.1). Compare "Their King, their Leader, and Supream on Earth" (*Paradise Regain'd* 1.99).

[53]Fletcher believes that there should be a comma here, since the compositor left a space for it, and that the compositor of the third edition left a space after "less" for a comma, but such reasoning presumes two similar mistakes and I disagree.

[54]A common verbal formula meaning "In very good or very bad fortune." Note that Satan makes a link between himself and Adam, in an attempt to capture an ally and thereby deny Adam free will.

[55]A use of italics to emphasize the word as word, or the word as quoted word. The meaning is "He who *calls* himself 'Almighty.'"

[56]It is at least amusing to speculate on where Satan got his information about how long it took God to create the world. Perhaps, as Fowler says, "Milton nodded" (9.136–38n). What is important is Satan's arrogance in saying God "styl'd" himself almighty: God's omnipotence is not a matter of propaganda or public relations.

[57]Satan's doubt here echoes his "perhaps" (4.112) in an earlier and similar soliloquy.

[58]As usual, Satan is stretching the truth, even to himself, since the figure was traditionally assumed to be one-third of the host of heaven, and Milton assumes it to be so at 4.869. Also, God is capable of vengeance, but not of spite, which, along with envy, is a Satanic motive (as at 2.384). Satan throughout the passage is imputing his own motives to God, and impugning God's motives.

[59]That is, into the place of the fallen angels in Heaven. Satan tries to deny that God created him or the angels (signaled by the "if" in 146), but the reader should remember that Satan has admitted that God created him (4.43). Also, the concept of "spoils" is alien to the way God conducts warfare, though the word can simply mean "possessions or offices" (*OED* 1) and the Son in Book 3 predicts the Resurrection in terms of contempt for Satan's spoils: " . . . I shall rise Victorious, and subdue / My vanquisher, spoild of his vanted spoile . . . " (250–51).

[60]The cherubim are associated with flames or flaming swords, as in 11.101 or 120, and, metaphorically, with flaming zeal.

Thir earthy Charge: Of these the vigilance
I dread, and to elude, thus wrapt in mist
Of midnight vapor glide obscure,[61] and prie
In every Bush and Brake,° where hap may finde   THICKET   160
The Serpent sleeping, in whose mazie foulds[62]
To hide me, and the dark intent I bring.
O foul descent! that I who erst contended
With Gods to sit the highest, am now constraind[63]
Into a Beast, and mixt with bestial slime,   165
This essence to incarnate and imbrute,
That to the hight of Deitie aspir'd;
But what will not Ambition and Revenge
Descend to? who aspires must down as low
As high he soard, obnoxious° first or last   TOOLS   170
To basest things. Revenge, at first though sweet,
Bitter ere long back on it self recoiles;[64]
Let it; I reck not, so it light well aim'd,
Since higher I fall short, on him who next
Provokes my envie, this new Favorite   175
Of Heav'n, this Man of Clay, Son of despite,
Whom us the more to spite his Maker rais'd
From dust: spite then with spite is best repaid.
    So saying, through each Thicket Danck or Drie,
Like a black mist[65] low creeping, he held on   180
His midnight search, where soonest he might finde
The Serpent: him fast sleeping soon he found
In Labyrinth of many a round self-rowld,
His head the midst, well stor'd with suttle wiles:
Not yet in horrid Shade or dismal Den,   185
Nor[66] nocent yet, but on the grassie Herbe[67]

---

[61]A deeply ironic contrast between statement and action, since Satan has just supposedly been taking the unfallen angels' part, as if inciting more of them to rebellion, in labeling them "subjected" to man, yet immediately he admits that he has run and hid out of fear of the angels he has been expressing concern for. Mists and fogs, both literal and figurative, are again presumed to be demonically inspired and to cause confusion or disorientation. See note 2 above.

[62]The twists and turns of the Serpent's body, expressed in mazes, in shifting shapes, and in duplicating folds, are fitting images of the Satanic mind, as is the recoiling cannon of 172 below. Only in such spiraling and recoiling or "rebounding" shapes can Satan find any hiding place. The ironic contrast is between angel of light, what Satan was as Lucifer, and lowly creature of earth and darkness. Since snakes and worms were associated, both were supposed to produce coatings of "bestial slime." And just as the Son will become incarnate as Jesus, Satan, in an ironic and perverse parallel, is incarnated in bestial slime as a snake.

[63]Probably "compressed" (*OED* 7), considering that Satan's body (his essence?) must have been dilated or compacted to fit into that of the Serpent. But Fowler is correct (9.164n) in suggesting "forced" or "produced in opposition to nature" (*OED* 2) as a valid alternative.

[64]The reader should probably keep in mind that the fallen angels invented gunpowder and cannonry as well as hollow military formations (the "hollow Cube / . . . [of] devilish Enginrie" in 6.552–53) and that Satan's hollowness corresponds to the tube of the weapons. His schemes are always backfiring and his trajectory always falls short. Satan's "I reck not" is almost infantile in its petulance.

[65]DuBartas's Satan moves in the same fashion toward the temptation of Eve:
    Sometimes me seemes (troubling *Eves* spirit) the fiend
    Made her this speaking fancy apprehend.
    For as in liquid cloudes exhaled thicklie
    Water and ayre (as moist) do mingle quickly:
    The evill Angels slide too-easily,
    As subtile spirits, into our fantasie.
        (*Divine Weekes* 2.1.2.135–40; Snyder 1: 342)

[66]The line in *1667* begins "Not." "Nor" may represent either a correction or another problem caused by foul case, since, "t" and "r" resemble one another closely; also, the compositor may have made an unconscious connection with the "Not" in the same position one line above. "Nor nocent" is Milton's characteristically inverted way of saying "not yet aware" or "not yet fallen." The Serpent is not yet aware of evil, but he is already "stor'd with suttle wiles." The Serpent in Genesis is also described as "subtle" before any temptation occurs.

[67]Editors since Newton (186n) have pointed out that the related phrase in Vergil is *graminis attigit herbam* (*Eclogue* 5.26).

Fearless unfeard he slept: in at his Mouth
The Devil enterd, and his brutal sense,
In heart or head, possessing soon inspir'd
With act intelligential;[68] but his sleep   190
Disturbd not, waiting close th' approach of Morn.
Now when as sacred Light began to dawne
In Eden on the humid° Flours, that breathd   MOIST
Thir morning incense, when all things that breathe,[69]
From th' Earths great Altar send up silent praise   195
To the Creator, and his Nostrils[70] fill
With grateful Smell, forth came the human pair
And joind thir vocal Worship to the Quire
Of Creatures wanting voice, that done, partake
The season, prime for sweetest Sents and Aires:[71]   200
Then commune[72] how that day they best may ply
Thir growing work: for much thir work outgrew
The hands dispatch of two Gardning so wide.°   WIDELY
And *Eve* first to her Husband thus began.[73]

    Adam, well may we labour still to dress   205
This Garden, still to tend Plant, Herb and Flour,[74]
Our pleasant task enjoyn'd, but till more hands
Aid us,[75] the work under our labour grows,
Luxurious° by restraint; what we by day   LUXURIANT
Lop overgrown, or prune, or prop, or bind,[76]   210
One night or two with wanton growth derides
Tending to wilde. Thou therefore now advise

---

[68]If animals could not normally act following a directive of the intellect, intelligent action will be exceptional (or perverse) coming from an animal. Satan's hiding in the Serpent's body will be nearly the first instance (see 4.396–408) of demonic possession. All serpents will therefore be symbolically punished after the Fall by the enmity placed by God between them and the descendants of Eve. In his act of possession, Satan "inspires" the Serpent's body, placing an intelligence within it that moves it to act above its beastly station. Satan causes the Serpent to talk either by creating sound waves vibrating the Serpent's tongue or by breathing air through the Serpent's mouth, which suggests the playing of a reed instrument.

[69]Both early editions have "breath," but I agree with Fletcher that the verb form should have an "e" as directed for Book 5.193 in the *1668 Errata*.

[70]Though the idea of an anthropomorphic God having nostrils may seem ludicrous, God is said to enjoy the "sweet savour" of the burnt offerings of Noah (Genesis 8.20–21) or of a priest (Leviticus 1.9).

[71]Very likely musical airs rather than breezes, "vocal Worship" to accompany the burnt offerings. "Quire" can have the sense that now only obtains to the ordered arrangement of pages of paper: "orderly group." It is as if voiceless nature and humankind, capable of song, gathered together at the hour of prime (the first canonical hour) to praise God through burnt offerings and song.

[72]Accented on the first syllable (see *OED* 1). Probably means "To hold intimate (chiefly mental or spiritual) intercourse [*with*]" (*OED* 7, citing *Paradise Regain'd* 2.261).

[73]As Fowler points out (9.204n), Eve speaks first here, something that has not happened before. Her speaking first, however, indicates that the distinctions between male and female decorum are not enforced before the Fall and that she has not violated any code of sexual conduct: no one tells her "Do not speak unless spoken to." Her speaking first, however, especially "to her Husband," may indicate the germ of rebellion against hierarchy. Her suggestion that they divide their labors, though wrong-headed, is not culpable: it is Adam's responsibility to correct it. Thus they act together in allowing Eve to face alone a danger they both have been warned about; Adam will be no less culpable than Eve. For an exposition of this passage along the lines that "Adam does the wrong thing for good reasons," see John Reichert, "'Against His Better Knowledge': A Case for Adam," *ELH* 48 (1981): 98.

[74]Eve makes the distinction among plants that can grow high above the ground, herbaceous growth near the surface, and flowers, presumably in the middle area. She will continue to be associated more closely than Adam with maintaining the garden. The word *dress* indicates her attention to controlling nature. The garden is on the verge of wildness and wantonness (like Eve's ringlets at 4.306) and it needs constant and intelligent care, as directed ("enjoyn'd") by God. The compositor of *1674* corrected a full stop in *1667* after "Flour."

[75]One of a number of references (compare 4.629) to the possibility of children, a question debated by theologians arguing about the transmission of original sin. If Adam and Eve had sex in Paradise while innocent, and Eve became pregnant (a certainty, according to St. Augustine in *City of God* 14.21, 22), their first child would have been Cain. Milton does not seem to believe what Augustine did, that "it was after they were expelled from it [Eden] that they came together to beget children . . ." (469, trans. Dods). On the question of intercourse without pregnancy, see Turner, *One Flesh* 287–89—his conclusion is that "Milton is entirely at a loss to explain why God has not allowed Eve to conceive" (287).

[76]The various duties of gardeners: cutting back overgrown branches, pruning, propping weakened or fruit-bearing branches or vines, or binding branches so that fruit receives more sun, as in espaliered fruit trees tied against a wall.

Or hear[77] what to my minde first thoughts present,[78]
Let us divide our labours, thou where choice
Leads thee, or where most needs, whether to wind   215
The Woodbine round this Arbour, or direct
The clasping Ivie where to climb,[79] while I
In yonder[80] Spring° of Roses intermixt   THICKET
With Myrtle, find what to redress° till Noon: PROP UP AGAIN
For while so near each other thus all day   220
Our taske we choose, what wonder if so near
Looks intervene and smiles, or object new
Casual discourse draw on, which intermits
Our dayes work brought to little, though begun
Early, and th' hour of Supper comes unearn'd.[81]   225
        To whom mild answer *Adam* thus return'd.[82]
Sole *Eve*, Associate sole,[83] to me beyond
Compare above all living Creatures deare,
Well hast thou motion'd,° well thy thoughts imployd   PROPOSED
How we might best fulfill the work which here   230
God hath assign'd us, nor of me shalt pass
Unprais'd: for nothing lovelier can be found
In Woman, then to studie houshold good,
And good workes in her Husband to promote.
Yet not so strictly hath our Lord impos'd   235
Labour, as to debarr° us when we need   PROHIBIT
Refreshment, whether food, or talk between,
Food of the mind, or this sweet intercourse
Of looks and smiles, for smiles from Reason flow,[84]
To brute deni'd, and are of Love the food,   240
Love not the lowest end of human life.
For not to irksom toile, but to delight
He made us, and delight to Reason joyn'd.
These paths & Bowers doubt not but our joynt hands
Will keep from Wilderness° with ease, as wide   WILDNESS   245
As we need walk, till younger hands ere long
Assist us: But if much converse° perhaps   CONVERSATION

---

[77]The "bear" of *1674* makes less sense than does the "hear" of *1667*. I assume the compositor had a problem seeing the shape of the letter.

[78]Modern punctuation usage might prefer a colon at this point.

[79]With irony that foreshadows what will help to cause the Fall, Eve suggests that Adam carry on duties of propping up or tying up weaker vines. When Eve separates herself from Adam, she will herself prop flowers but she will herself be described as a flower away from her "best prop" (433), Adam. The image of marriage often expressed in terms of elm tree and vine was a common one, and Milton may be allowing Eve to speak emblematically. See Todd Sammons, "'As the Vine Curls Her Tendrils': Marriage Topos and Erotic Countertopos in Paradise Lost," *Milton Quarterly* 20 (1986): 117–27.

[80]The word usually meant "within sight," though possibly at some distance. The possibility that Eve is within sight of Adam when she meets the Serpent is an enticing one, as Ann Torday Gulden has pointed out to me (e-mail 4 December 1997). It is possible that she is within sight yet he doesn't see her.

[81]Eve should probably not be thought of in the modern capacity of efficiency expert, though she does suggest division of labor based on work loss due to billing and cooing. She is arguing for the dignity and even the necessity for labor within household economy, a position taken by many of the Puritan books of marital instruction. Adam's praise for Eve's attention to studying "houshold good" indicates that Milton is seeing Adam and Eve in terms of ideal domestic economy. See Haller, "Hail Wedded Love."

[82]At this point Adam is not at all upset, as indicated by the adjective "mild." He will grow increasingly perturbed during the discussion. His mildness will be answered by her "Virgin Majestie" (270 below).

[83]The repetition of the adjective "sole" stresses not only the uniqueness of Eve (Latin *solus*, "alone") but the one-ness of Adam and Eve, who are "one Flesh, one Heart, one Soul" (8.499) and "Soul partner[s]" (4.411) quite literally. See Turner, *One Flesh*, for all the implications of these terms.

[84]A significant interpretation of the source of humor, which Adam extols as separating human from beast and for promoting or encouraging love. What Mikhail Bakhtin writes about late medieval laughter might be applicable here: "It was understood that fear never lurks behind laughter (which does not build stakes) and that hypocrisy and lies never laugh but wear a serious mask. Laughter created no dogmas and could not become authoritarian; it did not convey fear but a feeling of strength. It was linked with the procreating act, with birth, renewal, fertility, abundance" (*Rabelais* 95).

Thee satiate, to short absence I could yield.
For solitude somtimes is best societie.[85]
And short retirement urges sweet returne.   250
But other doubt° possesses me, least harm   FEAR
Befall thee sever'd from me; for thou knowst
What hath bin warn'd us, what malicious Foe
Envying our happiness, and of his own
Despairing, seeks to work us woe and shame   255
By sly assault; and somwhere nigh at hand
Watches, no doubt, with greedy hope to find
His wish and best advantage, us asunder,
Hopeless to circumvent us joynd, where each
To other speedie aide might lend at need;[86]   260
Whether his first design be to withdraw
Our fealtie[87] from God, or to disturb
Conjugal[88] Love, then which perhaps no bliss
Enjoy'd by us excites his envie more;
Or° this, or worse, leave not the faithful side   EITHER   265
That gave thee being, still shades thee and protects.
The Wife, where danger or dishonour[89] lurks,
Safest and seemliest by her Husband staies,
Who guards her, or with her the worst endures.
     To whom the Virgin Majestie of *Eve*,   270
As one who loves, and some unkindness meets,
With sweet austeer composure thus reply'd.[90]
     Ofspring of Heav'n and Earth, and all Earths Lord,
That such an Enemie we have, who seeks
Our ruin, both by thee informd I learne,   275
And from the parting Angel over-heard
As in a shadie nook I stood behind,
Just then returnd at shut of Evening Flours.[91]
But that thou shouldst my firmness therfore doubt
To God or thee, because we have a foe   280
May tempt it, I expected not to hear.
His violence thou fearst not, being such,
As wee, not capable of death or paine,
Can either not receave, or can repell.

don't doubt me Adam

---

[85]Adam is, for the sake of argument, allowing the philosophical position of Cicero and, to a lesser extent Horace, which had become a commonplace in the seventeenth century, that solitude is sometimes a more healthy condition than involvement in public life. For the context, see Andrew Marvell's poem "The Garden."

[86]The help in this case is mutual, though Adam does have superior physical strength. The idiom "at need" can be rendered "when needed."

[87]Originally the obligation of a medieval serf toward the landowner, but here with the transferred sense, "liberty" (see *OED* 3, which cites 3.204, "breaks his fealtie" [to God]).

[88]Apparently accented on the second syllable throughout *Paradise Lost*.

[89]Loss of domestic dignity in this case, but "honor" can also mean "chastity." Milton may be setting up an overtone with "Virgin" just below.

[90]The epithet "Virgin Majestie" suggests that Eve feels her regality threatened by being told that she should be guarded or protected by her husband. Dudley R. Hutcherson, in "Milton's Epithets for Eve," *University of Virginia Studies* ns 4 (1951): 253–60, discusses the progression from the Epic Voice's "Virgin Majestie" here to "immortal *Eve*" (291 below) to "O Woman" (343), as Adam becomes more and more angry or "fervent." Although a comma follows this line in *1674*, *1667* prints a period, the usual practice before a direct quotation.

[91]Eve has been listening—innocently—at the right moment and has heard Raphael warn Adam specifically about Satan, but discovering exactly when or even how she is listening is a puzzlement. She must have heard what is narrated in Book 7, since what Raphael says in Book 8 has little to do with Satan and she is described leaving Adam and Raphael voluntarily at 8.40–63. Raphael does use the word "enemie" at 8.234 to describe any fallen angel attempting to leave Hell, but Satan is not mentioned by name in Books 7 or 8. The last time Raphael calls Satan "envious Foe" is at 7.139. Eve does know of the prohibition against eating the fruit, since Raphael told Adam to warn her at 6.908–09; such knowledge is necessary for her part in the Fall, since otherwise she would not have been warned to avoid the fruit. Fowler writes that Eve was present at that time (9.276n), which is inaccurate.

His fraud is then thy fear, which plain inferrs   285
Thy equal fear that my firm Faith and Love
Can by his fraud be shak'n or seduc't;[92]
Thoughts, which how found they harbour in thy brest,[93]
Adam, misthought[94] of her to thee so dear?
   To whom with healing words *Adam* replyd.   290
2^d — Daughter of God and Man, immortal *Eve*,[95]
For such thou art, from sin and blame entire:
Not diffident° of thee do I dissuade   MISTRUSTFUL
Thy absence from my sight, but to avoid
Th' attempt it self, intended by our Foe.   295
For hee who tempts, though in vain, at least asperses[96]
The tempted with dishonour foul, suppos'd
Not incorruptible of Faith,° not prooff   FAITHFULNESS
Against temptation: thou thy self with scorne
And anger wouldst resent the offer'd wrong,   300
Though ineffectual found: misdeem not° then,   DON'T THINK BADLY
If such affront I labour to avert
From thee alone, which on us both at once
The Enemie, though bold, will hardly dare,
Or daring, first on mee th' assault shall light.   305
Nor thou his malice and false guile contemn;°   CONDEMN
Suttle he needs must be, who could seduce
Angels,[97] nor think superfluous others aid.
I from the influence of thy looks receave
Access[98] in every Vertue, in thy sight   310
More wise, more watchful, stronger, if need were
Of outward strength; while shame, thou looking on,
Shame to be overcome or over-reacht
Would utmost vigor raise, and rais'd unite.
Why shouldst not thou like sense within thee feel   315
When I am present, and thy trial choose
With me, best witness of thy Vertue tri'd.
   So spake domestick *Adam* in his care
And Matrimonial Love;[99] but *Eve*, who thought

---

[92]Literally "led aside [from God]" (compare "seduce / Angels" at 307–08 below), but the word did have sexual connotations in 1667 (*OED* 3 makes it synonymous with "debauch"). John Dryden, in his play adapted from *Paradise Lost*, *The State of Innocence*, discusses the "soft seducer, love" (4.2.33, cited in *OED seducer* 2).

[93]I have reinserted the comma of *1667*, omitted for no good reason in *1674*.

[94]The juxtaposition of "Thoughts" and "misthought" stresses Eve's pain at being misunderstood or thought badly of (*OED misthink* 4, citing this instance). At any rate, Eve appears to be wounded or hurt, since Adam must speak "healing words" when he replies.

[95]Adam has been put on the defensive. His epithets for Eve dignify her and remind her of her immortality, which may shortly be under siege, since, as the reader knows, "sin and blame" are not that far distant.

[96]As Ann Torday Gulden reminds me (e-mail 4 December 1997), the word contains an "asp." It also suggests aspersion in the Roman Catholic sense of ritual cleansing, and its ironic counterpart in the meanings of "besmattering" or "smearing," as in "cast aspersions."

[97]Adam describes Satan's powerful subtlety (the serpent is "subtle" in Genesis) in accurate terms of what it has accomplished in the past. His assessment underscores the superhuman but not invincible power of Satan to corrupt by fraud or guile.

[98]"The coming of anything as an addition" (*OED* 3.8). Adam's love for Eve helps to empower him. If love is treated in Platonic or Neoplatonic terms, Adam's love would strengthen him in the sense that it would lead him from the body to the soul, or from Eve's beauty on up to "the purely intellectual and divine beauty of God" (*Cambridge History of Renaissance Philosophy*, ed. Schmitt: 355). Eve's beauty would be treated as a "ray" emanating directly from God; thus her "looks" strengthen Adam and he feels a sense of shame when he does not act to defend her.

[99]Though in the 1990s "domestick" might suggest "domesticated" and hence put Adam in a comic or negative light, here the word seems to suggest the Puritan concept of "domestic honor," husband and wife pictured having proper mutual respect and practicing mutual support. "Care," derived from Latin *cura*, which suggests responsibility for someone else, is also a noun especially powerful for Milton, and of course "Matrimonial Love" has nothing negative about it, especially considering the high ideals for marriage that inform Milton's divorce tracts. The line in *1667* had only a comma after "Love."

Less attributed to her Faith sincere,[100]   320
Thus her reply with accent sweet renewd.[101]
   If this be our condition, thus to dwell
In narrow circuit strait'nd by a Foe,
Suttle or violent,[102] we not endu'd
Single with like defence, wherever met,   325
How are we happie, still° in fear of harm?
But harm precedes not sin: onely our Foe
Tempting affronts us with his foul esteem
Of our integritie: his foul esteeme
Sticks no dishonor on our Front,[103] but turns   330
Foul on himself; then wherefore shund or feard
By us? who rather double honour gaine[104]
From his surmise prov'd false, find peace within,[105]
Favour from Heav'n, our witness from th' event.
And what is Faith, Love, Vertue unassaid°   335
Alone, without exterior help sustaind?[106]
Let us not then suspect our happie State
Left so imperfet by the Maker wise,
As not secure to single or combin'd.[107]
Fraile is our happiness, if this be so,   340
And *Eden* were no *Eden* thus expos'd.
   To whom thus *Adam* fervently repli'd.[108]
O Woman, best are all things as the will
Of God ordain'd them, his creating hand
Nothing imperfet or deficient left   345
Of all that he Created, much less Man,
Or aught that might his happie State secure,

---

[100]Possibly "Eve, who gave too little thought to her sincere faith." Fowler points out that "*fides sincera* was a watchword or semitechnical theological term among the Reformers" (9.320n). Adam's intellect, at this point, seems more focused on the threat to both of them than does Eve's. The word *attributed* is accented on the first and third syllables.

[101]Though her accent is "sweet," Eve seems to begin in the middle of Adam's last sentence, as if she were cross-examining a witness in a courtroom or cutting off an opponent in an academic debate. The immediate result of her rhetorical tactic is to make Adam "fervent" the next time he speaks.

[102]Eve pictures herself and Adam as living in a place with narrow boundaries or circuits, restricted or "strait'nd" even more by the presence of a foe who can tempt them either by "violent" force or "Suttle" guile. Having the spectre of a "Foe" nearby limits their freedom of movement and their free will. She is also arguing that sexual difference ("Single" can be read as "Singly") inhibits their freedom.

[103]The image is one of a forehead or face ("Front") decorated by the horns of the cuckhold, or, in this case, perhaps distorted by a frown. Eve's strained pun between "affronts" and "Front" may indicate that she is unconsciously leaning toward an indefensible position. But her central argument will be close to that of the famous passage in *Areopagitica*: "I cannot praise a fugitive and cloister'd vertue, unexercis'd & unbreath'd, that never sallies out and sees her adversary, but slinks out of the race, where that immortall garland is to be run for, not without dust and heat" (Yale 2: 515). As many critics have pointed out, Milton puts one of his own most eloquent arguments against censorship or the restriction of human rights in the mouth of Eve just before she does meet an exceedingly strong adversary.

[104]The quantification of honor, as if double honor could be gained by brute force, is associated more with Satan in *Paradise Lost* than with any other character, since he is the great practitioner of duplicity whose sins always redound or recoil on him. Ironically, Eve's attempt at "double honour" will end in the "double terror" visited on Adam's imagination at 10.850, and Adam will refute Eve's argument for suicide after the Fall with the point that if they die they will "double [their punishment] upon [their] heads" (10.1040).

[105]Again, deeply ironic, since the Fall will "confound" "houshold peace," if Adam is correct in his projection of what marriage will be like after the Fall (10.908). Hell is also a place "where peace / And rest can never dwell" (1.65–66).

[106]Essentially Eve's argument is again that of Milton in *Areopagitica*, that an untested virtue is a blank or hollow one (Yale 2: 516). Both Eve and Adam accuse God of leaving them in an imperfect or defective state to challenge either Eve's beauty, in Adam's case when he is speaking with Raphael at 8.534–39, or here, when Eve accuses God of leaving them "not secure." Adam has an answer for Eve's accusation below (but no good answer for his own weakness in the presence of her beauty).

[107]The punctuation at this point is smeared in all copies Fletcher or I have examined, so that it could be either a comma or a period, but a period seems preferable to a comma, because a full stop seems indicated.

[108]Anger or fervor may not be proper before the Fall, but "fervently" (with its root in a Latin verb *fervere* meaning "to boil" or "to rage") suggests the beginning of anger and the epithet "O Woman" sounds harsh. Burden points out that if Adam is "first incenst" only at 9.1162, he cannot be genuinely angry here (92).

Secure from outward force; within himself
The danger lies, yet lies within his power:
Against his will he can receave no harme.   350
But God left free the Will, for what obeyes
Reason, is free, and Reason he made right,
But bid her well beware, and still erect,[109]
Least by some faire appeering good surpris'd
She dictate false, and misinforme the Will   355
To do what God expresly hath forbid.[110]
Not then mistrust, but tender love enjoynes,°
That I should mind thee oft, and mind thou me.[111]
Firm we subsist, yet possible to swerve,[112]
Since Reason not impossibly may meet
Some specious object by the Foe subornd,°   360
And fall into deception unaware,
Not keeping strictest watch, as she was warnd.[113]
Seek not temptation then, which to avoide
Were better, and most likelie if from mee   365
Thou sever not: Trial will come unsought.
Wouldst thou approve° thy constancie, approve
First thy obedience; th' other who can know,
Not seeing thee attempted, who attest?
But if thou think, trial unsought may finde   370
Us both securer then thus warnd thou seemst,
Go;[114] for thy stay, not free, absents thee more;
Go in thy native innocence, relie
On what thou hast of vertue, summon all,
For God towards thee hath done his part, do thine.   375
    So spake the Patriarch of Mankinde,[115] but *Eve*
Persisted, yet submiss, though last, repli'd.[116]

Margin glosses:
- PRESCRIBES AUTHORITATIVELY
- PROCURED BY UNDERHANDED MEANS
- PROVE, TEXT

[109]Milton may be reading "beware" in terms of its components, as if it were "be wary," so that the complements of the word "be" would be "ware" and "erect." Right reason is a Stoic concept, equivalent to the Christian conscience. See 3.98–99; 3.123–25; and 8.640–43 for evidence of the freedom of choice for Adam and Eve.

[110]The period of *1667* here seems preferable to the comma of *1674*. Adam predicts exactly what will happen to Eve: the Serpent, a "specious object by the Foe subornd," will appear good and fair, will surprise Eve's reason, and will dictate a false impression to Eve's will, causing her to disobey God's one commandment.

[111]The verb "mind" may carry the meanings "warn," "obey," and "care for" at the same time.

[112]Compare Samson's "Proudly secure, yet liable to fall" (*Samson Agonistes* 55).

[113]Note that "Reason" is a "she," as if Adam were asking the wrongly-leaning Eve to right herself with her fellow female entity Reason. The Latin noun *ratio*, "reason," is feminine. But Milton may also be associating Eve with Reason, "the faculty that chooses and directs the will" (Fowler 9.360–61n), though I do not agree with Fowler that Eve is clearly cast in the allegorical role of Reason.

[114]Both of Adam's "Go's" seem rhetorical, designed to make Eve rethink her plan and not leave at all, but she interprets the command literally and takes it as Adam's permission. There can be no sin in their lovers' quarrel, but there does seem to be at least a misunderstanding. The Augustinian problem of "evil will" or "concupiscence" may come up at this point. "But the first evil will, which preceded all man's evil acts, was rather a kind of falling away from the work of God to its own works than any positive work" (*City of God* 14.11; trans. Dods: 457). The problem for Augustine and for Milton was that, though Adam and Eve were innocent until they fell, the will to commit sin had to come from somewhere, and it could not come from God, "for the evil act had never been done had not an evil will preceded it" (*City of God* 14.13: 460). For various arguments whether Adam and Eve fell before they ate the fruit, see the articles on the subject of the "fortunate fall" by Tillyard, Bell, Shumaker, and Mollenkott. Hughes (371n) defines "securer" as "less careful," but it seems to mean the opposite; the two lines, 370–71, might better be read "But if you think that unsought trial might find us both less well-protected than you—even forewarned—seem to be . . . ", then go.

[115]Milton's epithet for Adam at this point, "Patriarch of Mankinde," ironically underscores his possible dereliction of duty: he is not being patriarchal, fatherly, or even "manly" enough to control his wife. Even before the Fall, Milton believed the husband had "greater authority" (*On Christian Doctrine* 1.10; Yale 6: 355) over the wife. After the Fall he will be asked "Was shee thy God, that her thou didst obey" (10.145) and "was shee made thy guide" (146), indicating that Adam abrogated his responsibility when he obeyed her, rather than acting as her guide and commanding her not to go (see 1155–56 below for Eve's accusation). His answer, of course, is to say that to stop her from going would have been to restrict her free will (1173–74 below).

[116]Eve, I take it, remains submissive yet persists and gets the last word. "It is not that, though seemingly submissive, she still managed to have the last word, but that, though having the last word, she still managed to stay submissive" (Burden 92).

With thy permission then, and thus forewarnd
Chiefly by what thy own last reasoning words
Touchd onely, that our trial, when least sought,   380
May finde us both perhaps farr less prepar'd,
The willinger I goe, nor much expect
A Foe so proud will first the weaker seek,
So bent, the more shall shame him his repulse.[117]
Thus saying, from her Husbands hand her hand   385
Soft she withdrew, and like a Wood-Nymph light
Oread or *Dryad*, or of *Delia*'s Traine,
Betook her to the Groves, but *Delia*'s self
In gate surpass'd and Goddess-like deport,
Though not as shee with Bow and Quiver armd,   390
But with such Gardning Tools as Art yet rude,
Guiltless of fire had formd, or Angels brought.[118]
To *Pales*, or *Pomona* thus adornd,
Likest[119] she seemd, *Pomona* when she fled
Vertumnus,[120] or to *Ceres* in her Prime,[121]   395
Yet Virgin of *Proserpina* from *Jove*.
Her long with ardent[122] look his Eye pursu'd
Delighted, but desiring more her stay.
Oft he to her his charge of quick returne
Repeated, shee to him as oft engag'd   400
To be returnd by Noon amid the Bowre,
And all things in best order to invite
Noontide repast, or Afternoons repose.[123]

---

[117]Her reasoning (which is Adam's as well) is the opposite of the truth, tragically, because Satan has been hoping against hope to find her separate from Adam (421–22 below).

[118]The images of Oreads (mortal mountain nymphs attendant on the goddess Diana, called "Delia" because of her origin on the island of Delos) or Dryads (nymphs supposed to live in trees) waiting on the goddess of chastity are deeply ironic and yet full of gentle but somewhat sardonic humor. Diana was armed and could at times be ferocious toward encroaching men, as when she transformed the hunter Actaeon into a stag and caused his own dogs to kill him, but Eve is armed only with the paradisal equivalent of gardening tools—and not even forged or metallic tools, but those "Guiltless of fire" (both in the sense of "innocent of the knowledge of fire" and "free of the use of fire brought about by the Fall"). The adjective "light" implies that Eve is somewhat giddy, the opposite of serious or thoughtful, at this point. Eve is treating an act with tragic consequences—the withdrawing of her hand from Adam's—far too lightly.

[119]"Likest" in *1667*, "Likeliest" in *1674*. I disagree with Fowler (9.394n) that "Likeliest" is the better choice. Eve is most like the goddesses named.

[120]For Milton, Vertumnus, god of spring and of orchards, was also the epitome of shifty thinking, in that he took many disguises to woo and win the goddess of fruit, Pomona (Ovid, *Metamorphoses* 14.622–99, in Humphries's lineation). Those who change arguments rapidly are "more difficult to pin down than Vertumnus" (*On Christian Doctrine* 1.5; Yale 6: 260). Milton chastises another shifty orator in *Tetrachordon* by saying " . . . let him trie which way he can wind in his *Vertumnian* distinctions and evasions" (Yale 2: 675). The comparison works for Satan, associated with deceitful metamorphoses, and Eve, associated with the cultivation of her garden.

[121]Pales was the Roman goddess of sheepfolds and pastures. Ceres, more important than Pomona or Pales as goddess of grain and harvests, gives her name to cereal. She is impregnated by Jove to bear, first, Pherephata, "fruit-bearer," and then Proserpine (there is a subtle and serious pun in Milton's choice of the name "Pro+serpina" rather than "Persephone"), who as a young woman is seized and carried away by Pluto, god of the underworld, causing Ceres to mourn for her daughter for half the year (fall and winter) when she is underground with Pluto and then bring spring when she is visiting her mother. Ceres and all the other women or demigods mentioned are pictured as innocent or virginal, "in [their] Prime," just before a fall. The word *prime* has nothing necessarily to do with youth, that I can see, nor is it a time-marker for Eve at the moment.

[122]Corresponds subtly with "fervent," since both words have to do with burning, but with quite different connotations in English, "ardent" being associated more with the emotional burning of love. There is a subtle balance here between love as a healthy emotion and love as a disease. For background, see Ferrand, *A Treatise*.

[123]Apparently we are to think the conversation goes on, but the crucial estrangement, the removal of her hand from his, has already occurred. Their "handedness" (see 4.739) has been an important emblem of their conjugal union, as it will continue to be after the Fall (12.648). Eve's single "rash hand" will also play an important part in the Fall (9.780), as will Adam's "liberal hand" (997 below); Adam's hand will become brutal after the Fall ("Her hand he seis'd" [1037 below]).

O much deceav'd, much failing, hapless *Eve*,[124]   405
Of thy presum'd return! event perverse!
Thou never from that houre in Paradise
Foundst either sweet repast,° or sound repose;   FOOD, DINING
Such ambush hid among sweet Flours and Shades[125]
Waited with hellish rancour° imminent   DEEP INFERNAL HATRED
To intercept thy way, or send thee back   410
Despoild of Innocence, of Faith, of Bliss.[126]
For now, and since first break of dawne the Fiend,
Meer Serpent in appearance,[127] forth was come,
And on his Quest, where likeliest he might finde
The onely two of Mankinde, but in them   415
The whole included Race,[128] his purposd prey.
In Bowre and Field he sought, where any tuft
Of Grove or Garden-Plot more pleasant lay,
Thir tendance or Plantation[129] for delight,
By Fountain or by shadie Rivulet   420
He sought them both, but wish'd his hap° might find   FORTUNE
Eve separate, he wish'd, but not with hope
Of what so seldom chanc'd, when to his wish,
Beyond his hope, *Eve* separate he spies,
Veild in a Cloud of Fragrance, where she stood,   425
Half spi'd, so thick the Roses bushing round
About her glowd, oft stooping to support
Each Flour of slender stalk, whose head though gay
Carnation, Purple, Azure, or spect with Gold,
Hung drooping unsustaind, them she upstaies   430
Gently with Mirtle band,[130] mindless the while,[131]
Her self, though fairest unsupported Flour,
From her best prop so farr, and storm so nigh.
Neerer he drew, and many a walk travers'd
Of stateliest Covert, Cedar, Pine, or Palme,   435
Then voluble° and bold, now hid, now seen   UNDULATING
Among thick-wov'n Arborets and Flours

---

[124]The three adjectives cover the possibilities for Eve's free will to act: she will be "deceived by the other first" (as according to 1 Timothy 2.14), she has failed Adam by not heeding his prophetic advice, and she is extraordinarily unfortunate, hapless, in her timing of this departure. Her "bad luck" should not be stressed, since what she does is of her own choosing, but it is the opposite of Satan's good "hap" mentioned in 421 below. Eve describes herself after the Fall as someone who "unweeting [has] offended," and someone who has been "Unhappilie deceav'd" (10.916–17). Disobedience of God and alliance with Satan are signaled by the word "perverse," which is used of the "Universe of death" (2.622, 625) that Satan's disobedience creates.
[125]The image of the snake in the grass was proverbial and used by Shakespeare often, as in Lady Macbeth's " . . . look like th' innocent flower, / But be the serpent under't" (1.5.65–6).
[126]Compare the other triad, "Faith, Love, Vertue" at 335 above.
[127]A rich phrase, since if the Serpent were just a phantasm the story of the Fall would be a simple allegory; if the Serpent were decorated with a human face (many commentators and visual artists, such as Andrew Willet and the painter Raphael, acknowledged that the Serpent may have had the face of a virgin—mirroring Eve's face narcissistically), Eve would have been reacting to a fellow human. Milton allows his Serpent to be a serpent without human characteristics, though his carbuncular eyes and crest make him at the least a very exotic serpent. Such serpents, usually associated with Syria, were assumed to exist by contemporary naturalists.
[128]Stresses the fact that sin becomes what might today be described as a genetic inheritance—the "mortal Sin / Original" of 1003-04 below—to all of humankind through Adam and Eve: such was accepted belief among biblical commentators, Protestant and Roman Catholic, of the seventeenth century.
[129]One would tend a garden-plot (hence "tendance") and treat a grove as a "Plantation," or considerable amount of land under cultivation.
[130]Fowler sees the picture of Eve propping the rose with myrtle (he does not include the carnation) as "an emblem of the dependence of unfallen bliss upon conjugal virtue" (9.426–31n), but I see the roses as roses, "Carnation" as the color of carnations, and myrtle as myrtle, especially considering that Milton generally avoided emblems or icons (but see the Sammons article mentioned in the note to 217 above).
[131]Adam's "vehemence" in the Fall is thus matched by Eve's being "mindless" before it, which I take to mean "careless in the face of being warned against imminent danger."

Imborderd[132] on each Bank, the hand° of *Eve*:   HANDIWORK, CRAFTSMANSHIP
Spot more delicious then those Gardens feign'd
Or of reviv'd *Adonis*, or renownd   440
Alcinous, host of old *Laertes* Son,[133]
Or that, not Mystic,[134] where the Sapient King
Held dalliance with his faire *Egyptian* Spouse.[135]
Much hee the Place admir'd, the Person more.
As one who long in populous City pent,   445
Where Houses thick and Sewers[136] annoy the Aire,
Forth issuing on a Summers Morn to breathe
Among the pleasant Villages and Farmes
Adjoynd,[137] from each thing met conceaves delight,
The smell of Grain, or tedded Grass,[138] or Kine,°   CATTLE   450
Or Dairie, each rural sight, each rural sound;
If chance with Nymphlike step fair Virgin pass,
What pleasing seemd, for her now pleases more,
She most, and in her look summs all Delight.[139]
Such Pleasure took the Serpent to behold   455
This Flourie Plat,° the sweet recess of *Eve*   PLOT, GARDEN
Thus earlie, thus alone; her Heav'nly forme[140]
Angelic, but more soft,[141] and Feminine,   LIKE ANGELS
Her graceful Innocence, her every Aire
Of gesture or lest° action overawd   LEAST   460
His Malice, and with rapine sweet bereav'd
His fierceness of the fierce intent it brought:
That space the Evil one abstracted stood

---

[132]May be heraldic, since "Imborderd" in heraldic terms means decorated with an ornamental border.
[133]Odysseus, Laertes son, is entertained by Alcinous, a king famous for his gardens, in *Odyssey* 7.
[134]In this case "Mystic" means something like "mythical," "superstitious," or "fictional," with the implication that Homer's account of the gardens of Alcinous is "feign'd" and the account of Solomon's gardens in the Song of Solomon is true, the difference between pagan and Christian. Solomon, the wise king, is rendered uxorious and weakened by his connection with the Queen of Sheba, "his faire *Egyptian* Spouse," who was believed to have seduced him into worshiping her false gods and building a temple to them. But the old Solomon had 700 wives and 300 concubines, "and his wives turned away his heart" from the God of Israel (1 Kings 11.3); he became an idolater with many of the gods of his wives, notably Ashtoreth, Chemosh, and Molech (11.5–7). Milton was very interested in the theme of wise men weakened by love, as with Samson, and Solomon was one biblical prototype. Adam was considered uxorious ("wife-following" in a way similar to Solomon's idolatrous love or the love of Samson for a Philistine woman in Delilah). Milton considered both Solomon and Samson as potential subjects for tragedy. Fowler cites the tradition that Adam was similar to Solomon in that both wise men gave in to their wives and Adam "by the drawings of kindred yielded to the woman" (*City of God* 14.11, trans. Dods: 459). In the Trinity Manuscript, amongst other outlines for tragedies, Milton listed "Solomon, Idolomargus, or Gynaecocratumenus, aut Thysiazusae" (Yale 8: 563n); the Greek words have been translated variously to mean that Solomon is to be considered "idol-mad," "woman-governed," or among the "Women-sacrificers." Milton thus labeled Solomon as driven into mad idolatry because he allows himself to be governed by women who sacrifice to false gods.
[135]Described in Song of Solomon 6.2: "My beloved is gone down into his garden, to the beds of spices, to feed in the gardens, and to gather lilies." Solomon, the "Sapient King" (best known for his wisdom), is here pictured as husband to the daughter of Pharaoh and singing the Song of Solomon to her, "the fairest among women" (1.7).
[136]Sewers in Milton's era could be open ditches or the more familiar drainage pipes for sewage (see *OED* 1). That they produced odor aboveground is attested to by Michael Drayton, as cited in the *OED* : "Vnder whose Floore, the common Sewer past Vp to the same, a loathsome stench. . . ."
[137]It may be worth noting here that in the course of writing *Paradise Lost*, Milton himself moved out of the city of London to the rural Buckinghamshire village of Chalfont St. Giles; hence the precise sensual impressions may be derived from experience. Contrast this simile with the "Towred Cities please us then, / And the busie humm of men" passage in "L'Allegro" (117–52), in which cities are viewed positively as seats of civilization and art, and compare it with the whole of "Elegy 7," which discusses the poet's pleasant encounter with a country lass.
[138]Tedded grass, a technical phrase from haymaking, is hay which has been fluffed or tossed while on the ground, to aid in the drying process. It does smell good (unless, of course, one suffers from hayfever).
[139]"In her appearance Eve sums up all pleasure." Eve is, in other words, like a little Garden of Eden in herself. Milton emphasizes her virginal purity and her innocence, in the midst of terrible danger.
[140]The word can simply mean "beauty, comeliness" (*OED* I.1.e), though Milton was well aware of its Aristotelian or scholastic (referring to medieval methods of disputation) overtone, "the essential determinant principle of a thing" (*OED* I.4.a), since Eve's beauty is close to an ideal.
[141]Bentley's rude conjecture that if Eve were softer than angels she would melt into fluid is not applicable. Fowler (9.457–58) is correct to assume that "soft" (a word often applied to Eve) suggests "gentle, free from severity or rigour" (*OED* II.8).

From his own evil, and for the time remain
Stupidly good, of enmitie disarm'd,

Great phrase - "stupidly good"

Of guile, of hate, of envie, of revenge;[142]   465
But the hot Hell that alwayes in him burnes,
Though in mid Heav'n, soon ended his delight,
And tortures him now more, the more he sees[143]
Of pleasure not for him ordain'd: then soon

he reassembles himself + all his hatred   470

Fierce hate he recollects, and all his thoughts
Of mischief, gratulating,[144] thus excites.°

INCITES HIMSELF

　　Thoughts, whither have ye led me, with what sweet
Compulsion thus transported to forget
What hither brought us, hate, not love, nor hope   475
Of Paradise for Hell, hope here to taste
Of pleasure, but all pleasure to destroy,
Save what is in destroying, other joy
To me is lost. Then let me not let pass
Occasion which now smiles, behold alone   480
The Woman, opportune[145] to all attempts,
Her Husband, for I view far round, not nigh,
Whose higher intellectual[146] more I shun,
And strength, of courage hautie,[147] and of limb

SARCASM

Heroic built,[148] though of terrestrial mould,°

CLAY   485

Foe not informidable, exempt from wound,
I not;[149] so much hath Hell debas'd, and paine
Infeebl'd me, to what I was in Heav'n.
Shee fair, divinely fair, fit Love for Gods,
Not terrible, though terrour be in Love   490
And beautie,[150] not approach't by stronger hate,
Hate stronger, under shew of Love well feign'd,

---

[142]With deep irony, Eve's goodness embodied in her outward form is said to have suspended Satan's malice "with rapine sweet." The potential rapist becomes the victim of the good power of Eve's beauty. Her beauty renders his evil "Stupidly good." She is like Proserpina—he is about to "rape" (i.e., seize) her—yet her beauty seizes him instead. What happens to Satan also seems to happen to evil beings who come up against the force of chastity in *Comus*, where "rigid looks of Chast austerity, / And noble grace" have the power to "dash" "brute violence / With sudden adoration, and blank aw" (450–52). Satan being "abstracted" suggests "Withdrawn from the contemplation of present objects; absent in mind" (*OED* 2), but he is also abstracted in the sense that his mind is uplifted.

[143]Milton characteristically shifts tenses, from "burnes" to "ended" to "tortures" to "ordain'd" to "recollects." Satan's problem is eternal but at the same time immediate.

[144]"Congratulating," in this case congratulating himself, exulting in the discovery of Eve separate from Adam.

[145]One of the less common definitions for the Latin word *opportunus* is "liable, exposed," which seems to be what Milton intends here, since Eve is not actively "ready" for Satan's temptation.

[146]The "intellect, mind" (*OED* B.1, citing this instance). Satan considers Adam's intellect more powerful than Eve's; together, each member of the couple gains strength from the union, but Eve is less powerful alone than she is with Adam present, especially while she is being tempted by an extremely crafty and guileful Serpent, and Adam is less powerful having been separated from unfallen Eve and then subjected to Eve as temptress. Milton himself acknowledged that a woman's intellect sometimes is more powerful than that of a man; in marriage, the less intelligent, he felt, should acquiesce to the more intelligent: " . . . if she exceed her husband in prudence and dexterity, and he contentedly yeeld, . . . then a superior and more naturall law comes in, that the wiser should govern the lesse wise, whether male or female" (*Tetrachordon*; Yale 2: 589).

[147]High in his own estimation (see *OED* 1). Satan is imputing his own bad character to Adam; in fact he is the being like a "proud steed reind" who "went haughtie on" (4.858).

[148]One of the few instances when Adam is described as being of heroic stature and as strong or stronger than the conventional epic hero like Achilles, Aeneas, or Orlando.

[149]Adam is still immortal and thus exempt from wounds; Satan knows he has been wounded by Michael in the War in Heaven (6.323–34), and he knows that his appearance has been debased compared to what it was in Heaven.

[150]The question is whether Satan is speaking Satanically or Miltonically. Does terror exist in love universally, or only from the perception of Satan, who knows only "jealousie / . . . the injur'd Lovers Hell" (5.449–50). Though love, and beauty, can be terribly destructive, there is no evidence that Milton wants us to see either in such a negative light.

The way which to her ruin now I tend.[151]
    So spake the Enemie of Mankind, enclos'd
In Serpent, Inmate bad, and toward *Eve*
Address'd his way, not with indented° wave,   WRIGGLING, BENDING   495
Prone on the ground, as since, but on his reare,
Circular base of rising foulds, that tour'd°   TOWERED
Fould above fould a surging Maze, his Head
Crested aloft, and Carbuncle[152] his Eyes;   500
With burnisht Neck of verdant Gold, erect
Amidst his circling Spires,° that on the grass   SPIRALS, COILS
Floted redundant:[153] pleasing was his shape,
And lovely, never since of Serpent kind
Lovelier, not those that in *Illyria* chang'd   505
Hermione and *Cadmus*, or the God
In *Epidaurus*; nor to which transformd
Ammonian Jove, or *Capitoline* was seen,
Hee with *Olympias*, this with her who bore
Scipio the highth of *Rome*.[154] With tract oblique   510
At first, as one who sought access, but feard
To interrupt,[155] side-long he works his way.
As when a Ship by skilful Stearsman wrought
Nigh Rivers mouth or Foreland,[156] where the Wind[157]
Veres oft, as oft so steers, and shifts her Saile;   515
So varied hee, and of his tortuous Traine

---

[151]The verb "tend" means "turn one's steps toward" (*OED* III.8) with a possible overtone of "set a trap" (*OED* III.7). Satan's idiom in speaking of Eve approaches that of the Petrarchan love poet, finding terror in Eve's beauty and in love itself, calling her "fair" and worshiping her beauty.

[152]Red like the various precious stones like the ruby that were associated with the carbuncles (see Ezekiel 28.13); but the noun also is associated with the redness of inflammation caused by disease—a carbuncle is also a cancerous, inflamed lump similar to a boil. Milton seems to be aiming toward the effect of a sick beauty, when one adds to the carbuncular eyes and the shining neck of greenish gold. A Freudian critic (compare Kerrigan or Boyette) would also be quick to point out a double meaning in terms like "surging" and "erect," and the temptation is undoubtedly meant to be taken as erotic, but perversely so.

[153]Probably both "wavelike" and "unnecessarily repetitive," as with Satan's rhetoric, which is florid and rebounds on itself.

[154]A catalogue of classical serpents. According to Ovid, the old Cadmus asks to become a serpent in order to atone for killing a sacred serpent and sowing the serpent's teeth to breed up warriors. When he is changed into a serpent, his wife Hermione asks to be transformed as well, and, while their attendants watch in horror, they become benign serpents—but not necessarily "lovely" ones (*Metamorphoses* 4.572–603). Osgood finds a source in Nonnus, *Dionysiaca* 44.107–118, which describes serpents seen in a dream by Agave, daughter of Cadmus, as circling the heads of Cadmus and Harmonia (interchangeably used for Hermione by Ovid and Nonnus) and caressing them (Osgood 18), but Starnes and Talbert cite Stephanus's *Dictionary* as Milton's source for Hermione (243–44). The God in Epidaurus was the father of medicine, Aesculapius, who had the power to change himself into a serpent like those two serpents twined about his famous rod, the caduceus, while accompanying a Roman embassy from Epidaurus to Italy. Aesculapius, like Satan, takes the form of a serpent "all crested / With gold" (*Metamorphoses* 15.669–70; trans. Humphries: 386). Jupiter Ammon (named after an Egyptian goat-headed god supposedly based at the oasis of Siwa in the Libyan desert) is the "*Lybian Jove*" of 4.277. Alexander the Great, according to Plutarch, believed that his father Philip of Macedonia shunned his wife Olympias because she was sleeping with a serpent, only to find that the serpent was Jupiter Ammon. "*Capitoline*" Jove was named after his temple on the Capitoline Hill at Rome, giving the reader a skeptical choice among the various manifestations of the pagan god. Scipio Africanus, at his height as consul of Rome, was supposed to have been engendered by a serpent who copulated with Scipio's mother. Svendsen cites Camerarius's *The Living Librarie* (London, 1595) as showing the links between the cases of serpentine miscegenation: after alleging that "Serpents have been noted to desire the companie of women" and that "by an Allegorie Satan is meant the Serpent" and that "Philo and the Hebrews say, That the Serpent signifieth allegorically, Lecherie," Camerarius goes on to say that Alexander saluted his mother as the son of Jupiter Ammon and that "a great Serpent lay with Scipios mother . . . " (249; qtd. in Svendsen, 169). Milton seems to be relying on classical and Christian gossip to construct a number of wild tales of relations between famous men and women and serpents in order to discredit pagan civilization for its superstitiousness.

[155]Satan in the gaudily and perversely handsome Serpent is acting like a courtier flattering the king or queen to whom he wants access. He is no common Serpent but "erect" and "Crested," "lovely," and hence seductive. His appearance and sound both have a shock value for Eve, since he is a handsome talking snake. The mythology of serpents would give Milton access to traditions of the Serpent as erect before the Fall but prone and groveling after it; the first illustrators of *Paradise Lost* in 1688 show the Serpent before the Fall erect, balanced on the tip of its tail. For folklore and mythology current in Milton's era, see Edward Topsell, *Historie of Serpents* (London, 1608).

[156]A cape or headland, around which, as with the river's mouth, the steering would require great navigational skill.

[157]Paul Klemp has pointed out that the beginning letters in the last five lines appropriately spell out "SATAN." See "'Now Hid, Now Seen': An Acrostic in *Paradise Lost*," *Milton Quarterly* 11 (1977): 91–92.

Curld many a wanton wreath[158] in sight of *Eve*,
To lure her Eye; shee busied heard the sound
Of rusling° Leaves, but minded not, as us'd   RUSTLING
To such disport before her through the Field,   520
From every Beast, more duteous at her call,
Then at *Circean* call the Herd disguis'd.[159]
Hee boulder now, uncall'd before her stood;
But as in gaze admiring: Oft he bowd
His turret Crest, and sleek enamel'd[160] Neck,   525
Fawning, and lick'd the ground whereon she trod.[161]
His gentle dumb expression turnd at length
The Eye of *Eve* to mark his play; he glad
Of her attention gaind, with Serpent Tongue
Organic,[162] or impulse of vocal Air,   530
His fraudulent temptation thus began.
    Wonder not, sovran Mistress, if perhaps
Thou canst, who art sole Wonder, much less arm
Thy looks, the Heav'n of mildness, with disdain,[163]
Displeas'd that I approach thee thus, and gaze   535
Insatiate, I thus single, nor have feard
Thy awful brow, more awful thus retir'd.
Fairest resemblance of thy Maker faire,
Thee all things living gaze on, all things thine
By gift, and thy Celestial Beautie[164] adore   540
With ravishment beheld, there best beheld
Where universally admir'd; but here
In this enclosure wild, these Beasts among,
Beholders rude, and shallow to discerne
Half what in thee is fair, one man except,   545
Who sees thee? (and what is one?) who shouldst be seen
A Goddess among Gods, ador'd and serv'd

---

[158]Either a knot or a maze or convolutions formed by his body, corresponding in a sinister way to Eve's "wanton ringlets" (4.306); compare "bent" above at 55 and 384. Though the adjective "wanton" can be applied to natural overgrowth, it often has a sexual overtone, as with "wanton passions" at 1.454. The next wreath we will see will be the "Garland wreath'd for *Eve*" (892 below) woven innocently by Adam while Eve is in the process of falling.

[159]The comparison seems to be deeply ironic, since Eve is not a Circe who has turned men into beasts but an innocent being (at this point) who can still communicate with animals. Satan has turned himself into a beast in order to gain access to her. The question for critics has been whether or not Eve is made guilty here by association with Homer's sorceress Circe with her rout of men turned into beasts (*Odyssey* 10.210–19). Only after the Fall will Adam, his own motives tainted by his sin, call Eve a "Serpent" (10.867). For the tradition associating Eve with various sorceresses, see Hughes, "Acrasia" and Brodwin, "Renaissance Circe." But notice that whereas Circe calls the herd, Eve does not call the Serpent: she addresses the animals in general.

[160]Of varied coloration, as with the "gay enameld colours" of 4.149. Willet cites the commentary of Pererius that the Serpent of Eden "is most like to be the serpent called *Scytala*, which hath a backe of divers colours" (47).

[161]Certainly the most perverse demonstration of Satan's fawning mock-idolatry, since the upright Serpent would have had to bend double to lick the ground. Snake lore of Milton's era might have associated the flicking of the snake's tongue with flattery's "licking up to" its victim.

[162]Satan uses the Serpent's tongue as an organ of speech, emitting air through the throat to create sound. As Fowler points out (9.530n), there may be a pun in "impulse," since it means both "motion" and "strong suggestion from a spirit" (*OED* I.3.a).

[163]Satan's language is that of an insincere Petrarchan love-poet, in "sovran Mistress," "sole Wonder," or "arm[ed] / . . . with disdain." His flattery elevates her to heavenly or celestial status, tempting her with a vision of angelic, superhuman beauty. His temptation will help her aspire to godhead; compare " . . . nor was God-head from her thought" (790).

[164]Eve's beauty is not celestial—it is earthly—and the creatures around her may gaze on her but they should not adore or worship her; certainly they should not be "ravished" by her beauty, since the word does suggest rape. Satan's flattery is very close in spirit and rhetoric to Comus's "well-plac't words of glozing courtesie" (*Comus* 161). Like Comus's argument, it relies on the copiousness of nature to suggest that excess is better than moderation, or, in this case, that a multitude of admirers is better than one. Satan is quite carefully stroking Eve's potential vanity, at the same time leading her to aspire to godhead.

By Angels numberless, thy daily Train.[165]
   So gloz'd[166] the Tempter, and his Proem[167] tun'd;
Into the Heart of *Eve* his words made way,   550
Though at the voice much marveling; at length
Not unamaz'd she thus in answer spake.[168]
What may this mean? Language of Man pronounc't
By Tongue of Brute, and human sense exprest?
The first at lest° of these I thought deni'd[169]   555
To Beasts, whom God on thir Creation-Day
Created mute to all articulat sound;
The latter I demurre, for in thir looks
Much reason, and in thir actions oft appeers.
Thee, Serpent, suttlest beast of all the field   560
I knew, but not with human voice endu'd;
Redouble° then this miracle, and say,
How cam'st thou speakable[170] of mute, and how
To me so friendly grown above the rest
Of brutal kind, that daily are in sight?   565
Say, for such wonder claims attention due.
   To whom the guileful Tempter thus reply'd.
Empress of this fair World,[171] resplendent *Eve*,
Easie to mee it is to tell thee all
What thou commandst, and right thou shouldst be obeyd: 570
I was at first as other Beasts that graze
The trodden Herb, of abject thoughts and low,
As was my food, nor aught but food discern'd
Or Sex, and apprehended nothing high:
Till on a day roaving the field, I chanc'd   575
A goodly Tree farr distant to behold
Loaden with fruit of fairest colours mixt,
Ruddie and Gold: I nearer drew to gaze;
When from the boughes a savorie odour blow'n,
Grateful to appetite, more pleas'd my sense   580
Then smell of sweetest Fenel or the Teats

---

[165]Milton here and elsewhere emphasizes in the word "Train" the need for false pomp to have attendants, strongly implying that true magnificence needs no train. The Serpent has a "Traine" at 516 above. It may be significant, in the realm of sexual politics, that Adam needs no attendants, whereas Eve even in Eden is always attended by graces or invisible servants. In the judgment of Adam and Eve, "Attendance none shall need, nor Train, where none / Are to behold the Judgment, but the judg'd, / Those two" (10.80–82).

[166]The word carries the overtones of "intentionally misinterpreting" or "lying in an elaborate way." As with Comus's flattering courtesy, Satanic lies are "glozing lyes" (3.93).

[167]Usually a brief introduction to a longer poem, as in the proem to Milton's Nativity Ode.

[168]To Eve's credit, she questions the identity and the linguistic ability of the Serpent. Willet paraphrases the early Church Father St. John Chrysostom to the effect that "the sight of the serpent, which after sinne became terrible and hatefull to man, was nowe not abhorred, neither were any creatures as yet in the state of mans innocencie, loathsome unto man, and therefore Eva might well indure the sight of the serpent" (47).

[169]There is a space in *1674* between the last two letters of "deni'd" but no identifiable apostrophe. Since the apostrophe is there in *1667*, editors safely assume that it should have been in *1674*, especially since "denid" would have been awkward, then or now.

[170]Capable of speaking.

[171]No one before this has elevated Eve to the status of empress. The word *empire* almost always has a negative connotation in Milton's poetry, because he associates it with pagan aspirations for worldly glory (see J. Martin Evans, *Milton's Imperial Epic: Paradise Lost and the Discourse on Colonialism*, Chapter 3 [Ithaca, NY: Cornell UP, 1996]). There has been no need up to now for Eve to command the animals or to be obeyed by them. If there has been worship, it has been undemonstrative.

Of Ewe or Goat dropping with Milk at Eevn,[172]
Unsuckt of Lamb or Kid, that tend thir play.
To satisfie the sharp desire I had
Of tasting those fair Apples,[173] I resolv'd   585
Not to deferr; hunger and thirst at once,
Powerful perswaders, quick'nd at the scent
Of that alluring fruit, urg'd me so keene.[174]
About the mossie Trunk I wound me soon,
For high from ground the branches would require   590
Thy utmost reach or *Adams*: Round the Tree
All other Beasts that saw, with like desire
Longing and envying stood, but could not reach.[175]
Amid the Tree now got, where plenty hung
Tempting so nigh, to pluck and eat[176] my fill   595
I spar'd not, for such pleasure till that hour
At Feed or Fountain never had I found.
Sated at length, ere long I might perceave
Strange alteration in me, to degree
Of Reason in my inward Powers, and Speech   600
Wanted not long, though to this shape retain'd.°   RESTRAINED, CONFINED
Thenceforth to Speculations high or deep
I turnd my thoughts, and with capacious mind
Considerd all things visible in Heav'n,
Or Earth, or Middle, all things fair and good;   605
But all that fair and good in thy Divine
Semblance, and in thy Beauties heav'nly Ray[177]
United I beheld; no Fair to thine
Equivalent or second, which compel'd
Mee thus, though importune[178] perhaps, to come   610
And gaze, and worship thee of right declar'd
Sovran of Creatures, universal Dame.[179]

[handwritten: Please eat the Fruit! With me!]

---

[172] Serpents were traditionally supposed to be attracted to the scent of fennel (the plant is related to licorice), and they were supposed to drink milk at night from ewes or nanny goats. See Pliny, *Natural History* 8.99. Milton himself seems to have subscribed to the belief that fennel made serpents (or humans like himself) quick-sighted, since he used the idiom "to see clearer then any fenell rub'd Serpent" (*Apology against a Pamphlet*; Yale 1: 909). There was a comma at this point in *1667* and a space in *1674* which might have been intended for a comma that did not ink properly or fell below the surface of the line.

[173] Milton characteristically allows Satan to name the fruit and thus trivialize it. As Epic Voice, Milton will avoid naming either muse or fruit, since it is the meaning of inspiration or disobedience, not the name, that he is concerned with in both cases. It does not matter what Adam and Eve eat, if the act of eating constitutes disobedience.

[174] Satan plants the suggestion in Eve's mind of satisfying a natural noon-time hunger by eating the forbidden fruit, just as he has planted in her subconscious mind by means of her dream the fantasy of eating the fruit and then flying. Again, the fruit does not allure or seduce on its own: Satan must suggest that it is alluring and thus manufacture the temptation. Suggesting that Eve might be hungry is part of his (not the fruit's) temptation.

[175] Satan even tries to create a kind of group hysteria, by picturing a crowd of animals around the Tree of the Knowledge of Good and Evil envying what never has happened: his eating of the fruit. Here Satan is a kind of confidence man. If Eve believes that he has eaten the fruit and thereby gained the ability to speak, then she will believe that she can climb the ladder of creation to become "more equal" (823 below) than Adam. Such "coney-catching" confidence games did exist in Elizabethan and Caroline England: see Arthur F. Kinney, ed. *Rogues, Vagabonds & Sturdy Beggars: A New Gallery of Tudor and Early Stuart Rogue Literature Exposing the Lives, Times, and Cozening Tricks of the Elizabethan Underworld* (Amherst: U of Massachusetts P, 1990).

[176] By now this verbal formula involving plucking and eating is familiar, from Eve's dream (5.65, 84), and it will be repeated at 781 below.

[177] Satan is beginning from the Neoplatonic notion that beauty does indeed produce a heavenly ray that should inspire the contemplative person to seek the God behind the ray, but as usual he pictures beauty or the beautiful woman—the "fair," as in the Petrarchan verbal formula—as an object to be worshiped idolatrously.

[178] The verb carries several senses: "To burden; to be troublesome or wearisome to; to trouble, worry, pester, annoy" (*OED* 1), with the secondary meaning of "To press, urge, impel." Here the adverb might be read as "irksomely persistent."

[179] It should not need to be pointed out that everything Satan has been saying is a lie: there was no eating of the fruit; there were no animals looking on and envying; no one gained knowledge and speech. But given the fact that Eve is confronted with a talking snake, the argument is cohesive and convincing. It is a beautifully constructed lie, ending in flattery of Eve as empress or mistress ("Dame" as in *OED* I.1) of the universe.

So talk'd the spirited[180] sly Snake; and *Eve*
Yet more amaz'd unwarie[181] thus reply'd.
   Serpent, thy overpraising leaves in doubt   615
The vertue° of that Fruit, in thee first prov'd:[182]   POTENCY
But say, where grows the Tree, from hence how far?
For many are the Trees of God that grow
In Paradise, and various, yet unknown
To us, in such aboundance lies our choice,   620
As leaves a greater store of Fruit untoucht,
Still hanging incorruptible, till men
Grow up to thir provision,[183] and more hands
Help to disburden Nature of her Bearth.
To whom the wilie Adder,[184] blithe and glad.
Empress, the way is readie, and not long,[185]   625
Beyond a row of Myrtles,[186] on a Flat,
Fast by° a Fountain, one small Thicket past   VERY NEAR
Of blowing° Myrrh and Balme; if thou accept   BLOOMING
My conduct,° I can bring thee thither soon,   GUIDANCE   630
   Lead then, said *Eve*. Hee leading swiftly rowld
In tangles, and made[187] intricate seem strait,
To mischief swift. Hope elevates, and joy
Bright'ns his Crest, as when a wandring Fire,[188]
Compact° of unctuous vapor,[189] which the Night   COMPOSED   635
Condenses, and the cold invirons round,
Kindl'd through agitation to a Flame,
Which oft, they say, some evil Spirit attends
Hovering and blazing with delusive° Light,   DELUDING
Misleads th' amaz'd Night-wanderer from his way   640
To Boggs and Mires, and oft through Pond or Poole,
There swallow'd up and lost, from succour farr.

[Handwritten marginalia: "Eve's hesitance"; "Let me show you!"; "Satan guides her to the tree."]

---

[180]He is spirited in that he has breathed his essence into, or inspired, the Serpent's body to speak, a usage initiated by Milton (*OED* 4). The word also had connotations of "excited" or "energetic," as it still does.

[181]Eve is not less culpable but she is both amazed, or utterly confused, and unwary, which is unaware, unthoughtful, or careless. She will be deceived in the Fall, as according to 1 Timothy 2.14. Adam will be "not deceav'd" (998 below; but compare 3.130). The qualification of her state of mind is very important here, since it helps to establish her freedom of will in the act of falling.

[182]Eve has doubts based on the Serpent's overpraising of the fruit, but she has believed the story of his increase in knowledge as a result of eating the fruit. She is "amaz'd" that a snake has been made to talk and seriously confused by what he has said, but she is also "unwarie." Adam has specifically warned her about "Some specious object by the Foe subornd" (361 above), which is exactly what she is faced with. To her credit, she does not yet know what fruit the Serpent is talking about.

[183]Until humankind reaches its full potential or fulfils prophecy, in this case the prophecy to be abundant and replenish the earth (Genesis 1.28).

[184]The epithets for the Serpent have become progressively more colorful, in a sinister way, each time he gains toward his goal of seducing Eve. From "spirited sly Snake" he has become "wilie Adder," and he will become the "dire Snake" of 643 below.

[185]Recalls "ready and easy way," one of Milton's favorite phrases for what Shakespeare calls "the primrose path of dalliance" (*Hamlet* 1.3.50), and part of the title of Milton's pamphlet on the removal of hireling ministers from the Church of England.

[186]I see no need to read the emblematic significance in myrtles that Fowler finds (9.627n). If myrtle indicates the female pudendum, what should we make of the blooming myrrh and balm, or the fountain? The existence of the grove of myrtles has already been firmly established (4.262, 694; compare also the myrrh at 5.23, 292); Milton has not given any signal to the reader that the vegetation should be thought symbolic.

[187]The "make" of *1667* is corrected here by *1674*.

[188]The simile compares Satan to swamp fire, a natural phenomenon associated either with phosphorescence or with electrical or gaseous "balls of fire." The artificial fire or light was thought to be the *ignis fatuus*, a demonic beacon that led the unaware to their damnation. Milton alternates between naturalistic description ("unctuous vapor" would be oil and volatile gas, easily ignited by a spark generated by friction or "agitation") and Christian interpretation. His qualification "they say" indicates skepticism, but his descriptions of origins and sources are very precise. The "fool's fire" was supposed to be an exhalation of earthly vapors, hot, oily, and glutinous, often seen by simple people in fens or swamps and interpreted as evil spirits (see John Swan, *Speculum Mundi; or, A Glasse Representing the Face of the World* [London: enlarged ed. 1643]: 87–89).

[189]The apparition of swamp fire would lead and entrap simple-minded travelers into falling into a pond or pool unconfessed or unshriven (the threat brought about by the apparition of Hamlet's father's ghost, which could be "a spirit of health, or goblin damn'd" [1.4.40]) and hence being damned for eternity. Thus the comparison between the "amaz'd Night-wanderer" and Eve is apt, as long as she does not realize where she is being led.

So glister'd[190] the dire Snake, and into fraud[191]
Led *Eve* our credulous Mother,[192] to the Tree
Of prohibition, root[193] of all our woe;   645
Which when she saw, thus to her guide she spake.

 Serpent, we might have spar'd our coming hither,
Fruitless[194] to mee, though Fruit be here to excess,
The credit of whose vertue rest[195] with thee,
Wondrous indeed,[196] if cause of such effects.   650
But of this Tree we may not taste nor touch;
God so commanded, and left that Command
Sole Daughter of his voice;[197] the rest, we live
Law to our selves, our Reason is our Law.

 To whom the Tempter guilefully repli'd.   655
Indeed? hath God then said that of the Fruit
Of all these Garden Trees ye shall not eate,
Yet Lords declar'd of all in Earth or Aire?

 To whom thus *Eve* yet sinless.[198] Of the Fruit
Of each Tree in the Garden we may eate,   660
But of the Fruit of this fair Tree amidst
The Garden, God hath said, Ye shall not eate
Thereof, nor shall ye touch it, least ye die.[199]

 She scarse had said, though brief, when now more bold
The Tempter, but with shew of Zeale and Love   665
To Man, and indignation at his wrong,
New part puts on,[200] and as to passion mov'd,
Fluctuats disturbd, yet comely and in act

---

[190]"So argued the deadly snake, brilliantly." The verb "glister," meaning "glitter" or "sparkle," was used figuratively of brilliant oratory, as in Thomas Fuller's image "he glistered in the oratoric and poetic sphere" (qtd. *OED* "glister" a).

[191]"State of being defrauded or deluded" (*OED* 5, citing this instance). The word here is used passively, as with the Latin *fraus*, "fraud." The line is itself a brilliant mixture of linguistic and etymological traditions, mixing "glister'd," "dire," and "fraud"—and the unexpectedly brutal and common Anglo-Saxon "Snake" is highlighted by more brilliant or showy words before and after it.

[192]Lest the reader blame Eve too much for being credulous, too easily convinced by a specious object, the Serpent, Milton appends the adjective to "our . . . Mother," uniting us with her in blood and sympathies.

[193]An irresistible but silent pun, since the tree is the root of all the problems that issue from Original Sin. But the tree is not most important for the fruit it bears: it is important because it is prohibited and to eat from it is disobedient.

[194]One of many buried and often serious puns (like that on "root"; and see 1188 below) in Milton's poetry: Eve says the trip is fruitless, implying that she will refuse the fruit. The play on "fruit" and "fruitless" (see Shoaf 144–53) here may indicate Eve's uneasiness—joking to cover fear—or her unwariness.

[195]The singular noun "credit" (it means "trustworthiness" here, as Shawcross points out) would seem to ask for a singular verb "rests," but neither *1667* nor *1674* has that reading.

[196]At this precise point Eve is wavering, since at the same time she acknowledges the prohibition she is still wondering at the supposed effects of eating the fruit on the stature and voice of the Serpent. God's commandment is the "Sole Daughter of his voice," indicating perhaps that obedience can be feminine even though Eve will be disobedient.

[197]Identified by Hunter as not only the Hebraism based on a phrase transliterated as *Bath kol*, but "one of the lowest recognizable forms of prophecy" (*Descent* 23).

[198]An important distinction for the narrator to make, since many critics have fallen into the trap of believing that either or both Adam and Eve sinned before the eating of the fruit. See articles by Lovejoy, Bell, Shumaker, Mollenkott, and Ulreich on the pros and cons of finding the Fall "fortunate."

[199]Eve's words carefully paraphrase God's prohibition in Genesis: "And the Lord God commanded the man, saying, Of every tree of the garden thou mayest freely eat: But of the tree of the knowledge of good and evil, thou shalt not eat of it: for in the day that thou eatest thereof thou shalt surely die" (2.16–17). Even though that command was spoken in Genesis to Adam only and before Eve was created, it is important to Milton to establish that Eve knows it word for word. Also, in antifeminist readings of Genesis, commentators pictured Eve adding to the command, "lest perhaps ye die" (the *ne forte moriamini* of the Vulgate Bible), a position Milton takes pains to avoid. Fowler nevertheless finds it to Eve's discredit that she says "least ye die" instead of "lest ye shall surely die" (9.663n). See Cheryl Guilfoyle, "The Addition."

[200]Satan in the Serpent, here defined in the general role of tempter, is putting on a show, or acting, in a hypocritical manner that allows him to keep assuming new parts, just as Satan has inhabited the bodies of different beasts—toad, cormorant, leopard—in his movements around Eden. Qualifying phrases like "as to" indicate that the passion he is supposed to be feeling is all an act; the words "comely," "act," and "matter" all show Satan acting or pretending in order to deceive Eve. At one moment he expresses zeal or love, either as a religious zealot or as a suitor, and in the next he is an orator. The multiple personalities or metamorphoses of a Vertumnus or Proteus may be part of his character at present; at any rate, Eve is not allowed to focus on his personality because it is shifting so rapidly.

Rais'd, as of som great matter to begin.
As when of old som Orator renound   670
In *Athens* or free *Rome*, where Eloquence
Flourishd, since mute,[201] to som great cause addrest,
Stood in himself collected, while each part,
Motion,[202] each act won audience ere the tongue,
Somtimes in highth[203] began, as no delay   675
Of Preface brooking through his Zeal of Right.
So standing, moving, or to highth upgrown
The Tempter all impassiond thus began.
    O Sacred, Wise, and Wisdom-giving Plant,
Mother of Science,[204] Now I feel thy Power   680
Within me cleere,° not onely to discerne   CLEARLY, DISTINCTLY
Things in thir Causes, but to trace the wayes
Of highest Agents, deemd however wise.[205]
Queen of this Universe, doe not believe
Those rigid threats of Death; ye shall not Die: 685
How should ye? by the Fruit? it gives you Life
To Knowledge.[206] By the Threatner? look on mee,
Mee who have touch'd and tasted, yet both live,
And life more perfet have attaind then Fate
Meant mee,[207] by ventring higher then my Lot.   690
Shall that be shut to Man, which to the Beast
Is open? or will God incense his ire°   KINDLE HIS ANGER
For such a petty Trespass, and not praise
Rather your dauntless vertue,[208] whom the pain
Of Death denounc't, whatever thing Death be,[209]   695
Deterrd not from atchieving what might leade
To happier life, knowledge of Good and Evil;
Of good, how just? of evil, if what is evil
Be real, why not known, since easier shunnd?[210]

---

[201]Authorial comment on the sad state of contemporary oratory. Great oratory belongs, in Milton's opinion, to ancient Greece and Rome. I do not agree with Fowler (9.670–76n) that the phrase "since mute" refers to the Serpent, since he is no longer speaking.

[202]Again, the theatrical imagery in "part," "motion" (which can mean "gesture," "mime," or "puppet show"), "act," and "audience" might lead a reader not only to distrust Satan's acting but the process of acting in general. As soon as Eve has fallen, she too begins the process of putting on parts and playing hypocritically to her audience, Adam.

[203]A phrase from oratory indicating the beginning of a speech without introduction or prefatory remarks. Satan is animated, moving like a spirited or passionate orator, brooking no delays because he wants to seem to have the courage of his convictions or "Zeal of Right."

[204]Milton has Satan address the tree as feminine and the mother of science (knowledge), as if it is kin to Eve through gender, but he is also plainly asking her to worship the tree, which really has no wonder-working power in itself, in an act of idolatry.

[205]Again Satan lies in order to show that, because he has eaten the fruit, he has gained the power to obtain forbidden knowledge and "be as gods" (Genesis 3.5). Tracing the ways of highest agents (presumably angels acting on God's behalf) should therefore be easy to him.

[206]The question marks are obviously misplaced in both editions, perhaps because the compositor of *1667* transposed punctuation marks in his composing stick and, because the page the compositor of *1674* was beginning to compose was just beginning, he apparently did not notice the mistake and blindly followed his copy. Editors since Fenton (1725) and Newton (1749) have changed the question mark after "Knowledge" to a period and changed the comma after "Threatner" to a question mark, since that phrase is interrogatory. The phrase "it gives you Life / To Knowledge" I take to mean "it gives you life in addition to knowledge," following Loh 687n.

[207]Supply "to attain" after "mee." Satan's fatalism is heretical.

[208]The adjective "dauntless" twists virtue to become something quantifiable and something tainted with the flavor of romantic epic, which (even in the hands of Spenser) is full of dauntless or undaunted heroics.

[209]Perhaps an intentional echo, on Milton's part, of Adam's speculation that death is "Som dreadful thing no doubt" (4.426). But Satan knows very well what Death is, since Sin has explained to Satan the nature of her son in detail (2.781-814). Here he heretically questions the commandment.

[210]Of course Satan has a valid point about the knowledge of good and evil (he is characteristically mixing truth and falsehood in order to confuse a potential sinner), but in this case the "Knowledge of Good [will be] bought dear by [Adam and Eve's] knowing ill" (4.222). However much Satan's impressive control of logic ("Not just, not God") may appeal to a reader aesthetically, his rhetoric, his ethics, and his theological position are always suspect. He argues *ad hominem*, for instance, when he labels an omnipotent God as "the Threatner," since omnipotence should not need to threaten its enemies. And

God therefore cannot hurt ye, and be just;   700
Not just, not God; not feard then, nor obeyd:
Your feare it self of Death removes the feare.[211]
Why then was this forbid? Why but to awe,
Why but to keep ye low and ignorant,
His worshippers; he knows that in the day   705
Ye Eate thereof, your Eyes that seem so cleere,
Yet are but dim,[212] shall perfetly be then
Op'nd and cleerd, and ye shall be as Gods,[213]
Knowing both Good and Evil as they know.
That ye should be as Gods, since I as Man,   710
Internal Man, is but proportion meet,°   FITTING PROPORTION
I of brute human, yee of human Gods.[214]
So ye shall die perhaps, but putting off
Human, to put on Gods, death to be wisht,
Though threat'nd, which no worse then this can bring.   715
And what are Gods that Man may not become
As they, participating° God-like food?   SHARING
The Gods are first,[215] and that advantage use
On our belief, that all from them proceeds;
I question it, for this fair Earth I see,   720
Warm'd by the Sun, producing every kind,°   SPECIES
Them nothing: If they[216] all things, who enclos'd
Knowledge of Good and Evil in this Tree,
That whoso eats thereof, forthwith attains
Wisdom without their leave? and wherein lies   725
Th' offence, that Man should thus attain to know?
What° can your knowledge hurt him, or this Tree   HOW
Impart[217] against his will if all be his?
Or is it envie, and can envie dwell
In heav'nly brests? these,[218] these and many more   730
Causes import[219] your need of this fair Fruit.

[handwritten annotation: that Eve needs this]

---

when Satan, the author of evil, argues that evil is nonexistent, a morally insecure reader will be left squirming. Questioning the reality of evil is itself heretical.

[211]This conjecture, while it sounds sententious, makes no sense at all, since fear of something cannot remove that something (particularly fear itself). Satan, in other words, is speaking high-sounding nonsense.

[212]The obverse is true: with sin their vision will be dimmed. One result of Satan's sin is that his face is "dimm'd" (4.114). Satan is arguing from a pagan perspective in which priests invent gods in order to keep people in awe.

[213]Satan's temptation of "the woman" in Genesis includes "Ye shall not surely die: For God doth know that in the day ye eat thereof, then your eyes shall be opened, and ye shall be as gods, knowing good and evil" (3.4–5). The Geneva Bible marginalia glosses this passage "As thogh he shulde say, God doeth not forbid you to eat of the frute, save that he knoweth that if you shulde eat therof, you shulde be like to him" (1560 ed.). What puzzled theologians and commentators, Milton among them, was the phrase "as gods," in the plural. Milton took "gods" to mean "angels," and he often took "gods" in the Old Testament as meaning "angels," both unfallen and fallen, or just "wicked spirits." Andrew Willet's interpretation is similar: "as gods" means "either as angels, or like unto us, sinnefull and wicked spirits" (48). Satan also postulates the existence of a plurality of gods (polytheism).

[214]The logic would be irrefutable, if he were telling the truth. But Eve should be able to see that though he speaks like a man, he is not one, unless she allows that he is an "Internal Man." Notice that Satan does add the "perhaps" to God's prohibition, as in the Vulgate passage cited above. The image of "putting off" and "put[ting] on" suggests that godhead is like clothing and can be quickly put on or taken off. In like manner, Satan will argue even more fallaciously that eating "God-like food," which suggests "idol food," makes one God.

[215]"The gods came first in creation, and therefore can use their primogeniture to fool those who come after into thinking that everything proceeds from them."

[216]Supply "produce."

[217]"Give away [the knowledge of good and evil]."

[218]Unusual lack of capitalization at the beginning of a sentence (see 1062 below and 8.350 for the opposite usage), which most editors correct to capital "These," but here beginning the sentence as if it followed a colon or semicolon might be an attempt to represent Satan's breathlessness. Beeching, Hughes, Shawcross, and Campbell allow the line to stand as it was written in *1667* and *1674*; Fowler and Elledge "correct" to capital "These." Compare 764 below.

[219]"Occasion" (*OED* I.4). "Many more causes bring about your need for this fair fruit."

Goddess humane,[220] reach then, and freely taste.
　　He ended, and his words replete with guile[221]
Into her heart too easie entrance won:
Fixt on the Fruit she gaz'd, which to behold　　　　　　　735
Might tempt alone, and in her ears the sound
Yet rung of his perswasive words, impregn'd
With Reason, to her seeming, and with Truth;[222]
Mean while the hour of Noon drew on, and wak'd
An eager appetite, rais'd by the smell　　　　　　　740
So savorie of that Fruit, which with desire,
Inclinable° now grown to touch or taste,　　　　INCLINED
Sollicited her longing eye; yet first
Pausing a while, thus to her self she mus'd.[223]
　　Great are thy Vertues, doubtless, best of Fruits,[224]　　745
Though kept from Man, and worthy to be admir'd,
Whose taste, too long forborn, at first assay
Gave elocution to the mute, and taught
The Tongue not made for Speech to speak thy praise:[225]
Thy praise hee also who forbids thy use,　　　　750
Conceales not from us, naming thee the Tree
Of Knowledge, knowledge both of good and evil;
Forbids us then to taste, but his forbidding
Commends thee more, while it inferrs the good
By thee communicated, and our want:°　　　　LACK　　755
For good unknown, sure is not had, or had
And yet unknown, is as not had at all.
In plain° then, what forbids he but to know,　　PLAINLY
Forbids us good, forbids us to be wise?
Such prohibitions binde not. But if Death　　　760
Bind us with after-bands,[226] what profits then
Our inward freedom? In the day we eate
Of this fair Fruit, our doom° is, we shall die.　　FATE
How dies the Serpent? hee hath eat'n and lives,
And knows, and speaks, and reasons, and discerns,　765
Irrational till then. For us alone
Was death invented?[227] or to us deni'd
This intellectual food, for beasts reserv'd?

---

[220]As Fowler points out, "Satan must now be very sure to risk so wild an oxymoron" (9.732n). According to *A Treatise of Stops*, the spelling with an "e" and the position of the word after a substantive ("Goddess," in this case) indicates that it should be pronounced like the modern "humane" (11). The compositors of *Paradise Lost* are consistent in this usage.

[221]"Force and guile" (for the latter as a motif, see 306, 466, 567, and 655 above) are Satan's two methods of gaining his objectives, traditionally and throughout *Paradise Lost*, with "fraud" being a synonym for "guile." In his dealings with Eve, not even the threat of force has been necessary.

[222]"His persuasive words were full of reason, to her way of thinking, and with truth." Eve is deceived by Satan's mixing truth with lies and Satan has appealed deceitfully to her sight, sound, smell, touch, and taste. Even her lunchtime hunger has been used to make her desire the fruit. The word "impregn'd," meaning "impregnated," suggests a perverse kind of engendering.

[223]Her pause signifies the difference between a completely careless act and one endorsed by thought. Thus she is culpable, because she has "mus'd" about eating the fruit. Her sin is mortal, not venial.

[224]At this point Eve has become idolatrous, in that in her soliloquy she addresses the Fruit itself as a worshipful entity; soon she will be calling it "Fruit Divine" (776). The period after "Fruits" replaced a comma in *1667*, but the comma of the first edition seems to provide the better reading.

[225]She has accepted Satan's lie that eating the fruit gives the Serpent the power to speak. She is thinking and speaking Satanically, from now until the point when she eats, and forever after. Her evil will has caused her to endorse the act of disobedience and sin in the few moments left before she eats the fruit. For the process leading from the suggestion of sin, then to the relishing of it, then to evil will and consent, see Augustine, *City of God* 14.13, "That in Adam's sin an evil will preceded the evil act."

[226]This may be the first instance of the compound form, meaning "a subsequent band or bond after a release" (see *OED* II).

[227]The answer to this rhetorical question, if one believes Adam at 4.427, is "yes": death is decreed by God as punishment for those who taste the fruit.

For Beasts it seems: yet that one Beast which first
Hath tasted, envies not, but brings with joy
The good befall'n him, Author unsuspect,
Friendly to man, farr from deceit or guile.[228]
What fear I then, rather what know to feare
Under this ignorance of good and Evil,
Of God or Death, of Law or Penaltie?
Here grows the Cure of all,[229] this Fruit Divine,
Fair to the Eye, inviting to the Taste,
Of vertue[230] to make wise: what hinders then
To reach, and feed at once both Bodie and Mind?
   So saying, her rash hand in evil[231] hour
Forth reaching to the Fruit, she pluck'd, she eat:[232]
Earth felt the wound, and Nature from her seat
Sighing through all her Works gave signs of woe,
That all was lost.[233] Back to the Thicket slunk[234]
The guiltie Serpent, and well might, for *Eve*
Intent now wholly on her taste, naught else
Regarded, such delight till then, as seemd,
In Fruit she never tasted, whether true
Or fansied so, through expectation high
Of knowledg, nor was God-head from her thought.
Greedily she ingorg'd without restraint,[235]
And knew not eating Death: Satiate at length,
And hight'nd as with Wine, jocond and boon,
Thus to her self she pleasingly began.
   O Sovran, vertuous, precious[236] of all Trees
In Paradise, of operation blest
To Sapience,[237] hitherto obscur'd, infam'd,
And thy fair Fruit let hang, as to no end
Created; but henceforth my early care,

770

775

780

785

790

795

---

[228]While saying this, of course, Eve is completely deceived by Satan's deceit and guile. Far from being an innocent "Author unsuspect," Satan is author or instigator of sin and thus always suspicious.

[229]Though the word "cure-all," meaning panacea or medicine that cures all diseases, is not recorded for the seventeenth century, that meaning seems close to what Milton intended, with overtones of fraudulent representaton of its curative powers, as if the fruit were a kind of snake-oil remedy. There may be a buried pun in "Cure" and "Care," since the fruit creates a wound that will need constant attention.

[230]Eve seems to be using the word in the Satanic sense of "power," without any overtones of "righteousness."

[231]Perhaps with a pun on Eve/evil. See 1067 below.

[232]Probably as in the obsolete English pronunciation of the past tense, "et."

[233]Though all is lost at this point, Adam will still be said to be "compleating" the "mortal sin / Original" (1003–04 below). The proverbial sympaty of all of nature to the Fall is made poignantly intimate by the withering of Adam's garland (892–93 below). The pathetic fallacy expressed here by nature reflects the belief that in the Fall of humankind all nature fell (was no longer "good" as the Genesis formula expresses it). Notice how rapidly Eve's fall and the retreat of the Serpent are described: the preamble is much more important than the act itself.

[234]A wonderfully apt verb, one which provides a picture of Satan in the Serpent, his horrible job done, slinking off into a thicket, like a snake who has just bitten someone, its cowardly retreat summed up in the undignified slunk. The Serpent is no longer important to Satan (or to Eve, for that matter), since its function is complete.

[235]In *On Christian Doctrine* Milton listed one of the "SPECIAL VIRTUES" as "SOBRIETY," opposite which are placed "drunkenness and gluttony" (2.9; Yale 6: 724–25). Eve's gluttony in this case also has an intoxicating effect on her, making her "high" as if she were drinking wine to excess. She is satiated in the bad sense of the word, and she is almost hysterically mirthful and companionable ("jocond and boon"). Milton takes pains to incorporate as many sins in the act of disobedience as could be imagined, so that gluttony and drunkenness are just two among many. See *On Christian Doctrine* 1.11, which lists being "greedy," among other sins for the pair, and comments "For what fault is there which man did not commit in committing this sin?" (Yale 6: 383).

[236]"O most sovereign, most virtuous, and most precious," an imitation of linguistic use of the positive for the superlative, in Greek, Latin, or Italian.

[237]If one remembers the ironic application of "Sapient" to the wise King Solomon, pictured in the act of idolatry to the false gods of his wives (442 above), then Eve will not be wise to worship the fruit, nor will Adam be wise in worshiping Eve. Compare the positive uses of wisdom, as at 7.9–10.

Not without Song, each Morning,[238] and due praise   800
Shall tend thee, and the fertil burden ease
Of thy full branches offer'd free to all;
Till dieted° by thee I grow mature   FED
In knowledge, as the Gods who all things know;[239]
Though others envie what they cannot give;   805
For had the gift bin theirs, it had not here
Thus grown. Experience,[240] next to thee I owe,
Best guide; not following thee, I had remain'd
In ignorance, thou op'nst Wisdoms way,
And giv'st access, though secret she retire.   810
And I perhaps am secret;[241] Heav'n is high,
High and remote to see from thence distinct
Each thing on Earth; and other care perhaps
May have diverted from continual watch
Our great Forbidder,[242] safe with all his Spies   815
About him. But to *Adam* in what sort[243]
Shall I appeer? shall I to him make known
As yet my change,[244] and give him to partake
Full happiness with mee, or rather not,
But keep the odds of Knowledge in my power   820
Without Copartner? so to add what wants
In Femal Sex, the more to draw his Love,
And render me more equal, and perhaps,
A thing not undesireable, somtime
Superior; for inferior who is free?   825
This may be well: but what if God have seen,
And Death ensue? then I shall be no more,
And *Adam* wedded to another *Eve*,
Shall live with her enjoying, I extinct;[245]
A death to think. Confirm'd then I resolve,   830
Adam shall share with me in bliss or woe:
So dear I love him, that with him all deaths

---

[238]Eve, already speaking with a Satanic style and with Satanic perversity and fogginess, promises to replace the couple's morning hymn to God with a hymn to the tree, together with early morning attendance at the shrine ("my early care"). Compare the use of "not without Song" applied to angelic hymning at 5.178.

[239]Eve suggests polytheism even as Satan had frequently done. The coy usage of "others" and "envie" probably indicates her hesitancy to name God.

[240]Discussing her sin in terms of experience again allows Eve to try to escape from responsibility for what she has done. The use of "experience" is comparable to the use of "doom," as something separate from God, free will, or fate. Both "experience" and "authority" have a heavy weight of theological tradition behind them; Milton might well have have remembered the Wife of Bath on the subject: "Experience, though noon auctoritee / Were in this world, is right ynough for me / To speke of wo that is in mariage" ("Wife of Bath's Prologue" 1–3, in The Riverside Chaucer, ed. Larry D. Benson [Boston: Houghton Mifflin, 1987]: 105).

[241]Eve's desire to be hidden foreshadows Adam's hiding from God after his fall; within the Christian system as Milton constructs it, Eve's desire to be not seen by an omnipresent and omniscient God is at best foolish: hence her Satanic "perhaps" (Satan introduces the word to the epic at 1.166 and uses it very often thereafter). She hints that God in Heaven is nearsighted, not capable of seeing things on Earth distinctly.

[242]Adopting even Satan's modes of address, Eve echoes "Threatner" (687 above) with "Forbidder."

[243]A very rich word, implying "rank" (*OED* 2.b and, without article, 15; compare *Samson Agonistes* 1608) or "variety" (*OED* 12). The word also suggests the theatrical, as in Samuel Johnson's definition, "A manner; a form of being or acting," citing this passage for support (*Dictionary*, 1769 ed.).

[244]She assumes she has changed for the better and put on godhead.

[245]Supply "life" or "existence" or "matrimony" after "enjoying"; before "extinct," supply "being." "A death to think" is equivalent to "I wouldn't think of it," though the fact that she has brought mortality on herself and humankind loads a colloquial phrase with heavy irony. Eve is considering the rabbinical tradition that God might make a second Eve or the equivalent of a Lilith to replace her (see Svendsen 168).

I could endure, without him live no life.[246]
   So saying, from the Tree her step she turnd,
But first low Reverence don, as to the power   835
That dwelt within, whose presence had infus'd
Into the plant scientialᵒ sap, deriv'd   WISDOM-GIVING
From Nectar, drink of Gods. *Adam* the while
Waiting desirous her return, had wove
Of choicest Flours a Garland to adorne   840
Her Tresses, and her rural labours crown,
As Reapers oft are wont thir Harvest Queen.[247]
Great joy he promis'd to his thoughts, and new
Solace in her return, so long delay'd;
Yet oft his heart, divineᵒ of somthing ill,   FORETELLING   845
Misgave him; hee the faultring measure[248] felt;
And forth to meet her went, the way she took
That Morn when first they parted; by the Tree
Of Knowledge he must pass, there he her met,
Scarse from the Tree returning; in her hand   850
A bough of fairest fruit that downie smil'd,[249]
New gatherd, and ambrosial smell diffus'd.
To him she hasted, in her face excuse
Came Prologue, and Apologie to prompt,[250]
Which with bland words at will she thus addrest.   855
   Hast thou not wonderd, *Adam*, at my stay?
Thee I have misst, and thought it long, depriv'd
Thy presence, agonie of love till now
Not felt,[251] nor shall be twice, for never more
Mean I to trie, what rash untri'd I sought,   860
The pain of absence from thy sight. But strange
Hath bin the cause, and wonderful to heare:
This Tree is not as we are told, a Tree
Of danger tasted, nor to evil unknown
Op'ning the way, but of Divine effect   865
To open Eyes, and make them Gods who taste;
And hath bin tasted such: the Serpent wise,

---

[246]Despite her declaration of love, Eve has made the decision to share the sin with Adam and thereby bring about his death. The sin could be defined as murder, or more specifically as parricide, since Eve in killing Adam is killing not only her mate but her father. At any rate, her "So dear I love him" is highly suspect. Fowler adduces Horace's ode 3.9 (especially line 24) as a possible influence, but even if Eve is in any way considering suicide (and she seems to want to take Adam down with her rather than die alone), Milton's passage is a parody of Horace's ode, which deals with rivalry between lovers and the potential for dying for love.

[247]Adam's weaving a garland for his harvest queen is horribly ironic, partly because there will never again be true pastoral bliss after the sin has ruined the natural balance in Eden. Also, Adam and Eve's labor will be tainted with necessity after the Fall, since Adam will be specifically punished to labor with sweat and bring forth as many "thorns . . . and thistles" as fruits and vegetables (Genesis 3.17–19).

[248]The rhythmic discord may indicate the imbalance of world harmony or rhythmic measure, since Milton often uses the noun "measure" to indicate a dance. Compare "Celestial measures" in *Paradise Regain'd* 1.170.

[249]Probably Burden is correct in the supposition that the bough of fruit can seem to be smiling to Adam, since Adam so far knows no harm from it (138). Its ambrosial smell, however, may be sinister, since ambrosia is the food of the pagan gods. References to ambrosia, nectar, and the "drink of Gods" (838 above) are suspect after the Fall.

[250]The theatrical image of Eve, who comes with what seems to be an allegorical Excuse announced by Prologue (the actor playing Prologue) accompanied with Apology acting as a prompt. Eve is two-faced, with a playlet going on in her facial expressions. The series of images shows Eve as a Satanic hypocritical actress. Her "bland words" indicate her artificiality and insincerity.

[251]Love has already become a sickness, an agony rather than a simple pleasure, flourishing on wonder and synthetic deprivation. For background on love considered as an illness allied with the complex of diseases associated with melancholy, see Ferrand, *A Treatise on Lovesickness*, and the classic of Milton's generation, Robert Burton's *Anatomy of Melancholy*. As Paul Klemp points out to me, Eve has been deprived of Adam's presence before, when Raphael visits, and she should have felt the "agonie of love" then (letter, October 1991).

Or not restraind as wee, or not obeying,
Hath eat'n of the fruit, and is become,
Not dead, as we are threatn'd, but thenceforth   870
Endu'd with human voice and human sense,
Reasoning to admiration,[252] and with mee
Perswasively hath so prevaild, that I
Have also tasted, and have also found
Th' effects to correspond, opener mine Eyes,   875
Dimm erst, dilated Spirits, ampler Heart,
And growing up to Godhead; which for thee
Chiefly I sought, without thee can despise.[253]
For bliss, as thou hast part, to me is bliss,
Tedious, unshar'd with thee, and odious soon.   880
Thou therefore also taste, that equal Lot
May joyne us, equal Joy, as equal Love;
Least thou not tasting, different degree
Disjoyne us, and I then too late renounce
Deitie for thee, when Fate[254] will not permit.   885

    Thus *Eve* with Countnance blithe her storie told;
But in her Cheek distemper flushing glowd.[255]
On th' other side, *Adam*, soon as he heard
The fatal Trespass don by *Eve*, amaz'd,
Astonied stood and Blank,° while horror chill   WHITE   890
Ran through his veins, and all his joynts relax'd;[256]
From his slack hand the Garland wreath'd for *Eve*
Down drop'd, and all the faded Roses shed:
Speechless he stood and pale, till thus at length
First to himself he inward silence broke.[257]   895
   O fairest of Creation, last and best
Of all Gods works, Creature in whom excell'd
Whatever can to sight or thought be formd,
Holy, divine, good, amiable, or sweet!
How art thou lost, how on a sudden lost,   900
Defac't, deflourd,[258] and now to Death devote?

---

[252]Demonstrating reason to the point of causing wonder in those who hear him. In reacting to what Eve has to say, Adam cannot share her wonder at hearing the Serpent speak, since Adam is "not deceav'd" (998 below). So much of what Eve says must seem to be nonsense to Adam, yet Eve's demeanor while speaking it causes him to be "fondly overcome with Femal charm" (999 below).

[253]Since Eve was discussing the possibility of being "more equal" and "keep[ing] the odds of Knowledge in [her] power" (823, 820 above), she can hardly claim to have eaten the fruit for Adam's sake. Taught by Satan, she has learned how to lie. She is, however, clearly deceived by Satan in the Serpent, since she does believe that the Serpent has risen to human nature by eating the fruit.

[254]Eve has become a pagan fatalist, at least for the time being.

[255]Eve's unhealthy flush should give away her dis-tempered or unbalanced temperament, which has also been unbalanced by her sin. Her carelessness here is truly despicable, since it is as if she were giving away the prospect of eternal death like a trinket.

[256]Adam's body language—his slump and his "slack hand"—demonstrate the "effeminate slackness" that Michael will accuse him of in 11.634. He is dumb-founded, amazed, and astonished but at the same time powerless against Eve's beauty and charm. In no way, however, is he less culpable than she. Her flush is answered by his pallor: neither is healthy.

[257]What follows is a soliloquy, corresponding to Eve's earlier inward speech just before she ate the fruit, which reinforces the dramatic setting of the book but also comments negatively on the need after the Fall for private conversations with oneself expressing internal contradictions. Adam here is curiously talking to himself, but about Eve; though he is not fallen, his anxiety projects his own fall.

[258]Eve has not been raped, nor has she lost her virginity to Satan, but she has lost her innocence, and she has even lost her garden (or she has been de-flowered). She has also been "seized" or "carried away" (the meaning of the Latin verb *rapere*), both from Adam and from God, by Satan in the Serpent. Eve has also been "de-faced" not only in "losing face" but in a theological sense that Arnold Stein (8) noticed in a definition of sin in *On Christian Doctrine*: "the lessening of the majesty of the human countenance" (1.12; Yale 6: 394). She is "devote[d]" to death in the religious sense of being a devotee (compare 3.208), but "devote" also carries the meaning of "given over to the powers of darkness" (*OED* verb sense 3).

Rather how hast thou yeelded to transgress[259]
The strict forbiddance, how to violate
The sacred Fruit forbidd'n! som cursed fraud
Of Enemie[260] hath beguil'd thee, yet unknown,
And mee with thee hath ruind, for with thee   905
Certain my resolution is to Die;[261]
How can I live without thee, how forgoe
Thy sweet Converse and Love so dearly joyn'd,
To live again in these wilde Woods forlorn?[262]   910
Should God create another *Eve*, and I
Another ~~Rib afford,~~° yet loss of thee
Would never from my heart; no no, I feel
The Link of Nature draw me: Flesh of Flesh,
Bone of my Bone thou art, and from thy State   915
Mine never shall be parted, bliss or woe.[263]

   So having said, as one from sad dismay
Recomforted, and after thoughts disturbd
Submitting to what seemd remediless,[264]
Thus in calm mood his Words to *Eve* he turnd.   920
   Bold deed thou hast presum'd, adventrous[265] *Eve*,
And peril great provok't, who thus hath[266] dar'd
Had it been onely coveting to Eye
That sacred Fruit, sacred to abstinence,[267]
Much more to taste it under banne to touch.[268]   925
But past who can recall, or don undoe?
Not God Omnipotent, nor Fate, yet so
Perhaps[269] thou shalt not Die, perhaps the Fact[270]
Is not so hainous° now, foretasted Fruit,

PROVIDE

HEINOUS, HORRIBLY EVIL

Handwritten marginalia: "Will rather die than leave Eve"; "internal monologue"; "HE NEEDS HER"; "Adam talking to Eve"; "SHE DID WHAT MILTON DID"

---

[259] According to the translation in the Authorized Version of 1 Timothy 2.14, "the woman being deceived was in the transgression," a clause which theologians glossed in many ways. Milton seems to be separating the first event of the transgression (Eve's eating the fruit) from its completion (Adam's eating); thus Eve could yield to transgression before Adam has eaten, yet neither she nor Adam be more culpable in the process.

[260] "Some cursed fraud or guile promulgated by an enemy" (with the implication that "Enemie" must mean "Satan").

[261] Adam may be resolved to die with her, but in no way is his decision to die fated to be: it is based on his free choice. Though his decision to die may seem a noble gesture in the name of love, it will only complete and endorse her sin. See Danielson, "The Fall of Man."

[262] If he were doomed by Eve's exile or death to remain in the wild woods of Eden, he would be lost without her, especially since, because she is his rib, she is part of him. Though the woods may indeed be innocently wild ("forlorn" here retains its Anglo-Saxon force of "utterly abandoned," "lost"), he would be lost without her, especially since, because she is his rib, she is part of him. As Adam sees it at this moment, he has no choice but to fall with her. After he has fallen, he will question his own choice and accuse Eve of having caused his fall. By hindsight he will also consider the possibility of a second Eve being created, a possibility that had been cultivated in the legend of Lilith, the possible first wife for Adam (for information about Lilith, see Louis Ginzberg, *The Legends of the Jews* [Philadelphia: The Jewish Publication Society of America, c. 1909–38] 1: 64–66, "Woman").

[263] Burden (164–65) and Fowler are quite right to use Milton's divorce tracts as commentary: "In a sense Adam becomes corrupt because he refuses to divorce Eve: because he wants solace at any price" (Fowler, 9.908–909n). But Leonard responds, "Is Eve's case then hopeless when she returns to Adam's side, having eaten the forbidden fruit?" Though Leonard concedes "that divorce is one possible remedy (for Adam)," he adds "but we cheapen the grace and delicacy of Milton's words if we refer them to Adam and divorce alone" (216). Despite the fact that she is part of his flesh, Adam still does have the choice to divorce Eve, but his dilemma only seems remediless.

[264] The key word here is "seemd," since Adam is still free to reject Eve. Her selfish denial of Adam is mirrored by his apparently altruistic acceptance of his fate with her, but he is still giving in to what seems to be a hopeless situation. What Adam says out loud after his decision to fall with Eve is culpable and Satanic. He is "in calm mood" when he says it because he is not deceived.

[265] Milton uses the same idiom for his own "adventrous Song" (1.13), but here the sense is that Eve has been an "adventurer" or that she has "ventured higher than her lot" (690 above).

[266] *1667* "hast." Despite Adams's argument in *Ikon* 92, "hath" seems to me to be a correction.

[267] Adam diminishes the value of the fruit while in the process of beginning to worship it, reducing asceticism to a pagan duty. Because one must make a sacred vow of abstinence, breaking the vow is that much more exciting.

[268] "How much more perilous is it then to *taste* the thing which we are forbidden to *touch*" (Loh's paraphrase, 921–25n).

[269] Adam's speech is starting to fill with "perhapses," a sure indication that he is thinking like Satan or Belial (compare 2.211, among many other passages in which the qualification indicates demonic uncertainty).

[270] As Fowler points out (9.928n), the customary sense of "fact" in the seventeenth century was "crime" (*OED* 1.c).

Profan'd first by the Serpent, by him first   930
Made common and unhallowd ere our taste;
Nor yet on him found deadly,[271] he yet lives,
Lives, as thou saidst,[272] and gaines to live as Man
Higher degree of Life, inducement strong
To us, as likely tasting to attaine   935
Proportional ascent, which cannot be
But to be Gods, or Angels Demi-gods.
Nor can I think that God, Creator wise,
Though threatning, will in earnest so destroy
Us his prime Creatures, dignifi'd so high,   940
Set over all his Works, which in our Fall,
For us created, needs with us must faile,
Dependent made; so God shall uncreate,
Be frustrate, do, undo, and labour loose,[273]
Not well conceav'd of God, who though his Power   945
Creation could repeate, yet would be loath
Us to abolish, least the Adversary
Triumph[274] and say; Fickle their State whom God
Most Favors, who can please him long?[275] Mee first
He ruind, now Mankind; whom will he next?   950
Matter of scorne, not to be given the Foe,
However I with thee have fixt my Lot,
Certain to undergoe like doom, if Death
Consort with thee, Death is to mee as Life;[276]
So forcible within my heart I feel   955
The Bond of Nature[277] draw me to my owne,
My own in thee, for what thou art is mine;
Our State cannot be severd, we are one,
One Flesh; to loose thee were to loose my self.
   So *Adam*, and thus *Eve* to him repli'd.   960
O glorious trial of exceeding Love,
Illustrious evidence, example high![278]
Ingaging me to emulate, but short
Of thy perfection, how shall I attaine,
Adam, from whose deare side I boast me sprung,   965

---

[271]"Nor yet found to have deadly effects on him." Adam is grabbing at as many straws as he can, in order to be able to justify what he is about to do. The argument that the fruit has been desecrated ("the serpent has already taken the spell off the fruit; therefore it is less hallowed and more common than it was before") is especially lame.

[272]Adam accepts Eve's word though he knows she is fallen and has been seduced by the specious object, the Serpent. Adam deceives himself willfully, if he is not lying outright.

[273]The word is genuinely ambiguous, since it could represent the modern lose or loose; thus it could mean either "undo" or "lose" (see 959 below). In losing His labor, God would not benefit from work performed in the Creation. The pun on "well conceav'd" is low and Satanic.

[274]Apparently accented on the second syllable.

[275]*1674* has a semicolon here, replacing the question mark of *1667*; I agree with Fletcher that foul case is the probable cause for the obvious mistake. Adam's argument against God being able to undo His creation seems a perverse echo of the Son's "wilt thou thy self / Abolish thy Creation, and unmake, / For him [Satan], what for thy glorie thou hast made?" (3.162–64).

[276]Like Eve and Satan, Adam is now talking in terms of fixed lot or fixed fate (compare the fallen angels when they are arguing the same point just as fruitlessly at 2.560) or doom. His selection of nouns like "doom" indicates what he thinks might be a loss of free will. He also uses the word "Consort" (even the verb, accented on the second syllable) in a way which suggests that Eve is married (like Sin?) to Death. Marriage has already been desecrated or made perverse.

[277]In an especially sinister, almost subliminal change, the "Link of Nature" (914 above) has become a bond, or band, strapping Adam's heart to Eve's flesh. Given Milton's mercantile and legal interests, he may also be speaking of a somewhat unpleasant new contract between Adam and Eve.

[278]Eve's hyperbolic apostrophe "O . . . trial" is a sign of her insincerity and hypocrisy; it also seems to be a parody of the reaction of a romantic heroine, say, to a hero returning with a talisman a damsel had asked him for.

And gladly of our Union heare thee speak,
One Heart, one Soul in both; whereof good prooff
This day affords, declaring thee resolvd,
Rather then Death or aught then Death more dread
Shall separate us, linkt in Love so deare,   970
To undergoe with mee one Guilt, one Crime,
If any be, of tasting this fair Fruit,
Whose vertue, for of good still good proceeds,
Direct, or by occasion hath presented
This happie trial of thy Love, which else   975
So eminently never had bin known.[279]
Were it I thought Death menac't would ensue
This my attempt, I would sustain alone
The worst, and not perswade thee rather° die   RATHER TO
Deserted, then oblige thee with a fact[280]   980
Pernicious to thy Peace, chiefly assur'd
Remarkably so late of thy so true,
So faithful Love unequald; but I feel
Farr otherwise th' event, not Death, but Life
Augmented, op'nd Eyes, new Hopes, new Joyes,   985
Taste so Divine, that what of sweet before
Hath toucht my sense, flat seems to this, and harsh.
On my experience, *Adam*, freely taste,
And fear of Death deliver to the Windes.[281]
    So saying, she embrac'd him, and for joy   990
Tenderly wept, much won that he his Love
Had so enobl'd, as of choice to incurr
Divine displeasure for her sake, or Death.
In recompence (for such compliance bad
Such recompence best merits) from the bough   995
She gave him of that fair enticing Fruit
With liberal hand: he scrupl'd not to eat
Against his better knowledge, not deceav'd,
But fondly overcome with Femal charm.[282]
Earth trembl'd from her entrails, as again   1000
In pangs, and Nature gave a second groan,
Skie lowr'd[283] and muttering Thunder, som sad drops

---

[279]Eve is not only hyperbolic, she is verbose ("Ingaging me to emulate"), vague, and repetitious, gushing meaningless and redundant patter.

[280]Eve not only binds herself to Adam in her imagery but she renders herself "obnoxious to guilt and punishment" (Newton's definition of "oblige" according to the Latin sense of *obligo* [978n]). Her strained alliteration in "Pernicious . . . Peace" is a sign of her insincerity. Fowler transliterates "chiefly assur'd" as "especially since I have been assured" (9.981n). I read most of the rest of this speech as convoluted gobbledegook, designed to shovel praise on Adam at the last minute.

[281]There may indeed be a horrible connection between Eve using a variant of the trite phrase "throw to the winds" and the emission of the odor of mortality, by which Death himself "snuff'd the smell / Of mortal change on Earth" (10.272-73; see Fowler 9.989n). When Eve embraces Adam, she has, like the damsel of romantic epic, been "won" by his "enobl'd" love, because he has risked so much of God's wrath just for her sake. She has, in other words, dared him to defy God—and he has taken the dare.

[282]The distinction Milton makes is again that of the author of 1 Timothy 2.14: "And Adam was not deceived, but the woman being deceived was in the transgression." Milton glosses Adam being "not deceav'd," adding that Adam scrupled not to eat—he knew in his fundamental moral principles that he should not eat—but that nevertheless he was fondly, foolishly overcome by female charm, which I take to mean the intoxicating and enervating effect of Eve's beauty. The passage is rich and evocative, since it would differentiate and define gender roles after the Fall, "instituting . . . a patriarchal society" (Northrop Frye, *Words with Power* [NY: Harcourt Brace, 1990]: 208).

[283]The sky itself acts in sympathy with the effects of sin, now both muttering and weeping "sad drops" in the world's first thunderstorm. As with Eve's fall, Adam's redounds through all creation. The text of *1667* has a comma here, which Fletcher thinks is needed; I am not sure enough to emend *1674*.

Wept at compleating of the mortal Sin[284]
Original; while *Adam* took no thought,
Eating his fill, nor *Eve* to iterate
Her former trespass fear'd, the more to soothe
Him with her lov'd societie, that now
As with new Wine[285] intoxicated both   1010
They swim in mirth, and fansie that they feel
Divinitie within them breeding wings
Wherewith to scorne the Earth:[286] but that false Fruit
Farr other operation first displaid,
Carnal desire enflaming, hee on *Eve*
Began to cast lascivious Eyes, she him
As wantonly repaid; in Lust they burne: 1015
Till *Adam* thus 'gan *Eve* to dalliance move.[287]
     Eve, now I see thou art exact of taste,
And elegant, of Sapience[288] no small part,
Since to each meaning savour we[289] apply,
And Palate call judicious; I the praise   1020
Yeild thee, so well this day thou has purvey'd.
Much pleasure we have lost, while we abstain'd
From this delightful Fruit, nor known till now
True relish, tasting; if such pleasure be
In things to us forbidden, it might be wish'd,   1025
For this one Tree had bin forbidden ten.[290]
But come, so well refresh't, now let us play,
As meet is, after such delicious Fare;
For never did thy Beautie since the day
I saw thee first and wedded thee, adorn'd   1030
With all[291] perfections, so enflame my sense
With ardor to enjoy thee,[292] fairer now
Then ever, bountie of this vertuous Tree.

---

[284]The only place in *Paradise Lost* where the phrase "original sin" is used, though Milton did use it in *On Christian Doctrine*, citing Augustine as his source but finding Augustine's term "too narrow, because this evil desire, this law of sin, was not only inbred in us, but also took possession of Adam after his fall, and from his point of view it could not be called original" (1.11; Yale 6: 389). Adam completes the sin, but his completing of it does not relieve him of any of the responsibility for the sin, which is mortal in that it induces death or mortality not only on Adam and Eve but on all humankind. It is a mortal as compared with a venial sin in that it is done in full awareness that the command is being broken. Adam taking no thought, when combined with Eve's "mindlessness" and his own "vehemence of love," represents deadly triviality or thoughtlessness on the part of both Adam and Eve. Both Adam and Eve "muse" about the act, but apparently the process of thinking is vehement or mindless.

[285]New or unseasoned wine has always been infamous for inducing quick drunkenness and causing bad hangovers.

[286]Both Adam and Eve feel "high" and have the false sensation of flying, perhaps taking a cue from what Eve has described in her dream, when the stripling cherub took her flying above the Earth after she had eaten the dream fruit (5.86–90). The image also evokes that of Icarus flying too near the sun, melting his wings, and falling to his death.

[287]Quite simply, sin turns love to lust. Instead of flying above the Earth, Adam and Eve are driven by their bodily and earthly lust. Eve's innocent "wanton ringlets" (4.306) have been replaced with wanton desire. I have reinstated the period after "move" as in *1667*, on the grounds that house style in printing houses of the time dictated a period before any quotation; the comma of *1674* is therefore obviously incorrect.

[288]As usual, sapience in a state of sin is dangerous "wisdom" or forbidden knowledge. Adam in praising Eve's elegance and good taste is really praising her inelegant excess, and the sapience is like that of Solomon when he in his dotage seeks after false gods. Everything Adam says is deeply ironic: the trivial food imagery suggests that eating this fruit discriminatingly is more valuable than gaining eternal life. The bad puns go on, with "let us play" replacing "let us pray."

[289]*1674* changes the "we" of *1667* to "me," which may be the result of foul case in that an inverted letter was selected. Only "we" makes sense.

[290]Adam is counting again, in alliance with Satan's materialism and quantification. They have not eaten well, they are not refreshed, and they cannot play innocently, ever again.

[291]Perhaps a buried pun on "Pandora," "*all*-gifted."

[292]In this context, "enjoy" is a vicious and amoral verb, something one would do in a brothel. Adam's images are of burning with lust, and the mutual lust is a kind of vicious game including "toy"-ing, leading to something like mutual rape when Adam "seis'd" Eve's hand. Before the Fall, the tenderest and most compassionate love is expressed in handholding, as at 4.321; thus the seizure of Eve's hand is by contrast (see also 12.648) a shocking image.

    So said he, and forbore not glance or toy   1035
Of amorous intent, well understood
Of *Eve*, whose Eye darted contagious Fire.[293]
Her hand he seis'd, and to a shadie bank,
Thick overhead with verdant roof imbowr'd
He led her nothing loath; Flours were the Couch,   1040
Pansies, and Violets, and Asphodel,
And Hyacinth, Earths freshest softest lap.[294]
There they thir fill of Love and Loves disport
Took largely, of thir mutual guilt the Seale,°   AGREEMENT
The solace of thir sin, till dewie sleep
Oppress'd them, wearied with thir amorous play.[295]   1045
Soon as the force of that fallacious Fruit,
That with exhilerating vapour bland[296]
About thir spirits had plaid, and inmost powers
Made erre, was now exhal'd, and grosser sleep
Bred of unkindly fumes,[297] with conscious dreams   1050
Encumberd,° now had left them, up they rose   BURDENED
As from unrest, and each the other viewing,
Soon found thir Eyes how op'nd, and thir minds
How dark'nd;[298] innocence, that as a veile
Had shadow'd them from knowing ill, was gon,   1055
Just confidence, and native righteousness
And honour from about them, naked left
To guiltie shame hee cover'd,[299] but his Robe
Uncover'd more, so rose the *Danite* strong
Herculean Samson from the Harlot-lap   1060
Of *Philistean Dalilah*,[300] and wak'd
Shorn of his strength,[301] They destitute and bare
Of all thir vertue:[302] silent, and in face

---

[293]Before the Fall, her eyes have given off the proverbial "Darts of desire" (8.62), but they were presumed to be innocent; here her eyes are actively darting dangerous fire that kindles burning ("ardor") in him.

[294]The flowers that provide Adam and Eve's couch are apparently still innocent and of no emblematic significance; the "lap" they provide does suggest complicity.

[295]Addison finds the passage beginning with "For never did thy beauty" (1029) "an exact copy of that between Jupiter and Juno in the fourteenth Iliad" (qtd. in Newton 1029n). Hera seduces Zeus in order to divert his attention from a battle, forearmed with the belt of Aphrodite and the promise of sleep after sex from Morpheus. The most obvious resemblances are in the "Never since I first saw you" formula (*Iliad* 14.315-17) and in the beds of similar flowers (clover, crocus, and hyacinth) that sprout under Zeus and Hera, to cushion them as they make love (346-51).

[296]Echoing Eve's "bland words" at 855 above. *Bland* may mean "pleasing to the senses" (*OED* 2, citing 5.5 as the first instance of the usage), but Milton obviously has something sinister in mind.

[297]Sin actually disrupts the digestive process and causes not only bad dreams but the gaseous and unnatural ("unkindly") fumes thought to engender evil fantasies.

[298]"And the eyes of them both were opened, and they knew that they were naked; and they sewed fig leaves together, and made themselves aprons" (Genesis 3.7). But Milton interprets the passage from Genesis with deep irony: "since [Adam says] our Eyes / Op'nd we find indeed, and find we know / Both Good and Evil, Good lost, and Evil got . . . " (1070-72 below).

[299]Eve has needed no veil before the Fall to cover her innocent nudity; she and Adam have been clothed metaphorically with domestic honor, confidence in their own justice, and inherent righteousness (4.288-324). Now, sadly, a kind of striptease is born: the "apron" of figleaves will uncover more than it covers, like the cloak shamefully applied to the naked, drunken Noah by his sons (Genesis 9.22-24).

[300]Milton summarizes his own *Samson Agonistes* (presumably imagined but not yet written) in three lines which compare Adam and Eve (together, interestingly) with Samson after being shorn by Delilah. Here, though, Delilah is pictured as Samson's harlot, not his wife. Samson was literally "shorn" (he had a haircut), but he was also shorn as sheep are shorn—deprived of their valuable covering, or "fleeced." According to *Samson Agonistes*, he also became a "tame Weather" (538; a wether being a castrated ram) in the process. Again it should be stressed that the comparison is between Samson and Adam and Eve, not between Samson and Adam, since Eve is not Milton's Dalila.

[301]Both editions have a comma after "strength" followed by the capital "T," not the customary practice of ending one sentence and beginning another (but look at the comma after "more," just above). My choice breaks with Shawcross's and agrees with Fowler's. Campbell supplies a semicolon.

[302]This is real virtue, which exists only in sentient beings, as opposed to the imagined power either of the tree (1033 above) or of the fruit itself (778 above).

Confounded[303] long they sate, as struck'n mute,
Till *Adam*, though not less then *Eve* abash't,[304]   1065
At length gave utterance to these words constraind.

    O *Eve*, in evil hour thou didst give eare
To that false Worm,[305] of whomsoever taught
To counterfet Mans voice, true in our Fall,
False in our promis'd Rising; since our Eyes   1070
Op'nd we find indeed, and find we know
Both Good and Evil, Good lost, and Evil got,
Bad Fruit of Knowledge, if this be to know,
Which leaves us naked thus, of Honour void,
Of Innocence, of Faith, of Puritie,   1075
Our wonted Ornaments now soild and staind,
And in our Faces evident the signes
Of foul concupiscence;[306] whence evil store;°   ABUNDANCE OF EVIL
Even shame, the last of evils; of the first
Be sure then. How shall I behold the face   1080
Henceforth of God or Angel, earst with joy
And rapture so oft beheld? those heav'nly shapes
Will dazle now this earthly,[307] with thir blaze
Insufferably bright. O might I here
In solitude live savage, in some glade   1085
Obscur'd, where highest Woods impenetrable
To Starr or Sun-light, spread thir umbrage broad
And brown as Evening:[308] Cover me ye Pines,
Ye Cedars, with innumerable boughs
Hide me, where I may never see them more.   1090
But let us now, as in bad plight, devise
What best may for[309] the present serve to hide
The Parts[310] of each from other, that seem most
To shame obnoxious,° and unseemliest seen.[311]   EXPOSED
Some Tree whose broad smooth Leaves together sowd,°   SEWED   1095
And girded on our loyns, may cover round
Those middle parts, that this new commer, Shame,
There sit not, and reproach us as unclean.

    So counsel'd hee, and both together went
Into the thickest Wood, there soon they chose   1100
The Figtree, not that kind for Fruit renown'd,
But such as at this day to *Indians* known

---

[303]Their sin shows in their being "de-faced," and their faces reflect at least the possibility of being "confounded," or damned.

[304]The reader might remember that Adam was only "half abash't" when admonished about his over-admiration of Eve by Raphael (8.595).

[305]Snake, worm, and dragon were all associated in the minds of Milton's contemporaries, but of all the epithets for Satan or Satan in the Serpent, this is the most demeaning. The assonance Adam sets up with "*Eve*," "evil," and "eare" builds a false etymology promoting guilt by association. Though in Genesis Eve was first named after the Fall, Adam has named her a number of times before in *Paradise Lost*.

[306]An important word, theologically speaking, meaning "evil desire." Augustine's *City of God* discusses *concupiscentia*, the state of mind which reflects evil desire either in angels or in human beings, often and in great detail, as in 12.6–8.

[307]Because of their distance from God as a result of the separating effect of sin, Adam and Eve will find the brightness of angels too intense for earthly senses to endure.

[308]Fowler sees Adam's request for solitude as the archetypal poem of retirement, as with Marvell's "The Garden," but "Adam's guilty impulse to retirement is by no means approved of by M[ilton]" (9.1085–90n). His guilt is reiterated by his desire to be covered by "umbrage" or to live in darkness where God cannot see him. In Genesis 3, Adam and Eve hide from the Lord.

[309]The compositor of *1674* transposed the "for" of this line with the "from" of the next; I have restored the correct order of *1667*.

[310]Sexual organs, called in later Latin either male *pudendum* or female *pudenda* from the verb *pudere*, "to be ashamed of."

[311]I have substituted the period of *1667* for the incorrect comma of *1674*.

In *Malabar* or *Decan*[312] spreds her Armes
Braunching so broad and long, that in the ground
The bended Twigs take root, and Daughters grow   1105
About the Mother Tree, a Pillard° shade   COLUMNED
High overarch't, and echoing Walks between;
There oft the *Indian* Herdsman shunning heate
Shelters in coole, and tends his pasturing Herds
At Loopholes cut through thickest shade:[313] Those Leaves   1110
They gatherd, broad as *Amazonian* Targe,[314]
And with what skill they had, together sowd,
To gird thir waste,° vain Covering if to hide   WAIST
Thir guilt and dreaded shame; O how unlike
To that first naked Glorie. Such of late   1115
Columbus found th' *American* so girt
With featherd Cincture,[315] naked else and wilde
Among the Trees on Iles and woodie Shores.
Thus fenc't, and as they thought, thir shame in part
Coverd, but not at rest or ease of Mind,   1120
They sate them down to weep, nor onely Teares
Raind at thir Eyes, but high Winds[316] worse within
Began to rise, high Passions, Anger, Hate,
Mistrust, Suspicion, Discord,[317] and shook sore
Thir inward State of Mind, calm Region once   1125
And full of Peace, now tost and turbulent:
For Understanding rul'd not, and the Will
Heard not her lore, both in subjection now
To sensual Appetite,[318] who from beneathe
Usurping over sovran Reason claimd   1130
Superior sway: from thus distemperd° brest,   DISEASED

---

[312]The Sultanate of the Deccan was in the southern half of India. A British outpost was established near what is now Calcutta in 1650. Malabar is on the west coast of the Indian peninsula. For possible sources for Milton's reference to the banyan or Indian figtree, see S. Viswanathan, "Milton and Purchas' Linschoten: An Additional Source for Milton's Indian Figtree," *Milton Newsletter* 2 (1968): 43–45. The Indian figtree as known through Purchas's *Pilgrimage* and through Pliny's *Natural History* and Ralegh's *History of the World* seems to have a figurative meaning based on what was known of its physical property. The tree was thought to be enormous, providing large amounts of shade and shelter through its growth habit of spreading daughter plants outward from a central mother plant. The word "overarch't" echoes the Vallombrosa simile (1.302–04), which also suggests the potential for shade in which to hide sin. The Indian herdsman may be included in the simile for no reason other than to prove that the figtree really existed in what was to Milton's audience a place where the British maintained an outpost. According to Viswanathan, the leaves supposed by Pliny to be of the figtree are really from a species of banana; thus their breadth. Those leaves are compared with the shields of the Amazon warriors possibly because the Amazons were famous for the quality of their weaponry, bows or, in this case, shields. As Fowler points out, the introduction of weaponry suggests that "before the Fall man never thought of fighting, let alone woman" (1100–10n). Though the Indian figtree is not evil in any obvious way, it is contrasted in all its properties with the innocent bower of Adam and Eve.
[313]The image seems to be of the herdsman within the structure provided by the figtree peeping out through loopholes cut through the foliage.
[314]"Broad as the shield of an Amazon."
[315]The costumes of some of the Indians that Columbus and his crew reported seeing in the Caribbean during the 1492 voyage did indeed use belts (cinctures) constructed of feathers. Camoëns had written the most widely recognized epic of exploration, *The Lusiads*, which dealt with the voyages of Vasco da Gama to various seductive island civilizations, in 1572. One can treat people discovered on a remote island either as linear descendants of Adam and Eve, hence as an innocent and unspoiled civilization, or as a group of naked savages linked by superstition with devil-worship. Perhaps the problem can best be seen in the nature of Shakespeare's Caliban. What Christians were to do with such civilizations was forever complicated by Montaigne's famous essay, "Of Cannibals," which suggested that a "primitive" and "savage" tribe of cannibals might give an example of how to improve western European laws and customs. Milton's simile shows the ambivalence of attitudes toward the Americans he pictures: they are clothed only with feather belts but otherwise are naked and wild, completely untutored in Christianity (see Evans *Milton's Imperial* for background).
[316]The microcosm of Adam and Eve, their tears now streaming down like rain and their passions blowing up like wind, matches the sinful macrocosm of all nature; before the Fall only innocent tears came down (5.130) and only gentle winds blew in Paradise (4.156).
[317]These seem to be vestiges of the allegorical figures Milton had designed into several of his earlier drafts of the epic in the Trinity College manuscript: the second draft, for instance, includes "Conscience, Labour, Sicknesse, Discontent, Ignorance, Feare, Death" (see Introduction, "The Fable").
[318]The same process that enslaves the animal-headed rout under the control of Comus, those who "roule with pleasure in a sensual stie" (77). The reference again is to the Scale of Nature, which should govern human faculties, with reason as rightful monarch.

Adam, estrang'd in look and alterd stile,
Speech intermitted thus to *Eve* renewd.
    Would thou hadst heark'nd to my words, and stai'd
With me, as I besought thee, when that strange
Desire of wandring this unhappie Morn,   1135
I know not whence possessd thee;[319] we had then
Remaind still happie, not as now, despoild
Of all our good, sham'd, naked, miserable.
Let none henceforth seek needless cause to approve°   TEST   1140
The Faith they owe;° when earnestly they seek   PROFESS
Such proof, conclude, they then begin to faile.
    To whom soon mov'd with touch of blame thus *Eve*.
What words have past thy Lips, *Adam* severe,
Imput'st thou that to my default, or will   1145
Of wandring, as thou call'st it, which who knows
But might as ill have happ'nd[320] thou being by,
Or to thy self perhaps: hadst thou been there,
Or here th' attempt, thou couldst not have discernd
Fraud in the Serpent, speaking as he spake;   1150
No ground of enmitie between us known,
Why hee should mean me ill, or seek to harme.
Was I to have never parted from thy side?
As good have grown there still a livelesse° Rib.   LIFELESS
Being as I am, why didst not thou the Head   1155
Command me absolutely not to go,
Going into such danger as thou saidst?
Too facil[321] then thou didst not much gainsay,
Nay didst permit, approve, and fair dismiss.
Hadst thou bin firm and fixt in thy dissent,[322]   1160
Neither had I transgress'd, nor thou with mee.
    To whom then first incenst[323] *Adam* repli'd.
Is this the Love, is this the recompence
Of mine to thee, ingrateful *Eve*, exprest
Immutable when thou wert lost, not I,   1165
Who might have liv'd and joyd° immortal bliss,   ENJOYED
Yet willingly chose rather Death with thee:[324]
And am I now upbraided, as the cause

---

[319]Mutual accusation continues. Reconstructing Eve's crime, Adam professes not to know where her strange desire to leave him comes from (he should: he listened to her dream). He lays all the blame on her, beginning to sound like one of the many antifeminist diatribes popular after John Knox had set the tone in *The First Blast of the Trumpet against the Monstrous Regiment* [i.e., rule] *of Women* (Geneva, 1558), the point of which had been that Mary Queen of Scots should not be allowed to rule either Scotland or England, because she was a woman. For the worst of the genre, see Joseph Swetnam, *The Arraignment of Lewde, Idle, Froward, and Unconstant Women* (London, 1615). Most of the antifeminist tracts used Eve as the prime example of a bad woman.

[320]Burden (81) notes that "happ'nd" again signals Eve's new dependence on Satan's determinism, in which fate becomes more important than God's will or providence. Eve has a point that Adam does not know what might have happened had the Serpent tempted him rather than her, but we do know that the Serpent preferred facing Eve separate from Adam (9.422).

[321]The question of just who is the more facile, Adam or Eve, can provide as lively a debate among Milton scholars as between Adam and Eve, especially because Eve is called Adam's "facil consort" by Satan in *Paradise Regain'd* 1.51. In both cases, the speakers who try to summarize character are suspect. In seventeenth-century usage, facile can mean "courteous" or "mild" (*OED* 4) or "easily led, compliant" (*OED* 5), but the Latin adverb *facile* means "easily," which suggests that facile in English might mean "easily persuaded" to Milton.

[322]"Disagreement," but with theological overtones, since if Adam had dissented more strongly, Eve would not have transgressed.

[323]Notice that Adam is first incensed at this point and that therefore he cannot be said to have been angry before the Fall. In the punctuation of the line, the compositor of *1674* has again substituted a comma for the period normally put before a direct quotation; I have reverted to the earlier text.

[324]Adam has a valid point, although a bitter one, about Eve's willingness to share her misery when she was doomed to die and he was not.

Of thy transgressing? not enough severe,
It seems, in thy restraint: what could I more?   1170
I warn'd thee, I admonish'd thee, foretold
The danger, and the lurking Enemie
That lay in wait; beyond this had bin force,
And force upon free will hath here no place.
But confidence[325] then bore thee on, secure°   CARELESS   1175
Either to meet no danger, or to finde
Matter of° glorious trial; and perhaps   PRETEXT FOR
I also err'd in overmuch admiring
What seemd in thee so perfet, that I thought
No evil durst attempt thee,[326] but I rue   1180
That errour now, which is become my crime,
And thou th' accuser. Thus it shall befall
Him who to worth in Women[327] overtrusting
Lets her will rule; restraint she will not brook,
And left to her self, if evil thence ensue,   1185
Shee first his weak indulgence will accuse.[328]
    Thus they in mutual accusation spent
The fruitless hours, but neither self-condemning,
And of thir vain contest appeer'd no end.[329]

The End of the Ninth Book.

---

[325]Slightly different in meaning from the modern word, confidence could suggest its opposite, overconfidence, or "excess of assurance, overboldness" (*OED* 4). Compare 6.343, where Satan's overconfidence is described.

[326]Adam at this point begins the process of confession, not to God but to Eve, in admitting that he was wrong to admire her ("wonder at" her) too much in his "vehemence of love."

[327]Richard Bentley (see Newton 1183n) wanted to emend this to read "Woman," since Adam immediately after begins to use the singular with "her." The plural is defensible on the grounds that it is generic, in which case the choice of singular or plural form would be optional.

[328]Since Adam has been headed on the path of "good" confession, the reader may well wonder at this point if Milton intends what Adam has said to be considered vindictive and fallen, because a fallen Adam says it, or whether he intends it to be considered the truth. The interpretive phrase "mutual accusation" suggests that Adam is still speaking wrong-headedly.

[329]The word "contest" is apparently accented on the second syllable. In his outline for "Adam unparadiz'd," Milton had described the aftermath of the Fall: "Adam then & Eve returne[,] accuse one another but especially Adam layes the blame to his wife, is stubborn in his offence[.]" The "fruitless hours" (another of the series of thematic puns) of "mutual accusation" are the results of the Fall on the relationship between Adam and Eve. Adam's stubbornness in his offence is beginning to show at the end of this book, but his excessive anger, and Eve's earlier repentance, will be demonstrated toward the end of Book 10.

Paradise Lost.

BOOK X.

THE ARGUMENT.

Mans transgression known, the Guardian Angels forsake Paradise, and return up to Heaven to approve thir vigilance, and are approv'd,[1] God declaring that The[2] entrance of Satan could not be by them prevented. He sends his Son to judge the Transgressors, who descends and gives Sentence accordingly: then in pity cloaths them both, and reascends. Sin and Death sitting till then at the Gates of Hell, by wondrous sympathie feeling[3] the success of Satan in this new World, and the sin by Man there committed, resolve to sit no longer confin'd in Hell, but to follow Satan thir Sire up to the place of Man: To make the way easier from Hell to this World to and fro, they pave a broad Highway or Bridge over Chaos, according to the Track that Satan first made; then preparing for Earth, they meet[4] him proud of his success returning to Hell; thir mutual gratulation. Satan arrives at Pandemonium, in full assembly[5] relates with boasting his success against Man; instead of applause is entertained with a general hiss by all his audience, transform'd with himself also suddenly into Serpents, according to his doom giv'n in Paradise; then deluded with a shew of the forbidden Tree springing up before them, they greedily reaching to take[6] of the Fruit, chew dust and bitter ashes. The proceedings of Sin and Death; God foretels the final Victory of his Son over them, and the renewing of all things; but for the present commands his Angels to make several alterations in the Heavens and Elements.[7] Adam more and more perceiving his fall'n condition heavily bewailes, rejects the condolement of Eve; she persists and at length appeases him: then to evade the Curse likely to fall on thir Ofspring, proposes to Adam violent wayes[8] which he approves not, but conceiving better hope, puts her in mind of the late Promise made them, that her Seed should be reveng'd on the Serpent, and exhorts her with him to seek Peace of the offended Deity, by repentance and supplication.

M Eanwhile the hainous and despightfull[9] act
　　Of *Satan* done in Paradise, and how
　　Hee in the Serpent,[10] had perverted *Eve*,
Her Husband shee, to taste the fatall fruit,[11]
Was known in Heav'n; for what can scape the Eye
Of God All-seeing,[12] or deceave his Heart

5

---

[1]"The Fall having become general knowledge, the angels who had been assigned to guard Paradise leave it and return to Heaven, to be assured that they had indeed been vigilant in their watch, and they are assured. . . ."

[2]The capitalization of "*The*" at the beginning of the line suggests that the compositor was looking ahead to setting poetry.

[3]Though they are far distant from Satan and Paradise, Sin and Death can detect the Fall by amazing empathy (in fact they smell the existence of death). The phrase "*new World*" begins the image of perverse exploration, and Satan will become a pathfinder and tracker a few lines later, when he lays down a track that will soon become a bridge and highway between Earth and Hell.

[4]Corrects the "*met*" of the first state of *1674*.

[5]Corrected from "*in full of assembly*" of *1674*.

[6]*1668* has "*taste*." The biblically-correct "*take*" apparently represents an authorial correction in *1674*. A typographical mistake "*rejccts*," below, was also corrected, and several commas removed—all representing subtle but authoritative corrections. For some reason, however, "*in full of assembly*" was not corrected.

[7]Changes in the arrangement of the poles of the Earth and the relationships between heavenly bodies, resulting in malign astrological arrangements. The macrocosm is again reacting to what has happened to the microcosm of Adam and Eve.

[8]Specifically suicide.

[9]"Hainous" (spelled with an "a" like the French *haineux*, rather than with an "e," as in the modern "heinous") suggests "infamous" (*OED* 1, citing this instance), whereas "despightfull" suggests "cruel" or "malignant" (*OED* 2, citing this instance). See also 9.929.

[10]This comma was omitted in *1667*.

[11]In what is an introduction or proem for the book rather than an invocation (1–16), the Epic Voice, sounding very much like God in Book 3, sums up the process of the Fall: Eve has been completely turned aside in an evil direction ("perverted") from God by Satan in the Serpent, and she has in turn perverted Adam to commit the sin. See Steadman, "'Man's First Disobedience.'"

[12]One popular emblem representing God shows the Deity in terms of the all-seeing eye. George Wither, *A Collection of Emblemes, Ancient and Moderne* (London, 1635), in his Illustration 31, pictures what seems to be divine wisdom standing king-like on the Earth, with an eye in the middle of his chest. See also Wind, figures 84–86. The image has persisted through freemasonry and is still present in the eye at the top of the pyramid on the American dollar bill. See 3.614 for an additional description of God's eye.

Omniscient, who in all things wise and just,
Hinder'd not *Satan* to attempt the minde
Of Man, with strength entire,[13] and free will arm'd,
Complete° to have discover'd and repulst   STRONG ENOUGH   10
Whatever wiles of Foe or seeming Friend.
For still° they knew, and ought to have still° remember'd   ALWAYS
The high Injunction not to taste that Fruit,
Whoever tempted; which they not obeying,
Incurr'd, what could they less, the penaltie,   15
And manifold in sin,[14] deserv'd to fall.
Up into Heav'n from Paradise in haste
Th' Angelic Guards ascended, mute and sad[15]
For Man, for of his state by this they knew,
Much wondring how the suttle Fiend had stoln   20
Entrance unseen.[16] Soon as th' unwelcome news
From Earth arriv'd at Heaven Gate, displeas'd
All were who heard, dim sadness did not spare
That time Celestial visages, yet mixt
With pitie, violated not thir bliss.   25
About the new-arriv'd, in multitudes
Th' ethereal People[17] ran, to hear and know
How all befell: they towards the Throne Supream
Accountable[18] made haste to make appear
With righteous plea, thir utmost vigilance,   30
And easily approv'd; when the most High
Eternal Father from his secret Cloud,
Amidst in Thunder utter'd thus his voice.[19]
    Assembl'd Angels, and ye Powers[20] return'd
From unsuccessful charge, be not dismaid,   35
Nor troubl'd at these tidings from the Earth,
Which your sincerest care could not prevent,
Foretold so lately what would come to pass,
When first this Tempter cross'd the Gulf from Hell.[21]
I told ye then he should prevail and speed°   SUCCEED   40
On his bad Errand, Man[22] should be seduc't

---

[13]"Unimpaired, undiminished," used of immaterial things (*OED* 4.c, citing this instance).

[14]"Manifold in the numbers and varieties of sin incorporated into their one act of disobedience." See *On Christian Doctrine* 1.11 (Yale 6: 382–85) for the many sins Milton and other theologians thought were incorporated in the Fall. The prayer service of the *Book of Common Prayer*, which Milton would have heard every morning he went to chapel as a schoolboy at St. Paul's school, contains the priest's injunction to general confession of the congregation, which begins "Dearly beloved brethren, the Scripture moveth us in sundry places, to acknowledge and confess our manifold sins and wickedness . . . " (1559 ed.).

[15]Perhaps Milton is leading us here to a proper or decorous reaction to the tragedy of Adam and Eve, silent solemnity.

[16]Satan's underground entrance is described at 9.69–76.

[17]Angels, resembling human beings but made of the quintessence ether. By calling them "people" Milton calls attention to their humanity.

[18]Probably both in the sense of "responsible for" and "reported accurately." The angels ran to the throne responsibly or they hastened to report on exactly how vigilant they had been. Since they were not at fault, they were hastily "approv'd" or vindicated.

[19]God speaks in thunder and out from amidst burning lamps in Revelation 4.5. See also 1 Samuel 7.10 for God in thunder and Exodus 19.9 for God in cloud. Fletcher would have this clause punctuated with commas after "Father" and "Amidst," which many editors after 1719 have adopted, but the change has no authority in the early texts.

[20]The angelic rank, but the military sense of "armies" may also be present.

[21]Probably based on the gulf between the rich man in Hell and Lazarus in Heaven described in Luke 16.26. In Milton's geographical scheme, however, what is being described is Chaos.

[22]Here "Man" seems to be a collective noun that includes both Adam and Eve, since the sins that Eve committed in the Fall are not differentiated from those Adam committed. In the final analysis, in other words, they are one in the Fall, and they both are "seduc't" into "believing lies": "His free Will" and "her own inclining" in 46 below reinforce the roles of both sexes in the sin.

And flatter'd out of all, believing lies
Against his Maker; no Decree of mine
Concurring to necessitate his Fall,
Or touch with lightest moment of impulse[23]   45
His free Will, to her own inclining left
In eevn scale.[24] But fall'n he is, and now
What rests° but that the mortal Sentence[25] pass   REMAINS
On his transgression, Death denounc't that day,
Which he presumes already vain and void,   50
Because not yet inflicted, as he fear'd,
By some immediate stroak; but soon shall find
Forbearance no acquittance ere day end.[26]
Justice shall not return as bountie scorn'd.[27]
But whom send I to judge them? whom but thee   55
Vicegerent[28] Son, to thee I have transferr'd
All Judgement, whether in Heav'n, or Earth, or Hell.
Easie it might[29] be seen that I intend
Mercie collegue° with Justice,[30] sending thee   ALLIED
Mans Friend, his Mediator, his design'd   60
Both Ransom and Redeemer voluntarie,[31]
And destin'd Man himself to judge Man fall'n.[32]
    So spake the Father, and unfoulding bright
Toward the right hand his Glorie, on the Son
Blaz'd forth unclouded Deitie; he full   65
Resplendent all his Father manifest
Express'd, and thus divinely answer'd milde.[33]
    Father Eternal, thine is to decree,

---

[23]The balance of Adam and Eve's decision to fall was in no way tipped by God, not even in the slightest increase in weight ("moment" is "an infinitesimal portion of weight") that might unbalance a scale. An impulse is a push—in this case a very light one. The scales remain an important image throughout the poem, with the phrase "Thou art weighed in the balance, and art found wanting" (the "handwriting on the wall" for Belshazzar in Daniel 5.27) always echoing as Satan's self-inflicted fate. For the image of Satan being weighed by the heavenly scales, see 4.997–1004.

[24]Again, God *"clears his own Justice and Wisdom from all imputation, having created Man free and able enough to have withstood his Tempter"* (Book 3 Argument).

[25]"Sentence of mortality," or "death sentence."

[26]Because death has not been instantaneous, Adam presumes that there has been no transgression, but he will soon find that his debt will be settled (an "acquittance" being the settling of a debt) before the end of the day on which he has sinned. One problem theologians and skeptics alike had found in the Genesis account of the aftermath of eating the fruit was that, though punishment had been specified as "in the day that thou eatest thereof, thou shalt surely die" (2.17), Adam and Eve do eat and they do not immediately die. The Protestant explanation for "death" was that it had a figurative meaning, as in the Geneva Bible: "By this death he meaneth the separacion of man from God, who is our life and chief felicite: and also that our disobedience is the cause thereof" (1560 ed.).

[27]The image is financial, following "acquittance." Since justice is given freely, it is unearned bounty and therefore should be welcomed, not scorned. Metaphorically, "bountie" connects with "Ransom" just below.

[28]A deputy who takes the place of a ruler in his absence. In this case the noun used as an adjective has theological meaning, since it implies that the Son can act for the Father with no loss of authority. Milton anticipates the Son of Man's role in the Last Judgment as depicted in Revelation 14.14.

[29]The text in *1667* reads "may." The reading "might" seems more nearly correct in that the mood should be conditional.

[30]In Christian orthodoxy, the Son was often associated with mercy and the Father with justice. See the Nativity Ode stanza fifteen.

[31]Though the Son is by God's design both ransom and mediator for humankind in a state of sin, His sacrifice is voluntary. (The interaction of providence and free will can be seen in "design'd" in company with "voluntarie" and "destin'd.")

[32]It is only appropriate, in other words, for the Son, who will become incarnate as Christ, will become the ransom (for humankind, held hostage by sin) and redeemer, to pass judgment on this first sin. For a visual representation of Christ in judgment, see the apocalyptic end-panel of Michelangelo's Sistine Chapel. For the apportionment of roles between Father and Son, compare John 5.22: "The Father judgeth no man, but hath committed all judgment unto the Son," a division of roles which Milton supported in *On Christian Doctrine* 1.5, in which the Son is responsible not only for judgment but for "The remission of sins: given to him even as man" (Yale 6: 268).

[33]The Father freely confers His glory on His Son in the image of unclouded light, so that the Son's "effulgence" will be no less resplendent than His Father's. After the Fall, at least, the glory of God must always be wrapped in clouds, since human perception would not be able to tolerate being exposed to God in all His glory. Compare Hebrews 1.3: "Who being the brightness of his glory, and the express image of his person, . . . [Christ] sat down on the right hand of the Majesty on high."

Mine both in Heav'n and Earth to do thy will
Supream, that thou in mee thy Son belov'd
Mayst ever rest well pleas'd.[34] I go to judge   70
On Earth these thy transgressors, but thou knowst,
Whoever judg'd, the worst on mee[35] must light,
When time shall be, for so I undertook
Before thee; and not repenting,[36] this obtaine   75
Of right, that I may mitigate thir doom
On me deriv'd,[37] yet I shall temper so
Justice with Mercie, as may illustrate[38] most
Them fully satisfied, and thee appease.
Attendance none shall need, nor Train, where none   80
Are to behold the Judgment, but the judg'd,
Those two; the third best absent is condemn'd,[39]
Convict[40] by flight, and Rebel to all Law
Conviction to the Serpent none belongs.[41]

    Thus saying, from his radiant Seat he rose   85
Of high collateral glorie:[42] him Thrones and Powers,
Princedoms, and Dominations[43] ministrant
Accompanied to Heaven Gate, from whence
Eden and all the Coast in prospect lay.[44]
Down he descended strait;° the speed of Gods   AS FAST AS POSSIBLE   90
Time counts not, though with swiftest minutes wing'd.
Now was the Sun in Western cadence[45] low
From Noon, and gentle Aires due at thir hour
To fan the Earth now wak'd, and usher in
The Eevning coole when he from wrauth more coole   95
Came the mild Judge and Intercessor both
To sentence Man: the voice of God they heard
Now walking in the Garden, by soft windes
Brought to thir Ears, while day declin'd, they heard,
And from his presence hid themselves among   100
The thickest Trees, both Man and Wife, till God
Approaching, thus to *Adam* call'd aloud.[46]

---

[34]Anticipating the voice from Heaven, after John the Baptist has baptized Christ: "This is my beloved Son, in whom I am well pleased" (Matthew 3.17).
[35]The verbal formula represented in "upon me . . . from mee . . . on me" will echo among the Son, Adam (739, 832), and Eve (936), as each assumes part of the responsibility for atoning for or mediating Original Sin. When the Son says that the worst will light (i.e., "alight") on Him, He is anticipating the Crucifixion. The phrase "When time shall be" suggests "when the time is appropriate" or "in the fullness of time" (Galatians 4.4).
[36]"So I undertook this responsiblity, in your presence, and I do not repent the choice."
[37]The word seems to be used very richly, to mean that the fate of Adam and Eve is channeled through or diverted by (Latin *derivare*, "to draw off," "divert") the Son's mediation. When the Son becomes incarnate, assuming a human body, He will also become a descendant of Adam and Eve, the "Seed" who will avenge the wrong done them by the Serpent (180–81 below).
[38]Accent should fall on the second syllable. The word suggests "illuminate" or "make clear." Those things being illuminated or glorified are "Justice" and "Mercie."
[39]The third guilty party, Satan, is best absent from the condemnation of Adam and Eve, presumably because their sin is of a much lower degree.
[40]Accented on the second syllable, the adjectival form from "convicted."
[41]The Son will pass judgment only on Adam and Eve; Satan has convicted himself by the guilty action of taking flight, but the Serpent has not committed any crime: his body has been used by Satan.
[42]Milton uses the word "collateral" rather than "equal" to define the subtle difference he finds between the Father and Son. For the relationship, see Adamson, Patrides, and Hunter, *Bright Essence*, and MacCallum, *Milton*.
[43]"The fourth of the nine orders of angels in the Dionysian hierarchy; a conventional representation of these in art. Cf. dominion 4, and see note s.v. cherub" (*OED* 3). See West 77.
[44]The word "Coast" could mean "region," but Milton may be picturing all of Mesopotamia from such a height, including the Mediterranean coast.
[45]"The rising and (esp.) falling of elemental sounds, as of a storm, the sea, etc." (*OED* 3), but here it seems to mean the fall or inclining motion of the sun.
[46]"God" is manifested here as the Son. The scene is that of Genesis 3.8: "And they heard the voice of the Lord God walking in the garden in the cool of the day: and Adam and his wife hid themselves from the presence of the Lord God amongst the trees of the garden."

Where art thou *Adam*, wont with joy to meet
My coming seen far off? I miss thee here,
Not pleas'd, thus entertaind with solitude,　　　　　　　　　　　105
Where obvious[47] dutie erewhile appear'd unsaught:
Or come I less conspicuous, or what change
Absents thee, or what chance detains?[48] Come forth.
He came, and with him *Eve*, more loth,[49] though first
To offend, discount'nanc't both, and discompos'd;　　　　　110
Love was not in thir looks, either to God
Or to each other, but apparent guilt,[50]
And shame, and perturbation, and despaire,
Anger, and obstinacie, and hate, and guile.
Whence *Adam* faultring long, thus answer'd brief.[51]　　　115
　　I heard thee in the Garden, and of thy voice
Affraid, being naked, hid my self. To whom
The gracious Judge without revile[52] repli'd.
　　My voice thou oft hast heard, and hast not fear'd.
But still rejoyc't, how is it now become　　　　　　　　　　120
So dreadful to thee? that thou art naked, who
Hath told thee? hast thou eaten of the Tree
Whereof I gave thee charge thou shouldst not eat?[53]
　　To whom thus *Adam* sore beset repli'd.
O Heav'n! in evil strait[54] this day I stand　　　　　　　　　125
Before my Judge, either to undergoe
My self the total Crime, or to accuse
My other self, the partner of my life;
Whose failing, while her Faith to me remaines,
I should conceal, and not expose to blame　　　　　　　　　130
By my complaint; but strict necessitie
Subdues me,[55] and calamitous constraint[56]
Least on my head both sin and punishment,
However insupportable, be all
Devolv'd;[57] though should I hold my peace,[58] yet thou　　135
Wouldst easily detect what I conceale.

---

[47]Retains the Latin meaning of "in the way" or in this case "coming out to meet."

[48]"Is it that I am less noticeable, or what change is it in you that causes you to be absent, or what chance event keeps you from coming to see me?"

[49]The reader might remember that she went to the "couch" with Adam "nothing loath" immediately after his Fall (9.1039). The Epic Voice describes her as being more hesitant than Adam to appear before God, even though she was first to sin.

[50]That is, guilt was obvious in their whole demeanor. Just as Eve was described as "Defac't" (9.901), they both are "discount'nanc't." Their faces indicate a distemper or discord of humors which at least outwardly resembles a disease. Their faces also show a parade of all the ills brought into the character and life of humankind as a result of the Fall, some of which are listed in the outlines for "Adam Unparadiz'd": "Labour greife hatred Envie warre famine Pestilence" (see Introduction, "The Fable").

[51]The answers of Adam and Eve in Genesis (the Serpent says nothing) are remarkable for their brevity.

[52]Without reviling (abusing or reproaching) them.

[53]"And [God] said, Who told thee that thou wast naked? Hast thou eaten of the tree, whereof I commanded thee that thou shouldest not eat?" (Genesis 3.11).

[54]"Narrowed or restricted condition." Milton adds considerably to Adam's dialogue in Genesis, which is only "The woman whom thou gavest to be with me, she gave me of the tree, and I did eat" (3.12). In Milton's dramatic rendering, Adam speaks as if in soliloquy, talking about the Son in the third person as "my Judge" and talking about Eve as if she were not there, perhaps because he does not want Eve to hear his ideas and because he knows that the Son in His omniscience ("thou / Wouldst easily detect what I conceale") can read his thoughts. When he first mentions Eve out loud, she will become "This Woman."

[55]Adam complains of his fate as "strict necessitie," but the reader may be asked to remember that "necessitie" is "The Tyrants plea" (4.394).

[56]The text of *1667* prints a comma here, which may be the preferable reading.

[57]"To cause to fall or alight (on someone)" (*OED* 3, citing this instance). Adam is using the "misery loves company" argument that Eve also has used, with Adam saying, in effect, "Why should I be the only one being punished, when Eve is available?"

[58]"Though even if I remain silent about it."

This Woman whom thou mad'st to be my help,
And gav'st me as thy perfet gift, so good,
So fit, so acceptable, so Divine,
That from her hand I could suspect no ill,   140
And what she did, whatever in it self,
Her doing seem'd to justifie the deed;[59]
Shee gave me of the Tree, and I did eate.
    To whom the sovran Presence thus repli'd.
Was shee thy God, that her thou didst obey   145
Before his voice,[60] or was shee made thy guide,
Superior, or but equal, that to her
Thou did'st resigne thy Manhood, and the Place
Wherein God set thee above her made of thee,
And for thee, whose perfection farr excell'd   150
Hers in all real dignitie.[61] Adornd
Shee was indeed, and lovely to attract
Thy Love, not thy Subjection, and her Gifts[62]
Were such as under Government well seem'd,
Unseemly to beare rule, which was thy part   155
And person,[63] had'st thou known thy self aright.
    So having said, he thus to *Eve* in few:[64]
Say Woman,[65] what is this which thou hast done?
    To whom sad *Eve* with shame nigh overwhelm'd,
Confessing soon, yet not before her Judge   160
Bold or loquacious, thus abasht[66] repli'd.
    The Serpent me beguil'd and I did eate.
    Which when the Lord God heard, without delay
To Judgement he proceeded on th' accus'd
Serpent though brute, unable to transferre   165
The Guilt on him who made him instrument
Of mischief, and polluted from the end°   PURPOSE
Of his Creation; justly then accurst,

---

[59]Reiterates Adam's complaint to Raphael that his wisdom "Looses discount'nanc't" in the presence of Eve (8.553); he is wrong to let that happen in either case. Milton's additions to Adam's dialogue seem to blame God even more for having created Eve, which indicates once again that Adam is being "stubborn in his offence" before "Justice" addresses him (see "Adam Unparadiz'd" in the Introduction).

[60]The charge here relates to idolatry, since Adam in worshiping Eve's outside was following a false god. Again, Milton follows the implications of 1 Corinthians 11.8–9, that since woman was made for man, man should not worship woman.

[61]Here if anywhere modern feminist critics and all who believe in an ideal of equality between the sexes have a strong case against Milton, who clearly believed and puts in the mouth of the Son the belief that, though both Adam and Eve are perfect, Eve is created from Adam's flesh in order to be a helpmeet for him: Adam's perfection outranks Eve's in the hierarchy of nature. Therefore she should obey him; if he obeys her, he resigns his manhood and violates his position in nature and she becomes his god, worshiped like an idol.

[62]Milton may well be thinking of Pandora, the gift of Jove to "th' unwiser son / Of *Japhet*" (4.716–17), Epimetheus, since her name means "all gifts," and he has already compared Eve to her (4.714).

[63]The two words "part" and "person" both emphasize Adam's role in marriage, since "part" suggests a dramatic role, and "person" in the Latin sense of *persona* (a mask for a stage performer or a dramatic character) also suggests a dramatic role.

[64]"In few words." The idiom also suggests a summary statement.

[65]The Son's epithet "Woman" may echo Adam's "O Woman" at 9.343 and "This Woman" at 137 above. The mild anger implied in the Son's epithet, which is not in the biblical dialogue, is answered by genuine (and sympathetic) remorse on Eve's part—a marked change from Adam's bold loquaciousness. If Adam has been unabashed and bold, Eve is sad or seriously repentant, and she is genuinely abashed, ready for heartfelt confession before her judge. After the Fall, Eve is quicker to repent (though she is also quicker to lapse into suicidal despair). Her answer here, unlike Adam's, follows Genesis word for word, with Milton changing the word order only to fit the iambic rhythm. Her reply is notably short, simple, and honest.

[66]Perhaps it would be good to remember here that when Adam was chastised by Raphael for overvaluing Eve's beauty at 8.595, he was only "half abash't."

As vitiated in Nature:[67] more to know
Concern'd not Man (since he no further knew)   170
Nor alter'd his offence; yet God at last
To Satan first in sin his doom apply'd,
Though in mysterious terms, judg'd as then best:
And on the Serpent thus his curse let fall.

  Because thou hast done this, thou art accurst   175
Above all Cattle, each Beast of the Field;
Upon thy Belly groveling thou shalt goe,
And dust shalt eat all the dayes of thy Life.[68]
Between Thee and the Woman I will put
Enmitie, and between thine and her Seed;   180
Her Seed shall bruse thy head, thou bruise his heel.

  So spake this Oracle, then verifi'd
When *Jesus* son of *Mary* second *Eve*,[69]
Saw *Satan*[70] fall like Lightning down from Heav'n,[71]
Prince of the Aire;[72] then rising from his Grave   185
Spoild Principalities and Powers,[73] triumpht
In open shew, and with ascension bright
Captivity led captive through the Aire,[74]
The Realm it self of Satan long usurpt,
Whom he shall tread at last under our feet;   190
Eevn hee who now foretold his fatal bruise,[75]
And to the Woman thus his Sentence turn'd.

  Thy sorrow I will greatly multiplie
By thy Conception; Children[76] thou shalt bring
In sorrow forth, and to thy Husbands will   195
Thine shall submit, hee over thee shall rule.[77]

  On *Adam* last thus judgement he pronounc'd.

---

[67]The problem of the Serpent is that its body is used for evil purposes by Satan. In Milton's careful wording he is not yet "nocent" (9.186) and a "Brute" (9.554), but his body is nevertheless used by Satan. The problem had become a theological puzzle for commentators on Genesis by Milton's era. Milton tries to solve the puzzle by making the Serpent "vitiated in Nature." The Serpent's natural "subtlety" made him a fit instrument for Satan to use; thus all serpents become at least apt symbols of the curse of sin, and there is a natural enmity between the sons of Eve and serpents. Serpents will try to bruise our heels, and we will try to step on them. Eventually Christ, Eve's "Seed," will tread on the Serpent when He kills the "old Dragon" at the Last Judgment, as in Caravaggio's painting *Madonna delle Serpe*. Here God's punishment of the Serpent is "mysterious": it prefigures His punishment of Satan, who has slunk off (9.784) before Adam and Eve are judged.

[68]"And the Lord God said unto the serpent, Because thou has done this, thou art cursed above all cattle, and above every beast of the field; upon thy belly shalt thou go, and dust thou shalt eat all the days of thy life. And I will put enmity between thee and the woman, and between thy seed and her seed; it shall bruise thy head, and thou shalt bruise his heel" (Genesis 3.14–15). Milton adds only "groveling" to the words of Genesis. The Geneva Bible's gloss on God's address to the Serpent is "He chiefly meaneth Satan, by whose motion & craft the serpent deceiveth the woman" (1560 ed.). The Son is speaking prophetically as an "Oracle," predicting the future enmity between Eve's "Seed" or the generations she will be mother to and the Serpent, or Satan, until Jesus, rising from the grave, will overcome death and Satan, avenging the "fatal bruise" by treading on the Serpent.

[69]Compare 5.387. The "second *Eve*" is Mary, mother of Christ. Since to amplify her importance would have seemed pro-Catholic, Milton seems to underplay the role of Mary here and in *Paradise Regain'd*. For a thorough discussion of the theological deemphasis on Mary, see Pecheux, "The Concept."

[70]The compositor for *1674* atypically added the italics for *Satan*, slavishly following the mistake of *1667*, as he will do also in lines 189, 236, and 258 below.

[71]"I beheld Satan as lightning fall from heaven" (Jesus speaking of his disciples casting out devils in Luke 10.18).

[72]More specifically, Satan seems to be the prince of the "middle Region of thick Air" (*Paradise Regain'd* 2.117), not the highest of heavens. The Son's phrase echoes ". . . the prince of the power of the air . . ." (Ephesians 2.2).

[73]In Colossians 2.14, Jesus is said to have "spoiled principalities and powers, [making] a shew of them openly, triumphing over them in it."

[74]"Thou hast ascended on high, thou has led captivity captive" (Psalm 68.18) was applied to Jesus at Ephesians 4.8: "he led captivity captive. . . ."

[75]"And the God of peace shall bruise Satan under your feet shortly" (Romans 16.20; the Geneva Bible reads "treade Satan"). The passage gave interpreters of the Bible an opportunity to read the enmity between Eve's descendants and the serpent of Genesis as a prophecy or oracle.

[76]The "Childern" of *1667* may represent Milton's spelling usage; in *1674*, it is normalized to the more familiar spelling. Shawcross restores the reading of *1667*.

[77]Reiterates the position that the husband's authority over the wife increased, unpleasantly, after and as a result of the fall (see *On Christian Doctrine* 1.10; Yale 6: 355). Milton added that the Hebrew word for husband was the same as "lord" in English (355).

Because thou hast heark'nd to the voice of thy Wife,[78]
And eaten of the Tree concerning which
I charg'd thee, saying: Thou shalt not eate thereof,   200
Curs'd is the ground for thy sake, thou in sorrow
Shalt eate thereof all the days of thy Life;
Thorns also and Thistles it shall bring thee forth
Unbid, and thou shalt eate th' Herb of th' Field,
In the sweat of thy Face shalt thou eat Bread,   205
Till thou return unto the ground, for thou
Out of the ground wast taken, know thy Birth,
For dust thou art, and shalt to dust returne.[79]
    So judg'd he Man, both Judge and Saviour sent,
And th' instant stroke of Death denounc't[80] that day   210
Remov'd farr off; then pittying how they stood
Before him naked to the aire, that now
Must suffer change,[81] disdain'd not to begin
Thenceforth the form of servant to assume,
As when he wash'd his servants feet[82] so now   215
As Father of his Familie[83] he clad
Thir nakedness with Skins of Beasts, or° slain,   EITHER
Or as the Snake with youthful Coate repaid;[84]
And thought not much to cloath his Enemies:
Nor hee thir outward onely with the Skins   220
Of Beasts, but inward nakedness, much more
Opprobrious,° with his Robe of righteousness,   UTTERLY SHAMEFUL
Araying cover'd from his Fathers sight.[85]
To him with swift ascent he up returnd,
Into his blissful bosom reassum'd   225
In glory as of old, to him appeas'd
All, though all-knowing, what had past with Man

---

[78]Because he reproduces Genesis so exactly, Milton creates one of the few lines in the poem that cannot be scanned as blank verse.

[79]"And unto Adam he said, Because thou hast hearkened unto the voice of thy wife, and hast eaten of the tree, of which I commanded thee, saying, Thou shalt not eat of it: cursed is the ground for thy sake; in sorrow shalt thou eat of it all the days of thy life; Thorns also and thistles shall it bring forth to thee; and thou shalt eat the herb of the field; In the sweat of thy face shalt thou eat bread, till thou return unto the ground; for out of it wast thou taken: for dust thou art, and unto dust shalt thou return" (Genesis 3.17–19).

[80]"Proclaimed," but in the negative sense, as a warning (*OED* 3). The Son countermands what seems to most untutored readers of Genesis to be a clear enough threat—that if Adam and Eve eat they will die that same day. Since Adam and Eve do eat in Genesis and since they do not die, Christian commentators had to account differently for the meaning of the word day. "Day" is "Remov'd farr off" and comes to mean "all the days" of Adam's life, as reported at 202 above.

[81]The temperate seasons of Paradise are now replaced by the stormy or icy seasons of a fallen world.

[82]The line in *1667* has a comma at this point.

[83]Jesus is described as taking on the role of a servant in Philippians 2.7, and he washes his disciples' feet in John 13.5–17, in order to demonstrate that "The servant is not greater than his lord; neither is he that is sent greater than he that sent him." Milton stresses the father-to-family and even the servant-to-master relationship here between the Son as judge of His children, Adam and Eve, and as "servant of God," and as Savior of God's children, when He is incarnated and dies for the sake of humankind. The simple act of a father clothing his children becomes the emblem of parental care and love—even though Adam and Eve, in allying themselves with Satan, have at least temporarily become His "Enemies." For the biblical context, compare Romans 5.10: "For if, when we were enemies, we were reconciled to God by the death of his Son, much more, being reconciled, we shall be saved by his life."

[84]Milton gives us a choice of possibilities (Mollenkott, "Milton's Technique"), as did most biblical commentators such as Willet (54). When the Son clothes Adam and Eve, he covers their nakedness with either the coats of slain beasts or something like the sloughed-off skin of a serpent. In other words, God does not need to kill the beasts to produce their skins for human clothing. Besides, He is metaphorically clothing their "inward nakedness . . . with his Robe of righteousness."

[85]As always with Milton, the inward or spiritual is more important than the outward or physical. Here the Son is acting as mediator "mixing intercession sweet" when he recounts the act of clothing Adam and Eve in the biblical robe of righteousness (Isaiah 61.10), which He does partly to help protect them against the wrath of the Father.

Recounted, mixing intercession sweet.[86]
Meanwhile ere thus was sin'd° and judg'd[87] on Earth,   SINNED
Within the Gates of Hell sate Sin and Death,   230
In counterview° within the Gates, that now   FACING EACH OTHER
Stood open wide, belching outrageous flame[88]
Farr into *Chaos*, since the Fiend pass'd through,
Sin opening,[89] who thus now to Death began.

    O Son, why sit we here each other viewing   235
Idlely, while Satan our great Author[90] thrives
In other Worlds, and happier Seat provides
For us his ofspring deare? It cannot be
But that success attends him; if mishap,
Ere this he had return'd, with fury driv'n   240
By his Avengers,[91] since no place like this
Can fit his punishment, or their revenge.
Methinks° I feel new strength within me rise,   IT SEEMS TO ME
Wings growing,[92] and Dominion giv'n me large
Beyond this Deep; whatever drawes me on,   245
Or° sympathie, or som connatural° force   EITHER   INHERENT
Powerful at greatest distance to unite
With secret amity things of like kinde
By secretest conveyance.[93] Thou my Shade[94]
Inseparable must[95] with mee along: 250
For Death from Sin no power can separate.
But least the difficultie of passing back
Stay his return perhaps over this Gulfe
Impassable, Impervious,[96] let us try
Adventrous[97] work, yet to thy power and mine   255
Not unagreeable, to found a path
Over this Maine° from Hell to that new World   EXPANSE OF OCEAN
Where Satan now prevailes, a Monument
Of merit high[98] to all th' infernal Host,
Easing thir passage hence, for intercourse,   260

---

[86]The Son's role as intercessor makes Him tell of Adam and Eve's redemption sympathetically. The Son will, in the Incarnation, become both son and brother to Adam and Eve, as well as the prophesied "Seed."

[87]"Meanwhile, before all this [sin] was thus committed and judged on Earth." For the similar use of the verb, see "was swum" at 7.503.

[88]Apparently Milton has in mind the image in medieval morality plays, a Hell-mouth belching enormous ("outrageous") amounts of flame standing ready to devour sinners. See 288 below as well.

[89]"Sin having opened them."

[90]The word "Author" is ironic since it is used elsewhere of God and of Adam as creators or life-givers. Satan's infernal trinity gives birth, of course, to death. The phrase "happier Seat" parodies that used of Eden: "happie rural seat of various view" (4.247). The word of affection "deare" is also ironic at 2.817 and 5.673.

[91]Corrects the singular "Avenger" of *1667*, to match the plural pronoun "their" in the next line.

[92]So also do Adam and Eve grow at least metaphorical wings as they become intoxicated after their fall (9.1009–11). Sin and Death are pictured here in actions that occurred at the same time as the Fall (see 229 above). As Fowler points out (9.244n), Sin rises and Adam falls simultaneously.

[93]Evidence of the "*wondrous sympathie*" reported in the Argument for this book. By a kind of telepathy, Sin could detect Death. "Conveyance" is any form of communication, but the word also suggested furtive communication or even theft (*OED* 3).

[94]Her epithet for Death gives us some idea of what he should look like: he is either shapeless or a constantly shifting shadow of his mother Sin. The word "Shade" also means "ghost," but here it seems to retain its literal meaning, since Death must always shadow his mother Sin (see 264 below).

[95]Supply "go" or "come."

[96]The two adjectives differ in shade of meaning, since "Impassable" suggests not only "incapable of providing passage" but "incapable of suffering or injury" and "incapable of feeling or emotion" (*OED* 1–3), and "Impervious" suggests "not affording passage at all."

[97]Milton has used the adjective "adventrous" of his own song in the epic (1.13), and Adam used it of Eve at 9.921, perhaps prophetically, but here the noun form of the word might suggest the modern "adventurer" or "soldier of fortune"—an explorer but only for the sake of adventure or booty.

[98]Presumably the same as the "merit" that raises Satan to his "bad eminence" (2.5–6).

Or transmigration,[99] as thir lot shall lead.[100]
Nor can I miss the way, so strongly drawn
By this new felt attraction and instinct.°   IMPULSE
    Whom thus the meager° Shadow answerd soon.   EMACIATED
Goe whither Fate and inclination strong   265
Leads thee, I shall not lag behinde, nor erre°   WANDER OFF
The way, thou leading, such a sent I draw°   INHALE
Of carnage, prey innumerable, and taste
The savour of Death from all things there that live:
Nor shall I to the work thou enterprisest[101]   270
Be wanting, but afford thee equal aid.[102]
    So saying, with delight he snuff'd° the smell   SNIFFED
Of mortal change on Earth.[103] As when a flock
Of ravenous Fowl, though many a League remote,
Against the day of Battel, to a Field,[104]   275
Where Armies lie encampt, come flying, lur'd
With sent° of living Carcasses design'd   SCENT
For death, the following day, in bloodie fight.
So sented the grim Feature,[105] and upturn'd
His Nostril wide into the murkie Air,   280
Sagacious of[106] his Quarry from so farr.
Then Both from out Hell Gates into the waste
Wide Anarchie of *Chaos* damp and dark
Flew divers,° and with Power (thir Power was great)   SEPARATELY
Hovering upon the Waters;[107] what they met   285
Solid or slimie, as in raging Sea
Tost up and down, together crowded drove
From each side shoaling[108] towards the mouth of Hell.
As when two Polar Winds blowing adverse
Upon the *Cronian* Sea,[109] together drive   290
Mountains of Ice, that stop th' imagin'd way
Beyond *Petsora* Eastward, to the rich
Cathaian Coast. The aggregated Soyle[110]

---

[99]The contrast is between easy and frequent commerce (intercourse) and permanent relocation or settlement in another place (transmigration). Fowler notes the fatalistic word "lot" (10.260–61n), a word used eleven times in *Paradise Lost*, sometimes in reference to the process of the Fall. Compare "Fate" in the vocabulary of Death, just below.

[100]The bridge constructed now becomes a landmark, an infernal edifice analogous to the city of Pandemonium.

[101]The verb "enterprise" suggests "to undertake an operation," with the implication that the operation is a military attack (*OED* 3).

[102]The line in *1674* wrongly includes a comma; *1667* has a period here, the standard usage of both editions before a quotation.

[103]In other words, Death can detect the smell of death or even the smell of mortality, like a vulture, from great distance. Milton's flock may be of ravens, also carrion birds, or of ravenous vultures. The carrion birds in this case have the paranormal or at least supernatural ability to smell death before it occurs. The eagle is reported to have a similar ability in Job 39.30.

[104]There would seem to be no comma necessary here since the next clause is restrictive, but the usage is arbitrary.

[105]"Form, shape, creation" (*OED* 1.c); in other words, a form that shifts its shape.

[106]"Acutely sensitive to the smell of." There was a Latin idiom built around the adjective *sagax* and associated with dogs used for tracking, which Hume noted as "A fit comparison for the *chief hell-hound*" (qtd. in Todd 281n).

[107]Another parody of the Spirit which "Dove-like satst brooding on the vast Abyss" (1.21) at Creation.

[108]Building up sand-bars. As William B. Hunter reminds me (letter, October 1991), "Sin and Death are not creating (only God can do that) but are aggregating materials for their bridge out of Chaos."

[109]The Arctic Ocean, which of course is pictured as solid with ice. There is a possible allusion to Pliny (*Natural History* 4.16), who uses the name *Cronium*. As Fowler points out, Henryk Hudson in 1608 tried to break through the polar ice in an unsuccessful attempt to find a northeast passage to China or Cathay. Milton would have been interested in the exploration for his *Brief History of Muscovia*, in which he mentions Petzora or Pechora, a river in northern Russia (Yale 8: 479). Cathay was thought to be a separate kingdom to the north of China bounded by the Great Wall and discovered only recently by the Russians (Yale 8: 576).

[110]The soil is hard-packed, made into an aggregate or turned to stone by the power of Death's mace or scepter, which apparently has Medusa's "*Gorgonian*" power to calcify.

Death with his Mace petrific,[111] cold and dry,[112]
As with a Trident smote, and fix't as firm   295
As *Delos* floating once; the rest his look
Bound with *Gorgonian* rigor not to move,
And with *Asphaltic* slime;[113] broad as the Gate,
Deep to the Roots of Hell the gather'd beach
They fasten'd, and the Mole[114] immense wraught on   300
Over the foaming deep high Archt, a Bridge
Of length prodigious joyning to the Wall
Immovable of this now fenceless world[115]
Forfeit to Death; from hence a passage broad,
Smooth, easie, inoffensive down to Hell.[116]   305
So, if great things to small may be compar'd,
Xerxes, the Libertie of *Greece* to yoke,
From *Susa* his *Memnonian* Palace high
Came to the Sea, and over *Hellespont*
Bridging his way, *Europe* with *Asia* joyn'd,   310
And scourg'd with many a stroak th' indignant waves.[117]
Now had they brought the work by wondrous Art
Pontifical,[118] a ridge of pendent Rock
Over the vext Abyss,[119] following the track
Of *Satan*,[120] to the self same place where hee   315
First lighted° from his Wing, and landed safe   ALIGHTED
From out of *Chaos* to the out side bare

[111]Quite possibly a sardonic anti-Roman-Catholic joke, because the Pope carries a mace as a symbol of his power and is said to be *Pontifex maximus*, the greatest of bridge-builders. See 313 below. The pun on St. Peter's name, which suggests "rock" in its Greek original, was first made by Christ in Matthew 16.18: ". . . thou art Peter, and upon this rock I will build my church. . . ."

[112]In the act of creation, God uses warm and wet elements (7.236–37). Pictured by Marlowe as "pale Death's stony mace" (*Dido* 2.1.115; ed. J. B. Steane), Death's scepter is also analogous to the "little tridents" Milton makes fun of as pagan artifacts in *Comus* 27. Neptune or Poseidon would have used his trident traditionally to cause earthquakes or tidal waves or to raise islands like Delos, the smallest of the Cyclades, which was supposed to be left a floating island by Poseidon until Zeus fixed it by means of a chain of adamant to the floor of the sea.

[113]Asphalt was often synonymous with pitch, bitumen, or the biblical "slime" (see *OED 1*). It became hellish by its association with such asphalt pits as the Phlegrean ("burning") Fields near Naples alluded to in 1.577, or with the pitch of the apocryphal Ecclesiasticus 13.1: "He that toucheth pitch, shalbe defiled with it" (Geneva Bible, 1560 ed.).

[114]"A massive structure . . . serving as a pier or breakwater; . . . an artificial harbor [by metonymy]" (*OED* substantive 3.2). Still current usage in Great Britain but not in the United States.

[115]The wall of this world is the orb of the Earth, which is not only fenceless but defenseless, since Death has been allowed in. As the island of Delos is anchored to the bottom of the sea, the bridge is anchored to the base of Hell—just as Milton's universe is anchored to Heaven (2.1051). The path to Hell is inoffensive not only in that it does not cause one to stumble but in that those who conform to a life that does not offend the authorities may well take the easy road to damnation.

[116]"Enter ye at the strait gate; for wide is the gate, and broad is the way, that leadeth to destruction, and many there be which go in thereat: Because strait is the gate, and narrow is the way, which leadeth unto life, and few there be that find it" (Matthew 7.13–14). Milton builds metaphors and puns on gates and fences.

[117]In the six-line comparison, Milton sums up the futility of military conquest. Even bridging the Hellespont at Susa (also called Memnonia because Memnon, son of the dawn, Aurora, and Tithonus, was supposed to have lived there) could not satisfy the greed of the Persian king Xerxes in his attempt to subdue the Greeks. Xerxes had had the Hellespont scourged or beaten because his first pontoon bridge between Europe (Chersonasus or Turkey) and Asia Minor had been destroyed in a storm. The comparison is between Death, building a bridge that will be successful only until Judgment Day, and Xerxes, building one that is much more temporary; both beings are megalomaniacs and both are ultimately defeated, their arrogant actions proven to be futile. Herodotus's description of Xerxes ordering his men "to lay three hundred lashes on the Hellespont" (*The History* 7.35, 482) is indeed ridiculous; Milton makes even the waves indignant at the outrage done them.

[118]Deeply ironic and probably satirical, since "Art" is a word Milton often associates with witchcraft, and "Pontifical" would be associated by any seventeenth-century reader with the Pope. It means, literally, "bridge maker." "The joke seems so good that unusually he [Milton] shortly afterwards repeats it, coining on the model of ` edifice' a new word 'pontifice,' 'bridge,' which once more offers a quibble with the already current word 'pontifice,' an epithet of the Pope . . ." (Corns 90–91).

[119]Parts of the bridge are apparently suspended ("pendent") and the "Abyss" (1.21) of Chaos is vexed with turbulent weather.

[120]The name is italicized again, in both *1667* and *1674*, perhaps signifying a change of compositors in the first edition and more slavish copying in the second. Satan is like an animal here, not only leaving a track but alighting like a bird.

Of this round World:[121] with Pinns of Adamant
And Chains they made all fast, too fast they made
And durable; and now in little space   320
The confines met of Empyrean Heav'n
And of this World, and on the left hand Hell[122]
With long reach interpos'd; three sev'ral° wayes   DIFFERENT
In sight, to each of these three places led.[123]
And now thir way to Earth they had descri'd,   325
To Paradise first tending, when behold
Satan in likeness of an Angel bright
Betwixt the *Centaure* and the *Scorpion* stearing
His *Zenith*, while the Sun in *Aries* rose:[124]
Disguis'd he came, but those his Children[125] dear   330
Thir Parent soon discern'd,[126] though in disguise.
Hee[127] after *Eve* seduc't, unminded slunk
Into the Wood fast by, and changing shape
To observe the sequel,° saw his guileful act   CONSEQUENCE
By *Eve*, though all unweeting,[128] seconded[129]   335
Upon her Husband, saw thir shame that sought
Vain covertures;[130] but when he saw descend
The Son of God to judge them,[131] terrifi'd
Hee fled, not hoping to escape, but shun
The present, fearing guiltie what his[132] wrauth   340
Might suddenly inflict; that past, return'd
By Night, and listening[133] where the hapless Paire
Sate in thir sad discourse, and various plaint,[134]
Thence gatherd his own doom, which understood
Not instant, but of future time.[135] With joy   345

---

[121]We are asked to remember Satan's landing described at 3.418-26. Just as the island of Delos was attached by chains of adamant, the bridge is anchored by the same durable legendary metal, as Satan will be bound by "Adamantine Chains" (1.48) in Hell. Apparently Milton considered adamant a rock (2.646) as well as a metal. The point here is that the bridge is made of frighteningly durable and inflexible material.

[122]Just as Sin is born from the left ("sinister") side of Satan's head and Eve from the left side of Adam's ribcage (the seat of the "cordial spirits" [8.466]), Hell is on the lefthand side. In the division of sheep and goats in the parable of final judgment, the sinner goats are put on the lefthand side (Matthew 25.33).

[123]The three landmarks alluded to are the stairway to Heaven, "Jacob's Ladder," of 3.510-15, the passageway from the outer sphere of the universe to Earth at 3.528-37, and this bridge.

[124]Satan steers a straight line between the constellations of the Centaur Sagittarius and Scorpio, while the sun rises in Aries. Fowler notes, "The real reason for steering [between the two] is . . . that the only constellation noticeably spread over these two signs is Anguis, the serpent held by Ophiuchus. . . . Anguis has its head in Libra, and extends through Scorpio into Sagittarius. Accordingly, Satan enters the world in Libra . . . but leaves it between Scorpio and Sagittarius" (10.328-29n).

[125]The reading of *1667*, "Childern," again may represent a spelling closer to Milton's preference.

[126]Compare the Son as a genuinely affectionate parent (as well as brother and future descendant) to Adam and Eve (216). Sin and Death need to see through their father's disguise (left over from deceiving Eve?) in order to recognize him.

[127]The line in *1667* has a comma after "Hee," but the removal of the comma may be a thoughtful correction (see Fletcher for the opposite opinion). The phrase "after *Eve* seduc't" means "after *Eve* had been seduced."

[128]The word "unweeting" ("unwitting," probably meaning "unthoughtful" or "careless" [compare *OED* "Unwitting" 1]) again suggests that Eve was "deceived," following 1 Timothy 2.14. Before the Fall, Eve is unwary; in the Fall, she is beguiled; after it, she is unweeting (for the connection between being unwary and unweeting, see *Comus* 539). Through it all, however, she remains responsible for her own actions.

[129]The word is very carefully chosen for its neutrality, since the sin is not "visited" on Adam, nor is it "inflicted": it is only seconded.

[130]When Adam and Eve discover their nakedness, their shame, personified, seeks to cover them, but the coverings of leaves (9.1110-14) were in vain (since their nakedness and vulnerability to death are spiritual, not physical).

[131]The comma of *1667* seems a better reading here than the absence of punctuation after "them" in *1674*.

[132]That is, the Son's.

[133]Satan gains most of his information about Adam and Eve by eavesdropping, and his relationship to them, especially to Eve, is often that of a voyeur, the two processes humiliating the objects of his "scopophilia" (see Schwartz, *Remembering* 54-59).

[134]Their separate complaints. The implication is that each has a sad tale to tell, but the word "plaint" often has a negative association with whining complaint in *Paradise Lost*, as in 9.98 above or 2.29.

[135]Satan will not die instantly, either, but his doom will be reserved for Judgment Day, when Death itself will die.

And tidings fraught,[136] to Hell he now return'd,
And at the brink of *Chaos*, neer the foot
Of this new wondrous Pontifice,° unhop't   BRIDGE
Met who to meet him came, his Ofspring dear.
Great joy was at thir meeting, and at sight   350
Of that stupendious Bridge his joy encreas'd.
Long hee admiring stood, till Sin, his faire
Inchanting Daughter,[137] thus the silence broke.
      O Parent, these are thy magnific[138] deeds,
Thy Trophies, which thou view'st as not thine own,   355
Thou art thir Author and prime Architect:[139]
For I no sooner in my Heart divin'd,
My Heart, which by a secret harmonie[140]
Still° moves with thine, join'd in connexion sweet,   ALWAYS
That thou on Earth hadst prosper'd, which thy looks   360
Now also evidence, but straight° I felt   IMMEDIATELY
Though distant from thee Worlds between, yet felt
That I must[141] after thee with this thy Son;
Such fatal consequence[142] unites us three:
Hell could no longer hold us in her bounds,   365
Nor this unvoyageable Gulf obscure
Detain from following thy illustrious track.
Thou hast atchiev'd our libertie, confin'd
Within Hell Gates till now, thou us impow'rd
To fortifie thus farr, and overlay   370
With this portentous[143] Bridge the dark Abyss.
Thine now is all this World, thy vertue[144] hath won
What thy hands builded not, thy Wisdom gain'd
With odds what Warr hath lost, and fully aveng'd
Our foile° in Heav'n; here thou shalt Monarch reign,   DEFEAT   375
There didst not; there let him still Victor sway,
As Battel hath adjudg'd, from this new World
Retiring, by his own doom alienated,
And henceforth Monarchie with thee divide
Of all things[145] parted by th' Empyreal bounds,   380
His Quadrature, from thy Orbicular World,[146]
Or trie° thee now more dang'rous to his Throne.   TEST
      Whom thus the Prince of Darkness answerd glad.

---

[136]"Filled with joy and with [what he believes to be] good news."

[137]Sin is given some of the attributes of the sorceress in Renaissance romantic epic, since she is both fair and enchanting. See Brodwin; Hughes, "Acrasia"; Browning.

[138]The word is suspicious, since it suggests inflated values, here and with "magnific Titles" (5.773).

[139]A parody of God's actions and achievements, since God is the only author of all and is also the *deus artifex* or celestial architect.

[140]The same as the "sympathie" or "connatural force" that is said to exist at 246 above; Satan believes there is a kind of secret harmony or telepathy among them.

[141]Supply "follow."

[142]"Such a fated relationship between cause and effect" (*OED* 2, citing this instance).

[143]Capable of carrying great traffic, but also signifying evil portents or predictions of future ills to plague humankind.

[144]"Raw power," rather than any normal positive sense of the word.

[145]The unnecessary comma of *1667* has apparently been edited out in *1674*.

[146]"This *world* is *orbicular* or round; *the empyreal Heaven* is a *quadrature* or square" (Newton 381n). What was interpreted as the Empyrean or Heaven of Heavens is described in Revelation 21.16 as a square. The cubic Heaven is forbidden to the fallen angels, but now the "Orbicular World" is open to them. The circle was generally thought to be perfect because it contained its own beginning and end.

Fair Daughter, and thou Son and Grandchild both,[147]
High proof ye now have giv'n to be the Race   SATAN   385
Of *Satan* (for I glorie in the name,
Antagonist of Heav'ns Almightie King)[148]
Amply have merited of me, of all
Th' infernal Empire, that so neer Heav'ns dore
Triumphal with triumphal act have met,   390
Mine with this glorious Work, and made one Realm
Hell and this World, one Realm, one Continent
Of easie thorough-fare. Therefore while I
Descend through Darkness, on your Rode° with ease   ROAD
To my associate Powers, them to acquaint   395
With these successes, and with them rejoyce,
You two this way, among these[149] numerous Orbs
All yours, right down to Paradise descend;
There dwell and Reign in bliss, thence on the Earth
Dominion exercise and in the Aire,   400
Chiefly on Man, sole Lord of all declar'd,
Him first make sure your thrall, and lastly kill.
My Substitutes I send ye, and Create
Plenipotent[150] on Earth, of matchless might
Issuing from mee: on your joynt vigor now   405
My hold of this new Kingdom all depends,
Through Sin to Death expos'd by my exploit.
If your joynt power prevailes,[151] th' affaires of Hell
No detriment need feare, goe and be strong.[152]

    So saying he dismiss'd them, they with speed   410
Thir course through thickest Constellations held
Spreading thir bane;° the blasted[153] Starrs lookt wan,[154]   POISON
And Planets, Planet-strook,[155] real Eclips[156]
Then sufferd. Th' other way *Satan* went down
The Causey° to Hell Gate; on either side   CAUSEWAY   415
Disparted *Chaos* over built exclaimd,[157]
And with rebounding surge the barrs assaild,
That scorn'd his indignation:[158] through the Gate,
Wide open and unguarded, *Satan* pass'd,
And all about found desolate; for those   420

---

[147]Satan seems to be investigating all avenues of incest in the epithets he applies to his children, since Sin becomes not only his daughter but his concubine, whereas Death becomes both his son (by Sin) and his grandchild (since Sin is his daughter and Death is the third generation). Together they represent the "Race / Of *Satan*," not very good evidence of his ability to produce a master race.

[148]We are reminded again by what is in the parenthesis that "Satan" means "Adversary" or "Antagonist."

[149]The line in *1667* reads "those"; the change seems an improvement.

[150]"Full of power," taking the Latin etymology of *plenus* (full of) and *potentia* (power) to its fullest.

[151]The "prevaile" of *1667*, which might have responded either to the subjunctive (Adams 103) or to the dual subject implied in "joynt power" has apparently been corrected to make it agree with "power" as a singular noun.

[152]Satan quotes scripture to his purpose, and in this case he is quoting the words of a patriarch: Moses adjures Joshua, "Be strong and of a good courage . . . " (Deuteronomy 31.7) and then "fear not, neither be dismayed" (31.8).

[153]"Breathed on in a malign way," but here used in the astrological sense of "exerting an evil influence on." See *OED* s.v. "blast" II.7.

[154]The stars they pass among are "blasted," some of their shine is diminished, and they are rendered "malign" in the astrological sense. It appears that the negative influences of astrology are born at this moment. Planetary influence becomes malignant, and the portents of eclipses and planetary oppositions are realized as evil. See Edmund's mocking speech about astrological influence on character in *King Lear* 1.2.129–45.

[155]"Stricken by the supposed malign influence of an adverse planet" (*OED* 1, citing this instance).

[156]Presumably any perceived eclipse but here the time discussed exists before eclipses might portend evil (as a result of the Fall).

[157]"Chaos, which has been divided and then had the bridge built over it, exclaims."

[158]In Vergil's *Georgics* 2.161, the ocean is said to be *indignatum* at having a breakwater imposed on it.

Appointed to sit there, had left thir charge,
Flown to the upper World;[159] the rest were all
Farr to the inland[160] retir'd, about the walls
Of *Pandæmonium*, Citie and proud seate
Of *Lucifer*, so by allusion calld,   425
Of that bright Starr to *Satan* paragond.[161]
There kept thir Watch the Legions, while the Grand[162]
In Council sate, sollicitous what chance
Might intercept thir Emperour sent, so hee
Departing gave command, and they observ'd.°   OBEYED   430
As when the *Tartar* from his *Russian* Foe
By *Astracan*[163] over the Snowie Plaines
Retires, or *Bactrian* Sophi[164] from the hornes
Of *Turkish* Crescent, leaves all waste beyond
The Realm of *Aladule*, in his retreate   435
To *Tauris* or *Casbeen*.[165] So these the late
Heav'n-banisht Host, left desert utmost Hell
Many a dark League, reduc't° in careful Watch   DRAWN TOGETHER
Round thir Metropolis, and now expecting
Each hour their great adventurer from the search   440
Of Forrein Worlds: he through the midst unmarkt,
In shew Plebeian Angel militant
Of lowest order, past;[166] and from the dore
Of that *Plutonian* Hall, invisible
Ascended his high Throne, which under state[167]   445
Of richest texture spred, at th' upper end
Was plac't in regal lustre. Down a while
He sate, and round about him saw unseen:
At last as from a Cloud his fulgent head[168]
And shape Starr bright[169] appeer'd, or brighter, clad   450
With what permissive glory[170] since his fall
Was left him, or false glitter: All amaz'd

---

[159]Sin and Death have already flown to Earth.

[160]In *1667* the word was divided into two, as "in land," but in my copy of *1674*, at least, there is no sign of separation and no sign of a conjectural hyphen.

[161]Hume brings to bear the now archaic French verb *paragonnér*, "to be equal or to be like"; thus "paragond" would be close in meaning to "compared." Milton emphasizes what he considers to be a fact here and elsewhere: Satan may be compared with the star, but the star (actually planet) is quite separate from him, since the comparison only held while Satan was one of the "Sons of light" (5.160).

[162]The "Grand" are those fallen angels who think themselves grand, probably the same as "The great Seraphic Lords and Cherubim / [who 'sat'] In close recess and secret conclave" (1.794–95).

[163]Both the Tartar kingdom and capital city near the mouth of the Volga on the Caspian Sea. Milton seems to be basing the simile on his memories of Russian history gleaned for his *Brief History of Muscovia*. For Astracan (modern Astrakhan), see Yale 8: 536.

[164]The Persian Shah, whose armies might fight in a crescent formation and whose flag contains a crescent moon. "Sophi" can mean "Sage" as in "Wise Man" as well as "Shah."

[165]Aladule is the greater part of modern Armenia, and Tauris is the modern Tabriz in northwestern Iran (Persia). Casbeen is now Kazvin, north of Teheran. Milton may be naming cities along seventeenth-century trade routes.

[166]Satan is still pictured as a soldier of fortune or adventurer. He sneaks through the midst of the council disguised and undetected as usual, but in this case in the undignified guise of a plebeian footsoldier, in order to make a grand entrance first as a shining head then as an entire "shape." The effect is comic-pretentious. The hall is *"Plutonian"* because it would be associated with Pluto, the Roman god of the underworld.

[167]Canopy, possibly as opulent as that designed to cover Bernini's baldacchino over the central altar in St. Peter's in Rome.

[168]His head at first appears, sparkling from out of the cloud. The image apparently parodies that of the real star Lucifer, and its "false glitter" or "fulgence" should be contrasted with the genuine "Effulgence" (6.680) of the Son. Satan's glitter (compare the modern term "glitz") is, as usual, a false or distorted mirror image of godhead. Hunter believes that his appearance is that of a supernova, for Milton's day an evil omen (*Descent* 63–64).

[169]The phrase was hyphenated "Starr-bright" in *1667*.

[170]All that remains of Satan's glory as Lucifer is what is allowed or permitted him by God (compare 3.685, where God also allows Satan's hypocrisy to exist).

At that so sudden blaze the *Stygian*[171] throng
Bent thir aspect,[172] and whom they wish'd beheld,[173]
Thir mighty Chief returnd: loud was th' acclaime: 455
Forth rush'd in haste the great consulting Peers,
Rais'd from thir Dark *Divan*,[174] and with like joy
Congratulant approach'd him, who with hand
Silence, and with these words attention won.

    Thrones, Dominations, Princedoms, Vertues, Powers,   460
For in possession such, not onely of right,
I call ye and declare ye now, returnd
Successful beyond hope,[175] to lead ye forth
Triumphant out of this infernal Pit
Abominable, accurst, the house of woe,   465
And Dungeon of our Tyrant: Now possess,
As Lords, a spacious World, to our native Heaven
Little inferiour, by my adventure hard
With peril great atchiev'd. Long were to tell[176]
What I have don, what sufferd, with what paine   470
Voyag'd th' unreal, vast, unbounded deep
Of horrible confusion, over which
By Sin and Death a broad way now is pav'd
To expedite your glorious march; but I
Toild out my uncouth passage,[177] forc't to ride   475
Th' untractable Abysse, plung'd in the womb
Of unoriginal *Night* and *Chaos* wilde,[178]
That jealous of thir secrets fiercely oppos'd
My journey strange, with clamorous uproare
Protesting Fate supreme; thence how I found   480
The new created World, which fame in Heav'n
Long had foretold, a Fabrick[179] wonderful
Of absolute perfection, therein Man
Plac't in a Paradise, by our exile
Made happie: Him by fraud I have seduc'd   485
From his Creator, and the more to increase
Your wonder, with an Apple;[180] he thereat
Offended, worth your laughter, hath giv'n up

[Handwritten annotation: SATAN ADDRESSING HIS MINIONS]

---

[171]Associated with the Styx, the Greek and Roman river of the underworld. Thus the "*Stygian* throng" are Satan's followers.
[172]"Turned their face toward."
[173]They see him whom they wanted to appear: Satan.
[174]Since the "*Divan*," in this sense an Oriental council of state (*OED* 1), was associated with Persian rulers (the word is Arabic and came to indicate the types of cushioned steps on which business was conducted), the image of the conquering sophy or sultan is re-invoked, along with its barbarism. The word "*Divan*" may be italicized because it was not yet accepted as English.
[175]Another way of saying "beyond hope" is "in despair"; a serious pun may be planted here, one which undercuts all that Satan says.
[176]All during this speech, Satan is posing as an epic hero, the subject of a potential *Sataniad*. Burden perhaps introduced the idea of a "satanic epic" (64). See also Neil Harris, "Milton's 'Sataneid': The Poet and the Devil in 'Paradise Lost,'" dissertation, University of Leicester, 1985, for development of this thesis in comparison with the practice of Dante, Boiardo, Ariosto, and Tasso. See also Lewalski, *Paradise Lost*.
[177]"My journey through uncharted territory."
[178]The image might be grotesquely sexual, since "womb" could mean "vagina" as well as "uterus." Night is "unoriginal" because it did not exist before God created it: thus Satan is unconsciously admitting God's creation, having publicly denied (5.856-58) that he was a created being in the past and then privately affirmed it (4.43). Needless to say, most of what he asserts to his followers is gross exaggeration, if not outright lying (except that Chaos did indeed give him a bumpy ride). He was not a great and brave adventurer, for instance, when he slunk out of Eden. His speech is made up of bits of self-inflating nonsense, and it will be greeted with a proper audience response.
[179]An architectural product of skilled workmanship (*OED* I.1) or the workmanship itself (*OED* II.5).
[180]As always, Satan diminishes or reduces symbols to material objects, as he also reduced the fruit of the Tree of the Knowledge of Good and Evil to "fair Apples" at 9.585.

Both his beloved Man and all his World,
To Sin and Death a prey, and so to us,   490
Without our hazard, labour, or allarme,
To range in, and to dwell, and over Man
To rule, as over all he should have rul'd.
True is, mee also he hath judg'd, or rather
Mee not, but the brute Serpent in whose shape   495
Man I deceav'd: that which to mee belongs,[181]
Is enmity, which he will put between
Mee and Mankinde; I am to bruise his heel;
His Seed, when is not set,[182] shall bruise my head:
A World who would not purchase with a bruise,[183]   500
Or much more grievous pain? Ye have th' account
Of my performance: What remains, ye Gods,
But up and enter now into full bliss.
     So having said, a while he stood, expecting
Thir universal shout and high applause   505
To fill his eare, when contrary he hears
On all sides, from innumerable tongues
A dismal[184] universal hiss, the sound
Of public scorn; he wonderd, but not long
Had leasure, wondring at himself now more;   510
His Visage drawn he felt to sharp and spare,[185]
His Armes clung to his Ribs, his Leggs entwining
Each other, till supplanted[186] down he fell
A monstrous Serpent on his Belly prone,
Reluctant,[187] but in vaine, a greater power   515
Now rul'd him, punisht in the shape he sin'd,
According to his doom:[188] he would have spoke,
But hiss for hiss returnd with forked tongue
To forked tongue, for now were all transform'd
Alike, to Serpents all,[189] as accessories   520
To his bold Riot: dreadful was the din
Of hissing through the Hall, thick swarming now

---

[181]"That part of the curse which belongs to me." Satan wants God's wrath to be misplaced on the Serpent, rather than on himself.

[182]"The date for which is not yet set or made known [by God]."

[183]Satan's reduction of his doom at Judgment Day, to be crushed under the heel of the Son, to a "bruise" is witty but fallacious. He is correct, as he will be questioning Jesus's "Real or Allegoric" kingdom in *Paradise Regain'd* 4.390, but he lacks the divine perspective—a bruise will occur and a world [of redemption] will be purchased [but not by Satan]. My thanks to Paul Klemp for pointing this out. Satan's gross materialism is again shown in his choice of the verb *purchase*.

[184]Considering all of Milton's other negative compounds, one would expect another on "dis-mal," and there is certainly onomatopoeia with "dis-" and "hiss." The word originated in *dies mali*, or evil days, but as an adjective it came to mean "unlucky," "cheerless," "Boding . . . disaster" (*OED* 2). The noun *dismal* also could mean "devil" (*OED* C.1.a).

[185]In the grotesque process of changing into a serpent, Satan feels his face draw up to become sharper and thinner than a human face. Milton probably intends a comparison to the transformation of Cadmus in Ovid, *Metamorphoses* 4: "Even as he spoke / He stretched out full-length forward, felt his skin / Harden, and scales increase, and mottled markings / Sprinkle his blackening body. He fell forward, / Crawled on his belly, with his legs behind him / Drawn in, and tapering" (576–81; see also DuRocher).

[186]Satan is tripped up by his feet becoming entwined as he is being transformed, since "supplant" in its primary sense means "cause to trip up" (*OED* 1), but as Fowler points out (10.511–14n, citing Ricks 64–65), Satan is also the great supplanter in that he ousts Adam and Eve from Paradise in order to replace them.

[187]Probably "struggling" or "resisting," from Latin *reluctans*.

[188]It is almost too appropriate that Satan's punishment would be that he be changed back into the shape of the Serpent. As Fowler neatly points out, "just when the devils seem about to become heroes in Satan's epic . . . they turn out instead to be monsters in God's" (10.517n).

[189]I have inserted a comma after "all," following the speculation of Fletcher that early penned corrections in copies of *1674* probably indicate a correction that should have been but was never made in print.

With complicated[190] monsters head and taile,
Scorpion and Asp, and *Amphisbæna*[191] dire,
Cerastes hornd, *Hydrus*, and *Ellops* drear,[192]   525
And *Dipsas* (not so thick swarm'd once the Soil
Bedropt with blood of *Gorgon*, or the Isle
Ophiusa)[193] but still greatest hee the midst,
Now Dragon grown, larger then whom the Sun
Ingenderd in the *Pythian* Vale on slime,   530
Huge *Python*,[194] and his Power no less he seem'd
Above the rest still to retain; they all
Him follow'd issuing forth to th' open Field,
Where all yet left of that revolted Rout
Heav'n-fall'n, in station stood or just array,[195]   535
Sublime[196] with expectation when to see
In Triumph issuing forth thir glorious Chief;
They saw, but other sight instead, a crowd
Of ugly Serpents; horror on them fell,
And horrid sympathie; for what they saw,   540
They felt themselvs now changing;[197] down thir arms,
Down fell both Spear and Shield, down they as fast,
And the dire hiss renew'd, and the dire form
Catcht by Contagion,[198] like in punishment,
As in thir crime. Thus was th' applause they meant,   545
Turnd to exploding hiss,[199] triumph to shame
Cast on themselves from thir own mouths. There stood
A Grove hard° by, sprung up with this thir change,   VERY NEAR
His will who reigns above, to aggravate
Thir penance, laden with Fruit like that   550

---

[190]Probably "tangled" (*OED* 2), since head and tail seem tied together. The emblem of the snake with its tail in its mouth, signifying an endless Satanic circle, comes to mind (George Wither, *A Collection of Emblemes* [London, 1634]: 157).

[191]A "dangerous" serpent with a head at either end of its body, described by Lucan in the *Pharsalia* 9.798–99 as having the ability to move in either direction its heads are pointing. As Milton moves through his catalogue of serpents, he seems to be imitating Lucan's extended digression (9.700–33) on all the varieties of serpents that were supposed to flourish in Libya. The severed head of the Gorgon Medusa was supposed to have been the "source [in Libya] of Serpents, which swarmed and hissed with flickering tongues from the spilt blood" (699–70; trans. Widdows 231). In the Sixth Day of the First Week of the *Divine Weekes*, DuBartas also catalogues everything from the Python conquered by Hercules to dragons, "aspics" (asps), and basilisks, asking God why such creatures were made, even before the Fall, to plague humankind:

> O, weart thou pleas'd to forme
> Th' innammel'd Scorpion, and the Viper-worme,
> Th' horned *Cerastes*, th' *Alexandrian* Skink,
> Th' Adder, and *Drynas* (full of odious stinke)
> Th' Eft, Snake, and *Dipsas* (causing deadly thirst)
> Why has thou arm'd them with a rage so curst. (ed. Snyder, 1: 267)

One can see, then, that the catalogue of serpents was at least a minor epic tradition.

[192]Cerastes was supposed to have four curled horns on its head, and the hydrus was a water snake (not the Hydra, which is the many-headed monster Hercules dispatched) that was supposed to attack crocodiles.

[193]The name means "full of snakes" and was in ancient Greece given to several different islands, including what is now called Formentara (in the Balearics, off the coast of Spain) and the island of Rhodes.

[194]General belief about snakes included the notion that some types were engendered spontaneously in mud heated by the sun. The belief probably originated in Ovid, *Metamorphoses* 1, where the Nile mud, heated by the sun, swelled "as seed / Swells in a mother's womb to shape and substance, / So new forms came to life" (421–23). The Nile bears Python "unwanted, a gigantic serpent, / ... whom the new people dreaded, / A huge bulk on the mountain-side" (438–40). As Milton acknowledges, Apollo himself has to use hundreds of arrows to bring down the huge snake. The memorial to the combat was the Pythian games.

[195]They either stood at their post or they were arranged in proper ranks.

[196]Literally or emotionally uplifted. Probably used in the negative sense of "haughty, proud" (*OED* 3, citing 4.300).

[197]Supply "into."

[198]Sin, therefore, is a contagious disease.

[199]The primary meaning of "explode" is "To clap and hoot [a player] off the stage" (*OED* 1), which makes "exploding" an appropriate adjective for "hiss."

Which grew in Paradise, the bait of *Eve*[200]
Us'd by the Tempter: on that prospect strange
Thir earnest eyes they fix'd, imagining
For one forbidden Tree a multitude
Now ris'n, to work them furder° woe or shame;   FURTHER   555
Yet parcht with scalding thurst and hunger fierce,
Though to delude them sent, could not abstain,
But on they[201] rould in heaps, and up the Trees
Climbing, sat thicker then the snakie locks
That curld *Megæra*:[202] greedily they pluck'd   560
The Frutage fair to sight, like that which grew
Neer that bituminous Lake[203] where *Sodom* flam'd;
This more delusive, not the touch, but taste
Deceav'd; they fondly thinking to allay
Thir appetite with gust,° instead of Fruit   RELISH   565
Chewd bitter Ashes, which th' offended taste
With spattering noise rejected:[204] oft they assayd,
Hunger and thirst constraining, drugd as oft,
With hatefullest disrelish writh'd thir jaws
With soot and cinders fill'd; so oft they fell   570
Into the same illusion, not as Man
Whom they triumph'd once lapst.[205] Thus were they plagu'd
And worn with Famin, long and ceasless hiss,
Till thir lost shape, permitted, they resum'd,
Yearly enjoynd, some say, to undergo   575
This annual humbling certain number'd days,
To dash thir pride, and joy for Man seduc't.
However some tradition they dispers'd
Among the Heathen of thir purchase got,
And Fabl'd how the Serpent, whom they calld   580
Ophion with *Eurynome*,[206] the wide-[207]
Encroaching *Eve* perhaps,[208] had first the rule

---

[200]The imagery of entrapment throws a new light on what has happened to Eve, if the fruit she ate was a bait used by Satan to capture her. "Bait" has always been used in the sense of "food designed to trick animals into entrapment" (see *OED* noun 1).

[201]On the page where these lines appear in *1674*, it looks as if type has been squeezed out of the printer's forme. Several lines have pushed-up letters, and the "e" in "they," present in *1667*, seems to have been lost.

[202]One of the three Furies, who as a group are often depicted as having snakes instead of hair on their heads. In Hades they were pictured sitting around Pluto's throne, as messengers of his vengeance. Just as serpents were born from the blood dropped by Medusa's snaky head, the Furies were supposed to have been born either from the blood of Coelus (god of the heavens) or from that of his son Saturn.

[203]The Dead Sea, on the shores of which was the city notorious for its vices, Sodom. The potential flames of the inflammable bitumen are comparable to the flames of Sodom, as God was destroying it for its wickedness. The story of the destruction of Sodom and Gomorrah is told in Genesis 13.12–19.28. For the fruit of Sodom, see Deuteronomy 32.32: "For their vine is of the vine of Sodom, and of the fields of Gomorrah: their grapes are grapes of gall, their clusters are bitter." It may be worth noting here that Milton equated the court of Charles I with Sodom in *Eikonoklastes* (Yale 3: 342).

[204]The fallen angels reject the apples with a spattering, or spitting-out, noise.

[205]Loh's paraphrase is helpful here: "i.e., they fell repeatedly under the same illusion, and did not fall just once, like man whom they triumphed (over)" (570–72n). The verb "triumph'd" could, as Loh's paraphrase indicates, signify "triumph over" (see *OED* c., which cites this instance).

[206]Milton's probable source for the story of Ophion (the name signifies a serpent) and Eurynome ("wide-encroaching" provides a translation for that name) is Apollonius of Rhodes, *Argonautica* 1.503. But Fowler (10.578–84n) also cites Claudian, *De Raptu Proserpinae* 3.332–56, for the image of Ophion as a serpent defeated by Jupiter in the war with the Giants and his skin hung out to rot. From Apollonius, Milton could have drawn the story, supposedly sung by Orpheus, of the rule of Ophion and Eurynome (daughter of Oceanus) over the Titans, while Zeus was still living in a cave on the mountain of Dictae in Crete (thus the epithet "*Dictæan Jove*"). In that version, Ophion, despite his name, was not associated with serpents.

[207]The only line in the poem joined with the next by a hyphen.

[208]Annotators even as early as Pearce (1733) have been troubled with the punctuation of this passage, since (1) there should be no comma after "*Eurynome*" but there should be a comma after "Encroaching," if the epithet should be applied to Eurynome; and (2) the name "Eurynome" already means "wide-encroaching," and thus Milton might be accused of redundancy, if he is applying the epithet to Eurynome. But I see no problem with the punctuation as it is in both early editions, since Milton seems to be taking Eurynome as part of the "fable" and applying her epithet "wide-encroaching," by the light

Of high *Olympus*, thence by *Saturn* driv'n
And *Ops*, ere yet *Dictæan Jove* was born.[209]
Mean while in Paradise the hellish pair   585
Too soon arriv'd, *Sin* there in power before,
Once actual, now in body,[210] and to dwell
Habitual habitant; behind her *Death*
Close following pace for pace, not mounted yet
On his pale Horse:[211] to whom *Sin* thus began.   590
    Second of *Satan* sprung,[212] all conquering *Death*,
What thinkst thou of our Empire now, though earnd
With travail difficult, not better farr
Then stil at Hels dark threshold to have sate watch,[213]
Unnam'd, undreaded, and thy self half starv'd?[214]   595
    Whom thus the Sin-born Monster answerd soon.
To mee, who with eternal Famin pine,
Alike is Hell, or Paradise, or Heaven,
There best, where most with ravin° I may meet;
Which here, though plenteous, all too little seems   600
To stuff this Maw, this vast unhide-bound Corps.[215]
    To whom th' incestuous Mother thus repli'd.
Thou therefore on these Herbs, and Fruits, and Flours
Feed first, on each Beast next, and Fish, and Fowle,
No homely morsels, and whatever thing   605
The Sithe of Time mowes down,[216] devour unspar'd,[217]
Till I in Man residing through the Race,
His thoughts, his looks, words, actions all infect,
And season him thy last and sweetest prey.
    This said, they both betook them several wayes,   610
Both to destroy, or unimmortal[218] make
All kinds, and for destruction to mature
Sooner or later; which th' Almightie seeing,
From his transcendent Seat the Saints among,
To those bright Orders utterd thus his voice.   615
    See with what heat these Dogs of Hell advance

°STARVATION

---

of Christian "shadowy types," to Eve, cautiously adding "perhaps."

[209]In Apollonius's version of the story, Ophion was defeated by Cronos or Saturn, while Eurynome gave her throne to Rhea or Ops. Christianizing the story made Ophion, when he was associated with the Titans or Giants, a shadowy type of Satan.

[210]A theological distinction based on the concepts of evil desire and evil action, the second being realized or "'actual' sin" (*On Christian Doctrine* 1.11; Yale 6: 391). Once empowered and then activated by the sin of Adam and Eve, Sin is actualized and has a body. The phrase "body of sin" (Romans 6.6) would have given Milton authority for making the distinction between Sin before she had a body and after.

[211]"And I looked, and behold a pale horse: and his name that sat on him was Death, and Hell followed with him. And power was given unto them over the fourth part of the Earth, to kill with sword, and with hunger, and with death, and with the beasts of the earth" (Revelation 6.8).

[212]"Second-born to Satan." Her genealogical title is matched by the Epic Voice's "Sin-born Monster" below.

[213]The length of this line might have caused the compositors both of *1667* and *1674* to set the unusual spellings "stil" and "Hels," but they did use the long form "sate," a choice which could conceivably indicate a directive from publisher or author. The line is identically spelled in both editions. Two lines above in *1667* the word "earnd" had to be wrapped under because of that line's length.

[214]Again, Milton is defining negativity with the help of the negative prefix "un-." Death is unnamed until Sin names him at 2.787 (see Leonard 165 for the context). Since "starv'd" also meant "dead," the word seems to carry the modern meaning of "half-starved" (Death is hungry to eat the sinful) or "half-dead."

[215]Because Death is a shape-shifter, he can be represented as a mouth, a huge "Maw," one second and an "unhide-bound Corps" the next. His "skin" seems to be so loosely attached it is hiding the body under it.

[216]"Old Father Time" is pictured as he still is, with a scythe used to mow down humans in death.

[217]Sin advises Death to eat from the bottom of the food chain up, from grass to fruits to flower and thence to land beasts, fish, and fowls, because plants and animals are already dying as a result of the Fall. She in turn will gradually infect all of humankind, so that the meat course for Death's dinner will be man. Death is a carrion-eater, so he would look forward to his food being "seasoned" in the sense of being overly ripe as well as preceded by spices.

[218]One in the series of negative compounds, in this case the first instance of the word reported by the *OED*.

To waste and havoc yonder World,[219] which I
So fair and good created, and had still
Kept in that State, had not the folly of Man
Let in these wastful Furies, who impute   620
Folly to mee,[220] so doth the Prince of Hell
And his Adherents, that with so much ease
I suffer them to enter and possess[221]
A place so heav'nly, and conniving[222] seem
To gratifie my scornful Enemies,   625
That laugh, as if transported with some fit
Of Passion, I to them had quitted° all,   HANDED OVER
At random yielded[223] up to their misrule;
And know not that I call'd and drew them thither
My Hell-hounds, to lick up the draff[224] and filth   630
Which mans polluting Sin with taint hath shed
On what was pure, till cramm'd and gorg'd, nigh burst
With suckt and glutted offal,[225] at one sling[226]
Of thy victorious Arm, well-pleasing Son,
Both *Sin*, and *Death*, and yawning *Grave*[227] at last   635
Through *Chaos* hurld, obstruct the mouth of Hell
For ever, and seal up his ravenous Jawes.
Then Heav'n and Earth renewd shall be made pure
To sanctitie that shall receive no staine:[228]
Till then the Curse[229] pronounc't on both precedes.   640
    He ended, and the heav'nly Audience loud
Sung *Halleluia*, as the sound of Seas,
Through multitude that sung:[230] Just are thy ways,
Righteous are thy Decrees on all thy Works;
Who can extenuate thee?[231] Next, to the Son,   645
Destin'd restorer of Mankind, by whom

---

[219]To wreak havoc was to allow an army to pillage at will, and to cry havoc was a military invitation to give no quarter. Milton may have allowed God to echo *Julius Caesar*: "And Caesar's spirit, ranging for revenge, / With Ate by his side come hot from hell, / Shall in these confines with a monarch's voice / Cry 'Havoc!' and let slip the dogs of war . . . " (3.1.270–73).

[220]God pictures the Furies, representative of the workings of a pagan fate, as mocking Him; the Furies are equated with the fallen angels.

[221]Like the modern "breaking and entering," a legal term.

[222]Pretending ignorance (*OED* 1).

[223]The "yeilded" of *1667* may be closer to Milton's spelling preference, but "their" in this line violates Milton's customary spelling in both editions.

[224]Disgusting leftovers of one sort or another: refuse, garbage, dregs.

[225]Again, the image is of eating dead and decaying matter. As in "leprous sin" (Nativity Ode 138). It is meant to be disgusting, to nurture a disgust for sin in the reader.

[226]The image is of a slingshot, as in the story of David and Goliath, but more specifically from 1 Samuel 25.29: " . . . and the souls of thine enemies, them shall he sling out, as out of the middle of a sling."

[227]This word may have been italicized by inertia, the compositor of *1667* and then of *1674* reflexively returning to the italic letters after having set "*Sin*" and then "*Death*," unless we are meant to read "*Grave*" as a personified entity. The Richardsons believed that Hell "signifies also the Grave" in a pleonasm or deliberate redundancy (qtd. in Newton 635n) in scriptural passages such as Hosea 13.14. If the latter is true, then "*Grave*" should at least be capitalized by editors who modernize the text. At the Last Judgment, the grave will "lose" its "sting" and death will be asked "where is thy victory?" (1 Corinthians 15.55). "Jaws of death" was then, as now, proverbial.

[228]Compare the image of the "last days" in 2 Peter 3.7: "But the heavens and the earth, which are now [i.e., which now exist], by the same word are kept in store, reserved unto fire against the day of judgment and perdition of ungodly men." The biblical phrase "Heav'n and Earth" means "the entire universe."

[229]Probably the curses pronounced on both Adam and Eve—to till the ground in hard and sometimes fruitless labor and to give birth in pain.

[230]A paraphrase of Revelation 19.6: "And I heard as it were the voice of a great multitude, and as the voice of many waters, and as the voice of mighty thunderings, saying, Alleluia: for the Lord God omnipotent reigneth." The general practice throughout *Paradise Lost* is to italicize "Halleluiah," but there is an exception at 2.243, and the word more often is spelled with an "h" at the end than not. Here "*Halleluia*" represents a direct quotation, and significant quotations can sometimes be set in italics, as with "*Encrease and multiply*," 730 below, or "*Wo to the inhabitants on Earth!*" at 4.5.

[231]"Who can diminish the honor due you?" (see *OED* II.5).

New Heav'n and Earth shall to the Ages rise,
Or down from Heav'n descend.[232] Such was thir song,
While the Creator calling forth by name
His mightie Angels gave them several charge,
As sorted best with° present things. The Sun   BEST ACCOMPANIED   650
Had first his precept° so to move, so shine,   COMMANDMENT
As might affect the Earth with cold and heat
Scarce tollerable, and from the North to call
Decrepit Winter,[233] from the South to bring   655
Solstitial summers heat.[234] To the blanc[235] Moone
Her office they prescrib'd, to th' other five
Thir planetarie motions and aspects[236]
In *Sextile*, *Square*, and *Trine*, and *Opposite*,[237]
Of noxious efficacie, and when to joyne   660
In Synod[238] unbenigne, and taught the fixt[239]
Thir influence malignant when to showre,
Which of them rising with the Sun, or falling,
Should prove tempestuous: To the Winds they set
Thir corners,[240] when with bluster to confound   665
Sea, Aire, and Shoar, the Thunder when to rowle
With terror through the dark Aereal Hall.
Some say[241] he bid his Angels turne ascanse
The Poles of Earth twice ten degrees and more
From the Suns Axle; they with labour push'd   670
Oblique the Centric Globe:° Som say the Sun   THE EARTH
Was bid turn Reines[242] from th' Equinoctial Rode°   ROAD
Like distant breadth to *Taurus*[243] with the Seav'n
Atlantick Sisters, and the *Spartan* Twins
Up to the *Tropic* Crab; thence down amaine   675

---

[232]In Revelation 21.10 " . . . that great city, the holy Jerusalem, [is pictured] descending out of heaven from God. . . ."

[233]A popular characterization, as in the modern "Old Man Winter."

[234]"The heat of the summer solstice. As Fowler points out, "the cosmic system used throughout most of the poem is not—in spite of many scholarly statements to the contrary—the Ptolemaic system. Instead, it is a theoretical system, of ideal simplicity, in which the ecliptic and the equatorial circles coincide" (10.651–706n). According to Babb, " . . . Milton did not become really well acquainted with or did not see the full significance of the new astronomy until *Paradise Lost* was already in some state of composition" and that "he became a reluctant Copernican, possibly without admitting even to himself that he was convinced" (92). Such speculation about changes of mind unfortunately cannot be proved, but Milton's "Some say," repeated, does indicate uncertainty. See Grant McColley, "The Astronomy of *Paradise Lost*," *Studies in Philology* 34 (1937): 209–47.

[235]The word means "white" as in French *blanc*, but also "morally vacant."

[236]Accented on the second syllable.

[237]The planets are lined up in relation to one another by degrees, sextile being 60 degrees, square or quartile being 90, trine 120, and opposite 180. As in a musical system of harmonics, "trine and sextile are harmonious, quartile and opposition disharmonious" (Fowler 658–61n). A "Synod" here would be a conjunction of planetary influences, but after the Fall a synod or conjunction of planets (*OED* 3) would have an "unbenigne" influence on the Earth. Placing the various aspects in italics throws emphasis on their astrological significance.

[238]Normally a synod, a formal meeting of church officials, would be benign.

[239]I.e., the "fixed stars." Stars and planets after the Fall may have "influence malignant" on human affairs through astrological power, and intemperate winds are allowed to bluster and thunder to roll. The phrase "Rain influence" ("L'Allegro" 122) is here interpreted astrologically: before the Fall, the influence was "sweet" (7.375).

[240]Winds are pictured as on a seventeenth-century map, at least at the four corners (if not all the points of the compass) of the Earth. The three elements are confounded or mixed in a chaotic manner to form inclement weather.

[241]The qualification here and again at 671 indicates some lingering uncertainty between a heliocentric and a geocentric order in the universe. Either the Earth was pushed off its axis more than twenty degrees or the sun's course shifted off the equator.

[242]The sun is pictured as Apollo's chariot, with horses drawing and reins by which to guide them. Thus "Axle" has a literal equivalent, as in the "burning Axletree" of the Nativity Ode 84, together with a mathematical value as an axis with degrees.

[243]Taurus is the constellation signified by a bull, the "*Atlantick* Sisters" the Pleiades (in the constellation Taurus), and the Spartan twins the constellation Gemini, or Twins, pictured as the Spartans Castor and Pollux. The Tropic of Cancer is the Crab, and Leo, Virgo, and Libra round out the constellations as far south as the Tropic of Capricorn. Milton very precisely sketches the relationship between the constellations in winter and summer, afterward turning to the distribution of weather patterns.

By *Leo* and the *Virgin* and the *Scales*,
As deep as *Capricorne*, to bring in change
Of Seasons to each Clime;[244] else had the Spring
Perpetual smil'd on Earth with vernant[245] Flours,
Equal in Days and Nights, except to those   680
Beyond the Polar Circles; to them Day
Had unbenighted shon, while the low Sun
To recompence his distance, in thir sight
Had rounded still th' *Horizon*, and not known
Or East or West, which had forbid the Snow   685
From cold *Estotiland*,[246] and South as farr
Beneath *Magellan*.[247] At that tasted Fruit
The Sun, as from *Thyestean* Banquet,[248] turn'd
His course intended; else how had the World
Inhabited, though sinless, more then now,   690
Avoided pinching cold and scorching heate?
These changes in the Heav'ns, though slow, produc'd
Like change on Sea and Land, sideral blast,[249]
Vapour, and Mist, and Exhalation hot,
Corrupt and Pestilent:[250] Now from the North   695
Of *Norumbega*, and the *Samoed*[251] shoar
Bursting thir brazen Dungeon,[252] armd with ice
And snow and haile and stormie gust and flaw,[253]
Boreas and *Cæcias* and *Argestes* loud
And *Thrascias* rend the Woods and Seas upturn;[254]   700

---

[244]"Region" (*OED* 2.b, citing 11.708) with the attendant weather ascribed to each region.

[245]"Flourishing or growing in spring" (*OED* 2.b, citing this instance), in the time of the vernal equinox.

[246]Territory adjacent to the Arctic Circle in North America, perhaps interesting to Milton because of the seventeenth-century quest for a northwest passage to China.

[247]Not the Straits of Magellan but what is now Argentina, called Magellonica (in Peter Heylyn's map of North and South America, published in *Cosmographie in Four Bookes* [1652]) after Ferdinand Magellan (Fowler 687n).

[248]Through a sympathetic reaction, at the Fall the sun turns away from the Earth with revulsion just as the sun was supposed to have turned off its axis at the sight of Atreus feeding his brother Thyestes one of his own children. After reflecting that an evil time in Roman history was "like the time of the feast of Thyestes," Lucan lists as one of the evil portents, "Earth slipped off from its axis anew" (*Civil War* 1.601, 612; trans. Widdows 18).

[249]A negative astrological influence caused by the stars (Latin *siderus*, "starry") or in this case by the Sun. The word "sideral" was an established synonym for "starry" in English.

[250]Probably the best definition for "Exhalation hot" would be "meteor," since meteors were thought by some to be vapors exhaled by the sun, and they also might portend corruption or pestilence, as evil omens.

[251]Norumbega was the name given to the general region of what is now southeastern Canada together with parts of the United States (as in Pietro Plancio's world map of 1594); Samoedia (the name is now preserved in the name of the "Samoyed" breed of dog) was the corresponding extreme northeast territory of what is now Siberia. Milton thought of the Samoeds as one of the nomadic tribes of Russia (Yale 8: 500); thus the adjective might be "the area where the Samoeds roam."

[252]The god of the winds, Aeolus, was thought to entrap the winds when they were not in use in a cave with mountains heaped on it—as in the magnificent description of Aeolus unleashing the winds to torment Aeneas in the *Aeneid* 1.56–123. The cave of the winds is not said to be "brazen" in Vergil.

[253]"A sudden burst or squall of wind" (*OED* substantive 2.1.b). Milton's use antedates any entry in the *OED*, and Shakespeare had used the gust and flaw comparatively in *Venus and Adonis:* " . . . Sorrow to shepherds, woe unto the birds, / Gust and fowl flaws to herdmen and to herds" (455–56). Apparently a flaw was considered more powerful than a gust.

[254]A catalogue of the winds from all corners of the Earth, at war for the first time. The atlas of Jan (or Johannes) Jansson, *Novus Atlas* in eleven volumes, included in its *Atlas Maritimus* volume, published in 1650 (when Milton still had his sight), showed the winds as demigods, of different racial types and ages depending on regions, with cheeks puffed in the act of blowing. See Amy Lee Turner, "Milton and Jansson's Sea Atlas," *Milton Quarterly* 4 (1970): 36–38: "The north-northeast (Boreas) and the east-north-east (Caecias) winds—armed with ice, snow, hail, and hurricane force—burst out of their prison at Samoedia. The west-north-west (Argestes) and the north-a-quarter-to-the-northwest (Thrascias) winds burst out of their dungeon at Norumbega. They are attacked by powerful southern winds from the South Pole region of Terra Australis Incognita, 'black with thunderous clouds.' The onslaught takes place near the equator at Siera Liona. Then the east and west winds interpose 'with thir lateral noise' and try to thwart the warring of the newly released north and south winds" (38). Milton's names for the winds, some ancient and some modern, all correspond very closely with those of Jansson. Newton thought the catalogue "needless ostentation of learning, and a strange mixture of ancient and modern, Latin and Italian names together" (699n), but with the help of Jansson's atlas one can see exactly how scrupulous Milton was in his details. For a corrective of Turner's identification, see Gordon Campbell, "Milton's Catalogue of the Winds," *Milton Quarterly* 18 (1984): 125–28.

With adverse blasts up-turns them from the South
Notus and *Afer* black with thundrous Clouds
From *Serraliona*; thwart of these as fierce
Forth rush the *Levant* and the *Ponent* Windes
Eurus and *Zephir* with thir lateral noise,   705
Sirocco, and *Libecchio*.²⁵⁵ Thus began
Outrage from liveless° things; but Discord first   LIFELESS
Daughter of Sin,²⁵⁶ among th' irrational,
Death introduc'd through fierce antipathie:
Beast now with Beast gan war, and Fowle with Fowle,   710
And Fish with Fish; to graze the Herb all leaving,²⁵⁷
Devour each other; nor stood much in awe
Of Man, but fled him, or with count'nance grim
Glar'd on him passing: these were from without
The growing miseries, which *Adam* saw   715
Alreadie in part, though hid in gloomiest shade,
To sorrow abandond, but worse felt within,
And in a troubl'd Sea of passion tost,
Thus to disburd'n sought with sad complaint.²⁵⁸

   O miserable of happie! is this the end   720
Of this new glorious World, and mee so late
The Glory of that Glory, who now becom
Accurst of blessed, hide me from the face
Of God, whom to behold was then my highth
Of happiness: yet well, if here would end   725
The miserie, I deserv'd it, and would beare
My own deservings; but this will not serve;
All that I eat or drink, or shall beget,
Is propagated curse.²⁵⁹ O voice once heard
Delightfully, *Encrease and multiply*,   730
Now death to heare! for what can I encrease
Or multiplie, but curses on my head?
Who of all Ages to succeed, but feeling
The evil on him brought by me, will curse
My Head, Ill fare our Ancestor impure,   735

---

²⁵⁵The line in *1674* has a comma here which Fletcher believed was due to foul case. Since "Thus" is capitalized and begins what seems to be a new sentence, most editors since the third edition in 1678 have substituted the period.

²⁵⁶Discord is usually pictured in Greek mythology as the goddess Eris or Discordia. The best-known act of Discord was the throwing of the apple addressed "To the Fairest" among the goddesses of Mt. Olympus. The discordant act caused a contest which the shepherd Paris decided in favor of Aphrodite, for which he was rewarded by being given the most beautiful woman in the world, Helen, who was already married to Menelaus. Helen's abduction was supposed to have been a major cause for the Trojan War. In making Discord daughter of Sin, Milton Christianizes the myth, but Vergil had already made Eris into a grotesque deity whose companions in creating panic were Mars, the god of war, and "serpents of death" (*Aeneid* 8.696–702). Thus Milton pictures her here as "among th' irrational."

²⁵⁷"All of them leaving off a vegetarian diet," the English equivalent of a Latin absolute construction.

²⁵⁸Using the imagery of Hamlet, taking arms against a sea of troubles (3.1.58), Adam begins to contemplate whether to be or not to be. Adam's soliloquy may be a sign of his fallenness, in the sense that he now "talks to himself." Broadbent's generalization (*Some* 80) that unfallen characters in *Paradise Lost* do not soliloquize is misleading, since fallen characters are not always wrong-headed: Adam's soliloquy here correctly analyzes his cursed position. See David Robertson, *"My self / Before me": Self-Love in the Works of John Milton* (Tampere, Finland: Tampere English Studies): 211–12. Though Adam's complaint does become extreme when he asks why he was made and when he accuses God of making the terms of the command "too hard" (it was easy to abstain from eating from one out of many trees), Adam's debate with himself is different from any of Satan's soliloquies, even though it does lead to human despair. It presents a dialectic that moves toward reconciliation with God, repentance, and atonement. Adam's language is notably simple and straightforward as he gropes for the truth. His soliloquy is no more reprehensible or unsympathetic than Hamlet's "To be or not to be" soliloquy.

²⁵⁹The potential for causing sin or bringing about some sort of curse in the acts of eating or of sexual intercourse has been increased horribly by the Fall, because both eating and sex now involve concupiscence or evil inclination; thus the food that Adam eats will represent the oppressive toil he has been cursed with, and propagation will be answered by the curse of pain in childbirth for Eve.

For this we may thank *Adam*; but his thanks
Shall be the execration;[260] so besides
Mine own that bide upon me,[261] all from mee
Shall with a fierce reflux on mee redound,
On mee as on thir natural center light   740
Heavie, though in thir place.[262] O fleeting joyes
Of Paradise, deare bought with lasting woes!
Did I request thee, Maker, from my Clay
To mould me Man, did I sollicite thee
From darkness to promote me, or here place   745
In this delicious Garden? as my Will
Concurd not to my being, it were but right
And equal[263] to reduce me to my dust,
Desirous to resigne, and render back
All I receav'd, unable to performe   750
Thy terms too hard, by which I was to hold
The good I sought not. To the loss of that,
Sufficient penaltie, why hast thou added
The sense of endless woes? inexplicable
Thy Justice seems; yet to say truth, too late,   755
I thus contest; then should have been refusd
Those terms whatever, when they were propos'd:
Thou didst accept them; wilt thou enjoy the good,
Then cavil° the conditions? and though God   DISPUTE, ARGUE
Made thee without thy leave, what if thy Son   760
Prove disobedient, and reprov'd, retort,
Wherefore didst thou beget me? I sought it not:[264]
Wouldst thou admit for his contempt of thee
That proud excuse? yet him not thy election,[265]
But Natural necessity begot.   765
God made thee of choice his own, and of his own
To serve him, thy reward was of his grace,
Thy punishment then justly is at his Will.
Be it so, for I submit, his doom° is fair,   JUDGMENT
That dust I am, and shall to dust returne: 770
O welcom hour whenever! why delayes
His hand to execute what his Decree
Fixd on this day? why do I overlive,
Why am I mockt with death, and length'nd out
To deathless pain? how gladly would I meet   775
Mortalitie my sentence, and be Earth

---

[260]Among the voices in his head, Adam hears future generations curse him for the inheritance of sin. Thus Adam is not merely talking to himself but, indirectly, to the reader. He also talks of himself as "Son" in the third person (760 below), which sets up a resonance between Adam as a son of God and the Son of God. Milton may have in mind St. Paul's comparison between the two sons: "For as in Adam all die, even so in Christ shall all be made alive" (1 Corinthians 15.22).

[261]"Besides the sins that abide with me now, all those sins that are carried into future generations will redound on me as well." The word "reflux" suggests the return of an enormous wave (*OED* 1.a).

[262]The repetition of "Mine own . . . mee . . . mee" will be echoed by Eve and then the Son, as each takes on responsibility for the sin or responsibility for atonement for the sin. See 832 below.

[263]"Just," in terms of a balanced judgment in which the punishment weighs the same as the crime.

[264]There is no punctuation at the end of the line in *1674*. Because a full stop is needed, I have restored the colon of *1667*, even though the colon is comparatively rare at the end of a line.

[265]"Selection" or "choice," but with the theological meaning, "predestination," in the near background. Compare the use of the noun "elect" at 3.136, 184. The word "necessity" suggests God's will, which is fate, and grace is given freely to regenerate sinners without their asking for it.

Insensible, how glad would lay me down
As in my Mothers lap?[266] there I should rest
And sleep secure; his dreadful voice no more
Would Thunder in my ears, no fear of worse   780
To mee and to my ofspring would torment me
With cruel expectation. Yet one doubt
Pursues me still, least all I cannot die,[267]
Least that pure breath of Life, the Spirit of Man
Which God inspir'd, cannot together perish   785
With this corporeal° Clod; then in the Grave,   BODILY
Or in some other dismal place,[268] who knows
But I shall die a living Death?[269] O thought
Horrid, if true! yet why? it was but breath
Of Life that sinn'd; what dies but what had life   790
And sin? the Bodie properly hath neither.
All of me then shall die:[270] let this appease
The doubt, since humane[271] reach no further knows.
For though the Lord of all be infinite,
Is his wrauth also? be it, man is not so,   795
But mortal doom'd. How can he exercise
Wrath[272] without end on Man whom Death must end?
Can he make deathless Death? that were to make
Strange contradiction, which to God himself
Impossible is held, as Argument°   EVIDENCE   800
Of weakness, not of Power. Will he[273] draw out,
For angers sake, finite to infinite
In punisht man,[274] to satisfie his rigour
Satisfi'd never; that were to extend
His Sentence beyond dust and Natures Law,   805
By which all Causes else according still
To the reception of thir matter act,[275]
Not to th' extent of thir own Spheare. But say
That Death be not one stroak, as I suppos'd,
Bereaving sense, but endless miserie   810
From this day onward, which I feel begun
Both in me, and without me, and so last
To perpetuitie; Ay me, that fear
Comes thundring back with dreadful revolution
On my defensless head; both Death and I   815

---

[266]"As in the lap of Mother Earth."
[267]"Lest I cannot die in every way conceivable." Compare "All of me" at 792 below.
[268]Again I have restored the punctuation of *1667*, the comma, because the phrase within the comma offers an alternative to "Grave."
[269]The final death of eternal damnation and thus a living death.
[270]This is the doctrine of mortalism, that both soul and body die, an idea supported in *On Christian Doctrine* and by various sects in Milton's time called "mortalists" or "soul sleepers." Mortalism was developed to answer the question of the physical location of the soul between death and the Last Judgment (a problem resolved by Roman Catholics in the doctrine of Purgatory). See Burns, *Christian Mortalism*.
[271]Probably pronounced "human." See 9.732.
[272]The change to the less common spelling (from "wrauth") might represent economy in *1667* because the line as it was printed extends from margin to margin; the compositor of *1674* here follows the copy-text in reproducing the spelling variant.
[273]"If he were to draw out." A comma was inserted here in both early editions, but virtually all editors remove it.
[274]"In man having been punished."
[275]This is the Aristotelian idea of form exerted in the proper matter, part of the theory underlying the Scale of Nature mentioned at 5.509. See Hunter, *The Descent* 137–48.

Am found Eternal, and incorporate[276] both,
Nor I on my part single, in mee all
Posteritie stands curst: Fair Patrimonie
That I must leave ye, Sons; O were I able[277]
To waste it all my self, and leave ye none!   820
So disinherited how would ye bless
Me now your curse! Ah, why should all mankind
For one mans fault thus guiltless be condemn'd,
If guiltless? But from me what can proceed,
But all corrupt, both Mind and Will deprav'd,[278]   825
Not to do onely, but to will the same
With me?[279] how can they then[280] acquitted stand
In sight of God? Him after all Disputes
Forc't I absolve:[281] all my evasions vain,
And reasonings, though through Mazes,[282] lead me still   830
But to my own conviction: first and last
On mee, mee onely, as the sourse and spring
Of all corruption, all the blame lights due;[283]
So might the wrauth. Fond wish! couldst thou support
That burden heavier then the Earth to bear[284]   835
Then all the World much heavier, though divided
With that bad Woman? Thus what thou desir'st[285]
And what thou fearst, alike destroyes all hope
Of refuge, and concludes thee miserable
Beyond all past example and future,   840
To *Satan* only like both crime and doom.[286]
O Conscience, into what Abyss of fears
And horrors hast thou driv'n me; out of which
I find no way, from deep to deeper plung'd![287]

        Thus *Adam* to himself lamented loud   845
Through the still Night, not now, as ere man fell,
Wholsom and cool, and mild, but with black Air
Accompanied, with damps[288] and dreadful gloom,

---

[276]Combined in one body (*OED* I.1).

[277]"O would that I were able."

[278]All humankind after Adam's sin lives in a general (but not a total) state of moral depravity, what Milton calls "The depravity which all human minds have in common, . . . [which] Our first parents implanted . . . in us" (*On Christian Doctrine* 1.11; Yale 6: 389).

[279]The reprobate are defined in Romans 1.32 as those "Who knowing the judgment of God, that they which commit such things are worthy of death, not only do the same, but have pleasure in them that do them."

[280]The word "then" was omitted in *1667* and added in *1674*.

[281]"After all these disputes (i.e., arguments), I must perforce (i.e., be 'forced to') absolve him" (Loh 828–29n).

[282]Recognizable as the mazes of Satanic error, as in the "mazie foulds" (9.161) of Satan in the Serpent's body or in the "wandring mazes" (2.561) of the fallen angels' disputation. Adam's syntax is at this moment mazy as well.

[283]Compare with Adam's ignorance of the Son's true assumption of responsibility for sin at 3.236–37: "Behold mee then, mee for him, life for life / I offer, on mee let thine anger fall," and compare Eve's falsely taking on the responsibility at 935–36 below. Despite Adam and Eve's complaints and what might now be called their self-pity, the full burden of sin will rest on the Son in the process of atonement. "CHRIST, AS . . . GOD-MAN, SUBMITTED HIMSELF VOLUNTARILY, BOTH IN LIFE AND IN DEATH, TO THE DIVINE JUSTICE, IN ORDER TO SUFFER ALL THE THINGS WHICH WERE NECESSARY FOR OUR REDEMPTION" (*On Christian Doctrine* 1.16; Yale 6: 438).

[284]The line in *1667* has a comma here. Fletcher thinks it is needed; I am not at all sure.

[285]Again, *1667* has a comma after "desir'st." Fletcher speculates that it "seems to be needed." I disagree and have omitted it.

[286]But we know that God distinguishes between Satan's sin and that of Adam and Eve. "Man falls deceiv'd / By the other first: Man therefore shall find grace, / The other [Satan] none" (3.130–32).

[287]Adam unaided can find no help within himself. That can come only after God extends His grace, described as having happened in the opening lines of Book 11.

[288]A damp was "An exhalation, a vapour or gas, of a noxious kind" (*OED* 1, citing Dekker [1606]), with the assumption that "damps" might be "contagious."

Which to his evil Conscience represented
All things with double terror:[289] On the Ground   850
Outstretcht he lay, on the cold ground, and oft
Curs'd his Creation, Death as oft accus'd
Of tardie execution, since denounc't[290]
The day of his offence. Why comes not Death,
Said hee, with one thrice acceptable[291] stroke   855
To end me? Shall Truth fail to keep her word,
Justice Divine not hast'n to be just?
But Death comes not at call, Justice Divine
Mends not her slowest pace for prayers or cries.[292]
O Woods, O Fountains, Hillocks, Dales and Bowrs,   860
With other echo late I taught your Shades
To answer, and resound farr other Song.
Whom thus afflicted when sad *Eve* beheld,
Desolate where she sate, approaching nigh,
Soft words to his fierce passion she assay'd: 865
But her with stern regard he thus repell'd.[293]

    Out of my sight, thou Serpent, that name best
Befits thee with him leagu'd, thy self as false
And hateful; nothing wants,° but that thy shape,   LACKS
Like his, and colour Serpentine may shew   870
Thy inward fraud, to warn all Creatures from thee
Henceforth; least that too heav'nly form, pretended
To hellish falshood, snare them.[294] But for thee
I had persisted happie, had not thy pride
And wandring vanitie, when lest was safe,   875
Rejected my forewarning, and disdain'd
Not to be trusted, longing to be seen
Though by the Devil himself, him overweening°   ARROGANT

---

[289]The Epic Voice gives us some keys to understanding Adam's lamentation. Conscience is elsewhere God's "Umpire" (3.195); hence what is speaking through him is not evil in itself, but "evil Conscience," Adam's conscience as it reflects on the evil he has done.

[290]The syntax is confusing. I take it that Death is denounced as well as accused by Adam because it doesn't come in the day when it was supposed to come, the day in which the first sin occurred. There is the slim possibility that "denounc't" means simply "announced," based upon the Latin noun *denuntiatio*, meaning "announcement," a possibility that Fowler takes as a sure thing.

[291]"Acceptable" seems to have been accented on the first and third syllables. The "double terror" of 850 above seems to be answered by Adam's asking for "one thrice acceptable stroke," a verbal formula suggesting intensity of feeling.

[292]The sentence sounds proverbial but I have not been able to locate a similar reference to justice in collections of proverbs or in the Bible. Compare Milton's phrasing in *Eikonoklastes*: ". . . Justice in her very essence is all strength and activity" (Yale 3: 584).

[293]Eve is repentant, sad, desolate, speaking soft words to allay his fierce passion. At this point she is much closer to atonement and repentance than Adam. His fierce passion underlies what he has to say in the following passage, which is an antifeminist diatribe borrowed from sources like the *Malleus Maleficarum* (literally "the hammer of witches," written as an inquisitor's handbook in 1489 by Heinrich Kramer and Jakob Sprenger) and other antifeminist books which attributed the origins of all sins in great part to Eve. See Utley, *The Crooked Rib*, for a general report on the tradition. For the best recent summary of opinion on modern attitudes toward Milton's position with respect to women, see Shullenberger; see also Lewalski, "Milton on Women—Yet Again," in *Problems for Feminist Criticism*, ed. Sally Minogue (London: Routledge, 1990): 46–69.

[294]The extreme expression of the woman who is also bait or snare and who defiles man by enchantment can be seen in William Prynne, *Histrio-Mastix: The Players Scourge, or Actors Tragedie* (London, 1633):

    such Songs [of lascivious women], such Poems as these [should be] abundantly condemned as *filthy, and unchristian defilements, which contaminate the soules, effeminate the mindes, deprave the manners, of those that heere or sing them, exciting, entising them to lust, to whoredome, adultery, prophanes, wantonesse, scurility, luxury, drunkennesse, excese: alienating their mindes from God, from grace and heavenly things; and Syren like, with their sweet enchantments entrap, ensnare, destroy mens soules, proving bitter portions to them at the last, though they seeme sweet and pleasant for the present.* (267)

I am indebted for this reference to Linda Phyllis Austern, "'Sing Againe Syren.'" Prynne's extreme statement provides a cluster of suggestive words that will also be used both ironically and with direct meaning for Adam's sin, as with *defilement, effeminate, wantonness, luxury, sweet, enchantment*, and *ensnare*, all of which are used seriously and ironically for what happens to and is caused by Adam in his idolatrous worship of Eve's beauty. Prynne is unquestionably blaming the moral lapse on the "Syren like" woman; Milton is unquestionably blaming the lapse on man's effeminate slackness. One should be aware that professionally Milton would have despised Prynne, who attacked Milton as a divorcer (Parker 1: 275) and generally was his opponent in the pamphlet wars of the 1640s. Milton almost surely read *Histrio-Mastix* [see Parker 1: 124]).

To over-reach, but with the Serpent meeting
Fool'd and beguil'd, by him thou, I by thee,   880
To trust thee from my side, imagin'd wise,
Constant, mature, proof against all assaults,
And understood not all was but a shew
Rather then solid vertu, all but a Rib
Crooked by nature, bent, as now appears,   885
More to the part sinister[295] from me drawn,
Well if thrown out, as supernumerarie
To my just number found.[296] O why did God,
Creator wise, that peopl'd highest Heav'n
With Spirits Masculine, create at last   890
This noveltie[297] on Earth, this fair defect
Of Nature, and not fill the World at once
With Men as Angels without Feminine,[298]
Or find some other way to generate
Mankind? this mischief had not then befall'n,   895
And more that shall befall, innumerable
Disturbances on Earth through Femal snares,
And straight conjunction° with this Sex: for either   YOKING, CLOSE CONFINEMENT
He never shall find out fit Mate,[299] but such
As some misfortune brings him, or mistake,   900
Or whom he wishes most shall seldom gain
Through her perverseness, but shall see her gaind
By a farr worse, or if she love, withheld
By Parents, or his happiest choice too late
Shall meet, alreadie linkt and Wedlock-bound   905
To a fell Adversarie, his hate or shame:
Which infinite calamitie shall cause
To Humane[300] life, and houshold peace confound.[301]

---

[295]"The stressing shown by examples in verse down to the time of Pope is sinis′ter" (*OED*).

[296]Milton may be making fun of the antifeminist (I use a word that did not exist in the seventeenth century) arguments that Eve, having been created from a rib, was therefore crooked by nature, and that the rib from which Eve was made was an extra or even superfluous ("supernumerarie") part of Adam's body. The rib could also be taken as an evil omen if it is considered to be like the "bar sinister" of heraldry, that is taken from Adam's lefthand or sinister side (the answering argument is that the left side of the body is also where the heart is, and hence is "cordial" [see 8.466]). Aristotle may have been the first man to consider woman to be a "defect of nature" or a defective male ("On Generation" 735.25 and elsewhere). There are no indications that Milton himself took this indictment of women seriously, though the Chorus's antifeminist arguments in *Samson Agonistes* 1034–60, closely echo 895–908. In his divorce tracts, Milton often focused on the problem of a potential wife being "withheld / By Parents" (see, for instance, *Tetrachordon* [Yale 2: 612]), and he did consider the possibility that the "rib" in marriage might become "not a true limb so much, though that be lawfull, but an adherent, a sore, the gangrene of a limb" (Yale 2: 602). His better-balanced view of an ideal marriage was that it should be "a blessing not a curse, a gift of God not a snare" (2: 613). Differentiating between Milton's personal opinions and Adam's irrational diatribe in this passage is extremely difficult.

[297]Eve was created last (antifeminists argued that her creation was a mistake; profeminists that the last created would have been the best, since even God would have learned from His mistakes), and here Adam argues that in creating her God only created an unnecessary novelty, rather than anything of real value.

[298]We know this argument is fallacious, because angels, according to Raphael, do love and do enjoy sexuality, though they can "either Sex assume, or both" (1.424). Adam's "Spirits Masculine" (890 above) is therefore misleading, even distorted.

[299]Another way of saying "help-meet" (Genesis 2.18), a phrase meaning "fitting companion" which Milton often emphasizes in *Doctrine and Discipline of Divorce*, *Tetrachordon*, and *Colasterion*. See, for instance, *Doctrine and Discipline* in Yale 2: 245–46: "a meet and happy conversation is the chiefest and the noblest end of mariage."

[300]Probably pronounced "human."

[301]Lines 898–908 are especially difficult to interpret because Adam has before that point been rehearsing clichés of antifeminist literature. His argument has been demonstrably wrong-headed and Satanic in its reasoning; it is obvious from what follows Adam's tirade that he is in the wrong in his passion and Eve is his victim. Adam's emphasis turns at 898, however, to unhappy marriages, and his arguments begin to run very close to Milton's in the various divorce tracts, as with *Tetrachordon*: "While man and woman were both perfet each to other, there needed no divorce; but when they both degenerated to imperfection, & oft times grew to be an intolerable evil each to other, then law more justly did permit the alienating of that evil which mistake made proper, then it did the appropriating of that good which Nature at first made common" (Yale 2: 665). The autobiographical inferences are hard to avoid, since Milton had a long running battle with his in-laws from his first marriage, the Powell family. Mary Powell indeed left him for a time, during which

He added not, and from her turn'd, but *Eve*
Not so repulst, with Tears that ceas'd not flowing,   910
And tresses all disorderd, at his feet
Fell humble, and imbracing them, besaught
His peace, and thus proceeded in her plaint.[302]
    Forsake me not thus, *Adam*, witness Heav'n
What love sincere, and reverence in my heart   915
I beare thee, and unweeting have offended,
Unhappilie deceav'd;[303] thy suppliant
I beg, and clasp thy knees; bereave me not,
Whereon I live,[304] thy gentle looks, thy aid,
Thy counsel in this uttermost distress,   920
My onely strength and stay: forlorn of° thee,   ABANDONED BY
Whither shall I betake me, where subsist?
While yet we live, scarse one short hour perhaps,
Between us two let there be peace, both joyning,
As joyn'd in injuries, one enmitie   925
Against a Foe by doom express assign'd us,
That cruel Serpent: On me exercise not
Thy hatred for this miserie befall'n,
On me alreadie lost, mee then thy self
More miserable; both have sin'd, but thou   930
Against God onely, I against God and thee,
And to the place of judgment will return,
There with my cries importune[305] Heaven, that all
The sentence from thy head remov'd may light
On me, sole cause to thee of all this woe,   935
Mee mee onely just object of his ire.
    She ended weeping, and her lowlie plight,
Immoveable[306] till peace obtain'd from fault
Acknowledg'd and deplor'd, in *Adam* wraught
Commiseration; soon his heart relented[307]   940
Towards her, his life so late and sole delight,
Now at his feet submissive in distress,
Creature so faire his reconcilement seeking,
His counsel whom she had displeas'd, his aide;[308]
As one disarm'd, his anger all he lost,   945

---

abandonment he apparently considered the possibility either of divorcing (impossible given English law at the time, which permitted divorce only on the grounds of adultery or sexual dysfunction) or marrying a second wife (see Miller, *John Milton*). Nevertheless, dramatic decorum does suggest that Adam should be speaking angrily, even Satanically, at this point.

[302]Eve's position at Adam's feet with "tresses all disorderd" recalls the figure of Mary, sister of Martha, annointing Christ with ointment and wiping his feet with her hair (John 11.2; compare Luke 7.37–38) and the *mater dolorosa*, Mary the mother of Christ pictured together with Mary Magdalene weeping after the Crucifixion (Matthew 27.56; Mark 15.40–41; Luke 23.27). In other words, the image of Eve in sorrow is completely sympathetic and represents genuine sorrow and repentance. It should be contrasted with Adam's overly dramatic flinging himself on the ground. What Eve is practicing here is embodied in the phrase "A soft answer turneth away wrath" (Proverbs 15.1).

[303]Eve begs Adam's forgiveness on the grounds that she has fallen unwittingly, having been deceived by the Serpent. See 1 Timothy 2.13–14.

[304]"You on whose life I depend."

[305]Accented on the second syllable.

[306]Presumably it is Adam whose heart has been unmoveable until Eve acknowledges her fault, but her plight also is immobile until she is reconciled with Adam.

[307]The capacity for returning to tenderheartedness helps to separate Adam from Satan, whose heart, like that of Pharaoh (Exodus 14), remains hard.

[308]His helpmeet, in other words. Adam has returned to his senses and can see Eve as he should see her, since she was created to aid or help him. According to Lewalski, Eve's "essential role . . . builds upon but goes beyond the idea of marital partnership in Puritan marriage theory, and contributes to the evolving concept of companionate marriage. . . . Eve's fundamental social role is quite simply to share with Adam in the entire range of human activities" ("Milton on Women" 53).

And thus with peaceful words uprais'd her soon.
    Unwarie, and too desirous, as before,[309]
So now of what thou knowst not, who desir'st
The punishment all on thy self; alas,
Beare thine own first, ill able to sustaine   950
His full wrauth whose thou feelst as yet lest part,
And my displeasure bearst so ill.[310] If Prayers
Could alter high Decrees, I to that place
Would speed before thee, and be louder heard,
That on my head all might be visited,   955
Thy frailtie and infirmer Sex forgiv'n,
To me committed and by me expos'd.[311]
But rise, let us no more contend, nor blame
Each other, blam'd enough elsewhere,[312] but strive
In offices° of Love, how we may light'n   DUTIES   960
Each others burden in our share of woe;
Since this days Death denounc't,[313] if ought I see,
Will prove no sudden, but a slow-pac't evill,
A long days dying to augment our paine,[314]
And to our Seed (O hapless Seed!) deriv'd.[315]   965
    To whom thus *Eve*, recovering heart, repli'd.
Adam, by sad experiment° I know   TRIAL
How little weight my words with thee can finde,
Found so erroneous, thence by just event[316]
Found so unfortunate; nevertheless,   970
Restor'd by thee, vile as I am, to place
Of new acceptance, hopeful to regaine
Thy Love, the sole contentment of my heart
Living or dying, from thee I will not hide
What thoughts in my unquiet brest are ris'n,   975
Tending to some relief of our extremes,
Or end, though sharp and sad, yet tolerable,
As in[317] our evils, and of easier choice.
If care of our descent perplex us most,
Which must be born to certain woe, devourd   980
By Death at last, and miserable it is
To be to others cause of misery,
Our own begotten, and of our Loines to bring
Into this cursed World a woful Race,

---

[309]Without condescending to Eve, and remaining tender toward her, Adam says she is again unwary—as she was in the process of the Fall—and that she is blaming herself too greatly.

[310]"You are hardly able to bear my displeasure, much less God's wrath."

[311]Confessing to her, Adam admits that in allowing her to go out he exposed her to danger. In alluding to her "frailtie and infirmer Sex," Adam is supposed to be speaking what the reader should perceive as the absolute truth about Eve's nature, even given more recent opinions about sexual roles to the contrary.

[312]They are blamed by God's justice, thus they need not compound their problems by mutual accusation.

[313]Read "days" as the possessive "day's." Since the death proclaimed as occurring this day must be reinterpreted, Adam asks Eve to reconsider it as slow-paced, a "long days dying."

[314]Adam now understands that they will not die in the actual day that they have sinned, but that they are already infected by sin with mortality.

[315]Transmitted by descent, as in 77 above.

[316]"By an outcome or consequence judged fairly." God has judged or is in the process of judging their disobedience fairly; they have been "unfortunate" in a much stronger sense than is current in the twentieth century. Eve is exaggerating how "vile" she thinks she is in Adam's sight; in fact, he has already forgiven her.

[317]"Considering our ill situation" (Richardson, qtd. in Newton 978n), a possible Latinism built on the usage of *ut*.

That after wretched Life must be at last   985
Food for so foule a Monster,[318] in thy power
It lies, yet ere Conception to prevent[319]
The Race unblest, to being yet unbegot.[320]
Childless thou art, Childless remaine: So Death[321]
Shall be deceav'd his glut,[322] and with us two   990
Be forc'd to satisfie his Rav'nous Maw.
But if thou judge it hard and difficult,
Conversing, looking, loving, to abstain
From Loves due Rites, Nuptial imbraces sweet,
And with desire to languish without hope,[323]   995
Before the present object languishing
With like desire, which would be miserie[324]
And torment less then none of what we dread,
Then both our selves and Seed at once to free
From what we fear for both, let us make short,   1000
Let us seek Death, or he not found, supply
With our own hands his Office[325] on our selves;
Why stand we longer shivering under feares,
That shew no end but Death, and have the power,
Of many ways to die the shortest choosing,[326]   1005
Destruction with destruction to destroy.
    She ended heer, or vehement despaire
Broke off the rest;[327] so much of Death her thoughts
Had entertaind, as di'd[328] her Cheeks with pale.
But *Adam* with such counsel nothing° sway'd,   IN NO WAY   1010
To better hopes his more attentive minde[329]
Labouring had rais'd, and thus to *Eve* repli'd.
    Eve, thy contempt of life and pleasure seems

---

[318]Death, who will devour all mortal things.

[319]"It lies in your power, before conception, to cut off beforehand or render impossible future generations" (*OED* sb. *prevent* II.6).

[320]A reference to the apparent fact that so far no children have been begotten in Eden. Critics generally agree that Milton's Adam and Eve had sexual intercourse before the Fall. Since in a perfect world, intercourse would automatically engender children (at least according to Augustine, who wrote that "it was after they were expelled from [Paradise] that they came together to beget children, and begot them" [*The City of God* 14.21; Dods trans. 469]), it would be embarrassing that a child conceived in Eden before the Fall would turn out to be Cain.

[321]"So Death" appears in *1674* at the beginning of 990, but since it is in 990 in *1667* and since to move it below would unbalance the pentameter of both lines, editors universally restore the two words in 989. Fowler leaves the line as it was, arguing that the line discussing defective childbirth is meant itself to be defective (10.989–90n), but I think that his is too precise an interpretation in that Milton nowhere else that I know of makes a defective line parallel with a defective sentiment (but see 550 above, and Fletcher's note to that passage).

[322]Death will, in effect, be deceived in his hope to eat and then be denied his gluttonous feast on future generations.

[323]Probably recalling Dante, *Inferno* 4.42: "sanza speme vivemo in disio" ("without hope we live in desire").

[324]Printed as "miserie" in *1667*, then "meserie" in *1674*. Following editorial practice that began in 1678, I restore the reading of *1667*.

[325]His official position or duties as executioner. Adam will advise against mutual suicide, even though (to the classical Romans) it might suggest a Stoic "contempt of life."

[326]Newton constructs the syntax of the sentence as "*and have the power to destroy destruction with destruction, choosing the shortest of many ways to die*" (1004n). If one reads the sentence that way, the placement of commas makes perfect sense. Loh calls the use of "Destruction" a "triple play of the word" (1006n).

[327]The word "vehement" appears again, indicating that mindless passion is governing her behavior. Milton would have viewed Eve's inclination toward suicide as a "perverse hatred of oneself" (*On Christian Doctrine* 2.8; Yale 6: 719; citing Ephesians 5.29, "For no man ever yet hated his own flesh; but nourisheth and cherisheth it, even as the Lord the church.").

[328]Her thoughts of death dyed her cheeks with pallor; in other words, she turned pale with fear of death. For a comparable image, see Vergil, *Aeneid* 4.499, "her face going deadly white."

[329]Adam's mind is more attentive (perhaps "focused" in the modern sense), concentrates on faith, and wanders less than Eve's: he has the "higher intellectual" (9.483) that Satan wants to avoid, in the sense that his intellectual faculties are more acute and in this case quicker to perceive what is wrong with suicide. He sees that what she says might look good from the perspective of representing contempt for worldliness or bodily pleasure, but it is wrongheaded in that it would deny God's providence in punishing Satan in the Serpent and would instead bring down a double punishment on them for becoming suicides.

To argue in thee somthing more sublime
And excellent then what thy minde contemnes;°　　　　　　DESPISES　　　1015
But self-destruction therefore saught, refutes
That excellence thought in thee, and implies,
Not thy contempt, but anguish and regret
For loss of life and pleasure overlov'd.
Or if thou covet death, as utmost end　　　　　　　　　　　　　　　1020
Of miserie, so thinking to evade
The penaltie pronounc't, doubt not but God
Hath wiselier arm'd his vengeful ire then so
To be forestall'd; much more I fear least Death
So snatcht will not exempt us from the paine　　　　　　　　　　　　1025
We are by doom° to pay; rather such acts　　　　　　　JUDGMENT
Of contumacie° will provoke the highest　　　　　　　PRIDE
To make death in us live:³³⁰ Then let us seek
Some safer resolution, which methinks
I have in view, calling to minde with heed　　　　　　　　　　　　　1030
Part of our Sentence, that thy Seed shall bruise³³¹
The Serpents head; piteous amends, unless
Be meant, whom I conjecture, our grand Foe
Satan, who in the Serpent hath contriv'd
Against us this deceit: to crush his head　　　　　　　　　　　　　1035
Would be revenge indeed; which will be lost
By death brought on our selves, or childless days
Resolv'd, as thou proposest; so our Foe
Shall scape his punishment ordain'd, and wee
Instead shall double ours upon our heads.　　　　　　　　　　　　1040
No more be mention'd then of violence
Against our selves, and wilful barrenness,
That cuts us off from hope, and favours onely
Rancor and pride, impatience and despite,
Reluctance° against God and his just yoke　　　　　　RESISTANCE　　1045
Laid on our Necks.³³² Remember with what mild
And gracious temper he both heard and judg'd
Without wrauth or reviling; wee expected
Immediate dissolution, which we thought
Was meant by Death that day, when lo, to thee　　　　　　　　　　1050
Pains onely in Child-bearing were foretold,³³³
And bringing forth, soon recompenc't with joy,
Fruit of thy Womb:³³⁴ On mee the Curse aslope

---

³³⁰Refers to the "living Death" in 788 above.
³³¹"The future perfect "shall bruse" (see 181 above) is more nearly certain than "will bruise" and carries the weight here of prophecy. Also, Adam is arguing with the position we have seen in Satan's boast that he will have achieved his purpose of corrupting humankind with only a bruise to show for it (500 above). Crushing the Serpent's head is much worse than giving him a bruise, and, Adam argues, unless they remain alive, the prophecy that the Seed (that is, the Son) will crush the head of the Serpent will not be fulfilled. Adam gently but firmly asserts his authority over Eve and corrects her "vehement despaire."
³³²Marriage was often illustrated by the seventeenth century emblem of a yoke, the mechanism binding oxen or other work animals together for life, but the image was in general not a negative one, suggesting, as it does, that married partners must work closely in harmony with each other.
³³³Eve's curse for her part in the Fall is bearing children in the pain of labor, the general interpretation of "in sorrow thou shalt bring forth children" (Genesis 3.16). What is being demonstrated with Adam's gentle reprimand is also part of God's judgment that Eve's "desire shall be to [her] husband, and he shall rule over [her]" (3.16).
³³⁴"A woman when she is in travail hath sorrow, because her hour is come: but as soon as she is delivered of the child, she remembereth no more the anguish, for joy that a man is born into the world" (John 16.21, alluding to the birth of Christ). The phrase "Fruit of thy Womb" is taken from another allusion to the coming of Christ in Luke 1.42.

Glanc'd on the ground,[335] with labour I must earne
My bread; what harm? Idleness had bin worse;
My labour will sustain me; and least Cold
Or Heat should injure us, his timely care
Hath unbesaught provided, and his hands
Cloath'd us unworthie, pitying while he judg'd;
How much more, if we pray him, will his ear
Be open, and his heart to pitie incline,[336]
And teach us further by what means to shun
Th' inclement Seasons, Rain, Ice, Hail and Snow,
Which now the Skie with various Face begins
To shew us in this Mountain, while the Winds
Blow moist and keen, shattering the graceful locks
Of these fair spreading Trees; which bids us seek
Som better shroud,[337] som better warmth to cherish
Our Limbs benumm'd, ere this diurnal Starr
Leave cold the Night,[338] how we his gather'd beams,
Reflected, may with matter sere foment,[339]
Or by collision of two bodies grinde
The Air attrite to Fire,[340] as late the Clouds
Justling° or pusht with Winds rude in thir shock
Tine° the slant Lightning, whose thwart° flame driv'n down
Kindles the gummie bark of Firr or Pine,
And sends a comfortable heat from farr,
Which might supplie[341] the Sun: such Fire to use,
And what may else be remedie or cure
To evils which our own misdeeds have wrought,
Hee will instruct us praying, and of Grace
Beseeching him, so as we need not fear
To pass commodiously[342] this life, sustain'd
By him with many comforts, till we end
In dust, our final rest and native home.
What better can we do, then to the place
Repairing where he judg'd us, prostrate fall

1055

1060

1065

1070

JOSTLING, COLLIDING

IGNITE   SLANTING   1075

1080

1085

---

[335]"God's curse glanced off me and hit the ground instead." Adam is trying to make the best of a bad thing, God's curse on his future labor to till the soil, but he is also reminding Eve that God has already demonstrated not only justice but pity and mercy, in clothing them as well as cursing them. Milton would have endorsed Adam's opinion that hard labor is better than idleness, since he defined industry as "the virtue which enables one to make an honest living," citing Genesis 3.19, "you shall eat your food in the sweat of your face." He defined its opposite as "Laziness in providing for one's needs" (*On Christian Doctrine* 2.9; Yale 6: 731, 732).

[336]Phrases common in the Bible and sometimes entered into church services in the Book of Common Prayer, as in "Give ear, O my people, to my law: incline your ears to the words of my mouth" (Psalm 78.1) or "Incline my heart unto thy testimonies, and not to covetousness" (Psalm 119.36).

[337]The word was neutral and meant "covering" or "shelter," not just "grave cloth."

[338]The diurnal (daily) star is the sun, which, when it leaves the sky, creates the colder evening.

[339]With dry tinder they may be able to engender ("foment" is from Latin *fomes*, "tinder") fire, to keep themselves warm in the changing seasons. A concave glass lens would refract ("reflect" in Milton's optics). Very dry ("sere") matter is necessary to start such a fire. In the transitive sense, "reflect" meant "To turn or direct in a certain course, to divert; to turn away or aside, to deflect" (*OED* I.1); thus the light could be directed through the lens to intensify it to produce fire.

[340]Adam continues to discuss the newly necessary technology of producing fire, either by focusing sunlight with a parabolic mirror or magnifying glass on tinder or by friction—the rubbing of sticks together or the striking of flint on steel. The word "attrite" means "ground down by friction" (*OED* 1), but one should also perhaps keep in mind the moral process of attrition, which would lead to contrition and thence to repentance (*OED attrite* 2 and *attrition* 4). Adam likens the technology of man creating fire to the heavenly process of creating fire by lightning, enkindling and driving a transverse ("thwart") flame down to Earth and catching pitchy trees such as the pine or fir on fire.

[341]"Replace the heat of." Before the Fall, humankind was "Guiltless of fire" (9.392): the phrase suggests that technology or "science" (the Greek word transliterated as *techne*) was in part compensation ("remedie or cure") for the inherent understanding humankind previously had of natural processes.

[342]"To enjoy to the fullest extent."

Before him reverent, and there confess
Humbly our faults,[343] and pardon beg, with tears
Watering the ground, and with our sighs the Air   1090
Frequenting,°[344] sent from hearts contrite, in sign   SUPPLYING ABUNDANTLY
Of sorrow unfeign'd, and humiliation meek.
Undoubtedly he will relent and turn
From his displeasure; in whose look serene,
When angry most he seem'd and most severe,   1095
What else but favor, grace, and mercie shon?[345]
    So spake our Father penitent, nor *Eve*
Felt less remorse: they forthwith to the place
Repairing where he judg'd them prostrate fell
Before him reverent, and both confess'd   1100
Humbly thir faults, and pardon beg'd, with tears
Watering the ground, and with thir sighs the Air
Frequenting, sent from hearts contrite, in sign
Of sorrow unfeign'd, and humiliation meek.[346]

The End of the Tenth Book.

---

[343]The Book of Common Prayer comes to mind, as in what the priest says "to them that come to receive the Holy Communion": "Draw near, and take this holy Sacrament to your comfort; make your humble confession to Almighty God before this congregation here gathered together in his holy name, meekly kneeling upon their knees" (1559 ed.). Milton reconstitutes the process of confession, free of the ritual of the church.
[344]Apparently accented on the second syllable.
[345]Again, in the Anglican communion service, after confession, the priest says that God "hath promised forgiveness of sins to all them which with hearty repentance and true faith turn unto him" (*Book of Common Prayer* 1559 ed., ed. Booty 260).
[346]One wonders why the passage needed to be repeated almost verbatim from 1089–1092 to 1099–1104, but the reiteration does provide a kind of coda to the book and to the scene of penitence. God does something similar in miniature in 3.190–91.

Paradise Lost.

BOOK XI.

THE ARGUMENT.

The Son of God presents to his Father the Prayers of our first Parents now repenting, and intercedes for them: God accepts them, but¹ declares that they must no longer abide in Paradise; sends Michael with a Band of Cherubim to dispossess them; but first to reveal to Adam future things: Michaels coming down. Adam shews to Eve certain ominous signs; he discerns Michaels approach, goes out to meet him: the Angel denounces thir departure. Eve's Lamentation. Adam pleads, but submits: The Angel leads him up to a high Hill, sets before him in vision what shall happ'n till the Flood.

T Hus they in lowliest plight repentant stood²
    Praying, for from the Mercie-seat above
    Prevenient Grace³ descending had remov'd
    The stonie from thir hearts, & made new flesh
Regenerate grow instead,⁴ that sighs now breath'd   5
Unutterable, which the Spirit of prayer
Inspir'd,⁵ and wing'd for Heav'n with speedier flight
Then loudest Oratorie: yet thir port°   DEPORTMENT
Not of mean suiters, nor important less
Seem'd thir Petition, then when th' ancient Pair   10
In Fables old, less ancient yet then these,
Deucalion and chaste *Pyrrha* to restore
The Race of Mankind drownd,⁶ before the Shrine
Of *Themis* stood devout. To Heav'n thir prayers
Flew up, nor missd the way, by envious windes   15
Blow'n vagabond or frustrate:⁷ in they passd

---

¹The text of *1668* reads "*and*"; the contrasting "*but*" of *1674* is stronger and more logical. In *1668*, "*Cherubim*" in line 5 of the Argument was "*Cherubims*," an obviously incorrect plural, according to Milton's preferred usage. The Argument of *1674* also seems to correct punctuation, changing the comma after "signs" in line 7 to a semicolon.

²The word "stood" may just mean "remained," since at the end of the previous book Adam and Eve were prostrate, though various editors have made the case that as soon as they repent Adam and Eve become morally and even physically upright.

³Prevenient grace was a central doctrine of the Arminian dissenters from Calvinism. Humankind cannot save itself unaided—cannot even initiate it alone. God must have previously extended His grace (hence it is prevenient), which the Arminian thought could be accepted or rejected. For the Calvinist the extension of grace was thought to be irresistible.

⁴In promising that the Seed will redeem humankind before passing judgment, God "prefaced man's condemnation with a free redemption" (*On Christian Doctrine* 1.14; Yale 6: 416). Removing the stoniness from the heart is described in Ezekiel 11.19: ". . . I [God] will take the stony heart out of their flesh, and will give them an heart of flesh."

⁵As Milton used it, "Spirit" could mean "a divine impulse, light, voice or word sent from above, either through Christ, who is the word of God, or through some other channel" (*On Christian Doctrine* 1.6; Yale 6: 284); hence the Spirit described here can inspire prayer and then transport it to Heaven. Compare Romans 8.26: ". . . the Spirit itself maketh intercession for us with groanings which cannot be uttered." The Spirit, in other words, acts as instigator of prayer and intercessor with God, "Inciting and urging us . . . to address God as our Father, through faith" (1.15; Yale 6: 435).

⁶Milton compares Adam and Eve after the Fall to Ovid's good married couple Deucalion and Pyrrha after the catastrophic flood that was said to have drowned all of humankind in *Metamorphoses* 1.314–449. Like Deucalion and Pyrrha, Adam and Eve will become the progenitors of all living human beings after them. Like Ovid's pair, Adam and Eve also petition the deity (Themis, in the case of Deucalion and Pyrrha) for the benefit of future generations. It seems important that Ovid's pair are inherently good people (like their Old Testament analogues, Noah and his wife), whereas Adam and Eve are newly regenerate. Also, Pyrrha is described as "chaste," which suggests that Eve may have regained what Milton regarded as a kind of chastity or purity within the state of marriage (compare 4.761, where the marriage bed is pronounced chaste).

⁷Probably the same as the "violent cross wind" in 3.487, which blows souls into Milton's Limbo of Vanity. The noun *vagabond*, used here as an adjective, would suggest aimless wandering, and "frustrate" was a common variant form of "frustrated."

Dimentionless[8] through Heav'nly dores; then clad
With incense, where the Golden Altar fum'd,[9]
By thir great Intercessor, came in sight
Before the Fathers Throne: Them the glad Son   20
Presenting, thus to intercede began.[10]
   See Father, what first fruits on Earth are sprung
From thy implanted Grace in Man, these Sighs
And Prayers, which in this Golden Censer, mixt
With Incense, I thy Priest before thee bring,   25
Fruits of more pleasing savour from thy seed
Sow'n with contrition in his heart, then those
Which his own hand manuring° all the Trees   FERTILIZING
Of Paradise could have produc't, ere fall'n
From innocence. Now therefore bend thine eare   30
To supplication, heare his sighs though mute;
Unskilful with what words to pray, let mee
Interpret for him, mee his Advocate
And propitiation,[11] all his works on mee
Good or not good ingraft,[12] my Merit[13] those   35
Shall perfet, and for these my Death shall pay.
Accept me, and in mee from these receave
The smell of peace[14] toward Mankinde, let him live
Before thee reconcil'd, at least his days
Numberd, though sad, till Death, his doom[15] (which I   40
To mitigate thus plead, not to reverse)
To better life shall yeeld him, where with mee
All my redeemd may dwell in joy and bliss,
Made one with me as I with thee am one.
   To whom the Father, without Cloud,[16] serene.   45
All thy request for Man, accepted° Son,   APPROVED
Obtain, all thy request was my Decree:
But longer in that Paradise to dwell,
The Law I gave to Nature him forbids:
Those pure immortal Elements that know   50
No gross, no unharmoneous mixture foule,
Eject him tainted now, and purge him off

---

[8]Without the extension or dimension of a human body (*OED* 1.a, the first recorded instance). Corns comments on "dimentionless" that it "emphasizes with a peculiar precision the immateriality of prayer" (100).
[9]This is not the incense that Milton knew was used in Roman Catholic and in high Anglican ceremony but the "sweet savor" often used of sacrifices described in the Old Testament, as in Ezekiel 20.41.
[10]For Milton the only approach to the Father by humankind is through the Son, the only true priest.
[11]"And if any man sin, we have an advocate with the Father, Jesus Christ the righteous: And he is the propitiation for our sins: and not for ours only, but also for the sins of the whole world" (1 John 2.1–2). The repetition of "mee" again represents the Son's assumption of the burden of the sins of Adam and Eve.
[12]The continuing images are of God or the Son as gardeners, attentive to fertilizing the ground around their trees and attentive to the grafting process. Romans 11.16–24 develops the metaphor of grafting wild "scions," potential unbelievers, onto the "tree" of the early church.
[13]The Son is raised to His eminence by His own merit, not by any undeserved elevation of Him by the Father.
[14]Peace offerings may have the sweet savor of Noah's burnt offering that pleases God's sense of smell in Genesis 8.21.
[15]God's judgment on humankind, the sentence of death, which is viewed here as leading to eternal life.
[16]In speaking with the Son, God has no need to provide clouds to protect the viewer, whereas in revealing Himself to Abraham and others in the Old Testament, God is apt to appear in cloud (Exodus 16.10) or pillar of fire (Exodus 13.21) or burning bush (Exodus 3.4). Also, a cloudy countenance would indicate anger. The preposition without should be accented on the first syllable, an emphatic form (compare 2.892).

As a distemper, gross to aire as gross,[17]
And mortal food, as may dispose him best
For dissolution wrought by Sin, that first   55
Distemperd[18] all things, and of incorrupt
Corrupted. I at first with two fair gifts
Created him endowd, with Happiness
And Immortalitie: that fondly° lost,   FOOLISHLY
This other serv'd but to eternize woe;[19]   60
Till I provided Death; so Death becomes
His final remedie, and after Life
Tri'd in sharp tribulation, and refin'd
By Faith and faithful works,[20] to second Life,
Wak'd in the renovation of the just,   65
Resignes him up with Heav'n and Earth renewd.[21]
But let us call to Synod all the Blest
Through Heav'ns wide bounds;[22] from them I will not hide
My judgments, how with Mankind I proceed,
As how with peccant° Angels late they saw;   SINFUL   70
And in thir state, though firm, stood more confirmd.

    He ended, and the Son gave signal high
To the bright Minister that watchd, hee blew
His Trumpet, heard in *Oreb* since perhaps
When God descended,[23] and perhaps once more   75
To sound at general Doom. Th' Angelic blast
Filld all the Regions: from thir blissful Bowrs
Of *Amarantin* Shade,[24] Fountain or Spring,
By the waters of Life,[25] where ere they sate
In fellowships of joy: the Sons of Light   80
Hasted, resorting to the Summons high,
And took thir Seats; till from his Throne supream
Th' Almighty thus pronouncd his sovran Will.

---

[17]Adam and Eve have been intemperate; their physical and moral distemper can no longer be accepted in the pure soil of Paradise. They are too crude to be there and, like toxic elements in the digestive tract, they must be purged. Belial predicts the same problem for fallen angels trying to return to Heaven: "th' Ethereal mould / Incapable of stain would soon expel / Her mischief, and purge off the baser fire / Victorious" (2.139–42).

[18]To distemper is to disarrange the natural order of the four humors, so that a serious imbalance occurs in the human body. When the elements are balanced, the organism is healthy, but when they are distempered and tend toward dissolution, the body is ill, either with sin or disease (the two were closely allied in seventeenth-century medical theory). The repeated word "gross" here probably refers to "him" (Adam) rather than to "distemper"; thus the comma after "distemper" at line 53 is important to the syntax (see Newton 53n).

[19]"When humankind lost the happiness of innocence, immortality would provide only eternal woe." The verb "eternize" is accented on the second syllable.

[20]For Milton as with most Protestants, "Faith not void of workes" (12.427) was necessary for salvation after death. "Faith has its own works, which may be different from the works of the law. We are justified, then, by faith, but a living faith, not a dead one, and the only living faith is a faith which acts. . . . a true and living faith cannot exist without works, though these may be different from the works of the written law" (*On Christian Doctrine* 1.22; Yale 6: 490).

[21]When the just are regenerate and faith and good works balance each other, the universe is renewed and humankind can be admitted to a second life, after death, in Heaven. Compare the apocalyptic vision in 2 Peter 3.13: "Nevertheless we, according to his promise, look for new heavens and a new earth, wherein dwelleth righteousness."

[22]"Let us call a meeting of all those in Heaven."

[23]Referring to Exodus 20.18, where the Ten Commandments were given to Moses amidst "the noise of the trumpet," and to the apocalyptic passage in 1 Thessalonians 4.16 in which "the Lord himself shall descend from heaven with a shout, with the voice of the archangel, and with the trump of God: and the dead in Christ shall rise first." So the trumpet heralds both the giving of the Law and the Day of Judgment.

[24]Amaranth is, for Milton, the unwithering flower of Paradise and thus a symbol of immortality. See 3.353–57, where the amaranth is described as a flower too good to remain on earth after the Fall: it had to be transported to Heaven.

[25]"And he said unto me, It is done. I am Alpha and Omega, the beginning and the end. I will give unto him that is athirst of the fountain of the water of life freely" (Revelation 21.6).

    O Sons,[26] like one of us Man is become
To know both Good and Evil, since his taste
Of that defended° Fruit; but let him boast   FORBIDDEN   85
His knowledge of Good lost, and Evil got,
Happier, had it suffic'd him to have known
Good by it self, and Evil not at all.[27]
He sorrows now, repents, and prayes contrite,[28]   90
My motions in him, longer then they move,[29]
His heart I know, how variable and vain
Self-left.[30] Least therefore his now bolder hand
Reach also of the Tree of Life, and eat,
And live for ever, dream at least to live   95
For ever, to remove him I decree,
And send him from the Garden forth to Till
The Ground whence he was taken, fitter soile.[31]
    Michael,[32] this my behest have thou in charge,
Take to thee from among the Cherubim   100
Thy choice of flaming[33] Warriours, least the Fiend
Or° in behalf of Man, or to invade   EITHER
Vacant possession[34] som new trouble raise:
Hast thee, and from the Paradise of God
Without remorse[35] drive out the sinful Pair,   105
From hallowd ground th' unholie, and denounce°   ANNOUNCE OMINOUSLY
To them and to thir Progenie from thence
Perpetual banishment. Yet least they faint°   BECOME FAINT-HEARTED
At the sad Sentence rigorously urg'd,
For I behold them softn'd and with tears   110

---

[26]The mode of address helps explain such troubling phrases as the Serpent's "ye shall be as gods" in Genesis 3.5 and God's "Behold, the man is become as one of us, to know good and evil" in Genesis 3.22. If "gods" as used by the Serpent and "us" as used by God both mean "angels," then there is no real plurality of gods in Genesis, and we are safely within a monotheistic system. Also, Milton (together with Willet 55) seems to have believed that God was speaking ironically, since the "knowledge of Good lost, and Evil got" is nothing for humankind to triumph about.

[27]This passage has been used by Virginia Mollenkott ("Milton's Rejection") to suggest that Milton did not endorse the belief often ascribed to him that the Fall was fortunate in its outcome. For the scholarly debate, see the various articles by Bell, Shumaker, and Pecheux.

[28]Having a contrite heart was one of the traditional Christian conditions for being granted forgiveness. "A sorrowful spirit is a sacrifice to God: despise not, O Lord, humble and contrite hearts" (Psalm 51.17), as in the *Book of Common Prayer*; the Authorized Version translates "The sacrifices of God are a broken spirit: a broken and a contrite heart, O God, thou wilt not despise"; Milton used the passage in *On Christian Doctrine* to illustrate humility (2.3; Yale 6: 661–62). Here the word *contrite* should be accented on the second syllable.

[29]Loh paraphrases: "After my impulses have moved in him (i.e., when they have stopped), I know how variable and vain his heart is, when left to itself" (91–93n).

[30]God's "motions" in Adam and Eve are promptings to repentance; motion is used in the theological context of "A working of God in the soul" (*OED* spec. 9.b). As Samson moves toward reconciliation with God in *Samson Agonistes*, he feels "rouzing motions" coming from God (1382). God knows Adam's weaknesses, that he is fickle (variable) and vain if left to his own devices.

[31]"And the Lord God said, Behold, the man is become as one of us, to know good and evil: and now, lest he put forth his hand, and take also of the tree of life, and eat, and live for ever: Therefore the Lord God sent him forth from the garden of Eden, to till the ground from whence he was taken" (Genesis 3.22–23).

[32]The Archangel Michael is identified much more with war and the Last Judgment (Revelation 12) than is the softer and more "sociable spirit" Raphael; hence it is appropriate that he is appointed to help carry out the sentence on Adam and Eve.

[33]Cherubim were often associated with flame or with flaming swords or the wheels of Ezekiel's chariot (West 134, 157–58). Milton has in mind the upcoming duty of the cherubim that Michael will leave at the gates of Eden, with the "brandisht Sword of God before them" (12.633).

[34]Fletcher comments that a comma might be added here and that in one copy of *1674* he examined someone (perhaps at the press itself) had added the comma in ink by hand. "Vacant possession" is a legal term having to do with taking possession of apparently abandoned property (*OED vacant* A.1.c). Thus Satan is realized as a threat to the vacated Eden. Also, Satan is supposed to be acting "in behalf of" man in the sense of "with regard to": there may now be some sympathy between the fallen angel and the fallen couple, but Satan might still try to invade Eden just in order to possess it or gain revenge on God. Fowler (11.102n) sees this passage as ironic, but I think it can be read as a part of a series of straight directives to Michael.

[35]God does not command the angels to be remorseless, and angels are said to display remorselessness elsewhere (5.566), but here it would not be appropriate, because God's justice is being fulfilled in the sentencing of Adam and Eve.

Bewailing thir excess,[36] all terror hide.
If patiently thy bidding they obey,
Dismiss them not disconsolate; reveale
To *Adam* what shall come in future dayes,
As I shall thee enlighten,[37] intermix   115
My Cov'nant in the womans seed renewd;
So send them forth, though sorrowing, yet in peace:
And on the East side of the Garden place,
Where entrance up from *Eden* easiest climbes,
Cherubic watch, and of a Sword the flame   120
Wide waving, all approach farr off to fright,
And guard all passage to the Tree of Life:[38]
Least Paradise a receptacle prove
To Spirits foule, and all my Trees thir prey,
With whose stol'n Fruit Man once more to delude.   125
   He ceas'd; and th' Archangelic Power prepar'd
For swift descent, with him the Cohort° bright   BAND OF WARRIORS
Of watchful Cherubim; four faces each
Had, like a double *Janus*,[39] all thir shape
Spangl'd with eyes more numerous then those   130
Of *Argus*, and more wakeful then to drouze,
Charm'd with *Arcadian* Pipe, the Pastoral Reed
Of *Hermes*, or his opiate Rod.[40] Mean while
To resalute the World with sacred Light
Leucothea[41] wak'd, and with fresh dews imbalmd°   INFUSED WITH BALM   135
The Earth, when *Adam* and first Matron *Eve*
Had ended now thir Orisons,° and found[42]   PRAYERS
Strength added from above, new hope to spring
Out of despaire, joy, but with fear yet linkt;[43]
Which thus to *Eve* his welcome words renewd.   140
   Eve, easily may Faith admit, that all
The good which we enjoy, from Heav'n descends;[44]

---

[36]Possibly their transgression (*OED* 3), though excess was certainly part of the act of sinning.

[37]God must enlighten Michael with information before he can enlighten Adam, who in turn and at times will do the same for Eve (12.597-605)—though Eve overhears at times (9.276) or receives information via dreams (12.595-97). God will fill Michael's mind with the prophecy of future history that Michael will pass on to Adam and Eve. Also, God demonstrates mercy in His instructions to Michael to watch for signs of repentance and the newly-instated virtue of patience. The word *Covenant* looks forward to the pact made between God and Noah that there will be no more catastrophic floods (Genesis 9.11), but God's covenant was also a general sign of the workings of providence in the affairs of humankind (*On Christian Doctrine* 1.8; Yale 6: 329). Here the evidence of God's covenant is in the generations from Eve (the "Seed") that will eventually lead to Christ.

[38]The passage looks forward to events described in Genesis 3.24: "So he [God] drove out the man; and he placed at the east of the garden of Eden Cherubims, and a flaming sword which turned every way, to keep the way of the tree of life."

[39]Though the ancient god of Rome and its gateways, Janus, is usually represented with two faces (the month January, like its namesake, looks backward at the old and forward at the new), there were statues in Rome showing Janus with four faces, *Janus Quadrifrons*, and Christian commentary associated the four-faced Janus with the cherubim having faces of their own plus the faces of a man, a lion, and an eagle pictured forming the wheels of the chariot of God in Ezekiel 10.14.

[40]Not satisfied with one classical foreshadowing, Milton adds the story of the hundred-eyed watchman Argus, set by Juno to guard the chastity of Io against the lechery of her husband Zeus. Zeus, however, sent Mercury to lull Argos to sleep with his reed panpipe and "With movements of the ['sleep-producing'] wand" (Ovid, *Metamorphoses* 1.673, 715; trans. Humphries), and then kill him. Though Juno was supposed to have translated Argus's eyes into the tail of the peacock, Christian interpretation might allegorize his eyes into an astrological sign (Fowler 11.129-33n).

[41]Leucothea or Ino was a minor Roman sea deity invoked by women on behalf of the children of their brothers and called *Mater Matuta*, a name which associated her with Aurora, goddess of the dawn, since *Matuta* was another name for Aurora (hence the French *matin*, "morning"). For Leucothea in the context of fleeing rape, see *Comus* 866-75.

[42]The comma present at this point in *1667* has been judiciously removed in *1674*.

[43]Adam and Eve's "fear" is not necessarily a bad thing, since "The fear of the Lord is the beginning of knowledge" (Proverbs 1.7).

[44]"Every good gift and every perfect gift is from above, and cometh down from the Father of lights, with whom there is no variableness, neither shadow of turning" (James 1.17). There is no mark of punctuation after "descends" in *1667*.

But that from us ought° should ascend to Heav'n   AUGHT, ANYTHING
So prevalent° as to concerne the mind   POWERFUL
Of God high-blest, or to incline his will,
Hard to belief may seem; yet this will Prayer,   145
Or one short sigh of humane[45] breath, up-borne
Ev'n to the Seat[46] of God. For since I saught
By Prayer th' offended Deitie to appease,
Kneel'd and before him humbl'd all my heart,
Methought I saw him placable and mild,   150
Bending his eare;[47] perswasion in me grew
That I was heard with favour; peace returnd
Home to my Brest, and to my memorie
His promise, that thy Seed shall bruise our Foe;[48]
Which then not minded° in dismay,[49] yet now   155
Assures me that the bitterness of death   ATTENDED TO
Is past, and we shall live. Whence Haile[50] to thee,
Eve rightly call'd, Mother of all Mankind,
Mother of all things living, since by thee
Man is to live, and all things live for Man.   160

     To whom thus *Eve* with sad° demeanour meek.
Ill worthie I such title should belong[51]   SERIOUS
To me transgressour, who for thee ordaind
A help, became thy snare;[52] to mee reproach
Rather belongs, distrust and all dispraise: 165
But infinite in pardon was my Judge,
That I who first brought Death on all,[53] am grac't°
The sourse of life; next favourable thou,[54]   FAVORED TO BE
Who highly thus to entitle me voutsaf'st,
Farr other name deserving. But the Field   170
To labour calls us now with sweat impos'd,
Though after sleepless Night;[55] for see the Morn,
All unconcern'd with our unrest, begins

---

[45]Probably pronounced "human." Books 9–11 always use this spelling, which may indicate a compositor's preference. Before Book 9, the compositors had always used "human," except when the word followed a substantive.

[46]The Mercy Seat, mentioned in 2 above.

[47]Though God is not said to have "bended his ear" in the Bible, he is often said to have "inclined his ear" toward the prayers of supplicants, as in the request "I have called upon thee, for thou wilt hear me, O God: incline thine ear unto me" in Psalm 17.6.

[48]The by-now-familiar image of the Seed (Christ) bruising or crushing the head of the Serpent, as in the curse imposed in 10.175–81.

[49]"Because we were in dismay, we could not in the midst of sin focus on ('mind') God's promise." Adam is premature in thinking that God's promise that the head of the Serpent will be bruised means that death will not be forthcoming.

[50]The unusual capitalization of the verb may come from the biblical and ritualistic importance (at least within Roman Catholic ritual) of the *Ave Maria* which Adam's phrase foreshadows. Compare 5.385–87, where Eve is she "On whom the Angel *Haile* / Bestowd, the holy salutation us'd / Long after to blest *Marie*, second *Eve*." Notice that the salutation is italicized for emphasis. Like Adam, Raphael addresses Eve as "Mother of Mankind," a reference to Genesis 3.20, "And Adam called his wife's name Eve; because she was the mother of all living."

[51]"Ill worthie" should be read as an adjectival construction modifying "I": this line and the next might be paraphrased as "I am one not worthy to have such a title, since I am a transgressor."

[52]Eve was created to be Adam's "help-meet." Here she admits to having become his "snare" instead, a snare being a kind of trap or net used by hunters to catch animals unawares. The word *snare* is resonant throughout Milton's works: Dalila, for instance, is Samson's "accomplist snare" (*Samson Agonistes* 230), and Comus wants to "hug" his victim into "snares" (*Comus* 164). Eve pictures herself as a snare because she (or, more properly, her body) has been used by Satan to entrap Adam.

[53]Milton does not often stress the fact that Eve fell first; here it is Eve who notes her precedence in the Fall. Antifeminist literature always interpreted her being first as indicating that women were more inclined, or more quickly inclined, to sin than men.

[54]In effect, "You were the second person who has favored me by addressing me with the salutation 'Hail.'" Eve, incriminating herself in her humility, thinks that she deserves a far worse title.

[55]The punishments imposed are now enforced: even after a sleepless night, Adam and Eve must begin laboring not pleasantly as before but by the sweat of their brow. *Both* Adam and Eve are called forth to labor.

Her rosie progress smiling;[56] let us forth,   175
I never from thy side henceforth to stray,
Wherere our days work lies, though now enjoind
Laborious, till day droop; while here we dwell,
What can be toilsom in these pleasant Walkes?
Here let us live, though in fall'n state, content.   180
    So spake, so wish'd much-humbl'd *Eve*, but Fate
Subscrib'd not; Nature first gave Signs, imprest
On Bird, Beast, Aire, Aire suddenly eclips'd
After short blush of Morn;[57] nigh in her sight
The Bird of *Jove*, stoopt from his aerie tour,°   TOWER   185
Two Birds of gayest plume before him drove:[58]
Down from a Hill the Beast that reigns in Woods,
First hunter then, pursu'd a gentle brace,°   PAIR
Goodliest of all the Forrest, Hart and Hinde;[59]
Direct to th' Eastern Gate was bent thir flight.   190
Adam observ'd, and with his Eye the chase
Pursuing, not unmov'd to *Eve* thus spake.
    O *Eve*, some furder change awaits us nigh,
Which Heav'n by these mute signs in Nature shews
Forerunners of his purpose, or to warn   195
Us haply° too secure of our discharge   POSSIBLY, PERHAPS
From penaltie, because from death releast
Some days; how long, and what till then our life,
Who knows, or more then this, that we are dust,
And thither must return and be no more.   200
Why else this double object in our sight[60]
Of flight pursu'd in th' Air and ore the ground
One way the self-same hour? why in the East
Darkness ere Dayes mid-course, and Morning light
More orient[61] in yon Western Cloud that draws   205
O're the blew Firmament a radiant white,
And slow descends, with somthing heav'nly fraught.
    He err'd not, for by this the heav'nly Bands
Down from a Skie of Jasper[62] lighted° now   ALIGHTED
In Paradise, and on a Hill made alt,°   A HALT   210
A glorious Apparition, had not doubt

---

[56]The dawn is pictured in terms that seem to suggest Homer's famous rosy-fingered dawn but perhaps comes closer to Horatio's description of the morning in *Hamlet*: "But look, the morn in russet mantle clad / Walks o'er the dew of yon high eastward hill" (1.1166–67).

[57]As Fowler points out, these are portents, not the first signs of the Fall in nature (as Hughes's note on "signs" would indicate); the signs of the Fall were perceptible to Adam at 10.715 (Fowler 11.182–90n). Portents might manifest themselves not only in the arrangement of heavenly bodies (as with eclipses) but in the behavior of beasts of the earth or in the flight of birds.

[58]In this omen an eagle (the bird associated with Jove) swoops down on (the technical term *stoop* is brought in from falconry) two other birds that may be peacocks. The situation may foreshadow male and female quarreling after the Fall, since Jove's eagle might be pursuing Juno's peacocks, or it may foreshadow the Expulsion as an emblem of pursuit.

[59]The lion, king of the beasts, now for the first time becomes a hunter and pursues a mated hart and hind, male and female deer, pictured here as aristocratic ("gentle") and good. Before the Fall, the lion was peaceable (4.343–44). In the illustration to Book 11 in the 1699 Folio, one can see the lion chasing hart and hind and a bird of prey pursuing smaller birds through the air.

[60]Probably because of foul case or the attraction of "flight" in the next line, the compositor of *1674* used the long "ſ" form and the word became "fight," which would obviously be inappropriate. The "sight" of *1667* is surely correct.

[61]Both "eastern" and "bright."

[62]The sky seems to be the various or marbled colors of the semiprecious stone jasper—red, green, yellow, and brown. Milton's allusion here may well be to God pictured in judgment in Revelation 4.3: "And he that sat was to look upon like a jasper and a sardine stone" ("sardine stone" probably being the semiprecious sardonyx).

And carnal fear that day dimm'd *Adams* eye.[63]
Not that more glorious, when the Angels met
Jacob in *Mahanaim*,[64] where he saw
The field Pavilion'd with his Guardians bright;   215
Nor that which on the flaming Mount appeerd
In *Dothan*,[65] cover'd with a Camp of Fire,
Against the *Syrian* King, who to surprize
One man, Assassin-like had levied Warr,
Warr unproclam'd.[66] The Princely Hierarch[67]   220
In thir bright stand,[68] there left his Powers to seise
Possession of the Garden;[69] hee alone,
To find where *Adam* shelterd, took his way,
Not unperceav'd of *Adam*, who to *Eve*,
While the great Visitant approachd, thus spake.   225
    Eve, now expect great tidings, which perhaps
Of us will soon determin,[70] or impose
New Laws to be observ'd; for I descrie
From yonder blazing Cloud that veils the Hill
One of the heav'nly Host, and by his Gate°   GAIT   230
None of the meanest, some great Potentate
Or of the Thrones above,[71] such Majestie
Invests him coming;[72] yet not terrible,
That I should fear, nor sociably mild,
As *Raphael*, that I should much confide,[73]   235
But solemn and sublime, whom not to offend,
With reverence I must meet, and thou retire.[74]
He ended; and th' Arch-Angel[75] soon drew nigh,

---

[63]Adam's jaded or "carnal" eye has noticed the dark or fearful omens but not the bright presence of the angels.

[64]Because Jacob in Genesis 32.1 sees a place covered with tents of angels, he calls it "Mahanaim," which means "tents," a word also accommodated by Milton's "Pavilion'd." See the marginal definition in the Geneva Bible (1560 ed.).

[65]The story told in 2 Kings 6 is that of the "one man": the prophet Elisha in the city of Dothan performing miracles, such as making iron ax-heads rise to the surface of water. The King of Aram (Syria), at war with Israel, sends troops to surround the city and fetch him. When Elisha's servant expresses fear, Elisha prays that God would open the servant's eyes, and "behold, the mountain was full of horses and chariots of fire round about Elisha" (17). Milton cites the passage in *On Christian Doctrine* as an illustration of the fact that angels "often appeared looking like soldiers" (1.9; Yale 6: 347). The phrase "One man" suggests that Milton wants the reader to include Elisha among the select group of "just men" distinguished by their singularity, good deeds, and spiritual power—those few who were examples or role models for human behavior.

[66]According to the Geneva Bible marginalia, the King of Syria planted his men to "lie in ambushe & take the Israelites at unwares" (1560 ed., referring to 2 Kings 6.9). The customary spelling of the past participle form would be "unproclaim'd," but here *1674* follows *1667* by rote, as in the unusual capitalization of "Pavilion'd" above and "Princely" below.

[67]That is, Michael. Milton seems to have used the term "Hierarch" vaguely for "high-ranking angel," since he applies it to Raphael as well (5.468; see 5.587).

[68]The word *stand* suggests battle station or position in a hunt (*OED* II.12, 13), though Fowler thinks there may also be an allusion to the "elevated resting place of a hawk" (*OED* II.14; Fowler 11.221n), echoing the omen of the eagle.

[69]Michael has given orders to his troops to secure and take possession of the entire garden, while he seeks out Adam and Eve alone.

[70]Though "determin" may be defined as "make an end" (Fowler 11.227n), I would prefer "decree" (*OED* 7), signifying God's control over the fate of Adam and Eve. In other words, the news from the angel may make them aware of the full extent of God's judgment of death on them. The idiom "determine of us" would then mean "determine our fates."

[71]Adam perceives that Michael is either a great Potentate or a Throne, one of two of the higher ranks in the hierarchy of angels (West 134). There are Potentates in Hell as well (1.315)—or at least Satan wants the fallen angels to think that the titles still have importance after the War in Heaven.

[72]In his appearance as he comes toward Adam and Eve, Michael is invested with majesty. The line in *1674* has a question mark here, which seems inappropriate and probably represents foul case, as Fletcher suggests.

[73]Adam contrasts the demeanor of Michael with that of Raphael. Raphael, being "sociably mild" (compare "sociable Spirit" at 5.221) was easy to confide in; Michael is much more formidable, since he is both solemn and sublime. Adam does not fear Michael, just as he is "not awd" by Raphael in 5.358, but the warlike angel is not easy to talk to, especially not after the Fall.

[74]Before the Fall, Eve retired from the conversation of Adam and Raphael voluntarily; now she must be firmly requested to leave, since Adam's dominion over her has increased after and because of the Fall.

[75]Michael is revealed as the archangel he is, but, in order not to intimidate Adam, he comes as a richly-dressed soldier. His angelic nature is revealed only in the celestial components of his dress, some of which seem to be taken from the astrological figures in the Zodiac.

Not in his shape Celestial, but as Man
Clad to meet Man; over his lucid° Armes   BRIGHT, DAZZLING   240
A militarie Vest° of purple flowd   GARMENT
Livelier then *Meliboean*,[76] or the graine
Of *Sarra*,[77] worn by Kings and Hero's old
In time of Truce; *Iris* had dipt the wooff;[78]
His starrie Helme unbuckl'd[79] shew'd him prime   245
In Manhood where Youth ended; by his side
As in a glistering *Zodiac*[80] hung the Sword,
Satans dire dread,[81] and in his hand the Spear.
Adam bowd low, hee Kingly from his State
Inclin'd not,[82] but his coming thus declar'd.   250
    Adam, Heav'ns high behest no Preface needs:
Sufficient that thy Prayers are heard, and Death,
Then due by sentence when thou didst transgress,
Defeated of his seisure many dayes[83]
Giv'n thee of Grace, wherein thou may'st repent,   255
And one bad act with many deeds well done
Mayst cover:[84] well may then thy Lord appeas'd
Redeem thee quite° from Deaths rapacious claime;   COMPLETELY, UTTERLY
But longer in this Paradise to dwell
Permits not;[85] to remove thee I am come,   260
And send thee from the Garden forth to till
The ground whence thou wast tak'n, fitter Soile.[86]
    He added not, for *Adam* at the newes
Heart-strook with chilling gripe[87] of sorrow stood,
That all his senses bound; *Eve*, who unseen   265
Yet all had heard, with audible lament
Discover'd soon the place of her retire.[88]
    O unexpected stroke, worse then of Death!
Must I thus leave thee Paradise? thus leave
Thee Native Soile, these happie Walks and Shades,   270
Fit haunt of Gods? where I had hope to spend,

---

[76]The purple dye, famous in antiquity, manufactured in Meliboea on the coast of Thessaly (at the foot of Mt. Ossa). A cloak dyed in Meliboean purple is a prize in the *Aeneid* 5.251.

[77]Sarra is the less familiar name for the city of Tyre, famous for the dye commonly known as "Tyrean purple" or *purpura sarranus*. Tyrian dye-work is mentioned in 2 Chronicles 2.14. The word *grain* is used in the sense of "ingrained" or "dyed in the grain" (the dye is ingrained deeply into the fabric).

[78]Above the mortal efforts of Meliboean or Tyrian dye, the fabrics Michael wears have been dyed in the woof (the warp and the woof being the two possible directions the weave takes in a woven fabric) by the goddess of the rainbow, Iris. The Attendant Spirit in *Comus* also has "skie robes spun out of *Iris* Woofe" (83).

[79]Michael's military helmet is also celestial ("starrie"), but it is unbuckled, showing that he comes in peace. As any ideal soldier should be, he is beyond youth but still in the prime of manhood.

[80]The sword hanging on Michael's belt might remind the reader of Orion's belt and sword in the Zodiac. Apparently Michael is as radiant in appearance in daylight as the stars would be on a clear night.

[81]Satan would dread the dire effects of Michael's sword because it cut his sword in half, wounding him deeply in the War in Heaven (6.320–27).

[82]Adam bows deeply to the angel's kingly state or inherent dignity, but Michael does not need to return the obeisance—he does not even incline his head in return. The small gesture (or lack of it) shows the changing relationships between humankind and the angels. Adam is now deferential because his sin has lowered him with respect to the angels. Also, Michael begins his dialogue abruptly, with no polite preamble.

[83]Michael's diction is legal: Death, like a magistrate, has been cheated of carrying out the sentencing of Adam and Eve and seizing them (considering who Death is, "seizing" would mean "killing"). God's grace has extended the sentence and cheated Death.

[84]"And above all things have fervent charity among yourselves: for charity shall cover the multitude of sins" (1 Peter 4.8). Milton uses the passage also to support the idea that charitable deeds will help mask unpleasantness in human actions in *On Christian Doctrine* (2.11; Yale 6: 749).

[85]"It is no longer permitted for you to live in this Paradise."

[86]Michael does not change the wording of God's decree at 96–98 above.

[87]The word spelled "gripe" could indicate either the modern "grip" or "grippe," the second in the sense of "ailment."

[88]Here *retire* combines verb and noun senses to become "retirement" or "withdrawal" (*OED* 1, citing this instance).

Quiet though sad, the respit° of that day
That must be mortal to us both. O flours,
That never will in other Climate grow,[89]
My early visitation, and my last   275
At Eev'n, which I bred up with tender hand
From the first op'ning bud, and gave ye Names,[90]
Who now shall reare ye° to the Sun, or ranke
Your Tribes,[91] and water from th' ambrosial Fount?[92]
Thee lastly nuptial Bowre, by mee adornd   280
With what to sight or smell was sweet; from thee
How shall I part, and whither wander down
Into a lower World, to this obscure
And wilde,[93] how shall we breath in other Aire
Less pure, accustomd to immortal Fruits?[94]   285
   Whom thus the Angel interrupted milde.
Lament not *Eve*, but patiently resigne
What justly thou hast lost; nor set thy heart,
Thus over-fond, on that which is not thine;
Thy going is not lonely, with thee goes   290
Thy Husband, him to follow thou art bound;
Where he abides, think there thy native soile.
   Adam by this from the cold sudden damp[95]
Recovering, and his scatterd spirits returnd,[96]
To *Michael* thus his humble words addressd.   295
   Celestial, whether among the Thrones, or nam'd
Of them the Highest,[97] for such of shape may seem
Prince above Princes, gently hast thou tould
Thy message, which might else in telling wound,
And in performing end us; what besides   300
Of sorrow and dejection and despair
Our frailtie can sustain, thy tidings bring,
Departure from this happy place, our sweet
Recess,[98] and onely consolation left
Familiar to our eyes, all places else   305

---

[89]The amaranth (3.353–54) is the only example given of a flower that would grow in Eden but not on what Milton referred to as "mortal soil" ("Lycidas" 78).

[90]If Adam had the responsibility for naming the animals, Eve had that of naming at least some of the plants (Leonard 46–47). As Northrop Frye ("Revelation to Eve" 23–24) and others have pointed out, Eve is associated with plant life, fertility, and gardening.

[91]Eve pictures herself not only naming the flowers but establishing a classification system according to something like an hierarchical series of genus and species.

[92]The Fountain of Life in Paradise was supposed to run nectar (4.240) and flow outward in four different rivers, though the entire landscape of the Mount of Paradise is altered as a result of the Fall (829–35 below). Satan rides into Eden through the underground passage of the river Tigris (9.71–75). For the overall typography of the rivers, see 4.223–46.

[93]The lower world (beneath the Mount of Paradise) will be more dark and wild in comparison with the Garden of Eden, where all has been well-lighted and under cultivation.

[94]Eve has been accustomed to breathing the pure air of Paradise and eating of its fruits, but the word "Fruits" at this point, even if paired respectfully with "immortal," would provide a kind of red flag to Michael, who will interrupt Eve as soon as she uses the phrase. Since they have just eaten of a fruit whose taste will bring mortality into the world, Eve seems to be saying the wrong thing at the wrong time, and she needs to be corrected, at least mildly, by Michael. His adjective for Eve is "over-fond," which here indicates that she has been somewhat foolish in overvaluing what she has irretrievably lost.

[95]Adam is recovering from what might be called a temporary depression, a figurative dampening of his spirits, thought to be allied with damp air at night and the warm and wet humor produced by melancholia in old age. "In old age, melancholy, the cold and dry humor, increases at the expense of blood, the warm and moist humor. From melancholy arises a 'damp,' a dry, noxious vapor. 'The Balm of Life' is the natural heat-moisture which resides in the blood" (Babb 38, commenting on 11.542–46).

[96]Adam's animal spirits had become scattered; thus they "bound" his senses at 265. Now his senses are collected.

[97]Fowler points out (11.296–98n) that it is only after the Fall that Adam begins to bother about the social status of different ranks of angels.

[98]Eve's privately cultivated plat in Eden has been called her "sweet recess" at 9.456.

Inhospitable appeer and desolate,
Nor knowing us nor known: and if by prayer
Incessant I could hope to change the will
Of him who all things can,° I would not cease   KNOWS, OR IS CAPABLE OF   310
To wearie him with my assiduous cries:
But prayer against his absolute Decree
No more availes then breath against the winde,
Blown stifling back on him that breaths it forth:
Therefore to his great bidding I submit.
This most afflicts me, that departing hence,   315
As from his face I shall be hid, deprivd
His blessed count'nance; here I could frequent,[99]
With worship, place by place where he voutsaf'd°   CONDESCENDED TO GRANT
Presence Divine, and to my Sons relate;
On this Mount he appeerd, under this Tree   320
Stood visible, among these Pines his voice
I heard, here with him at this Fountain talk'd:
So many grateful Altars I would reare
Of grassie Terfe, and pile up every Stone
Of lustre[100] from the brook, in memorie,   325
Or monument to Ages, and thereon
Offer sweet smelling Gumms and Fruits and Flours:[101]
In yonder nether° World where shall I seek   LOWER
His bright appearances, or footstep[102] trace?
For though I fled him angrie, yet recall'd   330
To life prolongd and promisd Race,[103] I now
Gladly behold though but his utmost skirts[104]
Of glory, and farr off his steps adore.
    To whom thus *Michael* with regard benigne.
Adam, thou know'st Heav'n his, and all the Earth,[105]   335
Not this Rock onely;[106] his Omnipresence fills
Land, Sea, and Aire, and every kinde that lives,
Fomented[107] by his virtual power and warmd:
All th' Earth he gave thee to possess and rule,

---

[99]Apparently accented on the second syllable.

[100]"Every shining stone."

[101]Since God is omnipresent, it is improper of Adam to think that setting up monuments or memorial places in various locales in Eden would be a proper way of honoring him. Such a practice, though emulating that of the Old Testament prophets who erected altars wherever God manifested himself, denies the ubiquity of God.

[102]A hyphen appears in *1674* between "step" and "trace" and in *1674* "foot" and "step" are two separate words. I agree with Fletcher that the hyphen belongs one word before it appears, a mechanical error on the part of the compositor. I have restored the "footstep" of *1674*, as most modern editors do.

[103]The same as the promised "Seed" of 10.1031 and elsewhere.

[104]The skirts of God are bright at 3.375–82: their origin in scripture may be God saying "I spread my skirt over thee, and covered thy nakedness" as quoted in Ezekiel 16.8. Here, however, the plural "utmost skirts" suggests "outer boundaries."

[105]There is a period at this point in *1674*, for which there can be no justification in the syntax of the sentence. Almost all modern editors (with the exception of Fowler) emend it to a comma, as did *1668*.

[106]A probable allusion to Christ's warning to the woman of Samaria in John 4.21: "Woman, believe me, the hour cometh when ye shall neither in this mountain, nor yet at Jerusalem, worship the Father." Milton has Michael caution Adam against localizing worship, which would be in keeping with Milton's general belief that worship should not be focused on churches or even assigned to a certain terrain. The possibly contemptuous reference to "this Rock" suggests that Adam's effort to pile up stones in holy places would trivialize or localize his religion and that Adam should not endorse the building of the church on any "rock," especially if he were to follow the Roman Catholic tradition of venerating St. Peter (*petra* meaning rock first in Greek and then in Latin) as the only foundation of the church.

[107]Nurtured, in the sense of bringing to fruition by providing heat and moisture to stimulate growth (*OED* 4.a, which cites 10.1071). God causes the fomentation by providing the life-giving ("virtual") power and the warmth.

No despicable[108] gift; surmise not then   340
His presence to these narrow bounds confin'd
Of Paradise or *Eden*: this had been
Perhaps thy Capital Seate, from whence had spred
All generations, and had hither come
From all the ends of th' Earth, to celebrate   345
And reverence thee thir great Progenitor.
But this præeminence thou hast lost, brought down
To dwell on eeven ground now with thy Sons:[109]
Yet doubt not but in Vallie and in plaine
God is as here, and will be found alike   350
Present, and of his presence many a signe
Still following thee, still compassing thee round
With goodness and paternal Love, his Face
Express,[110] and of his steps the track Divine.[111]
Which that thou mayst beleeve, and be confirmd[112]   355
Ere thou from hence depart, know I am sent
To shew thee what shall come in future dayes
To thee and to thy Ofspring; good with bad
Expect to hear, supernal Grace[113] contending
With sinfulness of Men; thereby to learn   360
True patience,[114] and to temper joy with fear
And pious sorrow,[115] equally enur'd
By moderation[116] either state to beare,
Prosperous or adverse: so shalt thou lead
Safest thy life, and best prepar'd endure   365
Thy mortal passage° when it comes. Ascend   I.E., DEATH
This Hill; let *Eve* (for I have drencht[117] her eyes)
Here sleep below while thou to foresight[118] wak'st,
As once thou slepst, while Shee to life was formd.
    To whom thus *Adam* gratefully repli'd.   370

---

[108]Apparently accented on the first and third syllables.

[109]Adam has been living in a mountain plateau in Paradise: now he will be forced to live with future generations in a nether world on "eeven ground."

[110]In the sense of "express image," the exact or true image (*OED* I.1.a) of God's face, not represented in any cloud or burning bush. Compare 7.526–28: " . . . in his own Image hee / Created thee, in the Image of God / Express." The source of the usage is Hebrews 1.3, discussing the Son, "Who being the brightness of his glory, and the express image of his person, and upholding all things by the word of his power, when he had by himself purged our sins, sat down on the right hand of the Majesty on high."

[111]Perhaps alluding to 1 Peter 2.21: " . . . because Christ also suffered for us, leaving us an example, that ye should follow his steps."

[112]The compositor of *1674* removes a comma at this point that was present in *1667*.

[113]Grace issuing from heaven. Compare 7.572–73, where "winged Messengers" are "On errands of supernal Grace."

[114]"PATIENCE is the virtue which shows itself when we peacefully accept God's promises, supported by confidence in the divine providence, power and goodness: also when we bear any evils that we have to bear calmly, as things which our supreme Father has sent for our good" (*On Christian Doctrine* 2.3; Yale 6: 662).

[115]In discussing the process of repentance in *On Christian Doctrine*, Milton notes that man, "SEEING WITH SORROW THAT HE HAS OFFENDED GOD BY HIS SINS," "TURNS TO GOD WITH ALL HUMILITY" (1.19; Yale 6: 466). One of Milton's proof texts for "seeing with sorrow" is 2 Corinthians 7.10: *"sadness which is according to God causes repentance for salvation, which is never to be repented"* (I quote from his rendition as translated by Carey). In other words, sadness (or "pious sorrow") that accords with God's desire for our repentance helps bring about salvation, which never needs to be repented for.

[116]Milton also lists moderation as one of the virtues one should cultivate with respect to one's neighbor: " . . . it entails insisting upon less than one's full legal rights, or even resigning one's rights altogether" (*On Christian Doctrine* 2.14; Yale 6: 778). Moderation would cultivate the ability to bear prosperity or adversity.

[117]Michael had applied something like a sleeping potion (a "drench" as "soporific . . . draught" or "potion," as in *OED* sb. spec. 2), in this case to Eve's eyes. An apt comparison might be to the herb that Oberon directs Puck to apply to the eyes of Titania and others in *Midsummer Night's Dream*, though a drench was normally administered by mouth.

[118]"Prophetic sight" or vision of the future. Michael makes the parallel between Eve being educated while sleeping and Adam being shown a series of visions of the future while awake—just as he once was put to sleep or anesthetized while still observing the creation of Eve from his side (8.460–78). For the various degrees of prophecy then recognized, see Hunter, *Descent* 21–30.

Ascend, I follow thee, safe Guide, the path
Thou lead'st me, and to the hand of Heav'n submit,
However chast'ning, to the evil turne
My obvious° breast, arming to overcom   VULNERABLE
By suffering,[119] and earne rest from labour won,   375
If so I may attain. So both ascend
In the Visions of God:[120] It was a Hill
Of Paradise the highest, from whose top
The Hemisphere of Earth in cleerest Ken°   VIEW
Stretcht out to amplest[121] reach of prospect lay.   380
Not higher that Hill nor wider looking round,
Whereon for different cause the Tempter set
Our second *Adam* in the Wilderness,
To shew him all Earths Kingdomes and thir Glory.[122]
His Eye might there command wherever stood   385
City of old or modern Fame, the Seat
Of mightiest Empire, from the destind Walls
Of *Cambalu*, seat of *Cathaian Can*[123]
And *Samarchand* by *Oxus*,[124] *Temirs* Throne,
To *Paquin* of *Sinæan* Kings,[125] and thence   390
To *Agra* and *Lahor* of great *Mogul*[126]
Down to the golden *Chersonese*,[127] or where
The *Persian* in *Ecbatan* sate,[128] or since
In *Hispahan,* or where the *Russian Ksar*
In *Mosco*,[129] or the Sultan in *Bizance*,   395
Turchestan-born;[130] nor could his eye not ken°   PERCEIVE

[119]Using the Christian paradoxes that patient resolution may overcome fierce action or that suffering (endurance) may also bring about victory, Adam argues that, in becoming a good Christian soldier, he will expose his breast to the enemy (evil) and by being passive overcome aggressive evil. Adam also anticipates that witnessing the future evil wrought by his sin, though it will be a passive experience, will also be hard work and, perhaps, earn him a well-justified rest. See Richard Jordan, *The Quiet Hero*, especially 1–27 and 122–45, for the connection between the virtue of temperance and the ideal of the passive hero.

[120]The use of the plural "Visions" and the mountain setting are in deference to the account of the series of visions in Ezekiel 40.2: "In the visions of God brought he me into the land of Israel, and set me upon a very high mountain, by which was as the frame of a city on the south."

[121]The word "the" before "amplest" was omitted in *1667*. Following Shawcross, I have restored the line as in *1667*. As Fletcher points out, one possible emendation would be "th' amplest." The "amplest reach of prospect" would be the widest and deepest angles of perspective the eye might perceive.

[122]The biblical reference is to Christ being tempted by the devil in Matthew 4.8: "Again, the devil taketh him up into an exceeding high mountain, and sheweth him all the kingdoms of the world, and the glory of them."

[123]The Chinese (Cathayan) Khan would be destined to rule in Cambaluc, the capital of Cathay.

[124]Samarkand is near the Oxus river, in what is now Iran. Temir (Marlowe's Tamburlaine) once ruled there. Milton may have noted it as being along a trade route, but his organization here is built on circles of power radiating from czars, khans, moguls, or shahs.

[125]Sinaean (Chinese) kings would have ruled in Peking (Paquin).

[126]Two regions and cities in northern India, both prominent in the affairs of England in the sixteenth and seventeenth centuries, Lahore to the north and Agra to the south (the city of Delhi lies between). Agra was known to Peter Heylyn as the seat of "the Great Monguls" (Fowler 11.391n). Milton would have associated "Moguls" with emperors of eastern India.

[127]The "golden" Chersonese is "Malacca the most southern promontory of the East Indies, so called on account of its riches to distinguish it from the other Chersoneses or peninsula's" (Newton 387n). As Fowler points out (11.392n), Josephus associated the peninsula, perhaps wrongly, with "the Ophir which supplied King Solomon with gold (*Antiq*. VIII vi 4)."

[128]Ecbatana (Hamadan) was the earlier, ancient summer capital of the Persian kings; Isfahan was the capital in the seventeenth century. (The better-known Persepolis was the Persian capital during the winter months.)

[129]The Russian czar, in Moscow. In seventeenth-century geography, Russia was the kingdom of Moscovia, about which Milton wrote in his *Brief History of Moscovia* (1682).

[130]"*Bizance*" is Byzantium or Istanbul, ruled by the Sultan of Turkey, whose lineage derived from the province of Turkestan, the Tartary region in central Asia between Mongolia and the Caspian Sea.

Th' Empire of *Negus*[131] to his utmost Port
Ercoco and the less *Maritim* Kings
Mombaza, and *Quiloa*, and *Melind*,[132]
And *Sofala* thought *Ophir*,[133] to the Realme   400
Of *Congo*, and *Angola* fardest South;[134]
Or thence from *Niger* Flood to *Atlas* Mount[135]
The Kingdoms of *Almansor*, *Fez* and *Sus*,[136]
Marocco and *Algiers*, and *Tremisen*;
On *Europe* thence, and where *Rome* was to sway   405
The World: in Spirit perhaps he also saw
Rich *Mexico* the seat of *Motezume*,[137]
And *Cusco* in *Peru*, the richer seat
Of *Atabalipa*, and yet unspoil'd
Guiana, whose great Citie *Geryons* Sons   410
Call *El Dorado*: but to nobler sights
Michael from *Adams* eyes the Filme remov'd[138]
Which that false Fruit that promis'd clearer sight
Had bred; then purg'd with Euphrasie and Rue[139]
The visual Nerve, for he had much to see;   415
And from the Well of Life three drops instill'd.[140]
So deep the power of these Ingredients pierc'd,
Eevn to the inmost seat of mental sight,[141]
That *Adam* now enforc't° to close his eyes,   FORCED

---

[131]We are (or Adam now is) in Africa, which Milton pictures as being composed of nine kingdoms mirroring those of Asia Minor and Russia. In northern Ethiopia or Abyssinia, the king was called the Negus. "Ercoco" is the modern port Arkiko, on the Red Sea. The word now spelled "maritime" was "Maritine" in *1667* and "*Maritim*" in *1674*, both of which were currently acceptable spellings; the italics used with "*Maritim*" may indicate that the compositor at least in *1674* found the word unfamiliar and thus treated it as if it were a place name. The metrics of the line indicate it should be accented on the second syllable.

[132]Mombasa and Malindi, both on the coasts of Kenya, and Kilwa, on the coast of Tanzania.

[133]Sofala was a port city in what is now Mozambique. More important, it was thought to be the biblical land of Ophir, from which Solomon received gold for the building of the Temple. The phrase "gold of Ophir" throughout the Old Testament always defines the purest form of gold.

[134]The regions of Congo and Angola are farthest south in Ethiopia, as Milton pictures them, with Angola south of Congo.

[135]From the river Niger (in what is now Nigeria) in the south to Mt. Atlas, near the northwestern coast of Africa in Mauritania.

[136]The best-known "*Almansor*" (the title "Al-mansur" meant "victorious" and was assumed by many Muslim rulers) was Amir Mohammed of Cordova, king of Andalusia in Spain in the tenth century, who was to become the subject of an heroic drama, John Dryden's *The Conquest of Granada*, written in 1668-69. Almansor's empire would have included the territories of Fez and Sus (in the province of Morocco), Morocco, Algiers, and Tremisen (now Tlemcen, in Algeria), all kingdoms arranged along the Barbary Coast of northern Africa.

[137]Montezuma, ruler of Mexico, whose kingdom had been despoiled by Cortez. Fowler points out that "*Motezume*" was "A more correct form than the Spanish Montezuma" (11.407-11n). Cuzco, in Peru, was plundered by Pizarro, who overcame Atahuallpa, Milton's "*Atabalipa*." Geryon is Dante's monster of fraud in Canto 17 of the *Inferno*, the descendant of the monster Geryon (usually thought to have lived in Cades or the modern Cadiz) that Hercules had slain, which had three bodies and three heads. The Spanish *conquistadores* would therefore be sons of Geryon because they proceeded by fraud and were rapacious. England was in active trade with Guiana, identified as the potential area where the rich city the Spanish called El Dorado should have been located. Milton has covered the entire continent of South America in the series of images.

[138]A succession of epic heroes had had their eyes rinsed to clear their vision, including Diomedes, whose eyes were cleared by Pallas Athene (*Iliad* 5.127); Aeneas, cleansed by Venus (*Aeneid* 2.604-05); and Goffredo, cleansed by the Archangel Michael (*Jerusalem Delivered* 18.92-93). But Milton may also be thinking of St. Paul, who had the "scales" fall from his eyes in Acts 9.18 after having been "filled with the Holy Ghost" through the laying on of Ananias's hands. The visions that follow those of contemporary conquest will be of "nobler sights."

[139]The false fruit of the Tree of the Knowledge of Good and Evil had promised clearer sight—an effect similar to that supposedly produced with the herb fennel (mentioned in 9.581)—but actually had imposed a film over the eyes of Adam. The two herbs Michael chooses to remove the film are among the many Milton would have known as medicines for restoring or quickening eyesight. As Fowler points out, "euphrasy" is not only known in herbal lore as "eyebright," its name in Greek means "cheerfulness"; whereas rue (as in "ruefulness") means "sorrow" (11.413-15n).

[140]Proverbs 10.11 may give a context: "The mouth of a righteous man is a well of life: but violence covereth the mouth of the wicked." Milton uses the passage in *On Christian Doctrine* to illustrate duties toward our neighbor affecting either his internal or external well-being. "They relate to his internal well-being when they affect his LIFE or HONOR, and to his external well-being when they affect his REPUTATION or FORTUNE. 'Life' here means not only his present but his eternal life and safety" (2.12; Yale 6: 753). Thus when Michael purges the visual nerve and then instills or slowly applies the healing drops from the well of life, he is not only being a healing angel, he may be instructing Adam how to be a good neighbor. Michael is also casting a medicinal spell, like Sabrina in *Comus* when she sprinkles the breast of the Lady three times (911-15).

[141]One of many references in the poem to spiritual insight or what became to the Puritan sects the "inner light" (though that phrase is not used by Milton). Compare "the inner man, the nobler part" in *Paradise Regain'd* 2.477, or Milton's appeal to the muse to "Shine inward" (*Paradise Lost* 3.52).

Sunk down and all his Spirits became intranst: 420
But him the gentle Angel by the hand
Soon rais'd, and his attention thus recall'd.[142]
    Adam, now ope thine eyes, and first behold[143]
Th' effects which thy original crime[144] hath wrought
In some to spring from thee, who never touch'd   425
Th' excepted Tree, nor with the Snake conspir'd,
Nor sinn'd thy sin,[145] yet from that sin derive
Corruption to bring forth more violent deeds.
    His eyes he op'nd, and beheld a field,
Part arable and tilth,[146] whereon were Sheaves   430
New reapt, the other part sheep-walks and foulds;
Ith' midst an Altar as the Land-mark stood
Rustic, of grassie sord;° thither anon°   SWARD, TURF   IMMEDIATELY
A sweatie Reaper[147] from his Tillage brought
First Fruits, the green Eare, and the yellow Sheaf,   435
Uncull'd, as came to hand; a Shepherd next
More meek[148] came with the Firstlings of his Flock
Choicest and best; then sacrificing, laid
The Inwards and thir Fat, with Incense strew'd,
On the cleft Wood, and all due Rites perform'd.[149]   440
His Offring soon propitious Fire from Heav'n[150]
Consum'd with nimble glance, and grateful steame;[151]
The others[152] not, for his was not sincere;
Whereat hee inlie rag'd, and as they talk'd,
Smote him into the Midriff with a stone   445

---

[142]Recalls scenes of visions and prophecies in the Old Testament, specifically the "great vision" of Daniel reported in Daniel 10, where an angel-like being comes to Daniel, is manifested to him alone and tells of being helped by "Michael, one of the chief princes" (10.13). Daniel's vision is, like Adam's, of "what shall befall [his] people in the latter days" (10.14). Michael will show Adam six scenes, each one of which might be regarded as a *tableau vivant* or as a short tragedy (Fowler 11.429–47n). I do not detect enough generic hints (as with "change / Those Notes to Tragic" at 9.5–6) to say for sure that Michael's scenes are meant to be considered as miniature tragedies; they are more apt to be the "mask of all the evills of this life & world" described in the outline "Adam unparadiz'd" in Milton's notes. The first outline for *Paradise Lost,* however, concluded with "other Tragedies," such as "Adam in Banishment," "The flood," and "Abram in Egypt."

[143]The point of the history of the world up to the appearance of Christ in the remainder of the poem is to show Adam how God's will affects history. Historical time is goal-oriented, not circular as philosophers following Plato had argued (see Patrides's monograph on the subject, *The Phoenix and the Ladder*). It is part of Adam's salvation thus to discover hope as he contemplates God's power as it works out purposefully in history.

[144]The sin is now being considered as a crime (or a complex of criminal acts) either against nature or against future generations who will be subject to mortality as a result of the disobedience of Adam and Eve.

[145]The word "sin" is not in *1674,* but is necessary for meter, as Fletcher points out. "Sinned thy sin" is a biblical idiom, as in Exodus 32.30, "Ye have sinned a great sin."

[146]Part of the field is plowable (arable) land and part is already under cultivation (tilth), having produced the sheaves that are being gathered. "Tilth" may carry the meaning "crop" or "harvest" (*OED* 3). A second part of the field is laid aside for the sheep pens.

[147]The reaper is sweaty as a result of the curse on Adam that he and future generations will have to earn their bread by the sweat of their brow (10.205). As a reaper, this man will have just cut down sheaf and ear. The sheaf is unculled because it has not yet been threshed from the ear. Fowler helpfully points out that the laborer—Cain—is anonymous because Adam should not be told which of his sons will turn out to be the murderer of the other (11.434n).

[148]The adjective never has negative connotations in Milton's poetry. Raphael, for instance, is "heav'nly meek" (8.217), and in *Paradise Regain'd* the "Son of God" is "our Saviour meek" (4.636). Milton evidently took the Beatitude "Blessed are the meek" (Matthew 5.5) quite seriously, though for the Authorized Version's "meek" he preferred the translation *mansuetudo,* in Latin closer to "gentleness" than to "meekness." In *On Christian Doctrine,* Milton contrasts gentleness and placidness with murder, using Cain's murder of Abel as his first example (2.12; Yale 6: 754).

[149]Abel, being meek, gentle, and obedient, follows the prescribed rituals of burnt offerings or the sacrifice of peace offerings as outlined in Leviticus 6.9–14 and 7.16–127, 29–34. The detail of the cleft pieces of wood comes from Abraham's cleaving wood for his burnt offering in Genesis 22.3.

[150]Abel's sacrifice is answered by the customary sign of approval from God, fire from heaven (see, among other examples, Leviticus 9.24).

[151]The rapid igniting flash ("nimble glance," meaning "A sudden movement producing a flash or gleam of light" [*OED* 3]) and the steam indicate God's auspicious gratitude for the sacrifice.

[152]A possessive, not a plural. The "other" is Cain, and his sacrifice is not acceptable because it is not sincere. The Geneva Bible marginalia give the reason for God's rejection of Cain's sacrifice: "Because he was an hypocrite and offred onely for an outwarde shew without sinceritie of heart" (1560 ed; see Genesis 4.5).

That beat out life;[153] he fell, and deadly pale
Groand out his Soul with gushing bloud effus'd.
Much at that sight was *Adam* in his heart
Dismai'd, and thus in haste to th' Angel cri'd.
   O Teacher, some great mischief[154] hath befall'n   450
To that meek man, who well had sacrific'd;
Is Pietie thus and pure Devotion paid?
   T' whom *Michael* thus, hee also mov'd,[155] repli'd.
These two are Brethren, *Adam,* and to come
Out of thy loyns; th' unjust the just hath slain,   455
For° envie that his Brothers Offering found   OUT OF
From Heav'n acceptance; but the bloodie Fact°   CRIME
Will be aveng'd, and th' others Faith approv'd
Loose no reward,[156] though here thou see him die,
Rowling in dust and gore. To which our Sire.   460
   Alas, both for the deed and for the cause!
But have I now seen Death? Is this the way
I must return to native dust? O sight
Of terrour, foul and ugly to behold,
Horrid to think, how horrible to feel!   465
   To whom thus *Michael.* Death thou hast seen
In his first shape on man; but many shapes
Of Death, and many are the wayes that lead
To his grim Cave,[157] all dismal; yet to sense
More terrible at th' entrance then within.   470
Some, as thou saw'st, by violent stroke shall die,
By Fire, Flood, Famin, by Intemperance more
In Meats and Drinks, which on the Earth shall bring
Diseases dire, of which a monstrous crew
Before thee shall appear; that thou mayst know   475
What miserie th' inabstinence[158] of *Eve*
Shall bring on men. Immediately a place
Before his eyes appeard, sad, noysom, dark,
A Lazar-house[159] it seemd, wherein were laid
Numbers of all diseas'd, all maladies   480
Of gastly Spasm, or racking torture, qualmes
Of heart-sick Agonie, all feavorous kinds,

---

[153]Genesis does not specify a weapon in Cain's murder of Abel, though Milton and Cowley (*Davideis* 1.16n) concluded independently that a stone would have been appropriate (since the murder weapon could then be used as tombstone).

[154]A stronger word in the seventeenth century than now, meaning "evil plight" (*OED* 1.a) and often being applied to demonic behavior. The word also had legal implications: "A condition in which a person suffers a wrong" (*OED* 3.a), a sense pertinent here, since Cain's is the first lawless deed reported after the Fall.

[155]The fact that Michael is moved with emotion at seeing the murder of Abel may be an indication that the scene is tragic, but it also indicates that in the midst of Michael's stern and warlike demeanor is deep sympathy for the human condition: he is also the "gentle Angel" of 421 above. Compare the angelic pity expressed in 10.25.

[156]The faith of Abel, of course, will be rewarded in Heaven, as with Lycidas, who is awarded fame not on Earth but in Heaven (84).

[157]Access to Vergil's Avernus, a river thought to lead to the underworld, is through a "deep, deep cave," "its mouth enormously gaping" (*Aeneid* 6.237; trans. Lewis). The word "dismal" not only means "dreadful" or "derived from evil days" (*dies mali*): Milton may also be using the buried pun in "dis" and "Dis" as an alternative Greek name for Hades.

[158]Eve is the first to eat the wrong food greedily (no extra blame is applied here, since Adam shortly follows suit). Milton seems to have coined the word *inabstinence*, since the first use of the word recorded in the *OED* was this instance.

[159]A hospital which was apt to be devoted to the care of lepers, though more broadly permitted to all those with infectious diseases—named for Lazarus, the beggar ill from some loathsome disease named in Luke 16.20.

Convulsions, Epilepsies, fierce Catarrhs,[160]
Intestin Stone and Ulcer, Colic pangs,[161]
Dæmoniac Phrenzie,[162] moaping Melancholie   485
And Moon-struck madness,[163] pining Atrophie,[164]
Marasmus,[165] and wide-wasting Pestilence,[166]
Dropsies,[167] and Asthma's, and Joint-racking Rheums.[168]
Dire was the tossing, deep the groans, despair
Tended the sick busiest from Couch to Couch;[169]   490
And over them triumphant Death his Dart
Shook, but delaid to strike, though oft invok't
With vows,[170] as thir chief good, and final hope.
Sight so deform what heart of Rock could long
Drie-ey'd behold? *Adam* could not, but wept,   495
Though not of Woman born; compassion quell'd
His best of Man,[171] and gave him up to tears
A space, till firmer thoughts restraind excess,
And scarce recovering words his plaint renew'd.
    O miserable Mankind, to what fall   500
Degraded, to what wretched state reserv'd!
Better end heer unborn.[172] Why is life giv'n
To be thus wrested from us? rather why
Obtruded° on us thus? who if we knew   FORCED
What we receive, would either not accept   505
Life offer'd, or soon beg to lay it down,
Glad to be so dismist in peace. Can thus
Th' Image of God[173] in man created once
So goodly and erect, though faultie since,
To such unsightly sufferings be debas't   510

---

[160]Diseases characterized by congestion, violent coughs, generation of fluids, and spitting.

[161]The intense pangs of colic are more noted today in infants, but Milton's disease is not age-specific. Lines 485–87 are lacking in *1667*. One can only speculate why Milton added more diseases to his dismal catalogue: perhaps (and this is only conjecture) he had encountered more himself between 1667 and 1674.

[162]A mania, dementia, or psychosis caused by demonic possession.

[163]Melancholy as a mental illness would be characterized by its sympathy with the waxing and waning moon (as in lunacy or the state of being "moon-struck") and its moping about or deep manic mood-swings into depression or elation. The moon was believed to operate on the brain, which was thought to be watery and thus comparable to the tides. For the definition of melancholy as a disease, see Robert Burton, *Anatomy of Melancholy*, ed. Thomas C. Faulkner et al. (2 vols.; Oxford: Clarendon, 1989): 1.1.3.1 and compare Ferrand.

[164]A wasting away of limbs or vital organs caused by depression, akin to modern anorexia. Milton may want us to think of the disease as psychogenic or in this case brought about by sinful pining.

[165]Another kind of atrophy due to complete lack of nourishment.

[166]As with the bubonic plague or any large-scale epidemic disease that caused large percentages of fatalities in those ill with the disease.

[167]Diseases characterized by excessive fluid levels in the body, as with edemas or ascites (excess fluids in body cavities). Excess drinking or alcoholism was supposed, quite rightly, to cause dropsy. When Donne satirizes the "spungie hydroptique Dutch" ("On His Mistress" 42, ed. Gardner), he is referring to their supposed wholesale alcoholism.

[168]Rheumatism or rheumatoid arthritis, which Milton might have associated with the gout which afflicted him in his later years (Parker, *Milton* 1: 638–39).

[169]Instead of nurse or doctor, Despair tends the sick, visiting each ill person, until all beg for Death's dart to finish them off quickly (see the illustration at Book 2, in which Death's dart is recognizable as a hand-propelled arrow, and compare 2.672).

[170]Death is often invoked in classical literature, from Sophocles, *Philoctetes* 797–98, through Horace, *Odes* 2.18.38–40 and Pliny, *Natural History* 7.1.167.

[171]Compassion here is proverbially associated with women's tears, which men were not supposed to shed, since irrational hysteria was supposed to have been provoked by vapors rising from the uterus. Babb outlines the way men were supposed to react emotionally in the seventeenth century, "A man who allows his emotions to overrule his reasonable will sacrifices his freedom and his virtue" (47), though Milton was certainly aware of the irony in the image of men "normally" lacking compassion and thus not having the ability to cry, especially having called attention to the angel Michael's being moved by the tragedy of Cain and Abel (at 453 above).

[172]Not the proper response, since Milton viewed the cause of suicide as "a perverse hatred of oneself" (*On Christian Doctrine* 2.8; Yale 6: 719).

[173]For Milton, the image of God remained at least a vestige in humankind: " . . . it cannot be denied that some traces of the divine image still remain in us, which are not wholly extinguished by this spiritual death" (*On Christian Doctrine* 1.12; Yale 6: 396). But Michael reminds Adam that the more humans sin, the more God's image forsakes them. An obvious parallel is the brutish groveling of demonic serpents (10.538–45).

Under inhuman pains? Why should not Man,
Retaining still Divine similitude
In part, from such deformities be free,
And for his Makers Image sake[174] exempt?
    Thir Makers Image, answerd *Michael,* then   515
Forsook them, when themselves they villifi'd[175]
To serve ungovern'd appetite, and took
His Image whom they serv'd, a brutish vice,
Inductive[176] mainly to the sin of *Eve.*
Therefore so abject is thir punishment,   520
Disfiguring not Gods likeness, but thir own,
Or if his likeness, by themselves defac't
While they pervert pure Natures healthful rules
To loathsom sickness, worthily, since they
Gods Image did not reverence in themselves.   525
    I yield[177] it just, said *Adam,* and submit.
But is there yet no other way, besides
These painful passages,° how we may come
To Death, and mix with our connatural dust?
    There is, said *Michael,* if thou well observe   530
The rule of not too much,[178] by temperance taught
In what thou eatst and drinkst, seeking from thence
Due nourishment, not gluttonous delight,
Till many years over thy head return:[179]
So maist thou live, till like ripe Fruit thou drop   535
Into thy Mothers lap,[180] or be with ease
Gatherd, not harshly pluckt, for death mature*:*
This is old age; but then thou must outlive
Thy youth, thy strength, thy beauty, which will change
To witherd weak and gray; thy Senses then   540
Obtuse, all taste of pleasure must forgoe,
To what thou hast, and for the Aire of youth
Hopeful and cheerful,[181] in thy blood will reigne
A melancholly damp of cold and dry
To weigh[182] thy Spirits down, and last consume   545
The Balme[183] of Life. To whom our Ancestor.

THE VARIOUS WAYS OF DYING

---

[174]Supply "be."

[175]Lowered themselves to a vile position, socially and morally.

[176]Leading toward or giving rise to (*OED* 1).

[177]The "yeild" of *1667* may represent Milton's preferred spelling.

[178]Not just a Christian axiom, the "rule of not too much"— sometimes paraphrased "all things in moderation"—had great appeal for Milton: "The virtue which regulates our appetite for the pleasures of the flesh is called TEMPERANCE," which also "includes sobriety and chastity, modesty and decency" (*Christian Doctrine* 2.9; Yale 6: 724).

[179]In other words, until many revolutions of the earth have occurred, with the years pictured as if they were astral bodies marking time. Compare "many moons ago" or "many happy returns of the day."

[180]A pleasant picture of ripe old age. Death is a fall like that of ripe fruit into the lap of Mother Earth. Shoaf writes about the metaphor that " . . . it *is* what Adam can expect: he will die, his old significance will die, into a new significance, a new life" (47). The image seems a beautiful compensation for someone who has fallen (by eating fruit!) but then has learned his lesson and repented. Parker's comment on Milton's death might be pertinent here: "Death, when it came to this man, would be the end of a song" (1: 639).

[181]The humor prevalent in youth, the sanguine or hopeful and airy humor, will be replaced in age by the morbid melancholy, associated with "damps" or "noxious exhalations" (*OED damp* as adjective, 1). A damp is also a stupor (*OED* 4) or a state of mental depression (*OED* 5). It should also be pointed out that melancholy damps were indeed "cold and dry"; they were in no way damp in the modern sense of "moist."

[182]The "waigh" of *1667* may represent Milton's spelling preference.

[183]The balm or balsam of life would be the last bit of vital essence, in alchemical usage "A healthful preservative essence, of oily and softly penetrative nature, conceived by Paracelsus to exist in all organic bodies" (*OED* 4 *balsam*).

    Henceforth I flie not Death, nor would prolong
Life much, bent rather how I may be quit°
Fairest and easiest of this combrous° charge,
Which I must keep till my appointed day   550
Of rendring up, and patiently attend
My dissolution.[184] *Michael* repli'd.[185]
    Nor love thy Life, nor hate; but what thou livst
Live well, how long or short permit[186] to Heav'n:
And now prepare thee for another sight.   555
    He lookd and saw a spacious Plaine, whereon
Were Tents of various hue;[187] by some were herds
Of Cattel grazing: others, whence the sound
Of Instruments that made melodious chime
Was heard, of Harp and Organ; and who moovd   560
Thir stops and chords was seen: his volant° touch
Instinct°[188] through all proportions[189] low and high
Fled[190] and pursu'd transverse the resonant fugue.
In other part stood one who at the Forge
Labouring, two massie° clods of Iron and Brass   565
Had melted (whether found where casual° fire
Had wasted woods on Mountain or in Vale,
Down to the veins of Earth, thence gliding hot
To som Caves mouth, or whether washt by stream
From underground) the liquid Ore he dreind   570
Into fit moulds prepar'd; from which he formd
First his own Tooles; then, what might else be wrought
Fusil° or grav'n in mettle. After these,
But on the hether° side a different sort
From the high neighbouring Hills, which was thir Seat,   575
Down to the Plain descended: by thir guise
Just men they seemd,[191] and all thir study bent
To worship God aright, and know his works

             PARDONED, ABSOLVED
             CUMBERSOME

             NIMBLE, FLYING
             IMPELLED

             MASSIVE, SOLID
             ACCIDENTAL

             CAST, MOLDED
             HITHER, NEARER

---

[184]Probably "Termination of life; death, decease. Variously understood as 'departure or release from life,' 'separation of the soul from the body,' and 'disintegration of the body'" (*OED* 8).

[185]The text of *1667* reads "*Michael* to him repli'd"; but *1674* has a comma after "*Michael* repli'd," which is an obvious error. The words "and patiently attend / My dissolution" are omitted in *1667*. Adam has not quite got it right yet: his over-willing acceptance of death is corrected by Michael's next statement.

[186]The idiom "permit to" means "To ... allow to pass, out of one's own ... power," here used with an indirect object (*OED* II.4, citing this instance). Adam should, in other words, allow the decision for his life or death to pass into the hands of Heaven.

[187]This vision, the third, seems at first to be a positive one, both to Adam and to the reader, but the tents here pictured will become the tents of wickedness, and the arts here practiced will become the arts that polish life. Adam's eyes and ears seduce him with pleasure; as he recently was seduced by the beauty of Eve, he is once again guilty of concupiscence or potentially evil desire. That the process is reiterated throughout *Paradise Lost* is testified by the whole of Stanley Fish's *Surpris'd by Sin.*

[188]Satan's motion, when he is in flight and propelled by a lightning blast, is "Instinct with Fire and Nitre" (2.937), although at that point "Instinct" seems to mean "instilled."

[189]In musical usage of Milton's time, proportion meant "arrangement according to mathematical balance" and was connected with a Pythagorean system of mathematically arranged harmonic scales, " . . . the system of time signatures which indicate proportional alteration of note values . . . " (*The Norton/Grove Concise Encyclopedia of Music,* ed. Stanley Sadie [New York: Norton, 1988]).

[190]Since the word fugue is built on Latin *fugare,* "to flee," the verb "Fled" is apt, but it also suggests the flight of the guilty. The process of fleeing and pursuing suggests a fallen hunting scene rather than unfallen peaceful coexistence.

[191]The key words for interpretation here are "guise" and "seemd." The men are the "Sons of Seth," or "Sethites," not the descendants of Cain. Milton used Genesis 6.2—"the sons of God saw that the daughters of men were beautiful, and took them . . . "—to illustrate his own belief that "Love is to be controlled so that we love most the things which are most worthy of love, and hate most the things which are most hateful" (*On Christian Doctrine* 2.8; Yale 6: 720). Behind his use of the passage was a long interpretive tradition concerning the "sons of God" (read as angels) and the "daughters of men" (read as seductresses desiring miscegenation between the divine and human). The unholy union of the sons of God and daughters of men produced what might now be called artistes or false artisans. For an explanation of the tradition, see Williams, *Common Expositor.*

Not hid, nor those things last[192] which might preserve
Freedom and Peace to men: they on the Plain   580
Long had not walkt, when from the Tents behold
A Beavie of fair Women, richly gay
In Gems and wanton dress; to the Harp they sung
Soft amorous Ditties, and in dance came on:
The Men though grave, ey'd them, and let thir eyes   585
Rove without rein, till in the amorous Net
Fast caught, they lik'd, and each his liking chose;
And now of love they treat° till th' Eevning Star[193]   CONCERN THEMSELVES
Loves Harbinger appeerd; then all in heat[194]
They light the Nuptial Torch, and bid invoke   590
Hymen, then first to marriage Rites invok't;
With Feast and Musick all the Tents resound.
Such happy interview and fair event
Of love and youth not lost, Songs, Garlands, Flours,
And charming Symphonies[195] attach'd° the heart   SEIZED   595
Of *Adam,* soon enclin'd to admit delight,
The bent° of Nature; which he thus express'd.   INCLINATION

    True opener[196] of mine eyes, prime Angel blest,
Much better seems this Vision, and more hope
Of peaceful dayes portends, then those two past;   600
Those were of hate and death, or pain much worse,
Here Nature seems fulfilld in all her ends.[197]

    To whom thus *Michael.* Judg not what is best
By pleasure, though to Nature seeming meet,°   PROPER
Created, as thou art, to nobler end   605
Holie and pure, conformitie divine.
Those Tents thou sawst so pleasant, were the Tents
Of wickedness,[198] wherein shall dwell his Race
Who slew his Brother; studious they appere
Of Arts[199] that polish Life, Inventers rare,   610
Unmindful of thir Maker, though his Spirit
Taught them, but they his gifts acknowledg'd none.
Yet they a beauteous ofspring shall beget;
For that fair femal Troop thou sawst, that seemd
Of Goddesses, so blithe, so smooth, so gay,   615
Yet empty of all good wherein consists

---

[192]The text in *1667* reads "lost," which was corrected in the *1668 Errata* list.

[193]Hesperus or Venus (planets were treated as stars in seventeenth-century cosmologies). At 8.519, the nightingale not only sings wedding hymns but it "bid[s] haste the Eevning Starr." As Fowler points out (11.588–89n), however, nowhere before the Fall is the pagan Hymen, god of marriage, invoked on behalf of Adam and Eve: Milton's "first . . . invok't" calls attention to the encroaching paganism.

[194]The animal nature of the men's lust is emphasized, since they are, like animals, "in heat." The phrase "youth not lost" may offer one reason for Adam to react positively, since he has been told by Michael (538–39 above) that he will lose his youth as a result of the Fall.

[195]The operative word here may be "charming," since for Milton the word always carries at least the faint odor of witchcraft. Symphonies were vocal or orchestral works in harmony or part-songs, not extended orchestral works.

[196]As opposed to the false "opener," the Tree of Knowledge of Good and Evil, which Eve had praised in 9.875.

[197]Adam is wrong-headed again, and, since his nature inclines toward pleasure, he accepts the "goodness" of the scene uncritically (or immorally). Michael will caution him not to treat pleasure as the greatest good and not to judge by appearances (outsides) again.

[198]Probably derived from Psalm 84.10: "I had rather be a doorkeeper in the house of my God, than to dwell in the tents of wickedness."

[199]Milton generally uses the words *art* and *artist* negatively, as if both were allied more closely than they are today with artifice and artisan. Here the phrase "studious . . . / Of Arts that polish Life" seems to define "artist" as in *OED* IV.9: "One who practices artifice, stratagem, or cunning contrivance; a schemer, a contriver." The Devil, by this definition, was described by Bishop Hall as cited in the *OED* as "a most skillfull Artist." See my "Art, Artists, Galileo and Concordances."

Womans domestic honour and chief praise;
Bred onely and completed° to the taste   POLISHED
Of lustful appetence,° to sing, to dance,   APPETITE
To dress, and troule the Tongue,²⁰⁰ and roule the Eye.   620
To these that sober Race of Men, whose lives
Religious titl'd them the Sons of God,²⁰¹
Shall yield²⁰² up all thir virtue, all thir fame
Ignobly, to the traines²⁰³ and to the smiles
Of these fair Atheists,²⁰⁴ and now swim in joy,   625
(Erelong° to swim at large) and laugh; for which   BEFORE LONG
The world erelong a world of tears must weepe.
　　To whom thus *Adam* of short joy bereft.
O pittie and shame, that they who to live well
Enterd so faire,²⁰⁵ should turn aside to tread   630
Paths indirect, or in the mid way faint!
But still I see the tenor of Mans woe
Holds on the same, from Woman to begin.²⁰⁶
　　From Mans effeminate slackness²⁰⁷ it begins,
Said th' Angel, who should better hold his place   635
By wisdome, and superiour gifts receav'd.
But now prepare thee for another Scene.
　　He lookd and saw wide Territorie spred
Before him, Towns, and rural works between,
Cities of Men with lofty Gates and Towrs,   640
Concours in Arms,²⁰⁸ fierce Faces threatning Warr,
Giants of mightie Bone, and bould emprise;²⁰⁹
Part wield thir Arms, part courb²¹⁰ the foaming Steed,
Single or in Array of Battel rang'd

---

²⁰⁰"To move (the tongue) volubly" (*OED* II.4.b, citing this as the first instance). The verb also carries the idea of wagging the tongue or even whirling it; the gesture is analogous with rolling the eyes.

²⁰¹"And it came to pass, when men began to multiply on the face of the earth, and daughters were born unto them, That the sons of God saw the daughters of men that they were fair; and they took them wives of all which they chose" (Genesis 6.1–2). The Geneva Bible glossed "sons of God" as "the children of the godlie, which began to degenerate," and "daughters of men" as "Those that came of wicked parents as of Kain" (1560 ed.).

²⁰²Again the *1674* compositor does not follow the spelling of *1667*, "yeild," one of the few instances when at least one of the compositors of the second edition altered his copy text.

²⁰³Here the word seems to mean "attractive traps," and it may be derived from the meaning "A drag-net, a seine" (*OED* 20.c). Compare "venereal trains" in *Samson Agonistes*, 533. In *Comus* 151, in an emendation, Milton replaces "traines" with "charmes."

²⁰⁴If the bevy of women is a group of sycophants worshiping the pagan god Hymen, they are atheists from a Christian point of view. The phrase "swim in joy," though proverbial, is deeply sardonic, and looks forward to the destruction of most of the human race in the Flood. The tears that future generations will shed will also add up to a world of tears.

²⁰⁵The image is one of a journey into a pleasant place: the men enter agreeably ("faire" is used as an adverb, *OED* 1) or prosperously (*OED* 6), but turn aside (the English translation of transgress) to follow indirect paths or, if they remained in the midway, they became faint-hearted. Adam's image is built on that of life as a highway.

²⁰⁶Adam is wrong again, this time to blame women in a standard antifeminist cliché—the false etymology that "woman" is derived from "woe"+ "man." Michael is very quick to blame Adam instead, because of his weakness for feminine beauty.

²⁰⁷Michael charges Adam with allowing the weakness supposedly characteristic of women to cause him to be slack. When he abrogated his male responsibility to guard and protect the woman, he himself was guilty of "effeminate slackness." Notice that what would have enabled Adam to "hold his place" would have been the wisdom that is higher than sexuality and the "superiour gifts" that men were supposed to have been given to reinforce their authority and protective role with respect to women. Compare Adam's "superior Love" (4.499) and Eve's realization that "beauty is excelld by manly grace / And wisdom, which alone is truly fair" (4.490–91).

²⁰⁸Probably soldiers simulating combat, since at this point the faces are only "threatning." "Concours" has the sense of "hostile encounter" (*OED* 1.b, citing this instance).

²⁰⁹The giants are at least associated with the "giants in the earth" of Genesis 6, presumed offspring of the "sons of God" and the "daughters of men." The chivalric words "emprise" ("bold deed in arms") and "Tournament" (652 below) may associate the giants satirically with the exaggerated heroism of Renaissance romantic epics. The giants of mighty bone might indeed be boneheads.

²¹⁰A technical term from horsemanship, since one would rein in or curb the horse by means of the bit in its mouth. The horses ("steeds" as in romantic epic) are foaming because they are overheated by exertion in battle. With horses heavily exercised, perspiration is expressed as foam.

Both Horse and Foot,[211] nor idely mustring stood;   645
One way a Band select from forage drives
A herd of Beeves, faire Oxen and faire Kine
From a fat° Meddow ground; or fleecy Flock,   FERTILE
Ewes and thir bleating Lambs over the Plaine,
Thir Bootie; scarce with Life the Shepherds flye,   650
But call in[212] aide, which makes[213] a bloody Fray;
With cruel Tournament the Squadrons joine;
Where Cattle[214] pastur'd late, now scatterd lies
With Carcasses and Arms th' ensanguind[215] Field
Deserted: Others to a Citie strong   655
Lay Seige, encampt; by Batterie, Scale, and Mine,
Assaulting;[216] others from the wall defend
With Dart and Jav'lin,[217] Stones and sulfurous Fire;
On each hand slaughter and gigantic deeds.
In other part the scepter'd Haralds call   660
To Council in the Citie Gates:[218] anon°   SOON
Grey-headed men and grave, with Warriours mixt,
Assemble, and Harangues[219] are heard, but soon
In factious opposition, till at last
Of middle Age one rising,[220] eminent   665
In wise deport, spake much of Right and Wrong,
Of Justice, of Religion, Truth and Peace,
And Judgment from above: him old and young
Exploded[221] and had seiz'd with violent hands,
Had not a Cloud descending snatch'd him thence   670

---

[211]Both cavalry and infantry or foot soldiers. The term "muster" is military usage for "to assemble under command." Here the soldiers are purposefully gathered to remove their booty—sheep and cattle—but the shepherds being robbed are crying for aid as they run away. Plundering is of course one of the least heroic actions of warfare.

[212]The two words "call in" were printed as one in *1674*.

[213]The word was printed "tacks" in *1667*. The printer or Milton may have ordered a change here from the less familiar "tacks" (tack was—among other senses—a military verb meaning "join in battle") to the more familiar "makes," but the verb form of tack was not in common use. Milton's usage of the verb tack is not documented in the *OED*. As Fletcher points out, tack also appears as a noun in *Of Reformation* (Yale 1: 530). Shawcross allows "tacks" to stand (perhaps following Adams's argument that "tacks" is idiomatic [99]), as did Darbishire and Beeching. Bush, Hughes, Fowler, Elledge, and Campbell all choose "makes." Despite the argument among bibliographers that the less familiar usage is more apt to be ignorantly corrected by a compositor, I believe that "makes" makes more sense and is the better reading.

[214]The spelling of *1667*, "Cattel," has been altered to "Cattle." The spelling in the first edition may represent Milton's preference. Shawcross assumes so and admits "Cattel" silently.

[215]The first instance of the word *ensanguined* (meaning "bloodied") recorded in the *OED*.

[216]Three standard military procedures used in assault or siege: the firing of ordnance ("Batterie"), the scaling of walls, and the undermining of fortifications (see *Henry V* 3.2.61).

[217]The distinction is between short spear and long, apparently, although dart could specify "arrow" as well as "pointed missiles in general, including arrows" (*OED* 1).

[218]Councils were often held and judges often sat at city gates in the Old Testament (Genesis 34.20; 2 Samuel 19.8; Jeremiah 38.7).

[219]Originally a speech given to any assembly, but the word came to mean a tirade or at least a pompous public utterance (*OED* 1.a).

[220]Enoch is the man "Of middle Age," an example of the "one just man" in the midst of multitudes of wrongdoers. Enoch's lifespan was 365 years (Genesis 5.23), less than half of that assigned to most patriarchs, when he was translated by God to Heaven. "As to inquire where he became [when God 'toke him away'], is mere curiositie," according to the Geneva Bible marginalia (1560 ed.). Though the story of Enoch was popular in legend and visual art, Milton probably drew most of his narrative from passages in the apocryphal Book of Enoch, to which he would have had access only through quotations of fragments introduced into biblical commentary. Enoch 14.8, for instance, describes the translation of Enoch from his own point of view: " . . . clouds invited me and a mist summoned me, and the course of the stars and the lightnings sped and hastened me, and the winds in the vision caused me to fly and lifted me upward, and bore me into heaven" (R. H. Charles, ed., *The Apocrypha and Pseudepigrapha of the Old Testament* [Oxford: Oxford UP, 1913]). See Hebrews 11.5 for an allusion to Enoch being translated "by faith" and Jude 14 for a reference to Enoch as prophet of the Second Coming. Milton takes the idea of "Let us now commende the famous men" from the often-quoted passage in the apocryphal Book of Ecclesiasticus 44, which commends Enoch, Noah, and Abraham, among others. That book was included in the apocryphal section of the Geneva Bible, from which I have quoted.

[221]"To drive off the stage by hooting" is the translation of the Latin verb *explodere*. The comma here in *1667* may be the better reading, though no modern editors I know of retain it.

Unseen amid the throng: so violence
Proceeded, and Oppression, and Sword-Law
Through all the Plain, and refuge none was found.
Adam was all in tears, and to his guide
Lamenting turnd full sad; O what are these,   675
Deaths Ministers, not Men, who thus deal Death
Inhumanly to men, and multiply
Ten thousandfould the sin of him who slew
His Brother; for of whom such massacher
Make they but of thir Brethren, men of men?   680
But who was that Just Man, whom had not Heav'n
Rescu'd, had in his Righteousness bin lost?
    To whom thus *Michael*. These are the product
Of those ill-mated[222] Marriages thou saw'st:
Where good with bad were matcht, who of themselves   685
Abhor to joyn; and by imprudence mixt,
Produce prodigious Births of bodie or mind.
Such were these Giants, men of high renown;
For in those dayes Might onely shall be admir'd,
And Valour and Heroic Vertu call'd;   690
To overcome in Battle,[223] and subdue
Nations, and bring home spoils with infinite
Man-slaughter, shall be held the highest pitch
Of human Glorie, and for Glorie done
Of triumph, to be styl'd great Conquerours,   695
Patrons of Mankind, Gods, and Sons of Gods,
Destroyers rightlier call'd and Plagues of men.[224]
Thus Fame shall be atchiev'd, renown on Earth,
And what most merits fame in silence hid.
But hee the seventh from thee,[225] whom thou beheldst   700
The onely righteous in a World perverse,[226]
And therefore hated, therefore so beset
With Foes for daring single to be just,
And utter odious Truth, that God would come
To judge them with his Saints: Him the most High   705
Rapt in a balmie Cloud with winged Steeds
Did, as thou sawst, receave, to walk with God
High in Salvation and the Climes of bliss,
Exempt from Death;[227] to shew thee what reward

---

[222]I have restored the "ill-mated" of *1667* as opposed to the unhyphenated form of *1674*. The ill-mated marriages of the sons of God and daughters of men were also treated at length in Enoch 6 and 7.

[223]The compositor again changes the spelling from *1667* "Battel."

[224]Milton's interpretation of Genesis 6.4–5: "There were giants in the earth in those days; and also after that, when the sons of God came in unto the daughters of men, and they bare children to them, the same became mighty men which were of old, men of renown. And God saw that the wickedness of man was great in the earth, and that every imagination of the thoughts of his heart was only evil continually."

[225]Enoch is called the "seventh from Adam" (the seventh in line of descent) in Jude 14.

[226]Resembling the "Universe of death," where "Nature breeds, / Perverse" (2.622, 624–25), the world of the fallen angels, against which only Abdiel holds out.

[227]The clouds may be associated with the translation of Elijah (2 Kings 2.11), who in turn was often associated with Enoch. Perhaps the end of the *Epitaphium Damonis*, with its vision of the apotheosis of Damon in *aethera purus* (204) or the pure air of Heaven surrounded by saints according to Revelation 14.4, should be read as partial commentary on "balmie Cloud." Enoch's translation was designed, according to the editors of the Geneva Bible, "To shewe that there was a better life prepared, & to be a testimonie of the immortalitie of souls & bodies" (gloss to Genesis 5.24; 1560 ed.). Genesis 5.24 describes Enoch as having "walked with God."

Awaits the good, the rest what punishment;[228]   710
Which now direct thine eyes and soon behold.
     He look'd, and saw the face of things quite chang'd,
The brazen Throat of Warr[229] had ceast to roar,
All now was turn'd to jollitie and game,
To luxurie and riot, feast and dance,[230]   715
Marrying or prostituting, as befell,
Rape or Adulterie, where passing faire[231]
Allurd them; thence from Cups to civil Broiles.[232]
At length a Reverend Sire[233] among them came,
And of thir doings great dislike declar'd,   720
And testifi'd against thir wayes; hee oft
Frequented[234] thir Assemblies, whereso° met,   WHERESOEVER
Triumphs or Festivals, and to them preachd
Conversion and Repentance, as to Souls
In Prison[235] under Judgements imminent: 725
But all in vain: which when he saw, he ceas'd
Contending, and remov'd his Tents farr off;
Then from the Mountain hewing Timber tall,
Began to build a Vessel of huge bulk,[236]
Measur'd by Cubit, length, and breadth, and highth,   730
Smeard round with Pitch, and in the side a dore
Contriv'd, and of provisions laid in large
For Man and Beast: when loe a wonder strange![237]
Of every Beast, and Bird, and Insect[238] small
Came seavens, and pairs,[239] and enterd in, as taught   735
Thir order:[240] last the Sire, and his three Sons
With thir four Wives; and God made fast the dore.[241]
Meanwhile the Southwind rose, and with black wings
Wide hovering, all the Clouds together drove

---

[228]The line in *1674* ends with an incorrect question mark, a choice which probably represents foul case, since the two marks of punctuation—the semicolon of *1667* and the exclamation point of *1674*—resemble one another when viewed from a distance.

[229]The throat of war is brazen most probably because war is heralded by the sounds of trumpets and other brass instruments, though shields and spears are also brazen in *Samson Agonistes* 132.

[230]All the terms in the last two lines have to do with licentious sexual behavior. The words jollity, luxury (licentiousness), and riot almost always have negative overtones in Milton's usage.

[231]The damsel who is surpassing fair or "passing faire" would have been a stock feature of romantic epic.

[232]What in modern terms would be called "spouse abuse," the sad process described is from drunkenness (as in "in his cups") to violence in the home ("civil Broiles") might indicate everything from domestic violence to civil war.

[233]Noah, who is the second of the just men presented. Milton follows closely the account of the Flood in Genesis 6.9–9.17. Luke 17.27 quotes Jesus as comparing present wicked times with the time before the Flood: "They did eat, they drank, they married wives, they were given in marriage, until the day that Noe entered into the ark, and the flood came, and destroyed them all." Josephus's *Antiquities* 1.3.1 is Milton's source for the detail of Noah's accusation of the rioters. The story of the Flood, the loss of a world through sin, provides an obvious echo of the story of the Fall; Noah's righteousness helps balance the sin of Adam.

[234]Presumably accented on the second syllable.

[235]As Christ will be said to have "preached unto the spirits in prison" (1 Peter 3.19). Noah was widely interpreted as a "type" of Christ.

[236]Interpreting the story of the Flood, the author of Hebrews wrote: "By faith Noah, being warned of God of things not seen as yet, moved with fear, prepared an ark to the saving of his house; by the which he condemned the world, and became heir of the righteousness which is by faith" (11.7).

[237]Though the punctuation appears to be a capital "I" in *1674*, the exclamation point of *1667* seems intended.

[238]As Fowler points out (11.734n), Milton's inclusion of insects on the Ark may represent what was in his time an up-to-date addition, since traditional commentary left insects off the Ark on the grounds that they were supposed to be generated spontaneously when heat is applied to mud or they were supposed to arise spontaneously out of putrefying meat (see *Hamlet* 2.2.181).

[239]God instructs Noah which kinds and numbers of each beast should be taken into the Ark: "Of every clean beast thou shalt take to thee by sevens, the male and his female: and of beasts that are not clean by two, the male and his female" (Genesis 7.2).

[240]Changed from the semicolon of *1667*, though the change may have no significance.

[241]To the terse comment "the Lord shut him in" of Genesis 7.16, Milton adds the homely detail of God's closing the door of the Ark.

From under Heav'n; the Hills to their supplie°   ASSISTANCE   740
Vapour, and Exhalation dusk and moist,²⁴²
Sent up amain;²⁴³ and now the thick'nd Skie
Like a dark Ceeling stood; down rush'd the Rain
Impetuous, and continu'd till the Earth
No more was seen; the floating Vessel swum   745
Uplifted; and secure with beaked prow
Rode tilting o're the Waves, all dwellings else
Flood overwhelmd, and them with all thir pomp
Deep under water rould; Sea cover'd Sea,
Sea without shoar;²⁴⁴ and in thir Palaces   750
Where luxurie late reign'd, Sea-monsters whelp'd
And stabl'd;²⁴⁵ of Mankind, so numerous late,
All left, in one small bottom swum imbark't.²⁴⁶
How didst thou grieve then, *Adam,* to behold
The end of all thy Ofspring, end so sad,   755
Depopulation; thee another Floud,
Of tears and sorrow a Floud thee also drown'd,
And sunk thee as thy Sons; till gently reard
By th' Angel, on thy feet thou stoodst at last,
Though comfortless, as when a Father mourns   760
His Children, all in view destroyd at once;
And scarce²⁴⁷ to th' Angel utterdst thus thy plaint.
    O Visions ill foreseen! better had I
Liv'd ignorant of future, so had borne
My part of evil onely, each dayes lot   765
Anough to beare;²⁴⁸ those now, that were dispenst°   GIVEN
The burd'n of many Ages, on me light
At once, by my foreknowledge gaining Birth
Abortive, to torment me ere thir being,
With thought that they must be. Let no man seek   770
Henceforth to be foretold what shall befall
Him or his Childern,²⁴⁹ evil he may be sure,
Which neither his foreknowing can prevent,
And hee the future evil shall no less
In apprehension then in substance feel   775
Grievous to bear: but that care now is past,

---

²⁴²"Mist [an "Exhalation" of the earth], dark and moist."

²⁴³A wind comes up from the south, pictured (as on contemporary wind charts) the color of the peoples of Africa, the wind Afer being black and looking somewhat like a cherub, with wings and cheeks puffed with the act of blowing. Milton's description of the Flood is based closely on Ovid's details from the flood of Deucalion and Pyrrha. Hence "the South-wind came out streaming / With dripping wings, and pitch-black darkness veiling / His terrible countenance" (*Metamorphoses* 1.264–66; trans. Humphries). In this account, the south wind squeezes rain out of the clouds.

²⁴⁴Again, Milton closely follows Ovid, with the emulation in this case being just as successful as the glorious original: " . . . everything is ocean, / An ocean with no shore-line" (1.291–92; trans. Humphries).

²⁴⁵The sea monsters—more grotesque and threatening than the normal sea-creatures pictured in Ovid's flood—seem to be mocking the behavior of the dissolute humans they replace. Their children are "whelp'd" (suggesting that they have many litters of offspring) and they stable themselves in palaces. Fowler sees a pun in "stabl'd" as meaning both "lived in a stable" and "stuck in the mud" (*OED* verb 2.2.b, verb 3; 11.738–53n).

²⁴⁶"In one small boat ('bottom') floated, having embarked."

²⁴⁷"Barely, only just" (*OED* B.2), an adverb rather than an adjective.

²⁴⁸Perhaps an echo of Matthew 6.34: "Take therefore no thought for the morrow: for the morrow shall take thought for the things of itself. Sufficient unto the day is the evil thereof."

²⁴⁹Milton's preferred spelling seems to have influenced the printed text in this rare case, since "Children" was printed "Childern" in *1667* and here the *1674* compositor uncharacteristically follows the spelling of his copy text.

Man is not[250] whom to warne:[251] those few escap't
Famin and anguish will at last consume[252]
Wandring that watrie Desert: I had hope
When violence was ceas't, and Warr on Earth,
All would have then gon well, peace would have crownd   780
With length of happy dayes the race of man;
But I was farr deceav'd; for now I see
Peace to corrupt no less then Warr to waste.[253]
How comes it thus? unfould, Celestial Guide,
And whether here the Race of man will end.[254]   785
    To whom thus *Michael*.[255] Those whom last thou sawst
In Triumph and luxurious wealth, are they
First seen in acts of prowess eminent
And great exploits, but of true vertu void;
Who having spilt much blood, and don much waste   790
Subduing Nations, and achievd thereby
Fame in the World, high titles, and rich prey,
Shall change thir course to pleasure, ease, and sloth,
Surfet, and lust, till wantonness and pride
Raise out of friendship hostil deeds in Peace.   795
The conquerd also, and enslav'd by Warr
Shall with thir freedom lost all vertu loose
And fear of God, from whom thir pietie feign'd
In sharp contest[256] of Battel found no aide
Against invaders; therefore coold in zeale   800
Thenceforth shall practice how to live secure,
Worldlie or dissolute, on what thir Lords
Shall leave them to enjoy;[257] for th' Earth shall bear
More then anough, that temperance may be tri'd:
So all shall turn degenerate, all deprav'd,   805
Justice and Temperance, Truth and Faith forgot;
One Man except, the onely Son of light
In a dark Age, against example good,
Against allurement, custom, and a World
Offended;° fearless of reproach and scorn,   810
            SINNED AGAINST
Or violence, hee of thir wicked wayes
Shall them admonish, and before them set
The paths of righteousness, how much more safe,
And full of peace, denouncing° wrauth to come
            PROCLAIMING   815
On thir impenitence; and shall returne
Of them derided, but of God observd

---

[250]Supply "him" or "the person."

[251]"There lives no man who can be warned." Adam believes that Noah and his company will die in the Flood.

[252]Famine and anguish will eventually consume those few who have escaped the Flood.

[253]Complementing "peace hath her victories / No less renown'd then warr" in Milton's Sonnet 16.

[254]There is no punctuation at this point in *1674*; editors supply what seems to have been a non-inking period. The syntax is difficult, but Adam is asking Michael to answer or unfold both the questions "How comes it thus?" and "whether here the Race of man will end[?]"

[255]Though neither of the early editions indents at this point, it was accepted practice to begin a verse paragraph with a new quoted speech, and I have emended correspondingly, as do Hughes, Shawcross, Elledge, and Campbell, but not Orgel or Fowler. The compositor seems to have had some problem between two pages, since "To whom thus *Michael*" begins a new page.

[256]Apparently accented on the second syllable, as seems to be Milton's consistent practice (see 4.872, for instance).

[257]Various editors find topical allusions here to life in England after the Restoration of Charles II in 1660. Milton seems to be castigating his countrymen for lacking the courage of religious convictions expressed publicly during the Interregnum.

The one just Man alive; by his command
Shall build a wondrous Ark, as thou beheldst,
To save himself and houshold from amidst
A World devote to universal rack.°   820
No sooner hee with them of Man and Beast   DESTRUCTION
Select for life shall in the Ark be lodg'd,
And shelterd round, but all the Cataracts[258]
Of Heav'n set open on the Earth shall powre   825
Raine day and night, all fountains of the Deep
Broke up, shall heave the Ocean to usurp
Beyond all bounds, till inundation rise
Above the highest Hills: then shall this Mount
Of Paradise by might of Waves be moovd   830
Out of his place, pushd by the horned floud,[259]
With all his verdure spoil'd, and Trees adrift
Down the great River to the op'ning Gulf,
And there take root an Iland salt and bare,
The haunt of Seales and Orcs,[260] and Sea-mews clang.[261]   835
To teach thee that God attributes to place
No sanctitie, if none be thither brought
By Men who there frequent,[262] or therein dwell.
And now what further shall ensue, behold.

    He lookd, and saw the Ark hull[263] on the floud,   840
Which now abated, for the Clouds were fled,
Drivn by a keen North-winde,[264] that blowing drie
Wrinkl'd the face of Deluge, as decai'd;[265]
And the cleer Sun on his wide watrie Glass[266]
Gaz'd hot, and of the fresh Wave largely drew,   845
As after thirst, which made thir flowing shrink
From standing lake to tripping[267] ebbe, that stole
With soft foot towards the deep, who now had stopt
His Sluces, as the Heav'n his windows shut.[268]
The Ark no more now flotes, but seems on ground   850
Fast on the top of som high mountain fixt.[269]

---

[258]Fowler points out that, though the Authorized Version has "windows"—with a marginal note indicating that that meant "flood-gates"—both the Vulgate and Junius-Tremelius Latin versions have *cataractae* (824–27n).

[259]The headwaters of the Flood become something like a bull, pushing the mountain of Paradise to become an island. Fowler notes that the phrase "horned floud" might be derived not from Vergil's description of the Tiber River (*Aeneid* 8.77) but from similar images in Ben Jonson's plays or William Browne's *Brittania's Pastorals* (2.5; Fowler 829–38n).

[260]Orcs could be various kinds of sea and land monsters, as in Ariosto's *Orlando Furioso* 8.51, where Proteus, a sea-god, in his wrath "sent onshore his orcs and sea-lions and all his watery flock to ravage the sheep and cattle, yes, and the hamlets and farms and those who toiled there" (trans. Waldman). Milton's Satan is metaphorically allied with orcs through his association with Leviathan at 1.201–02, though "orc" should not be read only as "Leviathan."

[261]"Sea-mews" are gulls, their harsh cries a "clang," as at 7.422. The same word was used of the sound of a trumpet (*OED* verb 1, 3).

[262]Apparently accented on the second syllable, as it seems to be in most occurrences in *Paradise Lost* (but see 3.534).

[263]Floating adrift, led by prevailing currents or winds, a nautical term (*OED* verb 2). A ship was said to be "hulling" in the calm before a storm.

[264]Matching the action of the south wind in bringing in the rain and flood, and echoing Ovid, *Metamorphoses* 1.328.

[265]The face of the flood was wrinkled by the action of the wind upon it, as if it were the face of an old person.

[266]The calm surface of the sea has now become a mirror (as in "looking glass") in which the sun can see its clear (not wrinkled) reflection (*OED* 8.c, citing this instance). I disagree with Fowler's conjecture that "Glass" means "drinking vessel" and that the sun is being pictured as scooping up what he drinks (844–46n). Nevertheless, the sun does drink the sea down to abate the flood.

[267]The standing or stable body of water is made to dance or "trip" by the process of displacement: the small amount of water left dances toward the lowest point.

[268]"The fountains also of the deep and the windows of heaven were stopped, and the rain from heaven was restrained" (Genesis 8.2).

[269]Milton carefully avoids localizing the resting place of the Ark as the mountains of Ararat (Genesis 8.4). (If he had done so, the place would have become improperly sacred; humankind would have worshiped the place rather than celebrated the covenant between God and humankind that Milton considered more important.)

And now the tops of Hills as Rocks appeer;
With clamor thence the rapid Currents drive
Towards the retreating Sea thir furious tyde.
Forthwith from out the Arke a Raven flies,   855
And after him, the surer messenger,
A Dove sent forth once and agen[270] to spie[271]
Green Tree or ground whereon his foot may light;
The second time returning, in his Bill
An Olive leafe he brings, pacific signe:°   SIGN OF PEACE   860
Anon drie ground appeers, and from his Arke
The ancient Sire descends with all his Train;
Then with uplifted hands, and eyes devout,
Grateful[272] to Heav'n, over his head beholds
A dewie Cloud, and in the Cloud a Bow   865
Conspicuous with three listed colours gay,[273]
Betok'ning peace from God, and Cov'nant new.
Whereat the heart of *Adam* erst° so sad   PREVIOUSLY
Greatly rejoyc'd, and thus his joy broke forth.
    O thou who[274] future things canst represent   870
As present, Heav'nly instructer, I revive
At this last sight, assur'd that Man shall live
With all the Creatures, and thir seed preserve.
Farr less I now lament for one whole World
Of wicked Sons destroyd, then I rejoyce   875
For one Man found so perfet and so just,
That God voutsafes to raise another World
From him, and all his anger to forget.
But say, what mean those colour'd streaks in Heavn,
Distended[275] as the Brow of God appeas'd,   880
Or serve they as a flourie verge[276] to binde
The fluid skirts of that same watrie Cloud,
Least it again dissolve and showr the Earth?
    To whom th' Archangel. Dextrously thou aim'st;
So willingly doth God remit his Ire,   885
Though late repenting him of Man deprav'd,[277]
Griev'd at his heart, when looking down he saw
The whole Earth fill'd with violence, and all flesh
Corrupting[278] each thir way; yet those remoov'd,
Such grace shall one just Man find in his sight,   890

[handwritten: A BEGINNING NOT AN ENDING]

---

[270]The dove (a better messenger than a raven) released by Noah the first time returned to the Ark, indicating that the flood waters had not abated. Seven days later, Noah released it again, this time the dove made landfall successfully.

[271]Not "spy on" but "espy" or "see," as in "spyglass."

[272]Ricks finds a pun here between the meanings of "grateful," as in "feeling gratitude" and "pleasing" (*Milton's* 114).

[273]The rainbow is the sign of God's covenant with humankind, the agreement never again to "curse the ground" or "smite any more every living thing" (Genesis 8.21; see also 9.8–17). The three primary colors of the rainbow are red, yellow, and blue, they are arranged in lists, or bands, as if they were arranged by military discipline, and the colors are "gay" because they are bright and joyous.

[274]"Who" seems preferable to the "that" of *1667*.

[275]Expanded, rather than being contracted in anger.

[276]Border, as in a flower border which serves to demarcate part of a piece of property; the image of "verge" is matched by "skirts" (as in "outskirts"), which are the fluid borders of the cloud.

[277]The verbs echo those of Genesis 6.6: "And it repented the Lord that he had made man on the earth, and it grieved him at his heart." That sentiment was voiced before "Noah found grace in the eyes of the Lord" (Genesis 6.8).

[278]"The earth also was corrupt before God, and the earth was filled with violence. And God looked upon the earth, and, behold, it was corrupt; for all flesh had corrupted his way upon the earth" (Genesis 6.11–12).

That he relents, not to blot out mankind,
And makes a Covenant never to destroy
The Earth again by flood, nor let the Sea
Surpass his bounds, nor Rain to drown the World
With Man therein or Beast; but when he brings   895
Over the Earth a Cloud, will therein set
His triple-colour'd Bow, whereon to look
And call to mind his Cov'nant: Day and Night,
Seed time and Harvest, Heat and hoary Frost
Shall hold thir course, till fire purge all things new,   900
Both Heav'n and Earth, wherein the just shall dwell.[279]

The End of the Eleventh Book.

---

[279]The image of Judgment Day is appropriately taken from 2 Peter, in which the Flood is remembered as Peter looks forward to "the day of judgment and perdition of ungodly men" (3.7) during "which the heavens shall pass away with a great noise, and the elements shall melt with fervent heat, the earth also and the works that are therein shall be burned up" (3.10). The righteous, however, "look for new heavens and a new earth, wherein dwelleth righteousness" (3.13). In *On Christian Doctrine* Milton discussed "the fourth and last degree of death, namely, eternal death or the punishment of the damned," under which heading "can be included the death of this foul and polluted world itself, that is, its end and conflagration" (1.33; Yale 6: 627). Milton expressed doubt whether the "abolition of the world's substance, or only a change in its qualities" (627) was meant. On the positive side, "Our glorification will be accompanied by the renovation of, and our possession of, heaven and earth and all those creatures in both which may be useful or delightful to us" (632). For the most recent full-length studies dealing with Milton and his contemporaries' attitudes toward the Apocalypse, see Ryken, *Apocalyptic*, and Patrides and Wittreich, eds., *Apocalypse*.

Paradise Lost.

BOOK XII.

THE ARGUMENT.

The Angel Michael *continues from the Flood to relate what shall succeed;*[1] *then, in the mention of* Abraham, *comes by degrees to explain, who that Seed of the Woman shall be, which was promised* Adam *and* Eve *in the Fall; his Incarnation, Death, Resurrection, and Ascension; the state of the Church till his second Coming.* Adam *greatly satisfied and recomforted by these Relations*[2] *and Promises descends the Hill with* Michael; *wakens* Eve, *who all this while had slept, but with gentle dreams compos'd to quietness of mind and submission.*[3] Michael *in either hand leads them out of Paradise, the fiery Sword waving behind them, and the Cherubim taking thir Stations to guard the Place.*[4]

AS one who in his journey bates° at Noone,	ABATES, TEMPORARILY SUSPENDS

AS one who in his journey bates° at Noone,
    Though bent on speed, so heer the Archangel paus'd
    Betwixt the world destroy'd and world restor'd,
    If *Adam* aught perhaps might interpose;[5]
Then with transition sweet new Speech resumes.[6]   5
Thus thou hast seen one World begin and end;
And Man as from a second stock proceed.
Much thou hast yet to see, but I perceave
Thy mortal sight to faile; objects divine
Must needs impaire[7] and wearie human sense: 10
Henceforth what is to com I will relate,
Thou therefore give due audience, and attend.
This second sours of Men, while yet but few,[8]
And while the dread of judgement past remains
Fresh in thir mindes, fearing the Deitie,   15
With some regard to what is just and right
Shall lead thir lives, and multiplie apace,
Labouring the soile, and reaping plenteous crop,

---

[1]"To follow or come *after* in the course of events, . . . come into being subsequently" (*OED* 6.a). Compare " . . . enjoy, till I return, / Short pleasures, for long woes are to succeed" (4.534-35). After the vision of the future up to the time of Noah and the Flood in Book 11, the narrative becomes oral prophecy, another form of divine revelation to humankind. See Hunter, *Descent* 21-30.

[2]Narratives, extended stories.

[3]At 608 below, Adam finds Eve awake and does not have to awaken her.

[4]The text of *1674* has a comma here, which is obviously incorrect; I restore the period of *1667*. Lines 1-5 (of the book proper, not of the Argument) were added in *1674*, allowing Michael a pause in his narrative. Fowler notes, however, that there is no new paragraph at the beginning of this book "to mark the pause in the archangel's journey" (1-5n). In Genesis the flaming sword accompanies the cherubim left behind to guard the east of the Garden of Eden: it "turned every way, to keep the way of the tree of life" (3.24). Milton seems here to allow the sword to threaten Adam and Eve from behind or to warn them against turning back.

[5]Michael pauses, politely, to see if Adam has anything to interject. The noon hour (if the "Noone" in line 1 is more than metaphorical—see Cirillo) may be pivotal again, as it was in the Fall. As the sixth hour of the day, noon provides a turning point from the description of the world destroyed in the Flood and the world as it was restored after the covenant with Noah.

[6]The last book of *1667*, Book 10, numbers the next line 898.

[7]Probably the visions that Michael has offered have been so strong and clear that Adam is exhausted and weakened (using impair as in *OED* 2, "grow . . . weaker") by having beheld them.

[8]The second source of humankind would be the generations issuing from Noah's family, which are of course "yet but few." The text of *1674* has a semicolon here, which probably came from the compositor's misreading a broken comma in *1667*. I have restored the comma.

Corn, wine[9] and oyle; and from the herd or flock,
Oft sacrificing Bullock, Lamb, or Kid,   20
With large Wine-offerings pour'd, and sacred Feast,
Shal spend thir dayes in joy unblam'd, and dwell
Long time° in peace by Families and Tribes   FOR A LONG TIME
Under paternal rule; till one shall rise
Of proud ambitious heart, who not content   25
With fair equalitie, fraternal state,
Will arrogate Dominion undeserv'd
Over his brethren, and quite dispossess
Concord and law of Nature from the Earth;[10]
Hunting (and Men not Beasts shall be his game)   30
With Warr and hostile snare such as refuse
Subjection to his Empire tyrannous:
A mightie Hunter thence he shall be styl'd
Before the Lord, as in despite of Heav'n,[11]
Or from Heav'n claiming[12] second Sovrantie;   35
And from Rebellion shall derive his name,[13]
Though of Rebellion others he accuse.
Hee with a crew, whom like Ambition joyns
With him or under him to tyrannize,
Marching from *Eden* towards the West, shall finde   40
The Plain,[14] wherein a black bituminous gurge
Boiles out from under ground, the mouth of Hell;
Of Brick, and of that stuff they cast to build
A Citie and Towre, whose top may reach to Heav'n;
And get themselves a name, least far disperst   45

---

[9]If "corn" can be "The seed or fruit of . . . an apple, a grape" (*OED* 2.b), then "corn wine" is possible, but the punctuation of the first two editions, with no comma between "Corn" and "wine," is very unlikely. Variants of the formula "corn and wine and oil" are extremely common in the Old Testament, as with "the tithe of thy corn, or of thy wine, or of thy oil" in Deuteronomy 12.17, which Milton cited in *Likeliest Means* (Yale 7: 282), but "corn wine" never appears. Darbishire assumes that a comma should be there and adds it silently. Shawcross does not and Fowler does not (but Fowler says nothing about the problem with "corn wine"). The editors or compositors of the 1688 Folio were the first to add the comma after "Corn." I have added the comma, not on the grounds that it has early authority, but because "Corn wine" seems to be nonsense.

[10]The semicolon clearly printing in *1667* (at what is in that edition 10.920) seems to be a better reading than what looks like a comma in *1674*. Nimrod is the "mighty hunter before the Lord" of Genesis 10.8. Though Babel is mentioned in the sentence following, the connection between Nimrod and the Tower of Babel had to be established by commentators who based their interpretation on Josephus, *Antiquities* 1.4.2–3, which had set the meaning of the name Babel and established Nimrod as a tyrant. The Geneva Bible glossed "mighty" as meaning "a cruel oppressor & tyrant" and it glossed "He was a mighty hunter before the Lord, wherfore it was said, As Nimrod the mighty hunter before the Lord" as signifying "His tyrannie came into a proverbe as hated bothe of God and man: for he passed not to commit crueltie even in Gods presence" (1560 ed.). Milton described Nimrod wittily in *Eikonoklastes*: "The Bishops could have told . . . that *Nimrod*, the first that hunted after Faction is reputed, by ancient Tradition, the first that founded Monarchy; whence it appeares that to hunt after Faction is more properly the Kings game" (Yale 3: 598). Milton contrasts familial "paternal rule" or the "fair equalitie" of a "fraternal state" with Nimrod's proverbial tyranny and his need to "arrogate [claim unjustly] Dominion." See Richard F. Hardin, "Milton's Nimrod," *Milton Quarterly* 22 (1988): 38–44, which concludes that Nimrod was, in Milton's eyes, "yet another hunter of men who is self-tempted, self-depraved, and self-deceived" (43).

[11]Milton glosses the puzzling phrase "Before the Lord" of Genesis 10.9 as meaning "To say Kings are accountable to none but God, is the overturning of all Law" (*Tenure*; Yale 3: 204). Milton by contrast made kings out to be accountable not only to God but to the people who commit trust to them (Yale 3: 212).

[12]The "claming" of *1674* seems to be a misprint.

[13]According to Hardin, "Nimrod's name was also linked with a happy etymological fault in its mistaken derivation from the Hebrew *marad* (rebel), an error that appears in Philo Judaeus (70) [Philo of Alexander, *Two Treatises of Philo of Alexandria*, ed. David Winston and John Dillon (Brown U Judaic Studies. Chico, CA: Scholars' Press, 1983)], who did not know Hebrew" (39). Nimrod's name, then, and his tyranny identified him as a type of Satan.

[14]The plain of Shinar described as the site of the Tower of Babel in Genesis 11. Journeying "from the east," the families of the sons of Noah settled on the plain in the land of Shinar, "And they said one to another, Go to, let us make brick, and burn them thoroughly. And they had brick for stone, and slime had they for mortar" (11.3). The "slime" of the Authorized Version translated the *bitumen* of the Latin Vulgate. Milton pictures a whirlpool ("gurge" in its first use in English) of bitumen at one of the traditional earthly entrances to the classical underworld, which would have provided hellish mortar for the bricks of the Tower of Babel. Boiling pitch would have been associated with the torments of the Christian Hell, but Milton does not place that Hell beneath the earth. The verb *cast* suggests both to scheme (*OED* VII.43) and to put into shape (VIII), as well as "place . . . with . . . violence" (V).

In foraign Lands thir memorie be lost
Regardless whether good or evil fame.[15]
But God who oft descends to visit men
Unseen, and through thir habitations walks
To mark thir doings, them beholding soon,   50
Comes down to see thir Citie, ere the Tower
Obstruct Heav'n Towrs, and in derision[16] sets
Upon thir Tongues a various° Spirit to rase°   CONFUSING, DIVIDING   ERASE
Quite out thir Native Language, and instead
To sow a jangling noise of words unknown: 55
Forthwith a hideous gabble rises loud
Among the Builders; each to other calls
Not understood, till hoarse, and all in rage,
As mockt they storm;° great laughter was in Heav'n   RAGE
And looking down, to see the hubbub° strange   BARBARIC CONFUSION   60
And hear the din; thus was the building left
Ridiculous, and the work Confusion nam'd.[17]
    Whereto thus *Adam* fatherly[18] displeas'd.
O execrable Son so to aspire
Above his Brethren, to himself assuming   65
Authoritie usurpt, from God not giv'n:
He gave us onely over Beast, Fish, Fowl
Dominion absolute; that right we hold
By his donation;[19] but Man over men
He made not Lord; such title to himself   70
Reserving, human left from human free.
But this Usurper his encroachment proud
Stayes not on Man; to God his Tower intends°   MEANS
Siege and defiance: Wretched man! what food
Will he convey up thither to sustain   75
Himself and his rash Armie, where thin Aire[20]
Above the Clouds will pine his entrails gross,[21]
And famish him of Breath, if not of Bread?
    To whom thus *Michael*. Justly thou abhorr'st
That Son, who on the quiet state of men   80
Such trouble brought, affecting to subdue
Rational Libertie; yet know withall,

---

[15]The process of getting themselves a name (and losing their good names in the process) ties the builders of the Tower even more firmly to the fallen angels who had their names blotted out in the Book of Heaven (see 54 below). Genesis 11.4 quotes the builders as saying "let us make us a name, lest we be scattered abroad upon the face of the whole earth," but Milton probably stresses the irony by not allowing Michael even to name Nimrod (or Babel, for that matter) in this passage. Leonard asks, rhetorically, "Can it be that Nimrod's name is also razed out?" (54); the answer is obviously yes: instead of gaining fame and reputation, those who built the Tower of Babel become infamous, their names blotted out.

[16]Another instance of God's justly holding his foes "in derision" (compare 5.735–36 and Psalm 2.4).

[17]Words like *gabble hubbub, jangling*, and *din* echo the babble of confused languages. The scene is analogous to that of the grotesque metamorphoses of the fallen angels attending Satan's speech in Book 10, and Satan himself, when they are all changed into varieties of writhing serpents, scorpions, and dragons (504–32). As Fowler points out (12.62n), "Babel" in Genesis 11.9 was glossed in the Authorized Bible as "Confusion." The Geneva Bible had also committed the etymological error.

[18]The word is carefully chosen, since Michael's narrative here and below concentrates on the proper and improper relations between fathers and sons.

[19]Simply, the word means "gift," but the Latin *donatio* suggests more of a formal presentation (not the modern sense of "charitable gift").

[20]The air high above the Earth was rightly thought too thin for humans to endure, whereas spirits could vanish into "thin air" (Shakespeare, *Tempest* 4.1.150).

[21]The thin air will cause his entrails to waste away or be tormented by pain ("pine" means not only to be in torment but also to waste away, as in *OED* 1, 2, 5) and deprive him not only of breath (and the air to breathe) but of bread as well, since no wheat or other source of bread would grow at that elevation.

Since thy original lapse, true Libertie
Is lost, which always with right Reason dwells
Twinn'd, and from her hath no dividual° being:[22]   SEPARATE   85
Reason in man obscur'd, or not obeyd,
Immediately inordinate desires
And upstart Passions catch the Government[23]
From Reason, and to servitude reduce
Man till then free. Therefore since hee permits   90
Within himself unworthie Powers to reign
Over free Reason, God in Judgement just
Subjects him from without to violent Lords;
Who oft as undeservedly enthrall
His outward freedom: Tyrannie must be,   95
Though to the Tyrant thereby no excuse.[24]
Yet somtimes Nations will decline so low
From vertue, which is reason,[25] that no wrong,
But Justice, and some fatal curse annext
Deprives them of thir outward libertie,   100
Thir inward lost: Witness th' irreverent Son[26]
Of him who built the Ark, who for the shame
Don to his Father, heard this heavie curse,
Servant of Servants,[27] on his vitious° Race.   DEPRAVED
Thus will this latter, as the former World,   105
Still tend from bad to worse, till God at last
Wearied with their iniquities, withdraw
His presence from among them, and avert
His holy Eyes; resolving from thenceforth
To leave them to thir own polluted wayes;   110
And one peculiar Nation[28] to select
From all the rest, of whom to be invok'd,
A Nation from one faithful man[29] to spring:
Him on this side *Euphrates* yet residing,

---

[22]Sin caused servitude. Nimrod is linked by the word "Son" with the ironically named "Sons of God" (5.447) who in breeding with the "daughters of men" (*Paradise Regain'd* 2.154) produced "Devils to adore for Deities" (*Paradise Lost* 1.373). When the Satanic Nimrod enslaved his followers, he had to defeat in them that "rational liberty" or "true liberty" that humankind naturally possessed before the Fall. Since Milton spent much of his political career trying to define civil and domestic liberty, Michael's explanation here is resonant with terms that had special meaning for Milton. Milton saw liberty as a God-given birthright subject to conscience ("right Reason"; for the connection between liberty and conscience, see *The Digression*, in Yale 5: 449). Liberty could be easily lost after and because of the Fall. The Stoic right reason is again equated with Christian conscience.

[23]Used both in the sense of "control" (as in the "governor" of an engine) and "civil rule." The analogy is between the human body and the body politic: if passions rule the body, it becomes slave to its passions, and if unreason rules or seizes ("catches") the state, slavery results.

[24]Sadly, tyranny must exist after the Fall, but admitting that does not give license or approval to the actions of a tyrant.

[25]Milton equated virtue with truth, nobleness of mind, and wisdom, and he labeled temperance as an important virtue. To equate virtue with reason, then, was no large extension of its meaning.

[26]Again the word "Son" is used sardonically, since Ham, who is not named here, did a disservice to his father Noah (observing his nakedness) and thereby subjected his sons to the curse of servitude. "And [Noah] said, Cursed be Canaan; a servant of servants shall he be unto his brethren" (Genesis 9.25). The passage was sadly used in support of the subjection of Hamitic peoples to slavery, as Milton uses it here to condemn what he calls a "vitious Race." The Geneva Bible glossed "servant of servants" as "a most vile slave" (1560 ed.). With the sons of Abraham (145 below), the words *son* and *sons* will return to their normal positive value.

[27]As a direct quotation from Noah, the phrase is italicized.

[28]The nation of the tribes of Israel, which is described in Deuteronomy 14.2 as "an holy people unto the Lord thy God, and the Lord hath chosen thee to be a peculiar people unto himself, above all the nations that are upon the earth." As *On Christian Doctrine* states, Milton did not "understand by the term election that general or, so to speak, national election by which God chose the whole nation of Israel as his own people" (1.4; Yale 6: 172). The election of the nation of Israel, in other words, is taken for granted, and the proof text Milton cites is Deuteronomy 7.6: "Jehovah selected you to be a people peculiar to him" (qtd. from Milton's Latin as translated by John Carey; the Authorized Version translates: "the Lord thy God hath chosen thee to be a special people unto himself," and the Geneva Bible translates "the Lord thy God hathe chosen thee, to be a precious people unto him selfe . . . ").

[29]Abraham, called "a father of many nations" in Genesis 17.5. Abraham's father, according to Joshua 24.2, was Terah, who "served other gods."

Bred up in Idol-worship; O that men
(Canst thou believe?) should be so stupid grown,
While yet the Patriark[30] liv'd, who scap'd the Flood,
As to forsake the living God, and fall
To worship thir own work in Wood and Stone
For Gods![31] yet him God the most High[32] voutsafes
To call by Vision from his Fathers house,[33]
His kindred and false Gods, into a Land
Which he will shew him, and from him will raise
A mightie Nation, and upon him showre
His benediction so, that in his Seed
All Nations shall be blest; he straight obeys,
Not knowing to what Land, yet firm believes:[34]
I see him, but thou canst not,[35] with what Faith
He leaves his Gods, his Friends, and native Soile
Ur of *Chaldæa*, passing now the Ford[36]
To *Haran*, after him a cumbrous Train
Of Herds and Flocks, and numerous servitude;[37]
Not wandring poor, but trusting all his wealth
With God, who call'd him, in a land unknown.
Canaan he now attains, I see his Tents
Pitcht about *Sechem*, and the neighbouring Plaine
Of *Moreh*;[38] there by promise he receaves
Gift to his Progenie of all that Land;[39]
From *Hamath* Northward[40] to the Desert South
(Things by thir names I call, though yet unnam'd)
From *Hermon*[41] East to the great Western Sea,°   I.E., THE MEDITERRANEAN
Mount *Hermon*, yonder Sea, each place behold
In prospect, as I point them; on the shoare
Mount *Carmel*;[42] here the double-founted stream
Jordan,[43] true limit Eastward; but his Sons

115

120

125

130

135

140

145

---

[30]"And Noah lived after the flood three hundred and fifty years. And all the days of Noah were nine hundred and fifty years; and he died" (Genesis 9.28–29).

[31]In other words, the unfaithful are making graven images out of wood or stone, which would fit with the image of the time "When all our Fathers worship't Stocks and Stones" (Sonnet 18; see Jeremiah 2.27).

[32]Melchizedek, both King of Salem and a priest, "blessed [Abram], and said, Blessed be Abram of the most high God, possessor of heaven and earth" (Genesis 14.19).

[33]The narrative here follows closely what is described in Genesis 11 and 12, where the Lord tells Abram to leave his father's house so that he can become "a great nation" (12.2). Abram takes Sarai, his wife, and Lot, his brother's son, "and the souls they had gotten in Haran" (12.5) and the entourage leaves Ur of the Chaldees (11.31) and travels into the land of Canaan, which the Lord gives to the "Seed" (12.7) of Abram.

[34]Hebrews 11.8 stresses Abraham's faith in journeying forth without being sure of where he was being directed. Fowler points out the irony for Adam, since "he will shortly be challenged by the need to have a similar faith" (121–34n).

[35]Michael's inner vision of the future is not visible to Adam, who must accept the narrative on faith.

[36]Since Ur was on one bank of the Euphrates and Haran on the other, Milton assumes a ford that would allow the band to cross over.

[37]A train of servants, illustrating the fact that servitude was instituted after the Fall.

[38]"And Abram passed through the land [Canaan] unto the place of Sichem, unto the plain of Moreh" (Genesis 12.6). Milton may have derived the spelling "Sechem" from the "Shechem" of the Geneva Bible.

[39]The Lord promises a carefully demarcated land of Canaan to Moses and the children of Israel in Numbers 34.1–12.

[40]The coast of Hamath is identified as a northern border in Ezekiel 47.17.

[41]Joshua 13.5–6 mentions Hermon as a border, associating it with Hamath as well.

[42]Mt. Carmel, next to the sea according to Jeremiah 46.18, is named as a westward border at Joshua 19.26.

[43]The river Jordan is named as an "east border . . . [on] the salt sea, even unto the end of Jordan" in Joshua 15.5. As Fowler points out (135–51n), the false assumption that the river Jordan is formed by the confluence of two fountains named Jor and Dan may be derived from George Sandys's *Relation of a Journey Begun An. Dom. 1610* (1615). See also Cawley, *Milton* 102–08.

Shall dwell to *Senir*,[44] that long ridge of Hills.
This ponder, that all Nations of the Earth
Shall in his Seed be blessed; by that Seed
Is meant thy great deliverer, who shall bruise
The Serpents head;[45] whereof to thee anon   150
Plainlier shall be reveald. This Patriarch blest,
Whom *faithful Abraham*[46] due time shall call,
A Son, and of his Son a Grand-childe[47] leaves,
Like him in faith, in wisdom, and renown;
The Grandchilde with twelve Sons increast, departs   155
From *Canaan*, to a Land hereafter call'd
Egypt, divided by the River *Nile*;[48]
See where it flows, disgorging at seaven mouthes[49]
Into the Sea: to sojourn in that Land
He comes invited by a yonger Son   160
In time of dearth, a Son whose worthy deeds
Raise him to be the second in that Realme
Of *Pharao*: there he dies, and leaves his Race
Growing into a Nation, and now grown
Suspected to a sequent King,[50] who seeks   165
To stop thir overgrowth, as inmate guests
Too numerous; whence of guests he makes them slaves
Inhospitably, and kills thir infant Males:[51]
Till by two brethren (those two brethren call
Moses and *Aaron*) sent from God to claime   170
His people from enthralment,° they return   SERVITUDE
With glory and spoile back to thir promis'd Land.
But first the lawless Tyrant,[52] who denies
To know thir God, or message to regard,
Must be compelld by Signes and Judgements dire;[53]   175
To blood unshed the Rivers must be turnd,
Frogs, Lice and Flies must all his Palace fill
With loath'd intrusion, and fill all the land;

---

[44]"Shenir" is identified by the marginalia of the Geneva Bible for Ezekiel 27.5 as Mt. Hermon: "This mountaine was called Hermon, but the Amorites called it Shenir." Deuteronomy 3.9 (1560 ed.) attempts to clear up the discrepancies in naming Mt. Hermon: "Which Hermon the Sidonians call Shirion, but the Amorites call it Shenir." Milton seems to be thinking of "Senir" as the ridge of which Mt. Hermon formed a part. See 1 Chronicles 5.23, where the two are associated.

[45]The "Seed" of Abraham will eventually lead to Jesus, who will at the end of time crush the head of the Serpent under his heel, fulfilling the curse alluded to in 10.179–81.

[46]The italics seem to be used to give special emphasis to a phrase supposedly instituted by God (see Galatians 3.9): Abraham is an epitome of faithfulness.

[47]The son is Isaac and the grandchild Jacob.

[48]Genesis 45–46 tells of Jacob's journey with the rest of his family to Egypt at the bidding of his younger son Joseph, who is the trusted second in command to Pharaoh. The twelve sons of Jacob are the respective founders of the twelve tribes of Israel.

[49]Classical poetry often mentions the seven mouths disgorging into the Mediterranean from the Nile, as in *Aeneid* 6.800: "And the seven mouths of the Nile are in a lather of fright" (trans. Lewis). Sylvester's DuBartas uses the formula "O seven-horn'd *Nile*" (2: 554).

[50]The king or pharaoh, called Busiris in 1.307, is "sequent" in the sense that he is a successor of Joseph's Pharaoh, but he is also a pursuer of the Israelites under Moses, and his "*Memphian* Chivalry" will pay for the pursuit by having the Red Sea close over its head. For the narrative, see Exodus 14.

[51]Pharaoh commands the Hebrew midwives to kill all the male infants of the Israelites in Exodus 1.15–16.

[52]This Pharaoh, the pursuer of Moses and his people, was a type of the hard-hearted tyrant for Milton, not being persuaded by plagues or portents to let Moses's people go: " . . . when God incites to sin he is nevertheless not the cause of anyone's sinning, so when he hardens the heart of a sinner or blinds him, he is not the cause of sin. . . . Thus Pharaoh became more obstinate and more furious when God's commands ran counter to his will" (1.8; Yale 6: 336). For a comparison of Pharaoh and King Charles I, see *Eikonoklastes* in Yale 3: 516.

[53]For the ten plagues of Egypt, see Exodus 7–15. Fowler believes that Milton adds an image of a chariot in 183, invoking a parallel with the "Chariot of Paternal Deitie" of 6.750. But what Fowler sees as a chariot may be fireballs generated by a severe electrical storm, rolling across the land and setting vegetation on fire: "the fire ran along upon the ground" in Exodus 9.23.

His Cattel must of Rot and Murren[54] die,
Botches[55] and blaines must all his flesh imboss,   180
And all his people; Thunder mixt with Haile,
Haile mixt with fire must rend th' *Egyptian* Skie
And wheel on th' Earth, devouring where it rouls;
What it devours not, Herb, or Fruit, or Graine,
A darksom Cloud of Locusts swarming down   185
Must eat, and on the ground leave nothing green:
Darkness must overshadow all his bounds,
Palpable darkness,[56] and blot out three dayes;[57]
Last with one midnight stroke all the first-born
Of *Egypt* must lie dead. Thus with ten wounds   190
The River-dragon[58] tam'd at length submits
To let his sojourners[59] depart, and oft
Humbles his stubborn heart, but still as Ice
More hard'nd after thaw, till in his rage
Pursuing whom he late dismissd, the Sea   195
Swallows him with his Host, but them lets pass
As on drie land between two christal walls,[60]
Aw'd by the rod of *Moses* so to stand
Divided, till his rescu'd[61] gain thir shoar:
Such wondrous power God to his Saint[62] will lend,   200
Though present in his Angel,[63] who shall goe
Before them in a Cloud, and Pillar of Fire,[64]
By day a Cloud, by night a Pillar of Fire,
To guide them in thir journey, and remove[65]
Behinde them, while th' obdurat° King pursues: HARDHEARTED   205
All night he will pursue, but his approach

---

[54]Murrain, now called foot-and-mouth disease in cattle (and by "cattle" is understood all domesticated animals). The spelling here is a better phonetic description of the way the word is still pronounced (*mur'in*). "Rot" could be any wasting or putrefying affliction of sheep or cattle, including murrain.
[55]Not blotches but swellings on the skin, pimples, or sores. A blain is a boil or a blister. Both terms are taken from the account in Exodus; both afflictions would "imboss" the skin in the sense of causing raised lesions.
[56]As Fowler points out (188n), Milton follows the Vulgate *tenebrae . . . ut palparit queant*, which the Authorized Version translates "even darkness which may be felt" (Exodus 10.21).
[57]Following closely the account in Exodus 10.12–19, which includes the detail of the clouds of locusts darkening the whole face of the earth.
[58]Pharaoh at the center of the mouths of the Nile, with Milton's image depending on an allusion to Ezekiel 29.3, wherein the Son of Man prophesies against Pharaoh as "the great dragon that lieth in the midst of his rivers, which hath said, My river is mine own, and I have made it for myself." The dragon in Ezekiel is caught by means of hooks in his jaws and then thrown into the wilderness to rot. The allusion leads inevitably to a comparison between Pharaoh and "the dragon, that old serpent, which is the Devil, and Satan" (Revelation 20.2). Milton calls attention to the typology of the hardhearted Pharaoh standing for Satan. The ten wounds are the ten plagues.
[59]The term emphasizes the role of the tribes of Israel as travelers or sojourners until they reach the Promised Land.
[60]Compare Milton's youthful translation of Psalm 136.49–50: "The floods stood still like Walls of Glass, / While the Hebrew Bands did pass." Exodus reads "the waters were a wall unto them on their right hand, and on their left" (14.22). Milton makes the walls out of glass or crystal, perhaps remembering Sylvester's translation of DuBartas's *Divine Weekes and Works*: "Th' *Egiptian* Troopes pursue them by the track; / Yet waites the patient Sea, and still stands back, / Till all the Hoast bee marching in their Ranks / Within the Lane betweene his cristall Banks" (2: 564). Compare also the division of waters in the Creation "in crystal Wall" (7.293).
[61]The sea, in awe of Moses's rod, stands divided, until those he has rescued can reach the shore.
[62]Moses is a saint in Milton's usage, which is that of seventeenth-century English Puritan writings, suggesting any holy (*sanctus*) person. See Christopher for general background for the usage.
[63]In Exodus 33.2–4, God in speaking to Moses says, "And I will send an angel before thee; . . . for I will not go up in the midst of thee; . . . lest I consume thee in the way. And when the people heard these evil tidings, they mourned." Milton used the passage exactly as quoted to establish that though he spoke for Jehovah or Christ, the angel was the divinity in name only, "the representation of [God's] name and glory in some angel" (*On Christian Doctrine* 1.5; Yale 6: 254).
[64]The pilliar of fire of Exodus 13.21.
[65]Probably "To take or convey away from a place" (*OED* I.1.c), since the pillar of fire is leading the Israelites.

Darkness defends between[66] till morning Watch;
Then through the Firey Pillar and the Cloud
God looking forth will trouble all his Host
And craze° thir Chariot wheels: when by command   SHATTER   210
Moses once more his potent Rod extends
Over the Sea; the Sea his Rod obeys;
On thir imbattelld ranks the Waves return,
And overwhelm thir Warr:[67] the Race elect[68]
Safe towards *Canaan* from the shoar advance   215
Through the wilde Desert, not the readiest way,
Least entring on the *Canaanite* allarmd
Warr terrifie them inexpert, and feare
Return them back to *Egypt*, choosing rather
Inglorious life with servitude; for life   220
To noble and ignoble is more sweet
Untraind in Armes,[69] where rashness leads not on.
This also shall they gain by thir delay
In the wide Wilderness,[70] there they shall found
Thir government, and thir great Senate[71] choose   225
Through the twelve Tribes, to rule by Laws ordaind:
God from the Mount of *Sinai*, whose gray top[72]
Shall tremble, he descending, will himself
In Thunder[73] Lightning and loud Trumpets sound
Ordaine them Lawes;[74] part such as appertaine   230
To civil Justice, part religious Rites
Of sacrifice, informing them, by types
And shadows,[75] of that destind Seed to bruise
The Serpent, by what means he shall achieve
Mankinds deliverance. But the voice of God   235
To mortal eare is dreadful;[76] they beseech

---

[66]Darkness defends or stands between the Israelites and Pharaoh until the first military watch of the morning. Milton does not use the idiom "defends between" elsewhere.

[67]The first instance recorded in the *OED* of the word being used as a collective noun, meaning "the sum total of fighting forces."

[68]The Israelites. In the phrasing here and in "not the readiest way," Milton calls attention to the typology associated with the warfaring Christian: the elect (Israelites) must not take the ready and easy way toward the truth or the Promised Land but instead must venture through the dangerous desert. As Fowler points out (216–19n), Milton compared the tribes of Israel wandering in the desert to the English wandering toward truth by the harsh trials of the Civil Wars (in *Eikonoklastes* Yale 3: 580). Thomas Corns informs me that the image was common in Civil War literature of all kinds (letter, September 1991).

[69]Loh rearranges the difficult syntax: "for, where rashness does not lead on (i.e., when people are not led on by rashness), life untrained in arms is more sweet to the noble and ignoble (i.e., all people, high and low) alike" (220–22n).

[70]Exodus 16.35 and Numbers 14.33 mention the forty years the Israelites wandered in the wilderness.

[71]By now the political analogy is becoming clear. While undergoing the trials of the desert, the tribes of Israel forged their political system, just as England had forged its parliamentary system during the Civil Wars. Milton is more than likely alluding to his own *Readie and Easy Way*, in which he discusses the establishment of senates or sanhedrins in Israel and in Rome (Yale 7: 435–42).

[72]Mt. Sinai has a gray top because God comes to Moses there "in a thick cloud" (Exodus 19.9). It is actually the people who are described as trembling, not the mountain (19.16).

[73]One would normally expect a comma here (as with "Corn wine" at 19 above), but none of the first three editions supplies one. The 1688 Folio does correct what looks like an error. Fowler calls attention to the lack of apostrophe with "Trumpets" as possible "double syntax" (229n), but the compositors of *1667* and *1674* generally left out apostrophes with possessives, and the decision was, so far as I can determine, arbitrary. The word "Trumpets," however lacking an apostrophe, is meant to be taken as a possessive and not a simple plural form.

[74]"Ordain laws for them." God, in other words, speaking in thunder and lightning, will ordain the Ten Commandments and the rest of their laws for the tribes of Israel.

[75]For background to the regarding of Old Testament figures as either "types" or "shadows," see Madsen, *From Shadowy Types.*

[76]The voice of God is too awe-inspiring or full of dread for the average ear to hear; therefore Moses must interpret and deliver the tablets for God. Typology is again at work here, as Milton reminds us of with "types / And shadows." Hebrews 8.5 discusses Moses in terms of high priests "Who serve unto the example and shadow of heavenly things, as Moses was admonished of God when he was about to make the tabernacle. . . ." Moses (or Jesus) is necessary as mediator. In Exodus 20.19, the Israelites plead with Moses to speak to them in place of God, since if God speaks to them directly the

That *Moses* might report to them his will,
And terror cease; he grants what they besaught
Instructed that to God is no access
Without Mediator, whose high Office now   240
Moses in figure° beares, to introduce   FIGURATIVELY
One greater, of whose day he shall foretell,
And all the Prophets in thir Age the times
Of great *Messiah* shall sing.[77] Thus Laws and Rites
Establisht, such delight hath God in Men   245
Obedient to his will, that he voutsafes
Among them to set up his Tabernacle,[78]
The holy One with mortal Men to dwell:
By his prescript a Sanctuary is fram'd
Of Cedar, overlaid with Gold,[79] therein   250
An Ark, and in the Ark his Testimony,
The Records of his Cov'nant, over these
A Mercie-seat of Gold[80] between the wings
Of two bright Cherubim, before him burn
Seaven Lamps as in a Zodiac representing   255
The Heav'nly fires;[81] over the Tent a Cloud
Shall rest by Day, a fiery gleame by Night,
Save when they journie, and at length they come,
Conducted by his Angel to the Land
Promisd to *Abraham*[82] and his Seed: the rest   260
Were long to tell, how many Battels fought,
How many Kings destroyd, and Kingdoms won,
Or how the Sun shall in mid Heav'n stand still
A day entire, and Nights due course adjourne,
Mans voice commanding, Sun in *Gibeon* stand,[83]   265
And thou Moon in the vale of *Aialon*,
Till *Israel*[84] overcome; so call the third
From *Abraham*, Son of *Isaac,* and from him
His whole descent, who thus shall *Canaan* win.

  Here *Adam* interpos'd. O sent from Heav'n,   270
Enlightner of my darkness, gracious things
Thou hast reveald, those chiefly which concerne

---

experience would kill them.

[77]Thus Jesus is called "high priest" and compared with Moses in Hebrews 8.1–13. Moses would have formed the "covenant with the house of Israel" (10), whereas Jesus would have formed "A new covenant" (13). And Moses is a type of Christ in his function as mediator: "The name and, in a sense, the office of mediator is also ascribed to Moses, as a type of Christ" (*On Christian Doctrine* 1.15; Yale 6: 431). See Jason P. Rosenblatt, "The Mosaic Voice in *Paradise Lost*," *Milton Studies* 7 (1975): 207–32.

[78]The tabernacle was the holiest of shrines for Israel; God speaks to Moses, in the form of a "cloudy pillar" at the door of the tabernacle, in Exodus 33.9.

[79]For the construction of the tabernacle, see Exodus 25–27. According to the Geneva Bible, the "wood Shittim" mentioned at 25.5 is "thoght to be a kind of cedar, which wil not rot" (1560 ed.).

[80]See the "Mercie-seat above" (11.2), which is described as being made of gold and resting above the Ark of the Covenant, with statues of cherubim on its "ends," at Exodus 25.17–20.

[81]The seven lamps or seven-branched candlesticks still used in Jewish ceremony would provide an echo of or correspondence with planetary numbers. Fowler cites Josephus, *Antiquities* 3.6.7 on the symbolism in the arrangement of groups of seven (247–56n).

[82]Though the name is not spelled "Abram" here, it should be a disyllable if the scansion of the line is regular, which might be significant since God adds the third syllable to "Abram" at Genesis 17.5 to establish that he has become "a father of many nations." God establishes his covenant with Abram at ninety-nine years of age, commands him to be "perfect" thereafter, and promises to "multiply" him "exceedingly"; then his name is changed.

[83]"Then spake Joshua to the Lord in the day when the Lord delivered up the Amorites before the children of Israel, and he said in the sight of Israel, Sun, stand thou still upon Gibeon; and thou, Moon, in the valley of Ajalon" (Joshua 10.12). The "voice of a man" unto which God hearkened is in 10.14. One of the possible choices for a biblical drama that Milton listed in the Trinity Manuscript is "Josuah in Gibeon. Josu. 10" (Yale 8: 555).

[84]See Genesis 32.28, where Jacob is given the name Israel by the angel with whom he has wrestled.

Just *Abraham* and his Seed: now first I finde
Mine eyes true op'ning,[85] and my heart much eas'd,
Erwhile perplext with thoughts what would becom   275
Of mee and all Mankind; but now I see
His day, in whom all Nations shall be blest,
Favour unmerited by me, who sought
Forbidd'n knowledge by forbidd'n means.
This yet I apprehend not, why to those   280
Among whom God will deigne to dwell on Earth
So many and so various Laws are giv'n;
So many Laws argue so many sins
Among them; how can God with such reside?
   To whom thus *Michael*. Doubt not but that sin   285
Will reign among them, as of thee begot;
And therefore was Law given them to evince°   DEMONSTRATE, MAKE CLEAR
Thir natural pravitie,° by stirring up   DEPRAVITY
Sin against Law to fight; that when they see
Law can discover sin,[86] but not remove,   290
Save by those shadowie expiations weak,
The bloud of Bulls and Goats,[87] they may conclude
Some bloud more precious must be paid for Man,
Just for unjust,[88] that in such righteousness
To them by Faith imputed,[89] they may finde   295
Justification[90] towards God, and peace
Of Conscience,[91] which the Law by Ceremonies
Cannot appease, nor Man the moral part
Perform, and not performing cannot live.
So law appears imperfet, and but° giv'n   ONLY   300
With purpose to resign[92] them in full time
Up to a better Cov'nant,[93] disciplin'd

---

[85]Adam is comparing the true opening of his eyes with the false promise of the Serpent at Genesis 3.5; compare 11.412–20, where Michael actually purges Adam's eyes with herbal medicine.

[86]"Law" is used in the biblical or Pauline sense: "For I delight in the law of God after the inward man: But I see another law in my members, warring against the law of my mind, and bringing me into captivity to the law of sin which is in my members" (Romans 7.22–23). Since "by the law is the knowledge of sin" (Romans 3.20), "all the world may become guilty before God" (3.19). Milton explains the context of 3.19 in *On Christian Doctrine* 1.11: "Thus as soon as the fall occurred, our first parents became guilty, though there could have been no original sin in them. Moreover all Adam's descendants were included in the guilt, though original sin had not yet been implanted in them. Finally, guilt is taken away from the regenerate, but they still have original sin" (Yale 6: 390).

[87]The blood sacrifices, even those of the faithful Old Testament patriarchs, were but a shadowy type of Christian sacrifice: "For the law having a shadow of good things to come, and not the very image of the things, can never with those sacrifices which they offered year by year continually make the comers thereunto perfect" (Hebrews 10.1).

[88]The blood of the just, that of Christ in the Crucifixion, must be shed for the unjust, sinful humankind, redeemed "with the precious blood of Christ, as of a lamb without blemish and without spot" (1 Peter 1.19). "For Christ also hath once suffered for sins, the just for the unjust, that he might bring us to God, being put to death in the flesh, but quickened by the Spirit" (1 Peter 3.18).

[89]A word charged with theological meaning, as in *OED* 2: "Ascribed by vicarious substitution" with an example taken from a 1620 textbook of logic: "Imputed justice by which we are justified before God, is inherent in Christ." The word *imputation* has generally negative connotations when used by Milton, as in "a horrid imputation laid upon the law" (*Tetrachordon*; Yale 2: 659).

[90]Again, "Justification" is used in the theological sense: "Before faith came, we were kept under the law, shut up unto the faith which should afterwards be revealed. Wherefore the law was our schoolmaster to bring us unto Christ, that we might be justified by faith" (Galations 3.23–24).

[91]Although those who do not have the law are "a law unto themselves," they nevertheless "shew the work of the law written in their hearts, their conscience also bearing witness, and their thoughts the mean while accusing or else excusing one another" (Romans 2.14–15).

[92]To "yield up . . . with confidence" (*OED* 2b).

[93]In time, the law will give them to a better covenant than that made with the house of Israel "when [God] took them by the hand to lead them out of the land of Egypt" (Hebrews 8.9), since Christ, who is "an high priest, who is set on the right hand of the throne of the Majesty in the heavens" (Hebrews 8.1), is also "mediator of a better covenant, which was established upon better promises" (8.6). The high priests of the Old Testament were "the example and shadow of heavenly things" (8.5), fulfilled "according to the pattern shewed to thee in the mount" (8.5).

From shadowie Types to Truth, from Flesh to Spirit,
From imposition of strict Laws, to free
Acceptance of large Grace, from servil fear   305
To filial, works of Law to works of Faith.[94]
And therefore shall not *Moses*, though of God
Highly belov'd, being but the Minister
Of Law, his people into *Canaan* lead;
But *Joshua* whom the Gentiles *Jesus* call,[95]   310
His Name and Office bearing, who shall quell
The adversarie Serpent, and bring back
Through the worlds wilderness long wanderd man
Safe to eternal Paradise of rest.
Meanwhile they in thir earthly *Canaan* plac't   315
Long time shall dwell and prosper, but° when sins   EXCEPT
National interrupt thir public peace,
Provoking God to raise them enemies:[96]
From whom as oft he saves them penitent
By Judges first, then under Kings;[97] of whom   320
The second, both for pietie renownd
And puissant° deeds, a promise shall receive   POWERFUL
Irrevocable, that his Regal Throne
For ever shall endure; the like shall sing
All Prophecie, That of the Royal Stock   325
Of *David* (so I name this King) shall rise
A Son, the Womans Seed to thee foretold,
Foretold to *Abraham*, as in whom shall trust
All Nations, and to Kings foretold, of Kings
The last, for of his Reign shall be no end.   330
But first a long succession must ensue,
And his next Son for Wealth and Wisdom fam'd,[98]
The clouded Ark of God till then in Tents
Wandring, shall in a glorious Temple enshrine.
Such follow him, as shall be registerd   335
Part good, part bad, of bad the longer scrowle,°   SCROLL, LIST
Whose foul Idolatries, and other faults
Heapt to the popular summe,[99] will so incense

---

[94]The passages about the old law and the new, the new covenant, the Old Testament priests foreshadowing the New Testament Christ, the movement from flesh up to spirit, the movement also from the servile fear of the Old Testament to the filial acceptance of the New, are all essential to Milton's understanding of Christianity, as evidenced by Madsen's full treatment of the theme. The Old Testament Joshua becomes the New Testament Jesus, which is appropriate because *Jesus* is the Greek equivalent of Hebrew *Joshua*.

[95]"The imperfection of the law was made apparent in the person of Moses himself. For Moses, who was the type of the law, could not lead the children of Israel into the land of Canaan, that is, into eternal rest. But an entrance was granted to them under Joshua, that is, Jesus" (*On Christian Doctrine* 1.26; Yale 6: 519). The Old Testament is to be read typologically, with figures like Joshua meant to be read as shadowy types of Christ and Moses as the type of the law the obedience of which leads to eternal rest. See H. R. MacCallum, "Milton and Figurative Interpretation of the Bible," *University of Toronto Quarterly* 31 (1962): 397–415.

[96]"To raise up enemies against them," in order to punish them for wrongdoing. The book of Joshua details the Jewish conquest of Canaan.

[97]Following the order of the books of the Bible, from Judges through 1 and 2 Samuel (then viewed as the first and second books of Kings) through what are now known as 1 and 2 Kings. The Book of Judges explains the purposes of the judges of Israel: "the Lord raised up judges, which delivered them out of the hand of those that spoiled them" (2.16). 1 Kings begins with the death of King David, who is promised by the prophet Nathan at 2 Samuel 7.16: "thine house and thy kingdom shall be established for ever before thee: thy throne shall be established for ever." The reign of King David, second after Saul's, foreshadows in its greatness the fulfilling of the Old Testament shadowy type of David with the New Testament truth of the "Seed," Jesus.

[98]Solomon, famous for wise judgments, for his wealth, and for his building of the Temple (1 Kings 5–8, retold in 2 Chronicles 2–5) to house the ark, which is pictured here as clouded because God while speaking from it surrounded it with clouds and mist (as at 1 Kings 8.10). As Fowler points out (332–34n), the building of the Temple was the occasion of another divine covenant (1 Kings 9.1–9), thus making it a pivotal point in Hebrew and Christian history.

[99]"Added to the sum total of the people's offenses." "Heapt to the . . . summe" would have meant something close to "heaped to the brim."

God, as to leave them, and expose thir Land,   340
Thir Citie, his Temple, and his holy Ark
With all his sacred things, a scorn and prey
To that proud Citie, whose high Walls thou saw'st
Left in confusion, *Babylon* thence call'd.[100]
There in captivitie he lets them dwell   345
The space of seventie years, then brings them back,
Remembring mercie, and his Cov'nant sworn
To *David*, stablisht as the dayes of Heav'n.
Returnd from *Babylon* by leave of Kings
Thir Lords, whom God dispos'd, the house of God   350
They first re-edifie,[101] and for a while
In mean estate live moderate, till grown
In wealth and multitude, factious they grow;
But first among the Priests dissension springs,[102]
Men who attend the Altar, and should most
Endeavour° Peace: thir strife pollution brings   ATTEMPT   355
Upon the Temple it self: at last they seise
The Scepter, and regard not *Davids* Sons,°   DESCENDANTS
Then loose it to a stranger,[103] that the true
Anointed King *Messiah* might be born
Barr'd° of his right; yet at his Birth a Starr   DISPOSSESSED   360
Unseen before in Heav'n proclaims him com,
And guides the Eastern Sages, who enquire
His place, to offer Incense, Myrrh, and Gold;[104]
His place of birth a solemn Angel tells
To simple Shepherds, keeping watch by night;[105]   365
They gladly thither haste, and by a Quire
Of squadrond Angels hear his Carol sung.[106]
A Virgin is his Mother, but his Sire

---

[100]The captivity of the tribes of Israel in Babylon under King Nebuchadnezzar was brought about by the "abominations" of Jehoiachim (2 Chronicles 36.8) and the "evil in the sight of the Lord" of Zedekiah (36.12). The chief priests and the people of Israel had angered the Lord God of Israel by polluting the Temple with heathen worship, until God allowed the Temple to be burnt and the people delivered into captivity in Babylon for seventy years. The "perpetual covenant that shall not be forgotten" (Jeremiah 50.5) is agreed upon after Babylon is defeated by "a nation" "out of the north" and her idols are broken (50.3). Since "Babylon" is derived from Hebrew "Babel," a proper noun in the Old Testament often associated with a state of confusion, the confusion of languages in the Tower of Babel in Genesis 11 is imputed to Babylon.

[101]Ezra rebuilds or re-edifies the Temple, as commanded by God through Cyrus, King of Persia, in Ezra 1.1–4.

[102]Perhaps because Milton had argued against the civil power of prelates in the pamphlet wars of the 1640s, he here emphasizes the dissension and squabbling intrigue of the priests described in the apocryphal 2 Maccabees 4–6. Such unpriestly behavior could lead to the reinstatement of pagan religions, as when Antiochus sacked Jerusalem and desecrated the Temple, rededicating it to Jupiter. Aristobolus, eldest son of Hyrcanus, a Jewish high priest, was the first to assume the title of king after the Babylonian captivity (Newton 355n).

[103]Fowler (following Newton) identifies the stranger as Antipater the Idumean, father of Herod the Great, whom Julius Caesar made Procurator of Judaea in 47 BC. Herod was tetrarch when Christ was born (358n). Milton has been reading in Josephus, *Antiquities* 14.8.5, but the accounts of the portents of Christ's birth combine details from Matthew 2 and Luke 2.

[104]When the wise men ("Eastern Sages") arrived in Bethlehem at the nativity of Jesus and when they saw the young child, "they presented unto him gifts; gold, and frankincense, and myrrh" (Matthew 2.11).

[105]"And, lo, the angel of the Lord came upon them, and the glory of the Lord shone round about them: and they were sore afraid. And the angel said unto them, Fear not: for, behold, I bring you good tidings of great joy, which shall be to all people" (Luke 2.9–10). The angel is solemn in the possible senses of "sacred" (*OED* 1), "of a ceremonious character" (*OED* 3), or awe-inspiring (*OED* 7).

[106]Compare the description in the Nativity Ode stanzas 9–13 of the music of angels "Harping in loud and solemn quire, / With unexpressive notes to Heav'ns new-born Heir" (115–16). Milton pictures the angels there, as here, in a state of military preparedness, ready to fight as Christian soldiers. Compare 4.946, 6.537, among other references to angels as warriors.

The Power[107] of the most High; he shall ascend
The Throne hereditarie, and bound his Reign[108]   370
With earths wide bounds, his glory with the Heav'ns.
    He ceas'd, discerning *Adam* with such joy
Surcharg'd,° as had like grief bin dew'd in tears,   OVERWHELMED
Without the vent of words, which these he breathd.
    O Prophet of glad tidings, finisher   375
Of utmost hope! now clear I understand
What oft my steddiest thoughts have searcht in vain,
Why our great expectation should be call'd
The seed of Woman: Virgin Mother, Haile,[109]
High in the love of Heav'n, yet from my Loynes   380
Thou shalt proceed, and from thy Womb the Son
Of God most High; So God with man unites.
Needs must the Serpent now his capital bruise[110]
Expect with mortal paine: say where and when
Thir fight, what stroke shall bruise the Victors heel.[111]   385
    To whom thus *Michael*. Dream not of thir fight,
As of a Duel, or the local wounds
Of head or heel: not therefore joynes the Son
Manhood to God-head, with more strength to foil
Thy enemie; nor so is overcome   390
Satan, whose fall from Heav'n, a deadlier bruise,
Disabl'd not to give thee thy deaths wound:
Which hee, who comes thy Saviour, shall recure,°   HEAL
Not by destroying *Satan*, but his works
In thee and in thy Seed:[112] nor can this be,   395
But by fulfilling that which thou didst want,°   LACK
Obedience to the Law of God, impos'd
On penaltie of death, and suffering death,
The penaltie to thy transgression due,
And due to theirs which out of thine will grow: 400
So onely can high Justice rest appaid.°   SATISFIED
The Law of God exact he shall fulfill
Both by obedience and by love, though love
Alone fulfill the Law;[113] thy punishment
He shall endure by coming in the Flesh   405

---

[107]The word "Power" is very carefully chosen, perhaps to avoid the word "Spirit," since Milton seems at pains not to associate the entity usually called Holy Ghost or Holy Spirit with the conception of Christ, since he believes that there is "not a single word in the Bible about the mystery of the Trinity" (*On Christian Doctrine* 1.14; Yale 6: 420). Milton read the passage in Luke 1.35—"the Holy Spirit shall come upon you, and the power of the Highest shall overshadow you"—as an indicattion of the power and spirit of the Father: "I should say that these words refer to the power and spirit of the Father himself" (6: 428).

[108]"Set the boundaries of his kingdom." Christ's kingdom, in other words, is bound only by the boundaries of Earth or Heaven.

[109]Adam paraphrases the terminology of the angel venerating Mary at the Annunciation (Luke 1.31–35).

[110]The bruise on his head (*capitalis*, Latin "of or related to the head"), but also his capital bruise in the sense that it will be punishment for his capital crime, and it will also be fatal, as in "capital punishment."

[111]Adam is mistaken to see the Son as an epic hero or a St. George overcoming a fictitious dragon in a duel. The fight that Milton imagines is much more subtle and psychological. It is the battle of wits and souls between Satan and Jesus in *Paradise Regain'd*. But there will also be real battles, as Michael has described them (11.691; 12.261 above), to destroy the works of Satan in Adam and in his "Seed." These battles will be won by the Son's reinstatement of obedience and reaffirmation of love, proven by the sacrifice of the Crucifixion. Again, Michael has to correct Adam's misperception gently.

[112]"He that committeth sin is of the devil; for the devil sinneth from the beginning. For this purpose the Son of God was manifested, that he might destroy the works of the devil" (1 John 3.8).

[113]After repeating the Ten Commandments and ending with Christ's summary of the law, "Thou shalt love thy neighbour as thyself," Romans 13 comments on all the law and the commandments: "Love worketh no ill to his neighbour: therefore love is the fulfilling of the law" (10).

To a reproachful life and cursed death,[114]
Proclaiming Life to all who shall believe
In his redemption, and that his obedience
Imputed becomes theirs by Faith,[115] his merits
To save them, not thir own, though legal works.   410
For this he shall live hated, be blasphem'd,
Seis'd on by force, judg'd, and to death condemnd
A shameful and accurst,[116] naild to the Cross
By his own Nation,[117] slaine for bringing Life;
But to the Cross he nailes thy Enemies,   415
The Law that is against thee, and the sins
Of all mankinde, with him there crucifi'd,[118]
Never to hurt them more who rightly trust
In this his satisfaction;[119] so he dies,
But soon revives, Death over him no power   420
Shall long usurp; ere the third dawning light
Returne, the Starres of Morn[120] shall see him rise
Out of his grave, fresh as the dawning light,
Thy ransom paid,[121] which Man from death redeems,
His death for Man, as many as offerd Life   425
Neglect not,[122] and the benefit imbrace
By Faith not void of workes:[123] this God-like act
Annuls thy doom, the death thou shouldst have dy'd,
In sin for ever lost from life; this act
Shall bruise the head of *Satan*, crush his strength   430
Defeating Sin and Death, his two maine armes,
And fix farr deeper in his head thir stings[124]
Then temporal death[125] shall bruise the Victors heel,
Or theirs[126] whom he redeems, a death like sleep,
A gentle wafting to immortal Life.   435

---

[114]Christ is often reproached during His career on earth, as when the Philistines accuse Him of violating the Sabbath. His death on the Cross is cursed, as in Galatians 3.13: "for it is written, Cursed is everyone that hangeth on a tree."

[115]If humankind is justified by faith, the imputing (attributing vicariously) of Christ's merits to humanity is necessary for humankind to be saved. Humankind gets what it does not deserve, by imputation, if it is faithful.

[116]Loh reads the construction to be rearranged as "and condemned to a shameful and accursed death" (412–13n).

[117]The Jews were traditionally blamed for the Crucifixion of their own Messiah in Christ, but there is no evidence in Milton's works that he condemned Jews for having allowed the Crucifixion.

[118]Michael envisions the old law dying, along with the enemies of Christ and the sins of humankind, on the Cross. Christ's death takes away the sins of the world and represents a defeat for the enemies of Christianity. The entire scene of Christ meeting an ignominious defeat with triumph is ironic.

[119]Compare the phrase from the 1644 edition of the *Doctrine and Discipline of Divorce*: "the prime end of the Gospel is not so much to exact our obedience, as to reveal grace and the satisfaction of our disobedience" (Yale 2: 304–05).

[120]The stars of morning are probably the "morning stars [who] sang together," when "all the sons of God shouted for joy" at the Creation as described by the Lord speaking from the whirlwind in Job 38.7. Those real "sons of God" are to be differentiated from the false "sons of God" who bred with the "daughters of men" at Genesis 6.2. In the image in question, "Starres of Morn" may represent those angels who, like the morning and the evening star, set and then rise again in a kind of resurrection. If Milton is alluding to Job 38.7, the same angels were present at the beginning of the world who will be present at the Resurrection. The morning stars also complement the Son as the sun: they witness the dawning light of the Resurrection.

[121]Matthew 20.28 describes Christ as "Son of man" offering His life as ransom when He dies on the Cross. See also Mark 10.45.

[122]The "many as offerd Life" suggests an elect, those who are saved by God's election at 3.173 or 3.183–84.

[123]Salvation is more by faith than by works, though faith itself is a kind of action: "Obviously if to believe is to act then faith is an action, or rather a habit acquired by frequent actions, not merely infused. It is by this that we are justified . . ." (*On Christian Doctrine* 1.22; Yale 6: 489).

[124]The imagery of "O death, where is thy sting" (1 Corinthians 15.55) here pictures the stings of Sin and Death in the head of Satan (from whence Sin originally issued).

[125]The death of the body occurs in time as humans perceive it and is therefore "temporal" or temporary, since Milton believed that death was a kind of going to sleep until the Second Coming of the Messiah. Technically, the heresy was known as "thnetopsychism" and more popularly as the "sleeper heresy." See Kelley's introduction to *On Christian Doctrine*: Yale 6: 91–95.

[126]Perhaps this anomalous spelling is worth noting, since "thir" is preferred in the great majority of instances. By 497 below the compositor is back to the normal "thir."

Nor after resurrection shall he stay
Longer on Earth then certaine times to appeer
To his Disciples, Men who in his Life
Still° follow'd him; to them shall leave in charge   ALWAYS
To teach all nations what of him they learn'd   440
And his Salvation, them who shall beleeve
Baptizing in the profluent stream,[127] the signe
Of washing them from guilt of sin to Life
Pure, and in mind prepar'd, if so befall,
For death, like that which the redeemer dy'd.   445
All Nations they shall teach;[128] for from that day
Not onely to the Sons of *Abrahams*[129] Loines
Salvation shall be Preacht, but to the Sons
Of *Abrahams* Faith wherever through the world;
So in his seed all Nations shall be blest.   450
Then to the Heav'n of Heav'ns he shall ascend
With victory, triumphing[130] through the aire
Over his foes and thine; there shall surprise
The Serpent, Prince of aire,[131] and drag in Chaines[132]
Through all his Realme, and there confounded° leave;   DAMNED   455
Then enter into glory, and resume
His Seat at Gods right hand, exalted high
Above all names in Heav'n; and thence shall come,
When this worlds disolution shall be ripe,
With glory and power to judge both quick and dead,[133]   460
To judge th' unfaithful dead, but to reward
His faithful, and receave them into bliss,
Whether in Heav'n or Earth,[134] for then the Earth
Shall all be Paradise, far happier place
Then this of *Eden*, and far happier daies.[135]   465

---

[127]Milton believed, along with some Protestant sects still existing, that baptism should be performed in running water (a close translation of the Latin phrase *aqua profluens* which Milton used in *On Christian Doctrine* as *in profluentem aquam* [1.28; Yale 6: 544n]). As Maurice Kelley summarizes in the Yale *Complete Prose*, "Milton's position on this sacrament may be described as Socinian-Anabaptist immersionism, with the further stipulation that the rite must be performed in running water" (6: 544n6).

[128]The book of Acts describes the spread of Christ's word by apostles, "a fewe simple men of no reputation, who replenished all the world with the sounde of his Gospel" (Geneva Bible, 1560 ed., the "Argument" to Acts).

[129]Abraham was interpreted as an ancestor of all races, not merely the Jews. Milton speaks of the fulfilment of God's promise "to *Abraham* and his seed in the *Messiah*" (*Apology Against a Pamphlet*, Yale 1: 950).

[130]Probably accented on the second syllable, as in every other instance in Milton's poetry, although the word triumph may be accented on the first or second syllable, as in 9.948 vs. 10.537.

[131]Ephesians 2.2 describes a tempting spirit which commentators interpreted as Satan: "the prince of the power of the air, the spirit that now worketh in the children of disobedience." Milton cited the passage in order to show that the "Bad angels" "are able to wander all over the earth, the air, and even heaven, to carry out God's judgments" (*On Christian Doctrine* 1.9; Yale 6: 348).

[132]"And I saw an angel come down from heaven, having the key of the bottomless pit and a great chain in his hand. And he laid hold on the dragon, that old serpent, which is the Devil, and Satan, and bound him a thousand years, And cast him into the bottomless pit . . . " (Revelation 20.1–2). Thus Satan is chained when he is cast into Hell, so it is assumed that at the Last Judgment he will still be in chains as he is dragged through his realm.

[133]The phrase "to judge both the quick and the dead" is part of the Apostles' Creed (and the Bible, as in 2 Timothy 4.1), but Milton quickly qualifies "the dead" to mean "th' unfaithful dead" and thus emends the Creed. The "quick" are those who are living or those who still have the power of motion.

[134]The question is what is meant by "the new heaven and the new earth" in Revelation 21.1, which was interpreted to mean "All things shalbe renued and restored into a moste excellent and perfect estate, and therefore the day of the resurrection is called, The day of restauracion of all things, Acts 5.21" (Geneva Bible, 1560 ed., marginal note to 21.1). Milton hesitates to interpret the passage in Revelation 21.1.

[135]The "far happier" place will be "A paradise within thee [Adam and his descendants], happier farr" of 587 below.

So spake th' Archangel *Michael*, then paus'd,[136]
As at the Worlds great period;[137] and our Sire
Replete with joy and wonder thus repli'd.
    O goodness infinite, goodness immense!
That all this good of evil shall produce,
And evil turn to good;[138] more wonderful   470
Then that which by creation first brought forth
Light out of darkness! full of doubt I stand,
Whether I should repent me now of sin
By mee done and occasiond, or rejoyce
Much more, that much more good thereof shall spring,   475
To God more glory, more good will to Men
From God, and over wrauth grace shall abound.[139]
But say, if our deliverer up to Heav'n
Must reascend, what will betide the few
His faithful, left among th' unfaithful herd,   480
The enemies of truth; who then shall guide
His people, who defend? will they not deale
Wors with his followers then with him they dealt?[140]
    Be sure they will, said th' Angel; but from Heav'n
Hee to his own a Comforter[141] will send,   485
The promise of the Father, who shall dwell
His Spirit within them, and the Law of Faith
Working through love,[142] upon thir hearts shall write,
To guide them in all truth, and also arme   490
With spiritual Armour,[143] able to resist

---

[136]As Fowler points out (466–67n), this pause is carefully timed, corresponding with Michael's first pause at 12.2. The pauses will divide Adam's instruction into three parts corresponding to the three drops of the well of life that have been infused into his eyes (11.416). The three instruction periods may be divided into 11.429–901, 12.1–467, and 12.468–605. See Raymond Waddington, "The Death of Adam: Vision and Voice in Books XI and XII of *Paradise Lost*," *Modern Philology* 70 (1972): 9–21.

[137]"Period" is used in the sense of "termination," or in this case "Last Judgment." If Fowler is correct, Michael's first pause was after six thousand years of human history and the second pause comes at the Millenium (usually defined as the thousand years after the Second Coming of Christ). The divine weeks and works, as in DuBartas's title, could therefore represent all history as known to humankind. In *The City of God*, St. Augustine outlines the seven ages of humankind as days: "The first age, as the first day, extends from Adam to the deluge; the second from the deluge to Abraham, equalling the first, not in length of time, but in the number of generations, there being ten in each. From Abraham to the advent of Christ there are, as the evangelist Matthew calculates, three periods, in each of which are fourteen generations—one period from Abraham to David, a second from David to the captivity, a third from the captivity to the birth of Christ in the flesh. There are thus five ages in all. The sixth is now passing and cannot be measured by any number of generations . . . . After this period God shall rest as on the seventh day, when He shall give us (who shall be the seventh day) rest in Himself" (22.30; trans. Dods 867).

[138]Adam celebrates, perhaps prematurely, what has often been labeled by modern critics "the Paradox of the Fortunate Fall" (the term "O felix culpa," "O happy sin," is taken from the Exultet for Holy Saturday in the Catholic missal), that out of sin a greater good should proceed. Lovejoy outlines the history of the idea, and Mollenkott ("Milton's Rejection") questions Milton's subscription to it: Michael does describe a Paradise within Adam and Eve that is happier than that which they leave in Eden, but whether it would have been better for the couple never to have given in to temptation certainly has always been open to dispute. John Ulreich addresses the issue brilliantly in "A Paradise Within: The Fortunate Fall in *Paradise Lost*," *Journal of the History of Ideas* 32 (1971): 351–66. Michael, however, is not quite at the point of agreeing with everything Adam has just said (he will be at 575–76 below).

[139]As indicated by John Bunyan's title *Grace Abounding to the Chief of Sinners* (1666), the phrase derived from "where sin abounded, grace did much more abound" (Romans 5.20) was popular at least among Nonconformists.

[140]The passage suggests that the righteous followers of the "deliverer" will undergo punishments, as they imitate Christ, that are even worse than crucifixion.

[141]Milton interprets John 15.25: "But when the Comforter is come, whom I will send unto you from the Father, even the Spirit of truth, which proceedeth from the Father, he shall testify of me."

[142]Compare the "faith which worketh by love" of Galatians 5.6. See also Romans 3.27 and Hebrews 8.10.

[143]Following very closely the imagery of Ephesians 6.11–17, which is concerned with Christians putting on the "whole armour of God" to defend themselves "against the wiles of the devil" (11; compare the behavior of Spenser's Red Cross Knight in Book 1 of the *The Faerie Queene*). Their loins should be girded with truth, they wear the "breastplate of righteousness" (14), but above all, they should be "taking the shield of faith, wherewith [they] shall be able to quench all the fiery darts of the wicked" (16). There are so many echoes of the Pauline epistles through line 508 that Michael's speech becomes a tissue of quotations.

Satans assaults, and quench his fierie darts,
What man can do against them, not affraid,
Though to the death, against such cruelties
With inward consolations recompenc't,   495
And oft supported so as shall amaze
Thir proudest persecuters: for the Spirit
Powrd first on his Apostles,[144] whom he sends
To evangelize the Nations, then on all
Baptiz'd, shall them with wondrous gifts endue   500
To speak all Tongues,[145] and do all Miracles,
As did thir Lord before them. Thus they win
Great numbers of each Nation to receave
With joy the tidings brought from Heav'n: at length
Thir Ministry perform'd, and race well run,[146]   505
Thir doctrine and thir story written left,
They die; but in thir room, as they forewarne,
Wolves shall succeed for teachers, grievous Wolves,[147]
Who all the sacred mysteries of Heav'n
To thir own vile advantages shall turne   510
Of lucre[148] and ambition, and the truth
With superstitions and traditions taint,
Left onely in those written Records pure,
Though not but by the Spirit understood.
Then shall they seek to avail themselves of names,   515
Places and titles, and with these to joine
Secular power, though feigning still to act
By spiritual, to themselves appropriating
The Spirit of God, promisd alike and giv'n
To all Beleevers;[149] and from that pretense,   520
Spiritual Lawes by carnal power shall force
On every conscience;[150] Laws which none shall finde

---

[144]Pentecost, as reported in Acts 2.

[145]Referring to the abilities of St. Paul and other apostles who miraculously could speak in the tongues or languages of peoples that they were trying to convert to Christianity. The practice is first alluded to in Mark 16.17, then shown in action in Acts 2.4–7.

[146]The race is described in 1 Corinthians 9.24–26: "Know ye not that they which run in a race run all, but one receiveth the prize? So run, that ye may obtain. And every man that striveth for the mastery is temperate in all things. Now they do it to obtain a corruptible crown; but we an incorruptible." For Milton's use of the same image, compare the race for the "immortall garland" in *Areopagitica* (Yale 2: 515).

[147]Perhaps thinking that the King's censor will not read as far as Book 12, Milton dares here to excoriate the negligent clergy that he had first attacked with the same imagery in the "grim Woolf with privy paw" of "Lycidas" 128. The wolf simile of 4.183–87 is not so obviously polemical. But Fowler believes the passage to be attacking "everything in the Church that is not built by Faith" (507–08n), and Schultz argues that Milton's portrayal of the Antichrist is directed at the Roman Catholic Church (127). The wolf imagery of the entire passage is based on Acts 20.29: "For I know this, that after my departing shall grievous wolves enter in among you, not sparing the flock."

[148]"Feed the flock of God which is among you, taking the oversight thereof, not by constraint, but willingly; not for filthy lucre, but of a ready mind" (1 Peter 5.2). Milton's tract *Considerations Touching the Likeliest Means To Remove Hirelings out of the Christian Church* (1659) focuses on getting rid of prelates working only for the wages. "Filthy lucre" is proverbial in the Pauline epistles, meaning something like "tainted money."

[149]The "inner light" of understanding scripture that Milton and other Puritans believed to be given to "all Beleevers" is contrasted with the proprietary claim of the Roman Catholic clergy to "The Spirit of God."

[150]Milton seems to be expressing his own anger at reliance on tradition and temporal rather than spiritual laws within the church. He often attacked the Roman Catholic or English church's quest for secular power in his prose tracts, as in *Of Reformation* (1641): "Let us not be so overcredulous, unless God hath blinded us, as to trust our deer Soules into the hands of men that beg so devoutly for the pride, and gluttony of their owne backs, and bellies, that sue and sollicite so eagerly, not for the saving of Soules, the consideration of which can have heer no place at all, but for their Bishopricks, Deaneries, Prebends, and Chanonies [possibly 'canonries']" (Yale 1: 610).

Left them inrould,[151] or what the Spirit within
Shall on the heart engrave. What will they then
But force the Spirit of Grace[152] it self, and binde   525
His consort Libertie; what, but unbuild
His living Temples, built by Faith to stand,
Thir own Faith not anothers: for on Earth
Who against Faith and Conscience can be heard
Infallible?[153] yet many will presume: 530
Whence heavie persecution shall arise
On all who in the worship persevere
Of Spirit and Truth;[154] the rest, farr greater part,
Well[155] deem in outward Rites and specious formes
Religion satisfi'd; Truth shall retire   535
Bestuck with slandrous darts, and works of Faith[156]
Rarely be found: so shall the World goe on,
To good malignant, to bad men benigne,
Under her own waight groaning[157] till the day
Appeer of respiration[158] to the just,   540
And vengeance to the wicked,[159] at return
Of him so lately promiss'd to thy aid[160]
The Womans seed, obscurely then foretold,
Now amplier known thy Saviour and thy Lord,[161]
Last in the Clouds from Heav'n to be reveald   545
In glory of the Father, to dissolve[162]
Satan with his perverted World, then raise

---

[151]"Enrolled," or inscribed in written legal or spiritual records. Compare Jeremiah 31.33: "I will put my law in their inward parts, and write it in their hearts." The syntax is puzzling, especially if one reads the line as Loh does (522–24n), to have eleven syllables (if "Spirit" is read as a monosyllable, however, the line is regular). Loh would prefer to omit the pronoun "them" (522–24n). Newton does not have the trouble Loh has; he paraphrases, "Laws neither agreeable to reveal'd or natural religion, neither to be found in holy Scripture, or written on their hearts by the Spirit of God, according to that divine promise [ciding Jeremiah 31.33]" (522n).

[152]The association between Spirit and liberty is made in 2 Corinthians 3.17: "Now the Lord is that Spirit: and where the Spirit of the Lord is, there is liberty." Milton clarifies his meaning in *On Christian Doctrine*: " . . . our liberty could not be perfect or manifest before the advent of Christ, our liberator. Therefore liberty is a matter relevant chiefly to the gospel, and is associated with it. This is so, first, because truth exists chiefly under the gospel . . . " (1.27; Yale 6: 536).

[153]Though Fowler reminds us that the doctrine of Papal Infallibility was not instituted until 1870 (528–30n), Milton had attacked the Pope for claiming "this infallibilitie over both the conscience and the scripture" (*A Treatise on Civil Power*; Yale 7: 248).

[154]"But the hour cometh, and now is, when the true worshipers shall worship the Father in spirit and in truth: for the Father seeketh such to worship him" (John 4.23).

[155]The text of *1667* has "Will," and either of the two readings might be acceptable. Darbishire chooses "Will" and so does Shawcross, but Fowler chooses "Well." On the grounds that in this case "Well" may indicate a correction, "Well" is my choice, especially since it would express sardonically the action of "the rest." As Fletcher writes, after expressing his preference for "Well," " . . . who can tell exactly what Milton wanted here?"

[156]Compare "Faith not void of workes" in 427 above.

[157]The text of *1667* has a comma here. The participle "groaning" is derived from Romans 8.22, which looks forward to a future deliverance from "the sufferings of this present time" (8.18): "For we know that the whole creation groaneth and travaileth in pain together until now." The reader is meant to remember that the entire creation groaned at the completion of the original sin at 9.1001.

[158]Opportunity to breathe again (*OED* 3), as in the modern "breather." Acts 3.19 is probably the source for the concept of atonement being followed by refreshment: "Repent ye therefore, and be converted, that your sins may be blotted out, when the times of refreshing shall come from the presence of the Lord." As Fowler points out, the Greek word ἀνάψυξις of the Septuagint is sometimes translated with the Latin *respiratio* (539–51n).

[159]Discussing the fate of the wicked, Psalm 58 predicts "The righteous shall rejoice when he seeth the vengeance: he shall wash his feet in the blood of the wicked. So that a man shall say, Verily there is a reward for the righteous: verily he is a God that judgeth in the earth" (10–11).

[160]The text of *1667* has a comma here, which would place "The Womans seed" in apposition with "him," though the phrase seems to be restrictive, to modern ears, and seems not to need a comma.

[161]The "Seed" is now more fully revealed to be the Son, who is both Lord and Savior.

[162]Annihilate or utterly destroy (*OED* 7), almost in the modern sense of "vaporize." Perhaps we are asked to remember that spirits "Cannot but by annihilating die" (6.347). "After a thousand years," Milton writes in *On Christian Doctrine*, "Satan will come again, raging, and will besiege the church with huge forces, with all the enemies of the church collected together. But he will be thrown down by fire from heaven and condemned to everlasting punishment" (1.33; Yale 6: 625).

From the conflagrant mass,[163] purg'd and refin'd,
New Heav'ns, new Earth, Ages of endless date
Founded in righteousness and peace and love[164]
To bring forth fruits[165] Joy and eternal Bliss.   550
    He ended; and thus *Adam* last reply'd.
How soon hath thy prediction, Seer blest,
Measur'd this transient World, the Race of time,[166]
Till time stand fixt:[167] beyond is all abyss,   555
Eternitie, whose end no eye can reach.
Greatly instructed I shall hence depart,
Greatly in peace of thought, and have my fill
Of knowledge, what this Vessel[168] can containe;
Beyond which was my folly to aspire.   560
Henceforth I learne, that to obey[169] is best,
And love with fear[170] the onely God, to walk
As in his presence, ever to observe
His providence, and on him sole depend,
Mercifull over all his works,[171] with good   565
Still overcoming evil,[172] and by small
Accomplishing great things, by things deemd weak[173]
Subverting worldly strong, and worldly wise
By simply meek; that suffering for Truths sake
Is fortitude to highest victorie,[174]   570
And to the faithful Death the Gate of Life;
Taught this by his example whom I now
Acknowledge my Redeemer ever blest.
    To whom thus also th' Angel last repli'd:
This having learnt, thou hast attain the summe   575
Of wisdom; hope no higher, though all the Starrs
Thou knewst by name, and all th' ethereal Powers,
All secrets of the deep, all Natures works,
Or works of God in Heav'n, Aire, Earth, or Sea,
And all the riches of this World enjoydst,   580
And all the rule, one Empire; onely add
Deeds to thy knowledge answerable, add Faith,

---

[163]Compare the last two lines of Book 11. Milton believed that eternal death came not only to the damned but to "this foul and polluted world itself, . . . its end and conflagration" (*On Christian Doctrine* 1.33; Yale 6: 627), but theologians argued over whether the conflagration would come to the world's substance or only to its qualities (Yale 6: 627n).

[164]The text of *1667* has a comma here.

[165]This is another series that would seem to demand a comma, in this case after "fruits." Notably, the 1688 Folio does not attempt to correct the punctuation, though some modern editors, like B. A. Wright and Douglas Bush, add the comma as a silent emendation.

[166]For the full implications of the term in Renaissance historiography, see Baker, *The Race of Time.*

[167]In Revelation 10.6, an angel swears by the Creator "that there should be time no longer."

[168]Not the body but the intellect. Possibly Milton has in mind St. Paul's advice to Timothy: "If a man therefore purge himself from ['vessels of gold and of silver'], he shall be a vessel unto honour, sanctified, and meet for the master's use, and prepared unto every good work" (2 Timothy 2.21).

[169]Obviously answering his crime of man's first disobedience.

[170]"Fear of the Lord" is a formula of the Old Testament, almost never used in a negative context: "the fear of the Lord is the beginning of wisdom" (Psalm 111.10) is typical usage. The Lord is quoted in Deuteronomy 10.12 as saying " . . . what doth the Lord thy God require of thee, but to fear the Lord thy God, to walk in all his ways, and to love him, and to serve the Lord thy God with all thy heart and with all thy soul. . . ."

[171]"The Lord is good to all: and his tender mercies are over all his works" (Psalm 145.9).

[172]The phrase may be taken from Romans 12.21, "overcome evil with good."

[173]" . . . God hath chosen the weak things of the world to confound the things which are mighty" (1 Corinthians 1.27).

[174]Compare other passages that deal with patience and heroic martyrdom, in *Paradise Lost* and elsewhere, as with 9.31–33, *Paradise Regain'd* 1.426, and *Samson Agonistes* 654.

Add vertue, Patience, Temperance, add Love,[175]
By name to come call'd Charitie, the soul
Of all the rest: then wilt thou not be loath   585
To leave this Paradise, but shalt possess
A paradise within thee,[176] happier farr.
Let us descend now therefore from this top
Of Speculation;[177] for the hour precise
Exacts our parting hence;[178] and see the Guards,   590
By mee encampt on yonder Hill, expect
Thir motion,[179] at whose Front a flaming Sword,
In signal of remove, waves fiercely round;
We may no longer stay: go, waken *Eve*;
Her also I with gentle Dreams have calm'd   595
Portending good, and all her spirits[180] compos'd
To meek submission:[181] thou at season fit
Let her with thee partake what thou hast heard,
Chiefly what may concern her Faith to know,
The great deliverance by her Seed to come   600
(For by the Womans Seed)[182] on all Mankind,[183]
That ye may live, which will be many dayes,[184]
Both in one Faith unanimous though sad,
With cause for evils past, yet much more cheer'd
With meditation on the happie end.   605

    He ended, and they both descend the Hill;
Descended, *Adam* to the Bowre where *Eve*
Lay sleeping ran before, but found her wak't;[185]
And thus with words not sad[186] she him receav'd.

    Whence thou returnst, and whither wentst, I know;   610

[handwritten margin notes: "Adam wakes up Eve" and "Eves lost words start here"]

---

[175]"Add to your faith virtue; and to virtue knowledge; And to knowledge temperance; and to temperance patience; and to patience godliness; And to godliness brotherly kindness; and to brotherly kindness charity" (2 Peter 1.5–7). Notice that Milton omits mention of godliness and brotherly love and adds deeds. He cites 2 Peter 1.5 as evidence that "What chiefly constitutes the true worship of God is eagerness to do good works" (*On Christian Doctrine* 2.1; Yale 6: 637).

[176]Corresponding to Satan's "Hell within" at 4.20. G. C. Taylor 208 cites Robert Croft, *A Paradice within us; or the Happie Mind* (1640), which uses much of the terminology Milton uses to give advice about how to obtain an internal paradise based on tranquility of mind. If this line is compared with the injunction to Jesus at the close of the temptations in *Paradise Regain'd*—"by vanquishing / Temptation, [thou] hast regain'd lost Paradise, / And frustrated the conquest fraudulent" (4.607–09)—one may argue that the true subject of *Paradise Lost* is that inner order and that the whole poem can be read on one level as a symbolic depiction of this inward loss. See Martz, *The Paradise Within*, 103–67.

[177]Vantage point or place from which things can be seen clearly.

[178]It is (as far as we can tell) once again the noon hour, the hour when Eve had eaten the fruit (see Cirillo). Since one full day has passed, it is appropriate that Adam and Eve be punished at least figuratively with the "death" of leaving Eden in the sense that God's promise to punish them "in the day that ye eat thereof" will be fulfilled. Not only the Fall and the Expulsion but also the Crucifixion were all supposed to occur at the noon hour.

[179]"Expect their orders to deploy," using *motion* as a military term, to be followed by another word, *remove*, which had the military sense of an ordered departure. The angels are still under Michael's command, though the flaming sword does give the command.

[180]Apparently a monosyllable here.

[181]There is no evidence in *Paradise Lost* that Eve's proper role according to Milton is anything other than "meek submission," especially after the Fall. Nevertheless, she is the participant in the Fall who has the last word in the epic.

[182]The phrase seems awkward and perhaps redundant, since the "Seed" has been mentioned as recently as 543, and Fowler's gloss, "for it will be by one born of a virgin," does not quite seem to fit the sense, unless Michael is projecting "Woman" as the Virgin Mary, alluded to (but not with the title "Woman") at 368.

[183]Some copies of *1667* have a comma here, even though *1674* does not. I restore the comma on the grounds that the next four lines represent a fragment without it. My thanks for pointing this out go to an anonymous copyeditor for Macmillan.

[184]According to Genesis 5.5, Adam lived to be 930, an average age for a patriarch. Renaissance paintings sometimes show Adam and Eve in extreme old age.

[185]Newton was the first editor to point out the inconsistency with the Argument of this book, which states clearly that Adam "*wakens* Eve, *who all this while had slept*" (608n).

[186]Eve's dream has refreshed her, so that Adam's enthusiasm in running to see her is matched by her encouraging words: they both are "cheer'd" and "not sad." The rapid changes in tense in the verb forms used from 605 through 608 help indicate their excitement.

For God is also in sleep, and Dreams advise,[187]
Which he hath sent propitious, some great good
Presaging, since with sorrow and hearts distress
Wearied I fell asleep: but now lead on;
In mee is no delay; with thee to goe,   615
Is to stay here;[188] without thee here to stay,
Is to go hence unwilling; thou to mee
Art all things under Heav'n, all places thou,
Who for my wilful crime[189] art banisht hence.
This further consolation yet secure   620
I carry hence; though all by mee is lost,
Such favour I unworthie am voutsaft,
By mee the Promis'd Seed shall all restore.
    So spake our Mother *Eve*, and *Adam* heard
Well pleas'd, but answer'd not; for now too nigh   625
Th' Archangel stood, and from the other Hill
To thir fixt Station, all in bright array
The Cherubim descended; on the ground
Gliding meteorous,[190] as Ev'ning Mist
Ris'n from a River o're the marish° glides,   MARSH   630
And gathers ground fast at the Labourers heel
Homeward returning.[191] High in Front advanc't,
The brandisht Sword of God before them blaz'd
Fierce as a Comet;[192] which with torrid heat,
And vapour as the *Libyan* Air adust,   635
Began to parch that temperate Clime; whereat
In either hand the hastning Angel caught
Our lingring Parents,[193] and to th' Eastern Gate
Led them direct, and down the Cliff as fast
To the subjected Plaine; then disappeer'd.   640
They looking back, all th' Eastern side beheld
Of Paradise, so late thir happie seat,

---

[187]Eve acknowledges the fact that her dream is a vision of the future, as in Numbers 12.6: "I the Lord will make myself known unto him in a vision, and will speak to him in a dream."

[188]May echo the famous oath of loyalty spoken by Ruth to her mother-in-law Naomi: " . . . for whither thou goest, I will go; and where thou lodgest, I will lodge: thy people shall be my people, and thy God my God" (Ruth 1.16). Ruth's loyalty so attracts Boaz that he marries her. By Milton's era, the phrase "whither thou goest" was understood to mean a wife (Tilley W316). As Newton first pointed out, Eve is following Michael's injunction at 11.292, "Where he abides, think there thy native soile." Newton comments, "So that the Author makes Woman's Paradise to be in company with her husband, but Man's to be in himself" (616n).

[189]Eve is perhaps taking too much of the blame for what has previously been called her "inabstinence" (11.476): though she has taken part in a great crime, all is not lost just because of her, and Adam did have to complete the "mortal Sin / Original" (9.1003–04).

[190]A picture of cherubim walking as if above the ground, like a mist. "Meteorous" is Milton's coined version (the *OED* cites this as the first instance of the adjectival form) of "meteoric." A meteor might be any volatile exhalation of the earth, from mist and *ignis fatuus* near the surface on up to fireballs or comets and shooting stars in the sky.

[191]Is the mist sinister (like Satan when he appears in Eden "Like a black mist low creeping" in 9.180) or is it positive because it is here associated with the cherubim? The answer is probably yes and no. All the various exhalations of the earth—the *ignis fatuus*, the comet of 634 below and the torrid heat of Libya—all have negative connotations, at least two out of the three being closely associated with Satanic evil omens. But here the cherubim and the emblematic sword are all doing their duty in threatening Adam and Eve the way that an incoming mist might threaten a laborer heading home at dusk. The subtexts buried carefully in the imagery remind us that Adam is indeed a laborer now, one who must live by the sweat of his brow, and that his heel is made not only for running away but for crushing the head of the Serpent. Also, not only the cherubim and the sword are menacing: the very seasons and climate of the place that was Eden are becoming torrid, "adust"—scorched or utterly dried up.

[192]Again, the comet is an omen of disaster.

[193]If one contrasts the image of the angel hand-in-hand with Adam and Eve with the menacing natural images, one is still left with hope. Fowler, following Addison, sees the angel's conduct of Adam and Eve out of Eden as being like that of the two angels who lead Lot and his wife and daughters out of Sodom (Genesis 19.16). I do not see many grounds for comparison, since Lot's family is being led from an evil place to a good place (though both Sodom and Eden are being destroyed and an angel leads both families). Usually Milton draws his biblical analogies so that there are more exact correspondences.

Wav'd over by that flaming Brand,[194] the Gate
With dreadful Faces throng'd and fierie Armes:[195]
Som natural tears they drop'd, but wip'd them soon;
The World was all before them, where to choose[196]
Thir place of rest, and Providence thir guide:
They hand in hand with wandring steps and slow,[197]
Through *Eden* took thir solitarie way.

645

THE END.

---

[194]The word "Brand" works in several senses, since the Italian poetic word for sword is *brando*, but the sense as in "firebrand" was also current (*OED* 2). Spenser had used the word to mean "sword" (as in "steely brand" [*The Faerie Queene* 5.1.9]). The *OED* does record the usage of "brand" as "sword" in II.8.b.
[195]The cherubim are at the gate along with the sword, which seems to be oscillating, a sufficiently menacing vision to keep Adam and Eve from thinking of re-entry. The dreadfulness of the angelic guard and the sword seems to represent justice rather than horror. Although there is no suggestion of this in Genesis 3, William B. Hunter has shown that there was a tradition among commentators that the angelic guards were frightening, citing Milton's near-contemporary Henry More. See *Modern Language Review* 44 (1949): 90–91.
[196]Fowler points out acutely that "Providence" can be the object of "choose." Not only do "decisions of faith lie ahead" (647n), the verb *choose* indicates that free will is again in operation with Adam and Eve; God's providence always has been in effect. Images of near despair ("dreadful Faces") are carefully balanced against images of great hope ("hand in hand").
[197]The fact that their steps are wandering and slow should not be taken as an indication that Adam and Eve are in error or that they are hesitant. Psalm 107.4 helps establish a context: "They ['the redeemed of the Lord' of 107.2] wandered in the wilderness in a solitary way; they found no city to dwell in." Here Adam and Eve are still wandering in the country around Paradise, that of Eden, and of course they find no city. The psalm goes on to offer hope to the same wanderers: "Then they cried unto the Lord in their trouble, and he delivered them out of their distresses" (6). The message of the entire psalm is one of hope in the goodness and mercy of God.

Paradise Regain'd (1671)

Introduction

It has not the harmony of numbers, the sublimity of thought, and the beauties of diction, which are in *Paradise Lost*. It is composed in a lower and less striking stile, a stile suited to the subject. Artful sophistry, false reasoning, set off in the most specious manner, and refuted by the Son of God with strong unaffected eloquence, is the peculiar excellence of this poem. Satan there defends a bad cause with great skill and subtlety, as one thoroughly versed in that craft.

> —John Jortin, as quoted by Thomas Newton
> in his 1766 edition of the poem.

POSSIBLE OCCASION: ELLWOOD'S QUESTION

"Thou hast said much here [in *Paradise Lost*] of *Paradise lost*; but what hast thou to say of *Paradise found*?" (Shawcross, *John Milton* 148), asked Milton's somewhat presumptuous Quaker friend and amanuensis Thomas Ellwood, in 1665, after Ellwood had read the manuscript. Ellwood had helped Milton find a brick cottage in Chalfont-St.Giles, northwest of London, to avoid the plague then raging in the city. According to Ellwood, Milton's initial response was silence (for an account of what happened, preserved only from Ellwood's perspective, see Parker 597–98 and McLaughlin). Then more than a year passed, until Milton had produced *Paradise Regain'd* and could show it to Ellwood. Milton acknowledged, perhaps condescendingly, that the production of the brief epic was all due to Ellwood's question. Ellwood quotes Milton as saying: *"This is owing to you: for you put it into my head by the question you put to me at* Chalfont, *which before I had not thought of"* (Shawcross, *John Milton* 148). Milton was fifty-four, Ellwood twenty-three, and the exchange between them might have been made in good spirits between master and pupil, though Christopher Ricks makes a good case for taking Ellwood seriously (*English Poetry* 293–94).

There is evidence, however, that Milton had been planning a brief epic on the subject of the temptation of Christ long before he met Ellwood. As Shawcross writes, "*Paradise Regain'd* was perhaps a result of further cogitation about a drama on Christ as first suggested for different 'plots' in the [Trinity Manuscript], . . . dated in early 1642." Shawcross believes that work on a drama that became the short epic may have begun "in the pre-1649 period" (*John Milton* 151). Certainly Milton was using Christ as a subject of a poem as early as "The Passion," which was probably written in March 1630, and "Upon the Circumcision," written some time in the 1630s—not to mention the Nativity Ode of 1629.

Topics listed in the outlines for biblical tragedies of the Trinity Manuscript include "Christ born," "Christ bound," "Christ Crucifi'd" (Yale 8: 559). There is even a short plot-summary for a projected play called "Christus patiens": "The Scene in yᵉ garden beginning fro[m] yᵉ comming thither till Judas betraies & yᵉ officers lead him away yᵉ rest by message & chorus, his agony may receiv noble expressions" (Yale 8: 580).

AUTHORIAL INTRUSION?

It may represent a critical fallacy to say that Milton identified closely with the character he called the Son of God in *Paradise Regain'd*, but I will do it anyway. Would Milton have dared to compare himself as he was in his youth to the young Christ? Many modern critics and some biographers might secretly respond "Certainly," though publically disavowing the biographical fallacy. In the 1950s, James Holly Hanford wrote unashamedly, "Yet Milton as certainly identifies himself with his calm philosophically triumphant Christ, as he had earlier identified himself with the rebellious Satan or the distraught and impassioned Adam, and the portrait is equally valid and important as a record of his inner life" (*John Milton* 201). The older Milton pictured the young Son of God like himself as he once was, the "Lady of Christ's [College]," in passive resistance to evil and degeneracy. When he signed a friend's autograph album on November 19, 1651, not long after his blindness became permanent, Milton dictated to an amanuensis a modified Greek quotation from Luke or more likely from 2 Corinthians, a phrase translated in the King James Bible as "I shall be perfected" (Luke 13.32) or "my strength is made perfect in weakness" (2 Corinthians 13.9). Then Milton signed his name (see Parker 389, and Campbell's correcting note). In other words, in 1651, Milton was closely identifying himself with the words of Christ.

At many points in the poem, Milton seems to be fitting the Son of God's character like a second skin over his own, or vice versa. The Son mirrors Milton in his seriousness and studious nature as a youth, his rejection of the temptation of sensuality and his "puritan" asceticism, his rejection of riches over education, his rejection of the mass of people in favor of an educated elite, and his rejection of tyrannical kingship or the theory of the divine right of kings. The Son even seems to have come from a hard-working bourgeois background, and he seems to be fighting for all the things Milton had fought for all his life—with the single exception of divorce. I do not want to go as far as A. L. Rowse, who proclaimed that for Milton "'God' was but a projection of his own ego" (58), but Milton's Son of God certainly resembles his creator, Milton.

Allied with the critical problem of determining if Milton identified with Christ, Milton's Son of God seems "cold" to a number of readers (Fisher, answered by Rushdy, "Frigorifick"). He may be perceived by modern readers as priggish or puritanical, since he so easily rejects temptations of the flesh, the devil, and the world. But how is a perfect man to talk, if not with simple, clear logic? Christopher Hill defines what some readers see as the "excessively negative attitude of Jesus" as the Son of God "rejecting, one by one, temptations which had led the English revolutionaries a-stray—avarice and ambition, the false politics of compromise with evil, clerical pride or ivory-tower escapism, the urge for instant solutions" (421).

DEFENSIVENESS ABOUT COMPARING *PARADISE REGAIN'D* WITH *PARADISE LOST*

Milton was protective and defensive about *Paradise Regain'd*. Apparently he could not tolerate hearing it dispraised. Edward Phillips wrote that "however it [*Paradise Regain'd*] is generally censur'd to be much inferiour to the other [*Paradise Lost*], . . . he could not hear with any patience any such thing when related to him," and Phillips added his own words in its defense, "but it is thought by the most judicious to be little or nothing inferiour to the other for stile and decorum" (Darbishire 76).

BIBLICAL SOURCES IN LUKE AND MATTHEW

Different biblical scholars have identified the Gospel of Luke as Milton's primary source for the most elaborate details of the story of the temptation of Christ (see, for instance, Radzinowicz "How Milton" 210), though Matthew offers most of the same details. The Gospel of Mark, however, takes only two verses to sum up the temptation, and John ignores it completely. Pope points out that Milton "follows the lead of Matthew" in assuming that "Satan appears in the wilderness and the temptations begin only at the expiration of the forty days, during which Christ has not been molested" (5).

The contrast between *Paradise Lost* and *Paradise Regain'd* implied in Milton's theme is easily supported in Scripture: "For as by one man's disobedience many were made sinners, so by the obedience of one shall many be made righteous" (Romans 5.19). The brief epic focuses on obedience. The contrast in Romans thus allows Milton to establish coherence between *Paradise Lost* and *Paradise Regain'd*.

THE DIFFICULTY OF CHARACTERIZING CHRIST

Sims finds the characterization of the Son of God to be "heightened dramatically by Biblical allusions which associate him with Abraham, Moses, and especially with the Christ of the New Testament . . ., [with] his unassuming, humble patience and his calm, fearless passivity under the hand of his Father, characteristics which are based on his assurance of who he is, what his mission is, and what the limitations of his adversary are" (200).

Yet anyone who dares characterize Christ on stage or in any medium which is subject to public scrutiny will be open to being criticized for making him seem a self-righteous prig. The Italian film director Pier Luigi Pasolini was criticized for making his Christ into a priggish twit; Hollywood movies like *The King of Kings* or *The Bible* must impose soaring and romantic music over the scene during which Christ delivers the Beatitudes; and a movie like *Monty Python's The Life of Brian* may be refreshing just for its destruction of the cinematic clichés surrounding the depiction of Christ. In other words, presenting the character Christ in a public medium is often a difficult and thankless job.

STYLE, IMAGERY, AND RHETORIC

When discussing his own prose style versus that of the earlier chroniclers of English history such as Matthew of Westminster, Milton wrote that, instead of imitating them, he would "choose to represent the truth naked, though as lean as a plain Journal" (*History of Britain*; Yale 5: 230). Milton seems to be representing the truth naked in his poetic style of *Paradise Regain'd*. Everything the Son of God says seems to epitomize Milton's ideal oratorical style as:

> As men divinely taught, and better teaching
> The solid rules of Civil Government
> In thir majestic unaffected stile
> Then all the Oratory of *Greece* and *Rome*.
> (4.357–60)

The "majestic unaffected stile" is the ideal style of *Paradise Regain'd*, the style by which all others are measured. The "perswasive Rhetoric / That sleek't [Satan's] tongue, and won so much on *Eve*" (4.4–5) has no place in the Son of God's mouth.

Like the speech of the Son of God within it, the style of *Paradise Regain'd* seems cold, distant, godlike, objective. Even Satan does not seem such a colorful or enticing character when his rhetoric faces the cold light of the Son's arguments. Some adjectives used of Milton's poetic style in the brief epic are "plain," "bald," "unadorned," "flat," "colorless," "dry," "muted," or "bleak" (Burnett 112). Ricks finds the style "repetitious and over-emphatic" even when it represents words in the mouth of God or the Son of God (297). On the other hand, Corns believes that the "sportive use of language" is "much more powerfully present in *Paradise Regained* [than in *Comus* and *Samson Agonistes*], both the tone and texture of which [i.e., those of *Paradise Regain'd*] have been rather undervalued by critical orthodoxy" (65). It may be useful to a modern reader to think of Milton moving away from the style of the earlier Shakespeare and Edmund Spenser and toward the style of Samuel Beckett, who owes more to Milton (Labriola, "Insuperable") than is generally acknowledged.

Milton's imagery often seems recycled from *Paradise Lost*, especially considering that he must reconstruct the character of Satan, now doomed to be defeated by the "one greater man" mentioned at the beginning of the longer epic. Satan is even more of a cosmic loser, and I mean that in a universal, not a colloquial, sense. He cannot flatter the Son of God as he did Eve, he cannot touch Christ with any temptation of the flesh as he did Adam with the beauty of Eve. Nor can Satan deceive Christ with disguises, the way even Comus could momentarily fool the Lady into thinking he was a simple cottager.

CHARACTERIZATION

There are only two characters emphasized in the brief epic, the Son of God and Satan, with brief appearances by Belial and Mary. We should not forget God the Father. Those are all the speaking parts, as if Milton were paring away dramatic elements to restore the purity of Aeschylus's limited number of characters in the earliest form of Greek tragedy. God the Father is a speaking character, as is the narrator, though, unlike the Epic Voice in *Paradise Lost*, the narrator of the brief epic has no personality or role that would allow him conversation with a divine muse. The character of God the Father seems to be allowed in *Paradise Regain'd* only to prove that the Son of God is not the same as his Father, almost as if the Son had been left on Earth on his own, to fend for himself.

Milton does not use a chorus or a narrating angel, unless we see the last antiphonal chorus of angels as the remnant of an earlier dramatic format. He certainly underplays his own participatory role as narrator or commentator on the action, largely eliminating the structure and authorial control that invocations impose on epic. At the beginning of the poem he only once invokes the Muse who (the reader is supposed to remember) inspired him to write *Paradise Lost*; then Milton is

done with muses for the duration of the poem. As Martz points out, Milton conflates the Son of God with the narrator, whose plain style governs that of the poem: both "Satan and the Son of God in this poem speak within the mind of one who hopes to be himself a Son of God; both of these actors use the human voice that this particular possible Son of God, John Milton, possesses" (261). I should point out, however, that Martz notes Satan's separate "sardonic commentary" on the Baptism (253). I would add that that same commentary is full of the involution and the lies inherent in Satan's character as displayed in his rhetoric.

Belial and Mary may be in the poem in order to point the contrast between the two of them. In modern parlance, Milton does not empower Mary in the sense used by feminist criticism when he gives her a speaking part, but at least he includes her; her role in the life of the Son of God is not trivialized or sentimentalized. She is the opposite of a *mater dolorosa*—she neither weeps nor whines—but she does add a human feminine element to the poem. Surely Milton is reacting against Roman Catholic "Mariolatry" that he might have observed on his trip to Italy in the late 1630s by making Mary into a simple mother with nothing unusual about her. It may be that the absence of a mother in *Samson Agonistes* is compensated for by the presence of Mary in *Paradise Regain'd*. Mary is not just the Blessed Virgin Mary to whom one was supposed to say "Hail Mary." She is a woman fairly amazed with what happened to her when the angel said *Hail Mary* (which Milton as a fervid Protestant may have felt was the only true and authentic time it should have been said).

"Mother" and "Son" and "Father" tie the poem together: being part of the family is the foundation of any character's strength. The perversity of Belial's lack of a family (he has only Satan as a "mate") demonstrates his contrasting weakness. The poem even closes on a quiet domestic scene: the Son returning to his mother's house. The biblical Belial, by contrast, is a person of the streets, without a home or family.

Belial is there for the perversity he represents and for the contrast he offers to the more clever Satan. As Milton pointed out in the *Doctrine and Discipline of Divorce* in 1644, there is "incommunicable antagony . . . between Christ and *Belial*" (Yale 2: 265). Belial's vision is limited to fleshly temptation. Satan understands Belial's methods of temptation but he disdains using them: he uses Belial's fleshly temptation (in the form of Ganymede and Hylas—for homosexual—and the nymphs—for heterosexual—temptation). But he adds flattery, competitiveness, and other intellectual temptations.

NOMENCLATURE: WHAT TO CALL JESUS, WHAT TO CALL GOD

One critical method used to discover Milton's meanings, even intentions, in *Paradise Regain'd* is to study his titles and epithets, as John Leonard has amply demonstrated in *Naming in Paradise*. Tracking the names used for Jesus Christ in the brief epic is a lesson in naming. He is most often called the Son or the Son of God (fifty-six times, forty of them in the epithet "Son of God"), but he is also identified once as the "Son of *David*" (4.500), once as "Son of the most High" (4.633), and once as "Morning Star" (1.294). He is simply "our Saviour" twenty-one times, and he is once given all his titles in a lump, as "Jesus Messiah Son of God declar'd" (2.4; notice the ambiguity in "declar'd"). In the end he is simply "our Saviour meek" (4.636). Six times he is called Jesus, probably not strategically, and he is never called Christ (which Milton took to mean merely "the anointed one"; see 2.50 and Martz 252) in *Paradise Regain'd* or, for that matter, in any of Milton's major poetry. "Christ" seems to Milton to be a generic title to be avoided, whereas the generic "Messiah," meaning God's anointed one but also meaning that semidivine being prophesied in the Old Testament, is used seven times. Milton seems to want Jesus to be identified most clearly in his role as Son of God. The Savior, despite his meekness, has the last word. In this introduction, and in my notes, I will refer to Milton's character as the Son of God, in order to try to fix his character's name as Milton preferred it.

In *On Christian Doctrine*, in the long chapter on the Son of God (1.5), Milton spends much of his time arriving at a description of the Son that will not confuse his reader about the distinction between the Son and the Father. He asks, aggressively, "What name, if not 'Son'?" (Yale 6: 206). Just as aggressively, as he skirts the borders of heresy, Milton states "The Father and the Son are certainly not one in essence" (219). The "Son receives his name from the Father" (260) as well as "his very being" (261). Milton's logic ultimately runs in this way:

> The name "Son," upon which my opponents chiefly build their theory of his supreme divinity, is in fact itself the best refutation of their theory. For a supreme God is self-existent, but a god who is not self-existent, who did not beget but was begotten, is not a first cause but an effect, and is therefore not a supreme God. (263–64)

The Father grants the Son the qualities of omnipresence, omniscience, and omnipotence, but "Even the Son . . . does not know absolutely everything, for there are some secrets which the Father has kept to himself alone"

(265). A valid question to ask of Milton's characterization of the Son would be "Does he really know who he is, at least at the beginning?"

THE CENTRAL DEBATE (OR IS IT THAT?) AND THE DEBATERS

Satan proceeds in his debate with the Son of God—no debate is possible, really, with omniscience and omnipotence—by insinuation and innuendo. He murmurs like a malcontent, he infers things that don't exist, he insults while appearing to flatter. His stance is that of a corrupt lawyer pleading his own case, a lawyer who does not believe in himself but is nevertheless pleading as client. He repeats words like "glory" and "reign" until they mean little or nothing: his echoing words are hollow, in phrases like "My error was my error and my crime / My crime" (3.212–13). Satan will not give up. As well as being like a corrupt lawyer, he is like an annoying salesman who will not take his foot out of the door. Toward the end of the debate he is finally "Quite at a loss, for all his darts were spent," and he has to display his anger "with stern brow" (4.366–67). Evil is impotent and ineffectual, though it may seem at least temporarily strong and efficient.

The Son of God defines false argumentation in a few memorable phrases as "fabling . . . and smooth conceits," and he substitutes "plain sence" as being the morally best way to argue (4.295–96). *Fabling* is substituting pleasant falsehoods for the truth, and *smooth conceits* are falsely pleasing images that lull one into believing that what one hears is the truth when it isn't.

Nevertheless, there are long stretches in Book 4 when Satan speaks almost nothing but the truth. If a reader is not listening closely for occasional lies, there may be a tendency to forget who is talking, the Son of God or Satan. When Satan reports the vices of the emperor Tiberius, for instance, his opinion seems to be close to Milton's opinion—or that of the Son of God. Satan's description of Jesus's youth is also not distorted or colored. Even his description of the wisdom of the Gentiles, including Socrates and Aristotle, seems even-handed and just. The Savior must reply to it "sagely" (4.285), because Satan's presentation of history is acceptable as common knowledge.

THE SON OF GOD'S DEBATING STYLE

The Son of God is a plain speaker, like a Quaker lay-preacher. His most typical utterances are phrases like "I never lik'd thy talk, thy offers less" (4.171). This simple style indicates that, in the context of the brief epic, "flowery" is evil and "simple" or "plain" is good. What the Son of God says may have overtones or reverberations (in the sense of words or phrases including echoes or allusions), and even an occasional serious pun, but it has no hollow echoes and no circumlocutions. Perhaps the emphasis of the Royal Society on concrete, specific language, exemplified in the writings of Thomas Sprat, had an effect on Milton's endorsement of plain speaking, but Quaker modes of address might also have influenced him in his later writings.

THE GENRE OF THE BRIEF EPIC

The brief epic is a subgenre, differentiated from the more diffuse epic, pastoral, or georgic. Martz does find georgic elements in the style of the poem (*Poet of Exile* 293–304), a view ably seconded by Anthony Low ("Milton"). Milton's brief epic can be said to be georgic in the sense that its size is not far off that of Vergil's *Georgics*, which is also in four books. Like Vergil's bucolic poetry, *Paradise Regain'd* is didactic, homely, mundane, and rustic in the sense that the Son's temptation occurs mostly in the desert. The Son does seem to be a kind of georgic hero in that he is hard-working and thoughtful, a born leader who might go from a rustic, unknown life to a position of world importance. The comparison with Vergil's *Georgics*, however, should not be pushed too far.

The genre of brief epic, as Milton conceives it, is biblical, modeled on the Book of Job as *Paradise Lost* is modeled on Genesis. The definitive work on the genre of *Paradise Regain'd* is Barbara Lewalski's *Milton's Brief Epic: The Genre, Meaning, and Art of* Paradise Regained. The closest analogue to *Paradise Regain'd* is Marco Girolamo Vida's brief epic *The Christiad*, first published in Cremona, Italy, in 1535. Milton alluded to Vida's work in "The Passion," with "Loud / O'er the rest Cremona's trump doth sound." Though the *Christiad* is concerned more with events surrounding the Crucifixion, a subject that Milton generally avoided (perhaps because it had been overemphasized in Renaissance Catholic art), Vida's six-book Vergilian epic dealing with significant events in the life of Christ appealed to Milton in his youth (DiCesare). Vida's model poet Vergil remained a model for Milton as well (Campbell, "Milton") throughout his career. There were such details as a demonic consult in Vida, a setting Milton used in both his epics, but *The Christiad* was a Catholic minor epic and thus off-limits for Milton to emulate.

Another generically odd comparison with *Paradise Regain'd* is the epyllion, the short erotic epic, as with Christopher Marlowe's *Hero and Leander*, which, like Shakespeare's *Venus and Adonis*, mixes seduction with heroic action. An erotic epyllion is a miniature epic, using heroic characters often in dialogue with one another, and it is erotic because it derives its dramatic tension from a love conquest. Marlowe's poem con-

centrates on Leander's love for and pursuit of Hero, during which he performs the heroic task of swimming the Hellespont to join his lover. Marlowe's poem is in iambic pentameter, like Milton's, but it is in couplets, the same iambic couplets that would later be called "heroic" and identified for no good reason with classical epic. Milton, if he imitated Marlowe in any sense, kept only the extravagant imagery (in the mouths of fallen angels), and he kept the erotic theme, in the suggestions of Belial, only to reject it as being not worthy of the Son of God.

Giles Fletcher's *Christs Victorie and Triumph* (London, 1610), an erotic (in the way that Donne's devotional poetry is erotic) short epic on the subject of Christ's temptation, was nearer to home in its subject matter but hardly to Milton's stylistic taste in his older years. In it Christ has "small curls" and "lovely locks" and his eyes cause "sweete wounds" to occur in the hearts of allegorical Graces (Kirkconnell 291).

COMPETITION WITH THE CLASSICAL

Milton is in self-conscious competition with classical epic throughout *Paradise Lost* and *Paradise Regain'd*. Classical epic and philosophy have clearly lost the battle, though they appear often in the form of mocked classical similes. Martz may be right: like Nicholas Ferrar on his deathbed, Milton may in the short epic be renouncing all classical literature and history, by its nature "full of Idolatry, and especially [all of its forms] tend to the Overthrow of Christian Religion, undermining the very Foundations thereof, and corrupt and pollute the minds of the Readers, with filthy lusts, as woe is me, I have proved myself" (quoted in Martz 268).

Probably the greatest dramatic tension of the brief epic is caused by the temptations of Greece and Rome, not just for imperial power but for the civilization of art and literature, what Satan says "The *Gentiles* also know, and write, and teach / To admiration" (4.227–28). The Son of God must reject the work of Plato, Homer, and the Greek tragedians as "false, or little else but dreams, / Conjectures, fancies, built on nothing firm" (4.291–92). Such a necessary rejection of "pagan" philosophy and art must have been hard for Milton to endorse. It also may be difficult for later readers to reject the wisdom of Athens or Rome.

DRAMATIC ELEMENTS

The poem is not a Shakespearean drama (though it is closer to Shakespeare's declamatory *Troilus and Cressida* which, like *Samson Agonistes*, may not have been intended for the popular stage, than it is even to *Hamlet*, which has plenty of action). *Paradise Regain'd*, like *Paradise Lost*, has some dramatic devices, from stage directions to soliloquies to a choral speech, but its dramatic style is more declamatory than dialogic. The cutting from speech to speech, on the other hand, can be quite rapid. In Book 1, jumps from speech to speech occur so rapidly that they can be confusing. Passages of dialogue, however, remain declamatory. Characters make pronouncements more than they exchange repartee.

STRUCTURE

Exactly how the poem is structured (Hunter), especially with respect to the number of temptations, is still hotly debated. Shawcross believes that parts of the brief epic were composed as early as the 1640s and other parts composed later: his conclusion, summarized briefly, is "that in 1665–66, if Milton had his manuscripts with him at Chalfont St. Giles, or in 1666 through mid–1669, the original dramatic fragment received alterations and additions because of an epic shift prompted by Ellwood's question" (*Paradise Regain'd* 15). Burton Jasper Weber's book, though detailed, is not really satisfying in its clever working out of structure, but it still might be consulted. Elizabeth Pope earlier surveyed the structure of the poem against the tradition of theology and literature devoted to the temptation of Christ; Radzinowicz and Patrides place it against biblical and Christian tradition; and Rushdy interprets it by means of modern critical perspectives.

STRUCTURE ACCORDING TO
BRIEF EPIC AND ALLEGORY

Paradise Regain'd is a brief epic which does not emphasize the conventional heroic attributes of a ferocious, clever, skilled general like Achilles, Odysseus, Aeneas, or Julius Caesar. Instead it emphasizes the Christian virtues of temperance, patience, meekness, wisdom, and magnanimity—virtues of a Job or Christ (Hamilton has graphed out an orderly arrangement of these from book to book). Its hero is passive, stationary, alone much of the time, and sufficient unto himself to resist temptation. "Patience" is one of the key words for interpreting the poem; it should be defined as "the endurance of evils and injuries" (*On Christian Doctrine* 2.10; Yale 6: 739), though it is more than that. Labriola ("*Christus*") establishes the solid medieval tradition behind the patience of Milton's Son. Richard Jordan writes that "The Christ of Milton's *Paradise Regained* is a direct imitation of the archetypal idea of Heroic Temperance as it exists in Christian tradition," with a direct reference to Guyon in Book 2 of Spenser's *The Faerie Queene* (122). Treip notes that Milton uses the word "allegory" only once, and that is in *Paradise Regain'd* 4.390 (181). Though Satan dismisses allegory in the brief epic, his dismissal of

the mode may represent an endorsement by the author (182). If any character in Milton represents an allegorical entity that might be called Heroic Patience, it is the Son of God in *Paradise Regain'd*.

Shawcross sees "[t]he basic structure of *Paradise Regain'd*" as "that of the triple equation of the flesh, the world, and the devil," expressed as "*concupiscentia carnis, concupiscentia oculorum,* and *superbia vitæ*; or hunger, kingdoms, and the tower; or necessity, fraud, and violence; or the role of the Son as prophet, as king, and as priest" (*Paradise Regain'd* 45). The division into units of three is useful, but imposing the rule of three may be too precise, since Satan's motives, to take one example, are not just based on his plea from necessity, or the fraud of his disguise, or the potential violence of his ability to push the Son off the pinnacle.

WHY *PARADISE REGAIN'D* MIGHT HAVE BEEN
PAIRED WITH *SAMSON AGONISTES*

The most obvious answer to the question of why the brief epic was paired with the dramatic poem in the volume of 1671 is that we don't know and we aren't likely to find out. The title page tells us only that *Samson Agonistes* is "added." The title page seems to further downplay the importance of the tragedy by calling *Paradise Regain'd* "A POEM" but not giving *Samson Agonistes* a generic tag, and by putting its title in a smaller point size. Of course Milton was blind in 1671: he may have had nothing whatsoever to do with the title page.

The brief epic might have been put first in the slender 1671 edition because it did form a sequel to *Paradise Lost*, but economic considerations might also have dictated the twin publication. Putting the two together as a package might help sell the work of a discredited regicide. Wittreich has summarized the opinions about the context of the two works, "The wisdom of putting *Paradise Regained* and *Samson Agonistes* together in the same volume" (329) in the last chapter of *Interpreting Samson Agonistes*, citing Shawcross and Rajan as the main proponents of the theory that the juxtaposition of the two works was intended by Milton to have meaning. The critical question was decided by William Kerrigan, at least for himself: the twin publication "was no accident: the two works complement each other almost as perfectly as 'L'Allegro' and 'Il Penseroso' " (*Prophetic* 268).

THE TEXT

We know that the manuscript containing both *Paradise Regain'd* and *Samson Agonistes* was in the hands of the publisher by spring of 1670. Lacking the manuscript itself, we have only one authoritative text for *Paradise*

Regain'd, that of 1671, and it isn't a very good one. The 1678 edition does not improve on *1671*: it is inferior in every detail, as are all the many editions derived from it.

The 1671 text is all we have, and it was not as well prepared as the 1667 and 1674 editions of *Paradise Lost*. It is in some places sloppily printed. The Errata list added at the end of the 1671 edition was itself misprinted ("knowledge" appeared as "knowlege" and "after" as "afrer" in the earlier state); the errata do not necessarily indicate authorial intervention. Book 1.226 "destroy" is changed to "subdue" by the direction of the Errata, as is 1.417 where "Imports" is changed to "Imparts," 2.128 "Threat'ns" to "Threat'ns then," 2.341 "pill'd" to "pil'd," 3.238 "insight" to "in sight," and 3.324 "shower" to "showers." The list of errata, with the exception of "destroy" being changed to "subdue," seems more likely to have been the result of in-press corrections following consultation of a manuscript than authorial corrections after proofreading.

The compositor of *1671* (judging by the even and consistent distribution of colons and semicolons there seems to have been only one person setting type) seems to have been following a manuscript which preserved some of Milton's spelling habits (for some examples from Book 1, see "battel" as opposed to "battle," "dore" for "door," "wast" for "waste," "aw" for "awe," "stroak" for "stroke," "flowr" for "flower," "supream" for "supreme," and "perfet" for "perfect") while it neglected others ("their" is substituted for "thir" three-fifths of the time; "sov'raign" is substituted for "sovran"). The persistence of "their" in preference to "thir" may well indicate that no one was strongly imposing a system of spelling on the compositor. The un-Miltonic spelling "their" is scattered through the four books almost at random, as if the compositor were following the manuscript part of the time—for that common word at least—but following his own inclination most of the time, although there is one instance at 4.424 when "thir" was substituted for "their" on a page that had been poorly inked and had to be run again.

The compositor kept some of the hyphenated compounds that Milton was fond of, but in general he avoided them. The compositor also generally honored the system of stresses in Milton's fairly regular iambic line, keeping past participles in strict adherence to syllable count, as with "defeated and repuls't" in 1.6 or "giv'n" (monosyllable) in 1.37 versus "woven" (disyllable) in 1.97. The compositor was not consistent in usage with "Heaven" versus "Heav'n." Shawcross's edition attempts to restore all monosyllabic "Heav'ns," consistently, but mine does not take that risk. Imposing modern consistency on spelling practices in seventeenth-century texts, to a practiced eye, looks anachronistic,

since late seventeenth-century printing, by its nature, was imprecise and erratic.

The printing of *1671* is neither very good nor very bad, as far as it can be said to have represented any of Milton's known habits of phonetic spelling, meaningful punctuation, or emphatic capitalization or other forms of emphasis. "The resulting texts are not more than fair approximations of what Milton must have wanted" (Fletcher 4: 43).

The printed text does tell us how Milton's contemporaries intended the words on the page to be viewed: the phonetic spelling helps show us how the words are to be pronounced; the italics show us something about emphasis on proper names ("Satan" is not italicized, neither is "Serpent," nor is "Messiah," and the "John" in "*John* the Baptist" is the only part of John's honorific title in italics); and the elisions tell us—approximately—how the lines are to be counted as iambic pentameter. The italics in a sequence of names such as "*Apollo, Neptune, Jupiter*, or *Pan*, / Satyr, or Fawn, or Silvan" (2.90–91) can show us usefully the difference between a proper name and a generic title; titles of religions or nations, when they are generic, are not often italicized, as with "Jew, or Greek, / Or Barbarous" (3.118–19). We cannot be sure that such choices represent the author's intentions (though Milton's apparent control over the text of the 1671 *Poems*, as far as the Latin poetry and its accents are concerned, is remarkable for any author in that era, much less a blind one), but we do know they represent the printing conventions of Milton's time.

BIBLIOGRAPHY

Editions are marked with an asterisk.

Barker, Arthur E. "Calm Regained through Passion Spent: The Conclusions of the Miltonic Effort." *The Prison and the Pinnacle. Papers To Commemorate the Tercentenary of* Paradise Regained *and* Samson Agonistes. Ed. Balachandra Rajan. Toronto: U of Toronto P, 1973. 3–48.

Burnett, Archie. *Milton's Style: The Shorter Poems,* Paradise Regained, *and* Samson Agonistes. London: Longman, 1981.

Cawley, Robert R. *Milton and the Literature of Travel.* Princeton: Princeton UP, 1951.

Chambers, A. B. "The Double Time Scheme in *Paradise Regained.*" *Milton Studies* 7 (1975): 189–205.

Clark, Ira. "Christ on the Tower in *Paradise Regained.*" *Milton Quarterly* 8 (1974): 104–07.

——. "*Paradise Regained* and the Gospel According to John." *Modern Philology* 71 (1973): 1–15.

Condee, Ralph W. *Structure in Milton's Poetry: From the Foundation to the Pinnacles.* University Park: Pennsylvania State UP, 1974.

Corns, Thomas N. *Milton's Language.* Oxford: Blackwell, 1990.

Cullen, Patrick. *Infernal Triad: The Flesh, the World, and the Devil in Spenser and Milton.* Princeton, NJ: Princeton UP, 1974.

DiCesare, Mario. *Vida's* Christiad *and the Vergilian Epic.* New York: Columbia UP, 1964.

Elliot, Emory. "Milton's Biblical Style in *Paradise Regained.*" *Milton Studies* 6 (1974): 227–42.

Fallon, Robert Thomas. *Milton in Government.* University Park: Pennsylvania State UP, 1993.

Ferry, Anne Davidson. *Milton's Epic Voice.* Cambridge, MA: Harvard UP, 1963.

Fish, Stanley. "Inaction and Silence: The Reader in *Paradise Regained.*" *Calm of Mind: Tercentenary Essays on "Paradise Regained" and "Samson Agonistes" in Honor of John S. Diekhoff.* Ed. Joseph A. Wittreich. Cleveland: P of Case Western Reserve U, 1971.

——. "Things and Actions Indifferent: The Temptation of Plot in *Paradise Regained.*" *Milton Studies* 17 (1983): 163–85.

Fisher, Alan. "Why is *Paradise Regain'd* So Cold?" *Milton Studies* 14 (1980): 195–217.

Flannagan, Roy. "Art, Artists, Galileo and Concordances." *Milton Quarterly* 20 (1986): 103–05.

*Fletcher, Harris F. *John Milton's Complete Poetical Works Reproduced in Photographic Facsimile: A Critical Text Edition Compiled and Edited by Harris Francis Fletcher.* Vol. 4. Urbana: U of Illinois P, 1948.

Forsyth, Neil. "Having Done All To Stand: Biblical and Classical Allusion in *Paradise Regained.*" *Milton Studies* 21 (1985): 199–214.

Fortin, René. "The Climactic Similes of *Paradise Regained.*"*Gaining upon Certainty: Selected Literary Criticism.* Providence, RI: Providence College P, 1995. 271–79.

Fowler, Alastair. "*Paradise Regained*: Some Problems of Style." *Medieval and Pseudo-Medieval Literatures.* Ed. Piero Boitano and Anna Torli. Cambridge: Cambridge UP, 1984.

Freeman, James. *Milton and the Martial Muse: "Paradise Lost" and European Traditions of War.* Princeton, NJ: Princeton UP, 1980.

Frye, Northrop. *The Return of Eden: Five Essays on Milton's Epics.* Toronto: U of Toronto P, 1965.

Gilbert, Allen H. *A Geographical Dictionary of Milton.* New Haven, CT: Yale UP, 1919.

Hamilton, Gary D. "Creating the Garden Anew: The Dynamics of *Paradise Regained.*" *Philological Quarterly* 50 (1971): 567–81.

Hanford, James Holly. *John Milton, Englishman.* New York: Crown, 1949.

Hendrix, Howard V. *The Ecstasy of Catastrophe: A Study of Apocalyptic Narrative from Langland to Milton.* New York: Lang, 1990.

Hieatt, A. Kent. *Chaucer, Spenser, Milton: Mythopoeic Continuities and Transformations.* Montreal: McGill-Queens UP, 1975.

Hughes, Merritt Y. "The Christ of *Paradise Regained* and the Renaissance Heroic Tradition." *Studies in Philology* 35 (1938): 254–77.

Hunter, William B., ed. *The English Spenserians.* Salt Lake City: U of Utah P, 1977.

Jordan, Richard Douglas. *The Quiet Hero: Figures of Temperance in Spenser, Donne, Milton, and Joyce.* Washington, DC: Catholic U of America P, 1989.

Kerrigan, William. *The Prophetic Milton.* Charlottesville: UP of Virginia, 1974.

——. *The Sacred Complex: On the Psychogenesis of* Paradise Lost. Cambridge, MA: Harvard UP, 1983.

Kirkconnell, G. Watson. *"Awake the Courteous Echo": The Themes and Prosody of* Comus, Lycidas, *and* Paradise Regained *in World Literature with Translations of the Major Analogues.* Toronto: U of Toronto P, 1973.

Labriola, Albert C. "*Christus Patiens*": The Virtue Patience and *Paradise Lost* I–II." *The Triumph of Patience: Medieval and Renaissance Studies.* Ed. Gerald J. Schiffhorst. Orlando: U Presses of Florida: 1978. 138–46.

——. "'Insuperable Highth of Loftiest Shade': Milton and Samuel Beckett." *Milton's Legacy in the Arts.* Ed. Labriola and Edward Sichi, Jr. University Park: Pennsylvania State UP, 1988. 205–17.

Leonard, John. *Naming in Paradise: Milton and the Language of Adam and Eve.* Oxford: Clarendon, 1990.

Lewalski, Barbara K. *Milton's Brief Epic: the Genre, Meaning, and Art of* Paradise Regained. Providence, RI: Brown UP, 1966.

Low, Anthony. "Milton and the Georgic Ideal." *The Georgic Revolution.* Princeton, NJ: Princeton UP, 1985. 296–352.

MacCallum, Hugh. *Milton and the Sons of God: The Divine Image in*

Milton's Epic Poetry. Toronto: U of Toronto P, 1986.

*MacKellar, Walter, ed. *A Variorum Commentary on the Poems of John Milton: Volume 4*. Paradise Regained. New York: Columbia UP, 1975.

McLaughlin, Elizabeth T. "Milton and Thomas Ellwood." *Milton Newsletter* 1 (1967): 17–28.

Martz, Louis. *The Paradise Within: Studies in Vaughan, Traherne, and Milton*. New Haven, CT: Yale UP, 1964.

—. *Poet of Exile: A Study of Milton's Poetry*. New Haven, CT: Yale UP, 1980.

*Newton, Thomas, ed. Paradise Regain'd. *A Poem, in Four Books. To Which is Added* Samson Agonistes. 2 vols. London, 1766.

Parker, William Riley. *Milton: A Biography*. 2 vols. Oxford: Clarendon, 1968.

Pope, Elizabeth M. *"Paradise Regained": the Tradition and the Poem*. Baltimore, MD: Johns Hopkins UP, 1947. Reprinted New York: Russell and Russell, 1962.

Quint, David. "David's Census: Milton's Politics and *Paradise Regained*." *Re-membering Milton: Essays on the Texts and Traditions*. Ed. Mary Nyquist and Margaret W. Ferguson. London: Methuen, 1987. 128–47.

Radzinowicz, Mary Ann. "How Milton Read the Bible: the Case of *Paradise Regained*." *The Cambridge Companion to Milton*. Ed. Dennis Danielson. Cambridge: Cambridge UP, 1989.

———. *Milton's Epics and the Book of Psalms*. Princeton: Princeton UP, 1989.

Rajan, Balachandra, ed. *The Prison and the Pinnacle*. Toronto: U of Toronto P, 1973.

Revard, Stella. "The Gospel of John and *Paradise Regained*: Jesus as 'True Light.'" *Milton and Scriptural Tradition: The Bible into Poetry*. Ed. James H. Sims and Leland Ryken. Columbia: U of Missouri P, 1984. 142–59.

Ricks, Christopher. *English Poetry and Prose, 1540–1674*. London: Peter Bedrick, 1987.

Rowse, A. L. *Milton the Puritan: Portrait of a Mind*. London: Macmillan, 1977.

Rushdy, Ashraf H. A. *The Empty Garden: The Subject of Late Milton*. Pittsburgh, PA: U of Pittsburgh P, 1992.

-----. "'The Fatal Influence of Frigorifick Wisdom': Warming Up to *Paradise Regained*." *Milton Quarterly* 24 (1990): 49–57.

Shawcross, John T. *John Milton: The Self and the World*. Lexington: UP of Kentucky, 1993.

---------. *Paradise Regain'd: Worthy t'have not remain'd so long unsung*. Pittsburgh, PA: Duquesne UP, 1989.

Shoaf, R. A. *Milton, Poet of Duality*. New Haven, CT: Yale UP, 1985.

Stein, Arnold. *Heroic Knowledge: An Interpretation of* Paradise Regained *and* Samson Agonistes. Minneapolis: U of Minnesota P, 1957.

Vida, Marco Girolamo. *The Christiad: A Latin-English Edition*. Ed. and trans. Gertrude C. Drake and Clarence A. Forbes. Carbondale: Southern Illinois UP, 1978.

Weber, Burton Jasper. *Wedges and Wings: The Patterning of* Paradise Regained. Carbondale: Southern Illinois UP, 1975.

Wittreich, Joseph. *Interpreting* Samson Agonistes. Princeton: Princeton UP, 1986.

Woodhouse, A. S. P. *The Heavenly Muse: A Preface to Milton*. Ed. Hugh MacCallum. Toronto: U of Toronto P, 1972.

PARADISE
REGAIN'D.

A

POEM.

In IV *Books.*

To which is added

SAMSON AGONISTES.

The Author
JOHN MILTON.

LONDON,

Printed by *J. M.* for *John Starkey* at the
Mitre in *Fleetstreet*, near *Temple-Bar.*
MDCLXXI.[1]

---

[1]If Milton did have any control over the typography of the 1671 edition of *Paradise Regain'd* and *Samson Agonistes*, the fact that "Regain'd." is set in a larger type size may be significant, as if he wanted to emphasize the regaining or finding of Paradise after Thomas Ellwood had asked him the question "Thou hast said much here [in *Paradise Lost*] of paradise lost, but what hast thou to say of paradise found" (for the complete story, see Parker 616).

PARADISE REGAIN'D,

A POEM.

The First BOOK.

I Who e're while the happy Garden sung,
By one mans disobedience[2] lost, now sing
Recover'd Paradise to all mankind,
By one mans firm obedience fully tri'd
Through all temptation, and the Tempter foil'd   5
In all his wiles, defeated and repuls't,
And *Eden* rais'd[3] in the wast° Wilderness.[4]   WASTE
  Thou Spirit who ledst this glorious Eremite[5]
Into the Desert, his Victorious Field[6]
Against the Spiritual Foe, and broughtst him thence   10
By proof° the undoubted Son of God, inspire,   TEST
As thou art wont, my prompted Song else mute,[7]
And bear through highth or depth of natures bounds
With prosperous wing full summ'd[8] to tell of deeds
Above Heroic,[9] though in secret done,   15
And unrecorded left through many an Age,
Worthy t' have not remain'd so long unsung.
  Now had the great Proclaimer[10] with a voice

---

[2]The opening probably echoes the opening phrase of Vergil's *Aeneid* as it existed in editions that Milton might have consulted—"Ille ego, qui quondam gracili modulatus avena / carmen . . . "—which Spenser paraphrased as "Lo! I, the man whose Muse whylome did maske, / As time her taught, in lowly Shephards weeds, / Am now enforst, a farre unfitter taske, / For trumpets sterne to chaunce mine Oaten reeds" (*The Faerie Queene* 1, proem, 1–4). Milton expects the reader to remember the opening phrase of *Paradise Lost*, "Of Mans First Disobedience," in order to contrast Adam's disobedience and the consequent loss of Paradise with Jesus's obedience and consequent recovery of Paradise. In placing his song about the "happy Garden" firmly in the past, Milton may be announcing that he has "graduated from pastoral apprentice work to the true epic subject" (Lewalski, *Brief Epic* 6), though to do so might put *Paradise Lost* in an inferior position generically.
[3]The figurative or typographical Eden, like the "paradise within" (*Paradise Lost* 12.587) that Michael finds in the regenerate Adam and Eve. Here Eden becomes a type of the city of God that Jesus will raise from the desert.
[4]"For the Lord shall comfort Zion: he will comfort all her waste places; and he will make her wilderness like Eden, and her desert like the garden of the Lord; joy and gladness shall be found therein, thanksgiving, and the voice of melody" (Isaiah 51.3).
[5]Hermit, from the classical Greek word meaning "desert-dweller." In this case the word does not signify a Christian living alone in a fixed habitation but Jesus wandering alone in the desert. The Spirit, we can presume, is the same entity as the Holy Spirit or Heavenly Muse Milton invoked in *Paradise Lost*, though she is never named in *Paradise Regain'd*.
[6]The word "Field" strongly suggests a military metaphor. Though the victory gained here by the Son of God, like his foe, is "spiritual," Milton avoided the notion that Jesus fought Satan in anything other than a psychomachia or spiritual war. He does, however, make God the Father describe the Son of God as "lay[ing] down the rudiments / Of his great warfare" and "conquer[ing] Sin and Death the two grand foes" (below, 157–59).
[7]If his song were not prompted by the Heavenly Muse, he would be mute. Milton takes the same position he has taken in *Paradise Lost*: his "Celestial Patroness . . . deignes / Her nightly visitation" to him "unimplor'd, / And dictates to [him] slumbring" (9.21–23); all would be lost "if all be [his], / Not Hers who brings it nightly to [his] Ear" (46–47).
[8]The wing is fully extended, with all its feathers spread, the technical word "summ'd" having been borrowed from falconry. The adjective "prosperous" suggests that the narrator, with the aid of the flight of the Heavenly Muse, will present a divine comedy which will end happily.
[9]For Milton, the best heroism is consistently private and without outward display; here it is also undocumented until his epic. As Carey points out (1.16n), the word "record" was used of the song of birds in the seventeenth century; hence Milton may be using it to signify unpremeditated or spontaneous, inspired song.
[10]John the Baptist, the voice crying in the wilderness of Isaiah 40.3, echoed in Matthew 3.3 and Mark 1.3.

More awful then the sound of Trumpet, cri'd
Repentance, and Heavens Kingdom nigh at hand   20
To all Baptiz'd: to his great Baptism flock'd
With aw the Regions round, and with them came
From *Nazareth* the Son of *Joseph* deem'd
To the flood *Jordan*,[11] came as then obscure,
Unmarkt, unknown; but him the Baptist soon   25
Descri'd, divinely warn'd,[12] and witness bore
As to his worthier, and would have resign'd
To him his Heavenly Office, nor was long
His witness unconfirm'd: on him baptiz'd
Heaven open'd, and in likeness of a Dove   30
The Spirit descended, while the Fathers voice
From Heav'n pronounc'd him his beloved Son.[13]
That heard the Adversary,[14] who roving still
About the world, at that assembly fam'd
Would not be last,[15] and with the voice divine   35
Nigh Thunder-struck, th' exalted man, to whom
Such high attest° was giv'n, a while survey'd   WITNESS
With wonder, then with envy fraught and rage
Flies to his place,° nor rests, but in mid air[16]   HOME
To Councel summons all his mighty Peers,   40
Within thick Clouds and dark ten-fold involv'd,
A gloomy Consistory;[17] and them amidst
With looks agast and sad[18] he thus bespake.°   SPOKE
  O ancient Powers of Air and this wide world,   *Satan*
For much more willingly I mention Air,   45
This our old Conquest, then° remember Hell   THAN
Our hated habitation; well ye know
How many Ages, as the years of men,[19]
This Universe we have possest, and rul'd
In manner at our will th' affairs of Earth,   50
Since *Adam* and his facil consort *Eve*[20]
Lost Paradise deceiv'd by me, though since
With dread attending° when that fatal wound   FEARFUL ATTENTION

---

[11]"With them came from Nazareth him who was supposed to be the son of Joseph, to the river Jordan." The word "flood" signifies only "large river" (*OED* 2). Compare Luke 3.

[12]John the Baptist reports that when he first sees the Son of God "he that sent me to baptize with water, the same said unto me, Upon whom thou shalt see the Spirit descending, and remaining on him, the same is he which baptizeth with the Holy Ghost" (John 1.33).

[13]When Jesus is baptized and rises out of the water, "lo, the heavens were opened unto him, and he saw the Spirit of God descending like a dove, and lighting upon him: And lo a voice from heaven, saying, This is my beloved Son, in whom I am well pleased" (Matthew 3.16–17).

[14]Satan is, as always, defined by his name, which in Hebrew signifies "Enemy" or "Adversary." He is pictured in restless and perpetual motion ("roving still" means "always roaming"). Satan reports to the Lord in Job that he has been ". . . going to and fro in the earth, and from walking up and down in it" (1.7).

[15]Pride of place makes Satan envious of the exaltation of the Son of God at the baptism: Satan cannot stand to be in second place. The voice of God, meanwhile, strikes him like a thunderbolt.

[16]The middle of the air was the region where fallen angels traditionally met. Ephesians 2.2 calls Satan "the prince of the power of the air." Compare the battle between Satan and Death in *Paradise Lost*, during which they "joyn thir dark Encounter in mid air" (2.718).

[17]The word normally meant a gathering of church officials, as in *Tenure of Kings and Magistrates*: "Let them assemble in Consistory with thir Elders and Deacons" (Yale 3: 241). Here it is used with heavy irony.

[18]The word "sad" was used more forcefully by Milton than it is today, meaning "very serious, solemn"; thus it can be paired with "agast."

[19]"As counted according to human years."

[20]Satan's presentation of the events of the Fall will mix truth with falsehood and will exaggerate his role. He unfairly demeans Eve as "facil" ("easily led"), though she was indeed deceived (is that "dis-Eved"?) and she was indeed Adam's "consort" (wife).

Shall be inflicted by the Seed of *Eve*[21] ~~SERPENT~~

Upon my head, long the decrees of Heav'n 55

Delay, for longest time to him is short;[22]

And now too soon for us the circling hours[23]

This dreaded time have compast, wherein we

Must bide the stroak of that long threatn'd wound,

At least if so we can, and by the head 60

Broken be not intended all our power

To be infring'd,[24] our freedom and our being[25]

In this fair Empire won of Earth and Air;

For this ill news I bring, the Womans seed

Destin'd to this, is late of woman born, 65

His birth to our just fear gave no small cause,

But his growth now to youths full flowr, displaying

All vertue, grace and wisdom[26] to atchieve

Things highest, greatest, multiplies my fear.

Before him a great Prophet, to proclaim 70

His coming, is sent Harbinger, who all

Invites, and in the Consecrated stream

Pretends° to wash off sin, and fit them so CLAIMS

Purified to receive him pure, or rather

To do him honour as their King; all come, 75

And he himself among them was baptiz'd,

Not thence to be more pure, but to receive

The testimony of Heaven, that who he is

Thenceforth the Nations may not doubt; I saw

The Prophet do him reverence, on him rising[27] 80

Out of the water, Heav'n above the Clouds

Unfold her Crystal Dores,[28] thence on his head

A perfect Dove[29] descend, what e're it meant,

And out of Heav'n the Sov'raign voice I heard,

This is my Son belov'd, in him am pleas'd. 85

His Mother then is mortal, but his Sire,

He who obtains[30] the Monarchy of Heav'n,

---

[21] "And I will put enmity between thee and the woman, and between thy seed and her seed; it shall bruise thy head, and thou shalt bruise his heel" (Genesis 3.15). The "Seed" was interpreted as being both the descendants of Eve and the Son of God. At the end of time, the Son will trample the Serpent under his foot, as in Caravaggio's painting *Madonna delle Serpe*.

[22] Based on 2 Peter 3.8: ". . . one day is with the Lord as a thousand years, and a thousand years as one day."

[23] The hours are pictured in an endless dancing round, as in a Renaissance town clock. The image also recalls the motion of the Zodiac or any heavenly body that marks time. For Satan, time is dreadful, since his destruction is inevitable.

[24] "If our (or my) head is broken under the heel of the Seed, as prophesied ('intended'), perhaps our power will not be broken (Latin *infringere*, meaning 'to break')." Satan is snatching hope from despair.

[25] There is a period at this point in the 1671 text, but the *Errata* specify "after being no stop."

[26] "And Jesus increased in wisdom and stature, and in favor with God and man" (Luke 2.52).

[27] "On him when he arose."

[28] Milton's Heaven has crystal battlements (*Paradise Lost* 1.742), crystal walls (*Paradise Lost* 6.860), and here crystal doors.

[29] The descending dove is described in all four Gospels: Matthew 3.16; Mark 1.10; Luke 3.22; John 1.32. "Let no one object," Milton wrote in *On Christian Doctrine*, "that a dove is not a person: any intelligent substance, whatever shape it takes, is a person" (Yale 6: 285). Likewise the term "spirit" "can mean the actual person of the Holy Spirit, or its symbol" (Yale 6: 285). Satan's qualifying phrase, "what e're it meant," may also ironically indicate the indecision Milton expressed about the "Holy Spirit" in *On Christian Doctrine*: ". . . the descent and the dove-like appearance of the Holy Spirit seems to have been nothing more than a sort of representation of the Father's supreme love and affection for the Son, communicated by the Holy Spirit in the very appropriate guise of a dove, and explained at the same time by a voice from the sky" (Yale 6: 284). God knows what the image of the dove meant, but neither Satan nor Milton is sure of what it meant.

[30] "Holds," from Latin *obtinere*, "to lay hold of anything"

And what will he not do to advance[31] his Son?
His first-begot we know, and sore have felt,[32]
When his fierce thunder drove us to the deep;   90
Who this is we must learn, for man he seems   CATCHES
In all his lineaments, though in his face   ATTENTION
The glimpses of his Fathers glory shine.[33]
Ye see our danger on the utmost edge
Of hazard,[34] which admits no long debate,   95
But must with something sudden be oppos'd,
Not force, but well couch't° fraud, well woven snares,[35]   CONCEALED
E're in the head of Nations he appear
Their King, their Leader, and Supream on Earth.
I, when no other durst,[36] sole undertook   100
The dismal[37] expedition to find out
And ruine *Adam*, and the exploit[38] perform'd
Successfully; a calmer voyage now
Will waft me; and the way found prosperous[39] once
Induces° best to hope of like success.   ARGUES   105
    He ended,[40] and his words impression left
Of much amazement[41] to th' infernal Crew,
Distracted and surpriz'd with deep dismay
At these sad tidings; but no time was then[42]
For long indulgence to their fears or grief: 110
Unanimous they all commit the care
And management of this main° enterprize
To him their great Dictator,[43] whose attempt   MOST IMPORTANT
At first against mankind so well had thriv'd
In *Adam*'s overthrow, and led thir march   115
From Hell's deep-vaulted Den to dwell in light,
Regents and Potentates, and Kings, yea gods[44]

---

[31]Surely "to advance" should be read "t' advance," with the syllable elided, in order to make an iambic line. Shawcross emends "t' advance" without noting the change. Compare "t' have" in 17, versus "the utmost," 94, for which "the" should indeed be read as an independent syllable.

[32]"Sorely have felt," or "have felt with pain."

[33]Satan may not be telling the truth here. Does he know that the Son as manifested as Jesus is the same as the being who drove the rebel angels out of Heaven? At this point we cannot tell for sure if he is lying to his council.

[34]On the utmost edge of a wager, the verge, say, of throwing the dice (though in metaphorical usage the word might have meant only "severe danger"). The imagery suggests that Satan would wish that chance ruled the universe, not God's will controlling fate. Satan is also pushing the issue, making the council decide something before thoughtful debate has occurred.

[35]The word "snare" has a deep resonance throughout Milton's works, suggesting, as it does, demonic entrapment. Compare "mortal snare" in *Paradise Lost* 4.8 and "hugg him into snares" in *Comus* 164.

[36]Satan is recalling the demonic consult described in *Paradise Lost* 2.430–66, during which he "volunteers" to seek out humankind to corrupt, seeking what the narrator calls "the high repute / Which he through hazard huge must earn" (2.472–73).

[37]Literally an expedition beginning on an evil day. Compare *OED* n. 1.

[38]Read as "th' exploit," with the syllable elided, as Shawcross prints it.

[39]Pronounce as a disyllable; it is spelled "prosp'rous" in the 1680 edition. Compare the pronunciation and the usage of the word at 14.

[40]The formula "He ended," as with "he thus bespake" (43), together with the ending or beginning of a verse paragraph, is an indicator that a passage of dialogue has ended or is beginning—replacing quotation marks.

[41]The word has a stronger meaning than it does in modern English. *OED* 1 defines it as "The condition of being mentally paralyzed, mental stupefaction, frenzy," using 4.562, "Satan smitten with amazement fell" as an instance.

[42]"There was no time then."

[43]Milton used the term quite specifically of Julius Caesar in his prose (*History of Britain*, Yale 5: 65, 70); the word "dictator" in classical Latin meant "one elected by the Romans only in emergencies, with absolute authority, for six months." Here it seems to be synonymous with "tyrant," although, if the fallen angels are considered to have given Satan only temporary absolute power, their self-deception may have allowed the tyranny to persist.

[44]Following Genesis 3.5, the words of the Serpent, "ye shall be as gods, knowing both good and evil." Milton and other commentators on Genesis took the gods mentioned here as "fallen angels."

Of many a[45] pleasant Realm and Province wide.
So to the Coast of *Jordan*[46] he directs
His easie[47] steps; girded with snaky wiles,[48] 120
Where he might likeliest find this new-declar'd,
This man of men,[49] attested Son of God,
Temptation and all guile[50] on him to try;
So to subvert[51] whom he suspected rais'd
To end his Raign on Earth so long enjoy'd: 125
But contrary unweeting[52] he fulfill'd
The purpos'd Counsel pre-ordain'd and fixt
Of the most High, who in full frequence° bright COMPANY
Of Angels, thus to *Gabriel* smiling[53] spake.
 Gabriel this day by proof° thou shalt behold, TRIAL 130
Thou and all Angels conversant[54] on Earth
With man or mens affairs, how I begin
To verifie that solemn message late,° MESSAGE ISSUED RECENTLY
On which I sent thee to the Virgin pure
In *Galilee*, that she should bear a Son 135
Great in Renown, and call'd the Son of God;
Then toldst her doubting how these things could be
To her a Virgin, that on her should come
The Holy Ghost, and the power of the highest
O're-shadow her:[55] this man born and now up-grown, 140
To shew him worthy of his birth divine
And high prediction, henceforth I expose[56]
To Satan; let him tempt and now assay° TRY OUT
His utmost subtilty, because he boasts
And vaunts of his great cunning to the throng 145
Of his Apostasie;[57] he might have learnt
Less over-weening, since he fail'd in *Job*,[58]

---

[45]Elide the two words to pronounce them as two syllables, as "many-ya," as in the proverbial "many a man" or "many a maid." Though seventeenth-century spelling did not normally show the elided syllable, regular iambic scansion reveals it. The prosodic term for this is enclitic elision.

[46]The baptismal river Jordan is associated with Leviathan or Satan in Job 40.23.

[47]"His easie steps" are his steps while at liberty or while he is permitted by God to roam.

[48]Satan has not only taken on the form of the Serpent in the past, he has taken on the character of the "subtle" Serpent (see Genesis 3.1) as part of his own character; hence he wears the wiles of the Serpent as if they were part of his costume. The good person, by contrast, was biblically girded with righteousness (Isaiah 11.5) or with truth (Ephesians 6.14).

[49]Stresses the mortality of the Son in the incarnation by making him a man of men rather than a man of God.

[50]The kind of "[i]nsidious cunning, deceit, treachery" (*OED* 1) characteristic of Satan.

[51]Completely overthrow.

[52]The adjective is also used of Eve (*Paradise Lost* 10.335, 916), when she unwittingly is seduced by Satan in the Serpent. Here Satan is being used by God providentially but unwittingly.

[53]God's smile here need not be sadistic. The happy outcome of the Son's combat with Satan is providential (under the control of God). Compare *Paradise Lost* 5.718. In the Bible, the angel Gabriel is often used by God as ambassador or messenger. An emblem of mercy, as compared with Michael's severity, Gabriel becomes "the guardian Angel of Paradise" (Newton 129n).

[54]The word should be emphasized on the first and third syllables. "Conversant" angels are allowed to have conversation with human beings. We observe Raphael and Michael in that office in *Paradise Lost*. Carey, following Newton, points out that Gabriel is guardian of Eden in *Paradise Lost* and the angel of the Annunciation (1.129n).

[55]"And the angel answered and said unto [Mary], The Holy Ghost shall come upon thee, and the power of the Highest shall overshadow thee: therefore also that holy thing which shall be born of thee shall be called the Son of God" (Luke 1.35).

[56]"Expose" in the sense of allowing out alone, undefended.

[57]The unthinking followers ("throng" implies mindlessness or carelessness) of Satan's rebellion against God: the fallen angels.

[58]If the book of Job is the model for the brief epic, the comparison between the Son of God as hero of this epic and Job as his hero in turn is here first made explicit. It will be reinforced with four other references, at 1.369, 425; and 3.64–67, 95. The word "servant" as it is used of Job in 3.67 below is in no way negative, since service to God is an honor, as in Matthew 25.21, "Well done, thou good and faithful servant." Lewalski shows there was a precedent in Gregory the Great's *Moralia in Job* for "relating Job and Christ in this way as heroes exhibited by God" (112).

Whose constant perseverance overcame
Whate're his cruel malice could invent.
He now shall know I can produce a man   150
Of female Seed,[59] far abler to resist
All his sollicitations, and at length
All his vast force, and drive him back to Hell,
Winning by Conquest what the first man lost
By fallacy surpriz'd.[60] But first I mean   155
To exercise[61] him in the Wilderness,
There he shall first lay down the rudiments°   INITIAL STRATEGIES
Of his great warfare, e're I send him forth
To conquer Sin and Death the two grand foes,
By Humiliation and strong Sufferance:[62]   160
His weakness[63] shall o'recome Satanic strength   GOD
And all the world, and mass of sinful flesh;[64]   SPEAKING
That all the Angels and Ætherial Powers,[65]
They now, and men hereafter may discern,
From what consummate vertue I have chose   165
This perfect Man, by merit[66] call'd my Son,
To earn Salvation for the Sons of men.

   So spake the Eternal Father, and all Heaven
Admiring stood a space, then into Hymns
Burst forth, and in Celestial measures mov'd,   170
Circling the Throne and Singing, while the hand
Sung with the voice,[67] and this the argument.°   SUBJECT MATTER
   Victory and Triumph to the Son of God
Now entring his great duel,[68] not of arms,

---

[59]Progeny descended from Eve's line. After Adam and Eve eat the fruit in Genesis, God punishes the serpent, saying "And I will put enmity between thee and the woman, and between thy seed and her seed; it shall bruise thy head, and thou shalt bruise his heel" (3.15). Milton, as well as other commentators and theologians of his era and long before, identified the Seed as Christ.

[60]The Son of God will win back by direct battle what Adam and Eve had lost by Satan's guile and deceit. One should see the battle as moral rather than physical, though something like a physical struggle occurs during the storm when Jesus is on the pinnacle of the Temple (4.436, 549; note that the Son does not resist). For the implications of "fallacy," compare "fair fallacious looks, and venereal trains" (*Samson Agonistes* 533), where the word "fallacious" implies calculated deception rather than logical error.

[61]Again, not a negative term, but positively used, as in exercising a horse in order to help keep it healthy and well-conditioned. The Son of God will also exercise free will in resisting Satan's temptations. As Carey notes, Milton writes of such a "good temptation . . . exercising ['exercendam'] . . . faith or patience" (156n, quoted from Columbia 15: 86–87).

[62]Close to the "Patience and Heroic Martyrdom" advocated in *Paradise Lost* 9.32. See Jordan, *The Quiet Hero*, for the figure of the patient and temperate hero. See also Albert C. Labriola, "Christus Patiens: The Virtue Patience and *Paradise Lost*, 1–2," in *The Triumph of Patience: Medieval and Renaissance Studies*, ed. Gerald J. Schiffhorst (Orlando: U Presses of Florida, 1978): 138–46.

[63]Alludes to 2 Corinthians 12.9, " . . . for my [i.e., the Lord's] strength is made perfect in weakness," a passage that might be especially close to Milton in his affliction of blindness. Compare also 1 Corinthians 1.25: "Because the foolishness of God is wiser than men; and the weakness of God is stronger than men."

[64]"Flesh considered as a huge sinful mass, as in "the body of sins of the flesh" (Colossians 2.11).

[65]"Armed forces or ranks of angels formed out of aether, the rarefied air the gods breathe and of which they are made." Ether was sometimes identified with the fifth element, whatever rarefied medium there was that existed in the heavens, above earth, air, fire, and water.

[66]Jesus must earn by merit the title of Son of God. As God says in *Paradise Lost*, the Son "hast been found / By Merit more then Birthright Son of God" (3.308–09). The contrast is between inherited privileges and earned privileges, as in the phrase "both by birth and merit the prime leader" (*History of Britain*, Yale 5: 89).

[67]The angels compose hymns spontaneously and sing them while dancing. See John G. Demaray, *Cosmos and Epic Representation: Dante, Spenser, Milton and the Transformation of Renaissance Heroic Poetry* (Pittsburgh, PA: Duquesne UP, 1991) for a discussion of this expression of celestial harmony and harmonic movement.

[68]The duel is what would now be called a psychological combat or in the middle ages would have been called a psychomachia between Jesus and Satan. It does have to do with force, but force of wit or force of goodness rather than physical force. In *Paradise Lost*, Michael admonishes Adam not to think of the combat between the Seed (Christ) and the Serpent or Dragon (Satan) in terms of physical combat: "Dream not of thir fight, / As of a Duel, or the local wounds / Of head or heel" (12.386–88). In such a test of mental strength, heroic passivity or resistance to evil may win out over the feverish activity of evil. An early reader of one copy Fletcher examined showed annoyance with the word "duel" by crossing it out and replacing it with "Conflict" (64n).

But to vanquish by wisdom hellish wiles.   175
The Father knows the Son;[69] therefore secure
Ventures his filial Vertue,° though untri'd,   INNER STRENGTH
Against whate're may tempt, whate're seduce,
Allure, or terrifie, or undermine.
Be frustrate° all ye stratagems of Hell,   FRUSTRATED   180
And devilish machinations come to nought.
  So they in Heav'n their Odes and Vigils[70] tun'd:
Mean while the Son of God, who yet some days
Lodg'd in *Bethabara* where *John* baptiz'd,[71]
Musing and much revolving in his brest,   185
How best the mighty work he might begin
Of Saviour to mankind, and which way first
Publish his God-like office now mature,[72]
One day forth walk'd alone, the Spirit leading;[73]
And his deep thoughts, the better to converse   190
With solitude, till far from track[74] of men,
Thought following thought, and step by step led on,
He entred now the bordering Desert wild,[75]
And with dark shades and rocks environ'd round,
His holy Meditations thus persu'd.   195
  O what a multitude of thoughts at once
Awakn'd in me swarm,[76] while I consider
What from within I feel my self, and hear
What from without comes often to my ears,
Ill sorting° with my present state compar'd.   MATCHING   200
When I was yet a child,[77] no childish play
To me was pleasing, all my mind was set
Serious to learn and know, and thence to do
What might be publick good;[78] my self I thought
Born to that end, born to promote all truth,   205
All righteous things: therefore above my years,
The Law of God I read, and found it sweet,[79]
Made it my whole delight, and in it grew

---

[69]"As the Father knoweth me, even so know I the Father" (John 10.15).

[70]The angels are poetical and musical, composing and singing heroic odes and night hymns or vigils.

[71]"These things were done in Bethabara beyond Jordan, where John was baptizing" (John 1.28).

[72]"Make known his godlike obligation now ready to be put into effect." Christ will effect the will of God and make his mission known at his baptism.

[73]Carey, silently following Newton, thinks this semicolon is in error and removes it (1.189n), but I see no problem with the stronger punctuation. The Spirit leads Jesus, not his thoughts, though it is true that the clause that follows the semicolon seems to provide no verb for "thoughts."

[74]"Far from traveled roads," as in "beaten track."

[75]The desert near Bethabara—presumably the "Arabia the deserte" shown adjacent to Bethabara and beyond the land of the Moabites in the 1560 Geneva Bible's "description of the holie land and of the places mencioned in the foure Evangelistes," according to the illustrationwhich precedes the first book of the New Testament.

[76]Thoughts swarming like bees, an image that suggests productivity, since a bee swarm heralds the division of a hive. But compare Samson's references to "thoughts, that like a deadly swarm / Of Hornets arm'd," that "rush upon [him] thronging" (*Samson Agonistes* 19–21).

[77]Echoing the famous phrasing from 1 Corinthians 2.13: "When I was a child, I spake as a child, I understood as a child, I thought as a child: but when I became a man, I put away childish things."

[78]What has fascinated biographers and critics who have commented on this passage is that Jesus's goals—his civic-mindedness, his asceticism or temperance, his high seriousness—all mirror those of Milton as he portrayed himself in his youth, though, as Parker reminds us, "We must not assume that self-idealization either crept in or was a compelling motive," even though in defining a perfect man Milton would have defined "his personal notions of perfect behaviour" (1: 617). For the opinion that Parker was trying to correct, consider James Holly Hanford's assertion that "Milton as certainly identifies himself with his calm, philosophically triumphant Christ, as he had earlier identified himself with the rebellious Satan or the distraught and impassioned Adam, and the portrait is equally valid and important as a record of his early life" (*John Milton, Englishman* 201).

[79]Words are often sweet in the Bible (Psalms 141.6 and 119.103), but the idiom does not involve the Law. Milton may be inferring sweetness from the "delight" in "But his delight is in the law of the Lord" (Psalm 1.2); hence the use of the word in the next line.

To such perfection, that e're yet my age
Had measur'd twice six years, at our great Feast   210
I went into the Temple, there to hear
The Teachers of our Law,[80] and to propose
What might improve my knowledge or their own;
And was admir'd° by all, yet this not all   WONDERED AT
To which my Spirit aspir'd, victorious deeds   215
Flam'd in my heart, heroic acts, one while°   ONE TIME
To rescue *Israel* from the *Roman* yoke,
Then to subdue and quell o're all the earth
Brute violence and proud Tyrannick pow'r,
Till truth were freed, and equity° restor'd: FAIR DEALING   220
Yet held it more humane, more heavenly first
By winning words to conquer willing hearts,
And make perswasion do the work of fear;
At least to try, and teach the erring Soul
Not wilfully mis-doing, but unware   225
Misled; the stubborn only to subdue.[81]
These growing thoughts my Mother[82] soon perceiving
By words at times cast forth inly rejoyc'd,
And said to me apart,° high are thy thoughts   PRIVATELY
O Son, but nourish them and let them soar   230
To what highth sacred vertue and true worth
Can raise them, though above example high;
By matchless Deeds express° thy matchless Sire.   DISPLAY
For know, thou art no Son of mortal man,
Though men esteem thee low of Parentage,[83]   235
Thy Father is the Eternal King, who rules
All Heaven and Earth, Angels and Sons of men,
A messenger from God fore-told thy birth
Conceiv'd in me a Virgin, he fore-told
Thou shouldst be great and sit on *David*'s Throne,   240
And of thy Kingdom there should be no end.[84]
At thy Nativity a glorious Quire
Of Angels in the fields of *Bethlehem*[85] sung

---

[80]In Luke 2.46–50, Jesus, at the age of twelve and during the feast of Passover, separates himself from his parents, visits the Temple, and amazes the "doctors" with his "understanding and answers."

[81]The 1671 *Errata* call for replacement of the original "destroy," softening the force of the image Jesus uses and thus showing him in a more humane light.

[82]It seems necessary here to mention that Milton downplays the role of Mary in the life of Jesus (perhaps as a reaction to what was perceived by Protestants as the idolatrous worship of Mary by Roman Catholics), giving her here only a short speech as quoted by Jesus. Because the quotation is indirect, the first word of Mary's speech is neither capitalized nor indented and the last line (258) is hard to spot. Clearly she is subordinated to her son, in hierarchical importance as well as grammatical (he speaks for her and she speaks through him, indirectly), just as she is the mortal mother of an immortal son. Milton does, however, allow Mary to speak at some length with her son, something she does not do in the New Testament—there she is reported merely to say to her precocious son, while he is in the company of the "doctors" in the Temple, "Son, why hast though thus dealt with us? behold, thy father and I have sought thee sorrowing" (Luke 2.48), to which Jesus makes the famous reply that he must be about his Father's business. Kerrigan reads Milton's scene in a Freudian context: "She initiates his separation from her, a mother who does not tempt or retard, but rather propels her son to the paternal identification that resolves the oedipus complex and organizes his autonomy" (*Sacred* 108).

[83]As the son of a carpenter, Jesus might have been considered of a menial class—if his father had not been King of Heaven. Compare 2.412–15 below, where Satan attempts to lower Jesus's self-esteem.

[84]The angel messenger says to Mary, "He shall be great, and shall be called the Son of the Highest: and the Lord God shall give unto him the throne of his father David: And he shall reign over the house of Jacob for ever; and of his kingdom shall be no end" (Luke 1.32–33).

[85]Milton scans the word both as a trisyllable (2.78), following the modern pronunciation, and as a disyllable here (compare 4.505), as in "bedlam" (*Apology*; Yale 1: 895).

To Shepherds watching at their folds[86] by night,
And told them the Messiah now was born, 245
Where they might see him, and to thee they came;[87]
Directed to the Manger where thou lais't,
For in the Inn was left no better room:
A Star, not seen before in Heaven appearing
Guided the Wise Men thither from the East, 250
To honour thee with Incense, Myrrh, and Gold,
By whose bright course led on they found the place,
Affirming it thy Star new grav'n[88] in Heaven,
By which they knew thee King of *Israel* born.
Just *Simeon*[89] and Prophetic *Anna*, warn'd 255
By Vision, found thee in the Temple, and spake
Before the Altar and the vested[90] Priest,
Like things of thee to all that present stood.
This having heard, strait I[91] again revolv'd
The Law and Prophets,[92] searching what was writ 260
Concerning the Messiah, to our Scribes[93]
Known partly, and soon found of whom they spake
I am; this chiefly, that my way must lie
Through many a hard assay° even to the death, °TRIAL
E're I the promis'd Kingdom can attain, 265
Or work Redemption[94] for mankind, whose sins[95]
Full weight must be transferr'd upon my head.
Yet neither thus disheartn'd or dismay'd,
The time prefixt° I waited, when behold °PROPHESIED, FIXED
The Baptist,[96] (of whose birth I oft had heard, 270
Not knew by sight) now come, who was to come
Before Messiah[97] and his way prepare.
I as all others to his Baptism came,
Which I believ'd was from above; but he
Strait° knew me, and with loudest voice proclaim'd °IMMEDIATELY 275
Me him (for it was shew'n him so from Heaven)
Me him whose Harbinger° he was; and first °FORERUNNER

---

[86]Varies the reading of the King James Bible, Luke 2.8, "flocks" to "folds." The Geneva Bible translates "keping watch by night because of their flocke" (1560 ed.).

[87]For these and the following details, see the first two chapters of Matthew and Luke.

[88]The idea that the Creator engraved the stars in Heaven helps personalize the cosmos the way that the hand that Robert Fludd (or his engraver) pictured adjusting the tuning of the harmonic universe in the oft-reproduced illustration of *Utriusque Cosmi Historia* (London, 1617–19).

[89]Simeon is described as both "just and devout" in Luke 2.25. The Holy Ghost reveals to him "that he should not see death, before he had seen the Lord's Christ" (26). Anna's separate prophecy is described in Luke 2.36–38. The separate prophecies authenticate the birth of Jesus as the Son of God.

[90]Invested, or dressed in a priestly vestment or robe. *OED* cites Milton as the first to have used the past participle in the sense of "clothed" specifically "in ecclesiastical vestments."

[91]Mary has finished speaking on the word "stood," and the "I" once again is Jesus. "This having heard" serves the purpose of a set of quotation marks.

[92]The phrase "the law and the prophets" is familiar from Matthew 5.17 and 7.12. Study of the Old Testament, for Jesus and for Paul, would have divided it among the Law of Moses and the prophetic books as of Isaiah and the Psalms. If one studied the "Law and the Prophets," one covered most of the legal structure underlying Judaism.

[93]Members of a select group of professional interpreters of the Law, often grouped with Pharisees as sticklers for traditional ceremony.

[94]"Cause redemption to happen."

[95]Possessive "sin's" or "sins'."

[96]Compare the accounts of the coming of John the Baptist in Matthew 3, Luke 3, and Mark 1. Milton uses his title rather than his name, defining him by the nature of his task, which is to announce that "one mightier than I cometh, the latchet of whose shoes I am not worthy to unloose: he shall baptize you with the Holy Ghost and with fire" (Luke 3.16).

[97]The title Messiah is rarely used in the New Testament (see John 1.41 and 4.25), but Milton used it to name the military conqueror in *Paradise Lost* (see 6.881, among other instances), and he will combine Jesus's various titles in "Jesus Messiah Son of God" in 2.4 below. The lack of commas between names may be instructive here.

Refus'd on me his Baptism to confer,[98]
As much his greater, and was hardly° won;   WITH DIFFICULTY
But as I rose out of the laving[99] stream,   280
Heaven open'd her eternal doors, from whence[100]
The Spirit descended on me like a Dove,[101]
And last the sum of all, my Father's voice,
Audibly[102] heard from Heav'n, pronounc'd me his,
Me his beloved Son, in whom alone   285
He was well pleas'd; by which I knew the time
Now full,° that I no more should live obscure,   RIPE, READY
But openly begin, as best becomes
The Authority[103] which I deriv'd from Heaven.
And now by some strong motion[104] I am led   290
Into this Wilderness, to what intent
I learn not yet, perhaps I need not know;[105]
For what concerns my knowledge God reveals.
   So spake our Morning Star[106] then in his rise,
And looking round on every side beheld   295
A pathless Desert, dusk° with horrid shades;   DUSKY, DARK
The way he came not having mark'd, return
Was difficult, by humane[107] steps untrod;
And he still on was led, but with such thoughts
Accompanied of things past and to come   300
Lodg'd in his brest, as well might recommend
Such Solitude before choicest Society.
Full forty days he pass'd, whether on hill
Sometimes, anon° in shady vale, each night   PRESENTLY
Under the covert° of some ancient Oak,   COVERING   305
Or Cedar, to defend him from the dew,[108]
Or harbour'd in one Cave, is not reveal'd;
Nor tasted humane food, nor hunger felt
Till those days ended, hunger'd then at last
Among wild Beasts: they at his sight grew mild,   310

---

[98]John refuses to baptize Jesus, saying "I have need to be baptized of thee, and comest thou to me" (Matthew 2.14), but Jesus nonetheless asks for and receives baptism of John.

[99]The root of the word is Latin *lavare*, "to wash," but John's baptism of Jesus is not only a physical washing but a symbolic washing away of sins.

[100]In order to read the line as iambic, one should scan it "Heav'n open'd her eternal doors, from whence," with "Heaven" treated as a monosyllable and the stress placed on the first syllable of "open'd."

[101]The "like" is important, since it allows both Holy Spirit and dove to be interpreted more loosely, in accord with Milton's anti-Trinitarian views.

[102]Perhaps the "voice [that] came from heaven" (Luke 3.22) is described as audible because it proclaims that Jesus is God's Son not to him alone but to the multitude gathering to watch John baptize him.

[103]Read as "Th' Authority."

[104]When it does not mean physical movement, motion is Milton's word for inward or even instinctive prompting from God, as in Samson's "rouzing motions" (*Samson Agonistes* 1382; compare *Paradise Lost* 11.91). The *OED* defines this sense as "A working of God in the soul" (9), but without citing Milton's usage.

[105]The interjected phrase shows that Jesus need not be omniscient, nor is his knowledge equal to that of the Father. "Even the Son, however, does not know absolutely everything, for there are some secrets which the Father has kept to himself alone" (*On Christian Doctrine* 1.5; Yale 6: 265).

[106]The narrator is making the common contrast between Lucifer, the morning star, and Jesus, the morning star (possibly) of Revelation 22.16, or harbinger of the coming of Christian truth. Revelation 8.10 pictured a "great star" fallen from Heaven, often interpreted as Satan. Milton classified such planets as "those stars of brightest magnitude that rise and set with the Sun, untill the opposite motion of their orbs bring them to such a place in the firmament, where they may be seen evning or morning" (*Areopagitica*; Yale 2: 550). Milton also wrote of the Court of Star Chamber, having been abolished, as "now fall'n from the starrs with *Lucifer*" (Yale 2: 570).

[107]Here the word seems to be equivalent to the modern "human," which unfortunately could be spelled with or without the "e" that makes it ambiguous to a modern reader. Compare "humane" at 221 above and *Paradise Lost* 2.109.

[108]Perhaps, in this case, "unhealthy clamminess." Evening dews were thought to carry disease, at which Shakespeare may be hinting in "Our day is gone, / Clowds, dews, and dangers come" (*Julius Caesar* 5.3.64–65).

Nor sleeping him nor waking harm'd,[109] his walk
The fiery Serpent fled, and noxious Worm,[110]
The Lion and fierce Tiger glar'd aloof.° FROM A DISTANCE
But now an aged man in Rural weeds,[111]
Following, as seem'd, the quest of some stray Ewe, 315
Or wither'd sticks to gather; which might serve
Against a Winters day when winds blow keen,
To warm him wet return'd from field at Eve,
He saw approach, who first with curious eye
Perus'd him, then with words thus utter'd[112] spake. 320
    Sir, what ill chance hath brought thee[113] to this place
So far from path or road of men, who pass
In Troop or Caravan, for single none
Durst ever, who return'd, and dropt not here
His Carcass, pin'd with hunger and with droughth?[114] 325
I ask the rather, and the more admire,
For that to me thou seem'st the man, whom late
Our new baptizing Prophet at the Ford
Of *Jordan* honour'd so, and call'd thee Son
Of God; I saw and heard, for we sometimes 330
Who dwell this wild,[115] constrain'd by want, come forth
To Town or Village nigh (nighest° is far) THE NEAREST
Where ought° we hear, and curious are to hear, AUGHT, ANYTHING
What happ'ns new; Fame also finds us out.[116]
    To whom the Son of God. Who brought me hither 335
Will bring me hence, no other Guide I seek.[117]
    By Miracle he may, reply'd the Swain,
What other way I see not, for we here
Live on tough roots and stubs,° to thirst inur'd SHOOTS
More then the Camel, and to drink go far,[118] 340
Men to much misery and hardship born;
But if thou be the Son of God, Command
That out of these hard stones be made thee bread;[119]
So shalt thou save thy self and us relieve
With Food, whereof we wretched seldom taste. 345

---

[109]"Nor did they harm him when he was either sleeping or awake." Mark 1.13 mentions the wild beasts but not that Jesus was safe among them.

[110]Both fiery serpent (dragon) and noxious worm (snake) are inherently fearful of the Son's goodness—probably because both are associated with Satan.

[111]One of a succession of innocent looking hypocrites in Spenser and Milton who attempt to corrupt good people. The venerable age and pastoral occupation of the man should imply freedom from guile, but Milton's readers would know from Archimago's appearance as "An aged Sire, in long blacke weedes yclad" (*The Faerie Queene* 1.1.29) that evil magicians can assume any shape they desire. Comus appears to the Lady in a similar pastoral disguise, as a "harmles Villager" (166).

[112]I have corrected from the unusual form "utt'red," which appears nowhere else in Milton's published poetry and was most likely a compositor's error.

[113]The "aged sire" uses the possibly less respectful "thee" rather than the more formal "you." As Ronberg puts it, "In the sixteenth and early seventeenth centuries, singular *you* (and of course *ye*) was employed by inferiors to superiors, e.g., children to parents, servants to masters, ordinary men to noblemen; and *thou/thee* were used in the reverse manner, but also when addressing God because of the wish for intimacy" (*A Way with Words: The Language of English Renaissance Literature* [London: Edward Arnold, 1992]: 76).

[114]"Exhausted by hunger and thirst."

[115]"Who live in this wild place."

[116]"Fame [Latin *Fama*, 'rumor'] also gets to us."

[117]The Son's curt answer may indicate skepticism. Satan in the "aged sire" has already implied that his fame, not his proper identity, has spread because of the notoriety of John the Baptist.

[118]Satan seems to be attempting to plant the desire for something to drink subliminally—a ruse that doesn't work. He seems to be appealing to Jesus's charity in asking for bread for his hungry fellow countrymen.

[119]"Command that bread be made out of these stones for you." In Luke 4.3–4, the devil says "If thou be the Son of God, command this stone that it be made bread" and Jesus answers him, "It is written, That man shall not live by bread alone, but by every word of God."

He ended, and the Son of God reply'd.
Think'st thou such force in Bread? is it not written
(For I discern thee other then thou seem'st)
Man lives not by Bread only, but each Word
Proceeding from the mouth of God; who fed   350
Our Fathers here with Manna; in the Mount
Moses was forty days, nor eat[120] nor drank,
And forty days *Eliah*[121] without food
Wandred this barren waste, the same I now:
Why dost thou then suggest to me distrust,   355
Knowing who I am, as I know who thou art?
    Whom thus answer'd th' Arch Fiend now undisguis'd.
'Tis true, I am that Spirit unfortunate,
Who leagu'd with millions more in rash revolt
Kept not my happy Station, but was driv'n   360
With them from bliss to the bottomless deep,
Yet to that hideous place not so confin'd
By rigour unconniving,[122] but that oft
Leaving my dolorous Prison I enjoy
Large liberty to round[123] this Globe of Earth,   365
Or range in th' Air, nor from the Heav'n of Heav'ns
Hath he excluded my resort[124] sometimes.
I came among the Sons of God, when he
Gave up into my hands *Uzzean Job*[125]
To prove him, and illustrate[126] his high worth;   370
And when to all his Angels he propos'd
To draw the proud King *Ahab* into fraud[127]
That he might fall in *Ramoth*, they demurring,[128]
I undertook that office, and the tongues
Of all his flattering Prophets glibb'd[129] with lyes   375
To his destruction, as I had in charge.
For what he bids I do; though I have lost
Much lustre of my native brightness,[130] lost
To be belov'd of God, I have not lost
To love, at least contemplate[131] and admire   380
What I see excellent in good, or fair,
Or vertuous, I should so have lost all sense.

---

[120]Pronounced "et."

[121]The prophet Elijah, who fasted like Moses and wandered like the tribes of Israel in the desert. Finding such parallel structures reinforces the typology that might identify Christ with Moses or Elijah.

[122]With unwinking alertness. "To connive" originally meant "to wink at or overlook." Milton's usage of the past-participial adjective is unique. Satan may be playing on the sounds of "confin'd" and "unconniving" in a meaningless echo. The result is weak rhetoric and poor poetry.

[123]"To make the complete circuit of, to pass or travel round (the world, a place, etc.)" (*OED* II.9a).

[124]A resort here would be a place to which God allows Satan to go.

[125]Job is from the land of Uz (Job 1.1). What God says to Satan about Job is "Behold, he is in thine hand; but save his life" (Job 2.6).

[126]Accented on the second syllable.

[127]Ahab was caused by his wife Jezebel to defraud Naboth of his vineyard and have Naboth killed in 1 Kings 21: ". . . there was none like unto Ahab, which did sell himself to work wickedness in the sight of the Lord, whom Jezebel his wife stirred up" (25). Ahab dies of a wound inflicted at a battle in Ramoth-gilead, and the dogs lick the blood of the dead Ahab in the same way they had licked the blood of Naboth (19), fulfilling the prophecy. As Carey points out, the sense of "fraud" as "the state of being defrauded or deluded" seems to be unique to Milton (372n). For the "flattering Prophets," see 1 Kings 22.19–23.

[128]Corrected by the *Errata* from "demuring."

[129]"Greased," or "made to flow easily." The adjective suggests that the prophets are hollow and glib. Milton's usage is not recorded in the *OED*.

[130]Compare *Paradise Lost* 1.591–92: "his form had yet not lost / All her Original brightness. . . ."

[131]Accented on the second syllable.

What can be then less in me[132] then desire
To see thee and approach thee, whom I know
Declar'd the Son of God, to hear attent°　　　　　ATTENTIVELY　　　385
Thy wisdom, and behold thy God-like deeds?
Men generally think me much a foe
To all mankind: why should I?[133] they to me
Never did wrong or violence, by them
I lost not what I lost, rather by them　　　　　390
I gain'd what I have gain'd, and with them dwell
Copartner in these Regions of the World,
If not disposer;° lend them oft my aid,　　　　　RULER
Oft my advice by presages and signs,
And answers, oracles, portents and dreams,　　　　　395
Whereby they may direct their future life.[134]
Envy they say excites me, thus to gain
Companions of my misery and wo.
At first it may be; but long since with wo
Nearer[135] acquainted, now I feel by proof,　　　　　400
That fellowship in pain divides not smart,[136]
Nor lightens aught each mans peculiar load.
Small consolation then, were Man adjoyn'd:°　　　　　ADDED
This wounds me most (what can it less) that Man,
Man fall'n shall be restor'd, I never more.　　　　　405

　　To whom our Saviour sternly thus reply'd.
Deservedly thou griev'st, compos'd of lyes
From the beginning, and in lies wilt end;[137]
Who boast'st release from Hell, and leave to come
Into the Heav'n of Heavens; thou com'st indeed,　　　　　410
As a poor miserable captive thrall,
Comes to the place where he before had sat
Among the Prime° in Splendour, now depos'd,　　　　　FOREMOST
Ejected, emptyed,[138] gaz'd, unpityed, shun'd,[139]
A spectacle of ruin or of scorn　　　　　415
To all the Host of Heaven; the happy place
Imparts[140] to thee no happiness, no joy,
Rather inflames thy torment, representing
Lost bliss, to thee no more communicable,[141]
So never more in Hell then when in Heaven.　　　　　420
But thou art serviceable to Heaven's King.

---

[132]Satan's involuted syntax suggests a hidden ironic message. While he says he would rather see and approach the Son of God than do anything else, the reader might sense his true desire is to avoid the confrontation. Lewalski argues "there can be nothing Satan desires less than thus to confront and listen to Christ" (351).

[133]Supply "be [such a foe]."

[134]Satan has just described the means by which Satanic religions might propagate themselves—by false prophecies, false dreams, and the worship of pagan gods—a process Milton labeled creating "devils to adore for deities" (*Paradise Lost* 1.373). "Whereby" is corrected from "Wherbey" in *1671*.

[135]The *1671 Errata* correct from "Never."

[136]Building on the idea that "misery loves company," Satan here concedes that having fellows in pain does not lessen the pain for each fellow.

[137]Satan is "a liar, and the father of it" in John 8.44. The Son of God at this point may or may not remember having encountered Satan in Heaven.

[138]Emptied, that is, of all their contents, or all that matters.

[139]The line should be scanned as "Ejected, empti'd, gaz'd, unpiti'd, shunn'd" in order to maintain an iambic pattern. The problem for the compositor is that an "i" before an "ed" elision was not generally permitted; neither modernized nor original spelling is much help, at this point, at least, with the problem of scanscion.

[140]Corrected by the *1671 Errata* from "Imports."

[141]Good is no longer communicable to Satan, though he carries Hell around with him. Compare *Paradise Lost* 1.254–55 and 4.78.

Wilt thou impute to obedience what thy fear
Extorts, or pleasure to do ill excites?
What but thy malice mov'd thee to misdeem°   THINK ILL
Of righteous[142] *Job*, then cruelly to afflict him   425
With all inflictions, but his patience won?[143]
The other service was thy chosen task,
To be a lyer in four hundred mouths;[144]
For lying is thy sustenance, thy food.
Yet thou pretend'st to truth; all Oracles   430
By thee are giv'n,[145] and what confest more true
Among the Nations? that hath been thy craft,
By mixing somewhat true to vent more lyes.[146]
But what have been thy answers, what but dark
Ambiguous and with double sense deluding,   435
Which they who ask'd have seldom understood,
And not well understood as good not known?
Who ever by consulting at thy shrine
Return'd the wiser, or the more instruct
To flye or follow what concern'd him most,   440
And run not sooner to his fatal snare?
For God hath justly giv'n the Nations up
To thy Delusions; justly, since they fell
Idolatrous, but when his purpose is
Among them to declare his Providence   445
To thee not known, whence hast thou then thy truth,
But from him or his Angels President°   PRESIDING
In every Province, who themselves disdaining
To approach thy Temples, give thee in command
What to the smallest tittle thou shalt say   450
To thy Adorers; thou with trembling fear,
Or like a Fawning Parasite obey'st;
Then to thy self ascrib'st the truth fore-told.
But this thy glory shall be soon retrench'd;°   CUT SHORT, REPRESSED
No more shalt thou by oracling abuse[147]   455
The Gentiles; henceforth Oracles are ceast,[148]
And thou no more with Pomp and Sacrifice
Shalt be enquir'd at *Delphos* or elsewhere,
At least in vain, for they shall find thee mute.
God hath now sent his living Oracle[149]   460

---

[142]Corrected from "irghteous" in *1671*.

[143]Hughes and Campbell significantly alter the punctuation of the last two lines, making them read ". . . Of righteous Job, then cruelly to afflict him /
With all inflictions? But his patience won." I must admit that moving the question mark back to where the comma is and turning the last clause into a
short sentence both help the lines make sense. If one reads the "But" as "except," however, as does Loh, sense is restored to the sentence without altering
the original punctuation.

[144]Perhaps a reference to 1 Kings 22.6: "Then the King of Israel [Ahab] gathered the prophets together, about four hundred men." There is a "lying spirit
in the mouth of all his prophets" (22.22), which Milton may have presumed to be Satan and that lying spirit causes the death of Ahab.

[145]Greek oracles in the classical era often spoke ambiguously, a fact not ignored by Christian Church Fathers: "Patristic writers almost universally
condemned oracles, not only because they were false or ambiguous, but also because they were the work of demons hostile to man" (MacKellar 96n).

[146]A key passage in understanding Satan's rhetoric or methods of persuasion. He mixes enough truth into each argument to make it persuasive, even though
most of the argument may be built on lies.

[147]"No longer will you be able to deceive [the Gentiles] by lying through oracles."

[148]One of the subjects of Milton's Nativity Ode is the cessation of the oracles at the birth of Christ.

[149]Christ by virtue of speaking truth, sometimes prophetically, becomes a true oracle, as compared to the demonically inspired false oracles of pagan
religions.

Into the World, to teach his final will,
And sends his Spirit of Truth[150] henceforth to dwell
In pious Hearts, an inward Oracle
To all truth requisite for men to know.
 So spake our Saviour; but the subtle[151] Fiend,   465
Though inly stung with anger and disdain,°   SCORN
Dissembl'd, and this Answer smooth return'd.
 Sharply thou hast insisted on rebuke,
And urg'd me hard with doings, which not will
But misery hath rested° from me; where   WRESTED, TAKEN BY FORCE   470
Easily canst thou find one miserable,
And not inforc'd oft-times to part from truth;
If it may stand him more in stead° to lye,   TO HIS BENEFIT
Say and unsay, feign, flatter, or abjure?
But thou art plac't above me, thou art Lord;   475
From thee I can and must submiss[152] endure
Check or reproof, and glad to scape so quit.[153]
Hard are the ways of truth, and rough to walk,[154]
Smooth on the tongue discourst, pleasing to th' ear,
And tuneable as Silvan Pipe or Song;   480
What wonder then if I delight to hear
Her dictates from thy mouth? most men admire
Vertue, who follow not her lore:° permit me   TEACHING
To hear thee when I come (since no man comes)
And talk at least, though I despair to attain.   485
Thy Father, who is holy, wise and pure,
Suffers the Hypocrite or Atheous° Priest   ATHEISTIC
To tread his Sacred Courts, and minister
About his Altar, handling holy things,
Praying or vowing, and vouchsaf'd his voice   490
To *Balaam*[155] Reprobate, a Prophet yet
Inspir'd; disdain not such access to me.
 To whom our Saviour with unalter'd brow.[156]
Thy coming hither, though I know thy scope,°   GOAL, AIM
I bid not or forbid; do as thou find'st   495
Permission from above; thou canst not more.[157]
 He added not; and Satan bowing low

---

[150]Christ comforts his disciples in John 16.13, promising them that "when he, the Spirit of truth, is come, he will guide you into all truth." In the seventeenth century the passage might be used to convince followers of various Puritan sects to believe in personal inspiration or in each pious person's inner light.

[151]The adjective was applied to the serpent in Genesis 3.1 and hence was used to define one aspect of Satan's character. "Fiend" is one of the degrading or diminutive titles of Satan: he is both the Fiend (the Devil himself) and lord of fiends.

[152]"Placed under," a passive process rather than an active one, which suggests the loss of free will (a lie).

[153]"Glad to escape from the charge." "Quit" here carries the modern sense of "acquitted."

[154]Compare Matthew 7.13, "strait is the gate, and narrow is the way, which leadeth unto life, and few there be that find it," one of Milton's favorite passages from the words of Jesus.

[155]"Thus did the Reprobate hireling Preist *Balaam* seeke to subdue the Israelites to *Moab*, if not by force, then by this divellish *Pollicy*, to draw them from the Sanctuary of God to the luxurious, and ribald feasts of *Baal-peor*" (*Of Reformation*; Yale 1: 589). "Reprobate" carries the meaning "utterly depraved" or "unredeemable." For the complete story of Balaam, see Numbers 22–24.

[156]The Son's unaltered brow (a frown or a smile would have altered it) shows that he is unmoved by or indifferent to Satan's flattery and hypocritical lies.

[157]Compare Gabriel's similar reply to Satan in *Paradise Lost*:
 Satan, I know thy strength, and thou knowst mine,
 Neither our own but giv'n; what follie then
 To boast what Arms can doe, since thine no more
 Then Heav'n permits, nor mine. . . .   (4.1006–09)

His gray dissimulation, disappear'd
Into thin Air[158] diffus'd: for now began
Night with her sullen wing[159] to double-shade
The Desert, Fowls in thir clay nests were couch't;°   LYING DOWN HIDDEN   500
And now wild Beasts came forth the woods to roam.

    The End of the First Book.

---

[158]Spirits vanish into thin air in *The Tempest* 4.1.150.
[159]The "wings of night" are proverbial, though Milton may be remembering Vergil, *Aeneid* 8.369: "Night came down, enfolding the earth with her dusky wings . . ." (trans. C. Day Lewis).

PARADISE REGAIN'D.

The Second BOOK.

MEan while the new-baptiz'd, who yet remain'd
At *Jordan* with the Baptist, and had seen
Him whom they heard so late expressly call'd
Jesus Messiah Son of God declar'd,[1]
And on that high Authority had believ'd,   5
And with him talkt, and with him lodg'd,[2] I mean
Andrew and *Simon*, famous after known
With others though in Holy Writ not nam'd,
Now missing him thir joy so lately found,
So lately found, and so abruptly gone,   10
Began to doubt, and doubted many days,
And as the days increas'd, increas'd thir doubt:
Sometimes they thought he might be only shewn,
And for a time caught up to God, as once
Moses was in the Mount, and missing long;[3]   15
And the great *Thisbite*[4] who on fiery wheels
Rode up to Heaven,[5] yet once again to come.
Therefore as those young Prophets[6] then with care
Sought lost *Eliah*, so in each place these
Nigh to *Bethabara*;[7] in *Jerico*   20
The City of Palms, *Ænon*, and *Salem* Old,

---

[1]Though the Apostles may have believed that Jesus was the Messiah, he was not given the title by the voice from Heaven in any of the Gospel accounts of the baptism. Andrew does, however, label him the Messiah in John 1.41: "We have found the Messias, which is, being interpreted, the Christ." Both "Messiah" and "Christ" both mean "the anointed one."

[2]Jesus "entered into the house of Simon and Andrew" in Mark 1.29.

[3]Moses is missing such a long time when he is in the process of receiving the Ten Commandments that the people below "gathered themselves together unto Aaron and said . . . we wot not what is become of him" (Exodus 32.1). The delay causes the people and Aaron to conspire to make the idolatrous golden calf.

[4]The prophet Elijah is called the "Tishbite" in the Authorized Version of 1 Kings 17.1. MacKellar speculates that Milton followed the Greek of the Septuagint in forming his own version of the name and that he disliked the "sh" sound in general, as when he avoided it in Basan for Bashan, Sittim for Shittim (*Paradise Lost* 1.398–413), and Silo for Shiloh (see *Samson Agonistes* 1674; MacKellar 105n16).

[5]Elijah is translated to Heaven in 2 Kings 11: " . . . behold, there appeared a chariot of fire, and horses of fire, and parted them both [Elisha is present as well] asunder; and Elijah went up by a whirlwind into heaven. "The second coming of Elijah is predicted in Malachi 4.5: "Behold, I will send you Elijah the prophet before the coming of the great and dreadful day of the Lord." Jesus compares John the Baptist with Elias (the Greek form of Elijah) in Matthew 11.14.

[6]After Elijah has been translated to Heaven, "fifty strong men" searched for him "three days, but found him not" (2 Kings 2.15-17).

[7]Each of the places named are associated with John or are near the river Jordan, where he practiced baptism. Betharaba is mentioned in John 1.28, Jericho is called the "city of palm trees" in Deuteronomy 34.3, and Aenon and Salem are mentioned in John 3.23. Salem is "old," as Campbell points out, "in deference to a patristic tradition which identified the 'Salim' of John the Baptist with the Salem of Melchizedek (Gen. xiv. 18, Heb. vii. 102)" (458n20–24).

Machærus[8] and each Town or City wall'd
On this side the broad lake *Genezaret*,
Or in *Perea*, but return'd in vain.
Then on the bank of *Jordan*, by a Creek: 25
Where winds with Reeds, and Osiers whisp'ring play
Plain Fishermen,[9] no greater men them call,
Close in a Cottage low together got
Thir unexpected loss and plaints° outbreath'd.[10]   LAMENTATIONS
    Alas, from what high hope to what relapse   30
Unlook'd for are we fall'n, our eyes beheld
Messiah certainly now come, so long
Expected of our Fathers; we have heard
His words, his wisdom full of grace and truth,
Now, now, for sure, deliverance is at hand,   35
The Kingdom shall to *Israel* be restor'd:
Thus we rejoyc'd, but soon our joy is turn'd
Into perplexity and new amaze:
For whither is he gone, what accident
Hath rapt him from us?[11] will he now retire   40
After appearance, and again prolong
Our expectation? God of *Israel*,
Send thy Messiah forth, the time is come;
Behold the Kings of the Earth[12] how they oppress
Thy chosen, to what highth thir pow'r unjust   45
They have exalted, and behind them cast
All fear of thee, arise and vindicate
Thy Glory, free thy people from thir yoke,
But let us wait; thus far he hath perform'd,
Sent his Anointed, and to us reveal'd him,   50
By his great Prophet, pointed at and shown,[13]
In publick, and with him we have convers'd;
Let us be glad of this, and all our fears
Lay on his Providence; he will not fail
Nor will withdraw him° now, nor will recall,   HIMSELF   55
Mock us with his blest sight, then snatch him hence,
Soon we shall see our hope, our joy return.
    Thus they out of their plaints new hope resume
To find whom at the first they found unsought:
But to his Mother *Mary*, when she saw   60
Others return'd from Baptism, not her Son,

---

[8]John the Baptist was imprisoned and executed at the fortress of Machaerus. Genezaret is the same as the Sea of Galilee (Luke 5.1); Perea was the name given to the district "beyond Jordan" (Matthew 11.1).

[9]Milton couches the description of the biblical fishermen in pastoral language: in *Comus* 319-20, for instance, Comus would like to lead the Lady to a "low / But loyal cottage." The reeds and osiers along the stream also seem to have been recycled by Milton from similar reeds in *Comus* 345 (or *Paradise Lost* 11.132) or "Osier dank" in *Comus* 891.

[10]What follows is a short piscatory eclogue, fisherman's song, or "plaint." "Introduced by language borrowed from Spenser's *Shepheardes Calender*, as with "A shepheards boye, (no better doe him call)" or from Phineas Fletcher's *Piscatory Eclogues* 3.1, "A fisher-lad (no higher dares he look)," the plaint continues from line 30 to line 57 and follows the original model of Jacopo Sannazaro (see *The Piscatory Eclogues of Jacopo Sannazaro*, ed. W. P. Mustard [London, 1914]). Though *1671* does not indent the beginning of the speech, I have done so, as do most modern editors (Campbell adds quotation marks around the "plaints"). Milton adds dramatic variety with what is also a short chorus, followed by a soliloquy given by Mary, mother of Jesus.

[11]"What trick of fate has taken him (violence is implied in 'rapt') from us?"

[12]Compare Psalm 2.2: "The kings of the earth set themselves . . . against the Lord, and against his anointed, ..."

[13]Most of the representations of John the Baptist and Jesus painted from about 1400 to 1700 show John pointing with his finger toward Jesus.

Nor left at *Jordan*, tydings of him none;[14]
Within her brest, though calm; her brest though pure,
Motherly cares and fears got head,[15] and rais'd
Some troubl'd thoughts, which she in sighs thus clad.   65
    O what avails me now that honour high
To have conceiv'd of God, or that salute[16]
Hale highly favour'd, among women blest;
While I to sorrows am no less advanc't,
And fears as eminent, above the lot   70
Of other women, by the birth I bore,
In such a season born when scarce a Shed
Could be obtain'd to shelter him or me
From the bleak air; a Stable was our warmth,
A Manger his, yet soon enforc't to flye   75
Thence into *Egypt*, till the Murd'rous King[17]
Were dead, who sought his life, and missing fill'd
With Infant blood the streets of *Bethlehem*;
From *Egypt* home return'd, in *Nazareth*
Hath been our dwelling many years, his life   80
Private, unactive, calm, contemplative,
Little suspicious to any King;[18] but now
Full grown to Man, acknowledg'd, as I hear,
By *John* the Baptist, and in publick shown,
Son own'd[19] from Heaven by his Father's voice;   85
I look't for some great change; to Honour? no,
But trouble, as old *Simeon* plain fore-told,[20]
That to the fall and rising he should be
Of many in *Israel*, and to a sign
Spoken against,° that through my very Soul   DENIGRATED   90
A sword shall pierce, this is my favour'd lot,
My Exaltation[21] to Afflictions high;
Afflicted I may be, it seems, and blest;
I will not argue that, nor will repine.°   COMPLAIN
But where delays he now? some great intent   95
Conceals him:[22] when twelve years he scarce had seen,
I lost him, but so found, as well I saw
He could not lose himself; but went about
His Father's business;[23] what he meant I mus'd,

---

[14]Milton dramatizes what is not depicted in the Gospels, the demonstration of "Motherly cares and fears" on Mary's part, as she worries about the return of her son, and in so doing humanizes Mary.

[15]"Assumed control." *Head* is used as in "got up a head of steam."

[16]The greeting which the angel Gabriel bestowed on her at Luke 1.28: "Hail, thou that art highly favoured, the Lord is with thee: blessed art thou among women."

[17]Herod, who sought to stamp out the prophesied "King of the Jews" by having all the children under the age of two in Bethlehem and surrounding towns killed (Matthew 2), the "slaughter of the innocents" so often painted in the Renaissance.

[18]Though it is true that Joseph and his family felt it necessary to avoid Archilaus, the son of Herod, Milton adds the supposition that the young Jesus's life was "Private, unactive, calm, [and] contemplative."

[19]"Named as heir" (the opposite of "disowned").

[20]"And Simeon blessed them, and said unto Mary his mother, Behold, this child is set for the fall and rising again of many in Israel; and for a sign which shall be spoken against; (Yea, a sword shall pierce through thy own soul also,) that the thoughts of many hearts may be revealed" (Luke 2.34–35).

[21]As Campbell notes, "Miriam, the Hebrew form of Mary, is of uncertain etymology, but was sometimes believed to mean 'exaltation' (92n)."

[22]"Some great purpose conceals his identity [for the present]."

[23]In Luke 2.49, Jesus replies to his mother's and father's amazement and sorrow in finding him, after three days' absence from them, among the "doctors" in the Temple: "And he said unto them, How is it that ye sought me? wist ye not that I must be about my Father's business."

Since understand; much more his absence now   100
Thus long to some great purpose he obscures.
But I to wait with patience am inur'd;
My heart hath been a store-house long of things
And sayings laid up, portending strange events.
    Thus *Mary* pondering[24] oft, and oft to mind   105
Recalling what remarkably had pass'd
Since first her Salutation heard, with thoughts
Meekly compos'd awaited the fulfilling:
The while her Son tracing the Desert wild,
Sole but with holiest Meditations fed,[25]   110
Into himself descended, and at once
All his great work to come before him set:
How to begin, how to accomplish best
His end of being on Earth, and mission high:
For Satan[26] with slye preface to return[27]   115
Had left him vacant,° and with speed was gon   AT LEISURE
Up to the middle Region of thick Air,[28]
Where all his Potentates in Council sate;
There without sign of boast, or sign of joy,
Sollicitous and blank[29] he thus began.   120
    Princes, Heavens antient Sons,[30] Æthereal Thrones,[31]
Demonian[32] Spirits now, from the Element
Each of his reign allotted, rightlier call'd,
Powers of Fire, Air, Water, and Earth beneath,
So may we hold our place and these mild° seats   LESS SEVERE   125
Without new trouble; such an Enemy
Is ris'n to invade us, who no less
Threat'ns then[33] our expulsion down to Hell;
I, as I undertook, and with the vote
Consenting in full frequence° was impowr'd,   ASSEMBLY   130
Have found him, view'd him, tasted[34] him, but find
Far other labour to be undergon
Then when I dealt with *Adam* first of Men,
Though *Adam* by his Wives° allurement fell,[35]   WIFE'S
However to this Man inferior far,   135
If he be Man by Mothers side at least,

[24]The word should be pronounced as a disyllable, as in the "pondring" of *1680*.

[25]"Alone, but inspired by God with the holiest of ideas."

[26]The proper name is not italicized, most likely because it is a generic term, like "Jesus Messiah Son of God" of line 4 above, or the references to "the Baptist."

[27]Slyly, Satan has insinuated that he will return. I agree with Carey that Milton "means that before Satan left he said he would return" (2.115n).

[28]The middle of the air, "thick air" as compared to the thin air mentioned earlier—traditionally the region of devils.

[29]Always negative in Milton's usage, the word literally meant "white" or in a transferred sense "empty" or "devoid of emotion." Carey notes its meaning as "resourceless, nonplussed" (2.120n), which may be accurate, following *OED* 5: "Of persons: (Looking) as if deprived of the faculty of speech or action; 'shut up,' utterly disconcerted, discomfited, resourceless, or non-plussed; now chiefly in to look blank."

[30]The "Sons of God" mentioned in Genesis 6.2, whose meaning is amplified in *Paradise Lost* 5.447 and 11.622–99. See Hughes, "Devils."

[31] "Thrones" was one of the angelic orders. Satan is inflating the title and the substance of the fallen angels by reconstituting their rank and reinstituting their original creation out of ether (the fifth essence or quintessence).

[32]Milton's is the first usage recorded of this unusual adjective, the same as "demonic."

[33]The word "then" is inserted on the instructions of the *1671 Errata*.

[34] "Attempted to understand what makes him work," or "sounded him."

[35]Perhaps not an outright lie, but at best a half-truth. Adam's susceptibility to Eve's beauty in *Paradise Lost*, his "effeminate slackness" (11.634), seems more important as a cause of his fall than her aggressive "allurement."

With more then humane gifts from Heaven adorn'd,
Perfections absolute, Graces divine,
And amplitude of mind° to greatest Deeds.[36]   MAGNANIMITY
Therefore I am return'd, lest confidence   140
Of my success with *Eve* in Paradise
Deceive ye to perswasion over-sure
Of like succeeding here;[37] I summon all
Rather to be in readiness, with hand
Or counsel to assist; lest I who erst   145
Thought none my equal, now be over-match'd.
    So spake the old Serpent doubting,[38] and from all
With clamour[39] was assur'd thir utmost aid
At his command; when from amidst them rose
Belial[40] the dissolutest Spirit that fell,   150
The sensuallest, and after *Asmodai*[41]
The fleshliest Incubus, and thus advis'd.
    Set women in his eye and in his walk,
Among daughters of men[42] the fairest found;
Many are in each Region passing fair°   SURPASSINGLY ATTRACTIVE   155
As the noon Skie; more like to Goddesses
Then Mortal Creatures, graceful and discreet,
Expert in amorous Arts, enchanting tongues
Perswasive, Virgin majesty with mild
And sweet allay'd,[43] yet terrible to approach,   160
Skill'd to retire, and in retiring draw
Hearts after them tangl'd in Amorous Nets.[44]
Such object hath the power to soft'n and tame
Severest temper, smooth the rugged'st brow,
Enerve, and with voluptuous hope dissolve,[45]   165

---

[36]About a Roman commander he admired, Milton wrote "He [was] a man endu'd with all nobleness of mind, frugal, temperate, mild, and magnanimous, in Warr bold and watchful, invincible against lucre, and the assault of bribes . . . " (*History of Britain*; Yale 5: 99). The admirable qualities Milton found in Ulpius Marcellus all exist in the Son of Man. Satan is speaking the truth.

[37]Satan does not, in other words, want his audience to be overconfident of his success with Jesus because of his success in tempting Eve.

[38]The epithet "old Serpent doubting" puts Satan in his place, making him seem feeble and indecisive, though what seems to be a reference to the serpent's age may be confusing to a reader who has not read Revelation 12.9, which describes "that old serpent, called the Devil, and Satan, which deceiveth the whole world."

[39]The choice of the noun may indicate authorial disapproval, since the word could mean "an outburst of noisy utterance" (*OED* 1.b). The fallen angels approve, but their approval is indicated by noisy, discordant murmurs.

[40]In *Paradise Lost*, Belial is timorous and slothful, but his words are pleasing to the ear (2.108–19); here another set of characteristics built on the name "Belial" as indicating "worthless" emerges. Biblical commentary made Belial and the Sons of Belial representative of perverse or violent lust pursuing rape or sodomy. See Hunter, "Belial" and Flannagan, "Belial."

[41]The same as *Asmodeus* (*Paradise Lost* 4.168 and 6.365), mentioned in the apocryphal book Tobit 3.8. Because Asmodeus is "the evil spirit" who killed the seven husbands of Sarah before each could sleep with her, he gained a reputation in folklore for being hostile to marriage and for being a promoter of lust (*Variorum* 115n151). An incubus is a male spirit who deceives and seduces women while they are sleeping, usually by inhabiting the body of an attractive young man; the female counterpart is a succubus.

[42]This description closely corresponds to that of the "Daughters of Men" in *Paradise Lost* 11.581–627.

[43]The phrase "Virgin Majesty" is applied to Eve's demeanor before the Fall in *Paradise Lost* (9.270), as are the adjectives "mild" (4.479) and "sweet" (4.298).

[44]An "amorous Net" appears in the Tents of Wickedness tableau in *Paradise Lost* at 11.586; similar nets or snares appear in *Comus* 164.

[45]The supposedly enervating effects of illicit sexuality on men, expressed perhaps most cogently in Ariosto's picture in the *Orlando Furioso* of the hero Ruggiero captivated by the witch Alcina:

> His locks, bedewed with waters of sweet savor,
> Stood curlèd round in order on his head;
> He had such wanton womanish behavior
> As though in Valence he had long been bred;
> So changed in speech, in manners, and in favor,
> So from himself beyond all reason led
> By these enchantments of this am'rous dame

Draw out with credulous[46] desire, and lead
At will the manliest, resolutest brest,
As the Magnetic[47] hardest Iron draws.
Women, when nothing else, beguil'd the heart
Of wisest *Solomon*,[48] and made him build,   170
And made him bow to the Gods of his Wives.
    To whom quick answer Satan thus return'd.
Belial, in much uneven scale thou weigh'st
All others by thy self; because of old
Thou thy self doat'st on womankind, admiring   175
Thir shape, thir colour, and attractive grace,[49]
None are, thou think'st, but taken with such toys.°   EROTIC DIVERSIONS
Before the Flood thou with thy lusty Crew,
False titl'd Sons of God,[50] roaming the Earth
Cast wanton eyes on the daughters of men,   180
And coupl'd with them, and begot a race.
Have we not seen, or by relation heard,
In Courts and Regal Chambers how thou lurk'st,[51]
In Wood or Grove by mossie Fountain side,
In Valley or Green Meadow to way-lay   185
Some beauty rare, *Calisto*, *Clymene*,
Daphne, or *Semele*, *Antiopa*,
Or *Amymone*, *Syrinx*,[52] many more
Too long, then lay'st thy scapes° on names ador'd,   OUTRAGEOUS SINS
Apollo, *Neptune*, *Jupiter*, or *Pan*,   190
Satyr, or Fawn, or Silvan?[53] But these haunts
Delight not all; among the Sons of Men,
How many have with a smile made small account
Of beauty and her lures, easily scorn'd
All her assaults, on worthier things intent?   195

He was himself in nothing but in name. (Canto 7.53; Harington trans.)

[46]Credulousness, ease of belief, can be fallen or unfallen in Milton's moral structure of words. Just before the Fall, Eve is "our credulous Mother" in *Paradise Lost* 9.644.

[47]"Magnetic" was used as a noun as well as an adjective in seventeenth-century usage.

[48]In King Solomon's old age "his wives [he had 700] turned away his heart after other gods: and his heart was not perfect with the Lord his God, as was the heart of David his father" (1 Kings 11.4). His idolatry caused him to worship Astoreth, Milcom, Chemosh, and Molech, among other "abominations."

[49]The same phrase is used of Eve in *Paradise Lost* before the Fall, where she is described as having been created "For softness . . . and sweet attractive Grace" (4.298).

[50]Milton associates the Sons of Belial with both the descendants of Seth mentioned several times in Genesis and the "sons of God" who "saw the daughters of men" in Genesis 6.2 and somehow begot "giants in the earth in those days" (6.4). Biblical commentary associated the passage with the proliferation of evil spirits (see *Paradise Lost* 11.574-92 for Milton's expansion of the story). As MacKellar summarizes, "Belial and his associates have cloaked their amorous activities under the name of Sons of God, to which they have no right; but actually they are pagan gods, as the names Apollo, Neptune, Jupiter, and Pan in line 190 make plain" (n178-81).

[51]Milton seems to be expanding the influence of Belial into the realm of courtier and then pastoral poet, as he does with the "Court Amours" in *Paradise Lost* 4.767, courtly flirtations which in the same line are associated with "Casual fruition." In this context, courtly love, and the poetry brought about because of it, arises out of the kind of evil Belial represents.

[52]All of these women, most of them nymphs, are victims of godly rape or attempted rape, most of them being found in Ovid's *Metamorphoses*. Callisto is an Arcadian nymph and huntress seduced by Jupiter posing as Diana (*Metamorphoses* 2.409-40). Clymene, who became the wife of Merops, was first impregnated by Apollo and became the mother of Phaeton (*Metamorphoses* 1.765-75). Daphne is the first love of Apollo; in trying to escape from him, she prays to her father, the river god Peneus, who transforms her into the laurel, whose leaves would be used to crown laureate artists thereafter. Due to a ruse of Juno, Jupiter's jealous wife, Semele asks him to reveal himself to her as they make love and is incinerated as a result; Jupiter must take the seed of his child Bacchus from her and nurture it in his own thigh (Hesiod, *Theogony* 940-42). Amymone is a nymph carried away by Neptune; the rape engenders a son, Nauplius (Ovid, *Amores* 1.5.515). Syrinx is the victim of a rape intended by the god Pan, but she is changed by other gods into the reed syrinx, from which Pan is supposed to have made panpipes (*Metamorphoses* 1.5.691). Jupiter seduces Antiopa in the form of a satyr (*Metamorphoses* 6.110).

[53]All three fit the definition for *sylvan*: "An imaginary being supposed to haunt woods or groves; a deity or spirit of the woods" (*OED* A.n.).

Remember that *Pellean* Conquerour,[54]
A youth, how all the Beauties of the East
He slightly view'd, and slightly over-pass'd;
How hee sirnam'd of *Africa*[55] dismiss'd
In his prime youth the fair *Iberian* maid.   200
For *Solomon* he liv'd at ease,[56] and full
Of honour, wealth, high fare, aim'd not beyond
Higher design then to enjoy his State;
Thence to the bait of Women lay expos'd;
But he whom we attempt is wiser far   205
Then *Solomon*,[57] of more exalted mind,
Made and set wholly on the accomplishment
Of greatest things; what woman will you find,
Though of this Age the wonder and the fame,
On whom his leisure° will vouchsafe an eye   UNOCCUPIED TIME   210
Of fond desire? or should she confident,
As sitting Queen ador'd on Beauties Throne,
Descend with all her winning charms begirt
To enamour, as the Zone of *Venus* once[58]
Wrought that effect on *Jove*, so Fables tell;   215
How would one look from his Majestick brow
Seated as on the top of Vertues hill,[59]
Discount'nance her despis'd, and put to rout
All her array; her female pride deject,
Or turn to reverent awe? for Beauty stands   220
In the admiration only of weak minds
Led captive;[60] cease to admire, and all her Plumes
Fall flat and shrink into a trivial toy,
At every sudden slighting° quite abasht: REBUFFING
Therefore with manlier objects we must try   225
His constancy, with such as have more shew
Of worth, of honour, glory, and popular praise;
Rocks whereon greatest men have oftest wreck'd;
Or that which only seems to satisfie
Lawful desires of Nature, not beyond;   230
And now I know he hungers where no food
Is to be found, in the wide Wilderness;
The rest commit to me, I shall let pass
No advantage, and his strength as oft assay.°   TEST
    He ceas'd, and heard thir grant° in loud acclaim; AGREEMENT   235
Then forthwith to him takes a chosen band

---

[54]Alexander the Great is identified by his place of origin, Pella, in Macedonia. As MacKellar points out, "Milton probably refers to the treatment of the mother, wife, and daughters of Darius, whom [Alexander] captured after the battle of Issus" (n196–98).

[55]The Roman general Scipio, called Africanus after he defeated the Carthaginians (Livy 30.45.6). Scipio was supposed, earlier in his military career, to have returned a beautiful woman captured in New Carthage in Spain (Iberia)—a woman to whom he himself was attracted—to her princely lover (Livy 26.50).

[56]Not a complimentary phrase; "at ease" suggests "easy," or "morally casual." Solomon is pictured, by Satan at least, as being morally compromised in his dotage.

[57]The epithet is based on Matthew 12.42: "Behold, a greater than Solomon is here." In the passage, Christ is presumably referring to himself.

[58]In the *Iliad*, Hera obtains the enchanted belt or girdle of Aphrodite, under false pretenses, to help her entice Zeus to make love to her (14.214–21).

[59]The Son is contrasted implicitly with Zeus, who is overcome with desire as a result of Hera's trickery. In contrast, the Son dismisses insincere desire with one look from his majestic brow: in other words, unlawful desire is beneath his contempt.

[60]A summary of Milton's opinions about the enervating effects of beauty and how they can be overcome by strength of mind. Compare *Samson Agonistes* 1003–07.

Of Spirits likest to himself in guile[61]
To be at hand, and at his beck° appear,   SUMMONING
If cause were to unfold some active Scene
Of various persons each to know his part;[62]   240
Then to the Desert takes with these his flight;
Where still from shade to shade[63] the Son of God
After forty days fasting had remain'd,
Now hungring first, and to himself thus said.

    Where will this end? four times ten days I have pass'd   245
Wandring this woody maze, and humane food
Nor tasted, nor had appetite; that Fast
To Vertue I impute not, or count part
Of what I suffer here; if Nature need not,
Or God support Nature without repast   250
Though needing, what praise is it to endure?
But now I feel[64] I hunger, which declares,
Nature hath need of what she asks; yet God
Can satisfie that need some other way,
Though hunger still remain: so it remain   255
Without this bodies° wasting, I content me,   BODY'S
And from the sting of Famine fear no harm,
Nor mind° it, fed with better thoughts that feed   PAY ATTENTION TO
Mee hungring more to do my Fathers will.

    It was the hour of night,[65] when thus the Son   260
Commun'd in silent walk, then laid him down
Under the hospitable covert nigh
Of Trees thick interwoven; there he slept,
And dream'd, as appetite is wont to dream,[66]
Of meats and drinks, Natures refreshment sweet;   265
Him thought, he by the Brook of *Cherith* stood[67]
And saw the Ravens with their horny beaks
Food to *Elijah* bringing Even and Morn,
Though ravenous, taught to abstain from what they brought:
He saw the Prophet also how he fled   270
Into the Desert, and how there he slept
Under a Juniper;[68] then how awakt,
He found his Supper on the coals prepar'd,
And by the Angel was bid rise and eat,

---

[61]Guile (as opposed to force) is Satan's characteristic device, employing insidious cunning or treachery. Presumably others among the fallen angels are selected because their guile resembles that of their leader.

[62]The image is that of a part in a play: drama is assumed to be almost inherently deceitful because it can easily be used to promote a demonic illusion.

[63]Probably "from one evening to the next," though MacKellar, I think erroneously, agrees with Jerram's "passing from one shelter to another" (n242).

[64]The second edition adds a comma here, but the syntax of the sentence seems to indicate that the Son of Man perceives his own hunger; no pause is needed. Loh paraphrases 255–57 as "so long as my hunger does not weaken my body, I content me (i.e., am satisfied) and fear no harm from the sting of famine (i.e., hunger)" (396n255–57).

[65]Presumably the hour of nightfall.

[66]Conscious desire, for food, is played out in the unconscious action of dreams.

[67]"It seemed to him that he stood by the brook of Cherith." The reflexive idiom "Him thought" is close to "methinks": both were derived from a confusion between the Anglo-Saxon words for "think" and "seem." The Son of God is establishing a link between himself and the prophet Elijah, who in 1 Kings 17 is directed by God to hide himself from the tyrannical Ahab by the brook Cherith, from which he can drink the water while ravens are commanded by God to bring him food. The miracles surrounding the feeding and housing of Elijah closely resemble miracles to be performed by Christ: nourishment in a wilderness, endless replenishment of stored food, and the revival of one near death.

[68]On a second trip into the wilderness to avoid the wrath of Ahab, Elijah sleeps under a juniper tree and is awakened twice by an angel who provides him with cake and water. The two meals are enough to sustain him for forty days and nights in the wilderness (1 Kings 19).

And eat the second time after repose, 275
The strength whereof suffic'd him forty days;
Sometimes that with *Elijah* he partook,
Or as a guest with *Daniel* at his pulse.[69]
Thus wore out night, and now the Herald Lark[70]
Left his ground-nest, high towring to descry 280
The morns approach, and greet her with his Song:
As lightly from his grassy Couch up rose
Our Saviour, and found all was but a dream,
Fasting he went to sleep, and fasting wak'd.
Up to a hill anon his steps he rear'd, 285
From whose high top to ken[71] the prospect round,
If Cottage were in view, Sheep-cote or Herd;
But Cottage, Herd or Sheep-cote none he saw,
Only in a bottom saw a pleasant Grove,
With chaunt of tuneful Birds resounding loud; 290
Thither he bent his way, determin'd there
To rest at noon, and entr'd soon the shade
High rooft[72] and walks beneath, and alleys brown
That open'd in the midst a woody Scene,
Natures own work it seem'd (Nature taught Art) 295
And to a Superstitious eye the haunt
Of Wood-Gods and Wood-Nymphs; he view'd it round,
When suddenly a man before him stood,
Not rustic as before, but seemlier clad,
As one in City, or Court, or Palace bred,[73] 300
And with fair speech these words to him address'd.

　　With granted leave officious° I return, *EAGER TO PLEASE*
But much more wonder that the Son of God
In this wild solitude so long should bide
Of all things destitute, and well I know, 305
Not without hunger. Others of some note,
As story tells, have trod this Wilderness;
The Fugitive Bond-woman[74] with her Son
Out cast *Nebaioth*, yet found she[75] relief
By a providing Angel; all the race 310
Of *Israel* here had famish'd, had not God
Rain'd from Heaven Manna, and that Prophet bold
Native of *Thebez*[76] wandring here was fed
Twice by a voice inviting him to eat.
Of thee these forty days none hath regard, 315

---

[69]"The edible seeds of leguminous plants cultivated for food, as peas, beans, lentils, etc." (*OED* 1). Milton uses the term to signify basic and simple food (see *Comus* 721, where Milton replaces "fetches" [i.e., vetch] in the Trinity Manuscript with "pulses" in the printed text). Daniel is given pulse to eat in Daniel 1.12; again, Milton is establishing a typological link between a prophetic figure in the Old Testament and Christ.
[70]The lark is a herald because it announces the coming of the day.
[71]"To descry, see; to catch sight of, discover by sight; to look at, scan" (*OED* 6, citing this passage).
[72]The canopy of trees creates a high arch, in other words, under which is comfortable shade from the sun.
[73]The implication is that city, court, and palace all breed corruption, as with the reference in 2.183 to "Courts and Regal Chambers" where evil lurks. Compare *Paradise Lost* 9.445.
[74]Hagar, in Genesis 21.14-19; but her son is Ishmael, and his son is Nebaioth.
[75]I have emended from "he," following other editors convinced that the pronoun should modify the understood "Hagar."
[76]Corrected from "Thebes" by the *Errata* list of *1671*, to make sure the city is not connected with the Greek city and perhaps to emphasize the fact that the name should be pronounced with two syllables. Milton is referring to Elijah's place of origin—he is a Tishbite—but "Milton is apparently without authority for making this city, rather than Thisbe across the Jordan, the city of Eliha the Tishbite" (Gilbert, *A Geographical Dictionary of Milton* 294–95).

Forty and more deserted here indeed.
    To whom thus Jesus; what conclud'st thou hence?
They all had need, I as thou seest have none.
    How hast thou hunger then? Satan reply'd,
Tell me if Food were now before thee set,   320
Would'st thou not eat? Thereafter as I like
The giver, answer'd Jesus. Why should that
Cause thy refusal, said the subtle Fiend,
Hast thou not right to all Created things,
Owe not all Creatures by just right to thee   325
Duty and Service, nor to stay till bid,
But tender all their power? nor mention I
Meats by the Law unclean, or offer'd first
To Idols, those young *Daniel* could refuse;
Nor proffer'd by an Enemy, though who   330
Would scruple that, with want opprest? behold
Nature asham'd, or better to express,
Troubl'd that thou shouldst hunger, hath purvey'd
From all the Elements her choicest store
To treat thee as beseems, and as her Lord   335
With honour, only deign to sit and eat.
    He spake no dream, for as his words had end,
Our Saviour lifting up his eyes beheld
In ample space under the broadest shade
A Table richly spred, in regal mode,   340
With dishes pil'd,[77] and meats of noblest sort
And savour, Beasts of chase, or Fowl of game,
In pastry built,[78] or from the spit, or boyl'd,
Gris-amber-steam'd;[79] all Fish from Sea or Shore,
Freshet,[80] or purling Brook, of shell or fin,   345
And exquisitest name, for which was drain'd[81]
Pontus[82] and *Lucrine* Bay,[83] and *Afric* Coast.[84]
Alas how simple, to these Cates° compar'd,   FANCY DISHES
Was that crude° Apple that diverted *Eve*!   RAW, UNPREPARED
And at a stately side-board[85] by the wine   350
That fragrant smell diffus'd, in order stood
Tall stripling youths rich clad, of fairer hew°   FORM, COMPLEXION

---

[77]Corrected in the *1671 Errata* from "pill'd." Compare "trip'd" at 354 below, which may have offered less of a problem to a seventeenth-century reader.
[78]Wild poultry or other game such as venison, cooked in a pastry shell. Extravagant pastries, as with the nursery rhyme's "Four and twenty blackbirds, baked in a pie," were popular in court circles in the seventeenth century. The context here is contemporary courtly excess in cooking as compared with Roman luxury, which scoured the Roman provinces to find exotic seafood or give exquisite names to elaborate cooked dishes. See Juvenal, *Satires* 5.76–105, for some of the excessive luxury in Roman eating habits. The Son of Man, on the other hand, needs only pulse and water for sustenance.
[79]Ambergris, same as grisamber, "A wax-like substance of marbled ashy colour, found floating in tropical seas, and as a morbid secretion in the intestines of the sperm-whale. It is odoriferous and used in perfumery; formerly in cookery." (*OED*). The food is being steamed in a bath flavored by ambergris.
[80]A fast-running, temporary stream (as formed after a quick rain), as compared to the slower-moving ("purling" suggests "undulating") brook.
[81] "Strained," as through a net (see *OED* 1.1). The various bodies of water were filtered through nets or sieves in order to capture their fish. For a comparable usage, see *Paradise Lost* 3.605: there the changeable Proteus is strained through a limbeck (the alchemical vessel, shaped like a gourd, also called an alembic; see *Paradise Lost* 3.605), in order to discover his original or essential form.
[82]The Black Sea, the Pontus Euxinus, supposed by Pliny (9.19–2) to produce abundant seafood quickly.
[83]A saltwater bay near Naples that produced noted oysters, treasured by the ancient Romans (see Juvenal 4.141).
[84]The Nile was another major source for fish for the Romans.
[85] "A piece of dining-room furniture for holding side-dishes, wine, plate, etc., and often having cupboards and drawers" (*OED* 1.b, citing this usage as the first recorded instance).

Then *Ganymed*[86] or *Hylas*, distant more
Under the Trees now trip'd,[87] now solemn stood
Nymphs of *Diana*'s train, and *Naiades* 355
With fruits and flowers from *Amalthea*'s horn,[88]
And Ladies of th' *Hesperides*,[89] that seem'd
Fairer then feign'd of old, or fabl'd since
Of Fairy Damsels[90] met in Forest wide
By Knights of *Logres*,[91] or of *Lyones*,[92] 360
Lancelot or *Pelleas*, or *Pellenore*,[93]
And all the while Harmonious Airs were heard
Of chiming strings, or charming pipes and winds
Of gentlest gale *Arabian* odors fann'd
From their soft wings,[94] and *Flora*'s[95] earliest smells. 365
Such was the Splendour, and the Tempter now
His invitation earnestly renew'd.
  .What doubts the Son of God to sit and eat?[96]
These are not Fruits forbidden,[97] no interdict° PROHIBITION
Defends° the touching of these viands° pure, FORBIDS FOODS 370
Thir taste no knowledge works,[98] at least of evil,
But life preserves, destroys life's enemy,
Hunger, with sweet restorative delight.
All these are Spirits of Air, and Woods, and Springs,
Thy gentle Ministers, who come to pay 375
Thee homage, and acknowledge thee thir Lord:
What doubt'st° thou Son of God? sit down and eat. WHAT DO YOU FEAR

---

[86]In Elegy 7, Milton pictures Ganymede, whom Ovid describes as a beautiful youth seized by Jupiter to be his cupbearer (see *Metamorphoses* 10.155-61), and Hylas, also a beautiful young man dragged into a fountain by a nymph who falls in love with him and steals him away from Hercules, his male lover (Propertius 1.20.6). Bredbeck conjectures that the "manlier objects" Satan has mentioned in 225 above, "are figured homoerotically through the allusion to Ganymede and Hylas" (224) and that Milton is using the allusions "as a means of condemning patriarchal sexual decorum to a *limited* status" (224).

[87]"Tripped," stepped lightly, as in a dance.

[88]The cornucopia, or horn of plenty. Ovid, *Fasti* 5.115-26, tells of the nymph Amalthea, who possessed a goat that had suckled Jupiter as an infant on Mt. Ida. When the goat broke off a horn, Amalthea carried it full of fruit to Jupiter for nourishment. As a reward to his nurse, Jupiter set the cornucopia among the stars. According to other versions, Jupiter gave the horn the miraculous capacity to remain filled with whatever its owner might desire.

[89]"The nymphs (variously reckoned as three, four, and seven), daughters of Hesperus, who were fabled to guard, with the aid of a watchful dragon, the garden in which golden apples grew in the Isles of the Blest, at the western extremity of the earth" (*OED*). Milton here gives them an aristocratic heritage as "Ladies," the irony of which suggests that they should be taken lightly as emblems of pagan superstition, as in *Paradise Lost* 4.250-51.

[90]Another disparaging reference, this time to the damsels of romantic epic. The key word is "seems," since the damsels of romance are in fact no better than the nymphs of pagan tradition.

[91]The medieval demarcation of an area of England, the same as Loegria, east of the Severn River (near where Milton's *Comus* is set) and south of the Humber River. Milton uses Loegria to demarcate a portion of medieval England ruled by Locrine, who named it, in his *History of Britain* (Yale 5: 17-18).

[92]Lyonesse, a mythical country associated with Arthurian legend, was supposed to be off the southwestern coast of England, between Land's End and the Scilly Islands. It is mentioned by Spenser as the birthplace of Tristan; it is also supposed to have been the birthplace of Arthur; and Tennyson makes it the place where Arthur dies. It was also supposed by William Camden to have submerged in the sea (MacKellar 132n).

[93]In Malory's *Morte d'Arthur*, Lancelot, usually a champion of virtue, becomes so drunk that he sleeps with Elaine twice, thinking that she is Queen Gueneuere (21.13). Pelleas, despite being one of the four knights of the Round Table to achieve the Grail, is also corrupted in a love affair with Ettard. Lewalski (225) believes that the allusion should not be to Pellenore, King of the Isles, who is killed by Sir Gawain, but to his son Percivale, who resists sexual temptation in the form of a she-demon posing as a fair gentlewoman by making the sign of the cross (Malory 14.9-10). It is not characteristic of Milton, however, to get his characters wrong.

[94]Whose wings? Perhaps we are in the realm of fairies with wings, or, more likely, the airs and winds have wings, as in *Paradise Lost* 4.156-57, where gales have wings that dispense odors by means of fanning motions. Perfumes of Arabia were proverbially rich, as with frankincense and myrrh.

[95]The Roman goddess of flowers, who presided over a licentious festival, the Floralia. With the tempting odors and charming (in both senses) music, Milton probably here represents nature and art misused for temptation.

[96]"Why does the Son of God fear [or hesitate] to sit and eat?" The Latin idiom is *quid dubitas*.

[97]An allusion to the fall of Adam and Eve (compare 324 above). The command not to eat the fruit recorded in Genesis 3 is also an interdict or interdiction (*Paradise Lost* 7.46, 8.334). Though the devil of Matthew says only "If thou be the Son of God, command that these stones be made bread" (4.3), Milton has Satan repeat the temptation of appealing food that worked with Eve.

[98]In the sense "brings about" or "causes to happen," as in the idiom "he works magic." I have moved the comma from after "knowledge," in *1671*, to its present position.

To whom thus Jesus temperately[99] reply'd:
Said'st thou not that to all things I had right?
And who withholds my pow'r that right to use?   380
Shall I receive by gift what of my own,
When and where likes me best,[100] I can command?
I can at will, doubt not, as soon as thou,
Command a Table in this Wilderness,
And call swift flights of Angels ministrant
Array'd in Glory on my cup to attend: 385
Why shouldst thou then obtrude° this diligence,   THRUST FORWARD
In vain, where no acceptance it can find,
And with my hunger what hast thou to do?
Thy pompous Delicacies I contemn,   390
And count thy specious gifts no gifts but guiles.
    To whom thus answer'd Satan malecontent:[101]
That I have also power to give thou seest,
If of that pow'r I bring thee voluntary
What I might have bestow'd on whom I pleas'd,   395
And rather opportunely in this place
Chose to impart to thy apparent need,
Why shouldst thou not accept it? but I see
What I can do or offer is suspect;
Of these things others quickly will dispose   400
Whose pains have earn'd the far fet[102] spoil. With that
Both Table and Provision vanish'd quite
With sound of Harpies wings, and Talons heard;[103]
Only the importune[104] Tempter still remain'd,
And with these words his temptation pursu'd.   405
    By hunger, that each other Creature tames,
Thou art not to be harm'd, therefore not mov'd;
Thy temperance invincible besides,
For no allurement yields to appetite,
And all thy heart is set on high designs,   410
High actions; but wherewith to be atchiev'd?
Great acts require great means of enterprise,
Thou art unknown, unfriended, low of birth,[105]
A Carpenter thy Father known, thy self
Bred up in poverty and streights[106] at home;   415
Lost in a Desert here and hunger-bit:[107]
Which way or from what hope dost thou aspire
To greatness? whence Authority deriv'st,

---

[99]MacKellar points to the various adverbs applied to Jesus's replies—"patiently" (432); "calmly" (3.43); "fervently" (3.121)—and concludes "Although in the course of temptations Christ's temper becomes more and more strained, it is always firmly controlled" (133n).

[100]"When and where it seems best to me."

[101]"Intensely frustrated." The word was spelled and perhaps pronounced "male-content" more often than not in the sixteenth and seventeenth centuries.

[102]Literally "fetched from afar," brought here from exotic places. The form "far fet" was acceptable in seventeenth-century usage.

[103]Harpies, female winged beasts who despoil a banquet in the *Aeneid* 3.225–28 and cause a banquet to disappear in *The Tempest* 3.3.83.

[104]"Irksome," with the overtone of "inopportune" ("no longer needed," "supernumary"). The adjective is pronounced here with emphasis on the second syllable, and there should be elision with "th' importune," despite its not being spelled that way.

[105]Satan is insulting Jesus's ancestry and parentage on earth, as if he were the aristocrat looking down on a base-born person; he implies that Jesus had to purchase respect with money.

[106]"Straits," hardships, deprivations.

[107]Milton may well have taken this unusual adjective from the only recorded usage previous to his own, that of the Sternhold and Hopkins 1549 translation of Psalm 34.10: "The Lions shall be hungerbit, and pinde with famine much."

What Followers, what Retinue canst thou gain,
Or at thy heels the dizzy Multitude, 420
Longer then thou canst feed them on thy cost?
Money brings Honour, Friends, Conquest, and Realms;
What rais'd *Antipater* the *Edomite*,[108]
And his Son *Herod* plac'd on *Juda*'s[109] Throne;
(Thy throne) but gold that got him puissant[110] friends? 425
Therefore, if at great things thou wouldst arrive,
Get Riches first, get Wealth, and Treasure heap,
Not difficult, if thou hearken to me,
Riches are mine, Fortune is in my hand;
They whom I favour thrive in wealth amain, 430
While Virtue, Valour, Wisdom sit in want.[111]
    To whom thus Jesus patiently reply'd;
Yet Wealth without these three is impotent,°   HAS NO POWER
To gain dominion or to keep it gain'd.
Witness those antient Empires of the Earth, 435
In highth of all thir flowing wealth dissolv'd:
But men endu'd with these have oft attain'd
In lowest poverty to highest deeds;
Gideon and *Jephtha*, and the Shepherd lad,[112]
Whose off-spring on the Throne of *Juda* sat 440
So many Ages, and shall yet regain
That seat, and reign in *Israel* without end.
Among the Heathen, (for throughout the World
To me is not unknown what hath been done
Worthy of Memorial) canst thou not remember 445
Quintius, Fabricius, Curius, Regulus?[113]
For I esteem those names of men so poor
Who could do mighty things, and could contemn
Riches though offer'd from the hand of Kings.
And what in me seems wanting, but that I 450
May also in this poverty as soon
Accomplish what they did, perhaps and more?
Extol not Riches then, the toyl° of Fools,   TRAP, HUNTER'S NET
The wise mans cumbrance if not snare, more apt
To slacken Virtue, and abate her edge, 455

---

[108]Antipater is an Edomite or Idumean, appointed by Julius Caesar as Procurator of Judaea; his son is Herod the Great, known for tyrannical acts of cruelty like with the slaughter of innocent children in the attempt to kill the infant Christ (Matthew 2.16). Satan's examples are ironically chosen, since the Son of Man knows full well that the wealthy and powerful family of Antipater has already attempted to kill him.

[109]More often called "Judea," but the two names are identical, standing for the region in which Bethlehem and Jerusalem are located.

[110]One of the few words of obvious French origin that Milton uses. "Puissant," meaning "powerful," is associated with romantic epic and is used disparagingly here: gold buys powerful friends.

[111]Compare the last lines of Milton's Sonnet 15.

[112]Jesus answers Satan's pompous aristocratic examples with the example of men upraised by the people (a theory of natural nobility and of elected monarchy may be a subtext at this point). Gideon came from a poor family and was the youngest of his household, yet he gathered an army and routed the Midianite forces (Judges 6–7). Jephtha, the son of a harlot exiled by the elders of Gilead, was asked by those same elders to lead his people to victory against the Ammonites, after which he was elected head and captain over them (Judges 11.1–33).

[113]MacKellar summarizes: "The four men here commended for their integrity belonged to the period of the Roman Republic when the Romans were celebrated for their frugality and austere virtue" (138n). Lucius Quintus Cincinnatus was called from his small farm near Rome to lead the Romans against the Aequans (Livy 3.26). Caius Faricius Luscinus, although he was poor, refused to accept gifts from Pyrrhus (Claudian 3.200–01). Marcus Curius Dentatus, after defeating Pyrrhus in addition to the Samnites and the Sabines, gave all the spoils of various battles to the Roman Republic and retired to his farm (Cicero, "De Senectute," 16.55–56). Marcus Attilius Regulus, captured by the Carthaginians in the first Punic War, was released on the promise of return; he persuaded the Roman Senate not to accept Carthaginian terms, he did return to Carthage, and he was tortured to death (Cicero, "De Officiis" 1.100.13).

Then prompt her to do aught may merit praise.[114]
What if with like aversion I reject
Riches and Realms; yet not for that a Crown,
Golden in shew, is but a wreath of thorns,[115]
Brings dangers, troubles, cares, and sleepless nights   460
To him who wears the Regal Diadem,[116]
When on his shoulders each mans burden lies;
For therein stands the office of a King,
His Honour, Vertue, Merit and chief Praise,
That for the Publick all this weight he bears.   465
Yet he who reigns within himself, and rules
Passions, Desires, and Fears, is more a King;[117]
Which every wise and vertuous man attains:
And who attains not, ill aspires to rule
Cities of men or head-strong Multitudes,   470
Subject himself to Anarchy within,
Or lawless passions in him which he serves.
But to guide Nations in the way of truth
By saving Doctrine,[118] and from errour lead
To know, and knowing worship God aright,   475
Is yet more Kingly, this attracts the Soul,
Governs the inner man, the nobler part,
That other o're the body only reigns,
And oft by force, which to a generous mind
So reigning can be no sincere delight.   480
Besides to give a Kingdom hath been thought
Greater and nobler done, and to lay down
Far more magnanimous,[119] then to assume.
Riches are needless then, both for themselves,
And for thy reason why they should be sought,   485
To gain a Scepter, oftest better miss't.[120]

The End of the Second Book.

---

[114]"Than prompt her to do anything that might deserve praise."

[115]The crown of thorns Christ will wear during crucifixion (Matthew 27.29).

[116]The passage at least sounds like "Uneasy lies the head that wears a crown" (2 *Henry VI* 3.1.31) and similar passages in *Henry V* (4.1.235–42) and *Richard II* (3.3.143–57).

[117]A dangerous sentiment in an age of monarchy and specifically at a time shortly after the restoration of the English monarchy. Milton skirts close to the idea "Every man a king," but he also suggests that men who reign should have kingly qualities, qualities that are found only in just men.

[118]Perhaps closer to the meanings associated with the Latin word *doctrina*, not only teaching and instruction, but its products science, erudition, and learning.

[119]Again, the magnanimity of Jesus is emphasized through the fact that he admires the quality in others. MacKellar believes that "Milton's views of humility and magnanimity are essentially the same as those of Aquinas, and that he accepts what had long been the orthodox teaching of the Church" (42).

[120]Satan's reasoning for buying a scepter (earthly rule) is fallacious; it would be better not to have the position, if one had to buy it.

PARADISE REGAIN'D.

The Third BOOK.

SO spake the Son of God, and Satan stood
A while as mute confounded what to say,
What to reply, confuted and convinc't
Of his weak arguing, and fallacious drift;°   FALSE CONCLUSION
At length collecting all his Serpent wiles,   5
With soothing words renew'd, him thus accosts.°   COMES ALONGSIDE
   I see thou know'st what is of use to know,
What best to say canst say, to do canst do;
Thy actions to thy words accord, thy words
To thy large heart give utterance due, thy heart   10
Conteins of good, wise, just, the perfect shape.
Should Kings and Nations from thy mouth consult,
Thy Counsel would be as the Oracle
Urim and Thummim,[1] those oraculous gems
On <i>Aaron</i>'s breast: or tongue of Seers old   15
Infallible; or wert thou sought to° deeds   CALLED UPON TO DO
That might require th' array of war, thy skill
Of conduct would be such, that all the world
Could not sustain thy Prowess, or subsist
In battel, though against thy few in arms.   20
These God-like Vertues wherefore dost thou hide?
Affecting private life, or more obscure
In savage Wilderness, wherefore deprive
All Earth her wonder at thy acts, thy self
The fame and glory, glory the reward   25
That sole excites to high attempts the flame
Of most erected° Spirits, most temper'd pure   ELEVATED, EXALTED
Ætherial, who all pleasures else despise,
All treasures and all gain esteem as dross,
And dignities and powers all but the highest?[2]   30
Thy years are ripe, and over-ripe, the Son

---

[1]Two sacred objects of uncertain nature that Moses put in the breastplate of Aaron, used in the process of divination like sacred dice (Exodus 28). Urim means "light" and Thummim "Truth." For further discussion, see Michael Lieb, *Poetics of the Holy: A Reading of* Paradise Lost (Chapel Hill: U of North Carolina P, 1981): 56–57.

[2]The temptation to glory is a subtle one with the Son of God, who deeply deserves to be glorified. Milton had written eloquently of the need for fame and glory in "Lycidas": "Fame is the spur that the clear spirit doth raise / (That last infirmity of noble mind) / To scorn delights and life laborious days" (70–72).

Of *Macedonian Philip*[3] had e're these
Won *Asia* and the Throne of *Cyrus* held
At his dispose,° young *Scipio* had brought down   DISPOSAL
The *Carthaginian* pride, young *Pompey* quell'd   35
The *Pontic* King and in triumph had rode.
Yet years, and to ripe years judgment mature,
Quench not the thirst of glory, but augment.
Great *Julius*, whom now all the world admires
The more he grew in years, the more inflam'd   40
With glory, wept that he had liv'd so long
Inglorious: but thou yet art not too late.
    To whom our Saviour[4] calmly thus reply'd.
Thou neither dost perswade me to seek wealth
For Empires sake, nor Empire to affect   45
For glories sake by all thy argument.
For what is glory but the blaze of fame,
The peoples praise, if always praise unmixt?
And what the people but a herd confus'd,[5]
A miscellaneous rabble, who extol   50
Things vulgar, & well weigh'd, scarce worth the praise,
They praise and they admire they know not what;
And know not whom, but as one leads the other;
And what delight to be by such extoll'd,
To live upon thir tongues and be thir talk,   55
Of whom to be disprais'd were no small praise?[6]
His lot who dares be singularly° good.   UNIQUELY
Th' intelligent among them and the wise[7]
Are few, and glory scarce of few is rais'd.
This is true glory and renown, when God   60
Looking on the Earth, with approbation marks
The just man, and divulges° him through Heaven   MAKES HIM KNOWN
To all his Angels, who with true applause
Recount his praises; thus he did to *Job*,[8]
When to extend his fame through Heaven & Earth,   65
As thou to thy reproach mayst well remember,
He ask'd thee, hast thou seen my servant *Job*?[9]
Famous he was in Heaven, on Earth less known;

---

[3]Satan seems to be attempting to create jealousy in the Son of God by comparing his achievements at his age (about thirty, according to Luke 3.23) with those of Alexander the Great defeating the Persian king Cyrus at Arbala when he was twenty-five; then of Scipio, who, at twenty-seven, drove the Carthaginians out of Spain; of Pompey, who was forty (Carey says "Satan exaggerates" [3.35–36n]) when he defeated Mithridates; and finally with Julius Caesar, who was said by Plutarch to have burst into tears when reading of the achievements of Alexander at his age (*Life of Caesar* 11.3).

[4]The epithet may call the reader's attention to the difference between how Satan must perceive Christ as "Son of God" and how we are allowed to call him "our Saviour." The title endows Christ with humanity and that together with his calmness in the face of dangerous flattery ally us with him.

[5]The Savior's rejection of the mob as an ignorant herd echoes Milton's when he labels the average run of people "a credulous and hapless herd, begott'n to servility," in *Eikonoklastes* (Yale 3: 601). The perspective is that of the "one just man" as Milton pictures his type here and throughout *Paradise Lost* (see my introduction under that heading).

[6]Proverbial wisdom, going back at least to Seneca, *De remediis fortuitorum* 7.1: "To be dispraised by the malicious is to be praised."

[7]An aristocracy or meritocracy based on intelligence and wisdom, not on wealth or the primogeniture of kings or princely families. According to Robert Fallon, Milton founded his own design of government on "two principles, the rejection of kingship and the delegation of sovereignty to a permanent senate" (*Milton in Government* 205).

[8]"And the Lord said unto Satan, Hast thou considered my servant Job, that there is none like him in the earth, a perfect and an upright man, one that feareth God, and escheweth evil?" (Job 1.8).

[9]As Lewalski and many others have pointed out, the book of Job offered to Milton a pattern of a brief epic, which means that the Son of God will become like the character of Job—especially since Satan appears in that book for the first time as a temptor in the Bible.

Where glory is false glory, attributed
To things not glorious, men not worthy of fame.   70
They err who count it glorious to subdue
By Conquest far and wide, to over-run
Large Countries, and in field great Battels win,
Great Cities by assault:[10] what do these Worthies,[11]
But rob and spoil, burn, slaughter, and enslave   75
Peaceable Nations, neighbouring, or remote,
Made Captive, yet deserving freedom more
Then those thir Conquerours, who leave behind
Nothing but ruin wheresoe're they rove,
And all the flourishing works of peace destroy,   80
Then swell with pride, and must be titl'd Gods,[12]
Great Benefactors[13] of mankind, Deliverers,
Worship't with Temple, Priest and Sacrifice;
One is the Son of *Jove*, of *Mars* the other,
Till Conquerour Death discover them scarce men,   85
Rowling in brutish vices,[14] and deform'd,
Violent or shameful death thir due reward.
But if there be in glory aught of good,
It may by means far different be attain'd
Without ambition, war, or violence;   90
By deeds of peace, by wisdom eminent,
By patience, temperance; I mention still
Him whom thy wrongs with Saintly patience born,°   BORNE
Made famous in a Land and times obscure;
Who names not now with honour patient *Job*?   95
Poor *Socrates* (who next more memorable?)
By what he taught and suffer'd for so doing,[15]
For truths sake suffering death unjust, lives now
Equal in fame to proudest Conquerours.
Yet if for fame and glory aught be done,   100
Aught suffer'd; if young *African*[16] for fame
His wasted Country freed from *Punic* rage,
The deed becomes unprais'd, the man at least,
And loses, though but verbal, his reward.
Shall I seek glory then, as vain men seek   105
Oft not deserv'd? I seek not mine, but his
Who sent me, and thereby witness whence I am.

[10]An indictment of the destructive power of war. For the various opinions about whether Milton supported holy war, revolution, or the maintenance of a standing army, see Fallon, *Captain*; Freeman; and Revard.

[11]Ironic use of a word associated with romantic heroism, as in the Nine Worthies, "composed of three Jews (Joshua, David, and Judas Maccabæus), three Gentiles (Hector, Alexander, and Julius Cæsar), and three Christians (Arthur, Charlemagne, and Godfrey of Bouillon)" (*OED* C.n.1.c).

[12]Roman emperors such as Nero and Caligula declared themselves or were declared by the Senate to be gods. Carey points out as well that the deification of rulers extended to "Herod [who] made an oration unto them. And the people gave a shout, saying, It is the voice of a god, and not of a man" (Acts 12.21–22). For his presumptuous behavior, though, Herod was struck dead.

[13]"The kings of the Gentiles . . . are called benefactors" (Luke 22.25).

[14]Like the subhuman creatures of *Comus*, who "roul with pleasure in a sensual stie" (77). It may or may not be relevant, but Carey reports that Alexander the Great was supposed to have died at thirty-three due to alcoholism (3.84n). Modern historians connect his death more with what may have been malaria than with his legendary carousing.

[15]Socrates might have escaped death after being falsely charged with corrupting the youth of Athens but instead chose to meet his execution with patience and dignity (see Plato's account in *Crito*). His noble death was often compared with Christ's and was a potential subject of tragedy (see Newton 98n).

[16]Scipio Africanus, whose attack on Carthage in 204 BCE caused Hannibal to be recalled from Italy. This Scipio is described as "younger" because older members of his family had been killed in the Punic Wars and because he was indeed in his twenties.

To whom the Tempter murmuring[17] thus reply'd.
Think not so slight of glory; therein least
Resembling thy great Father: he seeks glory,
And for his glory all things made, all things
Orders and governs, nor content in Heaven
By all his Angels glorifi'd, requires
Glory from men, from all men good or bad,
Wise or unwise, no difference, no exemption;
Above all Sacrifice, or hallow'd gift
Glory he requires, and glory he receives
Promiscuous from all Nations, Jew, or Greek,
Or Barbarous, nor exception hath declar'd;
From us his foes pronounc't glory he exacts.
   To whom our Saviour fervently[18] reply'd.
And reason; since his word all things produc'd,
Though chiefly not for glory as prime end,
But to shew forth his goodness, and impart
His good communicable to every soul
Freely; of whom what could he less expect
Then glory and benediction, that is thanks,
The slightest, easiest, readiest recompence
From them who could return him nothing else,[19]
And not returning that would likeliest render
Contempt instead, dishonour, obloquy?°
Hard recompence, unsutable return
For so much good, so much beneficence.
But why should man seek glory? who of his own
Hath nothing, and to whom nothing belongs
But condemnation, ignominy, and shame?
Who for so many benefits receiv'd
Turn'd recreant[20] to God, ingrate and false,
And so of all true good himself despoil'd,
Yet, sacrilegious, to himself would take
That which to God alone of right belongs;
Yet so much bounty is in God, such grace,
That who advance his glory, not thir own,
Them he himself to glory will advance.[21]
   So spake the Son of God; and here again
Satan had not to answer,[22] but stood struck°
With guilt of his own sin, for he himself
Insatiable of glory had lost all,

DISGRACE

STRICKEN

110
115
120
125
130
135
140
145

[17]The word probably carries all the meanings current in 1671: grumbling, repeating indistinguishable sounds, and emitting a low and continuous noise. What Satan says echoes in a hollow way, recoils on itself, and in its repetitiveness, as with the word "glory," it constitutes doubletalk.
[18]Probably not "passionately," but "rightfully angry." The Savior at this point is justifiably angry because Satan has mocked the Father's glorification, has mocked wisdom, and has implied that those who give the Father glory give it "promiscuously" and that the Father "exacts" or forces that glorification out of his followers. The Savior quickly cuts Satan off, finishing his sentence for him.
[19]Compare Satan's description of the easy service angels give to God in *Paradise Lost* 4.44–48.
[20]Probably "Unfaithful to duty; false, apostate" (*OED* 2.a, citing this instance).
[21]For the context of the Son of God's doctrine, see *On Christian Doctrine* 1.4 (Yale 6: 194–95), on grace, justice, penitence, and reprobation. Satan and similar reprobate human beings have what Milton calls "the absence of penitence; the contempt for grace; and the refusal to listen to God's repeated call" (195).
[22]"Satan had nothing to answer." He is pictured as a corrupt lawyer, copping a plea even though he really has nothing further legitimate to say. Milton's opinion of the legal profession was not high: compare the phrase "shameless, . . . bestial plea" in *Reason of Church-Government* (Yale 1: 856).

Yet of another Plea° bethought him soon.   LEGAL PLOY

    Of glory as thou wilt, said he, so deem,   150
Worth or not worth the seeking, let it pass:
But to a Kingdom thou art born,[23] ordain'd
To sit upon thy Father° *David*'s Throne;   ANCESTOR
By Mothers side thy Father,[24] though thy right
Be now in powerful hands, that will not part   155
Easily from possession won with arms;
Judæa now and all the promis'd land
Reduc't a Province under *Roman* yoke,[25]
Obeys *Tiberius*; nor is always rul'd
With temperate sway; oft have they violated   160
The Temple, oft the Law with foul affronts,
Abominations rather, as did once
Antiochus:[26] and think'st thou to regain
Thy right by sitting still or thus retiring?
So did not *Machabeus*:[27] he indeed   165
Retir'd unto the Desert, but with arms;
And o're a mighty King so oft prevail'd,
That by strong hand his Family obtain'd,
Though Priests, the Crown, and *David*'s Throne usurp'd,
With *Modin* and her Suburbs once content.   170
If Kingdom move thee not, let move thee Zeal,
And Duty; Zeal and Duty are not slow;
But on Occasions forelock[28] watchful wait.
They themselves rather are occasion best,[29]
Zeal of thy Fathers house, Duty to free   175
Thy Country from her Heathen servitude;
So shalt thou best fullfil, best verifie
The Prophets old, who sung thy endless raign,
The happier raign the sooner it begins,
Raign then; what canst thou better do the while?   180
    To whom our Saviour answer thus return'd.
All things are best fullfil'd in their due time,
And time there is for all things, Truth hath said:[30]
If of my raign Prophetic Writ hath told
That it shall never end,[31] so when begin   185

---

[23]"You are born to inherit a kingdom." Satan continues to use the respectful "thou."

[24]Satan may be insulting the Son of God's ancestry by implying that it is only through his mother's lineage that he could claim descent from David, even though Christ is often referred to as "Son of David" in the New Testament, and David is Christ's "father" in Luke 1.32.

[25]"Reduced to the status of a province under Roman rule." The Roman governor Quirinus annexed Judea to Syria in AD 6. Pontius Pilate served as governor of Judea from AD 26–36 under the emperor Tiberius (AD 14–37). Pilate is first noted in the New Testament for his atrocities, in Luke 13.1. Though the adjective "Roman" is not italicized at this point in *1671*, it is so at all other instances, and I have therefore restored the italics.

[26]Antiochus is described in the apocryphal First Book of Macabees as conquering Israel, entering the sanctuary, and taking away all holy objects that were silver or gold (22–24). The historical Antiochus IV probably looted the Temple in 168 BCE.

[27]Judas Maccabeus (his epithet "Maccabeus" means "hammer-like") led a rebellion against Antiochus (1 Maccabees 20–63). He was from the obscure town of Modin, northwest of Jerusalem. Lewalski (262) notes that commentators like Giovanni Diodati made Judas Maccabeus into a type of Christ fighting Antiochus as Antichrist. Judas Maccabeus's sojourn in the desert is described in 1 Maccabees 5.24–28.

[28]To "catch occasion by her forelock" was proverbial for seizing an opportunity quickly. Spenser uses the image in *Amoretti* 70: "The ioyous time wil not be staid, Unlesse she doe him by the forelock take" (quoted in *OED* "forelock" n.2.2). Carey points out that Guyon actually grasps occasion's forelock in the *The Faerie Queene* 2.4.12 (3.172–74n).

[29]The two occasions or causes are listed after the comma. When Jesus drove the moneychangers from the Temple, "his disciples remembered it was written [in Psalm 69.9], The zeal of thine house hath eaten me up" (John 2.17).

[30]"Truth" apparently is quoting Ecclesiastes 3.1: "To every thing there is a season, and a time to every purpose under the heaven."

[31]"Of the increase of his government and peace there shall be no end" (Isaiah 9.7).

The Father in his purpose hath decreed,
He in whose hand all times and seasons roul.°   COLLECT
What if he hath decreed that I shall first
Be try'd in humble state,[32] and things adverse,
By tribulations, injuries, insults,   190
Contempts, and scorns, and snares, and violence,
Suffering, abstaining, quietly expecting
Without distrust or doubt, that he may know
What I can suffer, how obey? who best
Can suffer, best can do;[33] best reign, who first   195
Well hath obey'd; just tryal e're I merit
My exaltation without change or end.
But what concerns it thee when I begin
My everlasting Kingdom, why art thou
Sollicitous, what moves thy inquisition?   200
Know'st thou not that my rising is thy fall,
And my promotion° will be thy destruction?   ADVANCEMENT

    To whom the Tempter inly rackt[34] reply'd.
Let that come when it comes; all hope is lost
Of my reception into grace; what worse?   205
For where no hope is left, is left no fear;
If there be worse, the expectation more
Of worse torments me then the feeling can.
I would be at the worst; worst is my Port,
My harbour and my ultimate repose,   210
The end I would attain, my final good.
My error was my error, and my crime
My crime; whatever for it self condemn'd,
And will alike be punish'd; whether thou
Raign or raign not; though to that gentle brow   215
Willingly I could flye,[35] and hope thy raign,
From that placid aspect and meek regard,°   FROM THE EVIDENCE OF YOUR PEACEFUL APPEARANCE
Rather then aggravate my evil state,
Would stand between me and thy Fathers ire,
(Whose ire I dread more then the fire of Hell)   220
A shelter and a kind of shading cool
Interposition, as a summers cloud.[36]
If I then to the worst that can be hast,[37]
Why move thy feet so slow to what is best,
Happiest° both to thy self and all the world,   MOST FORTUNATE   225
That thou who worthiest art should'st be thir King?
Perhaps thou linger'st in deep thoughts detain'd
Of the enterprize° so hazardous and high;   DIFFICULT UNDERTAKING
No wonder, for though in thee be united

---

[32]"Be tested in a humble state [incarnation]."
[33]The words "do" and "suffer" represent opposites, expressing action or passive endurance.
[34]In *Paradise Lost*, when we first hear Satan speak, he is described as "in pain, / Vaunting aloud, but rackt with deep despare" (1.125–26).
[35]Just as Satan is attracted to the beauty of Eve and rendered "Stupidly good, of enmitie disarm'd" (*Paradise Lost* 9.465), he is here genuinely attracted to the Son of God's gentleness as expressed in his face and to his placidity and meekness.
[36]Satan may be quoting scripture to his own purposes here: "For thou hast been . . . a refuge from the storm, a shadow from the heat . . . " (Isaiah 25.4). He may seek the comfort available from God but he cannot attain it.
[37]Loh rearranges the sentence to read "If I then haste to the worst that can be" and suggests that we read "'I' 223 and 'thy' 224 to bring out the meaning" (223n).

What of perfection can in man be found,   230
Or human nature can receive, consider
Thy life hath yet been private, most part spent
At home, scarce view'd the *Gallilean* Towns,
And once a year *Jerusalem*,[38] few days
Short sojourn; and what thence could'st thou observe?   235
The world thou hast not seen, much less her glory,
Empires, and Monarchs, and thir radiant Courts,
Best school of best experience, quickest in sight
In all things that to greatest actions lead.
The wisest, unexperienc't, will be ever   240
Timorous and loth,[39] with novice modesty,[40]
(As he who seeking Asses found a Kingdom)[41]
Irresolute, unhardy, unadventrous:[42]
But I will bring thee where thou soon shalt quit°   LEAVE BEHIND
Those rudiments,[43] and see before thine eyes   245
The Monarchies of the Earth, thir pomp° and state,   SPLENDID DISPLAY
Sufficient introduction to inform
Thee, of thy self so apt, in regal Arts,[44]
And regal Mysteries;[45] that thou may'st know
How best their opposition[46] to withstand.   250
  With that (such power was giv'n him[47] then) he took
The Son of God up to a Mountain high.[48]
It was a Mountain at whose verdant° feet   GREEN WITH VEGETATION
A spatious plain outstretch't in circuit wide
Lay pleasant; from his[49] side two rivers flow'd,   255
Th' one winding, the other strait and left between
Fair Champain° with less rivers interveind,   FLAT, OPEN TRACT OF LAND
Then meeting joyn'd thir tribute to the Sea:
Fertil of corn the glebe,[50] of oyl and wine,
With herds the pastures throng'd, with flocks the hills,   260
Huge Cities and high towr'd, that well might seem
The seats of mightiest Monarchs, and so large
The Prospect was, that here and there was room

---

[38]Satan knows the movements of the family: "Now his parents went to Jerusalem every year at the feast of the passover" (Luke 2.41).

[39]In the first state of *1671*, the word was printed "loah," which was corrected to "loth" while the F2 gathering (the section of the book identified by "F2," "F3," etc., at the bottom of the page) was in production.

[40]"With modesty employed for the first time." "Novice" is rarely recorded in the *OED* as an adjective.

[41]In search of his father's lost asses, Saul is sought out by the prophet Samuel, having been instructed in advance by the Lord to "anoint him to be captain over my people Israel, that he may save my people out of the hands of the Philistines" (1 Samuel 9.16).

[42]Milton invented this negative form of "adventurous," and the trisyllabic form represents his preferred spelling of the word (see *Paradise Lost* 1.13 and every other use of the word in that poem).

[43]Initial, imperfect stages; beginnings.

[44]A potentially negative term, especially in Satan's mouth. See my "Art, Artists."

[45]Perhaps "secrets of state," as MacKellar suggests (249n).

[46]The opposition of the "Monarchies of the Earth."

[47]The authorial comment indicates that Satan's power is not self-generated but permitted by God. See above 1.493–96. The "proper place" of the fallen angels "is hell, which they cannot leave without permission" (*On Christian Doctrine* 1.9; Yale 6: 348–49).

[48]The "exceedingly high mountain" or merely "high mountain" is that found in Matthew 4.8 and Luke 4.5, respectively. Carey (3.252n), following Gilbert (210), identifies the mountain as Mt. Niphates, the same that Satan alights on in *Paradise Lost* 3.742. The two rivers alluded to, therefore, might be the Tigris and the Euphrates, issuing from the base of Mt. Niphates. The Tigris was supposed to be straight (its name is the Persian word for arrow), and the Euphrates winding. The two rivers come together and flow into the Persian Gulf.

[49]Perhaps because the Latin noun *mons* is masculine, Milton gives the mountain a masculine pronoun, "his." The gendering of nouns can be difficult to assess in Milton's poetry: Egypt is a she in *Paradise Lost* 1.480 and the moon a she in 1.291, as is the mind in 3.52. The pronoun "its" was just coming into use in the seventeenth century: Milton probably used it less than five times.

[50]"Fertile with grain is the land."

For barren desert fountainless[51] and dry.
To this high mountain top the Tempter brought   265
Our Saviour, and new train[52] of words began.

    Well have we speeded, and o're hill and dale,[53]
Forest and field, and flood, Temples and Towers
Cut shorter many a league; here thou behold'st
Assyria and her Empires antient bounds,[54]   270
Araxes and the *Caspian* lake, thence on
As far as *Indus* East, *Euphrates* West,
And oft beyond; to South the *Persian* Bay,
And inaccessible the *Arabian* drouth:°   DESERT
Here *Ninevee*,[55] of length within her wall   275
Several days journey,[56] built by *Ninus* old,[57]
Of that first golden Monarchy the seat,
And seat of *Salmanassar*,[58] whose success
Israel in long captivity still mourns;
There *Babylon*[59] the wonder of all tongues,   280
As antient, but rebuilt by him who twice
Judah and all thy Father *David*'s house
Led captive, and *Jerusalem* laid waste,[60]
Till *Cyrus* set them free; *Persepolis*[61]
His City there thou seest, and *Bactra* there;   285
Ecbatana her structure vast there shews,
And *Hecatompylos*[62] her hunderd[63] gates,
There *Susa* by *Choaspes*,[64] amber stream,
The drink of none but Kings;[65] of later fame

---

[51]"Without springs or sources of water." Milton invented this adjective form.

[52]"New string of words." "Train" is always a negative word in Milton's usage, suggesting everything from "useless ornamental attachment" (compare "gay Traine" in *Paradise Lost* 7.444) to "sinister tail" (as with "bestial train" in *Paradise Lost* 2.873).

[53]Satan, always diverting, is talking like Shakespeare's Puck, who also travels "Over hill, over dale, / Thorough bush, thorough brier" (*Midsummer Night's Dream* 2.1.2–3).

[54]The Assyrian empire at its height took the form of a large crescent extending in the north to the Caspian Sea, in the southeast horn to the Persian Gulf, and in the southwest horn down into Israel. The river Araxes, running into the Caspian Sea, formed the north border, the Indus River the eastern, and the Euphrates the western. The Arabian desert would create a border in the south due to its inaccessibility.

[55]I am presuming that Milton chose the form of the place name based on its spelling in Latin, *Ninive*. Most editors emend to the customary "Nineveh."

[56]So large that it took several days to walk the circuit of the walls: 4080 furlongs (a furlong is the length of a spearthrow, about 1/8 mile), according to Diodorus Siculus 2.3.2.

[57]Ninus, King of Assyria, legendary founder of the city of Nineveh (see Diodorus Siculus 2.3.2–4), husband of Semiramis, "old" because he was supposed to have been of the generation of Abraham (MacKellar 276n).

[58]The same as Shalmaneser in 2 Kings 17.31, king of Assyria from 727 to 722 BC. In 2 Kings 17.3–6 he made Hoshea, the King of Israel, his servant, but when Hoshea led a conspiracy against him, he besieged Samaria and carried the Israelites into captivity in various cities in Assyria. Milton may have preferred the spelling of the name found in the Authorized Version's apocryphal 2 Esdras 13.40.

[59]The city that straddled the Euphrates river, one of the wonders of the ancient world, with the famous landmarks of the hanging gardens and the temple of Zeus Belus or Bel (Herodotus 1.178–81). Babylon was a seat of Mesopotamian civilization from 604 to 539 BCE, when it fell to the Persians under Cyrus.

[60]Nebuchadnezzar, King of Babylon from 604–562 BCE, who captured Jerusalem in 597 BCE and carried most of the Jews as captives to Babylon (2 Kings 24.10–17), from which they were eventually rescued by Cyrus, King of Persia, who captured Babylon and returned them to their homeland in 538 BC (see Ezra 1–2).

[61]A great city of the Persian empire, inland and northeast of the Persian Gulf, known for its wealth and monuments, destroyed by Alexander the Great in 339 BC. The court of Darius was based in winter at Persepolis or Susa and in summer at Ecbatana. Bactra or Bactria was a city in the grand satrapy of Bactria, northeast of Persepolis between the Hindu Kush mountain range and the Oxus River.

[62]The capital of Parthia, southeast of the Caspian Sea. Its name in Greek indicates it was a city of a "hundred gates."

[63]A spelling preferred by Milton which in this case may have slipped through via a manuscript into print.

[64]Susa is Shushan in the Old Testament (Esther 1.2), capital of Susiana, located near the northwest tip of the Persian Gulf. Its river is Choaspes, and apparently "amber" streams were lucid or clear or shining like amber.

[65]An ancient rumor, often discussed by early editors of Milton, begun by Herodotus (1.188), that kings of Persia took with them to battle only the water of the Choaspes. As MacKellar points out, Milton's associate Peter Heylyn, in his *Cosmographie* (London, 1667), "does *not* say that only kings drank the water" (289n).

Built by *Emathian*,[66] or by *Parthian* hands,   290
The great *Seleucia*,[67] *Nisibis*,[68] and there
Artaxata,[69] *Teredon*,[70] *Tesiphon*,[71]
Turning with easie eye thou may'st behold.
All these the *Parthian*,[72] now some Ages past,
By great *Arsaces*[73] led, who founded first   295
That Empire, under his dominion holds
From the luxurious Kings of *Antioch*[74] won.
And just in time thou com'st to have a view
Of his great power; for now the *Parthian* King[75]
In *Ctesiphon* hath gather'd all his Host   300
Against the *Scythian*,[76] whose incursions wild
Have wasted *Sogdiana*; to her aid
He marches now in hast; see, though from far,
His thousands, in what martial equipage
They issue forth, Steel Bows, and Shafts their arms   305
Of equal dread in flight, or in pursuit;
All Horsemen, in which fight they most excel;
See how in warlike muster they appear,
In Rhombs and wedges, and half moons, and wings.[77]

    He look't and saw what numbers numberless   310
The City gates out powr'd,° light armed Troops   POURED FORTH
In coats of Mail and military pride;°   DISPLAY
In Mail thir horses clad, yet fleet and strong,
Prauncing their riders bore, the flower and choice
Of·many Provinces from bound to bound;   315
From *Arachosia*,[78] from *Candaor*[79] East,
And *Margiana*[80] to the *Hyrcanian* cliffs

---

[66]The Emathians were Macedonian peoples that succeeded Alexander, and the Parthian warriors, famous for the practice of firing arrows at their enemies while retreating, were famous as well for erecting cities.

[67]Seleucus Nicator, another of Alexander the Great's successors, founded the Seleucid empire and built seven cities in the area of what is now Syria carrying the name Seleucia. Seleucia the Great was on the Tigris, about ninety miles from Babylon, and its eminence helped to eclipse that of Babylon.

[68]A city in western Mesopotamia, south of the Tigris, also known as Antioch in Mygdonia.

[69]A city in Armenia southeast of the Black Sea, which Hannibal was said to have built for King Artaxias.

[70]A town near the beginning of the river formed by the joining of the Tigris and the Euphrates, near the Arabian gulf.

[71]Usually spelled Ctesiphon, as it is eight lines below. A city on the Tigris near Seleucia, winter home of the kings of Parthia, said by Pliny to have been built with the idea of ruining Seleucia, as Seleucia had ruined Babylon (*Natural History* 6.30.122).

[72]I.e., the Parthian army, spoken of in the collective singular.

[73]Founder of the dynasty of the Arsacidae, kings of Parthia.

[74]Arsaces or his descendants made war on the people of Antioch, a city on the Orontes River; perhaps Milton has in mind Arsaces's son by the same name, who conquered Antiochus, the son of Seleucus.

[75]David Quint finds that the allusion to Pompey's action in Lucan's *Civil War* in seeking the aid of the Parthian king in order to continue the war against Julius Caesar (8.162f) puts Jesus "in the position of a defeated republican, the loser of the civil war who now considers what form of resistance to pursue against the new Caesarian monarchy—that is to say, roughly in the same position of John Milton himself during the Restoration" (128).

[76]Ctesiphon was the winter residence of the Parthian kings and an ample stronghold from which the Parthians might well muster an army to go against the Scythians attacking Sogdiana, a province bordering Scythia. Milton seems to have no special excursion in mind, just a bit of border warfare (see MacKellar 298–336n).

[77]Milton taught his own pupils the rudiments of military formations such as the geometric shapes of armies he here describes. See James H. Hanford, "Milton on the Art of War" (*John Milton, Poet and Humanist* [Cleveland: Case Western Reserve P, 1966]: 216–18). The rhomb would be a lozenge-shaped formation, the wedge a half-rhomb, the half-moon formation would be presented with the main body of an army in the middle, thick portion of the half-moon, with the flanks rounding out the semicircle.

[78]The district forming the eastern boundary of Parthia, itself bordered by the Indus River.

[79]The usual spelling is Candahar, a city in what is now Afghanistan.

[80]Northern border of Parthia, an extensive region between Bactria and Parthia.

Of *Caucasus*,[81] and dark *Iberian*[82] dales,
From *Atropatia*[83] and the neighbouring plains
Of *Adiabene*,[84] *Media*, and the South   320
Of *Susiana*[85] to *Balsara*'s hav'n.
He saw them in thir forms of battell rang'd,
How quick they wheel'd, and flying behind them shot
Sharp sleet of arrowie showers[86] against the face
Of thir pursuers, and overcame by flight;   325
The field all iron cast a gleaming brown,
Nor wanted clouds of foot, nor on each horn,[87]
Cuirassiers° all in steel for standing fight;   ARMORED TROOPS
Chariots or Elephants endorst° with Towers   INSCRIBED ON THE BACK
Of Archers, nor of labouring Pioners[88]   330
A multitude with Spades and Axes arm'd
To lay hills plain,° fell woods, or valleys fill,   FLAT
Or where plain was raise hill, or over-lay
With bridges rivers proud, as with a yoke;
Mules after these, Camels and Dromedaries,   335
And Waggons fraught with Utensils[89] of war.
Such forces met not, nor so wide a camp,
When *Agrican*[90] with all his Northern powers
Besieg'd *Albracca*, as Romances tell;
The City of *Gallaphrone*, from thence to win   340
The fairest of her Sex *Angelica*[91]
His daughter, sought by many Prowest[92] Knights,
Both *Paynim*,[93] and the Peers of *Charlemane*.
Such and so numerous was thir Chivalrie;
At sight whereof the Fiend yet more presum'd,   345
And to our Saviour thus his words renew'd.

---

[81]Milton may be conflating the Caspian Sea, also called the Hyrcanian Sea, with the region of the Caucasus Mountains, some distance northeast of it.
[82]Not the Iberian peninsula (Spain) but the region now known as Georgia, between the Black Sea and the Caspian Sea. Milton probably took the notion of the dark region from Samuel Purchas, *Purchas his Pilgrimes* 3.110: "in those parts [Georgia] there is a Province or Country called *Hamsen* . . . whose whole extent is all covered over with such thicke and palpable darknesse, that none can see any thing therein, neither doe any dare to goe into that Land, because they know not the way out againe" (quoted in MacKellar 317n).
[83]Media-Atropatenia was a province west of Parthia, between the Caspian Sea and Armenia.
[84]One of the plains near Nineveh, south of Armenia on the Tigris. Media, which became northern Persia (now Iran), was divided into Media Magna and Media Atropatia.
[85]A province in southeastern Persia, the capital of which is Susa. Balsara is a city on the river formed by the union of the Tigris and the Euphrates, due south of Susa.
[86]The *1671 Errata* corrected the singular "shower" to the plural. What is being described is the famous "Parthian shot," the backward firing of arrows as the Parthian army was supposedly in retreat. The image of arrows as rain, sleet, or snow appears in Pindar, Vergil, Statius, and Spenser (see MacKellar 324n).
[87]I.e., each wing of the army.
[88]Those who dig military fortifications such as trenches or ramparts, or undermine enemy fortifications. Probably pronounced with three syllables, as it is spelled here, with the stress on the first syllable, as in Shakespeare (see *Henry V* 3.2.87). The word is allied with both peon and pawn.
[89]Stressed on the first syllable, as was common before the eighteenth century (see *OED*).
[90]A curious segue (what I mean by that is an uninterrupted musical shift from one set of images to another) by means of a simile to Renaissance romance, specifically to Matteo Boiardo, *Orlando Innamorato* 1.10. The Tartar king Agrican besieges Albracca, in quest of the beautiful but faithless Angelica on behalf of Orlando, who is driven mad for love of her. Despite MacKellar's and Steadman's warning that Milton's choice here was not gratuitous, the introduction of warfare according to Renaissance Italian epic seems to trivialize history (see MacKellar 337–42n and Steadman, *Milton* 26). Thyer's judgment was probably just: "It must be acknowledged, I think, by the greatest admirers of Milton, that the impression which romances had made upon his imagination in his youth, has in this place led him into a blameable excess" (Newton 337n).
[91]It may be significant that Angelica, the fickle and flighty heroine not only of Boiardo's *Orlando Innamorato* but of Ariosto's *Orlando Furioso*, is described in terms reminiscent of Milton's Eve, who is "the fairest of [her] daughters" (*Paradise Lost* 4.324; see above, 2.154).
[92]"Valiant." The noun *prowess* should, theoretically, not be made into a superlative adjective, but both Spenser and Milton did it.
[93]A standard alternative in the seventeenth century for "pagan," but one peculiar to romances. With "Prowest" and "Paynim" and "Chivalrie," Milton mocks the language of the romantic epics he is belittling. Chivalry can mean "cavalry," or it can be applied to an entire army.

That thou may'st know I seek not to engage°　　　　CHALLENGE
Thy Vertue,[94] and not every way secure
On no slight grounds thy safety;[95] hear, and mark
To what end I have brought thee hither and shewn
All this fair sight; thy Kingdom though foretold　　　350
By Prophet or by Angel, unless thou
Endeavour, as thy Father° *David* did,　　　ANCESTOR
Thou never shalt obtain; prediction still
In all things, and all men, supposes means,
Without means us'd, what it predicts revokes.°　　　355
But say thou wer't possess'd of *David*'s Throne　　　REVERSES
By free consent of all, none opposite,°　　　OPPOSING
Samaritan or *Jew*;[96] how could'st thou hope
Long to enjoy it quiet and secure,
Between two such enclosing enemies　　　360
Roman and *Parthian*?[97] therefore one of these
Thou must make sure thy own, the *Parthian* first
By my advice, as nearer and of late
Found able by invasion to annoy°　　　HARM IN A MILITARY SENSE　　　365
Thy country, and captive lead away her Kings
Antigonus, and old *Hyrcanus* bound,
Maugre° the *Roman*:[98] it shall be my task　　　IN SPITE OF
To render thee the *Parthian* at dispose;[99]
Chuse which thou wilt by conquest or by league.°　　　DIPLOMATIC ALLIANCE　　　370
By him thou shalt regain, without him not,
That which alone can truly reinstall thee
In *David*'s royal seat, his true Successour,
Deliverance of thy brethren, those ten Tribes
Whose off-spring in his Territory yet serve　　　375
In *Habor*,[100] and among the *Medes* dispers't,
Ten Sons of *Jacob*, two of *Joseph*[101] lost
Thus long from *Israel*; serving as of old
Thir Fathers in the land of *Egypt* serv'd,
This offer sets before thee to deliver.　　　380
These if from servitude thou shalt restore
To thir inheritance, then, nor till then,
Thou on the Throne of *David* in full glory,

---

[94]Probably both "strength" and "moral excellence" are implied in the word, which is derived from the very rich and meaningful Latin word *virtus*, part of the character of heroes like Aeneas.

[95]The syntax is difficult, but Satan seems to be saying that he will make every effort to see that the Savior is safe from harm, in an offer of something like diplomatic immunity.

[96]Normally the generic term would not be italicized, but here it seems to be because of the proximity of "*Samaritan*." Jews had "no dealings with the Samaritans," according to a Samaritan woman speaking with Jesus (John 4.9); hence the force of the parable of the good Samaritan (Luke 10.30–37).

[97]Posing as a diplomatic envoy, Satan is tempting the Savior to side with the Parthians to overthrow Roman rule in Palestine. Satan's hidden agenda is to tempt the Savior with the presumably inevitable corruption caused by assuming worldly power.

[98]Carey says definitively, "Satan is inaccurate. The Parthians were allies of Antigonus" with their support he overran Judaea and captured Jerusalem. He took prisoner his uncle, the seventy-year-old Hyrcanus II and Herod's brother, Phasaelus; killed the latter; and cut off the ears of the former to disqualify him from priestly office, carrying him off to Seleucia. The events are narrated in Josephus's *Antiquities* 14.13–16. The nagging question remains: Is it Satan who is wrong or Milton? Newton's note begins "Here seems to be a slip of memory in our author" (366n). MacKellar believes "It suits Satan's purpose . . . to represent this exhibition of Parthian power as a recent occurrence, and hence his historical inaccuracies" (364–68n).

[99]"At my beck and call," "at my disposal."

[100]Habor (together with the cities of the Medes) is described as a place of captivity for the Israelites near the river Gazan (2 Kings 18.11).

[101]The two directly descended from Joseph are those named after his sons Ephraim and Manasses.

From *Egypt* to *Euphrates* and beyond[102]
Shalt raign, and *Rome* or *Cæsar* not need fear.   385
    To whom our Saviour answer'd thus unmov'd.
Much ostentation vain of fleshly arm,[103]
And fragile arms, much instrument of war
Long in preparing, soon to nothing brought,   390
Before mine eyes thou hast set; and in my ear
Vented[104] much policy,° and projects° deep   POLITICAL INTRIGUE   SCHEMES
Of enemies, of aids,[105] battels and leagues,
Plausible to the world, to me worth naught.
Means I must use thou say'st, prediction else   395
Will unpredict[106] and fail me of the Throne:
My time I told thee, (and that time for thee
Were better farthest off) is not yet come;[107]
When that comes think not thou to find me slack
On my part aught endeavouring, or to need   400
Thy politic maxims, or that cumbersome
Luggage of war there shewn me, argument
Of human weakness rather then of strength.
My brethren, as thou call'st them; those Ten Tribes
I must deliver, if I mean to raign   405
David's true heir, and his full Scepter sway
To just extent over all *Israel*'s Sons;
But whence to thee this zeal, where was it then
For *Israel*, or for *David*, or his Throne,
When thou stood'st up his Tempter to the pride   410
Of numbring *Israel*, which cost the lives
Of threescore and ten thousand *Israelites*
By three days Pestilence?[108] such was thy zeal
To *Israel* then, the same that now to me.
As for those captive Tribes, themselves were they   415
Who wrought their own captivity, fell off
From God to worship Calves,[109] the Deities
Of *Egypt*, *Baal* next[110] and *Ashtaroth*,[111]

---

[102]The promise to Abram that his sons be rulers from the Nile to the Euphrates is made in Genesis 15.18.

[103]The Savior is punning on the two senses of arm (of flesh) and arms (as in "bear arms"), with allusions to 2 Chronicles 32.8, "With him is an arm of flesh; but with us is the Lord our God to help us, and to fight our battles"; and to Jeremiah 17.5: "Thus saith the Lord; Cursed be the man that trusteth in man, and maketh flesh his arm, and whose heart departeth from the Lord."

[104]Implied in the verb is the idea of letting out hot air or gas. Milton used the verb elsewhere in the sense of excreting unhealthy fumes, literally or figuratively (see *Of Reformation*; Yale 1: 615).

[105]Probably used in a legal sense: "Eng. Law. Help or assistance in defending an action, legally claimed by the defendant from some one who has a joint-interest in the defence" (*OED* 2.a).

[106]Thyer found the play on words "rather too light and familiar for the dignity of the speaker" (quoted in Newton 394n), but the Savior seems to be expressing contempt for Satan even in his manner of speech.

[107]"And Jesus said unto them, My time is not yet come . . . " John 7.6.

[108]Reminding Satan of his hypocrisy in expressing concern for a people he had earlier undermined. His treachery is documented in 1 Chronicles 21.1: "And Satan stood up against Israel, and provoked David to number Israel." The census provokes a revolt that God punishes by a plague: it kills 70,000. The marginalia of the Geneva Bible comment: "He [Satan] tempted David in setting before his eyes his excellencie & glorie, his power & victories" (1560 ed.).

[109]Jereboam, fearing that the Israelites would return to Rehoboam, King of Judah, "took counsel, and made two calves of gold, and said unto them [the Israelites], It is too much for you to go up to Jerusalem: behold thy gods, O Israel, which brought thee up out of the land of Egypt" (1 Kings 12.28)." Of their own will, the Israelites sinfully accept the worship of the calves, placed in Bethel and Dan respectively.

[110]Worshiped by Ahab in 1 Kings 16.31–32, following the practice of his wife Jezebel, daughter of the King of Zidon.

[111]The plural form of Ashtoreth (see *Paradise Lost* 1.422, 438), the Zidonian equivalent of Venus. Baals and Astartes (Ashtaroth) are worshipped idolatrously by the Israelites in Judges 2.13–14 and 10.6–7.

And all the Idolatries of Heathen round,[112]
Besides thir other worse then heathenish crimes;[113]
Nor in the land of their captivity   420
Humbled themselves, or penitent besought
The God of their fore-fathers; but so dy'd
Impenitent, and left a race behind
Like to themselves, distinguishable scarce
From Gentils,[114] but by Circumcision vain,[115]   425
And God with Idols in their worship joyn'd.
Should I of these the liberty regard,[116]
Who freed, as to their antient Patrimony,
Unhumbl'd, unrepentant, unreform'd,
Headlong would follow; and to thir Gods perhaps   430
Of *Bethel* and of *Dan*?[117] no, let them serve
Thir enemies, who serve Idols with God.
Yet he at length, time to himself best known,
Remembring *Abraham* by some wond'rous call
May bring them back repentant and sincere,   435
And at their passing cleave the *Assyrian* flood,[118]
While to their native land with joy they hast,
As the Red Sea and *Jordan* once he cleft,
When to the promis'd land thir Fathers pass'd;
To his due time and providence I leave them.   440

So spake *Israel*'s true King, and to the Fiend
Made answer meet, that made void all his wiles.
So fares it when with truth falshood contends.

The End of the Third Book.

---

[112]As Milton did in the Nativity Ode, 197–201, the Savior belittles the people of Egypt for worshiping gods in the forms of animals.
[113]Worship of Baal involving "the blood of innocents" and "slaughter" is mentioned in Jeremiah 19.4–6.
[114]Gentiles (not members of the tribes of Israel).
[115]Alluding to Galatians 5.6: "For in Jesus Christ neither circumcision availeth any thing, nor uncircumcision; but faith which worketh by love." Compare Romans 2.25: "If thou be a breaker of the law, thy circumcision is made uncircumcision."
[116]"Should I have a regard for the liberty of those."
[117]Referring once again to the calves erected in Bethel and Dan by Jereboam.
[118]The miraculous parting of the Red Sea, to deliver the tribes of Israel out of bondage in Egypt (Exodus 14.21–22). The Jordan River is similarly divided in Joshua 3.14–17. The word "flood" was used of any large body of flowing water (*OED* 2).

PARADISE REGAIN'D.

The Fourth BOOK.

PErplex'd and troubl'd at his bad success°
The Tempter stood, nor had what° to reply,
Discover'd in his fraud, thrown from his hope,
So oft, and the perswasive Rhetoric
That sleek't his tongue, and won so much on *Eve*, 5
So little here, nay lost;[1] but *Eve* was *Eve*,
This far his over-match, who self deceiv'd[2]
And rash, before-hand had no better weigh'd
The strength he was to cope with, or his own:
But as a man who had been matchless held 10
In cunning, over-reach't where least he thought,
To salve his credit,[3] and for very spight
Still° will be tempting him who foyls him still,
And never cease, though to his shame the more;
Or as a swarm of flies in vintage time,[4] 15
About the wine-press where sweet moust is powr'd,
Beat off, returns as oft with humming sound;
Or surging waves against a solid rock,
Though all to shivers dash't, the assault renew,[5]
Vain battry,[6] and in froth or bubbles end; 20
So Satan, whom repulse upon repulse
Met ever; and to shameful silence brought,
Yet gives not o're° though desperate of success,
And his vain importunity pursues.
He brought our Saviour to the western side 25
Of that high mountain, whence he might behold
Another plain, long but in bredth not wide;
Wash'd by the Southern Sea, and on the North
To equal length back'd with a ridge of hills
That screen'd the fruits of the earth and seats of men 30

ILL-SUCCESS, FAILURE

ANYTHING

ALWAYS, PERPETUALLY

YET DOESN'T GIVE IN

---

[1] "[Won] so little here—no, lost."
[2] Adam and Eve were "deceiv'd / By the other first" and "shall find grace," whereas Satan shall find none, because he and the other fallen angels were "Self-tempted, self-deprav'd" (*Paradise Lost* 3.130–31).
[3] "To heal his wounded credibility." The second edition substituted "save" for "salve," which would destroy the image of wounding and healing.
[4] An epic simile, the image of flies swarming around the sweet must fermenting in a wine press resembles Homer's image of insects swarming to fresh sheep's milk in the *Iliad* 2.469–70.
[5] Perhaps imitating the shorter simile in the *Iliad* 15.618–21:
                   like some towering
     huge sea-cliff that lies close along the grey salt water
     and stands up against the screaming winds and their sudden directions
     and against the waves that grow to bigness and burst up against it. (Lattimore trans.)
[6] Battery: physical attack or bombardment, as in "assault and battery."

From cold *Septentrion*[7] blasts, thence in the midst
Divided by a river,[8] of whose banks
On each side an Imperial City stood,
With Towers and Temples proudly elevate
On seven small Hills, with Palaces adorn'd,　　　　　　35
Porches and Theatres, Baths, Aqueducts,
Statues and Trophees, and Triumphal Arcs,[9]
Gardens and Groves presented to his eyes,
Above the highth of Mountains interpos'd.
By what strange Parallax[10] or Optic skill　　　　　　40
Of vision multiplyed through air,[11] or glass
Of Telescope, were curious to enquire:
And now the Tempter thus his silence broke.
　　The City which thou seest no other deem
Then great and glorious *Rome*, Queen of the Earth　　45
So far renown'd, and with the spoils enricht
Of Nations; there the Capitol thou seest
Above the rest lifting his[12] stately head
On the *Tarpeian* rock, her Cittadel
Impregnable, and there Mount *Palatine*[13]　　　　　　50
The Imperial Palace, compass huge, and high
The Structure, skill of noblest Architects,
With gilded battlements, conspicuous far,
Turrets and Terrases, and glittering Spires.
Many a fair Edifice besides, more like　　　　　　　　55
Houses of Gods (so well I have dispos'd
My Aerie Microscope)[14] thou may'st behold
Outside and inside both, pillars and roofs
Carv'd work, the hand of fam'd Artificers
In Cedar, Marble, Ivory or Gold.　　　　　　　　　　60
Thence to the gates cast round thine eye, and see
What conflux[15] issuing forth, or entring in,
Pretors,[16] Proconsuls[17] to thir Provinces
Hasting or on return, in robes of State;
Lictors[18] and rods the ensigns of thir power,　　　　65

---

[7]Northerly, from the constellation of the Great Bear, seven stars encircling northern regions.

[8]The Tiber. The city, of course, is Rome.

[9]Not arches but arcs, here used perhaps for the monosyllable. Carey and Campbell wisely choose not to modernize the spelling in this instance.

[10]"(Astron.) Apparent displacement, or difference in the apparent position, of an object, caused by actual change (or difference) of position of the point of observation" (*OED* 1.a). Commentators argued about how Satan could project all the kingdoms of the Earth from one perspective: Milton here gives the reader a choice of several explanations.

[11]A mirage, a delusory image caused by atmospheric conditions, as in a desert.

[12]A curious choice of gender for the word "Capitol," since *caput*, the Latin word for "head" is neuter, as is *Capitolium*. According to one fanciful etymology, however, the Capitoline hill was so named because a man's head was found there when the foundations were being dug for the temple of Jupiter (Livy 1.55). The citadel was built adjacent to the Tarpeian rock, on the northern summit of the Capitoline hill.

[13]The Palatine hill is that adjacent to the Capitoline, separated from it by the Forum. The word "Mount" is being used loosely, perhaps on purpose by Satan, to amplify the importance of Rome.

[14]The use of the adjective "Aerie" would suggest that Satan's instrument, whether microscope in the modern sense or telescope, is designed to produce an illusion or to fool the eye.

[15]Flowing together (of people).

[16]Magistrates working directly under Roman consuls.

[17]Governors of senatorial provinces.

[18]Twelve lictors served a consul, and each was supposed to carry the fasces, or bundle of sticks and axes that symbolized Roman authority and discipline (as pictured on the U.S. dime). Milton may be reducing the fasces to "rods," the willow or birch switches schoolmasters would use to discipline poor or disobedient pupils.

Legions and Cohorts,[19] turmes[20] of horse and wings:
Or Embassies from Regions far remote
In various habits on the *Appian* road,[21]
Or on the *Æmilian*, some from farthest South,
Syene,[22] and where the shadow both way falls,   70
Meroe Nilotic Isle,[23] and more to West,
The Realm of *Bocchus*[24] to the Black-moor Sea;
From the *Asian* Kings and *Parthian* among these,
From *India* and the golden *Chersoness*,[25]
And utmost *Indian* Isle *Taprobane*,[26]   75
Dusk° faces with white silken Turbants[27] wreath'd: DUSKY, DARK
From *Gallia*,[28] *Gades*, and the *Brittish* West,
Germans[29] and *Scythians*, and *Sarmatians* North
Beyond *Danubius* to the *Tauric* Pool.[30]
All Nations now to *Rome* obedience pay,   80
To *Rome*'s great Emperour, whose wide domain
In ample Territory, wealth and power,
Civility of Manners, Arts, and Arms,
And long Renown thou justly may'st prefer
Before the *Parthian*; these two Thrones except,   85
The rest are barbarous, and scarce worth the sight,
Shar'd among petty Kings too far remov'd;
These having shewn thee, I have shewn thee all
The Kingdoms of the world, and all thir glory.
This Emperour[31] hath no Son, and now is old,   90
Old, and lascivious, and from *Rome* retir'd
To *Capreæ* an Island small but strong
On the *Campanian* shore,[32] with purpose there
His horrid lusts in private to enjoy,

---

[19]Ten cohorts, bodies of infantry, made up a legion.

[20]Squadrons of thirty or so horsemen, from the Latin *turma*.

[21]The Via Appia ("Appian Way"), named for Appius Claudius, led southward from Rome to Brundusium (the modern Brindisi) and the Via Æmelia, named after the Consul Æmilius, stretched from Placentia in north central Italy to Ariminum on the Adriatic coast.

[22]Egyptian city on the lower Nile, the modern Aswan.

[23]Supposedly an island region but really land surrounded by the White and Blue Nile, toward the lower ends of the rivers. The city Meroe "in the third century BC . . . became the capital of the country known to the Greeks as Ethiopia" (Nicholas Grimal, *A History of Ancient Egypt* [London: B.H. Blackwell, 1992]: 387). The adjective "*Nilotic*" means, simply, "of the region of the Nile."

[24]Bocchus was the father-in-law of the better known Jugurtha, king of the ancient Mauretania on the northern coast of Africa. The "Black-moor Sea" would be the area of the Mediterranean off the Barbary coast, land of the Moors or Blackamoors. In the Elizabethan era, any person with black skin might be labeled a blackamoor or an "Ethiop."

[25]A chersonese is simply a peninsula, but the Golden Chersonese was usually identified as the peninsula of Malacca or the Malay Peninsula. MacKellar speculates that Milton used the form "*Chersoness*" in order to avoid a rhyme with "these" (74n). In the *Orlando Furioso*, Ariosto associates "*l'aurea Chersonesso*" with Taprobane in the same stanza (15.17), and Michael Drayton, in his *Poly-Olbion* (1622), applies the word *chersonese* often to English peninsulas (as in 1.84).

[26]Probably Ceylon, off the southern tip of India, or possibly Sumatra, thought by seventeenth-century mapmakers to be the last island toward the east.

[27]The more familiar forms of "turban" in the seventeenth century were "turbant" and "tulibant."

[28]"*Gallia*" is Gaul or France, "*Gades*" is Cadiz, in Spain, and the "*British* West" is probably Brittany, in northern France, viewed as a Roman province.

[29]Beginning a list of three barbarian tribes with the Germans (Germanic tribes probably living around the North Sea), Satan proceeds to the Scythians, who lived on the shore of the Caspian Sea, and the Sarmathians, who lived north of the Scythians in what is now Poland.

[30]The Tauric pool is the Sea of Azov, north of the Black Sea. Scythian tribes lived just north of the Sea of Azov, and Sarmathian tribes to the north of them. In the Crimean peninsula, surrounded by the Black Sea and the Sea of Azov, lived the Tauri, whence the adjective "*Tauric*."

[31]Tiberius Caesar, whose three sons were all dead by the time he retired to the island of Capri, off Naples. Suetonius (*Caesars* 3.40) gives a vivid picture of the old emperor's vices with young boys in the grottoes of Capri. The island was strong and defensible because it is composed of high cliffs and inaccessible except from one small beach.

[32]Off the shores of Campania, the Roman province that included Naples and Pompeii.

Committing to a wicked Favourite[33]　　　　　　　　　　95
All publick cares, and yet of him suspicious,
Hated of all, and hating; with what ease
Indu'd with Regal Vertues as thou art,
Appearing, and beginning noble deeds,
Might'st thou expel this monster from his Throne　　　100
Now made a stye, and in his place ascending
A victor[34] people free from servile yoke?
And with my help thou may'st; to me the power
Is given,[35] and by that right I give it thee.
Aim therefore at no less then all the world,　　　　105
Aim at the highest, without the highest attain'd
Will be for thee no sitting, or not long
On *David*'s Throne, be propheci'd what will.
　To whom the Son of God unmov'd reply'd.
Nor doth this grandeur and majestic show　　　　110
Of luxury,[36] though call'd magnificence,
More then of arms before, allure mine eye,
Much less my mind; though thou should'st add to tell
Thir sumptuous gluttonies, and gorgeous feasts
On *Cittron*[37] tables or *Atlantic* stone;　　　　115
(For I have also heard, perhaps have read)
Their wines of *Setia*, *Cales*, and *Falerne*,[38]
Chios and *Creet*,[39] and how they quaff° in Gold,　　DRINK DEEPLY
Crystal and Myrrhine[40] cups imboss'd with Gems
And studs of Pearl, to me should'st tell who thirst　　120
And hunger still: then Embassies thou shew'st
From Nations far and nigh; what honour that,
But tedious wast of time to sit and hear
So many hollow complements and lies,
Outlandish flatteries?[41] then proceed'st to talk　　　125
Of the Emperour, how easily subdu'd,
How gloriously; I shall, thou say'st, expel
A brutish monster: what if I withal
Expel a Devil who first made him such?
Let his tormenter Conscience find him out,　　　　130
For him I was not sent, nor yet to free
That people victor once, now vile and base,
Deservedly made vassal, who once just,

---

[33]Sejanus, who in his own quest for power fed Tiberius's vices. For his pains, he was betrayed by Tiberius to the Roman Senate, which condemned him to death in AD 31.

[34]There is a comma at this point in *1671*, but it is canceled by the *Errata*.

[35]"And the devil said unto him, All this power will I give thee, and the glory of them: for that is delivered unto me; and to whomsoever I will I give it" (Luke 4.6).

[36]The word had more to do with vice than riches in the seventeenth century: synonyms for it would be "lechery" and "voluptuousness."

[37]The aromatic wood of the North African citron tree, known in Latin as *citrum*. See Pliny, *Natural History* 13.15.29, for the use of the wood in making prized furniture. "*Atlantic* stone" may be marble from the region around Mt. Atlas, but so far no scholar has been able to identify its source, nor is there any reference to the phrase in the *OED*.

[38]Three regions famous for their wines: Sezza, near Rome, and Cales and Falernia, in the Campania, near Mt. Vesuvius.

[39]Islands associated with Greek wines, prized by Romans such as Horace (*Odes* 3.19.5).

[40]"Made of or pertaining to murra. [M]urrhine glass: a modern fancy name for a delicate ware brought from the East, and made of fluor-spar" (*OED* A. adj.). Possibly the same as Chinese porcelain.

[41]It is difficult not to think in terms of Milton's career as a diplomatic translator at this point, as Fallon reminds us by quoting from this passage in *Milton in Government* 105–06.

Frugal, and mild, and temperate, conquer'd well,
But govern ill the Nations under yoke,
Peeling thir Provinces,[42] exhausted all   135
By lust and rapine; first ambitious grown
Of triumph[43] that insulting vanity;
Then cruel, by thir sports to blood enur'd°   ACCUSTOMED
Of fighting beasts, and men to beasts expos'd,   140
Luxurious by thir wealth, and greedier still,
And from the daily Scene effeminate.[44]
What wise and valiant man would seek to free
These thus degenerate, by themselves enslav'd,[45]
Or could of inward slaves make outward free?   145
Know therefore when my season comes to sit
On *David*'s Throne, it shall be like a tree
Spreading and over-shadowing all the Earth,[46]
Or as a stone that shall to pieces dash
All Monarchies besides throughout the world,[47]   150
And of my Kingdom there shall be no end:[48]
Means there shall be to this, but what the means,
Is not for thee to know, nor me to tell.
    To whom the Tempter impudent repli'd.
I see all offers made by me how slight   155
Thou valu'st, because offer'd, and reject'st:
Nothing will please the difficult and nice,°   OVERLY FASTIDIOUS
Or nothing more then still to contradict:
On the other side know also thou, that I
On what I offer set as high esteem,   160
Nor what I part with mean to give for naught;
All these which in a moment thou behold'st,
The Kingdoms of the world to thee I give;[49]
For giv'n to me, I give to whom I please,
No trifle; yet with this reserve, not else,   165
On this condition, if thou wilt fall down,
And worship me as thy superior Lord,

---

[42]Robbing, despoiling, plundering their colonies (see *OED* 1.a).

[43]"First becoming ambitious from their triumphs" (see Loh's paraphrase 137–38n). Read "insulting vanity" as in apposition with "triumph." A comma after "triumph" might have helped, but there is none in the early editions. Campbell nevertheless inserts it, though Shawcross, Carey, and Orgel and Strong do not.

[44]The word *scene* meant "stage performance" in the seventeenth century, as Carey points out (142n), but here Milton is referring to the spectacles frequently occurring in the Roman Colosseum—gladiatorial combat, living victims sacrificed to fierce animals—that might cause the so-called military virtues to crumble in the Roman populace and "effeminacy" to settle on erstwhile warriors. The perspective here is very close to the angel Michael's accusation of "effeminate slackness" applied to men who succumb too easily to pleasure and vice in *Paradise Lost* 11.634. Compare *Samson Agonistes* 410 "foul effeminacy held me yok't" and 562 "Effeminatly vanquish't." The moral point of view is hierarchical: when men violate their place in the natural hierarchy and become effeminate, they become vicious, luxurious, weak, and slack in duty. Compare *OED* 2, "To make womanish or unmanly; to enervate" and the citation from Thomas Hanmer, *Ancient Ecclesiastical History* (1577), "He effeminated his souldiers with all kind of delicacy and lasciviousnesse."

[45]Sin enslaves by distancing people or angels from God; and, Milton implies, those who enslave themselves by vices deserve to be slaves. Compare *Paradise Lost* 3.125, "Till they enthrall themselves" and 6.181, "Thy self not free, but to thy self enthrall'd."

[46]In Daniel 4.10–12, Nebuchadnezzar has a prophetic dream of "a tree in the midst of the Earth, . . . and the height thereof reached unto heaven, and the sight thereof to the end of all the earth." The dream is interpreted by Daniel; it is fulfilled; and it helps Nebuchadnezzar return to the God of Israel. Christian exegetes could see the dream sequence as a prophecy of Jesus's rule of earth, especially considering the genealogical images of trees issuing from Adam and Eve or David and flowering in Jesus, as they were represented in many sixteenth- and seventeenth-century Bibles.

[47]Another of the dreams of Nebuchadnezzar intepreted by Daniel is of the idol with feet of clay, destroyed by "a stone . . . cut out without hands" (Daniel 2.34). Again the image of "a king of kings . . . given . . . a kingdom, power, and strength, and glory" (2.37) that Daniel attributes to Nebuchadnezzar fits Jesus as king of kings.

[48]"And of his kingdom there shall be no end" (Luke 1.33).

[49]Again, see Luke 4.6.

Easily done, and hold them[50] all of me;
For what can less so great a gift deserve?
　　Whom thus our Saviour answer'd with disdain.　　　　170
I never lik'd thy talk, thy offers less,
Now both abhor, since thou hast dar'd to utter
The abominable terms, impious condition;
But I endure the time, till which expir'd,
Thou hast permission on me.[51] It is written　　　　175
The first of all Commandments, Thou shalt worship
The Lord thy God, and only him shalt serve;
And dar'st thou to the Son of God propound
To worship thee accurst, now more accurst
For this attempt bolder then that on *Eve*,　　　　180
And more blasphemous?[52] which expect to rue.°　　　REGRET
The Kingdoms of the world to thee were giv'n,
Permitted rather, and by thee usurp't,
Other donation° none thou canst produce:　　　GIFT
If given, by whom but by the King of Kings,　　　　185
God over all supreme? if giv'n to thee,
By thee how fairly is the Giver now
Repaid? But gratitude in thee is lost
Long since.[53] Wert thou so void of fear or shame,
As offer them to me the Son of God,　　　　190
To me my own, on such abhorred pact,
That I fall down and worship thee as God?
Get thee behind me;[54] plain thou now appear'st
That Evil one, Satan for ever damn'd.
　　To whom the Fiend with fear abasht reply'd.　　　　195
Be not so sore offended, Son of God;
Though Sons of God both Angels are and Men,[55]
If I to try whether in higher sort
Then these thou bear'st that title,[56] have propos'd
What both from Men and Angels I receive,　　　　200
Tetrarchs[57] of fire, air, flood, and on the earth
Nations besides from all the quarter'd winds,[58]
God of this world invok't and world beneath;
Who then thou art, whose coming is foretold

---

[50]I.e., all the kingdoms of the world.

[51]I.e., "You are at liberty to try to tempt me." The permission involved is that of God the Father.

[52]Accented on the second syllable. Satan's attack on the incarnate God is more blasphemous than any attack on a purely human being.

[53]I.e., "You have not understood the meaning of gratitude for some time now."

[54]"And Jesus answered and said unto him, Get thee behind me, Satan: for it is written, Thou shalt worship the Lord thy God, and him only shalt thou serve" (Luke 4.8).

[55]Angels are called "sons of God" at Job 38.7; men are called "sons of God" in 1 John 1, 2 and elsewhere throughout the New Testament. They are alluded to in this way only indirectly in Isaiah 64.8, then the angels address God: "But now, O Lord, thou art our father." Thanks to Jim Orrick for pointing these out to me. Hugh MacCallum, *Milton and the Sons of God: The Divine Image in Milton's Epic Poetry* (Toronto: U of Toronto P, 1986) investigates the image very thoroughly.

[56]"If I, to test whether or not you bear the title 'Son of God' in any higher sense of rank than those other beings titled 'Sons of God.'" Satan presumptuously has been testing the true Son of God against the devils who posed as Sons of God and whose nomenclature is false and misleading.

[57]"A ruler of a fourth part, or of one of four parts, divisions, elements, etc.; also a subordinate ruler generally" (*OED* trans. and fig. 2.a, citing this passage). Herod the Tetrarch had been the ruler who pursued Jesus as an infant. Here Satan divides the four elements into a tetrarchy and gives demons control over both elements and winds from the four corners of the Earth.

[58]North, south, east, and west winds were often pictured on Renaissance world maps as blowing from four corners. See Gordon Campbell, "Milton's Catalogue of the Winds," *Milton Quarterly* 18 (1984): 125–28.

To me so fatal, me it most concerns.   205
The tryal hath indamag'd thee° no way,   HURT YOUR REPUTATION
Rather more honour left and more esteem;
Me naught° advantag'd, missing what I aim'd.   IN NO WAY
Therefore let pass, as they are transitory,
The Kingdoms of this world; I shall no more   210
Advise thee, gain them as thou canst, or not.
And thou thy self seem'st otherwise inclin'd
Then to a worldly Crown, addicted° more   DESTINED
To contemplation and profound dispute,
As by that early action may be judg'd,   215
When slipping from thy Mothers eye thou went'st
Alone into the Temple;[59] there was found
Among the gravest Rabbies[60] disputant
On points and questions fitting *Moses* Chair,[61]
Teaching not taught; the childhood shews the man,   220
As morning shews the day. Be famous then
By wisdom; as thy Empire must extend,
So let extend thy mind o're all the world,
In knowledge, all things in it comprehend,
All knowledge is not couch't° in *Moses* Law,   HIDDEN   225
The *Pentateuch*[62] or what the Prophets wrote,
The *Gentiles* also know, and write, and teach
To admiration,[63] led by Natures light;[64]
And with the *Gentiles* much thou must converse,
Ruling them by perswasion as thou mean'st,   230
Without thir learning how wilt thou with them,
Or they with thee hold conversation meet?
How wilt thou reason with them, how refute
Thir Idolisms,[65] Traditions, Paradoxes?
Error by his own arms is best evinc't.[66]   235
Look once more e're we leave this specular[67] Mount
Westward, much nearer by Southwest, behold
Where on the *Ægean* shore a City stands
Built nobly, pure the air, and light[68] the soil,
Athens the eye of *Greece*,[69] Mother of Arts   240
And Eloquence, native to famous wits[70]

---

[59]According to Luke 2, "the child Jesus tarried behind in Jerusalem; and Joseph and his mother knew not of it" (43).

[60]"And it came to pass, that after three days they found him in the temple, sitting in the midst of the doctors, both hearing them, and asking them questions. And all that heard him were astonished at his understanding and answers" (Luke 2.46–47). Milton quite appropriately makes the "doctors," learned men, into rabbis.

[61]The chair in which the doctors expounded the truth, as in Jesus's scornful statement, "The scribes and the Pharisees sit in Moses' seat" (Matthew 23.2).

[62]The first five books of the Bible, supposed to have been written by Moses.

[63]"Teach to the point of being awe-inspiring." "Admiration" was a stronger word than it is at present, meaning "astonishment" (*OED* 1).

[64]The "light of nature" was supposed to be "the capacity given to man of discerning certain divine truths without the help of revelation" (*OED* 6.b). Though Christians generally acknowledged that ancient wise men such as Socrates or Plato (labeled here as "Gentiles") might possess a certain amount of "truth," it is presumptuous of Satan to ask the Son of God to rely on pagan wisdom as compared to divine truth revealed in Scripture.

[65]"Idolatries." First used in Sylvester's translation of DuBartas's *Divine Weekes* 2.4.5.

[66]"Error is best conquered by one wearing his armor."

[67]This mountain being used as a lookout or watchtower. Implicit in the word "specular" are the meanings for Latin *speculum*, "mirror," and *specula*, "watch tower." In other words, the vision from the Mount may not be a true one, but a mirage or mirror image.

[68]I.e., tillable, fertile.

[69]Aristotle, *Rhetoric* 3.10.7, defines Athens and Sparta as the eyes (seats of intelligence, centers of wisdom) of Greece.

[70]Intelligent people who expressed their thoughts in verbal art. (John Donne was considered a wit.) But the word also contains overtones of "useless display of book learning."

Or hospitable, in her sweet recess,
City or Suburban, studious walks and shades;
See there the Olive Grove of *Academe*,[71]
Plato's retirement, where the *Attic* Bird[72]   245
Trills her thick-warbl'd notes the summer long,
There flowrie hill *Hymettus*[73] with the sound
Of Bees industrious murmur[74] oft invites
To studious musing; there *Ilissus*[75] rouls
His whispering stream; within the walls then view   250
The schools of antient Sages;[76] his who bred
Great *Alexander* to subdue the world,[77]
Lyceum there, and painted *Stoa*[78] next:
There thou shalt hear and learn the secret power
Of harmony[79] in tones and numbers hit   255
By voice or hand, and various-measur'd verse,
Æolian charms and *Dorian Lyric* Odes,[80]
And his who gave them breath, but higher sung,
Blind *Melesigenes* thence *Homer* call'd,[81]
Whose Poem *Phœbus* challeng'd for his own.[82]   260
Thence what the lofty grave Tragœdians taught
In *Chorus* or *Iambic*,[83] teachers best
Of moral prudence, with delight receiv'd
In brief sententious precepts, while they treat
Of fate, and chance, and change in human life;   265
High actions, and high passions best describing:[84]

[71]The famous Grove of Academe, a public park and exercise area about a mile northwest of Athens, which contained groves of olive trees. In walking there with his pupils, Plato established a method of teaching and gave the word *academy* to western civilization.

[72]The nightingale, called *Attica avis* in Martial *Epodes* 1.46. As Newton pointed out, "Milton was delighted with the nightingale; no poet has introduc'd it so often, or spoken of it with such rapture as he . . . " (245n).

[73]Hymettus is a mountain about two miles from Athens whose flower-covered slopes encourage bees to produce famous honey, flavored by the thyme that grows there.

[74]The word in this case echoes the sounds of bees and is in no way like Satan's earlier murmuring. The industriousness of the bees not only produces a comforting sound but gives an example of productive labor to humanity and thus provokes thought while providing a kind of music.

[75]A small river originating on Hymettus and flowing south of Athens into the sea.

[76]The nature of being sagacious is being argued here, and the Son of God will have to answer Satan "sagely" after this speech is done, as if Christian wisdom must inevitably replace pagan wisdom.

[77]The school of Aristotle, tutor of Alexander the Great. The Lyceum was a park east of Athens (and not, precisely, "within the walls," as Carey reminds us [253n]), where Aristotle and his pupils used to stroll and discuss various topics. Hence they were called "peripatetics" ("strollers") and the school of philosophy "peripatetic."

[78]The covered porch of the market of Athens, painted with famous frescoes by Polygnotus (Pausanias 1.15), used as a place of public debate by various schools of philosophers, among them the Stoics led by the philosopher Zeno.

[79]Harmony seems to be used in a broader educational sense, as Milton uses it in "L'Allegro," "the hidden soul of harmony" (144), or in a religious sense as in *Comus*: "And give resounding grace to all Heav'ns Harmonies" (243). The soul of music has meaning hidden in its mathematical structure, or numbers.

[80]Two schools of Greek lyric poetry were the Aeolian, exemplified in the passionate love poetry of Sappho and Alcaeus ("charm" is etymologically related to *carmen*, Latin for song), and Dorian, for which Pindar with his heroic odes was the chief example.

[81]According to two early lives of Homer, that attributed to Herodotus and that of Pseudo-Plutarch, Homer's mother, Critheis, named him Melesigenes, because he was born near the river Meles in Ionia, on the coast of Asia Minor. When he went blind, the Cumaeans called him Ὅμηρος, their word for blind (see MacKellar 259). Birthplaces for Homer, however, were located all over the Aegean Sea.

[82]There is an epigram in the *Greek Anthology* quoting Phoebus Apollo as saying "The song is mine, but divine Homer wrote it down" (9.455; quoted by MacKellar 260n).

[83]Iambic trimeter was the meter most often used during dramatic scenes, whereas during choral scenes the meter might vary quite widely. Compare Milton's practices in the choruses of *Samson Agonistes*. The function of the chorus was also varied: it might give advice, castigate wrongdoers, pray to the gods, or cheer the victories of heroes.

[84]Compare *Paradise Lost* 2.559–60, for other fallen angels discussing the subjects of tragedy. Milton paraphrases Aristotle's *Poetics* in his own preface to *Samson Agonistes*: tragedy is "to be of power by raising pity and fear, or terror, to purge the mind of those and such like passions, that is to temper and reduce them to just measure with a kind of delight, stirr'd up by reading or seeing those passions well imitated." There is a question in this passage of whether Milton has Satan speaking from the perspective of Satan or from the perspective of Milton. MacKellar finds that this analysis of tragedy represents

Thence to the famous Orators repair,
Those antient, whose resistless eloquence
Wielded[85] at will that fierce Democratie,°   DEMOCRACY
Shook the Arsenal and fulmin'd° over *Greece*,[86]   SPOKE THUNDEROUSLY   270
To *Macedon*, and *Artaxerxes* Throne;
To sage Philosophy next lend thine ear,
From Heaven descended to the low-rooft house[87]
Of *Socrates*, see there his Tenement,
Whom well inspir'd the Oracle pronounc'd[88]   275
Wisest of men; from whose mouth issu'd forth
Mellifluous streams that water'd all the schools
Of Academics old and new, with those
Sirnam'd[89] *Peripatetics*, and the Sect
Epicurean, and the *Stoic* severe;[90]   280
These here revolve, or, as thou lik'st, at home,
Till time mature thee to a Kingdom's waight;[91]
These rules will render thee a King compleat
Within thy self, much more with Empire joyn'd.

  To whom our Saviour sagely thus repli'd.   285
Think not but that I know these things, or think
I know them not; not therefore am I short
Of knowing what I aught: he who receives
Light from above, from the fountain of light,[92]
No other doctrine needs, though granted true;   290
But these are false, or little else but dreams,
Conjectures, fancies, built on nothing firm.
The first and wisest of them all profess'd
To know this only, that he nothing knew;[93]
The next to fabling fell and smooth conceits,[94]   295

Satan as "a kind of fatalist" (265n), but the summary is, I believe, a fair representation of Milton's opinion of Greek tragedy and does not represent a distorted Satanic perspective.

[85]"Ruled," a sense implied in a phrase like "wielded a kingdom."

[86]The eloquent opinions of orators like Demosthenes or political leaders like Pericles, in other words, had the power of thunder and lightning. E.C. Baldwin, in "'Shook the Arsenal': A Note on *Paradise Regained*," *Philological Quarterly* 18 (1939): 218–22, points to Aristophanes's *Acharnians* 531 for the Greek sense of "shake," and MacKellar adds that an oration of Demosthenes was said to have interrupted the building of the Arsenal, the naval storehouse of the Piraeus, port of Athens, a very famous landmark (270n). In Aristophanes's comedy, Pericles is pictured satirically as he attempts to inspire the Athenians while Sparta was attacking the city and while ships of the Athenian fleet were warring, together with those of the Egyptians, against the Persian king, Artaxerxes. Milton's reference is obscure enough so that it was not identified until Baldwin's article.

[87]Socrates is pictured as a poor but honest man whose house is humble and small. "Low-rooft" is a compound used in Sylvester's DuBartas 2.1.4.90: "The low-rooft broken wals (In stead of Arras) hang with Spiders' cauls." The word "low" indicates social rank as well as poverty, but not necessarily poverty of spirit, as in Milton's "Passion" 18, where "low-rooft" is applied to Christ's body. The word "Tenement" might indicate a rented portion of a larger house (OED 4.a), but it does not carry the modern American sense of "overcrowded apartment house."

[88]In Plato's *Apology* 21, Socrates reports that Chaerephon had asked the Delphic orator if there were any wiser man than Sophocles and was answered that there was no one wiser. The report became the impetus behind Socrates's questioning of other men reputed to be wise.

[89]Surname, in modern standard English spelling. In the usage of Milton's printers, the two spellings are equally divided, with a slight edge to "surname." One false etymology for the word as used in English made it derive from "sire" plus "name"; hence the spelling.

[90]Peripatetics, as explained in n. 76 above, were followers of Aristotle; Epicureans of Epicurus, whose hedonistic, pleasure-seeking philosophy Milton identified with libertinism (see Yale 2: 495); and Stoics became "the budge doctors of the *Stoic* fur" that the evil Comus makes fun of in *Comus* 707 .

[91]"Until time matures you enough to take on the heavy responsibility of a kingdom."

[92]See Roland Swardson's work on the subject, *Poetry and The Fountain of Light; Observations on the Conflict between Christian and Classical Traditions in Seventeenth-Century Poetry* (Columbia: U of Missouri P, 1962) and *Paradise Lost* 3.375.

[93]A paraphrase of what is probably Socrates's most famous saying about himself, that he knew only that he knew nothing.

[94]A rejection of Plato for mythologizing and making false parables, as in the story of Atlantis, which Milton never mentioned, or, for that matter, the construct of the entire *Republic*. Critics have had difficulties with the rejection of what Milton had called "the divine volumes of *Plato*" (*Apology against a Pamphlet;* Yale 1: 891), but he was just as capable of labeling the philosopher "*Plato* . . . in his heathenism" (*Tetrachordon;* Yale 2: 593), even in 1644.

A third sort doubted all things, though plain sence;[95]
Others in vertue plac'd felicity,
But vertue joyn'd with riches and long life,
In corporal pleasure he, and careless ease,
The *Stoic*[96] last in Philosophic pride,　　　　　　　　　　　300
By him call'd vertue; and his vertuous man,
Wise, perfect in himself, and all possessing
Equal to God, oft shames not to prefer,
As fearing God nor man, contemning all
Wealth, pleasure, pain or torment, death and life,　　　　305
Which when he lists,° he leaves, or boasts he can,　　IS INCLINED TO
For all his tedious talk is but vain boast,
Or subtle shifts conviction to evade.
Alas what can they teach, and not mislead;
Ignorant of themselves, of God much more,　　　　　　　310
And how the world began, and how man fell
Degraded by himself, on grace depending?
Much of the Soul they talk, but all awrie,
And in themselves seek vertue, and to themselves
All glory arrogate,° to God give none,　　LAY CLAIM TO　　315
Rather accuse him under usual names,
Fortune and Fate, as one regardless quite
Of mortal things. Who therefore seeks in these
True wisdom, finds her not, or by delusion
Far worse, her false resemblance only meets,　　　　　320
An empty cloud. However many books
Wise men have said are wearisom; who[97] reads
Incessantly, and to his reading brings not
A spirit and judgment equal or superior,
(And what he brings, what needs he elsewhere seek)　　325
Uncertain and unsettl'd still remains,
Deep verst in books and shallow in himself,[98]
Crude° or intoxicate, collecting toys,　　INDIGESTIBLE
And trifles for choice matters, worth a spunge;[99]
As Children gathering pibles[100] on the shore.　　　　330
Or if I would delight my private hours
With Music or with Poem, where so soon
As in our native Language can I find
That solace? All our Law and Story strew'd

---

[95]The Skeptics, followers of Pyrrho of Elis (c. 360–270 BCE), who believed that it was impossible to know anything for sure and that therefore one should remain unflappable and aloof from opinion.

[96]I have restored the italics on a proper noun normally italicized. There was a long tradition of attacking Stoicism, which disavowed reliance on worldly goods but permitted suicide, among Christian Church Fathers such as Lactantius. Milton opposed "the apathy of Stoics" in *On Christian Doctrine*, because "sensibility to pain, and complaints and lamentations, are not inconsistent with true patience, as may be seen from the example of Job and of other holy men in adversity" (2.10; Yale 6: 740). Stoic patience, in other words, is of little value when compared with Christian patience.

[97]Substitute "He who reads."

[98]Speaking for the value of inspiration or inner light over shallow book learning, or, as Lewalski (291–95) points out, the value of wisdom (*sapientia*) over knowledge (*scientia*).

[99]"Worth using a sponge on, or erasing."

[100]Pebbles. The word was also spelled "peebles" and "poppels" in the sixteenth and seventeenth centuries.

With Hymns, our Psalms with artful terms inscrib'd,[101]   335
Our Hebrew Songs and Harps in *Babylon*,[102]
That pleas'd so well our Victors ear, declare
That rather *Greece* from us these Arts deriv'd;
Ill imitated, while they loudest sing
The vices of thir Deities, and thir own   340
In Fable, Hymn, or Song, so personating°   PLAYING THE PART OF
Thir Gods ridiculous, and themselves past shame.[103]
Remove their swelling Epithetes thick laid
As varnish on a Harlots cheek,[104] the rest,
Thin sown with aught of profit or delight,   345
Will far be found unworthy to compare
With *Sion*'s songs, to all true tasts[105] excelling,
Where God is prais'd aright, and Godlike men,
The Holiest of Holies,[106] and his Saints;
Such are from God inspir'd, not such from thee;   350
Unless where moral vertue is express't
By light of Nature not in all quite lost.
Thir Orators thou then extoll'st, as those
The top of Eloquence, Statists[107] indeed,
And lovers of thir Country, as may seem;   355
But herein to our Prophets far beneath,
As men divinely taught, and better teaching
The solid rules of Civil Government
In thir majestic unaffected stile[108]
Then all the Oratory of *Greece* and *Rome*.   360
In them is plainest taught, and easiest learnt,
What makes a Nation happy, and keeps it so,
What ruins Kingdoms, and lays Cities flat;
These only with our Law best form a King.

    So spake the Son of God; but Satan now   365
Quite at a loss, for all his darts were spent,
Thus to our Saviour with stern brow reply'd.

---

[101]The Bible, in other words, has all the expressions of art necessary for the fulfillment of the Christian artist: songs, hymns, psalms, fables (extended narratives). In this view, later Greek arts expressed in the genres of lyrical poetry, epic, or drama are derived from and imitative of the kind of poetry and generic expression found in the Bible. Psalms are the best of lyric poetry and the book of Job the model for the brief epic that Milton is writing. Concentrating on the Psalms and their influence on *Paradise Regain'd*, Radzinowicz summarizes "Milton thought Hebrew poetry worthiest of imitation because it was 'the most beautiful and skillful poetry ever composed'" and therefore "he imitated it comprehensively too, without respect to speaker, as a fluent medium recognizably scriptural, a verse on which to play variations" (*Milton's Epics* 85).

[102]"By the rivers of Babylon, there we sat down, yea, we wept, when we remembered Zion. We hanged our harps upon the willows in the midst thereof. For there they that carried us away captive required of us a song; and they that wasted us required of us mirth, saying, Sing us one of the songs of Zion" (Psalm 137.1–3).

[103]The often lewd or ridiculous comic presentation of the Greek stage, in other words, was only a pale echo of the high seriousness of the proto-Christian art of the tribes of Israel.

[104]Their imagery is like heavily applied makeup on a whore's cheek. Compare Claudius's description of his own sinful state as "The harlot's cheek, beautied with plast'ring art" (*Hamlet* 3.1.50). Radzinowicz reminds us that Satan's florid style is like the harlot's cheek, as compared with "the Son's plain style" (*Milton's Epics* 85).

[105]The first use recorded of the word "taste" in the sense of "good taste": "The sense of what is appropriate, harmonious, or beautiful; esp. discernment and appreciation of the beautiful in nature or art; spec. the faculty of perceiving and enjoying what is excellent in art, literature, and the like" (*OED* 8.a).

[106]Milton makes the individual soul the Holy of Holies, removing significance from any particular shrine. In *Reason of Church-Government*, as elsewhere, Milton mentions priestly imitation of Christ as blasphemous: the "type of Christ in some one particular, as of entring yearly into the Holy of holies and such like, rested upon the High Priest only as more immediately personating our Saviour" (Yale 2: 773).

[107]In 1641, Milton put statists (politicians) in an equally unattractive context: the English Bishops, he writes "suffer'd themselvs to be the common stales [inexpensive prostitutes] to countenance with their prostituted Gravities every Politick Fetch [trick, ruse] that was then on foot, as oft as the Potent *Statists* pleas'd to employ them" (*Of Reformation*; Yale 1: 531).

[108]The Old Testament prophets, such as Moses, are to be considered better stylists in rhetoric than classical orators.

Since neither wealth, nor honour, arms nor arts,
Kingdom nor Empire pleases thee, nor aught
By me propos'd in life contemplative,   370
Or active, tended on° by glory, or fame,   ATTENDED
What dost thou° in this World? the Wilderness   WHAT ARE YOU DOING
For thee is fittest place, I found thee there,
And thither will return thee, yet remember
What I foretell thee, soon thou shalt have cause   375
To wish thou never hadst rejected thus
Nicely° or cautiously my offer'd aid,   FASTIDIOUSLY
Which would have set thee in short time with ease
On *David*'s Throne; or Throne of all the world,
Now at full age,[109] fulness of time, thy season,   380
When Prophesies of thee are best fullfill'd.
Now contrary, if I read aught in Heaven,[110]
Or Heav'n write aught of Fate, by what the Stars
Voluminous, or single characters,[111]
In their conjunction met, give me to spell,[112]   385
Sorrows, and labours, opposition, hate,
Attends thee, scorns, reproaches, injuries,
Violence and stripes,[113] and lastly cruel death,
A Kingdom they portend thee, but what Kingdom,
Real or Allegoric[114] I discern not,   390
Nor when, eternal sure, as without end,
Without beginning; for no date prefixt
Directs me in the Starry Rubric[115] set.
So saying he took (for still he knew his power
Not yet expir'd) and to the Wilderness   395
Brought back the Son of God, and left him there,
Feigning° to disappear. Darkness now rose,   PRETENDING
As day-light sunk, and brought in lowring° night   FROWNING
Her shadowy off-spring unsubstantial both,[116]
Privation meer of light and absent day.   400
Our Saviour meek and with untroubl'd mind
After his aerie jaunt,[117] though hurried sore,°   SORELY HURRIED
Hungry and cold[118] betook him to his rest,

---

[109]"Full age" is, in English law, the twenty-first year, supposedly the age of emotional maturity (*OED* 1.1.3).
[110]Satan is reading Christ's horoscope, a practice that Milton felt was valid at least for Christ: "However, both the wise men who came to Jerusalem from the east, and the star itself, which shone at Christ's birth, Matt. ii.1.2, show that there is some astrology which is neither useless nor unlawful" (*On Christian Doctrine* 2.5; Yale 6: 696). Milton apparently had his own horoscope taken (Parker 951; and Harry Rusche, "A Reading of John Milton's Horoscope," *Milton Quarterly* 13 [1979]: 6–11).
[111]"In many volumes of lore or in single letters."
[112]Either in the conventional sense of discovering the sense of words by spelling them out or in the magical sense of interpreting mystical messages or divining.
[113]The stripes incurred when Christ is scourged or whipped (see Matthew 20.19, predicting that the scribes "shall deliver him to the Gentiles to mock, and to scourge, and to crucify him").
[114]Milton's use of the word, juxtaposing it with "Real," suggests that he had indeed rejected allegory as a valid mode and that, at least at this point, "Allegoric" means something like "fabulous." But Milton's customary use of the word relates it to biblical types (see Yale 1: 714) and hence is not pejorative.
[115]The rubric of the stars would resemble the rubric (red-lettered text) in the margins of prayer books, instructing the reader in what to do or how to interpret the ceremony.
[116]I.e., both darkness and her offspring night are unsubstantial (lack substance and value).
[117]"A fatiguing or troublesome journey" (*OED* 1), in this case through the air.
[118]Campbell adds a comma here (there is no authority for it in the early texts); in this case, the comma might help the modern reader with the syntax of the sentence, since "Hungry and cold" modify "Our Saviour."

Wherever, under some concourse[119] of shades
Whose branching arms thick intertwind might shield
From dews and damps of night his shelter'd head,   405
But shelter'd slept in vain, for at his head
The Tempter watch'd, and soon with ugly dreams
Disturb'd his sleep;[120] and either Tropic[121] now
Gan thunder,° and both ends of Heav'n, the Clouds   DID THUNDER
From many a horrid rift abortive[122] pour'd   410
Fierce rain with lightning mixt, water with fire
In ruine reconcil'd: nor slept the winds
Within thir stony caves, but rush'd abroad
From the four hinges of the world,[123] and fell
On the vext Wilderness, whose tallest Pines,   415
Though rooted deep as high, and sturdiest Oaks
Bow'd their Stiff necks, loaden with stormy blasts,
Or torn up sheer: ill wast thou shrouded° then,   SHELTERED
O patient Son of God, yet only stoodst
Unshaken; nor yet staid the terror there,[124]   420
Infernal Ghosts, and Hellish Furies, round
Environ'd thee, some howl'd, some yell'd, some shriek'd,
Some bent at thee thir fiery darts,[125] while thou
Sat'st unappall'd in calm and sinless peace.
Thus pass'd the night so foul till morning fair   425
Came forth with Pilgrim steps in amice gray;[126]
Who with her radiant finger[127] still'd the roar
Of thunder, chas'd the clouds, and laid° the winds,   LAID TO REST
And grisly Spectres, which the Fiend had rais'd   430
To tempt the Son of God with terrors dire.
And now the Sun with more effectual beams
Had chear'd the face of Earth, and dry'd the wet°   MOISTURE
From drooping plant, or dropping tree; the birds
Who all things now behold more fresh and green,   435
After a night of storm so ruinous,
Clear'd up° their choicest notes in bush and spray   BRIGHTENED
To gratulate° the sweet return of morn;   EXPRESS JOY AT
Nor yet amidst this joy and brightest morn
Was absent, after all his mischief[128] done,   440
The Prince of darkness, glad would also seem
Of this fair change, and to our Saviour came,
Yet with no new device,° they all were spent,   CONTRIVANCE, TRICK
Rather by this his last affront° resolv'd,   OPEN INSULT

---

[119]"An assemblage of things brought together" (*OED* 4, citing this instance).
[120]Following the procedure of *Paradise Lost*, in which Satan is discovered "Squat like a Toad, close at the eare of *Eve*, / Assaying by his Devilish art to reach / The Organs of her Fancie" (4.800–02).
[121]Probably "from either side of the sky," since the tropics of Capricorn or Cancer have no relevance to where Satan and the Son are situated.
[122]"Rendering fruitless or barren" (compare *OED* A.1.b, which cites *Paradise Lost* 2.441 "abortive gulf").
[123]The four cardinal points of the compass, deriving "hinges" from Latin *cardo*, "hinge," if Carey, following Newton, is correct (413n).
[124]"Nor did the [T]error remain satisfied with that." Compare the use of "terror" as something like an allegorical entity in *Paradise Lost* 2.704 (meaning Death) and 6.859 "terrours" (see 6.859n).
[125]I.e., some bent their bows, aiming their fiery darts (arrows) at him.
[126]"An article of costume of the religious orders, made of, or lined with grey fur" (*OED* 1).
[127]I.e., the rays of the sun.
[128]Not just pranks but evil deeds (the word had a stronger sense of wrongdoing and was often associated with evil spirits).

Desperate of better course, to vent his rage, 445
And mad despight to be so oft repell'd.
Him walking on a Sunny hill he found,
Back'd on the North and West by a thick wood,
Out of the wood he starts in wonted shape;[129]
And in a careless[130] mood thus to him said. 450

 Fair morning yet betides thee Son of God,
After a dismal night; I heard the rack[131]
As Earth and Skie would mingle;[132] but my self
Was distant; and these flaws,° though mortals fear them SQUALLS
As dangerous to the pillard frame of Heaven,[133] 455
Or to the Earths dark basis° underneath, BASE, FOUNDATION
Are to the main[134] as inconsiderable,
And harmless, if not wholsom, as a sneeze
To mans less universe,[135] and soon are gone;
Yet as being oft times noxious° where they light INJURIOUS, HARMFUL 460
On man, beast, plant, wastful and turbulent,
Like turbulencies in the affairs of men,
Over whose heads they rore, and seem to point,
They oft fore-signifie and threaten ill:
This Tempest at this Desert most was bent;° AIMED 465
Of men at thee, for only thou here dwell'st.
Did I not tell thee, if thou didst reject
The perfet[136] season° offer'd with my aid OPPORTUNE TIME
To win thy destin'd seat, but wilt prolong
All to the push of Fate,° persue thy way THE PRESSURE OF DESTINY 470
Of gaining *David*'s Throne no man knows when,
For both the when and how is no where told,
Thou shalt be what thou art ordain'd, no doubt;
For Angels have proclaim'd it, but concealing
The time and means: each act is rightliest done, 475
Not when it must, but when it may be best.
If thou observe not this, be sure to find,
What I foretold thee, many a hard assay° TEST, ORDEAL
Of dangers, and adversities and pains,
E're thou of *Israel*'s Scepter[137] get fast hold; 480
Whereof this ominous night that clos'd thee round,
So many terrors, voices, prodigies
May warn thee, as a sure fore-going sign.
 So talk'd he, while the Son of God went on

---

[129]This would seem to be his customary ("wonted") shape, with cloven hooves and a tail, but, as Pope 49–50 points out, he will be described later as "without wing / Of *Hippogrif*" (541–42). She would have us read "his usual disguise."

[130]Considering what has passed and will pass between them—all but eternal mortal combat—Satan's hypocritical carelessness at this point seems funny. Much of what he does, however, seems to be whistling in the dark.

[131]Probably "crash," or loud noise (see *OED* 1), but with the destructive force implied in the phrase "rack and ruin."

[132]Compare *Aeneid* 1.133–34, *caelum terramque . . . miscere.*

[133]"The pillars of heaven tremble" in Job 26.11.

[134]The broad expanse on the surface of the earth, rather than its underpinnings. See *OED* 5.b. It may help to see "main" as short for "mainland."

[135]"Humankind's smaller universe," i.e., the body.

[136]The spelling may indicate a preference of Milton, slipping through the process of composition. The *OED* editors point out, somewhat imprecisely, that "The words perfect and imperfect occur 34 times in Milton's Poems, and in 22 instances the spelling is perfet, imperfet (A. J. Wyatt Note to P.R. iv. 468)." See Shawcross, "Milton's Spelling," in *A Milton Encyclopedia.*

[137]"[T]here shall come a Star out of Jacob, and a Sceptre shall rise out of Israel, and shall smite the corners of Moab, and destroy all the children of Sheth" (Numbers 25.17).

And staid not,° but in brief him answer'd thus.   DID NOT HESITATE   485
    Mee worse then wet thou find'st not;[138] other harm
Those terrors which thou speak'st of, did me none;
I never fear'd they could, though noising loud
And threatning nigh; what they can do as signs
Betok'ning, or ill boding, I contemn   490
As false portents,[139] not sent from God, but thee;
Who knowing I shall raign past thy preventing,
Obtrud'st thy offer'd aid, that I accepting
At least might seem to hold all power of thee,
Ambitious spirit, and wouldst be thought my God,   495
And storm'st refus'd,[140] thinking to terrifie
Mee to thy will; desist, thou art discern'd
And toil'st in vain, nor me in vain molest.°   ANNOY, VEX
    To whom the Fiend now swoln with rage reply'd:
Then hear, O Son of *David*, Virgin-born;   500
For Son of God to me is yet in doubt,
Of the Messiah I have heard foretold
By all the Prophets; of thy birth at length
Announc't by *Gabriel* with the first I knew,
And of the Angelic Song in *Bethlehem* field,   505
On thy birth-night, that sung thee Saviour born.[141]
From that time seldom have I ceas'd to eye
Thy infancy, thy childhood, and thy youth,
Thy manhood last, though yet in private bred;
Till at the Ford of *Jordan* whither all   510
Flock'd to the Baptist, I among the rest,
Though not to be Baptiz'd, by voice from Heav'n
Heard thee pronounc'd the Son of God belov'd.
Thenceforth I thought thee worth my nearer view
And narrower Scrutiny, that I might learn   515
In what degree° or meaning thou art call'd   APPROPRIATE RANK
The Son of God, which bears no single sence;
The Son of God I also am, or was,
And if I was, I am; relation stands;
All men are Sons of God;[142] yet thee I thought   520
In some respect far higher so declar'd.
Therefore I watch'd thy footsteps from that hour,
And follow'd thee still on to this wast wild;
Where by all best conjectures[143] I collect°
Thou art to be my fatal enemy.   GATHER, RECALL   525

---

[138]The simplicity of the image and terseness of the reply show the honesty and directness—not without sarcasm—of the Son of God's answer. Corns admires its "bluntness," asking the modern reader to "consider how much more striking it would have been for a contemporary audience attuned to the grandiloquent civilities of formal address." Satan's forms of address by contrast represent "the insidious politeness of treacherous figures" (*Milton's Language* 20–21).

[139]Tempestuous weather was thought to be brought by demons and witches riding the whirlwind; thus a heavy storm was a demonic portent of evil things to come.

[140]"And, when you were refused, you stormed [raged] yourself."

[141]Satan's narrative places him as an observer of Christ's birth and seats the beginning of his thoughts of envy and revenge at Christ's incarnation.

[142]By identifying himself as a Son of God (see Job 1.6), Satan attempts to usurp Jesus's title. But, "[b]ecause he is himself confused and forever 'despoiled' (*PR* 3.139) of singularity, because ambiguity is part of his diet, Satan cannot penetrate the coverings of signs to the 'single sense' of the 'Son of God'" (Shoaf 166).

[143]Probably "The interpretation of signs or omens; interpretation of dreams; divining; a conclusion as to coming events drawn from signs or omens; a forecast, a prognostication" (*OED* 1).

Good reason then, if I before-hand seek
To understand my Adversary,[144] who
And what he is; his wisdom, power, intent,
By parl, or composition, truce, or league[145]
To win him, or win from him what I can.   530
And opportunity I here have had
To try thee, sift[146] thee, and confess have found thee
Proof against all temptation as a rock
Of Adamant,[147] and as a Center, firm
To the utmost of meer man both wise and good,   535
Not more; for Honours, Riches, Kingdoms, Glory
Have been before contemn'd, and may agen:
Therefore to know what more thou art then man,
Worth naming Son of God by voice from Heav'n,
Another method° I must now begin.   MODE OF DISCOURSE   540
    So saying he caught him up, and without wing
Of *Hippogrif*[148] bore through the Air sublime[149]
Over the Wilderness and o're the Plain;
Till underneath them fair *Jerusalem*,
The holy City lifted high her Towers,   545
And higher yet the glorious Temple[150] rear'd
Her pile,° far off appearing like a Mount   STRUCTURE
Of Alabaster, top't with Golden Spires:[151]
There on the highest Pinacle he set
The Son of God; and added thus in scorn: 550
    There stand, if thou wilt stand;[152] to stand upright
Will ask thee skill; I to thy Fathers house
Have brought thee, and highest plac't, highest is best,
Now shew thy Progeny;[153] if not to stand,
Cast thy self down; safely if Son of God: 555
For it is written, He will give command
Concerning thee to his Angels, in thir hands
They shall up lift thee, lest at any time
Thou chance to dash thy foot against a stone.[154]
    To whom thus Jesus:[155] also it is written,   560

---

[144]Again, the key word is twisted, since Satan is the Adversary—by the etymology of his name in Hebrew.

[145]All are military and diplomatic terms: "parl" is parley, or diplomatic meeting between representatives of armies; "composition" is a truce or treaty; and "league" is a military or diplomatic alliance.

[146]Subject to close questioning (see *OED* 2.b fig.).

[147]The hardest material imaginable, sometimes identified with diamond, sometimes with a lodestone, sometimes with steel.

[148]As contrasted with other Renaissance epics in which heroes or heroines rode through the air on monsters like Geryon in Dante's *Inferno* Canto 17 or the hippogriff in Ariosto's *Orlando Furioso* 4.18.

[149]"Through the highest atmosphere."

[150]Curiously, Milton makes the Temple feminine, though Solomon was thought to be its architect and the Latin original of the English word, *templum*, is neuter.

[151]Milton interpreted the "pinnacle" of Matthew 4.5 as a "spire," though there are no spires in the Authorized Version. Nor is there mention of the Temple as being constructed of alabaster. As Carey notes (545, 548n), however, Josephus reports that there were sharp points on the roof of the Temple and that the Temple appeared gold and white, "like a mountain covered with snow" (*Jewish War* 5.5.6). Commentators argued whether the Son of God needed to balance, somewhat precariously, on some point of the Temple.

[152]His words in Luke 4.9 are "If thou be the Son of God, cast thyself down from hence," which follows Matthew 4.6 closely.

[153]"Display the force of your parentage." See *OED* 5.

[154]Following Luke 4.10–11 and Matthew 4.6 precisely.

[155]The first and only time he is called by this name in this book.

Tempt not the Lord thy God,[156] he said and stood.
But Satan smitten with amazement fell
As when Earths Son *Antæus* (to compare
Small things with greatest) in *Irassa* strove
With *Joves Alcides*,[157] and oft foil'd still rose, 565
Receiving from his mother Earth new strength,
Fresh from his fall, and fiercer grapple joyn'd,
Throttl'd at length in the Air, expir'd and fell;
So after many a foil the Tempter proud,
Renewing fresh assaults, amidst his pride 570
Fell whence he stood to see his Victor fall.
And as that *Theban* Monster[158] that propos'd
Her riddle, and him, who solv'd it not, devour'd;
That once found out and solv'd, for grief and spight
Cast her self headlong from th' *Ismenian* steep, 575
So strook with dread and anguish fell the Fiend,
And to his crew, that sat consulting, brought
Joyless triumphals of his hop't success,
Ruin, and desperation, and dismay,
Who durst so proudly tempt the Son of God.[159] 580
So Satan fell and strait a fiery Globe[160]
Of Angels on full sail of wing flew nigh,
Who on their plumy Vans° receiv'd him[161] soft   WINGS
From his uneasie station, and upbore
As on a floating couch through the blithe° Air,   SYMPATHETIC 585
Then in a flowry valley set him down
On a green bank, and set before him spred
A table of Celestial Food, Divine,
Ambrosial,[162] Fruits fetcht from the tree of life,[163]
And from the fount of life Ambrosial drink, 590
That soon refresh'd him wearied, and repair'd
What hunger, if aught hunger had impair'd,

---

[156]From Luke 4.12. Milton adds the business of standing—as contrasted with the fall of Satan, which is also extra-Biblical—since Luke 4.13 says merely that Satan "departed from him for a season."

[157]Antaeus was the son of Gaiea, Earth, and Hercules was called Alcides after his grandfather Alcaeus. He is labeled as "*Joves*" because he was the son of Jove. In their wrestling match to the death, Antaeus drew double strength each time he touched his mother Earth. Hercules therefore had to hold him off the ground until he lost his strength and could be strangled. The story was easily allegorized, as in Sandys's version of Ovid's *Metamorphoses* 9: " . . . the morall is more fruitfull: *Hercules* being the symbol of the Soul, and *Antaeus* of the Body; Prudence the essence of the one, and sensual Pleasure of the other; betweene whom there is a perpetuall conflict. For the Appetite alwaies rebells against Reason: nor can Reason prevaile; unlesse it so raise the body, and hold it aloft from the contagion of earthly thinges, that it recover no more force from the same, till the desires and affections thereof, which are the sons of the Earth, be altogether suffocated" (428). The linking of Antaeus and the Libyan town Irassa (or Iresus) could only have been through Pindar's *Pythian Ode* 9.106, according to L. R. Farnell, in *Times Literary Supplement* 1 October 1931, 754.

[158]The Sphinx; a monster because it had the head and breasts of a woman, the body of a dog, the tail of a serpent, the wings of a bird, the paws of a lion, and the voice of a human (see Hesiod, *Theogony* 326). Juno sent the Sphinx to Thebes to punish descendants of Cadmus by posing riddles and then destroying those who could not answer them. Oedipus answered the riddle concerning the creature that walked on four legs in the morning, two at noon, and three in the evening with the proper reply, "Man," and the Sphinx was supposed to have thrown herself from the acropolis at Thebes into the river Ismenus as a result (Pausanias, *History of Greece* 9.10).

[159]Compare *Paradise Lost* 1.44–49 for a similar diminuendo effect describing the fall of Satan.

[160]From the Latin *globus*, a full assembly of people in a compact body. Giles Fletcher had used the similar construction, "A globe of winged Angels, swift as thought," in *Christs Triumph* 13 (see *OED* 8).

[161]The Son of God, not Satan.

[162]Though based on the meaning of ambrosia, the supposed food of the Greek gods, the adjective "Ambrosial" here seems to mean "pertaining to things fit for God," as with the "Ambrosial weeds [clothing]" of *Comus* 16 or the "Ambrosial Odours and Ambrosial Flowers" of *Paradise Lost* 2.245.

[163]Milton makes nothing special of the tree of life mentioned in Genesis 2.9, but eating from it was supposed to confer immortality (Genesis 3.22). In *On Christian Doctrine*, he admits "I do not know whether the tree of life ought to be called a sacrament, rather than a symbol of eternal life or even perhaps the food of eternal life" (1.10; Yale 6: 353). See C. A. Patrides, "The Tree of Knowledge in the Christian Tradition," *Studia Neophilologica* 34 (1962): 240–42.

Or thirst, and as he fed, Angelic Quires
Sung Heavenly Anthems[164] of his victory
Over temptation, and the Tempter proud.[165]   595
    True Image of the Father[166] whether thron'd
In the bosom of bliss, and light of light
Conceiving, or remote from Heaven, enshrin'd
In fleshly Tabernacle, and human form,
Wandring the Wilderness, whatever place,   600
Habit, or state, or motion, still expressing
The Son of God, with Godlike force indu'd
Against th' Attempter of thy Fathers Throne,
And Thief of Paradise; him long of old
Thou didst debel,[167] and down from Heav'n cast   605
With all his Army, now thou hast aveng'd
Supplanted[168] *Adam*, and by vanquishing
Temptation, hast regain'd lost Paradise,
And frustrated the conquest fraudulent:
He never more henceforth will dare set foot   610
In Paradise to tempt; his snares are broke:[169]
For though that seat of earthly bliss[170] be fail'd,
A fairer Paradise is founded now
For *Adam* and his chosen Sons,[171] whom thou
A Saviour art come down to re-install.   615
Where they shall dwell secure, when time shall be
Of Tempter and Temptation without fear.[172]
But thou, Infernal Serpent, shalt not long
Rule in the Clouds; like an Autumnal Star[173]
Or Lightning thou shalt fall from Heav'n trod down   620
Under his feet: for proof, e're this thou feel'st
Thy wound,[174] yet not thy last and deadliest wound
By this repulse receiv'd, and hold'st in Hell
No triumph; in all her gates *Abaddon*[175] rues
Thy bold attempt; hereafter learn with awe   625
To dread the Son of God: he all unarm'd
Shall chase thee with the terror of his voice
From thy Demoniac holds,[176] possession foul,

---

[164]Presumably the choirs are singing antiphonally (*antiphon* being the root of the English *anthem*), with one choir answering the other musically.

[165]What follows in the next verse paragraph is the anthem sung by the heavenly choirs. The chorus ends the short epic with a song of praise and a final narrative. The eighteenth-century editor Calton thought the choral anthem provided "grandeur [in] its close": "The Demon falls with amazement and terror, on this full proof of his being that very Son of God, whose thunder forced him out of Heaven. The blessed Angels receive new knowledge. They behold a sublime truth establish'd, which was a secret to them at the beginning of the temptation; and the great discovery gives a proper opening to their hymn on the victory of Christ, and the defeat of the Tempter" (quoted in Newton 596n).

[166]Exactly how the Son is an image of the Father is often discussed in *On Christian Doctrine*, especially in 1.5, "Of the Son of God" (Yale 6: 204–80). The Son of God is one with the Father "not in essence but in love, in communion, in agreement, in charity, in spirit, and finally in glory" (220).

[167]Subdue in warfare (Latin *bellus*).

[168]Tripped up, turned head over heels (Latin *planta*, "sole of the foot").

[169]"Our soul is escaped as a bird out of the snare of the fowlers: the snare is broken, and we are escaped" (Psalm 124.7).

[170]Eden, to be replaced by a "paradise within . . . happier farr" (*Paradise Lost* 12.587).

[171]See *Paradise Lost* 3.183–84 for a reference to the election of certain human beings, and see *On Christian Doctrine* 1.4 (Yale 6: 176).

[172]"When there will be a time in which fear of Tempter or temptation will no longer exist."

[173]Probably a comet or meteor or shooting star as bright as the very fiery star, Sirius, plainly visible in autumn.

[174]The wound or bruise promised to the serpent in Genesis 3.15.

[175]"Used in Rev. ix. 11 as equivalent to the Gr. Ἀπολλύων, destroyer, as the name of 'the angel of the bottomless pit.' Hence applied by Milton to the bottomless pit, or abyss of hell, itself" (*OED* "Abaddon").

[176]Probably "A place of refuge, shelter, or temporary abode; a lurking-place (of animals)" (*OED* 9), if not a stronghold or fortified place.

Thee and thy Legions, yelling they shall flye,
And beg to hide them in a herd of Swine,[177]
Lest he command them down into the deep
Bound, and to torment sent before thir time.
Hail Son of the most High, heir of both worlds,
Queller of Satan, on thy glorious work
Now enter, and begin to save mankind.

    Thus they the Son of God our Saviour meek[178]
Sung Victor, and from Heavenly Feast refresht
Brought on his way with joy; hee unobserv'd
Home to his Mothers house private return'd.[179]

The END.

630

635

---

[177]The herd of swine in Matthew 8.28–32, into which Christ casts the devils from two people, after the devils request it; the swine "ran violently down a steep place into the sea, and perished in the waters" (32). Compare the account of the Gaddarene swine in Luke 8.26–33, in which the devils again beseech Jesus to enter the swine.

[178]The quality of meekness, the opposite of Satanic pride, continues to be important for Milton, as it was as early as in *Of Reformation* (1641), where Christ is "the meeke *Lord*" (Yale 1: 524). Perhaps the closest Milton comes to meekness in his own delineation of special virtues or duties toward one's neighbor is with "GENTLENESS," which "treats all men in a peaceful and friendly way, as far as possible," for the support of which virtue he quotes Jesus in Matthew 11.29: ". . . I am meek and lowly in heart . . . ." See *On Christian Doctrine* 2.12 (Yale 6: 754.).

[179]A quiet, domestic ending to the brief epic. The Son of God is pictured returning to his home and to his mother, reiterating the importance of his humanity and his relationship with his human family as well as with his Father.

SAMSON AGONISTES,

A

DRAMATIC POEM.

The Author

JOHN MILTON.

Aristot. Poet. Cap. 6.

Τραγωδια μίμησις πράξεοις σπυδαίας, &c.

*Tragœdia est imitatio actionis seriæ, &c. Per misericordiam &
metum perficiens talium affectuum lustrationem.*

LONDON,

Printed by *J. M.* for *John Starkey* at the
Mitre in *Fleetstreet*, near *Temple-Bar.*
MDCLXXI.

Samson Agonistes

Introduction

MILTON'S EARLIER REFERENCES TO SAMSON

After the Fall in Book 9 of *Paradise Lost*, the narrator describes Adam and Eve in terms of Samson:

> so rose the *Danite* strong
> *Herculean Samson* from the Harlot-lap
> Of *Philistean Dalilah*, and wak'd
> Shorn of his strength, they destitute and bare
> Of all thir vertue . . . (1059–63)

The passage helps us interpret Milton's dramatic poem, *Samson Agonistes*. It seems to have been written before Milton finished, possibly before he began, *Samson Agonistes*, because it represents the story as Milton conceived it before he made important final changes. The action described in *Paradise Lost* precedes the action of the dramatic poem. Samson, of the tribe of Dan and resembling the Greek and Roman hero Hercules, rises from Dalila's lap—that of a harlot, not of the wife Dalila is made to be in *Samson Agonistes*. It is Adam and Eve together who are pictured as being like Samson shorn of his strength in Dalila's lap, and thus the weakness the man and the woman display is not confined to male effeminacy or female guilefulness (Revard 271). Though Samson's identity as a Danite or a member of the tribe of Dan is preserved in the dramatic poem, the comparison with Hercules (in various myths also strong and susceptible to women) is dropped or rendered implicit.

Milton did make Dalila (Milton's insistent spelling of her name) a wife instead of a harlot (prostitute). Because Milton's Samson has married his Dalila (Stollman), her treachery betrays the institution of marriage, and her nearness to Samson—as a bosom snake—is reinforced by the marriage bond. To Samson, she is "My Wife, my Traytress" (725). Her very name is possibly related to a Hebrew word meaning "flirtatious" (*Harper Collins Study Bible* Judges 16.4n) or "weakness" (Lieb 125).

I use the passage from *Paradise Lost* to introduce Milton's longstanding concern with the image and story of Samson. Allusions to the Samson story also appear in *Doctrine and Discipline of Divorce* (Book 1, Ch. 6), *Areopagitica*, *Reason of Church Government*, and *Eikonoklastes*, showing that "The ideas and the imagery of *Samson Agonistes* evolved over many years" (Kranidas 144). In his list of potential subjects for plays on themes or stories derived from the Bible or from English or Scottish history in the Trinity Manuscript, Milton included "Samson marriing [marrying] or in Ramath Lechi Jud. 15." and "Dagonalia. Jud. 16." In the margin to the left of the first title, he wrote "Samson pursophorus or

Hybristes, or," apparently to be inserted in front of "Samson in Ramath Lechi Jud. 15," which itself had "marriing or" inserted in it: in other words, Milton was at that point also interested in Samson's marriages. The Greek word "pursophorus" may be translated as "violent" (as in Masson), and "Hybristes" as in its Greek form "violent, wanton, licentious, insolent" (Liddell and Scott; see Yale 8: 562n.34), with a nod toward the term *hybris* as used by Aristotle for the principal fault to be found in tragic heroes.

The brief notes about subjects for dramas show Milton concentrating on the subject of Samson's marriage to the Woman of Timna described in Judges 15 and 16, and then on the festival of Dagon, in Judges 16.23–30, during which Samson violently pulls down the pillars of the Philistine "house." When, exactly, Milton jotted down the list of subjects is debatable, though most editors agree that it was in the early 1640s (Yale 8: 539). Parker believes Milton's notes on the Samson story indicate his concern from the beginning to make Samson's domestic struggle and catastrophic death fit the Aristotelian and Italian critical formulas for a Greek tragedy ("The Trinity Manuscript"). I would add that the domestic problems of Samson seem to have been allied with those of Solomon, who was described in the outlines for tragedies as "Gynaecocratomenus or Idolmargus or Thysiazusae," that is as "woman-governed," "idol-mad," and "sacrificer to women" (Yale 8: 563n; the translation of the last word is arguable). Like King Solomon, Samson married infidels and was ruled by them. In doing so, he became idolatrous, following after the gods of the women to whom he attached himself in his old age (1 Kings 11). Like Milton's Adam, his Samson allowed himself to be led by a woman, even perhaps to make an idol of a woman, to his downfall. Uxoriousness—a weak and susceptible man's degrading of himself on behalf of a power-hungry woman—is also a major theme in Milton's divorce tracts:

> What an injury is it after wedlock not to be belov'd, what to be slighted, what to be contended with in point of house-rule who shall be the head, not for any parity of wisdome, for that were something reasonable, but out of a female pride.
>
> (*Doctrine and Discipline of Divorce*; Yale 2: 324)

ADDITIONS TO THE BIBLICAL SAMSON STORY

Milton's dramatic poem *Samson Agonistes* has as its hero an inspired prophet and a keen judge of human character, yet the biblical Samson in Judges 16 and 17 might seem, to a modern reader brought up on anthropology and comparative folklore, to be a lout, a trickster, a stooge—the type of a stupid athlete—defined by his action of tying foxes' tails together and using them to set fields on fire. "There is nothing in Scripture to suggest the inwardness of Samson's thought. The simple folklore hero of the Bible tale is transformed [in *Samson Agonistes*] at once into the spiritual image of his creator" (Hanford, *John Milton* 213). When transformed into a hero of the popular medium of the Hollywood biblical epic movie, Samson becomes a thick-brained muscleman with long hair and a diseased yearning for fatal women. Though in the Bible he is described as a judge (MacCallum), he is also the physically strong man overcome by the wiles of a physically weaker but wily and clever woman. He is the trickster tricked and the uxorious lover. Delilah (in the biblical spelling) has become the prototype of the fatal woman who snares her man and brings him down (Demetrakopoulos).

What Milton leaves out in his retelling of the Bible story may be significant. Though the Chorus describes Samson as being one of the elect to God (678), he does not stress his affiliation with the Nazarite sect, though the Chorus does at least use the name Nazarite (318). This is puzzling, since Samson's vows, which he breaks with great regularity, could have been used to portray him as a type of John the Baptist. The vows included the famous uncut hair, abstinence from strong drink, and a promise to "separate themselves unto the Lord" (Numbers 6.2). Milton neglects on purpose to tell us that the Woman of Timna, after betraying Samson to the Philistines, is first "given" to an anonymous friend of Samson; then she is, with her father, burned to death. Like Samson's mother, the Woman of Timna represents a significant omission from the biblical plot, and another meaningful female absence in the dramatic poem. Milton also refuses to have Samson emphasize the famous jawbone of an ass, which he reduces in stature to his "trivial" weapon (142) against the Philistines. Oddly enough, the taking of foreskins in battle is what is emphasized. Samson's hair, what seems in the Bible to be the magical evidence of his strength, is also not important in Milton's version. Milton seems not to want to make an ikon or fetish of any part of Samson's person or identity.

Delilah in Judges is merely a woman with whom Samson falls in love, after the death of the Woman of Timna. Biblical commentaries make her either a harlot or a wife (Krouse 101). Milton calls her Samson's wife, but he gives her many of the characteristics of a prostitute, most notably her garish costume. She does, of course, sell him for silver. Knoppers investigates all the implications of Dalila as harlot based on a comparison between Milton's Samson and Dalila and the harlot and fool of Proverbs 7, a passage to which Milton refers elsewhere and a passage about which there was a great deal of discussion in seventeenth-century marriage manuals ("Sung" 239–46).

Milton adds significant details to the biblical account. Manoa offers to ransom Samson from the Philistines, but the biblical Samson was not ransomed. The potential for Samson to be ransomed seems to have been added to Milton's account as another form of temptation—Manoa's selling out of Samson, in order to buy him a life of inactive ease. The priest at Dalila's ear (857) is another detail not in the account in Judges, though the priest clearly represents Milton's mistrust of any politicized clergyman, a major theme in his anti-prelatical tracts (Shawcross, "Misreading" 199). By his additions, Milton may be indicating his contempt for the English after the Restoration (Knoppers, *Historicizing* Ch. 2), for the English clergy during the time of Archbishop Laud (Hill 428–31), or for the English aristocracy. The priest at her ear tempts Dalila; the Israelites are content with bondage instead of liberty; and the Philistine lords are drunken, cowardly, insolent, and effete. Those Philistine lords have often been compared by critics to the courtiers attendant on Charles I as pictured by Milton in his antimonarchical tracts, or those dissolute rakes who attended Charles II notoriously after the Restoration, who often qualified as "sons of Belial."

The keeping of secrets also figures into the plot of *Samson Agonistes* (Landy). As Robert Fallon notes, "Though there is no mention of a divine prohibition in the biblical account, the drama repeats time and time again that Samson was forbidden to reveal the source of his strength" (170). The prohibition, and Samson's betrayal of it, allies him with Adam and Eve. Haskin makes the connection between Samson not keeping secrets and Christ asking those on whom he performed miracles not to reveal what happened (Chapter 6).

SAMSON AND GIDEON

Another intriguing biblical type associated with Samson, the figure of "Gideon Idoloclastes," like that of Solomon (Steadman, "Causality" 218), remains active in the background of the poem. Radzinowicz points out that St. Paul and the Chorus in *Samson Agonistes* group Samson "with Gideon and Jephtha as elect saints who were potential, but disregarded, believers" (*Towards* 30–31). In Hebrews 11.32–34, the author, in Milton's era thought to be St. Paul, connects the warrior Gideon with Barak, Samson, Jephtha, David, and Samuel. The Epistle's earlier lists of those victorious through faith mention Abel, Enoch, Noah, Abraham, Sarah, Isaac,

Jacob, Joseph, Moses, and Rahab—a list that comes close to Milton's nominees for "just men" in *Paradise Lost*. In line 280 of *Samson Agonistes*, the Chorus mentions the "matchless *Gideon*" together with Jephthah, both of whose deeds are compared with Samson's. What also might have interested Milton in Gideon, however, might have been his idolatry.

The story of Gideon is complicated—as is the process of working out what Gideon might mean to a seventeenth-century reader. Gideon's family, living under the oppressive rule of the Midianites (Judges 6–8) is visited by an angel, like Samson's family, and the angel announces that Gideon will deliver his people from the Midianites. Gideon first destroys an idol of Baal and then routs the Baal-worshipers, the Midianites, with his famous army of 300 hand-picked men. But, after the Midianites are defeated, Gideon makes an ephod (in this case, a graven image) of gold, and "all Israel went thither a whoring after it: which thing became a snare unto Gideon, and to his house" (8.9). Thus Gideon, like Samson, was both an idol-breaker and an idol-worshiper.

MARITAL COMBAT

Milton's Samson and his Dalila are much deeper emotionally than either the stereotype of the strong, thick-headed man or that of the fatal woman. But together they do represent male and female combat. Dalila is a foreigner, an infidel, a heathen Philistine whom Samson marries against the wisdom of his father, far outside the tribe of Dan. As Manoa points out, Samson continues in his own tradition of bad marriage choices from the Woman of Timna to Dalila, even if he did have what the Bible calls an "intimate impulse" for the first marriage. Dalila has been defended by Irene Samuel as a sincere wronged woman who "lacks minimal logic" (248) and by John Ulreich as "a woman desperately seeking love" (189), but the fact remains that she is excoriated by her husband as a serpent, an hyena, and a traitress, not to mention the bad names the Chorus smears her with. In the terms of feminist criticism, she may very well represent the muted woman who seeks a justifiable revenge or a violation of the stereotype (Lewalski, "Milton" 64–65), but the reader of the poem must take sides for or against her. The side for her is well-represented by Samuel and Ulreich, the side against by Kranidas and Lieb. It is hard not to agree with Lewalski that "Milton represents Dalila as a bad woman, but in terms which honour women more in the harshness of that representation than do the critics who seek to excuse her on her terms" ("Milton" 63).

SAMSON AS A TYPE OF CHRIST

Krouse has proven conclusively that the Samson of Renaissance biblical commentary was a complicated type of Christ. Critics have sometimes linked the two works published together—*Samson Agonistes* and *Paradise Regain'd*—through typology. But what could the lout Samson and Jesus have in common? Ultimately, they both resist temptation. Both get their great strength directly from God, though both are tested in their human state. Both are subject to "motions" and inspiration engineered by God. Both ultimately sacrifice their lives for the sake of their people, overcoming many evil enemies in the process. Milton characterizes both as self-questioning adults who must put aside childish behavior in order to accomplish great deeds. Both, according to Hill, are men of action, "not merely suffering" (446). As Wittreich and others have pointed out, the pairing of *Paradise Regain'd* and *Samson Agonistes* seems to be no accident, though Wittreich does see a contrast between Christ and Samson.

ANALOGUES AND PRECEDENTS

Kirkconnell has collected translations or bibliographical citations to over 100 variants of the Samson story, most in dramatic or operatic form, before and after Milton's version. The most subtle, Kirkconnell believes, is the 1660 play written by the Dutch Joost van den Vondel, *Samson, of Heilige Wraeck, Treurspel*, whose title Kirkconnell translates as "Samson, or Holy Revenge." Dagon is a speaking character in Vondel's play, there is a chorus of Jewish women, a Princess of Gaza, temple musicians, and Fadaël, the angel who presided over Samson's birth. Samson's chains include a neck-ring, like a dog collar, and a beggar's bell, to help him beg for food. He is covered with flour, because the mill he operates grinds and pulverizes wheat. The chorus of Jewish women address him as "Prince Samson" and call attention to the power of inner light within him, despite his outward blindness (85). Samson and Delilah have a long bedtime talk reported by Samson, during which "she . . . grappled me and boarded me" (86). Vondel's Dalilah is much more explicit in using both her overt sexuality and her tears to overcome Samson.

A GREEK TRAGEDY ON A BIBLICAL THEME

Parker found, as the title of his 1937 book urges, that *Samson Agonistes* owed a debt to Greek tragedy, especially to those tragedies written by Milton's favorite of the three great tragedians, Euripides. Parker points out that Milton's epithet "Agonistes" could mean wrestler, advocate, actor, and champion (*Milton's Debt* 13). Le Comte reminds us, however, that "'Agonize' in the 17th century meant to 'play the champion' and had nothing to do with inner torment" (*A Milton Dictionary*, "Samson"). Parker finds Aeschylus an influence on

Milton's uncomplicated plot structure and Sophocles a tasteful influence on Milton's choice to reject the spectacular. Like Sophocles's heroes, Samson has dignity and grandeur, but, like Euripides's heroes, he has a mind divided against itself. Milton's characterization of Samson also adds the Christian dimension of his being inspired directly by a merciful God, which means that Christian grace and forgiveness of sin will be available to him, as it was not for Greek tragic heroes. Parker believes that the form and spirit of the dramatic poem is Greek and its content Judeo-Christian (*Milton's Debt* 207–08). Radzinowicz also concludes "the tragedy is Christian, and the matter for serious and pained regret is the mystery of iniquity" ("Distinctive" 253). Steadman defines the major "agon" of the poem as a *theomachia*, a contest between the false god Dagon and the true "living God" (1140) of Samson ("Causality" 219–20). Keeping in mind the punning often buried in Milton's poetry, he might even be suggesting that "agon" is part of the name of Dagon.

Michael Spiller writes that Milton did respect the "Greek tragic form by refraining from authorial intrusion, but he did not on that account refrain also from indicating to his readers how they should respond" (129). The problem, as with Greek tragedy, is when the audience might safely believe what the Chorus says, or Manoa, or the Messenger, or any possible mouthpiece for Milton, in the dramatic poem. Arthur Barker labels Manoa "stupid" though well-meaning (41) and defines the Chorus as "the neo-classical chorus of enslaved and unredeemed Hebrews" (39) until the end.

Milton's Chorus keeps in character as a group of Danite men, "friends and neighbours" (180), who don't know quite how to interpret the past and present actions of their hero. Toward the end, Manoa and the Chorus do seem to speak Miltonic truth or, as Spiller puts it, they "speak in an authorial fashion, and guide us to the delight that accompanies wisdom" (129). Bennett, however, believes that the Chorus is wrong when they speak against Samson's rational interpretation of Old Testament law (*Reviving* 124). The Chorus's evaluation of Harapha seems just. Most of what the Chorus says about bad women seems accurate for the character of Dalila, but enough bits of Choral opinion seem morally offbase for us to agree with Bennett and find them occasionally dead wrong.

GAMES WITH NAMES: ETYMOLOGY, SPELLING, AND PHONETIC PRONUNCIATION

Some critics argue from Samson's name, which is sometimes associated with the sun (*Shemesh* in transliterated Hebrew) and sometimes with the idea of "a second chance," that he has the potential for regenera-

tion. "Like a bird of God," Lieb argues, "he is able to behold the sun, the fountain of celestial radiance. He is, in effect, reborn in the sun. All this is implicit in the return of strength from weakness (cf. Heb. 11:34)" (*Milton* 232). The Phoenix, to whom Samson is compared, was also said to be capable of gazing at the sun without harm (Hill 445–48). The entire dramatic poem, Lieb believes, examines the Christian paradox that strength can arise from weakness, a concept that fascinated Milton even before he became blind. Samson was one of those who, through faith, "Quenched the violence of fyre, escaped the edge of the sworde, of weake were made strong, waxed valiant in battel, turned to flight the armies of the aliantes" (Hebrews 11.34; Geneva Bible; the Authorized Version substitutes "aliens" for "aliantes").

Milton chooses versions of names quite carefully, most probably because of his philological knowledge as a polyglot, a person conversant in many languages, but also because of the necessities of iambic pentameter.

Here is a list of names as recorded in the Authorized Version of the Bible, together with the Miltonic version of each:

AV	Milton
Delilah	Dálila
Goliath	Goliah
Manoah	Mánoa
Philistine (adj.)	Philistian
Timnah	Timna
Sorek	Sorec
Palestine	Palestin
Hebrews	Ebrews
Shiloh	Silo

BELLIGERENT PREFATORY MATTER

Milton's preface "*Of that sort of Dramatic Poem which is call'd Tragedy*" is just as belligerent and revolutionary in spirit as his testy note on the verse written for *Paradise Lost*. He seems always to have believed that the best defense is a good offense. In his short preface he attacks the idea that tragedy might be considered an inferior art form, as if his dramatic poem (he insists we call it that, or "tragedy") were under attack already, and he seems to deny the possibility of performance when he says the work was never intended for the stage. Because it was never intended for the stage, he denies it acts and scenes, though he suggests that they may have been part of the structure when he writes "It suffices if the whole Drama be found not produc't beyond the fift Act." He does enclose the action of the dramatic poem "within the space of 24 hours." In other words, he somewhat cantankerously gives the reader a playable Greek tragedy and then takes it away. He may conceivably be reacting against the Restoration stage, though it is hard to tell if he would have been at all inclined to experience it firsthand. Productions of the play within the last twenty years as "readers' theater," however, argue for the possibility of its working on stage (Shaw). As would be appropriate for a blind man, perhaps radio is the best medium for performance for *Samson Agonistes*. Recordings such as that made by Tony Church and Margaret Rawlings playing Samson and Dalila indicate how successful the drama can be when an audience can listen to it (Argo mono RG544/5).

In the spirit of puritanism embodied in the word *purify*, Milton restores an ancient, ritualistic, morally valuable art form to its original purity; his tragedy will be "coming forth after the antient manner, much different from what among us passes for best." As if that were not enough to annoy his present, unworthy reader, Milton identifies himself as author with the likes of St. Paul, Gregory Nazianzen, and, finally, with "*Æschulus, Sophocles,* and *Euripides.*" In other words, he identifies himself with the most astute Christian commentators on drama and the best writers of tragedy.

"The ARGUMENT," Milton's outline of his own plot, is not quite so testy. Milton had apparently been asked by his publisher to provide arguments for each book of *Paradise Lost* after the first edition of the epic appeared, together with his annoyed note on "why the poem rhymes not." By contrast, for *Samson Agonistes* he seems to have been quite willing to supply the argument and the note on tragedy. *Paradise Regain'd* seems to have needed no defense for the genre of short biblical epic, in his mind, and no arguments or plot summaries to make it understandable, but *Samson Agonistes* as a Christian Greek tragedy on a Hebrew theme needed a defense, first, then an argument.

Milton's early readers seem to have accepted his terms. Francis Atterbury writes to Alexander Pope on June 15, 1722, saying the poem is "Written in the very Spirit of the Ancients, [and thus] it deserves your care and is capable of being improv'd, with little trouble, into a perfect Model and Standard of Tragic Poetry, always allowing for its being a Story taken out of the Bible which is an Objection that at this time of day, I know is not to be got over" (quoted in Shawcross, *Milton* 243). Atterbury's focus is on Milton's tragedy as no less worthy than the tragedy of Aeschylus, Sophocles, and Euripides. Elijah Fenton, in his 1725 life of Milton, likewise saw the dramatic poem as "a tragedy not unworthy the Grecian stage when Athens was in her glory" (quoted in Shawcross, *Milton* 246).

CHARACTERIZATION

Despite his stated desire to avoid the trappings of the stage, Milton does give us some stage directions that tell us what Samson, Dalila, Manoa, and Harapha should look like or do on stage. If Dalila resembles a fully-rigged ship (she also has a train of attendants), and Manoa has white hair, Samson is in chains, his worn-out and soiled clothing that of the lowest rank of bondslave. Harapha, who seems over-fastidious and perhaps is overdressed even for a giant, hints that Samson is too dirty to touch (1107). Samson's body language at least when we first see him suggests impotence and defeat. He describes himself as a "moving Grave" (102). According to the Chorus, "he lies at random, carelessly diffus'd, / With languish't head unprop't" (118–19). He is weak-minded as well at the beginning of the poem, and his career to date illustrates his own great maxim "All wickedness is weakness" (834). His thoughts and memories are like hornets stinging him. He has become his own dungeon, in the absence even of inner light to compensate for his blindness. He longs for death during much of the poem. His characteristic song is a lament (Grose 160). But, in the end, he is a predatory dragon overcoming the enemies of his people and his God, and he is a phoenix rising from the ashes of his former self into everlasting life. The imagery gives us a series of tools to use in assessing Samson's motives and character.

Like Eve in *Paradise Lost*, Milton's Dalila is perhaps a more fascinating character than her male counterpart—even though Milton doesn't even mention her in his Argument. Perhaps Dalila is meant to attract and seduce the audience as well as Samson. She is a clothes-horse, overdressed, as garish as the pictorial stereotype of the Venetian courtesan advertising her wares. She is also a fully-rigged sailing vessel, all decked out and be-ribboned, superficially attractive but with the suggestion of the "sting" of a serpent or scorpion hidden beneath the fancy clothing. She still seems attractive enough for Samson to have to say "let her not come near me" (725), possibly protesting so loudly out of fear of her charms. But "[w]hat he rejects," writes Rumrich, "is not a sexual temptation, at least not in the usual sense, but her desire to dominate him through caretaking" (90). Her care for her former husband is that of a smothering mother or nurse.

Though she relies on sensory trappings to overcome or tempt Samson, Dalila is a formidable adversary, still tempting after all she has done to him. She is made to seem very close to Samson in that she wants for herself what he will actually achieve—honor and a posthumous monument—and she is linked to him within the subtext of imagery, especially that connected with ships (see 198–200 for him, 713–14 for her).

Harapha on the surface is a stupid and cowardly giant, resembling the giant in the Jack and the Beanstalk story, full of vainglory and posturing. Many critics have pointed out that he is a mirror image of the earlier Samson as he walked about like a "petty god." His hollow rhetoric and shambling gait might give him away, as would his self-important announcement, "Men call me *Harapha*." Though Harapha is a parody of an aristocrat, his nobility is real, "though it does embody a false criterion of nobility" (Steadman, "Men of Renown" 182). In the description of Harapha's armor, however, there is one very important bit of characterization, namely his resemblance to Goliath, who

> . . . had an helmet of brasse upon his head, and a brigandine upon him: and the weight of his brigandine was five thousand shekels of brasse.
>
> And he had bootes of brasse upon his legges, & a shilde of brasse upon his shoulders.
>
> And the shafte of his speare was like a weavers beame: and his speare head weyed six hundreth shekels of yron: and one bearing a shilde went before him.
>
> (1 Samuel 17.5–7; Geneva Bible)

If Milton's Harapha resembles the biblical Goliath in so many details of his armor, then Samson must resemble David. Milton makes the comparison between David and Samson implicit by discussing David as an example of the way God might incline the heart of someone who has conceived evil to act in a way that demonstrates his own pride and wickedness (Labriola 101). Like David, Samson is inclined to act in response to his own temptation to do evil, especially in his two marriages. Labriola finds that "David's pride and the way in which God 'impelled him to display' it, parallel remarkably Samson's pride and the 'divine impulsion' in him" (102; "Divine impulsion" is Manoa's term at 422). And Lieb observes that from the perspective of the struggle between Samson and Harapha, "the David–Goliath battle assumes importance as a profound symbol of the way faith in the power of God is sufficient to overcome the mightiest of enemies" (*Milton* 248).

Harapha's aristocratic background and hollow posturing also offer play for the imagination, especially since Harapha is a generic giant (the Hebrew word in 2 Samuel 21.16 was left as the transliterated "Haraphah" in the Geneva Bible but altered to "giant" in the AV) and a character Milton made up. In facing him down, Samson, not a Philistine and not noble except in the gifts he has been given by God, overcomes a hollow aristocratic braggart, a gigantic upper-class twit. Patrides rightly points to the braggart soldier of Greek and Roman co-

medy as Harapha's dramatic ancestor. Though Berkeley and Khoddam argue that Samson's Tribe of Dan was not highly esteemed and hence Samson's social position is lower than that of Harapha, their characterization of the Tribe of Dan has been disputed by Miller, and the tribe of Dan does not seem to be disparaged in Milton's work. Harapha does talk condescendingly to Samson, and Samson offers to fight him with an oak staff, a humble and unaristocratic weapon.

Biographical echoes have also been found in the character of Harapha, who has been compared by a number of critics to Milton's chief international intellectual opponent in the pamphlet wars concerning monarchy, Claude de Saumaise, better known by his Latin name Salmasius (Lieb, *Milton* 244–46). If Harapha equals Salmasius, obviously Samson is meant to echo Milton, in his struggle against another intellectual giant.

Manoa means well and is overly solicitous for the comfort of a son brought to him by a miraculous birth out of a wife hitherto barren. The unnamed person we might call "Mrs. Manoa," Samson's mother, plays a part in the story in Judges 15, but she is never named by Milton, and the word "mother" is never used in the dramatic poem, though Samson at least mentions "both [his] Parents" (25). Manoa wants to buy his son out of slavery, even if it takes the last bit of his savings. Though Samson himself seems old, Manoa must be older, though he is not quite doddering; his durability is shown in the fact that he gets what is very nearly the last word in the play, after having outlived his son. His gait is that of "Old *Manoah*" (328), though the good news about the Philistines' taking his ransom seriously does indeed make him walk with more bounce (1441–42).

SAMSON'S AGE

A debate recently flourished on the discussion list Milton-L, which can be found on the World Wide Web at the following address:

http://www.richmond.edu/~creamer/milton.html

John Leonard questioned my assumption, which he noticed while reading a draft of this introduction, that Samson might be considered as old. Leonard had also believed that Samson was old, until a professor of his at Cambridge had asked him to question his assumption. In fact we have no precise or definitive evidence of Samson's age, either from Judges or the Bible. He is certainly old enough to have married twice, and he and Dalila "long since are twain" (929). He has served as a judge for twenty years, and, if his father is seventy or so, he should be about fifty. But he is young enough to be quite strong: he works at the mill, is a threat to the giant Harapha, and he does bring down the temple of Dagon.

On Milton-L, I wrote,

Consider this passage, though, from the Chorus:

See how he lies at random, carelessly diffus'd,
With languish'd head unprop,
As one past hope, abandon'd,
And by himself given over.

Is he old-thinking or just morally weak? The way he puts it is "O impotence of mind, in body strong!" If he is not old, the way he lives is "worse then chains, / Dungeon, or beggery, or decrepit age!" So he talks old, even if he isn't that old. He is humiliatingly "In power of others, never in [his] own." And he is "dead more then half," which I take to mean that he thinks he has one foot in the grave. He refers to a time when "length of years / And sedentary numness craze my limbs / To a contemptible old age obscure." He's not there yet, but he's well on the way. Doesn't he seem old, as he lives "a life half dead, a living death, / And buried?" Manoa says he is "ever failing / In mortal strength," though weakness of course does not necessarily denote old age. Samson says the experience with Dalila has caused him to be "Softn'd with pleasure and voluptuous life."

Joseph Wittreich's *Interpreting Samson Agonistes* attempts to answer the age question, definitively: "By Milton's time, it was understood that Samson was born in 1155 BC, married in 1137 BC, sent the foxes through the fields a year later, and died in the temple holocaust of 1117 BC. That is, Samson married at the age of eighteen and died when he was thirty-eight, with all events in that twenty-year period pertaining to his judgeship" (117). That would make him thirty-eight, an old-thinking thirty-eight.

Through images of degeneracy and dying, Milton certainly brings us to believe that Samson is near death, already a "walking grave." He has, according to Manoa, aged prematurely; he is "Made older then [his] age through eye-sight lost" (1489). But estimates of his age during the play vary—among the various well-respected contributors on Milton-L—from "35 tops" to mid- or late-fifties. Then there is the question of what age was "old" in 1671. The age of thirty-five might have been considered late middle-age.

IMAGERY

As Carey has cleverly pointed out and Lewalski has reiterated, the imagery of the dramatic poem is often nautical (Carey summarizes on 337–39), as is the imagery connected with Satan in *Paradise Lost*. It may have something to do very indirectly with the emerging naval power of England, or with its mercantile fleet. Samson is a wrecked pilot, because he has allowed his vessel to be steered by Dalila and others who have betrayed him. As if she were a Petrarchan object of desire, Dalila uses the tempest of her tears and the wind of her sighs and supplications to take him off course and wreck him. She herself is a stately ship of Tarsus ("Tarshish" is proverbial in the Bible as a naval power), decked out with streamers flowing behind her. Cox labels the imagery of water, fire, air, and earth as "elemental," rather than just nautical (253–54); if that is true, Dalila is like a rough sea that causes Samson's ship to wreck.

In imagery, Dalila is also a monster, a sorceress, a snare for men, a bosom snake, a viper. In another possible subtext, her viper might be related to Samson's dragon, since both were thought to be in the family of snakes and "worms," though his dragon is heroic, immense, open, and aggressive, and her bosom snake is hidden and passive-aggressive by nature.

Samson is the deliverer of Israel and, lest we forget, one of the judges of the tribes of Israel (see MacCallum for all this might imply in Renaissance theology). Yet as the play begins Samson needs a doctor for his own catharsis. In his youth, Samson has been nurtured by Manoa like a precious and holy plant (362), but he is ill, his illness having been caused by his own degeneracy (Hawkins). From Milton's introduction, we have some idea that the play is about sickness, the kind of sickness cured (at least in an audience) by the homeopathic medicine of witnessing a tragedy and being purged of dangerous emotions. As Joan Bennett puts it, "We should expect, then, that by Samson's experience we will emerge strengthened in mind and spirit to meet such suffering directly in its full and complicated force in our world and in ourselves" ("A Reading" 227) The Chorus tells us that they wish Samson cured by words that are "Salve to thy Sores, [and] apt . . . to swage / The tumors of a troubl'd mind, / And are as Balm to fester'd wounds" (184–86). The sores may be literal, through whippings Samson may have received as a slave, but they are more likely to be psychological sores, tumors, and festered wounds.

Manoa has thought that, when he conceived Samson in his own partnership with a hitherto barren wife, it was fortunate, but that even the gift of Samson from God contained a "Scorpions tail behind" (360), something not unlike the serpent's sting revealed by Dalila when she last leaves Samson (997).

Samson is attacked by the Woman of Timna with

"wiles[,] . . . blandisht parlies, feminine assaults, / Tongue-batteries" (402–04), as if he were some sort of fortress under siege. Samson the muscleman tends to become effeminate in the process of following bad women. As he is shorn of his hair, in which lies his strength, he is also emasculated, made into a "tame Weather" (538: a wether is a castrated ram) or a drone (567) by Dalila's shears. (Vondel had made him "The lion-tamer, by a woman tamed, / [who] Lies meekly, like a lamb, within his cage" [Kirkconnell 79].) More than Adam in *Paradise Lost*, he is guilty of effeminate slackness, uxoriousness, and something like idolatry, in associating with women of Philistia who worship Dagon, rather than women of Israel, who worship the "living God" (1140). Milton makes a large point in the divorce tracts of asking the husband not to marry outside of his faith or political sphere, something close to what Milton the Parliamentarian had done when he married the daughter of a Royalist, Mary Powell. Milton wrote that " . . . a right beleever ought to divorce an idolatrous heretick" because unbelievers will "perpetually at our elbow seduce us from the true worship of God, or defile and daily scandalize our conscience by their hopeles continuance in misbelief" (*Doctrine and Discipline of Divorce*; Yale 2: 263, 264–65). We don't know what Mary Powell believed, but certainly her parents were in the Royalist, high-church camp. Dalila is not Mary Powell, but she is an unbeliever, and Samson has good reason, within the boundaries that Milton set in the divorce tracts, for divorcing her and her equally traitorous predecessor, the Woman of Timna. As Haskin puts it, in his exchange with Dalila, Samson "replies in tones that anticipate the prophetic literature, where the Lord will complain about Israel's idolatry under the figure of marital infidelity" (180).

Yet Solomon, not Samson, was the chief example of uxoriousness in the Bible. Another subject for a biblical play in Milton's list was Solomon "governed by women" (Yale 8: 563n). The Chorus more than Samson is savage in indicting marriage contracted with inappropriate women, echoing Milton's divorce tracts and parts of *Paradise Lost* (9.1025–60). Whether the Chorus is to be trusted, however, is difficult to determine.

PERSONAL, POLITICAL, AND RELIGIOUS IMPLICATIONS

A recent study by Sharon Achinstein leads us to believe that Milton had sympathy after the Restoration for Dissenters such as the Quakers Thomas Ellwood, William Penn, or Isaac Penington the elder or the younger (see Hill 216). Such a sympathy is demonstrated in Samson's refusal to violate his conscience in public. Labriola, Steadman, and Wittreich have looked to Milton's anti-prelatical or theological writings to find structure in Samson's spiritual renovation and reconciliation with God. Critics have looked long and hard in order to justify Samson's act of vengeance.

Probably some of the problems of a politically outcast blind man in care of his wife, children, and servants (Milton, in other words) are demonstrated in Samson's frustration and helplessness in Gaza and in his temptation to domestic comfort or luxury as offered to him by Dalila. Parker may have been right in the general principle "to objectify personal feeling was a necessity with Milton" and its application: "In poetry he achieved it by pouring emotion into a rigid form and by ordering its expression in terms of rhetorical convention" (237). *Samson Agonistes* certainly represents an attempt to objectify deep personal feelings. Samson's "O dark, dark, dark amidst the blaze of noon" (80) seems deeply felt, by the author, as does Samson's blind helplessness.

There are also social and political attitudes demonstrated in the poem. Harapha is an inflated, godless aristocrat outwitted or at least out-punned and physically cowed by a powerful and godly, well-educated member of the bourgeoisie. The Philistine drunkenness and debauchery parallel that of the Sons of Belial so highly visible in the streets of London after the Restoration—the rakish and dissolute followers of Charles II. Contemporary Marxist critics such as Tony Davies point out some of the possible political implications of the entire poem: "If Satan is Milton's critique of kingly power, *Samson* may voice, no less searchingly and with a more personal involvement, his doubts about the cause he had made his own, its historical certainty, its anger and frustration, its dreams of a final, victorious reckoning" (266). Curiously, Davies does not explore the social implications in the character of Harapha, but Christopher Hill does:

> Harapha, with his "feudal" notions of honour, could relate to the restored Cavaliers who mocked Milton and his cause, though he may also contain something of the ostentatiously heroic fire-eaters of the New Model Army whom Milton had warned not to turn into Royalists themselves—part of his rejection of romantic revolutionism. (*Milton* 435)

Also, Milton himself, in his international pamphlet war with Salmasius, had been compared with David and Salmasius with Goliath (Hill 182 cites Marchamont Nedham and Edward Phillips's biography). The comparison between Harapha/Goliath and the gigantic intellect Salmasius, whose death Milton thought he had caused, again makes Milton into the biblical David or Samson.

Michael Wilding sees a radical shift from old order to new in the poem: "The public world of ceremony and violence, the attempts to create a juster world by the Satanic ethos of war—this has been replaced by the quietest ethic of private moral victories, the preparation of the individual soul for the eternal kingdom of heaven" ("Regaining" 140–41). Wilding's point, however, might be undercut by Samson's slaughter of the Philistines.

Hill sees hope for future democracies in the common people who escape the ruin of the temple of Dagon: "The most one can hope for the vulgar who stand outside the Temple is that they will escape the destruction of the Philistine aristocracy in the day of Babylonian woe, and that they too will learn to take advantage of their second chance" (441). From a sociological perspective, John Guillory sees *Samson Agonistes* as "the prototype of the bourgeois career drama" (120), with Samson developing grounds for divorce from Dalila when he is faced with the choice between going to her house or that of his father.

The priest at Dalila's ear prompting her to do evil to Samson might very easily be seen as reflecting Milton's distrust or even hatred of corrupt English prelates. In *Reason of Church-Government* (1642), Milton had specifically compared the biblical Dalilah's perfidy to the "strumpet flatteries of Prelats" (Yale 1: 858; see Lieb, *Milton* 229). Milton's hatred of a priesthood tied to princely authority remained constant throughout his political career.

Milton alters the "house" in which Samson brings down the roof upon the Philistines to a "theatre" which seems to be designed like a Roman amphitheater, except that it is partly under roof. What should we make of this? Perhaps (and that is a big perhaps), the conversion indicates Milton's disgust for what theater had become during the Restoration, a place for puppet-shows and freak performances like those demonstrations of Samson's strength for the Philistines—not a place for plays of high moral seriousness whose themes were exemplary for a nation.

The physical surroundings of theater as Milton describes it are architecturally precise:

> The building was a spacious Theatre
> Half round on two main Pillars vaulted high,
> With seats where all the Lords and each degree
> Of sort, might sit in order to behold,
> The other side was op'n, where the throng
> On banks and scaffolds under Skie might stand.
>   (1605–10)

Milton divides the amphitheater into covered seats and

cheap open seats, perhaps standing room only, and he allows Samson to kill the aristocrats while allowing the vulgar to survive. Is the implied lesson in the slaughter that the privileged few who buy expensive tickets in theaters deserve to die? Samson's resentment for having to perform games and tricks for the Philistines does sound like a condemnation of tasteless and immoral entertainment—and the people who sponsor it. Milton's interpretation of the word *theatre* (see *OED* 2a) might imply the partly covered Elizabethan theater, with the groundlings exposed to the weather, since no Roman theater that I know of (unless one counts the Coliseum) offered seating under roof for rich patrons.

THE THORNY QUESTION OF DATING

We do not know for sure when *Samson Agonistes* was written or, more specifically, when it was started and when finished. William Riley Parker dropped the bomb of early dating in a paper first read in 1937, and he confirmed it in his biography of Milton. Many kinds of arguments have been advanced by Parker, Lewalski ("*Samson*"), Radzinowicz, Patrick, and other scholars. Radzinowicz neatly summarizes conjectures about dates in her Appendix E, "1649–51, 1647–1653, 1660–1661, and 1667–1670," "four dates, or a combination of some of them" (387). The dating game quickly becomes a futile exercise, though one can use empirical data derived from a close study of metrics (Patrick), neologisms (Corns), or stylistics (Evans) to help date a poetic style.

I can only report that the consensus now favors a late date, near or after the Restoration, largely because of the kinds of evidence critics have advanced about the politics of the dramatic poem. Radzinowicz's opinion seems to be that of most Milton scholars: "none of the newer critics crudely identify Samson and Milton but they do discern latent patterns pointing toward a poem of Milton's old age" (407). For Lieb, it is a foregone conclusion: "Here [in the *Defensio Prima*], as elsewhere, Milton projects himself into the figure of Samson . . ." (*Milton* 236). Though Lieb and I are just two of the many "late date" advocates, Parker's arguments remain forceful and difficult to refute, and stylometric arguments based, say, on the incidence of compound constructions might also indicate that an earlier date should be considered.

STRUCTURE

In his famous critique of *Samson Agonistes*, Samuel Johnson found that the poem "must be allowed to want a middle, since nothing passes between the first act and the last, that either hastens or delays the death of Samson" (*Rambler* 139; 376) and critics have fought with Johnson, arguing that Samson grows in stature as he faces Manoa, Dalila, and Harapha. Modern critics find those confrontational scenes more arresting than the introduction or the catastrophe. Johnson maliciously attacks the presence of Dalila, who is "no more seen or heard of; nor has her visit any effect but that of raising the character of Samson" (374), and Harapha, "whose name had never been mentioned before, and who has no other motive of coming than to see the man whose strength and actions are so loudly celebrated" (374).

The endings of *Paradise Regain'd* and *Samson Agonistes* are written so as to parallel one another: the Son of God "unobserv'd / Home to his Mothers house private return'd" (4.638–39) and Manoa will take Samson's body "Home to his Fathers house" (1733), something that doesn't happen in the biblical account in Judges. Such echoing ties the two poems together. Critics have argued often about the significance of the phrase "To which is added *SAMSON AGONISTES*" on the title page of the 1671 edition that paired the two poems (see, for instance, Wittreich, "Strange"). Likewise, as Christopher Hill points out, the ending of *Paradise Lost*, the image of Adam and Eve leaving Eden "with wandering steps and slow," is picked up by the beginning of *Samson Agonistes*, "A little onward lend thy guiding hand" (see Hill, *Milton* 431–32). The two epics and the tragedy are also linked by the quietness of their endings.

SIGNIFICANT OMISSIONS

Milton is remarkably restrained for what he leaves out or what he rejects from previous poetic devices or banks of allusion. He does not refer to the New Testament or to Christ at all, and he does not refer to classical mythology, though Samson does mention "the Gentiles" twice (150, 500), meaning (we presume) the Greeks living within his own time. Given that Samson was considered a type of Christ and that Hercules was his mythic parallel, Milton's restraint in not alluding to either explicitly is remarkable. Despite Samuel Johnson's accusation that Milton was anachronistic in using "Chalybean Steel" or "Alp [as] the general name of a mountain" (*Rambler* 140; 377), the dramatic poem is remarkably free of time-tied baggage. If one looks at most of the analogues—plays or operas dealing with Samson—collected by Kirkconnell, their imagery is Christian, their allusions are to the Greek and Roman classics, and they are indebted to other contemporary works. Milton's topical or timely allusions—to decadent aristocrats or priests, for instance—would have had to be kept under veil, considering that Milton in 1671 was labeled a regicide and might have been imprisoned or even executed for such "treason." His imagery is not Christian; his dramatic poem is parallel to a number of Greek tragedies, but not slavishly imitative of any other

play; and he is too proud to imitate any contemporary tragedy, not even *Hamlet* or *King Lear*. His "Dramatic Poem" is an affront and a rebuttal to the entire world of the Restoration stage.

POETIC STYLE

Though it is not quite so terse as *Paradise Regain'd*, the style of *Samson Agonistes* is elliptical, spare (this is why the comparatively few images like that of the phoenix stand out), and enigmatic. It is almost as if Milton wants to withhold meaning from his reader. Una Ellis-Fermor sees the prosody of the drama in musical terms, as a "heavy, dragging" cadence in the beginning, followed by "sharp and restless, more often irresolute, wavering, uncertain" movement by lines 74–82 (148–49). She sees the most significant musical units—verse paragraphs—as reflecting meaning and mood as well as rhythm and internal harmony.

On the level of word-choice, Corns notes that "words of Miltonic coining [are] much rarer in *Samson Agonistes* than in *Comus*" (58), and he notices the high incidence within the poem of "words containing or cognate with the element 'self'" (59), indicating Samson's self-absorption. Sentence length and number of syllables per sentence are distinctively lower in *Samson Agonistes* than in all of Milton's other long poetic works (14), indicating an elliptical, plain-speaking mode of discourse.

PROSODY: SCANSION AND STROPHIC PATTERNS

Just observing the shapes of the variable lines in Milton's verse drama tells us something about his experimentation with measure—the mathematical counting of syllables within the line, and the length of the line on the page as compared with the length of time it takes to say the line aloud. Milton is concerned with declamation and breathing at the same time, by which I mean that his speeches are rarely naturalistic, as are the speeches in Shakespeare's comedies or his late tragedies. Each character declaims at length, developing ideas as if debating in public, and breath control becomes as important to an actor reading the lines as does any reaction to another character's lines. Strophes and epistrophes, the classical drama's turns and counter turns, are set up within the speeches that allude to the movements of the chorus in Greek drama without mimicking them. The words do the dancing. The verse-forms within the strophes may imply emotion more than motion. By definition, the term allaeostrophe meant "verse which does not exhibit a repeated pattern of any sort" (*The New Princeton Encyclopedia of Poetry and Poetics*); thus Milton was free to vary rhythms and line lengths as he wished.

Line lengths are highly irregular, on purpose—a

practice that looks back at least as far as "Lycidas"—and the strophic patterns clearly allude to the Latin ode to Rouse. Not all lines can be safely scanned as regularly iambic (compare Hamlet's "To be or not to be" soliloquy for similar metrical play). Lines convey intense emotion: they are packed but terse. The lengths of lines vary without recognizable patterns, yet the reader might feel as if he or she is being led along, mathematically and rhythmically, by how the line lengths are being regulated or manipulated.

We can't be sure precisely what Milton means in the head note to the poem:

> . . . *Chorus* is here introduc'd after the Greek manner, not antient only but modern, and still in use among the *Italians*. In the modelling therefore of this Poem, with good reason, the Antients and *Italians* are rather follow'd, as of much more authority and fame. The measure of Verse us'd in the Chorus is of all sorts, call'd by the Greeks *Monostrophic*, or rather *Apolelymenon*, without regard had to *Strophe*, *Antistrophe* or *Epod*, which were a kind of Stanza's fram'd only for the Music, then us'd with the Chorus that sung; not essential to the Poem, and therefore not material; or being divided into Stanza's or Pauses, they may be call'd *Allæostropha*.

Milton seems to be replacing the echoing strophe and antistrophe of Greek tragedy with monostrophes, and incorporating internal variety of line lengths, or allaeostrophes, with strophes of irregular length and without any recognizable rhythmic pattern. He discards the use of strophes, stanzas with pauses between them. He also discards lyrics, since his dramatic poem is not meant to be sung (though lines may have musical structure); certain lines—especially choral lines or lines conveying intense emotion—might be chanted. Choruses in Milton's dramatic poem are close to the Greek models in Euripides and Sophocles, but they also have an integrity in English. They may look on the page like Greek choruses, but they do not try to sound like Greek choruses, either quaintly or anachronistically.

What Milton arrives at in his metrics is quite original for his time, something not far from free verse as advocated by Ezra Pound and practiced, say, in "The Love Song of J. Alfred Prufrock," by T. S. Eliot. It is no accident that Eliot wrote his own parody of Milton's verse forms and subject matter in a poem called "Sweeney Agonistes." The great predecessors of Pound and Eliot, Gerard Manley Hopkins and Robert Bridges, examined the metrics of *Samson Agonistes* closely as a model for their own.

STRUCTURE AND GENRE: NOT THAT OF ELIZABETHAN TRAGEDY

Milton completely rejected Elizabethan tragedy while writing a dramatic poem not intended for the stage. Though he might have looked profitably at Shakespeare's apocalyptic and baroque *King Lear* (it is very unlikely that he did) as an example of how to write a tragedy about Samson, he did not model his tragedy on Shakespearean tragedy—not for structure, not for verse forms, not for dialogue, not for characterization, not for dramatic devices.

Samson Agonistes does have a dramatic structure, one which Low meticulously lays out:

> Making use of Parker's findings, and realizing that precise lineation is made difficult by brief transitional passages that join the episodes, one may tabulate the play's divisions as follows:
>
> prologos, 1–114, Samson's soliloquy
> parados (Chorus' entry song), 115–75, Chorus
> 1 epeisodion (episode), 176–292, Samson and Chorus
> 1 stasimon (chorus), 293–329, Chorus
> 2 epeisodion, 330–651, Samson and Manoa
> 2 stasimon, 652–724, Chorus
> 3 epeisodion, 725–1009, Samson and Dalila
> 3 stasimon, 1010–61, Chorus
> 4 epeisodion, 1062–1267, Samson and Harapha
> 4 stasimon, 1268–1307, Chorus
> 5 epeisodion, 1308–1426, Samson and Public Officer
> 5 stasimon, 1427–44, Chorus
> exodos (exit song), 1445–1758; Manoa, Messenger, Chorus
>
> Milton's plan includes
>
> kommos (dirge), 1660–1758, Manoa, Chorus, and Semichoruses
>
>   (*Blaze* 6–7)

It is to Milton's credit that, though the Greek organizational plan that Low catalogues seems to be there, the audience or reader does not notice it at all, just as one does not notice similar classical rhetorical divisions in *Areopagitica*. The dramatic poem is unobtrusively organized and has no interruptions for definitive act and scene division: it flows smoothly from one scene into the next, with very few stage directions. The rising action of the play does not depend on action but on spiritual growth or the growth of emotional intensity.

UNPLEASANTNESS AND UNCERTAINTY

Recent critics have avoided the question of the play

being unpleasant to read (with the notable exception of John Carey, who calls the ending "morally disgusting" [333]), at least in the twentieth century, though they have commented on its brutal starkness or its antifeminism, which Kirkconnell does not believe is extreme within the tradition of writing about Samson (vi–vii). The characters in the play, including Samson, are not heroic in most senses of the word. Samson commits suicide, vengefully taking the life of many Philistines; one of the key words in the play is *vengeance*. Zagorin argues, tentatively, that "the poem may even be a revenge fantasy" on Milton's part (144). Samson hasn't many good things to say about anyone—not even himself. Even if he is young enough to be strong and vigorous, he seems old and bitter, devoted more to death than life. I do not wish to oversimplify our definition of the character or the play, but, compared with *Hamlet*, where is the tragic hero or the model of nobility or magnanimity in Milton's dramatic poem? Samson isn't shown to have done anything clearly heroic until the Chorus and Manoa discuss the meaning of his cataclysmic act, after his death.

Consider all these depressing facts: the Chorus is often wrong and wrong-headed; Manoa is wrong in his assessment of his son's needs; Dalila is a manifest serpent and a viper; Harapha is a cowardly braggart; and the Public Servant is duped by Samson into thinking that Samson is coming with him for the common good. Samson has been a riddler and a trickster, and a dupe for women, which makes him more of a "fool," as he admits, than a tragic hero. Samson's and the Chorus's riddles, necessary to cover their subversive plots (Jackie DiSalvo called Samson a "terrorist" at an International Milton Seminar in 1994; and Empson had called him a "Nihilist," which is not much better) against the Philistines, create problems for the reader in uncovering truth. Steadman is probably right that we don't know for sure who is telling the truth until the end of the poem ("Causality" 220).

Samson is also a kind of recovering addict, having succumbed repeatedly to the blandishments of infidel women. Are we to believe that Milton wanted to ennoble the character by remaking Samson into a champion oddly chosen by God, or by layering his own autobiographical and political concerns on top of the character of a negative, blind former champion, an overmuscular, testosterone-filled goon, who, after being duped by one Philistine bride, immediately goes out and finds her soulmate in another? The image of the phoenix, rising from its own ashes, must carry much weight if we are to believe in Samson's redemption and reconciliation with God in the end. We also must believe, as Carey does, in the "triumphant upward arc"

(341) of the plot in order to see a message of hope in the tragedy. Whether or not Samson is redeemed in his act of suicide and wholesale destruction is still argued hotly by critics such as Wittreich and Radzinowicz.

THE TRAGIC ISOLATION OF SAMSON

The audience or reader may be struck with the utter loneliness of Samson's position (he is "excluded / All friendship, and avoided as a blab" [494–95]), since no one else knows what the truth is, and no one in the poem but Samson is subject to inspiration directly from God, or "rouzing motions" (1382). The plot portrays the withdrawal of the main character from life, and his denial of many forms of meaning. Certainly Samson feels no comfort in his domestic life: he doesn't even have children or a surviving mother. Milton calculatedly removes even the "breathren" who in Judges were supposed to have recovered Samson's body and to have given it decent burial (Judges 16.31). His own people are servile to the Philistines; his two wives, infidels, have betrayed him for money or fame; his father thinks the best freedoms are those bought with a ransom; his friends (the Chorus) are often of shallow opinion; in public he is humiliated by his position as a bondslave and taunted by braggarts like Harapha. He is not sure of the truth about himself: if he is a fool and a blab. He often wonders how could God have divinely appointed him and given him a mission. Critics have long argued whether or not he is regenerated at the end. Does he have anything like redemption or inner peace when he murders thousands of God's enemies and commits suicide at the same time? No other tragedy ends with such a desolate event: could Milton have been celebrating the glory of an isolated terrorist?

THE TEXT

Paradise Regain'd and *Samson Agonistes* are part of the same printed book, the 1671 volume with the title page that begins with the words emphasized as

PARADISE
REGAIN'D.

and then, almost seeming to be an afterthought,

To which is added
SAMSON AGONISTES.

with the second title in italics but not in so large a font. Shawcross comments "Yet *Samson* is not lost on the title page, and its own title page [when its text begins] with separate pagination for the poem implies a twofold, balanced volume, similar to Sir Thomas Browne's 1658 *Hydrotaphia Together With The Garden of Cyrus*" ("Genres" 226). A title page for a seventeenth-century volume should be studied closely, since "each feature [on the title page] was a site of contestation and negotiation," and "such features as frontispieces, title pages, dedications, epistles, and commendatory verse historically mediate texts in revealing ways" (Marotti 67). But what should we make of the emphases on the title page? Shawcross, Wittreich, Rajan, and others have made a great deal out of that phrase "To which is added."

Neither *Samson Agonistes* nor *Paradise Regain'd* is very faithfully printed, for what we know about the preferences of the author. Though some of Milton's spelling preferences creep through into the printed text, the *Errata* list, the *Omissa* (lines of text for some reason left out of the printed version and listed at the end), and mis-lineation all argue that whoever controlled the printing was not scrupulously accurate. If they had been, pages would have been corrected in press, rather than being retrofit with an *Omissa* list. Orthography (I am speaking specifically of punctuation and capitalization) is inconsistent: a vocative might not be set off by commas, for instance, or a capitalized adjective might appear for no good reason in a series of uncapitalized adjectives. The speech prefix for Samson is sometimes "*Sam.*", sometimes "*Sa.*", and sometimes "*Sams.*".

One test for telling whether the printer was honoring Milton's spelling preferences, at least, could be found in the choice between "their," a spelling preferred in most printing houses of the era, and "thir" or "thire," Milton's preferred spellings. "Thir" appears regularly until line 190, where "their" first appears; thereafter one cannot predict when an aberrant "their" will slip in. Distribution of "theirs" might tell us something about how the poem was set into type or about how someone acting for the printer or for Milton might have influenced a compositor.

John Shawcross summarized his opinions about the text of *Samson Agonistes* in an e-mail message to me written in June of 1997:

> I think the composing was most unreliable, but that elements from the copy text got into the 1671 volume in spite of carelessness in setting spellings, etc., and we must not forget that the copy text must have gone through at least one scribe's hands if not more. But since SA gives us loads of Miltonic spellings (whether because an original text by Milton lay in the background, allowing an early date for some of it, or because the scribe knew how Milton spelled certain

words, or because Milton gave specific instructions on the spellings—specifically or generally), the compositor was pretty clearly inconsistent. There are 80 examples of "thir" (one in a second state of text), for instance, and words like "unwholsom," "burdensom," "welcom," "highth," "degenerately," "perfet," "anough."

Fletcher concluded unequivocally that John Macocke (or Macock) was the "J. M." listed as printer for the two poems on the title page and that John Starkey apparently owned the rights to reproduce the book, presumably sold to him by Milton, though no agreement has survived (Fletcher 12). The typeface used was the equivalent of 14-point Garamond, with enough leading provided between the lines (Fletcher 28) to give a very legible distribution of lines of type. I have chosen in this edition to reduce the size of the Garamond font to 9-point but to use conventional modern leading.

Intriguingly, Francis Atterbury in his letter to Pope mentions a manuscript of *Samson Agonistes* belonging to the printer Jacob Tonson (Shawcross *Milton* 243), but if a manuscript ever existed, we have no witness by anyone who saw it.

Works Cited
Editions are marked with an asterisk

Achinstein, Sharon. *Milton and the Revolutionary Reader*. Princeton, NJ: Princeton UP, 1994.

Barker, Arthur E. "Calm Regained through Passion Spent: The Conditions of the Miltonic Effort." *The Prison and the Pinnacle*. Ed. Balachandra Rajan. Toronto: U of Toronto P, 1973. 3-48.

Bennett, Joan S. "A Reading of *Samson Agonistes*." *The Cambridge Companion to Milton*. Ed. Dennis Danielson. Cambridge: Cambridge UP, 1989. 225-41.

——. "Liberty under the Law: The Chorus and the Meaning of *Samson Agonistes*." *Milton Studies* 12 (1978): 141-63.

——. *Reviving Liberty: Radical Christian Humanism in Milton's Great Poems*. Cambridge, MA: Harvard UP, 1989.

Berkeley, David, and Salwa Khoddam. "Samson the Base versus Harapha the Gentle." *Milton Quarterly* 17 (1983): 1-7.

*Broadbent, John, and Robert Hodge, eds. *John Milton*: Samson Agonistes, *Sonnets, &c.* Cambridge: Cambridge UP, 1977.

*Bullough, Geoffrey, and Margaret Bullough, eds. *Milton's Dramatic Poems*. Rev. ed. London: Athlone, 1973.

Burnett, Archie. *Milton's Style: The Shorter Poems*, Paradise Regained, *and* Samson Agonistes. London: Longman, 1981.

Cable, Lana. *Carnal Rhetoric: Milton's Iconoclasm and the Poetics of Desire*. Durham, NC: Duke UP, 1995.

*Campbell, Gordon, ed. *John Milton. Complete English Poems*, Of Education, Areopagitica. London: Dent, 1993.

*Carey, John, ed. *Milton. Complete Shorter Poems*. Fourth impression, with corrections. London: Longman, 1981.

Christopher, Georgia B. *Milton and the Science of the Saints*. Princeton, NJ: Princeton UP, 1982.

Corns, Thomas N. *Milton's Language*. London: Basil Blackwell, 1990.

Cox, Lee Sheridan. "Natural Science and Figurative Design in *Samson Agonistes*." *ELH* 35 (1968): 51–74. Reprinted in *Critical Essays on Milton from ELH*. Baltimore, MD: Johns Hopkins UP, 1969. 253–76.

*Davies, Tony, ed. *John Milton: Selected Longer Poems and Prose*. London: Routledge, 1992.

Demetrakopoulos, S. A. "Eve as a Circean and Courtly Fatal Woman." *Milton Quarterly* 9 (1975): 99–107.

Dobson, E. J. "Milton's Pronunciation." *Language and Style in Milton: A Symposium in Honor of the Tercentenary of *Paradise Lost. Ed. Ronald David Emma and John T. Shawcross. New York: Ungar, 1967. 154–92.

Ellis-Fermor, Una. "A Note on the Dramatic Function of the Prosody of *Samson Agonistes*." *The Frontiers of Drama*. London: Methuen, 1948. 148–52.

Evans, Robert O. *Milton's Elisions*. Gainesville: U of Florida P, 1966.

Grose, Christopher. *Milton and the Sense of Tradition*. New Haven, CT: Yale UP, 1988.

Guillory, John. "Dalila's House: *Samson Agonistes* and the Sexual Division of Labor." *Rewriting the Renaissance: The Discourses of Sexual Difference in Early Modern Europe*. Ed. Margaret W. Ferguson, Maureen Quilligan, and Nancy J. Vickers. Chicago: U Chicago P, 1986. 106–22.

Hanford, James Holly. *John Milton, Englishman*. New York: Crown, 1949.

——. "*Samson Agonistes* and Milton in Old Age." *John Milton, Poet and Humanist: Essays by James Holly Hanford*. Cleveland, OH: P of Western Reserve U, 1966. 264–86.

Haskin, Dayton. *Milton's Burden of Interpretation*. Philadelphia: U of Pennsylvania P, 1994.

Hawkins, Sherman. "Samson's Catharsis." *Milton Studies* 2 (1970): 211–30.

Hill, Christopher. *Milton and the English Revolution*. New York: Viking, 1977.

*Hone, Ralph E., ed. *John Milton's* Samson Agonistes: *The Poem and Materials for Analysis*. San Francisco, CA: Chandler, 1966.

Johnson, Samuel. *Rambler* 139, 140. *The Yale Edition of the Works of Samuel Johnson*. Ed. W. J. Bate and Albrecht B. Strauss. New Haven, CT: Yale UP, 1969.

Kirkconnell, G. Watson. *That Invincible Samson: The Theme of *Samson Agonistes *in World Literature with Translations of the Major Analogues*. Toronto: U of Toronto P, 1964.

Knoppers, Laura Lunger. *Historicizing Milton: Spectacle, Power, and Poetry in Restoration England*. Athens: U of Georgia P, 1994.

——. "'Sung and proverb'd for a Fool': *Samson Agonistes* and Solomon's Harlot." *Milton Studies* 26 (1990): 239–51.

Kranidas, Thomas. "Dalila's Role in *Samson Agonistes*." *Studies in English Literature, 1500–1900* 6 (1966): 125–37.

——."*Samson Agonistes*." *A Milton Encyclopedia*. Gen. ed. William B. Hunter. Lewisburg, PA: Bucknell UP, 1979.

Krouse, F. Michael. *Milton's Samson and the Christian Tradition*. Princeton, NJ: Princeton UP, 1949.

Labriola, Albert C. "Divine Urgency as a Motive for Conduct in *Samson Agonistes*. *Philological Quarterly* 50 (1971): 99–107.

Landy, Marcia. "Language and the Seal of Silence in *Samson Agonistes*." *Milton Studies* 2 (1970): 175–94.

Lewalski, Barbara. "Milton on Women—Yet Again." *Problems for Feminist Criticism*. Ed. Sally Minogue. London: Routledge, 1990. 46–69.

——. "*Samson Agonistes* and the 'Tragedy' of the Apocalypse." PMLA 85 (1970): 1050–62.

Lieb, Michael. *Milton and the Culture of Violence*. Ithaca, NY: Cornell UP, 1994.

——."The Theology of Strength." *The Sinews of Ulysses: Form and Convention in Milton's Works*. Pittsburgh, PA: Duquesne UP, 1989.

Low, Anthony. *The Blaze of Noon: A Reading of *Samson Agonistes. New York: Columbia UP, 1974.

MacCallum, Hugh. "*Samson Agonistes*: The Deliverer as Judge." *Milton Studies* 23 (1987): 259–90.

Marotti, Arthur F. "Manuscript, Print, and the Social History of the Lyric." *The Cambridge Companion to English Poetry, Donne to Marvell*. Ed. Thomas N. Corns. Cambridge: Cambridge UP, 1993. 52–79.

Miller, Leo. "Milton's Heroic Samson: In Response to Berkeley and Khoddam." *Milton Quarterly* 18 (1984): 25–27.

*Milton, John. *Paradise Regained, Samson Agonistes 1671*. A Scolar Press Facsimile. Menston, Eng.: Scolar, 1968.

Mollenkott, Virginia R. "Relativism in *Samson Agonistes*." *Studies in Philology* 67 (1970): 89–102.

Parker, William Riley. *Milton: A Biography*. Oxford: Clarendon, 1968.

——. *Milton's Debt to Greek Tragedy in *Samson Agonistes. Baltimore, MD: Johns Hopkins UP, 1937.

——. "The Trinity Manuscript and Milton's Plans for a Tragedy." *JEGP* 34 (1935): 225–32.

Patrick, J. Max. "Milton's Revolution against Rime, and Some of Its Implications." *Milton and the Art of Sacred Song*. Ed. Patrick and Roger H. Sundell. Madison: U of Wisconsin P, 1979. 99–115.

Patrides, C. A. "The Comic Dimension in Greek Tragedy and *Samson Agonistes*." *Milton Studies* 10 (1977): 3–21.

*Prince, F. T., ed. *Milton:* Samson Agonistes. Oxford: Oxford UP, 1960.

Radzinowicz, Mary Ann. "The Distinctive Tragedy of *Samson Agonis-*

tes." *Milton Studies* 17 (1983): 249–80.

———. *Toward "Samson Agonistes": The Growth of Milton's Mind.* Princeton, NJ: Princeton UP, 1978.

Rajan, Balachandra. "To Which Is Added *Samson Agonistes—*." *The Prison and the Pinnacle.* Ed. Rajan. Toronto: U of Toronto P, 1973. 82–110.

Revard, Stella P. "Milton's Dalila and Eve: Filling in the Spaces in the Biblical Text." *Arenas of Conflict: Milton and the Unfettered Mind.* Ed. Kristin Pruit McColgan and Charles W. Durham. Cranbury, NJ: Associated UP, 1997. 271–81.

Rogers, John. *The Matter of Revolution: Science, Poetry, and Politics in the Age of Milton.* Ithaca, NY: Cornell UP, 1996.

Rudrum, Alan. *A Critical Commentary on Milton's* Samson Agonistes. London: Macmillan, 1969.

Rumrich, John. *Milton Unbound: Controversy and Reinterpretation.* Cambridge: Cambridge UP, 1996.

Rushdy, Ashraf. *The Empty Garden: The Subject of Late Milton.* Pittsburgh, PA: U of Pittsburgh P, 1992.

Samuel, Irene. "*Samson Agonistes* as Tragedy." *Calm of Mind: Tercentenary Essays on* Paradise Regained *and* Samson Agonistes *in Honor of John S. Diekhoff.* Ed. Joseph A. Wittreich, Jr. Cleveland, OH: P of Case Western Reserve U, 1971. 235–57.

Sellin, Paul R. "Milton's Epithet *Agonistes*." *Studies in English Literature, 1500–1900* 4 (1964): 137–62.

Shaw, William P. "Producing *Samson Agonistes*." *Milton Quarterly* 13 (1979): 69–79.

*Shawcross, John T., ed. *The Complete Poetry of John Milton.* New York: Doubleday Anchor, 1971.

———. "The Genres of *Paradise Regain'd* and *Samson Agonistes*: The Wisdom of Their Joint Publication." *Composite Orders: The Genres of Milton's Last Poems.* Ed. Richard S. Ide and Joseph A. Wittreich. *Milton Studies* 17 (1983). 225–48.

———. *John Milton: The Self and the World.* Lexington: UP of Kentucky, 1993.

———. "Misreading Milton." *The Miltonic Samson. Milton Studies* 33. Ed. Albert C. Labriola and Michael Lieb. Pittsburgh: U Pittsburgh P, 1997.

Spiller, Michael. "Directing the Audience in *Samson Agonistes*." *Of Poetry and Politics: New Essays on Milton and His World.* Ed. Paul Stanwood. Binghamton, NY: Medieval and Renaissance Texts and Studies, 1995. 121–29.

Steadman, John M. "Causality and Catastrophe in *Samson Agonistes*." *Milton Studies* 28 (1992): 211–26.

Stollman, Samuel S. "Milton's Samson and the Jewish Tradition." *Milton Studies* 3 (1971): 185–200.

Swaim, Kathleen. "The Doubling of the Chorus in *Samson Agonistes*." *Milton Studies* 20 (1984): 225–45.

Ulreich, John C., Jr. "Incident to All Our Sex: The Tragedy of Dalila." *Milton and the Idea of Woman.* Ed. Julia M. Walker. Urbana: U of Illinois P, 1988. 185–210.

Wilding, Michael. "Regaining the Radical Milton." *The Radical Reader.* Ed. Stephen Knight and Michael Wilding. Sydney, Australia: Wild & Woolley, 1977.

Wittreich, Joseph. *Interpreting* Samson Agonistes. Princeton, NJ: Princeton UP, 1986.

———. "Strange Text! *Paradise Regain'd . . . To Which is Added Samson Agonistes*." *Poems in Their Place: The Intertextuality and Order of Poetic Collections.* Ed. Neil Fraistat. Chapel Hill: U of North Carolina P, 1986. 164–94.

Zagorin, Perez. *Milton: Aristocrat & Rebel.* Rochester, NY: D. S. Brewer, 1992.

Of that sort of Dramatic Poem which is call'd Tragedy.[1]

Tragedy, as it was antiently compos'd, hath been ever held the gravest, moralest, and most profitable of all other Poems: therefore said by *Aristotle* to be of power by raising pity and fear, or terror, to purge the mind of those and such like passions, that is to temper and reduce them to just measure[2] with a kind of delight, stirr'd up by reading or seeing those passions well imitated.[3] Nor is Nature wanting in her own effects to make good his assertion: for so in Physic[4] things of melancholic hue and quality[5] are us'd against melancholy, sowr against sowr, salt to remove salt humours.[6] Hence Philosophers and other gravest Writers, as *Cicero*, *Plutarch* and others, frequently cite out of Tragic Poets, both to adorn and illustrate thir discourse. The Apostle *Paul* himself thought it not unworthy to insert a verse of *Euripides* into the Text of Holy Scripture, 1 *Cor.* 15.33.[7] and *Paræus*[8] commenting on the Revelation, divides the whole Book as a Tragedy, into Acts distinguisht each by a Chorus of Heavenly Harpings and Song between. Heretofore Men in highest dignity have labour'd not a little to be thought able to compose a Tragedy. Of that honour *Dionysius* the elder[9] was no less ambitious, then before of his attaining to the Tyranny. *Augustus Cæsar* also had begun his *Ajax*,[10] but unable to please his own judgment with what he had begun, left it unfinisht. *Seneca* the Philosopher is by some thought the Author of those Tragedies (at lest the best of them) that go under that name.[11] *Gregory Nazianzen*[12] a Father of the Church, thought it not unbeseeming the sanctity of his person to write a Tragedy, which he entitl'd, *Christ suffering*.[13] This is mention'd to vindicate Tragedy from the small esteem, or rather infamy, which in the account of many it undergoes at this day with other common Interludes;[14] hap'ning through the Poets error of intermixing Comic stuff with Tragic sadness[15] and gravity; or introducing trivial and vulgar persons, which by all judicious hath bin counted absurd;[16] and brought in without discretion, corruptly to gratifie the people. And though antient Tragedy use no Prologue, yet using sometimes, in case of self defence, or explanation, that which *Martial* calls an Epistle;[17] in behalf of this Tragedy coming forth after the antient manner, much different from what among us passes for best, thus much

---

[1]For the context of the debate over the nature of tragedy—a debate that involved Milton, Andrew Marvell, and John Dryden—see Morris Freedman, "Milton and Dryden on Tragedy," *English Writers of the Eighteenth Century*, ed. John H. Middendorf (New York: Columbia UP, 1971): 158–71.

[2]Proper proportion.

[3]Aristotle's *Poetics* 6 discusses the purgation or catharsis of pity and fear supposed to be effected on the audience of tragedies. Milton had called attention to that chapter by quoting from it in Greek, then translating into Latin, on his title page.

[4]Medical practice.

[5]Outward appearance and inner nature. Aristotle's discussion did not include a theory of medical (or what we might call psychogenic) purgation, discussed in Sherman Hawkins, "Samson's Catharsis," *Milton Studies* 2 (1970): 211–30. For the most complete discussion of the influence of the Italian critics on Milton's theory of tragedy, see John M. Steadman, *Epic and Tragic Structure in* Paradise Lost (Chicago, IL: U of Chicago P, 1976), Chapters 6 and 7.

[6]"Humour" here is "Used for the peculiar constitution or quality (e.g. saltness, sourness) of a material substance" (*OED* 2.d).

[7]The verse, "Evil communications corrupt good manners," which Milton also cites in *Areopagitica* (Yale 2: 508), is from Menander's *Thais*, rather than from anything written by Euripides, but "the fragment in which it has survived is found in editions of both Menander and Euripides" (Yale 8: 134n).

[8]The Calvinist David Paraeus is one of Milton's favorite commentators on scripture, judging by the number of citations in various prose works. Milton used his ideas more than once to justify the existence of Christian tragedy: "And the Apocalyps of Saint *John* is the majestick image of a high and stately Tragedy, shutting up and intermingling her solemn Scenes and Acts with a sevenfold *Chorus* of halleluja's and harping symphonies: and this my opinion the grave autority of *Pareus* commenting that booke is sufficient to confirm" (*Reason of Church Government*; Yale 1: 815).

[9]Dionysius I of Syracuse (his precise title was "strategos," and he ruled from 405 to 367 BCE), oppressive ruler but patron of the arts. He was supposed to have purchased the writing tablets of Aeschylus and to have been patron to Plato before attempting to have him sold into slavery. His tragedy *The Ransoming of Hector* won a prize at a festival of Lenaea in Athens in 367 BCE, but he was supposed to have died in a drinking bout afterward ("Syracuse," *The Oxford Companion to Classical Literature*, ed. M.C. Howatson [Oxford: Oxford UP, 1989]).

[10]Suetonius, *Lives of the Caesars* 2.85, tells the story of Augustus beginning a play about the Homeric hero Ajax with great enthusiasm but erasing it because he did not like his own style.

[11]The Stoic philosopher and the playwright were one and the same. Carey points out where the mistaken identification began, in Sidonius Apollinaris, *Carmen* 9.230–38 (*Samson Agonistes*, Introduction 21n).

[12]Milton was again deceived by author attribution. We know that the tragedy Milton calls *Christ suffering* was probably written by Apollinaris the Elder rather than by Gregory Nazianzen (325?–390?), Church Father and Bishop of Constantinople.

[13]Milton himself mentioned the subjects "Christ born," "Christ bound," "Christ Crucifi'd," and "Christ risen" as four potential subjects for tragedies he himself might write (Yale 8: 559), though of course he was to concentrate on Christ's temptation by Satan in the wilderness (Matthew 4) in *Paradise Regain'd*.

[14]Technically a comic play inserted between acts of a serious morality play (*OED* 1), but by Milton's time any popular, possibly scurrilous or bawdy comedy, an opinion he endorses in *Reason of Church Government* (Yale 1: 818).

[15]High seriousness.

[16]Milton must not have considered the introduction of Harapha, who can be interpreted as a comic figure, to be an intrusion into a tragic plot.

[17]The Roman poet Martial, in his own epistle included in *Epigrams* 2, speaks of tragedies needing prefaces because they cannot speak in their own defense.

before-hand may be Epistl'd; that *Chorus* is here introduc'd after the Greek manner, not antient only but modern, and still in use among the *Italians*.[18] In the modelling therefore of this Poem, with good reason, the Antients and *Italians* are rather follow'd, as of much more authority and fame. The measure of Verse us'd in the Chorus is of all sorts, call'd by the Greeks *Monostrophic*,[19] or rather *Apolelymenon*, without regard had to *Strophe, Antistrophe* or *Epod*, which were a kind of Stanza's fram'd only for the Music, then us'd with the Chorus that sung; not essential to the Poem, and therefore not material; or being divided into Stanza's or Pauses, they may be call'd *Allæostropha*. Division into Act and Scene referring chiefly to the Stage (to which this work never was intended) is here omitted.

It suffices if the whole Drama be found not produc't beyond the fift Act,[20] of the style and uniformitie, and that commonly call'd the Plot, whether intricate or explicit,[21] which is nothing indeed but such œconomy, or disposition of the fable[22] as may stand best with verisimilitude and decorum; they only will best judge who are not unacquainted with *Æshulus, Sophocles,* and *Euripides,* the three Tragic Poets unequall'd yet by any, and the best rule to all who endeavour to write Tragedy. The circumscription of time wherein the whole Drama begins and ends, is according to antient rule, and best example, within the space of 24 hours.[23]

HOMEOPATHIC

The ARGUMENT.

SAmson *made Captive, Blind, and now in the Prison at* Gaza,[24] *there to labour as in a common work-house,*[25] *on a Festival day, in the general cessation from labour, comes forth into the open Air, to a place nigh, somewhat retir'd there to sit a while and bemoan his condition. Where he happens at length to be visited by certain friends and equals of his tribe,*[26] *which make the Chorus, who seek to comfort him what*[27] *they can; then by his old Father* Manoa, *who endeavours the like, and withal tells him his purpose to procure his liberty by ransom; lastly, that this Feast was proclaim'd by the* Philistins *as a day of Thanksgiving for thir deliverance from the hands of* Samson, *which yet more troubles him.* Manoa *then departs to prosecute his endeavour with the* Philistian[28] *Lords for* Samson's *redemption;*[29] *who in the mean while is visited by other persons;*[30] *and lastly by a publick Officer to require his coming to the Feast before the Lords and People, to play or shew his strength in thir presence; he at first refuses, dismissing the publick Officer with absolute denyal to come; at length perswaded inwardly that this was from God, he yields to go along with him, who came now the second time with great threatnings to fetch him; the Chorus yet remaining on the place,* Manoa *returns full of joyful hope, to procure e're long his Sons deliverance: in the midst of which discourse an Ebrew comes in haste confusedly at first; and afterward more distinctly relating the Catastrophe, what* Samson *had done to the* Philistins, *and by accident*[31] *to himself; wherewith the Tragedy ends.*

---

[18]In *Of Education,* Milton mentions "the *Italian* commentaries of *Castelvetro, Tasso, Mazzoni,* and others, [which teach] what the laws are of a true *Epic* poem, what of a *Dramatic,* what of a *Lyric,* what decorum is, which is the grand master peece to observe" (Yale 2: 404–405).

[19]Including only one strophe ("turn" or change in direction of the chorus) within a stanza. "Apolelymenon" ("freed"), because the chorus in Milton's dramatic poem will not be bound to make the change of direction required by the Greek stage. Strophes were sung originally while moving from right to left, antistrophes while moving from left to right, and epodes while standing still. Allaeostropha was one type of apolelymena. "Milton uses the term, spelled *allæostropha* (for reasons unknown), in the preface to *Samson Agonistes* to describe verse in irregular stanzas" (*New Princeton Encyclopedia of Poetry and Poetics,* ed. Alex Preminger and T. F. F. Brogan [Princeton, NJ: Princeton UP, 1993]: "Allæostropha").

[20]"It is enough that the entire play should not take up more than five acts." "Produced" has the sense of "extended."

[21]Aristotle divides tragic plots into the simple (here "explicit") or complex (here "intricate") in the *Poetics* 6.

[22]Plot, story.

[23]What has been more recently called the "unity of time"; when it is paired with "unity of place" and "unity of action," the three unities are in place. According to Aristotle, tragic plots were supposed to confine themselves to one day, but there were exceptions among the plays of the three great Greek tragedians, as in Euripides's *Suppliants,* which Milton knew and cited more than once.

[24]Chief of the five principal cities of the Philistine confederation, southwest of Jerusalem. For the Philistines, see Judges 13–16 and 1 Samuel.

[25]Workshop for the poor.

[26]The tribe of Dan or the Danites (see *Paradise Lost* 9.1059). Manoa will later call the Chorus "Brethren and men of *Dan*" (332). We might assume that the Chorus is comprised of men about the same age as Samson, if John Leonard and Robert Wickenheiser are correct in assuming that "equals" conforms to the *OED* definition "people of about the same age" (B.1c).

[27]"In whatever way."

[28]Milton writes the adjective form consistently as "Philistian" and the noun as "Philistine." According to the *OED,* he is the first in English to make such a distinction.

[29]Freedom gained by ransom.

[30]The "other persons" include Dalila and Harapha, in the Argument not important enough to be given names.

[31]"By chance," an important distinction to make, since the phrase implies that Samson is not suicidal when he brings down the temple.

The Persons.

Samson.
Manoa *the Father of* Samson.
Dalila *his Wife.*[1]
Harapha *of* Gath.[2]
Publick Officer.
Messenger.
Chorus *of* Danites.
The Scene before the Prison in Gaza.

---

[1]Delilah is never Samson's wife in the account in Judges 14–16; she is mentioned only as a woman from the valley of Sorek whom Samson loved. In making Dalila Samson's wife, Milton intensifies her betrayal of him to the Philistines.

[2]A fictional giant, not a part of the biblical account of the life of Samson, conceived by Milton as a relative of Goliath, the giant killed by David. Harapha is named as Goliath's father at 1248–49. The David and Goliath story is in 1 Samuel 17–22. Other giants from Gath are mentioned in 2 Samuel 18–22. Jewish biblical commentary makes Goliath a descendent of Samson who wears the insignia of Dagon in battle; Christian commentary makes him into a type of Satan, fighting against Christ (see "Goliath," in *A Dictionary of Biblical Tradition in English Literature*, gen. ed. David Lyle Jeffrey [Grand Rapids, MI: Eerdmans, 1992]).

[handwritten: CLOSET DRAMA MEANT TO BE READ & NOT PERFORMED]

SAMSON
AGONISTES.

[handwritten: SAMSON THE STRUGGLER / HEBREW & GREEK]

Sams.

ALittle onward lend thy guiding hand
  To these dark steps, a little further on;[3]
For yonder bank hath choice of Sun or shade,
There I am wont° to sit, when any chance   ACCUSTOMED
Relieves me from my task of servile toyl,   5
Daily in the common Prison else enjoyn'd me,[4]
Where I a Prisoner chain'd, scarce freely draw
The air imprison'd also, close and damp,
Unwholsom draught:[5] but here I feel amends,[6]
The breath of Heav'n fresh-blowing, pure and sweet,
With day-spring° born; here leave me to respire.[7]   DAYBREAK   10
This day a solemn Feast the people hold
To *Dagon*[8] thir Sea-Idol, and forbid
Laborious works, unwillingly this rest
Thir Superstition[9] yields me; hence with leave   15
Retiring from the popular noise,[10] I seek
This unfrequented place to find some ease,
Ease to the body some, none to the mind
From restless thoughts, that like a deadly swarm
Of Hornets arm'd,[11] no sooner found alone,   20
But rush upon me thronging, and present
Times past, what once I was, and what am now.
O wherefore° was my birth from Heaven foretold   WHY
Twice by an Angel,[12] who at last in sight
Of both my Parents all in flames ascended   25
From off the Altar, where an Off'ring burn'd,

[handwritten: SAMSON AS A TYPE OF CHRIST]

---

[3]Though the person leading Samson is anonymous, the situation may be intended to recall the similar beginning of Sophocles's *Oedipus at Colonus*, with Antigone leading her blind father Oedipus. Samson, of course, has no children to depend on in his blindness.

[4]"Otherwise forced on me."

[5]"Drawing of smoke or vapour into the mouth, inhaling; that which is inhaled at one breath" (*OED* 16, citing this instance).

[6]"Improvement in health, recovery" (*OED* 4b, "amends," citing this instance).

[7]"Leave me here to catch my breath." Phineas Fletcher had used the same phrase, "here leave me to respire," in *The Purple Island* (1633) 11.1.

[8]The national god of the Philistines, called "Philistims" in the Geneva Bible, which identifies Dagon as "their chief idole, & as some write, from the navil downwarde was like a fishe, and upwarde like a man" (1 Samuel 5.2n), which Milton echoes in *Paradise Lost*: "*Dagon* his Name, Sea Monster, upward Man / And downward Fish . . . " (1.462–63).

[9]Probably "An irrational religious system; a false, pagan, or idolatrous religion" (*OED* 2, citing this instance).

[10]Presumably from the noise of people speaking, with a disparaging reference to the Philistine people implied: Samson considers what they say as noise.

[11]A simile taken from natural observation of aggressive hornet behavior, as with bees, yellow jackets, or wasps defending nests or hives. Milton not only constructs an emotional state, he defines the attack of hornets as potentially deadly.

[12]In Judges 13, an angel appears once to Samson's mother, who had been barren, and announces to her that she would bear a son, "and no rasor shal come on his head: for the childe shalbe a Nazarite unto God from his birth: and he shal begin to save Israel out of the hands of the Philistims" (Geneva). Samson is a Nazarite because he has been dedicated to God's service by his parents' vow. Both his mother and Samson had to abstain from wine and follow other dietary restrictions, and Samson was supposed to avoid defilement by contact with a dead body and not to allow a razor to cut his hair. As Mary Joan Winn Leith points out in *The Oxford Companion to the Bible*, "Part of the irony of the Samson story is that Samson appears not to keep any of his vows. He attended drinking feasts (Judg. 16.17), touched the carcass of a dead lion (Judg. 14.9–9), and allowed his hair to be cut by Delilah (Judg. 16.15–19)" ("Nazirite"). Nevertheless, Samson in seventeenth-century biblical commentary was constantly referred to as a type of Christ (see the table of comparisons between Samson and Christ from Thomas Hayne, *The Generall View of the Holy Scriptures* [1640]: 217–18, reproduced facing page 69 in Krouse).

As in a fiery column charioting
His Godlike presence, and from some great act
Or benefit reveal'd to *Abraham*'s[13] race?
Why was my breeding order'd and prescrib'd   30
As of a person separate to[14] God,
Design'd for great exploits;[15] if I must dye
Betray'd, Captiv'd,[16] and both my Eyes put out,
Made of my Enemies the scorn and gaze;
To grind in Brazen Fetters under task[17]   35
With this Heav'n-gifted strength? O glorious strength
Put to the labour of a Beast, debas't
Lower then bondslave![18] Promise was that I
Should *Israel* from *Philistian* yoke deliver;
Ask for this great Deliverer now, and find him   40
Eyeless in *Gaza*[19] at the Mill with slaves,
Himself in bonds under *Philistian* yoke;[20]
Yet stay, let me not rashly call in doubt
Divine Prediction; what if all foretold
Had been fulfilld but° through mine own default,°   ONLY   FAULT   45
Whom have I to complain of but my self?
Who this high gift of strength committed to me,
In what part lodg'd, how easily bereft me,°   TAKEN FROM ME
Under the Seal of silence[21] could not keep,
But weakly to a woman must reveal it,   50
O'recome with importunity and tears.[22]
O impotence of mind, in body strong!
But what is strength without a double share
Of wisdom, vast, unwieldy, burdensom,
Proudly secure, yet liable to fall[23]   55
By weakest suttleties, not made to rule,
But to subserve where wisdom bears command.[24]
God, when he gave me strength, to shew withal

---

[13]Pronounce as a disyllable ("Abram" is the first form of the name found in Genesis 11.27 through 17.5; then it is altered to "Abraham" as the name comes to mean "father of many").

[14]Separated from common humanity, for service to God (as a Nazarite).

[15]Accented on the second syllable.

[16]Accented on the second syllable, with a broad vowel sound, as in "ivy."

[17]Milton adds the detail that the simple "fetters" mentioned in Judges 16.21 be made of brass, thus "brazen." The idiom "under task" means "under the command of a taskmaster, under compulsion" (see *OED* "under task").

[18]A more emphatic form than "slave" by itself (*OED* 1), hence a doubly debased person.

[19]City in Philistia. Ashkelon and Ashdod were the major cities of the region; one temple devoted to Dagon was located at Ashdod (1 Samuel 5.1-2).

[20]Restrained by the kind of yoke one would use on oxen.

[21]Under a vow of silence, which Samson identifies here as having been given his personal bond, as if he had set his seal to the promise of silence (Landy). There is no vow of silence in Judges, though Samson is moved by Delilah's insistence: "because she was importunate upon him with her wordes continually, and vexed him, his soule was peined unto the death" (16.15). The Geneva marginalia comments, at that point, "Thus his immoderate affections toward a wicked woman caused him to lose God's excellent gifts, & become slave unto them, whome he shulde have ruled." For the vows and duties of a Nazarite, see Numbers 6.1–21. Milton seems to have been more interested in the sources of Samson's power and the growth of his power while he is disabled (having his head shorn, being blinded, and being held captive in Gaza). As Samson grows in understanding of himself, his physical and emotional strength returns. For biblical traditions, Jewish and Christian, surrounding Samson's strength in weakness, see Michael Lieb, *The Sinews of Ulysses* [Pittsburgh, PA: Duquesne UP, 1989]: Chapter 7.

[22]Milton adds "and tears," significantly, to the biblical account.

[23]Echoes "Sufficient to have stood, though free to fall" in *Paradise Lost* 3.99.

[24]"Where wisdom is in control."

How slight the gift was, hung it in my Hair.[25]
But peace, I must not quarrel with the will   60
Of highest dispensation,[26] which herein
Happ'ly had ends above my reach to know:
Suffices that to me strength is my bane,°   DOWNFALL, RUIN
And proves the sourse of all my miseries;
So many, and so huge, that each apart°   SEPARATELY   65
Would ask a life to wail,[27] but chief of all,
O loss of sight, of thee I most complain!
Blind among enemies, O worse then chains,
Dungeon, or beggery, or decrepit age!
Light the prime work of God to me is extinct,°   EXTINGUISHED, PUT OUT   70
And all her various objects of delight
Annull'd,° which might in part my grief have eas'd,   ANNIHILATED
Inferiour to the vilest now become
Of man or worm;[28] the vilest here excel me,
They creep, yet see, I dark in light expos'd   75
To daily fraud, contempt, abuse and wrong,
Within doors, or without, still° as a fool,   ALWAYS
In power of others, never in my own;
Scarce half I seem to live, dead more then half.
O dark, dark, dark, amid the blaze of noon,   80
Irrecoverably dark, total Eclipse
Without all hope of day!
O first created Beam, and thou great Word,
Let there be light, and light was over all;[29]
Why am I thus bereav'd thy prime decree?   85
The Sun to me is dark
And silent as the Moon,
When she deserts the night
Hid in her vacant interlunar cave.[30]
Since light so necessary is to life,   90
And almost life it self, if it be true
That light is in the Soul,
She all in every part;[31] why was the sight
To such a tender ball as th' eye confin'd?
So obvious and so easie to be quench't,[32]   95
And not as feeling through all parts diffus'd,
That she might look at will through every pore?
Then had I not been thus exil'd from light;

---

[25]Since part of the Nazarite's vow was not to apply a razor to his hair, Samson's identity and power as a devotee of God are bound up, quite literally, with his hair. The simple and colloquial diction of "hung it," as if Samson's hair were a hat rack for God's gift, reinforces the irony of the situation and demonstrates Samson's bitter wit.

[26]The order instituted by divine providence, or God's will.

[27]"Would ask a lifetime to bewail."

[28]He is lower, in other words, than the lowliest or most despicable man or snake ("worm" usually carried that meaning).

[29]The character Samson was often identified in revolutionary literature (as a type of Christ) having "sunny locks waving and curling about his godlike shoulders" (quoted in Hill 430–31). Samson's exile into the darkness of being blind is thus bitterly ironic, if his head emanates light or if he himself possesses inner light.

[30]The moon was referred to in classical literature as *silens luna* during the interlunar night, the period during the month when the moon is not visible. Compare the "cave / Within the Mount of God, fast by his Throne, / Where light and darkness in perpetual round / Lodge and dislodge by turns, which makes through Heav'n / Gratefull vicissitude, like Day and Night" (*Paradise Lost* 6.4–8).

[31]Samson refers to a theological commonplace that the soul exists in every part of the body (see Augustine, *De Trinitate* 6.6). The soul in Latin is *anima*, a feminine noun, thus the use of the feminine pronoun "she."

[32]"So exposed and so easy to be extinguished."

As in the land of darkness yet in light,
To live a life half dead, a living death,   100
And buried; but O yet more miserable!
My self, my Sepulcher, a moving Grave,
Buried, yet not exempt
By priviledge of death and burial
From worst of other evils, pains and wrongs,   105
But made hereby obnoxious° more   SUSCEPTIBLE
To all the miseries of life,
Life in captivity
Among inhuman foes.
But who are these? for with joint pace I hear   110
The tread of many feet stearing this way;
Perhaps my enemies who come to stare
At my affliction, and perhaps to insult,°   EXULT PROUDLY
Thir daily practice to afflict me more.
   Chor. This, this is he; softly a while,   115
Let us not break in upon him;
O change beyond report, thought, or belief!
See how he lies at random, carelesly diffus'd,°   SPREAD OUT
With languish't head unpropt,
As one past hope, abandon'd,   120
And by himself given over;[33]
In slavish habit, ill-fitted weeds°   CLOTHES
O're worn° and soild;   WORN OUT
Or do my eyes misrepresent? Can this be hee,
That Heroic, that Renown'd,   125
Irresistible[34] *Samson?*[35] whom unarm'd
No strength of man, or fiercest wild beast could withstand;
Who tore the Lion, as the Lion tears the Kid,
Ran on embattelld Armies clad in Iron,
And weaponless himself,   130
Made Arms ridiculous, useless the forgery°   FORGING
Of brazen shield and spear, the hammer'd Cuirass,°   BREASTPLATE
Chalybean[36] temper'd steel, and frock of mail°   COAT OF MAIL
Adamantean Proof;[37]
But safest he who stood aloof,   135
When insupportably° his foot advanc't,   IRRESISTIBLY
In scorn of thir proud arms and warlike tools,
Spurn'd them to death by Troops. The bold *Ascalonite*[38]
Fled from his Lion ramp,[39] old Warriors turn'd
Thir plated backs under his heel;   140
Or grovling° soild thir crested helmets in the dust.   LYING FACE DOWNWARD
Then with what trivial weapon came to hand,

---

[33]Probably meant to be read as a monosyllable, "o'er," together with "giv'n," judging by the metrics of the line and the general absence of unstressed endings on the last syllables of lines.

[34]Corrected by the *Errata* from "Irisistable."

[35]The "a" was printed upside down in *1671* and has been corrected.

[36] The Chalybeans, who lived on the Black Sea coast in northern Turkey were famous metal-smiths, as in Vergil, *Georgics* 1.58.

[37]Resistant to the hardest of metals, adamant. Milton apparently made up the adjective form, *adamantean*, used here for the first and only instance recorded in the *OED*.

[38]Someone from the Philistine city of Ascalon.

[39]Lion in the act of rising on his hindquarters, as in heraldry, "a lion rampant."

The Jaw of a dead Ass, his sword of bone,
A thousand fore-skins fell,[40] the flower of *Palestin*
In *Ramath-lechi*[41] famous to this day: 145
Then by main° force pull'd up, and on his shoulders bore   ENORMOUS
The Gates of *Azza*,[42] Post, and massie° Bar   SOLID, HEAVY
Up to the Hill by *Hebron*, seat of Giants[43] old,
No journey of a Sabbath day,[44] and loaded so;
Like whom the Gentiles feign to bear up Heav'n.[45]   150
Which shall I first bewail,
Thy Bondage or lost Sight,
Prison within Prison
Inseparably dark?
Thou art become (O worst imprisonment!)   155
The Dungeon of thy self; thy Soul
(Which Men enjoying sight oft without cause complain)[46]
Imprison'd now indeed,
In real[47] darkness of the body dwells,
Shut up from outward light   160
To incorporate° with gloomy night;   FORM ONE BODY
For inward light alas
Puts forth no visual beam.[48]
O mirror of our fickle state,
Since man on earth unparallel'd![49]   165
The rarer thy example stands,
By how much from the top of wondrous glory,
Strongest of mortal men,
To lowest pitch of abject fortune thou art fall'n.[50]
For him I reckon not in high estate   170

---

[40]It was the custom of the tribes of Israel, themselves circumcised, to cut off and display the foreskins of enemies like the Philistines slain in battle. In 1 Samuel 18.27, David brings the foreskins of 200 slain Philistines to Saul as evidence of how many were killed in battle. In Judges 15.18, Samson expresses to God the fear that he might "fall into the hands of the uncircumcised."

[41]See Judges 15.17, for Samson's naming of Ramath-Lechi, or Ramath-Lehi (in the AV).

[42]A variant spelling of Gaza.

[43]Perhaps the giants are introduced at this point to foreshadow the existence of giants such as Harapha.

[44]A reference to the Jewish law that human travel on the Sabbath should be restricted to less than a mile measured out in steps (compare Exodus 16.29). Possibly in defiance of the law, Samson carries the gates from Gaza to Hebron, a distance of about forty miles.

[45]The Titan Atlas (or the mountain in Africa with the same name) was supposed to have held the world on his shoulders. Milton allows Samson as one of the chosen Israelites to belittle the beliefs of the Gentiles (in this case, the Greeks and Romans).

[46]Corrected by the *Errata* from "complain'd."

[47]Pronounced as a disyllable.

[48]An eye beam was thought to issue from the eye, as a ray (*Paradise Lost* 3.620). John Donne's famous image from "The Extasie" gives a memorable picture of the phenomenon: "Our eye-beames twisted, and did thred / Our eyes, upon one double string" (*The Poems of John Donne*, ed. Herbert J. C. Grierson [Oxford: Oxford UP, 1958]).

[49]"Unsurpassed since man first came to be on the earth."

[50]Milton is perhaps suggesting that the Chorus endorses the medieval conception of tragedy, according to which the goddess Fortuna spins a wheel which throws the person of high estate (a king or important personage) quickly into the dirt, showing how fragile human importance may be. Such a view was derived from Giovanni Boccaccio's *De casibus virorum illustrium*, written in the 1360s, which catalogues the rapid rise and fall of various princes and was outlined in Chaucer's "Monk's Tale," which in turn outlines the falls of Lucifer, Adam, and Samson. The Monk outlines his tragic tales in this way:

   I wol biwaille in manere of tragedie
  The harm of hem that stoode in heigh degree,
  And fillen so that ther nas no remedie
  To brynge hem out of hir adversitee.
  For certain, whan that Fortune list to flee,
  Ther may no man the cours of hire withholde.
  Lat no man truste on blynd prosperitiee;
  Be war by thise ensamples trewe and olde.
    The Riverside Chaucer, ed. Larry D. Benson (Boston: Houghton Mifflin, 1987): 241

Whom long descent of birth
Or the sphear of fortune raises;
But thee whose strength, while vertue was her mate,
Might have subdu'd the Earth,
Universally crown'd with highest praises.   175
    Sam. I hear the sound of words, thir sense the air
Dissolves unjointed e're it reach my ear.
    Chor. Hee speaks, let us draw nigh. Matchless in might,
The glory late of *Israel,* now the grief;
We come thy friends and neighbours not unknown   180
From *Eshtaol* and *Zora's*[51] fruitful Vale
To visit or bewail thee, or if better,
Counsel or Consolation we may bring,
Salve to thy Sores, apt words have power to swage°   ASSUAGE, HEAL
The tumors° of a troubl'd mind,   SWELLINGS, OUTBURSTS   185
And are as Balm[52] to fester'd wounds.
    Sam. Your coming, Friends, revives me, for I learn
Now of my own experience, not by talk,
How counterfeit a coin they are who friends
Bear in their Superscription[53] (of the most   190
I would be understood)[54] in prosperous days
They swarm, but in adverse withdraw their head
Not to be found, though sought. Yee see, O friends,
How many evils have enclos'd me round;
Yet that which was the worst now least afflicts me,   195
Blindness, for had I sight, confus'd with shame,
How could I once look up, or heave the head,
Who like a foolish Pilot[55] have shipwrack't,
My Vessel trusted to me from above,
Gloriously rigg'd; and for a word, a tear,   200
Fool, have divulg'd the secret gift of God[56]
To a deceitful Woman: tell me Friends,
Am I not sung and proverbd[57] for a Fool
In every street, do they not say, how well
Are come upon him his deserts? yet why?   205
Immeasurable strength they might behold
In me, of wisdom nothing more then mean;°   AVERAGE, MEDIOCRE
This with the other should, at least, have paird,
These two proportiond ill drove me transverse.°   OFF COURSE
    Chor. Tax not divine disposal,[58] wisest Men   210
Have err'd, and by bad Women been deceiv'd;

---

[51]What might be called Samson's neighborhood: he was born at Zora (Judges 13.2) and he will be buried in Manoa's burial plot between the two towns (Judges 16.31).

[52]Soothing ointment, as in the famous "balm of Gilead" (Jeremiah 8.22).

[53]The image of coining carries over from the previous line, since a superscription was an inscription on a coin, literally something written to identify what is below. The image of counterfeit friends compared with counterfeit money is still in use.

[54]"Understand that what I say applies to most (but not all) people."

[55]Ship's pilot, in charge of steering the ship. Samson's body is his ship, and he wrecks it by allowing his lust for Dalila to take him off course. The nautical imagery ties Samson as ship with Dalila as the imitation of a "stately Ship / Of *Tarsus*" (714–15).

[56]Samson has, after many evasive answers, divulged to Dalila that his strength is attached to the length of his hair by virtue of his having taken the Nazarite vow (Judges 16.17).

[57]Made into a proverbial object of ridicule.

[58]"Don't blame the way that God has managed the course of your life."

And shall again, pretend they ne're so wise.[59]
Deject not then so overmuch thy self,[60]
Who hast of sorrow thy full load besides;
Yet truth to say, I oft have heard men wonder   215
Why thou shouldst wed *Philistian*[61] women rather
Then of thine own Tribe fairer, or as fair,
At least of thy own Nation, and as noble.[62]
    Sam. The first I saw at *Timna*,[63] and she pleas'd
Mee, not my Parents, that° I sought to wed,   SHE WHOM   220
The daughter of an Infidel: they knew not
That what I motion'd[64] was of God; I knew
From intimate impulse, and therefore urg'd
The Marriage on; that by occasion hence
I might begin *Israel*'s Deliverance,   225
The work to which I was divinely call'd;[65]
She proving false,[66] the next I took to Wife
(O that I never had! fond wish too late.)
Was in the Vale of *Sorec, Dalila*,[67]
That specious Monster, my accomplisht snare.[68]   230
I thought it lawful from my former act,[69]
And the same end; still watching to oppress
Israel's oppressours: of what now I suffer
She was not the prime cause, but I my self,[70]
Who vanquisht with a peal[71] of words (O weakness!)   235
Gave up my fort of silence to a Woman.
    Chor. In seeking just occasion to provoke
The *Philistine*, thy Countries Enemy,
Thou never wast remiss, I bear thee witness:

---

[59]"However intelligent they claim to be."

[60]A similar modern idiom might be "Don't put yourself down so much." The verb "deject" carries its literal meaning of "throw down."

[61]The Woman of Timna, Samson's first wife, was a Philistine (Judges 14.1), and Milton interpreted Dalila's origins as Philistine, though the Bible does not say specifically what they were. Milton may have thought it important to establish that his Dalila was a member of an alien and idolatrous sect of Dagon-worshipers (compare *Doctrine and Discipline of Divorce*, Chs. 7 and 8). The Geneva Bible does not assign Delilah a race or religion, but it summarizes Samson's relationship to her: "Thus his immoderate affections towarde a wicked woman caused him to lose Gods excellent gifts, & become slave unto them, whome he shulde have ruled" (Judges 16 margin), a position that Milton probably shared.

[62]Implied in "fair" and "noble" would be good-looking, wealthy, and well-born or well-connected.

[63]The Woman of Timna betrayed Samson to her people, the Philistines, by forcing him (she "lay sore upon him" [Judges 14.17]) to reveal the answer to his riddle concerning honey to be found in the carcass of a lion.

[64]Corrected from "mention'd" by the *Errata*. The word "motion'd" is loaded, in the sense that it will later carry into the "rouzing motions" (1382) that will inspire Samson to bring down the temple of Dagon. Here it can mean "recommended as a marriage partner" (Leonard 222n). As in the usage later in the poem, it can also mean the working of God in the soul (*OED* 9b).

[65]See Judges 14. Samson marries the infidel Philistine Woman of Timna, against his parents' wishes, because to do so helps fulfill what he knew were God's plans (the plans were "of the LORD, that he sought an occasion against the Philistines," according to the AV) for him; still, the woman betrayed him to the Philistines.

[66]What Milton does not tell us is that the Woman of Timna, having betrayed Samson, "was given to his companion" (Judges 14.20), called a "Paranymph" (see 1020), by her Timnite father. In his answer to this action, Samson attaches torches to the tails of foxes and sets Philistine wheat fields on fire. The Philistines, in retaliation for that, "burnt [Samson's wife] and her father with fire" (15.6).

[67]"And it came to pass afterward [after he had 'judged Israel in the days of the Philistines twenty years'], that he loved a woman in the valley of Sorek, whose name was Delilah" (Judges 16.4). Notice how much more seductively beautiful is Milton's "in the Vale of *Sorec, Dalila*."

[68]Samson summarizes her character in two memorable phrases. She is a monster whose distorted personality makes her resemble a fully-rigged ship, a venomous snake, or a hyena; she is also a man-trap, a snare, a limed twig or a net laid to trap a man made temporarily weak by worshiping her outward beauty. Comus employs similar snares to trap his victims (164), and Eve after the Fall calls herself Adam's snare (11.165). Dalila is specious in the same way Satan in the Serpent is specious (*Paradise Lost* 9.361) and tainted gifts are specious in *Paradise Regain'd* (2.391).

[69]Because he married one Philistine woman acting under the "motion" of God, Samson can justify his marriage to a second, but Leonard asks us to "Notice that Samson does not say that he received a divine 'motion' to marry Dalila" (231n).

[70]Like Adam and Eve, Samson takes full responsibility for his own individual fall and does not blame it on the other gender.

[71]Probably "A discharge of guns or cannon so as to produce a loud sound; esp. as an expression of joy, a salute, etc. " (*OED* 2.5). The noisy word-attack is a fusillade that breaks down his fort of silence (one of his Nazarite vows).

Yet *Israel* still serves with all his Sons.   240
   Sam. That fault I take not on me, but transfer
On *Israel*'s Governours, and Heads of Tribes,[72]
Who seeing those great acts which God had done
Singly by me against their Conquerours
Acknowledg'd not, or not at all consider'd   245
Deliverance offerd: I on th' other side
Us'd no ambition[73] to commend my deeds,
The deeds themselves, though mute, spoke loud the dooer;
But they persisted deaf, and would not seem
To count them things worth notice, till at length   250
Thir Lords the *Philistines* with gather'd powers
Enterd *Judea* seeking mee, who then
Safe to the rock of *Etham* was retir'd,[74]
Not flying,° but fore-casting in what place   FLEEING, RUNNING AWAY
To set upon them, what advantag'd best;[75]   255
Mean while the men of *Judah* to prevent
The harrass° of thir Land, beset me round;[76]   HARASSMENT
I willingly on some conditions came
Into thir hands,[77] and they as gladly yield me
To the uncircumcis'd[78] a welcom prey,   260
Bound with two cords; but cords to me were threds
Toucht with the flame: on thir whole Host I flew
Unarm'd, and with a trivial weapon fell'd
Their choicest youth; they only liv'd who fled.[79]
Had *Judah* that day join'd,° or one whole Tribe,   ENTERED THE BATTLE 265
They had by this possess'd the Towers of *Gath*,
And lorded over them whom now they serve;
But what more oft in Nations grown corrupt,
And by thir vices brought to servitude,
Then to love Bondage more then Liberty,   270
Bondage with ease then strenuous liberty;[80]
And to despise, or envy, or suspect
Whom God hath of his special favour rais'd
As thir Deliverer; if he aught° begin,   ANYTHING
How frequent to desert him, and at last   275
To heap ingratitude on worthiest deeds?
   Cho. Thy words to my remembrance bring
How *Succoth* and the Fort of *Penuel*[81]
Thir great Deliverer contemn'd,

---

[72]The bondage imposed on the people of Israel resembles the "double bondage under prelatical and regal tyrannie" that Milton defines in *The Likeliest Means to Remove Hirelings out of the Church* (1659; Yale 7: 274). Samson's political position is analogous to that of Milton in 1659: he is gadfly, prophet, warning voice to the tribes of Israel, and "divinely appointed liberator" (Lewalski, "Samson" 242).

[73]Probably "Canvassing, personal solicitation of honours. (L. ambitio.)" (*OED* 5, citing this instance).

[74]After the Philistines had burnt the Woman of Timnath (the name used in the AV) and her father, Samson "smote them hip and thigh with a great slaughter: and he went down and dwelt in the top of the rock Etam" (Judges 15.8).

[75]"What gave the best advantage [militarily speaking]."

[76]"Attacked me from all sides."

[77]For the events described, see Judges 15.9–15.

[78]As an Israelite, Samson classifies other peoples as uncircumcised, to distinguish between the "civilized" religious practices of the Tribes of Israel and the barbaric customs of other nations. Compare the exclusion of the uncircumcised from the passover in Exodus 12.48.

[79]The trivial weapon is the famous jawbone of an ass, with which Samson kills a thousand men (Judges 15.15–16).

[80]A reiterated theme in Milton's political and poetic writing—that liberty is strenuous and bondage easy.

[81]The Chorus provides examples of ingratitude. In Judges 8, ungrateful Ephraimites from Succoth and Penuel refuse to give bread to Gideon's select group of soldiers as they are pursuing Zebah and Zalmunna, the "vanquished kings" of Midian.

The matchless *Gideon* in pursuit   280
Of *Madian* and her vanquisht Kings:
And how ingrateful *Ephraim*[82]
Had dealt with *Jephtha*, who by argument,
Not worse then by his shield and spear
Defended *Israel* from the *Ammonite*,   285
Had not his prowess quell'd thir pride
In that sore° battel when so many dy'd   GRIEVOUS, DEADLY
Without Reprieve adjudg'd to death,
For want of well pronouncing *Shibboleth*.[83]
     Sam. Of such examples adde mee to the roul,°   ROLL   290
Mee easily indeed mine[84] may neglect,
But Gods propos'd deliverance not so.
     Chor. Just are the ways of God,
And justifiable to Men;[85]
Unless there be who think not God at all,[86]   295
If any be, they walk obscure;°   IN DARKNESS
For of such Doctrine never was there School,
But the heart of the Fool,
And no man therein Doctor° but himself.   LEARNED PERSON
     Yet more there be who doubt his ways not just,[87]
As to his own edicts, found contradicting,   300
Then give the rains° to wandring thought,   REINS
Regardless of his glories diminution;
Till by thir own perplexities involv'd
They ravel[88] more, still less resolv'd,   305
But never find self-satisfying solution.
     As if they would confine th' interminable,
And tie him to his own prescript,°   RULE
Who made our Laws to bind us, not himself,
And hath full right to exempt   310
Whom so it pleases him by choice
From National obstriction,[89] without taint
Of sin, or legal debt;
For with his own Laws he can best dispence.°   ADMINISTER JUSTICE
     He would not else who never wanted means,   315
Nor in respect of the enemy just cause
To set his people free,
Have prompted this Heroic *Nazarite*,
Against his vow of strictest purity,

---

[82]Once again the Ephraimites are ungrateful, this time to the warrior Jephtha, in Judges 12.1–6. As Leonard points out, "St. Paul names Gideon and Jephtha alongside Samson as examples of exemplary faith (Heb. 11.32)" (282n).

[83]The Ephraimites could not pronounce the word "Shibboleth." The word was therefore used as a test when Jephtha's men of Gilead were screening escaped Emphraimites; a "shibboleth" today represents any similar linguistic test word.

[84]"My own people," the Israelites, whom Samson has often neglected.

[85]The Chorus seems to be speaking oracular truth here, since the lines echo Revelation 15.3 and *Paradise Lost* 1.26.

[86]Those who do not believe in God.

[87]The indented lines indicate choral movement. As Carey points out, line 306 (as well as 307) was indented in some states of *1671*, but obviously an indented part of the text should not begin in mid-sentence.

[88]Probably "to entangle, confuse, perplex" (*OED* 5.a), another image of a snare or maze of error, for the unsuspecting to become entangled in.

[89]National law or ordinance. Deuteronomy 7.4 hints that a marriage between a Jew and a Gentile amounts to idol-worship. Milton in *On Christian Doctrine* uses that text to support the opinion that "Under the gospel, marriage between those who differed in their religious opinions was avoided with equal care" (Yale 6: 369).

To seek in marriage that fallacious Bride,[90]   320
Unclean, unchaste.
   Down Reason then, at least vain reasonings down,
Though Reason here aver
That moral verdit° quits her of unclean: VERDICT
Unchaste was subsequent,[91] her stain not his.   325
   But see here comes thy reverend Sire
With careful° step, Locks white as doune,[92]   FULL OF CARE, WORRIED
Old *Manoah*: advise
Forthwith how thou oughtst to receive him.
   Sam. Ay me, another inward grief awak't,   330
With mention of that name renews th' assault.[93]
   Man. Brethren and men of *Dan*, for such ye seem,
Though in this uncouth° place; if old respect,   OBSCURE, UNFAMILIAR
As I suppose, towards your once gloried friend,
My Son now Captive, hither hath inform'd°   GUIDED   335
Your younger feet, while mine cast back° with age   WORN OUT
Came lagging after; say if he be here.
   Chor. As signal° now in low dejected° state,   CONSPICUOUS   THROWN DOWN
As earst° in highest, behold him where he lies.   FORMERLY
   Man. O miserable change![94] is this the man,   340
That invincible *Samson*, far renown'd,
The dread of *Israel*'s foes, who with a strength
Equivalent to Angels walk'd thir streets,
None offering fight; who single combatant
Duell'd thir Armies[95] rank't in proud array,   345
Himself an Army, now unequal match
To save himself against a coward arm'd
At one spears length. O ever failing trust
In mortal strength! and oh what not in man
Deceivable and vain![96] Nay what thing good   350
Pray'd for, but often proves our woe, our bane?
I pray'd for Children, and thought barrenness
In wedlock a reproach; I gain'd a Son,
And[97] such a Son as all Men hail'd me happy;
Who would be now a Father in my stead?   355
O wherefore did God grant me my request,
And as a blessing with such pomp adorn'd?
Why are his gifts desirable, to tempt
Our earnest Prayers, then giv'n with solemn hand
As Graces, draw a Scorpions tail behind?[98]   360

---

[90]The Woman of Timna, who was "fallacious" in that she, like Dalila, deceived and betrayed Samson. She is "unclean" because she is not an Israelite.

[91]Apparently she is unchaste because she was given to Samson's friend (Judges 14.20). If she were treated as property, of course, she would have no say in the matter, and the Chorus's label "Unchaste" seems not to ring true.

[92]"Hair white as down [as in feathers]."

[93]Samson imagines himself as under assault or besieged by the memory of his father. Or he expresses his shame at having to confront him.

[94]In emphasizing Samson's present miserable state and fall from his former glory, Manoa seems to be reinforcing the notion of a tragic hero as someone who has fallen from a high estate into wretchedness, as in Chaucer's "Monk's Tale."

[95]Samson alone could fight entire armies by himself, as if in a duel.

[96]"And what is there in man that is not capable of being deceived, or vain?"

[97]"And" is added at the direction of the *Errata*.

[98]Perhaps an allusion to Luke 11.11–12: "If a son shall ask bread of any of you that is a father, will he give him a stone? Or if he ask a fish, will he for a fish give him a serpent? Or if he shall ask an egg, will he offer him a scorpion." But the imagery here is essentially similar to that used of Dalila, described by the Chorus as "a manifest Serpent by her sting" (997). Milton's natural history includes serpents which, like stingrays, have a poison dart in their tails.

For this did the Angel twice descend? for this
Ordain'd thy nurture[99] holy, as of a Plant;
Select, and Sacred,[100] Glorious for a while,
The miracle of men: then in an hour
Ensnar'd, assaulted, overcome, led bound,   365
Thy Foes derision, Captive, Poor, and Blind
Into a Dungeon thrust, to work with Slaves?
Alas methinks° whom God hath chosen once   IT SEEMS TO ME
To worthiest deeds, if he through frailty err,
He should not so o'rewhelm, and as a thrall   370
Subject him to so foul indignities,
Be it but for honours sake of former deeds.

    Sam. Appoint not heavenly disposition,[101] Father,
Nothing of all these evils hath befall'n me
But justly; I my self have brought them on,   375
Sole Author I, sole cause:[102] if aught seem vile,
As vile hath been my folly,[103] who have profan'd
The mystery of God giv'n me under pledge
Of vow, and have betray'd it to a woman,
A *Canaanite*,[104] my faithless enemy.   380
This well I knew, nor was at all surpris'd,
But warn'd by oft° experience: did not she   OFTEN-OCCURRING
Of *Timna* first betray me, and reveal
The secret wrested from me in her highth
Of Nuptial Love profest, carrying it strait°   IMMEDIATELY   385
To them who had corrupted her, my Spies,[105]
And Rivals? In this other was there found
More Faith? who also in her prime of love,
Spousal embraces, vitiated° with Gold,   CORRUPTED
Though offer'd only, by the sent° conceiv'd   SCENT   390
Her spurious first-born;[106] Treason against me?
Thrice she assay'd with flattering prayers and sighs,
And amorous reproaches to win from me
My capital[107] secret, in what part my strength
Lay stor'd, in what part summ'd, that she might know: 395
Thrice I deluded[108] her, and turn'd to sport
Her importunity, each time perceiving
How openly, and with what impudence
She purpos'd[109] to betray me, and (which was worse
Then undissembl'd hate) with what contempt   400
She sought to make me Traytor to my self;

---

[99]Samson is meant by God to be nurtured by his parents, pictured as priest-like tenders of a sacred plant.
[100]Selected by God to be a Nazarite.
[101]Samson reproaches his father for blaming God for the misfortune he has brought on himself.
[102]Compare Eve's repentant phrase "sole cause to thee of all this woe" in *Paradise Lost* 10.935.
[103]"If anything seems vile, my foolishness would seem just as vile."
[104]The Philistines were not native to Caanan, but immigrants from Caphtor (Amos 9.7).
[105]Presumably spies hired by Philistines to observe Samson's activities, the "thirty companions" the Philistines "brought" "to be with him" (Judges 14.11).
[106]Dalila corrupted the marriage bed when she smelled the wealth offered her to betray Samson by the Philistines (Judges 16.5). With the phrase "in her prime of love," Samson admits her sexual attractiveness as he perceived it. The smell of money perversely caused Dalila to conceive, but only spuriously.
[107]An etymological pun, meaning "very important" and "pertaining to the head" (or his hair, in this case).
[108]"Tricked her by joking," Samson's characteristic riddling also implied in "sport."
[109]Accented on the first syllable. Her purpose was to betray him, or she was determined to betray him ("propose" and "purpose" as verbs began usage as doublets, with no distinction in meaning between them—see *OED* 1).

Yet the fourth time, when mustring all her wiles,
With blandisht parlies,[110] feminine assaults,
Tongue-batteries, she surceas'd not day nor night
To storm° me over-watch't, and wearied out.[111]   OVERCOME QUICKLY, IN WAR   405
At times when men seek most repose and rest,
I yielded, and unlock'd her all my heart,
Who with a grain° of manhood well resolv'd   THE SMALLEST MEASURE
Might easily have shook off all her snares:
But foul effeminacy[112] held me yok't   410
Her Bond-slave; O indignity, O blot
To Honour and Religion! servil mind
Rewarded well with servil punishment!
The base degree° to which I now am fall'n,   LOW SOCIAL STATUS
These rags, this grinding,[113] is not yet so base   415
As was my former servitude, ignoble,
Unmanly, ignominious, infamous,
True slavery, and that blindness worse then this,
That saw not how degenerately I serv'd.
     Man. I cannot praise thy Marriage choises, Son,[114]   420
Rather approv'd them not; but thou didst plead
Divine impulsion[115] prompting how thou might'st
Find some occasion to infest° our Foes.   ATTACK
I state[116] not that; this I am sure; our Foes
Found soon occasion thereby to make thee   425
Thir Captive, and thir triumph;[117] thou the sooner
Temptation found'st, or over-potent charms[118]
To violate the sacred trust of silence
Deposited within thee; which to have kept
Tacit, was in thy power; true; and thou bear'st   430
Enough, and more the burden of that fault;
Bitterly hast thou paid, and still art paying
That rigid° score. A worse thing yet remains,   UNYIELDING
This day the *Philistines* a popular Feast
Here celebrate in *Gaza*; and proclaim   435

---

[110]"Flattering word games." Samson's summary of Dalila's behavior sounds like stock antifeminist rhetoric. Joseph Swetnam, in *The Araignment Of Lewd, Idle, Froward, and unconstant women* (London, 1615), discussed the epitome of the bad wife in similar terms: "Her husband being overcome by her flattering speech, partly he yeeldeth to her request, although it be a greefe to him . . . " (C2ᵛ; quoted in Louis B. Wright, *Middle-Class Culture in Elizabethan England* [Ithaca, NY: Cornell UP, 1958]: 487).

[111]Milton's Samson exaggerates or embellishes the biblical account, which says only that "Samson's wife wept before him seven days, . . . ; and when the seventh day came, he tolde her, because she was importunate upon him" (14.17). She is instructed to "Entise" her husband, and she does accuse him of not loving her because he "put forthe a riddle unto the children of my people, and hast not tolde it me" (14.16; Geneva Bible). Samson's imagery again refers to himself as a castle under siege, "over-watch't" in the sense of needing a perpetual guard on duty, day or night, then "stormed."

[112]Enslavement to a woman. Compare the angel Michael's description of Adam's "effeminate slackness" in *Paradise Lost* 11.634. Effeminacy in this sense would have nothing to do with male homosexuality but with a man violating a God-given gender role by being perceived as allowing himself to become as weak as a woman. It is "foul" because it represents a violation of a role assigned by God at the creation of the sexes, Eve having been made from Adam's rib in order to be his "help-meet." Samson has, unnaturally, become the bondslave of Dalila just as he is the more legitimate bondslave of the Philistines.

[113]The work he is performing at the mill, which is as degrading as the rags he is forced to wear.

[114]Surely this is one of the greatest understatements in all tragedy, to the point of provoking laughter occasionally in modern audiences listening to a performance. The humor in it is probably intentional.

[115]Samson had claimed "intimate impulse" from God in his first marriage (223). Manoa doubts Samson's divine guidance. If Manoa is right, then the "rouzing motions" that Samson says propel him toward his fate in pulling down the temple of Dagon (1382) are also called into doubt. The reader needs to determine how reliable a witness Manoa might be.

[116]? To assign a value to, have an opinion upon" (*OED* 2.b), but the question mark indicates puzzlement at Milton's unique usage. The verb "I state" might mean only "I say."

[117]"The subject of triumph" (the only use of the word with this sense, according to *OED* 2b).

[118]"Charms" apparently in the sense of "female charms," though Milton often uses the word with its force from "magic charms."

Great Pomp, and Sacrifice, and Praises loud
To *Dagon*, as their God who hath deliver'd
Thee *Samson* bound and blind into thir hands,
Them out of thine, who slew'st them many a slain.[119]
So *Dagon* shall be magnifi'd,° and God,   EXALTED   440
Besides whom is no God, compar'd with Idols,
Disglorifi'd,[120] blasphem'd, and had in scorn
By th' Idolatrous rout amidst thir wine;
Which to have come to pass by means of thee,
Samson, of all thy sufferings think the heaviest,   445
Of all reproach the most with shame that ever
Could have befall'n thee and thy Fathers house.
　　Sam. Father, I do acknowledge and confess[121]
That I this honour, I this pomp[122] have brought
To *Dagon*, and advanc'd his praises high   450
Among the Heathen round;[123] to God have brought
Dishonour, obloquie,° and op't° the mouths   SHAME   OPENED
Of Idolists, and Atheists; have brought scandal
To *Israel*, diffidence of° God, and doubt   DISTRUST FROM
In feeble hearts, propense° anough before   INCLINED   455
To waver, or fall off and joyn with Idols;
Which is my chief affliction, shame and sorrow,
The anguish of my Soul, that suffers not
Mine eie to harbour sleep, or thoughts to rest.
This only hope relieves me, that the strife   460
With me hath end; all the contest is now
'Twixt God and *Dagon*; *Dagon* hath presum'd,
Me overthrown, to enter lists[124] with God,
His Deity comparing and preferring
Before the God of *Abraham*. He, be sure,   465
Will not connive,[125] or linger, thus provok'd,
But will arise and his great name assert:
Dagon must stoop,[126] and shall e're long receive
Such a discomfit, as shall quite despoil him[127]
Of all these boasted Trophies won on me,   470
And with confusion blank[128] his Worshippers.
　　Man. With cause this hope relieves thee, and these words
I as a Prophecy receive: for God,
Nothing more certain,[129] will not long defer
To vindicate the glory of his name   475

---

[119]This phrase sounds as if it should be biblical, but it is not. It seems to mean "You killed many of those who were slain."

[120]Milton apparently made up the negative compound, the opposite of "glorified." The word is not in the *OED*.

[121]The phrasing seems to echo the minister's call for confession, "to acknowledge and confess our manifold sins and wickedness" from the Morning Prayer service of the *Book of Common Prayer 1559: The Elizabethan Prayer Book*, ed. John E. Booty (Charlottesville: UP of Virginia, 1976): 50.

[122]Ceremonial (and therefore meaningless) display, public glory. Compare "After a long pomp and tedious preparation out of heathen authors" (*Likeliest Means;* Yale 7: 290).

[123]"Among the surrounding heathen tribes."

[124]Places of armed combat or, by extension, of public debate.

[125]"Shut his eyes to wrongdoing," from the Latin *conivere*, to wink or shut one's eyes. The *OED* defines "connive" here as "To remain dormant or inactive" (5), citing only two instances from Milton, but I see no reason why the idiom of winking would not be acceptable.

[126]"Bow down" or "submit," but with the prophetic implication of "fall on his face" (see the various meanings of the verb in the *OED*).

[127]"Take away his spoils—what he has won from me in battle."

[128]Put them out of countenance, make them turn pale with fear or confusion, leave them at a loss for words. By extension, the Philistines are also "blank" in the sense that they have no moral direction.

[129]"There is nothing more certain than this" (expressing certainty about what God's action should be).

Against all competition, nor will long
Endure it, doubtful whether God be Lord,
Or *Dagon*. But for thee what shall be done?
Thou must not in the mean while here forgot
Lie in this miserable loathsom plight   480
Neglected. I already have made way
To some *Philistian* Lords, with whom to treat°   ENTREAT
About thy ransom:[130] well they may by this°   BY NOW
Have satisfi'd thir utmost of revenge[131]
By pains and slaveries, worse then death inflicted   485
On thee, who now no more canst do them harm.
    Sam. Spare that proposal, Father, spare the trouble
Of that sollicitation; let me here,
As I deserve, pay on° my punishment;   CONTINUE TO PAY FOR
And expiate, if possible, my crime,   490
Shameful garrulity.[132] To have reveal'd
Secrets of men, the secrets of a friend,
How hainous had the fact° been, how deserving   DEED, ACT
Contempt, and scorn of all, to be excluded
All friendship, and avoided as a blab,[133]   495
The mark of fool set on his front?[134]
But I Gods counsel have not kept, his holy secret
Presumptuously have publish'd, impiously,[135]
Weakly at least, and shamefully: A sin
That Gentiles in thir Parables condemn   500
To thir abyss and horrid pains confin'd.[136]
    Man. Be penitent and for thy fault contrite,
But act not in thy own affliction, Son,
Repent the sin, but if the punishment
Thou canst avoid, self-preservation bids;[137]   505
Or th' execution leave to high disposal,
And let another hand, not thine, exact
Thy penal forfeit from thy self; perhaps
God will relent,[138] and quit thee all his debt;
Who evermore approves and more accepts   510
(Best pleas'd with humble and filial submission)
Him who imploring mercy sues for life,
Then who self-rigorous chooses death as due;
Which argues over-just, and self-displeas'd
For self-offence, more then for God offended.   515

---

[130]Neither the Bible nor the extra-biblical Samson tradition, as recorded by Krouse, includes a ransom.
[131]"Their utmost desire for revenge."
[132]It is bad enough to blab confidences about oneself or one's friends to someone else: Samson has blabbed God's secrets. But the Nazarite vows did not contain a vow of silence (see Labriola); Milton adds this detail perhaps to emphasize Samson's garrulity or his betrayal of God's trust.
[133]Someone who talks too much, reveals secrets, or practices "shameful garrulity."
[134]Presumably Milton is thinking of Samson as being punished by having the word "Fool" written on his forehead ("front").
[135]"With overweening self-confidence, I have made [my secret] known to the public, irreverently."
[136]Samson makes a distinction between Jews and what seem to be proto-Christians, "Gentiles," who have a version of Hell in their myths or "Parables." Presumably he is talking about Greek and Roman myths of the underworld, as ruled by Hades or Pluto, where those who, like Tantalus, sin against the gods are punished. Such myths are shadowy types of the Christian Hell.
[137]Presumably Manoa is tempting Samson with "liberty, ease, and peace in retirement," if Krouse is correct (126). If Samson sought self-preservation only, however, he would not exert God's vengeance on the Philistines.
[138]This sounds like Mammon's ignoble suggestion "Suppose he [God] should relent / And publish Grace to all, on promise made / Of new subjection" (*Paradise Lost* 2.237–39).

Reject not then what offerd means, who knows
But God hath set before us, to return thee
Home to thy countrey and his sacred house,[139]
Where thou mayst bring thy off'rings, to avert
His further ire, with praiers and vows renew'd.   520
    Sam. His pardon I implore; but as for life,
To what end should I seek it? when in strength
All mortals I excell'd, and great in hopes
With youthful courage and magnanimous thoughts
Of birth from Heav'n foretold and high exploits,[140]   525
Full of divine instinct,[141] after some proof
Of acts indeed heroic, far beyond
The Sons of *Anac*,[142] famous now and blaz'd,[143]
Fearless of danger, like a petty God[144]
I walk'd about admir'd of all and dreaded   530
On hostile ground, none daring my affront.
Then swoll'n with pride into the snare I fell
Of fair fallacious looks, venereal trains,[145]
Softn'd with pleasure and voluptuous life;
At length to lay my head and hallow'd pledge[146]   535
Of all my strength in the lascivious lap
Of a deceitful Concubine who shore me
Like a tame Weather,[147] all my precious fleece,
Then turn'd me out ridiculous, despoil'd,
Shav'n, and disarm'd among my enemies.   540
    Chor. Desire of wine and all delicious drinks,
Which many a famous Warriour overturns,[148]
Thou couldst repress, nor did the dancing Rubie[149]
Sparkling, out-pow'rd,° the flavor, or the smell,   POURED
Or taste that cheers the heart of Gods and men,   545
Allure thee from the cool Crystalline stream.[150]
    Sam. Where ever fountain or fresh current flow'd
Against the Eastern ray, translucent, pure.
With touch ætherial of Heav'ns fiery rod
I drank,[151] from the clear milkie juice allaying   550
Thirst, and refresht; nor envy'd them the grape

---

[139]Probably the Tabernacle, the tent in which the Ark of the Covenant was stored before Solomon built his famous Temple (Exodus 26).
[140]Accented on the second syllable.
[141]Inward promptings inspired by God. Samson responds to Manoa's fear that his instinct is not divinely inspired. Also accented on the second syllable.
[142]Proverbial race of giants to whom Goliath and Harapha were presumably related (see Numbers 13.33).
[143]Published to the world, made famous. Milton may be making the distinction between being famous and advertising one's own fame beyond the bounds of good taste.
[144]"Small-natured," "puny" (as compared with a real god, or God).
[145]Traps ("trains") like those set by the goddess of love, Venus, and hence venereal. "Train" contains the meanings of "trick," "deceitful ploy," "enticement," as well as "snare."
[146]In this case, his hair is his pledge, since his strength is stored there, according to God's will.
[147]Wether, castrated male sheep. A recently-shorn sheep, male or female, looks ridiculously naked and vulnerable and is a proverbial object of scorn, as in the idiom "he had been fleeced."
[148]That is, wine causes many a famous hero to fall or become besotted. As a Nazarite, Samson was supposed to avoid wine (Numbers 6.3).
[149]Sparkling red wine.
[150]In other words, Samson found it easy to resist drink but not the temptations of sex. We are close to the kinds of temptation that Comus and his mother Circe use, "a thick intoxicating potion which a certain Sorceress the abuser of loves name carries about" (Yale 1: 892). In contrast to that perverse use of wine, love's "charming cup is only vertue which she bears in her hand to those who are worthy" (891).
[151]Leonard reminds us that "Ancient belief held that the most wholesome water was that which rose from a spring in the face of the rising sun" (547–48n), citing Torquato Tasso, *Il Mondo Creato*, Terzo Giorno, 133–40.

Whose heads that turbulent liquor fills with fumes.
   Chor. O madness, to think use of strongest wines
And strongest drinks our chief support of health,
When God with these forbid'n made choice to rear   555
His mighty Champion, strong above compare,°   COMPARISON
Whose drink was only from the liquid brook.
   Sam. But what avail'd this temperance, not compleat°   FULLY PROTECTED
Against another object more enticing?
What boots it° at one gate to make defence,   WHAT GOOD DOES IT DO   560
And at another to let in the foe
Effeminatly vanquish't?[152] by which means,
Now blind, disheartn'd, sham'd, dishonour'd, quell'd,°   REDUCED TO SUBJECTION
To what can I be useful, wherein serve
My Nation, and the work from Heav'n impos'd,   565
But to sit idle on the houshold hearth,
A burdenous drone; to visitants a gaze,°   OBJECT TO BE STARED AT
Or pitied object, these redundant° locks   OVERLY ABUNDANT
Robustious° to no purpose clustring down,   HEALTHY-LOOKING
Vain monument of strength; till length of years   570
And sedentary numness craze my limbs
To a contemptible old age obscure.[153]
Here rather let me drudge and earn my bread,
Till vermin or the draff of servil food
Consume me,[154] and oft-invocated death   575
Hast'n the welcom end of all my pains.
   Man. Wilt thou then serve the *Philistines* with that gift
Which was expressly giv'n thee to annoy° them?   VEX, INJURE
Better at home lie bed-rid, not only idle,
Inglorious, unimploy'd,[155] with age out-worn.°   WORN-OUT, EXHAUSTED   580
But God who caus'd a fountain at thy prayer
From the dry ground to spring,[156] thy thirst to allay
After the brunt of battel, can as easie
Cause light again within thy eies to spring,
Wherewith to serve him better then thou hast;   585
And I perswade me so; why else this strength
Miraculous[157] yet remaining in those locks?
His might continues in thee not for naught,
Nor shall his wondrous gifts be frustrate° thus.   USELESS
   Sam. All otherwise to me my thoughts portend,   590
That these dark orbs[158] no more shall treat with° light,   HAVE TO DO WITH

---

[152]"Defeated by one's susceptibility to female charm." Compare "effeminate slackness" as a charge against Adam in *Paradise Lost* 11.634 and "foul effeminacy" (above, 410).

[153]It is hard not to hear self-pitying autobiography in these lines, with very little distance between the plight of Milton after the Restoration and Samson in captivity. See Hanford, "*Samson Agonistes* and Milton in Old Age," but with the caution that William Riley Parker and John Shawcross have disputed Hanford's conclusions.

[154]"Until vermin [such as lice] or the garbage that slaves have to eat causes him to waste away or die."

[155]According to the *OED*, Milton invented the word in the modern sense, "Not engaged in any work or occupation; idle; spec. temporarily out of work" (2a).

[156]Judges 15.18–19 describes a miracle by which Samson is provided water after using the jawbone to kill Philistines in battle. Depending on which way the Hebrew is translated, the water is made to issue either from a "great toothe in the jaw" (Geneva gloss) or from the dry ground (Milton's preference).

[157]Supply "strength" after "miraculous."

[158]The reference to orbs, as Carol Bisbee reminds me (e-mail message, August 1997), indicates that Milton identifies Samson's blindness with his own, since the historical Samson, having had his eyes removed (?), would have no "orbs," whereas Milton was proud of the fact that his eyes appeared to be normal even after he became blind. Even though Samson is "Eyeless in *Gaza*" (41), Manoa later expresses hope that eyesight will be miraculously restored by God (1502–27). Milton expressed hope for being healed of his blindness, through a physician's knowledge, in his second letter to Leonard Philaras.

light of life continue long,
double darkness[159] nigh at hand:
el my genial spirits° droop,   VITAL SPIRITS
l flat, nature within me seems   595
nctions weary of her self;
may glory run, and race of shame,
And I shall shortly be with them that rest.
    Man. Believe not these suggestions which proceed
From anguish of the mind and humours black,[160]   600
That mingle with thy fancy.° I however   IMAGINATION
Must not omit a Fathers timely care
To prosecute° the means of thy deliverance   PURSUE, FOLLOW UP
By ransom or how else: mean while be calm,
And healing words from these thy friends admit.°   ALLOW   605
    Sam. O that torment should not be confin'd
To the bodies wounds and sores
With maladies innumerable
In heart, head, brest, and reins;°   KIDNEYS
But must secret passage find   610
To th' inmost mind,
There exercise all his fierce accidents,°   SYMPTOMS
And on her purest spirits prey,
As on entrails, joints, and limbs,
With answerable pains, but more intense,[161]   615
Though void of corporal sense.
    My griefs not only pain me
As a lingring disease,
But finding no redress, ferment and rage,
Nor less then wounds immedicable[162]   620
Ranckle, and fester, and gangrene,[163]
To black mortification.
Thoughts[164] my Tormenters arm'd with deadly stings
Mangle my apprehensive tenderest parts,
Exasperate, exulcerate, and raise   625
Dire inflammation[165] which no cooling herb
Or medcinal liquor can asswage,
Nor breath of Vernal Air from snowy *Alp*.[166]
Sleep hath forsook[167] and giv'n me o're
To deaths benumming Opium as my only cure.   630
Thence faintings, swoonings[168] of despair,
And sense of Heav'ns desertion.
    I was his nursling once and choice delight,
His destin'd from the womb,

---

[159]The darkness of being blind, first, and then of death.
[160]Vapors emanating from an excess of black bile in the system, causing melancholy or depression.
[161]The mental torments correspond to the physical ones, but they are more intense.
[162]Remediless, without cure.
[163]Used as a verb here, meaning "become necrotic, or gangrenous."
[164]"Thoughts" is the subject of the verb "Mangle." Also, supply "who" after "Thoughts." Milton seems to be torturing syntax in order to show the physical pain of mental and physical disease.
[165]"Increase the fierceness of a disease, cause ulcers, or cause deadly inflammation."
[166]"No springlike breeze from a snow-capped mountain." An "alp" was any tall mountain.
[167]Sleep has left him. Samson has mentioned loss of sleep before (459), indicating what then might be called melancholy or now would be called depression.
[168]Since swoonings were fainting fits (*OED* 2, citing this instance), Samson seems to be redundant.

Promisd by Heavenly message[169] twice descending.   635
Under his special eie
Abstemious I grew up and thriv'd amain;°   EXCEEDINGLY
He led me on to mightiest deeds
Above the nerve° of mortal arm   STRENGTH, MUSCLE
Against the uncircumcis'd, our enemies.   640
But now hath cast me off as never known,
And to those cruel enemies,
Whom I by his appointment° had provok't,   INSTRUCTION
Left me all helpless with th' irreparable loss
Of sight, reserv'd alive to be repeated[170]   645
The subject of thir cruelty, or scorn.
Nor am I in the list of them that hope;
Hopeless are all my evils, all remediless;[171]
This one prayer yet remains, might I be heard,
No long petition, speedy death,   650
The close of all my miseries, and the balm.
   Chor. Many are the sayings of the wise
In antient and in modern books enroll'd;
Extolling Patience as the truest fortitude;[172]
And to the bearing well of all calamities,   655
All chances incident to mans frail life[173]
Consolatories[174] writ[175]
With studied argument, and much perswasion sought
Lenient of° grief and anxious thought,   CONSOLATION TO
But with[176] th' afflicted in his pangs thir sound   660
Little prevails, or rather seems a tune,
Harsh, and of dissonant mood[177] from his complaint,
Unless he feel within
Some sourse of consolation from above;
Secret refreshings, that repair his strength,   665
And fainting spirits uphold.
    God of our Fathers, what is man![178]
That thou towards him with hand so various,
Or might I say contrarious,
Temperst thy providence through his short course,   670
Not evenly, as thou rul'st
The Angelic orders and inferiour creatures mute,
Irrational and brute.
Nor do I name of men the common rout,
That wandring loose about   675

---

[169]Prophetic news from God carried by an angel in Judges 13.

[170]Supply "as." As Swaim points out, "*Samson Agonistes* is riddled with doubleness from its smallest details to its largest issues" (225).

[171]Probably accented on the first and last syllables, as in *Paradise Lost* 9.919.

[172]The fact that the Chorus is recommending patience, a virtue emphasized heavily by Milton in *Paradise Lost* and *Paradise Regain'd*, suggests that they perceive Samson as having fallen into suicidal despair.

[173]There was a period here in *1671*, corrected to "no stop" (no period) by the *Errata*.

[174]"'A speech or writing containing topicks of comfort'" (Samuel Johnson, quoted in *OED* 1.b.n).

[175]The period present here in *1670* is removed, as the *Errata* instructs.

[176]Corrected from "to" in the original by the *Errata*.

[177]Probably used in the musical sense of "mode," here seen as using a dissonant scale in the composition of a piece of music (see "Mode" in *The Norton/Grove Concise Encyclopedia of Music*, ed. Stanley Sadie [New York: Norton, 1988]).

[178]Formulaic biblical speech, as in "we cried unto the Lord God of our fathers" (Deuteronomy 26.7) and "What is man, that thou shouldest magnify him?" (Job 7.17).

Grow up and perish, as the summer flie,
Heads without name no more rememberd,
But such as thou hast solemnly elected,
With gifts and graces eminently adorn'd
To some great work, thy glory,   680
And peoples safety, which in part they effect:
Yet toward these thus dignifi'd, thou oft
Amidst thir highth of noon,
Changest thy countenance, and thy hand with no regard
Of highest favours past   685
From thee on them, or them to thee of service.
   Nor only dost degrade them, or remit
To life obscur'd, which were a fair dismission,°   REMOVAL FROM A POSITION OF IMPORTANCE
But throw'st them lower then thou didst exalt them high,
Unseemly falls in human eie,   690
Too grievous for the trespass or omission,
Oft leav'st them to the hostile sword
Of Heathen and prophane, thir carkasses
To dogs and fowls a prey, or else captiv'd:°   MADE CAPTIVE
Or to the unjust tribunals, under change of times,   695
And condemnation of the ingrateful multitude.
If these they scape, perhaps in poverty
With sickness and disease thou bow'st them down,
Painful diseases and deform'd,
In crude old age;   700
Though not disordinate, yet causless suffring
The punishment of dissolute days, in fine,°   TO SUMMARIZE
Just or unjust, alike seem miserable,
For oft alike, both come to evil end.
   So deal not with this once thy glorious Champion,   705
The Image of thy strength, and mighty minister.
What do I beg? how hast thou dealt already?
Behold him in this state calamitous, and turn
His labours, for thou canst, to peaceful end.
   But who is this,[179] what thing of Sea or Land?   710
Femal of sex it seems,
That so bedeckt, ornate, and gay,°   GAUDY, BRIGHTLY DRESSED
Comes this way sailing
Like a stately Ship
Of *Tarsus*,[180] bound for th' Isles   715
Of *Javan* or *Gadier*[181]
With all her bravery on, and tackle trim,
Sails fill'd, and streamers waving,
Courted by all the winds that hold them play,
An Amber sent of odorous perfume[182]   720
Her harbinger, a damsel train behind;
Some rich *Philistian* Matron she may seem,

---

[179]The quick change of topic is a buried stage direction or cue in that it announces the arrival of Dalila.
[180]"Ship of Tarshish" is proverbial in the Bible, as in Isaiah 23.1 and 14, though "Tarshish" is probably not Tarsus in Asia Minor but Tarshish at the mouth of the Guadalquiver River in southern Spain.
[181]The islands of Javan would be Ionian islands, since Javan, the son of Japhet (Genesis 10.2) was supposed to have founded Ionia; from Javan, says the Geneva Bible marginalia, "came the Medes [Persians] and Grekes." "*Gadier*" is a euphonic form of the Phoenician and Roman name for Cadiz, "Gades."
[182]A perfumed scent derived from ambergris, the discarded excrescence of a whale.

And now at nearer view, no other certain
Then *Dalila* thy wife.
   Sam. My Wife, my Traytress, let her not come near me.   725
   Cho. Yet on she moves, now stands & eies thee fixt,
About t' have spoke, but now, with head declin'd
Like a fair flower surcharg'd with dew,[183] she weeps
And words addrest seem into tears dissolv'd,
Wetting the borders of her silk'n veil: 730
But now again she makes address to speak.
   Dal. With doubtful° feet and wavering resolution   UNCERTAIN
I came, still dreading thy displeasure, *Samson*,
Which to have merited, without excuse,
I cannot but acknowledge; yet if tears   735
May expiate (though the fact more evil drew
In the perverse event then I foresaw)[184]
My penance hath not slack'n'd, though my pardon
No way assur'd. But conjugal affection
Prevailing over fear, and timerous doubt   740
Hath led me on desirous to behold
Once more thy face, and know of thy estate.
If aught in my ability may serve
To light'n what thou suffer'st, and appease
Thy mind with what amends° is in my power, EASES, FREES FROM FAULTS 745
Though late, yet in some part to recompense
My rash but more unfortunate misdeed.[185]
   Sam. Out, out *Hyæna*;[186] these are thy wonted arts,
And arts of every woman false like thee,[187]
To break all faith, all vows, deceive, betray,   750
Then as repentant to submit, beseech,
And reconcilement move with feign'd remorse,
Confess, and promise wonders in her change,
Not truly penitent, but chief to try
Her husband, how far urg'd his patience bears,   755
His vertue or weakness which way to assail:
Then with more cautious and instructed skill
Again transgresses, and again submits;
That wisest and best men full oft beguil'd
With goodness principl'd not to reject   760
The penitent, but ever to forgive,
Are drawn to wear out miserable days,
Entangl'd with a poysnous bosom snake,[188]
If not by quick destruction soon cut off

---

[183]Perhaps a reference to the daffodil or narcissus, whose head was supposed to fill with water during rain and thus "weep" when it overflowed ("Lycidas" 150).

[184]The deed ("fact") of betraying Samson caused more of an unexpected and evil outcome ("event") than she expected.

[185]The audience cannot be sure that Dalila is not telling the truth. She has no other reason to betray Samson further. She will offer him the temptation of a soft life at her home, something he will vehemently decline. For a sympathetic view of Dalila at this point, see Samuel and Ulreich.

[186]Superstition in Milton's day, following Pliny's *Natural History* 8.44, held that the hyena could change sex and that it lured men to their deaths by imitating human voices. For some speculations on choice of the animal as compared with Dalila, see Samuel Hornsby, "Penance of the Hyena in *Samson Agonistes*," *Philological Quarterly* 57 (1978): 353–58.

[187]The marginalia for Judges 16.17 in the Geneva Bible would give Milton an excuse for putting such extreme words in the mouth of Samson: "Thus [Samson's] immoderate affections towarde a wicked woman caused him to lose Gods excellent gifts, & become slave unto them, whome he shoulde have ruled."

[188]For the history of the image, as with Cleopatra's famous asp, see Jackson Campbell Boswell, "Samson's Bosom Snake," *Milton Quarterly* 8 (1974): 77–80.

As I by thee, to Ages an example.   765
   Dal. Yet hear me *Samson*; not that I endeavour
To lessen or extenuate my offence,
But that on th' other side if it be weigh'd
By it self, with aggravations not surcharg'd,
Or else with just allowance counterpois'd,   770
I may, if possible, thy pardon find
The easier towards me, or thy hatred less.
First granting, as I do, it was a weakness
In me, but incident to all our sex,
Curiosity, inquisitive, importune   775
Of secrets, then with like infirmity
To publish them, both common female faults:
Was it not weakness also to make known
For importunity,° that is for naught,   TROUBLESOMENESS
Wherein consisted all thy strength and safety?   780
To what I did thou shewdst me first the way.[189]
But I to enemies reveal'd, and should not.
Nor shouldst thou have trusted that to womans frailty
E're I to thee, thou to thy self wast cruel.
Let weakness then with weakness come to parl°   NEGOTIATE   785
So near related, or the same of kind,
Thine forgive mine; that men may censure thine
The gentler, if severely thou exact not
More strength from me, then in thy self was found.
And what if Love, which thou interpret'st hate,   790
The jealousie of Love, powerful of sway
In human hearts, nor less in mine towards thee,
Caus'd what I did? I saw thee mutable°   FICKLE
Of fancy, feard lest one day thou wouldst leave me
As her at *Timna*,[190] sought by all means therefore   795
How to endear, and hold thee to me firmest:
No better way I saw then by importuning
To learn thy secrets, get into my power
Thy key of strength and safety: thou wilt say,
Why then reveal'd? I was assur'd by those   800
Who tempted me, that nothing was design'd
Against thee but safe custody, and hold:
That made for me,[191] I knew that liberty
Would draw thee forth to perilous[192] enterprises,
While I at home sate full of cares and fears   805
Wailing thy absence in my widow'd bed;
Here I should still enjoy thee day and night
Mine and Loves prisoner,[193] not the *Philistines*,
Whole to my self, unhazarded abroad,[194]
Fearless at home of partners in my love.   810

---

[189]She implies that her blabbing imitated that of Samson.
[190]Samson's father-in-law did give away his first wife, the Woman of Timna, to the "Paranymph" friend of Samson's, after she betrayed him (Judges 14.20).
[191]"That made for my advantage."
[192]Probably a disyllable, and pronounced "parlous," which was an independent spelling variant so strongly entrenched that the *OED* allows it to be a separate word.
[193]She implies that Samson was or would be her captive and love slave.
[194]"Not put to risk by being allowed out."

These reasons in Loves law have past for good,
Though fond and reasonless to some perhaps;
And Love hath oft, well meaning, wrought much wo,
Yet always pity or pardon hath obtain'd.
Be not unlike all others, not austere   815
As thou art strong, inflexible as steel.
If thou in strength all mortals dost exceed,
In uncompassionate anger do not so.

   Sam. How cunningly the sorceress[195] displays
Her own transgressions, to upbraid me mine?[196]   820
That malice not repentance brought thee hither,
By this appears: I gave, thou say'st, th' example,
I led the way; bitter reproach, but true,
I to my self was false e'er thou to me,
Such pardon therefore as I give my folly,   825
Take to thy wicked deed: which when thou seest
Impartial, self-severe, inexorable,
Thou wilt renounce thy seeking, and much rather
Confess it feign'd, weakness is thy excuse,
And I believe it, weakness to resist   830
Philistian gold: if weakness may excuse,
What Murtherer,[197] what Traytor, Parricide,
Incestuous, Sacrilegious, but may plead it?
All wickedness is weakness: that plea therefore
With God or Man will gain thee no remission.   835
But Love constrain'd thee; call it furious rage
To satisfie thy lust: Love seeks to have Love;
My love how couldst thou hope, who tookst the way
To raise in me inexpiable hate,
Knowing, as needs I must, by thee betray'd?[198]   840
In vain thou striv'st to cover shame with shame,
Or by evasions thy crime uncoverst more.

   Dal. Since thou determinst weakness for no plea
In man or woman, though to thy own condemning,
Hear what assaults I had, what snares besides,   845
What sieges girt me round, e're I consented;
Which might have aw'd° the best resolv'd of men,   INTIMIDATED
The constantest to have yielded without blame.
It was not gold,[199] as to my charge thou lay'st,
That wrought with me: thou know'st the Magistrates   850
And Princes of my countrey came in person,
Sollicited, commanded, threatn'd, urg'd,
Adjur'd by all the bonds of civil Duty
And of Religion, press'd how just it was,
How honourable, how glorious to entrap   855
A common enemy, who had destroy'd

---

[195]The word suggests that Dalila practices black magic, but she is less a sorcerer than Comus. Samson perceives her as inherently deceitful and therefore a moral conjurer if not a necromancer.

[196]The question mark was used more loosely in seventeenth-century printing practice than it is today; in this case it might have been dictated by the use of the interrogatory "How" at the beginning of the sentence.

[197]Pronounced as the modern "murderer."

[198]"Understanding, as it became obvious, that I was betrayed by you."

[199]Her costume might belie this, since it is very rich; she seems to be flaunting her newfound wealth (from selling Samson) in wearing silk and other finery.

Such numbers of our Nation: and the Priest[200]
Was not behind, but ever at my ear,
Preaching how meritorious with the gods
It would be to ensnare an irreligious   860
Dishonourer of *Dagon*: what had I
To oppose against such powerful arguments?
Only my love of thee held long debate;
And combated[201] in silence all these reasons
With hard contest:[202] at length that grounded maxim   865
So rife° and celebrated in the mouths   WIDESPREAD
Of wisest men; that to the public good
Private respects must yield; with grave authority
Took full possession of me and prevail'd;
Vertue, as I thought, truth, duty so enjoyning.   870
    Sam. I thought where all thy circling wiles would end;[203]
In feign'd Religion, smooth hypocrisie.
But had thy love, still odiously pretended,
Bin, as it ought, sincere, it would have taught thee
Far other reasonings, brought forth other deeds.   875
I before° all the daughters of my Tribe   IN PREFERENCE TO
And of my Nation chose thee from among
My enemies, lov'd thee, as too well thou knew'st,
Too well, unbosom'd° all my secrets to thee,   REVEALED
Not out of levity, but over-powr'd   880
By thy request, who could deny thee nothing;
Yet now am judg'd an enemy. Why then
Didst thou at first receive me for thy husband?
Then, as since then, thy countries foe profest:
Being once a wife, for me thou wast to leave   885
Parents and countrey; nor was I their subject,
Nor under their protection but my own,
Thou mine, not theirs: if aught against my life
Thy countrey sought of thee, it sought unjustly,
Against the law of nature, law of nations,[204]   890
No more thy countrey, but an impious crew
Of men conspiring to uphold thir state
By worse then hostile deeds, violating the ends
For which our countrey is a name so dear;
Not therefore to be obey'd. But zeal[205] mov'd thee;   895
To please thy gods thou didst it; gods unable
To acquit themselves and prosecute their foes
But by ungodly deeds, the contradiction
Of their own deity, Gods cannot be:
Less therefore to be pleas'd, obey'd, or fear'd,   900

---

[200]No priest is mentioned in the account in Judges.
[201]Accented on the first syllable.
[202]Accented on the second syllable.
[203]"I suspected that was where all your serpentine tricks would end, with religion." The distant allusion seems to be to serpentine or circular movement in reasoning or rhetoric, designed to confuse the audience. Satan in the serpent makes "intricate seem straight" in *Paradise Lost* 9.632; compare 9.510–15, for the moral implications in such physical movement.
[204]Milton studied the law of nations with the help of John Selden's *De Jure Naturali* (1640); he commended "that noble volume written by our learned Selden, *Of the law of nature & of Nations*" (*Doctrine and Discipline of Divorce*; Yale 2: 350; compare Yale 2: 513).
[205]Enthusiastic worship of gods like Dagon.

These false pretexts and varnish'd colours failing,
Bare in thy guilt how foul must thou appear?
  Dal. In argument with men a woman ever
Goes by the worse,[206] whatever be her cause.
  Sam. For want of words no doubt, or lack of breath,   905
Witness when I was worried with thy peals.[207]
  Dal. I was a fool, too rash, and quite mistaken
In what I thought would have succeeded best.
Let me obtain forgiveness of thee, *Samson*,
Afford me place to shew what recompence   910
Towards thee I intend for what I have misdone,
Misguided; only what remains past cure
Bear not too sensibly, nor still insist
To afflict thy self in vain: though sight be lost,
Life yet hath many solaces, enjoy'd   915
Where other senses want not their delights
At home in leisure and domestic ease,°   COMFORT
Exempt from many a care and chance to which
Eye-sight exposes daily men abroad.
I to the Lords will intercede, not doubting   920
Thir favourable ear,[208] that I may fetch thee
From forth° this loathsom prison-house, to abide   OUT OF
With me, where my redoubl'd love and care
With nursing diligence, to me glad office,
May ever tend about thee to old age   925
With all things grateful chear'd, and so suppli'd,
That what by me thou hast lost thou least shalt miss.
  Sams. No, no, of my condition take no care;
It fits not;° thou and I long since are twain;[209]   IT DOES NOT SUIT YOUR POSITION
Nor think me so unwary or accurst   930
To bring my feet again into the snare
Where once I have been caught; I know thy trains
Though dearly to my cost, thy ginns, and toyls;[210]
Thy fair enchanted cup, and warbling charms[211]
No more on me have power, their force is null'd,   935
So much of Adders wisdom I have learn't
To fence° my ear against thy sorceries.   PROTECT
If in my flower of youth and strength, when all men
Lov'd, honour'd, fear'd me, thou alone could hate me
Thy Husband, slight me, sell me, and forgo me;   940
How wouldst thou use me now, blind, and thereby
Deceiveable, in most things as a child
Helpless, thence easily contemn'd,° and scorn'd,   TREATED WITH CONTEMPT

---

[206]The idiom "go by the worse" means "to be defeated or worsted, fail, miscarry." "In arguments with men," Dalila is saying, "women always lose." Feminist critics have taken her accuracy in describing the oppression of women to indicate that the audience should develop sympathy for her. As Lewalski puts it, "She also asserts her female weakness before the concerted pressure and strong arguments of civil and religious authority, and the authoritative maxims of 'wisest men'" ("Milton on Women" 64).
[207]"Loud outburst[s] of sound" (*OED* 6, citing 235 above).
[208]"Not fearing that they will listen sympathetically to my plea."
[209]In his mind, at least, Samson has long since divorced Dalila, although in 958 below he refers to her pending widowhood. Given Milton's long-term interest in divorce, one wonders what Samson's grounds were for divorce.
[210]Trains, gins, and toils are all types of snares or traps for wild animals. The terms are also used for human deceitful devices, as in *Comus* 150, where "charmes" was substituted for "traines" in the Trinity Manuscript, and 164, where "snares" was substituted for "nets."
[211]The cup would be that of Circe, alluded to earlier in *Comus* 51 and 525. A sorceress is pictured chanting mystically, warbling, over the toxic cup.

And last neglected? How wouldst thou insult[212]
When I must live uxorious° to thy will   WIFE-ENSLAVED   945
In perfet[213] thraldom, how again betray me,
Bearing my words and doings to the Lords
To gloss upon,° and censuring, frown or smile?   INTERPRET SCORNFULLY
This Gaol° I count the house of Liberty   JAIL
To thine whose doors my feet shall never enter.   950
    Dal. Let me approach at least, and touch thy hand.
    Sam. Not for thy life, lest fierce remembrance wake
My sudden rage to tear thee joint by joint.
At distance I forgive thee, go with that;
Bewail thy falshood, and the pious works   955
It hath brought forth to make thee memorable
Among illustrious women, faithful wives:
Cherish thy hast'n'd widowhood with the gold
Of Matrimonial treason: so farewel.
    Dal. I see thou art implacable, more deaf   960
To prayers, then winds and seas, yet winds to seas
Are reconcil'd at length, and Sea to Shore:
Thy anger, unappeasable, still rages,
Eternal tempest never to be calm'd.
Why do I humble thus my self, and suing   965
For peace, reap nothing but repulse° and hate?   REJECTION
Bid go with evil omen and the brand
Of infamy upon my name denounc't?
To mix with thy concernments° I desist   WHATEVER INTERESTS YOU
Henceforth, nor too much disapprove my own.[214]   970
Fame if not double-fac't is double-mouth'd,
And with contrary blast[215] proclaims most deeds,
On both his wings, one black, th' other white,
Bears greatest names in his wild aerie flight.
My name perhaps among the Circumcis'd   975
In *Dan*, in *Judah*, and the bordering Tribes,
To all posterity may stand defam'd,
With malediction mention'd, and the blot
Of falshood most unconjugal traduc't.
But in my countrey where I most desire,   980
In *Ecron*, *Gaza*, *Asdod*, and in *Gath*[216]
I shall be nam'd among the famousest
Of Women, sung at solemn festivals,
Living and dead recorded, who to save
Her countrey from a fierce destroyer, chose   985
Above the faith of wedlock-bands, my tomb
With odours° visited and annual flowers.   PERFUMES OR SWEET-SMELLING SACRIFICES
Not less renown'd then in Mount *Ephraim*,

---

[212]"To manifest arrogant or scornful delight by speech or behaviour; to exult proudly or contemptuously; to boast, brag, vaunt, glory, triumph, esp. in an insolent or scornful way" (*OED* 1, citing 113 above).

[213]A Miltonic spelling (for "perfect") seems to have slipped by the compositor.

[214]Dalila turns almost immediately from placating Samson and asking for his forgiveness to renouncing him and announcing her own fame. She is probably meant to betray herself in an unconscious slip with the terms "double-fac't" and "double-mouth'd."

[215]Possibly with the literal sense of "powerful trumpet call, backwards from its normal direction," with the figurative sense of "behind-hand rumor [the Latin goddess *Fama*]." Compare Vergil's famous description of Rumor traveling over the roof tops in *Aeneid* 4.173–88.

[216]The four principal cities of Philistia.

Jael, who with inhospitable guile
Smote *Sisera* sleeping through the Temples nail'd.[217]   990
Nor shall I count it hainous to enjoy
The public marks of honour and reward
Conferr'd upon me, for the piety
Which to my countrey I was judg'd to have shewn.
At this who ever envies or repines   995
I leave him to his lot, and like my own.[218]

    Chor. She's gone, a manifest Serpent by her sting
Discover'd in the end, till now conceal'd.

    Sam. So let her go, God sent her to debase me,
And aggravate my folly who committed   1000
To such a viper his most sacred trust
Of secresie, my safety, and my life.

    Chor. Yet beauty, though injurious, hath strange power,
After offence returning, to regain
Love once possest, nor can be easily   1005
Repuls't, without much inward passion felt
And secret sting of amorous remorse.

    Sam. Love-quarrels oft in pleasing concord end,
Not wedlock-trechery endangering life.

    Cho. It is not vertue, wisdom, valour, wit,   1010
Strength, comliness of shape, or amplest merit
That womans love can win or long inherit;
But what it is, hard is to say,
Harder to hit,
(Which way soever men refer it)   1015
Much like thy riddle, *Samson*, in one day
Or seven, though one should musing sit;[219]
    If any of these or all, the *Timnian* bride
Had not so soon preferr'd
Thy Paranymph,[220] worthless to thee compar'd,   1020
Successour in thy bed,
Nor both so loosly disally'd°   FREED FROM A UNION
Thir nuptials, nor this last so trecherously
Had shorn the fatal harvest of thy head.
Is it for that such outward ornament   1025
Was lavish't on thir Sex, that inward gifts
Were left for hast unfinish't, judgment scant,
Capacity not rais'd to apprehend
Or value what is best
In choice, but oftest to affect the wrong?   1030
Or was too much of self-love mixt,

---

[217]In a time of war between the tribes of Israel and the Canaanites, a Canaanite captain, Sisera, has harassed the children of Israel for many years. The prophetess Deborah tells the Israelite commander Barak to gather forces from the tribe of Zebulun and pursue Sisera, whom she will deliver into their hands. Sisera flees to the tent of Jael, the wife of Heber the Kenite—supposedly a friend to the Canaanites. But Jael lures Sisera to bed and then, when he is asleep, drives a nail through his head (Judges 4).

[218]The end of her speech seems to reveal the real Dalila, who has sought fame for overcoming an enemy of her people. The Chorus's opinion in the next two lines seems to be accurate. Her self-declared reward for her heroism should be compared with Manoa's plans for a memorial to Samson (1733–44). She thinks she is heroic like Jael when she kills Sisera (Judges 4 and 5), and that like Jael, she will have hymns sung in her honor (Judges 5.24–31; the hymn to Jael is sung by an angel).

[219]The indented paragraphs below are manifestations of the Chorus's "turns" or strophes.

[220]"Friend of the bridegroom," as with the modern "best man." Samson's father-in-law gave the Woman of Timna to his friend after he had discovered her treachery (Judges 14.20). The Paranymph, Samson's rival, is described as "worthless."

Of constancy no root infixt,
That either they love nothing, or not long?
    What e're it be, to wisest men and best
Seeming at first all heavenly under virgin veil,[221]   1035
Soft, modest, meek, demure,
Once join'd, the contrary she proves, a thorn[222]
Intestin, far within defensive arms
A cleaving° mischief, in his way to vertue   CLINGING
Adverse and turbulent, or by her charms   1040
Draws him awry enslav'd
With dotage, and his sense deprav'd
To folly and shameful deeds which ruin ends.
What Pilot so expert but needs must wreck
Embarqu'd° with such a Stears-mate at the Helm?   ON BOARD A SHIP   1045
    Favour'd of Heav'n who finds
One vertuous rarely found,
That in domestic good combines:
Happy that house! his way to peace is smooth:
But vertue which breaks through all opposition,   1050
And all temptation can remove,
Most shines and most is acceptable above.
    Therefore Gods universal Law
Gave to the man despotic power[223]
Over his female in due awe,   1055
Nor from that right to part an hour,
Smile she or lowre:
So shall he least confusion draw
On his whole life, not sway'd
By female usurpation, nor dismay'd.   1060
    But had we best retire, I see a storm?
    Sam. Fair days have oft contracted wind and rain.
    Chor. But this another kind of tempest brings.
    Sam. Be less abstruse, my riddling days are past.[224]
    Chor. Look now for no inchanting voice, nor fear   1065
The bait of honied words; a rougher tongue
Draws hitherward, I know him by his stride,
The Giant *Harapha* of *Gath*,[225] his look
Haughty as is his pile[226] high-built and proud.
Comes he in peace? what wind hath blown him hither   1070
I less conjecture then when first I saw

---

[221]Compare the similar passage from Milton's *Doctrine and Discipline of Divorce* (1644 ed.): "who knowes not that the bashfull mutenes of a virgin may oft-times hide all the unlivelines & naturall sloth which is really unfit for conversation . . ." (Yale 2: 249).
[222]Compare *Tetrachordon*, in a passage concerning Adam and Eve: Adam "might well know if God took a rib out of his inside, to form of it a double good to him, he would far sooner dis-joyn it from his outside, to prevent a treble mischief to him: and far sooner cut it quite off from all relation for his undoubted ease, then nail it into his body again, to stick for ever there a thorn in his heart" (Yale 2: 602).
[223]There is no evidence that Milton himself believed that the man's power over the wife, after the fall of Adam and Eve, should have to be despotic or tyrannical; though he certainly believed that the husband's authority increased after and because of the Fall.
[224]There may be more to Samson's riddling, or the theme of riddling in Judges, than modern readers could guess. Michael Lieb calls attention to the riddle in the original passage as "a speech act that encodes both power relations and acts of violence" (*Milton* 245n), citing Mieke Bal, *Death and Dissymmetry: The Politics of Coherence in the Book of Judges* (Chicago: U of Chicago P, 1988): 75–80, 135–43.
[225]Building on the identification of "Haraphah," named in the Geneva Bible at 2 Samuel 21.16, as "one of the race of Gyants," according to the Geneva marginalia, but who does not enter into the book of Judges. Milton makes Harapha the father of Goliath, with whom he is tied by similarities in armor.
[226]Literally an architectural structure, the word "pile" being used to mean everything from a small castle to any "heap," but here the word might suggest something like a hollow monument to vainglory, since Harapha is all style and appearance, without substance.

The sumptuous *Dalila* floating this way:
His habit carries peace,[227] his brow defiance.
   Sam. Or peace or not, alike to me he comes.[228]
   Chor. His fraught[229] we soon shall know, he now arrives.   1075
   Har. I come not *Samson*, to condole thy chance,[230]
As these perhaps, yet wish it had not been,
Though for no friendly intent. I am of *Gath*,[231]
Men call me *Harapha*, of stock renown'd
As *Og* or *Anak* and the *Emims* old   1080
That *Kiriathaim* held,[232] thou knowst me now
If thou at all art known.[233] Much I have heard
Of thy prodigious might and feats perform'd
Incredible to me, in this displeas'd,
That I was never present on the place   1085
Of those encounters, where we might have tri'd
Each others force in camp or listed field:[234]
And now am come to see of whom such noise
Hath walk'd about, and each limb to survey,
If thy appearance answer loud report.°   OBVIOUS RUMOR   1090
   Sam. The way to know were not to see but taste.°   EXPERIENCE
   Har. Dost thou already single[235] me; I thought
Gives° and the Mill had tam'd thee? O that fortune   GYVES, MANACLES
Had brought me to the field where thou art fam'd
To have wrought such wonders with an Asses Jaw;   1095
I should have forc'd thee soon wish other arms,
Or left thy carkass where the Ass lay thrown:
So had the glory of Prowess been recover'd
To *Palestine*, won by a *Philistine*
From the unforeskinn'd race, of whom thou bear'st   1100
The highest name for valiant Acts, that honour
Certain to have won by mortal duel from thee,
I lose, prevented by thy eyes put out.[236]
   Sam. Boast not of what thou wouldst have done, but do
What then thou would'st, thou seest it in thy hand.   1105
   Har. To combat with a blind man I disdain,
And thou hast need much washing to be toucht.
   Sam. Such usage as your honourable Lords
Afford me assassinated° and betray'd,   WOUNDED BY TREACHERY
Who durst not with thir whole united powers   1110
In fight withstand me single and unarm'd,
Nor in the house with chamber Ambushes[237]

---

[227]Apparently, Harapha is not dressed in armor and, therefore, has not come to fight.

[228]"Whether he comes in peace or not, it is all the same to me."

[229]Literally his freight or cargo (keeping up the nautical imagery), but metaphorically whatever is on his mind.

[230]"Express sympathy with your lot."

[231]The first state of *1671* had no comma here.

[232]Og is mentioned as the last of the giants in Deuteronomy 3.11; giants are described as the "sons of Anak" in Numbers 13.33; and the Emims, "accounted giants" (Deuteronomy 2.11), live in the plain of Kiriathaim (Genesis 14.5).

[233]Compare Satan's "Not to know mee argues your selves unknown" in *Paradise Lost* 4.830.

[234]Fields where ritualized combat was performed in enclosures (lists).

[235]"To pick out or distinguish from others. . . . with allusion to a challenge" (*OED* 4, with a reference to this passage).

[236]Because Samson's eyes have been put out earlier, "prevented" in the sense of "anticipated" or "forestalled," Harapha can win no honor now in fighting him.

[237]Ambushes inside rooms of a house.

Close-banded[238] durst attaque me, no not sleeping,
Till they had hir'd a woman with their gold
Breaking her Marriage Faith to circumvent me.   1115
Therefore without feign'd shifts let be assign'd
Some narrow place enclos'd, where sight may give thee,
Or rather flight, no great advantage on me;
Then put on all thy gorgeous arms, thy Helmet
And Brigandine[239] of brass, thy broad Habergeon,   1120
Vant-brass and Greves,[240] and Gauntlet, add thy Spear
A Weavers beam,[241] and seven-times-folded shield,
I only with an Oak'n staff will meet thee,
And raise such out-cries on thy clatter'd Iron,°   CLANGING ARMOR
Which long shall not with-hold mee from thy head,   1125
That in a little time while breath remains thee,
Thou oft shalt wish thy self at *Gath* to boast
Again in safety what thou wouldst have done
To *Samson*, but shalt never see *Gath* more.
    Har. Thou durst not thus disparage glorious arms   1130
Which greatest Heroes have in battel worn,
Thir ornament and safety, had not spells
And black enchantments, some Magicians Art
Arm'd thee or charm'd thee strong, which thou from Heaven
Feigndst at thy birth was giv'n thee in thy hair,   1135
Where strength can least abide, though all thy hairs
Were bristles rang'd like those that ridge the back
Of chaf't° wild Boars, or ruffl'd Porcupines.   ANGERED, IRRITATED
    Sam. I know no Spells, use no forbidden Arts;
My trust is in the living God who gave me   1140
At my Nativity this strength, diffus'd
No less through all my sinews, joints and bones,
Then thine, while I preserv'd these locks unshorn,
The pledge of my unviolated vow.
For proof hereof, if *Dagon* be thy god,   1145
Go to his Temple, invocate[242] his aid
With solemnest devotion, spread before him
How highly it concerns his glory now
To frustrate and dissolve these Magic spells,
Which I to be the power of *Israel*'s God   1150
Avow, and challenge *Dagon* to the test,
Offering to combat thee his Champion bold,
With th' utmost of his Godhead seconded:
Then thou shalt see, or rather to thy sorrow
Soon feel, whose God is strongest, thine or mine.   1155

---

[238]The ambushes would be conducted, as he pictures them, by a closed rank of assailants.
[239]Brigandine or brigantine was body armor, a kind of chain mail sewn on to leather or cloth. A habergeon (accented on the first and third syllables) was a vest covered with scale armor or chain mail.
[240]A vambrace was defensive armor for the forearm; Milton seems to be emphasizing the connection with brass by the spelling variant "Vant-brass." Greves or greaves were armor for below the knee. A gauntlet was an armed glove, as in the phrase "throw down the gauntlet," which means "challenge to a duel."
[241]Proverbial phrase, used in English Bibles from the Great Bible of 1539 ("Ye shafte of his spere was like a weuers beame" [1 Samuel 17.7]) throughout the Geneva Bible and the AV. The description of Harapha's armor is derived from the armor of Goliath, who is also a Philistine of Gath (17.4–7; Milton makes Goliath one of Harapha's children, for a hint of which see 2 Samuel 21.16–22). His shield, however, seems to be derived from that of Ajax in the *Iliad* 7.219–23, which is made from seven layers of bull hide.
[242]Accent on the first syllable.

Har. Presume not on thy God, what e're he be,
Thee he regards not, owns not,° hath cut off   DOES NOT ACKNOWLEDGE
Quite from his people, and delivered up
Into thy Enemies hand, permitted them
To put out both thine eyes, and fetter'd send thee   1160
Into the common Prison, there to grind
Among the Slaves and Asses thy comrades,[243]
As good for nothing else, no better service
With those thy boyst'rous° locks, no worthy match   COARSE-GROWING, RANK
For valour to assail, nor by the sword   1165
Of noble Warriour, so to stain his honour,
But by the Barbers razor best subdu'd.
    Sam. All these indignities, for such they are
From thine,° these evils I deserve and more,   YOUR PEOPLE
Acknowledge them from God inflicted on me   1170
Justly, yet despair not of his final pardon
Whose ear is ever open; and his eye
Gracious to re-admit the suppliant;[244]
In confidence whereof I once again
Defie thee to the trial of mortal fight,   1175
By combat to decide whose god is God,[245]
Thine or whom I with *Israel*'s Sons adore.
    Har. Fair honour that thou dost thy God, in trusting
He will accept thee to defend his cause,
A Murtherer, a Revolter, and a Robber.[246]   1180
    Sam. Tongue-doubtie[247] Giant, how dost thou prove me these?
    Har. Is not thy Nation subject to our Lords?
Thir Magistrates confest it, when they took thee
As a League-breaker and deliver'd bound
Into our hands: for hadst thou not committed   1185
Notorious murder on those thirty men
At *Askalon*, who never did thee harm,
Then like a Robber stripdst them of thir robes?[248]
The *Philistines*, when thou hadst broke the league,
Went up with armed powers thee only seeking,   1190
To others did no violence nor spoil.
    Sam. Among the Daughters of the *Philistines*
I chose a Wife, which argu'd me no foe;
And in your City held my Nuptial Feast:
But your ill-meaning Politician Lords,   1195
Under pretence of Bridal friends and guests,
Appointed to await me thirty spies,
Who threatning cruel death constrain'd the bride
To wring from me and tell to them my secret,
That solv'd the riddle which I had propos'd.   1200

---

[243]Accent on the last syllable.

[244]Samson is following Milton's outline in *On Christian Doctrine* for the process of regeneration or spiritual renovation (see Columbia 15: 354–57). See Albert C. Labriola, "Divine."

[245]The capitalization of the two types of god seems significant here, as it would be in modern usage.

[246]Harapha tries to put Samson in his place, as a villain, by labeling him loosely according to his crimes against the Philistines. "Murtherer" would have been pronounced like the modern "murderer."

[247]"Valiant only in the use of your tongue." Harapha can blow hard, like any bully, but he hasn't the courage to fight against equal odds.

[248]In Judges 14.19, with "the Spirit of the Lord . . . upon him," Samson kills thirty men of Ashkelon and despoils them.

When I perceiv'd all set on enmity,
As on my enemies, where ever chanc'd,
I us'd hostility,° and took thir spoil   HOSTILE ACTS
To pay my underminers in thir coin.   1205
My Nation was subjected to your Lords.
It was the force of Conquest; force with force
Is well ejected when the Conquer'd can.
But I a private person, whom my Countrey
As a league-breaker gave up bound, presum'd   1210
Single Rebellion and did Hostile Acts.
I was no private but a person rais'd
With strength sufficient and command from Heav'n[249]
To free my Countrey; if their servile minds
Me their Deliverer sent would not receive,   1215
But to thir Masters gave me up for nought,
Th' unworthier they; whence to this day they serve.
I was to do my part from Heav'n assign'd,
And had perform'd it if my known offence
Had not disabl'd me, not all your force: 1220
These shifts° refuted, answer thy appellant   DODGY ARGUMENTS
Though by his blindness maim'd for high attempts,
Who now defies thee thrice to single fight,
As a petty enterprise of small enforce.
    Har. With thee[250] a Man condemn'd, a Slave enrol'd,   1225
Due by the Law to capital punishment?
To fight with thee no man of arms will deign.[251]
    Sam. Cam'st thou for this, vain boaster, to survey me,
To descant[252] on my strength, and give thy verdict?°   VERDICT
Come nearer, part not hence so slight inform'd;   1230
But take good heed my hand survey not thee.[253]
    Har. O *Baal-zebub*! can my ears unus'd
Hear these dishonours, and not render death?
    Sam. No man with-holds thee, nothing from thy hand
Fear I incurable;[254] bring up thy van,[255]   1235
My heels are fetter'd, but my fist is free.
    Har. This insolence other kind of answer fits.
    Sams. Go baffl'd° coward, lest I run upon thee,   DISHONORED
Though in these chains, bulk without spirit vast,
And with one buffet lay thy structure low,   1240
Or swing thee in the Air, then dash thee down
To the hazard of thy brains and shatter'd sides.[256]
    Har. By *Astaroth*[257] e're long thou shalt lament
These braveries in Irons loaden on thee.[258]

---

[249]Compare the "rouzing motions" at 1382, or the various other evidences that God often speaks through Samson.

[250]Modern punctuation would supply a dash, or at least a comma, at this point.

[251]Harapha claims to be above the rank required to fight with someone of such a low status as Samson: he would not deign combat with a common criminal.

[252]"To talk at length (and without substance) about."

[253]"Beware if my hand takes measure of you." Samson implies that if he is allowed to touch Harapha, Harapha will be a dead man.

[254]"There is nothing that you can do with your hands that I could not find an answer for."

[255]"Bring in your vanguard," as in modern United States slang, "Take your best shot."

[256]Wrestling tactics appropriate to Samson as agonist (wrestler, contender for prizes).

[257]His cursing by Beelzebub and by Ashtaroth represents the last effort of Harapha to seem brave.

[258]By the next lines we know he exits at this point.

Chor. His Giantship is gone somewhat crest-fall'n,[259]
Stalking with less unconsci'nable strides,
And lower looks, but in a sultrie chafe.°   ROUT   1245
    Sam. I dread him not, nor all his Giant-brood,
Though Fame divulge[260] him Father of five Sons
All of Gigantic size, *Goliah* chief.[261]
    Chor. He will directly to the Lords, I fear,   1250
And with malitious counsel stir them up
Some way or other yet further to afflict thee.
    Sam. He must allege some cause, and offer'd fight
Will not dare mention, lest a question rise
Whether he durst accept the offer or not,   1255
And that he durst not plain enough appear'd.
Much more affliction then already felt
They cannot well impose, nor I sustain;
If they intend advantage of my labours
The work of many hands, which earns my keeping   1260
With no small profit daily to my owners.
But come what will, my deadliest foe will prove
My speediest friend, by death to rid me hence,
The worst that he can give, to me the best.
Yet so it may fall out, because thir end   1265
Is hate, not help to me, it may with mine
Draw thir own ruin who attempt the deed.
    Chor. Oh how comely it is and how reviving
To the Spirits of just men long opprest!
When God into the hands of thir deliverer   1270
Puts invincible might
To quell the mighty of the Earth, th' oppressour,
The brute and boist'rous force of violent men
Hardy and industrious to support
Tyrannic power, but raging to pursue   1275
The righteous and all such as honour Truth;
He all thir Ammunition°   MILITARY SUPPLIES
And feats of War defeats
With plain Heroic magnitude of mind
And celestial vigour arm'd,   1280
Thir Armories and Magazins[262] contemns,
Renders them useless, while
With winged expedition
Swift as the lightning glance he executes
His errand on the wicked, who surpris'd   1285
Lose thir defence distracted and amaz'd.
    But patience is more oft the exercise
Of Saints,[263] the trial of thir fortitude,
Making them each his own Deliverer,
And Victor over all   1290

---

[259]The image embodied in the cliché is appropriate here: Harapha's knightly crest has been toppled when faced with Samson's genuine strength.
[260]Corrected by the *Errata* from "divulg'd."
[261]Establishes the fact (for the purposes of this play) that Harapha is the father of Goliath.
[262]Storehouses for gunpowder or weaponry.
[263]The word is used in the Old Testament, often in Psalms. Here it seems to mean something like "very good men," the Protestant and Puritan sense.

That tyrannie or fortune can inflict,
Either of these is in thy lot,
Samson, with might endu'd
Above the Sons of men; but sight bereav'd[264]
May chance to number thee with those   1295
Whom Patience finally must crown.
This Idols day hath bin to thee no day of rest,
     Labouring° thy mind   BELABORING, WORKING
More then the working day thy hands,
And yet perhaps more trouble is behind.   1300
For I descry° this way   DISCERN, SPOT
Some other tending, in his hand
A Scepter or quaint° staff he bears,   SKILLFULLY MADE
Comes on amain, speed in his look.
By his habit I discern him now   1305
A Public Officer, and now at hand.
His message will be short and voluble.[265]
     Off. Ebrews, the Pris'ner *Samson* here I seek.
     Chor. His manacles remark° him, there he sits.   IDENTIFY
     Off. Samson, to thee our Lords thus bid me say;[266]   1310
This day to *Dagon* is a solemn Feast,
With Sacrifices, Triumph, Pomp, and Games;
Thy strength they know surpassing human rate,[267]
And now some public proof thereof require
To honour this great Feast, and great Assembly;   1315
Rise therefore with all speed and come along,
Where I will see thee heartn'd[268] and fresh clad
To appear as fits° before th' illustrious Lords.   AS IS FITTING
     Sam. Thou knowst I am an *Ebrew*, therefore tell them,
Our Law[269] forbids at thir Religious Rites   1320
My presence; for that cause I cannot come.
     Off. This answer, be assur'd, will not content them.
     Sam. Have they not Sword-players,° and ev'ry sort   GLADIATORS
Of Gymnic Artists, Wrestlers, Riders, Runners,
Juglers and Dancers, Antics,° Mummers, Mimics,[270]   CLOWNS   1325
But they must pick me out with shackles tir'd,°   DRESSED
And over-labour'd at thir publick Mill,
To make them sport° with blind activity?   TO AMUSE THEM
Do they not seek occasion of new quarrels
On my refusal to distress me more,   1330
Or make a game of my calamities?
Return the way thou cam'st, I will not come.
     Off. Regard thy self,[271] this will offend them highly.
     Sam. My self? my conscience and internal peace.

---

[264]Bereaved of sight, answering "with might endu'd," above.
[265]Probably "easy of utterance," rather than "deceitful." The Public Servant may be speaking breathlessly in order to get the conversation over with.
[266]The semicolon is probably used the same way that a modern colon would be used—to introduce indirect discourse.
[267]Correcting "human race," by instruction of the *Errata*.
[268]"Given a fresh spirit," "enheartened."
[269]It should probably be stressed that this law is derived from Old Testament codes rather than those of the New Testament. See Calum M. Carmichael, *The Origins of Biblical Law: The Decalogue and the Book of the Covenant* (Ithaca, NY: Cornell UP, 1992).
[270]Corrected from the nonsensical "Mimirs" of the original, by instruction of the *Errata*.
[271]"Watch yourself," "watch out for what you say."

Can they think me so broken, so debas'd   1335
With corporal servitude, that my mind ever
Will condescend to such absurd commands?[272]
Although thir drudge, to be thir fool or jester,
And in my midst of sorrow and heart-grief
To shew them feats,[273] and play before thir god,   1340
The worst of all indignities, yet on me
Joyn'd with extream contempt? I will not come.
    Off. My message was impos'd on me with speed,
Brooks no delay: is this thy resolution?
      Sam. So take it with what speed thy message needs.   1345
      Off. I am sorry what this stoutness° will produce.   OBSTINACY
      Sa. Perhaps thou shalt have cause to sorrow indeed.[274]
      Chor. Consider, *Samson*; matters now are strain'd
Up to the highth, whether to hold or break;
He's gone, and who knows how he may report   1350
Thy words by adding fuel to the flame?
Expect another message more imperious,
More Lordly thund'ring then thou well wilt bear.
      Sam. Shall I abuse this Consecrated gift
Of strength, again returning with my hair   1355
After my great transgression, so requite
Favour renew'd, and add a greater sin
By prostituting holy things to Idols;
A *Nazarite* in place abominable
Vaunting my strength in honour to thir *Dagon*?   1360
Besides, how vile, contemptible, ridiculous,
What act more execrably unclean, prophane?
      Chor. Yet with this strength thou serv'st the *Philistines*,
Idolatrous, uncircumcis'd, unclean.
      Sam. Not in thir Idol-worship, but by labour   1365
Honest and lawful to deserve my food
Of those who have me in thir civil power.[275]
      Chor. Where the heart joins not, outward acts defile not.
      Sam. Where outward force constrains, the sentence holds
But who constrains me to the Temple of *Dagon*,   1370
Not dragging? the *Philistian* Lords command.
Commands are no constraints. If I obey them,
I do it freely; venturing to displease
God for the fear of Man, and Man prefer,
Set God behind: which in his jealousie   1375
Shall never, unrepented, find forgiveness.
Yet that he may dispense with me or thee
Present in Temples at Idolatrous Rites
For some important cause, thou needst not doubt.
      Chor. How thou wilt here come off surmounts my reach.   1380
      Sam. Be of good courage, I begin to feel

---

[272]In its earlier state, *1671* has a period, not a question mark.
[273]The comma was omitted in the first state of *1671*.
[274]The "cause to sorrow" here may be prophetic of the downfall of the temple of Dagon. In other words, Samson may have a presentiment of what God will bid him to do.
[275]Samson makes a logical distinction between the honest labor at the mill that he as a war captive has been asked to perform and a humiliating public display of strength. We are in the realm of international law governing prisoners taken in battle.

Some rouzing motions in me which dispose
To something extraordinary my thoughts.
I with this Messenger will go along,
Nothing to do, be sure, that may dishonour   1385
Our Law, or stain my vow of *Nazarite.*
If there be aught of presage in the mind,[276]
This day will be remarkable in my life
By some great act, or of my days the last.
   Chor. In time thou hast resolv'd, the man returns.   1390
   Off. Samson, this second message from our Lords
To thee I am bid say. Art thou our Slave,
Our Captive, at the public Mill our drudge,
And dar'st thou at our sending and command
Dispute thy coming? come without delay;   1395
Or we shall find such Engines[277] to assail
And hamper thee, as thou shalt come of force,°   BY BEING FORCED
Though thou wert firmlier fastn'd then a rock.
   Sam. I could be well content to try thir Art,
Which to no few of them would prove pernicious.   1400
Yet knowing thir advantages too many,
Because they shall not trail me through thir streets
Like a wild Beast, I am content to go.
Masters commands come with a power resistless
To such as owe them absolute subjection;   1405
And for a life who will not change his purpose?
(So mutable are all the ways of men)
Yet this be sure, in nothing to comply
Scandalous or forbidden in our Law.
   Off. I praise thy resolution, doff these links: 1410
By this compliance thou wilt win the Lords
To favour, and perhaps to set thee free.
   Sam. Brethren farewel, your company along
I will not wish, lest it perhaps offend them
To see me girt° with Friends; and how the sight   SURROUNDED   1415
Of me as of a common Enemy,
So dreaded once, may now exasperate them
I know not. Lords are Lordliest in thir wine;
And the well-feasted Priest then soonest fir'd
With zeal, if aught Religion seem concern'd:[278]   1420
No less the people on thir Holy-days
Impetuous, insolent, unquenchable;
Happ'n what may, of me expect to hear
Nothing dishonourable, impure, unworthy
Our God, our Law, my Nation, or my self,   1425
The last of me or no I cannot warrant.
   Chor. Go, and the Holy One
Of *Israel* be thy guide
To what may serve his glory best, & spread his name
Great among the Heathen round: 1430

---

[276]"If the mind has any prophetic power."
[277]Perhaps instruments of torture.
[278]"If religion in any way plays a part in this celebration."

Send thee the Angel of thy Birth, to stand
Fast by° thy side, who from thy Fathers field   RIGHT NEXT TO
Rode up in flames after his message told
Of thy conception,[279] and be now a shield
Of fire; that Spirit that first rusht on thee   1435
In the Camp of *Dan*[280]
Be efficacious in thee now at need.
For never was from Heaven imparted
Measure of strength so great to mortal seed,
As in thy wond'rous actions hath been seen.   1440
But wherefore comes old *Manoa* in such hast
With youthful steps? much livelier then e're while
He seems: supposing here to find his Son,
Or of him bringing to us some glad news?
    Man. Peace with you brethren; my inducement hither   1445
Was not at present here to find my Son,
By order of the Lords new parted hence
To come and play before them at thir Feast.
I heard all as I came, the City rings
And numbers thither flock, I had no will,   1450
Lest I should see him forc't to things unseemly.
But that which mov'd my coming now, was chiefly
To give ye part with me what hope I have
With good success to work his liberty.[281]
    Cho. That hope would much rejoyce us to partake   1455
With thee; say reverend Sire, we thirst to hear.
    Man. I have attempted one by one the Lords
Either at home, or through the high street° passing,   MAIN STREET
With supplication prone° and Fathers tears   LYING FACE DOWN
To accept of ransom for my Son thir pris'ner,   1460
Some much averse I found and wondrous harsh,
Contemptuous, proud, set on revenge and spite;
That part most reverenc'd *Dagon* and his Priests,[282]
Others more moderate seeming, but thir aim
Private reward, for which both God and State   1465
They easily would set to sale, a third
More generous far and civil, who confess'd
They had anough reveng'd, having reduc't
Thir foe to misery beneath thir fears,
The rest was magnanimity to remit,   1470
If some convenient ransom were propos'd.
What noise or shout was that? it tore the Skie.
    Chor. Doubtless the people shouting to behold
Thir once great dread,° captive, & blind before them,   PERSON TO BE FEARED
Or at some proof of strength before them shown.   1475
    Man. His ransom, if my whole inheritance
May compass° it, shall willingly be paid   ENCOMPASS, EXTEND TO
And numberd down:° much rather I shall chuse   COUNTED OUT

---

[279]The angel ascends in a flame that issues from the altar up to heaven in Judges 13.30.
[280]See Judges 13.25; 14.6, where "the Spirit of the LORD came mightily upon him"; and 19.
[281]In other words, Manoa has hopes to effect Samson's release, with a good outcome ("success") to reward his effort.
[282]Gratuitous priest-bashing, sounding more like Milton's anti-prelatical tracts than the account in Judges.

To live the poorest in my Tribe, then richest,
And he in that calamitous° prison left.   DISTRESSFUL   1480
No, I am fixt not to part hence without him.
For his redemption all my Patrimony,
If need be, I am ready to forgo
And quit:° not wanting him, I shall want° nothing.   GIVE UP, RELEASE   LACK
   Chor. Fathers are wont to lay up for thir Sons,   1485
Thou for thy Son art bent to lay out all;
Sons wont to nurse thir Parents in old age,
Thou in old age car'st how to nurse thy Son,[283]
Made older then thy age through eye-sight lost.
   Man. It shall be my delight to tend his eyes,   1490
And view him sitting in the house,[284] enobl'd
With all those high exploits by him atchiev'd,
And on his shoulders waving down those locks,
That of a Nation arm'd the strength contain'd:
And I perswade me° God had not permitted   I AM PERSUADED   1495
His strength again to grow up with his hair
Garrison'd round about him like a Camp
Of faithful Souldiery, were not his purpose
To use him further yet in some great service,
Not to sit idle with so great a gift   1500
Useless, and thence ridiculous about him.
And since his strength with eye-sight was not lost,
God will restore him eye-sight to his strength.[285]
   Chor. Thy hopes are not ill founded nor seem vain
Of his delivery, and thy joy thereon   1505
Conceiv'd, agreeable to a Fathers love,
In both which we, as next participate.[286]
   Man. I know your friendly minds and——O what noise!
Mercy of Heav'n what hideous noise was that!
Horribly loud unlike the former shout.   1510
   Chor. Noise call you it or universal groan
As if the whole inhabitation perish'd,
Blood, death, and deathful deeds are in that noise,
Ruin, destruction at the utmost point.
   Man. Of ruin indeed methought I heard the noise,   1515
Oh it continues, they have slain my Son.
   Chor. Thy Son is rather slaying them, that outcry
From slaughter of one foe could not ascend.
   Man. Some dismal accident it needs must be;
What shall we do, stay here or run and see?   1520
   Chor. Best keep together here, lest running thither
We unawares run into dangers mouth.
This evil on the *Philistines* is fall'n,
From whom could else a general cry be heard?
The sufferers then will scarce molest us here,   1525

---

[283]The period here in *1671* was, as Fletcher speculates, probably foul case (mixed in the wrong compositor's case) for a comma.
[284]Contrast Manoa's care for his invalid son with that of Dalila, "Here I should still enjoy thee day and night / Mine and Loves prisoner" (807–08).
[285]There is no evidence that God restores Samson's eyesight with his strength, though of course God could effect such a miracle.
[286]They are near Samson in affection and in kinship, being of the tribe of Dan.

From other hands we need not much to fear.[287]
What if his eye–sight (for to *Israels* God
Nothing is hard) by miracle restor'd,
He now be dealing dole among his foes,
And over heaps of slaughter'd walk his way?   1530
   Man. That were a joy presumptuous to be thought.
   Chor. Yet God hath wrought things as incredible
For his people of old; what hinders now?
   Man. He can I know, but doubt to think he will;[288]
Yet Hope would fain subscribe, and tempts Belief.[289]   1535
A little stay will bring some notice hither.[290]
   Chor. Of good or bad so great, of bad the sooner;
For evil news rides post, while good news baits.°   ABATES, HESITATES
And to our wish I see one hither speeding,
An *Ebrew*, as I guess, and of our Tribe.   1540
   Mess. O whither shall I run, or which way flie
The sight of this so horrid spectacle
Which earst° my eyes beheld and yet behold;   EARLIER
For dire imagination° still persues me.   A VISION OF CATASTROPHE
But providence or instinct of nature[291] seems,   1545
Or reason though disturb'd, and scarse consulted
To have guided me aright, I know not how,
To thee first reverend *Manoa*, and to these
My Countreymen, whom here I knew remaining,
As at some distance from the place of horrour,   1550
So in the sad event° too much concern'd.   OUTCOME
   Man. The accident was loud, & here[292] before thee
With rueful cry, yet what it was we hear not,
No Preface needs, thou seest we long to know.
   Mess. It would burst forth, but I recover breath   1555
And sense distract,° to know well what I utter.   CONFUSED
   Man. Tell us the sum, the circumstance defer.[293]
   Mess. Gaza yet stands, but all her Sons are fall'n,
All in a moment overwhelm'd and fall'n.
   Man. Sad, but thou knowst to *Israelites* not saddest   1560
The desolation of a Hostile City.
   Mess. Feed on that first, there may in grief be surfet.°   SATISFACTION
   Man. Relate by whom. *Mess.* By *Samson. Man.* That still lessens
The sorrow, and converts it nigh to joy.
   Mess. Ah *Manoa* I refrain, too suddenly   1565

---

[287]Nine lines plus one were added here and after "A little stay," from the *Omissa*. The *Omissa* were introduced with these words:
    Omissa.
   Page 89 after verse 1537. which ends,
   Not so much to fear, insert these.
Carey points out "thus in the uncorrected state of *1671* l. 1536 was given to the chorus, not Manoa. In the corrected state the chorus take up and finish what Manoa is saying, thus: '(*Manoa*) a little wait will bring some information (*Chorus*) about such a great good or evil as—judging from the noise—has just occurred: and that information will come all the quicker if the occurrence is evil" (1536–37n).
[288]"God could do such a thing, but I do not think that He will."
[289]The capitalization might conceivably indicate that the reader is to take Hope and Belief allegorically, but the argument would be tenuous at best.
[290]The second line from the *Omissa* was inserted here with the words "After the next verse which begins, *A little stay,* insert this."
[291]Probably "innate impulse," based on God's control over the individual through inner promptings or "rouzing motions," as compared with God's ordering of history (God's Providence).
[292]Corrects "heard" by instruction of the *Errata.*
[293]"Please summarize, and leave out the details."

To utter what will come at last too soon;
Lest evil tidings with too rude irruption°   VIOLENT BREAK-IN
Hitting thy aged ear should pierce too deep.
   Man. Suspense in news is torture, speak them out.
   Mess. Then take the worst in brief, *Samson* is dead.   1570
   Man. The worst indeed, O all my hope's[294] defeated
To free him hence! but death who sets all free
Hath paid his ransom now and full discharge.
What windy° joy this day had I conceiv'd   LONG-WINDED, INFLATED
Hopeful of his Delivery, which now proves   1575
Abortive as the first-born bloom of spring
Nipt with the lagging rear of winters frost.
Yet e're I give the rains[295] to grief, say first,
How dy'd he? death to life is crown or shame.
All by him fell thou say'st, by whom fell he,   1580
What glorious hand gave *Samson* his deaths wound?
   Mess. Unwounded of his enemies he fell.
   Man. Wearied with slaughter then or how? explain.
   Mess. By his own hands. *Man.* Self-violence? what cause
Brought him so soon at variance with himself   1585
Among his foes? *Mess.* Inevitable cause
At once both to destroy and be destroy'd;
The Edifice where all were met to see him
Upon thir heads and on his own he pull'd.
   Man. O lastly over-strong against thy self!   1590
A dreadful way thou took'st to thy revenge.
More then anough we know; but while things yet
Are in confusion, give us if thou canst,
Eye-witness of what first or last was done,
Relation more particular and distinct.   1595
   Mess. Occasions° drew me early to this City,   BUSINESS ENGAGEMENTS
And as the gates I enter'd with Sun-rise,
The morning Trumpets Festival proclaim'd
Through each high street: little I had dispatch't
When all abroad was rumour'd that this day   1600
Samson should be brought forth to shew the people
Proof of his mighty strength in feats and games;
I sorrow'd at his captive state, but minded°   WAS DISPOSED
Not to be absent at that spectacle.
The building was a spacious Theatre[296]   1605
Half round on two main Pillars vaulted high,
With seats where all the Lords and each degree
Of sort,° might sit in order to behold,   CONDITION, RANK
The other side was op'n, where the throng°   CROWD OF ORDINARY PEOPLE
On banks° and scaffolds under Skie might stand;   BENCHES   1610

---

[294]Probably this represents the plural form of the word and not the contraction for "hope is." A modern-spelling edition must make the choice between the two word forms, as in Carey.

[295]"Give the reins to," "allow myself to be overcome by."

[296]In Judges it is a "house," but large enough to be supported by central pillars, and large enough to hold a greater quantity of Philistines than Samson had killed up to this point in his life. Carey points to George Sandys's description of the ruins of a "theater of Samson" on a hill above Gaza (*A Relation of a Journey* [London, 1615]: 149), which might well have been Milton's source.

I among these aloof obscurely stood.[297]
The Feast and noon grew high, and Sacrifice
Had fill'd thir hearts with mirth, high chear, & wine,
When to thir sports they turn'd. Immediately
Was *Samson* as a public servant brought,   1615
In thir state Livery clad; before him Pipes
And Timbrels,[298] on each side went armed guards,
Both horse and foot before him and behind
Archers, and Slingers, Cataphracts and Spears.[299]
At sight of him the people with a shout   1620
Rifted the Air clamouring thir god with praise,[300]
Who had made thir dreadful enemy thir thrall.
He patient but undaunted where they led him,
Came to the place, and what was set before him
Which without help of eye, might be assay'd,   1625
To heave, pull, draw, or break, he still° perform'd   CONSTANTLY
All with incredible, stupendious[301] force,
None daring to appear Antagonist.[302]
At length for intermission sake they led him
Between the pillars; he his guide requested   1630
(For so from such as nearer stood we heard)
As over-tir'd to let him lean a while
With both his arms on those two massie° Pillars   SOLID
That to the arched roof gave main support.
He unsuspitious led him; which when *Samson*   1635
Felt in his arms, with head a while enclin'd,
And eyes fast fixt he stood, as one who pray'd,[303]
Or some great matter in his mind revolv'd.
At last with head erect thus cryed[304] aloud,
    Hitherto, Lords, what your commands impos'd   1640
I have perform'd, as reason was,° obeying,   AS WAS REASONABLE
Not without wonder or delight beheld.
Now of my own accord[305] such other tryal
I mean to shew you of my strength, yet greater;
As with amaze° shall strike all who behold.   WONDER, AMAZEMENT   1645
This utter'd, straining all his nerves° he bow'd,   MUSCLES
As with the force of winds and waters pent,
When Mountains tremble,[306] those two massie° Pillars   HUGE
With horrible convulsion to and fro,
He tugg'd, he shook, till down they came and drew   1650

---

[297]Apparently the Messenger has been situated in the equivalent of the cheap seats, which allowed him to escape destruction. He is "aloof" perhaps in the sense that he has kept his distance from the Philistines (*OED* 7.C).

[298]The biblical equivalent of the tabor or tambourine.

[299]"Those in full armor and those carrying only spears." Milton seems to have been the first to use "cataphract" in this sense in English, though the Greek word from which it is derived means "man in armor."

[300]They split the air with their outcries to their god.

[301]The preferred form of "stupendous," until the late seventeenth century.

[302]Someone to challenge him in an athletic contest.

[303]Samson's appearance as if in prayer might help lend Christian dignity to an act of suicidal slaughter. Krouse shows the problems that Samson's "Let me die with the Philistines" (Judges 16.26) caused for Christians who wanted to consider Samson a saint (51).

[304]A monosyllable here, probably incorrectly set for "cry'd."

[305]The phrase "of my own accord" may have legal implications, because, though a prisoner, Samson at this point is speaking his conscience, as if he were a Quaker under oath (see Achinstein, at various points, discussing Quaker oaths or speaking one's conscience in the courtroom).

[306]Apparently volcanoes are pictured in the process of erupting.

The whole roof after them, with burst of thunder
Upon the heads of all who sate beneath,
Lords, Ladies, Captains, Councellors, or Priests,[307]
Thir choice nobility and flower, not only
Of this but each *Philistian* City round   1655
Met from all parts to solemnize this Feast.
Samson with these immixt, inevitably
Pulld down the same destruction on himself;
The vulgar only scap'd who stood without.
    Chor. O dearly-bought revenge, yet glorious!   1660
Living or dying thou hast fulfill'd
The work for which thou wast foretold
To *Israel*, and now ly'st victorious
Among thy slain self-kill'd
Not willingly, but tangl'd in the fold,   1665
Of dire necessity,[308] whose law in death conjoin'd
Thee with thy slaughter'd foes in number more
Then all thy life had slain before.
    Semichor. While thir hearts were jocund and sublime,
Drunk with Idolatry, drunk with Wine,   1670
And fat regorg'd[309] of Bulls and Goats,
Chaunting thir Idol, and preferring
Before our living Dread[310] who dwells
In *Silo*[311] his bright Sanctuary:
Among them he a spirit of phrenzie° sent,   DEMONIC POSSESSION   1675
Who hurt thir minds,[312]
And urg'd them on with mad desire
To call in hast for thir destroyer;
They only set on sport and play
Unweetingly importun'd°   BEGGED   1680
Thir own destruction to come speedy upon them.
So fond are mortal men
Fall'n into wrath divine,
As thir own ruin on themselves to invite,
Insensate left, or to sense reprobate,°   MORALLY CORRUPT   1685
And with blindness internal struck.
    Semichor. But he though blind of sight,
Despis'd and thought extinguish't quite,[313]
With inward eyes illuminated
His fierie vertue rouz'd   1690
From under ashes into sudden flame,
And as an ev'ning Dragon came,

---

[307]The list does not seem to be gratuitous, covering as it does the aristocracy, the legal establishment, and the priesthood. Contrast them with the "vulgar" or the "throng," those in standing-room-only who were the only ones to have escaped the devastation. Again, Milton adds to the account in Judges, which mentions only "lords" and "people" having been destroyed together (16.30, in the AV wording).
[308]We are probably being led, by Milton through the Chorus, to think of fate or necessity in terms of classical Greek tragedy, as with the ironies of the fate of Sophocles's Oedipus. Samson brings about his own heroic death, but accidentally, in carrying out God's mission to destroy the Philistines. For the phrase "dire necessity," see Horace, *Odes* 3.26.6.
[309]Carey believes that the allusion is to food regurgitated by ruminants (1671n), but there would be no reasons for ruminant animals to be eating fat. The fat seems more likely to be that used in ritual burning, as in Leviticus 9.10 and 19: "He slew also the bullock and the ram for a sacrifice of peace offerings."
[310]The word "dread" ties Samson, who has been called the dread of the Philistines (1474), with the living God.
[311]Shiloh, where the Ark of the Covenant was kept before it was removed, according to 1 Samuel 4.4.
[312]The spirit is the one which affects their minds and drives them crazy temporarily.
[313]"As ineffective as if he were dead (extinguished)."

Assailant on the perched roosts,
And nests in order rang'd
Of tame villatic Fowl;[314] but as an Eagle　　　　1695
His cloudless thunder° bolted on thir heads.　　　　LIGHTNING
So vertue giv'n for lost,
Deprest, and overthrown, as seem'd,
Like that self-begott'n bird
In the *Arabian* woods embost,[315]　　　　1700
That no second knows nor third,
And lay e're while a Holocaust,[316]
From out her ashie womb now teem'd,°　　　　IS BORN
Revives, reflourishes, then vigorous most
When most unactive deem'd,　　　　1705
And though her body die, her fame survives,
A secular[317] bird ages of lives.[318]

　　Man. Come, come, no time for lamentation now,
Nor much more cause, *Samson* hath quit° himself　　　　CONDUCTED, ACQUITTED
Like *Samson*, and heroicly hath finish'd　　　　1710
A life Heroic, on his Enemies
Fully reveng'd, hath left them years of mourning,
And lamentation to the Sons of *Caphtor*
Through all *Philistian* bounds.° To *Israel*　　　　BOUNDARIES
Honour hath left, and freedom, let but them　　　　1715
Find courage to lay hold on this occasion,
To himself and Fathers house eternal fame;
And which is best and happiest yet, all this
With God not parted from him, as was feard,
But favouring and assisting to the end.　　　　1720
Nothing is here for tears, nothing to wail
Or knock the breast, no weakness, no contempt,
Dispraise, or blame, nothing but well and fair,
And what may quiet us in a death so noble.
Let us go find the body where it lies　　　　1725
Sok't in his enemies blood, and from the stream
With lavers° pure and cleansing herbs wash off　　　　RITUAL WASH BASINS
The clotted gore. I with what speed the while

---

[314]The image seems out of place, since it represents the dragon as a bird of prey attacking tame and domestic fowl ("villatic" being derived from villa, country house). Perhaps the audience is meant to think "They had it coming" of the Philistines, but the image of a dragon attacking chickens in a rural house or village does not sit well in terms of the rules of hunting or of husbandry. Perhaps Shawcross's note describing the dragon as "winged serpent emitting fire" (618n30) is most nearly correct (compare Genesis 49.16–18). It may be worth noting that Newton described the dragon as a serpent with no apparent problem with the combination.

[315]Perhaps "swollen, about ready to burst" (*OED* 4), but the meaning here is uncertain, and the *OED* does not record Milton's usage. Shawcross's "sheltered" echoes Hughes's note, as does Campbell's and Carey's. Hughes adds "The word originally applied to hunted animals." What the *OED* reports is "Of a hunted animal: Driven to extremity; foaming at the mouth from exhaustion. Also transf. of persons." I find no evidence in the passage that the phoenix has been hunted to exhaustion. Richardson's note to Spenser's *The Faerie Queene* 1.3.24 ("A knight her met in mighty arms imbost") with "imbost" made to mean "concealed, covered," makes more sense (Newton 1700n).

[316]Something completely consumed by fire (apparently Milton's coinage, in this sense, according to *OED* 2c).

[317]Carey provides "Lasting for ages," as a seventeenth-century usage having nothing to do with the usual contrast between secular and clerical (outside or inside the boundaries of the church) but everything to do with Latin *sæculum*, meaning "age" or "generation." Early editors wanted to remove the comma after "survives," because of the potential ambiguity.

[318]The *OED* provides a full and useful description of the phoenix: "A mythical bird, of gorgeous plumage, fabled to be the only one of its kind, and to live five or six hundred years in the Arabian desert, after which it burnt itself to ashes on a funeral pile of aromatic twigs ignited by the sun and fanned by its own wings, but only to emerge from its ashes with renewed youth, to live through another cycle of years. (Variations of the myth were that the phœnix burnt itself on the altar of the temple at Heliopolis: and that a worm emerged from the ashes and became the young phœnix.)" Milton has made the gender of the phœnix feminine, perhaps on the evidence of the Italian *fenice*.

(*Gaza* is not in plight to say us nay)[319]
Will send for all my kindred, all my friends   1730
To fetch him hence and solemnly attend
With silent obsequie and funeral train
Home to his Fathers house:[320] there will I build him
A Monument, and plant it round with shade
Of Laurel ever green,[321] and branching Palm,   1735
With all his Trophies hung, and Acts enroll'd[322]
In copious Legend, or sweet Lyric Song.
Thither shall all the valiant youth resort,
And from his memory inflame thir breasts
To matchless valour, and adventures high: 1740
The Virgins also shall on feastful days
Visit his Tomb with flowers, only bewailing
His lot unfortunate in nuptial choice,
From whence captivity and loss of eyes.[323]

    Chor. All is best, though we oft doubt,[324]   1745
What th' unsearchable dispose°   DISPOSITION
Of highest wisdom brings about,
And ever best found in the close.[325]
Oft he seems to hide his face,
But unexpectedly returns   1750
And to his faithful Champion hath in place
Bore witness gloriously; whence *Gaza* mourns
And all that band them° to resist   ALL THOSE WHO COME TOGETHER
His uncontroulable intent,
His servants he with new acquist°   ACQUISITION, GAIN   1755
Of true experience from this great event
With peace and consolation hath dismist,
And calm of mind all passion spent.[326]

      THE END.

---

[319]"Gaza is not in a position to deny us."
[320]Compare the ending of *Paradise Regain'd*, when Jesus "Home to his Mothers house private return'd" (4.639).
[321]The echo of "Lycidas" 2, "Ye myrtles brown, with ivy never sere," would seem to reinforce what Manoa proposes—to set up a shrine to the memory of Samson, though Milton as an iconoclastic Protestant would normally be wary of shrines to the memory of saints or national heroes.
[322]Perhaps scrolls on display at Manoa's monument, listing the achievements of Samson.
[323]Milton seems to want us to note, somewhat vengefully, that Dalila has left Samson with the image of a very similar monument to her memory, with attendants, flowers, and services on feast days, for her service to her country; see 980–87. Anonymous "women" are to sing for her, but "virgins" sing for Samson, in the monument as designed by Manoa. If she has been among the Philistine dead, no such monument would be likely to be erected.
[324]The last choral speech is a Petrarchan sonnet rhyming ABAB, CDCD, EFEFEF, with four irregular feet to each line.
[325]The end, usually of a piece of music.
[326]Suggests the Aristotelian catharsis or purging that was supposed to accompany the experience of witnessing a tragedy: a potentially harmful passion is purged, for the betterment of the citizen and the state.

Prolusions (Academic Essays)

Prolusions were, by the definition of *prolusio* in Latin, preliminary exercises or essays. They also conformed to the classical definition of *oration*, with all or most of the parts in place: exordium, proposition, proof (confirmation and refutation), and epilogue or conclusion. Milton's Prolusions, delivered while he was a student at Christ College, Cambridge, between 1625 and 1632, must have seemed erudite even for college exercises, since they display his budding talents as a mythographer, lexicographer, educational reformer, historian, and poet.

Milton thought enough of them to publish them together with Latin personal correspondence in 1674, as if he knew how prophetic the Prolusions were concerning his later career. The printer's preface makes it clear that the Prolusions were used to pad the slender volume, to help make the book profitable (Yale 1: 211). It was not until the 1880s and Masson's great biography that scholars became aware of the value of the Prolusions as commentary on Milton's later work.

At times, the Prolusions represent a tired effort by an exasperated undergraduate who fears he is boring his auditors. For the Fourth Prolusion, he unashamedly cribbed most of his information from the Jesuit scholastic philosopher Francis Suarez (Hartman 4), without mentioning his source. When he does mention a source, Chrysostom Javello, in the Fifth Prolusion, it is to criticize Javello's monkish style. Technical and jargon-ridden, the Fourth and Fifth Prolusions are tiresome. The other five Prolusions are more original in their style and choice of authorities, and the Sixth, the funny one on "sportive exercises," is notable both as Milton's first ambitious essay in prose and as proof that he possessed a healthy, if sometimes bawdy, sense of humor. Considering how important learning was to his prose and poetry, or how important heavenly inspiration, the Second Prolusion, on the music of the spheres, and the Seventh Prolusion, on the importance of learning, both prophesy where his career will lead him.

The Third Prolusion, against scholastic philosophy, shows Milton's revolutionary reaction against the educational system of his time; it is important as a precursor to Milton's *Of Education*. Milton may have lumped the outmoded scholastic curriculum of Cambridge together with the attitudes of his first tutor, William Chappell. The conflict between the two men is perhaps reflected in this and in the Seventh Prolusion (Miller). The attack on scholasticism gives coherence to the whole set of Prolusions. Woodhouse provides a tentative chronology, which is useful because we do not know if the numbers present in the first printed edition indicate order of composition.

The debating technique used in the Prolusions is familiar as it is in today's undergraduate forensic teams: take a moot question and argue it with force and authority on one side or the other. Milton in his first Prolusion argues that Day is better than Night. For practical application of the debating technique to the same subject matter, we can look at *Paradise Lost*, where Satan, the evil orator, will argue in Eve's ear in a dream that Night is better than Day (*Paradise Lost* 5.38–47).

Milton seems to enjoy the intellectual wrestling match that the format of the debate allows him. Even if his opponents are at times only straw men, the contest, the *agon*, the struggle, is everything. He will use the same debating skills in writing various orations and essays advocating one point of view, with his early prose tracts *Of Education* and *Areopagitica*; and he will speak to both sides of a question most notably in "L'Allegro" and "Il Penseroso," poems probably contemporary with the Prolusions. Even with the last poems he wrote, if one believes that *Paradise Regain'd* and *Samson Agonistes* are his last works, debate between formidable opponents creates dramatic tension; and the same sort of straw men are set up and knocked down by Milton's arguments in *On Christian Doctrine*.

TEXT AND TRANSLATION

The Latin text of the prolusions was first printed in *Joannis Miltonii Angli, Epistolarum Familiarium Liber Unus: Quibus Accesserunt, Ejusdem, jam olim in Collegio Adolescentis, Prolusiones Quaedam Oratoriae* (London, 1674). The translation Parker offers is "a book of the familiar letters of John Milton, Englishman, to which have been added certain oratorical exercises of the same writer, done when he was still a youth in college" (637). Brabazon Aylmer was the cautious printer: neither he nor Milton would be allowed to publish any of Milton's state letters while he was still alive, because of problems with the Restoration censors.

The translation used here is that of Phyllis B. Tillyard preserved in the Yale edition of Milton's complete prose, with occasional small corrections or modernizations (as with "calloused" for "horny"). The Latin text, with an English translation on facing pages, is readily available in the Columbia edition of Milton's complete works (12: 118–285), but the translation is dated. Kathryn A. McEuen's notes to the Yale edition are still the most complete. Hartman's "Foreword" is useful as well, and both Patterson and Hughes include all the Prolusions, with notes, though Hartman includes the text of only the Seventh.

Works Cited
Editions are identified with an asterisk.

Cavanaugh, Sister Mary Hortense, S. S. J. "John Milton's *Prolusions* Considered in the Light of his Rhetorical and Dialectical Education at St. Paul's Grammar School and Cambridge University." Doctoral diss., Fordham U, 1968.

*Hartmann, Thomas R., ed. "The Prolusions, Prolusiones Quaedam Oratoriae, Some Academic Exercises, 1628–1632." *The Prose of John Milton*. Gen. Ed. J. Max Patrick. New York: New York UP, 1968.

Miller, Leo. "Milton's Clash with Chappell: A Suggested Reconstruction." *Milton Quarterly* 14 (1980): 77–87.

*Tillyard, Phyllis B., trans. *Milton: Private Correspondence and Academic Exercises*. Folcroft, PA: Folcroft Library Editions, 1969.

Woodhouse, A. S. P. "Notes on Milton's Early Development." *University of Toronto Quarterly* 13 (1943–44): 66–101.

I.

DELIVERED IN COLLEGE
Whether Day or Night is the More Excellent

It is a frequent maxim of the most eminent masters of rhetoric, as you know well, Members of the University, that in every style of oration, whether demonstrative, deliberative, or judicial, the speaker must begin by winning the good-will of his audience; without it he cannot make any impression upon them, nor succeed as he could wish in his cause. If this be so (and, to tell the truth, I know that the learned are all agreed in regarding it as an established axiom), how very unfortunate I am and to what a pass I am brought this day! At the very outset of my oration I fear I shall have to say something contrary to all the rules of oratory, and be forced to depart from the first and chief duty of an orator. For how can I hope for your good-will, when in all this great assembly I encounter none but hostile glances,[1] so that my task seems to be to placate the implacable? So provocative of animosity, even in the home of learning, is the rivalry of those who pursue different studies or whose opinions differ concerning the studies they pursue in common. However, I care not if "Polydamas and the women of Troy prefer Labeo to me;—a trifle, this."[2]

Yet to prevent complete despair, I see here and there, if I do not mistake, some who show clearly by their looks how well they wish me. The approval of these, few though they be, is more precious to me than that of the countless hosts of the ignorant, who lack all intelligence, reasoning power, and sound judgment, and who pride themselves on the ridiculous effervescing froth of their verbiage. Stripped of their covering of patches borrowed from new-fangled authors, they will prove to have no more in them than a serpent's slough,[3] and once they have come to the end of their stock of phrases and platitudes you will find them unable to utter so much as a syllable, as dumb as the frogs of Seriphus.[4] How difficult even Heraclitus[5] would find it, were he still alive, to keep a straight face at the sight of these speechifiers (if I may call them so without offence), first grandly spouting their lines in the tragic part of Euripides' Orestes,[6] or as the mad Hercules in his dying agony, and then, their slender stock of phrases exhausted and all their glory gone, drawing in their horns and crawling off like snails.

But to return to the point, from which I have wandered a little. If there is anyone who has refused peace on any terms and declared war *à mort* against me, I will for once stoop to beg and entreat him to lay aside his animosity for a moment and show himself an unbiased judge in this debate, and not to allow the speaker's fault (if such there be) to prejudice the best and most deserving of causes. If you consider that I have spoken with too much sharpness and bitterness, I confess that I have done so intentionally, for I wish the beginning of my speech to resemble the first gleam of dawn, which presages the fairest day when overcast.

The question of whether Day or Night is preferable is no common theme of discussion, and it is now my duty, the task meted out to me this morning, to probe the subject thoroughly and radically, though it might seem better suited to a poetical exercise than to a contest of rhetoric.

Did I say that Night had declared war on Day? What should this portend? What means this daring enterprise? Are the Titans waging anew their ancient war, and renewing the battle of Phlegra's plain?[7] Has Earth

---

[1]Biographers take this statement to mean that, at this point in his academic career, Milton was unpopular, perhaps because of the kind of arrogance he displays at the end of this very paragraph (see Yale 1: 220n3).
[2]From Persius, *Satires* 1.4–5, a description of a very poor poet, Attius Labeo, who attempted to translate Homer. Even at this point in his career, Milton seems to be searching for a "fit audience . . . though few" (*Paradise Lost* 7.31).

[3]The cast-off skin of a snake; thus anything useless or empty.
[4]On this small island in the Aegean, to which Roman criminals were exiled, the frogs were not supposed to be able to croak. The phrase *seriphia rana* was applied to men who could neither speak nor sing.
[5]The philosopher (540–475 BCE), who had a reputation for antisocial behavior.
[6]Actors (possibly from Cambridge) described overacting in roles created by playwrights like the Greek Euripides and the Roman philosopher Seneca (*Hercules Furens*, or "Hercules Insane").
[7]The Titans, who declared war on the Olympian gods and were consequently imprisoned, included Saturn, Hyperion, Iapetus, and Briareus, according to Hesiod, *Theogony* 135, etc. For Phlegra in Macedonia and in Italy, places where the combat between gods and giants began and ended, see *Paradise Lost* 1.577.

brought forth new offspring of portentous stature to flout the gods of heaven? Or has Typhoeus[8] forced his way from beneath the bulk of Etna piled upon him? Or last, as Briareus eluded Cerberus and escaped from his fetters of adamant? What can it possibly be that has now thrice roused the hopes of the gods of hell to rule the empire of the heavens? Does Night so scorn the thunderbolt of Jove? Cares she nothing for the matchless might of Pallas, which wrought such havoc in days of old among the earth-born brothers? Has she forgotten Bacchus' triumph over the shattered band of Giants, renowned through all the space of heaven? No, none of these. Full well she remembers, to her grief, how of those brothers most were slain by Jove, and the survivors driven in headlong flight even to the furthest corners of the underworld. Not for war, but for something far other, does she now anxiously prepare. Her thoughts now turn to complaints and accusations, and, woman-like, after a brave fight with tooth and nail, she proceeds to argument, or rather abuse, to try, I suppose, whether her hands or her tongue are the better weapon.[9] But I will soon show how unadvised, how arrogant, and how ill-founded is her claim to supremacy, compared with Day's. And indeed I see Day herself, awakened by the crowing of the rooster, hastening hither more swiftly than is her wont, to hear her own praise.

Now since it is generally agreed that to be of noble lineage and to trace one's descent back to kings and gods of old is an essential qualification for honors and dignity, it behoves us to enquire, first, which of the two is of nobler birth, secondly, which can trace back her descent the furthest, and thirdly, which is of greater service to mankind?

I find it stated by the most ancient authorities on mythology that Demogorgon, the ancestor of all the gods (whom I supposed to be identical with the Chaos of the ancients), was the father of Earth, among his many children. Night was the child of Earth, by an unknown father (though Hesiod gives a slightly different pedigree and calls Night the child of Chaos, in the line "From Chaos sprang Erebus and black Night").[10] Whatever her parentage, when she had reached marriageable age, the shepherd Phanes asked her to wife. Her mother consented, but she herself opposed the match, refusing

to contract an alliance with a man she did not know and had never seen, and one moreover whose style of life was so different from her own. Annoyed at the rebuff, and with his love turned to hatred, Phanes in his indignation pushed this dusky daughter of Earth through all the length and breadth of the world to slay her. She now feared his enmity as much as she had previously scorned his love. Therefore she did not feel secure enough even among the most distant peoples or in the most remote places, not even in the very bosom of her mother, but fled for refuge, secretly and by stealth, to the incestuous embrace of her brother Erebus. Thus she found at once release from her pressing fears and a husband who was certainly very like herself. From this pretty pair Aether and Day are said to have sprung, according to Hesiod, whom I have already quoted:

> From Night again sprang Aether and Day
> Whom she conceived and bore by Erebus' embrace.[11]

But the more cultured Muses and Philosophy herself, the neighbor of the gods, forbid us to place entire confidence in the poets who have given the gods their forms, especially the Greek poets; and no one should regard it as a reproach to them that in a question of such importance they hardly seem sufficient and reliable authorities. For if any of them has departed from the truth to some slight extent, the blame should not be laid upon their genius, which is most divine, but upon the perverse and blind ignorance of the age, which at that time was all-pervading. They have attained an ample meed of honor and glory by gathering together in one place and forming into organized communities men who previously roamed like beasts at random through the forests and mountains, and by being the first to teach, by their divine inspiration, all the sciences which are known today, arraying them in the charming cloak of fable; and their best title to everlasting fame (and that no mean one) is that they have left to their successors the full development of that knowledge of the Arts which they so happily began.

Do not then, whoever you are, hastily accuse me of arrogance, in shattering or altering the statements of all the ancient poets, without any authority to support me. For I am not taking upon myself to do that, but am only attempting to bring them to the test of reason, and thereby to examine whether they can bear the scrutiny of strict truth.

First, then, the story that makes Night the child of

---

[8] In what might have been a separate war with Olympus, the fire-breathing giant Typhon frightened the gods so thoroughly that as punishment he was crushed under Mount Etna by Jupiter, to produce the volcanic eruptions there.

[9] Something of a cheap joke at the expense of the female Night, who, Milton implies, fights with her tongue rather than with the physical strength displayed by Pallas Athene (the female goddess of wisdom and war), Bacchus (whose name is Liber ["free"] at times in Latin), or Jupiter.

[10] Hesiod, *Theogony* 123.

[11] *Theogony* 124–25.

Earth is a learned and elegant allegory[12] of antiquity; for what is it that makes night envelop the world but the dense and solid earth, coming between the sun's light and our horizon?

Then, as to the statements of the mythologists, calling Night sometimes fatherless, sometimes motherless, these too are pleasing fictions, if we understand them to signify that she was a bastard or a changeling, or else that her parents refused for very shame to acknowledge so infamous and ignoble a child. But why they should believe that Phanes, endowed as he was with a wondrous and superhuman beauty, was so much in love with Night, a mere mulatto or silhouette, as even to wish to marry her, seems a problem hopelessly difficult to solve, unless the phenomenal scarcity of females at that time left him no choice.

But now let us come to close quarters with our subject. The ancients interpret Phanes as the sun or the day, and in relating that he first sought Night in marriage and then pursued her to avenge his rejection, they mean only to signify the alternation of day and night. But why should they have thought it necessary, in order to show this, to represent Phanes as a suitor for the hand of Night, when their perpetual alternation and mutual repulsion, as it were, could be indicated far better by the figure of an innate and unremitting hatred? for it is well known that light and darkness have been divided from one another by an implacable hatred from the very beginning of time. It is in fact my opinion that Night got her Greek name of εὐφρόνη[13] for the very reason that she showed caution and good sense in refusing to bind herself in wedlock to Phanes; for if she had once submitted to his embrace she would doubtless have been destroyed by his beams and by his unendurable radiance, or utterly consumed by fire; like Semele,[14] who, legend says, perished by fire, against the will of her lover, Jove. For this reason, with a proper regard for her security, she preferred Erebus to Phanes. With reference to this, Martial aptly and wittily says, "Worst of husbands, worst of wives, I wonder not that you agree so well."[15]

It is, I think, proper to mention with what a handsome family, how like their mother, she presented her husband—namely, Misery, Envy, Fear, Deceit, Fraud, Obstinacy, Poverty, Want, Hunger, Fretfulness, Sick-ness, Old Age, Pallor, Darkness, Sleep, Death, and Charon, her last child;[16] so that the proverb *from a bad crow a bad egg* is exactly applicable to this case.

There are, however, some who maintain that Night also bore Aether and Day to her husband Erebus. But who in his senses would not howl and turn down the advocate of such a theory, as he would anyone who seriously propounded Democritus' notions or the fairy-tales of childhood? Is it indeed probable on the face of it that black and gloomy Night should be the mother of a child so comely, so sweet, so universally beloved and desired? Such a child, as soon as conceived, would have caused her mother's death by her birth before due time, would have driven her father Erebus into headlong flight, and forced old Charon to hide his dazzled eyes beneath the waters of the Styx and flee to seek what refuge he might in the realms below, as fast as his oars and sails could carry him. No, so far from being born in Hades, Day has never even shown her face there, nor can she find entrance even through a chink or cranny, except in defiance of Fate's decree. No, I would rather declare that Day is older than Night, and that when the world had but newly emerged from Chaos, Day shed her wide-spreading rays over it, before ever the turn of Night had come—unless indeed we are so perverse as to call by the name of Night that foul and murky darkness, or regard it as identical with Demogorgon.[17]

Therefore I hold that Day is the eldest daughter of Heaven, or rather of his son, begotten by him, it is said, to be the comfort of the race of men and the terror of the infernal gods, for fear lest Night should rule unopposed, lest Ghosts and Furies and all that loathsome brood of monsters, unchecked by any barrier between Earth and Hades, should leave the pit of Hell and make their way even to the upper world, and lest wretched Man, enveloped and surrounded by murky darkness, should suffer even in this life the tortures of the damned.

So far, Members of the University, I have endeavored to drag from their deep and dark hiding-places the obscure children of Night; you will immediately perceive how worthy they are of their parentage—especially if I should first devote the best of my small powers to the praise of Day, though Day herself must far transcend the eloquence of all who sing her praise.

In the first place, there is assuredly no need to de-

---

[12]The Latin word translated here is *fabulata.* Hughes translates it as "story."

[13]Possibly meaning "sensible," as Tillyard's note suggests (Yale 1: 225n), but night was also described as "the kindly time," which translates the Greek word.

[14]Semele was incinerated due to the jealousy of Juno, for being exposed to Jupiter in his full glory, as mentioned in the *Iliad* 14.323.

[15]Martial, *Epigrams* 8.35, altered to fit Milton's context.

---

[16]Cicero, *De Natura Deorum* 3.17, provides a catalogue of the unpleasant offspring of Night and Erebus.

[17]Convenient deity to assign as the father of all gods. Boccaccio's *Genealogy of the Gods* put Demogorgon, supposedly the father of Night, at the top of a genealogical chart from which issued such deities as Noctem and Tenebram, Night and Darkness.

scribe to you how welcome and how desirable Day is to every living thing. Even the birds cannot hide their delight, but leave their nests at peep of dawn and noise it abroad from the tree-tops in sweetest song, or darting upwards as near as they may to the sun, take their flight to welcome the returning day. First of all these the wakeful rooster acclaims the sun's coming, and like a herald bids mankind shake off the bonds of sleep, and rise and run with joy to greet the new-born day. The kids skip in the meadows, and beasts of every kind leap and gambol in delight. The sad heliotrope, who all night long has gazed toward the east, awaiting her beloved Sun, now smiles and beams at her lover's approach. The marigold too and rose, to add their share to the joy of all, open their petals and shed abroad their perfume, which they have kept for the Sun alone, and would not give to Night, shutting themselves up within their little leaves at fall of evening. And all the other flowers raise their heads, drooping and weighed down with dew, and offer themselves to the Sun, mutely begging him to kiss away the tear-drops which his absence brought. The Earth too decks herself in lovelier robes to honor the Sun's coming, and the clouds, arrayed in garb of every hue, attend the rising god in festive train and long procession. And last, though nothing may be lacking to proclaim his praise, the Persians and Libyans give him divine honors; the Rhodians too have dedicated to his glory that far-famed Colossus of astounding size, created by the miraculous art of Chares of Lindus;[18] to the Sun, too, we are told, the American Indians even to this day make sacrifice with incense and every kind of ritual.[19] You yourselves, members of the University, must bear witness how delightful, how welcome, how long-awaited is the light of morning, since it recalls you to the cultured Muses from whom cruel Night parted you still unsatisfied and athirst. Saturn, hurled down to Hades from highest heaven, bears witness how gladly he would return to the light of day from that dread gloom, would Jove but grant the favor. Lastly, it is manifest that Pluto himself far preferred light to his own kingdom of darkness, since he so often strove to gain all the realm of heaven. Thus Orpheus says with truth and with poetic skill in his hymn to Dawn—"Then of a truth do mortal men rejoice, nor is there one who flees thy

face which shines above, when thou dost shake sweet sleep from their eyes. Every man is glad, and every creeping thing, all the tribes of beast and bird, and all the many creatures of the deep."

Nor is this to be wondered at, when we reflect that Day serves for use as well as pleasure, and is alone fitted to further the business of life; for who would have the hardihood to sail the wide and boundless seas, without a hope that Day would dawn? He would cross the ocean even as the ghosts cross Lethe and Acheron, beset on every hand by fearsome darkness. Every man would then pass his life in his own mean hovel, hardly daring to creep outside, so that the dissolution of human society must needs follow. To no purpose would Apelles[20] have pictured Venus rising from the waves, in vain would Zeuxis have painted Helen, if dark, dense night hid from our eyes these wondrous sights. In vain too would earth bring forth in abundance vines twining in many a winding trail, in vain nobly towering trees; in vain would she deck herself anew with buds and blossoms, as with stars, striving to imitate the heaven above.[21] Then indeed the noblest of the senses, sight, would lose its use to every creature; yes, and the light of the world's eye being quenched, all things would fade and perish utterly; nor would the men who lived on the darkened earth long survive this tragedy, since nothing would be left to support their life, nor any means of delaying the lapse of all things into the primeval Chaos.

One might continue in this strain with unabating flow, but Day herself in modesty would not permit the full recital, but would hasten her downward course toward the sunset to check her advocate's extravagances. My day is now indeed already drawing to its close, and will soon give place to night, to prevent your saying in jest that this is the longest day though the season is midwinter. This alone I ask, that by your leave I may add a few words which I cannot well omit.

With good reason, then, have the poets declared that Night springs from Hell, since by no means whatever could so many grievous ills descend upon mankind from any other quarter. For when night falls all things grow foul and vile, no difference can then be seen between a Helen and a Canidia,[22] a precious jewel and a common stone (but that some gems have the power to outshine the darkness). Then too the loveliest spots strike horror

---

[18]The Colossus of Rhodes, a giant brass statue, erected about 300 BCE, that guarded the entrance to a harbor of the capital city on the Island of Rhodes; Chares was its sculptor.

[19]For their worship of the sun or any deity other than the Christian God, American Indians would be treated as "brutish savages, which by reason of their godless ignorance and blasphemous Idolatrie, are worse than those beasts which are of most wilde and savage nature" (Robert Gray, *A Good Speed to Virginia* [London, 1609], sig. B1ʳ, quoted in J. Martin Evans, *Milton's Imperial Epic* [Ithaca, NY: Cornell UP]: 19.

---

[20]Apelles and Zeuxis were the most famous of the painters at work during the reign of Alexander the Great. The theme of Venus rising from the sea was celebrated in the Renaissance by the famous painting of Botticelli, in the Uffizi in Florence.

[21]This argument is essentially the same as that of Comus 710–36: what is the abundance of nature for, if not to be used by human beings?

[22]A witch-like hag mentioned by Horace in the *Epodes* 3, 5, and 17.

to the heart, a horror gathering force from a silence deep and sad. All creatures lingering in the fields, be they man or beast, hasten to house or lair for refuge; then, hiding their heads beneath their coverings, they shut their eyes against the dread aspect of night. None may be seen abroad except thieves and rogues who fear the light, who, breathing murder and rapine, lie in wait to rob honest folks of their goods, and wander forth by night alone, lest day betray them. For Day lays bare all crimes, nor ever suffers wrongdoing to pollute her light. None will you meet save ghosts and specters, and fearsome goblins who follow in Night's train from the realms below; it is their boast that all night long they rule the earth and share it with mankind. To this end, I think, night sharpens our hearing, that our ears may catch the sooner and our hearts perceive with greater dread the groans of specters, the screeching of owls and nightbirds, and the roaring of lions that prowl in search of prey. Hence clearly is revealed that man's deceit who says that night brings respite from their fears to men and lulls every care to rest. How false and vain is this opinion they know well from their own bitter experience who have ever felt the pangs of guilty consciences; they are beset by Sphinxes and Harpies, Gorgons and Chimeras,[23] who hunt their victims down with flaming torches in their hands; those poor wretches too know it full well who have no friend to help or succor them, none to assuage their grief with words of comfort, but must pour out their useless plaints to senseless stones, longing and praying for the dawn of day. For this reason did that choicest poet Ovid rightly call Night the mighty foster-mother of cares.[24]

Some indeed say that it is above all by night that our bodies, broken and worn out by the labors of the day, are revived and restored. But this is the merciful ordinance of God, for which we owe no gratitude to Night. But even were it so, sleep is not a thing so precious that Night deserves the honor for the bestowal of it. For when we betake ourselves to sleep, we do in truth but confess ourselves poor and feeble creatures, whose puny frames cannot endure even a little while without repose. And, to be sure, what is sleep but the image and semblance of death? Hence in Homer Sleep and Death are twins, conceived together and born at a single birth.[25]

Lastly, it is thanks to the sun that the moon and the other stars display their fires by night, for they have no light to radiate but such as they borrow from the sun.

Who then but a son of darkness, a robber, a gamester, or one whose wont is to spend his nights in the company of harlots and snore away his days—who, I ask, but such a fellow would have undertaken to defend a cause so odious and discreditable? I wonder that he dare so much as look upon this sun, or share with other men, without a qualm, that light that he is slandering so ungratefully. He deserves to share the fate of Python, slain by the stroke of the sun's hostile rays.[26] He deserves to pass a loathsome life imprisoned in Cimmerian darkness.[27] He deserves, above all, to see sleep overcoming his hearers even as he speaks, so that his best eloquence affects them no more than an idle dream, till, drowsy himself, he is cheated into taking his hearers' nods and snores for nods of approval and murmurs of praise as he ends his speech.

But I see the black brows of Night, and note the advance of darkness; I must withdraw, lest Night overtake me unawares.

I beg you then, my hearers, since Night is but the passing and the death of Day, not to give Death preference over Life, but graciously to honor my cause with your votes; so may the Muses prosper your studies, and Dawn, the friend of the Muses, hear your prayers; and may the Sun, who sees and hears all things, hearken to all in this assembly who honor and support his cause. I have done.

II.
DELIVERED IN THE PUBLIC SCHOOLS
On the Harmony of the Spheres

If there is any room for an insignificant person like myself, Members of the University, after you have heard so many eminent speakers, I too will attempt, to the best of my small powers, to show my appreciation of this day's appointed celebrations, and to follow, though at a distance, the festal train of eloquence today. And so, though I should in any case shun and avoid the usual trite and hackneyed topics, I am fired and aroused to do my utmost to find some novel theme by the thought of this day's importance and of our speakers who, as I rightly expected, have already paid such worthy tribute to it. These two considerations might well suffice to stimulate and spur on even a dull and sluggish brain. So I conceived the idea of making a few prelimi-

---

[23]Assorted monsters of the classical world, assumed here to be proper inhabitants of the Christian Hell. Compare the "*Gorgons, and Hydra's, and Chimera's dire*" of *Paradise Lost* 2.628.
[24]*Metamorphoses* 8.81.
[25]Hughes cites the *Iliad* 14.231, 672, and 682.

[26]Usually the death of the Python is supposed to have been by the arrows of Apollo (Ovid, *Metamorphoses* 1.438).
[27]Proverbially, Cimmeria was a place where humans lived in caves and hence the darkest place imaginable, as in "L'Allegro" 10: "In dark *Cimmerian* desert ever dwell."

nary remarks with open hand,[28] as we say, and rhetorical exuberance, on the subject of that heavenly harmony which is presently to be discussed as it were with closed fist—but with an eye to the time at my disposal, which is now strictly limited.

Now I beg you, my hearers, not to take this theory as seriously intended. For who in his senses would suppose that Pythagoras,[29] a very god among philosophers, whose name all men of that time hailed with the most profound reverence—who, I ask, would suppose that he ever put forward a theory based on such very poor foundations? Surely, if he held any doctrine of the harmony of the spheres, or taught that the heavens revolve in unison with some sweet melody, it was only as a means of suggesting allegorically the close interrelation of the orbs and their uniform revolution in accordance with the laws of destiny for ever. In this he followed the example of the poets, or (what is almost the same thing) of the divine oracles, who never display before the eyes of the vulgar any holy or secret mystery unless it be in some way cloaked or veiled.[30]

Pythagoras was followed by Plato, that best interpreter of Mother Nature; he tells us that upon each one of the celestial orbs is seated a being called a Siren, at whose mellifluous song both gods and men are rapt in wonder.

Homer moreover used the remarkable and apt metaphor of the golden chain suspended by Jove from heaven to represent this universal concord and sweet union of all things which Pythagoras poetically figures as harmony.[31]

Then Aristotle, the rival and constant detractor of Pythagoras and Plato, wishing to construct a road to fame on the ruin of these great masters' theories, foisted on Pythagoras a literal doctrine of the unheard symphony of heaven and the melody of the spheres. But if only fate or chance had allowed your soul, O Father Pythagoras, to transmigrate into my body, you would not have lacked a champion to deliver you without difficulty, under however heavy a burden of obloquy you might be laboring!

After all, we may well ask, why should not the heavenly bodies give forth musical tones in their annual revolutions? Does it not seem reasonable to you, Aristotle? Why, I can hardly believe that those Intelligences[32] of yours could have endured through so many centuries the sedentary toil of making the heavens rotate, if the ineffable music of the stars had not prevented them from leaving their posts, and the melody, by its enchantment, persuaded them to stay. If you rob the heavens of this music, you devote those wonderful minds and subordinate gods of yours to a life of drudgery, and condemn them to the treadmill. And even Atlas[33] himself would have long since cast down the burden of the skies from his shoulders to its ruin, had not that sweet harmony soothed him with an ecstasy of delight as he panted and sweated beneath his heavy load. Again, the Dolphin would long since have wearied of the stars and preferred his proper element of the sea to the skies, had he not well known that the singing spheres of heaven far surpassed Arion's lyre[34] in sweetness. And we may well believe that it is in order to tune their own notes in accord with that harmony of heaven to which they listen so intently, that the lark takes her flight up to the clouds at daybreak and the nightingale passes lonely hours in song.

Hence arose the story, which has prevailed since the earliest times, of how the Muses dance before Jove's altar day and night;[35] hence too the attribution to Phoebus, in the remote past, of musical skill. Hence the belief held by revered antiquity that Harmonia was the daughter of Jove and Electra, and that at her marriage to Cadmus all the choirs of heaven sang in concert.

What if no one on earth has ever heard this symphony of the stars? It does not therefore follow that everything beyond the sphere of the moon is mute and utterly benumbed in silence. The fault is in our own deaf ears, which are either unable or unworthy to hear these sweet strains.[36]

[28]Rhetoric was supposed to deal with an open hand, and logic with a closed fist.

[29]Greek mystical philosopher from the sixth century BCE, whose cryptic teachings included a belief in reincarnation and transmigration of souls, and in a notion of the mathematical precision of celestial harmony and music-making. Pythagoreans came to believe that the Earth is a sphere and that Earth and planets revolve around a central fire.

[30]Poets like Chaucer and Spenser, for Milton, sing songs "Where more is meant than meets the ear" ("Il Penseroso" 120).

[31]In the *Iliad* 8.18–29, Homer recounts the tug of war suggested by Zeus to the rest of the Olympian gods, using a golden chain, a contest which he would of course win. The chain was adopted by various philosophers as evidence of a great chain of being and of hierarchy within that chain.

[32]Planetary "intelligences," or something like angels controlling the motion of heavenly bodies, was supposed to have been derived from the teachings of Aristotle, whom Milton is roasting at this point. In *Paradise Lost* 8.180–81, Milton has Adam address Raphael as "pure / Intelligence of Heav'n, Angel serene!" For Aristotle's refutation of the Pythagorean harmony of the spheres, see his *De Caelo*, 2.9.

[33]The Titan Atlas, supposedly tricked by Hercules into assuming the burden of holding up the heavens.

[34]For taking the poet Arion on his back after listening to his harp, a dolphin was translated to the skies to become a constellation near Capricorn.

[35]The image of the Muses dancing and singing in front of the altar of Jove is from the opening of Hesiod, *Theogony*.

[36]The Lady in *Comus* is evidently capable of hearing the Music of the Spheres, and addressing Echo, who is "Sweet Queen of Parly, Daughter of the Sphere," who gives "resounding grace to all Heav'ns harmonies" (241–43); the subject comes up again in "Arcades" 72–73.

But this melody of the heavens is not all unheard. For who, O Aristotle, could believe that those "goats"[37] you tell of keep skipping in the midmost tracts of air for any other reason than that when they plainly hear the orchestra of heaven, being so near at hand, they cannot choose but dance?

Again, Pythagoras alone among men is said to have heard this music—if indeed he was not rather some good spirit and denizen of heaven, sent down perchance by the gods' behest to instruct mankind in holiness and lead them back to righteousness; at the least, he was assuredly a man endowed with a full meed of virtue, worthy to hold converse with the gods themselves, whose like he was, and to partake of the fellowship of heaven. Therefore I wonder not that the gods, who loved him well, permitted him to share the most secret mysteries of nature.

The fact that we are unable to hear this harmony seems certainly to be due to the presumption of that thief Prometheus,[38] which brought so many evils upon men, and robbed us of that happiness which we may never again enjoy so long as we remain buried in sin and degraded by brutish desires; for how can we become sensitive to this heavenly sound while our souls are, as Persius says,[39] bowed to the ground and lacking in every heavenly element? But if our souls were pure, chaste, and white as snow, as was Pythagoras' of old, then indeed our ears would ring and be filled with that exquisite music of the stars in their orbits; then would all things turn back to the Age of Gold,[40] and we ourselves, free from every grief, would pass our lives in a blessed peace which even the gods might envy.

At this point time cuts me short in mid career, and luckily too, for I am afraid that by my confused and unmelodious style I have been all the while offending against that very harmony of which I speak, and have myself been an obstacle to your hearing it. And so I have done.

---

[37]Meteorological phenomena resembling torches, which apparently skipped through the sky like young goats (Aristotle, *Meteorologica* 1.4.341).

[38]Milton is probably treating Prometheus, whose theft of fire from the gods was generally thought to have a civilizing effect on humankind, with tongue-in-cheek humor. It is Pandora, given to Prometheus by Jupiter and later married to his "unwiser" brother Epimetheus (*Paradise Lost* 4.716–17), who brings evil into the world through opening a box containing all the evils that will afflict the human race. Later in this Prolusion, Milton will allude to the further punishment of Prometheus, banished to a peak in the Caucasus mountains, with an eagle consuming his liver, which was restored each night.

[39]*Satires* 2.61, "O Souls bowed down to earth, and void of all heavenly thoughts" (*Juvenal and Persius*, trans. G. G. Ramsay [New York: Loeb Classical Library, 1930]: 340).

[40]Compare "Time will run back, and fetch the age of gold" (Nativity Ode 135).

III.
DELIVERED IN THE PUBLIC SCHOOLS
An Attack on the Scholastic Philosophy

I have been deeply occupied of late, gentlemen, in seeking, and indeed one of my chief anxieties has been to find, what device of rhetoric would best enable me to engage my hearer's attention: when of a sudden there came into my mind the precept often inculcated in his writings by Cicero (with whose name my speech auspiciously begins)—namely that the fundamental duties of an orator are first to instruct, secondly to delight, and thirdly to persuade. And so I have made it my chief objective to fulfil as nearly as possible this threefold function of a speaker.

Now for instruction, it ill befits me to take upon myself to give it to men so erudite in every branch of learning as yourselves, or you to receive it; still, it may be permissible for me to take the nearest course and bring to your notice a matter which may prove to be not altogether without interest. Secondly for delight, though I greatly fear it is beyond my poor abilities, yet it shall be my chief wish to afford this also: but even if I attain this, it will not be enough unless I succeed also in persuading you. Thirdly, for persuasion, I shall attain the height of my ambition for the present if I can induce you who hear me to turn less assiduously the pages of those vast and ponderous tomes of our professors of so-called exactitude, and to be less zealous in your study of the crabbed arguments of wiseacres.

Now to make it plain to all how proper and reasonable is my theme, I will show briefly, in the short half hour at my disposal, that these studies promote neither delight nor instruction, nor do they indeed serve any useful purpose whatsoever.

First I will issue a challenge, gentlemen. If I can at all judge your feelings by my own, what pleasure can there possibly be in these petty disputations of sour old men, which reek, if not of the cave of Trophonius,[41] at any rate of the monkish cells in which they were written, exude the gloomy severity of their writers, bear the traces of their authors' wrinkles, and in spite of their condensed style produce by their excessive tediousness only boredom and distaste; and if ever they are read at length, provoke an altogether natural aversion and an utter disgust in their readers. Many a time, when the duty of tracing out these petty subtleties for a while has been laid upon me, when my mind has been dulled and my sight blurred by continued reading—many a time, I

---

[41]The cave of Trophonius, a Greek oracle whose sour predictions always left those who visited it in a melancholy state.

say, I have paused to take a breath, and have sought some slight relief from my boredom in looking to see how much yet remained of my task. When, as always happened, I found that more remained to be done than I had as yet got through, how often I have wished that instead of having these fooleries forced upon me, I had been set to clean out the stable of Augeas again, and I have envied Hercules his luck in having been spared such labors as these by a kindly Juno.[42]

And then this dull feeble subject-matter, which as it were crawls along on the ground, is never raised or elevated by the ornaments of style, but the style itself is dry and lifeless, so exactly suited to the barrenness of the subject that it might well have been composed in the reign of the gloomy king Saturn, but that the innocent simplicity of those days would have known nothing of the delusions and digressions with which these books abound in every part. Believe me, my learned friends, when I go through these empty quibbles as I often must, against my will, it seems to me as if I were forcing my way through rough and rocky wastes, desolate wildernesses, and precipitous mountain gorges. And so it is not likely that the dainty and elegant Muses preside over these ragged and tattered studies, or consent to be the patrons of their maudlin partisans; and I cannot believe that there was ever a place for them on Parnassus unless it were at some waste corner at the very foot of the mountain, some spot with nothing to recommend it, tangled and matted with thorns and brambles, overgrown with thistles and nettles,[43] remote from the dances and company of the goddesses, where no laurels grow nor flowers bloom, and to which the sound of Apollo's lyre can never penetrate.

Now surely divine poetry, by that power with which it is by heavenly grace indued, raises aloft the soul smothered by the dust of earth and sets it among the mansions of heaven, and breathing over it the scent of nectar and bedewing it with ambrosia instils into it heavenly felicity and whispers to it everlasting joy. Rhetoric, again, so captivates the minds of men and draws them after it so gently enchained that it has the power now of moving them to pity, now of inciting them to hatred, now of arousing them to warlike valor, now of inspiring them beyond the fear of death. History, skillfully narrated, now calms and soothes the restless and troubled mind, now fills it with delight, and now brings

tears to the eyes; soft and gentle tears, tears which bring with them a kind of mournful joy. But these useless and barren controversies and bickerings lack all power to affect the emotions in any way whatever; they merely dull and stupefy the intellect. Further, they bring delight to none but those of a rude and boorish disposition, inclined by some innate tendency to quarrels and dissension, prating fellows moreover, and such as detest and ever turn away from sound and wholesome wisdom. Let us then banish such an one with all his quibbles to the Caucasus or wheresoever blind Barbarity holds sway; there let him set up his workshop of tricks and fallacies, and vex and torment himself to his heart's content about questions of no importance, until excessive fretting, like Prometheus' eagle, eats out his heart and consumes him altogether.

These studies are as fruitless as they are joyless, and can add nothing whatever to true knowledge. If we set before our eyes those hordes of old men in monkish garb, the chief authors of these quibbles, how many among them have ever contributed anything to the enrichment of literature? Beyond a doubt, by their harsh and uncouth treatment they have nearly rendered hideous that philosophy which was once cultured and well-ordered and urbane, and like evil genii they have implanted thorns and briars in men's hearts and introduced discord into the schools, which has notably retarded the happy progress of our scholars. For these quick-change would-be philosophers of ours argue back and forth, one bolstering up his thesis on every side, another laboring hard to cause its downfall, while what one would think firmly established by irrefragable arguments is forthwith shattered by an opponent with the greatest ease. Between them all the student hesitates, as at a cross-roads, in doubt whither to turn or what direction to choose, and unable to make any decision, while such a host of weapons is hurled against him from every side that they hide the light and shed deep darkness over the whole question; so that in the end the reader is reduced to imitating the weary toils of Ceres and seeking for Truth through all the world by the light of a torch without ever finding it:[44] at last he reaches such a pitch of madness as to believe himself utterly blind when in fact there is nothing for him to see.

Besides all this, it not infrequently happens that those who have entirely devoted and dedicated themselves to this blight of disputation lamentably betray their ignorance and absurd childishness when faced with a new

[42]Cleaning out the stables of Augeas (diverting the river Alpheus in the process) is proverbially one of the most difficult of the twelve legendary labors of Hercules (Apollodorus, *The Library* 2.5.1–12).

[43]Compare the almost identical image in English of "that asinine feast of sowthistles and brambles" usually set before the English student as Milton pictures him in *Of Education* (Yale 2: 377).

[44]Ceres, goddess of grain and the harvest, is usually pictured in search of her daughter Proserpina (rather than Truth), who was seized by Pluto and carried off to his kingdom under the Earth (for one account, see Ovid, *Metamorphoses*, 5.534-51).

situation outside their usual idiotic occupation. Finally, the supreme result of all this earnest labor is to make you a more finished fool and cleverer contriver of conceits, and to endow you with a more expert ignorance: and no wonder, since all these problems at which you have been working in such torment and anxiety have no existence in reality at all, but like unreal ghosts and phantoms without substance obsess minds already disordered and empty of true wisdom.

For the rest, even if I were silent, it is amply clear to you how little these trivialities contribute to morality or purity of life, which is the most important consideration of all. From this obviously follows my final point, namely that this unseemly battle of words tends neither to the general good nor to the honor and profit of our country, which is generally considered the supreme purpose of all sciences.

Now there are, as I have remarked, two things which most enrich and adorn our country: eloquent speech and noble action. But this contentious duel of words has no power either to teach eloquence or to inculcate wisdom or to incite to noble acts. Then away with these ingenious praters, with all their forms and phrases, who ought to be condemned after death to twist the rope in Hades in company with the Ocnus of legend.[45]

But how much better were it, gentlemen, and how much more consonant with your dignity, now to let your eyes wander as it were over all the lands depicted on the map, and to behold places trodden by the heroes of old, to range over the regions made famous by wars, by triumphs, and even by the tales of poets of renown, now to traverse the stormy Adriatic, now to climb unharmed the slopes of fiery Etna, then to spy out the customs of mankind and those states which are well ordered; next to seek out and explore the nature of all living creatures, and after that to turn your attention to the secret virtues of stones and herbs. And do not shrink from taking your flight into the skies and gazing upon the manifold shapes of the clouds, the mighty piles of snow, and the source of the dews of the morning; then inspect the coffers wherein the hail is stored and examine the arsenals of the thunderbolts. And do not let the intent of Jupiter or of Nature elude you, when a huge and fearful comet threatens to set the heavens aflame, nor let the smallest star escape you of all the myriads which are scattered and strewn between the poles: yes, even follow close upon the sun in all his journeys, and ask account of time itself and

demand the reckoning of its eternal passage.[46]

But let not your mind rest content to be bounded and cabined by the limits which encompass the earth, but let it wander beyond the confines of the world, and at the last attain the summit of all human wisdom and learn to know itself, and therewith those holy minds and intelligences whose company it must hereafter join.

What need I say more? In all these studies take as your instructor him who is already your delight—Aristotle, who has recorded all these things with learning and diligence for our instruction. I see that the mention of his name at once arouses you,[47] Members of the University, and that you are gradually being won over to my side, and following apace, as it were, at his invitation. If this be so, it is to him that you must render praise and thanks for any profit my words have brought; so far as concerns myself, I shall be well satisfied if you of your goodness grant me pardon for the length of my address. I have done.

IV.
DELIVERED IN COLLEGE
A THESIS
In the Destruction of any Substance there can be no Resolution into First Matter[48]

This is not the place to enquire too nicely whether Error escaped from Pandora's box, or from the depths of the Styx, or lastly whether he is to be accounted one of the sons of Earth who conspired against the gods. This much, however, is clear to the least observant, that by imperceptible degrees, like Typhon[49] of old or Neptune's son Ephialtes, he has grown to such a portentous size that I believe Truth itself to be menaced by him. For I see that he often fights on equal terms against the goddess Truth, I see that after sustaining losses he is

---

[45]The labor of Ocnus in weaving a cord that is immediately consumed by a donkey (Ocnus's wife also consumed all he earned) was proverbial for any wasted hard work (Propertius 4.3.21).

[46]The last paragraph is a manifesto listing subjects that Milton believed should be taught in school—practical, experimental, and scientific subjects, as compared with theoretical and useless scholastic knowledge. His own curriculum as laid out for his pupils or in *Of Education* answers that of the universities as they existed when he attended Cambridge.

[47]Any attack on Aristotle would have been an attack on the academic curriculum of Cambridge. Milton knows what he is doing in annoying his audience.

[48]It may be that Milton's original audience understood the philosophical subtleties of this oration, but neither David Masson nor E. M. W. Tillyard felt qualified to judge the frame of reference for the oration (Yale 1: 248). Of course, the oration may have been intended to illustrate the evils of scholasticism Milton had delineated in Prolusion 3.

[49]Typhon, Ephialtes, and Antaeus were all classical monsters or giants that a Christian of Milton's time might have been constrained to see as Error, a figure foreshadowing the various manifestations of Satan. Leviathan would be another obvious candidate for the group.

richer, after being wounded he is sound and whole, after being vanquished he is triumphant over his vanquishers, like the Libyan Antaeus in the ancient tale. So far has this gone, that one might with good reason doubt the correctness of Ovid's well-known poem, and question whether Astraea was really the last of the immortals to quit the earth;[50] for I fear that many centuries later Peace and Truth too came to loathe mankind and abandoned it. For assuredly no one could be persuaded into believing that if Truth were still a visitor to the earth, one-eyed and near-sighted Error could look upon her, the co-equal of the sun, without being altogether blinded and cast back once more into that lower world from which he originally came forth. But there can in fact be no doubt that Truth has fled away to her home in heaven, never to return to hapless man; and now foul Error reigns supreme in all the schools, and has seized the power, as it were, with the help of a strong and active body of supporters. With this added strength, and swollen past endurance, he has assailed every particle and fragment of natural philosophy and outraged it with impious claws, even as, we are told, the Harpies defiled the table of Phineus, King of Arcady.[51]

The thing has come to such a pass that the richest dainties of philosophy, sumptuous as the feasts which the gods enjoy, now only disgust those who partake of them. For it often happens that a student who turns the pages of the philosophers' books and is busied about them day and night departs more puzzled than he came. For whatever one writer has affirmed and believes that he has established by a sufficient argument, another confutes, or at least seems to confute, with the greatest ease, and both are able almost indefinitely the one to find objections, the other replies. The wretched reader meanwhile, continually rent and torn in pieces as if between two wild beasts, and half dead with boredom, is at last left as at a cross-roads, without any idea which way to turn. But, to be quite candid, it may not be worthwhile to spend the trouble which is demanded in finding out on which side the truth really lies; for in fact it is very often about questions of the most trifling importance that the most heated disputes of philosophy occur.

But I seem to catch a whisper of "What is he driving at now? He attacks Error, while he himself wanders erratically all over the world." I confess that I have indeed erred and strayed, which I should not have done had I not hoped much from your kindness.

Well, I must now gird myself up to the task before me; and may the goddess Lua (as Lipsius says)[52] grant me a happy deliverance from all my difficulties.

The problem which is set us to thrash out today is whether in the destruction of any substance there can be a resolution into first matter. This is usually expressed in other words, "whether any accidents which were in the corrupted substance remain also in that generated from it"—that is to say, whether when the form perishes all accidents which had previously existed in the composite perish also.

There is a wide divergence of opinion about this on the part of philosophers of great repute. Some vehemently assert that such a resolution does take place, others fight tooth and nail against its possibility. I am inclined to agree with these last, and am led to differ fundamentally from the former first by reason, as I believe, and secondly by the authority of so many eminent men. It remains for me shortly to attempt to supply a proof. I shall do so as briefly as possible, and first of all as follows.

If there is resolution into primary matter, it follows that we are wrong in asserting the essential proposition with regard to primary matter, namely that it is never found pure. Our opponents will hasten to reply: This is said in respect of form. Well, let us grant these sciolists that substantial forms are never found apart from accidental ones.

But this is a minor point, and does not go to the root of the question; we must use stronger arguments.

First then let us see whether we have any of the ancient philosophers on our side. Even as we ask, here comes Aristotle of his own accord to meet us, and ranges himself on our side, together with a chosen band of his commentators. And pray note, my hearers, that it was at Aristotle's own instance and instigation that this battle was begun, and that, I hope, under good auspices. He does in fact himself seem to hint exactly at our view, in *Metaph. 7, Text 8*, where he says that quantity is first of all inherent in matter. If anyone refuses to accept this dictum, I shall not hesitate to indict him for

---

[50]Ovid's description of the Iron Age and the departure of Astraea (Justice) is made parallel to the loss of innocence in the Christian universe. Sandys summarizes "The Brazen Age [leading to the Iron Age] succeeded the Silver: for man grew not instantly superlative wicked, but degenerated by degrees, till imboldned by custome, through his insolencie and out-rage, he affrighted *Astraea* or Justice from the earth" (Sandys 60). Sandys reinforces the comparison by referring to the prophet Enoch's translation to Heaven as evidence of the corruption of humankind.

[51]See Vergil, *Aeneid* 3.226–30, for the typical picture of the Harpies befouling food. The Harpies appear often as symbols of ravenousness or spoliation in the Latin and English poetry and prose of Milton.

[52]An ancient Roman goddess. Justus Lipsius (1547–1606) was a Belgian humanist reformer and scholar. Hughes discovered Lipsius's description of Lua presiding over religious rites connected with the census, in his *De censura et censu* (*Opera Omnia* [Vesaliae, 1625]: 1483. McEuen's note in the Yale edition is misleading.

heresy, in accordance with the laws of all the sages. Moreover, he elsewhere plainly regards quantity as a property of primary matter, which most of his followers also assert; but who would tolerate the forcible separation of a property from its subject, even on the pronouncement of a judge appointed by themselves? But now, let us come to close grips with the question, and weigh carefully what reason suggests.

The assertion, then, is proved first by the argument that matter has an actual proper entity in consequence of its own proper existence, and is therefore capable of having quantity, at any rate the quantity called indeterminate. There is also the argument sometimes confidently put forward that form is only received into matter through the medium of quantity.

Secondly, if an accident is destroyed, it can only be destroyed in one of the following ways—either by the introduction of a contrary, or by cessation of its term, or by the absence of some other conserving cause, or lastly, by the defect of the proper subject in which it inheres. Quantity cannot be destroyed in the first way, since it has no contrary; and although quality has, this must not be substituted here: the second way does not apply, since it is proper to relatives; nor by the absence of a conserving cause, for that which my opponents assign is form. Now accidents are conceived to depend upon form in two ways—in the genus of formal cause, or in that of efficient cause; the first kind of dependence is not immediate, for the substantial form does not inform accidents, nor is it conceivable that a cause can have any other function in regard to them in this genus. Therefore it is only mediate, that is to say in so far as matter is dependent upon form, and form in turn on matter. The second kind of dependence is in the genus of efficient cause; but whether accidents are dependent on form or not in this genus is doubtful. But even if we grant that it is so, it still does not follow that when the form perishes the accidents also perish with it, because when that cause fails another similar one succeeds it immediately, which is completely sufficient to maintain precisely the same effect, and that without interruption. Finally, that quantity and other similar accidents are not annihilated by the defect of the proper subject is proved thus—the subject of quantity is either a composite form or matter; now it is clear that it is not a composite, because an accident which is in a composite attains by its union both matter and form by means of one thing; but quantity cannot by any means attain a rational soul, for this is spiritual and entirely incapable of the formal effect of quantity, that is to say, of quantitative extension. Further, it is sufficiently clear from what has been said that form is not the subject of quantity. It follows therefore that only matter can be the subject of quantity, and

so all inference of destruction is excluded in regard to quantity.

As regards the example of a scar commonly adduced, I consider it to be a very cogent argument; for no one could so force my credulity as to make me believe that it is quite other in the corpse than what it was just before in the living body, since there is neither reason nor necessity to correct our sense, which is indeed rarely deluded concerning its proper object. I would far rather listen to marvelous stories of ghosts and hobgoblins than to the foolish and futile pratings of these crazy would-be philosophers about the re-creation *de novo* of these accidents of theirs. Now we know for certain that heat and those other qualities of an animal which are capable of increase and decrease are precisely the same at the moment of death, and also after death; why then should these be destroyed when others like them are to be produced? Besides, if they were to be produced newly they would not last so short a time, for they would not reach their utmost intensity suddenly, but only gradually and little by little. Remember too that it is a very ancient axiom that quantity follows matter and quality form.

I might, indeed I ought, to have dwelt longer on this question. I cannot tell whether I have bored you, but I have certainly bored myself to extinction. It remains for me to deal with my opponents' arguments. May the Muses grant that I reduce them to primary matter, if that be possible, or rather to nothing at all.

As to their first point, Aristotle's testimony in saying that no sensitive subject remains in generation, we reply that this should be understood as applying to the complete and integral subject, that is to say, to the substantial composite, as the ancient and learned author Philoponus[53] bears witness. Secondly, regarding Aristotle's statement that matter is neither what, nor how much, nor of what kind; by this it is not meant that matter has no quantity or quality, but that it does not include either quantity or quality of itself or in its own essence. Thirdly, Aristotle says that when primary substances are destroyed all accidents are destroyed. We do not deny that this will happen, provided you grant that another may immediately succeed that which was destroyed.

Finally, he says that form is received into bare matter; that is, bare of the substantial form.

Now the fight grows fierce, and victory hangs in the balance, for they renew the battle and attack us as follows: Since matter is pure potentiality, it has no being except that which it gains through the form it has borrowed;

---

[53]Seventh-century commentator on the works of Aristotle.

hence it also has no power of itself to support accidents, unless at the least it is conjoined by nature to form, to which it is indebted for its being. This error they usually amend thus—that primary matter has its own proper being, which may indeed be incomplete in the genus of substance, but as compared with accident may not unreasonably be called absolute being. They object moreover that matter has regard to substantial form as its first act, but no accidents as its second act. I reply that matter has regard to form, first in the order of intention, but not of generation or execution. Our argument now begins to bubble and boil, and our opponents press harder upon us, as in mortal combat, thus: Every property flows actively from the essence of that of which it is property; but quantity cannot do so, for this flow is a form of activity, but matter itself has no activity, being merely passive; therefore, etc., etc. I reply that the natural combination of matter with quantity can be understood in two ways, first by reason of the passive potentiality alone within its own nature, which demands such an affection: for there is no necessity that every innate property should be attributed to a subject by reason of its own active principle; since sometimes the passive suffices, in the way in which many consider that motion is natural to the heavens. Secondly, it can also be understood as being due to its intrinsic active flowing forth, since it contains in itself true and actual being.

But my opponents have not even yet lost all hope of victory; for they are making a second attack, inferring from this that form is combined with matter through the medium of quantity as a disposition or necessary condition, but not at all as a potentiality immediately receptive of form.

Finally, they argue thus: if quantity is inherent in matter alone, it follows that it is ingenerable and incorruptible; which seems to be contradictory, since movement in itself is toward quantity. However, we grant the inference, since in fact quantity is incorruptible as regards its own entity, but as regards its various terms it can begin and cease to be, by the conjunction and division of quantity; nor is motion in itself related to production of quantity, but to its accretion; and it does not exist by virtue of one quantity being subjoined to another, and by the quantity which was alien becoming proper to itself.

I might bring forth arguments on both sides but will refrain, to spare you boredom. At this point, then, it is best for me to beat a retreat.

V.
DELIVERED IN THE PUBLIC SCHOOLS
There are no partial Forms in an Animal in addition to the Whole[54]

The Romans, masters of the world in ancient times, attained the highest summit of power, which neither the vastness of Assyria nor the martial prowess of Macedon could reach, and to which the majesty of kings in time to come will never be able to exalt itself. This position they attained, either because Jupiter, feeling the burden of his age and finding it enough for himself to rule over the heavens alone, wished to retire into private life, and therefore entrusted the reins of government over mankind to the Roman people, as being in some sort gods on earth; or because, when he cast his father Saturn down into Italy, he granted him this favor to console him for the loss of heaven, namely that his descendants the Romans should have dominion over the whole extent of land and ocean.

However this may be, he certainly did not allow them to enjoy this privilege without earning it, but only granted it to them after constant wars and prolonged toil; his intention being, I suppose, to prove whether the Romans were the only nation worthy to be the vicegerents of supreme Jove on earth. And so they were compelled to live a life of abstinence and hardship, and to find the new pleasures of peace always cut short by war's alarms and the clash of arms around them. In addition to this, they were under the necessity of providing garrisons, which they had frequently to renew, for the various cities and provinces they had conquered, and of sending nearly all their young men either to distant wars or to their colonies. Moreover, the victories they gained were not always bloodless; on the contrary, they often suffered grievous disasters. So for example Brennus,[55] the leader of the Gauls, almost succeeded in destroying the glory of Rome in its early bloom, and the noble city of Carthage came within a little of wresting from Rome the governance of the world with which she had been divinely entrusted. Lastly, the Goths and Vandals under their king Alaric, and the Huns and Pannonians under their leaders Attila and Bleda passed in a torrent over the whole of Italy, cruelly plundered the abounding riches of the empire, the accumulated spoils of so many wars, overwhelmed in shameful flight the Romans, who were but now the lords of mankind, and captured the city, captured Rome herself, by the mere terror of their name. No deed in fact or fable could be

[54]For a useful summary of what Prolusions 4 and 5 say as a unit, see McEuen's notes in Yale 1: 255–57.
[55]Milton comments on Brennus in the *History of Britain* (Yale 5: 28).

more remarkable than this. It is as if victory herself had either fallen in love with them or been panic-stricken by their prowess in arms, so as to be completely at their command.

You have been wondering long enough, my hearers, what can be my reason for enlarging on all this; I will tell you. Whenever I consider and reflect upon these events, I am reminded afresh of the mighty struggle which has been waged to save Truth, and of the universal eagerness and watchfulness with which men are striving to rescue Truth, already tottering and almost overthrown, from the outrages of her foes. Yet we are powerless to check the inroads which the vile horde of errors daily makes upon every branch of learning. Error has indeed, by force or fraud,[56] gained such ascendancy as to be able to impose its own likeness on the snowwhite form of Truth, or by I know not what artifice to assume her heavenly similitude. By this device, it seems, it has often deceived even great philosophers, and has laid claim to the honors and reverence which are due to Truth alone. This you will have an opportunity of seeing in the question at issue today, in which we find champions of no mean ability engaged, men who might win fair fame, if they would but abandon their present allegiance and serve under the banner of Truth.

So it is now my task to lay Error bare and so strip it of its borrowed plumes, thus reducing it to its native hideousness. To accomplish this the more readily, I think it best to follow in the footsteps of the weightiest authorities; for it is not to be expected that I should add anything of my own—anything, that is, which has escaped the notice and attention of so many men eminent for their learning. Therefore I will set forth briefly so much as is needed to elucidate the subject, and will add one or two arguments to fortify my position like a rampart. Then if there is any opposition or objection to my opinion, I will resolve it as best I may; but I will touch on it as with the tips of my wings.

We read that various opinions have been advanced in opposition to the idea of the idea of the unity of form which the more discerning philosophers have always held to exist in one and the same matter. For some hotly assert that in an animal there may be several total forms, and this they maintain each according to his capacity; others roundly declare that though only one total form can be readily received by one and the same matter, yet several partial forms may be. For the moment I will make a truce with the former party, according to the usage of war, while I concentrate the whole strength and force of my attack upon the latter.

In the forefront let me set Aristotle, who is entirely on our side, and who, towards the end of the first book of the *De Anima*, unequivocally lends his support to our assertion.

No long investigation is needed to find a few more arguments to add to this authority. Chrysostom Javello is the first to come to my help; from the dung-heap of his rude and unpolished style we may dig out gold and pearls; if anyone is so refined as to despise these, Aesop's fable of the rooster will fit him very neatly. His argument runs much as follows: The distinction and organization of dissimilar parts must precede the introduction of the soul, since this is the act not of any body at random, but of a physically organic body; therefore these partial forms must be corrupted immediately before the production of the total form, unless we are to disregard entirely the universally accepted axiom that "the generation of one thing is the corruption of another." The production of these partial forms is not followed by the instantaneous production of others similar to them; for this would be purposeless and at variance with the wisdom of Mother Nature. Secondly, since every form, whether perfect or imperfect, contributes its specific being, it necessarily follows that, as long as that form remains, that object also remains the same, not varied according to its substance; therefore the total form will supervene like an accident, that is to say not by generation but by alteration. It follows moreover that the soul of the whole, whether divisible or indivisible, is not sufficient to inform every part of the living creature fully and perfectly; this no reason can persuade us to grant. It also follows that one substantial form is as it were a proximate and permanent disposition toward another, which is contrary to truth, since every form constitutes an essence complete in the genus of substance. Finally, if there is a plurality of partial forms in every part, of a man for example, from them there will certainly arise one complete form distinct from the rational soul; hence this form will be the form either of an inanimate thing or corporeity, or of a mixture (which in fact is most unlikely to exist in man in addition to the soul) or else it will be a sensitive or vegetative soul. This latter assertion would be absolutely rejected by the more learned among the philosophers. I will refrain from further proof of this, since it is generally admitted and moreover does not go to the root of the matter.

Again, our opponents bring forward the objection (and this is the crux of the discussion) that when a part of an animal has been cut off it remains in act after the separation, not through the proper form of the whole, since it is outside the whole, nor through the form re-

---

[56]The phrasing allies Error with Satan, who also proceeds by force or guile (*Paradise Lost* 1.121, 646).

cently acquired, since there is no agent, no perceptible action, and no previous alteration; therefore it exists in act through the proper form which it had before, while it still formed a part of the whole. By this argument they consider that they batter down and utterly demolish our position. The reply which is commonly made is perfectly valid, that a form generated *de novo*, since it is very frequent, as pertaining to a corpse and being as it were a way to resolution, certainly requires neither a long time, nor many dispositions, nor ordered alteration to be so generated. Besides, what if some other universal cause were to combine with the previous mixture to induce some kind of form, that there may not be pure and unqualified matter? Moreover, the fact that we can perceive manifold operations in a animal is not due to distinct partial forms but to the preponderance of the total soul, which is of equal importance with the forms distinct in appearance.

I would prefer to pass over, by agreement, the other minor objections which are put forward, for they are not vital, and will be more easily countered and more satisfactorily disproved if they chance to be brought forward in the course of the disputation.

Whatever the outcome may be, even if I fail in my cause, the cause itself will never fail. For invincible Truth has within herself strength enough and to spare for her own defense, and has no need of any other help; and though she may seem to us at times to be hard pressed and beaten to the ground, yet she maintains herself ever inviolate and uninjured by the claws of Error, even as the sun, who often shows himself to human eyes obscured and darkened by clouds, but then drawing in his beams and gathering together all his splendor, shines forth again in blazing glory without spot of stain.

VI.

DELIVERED IN THE COLLEGE SUMMER VACATION, BUT IN THE PRESENCE OF ALMOST THE WHOLE BODY OF STUDENTS, AS IS CUSTOMARY

(i) The Oration

Sportive Exercises on occasion are not inconsistent with philosophical Studies

On my return from that city which is the chief of all cities, Members of the University, filled (I had almost said "to repletion") with all the good things which are to be found there in such abundance, I looked forward to enjoying once more a spell of cultured leisure, a mode of life in which, it is my belief, even the souls of the blessed find delight. I fully intended at last to bury myself in learning and to devote myself day and night to the charms of philosophy; for the alternation of toil and pleasure usually has the effect of annihilating the boredom brought about by satiety and of making us the more eager to resume our interrupted tasks. Just as I was warming to my work there came a sudden summons and I was dragged away by the yearly celebration of our ancient custom, and commanded to transfer that zeal, which I had intended to devote to the acquisition of knowledge, to foolery and the invention of new jests—as if the world were not already full of fools, as if that famous Ship of Fools,[57] as renowned in song as the Argo[58] herself, had been wrecked, or finally as if there were not matter enough already to make Democritus laugh.[59]

But I ask your pardon, my hearers; for although I have spoken somewhat too freely, the custom which we celebrate today is assuredly no foolish one, but on the contrary most commendable, as I intend to make plain forthwith. And if Junius Brutus,[60] that second founder of Rome and great avenger of the lusts of kings, could

---

[57]I quote from the *OED*: "after the title of Sebastian Brant's satirical work *Das Narrenschiff* (1494), translated into English by Alexander Barclay as *The shyp of folys of the worlde* (1509), a ship whose passengers represent various types of vice or folly." Dekker used the phrase in 1609, indicating that it would still be current when Milton appropriated it.

[58]The ship carrying the Argonauts, subject of Apollonius of Rhodes short epic the *Argonautica*, which Milton would later include as part of his students' curriculum.

[59]Democritus (b. c. 460 BCE) was known as the laughing philosopher for his habit of laughing at the general follies of humankind.

[60]The nephew of the tyrant Tarquinius Superbus, Lucius Junius Brutus pretended insanity in order not to be put to death by Tarquin, but when Tarquin raped Lucretia (Shakespeare's Lucrece) and she committed suicide in 509 BCE, the outraged Brutus led a revolt against the Tarquin family, became a consul, and helped found the Roman Republic. His life is recorded in Livy 1, Ch. 56.

bring himself to disguise his almost godlike mind and wonderful natural talents under the semblance of idiocy, there is assuredly no reason why I should be ashamed to play the wise fool for a while, especially at the bidding of him whose duty it is, like the aediles' at Rome,[61] to organize these shows, which are almost a regular custom. I was further strongly induced and persuaded to undertake this office by the new-found friendliness towards me of you who are fellow students of my own college.[62] For when, some months ago, I was to make an academic oration before you, I felt sure any effort of mine would have but a cold reception from you, and would find in Aeacus or Minos a more lenient judge than any one of you.[63] But quite contrary to my expectation, contrary indeed to any spark of hope I may have entertained, I heard, or rather I myself felt, that my speech was received with quite unusual applause on every hand, even on the part of those who had previously shown me only hostility and dislike, because of disagreements concerning our studies. A generous way indeed of displaying rivalry, and one worthy of a royal nature! For while friendship itself is often apt to misinterpret what is really free from faults, on this occasion keen and biting enmity was kind enough to construe in a more gentle and lenient spirit than I deserved both my mistakes, which may have been many, and my rhetorical failures, which were doubtless not a few. On this one occasion and in this one instance mad fury seemed to become sane, and by this action to free itself from the imputation of lunacy.

I am quite overcome with pride and joy at finding myself surrounded on all sides by such an assembly of learned men; and yet, when I take stock of myself and turning my eyes inward consider in my own heart the meager powers I possess, I blush to myself and a sudden uprush of sadness overwhelms and chokes my rising joy.

But gentlemen, do not, I beg of you, desert me as I lie here fallen, and stricken by your eyes as by lightning.[64] Let the soft breeze of your goodwill refresh my fainting spirit, as well as it can, and warm it into life again; so shall my sickness, thanks to you, be less acute, and the remedy, since it is you who apply it, the more willingly and gladly accepted; so that it would be a true pleasure to me often to faint thus, if I might as often be revived

and restored by you. But what matchless power, what marvelous virtue is yours, which like Achilles's spear, the gift of Vulcan, at once inflicts the wound and heals it![65] For the rest, let no one wonder that I triumph, as though exalted to heaven, at finding so many men eminent for their learning, the very flower as it were of the University, gathered together here; for I can scarce believe that a greater number flocked of old to Athens to hear those two supreme orators, Demosthenes and Aeschines,[66] contending for the crown of eloquence, or that such felicity ever fell to the lot of Hortensius[67] at any declamation of his, or that so great a company of cultured men ever graced a speech of Cicero's. So that with however poor success I perform my task, it will be yet no mean honor to me merely to have opened my lips before so large and crowded an assembly of our most eminent men. And by heaven I cannot help flattering myself a little that I am, as I think, far more fortunate than Orpheus or Amphion;[68] for they did but supply the trained and skillful touch to make the strings give forth their sweet harmony, and the exquisite music was due as much to the instrument itself as to their apt and dexterous handling of it. But if I win any praise here today, it will be entirely and truly my own, and the more glorious in proportion as the creations of the intellect are superior to manual skill. Besides, Orpheus and Amphion used to attract an audience consisting only of rocks and wild beasts and trees, and if any human beings came, they were at best but rude and rustic folk; but I find the most learned men altogether engrossed in listening to my words and hanging on my lips. Lastly, like those rustics and wild beasts used to follow after the stringed music which they already knew well and had often heard before; you have been drawn hither and held fast here by expectation alone.

But, Members of the University, I would before all have you know that I have not spoken thus in a spirit of boastfulness. For I only wish that such a stream of ho-

---

[61]Civic magistrates in imperial Rome who were in charge of public occasions.

[62]Milton's stance here is of someone who has buried his feuds with his classmates and the university community, quite unlike his stance in the first Prolusion.

[63]Proverbially fair human beings who were supposed to have been made judges in the classical underworld as a reward for their justness.

[64]The power of the human glance, as in "Lightning glimps" of *Paradise Lost* 6.642, or "lightning glance" of *Samson Agonistes* 1284.

[65]Achilles miraculously cures the wound of Telephus by applying rust scraped off the point of the spear he has just used to wound him (Ovid, *Metamorphoses* 13.171).

[66]Famous as rival orators flourishing in Athens in about 350 BCE.

[67]Roman orator celebrated by Cicero in *De Oratore* 3.61. Hughes points out that the two were also rivals, "especially when Cicero prosecuted Verres in 70 B.C." (614n).

[68]Orpheus is an important fixture in Milton's poetry and prose, and a representative of the divine poet, and poet as role-model for Milton himself. His power to charm by his music is recorded in Ovid *Metamorphoses*, at the beginning of Book 11. Likewise, Amphion was said to have such a power in his playing of the lyre that its kinetic energy was supposed to have erected the walls of Thebes. For both poets mentioned simultaneously, see Ovid, *Ars Amatoria* 3.321–23.

neyed, or rather nectared,[69] eloquence might be granted me, if but for this once, as of old ever steeped and as it were celestially bedewed the great minds of Athens and Rome; would that I could suck out all the innermost marrow of persuasion, pilfer the notebooks of Mercury himself,[70] and empty all the coffers of wit, that I might produce something worthy of such great expectations, so notable a concourse, and so polished and refined an audience. So behold, my hearers, whither my consuming desire and longing to please you drives me and carries me away: all unexpectedly I find myself wafted in an ambition which is, however, a righteous one, and a virtuous sacrilege, if there can be such a thing.

Certainly I do not consider that I need beg and implore the help of the Muses, for I find myself surrounded by men in whom the Muses and the Graces are incarnate,[71] and it seems to me that Helicon and all the other shrines of the Muses have poured forth their nurslings to celebrate this day, so that one might well believe that the laurels of Parnassus pine and fade for lack of them. Therefore it will surely be useless to seek the Muses, the Graces, and the Loves[72] in any other spot in all the world than this. If so, Barbarity, Error, Ignorance, and all that tribe which the Muses loathe must needs take flight with all speed at the sight of you, and hide themselves in a far distant region. And then, why should not ever barbarous, vulgar, or outworn word or phrase be forthwith banished from my speech, and I myself become straightaway eloquent and accomplished, through the working of your influence and secret inspiration?

However that may be, I entreat you, my hearers, not to grudge a little of your time to my frivolities, for even the gods themselves are said often to have laid aside for the moment the cares of the commonwealth of heaven and to have been present as spectators of the wars of puny man. Sometimes, indeed, the stories tell, they did not disdain humble homes, but accepted the hospitality of the poor and gladly made a meal of beans and herbs.[73] So too I beg and beseech you, my kind hearers, to accept what I can offer as in some sort a humble banquet for your delicate and discerning taste.

I am indeed well aware that many sciolists[74] are in the habit of arrogantly and stupidly belittling in others any subject of which they happen to know nothing themselves, as if it were not worth spending trouble upon; so for instance one foolishly rails at Dialectic, because he could never master it; another despises Natural Philosophy, because, to be sure, the fairest of the goddesses, Nature, never so honored him as to show herself naked to his eyes.[75] But for my part I will not shrink from singing the praises of jests and merriment to the best of my powers, even though I must admit that I have but very slight aptitude for them. I must however first point out that I am today to praise mirth in a serious style,[76] which seems an arduous task indeed and far from easy. Nor are these praises undeserved. For what is more likely to win friendship quickly and retain it long, than a pleasant and gay disposition? while if a man is devoid of wit and humor and elegant pleasantry, hardly anyone will find him agreeable or welcome. But in our own case, Members of the University, if we made it our daily custom to go to sleep and, so to speak, die in philosophy and grow old among the thorns and brambles of logic, without any relaxation or breathing-space, what, I ask, would the pursuit of philosophy amount to but prophesying in the cave of Trophonius and following the overrigid rule of Cato?[77] Why, the very rustics would say that we live on mustard. Besides, just as those who exercise themselves in wrestling and other sports grow much stronger than others and more ready for all emergencies, even so we usually find that these mental gymnastics strengthen the sinews of the mind and tone up its whole system, and polish and sharpen the intellect, making it versatile and adaptable. But if a man does not desire to be considered cultured and witty, he must not be annoyed if he is called a clown and a boor. There is, too, a certain low kind of fellow, often enough met with, who, being themselves incapable of wit or gaiety, and conscious of their own dullness and stupidity, always conclude that any witty remark they may hear is at their expense.[78] It would indeed serve them right if their unreasonable suspicions were to be realized, and if they

---

[69]"Nectared" because derived from classical sources of inspiration, associated with gods whose food was nectar and ambrosia.

[70]Since Mercury was the god of thieves, pilfering his notebook would be appropriate.

[71]Milton thought of the English universities as natural homes to the Muses, as in the ode to Rouse 62.

[72]Three groupings of gods or demigods who might inspire grace itself, dance, or varying kinds of artistic inspiration.

[73]The story of Baucis and Philemon in Ovid, *Metamorphoses* 8 records a godly visit to a humble cottage. Milton may have had that in mind when Raphael visits Adam and Eve in Books 5–8 of *Paradise Lost*.

[74]Pretenders to knowledge.

[75]In *Ad Patrem* 90–92, Milton pictures himself as embracing "scientia," or knowledge, pictured as a nude goddess.

[76]Very similar to what Milton did in "L'Allegro."

[77]For Trophonius, see Prolusion 3. Cato is likely to be the censor Marcus Portius Cato, legendary for his ascetic or Stoic personal habits. He drank only water, was satisfied with any food put before him, and attempted never to become angry. He fills, in other words, the stereotype of the Puritan prude (as with Shakespeare's Malvolio). Plutarch wrote his biography. Milton seems to have subscribed to some of Cato's personal habits, if one is to take the verse letter to Diodati, Elegy 6, seriously.

[78]A hint at what Milton considered a valuable asset: a sense of humor.

could find themselves the butt of everyone's witticisms, till they were almost driven to suicide. But such dregs of mankind as these cannot stand in the way of the pleasantry of polite society.

Would you now, gentlemen, have me build up a structure of proof from instances on this foundation of reason? I can indeed find plenty of such instances. First of all comes Homer, the rising sun or morning star of cultured literature, at whose birth all learning was born also, his twin. He sometimes withdrew his divine mind from the councils of the gods and the doings of heaven and diverted it to comic subjects, such as that most amusing description of the battle of frogs and mice. Moreover Socrates, according to the Pythian Apollo, the wisest of men, is said often to have bridled his wife's shrewish tongue with a jesting word.[79] Besides, we read that the conversation of the ancient philosophers was always sprinkled with witty sayings and enlivened by a pleasant sparkle; and it was certainly this quality about all which conferred an immortal fame upon all the ancient writers of comedies and epigrams, whether Greek or Latin. Moreover we are told that Cicero's jokes and witticisms, collected by Tiro,[80] filled three volumes. And we are all familiar with that sprightly encomium of Folly composed by an author of no small repute,[81] while we have many other diverting essays on comic subjects by famous authors of our own times.

Would you have me cite great generals, kings, and heroes? Take then Pericles, Epaminondas, Agesilaius, and Philip of Macedon, who, if I may speak in Gellius's[82] manner, overflowed with humorous and witty sayings, according to the statements of historians. Take too Laelius, Scipio, Pompey, Julius Caesar and Augustus, all of whom were, according to Cicero, pre-eminent among their contemporaries for wit. Would you have yet greater names? Jove himself and the other deities are represented by the poets, who give us the best pictures of the truth, as giving themselves up

to merriment at their feasts and carouses. Finally, gentlemen, I invoke the seal of approval set by yourselves, which I consider worth all the rest. For that jests and jollity are far from displeasing to you is proved clearly enough by your coming here in crowds to-day, and to this every one of you seems to nod assent. Nor, I swear, is it to be wondered at that all honest and all eminent men find pleasure in this lively and elegant pleasantry, since it too has a place of honor in the famous Aristotelian classification of virtues,[83] and as in some Pantheon shines in splendor like a goddess among her sister deities.

But perhaps there may be some bearded Masters of crabbed and surly nature, who, thinking themselves Catos[84] not merely in a small way but on a grand scale, and composing their countenances to a Stoic severity, shake their obstinate heads and uneasily complain that nowadays everything is confusion and going from bad to worse, and that the newly-created Bachelors, instead of expounding the Prior Analytics of Aristotle, shamelessly and unseasonably bandy about scurrilous and empty trivialities, and that today's exercises, which our forbears undoubtedly instituted with the proper and honest purpose of winning some solid gain either of rhetoric or philosophy, have of late been perverted into a show of feeble witticism. But I have an answer to them ready to hand. Let them know, if they do not know already, that when the laws of our Republic of Letters were first laid down, learning had only just penetrated from foreign lands to our country; therefore, since the knowledge of Greek and Latin was exceedingly rare and unusual, it was necessary to strive and struggle toward them with the more intensive study and more unremitting efforts. We, however, though inferior to our predecessors in morals, are superior to them in learning, and ought to turn our backs on those studies which offer but little difficulty, and betake ourselves to those to which they too would have turned their attention, had they had leisure to do so. And you are well aware that the earliest lawgivers were always wont to issue ordinances rather harder and more severe than men could endure, in order that as men grew less strict and accurate in their observance of them they might hit upon the right kind of moderate behavior. Finally, since the circumstances are now entirely different, we must necessarily allow many laws and customs, if not to lapse and fall into disuse, at least to be narrowed in their appli-

---

[79]Socrates' almost legendarily shrewish wife was Xantippe, who was famous for, among other things, dumping the contents of a chamber pot on her husband's head..

[80]Cicero's freed slave, secretary, and friend. He edited some of the *Letters to His Friends* collected in the three volumes in the Loeb series (ed. W. G. Williams [New York: Loeb Classical Library, 1927]).

[81]It may be odd that Milton does not mention Desiderius Erasmus by name, but he does allude to the great humanist and educational reformer by reference to the title of his best-known work, translated as *In Praise of Folly* (1509).

[82]Aulus Gellius (fl. c. 130 AD), Roman grammarian, compiled a large series of anecdotal essays, collected as the *Noctes Atticae*, or *Attic Nights*, which were full of good-humored commentary on a wide variety of subjects. Gellius's gossipy information would provide a modern speaker, in Milton's day, with colorful and funny details concerning Roman and Greek language, customs, and personalities.

[83]Urbanity, as in the *Nicomachean Ethics* 2.1–6. Hughes points out that for Milton urbanity was more than just a "superficially pleasant disposition"; it implied "acuteness, candor, and purity of mind" (616n; compare Columbia 17: 322).

[84]In other words censors of public behavior, as Cato was.

cation and disregarded in some details. But, they say, raising their eyebrows, if such frivolities are to be openly tolerated and approved and to win public praise, every student will straightaway turn his attention away from sound and solid learning and devote it to shows and stage frivolity, so that the very training schools of philosophy will send out, instead of learned and prudent men, fools more shameless than buffoons and play-actors.

For my part, I consider that a man who can be so given up to foolish jests as altogether to neglect for them his serious and really useful work, is incapable of distinguishing himself in either of these spheres: not in that of serious work, for if he were by nature adapted and suited to dealing with serious matters he would not, I am sure, allow himself to be so easily led away from them; nor yet in that is frivolity, because no one can be master of a fine and clever wit who has not first learnt how to behave seriously.

But I am afraid, gentlemen, that I have been spinning out my speech too long. I will not make excuses for this as I might, lest in excusing it I should aggravate my fault. In a moment we shall shake off the fetters of rhetoric and throw ourselves into comic license. If in the course of this I outgo by a finger's breadth, as they say, my usual custom of strict rules of modesty, I beg you, gentlemen, to accept this explanation: it is to give you pleasure that I have put off and for the moment laid aside my usual habit, and if anything I may say is loose or licentious, put it down to the suggestion, not of my real mind and character, but of the needs of the moment and the genius of the place. And so I entreat at the beginning of my entertainment the favor which actors beg at the end of theirs: give me your laughter and applause.

(ii) The Prolusion

At the moment when the commonwealth of fools is, as it seems, tottering and on the brink of disaster, I have been made its Dictator, though I know not how I have deserved the honor. Why should the choice fall on me, when that famous leader and commander of all the Sophisters[85] was an eager candidate for the post, and would have fulfilled his duties valiantly; for that seasoned warrior on a previous occasion boldly led some fifty Sophisters, armed with short staves, across Barnwell Field,[86] and, as a step toward laying siege to the town in the approved military style, destroyed the aqueduct, in order

to force the townsfolk to surrender through shortage of water. I am deeply distressed at this hero's recent departure, since his going leaves all us Sophisters not merely headless but beheaded.

I ask you now to imagine, gentlemen, though it is not the first of April, that we are celebrating the Hilaria in honor of the Mother of the Gods,[87] or a festival sacred to the god Laughter. Laugh, then, and raise a roar from your saucy lungs, smooth out the wrinkles of your brow, make a long nose, if you like, but don't turn it up at anything; let the whole place resound with shouts of mirth, let unbridled hilarity make the tears of merriment flow freely, so that laughter may drain them dry, leaving not a drop to grace the triumph of grief.[88] For my part, if I see anyone not opening his mouth as wide as he should to laugh, I shall say that he is trying to hide teeth which are foul and decayed, and yellow from neglect, or misplaced and projecting, or else that at today's feast he has so crammed his belly that he dares not put any extra strain on it by laughing, for fear not the Sphinx but his sphincter anus should sing a second part to his mouth's first and accidentally let out some enigmas, of which I leave to the doctors instead of to Oedipus to explain. For I should not like the cheerful sound of laughter to be drowned by groans from the posterior in this assembly. I leave it to the doctors, who can loosen the bowels, to loosen up all this. If anyone does not raise his voice loud and clear enough, I shall swear that his breath is so foul and poisonous that the fumes of Etna or Avernus could not be more noisome, or at any rate that he has just been eating onions and leeks so that he dare not open his mouth for fear of making his neighbors choke with his evil-smelling breath. Next, there must be no trace of that dreadful infernal sound, a hiss, anywhere in this assembly; for if it is heard here today, I shall believe that the Furies and Eumenides are skulking somewhere among you, that their snakes and serpents have found their way into your bosoms, and that the madness of Athamas[89] has come upon you.

To be sure, gentlemen, I am quite overcome with wonder and admiration at the favor you have shown me, in forcing your way through flame and fire into this place to hear me speak. For at the very threshold there

---

[85]College students mostly in their second year.
[86]A mock-heroic description of a recent college prank. Barnwell Meadows were owned by the University.

---

[87]Cybele, whose feast, the Hilaria, was celebrated in March.
[88]Compare the image of "Laughter holding both his sides" in "L'Allegro" 32.
[89]Ovid, *Metamorphoses* 4.452–542, tells the story of the madness of King Athamas of Thebes, inspired by the Furies to kill one of his children and to force his wife to drown herself holding the other.

stands on one hand our fiery Cerberus[90] barking forth smoke to terrify us, laying about him with his blazing staff, and puffing out mouthfuls of glowing embers. On the other hand that burning and all-consuming furnace of ours belches forth lurid flames and pours out coiling wreaths of smoke, so that it would be as easy to force one's way past him as to traverse the road to Hades, and that against the will of Pluto; and certainly Jason himself encountered no greater danger in his attempt upon the fire-breathing oxen of Mars. But now, gentlemen, you may well believe yourselves to be in heaven, after having passed through purgatory, and come safe and sound out of the fiery furnace by some new miracle. I cannot think of any hero whose valor can be fairly compared with yours; for the renowned Bellerophon showed no greater courage in subduing the fire-vomiting Chimera, nor did the valiant champions of King Arthur more easily overcome and destroy the enchantments of the flaming, fiery castle. Hence I feel justified in promising myself a choice and select audience; for if any rubbish has passed through the furnaces and penetrated to this place, I can only say that our porters are mere jack-o'-lanterns, or "foolish fires."

But how happy and secure we are and always shall be! For at Rome it was the custom to guard the eternal fire most carefully and scrupulously, to secure the permanence of the empire; but we are ourselves guarded by living and watchful fires. Living and watchful, did I say? that expression slipped from my tongue unawares, for now that I come to think of it, they go out at the approach of dusk, and only rekindle in broad daylight. Still there is good hope that our House may shine once more, since none would deny that two of the greatest Luminaries of the University preside over our college; yet they would not be more highly honored anywhere than at Rome, for there Vestal Virgins would keep them aglow and awake all night long. Or, it may be, these flaming brothers might be initiated into the seraphic order. Lastly, that half-line of Vergil applies exactly to them, "They have the vital force of fire."[91] Indeed, I am inclined to believe that Horace referred to these Lights of ours, for the elder of them, as he stands among his wife and children, "shines among them all, like the moon among lesser lights."[92] But I cannot pass over Ovid's egregious error in saying, "No creatures do we

know which are born of flame." For we see flitting all around us little Sparks, the offspring of this Spark of ours. If Ovid denies this, he will necessarily be casting aspersions on their mother's good name.

To return to yourselves, gentlemen. That you may not regret having taken so difficult and dangerous a journey, here is a banquet ready prepared for you! Here are tables decked with all the luxury of Persia and loaded with rarest dainties, fit to delight and captivate the palate of a very Apicius. For it is said that eight whole boars were set before Antony and Cleopatra at a banquet, but behold, before you are set, as a first course, fifty fatted boars which have been pickled in beer for three years, and yet are still so tough that they may well tire out even our dog-teeth. Next, the same number of excellent oxen with magnificent tails, just roasted before the door by our fiery servant; only I am afraid all of the juice has gone into the dripping-pan. After them come as many calves' heads, fat and fleshy enough, but with so little brains as not to be enough for seasoning. Then again a hundred kids, more or less, but too lean, I think, from over-indulgence in the pleasures of love. We expected a few fine rams with fine spreading horns, but our cooks have not yet brought them from the town. If anyone prefers birds, we can provide any number of them, long fattened on dough and flour and grated cheese. First of all, any kind of bird as green in character as plumage, which, I fancy, must have come from the same part of the world as parrots; as they always fly about in flocks and nest in the same place, they will be served up all on one dish. I would advise you to partake of them sparingly, for besides being rather underdone and lacking in solid nutriment, they are apt to produce a rash in those who eat them, if our epicure is right. Now enjoy your feast with a right good will, for here comes a dish which I can most heartily recommend, namely an enormous turkey, so fat and stout after three years' fattening that one vast dish is scarcely big enough for it, and with such a long and horny beak that it could attack an elephant or a rhinoceros with impunity; but we have had it killed for today, just at the right moment since it was beginning to be a danger to young girls and to attack women, like the large apes.

This is followed by some Irish birds (of which I do not know the name but which are very like cranes in their gait and lanky figures), though as a rule they are kept for the last course. This is a novel and rare, rather than wholesome dish, and I would therefore warn you not to taste them, for they are very apt, if our epicure is right, to produce lice. I consider that they are more likely to be useful to grooms, for they are naturally lively, spirited, and prancing, so that if they are given as a clyster to clean horses they make them more lively

---

[90]Like Milton's other subsequent plays on names, "Cerberus" puns on a name of a college servant, in this case Sparks (278–79), whose name might associate him with the flames of the classical underworld and hence with its entrance-keeper Cerberus. He may also be working on names like Furness or Cole, as he will later play on river and Rivers.

[91]Half-lines in the *Aeneid* may indicate Vergil's care in composition. The line referred to is 6.730.

[92]*Epodes* 15.1–2. The reference to Ovid is to the *Fasti* 6.292.

and fleet than they would be even if they had swallowed a dozen live eels.

You see also several geese, some of this year's hatching and some older; they have good loud voices noisier than the frogs of Aristophanes. You will easily recognize them—in fact it is a wonder that they have not already betrayed themselves by hissing, and perhaps you will hear them in a moment.

We have besides a few eggs, but they are "bad eggs." Of fruits we have only apples and medlars, and they are gallows-fruit and are not quite ripe, so that it would be better to hang them up again to ripen in the sun.

You see what we have provided, so I beg you to help yourselves to what you fancy. But I expect you will say that this banquet, like the nocturnal feasts offered by the devil to witches, is cooked without salt, and I am afraid you will go away hungrier than you came.

I will now turn to what concerns me more closely. The Romans had their Floralia,[93] the rustics their Palilia, the bakers their Fornacalia, and we too keep the custom of amusing ourselves as Socrates advised, especially at this season when we find ourselves released from cares and business. Now the Inns of Court[94] have their Lords, as they call them, showing how ambitious they are of rank. But we, gentlemen, in our desire to come as near as may be to paternity, are eager to play in pretense a part which we should not dare really to play unless in secret; even as girls are wont to invent games of weddings and births, striving to catch and hold the shadows of those things for which they long and yearn.

Why this custom should have been neglected last year I cannot imagine, unless it was because those who were to be Fathers had shown such activity in the town that the master of the ceremonies, out of consideration for the labors they had already undergone, voluntarily excused them this duty.

But, I ask, how does it happen that I have so quickly become a Father? Good heavens, what a prodigy is this, more astonishing than any recorded by Pliny![95] Have I slain some serpent and incurred the fate of Tiresias?[96] Has some Thessalian witch poured magic ointment over me?[97] Or have I been violated by some god, like Caeneus[98] of old, and won my manhood as the price of my dishonor, that I should be suddenly thus changed from woman into man? Some of late called me "the Lady."[99] But why do I seem to them too little of a man? Have they no regard for Priscian?[100] Do these bungling grammarians attribute to the feminine gender what is proper to the masculine, like this? It is, I suppose, because I have never brought myself to toss off great bumpers like a prize-fighter,[101] or because my hand has never grown calloused with driving the plough, or because I was never a farm hand at seven or laid myself down full length in the midday sun; or at last perhaps because I never showed my virility in the way these brothellers do. But I wish they could leave playing the ass as readily as I the woman.

But see how stupid and ill-advised they are to reproach me with a thing upon which I can most justly pride myself. For Demosthenes[102] himself was said to be too little of a man by his rivals and opponents. Hortensius also, the most eminent orator after Cicero, was called by Torquatus the lyre-player. His reply was, "I would rather be Dionysia indeed than a man without taste, culture, or urbanity, like you, Torquatus." (But indeed as to any such nickname as "Lord" or "Lady" I utterly reject and repudiate it; for, gentlemen, it is only in your courts and on your platforms that I have any ambition to lord it.) Who will forbid me to rejoice at so auspicious and happy an omen, and to exult at sharing a reproach aimed at such great men? In the meantime, as I consider all good and excellent men to be above envy, even so I hold these spiteful fellows to be so far beneath all others that those who revile them are unworthy. And so I take up my role of Father and

---

[93]There was a Roman Floralia, a game-festival in honor of the goddess of flowers, Flora, held in April and May; the Palila was a festival celebrated in April honoring Pales, goddess of sheepfolds and pastures (she appears in comparison with Eve in *Paradise Lost* 9.393); and the Fornacalia were festivals celebrating Fornax, goddess of baking and bake-ovens, held in early February.

[94]Center of legal activities, the equivalent of law school, in Milton's London. Milton would be closely in touch with the Inns of Court through his own legal training as a scrivener's son and through his brother Christopher's education as a lawyer.

[95]Pliny the Elder's (23–79 AD) *Naturalis Historia* recorded much "unnatural natural history," accounts of wonderful and fanciful monsters.

[96]Tiresias was supposed to have un-knotted two snakes mating and to have been punished by having his sex changed to that of a woman for eight years (Ovid, *Metamorphoses* 3.322–31).

[97]Something like that happened to the character assumed by Apuleius in *The Golden Ass*: a witch's potion transformed him into a donkey.

[98]The Thessalian virgin Caenis was raped by Neptune and was granted one wish: she asked to be changed into a man (Ovid, *Metamorphoses* 12: 191–210).

[99]A reference to his nickname, "the Lady," at Christ's College, perhaps because of his precise manners or pale complexion. Here Milton's objection to being labeled seems to be made in good humor.

[100]Sixth-century AD Roman who compiled the most famous Latin grammar.

[101]As McEuen points out, Milton uses the word *pancratice*, which signified a rough combination of wrestling and boxing (Yale 1: 284n).

[102]Both the famous orators, the Greek Demosthenes and the Roman Hortalus Quintus Hortensius, seemed to their contemporaries to be effeminate in manner or in sexual inclination, and Hortensius, like Milton, was given a female nickname, Dionysia.

address myself to my sons, of whom I perceive a goodly number, and I see that the jolly rascals acknowledge me as their father by a furtive nod.

Do you ask their names?[103] I should not like my sons to be given the names of various dishes, and to furnish forth a banquet for you, for that would be too like the savagery of Tantalus and Lycaon;[104] and I will not give them the names of the parts of the body, lest you should think me the father of so many bits of men instead of whole ones; nor do I fancy calling them after the various kinds of meat lest in my remarks I should not keep to my muttons, as the proverb says. No, I will have them called after the Predicaments of Aristotle,[105] to indicate the nobility of their birth and the liberality of their habits; and I shall take good care, too, that all of them are promoted to some degree before I die.

As for my jokes, I don't want them to have no bite in them, or you may well say they are hackneyed and stale, and that some wheezy old woman has spat them out. At the same time I do not think that anyone will accuse my jokes of being too biting, unless he has no teeth himself and finds fault with them because they are not like his own. Certainly on this occasion I could wish that my lot were the same as Horace's, and that I were a fish-monger's son, for then I should have just the right amount of salt, and I should send you all off so nicely pickled that you would be as sick of salt water as were those soldiers of ours who lately managed to escape from the island of Ré.[106]

I want to avoid being heavily sententious in my advice to you, my sons, so as not to seem to have taken more pains in educating than in begetting you. Only take care you do not turn prodigal sons, and mind you all keep off Bass,[107] or I will disown you as bastards. Any other advice I may have to offer had best be given in our native language; and I will do my utmost to make my meaning plain.

For the rest, I must pray to Neptune, Apollo, Vulcan, and all the artificer-gods to strengthen my ribs with wooden supports or to bind them round with iron plates. And I must beseech the goddess Ceres also, who gave Pelops a shoulder-blade of ivory, to be so good as to repair my sides, which are nearly worn out, in a similar way. It is not surprising after so much shouting and after begetting so many sons they are the worse for wear.

I have "dallied" (in the Neronian sense of the word) more than long enough over these things. Now I will overleap the University Statutes as if they were the wall of Romulus and run off from Latin into English.[108] Lend me attentive ears and minds, you whom such things amuse.

VII.
DELIVERED IN THE COLLEGE CHAPEL IN DEFENCE OF LEARNING AN ORATION[109]
Learning brings more Blessings to Men than Ignorance

ALTHOUGH, gentlemen, nothing could give me greater pleasure and satisfaction than your presence here, than this eager crowd in cap and gown, or than the honorable office of speaker, which I have already once or twice discharged before you gladly enough, I must, to be candid, confess that I scarcely ever undertake these speeches of my own free will; even though my own disposition and the trend of my studies make no impediment. In fact, if the choice had been offered me, I could well have dispensed with this evening's task. For I have learnt from the writings and sayings of wise men that nothing common or mediocre can be tolerated in an orator any more than in a poet, and that he who would be an orator in reality as well as by repute must first acquire a thorough knowledge of all the arts and sciences to form a complete background

---

[103]For some of the plays on the names of his fellow students, see Masson 1: 261.

[104]Both Tantalus and Lycaon performed crimes involving cannibalism or human sacrifice. For Tantalus and his cannibalized son Pelops, see Ovid's *Metamorphoses* 6.401, and for Lycaon 1.216.

[105]The Predicaments were categories devised by Aristotle, with Ens (Being) as their father. The ten Predicaments were substance, quantity, quality, relation, place, time, action, passion, posture, and habit; they have to do with the relations between subject and predicate in grammar.

[106]A naval expedition in 1627, used as a diversion to regain popular support by Charles I and under the command of Buckingham, to aid the Huguenots.

[107]A reinstated pun in the English translation, working with the modern beer, Bass, as compared with Milton's actual pun on the etymology of Liber (god of wine, Bacchus) and *liberi* (children).

[108]At this point "Lines at a Vacation Exercise" were inserted.

[109]This last and perhaps best of the Prolusions probably represents Milton's farewell to Cambridge, the declamation required of students about to take a master's degree (Masson 1: 266), which for him would like have been presented in the summer of 1632. Perhaps annoyed with an assignment that required that he interrupt his own personal quest for knowledge through intensive reading, he had proposed the topic "Ignorance is more rewarding than *Ars*," here translated as "Knowledge" or "Learning." But, to his apparent delight, he was asked to defend learning instead. The result was "a piece which must rank today among Milton's major works in prose" (Parker 109). McEuen describes the effects of Francis Bacon's *Advancement of Learning* on Milton's oration, and she summarizes the various topics Milton emphasizes, as with "the three types of learning—history, poetry, and philosophy" (Yale 1: 287). The Seventh Prolusion is obviously a personal credo and a plan for his vocation as a poet, orator, historian representing his native country. In effect it prophesies his entire public career with great accuracy.

to his own calling. Since however this is impossible at my age, I would rather endeavor truly to deserve that reputation by long and concentrated study and by the preliminary acquisition of that background, than snatch at a false repute by a premature and hastily acquired eloquence.

Afire and aglow with these plans and notions, I found that there was no more serious hindrance or obstacle than the loss of time caused by these constant interruptions, while nothing better promoted the development and well-being of the mind, contrary to what is the case with the body, than a cultured and liberal leisure. This I believe to be the meaning of Hesiod's holy sleep[110] and Endymion's nightly meeting with the moon;[111] this was the significance of Prometheus' withdrawal, under the guidance of Mercury, to the lofty solitude of the Caucasus, where at last he became the wisest of gods and men, so that his advice was sought by Jupiter himself concerning the marriage of Thetis. I can myself call to witness the woods and rivers and the beloved village elms,[112] under whose shade I enjoyed in the summer just past (if I may tell the secrets of the goddesses) such sweet intercourse with the Muses, as I still remember with delight. There I too, amid rural scenes and woodland solitudes, felt that I had enjoyed a season of growth in a life of seclusion.

I might indeed have hoped to find here also the same opportunity for retirement, had not the distressing task of speaking been unseasonably imposed on me. This so cruelly deprived me of my holy slumbers, so tormented my mind, intent upon other things, and so hindered and hampered me in the hard and arduous pursuit of learning, that I gave up all hope of finding any peace and began sadly to think how far removed I was from that tranquillity which learning had at first promised me, how hard my life was like to be amid this turmoil and agitation, and that all attempts to pursue Learning had best be abandoned. And so, almost beside myself, I rashly determined on singing the praise of Ignorance, since that was not subject to these disturbances, and I proposed as the theme of dispute the question whether Art or Ignorance bestowed greater blessings on its devotees. I know not how it is, but somehow either my destiny or my disposition forbade me to give up my old devotion to the Muses; indeed, blind chance itself seemed of a sudden to be endowed with prudence and

foresight and to join in the prohibition. Sooner than I could have expected, Ignorance found her champion, and the defence of Learning devolved on me. I am delighted thus to have been played with, and am not ashamed that I owe the restoration of my sight to Fortune, who is herself blind. For this she deserves my gratitude. Now I may at any rate be permitted to sing the praises of Learning, from whose embrace I have been torn, and as it were assuage my longing for the absent beloved by speaking of her. This can now hardly be called an interruption, for who would regard it as an interruption when he is called upon to praise or defend the object of his affection, his admiration, and his deepest desire?

But, gentlemen, it is my opinion that the power of eloquence is most manifest when it deals with subjects which rouse no particular enthusiasm. Those which most stir our admiration can hardly be compassed within the bounds of a speech: the very abundance of material is a drawback, and the multiplicity of subjects narrows and confines the swelling stream of eloquence. I am now suffering from this excess of material: that which should be my strength makes me weak, and that which should be my defence makes me defenceless. So I must make my choice, or at least mention only in passing rather than discuss at length the numerous arguments on whose powerful support our cause relies for its defence and security. On this occasion it seems to me that my efforts must be directed entirely to showing how and to what extent Learning and Ignorance respectively promote that happiness which is the aim of every one of us. With this question I shall easily deal in my speech, nor need I be over-anxious about what objections Folly may bring against Knowledge, or Ignorance against Learning. Yet the very ability of Ignorance to raise any objection, to make a speech, or even to open her lips in this great and learned assembly, she has received as a favor, or rather an alms, from Learning.

It is, I think, a belief familiar and generally accepted that the great Creator of the world, while constituting all else fleeting and perishable, infused into man, besides what was mortal, a certain divine spirit, a part of Himself, as it were, which is immortal, imperishable, and exempt from death and extinction. After wandering about the earth for some time, like some heavenly visitant, in holiness and righteousness, this spirit was to take its flight upward to heaven whence it had come and to return once more to the abode and home which was its birthright. It follows that nothing can be reckoned as a cause of our happiness which does not somehow take into account both everlasting life and our ordinary life here on earth. This eternal life, as almost everyone admits, is to be found in contemplation alone, by which

---

[110]The sleep of inspiration by the Muses of Helicon described by Hesiod in the *Theogony* 22–23.

[111]Endymion met with his lover Diana, the Moon, each night—a convenient myth for nocturnal inspiration.

[112]This might well describe Milton's studious retreat to the family home in the little village of Horton, in Buckinghamshire.

the mind is uplifted, without the aid of the body, and gathered within itself so that it attains, to its inexpressible joy, a life akin to that of the immortal gods. But without Art, the mind is fruitless, joyless, and altogether null and void. For who can worthily gaze upon and contemplate the Ideas of things human or divine, unless he possesses a mind trained and ennobled by learning and study, without which he can know practically nothing of them: for indeed, every approach to the happy life seems barred to the man who has no part in Learning. God would indeed seem to have endowed us to no purpose, or even to our distress, with this soul which is capable and indeed insatiably desirous of highest wisdom, if he had not intended us to strive with all our might toward the lofty understanding of those things, for which he had at our creation instilled so great a longing into the human mind. Survey from every angle the entire aspect of these things and you will perceive that the great Artificer of this mighty fabric established it for His own glory. The more deeply we delve into the wondrous wisdom, the marvelous skill, and the outstanding variety of its creation (which we cannot do without the aid of Learning), the greater grows the wonder and awe we feel for its Creator and the louder the praises we offer Him, which we believe and are fully persuaded that He delights to accept. Can we indeed believe, my hearers, that the vast spaces of boundless air are illuminated and adorned with everlasting lights, that these are endowed with such rapidity of motion and pass through such intricate revolutions, merely to serve as a lantern for base and slothful men, and to light the path of the idle and the sluggard here below? Do we perceive no purpose in the luxuriance of fruit and herb beyond the short-lived beauty of verdure? Of a truth, if we are so little able to appraise their value that we make no effort to go beyond the crass perceptions of the senses, we shall show ourselves not merely servile and abject, but ungracious and wicked before the goodness of God; for by our unresponsiveness and grudging spirit He is deprived of much of the glory which is His due, and of the reverence which His mighty power exacts. If then Learning is our guide and leader in the search after happiness, if it is ordained and approved by almighty God, and most conformable to His glory, surely it cannot but bring the greatest blessings upon those who follow after it.

I am well aware, gentlemen, that this contemplation, by which we strive to reach the highest goal, cannot partake of true happiness unless it is conjoined with integrity of life and uprightness of character. I know, too, that many men eminent for learning have been of bad character, and slaves to anger, hatred, and evil passions, while on the other hand many utterly ignorant men have shown themselves righteous and just. What of

it? Does it follow that Ignorance is more blessed? By no means. For the truth is, gentlemen, that though the corrupt morals of their country and the evil communications of the illiterate have in some instances lured into wicked courses a few men distinguished for their learning, yet the influence of a single wise and prudent man has often kept loyal to their duty a large number of men who lacked the advantages of Learning. And indeed a single household, even a single individual, endowed with the gifts of Art and Wisdom, may often prove to be a great gift of God, and sufficient to lead a whole state to righteousness. But where no Arts flourish, where all scholarship is banished, there you will find no single trace of a good man, but savagery and barbarity stalk abroad. As instances of this I adduce no one country, province, or race alone, but Europe itself, forming as it does one fourth of the entire globe. Throughout this continent a few hundred years ago all the noble arts had perished and the Muses had deserted all the universities of the day, over which they had long presided; blind illiteracy had penetrated and intrenched itself everywhere, nothing was heard in the schools but the absurd doctrines of drivelling monks, and that profane and hideous monster, Ignorance, assumed the gown and lorded it on our empty platforms and pulpits and in our deserted professorial chairs.[113] Then Piety went in mourning, and Religion sickened and flagged, so that only after prolonged suffering, and hardly even to this day, has she recovered from her grievous wound. But, gentlemen, it is, I believe, an established maxim of philosophy that the cognisance of every art and science appertains to the Intellect only and that the home and sanctuary of uprightness is the Will. But all agree that while the human Intellect shines forth as the lord and governor of all the other faculties, it guides and illuminates with its radiance the Will also, which would else be blind, and the Will shines with a borrowed light, even as the moon does. So, even though we grant and willingly concede that Virtue without Learning is more conducive to happiness than Learning without Virtue, yet, when these two are once wedded in happy union as they surely ought to be, and often are, then indeed Knowledge raises her head aloft and shows herself far superior, and shining forth takes her seat on high beside the king and governor, Intellect, and gazes upon the doings of the Will below as some object lying far beneath her feet; and thereafter for evermore she claims as her right all excellence and splendor and a majesty next to that of God Himself.

---

[113]Milton assumes a Protestant interpretation of medieval history, blaming Roman Catholic monkishness for the "Dark Ages."

Let us now leave these heights to consider our ordinary life, and see what advantages Learning and Ignorance respectively can offer in public and private life. I will say nothing of the argument that Learning is the fairest ornament of youth, the strong defence of manhood, and the glory and solace of age. Nor will I mention that many men highly honored in their day, and even some of the greatest men of ancient Rome, after performing many noble deeds and winning great glory by their exploits, turned from the strife and turmoil of ambition to the study of literature as into a port and welcome refuge. Clearly these honored sages realized that the best part of the life which yet remained to them must be spent to the best advantage. They were first among men; they wished by virtue of these arts not to be the last among gods. They had once striven for glory, and now strove for immortality. Their warfare against the foes of their country had been far other, but now that they were facing death, the greatest enemy of mankind, these were the weapons they took up, these the legions they enrolled, and these the resources from which they derived their strength.

But the chief part of human happiness is derived from the society of one's fellows and the formation of friendships, and it is often asserted that the learned are as a rule hard to please, lacking in courtesy, odd in manner, and seldom gifted with the gracious address that wins men's hearts. I admit that a man who is almost entirely absorbed and immersed in study finds it much easier to converse with gods than with men, either because he habitually associates with gods but is unaccustomed to human affairs and a stranger among them, or because the mind, expanding through constant meditation on things divine and therefore feeling cramped within the narrow limits of the body, is less expert in the nicer formalities of social life. But if such a man once forms a worthy and congenial friendship, there is none who cultivates it more assiduously. For what can we imagine more delightful and happy than those conversations of learned and wise men, such as those which the divine Plato is said often to have held in the shade of that famous plane-tree, conversations which all mankind might well have flocked to hear in spell-bound silence? But gross talk and mutual incitement to indulge in luxury and lust is the friendship of ignorance, or rather the ignorance of friendship.

Moreover if this human happiness consists in the honorable and liberal joys of the mind, such a pleasure is to be found in Study and Learning as far surpasses every other. What a thing it is to grasp the nature of the whole firmament and of its stars, all the movements and changes of the atmosphere, whether it strikes terror into ignorant minds by the majestic roll of thunder or by fiery comets, or whether it freezes into snow or hail, or

whether again it falls softly and gently in showers of dew; then perfectly to understand the shifting winds and all the exhalations and vapors which earth and sea give forth; next to know the hidden virtues of plants and metals and understand the nature and the feelings, if that may be, of every living creature; next the delicate structure of the human body and the art of keeping it in health; and, to crown all, the divine might and power of the soul, and any knowledge we may have gained concerning those beings we call spirits and genii and daemons. There is an infinite number of subjects besides these, a great part of which might be learnt in less time than it would take to enumerate them all. So at length, my hearers, when universal learning has once completed its cycle, the spirit of man, no longer confined within this dark prison-house, will reach out far and wide, till it fills the whole world and the space far beyond with the expansion of its divine greatness. Then at last most of the chances and changes of the world will be so quickly perceived that to him who holds this stronghold of wisdom hardly anything can happen in his life which is unforeseen or fortuitous. He will indeed seem to be one whose rule and dominion the stars obey, to whose command the earth and sea hearken, and whom winds and tempests serve; to whom, lastly, Mother Nature herself has surrendered, as if indeed some god had abdicated the throne of the world and entrusted its rights, laws, and administration to him as governor.

Besides this, what delight it affords to the mind to take its flight through the history and geography of every nation and to observe the changes in the conditions of kingdoms, races, cities, and peoples, to the increase of wisdom and righteousness. This, my hearers, is to live in every period of the world's history, and to be as it were coeval with time itself. And indeed, while we look to the future for the glory of our name, this will be to extend and stretch our lives backward before our birth, to wrest from a grudging Fate a kind of retrospective immortality. I pass over a pleasure with which none can compare—to be the oracle of many nations, to find one's home regarded as a kind of temple, to be a man whom kings and states invite to come to them, whom men from near and far flock to visit, while to others it is a matter for pride if they have but set eyes on him once. These are the rewards of study, these are the prizes which learning can and often does bestow upon her votaries in private life.[114]

What, then, of public life? It is true that few have been raised to the height of majesty through a reputa-

---

[114]Compare the image of the contemplative man attaining old age and wisdom "with something like prophetic strain" in "Il Penseroso" 174.

tion for learning, and not many more through a reputation for uprightness. Such men certainly enjoy a kingdom in themselves far more glorious than any earthly dominion;[115] and who can lay claim to a twofold sovereignty without incurring the charge of ambition? I will, however, add this one thing more: that there have hitherto been but two men who have ruled the whole world, as by divine right, and shared an empire over all kings and princes equal to that of the gods themselves; namely Alexander the Great and Augustus, both of whom were students of philosophy. It is as though Providence had specially singled them out as examples to humanity, to show to what sort of man the helm or reins of government should be entrusted.

But, it may be objected, many nations have won fame by their deeds or their wealth, without owing anything to learning. We know of but few Spartans, for example, who took any interest in liberal education, and the Romans only admitted philosophy within the walls of their city after a long time. But the Spartans found a law-giver in Lycurgus. who was both a philosopher and so ardent a student of poetry that he was the first to gather together with extreme care the writings of Homer, which were scattered throughout Ionia. The Romans, hardly able to support themselves after the various risings and disturbances which had taken place in the city, sent ambassadors to beg for the Decemviral Laws, also called the Twelve Tables, from Athens, which was at that time foremost in the study of liberal Arts.

How are we to answer the objection that the Turks of today have acquired an extensive dominion over the wealthy kingdoms of Asia in spite of being entirely devoid of culture? For my part, I have certainly never heard of anything in that state which deserves to be regarded as an example to us—if indeed one should dignify with the name of "state" the power which a horde of utter barbarians united by complicity in crime has seized by violence and murder. The provision of the necessaries of life, and their maintenance when acquired, we owe not to Art but to Nature; greedy attacks on the property of others, mutual assistance for purposes of plunder, and criminal conspiracy are the outcome of the perversion of Nature. Some kind of justice indeed is exercised in such states, as might be expected; for while the other virtues are easily put to flight, Justice from her throne compels homage, for without her even the most unjust states would soon fall into decay. I must not, however, omit to mention that the Saracens, to whom the Turks are indebted almost for their existence, en-

larged their empire as much by the study of liberal culture as by force of arms.

If we go back to antiquity, we shall find that some states owed not merely their laws but their very foundation to culture. The oldest progenitors of every race are said to have wandered through the woods and mountains, seeking their livelihood after the fashion of wild beasts, with head erect but stooping posture. One might well think that they shared everything with the animals, except the dignity of their form; the same caves, the same dens, afforded them shelter from rain and frost. There were then no cities, no marble palaces, no shining altars or temples of the gods; they had no religion to guide them, no laws or law-courts, no bridal torches, no festal dance, no song at the joyful board, no funeral rites, no mourning, hardly even a grave paid honor to the dead. There were no feasts, no games; no sound of music was ever heard: all these refinements were then lacking which idleness now misuses to foster luxury. Then of a sudden the Arts and Sciences breathed their divine breath into the savage breasts of men, and instilling into them the knowledge of themselves, gently drew them to dwell together within the walls of cities. Therefore surely cities may well expect to have a long and happy history under the direction of those guides by whom they were first of all founded, then firmly based on laws, and finally fortified by wise counsels.

What now of Ignorance? I perceive, gentlemen, that Ignorance is struck blind and senseless, skulks at a distance, casts about for a way of escape, and complains that life is short and Art long. But if we do but remove two great obstacles to our studies, namely first our bad methods of teaching the Arts, and secondly our lack of enthusiasm, we shall find that, with all deference to Galen, or whoever may have been the author of the saying, quite the contrary is the truth, and that life is long, and Art short. There is nothing so excellent and at the same time so exacting as Art, nothing more sluggish and languid than ourselves. We allow ourselves to be outdone by laborers and husbandmen in working after dark and before dawn; they show greater energy in a mean occupation, to gain a miserable livelihood, than we do in the noblest of occupations, to win a life of true happiness. Though we aspire to the highest and best of human conditions we can endure neither hard work nor yet the reproach of idleness; in fact we are ashamed of owning the very character which we hate not to have imputed to us. But, we object, our health forbids late hours and hard study. It is a shameful admission that we neglect to cultivate our minds out of consideration to our bodies, whose health all should be ready to impair if thereby their minds might gain the more. Yet those who make this excuse are certainly for the most part worthless fel-

---

[115]Compare the famous "paradise within thee, happier farr" of *Paradise Lost* 12.587.

lows; for though they disregard every consideration of their time, their talents, and their health, and give themselves up to gluttony, to drinking like whales, and to spending their nights in gaming and debauchery, they never complain that they are any the worse for it. Since, then, it is their constant habit and practice to show eagerness and energy in the pursuit of vice, but listlessness and lethargy where any activity of virtue or intelligence is concerned, they cannot lay blame on Nature or the shortness of life with any show of truth or justice. But if we were to set ourselves to live modestly and temperately, and to tame the impulses of headstrong youth by reason and steady devotion to study, keeping the divine vigor of our minds unstained and uncontaminated by any impurity or pollution, we should be astonished to find, gentlemen, looking backward over a period of years, how great a distance we had covered and across how wide a sea of learning we had sailed, without a check on our voyage.

This voyage, too, will be much shortened if we know how to select branches of learning that are useful, and what is useful within them. In the first place, how many despicable quibbles there are in grammar and rhetoric! One may hear the teachers of them talking sometimes like savages and sometimes like babies. What about logic? That is indeed the queen of the Arts, if taught as it should be, but unfortunately how much foolishness there is in reason! Its teachers are not like men at all, but like finches which live on thorns and thistles. "O iron stomachs of the harvesters!" What am I to say of that branch of learning which the Peripatetics call metaphysics? It is not, as the authority of great men would have me believe, an exceedingly rich Art; it is, I say, not an Art at all, but a sinister rock, a Lernian bog[116] of fallacies, devised to cause shipwreck and pestilence. These are the wounds, to which I have already referred, which the ignorance of gownsmen inflicts; and this monkish disease has already infected natural philosophy to a considerable extent; the mathematicians too are afflicted with longing for the petty triumph of demonstrative rhetoric. If we disregard and curtail all these subjects, which can be of no use to us, as we should, we shall be surprised to find how many whole years we shall save. Jurisprudence in particular suffers much from our confused methods of teaching, and from what is even worse, a jargon which one might well take for some Red Indian dialect, or even no human speech at all. Often, when I have heard our lawyers shouting at each other in this lingo,[117] it has occurred to me to wonder whether men who had neither human tongue nor human speech could have any human feelings either. I do indeed fear that sacred Justice will pay no attention to us and that she will never understand our complaints and wrongs, as she cannot speak our language.

Therefore, gentlemen, if from our childhood onward we never allow a day to pass without its lesson and diligent study, if we are wise enough to rule out of every art what is irrelevant, superfluous, or unprofitable, we shall assuredly, before we have attained the age of Alexander the Great, have made ourselves masters of something greater and more glorious than that world of his. And so far from complaining of the shortness of life and the slowness of Art, I think we shall be more likely to weep and wail, as Alexander did, because there are no more worlds for us to conquer.

Ignorance is breathing her last, and you are now watching her final efforts and her dying struggle. She declares that glory is mankind's most powerful incentive, and that whereas a long succession and course of years has bestowed glory on the illustrious men of old, we live under the shadow of the world's old age and decrepitude,[118] and of the impending dissolution of all things, so that even if we leave behind us anything deserving of everlasting fame, the scope of our glory is narrowed, since there will be few succeeding generations to remember us. It is therefore to no purpose that we produce so many books and noble monuments of learning, seeing that the approaching conflagration of the world will destroy them all. I do not deny that this may indeed be so; but yet to have no thought of glory when we do well is above all glory. The ancients could indeed derive no satisfaction from the empty praise of men, seeing that no joy or knowledge of it could reach them when they were dead and gone. But we may hope for an eternal life, which will never allow the memory of the good deeds we have performed on earth to perish; in which, if we have done well here, we shall ourselves be present to hear our praise; and in which, according to a wise philosophy held by many, those who have lived temperately and devoted all their time to noble arts, and have thus been of service to mankind, will be rewarded by the bestowal of a wisdom matchless and supreme over all others.

Let the idle now cease to upbraid us with the un-

---

[116]Gruesome lake into which the fifty daughters of Danaus, king of Argos, threw the heads of their husbands whose existence represented a threat to their father (Apollodorus 2.1).

[117]Not the only jibe at his brother's chosen profession or at misuse of law Latin; see Elegy 1, 31–32.
[118]Reference to the then-current debate in works of Francis Bacon and George Hakewill over whether or not the Earth is in a decline or "Nature" decayed, exemplified in Hakewill's *An Apologie of the Power and Providence of God in the Government of the World* (1627).

certainties and perplexities of learning, which are indeed not the fault so much of learning as of the frailty of man. It is this consideration, gentlemen, which disproves or mitigates or compensates for Socrates' famous ignorance and the Sceptics' timid suspension of judgment.

And finally, we may well ask, what is the happiness which Ignorance promises? To enjoy what one possesses, to have no enemies, to be beyond the reach of all care and trouble, to pass one's life in peace and quiet so far as may be—this is but the life of a beast, or of some bird which builds its little nest in the farthest depths of the forest as near to the sky as it can, in security, rears its offspring, flits about in search of sustenance without fear of the fowler, and pours forth its sweet melodies at dawn and dusk. Why should one ask for that divine activity of the mind in addition? Well, if such is the argument, we will offer Ignorance Circe's cup, and bid her throw off her human shape, and walk no longer erect, and betake her to the beasts. To the beasts, did I say? they will surely refuse to receive so infamous a guest, at any rate if they are either endowed with some kind of inferior reasoning power, as many maintain, or guided by some powerful instinct, enabling them to practice the Arts, or something resembling the Arts, among themselves. For Plutarch[119] tells us that in the pursuit of game, dogs show some knowledge of dialectic, and if they chance to come to cross-roads, they obviously make use of a disjunctive syllogism. Aristotle[120] points out that the nightingale in some sort instructs her offspring in the principles of music. Almost every animal is its own physician, and many of them have given valuable lessons in medicine to man; the Egyptian ibis teaches us the value of purgatives, the hippopotamus of blood-letting.[121] Who can maintain that creatures which so often give us warning of coming wind, rain, floods, or fair weather, know nothing of astronomy? What prudent and strict ethics are shown by those geese which check their dangerous loquacity by holding pebbles in their beaks as they fly over Mount Taurus! Our domestic economy owes much to the ants, our commonwealth to the bees, while military science admits its indebtedness to the cranes for the practice of posting sentinels and for the triangular formation in battle. The beasts are too wise to admit Ignorance to their fellowship and society; they will force her to a lower station. What then? To stocks and stones? Why even the trees, bushes,

and whole woods once tore up their roots and hurried to hear the skillful strains of Orpheus. Often, too, they were endowed with mysterious powers and uttered divine oracles, as for instance did the rocks of Dodona.[122] Rocks, too, show a certain aptitude for learning in that they reply to the sacred words of poets; will not these also reject Ignorance? Therefore, driven lower than any kind of beast, lower than stocks and stones, lower than any natural species, will Ignorance be permitted to find repose in the famous "non-existent" of the Epicureans? No, not even there; for Ignorance must be something yet worse, yet more vile, yet more wretched, in a word the very depth of degradation.

I come now to you, my clever hearers, for even without any words of mine I see in you not so much arguments on my side as darts which I shall hurl at Ignorance until she is slain. I have sounded the attack, do you rush into battle; put this enemy to flight, drive her from your porticos and walks. If you allow her to exist, you yourselves will be that which you know to be the most wretched thing in the world. This cause is the personal concern of you all. So, if I have perchance spoken at much greater length than is customary in this place, not forgetting that this was demanded by the importance of the subject, you will, I hope, pardon me, my judges, since it is one more proof of the interest I feel in you, of my zeal on your behalf, and of the nights of toil and wakefulness I consented to endure for your sakes. I have done.

---

[119]*Morals*, ed. William W. Goodwin (Boston, 1870): 5: 179-80.
[120]In the *Historia Naturalium* (4.9.536[b]).
[121]Cicero in the De Natura Deorum 2.1.126-27 discusses the self-purgation of the ibis; Pliny discusses the hippopotamus in the act of wounding itself in specific veins in order to let blood and thereby purge itself of disease (*Natural History* 8.40-41.96-97, in the Loeb ed.).

[122]The sacred grove of oak trees at Dodona was supposed to issue prophecies (see *Paradise Lost* 1.518).

Of Reformation (1641)

OCCASION

The ninety-page pamphlet *Of Reformation* was the first of Milton's English prose tracts on the subject of church hierarchy. As David Norbrook writes, "He was moved to publish his first pamphlet . . . at a time when some kind of compromise, the 'reduced episcopacy' advocated by Ussher and supported by Quarles, seemed to be likely to prevail. Milton fiercely attacked such lukewarm compromises and urged the need for a radical break with the past" (60).

Milton had a strong ideal of what the role of a churchman should be; even a bishop should provide

> . . . the fellowly and friendly yoke of a teaching and laborious Ministery, the Pastorlike and Apostolick imitation of meeke and unlordly Discipline, the gentle and benevolent mediocritie of Church-maintenance . . . .

The prelates of the 1640s, according to Milton, were not pastors, they were not meek, they spent very little time ministering to the Church without expecting reward. Instead, the twenty-four bishops of the Church of England were wealthy and lordly; they sometimes lived in palaces; and they dressed in expensive and rare silks and satins even as they represented the Church. They had temporal power in the distribution of land and benefices—church livings granted often to the younger sons of nobility—and they had legal power in ecclesiastical courts that operated independently of their civil counterparts.

What the prelates represented to Milton was the abuse of aristocratic power and wealth, though at the time when he wrote this tract he could see nothing wrong with being wealthy or with being an aristocrat: he conceived of himself as being one of the educated elite. But the ceremonies of the Church, the rituals, the costumes, the formal recitation presided over by the prelates, all represented an excrescence on the state, and manacles on the people. Like most emerging Puritans, Milton believed in the liberty of the individual conscience to learn at home from the Bible. Instead, the prelates represented compulsory church attendance, ceremonies enforced on people from birth through death, and a code of private behavior that might dictate whether or not one might be allowed to pray or hold a religious service at home, or enjoy sports in public (Marcus).

At this point in his political career, Milton seems still to believe strongly in monarchy as the best form of government (he was never against the institution of kings, though he opposed tyranny). One can see the beginnings of democratic or representative church government, at least, in his suggestion that bishops should be elected officials, as they were in the early church. In other words, a bishop should, he thought, be voted into office, and not appointed for life by a king or an archbishop.

AUDIENCE

It is difficult to say for sure that the "Sir" addressed constantly in the tract is any individual being. Tony Davies writes, confidently, that the tract is a letter to a friend, but, if it is, that friend is kept at a formal distance by the respectful "Sir," as Samuel Hartlib is kept at a distance by being called "Master" as he is addressed in *Of Education*. At times, toward the end, the "Sir" addressed by Milton seems to be God, to whom a prayer is offered; with God's help, Milton will "lift up [his] hands to that Eternall and Propitious *Throne*, where nothing is readier then *grace* and *refuge* to the distresses of mortall Suppliants . . . ."

For Milton, quoting the Bible was a political act. His polemic against corruption within the English church took a vivid biblical image—"So then because thou art lukewarm, and neither hot nor cold, I will spue thee out of my mouth" (Revelation 3.16)—to make it into the "queasy temper of luke-warmnesse" that would cause even God to vomit (877 below). What the modern reader can't know is that such queasiness was one of the "commonplace tropes which evoked the power and fatal destiny of the wicked" (Tuttle 69), and that Elizabeth I had used the same image for religious indecision.

ORGANIZATION

What Elizabeth Skerpan writes about *The Tenure of Kings and Magistrates* applies equally well to *Of Reformation*: "Milton is one of the very few Independents to present a full rereading of history, law, and religion in one tract" (128). Milton, with his rhetorical control, undertakes a complete transformation of his reader's attitudes toward life. He has a plan for England that will include reformation of its church, altering its education, changing its form of government, and even improving its poetry.

IMAGERY

Images run wild in *Of Reformation*. The reader often is carried along on waves of imagery, and I do mean that seriously. The one extended metaphor—prelacy as a wen next to the head of the state—is a prose poem built on an image, an amazing feat of creative rhetoric. It is the "noysom, and diseased tumor of Prelacie" that Milton attacks, as compared with the image of the true church as "members of the mystical body of Christ" (Yale 1: 519n). That tumor becomes the famous "Wen" of the Tale that Milton inserts into his argument (859). What ought to be a mystical body has developed a very real-looking excrescence, an exterior tumor, that is repulsive and funny at the same time. Grotesqueness serves Milton's satire well.

Milton also frames the organization of the tract with allegorical entities waging an everlasting war between good and evil. When an early Christian Emperor, Theodosius, is found capable of "heroick *humility*," he is indeed an ideal human being, as are those men capable of meekness or largeness of mind—magnanimity, a virtue that Milton never stopped emphasizing in his prose and his poetry: "to govern well is to train up a Nation in true wisdom and vertue, and that which springs from thence magnanimity, (take heed of that) and that which is our beginning, regeneration, and happiest end, likenes to *God* . . . ."

TEXT

Of Reformation is well-printed by the standards that usually apply to the ephemeral or temporary world of the seventeenth-century political or religious pamphleteer. By modern standards, the text is presented as overemphatic: many nouns and some adjectives are capitalized; italicized words and phrases are used in almost every sentence; even punctuation marks like colons and semicolons seem to be used too often for modern tastes. But the italics seem to tell us what words the author wants to be emphasized, or how they might be pronounced. In a phrase like "guegaw's fetcht from *Arons* old wardrope, or the *Flamins vestry*," the phonetic spellings of "guegaw's," "*Arons*," "wardrope," even "fetcht," indicate how we are to say the words (Milton's headmaster at St. Paul's School, Alexander Gil the Elder, emphasized phonetic spelling in his own grammar book). The italics on "*Flamins vestry*" give us a hint that Milton wants us to take the phrase satirically, picturing the Roman priests hanging their robes in an English church vestry. And of course printers in the 1640s did not prefer to use quotation marks, so that quotations, even from the Bible, would be indicated by italics.

Italics also mark a darker side of language, as when *Rome* is italicized, but not "Jew," "Sarazen," or "Turk." More positively, italics indicate something like allegorical status, as with deified words like *God*. On one pair of pages selected at random, here are the words italicized:

pure worship	*envie*
God	*craft*
justice	*malice*
vertue	*Aphorismers*
wisdome	*Politicasters*
unity	
peace	
pure doctrine	
gratulation	
union	
salvation	

I have arranged the "good" words and phrases, in the left column, and lined them up against the "bad" ones in the right. Even in the italics, good wins over evil with greater numbers. With such an arrangement it becomes easy to see that Milton, in cahoots with the compositor, has set a moral or ethical structure in the very appearance of the emphasized words on the page. In terms of italics, good is winning out over evil.

Throughout most of the tract, if I am right about the type-setting of the pamphlet, the compositor who set most of the text was collaborating closely with Milton, using what might be called rhetorical italics to emphasize words meant to be read emphatically. He was not following Milton's preferred spelling of some important words, such as "Parliament" (Milton spelled it "Parlament" almost invariably), or "chief" (Milton generally preferred "ei" in that group of words), or "their" (Milton spelled it "thir" or "thire," not in the preferred form of his day and ours). I should point out that printing styles for italics, spelling, and punctuation were far from standardized in the seventeenth century.

As copy-text I will use the Bodleian copy of *Of Reformation*, which was included in the group of eleven pamphlets that Milton gave to the library apparently at the request of John Rouse, the Librarian. Rouse's "claim that he did not know how to tell a lie and was unable to praise a bad book was perhaps echoed when John Milton in 1646 sent copies of some of his polemical writings to the Library, a gift he addressed personally to Rouse as a most learned man and a good judge of books. Rouse had possibly shown his judgement in this instance by soliciting the gift" (Philip 42–43).

Works Cited

Editions are identified with an asterisk

*Davies, Tony, ed. *John Milton: Selected Shorter Poems and Prose.* London: Routledge, 1988.

*Hale, Will T., ed. *Of Reformation.* New Haven: Yale UP, 1916.

Kranidas, Thomas. "Milton's *Of Reformation*: The Politics of Vision." *ELH* 49 (1982): 497–513.

Lieb, Michael. "Milton's *Of Reformation* and the Dynamics of Controversy." *Achievements of the Left Hand: Essays on the Prose of John Milton,* ed. Michael Lieb and John T. Shawcross. Amherst: U of Massachusetts P, 1974. 55–82.

Loewenstein, David. *Milton and the Drama of History: Historical Vision, Iconoclasm, and the Literary Imagination.* Cambridge: Cambridge UP, 1990.

Marcus, Leah S. *The Politics of Mirth: Jonson, Herrick, Milton, Marvell, and the Defense of Old Holiday Pastimes.* Chicago, IL: U of Chicago P, 1986.

Mueller, Janel. "Embodying Glory: the Apocalyptic Strain in Milton's *Of Reformation,* in *Politics, Poetics, and Hermeneutics in Milton's Prose.* Ed. David Loewenstein and James Grantham Turner. Cambridge: Cambridge UP, 1990. 9–40.

Philip, Ian. *The Bodleian Library in the Seventeenth & Eighteenth Centuries.* Oxford: Clarendon, 1983.

Skerpan, Elizabeth. *The Rhetoric of Politics in the English Revolution, 1642–1660.* Columbia: U of Missouri P, 1992.

Stavely, Keith. *The Politics of Milton's Prose Style.* New Haven, CT: Yale UP, 1975.

Tuttle, Elizabeth. "Biblical Reference in the Political Pamphlets of the Levelers and Milton, 1638–1654." *Milton and Republicanism.* Ed. David Armitage, Armand Himy, and Quentin Skinner. Cambridge: Cambridge UP, 1995. 63–81.

OF
REFORMATION
IN
ENGLAND,

And the CAVVSES that hitherto have hindred it.

Sir,

Amidst those deepe and retired thoughts, which with every man Christianly instructed, ought to be most frequent, of *God,* and of his miraculous *ways,* and *works,* amongst men, and of our *Religion* and *Worship,* be perform'd to him; after the story of our Saviour *Christ,* suffering to the lowest bent of weakness, in the *Flesh,* and presently triumphing to the highest pitch of *glory,* in the *Spirit,* which drew up his body also, till we in both be united to him in the Revelation of his Kingdome: I do not know of any thing more worthy to take up the whole passion of pitty, on the one side, and joy on the other: then to consider first, the foule and sudden corruption, and then after many a tedious age, the long-deferr'd; but much more wonderfull and happy reformation of the *Church* in these latter days. Sad it is to thinke how that Doctrine of the *Gospel,* planted by teachers Divinely inspir'd, and by them winnow'd,[1] and sifted, from the chaffe of overdated Ceremonies, and refin'd to such a Spirituall height, and temper of purity, and knowledge of the Creator, that the body, with all the circumstances of time and place, were purifi'd by the affections of the regenerat Soule, and nothing[2] left impure, but sinne; *Faith* needing not the weak, and fallible office of the Senses, to be either the Ushers, or Interpreters, of heavenly Mysteries, save where our Lord himselfe in his Sacraments ordain'd; that such a Doctrine should through the grossenesse, and blindnesse, of her Professors, and the fraud of deceivable traditions, drag so downwards, as to backslide one way into the Jewish beggery, of old cast rudiments, and

---

[1] The image is of the sifting and winnowing of wheat, during which the chaff is allowed to blow away. "To separate the wheat from the chaff" is still proverbial.

[2] "In no way."

stumble forward another way into the new-vomited Paganisme, of sensuall[3] Idolatry, attributing purity, or impurity, to things indifferent, that they might bring the inward acts of the *Spirit* to the outward, and customary ey-Service[4] of the body, as if they could make *God* earthly, and fleshly, because they could not make themselves *heavenly*, and *Spirituall*: they began to draw downe all the Divine intercours,[5] betwixt *God*, and the Soule, yea, the very shape of *God* himselfe, into an exterior, and bodily forme, urgently pretending a necessity, and obligement of joyning the body in a formall reverence, and Worship circumscrib'd they hallow'd it, they fum'd it,[6] they sprinkel'd it, they be deck't it, not in robes of pure innocency, but of pure Linnen, with other deformed, and fantastick dresses in Palls, and Miters, gold, and guegaw's[7] fetcht from *Arons* old wardrope, or the *Flamins vestry*: then was the *Priest* set to *con his motions*, and his *Postures* his *Liturgies*, and his *Lurries*, till the Soule by this meanes of over-bodying her selfe, given up justly to fleshly delights, bated her wing apace downeward: and finding the ease she had from her visible, and sensuous collegue the body in performance of *Religious* duties her pineons now broken, and flagging, shifted off from her selfe, the labour of high soaring any more, forgot her heavenly flight, and left the dull, and droyling[8] carcas to plod on in the old rode, and drudging Trade of outward conformity. And here out of question from her pervers conceiting of *God*, and holy things, she had faln to beleeve no *God* at all, had not custome and the worme of conscience nipt her incredulity hence to all the duty's of evangelicall grace instead of the adoptive and cheerefull boldnesse which our new alliance with *God* requires, came Servile, and thrallike feare: for in very deed, the superstitious man by his good will is an Atheist; but being scarr'd from thence by the pangs, and gripes of a boyling conscience, all in a pudder shuffles up to himselfe such a *God*, and such a worship as is most agreeable to remedy his feare, which feare of his, as also is his hope, fixt onely upon the *Flesh*, renders likewise the whole faculty of his apprehension, carnall, and all the

inward acts of *worship* issuing from the native strength of the SOULE, run out lavishly to the upper skin, and there harden into a crust of Formallitie. Hence men came to scan the *Scriptures*, by the letter, and in the Covenant of our Redemption, magnifi'd the external signs more then the quickning power of the *Spirit*, and yet looking on them through their own guiltinesse with a Servile feare, and finding as little comfort, or rather terror from them againe, they knew not how to hide their Slavish approach to *Gods* behests by them not understood, nor worthily receav'd, but by cloaking their Servile crouching to all *Religious* Presentments, somtimes lawfull, somtimes Idolatrous, under the name of *humility*, and terming the Py-bald frippery, and ostentation of Ceremony's, decency.[9]

Then was Baptisme chang'd into a kind of exorcisme, and water Sanctifi'd by *Christs* institute, thought little enough to wash off the originall Spot without the Scratch, or crosse impression of a Priests fore-finger:[10] and that feast of free grace, and adoption to which *Christ* invited his disciples to sit as Brethren, and coheires of the happy Covenant, which at that Table was to be Seal'd to them, even that Feast of love and heavenly-admitted fellowship, the Seale of filiall grace became the Subject of horror, and glouting[11] adoration, pageanted about, like a dreadfull[12] Idol: which sometimes deceve's wel-meaning men, and beguiles them of their reward, by their voluntary humility, which indeed, is fleshly pride, preferring a foolish Sacrifice, and the rudiments of the world, as Saint *Paul* to the *Colossians* explaineth, before a savory obedience to *Christs* example. Such was *Peters* unseasonable Humilitie, as then his Knowledge was small, when *Christ* came to wash his feet; who at an impertinent time would needs straine courtesy with his Master, and falling troublesomly upon the lowly, alwise, and unexaminable intention of *Christ*[13] in what he went with resolution to doe, so provok't by his interruption the meeke *Lord*, that he threat'nd to exclude him from his heavenly Portion, unlesse he could be content to be lesse arrogant, and stiff neckt in his humility.

But to dwell no longer in characterizing the *Depravities* of the *Church*, and how they sprung, and how they tooke increase; when I recall to mind at last, after so many darke Ages, wherein the huge overshadowing

---

[3]The "n" in "sensuall" had been turned upside down by the compositor. Presumably it was Milton himself who called attention to this mistake in the Bodleian copy by putting a dot over what appears to be a "u."

[4]"The action or conduct of an eye-servant; service performed only under inspection or under the master's eye" (*OED* 1a).

[5]They begin to bring to bear, in the argument, supposed dialogue or negotiation ("intercours") between God and the spirit.

[6]The series of verbs describes part of the rituals of the Roman Catholic Church, among them the use of holy water and of incense, and part of the rich costuming.

[7]Variant spelling of "gewgaw," "A gaudy trifle, plaything, or ornament, a pretty thing of little value, a toy or bauble" (*OED* 1).

[8]Drudging, working in slave-labor.

---

[9]"Calling the frippery of multicolored robes and ostentatious ceremony decency." The word "piebald" suggests "mongrel" or "incongruous."

[10]The marking of the cross in holy water on the infant's head in the baptism service is supposed to wash off original sin.

[11]"Glowering," "sullen." Ominous clouds were said to be glouting.

[12]"Awe-inspiring," "frightening."

[13]"The humble, all-wise, and unquestionable intention of Christ."

traine of *Error* had almost swept all the Starres out of the Firmament of the *Church*; how the bright and blissfull *Reformation* (by Divine Power) strook through the black and settled Night of *Ignorance* and *Anti-christian Tyranny*, me thinks a soveraigne and reviving joy must needs rush into the bosome of him that reads or heares; and the sweet Odour of the returning *Gospell* imbath his Soule with the fragrancy of Heaven. Then was the Sacred BIBLE sought out of the dusty corners where prophane *Falshood* and *Neglect* had throwne it, the *Schooles* opened, *Divine* and *Humane Learning* rak't out of the embers of *forgotten Tongues*, the *Princes* and *Cities* trooping apace to the new erected Banner of *Salvation*; the *Martyrs*, with the unresistable *might* of *Weaknesse*, shaking the *Powers* of *Darknesse*, and scording the *fiery rage* of the old *red Dragon*.

The pleasing pursuit of these thoughts hath oft-times led mee into a serious question and debatement with my selfe, how it should come to passe that *England* (having had this *grace* and *honour* from GOD to be the first that should set up a Standard for the recovery of *lost Truth*,[14] and blow the first *Evangelick Trumpet* to the *Nations*, holding up, as from a Hill, the new Lampe of *saving-light* to all Christendome should now be last, and most unsettl'd in the enjoyment of that *Peace*, whereof she[15] taught the way to others' although indeed our *Wicklefs* preaching, at which all the succeding *Reformers* more effectually lighted their *Tapers*, was to his Countrey-men but a short blaze soone dampt[16] and stifl'd by the *Pope*, and *Prelates* for sixe or seven Kings Reignes; yet me thinkes the *Precedencie* which GOD gave this *Iland*, to be the first *Restorer* of *buried Truth*, should have beene followed with more happy success, and sooner attain'd Perfection; in which, as yet we are amongst the last: for, albeit in *purity* of *Doctrine* we agree with our Brethren; yet in discipline[17] which is the *execution* and *applying* of *Doctrine* home, and laying the *salve* to the very *Orifice* of the *wound*; yea tenting[18] and searching to the *Core*, without which *Pulpit Preaching* is but shooting at Rovers;[19] in this we are no better than a *Schisme*, from all

the *Reformation*, and a sore scandall to them, for while wee hold *Ordination* to belong onely to *Bishops*, as our *Prelates* doe, wee must of necessity hold also their *Ministers* to be no *Ministers*, and shortly after their *Church* to be no *Church*. Not to speake of those sence-lesse *Ceremonies* which wee onely retaine, as a dangerous earnest[20] of sliding back to *Rome*, and serving meerely, either as a mist to cover nakednesse where true *grace* is extinguisht; or as an Enterlude[21] to set out the *pompe* of *Prelatisme*. Certainly it would be worth the while therefore and the paines, to enquire more particularly, what, and how many the chiefe causes have been that have still hindred our *Uniforme Consent* to the rest of the *Churches* abroad, (at this time especially) when the *Kingdome* is in a good *propensity* thereto; and all Men in Prayers, in Hopes, or in Disputes, either for or against it.

Yet will I not insist on that which may seeme to be the cause on GODS part; as his judgement on our sinnes, the tryall of his owne, the unmasking of Hypocrites; nor shall I stay to speake of the continuall eagernes and extreame diligence of the *Pope* and *Papists* to stop the furtherance of *Reformation*, which know they have no hold or hope of *England* their lost Darling, longer then the *goverment* of *Bishops* bolsters them out; and therefore plot all they can to uphold them, as may bee seene by the *Book of Santa Clara*[22] the Popish *Preist*[23] in defence of *Bishops*, which came out piping hot much about the time that one of our own *Prelats* out of an ominous feare had writ on the same *Argument*; as if they had joyn'd their forces like good Confederates to support one falling *Babel*.

But I shall cheifly indeavour to declare those Causes that hinder the forwarding of *true Discipline*, which are among our selves. Orderly proceeding will divide our inquirie into our *Fore-Fathers dayes*, and into *our Times*. HENRY the 8. was the first that rent this *Kingdome* from the *Popes* Subjection totally; but his Quarrell being more about *Supremacie*, then other faultinesse in *Religion* that he regarded, it is no marvell if hee stuck where

---

[14]Before the phrase "*lost Truth*," the Bodleian copy had had the word "else," which has been struck through, again presumably by the pen of Milton.

[15]The Bodleian text has "we," which has a mark of correction over it, with "she" written in the margin with a similar mark, indicating that the "we" should be corrected. "Christendome" thus assumes a gender and not a collective identity.

[16]Extinguished.

[17]The text in the Bodleian copy read "in the *execution*," but Milton crossed out "the" and added "discipline wch is the" in the right margin.

[18]"Probing," here extending the image of the wound (see *OED* "tent" 1a, b).

[19]Shooting arrows at random targets, as compared with shooting at "butts," which are at a fixed distance.

[20]Pledge.

[21]Milton uses the theatrical term sardonically, since an interlude was usually a short comic piece in the middle of a morality play, another kind of senseless ceremony.

[22]Franciscus Sancta Clara, whose *Apologia Episcoporum seu Sacri Magistratus* (1640) may be referred to. This renegade convert to Roman Catholicism was born in Coventry, England, as Christopher Davenport. Milton may have known that Sancta Clara (his name seems to be a conflation of the names of St. Francis and St. Clare) had met Archbishop Laud at the court of Charles I and that Francis Rous had accused him of trying to emend the Articles of Religion to make them conform with Catholic beliefs (Yale 1: 528–29n39).

[23]One of Milton's preferred spellings seems to have crept in through the compositor. See "cheifly" at the beginning of the next paragraph.

he did. The next default was in the *Bishops*, who though they had renounc't the *Pope*, they still hugg'd the *Pope-dome*, and shar'd the Authority among themselves, by their sixe bloody Articles persecuting the *Protestants* no slacker then the *Pope* would have done. And doutles, when ever the Pope shall fall, if his ruine bee not like the sudden-down-come of a Towre, the *Bishops*, when they see him tottering, will leave him, and fall to scrambling, catch who may, hee a Patriarch-dome, and another what comes next hand; as the French Cardinall of late, and the *See* of *Canterbury* hath plainly affected.

In *Edward* the 6. Dayes, why a compleate *Reform* was not effected, to any considerate man may appease. First, he no sooner entred into his Kingdome, but into a Warre with *Scotland*; from whence the Protector returning with Victory had but newly put his hand to repeale the 6. *Articles*, and throw the Images out of *Churches*, but Rebellions on all sides stir'd up by obdurate Papists, and other Tumults[24] with a plaine Warre in *Norfolke*, holding tack[25] against two of the Kings *Generals*, made them of force content themselves with what they had already done. Hereupon follow'd ambitious Contentions among the *Peeres*, which ceas'd not but with the Protectors death, who was the most zealous in this point: and then *Northumberland* was hee that could doe most in *England*, who little minding *Religion*, (as his Apostacie well shew'd at his death, bent all his wit how to bring the Right of the *Crowne* into his owne Line. And for the *Bishops*, they were so far from any such worthy Attempts, as that they suffer'd themselvs to be the common[26] stales[27] to countenance with their prostituted Gravities every Politick Fetch that was then on foot, as oft as the Potent *Statists* pleas'd to employ them. Never do we read that they made use of their Authority and high Place of accesse, to bring the jarring Nobility to *Christian peace*, or to withstand their disloyall Projects; but if a Toleration for *Masse* were to be beg'd of the King for his Sister MARY, lest CHARLES the Fifth should be angry; who but the grave Prelates *Cranmer* and *Ridley* must be sent to extort it from the young King? But out of the mouth of that godly and Royall *Childe*, Christ himselfe return'd such an awfull repulse to those halting and time-serving *Prelates*, that after much bold importunity, they went their way not without shame and teares.

Nor was this the first time that they discover'd[28] to bee followers of this World; for when the Protectors Brother, Lord *Sudley*, the Admirall through private malice and mal-engine[29] was to lose his life, no man could bee found fitter then Bishop *Latimer* (like another Doctor *Shaw*) to divulge in his Sermon the forged Accusations laid to his charge, thereby to defame him with the People, who else was thought would take ill the innocent mans death, unlesse the Reverend *Bishop* could warrant them there was no foule play. What could be more impious then to debarre the Children of the King from their right to the Crowne? To comply with the ambitious Usurpation of a Traytor; and to make void the last Will of HENRY 8. To which the Breakers had sworne observance? Yet Bishop *Cranmer*, one of the Executors, and the other *Bishops* none refusing, (lest they should resist the Duke of *Northumberland*) could find in their Consciences to set their hands to the disinabling and defeating not onely of Princesse MARY the *Papist*, but of ELIZABETH the *Protestant*, and (by the Bishops judgement) the Lawfull Issue of King HENRY.

Who then can thinke, (though these *Prelates* had sought a further *Reformation*) that the least wry[30] face of a *Politician* would not have hush't them. But it will be said, These men were *Martyrs*: What then? Though every true Christian will be a *Martyr* when he is called to it; not presently does it follow that every one suffering for Religion, is without exception. Saint *Paul* writes, that *A man may give his Body to be burnt*, (meaning for Religion) *and yet not have Charitie*: He is not therfore above all possibility of erring, because hee burnes for some Points of Truth.

Witnes the *Arians* and *Pelagians* which were slaine by the Heathen for *Christs* sake; yet we take both these for no true friends of *Christ*. If the *Martyrs* (saith *Cyprian* in his 30. Epistle) decree one thing, and the *Gospel* another, either the *Martyrs* must lose their Crowne by not observing the *Gospel* for which they are *Martyrs*; or the Majestie of the *Gospel* must be broken and lie flat, if it can be overtopt by the *novelty* of any other *Decree*.

And heerewithall I invoke the *Immortall* DEITIE *Reveler*[31] and *Judge* of Secrets, That wherever I have in this BOOKE plainely and roundly[32] (though worthily and truly) laid open the faults and blemishes of *Fathers*,[33]

---

[24]Public disturbances, riots, as contrasted with full-scale war.

[25]Perhaps holding to a zig-zag or circuitous course, as in nautical language (compare *OED* 2.b).

[26]I have expanded the word from "commõ," as it was printed in the Bodleian copy.

[27]Prostitutes of a lower order, fitting with "prostituted," "Fetch" (probably "decoy" or pimp—see *OED* 5), and "Potent."

[28]"They revealed themselves to be."

[29]Fraud, deceitfulness. Spenser used the word in *The Faerie Queene* 3.1.53.

[30]Contorted, grotesque.

[31]Revealer (through prophecies).

[32]Thoroughly, completely.

[33]The early Fathers of the Christian Church, such as Augustine, Tertullian, or Jerome.

Martyrs, or Christian *Emperors*; or have otherwise inveighed against Error and Superstition with vehement Expressions: I have done it, neither out of malice, nor list to speak evill, nor any vaine-glory; but of meere necessity, to vindicate the spotlesse *Truth* from an ignominious bondage, whose native worth is now become of such a low esteeme, that shee is like to finde small credit with us for what she can say, unlesse shee can bring a Ticket from *Cranmer*, *Latimer*, and *Ridley*; or prove her selfe a retainer to *Constantine*, and weare his *badge*. More tolerable it were for the *Church* of GOD that all these Names were utterly abolisht, like the *Brazen Serpent*; then that mens fond opinions should thus idolize them, and the Heavenly *Truth* be thus captivated.

Now to proceed, whatsoever the *Bishops* were, it seemes they themselves were unsatisfi'd in matters of *Religion*, as they then stood, by that Commission granted to 8. *Bishops*,[34] 8. Other *Divines*, 8. *Civilians*, 8. common *Lawyers*, to frame *Ecclesiasticall Constitutions*; which no wonder if it came to nothing; for (as *Hayward* relates) both their Professions and their Ends were different. Lastly, we all know by Examples, that exact *Reformation* is not perfited[35] at the first push, and those unweildy Times of *Edward* 6. May hold some Plea by this excuse: Now let any reasonable man judge whether that *Kings Reigne* be a fit time from whence to patterne out the Constitution of a *Church Discipline*, much lesse that it should yeeld occasion from whence to foster and establish the continuance of Imperfection with the commendatory subscriptions of *Confessors* and *Martyrs*, to intitle and ingage a glorious *Name* to a grosse corruption. It was not *Episcopacie* that wrought in them the Heavenly Fortitude of *Martyrdome*; as little is it that *Martyrdome* can make good *Episcopacie*: But it was *Episcopacie* that let the good and holy Men through the temptation of the *Enemie*, and the snare of this present world to many blame-worthy and opprobrious *Actions*. And it is still *Episcopacie* that before all our eyes worsens and sluggs[36] the most learned, and seeming religious of our *Ministers*, who no sooner advanc't to it, but like a seething pot set to coole, sensibly exhale and reake out the greatest part of that zeale, and those Gifts which were formerly in them, settling in a skinny congealment of ease and sloth at the top:[37] and if they keep their

Learning by some potent sway of Nature, 'tis a rare chance; but their *devotion* most commonly comes to that queazy temper of luke-warmnesse, that gives a Vomit to GOD himselfe.[38]

But what doe wee suffer mis-shapen and enormous *Prelatisme*, as we do, thus to blanch[39] and varnish her deformities with the faire colours, as before of *Martrdome*, so now of *Episcopacie*? They are not *Bishops*, GOD and all *good Men* know they are not, that have fill'd this Land with late confusion and violence; but a Tyrannicall crew and Corporation of Imposters, that have blinded and abus'd the World so longer under that Name. He that inabl'd with *gifts* from *God*, and the lawfull and Primitive choyce of the *Church* assembl'd in convenient number, faithfully from that time forward feeds his Parochiall *Flock*, ha's his coequall and compresbyteriall Power to ordaine *Ministers* and *Deacons* by publique Prayer, and *Vote* of *Christs* Congregation in like sort as he himselfe was ordain'd, and is a true *Apostolick Bishop*. But when hee steps up into the Chayre of *Pontificall* Pride, and changes a moderate and exemplary House, for a mis-govern'd and haughty *Palace, spirituall Dignity* for carnall *Precedence*, and *secular high Office* and *employment* for the high *Negotiations* of his Heavenly *Embassage*, Then he *degrades*, then hee *un-Bishops* himself; hee that makes him *Bishop* makes him no *Bishop*. No marvell therfore if S. *Martin* complain'd to *Sulpitius Severus* that since hee was *Bishop* he felt inwardly a sensible decay of those *vertues* and *graces* that *God*[40] had given him in great measure before; Although the same *Sulpitius* write that he was nothing tainted, or alter'd in his *habit, dyet*, and personall *demeanour* from that simple plainnesse to which he first betook himselfe. It was not therfore that thing alone which *God* took displeasure at the *Bishops* of those times, but rather an universall rottennes, and gangrene in the whole *Function*.

From hence I pass to Qu. ELIZABETH, the next *Protestant* Prince, in whose Dayes why Religion attain'd not a perfect reducement in the beginning of her Reigne, I suppose the hindring Causes will be found to bee common with some formerly alledg'd for King EDWARD 6. The greennesse of the Times, the weake Estate which

---

[34]The printing house convention was to include periods after each number; this is a series of offices all gathered in groups of eight.
[35]Perfected, or brought to a conclusion or proper end. "Perfect" could be spelled "perfite" or "perfait."
[36]Probably "causes to slow down or become lazy." The more familiar form of the word now would be "slogs."
[37]The thin layer of "grease," in other words, comes to the top of the pot as the broth cools. As the steam of zeale is wasted, greasy sloth and ease remain behind.

[38]A striking, and perhaps disgusting image, but an effective one, derived from Revelation: "I know thy works, that thou art neither cold nor hot: I would thou wert cold or hot. So then because thou art lukewarm, and neither cold nor hot, I will spue thee out of my my mouth" (3.15–18). It is characteristic of the Old Testament as well to allow to God human characteristics such as anger, love, and the sensual abilities to smell odors (see *Paradise Lost* 9.197) or feel nausea.
[39]Color white with make-up such as ceruse or lead arsenate.
[40]It may not be significant, but the compositor has switched from setting the name "God" from small capital letters to italics.

Qu. MARY left the Realme in, the great Places and Office executed by *Papists*, the *Judges*, the *Lawyers*, the *Justices* of Peace for the most part *Popish*, the *Bishops* firme to *Rome*, from whence was to be expected the furious flashing of Excommunications, and absolving the *People* from their Obedience. Next, her private *Councellours*, whosoever they were, perswaded her (as *Camden* writes) that the altering of *Ecclesiasticall Politie*, would move sedition. Then was the *Liturgie* given to a number of moderate *Divines*, and Sir *Tho. Smith* a Statesman to bee purg'd, and Physick't: And surely they were moderate *Divines* indeed, neither hot nor cold; and *Grindall* the best of them, afterwards *Arch-Bishop* of *Canterbury* lost favour in the Court, and I think was discharg'd the goverment of his *See* for favouring the *Ministers*, though *Camden* seeme willing to finde another Cause: therefore about her second Yeare in a *Parliament* of Men and Minds some scarce well grounded, others belching the soure Crudities of yesterdayes *Poperie*, those Constitutions of EDW. 6. Which as you heard before, no way satisfi'd the men that made them, are now establish't for best, and not to be mended. From that time follow'd nothing but Imprisonments, troubles, disgraces on all those that found fault with the *Decrees* of the Convocation, and strait were they branded with the Name of *Puritans*. As for the Queene herselfe, shee was made beleeve that by putting down *Bishops* her *Prerogative* would be infring'd, of which shall be spoken anon, as the course of Method brings it in. And why the *Prelats* labour'd it should be so thought, ask not them, but ask their Bellies. They had found a good Tabernacle, they sate under a spreading Vine, their Lot was fallen in a faire Inheritance. And these perhaps were the cheife impeachments of a more sound rectifying the *Church* in the Queens time.

From this Period I count to begin our Times, which, because they concerne us more neerely, and our owne eyes and eares can give us the ampler scope to judge, will require a more exact search; and to effect this the speedier, I shall distinguish such as I esteeme to be the hinderers of *Reformation* into 3. Sorts, *Antiquarians* (for so I had rather call them then *Antiquaries*,[41] whose labours are usefull and laudable) 2. *Libertines*, 3. *Politi-tians*.

To the votarists of Antiquity I shall think to have fully answer'd, if I shall be able to prove out of

Antiquity, First, that if they will conform our Bishops[42] to the purer times, they must mew their feathers, and their pounces,[43] and make but curtail'd Bishops of them; and we know they hate to be dockt and clipt, as much as to be put down outright. Secondly, that those purer times were corrupt, and their Books corrupted soon after. Thirdly, that the best of those that then wrote, disclaim that any man should repose on them, and send all to the Scriptures.

First therfore, if those that over-affect Antiquity, will follow the square therof, their Bishops must be elected by the hands of the whole *Church*. The ancientest of the extant Fathers *Ignatius*, writing to the Philadelphians saith, *that it belongs to them as to the Church of God to choose a Bishop.* Let no man cavill,[44] but take the Church of *God* as meaning the whole consistence of Orders and Members, as S. *Pauls* Epistles express, and this likewise being read over: Besides this, it is there to be mark'd, that those Philadelphians are exhorted to choose a Bishop of *Antioch*. Whence it seems by the way that there was not that wary limitation of Dioces in those times, which is confirm'd even by a fast friend of Episcopacie, *Camden*,[45] who cannot but love Bishops, as well as old coins, and his much lamented Monasteries for antiquities sake. He writes in his description of *Scotland, that over all the world Bishops had no certaine Dioces, till Pope* Dionysius *about the yeare* 268, *did cut them out, and that the Bishops of Scotland executed their function in what place soever they came indifferently, and without distinction till King* Malcolm *the third, about the yeare* 1070, whence may be guest what their function was: was it to goe about circl'd with a band of rooking[46] Officials, with cloke bagges[47] full of Citations, and Processes to be serv'd by a corporalty of griffonlike Promooters, and Apparitors?[48] Did he goe about to pitch down his Court, as an Empirick[49] does his banck, to inveigle in all the mony of the Countrey?[50] no certainly it

---

[41]A collector of antique things, as compared with Milton's coined word "Antiquitarian," which the *OED* defines as "One attached to the practices or opinions of antiquity," citing this as the first instance.

[42]For some reason, the compositor stops italicizing the word "bishop" at this point, except in quotations, and he does not resume italicizing the word for some time.

[43]Apparently we are in the world of falconry, in which both feathers and claws (pounces) might be contained (mewed) or clipped. Since Milton's application of the word *pounce* to humans is the first recorded in the *OED*, it seems impossible to determine exactly how he meant it.

[44]Quibble; argue in a petty way.

[45]The Elizabethan antiquary and historian William Camden, whose *Brittania* is full of drawings of Roman coins.

[46]"Cheating," "swindling," as in "He was rooked out of his money."

[47]Presumably bags or pockets in their ecclesiastical cloaks.

[48]Probably in this case the griffon refers to a griffon-vulture (see *OED* "griffon" 4, which cites this instance). The "Apparitor" seems to be an official in an ecclesiastical court. The image is one of rapacious public church officials.

[49]Apparently a charlatan with a money-lending scheme (see *OED* 2.b).

[50]I have silently expanded the spelling "Coũtrey" in the Bodleian copy.

would not have bin permitted him to exercise any such function indifferently wherever he came. And verily some such matter it was as want of a fat Dioces that kept our Britain Bishops so poore in the Primitive times, that being call'd to the Councell of *Ariminum* in the yeare 359. they had not wherewithall to defray the charges of their journey, but were fed, and lodg'd upon the Emperors cost, which must needs be no accidentall, but usuall poverty in them, for the author *Sulp. Severus* in his 2 Booke of Church History praises them, and avouches it praise-worthy in a Bishop, to be so poore as to have nothing of his own. But to return to the ancient election of Bishops that it could not lawfully be without the consent of the people is so expresse in *Cyprian*, and so often to be met with, that to cite each place at large, were to translate a good part of the volume, therfore touching the chief passages, I referre the rest to whom so list peruse the Author himselfe: in the 24. Epist. *If a Bishop* saith he, *be once made and allow'd by the testimony and judgement of his collegues, and the people, no other can be made.* In the 55. *When a Bishop is made by the suffrage of all the people in peace.* In the 68. Marke but what he saies, *The people chiefly hath power, either of choosing worthy ones, or refusing unworthy*: this he there proves by authorities out of the old and new Testament, and with solid reasons these were his antiquities.

This voyce of the people to be had ever in Episcopal elections was so well known, before *Cyprians* time, even to those that were without the Church, that the Emperor *Alexander Severus* desir'd to have his governours of Provinces chosen in the same manner, as *Lampridius* can tell: So little thought it he offensive to Monarchy; and if single authorities perswade not, hearken what the whole generall Council of *Nicæa* the first and famousest of all the rest determines, writing a Synodal *Epist.* To the African Churches, to warn them of *Arrianisme*, it exhorts them to choose orthodox Bishops in the place of the dead so they be worthy, and the people choose them, whereby they seem to make the peoples assent so necessary; that merit without their free choyce were not sufficient to make a Bishop. What would ye say now grave Fathers if you should wake and see unworthy Bishops, or rather no Bishops, but Egyptian task-masters of Ceremonies thrust purposely upon the groaning Church to the affliction, and vexation of *Gods* people? It was not of old that a Conspiracie of Bishops could frustrate and fob off the right of the people, for we may read how S. *Martin* soon after *Constantine* was made Bishop of *Turon* in *France* by the peoples consent from all places thereabout

maugre all the opposition[51] that the Bishops could make. Thus went matters of the Church almost 400. yeare after *Christ*, and very probably farre lower, for *Nicephorus Phocas* the Greek Emperour, whose reign fell neare the 1000. year of our Lord, having done many things tyranically, it is said by *Cedrenus* to have done nothing more grievous and displeasing to the people, then to have inacted that no Bishop should be chosen without his will; so long did this right remain to the people in the midst of other palpable corruptions: Now for Episcopall dignity, what it was, see out of *Ignatius*, who in his Epistle to those of *Trallis* confesseth *that the Presbyters, are his fellow Counsellers, and fellow benchers.* And *Cyprian* in many places, as in the 6.41.52. Epist. speaking of *Presbyters*, calls them his *Compresbyters*, as if he deem'd himselfe no other, whenas by the same place it appeares he was a Bishop, he calls them Breathren; but that will be thought his meeknesse: yea, but the *Presbyters* and Deacons writing to him think they doe him honour enough when they phrase him to higher than Brother *Cyprian*, and deare *Cyprian* in the 26. Epist. For their Authority 'tis evident not to have bin single, but depending on the counsel of the *Presbyters*, as from *Ignatius* was erewhile alledg'd; and the same *Cyprian* acknowledges as much in the 6 Epist. And addes therto that he had determin'd from his entrance into the Office of Bishop to doe nothing without the consent of his people, and so in the 31. Epist, for it were tedious to course through all his writings which are so full of the like assertions, insomuch that ev'n in the womb and center of Apostacy *Rome* it selfe, there yet remains a glimps of this truth, for the Pope himselfe, as a learned English writer notes well, performeth all Ecclesiasticall jurisdiction as in Consistory[52] amongst his Cardinals, which were originally but the Parish Priests of *Rome*. Thus then did the Spirit of unity and meekness inspire, and animate every joynt, and sinew of the mysticall body, but now the gravest, and worthiest Minister, a true Bishop of his fold shall be revil'd, and ruffl'd by an insulting, and only-Canon-wise Prelate, as if he were some slight paltry companion: and the people of *God* redeem'd, and wash'd with *Christs* blood, and dignify'd with so many glorious titles of Saints, and sons in the Gospel, are now no better reputed then impure ethnicks,[53] and lay dogs; stones & Pillars, and Crucifixes have now the honour, and the almes due to *Christs*

---

[51]"In spite of all the opposition."

[52]"The ecclesiastical senate in which the Pope, presiding over the whole body of Cardinals, deliberates upon the affairs of the church. Also, a meeting of this body" (*OED* 2.6).

[53]People other than Christians; pagans.

living members;[54] the Table of Communion now become a Table of separation stands like an exalted platforme upon the brow of the quire, fortifi'd with bulwark, and barricado, to keep off the profane touch of the Laicks, while the obscene, and surfeted Priest scruples not to pay, and mammock the sacramentall bread, as familiarly as his Tavern Bisket. And thus the people vilifi'd and rejected by them, give over the earnest study of vertue, and godlinesse as a thing of greater purity then they need, and the search of divine knowledge as a mystery too high for their capacity's, and only for Churchmen to meddle with, which is that the Prelates desire, that when they have brought us back to Popish blindnesse we might commit to their dispose the whole managing of our salvation, for they think it was never faire world with them since that time: But he that will mould a modern Bishop into a primitive, must yeeld him to be elected by the popular voyce, undiocest, unrevenu'd, unlorded, and leave him nothing but brotherly equality, matchles temperance, frequent fasting, incessant prayer, and preaching, continual watchings, and labours in his Ministery, which what a rich bootie it would be, what a plump endowment to the many-benefice-gaping mouth of a Prelate, what a relish it would give to his canary-sucking,[55] and swan-eating palat, let old Bishop *Mountain* judge for me.

How little therfore those ancient times make for modern Bishops hath bin plainly discours'd, but let them make for them as much as they will, yet why we ought not stand to their arbitrement shall now appeare by a threefold corruption which will be found upon them. 1. The best times were spreadingly infected. 2. The best men of those times fouly tainted. 3. The best writings of those men dangerously adulterated. These Positions are to be made good out of those times witnessing of themselves. First, *Ignatius* in his early dayes testifies to the Churches of *Asia*, that even then Heresies were sprung up, and rife every where, as *Eusebius* relates in his 3. Book, 35. chap. After the Greek number. And *Hegesippus* a grave Church writer of prime Antiquity affirms in the same Book of *Euseb.* c. 32. *that while the Apostles were on earth the depravers of doctrine did but lurk, but they once gon, with open forehead*[56] *they durst preach down the truth with falsities:* yea those that are reckon'd for orthodox began to make sad, and shameful rents in the Church about the trivial celebration of Feasts, not agreeing when to keep Easter

day, which controversie grew so hot, that *Victor* the Bishop of *Rome* Excommunicated all the Churches of *Asia* for no other cause, and was worthily therof re-prov'd by *Irenæus*. For can any sound Theologer[57] think that these great Fathers understood what was Gospel, or what was Excommunication? doubtlesse that which led the good men into fraud and error was, that they attended more to the neer tradition of what they heard the Apostles somtimes did, then to what they had left written, not considering that many things which they did, were by the Apostles themselves profest to be done only for the present, and of meer indulgence to some scrupulous converts of the Circumcision, but what they writ was of firm decree to all future ages. Look but a centur lower in the 1. *cap.* of *Eusebius* 8. Book. What a universal tetter[58] of impurity had invenom'd every part, order, and degree of the Church, to omit the lay herd which will be little regarded, *those that seem'd to be our Pastors,* saith he, *overturning the Law of Gods worship, burnt in contentions one towards another, and incresing in hatred and bitternes, outragiously sought to uphold Lord-ship, and command as it were a tyranny.* Stay but a little, magnanimous Bishops, suppresse your aspiring thoughts, for there is nothing wanting but *Constantine* to reigne, and then Tyranny her selfe shall give up all her cittadels into your hands, and count ye thence forward her trustiest agents. Such were these that must be call'd the ancientest, and most virgin times between *Christ* and *Constantine*. Nor was this general contagion in their actions, and not in their writings: who is ignorant of the foul errors, the ridiculous wrestling of Scripture, and the Heresies, the vanities thick sown through the volums of *Justin Martyr, Clemens, Origen, Tertullian* and others of eldest time? Who would think him fit to write an Apology for Christian Faith to the Roman Senat, that would tell them how of the Angels, which he must needs mean those in *Gen.* call'd the *Sons of God,* mixing Women were begotten the Devills, as good *Justin Martyr* in his Apology told them. But more indignation would it move to any Christian that shall read *Tertullian* terming S. *Paul* a novice and raw in grace, for reproving S. *Peter* at *Antioch,* worthy to be blam'd if we beleeve the Epistle to the *Galatians*: perhaps from this hint the blasphemous Jesuits presum'd in *Italy* to give their judgement of S. *Paul,* as of a hot headed person, as *Sandys* in his Relations tells us.

Now besides all this, who knows not how many surreptitious works are ingraff'd[59] into the legitimate

---

[54]The members are the members of the Christian Church; the point is that things or objects of devotion have become more important than people.
[55]Gluttonous drinker of the sweet wine made in the Canary Islands.
[56]Open (honest-looking) countenance, as in "bold-face lies."

[57]Theologian, though Milton may be using the less-familiar term as a diminutive to downgrade or belittle the occupation.
[58]Literally a rash-like, pustular eruption of the skin.
[59]Grafted, as in implanting grafts on fruit trees.

writings of the Fathers, and of those Books that passe for authentick who knows what hath bin tamper'd withall, what hath bin raz'd out, what hath bin inferred, besides the late legerdemain of the Papists, that which *Sulpitious* writes concerning *Origens* Books gives us cause vehemently to suspect, there hath bin packing of old. In the third chap. of his 1. Dialogue, we may read what wrangling the Bishops and Monks had about the reading, or not reading of *Origen*, some objecting that he was corrupted by Hereticks, others answering that all such Books had bin so dealt with. How then shall I trust these times to lead me, that testifie so ill of leading themselvs, certainly of their defects their own witnesse may be best receiv'd, but of the rectitude, and sincerity of their life and doctrine to judge rightly, wee must judge by that which was to be their rule.

But it will be objected that this was an unsetl'd state of the Church wanting the temporall Magistrate to suppresse the licence of false Brethren; and the extravagancy of still-new opinions, a time not imitable for Church government, where the temporall and spirituall power did not close in one beleife, as under *Constantine*. I am not of opinion to thinke the Church a *Vine* in this respect, because, as they take it, she cannot subsist without clasping about the Elme of worldly strength, and felicity, as if the heavenly City could not support it selfe without the props and buttresses of secular Authoritie. They extoll *Constantine* because he extol'd them; as our homebred Monks in their Histories blanch[60] the Kings their Benefactors, and brand those that went about to be their Correctors. If he had curb'd the growing Pride, Avarice, and Luxury of the *Clergie*, then every Page of his Story should have swel'd with his Faults, and that which *Zozimus* the Heathen writes of him should have come in to boot: wee should have heard then in every Declamation how hee slew his Nephew *Commodus* a worthy man, his noble and eldest Son *Crispus*, his Wife *Fausta*, besides numbers of his Friends; then his cruell exactions, his unsoundness in Religion, favoring the *Arrians* that had been condemn'd in a Counsell, of which himselfe sate as it were President, his hard measure and banishment of the faithfull and invincible *Athanasius*, his living unbaptiz'd almost to his dying day; these blurs are too apparent in his Life. But since hee must needs bee the Load-starre of *Reformation* as some men clatter,[61] it will be good to see further his knowledge of *Religion* what it was, and by that we may likewise guesse at the sincerity of his Times in those that were not Hereticall, it being likely that he

would converse with the famosest *Prelates* (for so he had made them) that were to be found for learning.

Of his *Arianisme* we heard, and for the rest, a pretty scantling[62] of his Knowledge may be taken by his deferring to be baptiz'd so many yeares, a thing not unusuall, and repugnant to the Tenor of *Scripture*, *Philip* knowing nothing that should hinder the *Eunuch* to be *baptiz'd* after *profession* of his *beleife*. Next, by the excessive devotion, that I may not say Superstition both of him and his Mother *Helena* to find out the Crosse on which *Christ* suffer'd, that had long lien[63] under the rubbish of old ruines, (a thing which the Disciples and Kindred of our Saviour might with more ease have done, if they had thought it a pious duty:) some of the nailes whereof hee put into his Helmet, to beare off blowes in battell, others he fasten'd among the studds of his bridle, to fulfill (as he thought, or his Court *Bishops* perswaded him) the Prophesie of *Zachariah*; *And it shall be that that which is in the bridle shall be holy to the Lord.* Part of the Crosse, in which he thought such Vertue to reside, as would prove a kind of *Palladium* to save the *Citie* where ever it remain'd, he caus'd to be laid up in a Pillar of Porphyrie by his Statue. How hee or his Teachers could trifle thus with half an eye open upon Saint *Pauls* principles, I know not how to imagine.

How should then the dim Taper of this Emperours age that had such a need of snuffing, extend any beame to our Times wherewith wee might hope to be better lighted, then by those Luminaries that God hath set up to shine to us far neerer hand. And what *Reformation* he wrought for his owne time it will not be amisse to consider, hee apointed certain times for Fasts, and Feasts, built stately Churches, gave large Immunities[64] to the Clergie, great Riches and Promotions to *Bishops*, gave and minister'd occasion to bring in a Deluge of Ceremonies, thereby either to draw in the Heathen by a resemblance of their rites, or to set a glosse upon the simplicity, and plainnesse of Christianity which to the gorgeous solemnities of *Paganisme*, and the sense of the Worlds Children seem'd but a homely and Yeomanly *Religion*, for the beauty of inward Sanctity was not within their prospect.

So that in this manner the *Prelates* both then and ever since comming from a meane, and Plebeyan *Life* on a sudden to be Lords of stately Palaces, rich furniture, delicious fare, and *Princely* attendance, thought the plaine and homespun verity of *Christs* Gospell unfit any longer to hold their Lordships acquaintance, unlesse the poore thred-bare Matron were put into better clothes;

---

[60]"Whiten," as in "white-wash."
[61]"To talk rapidly and noisily; to talk idly; to chatter, prattle, babble" (*OED* 3).

[62]Measure, measurement.
[63]"Lain." "Lien" is an obsolete past participle of "lie."
[64]Exemptions, most probably, from public service or taxation.

her chast and modest vaile surrounded with celestiall beames they overlai'd with wanton *tresses*, and in a flaring tire[65] bespekkl'd her with all the gaudy allurements of a Whore.

Thus flourish't the Church with *Constantines* wealth, and thereafter were the effects that follow'd; his Son *Constantius* prov'd a flat *Arian*, and his Nephew *Julian* an Apostate, and there his Race ended; the Church that before by insensible degrees welk't[66] and impair'd, now with large steps went downe hill decaying; at this time *Antichrist* began first to put forth his horne, and that saying was common that former times had woodden Chalices and golden *Preists*; but they golden Chalices and woodden *Preists*. Formerly (saith *Sulpitius*) *Martyrdome* by glorious death was sought more greedily, then now Bishopricks by vile Ambition are hunted after (speaking of these Times) and in another place; they gape after possessions, they tend Lands and Livings, they coure over[67] their gold, they buy and sell: and if there be any that neither possesse nor traffique, that which is worse, they sit still, and expect guifts, and prostitute every induement[68] of grace, every holy thing to sale. And in the end of his History thus he concludes, all things went to wrack by the *faction, wilfulnesse*, and *avarice* of the *Bishops*, and by this means *Gods people,* & every *good man* was had in scorn and derision; which S. *Martin* found truly to be said by his friend *Sulpitius*; for being held in admiration by all men, he had onely the *Bishops* his enemies, found God lesse favorable to him after he was *Bishop* then before, & for his last 16. yeares would come at no *Bishops* meeting. Thus you see Sir what *Constantines* doings in the Church brought forth, either in his own or in his Sons Reigne.

Now lest it should bee thought that somthing else might ayle this Author thus to hamper the Bishops of those dayes; I will bring you the opinion of three the famousest men for wit and learning, that *Italy* at this day glories of, whereby it may be concluded for a receiv'd opinion even among men professing the Romish Faith, that *Constantine* marr'd all in the Church. *Dante* in his 19 *Canto* of *Inferno* hath thus, as I will render it you in English blank Verse.[69]

Ah Constantine, *of how much ill was cause*
Not thy Conversion, but those rich demaines
That the first wealthy Pope *receiv'd of thee.*

So in his 20. Canto of *Paradise* hee makes the like complaint, and *Petrarch* seconds him in the same mind in his 108. Sonnet which is wip't out by the Inquisitor in some Editions;[70] speaking of the Roman *Antichrist* as meerely bred up by *Constantine.*

Founded in chast and humble Povertie,
'Gainst them that rais'd thee dost thou lift thy horn,
Impudent whore, where hast thou plac'd thy hope?
In thy Adulterers, or thy ill got wealth?
Another Constantine *comes not in hast.*

Ariosto of *Ferrara* after both these in time, but equall in fame, following the scope of his Poem in a difficult knot how to restore *Orlando* his chiefe Hero to his lost senses, brings *Astolfo* the English Knight up into the moone, where S. *John*, as he feignes, met him. *Cant.* 34.

And to be short; at last his guid him brings
Into a goodly valley, where he sees
A mighty masse of things strangely confus'd,
Things that on earth were lost, or were abus'd.

And amongst these so abused things listen what hee met withall, under the Conduct of the *Evangelist.*

Then past hee to a flowry Mountaine greene,
Which once smelt sweet, now stinks as odiously;
This was that gift (if you the truth will have)
That Constantine *to good* Svlvestro *gave.*

And this was a truth well knowne in *England* before this *Poet* was borne, as our *Chaucers* Plowman shall tell you by and by upon another occasion. By all these circumstances laid together, I do not see how it can be disputed what good this Emperour *Constantine* wrought to the Church, but rather whether ever any, though perhaps not wittingly, set open a dore to more mischiefe in Christendome. There is just cause therefore that when the *Prelates* cry out Let the Church be reform'd according to *Constantine*, it should sound to a judicious eare no otherwise, then if they should say Make us rich, make us lofty, make us lawlesse, for if any under him were not so, thanks to those ancient remains of

---

[65]"Gaudy dress," "flaunting attire."

[66]"Faded," "withered."

[67]"Cower over," "crouch over," presumably to protect it.

[68]Probably close to the meaning of the modern "endowment," though the word "indument" could mean "clothes," or "vestment." The Latin verb *induere* means "to put on."

[69]Milton tries his hand at the poetic medium of Elizabethan tragedy, blank verse, not attempting to reproduce the *terza rima* of Dante. In the translations from Dante and Ariosto, Milton is demonstrating his knowledge of Italian and his virtuosity as an English poet and translator.

[70]Milton, probably while in Italy, had noticed the effect of Church censorship on poetry, as he will satirize it in *Areopagitica*. One wonders how or where he compared a number of modern editions of Petrarch, to discover which poems had been expurgated.

integrity, which were not yet quite worne out, and not to his Government.

Thus finally it appears that those purer Times were no such as they are cry'd up, and not to be follow'd without suspicion, doubt and anger. The last point wherein the *Antiquary* is to bee dealt with at his owne weapon, is to make it manifest, that the ancientest, and best of the Fathers have disclaim'd all sufficiency in themselves that men should rely on, and sent all commers to the Scriptures, as all sufficient; that this is true, will not be unduly gather'd by shewing what esteeme they had of Antiquity themselves, and what validity they thought in it to prove Doctrine, or Discipline. I must of necessitie begin from the second ranke of Fathers, because till then Antiquitie could have no Plea. *Cyprian* in his 63. *Epistle.* If any, saith he, of our Auncestors either ignorantly or out of simplicity hath not observ'd that which the Lord taught us by his example (speaking of the Lords Supper) his simplicity *God* may pardon of his mercy, but wee cannot be excus'd for following him, being instructed by the Lord. And have not we the same instructions, and will not this holy man with all the whole Consistorie of Saints and Martyrs that liv'd of old rise up and stop our mouthes in judgement, when wee shall goe about to Father our Errors, and opinions upon their Authority? in the 73. *Epist.* Hee adds, in vaine doe they oppose custome to us if they be overcome by reason; as if custome were greater then Truth, or that in spirituall things that were better by the holy Ghost. In the 74. neither ought Custome to hinder that Truth should not prevaile, for Custome without Truth is but agednesse of Error.

Next *Lactantius*, he that was prefer'd to have the bringing up of *Constantines* children in his second Booke of *Institutions*, Chap. 7. & 8. disputes against the vaine trust in Antiquity, as being the cheifest Argument of the Heathen, against the Christians, they doe not consider, saith he, what Religion is, but they are confident it is true, because the Ancients deliver'd it, they count it a trespasse to examine it. And in the eighth, not because they went before us in time, therefore in wisdome, which being given alike to all Ates, cannot be prepossest by the Ancients; wherefore seeing that to seeke the Truth is inbred to all, they bereave themselves of wisedome the gift of God who without judgement follow the Ancients, and are led by others like bruit beasts. St. *Austin* writes to *Fortunatian* that he counts it lawfull in the bookes of whomsoever to reject that which he finds otherwise then true, and so hee would have others deale by him. He neither accounted, as it seems, those Fathers that went before, nor himselfe, nor others of his rank, for men of more

then ordinary spirit, that might equally deceive, and be deceiv'd. and oftimes, setting our servile humors aside, yea *God* so ordering, we may find Truth with one man, as soon as in a Counsell, as *Cyprian* agrees 71. Epist. *Many things*, saith he, *are better reveal'd to single persons.* At *Nicæa* in the first, and best reputed Counsell of all the world, there had gon out a Canon to divorce married Priests, had not one old man *Paphnutius* stood up and reason'd against it.[71]

Now remains it to shew clearly that the Fathers referre all decision of controversie to the Scriptures, as all-sufficient to direct, to resolve, and to determine. *Ignatius* taking his last leave of the Asian Churches, as he went to martyrdome exhorted them to adhere close to the written doctrine of the Apostles, necessarily written for posterity: so farre was he from unwritten traditions, as may be read in the 36.c. of *Eusebius* 3.b. In the 74. Epist. of *Cyprian* against *Stefan* Bish. of *Rome* imposing upon him a tradition, *whence*, quoth he, *is this tradition? Is it fetcht from the authority of Christ in the Gospel, or of the Apostles in their Epistles: for God testifies that those things are to be done which are written:* and then thus: *what obstinacie, what presumption is this to preferre humane Tradition before divine ordinance?* And in the same Epist. *If we shall return to the head, and beginning of divine tradition* (which we all know he means the Bible) *humane error ceases, and the reason of heavenly misteries unfolded, whatsoever was obscure, becomes cleare.* And in the 14. Distinct. of the same Epist. directly against our modern fantasies of a still visible Church, he teaches, *that succession of truth may fail, to renew which we must have recourse to the fountaines,* using this excellent similitude, *if a Channel, or Conduit pipe which brought in water plentifully before, suddenly fail, doe we not goe to the fountaine to know the cause, whether the Spring affords no more, or whether the vein be stopt, or turn'd aside in the midcourse: thus ought we to doe, keeping Gods precepts, that if in ought the truth shall be chang'd, we may repaire to the Gospel, and to the Apostles, that thence may arise the reason of our doings, from whence our order, and beginning arose.* In the 75. he inveighs bitterly against Pope *Stefanus*, for that he could boast his Succession from *Peter*, and yet foist in[72] Traditions that were not Apostolicall. And in his Book of the unity of the Church he compares those that neglecting *Gods* Word, follow the doctrines of men, to *Coreh*, *Dathan*, and *Abiram*. The very first page of

[71]Paphnutius's behavior would suggest a model for the character of Abdiel in *Paradise Lost*, the one just angel who resisted Satan publicly.
[72] The term is from dicing: "To palm (a 'flat' or false die) so as to be able to introduce it when required. Also intr. to cheat by this means . . . ; to foist in: to introduce (the flat) surreptitiously when palmed" (*OED* 1.1).

Athanasius against the Gentiles, averres the the Scriptures to be sufficient of themselves for the declaration of Truth; and that if his friend *Macarius* read other Religious writers, it was but φιλοκάλως *come un virtuoso,* (as the Italians say,) as a lover of elegance: and in his 2*d* Tome the 39. pag, after he hath rekon'd up the Canonicall Books, *In these only,* saith he, *is the doctrine of godlinesse taught, let not man adde to these, or take from these*; and in his *Synopsis,* having again set down all the Writers of the old & new Testament, *these,* saith he, *be the anchors, and props of our Faith:* besides these, millions of other Books have bin written by great and wise men according to rule, and agreement with these, of which I will not now speak, as being of infinite number, and meer dependance on the canonical Books. *Basil* in his 2*d* Tome writing of true Faith, tells his auditors he is bound to teach them that which he hath learn't out of the Bible: and in the same Treatise, he saith, *That seeing the Commandments of the Lord, are faithfull and sure for ever; it is a plain falling from the Faith, and a high pride either to make void any thing therin, or to introduce any thing not there to be found:* and he gives the reason *for Christ saith, My Sheep heare my voyce, they will not follow another, but fly from him, because they know not his voyce.* But not to be endlesse in quotations, it may chance to be objected, that there be many opinions in the Fathers which have no ground in Scriptures; so much the lesse, may I say, should we follow them, for their own words shall condemn them, and acquit us, that lean not on them; otherwise these their words shall acquit them, and condemn us. But it will be reply'd, the Scriptures are difficult to be understood, and therfore require the explanation of the Fathers, 'tis true there be some Books, and especially some places in those Books that remain clouded; yet ever that which is most necessary to be known its most easie; and that which is most difficult, so farr expounds it selfe ever as to tell us how little it imports our *saving knowledge.* Hence to inferre a generall obscurity over all the text, is a meer suggestion of the Devil to disswade men from reading it, and casts an aspersion of dishonour both upon the *mercy, truth,* and *wisdome* of God: We count it no gentlenesse, or fair dealing in a man of Power among us, to require strict, and punctual obedience, and yet give out all his commands ambiguous and obscure, we should think he had a blot upon us, certainly such commands were no commands, but snares. The very essence of Truth is plainnesse, and brightnes; the darknes and crookednesse is our own. The *wisdome* of God created *understanding,* fit and proportionable to Truth the object, and end of it, as the eye to the thing visible. If our *understanding* have a film of *ignorance* over it, or be blear with gazing on other false glisterings,

what is that to Truth? If we will but purge with sovrain eyesalve that intellectual ray which *God* hath planted in us, then we would beleeve the Scriptures protesting their own plainnes, and perspecuity, calling to them to be instructed, not only the *wise,* and *learned,* but the *simple,* the *poor,* the *babes,* foretelling an extraordinary effusion of *Gods* Spirit upon every age, and sexe, attributing to all men, and requiring from them the ability of searching, trying, examining all things, and by the Spirit discerning that which is good; and as the Scriptures themselvs pronounce their own plainnes, so doe the Fathers testifie of them.

I will not run into a paroxysm of citations again in this point, only instance *Athanasius* in his fore-mention'd first page; *the knowledge of Truth,* saith he, *wants no humane lore, as being evident in it selfe, and by the preaching of Christ now opens brighter then the Sun.* If these Doctors who had scarse half the light that we enjoy, who all except 2 or 3 were ignorant of the Hebrew tongue, and many of the Greek, blundring upon the dangerous, and suspectifull translations of the Apostat *Aquila,* the Heretical Theodotion,[73] the Ju-daïz'd *Symmachus*; the erroneous *Origen*; if these could yet find the Bible so easie, why should we doubt, that have all the helps of Learning, and faithfull industry that man in this life can look for, and the assistance of *God* as neer now to us as ever. But let the Scriptures be hard; are they more hard, more crabbed, more abstruse then the Fathers? He that cannot understand the sober, plain, and unaffected stile of the Scriptures, will be ten times more puzzl'd with the knotty Africanisms, the pamper'd metafors; the intricat, and involv'd sentences of the Fathers; besides the fantastick, and declamatory flashes; the crosse-jingling periods[74] which cannot but disturb, and come thwart a setl'd devotion worse then the din of bells, and rattles.

Now Sir, for the love of holy *Reformation,* what can be said more against these importunat clients[75] of Antiquity, then she her selfe their patronesse hath said. Whether think ye would she approve still to dote upon immeasureable, innuberable, and therfore unnecessary,

---

[73]It is probably a typographical error that the compositor forgot to italicise this proper noun. Theodotion was an obscure theologician and a contemporary of Irenaeus, best known for his translations of scripture, especially for Isaiah 7:14, "Behold a young woman shall conceive," which was supposed to have countered the belief that it was Joseph who was the father of Jesus (Yale 1: 567n.171).

[74]"Discordant sentences." "Jingling," here, would be something like "rhythmical noise," and cross-jingling would be two strains of discordant noise working against each other.

[75]A plebian servant who was under an obligation to his master, in the Roman world, in return for which the patron would protect him (see *OED* 1).

and unmercifull volumes, choosing rather to erre with the specious name of the Fathers, or to take a sound Truth at the hand of a plain upright man that all his dayes hath bin diligently reading the holy Scriptures, and therto imploring *Gods* grace, while the admirers of Antiquity have bin beating their brains about their *Ambones*, their *Diptychs*, and *Meniaia's*? Now, he that cannot tell of Stations, and Indictions; nor has wasted his pretious howrs in the endles conferring of Councels and Conclaves that demolish one another, although I know many of those that pretend to be great Rabbies in these studies have scarce saluted them from the strings, and the titlepage, or to give 'em more, have bin but the Ferrets and Moushunts[76] of an Index: yet what Pastor, or Minister how learned, religious, or discreet soever does not now bring both his cheeks full blown with Oecumenical, and synodical, shall be counted a lank, shallow, unsufficient man, yea a dunce, and not worthy to speak about *Reformation* of *Church Discipline*. But I trust they for whom *God* hath reserv'd the honour of Reforming this Church will easily perceive their adversaries drift in this calling for Antiquity, they feare the plain field of the Scriptures, the chase is too hot; they seek the dark, the bushie, the tangled Forrest, they would imbosk: they feel themselvs strook in the transparent streams of divine Truth, they would plunge, and tumble, and thinke to ly hid in the foul weeds, and muddy waters, where no plummet can reach the bottome. But let them beat themselvs like Whales, and spend their oyl till they be dradg'd ashoar: though wherfore should the Ministers give them so much line for shifts, and delays? Wherfore should they not urge only the Gospel, and hold it ever in their faces like a mirror of Diamond, till it dazle, and pierce their misty ey balls? maintaining it the honour of its absolute sufficiency, and supremacy inviolable: For if the Scripture be for *Reformation*, and Antiquity to boot, 'tis but an advantage to the dozen, 'tis no winning cast: and though Antiquity be against it, while the Scriptures be for it, the Cause is as good as ought to be wisht, Antiquity it selfe fitting Judge.

But to draw to an end; the second sort of those that may be justly number'd among the hinderers of *Reformation*, are Libertines, these suggest that the Discipline sought would be intolerable: for one Bishop now in a Dioces we should then have a Pope in every Parish. It will not be requisite to Answer these men, but only to discover them, for reason they have none, but lust, and licentiousnes, and therfore answer can have none. It is not any Discipline that they could live under, it is the

corruption, and remisnes of Discipline. Episcopacy duly executed, yea the Turkish, and Jewish rigor against whoring, and drinking the dear, and tender Discipline of a Father; the sociable, and loving reproof of a Brother; the bosome admonition of a Friend is a *Presbytery* and a Consistory to them. 'Tis only the merry Frier in *Chaucer* can disple[77] them.

Full sweetly heard he confession
And pleasant was his absolution,
He was an easie man to give pennance.

And so I leave them: and referre the political discourse of Episcopacy to a Second Book.

OF
REFORMATION, &c.

The Second Book.

Sir,

IT is a work good, and prudent to be able to guide one man; of larger extended vertue to order wel one house; but to govern a Nation piously, and justly, which only is to say happily, is for a spirit of the greatest size, and divinest mettle. And certainly of no lesse a mind, nor of lesse excellence in another way, were they who by writing layd the solid, and true foundations of this Science, which being of greatest importance to the life of man, yet there is no art that hath bin more canker'd in her principles, more soyl'd, and slubber'd[78] with aphorising[79] pedantry then the art of policie; and that most, where a man would thinke should least be, in Christian Common-wealths. They teach not that to govern well is to train up a Nation in true wisdom and vertue, and that which springs from thence magnanimity, (take heed of that) and that which is our beginning, regeneration, and happiest end, likenes to *God*, which in one word we call *godlines*, & that this is the true florishing of a Land, other things to follow as the shadow does the substance: to teach thus were meer

---

[76]Mouse-hunters (ferrets would hunt rats).

[77]"Subject them to discipline" ("disple" is a verb).
[78]Soiled or smeared.
[79]Milton invented the word, meaning "making up wise sayings excessively." Coleridge is the only other author to use it, according to the *OED*.

pulpitry to them. This is the master-piece of a modern politician, how to qualifie, and mould the sufferance and subjection of the people to the length of that foot that is to tread on their necks, how rapine may serve it selfe with the fair, and honourable pretences of publick good, how the puny Law may be brought under the wardship, and controul of lust, and will, in which attempt if they fall short, then must a superficial colour of reputation by all means direct or indirect be gotten to wash over the unsightly bruse of honor. To make men governable in this manner their precepts mainly tend to break a nationall spirit, and courage by count'nancing open riot, lusury, and ignorance, till having thus disfigur'd and made men beneath men, as *Juno* in the Fable of *Iö*, they deliver up the poor trans-formed heifer of the Commonwealth to be stung and vext with the breese,[80] and goad of oppression under the custody of some *Argus* with a hundred eyes of jealousie. To be plainer Sir, how to soder,[81] how to stop a leak, how to keep up the floting carcas of a crazie, and diseased Monarchy, or State betwixt wind, and water,[82] swimming still upon her own dead lees, that now is the deepest design of a politician. Alas Sir! A Common-welth ought to be as one huge Christian personage, one mighty growth, and stature of an honest man, as big, and compact in vertue as in body; for looke what the grounds, and causes are of single happines to one man, the same yee shall find them to a whole state, as *Aristotle* both in his ethicks, and politiks, from the principles of reason layes down by consequence therfore, that which is good, and agreeable to monarchy, will appeare soonest to be so, by being good and agreeable to the true wel-fare of every Christian, and that which can be justly prov'd hurtfull, and offensive to every true Christian, wilbe evinc't to be alike hurtful to monarchy: for *God* forbid, that we should separate and distinguish the end, and good of a monarch, from the end and good of the monarchy, or of that, from Christianity. How then this third, and last sort that hinder reformation, will justify that it stands not with reason of state, I much muse? For certain I am the *Bible* is shut against them, as certaine that neither *Plato*, nor *Aristotle* is for their turnes.[83] What they can bring us now from the Schools of *Loyola* with his Jesuites, or their *Malvezzi* that can cut *Tacitus* into

slivers,[84] we shall presently hear. They alledge 1. That the Church government must be conformable to the ci-vill politie, next, that no forme of Church government is agreeable to monarchy, but that of Bishops. Must Church government that is appointed in the Gospel, and has chief respect to the soul, be conformable, and pliant to civil, that is arbitrary, and chiefly conversant about the visible and external part of man? This is the very maxim that moulded the Calvs of *Bethel* and of *Dan*, this was the quintessence of *Jeroboams* policy, he made Religion conform to his politick interests, & this was the sin that watcht over the Israelites till their final captivity. If this State principle come from the Prelates, as they affect to be counted statists, let them look back to *Elutherius* Bishop of *Rome*, and see what he thought of the policy of *England*; being requir'd by *Lucius* the first Christian King of this Iland to give his counsel for the founding of Religious Laws, little thought he of this sage caution, but bids him betake himselfe to the old, and new Testament, and receive direction from them how to administer both Church, and Common-wealth; that he was *Gods* Vicar, and therfore to rule by *Gods* Laws, that the Edicts of *Cæsar* we may at all times disallow, but the Statutes of *God* for no reason we may reject. Now certaine if Church-goverment be taught in the Gospel, as the Bishops dare not deny, we may well conclude of what late standing this Position is, newly calculated for the altitude of Bishop elevation, and lettice for their lips. But by what example can they shew that the form of Church Discipline must be minted, and modell'd out to secular pretences? The ancient Republick of the Jews is evident to have run through all the changes of civil estate, if we survey the Story from the giving of the Law to the *Herods*, yet did one manner of Priestly government serve without inconvenience to all these temporal mutations: it serv'd the mild Aristocracy of elective Dukes, and heads of Tribes joyn'd with them; the dictatorship of the Judges, the easie, or hard-handed Monarchy's, the domestick, or forrain tyrannies, Lastly the Roman Senat from without, the Jewish Senat at home with the Galilean Tetrarch, yet the Levites had some right to deal in civil affairs: but seeing the Evangelical precept forbids Churchmen to intermeddle with worldly imployments, what interweavings, or interworkings can knit the Minister, and the Magistrate in their several functions to the regard of any precise correspondency? Seeing that the Churchmans office is only to teach men the Christian Faith, to exhort all, to incourage the good, to

---

[80]Bruise, in this case the contusion that a goad or whip might make (see OED "bruise" 2).

[81]Solder, apply heated tin or lead to patch copper or other metals.

[82]Similar to Milton's image of the floating body of Lycidas being carried by wind or water, to "welter to the parching wind" ("Lycidas" 13).

[83]The comma present in Bodleian and other copies seems to be an obvious error, and I have corrected as did the Yale editors.

---

[84]The phrase "and steaks [probably a figurative sense of 'pieces of meat']" following "slivers" was scratched through in the Bodleian copy, presumably by Milton himself. The Yale editors retain it.

admonish the bad, privately the lesse offender, publickly the scandalous and stubborn; to censure, and separate from the communion of *Christs* flock, the contagious, and incorrigible, to receive with joy, and fatherly compassion the penitent, all this must be don, and more then this beyond any Church autority. What is all this either here, or there to the temporal regiment of Wealpublick,[85] whether it be Popular, Princely, or Monarchical? Where doth it intrench upon the temporal governor, where does it come in his walk? Where does it make inrode upon his jurisdiction? Indeed if the Ministers part be rightly discharg'd, it renders him the people more conscionable, quiet, and easie to be govern'd, if otherwise his life and doctrine will declare him. If therfore the Constitution of the Church be already set down by divine prescript, as all sides confesse, then can she not be a handmaid to wait on civil commodities, and respects: and if the nature and limits of Church Discipline be such, as are either helpfull to all political estates indifferently, or have no particular relation to any, then is there no necessity, nor indeed possibility of linking the one with the other in a speciall conformation.

Now for their second conclusion, *That no form of Church government is agreeable to Monarchy, but that of Bishops*, although it fall to pieces of it selfe by that which hath bin sayde: yet to give them play front, and reare, it shall be my task to prove that Episcopacy with that Autority which it challenges in *England* is not only not agreeable, but tending to the destruction of Monarchy. While the Primitive Pastors of the Church of *God* labour'd faithfully in their Ministery, tending only their Sheep, and not seeking, but avoiding all worldly matters as clogs,[86] and indeed derogations, and debasements to their high calling, little needed the Princes, and potentates of the earth, which way soever the Gospel was spread, to study ways how to make a coherence between the Churches politie, and theirs: therfore when *Pilate* heard once our Saviour *Christ* professing that *his Kingdome was not of this world*, he thought the man could not stand much in *Cæsars* light, nor much indammage[87] the Roman Empire: for if the life of *Christ* be hid to this world, much more is his Scepter unoperative, but in spirituall things. And thus liv'd, for 2 or 3 ages, the Successors of the Apostles. But when through *Constantines* lavish Supersition they

forsook their *first love*, and set themselvs up two Gods instead, *Mammon* and their Belly, then taking advantage of the spiritual power which they had on mens consciences, they began to cast a longing eye to get the body also, and bodily things into their command, upon which their carnal desires, the Spirit dayly quenching and dying in them, they knew no way to keep themselves up from falling to nothing, but by bolstering, and supporting their inward rottenes by a carnal, and outward strength. For a while they rather privily sought opportunity, then hastily disclos'd their project, but when *Constantine* was dead, and 3 or 4 Emperors more, their drift became notorious, and offensive to the whole world: for while *Theodosius* the younger reign'd, thus writes *Socrates* the Historian in his *7th* Book, 11. chap. now began an ill name to stick upon the Bishops of *Rome*, and *Alexandria*, who beyond their Priestly bounds now long agoe had stept into principality. and this was scarse 80. years since their raising from the meanest worldly condition. Of courtesie now let any man tell me, if they draw to themselves a *temporal* strength and *power* out of *Cæsars* Dominion, is not *Cæsars* Empire thereby diminisht? but this was a stolne bit, hitherto hee was a Caterpiller secretly gnawing at *Monarchy*, the next time you shall see him a Woolfe, a Lyon, lifting his paw against his raiser, as *Petrarch* exprest it, and finally an open enemy, and subverter of the Greeke Empire. *Philippicus* and *Leo*, with divers other Emperours after them, not without the advice of their *Patriarchs*, and at length of a whole Easterne Counsell of 3. hundred thirty eight *Bishops*, threw the Images out of *Churches* as being decreed idolatrous.

Upon this goodly occasion the *Bishop* of *Rome* not only seizes the City, and all the Territory about into his owne hands, and makes himselfe Lord thereof, which till then was govern'd by a Greeke Magistrate, but absolves all *Italy* of their Tribute, and obedience due to the Emperour, because hee obey'd Gods Commandement in abolishing Idolatry.

Mark Sir here how the Pope came by S. *Peters* Patrymony, as he feigns it, not the donation of *Constantine*, but idolatry and rebellion got it him. Yee need but read *Sigonius* one of his owne Sect to know the Story at large. And now to shroud himselfe against a storme from the Greek Continent, and provide a Champion to bear him out in these practises, hee takes upon him by Papall sentence to unthrone *Chilpericus* the rightfull K. of *France* and gives the Kingdome to *Pepin* for no other cause but that hee seem'd to him the more active man.

---

[85]Public welfare, what is usually called public weal. Milton did not invent the term, which was more often spelled "weal-public."

[86]Probably "A block or heavy piece of wood, or the like, attached to the leg or neck of a man or beast, to impede motion or prevent escape" (*OED* 2), though "clog" could mean any sort of impediment.

[87]Inflict damage upon.

If he were a freind[88] herein to *Monarchy* I know not, but to the *Monarch* I need not aske what he was.

Having thus made *Pepin* his fast freind, he cals him into *Italy* against *Aistulphus* the *Lombard*, that warr'd upon him for his late Usurpation of *Rome* as belonging to *Ravenna* which he had newly won. *Pepin*, not unobedient to the Popes call, passing into *Italy*, frees him out of danger, and wins for him the whole exarchat of *Ravenna*, which though it had beene almost immediately before, the hereditary possession of that *Monarchy* which was his cheife Patron, and Benefactor, yet he takes, and keepes it to himselfe as lawfull prize, and give to St. *Peter*. What a dangerous fallacie is this, when a spirituall man may snatch to himselfe any temporall Dignity, or Dominion under pretence of receiving it for the Churches use; thus he claims *Naples, Sicily, England*, and what not? To bee short, under shew of his zeale against the errors of the Greeke Church, hee never ceast baiting, and goring the Successors of his best Lord *Constantine* what by his barking curses, and Excommunications, what by his hindering the Westerne Princes from ayding them against the Sarazens, and Turkes, unlesse when they humour'd him; so that it may be truly affirm'd, he was the subversion, and fall of that *Monarchy*, which was the hoisting of him; this, besides *Petrarch*, whom I have cited, our *Chaucer* also hath observ'd, and gives from hence a caution to *England* to beware of her *Bishops* in time, for that their ends, and aymes are not more freindly to *Monarchy* then the Popes.

Thus hee brings in the Plow-man speaking, 2. *Part. Stanz.* 28.

The Emperour Yafe the Pope sometime
So high Lordship him above
That at last the silly Kime,
The proud Pope put him out,
So of this Realme is no doubt,
But Lords beware, and them defend,
For now these folks be wonders stout
The King and Lords now this amend

And in the next Stanza which begins the third part of the tale he argues that they ought not to bee Lords.

Moses Law forbode it tho
That Preists should not Lordships welde
Christs Gospell bitteth also,
That they should no Lordships held

Ne Christs Apostle were never so bold
No such Lordships to hem embrace
But smeren her Sheep, and keep her Fold.

And so forward. Whether the Bishops of *England* have deserv'd thus to bee fear'd by men so wise as our *Chaucer* is esteem'd, and how agreeable to our *Monarchy*, and *Monarchs* their demeanour ha's been, he that is but meanly read in our *Chronicles* needs not be instructed. Have they not been as the *Canaanites*, and *Philistims* to this Kingdom? what Treasons, what revolts to the Pope, what Rebellions, and those the basest, and most pretenselesse have they not been chiefe in? What could *Monarchy* think when *Becket* durst challenge the custody of *Rotchester Castle*, and the Tower of *London*, as appertaining to his Signory? To omit his insolencies and affronts to Regall Majestie, till the Lashes inflicted on the anointed bod of the King washt off the holy *Unction* with his *blood* drawn by the polluted hands of *Bishops, Abbots*, and *Monks*.

What good upholders of Royalty were the *Bishops*, when by their rebellious opposition against King *John*, *Normandy* was lost, he himselfe depos'd, and this Kingdom made over to the *Pope*? When the Bishop of *Winchester* durst tell the Nobles, the Pillars of the Realme, that there were no Peeres in *England*, as in *France*, but that the King might doe what hee pleas'd. What could Tyranny say more? it would bee petty now if I should insist upon the rendring up of *Tournay* by *Woolseyes* Treason, the Excommunications, Cursings, and Interdicts upon the whole Land. For haply I shall be cut of short by a reply, that these were the faults of the men, and their Popish errors, not of *Episcopacie*, that hath now renounc't the Pope, and is a Protestant. Yes sure; as wise and famous men have suspected, and fear'd the Protestant *Episcopacie* in *England*, as those that have fear'd the Papall.

You know Sir what was the judgement of *Padre Paolo* the great Venetian Antagonist of the *Pope*, for it is extant in the hands of many men, whereby he declares his feare, that when the Hierarchy of *England* shall light into the hands of busie and audacious men, or shall meet with Princes tractable to the Prelacy, then much mischiefe is like to ensue. And can it bee neerer hand, then when *Bishops* shall openly affirme that, No *Bishop*, no *King*? a trimme Paradox, and that yee may know where they have beene a begging for it, I will fetch you the Twin-brother to it out of the Jesuites Cell; they feeling the Axe of Gods reformation hewing at the old and hollow trunk of Papacie, and finding the Spaniard their surest friend, and safest refuge, to sooth him up in his dreame of a fift Monarchy, and withall to uphold the decrepit Papalty have invented this super-politick

---

[88]The spellings of "freind" and, a little later, "cheife" and then "freindly," may indicate that the compositor is following Milton's preferences for a time.

Aphorisme, as one termes it, One Pope, and one King.

Surely there is not any Prince in *Christendome* who hearing this rare Sophistry can choose but smile, and if we be not blind at home we may as well perceived that this worthy Motto, no *Bishop*, no *King* is of the same batch, and infanted out of the same feares, a meere ague-cake[89] coagulated of a certain Fever they have, presaging their time to be but short: and now like those that are sinking, they catch round at which is likeliest to hld them up. And would perswade Regall Power, that if they dive, he must after. But what greater debasement can there be to Royall Dignity, whose towring, and stedfast heighth rests upon the unmovable foundations of Justice, and Heroick vertue, then to chaine it in a dependance of subsisting, or ruining to the painted Battlements, and gaudy rottennesse of Prelatrie, which want but one puffe of the Kings to blow them down like a past-bord House built of *Court-Cards*. Sir the little adoe, which me thinks I find in untacking these pleasant Sophismes, puts me into the mood to tell you a tale ere I proceed further; and *Menenius Agrippa* speed us.

A Tale.[90]

Upon a time the Body summon'd all the Members to meet in the Guild for the common good (as *Æsops* Chronicles averre many stranger Accidents) the head by right takes the first seat, and next to it a hughe and monstrous Wen little lesse then the Head it selfe, growing to it by a narrower excrescency. The members amaz'd began to ask one another what hee was that took place next their cheif; none could resolve. Whereat the Wen, though unweildy, with much adoe gets up and bespeaks the Assembly to this purpose. That as in place he was second to the head, so by due of merit;[91] that he was to it an ornament, and strength, and of speciall neere relation, and that if the head should faile, none were fitter then himselfe to step into his place; therefore hee thought it for the honour of the Body, that such dignities and rich indowments should be decreed him as did adorne, and set out the noblest Members. To this was answer'd, that it should bee consulted. Then was a wise and learned Philosopher sent for, that knew all the Charters, Lawes, and Tenures of the Body. On him it is impos'd by all, as cheife Committee to examine, and discusse the claime and Petition of right put in by the Wen; who soone perceiving the matter, and wondring at the boldnesse of such a swolne Tumor, Wilt thou

(quoth he) that art but a bottle[92] of vitious and harden'd excrements, contend with the lawfull and free-borne members, whose certain number is set by ancient, and unrepealable Stature? head thou art none, though thou receive this huge substance from it, what office bearst thou? What good canst thou shew by thee done to the Common-weale? the Wen not easily dash't replies, that his Office was his glory, for so oft as the soule would retire out of the head from over the steaming vapours of the lwer parts to Divine Contemplation, with him shee found the purest, and quietest retreat, as being most remote from soile, and disturbance. Lourdan,[93] quoth the Philosopher, thy folly is as great as thy filth; know that all the faculties of the Soule are confin'd of old to their severall vessels, and *ventricles*, from which they cannot part without dissolution of the whole Body; and that thou containst no good think in thee, but a heape of hard, and loathsome uncleannes, and art to the head a foul disfigurment and burden, when I have cut thee off, and open'd thee, as by the help of these implements I will doe, all men shall see.

But to return, whence was digress't, seeing that the throne of a King, as the wise K. *Salomon* often remembers[94] us, *is establisht in Justice,* which is the universall *Justice* that *Aristotle* so much praises, containing in it all other vertues, it may assure us that the fall of Prelacy, whose actions are so farre distant from *Justice*, cannot shake the least fringe that borders the royal canopy: but that their standing doth continually oppose, and lay battery to[95] regal safety, shall by that which follows easily appear. Amongst many secondary, and accessory causes that support Monarchy, these are not of least reckning, though common to all other States: the love of the Subjects, the multitude, and valor of the people, and store of treasure. In all these things had the Kingdome bin of late sore weak'nd, and chiefly by the Prelates. First let any man consider, that if any Prince shall suffer under him a commission of autority to be exerciz'd, till all the Land grone, and cry out, as against a whippe of Scorpions, whether this be not likely to lessen, and keel[96] the affections of the Subject. Next what numbers of faithfull, and freeborn Englishmen, and good Christians have bin constrain'ed to forsake their dearest home, their friends, and kindred, whom nothing but the wide Ocean, and the savage deserts of *America* could hide and

---

[89]An enlargement of the spleen or other internal organ, due to a fever (ague). Milton's is the first recorded usage in the *OED*.

[90]In the 1641 edition, "*A Tale.*" is in the left margin.

[91]Compare "by merit rais'd / To that high eminence," as it is used of Satan in *Paradise Lost* 2.5–6.

[92]Apparently a glass container, though "bottle" was also used of a bundle (of hay).

[93]"Lazy fellow."

[94]"Reminds," or "teaches."

[95]To lay battery to is to beseige with heavy artillery.

[96]"Assuage," "lessen" (*OED* v. 1.2, citing this instance).

shelter from the fury of the Bishops. O Sir, if we could but see the shape of our deare Mother *England*, as Poets are wont to give a personal form to what they please, how would she appeare, think ye, but in a mourning weed,[97] with ashes upon her head, and teares abundantly flowing from her eyes, to behold so many of her children expos'd at once, and thrust from things of dearest necessity, because their conscience could not assent to things which the Bishops thought *indifferent*. What more binding then Conscience? what more free then *indifferency*? cruel then must that *indifferency* needs be, that shall violate the strict necessity of Conscience, merciles, and inhumane that free choyse, and liberty that shall break asunder the bonds of Religion. Let the Astrologers be dismay'd at the portentous blaze of comets, and impressions[98] in the aire as foretelling troubles and changes to states: I shall beleeve there cannot be a more ill-boding signe to a Nation (*God* turne the Omen from us) then when the Inhabitants, to avoid insufferable grievances at home, are inforc'd by heaps to forsake their native Country. Now wheras the only remedy, and amends against the depopulation, and thinnesse of a Land within, is the borrow'd strength of firme alliance from without, these Priestly policies of theirs having thus exhausted our domestick forces, have gone the way also to leave us as nake of our firmest, & faithfullest neighbours abroad, by disparaging, and alienating from us all Protestant Princes, and Common-wealths, who are not ignorant that our Prelats, and as many as they can infect, account them no better then a sort of sacrilegious, and puritanical Rebels, preferring the *Spaniard* our deadly enemy before them and set all orthodox writers at nought in comparison of the Jesuits, who are indeed the onely corrupters of youth, and good learning; and I have heard many wise, and learned men in *Italy* say as much. It cannot be that the strongest knot of confederacy should not dayly slak'n, when Religion which is the chiefe ingagement of our league shall be turn'd to their reproach. Hence it is that the prosperous, and prudent states of the united Provinces, whom we ought to love, if not for themselves, yet for our own good work in them, they having bin in a manner planted, and erected by us, and having bin since to us the faithfull watchmen, and discoverers of many a Popish, and Austrian complotted Treason, and with us the partners of many a bloody, and victorious battell, whom the similitude of manners and language, the commodity of traffick, which founded the old Burgundian league betwixt us, but chiefly Religion should

bind to us immortally, even such friends as these, out of some principles instill'd into us by the Prelates, have been often dismist with distastfull answers, and somtimes unfriendly actions: nor is it to be consider'd to the breach of confederate Nations whose mutual interest is of such high consequence, though their Merchants bicker in the East Indies, neither is it safe, or warie, or indeed Christianly, that the *French* king, of a different Faith, should afford our neerest Allyes as good protection as we. Sir, I perswade my selfe, if our zeale to true Religion, and the brotherly usage of our truest friends were as notorious to the world, as our *Prelatical Schism*, and captivity to *Rotchet Apothegms*,[99] we had here this seene our old Conquerours, and afterward Liege-men the *Normans*, together with the *Britains* our proper Colony, and all the *Gascoins* that are the rightfull *Dowry* of our ancient Kings, come with cap, and knee, desiring the shadow of the *English* Scepter to defend them from the hot persecutions and taxes of the *French*. But when they come thither, and see a Tympany of *Spanioliz'd Bishops*[100] swaggering in the fore-top of the State, and meddling to turne, and dandle the *Royall Ball*[101] with unskilfull and *Pedantick palmes*, no marvell though they think it as unsafe to commit Religion, and liberty to their arbitrating as to a Synagogue of Jesuites.[102]

But what doe I stand reck'ning upon advantages, and gaines lost by the mis-rule, and turbulency of the *Prelats*, what do I pick up so thriftily their scatterings and diminishings of the meaner Subject, whilst they by their seditious practises have indanger'd to loose the King one third of his main Stock, what they have not done to banish him from his own Native Countrey? but to speake of this as it ought would ask a Volume by it selfe.

Thus as they have unpeopl'd the Kingdome by expusion of so many thousands, as they have endeavor'd to lay the skirts of it bare by disheartning and

---

[97] A garment worn in mourning.

[98] Probably "An atmospheric influence, condition, or phenomenon. *fiery impression*, a comet, meteor, or the like" (*OED* 5).

[99] The word "rotchet" appears only as a spelling variant of "ratchet" in the *OED*, but a curious usage appears for "ratchet (? after brachet from brach)," with the following quotation: "1563 Becon Acts Christ & Antichr. Wks. III. 400 Antichrist hunteth the wilde dere . . . with houndes and ratchettes ronning." The word had, then, been used in a polemical and religious sense, whether or not it was connected with "brach," female dog.

[100] Playing delightfully on "Spagniol" meaning "Hispanic" and "spaniel," the lapdog. The pun had been used before, but it is still funny as a nationalistic slur in the context of seventeenth-century religious polemic.

[101] The orb carried by the monarch as a symbol of royal authority (over the world).

[102] Milton smears Jesuits and Jews by connecting them through the synagogue as a religious meeting place. "Synagogue of Satan" was a common phrase in polemic, and Milton himself was to label what he considered to be an "un-Christian" church in Scotland as a synagogue in 1648 (see Yale 3: 332).

dishonouring our loyallest Confederates abroad, so have they hamstrung the valour of the Subject by seeking to effeminate us all at home. Well knows every wise Nation that that their Liberty consists in manly and honest labours, in sobriety and rigorous honour to the Marriage Bed, which in both Sexes should be bred up from chast hopes to loyall Enjoyments; and when the people slacken, and fall to loosnes, and riot, then doe they as much as if they laid downe their necks for some wily Tyrant to get up and ride. Thus learnt *Cyrus* to tame the *Lydians*, whom by Armes he could not, whilst they kept themselves from Luxury; with one easy Proclamation to set up *Stews*,[103] dancing, feasting, & dicing he made them soone his slaves. I know not what drift the *Prelats* had, whose Brokers they were to prepare, and supple us either for a Forreigne Invasion or Domestick oppression; but this I am sure they took the ready way to despoile us both of *manhood* and *grace* at once, and that in the shamefullest and ungodliest manner upon that day which Gods law, and even our own reason hath consecrated, that we might have one day at least of seven set apart wherein to examin and encrease our knowledge of God, to meditate, and commune of our Faith, our Hope, our eternall City in Heaven, and to quick'n, withall, the study, and exercise of Charity; at such a time that men should be pluck't from their soberest and saddest thoughts, and by *Bishops* the pretended *Fathers of the Church* instigated by publique Edict, and with earnest indeavour push't forward to gaming, jigging, wassailing, and mixt dancing is a horror to think. Thus did the Reprobate hireling Preist *Balaam* seeke to subdue the Israelites to *Moab*, if not by force, then by this divellish *Pollicy*, to draw them from the Sanctuary of God to the luxurious, and ribald feasts of *Baal-peor*. Thus have they trespas't not onely against the *Monarchy* of *England*, but of Heaven also, as others, I doubt not, can prosecute against them.

I proceed within my own bounds to shew you next what good Agents they are about the Revennues and Riches of the Kingdome, which declares of what moment they are to *Monarchy*, or what availe. Two Leeches they have that still suck, and suck the Kingdome, their Ceremonies, and their Courts. If any man will contend that Ceremonies bee lawfull under the Gospell, hee may bee answer'd otherwere. This doubtlesse that they ought to bee many and over-costly, no true *Protestant* will affirme. Now I appeale to all wise men, what an excessive wast of Treasury hath beene within these few yeares in this Land not in the expedient, but in the Idolatrous erection of Temples beautified exquisitely to out-vie the Papists, the costly and deare-bought Scandals, and snares of Images, Pictures, rich Coaps, gorgeous Altar-clothes: and by the courses they tooke, and the opinions they held, it was not likely any stay would be, or any end of their madnes, where a pious pretext is so ready as hand to cover their insatiate desires. What can we supposed this will come to? What other materials then these have built up the *Spiritual* BABEL to the heighth of her Abominations? Beleeve it Sir right truly it may be said, that Antichrist is *Mammons* Son. The soure levin of humane Traditions mixt in one putrifi'd Masse with the poisonous dregs of hypocrisie in the hearts of *Prelates* that lye basking in the Sunny warmth of Wealth, and Promotion, is the Serpents Egge that will hatch an *Antichrist* wheresoever, and ingender the same Monster as big, or little as the Lump is which breeds him. If the splendor of *Gold* and *Silver* begin to Lord it once againe in the Church of *England*, wee shall see *Antichrist* shortly wallow heere, though his cheife Kennell be at *Rome*. If they had one thought upon *Gods glory* and the advancement of Christian Faith, they would be a means that with these expences thus profusely throwne away in trash, rather *Churches* and *Schools* might be built, where they cry out for want, and more added where too few are; a moderate maintenance distributed to every painful Minister, that now scarse sustaines his Family with Bread, while the *Prelats* revell like *Belshazzar* with their full carouses in *Goblets*, and *vessels* of *gold* snatcht from *Gods Temple*. Which (I hope) the Worthy Men of our Land will consider. Now then for their COURTS. What a Masse of Money is drawne from the Veines into the Ulcers of the Kingdome this way; their Extortions, their open Corruptions, the multitude of hungry and ravenous Harpies that swarme about their Offices declare sufficiently. And what though all this go not oversea? 'twere better it did: better a penurious Kingdom, then where excessive wealth flowes into the *gracelesse* and injurious hands of common sponges to the impoverishing of good and loyall men, and that by such execrable, such irreligious courses.

If the sacred and dreadfull works of holy *Discipline*, *Censure*, *Pennance*, *Excommunication*, and *Absolution*, where no prophane thing ought to have accesse, nothing to be assistant but sage and Christianly *Admonition*, brotherly *Love*, flaming *Charity*, and *Zeale*; and then according to the Effects, Paternall *Sorrow*, or Paternall *Joy*, milde *Severity*, melting *Compassion*, if such Divine *Ministeries* as these, wherin the Angel of the *Church* represents the Person of *Christ Jesus*, must lie prostitute to sordid Fees, and not passe to an fro betweene our Saviour that of free grace redeem'd us, and the submissive Penitent, without the truccage of perishing Coine,

---

[103]Cheap houses of prostitution.

and the Butcherly execution of Tormentors, Rooks, and Rakeshames sold to lucre, then have the Babilonish Marchants[104] of *Soules* just excuse. Hitherto Sir you have heard how the *Prelates* have weaken'd and withdrawne the externall Accomplishments of Kingly prosperity, the love of the People, their multitude, their valour, their wealth; mining, and sapping the out-works, and redoubts of *Monarchy*; now heare how they strike at the very heart, and vitals.

We know that *Monarchy* is made up of two parts, the Liberty of the subject, and the supremacie of the King. I begin at the root. See what gentle, and benigne Fathers they have beene to our liberty. Their trade being, by the same Alchymy that the *Pope* uses, to extract heaps of *gold*, and *silver* out of the drossie *Bullion* of the Peoples sinnes, and justly fearing that the quick-sighted *Protestants* eye clear'd in great part from the mist of Superstition, may at one time or other looke with a good judgement into these their deceitfull Pedleries, to gaine as many associats of guiltines as they can, and to infect the temporall Magistrate with the like lawlesse though not sacrilegious extortion, see a while what they doe; they ingage themselves to preach, and perswade an assertion for truth the most false, and to this *Monarchy* then a Popular Commotion, for the dissolution of *Monarchy* slides aptest into a *Democracy*; and what stirs the Englishmen, as our wisest writers have observ'd, sooner to rebellion, then violent, and heavy hands upon their goods and purses? Yet these devout *Prelates*, spight of our great Charter, and the soules of our Progenitors that wrested their liberties out of the *Norman* gripe with their dearest blood and highest prowesse, for these many years have not ceas't in their Pulpits wrinching, and spraining the *text*, to set at nought and trample under foot all the most sacred, and life blood Lawes, Statutes, and Acts of *Parliament* that are the holy Cov'nant of Union, and Marriage betweene the King and his Realme, by proscribing, and confiscating from us all the right we have to our owne bodies, goods and liberties. What is this, but to blow a trumpet, and proclaime a fire-crosse[105] to a hereditary, and perpetuall civill warre. Thus much against the Subjects Liberty hath been assaulted by them. Now how they have spar'd Supremacie, or likely are hereafter to submit to it, remaines lastly to bee consider'd.

The emulation that under the old Law was in the King toward the *Preist*, is now so come about in the Gospell, that all the danger is to be fear'd from the *Preist* to the *King*. Whilst the *Preists* Office in the Law was set out with an exteriour lustre of Pomp and glory, Kings were ambitious to be *Preists*; now *Priests*[106] not perceiving the heavenly brightness, and inward splendor of their more glorious *Evangelick Ministery* with as great ambition affect to be Kings; as in all their courses is easie to be observ'd. Their eyes ever imminent upon worldly matters, their desires ever thirsting after worldly employments, in stead of diligent and fervent studie in the Bible, they covet to be expert in Canons, and Decretals, which may inable them to judge, and interpose in temporall Causes, however pretended *Ecclesiasticall*. Do they not hord up *Pelfe*, seeke to bee potent in *secular Strength*, in *State Affaires*, in *Lands*, *Lordships*, and *Demeanes*, to *sway* and carry all before them in *high Courts*, and *Privie Counsels*, to bring into their grasp, the *high* and *principall Offices* of the Kingdom? have they not been bold of late to check the *Common Law*, to slight and brave the indiminishable Majestie of our highest Court the Law-giving and Sacred *Parliament*? Doe they not plainly labour to exempt *Church-men* from the *Magistrate*? Yea, so presumtuously as to question, and menace *Officers* that represent the *Kings Person* for using their Authority against drunken *Preists*? The cause of protecting *murderous Clergie-men* was the first heart-burning that swel'd up the audacious *Becket* to the pestilent, and odious vexation of *Henry* the second. Nay more, have not some of their devoted Schollers begun, I need not say to nibble, but openly to argue agains the Kings *Supremacie*? is not the Cheife of them accus'd out of his owne Booke, and his *late Canons* to affect a certaine unquestionable *Patriarchat*, independent and unsubordinate to the Crowne? From whence having first brought us to a servile *Estate of Religion*, and *Manhood*, and having predispos'd his conditions with the *Pope*, that layes claime to this *Land*, or some *Pepin* of his owne creating, it were all as likely for him to aspire to the *Monarchy* among us, as that the *Pope* could fine meanes so on the sudden both to bereave the Emperour of the *Roman Territory* with the favour of *Italy*, and by an unexpected friend out of *France*, while he was in danger to lose his *new-got Purchase*, beyond hope to leap in to the faire *Exarchat* of *Ravenna*.

A good while the *Pope* suttl'y acted the *Lamb*, writing to the Emperour, my Lord *Tiberius*, my Lord *Mauritius*, but no sooner did this his Lord pluck at the Images, and Idols, but hee threw off his Sheepes clothing, and started up a Wolfe; laying his pawes upon the Emperours right,

---

[104]The catchword between pages 63 and 64 begins the word "Mer-," a slight deviation in spelling.
[105]A fire-brand or cross dipped in pitch on one end and blood on the other, carried by one Scottish clan or another to proclaim the outbreak of war.

---

[106]After setting "*Preist*," with reversed "ei," three times, the compositor returns to the more normal spelling *Priest*. We might wonder mischievously if Milton was nagging him.

as forfeited to *Peter*. Why may not wee as well, having been forewarn'd at home by our renowned *Chaucer*, and from abroad by the great and learned *Padre Paolo*, from the like beginnings, as we see they are, feare the like events? Certainly a wise, and provident King ought to suspect a *Hierarchy* in his Realme, being ever attended, as it is, with two such greedy Purveyers, Ambition and Usurpation. I say hee ought to suspect a *Hierarchy* to bee as dangerous and derogatory from his Crown as a *Tetrarchy* or a *Heptarchy*. Yet now that the *Prelates* had almost attain'd to what their insolent, and unbridl'd minds had hurried them' to thrust the Laitie under the despoticall rule of the *Monarch*, that they themselves might confine the *Monarchy* to a kind of Pupillage under their *Hierarchy*, observe but how their own Principles combat one another, and supplant each one his fellow.

Having fitted us only for peace, and that a servile peace, by lessening our numbers, dreining our estates, enfeebling our bodies, cowing our free spirits by those wayes as you have heard, their impotent actions cannot sustaine themselves the least moment, unlesse they rouze us up to a *Warre* fit for *Cain* to be the Leader of; an abhorred, a cursed, a Fraternall *Warre*. ENGLAND and SCOTLAND dearest Brothers both in *Nature*, and in CHRIST must be set to wade in one anothers blood; and IRELAND our free Denizon upon the back of us both, as occasion should serve: a piece of Service that the *Pope* and all his Factors have beene compassing to doe ever since the *Reformation*.

But ever-blessed be he, and ever glorifi'd that from his high watch-Tower in the Heav'ns discerning the crooked wayes of perverse, and cruell men, hath hitherto maim'd, and infatuated all their damnable inventions, and deluded their great Wizzards with a delusion fit for fooles and children: had GOD been so minded hee could have sent a Spirit of *Mutiny* amongst us, as hee did between *Abimilech* and the *Sechemites*, to have made our Funerals, and slaine heaps more in number then the miserable surviving remnant, but he, when wee least deserv'd, sent out a gentle gale, and message of peace from the wings of those his Cherubims, that fanne his Mercy-seat. Nor shall the *wisdome*, the *moderation*, the *Christian Pietie*, the *Constancy* of our Nobility and Commons of *England* be ever forgotten, whose calme, and temperat connivence could sit still, and smile out the stormy bluster of men more audacious, and precipitant, then of solid and deep reach, till their own fury had run it selfe out of breath, assailing, by rash and heady *approches*, the impregnable situation of our Liberty and safety, that laught such weake enginry to scorne, such poore drifts to make a

Nationall *Warre* of a *Surplice Brabble*,[107] a *Tippet-scuffle*,[108] and ingage the unattanted Honour of *English* Knighthood, to unfurle the streaming *Red Crosse*, or to reare the horrid *Standard* of those fatall guly Dragons for so unworthy a purpose, as to force upon their *Fellow-Subjects*, that whiche themselves are weary of, the *Skeleton* of a *Masse-book*. Nor must the *Patience*, the *Fortitude*, the *firme Obedience* of the Nobles and People of *Scotland* striving against manifold Provocations, nor must their sincere and moderate proceedings hitherto, be unremember'd, to the shamefull Conviction of all their Detractors.

Goe on both hand in hand O NATIONS never to be dis-united, be the *Praise* and the *Heroic Song* of all POSTERITY; merit this, but seeke onely *Vertue*, not to extend your Limits; for what needs? to win a fading triumphant *Lawrell* out of the *teares* of *wretched Men*, but to settle the *pure worship* of *God* in his Church, and *justice*[109] in the State. then[110] shall the hardest difficulties smooth themselves before ye; *envie* shall sink to hell, *craft* and *malice* be confounded, whether it be homebred mischeif, or outlandish cunning: yea[111] other Nations will then cover to serve ye, for Lordship and victory are but the pages of *justice* and *vertue*. Commit securely to true *wisdome* the vanquishing and uncasing[112] of craft and suttletie, which are but her two runnagates: joyn your invincible might to doe worthy, and Godlike deeds, and then he that seeks to break your union, a cleaving curse be his inheritance to all generations.

Sir, you have now at length this question for the time, and as my memory would best serve me in such a copious, and vast theme, fully handl'd, and you your selfe may judge whether Prelacy be the only Church-goverment agreeable to MONARCHY. Seeing therfore the perillous, and confused estate into which we are faln, and that to the certain knowledge of all men through the irreligious pride and hatefull Tyranny of Prelats (as the innumerable, and grievous complaints of every shire cry out) if we will now resolve to settle affairs either according to pure Religion, or sound

---

[107]A petty dispute over what ecclesiastical garment (surplice) to wear.

[108]In ecclesiastical usage a tippet is "A band of silk or other material worn [by the priest] round the neck, with the two ends pendent from the shoulders in front" (*OED* 1c).

[109]The italics on such terms as "*justice*," and "*craft* and *malice*" seems to give them the status of allegorical figures.

[110]The Yale editors capitalize "then," presumably because it begins a new sentence, but often a sentence which carries on the idea of the previous sentence will begin with a lower-case letter.

[111]The word "all" (before "other Nations") has been scratched through in the Bodleian copy. The Yale editors omit "all" silently, but they and the Columbia editors include a comma after "Yea," which is not in the printed text.

[112]The taking out of a case (as in "letting the cat out of the bag").

Policy, we must first of all begin roundly to cashier, and cut away from the publick body the noysom, and diseased tumor of Prelacie, and come from Schisme to *unity* with our neighbour Reformed sister Churches, which with the blessing of *peace* and *pure* doctrine have now long time flourish'd; and doubtles with all hearty *joy*, and gratulation, will meet, and welcome our Christian *union* with them, as they have bin all this while griev'd at our strangenes and little better then separation from them. And for the Discipline propounded, seeing that it hath bin inevitably prov'd that the natural, and fundamental causes of political happines in all coverments are the same, and that this Church Discipline is taught in the Word of *God*, and, as we see, agrees according to wish with all such states as have receiv'd it, we may infallibly assure our selvs that it will as wel agree with Monarchy, though all the Tribe of *Aphorismers*, and *Politicasters* would perswade us there be secret, and misterious reasons against it. For upon the setling herof mark what nourishing and cordial restorements to the State will follow, the Ministers of the Gospel attending only to the work of *salvation* every one within his limited charge, besides the diffusive blessings of *God* upon all our actions, the King shall sit without an old disturber,[113] a dayly incroacher, and intruder; shall ridde his Kingdome of a strong sequester'd, and collateral power; a confronting miter, whose potent wealth, and wakefull ambition he had just cause to hold in jealousie: not to repeat the other present evills which only their removal will remove. And because things simply pure are inconsistent in the masse of nature, nor are the elements or humors in Mans Body exactly *homogeneall*, and hence the best founded Common-wealths, and least barbarous have aym'd at a certaine mixture and temperament, partaking the severall vertues of each other[114] State, that each part drawing to it selfe may keep up a steddy, and eev'n uprightnesse in common.

There is no Civill *Goverment* that hath beene known, no not the *Spartan*, nor the *Roman*, though both for this respect so much prais'd by the wise *Polybius*, more divinely and harmoniously tun'd, more equally ballanc'd as it were by the hand and scale of Justice, then is the Common-wealth of *England:* where under a free, and untutor'd *Monarch*, the noblest, worthiest, and most prudent men, with full approbation, and suffrage of the People have in their power the supreme, and finall determination of highest Affaires. Now if Conformity of Church *Discipline* to the Civill be so

desir'd, there can be nothing more parallel, more uniform, then when under the Soveraigne Prince *Christs* Vicegerent using the *Scepter* of *David*, according to *Gods Law*, the *godliest*, the *wisest*, the *learnedest* Ministers in their severall charges have the instructing and disciplining of *Gods people* by whose full and free Election they are consecrated to that holy and equall *Aristocracy*. And why should not the Piety, and Conscience of *Englishmen* as members of the Church be trusted in the Election of Pastors to Functions that nothing concerne a *Monarch*, as well as their worldly wisedomes are priviledg'd as *members* of the *State* in suffraging their Knights, and Burgesses to matters that concern him neerely? And if in weighing these severall Offices, their difference in time and qualitie be cast in, I know they will not turn the beame of equall Judgement the moity[115] of a scruple. Wee therfore having already a kind of Apostolicall, and ancient *Church* Election in our State, what a perversnesse would it be in us of all others to retain forcibly a kind of imperious, and stately Election in our *Church*? And what a blindnesse to thinke that what is already Evangelicall as it were by a happy chance in our *Politie*, should be repugnant to that which is the same by divine command in the Ministery? Thus then wee see that our Ecclesiall, and Politicall choyses may consent and sort as well together without any rupture in the STATE, as Christians, and Freeholders. But as for honour, that ought indeed to be different, and distinct as either Office looks a severall way, the Minister whose *Calling* and *end* is spirituall, ought to be honour'd as a Father and Physitian to the Soule (if he be found to be so) with a *Son*-like and *Disciple*-like reverence, which is indeed the dearest, and most affectionate *honour*, most to be desir'd by a wise man, and such as will easily command a free and plentifull provision of outward necessaries, without his furder care of this world.

The Magistrate whose Charge is to see to our Persons, and Estates, is to be honour'd with a more elaborate and personall Courtship, with large Salaries and Stipends, that hee himselfe may abound in those things whereof his legall justice and watchfull care gives us the quiet injoyment. And this discinction of Honour will bring forth a seemly and gracefull Uniformity over all the Kingdome.

Then shall the Nobles possesse all the Dignities and Offices of temporall honour to themselves, sole Lords without the improper mixture of Scholastick, and pusillanimous upstarts, the *Parliament* shall void her

---

[113]Presumably Archbishop William Laud.
[114]An "s" at the end of "other" was scratched out in the Bodleian copy. Both Yale and Columbia make the correction, silently.

---

[115]Small part. The image is from weighing with scales, with moral scruples bringing down the balance beam just a trifle.

Upper House of the same annoyances, the Common, and Civill *Lawes* shall be both set free, the former from the controule, the other from the meere vassalage and *Copy-hold*[116] of the *Clergie*.

And wheras *temporall Lawes* rather punish men when they have transgress't, then form them to be such as should transgresse seldomest, wee may conceive great hopes through the showres of Divine Benediction, watering the unmolested and watchfull paines of the *Ministery*, that the whole Inheritance of God will grow up so straight and blamelesse, that the Civill magistrate may with farre lesse toyle and difficulty, and far more ease and delight steare the tall and goodly *Vessell* of the Common-wealth through all the gusts and tides of the Worlds mutability.[117]

Here I might have ended, but that some Objections, which I have heard commonly flying about, presse mee to the endevour of an answere. We must not run they say into sudden extreams. This is a fallacious Rule, unlesse understood only of the actions of Vertue about things indifferent, for if it be found that those two extreames be *Vice* and *Vertue, Falshood* and *Truth*, the greater extremity of *Vertue* and superlative *Truth* we run into, the more *vertuous*, and the more *wise*, we become; and he that flying from degenerate and traditionall corruption, feares to shoot himselfe too far into the meeting imbraces of a Divinely-warranted *Reformation*, had better not have run at all. And for the suddennesse it cannot be fear'd. Who should oppose it? The *Papists*? They dare not. The *Protestants* otherwise affected. They were mad. There is nothing will be remoov'd but what to them is profess'dly indifferent. The long affection which the People have borne to it, what for it selfe, what for the odiousnes of *Prelates*, is evident: from the first yeare of Qu. *Elizabeth*, it hath still beene more and more propounded, desir'd, and be-seech't, yea sometimes favourably forwarded by the *Parliaments* themselves. Yet if it were sudden & swift, provided still it be from worse to better, certainly wee ought to hie us from evill like a torrent, and rid our selves of corrupt Discipline, as wee would shake fire out of our bosomes.

Speedy and vehement were the *Reformations* of all the good Kings of *Juda*, though the people had beene nuz-zl'd in Idolatry never so long before; they fear'd not the bug-bear danger, nor the Lyon in the way that the sluggish and timorous Politician thinks he sees; no more did our Brethren of the Reformed Churches abroad; they ventur'd (God being their guide) out of rigid POPERY, into that which wee in mockery call precise *Puritanisme*, and yet wee see no inconvenience befell them.

Let us not dally with God when he offers us a full blessing, to take as much of it as wee think will serve our ends, and turne him back the rest upon his hands, lest in his anger he snatch all from us again. Next they alledge the *antiquity* of *Episcopacy* through all *Ages*. What it was in the *Apostles* time, that questionless it must be still, and therin I trust the Ministers will be able to satisfie the *Parliament*. But if *Episcopacie* be taken for *Prelacie*, all the Ages they can deduce[118] it through, will make it no more venerable then *Papacie*.

Most certain it is (as all our *Stories*[119] beare witnesse) that ever since their coming to the See of *Canterbury* for neere twelve hundred yeares, to speake of them in gen-erall, they have been in *England* to our Soules a sad and dolefull succession of illiterate and blind guides: to our purses, and goods a wastfull band of robbers, a perpe-tuall havock, and rapine: To our state a continuall *Hy-dra* of mischiefe, and molestation, the forge of discord and Rebellion: This is the Trophey of their Antiquity, and boasted Succession through so many Ages. And for those *Prelat-Martyrs* they glory of, they are to bee judg'd what they were by the *Gospel*, and not the *Gospel* to be tried by them.

And it is to be noted that if they were for Bishopricks and Ceremonies, it was in their prosperitie, and fulnes of bread, but in their persecution, which purifi'd them, and neer their death, which was their garland, they plainely dislik'd and condemn'd the Ceremonies, and threw away those Episcopall ornaments wherein they were instal'd, as foolish and detestable, for so the words of *Ridley* at his degradment, and his letter to *Hooper* ex-pressly shew. Neither doth the Author of our Church History spare to record sadly the fall (for so he termes it) and infirmities of these Martyrs, though we would deify them. And why should their Martyrdom more countnance corrupt doctrine, or discipline, then their subscriptions justify their Treason to the Royall blood of this Relm by diverting and intaling[120] the right of the Crown from the true heires, to the houses of *Northum-berland* and *Suffolk*, which had it tooke effect, this pre-sent King had in all likelyhood never sat on this Throne, and the happy union of this Iland had bin frustrated.

Lastly, whereas they adde that some the learnedest of

---

[116]"A kind of tenure in England of ancient origin: tenure of lands being parcel of a manor, 'at the will of the lord according to the custom of the manor,' by copy of the manorial court-roll" (*OED* 1a).

[117]What Milton had to say originally ends here, on page 74 out of ninety in the original pamphlet.

[118]Close to the Latin *deducere*, "to lead downward," in this case to trace down through the ages (see *OED* 5).

[119]Histories, or chronicles.

[120]Entailing, legally binding an estate on an identifiable line of inheritors.

the reformed abroad admire our Episcopacy, it had bin more for the strength of the Argument to tell us that som of the wisest Statesmen admire it, for thereby we might guesse them weary of the present discipline, as offensive to their State, which is the bugge[121] we feare; but being they are Church-men, we may rather suspect them for some *Prelatizing-spirits* that admire our *Bishopricks*, not *Episcopacy*. The next objection vanishes of it selfe, propounding a doubt, whether a greater inconvenience would not grow from the corruption of any other discipline, then from that of *Episcopacy*. This seemes an unseasonable foresight, and out of order to deferre, and put off the most needfull constitution of one right *discipline*, while we stand ballancing the discommodity's of two corrupt ones. First constitute that which is right, and of it selfe it will discover, and rectify that which swervs, and easily remedy the pretended feare of having a *Pope* in every Parish, unlesse we call the zealous, and meek censure of the *Church*, a *Popedom*, which whoso does let him advise how he can reject the Pastorly *Rod*, and Sheep-hooke of CHRIST, and those cords of love, and not feare to fall under the iron *Scepter* of his anger that will dash him to peeces like a Potsherd.

At another doubt of theirs I wonder; whether this discipline which we desire, be such as can be put in practise within this Kingdom, they say it cannot stand with the common Law, nor with the Kings safety; the government of Episcopacy, is now so weav'd into the common Law: In *Gods* name let it weave out again; let not humain quillets[122] keep back divine authority. Tis not the common Law, nor the civil, but piety, and justice, that are our foundresses; they stoop not, neither change colour for *Aristocracy*, *democracy*, or *Monarchy*, nor yet at all interrupt their just courses, but farre above the taking notice of these inferior niceties with perfect sympathy, where ever they meet, kisse each other. Lastly, they are fearfull that the discipline which will succeed cannot stand with the Ks. safety. Wherefore? it is but *Episcopacy* reduc't to what it should be, were it not that the Tyranny of *Prelates* under the name of *Bishops* hath made our eares tender, and startling, we might call every good Minister a *Bishop*, as every *Bishop*, yea the *Apostles* themselves are call'd Ministers, and the *Angels ministring Spirits*, and the *Ministers* againe *Angels*. But wherein is this propounded government so shrewd? Because the goverment of assemblies will succeed. Did not the *Apostles* govern the Church by assemblies, how should it else be Catholik, how should it have Com-

munion? Wee count it Sacrilege to take from the rich *Prelates* their Lands, and revenu's which is Sacrilege in them to keep, using them as they doe, and can we think it safe to defraude the living Church of GOD of that right which GOD has given her in assemblies! O but the consequence: Assemblies draw to them the Supremacy of Ecclesiasticall jurisdiction. No surely, they draw no Supremacy, but that authority which CHRIST, and Saint *Paul* in his name conferrs upon them. The K. may still retain the same Supremacy in the Assemblies, as in the *Parliament*, here he can do nothing alone against the common Law, and there neither alone, nor with consent against the Scriptures. But is this all? No, this Ecclesiasticall Supremacy draws to it the power to excommunicate Kings; and then followes the worst that can be imagin'd. Doe they hope to avoyd this by keeping *Prelates* that have so often don it? Not to exemplifie the malapert insolence of our own *Bishops* in this kind towards our Kings: I shall turn back to the *Primitive*, and pure times, which the objecters would have the rule of reformation to us.

Not an assembly, but one *Bishop* alone, Saint AMBROSE of *Millan*, held *Theodosius* the most Christian Emperor under excommunication above eight moneths together, drove him from the Church in the presence of his Nobles, which the good Emperor bore with heroick *humility*, and never ceas't by prayers, and teares, till he was absolv'd, for which coming to the Bishop with *Supplication* into the *Salutory*, some out Porch of the Church, he was charg'd by him of tyrannicall madnes against GOD, for comming into holy ground. At last upon conditions absolv'd, and after great *humiliation* approaching to the Altar to offer (as those thrise pure times then thought meet) he had scarse with-drawne his hand, and stood awhile, when a bold Arch-deacon comes in the Bishops name, and chaces him from within the railes telling him peremptorily that the place wherein he stood, was for none but the *Priests* to enter, or to touch: and this is another peece of pure *Primitive Divinity*. Thinke yee then our Bishops will forgoe the power of excommunication on whomsoever? No certainly, unlesse to compasse sinister ends, and then revoke when they see their time. And yet this most mild, though withal dredfull, and inviolable Prerogative of *Christs* diadem excommunication servs for nothing with them, but to prog,[123] and pandar for fees, or to display their pride and sharpen their revenge, debarring men the protection of the Law, and I remember not whether in some cases it bereave not men all right to their worldly goods, and Inheritances besides the deniall

---

[121]I.e., bugbear.
[122]Quibbles, fruitless distinctions, petty arguments.

[123]Scrounge for, solicit.

of Christian buriall. But in the Evangelical, and reformed use of this sacred censure, no such prostitution, no such *Iscariotical* drifts are to be doubted, as that *Spiritual* doom, and sentence, should invade worldly possession, which is the rightfull lot and portion, even of the wickedest men, as frankly bestow'd upon them by the al-dispensing bounty, as *rain*, and *Sun-shine*. No, no, it seekes not to bereave or destroy the body, it seekes to save the Soule by humbling the body, not by Imprisonment, or pecuniary mulct,[124] much lesse by stripes or bonds, or disinheritance, but by Fatherly admonishment, and Christian rebuke, to cast it into godly sorrow, whose end is joy, and ingenuous bashfulnesse to sin: if that can not be wrought, then as a tender Mother takes her Child and holds it over the pit with scarring words, that it may learne to feare, where danger is, so doth excommunication as deerly, and as freely without money, use her wholsome and saving terrors, she is instant, she beseeches, by all the deere, and sweet promises of SALVATION she entices and woos, by all the threatnings, the thunders of the *Law*, and rejected *Gosspel* she charges, and adjures; this is all her Armory, her munition, her Artillery, then she awaites with long-sufferrence, and yet ardent zeale. In briefe, there is no act in all the errand of *Gods Ministers* to man-kind, wherein passes more loverlike contestation between CHRIST and the Soule of a regenerate man lapsing, then before, and in, and after the sentence of Excommunication. As for the fogging proctorage[125] of money, with such an eye as strooke *Gehezi* with Leprosy, and *Simon Magus* with a curse, so does she looke, and so threaten her firy whip against that banking den of theeves that dare thus baffle, and buy and sell the awfull, and majestick wrincles of her brow. He that is rightly and apostolically sped with her invisible arrow, if he can[126] be at peace in his Soule, and not smel within him the brimstone of Hell, may have faire leave to tell all his baggs over undiminish't of the least farding,[127] may eat his dainties, drinke his wine, use his delights, enjoy his Lands, and liberties, not the least skin rais'd, not the least haire misplac't for all that excommunication has done: much more may a King injoy his rights, and Prerogatives mundeflour'd, untouch'd, and be as absolute, and compleat a King, as all his royalties and revenu's can make him. And therefore little did *Theodosius* fear a plot upon his Empire when he stood excommunicat by Saint *Ambrose*, thought it

were done either with much hauty pride, or ignorant zeale. But let us rather look upon the reformed Churches beyond the seas, the *Grizons*, the *Suisses*, the *Hollanders*, the *French*, that have a Supremacy to live under as well as we, where do they clash and justle Supremacies with the Civil *Magistrate*? In *France* a more severe Monarchy then ours, the *Protestants* under this Church goverment carry the name of the best Subjects the King has; and yet *Presbytery*, if it must be so call'd, does there all that it desires to doe: how easie were it, if there be such great suspicion, to give no more scope to it in *England*. But let us not for feare of a scarre-crow, or else through hatred to be reform'd stand hankering and politizing, when GOD with spread hands testifies to us, and points us out the say to our peace.

Let us not be so overcredulous, unlesse GOD hath blinded us, as to trust our deer Soules into the hands of men that beg so devoutly for the pride, and gluttony of their owne backs, and bellies, that sue and sollicite so eagerly, not for the saving of Soules, the consideration of which can have heer no place at all, but for their Bishopricks, Deaneries, Prebends, and Chanonies;[128] how can these men not be corrupt, whose very cause is the bribe of their own pleading; whose mouths cannot open without the strong breath, and loud stench of avarice, Simony, and Sacrilege, embezling the treasury of the Church on painted, and guilded walles of Temples wherein GOD hath testified to have no delight, warming their Palace Kitchins, and from thence their unctuous, and epicurean paunches, with the almes of the blind, the lame, the impotent, the aged, the orfan, the widow, for with these the treasury of CHRIST ought to be, here must his jewels bestow'd, his rich Cabinet must be emptied heer; as the constant martyr Saint *Laurence* taught the *Roman Prætor*. Sir would you know that the remonstrance of these men would have, what their Petition imply's? They intreate us that we would not be weary of those insupportable greevances that our shoulders have hitherto cract under, they beseech us that we would think'em fit to be our Justices of peace, our Lords, our highest officers of State, though they come furnish't with no more experience then they learnt between the *Cook*, and the *manciple*, or more profoundly at the Colledge *audit*, or the *regent house*, or to come to their deepest insight, at their *Patrons Table*; they would request us to indure still the russling of their Silken Cassocks, and that we would burst our *midriffes* rather then laugh to see them under Sayl in all their

---

[124]Fine or penalty.

[125] Proctors were minor officials of the church who used underhanded methods to collect fees from people on trial in ecclesiastical courts (Yale 1: 608n).

[126]Expanded from "cã" in the Bodleian copy.

[127]Farthing, the smallest denomination of English coin.

---

[128]The *OED* assigns the word "Chanony" as Milton uses it to the meaning "canonry," the offices of the canons of the church.

Lawn, and Sarcenet, their shrouds, and tackle,[129] with a *geometricall rhomboides* upon their heads:[130] they would bear us in hand[131] that we must of duty wtill appear before them once a year in *Jerusalem* like good circumcizd *males*, and *Females* to be taxt by the poul, to be scons't[132] our head money, our tuppences in their Chaunlery Shop-book[133] of *Easter*. They pray us that it would please us to let them still hale us, and worrey us with their band-dogs and Pursivants;[134] and that it would please the *Parliament* that they may yet have the whipping, fleecing, and stealing of us in their diabolical Courts to tear the flesh from our bones, and into our wide wounds instead of balm, to power in the oil of Tartar, vitriol, and mercury; Surely a right reasonable, innocent, and soft-hearted Petition. O the relenting bowels of the Fathers. Can this bee granted them unlesse GOD have smitten us with frenzie[135] from above, and with a dazling giddinesse at noon-day? Should not those men rather be heard that come to plead against their own preferments, their worldly advantages, their owne abundance; for honour, and obedience to *Gods word*, the conversion of Soules, the *Christian peace* of the Land, and *union* of the reformed *Catholick Church*, the *unappropriating*, and *unmonopolizing* the rewards of *learning* and *industry*, from the greasie clutch of ignorance, and high feeding. We have tri'd already, & miserably felt what *ambition worldly glory & immoderat wealth* can do, what the boistrous & contradictional hand of a temporall, earthly, and corporeall Spiritualty can availe to the edifying of Christs holy *Church*; were it such a desperate hazard to put to the venture the universall Votes of *Christs* Congregation, the fellowly and friendly yoke of a teaching and laborious Ministery, the Pastorlike and Apostolick imitation of meeke and unlordly Discipline, the gentle and benevolent mediocritie of Church-maintenance, without the ignoble Hucsterage of pidling *Tithes*? Were it such an incurable

---

[129]The satirical image of the prelates under full sail in silk, lawn (fine linen), and sarcenet (silken cloth), is close in tone to the image of Dalila in *Samson Agonistes* 713-18.

[130]The bishop's mitre, shaped like a rhomboid or lozenge. The later Latin term was *rhomboides*, hence what looks like a plural form in a singular sense.

[131]"They would remind us."

[132]Fined or penalized (very specific to Oxford or Cambridge in Milton's time) for breaking a rule. The word "poul" refers to the head, as in "poll tax."

[133]Candle-maker's or petty shop-keeper's account book.

[134]The image is borrowed from Prynne's *Lord Bishops* (1640): "Nor wants he [Archbishop Laud] either *Canons* and *Ceremonies*, as snares to catch, nor *Pursuivants*, as Beagles to *hunt* out the *poor sheep* and to hale them to his Shambles, for refusing to be *fed* with such *hemlocke*, instead of *Gods* wholesome *word*" (chap. 6, p. [37], as reported in Yale 1: 612n).

[135]Probably prophetic ecstasy. For a biblical context of blindness at noon-day, see Isaiah 59.10.

mischiefe to make a little triall, what all this would doe to the flourishing and growing up of *Christs* mysticall body? As rather to use every poore shift, and if that serve not, to threaten uproare and combustion, and shake the brand[136] of Civill Discord?

O Sir, I doe now feele my selfe inwrapt on the sodaine into those mazes and *Labyrinths* of dreadfull and hideous thoughts, that which way to get out, or which way to end I know not, unless I turne mine eyes, and with your help lift up my hands to that Eternall and Propitious *Throne*, where nothing is readier then *grace* and *refuge* to the distresses of mortall Suppliants: and it were a shame to leave these serious thoughts lesse piously then the Heathen were wont to conclude their graver discourses.

Thou therefore that sits't in light & glory unapprochable, *Parent* of *Angels* and *Men*! next thee I implore Omnipotent King, Redeemer of that lost remnant whose nature thou didst assume, ineffable and everlasting *Love*! And thou the third subsistence of Divine Infinitude, *illumining Spirit*, the joy and solace of created *Things*! one *Tri-personall* GODHEAD! looke upon this thy poore and almost spent, and expiring *Church*, leave her not thus a prey to these importunate *Wolves*, that wait and thinke long till they devour thy tender *Flock*, these wilde *Boares* that have broke into thy *Vineyard*, and left the print of thir polluting hoofs on the Soules of thy Servants. O let them not bring about their damned *designes* that stand now at the entrance of the bottomless pit expecting the Watch-word to open and let out those dreadfull *Locusts* and *Scorpions*, to *reinvolve* us in that pitchy *Cloud* of infernall darknes, where we shall never more see the *Sunne* of thy *Truth* againe, never hope for the cheerfull dawne, never more heare the *Bird* of *Morning* sing. Be mov'd with pitty at the afflicted state of this our shaken *Monarchy*, that now lies labouring under her throwes, and struggling against the grudges of more dreaded Calamities.

O thou that after the impetuous rage of five bloody Inundations, and the succeeding Sword of intestine *Warre*, soaking the Land in her owne gore, didst pitty the sad and ceasles revolution of our swift and thick-coming sorrowes when wee were quite breathlesse, of thy *free grace* didst motion *Peace*, and termes of Cov'nant with us!, & having first welnigh freed us from *Antichristian* thraldome, didst built up this *Britannick Empire* to a glorious and enviable heighth with all her Daughter Ilands about her, stay us in this felicitie, let not the obstinacy of our halfe Obedience and will-Worship bring forth that *Viper* of *Sedition*, that for

---

[136]The fire-brand that might be carried by rioters or revolutionaries.

these Fourescore Yeares hath been breeding to eat through the entrals of our *Peace*; but let her cast her Abortive Spawne without the danger of this travailling & throbbing *Kingdome*. That we may still remember in our *solemne Thansksgivings*, how for us the *Northren Ocean* even to the frozen *Thule* was scatter'd with the proud Ship-wracks of the *Spanish Armado*, and the very maw of Hell ransack't, and made to give up her conceal'd destruction, ere shee could vent it in that horrible and damned blast.

O how much more glorious will those former Deliverances appeare, when we shall know them not onely to have sav'd us from greatest miseries past, but to have reserv'd us for greatest happinesse to come. Hitherto thou has but freed us, and that not fully, from the unjust and Tyrannous Claime of thy Foes, now unite us intirely, and appropriate us to thy selfe, tie us everlastingly in willing Homage to the *Prerogative* of thy eternall *Throne*.

And now wee knowe, O thou our most certain hope and defence, that thine enemies have been consulting all the Sorceries of the *great Whore*,[137] and have joyn'd their Plots with that sad Intelligencing Tyrant that mischiefes the World with his Mines of *Ophir*, and lies thirsting to revenge his Navall ruines that have larded our Seas; but let them all take Counsell together, and let it come to nought, let them Decree, and doe thou Cancell it, let them gather themselves and bee broken, let them imbattell, and be broken, for thou art with us.

Then amidst the *Hymns*, and *Hallelujahs* of *Saints* some one may perhaps bee heard offering at high *strains* in new and lofty *Measures* to sing and celebrate thy *divine Mercies*, and *marvelous Judgements* in this Land throughout all AGES; whereby this great and Warlike Nation instructed and inur'd to the fervent and continuall practice of *Truth* and *Righteousnesse*, and casting farre from her the *rags* of her old *vices* may presse on hard to that *high* and *happy* emulation to be found the *soberest, wisest,* and *most Christian People* at that day when thou the Eternall and shortly-expected King shalt open the Clouds to judge the severall Kingdomes of the World, and distributing *Nationall Honours* and *Rewards* to Religious and just *Common-wealths,* shall put an end to all Earthly *Tyrannies,* proclaiming thy universal and milde *Monarchy* through Heaven and Earth. Where they undoubtedly that by their *Labours, Counsels,* and *Prayers* have been earnest for the *Common good* of *Religion* and their *Countrey,* shall receive, above the inferiour *Orders* of the *Blessed,* the

Regall addition of *Principalities, Legions,* and *Thrones* into their glorious Titles, and in supereminence of *beatifick Vision* progressing the *datelesse* and *irrevoluble*[138] Circle of *Eternity* shall clasp inseparable Hands with *joy,* and *blisse* in over-measure for ever.

But they contrary that by the impairing and diminution of the true *Faith,* the distresses and servitude of their *Countrey* aspire to high *Dignity, Rule* and *Promotion* here, after a shamefull end in this *Life* (which *God* grant them) shall be thrown downe eternally into the *darkest* and *deepest Gulfe* of HELL, where under the *despightfull controule,* the trample and spurne of all the other *Damned,* that in the anguish of their *torture* shall have no other ease then to exercise a *Raving* and *Bestiall Tyranny* over them as their *Slaves* and *Negro's,* they shall remaine in that plight for ever, the *basest,* the *lowermost,* the *most dejected,* most *underfoot* and *downe-trodden Vassals of Perdition.*

The End.

---

[137]The Whore of Babylon as identified by Protestant English, the Papacy. Milton associates Jesuit plots with sorcery, in a kind of anti-Roman Catholic paranoia that sees all of Catholic continental Europe as plotting against Protestant England.

[138]"That has no finite period of revolution, whose revolution is never completed; of infinite circuit" (*OED*). Milton made up the word, apparently.

From *Reason of Church-Government*
(1642)

In his preface to the Yale edition of *The Reason of Church-Government*, Ralph Haug describes it as "the longest, and to a later age the most memorable, of the five pamphlets Milton wrote in 1641–1642 against the Anglican bishops" (Yale 1: 736). Haug points out that it is the first anti-prelatical tract to which Milton signed his name. Considering that Milton took great pride in signing his name to his later prose and poetry, the fact that this tract was the first in which he did so, as "Mr. John Milton" on the title page, does seem important. In Book 2, Milton would announce to the public his plans for becoming a great poet and a credit to his native country.

When Milton finished Book 1 of *The Reason of Church-Government*, he shifted gears, as if he were tired of what he was doing, and he began to talk about himself—his ambitions, his grand schemes, his insecurities when writing political prose. What does the digression at the beginning of Book 2 have to do with church government? Not very much at all, really. But, to a modern reader, looking for Milton the poet in the prose, what happens to the style in the pamphlet at that point is dramatic: it comes alive with passionately felt images. The invective becomes funny, the imagery becomes poetic in the sense that each image expands with allusive depth; newly coined words increase. For this reason, I have chosen in this edition to reproduce Book 1 and the preamble of Book 2. The autobiographical references in that preamble show Milton's astonishingly consistent plan for his own career: they are an announcement of his poetic ambitions to write in noble forms of poetry and in his native language, to glorify God and his country (for an outline of the principles presented, see Yale 1: 743). Though he protests that he is young to enter into such a contest with learned opponents, he hopes to overcome his youthfulness with precocious learning, and he seeks an "elegant & learned reader."

To attack the bishops, or in the specific language of his invective the prelates, was Milton's single stated purpose in writing *The Reason of Church-Government*. The *Reason* of his title has a rich and complicated meaning, something like the French *raison* in *raison d'être* or *raison d'état*. It is also a translation of the Latin *ratio*, meaning a reckoning or an account. A modern translation might be "The Rationale of Church-government," or "The Reasoning behind Church-government." For Milton, the rationale of how the church might govern itself should not allow prelates to rule, or at least not prelates who are greedy, "lordly" in the worst sense of the word, pretentious about their style of living, and obsessive in their antiquarian desire to defend custom against all reasonable objections. The difference between Milton's use of the word "Lord," meaning God the Father, and his use of "lordly," is instructive: "lordly" invariably suggests pretentious assumption of worldly power. Milton likewise cleverly uses the phrase "lording over" as in "Lording over their brethren in regard of their persons altogether unlike." By contrast, the word "minister," used today to mean the appointed leader of a congregation, for Milton had its original meaning of "servant" (see Hill 82), which, he thought, should represent the true role of the servants of the Church. For other perspectives on the imagery of the tract and its effects on its original and a modern audience, see Fish and Huntley.

A prelate was any high church official, a bishop, an archbishop, or just a patriarch (*OED* 1). In Milton's usage, the word becomes a label that allows him to avoid the words "bishop" or "archbishop," since to do so would be to launch an attack on someone as powerful as Archbishop William Laud. Laud's temporal power was dangerous to ordinary citizens. Milton's friend Alexander Gil the Younger was imprisoned for two years, having been denounced to Laud in 1628 for celebrating the assassin of King James's favorite Buckingham (Hill 28). Milton did not want to risk imprisonment, or the then customary loss of ears or nose for religious dissent.

Milton's audience, nevertheless, is Parliament, if not Archbishop Laud himself. Whenever Milton addresses "Lords and Commons," he is addressing both parties. The first instance of the form of address, incidentally, appears on p. 60 in the original printing, suggesting that Milton may have had another audience in mind to begin with. Milton's position is radical: he would, eventually, have limited church governors to elected officials (not those appointed by the King). Though his position is not anti-monarchical in this pamphlet, the power behind the bishops (in his hidden agenda) has to be the King. To attack the prelates in 1641 was not so indirectly to attack the King himself. It is probably true that "By the sixteen-forties he [Milton] was already questioning the institution of monarchy" (Hill 92), directly or indirectly. At any rate, Milton was accusing the prelates, collectively, of ripping the state apart (Loewenstein 44–45).

TEXT

The Reason of Church-Government was published only once during Milton's lifetime, in 1641. The sixty-five-page pamphlet, densely printed with few paragraphs, was presented to John Rouse, librarian of the Bodley, along with eleven other works. Milton listed it as "De ratione politicæ Ecclesiasticæ" in the table he gave to Rouse and noted that it had two books.

If the typography of the printed book tells a coherent

story, Milton seems to be jockeying for control of the process of composition, as evidenced by the use of italics and by spelling preferences. No biblical quotations are italicized until toward the end of Book 1 (p. 31 in *1641*); thereafter, quotations are italicized. The spelling of the word *authority* as "autority" also offers evidence: "Authority" appears consistently until p. 9, where "autority" first appears, never to change afterward. "Profet," a Miltonic spelling, first appears on p. 34; before that it was always "prophet." My tabulation is only sketchy at this point, but further work on the typography of the printed text may well indicate that Milton eventually broke down the resistance of the printer and the compositor, until his will was done.

My copy-text for this edition has been the copy of the 1641 edition that Milton donated to the Bodleian Library. Individual copies of *1641* used for collation in the Yale edition are listed in 1: 743–44. My text might be checked against Yale or any one of them.

Works Cited

Fish, Stanley. "Reasons That Imply Themselves: Imagery, Argument, and the Reader in Milton's *Reason of Church Government*." *Self-Consuming Artifacts: The Experience of Seventeenth-Century Literature*. Berkeley: U of California P, 1972. 265–302.

Hill, Christopher. *Milton and the English Revolution*. New York: Viking, 1977.

Huntley, John F. "The Images of Poet and Poetry in Milton's *The Reason of Church-Government*." *Achievements of the Left Hand: Essays on the Prose of John Milton*. Ed. Michael Lieb and John T. Shawcross. Amherst: U of Massachusetts P, 1974. 83–120.

Loewenstein, David. *Milton and the Drama of History: Historical Vision, Iconoclasm, and the Literary Imagination*. Cambridge: Cambridge UP, 1990.

THE
REASON
OF
Church-government
Urg'd against
PRELATY
By Mr. *John Milton*.
In two Books.[1]

The Reason of Church-government
urg'd against PRELATY.

THE PREFACE.

IN the publishing of humane lawes, which for the most part aime not beyond the good of civill society, to set them barely forth to the people without reason or Preface, like a physicall prescript,[2] or only with threatnings, as it were a lordly command, in the judgement of *Plato* was thought to be done neither generously nor wisely. His advice was, seeing that persuasion certainly is a more winning, and more manlike way to keepe men in obedience then feare, that to such lawes as were of principall moment, there should be us'd as an induction, some well temper'd discourse, shewing how good, how gainfull, how happy it must needs be to live according to honesty and justice, which being utter'd with those native colours and graces of speech, as true eloquence the daughter of vertue can best bestow upon her mothers praises, would so incite, and in a manner, charme the multitude into the love of that which is really good, as to imbrace it ever after, not of custome and awe, which most men do, but of choice

[1] In copying this title, I have used the 1641 title page as my model, in order to show the comparative sizes of type faces, which might indicate the weight of words like "Reason," "Church-government," and "Prelaty."
[2] Prescription or remedy for an ailment. Plato offers a prescription for how good doctors (lawgivers) might treat the state as compared with bad doctors in *Laws* 4.720a.

and purpose, with true and constant delight. But this practice we may learn, from a better & more ancient authority, then any heathen writer hath to give us, and indeed being a point of so high wisdome & worth, how could it be but we should find it in that book, within whose sacred context all wisdome is infolded? *Moses* therefore the only Lawgiver that we can believe to have beene visibly taught of God, knowing how vaine it was to write lawes to men whose hearts were not first season'd with the knowledge of God and of his workes, began from the book of Genesis, as a prologue to his lawes; which *Josephus*[3] right well hath noted. That the nation of the Jewes, reading therein the universall goodnesse of God to all creatures in the Creation, and his peculiar favour to them in his election of *Abraham* their ancestor, from whom they could derive so many blessings upon themselves, might be mov'd to obey sincerely by knowing so good a reason of their obedience. If then in the administration of civill justice, and under the obscurity of Ceremoniall rites, such care was had by the wisest of the heathen, and by *Moses* among the Jewes, to instruct them at least in a generall reason of that government to which their subjection was requir'd, how much more ought the members of the Church under the Gospell seeke to informe their understanding in the reason of that government which the Church claimes to have over them: especially for that the Church hath in her immediate cure those inner parts and affections of the mind where the seat of reason is; having power to examine our spirituall knowledge, and to demand from us in Gods behalfe a service intirely reasonable. But because about the manner and order of this government, whether it ought to be Presbyteriall,[4] or Prelaticall,[5] such endlesse question, or rather uproare is arisen in this land, as may be justly term'd, what the feaver is to the Physitians, the eternall reproach of our Divines;[6] whilest other profound Clerks of late greatly, as they conceive, to the advancement of Prelaty, are so earnestly meting out the Lydian proconsular Asia, to make good the prime metropolis of Ephesus,[7] as if some of our Prelates in all haste meant to change their soile, and become neighbours to the English Bishop of Chalcedon; and whilest good *Breerwood* as busily bestirres himselfe in our vulgar tongue to divide precisely the three Patriarchats, of Rome, Alexandria, and Antioch, and whether to any of these England doth belong, I shall in the meane while not cease to hope through the mercy and grace of Christ, the head and husband of his Church, that England shortly is to belong, neither to See[8] Patriarchall, nor See Prelaticall, but to the faithfull feeding and disciplining of that ministeriall order, which the blessed Apostles constituted throughout the Churches: and this I shall assay to prove can be no other, then that of Presbyters and Deacons. And if any man incline to thinke I undertake a taske too difficult for my yeares, I trust through the supreme inlightning assistances farre otherwise; for my yeares, be they few or many, what imports it? So they bring reason, let that be lookt on: and for the task, from hence that the question in hand is so needfull, to be known at this time chiefly by every meaner capacity, and containes in it the explication of many admirable and heavenly privileges reacht out to us by the Gospell, I conclude the task must be easie. God having to this end ordain'd his Gospell to be the revelation of his power and wisdome in Christ Jesus. And this is one depth of his wisdome, that he could so plainly reveale so great a measure of it to the grosse distorted apprehension of decay'd mankinde. Let others therefore dread and shun the Scriptures for their darknesse, I shall wish I may deserve to be reckon'd among those who admire and dwell upon them for their clearnesse. And this seemes to be the cause why in those places of holy writ, wherein is treated of Church-government, the reasons thereof are not formally, and prefestly set downe, because to him that heeds attentively the drift and scope of Christian profession,[9] they easily imply themselves, which thing further to explane, having now prefac'd enough, I shall no longer deferre.

---

[3]Flavius Josephus (37?–98? AD), historian of the Jews preface to the *Antiquities*. Instead of codifying laws, Moses pointed to God as the source of all inspiration and the creator of the world.

[4]Protestant hierarchy in which elders (elected lay-persons) and ministers rule each individual congregation, with selected presbyters and elders ruling a defined district presided over by a synod and, at the top, a general assembly.

[5]Roman Catholic hierarchy, followed closely in the 1640s by the English Church, by which the Archbishop of Canterbury had autocratic control over the bishops beneath him. The Anglican Church was defined by its opponents in terms of its reliance on ritual as laid out by the Book of Common Prayer, its lavish costumes and church decorations, and its politicized appointments—through a kind of old-boy network of aristocratic families with connections to the bishops.

[6]Ministers having authority within the church.

[7]Milton is attacking Archbishop James Ussher's essay, "A Geographical and Historicall Disquisition, Touching on the *Lydian* or *Proconsular Asia*, and *Seven* Metropoliticall Churches Contained Therein," in *Certain Brief Treatises* (Oxford, 1641). Theologians and church historians looked to the original division of congregations for guidance in creating a modern system of church government.

[8]Residence or seat of power for an archbishop.

[9]The professing of Christianity.

CHAP. I.

That Church-government is prescrib'd in the Gospell,
and that to say otherwise is unsound.

The first and greatest reason of Church-government, we may securely with the assent of many on the adverse part, affirme to be, because we finde it so ordain'd and set out to us by the appointment of God in the Scriptures; but whether this be Presbyteriall, or Prelaticall, it cannot be brought to the scanning, untill I have said what is meet to some who do not think it for the ease of their inconsequent opinions, to grant that Church discipline is platform'd in the Bible, but that it is left to the discretion of men. To this conceit[10] of theirs I answer, that it is both unsound and untrue. For there is not that thing in the world of more grave and urgent importance throughout the whole life of man, then is discipline. What need I instance?[11] He that hath read with judgement, of Nations and Commonwealths, of Cities and Camps, of peace and warre, sea and land, will readily agree that the flourishing and decaying of all civill societies, all the moments and turnings of humane occasions are mov'd to and fro as upon the axle of discipline. So that whatsoever power or sway in mortall things weaker men have attributed to fortune, I durst with more confidence (the honour of divine providence ever sav'd) ascribe either to the vigor, or the slacknesse of discipline. Nor is there any sociable perfection in this life civill or sacred that can be above discipline, but she is that which with her musicall cords preserves and holds all the parts thereof together. Hence in those perfect armies of *Cyrus* in *Xenophon*, and *Scipio* in the Roman stories, the excellence of military skill was esteem'd, not by the not needing, but by the readiest submitting to the edicts of their commander. And certainly discipline is not only the removall of disorder, but if any visible shape can be given to divine things, the very visible shape and image of vertue, whereby she is not only seene in the regular gestures and motions of her heavenly paces as she walkes, but also makes the harmony of her voice audible to mortall eares. Yea the Angels themselves, in whom no disorder is fear'd, as the Apostle that saw them in his rapture describes, are distinguisht and quaterniond into their celestiall Princedomes, and Satrapies, according as God himselfe hath writ his imperiall decrees through the great provinces of heav'n.[12] The state also of the blessed in Paradise, though never so perfect, is not therefore left without discipline, whose golden survaying reed marks out and measures every quarter and circuit of new Jerusalem. Yet is it not to be conceiv'd that those eternall effluences of sanctity and love in the glorified Saints should by this meanes be confin'd and cloy'd with repetition of that which is prescrib'd, but that our happinesse may orbe it selfe into a thousand vagancies[13] of glory and delight, and with a kinde of eccentricall equation be as it were an invariable Planet of joy and felicity, how much lesse can we believe that God would leave his fraile and feeble, though not lesse beloved Church here below to the perpetuall stumble of conjecture and disturbance in this our darke voyage without the card[14] and compasse of Discipline. Which is so hard to be of mans making, that we may see even in the guidance of a civill state to worldly happinesse, it is not for every learned, or every wise man, though many of them consult in common, to invent or frame a discipline, but if it be at all the worke of man, it must be of such a one as is a true knower of himselfe, and himselfe in whom contemplation and practice, wit, prudence, fortitude, and eloquence must be rarely met, both to comprehend the hidden causes of things, and span in his thoughts all the various effects that passion or complexion can worke in mans nature; and hereto must his hand be at defiance with gaine, and his heart in all vertues heroick. So far is it from the kenne of these wretched projectors of ours[15] that bescraull their Pamflets every day with new formes of government for our Church. And therefore all the ancient lawgivers were either truly inspir'd as *Moses,* or were such men as with authority anough might give it out to be so, as *Minos, Lycurgus, Numa,*[16] because they wisely forethought that men would never quietly submit to such a discipline as had not more of Gods hand in it then mans. To come within the narrownesse of houshold government, observation will shew us many deepe[17] counsellers of state and judges to demean themselves incorruptly in the setl'd course of affaires,

---

[10]Fanciful notion, idea.
[11]"Why do I need to give examples?"

[12]The military hierarchy of angels, as it was understood in Milton's time. Chapter 9 of Milton's *On Christian Doctrine* describes them as often appearing to be soldiers.
[13]"Wanderings." Milton may have invented the word; at least he is the first cited for the noun ("vagant" is the adjective form, built on Latin *vagans,* "wandering").
[14]Map. Specifically, "The circular piece of stiff paper on which the 32 points are marked in the mariner's compass" (*OED* 4.a).
[15]"So far is it removed from the understanding of those stupid, amateurish experimenters of ours."
[16]All proverbial judges of humankind, in this world or the Greek and Roman underworld.
[17]Wise.

and many worthy Preachers upright in their lives, powerfull in their audience; but look upon either of these men where they are left to their own disciplining at home, and you shall soone perceive for all their single knowledge and uprightnesse, how deficient they are in the regulating of their own family; not only in what may concerne the vertuous and decent composure of their minds in their severall places, but that which is of a lower and easier performance the right possessing of the outward vessell, their body, in health or sicknesse, rest or labour, diet, or abstinence, whereby to render it more pliant to the soule, and usefull to the Commonwealth: which if men were but as good to discipline themselves, as some are to tutor their Horses and Hawks, it could not be so grosse in most housholds. If then it appear so hard and so little knowne, how to governe a house well, which is thought of so easie discharge, and for every mans undertaking, what skill of man, what wisdome, what parts, can be sufficient to give lawes & ordinances to the elect houshold of God? If we could imagine that he had left it at randome without his provident and gracious ordering, who is he so arrogant so presumptuous that durst dispose and guide the living arke of the holy Ghost, though he should finde it wandring in the field of *Bethshemesh*,[18] without the conscious warrant of some high calling. But no profane insolence can paralell that which our Prelates dare avouch, to drive outragiously, and shatter the holy arke of the Church, not born upon their shoulders with pains and labour in the word, but drawne with rude oxen their officials, and their owne brute inventions. Let them make shewes of reforming while they will, so long as the Church is mounted upon the Prelaticall Cart, and not as it ought between the hands of the Ministers, it will but shake and totter, and he that sets to his hand though with a good intent to hinder the shogging[19] of it, in this unlawfull waggonry wherein it rides, let him beware it be not fatall to him as it was to *Uzza*.[20] Certainly if God be the father of his family the Church, wherein could he expresse that name more, then in training it up under his owne all-wise and dear Oeconomy,[21] not turning it loose to the havock of strangers and wolves that would ask no better plea then this to doe in the Church of Christ, what ever humour, faction, policy, or licentious will would prompt them

to. Againe, if Christ be the Churches husband expecting her to be presented before him a pure unspotted virgin;[22] in what could he shew his tender love to her more, then in prescribing his owne wayes which he best knew would be to the improvement of her health and beauty with much greater care doubtlesse then the Persian King could appoint for his Queene *Esther*,[23] those maiden dietings & set prescriptions of baths, & odors, which may render[24] her at last the more amiable to his eye. For of any age or sex, most unfitly may a virgin be left to an uncertaine and arbitrary education. Yea though she be well instructed, yet is she still under a more strait tuition, especially if betroth'd. In like manner the Church bearing the same resemblance, it were not reason to think she whould be left destitute of that care which is as necessary, and proper to her, as instruction. For publick preaching indeed is the gift of the Spirit working as best seemes to his secret will, but discipline is the practick work of preaching directed and apply'd as is most requisite to particular duty; without which it were all one to the benefit of souls, as it would be to the cure of bodies, if all the Physitians in London should get into the severall Pulpits of the City, and assembling all the diseased in every parish should begin a learned Lecture of Pleurisies, Palsies, Lethargies, to which perhaps none there present were inclin'd, and so without so much as feeling one puls, or giving the least order to any skilfull Apothecary, should dismisse 'em from time to time, some groaning, some languishing, some expiring, with this only charge to look well to themselves, and do as they heare. Of what excellence and necessity then Church-discipline is, how beyond the faculty of man to frame, and how dangerous to be left to mans invention who would be every foot turning it to sinister ends, how properly also it is the worke of God as father, and of Christ as Husband of the Church; we have by thus much heard.

CHAP. II.
That Church governement is set downe in holy Scripture,
and that to say otherwise is untrue.

AS therefore it is unsound to say that God hath not appointed any set government in his Church, so is it untrue. Of the time of the Law there can be no doubt; for to let passe the first institution of Priests and Levites, which is too cleare to be insisted upon, when the

---

[18]In 1 Samuel 6.14, the ark of the covenant, the sacred chest which held the stones on which were written the Ten Commandments, is brought by Philistines to the filed of Bethshemesh.
[19]"Shaking," "jolting."
[20]2 Samuel 6 describes God's punishment of Uzza for his arrogance in touching the ark.
[21]Management of a household.

---

[22]2 Corinthians 11.2.
[23]Rituals of purification for the bride of Ahasuerus (Ester 2.12).
[24]Corrected by the errata list from "tender."

Temple came to be built, which in plaine judgement could breed no essentiall change either in religion, or in the Priestly government; yet God to shew how little he could endure that men should be tampring and contriving in his worship, though in things of lesse regard, gave to *David* for *Solomon* not only a pattern and modell of the Temple, but a direction for the courses of the Priests and Levites, and for all the worke of their service. At the returne from the Captivity things were only restor'd after the ordinance of *Moses* and *David*; or if the least alteration be to be found, they had with them inspired men, Prophets, and it were not sober to say they did ought of moment without divine intimation. In the Prophesie of *Ezekiel* from the 40 Chapt. onward, after the destruction of the Temple, God by his Prophet seeking to weane the hearts of the Jewes from their old law to expect a new and more perfect reformation under Christ, sets out before their eyes the stately fabrick & constitution of his Church, with al the ecclesiasticall functions appertaining; indeed the description is as sorted best to the apprehension of those times, typicall and shadowie,[25] but in such manner as never yet came to passe, nor never must literally, unlesse we mean to annihilat the Gospel. But so exquisit and lively the description is in portraying the new state of the Church, and especially in those points where government seemes to be most active, that both Jewes and Gentiles might have good cause to be assur'd, that God when ever he meant to reforme his Church, never intended to leave the governement thereof delineated here in such curious architecture, to be patch't afterwards, and varnish't over with the devices and imbellishings of mans imagination. Did God take such delight in measuring out the pillars, arches, and doores of a materiall Temple, was he so punctuall and circumspect in lavers, altars, and sacrifices soone after to be abrogated, lest any of these should have beene made contrary to his minde? Is not a farre more perfect worke more agreeable to his perfection in the most perfect state of the Church militant, the new alliance of God to man? should not he rather now by his owne prescribed discipline have cast his line and levell[26] upon the soule of man which is his rationall temple, and by the divine square and compasse thereof forme and regenerate in us the lovely shapes of vertues and graces, the sooner to edifie and accomplsh that immortal stature of Christs body which is his Church, in all her glorious lineaments and proportions. And that this indeed God hath done

for us in the Gospel we shall see with open eyes, not under a vaile. We may passe over the history of the Acts and other places, turning only to those Epistles of S. *Paul* to *Timothy* and *Titus*: where the spirituall eye may discerne more goodly and gracefully erected then all the magnificence of Temple or Tabernackle, such a heavenly structure of evangelick discipline so diffusive of knowledge and charity to the prosperous increase and growth of the Church, that it cannot be wonder'd if that elegant and artfull symmetry of the promised new temple in *Ezechiel*,[27] and all those sumptuous things under the Law were made to signifie the inward beauty and splendor of the Christian Church thus govern'd. And whether this be commanded let it now be judg'd. S. *Paul* after his preface to the first of *Timothy* which hee concludes in the 17 Verse with Amen, enters upon the subject of his Epistle which is is to establish the Church-government with a command. This charge I commit to thee son *Timothy*: according to the prophecies which went before on thee, that thou by them might'st war a good warfare. Which is plain enough thus expounded. This charge I commit to thee wherein I now go about to instruct thee how thou shalt set up Church-discipline, that thou might'st warre a good warfare, bearing thy selfe constantly and faithfully in the Ministery, which in the 1 to the Corinthians is also call'd a warfare: and so after a kinde of Parenthesis concerning *Hymenæus* he returnes to his command though under the milde word of exhorting, Cap.2.v.1. I exhort therefore. As if he had interrupted his former command by the occasionall mention of *Hymenæus*. More beneath in the 14.V. of the 3 C. when he hath deliver'd the duties of Bishops or Presbyters and Deacons not once naming any other order in the Church, he thus addes. These thing write I unto thee hoping to come unto thee shortly (such necessity it seems there was) but if I tarry long, that thou mai'st know how thou ought'st to behave thy selfe in the house of God. From this place it may be justly ask'd, whether *Timothy* by this here written might know what was to be knowne concerning the orders of Church governours or no? If he might, then in such a cleere text as this may we know without further jangle; if he might not, then did S. *Paul* write insufficiently, and moreover said not true, for he saith here he might know, and I perswade my selfe he did know ere this was written, but that the Apostle had more regard to the instruction of us, then to the informing of him. In the fifth Chap. after some other Church precepts concerning discipline, mark what a

---

[25]The description, in other words, is accommodated to the understanding of the people at the time, and is therefore sorted according to Old and New Testament types (typical) and mystical (shadowy).
[26]The tools of the carpenter and architect.

---

[27]A Miltonic spelling for "Ezekial" seems to have gotten through the compositor.

dreadfull command followes, Verse 21. I charge thee before God and the Lord Jesus Christ, and the elect Angels, that thou observe these things, and as if all were not yet sure enough, he closes up the Epistle with an adjuring charge thus. I give thee charge in the sight of God who quickneth all things, and before Christ Jesus, that thou keepe this commandement: that is the whole commandement concerning discipline, being the maine purpose of the Epistle: although *Hooker*[28] would faine have this denouncement referr'd to the particular precept going before, because the word Commandement is in the singular number, not remembring that even in the first Chapt. of this Epistle, the word Commandement is us'd in a plurall sense, *Vers.* 5. Now the end[29] of the Commandement is charity. And what is more frequent then in like manner to say the Law of *Moses.* So that either to restraine the significance too much, or too much to inlarg it would make the adjuration either not so waighty, or not so pertinent. And thus we find here that the rules of Church-discipline are not only commanded, but hedg'd about with such a terrible impalement of commands, as he that will break through wilfully to violate the least of them, must hazard the wounding of his conscience even to death. Yet all of this notwithstanding we shall finde them broken wellnigh all by the faire pretenders even of the next ages. No lesse to the contempt of him whom they fain to be the archfounder of prelaty S. *Peter*, who by what he writes in the 5 Chap. of his first Epistle should seeme to be farre another man then tradition reports him: there he commits to the Presbyters only full authority both of feeding the flock, and Episcopating: and commands that obedience be given to them as to the mighty hand of God, wch is his mighty ordinance. Yet all this was as nothing to repell the ventrous boldnesse of innovation[30] that ensu'd, changing the decrees of God that is immutable, as if they had been breath'd by man. Neverthelesse when Christ by those visions of S. *John* foreshewes the reformation of his church, he bids him take his Reed[31] and meet it out againe after the first patterne, for he prescribes him no other. Arise, said the Angell, and measure the Temple of God and the Altar, and them that worship therein. What is there in the world can measure men but discipline? Our word ruling imports no lesse. Doctrine indeed is the measure, or at least the reason of measure, tis true, but unlesse the mea-

sure be apply'd to that which it is to measure, how can it actually doe its proper worke? Whether therefore discipline be all one with doctrine, or the particular application thereof to this or that person, we all agree that doctrine must be such only as is commanded; or whether it be something really differing from doctrine, yet was it only of Gods appointment, as being the most adequat measure of the Church and her children, which is here the office of a great Evangelist and the reed given him from heaven. But that part of the Temple which is not thus measur'd, so farre is it from being in Gods tuition or delight, that in the following verse he rejects it, however in shew and visibility it may seeme a part of his Church, yet in as much as it lyes thus unmeasur'd he leaves it to be trampl'd by the Gentiles, that is to be polluted with idolatrous and Gentilish rites and ceremonies. And that the principall reformation here foretold is already come to passe as well in discipline as in doctrine the state of our neighbour Churches afford us to behold. Thus through all the periods and changes of the Church it hath beene prov'd that God hath still reserv'd to himselfe the right of enacting Church-government.

CHAP. III.

That it is dangerous and unworthy the Gospell to hold that Church-government is to be pattern'd by the Law, as B. Andrews *and the Primat of* Armagh *maintaine.*

WE may returne now from this interposing difficulty thus remov'd, to affirme, that since Church-government is so strictly commanded in Gods Word, the first and greatest reason why we should submit thereto, is because God hath so commanded. But whether of these two, Prelaty or Presbytery can prove it selfe to be supported by this first and greatest reason, must be the next dispute. Wherein this position is to be first layd down is granted; that I may not follow a chase rather then an argument, that one of these two, and none other is of Gods ordaining, and if it be, that ordinance must be evident in the Gospell. For the imperfect and obscure institution of the Law, which the Apostles themselves doubt not oft-times to vilifie, cannot give rules to the compleat and glorious ministration of the Gospell, which lookes on the Law, as on a childe, not as on a tutor. And that the Prelates have no sure foundation in the Gospell, their own guiltinesse doth manifest: they would not else run questing up as high as *Adam* to fetch their originall, as tis said one of them lately did in publick. To which assertion, had I heard

---

[28]Richard Hooker, *Of the Laws of Ecclesiastical Polity* 3.11.11: "The very words themselves doe restraine themselves unto some one speciall commandement among many" (1611 ed., as quoted in Yale 1: 759n).
[29]Goal.
[30]The adventuresome or boldly dangerous quest for novelty.
[31]The measuring reed mentioned in Ezekial 42.16.

it,[32] because I see they are so insatiable of antiquity, I should have gladly assented, and confest them yet more ancient. For *Lucifer*[33] before *Adam* was the first prelat Angel, and both he, as is commonly thought, and our forefather *Adam*, as we all know, for aspiring above their orders, were miserably degraded. But others better advis'd are content to receive their beginning from *Aaron* and his sons, among whom B. *Andrews*[34] of late yeares, and in these times the Primat of *Armagh*[35] for their learning are reputed the best able to say what may be said in this opinion. The Primat in his discourse about the originall of Episcopacy newly revis'd begins thus. The ground of Episcopacy is fetcht partly from the pattern prescrib'd by God in the old Testament, and partly from the imitation thereof brought in by the Apostles. Herein I must entreat to be excus'd of the desire I have to be satisfi'd, how for example the ground of Episcop. is fetch't partly from the example of the old Testament, by whom next, and by whose authority. Secondly, how the Church-government under the Gospell can be rightly call'd an imitation of that in the old Testament? for that the Gospell is the end and fulfilling of the Law, our liberty also from the bondage of the Law I plainly reade. How then the ripe age of the Gospell should be put to schoole againe, and learn to governe her selfe from the infancy of the Law, the stronger to imitate the weaker, the freeman to follow the captive, the learned to be lesson'd by the rude, will be a hard undertaking to evince from any of those principles which either art or inspiration hath written. If any thing done by the Apostles may be drawne howsoever to a likenesse of something Mosaicall, if it cannot be prov'd that it was done of purpose in imitation, as having the right thereof grounded in nature, and not in ceremony or type, it will little availe the matter. The whole Judaick law is either politicall, and to take patter by that, no Christian nation ever thought it selfe oblig'd in conscience or morall, which containes in it the observation of whatsoever is substantially, and perpetually true and good, either in religion, or course of life. That which is thus morall, besides what we fetch from those unwritten lawes and Ideas which nature hath ingraven in us, the Gospell, as stands with her dignity most, lec-

tures to us from her own authentick hand-writing and command, not copies out from the borrow'd manuscript of a subservient scrowl,[36] by way of imitating. As well might be said in her Sacrament of water to imitate the baptisme of *John*. That though she retaine excommunication us'd in the Synagogue, retain the morality of the Sabbath, she does not therefore imitate the law her underling, but perfect her. All that was morally deliver'd from the law to the Gospell in the office of the Priests and Levites, was that there should be a ministery set a part to teach and discipline the Church, both which duties the Apostles thought good to commit to the Presbyters. And if any distinction of honour were to be made among them, they directed it should be to those not that only rule well, but especially to those that labor in the word and doctrine. By which[37] we are taught that laborious teaching is the most honourable Prelaty that one Minister can have above another in the Gospell: if therefore the superiority of Bishopship be grounded on the Priesthood as part of the morall law, it cannot be said to be an imitation; for it were ridiculous that morality should imitate morality, which ever was the same thing. This very word of patterning or imitating excludes Episcopacy from the solid and grave Ethicall law, and betraies it to be a meere childe of ceremony, or likelier some misbegotten thing, that having pluckt the gay feathers of her obsolet bravery to hide her own deformed barenesse, now vaunts and glories in her stolne plumes. In the mean while what danger there is against the very life of the Gospell to make in any thing the typical law her pattern, and how impossible in that which touches the Priestly government, I shall use such light as I have receav'd, to lay open. It cannot be unknowne by what expressions the holy Apostle S. *Paul* spares not to explane to us the nature and condition of the law, calling those ordinances which were the chiefe and essentiall offices of the Priests, the elements and rediments of the world both weake and beggarly. Now to breed, and bring up the children of the promise, the heirs of liberty and grace under such a kinde of government as is profest to be but an imitation of that ministery which engender'd to bondage the sons of *Agar*,[38] how can this be but a foul injury and derogation, if not a cancelling of that birthright and immunity which Christ hath purchas'd for us

---

[32]Milton may have heard John Williams, Bishop of Lincoln, make the statement during the week of November 1–8, 1641 (Yale 1: 762n).

[33]Milton is playing on the idea of Lucifer ('light-bearer') as an angel who questions hierarchy before the Fall who of course becomes Satan as a result. For biblical reinforcement, see Isaiah 14.12: "How art thou fallen from heaven, O Lucifer, son of the morning."

[34]Lancelot Andrews (1555–1626), Bishop of Winchester, for whom Milton had written a memorial poem in Latin.

[35]James Ussher (1581–1656), Archbishop (in this case "Primate") of the northern Irish diocese of Armagh.

---

[36]Scroll, roll of parchment for writing on. Apparently the image is of reading from a second-hand copy, rather than using the original manuscript from an author.

[37]Marginal note: "I Tim. 5," a reference to "Let the elders that rule well be counted worthy of double honour, especially they who labour in the word and doctrine" (1 Timothy 5.17).

[38]Hagar or Agar is the bondswoman or slave to Abraham and the mother of Ishmael, who is treated as a servant (Galatians 4.22–31).

with his blood. For the ministration of the law consisting of carnall things, drew to it such a ministery as consisted of carnall respects, dignity, precedence, and the like. And such a ministery establish't in the Gospell, as is founded upon the points and termes of superiority, and nests it selfe in worldly honours, will draw to it, and we see it doth, such a religion as runnes back againe to the old pompe and glory of the flesh. For doubtlesse there is a certaine attraction and magnetick force betwixt the religion and the ministeriall forme thereof. If the religion be pure, spirituall, simple, and lowly, as the Gospel most truly is, such must the face of the ministery be. And in like manner if the forme of the Ministery be grounded in the worldly degrees of autority, honour, temporall jurisdiction, we see it with our eyes it will turne the inward power and purity of the Gospel into the outward carnality of the law; evaporating and exhaling the internal worship into empty conformities, and gay shewes. And what remains then but that wee should runne into as dangerous and deadly apostacy as our lamented neighbours the Papists, who by this very snare and pitfall of imitating the ceremonial law, fel into that irrecoverable superstition, as must needs make void the cov'nant of salvation to them that persist in this blindnesse.

CHAP. IV.

That it is impossible to make the Priesthood of Aaron
a pattern whereon to ground Episcopacy.

THat which was promis'd next, is to declare the impossibility of grounding Evangelick government in the imitation of the Jewish Priesthood: which will be done by considering both the quality of the persons, and the office it selfe. *Aaron* and his sonnes were the Princes of their Tribe before they were sanctified to the Priesthood: that personall eminence which they held above the other *Levites*, they receav'd not only from their office, but partly brought it into their office: and so from that time forward the Priests were not chosen out of the whole number of the Levites, our Bishops, but were borne inheritors of the dignity. Therefore unlesse we shall choose our Prelats only out of the Nobility, and let them runne in a blood,[39] there can be no possible imitation of Lording over their brethren in regard of their persons altogether unlike. As

for the office w^ch[40] was a representation of Christs own person more immediately in the high Priest, & of his whole priestly office in all the other; to the performance of wch the Levits were but as servitors & Deacons, it was necessary there should be a distinction of dignity betweene two functions of so great ods. But there being no such difference among our Ministers, unlesse it be in reference to the Deacons, it is impossible to found a Prelaty upon the imitation of this Priesthood. For wherein, or in what worke is the office of a Prelat excellent above that of a Pastor? in ordination you'l say; but flatly against Scripture, for there we know *Timothy* receav'd ordination by the hands of the Presbytery, notwithstanding all the vaine delusions that are us'd to evade that testimony, and maintaine an unwarrantable usurpation. But wherefore should ordination be a cause of setting up a superior degree in the Church? is not that whereby Christ became our Saviour a higher and greater worke, then that whereby he did ordaine messengers to preach and publish him our Saviour? Every Minister sustains the person of Christ in his highest work of communicating to us the mysteries of our salvation, and hath the power of binding and absolving, how should he need a higher dignity to represent or execute that which is an inferior work in Christ? why should the performance of ordination which is a lower office exalt a Prelat, and not the seldome discharge of a higher and more noble office wch is administring much rather depresse him? Verily neither the nature, nor the example of ordination doth any way require an imparity betweene the ordainer and the ordained. For what more naturall then every like to produce his like, man to beget man, fire to propagate fire, and in examples of highest opinion the ordainer is inferior to the ordained; for the Pope is not made by the precedent Pope, but by Cardinals, who ordain and consecrate to a higher and greater office then their own.

---

[39] I cannot find the phrase among seventeenth-century idioms or in the *OED*, but I assume that it means "unless they seem to be blood-brothers."

[40] Towards the end of p. 13, the compositor of this volume seems to have been trying to squeeze more than the normal volume of words into the page, witness the "w^ch" in place of "which" and ampersand in place of "and." Even the spelling "Levits" for "Levites" seems to have been affected.

CHAP. V.

To the Arguments of B. Andrews *and the* Primat.

IT followes here to attend to certaine objections in a little treatise lately printed among others of like sort at *Oxford*, and in the title said to be out of the rude draughts of Bishop *Andrews*. And surely they bee rude draughts indeed, in so much that it is marvell to think what his friends meant to let come abroad such shallow reasonings with the name of a man so much bruited for learning. In the 12 and 23 pages he seemes most notoriously inconstant to himselfe; for in the former place he tels us he forbeares to take any argument of Prelaty from *Aaron*, as being the type of Christ. In the latter he can forbeare no longer, but repents him of his rash gratuity, affirming, that to say, Christ being come in the flesh, his figure in the high Priest ceaseth, is the shift of an Anabaptist; and stiffly argues that Christ being as well King as Priest, was as well fore-resembled by the Kings then, as by the high Priest. So that if his comming take away the one type, it must also the other. Marvellous piece of divinity! and well worth that the land should pay six thousand pound a yeare for, in a Bishoprick, although I reade of no Sophister among the Greeks that was so dear,[41] neither *Hippias* nor *Protagoras*,[42] nor any whom the Socratick school famously refuted without hire. Here we have the type of the King sow'd to the typet[43] of the Bishop, suttly to cast a jealousie upon the Crowne, as if the right of Kings, like *Meleager*[44] in the Metamorphosis, were no longer liv'd then the firebrand of Prelaty. But more likely the Prelats fearing (for their own guilty carriage protests they doe feare)[45] that their faire dayes cannot long hold, practize by possessing the King with[46] this most false doctrine, to ingage his power for them, as in his owne quarrell, that when they fall they may fall in a generall ruine, just as cruell *Tyberius* would wish,

When I dye, let the earth be roul'd in flames.[47]

But where, O Bishop, doth the purpose of the law set forth Christ to us as King? That which never was intended in the Law, can never be abolish't as part thereof. When the Law was made, there was not King: if before the law, or under the law God by a speciall type in any King would foresignifie the future kingdome of Christ, which is not yet visibly come, what was that to the law? The whole ceremoniall law, and types can be in no law else, comprehends nothing but the propitiatory office of Christs Priesthood, which being in substance accomplisht, both law and Priesthood fades away of it selfe, and passes into aire like a transitory vision, and the right of Kings neither stands by any type nor falls. We acknowledge that the civill magistrate weares an autority of Gods giving, and ought to be obey'd as his vicegerent. But to make a King a type, we say is an abusive and unskilfull speech, and of a morall solidity make it seeme a ceremoniall shadow. Therefore your typical chaine of King and Priest must unlink. But is not the type of Priest taken away by Christs comming? no saith this famous Protestant Bishop of Winchester; it is not, and he that saith it is, is an Anabaptist. What think ye Readers, do ye not understand him? What can be gather'd hence but that the Prelat would still sacrifice? conceave him readers, he would mistificate.[48] Their altars indeed were in a fair forwardnesse; and by such arguments as these they were setting up the molten Calfe of their Masse againe, and of their great Hierarch the Pope. For if the type of Priest be not taken away, then neither of the high Priest, it were a strange beheading; and high Priest more then one there cannot be, and that one can be no lesse then a Pope. And this doubtlesse was the bent of his career, though never so covertly. Yea but there was something else in the high Priest besides the figure, as is plain by S. *Pauls* acknowledging him. Tis true that in the 17 of *Deut.* whence this autority arises to the Priest in matters too hard for the secular judges, as must needs be many in the occasions of those times involv'd so with ceremoniall niceties, no wonder though it be commanded to enquire at the mouth of the Priests, who besides the Magistrates their collegues had the Oracle of Urim[49] to consult with. And whether the high Priest *Ananias* had not incroach't beyond the limits of his Priestly autority, or whether us'd it rightly, was no time them for S. *Paul* to contest about. But if this instance be able to assert any right of jurisdiction to the Clergy, it must impart it in common to all Ministers, since it were

---

[41]Expensive.

[42]Sophists were paid to teach virtue, as with Hippias and Protagoras, whom Socrates made fun of in Plato's *Protagoras*.

[43]A tippet is part of the bishop's costume. Milton's nephew Edward Phillips defined it as "a certain long Scarf which Doctors of Divinity wear when they go abroad in their Gowns" (see *OED* i.c). Milton's clever homonym is built on "type"/"tippet."

[44]Meleager lived only as long as the piece of wood that represented his life remained unburnt by the three Fates (Ovid, *Metamorphoses* 8.451–56).

[45]Their own guilty body-language demonstrates the fact that they do live in fear.

[46]"Putting this false information into possession of the King."

[47]Attributed to Nero by Suetonius, *Life of Nero* 38.

[48]A word obviously made up on the spot, one which has not made it into the *OED*.

[49]Compare *Paradise Regain'd* 3.14, and the note on Urim and Thummim.

a great folly to seeke for counsell in a hard intricat scruple from a Dunce Prelat, when there might be found a speedier solution from a grave and learned Minister, whom God hath gifted with the judgement of Urim more amply oft-times then all the Prelates together; and now in the Gospell hath granted the privilege of this oraculous Ephod alike to all his Ministers. The reason therefore of imparity in the Priests, being now as is aforesaid, really annull'd both in their person, and in their representative office, what right of jurisdiction soever can be from this place Levitically bequeath'd, must descend upon the Ministers of the Gospell equally, as it findes them in all other points equall. Well then he is finally content to let *Aaron* go. *Eleazar* will serve his turne, as being a superior of superiors, and yet no type of Christ in *Aarons* life time. O thou that would'st winde into any figment, or phantasme to save thy Miter! Yet all this will not fadge,[50] though it be cunningly interpolisht by some second hand with crooks[51] & emendations; Heare then; the type of Christ in some one particular, as of entring yearly into the Holy of holies and such like, rested upon the High Priest only as more immediately personating our Saviour: but to resemble his whole satisfactory office all the lineage of *Aaron* was no more then sufficient. And all, or any of the Priests, consider'd separately without relation to the highest, are but as a livelesse trunk[52] and signifie nothing. And this shewes the excellence of Christs sacrifice, who at once and in one person fulfill'd that which many hunderds of Priests many times repeating had anough to foreshew. What other imparity there was among themselves, we may safely suppose it depended on the dignity of their birth and family, together with the circumstances of a carnall service, which might afford many priorities. And this I take to be the summe of what the Bishop hath laid together to make plea for Prelaty by imitation of the Law. Though indeed, if it may stand, it will inferre Popedome all as well. Many other courses he tries, enforcing himselfe with much ostentation of endlesse genealogies, as if he were the man that S. *Paul* forewarnes us of in *Timothy*, but so unvigorously, that I do not feare his winning of many to his cause, but such as doting upon great names are either over-weake, or over sudden of faith. I shall not refuse therefore to leane so much prudence as I finde in the Roman Souldier that attended the crosse, not to stand breaking of legs, when the breath is quite out of the body, but passe to that which follows. The Primat of *Armagh* at the beginning

of his tractat seeks to availe himselfe of that place in the 66 of *Isaiah*, I will take of them for Priests and Levites, saith the Lord; to uphold hereby such a forme of superiority among the ministers of the Gospell, succeeding those in the law, as the Lords day did the Sabbath. But certain if this method may be admitted of interpreting those propheticall passages concerning Christian times in a punctuall correspondence, it may be with equall probability be urg'd upon us, that we are bound to observe some monthly solemnity answerable to the new moons, as well as the Lords day which we keepe in lieu of the Sabbath: for in the 23 v. the Prophet joynes them in the same manner together, as before he did the Priests and Levites, thus. And it shall come to passe that from one new moone to another, and from one Sabbath to another shall all flesh come to worship before me, saith the Lord. Undoubtedly with as good consequence may it be alledg'd from hence, that we are to solemnize some religious monthly meeting different from the Sabbath, as from the other any distinct formality of Ecclesiasticall orders may be inferr'd. This rather will appeare to be the lawfull and unconstrain'd sense of the text, that God in taking of them for Priests and Levites, will not esteeme them unworthy though Gentiles, to undergoe any function in the Church, but will make of them a full and perfect ministery, as was that of the Priests and Levites in their kinde. And Bishop *Andrews* himselfe to end the controversie, sends us a candid exposition of this quoted verse from the 24. page of his said book, plainly deciding that God by those legall names there of Priests and Levites means our Presbyters, and Deacons, for which either ingenuous confession, or slip of his pen we give him thanks, and withall to him that brought these treatises into one volume, who setting the contradictions of two learned men so neere together, did not foresee. What other deducements or analogies are cited out of S. *Paul* to prove a likenesse betweene the Ministers of the Old and New Testament, having tri'd their sinewes I judge they may passe without harme doing to our cause. We may remember then that Prelaty neither hath nor can have foundation in the law, nor yet in the Gospell, which assertion as being for the plainnesse thereof a matter of eye sight, rather then of disquisition I voluntarily omitt, not forgetting to specifie this note againe, that the earnest desire which the Prelates have to build their Hierarchy upon the sandy bottome of the law, gives us to set abundantly the little assurance which they finde to reare up their high roofs by the autority of the Gospell, repulst as it were from the writings of the Apostles, and driven to take sanctuary among the Jewes. Hence that open confession of the Primat before mention'd. Episcopacy is fetcht partly from the patterne of the Old

---

[50]Agree, be suitable.
[51]Bracketed items [as in this addition].
[52]Headless, lifeless body.

Testament, & partly from the New as an imitation of the Old, though nothing can be more rotten in Divinity then such a position as this, and is all one as to say Episcopacy is partly of divine institution, and partly of mans own carving. For who gave the autority to fetch more from the patterne of the law then what the Apostles had already fetcht, if they fetcht any thing at a'l, as hath beene prov'd they did not. So was *Jereboams*[53] Episcopacy partly from the patterne of the law, and partly from the patterne of his owne carnality; a parti-colour'd and a parti-member'd Episcopacy, and what can this be lesse then a monstrous? Others therefore among the Prelats perhaps not so well able to brook, or rather to justifie this foule relapsing to the old law, have condiscended at last to a plaine confessing that both the names and office of Bishops and Presbyters at first were the same, and in the Scriptures no where distinguisht. This grants the remonstrant in the fift Section of his defence, and in the Preface to his last short answer. But what need respect be had whether he grant or grant it not, when as through all antiquity, and even in the loftiest times of Prelaty we find it granted. *Jerome* the learned'st of the Fathers hides not his opinion, that custome only, which the Proverbe cals a tyrant, was the maker of Prelaty; before his audacious workmanship the Churches were rul'd in common by the Presbyters, and such a certaine truth this was esteem'd, that it became a decree among the Papall Canons compil'd by *Gratian*. *Anselme* also of Canturbury, who to uphold the points of his Prelatisme made himselfe a traytor to his country, yet commenting the Epistles to *Titus* and the *Philippians* acknowledges from the cleernesse of the text, what *Jerome* and the Church Rubrick hath before acknowledg'd. He little dreamt then that the weeding-hook of reformation would after two ages pluck up his glorious poppy from insulting over the good corne. Though since some of our Brittish Prelates seeing themselves prest to produce Scripture, try all their cunning, if the New Testament will not help them to frame of their own heads as it were with wax a kind of Mimick Bishop limm'ed out[54] to the life of a dead Priesthood. Or else they would straine us out a certain figurative Prelat, by wringing the collective allegory[55] of those seven Angels into seven single Rochets[56]

Howsoever since it thus appeares that custome was the creator of Prelaty being lesse ancient then the government of Presbyters, it is an extreme folly to give them the hearing that tell us of Bishops through so many ages: and if against their tedious muster of citations, Sees, and successions, it be reply'd that wagers[57] and Church antiquities, such as are repugnant to the plaine dictat of Scripture are both alike the arguments of fooles, they have their answer. We rather are to cite all those ages to an arraignment before the word of God, wherefore, and what pretending, how presuming they durst alter that divine institution of Presbyters, which the Apostles who were no various and inconstant men surely had set up in the Churches, and why they choose to live by custome and catalogue, or as S. *Paul* saith by sight and visibility, rather then by faith? But first I conclude from their owne mouthes that Gods command in Scripture, which doubtlesse ought to be the first and greatest reason of Church-government, is wanting to Prelaty. And certainly we have plenteous warrant in the doctrine of Christ to determine that the want of this reason is of it selfe sufficient to confute all other pretences that may be brought in favour of it.

CHAP. VI.

That Prelaty was not set up for prevention of Schisme, as is pretended, or if it were, that it performes not what it was first set up for, but quite the contrary.

YEt because it hath the outside of a specious reason, & specious things we know are aptest to worke with humane lightnesse and frailty, even against the solidest truth, that sounds not plausibly, let us think it worth the examining for the love of infirmer Christians, of what importance this their second reason may be. Tradition they say hath taught them that for the prevention of growing schisme the Bishop was heav'd above the Presbyter. And must tradition then ever thus to the worlds end be the perpetuall canker-worme to eat out Gods Commandements? are his decrees so inconsiderate and so fickle, that when the statutes of *Solon*, or *Lycurgus* shall prove durably good to many ages, his in 40 yeares shall be found defective, ill contriv'd, and for

---

[53]A king but not properly a priest, who "became one of the priests of the high places" in 1Kings 13.33. Jeroboam took advantage of the priestly office to institute temporary idolatry.

[54]Pictorially set out in a drawing or portrait by a limner or sculptor, who might use wax to create a likeness. This is one of the very few references to visual art in Milton's work.

[55]A rare instance of the word in Milton, but at least an indication that he knew what allegory was and how it might be used.

[56]Ecclesiastical vestments worn by bishops.

[57]The Yale editors posit a proverb that the fool uses wagers for arguments, citing Samuel Butler's "Hudibras" 2.1.298, " . . . fools for arguments use wagers" (1664 ed., quoted in Yale 1: 778n).

needfull causes to be alter'd? Our Saviour and his Apostles did not only foresee, but foretell and fore-warne us to looke for schisme. Is it a thing to be imagin'd of Gods wisdome, or at least of Apostolick prudence to set up such a government in the tendernesse of the Church, as should incline, or not be more able then any other to oppose it selfe to schisme? it was well knowne that a bold lurker schisme was even in the houshold of Christ betweene his owne Disciples and those of *John* the Baptist about fasting: and early in the Acts of the Apostles the noise of schisme had almost drown'd the proclaiming of the Gospell; yet we reade not in Scripture than thought was had of making Pre-lates, no not in those places where dissention was most rife. If Prelaty had beene then esteeem'd a remedy against schisme, where was it more needfull then in that great variance among the Corinthians which S. *Paul* so labour'd to reconcile? and whose eye could have found the fittest remedy sooner then his? and what could have made the remedy more available, then to have us'd it speedily? and lastly what could have beene more neces-sary then to have written it for our instruction? yet we see he neither commended it to us, nor us'd it himselfe. For the same division remaining there, or else bursting forth againe more then 20 yeares after S. *Pauls* death, wee finde in *Clements* Epistle of venerable autority writ-ten to the yet factious *Corinthians*, that they were still govern'd by Presbyters. And the same of other Churches out of *Hermas*, and divers other the scholers of the Apostles by the late industry of the learned *Sal-matius*[58] appeares. Neither yet did this worthy *Clement* S. *Pauls* disciple, though writing to them to lay aside schisme, in the least word advise them to change the Prebyteriall government into Prelaty. And therefore if God afterward gave, or permitted this insurrection of Episcopacy, it is to be fear'd he did it in his wrath, as he gave the Israelites a King. With so good a will doth he use to alter his own chosen government once estab-lish'd. For marke whether this rare device of mans braine thus preferr'd before the ordinance of God, had better successe then fleshly wisdome not counseling with God is wont to have. So farre was it from re-moving schisme, that if schisme parted the congrega-tions before, now it rent and mangl'd, now it rag'd, Heresie begat heresie with a certaine monstrous haste of pregnancy in her birth, at once borne and bringing forth. Contentions before brotherly were not hostile. Men went to choose their Bishop as they went to a

pitcht field,[59] and the day of his election was like the sacking of a City, sometimes ended with the blood of thousands. Nor this among hereticks only, but men of the same beliefe, yea confessors, and that with such odi-ous ambition, that *Eusebius* in his eighth book testifies he abhorr'd to write.[60] And the reason is not obscure, for the poore dignity or rather burden of a Parochial Presbyter could not ingage any great party, nor that to any deadly feud: but Prelaty was a power[61] of that ex-tent, and sway, that if her election were popular, it was seldome not the cause of some faction or broil[62] in the Church. But if her dignity came by favour of some Prince, she was from that time his creature, and obnox-ious to comply with his ends in state were they right or wrong. So that in stead of finding Prelaty an impeacher of Schisme or faction, the more I search, the more I grow into all perswasion to think rather that faction and she as with a spousall ring are wedded together, never to be divorc't. But here let every one behold the just, and dreadfull judgement of God meeting with the audacious pride of man that durst offer to mend the ordinances of heaven. God out of the strife of men brought forth by his Apostles to the Church that beneficent and ever distributing office of Deacons, the stewards and Min-isters of holy almes, man out of the pretended care of peace & unity being caught in the share of his impious boldnesse to correct the will of Christ, brought forth to himselfe upon the Church that irreconcileable schisme of perdition and Apostasy, the Roman Antichrist: for that the exaltation of the Pope arose out of the reason of Prelaty it cannot be deny'd. And as I noted before that the patterne of the High Priest pleaded for in the Gospel (for take away the head Priest the rest are but a carcasse) sets up with better reason a Pope, then an Archbishop, for if Prelaty must still rise and rise till it com to a Primat, why should it stay there? when as the catholick government is not to follow the division of kingdomes, the temple best representing the universall Church, and the High Priest the universall head; so I observe here, that if to quiet schisme there must be one head of Pre-laty in a land of Monarchy rising from a Provinciall to a nationall Primacy, there may upon better grounds of repressing schisme be set up one catholick head over the catholick Church. For the peace and good of the Church is not terminated in the schismelesse estate of one or two kingdomes, but should be provided for by the joynt consultation of all reformed Christendome:

---

[58]Salmasius, the learned Claude de Saumaise (1588–1653), here considered as "a great Protestant divine on the right side of the anti-Episcopal controversy" (Yale 1: 781n), will later become Milton's bitter opponent over questions having to do with the execution of Charles I.

[59]An organized battlefield; a battlefield where troops are dispersed in a planned order.
[60]The first great historian of the Christian church.
[61]Army.
[62]Loud argument, brawl.

that all controversie may end in the finall pronounce or canon of one Arch-primat, or Protestant Pope. Although by this meanes for ought I see, all the diameters of schisme may as well meet and be knit up in the center of one grand falshood. Now let all impartiall men arbitrate what goodly inference these two maine reasons of the Prelats have, that by a naturall league of consequence make more for the Pope then for themselves. Yea to say more home are the very wombe for a new subantichrist to breed in; if it be not rather the old force and power of the same man of sin counterfeiting protestant. It was not the prevention of schisme, but it was schisme it selfe, and the hatefull thirst of Lording in the Church that first bestow'd a being upon Prelaty; this was the true cause, but the pretence is stil the same. The Prelates, as they would have it thought, are the only mawls of schisme. Forsooth if they be put downe, a deluge of innumerable sects will follow; we shall be all Brownists,[63] Familists,[64] Anabaptists.[65] For the word Puritan[66] seemes to be quasht, and all that heretofore were counted such, are now Brownists. And thus doe they raise an evill report upon the expected reforming grace that God hath bid us hope for, like those faithlesse spie, whose carcasses shall perish in the wildernesse of their owne confused ignorance, and never taste the good of reformation. Doe they keep away schisme? if to bring a num and chil stupidity of soul, an unactive blindnesse of minde upon the people by their leaden doctrine, or no doctrine at all, if to persecute all knowing and zealous Christians by the violence of their courts, be to keep away schisme, they keep away schisme indeed; and by this kind of discipline all *Italy* and *Spaine* is as purely and politicly kept from schisme as *England* hath beene by them. With as good a plea might the dead palsie boast to a man, tis I that free you from stitches and paines, and the troublesome feeling of cold & heat, of wounds and stroke; if I were gone, all these would molest you. The Winter might as well vaunt it selfe against the Spring, I destroy all noysome and rank weeds, I keepe down all pestilent vapours. Yes and all wholesome herbs, and all

fresh dews, by your violent & hidebound frost; but when the gentle west winds shall open the fruitfull bosome of the earth thus over-girdled by your imprisonment, then the flowers put forth and spring, and then the Sunne shall scatter the mists, and the manuring hand of the Tiller shall root up all that burdens the soile without thank to your bondage. But farre worse then any frozen captivity is the bondage of Prelates, for that other, if it keep down any thing which is good, within the earth, so doth it likewise that which is ill, but these let out freely the ill, and keep down the good, or else keepe down the lesser ill, and let out the greatest. Be asham'd at last to tell the Parlament ye curbe Schismaticks, when as they know ye cherish and side with Papists, and are not as it were one party with them, and tis said they helpe to petition for ye. Can we believe that your government strains in good earnest at the petty gnats of schism, when as we see it makes nothing to swallow the Camel heresie of *Rome*; but that indeed your throats are of the right Pharisaical straine. Where are thos schismaticks with whom the Prelats hold such hot skirmish? shew us your acts, those glorious annals which your Courts of loathed memory lately deceas'd have left us? those schismaticks I doubt me wil be found the most of them such as whose only schisme was to have spoke the truth against your high abominations and cruelties in the Church; this is the schisme ye hate most, the removall of your criminous Hierarchy. A politick government of yours, and of a pleasant conceit, set up to remove those as a pretended schisme, that would remove you as a palpable heresie in government. If the schisme would pardon ye that, she might go jagg'd in as many cuts and slashes as she pleas'd for you. As for the rending of the Church, we have many reasons to thinke it is not that which ye labour to prevent so much as the rending of your pontificall sleeves: that schisme would be the sorest schisme to you, that would be Brownisme and Anabaptisme indeed. If we go downe, say you, as if *Adrians* wall were broke, a flood of sects will rush in. What sects? What are their opinions? give us the Inventory; it will appeare both by your former prosecutions and your present instances, that they are only such to speake of as are offended with your lawlesse government, your ceremonies, your Liturgy, an extract of the Masse book translated. But that they should be contemners of publick prayer, and Churches us'd without superstition, I trust God will manifest it ere long to be as false a slander, as your former slanders against the Scots. Noise it till ye be hoarse; that a rabble of Sects will come in, it will be answer'd ye, no rabble sir Priest, but a unanimous multitude of good Protestants will then joyne to the Church, which now because of you stand separated. This will be the

---

[63]Followers of Robert Browne (1550?–1633?), imprisoned countless times for his beliefs, in a sect that later was to evolve into those called Independents or Congregationists, because they believed that each congregation should set its own rules and that their believers operated independently of the state.

[64]The mystical believers in the Family of Love, who met secretly and were composed mostly of lower-class itinerants (see Hill, *Milton and the English Revolution* 70–79).

[65]Believers in adult baptism by total immersion, non-hierarchical church leadership, and the separation of church and state; ancestors of modern Baptists.

[66]Milton thought, at least, that the term *Puritan* was dying in usage.

dreadfull consequence of your removall. As for those terrible names of Sectaries and Schismaticks which he have got together, we know your manner of sight, when the quiver of your arguments which is ever thin, and weakly stor'd, after the first brunt[67] is quite empty, your course is to betake ye to your other quiver of slander, wherein lyes your best archery. And whom ye could not move by sophisticall arguing, them you thinke to confute by scandalous misnaming. Thereby inciting the blinder sort of people to mislike and deride sound doctrine and good christianity under two or three vile and hatefull terms. But if we could easily indure and dissolve your doubtiest[68] reasons in argument, we shall more easily beare the worst of your unreasonablenesse in calumny and false report. Especially being fortold by Christ, that if he our Master were by your predecessors call'd Samaritan and Belzebub,[69] we must not think it strange if his best Disciples in the reformation, as at first by those of your tribe they were call'd Lollards and Hussites, so now by you be term'd Puritans, and Brownists. But my hope is that the people of England will not suffer themselves to be juggl'd thus out of their faith and religion by a mist of names cast before their eyes, but will search wisely by the Scriptures, and look quite through this fraudulent aspersion of a disgracefull name into the things themselves: knowing that the Primitive Christians in their times were accounted such as are now call'd Familists and Adamites, or worse. And many on the Prelatickside like the Church of *Sardis* have a name to live, and yet are dead;[70] to be Protestants, and indeed Papists in most of their principles. Thus perswaded, this your old fallacy wee shall soone unmask, and quickly apprehend how you prevent schisme, and who are your schismaticks. But what if ye prevent, and hinder all good means of preventing schisme? that way which the Apostles us'd, was to call a councell; from which by any thing that can be learnt from the fifteenth of the *Acts*, no faithfull Christian was debarr'd, to whom knowledge and piety might give entrance. Of such a councell as this every parochiall Consistory is a right homogeneous and constituting part being in it selfe as it were a little Synod, and towards a generall assembly moving upon her own basis in an even and firme progression, as those smaller squares in battell unite in one great cube, the main phalanx, an

emblem of truth and steadfastnesse. Whereas on the other side Prelaty ascending by a graduall monarchy from Bishop to Arch-bishop, from thence to Primat, and from thence, for there can be no reason yeilded neither in nature, nor in religion, wherefore, if it have lawfully mounted thus high, it should not be a Lordly ascendent in the horoscope of the Church, from Primate to Patriarch, and so to Pope. I say Prelaty thus ascending in a continuall pyramid upon pretence to perfect the Churches unity, if notwithstanding it be found most needfull, yea the untmost helpe to dearn up[71] the rents of schisme [72]by calling a councell, what does it but teach us that Prelaty is of no force to effect this work which she boasts to be her maister-peice; and that her pyramid aspires and sharpens to ambition, not to perfection, or unity. This we know, that as often as any great schisme disparts the Church, and Synods be proclam'd, the Presbyters have as great right there, and as free vote of old, as the Bishops, which the Canon law conceals not. So that Prelaty if she will seek to close up divisions in the Church, must be forc't to dissolve, and unmake her own pyramidal figure,[73] which she affirmes to be of such united power, when as indeed it is the most dividing and schismaticall forme that Geometricians know of, and must be faine to inglobe, or incube her selfe among the Presbyters; which she hating to do, sends her haughty Prelates from all parts with their forked Miters, the badge of schisme or the stamps of his cloven foot whom they serve I think, who according to their hierarchies acuminating[74] still higher and higher in a cone of Prelaty, in stead of healing up the gashes of the Church, as it happens in such pointed bodies meeting, fall to gore one another with their sharpe spires for upper place, and precedence, till the councell it selfe prove the greatest schisme of all. And thus they are so farre from hindring dissention, that they have made unprofitable, and even noysome the chiefest remedy we have to keep Christendom at one, which is by councels: and these if wee rightly consider Apostolick example, are nothing else but generall Presbyteries. This seem'd so farre from the Apostles to think much of, as if hereby their dignity were impair'd, that, as we may gather by those Epistles of *Peter* and *John*, which are likely to be latest written when the Church grew to a setling, like those heroick patricians of Rome (if we may use such

---

[67]Violent attack.

[68]Most dubious (not recorded in the *OED*, though "doubty" is).

[69]Derived from Matthew 19.25, "If they have called the master of the house Beelzebub, how much more shall they call them of his household?"

[70]The Apocalypse was written for an audience that included the people of Sardis. Milton quotes from Revelation 3.1, "Thou hast a name that thou livest, and art dead."

[71]Patch up, mend.

[72]Since the Greek word *schism* means "tear," Milton can play on the meaning of tearing or ripping apart.

[73]Milton plays on the various symbolic meanings of geometrical structures such as pyramids and phalanxes, like that he describes in his memorial poem to Shakespeare for the pyramid that points to the stars or the strength usually attributed to the phalanx as a military formation.

[74]Tapering up to a point, like a pyramid.

comparison) hasting to lay downe their dictatorship, they rejoys't to call themselves and to be as fellow Elders among their brethren. Knowing that their high office was but as the scaffolding of the Church yet unbuilt, and would be but a troublesome disfigurement, so soone as the building was finisht. But the lofty minds of an age or two after, such was their small discerning, thought it a poore indignity, that the high rear'd government of the Church should so on a sudden, as it seem'd to them, squat into a Presbytery. Next or rather before councels the timeliest prevention of schisme is to preach the Gospell abundantly and powerfully throughout all the land, to instruct the youth religiously, to endeavour how the Scriptures may be easiest understood by all men; to all which the proceedings of these men have been on set purpose contrary. But how O Prelats should you remove schisme, and how should you not remove and oppose all the meanes of removing schisme: when Prelaty is a schisme it selfe from the most reformed and most flourishing of our neighbour Churches abroad, and a sad subject of discord and offence to the whole nation at home. The remedy which you alledge is the very disease we groan under; and never can be to us a remedy but by removing it selfe. Your predecessors were believ'd to assume this preeminence above their brethren only that they might appease dissention. Now God and the Church cals upon you, for the same reason to lay it down, as being to thousands of good men offensive, burdensome, intolerable. Surrender that pledge which unlesse you fowlely usurpt it, the Church gave you, and now claimes it againe, for the reason she first lent it. Discharge the trust committed to you, prevent schisme, and that ye can never do, but by discharging your selves. That government which ye hold, we confesse prevents much, hinders much, removes much; but what? the schisms and grievances of the Church? no, but all the peace and unity, all the welfare not of the Church alone, but of the whole kingdome. And if it be still permitted ye to hold, will cause the most sad I know not whether separation be anough to say, but such a wide gulph of distraction in this land as will never close her dismall gap, untill ye be forc't (for of your selvs ye wil never do as that Roman *Curtius* nobly did) for the Churches peace & your countries, to leap into the midst, and be no more seen. By this we shal know whether your be that ancient Prelaty wich you say was first constituted for the reducement of quiet & unanimity into the Church, for the[75] you wil not delay to prefer that above your own preferment. If otherwise, we must be confident that your Prelaty is nothing else but your ambition, an insolent preferring of your selves above your brethren, and all your leaned scraping in antiquity even to disturbe the bones of old *Aaron* and his sonnes in their graves, is but to maintain and set upon our necks a stately and severe dignity, which you call sacred, and is nothing in very deed but a grave and reverent gluttony, a sanctimonious avarice, in comparison of which, all the duties and dearnesses which ye owe to God or to his Church, to law, custome, or nature, ye have resolv'd to set at nought. I could put you in mind what counsell *Clement* a fellow labourer with the Apostles gave to the Presbyters of *Corinth*, whom the people though unjustly sought to remove. Who among you saith he, is noble minded, who is pittifull, who is charitable, let him say thus, if for me this sedition, this enmity, these differences be, I willingly depart, I go my wayes, only let the flock of Christ be at peace with the Presbyters that are set over it. He that shall do this, saith he, shall get him great honour in the Lord, and all places will receave him. This was *Clements* counsell to good and holy men that they should depart rather from their just office, then by their stay, to ravle[76] out the seamlesse garment of concord in the Church. But I have better counsell to give the Prelats, and farre more acceptable to their eares, this advice in my opinion is fitter for them. Cling fast to your Pontificall Sees, bate not, quit your selves like Barons, stand to the utmost for your haughty Courts and votes in Parliament. Still tell us that you prevent schisme, though schisme and combustion be the very issue of your bodies, your first born; and set your country a bleeding in a Prelaticall mutiny; to fight for your pompe, and that ill favour'd weed of temporall honour that sits dishonourably upon your laick shoulders, that he may be fat and fleshy, swoln with high thoughts and big with mischievous designes, when God comes to visit upon you all this forescore yeares vexation of his Church under your Egyptian tyranny. For certainly of all those blessed soules which you have persecuted, and those miserable ones which you have lost, the just vengeance does not sleepe.

CHAP. VII.

That those many Sects and Schismes by some suppos'd to be among us, and that rebellion in Ireland, *ought not to be a hindrance, but a hastning of reformation.*

---

[75]Abbreviation for "then."

[76]Unravel.

AS for those many Sects and divisions rumor'd abroad to be amongst us, it is not hard to perceave that they are partly the meere fictions and false alarmes of the Prelates, thereby to cast amazements and panick terrors into the hearts of weaker Christians that they should not venture to change the present deformity of the Church for fear of I know not what worse inconveniencies. With the same objected feares and supicions, we know that suttle Prelat *Gardner*[77] sought to divert the first reformation. It may suffice us to be taught by S. *Paul* that there must be sects for the manifesting of those that are sound hearted. These are but winds and flaws[78] to try the floting vessell of our faith whether it be stanch[79] and sayl well, whether our ballast be just, our anchorage and cable strong. By this is seene who lives by faith and certain knowledge, and who by credulity and the prevailing opinion of the age; whose vertue is of an unchangeable graine, and whose of a slight wash.[80] If God come to trie our constancy we ought not to shrink, or stand the lesse firmly for that, but passe on with more stedfast reesolution to establish the truth though it were through a lane of sects and heresies on each side. Other things men do to the glory of God: but sects and errors it seems God suffers to be for the glory of good men; that the world may know and reference their true fortitude and undaunted constancy in the truth. Let us not therefore make these things an incumbrance, or an excuse of our delay in reforming, which God sends us as an incitement to proceed with more honour and alacrity. For if there were no opposition on where were the triall of an unfained goodnesse and magnanimity? vertue that wavers is not vertue, but vice revolted from it selfe, and after a while returning. The actions of just and pious men do not darken in their middle course; but *Solomon* tels us they are as the shining light, that shineth more and more unto the perfet day. But if we shall suffer the trifling doubts and jealousies of future sects to overcloud the faire beginnings of purpos't[81] reformation, let us rather fear that another proverb of the same Wiseman be not upraided[82] to us, that the way of the wicked is as darknesse, they stumble at they know not what. If sects and schismes be turbulent in the unsetl'd estate of a Church, while it lies under the amending hand, it best beseems our Christian courage to think they are but as the throws and pangs that go before the birth of reformation, and that the work it selfe is now in doing. For if we look but in the nature of elementall and mixt things,[83] we know they cannot suffer any change of one kind, or quality into another without the struggl of contrarieties. And in things artificiall, seldome any elegance is wrought without a superfluous wast and refuse in the transaction. No Marble statue can be politely carv'd, no fair edifice built without almost as much rubbish and sweeping. Insomuch that even in the spirituall conflict of S. *Pauls* conversion there fell scales from his eyes that were not perceav'd before. No wonder then in the reforming of a Church which is never brought to effect without the fierce encounter of truth and falshood[84] together, if, as it were between the splinters and shares[85] of so violent a jousting, there fall from between the shock[86] many fond errors and fanatick opinions, which when truth has the upper hand, and the reformation shall be perfeted, will easily be rid out of the way, or kept so low, as that they shall be only the exercise of our knowledge, not the disturbance, or interruption of our faith. As for that which *Barclay*[87] in his image of minds writes concerning the horrible and barbarous conceits of Englishmen in their religion. I deeme it spoken like what hee was, a fugitive Papist traducing the Iland whence he sprung. It may be more judiciously gather'd from hence, that the Englishman of many other nations is least atheisticall, and bears a naturall disposition of much reverence and awe towards the Deity; but in his weaknesse and want of better instruction, which among us too frequently is neglected, especially by the meaner sort, turning the bent of his own wits with a scrupulous and ceaselesse care what he might do to informe himselfe aright of God and his worship, he may fall not unlikely sometimes as any otherland[88] man into an uncouth opinion. And verily if we look at his native towardliness in

---

[77]"Subtle" is not a good word here, since it is also used of the Serpent in Eden. Stephen Gardiner (c. 1485–1555), a Bishop of Winchester and Lord High Chancellor under Henry VIII, is on Milton's list of treacherous English churchmen because he aided Queen Mary in persecuting Protestants.

[78]Gusts, bursts of wind.

[79]Watertight.

[80]The contrast is between an ingrained dye, which is permanent, and a thin layer of color brushed on, a wash.

[81]Corrected from "purpos'st" in the Bodleian copy, following Yale.

[82]Upbraided, brought forward for censure.

[83]Though the science of Milton's time did not support atomic theory as it is known today, it did divide elements, earth, air, fire, water, from mixed substances such as metals in which the elements seem to make war.

[84]Printed as "fashood" in Bodleian, here corrected. There are so many odd spellings ("struggl," "upraided") and mistakes ("purpos'st") in the D3 page that one wonders if a new compositor began work here.

[85]Parings, parts cut off.

[86]Probably the image is from the shock or fierce encounter between two horsemen in a joust.

[87]John Barclay (1582–1621) at first made satirical fun of the Roman Catholic church in various pamphlets, but he converted to Catholicism and became an exile, living in Rome from 1616 until his death.

[88]Presumably someone from a land other than England, an outlander or foreigner, but the word is not in the *OED*.

the roughcast without breeding, some nation or other may haply be better compos'd to a naturall civility, and right judgement then he. But if he get the benefit once of a wise and well rectifi'd nurture, which must first come in generall from the godly vigilance of the Church, I suppose that where ever mention is made of countries,[89] manners, or men, the English people among the first that shall be prais'd, may deserve to be accounted a right pious, right honest, and right hardy nation. But thus while some stand dallying and deferring to reform for fear of that which should mainly hasten them forward, lest schism and error should encrease, we may now thank our selves and our delayes if instead of schism a bloody and inhumane rebellion be strook in between our slow movings. Indeed against violent and powerfull opposition there can be no just blame of a lingring dispatch. But this I urge against those that discourse it for a maxim, as if the swift opportunities of establishing, or reforming religion, were to attend upon the fleam[90] of state businesse. In state many things at first are crude and hard to digest, which only time and deliberation can supple, and concoct. But in religion wherein is no immaturity, nothing out of season, it goes farre otherwise. The doore of grace turnes upon smooth hinges wide opening to send out, but soon shutting to recall the precious offers of mercy to a nation: which unlesse Watchfulnesse and Zeale two quick-sighted and ready-handed Virgins be there in our behalfe to receave, we loose: and still the ofter we loose, the straiter the doore opens, and the lesse is offer'd. This is all we get by demurring in Gods service. Tis not rebellion that ought to be the hindrance of reformation, but it is the want of this which is the cause of that. The Prelats which boast themselves the only bridlers of schisme God knows have been so cold and backward both there and with us to represse heresie and idolatry, that either through their carelessnesse or their craft all this mischiefe is befaln. What can the Irish subject do lesse in Gods just displeasure against us, then revenge upon English bodies the little care that our Prelats have had of their souls. Nor hath their negligence been new in that Iland but ever notorious in Queen *Elizabeths* dayes, as *Camden*[91] their known friend forbears not to complain. Yet so little are they toucht with remorce of these their cruelties, for these cruelties are theirs, the bloody

revenge of those souls which they have famisht, that whenas against our brethren the Scots, who by their upright and loyall[92] deeds have now bought themselves an honourable name to posterity, whatsoever malice by slander could invent, rage in hostility attempt, they greedily attempted, toward these murdrous Irish the enemies of God and mankind, a cursed off-spring of their own connivence, no man takes notice but that they seeme to be very calmly and indifferently affected. Where then should we begin to extinguish a rebellion that hath his cause from the misgovernment of the Church, where? but at the Churches reformation, and the removall of that government which persues and warres with all good Christians under the name of schismaticks, but maintains and fosters all Papists and Idolaters as tolerable Christians. And if the sacred Bible may be our light, we are neither without example, nor the witnesse of God himselfe, that the corrupted estate of the Church is both the cause of tumult, and civill warres, and that to stint them, the peace of the Church must first be setl'd. *Now for a long season,* saith *Azariah* to King *Asa, Israel hath beene without the true God, and without a teaching Priest, and without law: and in those times there was no peace to him that went out, nor to him that came in, but great vexations were upon all the inhabitants of the countries. And nation was destroy'd of nation, and City of City, for God did vex them with all adversity. Be ye strong therefore,* saith he to the reformers of that age, *and let not your hands be weake, for your worke shal bee rewarded.* And in those Prophets that liv'd in the times of reformation after the Captivity often doth God stirre up the people to consider that while establishment of Church matters was neglected, and put off, there was *no peace to him that went out or came in, for I,* saith God, *had set all men every one against his neighbour.* But from the very day forward that they went seriously, and effectually about the welfare of the Church, he tels them that they[93] themselves might perceave the sudden change of things into a prosperous and peacefull condition. But it will here be said that the reformation is a long work, and the miseries of *Ireland* are urgent of a speedy redresse. They be indeed; and how speedy we are, the poore afflicted remnant of our martyr'd countrymen that sit there on the Sea-shore, counting the houres of our delay with their sighs, and the minuts with their

---

[89]The errata list adds this comma.

[90]Phlegm, slow-moving liquid, here compared with the slow movement of bureaucratic affairs.

[91]William Camden (1551–1623), the most prominent historian of the Elizabeth's time, who did criticize the prelates, complaining of their "careless negligence" (*Brittania* [1586] 82; see Yale 1: 798n).

[92]At this point, a compositor has entered the catchword "and," which is continued on the next page, but repetitiously, as "and loyall deeds." I have removed the duplicate phrase.

[93]A marginal note directs the reader to "Haggai 2." There God assures Zerubbabel and Joshua, "According to the word I covenanted with you when ye came out of Egypt, so my spirit remaineth among you: fear ye not" (2.5).

falling teares, perhaps with the destilling of their bloody wounds, if they have not quite by this time cast off, and almost curst the vain hope of our founder'd ships, and aids, can best judge how speedy we are to their reliefe. But let their succors be hasted, as all need and reason is, and let not therefore the reformation which is the chiefest cause of successe and victory be still procrastinated. They of the captivity in their greatest extremities could find both counsell and hands anough at once to build, and to expect the enemies assault. And we for our parts a populous and mighty nation must needs be faln into a strange plight either of effeminacy, or confusion, if *Ireland* that was once the conquest of one single Earle with his privat forces, and the small assistance of a petty Kernish Prince, should not take up all the wisdome and prowesse of this potent Monarchy to quell a barbarous crew of rebels, whom if we take but the right course to subdue, that is beginning at the reformation of our Church, their own horrid murders and rapes will so fight against them, that the very sutlers[94] and horse boyes of the Campe will be able to rout and chase them without the staining of any Noble sword. To proceed by other method in this enterprize, be our Captains and Commanders never so expert, will be as great an error in the art of warre, as any novice in souldiership ever committed. And thus I leave it as a declared truth, that neither the feare of sects no nor rebellion can be a fit plea to stay reformation, but rather to push it forward with all possible diligence and speed.

The second Book. [95]

HOw happy were it for this frail, and as it may be truly call'd, mortall life of man, since all earthly things which have the name of good and convenient in our daily use, are withall so cumbersome and full of trouble if knowledge yet which is the best and lightsomest possession of the mind, were as the common saying is, no burden, and that what it wanted of being a load to any part of the body, it did not with a heavie advantage overlay upon the spirit. For not to speak of that knowledge that rests in the contemplation of naturall causes and dimensions, which must needs be a lower wisdom, as the object is low, certain it is that he who hath obtain'd in more then the scantest measure to know any thing distinctly of God, and of his true worship, and what is infallibly good and happy in the state of mans life, what in it selfe evil and miserable, though vulgarly not so esteem'd, he that hath obtain'd to know this, the only high valuable wisdom indeed, remembring also that God even to a strictnesse requires the improvment of these his entrusted gifts, cannot but sustain a sorer burden of mind, and more pressing then any supportable toil, or waight, which the body can labour under; how and in what manner he shall dispose and employ those summes of knowledge and illumination, which God hath sent him into this world to trade with. And that which aggravats the burden more is, that having receiv'd amongst his allotted parcels certain pretious truths of such an orient luster[96] as no Diamond can equall, which never the lesse he has in charge to put off at any cheap rate, yea for nothing to them that will, the great Marchants of this world fearing that this cours would soon discover,[97] and disgrace the fals glitter of their deceitfull wares wherewith they abuse the people, like poor Indians with beads and glasses, practize by all means how they may suppresse the venting of such rarities and such a cheapnes as would undoe them, and turn their truth upon their hands. Therefore by gratifying the corrupt desires of men in fleshly doctrines, they stirre them up to persecute with hatred and contempt all those that seek to bear themselves uprightly in this their spiritual factory:[98] which they foreseeing, though they cannot but testify of Truth and the excellence of that heavenly traffick which they bring against what opposition, or danger soever, yet needs must it sit heavily upon their spirits, that being in Gods prime intention and their own, selected heralds of peace, and dispensers of treasure[99] inestimable without price to them that have no pence, they sinne in the discharge of their commission that they are made the greatest variance and offence, a very sword and fire both in house and City over the whole earth. This is that which the said Prophet *Jeremiah* laments, *Wo is me my mother, that thou has born me a man of strife, and contention.* And although divine inspiration must certainly have been sweet to those ancient profets, yet the irksomnesse of that truth which they brought was so unpleasant to them that every where they call it a burden. Yea that mysterious book of Revelation which the great Evangelist was bid

---

94 Petty tradesmen who followed an army to sell it provisions.
95 There is no heading above for the first book.

96 Bright shine.
97 Reveal.
98 Trading post.
99 The errata list corrects "treasures."

to eat, as it had been some eye-brightning electuary[100] of knowledge, and foresight, though it were sweet in his mouth, and in the learning, it was bitter in his belly; bitter in the denouncing. Nor was this hid from the wise Poet *Sophocles*,[101] who in that place of his Tragedy where *Tiresias* is call'd to resolve K. *Edipus* in a matter which he knew would be grievous, brings him in bemoaning his lot, that he knew more then other men. For surely to every good and peaceable man it must in nature needs be a hatefull thing to be the displeaser, and molester of thousands; much better would it like him doubtlesse to be the messenger of gladnes and contentment, which is his chief intended busines, to all mankind, but that they resist and oppose their own true happinesse. But when God commands to take the trumpet and blow a dolorous or a jarring blast, it lies not in mans will what he shall say, or what he shall conceal. If he shall think to be silent, as *Jeremiah* did, because of the reproach and derision he met with daily, and *all his familiar friends watcht for his halting* to be reveng'd on him, for speaking the truth, he would be forc't to confesse as he confest, *his word was in my heart as a burning fire shut up in my bones I was weary with forbearing, and could not stay.* Which might teach these times not suddenly to condemn all things that are sharply spoken, or vehemently written, as proceeding out of stomach, virulence and ill nature, but to consider rather that if the Prelats have leav to say the worst that can be said, and doe the worst that can be don, while they strive to keep to themselves to their great pleasure and commodity those things which they ought to render up, no man can be justly offended with him selfe those sharp, but saving words which would be a terror, and a torment in him to keep back. For me I have determin'd to lay us as the best treasure, and solace of a good old age, if God voutsafe it me, the honest liberty of free speech from my youth, where I shall think it available in so dear a concernment as the Churches good. For if I be either by disposition, or what other cause too inquisitive, or suspitious of my self and mine own doings, who can help it? but this I foresee, that should the Church be brought under heavy oppression, and God have given me ability the while to reason against that man that should be the author of so foul a deed, or should she by blessing from above on the industry and courage of faithfull men change this her distracted estate

into better daies without the lest furtherance or contribution of those few talents which God at that present had lent me,[102] I foresee what stories I should heare within my selfe, all my life after, of discourage and reproach. Timorous and ingratefull, the Church of God is now again at the foot of her insulting enemies: and thou bewailst, what matters it for thee or thy bewailing? when time was, thou couldst not find a syllable of all that thou hadst read, or studied, to utter in her behalfe. Yet ease and leasure was given thee for thy retired thoughts out of the sweat of other men. Thou hadst the diligence, the parts, the language of a man, if a vain subject were to be adorn'd or beautifi'd, but when the cause of God and his Church was to be pleased, for which purpose that tongue was given thee which thou hast, God listen'd if he could heare thy voice among his zealous servants, but thou wert domb[103] as a beast; from hence forward be that which thine own brutish silence hath made thee. Or else I should have heard on the other eare, slothfull, and ever to be set light by, the Church hath now overcom her late distresses after the unwearied labours of many her true servants that stood up in her defence; thou also wouldst take upon thee to share amongst them of their joy: but wherefore thou? where canst thou shew any word or deed of thine which might have hasten'd her peace; whatever thou dost now talke, or write, or look is the almes of other mens active prudence and zeale. Dare not now to say, or doe any thing better then thy former sloth and infancy,[104] or if thou darst, thou dost impudently to make a thrifty purchase of boldnesse to thy selfe out of the painfull merits of other men: what before was thy sin, is now thy duty to be, abject, and worthlesse. These and such like lessons as these, I know would have been my Matins duly, and my Even-song.[105] But now by this little diligence, mark what a privilege I have gain'd; with good men and Saints to clame my right of lamenting the tribulations of the Church, if she should suffer, when others that have ventur'd nothing for her sake, have not the honour to be admitted mourners. But if she lift up her drooping head and prosper, among those that have something more then wisht her welfare, I have my charter and freehold[106] of rejoycing to me and my heires. Concerning therefore this wayward subject against prelaty, the touching

---

[100]An electuary was a medicine made palatable by mixing with something sweet like honey or fruit preserves. In a metaphor, Milton can make it into an eye-brightening salve. The mention of an eye-brightening electuary might indicate the beginnings of Milton's eye problems.
[101]Sophocles, *Oedipus the King* 316–17.

[102]Compare "that one Talent which is death to hide" in Sonnet 19. Both images are based on the parable of the talents, Matthew 25.14–31.
[103]Dumb, silent.
[104]Speechlessness.
[105]The morning song and the evening song of the Church of England (and Roman Catholicism, as well), though Milton's meaning is probably generic.
[106]Legal rights.

whereof is so distastfull and disquietous to a number of men, as by what hath been said I may deserve of charitable readers to be credited, that neither envy nor gall hath enterd me upon this controversy, but the enforcement of conscience only, and a preventive fear least the omitting of this duty should be against me when I would store up to my self the good provision of peaceful hours,[107] So lest it should be still imputed to me, as I have found it hath bin, that some self-pleasing humor of vain-glory hath incited me to contest with men of high estimation, now while green yeers are upon my head, from this needlesse surmisall I shall hope to disswade the intelligent and equal auditor, if I can but say succesfully that which in this exigent behoovs me, although I would be heard only, if it might be, by the elegant & learned reader, to whom principally for a while I shal beg leav I may address my selfe. To him it will be no new thing though I tell him that if I hunted after praise by the ostentation of wit and learning, I should not write thus out of mine own season, when I have neither yet compleated to my minde the full circle of my private studies, although I complain not of any insufficiency to the matter in hand, or were I ready to my wishes, it were a folly to commit any thing elaborately compos'd to the carelesse and interrupted listening of these tumultuous times. Next if I were wise only to mine own ends, I would certainly take such a subject as of it self might catch applause, whereas this hath all the disadvantages on the contrary, and such a subject as the publishing whereof might be delayd at pleasure, and time enough to pencill it over with all the curious touches of art, even to the perfection of a faultlesse picture,[108] whenas in this argument the not deferring is of great moment to the good speeding, that if solidity have leisure to doe her office, art cannot have much. Lastly, I should not chuse this manner of writing wherin knowing my self inferior to my self, led by the genial power of nature to another task, I have the use, as I may account it, but of my left hand. And thou I shall be foolish in saying more to this purpose, yet since it will be such a folly as wisest men going about to commit, have only confest and so committed, I may trust with more reason, because with more folly to have courteous pardon. For although a Poet soaring in the high region of his fancies with his garland and singing robes about him might without apology speak more of himself then I mean to do, yet for me sitting here below in the cool

element of prose, a mortall thing among many readers of no Empyreall conceit, to venture and divulge unusual things of my selfe, I shall petition to the gentler sort, it may not be envy to me. I must say therefore that after I had from my first yeeres by the ceaselesse diligence and care of my father, whom God recompence, bin exercis'd to the tongues,[109] and some sciences, as my age would suffer, by sundry masters and teachers both at home and at the schools, it was found that whether ought was impos'd me by them that had the overlooking, or betak'n to of mine own choise in English, or other tongue, prosing or versing, but chiefly this latter, the stile by certain vital signes it had, was likely to live. But much latelier in the privat Academies of *Italy*, whither I was favor'd to resort, perceiving that some trifles which I had in memory, compos'd at under twenty or thereabout (for the manner is that every one must give some proof of his wit and reading there) me with acceptance above what was lookt for, and other things which I had shifted in scarsity of books and conveniences to patch up amongst them, were receiv'd with written Encomiums,[110] which the Italian is not forward to bestow on men of this side the *Alps*. I began this farre to assent both to them and divers of my friends here at home, and not lesse to an inward prompting which now grew daily upon me, that by labour and intent study (which I take to be my portion in this life) joyn'd with the strong propensity of nature, I might perhaps leave something so written to aftertimes, as they should not willingly let it die. These thoughts at once possest me, and these other. That if *I* were certain to write as men buy Leases, for three lives and downward,[111] there ought no regard be sooner had, then to Gods glory by the honour and instruction of my country. For which cause, and not only for that I knew it would be hard to arrive at the second rank among the Latins, *I* apply'd my selfe to that resolution which *Ariosto* follow'd against the perswasions of *Bembo*,[112] to fix all the industry and art I could unite to the adorning of my native tongue; not to make verbal curiosities the end, that were a toylsom

---

[107]The image of the peaceful old age of the poet in "Il Penseroso," waiting to arrive at "somthing like prophetic strain" (174) seems very close to what is pictured here.

[108]One of Milton's very few references to the art of portraiture, and one of the few uses of "art" in a positive sense.

---

[109]Languages. *Ad Patrem* mentions Latin, Greek, French, Italian, Hebrew (79–85), to which would be added Spanish, perhaps Portuguese, Syriac, Aramaic, and Dutch.

[110]The poems of tribute which Milton attached to the beginning of his *Elegiarum* and *Sylvarum*, the books of Latin poetry that made up the second half of the 1645 *Poems*.

[111]A lease written for three generations of owners of property.

[112]Pietro Bembo (1470–1547), himself a poet. John Harington's short life of Ariosto appended to his translation of *Orlando Furioso* (1591) repeats the often-told story of Bembo's advice to Ariosto that, for a wider audience, he should write in Latin. Ariosto did not take the advice, writing in Italian instead, choosing to be first-rate amongst his countrymen rather than second-rate among the poets who wrote in Latin (416–17).

vanity, but to be an interpreter & relater of the best and sagest things among mine own Citizens throughout this Iland in the mother dialect. That what the greatest and choycest wits of *Athens, Rome,* or modern *Italy,* and those Hebrew of old did for their country, I in my proportion with this over and above of being a Christian, might doe for mine: not caring to be once nam'd abroad, though perhaps I could attaine to that, but content with these British Ilands as my world, whose fortune hath hitherto bin, that if the Athenians, as some say, made their small deeds great and renowned by their eloquent writers, *England* hath had her noble atchievments made small by the unskilfull handling of monks and mechanicks.[113]

Time servs not now, and perhaps I might seem too profuse to give any certain account of what the mind at home in the spacious circuits of her musing hath liberty to propose to her self, though of highest hope, and hardest attempting, whether that Epick form whereof the two poems of *Homer,* and those other two of *Virgil* and *Tasso* are a diffuse,[114] and the book of *Job* a brief model: or whether the rules of *Aristotle* herein are strictly to be kept, or nature to be follow'd, which in them that know art, and use judgement is no transgression, but an inriching of art. And lastly what K. or Knight before the conquest might be chosen in whom to lay the pattern of a Christian *Heroe.* And as *Tasso* gave to a Prince of *Italy* his chois whether he would command him to write of *Godfreys* expedition against the infidels, or *Belisarius* against the Gothes, or *Charlemain* against the Lombards; if to the instinct of nature and the imboldning of art ought may be trustee, and that there be nothing advers in our climat,[115] or the fate of this age, it haply would be no rashnesse from an equal diligence and inclination to present the like offer in our own ancient stories. Or whether those Dramatic constitutions, wherein *Sophocles* and *Euripides* raigne shall be found more doctrinal and exemplary to a Nation, the Scripture also affords us a divine pastoral Drama in the Song of *Salomon* consisting of two persons and a double Chorus, as *Origen* rightly judges. And the Apocalyps of Saint *John* is the majestick image of a high and stately Tragedy, shutting up and intermingling her solemn Scenes and Acts with a sevenfold *Chorus* of halleluja's and harping symphonies:

and this is my opinion the grave autority of *Pareus*[116] commenting that booke is sufficient to confirm. Or if occasion shall lead to imitat those magnifick Odes and Hymns wherein *Pindarus* and *Callimachus*[117] are in most things worthy, some others in their frame judicious, in their matter most an end faulty:[118] But those frequent songs throughout the law and prophets[119] beyond all these, not in their divine argument alone, but in the very critical art of composition may be easily made appear over all the kinds of Lyrick poesy, to be incomparable. These abilities, wheresoever they be found, are the inspired guift of God rarely bestow'd, but yet to some (though most abuse) in every Nation: and are of power beside the office of a pulpit, to inbreed and cherish in a great people the seeds of vertu, and publick civility, to allay the perturbations of the mind, and set the affections in right tune, to celebrate in glorious and lofty Hymns the throne and equipage of Gods Almightinesse, and what he works, and what he suffers to be wrought with high providence in his Church, to sing the victorious agonies of Martyrs and Saints, the deeds and triumphs of just and pious Nations doing valiantly through faith against the enemies of Christ, to deplore the general relapses of Kingdoms and States from justice and Gods true worship. Lastly, whatsoever in religion is holy and sublime, in vertu amiable, or grave, whatsoever hath passion or admiration in all the change of that which is call'd fortune from without, or the wily suttleties and refluxes of mans thoughts from within, all these things with a solid and treatable smoothnesse to paint out and describe. Teaching over the whole book of sanctity and vertu through all the instances of example with such delight to those especially of soft and delicious temper who will not so much as look upon Truth herselfe, unlesse they see her elegantly drest, that whereas the paths of honesty and good life appear now rugged and difficult, though they be indeed easy and pleasant, they would then appeare to all men both easy and pleasant though they were rugged and difficult indeed. And what a benefit this would be to our youth and gentry, may be soon guest[120] by what we know of the corruption and bane which they suck in dayly from

---

[113]Vulgar people, with the implication that English history had been written by ignorant manual laborers.

[114]The extended and long, or diffuse, epics of Homer, Vergil, and Tasso are examples of that type, whereas the book of Job (on which Milton have modeled his *Paradise Regain'd*) is the model for brief epic.

[115]The general belief was that the more northern the climate, the weaker the poetic inspiration. Milton expresses essentially the same fear of a depressing cold climate in *Paradise Lost* 9.44–45.

[116]The biblical commentator David Paraeus, cited for his commentary on the Apocalypse by the Yale editors in *Operum Theologicorum* (1628), 2: 1077. Milton cites Paraeus on Revelation as tragedy again in his preface to *Samson Agonistes.*

[117]Classical Greek poets exemplary for hymns (Callimachus, born in 317 BCE) or for odes (Pindar, 522?–443 BCE).

[118]Faulty in their choice of subject matter because it was not (I assume) ultimately of sufficient religious or civic value. The idiom "an end" apparently is the same as "in the end" (*OED* 1).

[119]The Old Testament.

[120]Guessed.

the writings and interludes of libidinous and ignorant Poetasters, who having scars ever heard of that which is the main consistence of a true poem, the choys of such persons as they ought to introduce, and what is morall and decent to each one, doe for the most part lap us vitious principles in sweet pils to be swallow'd down, and make the tast of vertuous documents harsh and sowr. But because the spirit of man cannot demean it selfe lively[121] in this body without some recreating intermission of labour, and serious things, it were happy for the Common wealth, if our Magistrates, as in those famous governments of old, would take into their care, not only the deciding of our contentious Law cases and brauls, but the managing of our publick sports, and festival pastimes,[122] that they might be, not such as were autoriz'd a while since, the provocations of drunkennesse and lust, but such as may inure and harden our bodies by martial exercises to all warlike skil and performance, and may civilize, adorn and make discreet our minds by the learned and affable meeting of frequent Academies, and the procurement of wise and artfull recitations sweetned with eloquent and gracefull inticements to the love and practice of justice, temperance and fortitude, instructing and bettering the Nation at all opportunities, that the call of wisdom and vertu may be heard every where, as *Salomon* saith, *She crieth without, she uttereth her voice in the streets, in the top of high places, in the chief concours, and in the openings of the Gates.* Whether this may not be only in Pulpits, but after another persuasive method, at set and solemn Paneguries,[123] in Theaters, porches,[124] or what other place, or way may win most upon the people to receiv at once both recreation, & instruction, let them in autority consult. The thing which I had to say, and those intentions which have liv'd within me ever since I could conceiv my self any thing worth to my Countrie, I return to crave excuse that urgent reason hath pluckt from me by an abortive and foredated discovery.[125] And the accomplishment of them lies not but in a power above mans to promise; but that noe hath by more studious ways

endeavour'd, and with more unwearied spirit that none shall, that I dare almost averre of my self, as farre as life and free leasure will extend, and that the Land had once infranchis'd her self from this impertinent yoke of prelaty, under whose inquisitorious and tyrannical duncery no free and splendit wit can flourish. Neither do I think it shame to covnant with any knowing reader, that for some few yeers yet I may go on trust with him toward the payment of what I am not indebted, as being a work not to be rays'd from the heat of youth, or the vapours of wine, like that which flows at wast from the pen of some vulgar Amorist,[126] or the trencher fury of a riming parasite,[127] nor to be obtain'd by the invocation of Dame Memory and her Siren daughters,[128] but by devout prayer to that eternall Spirit who can enrich with all utterance and knowledge, and sends out his Seraphim with the hallow'd fire of his Altar to touch and purify the lips of whom he pleases:[129] to this must be added industrious and select reading, steddy observation, insight into all seemly and generous arts and affaires, till which in some measure be compast, at mine own peril and cost I refuse not to sustain this expectation from as many as are not loath to hazard so much credulity from the best pledges that I can give them. Although it nothing content me to have disclos'd thus much before hand, but that I trust hereby to make it manifest with what small willingnesse I endure to interrupt the pursuit of no lesse hopes then these, and leave a calme and pleasing solitarynes fed with cherful and confident thoughts, to imbark in a troubl'd sea of noises and hoars disputes, put from beholding the bright countenance of truth in the quiet and still air of delightfull studies to come into the dim reflexion of hollow antiquities sold by the seeming bulk, and there be fain to club quotations with men[130] whose learning and beleif lies in marginal stuffings, who when they have like good sumpters[131] laid ye down their hors load of citations and

---

[121]Maintain itself in good mental health; maintain a healthful demeanor.

[122]A reference to the current controversy within the church and state over whether ancient pastimes and sports should be allowed on holidays. Charles I *Book of Sports*, issued in 1633, declared "dancing . . . archery . . . May games, Whitsun-ales, and morris-dancers" legal for holidays (cited in Yale 1: 919n). Puritan factions considered such frivolities prophane.

[123]Panegyries (Milton's is the first recorded use of the term), religious festival days.

[124]Probably church gates or porches, where public and civic ceremonies were sometimes conducted or announced.

[125]Similar in tone to the opening image of "Lycidas." Not yet ready or ripe for performance, Milton has been summoned into print by the urgency of the situation.

[126]As compared with the erotic lyric poet, often inspired by lust and by wine, Milton endorses the sober, water-drinking, temperate-living poet, whom he pictured as being like Homer, capable of the force it would take to write an extended poem like an epic that would inspire humankind with its moral instruction.

[127]The artificially induced poetic furor of the kind produced by a court parasite, forced to rhyme for his plate of food (trencher).

[128]The reference here is demeaning, since "Dame Memory" suggests a pretentious middle-class appearance such as that of Chaucer's Dame Pertelotte, the gossipy wife of Chaunticleer. The daughters of Memory are usually the Muses, picturing them as sirens perched on the eight spheres and generating music.

[129]Alluding to the passage in Isaiah 6.1–7 in which God sends an angel with a live coal in his hand to touch and thereby purify the lips of the would-be faithful.

[130]To use quotations as clubs with which to beat learned opponents such as Ussher.

[131]Pack-horses, beasts of burden.

fathers at your dore, with a rapsody of who and who were Bishops here or there, ye may take off their pack-saddles, their days work is don, and episcopacy, as they think, stoutly vindicated. Let any gentle apprehension that can distinguish learned pains from unlearned drudgery, imagin what pleasure or profoundnesse can be in this, or what honour to deal against such adversaries. But were it the meanest under-service, if God by his Secretary conscience[132] injoyn it, it were sad for me if I should draw back, for me especially, now when all men offer their aid to help ease and lighten[133] the difficult labours of the Church, to whose service by the intentions of my parents and friends *I* was destin'd of a child,

and in mine own resolutions, till comming to some maturity of years and perceaving what tyranny had invaded the Church, that he who would take Orders must subscribe[134] slave, and take an oath withall,[135] which unlesse he took with a conscience that would retch he must either strait perjure, or split his faith, *I* thought it better to preferre a blameless silence before the sacred office of speaking bought, and begun with servitude and forswearing.[136] Howsoever thus Church-outed by the Prelats, hence may appear the right I have to meddle in these matters, as before, the necessity and constraint appear'd.

---

[134]I have corrected from "subscibe," as the errata list suggests.

[135]A candidate for ordination in the English church of 1641 (most graduates of Cambridge and Oxford would take orders), had to swear allegiance to the King, to the Book of Common Prayer and its thirty-nine Articles, to the hierarchy of bishops, priests, and deacons, and, in a recently added clause, to the "Government of the Church" (Yale 1: 823n).

[136]Taking the oath is pictured as a mercantile transaction: on giving the oath one purchased or bought into the priesthood. Milton's refusal to take the oath gives him the personal impetus and the moral obligation to write *Reason of Church-government.*

---

[132]God calls *"Conscience"* "My Umpire" in the memorable phrase in *Paradise Lost* 3.195.

[133]Corrected from "enlighten" by the errata.

Doctrine and Discipline of Divorce (1644)

In his title, Milton gives dignity to what was in the 1640s a disreputable subject, divorce, by giving it a doctrine—a set of invariable laws on the subject—and a discipline—a set of rules for effecting divorce. The word *doctrine* also has in its etymology the Latin verb *docere*, "to instruct." It was used in theology to identify the most sacred body of religious truths. *Discipline* suggests the process of learning or being a pupil. The word also suggests a code of religious rules or laws, in this case governing marriage or its dissolution. Milton used the phrase "Church Discipline" often, meaning the rules a Christian should live by within the church, and he used the Latin word *Doctrina* for his own theological treatise, *De Doctrina Christiana*. Modern readers will find part of the subtitle, "Restor'd to the good of both SEXES," instructive in that it hints of gender equality.

The strategy of Milton's title echoes that of his later *Judgement of Martin Bucer, Concerning Divorce* (August, 1644). The *"Judgement"* (meaning honored opinion) comes before the respected name of Bucer, followed at last by the more controversial *"Divorce."*

Historical perspectives change. From the present millenial vantage point, we can look back with approval on Milton's foresight in advocating divorce (we have in the U. S. recently preferred the label "dissolution") on the grounds of mutual incompatibility as reasonable and humane. But in Milton's England, where Church and State worked so closely together that their courts sometimes had conflicting jurisdictions, divorce was a violation of a legal and religious bond instituted in the Book of Common Prayer (though Puritan factions denigrated the very use of that book in church, it nevertheless had to have a strong influence over any churchgoer). Both the Roman Catholic and the English high Anglican churches forbade divorce except on the bases of failure to consummate the marriage, adultery, or impotence. English clerics, unlike Catholic monks, friars, or nuns, were allowed to marry.

What Milton advocates in the divorce tracts is "divorce and remarriage in cases of hopeless temperamental incompatibility" (Stone 102). He may have arrived at that position because his own wife, Mary Powell Milton, deserted him in mid-August 1642, not quite two months after their June (? scholars have suggested May, June, or July) wedding. She would not return until 1645. We cannot tell for sure if Milton was contemplating his own divorce as he was writing his pamphlets in favor of divorce. He may even have been contemplating the subject of divorce before he married (Shawcross *John Milton* 214), but whether this was the same sort of divorce he discussed in the divorce tracts has been debated (Vinovich 7). It does not seem reasonable to me that a semi-middle-aged man on the brink of marriage would be studying divorce yet. But a proud, rejected, middle-class man trying to marry into the landed gentry might. I should point out that Milton never emphasized in any of the divorce tracts his own most legally defensible grounds for divorce, which was desertion.

Before he met, married, and was deserted by Mary Powell, Milton apparently believed that there were legitimate alternatives to marriage for both men and women. Though it did not resemble monkish celibacy, which he abhorred, Milton's version of chastity had assumed something near a holy state in Milton's 1634 *Comus*, and both "Lycidas" and *"Epitaphium Damonis"* seem to honor the sexual abstinence of the young men they memorialize. Within the educational system of Milton's youth, a celibate don at Cambridge or Oxford, in something like a seminary, was more the rule than the exception. Milton had expressed some good-humored resistance to his being labeled as "the Lady of Christ's [College]" in Prolusion 6: obviously concerned about the label, he admitted to looking effeminate or at least pale, but he separated himself from the beer-guzzling contests of his fellow students, whom he described as behaving like donkeys.

Though he expressed vague desire for the young women of London he gazes at in his Latin elegies written with Charles Diodati as audience, Milton apparently remained celibate until he married: at least he bragged about resisting temptation when he traveled to such legendary places of dissolution as Venice and Naples during his European tour. He returned to England with the serious purposes of being a scholar and instructing young men at his home, then suddenly, at the age of thirty four "after a month's stay [with the Powell family], home he returns a Married-man, that went out a Batchelor" (according to Edward Phillips's gleeful account of his uncle's behavior, in Darbishire 63). Within the space of about two months in 1642, Mary had married him and left him, at first under pretense of returning home for a holiday. Phillips writes that Milton's messenger, asking about his Mary's return, was rebuffed or insulted. Mary would not return until after the point when King Charles's fortunes (hence those of the Royalist Powell family) looked very bleak (see Phillips in Darbishire 66).

Milton had taken his seventeen-year-old bride, who was used to a large country home at Forest Hill near Oxford, back to his house in London, in which his primary occupation was to teach and his secondary occupations were to be a scholar and poet. Mary had to listen to the silence of his reading and to the noise of his pupils being disciplined, since he was a strong believer in corporal punishment, at least for young male pupils.

Milton may have believed that he could not have obtained a divorce in his own country either on the grounds of adultery or desertion—witness this little aside in *The Doctrine and Discipline of Divorce*:

> Afterwards it [marriage] was thought so Sacramentall, that no adultery or desertion could dissolve it; and this is the sense of our Canon Courts in England to this day . . . .

Halkett writes, unequivocally, "The English church alone, which still followed canon law in matrimonial issues, did not yet recognize divorce *a vinculo* at all, for whatever cause. It merely allowed separation in cases of adultery, *a mensa et thoro* (*Milton* 3). The divorce, in other words, would not be from the bonds of marriage, but a separation from bed and board, without the comfort of remarriage.

Not to be defeated by the domestic reversal of Mary Powell's leaving, Milton fought back through his studies and his writing. He also began to think, at least, in terms of courting another woman. By 1645, he had "a design of Marrying one of Dr. *Davis's* Daughters, a very Handsome and Witty Gentlewoman" (Darbishire 66), if Edward Phillips's account is accurate. The anonymous biographer, most likely Cyriak Skinner, also writes that, because of Mary's desertion, Milton "thought upon a Divorce, that hee might bee free to marry another; concerning which hee also was in treaty" (Darbishire 23).

Between the desertion in 1642 and the return of his wife in 1645, Milton read all he could find having to do with the divorce, despite Christ's injunction "That whosoever shall put away his wife, saving for the cause of fornication, causeth her to commit adultery: and whosoever shall marry her that is divorced committeth adultery" (Matthew 5. 32). Milton also resisted the Old Testament tradition that divorce should be allowed in cases where the wife "find[s] no favour in his [her husband's] eyes, because he hath found some uncleanness in her; then let him write her a bill of divorcement, and give it in her hand, and send her out of his house" (Deuteronomy 24.1).

SCHOLARLY PREPARATION FOR THE DIVORCE TRACTS

Milton prepared to write his treatises by reading the contemporary legal philosophers Erasmus, Hugo Grotius, and Martin Bucer (whose work he discovered after he had begun writing on the subject), all of whose erudition might lend stature to what could easily be seen—and would be seen—as a disreputable argument that the law should allow divorce at will or on a whim.

Milton also read in the biblical commentaries of David Paraeus, John Calvin, Paul Fagius, André Rivetus, and others he calls "common expositors" (for the context of biblical commentary in the sixteenth and seventeenth centuries, see Williams). As was his custom in any of his arguments in print, he might combine passages from Old and New Testaments as proof texts, texts to prove a point he is making in this case about divorce.

THE MODEL MARRIAGE: ADAM AND EVE

Milton's case study for the perfect marriage, built on "a law out of Paradise giv'n in time of originall perfection" was that of Adam and Eve. Whenever Milton uses the term "original" in connection with marriage, he means the marriage of Adam and Eve. The marriage in Eden was "a fit and perfect mariage, with an interdict of ever divorcing such a Union." The horrible alternative, in a fallen world, was "instead of being one flesh, they will be rather two carkasses chain'd unnaturally together."

ORGANIZATION

Skinner has a clear grasp of what Milton emphasized in the three divorce tracts:

> In these hee taught the right use and design of Marriage; then the Original and practise of Divorces amongst the Jews, and show'd that our Savior, in those foure places of the Evangelists, meant not the abrogating, but rectifying the abuses of it; rendring to that purpose another Sense of the word Fornication (and wch is also the Opinion amongst others of Mr. Selden in his *Uxor Hebræa*) then what is commonly received. Martin Bucers Judgment in this matter he likewise translated into English. (Darbishire 23–24)

Milton did demand more for the civil right to divorce than did any previous reformer. Ernest Sirluck summarized Milton's demands for the institution of divorce:

> It was for the recognition of divorce *a vinculo* with the right of remarriage for both parties; the liberalization of grounds, particularly to include incompatibility; and the removal of divorce from public jurisdiction, whether ecclesiastical or civil, to private
> (Yale 2: 146)

Thus Milton wanted to make divorce by mutual consent a matter of private conscience, not public policy or religious mandate.

DISREPUTABLE RESULTS

For his pains in the cause of human rights within the family, Milton was labeled a "divorcer," or someone who advocated "divorce at pleasure," as the result of his impassioned and scholarly argument. Herbert Palmer, in a sermon given before Parliament and the Assembly on August 13, 1644, attacked the *Doctrine and Discipline of Divorce* as a "*wicked booke . . . deserving to be burnt, whose Author hath been so impudent as to set his name to it and dedicate it to your selves . . .*" (quoted Yale 2: 103). Milton answered Palmer by using his own rhetorical methods against him in *Tetrachordon*. The second of the divorce tracts is a long-winded (132 pp. in the Yale edition) exposition of four "chiefe places in Scripture which treat of Mariage, or nullities in Mariage" (Yale 2: 586). The tract is notable, like its predecessor, for what it says about the marriage of Adam and Eve.

Milton's bristly nature could not endure public criticism, and the third of his original divorce tracts, *Colasterion*, is a furious attack (the title word means "rod of correction") on the "serving-man" who had dared to write *An Answer to a Book, Intituled, The Doctrine and Discipline of Divorce, or, A Plea for Ladies and Gentlewomen, and all other Maried Women against Divorce* (licenced 14 November, 1644). Entitled to call himself a gentleman by virtue of having graduated from Cambridge, Milton looks down on the anonymous author, whom he smears with titles like "illiterat, and arrogant presumer in that which hee understands not; bearing us in hand [deceiving us] as if hee knew both Greek and Ebrew, and is not able to spell it" (Yale 2: 724).

CRITICAL RECEPTION: MILTON'S SELF-CREATION AND THE ROASTING OF HIS REPUTATION

Milton himself regretted publishing *The Doctrine and Discipline of Divorce* in English, because he wanted a reader above the common reader, and such a reader would be more likely to read a scholarly treatise in Latin. By hindsight, in the autobiographical sections of his prose defenses written in Latin, he saw the divorce tracts as his grand attempt to bring liberty to the home, just as he tried to bring it to the state, as with *Areopagitica*'s plea against state censorship, and to the church, as with *The Reason of Church-government*.

TEXT

The Doctrine and Discipline of Divorce was first published on August 1, 1643, as recorded by Thomason. "It [the first edition] was printed by Thomas Payne and Matthew Simmons; there is a long errata list. Claud A. Thompson suggests that Payne set sig[nature]s B and C, and Simmons sigs. D–H on the basis of orthography" (Shawcross, "A Survey" 296; see also Thompson). Sim-

mons, at least, was remarkably faithful to Milton's personal spelling system, and he is likely to be the only compositor of *1644*. Students of Milton's orthography turn to Simmons's work in *Colasterion* as representative of Milton's spelling system as most successfully enforced on a printed text.

The text here represented is the 1644 expanded second edition of the tract, eighty-two closely printed pages. "This revised, second edition is so different from the 1643 version that it almost constitutes a second volume on divorce" (Shawcross 296). But to conflate the 1643 and 1644 editions by means of bracketed text, as the Yale editors attempted to do, creates an ugly and confusing typographical jungle on the page. Perhaps the ideal text of the tract would be a hypertext edition that might allow discrete versions of each text to be viewed side-by-side in columns. But for the print medium one must make a choice, and mine is for the 1644 edition, and, very specifically, the Bodleian Library copy of the 1644 edition (Shelfmark 4o F 56 Th [kept as Arch. G e. 44]), which has corrections in what is probably the hand of a printing house scribe. It is part of a presentation volume, the eleven tracts given by Milton in 1645 or 1646 to the Bodleian apparently at the request of John Rouse, Bodley Librarian. A third edition, dated 1645, may be used by a modern editor to help determine if Miltonic orthography leaves traces in any of the later editions.

The 1644 edition of *The Doctrine and Discipline of Divorce* is carefully printed and well-produced. The pages look good and the layout of the quarto volume makes it easy to read, with chapters arranged neatly by author and printer so that they come in intervals designed not to try the reader's patience. Each chapter heading also provides a shorthand summary of its contents, using a style like that of most Bibles printed in the Renaissance. The presence of the headings indicates Milton's care in organizing his first pamphlet on divorce. The printer, in turn, was confident enough of the contents of the tract to use devices such as ornamented drop-capitals—devices that might identify the printer, rendering him liable to prosecution. The first edition identified the printers as "*T.P.* and *M.S.*" on its title page; the second edition gave no printer but identified the author as "*J.M.*" Milton, in other words, did not hazard his whole name in the publication, but he did allow himself to be identified by his initials.

The compositor of *1644* seems to have been faithful in general to Milton's orthography (for context, see McKenzie): the spelling of the word "mariage," Milton's preferred form, is a case in point; usually the compositor honored that spelling. Other preferences that are Miltonic, which are usually preserved, are "covnant," "beleeve," "carkasses," "vertue," "perswade," "anough," "cattel," "hainous," "Pharises" (plural of Pharisee), "somthing," and "autority" (at least on p. 34 of the original).

Capitalization also might tell us something about what Milton might want emphasized. The word "Law" is almost always capitalized throughout the tract, as are other related legal terms such as "Canon," "Commonwealth," "Magistrate," and "Minister," but the word "mariage" almost never is, and "divorce" is almost never capitalized.

Italics are substituted for modern quotation marks. They can be used subtly, so as not to distract the reader. For instance, when there is a quotation from Deuteronomy, the quotation itself may be italicized but the "Deut." left without its customary italics. Italics also affect meaning: the italics are consistently removed from "Pharises," which somehow lowers the status of the Pharisees. Italics can be used for rhetorical emphasis (see "*bondage*" on original p. 70), or as in the modern usage of identifying a word as word ("*fornication*" is identified this way). To remove italics in the process of modernizing the text is to remove part of its meaning.

Spelling affects pronunciation as well as meaning. Consider the following sentence:

> That the ordinance which God gave to our comfort, may not be pinn'd upon us to our undeserved thraldom; to be coopt up as it were in mockery of wedlock, to a perpetual betrothed lonelines and discontent, if nothing worse ensue.

The spelling "ordinance" tells us we should pronounce the word with three syllables (compare "covnant," which is always spelled with two); "pinn'd" is a monosyllable, but "undeserved" is read as "undeservèd"; "coopt" is a monosyllable and perhaps clipped in pronunciation, but "betrothed" is "betrothèd." The spelling, in this case devised according to a system Milton probably learned at the hand of the headmaster of at St. Paul's School, Alexander Gil, is consistent, despite the erratic usage of most printers of the period.

I have modernized only i/j, u/v, and short s/long s, all for the sake of not confusing the modern reader. For reference to the original pagination, I have added in brackets the letters and numbers of gatherings and page numbers, when they are present in the original.

Works Cited

Barker, Arthur E. "Christian Liberty in Milton's Divorce Pamphlets." *Modern Language Review* 35 (1940): 153–61.

Darbishire, Helen. *The Early Lives of Milton*. Oxford: Clarendon P, 1932.

Haley, Janet E. "Female Autonomy in Milton's Sexual Politics." *Milton and the Idea of Woman*, ed. Julia M. Walker. Urbana: U of Illinois P, 1988. 230–53.

Halkett, John G. *Milton and the Idea of Matrimony: A Study of the Divorce Tracts and* Paradise Lost. New Haven, CT: Yale UP, 1970.

Kingdon, Robert M. *Adultery and Divorce in Calvin's Geneva*. Cambridge, MA: Harvard UP, 1995.

LeComte. *Milton and Sex*. New York: Columbia UP, 1978.

McKenzie, Donald F. "Printers of the Mind." *Studies in Bibliography* 22 (1969): 1–75.

Patterson, Annabel. "No meer amatorious novel?" *John Milton*. Ed. Patterson. New York: Longman, 1992. 88–101.

Powell, Chilton Latham. *English Domestic Relations, 1487–1653*. New York: Columbia UP, 1917.

Shawcross, John T. *John Milton: The Self and the World*. Lexington: U of Kentucky P, 1993.

———. "A Survey of Milton's Prose Works." *Achievements of the Left Hand: Essays on the Prose of John Milton*. Ed. Michael Lieb and John T. Shawcross. Amherst: U of Massachusetts P, 1974. 291–391.

———. "Milton and Covenant: The Christian View of Old Testament Theology." *Milton and Scriptural Tradition: The Bible into Poetry*. Columbia: U of Missouri P, 1984.

Sims, James H. *The Bible in Milton's Epics*. Gainesville: U of Florida P, 1962.

Stone, Lawrence. *The Family, Sex and Marriage in England 1500–1800*. New York: Harper, 1979.

——. *Road to Divorce: England 1530–1987*. Oxford: Oxford UP, 1990.

Thompson, Claud. "Milton's *Doctrine and Discipline of Divorce*: A Bibliographical Study." Ph.D. diss., University of Wisconsin, 1971.

Treip, Mindele. *Allegorical Poetics & the Epic: The Renaissance Tradition to* Paradise Lost. Lexington: UP of Kentucky, 1994.

Turner, James. *One Flesh: Paradisal Marriage and Sexual Relations in the Age of Milton*. Oxford: Clarendon P, 1987.

Vinovich, J. Michael. "Protocols of Reading: Milton and Biography." *Early Modern Literary Studies* 1 (1995): 2.1–15.

Williams, Arnold. *The Common Expositor: An Account of the Commentaries on Genesis, 1527–1633*. Chapel Hill: U of North Carolina P, 1948.

Wright, Louis B. *Middle Class Culture in Elizabethan England*. Chapel Hill: U of North Carolina P, 1935.

TO THE
PARLAMENT
OF
ENGLAND,
with the ASSEMBLY.

I F it were seriously askt, and it would be no untimely question, Renowned Parlament,[1] select Assembly, who of all Teachers and Maisters that have ever taught, hath drawn the most Disciples after him, both in Religion, and in manners, it might bee not untruly answer'd, Custome. Though vertue be commended for the most perswasive in her *Theory*; and Conscience in the plain demonstration of the spirit, finds most evincing,[2] yet whether it be the secret of divine will, or the originall blindnesse we are born in,[3] so it happ'ns for the most part, that Custome still is silently receiv'd for the best instructer. Except it be, because her method is so glib and easie, in some manner like to that vision of *Ezekiel*, rowling up her sudden book of implicit knowledge, for him that will, to take and swallow down at pleasure;[4] which proving but of bad nourishment in the concoction, as it was heedlesse in the devouring, puffs up unhealthily, a certaine big face of pretended learning, mistaken among credulous men, for the wholsome habit of soundnesse and good constitution; but is indeed no other, then that swoln visage of counterfeit knowledge and literature,[5] which not onely in private marrs our education, but also in publick is the common climer into every chair, where either Religion is preach't, or Law reported: filling each estate of life and profession, with abject and servil principles; depressing the high and Heaven-born spirit of Man, farre beneath the condition wherein either God created him or sin hath sunke him. To persue the Allegory,[6] Custome being but a meer face, as Eccho is a meere voice, rests not in her unaccomplishment, untill by secret inclination, she accorporat[7] her selfe with error, who being a blind and Serpentine body without a head, willingly accepts what he wants, and supplies what her incompleatnesse went seeking. Hence it is, that Error supports Custome, Custome count'nances Error. And these two betweene them would persecute and chase away all truth and solid wisdome out of humane life, were it not that God, rather then man, once in many ages, cals together the prudent and Religious counsels of Men, deputed to represse the encroachments, and to worke off the inveterate blots and obscurities wrought upon our mindes by the suttle insinuating of Error and Custome: Who with the numerous and vulgar train of their followers make it their chiefe designe to envie and cry-down the industry of free reasoning, under the terms of humor,[8] and innovation; as if the womb of teeming Truth were to be clos'd up, if shee presume to bring forth ought, that sorts not with their unchew'd notions and suppositions. Against which notorious injury and abuse of mans free soul to testifie and oppose the utmost that study and true labour can attaine, heretofore the incitement of men reputed grave hath led me among others; and now the duty and the right of an instructed Christian cals me through the chance of good or evill report, to be the sole advocate of a discount'nanct truth: a high enterprise Lords and Commons, a high enterprise and a hard, and such as every seventh Son of a seventh Son[9] does not venture on. Nor have I amidst the clamor of so much envie and impertinence, whether[10] to appeal, but to the concourse of so much piety and wisdome heer assembl'd. Bringing in my hands an ancient and most necessary, most charitable, and yet most injur'd Statue

---

[1] Milton seems to have imposed his preferred spelling, "parlament," on the compositors, who follow the spelling with some consistency throughout the document.

[2] Convincing (Milton's is the first usage in this sense recorded in the *OED*).

[3] The result of original sin.

[4] In Ezekiel 2 and 3, a spirit speaking internally gives the prophet a book in the form of a scroll to eat. The prophet eats the book, which has a sweet taste despite being full of "lamentations, and mourning, and woe" (2.10), and gains God's wisdom in the act of eating. Milton's digested book is the bad book of Custom, and it causes indigestion.

[5] Acquaintance with books.

[6] Extended metaphor (with no necessity to give abstractions human qualities at this point). Treip concludes, from this passage and others in Milton's prose, "that Milton's uses of 'allegory' are numerous, are set in significant contexts, and *always* appear associated with a wider kind of figuration—as opposed to his personal uses of 'type' or 'types,' which imply strict Christological prediction only" (325).

[7] Incorporate, unite with in one body.

[8] Whimsical behavior; behavior according to the inclination of one's humors, whether melancholy, bilious, sanguine, or choleric.

[9] The seventh son of the seventh son is proverbially destined for greatness. The phrase sounds biblical but is not. Milton attached some significance in *Paradise Lost* 11.700 to Enoch's being the seventh in descent from Adam (see Jude 14).

[10] Anywhere.

of *Moses*:[11] not repeald ever by him who only had the authority, but thrown aside with much inconsiderat neglect, under the rubbish of Canonicall ignorance: as once the whole law was by some such like conveyance in *Josiahs* time. And hee who shall indeavour the amendment of any old neglected grievance in Church or State, or in the daily course of life, if he be gifted with abilities of mind that may raise him to so high an undertaking, I grant he hath already much whereof not to repent him; yet let mee arreed him,[12] not to be the foreman of any mis-judgd opinion, unlesse his resolutions be firmly seated in a square and constant mind, not conscious to it self of any deserved blame, and regardles of ungrounded suspicions. For this let him be sure he shall be boorded presently by the ruder sort, but not by discreet and well nurtur'd men, with a thousand idle descants and surmises. Who when they cannot confute the least joynt or sinew of any passage in the book; yet God forbid that truth should be truth, because they have a boistrous conceit of some pretences in the Writer. But were they not more busie and inquisitive then the Apostle commends, they would heare him at least, *rejoycing, so the Truth be preacht, whether of envie or other pretence whatsoever:* For Truth is as impossible to be soil'd by any outward touch, as the Sun beam. Though this ill hap wait on her nativity, that shee never comes into the world, but like a Bastard, to the ignominy of him that brought her forth: till Time the Midwife rather then the mother of Truth, have washt and salted the Infant, declar'd her legitimat, and Churcht the father of his young *Minerva*, from the needlesse causes of his purgation. Your selves can best witnesse this, worthy Patriots, and better will, no doubt, hereafter: for who among ye of the formost that have travail'd in her behalfe to the good of Church, or State, hath not been often traduc't to be the agent of his owne by-ends, under pretext of Reformation. So much the more I shall not be unjust to hope, that however Infamy, or Envy may work in other men to doe her fretfull will against this discourse, yet that the experience of your owne uprightnesse mis-interpreted, will put ye in mind to give it free audience and generous construction. What though the brood of Belial, the draffe of men, to whom no liberty is pleasing, but unbridl'd and vagabond lust without pale or partition, will laugh broad perhaps, to

see so great a strength of Scripture mustering up in favour, as they suppose, of their debausheries; they will know better, when they shall hence learne, that honest liberty is the greatest foe to dishonest licence. And what though others out of a waterish and queasy conscience because ever crasy[13] and never yet sound, will rail and fancy to themselves, that injury and licence is the best of this Book? Did not the distemper of their own stomacks affect them with a dizzy megrim,[14] they would soon tie up their tongues, and discern themselves like that *Assyrian* blasphemer all this while reproacing not man but the Almighty, *the holy one of Israel*,[15] whom they doe not deny to have belawgiv'n[16] his owne sacred people with this very allowance, which they now call injury and licence, and dare cry shame on, and will doe yet a while, till they get a little cordiall sobriety to settle their qualming zeale. But this question concerns not us perhaps: Indeed mans disposition though prone to search after vain curiosities, yet when points of difficulty are to be discusst, appertaining to the removall of unreasonable wrong and burden from the perplext life of our brother, it is incredible how cold, how dull, and farre from all fellow feeling we are, without the spurre of self-concernment. Yet if the wisdome, the justice, the purity of God be to be cleer'd from foulest imputations which are not yet avoided, if charity be not to be degraded and trodd'n down under a civil Ordinance, if Matrimony be not to be advanc't like that exalted perdition, writt'n of to the *Thessalonians, above all that is called God*,[17] or goodnesse, nay, against them both, then I dare affirm: there will be found in the Contents of this Booke, that which may concern us all. You it concerns chiefly, Worthies in Parlament, on whom, as on our deliverers, all our grievances and cares, by the merit of your eminence and fortitude are devolv'd: Me it concerns next, having with much labour and faithfull diligence first found out, or at least with a fearlesse and communicative candor first publisht to the manifest good of Christendome, that which calling to witnesse every thing mortall and immortall, I beleeve unfainedly to be true. Let not other men thinke their conscience bound to search continually after truth, to pray for enlightning from[18]

---

[11]Deuteronomy 24.1, which Milton supposes—as did most Bible scholars of his era—to have been written by Moses, sets out the Old Testament law of divorce: "When a man hath taken a wife, and married her, and it come to pass that she find no favour in his eyes, because he hath found some uncleanness in her: then let him write her a bill of divorcement, and give it in her hand, and send her out of his house."
[12]"Give him advice."

---

[13]Crazy.
[14]Migraine.
[15]God is often called "the holy one of [or in] Israel" in the Old Testament, beginning with 1 Kings 19.22.
[16]Milton probably made the word up (see *OED* be- [prefix] 7). Here it seems to be used contemptuously.
[17]2 Thessalonians 2.4.
[18]In the copy that he presented to the Bodleian library, Milton (his is the most likely hand) has corrected "rom" at the beginning of a line to "from."

above to publish what they think they have so obtain & debarr me from conceiving my self ty'd by the same duties. Yee have now, doubtlesse by the savour and appointment of God, yee have now in your hands a great and populous Nation to Reform; from what corruption, what blindnes in Religion yee know well; in what a degenerat and fal'n spirit from the apprehension of native liberty, and true manlines, I'am sure ye find: with what unbounded licence rushing to whordoms and adulteries needs not long enquiry: insomuch that the fears which men have of too strict a discipline, perhaps exceed the hopes that can bee in others, of ever introducing it with any great successe. What if I should tell yee now of dispensations and indulgences, to give a little the rains, to let them play and nibble with the bait a while;[19] a people as hard of heart as that Egyptian Colony that went to *Canaan*. This is the common doctrine that adulterous and injurious divorces were not conniv'd only, but with ey open allow'd of old for hardnesse of heart. But that opinion, I trust, by then this following argument hath been well read, will be left for one of the mysteries of an indulgent Antichrist, to farm out incest by, and those his other tributary pollutions. What middle way can be tak'n then, may some interrupt, if we must neither turne to the right nor to the left, and that the people hate to be reform'd: Mark then, Judges and Lawgivers, and yee whose Office is to be our teachers, for I will utter now a doctrine, if ever any other, though neglected or not understood, yet of great and powerfull importance to the governing of mankind. He who wisely would restrain the reasonable Soul of man within due bounds, must first know himself perfectly, how far the territory and dominion extends of just and honest liberty. As little must he offer to bind that which God hath loos'n'd, as to loos'n that which he hath bound. The ignorance and mistake of this high point, hath heapt up one huge half of all the misery that hath bin since *Adam*. In the Gospel we shall read a supercilious crew of masters, whose holinesse, or rather whose evill eye, grieving that God should be so facil to man, was to set straiter limits to obedience, then God had set; to inslave the dignity of man, to put a garrison upon his neck of empty, and overdignifi'd precepts. And we shall read our Saviour never more greev'd and troubl'd, then to meet with such a peevish madnesse among men against their own freedome. How can we expect him to be lesse offended with us, when much of the same folly shall be found yet remaining where it lest out, to the perishing of thousands. The greatest burden

in the world is superstition; not onely of Ceremonies in the Church, but of imaginary and scarcrow sins at home. What greater weakning, what more suttle stratagem against our Christian warfare, when besides the grosse body of real transgressions to encounter; wee shall bee terrify'd by a vain and shadowy meanacing of faults that are not: When things indifferent shall be set to over-front us, under the banners of sin, what wonder if wee bee routed, and by this art of our Adversary, fall into the subjection of worst and deadliest offences. The superstition of the Papist is, *touch not, taste not*, when *God* bids both: and ours is, *part not, separat not*, when God and charity both permits and commands. *Let all things be done with charity*, saith St. *Paul*: and his Master saith, *Shee is the fulfilling of the Law*. Yet now a civil, an indifferent, a somtime diswaded Law of mariage, must be forc't upon us to fulfill, not onely without charity, but against her. No place in Heav'n or Earth, except Hell, where charity may not enter: yet mariage the Ordinance of our solace and contentments, the remedy of our lonelinesse will not admit now either of charity or mercy to come in and mediate or pacifie the fiercenes[20] of this gentle Ordinance, the unremedied lonelinesse of this remedy. Advise yee well, supreme Senat, if charity be thus excluded and expulst, how yee will defend the untainted honour of your own actions and proceedings. He who marries intends as little to conspire his own ruine, as he that swears Allegiance: and as a whole people is in proportion to an ill Government, so is one man to an ill mariage. If they against any authority, Covnant, or Statue, may by the soveraign edict of charity, save not only their lives but honest liberties from unworthy bondage, as well may he against any private Covnant, which hee never enter'd to his mischief, redeem himself from unsupportable disturbances to honest peace, and just contentment: And much the rather, for that to resist the highest Magistrat though tyrannizing God never gave us expresse allowance, only he gave us reason, charity,[21] nature and good example to bear us out; but in this economical misfortune, thus to demean our selves, besides the warrant of those foure great directors, which doth as justly belong hither, we have an expresse law of *God*, and such a law, as wherof our Saviour with a solemn threat forbid the abrogating. For no effect of tyranny can sit more heavy on the Common-wealth, then this houshold unhappines on the family. And farewell all hope of true Reformation in the state, while such an evill as this lies

---

[19]Milton begins with an image from horsemanship, to give the horse free rein or loosen the reins, and moves to the image from fishing, to let the fish play with the bait and nibble it before taking the hook.

---

[20]Milton corrected "fiercnes" to "fiercenes" by inserting an "e," by means of a caret, in the Bodleian copy.
[21]I have added a comma here (following Yale) though there is none in the original.

undiscern'd or unregarded in the house. On the redresse whereof depends, not only the spiritfull and orderly life of our grwn men, but the willing, and carefull education of our children. Let this therefore be new examin'd, this tenure and free-hold of mankind, this native and domestick Charter giv'n us by a greater Lord then that *Saxon* king the Confessor. Let the statutes of God be turn'd over, be scann'd a new, and consider'd; not altogether by the narrow intellectuals of quotationists and common placers, but (as was the ancient right of Counsels) by men of what liberall profession soever, of eminent spirit and breeding joyn'd with a diffuse and various knowledge of divine and human things; able to ballance and define good and evill, right and wrong, throughout every state of life; able to shew us the waies of the Lord, strait and faithfull as they are, not full of cranks and contradictions, and pit falling dispences, but with divine insight and benignnity measur'd out to the proportion of each mind and spirit, each temper and disposition, created so different each from other, and yet by the skill of wise conducting, all to become uniform in vertue. To expedite these knots were worthy a learned and memorable synod; while our enemies expect to see the expectation of the Church tir'd out with dependencies and independencies how they will compound, and in what Calends. Doubt not, worthy Senators, to vindicate the sacred honour and judgment of *Moses* your predecessor, from the shallow commenting of Scholasticks and Canonists. Doubt not after him to reach out your steddy hands to the mis-inform'd and wearied life of man; to restore this his lost heritage, into the houshold state; wherwith be sure that peace and love the best subsistence of a Christian family will return home from whence they are now banisht; places of prostitution wil be lesse haunted, the neighbours bed less attempted, the yoke of prudent and manly discipline will be generally submitted to, sober and well order'd living will soon spring up in the Common-wealth. Ye have an author great beyond exception, *Moses*; and one yet greater, he who hedg'd in from abolishing, every smallest jot and tittle of precious equity contain'd in that Law, with a more accurat and lasting Masoreth, then either the Synagogue of *Ezra*, or the *Galilean* School at *Tiberias* hath left us. Whatever els ye can enact, will scarce concern a third part of the Brittish name: but the benefit and good of this your magnanimous example, will easily spread far beyond the banks of *Tweed* and the *Norman* Iles. It would not be the first, or second time, since our ancient *Druides*, by whom this Island was the Cathedrall of Philosophy to *France*, left off their pagan rites, that England hath had this honour vouchsaft from Heav'n, to give out reformation to the World. Who was it but our English *Constantine* that

baptiz'd the Roman Empire? who but the *Northumbrian Willibrode*, and *Winifrede* of *Devon* with their followers, were the first Apostles of *Germany*?[22] Who but *Alcuin* and *Wicklef* our Country men open'd the eyes of *Europe*, the one in arts, the other in Religion. Let not England, forget her precedence of teaching nations how to live.

Know, Worthies, know and exercise the privilege of your honour'd Country. A greater title I heer bring ye, then is either in the power or in the policy of *Rome* to give her *Monarchs*; this glorious act will stile ye as the defenders of Charity. Nor is this yet the highest inscription that will adorne so religious and so holy a defence as this; behold heer the pure and sacred Law of God, and his yet purer and more sacred name offring themselvs to you first, of all Christian reformers to be acquitted from the long suffer'd ungodly attribute of patronizing Adultery. Deferre not to wipe off instantly these imputative blurrs and stains cast by rude fancies upon the throne and beauty it selfe of inviolable holines: lest some other people more devout and wise then wee, bereav us this offer'd immortal glory, our wonted prerogative, of being the first asserters in every great vindication. For me, as farre as my part leads me, I have already my greatest gain, assurance and inward satisfaction to have don in this nothing unworthy of an honest life, and studies well employ'd. With what event among the wise and right understanding handfull of men, I am secure. But how among the drove of Custom and Prejudice this will be relisht, by such whose capacity, since their youth run ahead into the easie creek of a System or a Medulla, sayls there at will under the blown physiognomy of their unlabour'd rudiments, for them what their[23] tast will be, I have also surety sufficient, from the entire league that hath bin ever between formal ignorance and grave obstinacie. Yet when I remember the little that our Saviour could prevail about this doctrine of Charity against the crabbed textuists of his time, I make no wonder, but rest confident that who so preferrs either Matrimony, or other Ordinance before the good of man and the plain exigence of Charity, let him professe Papist, or Protestant, or what he will, he is no better then a Pharise, And understands not the Gospel: whom as a misinterpreter of Christ I openly protest against; and provoke him to the trial of this truth before all the world. and let him bethink him

---

[22] St. Willibrord (c. 657–c. 738), or Wilbrod, mentioned in Milton's *History of Britain* (1670 ed.: 64) as having spread Christianity to Germany and founded the first Bishopric in Frisia; Winfrid (c. 680–755), or St. Boniface, was martyred in Frisia.

[23] I have separated "what" and "their," since their joining together in the original has no precedent.

withall how he will soder up the shifting flaws of his ungirt permissions, his venial and unvenial dispences, wherwith the Law of God pardoning and unpardoning hath bin shamefully branded, for want of heed in glossing, to have eluded and baffl'd out all Faith and chastity from the mariagebed of that holy seed, with politick and judicial adulteries. I seek not to seduce the simple and illiterat; my errand is to find out the choisest and the learnedest, who have this high gift of wisdom to answer solidly, or to be convinc't. I crave it from the piety, the learning and the prudence which is hous'd in this place. It might perhaps more fitly have bin writt'n in another tongue; and I had don so, but that the esteem I have of my Countries judgement, and the love I beare to my native language to serv it first with what I endeavour, made me speak it thus, ere I assay the verdit of outlandish readers. And perhaps also heer I might have ended nameles, but that the addresse of these lines chiefly to the Parlament of *England* might have seem'd ingratefull not to acknowledge by whose Religious care, unwearied watchfulnes, couragious and heroick resolutions, I enjoy the peace and studious leisure to remain,

The Honourer and Attendant of their Noble worth and vertues,

John Milton

THE DOCTRINE AND DISCIPLINE
of *DIVORCE;*
Restor'd to the good of both Sexes.

---

1. BOOKE.

The Preface.
That Man is the occasion of his owne miseries, in most of those evills which hee imputes to Gods inflicting. The absurdity of our canonists in their decrees about divorce. The Christian imperiall Lawes fram'd with more Equity. The opinion of Hugo Grotius, *and* Paulus Fagius: *And the purpose in generall of this Discourse.*

Many men, whether it be their fate, or fond opinion, easily perswade themselves, if God would but be pleas'd a while to withdraw his just punishments from us, and to restrain what power either the devill, or any earthly enemy hath to work us woe, that then mans nature would find immediate rest and releasement from all evils. But verily they who think so, if they be such as have a mind large enough to take into their thoughts a generall survey of human things, would soon prove themselves in that opinion farre deceiv'd. For though it were granted us by divine indulgence to be exempt from all that can be harmful to us from without, yet the perversnesse of our folly is so bent, that we should never lin[24] hammering out of our owne hearts, as it were out of a flint, the seeds and sparkles of new misery to our selvs, till all were in a blaze againe. And no marvell if out of our own hearts, for they are evill; but ev'n out of those things which God meant us, either for a principall good, or a pure contentment, we are still hatching and contriving upon our selves matter of continuall sorrow and perplexitie. What greater good to man then that reaveled rule, whereby God vouchsafes to shew us how he would be worshipt? And yet that not rightly understood, became the cause that once a fa-

---

[24]Stop, cease.

mous man in *Israel*[25] could not but oblige his conscience to be the sacrificer, or if not, the jaylor of his innocent and only daughter. And was the cause ofttimes that Armies of valiant men have given up their throats to a heathenish enemy on the Sabbath day: fondly thinking their defensive resistance to be as then a work unlawfull. What thing more instituted to the solace and delight of man then marriage? and yet the mis-interpreting of some Scripture directed mainly against the abusers of the Law for divorce giv'n by *Moses*, hath chang'd the blessing of matrimony not seldome into a familiar and co-inhabiting mischiefe; at least into a drooping and disconsolate houshold captivity, without refuge or redemption. So ungovern'd and so wild a race doth superstition run us from one extreme of abused liberty into the other of unmercifull restraint. For although God in the first ordaining of marriage, taught us to what end he did it, in words expresly implying the apt and cheerfull conversation of man with woman, to comfort and refresh him against the evill of solitary life, not mentioning the purpose of generation till afterwards, as being but a secondary end in dignity, though not in necessity; yet now, if any two be but once handed in the Church, and have tasted in any sort the nuptiall bed, let them find themselves never so mistak'n in their dispositions through any error, concealment, or misadventure, that through their different tempers, thoughts, and constitutions, they can neither be to one another a remedy against lonelines, nor live in any union or contentment all their dayes, yet they shall, so they be but found suitable weapon'd to the least possibility of sensual enjoyment, be made, spight of *antipathy* to fadge[26] together, and combine as they may to their unspeakable wearisomnes and despaire of all sociable delight in the ordinance which God establisht to that very end. What a calamity is this, and as the Wise-man if he were alive, would sigh out in his own phrase, what a *sore evill is this under the Sunne!*[27] All which we can referre justly to no other author then the Canon Law and her adherents, not consulting with charitie, the interpreter and guide of our faith, but resting in the meere element of the Text; doubtles by the policy of the devill to make that gracious ordinance become unsupportable, that what with men not daring to venture upon wedlock, and what with men wearied out of it, all inordinate licence

might abound. It was for many ages that mariage lay in disgrace with most of the ancient Doctors, as a work of the flesh, almost a defilement, wholly deny'd to Priests, and the second time disswaded to all, as he that reads *Tertullian* or *Jerom* may see at large. Afterwards it was thought so Sacramentall, that no adultery or desertion could dissolve it; and this is the sense of our Canon Courts in England to this day, but in no other reformed Church els: yet there remains in them also a burden on it as heavie as the other two were disgracefull or superstitious, and of as much iniquity, crossing a Law not onely writt'n by *Moses*, but character'd in us by nature, of more antiquity and deeper ground then marriage it selfe; which Law is to force nothing against the faultles proprieties of nature: yet that this may be colourably[28] done, our Saviours words touching divorce, are as it were congeal'd into a stony rigor, inconsistent both with his doctrine and his office, and that which he preacht onely to the conscience, is by Canonicall tyranny snatcht into the compulsive censure of a judiciall Court; where Laws are impos'd even against the venerable and secret power of natures impression, to love what ever cause be found to loath. Which is a hainous barbarisme both against the honour of mariage, the dignity of man and his soule, the goodnes of Christianitie, and all the humane respects of civilitie. Notwithstanding that some the wisest and gravest among the Christian Emperours, who had about them, to consult with, those of the Fathers then living, who for their learning and holines of life are still with us in great renowne, have made their statutes and edicts concerning this debate, far more easie and relenting in many necessary cases, wherein the Canon is inflexible. And *Hugo Grotius*, a man of these times, one of the best learned, seems not obscurely to adhere in his perswasion to the equity of those Imperiall decrees, in his notes upon the *Evangelists*, much allaying the outward roughness of the Text, which hath for the most part been too immoderately expounded; and excites the diligence of others to enquire further into this question, as containing many points that have not yet been explain'd. Which ever likely to remain intricate and hopelesse upon the suppositions commonly stuck to, the autority[29] of *Paulus Fagius*, one so learned at so eminent in *England* once, if it might perswade, would strait acquaint us with a solution of these differences, no lesse prudent then compendious. He in his comment on the *Pentateuch* doubted not to maintain that divorces might be as lawfully permitted by the Magistrate to Christians,

---

[25]In order to conquer the Ammonites, the famous Israelite captain Jephthah promises to sacrifice "whatsoever cometh forth of the doors of [his] house to greet [him]" (Judges 11.31). Despite the fact that she is his only child, Jephthah honors his oath.

[26]Tolerate or put up with [one another].

[27]The wise man is Solomon; see Ecclesiastes 5.13: "There is a sore evil which I have seen under the sun, namely, riches kept for the owners thereof to their hurt."

[28]Speciously, fallaciously, hypocritically.

[29]A Miltonic spelling that seems to have passed through in the process of page-composition.

as they were to the Jewes. But because he is but briefe, and these things of great consequence not to be kept obscure, I shall conceave it nothing above my duty either for the difficulty or the censure that may passe thereon, to communicate such thoughts as I also have had, and do offer them now in this generall labour of reformation, to the candid view both of Church and Magistrate; especially because I see it is the hope of good men, that those irregular and unspirituall Courts have spun their utmost date in this Land;[30] and some better course must now be constituted. This therefore shall be the task and period of this discourse to prove, first that other reasons of divorce besides adultery, were by the Law of *Moses*, and are yet to be allow'd by the Christian Magistrate as a peece of justice, and that the words of Christ are not hereby contraried. Next, that to prohibit absolutely any divorce whatsoever except those which *Moses* excepted, is against the reason of Law, as in due place I shall shew out of *Fagius* with many additions. He therefore who by adventuring shall be so happy as with successe to light the way of such an expedient liberty and truth as this, shall restore the much wrong'd and over-sorrow'd state of matrimony, not onely to those mercifull and life-giving remedies of *Moses,* but, as much as may be, to that serene and blisfull condition it was in at the beginning; and shall deserv of all aprehensive men (considering the troubles and distempers which for want of this insight might have bin so oft in Kingdomes, in States, and Families) shall deserve to be reck'n'd among the publick benefactors of civill and humane life; above the inventors of wine and oyle; for this is a far dearer, far nobler, and more desirable cherishing to mans life, unworthily expos'd to sadness and mistake, which he shall vindicate. Not that licence and levity and unconsented breach of faith should herein be countnanc't, but that some conscionable and tender pitty might be had of those who have unwarily in a thing they never practiz'd before, made themselves the bondmen of a luckles and helples matrimony. In which Argument he whose courage can serve him to give the first onset, must look for two severall oppositions: the one from those who having sworn themselves to long custom and the letter of the Text, will not out of the road: the other from those whose grosse and vulgar apprehensions conceit but low[31] of matrimoniall purposes, and in the work of male and female think they have all. Neverthelesse, it shall be here sought by due wayes to be made appear, that those words of God in the institution, promising a meet help against lonelines; and those words of Christ,

That his yoke is easie and his burden light,[32] were not spoken in vain; for if the knot of marriage may in no case be dissolv'd but for adultery, all the burd'ns and services of the Law are not so intolerable. This onely is desir'd of them who are minded to judge hardly of thus maintaining, that they would be still and heare all out, nor think it equall to answer deliberate reason with sudden heat and noise; remembring this, that many truths now of reverend esteem and credit, had their birth and beginning once from singular and private thoughts while the most of men were otherwise possest; and had the fate at first to be generally exploded and exclaim'd on by many violent opposers; yet I may erre perhaps in soothing my selfe that this present truth reviv'd, will deserve on all hands to be not sinisterly receiv'd, in that it undertakes the cure of an inveterate[33] disease crept into the best part of humane society: and to doe this with no smarting corrosive, but with a smooth and pleasing lesson, which receiv'd hath the vertue to soften and dispell rooted and knotty sorrowes: and without inchantment if that be fear'd, or spell us'd, hath regard at once both to serious pitty, and upright honesty; that tends to the redeeming and restoring of none but such as are the object of compassion; having in an ill houre hamper'd themselves to the utter dispatch of all their most beloved comforts and repose for this lives term. But if we shall obstinately dislike this new overture of unexpected ease and recovery, what remains but to deplore the frowardnes[34] of our hopeles condition, which neither can endure the estate we are in, nor admit of remedy either sharp or sweet. Sharp we ourselves distast; and sweet, under whose hands we are, is scrupl'd and suspected as too lushious. In such a posture Christ found the *Jews*, who were neither won with the austerity of *John the Baptist*, and thought it too much licence to follow freely the charming pipe of him who sounded and proclaim'd liberty and reliefe to all distresses; yet Truth in some age or other will find her witnes, and shall be justify'd at last by her own children.

---

[30]Milton was hoping for the termination of ecclesiastical courts in England, not yet effected (see Yale 2: 239n19).
[31]"Have a low idea of."

[32]Matthew 11.30.
[33]The word *inveterate* had its "n" inverted in the Bodleian copy: Milton did not correct the error.
[34]Perversity, obstinacy.

CHAP. I.

The Position. Prov'd by the Law of Moses. That Law expounded and asserted to a morall and charitable use, first by Paulus Fagius; *next with other additions.*

TO remove therfore if it be possible, this great and sad oppression which through the strictnes of a literall interpreting hath invaded and disturb'd the dearest and most peaceable estate of houshold society, to the over-burdening, if not the over-whelming of many Christians better worth then to be so deserted of the Churches considerate care, this position shall be laid down; first proving then answering what may be objected either from Scripture or light of reason.

That indisposition, unfitnes, or contrariety of mind, rising from a cause in nature unchangeable, hindring and ever likely to hinder the main benefits of conjugall society, which are solace and peace, is a greater reason of divorce then naturall frigidity, especially if there be no children, and that there be mutuall consent.

This I gather from the Law in Deut. 24.1. *When a man hath tak'n a wife and married her, and it come to passe that she find no favour in his eyes, because he hath found some uncleanesse in her, let him write her a bill of divorcement, and give it in her hand, and send her out of his house, &c.* This Law, if the words of Christ may be admitted into our beleef, shall never while the world stands, for him be abrogated. First therfore I here set down what learned *Fagius* hat observ'd on this Law; *The Law of God,* saith he, *permitted divorce for the help of human weaknes. For every one that of necessity separats, cannot live single. That Christ deny'd divorce to his own, hinders not; for what is that to the unregenerated, who hath not attain'd such perfection? Let not the remedy be despis'd which was giv'n to weaknes. And when Christ saith, who marries the divorc't, commits adultery, it is to be understood if he had any plot in the divorce.* The rest I reserve untill it be disputed, how the Magistrate is to doe herein. From hence we may plainly discern a twofold consideration in this Law. First the end of the Lawgiver, and the proper act of the Law to command or to allow somthing just and honest, or indifferent. Secondly, his sufferance from some accidental result of evil by this allowance, which the Law cannot remedy. For if this Law have no other end of act buy onely the allowance of a sin, though never to so good intention, that Law is no Law but sin muffl'd in the robe of Law, or Law disguis'd in the loose garment of sin. Both which are to foul *Hypotheses* to save the *Phenomenon* of our Saviours answer to the Pharises about this matter. And I trust anon by the help of an infallible guide to perfet

such *Prutenick* tables[35] as shall mend the *Astronomy* of our wide expositors.[36]

The cause of divorce mention'd in the Law is translated *some uncleannesse;* but in the Hebrew it sounds *nakednes of ought, or any reall nakednes:* which by all the learned interpreters is refer'd to the mind, as well as to the body. And what greater nakednes or unfitnes of mind then that which hinders ever the solace and peacefull society of the maried couple, and what hinders that more then the unfitnes and defectivenes of an unconjugal mind. The cause therfore of divorce expres't in the position cannot but agree with that describ'd in the best and equalest sense of *Moses* Law. Which being a matter of pure charity, is plainly moral, and more now in force then ever: therfore surely lawfull. For if under the Law such was Gods gracious indulgence, as not to suffer the ordinance of his goodnes and favour, through any error to be ser'd[37] and stigmatiz'd upon his servants to their misery and thraldome, much lesse will he suffer it now under the covenant of grace, by abrogating his former grant of remedy and releef. But the first institution will be objected to have ordain'd mariage inseparable. To that a little patience untill this first part have amply discours't the grave and pious reasons of this divorsive Law; and then I doubt not but with one gentle stroking to wipe away ten thousand teares out of the life of man. Yet thus much I shall now insist on, that what ever the institution were, it could not be so enormous, nor so rebellious against both nature and reason as to exalt it selfe above the end and person for whom it was instituted.

CHAP. II.

The first reason of this Law grounded on the prime reason of matrimony. *That no cov'nant whatsoever obliges against the main end both of it self, and of the parties cov'nanting.*

FOr all sense and equity reclaims that any Law or Cov'nant how solemn or strait[38] soever, either between God and man, or man and man, though of Gods joyning, should bind against a prime and principall scope of its own institution, and of both or either party cov'nanting: neither can it be of force to

---

[35]Copernican planetary tables devised by Erasmus Reinhold for his patron Duke Albrecht of Prussia, hence "Prutenick."

[36]Expositors are those who interpreted the Bible; here they are "wide of the mark," or they miss the truth.

[37]Probably "seared," which might refer to the burning of the stigmata or to the process of drying up or withering (*OED* "seared" 1).

[38]Strict.

ingage a blameles creature to his own perpetuall sorrow, mistak'n for his expected solace, without suffering charity to step in and doe a confest good work of parting those whom nothing holds together, but this of Gods joyning, falsly suppos'd against the expresse end of his own ordinance. And what his chiefe end was of creating woman to be joynd with man, his own instituting words declare, and are infallible to informe us what is mariage and what is no mariage: unlesse we can think them set there to no purpose: *It is not good,* saith he, *that man should be alone; I will make him a help meet for him.* From which words so plain, lesse cannot be concluded, nor is by any learned Interpreter, then that in Gods intention a meet and happy conversation is the chiefest and the noblest end of mariage: for we find here no expression so necessarily implying carnall knowledge, as this prevention of lonlinesse to the mind and spirit of man. To this *Fagius, Calvin, Pareus, Rivetus,*[39] as willingly and largely assent as can be wisht. And indeed it is a greater blessing from God, more worthy so excellent a creature as man is, and a higher end to honour and sanctifie the league of marriage, whenas the solace and satisfaction of the mind is regarded and provided for before the sensitive pleasing of the body. And with all generous persons maried thus it is, that where the mind and person pleases aptly, there some unaccomplishment of the bodies delight may be better born with, then when the mind hangs off in an unclosing disproportion, though the body be as it ought; for there all corporall delight will soon become unsavoury and contemptible. And the solitarines of man, which God had namely and principally order'd to prevent by mariage, hath no remedy, but lies under a worse condition then the loneliest single life; for in single life the absence and remotenes of a helper might inure him to expect his own comforts out of himselfe, or to see with hope; but here the continuall sight of his deluded thoughts without cure, must needs be to him, if especially his complexion incline him to melancholy, a daily trouble and pain of losse in some degree like that which Reprobats feel. Lest therfore so noble a creature as man should be shut up incurably under a worse evill by an easie mistake in that ordinance which God gave him to remedy a lesse evill, reaping to himselfe sorrow while he went to rid away solitarines, it cannot avoid to be concluded, that if the woman be naturally so of disposition, as will not help to remove, but help to increase that same God-forbidd'n lonelines which will in time draw on with it a generall discomfort and

dejection of mind, not beseeming either Christian profession or morall conversation, unprofitable and dangerous to the Common-wealth, when the houshold estate, out of which must flourish forth the vigor and spirit of all publick enterprizes, is so ill contented and procur'd[40] at home, and cannot be supported; such a mariage can be no mariage whereto the most honest end is wanting: and the agrieved person shall doe more manly, to be extraordinary and singular in claiming the due right whereof he is frustrated, then to piece up his lost contentment by visiting the Stews,[41] or stepping to his neighbors bed, which is the common shift in this mis-fortune; or els by suffering his usefull life to wast away, and be lost under a secret affliction of an unconscionable size to humane strength. Against all which evills the mercy of this Mosaick Law was graciously exhibited.

CHAP. III.

The ignorance and iniquity of Canon Law, providing for the right of the body in mariage, but nothing for the wrongs and greevances of the mind. An objection, that the mind should be better lookt to before contract, answered.

HOw vain therfore is it, and how preposterous in the Canon Law to have made such carefull provision against the impediment of carnall performance, and to have had no care about the uncovering inability of mind, so defective to the purest and most sacred end of matrimony: and that the vessell of voluptuous enjoyment must be made good to him that has tak'n it upon trust without any caution, when as the mind from whence must flow the acts of peace and love, a far more pretious mixture then the quintessence of an excrement, though it be found never so deficient and unable to performe the best duty of marriage in a cheerfull and agreeable conversation: shall be though good anough, how ever flat and melancholious it be, and must serve, though to the eternall disturbance and languishing of him that complains him. Yet wisdom and charity waighing Gods own institution, would think that the pitting of a sad spirit wedded to lonelines should deserve to be free'd, aswell as the impatience of a sensuall desire so providently reliev'd. 'Tis read to us in the Liturgy, that *we must not marry to satisfie the fleshly appetite, like brute beast: that have no understanding;* but the Canon so runs, as if it dreamt of

---

[39]All authors of commentaries that include discussion of the passage under consideration, Genesis 2.18.

[40]Cared for, or, in this case, not cared for.
[41]Lower-class houses of prostitution.

no other matter then such an appetite to be satisfy'd; for if it happens that nature hath stopt or extinguisht the veins of sensuality, that mariage is annul'd. But though all the faculties of the understanding and conversing part after triall appeare to be so ill and so aversly met through natures unalterable working, as that neigher peace, nor any sociable contentment can follow, tis as nothing, the contract shall stand as firme as ever, betide what will. What is this but secretly to instruct us, that however many grave reasons are pretended to the maried life, yet that nothing indeed is thought worth regard therein, but the prescrib'd satisfaction of an irrational heat; which cannot be but ignominious to the state of mariage, dishonourable to the undervalu'd soule of man, and even to Christian doctrine it selfe. While it seems more mov'd at the disappointing of an impetuous nerve,[42] then at the ingenuous grievance of a mind unreasonably yoakt; and to place more of mariage in the channell of concupiscence, then in the pure influence of peace and love whereof the souls lawfull contentment is the onely fountain.

But some are ready to object, that the disposition ought seriously to be consider'd before. But let them know again, that for all the wariness can be us'd, it may yet befall a discreet man to be mistak'n in his choice, and we have plenty of examples. The sobrest and best govern'd men are least practiz'd in these affairs; and who knowes not that the bashfull mutenes of a virgin may oft-times hide all the unlivelines and natural sloth which is really unfit for conversation; nor is there that freedom of accesse granted or presum'd, as may suffice to a perfect discerning till too late: and where any indisposition is suspected, what more usuall then the perswasion of friends, that acquaintance, as it increases, will amend all. And lastly, it is not strange though many who have spent their youth chastly, are in some things not so quick-sighted, while they hast too eagerly to light the nuptiall torch; nor is it therefore that for a modest error a man should forfeit so great a happines, and no charitable means to release him. Since they who have liv'd most loosely by reason of their bold accustoming,[43] prove most succesfull in their matches, because their wild affections unsetling at will, have been as so many divorces to teach them experience. When as the sober man honouring the appearance of modesty, and hoping well of every sociall vertue under that veile, may easily chance to meet, if not with a body impenetrable, yet often with a mind to all other due conversation inaccessible, and to all the more estimable and superior

purposes of matrimony uselesse and almost liveles:[44] and what a solace, what a fit help such a consort would be through the whole life of a man, is lesse pain to conjecture then to have experience.

CHAP. IIII.

The Second Reason of this Law, because without it, mariage as it happ'ns oft is not a remedy of that which it promises, as any rationall creature would expect. That mariage, if we pattern from the beginning as our Saviour bids, was not properly the remedy of lust, but the fulfilling of conjugall love and helpfulnes.

ANd that we may further see what a violent and cruell thing it is to force the continuing of those together, whom God and nature in the gentlest end of mariage never joynd, divers evils and extremities that follow upon such a compulsion, shall here be set in view. Of evils the first and greatest is, that hereby a most absurd and rash imputation is fixt upon God and his holy Laws, of conniving and dispensing with open and common adultery among his chosen people; a thing which the rankest politician would think it shame and disworship, that his Laws should countenance; how and in what manner this comes to passe, I shall reserve, till the course of method brings on the unfolding of many Scriptures. Next the Law and Gospel are hereby made liable to more then one contradiction, which I referre also thither. Lastly, the supreme dictate of charitie is hereby many wayes neglected and violated. Which I shall forthwith address to prove. First we know St. *Paul* saith, *It is better to marry then to burn.* Mariage therfore was giv'n as a remedy of that trouble: but what might this burning mean? Certainly not the meer motion of carnall lust, not the meer goad of a sensitive desire; God does not principally take care for such cattell. What is it then but that desire which God put into *Adam* in Paradise before he knew the sin of incontinence; that desire which God saw it was not good that man should be left alone to burn in; the desire and longing to put off an unkindly solitarines by united another body, but not without a fit soule to his in the cheerfull society of wedlock. Which if it were so needfull before the fall, when man was much more perfect in himself, how much more is it needfull now against all the sorrows and casualties of this life to have an intimate and speaking help, a ready and reviving associate in marriage: whereof who misses by chancing on a mute and spiritles mate, remains more alone then

---

[42]Probably the penis (*OED* I.1.b), corresponding to the "channell of concupiscence," the vagina.
[43]Making themselves familiar with [loose living].

[44]Lifeless.

before, and in a burning lesse to be contain'd then that which is fleshly and more to be consider'd; as being more deeply rooted even in the faultles innocence of nature. As for that other burning, which is but as it were the venom of a lusty and over-abounding concoction, strict life and labour, with the abatement of a full diet may keep that low and obedient enough: but this pure and more inbred desire of joyning[45] to it selfe in conjugall fellowship a fit conversing soul (which desire is properly call'd love) *is stronger then death,* as the spouse of Christ thought, *many waters cannot quench it, neither can the floods drown it.* This is that rationall burning that mariage is to remedy, not to be allay'd with fasting, nor with any penance to be subdu'd, which how can he asswage who by mis-hap hath met the unmeetest and most unsutable mind? Who hath the power to struggle with an intelligible flame, not in paradice to be resisted, become now more ardent by being fail'd of what in reason it lookt for; and even then most unquencht, when the importunity of a provender[46] burning is well anough appeas'd; and yet the soule hath obtained nothing of what it justly desires. Certainly such a one forbidd'n to divorce, is in effect forbidd'n to marry, and compell'd to greater difficulties then in a single life; for if there be not a more human burning which mariage must satisfie, or els may be dissolv'd, then that of copulation, mariage cannot be honorable for the meer[47] reducing and terminating of lust between two: seeing many beasts in voluntary and chosen couples, live together as unadulterously, and are as truly maried in that respect. But all ingenuous men will see that the dignity & blessing of mariage is plac't rather in the mutual enjoyment of that which the wanting soul needfully seeks, then of that which the plenteous body would joyfully give away. Hence it is that *Plato* in his festival discours bings in[48] *Socrates* relating what he fain'd to have learnt from the Prophetesse *Diotima,* how *Love* was the sonne of *Penury,* begot of *Plenty* in the Garden of *Jupiter.* Which divinely sorts with[49] that which in effect *Moses* tells us, that *Love* was the son of *Lonelines,* begot in Paradise by that sociable and helpful aptitude which God implanted between man and woman toward each other. The same also is that burning mention'd by S. *Paul,* wherof mariage ought to be the remedy; the Flesh hath other mutuall and easie curbs which are in the power of any temperate man. When therfore this originall and sinles *Penury* or *Lonelines* of the soul cannot lay it selfe down by the side of such a meet and acceptable union as God ordain'd in marriage, at least in some proportion, it cannot conceive and bring forth *Love,* but remains utterly unmarried under a formall wedlock, and still burnes in the proper meaning of S. *Paul.* Then enters *Hate,* not that Hate that sins, but that which onely is naturall dissatisfaction, and the turning aside from a mistaken object: if that mistake have done injury, it fails not to dismisse with recompence; for to retain still, and not be able to love, is to heap up more injury. Thence this wise and pious Law of dismission now defended took beginning: He therfore who lacking of his due in the most native and human end of mariage, thinks it better to part then to live sadly and injuriously to that cheerfull covnant (for not to be belov'd, & yet retain'd, is the greatest injury to a gentle spirit) he I say, who therfore seeks to part, is one who highly honours the maried life, and would not stain it: and the reasons which[50] now move him to divorce, are equall to the best of those that could first warrant him to marry; for, as was plainly shewn, both the hate which now diverts him and the lonelinesse which leads him still powerfully to seek a fit help, hath not the least grain of a sin in it, if he be worthy to understand himselfe.

CHAP. V.

The Third Reason of this Law, because without it, he who has happn'd where he find nothing but remediles offences and discontents, is in more and greater temptations then ever before.

THirdly, Yet it is next to be fear'd, if he must be still bound without reason by a deafe rigor, that when he perceives the just expectance of his mind defeated, he will begin even against Law to cast about where he may find his satisfaction more compleat, unlesse he be a thing heroically vertuous, and that are not the common lump of men for whom chiefly the Laws ought to be made, though not to their

---

[45]The earlier state of the text represented by the Bodleian copy has "joying" at this point, and, a little later, "most unmeetest and unsutable mind." Though Milton did not correct them in his own handwriting, we presume that "joying" and "unmeetest and most unsutable mind" are correct. See Yale 2: 251n8.

[46]The editors of the *OED* guess that this apparent adjective form is in error. Provender (what is procured to feed someone or some animal) should nourish rather than be burned. The entire sentence is difficult to decipher.

[47]The Yale editors chose "meer" rather than "meet," silently, but probably on the grounds that *1643* has "meer." The Bodleian copy clearly prints "meet," but "meer" seems to be more logically consistent.

[48]The Yale editors choose the more common "brings in," which I believe is in error, since the first listed meaning of the verb "bing" listed in the *OED* has to do with tossing into a pile.

[49]Agrees with.

[50]Printed as "whch" in Bodleian.

sins yet to their unsinning weaknesses, it being above their strength to endure the lonely estate, which while they shunn'd, they are fal'n into. And yet there follows upon this a worse temptation; for if he be such as hath spent his youth unblamably, and layd up his chiefest earthly comforts in the enjoyment of a contented mariage, nor did neglect that furderance which was to be obtain'd therein by constant prayers, when he shall find himselfe bound fast to an uncomplying discord of nature, or, as it oft happens, to an image of earth and fleam, with whom he lookt to be the copartner of a sweet and gladsome society, and sees withall that his bondage is now inevitable, though he be almost the strongest Christian, he will be ready to despair in vertue, and mutin against divine providence: and this doubtles is the reason of those lapses and that melancholy despair which we see in many wedded persons, though they understand it not, or pretend other causes, because they know no remedy, and is of extreme danger; therfore when human frailty sur-charg'd, is at such a losse, charity ought to venture much, and use bold physick, lest an over-tost faith en-danger to shipwrack.

CHAP. VI.

The fourth Reason of this Law, that God regards Love and Peace in the family, more then a compulsive performance of mariage, which is more broke by a grievous continuance, then by a needful divorce.

Fourthly, Mariage is a cov'nant, the very beeing wherof consists, not in a forc't cohabitation, and counterfet performance of duties, but in unfained love and peace. And of matrimoniall love, no doubt but that was chiefly meant, which by the ancient Sages was thus parabl'd. That Love, if he be not twin-born, yet hath a brother wondrous like him, call'd *Anteros:* whom while he seeks all about, his chance is to meet with many fals and faining Desires that wander singly up and down in his likenes. By them in their borrow'd garb, Love, though not wholly blind, as Poets wrong him, yet having but one eye, as being born an Archer aiming, and that eye not the quickest in this dark region here below, which is not Love's proper sphere, partly out of the simplicity, and credulity which is native to him, often deceiv'd, imbraces and consorts him with these obvious and suborned striplings, as if they were his Mothers own Sons, for so he thinks them, while they suttly keep themselves most on his blind side. But after a while, as his manner is, when soaring up into the high Towr of his *Apogæum,* above the shadow of the earth, he darts out the direct rayes of his then most piercing eyesight upon the impostures, and trim disguises that were us'd

with him, and discerns that this is not his genuin brother, as he imagin'd, he has no longer the power to hold fellowship with such a personated mate. For strait his arrows loose their golden heads, and shed their purple feathers, his silk'n breades untwine, and slip their knots and that original and firie vertue giv'n him by Fate, all on a sudden goes out and leaves him undeifi'd, and despoil'd of all his force: till finding *Anteros* at last, he kindles and repairs the almost faded ammunition of his Deity by the reflection of a coequal & *homogeneal* fire. Thus mine author sung it to me; and by the leave of those who would be counted the only grave ones, this is no meer amatorious novel (though to be wise and skilful in these matters, men heretofore of greatest name in vertue, have esteemd it one of the highest arks that human contemplation circling upward, can make from the glassy Sea[51] wheron she stands) but this is a deep and serious verity, shewing us that Love in mariage cannot live nor subsist, unlesse it be mutual; and where love cannot be, there can be left of wedlock nothing, but the empty husk of an outside matrimony; as undelightfull and unpleasing to God, as any other kind of hypocrisie. So farre is his command from tying men to the obser-vance of duties, which there is no help for, but they must be dissembl'd. If *Salomons* advice be not overfrolick, *Live joyfully,* saith he, *with the wife whom thou lovest, all thy days, for that is thy portion.* How then, where we find it impossible to rejoyce or to love, can we obey this precept? how miserably do we defraud our selves of that comfortable portion which God gives us, by striving vainly to glue an error together which God and nature will not joyn; adding but more vexation and violence to that blisful society by our importunate superstition, that will not hearken to St. *Paul,* 1 *Cor.* 7. who speaking of mariage and divorce, determines plain enough in generall, that God therein *hath call'd us to peace,* and not *to bondage.* Yea, God himself commands in his Law more then once, and by his Prophet *Malachy,* as *Calvin* and the best translations read, that *he who hates let him divorce,* that is, he who cannot love: hence is it that the Rabbins and *Maimonides* famous among the rest in a Book of his set forth by *Buxtorsius,* tells us that *Divorce was permitted by* Moses *to preserve peace in mariage, and quiet in the family.* Surely the Jewes had their saving peace about them, as well as we, yet care was tak'n that this wholsom provision for houshold peace should also be allow'd them; and must this be deny'd to Christians? O perversnes! that the Law should be made more provident of peacemaking then the

---

[51]The *Errata* correct "the'globy sea," which may have been a misreading from the manuscript.

Gospel! that the Gospel should be put to beg a most necessary help of mercy from the Law, but must not have it: and that to grind in the mill of an undelighted and servil copulation, must be the only forc't work of a Christian mariage, oft times with such a yokefellow, from whom both love and peace, both nature and Religion mourns to be separated. I cannot therfore be so diffident, as not securely to conclude, that he who can receive nothing of the most important helps in mariage, being thereby disinabl'd to return that duty which is his, with a clear and hearty countnance; and thus continues to grieve whom he would not, and is no lesse griev'd, that man ought even for loves sake and peace to move Divorce upon good and liberall conditions to the divorc't. And it is a lesse breach of wedlock to part with wise and quiet consent betimes, then still to foile and profane that mystery of joy and union with a polluting sadnes and perpetuall distemper; for it is not the outward continuing of mariage that keeps whole that cov'nant, but whosoever does most according to peace and love, whether in mariage, or in divorce, he it is that breaks mariage least; it being so often written, that *Love only is the fullfilling of every Commandment.*

CHAP. VII.

The fifth Reason, that nothing more hinders and disturbs the whole life of a Christian, than a matrimony found to be uncurably unfit, and doth the same in effect that an Idolatrous match.

FIfthly, as those Priests of old were not to be long in sorrow, or if they were, they could not rightly execute their function; so every true Christian in a higher order of Priesthood is a person dedicate to joy and peace, offering himself a lively sacrifice of praise and thanksgiving, and there is no Christian duty that is not to be season'd and set off with cheerfulnes; which in a thousand outward and intermitting crosses may yet be done well, as in this vale of tears, but in such a bosome affliction as this, crushing the very foundation of his inmost nature, when he shall be forc't to love against a possibility, and to use a dissimulation against his soule in the perpetuall and ceaseles duties of a husband, doubtles his whole duty of serving God must needs be blurr'd and tainted with a sad unpreparednesse and dejection of spirit, wherin God has no delight. Who sees not therfore how much more Christianity it would be to break by divorce that which is more broken by undue and forcible keeping, rather then *to cover the Altar of the Lord with continuall teares, so that he regardeth not the offering any more* rather then that the whole worship of a Christian mans life should languish

and fade away beneath the weight of an immeasurable griefe and discouragement. And because some think the childre'n of a second matrimony succeeding a divorce, would not be a holy seed, it hinder'd not the Jews from being so, and why should we not think them more holy then the off-spring of a former ill-twisted wedlock, begotten only out of a bestiall necessitie, without any true love or contentment, or joy to their parents, so that in some sense we may call them the *children of wrath* and anguish, which will as little conduce to their sanctifying, as if they had been bastards; for nothing more then disturbance of mind suspends us from approaching to God. Such a disturbance especially as both assaults our faith and trust in Gods providence, and ends, if there be not a miracle of vertue on either side, not only in bitternes and wrath, the canker of devotion, but in a desperate and vitious carelesnes; when he sees himselfe without fault of his, train'd by a deceitfull bait into a snare of misery, betrai'd by an alluring ordinance,[52] and then made the thrall of heavines and discomfort by an undivorcing Law of God, as he erroneously thinks, but of mans iniquity, as the truth is; for that God preferres the free and cheerfull worship of a Christian, before the grievous and exacted observance of an unhappy marriage, besides that the generall maximes of Religion assure us, will be more manifest by drawing a parallell argument from the ground of divorcing an Idolatresse, which was, lest she should alienate his heart from the true worship of God: and what difference is there whether she pervert him to superstition by her enticing sorcery, or disinable him in the whole service of God through the disturbance of her unhelpfull and unfit society; and so drive him at last through murmuring and despair to thoughts of Atheisme; neither doth it lessen the cause of separating in that the one willingly allures him from the faith, the other perhaps unwillingly drives him; for in the account of God it comes all to one, that the wife looses him a servant; and therfore by all the united force of the *Decalogue* she ought to be disbanded, unless we must set mariage above God and charity, which is a doctrine of devils no lesse then forbidding to marry.

---

[52]The legal bond of marriage is perhaps viewed as a result of a religious or legal ordinance (not so authoritative as a statute).

CHAP. VIII.

That an idolatrous Heretick ought to be divorc't after a convenient space giv'n to hope of conversion. That place of I Corinth. 7. restor'd from a twofold erroneous exposition, and that the common expositers flatly contradict the morall law.

ANd here by the way to illustrate the whole question of divorce; ere this treatise end, I shall not be loath to spend a few lines in hope to give a full resolve of that which is yet so much controverted, whether an idolatrous heretick ought to be divorc't. To the resolving wherof we must first know that the *Jews* were commanded to divorce an unbeleeving Gentile for two causes: first, because all other Nations, especially the *Canaanites* were to them unclean. Secondly, to avoid seducement. That other Nations were to the *Jews* impure, even to the separating of mariage, will appear out of *Exod.* 34. 16. *Deut.* 7. 3, 6. compar'd with *Ezra* 9. 2. also chap. 10. 10, 11. *Nehem.* 13. 30. This was the ground of that doubt rais'd among the *Corinthians* by some of the Circumcision; Whether an unbeleever were not still to be counted an unclean thing, so as that they ought to divorce from such a person. This doubt of theirs S. *Paul* removes by an Evangelicall reason, having respect to that Vision of S. *Peter*, wherin the distinction of clean and unclean being abolisht, all living creatures were sanctified to a pure and Christian use, and mankind especially, now invited by a general call to the cov'nant of grace. Therefore saith S. *Paul*, *The unbeleeving wife is sanctify'd by the husband*; that is, made pure and lawfull to his use; so that he need not put her away for fear lest her unbelief should defile him; but that if he found her love stil towards him, he might rather hope to win her. The second reason of that divorce was to avoid seducement, as is prov'd by comparing those places of the Law, to that which *Ezra* and *Nehemiah* did by divine warrant in compelling the *Jews* to forgo their wives. And this reason is morall and perpetuall in the rule of Christian faith without evasion. Therfore saith the Apostle, 2 *Cor.* 6. *Mis-yoke not together with infidels*, which is interpreted of mariage in the first place. And although the former legall pollution be now don off, yet there is a spirituall contagion in Idolatry as much to be shun'd; and though seducement were not to be fear'd, yet where there is no hope of converting, there alwayes ought to be a certain religious aversation[53] and abhorring, which can no way sort[54] with Mariage: Therfore saith S. *Paul*, *What fellowship hath righteousnesse with unrighteousnesse? what communion hath light with darknes? what concord hath Christ with Belial? what part hath he that beleeveth with an infidel?* And the next verse but one he moralizes, and makes us liable to that command of *Isaiah*, *Wherefore come out from among them, and be ye separate, saith the Lord; touch not the unclean thing, and I will receive ye.* And this command thus Gospelliz'd to us, hath the same force with that wheron *Ezra* grounded the pious necessity of divorcing. Neither had he other commission for what he did, then such a generall command in *Deut.* as this, nay not so direct as this; for he is bid there not to marry, but not bid to divorce, and yet we see with what a zeal and confidence he was the author of a generall divorce between the faithfull and unfaithfull seed. The Gospell is more plainly on his side according to three of the Evangelists, then the words of the Law; for where the case of divorce is handled with such a severity as was fittest to aggravate the fault of unbounded licence; yet still in the same chapter when it comes into question afterwards whether any civill respect, or natural relation which is dearest, may be our plea to divide, or hinder, or but delay our duty to religion, we heare it determin'd, that father and mother, and wife also is not only to be hated, but forsak'n, if we mean to inherit the great reward there promis'd. Nor will it suffice to be put off by saying we must forsake them onely by not consenting or not complying with them, for that were to be don, and roundly too, though being of the same faith they should but seek, out of a fleshly tendernes to weak'n our Christian fortitude with worldly perswasions, or but to unsettle our constancie with timorous and softning suggestions: as we may read with what a vehemence *Job*, the patientest of men, rejected the desperat counsels of his wife; and *Moses* the meekest[55] being throughly offended with the prophane speeches of *Zippora*, sent her back to her father. But if they shall perpetually at our elbow seduce us from the true worship of God, or defile and daily scandalize our conscience by their hopeles continuance in misbelief, then ev'n in the due progresse of reason, and that ever-equall proportion which justice proceeds by, it cannot be imagin'd that this cited place commands lesse then a totall and finall separation from such an adherent; at least that no force should be us'd to keep them together: while we remember that God commanded *Abraham* to send away his irreligious wife and her son for the offences which they gave in a pious family. And it may be guest that *David* for the like

---

[53] "A moral turning away, estrangement" (OED 2).
[54] Agree.

[55] Piously humble. Patience and meekness are both characteristic of the Son of God in *Paradise Regain'd*.

cause dispos'd of *Michal* in such a sort, as little differ'd from a dismission. Therefore against reiterated scandals and seducements, which never cease, much more can no other remedy or retirement be found but absolute departure. For what kind of matrimony can that remain to be, what one dutie between such can be perform'd as it should be from the heart, when their thoughts and spirits flie asunder as farre as heaven from hell; especially if the time that hope should send forth her expected blossoms be past in vain? It will easily be true, that a father or brother may be hated zealously and lov'd civilly or naturally;[56] for those duties may be perfom'd at distance, and doe admit of any long absence: but how the peace and perpetuall cohabitation of mariage can be kept, how that benevolent and intimate communion of body can be held with one that must be hated with a most operative hatred, must be forsak'n and yet continually dwelt with and accompanied, he who can distinguish, hath the gift of an affection very odly divided and contriv'd: while others both just and wise, and *Salomon* among the rest, if they may not hate and forsake as *Moses* enjoyns, and the Gospell imports, will find it impossible not to love otherwise then will sort with the love of God, whose jealousie brooks no corrivall. And whether is more likely, that Christ bidding to forsake wife for religion, meant it by divorce as *Moses* meant it, whose Law grounded on morall reason, was both his office and his essence to maintain, or that he should bring a new morality into religion, not only new, but contrary to an unchangeable command, and dangerously derogating from our love & worship of God. As if when *Moses* had bid divorce absolutely, and Christ had said, hate & forsake, and his Apostle had said, no communion with Christ & *Belial*, yet that Christ after all this could be understood to say, divorce not, no not for religion, seduce, or seduce not. What mighty and invisible Remora[57] is this in matrimony able to demurre and to contemne all the divorsive engines in heaven or earth. Both which may now passe away if this be true, for more then many jots or tittles, a whole morall Law is abolisht. But if we dare beleeve it is not, then in the method of religion, and to save the honour and dignity of our faith, we are to retreat, and gather up our selves from the observance of an inferior and civill ordinance, to the strict maintaining of a generall and religious command, which is written, *Thou shalt make no cov'nant with them*, Deut. 7. 2, 3. and that cov'nant

which cannot be lawfully made, we have directions and examples lawfully to dissolve. Also 2 Chron. 19.2. *Shouldst thou love them that hate the Lord?* No doubtlesse: for there is a certain scale of duties, there is a certain Hierarchy of upper and lower commands, which for want of studying in right order, all the world is in confusion. Upon these principles I answer, that a right beleever ought to divorce an idolatrous heretick, unlesse upon better hopes: however that it is in the beleevers choice to divorce or not.

The former part will be manifest thus; first, an apostate idolater whether husband or wife seducing, was to die by the decree of God, Deut. 13. 6, 9. that mariage therfore God himselfe dis-joyns: for others born idolaters the morall reason of their dangerous keeping, and the incommunicable antagony[58] that is between Christ and *Belial*, will be sufficient to enforce the commandment of those two inspir'd reformers *Ezra* and *Nehemiah*, to put an idolater away as well under the Gospel.

The latter part, that although there be no seducement fear'd, yet if there be no hope giv'n, the divorce is lawfull, will appear by this, that idolatrous marriage is still hatefull to God, therfore still it may be divorc't by the patern of that warrant that *Ezra* had; and by the same everlasting reason: Neither can any man give an account wherefore, if those whom God joyns, no man may separate, it should not follow, that whom he joyns not, but hates to joyn, those man ought to separate. But saith the Lawyer, that which ought not to have been don, once don avails. I answer, this is but a crotchet of the Law, but that brought against it is plain Scripture. As for what Christ spake concerning divorce, tis confest by all knowing men, he meant onely between them of the same faith. But what shall we say then to S. *Paul*, who seemes to bid us not divorce an Infidell willing to stay? We may safely say thus; that wrong collections have been hitherto made out of those words by modern Divines. His drift, as was heard before, is plain: not to command our stay in mariage with an Infidel, that had been a flat renouncing of the religious and morall law; but to inform the *Corinthians* that the body of an unbeleever was not defiling, if his desire to live in Christian wedlock shewd any likelihood that his heart was opening to the faith: and therfore advises to forbeare departure so long, till nothing have been neglected to set forward a conversion: this I say he advises, and that with certain cautions; not commands: If we can take up so much credit for him, as to get him beleev'd upon his own word; for what is this els but his

---

[56]Even a family member might be zealously hated for religious reasons but loved as a brother or even as a neighbor.

[57]"The sucking-fish (*Echeneis remora*), believed by the ancients to have the power of staying the course of any ship to which it attached itself" (*OED* 1).

---

[58]Apparently Milton invented this variant on "antagonism."

counsell in a thing indifferent, *to the rest speak I, not the Lord*; for though it be true that the Lord never spake it, yet from S. *Pauls* mouth we should have took it as a command, had not himself forewarn'd us, and disclaim'd; which, notwithstanding if we shall still avouch to be a command, he palpably denying it, this is not to expound S. *Paul*, but to out-face him. Neither doth it follow, but that the Apostle may interpose his judgement in a case of Christian liberty, without the guilt of adding to Gods word. How doe we know mariage or single life to be of choice, but by such like words as these, *I speak this by permission, not of commandment, I have no command of the Lord, yet I give my judgement.* Why shall not the like words have leave to signifie a freedom in this our present question, though *Beza* deny. Neither is the Scripture hereby less inspir'd, because S. *Paul* confesses to have writt'n therin what he had not of command; for we grant that the Spirit of God led him thus to expresse himselfe to Christian prudence in a matter which God thought best to leave uncommanded. *Beza* therefore must be warily read, when he taxes S. *Austine* of *Blasphemy*, for holding that S. *Paul* spake heer as of a thing indifferent. But if it must be a command, I shall yet the more evince it to be a command that we should herein be left free: and that out of the Greek word us'd in the 12. v. which instructs us plainly, there must be a joynt assent and good liking on both sides; he that will not deprave the Text must thus render it; *If a brother have an unbeleeving wife, and she joyne in consent to dwell with him* (which cannot utter lesse to us than a mutuall agreement) let him not put her away for the meer surmise of Judaicall uncleannes: and the reason follows, for the body of an infidell is not polluted, neither to benevolence, nor to procreation. Moreover, this note of mutual complacencie forbids all offer of seducement; which to a person of zeal cannot be attempted without great offence: if therefore seducement be fear'd, this place hinders not divorce. Another caution was put in this supposed command, of not bringing the beleever into *bondage* heerby, which doubtles might prove extreme, if Christian liberty and conscience were left to the humor of a Pagan staying at pleasure to play with, or to vex and wound with a thousand scandals and burdens, above strength to bear: If therfore the conceived hope of gaining a soul, come to nothing, then charity commands that the beleever be not wearied out with endlesse waiting under many grievances sore to his spirit; but that respect be had rather to the present suffering of a true Christian, then the uncertain winning of an obdur'd heretick. The counsell we have from S. *Paul* to hope, cannot countermand the moral and Evangelick charge we have from God to feare seducement, to

separate from the misbeleever, the unclean the obdurat. The Apostle wisheth us to hope, but does not send us a wooll-gathering after vain hope: he saith, *How knowest thou, O man, whether thou shalt save thy Wife*, that is, till he try all due means, and set some reasonable time to himselfe, after which he may give over washing an Ethiope, if he will hear the advice of the Gospel. *Cast not pearls before swine*, saith Christ himself. *Let him be to thee as a heathen. Shake the dust off thy feet.* If this be not anough, *hate and forsake*, what relation soever. And this also that follows must appertain to the precept, *Let every man wherin he is call'd, therein abide*[59] *with God*, v. 24. that is, so walking in his inferior calling of mariage, as not by dangerous subjection to that ordinance, to hinder and disturb the higher calling of his Christianity. Last, and never too oft remembred, whether this be a command or an advice, we must looke that it be so understood, as not to contradict the least point of morall religion that God hath formerly commanded, otherwise what doe we but set the morall Law and the Gospel at civill war together: and who then shall be able to serve these two masters?

CHAP. IX.

That adultery is not the greatest breach of matrimony, that there may be other violations as great.

NOw whether Idolatry or Adultery be the greatest violation of mariage, if any demand, let him thus consider, that among Christian Writers touching matrimony, there be three chiefe ends therof agreed on; Godly society, next civill, and thirdly, that of the mariage-bed. Of these the first in name to be the highest and most excellent, no baptiz'd man can deny; nor that Idolatry smites directly against this prime end, nor that such as the violated end is, such is the violation: but he who affirms adultery to be the highest breach, affirms the bed to be the highest of mariage, which is in truth a grosse and borish opinion, now common soever; as farre from the countnance of Scripture, as from the light of all clean philosophy,[60] or civill nature. And out of question[61] the cheerfull help that may be in mariage toward sanctity of life, is the purest, and so the noblest end of that contract: but if the particular of each person be consider'd, then of those three ends which God appointed, that to him is greatest which is most necessary: and mariage is then most brok'n to him,

---

[59]The word was printed "abdie" on p. 23, but "abide" in the catchword on p. 22.
[60]Clear or pure philosophy.
[61]Unquestionably.

when he utterly wants[62] the fruition of that which he most sought therin, whether it were religious, civill, or corporall society. Of which wants to do him right by divorce only for the last and meanest, is a perverse injury, and the pretended reason of it as frigid as frigidity it selfe, which the *Code* and Canon are only sensible of. Thus much of this controversie. I now return to the former argument. And having shewn that disproportion, contrariety, or numnesse of minde may justly be divorc't, by proving already that the prohibition therof opposes the expresse end of Gods institution, suffers not mariage to satisfie that intellectuall and innocent desire which God himself kindl'd in man to be the bond of wedlock, but only to remedy a sublunary and bestial burning, which frugal diet, without mariage, would easily chast'n. Next that it drives many to transgresse the conjugall bed, while the soule wanders after that satisfaction which it had hope to find at home, but hath mis't. Or els it sits repining even to Atheism; finding it self hardly dealt with but misdeeming the cause to be in Gods Law, which is in mans unrighteous ignorance. I have shew'n also how it unties the inward knot of mariage, which is peace and love (if that can be unti'd which was never knit) while it aimes to keep fast the outward formalitie; how it lets perish the Christian man, to compel impossibly the maried man.

CHAP. X.

The sixth Reason of this Law, that to prohibit divorce sought for natural causes is against nature.

The sixth place declares this prohibition to be as respectlesse of human nature as it is of religion, and therfore is not of God. He teaches, that an unlawful mariage may be lawfully divorc't. And that those who having throughly discern'd each others disposition which oft-times cannot be till after matrimony, shall then find a powerful reluctance and recoile of nature on either side blasting all the content of their mutuall society, that such persons are not lawfully maried, (to use the Apostles words) *Say I these things as a man, or saith not the Law also the same? for it is writt'n,* Deut. 22. *Thou shalt not sowe thy vineyard with diverse seeds, lest thou defile both. Thou shalt not plow with an Oxe and an Asse together,* and the like. I follow the pattern of St. *Pauls* reasoning; *Doth God care for Asses and Oxen,* how ill they yoke together, *or is it not said altogether for our sakes? for our sakes no doubt this is writt'n.* Yea the Apostle himself, in the forecited *2 Cor. 6. 14.* alludes

from that place of Deut. to forbid mis-yoking mariage; as by the Greek word is evident, though he instance but in one example of mis-matching with an Infidell: yet next to that what can be a fouler incongruity, a greater violence to the reverend secret of nature, then to force a mixture of minds that cannot unite, and to sowe the furrow of mans nativity with seed of two incoherent and uncombining dispositions; which act being kindly and voluntarie, as it ought, the Apostle in the language he wrote call'd *Eunoia,* and the Latines *Benevolence,* intimating the original therof to be in the understanding and the will; if not, surely there is nothing which might more properly be call'd a malevolence rather; and is the most injurious and unnaturall tribute that can be extorted from a person endew'd with reason, to be made pay out the best substance of his body, and of his soul too, as some think, when either for just and powerfull causes he cannot like, or from unequall causes finds not recompence. And that there is a hidden efficacie of love and hatred in man as wel as in other kinds, not morall, but naturall, which though not alwayes in the choyce, yet in the successe of mariage wil ever be most predominant, besides daily experience, the author of *Ecclesiasticus,* whose wisedom hath set him next the Bible,[63] acknowledges, 13. 16. *A man,* saith he, *will cleave to his like.* But what might be the cause, whether each ones allotted *Genius* or proper Starre, or whether the supernall[64] influence of Schemes and angular aspects or this elemental *Crasis*[65] here below, whether all these jointly or singly meeting friendly, or unfriendly in either party, I dare not, with the men I am likest to clash, appear so much a Philosopher as to conjecture. The ancient proverb in *Homer* lesse abstruse intitles this worke of leading each like person to his like, peculiarly to God himselfe: which is plain anough also by his naming of a meet or like help in the first espousall instituted; and that every woman is meet for every man, none so absurd as to affirm. Seeing then there is a twofold Seminary or stock[66] in nature, from whence are deriv'd the issues of love and hatred distinctly flowing through the whole masse of created things, and that God's doing ever is to bring the due likenesses and harmonies of his workes together, except when out of two contraries met to their own destruction, he moulds a third existence, and that it is

---

[63]Since the apocryphal book of Ecclesiasticus was usually included in standard full-scale Bibles published in the sixteenth and seventeenth centuries, it was literally next to the authorized versions of the Bible, and next to the canonical books in authority as well.
[64]Higher, or heavenly.
[65]Combination of humors, temperament.
[66]Seed or root-stock (two types of planting cultures).

error, or some evil Angel which either blindly or maliciously hath drawn together, in two persons ill imbarkt in wedlock the sleeping discords and enmities of nature lull'd on purpose with some false bait, that they may wake to agony and strife, later then prevention could have wisht, if from the bent of just and honest intentions beginning what was begun, and so continuing, all that is equall, all that is fair and possible hath been tri'd, and no accommodation likely to succeed what folly is it still to stand combating and battering against invincible causes and effects, with evill upon evill, till either the best of our dayes be linger'd out, or ended with some speeding sorrow. The wise *Ecclesiasticus* advises rather, 37. 27. *My sonne, prove thy soule in thy life, see what is evill for it, and give not that unto it.* Reason he had to say so; for if the noysomnesse or disfigurement of body can soon destroy the sympathy of mind to wedlock duties, much more wil the annoyance and trouble of mind infuse it selfe into all the faculties and acts of the body, to render them invalid, unkindly, and even unholy against the fundamentall law book of nature, which *Moses* never thwarts, but reverences: therefore he commands us to force nothing against sympathy or naturall order, no not upon the most abject creatures; to shew that such an indignity cannot be offer'd to man without an impious crime. And certainly those divine meditating words of finding out a meet and like help to man, have in them a consideration of more then the indefinite likenesse of womanhood; nor are they to be made waste paper on, for the dulnesse of Canon divinity: no, nor those other allegorick precepts of beneficence fetcht out of the closet of nature to teach us goodnes and compassion in not compelling together unmatchable societies, or if they meet through mischance, by all consequence to disjoyn them, as God and nature signifies and lectures to us not onely by those recited decrees, but ev'n by the first and last of all his visible works; when by his divorcing command the world first rose out of Chaos, nor can be renewed again out of confusion but by the separating of unmeet consorts.

CHAP. XI.

The seventh Reason, That sometimes continuance in mariage may be evidently the shortning or endangering of life to either party; both Law and divinity concluding, that life is to be prefer'd before mariage the intended solace of life.

SEventhly, The Canon Law and Divines consent, that if either party be found contriving against anothers life, they may be sever'd by divorce; for a sin against the life of mariage, is greater then a sin against the bed: the one destroyes, the other but defiles: The same may be said touching those persons who being of a pensive nature and cours of life, have sum'd up all their solace in that free and lightsome conversation which God and man intends in mariage: wherof when they see themselves depriv'd by meeting an unsociable consort, they oft-times resent one another's mistake so deeply, that long it is not ere griefe end one of them. When therfore this danger[67] is foreseen, that the life is in perill by living together, what matter is it whether helples griefe or wilfull practice be the cause; This is certain, that the preservation[68] of life is more worth than the compulsory keeping of mariage; and it is no lesse then crueltie to force a man to remain in that state as the solace of his life, which he and his friends know will be either the undoing or the disheartning of his life. And what is life without the vigor and spiritfull exercise of life? how can it be usefull either to private or public employment? Shall it therfore be quite dejected, though never so valuable, and left to moulder away in heavines for the superstitious and impossible performance of an ill-driv'n bargain? Nothing more inviolable then vowes made to God, yet we read in *Numbers*, that if a wife had made such a vow, the meer will and authority of her husband might break it; how much more may he break the error of his own bonds with an unfit and mistak'n[69] wife, to the saving of his welfare, his life, yea his faith and vertue from the hazard of over-strong temptations; for if man be Lord of the Sabbath, to the curing of a Fevor, can he be lesse then Lord of mariage in such important causes as these?

CHAP. XII.

The eighth reason, It is probable, or rather certain, that every one who happ'ns to marry, hath not the calling, and therefore upon unfitnesse found and consider'd, force ought not to be us'd.

EIghthly, It is most sure that some ev'n of those who are not plainly defective in body, yet are destitut of all other mariageable gifts, and consequently have not the calling to marry: unlesse nothing be requisite therto but a meer instrumentall body; which to affirm, is to that unanimous Covenant a reproach: yet it is as sure that many such, not of their own desire, but by the perswasion of friends, or not knowing themselves, doe often enter into wedlock; where finding the difference at length between the duties of a married life, and the gifts of a single life; what unfitnes of mind, what

---

[67]Corrected from "dnager" in the Bodleian copy.
[68]In the Bodleian copy "peservation," here corrected.
[69]Mis-taken, or mistakenly taken.

wearisomnesse, what scruples and doubts to an incredible offence, and displeasure are like to follow between, may be soon imagin'd: whom thus to shut up and immure[70] and shut up together, the one with a mischosen mate, the other in a mistak'n calling, is not a cours that Christian wisedome and tendernesse ought to use. As for the custome that some parents and guardians have of forcing mariages, it will be better to say nothing of such a savage inhumanity, but only thus, that the Law which gives not all freedom of divorce to any creature endu'd with reason so assasinated, is next in cruelty.

CHAP. XIII.

The ninth reason, Because mariage is not a meer carnall coition, but a human Society, where that cannot reasonably be had, there can be no true matrimony. Mariage compar'd with all other cov'nants and vowes warrantably broken for the good of man. Mariage the Papists Sacrament, and unfit mariage the Protestants Idoll.

Ninthly, I suppose it will be allow'd us that mariage is a human Society, and that all human society must proceed from the mind rather then the body, els it would be but a kind of animall or beastish[71] meeting; if the mind therfore cannot[72] have that due company by mariage, that it may reasonably and humanly desire, that mariage can be no human society, but a certain formality; or guilding over of little better than a brutish congresse, and so in very wisdome and purenesse to be dissolv'd.

But mariage is more then human, *the Covenant of God*, Prov. 2. 17. therfore man cannot dissolve it. I answer, if it be more then human, so much the more it argues the chiefe society thereof to be in the soule rather than in the body, and the greatest breach therof to be unfitnesse of mind rather then defect of body: for the body can have least affinity in a covnant more then human, so that the reason of dissolving holds good the rather. Again, I answer, that the Sabbath is a higher institution, a command of the first Table, for the breach wherof God hath farre more and oftner testify'd his anger, then for divorces, which from *Moses* to *Malachy* he never took displeasure at, nor then neither, if we mark[73] the Text; and yet as oft as the good of man is concern'd, he not onely permits, but commands to break the Sabbath. What covnant more contracted with

God, and lesse in mans power, then the vow which hath once past his lips? yet if it be found rash, if offensive, if unfruitfull either to Gods glory or the good of man, our doctrine forces not error and unwillingnes irksomly to keep it, but counsels wisedome and better thoughts boldly to break it; therfore to enjoyn the indissoluble keeping of a mariage found unfit against the good of man both soul and body, as hath bin evidenc't, is to make an idol of mariage, to advance it above the worship of God and the good of man, to make it a transcendent command, above both the second and first Table, which is a most prodigious Doctrine.

Next, whereas they cite out of the *Proverbs*, that it is the *Covnant of God*, and therfore more then human, that consequence is manifestly false: for so the covnant which *Zedechiah* made with the Infidell King of *Babel*, is call'd the *Covenant of God*, Ezek. 17. 19. which would be strange to heare counted more then a human covnant. So every covnant between man and man, bound by oath, may be call'd the covnant of God, because God therin is attested. So of mariage he is the authour and the witnes; yet hence will not follow any divine astriction[74] more then what is subordinate to the glory of God, and the main good of either party; for as the glory of God and their esteemed fitnesse one for the other, was the motive which led them both at first to think without other revelation that God had joynd them together, So when it shall be found by their apparent unfitnesse, that their continuing to be man and wife is against the glory of God and their mutuall happinesse, it may assure them that God never joyn'd them; who hath reveal'd his gracious will not to set the ordinance above the man for whom it was ordain'd; not to canonize mariage either as a tyrannesse or a goddesse over the enfranchiz'd life and soul of man: for wherin can God delight, wherin be worshipt, wherein be glorify'd by the forcible continuing of an improper and ill-yoking couple? He that lov'd not to see the disparity of severall cattell at the plow, cannot be pleas'd with vast unmeetnesse in mariage. Where can be the peace and love which must invite God to such a house, may it not be fear'd that the not divorcing of such a helplesse disagreement, will be the divorcing of God finally from such a place? But it is a triall of our patience they say: I grant it: but which of *Jobs* afflictions were sent him with that law, that he might not use means to remove any of them if he could? And what if it subvert our patience and our faith too? Who shall answer for the perishing of all those soules perishing by stubborn expositions of particular and inferior precepts against the generall and

---

[70]Wall in.
[71]Beastly.
[72]Written "connot" in the Bodleian copy, and not corrected by Milton.
[73]Pay attention to.

---

[74]Moral or legal obligation; bond (*OED* 3 cites this instance).

supreme rule of charity? They dare not affirm that mariage is either a Sacrament, or a mystery, though all those sacred things give place to man, and yet they invest it with such an awfull sanctity, and give such adamantine chains[75] to bind with, as if it were to be worshipt like some Indian deity, when it can conferre no blessing upon us, but works more and more to our misery. To such teachers the saying of S. *Peter* at the Councell of *Jerusalem* will doe well to be apply'd: *Why tempt ye God to put a yoke upon the necks* of Christian men, which neither the *Jews*, Gods ancient people, *nor we are able to bear*: and nothing but unwary expounding hath brought upon us.

CHAP. XIV.
Considerations concerning Familisme, Antinomianisme; and why it may be thought that such opinions may proceed from the undue restraint of some just liberty, then which no greater cause to contemne Discipline.

TO these considerations this also may be added as no improbable conjecture: seeing that sort of men who follow *Anabaptism, Familism, Antinomianism*,[76] and other fanatic dreams (if we understand them not amisse) be such most commonly as are by nature addicted to Religion, of life also not debausht, and that their opinions having full swinge, do end in satisfaction of the flesh, it may be come with reason into the thoughts of a wise man, whether all this proceed not partly, if not chiefly, from the restraint of some lawfull liberty, which ought to be giv'n men, and is deny'd them. As by Physick we learn in menstruous bodies, where natures current hath been stopt, that the suffocation and upward forcing of some lower part, affects the head and inward sense with dotage and idle fancies. And on the other hand, whether the rest of vulgar men not so religiously professing do not give themselvs much the more to whoredom and adulteries, loving the corrupt and venial discipline of clergie courts, but hating to heare of perfect reformation: when as they foresee that then fornication shall be austerely censur'd, adultery punisht, and mariage the appointed refuge of nature, though it hap to be never so incongruous and displeasing, must yet of force be worn out, when it can be to no other purpose but of strife and hatred, a thing odious to God. This may be worth the study of skilfull

men in Theology, and the reason of things: and lastly to examine whether some undue and ill grounded strictnesse upon the blamelesse nature of man, be not the cause in those[77] places where already reformation is, that the discipline of the Church so often and so unavoidbly brok'n, is brought into contempt and derision. And if it be thus, let those who are still bent to hold this obstinate *literality*, so prepare themselves as to share in the account for all these transgressions, when it shall be demanded at the last day by one who will scan and sift things with more then a literall wisedome of equity; for, if these reasons be duly ponder'd, and that the Gospell is more jealous of laying on excessive burdens then ever the Law was, lest the soule of a Christian which is inestimable, should be over-tempted and cast away, considering also that many properties of nature, which the power of regeneration it selfe never alters, may cause dislike of conversing even between the most sanctify'd, which continually grating in harsh tune together, may breed some jarre and discord, and that end in rancor and strife, a thing so opposite both to mariage and to Christianity, it would perhaps be lesse schandall[78] to divorce a naturall disparity, then to link violently together an unchristian dissention, committing two ensnared soules inevitably to kindle one another, not with the fire of love, but with a hatred inconcileable, who were they dissevered, would be straight friends in any other relation. But if an alphabeticall servility must be still urged, it may so fall out, that the true Church may unwittingly use as much cruelty in forbidding to divorce, as the Church of Antichrist doth wilfully in forbidding to marry.

---

[75]Compare "Adamantine Chains and penal Fire" in *Paradise Lost* 1.48.
[76]"The Antinomianism idea of righteousness was idealism of the highest sort, holding that all the Mosaic law, moral as well as ceremonial, had been abrogated for Christians by the coming of Christ, whose spirit now dwelt in the heart of the believer and replaced the codified law as a moral guide (*De Doctrina, CPW* 6: 521–41)" (Bennett 97).

[77]Bodleian has "in those" repeated.
[78]Scandal.

THE SECOND BOOK.

CHAP. I.

The Ordinance of Sabbath and mariage compar'd. Hyperbole no unfrequent figure in the Gospel. Excesse cur'd by contrary excesse. Christ neither did, nor could abrogat the Law of divorce, but only reprove the abuse therof.

Hitherto the Position undertaken hath bin declar'd, and prov'd by a Law of God, that Law prov'd to be moral, and unabolishable for many reasons equal, honest, charitable, just, annext thereto. It follows now that those places of Scripture which have a seeming to revoke the prudence of *Moses*, or rather that mercifull decree of God, be forthwith explain'd and reconcil'd. For what are all these reasonings worth will some reply, whenas the words of Christ are plainly against all divorce, except *in case of fornication*. To whom he whose minde were to answer no more but this, *except also in case of charity*, might safely appeal to the more plain words of Christ in defence of so excepting. *Thou shalt doe no manner of worke* saith the commandment of the Sabbath. Yes saith Christ works of charity. And shall we be more severe in paraphrasing the considerat and tender Gospel, then he was in expounding the rigid and peremptory Law? What was ever in all appearance lesse made for man, and more for God alone then the Sabbath? yet when the good of man comes into the scales, we hear that voice of infinite goodnesse and benignity that *Sabbath was made for man, not man for Sabbath*. What thing ever was more made for Man alone and lesse for God then mariage? And shall we load it with a cruel and senceles bondage utterly against both the good of man and the glory of God? Let who so will now listen, I want neither pall nor mitre, I stay neither for ordination nor[79] induction, but in the firm faith of a knowing Christian, which is the best and truest endowment of the keyes, I pronounce, the man who shall bind so cruelly a good and gracious ordinance of God, hath not in that the Spirit of Christ. Yet that every text of Scripture seeming opposite may be attended with a due exposition, this other part ensues, and makes account to find no slender arguments for this assertion out of those very Scriptures, which are commonly urg'd against it.

First therfore let us remember as a thing not to be deny'd, that all places of Scripture wherin just reason of doubt arises from the letter, are to be expounded by considering upon what occasion every thing is set down: and by comparing other Texts. The occasion which induc't our Saviour to speak of divorce, was either to convince the extravagance of the Pharises in that point, or to give a sharp and vehement answer to a tempting question. And in such cases that we are not to repose all upon the literall terms of so many words, many instances will teach us: Wherin we may plainly discover how Christ meant not to be tak'n word for word, but like a wise Physician, administring one excesse against another to reduce us to a perfect mean:[80] Where the Pharises were strict, there Christ seems remisse; where they were too remisse, he saw it needfull to seem most severe: in one place he censures an unchast look to be adultery already committed: another time he passes over actuall adultery with lesse reproof then for an unchast look; not so heavily condemning secret weaknes, as open malice: So heer he may be justly thought to have giv'n this rigid sentence against divorce, not to cut off all remedy from a good man who finds himself consuming away in a disconsolate and uninjoy'd matrimony, but to lay a bridle upon the bold abuses of those over-weening *Rabbies*; which he could not more effectually doe, then by a countersway[81] of restraint curbing their wild exorbitance almost into the other extreme; as when we bow things the contrary way, to make them come to their naturall straitnesse. And that this was the only intention of Christ is most evident; if we attend but to his own words and protestation made in the same Sermon, not many verses before he treats of divorcing, that he came not to abrogate from the Law *one jot or tittle*, and denounces against them that shall so teach.

But S. *Luke*, the verse immediatly before going that of divorce, inserts the same caveat, as if the latter could not be understood without the former; and as a witnesse to produce against this our wilfull mistake of abrogating, which must needs confirm us that what ever els in the political law of more special relation to the Jews might cease to us, yet that of those precepts concerning divorce, not one of them was repeal'd by the doctrine of Christ, unlesse we have vow'd not to beleeve his own cautious and immediat profession; for if these our Saviours words inveigh against all divorce, and condemn it as adultery, except it be for adultery, and be not rather understood against the abuse of those divorces permitted in the Law, then is that Law of *Moses*, Deut. 24. 1. not only repeal'd and wholly annull'd against the promise of Christ and his known profession, not to

---

[79] The Errata corrects "or" to "nor" here.

[80] The good physician would try by medicine to create a perfectly balanced temperament.

[81] An opposing force. Milton seems to have invented the word; his use is the only recorded in the *OED*.

meddle in matters Judicial, but that which is more strange, the very substance and purpose of that Law is contradicted and convinc'd[82] both of injustice and impurity, as having authoriz'd and maintain'd legall adultery by statute. *Moses* also cannot scape to be guilty of unequall and unwise decrees, punishing one act of secret adultery by death, and permitting a whole life of open adultery by Law. And albeit Lawyers write that some politicall edicts, though not approv'd, are yet allow'd to the scum[83] of the people and the necessity of the times; these excuses have but a weak pulse: for first, we read, not that the scoundrel people, but the choicest, the wisest, the holiest of that nation have frequently us'd these lawes, or such as these in the best and holiest times. Secondly, be it yeelded, that in matters not very bad or impure, a human law giver may slacken something of that which is exactly good, to the disposition of the people and the times: but if the perfect, the pure, the righteous law of God, for so are all his statutes and his judgements, be found to have allow'd smoothly without any certain reprehension,[84] that which Christ afterward declares to be adultery, how can we free this Law from the horrible endightment of being both impure, unjust, and fallacious.

CHAP. II.

How divorce was permitted for hardnesse of heart, cannot be understood by the common exposition. That the Law cannot permit, much lesse enact a permission of sin.[85]

Neither wil it serve to say this was permitted for the hardnes of their hearts, in that sense as it is usually explain'd, for the Law were then but a corrupt and erroneous School-master, teaching us to dash against a vitall maxim of religion,[86] by doing foul evil[87] in hope of some certain good.

This onely Text not to be match't again throughout the whole Scripture, wherby God in his perfect Law should seem to have granted to the hard hearts of his holy people under his owne hand, a civill immunity and free charter to live and die in a long successive adultery, under a covenant of works, till the *Messiah*, and then that indulgent permission to be strictly deny'd by a covnant of grace; besides the incoherence of such a doctrine, cannot, must not be thus interpreted, to the raising of a paradox never known til then, onely hanging by the twin'd thred of one doubtfull Scripture, against so many other rules and leading principles of religion, of justice, and purity of life. For what could be granted more either to the fear, or to the lust of any tyrant, or politician, then this authority of *Moses* thus expounded; which opens him a way at will to damme up justice, and not onely to admit of any *Romish* or *Austrian* dispences, but to enact a statute of that which he dares not seeme to approve, ev'n to legitimate vice, to make sinne it selfe, the ever alien & vassal sin, a free Citizen of the Common-wealth, pretending onely these or these plausible reasons. And well he might, all the while that *Moses* shall be alledg'd to have done as much without shewing any reason at all. Yet this could not enter into the heart of David, *Psal.* 94. 20. how any such autority[88] as endevours *to fashion wickednes by a law,* should derive it selfe from God. And *Isaiah* layes *woe upon them that decree unrighteous decrees,* 10. 1. Now which of these two is the better Lawgiver, and which deserves most a woe, he that gives out an edict singly unjust, or he that confirms to generations a fixt and unmolested impunity of that which is not onely held to be unjust, but also unclean, and both in a high degree, not only as they themselves affirm, an injurious expulsion of one wife, but also an unclean freedom by more then a patent to wed another adulterously? How can we therfore with safety thus dangerously confine the free simplicity of our Saviours meaning to that which meerly amounts from so many letters, whenas it can consist neither with his former and cautionary words, nor with other more pure and holy principles, nor finally with the scope of charity, commanding by his expresse commission in a higher strain. But all rather of necessity must be understood as only against the abuse of that wise and ingenuous liberty which *Moses* gave, and to terrifie a roaving conscience from sinning under that pretext.

---

[82]Written "covinc't" in Bodleian, but here corrected.

[83]The worst sort.

[84]Misprinted "teprehension" in Bodleian.

[85]At the bottom of p. 33 in Bodleian, the compositor has tried to squeeze in the beginning of Chapter 2 without creating a widow or orphan line on this page or the next. He has left out the normal space between the end of the text one chapter and the heading of the next and he has altered the headnote so that it has no hanging indent. I have restored the style of the other chapters.

[86]Printed "reliegion" in Bodleian.

[87]Bodleian has "doing fou lvill." Obviously, the compositor was either tired or confused at this point (see Yale 2: 285n3, for another perhaps related problem in 1643).

---

[88]Apparently a Miltonic spelling preference has slipped through, though the word is usually spelled "authority" in Bodleian.

CHAP. III.

That to allow sin by Law, is against the nature of Law, the end of the law-giver and the good of the people. Impossible therfore in the Law of God. That it makes God the author of sin more than any thing objected by the Jesuits or Arminians against Predestination.

BUT[89] let us further examin upon what consideration a Law of licence could be thus giv'n to a holy people for the hardnesse of heart. I suppose all wil answer, that for some good end or other. But here the contrary shall be prov'd. First, that many ill effects, but no good end of such a sufferance can be shewn; next, that a thing unlawful can for no good end whatever be either don or allow'd by a positive law. If there were any good end aim'd at, that end was then good, either as to the Law, or to the lawgiver licencing; or as to the person licenc't. That it could not be the end of the Law, whether Moral or Judiciall, to licence a sin, I prove easily out of *Rom.* 5. 20. *The Law enter'd, that the offence might abound*, that is, that sin might be made abundantly manifest to be hainous and displeasing to God, that so his offer'd grace might be the more esteem'd. Now if the Law in stead of aggravating and terrifying sin, shall give out licence, it foils it selfe, and turns recreant from its own end: it forestalls the pure grace of Christ which is through righteousnesse, with impure indulgences which are through sin. And instead of discovering sin, for *by the Law is the knowledge therof,* saith S. *Paul,* and that by certain and true light for men to walk in safely, it holds out fals and dazling fires to stumble men: or like those miserable flies[90] to run into with delight and be burnt: for how many soules might easily think that to be lawfull, which the Law and Magistrate allow'd them? Again we read, 1 Tim. 1. 5. *The end of the Commandment is charity, out of a pure heart, and of a good conscience, and of faith unfained.* But never could that be charity to allow a people what they could not use with a pure heart, but with conscience and faith both deceiv'd, or els despis'd. The more particular end of the Judicial Law is set forth to us clearly, *Rom.* 13. that God hath giv'n to that Law *a Sword not in vain, but to be a terror to evil works, a revenge to execute wrath upon him that doth evil.* If this terrible commission should but forbeare to punish wickednes, were it other to be accounted then partial and unjust? but if it begin to write indulgence to vulgar uncleannes, can it doe more to corrupt and shame the end of its own being?

Lastly, if the Law allow sin, it enters into a kind of covnant with sin, and if it doe, there is not a greater sinner in the world then the Law it selfe. The Law, to use an allegory[91] somthing different from that in *Philo Judæus* concerning *Amaleck,* though haply more significant, the Law is the *Israelite,* and hath this absolute charge given it, Deut. 25. *To blot out the memory of* sin, *the Amalekite, from under heav'n, not to forget it.* Again, the Law is the *Israelite,* and hath this expresse repeated command *to make no cov'nant with* sin, the *Canaanite,* but to expell him, lest he prove a snare. And to say truth it were too rigid and reasonlesse to proclaime such an enmity between man and man, were it not the type of a greater enmity between law and sin. I spake ev'n now, as if sin were condemn'd in a perpetual *villenage*[92] never to be free by law, never to be *manumitted*: but sure[93] sin can have no tenure by law at all but is rather an eternal outlaw, and in hostility with law past all atonement: both *diagonial* contraries,[94] as much allowing one another, as day and night together in one hemisphere. Or if it be possible, that sin with his darknes may come to composition, it cannot be without a foul eclipse and twylight to the law, whose brightnesse ought to surpasse the noon. Thus we see how this unclean permittance[95] defeats the sacred and glorious end both of the Moral and Judicial Law.

As little good can the lawgiver propose to equity by such a lavish remissnes as this: if to remedy hardnes of heart *Paræus* and other divines confesse, it more encreases by this liberty, then is lessn'd: and how is it probable that their hearts were more hard in this, that it should be yeelded to, then in any other crime? Their hearts were set upon usury, and are to this day, no Nation more; yet that which was the endammaging only of their estates, was narrowly forbid; this which is thought the extreme injury and dishonour of their Wives and daughters with the defilement also of themselves, is bounteously allow'd. Their hearts were as hard under their best Kings to offer in high places, though to the true God; yet that but a small thing is strictly forwarn'd; this accounted a high offence against one of the greatest moral duties, is calmely permitted and establisht. How can it be evaded but that the heavy censure of Christ should fall worse upon this lawgiver

---

[89]At this point, the compositor gave over the normal style of the book and used a capital B instead of a dropped cap; I have restored the normal style as does Yale.
[90]Butterflies or moths led to a flame only to be burned up.

[91]An image, a figurative comparison, or an extended simile (not necessarily involving an abstraction personified). The "type" in the next sentence would represent something closer to the modern sense of an allegorical opposition ("Law" vs. "Sin"). For extended definitions of allegory and type, see Treip, *Allegorical Poetics.*
[92]Serfdom (near-slavery).
[93]Surely.
[94]Diametrically opposed logical arguments.
[95]Permission.

of theirs, then upon all the Scribes and Pharises? For they did but omit Judgement and Mercy to trifle in Mint and Cummin, yet all according to Law; but this their Law-giver, altogether as punctuall in such niceties, goes marching on to adulteries, through the violence of divorce by Law against Law. If it were such a cursed act of *Pilate* a subordinate Judge to *Cæsar*, over-swayd by those hard hearts with much a doe to suffer one transgression of Law but once, what is it then with lesse a doe to publish a Law of transgression for many ages? Did God for this come down and cover the Mount of *Sinai* with his Glory, uttering in thunder those his sacred Ordinances out of the bottomlesse treasures of his wisdome and infinit purenes to patch up an ulcerous and rott'n common-wealth with strict and stern injunctions, to wash the skin and garments for every unclean touch, and such easie permission giv'n to pollute the soule with adulteries by publick authority, without disgrace, or question? No, it had bin better that man had never known Law or matrimony, then that such foul iniquity should be fast'nd upon the holy One of *Israel*, the Judge of all the earth, and such a peece of folly as *Belzebub* would not commit, to divide against himself and pervert his own ends;[96] or if he to compasse more mischief, might yeild perhaps to fain[97] some good deed, yet that God should enact a licence of certain evill for uncertain good against His own glory and purenes, is abominable to conceive. And as it is destructive to the end of Law, and blasphemous to the honour of the lawgiver licensing, so it is as pernicious to the person licenc't. If a private friend admonish not, the Scripture saith *he hates his brother, and lets him perish*; but if he sooth him, and allow him in his faults, the Proverbs teach us *he spreads a net for his neighbours feet, and worketh ruin*. If the Magistrate or Prince forget to administer due justice and restrain not sin; *Eli* himself could say, *it made the Lords people to transgresse*. But if he count'nance them against law by his own example, what havock it makes both in Religion and vertue among the people, may be guest by the anger it brought upon *Hophni* and *Phineas*[98] not to be appeas'd with *sacrifice nor offring for ever*. If the Law be silent to declare sin, the people must needs generally goe astray,

for the Apostle himselfe saith, *he had not known lust but by the Law:* and surely such a Nation seems not to be under the illuminating guidance of Gods law, but under the horrible doom rather of such as despise the Gospel, *he that is filthy let him be filthy still*. But where the Law it selfe gives a warrant for sin, I know not what condition of misery to imagin miserable anough for such a people, unlesse that portion of the wicked, or rather of the damned, on whom God threatens in 11. Psalm, *to rain snares*: but that questionlesse[99] cannot be by any Law, which the Apostle saith is *a ministery ordain'd of God unto our good*, and not so many waies and in so high a degree to our destruction, as we have now bin graduating. And this is all the good can come to the person licenc't in his hardnesse of heart.

I am next to mention that which because it is a ground in Divinity, Rom. 3. will save the labour of demonstrating, unlesse her giv'n axioms be more doubted then in other Arts (although it be no lesse firm in the precepts of Philosophy) that a thing unlawfull can for no good whatsoever be done, much lesse allow'd by a positive law. And this is the matter why Interpreters upon that passage in *Hosea*[100] will not consent it to be a true story, that the Prophet took a Harlot to wife, because God being a pure Spirit could not command a thing repugnant to his own nature, no not for so good an end as to exhibit more to the life a wholsom and perhaps a converting parable to many an Israelite. Yet that he commanded the allowance of adulterous and injurious divorses for hardnes of heart, a reason obscure and in a wrong sense, they can very savourily[101] perswade themselves; so tenacious is the leven of an old conceit. But they shift it, he permitted only. Yet silence in the Law is consent, and consent is accessory; why then is not the Law being silent, or not active against a crime, accessory to its own conviction, it self judging? For though we should grant, that it approvs not, yet it wills; and the Lawyers maxim is, that the *will compell'd is yet the will*. And though *Aristotle* in his Ethicks call this *a mixt action*, yet he concludes it to be voluntary and inexcusable, if it be evill. How justly then might human law and Philosophy rise up against the righteousnesse of *Moses*, if this be true which our vulgar Divinity Fathers upon him, yea upon God himselfe, not silently and only negatively to permit, but in his law to divulge a written and generall priviledge to commit and persist in unlawfull divorces with a high hand, with security and no ill fame: for this is more then permitting

---

[96]The characterization (and even the spelling) of "*Belzebub*" sheds light on the character in *Paradise Lost*, who might be viewed as a piece of folly (viewed from God's perspective), divided against himself, and perverse against his own ends, feigning good deeds in order to accomplish evil purposes. Here, perhaps, Beelzebub should be taken as another name for Satan himself, and the name is spelled to be pronounced in three syllables, rather than the four syllables that better fit the iambic pentameter of *Paradise Lost*.

[97]Two characteristic Miltonic spellings, "fain" and "yeild."

[98]The sons of Eli (1 Samuel 3.14).

---

[99]Doubtlessly.

[100]Hosea 1.2–3.

[101]Heartily. Milton is credited in the *OED* for inventing the word.

or conniving,[102] this is maintaining; this is warranting, this is protecting, yea this is doing evill, and such an evil as that reprobat lawgiver did, whose lasting infamy is ingrav'n upon him like a surname, *he who made Israel to sin.* This is the lowest pitch cantrary to God that publick fraud and injustice can descend.

If it be affirm'd that God as being Lord may doe what he will; yet we must know that God hath not two wills, but one will, much lesse two contrary. If he once will'd adultery should be sinfull, and to be punisht by death, all his omnipotence will not allow him to will the allowance that his holiest people might as it were by his own *Antinomie*, or counter-statute, live unreprov'd in the same fact, as he himselfe esteem'd it, according to our common explainers. The hidden wayes of his providence we adore & search not; but the law is his reveled wil, his complete, his evident, and certain will; herein he appears to us as it were in human shape, enters into cov'nant with us, swears to keep it, binds himself like a just lawgiver to his own prescriptions, gives himselfe to be understood by men, judges and is judg'd, measures and is commensurat to right reason; cannot require lesse of us in one cantle[103] of his Law then in another, his legall justice cannot be so fickle and so variable, sometimes like a devouring fire, and by and by connivent[104] in the embers, or, if I may so say, oscitant[105] and supine. The vigor of his Law could no more remit, then the hallowed fire on his altar could be let goe out. The Lamps that burnt before him might need snuffing, but the light of his Law never. Of this also more beneath, is discussing a solution of *Rivetus.*

The Jesuits, and that sect among us which is nam'd of *Arminius*, are wont to charge us of making God the author of sinne in two degrees especially, not to speak of his permissions, 1. Because we hold that he hath decreed some to damnation,[106] and consequently to sinne, say they: Next, because those means which are of saving knowledge to others, he makes to them an occasion of greater sinne. Yet considering the perfection wherin man was created, and might have stood, no decree necessitating his free will but subsequent, though not in time yet in order to causes which were in his owne power, they might, methinks be perswaded to absolve both God and us. Whenas the doctrine of *Plato* and *Chrysippus* with their followers the *Academics* and

the *Stoics*, who knew not what a consummat and most adorned *Pandora* was bestow'd upon *Adam* to be the nurse, and guide of his arbitrary happinesse and perseverance, I mean his native innocence and perfection, which might have kept him from being our true *Epimetheus*, and though they taught of vertue and vice to be both the gift of *divine destiny*, they could yet find[107] reasons not invalid, to justifie the counsels of God and Fate from the insulsity[108] of mortal tongues: That mans own free will[109] self corrupted is the adequat and sufficient cause of his disobedience *besides fate*; as *Homer* also wanted not to expresse,[110] both in his *Iliad* and *Odyssei.* And *Manilius* the Poet, although in his fourth book he tells of some *created both to sinne and punishment*; yet without murmuring, and with an industroius cheerfulness he acquitts[111] the *Deity.* They were not ignorant in their heathen lore, that it is most God-like to punish those who of his creatures became his enemies with the greatest punishment; and they could attain also to think that the greatest, when God himselfe throws a man furthest from him; which then they held hee did, when he blinded, hard'n'd, and stirr'd up his offendors, to finish; and pile up their disperat work since they had undertak'n it. To banish for ever into a locall hell, whether in the aire or in the center, or in that uttermost and bottomlesse gulph of *Chaos*, deeper from holy blisse then the worlds diameter multiply'd, they thought not a punishing so proper and proportionat for God to inflict, as to punish sinne with sinne. Thus were the common sort of Gentiles wont to think, without any wry thoughts cast upon[112] divine governance. And therefore *Cicero*, not in his *Tusculan* or *Campanian* retirements among the learned wits of that age; but ev'n in the *Senat* to a mixt auditory (though he were sparing otherwise to broach his Philosophy among Statists and Lawyers) yet as to this point both in his Oration against *Piso*, and in that which is about the answers of the Soothsayers against *Clodius*, he declares it publikly as no paradox to common ears, that God cannot punish man more, nor make him more miserable,[113] then still by making him more sinnfull. Thus we see how in this controversie the justice of God stood upright ev'n among heathen disputers. But if any

---

[102]In a smudgy correction, Milton has crossed out what looks to be the "tr" in "contriving," substituting an "n," to make "conniving" in the Bodleian copy.
[103]Nook or corner.
[104]Overlooking errors or offences.
[105]Yawning, drowsy.
[106]Printed as "danmation" in Bodleian and here corrected.

[107]The *Errata* correct "give" to "find." For some reason, at least three errors occurred on this page (39) that had to be corrected in the Errata.
[108]Folly, stupidity (Latin *insulsitas*).
[109]The *Errata* correct "will" to "freewill."
[110]As Homer expressed.
[111]The "acquits" of the text at this point is corrected in the Errata to "he acquitts."
[112]Written "uopn" in Bodleian and here corrected.
[113]At this point, Bodleian has a comma followed by a colon; I retain just the comma.

one be truly, and not pretendedly zealous for Gods honour, here I call him forth before men and Angels, to use his best and most advised skill, lest God more unavoidably then ever yet, and in the guiltiest manner be made the author of sin: if he shall not onely deliver over and incite his enemies by rebuks to sin as a punishment, but shall by patent under his own broad seal[114] allow his friends whom he would sanctify and save, whom he would unite to himselfe, and not disjoyne, whom he would correct by wholsome chastning, and not punish as hee doth the damned by lewd sinning, if he shall allow these in his Law the perfect rule of his own purest wil, and our most edify'd conscience, the perpetrating of an odious and manifold sin without the lest contesting. Tis wonder'd how there can be in God a secret, and a reveal'd will; and yet what wonder, if there be in man two answerable causes. But here there must be two revealed wills grappling in a fraternall warre with one another without any reasonable cause apprehended. This cannot be lesse then to ingraft sin into the substance of the law, which law is to provoke sin by crossing and forbidding, not by complying with it. Nay this is, which I tremble in uttering, to incarnat sin into the unpunishing, and well-pleas'd will of God. To avoid these dreadfull consequences that tread upon the heels of those allowances to sin, will be a task of farre more difficulty then to appease those minds which perhaps out of a vigilant and wary conscience except against predestination. Thus finally we may conclude, that a Law wholly giving licence cannot upon any good consideration be giv'n to a holy people, for hardnesse of heart in the vulgar sense.

CHAP. IV.

That if Divorce be no command, no more is mariage. That divorce could be no dispensation if it were sinfull. The Solution of Rivetus, *that God dispenc't by some unknown way, ought not to satisfie a Christian mind.*

OThers[115] think to evade the matter by not granting any Law of divorce, but onely a dispensation, which is contrary to the words of Christ, who himselfe calls it a *Law*, Mark 10. 5. or if we speak of a command in the strictest definition, then mariage it selfe is no more a command then divorce, but onely a free permission to him who cannot contain. But as to dispensation I affirm, the same as before of the Law,

that it can never be giv'n to the allowance of sin, God cannot give it neither in respect of himselfe, nor in respect of man: not in respect of himselfe, being a most pure essence, the just avenger of sin; neither can he make that cease to be a sin, which is in it self injust and impure, as all divorces they say were which were not for adultery. Not in respect of man; for then it must be either to his good or to his evill; Not to his good; for how can that be imagin'd any good to a sinner whom nothing but rebuke and due correction can save, to heare the determinate oracle of divine Law louder than any reproof dispensing and providing for the impunity, and convenience of sin; to make that doubtfull, or rather lawfull, which the end of the law was to make most evidently hatefull? Nor to the evill of man can a dispence[116] be given; for *if the Law were ordaind unto life*, Ro. 7. 10. how can the same God publish dispences against that Law, which must needs be unto death? Absurd and monstrous would that dispence be, if any Judge or Law should give it a man to cut his own throat, or to damne himselfe. Dispence therefore presupposes full pardon, or els it is not a dispence, but a most baneful & bloody snare. And why should God enter covnant with a people to be holy, as the *Command is holy, and just, and good, Ro. 7. 12.* and yet suffer an impure and[117] treacherous dispence to mislead and betray them under the vizard[118] of Law to a legitimate practice of uncleannesse? God is no covnant breaker, he cannot doe this.

Rivetus, a diligent and learned Writer, having well waigh'd what hath been written by those founders of dispence, and finding the small agreement among them, would fain work himselfe aloof these rocks and quicksands, and thinks it best to conclude that God certainly did dispence, but by some way to us unknown, and so to leave it. But to this I oppose, that a Christian by no meanes ought rest himself in such an ignorance; whereby so may absurdities will strait reflect both against the purity, justice, and wisdome of God, the end also both of Law and Gospel, and the comparison of them both together. God indeed in some wayes of his providence, is high and secret past finding out: but in the delivery and execution of his Law, especially in the managing of a duty so daily and so familiar as this is wherof we reason, hath plain enough reveal'd himself, and requires the observance therof not otherwise then to the law of nature and of equity imprinted in us seems correspondent. And hee hath taught us to love and to extoll his Lawes, not onely as

---

[114]Probably the elect, chosen by God as if by injunction (patent) and signed, sealed, and delivered. Compare God's "guifts promis'd only to the elect" (*Apology*; Yale 1: 941).

[115]For some reason, the compositor has taken out the normal spacing between chapters and has not used a drop-capital. I have restored both.

[116]Dispensation, forgiveness of offence.

[117]Printed as "anc" in Bodleian and here corrected.

[118]Mask, disguise.

they are his, but as they are just and good to every wise and sober understanding. Therfore *Abraham*, ev'n to the face of God himselfe, seem'd to doubt of divine justice, if it should swerve from that irradiation wherwith it had enlight'ned the mind of man, and bound it selfe to observe its own rule. *Wilt thou destroy the righteous with the wicked? That be far from thee; shall not the Judge of the earth doe right?* Therby declaring that God hath created a righteousnesse in right it selfe, against which he cannot doe. So *David*, Psal. 119. *The testimonies which thou hast commanded are righteous and very faithfull; thy word is very pure, therfore thy servant loveth it.* Not only then for the authours sake, but for its owne purity. *He is faithful*, saith S. *Paul*, *he cannot deny himselfe*, that is, he cannot deny his own promises, cannot but be true to his own rules. How should we imitate him els to *be perfect as he is perfect.* If at pleasure hee can dispence with golden Poetick ages of such pleasing licence, as in the fabl'd reign of old *Saturn.* And this perhaps before the Law might have some covert, but under such an undispencing covenant as *Moses* made with them, and not to tell us why and wherfore indulgence cannot give quiet to the brest of an intelligent man. We must be resolv'd how the law can be pure and perspicuous, and yet throw a polluted skirt over these *Eleusinian* mysteries, that no man can utter what they mean: worse in this then the worst obscenities of heathen superstition; for their filthines was hid, but the mystick reason therof known to their Sages: But this Jewish imputed filthinesse was daily and open, but the reason of it is not known to our Divines. We know of no designe the Gospel can have to impose new righteousnes upon works, but to remit the old by faith without works, if we mean justifying works: we know no mystery our Saviour could have to lay new bonds upon mariage in the covnant of grace which himselfe had loosen'd to the severity of law. So that *Rivetus* may pardon us, if we cannot bee contented with his non-solution to remain in such a peck of incertainties and doubts so dangerous and gastly to the fundamentals of our faith.

CHAP. V.

What a Dispensation is.

THerfore to get some better satisfaction, we must proceed to enquire as diligently as we can, what a dispensation is, which I find to be either properly so call'd, or improperly. Improperly so call'd, is rather a particular and exceptive law absolving and disobliging from a more general command for some just and reasonable cause. As *Numb.* 9. they who were unclean, or in a journey, had leave to keep the passover, in the second moneth, but otherwise ever in the first. As for

that in *Leviticus* of marying the brothers wife, it was a penall statute rather than a dispense; and commands nothing injurious or in it selfe unclean, only preferres a speciall reason of charitie before an institutive decencie, and perhaps is meant for life time onely, as is exprest beneath in the prohibition of taking two sisters. What other edict of *Moses*, carrying but the semblance of a Law in any other kind, may beare the name of a dispence, I have not readily to instance. But a dispensation most properly is some particular accident rarely happ'ning, and therfore not specify'd in the Law, but left to the decision of charity, ev'n under the bondage of Jewish rites, much more under the liberty of the Gospel. Thus did *David enter into the house of God, and did eat the Shew bread, he and his followers, which was* ceremonially *unlawfull.* Of such dispenses as these it was that *Verdune* the *French* Divine so gravely disputed in the Councell of *Trent* against Friar *Adrian*, who held that the Pope might dispence with any thing. *It is a fond perswasion*, saith *Verdune*, *that dispencing is a favour, nay it is as good distributive justice, as what is most, and the Priest sins if he give it not: for it is nothing else but a right interpretation of law.* Thus farre that I can learn touching this matter wholsomly decreed. But that God, who is the giver of every good and perfect gift, *James* 1. should give out a rule and directory to sin by, should enact a dispensation as long liv'd as a law wherby to live in priviledg'd adultery for hardnes of heart, and yet this obdurat disease cannot bee conceiv'd how it was the more amended by this unclean remedy, is the most deadly and Scorpion like gift that the enemy of mankind could have given to any miserable sinner, and is rather such a dispence as that was which the serpent gave to our first parents. God gave Quails in his wrath, and Kings in his wrath, yet neither of these things evill in themselves; but that hee whose eyes cannot behold impurity, should in the book of his holy covnant, his most unpassionat law, give licence, and statute for uncontroul'd adultery, although it goe for the receiv'd opinion, I shall ever disswade my soul from such a creed, such an indulgence as the shop of Antichrist never forg'd a baser.

CHAP. VI.

That the Jew had no more right to this supposed dispence, then the Christian hath, and rather not so much.

BUt if we must needs dispence, let us for a while so far dispence with truth, as to grant that sinne may be dispenc't: yet there will be copious reason found to prove that the Jew had no more right to such a suppos'd indulgence, then the Christian, whether we look at the clear knowledge wherin he liv'd, or the strict performance of works wherto he was bound. Besides visions and prophesies, they had the Law of God, which in the Psalmes and Proverbs is chiefly prais'd for surenesse and certainty both easie and perfect to the enlightning of the simple. How could it be so obscure then, or they so sottishly blind in this plain morall and houshold duty? They had the same precepts about mariage, Christ added nothing to their clearnesse, for that had argu'd them imperfect; hee opens not the Law, but removes the Pharisaick mists rais'd between the law and the peoples eyes: the onely sentence which he addes, *What God hath join'd let no man put asunder*, is as obscure as any clause fetch't out of *Genesis*, and hath encreast a yet undecided controversie of *Clandestine* mariages. If we examine over all his sayings, we shall find him not so much interpreting the Law with his words, as referring his owne words to be interpreted by the Law, and oftner obscures his mind in short, and vehement, and compact sentences, to blind and puzzle them the more who would not understand the Law. The Jews therfore were as little to be dispens't with for lack of morall knowledge as we.

Next, none I think will deny, but that they were as much bound to perform the Law as any Christian. That severe and rigorous knife not sparing the tender fore-skin of any male infant, to carve upon his flesh the mark of that strict and pure covnant wherinto he enter'd, might give us to understand anough against the fancie of dispensing. S. *Paul* testifies, that every *circumcis'd man is a debtor to the whole law*, Gal. 5. or els *circumcision is in vain*, Rom, 2. 25. How vain then and how prepos-terous must it needs be to exact a circumcision of the Flesh from an infant unto an outward signe of purity, and to dispence an uncircumcision in the soul of a grown man to an inward and reall impurity? How vain again was that law to impose tedious expiations for every slight sinne of ignorance and error, and to priviledge without penance or disturbance an odious crime whether of ignorance or obstinacie? How unjust also inflicting death & extirpation for the mark of cir-cumstantial purenes omitted, and proclaiming all honest and liberall indemnity to the act of a substantial impurenesse committed, making void the covnant that was made against it? Thus if we consider the tenor of the Law, to be circumcis'd and to perform all, not pardoning so much as the scapes of error and ignorance, and compare this with the condition of the Gospel, beleeve and be baptiz'd; I suppose it cannot bee long ere we grant that the Jew was bound as strictly to the performance of every duty as was possible, and therefore could not be dispenc't with more then the Christian, perhaps not so much.

CHAP. VII.

That the Gospel is apter to dispence then the Law. Paræus *answer'd.*

IF then the Law wil afford no reason why the Jew should be more gently dealt with then the Christian, then surely the Gospel can afford as little why the Christian should be lesse gently dealt with than the Jew. The Gospell indeed exhorts to highest perfection but beares with weakest infirmity more then the Law. Hence those indulgencies, *All cannot receive this saying, Every man hath his proper gift*, with express charges not to lay on yokes which our fathers could not bear. The nature of man still is as weak and yet as hard, and that weaknesse and hardnesse as unfit and as unteachable to bee harshly us'd as ever. I but,[119] saith *Paræus*, there is a greater portion of Spirit powr'd upon the Gospel, which requires from us perfecter obedience. I answer, This does not prove that the law therfore might give allowance to sinne more then the Gospel; and if it were no sin, wee know it the work of the Spirit to *mortifie our corrupt desires and evill concupiscence*; but not to root up our naturall affections and disaffections moving to and fro ev'n in wisest men upon just and necessary reasons which were the true ground of that *Mosaic* dispence, and is the utmost extent of our pleading. What is more or lesse perfect we dispute not, but what is sinne or no sinne; and in that I still affirm the Law requir'd as perfect obedience as the Gospell: besides that the prime end of the Gospel is not so much to exact our obedience, as to reveal grace and the satisfaction of our disobedience. What is now exacted from us, it is the accusing Law that does it ev'n yet under the Gospell; but cannot bee more extreme to us now then to the Jewes of old: for the Law ever was of works, and the Gospell ever was of grace.

Either then the Law by harmlesse and needfull dispences which the Gospel is now made to deny, must have anticipated and exceeded the grace of the Gospel, or els must be found to have giv'n politick and superficial graces without real pardon, saying in general doe this and live, and yet deceiving and damning under hand, with unsound and hollow permissions, which is utterly abhorring from the end of all Law, as hath bin shewd. But if those indulgences were safe and sinles out of tendernes and compassion, as indeed they were, and yet shall be abrogated by the Gospel, then the Law, whose end is by rigor to magnifie Grace, shall it self give grace, and pluck a faire plume from the Gospel, instead of hastning us thither, alluring us from it. And

---

[119]"Ay [yes], but . . . ."

wheras the terror of the Law was as a servant to amplifie and illustrat the mildnesse of grace; now the unmildnesse of Evangelick grace shall turn servant to declare the grace and mildnesse of the rigorous Law. The Law was harsh to extoll the grace of the Gospel, and now the Gospel by a new affected strictnes of her own, shall extenuate the grace, which her self offers. For by exacting a duty which the Law dispens't, if we perform it, then is grace diminisht, by how much performance advances, unlesse the Apostle argue wrong: if we perform it not, and perish for not performing, then are the conditions of grace harder then those of rigor. If through Faith and Repentance we perish not, yet grace still remains the lesse, by requiring that which rigor did not require, or at least not so strictly. Thus much therfore to *Paræus*, that if the Gospel require perfecter obedience then the Law as a duty, it exalts the Law and debases it self, which is dishonourable to the work of our Redemption. Seeing therfore that all the causes of any allowance that the Jews might have, remain as well to the Christians, this is a certain rule, that so long as the causes remain the allowance ought. And having thus at length enquir'd the truth concerning Law and dispence, their ends, their uses, their limits, and in what manner both Jew and Christian stands liable to the one, or capable of the other, we may safely conclude, that to affirm the giving of any law, or law-like dispence to sin for hardnesse of heart, is a doctrine of that extravagance from the sage principles of piety, that who so considers throughly, cannot but admire how this hath been digested all this while.

CHAP. VIII.

The true sence how Moses suffer'd divorce for hardnesse of heart.

WHat[120] may we doe then to salve this seeming inconsistence? I must not dissemble that I am confident it can be don no other way than this.

Moses Deut. 24. 1. establisht a grave and prudent Law, full of moral equity, full of due consideration towards nature, that cannot be resisted; a Law consenting with the Laws of wisest men and civilest Nations. That when a man hath maried a wife, if it come to passe that he cannot love her by reason of some displeasing natural quality or unfitnes in her, let him write her a bill of divorce. The intent of which Law undoubtedly was this, that if any good and peaceable man should discover some helples disagreement or dislike either of mind or body, wherby he could not cheerfully perform the duty of a husband without the perpetual dissembling of offence and disturbance to his spirit, rather then to live uncomfortably and unhappily both to himself and to his wife, rather then to continue undertaking a duty which he could not possibly discharge, he might dismisse her whom he could not tolerably and so not conscionably retain. And this law the Spirit of God by the mouth of *Salomon*, Pro. 30. 21. 23. testifies to be a good and a necessary Law; by granting it that *a hated Woman* (for so the hebrew word signifies, rather than odious though it come all to one) *that a hated woman, when she is maried, is a thing that the earth cannot beare.* What follows then but that the charitable Law must remedy what nature cannot undergoe. Now that many licentious and hard hearted men took hold of this Law to cloak their bad purposes is nothing strange to beleeve. And these were they, not for whom *Moses* made the Law, God forbid, but whose hardnes of heart taking ill advantage by this Law he held it better to suffer as by accident, where it could not be detected, rather than good men should loose their just and lawfull priviledge of remedy: Christ therfore having to answer these tempting Pharises, according as his custom was, not meaning to inform their proud ignorance what *Moses* did in the true intent of the Law, which they had ill cited, suppressing the true cause for which *Moses* gave it, and extending it to every slight matter, tells them their own, what *Moses* was forc't to suffer by their abuse of his Law. Which is yet more plain if we mark that our Saviour the fifth of *Matth.* cites not the Law of *Moses*, but the Pharisaical tradition falsly[121] grounded upon that law. And in those other places, Chap. 19. and *Mark* 10. the Pharises cite the Law, but conceale the wise and human reason there exprest; which our Saviour corrects not in them, whose pride deserv'd not his instruction, only returns them what is proper to them; *Moses for the hardnesse of your heart suffer'd you*, that is, such as you *to put away your wives*; and *to you he wrote this precept* for this cause, which (*to you*) must be read with an impression, and understood limitedly of such as cover'd ill purposes under that Law: for it was seasonable that they should hear their own unbounded licence rebukt, but not seasonable for them to hear a good mans requisit liberty explain'd. But us he hath taught better, if we have eares to hear. He himselfe acknowledg'd it to be a Law, *Mark* 10. *and being a Law of God, it must have an undoubted end of charity, which may be us'd with a pure heart, a good conscience, and faith unfained*, as was heard: it cannot allow sin, but is purposely to resist sin,

[120]The compositor has eliminated the customary dropped capital in favor of capitalizing all four letters of "WHAT." For consistency's sake, I have made the style consistent with the other chapter headings.

[121]Written "fasly," here corrected to "falsly."

as by the same chapter to *Timothy* appears. There we learn also *that the Law is good, if a man use it lawfully.* Out of doubt then there must be a certain good in this Law which *Moses* willingly allow'd; and there might be an unlawfull use made therof by hypocrits; and that was it which *Moses* unwillingly suffer'd; foreseeing it in general, but not able to discern it in particulars. Christ therfore mentions not here what *Moses* and the Law intended: for good men might know that by many other rules: and the scornful Pharises were not fit to be told, untill they could imploy that knowledge they had lesse abusively. Only he acquaints them with what *Moses* by them was put to suffer.

CHAP. IX.
The words of the Institution how to be understood; and of our Saviours answer to his Disciples.

ANd to entertain a little their overweening arrogance as best befitted, and to amaze them yet furder, because they thought it no hard matter to fulfill the Law, he draws them up to that unseparable institution which God ordain'd in the beginning before the fall, when man and woman were both perfect, and could have no cause to separate: just as in the same Chap. he stands not to contend with the arrogant young man who boasted his observance of the whole Law, whether he had indeed kept it or not, but skrues him up higher to a task of that perfection, which no man is bound to imitate. And in like manner that pattern of the first institution he set before the opinionative Pharises to dazle them and not to bind us. For this is a solid rule, that every command giv'n with a reason, binds our obedience no otherwise then that reason holds. Of this sort was that command in *Eden; Therfore shall a man cleave to his wife, and they shall be one flesh*: which we see is no absolute command, but with an inference, *Therfore*: the reason then must be first consider'd, that our obedience be not mis-obedience. The first is, for it is not single, because the wife is to the husband *flesh of his flesh*, as in the verse going before. But this reason cannot be sufficient of it self: for why then should he for his wife leave his father and mother, with whom he is farre *more flesh of flesh, and bone of bone*, as being made of their substance? And besides it can be but a sorry and ignoble society of life, whose inseparable injunction depends meerly upon flesh and bones. Therfore we must look higher, since Christ himself recalls us to the beginning, and we shall finde that the primitive reason of never divorcing, was that sacred and not vain promise of God to remedy mans loneliness by *making him a meet help for him*, though not now in perfection, as at first, yet still in proportion as things now are. And this is

repeated vers. 20 when all other creatures were fitly associated and brought to *Adam*, as if the divine power had bin in some care and deep thought, because *there was not yet found an help meet for man.* And can we so slightly depresse[122] the all-wise purpose of a deliberating God, as if his consultation had produc't no other good for man but to joyn him with an accidentall companion of propagation, which his sudden[123] word had already made for every beast? nay a far lesse good to man it will be found, if she must at all aventures[124] be fasten'd upon him individually. And therfore even plain sense and equity, and, which is above them both, the all-interpreting voice of Charity her self cries loud that this primitive reason, this consulted promise of God *to make a meet help*, is the onely cause that gives authority to this command of not divorcing, to be a command. And it might be further added, that if the true definition of a wife were askt in good earnest, this clause of being a *meet help* would shew it self so necessary, and so essential in that demonstrative argument, that it might be logically concluded: therfore she who naturally and perpetually is no meet help, can be no wife; which cleerly takes away the difficulty of dismissing of such a one. If this be not thought anough, I answer yet furder, that mariage, unlesse it mean a fit and tolerable mariage, is not inseparable neither by nature nor institution. Not by nature for then those Mosaick divorces had bin against nature, if separable and inseparable be contraries, as who doubts they be: and what is against nature is against Law, if soundest Philosophy abuse us not: by this reckning *Moses* should bee most unmosaick, that is, most illegal, not to say most unnaturall. Nor is it inseparable by the first institution: for then no second institution in the same Law for so many causes could dissolve it: it being most unworthy a human (as *Plato's* judgement is in the fourth book of his Lawes) much more a divine Law-giver to write two several decrees upon the same thing. But what could *Plato* have deem'd if one of these were good, and the other evill to be done? Lastly, suppose it bee inseparable by institution, yet in competition with higher things, as religion and charity in mainest matters, and when the chiefe end is frustrat for which it was ordain'd, as hath been shown, if still it must remain inseparable, it holds a strange and lawlesse propriety from all other works of God under heaven. From these many considerations we may safely gather, that so much of the first institution as our Saviour mentions, for he mentions not all, was but to quell and put to non-plus the tempting Pharises; and to

---

[122]Devalue, disparage.
[123]Possibly unpremeditated (see *OED* 2.a).
[124]"By every bad chance."

lay open their ignorance and shallow understanding of the Scriptures. For, saith he, *have ye not read that he which made them at the beginning, made them male and female, and said, for this cause shall a man cleave to his wife?* which these blind usurpers of *Moses* chair could not gainsay: as if this single respect of male and female were sufficient against a thousand inconveniences and mischiefes, to clogge a rationall creature to his endlesse sorrow unrelinquishably, under the guilefull super-scription of his intended solace and comfort. What if they had thus answer'd, Master, if thou mean to make wedlock as inseparable as it was from the beginning, let it be made also a fit society, as God meant it, which we shall soon understand it ought to be, if thou recite the whole reason of the law. Doubtlesse our Saviour had applauded their just answer. For then they had expounded this command of Paradise, even as *Moses* himselfe expounds it by his lawes of divorce, that is, with due and wise regard had to the premises and reasons of the first command, according to which, without unclean and temporizing permissions he instructs us in this imperfect state what we may lawfully doe about divorce.

But if it be thought that the Disciples offended at the rigor of Christs answer, could yet obtain no mitigation of the former sentence pronounc't to the Pharises, it may be fully answer'd, that our Saviour continues the same reply to his Disciples, as men leaven'd with the same customary licence which the Pharises maintain'd, and displeas'd at the removing of a traditionall abuse wherto they had so long not unwillingly bin us'd: it was no time then to contend with their slow and prejudicial belief, in a thing wherin an ordinary measure of light in Scripture, with some attention might afterwards in-forme them well anough. And yet ere Christ had finish't this argument, they might have pickt out of his own concluding words, an answer more to their minds, and in effect the same with that which hath been all this while entreating audience. *All men,* said he, *cannot receive this saying, save they to whom it is given, he that is able to receive it let him receive it.* What saying is this which is left to a mans choice to receive or not receive? What but the married life. Was our Saviour then so mild and so favourable to the weaknesse of a single man, and is he turn'd on the sudden so rigorous and inexorable to the distresses and extremities of an ill wedded man? Did hee so graciously give leave to change the better single life for the worse maried life? Did he open so to us this hazardous and accidentall door of mariage to shut upon us like the gate of death without retracting or returning, without permitting to change the worst, most insup-portable, most unchristian mischance of mariage for all the mischiefes and sorrows that can ensue, being an

ordinance which was especially giv'n as a cordial and exhilarating cup of solace the better to beare our other crosses and afflictions? Questionlesse this were a hard-heartednesse of undivorcing, worse then that in the Jewes which they say extorted the allowance from *Moses,* and is utterly dissonant from[125] all the doctrine of our Saviour. After these considerations therfore to take a law out of Paradise giv'n in time of originall perfection, and to take it barely without those just and equall inferences and reasons which mainly establish it, nor so much as admitting those needfull and safe allowances wherwith *Moses* himselfe interprets it to the faln condition of man, argues nothing in us but rash-nesse and contempt of those meanes that God left us in his pure and chast Law without which it will not be possible for us to perform the strict imposition of this command: or if we strive beyond our strength, we shall strive to obay it otherwise then God commands it. And lamented experience daily teaches the bitter and vain fruits of this our presumption, forcing men in a thing wherin we are not able to judge either of their strength, or of their sufferance. Whom neither one vice nor other by natural addiction, but onely mariage ruins, which doubtlesse is not the fault of that ordinance, for God gave it as a blessing, nor alwayes of mans mis-choosing; it being an error above wisdom to prevent, as examples of wisest men so mistaken manifest: it is the fault therfore of a perverse opinion that will have it continu'd in despite of nature and reason, when indeed it was never truly joyn'd. All those expositers upon the first of *Matthew* confesse the Law of *Moses* to be the Law of the Lord wherin no addition or diminution hath place; yet coming to the point of divorce, as if they fear'd not to be call'd least in the kingdom of heav'n, any slight evasion will content them to reconcile those contradictions which they make between Christ and *Moses,* between Christ and Christ.

CHAP. X.

The vain shift of those who make the law of divorce to bee onely the premises of a succeeding law.

SOme will have it no Law, but the granted premises of another Law following, contrary to the words of Christ, *Mark* 10. 5. and all other translations of gravest authority, who render it in form of a Law; agreeable to *Malach.* 2. 16. as it is most anciently and modernly expounded. Besides the bill of divorce, and the particu-lar occasion therein mention'd, declares it to be orderly and legall. And what avails this to make the matter

---

[125]In disagreement with.

more righteous, if such an adulterous condition shal be mention'd to build a law upon without either punishment, or so much as forbidding; they pretend it is implicitly reprov'd in these words, *Deut.* 24. 4. *after she is defil'd*; but who sees not that this defilement is not onely in respect of returning to her former husband after an intermixt mariage; els why was not the defiling condition first forbidd'n, which would have sav'd the labour of this after law; nor is it seemly or piously attributed to the justice of God and his known hatred of sinne, that such a hainous fault as this through all the Law, should be only wip't with an implicit and oblique touch (which yet is falsly suppos'd) and that his peculiar people should be let wallow in adulterous mariages almost two thousand yeares, for want of a direct Law to prohibit them; 'tis rather to be confidently assum'd that this was granted to apparent necesities, as being of unquestionable right and reason in the Law of nature, in that it stil passes without inhibition, ev'n when greatest cause is giv'n to us to expect it should be directly forbidd'n.

CHAP. XI.
The other shift of saying divorce was permitted by Law, but not approv'd. More of the Institution.

But it was not approv'd. So much the worse that it was allow'd; as if sin had overmasterd the law of God, to conform her steddy and strait rule to sins crookednesse, which is impossible. Besides, what needed a positive grant of that which was not approv'd? it restrain'd no liberty to him that could but use a little fraud, it had bin better silenc't, unlesse it were approv'd in some case or other. but still it was not approv'd. Miserable excusers! He who doth evil that good may come thereby, approves not what he doth, and yet the grand rule forbids him, and counts *his damnation* just if he doe it. The Sorceresse *Medea* did not approve her owne evill doings, yet lookt not to be excus'd for that; and it is the constant opinion of *Plato* in *Protagoras*, and other of his dialogues agreeing with that proverbiall sentence among the *Greeks*, that no *man is wicked willingly*; which also the *Peripateticks* doe rather distingush then deny. What great thank then if any man reputed wise and constant will neither doe nor permit others under his charge to doe that which hee approves not, especially in matter of sinne. But for a Judge, but for a Magistrate the Shepheard of his people to surrender up his approbation against law & his own judgment, to the obstinacie of his heard, what more un-Judge-like, more un-Magistratelike, and in warre more un-commander-like? Twice in a short time it was the undoing of the Roman State, first when *Pompey*, next when *Marcus Brutus* had not magnanimity anough but to make so poore a resignation of what they approv'd, to what the boisterous Tribunes and Souldiers bawl'd for. Twice it was the saving of two the greatest Common-wealths in the world, of *Athens* by *Themistocles* at the Sea fight of *Salamis*; of *Rome* by *Fabius Maximus* in the *Punick* warre, for that these two matchlesse Generalls had the fortitude at home against the rashnes and the clamours of their own Captains and confederates to withstand the doing or permitting of what they could not approve in their duty of their great command. Thus farre of civill prudence. But when we speak of sinne, let us look againe upon the old reverend *Eli*; who in his heavie punishment found no difference between the doing and permitting of what he did not approve. If hardnesse of heart in the people may be any excuse, why then is *Pilate* branded through all memory? Hee approv'd not what he did, he openly protested, he washt his hands and laboured not a little, ere he would yeeld to the hard hearts of a whole people, both Princes and plebeians, importuning & tumulting ev'n to the fear of a revolt. Yet is there any will undertake his cause? If therfore Pilat for suffering but one act of cruelty against law, though with much unwillingnesse testify'd, at the violent demand of a whole Nation, shall stand so black upon record to all posterity? Alas for *Moses*! what shall we say for him, while we are taught to beleeve he suffer'd not one act onely both of cruelty and uncleannesse in one divorce, but made it a plain and lasting law against law, whereby ten thousand acts accounted both cruell and unclean, might be daily committed, and this without the least suit or petition of the people that wee can read of.

And can we conceive without vile thoughts, that the majesty and holines of God could endure so many ages to gratifie a stubborn people in the practice of a foul polluting sin, and could he expect they should abstain, he not signifying his mind in a plain command, at such time especially when he was framing their laws and them to all possible perfection? But they were to look back to the first institution, nay rather why was not that individual institution brought out of Paradise, as was that of the Sabbath, and repeated in the body of the Law, that men might have understood it to be a command? for that any sentence that bears the resemblance of a precept, set there so out of place in another world, at such a distance from the whole Law, and not once mention'd there, should be an obliging command to us, is very disputable, and perhaps it might be deny'd to be a command without further dispute: however, it commands not absolutely, as hath bin clear'd, but only with reference to that precedent promise of God, which is the very ground of his institution; if that appeare not in some tolerable sort, how can we affirm such a matrimony to be the same which God instituted! In such an accident it will best behove our sobernes to follow rather what moral *Sinai* prescribes equal to our strength, then fondly to think within our strength of all that lost Paradise relates.

CHAP. XII.
The third shift of them who esteem it a meer judicial Law.
Prov'd again to be a Law of moral equity.

ANother while it shall suffice them, that it was not a moral but a judicial Law, & so was abrogated. Nay rather not abrogated, because judicial: which Law the ministery of Christ came not to deal with. And who put it in mans power to exempt, where Christ speaks in general of not abrogating *the least jot or tittle*, and in special not that of divorce, because it follows among those Laws, which he promis'd expresly not to abrogate, but to vindicate from abusive traditions: which is most evidently to be seen in the 16. of *Luke*, where this caution of not abrogating is inserted immediatly, and not otherwise then purposely, when no other point of the Law is toucht, but that of divorce. And if we mark the 31. vers. of *Mat.* the 5. he there cites not the Law of *Moses*, but the licencious Glosse which traduc't the Law; that therfore which he cited, that he abrogated, and not only abrogated, but disallow'd and flatly condemn'd, which could not be the Law of *Moses*; for that had bin foulely to the rebuke of his great servant. To abrogate a Law made with Gods allowance, had bin to tell us only that such a Law was now to cease: but to refute it with an ignominious note of civilizing adultery, casts the reproof, which was meant only to the Pharises ev'n upon him who made the Law. But yet if that be judicial which belongs to a civil Court, this Law is lesse judicial then nine of the ten Commandements; for antiquaries affirm that divorces proceeded among the Jews without knowledge of the Magistrate, only with hands and seales under the testimony of some Rabbies to be then present. *Perkins* in a *Treatise of Conscience* grants, that what in the judicial Law is of common equity, binds also the Christian. And how to judge of this, prescribes 2. wayes. If wise Nations have enacted the like decree. Or if it maintain the good of family, Church, or Common-wealth. This therfore is a pure moral *economical* Law, too hastily imputed of tolerating sin; being rather so clear in nature and reason, that it was left to a mans own arbitrement to be determin'd between God and his own conscience; not only among the Jews, but in every wise nation; the restraint wherof, who is not too thick sighted, may see how hurtfull and distractive it is to the house, the Church, and Common-wealth. And that

power which Christ never took from the master of family, but rectify'd only to a right and wary use at home; that power the undiscerning Canonist hath improperly usurpt into his Court-leet,[126] and bescribbl'd with a thousand trifling impertinencies, which yet have fill'd the life of man with serious trouble and calamity. Yet grant it were of old a judicial Law, it need not be the lesse moral for that, being conversant, as it is, about vertue or vice. And our Saviour disputes not heer the judicature, for that was not his office, but the morality of divorce, whether it be adultery or no; if therfore he touch the law of *Moses* at all, he touches the moral part therof; which is absurd to imagine, that the cov'nant of grace should reform the exact and perfect law of works, eternal and immutable; or if he touch not the Law at all, then is not the allowance therof disallow'd to us.

CHAP. XIII.
The ridiculous opinion, that divorce was permitted from the custom in Ægypt. That Moses gave not this Law unwillingly. Perkins confesses this Law was not abrogated.

OThers are so ridiculous as to allege that this licence of divorcing was giv'n them because they were so accustom'd in Egypt. As if an ill custom were to be kept to all posterity; for the dispensation is both universal and of time unlimited, and so indeed no dispensation at all; for the over-dated dispensation of a thing unlawfull, serves for nothing but to encrease hardnes of heart, and makes men but wax more incorrigible, which were a great reproach to be said of any Law or allowance that God should give us. In these opinions it would be more Religion to advise well, lest we make our selves juster then God, by censuring rashly that for sin which his unspotted Law without rebuke allows, and his people without being conscious of displeasing him have us'd. And if we can think so of *Moses*, as that the Jewish obstinacy could compell him to write such impure permissions against the rule of God and his own judgement, doubtles it was his part to have protested publickly what straits he was driv'n to, and to have declar'd his conscience when he gave any Law against his mind; for the Law is the touch-stone of sin and of conscience, and must not be intermixt with corrupt indulgences; for then it looses the greatest praise it has, of being certain, and infallible, not leading into

---

[126]A court-leet was "A court of record held periodically in a hundred, lordship, or manor, before the lord or his steward, and attended by the residents of the district" (*OED*); Milton is suggesting that the Canonist is running a small-town court which produces petty or backward judgments.

error, as all the Jews were led by this connivence of Moses if it were a connivence. But still they fly back to the primitive institution, and would have us re-enter Paradise against the sword that guards it.[127] Whom I again thus reply to, that the place in Genesis contains the description of a fit and perfect mariage, with an interdict of ever divorcing such a union; but where nature is discover'd to have never joyn'd indeed, but vehemently seeks to part, it cannot be there conceiv'd that God forbids it; nay he commands it both in the Law and in the Prophet *Malachy*, which is to be our rule. And *Perkins* upon this chap. of *Matth.* deals plainly, that our Saviour heer confutes not *Moses* Law, but the false glosses that deprav'd the Law; which being true, *Perkins* must needs grant, that somthing then is left to that law which Christ found no fault with; and what can that be but the conscionable use of such liberty as the plain words import? So that by his owne inference, Christ did not absolutely intend to restrain all divorces to the onely cause of adultery. This therefore is the true scope of our Saviours will, that he who looks upon the law concerning divorce, should look also back upon the first institution, that he may endeavour what is perfectest: and he that looks upon the institution should not refuse as sinfull and unlawfull those allowances which God affords him in his following Law, lest he make himselfe purer then his maker; and presuming above strength, slip into temptations irrecoverably. For this is wonderfull, that in all those decrees concerning mariage, God should never once mention the prime institution to disswade them from divorcing; and that he should forbid smaller sinnes as opposite to the hardnesse of their hearts, and let this adulterous matter of divorce pass ever unreprov'd.

This is also to bee marvell'd, that seeing Christ did not condemn whatever it was that *Moses* suffer'd, and that therupon the Christian Magistrate permits usury and open stews, and here with us adultery to bee so slightly punisht, which was punisht by death to these hard hearted Jewes, why wee should strain thus at the matter of divorce, which may stand so much with charity to permit, and make no scruple to allow usury esteem'd to be so much against charity. But this it is to embroile our selves against the righteous and all-wise Judgements and Statutes of God; which are not variable and contrarious, as we would make them, one while permitting and another while forbidding, but are most constant and most harmonious each to other. For how can the uncorrupt and majestick Law of God, bearing in her hand the wages of life and death, harbour such a repugnance within herselfe, as to require an unexempted and impartiall obedience to all her decrees, either from us or from our Mediator, and yet debase her selfe to faulter so many ages with circumcis'd adulteries by unclean and slubbering[128] permissions.

CHAP. XIV.
That Beza's *opinion of regulating sinne by Apostolick law, cannot be sound.*

YEt[129] *Beza's* opinion is that a politick Law, but what politick Law, I know not, unlesse one of *Matchiavel's*,[130] may regulate sin; may bear indeed, I grant, with imperfection for a time, as those Canons of the Apostles did in ceremoniall things: but as for sinne, the essence of it cannot consist[131] with rule; and if the law fall to regulate sinne, and not to take it utterly away, it necessarily confirms and establishes sinne. To make a regularity of sinne by law, either the law must straiten sinne into no sinne, or sinne must crook the law into no law. The Judiciall law can serve to no other end then to be the protector and champion of Religion and honest civility, as is set down plainly, *Rom.* 13. and is but the arm of morall law, which can no more be separate from justice then justice from vertue: their office also in a different manner steers the same cours; the one teaches what is good by precept, the other unteaches what is bad by punishment. But if we give way to politick dispensations of lewd uncleannesse, the first good consequence of such a relaxe will bee the justifying of Papal stews, joyn'd with a toleration of epidemick whordom. Justice must revolt from the end of her authority, and become the patron of that wherof she was created the punisher. The example of usury which is commonly alleg'd, makes against the allegation which it brings, as I touch'd before. Besides that usury, so much as is permitted by the Magistrate and demanded by common equity, is neither against the word of God, nor the rule of charity, as hath been often discus't by men of eminent learning and judgement. There must be therefore some other example found out to shew us wherein civill policy may with warrant from God settle wickednes by law, and make that lawfull which is

---

[127]Compare "The brandisht Sword of God before them blaz'd / Fierce as a Comet" (*Paradise Lost* 12.633–34).

[128]Working in unclean or slovenly conditions.
[129]The compositor here seems not to have had access to a drop-capital for a Y; he has substituted all-caps "YET." For the sake of consistency, I have once again used the customary chapter opening.
[130]The spelling is interesting here, since Milton would have known full well the Italian spelling and pronunciation of Macchiavelli; for one reason or another—perhaps a printer's oversight—the spelling reflects the common English mispronunciation "Match-abel."
[131]To be consistent with, or harmonize with.

lawlesse. Although I doubt not but upon deeper consideration, that which is true in Physick, wil be found as true in policie: that as of bad pulses those that beat most in order, are much worse then those that keep the most inordinat circuit, so of popular vices those that may bee committed legally, will be more pernicious then those that are left to their own cours at perill, not under a stinted priviledge to sin orderly and regularly, which is an implicit contradiction, but under due and fearlesse execution of punishment.

The political law, since it cannot regulate vice, is to restrain it, by using all means to root it out: but if it suffer the weed to grow up to any pleasurable or contented height upon what pretext[132] soever, it fastens the root, it prunes and dresses vice, as if it were a good plant. Let no man doubt therfore to affirm that it is not so hurtfull or dishonourable to a Common wealth, nor so much to the hardning of hearts, when those worse faults pretended to be fear'd are committed, by who so dares under strict and executed penalty, as when those lesse faults tolerated for fear of greater harden their faces, not their hearts only, under the protection of publick authority. For what lesse indignity were this, then as if Justice her self, the Queen of vertues, descending from her scepter'd royalty, instead of conquering should compound and treat with sin her eternal adversary and rebel, upon ignoble terms. Or as if the judicial Law were like that untrusty steward in the Gospel and instead of calling in the debts of his moral master, should give out subtle and sly acquittances to keep him self from begging. Or let us person[133] him like some wretched itinerary Judge, who to gratifie his delinquents before him, would let them basely break his head, lest they should pull him from the bench, and throw him over the barre. Unlesse we had rather think both moral and judicial full of malice and deadly purpose conspir'd to let the debtor Israelite the seed of *Abraham*, run on upon a banckrout score, flatter'd with insufficient and insnaring discharges, that so he might be hal'd to a more cruel forfeit for all the indulgent arrears which those judicial acquitments had ingaged him in. No no, this cannot be, that the Law whose integrity and faithfulnesse is next to God, should be either the shamelesse broker of our impunities, or the intended instrument of our destruction. The method of holy correction such as became the Common wealth of *Israel*, is not to bribe sin with sin, to capitulate and hire out one crime with another: but with more noble and

gracefull severity then *Popilius* the *Roman legat*[134] us'd with *Antiochus*, to limit and level out the direct way from vice to virtue, with straightest and exactest lines on either side, not winding or indenting so much as to the right hand of fair pretences. Violence indeed and insurrection may force the Law to suffer what it cannot mend: but to write a decree in allowance of sin, as soon can the hand of Justice rot off. Let this be ever concluded as a truth that will outlive the faith of those that seek to bear it down.

CHAP. XV.
That divorce was not giv'n for wives only, as Beza *and* Paraeus *write. More of the institution.*

Lastly, If Divorce were granted, as *Beza* and others say, not for men but to release afflicted wives; certainly it is not only a dispensation, but a most mercifull Law: and why it should not yet be in force, being wholly as needfull, I know not what can be in cause but senselesse cruelty. But yet to say, divorce was granted for relief of wives, rather then of husbands, is but weakly conjectur'd, and is manifest[135] the extreme shift of a huddled exposition. Whenas it could not be found how hardnesse of heart should be lessen'd by liberty of divorce, a fancy[136] was devis'd to hide the flaw, by commenting that divorce was permitted only for the help of wives. Palpably uxorious! Who can be ignorant that woman was created for man, and not man for woman; and that a husband may be injur'd as insufferably in mariage as a wife. What an injury is it after wedlock not to be belov'd, what to be slighted, what to be contended with in point of house-rule who shall be the head, not for any parity of wisdome, for that were somthing reasonable, but out of a female pride. *I suffer not*, saith S. Paul, *the woman to usurp authority over the man.* If the Apostle could not suffer it, into what mould is he mortify'd that can? *Salomon* saith, *That a bad wife is to her husband as rott'nnesse to his bones, a continual dropping: better dwell in a corner of the house top, or in the wildernes* then with such a one. *Whoso hideth her hideth the wind, and one of the four mischiefs that the earth cannot bear.* If the Spirit of God wrote such aggravations as these, and as may be guest by these similitudes, counsels the man rather to divorce then to live with such a collegue, and yet on the other side expresses nothing of the wives suffering with a bad husband; is it not most likely that God in his Law had

---

[132]The Bodleian has "petext" here, which I have corrected.
[133]Represent. Milton seems to have invented the usage.

[134]This word is difficult to decipher as printed in Bodleian: it may be "*legal.*"
[135]Clearly shown to be.
[136]Fantasy, illusion.

more pitty towards man thus wedlockt, then towards the woman that was created for another. The same Spirit relates to us the cours which the *Medes* and *Persians* took by occasion of *Vashti*, whose meer denial to come at her husbands sending, lost her the being Queen any longer, and set up a wholesome Law, *that every man should beare rule in his own house.* And the divine relater shews us not the least signe of disliking what was done; how should he? if *Moses* long before was nothing[137] lesse mindful of the honour and preeminence due to man. So that to say divorce was granted for woman rather then man, was but fondly invented. Esteeming therfore to have asserted thus an injur'd law of *Moses*, from the unwarranted and guilty name of a dispensation, to be again a most equall and requisite law, we have the word of Christ himself, that he came not to alter the least tittle of it; and signifies no small displeasure against him that shall teach to do so. On which relying, I shall not much waver to affirm, that those words which are made to intimate, as if they forbad all divorce but for adultery (though *Moses* have constituted otherwise) those words tak'n circumscriptly, without regard to any precedent law of *Moses*, or attestation of Christ himself, or without care to preserve those his fundamental and superior laws of nature and charity, to which all other ordinances give up their seals, are as much against plain equity, and the mercy of religion, as those words of *Take, eat, this is my body*, elementally understood, are against nature and sense.

And surely the restoring of this degraded law, hath well recompenc't the diligence was us'd by enlightning us further to find out wherfore Christ took off the Pharises from alleging the law, and referr'd them to the first institution, not condemning, altering, or abolishing this precept of divorce, which is plainly moral, for that were against his truth, his promise, and his prophetick office; but knowing how fallaciously they had cited, and conceal'd the particular and natural reason of the Law, that they might justifie any froward reason of their own, he lets goe that sophistry unconvinc't, for that had bin to teach them else, which his purpose was not. And since they had tak'n a liberty which the law gave not, he amuses and repells their tempting pride with a perfection of Paradise, which the law requir'd not; not therby to oblige our performance to that wherto the law never enjoyn'd the fal'n estate of man: for if the first institution must make wedlock; what ever happen, inseparable to us, it must make it also as perfect, as meetly helpfull, and as comfortable, as God promis'd it should be, at least in some degree; otherwise it is not

equal or proportionable to the strength of man, that he should be reduc't into such indissoluble bonds to his assured misery, if all the other conditions of that cov'nant be manifestly alter'd.

CHAP. XVI.

How to be understood that they must be one flesh: and how that those whom God hath joyn'd man should not sunder.

NExt he saith, *they must be one flesh*; which, when all conjecturing is don, will be found to import no more but to make legitimate and good the carnal act, which els might seem to have somthing of pollution in it: and infers thus much over, that the fit union of their souls be such as may even incorporate them to love and amity; but that can never be where no correspondence is of the minde; nay instead of being one flesh, they will be rather two carkasses chain'd unnaturally together; or as it may happ'n, a living soule bound to a dead corps, a punishment too like that inflicted by the tyrant *Mezentius*; so little worthy to be receiv'd as that remedy of lonelinesse which God meant us. Since we know it is not the joyning of another body will remove lonelinesse, but the uniting of another compliable[138] mind; and that it is no blessing but a torment, nay a base and brutish condition to be one flesh, unless where nature can in some measure fix a unity of disposition. The meaning therfore of these words, *For this cause shall a man leave his father and his mother, and shall cleave to his wife*, was first to shew us the deer affection which naturally grows in every not unnatural mariage, ev'n to the leaving of parents, or other familiarity whatsoever: next, it justifies a man in so doing, that nothing is done undutifully to father or mother. But he that should be here sternly commanded to cleave to his error, a disposition which to his he finds will never cement a quotidian of sorrow and discontent in his house, let us be excus'd to pause a little and bethink us every way round ere wee lay such a flat solecisme upon the gracious, and certainly not inexorable, not ruthlesse and flinty ordinance of marriage. For if the meaning of these words must be thus blockt up within their owne letters from all equity and fair deduction, they will serve then well indeed their turn, who affirme divorce to have been granted onely for wives; whenas we see no word of this text bindes women, but men onely, what it binds. No marvell then if *Salomith* sister to *Herod*, sent a writ of ease[139] to *Costobarus* her husband; which, as *Josephus*

---

[137]In no way.

[138]Compliant, agreeable.
[139]"A certificate of discharge from employment; transf. a 'bill of divorcement'" (OED "writ" 9).

there attests, was lawfull onely to men. No marvell though *Placidia*, the sister of *Honorius* threat'n'd the like to Earle *Constantius*, for a triviall cause, as *Photius* relates from *Olympiodorus*. No marvell any thing if letters must be turn'd into palisadoes to stake out all requisite sense from entring to their due enlargement.

Lastly, Christ himselfe tells who should not bee put asunder, namely those whom God hath joyn'd. A plain solution of this great controversie, if men would but use their eyes; for when is it that God may bee said to joyn, when the parties and their friends consent? No surely, for that may concurre to lewdest ends. Or is it when Church rites are finisht? Neither; for the efficacie of those depends upon the presupposed fitnesse of either party. Perhaps after carnall knowledge? Least of all; for that may joyn persons whom neither law nor nature dares joyn: tis left, that only then, when the minds are fitly dispos'd, and enabl'd to maintain a cheerfull conversation, to the solace and love of each other, according as God intended and promis'd in the very first foundation of matrimony, *I will make him a help meet for him*, for surely what God intended and promis'd, that onely can be thought to bee his joyning, and not the contrary. So likewise the Apostle witnesseth, 1 *Cor.* 7. 15. that in mariage *God hath call'd us to peace.* And doubtlesse in what respect he hath call'd us to mariage, in that also hee hath joyn'd us. The rest whom either disproportion[140] or deadnesse of spirit, or something distastfull and averse in the immutable bent of nature renders conjugall, error may have joyn'd, but God never joyn'd against the meaning of his own ordinance. And if he joynd them not, then is there no power above their own consent to hinder them from unjoyning, when they cannot reap the sobrest ends of being together in any tolerable sort. Neither can it be said properly that such twain were ever divorc't, but only parted from each other, as two persons unconjunctive and unmariable together. But if, whom God hath made a fit help, frowardnesse or private injuries hath made unfit, that being the secret of mariage God can better judge then man, neither is man indeed fit or able to decide this matter: however it be, undoubtedly a peacefull divorce is a lesse evill, and lesse in scandall then a hatefull hard-hearted and destructive continuance of mariage in the judgement of *Moses* and of Christ, that justifies him in choosing the lesse evill, which if it were an honest and civill prudence in the law, what is there in the Gospell forbidding such a kind of legall wisdom, though wee should admit the common Expositers?

---

[140]A capital letter appears in "disproPortion" in Bodleian, here corrected.

CHAP. XVI.

The sentence of Christ concerning divorce how to be expounded. What Grotius *hath observ'd. Other additions.*

Having thus unfolded those ambiguous reasons, wherewith Christ, as his wont was, gave to the Pharises that came to sound him, such an answer as they deserv'd, it will not be uneasie to explain the sentence it selfe that now follows; *Whosoever shall put away his wife, except it be for fornication, and shall marry another, committeth adultery.* First therfore I will set down what is observ'd by *Grotius* upon this point, a man of generall learning. Next I produce what mine own thoughts gave me, before I had seen his annotations. *Origen,* saith he, notes that Christ nam'd adultery rather as one example of other like cases, then as one only exception. And that is frequent, not only in human but in divine Laws, to expresse one kind of fact, wherby other causes of like nature may have the like plea: as *Exod.* 21. 18, 19, 20, 26. *Deut.* 19. 5. And from the maxims of civil Law he shews that ev'n in sharpest penal laws, the same reason hath the same right: and in gentler Lawes, that from like causes to like the Law interprets rightly. But it may be objected, saith hee, that nothing destroyes the end of wedlock so much as adultery. To which he answers, that mariage was not ordaind only for copulation, but for mutuall help and comfort of life; and if we mark diligently the nature of our Saviours commands, wee shall finde that both their beginning and their end consists in charity; whose will is that wee should so be good to others, as that wee bee not cruell to our selves. And hence it appeares why *Marke,* and *Luke,* and S. *Paul* to the *Cor.* mentioning this precept of Christ, adde no exception: because exceptions that arise from naturall equity, are included silently under generall terms: it would bee consider'd therfore whether the same equity may not have place in other cases lesse frequent. Thus farre he. From hence, is what I adde: first, that this saying of Christ, as it is usually expounded, can be no law at all, that a man for no cause should separate but for adultery, except it bee a supernaturall law, not binding us as we now are had it bin the law of nature, either the Jews, or some other wise and civill nation would have pres't it: or let it be so; yet that law, *Deut.* 24. 1. wherby a man hath leave to part, when as for just and naturall cause discover'd he cannot love, is a law ancienter and deeper ingrav'n in blameles nature then the other: therfore the inspired Law-giver Moses took care that this should be specify'd and allow'd; the other he let vanish in silence, not once repeated in the volume of his law, ev'n as the reason of it vanisht with Paradise. Secondly, this can be no new command, for the Gospel enjoyns no new morality, save only the infinit enlargement of charity, which in this respect is call'd the *new commandement* by S. *John*; as being the accomplishment of every command. Thirdly, It is no command of perfection further then it partakes of charity, which is *the bond of perfection*. Those commands therfore which compell us to self cruelty above our strength, so hardly will help forward to perfection, that they hinder and set backward in all the common rudiments of Christianity, as was prov'd. It being thus clear, that the words of Christ can be no kind of command, as they are vulgarly tak'n, we shall now see in what sence they may be a command, and that an excellent one, the same with that of *Moses*, and no other. *Moses* had granted that only for a natural annoyance, defect, or dislike, whether in body or mind (for so the Hebrew words plainly note) which a man could not force himselfe to live with, he might give a bill of divorce, therby forbidding any other cause wherin amendment or reconciliation might have place. This Law the Pharises depraving, extended to any slight contentious cause whatsoever. Christ therfore seeing where they halted, urges the negative part of that law, which is necessarily understood (for the determinate permission of *Moses* binds them from further licence) and checking their supercilious drift, declares that no accidental, temporary, or reconcileable offence, except fornication, can justify a divorce: he touches not here those natural and perpetual hindrances of society, whether in body or mind, which are not to be remov'd; for such, as they are aptest to cause an unchangeable offence, so are they not capable of reconcilement because not of amendment; they do not break indeed, but they annihilate the bands of mariage more then adultery. For that fault committed argues not alwaies a hatred either natural or incidental[141] against whom it is committed; neither does it inferre a disability of all future helpfulnes, or loyalty, or loving agreement, being once past, and pardon'd, where it can be pardon'd: but that which naturally distasts, and *finds no favour in the eyes* of matrimony, can never be conceal'd, never appeas'd, never intermitted, but proves a perpetuall nullity of love and contentment, a solitude, and dead vacation[142] of all acceptable conversing. *Moses* therfore permits divorce, but in cases only that have no hands to joyn, and more need separating then adultery. Christ forbids it, but in matters only that may accord, and those lesse then fornication. Thus is *Moses* Law here plainly confirm'd, and those causes which he permitted, not a jot gainsaid. And that this is the true meaning of

this place I prove by no lesse an Author then S. *Paul* himself, 1 *Cor.* 7. 10, 11. upon which text Interpreters agree that the Apostle only repeats the precept of Christ: where while he speaks of *the wives reconcilement to her husband*, he puts it out of controversie, that our Saviour meant chiefly matters of strife and reconcilement: of which sort he would not that any difference should be the occasion of divorce, except fornication. And that we may learn better how to value a grave and prudent law of *Moses*, and how unadvisedly we smatter with our lips, when we talk of Christs abolishing any Judiciall law of his great Father, except in some circumstances which are Judaicall rather then Judicial, and need no abolishing, but cease of themselvs, I say again, that this recited law of *Moses* contains a cause of divorce greater beyond compare then that for adultery; and whoso cannot so conceive it, errs and wrongs exceedingly a law of deep wisdom for want of well fadoming. For let him mark no man urges the just divorcing of adultery, as it is a sin, but as it is an injury to mariage; and though it be but once committed, and that without malice, whether through importunity or opportunity, the Gospel does not therfore disswade him who would therfore divorce; but that natural hatred whenever it arises, is a greater evil in mariage, then the accident of adultery, a greater defrauding, a greater injustice, and yet not blameable, he who understands not after all this representing, I doubt his will like a hard spleen draws faster then his understanding can well sanguifie. Nor did that man ever know or feel what it is to love truly, nor ever yet comprehend in his thoughts what the true intent of mariage is. And this also will be somwhat above his reach, but yet no lesse a truth for lack of his perspective, that as no man apprehends what vice is, so well as he who is truly vertuous, no man knows hel like him who converses most in heav'n, so there is none that can estimate the evil and the affliction of a naturall hatred in matrimony, unlesse he have a soul gentle anough and spacious anough to contemplate what is true love.

And the reason why men so disesteem this wise judging Law of God, and count hate, or the *not finding of favour*, as it is there term'd, a humorous, a dishonest, and slight cause of divorce, is because themselves apprehend so little of what true concord means: for if they did they would be juster in their ballancing between natural hatred and casuall adultery;[143] this being but a transient injury, and soon amended, I mean as to the party against whom the trespasse is: but the other being an unspeakable and unremitting sorrow and

---

[141]Milton corrected the mispelling "indicental" in the Bodleian copy, in the margin, apparently to the "incidental" that I have printed.
[142]Cessation.

---

[143]Compare "Casual fruition" in *Paradise Lost* 4.767.

offence, wherof no amends can be made, no cure, no ceasing but by divorce, which like a divine touch in one moment heals all; and like the word of God, in one instant hushes outrageous tempests into a sudden stilnesse and peacefull calm. Yet all this so great a good of Gods own enlarging to us, is by the hard rains[144] of them that sit us, wholly diverted and imbezzl'd from us. Maligners of mankind! But who hath taught you to mangle thus, and make more gashes in the miseries of a blamelesse creature, with the leaden daggers of your literall decrees, to whose ease you cannot adde the tithe of one small atome, but by letting alone your unhelpfull Surgery. As for such as think wandring concupiscence to bee here newly and more precisely forbidd'n then it was before, if the Apostle can convince them; we know that we are to *know lust by the law*, and not by any new discovery of the Gospel. The Law of *Moses* knew what it permitted, and the Gospel knew what it forbid; hee that under a peevish conceit of debarring concupiscence, shall goe about to make a novice of *Moses*, (not to say a worse thing for reverence sake) and such a one of God himselfe as is a horror to think, to bind our Saviour in the default of a down-right promise breaking, and to bind the disunions of complaining nature in chains together, and curb them with a banon bit, tis he that commits all the whordom and adultery, which himselfe adjudges, besides the former guilt so manifold that lies upon him. And if none of these considerations with all their wait and gravity, can avail to the dispossessing him of his pretious literalism, let some one or other entreat him but to read on in the same 19. of *Math.* till he come to that place that sayes, *Some make themselves Eunuchs for the kingdom of heavns sake.* And if then he please to make use of *Origens* knife,[145] he may doe well to be his own carver.

CHAP. XVIII.

Whether the words of our Saviour be rightly expounded only of actual fornication to be the cause of divorce. The Opinion of Grotius, *with other reasons.*

BUt because we know that Christ never gave a Judiciall Law, and that the word *fornication* is variously significant in Scripture, it wil be much right done to our Saviours words, to consider diligently, whether it be meant heer that nothing but actuall fornication prov'd by witnes can warrant a divorce, for so our cannon law judges. Nevertheless as I find that *Grotius* on this place hath observ'd the Christian Emperours, *Theodosius* the second and *Justinian*, men of high wisdom and reputed piety, decreed it to bee a divorsive fornication, if the wife attempted either against the knowledge, or obstinatly against the will of her husband, such things as gave open suspicion of adulterizing: as the wilfull haunting of feasts, and invitations with men not of her neer kindred, the lying forth of her house without probable cause, the frequenting of Theaters against her husbands mind, her endeavour to prevent or destroy conception. Hence that of Jerom, *Where fornication is suspected, the wife may lawfully be divorc't*; not that every motion of a jealous mind should be regarded, but that it should not be exacted to prove all things by the visibility of Law witnessing, or els to hood-wink the mind: for the law is not able to judge of these things but by the rule of equity, and by permitting a wise man to walk the middle way of prudent circumspection, neither wretchedly jealous, nor stupidly and tamely patient. To this purpose hath *Grotius* in his notes. He shews also that fornication is tak'n in Scripture for such a continual headstrong behaviour, as tends to plain contempt of the husband: and proves it out of *Judges* 19. 2. where the Levites wife is said to have plaid the whoor against him; which *Josephus* and the *Septuagint*, with the *Chaldean*, interpret onely of stubbornesse and rebellion against her husband: and to this I adde that *Kimchi*, and the two other Rabbies who glosse the text, are in the same opinion. *Ben Gersom* reasons, that had it bin whoordom, a Jew and a Levit would have disdain'd to fetch her again. And this I shall contribute, that had it been whoordom, she would have chosen any other place to run to, then to her fathers house, it being so infamous for an Hebrew woman to play the harlot, and so opprobrious to the parents. Fornication then in this place of the *Judges* is understood for stubborn disobedience against the husband, and not for adultery. A sin of that sudden activity as to be already committed, when no more is done, but onely lookt unchastly: which yet I should bee loath to judge worthy a divorce, though in our Saviour's language it bee called adultery. Neverthelesse when palpable and frequent signs are giv'n, the law of God, *Numb.* 5. so far gave way to the jealousie of a man as that the woman set before the Sanctuary with her head uncover'd, was adjur'd by the Priest to swear whether she were false or no; and constrain'd to drink that *bitter water* with an undoubted *curse of rottennesse and tympany* to follow, unlesse she were innocent. And the jealous man had not bin guiltles before God, as seems by the last verse, if having such a suspition in his head, he should neglect his triall; which if to this day it be not to be us'd, or be thought as uncertain of effect as our antiquated law of *Ordalium*, yet all equity will judge that many

---

[144]Reins, as in the reins controlling a horse.
[145]Taking the biblical passage very seriously, the church father Origen castrated himself.

adulterous demeanors which are of lewd suspicion and example, may be held sufficient to incurre a divorce, though the act it selfe hath not been provd. And seeing the generosity of our Nation is so, as to account no reproach more abominable, then to bee nicknam'd the husband of an adultresse, that our law should not be as ample as the Law of God to vindicate a man from that ignoble sufferance, is our barbarous unskilfulnesse, not considering that the law should be exasperated according to our estimation of the injury. And if it must be suffer'd till the act be visibly prov'd, *Salomon* himselfe, whose judgement will be granted to surpasse the acutenesse of any Canonist, confesses, *Pro.* 30. 19. 20. that for the act of adultery it is as difficult to be found as the *track of an Eagle in the aire, or the way of a ship in the Sea*: so that a man may be put to unmanly indignities, ere it be found out. This therfore may bee anough to inform us, that divorsive adultery is not limited by our Saviour to the utmost act, and that to be attested alwayes by eye witnesse, but may bee extended also to divers obvious actions, which either plainly lead to adultery, or give such presumption, wherby sensible men may suspect the deed to bee already don. And this the rather may bee thought, in that our Saviour chose to use the word *Fornication*, which word is found to signifie other matrimoniall transgressions of main breach to that covnant besides actuall adultery. For that sinne needed not the riddance of divorce, but of death by the Law, which was active ev'n till then by the example of the woman tak'n in adultery; or if the law had been dormant, our Saviour was more likely to have told them of their neglect, then to have let a capitall crime silently scape[146] into a divorce; or if it bee said his businesse was not to tell them what was criminall in the civill Courts, but what was sinfull at the barre of conscience, how dare they then having no other ground then these our Saviours words, draw that into triall of law, which both by *Moses* and our Saviour was left to the jurisdiction of conscience? But wee take from our Saviour, say they, only that it was adultery and our Law of it selfe applies the punishment. But by their leave that so argue, the great Law-giver of all the world who knew best what was adultery both to the Jew and to the Gentile appointed no such applying, and never likes when mortall men will be vainly presuming to out-strip his justice.

CHAP. XIX.

Christs manner of teaching. S. Paul adds to the matter of divorce without command, to shew the matter to be of equity, not of rigor. That the bondage of a Christian may be as much, and his peace as little in some other mariages besides idolatrous: If those arguments therfore be good in that one case, why not in those other: therfore the apostle himselfe adds ν τω τοι τοις.[147]

THus at length wee see both by this and by other places, that there is scarce any one saying in the Gospel but must bee read with limitations and distinctions, to bee rightly understood; for Christ gives no full comments or continued discourses, but as *Demetrius* the Rhetoritian phrases it, speaks oft in Monosyllables, like a maister, scattering the heavenly grain of his doctrine like pearl heer and there, which requires a skilfull and laborious gatherer, who must compare the words he findes, with other precepts, with the end of every ordinance, and with the generall *analogie* of Evangelick doctrine: otherwise many particular sayings would bee but strange repugnant riddles; and the Church would offend in granting divorce for frigidity, which is not here excepted with adultery, but by them added. And this was it undoubtedly which gave reason to S. *Paul* of his own authority, as hee professes, and without command from the Lord, to enlarge the seeming construction of those places in the Gospel; by adding a case wherin a person deserted, which is somthing less then divorc't, may lawfully marry again. And having declar'd his opinion in one case, he leaves a furder liberty for Christian prudence to determine in cases of like importance; using words so plain as not to be shifted off, *that a brother or a sister is not under bondage in such cases*; adding also, that *God hath called us to peace* in mariage.

Now if it be plain that a Christian may be brought into unworthy *bondage*, and his religious *peace* not onely interrupted now and then, but perpetually and finally hinder'd in wedlock by mis-yoking with a diversity of nature as well as of religion, the reasons of S. *Paul* cannot be made speciall to that one case of infidelity, but are of equal moment to a divorce, wherever Christian liberty and peace are without fault equally obstructed. That the ordinance which God gave to our comfort, may not be pinn'd upon us to our undeserved thraldom; to be coopt up as it were in mockery of wedlock, to a perpetual betrothed lonelines and discontent, if nothing worse ensue. There being nought els of mariage left between such, but a dis-

---

[146]Escape, transform itself.

[147]"In such cases" (see 1 Corinthians 7.15).

pleasing and forc't remedy against the sting of a bruit desire: which fleshly accustoming without the souls union and commixture of intellectuall delight, as it is rather a soiling then a fulfilling of mariage-rites, so it is anough[148] to imbase the mettle[149] of a generous spirit, and sinks him to a low and vulgar pitch of endeavour in all his actions, or, which is wors, leavs him in a dispairing plight of abject & hardn'd thoughts: which condition rather then a good man should fal into a man usefull in the service of God and mankind, Christ himself hath taught us to dispence with the most sacred ordinance of his worship, even for a bodily healing to dispence with that holy and speculative rest of Sabbath, much more then with the erroneous observance of an ill-knotted mariage, for the sustaining of an overcharg'd faith and perseverance.

CHAP. XX.

The meaning of S. Paul, *that* Charity beleeveth all things. *What is to be said to the licence which is vainly fear'd will grow hereby. What to those who never have don prescribing patience in this case. The Papist most severe against divorce: yet most easie to all licence. Of all the miseries in mariage God is to be clear'd, and the faults to be laid on man's unjust laws.*

A Nd though bad causes would take licence by this pretext, if that cannot be remedied, upon their conscience be it, who shall so doe. This was that hardnes of heart, and abuse of a good law which *Moses* was content to suffer, rather then good men should not have it at all to use needfully. And he who to run after one lost sheep, left ninety nine of his own flock at random in the wildernes, would little perplex his thought for the obduring of nine hunder'd and ninety such as will daily take worse liberties, whether they have permission or not. To conclude, as without charity God hath giv'n no commandment to men, so without it, neither can men rightly beleeve any commandment giv'n. For every act of true faith, as well that wherby we beleeve the law, as that wherby we endeavour the law, is wrought in us by charity, according to that in the divine hymne of S. *Paul, 1 Cor. 13. Charity beleeveth all things*: not as if she were so credulous, which is the exposition hitherto current, for that were a trivial praise, but to teach us that charity is the high governesse of our beleefe, and that we cannot safely assent to any precept writt'n in the Bible, but as charity commends it to us. Which

agrees with that of the same Apostle to the *Ephes.* 4. 14. 15. where he tells us that the way to get a sure un-doubted knowledge of things, is to hold that for truth, which accords most with charity. Whose unerring guidance and conduct having follow'd as a load-starre,[150] with all diligence and fidelity in this question, I trust, through the help of that illuminating Spirit which hath favour'd me,[151] to have done no every days work: in asserting after many ages the words of Christ with other Scriptures of great concernment, from burdensom & remorsles obscurity, tangl'd with manifold repugnances, to their native lustre and consent between each other: hereby also dissolving tedious and *Gordian* difficulties, which have hitherto molested the Church of God, and are now decided, not with the sword of *Alexander,* but with the immaculate hands of charity, to the unspeak-able good of Christendome. And let the extreme lit-eralist sit down now and revolve whether this in all necessity be not the due result of our Saviours words: or if he persist to be otherwise opinion'd, let him well advise, lest thinking to gripe fast[152] the Gospel, he be found in stead with the canon law in his fist: whose boisterous edicts tyrannizing the blessed ordinance of mariage into the quality of a most unnatural and unchristianly yoke, have giv'n the flesh this advantage to hate it, and turn aside, oft times unwillingly, to all dissolute uncleannesse, even till punishment it self is weary, and overcome by the incredible frequency of trading lust and uncontroull'd adulteries. Yet men whose creed is custom, I doubt not but wil be still endeavouring to hide the sloth of their own timorous capacities with this pretext, that for all this tis better to endure with patience and silence this affliction which God hath sent. And I agree tis true, if this be exhorted and not enjoyn'd; but withall it will be wisely don to be as sure as may be, that what mans iniquity hath laid on, be not imputed to Gods sending, least under the colour of an affected patience we detain our selves at the gulphs mouth of many hideous temptations, not to be withstood without proper gifts, which, as *Perkins* well notes, God gives not ordinarily, no not to most earnest prayers. Therfore we pray, *Lead us not into Temptation,* a vain prayer, if having led our selves thither, we love to stay in that perilous condition. God sends remedies, as well as evills; under which he who lies and groans, that

---

[148]Spelled "anongh," with an inverted "u," in the Bodleian copy and here corrected.
[149]The phrase should be read as "embase (devalue) the metal," as in debasing coins by adding cheaper alloys (see *OED* "embase" 4).

[150]A loadstar or lodestar metaphorically was a guiding light, having associations with the pole star.
[151]Milton seems to be referring to a Spirit similar to that which he addresses in the invocations of *Paradise Lost*. The private search for "inner light," Puritan evidence of the presence of God in each individual, may be operant here.
[152]"To grip closely."

may lawfully acquit himselfe, is accessory to his own ruin: nor will it excuse him, though he suffer through a sluggish fearfulnes to search throughly what is lawfull, for feare of disquieting the secure falsity of an old opinion. Who doubts not but that it may be piously said, to him who would dismiss frigidity, bear your trial, take it, as if God would have you live this life of continence: if he exhort this, I hear him as an Angel, though he speak without warrant: but if he would compell me, I know him for Satan. To him who divorces an adulteresse, Piety might say; Pardon her; you may shew much mercy, you may win a soul: yet the law both of God and man leaves it freely to him. For God loves not to plow out the heart of our endeavours with over-hard and sad tasks. God delights not to make a drudge of vertue, whose actions must be al elective & unconstrain'd. Forc't *vertue* is as a *bolt* overshot it goes neither forward nor backward, and does no good as it stands. Seeing therfore that neither Scripture nor reason hath laid this unjust austerity upon divorce, we may resolve that nothing else hath wrought it, but that letter-bound servility of the Canon Doctors, supposing mariage to be a Sacrament, and out of the art they have to lay unnecessary burdens upon all men, to make a fair shew in the fleshly observance of matrimony, though peace and love with all other conjugall respects fare never so ill. And indeed the Papists who are the strictest forbidders of divorce, are the easiest libertines to admit of grosser uncleannesse; as if they had a designe by making wedlock a supportlesse yoke, to violate it most, under colour of preserving it most inviolable: and withall delighting, as their mystery is, to make men the day-labourers of their own afflictions, as if there were such a scarcity of miseries from abroad, that we should be made to melt our choycest home blessings, and coin them into crosses, for want wherby to hold commerce with patience. If any therfore who shall hap to read this discourse, hath been through misadventure ill ingag'd in this contracted evill here complain'd of, and finds the fits and workings of a high impatience frequently upon him, of all those wild words which men in misery think to ease themselves by uttering, let him not op'n his lips against the providence of heav'n, or tax the wayes of God and his divine truth: for they are equal, easie, and not burdensome; nor doe they ever crosse the just and reasonable desires of men, nor involve this our portion of mortall life, into a necessity of sadnesse and malecontent, by laws commanding over the unreducible *antipathies* of nature sooner or later found: but allow us to remedy and shake off those evills into which human[153] error hath led us through the midst of our best intentions; and to support our incident extremities by that authentick precept of soveran charity; whose grand commission is to doe and to dispose over all the ordinances of God to man; that love & truth may advance each other to everlasting. While we[154] literally superstitious through customary faintnesse of heart, not venturing to pierce with our free thoughts into the full latitude of nature and religion, abandon our selves[155] to serve under the tyranny of usurpt opinions, suffering those ordinances which were allotted to our solace and reviving, to trample over us and hale us into a multitude of sorrowes, which God never meant us. And where he sets us in a fair allowance of way, with honest liberty and prudence to our guard, we never leave subtilizing and casuisting till we have straitn'd and par'd that liberal path into a razors edge to walk on, between a precipice of unnecessary mischief on either side: and starting at every false Alarum we doe not know which way to set a foot forward with manly confidence and Christian resolution, through the confused ringing in our eares of *panick*[156] scruples and amazements.

CHAP. XXI.

That the matter of divorce is not to be try'd by law, but by conscience, as many other sins are. The Magistrate can only see that the condition of divorce be just and equall. The opinion of Fagius, *and the reasons of this assertion.*

ANother act of papall encroachment it was, to pluck the power and arbitrement of divorce from the master of family, into whose hands God and the law of all Nations had put it, and Christ so left it, preaching onely to the conscience, and not authorizing a judiciall Court to tosse about and divulge the unaccountable and secret reasons of disaffection between man and wife, as a thing most improperly answerable to any such kind of triall. But the Popes of *Rome* perceiving the great revenue and high authority it would give them ev'n over Princes, to have the judging and deciding of such a main consequence in the life of man as was divorce, wrought so upon the superstition of those ages, as to divest them of that right which God from the beginning

---

[153]There was an inverted letter in "hnman" in Bodleian, which I have corrected.

[154]In modern usage, a comma would help at this point; the text seems corrupt on this page, as evidenced in the note just below.

[155]Though Milton missed the inverted letter above, he did correct "seves" in this line to "selves" in the margin of Bodleian, after he had crossed out and put an X above "seves."

[156]Scruples caused by the god Pan, strictly speaking, though here the noun used as adjective seems to mean something like "chaotic."

had entrusted to the husband: by which meanes they subjected that ancient and naturally domestick prerogative to an externall and unbefitting Judicature. For although differences in divorce about Dowries, Jointures, and the like, besides the punishing of adultery, ought not to passe without referring, if need be, to the Magistrate, yet that the absolute and final hindring of divorce cannot belong to any civil or earthly power, against the will and consent of both parties, or of the husband alone, some reasons will be here urg'd as shall not need to decline the touch. But first I shall recite what hath bin already yeilded[157] by others in favour of this opinion. *Grotius* and many more agree, that notwithstanding what Christ spake therin to the conscience, the Magistrate is not therby enjoyn'd ought[158] against the preservation of civil peace, of equity, and of convenience. Among these *Fagius* is most remarkable, and gives the same liberty of pronouncing divorce to the Christian Magistrate as the Mosaick had. *For whatever* saith he, *Christ spake to the regenerat, the Judge hath to deal with the vulgar: if therfore any through hardnesse of heart will not be a tolerable wife to her husband, it will be lawfull as well now as of old to passe the bill of divorce, not by privat, but by publicke authority. Nor doth Man separate them then, but God by his law of divorce giv'n by* Moses. *What can hinder the Magistrate from so doing, to whose government all outward things are subject, to separate and remove from perpetual vexation and no small danger, those bodies whose minds are already separate: it being his office to procure peaceable and convenient living in the Common-wealth; and being as certain also, that they so necessarily separated cannot all receive a single life.* And this I observe that our divines doe generally condemn separation of bed and board, without the liberty of second choice: if that therfore in some cases be most purely necessary, as who so blockish[159] to deny, then is this also as needfull. Thus farre by others is already well stept,[160] to inform us that divorce is not a matter of Law but of Charity: if there remain a furlong yet to end the question, these following reasons may serve to gain it with any apprehension not too unlearned, or too wayward. First because ofttimes the causes of seeking divorce reside so deeply in the radical and innocent affections of nature, as is not within the diocese of Law to tamper with. Other relations may aptly anough be held together by a civil and vertuous love. But the duties of man and wife

are such as are chiefly conversant in that love, which is most ancient and meerly naturall; whose two prime statutes are to joyn it self to that which is good and acceptable and friendly; and to turn aside and depart from what is disagreeable, displeasing and unlike: of the two this latter is the strongest, and most equal to be regarded: for although a man may often be unjust in seeking that which he loves, yet he can never be unjust or blamable in retiring from his endles trouble and distast, whenas his tarrying can redound to no true content on either side. Hate is of all things the mightiest divider, nay, is division it self. To couple hatred therfore though wedlock try all her golden links, and borrow to her aid all the iron manacles and fetters of Law, it does but seek to twist a rope of sand, which was a task, they say, that pos'd[161] the divell. And that sluggish feind[162] in hell, *Ocnus,* whom the Poems tell of, brought his idle cordage to as good effect, which never serv'd to bind with, but to feed the Asse that stood at his elbow. And that the restrictive Law against divorce, attains as little to bind any thing truly in a disjoynted mariage, or to keep it bound, but servs only to feed the ignorance, and definitive impertinence of a doltish Canon, were no absurd allusion. To hinder therfore those deep and serious regresses of nature in a reasonable soul parting from that mistak'n help which he justly seeks in a person created for him, recollecting himself from an unmeet help which was never meant, and to detain him by compulsion in such a unpredestin'd misery as this, is in diameter against both nature and institution: but to interpose a jurisdictive power upon the inward and irremediable disposition of man, to command love and sympathy, to forbid dislike against the guiltles instinct of nature, is not within the Province of any Law to reach, and were indeed an uncommodious rudenesse, not a just power: for that Law may bandy with nature, and traverse her sage motions, was an error in *Callicles* the Rhetorician, whom *Socrates* from high principles confutes in *Plato's Gorgias.* If therfore divorce may be so naturall, and that law and nature are not to goe contrary, then to forbid divorce compulsively, is not only against nature, but against law.

Next it must be remember'd that all law is for some good that may be frequently attain'd without the admixture of a worse inconvenience; and therfore many grosse faults, as ingratitude and the like, which are too farre within the soul, to be cur'd by constraint of law, are left only to be wrought on by conscience and per-swasion. Which made *Aristotle* in the 10th of his *Ethicks*

---

[157]The rare occurrence of a Miltonic spelling in what would normally be an "-ie-" word.
[158]Aught, in any way.
[159]Blockheaded, stupid.
[160]Well-advanced (*OED* "Step" 3.d).

---

[161]Puzzled, confused.
[162]Another Miltonic spelling seems to have slipped through.

to *Nicomachus*, aim at a kind of division of law into private or perswasive, and publick or compulsive. Hence it is that the law forbidding divorce, never attains to any good end of such prohibition, but rather multiplies evil. For if natures resistlesse sway in love or hate bee once compell'd, it grows carelesse of it selfe, vitious, uselesse to friend, unserviceable and spiritlesse to the Common-wealth. Which Moses rightly foresaw, and all wise Law-givers that ever knew man, what kind of creature he was. The Parlament also and Clergy of England were not ignorant of this, when they consented that *Harry* the eighth might put away his Queen *Anne* of *Cleve*, whom he could not like after he had been wedded half a yeare; unlesse it were that contrary to the proverb, they made a necessity of that which might have been a vertue in them to doe. For even the freedome and eminence of mans creation gives him to be a Law in this matter to himselfe, being the head of the other Sex which was made for him: whom therefore though he ought not to injure, yet neither should he be forc't to retain in society to his own overthrow, nor to heare any judge therin above himselfe. It being also an unseemly affront to the sequestr'd and vail'd modesty of that sex, to have her unpleasingnesse and other concealments bandied up and down, and aggravated in open Court by those hir'd masters of tongue-fence. Such uncomely exigencies it befell no lesse a Majesty then *Henry* the eighth to be reduc't to; who finding just reason in his conscience to forgoe his brothers wife, after many indignities of being deluded, and made a boy of by those his two Cardinall Judges, was constrain'd at last, for want of other proof that she had been carnally known by Prince *Arthur*, ev'n to uncover the nakednesse of that vertuous Lady, and to recite openly the obscene evidence of his brothers Chamberlain. Yet it pleas'd God to make him see all the tyranny of *Rome*, by discovering this which they exercis'd over divorce; and to make him the beginner of a reformation to this whole Kingdome, by first asserting into his *familiary*[163] power the right of just divorce. Tis true, an adultresse cannot be sham'd anough by any publick proceeding: but that woman whose honour is not appeach't, is lesse injur'd by a silent dismission, being otherwise not illiberally dealt with, then to endure a clamouring debate of utterlesse[164] things, in a busines of that civill secrecy and difficult discerning, as not to bee over-much question'd by neerest friends. Which drew that answer from the greatest and worthiest *Roman* of his time,

Paulus Emilius, being demanded why hee would put away his wife for no visible reason? *This Shoo* said he, and held it out on his foot, *is a neat shoo, a new shoo, and yet none of you know where it wrings me*: much lesse by the unfamiliar cognisance of a fee'd Gamester can such a private difference be examin'd, neither ought it.

Again, if Law aim at the firm establishment and preservation of matrimoniall faith, wee know that cannot thrive under violent means, but is the more violated. It is not when two unfortunately met are by the Canon forc't to draw in that yoke an unmercifull dayes work of sorrow till death unharnesse 'em, that then the Law keeps mariage most unviolated and un-brok'n: but when the Law takes order that mariage be accountant and responsible to perform that society, whether it be religious, civill, or corporal, which may be consciationably requir'd and claim'd therein, or else to be dissolv'd if it cannot be undergone: This is to make mariage most indissoluble, by making it a just and equall dealer, a performer of those due helps which instituted the covnant, being otherwise a most unjust contract, and no more to be maintain'd under tuition[165] of law, then the vilest fraud or cheat, or theft that may be committed. But because this is such a secret kind of fraud or theft, as cannot bee discern'd by Law, but only by the plaintife himself therfore to divorce was never counted a politicall or civill offence neither to *Jew* nor *Gentile*, nor any judicial intendment of Christ, further then could be discern'd to transgresse the allowance of *Moses*, which was of necessity so large, that it doth all one as if it sent back the matter undeterminable at law, and intractable by rough dealing, to have instructions and admonitions bestow'd about it by them whose spirituall office is to adjure and to denounce, and so left to the conscience. The Law can onely appoint the just and equall conditions of divorce, and is to look how it is an injury to the divorc't, which in truth it can be none, as a meer separation; for if she consent, wherin has the Law to right her? or consent not; then is it either just, and so deserv'd; or if unjust, such in all likelihood was the divorcer, and to part from an unjust man is a happinesse, and no injury to bee lamented. But suppose it be an injury, the law is not able to amend it, unles she think it other then a miserable redress to return back from whence she was expell'd, or but intreated to be gone, or else to live apart still maried without mariage, a maried widow. Last, if it be to chast'n the divorcer, what Law punishes a deed which is not morall, but natural, a deed which cannot certainly be found to be an injury, or how can it be punisht by

---

[163]Milton made up the adjective, meaning something like "familial" or "domestic," from the Latin **familiarius**.
[164]Again, Milton made up the word, meaning "unutterable" or perhaps "unspeakable."

---

[165]Custody or protection.

prohibiting the divorce, but that the innocent must equally partake both in the shame and in the smart. So that which way soever we look the Law can to no rationall purpose forbid divorce, it can only take care that the conditions of divorce be not injurious. Thus then we see the trial of law how impertinent it is to this question of divorce, how helplesse next, and then how hurtfull.

CHAP. XXII.

The last Reason, why divorce is not to be restrain'd by Law, it being against the Law of nature and of Nations. The larger proof whereof referr'd to Mr. Seldens *Book* De jure naturali & gentium. *An objection of* Paræus *answer'd. How it ought to be order'd by the Church. That this will not breed any worse inconvenience nor so bad as is now suffer'd.*

THerfore the last reason why it should not be, is the example we have, not only from the noblest and wisest Common-wealths, guided by the clearest light of human knowledge, but also from the divine testimonies of God himself, lawgiving in person to a sanctify'd people. That all this is true, whoso desires to know at large with least pains, and expects not heer overlong rehersals of that which is by others already so judiciously gather'd, let him hast'n to be acquainted with that noble volume written by our learned *Selden, Of the law of nature & of Nations*, a work more useful and more worthy to be perus'd, whosoever studies to be a great man in wisdom, equity, and justice, then all those *decretals, and sumles sums*, which the *Pontificall Clerks* have doted on, ever since that unfortunat mother famously sinn'd thrice, and dy'd impenitent of her bringing into the world those two misbegott'n infants, & for ever infants, *Lombard* & *Gratian*, him the compiler of Canon iniquity, tother the *Tubalcain* of scholastick Sophistry, whose overspreading *barbarism* hath not only infus'd their own bastardy upon the fruitfullest part of human learning; not only dissipated and dejected the clear light of nature in us, & of nations but hath tainted also the fountains of divine doctrine, & render'd the pure and solid Law of God unbeneficial to us by their calumnious dunceries. Yet this Law which their unskilfulnesse hath made liable to all ignominy, the purity and wisdom of this Law shall be the buckler[166] of our dispute. Liberty of divorce we claim not, we think not but from this Law; the dignity, the faith, the authority therof is now grown among Christians, O astonishment! a labour of no mean

difficulty and envy to defend. That it should not be counted a faltring dispence a flattring permission of sin, the bil of adultery, a snare, is the expence of all this apology. And all that we solicite is, that it may be suffer'd to stand in the place where God set it amidst the firmament of his holy Laws to shine, as it was wont, upon the weaknesses and errors of men perishing els in the sincerity of their honest purposes: for certain there is no memory of whoredoms and adulteries left among us now, when this warranted freedom of Gods own giving is made dangerous and discarded for a scrowle of licence. It must be your suffrages and Votes, O English men, that this exploded decree of God and *Moses* may scape, and come off fair without the censure of a shamefull abrogating: which, if yonder Sun ride sure, and mean not to break word with us to morrow, was never yet abrogated by our Saviour. Give sentence, if you please that the frivolous Canon may reverse the infallible judgement of *Moses* and his great director. Or if it be the reformed writers, whose doctrine perswades this rather, their reasons I dare affirm are all silenc't, unlesse it be only this. *Paræus* on the Corinthians would prove that hardnes of heart in divorce is no more now to be permitted, but to be amerc't with fine and imprisonment. I am not willing to discover the for-gettings of reverend men, yet here I must. What article or clause of the whole new Cov'nant can Paræus bring to exasperat the judicial Law, upon any infirmity under the Gospel? (I say infirmity, for if it were the high hand of sin, the Law as little would have endur'd it as the Gospel) it would not stretch to the dividing of an inheritance; it refus'd to condemn adultery, not that these things should not be don at Law, but to shew that the Gospel hath not the least influence upon judicial Courts, much lesse to make them sharper, and more heavy, lest of all to arraine before a temporal judge that which the Law without summons acquitted. But saith he, the law was the time of youth, under violent affections, the Gospel in us is mature age, and ought to subdue affections. True, and so ought the Law too, if they be found inordinat, and not meerly natural and blameles. Next I distinguish that the time of the Law is compar'd to youth, and pupillage[167] in respect of the ceremonial part, which led the Jewes as children through corporal and garish rudiments, untill the fulnes of time should reveal to them the higher lessons of faith and redemption. This is not meant of the moral part, therin it soberly concern'd them not to be babies, but to be men in good earnest: the sad and awfull[168] majesty of

---

[166]Small shield, used to ward off blows as one fought with a sword.

[167]The state of being a minor in the sight of the law.
[168]Awe-inspiring.

the Law was not to be jested with, to bring a bearded nonage[169] with lascivious dispensations before that throne, had bin a leud affront, as it is now a grosse mistake. But what discipline is this Paræus to nourish violent affections in youth, by cockring[170] and wanton indulgences, and to chastise them in mature age with a boyish rod of correction. How much more coherent is it to Scripture, that the Law as a strict Schoolmaster should have punisht every trespasse without indulgence so banefull to youth, and that the Gospel should now correct that by admonition and reproof only, in free and mature age, which was punisht with stripes in the childhood and bondage of the Law. What therfore it allow'd then so fairly, much lesse is to be whipt now, especially in penal Courts: and if it ought now to trouble the conscience, why did that angry accuser and condemner Law repreev it? So then, neither from *Moses* nor from Christ hath the Magistrate any authority to proceed against it. But what? Shall then the disposal of that power return again to the master of family? Wherfore not? Since God there put it, and the presumptuous Canon thence bereft it. This only must be provided that the ancient manner be observ'd in the presence of the Minister and other grave selected Elders; who after they shall have admonisht and prest upon him the words of our Saviour, and he shall have protested in the faith of the eternal Gospel, and the hope he has of happy resurrection, that otherwise then thus he cannot doe, and thinks himself, and this his case not contain'd in that prohibition of divorce which Christ pronounc't, the matter not being of malice, but of nature, and so not capable of reconciling; to constrain him furder were to unchristen him, to unman him, to throw the mountain of *Sinai* upon him, with the weight of the whole Law to boot, flat against the liberty and essence of the Gospel, and yet nothing[171] available either to the sanctity of mariage, the good of husband, wife, or children, nothing profitable either to Church or Common-wealth, but hurtfull and pernicious to all these respects. But this will bring in confusion. Yet these cautious mistrusters might consider, that what they thus object, lights not upon this book but upon that which I engage against them, the book of God and *Moses*, with all the wisdome and providence which had forecast the worst of confusion that could succeed, and yet thought fit of such a permission. But let them be of good cheer, it wrought so little disorder among the Jews, that from *Moses* till after the captivity, not one of the Prophets thought it worth rebuking; for that of *Malachy* well lookt into, will

appeare to be not against divorcing but rather against keeping strange Concubines, to the vexation of their *Hebrew* wives. If therefore we Christians may be thought as good and tractable as the Jews were, and certainly the prohibiters of divorce presume us to be better, then lesse confusion is to bee fear'd for this among us, then was among them. If wee bee worse, or but as bad, which lamentable examples confirm we are, then have we more, or at least as much need of this permitted law, as they to whom God therfore gave it (as they say) under a harsher covnant. Let not therfore the frailty of man goe on thus inventing needlesse troubles to it self, to groan under the fals imagination of a strictnes never impos'd from above; enjoyning that for duty which is an impossible & vain supererogating. *Be not righteous overmuch*, is the counsell of *Ecclesiastes*; *why shouldst thou destroy thy selfe?* Let us not be thus over-curious to strain at *atoms*, and yet to stop every vent and cranny of permissive liberty; lest nature wanting those needful pores and breathingplaces which God hath not debar'd our weaknesse, either suddenly break out into some wide rupture of open vice, and frantick heresie, or else inwardly fester with repining and blasphemous thoughts, under an unreasonable and fruitlesse rigor of unwarranted law. Against which evills nothing can more beseem[172] the religion of the Church, or the wisedom of the State, then to consider timely and provide. And in so doing let them not doubt, but they shall vindicate the misreputed honour of God and his great Lawgiver, by suffering him to give his own laws according to the condition of man's nature best known to him, without the unsufferable imputation of dispencing legally with many ages of ratify'd adultery. They shall recover the misattended words of Christ to the sincerity of their true sense from manifold contradictions, and shall open them with the key of charity. Many helples Christians they shall raise from the depth of sadnes and distresse, utterly unfitted as they are to serve God or man: many they shall reclaime from obscure and giddy sects, many regain from dissolute and brutish licence, many from desperate hardnes, if ever that were justly pleaded. They shall set free many daughters of *Israel*, not wanting much of her sad plight *whom Satan had bound eighteen years*. Man they shall restore to his just dignity and prerogative in nature, preferring the souls free peace before the promiscuous draining of a carnall rage. Mariage from a perilous hazard and snare, they shall reduce to bee a more certain hav'n and retirement of happy society; when they shall judge according to God and *Moses*, and

---

[169]Someone below the legal age to assume a position.
[170]Spoiling or overindulging.
[171]In no way.

[172]Become (in the sense of "be becoming to").

how not then according to Christ? when they shall judge it more wisdom and goodnes to break that covnant seemingly and keep it really, then by compulsion of law to keep it seemingly, and by compulsion of blameles nature to break it really, at least if it were ever truly joyn'd. The vigor of discipline they may then turn with better successe upon the prostitute loosenes of the times, when men finding in themselves the infirmities of former ages, shall not be constrain'd above the gift of God in them, to unprofitable and impossible observances, never requir'd from the civilest, the wisest, the holiest Nations, whose other excellencies in morall vertue they never yet could equall. Last of all, to those whose mind still is to maintain textuall restrictions, wherof the bare sound cannot consist somtimes with humanity, much lesse with charity, I would ever answer by putting them in remembrance of a command above all commands, which they seem to have forgot, and who spake it; in comparison wherof, this which they so exalt, is but a petty and subordinate precept. *Let them goe* therfore with whom I am loath to couple them, yet they will needs run into the same blindnes with the Pharises, *let them goe therfore* and consider well what this lesson means, *I will have mercy and not sacrifice*; for on that *saying all the Law and Prophets depend*, much more the Gospel whose end and excellence is mercy and peace: Or if they cannot learn that, how will they hear this, which yet I shall not doubt to leave with them as a conclusion: That God the Son hath put all other things under his own feet; but his Commandments hee hath left all under the feet of Charity.   *The end.*[173]

---

[173]Below a bar-line beneath "*The end*" is the errata list: "Page 15, line 8. *read* it the glassy Sea. p.32.l.6. *for* or, *read* nor. p.39.l.32. *for* give, *read* find. lin.34. *For* will, freewil, lin. 38. *read* he acquitts. p.51. L.26. for without a comma."

Of Education
(1644)

Milton's eight-page pamphlet *Of Education* was presented as a letter to *"Master"* Samuel Hartlib. The Prussian emigré Hartlib was what the eighteenth century would call a projector or virtuoso, interested in improving society with a countless number of experiments and inventions. With all of his many projects, his method was to disseminate information "to an inner circle of trusted advisors who responded with analysis, criticism and queries which Hartlib framed into replies" (Raylor, "Samuel Hartlib" 96). Hartlib's network of advisors included people in the Netherlands and in New England. He was interested in everything from bee-keeping to the cultivation of tobacco, from raising silkworms to harvesting fish. His service to national industry won him a pension from Parliament (Hughes 630n).

In his educational research, Hartlib had a number of friends who published nothing about the topic except with his consultation and approval. Milton was not a member of that inner circle, but Hartlib did respect Milton as an author of many books, as a traveler, as a projector of schemes for social improvement, and perhaps as a fellow-supporter of a military engine designed by Edmond Felton, who printed a description of the machine at Hartib's request employing Thomas Underhill, the publisher who registered *Of Education* (Raylor, "New Light" 23).

What may be a sneering reference to "modern *Janua's* and *Didactics*" seems to insult Hartlib's favorite educational philosopher, the Moravian John Amos Comenius, who had visited England in 1641–42. Hartlib, who published most of the works on education that he himself solicited, did not publish Milton's work, though he may at least have purchased a copy and perhaps even supported the printer for the project (Raylor, "New Light" 23). The reactions to *Of Education* within the Hartlib circle were "[n]ot really favorable" (Shawcross, "A Survey" 30). Ernest Sirluck, in his general introduction to Milton's prose works of the 1640s in the Yale *Prose Works*, was the first to try to show that Milton was "fundamentally opposed" to Comenian policy (Yale 2: 187–205), but Raylor has taken exception to Sirluck's position, concluding that "There is . . . no substantive reason to believe that Hartlib refused to involve himself in the publication of the tractate *Of Education*, and no reason to assume that it caused a division between Milton and Hartlib in 1644" ("New Light" 23).

Yet, if one can hazard an educated guess, Milton's relationship with Hartlib may well have become an uneasy one with the publication of Milton's tract, in that Milton wanted endorsement from the man who championed Comenius, while he himself denied the validity of the most important of Comenius's ideas.

Edward LeComte, among others, has pointed out some of the similarities and some of the more obvious differences between Comenius's educational theory and Milton's:

> The two agreed that Latin could and should be taught faster, that foreign languages are means to an end, not ends in themselves, and that the general educational progression should be from the sensible to the abstract: as Bacon said, 'scholars . . . come too soon and too unripe to logic and rhetoric.' But Comenius was democratic (providing for the education of all classes, and girls as well as boys) and stressed vocational training, while slighting literature. (*Milton Dictionary* 218)

The differences between Milton and Comenius are profound. Milton wants education for the elite or well-born man, leading to a career as a statesman. Though he provided for the separate education of the elite, Comenius wanted something closer to universal vocational training, which Milton avoids discussing. Milton wants his pupils to read the best of Greek and Roman classics in each discipline; Comenius avoids citing pagan writers, to whom he is decidedly hostile. Comenius compiles phrases useful in trade, engineering, and diplomacy; his emphasis is on the practical and the mechanical, while Milton's is high-minded and not at all technological (though it does provide practical training, such as interviews with farmers and engineers). Milton's students might learn how military legions could be arranged in battle, but only in order to make those aristocratic pupils capable of being better commanding officers. Comenius's *Janua Linguarum Reserata* ("open door to languages") and *Didactica Magna* ("great didactic") were, we might say, both technical writing texts using Latin to advance business and industry. Milton instead claims to model his academies on those of Plato's *Republic* and Castiglione's *The Courtier*. It probably would not have occurred to Comenius to teach music, nor would his pupils have been allowed to study mathematics or poetic theory extensively, or exercise regularly, or ride out into the countryside in order to observe rural workers or architects at work.

It is no wonder that Hartlib did not publish Milton, even though Milton describes Hartlib as soliciting the work, at the very end: "Thus Master *Hartlib*, you have a generall view in writing, as your desire was, of that which at severall times I had discourst with you concerning the best and Noblest way of Education." As Lewalski points out, however, the terms of Milton's treatise "are in dialogue with, but not . . . in close agreement with the projects of the Hartlib Circle" (203). Milton in the end went on without Hartlib or Comenius, making practical suggestions about education based on his good experiences at St. Paul's School and on his bad experiences under his first tutor, William Chappell, at Cambridge.

Various scholars from LeComte to Lewalski have pointed out the influence of the ideas of Francis Bacon on Milton, Hartlib, and Comenius. Bacon had attempted to incorporate a system of education into his *Advancement of Learning* (1605) and *New Atlantis* (1627), building knowledge in young minds on the bases of first-hand observations, human self-awareness, and inductive reasoning.

Milton had tested his notions of how a curriculum might be formed, very practically, on his own small school, but he remained hostile to the educational philosophies of Oxford and Cambridge. As Lewalski puts it, "despite his own A.M. from Cambridge, [Milton] scornfully repudiated university education for arts students and ministers" (208). In *Of Education*, he was recommending that people practice what he had instituted in his own school, not what was inflicted on him at Cambridge. We have the testimonial of Edward Phillips, Milton's nephew and pupil, that Milton's little school, in operation from about 1640 to 1646, did accomplish what Milton intended for it to accomplish: it taught Latin and Greek in a remarkably short span of time, and it employed the best examples from Greek and Roman literature for everything from agricultural and military writing to epic poetry. In a reversal of the normal educational order imposed on Milton when he was a child, his students began reading simple but interesting works, the Greek and Roman equivalent of children's books, and ended with the study of the more theoretical fields of rhetoric and theology.

Milton would have done away with colleges altogether, since he wanted to teach pupils from their first learning age through the early twenties, allowing them separate postgraduate education only for the study of law or medicine. Milton would also suggest that a school should begin operation in a large house (as he used his own houses with his pupils), and he would have the state confiscate some of the large houses belonging to corrupt clergymen—just as Henry VIII had secularized the lands and buildings of the Catholic Church in the sixteenth century—and give them to his academies. He sees the position of the chief master of the school as that of a one-room schoolmaster, despite the existence of a large support staff, and he assigns absolute power to that one master, including the prerogative to whip students. There is evidence that Milton himself was whipped for insubordination by his tutor at Cambridge (Aubrey 200), and there is evidence that his young wife Mary was upset by hearing her husband's pupils being whipped (Parker 230). For him to accept or dole out such punishment only means that his disciplinary methods were typical of his time.

Always, however, Milton believed that "genuine education (and especially higher education) must be largely self-motivated and self-directed. He has no faith in perfect methods or systems, nor in epitomes and encyclopedias [such as those produced by Comenius and the Comenians]" (Lewalski 208).

PREPUBLICATION AESTHETIC AND CULTURAL BIASES

Milton attempts in *Of Education* to inculcate in his pupils his own love for poetry, which he believes should be "simple, sensuous, and passionate" (below, 984). One can see in his projected curriculum that he would not only be training his pupils in the best methods of scanning poems: he was himself preparing to write *Paradise Lost*. Since he is at the moment of writing *Of Education* caught up in thinking of military matters as the City of London prepared its defenses (Raylor, "New Light" 20–21), his academy would emphasize military discipline as well as practical training in swordsmanship and fortification.

Milton betrays cultural biases in *Of Education*: he can't stand the French "*Mounsieurs*" or even those English lawyers who can't even pronounce legal French or Latin well, but he loves Italian culture and literature to the point where he would have his pupils pronounce Latin with an Italian accent and to the point where he would have them study how to interpret classical epic as Italian Renaissance critics and epic-writers such as Castelvetro and Tasso interpreted them.

Milton had outlined his own reforms to the educational system—of Cambridge at least—in his Second and his Seventh Prolusions. These should be reread by any student who would like to understand *Of Education* in the context of Milton's undergraduate training.

Milton is a very humane teacher, more of a gentle encourager of his students than a severe disciplinarian: though he works his students hard, he cannot praise a school that does not mix physical exercise with intellectual exercise, and he does not see a school as a cloister, protecting its students from seeing what is going on outside its walls. He even implies that in springtime being in school is not worth as much to pupils as a visit to the countryside would be. We have Edward Phillips's sincere testimony that, despite his own predilections, Milton was never pedantic in his own teaching methods.

PUBLICATION HISTORY

Of Education was published twice in Milton's lifetime, first as a pamphlet without a title page, anonymously printed but legally registered on June 4, 1644, and second as a twenty-three page section of the 1673 *Poems*. The printer of the little pamphlet is unknown, though we know that it was registered to the bookseller/publisher Thomas Underhill. Parker assumes that Underhill made the arrangements for it to be printed, and that Milton had it printed at his own expense (256). A day after Underhill registered it, the pamphlet was marked as received into the collection of George Thomason, Milton's bookseller friend, who gathered a huge body of the pamphlets published during the 1640s and 1650s into a compendium now called the Thomason Tracts.

THE TEXT

I have chosen as my copy-text the first, 1644, edition of the pamphlet. The 1673 edition follows *1644* very closely, adding errors and making few significant corrections, which I note. The compositor who set *1644* incorporated into his text habits of spelling and capitalization that seem to approximate those of Milton more closely than those of the compositor of *1673* (the later edition was set, of course, long after Milton went blind in 1651). He prefers "ee" to "ie" in words that would today be spelled "peace" or "mere." He prefers much lighter capitalization than the compositor of 1673, saving capital letters for important nouns and rarely wasting them on adjectives. He prefers strongly to use the silent final "e" on words like "matchlesse," and he prefers doubled final consonants, as with "internall." He uses the Miltonic form "perfit" as well as "perfect" and he strongly prefers "dayly" to "daily." Like Milton, the compositor chooses "anough" over "enough," in a five to two ratio. He also prefers "choise" to "choice." One lonely "thir" made it into the first edition in one of the final pages, but its presence is not sufficient evidence to prove that the compositor was trying, at last, to be faithful to Milton's manuscript.

Allen Abbot presents the result of his collation of the two editions in Columbia 4: 360–61, but his work should be checked carefully for accuracy. Donald C. Dorian notes press corrections incorporated into a few copies: significantly, they are "Parliament" corrected to "Parlament" and "perfected" corrected to "perfeted" (360; see also 777).

Works Cited
Editions are marked with an asterisk.

Aubrey, John. *Aubrey's Brief Lives*. Ed. Oliver Lawson Dick. Ann Arbor: U of Michigan P, 1962.

Le Comte, Edward. *A Milton Dictionary*. New York: Philosophical Library, 1961.

Lewalski, Barbara. "Milton and the Hartlib Circle." *Literary Milton: Text, Pretext, Context*. Ed. Diana Treviño Benet and Michael Lieb. Pittsburgh: Duquesne UP, 1994. 202–19.

*Milton, John. *Of Education*. Ed. Donald C. Dorian. *Complete Prose Works of John Milton*. New Haven, CT: Yale UP, 1959.

*------. Areopagitica *and* Of Education, *With Autobiographical Passages from Other Prose Works*. Ed. George Sabine. Northbrook, IL: AHM Publishing, 1951.

*------. *The Tractate on Education, 1644*. Ed. Thomas R. Hartmann. *The Prose of John Milton*. Gen. Ed. J. Max Patrick. New York: New York UP, 1968. 217–43.

Parker, William Riley. *Milton: A Biography*. Oxford: Clarendon, 1968.

Raylor, Timothy. "New Light on Milton and Hartlib." *Milton Quarterly* 27 (1993): 19–31.

------. "Samuel Hartlib and the Commonwealth of Bees." *Culture and Cultivation in Early Modern England*. Ed. Michael Leslie and Timothy Raylor. Leicester, UK: Leicester UP, 1992. 91–129.

Rajan, Balachandra. "Simple, Sensuous and Passionate." *Review of English Studies* 21 (1945): 291–93.

Sadler, John Edward. *J.A. Comenius and the Concept of Universal Education*. New York: Barnes & Noble, 1966.

Shawcross, John T. *Milton: A Bibliography for the Years 1624–1700*. Binghamton, NY: MRTS, 1984.

------. *Milton: The Critical Heritage*. New York: Barnes & Noble, 1970.

Turnbull, G.H. *Samuel Hartlib: A Sketch of His Life and His Relations to J.A. Comenius*. Oxford: Oxford UP, 1920.

Of Education. To Master *Samuel Hartlib*.

Master Hartlib,

IAm long since perswaded, that to say, or doe ought worth memory, and imitation, no purpose or respect should sooner move us, then simply the love of God, and of mankinde. Neverthelesse to write now the reforming of Education, though it be one of the greatest and noblest designs, that can be thought on, and for the want whereof this nation perishes, I had not yet at this time been induc't, but by your earnest entreaties, and serious conjurements; as having my minde for the present halfe diverted in the pursuance of some other assertions, the knowledge and the use of which, cannot but be a great furtherance both to the enlargement of truth, and honest living, with much more peace. Nor should the lawes of any private friendship have prevail'd with me to divide thus, or transpose my former thoughts, but that I see those aims, those actions which have won you with me the esteem of a person sent hither by some good providence from a farre country to be the occasion and the incitement of great good to this Iland. And, as I hear, you have obtain'd the same repute with men of most approved wisdom, and some of highest authority among us. Not to mention the learned correspondence which you hold in forreigne parts, and the extraordinary pains and diligence which you have us'd in this matter both heer, and beyond the Seas; either by the definite will of God so ruling, or the peculiar sway of nature, which also is Gods working. Neither can I thinke that so reputed, and so valu'd as you are, you would to the forfeit of your own discerning ability, impose upon me an unfit and over ponderous argument, but that the satisfaction which you professe to have receiv'd from those incidentall discourses which we have wander'd into, hath prest & almost constrain'd you into a perswasion, that what you require from me in this point, I neither ought, nor can in conscience deferre beyond this time both of so much need at once, and so much opportunity to trie what God hath determin'd. I will not resist therefore, what ever it is either of divine, or humane obligement that you lay upon me; but will forthwith set down in writing, as you request me, that voluntary *Idea*,[1] which hath long in silence presented it self to me, of a better Education, in extent and comprehension farre more large, and yet of time farre shorter, and of attainment farre more certain, then hath been yet in practice. Brief I shall endeavour to be; for that which I have to say, assuredly this nation hath extreame need should be done sooner then spok'n. To tell you therefore what I have benefited herein among old renowned Authors, I shall spare; and to search what many modern *Janua's* and *Didactics*[2] more then ever I shall read, have projected, my inclination leads me not. But if you can accept of these few observations which have flowr'd off, and are as it were the burnishing of many studious and contemplative yeers altogether spent in the search of religious and civil knowledge, and such as pleas'd you so well in the relating, I here give you them to dispose of.

The end then of learning is to repair the ruins of our first parents by regaining to know God aright, and out of that knowledge to love him, to imitate him, to be like him, as we may the neerest by possessing our souls of true vertue, which being united to the heavenly grace of faith makes up the highest perfection. But because our understanding cannot in this body found it selfe but on sensible things, nor arrive so clearly to the knowledge of God and things invisible, as by orderly conning over the visible and inferior creature, the same method is necessarily to be follow'd in all discreet teaching. And seeing every nation affords not experience and tradition anough for all kinde of learning, therefore we are chiefly taught the languages of those people who have at any time been most industrious after wisdom; So that Language is but the Instrument convaying to us things usefull to be known. And though a linguist should pride himselfe to have all the Tongues that *Babel* cleft the world into, yet, if he have not studied the solid things in them as well as the words and lexicons, he were nothing so much to be esteem'd a learned man, as any yeoman or tradesman competently wise in his mother dialect only. Hence appear the many mistakes which have made learning generally so unpleasing and so unsuccessfull; first we do amisse to spend seven or eight years meerly in scraping together so much miserable Latin, and Greek, as might be learnt otherwise easily and delightfully in one year. And that which casts our proficiency therein so much behinde, is our time lost partly in too oft idle vacancies[3] given both to schools and Universities, partly in a preposterous exaction, forcing the empty wits of children to compose Theams, verses, and Orations, which are the acts of ripest judgment and the finall work of a head fill'd by long reading, and ob-

---

[1]The italics here might well suggest that Milton is attempting to highlight the term and ally it with the Greek word associated so closely with Plato.

[2]Short titles for two of Comenius's books. Hartlib had included an abstract of Comenius's *Great Didactic* for inclusion in *Pansophia* (1639).
[3]Suggests "empty spaces" as well as the short and longer vacations of the universities.

serving, with elegant maxims, and copious invention. These are not matters to be wrung from poor striplings, like blood out of the nose, or the plucking of untimely fruit: besides the ill habit which they get of wretched barbarizing against the Latin and Greek *idiom*, with their untutor'd *Anglicisms*,[4] odious to be read, yet not to be avoided without a well continu'd and judicious conversing[5] among pure Authors digested, which they scarce taste, wheras, if after some preparatory grounds of speech by their certain forms got into memory, they were led to the praxis[6] thereof in some chosen short book lesson'd throughly to them, they might then forthwith proceed to learn the substance of good things, and Arts in due order, which would bring the whole language quickly into their power. This I take to be the most rationall and most profitable way of learning languages, and whereby we may best hope to give account to God of our youth spent herein: And for the usuall method of teaching Arts, I deem it to be an old errour of universities not yet well recover'd from the Scholastick grosness of barbarous ages, that in stead of beginning with Arts most easie, and those be such as are most obvious to the sence, they present their young unmatriculated novices at first comming with the most intellective abstractions of Logick & metaphysicks: So that they having but newly left those Grammatick flats & shallows where they stuck unreasonably to learn a few words with lamentable construction, and now on the sudden transported under another climat to be tost and turmoild with their unballasted wits in fadomles and unquiet deeps of controversie, do for the most part grow into hatred and contempt of learning, mockt and deluded all this while with ragged notions and babblements,[7] while they expected worthy and delightfull knowledge; till poverty or youthfull years call them importunately their several wayes, and hasten them with the sway of friends either to an ambitious and mercenary, or ignorantly zealous Divinity;[8] Some allur'd to the trade of Law, grounding their purposes not on the prudent and heavenly contemplation of justice and equity which was never taught them, but on the promising and pleasing thoughts of litigious terms, fat contentions, and

flowing fees; others betake them to State affairs, with souls so unprincipl'd in vertue, and true generous breeding, that flattery, and court shifts and tyrannous aphorismes appear to them the highest points of wisdom; instilling their barren hearts with a conscientious slavery, if, as I rather think, it be not fain'd. Others lastly of a more delicious and airie spirit, retire themselves knowing no better, to the enjoyments of ease and luxury, living out their daies in feast and jollity; which indeed is the wisest and the safest course of all these, unless they were with more integrity undertak'n. And these are the errours, and these are the fruits of mispending our prime youth at the Schools and Universities as we do, either in learning meere words or such things chiefly, as were better unlearnt.

I shall detain you no longer in the demonstration of what we should not doe, but strait conduct ye to a hill side,[9] where I will point ye out the right path of a vertuous and noble Education; laborious indeed at the first ascent, but else so smooth, so green, so full of goodly prospect, and melodious sounds on every side, that the harp of *Orpheus* was not more charming. I doubt not but ye shall have more adoe to drive our dullest and laziest youth, our stocks and stubbs from the infinite desire of such a happy nurture, then we have now to hale[10] and drag our choisest and hopefullest wits to that asinine feast of sowthistles and brambles which is commonly set before them, as all the food and entertainment of their tenderest and most docible[11] age. I call therefore a compleate and generous Education that which fits a man to perform justly, skilfully and magnanimously all the offices both private and publike of peace and war. And how all this may be done between twelve, and one and twenty, lesse time then is now bestow'd in pure trifling at Grammar and *Sophistry*, is to be thus order'd.

First to finde out a spatious house and ground about it fit for an *Academy*, and big enough to lodge a hundred and fifty persons, whereof twenty or thereabout may be attendants, all under the government of one, who shall be thought of desert sufficient, and ability either to doe all, or wisely to direct, and oversee it done. This place should be at once both School and University, not needing a remove to any other house of Schollership, except it be some peculiar[12] Colledge of Law, or Physick, where they mean to be practitioners; but as for those generall studies which take up all our time from

---

[4]As a lexicographer and as a professional translator, Milton would hold a lifelong contempt for what he considered the barbarian invasion of later Latin usage.

[5]Holding a dialogue or reasonable conversation; learning rather than just reading; digesting as compared with the simple act of eating.

[6]Practice; action.

[7]Milton apparently invented this word, derived from Babel; he is, throughout the pamphlet, pushing the limits of meaning in most of the nouns he uses.

[8]Calling to the ministry. A Christian minister would be called a "divine" in England in the 1640s.

[9]The metaphorical Hill of Truth, usually pictured as steep and sometimes containing a maze, but with a beautiful prospect at the top.

[10]Summon; hail.

[11]Teachable.

[12]Discrete; dedicated.

Lilly[13] to the commencing, as they term it, Master of Art, it should be absolute. After this pattern, as many edifices may be converted to this use, as shall be needfull in every City throughout this land, which would tend much to the encrease of learning and civility every where. This number, lesse or more thus collected, to the convenience of a foot company,[14] or interchangeably two troops of cavalry should divide their daies works into three parts, as it lies orderly. Their studies, their exercise, and their diet.

For their studies, First they should begin with the chief and necessary rules of some good Grammar, either that now us'd, or any better: and while this is doing,[15] their speech is to be fashion'd to a distinct and cleer pronuntiation, as neer as may be to the *Italian*, especially in the vowels. For we Englishmen being farre northerly, doe not open our mouthes in the cold air, wide enough to grace a Southern tongue; but are observ'd by all other nations to speak exceeding close and inward: So that to smatter Latin with an English mouth, is as ill a hearing as law French. Next to make them expert in the usefullest points of grammar, and withall to season them, and win them early to the love of vertue and true labour, ere any flattering seducement, or vain principle seise them wandering, some easie and delightful book of Education would be read to them; whereof the Greeks have store as *Cebes*, *Plutarch*, and other Socratic discourses.[16] But in Latin we have none of classic authoritie extant, except the two or three first books of *Quintilian*,[17] and some select peeces elsewhere. But here the main skill and groundwork will be, to temper them such lectures and explanations upon every opportunity, as may lead and draw them in willing obedience, enflam'd with the study of learning, and the admiration of vertue; stirr'd up with high hopes of living to be brave men, and worthy patriots, dear to God, and famous to all ages. That they may despise and scorn all their childish, and ill taught qualities, to delight in manly, and liberall exercises: which he who hath the Art, and proper eloquence to catch them with, what with mild and effectuall perswasions, and what with the intimation of

some fear, if need be, but chiefly by his own example, might in a short space gain them to an incredible diligence and courage: infusing into their young brests such an ingenuous and noble ardor, as would not fail to make many of them renowned and matchlesse men. At the same time, some other hour of the day, might be taught them the rules of Arithmetick, and soon after the elements of Geometry even playing, as the old manner was. After evening repast, till bed time their thoughts will be best taken up in the easie grounds of Religion, and the story of Scripture. The next step would be to the Authors of *Agriculture*, *Cato*, *Varro*, and *Columella*,[18] for the matter is most easie, and if the language be difficult, so much the better, it is not a difficultie above their yeers. And here will be an occasion of inciting and inabling them hereafter to improve the tillage of their country, to recover the bad soil, and to remedy the wast that is made of good: for this was one of *Hercules*[19] praises. Ere half these Authors be read which will soon be with plying hard, and dayly,[20] they cannot chuse but be masters of any ordinary prose. So that it will be then seasonable for them to learn in any modern Author, the use of the Globes, and all the maps first[21] with the old names; and then with the new: or they might be then capable to read any compendious method of naturall Philosophy.[22] And at the same time might be entring into the Greek tongue, after the same manner as was before prescrib'd in the Latin; whereby the difficulties of Grammar being soon overcome, all the Historicall Physiology of *Aristotle* and *Theophrastus*[23] are open before them, and as I may say, under contribution. The like accesse will be to *Vitruvius*,[24] to *Senecas*[25] naturall questions, to *Mela*, *Celsus*, *Pliny*, or *Solinus*.[26] And having thus past the

---

[13]William Lily (1468?–1522). His *Beginning Book in Latin*, or in its familiar title *Lily's Latin Grammar*, was the standard Latin grammar in all English schools after it was authorized by Henry VIII.

[14]Infantry.

[15]Happening.

[16]The work by Cebes (thought to be a pupil of Socrates) that Milton recommends is *The Table*, which describes the ascent of children up to a garden inhabited by wise men. It was printed with the original Greek and a Latin translation in facing columns: the one column could act as a study aid for the other.

[17]The most famous of manuals of oratory, the *Institutio Oratoria* of Quintillian (d. AD 95) also contained a course of education for children, beginning at birth.

[18]Cato, *De re rustica*; Varro, *Rerum rusticarum*; and Columella, *De re rustica*.

[19]*1673* adds the italics to the proper name, and I correct likewise.

[20]*1673* puts the which clause in parentheses, as an aside.

[21]*1673* inserts a comma here and removes the semicolon after : "and all the maps, first with the old names and then with the new:" The punctuation seems to be an improvement.

[22]Natural philosophy was the study of the natural world, as with Aristotle's *Natural History of Animals*.

[23]Aristotle's pupil and his successor at the Peripatetic School in Athens.

[24]The first-century Roman author of *De Architectura*, Marcus Vitruvius Pollio, was the model for Renaissance architects like the Italian Palladio. I have restored italics to the name Vitruvius.

[25]As author of the *Natural Questions*, Lucius Annaeus Seneca (c. 5 BCE–AD 65) collected information on subjects such as the air itself or the nature of earthquakes.

[26]Pomponius Mela (first century AD)was the author of the geographical descriptions in *De Situ Orbis* of all the continents then known. Aulus Cornelius Celsus (first century AD) is the best-known Roman writer of a medical treatise; his *De Medicina* became a standard text for Renaissance physicians. Pliny the Elder's (c. AD 23–79) *Historiae Naturalis Libri XXXVII* was a hodgepodge of fascinating natural observations on

principles of *Arithmetick*, *Geometry*, *Astronomy*, and *Geography* with a generall compact of *Physicks*, they may descend in *Mathematicks* to the instrumentall science of *Trigonometry*, and from thence to Fortification, *Architecture*, *Enginry*,[27] or navigation. And in naturall Philosophy they may proceed leisurly from the History of *Meteors*, minerals, plants and living creatures as farre as Anatomy. Then also in course might be read to them out of some not tedious writer the institution of Physick; that they may know the tempers, the humors, the seasons, and how to manage a crudity:[28] which he who can wisely and timely doe, is not onely a great Physician to himselfe, and to his friends, but also may at some time or other, save an Army by this frugall and expenselesse meanes only; and not let the healthy and stout bodies of young men rot away under him for want of this discipline; which is a great pitty, and no lesse a shame to the commander.[29] To set forward all these proceedings in nature & mathematicks, what hinders, but that they may procure, as oft as shall be needfull, the helpfull experiences of Hunters, fowlers, Fishermen, Shepherds, Gardeners, *Apothecaries*; and in the other sciences, *Architects*, Engineers, Mariners, *Anatomists*; who doubtlesse would be ready some for reward, and some to favour such a hopefull Seminary.[30] And this will give them such a reall tincture of naturall knowledge, as they shall never forget, but dayly augment with delight. Then also those Poets which are now counted most hard, will be both facil and pleasant, *Orpheus*,[31] *Hesiod*,[32] *Theocritus*, *Aratus*, *Nicander*, *Oppian*, *Dionysius*, and in Latin *Lucretius*, *Manilius*, and the rurall part of *Virgil*.[33]

By this time, yeers and good generall precepts will

have furnisht them more distinctly with that act of reason which in *Ethics* is call'd *Proairesis*: that they may with some judgement contemplat upon morall good and evill. Then will be requir'd a speciall reinforcement of constant and sound endoctrinating to set them right and firm, instructing them more amply in the knowledge of vertue and the hatred of vice: while their young and pliant affections are led through all the morall works of *Plato*,[34] *Xenophon*, *Cicero*, *Plutarch*, *Laertius*,[35] and those *Locrian* remnants;[36] but still to be reduc't in their nightward studies wherewith they close the dayes work, under the determinat sentence of *David* or *Salomon*, or the Evangels and *Apostolic* Scriptures. Being perfit in the knowledge of personall duty, they may then begin the study of Economics. And either now, or before this, they may have easily learnt at any odde hour the *Italian* tongue. And soon after, but with warinesse and good antidote, it would be wholsome anough to let them tast some choise comedies, Greek, Latin, or *Italian:* Those tragedies also that treat of houshold matters, as *Trachiniæ*, *Alcestis*[37] and the like. The next remove must be to the study of *Politics*; to know the beginning, end, and reasons of politicall societies; that they may not in a dangerous fit of the common-wealth be such poor, shaken, uncertain reeds, of such a tottering conscience, as many of our great counsellers have lately shewn themselves, but stedfast pillars of the State. After this they are to dive into the grounds of law, and legal justice; deliver'd first, and with best warrant by *Moses*; and as farre as humane prudence can be trusted, in those extoll'd remains of Grecian Law-givers, *Licurgus*,[38] *Solon*, *Zaleucus*, *Charondas*, and thence to all the Romane *Edicts* and Tables with their *Justinian*;[39] and so down to the *Saxon* and common laws of England, and the Statutes. Sundayes also and every evening may be

---

sociological and geographical topics. The information has such a broad base that Pliny's work was translated by Philemon Holland as *The History of the World* (1601); Gaius Julius Solinus (third century AD) collected geographical descriptions of the known world, including information about the British Isles.

[27]The design of military engines.

[28]An indigestion caused by an imbalance of humors: "The state of being imperfectly digested, or the quality of being indigestible; indigestion; also, in old physiology, imperfect 'concoction' of the humours; undigested (or indigestible) matter in the stomach" (*OED* 6).

[29]Milton had undoubtedly discussed medical knowledge and practices with his friend Charles Diodati, who had prepared to become a physician like his father.

[30]Literally a seed-bed for ideas, not the conventional modern meaning of "school for seminarians."

[31]The legendary poet Orpheus was supposed to have written an extant work, the *Lithica*, on the properties of precious and other stones, but there is no evidence that Milton taught it to his pupils.

[32]All the poets listed wrote pastoral or agricultural poetry, astronomical or geographical poetry, or poetry related to medicine, hunting, fishing, or, in the case of Lucretius, *The Nature of Things*. For editions Milton might have used, see the Yale notes (2: 395–96).

[33]The *Georgics*. I have restored italics to the name of Vergil.

---

[34]Milton paired the works of Plato and Xenophon as "the divine volumes of *Plato*, and his equal *Xenophon*" in *An Apology* (Yale 1: 891). The "morall works" might have included a number of the dialogues of Plato and the *Apology*, plus works concerning Socrates by Xenophon.

[35]Diogenes Laertius (second or third century BCE), *Lives and Opinions of Eminent Philosophers*.

[36]Timaeus of Locri, supposed author of *On the Soul of the World and Nature*.

[37]The first is a domestic play by Sophocles dealing with the widow of Hercules, Dejanira, and the second focuses on Alcestis, the wife of Admetus, who sacrifices her own life to bring him back from the dead. She will appear in Milton's sonnet "Methought I Saw My Late Espoused Saint."

[38]Lycurgus was the legendary principal architect of the constitution of Sparta; Solon was the Greek legislator who framed the constitution of Athens; Zaleucus performed a similar service for a Greek colony in what is now southern Italy; and Charondas organized a legal system in Catana, in Sicily, about 500 BCE.

[39]Under the emperor Justinian (AD 527–65), the Eastern Empire codified Roman civil law.

now understandingly spent in the highest matters of *Theology*, and Church History ancient and modern: and ere this time the Hebrew Tongue at a set hour might have been gain'd, that the Scriptures may be now read in their own originall; whereto it would be no impossibility to add the *Chaldey*, and the *Syrian* Dialect.[40] When all these employments are well conquer'd, then will the choise[41] Histories, *heroic poems*, and *Attic* tragedies of statliest and most regal argument, with all the famous Politicall orations offer themselves; which if they were not only read; but some of them got by memory, and solemnly pronounc't with right accent, and grace, as might be taught, would endue them even with the spirit, and vigor of *Demosthenes* or *Cicero*,[42] *Euripides*, or *Sophocles*. And now lastly will be the time to read with them those organic arts which inable men to discourse and write perspicuously, elegantly, and according to the fitted stile of lofty, mean, or lowly. Logic therefore so much as is usefull, is to be referr'd to this due place withall her well couch't[43] heads and Topics, untill it be time to open her contracted palm[44] into a gracefull and ornate Rhetorick taught out of the rule of *Plato*, *Aristotle*, *Phalereus*,[45] *Cicero*, *Hermogenes*,[46] *Longinus*.[47] To which Poetry would be made subsequent, or indeed rather precedent, as being less suttle and fine, but more simple, sensuous and passionate.[48] I mean not here the prosody of a verse, which they could not but have hit on before among the rudiments of grammar; but that sublime Art which in *Aristotles poetics*, in *Horace*, and the *Italian* Commentaries of *Castelvetro*,[49] *Tasso*,[50]

Mazzoni,[51] and others, teaches what the laws are of a true *Epic* Poem, what of a *Dramatic*, what of a *Lyric*, what decorum is, which is the grand master peece to observe.[52] This would make them soon perceive what despicable creatures our common rimers and play-writes[53] be, and shew them, what Religious, what glorious and magnificent use might be made of Poetry both in divine and humane things. From hence and not till now will be the right season of forming them to be able writers and composers in every excellent matter, when they shall be thus fraught with an universall insight into things. Or whether they be to speak in Parliament or counsell, honour and attention would be waiting on their lips. There would then also appear in Pulpits other visages, other gestures, and stuffe otherwise wrought then what we now sit under,[54] oft times to as great a triall of our patience as any other that they preach to us. These are the studies wherein our noble and our gentle youth ought to bestow their time in a disciplinary way from twelve to one and twenty; unless they rely more upon their ancestors dead, then upon themselves living. In which methodicall course it is so suppos'd they must proceed by the steddy pace of learning onward, as at convenient times for memories sake to retire back into the middle ward, and sometimes into the rear of what they have been taught, untill they have confirm'd, and solidly united the whole body of their perfected knowledge, like the last embattelling of a Roman legion. Now will be worth the seeing what exercises, and what recreations[55] may best agree, and become[56] these Studies.

Their Exercise.

The course of Study hitherto briefly describ'd, is, what I can guesse by reading, likest to those ancient and

---

[40]Two of the ancient dialects of the Old Testament.

[41]I.e., "choice."

[42]Corrected from "*Cicere*" in *1644*, as in *1673*.

[43]Heads well-stuffed with knowledge, or ready for discussion on a higher level.

[44]The movement from logic to rhetoric was proverbially compared to moving from the closed fist to the open palm.

[45]Apparently Demetrius Phalereus (350-283 BCE), defender of the principle of liberty for the citizens of Athens, but Milton may be referring to a later Greek treatise *On Style*, written by another Demetrius living in the first century AD, which emphasizes a forcible rhetorical style (Yale 2: 403n).

[46]Hermogenes of Tarsus (first century AD), Greek grammarian and author of tracts on style that used classical texts for examples.

[47]Little is known of the actual author of *On The Sublime*, but the treatise was attributed to Dionysius Cassius Longinus, philosopher and critic of Athens who died in AD 273.

[48]Milton's phrasing here is very subtle and rich: see Balachandra Rajan, "Simple, Sensuous and Passionate," *Review of English Studies* 21 (1945): 289-301.

[49]Ludovico Castelvetro (1505-1571) translated Aristotle's *Poetics* into Italian and reformulated it to include the "three unities," of time, place, and setting.

[50]Torquato Tasso (1544-1595), whose two treatises on epic poetry, both of which are referred to as his *Discourses*, probably gave Milton a critical base for the poetic style of *Paradise Lost*. The edition of Tasso's *Discourses* translated and commented on by Mariella Cavalchini and Irene

Samuel (Oxford: Clarendon, 1973) is helpful for comparing the poetic styles of both epic writers.

[51]Giacomo Mazzoni (1548-98), author of two defenses of Dante's poetic style in the *Divine Comedy*. See John M. Steadman, "Milton and Mazzoni: The Genre of the *Divina Commedia*," *Huntington Library Quarterly* 23 (1960): 107-22.

[52]For all the implications in Milton's rich descriptions of decorum, see Thomas Kranidas, *The Fierce Equation: A Study of Milton's Decorum* (The Hague: Mouton, 1965).

[53]The statement seems to denigrate at least the dramatic production of the "sweetest" Shakespeare and the "learned" Jonson described in "L'Allegro" 131-33. *1673* has the word as "Play-writers," obviously incorrect.

[54]Probably a reference to the height of the pulpit, far above the heads of parishioners in seventeenth-century Anglican churches.

[55]*1673* has "what Exercises and Recreations," dropping the second "what" and modifying the punctuation, I think incorrectly.

[56]"May best become, or complement," with "become" used as in the modern phrase "The suit was becoming to him."

famous schools of *Pythagoras*, *Plato*, *Isocrates*,[57] *Aristotle* and such others, out of which were bred up such a number of renowned Philosophers, orators, Historians, Poets and Princes all over *Greece*, *Italy*, and *Asia*, besides the flourishing studies of *Cyrene* and *Alexandria*. But herein it shall exceed them, and supply a defect as great as that which *Plato* noted in the common-wealth of *Sparta*; whereas that City train'd up their youth most for warre, and these in their Academies and *Lyceum*, all for the gown,[58] this institution of breeding which I here delineate, shall be equally good both for Peace and warre. Therefore about an hour and a halfe ere they eat at noon should be allow'd them for exercise and due rest afterwards: But the time for this may be enlarg'd at pleasure, according as their rising in the morning shall be early. The exercise which I commend first, is the exact use of their weapon,[59] to guard and to strike safely with edge, or point; this will keep them healthy, nimble, strong, and well in breath, is also the likeliest means to make them grow large and tall, and to inspire them with a gallant and fearlesse courage, which being temper'd with seasonable lectures and precepts to them of true fortitude,[60] and patience, will turn into a native and heroick valour, and make them hate the cowardise of doing wrong. They must be also practiz'd in all the locks and gripes of wrastling, wherein English men were wont to excell, as need may often be in fight to tugge, to grapple,[61] and to close. And this perhaps will be anough, wherein to prove and heat their single strength.[62] The interim of unsweating themselves regularly,[63] and convenient rest before meat[64] may both with profit and delight be taken up in recreating and composing their travail'd spirits with the solemn and divine harmonies of musick heard,[65] or learnt; either while the skilfull *Organist* plies his grave and fancied descant, in lofty fugues, or the whole Symphony with artfull and unimaginable touches adorn and grace the well studied cords of some choise composer; some times the Lute, or soft organ stop waiting on elegant voices either to Religious, martiall, or civil ditties; which if wise men & prophets

be not extreamly out,[66] have a great power over dispositions and manners, to smooth and make them gentle from rustick harshnesse and distemper'd passions. The like also would not be unexpedient after meat to assist and cherish nature in her first concoction, and send their mindes backe to study in good tune and satisfaction. Where having follow'd it close under vigilant eyes till about two hours before supper, they are by a sudden alarum or watch word, to be call'd out to their military motions, under skie or covert,[67] according to the season, as was the Romane wont; first on foot, then as their age permits, on horse back, to all the art of cavalry; That having in sport, but with much exactnesse, and dayly muster,[68] serv'd out the rudiments of their Souldiership in all the skill of embattailling,[69] marching, encamping, fortifying, besieging and battering, with all the helps of ancient and modern stratagems, *Tactiks*[70] and warlike maxims, they may as it were out of a long warre come forth renowned and perfect Commanders in the service of their country. They would not then, if they were trusted with fair and hopefull armies, suffer them for want of just and wise discipline to shed away from about them like sick feathers,[71] though they be never so oft suppli'd: they would not suffer their empty & unrecrutible Colonells of twenty men in a Company to quaffe out, or convey into secret hoards, the wages of a delusive list, and a miserable remnant:[72] yet in the mean while to be overmaster'd with a score or two of drunkards, the only souldiery left about them, or else to comply with all rapines and violences. No[73] certainly, if they knew ought of that knowledge that belongs to good men or good governours, they would not suffer these things. But to return to our own institute, besides these constant exercises at home, there is another opportunity of gaining experience to be won from pleasure it self abroad; In those vernal seasons of the yeer, when the air is calm and pleasant, it were an injury and sullennesse against nature not to go out, and see her riches, and partake in her rejoycing with heaven and earth. I should not therefore be a perswader to them of studying much then, after two or three yeer that they have well laid their grounds, but to ride out in companies with pru-

---

[57]The Athenian orator (426–338 BCE) whom Milton seems to be emulating in *Areopagitica*.

[58]*1673* omits this comma.

[59]In effect, their rapier or personal sword, worn for self-defense by gentlemen

[60]*1674* omits this comma.

[61]*1673* has "to tugg or grapple" incorrectly.

[62]"The strength of each of them."

[63]For an analysis of Milton's opinions about the need for exercise, see Michael Lieb, "The Sinews of Ulysses: Exercise and Education in Milton," *Journal of General Education* 36 (1985): 245–56.

[64]"Before eating."

[65]1673 omits this comma.

---

[66]"If wise men and prophets are not utterly wrong."

[67]Outdoors or indoors.

[68]Assembling for military exercise.

[69]*1673* has "Embattelling."

[70]Underneath the "a" in 1643 is what appears to be underlining.

[71]Apparently when a bird was molting, shedding some of its feathers, it was considered to be ill.

[72]"Remnant" may mean "the leftovers of a badly damaged military force."

[73]*1644* has the word not capitalized, probably in error. I have corrected the capitalization.

dent and staid guides, to all the quarters of the land: learning and observing all places of strength, all commodities of building and of soil, for towns and tillage, harbours and Ports for trade. Somtimes taking sea as farre as to our Navy, to learn there also what they can in the practicall knowledge of sailing and of sea fight. These wayes would trie all their peculiar gifts of nature,[74] and if there were any secret excellence among them, would fetch it out, and give it fair opportunities to advance it selfe by, which could not but mightily redound to the good of this nation, and bring into fashion again those old admired vertues and excellencies, with farre more advantage now in this puritie of Christian knowledge. Nor shall we then need the *Mounsieurs* of *Paris* to take our hopefull youth into thir slight and prodigall custodies and send them over back again transform'd into mimics, apes & Kicshoes.[75] But if they desire to see other countries at three or four and twenty yeers of age, not to learn principles,[76] but to enlarge experience, and make wise observation, they will by that time be such as shall deserve the regard and honour of all men where they passe, and the society and friendship of those in all places who are best and most eminent. And perhaps then other Nations will be glad to visit us for their breeding, or else to imitate us in their own Country.

Now lastly for their diet there cannot be much to say, save only that it would be best in the same house; for much time else would be lost abroad, and many ill habits got; and that it should be plain, healthfull, and moderat I suppose is out of controversie. Thus Master[77] *Hartlib*, you have a generall view in writing, as your desire was, of that which at severall times I had discourst with you concerning the best and Noblest way of Education; not beginning as some have done from the cradle, which yet might be worth many considerations, if brevity had not been my scope, many other circumstances also I could have mention'd, but this to such as have the worth in them to make triall, for light and direction may be anough. Only I believe that this is not a bow for every man to shoot in that counts himself a teacher; but will require sinews almost equall to those which *Homer* gave *Ulysses*,[78] yet I am withall perswaded that it may prove much more easie in the assay, then it now seems at distance, and much more illustrious: howbeit not more difficult then I imagine, and that imagination presents me with nothing but very happy and very possible according to best wishes; if God have so decreed, and this age have spirit and capacity anough to apprehend.

The end.

---

[74]"Would test the individual capabilities of each student."
[75]A kickshaw, slangy term for useless trifle derived from the French *quelque chose*. The *OED* records Milton's use to be the first with the meaning of "A fantastical, frivolous person" (3).
[76]*1673* omits this comma.

[77]The "Master" was altered to "Mr." in the second edition, perhaps a meaningful demotion, although throughout the seventeenth century "Mr." stood for "Master."
[78]I have restored the italics for both proper names, not present in 1644.

Areopagitica (1644)

The Areopagus is a small hill near the Acropolis in Athens. The name "Areopagus" means "hill of Ares." Milton may have acknowledged the name of the god of war—Mars is the Latin equivalent—in his posture as a warfaring Christian in the tract. Areopagites, aristocratic judges of the court of the Areopagus, met regularly on the hill to hear cases. The judges were supposed to be the most virtuous and responsible citizens of Athens, and they were appointed for life. The famous orator Isocrates (436–338 BCE) used the title "Areopagitikos" for a speech he did not deliver in person because he had nervous and physical problems that prevented his speaking. Instead, it was to be read by the court and by the public at large. Isocrates's oration, usually translated as the "Areopagite Discourse" (c. 355 BCE), exhorted the people of Athens to restore to the Areopagus—a kind of Supreme Court—functions that had once made it a dominant moral force in Athenian life, "urging it to reclaim its former powers to control education and censor behaviour" (Orgel 821). As Ernest Sirluck and others have noted, Milton may have intended his audience to remember that St. Paul also delivered an oration on the Areopagus, reported in Acts 17.18–34 (Yale 2: 486n). There may be some friction or irony generated by rubbing the pagan Isocrates against the Christian St. Paul (Wittreich 111–12). Annabel Patterson would have us think of Isocrates's oration as "actually a reactionary document, urging the Areopagus to *institute* censorship" (115), but Isocrates's main point seems to be to ask that Athens be restored to the golden age he thought it had enjoyed when the Areopagus was in control of morality and education. The governing body had functioned as a kind of benign Big Brother, regulating conduct not with many written laws but with the virtuous example of the behavior of its judges, judges who not only became role models but also kept watch on the moral decisions of private citizens.

It is hard to say exactly what Milton wanted his readers to think of his associating himself with the Areopagus, with the Areopagite judges, or with Isocrates. If Milton meant by the allusion for us to think only in terms of Isocrates as eloquent orator and masterful prose stylist, that would be enough to create a rich relationship between the poet-orator and the ancient statesman who was also a master at oratory and the writing of beautiful prose. Milton's use of italics to emphasize words as words indicates that he does want the speech to be imagined as read out loud, as an oration as well as an essay.

Milton was fond of giving cryptic or esoteric Greek titles to his prose pamphlets, as one can see with the tract published next after *Areopagitica*, *Tetrachordon*, and, later, with *Colasterion*. The title *Areopagitica* certainly hints at the posture of its author as learned gentleman. Like Isocrates, Milton was offering his work to the state without delivering it in person. Milton sends off his silent oration while posing as a member of the intellectual elite, a Cambridge gentleman of means, writing from his home. The implication is that he, like Isocrates, is a brilliant orator even though he cannot, because of circumstances beyond his control, argue his case in person. Like Isocrates, Milton offers revolutionary reforms (Dowling). And, like St. Paul, Milton is an inspired orator, not just debating but recounting what he believes is Christian truth (Kendrick, "Ethics"). Since Milton's tract was unlicensed and unapproved by any state censor, and published by a printer who suppressed his name (Corns "Publication"), he may also be declaring his own courage in publishing it with his name (but not the printer's name or the licenser's approval) on the title page.

OCCASION

According to what is probably Skinner's biography,

> . . . *Areopagitica* [was] written in manner of an Oration, to vindicate the Freedom of the Press from the Tyranny of Licensers; Who either inslav'd to the Dictates of those that put them into Office, or prejudic'd by thir own Ignorance, are wont to hinder ye comming out of any thing which is not consonant to the common receiv'd Opinions, and by that means deprive the public of the benefit of many usefull labours.
>
> (above, 11)

The tract *Areopagitica* was directly a response to the Licensing Order of June 1643, which had banned the publication of any book or pamphlet not licensed by order of the Lords and Commons of Parliament and had empowered the Company of Stationers to enforce the licensing, to search out seditious presses, and to destroy any publication not duly licensed.

Here is the Licensing Order, in full:

> Whereas divers good Orders have bin lately made by both Houses of Parliament, for suppressing the great late abuses and frequent disorders in Printing many false forged, scandalous, seditious, libellous, and unlicensed Papers, Pamphlets, and Books to the great defamation of Religion and government. Which orders (notwithstanding the diligence of the Company of *Stationers*, to put them in full execution) have

taken little or no effect: By reason the bill in preparation, for redresse of the said disorders, hath hitherto bin retarded through the present distractions, and very many, as well *Stationers* and *Printers*, as others of sundry other professions not free of the *Stationers* Company and others being Delinquents (contrary to former orders and the constant custome used among the said Company) have taken liberty to Print, Vend and publish, the most profitable vendible Copies of Books, belonging to the Company and other *Stationers*, especially of such Agents as are imployed in putting the said Orders in Execution, and that by way of revenge for giveing information against them to the Houses for their Delinquences in Printing, to the great prejudice of the said Company of *Stationers* and Agents, & to their discouragement in this publik service.

It is therefore Ordered by the Lords and Commons in *Parliament*, That no Order or Declaration of both, or either House of *Parliament* shall be printed by any, but by order of one or both the said Houses: Nor other Book, Pamphlet, paper, nor part of any such Book, Pamphlet, or paper, shall from henceforth be printed, bound, stitched or put to sale by any person or persons whatsoever, unlesse the same be first approved of and licensed under the hands of such person or persons as both, or either of the said Houses shall appoint for the licensing of the same, and entred in the Register Book of the Company of *Stationers*, according to Ancient custom, and the Printer therof to put his name thereto. And that no person or persons shall hereafter print, or cause to be reprinted and Book or Books, or part of Book, or Books heretofore allowed of and granted to the said Company of *Stationers* for their relief and maintenance of their poore, without the license or consent of the Master, Wardens and Assistants of the said Company; Nor any Book or Books lawfully licensed and entred in the Register of the said Company for any particular member thereof, without the license and consent of the Owner or Owners therof. Nor yet import any such Book or Books, or part of Book or Books formerly Printed here, from beyond the Seas, upon paine of forfeiting the same to the Owner, or Owners of the Copies of the said Books, and such further punishment as shall be thought fit.

And for the Master and Wardens of the said Company, the Gentleman Usher of the House of *Peers*, the Sergeant of the Commons House and their deputies, together with the persons formerly appointed by the Committee of the House of Commons for Examinations, are hereby Authorized and required, from time to time, to make diligent search in all places where they shall think meete, for all unlicensed Printing Presses, and all Presses any way imployed in the printing of scandalous or unlicensed Papers, Pamphlets, Books, or any Copies of Books belonging to the said Company, or any members thereof, without their approbation and consents, and to seize and carry away such printing Presses Letters, together with the Nut, Spindle, and other materialls of every such irregular Printer, which they find so misimployed, unto the Common Hall of said Company, there to be defaced and made unserviceable according to Ancient Custom; And likewise to make diligent search in all suspected Printing-houses, Ware-houses, Shops and other places for such scandalous and unlicensed Books, papers, Pamphlets and all other Books, not entred, nor signed with the Printers name as aforesaid, being printed, or reprinted by such as have no lawfull interest in them, or any way contrary to this Order, and the same to seize and carry away to the said common hall, there to remain till both or either House of *Parliament* shall dispose thereof, And likewise to apprehend all Authors, Printers, and other persons whatsoever imployed in compiling, printing, stitching, binding, publishing and dispersing of the said scandalous, unlicensed, and unwarrantable papers, books and pamphlets as aforesaid, and all those who shall resist the said Parties in searching after them, and to bring them afore either of the Houses or the Committee of Examinations, that so they may receive such further punishments, as their Offences shal demerit, and not to be released untill they have given satisfaction to the Parties imployed in their apprehension for their paines and charges, and given sufficient caution not to offend in like sort for the future. And all Justices of the Peace, Captaines, Constables and other officers, are hereby ordered and required to be aiding, and assisting to the foresaid persons in the due execution of all, and singular the premisses and in the apprehension of all Offenders against the same. And in case of opposition to break open Doores and Locks.

And it is further ordered, that this Order be forthwith Printed and Published, to the end that notice be taken thereof, and all Contemners of it left inexcusable.

(Quoted in Yale 2: 797–98)

However brutal the Licensing Act may seem to a modern reader, with its endorsement of what we might consider illegal entry, search, and seizure, the tactics the act endorses were considered legal in 1643 when they were used against supposed sedition or treason. And

Milton's was only one of many pamphlets arguing issues to be considered by Parliament in a time of chaotic political upheaval (for the context, see Corns, *Uncloistered* 56–60, and Blum). There is no evidence that *Areopagitica* had much effect immediately after it was published, on November 23, 1644. It did appear without a printer's imprint, and "The printer is unknown" (Shawcross, "A Survey" 304), but Shawcross submits an educated guess that he may have been Augustine Matthews (*Milton: A Bibliography* 17). What the title page leaves out is also important. Not only does it omit the name of the publisher or bookseller (both used to direct the potential purchaser to a place of purchase), it also omits reference to the pamphlet's being licensed either by a state censor or by the Company of Stationers, the official guild-like licensing body that had already complained about what Milton wrote in favor of divorce (Parker 264). As one can see by reading the Licensing Order, the Stationers' Company was in the pocket of Parliament. *Areopagitica*, as Milton points out in the tract, has no "Imprimatur" from a church functionary, as had the Roman Catholic books he had seen when he went to Italy in 1638–39. Nor does it have any state or civic licensing. As he also reminds us inside the pamphlet, it will not be copyrighted, and it will not bring its author royalties after publication. One can see why it was published anonymously if one reads the Licensing Order, for fear that "in case of opposition" coming from printers, authorities would have the power "to break open Doores and Locks" and, indeed, deconstruct the entire printing operation, down to its nuts and bolts. As soon as *Areopagitica* was published, it could have become a wanted book, because it had been illegally published.

In the 1640s, Milton had already been a victim of attempts at censorship, and he was probably angry about his victimization. The second edition of his *Doctrine and Discipline of Divorce* (published 13 August 1644), was issued four months before *Areopagitica*. The M.P. Herbert Palmer, who appears not to have read the *Doctrine and Discipline,* declared it before both houses to be "a wicked booke . . . abroad and uncensored, though deserving to be burnt" (quoted in Blum 83). Book burning, of course, is one effective form of censorship. Some of Milton's later books, specifically those advocating the judicious execution of Charles I, were ordered burnt by the public hangman in Oxford, and others were burnt in monarchist communities on the Continent (Parker 984, 986). As Kranidas points out, "The urge to defend himself was immediate for Milton [because of the public censure of the *Doctrine and Discipline of Divorce*]; his movement to objectivity was one of the major achievements of the tract" (176).

Areopagitica came to be recognized as "the first work devoted primarily to freedom of the press" (Yale 2: 163), and, because of its eloquence and the power of its imagery and its arguments, it has become the best-known work on the subject in English. Yet "Milton's plea against censorship (noticed first in 1646) seems to have had little effect, and not to have been judged as it has by modern readers. It was appropriated as the source of Charles Blount's and William Denton's anti-licensing arguments in 1679 and 1681, respectively" (Shawcross, *Milton: The Critical* 13).

Despite the notable lack of attention to *Areopagitica* just after it was published, Christopher Hill corrects the earlier impression of William Riley Parker's *Milton's Contemporary Reputation* that Milton was unknown in parliamentary circles: " . . . among radical reformers—Baptists, Socinians, Levelers, Ranters and many others—there is evidence, if we look for it, that Milton was read and appreciated" (99). What Milton embraces and reflects in *Areopagitica* is the ". . . Utopian enthusiasm of the early forties, [when he] began to envisage the possibility of a reconstructed society in which the true poet could step forward as the acknowledged legislator of mankind" (159). *Areopagitica* is unabashed English chauvinism and egocentric optimism on Milton's part, with its "[p]oetry and politics . . . inextricably mixed " (159). The English are the chosen people, the new politicians will or should be epic poets, and *Areopagitica* is a kind of extended prayer that the English Christian poet should be allowed to produce (we presume) epic poetry without interference and with the approval of the state. Nigel Smith calls attention to the significant fact that "kings are simply not mentioned in the tract" (108), an omission implying that poets would be more important than kings in Milton's ideal England. In fighting censorship, Milton was allying himself with a Protestant and bourgeois movement: ". . . the printing industry was the principal natural ally of libertarian, heterodox, and ecumenical philosophers. Eager to expand markets and diversify production, the enterprising publisher was the natural enemy of narrow minds" (Eisenstein 419).

Any editor of *Areopagitica* should stress, however, that Milton's argument was not against all forms of censorship: it decries only "preventive censorship . . . , under which nothing was to be published except what had been approved in advance by an official license" (Yale 2: 163). Achsah Guibbory puts it succinctly: "Though his arguments against pre-publication censorship could be extended to include any censorship, Milton himself insisted that, once published, a book should be judged—even, like a person, punished if it is guilty of crimes" (286). John Illo and others have established that, closely examined, *Areopagitica* is "neither libertarian nor tolerationist" ("Euripides" 81–82). One irony that critics and biographers have not overlooked is that Milton himself became a kind of censor when he exercised control on behalf of the Commonwealth Parliament over the journal *Mercurius Politicus* in 1651 and 1652 (Shawcross, "Survey" 307). Francis Barker adds that "Milton was never opposed to censorship, in fact we know that in 1651 he served as a licenser of new books, a state censor" (67).

The point is that Milton was not a modern civil libertarian. He would come to believe, later in his career, in the rule of the intellectual elite (Trevor-Roper 257). When he wrote *Areopagitica*, Milton believed that theologically correct—that is, Protestant—literature should be allowed to be published. He would, of course, have preferred to censor or condemn Roman Catholic literature (Hill 155), and he believed in the power of the law to control libelous or scandalous publications—after they were published. Within his own pamphlet, Milton even praises the court of the Areopagus for burning libelous or atheistic books!

Stanley Fish has neatly summarized the problem of interpreting *Areopagitica*:

> . . . Milton is finally, and in a profound way, not [Fish believes] against licensing, and . . . he has almost no interest at all in the "freedom of the press" as an abstract or absolute good (and, indeed, does not unambiguously value freedom at all); and that his attitude towards books is informed by none of the reverence that presumably led the builders of the New York Public Library to have this sentence from the tract preside over their catalogue room: "A goode Booke is the pretious life blood of a master spirit, imbalm'd and tresur'd up on purpose to a life beyond life." (235)

Fish adds his own conclusions about the tract:

> Books are no more the subject of the *Areopagitica* than is free speech; both are subordinate to the process they make possible, the process of endless and proliferating interpretations whose goal is not the clarification of truth, but the making of us into members of her incorporate body so that we can be finally what the Christ of *Paradise Regained* is said already to be, a "living oracle" (*PR* I.460) (246–47).

RHETORIC AND STYLE

Areopagitica is a classical oration and can be divided into the conventional categories of that form of argumentation: a proem or exordium (introduction, before the argument begins), a proposition (statement of the position the tract will uphold), a confirmation together with proof and refutation of opposing opinions, a digression into related subjects, and a peroration or epilogue and conclusion (Dowling 50; Tsuji 77–78). C. A. Patrides wisely contrasts it with *Of Education*: whereas *Of Education* is "almost entirely devoid of rhetoric," *Areopagitica* "advances cumulatively in a series of waves, until the gathered force of argument and rhetorical patterns overwhelms our reservations and commands our assent" (29). Tsuji establishes the patterns of rhetoric derived from Isocrates, Aristotle, and Quintillian that Milton may have drawn on, and Steadman sets Milton's tract firmly in the tradition of Renaissance humanism (71). Although Milton does not embrace the plain style of Attic Greek oratory practiced by the elegant Isocrates, he does believe, like the Roman Quintillian, that the orator ought to be a good man, and that he ought to be a combination of statesman, poet, and priest (Tsuji 9). Of course he should have truth on his side, and he should not be sophistical (he should not argue without deep conviction on either side of an ethical question, as the Sophists were accused of doing, by Isocrates, among others). Milton compares himself to Isocrates, to Cicero, and to St. Paul, all exemplary orators who could argue passionately for what they considered to be the truth.

I should also mention the function of orator as teacher. Isocrates was himself a famous teacher of oratory as well as an orator. Milton is as eager to instruct the Houses of Parliament as he would be to instruct those who might follow his system of instruction in *Of Education*, published five months earlier than *Areopagitica*.

Beyond argumentation, perhaps in the role not of the orator and not of the teacher but of the poet, rhapsodist, and preacher, Milton includes passages of great lyrical strength unlike anything to be found in earlier English prose. He may have been imitating the much-admired poetic prose of Isocrates, though his English prose is richer and more finely woven than that of Isocrates in Greek. I am referring to images such as that of England emerging like a strong man or an eagle (below, 990), or like the famous passage that begins "For Books are not absolutely dead things." Such lyrical passages are quotable, but they are too long to be classified as "sententiae" (terse wise sayings) or the "apothegms" that Milton makes fun of in his references to "*Laconick* apothegms." Instead they are the prose equivalent of the epic similes in *Paradise Lost*. Their effect is emotional or sensual, as well as rhetorical.

Areopagitica is a hot blaze of learning, throwing off sparks in every direction. Its author might be thought a pedant if he weren't so obviously excited by what he has learned. One valid response that a modern reader might address to the author about the heaps of references and allusions is "You must be kidding," but Milton is not joking in most senses of the word: he just displays his remarkably memorious and eclectic mind at work, and in doing so he also shows off some of the most remarkable imagery ever put in prose. The imagery and the ideas are often radical for his own time, but they are prophetically radical, so that the modern reader may be seduced into agreeing with Milton ahistorically and seeing him as a mirror of ideas commonly accepted in modern democratic societies. The accepted role model of Roman manhood, Cato—as Milton pictures him—might become the dour Puritan not accepting liberal and progressive Greek ideas. The Inquisition, still granting imprimaturs or preventing publication of listed books in Milton's time, might be laughed at by a modern reader trained by Monty Python skits to think of it as an anachronism. Milton, however, knew the Inquisition first-hand as the agency that held Galileo under house arrest when he visited him in Florence (as Friedman reminds us), and he dwells on its stifling effects on literature and art throughout *Areopagitica*. In the 1630s and 1640s, there was a network of European presses publishing works forbidden or indexed by the Inquisition—works by Galileo, Francis Bacon, Comenius, and Grotius (see Eisenstein, Chs. 7 and 8). Milton may have had experience with such presses in Geneva, where he had visited in 1638, or in Amsterdam, famous for publishing religious and political tracts considered seditious in England.

There may be a conflict between style and content, or superficial meaning and subtext, in Milton's early political prose, as noted by Hugh Trevor-Roper:

Always we are dazzled by the sheer power of the writing: the incomparable richness of vocabulary, the exuberant metaphors, the buoyant spirits, the freshness and flexibility of style, the sudden colloquialism, the flashes of black wit. . . . But if we stay to look behind those winged words, at their meaning and intent, we can only be disgusted by the gross injustice, the hideous caricatures, the venomous, hysterical spite which they convey (253).

I would defend Milton against Trevor-Roper's reactionary charges of injustice: Milton's spite, directed self-righteously against the rule of the prelates in the hierarchy of the Church of England, does no more than reflect the bitterness between factions at the outbreak of civil war. It is revolutionary rhetoric, but, to its credit, it elevates the current political and theological debates to the international and even universal fight between good and evil. Sardonic and savage satire is used freely, especially against the Inquisitorial practices that Milton had observed first-hand when he had been in Italy in 1638–39. One of Samuel Hartlib's German correspondents complained that *Areopagitica* was "rather too satyrical throughout . . . and because of his all too highflown style in many places quite obscure" (translated in Norbrook). A modern reader might enjoy the satire, from this distance, and fight through the thick texture of learned allusions to enjoy the energy of the piece.

TEN YEARS LATER, MILTON COMMENTS ON *AREOPAGITICA* AND ITS IMAGERY

In 1654, in his *Second Defence*, Milton could reflect on the process of composing the speech:

Lastly I wrote, after the model of a regular speech, *Areopagitica*, on the liberty of printing, that the determination of true and false, of what ought to be published and what suppressed, might not be in the hands of the few who may be charged with the inspection of books, men commonly without learning and of vulgar judgement, and by whose license and pleasure, no one is suffered to publish any thing which may be above vulgar apprehension.

(Columbia 8: 133)

One can see Milton's intellectual elitism in the statement. He is not worried so much about being censored as he is about being censored by intellectual inferiors.

IMAGERY AND COMPOSITION

Areopagitica is full of images of violent and warlike Christianity (Raylor), of minutely observed human behavior, and of mercantile life in London. Milton's father and to some extent John Milton Jr. were both involved in the constant business of renting, contracting, selling, and suing necessary to the profession of scrivener which John Milton Sr. followed. The imagery makes the style at once colloquial and homely (nursing mothers, feet in the stirrup, and piddling accounts) and obtusely allusive. Biblical allusions may be especially oblique, connected with the chains of research and annotation that Milton makes fun of in the tract. Whenever the Roman Catholic Church or the Church of England under the control of Archbishop Thomas Laud is discussed, Milton adds layers of self-conscious and perhaps self-protecting irony—demonstrated in his making up words like "bejesuited." The end product of such layering of imagery is often deep and bitter laughter. And, as Lana Cable points out, *Areopagitica* "regularly points to the inadequacy of all signs to express the truths they serve" (117).

We have Milton's testimony in *Areopagitica* itself as to what his method might be in composing his tract:

> When a man writes to the world, he summons up all his reason and deliberation to assist him; he searches, meditats, is industrious, and likely consults and conferrs with his judicious friends; after all which done he takes himself to be inform'd in what he writes, as well as any that writ before him; if in this the most consummat act of his fidelity and ripenesse, no years, no industry, no former proof of his abilities can bring him to that state of maturity, as not to be still mistrusted and suspected, unlesse he carry all his considerat diligence, all his midnight watchings, and expence of *Palladian* oyl, to the hasty view of an unleasur'd licenser, perhaps much his younger, perhaps far his inferiour in judgement, perhaps one who never knew the labour of book-writing, and if he be not repulst, or slighted, must appear in Print like a punie with his guardian, and his censors hand on the back of his title to be his bayl and surety, that he is no idiot, or seducer, it cannot be but a dishonor and derogation to the author, to the book, to the priviledge and dignity of Learning.

This scholar and poet writes carefully, after consultation with thoughtful friends like Samuel Hartlib and after careful scholarly study, and he writes to display artfully what he has learned in his own reading. He wants no ignorant licenser to oversee such carefully composed work. He does not want to be treated like a child, or an idiot, or a seducer: he is more public-spirited and more mature, and he needs no guardian for his morality.

INFLUENCE IN THE HISTORY OF IDEAS: *AREOPAGITICA* AND THE U.S. FIRST AMENDMENT

Freedom of speech and freedom from prepublication censorship (in legal terms, "prior restraint") is taken for granted in the United States and in nations modeling their constitutions on that of the United States. Educated English and North American colonials in the eighteenth century such as James Madison, Benjamin Franklin, and Thomas Jefferson were expected to read Milton's prose as well as his poetry. Jefferson went so far as to try to analyze the metrics of *Paradise Lost* in his private memorabilia (Jefferson 596), and references to Milton outweigh those to all other poets in Jefferson's *Literary Commonplace Book* (Davies, "Borrowed" 258).

The real Milton might have despised the process of his becoming after his death a cultural icon in America, since he is the man who wrote *Eikonoklastes* and

thereby popularized the word "iconoclast." The fact remains that the prose works of a great poet demanded respect. *Areopagitica* has become part of the canon and part of that body of literature that still today defines cultural literacy. For the American founding fathers, *Areopagitica* would have been a kind of holy book just because it was written by Milton.

In yet another sense, Milton was an American in spite of not being involved directly in many colonial matters. In a paper I gave in 1988, I described Milton as "a kind of prototype American" (Flannagan 66). I discovered later that an American editor of Milton, Rufus W. Griswold, had said essentially the same thing in 1845 (Shawcross, *John Milton and Influence* 139). Milton as the author of *Areopagitica* in 1644 might be characterized as a prophet on the lunatic fringe, a "crackpot" as Parker put it, since he had in that year advocated divorce on paper, a position that most English people would have regarded as immoral, illegal, and perhaps even blasphemous, since Christ had not allowed for divorce except for adultery. Crank or not, prophet or not, Milton advocated freedom of speech, freedom of conscience (his work did have an influence on Jefferson's "Bill for Religious Freedom in Virginia" [Sensabaugh 145]), along with freedom to worship where and when one chooses, freedom of the will, and freedom to dissolve marriages by mutual consent, concepts which seem essential to political theory as practiced in the United States in the present age.

THE SUBVERSIVE TEXT

In the very typography of the title page is a powerful, subversive, freedom-loving, rabble-rousing (Hill 226; Parker 559; Kranidas 177), rebellious egocentrism or entrepreneurism. Milton is going it alone, proclaiming his own name, on a dangerous playing field, one in which he might have had his nose slit or his ears cut off next to his skull—the fate of the pamphleteer William Prynne. For writing things considered seditious, Prynne had his ears clipped once by the public hangman, then cropped even closer to his skull, when he wrote more things considered seditious (see Wilding 10–11); Milton probably alluded to such mutilation (Yale 1: 704), which was symbolic in that it denied Prynne the ability to hear the word of God, and he probably worried about enduring the same fate. Still, "*Areopagitica* carried his full name," as Thomas Corns puts it, "(though neither name nor initials of the printer) and constitutes a challenge to the new ascendancy to take him to court" (*Uncloistered* 56). Milton egregiously put his name on the marquee in lights. His printer's name is not there, but "London" and "1644" are. He may be protecting his printer against persecution, but he is declaring himself liable for what he has written. John Milton is advertising his own importance by making his name larger in font size than that of the "Parlament," and, if you notice the spelling of the word on the title page, Milton is even telling the Parliament how to spell its name (his preferred spelling, taken from the medieval Latin "parlamentum"). The author's name is even larger than "ENGLAND," typography that looks to me more than a bit seditious.

Areopagitica, though unlicensed and its printer and even its bookseller unacknowledged, is printed scrupulously, by which I mean that it seems to preserve many of the author's known habits of orthography. Shawcross has pointed out, however, how battered the typeface is, an indication that the printing process might have been not only surreptitious but quick and dirty ("Survey" 304). Though Milton may not have seen the work through the press (Sirluck 483), his concern for accuracy is shown in what were probably his corrections or corrections made on his behalf in presentation copies. All copies now preserved that Milton presented to libraries or individuals correct "wayfaring Christian" to "warfaring Christian," all corrections to "r's" having been inserted in what is possibly his hand. Shawcross believes that the corrections were more likely to have been made "in the print shop" ("Survey" 305). Milton also seems (and this is just informed speculation on my part) to have imposed his will on the printers and compositors who set type to use the less common spelling "parlament" throughout, from the title page on. Leo Miller has established that "Milton was a reviser" ("Milton" 576) and that he was punctilious about details like the spelling of a word with strong etymological associations (compare the English "parliament," the medieval Latin "parlamentum," the Italian "parlaménto," and the French "parlement"). Other Miltonic spellings include "voutsafe," "ventrous," "democraty," "anough" (or "anow"), "bin" (for "been"), "autority," and *Salomon*. Milton seems to be attending to details like the use of the accent mark with the Italian name "*Nicolò*," but he may also be guiding his readers toward correct pronunciation with the word he spells "Piatza"—perhaps he was instructing his reader in how to transliterate an Italian word, "piazza," to make pronouncing it easier for an English reader. Something similar happens with "Romanze," spelled after the Italian *romanzo*, along with "balcone" and "ghittarrs." The compositor may also have been instructed how to deal with some of the minutiae of capitalization, as with "new limbo's and new hells wherein they might include our Books," in which neither the words "limbo's" nor "hells" is given the dignity of capitalization, but "Books" is. The word "book" and all words beginning with "book" are almost invariably capitalized in the 1644 *Areopagitica* through folio

B2^v (p. 10), but as soon as folio B2^v ends and B3 begins the last instance of a capitalized "Books" occurs; thereafter in the tract "book" always begins with a lowercase "b." There is also a change of direction in the way in which personal names and place names are italicized, a de-emphasis on italicizing place names such as "Greece" (italicized only once) or adjectives made from place names such as "Chaldean" or "Roman." Such patterns may indicate that a first compositor was instructed to or had the habit of capitalizing "Book," but that a subsequent compositor, someone who set from gathering B3 to the end of the pamphlet, was either not instructed to capitalize the word or had the strong habit of not capitalizing it.

The orthographic usage in the tract is consistent. Italics are used for quotations and near paraphrases, and for emphasis on important words or phrases. Capitals are likewise used at times to indicate respect, as in "Your" when it applies to "Lords and Commons." In order to understand seventeenth-century orthography, consider the famous sentence "Many a man lives a burden to the Earth; but a good Booke is the pretious life-blood of a master spirit, imbalm'd and treasur'd up on purpose to a life beyond life." Choices are made to capitalize "Earth" and "Booke," to spell "pretious" rather than "precious," to hyphenate "life-blood," to spell the past participles "imbalm'd" and "treasur'd" (see Shawcross, "Orthography" 133). Those choices might all be influenced by Milton's holograph practices—how he wrote in his own handwriting—since the compositor would most likely be using Milton's manuscript as copy. The spelling of the adjective "pretious" (it appears twice in the tract) quite possibly indicates that one of Milton's preferences slipped through (Shawcross, "Orthography" 130) consistently; the hyphenation of "life-blood" is also typical of Milton's usage. I am inclined to believe that Milton—often talking about the process of seeing books through the press within the pamphlet—was himself closely overseeing the production of his own text. His italics tell too much about meaning to be accidental. They usually tell us that a word is a proper name or place name, or they tell us that a phrase is a quotation or that it is meant to be emphasized, as with "*Laconick Apothegms*," or ridiculed, as with "his brother *quadragesimal* and *matrimonial*" (Kranidas 179). At times the compositors may have been confused whether or not to italicize an adjective or noun form, as, for instance, when "Presbyter" is not italicized, but "Presbyterian" is. Italics also signal quotations, as when Milton quotes directly from the Licensing Order. It may also be that the italics, being a forerunner of modern quotation marks, were used for indirect quotations rather than verbatim quotations. An italicized quotation may include an unitalicized "&c," which seems to be designed to indicate an ellipsis in the passage being quoted.

Capitalization is less meaningful than italicization in seventeenth-century orthography: a capitalized initial letter signifies only that what follows are proper names or important nouns. Judging the importance of a noun was, I believe, usually up to the compositor and had little to do with the copy he was following (see Ronberg 13–15), but the noncapitalization of, say, "god" (meaning the Christian god), or "limbo," or "church" may have had political or theological implications in 1644. Also a capitalized initial letter in a word may indicate the beginning of a quotation, as with the capitalized "Rise" in "God . . . said without exception, Rise, *Peter*, kill and eat. . . ." Throughout the 1640s printers and even compositors in printing shops were closely watched, and foreigners were noted and carefully registered, for possibly seditious behavior (Lambert). A seditious compositor (or printer or author) might hide his religious or political agenda in capitalization and italics.

Milton's pamphlet as a whole is precisely but inexpensively printed. For instance, perhaps to save expense, the leading (spacing) between lines is narrowed to the point where lines are crowded and difficult to read. Some obvious new paragraphs are abutted with others, probably to conserve space (Campbell's edition, among others, introduces a number of new paragraphs). There are no internal headings or subheads, and there are no running headers. Economy and efficiency seem to govern house style.

I have normalized the 1644 text very little, changing long esses to their modern equivalent and changing the "J" that stood for the modern "I" (as in *Ionia*) or conversely the "I" that stood for the modern "J" (as in *Jove*). I have increased the leading between lines, to make the type on the page more legible, and I have normalized the spacing before and after punctuation marks. But I have not changed any spelling (including digraphs such as Æ or œ), or any capitalization, or punctuation, and I have preserved all italics.

It can be dangerous for an editor to emend, especially if the editor's emendation is silent. Campbell and Orgel both silently emend "Thus much may give us light after what sort Bookes were prohibited among the Greeks" to "what sort of books," without, I think, reading the idioms in the sentence or its syntax correctly (see below, n.52). Neither Hughes, Sirluck, nor Lutaud makes the emendation. Campbell silently emends "*Cataio*" to "Cathay," "*Delf*" to "Delft," and "*Jerom*" to "Jerome," each of which I think represents a distortion of what Milton probably wrote, and of a spelling that he might have used to indicate pronunciation. I have assumed

that, in cases other than obvious typographical errors (say an inverted "n" that becomes a "u"), the printers and compositors knew what they were doing. The paragraphing of the 1644 printing might be at times oppressive to a modern reader, because it forces on us large blocks of information to digest, but I have not redistributed the paragraphs, as did Hughes, Campbell, and Orgel. If twentieth-century readers can get used to reading pages of Faulkner or Proust without paragraph breaks, they can do the same with Milton.

Works Cited
(Editions are marked with an asterisk)

Armitage, David, Armand Himy, and Quentin Skinner, eds. *Milton and Republicanism*. Cambridge: Cambridge UP, 1995.

Barker, Arthur F. *Milton and the Puritan Dilemma, 1641–1660*. Toronto: U of Toronto P, 1942.

Barker, Francis. "*Areopagitica*: Subjectivity and the Moment of Censorship." *The Tremulous Private Body: Essays on Subjection*. New York: Methuen, 1984. Rpt. *John Milton*. Ed. Annabel Patterson. New York: Longman, 1992. 65–73.

Blum, Abbe. "The Author's Authority: *Areopagitica* and the Labour of Licensing." *Re-membering Milton: Essays on the Texts and Traditions*. Ed. Mary Nyquist and Margaret W. Ferguson. New York: Methuen, 1988. 74–96.

Boardman, John, Jasper Griffin, and Oswald Murray, eds. *The Oxford History of the Classical World*. Oxford: Oxford UP, 1986.

Cable, Lana. "'The Image of God in the Eye': *Areopagitica*'s Truth." *Carnal Rhetoric: Milton's Iconoclasm and the Poetics of Desire*. Durham, NC: Duke UP, 1995.

Camé, Jean-François "Images in Milton's *Areopagitica*," *Cahiers Elisabethains* 6 (1974): 23–37.

*Campbell, Gordon, ed. *John Milton: Complete English Poems*, Of Education, Areopagitica. 4th ed. London: J. M. Dent, 1990.

Christopher, Georgia B. *Milton and the Science of the Saints*. Princeton, NJ: Princeton UP, 1982.

Coiro, Ann Baynes. "Milton and Class Identity: The Publication of *Areoopagitica* and the 1645 Poems." *Journal of Medieval and Renaissance Studies* 22 (1992): 261–89.

Corns, Thomas N. *The Development of Milton's Prose Style*. Oxford: Clarendon, 1982.

—, ed. *The Literature of Controversy: Polemical Strategy from Milton to Junius*. London: Frank Cass, 1987.

—. "Publication and Politics 1640-1661: An SPSS-Based Account of the Thomason Collection of Civil War Tracts." *Literary and Linguistic Computing* 1 (1986): 74–84.

—. *Uncloistered Virtue: English Political Literature 1640-1660*. Oxford: Clarendon, 1992.

Davies, Tony. "Borrowed Language: Milton, Jefferson, Mirabeau." In

Armitage, *Milton and Republicanism*, 254–71.

*-----, ed. *John Milton: Selected Shorter Poems and Prose Writings*. New York: Routledge, 1988.

Dowling, Paul M. "*Areopagitica* and *Areopagiticus:* The Significance of the Isocratic Precedent." *Milton Studies* 21 (1986): 49–69.

Eisenstein, Elizabeth L. *The Printing Press as an Agent of Change: Communications and Cultural Transformations in Early-Modern Europe.* Cambridge: Cambridge UP, 1991.

Eusebius. *History of the Church from Christ to Constantine.* Trans. G. A. Williamson. New York: Dorset, 1984.

Evans, John X. "Imagery as Argument in Milton's *Areopagitica.*" *Texas Studies in Language and Literature* 8 (1969): 189–205.

Fish, Stanley. "Driving from the Letter: Truth and Indeterminacy in Milton's *Areopagitica.*" *Re-membering Milton: Essays on the Texts and Traditions.* Ed. Mary Nyquist and Margaret W. Ferguson. New York: Methuen, 1988.

Flannagan, Roy. "Look Homeward Angel: Milton Criticism in England and America." *Ringing the Bell Backward: The Proceedings of the First International Milton Symposium.* Ed. Ronald G. Shafer. Indiana U of P (the IUP Imprint Series), 1982.

Friedman, Donald. "Galileo and the Art of Seeing." *Milton and Italy: Contexts, Images, Contradictions.* Ed. Mario A. DiCesare. Binghamton, NY: Medieval & Renaissance Texts & Studies, 1991. 159–74.

Guibbory, Achsah. "Charles's Prayers, Idolatrous Images, and True Creation in Milton's *Eikonoklastes.*" *Of Poetry and Politics: New Essays on Milton and His World.* Ed. P.G. Stanwood. Binghamton, NY: Medieval & Renaissance Texts & Studies, 1995. 283–94.

*Hales, J. W., ed. *Milton's Areopagitica: Edited with Introduction and Notes by J. W. Hales.* Oxford: Clarendon, 1866. Rev. ed. 1882.

Hill, Christopher. *Milton and the English Revolution.* New York: Viking, 1978. Repr. Harmondsworth, Eng.: Penguin, 1979.

Illo, John. "Euripides, Milton, and Thomas Cooper." *Milton Quarterly* 27 (1993): 81–84.

---. "The Misreading of Milton's *Areopagitica.*" *Columbia University Forum* 8 (1965): 38–42. Rpt. *Radical Perspectives in the Arts.* Ed. Lee Baxendall. Harmondsworth, Eng.: Penguin, 1972. 178–92.

---. "*Areopagitica*s Mythic and Real." *Prose Studies* 11 (1988): 3–23.

Isocrates. *Areopagiticus.* Trans. George Norlin. New York: Putnam, 1929. 1: 100–57.

Jefferson, Thomas. *Memoirs, Correspondence, and Miscellanies, from the Papers of Thomas Jefferson.* Ed. Thomas Jefferson Randolph. Boston: Gray and Bowen, 1830. Vol. 3.

Kendall, Willmore. "How to Read Milton's *Areopagitica.*" *Journal of Politics* 22 (1960): 439–73.

Kendrick, Christopher. "Ethics and the Orator in *Areopagitica,*" *English Literary History* 50 (1983): 655–91.

------. *Milton: A Study in Ideology and Form.* New York: Methuen, 1986.

Kivette, Ruth. "The Ways and Wars of Truth." *Milton Quarterly* 6 (1972): 81–86.

Knoppers, Laura Lunger. *Historicizing Milton: Spectacle, Power, and Poetry in Restoration England.* Athens: U of Georgia P, 1994.

Kranidas, Thomas. "Polarity and Structure in Milton's *Areopagitica.*" *ELR: English Literary Renaissance* 14 (1984): 234-54.

Lambert, Sheila. "The Printers and the Government, 1604–1637." *Aspects of Printing from 1600.* Ed. Robin Myers and Michael Harris. Oxford: Oxford Polytechnic P, 1987. 1–29.

Le Comte, Edward S. "*Areopagitica* as a Scenario for *Paradise Lost.*" Lieb, *Achievements of the Left Hand.* 121–41.

Lieb, Michael, and John T. Shawcross, eds. *Achievements of the Left Hand: Essays on the Prose of John Milton.* Amherst, MA: U of Massachusetts P, 1974.

Lindenbaum, Peter. "John Milton and the Republican Mode of Literary Production." *Yearbook of English Studies* 21 (1991). 121–36.

Loewenstein, David A. "*Areopagitica* and the Dynamics of History." *Studies in English Literature* 28 (1988): 77–93.

----------. *Milton and the Drama of History: Historical Vision, Iconoclasm, and the Literary Imagination.* Cambridge: Cambridge UP, 1990.

--------, and James Grantham Turner, eds. *Politics, Poetics, and Hermeneutics in Milton's Prose.* Cambridge: Cambridge UP, 1990.

*Lutaud, Olivier, ed. *John Milton. Pour la Liberté de La Presse sans Autorisation ni Censure: Areopagitica.* Paris: Aubier-Flammarion, 1969.

Magnus, Elisabeth M. "Originality and Plagiarism in *Areopagitica* and *Eikonoklastes.*" *ELR: English Literary Renaissance* 21 (1991): 87–101.

Miller, Leo. "A German Critique of *Areopagitica* in 1647." *Notes & Queries* 234 (1989): 29–30.

----. "The Italian Imprimaturs in Milton's *Areopagitica.*" *Publications of the Bibliographical Society of America* 65 (1971): 345–55.

------. "Milton and Holstenius Reconsidered: An Exercise in Scholarly Practice." *Milton and Italy: Contexts, Images, Contradictions.* Ed. Mario A. DiCesare. Binghamton, NY: Medieval & Renaissance Texts & Studies, 1991. 573–87.

*Milton, John. *The Divorce Tracts,* Areopagitica, *and* Of Education *1644–45.* Menston, Eng.: Scolar, 1968.

Norbrook, David. "*Areopagitica:* Censorship, and the Early Modern Public Sphere." *The Administration of Aesthetics.* Ed. John Michael Archer and Richard Burt. Minneapolis: Minnesota UP, forthcoming.

*Orgel, Stephen, and Jonathan Goldberg, eds. *The Oxford Authors John Milton.* New York: Oxford UP, 1990. 236–73.

Parker, William Riley. *Milton: A Biography.* Oxford: Clarendon, 1966.

*Patrick, J. Max, ed. *Areopagitica. The Prose of John Milton.* New York: New York UP, 1968.

*Patrides, C. A. *John Milton: Selected Prose.* Harmondsworth, Eng.: Penguin, 1974.

Patterson, Annabel M. "The Hermeneutics of Censorship." *Censorship and Interpretation: The Conditions of Writing and Reading in Early Modern England*. Madison: U of Wisconsin P, 1984. 44–119.

Price, Alan F. "Incidental Imagery in *Areopagitica*," *Modern Philology* 49 (1952): 217–22.

Rapaport, Herman. *Milton and the Postmodern*. Lincoln: U of Nebraska P, 1983.

Raylor, Timothy. "New Light on Milton and Hartlib." *Milton Quarterly* 27 (1993): 19–23.

Ronberg, Gert. *A Way with Words: The Language of English Renaissance Literature*. London: Arnold, 1992.

Sensabaugh, George. *Milton in Early America*. Princeton: Princeton UP, 1964.

Shawcross, John T. *John Milton and Influence: Presence in Literature, History and Culture*. Pittsburgh: Duquesne UP, 1991.

———. *Milton: A Bibliography for the Years 1624–1700*. Binghamton, NY: Medieval & Renaissance Texts & Studies, 1984.

———. *Milton: The Critical Heritage*. New York: Barnes & Noble, 1970.

———. "Orthography and the Text of *Paradise Lost*." *Language and Style in Milton: A Symposium in Honor of the Tercentenary of *Paradise Lost. Ed. Ronald David Emma and John T. Shawcross. New York: Ungar, 1967. 120–53.

———. "A Survey of Milton's Prose Works." *Achievements of the Left Hand: Essays on the Prose of John Milton*. Ed. Michael Lieb and John Shawcross. Amherst: U of Massachusetts P, 1974. 291–391.

Shullenberger, William. "'Imprimatur': The Fate of Davanzati." *Milton and Italy: Contexts, Images, Contradictions*. Ed. Mario A. Di Cesare. Binghamton, NY: Medieval & Renaissance Texts & Studies, 1991. 175–96.

*Sirluck, Ernest, ed. *Areopagitica. Complete Prose Works of John Milton*. Vol. 2. New Haven: Yale UP, 1969.

Smallenburg, Henry M. "Contiguities and Moving Limbs: Style as Argument in *Areopagitica*," *Milton Studies* 9 (1976): 169–84.

Smith, Nigel. "*Areopagitica*: Voicing Contexts, 1643–5." *Politics, Poetics, and Hermeneutics in Milton's Prose*. Ed. David Loewenstein and James Grantham Turner. New York: Cambridge UP, 1990. 103–22.

Stavely, Keith W. *The Politics of Milton's Prose Style*. New Haven: Yale UP, 1975.

Steadman, John M. "The Dialectics of Temptation: Milton and the Idealistic View of Rhetoric." *The Hill and the Labyrinth: Discourse and Certitude in Milton and His Near-Contemporaries*. Berkeley: U of California P, 1984. 70–81.

Tsuji, Hiroko. *Rhetoric and Truth in Milton: A Conflict between Classical Rhetoric and Biblical Eloquence*. Kyoto, Japan: Yamaguchi, 1991.

Trevor-Roper, Hugh. "Milton in Politics." *Catholics, Anglicans and Puritans: Seventeenth Century Essays*. Chicago: U of Chicago P 1988. 231–82, 296–98.

Wilding, Michael. "Milton's *Areopagitica*: Liberty for the Sects." In Corns, *The Literature of Controversy* 7–38.

Wittreich, Joseph Anthony. "Milton's *Areopagitica*: Its Isocratic and Ironic Contexts." *Milton Studies* 4 (1972): 101–15.

Worden, Blair. "Literature and Censorship in Early Modern England." *Too Mighty to Be Free: Censorship and the Press in Britain and the Netherlands*. Zutphen: De Walburg P, 1988.

For the Liberty of unlicenc'd Printing.

THey who to States[1] and Governours of the Commonwealth direct their Speech, High Court of Parlament, or wanting[2] such accesse in a private condition, write that which they foresee may advance the publick good; I suppose them as at the beginning of no meane endeavour, not a little alter'd[3] and mov'd inwardly in their mindes: Some with doubt of what will be the successe,[4] others with feare of what will be the censure; some with hope, others with confidence of what they have to speake. And me perhaps each of these dispositions, as the subject was whereon I enter'd, may have at other times variously affected;[5] and likely might in these formost expressions now also disclose which of them sway'd most, but that the very attempt of this address thus made, and the thought of whom it hath recourse to, hath got the power within me to a passion, farre more welcome then incidentall to a Preface. Which though I stay not to confesse ere any aske, I shall be blamelesse, if it be no other, then the joy and gratulation which it[6] brings to all who wish and promote their Countries liberty; whereof this whole Discourse[7] propos'd will be a certaine testimony, if not a Trophey. For this is not the liberty which wee can hope, that no grievance ever should arise in the Commonwealth, that let no man in this World expect; but when complaints are freely heard, deeply consider'd, and speedily reform'd, then is the utmost bound of civill liberty attain'd, that wise men looke for. To which if I now manifest by the very sound of this which I shall utter, that wee are already in good part arriv'd, and yet from such a steepe disadvantage of tyranny and superstition grounded into our principles as was beyond the manhood of a *Roman* recovery,[8] it will bee attributed first, as is most due, to the strong assistance of God our deliverer, next to your faithfull guidance and undaunted Wisdome, Lords and Commons[9] of *England*. Neither is it in Gods esteeme the diminution of his glory,[10] when honourable things are spoken of good men and worthy Magistrates; which if I now first should begin to doe, after so fair a progresse of your laudable deeds, and such a long obligement upon the whole Realme to your indefatigable vertues, I might be justly reckn'd among the tardiest, and the unwillingest of them that praise yee. Neverthelesse there being three principall things, without which all praising is but Courtship[11] and flattery, First, when that only is prais'd which is solidly worth praise: next when greatest likelihoods are brought that such things are truly and really in those persons to whom they are ascrib'd, the other, when he who praises, by shewing that such his actuall perswasion is of whom he writes, can demonstrate that he flatters not; the former two of these I have heretofore endeavour'd, rescuing the employment from him who went about to impaire your merits with a triviall and malignant *Encomium*;[12] the latter as belonging chiefly to mine owne acquittall,[13] that whom I so extoll'd I did not flatter, hath been reserv'd opportunely to this occasion. For he who freely magnifies what hath been nobly done, and fears not to declare as freely what might be done better, gives ye the best cov'nant of his fidelity; and that his loyalest affection and his hope waits on your proceedings. His highest praising is not flattery, and his plainest advice is a kinde of praising; for though I should affirme and hold by argument, that it would fare better with truth, with learning, and the Commonwealth, if one of your publisht Orders[14] which I should name, were call'd in, yet at the same time it could not but much redound to the lustre of your milde and equall[15] Government, when as[16] private persons are hereby animated to thinke ye better pleas'd with publick advice, then other statists[17] have been delighted heretofore with publicke flattery. And men will then see what difference there is be-

---

[1]Heads of state, rulers.
[2]Being without; lacking.
[3]Affected emotionally, disturbed.
[4]Outcome.
[5]Showed a preference for.
[6]The whole oration is, most likely, the "it" in question.
[7]Probably the word means what it still means: "A spoken or written treatment of a subject, in which it is handled or discussed at length; a dissertation, treatise, homily, sermon, or the like" (*OED* 5).
[8]The phrase seems ironic. Roman manhood would ordinarily be connected with the virtues of bravery and civic-mindedness, but here it seems to be linked to Roman Catholic or "papist" practices suggested by "tyranny and superstition."
[9]Members of the House of Lords or the House of Commons in the English Parliament.

[10]God's glory is not, in other words, diminished when honorable things are spoken of such men.
[11]"Courtiership," or the flattering arts practiced by the courtier.
[12]Joseph Hall (1574–1656), Bishop of Norwich and Milton's adversary in pamphlet wars since 1641, when Hall's *Humble Remonstrance to the High Court of Parliament* set off a debate over episcopacy. Sirluck notes that "'Malignant' was a stock term by which the Parliamentary party designated its opponents" (Yale 2: 488n). Milton is arguing that Hall has been merely sending Parliament flattering documents—encomia.
[13]Performance.
[14]The Licensing Order of 1643, printed above in the Introduction.
[15]Fair, just, or impartial (meanings of the Latin "aequus" when it is applied to human beings).
[16]"At a time at which."
[17]Statesmen.

tween the magnanimity of a trienniall Parlament,[18] and that jealous hautinesse of Prelates[19] and cabin Counsellours that usurpt of late, when as they shall observe yee in the midd'st of your Victories and successes more gently brooking[20] writt'n exceptions against a voted Order, then other Courts, which had produc't nothing worth memory but the weake ostentation of wealth, would have endur'd the least signifi'd dislike at any sudden Proclamation. If I should thus farre presume upon the meek[21] demeanour of your civill and gentle greatnesse, Lords and Commons, as what your publisht Order hath directly said, that to gainsay, I might defend my selfe with ease, if any should accuse me of being new[22] or insolent, did they but know how much better I find ye esteem it to imitate the old and elegant humanity of Greece, then the barbarick pride of a *Hunnish* and *Norwegian* statelines. And out of those ages, to whose polite wisdom and letters we ow that we are not yet[23] *Gothes* and *Jutlanders*, I could name him who from his private house wrote that discourse to the Parlament of *Athens*,[24] that perswades them to change the forme of *Democraty*[25] which was then establisht. Such honour was done in those dayes to men who profest the study of wisdome and eloquence, not only in their own Country, but in other Lands, that Cities and Siniories[26] heard them gladly, and with great respect, if they had ought in publick to admonish the State. Thus did *Dion Prusæus* a stranger and a privat Orator counsell the *Rhodians*

against a former Edict:[27] and I abound with other like examples, which to set heer would be superfluous. But if from the industry of a life wholly dedicated to studious labours, and those naturall endowments haply not the worst for two and fifty degrees of northern latitude,[28] so much must be derogated,[29] as to count me not equall to any of those who had this priviledge, I would obtain to be thought not so inferior, as your selves are superior to the most of them who receiv'd their counsell: and how farre you excell them, be assur'd, Lords and Commons, there can no greater testimony appear, then when your prudent spirit acknowledges and obeyes the voice of reason from what quarter soever it be heard speaking; and renders ye as willing to repeal any Act of your own setting forth, as any set forth by your Predecessors.

If ye be thus resolv'd, as it were injury to thinke ye were not, I know not what should withhold me from presenting ye with a fit instance wherein to shew both that love of truth which ye eminently professe, and that uprightnesse of your judgement which is not wont to be partiall to your selves; by judging over again that Order which ye have ordain'd *to regulate Printing. That no Book, pamphlet, or paper shall be henceforth Printed, unlesse the same be first approv'd and licenc't by such*,[30] or at least one of such as shall be thereto appointed. For that part which preserves justly every mans Copy[31] to himselfe, or provides for the poor,[32] I touch not, only wish they be not made pretenses to abuse and persecute honest and painfull[33] Men, who offend not in either of these particulars. But that other clause of Licencing Books, which we thought had dy'd with his brother *quadragesimal* and *matrimonial*[34] when the Prelats expir'd, I shall now attend with such a Homily,[35] as shall

---

[18]"The Triennial Parliaments Act (February 16, 1641) provided for the automatic issue of writs for a new Parliament if the king failed to summon one within three years of the dissolution of the last" (Yale 2: 488n).

[19]Bishops or archbishops. William Laud, who was beheaded in 1647 after a long career purging the English church of puritans as privy counselor and Archbishop of Canterbury, would be the greatest example of a prelate. Milton never used the terms "prelate" or "prelacy" in a positive sense: compare "diseased tumour of Prelacie" in *Of Reformation* (Yale 1: 598). Likewise "cabin Counsellours" is a derogatory term for Charles I's cabinet ministers or privy counsellors.

[20]Enduring.

[21]Meekness is a quality Milton associates with Christ and with "Blessed are the meek"; hence it is almost always viewed positively in his prose or poetry.

[22]Probably "new-fangled" or "novel." Milton often uses the word "new" with negative associations, as in the phrase "re-ingendring Spirit of God with innovation, and that new creature for an upstart noveltie" (*Animadversions*; Yale 1: 703).

[23]Still. Milton knew that the English peoples were derived to a large extent from Scandinavian tribes.

[24]Isocrates.

[25]The less popular version of the word "democracy," based on the medieval Latin "democratia."

[26]Seniories, groups of church elders or city officials.

[27]The Greek orator Dio of Prusa (c. AD 40–117; Prusa is in Bithynia), also called Dion Chrysostom ("silver-tongued Dion"), upbraided the people of the island of Rhodes in his *Rhodiaca* for altering the names on their statuary to fit current rulers.

[28]Milton had a curious belief that living in a northern or damp latitude (i.e., in England) might cause retardation or loss of inspiration. Compare *Paradise Lost* 9.44–45.

[29]"Taken away from," with a hint of negative subtraction, or derogation stemming from aristocratic arrogance.

[30]The italics indicate that Milton is paraphrasing or quoting indirectly from the Licensing Order.

[31]Copyright, property "in copy" or protected by law.

[32]According to the Licensing Order, members of the Stationers Company were protected in their right to print any book that would benefit the poor.

[33]"Painstaking," "scrupulous."

[34]Milton is mocking dispensations from the law that could be granted by archbishops forbidding the eating of meat during Lent (called Quadragesima in the church calendar for its number of forty days) and to grant marriage licenses (normally the engaged would have to post banns announcing the marriage).

[35]Sermon.

lay before ye, first the inventors of it to bee those whom ye will be loath to own; next what is to be thought in generall of reading, what ever sort the Books be; and that this Order avails nothing to the suppressing of scandalous, seditious, and libellous Books, which were mainly intended to be supprest. Last, that it will be primely to the discouragement of all learning, and the stop of Truth, not only by disexercising[36] and blunting our abilities in what we know already, but by hindring and cropping[37] the discovery that might bee yet further made both in religious and civill Wisdome.

I deny not, but that it is of greatest concernment in the Church and Commonwealth, to have a vigilant eye how Bookes demeane[38] themselves as well as men; and thereafter to confine, imprison, and do sharpest justice on them as malefactors: For Books are not absolutely dead things, but doe contain a potencie of life in them to be as active as that soule was whose progeny they are; nay they do preserve as in a violl[39] the purest efficacie and extraction of that living intellect that bred them. I know they are as lively, and as vigorously productive, as those fabulous Dragons teeth;[40] and being sown up and down, may chance to spring up armed men. And yet on the other hand unlesse warinesse be us'd, as good almost kill a Man as kill a good Book; who kills a Man kills a reasonable creature, Gods Image; but hee who destroyes a good Booke, kills reason it selfe, kills the Image of God, as it were in the eye. Many a man lives a burden to the Earth; but a good Booke is the pretious life-blood of a master spirit, imbalm'd and treasur'd up on purpose to a life beyond life. 'Tis true, no age can restore a life, whereof perhaps there is no great losse; and revolutions of ages doe not oft recover the losse of a rejected truth, for the want of which whole Nations fare the worse. We should be wary therefore what persecution we raise against the living labours of publick men, how we spill[41] that season'd life of man preserv'd and stor'd up in Books; since we see a kinde of homicide may be thus committed, sometimes a martyrdome, and if it extend to the whole impression,[42] a kinde of massacre, whereof the execution ends not in the slaying of an elementall life, but strikes at that

ethereall and fift essence,[43] the breath of reason it selfe, slaies an immortality rather then a life. But lest I should be condemn'd of introducing licence,[44] while I oppose Licencing, I refuse not the paines to be so much Historicall, as will serve to shew what hath been done by ancient and famous Commonwealths, against this disorder, till the very time that this project of licencing crept out of the *Inquisition*,[45] was catcht up by our Prelates, and hath caught some of our Presbyters.[46]

In *Athens* where Books and Wits were ever busier then in any other part of *Greece*, I finde but only two sorts of writings which the Magistrate car'd to take notice of; those either blasphemous and Atheisticall, or Libellous. Thus the Books of *Protagoras* were by the Judges of *Areopagus* commanded to be burnt, and himselfe banisht the territory for a discourse begun with his confessing not to know *whether there were gods, or whether not*:[47] And against defaming, it was decreed that none should be traduc'd by name, as was the manner of *Vetus Comœdia*,[48] whereby we may guesse how they censur'd libelling: And this course was quick enough, as *Cicero* writes, to quell both the desperate wits of other Atheists, and the open way of defaming, as the event shew'd. Of other sects and opinions though tending to voluptuousnesse, and the denying of divine providence they tooke no heed. Therefore we do not read that

---

[36]As often happens with his negative compounds, Milton invented the word (as he did "disparaging" as well). His is the only use of the word recorded in the *OED*.

[37]Cutting short.

[38]Conduct themself, behave well (*OED* 1).

[39]Vial, container for precious liquids.

[40]The dragon's or viper's teeth sowed by Cadmus or Jason, that, once planted, sprung up as armed men, in the fables as told by Ovid in *Metamorphoses* 3.101–30 and 7.121–42.

[41]Destroy or kill.

[42]Entire printing run of a published work.

[43]The Quintessence or Fifth Element, beyond Earth, Air, Fire, and Water, often called ether. Since the angels were thought to be composed of ether, an "ethereall" nature would represent pure and immortal intellect, beyond earthly or bodily elements–-the "elementall."

[44]Licentious behavior, as compared with behavior conducted in the exercise of free will. Milton often makes the distinction between license and liberty, as in the 1644 edition of *Doctrine and Discipline of Divorce*: ". . . honest liberty is the greatest foe to dishonest licence" (Yale 2: 225).

[45]Though officially initiated by Torquemada in 1478, the Inquisition was still quite active in Milton's era; he uses it as the Roman Catholic instrument of enforcing policy and stifling dissent, as he will when he recalls seeing Galileo a prisoner of the Inquisition later in this tract.

[46]"Prelates" would be Church of England clergymen, whereas "Presbyters" would be church officials who identified their title (as in "Presbyterian") with that applied in the Old Testament to the elders of the Jewish Sanhedrin. The difference would resemble the modern choices among "priest," "pastor," and "minister," though both "prelate" and "presbyter" were loaded words, or fighting words, in 1644.

[47]Cicero's *On the Nature of the Gods* 1.23 reports on the banishment of Protagoras and the burning of his books because the opening statement of his treatise doubted the existence of the gods.

[48]The first known comic Greek plays, the best examples of which are the early plays of Aristophanes. The plots were crude, barely connecting skits; the costumes were limited; the chorus was overly important; personal invective and political satire was more the focus than the comedy of character; and and there was a phallus on stage in honor of Priapus. See M. C. Howatson, "Comedy," in *The Oxford Companion to Classical Literature* (2nd ed.; Oxford: Oxford UP, 1989).

either *Epicurus*,[49] or that libertine school of *Cyrene*,[50] or what the *Cynick* impudence[51] utter'd, was ever question'd by the Laws. Neither is it recorded that the writings of those old Comedians were supprest, though the acting of them were forbid; and that *Plato* commended the reading of *Aristophanes* the loosest of them all, to his royall scholler *Dionysius*,[52] is commonly known, and may be excus'd, if holy *Chrysostome*,[53] as is reported, nightly studied so much the same Author and had the art to cleanse a scurrilous vehemence into the stile of a rousing Sermon. That other leading City of *Greece*, *Lacedæmon*,[54] considering that *Lycurgus* their Lawgiver[55] was so addicted to elegant learning, as to have been the first that brought out of *Ionia* the scatter'd workes of *Homer*, and sent the Poet *Thales* from *Creet* to prepare and mollifie the *Spartan* surlinesse[56] with his smooth songs and odes, the better to plant among them law and civility, it is to be wonder'd how muselesse[57] and unbookish they were, minding nought but the feats of Warre. There needed no licencing of Books among them for they dislik'd all, but

their owne *Laconick Apothegms*,[58] and took a slight occasion to chase *Archilochus*[59] out of their City, perhaps for composing in a higher straine then their owne souldierly ballats and roundels[60] could reach to: Or if it were for his broad verses,[61] they were not therein so cautious, but they were as dissolute in their promiscuous conversing;[62] whence *Euripides* affirmes in *Andromache*,[63] that their women were all unchaste. Thus much may give us light after what sort[64] Bookes were prohibited among the Greeks. The Romans also for many ages train'd up only to a military roughnes, resembling most the *Lacedæmonian* guise, knew of learning little but what their twelve Tables,[65] and the *Pontifick* College[66] with their *Augurs* and *Flamins* taught them in Religion and Law, so unacquainted with other learning, that when *Carneades* and *Critolaus*, with the *Stoick Diogenes*[67] comming Embassadors to *Rome*, tooke

---

[49]As Sirluck points out, Milton's references to Epicurus, as with that in *The Reason of Church Government* (Yale 1: 856), are invariably negative, even though he taught his own students Lucretius's *On the Nature of Things*, an Epicurean poem, presumably for its scientific value (see Yale 2: 495n).

[50]Followers of Aristippus the Elder (c. 435–356 BC), who was born in Cyrene and had been a pupil of Socrates. His philosophy embraced hedonism and the pursuit of voluptuous pleasure as the main goals of life.

[51]The Cynic school was founded by Antisthenes (c. 440–c. 370 BC) in the school named Cynosarges, whence the name. Its most famous boorish practitioner was Diogenes the Cynic, famous for carrying around a wooden tub that served as his shelter; for asking Alexander the Great not to shade him from the sun; for practicing the most intimate acts in public; and for his search for an honest man by lamplight.

[52]There was a tradition reported on in a life of Aristophanes that Plato sent the tyrant Dionysius of Syracuse (the second of that name) a copy of works of Aristophanes to instruct him how the Athenian constitution worked (Yale 2: 495n).

[53]St. John Crysostom (c.347–407), Bishop of Constantinople, best known as an ascetic and as a defender of the poor, was supposed to have studied Aristophanes to discover how to use invective—funny direct attack—effectively in his sermons.

[54]Sparta, in the province of Laconia, known for fierce, brave, and churlish warriors.

[55]Lycurgus is a semimythical figure supposed by Plutarch in his life of Lycurgus to have codified the Spartan legal system. See Milton's reference to Lycurgus's collecting the Homeric fragments in Prolusion 7. The reference is to the poet and musician Thales or Thaletas, and not the better-known philosopher.

[56]Haughtiness. The Spartans were best known for their militarism, but here Milton associates them with insolence perhaps issuing out of their tradition for Laconic replies to questions.

[57]Milton invented this word, according to the *OED*, and it was not used again until Shelley picked it up. In the case of "unbookish," Shakespeare was first supposed to have used the word, in *Othello* 4.1.102.

[58]"Spartan wise sayings." The italics may indicate that we are to take the phrase as sarcasm (the Spartans had no wise sayings; or the Spartans could think of nothing to read but their own rules of behavior).

[59]Archilochus of Paros, a lyric and satiric poet of the seventh century BCE, rumored to be licentious (his poems were supposedly banned in Sparta) and cowardly, by Valerius Maximus 6.3 and Plutarch *Instituta Laconica* 239B respectively.

[60]Ballads and rondelays, short songs with lower-class or disreputable associations (a "roundel" was both a necromancer's circle and a country dance).

[61]I.e., obscene poems. "Broad" is used in a sense similar to that in the compound "broad-minded."

[62]Discoursing, talking or communicating.

[63]In 1.590–93, Euripides associates the public nudity of Spartan men and women athletes with inevitable immorality, though Plutarch ("Lycurgus" 13–14) defends the practice.

[64]Some modern editors add an "of" here, since it was Milton's common idiom, but there is none in the 1644 edition. The meaning of the sentence, however, seems to be "give us light ["enlighten us"] after what sort ["following what custom"] Bookes were prohibited. . . ."

[65]The twelve tables of Roman law codified in 451–450 BC, which thereafter were engraved in bronze and memorized by Roman schoolboys as the basis for all Roman law.

[66]Milton subtly compares ancient Roman theocracy, with its priestly class of augurs and flamens gathering in a pontific (literally "bridge-making") college, and the Roman Catholic power structure of his own time, with its "Pontifex Maximus," the pope, and the college of cardinals. Both the Roman Catholic bishops and the Roman priests would, in fact, have served a "Pontifex Maximus." The augurs were priests in charge of interpreting the relationship between the prophetic flight of birds and public ceremony; the Flamens were priests whose primary function was to keep sacred fires burning. Both classes are mentioned, again pejoratively, in the Nativity Ode 94.

[67]Carneades, the Greek philosopher born about 213, was sent by the city-state of Athens, along with Critolaus and Diogenes (the Stoic, as Milton points out, and not the Cynic), to Rome in 155 in order to try to persuade the Romans not to impose a fine on Athens. Proving his oratorical skills, Carneades argued one day in favor of justice as a commendable virtue and on the next that it was not a virtue but part of a civil compact. Cato the Censor (usually regarded as an exemplary statesman) on this occasion argued that Carneades should be sent back to Athens promptly because of his bad influence on Roman youth ("seducers" here might be read as "misleaders"). Marcus Porcius Cato,

thereby occasion to give the City a tast of their Philosophy, they were suspected for seducers by no lesse a man then *Cato* the Censor, who mov'd it in the Senat to dismisse them speedily, and to banish all such *Attick* bablers[68] out of *Italy*. But *Scipio* and others of the noblest Senators withstood him and his old *Sabin* austerity;[69] honour'd and admir'd the men; and the Censor himself at last in his old age fell to the study of that whereof before hee was so scrupulous. And yet at the same time *Nævius* and *Plautus* the first Latine comedians[70] had fill'd the City with all the borrow'd Scenes of *Menander* and *Philemon*. Then began[71] to be consider'd there also what was to be don to libellous books and Authors; for *Nævius*[72] was quickly cast into prison for his unbridl'd pen, and releas'd by the *Tribunes* upon his recantation: We read also that libels were burnt, and the makers punisht by *Augustus*. The like severity no doubt was us'd if ought were impiously writt'n against their esteemed gods. Except in these two points, how the world went in Books, the Magistrat kept no reckning. And therefore *Lucretius* without impeachment versifies his Epicurism to *Memmius*,[73] and had the honour to be set forth the second time by *Cicero*[74] so great a father of the Commonwealth; although[75] himselfe disputes against that opinion in his own writings. Nor was the Satyricall sharpnesse, or naked plainnes of

Lucilius, or *Catullus*, or *Flaccus*,[76] by any order prohibited. And for matters of State, the story of *Titus Livius*,[77] though it extoll'd that part which *Pompey* held, was not therefore supprest by *Octavius Cæsar* of the other Faction. But that *Naso*[78] was by him banisht in his old age, for the wanton Poems of his youth, was but a meer covert[79] of State over some secret cause: and besides, the Books were neither banisht nor call'd in. From hence we shall meet with little else but tyranny in the Roman Empire, that we may not marvell, if not so often bad, as good Books were silenc't. I shall therefore deem to have bin large enough in producing what among the ancients was punishable to write, save only which, all other arguments were free to treat on.

By this time[80] the Emperors were become Christians, whose discipline in this point I doe not finde to have bin more severe then what was formerly in practice. The Books of those whom they took to be grand Hereticks were examin'd, refuted, and condemn'd in the generall Councels; and not till then were prohibited, or burnt by autority of the Emperor. As for the writings of Heathen authors, unlesse they were plaine invectives against Christianity, as those of *Porphyrius*[81] and *Proclus*, they met with no interdict that can be cited, till about the year 400. in a *Carthaginian* Councel,[82] wherein Bishops

---

also known as the Elder to distinguish him from his nephew of the same name, is most famous as the political and military opponent of Julius Caesar; he committed suicide rather than fall into Caesar's hands in defeat, after re-reading Plato's *Phaedo*. The Roman title "Censor" designated two officials in charge of taking the census and protecting public morality by removing senators who had broken the law or offended public taste.

[68]"Greeks who speak nonsense." St. Paul is also labeled as a "babbler" in Acts 17.18.

[69]Scipio Africanus was opposed by Cato, who is described as "Sabine" because he was brought up in that remote—and thus austere—territory in central Italy. See Cicero, *On Old Age* 8.26.

[70]"The first two authors of comic plays in Latin." The four Roman comedists helped displace the Old Comedy Milton referred to earlier in the fourth and third centuries BCE (see Patrides 204n).

[71]Supply "there" before "began."

[72]Gnaeus Naevius (c. 270–190s BCE) was a Roman dramatist, specializing in Greek New Comedy but also the author of an epic on the Punic War that has survived only in fragments. He offended the Metelli family with one line in a comedy, concerning their becoming consuls by fate (rather than ability) and was possibly exiled for the offense.

[73]The Roman Epicurean poet Lucretius (c. 98–55 BCE) wrote the *De Rerum Natura* ("On the Nature of Things") at the time Memmius was praetor (58 BCE). Lucretius at least nominally dedicated the work to Memmius.

[74]Modern editors, as with Campbell and Orgel, often insert a comma here. The compositor of the 1644 edition may well have neglected a comma after setting the italic name "Cicero."

[75]Supply "he."

[76]Lucilius (fl. 130 BC) was a patrician satirical poet who attacked the follies of fellow aristocrats. Catullus was the most famous lyric poet of his time, but he could also attack even Julius Caesar in satirical rhymes (Boardman 485). Flaccus is Quintus Horatius Flaccus, best known as Horace, who, like Lucilius, wrote the gentler variety of satire (as opposed to the savage variety exemplified by those written by Juvenal). Horace did not attack his contemporaries in his satires.

[77]The history of Titus Livius (59 BCE–AD 17) is, together with those of Sallust and Suetonius, one of the best-known accounts of imperial Rome, which Livy observed from the court of Augustus Caesar. Livy was said by Tacitus (*Annals* 4.34) to have praised Pompey over Augustus, but with Augustus's approval.

[78]The poet Ovid, whose full name is Publius Ovidius Naso, was banished by Augustus in AD 8. His books were not suppressed but, as Campbell reminds us, "withdrawn from public libraries" (582n).

[79]"Cover-up." The circumstances of Augustus's banishment of Ovid have often been, and still are, the subject of much scholarly speculation. Milton's point is that Ovid was not banished for writing obscene poems but for some deeper political reason.

[80]The Emperor Constantine, who began his rule in AD 306, was the first to institute Christianity as the state religion, convening the Council of Nicea to establish official church policy in AD 325.

[81]The Neoplatonic philosopher (and former Christian) Porphyry wrote *Against the Christians*, which was burned publicly by order of Constantine before 325. Proclus (c. 412–85), an Athenian Neoplatonist, wrote against Christianity; his work may not have been banned but he himself fled to Asia Minor to avoid persecution.

[82]For the information concerning the council in Carthage held in AD 409 and for much of the information in the next few paragraphs, Milton drew very heavily on the account in Pietro Sarpi's *Istoria del Concilio Tridentino* (London, 1619), translated as *The Historie of the Councel of Trent* by Nathaniel Brent (London, 1620). Though Sarpi continued to live a monastic life until his death in 1623, he had considered voluntary

themselves were forbid to read the Books of Gentiles,[83] but Heresies they might read: while others long before them on the contrary scrupl'd more the Books of Hereticks, then of Gentiles. And that the primitive Councels and Bishops[84] were wont only to declare what Books were not commendable, passing no furder, but leaving it to each ones conscience to read or to lay by, till after the yeare 800. is observ'd already by *Padre Paolo*[85] the great unmasker of the *Trentine* Councel. After which time the Popes of *Rome* engrossing what they pleas'd of Politicall rule into their owne hands, extended their dominion over mens eyes,[86] as they had before over their judgements, burning and prohibiting to be read, what they fansied not; yet sparing in their censures, and the Books not many which they so dealt with: till *Martin* the 5.[87] by his Bull not only prohibited, but was the first that excommunicated[88] the reading of hereticall Books; for about that time *Wicklef*[89] and *Husse* growing terrible,[90] were they who first drove the Papall Court to a stricter policy of prohibiting. Which cours *Leo* the 10,[91] and his successors follow'd, untill the Councell of Trent, and the Spanish Inquisition engendring together brought forth, or perfeted[92] those

Catalogues, and expurging Indexes[93] that rake through the entralls of many an old good Author,[94] with a violation wors then any could be offer'd to his tomb. Nor did they stay in matters Hereticall, but any subject that was not to their palat, they either condemn'd in a prohibition, or had it strait into the new Purgatory of an Index. To fill up the measure of encroachment, their last invention was to ordain that no Book, pamphlet, or paper should be Printed (as if S. *Peter* had bequeath'd them the keys of the Presse also out of Paradise)[95] unlesse it were approv'd and licenc't under the hands of 2 or 3 glutton Friers. For example:

> Let the Chancellor *Cini* be pleas'd to see if in this present work be contain'd ought that may withstand the Printing,
> > *Vincent Rabatta* Vicar of *Florence*.

> I have seen this present work, and finde nothing athwart the Catholick faith and good manners: In witnesse whereof I have given, &c.
> > *Nicolò Cini* Chancellor of *Florence*.

> Attending the precedent relation, it is allow'd that this present work of *Davanzati* may be Printed,
> > *Vincent Rabatta*, &c.

> It may be Printed, *July* 15.
> > Friar *Simon Mompei d' Amelia* Chancellor of the holy office in *Florence*.[96]

Sure they have a conceit,[97] if he of the bottomlesse pit[98] had not long since broke prison, that this quadruple exorcism would barre him down. I feare their next designe will be to get into their custody the licencing of

---

exile in England, and Milton perceived him an enemy of the pope and thus an ally to Protestantism.

[83]Here used in the biblical sense of "heathens" or "nations without the benefit of religious truth."

[84]The councils and ruling bishops of the early Christian Church ("primitive" in the sense of "original").

[85]Paolo Sarpi, here addressed as a monk in the respectful title "Padre."

[86]Analogous to "pulling the wool over their eyes." Having the control of what they see, and censoring it.

[87]Pope Martin the Fifth (1368–1451), perhaps intentionally stripped of dignity here by being referred to by his first name.

[88]"To forbid (an action) under pain of excommunication" (*OED* 1.b, citing this instance).

[89]The religious reformer John Wycliffe (c. 1329–84) was especially important to incipient puritan revolutionaries because he had questioned the authority of kings, had emphasized the use of the Bible in the vernacular in the home, and had valued inward religion (what puritans were to call "inner light") rather than the formalism of the Roman Catholic Church of his time. Wycliffe's English followers were the Lollards mentioned in Chaucer. John Huss (c. 1369–1415) was Wycliffe's disciple, though from Bohemia; he was burned at the stake for his Wycliffite opinions.

[90]"Invoking fear" (in the pope).

[91]Milton follows Sarpi's account of the Council of Trent very closely: "*Martinus* 5. doth in a Bull excommunicate all the Sects of heretiques, especially *Wiglefists*, and *Hussites*, not mentioning those who read their bookes, though many of them went about. *Leo* the tenth condemning *Luther*, did withall forbid all his bookes, upon paine of excommunication. . . . The *Inquisitors*, being more diligent, made Catalogues of those which they knew" (quoted in Yale 2: 500n). For Milton's further use of Sarpi, see Yale 1: 396.

[92]"Perfected," "brought to a close." The word was often spelled "parfet" or "perfet."

[93]Indexes or lists of forbidden books compiled by Roman Catholic church officials.

[94]The image is one of the Indexes as laxatives that rake through the guts of good authors, purging good as well as bad writing.

[95]The licensers are pictured as encroaching on legislative or civil power: they use the power supposedly conferred on the popes by St. Peter who himself had received from Christ the keys to Heaven (Matthew 16.19). The sarcasm is in the contrast between the symbolic keys to the kingdom of Heaven vs. the keys to printing houses.

[96]The imprimaturs Milton quotes are from the flyleaf of *Scisma d'Inghilterra* (the title might be translated as "the division in the English Church") by Bernardo Davanzati Bostichi (1529–1606), a Florentine historian whose work was published posthumously and probably while Milton was in Florence (Yale 2: 504n). See Harris Fletcher, "Milton's Library—An Additional Title," *Philological Quarterly* 28 (1949): 72–76, for evidence that Milton purchased the book while in Florence (see also Miller, Shullenberger).

[97]"Conceit" could mean extravagant idea or notion (see *OED* III).

[98]Satan, thrust by an angel into the bottomless pit which is Hell (Revelation 20.1–3). Satan would have broken out of his prison first to seduce Adam and Eve; here the implication is that four superstitious exorcisms, the ones just cited, would not put him back.

that which they say *Claudius[99] intended, but went not through with. Voutsafe to see[100] another of their forms the Roman stamp:

Imprimatur,[101] If it seem good to the reverend
Master of the holy Palace,
     Belcastro Vicegerent.

Imprimatur
     Friar *Nicolò Rodolphi* Master of the
     holy Palace.

Sometimes 5 *Imprimaturs* are seen together dialoguewise in the Piatza of one Title page, complementing and ducking each to other with their shav'n reverences,[102] whether the Author, who stands by in perplexity at the foot of his Epistle, shall to the Presse or to the spunge. These are the prety responsories,[103] these are the deare Antiphonies[104] that so bewitcht of late our Prelats, and their Chaplaines with the goodly Eccho they made; and besotted us to the gay imitation of a lordly *Imprimatur*, one from Lambeth house, another from the West end of *Pauls*;[105] so apishly Romanizing,[106] that the word of command still was set downe in Latine; as if the learned Grammaticall pen that wrote it, would cast no ink without Latine: or perhaps, as they thought, because no vulgar tongue[107] was worthy to expresse the pure con-

ceit of an *Imprimatur*; but rather, as I hope, for that our English, the language of men ever famous, and formost in the atchievements of liberty, will not easily finde servile letters anow[108] to spell such a dictatorie presumption English. And thus ye have the Inventors and the originall of Book-licencing ript up,[109] and drawn as lineally as any pedigree. We have it not, that can be heard of, from any ancient State, or politie,[110] or Church, nor by any Statute left us by our Ancestors elder[111] or later; nor from the moderne custom of any reformed Citty, or Church abroad; but from the most Antichristian Councel, and the most tyrannous Inquisition that ever inquir'd. Till then Books were ever as freely admitted into the World as any other birth; the issue of the brain was no more stifl'd then the issue of the womb: no envious *Juno* sate cros-leg'd over the nativity of any mans intellectuall off-spring;[112] but if it prov'd a Monster, who denies, but that it was justly burnt, or sunk into the Sea. But that a Book in wors condition then a peccant[113] soul, should be to stand before a Jury ere it be borne to the World, and undergo yet in darknesse the judgement of *Radamanth*[114] and his Colleages, ere it can passe the ferry backward into light,[115] was never heard before, till that mysterious iniquity provokt and troubl'd at the first entrance of Reformation, sought out new limbo's and new hells wherein they might include our Books also within the number of their damned. And this was the rare morsell so officiously snatcht up, and so ilfavourdly imitated by

---

[99]Milton inserts a dirty joke by means of the asterick in the left margin of the 1644 edition, putting it discreetly in Latin: "*Quo veniam daret flatum cripitumque ventris in convivio emittendi. Sueton. in Claudio.*" The Emperor Claudius, having heard of a man who injured himself trying not to fart in public, was said by Suetonius to have thought about a regulation to allow such conduct. See Suetonius, *Divine Claudius* 32: "He is even said to have thought of an edict allowing the priviloege of breaking wind quietly or noisily at table, having learned of a man who ran some risk by restraining himself through modesty" (Loeb trans.). The implication is that it is ridiculous to try to regulate or censor bodily functions.

[100]"May it be granted for us to see."

[101]"Imprimatur," a neo-Latin verb, means "Let it be printed." Imprimaturs in the noun form were written authorizations, posted on the books themselves at times, that showed that they had permission to be in print.

[102]Two pictures at once: (1) the title-page of an Italian book, crowded with imprimaturs issued by a local church official, say in Florence, or coming from Rome by papal authority; (2) an Italian piazza with monks with tonsures (shaven crowns) bowing to each other and complimenting one another in insincere politeness. The author, present in his signature, is pictured below his dedicatory epistle, or letter to his patron. See Miller, "Italian."

[103]A responsory is "An anthem said or sung after a lesson by a soloist and choir alternately. Often applied to the gradual (which follows the epistle at mass)" (*OED* 1.a). Milton used it only to refer scornfully to Roman Catholic liturgy.

[104]"Antiphon" and "responsory" are used interchangeably.

[105]Lambeth House and the west end of St. Paul's Cathedral were the residences of the Archbishop of Canterbury and the Archbishop of London respectively, both of whom "had been appointed licensers of all books" by Star Chamber decrees of 1586 and 1637 (Wilding 8).

[106]Aping Roman Catholic behavior.

[107]"Native language," in this case English.

[108]A characteristic Milton spelling preference of "enough"—similar in seventeenth-century spelling practice to "anough," another of his preferred spellings—perhaps preserved from his manuscript.

[109]Possibly "To open up, lay bare, disclose, make known; also, to search into, examine" (*OED* 4.a).

[110]"Rule" or "internal order," as in Richard Hooker's famous title *Laws of Ecclesiastical Polity* (1594).

[111]"Older," or in this case "from an earlier era."

[112]The queen of the Roman gods, Juno, was said to preside over childbirth. She could retard the birth of a child by crossing her legs or by bidding her agent Ilythia, the goddess of delivery in childbirth, to do so (see Yale 2: 505n). Juno attempted by such a method to keep Alcmena from bearing Jupiter's child Hercules (Ovid, *Metamorphoses* 9. 281–323). The retarding of birth by sitting cross-legged seem to be regarded here as a superstition that might have been associated by Milton's generation with witchcraft, as Sandys infers: Juno "is here said by sitting crosleg'd, knitting her fingers within one an other, and muttering of charmes to have hindred *Alcmena's* delivery. Which in likelyhood hath a reference to the practice of Witches in former ages; and perhaps not unpractized in ours" (441).

[113]Sinful.

[114]The three judges who controlled admission to classical Hades were Rhadamanthus, Minos, and Aeacus. Milton is here condemning the practice of judging anything before birth.

[115]A reverse birth or reverse entrance to hell, since the normal procedure in entering hell would be to go from light forward into darkness. See Coiro's article for a context for the birth imagery.

our inquisiturient[116] Bishops, and the attendant minorites[117] their Chaplains. That ye like not now these most certain Authors of this licencing order, and that all sinister intention was farre distant from your thoughts, when ye were importun'd the passing it,[118] all men who know the integrity of your actions, and how ye honour Truth, will clear yee readily.

But some will say, What though the Inventors were bad, the thing for all that may be good? It may so;[119] yet if that thing be no such deep invention, but obvious, and easie for any man to light on, and yet best and wisest Commonwealths through all ages, and occasions have forborne to use it, and falsest seducers, and oppressors of men were the first who tooke it up, and to no other purpose but to obstruct and hinder the first approach of Reformation; I am of those who beleeve, it will be a harder alchymy then *Lullius*[120] ever knew, to sublimat[121] any good use out of such an invention. Yet this only is what I request to gain from this reason, that it may be held a dangerous and suspicious fruit, as certainly it deserves, for the tree that bore it, untill I can dissect[122] one by one the properties it has. But I have first to finish, as was propounded, what is to be thought in generall of reading Books, what ever sort they be, and whether be more the benefit, or the harm that thence proceeds?

Not to insist upon the examples of *Moses, Daniel* & *Paul*,[123] who were skilfull in all the learning of the Ægyptians, Caldeans,[124] and Greeks, which could not probably be without reading their Books of all sorts, in *Paul* especially, who thought it no defilement to insert into holy Scripture the sentences of three Greek Poets, and one of them a Tragedian,[125] the question was, notwithstanding sometimes controverted among the Primitive Doctors,[126] but with great odds on that side which affirm'd it both lawfull and profitable, as was then evidently perceiv'd, when *Julian* the Apostat,[127] and suttlest enemy to our faith, made a decree forbidding Christians the study of heathen learning: for, said he, they wound us with our own weapons, and with our owne arts and sciences they overcome us. And indeed the Christians were put so to their shifts[128] by this crafty means, and so much in danger to decline into all ignorance, that the two *Apollinarii*[129] were fain as a man may say, to coin all the seven liberall Sciences[130] out of the Bible, reducing it into divers forms of Orations, Poems, Dialogues, ev'n to the calculating of a new Christian Grammar. But saith the Historian *Socrates*,[131] The providence of God provided better then the industry of *Apollinarius* and his son, by taking away that illiterat[132] law with the life of him who devis'd it. So great an injury they then held it to be depriv'd of *Hellenick* learning;[133] and thought it a persecution more undermining, and secretly decaying the Church, then the open cruelty of *Decius* or *Dioclesian*.[134] And perhaps it was the same politick drift

---

[116]"Inquisitorial." Milton made up the adjective form, and his is the only use of the word recorded by the *OED*. Corns reminds us that Milton's coinage here and his use of "minorites" illustrate "how alien the activity of censorial investigation is to the English political tradition" (*Development* 72).

[117]A Minorite was "A friar minor or Franciscan" (*OED* 1.a). Milton is again condemning or satirizing high-church Anglicans under Archbishop Laud as being "papist" in their practices.

[118]"When you were begged to pass the licensing order."

[119] "It may be so."

[120]Raymond Lully (c. 1232–1315) was a Spanish-born chemist stoned to death for his attempts to convert Moslems in Mauretania to Christianity. His association with alchemy may be only legendary, but Milton accepts the legend here.

[121]"Sublimation" is a technical term from alchemy describing "Elevation to a higher state or plane of existence; transmutation into something higher, purer, or more sublime" (*OED* 5.a).

[122]"Examine minutely."

[123]Moses was supposed to be "learned in all the wisdoms of the Egyptians" (Acts 7.22), and Daniel was supposed to have knowledge and skill "in all wisdom" (1.17).

[124]The Chaldeans were proverbially associated with alchemy and other forms of mythical or magical learning, based on the associations created by Daniel 2.2: "The magicians, and the astrologers, and the sorcerers, and the Chaldeans." Milton makes the association between Chaldeans and magic in *An Apology* (Yale 1: 929). It is implied that there is nothing wrong with magic in the hands of good people.

[125]1 Corinthians 15.33 is quoted from Euripides, according to Socrates Scholasticus' *Ecclesiastical History* 3: 16, an opinion which will be echoed by Milton in his preface to *Samson Agonistes*. At 1 Corinthians 15.23 and 15.27 in the Geneva Bible, there is a note to "*Menander in Thaidi*," and St. Paul is supposed by modern biblical scholars to have quoted directly not from Euripides but from the Roman comic dramatist Menander in 1 Corinthians 15.33, "Evil communications corrupt good manners."

[126]Wise or learned men.

[127]Roman emperor from 361 to 363, called "the Apostate" by Christian church historians because he renounced Christianity and reinstituted "pagan" practices.

[128]"Were put in such a position that they had to shift for themselves."

[129]Plural because there were a father and a son named Apolinarius. The elder was a grammarian who composed a Christian grammar and then transposed much of the Old Testament into classical verse and dramatic form, and the younger formed the Gospels into Platonic dialogues. Milton is using the account of Socrates Scholasticus (c. 385–c. 440) that describes reaction to Julian's law forbidding Christians from studying Greek literature (Yale 2: 509n79).

[130] They were happy to arrange or set the biblical books in a counterfeit order according to the arrangement of the seven liberal arts (which would include rhetoric, philosophy, and mathematics).

[131]The historian of the early Christian Church, Socrates Scholasticus (c. 385–c. 440). Milton paraphrases a passage from Socrates' *Ecclesiastical History* 3.16 discussing how the Appolinares outwitted the imperial law forbidding Christians to study Greek literature by rendering the Mosaic books, the Old Testament histories, and the Gospels as Greek literature, until the death of Julian made the practice unnecessary.

[132]"Ignorant."

[133]Learning derived from Greek civilization.

[134]Both Decius Trajanus (201–251) and Diocletian (245–313) persecuted Christians systematically.

that the Divell whipt St. *Jerom*[135] in a lenten dream, for reading *Cicero*; or else it was a fantasm bred by the feaver which had then seis'd him. For had an Angel bin his discipliner, unlesse it were for dwelling too much upon Ciceronianisms, & had chastiz'd the reading, not the vanity,[136] it had bin plainly partiall; first to correct him for grave *Cicero*, and not for scurrill *Plautus* whom he confesses to have bin reading not long before; next to correct him only, and let so many more ancient Fathers wax[137] old in those pleasant and florid studies without the lash of such a tutoring apparition;[138] insomuch that *Basil* teaches how some good use may be made of *Margites* a sportfull Poem, not now extant, writ by *Homer*;[139] and why not then of *Morgante* an Italian Romanze much to the same purpose. But if it be agreed we shall be try'd by visions, there is a vision recorded by *Eusebius*[140] far ancienter then this tale of *Jerom* to the Nun *Eustochium*,[141] and besides has nothing of a feavor in it. *Dionysius Alexandrinus* was about the year 240, a person of great name in the Church for piety and learning, who had wont to avail himself much against hereticks by being conversant in their Books; untill a certain Presbyter laid it scrupulously to his conscience, how he durst venture himselfe among those defiling volumes. The worthy man loath to give offence fell into a new debate with himselfe what was to be thought; when suddenly a vision sent from God, it is his own Epistle that so averrs it, confirm'd him in these words: Read any books what ever come to thy hands, for thou art sufficient both to judge aright, and to examine each matter. To this revelation he assented the sooner, as he confesses, because it was answerable to[142] that of the Apostle to the Thessalonians, Prove all things, hold fast

that which is good. And he might have added another remarkable saying of the same Author; To the pure all things are pure,[143] not only meats and drinks, but all kinde of knowledge whether of good or evill; the knowledge cannot defile, nor consequently the books, if the will and conscience be not defil'd.[144] For books are as meats and viands are; some of good, some of evill substance; and yet God in that unapocryphall vision, said without exception, Rise *Peter*, kill and eat,[145] leaving the choice to each mans discretion. Wholesome meats[146] to a vitiated[147] stomack differ little or nothing from unwholesome; and best books to a naughty[148] mind are not unappliable to occasions of evill. Bad meats will scarce breed good nourishment in the healthiest concoction; but herein the difference is of bad books, that they to a discreet and judicious Reader serve in many respects to discover, to confute, to forewarn, and to illustrate. Wherof what better witnes can ye expect I should produce, then one of your own now sitting in Parlament, the chief of learned men reputed in this Land, Mr. *Selden*,[149] whose volume of naturall & national laws proves, not only by great autorities brought together, but by exquisite[150] reasons and theorems almost mathematically demonstrative, that all opinions, yea errors, known, read, and collated, are of main service & assistance toward the speedy attainment of what is truest. I conceive therefore, that when God did enlarge the universall diet of mans body, saving ever the rules of temperance, he then also, as before, left arbitrary the dyeting and repasting of our minds; as wherein every mature man might have to exercise his owne leading capacity. How great a vertue is temperance, how much of moment through the whole life of man? yet God committs the managing so great a

---

[135]Whether or not St. Jerome (c. 340–42), was whipped by an angel or devil in a dream for presuming to be a Christian while at the same time professing to love the writing of Cicero was a matter debated by Protestants like Paolo Sarpi (Yale 2: 510 n. 81).

[136]"Not the vanity or affectation of writing in Ciceronean Latin." The Latin prose of the Roman statesman Cicero is still considered to be the most elegant in style written in that language.

[137]"Become," or "grow."

[138]The ghostly presence of a schoolmaster, ready with a lash to beat pupils for misbehaving. Jerome's account of the whipping occurs in his eighteenth *Epistle*, but Paolo Sarpi interpreted the dream that occurred during Lent as being inspired by the Devil (see Yale 2: 510 n. 81).

[139]Basil the Great (c. 330–79), bishop of Caesarea, wrote the Basilian Rule for monks that adhered to his teaching. He recommended that his monks be allowed to read Homer among other classical writers in order to make good Christian use of pagan writings.

[140]Eusebius tells the story of Dionysius's dream vision, here ornamented and given a date out of Sarpi by Milton, in his *History of the Church* 7.7. Milton noted the passage in his Commonplace Book (see Yale 1: 377).

[141]Campbell's note is precise: "Julia Eustochium, the nun to whom Jerome addressed *Epistle* XXII (on virginity) in 385, had to flee Rome with Jerome because of the offence caused by the letter" (588n).

[142]"It corresponded with," "It was parallel to."

[143]"Unto the pure all things are pure: but unto them that are defiled and unbelieving is nothing pure; but even their mind and conscience is defiled" (Titus 1.15).

[144]Similar to the process of Eve's being tempted in her dream in *Paradise Lost* 5.117–19: the dream may enter and leave her mind, as long as it is unapproved, without staining her conscience.

[145]Acts 10.13. The process of digestion fascinated Milton as a parallel to the process of acquiring food without corruption (see 5.412), and good digestion in the pure Adam and Eve "Was Aerie light" (5.4).

[146]"Foodstuffs" (not just "meats" in the more recent sense).

[147]"Corrupted," "spoiled." The food may be good, but if the stomach itself is already upset or diseased, the food itself will be corrupted there.

[148]Literally a mind that thinks of nothing, but with the implication that thoughtlessness is evil. *OED* gives "thoroughly wicked" as one definition current in Milton's era.

[149]John Selden (1584–1654), famous in his own time as an erudite historian of natural law and a critic of unlimited power in the monarchy. Milton is alluding to Selden's *De Jure Naturali et Gentium justa Disciplinam Ebraeorum* (1640).

[150]"Abstruse," hard to find.

trust, without particular Law or prescription, wholly to the demeanour of every grown man. And therefore when he himself tabl'd[151] the Jews from heaven, that Omer[152] which was every mans daily portion of Manna, is computed to have bin more then might have well suffic'd the heartiest feeder thrice as many meals. For those actions which enter into a man, rather then issue out of him, and therefore defile not,[153] God uses not to captivat under a perpetuall childhood of prescription, but trusts him with the gift of reason to be his own chooser; there were but little work left for preaching, if law and compulsion should grow so fast upon those things which hertofore were govern'd only by exhortation. *Salomon*[154] informs us that much reading is a wearines to the flesh; but neither he, nor other inspir'd author tells us that such, or such reading is unlawfull: yet certainly had God thought good to limit us herein, it had bin much more expedient to have told us what was unlawfull, then what was wearisome. As for the burning of those Ephesian books by St. *Pauls* converts, tis reply'd the books were magick, the Syriack so renders them. It was a privat act, a voluntary act, and leaves us to a voluntary imitation: the men in remorse burnt those books which were their own; the Magistrat by this example is not appointed: these men practiz'd the books, another might perhaps have read them in some sort usefully. Good and evill we know in the field[155] of this World grow up together almost inseparably; and the knowledge of good is so involv'd and interwoven with the knowledge of evill, and in so many cunning resemblances hardly to be discern'd, that those confused seeds which were impos'd on *Psyche* as an incessant labour to cull out, and sort asunder, were not more intermixt. It was from out the rinde of one apple tasted, that the knowledge of good and evill as two twins cleaving together leapt forth into the World. And perhaps this is that doom which *Adam* fell into of knowing good and evill, that is to say of knowing good by evill. As therefore the state of man now is; what

wisdome can there be to choose, what continence to forbeare without the knowledge of evill? He that can apprehend and consider vice with all her baits and seeming pleasures, and yet abstain, and yet distinguish, and yet prefer that which is truly better, he is the true warfaring[156] Christian. I cannot praise a fugitive and cloister'd vertue, unexercis'd & unbreath'd,[157] that never sallies out and sees her adversary, but slinks out of the race, where that immortall garland is to be run for, not without dust and heat. Assuredly we bring not innocence into the world, we bring impurity much rather: that which purifies us is triall, and triall is by what is contrary. That vertue therefore which is but a youngling in the contemplation of evill, and knows not the utmost that vice promises to her followers, and rejects it, is but a blank vertue, not a pure; her whitenesse is but an excrementall[158] whitenesse; Which was the reason why our sage and serious Poet *Spencer*, whom I dare be known to think a better teacher then *Scotus* or *Aquinas*,[159] describing true temperance under the person of *Guion*, brings him in with his palmer through the cave of Mammon,[160] and the bowr of earthly blisse that he might see and know, and yet abstain. Since therefore the knowledge and survay of vice is in this world so necessary to the constituting of human vertue, and the scanning[161] of error to the confirmation of truth, how can we more safely, and with lesse danger scout into the regions of sin and falsity then by reading all manner of tractats, and hearing all manner of reason? And this is

[151]"Provided with meals." For the account of God's sending manna from Heaven to feed the Israelites, see Exodus 16.

[152]Biblical measure of volume: Moses instructs Aaron to fill jars for members of the tribes of Israel with "an omer full of manna" (Exodus 16.33).

[153]Christ makes the distinction between things that enter the body but do not defile it and sentiments that issue from the heart and do defile the spirit in Matthew 15: 18–20.

[154]Milton seems to have preferred the less-well-known spelling of "Solomon," judging by the number of times it appears with an "a" in his prose works, though the choice may at all times have been made by printer or compositor. The passage in Ecclesiastes here alluded to is 12: 12.

[155]"Large expanse." With the imagery of a field and seeds, there may be implied an allusion to the parable of the sower, Matthew 13.24–30.

[156]The general consensus of editorial opinion (see Yale 2: 515) is that the "wayfaring" of the printed text is wrong, since all presentation copies known to exist have made the correction of the one letter—a consistent correction made either in the printing house or by Milton himself. See the Introduction, "The Text," and Kivette.

[157]Although the *OED* offers "unexercised" as a synonym for "unbreathed," Milton may have intended to distinguish between "unexercised" and "not in good condition for aerobic exercise." Otherwise, his two adjectives would be redundant.

[158]"Of the nature of an outgrowth or excrescence," according to the *OED*, citing this instance as its first usage (adjective 2), although Milton may mean only that white is the color of some excrement. The adjective, when used of food, generally meant "supefluous to nutrition." See Sirluck's extensive note, however, on the possible legal meaning of "excrementals" (Yale 2: 516n).

[159]The two great medieval Christian theologians, Duns Scotus Erigina and St. Thomas Aquinas, representatives of the theological differences between the Franciscan and Domenican orders in the late middle ages.

[160]Curiously, this proper name is not in italics (as it is not in italics in the manuscript of the first book of *Paradise Lost*). The fallen angel Mammon, as Milton will picture him in the epic, is the epitome of materialism. Spenser pictures him as the god of "Riches, renowme, and principality" (*Faerie Queene* 2.7.8). Sirluck points out that Milton gets Spenser significantly wrong: the palmer does not accompany Guyon to the cave of Mammon (see Ernest Sirluck, "Milton Revises *The Faerie Queene*," *Modern Philology* 48 [1950]: 90–96).

[161]"Close investigation or consideration" (*OED* 2.a).

the benefit which may be had of books promiscuously[162] read. But of the harm that may result hence three kinds are usually reckn'd. First, is fear'd the infection that may spread; but then all human learning and controversie in religious points must remove[163] out of the world, yea the Bible it selfe; for that oftimes relates blasphemy not nicely,[164] it describes the carnall sense of wicked men not unelegantly, it brings in holiest men passionately murmuring against providence through all the arguments of *Epicurus*: in other great disputes it answers dubiously and darkly to the common reader: And ask a Talmudist what ails the modesty of his marginall Keri, that *Moses* and all the Prophets cannot perswade him to pronounce the textuall Chetiv. For these causes we all know the Bible it selfe put by the Papist into the first rank of prohibited books. The ancientest Fathers must be next remov'd, as *Clement* of *Alexandria*, and that *Eusebian* book of Evangelick preparation, transmitting our ears through a hoard of heathenish obscenities to receive the Gospel. Who finds not that *Irenæus, Epiphanius, Jerom*,[165] and others discover[166] more heresies then they well confute, and that oft for heresie which is the truer opinion. Nor boots it[167] to say for these, and all the heathen Writers of greatest infection,[168] if it must be thought so, with whom is bound up the life of human learning, that they writ in an unknown tongue, so long as we are sure those languages are known as well to the worst of men, who are both most able, and most diligent to instill the poison they suck, first into the Courts of Princes, acquainting them with the choisest delights, and criticisms of sin. As perhaps did that *Petronius* whom *Nero* call'd his *Arbiter*, the Master of his revels;[169] and that notorious ribald of *Arezzo*, dreaded, and yet dear to the Italian Courtiers. I name not him for posterities sake, whom *Harry* the 8. nam'd in merriment his Vicar of

hell.[170] By which compendious way all the contagion that foreine books can infuse, will finde a passage to the people farre easier and shorter then an Indian voyage, though it could be sail'd either by the North of *Cataio*[171] Eastward, or of *Canada* Westward, while our Spanish licencing gags the English Presse never so severely. But on the other side that infection which is from books of controversie in Religion, is more doubtfull and dangerous to the learned, then to the ignorant; and yet those books must be permitted untoucht by the licencer. It will be hard to instance where any ignorant man hath bin ever seduc't by Papisticall book in English, unlesse it were commended and expounded to him by some of that Clergy: and indeed all such tractats whether false or true are as the Prophesie of *Isaiah* was to the *Eunuch*,[172] not to be *understood without a guide*. But of our Priests and Doctors how many have bin corrupted by studying the comments of Jesuits and *Sorbonists*,[173] and how fast they could transfuse that corruption into the people, our experience is both late and sad. It is not forgot, since the acute and distinct *Arminius*[174] was perverted meerly by the perusing of a namelesse discours writt'n at *Delf*, which at first he took in hand to confute. Seeing therefore that those books, & those in great abundance which are likeliest to taint both life and doctrine, cannot be supprest without the fall of learning, and of all ability in disputation, and that these books of either sort are most and soonest catching to the learned, from whom to the common people what ever is hereticall or dissolute may quickly be convey'd, and that evill manners are as perfectly learnt without books a thousand other ways which cannot be stopt, and evill doctrine not with books can propagate, except a teacher guide,[175] which he might also doe without writing, and so beyond prohibiting, I am not able to

---

[162]"Indiscriminately."

[163]"Withdraw," perhaps following one sense of the Latin "removere." No reflexive was necessary in Milton's usage and that of his time (see Milton's translation of Psalm 88, l.69).

[164]"Not scrupulously, with attention to how it might corrupt the reader."

[165]Irenaeus (c. 130– c. 200), Bishop of Lyons, attacked Gnosticism in his Greek treatise usually presented in Latin as *Adversus omnes Haereses*. Epiphanius, bishop of Salmis (c. 315-403), refuted eighty heresies in *Panarion*. St. Jerome (c. 342-420), best known as the translator of the Bible into Latin, also passionately refuted many Greek heresies.

[166] "Reveal," rather than "discover through exploration."

[167] "Nor does it help."

[168]"Infection" in Old French theological usage was synonymous with "heresy" (see *OED* n. 1), but also with "poison," as Milton uses it below.

[169]Petronius, author of the *Satyricon*, served as Nero's "*arbiter elegantiarum*" or judge of entertainments, a post that Milton relates to the position of Master of the Revels or Lord Chamberlain, official censors of the Elizabethan or Jacobean court.

[170]Probably Sir Francis Bryan. See Starkey, David. "The Court: Castiglione's Ideal and Tudor Reality, Being a Discussion of Sir Thomas Wyatt's 'Satire Addressed to Sir Francis Bryan'." *Journal of the Warburg and Cortauld Institute* 45 (1982): 232-38.

[171]Cathay, or China. Canada was in 1644 a colony of France. Western European navigators searched for a "northwest passage" to the "Indies."

[172]The Apostle Philip explains the meaning of a passage in Isaiah to a eunuch of civil importance in Ethiopia, causing the eunuch to convert to Christianity and be baptized (Acts. 8: 27-39).

[173]The Jesuit order and the Roman Catholic center at the Sorbonne in Paris were recognized as seats of Catholic ("Papist") propaganda.

[174]The Dutch theologian Jacob Hermanns (1560-1609), known by his Latin name Arminius, was asked by Protestant theologians in Delft to refute views expressed in an anonymous pamphlet; out of his response in favor of general rather than particular predestination, free will, and toleration of religious diversity (Yale 2: 520n) came the set of beliefs called "Arminianism," to which Milton has been said in later years to subscribe (see *On Christian Doctrine* 1.4).

[175]"Unless a teacher guiding interpretation of the book infuse his students with evil."

unfold, how this cautelous[175] enterprise of licencing can be exempted from the number of vain and impossible attempts. And he who were pleasantly dispos'd,[176] could not well avoid to lik'n it to the exploit of that gallant man who thought to pound up[177] the crows by shutting his Parkgate. Besides another inconvenience, if learned men be the first receivers out of books, & dispredders[178] both of vice and error, how shall the licencers themselves be confided in, unlesse we can conferr upon them, or they assume to themselves above all others in the Land, the grace of infallibility, and uncorruptednesse? And again, if it be true, that a wise man like a good refiner can gather gold out of the drossiest volume, and that a fool will be a fool with the best book, yea or without book, there is no reason that we should deprive a wise man of any advantage to his wisdome, while we seek to restrain from a fool, that which being restrain'd will be no hindrance to his folly. For if there should be so much exactnesse always us'd to keep that from him which is unfit for his reading, we should in the judgement of *Aristotle*[179] not only, but of *Salomon*, and of our Saviour, not voutsafe him good precepts, and by consequence not willingly admit him to good books; as being certain that a wise man will make better use of an idle pamphlet, then a fool will do of sacred Scripture. 'Tis next alleg'd we must not expose our selves to temptations without necessity, and next to that, not imploy our time in vain things. To both these objections one answer will serve, out of the grounds already laid, that to all men such books are not temptations, nor vanities; but usefull drugs[180] and materialls wherewith to temper and compose effective and strong med'cins, which mans life cannot want. The rest, as children and childish men, who have not the art to qualifie and prepare these working minerals, well may be exhorted to forbear, but hinder'd forcibly they cannot be by all the licencing that Sainted Inquisition[181] could ever yet contrive; which is what I promis'd to deliver next, That this order of licencing conduces nothing[182] to the end for which it was fram'd; and hath almost

prevented[183] me by being clear already while thus much hath bin explaining. See[184] the ingenuity of Truth, who when she gets a free and willing hand, opens her self faster, then the pace of method[185] and discours can overtake her. It was the task which I began with, To shew that no Nation, or well instituted State, if they valu'd books at all, did ever use this way of licencing; and it might be answer'd, that this is a piece of prudence lately discover'd. To which I return,[186] that as it was a thing slight and obvious to think on, so if it had bin difficult to finde out, there wanted not among them long since, who suggested such a cours; which they not following, leave us a pattern of their judgement, that it was not the not knowing, but the not approving, which was the cause of their not using it. *Plato*,[187] a man of high autority indeed, but least of all for his Commonwealth, in the book of his laws, which no City ever yet receiv'd, fed his fancie with making many edicts to his ayrie Burgomasters, which they who otherwise admire him, wish had bin rather buried and excus'd in the *genial* cups of an *Academick*[188] night-sitting. By which laws he seems to tolerat no kind of learning, but by unalterable decree, consisting most of practicall traditions, to the attainment whereof a Library of smaller bulk then his own dialogues would be abundant. And there also enacts that no Poet should so much as read to any privat man, what he had writt'n, untill the Judges and Law-keepers had seen it, and allow'd it: But that *Plato*[189] meant this Law peculiarly to that Commonwealth which he had imagin'd, and to no other, is evident. Why was he not else a Law-giver to himself, but a transgressor, and to be expell'd by his own Magistrats; both for the wanton epigrams[190] and dialogues which he made, and his perpetuall reading of

---

[183]"Come before," "preceded in time."
[184]"Behold.
[185]Systematic treatment.
[186]"To which I answer."
[187]Plato's *Laws*, written after the *Republic*, also attempts to construct a city-state. Here Milton makes fun of Plato's impracticality in preaching of airy (read "air-headed" ?) bourgeois lawmakers and nightly drinking contests, symposia, in order to determine political policy. For what he is making fun of, see the *Laws* Book 7. The italics on "*genial*" and "*Academick*" seem to be used sardonically.
[188]Based on Plato's notion of an academy.
[189]See Irene Samuel, *Plato and Milton* (Ithaca, NY: Cornell UP, 1965), for an overview of Platonic influences on Milton.
[190]Presumably wanton because the epigrams collected by Diogenes Laertius (3: 23) deal with homosexual love, as would Plato's dialogues the *Symposium* and the *Phaedrus*.

---

[175]"Full of cautels [i.e., tricks]; deceitful, crafty, artful, wily" (*OED* 1).
[176]"Having a taste for pleasantries or jokes."
[177]Impound or pen up.
[178]Spreaders of news, distributers of information.
[179]Aristotle in the *Ethics* 1.3.1095; Solomon in Proverbs 23.9; and Jesus in Matthew 7.6: all have to do with the impossibility for learning to reach a fool.
[180]Both "drugs" and "materialls" have neutral meanings as "medicines," "materialls" coming from "materia medica."
[181]Probably a highly ironic phrase, since the Inquisition might create Protestant saints by tormenting them to death. As Campbell points out, the Spanish Inquisition was called "la Sancta Inquisición" (593n).
[182]Leads in no way.

Sophron Mimus,[191] and *Aristophanes*,[192] books of grossest infamy, and also for commending the latter of them though he were the malicious libeller of his chief friends, to be read by the Tyrant *Dionysius*, who had little need of such trash to spend his time on? But that he knew this licencing of Poems had reference and dependence to many other proviso's there set down in his fancied republic, which in this world could have no place: and so neither he himself, nor any Magistrat, or City ever imitated that cours, which tak'n apart from those other collaterall injunctions must needs be vain and fruitlesse. For if they fell upon one kind of strictnesse, unlesse their care were equall to regulat all other things of like aptnes to corrupt the mind, that single endeavour they knew would be but a fond labour; to shut and fortifie one gate against corruption, and be necessitated to leave others round about wide open. If we think to regulat Printing, thereby to rectifie manners, we must regulat all recreations and pastimes, all that is delightfull to man. No musick must be heard, no song be set or sung, but what is grave and *Dorick*.[193] There must be licencing dancers, that no gesture, motion, or deportment be taught our youth but what by their allowance shall be thought honest;[194] for such *Plato* was provided of;[195] It will ask more then the work of twenty licencers to examin all the lutes, the violins, and the ghittarrs[196] in every house; they must not be suffer'd to prattle as they doe, but must be licenc'd what they may say. And who shall silence all the airs and madrigalls, that whisper softnes in chambers? The Windows also, and the *Balcone's*[197] must be thought on,

there are shrewd[198] books, with dangerous Frontispices[199] set to sale; who shall prohibit them, shall twenty licencers? The villages also must have their visitors[200] to enquire what lectures the bagpipe and the rebbeck[201] reads ev'n to the ballatry,[202] and the gammuth[203] of every *municipal* fidler, for these are the Countrymans *Arcadia's* and his *Monte Mayors*. Next, what more Nationall corruption, for which England hears ill abroad, then houshold gluttony; who shall be the rectors of our daily rioting?[204] and what shall be done to inhibit the multitudes that frequent those houses where drunk'nes is sold and harbour'd? Our garments also should be referr'd to the licencing of some more sober workmasters to see them cut into a lesse wanton garb. Who shall regulat all the mixt conversation[205] of our youth, male and female together, as is the fashion of this Country, who shall still appoint what shall be discours'd, what presum'd, and no furder? Lastly, who shall forbid and separat all idle resort,[206] all evill company? These things will be, and must be; but how they shall be lest[207] hurtfull, how lest enticing, herein

---

[191]Sophron of Syracuse (fl. fifth century BCE) was called "Mimus" for his being author of mimes or realistic dramatic skits in Doric (popular and vital) vernacular.

[192]Aristophanes made fun of Socrates in the *Clouds*. Plato was supposed by some early biographers to have sent the tyrant Dionysius works by Aristophanes to read when Dionysius had asked for literature depicting life as it is.

[193]Based on the Greek Dorian mode. Milton uses it to signify music that is manly, perhaps warlike, dignified, measured, and reasonable. His own poetry in *Comus* had been described by Sir Henry Wotton as having "Dorick delicacy." Here Milton's usage also ironically indicates stuffiness.

[194]Chaste or virtuous.

[195]Plato's *Laws* 7.802 suggests methods for regulating movement in dances, words and phrases in poetry and music. Such regulation of the arts was seriously proposed by the poet and Puritan George Wither (see Yale 2: 534n).

[196]The spelling seems to imitate the Italian "ghitarra" or "chitarra," for the word that has become "guitar."

[197]The earlier spelling of "balcony" in English, from the Italian "balcone."

[198]"Of persons, their qualities, actions, etc.: Depraved, wicked; evil-disposed, malignant. Passing into a weaker sense: Malicious, mischievous" (*OED* 1.a). The sense may be associated with the actions of the animal, the shrew, which had a reputation for being bad-tempered and mischievous.

[199]The frontispiece (meaning an "illustrated title page") of books might be displayed in London bookstores to help sell a book it was part of. Sirluck believes that the spelling of the word indicates that Milton correctly alluded to an etymology combining "front" (Latin "frontem," "forehead") with the Latin "specio," "I look" (Yale 2: 524n). Milton may be referring to balconies or windows where prostitutes displayed themselves for sale. In any case, the word was used in the early seventeenth century in an architectural as well as a publishing sense.

[200]As Campbell points out, both "visitor" and "lecture" were emotive words to Milton's audience because of Archbishop Laud's "Metropolitan Visitation of his suffragen dioceses in 1634 and of the universities in 1636," during which the censorious visitors commented on the orthodoxy of sermons and "lectures" given by bourgeois clergy, "lecturers," who had been appointed not by the Church of England but by town officials, parishes, or even individuals. Most of these lecturers would be associated with Puritanism (see 595n1).

[201]The bagpipe and the rebeck, a simple two- or three-stringed fiddle (called the "jocund rebec" in "L'Allegro" 94), would be associated with the music-making of ordinary people. Such music, though, had political implications, because it might violate church decorum or ritual.

[202]"Balladry," the making of ballads. For the context of politicizing country pastimes, see Marcus, *The Politics*.

[203]A technical term from music, a "gamut" or "gammuth," derived from the Greek letter gamma, was "The first or lowest note in the mediæval scale of music, answering to the modern G on the lowest line of the bass stave" (*OED* 1).

[204]"Rectors" is another charged word because it would indicate a church official similar to a vicar, as well as someone who applies rules of behavior with godlike authority. Milton seems to be making fun of rectors by subjecting them to alliteration in "rectors . . . of rioting."

[205]Intimacy (usually used of married couples).

[206]An idle crowd, a bunch of ne'er-do-wells.

[207]Least.

consists the grave and governing wisdom of a State. To sequester out of the world into *Atlantick* and *Eutopian* polities,[208] which never can be drawn into use, will not mend our condition; but to ordain wisely as in this world of evil, in the midd'st whereof God hath plac't us unavoidably. Nor is it *Plato's* licencing of books will doe this, which necessarily pulls along with it so many other kinds of licencing, as will make us all both ridiculous and weary, and yet frustrat;[209] but those unwritt'n, or at least unconstraining laws of vertuous education, religious and civill nurture, which *Plato* there mentions,[210] as the bonds and ligaments of the Commonwealth, the pillars and the sustainers of every writt'n Statute; these they be which will bear chief sway in such matters as these, when all licencing will be easily eluded. Impunity and remissenes, for certain are the bane of a Commonwealth, but here the great art lyes to discern in what the law is to bid restraint and punishment, and in what things perswasion only is to work. If every action which is good, or evill in man at ripe years, were to be under pittance, and prescription, and compulsion, what were vertue but a name, what praise could be then due to well-doing, what grammercy[211] to be sober, just or continent? many there be that complain of divin Providence for suffering[212] *Adam* to transgresse, foolish tongues! when God gave him reason, he gave him freedom to choose, for reason is but choosing;[213] he had bin else a meer artificiall [214]*Adam*, such an *Adam* as he is in the motions. We our selves esteem not of that obedience, or love, or gift, which is of force: God therefore left him free, set before him a provoking object,[215] ever almost in his eyes; herein consisted his merit, herein the right of his reward, the praise of his abstinence. Wherefore did he creat passions within us, pleasures round about us, but that these rightly temper'd are the very ingredients of vertu? They are not skilfull considerers of human things, who

imagin to remove sin by removing the matter of sin; for, besides that it is a huge heap increasing under the very act of diminishing,[216] though some part of it may for a time be withdrawn from some persons, it cannot from all, in such a universall thing as books are; and when this is done, yet the sin remains entire. Though ye take from a covetous man all his treasure, he has yet one jewell left, ye cannot bereave him of his covetousnesse. Banish all objects of lust, shut up all youth into the severest discipline that can be exercis'd in any hermitage, ye cannot make them chaste, that came not thither so: such great care and wisdom is requir'd to the right managing of this point. Suppose we could expell sin by this means; look how much we thus expell of sin, so much we expell of vertue: for the matter of them both is the same; remove that, and ye remove them both alike. This justifies the high providence of God, who though he command us temperance, justice, continence, yet powrs[217] out before us ev'n to a profusenes all desirable things, and gives us minds that can wander beyond all limit and satiety. Why should we then affect a rigor contrary to the manner of God and of nature, by abridging or scanting those means, which books freely permitted are, both to the triall of vertue, and the exercise of truth. It would be better done to learn that the law must needs be frivolous which goes to restrain things, uncertainly and yet equally working to good, and to evill. And were I the chooser, a dram of well-doing should be preferr'd before many times as much the forcible hindrance of evill-doing. For God sure esteems the growth and compleating of one vertuous person, more then the restraint of ten vitious. And albeit what ever thing we hear or see, sitting, walking, travelling, or conversing may be fitly call'd our book, and is of the same effect that writings are, yet grant the thing to be prohibited were only books, it appears that this order hitherto is far insufficient to the end which it intends. Do we not see, not once or oftner, but weekly that continu'd Court-libell[218] against the Parlament and City, Printed, as the wet sheets can witnes, and dispers't among us, for all that licencing can doe? yet this is the prime service a man would think, wherein this order should give proof of it self. If it were executed, you'l say. But certain, if execution be remisse or blindfold now, and in this

---

[208]Fanciful Utopian or Atlantic commonwealths, as manufactured up by Sir Thomas More in *Utopia* (1516) or Plato in *Critias*, or Sir Francis Bacon in *The New Atlantis* (1627).

[209]"Frustrated."

[210]In *Laws* 1: 643–44, Plato has his dialoguists discuss childhood games as instruction for adult vocation and education in general as the preparation of the child to assume a life of passionate dedication to goodness and to civic duty.

[211]Thanks. "Grammercy," short for "Grant mercy" and analogous to "God-a-mercy," was a mild exclamation.

[212]Allowing.

[213]A short explanation of the doctrine of free will. See Milton's *On Christian Doctrine* 10 and 11 for the implications of Adam and Eve's choice of evil (disobedience) over good (obedience).

[214]"Made up by a craftsman or artificer," not real.

[215]The tree of the knowledge of good and evil in Genesis 3.2–3. It is provocative in that it is the cause of temptation (but not irresistible).

---

[216]Compare John Donne's "man was sour'd in the whole lump, poysoned in the fountain, perished at the chore, withered in the root, in the fall of *Adam*" (*The Sermons of John Donne*, ed. E.M. Simpson and G.R. Potter [Berkeley: U of Calfornia P, 1953–62]: 8: 176).

[217]Pours.

[218]*Mercurius Aulicus* ("Mercury [i.e., messages] from court," a Royalist news sheet issued from Oxford (and appointed by King Charles I) but reprinted and distributed—possibly with its sheets of paper still wet from the printing process—in London.

particular, what will it be hereafter, and in other books. If then the order shall not be vain and frustrat, behold a new labour, Lords and Commons, ye must repeal and proscribe all scandalous and unlicenc't books already printed and divulg'd;[219] after ye have drawn them up into a list, that all may know which are condemn'd, and which not; and ordain that no forrein books be deliver'd out of custody, till they have bin read over. This office will require the whole time of not a few overseers, and those no vulgar men. There be also books which are partly usefull and excellent, partly culpable and pernicious; this work will ask as many more officials, to make expurgations, and expunctions,[220] that the Commonwealth of learning be not damnify'd. In fine, when the multitude of books encrease upon their hands, ye must be fain to catalogue all those Printers who are found frequently offending, and forbidd the importation of their whole suspected *typography*. In a word, that this your order may be exact, and not deficient, ye must reform it perfectly according to the model of *Trent* and *Sevil*,[221] which I know ye abhorre to doe. Yet though ye should condiscend to this, which God forbid, the order still would be but fruitlesse and defective to that end whereto ye meant it. If to prevent sects and schisms, who is so unread or so uncatechis'd in story,[222] that hath not heard of many sects refusing books as a hindrance, and preserving their doctrine unmixt for many ages, only by unwritt'n traditions. The Christian faith, for that was once a schism, is not unknown to have spread all over *Asia*, ere any Gospel or Epistle was seen in writing. If the amendment of manners be aym'd at, look into Italy and Spain, whether those places be one scruple the better, the honester, the wiser, the chaster, since all the inquisitionall rigor that hath bin executed upon books.

Another reason, whereby to make it plain that this order will misse the end it seeks, consider by the quality which ought to be in every licencer. It cannot be deny'd but that he who is made judge to sit upon the birth, or death of books whether they may be wafted[223] into this world, or not, had need to be a man above the common measure, both studious, learned, and judicious; there may be else no mean[224] mistakes in the censure of what is passable or not; which is also no mean injury. If he be of such worth as behoovs him, there cannot be a more

tedious and unpleasing journey-work,[225] a greater losse of time levied upon his head, then to be made the perpetuall reader of unchosen books and pamphlets, oftimes huge volumes. There is no book that is acceptable unlesse at certain seasons; but to be enjoyn'd the reading of that at all times, and in a hand scars[226] legible, whereof three pages would not down[227] at any time in the fairest Print, is an imposition which I cannot beleeve how he that values time, and his own studies, or is but of a sensible nostrill should be able to endure. In this one thing I crave leave of the present licencers to be pardon'd for so thinking: who doubtlesse took this office up, looking on it through their obedience to the Parlament, whose command perhaps made all things seem easie and unlaborious to them; but that this short triall hath wearied them out already, their own expressions and excuses to them who make so many journeys to sollicit their licence, are testimony anough. Seeing therefore those who now possesse the imployment, by all evident signs wish themselves well ridd of it, and that no man of worth, none that is not a plain unthrift[228] of his own hours is ever likely to succeed them, except he mean to put himself to the salary of a Presse-corrector,[229] we may easily foresee what kind of licencers we are to expect hereafter, either ignorant, imperious, and remisse, or basely pecuniary. This is what I had to shew wherein this order cannot conduce to that end, whereof it bears the intention.

I lastly proceed from the no good it can do, to the manifest hurt it causes, in being first the greatest discouragement and affront, that can be offer'd to learning and to learned men. It was the complaint and lamentation of Prelats, upon very least breath of a motion to remove pluralities,[230] and distribute more equally Church revennu's, that then all learning would be for ever dasht and discourag'd. But as for that opinion, I never found cause to think that the tenth part of learning[231] stood or fell with the Clergy: nor could I ever but hold it for a sordid and unworthy speech of any Churchman who had a competency[232] left him. If therefore ye be loath to dishearten utterly and

---

[219]Published abroad, released to the common reader.
[220]Erasures.
[221]Two centers of the Inquisition, Trent being the seat of the Council of Trent in 1546 and Seville that of one of the most feared tribunals of the Spanish Inquisition (c. 1481).
[222]History.
[223]Conveyed safely.
[224]"Unimportant."

[225]Journeyman work, mechanical labor, drudgery.
[226]"Scarse," i.e., scarcely.
[227]"Would not go down," or be palatable.
[228]Wastrel, prodigal, spendthrift.
[229]Copy-editor working with sheets as they came directly from the press. Milton displays an extensive knowledge of how a printing press was run.
[230]Multiple church livings, whereby one clergyman might collect benefices from a number of parishes. Milton considers it to be one of the chief abuses of the Laudian church.
[231]Sardonic reference to the practice of tithing or giving one-tenth of one's income to support the church. Milton would return to the subject to discuss it fully in *Readie and Easy Way*.
[232]A competent or sufficient income or estate, a living.

discontent, not the mercenary crew of false pretenders to learning, but the free and ingenuous sort of such as evidently were born to study, and love lerning for it self, not for lucre, or any other end, but the service of God and of truth, and perhaps that lasting fame and perpetuity of praise which God and good men have consented shall be the reward of those whose publisht labours advance the good of mankind, then know, that so far to distrust the judgement & the honesty of one who hath but a common repute in learning, and never yet offended, as not to count him fit to print his mind without a tutor and examiner, lest he should drop a scism,[233] or something of corruption, is the greatest displeasure and indignity to a free and knowing spirit that can be put upon him. What advantage is it to be a man over it is to be a boy at school, if we have only scapt the ferular,[234] to come under the fescu[235] of an *Imprimatur?* if serious and elaborat writings, as if they were no more then the theam of a Grammar lad[236] under his Pedagogue must not be utter'd without the cursory eyes of a temporizing and extemporizing licencer. He who is not trusted with his own actions, his drift not being known to be evill, and standing to the hazard of[237] law and penalty, has no great argument to think himself reputed in the Commonwealth wherin he was born, for other then a fool or a foreiner. When a man writes to the world, he summons up all his reason and deliberation to assist him; he searches, meditats, is industrious, and likely consults and conferrs with his judicious friends; after all which done he takes himself to be inform'd in what he writes, as well as any that writ before him; if in this the most consummat act of his fidelity and ripenesse, no years, no industry, no former proof of his abilities can bring him to that state of maturity, as not to be still mistrusted and suspected, unlesse he carry all his considerat diligence, all his midnight watchings, and expence of *Palladian* oyl,[238] to the hasty view of an unleasur'd licencer, perhaps much his younger, perhaps far his inferiour in judgement, perhaps one who never knew the labour of book-writing, and if he be not repulst, or slighted, must appear in

Print like a punie[239] with his guardian, and his censors hand on the back of his title to be his bayl and surety,[240] that he is no idiot, or seducer, it cannot be but a dishonor and derogation to the author, to the book, to the priviledge and dignity of Learning. And what if the author shall be one so copious of fancie, as to have many things well worth the adding, come into his mind after licencing, while the book is yet under the Presse, which not seldom happ'ns to the best and diligentest writers; and that perhaps a dozen times in one book. The Printer dares not go beyond his licenc't copy; so often then must the author trudge to his leav-giver, that those his new insertions may be viewd; and many a jaunt will be made, ere that licencer, for it must be the same man, can either be found, or found at leisure; mean while either the Presse must stand still, which is no small damage,[241] or the author loose his accuratest thoughts, & send the book forth wors then he had made it, which to a diligent writer is the greatest melancholy and vexation that can befall. And how can a man teach with autority, which is the life of teaching, how can he be a Doctor in his book as he ought to be, or else had better be silent, whenas all he teaches, all he delivers, is but under the tuition, under the correction of his patriarchal[242] licencer to blot or alter what precisely accords not with the hidebound humor[243] which he calls his judgement. When every acute reader upon the first sight of a pedantick licence, will be ready with these like words to ding the book a coits distance from him,[244] I hate a pupil teacher, I endure not an instructer that comes to me under the wardship of an overseeing fist. I know nothing of the licencer, but that I have his own hand here for his arrogance; who shall warrant me his judgement?[245] The State Sir, replies the Stationer,[246] but has a quick return, The State shall be my governours, but not my criticks; they may be mistak'n in the choice of a licencer, as easily as this licencer may be mistak'n in

---

[233]"Allow religious dissent (schism) to slip through undetected."

[234]"Escaped the punishment of being hit with the teacher's rod" (a "feruler" was a rod made from the giant fennel plant used to whip students).

[235]Small piece of straw or grass (ineffectual, as contrasted with the "feruler").

[236]A pupil at a grammar school and thus at a lower level of learning.

[237]"Risking the consequences of."

[238]"Burning the midnight oil in order to gain wisdom." Pallas Athene was the goddess of wisdom: hence "*Palladian*."

[239]A junior student or someone whose smallness of stature or youth demanded a guardian or attendant.

[240]"Bayl" in the modern sense of "bail bond," guarantee or surety that a defendant will appear in court.

[241]Monetary loss, in the eyes of the law.

[242]Another loaded word, since it assumes that the licenser wants to become a "patriarch," a kind of junior pope, in his office. Archbishop Laud was accused by his enemies of desiring to be an English pope or patriarch (see Yale 2: 533 n. 167).

[243]Inflexible whim or disposition to do things a certain way.

[244]"To fling the book with great force a quoit's distance away." A coit or quoit would be a ring of metal used in athletic contests like a modern discus, and "a quoit's distance" was proverbial. In this case, the reader's anger toward a book licensed by a foolish academic causes him to fling it away in disgust.

[245]"Who will testify to his ability to judge?"

[246]Bookseller. Milton has started a kind of debate here, like a catechism, in which he is asking and answering his own questions dramatically.

an author: This is some common stuffe; and he might adde from Sir *Francis Bacon*, That *such authoriz'd books are but the language of the times.* For though a licencer should happ'n to be judicious more then ordnary, which will be a great jeopardy of the next succession, yet his very office, and his commission enjoyns him to let passe nothing but what is vulgarly receiv'd already. Nay, which is more lamentable, if the work of any deceased author, though never so famous in his life time, and even to this day, come to their hands for licence to be Printed, or Reprinted, if there be found in his book one sentence of a ventrous[247] edge, utter'd in the height of zeal, and who knows whether it might not be the dictat of a divine Spirit, yet not suiting with every low decrepit humor of their own, though it were *Knox*[248] himself, the Reformer of a Kingdom that spake it, they will not pardon him their dash:[249] the sense of that great man shall to all posterity be lost, for the fearfulnesse, or the presumptuous rashnesse of a perfunctory licencer. And to what an author this violence hath bin lately done, and in what book of greatest consequence to be faithfully publisht, I could now instance,[250] but shall forbear till a more convenient season. Yet if these things be not resented seriously and timely by them who have the remedy in their power, but that such iron moulds[251] as these shall have autority to knaw out the choisest periods[252] of exquisitest books, and to commit such a treacherous fraud against the orphan remainders of worthiest men after death, the more sorrow will belong to that haples race of men, whose misfortune it is to have understanding. Henceforth let no man care to learn, or care to be more then worldly wise; for certainly in higher matters to be ignorant and slothfull, to be a common stedfast dunce will be the only pleasant life, and only in request.

And as it is a particular disesteem of every knowing person alive, and most injurious to the writt'n labours and monuments of the dead, so to me it seems an undervaluing and vilifying of the whole Nation. I cannot set so light by all the invention, the art, the wit, the grave and solid judgement which is in England, as that it can be comprehended in any twenty capacities how good soever, much lesse that it should not passe except their superintendence be over it, except it be sifted and strain'd[253] with their strainers, that it should be uncurrant without their manuall stamp. Truth and understanding are not such wares as to be monopoliz'd[254] and traded in by tickets and statutes,[255] and standards. We must not think to make a staple commodity of all the knowledge in the Land, to mark and licence it like our broad cloath, and our wooll packs. What is it but a servitude like that impos'd by the Philistims,[256] not to be allow'd the sharpning of our own axes and coulters,[257] but we must repair[258] from all quarters to twenty licencing forges. Had any one writt'n and divulg'd erroneous things & scandalous to honest life, misusing and forfeiting the esteem had of his reason among men, if after conviction this only censure were adjudg'd him, that he should never henceforth write, but what were first examin'd by an appointed officer, whose hand should be annext[259] to passe his credit for him, that now he might be safely read, it could not be apprehended lesse then a disgracefull punishment. Whence to include the whole Nation, and those that never yet thus offended, under such a diffident and suspectfull prohibition, may plainly be understood what a disparagement it is. So much the more, when as dettors and delinquents may walk abroad without a keeper,[260] but unoffensive books must not stirre forth without a visible jaylor in thir title. Nor is it to the common people lesse then a reproach; for if we be so

---

[247]Adventurous or daring. Compare "adventrous Song" (*Paradise Lost* 1.13).

[248]John Knox (c. 1505–1572), reformer of the kingdom of Scotland and founder of Presbyterianism.

[249]Probably, as Campbell suggests (600n), an erasing line. Milton's practice of erasure in his own manuscripts was to draw a line or dash through any line he wanted expunged.

[250]So far as anyone knows, Milton never identified the author, though Edward Coke and John Knox have both been suggested, the first for his *Institutes* (1641), apparently mutilated by censors, and the second for his *History of the Reformation*, which had passages removed from its 1644 edition (Yale 2: 534n).

[251]Rust spots caused on cloth by a rusty iron; corrosive to the point of eating a hole through the fabric.

[252]Sentences.

[253]Constrained in a smaller space.

[254]Granting monopolies had traditionally been the prerogative of English monarchs, but it was especially resented by the subjects of Charles I after it was declared illegal in 1624.

[255]Tickets might be used to reinforce monopolies, as might local statutes that imposed strictures on trade. For instance, passage into a port might require tickets for certain goods, and statutes might forbid the importation or distribution of goods such as the broadcloth or wool that Milton mentions.

[256]Milton is using his variation on the Hebrew plural form of "Philistine." Israelites were required to go to the Philistines to have tools sharpened (1 Samuel 13.19–21).

[257]A coulter is the sharpened iron part of a plough, the part that cuts through the soil.

[258]Travel.

[259]Subjected; in other words, his handwriting should be licensed or his signature registered.

[260]May allude to the fact that members of Parliament and their families were not subject to being imprisoned for debt. Neither were those who lived in sanctuary, near the sites of dissolved monasteries. Those who supported the king in the Civil War and had therefore been sentenced to prison by Parliament in March 1643 were pardoned, if they confessed, in January of 1644. Thus they may or may not have been considered "delinquents."

jealous over them, as that we dare not trust them with an English pamphlet, what doe we but censure them for a giddy, vitious, and ungrounded people; in such a sick and weak estate of faith and discretion, as to be able to take nothing down but through the pipe[261] of a licencer. That this is care or love of them, we cannot pretend, whenas in those Popish places where the Laity are most hated and dispis'd the same strictnes is us'd over them. Wisdom we cannot call it, because it stops but one breach[262] of licence, nor that neither; whenas those corruptions which it seeks to prevent, break in faster at other dores which cannot be shut.

And in conclusion[263] it reflects to the disrepute of our Ministers also, of whose labours we should hope better, and of the proficiencie[264] which thir flock reaps by them, then that after all this light of the Gospel which is, and is to be, and all this continuall preaching, they should be still frequented with such an unprincipl'd, un-edify'd, and laick rabble,[265] as that the whiffe of every new pamphlet should stagger them out of thir cate-chism, and Christian walking. This may have much rea-son to discourage the Ministers when such a low con-ceit[266] is had of all their exhortations, and the benefiting of their hearers, as that they are not thought fit to be turn'd loose to three sheets of paper[267] without a licen-cer, that all the Sermons, all the Lectures preacht, print-ed, vented in such numbers, and such volumes, as have now well-nigh made all other books unsalable, should not be armor anough against one single *enchiridion*,[268] without the castle St. *Angelo*[269] of an *Imprimatur*.

And lest som should perswade ye, Lords and Com-mons, that these arguments of lerned mens discourage-ment at this your order, are meer flourishes, and not reall, I could recount what I have seen and heard in other Countries, where this kind of inquisition tyran-nizes; when I have sat among their lerned men, for that honor I had, and bin counted happy to be born in such

a place of *Philosophic* freedom, as they suppos'd England was, while themselvs did nothing but bemoan the servil condition into which lerning amongst them was brought; that this was which had dampt the glory of Italian wits;[270] that nothing had bin there writt'n now these many years but flattery and fustian. There it was that I found and visited the famous *Galileo* grown old, a prisner to the Inquisition, for thinking in Astronomy otherwise then the Franciscan and Dominican licencers thought. And though I knew that England then was groaning loudest under the Prelaticall yoak,[271] neverthe-lesse I took it as a pledge of future happines, that other Nations were so perswaded of her liberty. Yet was it beyond my hope that those Worthies were then breathing in her air, who should be her leaders to such a deliverance, as shall never be forgott'n by any revolu-tion of time that this world hath to finish. When that was once begun, it was as little in my fear, that what words of complaint I heard among lerned men of other parts utter'd against the Inquisition, the same I should hear by as lerned men at home utterd in time of Parla-ment against an order of licencing; and that so generally, that when I had disclos'd my self a companion of their discontent, I might say, if without envy, that he whom an honest *quæstorship* had indear'd to the *Sicilians*,[272] was not more by them importun'd against *Verres*, then the favourable opinion which I had among many who honour ye, and are known and respected by ye, loaded me with entreaties and perswasions, that I would not despair to lay together that which just reason should bring into my mind, toward the removal of an undeserved thraldom upon lerning. That this is not therefore the disburdning of a particular fancie, but the common grievance of all those who had prepar'd their minds and studies above the vulgar pitch to advance truth in others, and from others to entertain it, thus much may satisfie. And in their name I shall for neither friend nor foe conceal what the generall murmur is; that if it come to inquisitioning again, and licencing, and that we are so timorous of our selvs, and so suspicious of all men, as to fear each book, and the shaking of every leaf, before we know what the contents are, if some who but of late were little better then silenc't from preaching, shall come now to silence us from reading, except what they please, it cannot be guest[273] what is intended by

---

[261]A feeding pipe for patients not capable of swallowing food.

[262]One hole in the defensive wall of, as in "Once more unto the breach."

[263]Milton is nowhere near the end of the tract when he begins his con-clusion.

[264]Self-improvement.

[265]Expresses the anti-Laudian sentiment that the lay members of the church should not be treated like rabble or ignorant people but with respect (see Yale 2: 537n).

[266]Idea. (The word was neutral, close to the Italian "concetto," which is usually translated as "concept" or "opinion.")

[267]Possibly referring to a twentyfour-page pamphlet, composed of three eight-page gatherings each cut from one sheet of the size printers usually used for a quarto book.

[268]Handbook or concise treatise on one subject, but, as Sirluck points out (Yale 2: 537n), there is probably a pun on the other meaning of the Greek word, "hand-knife."

[269]The papal fortress across the Tiber from the Vatican, thus a proverbially strong defensive structure.

[270]"Intelligent Italian men."

[271]The civic and ecclesiastical power of the Laudian prelates created, in Milton's imagery, an insupportable yoke carried in universal bondage by the English.

[272]Cicero, who served as quaestor, or collector of public revenues, for Sicily in 75 BCE, and who attacked the Sicilian proconsul, Gaius Verres, for extortion and drove him from office.

[273]Guessed.

som but a second tyranny over learning: and will soon put it out of controversie that Bishops and Presbyters are the same to us both name and thing. That those evills of Prelaty which before from five or six and twenty Sees[274] were distributivly charg'd upon the whole people, will now light wholly upon learning, is not obscure to us: whenas now the Pastor of a small unlearned Parish, on the sudden shall be exalted Archbishop over a large dioces of books, and yet not remove, but keep his other cure[275] too, a mysticall pluralist. He who but of late cry'd down the sole ordination of every novice Batchelor of Art,[276] and deny'd sole jurisdiction over the simplest Parishioner, shall now at home in his privat chair assume both these over worthiest and excellentest books and ablest authors that write them. This is not, Yee Covnants and Protestations[277] that we have made, this is not to put down Prelaty, this is but to chop[278] an Episcopacy, this is but to translate the Palace *Metropolitan*[279] from one kind of dominion into another, this is but an old canonicall slight of *commuting* our penance. To startle thus betimes[280] at a meer unlicenc't pamphlet will after a while be afraid of every conventicle, and a while after will make a conventicle[281] of every Christian meeting. But I am certain that a State govern'd by the rules of justice and fortitude, or a Church built and founded upon the rock of faith and true knowledge, cannot be so pusillanimous. While things are yet not constituted in Religion, that freedom of writing should be restrain'd by a discipline imitated from the Prelats, and learnt by

them from the Inquisition to shut us up all again into the brest of a licencer, must needs give cause of doubt and discouragement to all learned and religious men. Who cannot but discern the finenes of this politic drift, and who are the contrivers; that while Bishops were to be baited down,[282] then all Presses might be open; it was the peoples birthright and priviledge in time of Parlament, it was the breaking forth of light. But now the Bishops abrogated and voided out of the Church, as if our Reformation sought no more, but to make room for others into their seats under another name, the Episcopall arts begin to bud again, the cruse of truth must run no more oyle,[283] liberty of Printing must be enthrall'd again under a Prelaticall commission of twenty, the privilege of the people nullify'd, and which is wors, the freedom of learning must groan again, and to her old fetters; all this the Parlament yet sitting. Although their own late arguments and defences against the Prelats might remember[284] them that this obstructing violence meets for the most part with an event utterly opposite to the end which it drives at: instead of suppressing sects and schisms, it raises them and invests them with a reputation: *the punishing of wits enhaunces their autority*, saith the Vicount St. *Albans, and a forbidd'n writing is thought to be a certain spark of truth that flies up in the faces of them who seeke to tread it out.*[285] This order therefore may prove a nursing mother to sects, but I shall easily shew how it will be a step-dame to Truth: and first by disinabling us to the maintenance of what is known already.

Well knows he who uses to consider, that our faith and knowledge thrives by exercise, as well as our limbs and complexion.[286] Truth is compar'd in Scripture to a streaming fountain; if her waters flow not in a perpetuall progression, they sick'n into a muddy pool of conformity and tradition. A man may be a heretick in the truth; and if he beleeve things only because his Pastor sayes so, or the Assembly so determins, without knowing other reason, though his belief be true, yet the very truth he holds, becomes his heresie. There is not any burden that som would gladlier post off to another, then the charge and care of their Religion. There be, who knows not that there be of Protestants and

---

[274]Seats of Bishops or dioceses over which bishops might have spiritual control.

[275]"Cure" or "curacy"; other living or position of responsibility within the church. The censor would hold a plurality of jobs; it would be "mysticall" because he would have the equivalent of an archbishop's spiritual control over the books he censored.

[276]Someone who has only taken the lowest academic decree. Most of the graduates of major British universities in the 1640s would be expected to take orders or become clergymen. Milton is alluding to the practice of allowing bishops arbitrarily to ordain any college graduate to a church living, a practice that the Presbyterians had opposed strongly (for the Presbyterian position, see *Animadversions*, Yale 1: 710–12).

[277]The Scottish National Covenant (established on February 28, 1638) drew battle lines with Charles I and Archbishop Laud, attempting to abolish episcopacy altogether. The Solemn League and Covenant between England and Scotland (ratified by the English Parliament September 25, 1643), based on the Scottish Covenant, created a military alliance between Scotland and the Long Parliament. The Protestation of 1641 attempted to protect Parliament against Charles's use of force.

[278]Exchange or barter for.

[279]The palace of Archbishop Laud at Canterbury. The word "*Metropolitan*" had an ecclesiastical meaning, since the "metropolitan see" would be the ecclesiastical realm of the bishop of the city of Canterbury or of London.

[280]At first, early.

[281]A meeting for the purpose of worship but outside of any church.

[282]Humbled, probably "abated" or cast down.

[283]In 1 Kings 17 the prophet Elijah miraculously causes a cruse (jar or pot or bottle of oil) and a barrel of meal to flow endlessly, through "the word of the Lord, which he spake by Elijah" (16).

[284]Remind.

[285]From the same passage in *A Wise and Moderate Dicourse* quoted above, note xx.

[286]Balance of humors in the body.

professors[287] who live and dye in as arrant an implicit faith, as any lay Papist of Loretto. A wealthy man addicted to his pleasure and to his profits, finds Religion to be a traffick so entangl'd, and of so many piddling accounts, that of all mysteries he cannot skill to[288] keep a stock going upon that trade. What should he doe? fain[289] he would have the name to be religious, fain he would bear up with his neighbours in that. What does he therefore, but resolvs to give over toyling, and to find himself out som factor,[290] to whose care and credit he may commit the whole managing of his religious affairs; som Divine of note and estimation that must be. To him he adheres, resigns the whole ware-house of his religion, with all the locks and keyes into his custody; and indeed makes the very person of that man his religion; esteems his associating with him a sufficient evidence and commendatory of his own piety. So that a man may say his religion is now no more within himself, but is becom a dividuall movable,[291] and goes and comes neer him, according as that good man frequents the house. He entertains him, gives him gifts, feasts him, lodges him; his religion comes home at night, praies, is liberally supt, and sumptuously laid to sleep, rises, is saluted, and after the malmsey,[292] or some well spic't bruage,[293] and better breakfasted then he whose morning appetite would have gladly fed on green figs between *Bethany* and *Jerusalem*,[294] his Religion walks abroad at eight, and leavs his kind entertainer in the shop trading all day without his religion.[295]

Another sort there be who when they hear that all things shall be order'd, all things regulated and setl'd; nothing writt'n but what passes through the custom-house of certain Publicans that have the tunaging and the poundaging[296] of all free spok'n truth, will strait give themselvs up into your hands, mak'em & cut'em out[297] what religion ye please; there be delights, there be re-creations and jolly pastimes that will fetch the day about from sun to sun, and rock the tedious year as in a delightfull dream. What need they torture their heads with that which others have tak'n so strictly, and so unalterably into their own pourveying. These are the fruits which a dull ease and cessation of our knowledge will bring forth among the people. How goodly, and how to be wisht were such an obedient unanimity as this, what a fine conformity would it starch[298] us all into? doubtles a stanch and solid peece of frame-work, as any January could freeze together.

Nor much better will be the consequence ev'n among the Clergy themselvs; it is no new thing never heard of before, for a *parochiall* Minister,[299] who has his reward, and is at his *Hercules* pillars[300] in a warm benefice, to be easily inclinable, if he have nothing else that may rouse up his studies, to finish his circuit in an English concordance and a *topic folio*,[301] the gatherings and savings of a sober graduatship, a *Harmony*[302] and a *Catena*, treading the constant round of certain common doctrinall heads, attended with their uses, motives, marks and means, out of which as out of an alphabet or sol fa by forming and transforming, joyning and disjoyning variously a little book-craft, and two hours meditation might furnish him unspeakably[303] to the

---

[287]Someone who openly professes his or her religion, but in the 1640s the term was often used of Puritans.

[288]Distinguish how to.

[289]Gladly.

[290]Business agent, purchasing agent.

[291]One of a number of portable goods, according to the law, which might be easily divided among heirs.

[292]A sweet Spanish wine, best known in literary circles for being the medium for the drowning of Clarence in Shakespeare's *Richard III* (1.4.161).

[293]Beer or other "bruage" was often spiced, as in the "Spicy Nut-brown Ale" of "L'Allegro" 100.

[294]"The "he" is Jesus, who caused a fig tree that did not feed him en route from Jerusalem to Bethany to wither away (see Matthew 21: 17–22).

[295]Religion personified is out of the house at eight in the morning, leaving his host the businessman to conduct his affairs all day, without the benefit of religious guidance. Milton's vignette of city business is brilliantly written, energetic, and precisely accurate.

[296]Publicans, probably tax-collectors here, imposed the ancient taxes of tunnage and poundage in the name of the Crown. The practice of collecting taxes on tuns or barrels of imported wine and on each pound sterling of the worth of other imported goods for the benefit of the

monarch was abolished at the accession of Charles I, but Parliament restored the right after Charles agreed in 1641 not to levy such taxes without the consent of Parliament.

[297]Possibly "flaunt" (*OED* "cut out" 1.n).

[298]In the figurative sense of "make rigid, formal, or precise; to frame (a discourse) in formal or pretentious terms" (*OED* 2.c, citing this instance).

[299]A minister appointed by a bishop or a parish priest. Sirluck comments on the emphasis indicated by the italics, used "to enforce the pun (minister of a parish, and parochially-minded minister" (Yale 2: 546n), but "parochial" meaning "narrow-minded" is a sense not recorded in the *OED* until the nineteenth century ("parochial" 2. fig.).

[300]The Pillars of Hercules, at the mouth of the Mediterranean Sea, would have represented the ancient limits of commercial enterprise. Here Milton seems to be using the image to represent the ultimate worldly goal of the greedy parish priest, to be warm and comfortable in an undeserved benefice.

[301]Probably a commonplace book or collection of axioms, personally maintained or designed for publication. The concordance, presumably to the Bible, would also be for private or public consumption.

[302]Milton's solitary parochial minister has the leisure (as did Milton) to collect materials for a "harmony" or a handbook of biblical passages made to complement one another or a "catena" or chain of quotations from the Church Fathers explaining passages of scripture. Milton satirizes the process of sermon-making by a lazy and inept parochial minister who might take doctrinal headings from manuals and handbooks, observe their motifs, their recognizable "marks" or signs, and their applications or uses ("means"). The process would be as predictable and dull as singing by the book (reciting an alphabet or singing a scale like "do-re-mi").

[303]Indescribably.

performance of more then a weekly charge of sermoning: not to reck'n up the infinit helps of inter-linearies,[304] breviaries, *synopses*, [305]and other loitering gear. But as for the multitude of Sermons ready printed and pil'd up, on every text that is not difficult, our London trading St. *Thomas* in his vestry, and adde to boot St. *Martin*, and St. *Hugh*,[306] have not within their hallow'd limits more vendible ware of all sorts ready made: so that penury he never need fear of Pulpit provision, having where so plenteously to refresh his magazin. But if his rear and flanks be not impal'd,[307] if his back dore be not secur'd by the rigid licencer, but that a bold book may now and then issue forth, and give the assault to some of his old collections in their trenches, it will concern him then to keep waking, to stand in watch, to set good guards and sentinells about his receiv'd opinions, to walk the round and counter-round with his fellow inspectors, fearing lest any of his flock be seduc't, who also then would be better instructed, better exercis'd and disciplin'd. And God send that the fear of this diligence which must then be us'd, doe not make us affect the lazines of a licencing Church.

For if we be sure we are in the right, and doe not hold the truth guiltily, which becomes not, if we our selves condemn not our own weak and frivolous teaching, and the people for an untaught and irreligious gadding rout, what can be more fair, then when a man judicious, learned, and of a conscience, for ought we know, as good as theirs that taught us what we know, shall not privily from house to house, which is more dangerous, but openly by writing publish to the world what his opinion is, what his reasons, and wherefore that which is now thought cannot be sound. Christ urg'd it as wherewith to justifie himself, that he preacht

in publick; yet writing is more publick then preaching; and more easie to refutation, if need be, there being so many whose businesse and profession meerly[308] it is, to be the champions of Truth; which if they neglect, what can be imputed but their sloth, or unability?

Thus much we are hinder'd and dis-inur'd by this cours of licencing toward the true knowledge of what we seem to know. For how much it hurts and hinders the licencers themselves in the calling of their Ministery, more then any secular employment, if they will discharge that office as they ought, so that of necessity they must neglect either the one duty or the other, I insist not, because it is a particular, but leave it to their own conscience, how they will decide it there.

There is yet behind of what I purpos'd to lay open, the incredible losse, and detriment that this plot of licencing puts us to, more then if som enemy at sea should stop up all our hav'ns and ports, and creeks, it hinders and retards the importation of our richest Marchandize, Truth: nay it was first establisht and put in practice by Antichristian malice and mystery on set purpose to extinguish, if it were possible, the light of Reformation, and to settle[309] falshood; little differing from that policie wherewith the Turk upholds his *Alcoran*,[310] by the prohibition of Printing. 'Tis not deny'd, but gladly confest, we are to send our thanks and vows to heav'n, louder then most of Nations, for that great measure of truth which we enjoy, especially in those main points between us and the Pope, with his appertinences the Prelats: but he who thinks we are to pitch our tent here, and have attain'd the utmost prospect of reformation, that the mortall glasse wherein we contemplate,[311] can shew us, till we come to *beatific* vision, that man by this very opinion declares, that he is yet farre short of Truth.

Truth indeed came once into the world with her divine Master, and was a perfect shape most glorious to look on: but when he ascended, and his Apostles after him were laid asleep, then strait arose a wicked race of deceivers, who as that story goes of the *Ægyptian Typhon*[312] with his conspirators, how they dealt with the

---

[304]Milton lists more reference works that might make sermonizing easier for a parish priest, including interlinear translations ("interlinears"), epitomes or compendia of religious observances ("breviaries"), synopses of the gospels or books of the Old Testament, and other "loitering gear" or shortcuts for intellectually lazy people. Milton uses the phrase "loitering books" in *An Apology against a Pamphlet* (Yale 1: 937) in a very similar context to condemn books that one should keep away from schoolchildren because they are a waste of time.

[305]A condensed version of something like the Old Testament, usually employing headings or tables. The *OED* records its first being used in 1611. Since it was a new word in English, derived from an identical word in later Latin, the compositor may have used italics to indicate its foreignness.

[306]Various local centers of book-selling, with at least one of them, St. Hugh, fabricated by Milton's imagination, perhaps on the theory that (1) shoemakers deserved a saint (there was a Welsh prince Hugh martyred and sainted, who had been a shoemaker), (2) the saint deserved a church, and (3) the churchyard deserved a book-selling establishment that might cater to tradespeople (see Yale 2: 547n).

[307]Fortified by palings or palisades.

[308]Utterly.

[309]Lay to rest, as in "The matter was settled."

[310]The Koran. "The Turk" may be understood to be representative of all Islamic nations in the Ottoman and Mughal empires.

[311]Presumably a dark mirror (1 Corinthians 13.12) whose image is limited by human mortality.

[312]Commentators agree that Plutarch's "On Isis and Osiris" is Milton's source for the allegory of the search for truth. Typhon (the Greek form for the Egyptian Set) tears up and scatters the sacred writings represented by the torn body of Osiris, and Isis searches out the pieces. The myth closely resembles another Greek myth that Milton often returns to, that of the trials of Psyche, who also has to collect the pieces of the truth. Sirluck points out that Milton is not friendly to the animal

good *Osiris*, took the virgin Truth, hewd her lovely form into a thousand peeces, and scatter'd them to the four winds. From that time ever since, the sad friends of Truth, such as durst appear, imitating the carefull search that *Isis* made for the mangl'd body of *Osiris*, went up and down gathering up limb by limb still as they could find them. We have not yet found them all, Lords and Commons, nor ever shall doe, till her Masters second comming;[313] he shall bring together every joynt and member, and shall mould them into an immortall feature[314] of lovelines and perfection. Suffer not these licencing prohibitions to stand at every place of opportunity forbidding and disturbing them that continue seeking, that continue to do our obsequies to the torn body of our martyr'd Saint. We boast our light; but if we look not wisely on the Sun it self, it smites us into darknes. Who can discern those planets that are oft *Combust*,[315] and those stars of brightest magnitude that rise and set with the Sun, untill the opposite motion of their orbs bring them to such a place in the firmament,[316] where they may be seen evning or morning. The light which we have gain'd, was giv'n us, not to be ever staring on, but by it to discover onward[317] things more remote from our knowledge. It is not the unfrocking of a Priest, the unmitring of a Bishop, and the removing him from off the *Presbyterian* shoulders that will make us a happy Nation, no, if other things as great in the Church, and in the rule of life both economicall and politicall be not lookt into and reform'd, we have lookt so long upon the blaze that *Zuinglius*[318] and *Calvin* hath beacon'd up to us, that we are stark blind. There be[319] who perpetually complain of

schisms and sects, and make it such a calamity that any man dissents from their maxims. 'Tis their own pride and ignorance which causes the disturbing, who neither will hear with meeknes, nor can convince, yet all must be supprest which is not found in their *Syntagma*. They are the troublers, they are the dividers of unity, who neglect and permit not others to unite those dissever'd peeces which are yet wanting to the body of Truth. To be still searching what we know not, by what we know, still closing up truth to truth as we find it (for all her body is *homogeneal*, and proportionall) this is the golden rule in *Theology* as well as in Arithmetick,[320] and makes up the best harmony in a Church; not the forc't and outward union of cold, and neutrall, and inwardly divided minds.

Lords and Commons of England, consider what Nation it is wherof ye are, and wherof ye are the governours: a Nation not slow and dull, but of a quick, ingenious, and piercing spirit, acute to invent, suttle and sinewy to discours, not beneath the reach of any point the highest that human capacity can soar to. Therefore the studies of learning in her deepest Sciences have bin so ancient, and so eminent among us, that Writers of good antiquity, and ablest judgement have bin perswaded that ev'n the school of *Pythagoras*, and the *Persian* wisdom took beginning from the old Philosophy of this Iland. And that wise and civill Roman, *Julius Agricola*,[321] who govern'd once here for *Cæsar*, preferr'd the naturall wits of Britain, before the labour'd studies of the French. Nor is it for nothing that the grave and frugal *Transilvanian*[322] sends out yearly from as farre as the mountanous borders of *Russia*, and beyond the *Hercynian* wildernes,[323] not their youth, but their stay'd[324] men, to learn our language, and our *theologic* arts. Yet that which is above all this, the favour and the love of heav'n we have great argument to think in a peculiar manner propitious and propending[325] towards us. Why else was this Nation chos'n before any other, that out of her as out of *Sion* should be proclam'd and sounded forth the first tidings and trumpet of Re-

---

gods Isis and Osiris in the Nativity Ode 211–23 and *Paradise Lost* 1.475–82.

[313]Milton shifts easily from Egyptian "shadowy type" to Christian "truth" in the theological premise that at the Second Coming Christ will cause all scattered bodies to reunite so that body and soul will meet judgment together. At the Second Coming, Milton came to believe, "It appears that each man will rise with the same identity as he had before," including the very same body he had in life (*On Christian Doctrine* 1.37, Yale 6: 620–21).

[314]Shape, or something formed and shaped (see *OED* 1.c).

[315] "Of the planets: Burnt up (as it were) by the sun in or near conjunction; (seemingly) extinguished by the sun's light" (*OED* 2; astrology). The theory was that planets would not be influential on human behavior if they were burned by being too close to the sun, as would be Venus, Mars, and Vulcan on occasion (see Yale 2: 550n).

[316]The canopy or vault of the heavens, in this case.

[317]"Situated in front, or in advance (in space, time, or succession generally); advanced" (*OED* 2).

[318]Ulrich Zwingli (1484–1531) and John Calvin (1509–64) together founded the Reformation, Zwingli obtaining the first legal sanction for the movement in Zurich in 1519 (see Yale 2: 550 n. 227). See Christopher for the effect of the spread of the Reformation on Milton's thought.

[319]"There are those who."

[320]Just as in mathematics the Pythagorean theorem is a kind of golden rule, in theology the perception of truth as homogeneous and based on harmonious proportions is golden.

[321]See Tacitus, *Agricola* 21. Agricola (AD 37–93) was proconsul of Britain under three different Caesars, Vespasian, Titus, and Domitian; Tacitus was his son-in-law. Milton uses Tacitus's account again in the *History of Britain* Book 2.

[322]The first mention of Transylvanians recorded in the *OED*. Transylvania, now part of Romania, was independent from 1535 to 1689 and was known as a center of Protestantism (see Yale 2: 552 n. 233).

[323]The *Hyrcania Sylva* was Julius Caesar's name for the mountainous forest regions of central and southern Germany (Yale 2: 552 n. 233).

[324]"Staid," respectable, stable.

[325]"Being well disposed toward."

formation to all *Europ*. And had it not bin the obstinat perversnes of our Prelats against the divine and admirable spirit of *Wicklef*, to suppresse him as a schismatic and *innovator*, perhaps neither the *Bohemian Husse*[326] and *Jerom*, no nor the name of *Luther*, or of *Calvin* had bin ever known: the glory of reforming all our neighbours had bin compleatly ours. But now, as our obdurat Clergy have with violence demean'd the matter, we are become hitherto the latest and the backwardest Schollers, of whom God offer'd to have made us the teachers. Now once again by all concurrence of signs, and by the generall instinct of holy and devout men, as they daily and solemnly expresse their thoughts, God is decreeing to begin some new and great period in his Church, ev'n to the reforming of Reformation it self: what does he then but reveal Himself to his servants, and as his manner is, first to his English-men; I say as his manner is, first to us, though we mark not the method of his counsels, and are unworthy. Behold now this vast City; a City of refuge, the mansion house of liberty, encompast and surrounded with his protection; the shop of warre hath not there more anvils and hammers waking, to fashion out the plates and instruments of armed Justice in defence of beleaguer'd Truth, then there be pens and heads there, sitting by their studious lamps, musing, searching, revolving new notions and idea's wherewith to present, as with their homage and their fealty the approaching Reformation: others as fast[327] reading, trying[328] all things, assenting to the force of reason and convincement. What could a man require more from a Nation so pliant and so prone to seek after knowledge. What wants there to such a towardly and pregnant[329] soile, but wise and faithfull labourers, to make a knowing people, a Nation of Prophets, of Sages, and of Worthies. We reck'n more then five months yet to harvest; there need not be five weeks, had we but eyes to lift up, the fields are white already. Where there is much desire to learn, there of necessity will be much arguing, much writing, many opinions; for opinion in good men is but knowledge in the making. Under these fantastic terrors of sect and schism, we wrong the earnest and zealous thirst after knowledge and understanding which God hath stirr'd up in this City. What some lament of, we rather should rejoyce at, should rather praise this pious forwardnes among men, to reassume the ill deputed care of their

Religion into their own hands again. A little generous prudence, a little forbearance of one another, and som grain of charity might win all these diligences to joyn, and unite into one generall and brotherly search after Truth; could we but forgoe this Prelaticall tradition of crowding free consciences and Christian liberties into canons and precepts of men. I doubt not, if some great and worthy stranger should come among us, wise to discern the mould[330] and temper of a people, and how to govern it, observing the high hopes and aims, the diligent alacrity of our extended thoughts and reasonings in the pursuance of truth and freedom, but that he would cry out as *Pirrhus*[331] did, admiring the Roman docility and courage, if such were my *Epirots*, I would not despair the greatest design that could be attempted to make a Church or Kingdom happy. Yet these are the men cry'd out against for schismaticks and sectaries; as if, while the Temple of the Lord was building, some cutting, some squaring the marble, others hewing the cedars, there should be a sort of irrationall men who could not consider there must be many schisms and many dissections made in the quarry and in the timber, ere the house of God can be built. And when every stone is laid artfully together, it cannot be united into a continuity, it can but be contiguous in this world; neither can every peece of the building be of one form; nay rather the perfection consists in this, that out of many moderat varieties and brotherly dissimilitudes[332] that are not vastly disproportionall arises the goodly and the gracefull symmetry that commends the whole pile[333] and structure. Let us therefore be more considerat builders, more wise in spirituall architecture, when great reformation is expected. For now the time seems come, wherein *Moses* the great Prophet may sit in heav'n rejoycing to see that memorable and glorious wish of his fulfill'd, when not only our sev'nty Elders, but all the Lords people are become Prophets. No marvell then though some men, and some good men too perhaps, but young in goodnesse, as *Joshua* then was, envy them. They fret, and out of their own weaknes are in agony, lest these divisions and subdivisions will undoe us. The adversarie again applauds, and waits the hour, when they have brancht themselves out, saith he, small anough into parties and partitions, then will be our

---

[326]Wycliff, Huss, and Jerome of Prague (c. 1365–1416) worked together in instituting an early form of reformation. Had Wycliff been successful, Milton says, England would have been the seat of the Reformation.
[327]Determinedly.
[328]Evaluating, weighing.
[329]Ready for planting.

[330]Mold, character.
[331]Pyrrhus (c. 318–272 BCE) military commander of Epirus, a country between Macedonia and Achaia, defeated a Roman army at Heracles in 280 BCE. He was reported by a number of historians to have said that if he had soldiers like the Romans, or the Romans had a general like him, he would conquer the world.
[332]Unlikeness, or in this case disagreement.
[333]Literally a small castle (*OED* 2), but Milton uses the word to signify any large building, or person resembling one (*Samson Agonistes* 1069).

time. Fool! he sees not the firm root, out of which we all grow, though into branches: nor will beware untill he see our small divided maniples[334] cutting through at every angle of his ill united and unweildy brigade. And that we are to hope better of all these supposed sects and schisms, and that we shall not need that solicitude honest perhaps though over timorous of them that vex[335] in this behalf, but shall laugh in the end, at those malicious applauders of our differences, I have these reasons to perswade me.

First, when a City shall be as it were besieg'd and blockt about, her navigable river infested,[336] inrodes and incursions round, defiance and battell oft rumor'd to be marching up ev'n to her walls, and suburb trenches,[337] that then the people, or the greater part, more then at other times, wholly tak'n up with the study of highest and most important matters to be reform'd, should be disputing, reasoning, reading, inventing, discoursing, ev'n to a rarity,[338] and admiration, things not before discourst or writt'n of, argues first a singular good will, contentednesse and confidence in your prudent foresight, and safe government, Lords and Commons; and from thence derives it self to a gallant bravery and well grounded contempt of their enemies, as if there were no small number of as great spirits among us, as his was, who when Rome was nigh besieg'd by *Hanibal*, being in the City, bought that peece of ground at no cheap rate, whereon *Hanibal* himself encampt his own regiment. Next it is a lively and cherfull presage[339] of our happy success and victory. For as in a body, when the blood is fresh, the spirits pure and vigorous, not only to vital, but to rationall faculties, and those in the acutest, and the pertest operations of wit and suttlety, it argues in what good plight and constitution the body is, so when the cherfulnesse of the people is so sprightly up, as that it has, not only wherewith to guard well its own freedom and safety, but to spare, and to bestow upon the solidest and sublimest points of controversie, and new invention, it betok'ns us not degenerated, nor dropping to a fatall decay, but casting off the old and wrincl'd skin of corruption to outlive these pangs and wax young again, entring the glorious waies of Truth and prosperous vertue destin'd to become great and

honourable in these latter ages. Methinks I see in my mind a noble and puissant Nation rousing herself[340] like a strong man after sleep, and shaking her invincible locks: Methinks I see her as an Eagle muing her mighty youth,[341] and kindling her undazl'd eyes at the full midday beam; purging and unscaling her long abused sight at the fountain it self of heav'nly radiance; while the whole noise of timorous and flocking birds, with those also that love the twilight, flutter about, amaz'd at what she means, and in their envious gabble would prognosticat a year of sects and schisms.

What should ye doe then, should ye suppresse all this flowry crop of knowledge and new light sprung up and yet springing daily in this City, should ye set an *Oligarchy* of twenty ingrossers[342] over it, to bring a famin upon our minds again, when we shall know nothing but what is measur'd to us by their bushel? Beleeve it, Lords and Commons, they who counsell ye to such a suppressing, doe as good as bid ye suppresse your selves; and I will soon shew how. If it be desir'd to know the immediat cause of all this free writing and free speaking, there cannot be assign'd a truer then your own mild, and free, and human government; it is the liberty, Lords and Commons, which your own valorous and happy counsels have purchast us, liberty which is the nurse of all great wits; this is that which hath rarify'd and enlightn'd our spirits like the influence of heav'n; this is that which hath enfranchis'd, enlarg'd and lifted up our apprehensions degrees above themselves. Ye cannot make us now lesse capable, lesse knowing, lesse eagarly pursuing of the truth, unlesse ye first make your selves, that made us so, lesse the lovers, lesse the founders of our true liberty. We can grow ignorant again, brutish, formall,[343] and slavish, as ye found us; but you then must first become that which ye cannot be, oppressive, arbitrary, and tyrannous, as they were from whom ye have free'd us. That our hearts are now more capacious, our thoughts more erected to the search and expectation of greatest and exactest things, is the issue of

---

[334]A maniple was a subdivision of a Roman legion consisting of 120 men. A brigade was a much larger force.

[335]Fret, worry, be vexed.

[336]Attacked.

[337]Defensive excavations on the perimeter of the city. A series of perimeter trenches had indeed been erected on a twelve-mile circuit around London in the summer of 1643 to protect it against attacks by royalist forces.

[338]Even to the point of discussing something rare and wondrous.

[339]Prediction, forecast.

---

[340]The noun "natio" in Latin is feminine, though Milton immediately shifts the sex of the nation to masculine when he compares England to Samson. The image of Samson resisting the various temptations of Delilah and the Philistines (Judges 16.6–14) is also used in *The Reason of Church-government* (Yale 1: 858–59).

[341]Probably an image from falconry, in which hunting activities must cease while the falcon molts or "mews" its feathers and thus renews its plumage. The *OED* comments on Milton's unique usage: "The precise sense intended is difficult to determine: perhaps 'to renew by the process of moulting'; some would render 'exchanging her mighty youth for the still mightier strength of full age'" (1.b).

[342]Wholesale purchasers. Exactly why "*Oligarchy*" is in italics is difficult to say, though the Greek-derived word had not been in use in English except for the last forty years, according to the *OED*.

[343]Bound by meaningless ritual.

your owne vertu propagated in us; ye cannot suppresse that unlesse ye reinforce an abrogated and mercilesse law, that fathers may dispatch[344] at will their own children. And who shall then stick closest to ye, and excite others? not he who takes up armes for cote and conduct,[345] and his four nobles of Danegelt. Although I dispraise not the defence of just immunities, yet love my peace better, if that were all. Give me the liberty to know, to utter, and to argue freely according to conscience, above all liberties.

What would be best advis'd then, if it be found so hurtfull and so unequall[346] to suppresse opinions for the newnes, or the unsutablenes to a customary acceptance, will not be my task to say; I only shall repeat what I have learnt from one of your own honourable number, a right noble and pious Lord, who had he not sacrific'd his life and fortunes to the Church and Commonwealth, we had not now mist and bewayl'd a worthy and undoubted patron of this argument. Ye know him I am sure; yet I for honours sake, and may it be eternall to him, shall name him, the Lord *Brook*. He writing of Episcopacy, and by the way treating of sects and schisms, left Ye[347] his vote, or rather now the last words of his dying charge, which I know will ever be of dear and honour'd regard with Ye, so full of meeknes and breathing charity, that next to his last testament, who bequeath'd love and peace to his Disciples, I cannot call to mind where I have read or heard words more mild and peacefull. He there exhorts us to hear with patience and humility those, however they be miscall'd, that desire to live purely, in such a use of Gods Ordinances, as the best guidance of their conscience gives them, and to tolerat them, though in some disconformity to our selves. The book it self will tell us more at large being publisht to the world, and dedicated to the Parlament by him who both for his life and for his death deserves, that what advice he left be not laid by without perusall.

And now the time in speciall[348] is, by priviledge to write and speak what may help to the furder discussing of matters in agitation. The Temple of *Janus*[349] with his two *controversal* faces might now not unsignificantly be set open. And though all the windes of doctrin[350] were let loose to play upon the earth, so Truth be in the field, we do injuriously by licencing and prohibiting to misdoubt[351] her strength. Let her and Falshood grapple; who ever knew Truth put to the wors, in a free and open encounter. Her confuting is the best and surest suppressing. He who hears what praying there is for light and clearer knowledge to be sent down among us, would think of other matters to be constituted beyond the discipline of *Geneva*,[352] fram'd and fabric't already to our hands. Yet when the new light which we beg for shines in upon us, there be[353] who envy, and oppose, if it come not first in at their casements. What a collusion is this, whenas we are exhorted by the wise man to use diligence, *to seek for wisdom as for hidd'n treasures*[354] early and late, that another order shall enjoyn us to know nothing but by statute. When a man hath bin labouring the hardest labour in the deep mines of knowledge, hath furnisht out his findings in all their equipage, drawn forth his reasons as it were a battell raung'd,[355] scatter'd and defeated all objections in his way, calls out his adversary into the plain, offers him the advantage of wind and sun, if he please; only that he may try the matter by dint of argument, for his opponents then to sculk, to lay ambushments, to keep a narrow bridge of licencing where the challenger should passe, though it be valour anough in shouldiership,[356] is but weaknes and cowardise in the wars of Truth. For who knows not that Truth is strong next to[357] the Almighty; she needs no policies, nor stratagems, nor licencings to make her victorious, those are the shifts and the defences that error uses against her power: give her but room, & do not bind her when she sleeps, for then she speaks not true, as the old *Proteus* did, who spake oracles only when he was caught & bound,[358] but then rather she turns herself into all shapes, except her own, and perhaps tunes her voice

---

[344]Dispose of or kill. By the "jus vitae et necis," Roman fathers had life or death power over their male children until 318 AD, at which point the law was abolished (Yale 2: 559n).

[345]"Money to provide a coat for each man furnished for military service" (*OED* "coat-money"), but here more specifically a tax levied by Charles I illegally in order to provide clothing and travel expenses for recruits in the royal army.

[346]Unjust.

[347]Capitalization of "Ye" is respectful usage to address "Ye Lords and Commons."

[348]In special, especially.

[349]The statuary of the Roman god Janus showed two faces aimed in opposite directions, or "contra-versial." His temple was left open during war and shut during peace.

[350]The phrase appears in Ephesians 4.14.

[351]Suspect, doubt.

[352]The Presbyterianism that emanated from the city of Geneva.

[353]Supply "some."

[354]Probably an amalgamation of two verses from Proverbs 2: "If thou seekest her [i.e., wisdom] as silver, and searchest for her as for hid treasures; then shalt thou understand the fear of the Lord, and find the knowledge of God" (4–5). Milton is not shy to offer his own translation of biblical passages.

[355]Ranged, spread out.

[356]"Soldiership," the discipline required of a soldier. Probably the word is misspelled, since "shouldier" is not listed by the *OED* as a variant spelling for "soldier."

[357]"Is almost as strong as."

[358]In the *Odyssey* 4.383–459, Proteus is described changing from one protean shape into another, to avoid being asked to divulge the truth.

according to the time, as *Micaiah* did before *Ahab*,[359] untill she be adjur'd[360] into her own likenes. Yet is it not impossible that she may have more shapes then one. What else is all that rank of things indifferent, wherein Truth may be on this side, or on the other, without being unlike her self. What but a vain shadow else is the abolition of *those ordinances, that hand writing nayl'd to the crosse*,[361] what great purchase is this Christian liberty which *Paul* so often boasts of. His doctrine is, that he who eats or eats not, regards a day, or regards it not, may doe either to the Lord. How many other things might be tolerated in peace, and left to conscience, had we but charity, and were it not the chief strong hold of our hypocrisie to be ever judging one another. I fear yet this iron yoke of outward conformity hath left a slavish print upon our necks; the ghost of a linnen decency[362] yet haunts us. We stumble and are impatient at the least dividing of one visible congregation from another, though it be not in fundamentalls; and through our forwardnes to suppresse, and our backwardnes to recover any enthrall'd peece of truth out of the gripe[363] of custom, we care not to keep truth separated from truth, which is the fiercest rent[364] and disunion of all. We doe not see that while we still affect by all means a rigid externall formality, we may as soon fall again into a grosse conforming stupidity, a stark and dead congealment of *wood and hay and stubble*[365] forc't and frozen together, which is more to the sudden degenerating of a Church then many *subdichotomies*[366] of petty schisms. Not that I can think well of every light separation, or that all in a Church is to be expected *gold and silver and pretious stones:* it is not possible for man to sever the wheat from the tares, the good fish from the other frie;[367] that must be the Angels Ministery at the end of mortall things. Yet if all cannot be of one mind, as who looks they should be? this doubtles is more wholsome, more prudent, and more Christian that many be tolerated, rather then all compell'd. I mean not tolerated Popery,[368] and open superstition, which as it extirpats all religions and civill supremacies, so it self should be extirpat, provided first that all charitable and compassionat means be us'd to win and regain the weak and the misled: that also which is impious or evil absolutely either against faith or maners no law can possibly permit, that intends not to unlaw it self: but those neighboring differences, or rather indifferences, are what I speak of, whether in some point of doctrine or of discipline, which though they may be many, yet need not interrupt *the unity of Spirit*, if we could but find among us *the bond of peace*. In the mean while if any one would write, and bring his helpfull hand to the slow-moving Reformation which we labour under, if Truth have spok'n to him before others, or but seem'd at least to speak, who hath so bejesuited[369] us that we should trouble that man with asking licence to doe so worthy a deed? and not consider this, that if it come to prohibiting, there is not ought more likely to be prohibited then truth it self; whose first appearance to our eyes blear'd and dimm'd with prejudice and custom, is more unsightly and unplausible then many errors, ev'n as the person is of many a great man slight and contemptible to see to. And what doe they tell us vainly of new opinions, when this very opinion of theirs, that none must be heard, but whom they like, is the worst and newest opinion of all others; and is the chief cause why sects and schisms doe so much abound, and true knowledge is kept at distance from us; besides yet a greater danger which is in it. For when God shakes a Kingdome with strong and healthfull commotions to a generall reforming,[370] 'tis not untrue that many sectaries and false teachers are then busiest in seducing; but yet more true it is, that God then raises to his own work men of rare abilities, and more then common industry not only to look back and revise what hath bin taught heretofore, but to gain furder and goe on, some new

---

[359]In 1 Kings 22.9–28, Michaiah speaks what King Ahab wants to hear, becoming one of a series of false prophets.

[360]"Solemnly charged, earnestly entreated or appealed to" (*OED* 2, citing Milton's usage in *Samson Agonistes* 853).

[361]In Colossians 2.13–14, Paul writes that Christ brought his followers to life, forgave their trespasses, and that He blotted out "the handwriting of ordinances that was against us, which was against us, which was contrary to us, and took it out of the way, nailing it to his cross."

[362]Laud had used the word "decency" in order to enforce conformity of dress or ceremony, hence the association between fine linen, such as Laud's bishops might wear, and decency. See Yale 2: 564n.

[363]Grip.

[364]Ripped or torn place in fabric or, metaphorically, in the church.

[365]In 1 Corinthians 3.10–13, Paul discusses the effects of fire on a foundation of "gold, silver, precious stones, wood, hay, stubble" (12), the point being that a fire would betray the materials used in construction, just as the fire of God's spirit will "try every man's work of what sort it is" (13).

[366]Milton invented this word, and, according to the *OED*, it hasn't been used since.

[367]Milton alludes to the whole series of images Christ makes for the likeness of the kingdom of heaven in Matthew 13.

[368]In other words, toleration might include many Protestant sects but not Roman Catholicism, which would be represented as "Popery" and thus superstition to Milton's audience. Roman Catholicism in this context would not tolerate any other religion or recognize any civic laws or hierarchies of command ("civill supremacies").

[369]"Oppressed by Jesuits." Because of their complicity in the Gunpowder Plot and their efforts to convert Protestants to Roman Catholicism, Jesuits were thought of as secret agents for the religious enemy. Milton not only made up the word—this usage is the first cited in the *OED*—but he removed the normal capital letter from the noun form.

[370]God shakes many nations in the Old Testament (see Isaiah 2.19, 21; 13.13, for example), but especially in Haggai 2.7, where the shaking seems to have a salutary effect.

enlightn'd steps in the discovery of truth. For such is the order of Gods enlightning his Church, to dispense and deal out by degrees his beam, so as our earthly eyes may best sustain it. Neither is God appointed and confin'd, where and out of what place these his chosen shall be first heard to speak; for he sees not as man sees, chooses not as man chooses, lest we should devote our selves again to set places, and assemblies, and outward callings of men; planting our faith one while in the old Convocation house, and another while in the Chappell at Westminster;[371] when all the faith and religion that shall be there canoniz'd, is not sufficient without plain convincement, and the charity of patient instruction to supple[372] the least bruise of conscience, to edifie the meanest Christian, who desires to walk in the Spirit, and not in the letter of human trust, for all the number of voices that can be there made; no though *Harry* the 7. himself there, with all his leige tombs[373] about him, should lend them voices from the dead, to swell their number. And if the men be erroneous who appear to be the leading schismaticks, what witholds us but our sloth, our self-will, and distrust in the right cause, that we doe not give them gentle meetings and gentle dismissions, that we debate not and examin the matter throughly with liberall and frequent audience; if not for their sakes, yet for our own? seeing no man who hath tasted learning, but will confesse the many waies of profiting by those who not contented with stale receits[374] are able to manage, and set forth new positions to the world. And were they but as the dust and cinders of our feet, so long as in that notion they may yet serve to polish and brighten the armoury of Truth,[375] ev'n for that respect they were not utterly to be cast away. But if they be of those whom God hath fitted for the speciall use of these times with eminent and ample gifts, and those perhaps neither among the Priests, nor among the Pharisees, and we in the hast of a precipitant zeal shall make no distinction, but resolve to stop their mouths, because we fear they come with new and dangerous opinions, as we commonly forejudge them ere we understand them, no lesse then woe to us, while

thinking thus to defend the Gospel, we are found the persecutors.

There have bin not a few since the beginning of this Parlament, both of the Presbytery and others who by their unlicenc't books to the contempt of an *Imprimatur* first broke that triple ice[376] clung about our hearts, and taught the people to see day: I hope that none of those were the perswaders to renew upon us this bondage which they themselves have wrought so much good by contemning. But if neither the check that *Moses* gave to young *Joshua*,[377] nor the countermand which our Saviour gave to young *John*,[378] who was so ready to prohibit those whom he thought unlicenc't, be not anough to admonish our Elders how unacceptable to God their testy mood of prohibiting is, if neither their own remembrance what evill hath abounded in the Church by this lett[379] of licencing, and what good they themselves have begun by transgressing it, be not anough, but that they will perswade, and execute the most *Dominican*[380] part of the Inquisition over us, and are already with one foot in the stirrup so active at suppressing, it would be no unequall distribution in the first place to suppresse the suppressors themselves; whom the change of their condition hath puft up, more then their late experience of harder times hath made wise.

And as for regulating the Presse, let no man think to have the honour of advising ye better then your selves have done in that Order publisht next before this,[381] that no book be Printed, unlesse the Printers and the Authors name, or at least the Printers be register'd. Those which otherwise come forth, if they be found mischievous and libellous, the fire and the executioner[382] will be the timeliest and the most effectuall remedy, that mans prevention can use. For this *authentic*[383] Spanish policy of licencing books, if I have said ought, will

---

[371]The assigning or sanctifying of a place of worship was an important issue between Puritan and Royalist factions. The Long Parliament had transferred the power of convocation from Laud's control to that of the Assembly of Divines, and the place of convocation from the Chapterhouse at Westminster to Henry VII's (i.e., that of "*Harry* the 7") Chapel, also in Westminster Abbey. See Yale 2: 567n.

[372]"To soften, mollify (the heart or mind); to cause to yield or be submissive; to make compliant or complaisant" (*OED* v. 1).

[373]The tombs of his liege lords or the lords who served him when he was king.

[374]Recipes or prescriptions of conduct.

[375]"To polish the armor of truth and make it shine."

[376]Perhaps, as Lutaud suggests, a near-echo of Horace's "aes triplex" (257 n. 229), or triple bronze layers, and possibly an oblique reference to Dante's Satan, buried to mid-breast in ice (*Inferno* 34.29).

[377]Moses checked or curbed the young Joshua as Milton has already mentioned.

[378]In Luke 9.49–50, Jesus asks John (here made young for the parallel with Joshua) not to forbid someone from casting out devils in his name, "for he that is not against us is for us" (50).

[379]Hindrance.

[380]The Dominican Friars were those most closely associated with the Spanish Inquisition, especially the infamous Dominican monk Torquemada (1420–98).

[381]The Order of January 29, 1642, actually issued as part of a series of orders and thus not "next before this."

[382]The public executioner in London was also in charge of burning seditious or libellous books, and at the same time punishing the offending author or publisher with humiliating mutilation such as ear cropping or nose slitting.

[383]Legally authorized. The italics here seem to emphasize the ironic illegality of the Inquisition.

prove the most unlicenc't book it self within a short while; and was the immediat image of a Star-chamber decree[384] to that purpose made in those very times when that Court did the rest of those her pious works, for which she is now fall'n from the Starres with *Lucifer*. Whereby ye may guesse what kinde of State prudence, what love of the people, what care of Religion, or good manners there was at the contriving, although with singular hypocrisie it pretended to bind books to their good behaviour. And how it got the upper hand of your precedent Order so well constituted before, if we may beleeve those men whose profession gives them cause to enquire most, it may be doubted there was in it the fraud of some old *patentees* and *monopolizers* in the trade of book-selling;[385] who under pretence of the poor in their Company not to be defrauded, and the just retaining of each man his severall copy,[386] which God forbid should be gainsaid, brought divers glosing[387] colours to the House, which were indeed but colours,

and serving to no end except it be to exercise a superiority over their neighbours, men who doe not therefore labour in an honest profession to which learning is indetted, that they should be made other mens vassalls. Another end is thought was aym'd at by some of them in procuring by petition this Order, that having power in their hands, malignant books might the easier scape abroad, as the event shews. But of these *Sophisms* and *Elenchs*[388] of marchandize I skill not: This I know, that errors in a good government and in a bad are equally almost incident; for what Magistrate may not be misinform'd, and much the sooner, if liberty of Printing be reduc't into the power of a few; but to redresse willingly and speedily what hath bin err'd,[389] and in highest autority to esteem a plain advertisement more then others have done a sumptuous bribe, is a vertue (honour'd Lords and Commons) answerable to Your highest actions, and whereof none can participat but greatest and wisest men.

The End.

---

[384]The Decree of July 11, 1637, which Sirluck labels as "the most elaborate instrument in English history for the suppression of undesired publication" (159).
[385]For patents and monopolies in book publishing, see Eisenstein 120, 557.
[386]"His own separate copy."
[387]Flattering (with overtones of "lying" or "being hypocritical").

[388]A sophism is a positive expression in logic, an elench a refutation. Evidently, Milton means, ironically, "lies proposed positively" and "lies that refute another logical proposition." He adds that he has no skill in determining the truth or falsity of how books may sell themselves. Publishers or booksellers might lie on a title page about place of publication, for instance, in order to avoid prosecution, or, in the case of *Areopagitica*, they may omit their own names from the title page.
[389]"What has been used erroneously."

Tetrachordon (Selections) (1645)

This longest of Milton's divorce tracts is devoted to harmonizing four different passages in scripture—hence the four chords of the title—to justify divorce. Milton made it a point to sign his name to it, with his initials on the title page and his name printed in full after his prefatory remarks to Parliament.

Though the subject matter, divorce, provokes an emotional response, the author maintains his objectivity in *Tetrachordon* by focusing on the biblical texts: Milton's private opinions rarely seem to intrude. He is interpreting Scripture, something his education had trained him to do very well, and his tone seems cool and impartial. He does not often seem to be describing himself as a deserted or wronged husband, as he did in both versions of *Doctrine and Discipline of Divorce*. He imagines what it might be like to live for years in a marriage in which husband and wife hated one another but had to remain together because of canon law—a situation he could only imagine or reconstruct from his own observation of other married couples.

Both *Tetrachordon* and *Colasterion*, the latter being Milton's beating (the word means something close to "cat-o-nine-tails") of a socially inferior "serving-man" who had dared to write against the *Doctrine and Discipline of Divorce*, were entered as published on or before March 4, 1645 (old style 1644), by Milton's friend the bookseller George Thomason.

Mary Powell Milton was to return later in 1645, after her deserted husband had apparently been courting Dr. Davis's daughter, with serious intentions of marrying her—if Edward Phillips is to be trusted.

ORGANIZATION

The bit of biblical text under scrutiny determines how Milton arranges his own argument. The Bible is seen as a collection of holy passages, any one of which is imagined to create a harmonious chord when harmonized with any other. A commonplace seventeenth-century phrase like "the harmony of the Gospels" expresses the desire to harmonize selected passages from the Bible. As the notes to the Yale edition make clear, Milton may select precise bits of evidence, even in his quotations from the Bible. If he does not like the way the Authorized Version translates a word or phrase, he will insert his own translation (Fletcher); if he does not want to use an entire passage, he will put the parts he is quoting in italics, but he will not indicate what he has left out (see the notes in Yale 2: 614–16 for various examples of changes in Biblical texts, and Fletcher, *Use* 34–36).

LOGIC

Milton seems almost fixated on his own logical methods, based on the logic theory dominant at Cambridge when he attended, that of Peter Ramus, and evidenced in Milton's own translation of Ramus's work in his *Art of Logic* (see Ong, Dahlø, Miller). It may well be that he was working on his translation of Ramus's *Logic* in preparation for teaching his nephews in 1645 (Yale 8: 145). Such terms as *method* and Milton's system of classifying topics in branches coming from more of a generalized tree are certainly derived from Ramus. A reader of the *Tetrachordon* might be well advised to read Milton's *Art of Logic* in order to understand how he organized and defined terms in his tract on divorce.

ADAM AND EVE: THE FIRST EXAMPLE OF A MARRIED COUPLE

I have selected the first of Milton's four expositions on passages of Scripture to reproduce here because it focuses on the creation and marriage of Adam and Eve. Milton pictures the first marriage as a "prime institution" and hence a model for what marriages might be, if we could get back to the garden. It is notable that he stresses the nature of woman as fitting help, or helpmeet, for the man whose loneliness she was created to relieve. Milton also stresses what he calls the fit conversation, the spiritual and intellectual communication, that was possible when man and woman were more nearly equal within the institution of marriage.

TEXT

The copy text for this edition is the 1645 edition and specifically the copy preserved in the Bodleian Library (Shelfmark 4° F 56 Th, kept as Arch. G e. 44).

The 98 pages of the tract are neatly produced and well printed, by the team of Thomas Payne and Samuel Simmons. As Shawcross points out ("Prose"), Payne's setting of earlier gatherings in the book is less precisely Miltonic than Simmons's. The pages are handsomely designed and the book has few typographical errors. The Errata list notes only two. The compositor who set the earlier portions, however, is not faithful to Milton's spelling practices. Occasionally the reader will notice that a Miltonic spelling like "freindship" creeps in, a sign that the compositor has been working from Milton's holograph manuscript, as would be customary at this stage of Milton's career. But there are conflicts that emerge, as with the Miltonic spelling "thir," which the compositor probably would have preferred not to use. In the excerpt printed below, for instance, he reproduces 28 of Milton's "thirs" but 41 "theirs," showing the more fashionable word form winning the battle. Milton's preference clearly loses with the word "onely":

that spelling appears only ten times, with "only" winning out 51 times. House style, and custom, in other words, defeat the author's habits, perceived as quirky.

Works Cited

Dahlø, Rolf. "The Date of Milton's *Artis Logicae* and the Development of the Idea of Definition in Milton's Works." *Huntington Library Quarterly* 43 (1979): 25–36.

Fletcher, Harris F. *The Use of the Bible in Milton's Prose.* New York: Haskell House, 1970.

Miller, Leo. "Milton Edits Freigius' *Life of Ramus.*" *Renaissance and Reformation* 8 (1972): 112–114.

Ong, Walter J., S.J. "Logic and the Epic Muse: Reflections on Noetic Structures in Milton's Milieu." *Achievements of the Left Hand: Essays on the Prose of John Milton.* Ed. Michael Lieb and John Shawcross. Amherst: U of Massachusetts P, 1974.

To the PARLAMENT.

That which I knew to be the part of a good Magistrate, aiming at true liberty through the right information of religious and civil life, and that which I saw, and was partaker, of your Vows and solemne Cov'nants, Parlament of England, your actions also manifestly tending to exalt the truth, and to depresse the tyranny of error, and ill custome, with more constancy and prowesse then ever yet any, since that Parlament which put the first Scepter of this Kingdom into his hand whom God and extraordinary vertue made thir Monarch, were the causes that mov'd me, one else not placing much in the eminence of a dedication, to present your high notice with a Discourse, conscious to it self of nothing more then of diligence, and firm affection to the publick good. And that ye took it so as wise and impartial men, obtaining so great power and dignitie, are wont to accept, in matters both doubtfull and important, what they think offer'd them well meant, and from a rational ability, I had no lesse then to perswade me. And on that perswasion am return'd, as to a famous and free Port, my self also bound by more then a maritime *Law*, to expose as freely what fraught age I conceave to bring of no trifles. For although it be generally known, how and by whom ye have been instigated to a hard censure of that former book entitl'd, The Doctrine, and Discipline of Divorce, an opinion held by some of the best among reformed Writers without scandal or confutement, though now thought new and dangerous by some of our Gnostics, whose little reading, and lesse meditating holds ever with hardest obstinacy that which it took up with easiest credulity, I do not find yet that ought, for the furious incitements which have been us'd, hath issu'd by your appointment, that might give the least inter-

ruption or disrepute either to the Author, or to the Book. Which he who will be better advis'd then to call your neglect, or connivence at a thing imagin'd so perilous, can attribute it to nothing more justly, then to the deep and quiet streame of your direct and calme deliberations; that gave not way either to the fervent rashnesse, or the immaterial gravity of those who ceas'd not to exasperate without cause. For which uprightnesse and incorrupt refusall of what ye were incensd to, Lords and Commons, (though it were don to justice, not to me, and was a peculiar demonstration how farre your waies are different from the rash vulgar) besides those allegiances of oath and duty, which are my public debt to your public labours, I have yet a store of gratitude laid up, which cannot be exhausted; and such thanks perhaps they may live to be, as shall more then whisper to the next ages. Yet that the Author may be known to ground himself upon his own innocence, and the merit of his cause, not upon the favour of a diversion, or a delay to any just censure, but wishes rather he might see those his detracters at any fair meeting, as learned debatements are privileg'd with a due freedome under equall Moderators, I shall here briefly single one of them (because he hath oblig'd me to it) who I perswade me having scarse read the book, nor knowing him who writ it, or at least faining the latter, hath not forborn to scandalize him, unconferr'd with, unadmonisht, undealt with by any Pastorly or brotherly convincement, in the most open and invective manner, and at the most bitter opportunity that drift or set designe could have invented. And this, when as the Canon Law, though commonly most favouring the boldnesse of their Priests, punishes the naming or traducing of any person in the Pulpit, was by him made no scruple. If I shall therfore take licence by the right of nature, and that liberty wherin I was born, to defend my self publicly against a printed Calumny, and do willingly appeal to those Judges to whom I am accus'd, it can be no immoderate, or unallowable course of seeking so just and needfull reparations. Which I had don long since, had not these employments, which are now visible, deferr'd me. It was preacht before ye, Lords and Commons, in August last upon a special day of humiliation, that there was a wicked Book abroad, *and ye were taxt of sin that it was yet* uncensur'd, the book deserving to be burnt, and impudence *also was charg'd upon the Author, who durst set his name to it, and dedicate it to* your selves. *First, Lords and Commons, I pray to that God, before whom ye then were prostrate, so to forgive ye those omissions and trespasses, which ye desire most should find forgivness, as I shall soon shew to the world how easily ye absolve your selves of that which this man calls your sin, and is indeed your wisdome, and your Noblenesse, where of to this day ye have don well not to repent.* He terms it a wicked book, *and why but* for allowing other causes of Divorce, then Christ and his Apostles mention; *and*

with the same censure condemns of wickednesse not onely
Martin Bucer *that elect Instrument of Reformation, highly
honour'd and had in reverence by* Edward *the sixth, and
his whole Parlament, whom also I had publisht in English
by a good providence, about a week before this calumnious
digression was preach'd; so that if he knew not* Bucer *then,
as he ought to have known, he might at least have known
him some months after, ere the Sermon came in print,
wherein notwithstanding he persists in his former sentence,
and condemnes again of wickednesse, either ignorantly or
wilfully, not onely* Martin Bucer, *and all the choisest and
holiest of our Reformers, but the whole Parlament and
Church of England in those best and purest times of* Edward *the sixth. All which I shall prove with good evidence,
at the end of these Explanations. And then let it be judg'd
and seriously consider'd with what hope the affairs of our
Religion are committed to one among others, who hath
now onely left him which of the twain he will choose, whether this shall be his palpable ignorance, or the same
wickednesse of his own book, which he so lavishly imputes
to the writings of other men: and whether this of his, that
thus peremptorily defames and attaints of wickednesse unspotted Churches, unblemisht Parlaments, and the most
eminent restorers of Christian Doctrine, deserve not to be
burnt first. And if his heat had burst out onely against the
opinion, his wonted passion had no doubt bin silently born*[1]
*with wonted patience. But since against the charity of that
solemne place and meeting, it serv'd him furder to inveigh
opprobriously against the person, branding him with no
lesse then impudence, onely for setting his name to what he
had writt'n, I must be excus'd not to be so wanting to the
defence of an honest name, or to the reputation of those
good men who afford me their society, but to be sensible of
such a foule endeavour'd disgrace: not knowing ought*[2]
*either in mine own deserts, or the Laws of this Land, why
I should be subject, in such a notorious and illegal manner,
to the intemperancies of this mans preaching choler. And
indeed to be so prompt and ready in the midst of his hum-
blenesse, to tosse reproaches of this bulk and size, argues as
if they were the weapons of his exercise, I am sure not of his
Ministery, or of that dayes work. Certainly to subscribe my
name at what I was to own,*[3] *was what the State had
order'd and requires. And he who lists not to be malicious,
would call it ingenuity, cleer conscience, willingnesse to
avouch what might be question'd, or to be better instructed.
And if God were so displeas'd with those,* Isa. 58. *who on
the solemne fast were wont to smite with the fist of
wickednesse, it could be no signe of his own humiliation
accepted, which dispos'd him to smite so keenly with a re-*

viling *tongue. But if onely to have writ my name must be
counted* impudence, *how doth this but justifie another,
who might affirm with as good warrant, that the late
Discourse of* Scripture and Reason, *which is certain to be
chiefly his own draught, was publisht without a name, out
of base fear, and the sly avoidance of what might follow to
his detriment, if the party at Court should hap to reach
him. And I, to have set my name, where he accuses me to
have set it, am so far from recanting, that I offer my hand
also if need be, to make good the same opinion which I
there maintain, by inevitable consequences drawn parallel
from his own principal arguments in that of* Scripture and
Reason; *which I shall pardon him, if he can deny, without
shaking his own composition to peeces. The* impudence
*therfore, since he waigh'd so little what a grosse revile that
was to give his equall, I send him back again for a* phylactery[4] *to stitch upon his arrogance, that censures not onely
before conviction so bitterly without so much as one reason
giv'n, but censures the Congregation of his Governors to
their faces, for not being so hasty as himself to censure.*

*And whereas my other crime is, that I address'd the De-
dication of what I had studied, to the* Parlament, *how
could I better declare the loyalty which I owe to that
supreme and majestick Tribunal, and the opinion which I
have of the high-entrusted judgement, and personall worth
assembl'd in that place. With the same affections therfore,
and the same addicted fidelity,* Parlament of England, *I
here again have brought to your perusal on the same argument these following Expositions of Scripture. The former
book, as pleas'd some to think, who were thought judicious,
had of reason in it to a sufficiencie; what they requir'd, was
that the Scriptures there alleg'd, might be discuss'd more
fully. To their desires, thus much furder hath been labour'd
in the Scriptures. Another sort also who wanted more autorities, and citations, have not been here unthought of. If
all this attain not to satisfie them, as I am confident that
none of those our great controversies at this day, hath had
a more demonstrative explaining, I must confesse to admire what it is, for doubtlesse it is not reason now adayes
that satisfies, or suborns the common credence of men, to
yeeld so easily, and grow so vehement in matters much
more disputable, and farre lesse conducing to the daily good
and peace of life. Some whose necessary shifts have long
enur'd them to cloak the defects of their unstudied yeers,
and hatred now to learn, under the appearance of a grave
solidity, which estimation they have gain'd among weak
perceivers, find the ease of slighting what they cannot
refute, and are determin'd, as I hear, to hold it not worth
the answering. In which number I must be forc'd to reck'n
that Doctor, who in a late equivocating Treatise plausibly*

[1] Borne.
[2] Aught; anything.
[3] Acknowledge.

[4] Useless religious ornament (in this case).

set afloat against the Dippers, *diving the while himself with a more deep prelatical malignance against the present state, & Church-government, mentions with ignominy the* Tractate of Divorce; *yet answers nothing, but instead thereof (for which I do not commend his marshalling) sets* Moses *also among the crew of his Anabaptists; as one who to a holy Nation, the Common-wealth of Israel, gave Laws breaking the bonds of mariage to inordinate lust. These are no mean surges of blasphemy, not onely dipping Moses the divine Lawgiver, but dashing with a high hand against the justice and purity of God himself as these ensuing Scriptures plainly and freely handl'd shall verifie to the launcing of that old* apostemated[5] *error. Him therefore I leave now to his repentance.*

Others, which is their courtesie, confesse that wit and parts may do much to make that seem true which is not (as was objected to Socrates *by them who could not resist his efficacy, that he ever made the worse cause seem the better) and thus thinking themselves discharg'd of the difficulty, love not to wade furder into the fear of a convincement. These will be their excuses to decline the full examining of this serious point. So much the more I presse it and repeat it, Lords and Commons, that ye beware while time is, ere this grand secret, and onely art of ignorance affecting tyrany, grow powerfull and rule among us. For if sound argument and reason shall be thus put of either by an undervaluing silence, or the maisterly censure of a rayling word or two in the Pulpit, or by rejecting the force of truth, as the meer cunning of eloquence, and Sophistry, what can be the end of this, but that all good learning and knowledge will suddenly decay: Ignorance, and illiterate presumption, which is yet but our disease, will turn at length into our very constitution, and prove the* hectic *evill of this age: worse to be fear'd, if it get once to reign over us, then any fift Monarchy. If this shall be the course, that what was wont to be a chief commendation, and the ground of other mens confidence in an Author, his diligence, his learning, his elocution whether by right, or by ill meaning granted him, shall be turn'd now to a disadvantage and suspicion against him, that what he writes though unconfuted, must therefore be mistrusted, therfore not receiv'd for the industry, the exactnesse, the labour in it, confess'd to be more then ordnary; as if wisdome had now forsak'n the thirstie and laborious inquirer to dwell against her nature with the arrogant and shallow babler, to what purpose all those pains and that continuall searching requir'd of us by* Solomon *to the attainment of understanding; why are men bred up with such care and expence to a life of perpetual studies, why do your selves with such endeavour seek to wipe off the imputation of intending to discourage the pro-*

gresse and advance of learning? He therfore whose heart can bear him to the high pitch of your noble enterprises, may easily assure himself that the prudence and farrejudging circumspectnesse of so grave a Magistracy sitting in Parlament, *who have before them the prepar'd and purpos'd Act of their most religious predecessors to imitate in this question, cannot reject the cleernesse of these reasons, and these allegations both here and formerly offer'd them; nor can over-look the necessity of ordaining more wholsomly and more humanly[6] in the casualties of Divorce, then our Laws have yet establisht: if the most urgent and excessive grievances hapning in domestick life, be worth the laying to heart, which, unlesse charity be farre from us, cannot be neglected. And that these things both in the right constitution, and in the right reformation of a Common-wealth call for speediest redresse, and ought to be the first consider'd, anough was urg'd in what was prefac'd to that monument of* Bucer *which I brought to your remembrance, and the other time before. Henceforth, except new cause be giv'n, I shall say lesse and lesse. For if the Law make not timely provision, let the Law, as reason is, bear the censure of those consequences, which her own default now more evidently produces. And if men want manlinesse to expostulate the right of their due ransom, and to second their own occasions, they may sit hereafter and bemoan themselves to have neglected through faintnesse the onely remedy of their sufferings, which a seasonable and well grounded speaking might have purchas'd them. And perhaps in time to come, others will know how to esteem what is not every day put into their hands, when they have markt events, and better weigh'd how hurtfull and unwise it is, to hide a secret and pernicious rupture under the ill counsell of a bashfull silence. But who would distrust ought, or not be ample in his hopes of your wise and Christian determinations? who have the prudence to consider, and should have the goodnesse like gods, as ye are call'd, to find out readily, and by just Law to administer those redresses which have of old, not without God ordaining, bin granted to the adversities of mankind, ere they who needed, were put to ask. Certainly, if any other have enlarg'd his thoughts to expect from this government so justly undertak'n, and by frequent assistances from heaven so apparently upheld, glorious changes renovations both in Church and State, he among the formost might be nam'd, who prayes that the fate of* England *may tarry for no other* Deliverers.

JOHN MILTON.

---

[5]The image is that of a festering boil ("apostem") needing to be lanced.

[6]Probably the word should be read as "humanely," though the two senses, "human" and "humane," were not clearly separated in the seventeenth century.

TETRACHORDON,

Expositions upon the foure chiefe places in
Scripture which treat of Mariage,
or nullities in Mariage.

Gen. 1. 27.

*So God created man in his owne image, in the image of
God created he him; male and female created he them.*
28. *And God blessed them, and God said unto them be
fruitfull, &c.*

Gen. 2.18.

And the Lord God said, It is not good that man should
be alone, I will make him a helpe meet for him.
23. *And Adam said, This is now bone of my bones, and
flesh of my flesh; she shall be called Woman, because she
was taken out of Man.*
24. *Therefore shall a man leave his father and his mother,
and shall cleave unto his wife, and they shall be one flesh.*

Gen. 1. 27.

SO *God created man in his owne image.*] To be inform'd aright in the whole History of Mariage, that
we may know for certain, not by a forc't yoke, but
by an impartial definition, what Mariage is, and what is
not Mariage; it will undoubtedly be safest, fairest, and
most with our obedience, to enquire, as our Saviours
direction is, how it was in the beginning. And that we
begin so high as man created after Gods owne Image,
there want not earnest causes. For nothing now adayes is
more degenerately forgott'n, then the true dignity of
man, almost in every respect, but especially in this prime
institution of Matrimony, wherein his native preeminence ought most to shine. Although if we consider
that just and naturall privileges men neither can rightly
seek, nor dare fully claime, unlesse they be ally'd to
inward goodnesse, and stedfast knowledge, and that the
want of this quells them to a servile sense of their own
unworthinesse, it may save the wondring why in this age
many are so opposite both to human and to Christian
liberty, either while they understand not, or envy others
that do; contenting, or rather priding themselves in a
specious humility and strictnesse bred out of low ignorance that never yet conceiv'd the freedome of the
Gospel; and is therefore by the Apostle to the Colossians
rankt with no better company, then Will-worship and the
meer shew of wisdome. And how injurious herein they
are, if not to themselves, yet to their neighbours, and not
to them only, but to the allwise and bounteous grace
offer'd us in our redemption, will orderly appear.
[*In the Image of God created he him.*] It is anough deter-

min'd, that this Image of God wherin man was created,
is meant Wisdom, Purity, Justice, and rule over all
creatures. All which being lost in *Adam*, was recover'd
with gain by the merits of Christ. For albeit our first
parent had lordship over sea, and land, and aire, yet
there was a law without him, as a guard set over him.
But Christ having cancell'd the hand writing of ordinances which was against us, *Coloss.* 2. 14. and interpreted the fulfilling of all through charity, hath in that respect set us over law, in the free custody of his love, and
left us victorious under the guidance of his living spirit,
not under the dead letter; to follow that which most
edifies, most aides and furders a religious life, makes us
holiest and likest to his immortall Image, not that which
makes us most conformable and captive to civill and
subordinat precepts; whereof the strictest observance
may oftimes prove the destruction not only of many
innocent persons and families, but of whole Nations.
Although indeed no ordinance human or from heav'n
can binde against the good of man; so that to keep them
strictly against that end, is all one with to breake them.
Men of most renowned vertu have sometimes by
transgressing, most truly kept the law; and wisest Magistrates have permitted and dispenc't it; while they lookt
not peevishly at the letter, but with a greater spirit at
the good of mankinde, if always not writt'n in the
characters of law, yet engrav'n in the heart of man by a
divine impression. This Heathens could see, as the
well-read in story[7] can recount of *Solon* and *Epaminondas*, whom *Cicero* in his first booke of *invention* nobly
defends.[8] *All law,* saith he, *we ought referr to the common
good, and interpret by that, not by the scrowl of letters. No
man observes law for laws sake, but for the good of them
for whom it was made.* The rest might serv well to lecture these times, deluded through belly-doctrines into a
devout slavery. The Scripture also affords us *David* in
the shew-bread, *Hezechiah* in the passeover sound and
safe transgressors of the literall command, which also
dispenc'd not seldom with it self; and taught us on what
just occasions to doe so: untill our Saviour for whom
that great and God-like work was reserv'd, redeem'd us
to a state above prescriptions by dissolving the whole
law into charity. And have we not the soul to understand this, and must we against this glory of Gods transcendent love towards us be still the servants of a literall
indightment?

[*Created he him.*] It might be doubted why he saith, *In
the Image of God created he him,* not them, as well as
male and female them; especially since that Image might

---

[7]History.
[8]Cicero, *De Inventione* 1.38.

be common to them both, but *male and female* could not, however the Jewes fable, and please themselvs with the accidentall concurrence of *Plato's* wit, as if man at first had bin created *Hermaphrodite:* but then it must have bin male and female created he him. So had the Image of God bin equally common to them both, it had no doubt bin said, In the image of God created he them. But St. *Paul* ends the controversie by explaining that the woman is not primarily and immediatly the image of God, but in reference to the man. *The head of the woman,* saith he, 1 *Cor.* 11. *is the man: he the image and glory of God, she the glory of the man:* he not for her, but she for him. Therefore his precept is, *Wives be subject to your husbands as is fit in the Lord, Coloss.* 3.18. *In every thing, Eph.* 5.24. Neverthelesse man is not to hold her as a servant, but receives her into a part of that empire which God proclaims him to, though not equally, yet largely, as his own image and glory: for it is no small glory to him, that a creature so like him, should be made subject to him. Not but that particular exceptions may have place, if she exceed her husband in prudence and dexterity, and he contentedly yeeld, for then a superior and more naturall law comes in, that the wiser should govern the lesse wise, whether male or female. But that which far more easily and obediently follows from this verse, is that, seeing woman was purposely made for man, and he her head, it cannot stand before the breath of this divine utterance, that man the portraiture of God, joyning to himself for his intended good and solace an inferiour sexe, should so becom her thrall, whose wilfulnes or inability to be a wife frustrates the occasionall[9] end of her creation, but that he may acquitt himself to freedom by his naturall birth-right, and that indeleble character of priority which God crown'd him with. If it be urg'd that sin hath lost him this, the answer is not far to seek, that from her the sin first proceeded,[10] which keeps her justly in the same proportion still beneath. She is not to gain by being first in the transgression, that man should furder loose to her, because already he hath lost by her means. Oft it happens that in this matter he is without fault; so that his punishment herein is causeles: and God hath the praise in our speeches of him, to sort his punishment in the same kind with the offence. Suppose he err'd; it is not the intent of God or man, to hunt an error so to the death with a revenge beyond all measure and proportion. But if we argue thus, this affliction is befaln him for his sin, therefore he must bear it, without

seeking the only remedy, first it will be false that all affliction comes for sin, as in the case of *Job,* and of the man born blind, *Joh.* 9.3, was evident: next by that reason, all miseries comming for sin, we must let them all lye upon us like the vermin of an Indian *Catharist,*[11] which his fond religion forbids him to molest. Were it a particular punishment inflicted through the anger of God upon a person, or upon a land, no law hinders us in that regard, no law but bids us remove it if we can: much more if it be a dangerous temptation withall, much more yet, if it be certainly a temptation, and not certainly a punishment, though a pain. As for what they say we must bear with patience, to bear with patience, and to seek effectuall remedies, implies no contradiction. It may no lesse be for our disobedience, our unfaithfulnes, and other sins against God, that wives becom adulterous to the bed, and questionles we ought to take the affliction as patiently, as christian prudence would wish; yet hereby is not lost the right of divorcing for adultery. No you say, because our Saviour excepted that only. But why, if he were so bent to punish our sins, and try our patience in binding on us a disastrous mariage, why did he except adultery? Certainly to have bin bound from divorce in that case also had bin as plentifull a punishment to our sins, and not too little work for the patientest. Nay perhaps they will say it was too great a sufferance: And with as slight a reason, for no wise man but would sooner pardon the act of adultery once and again committed by a person worth pitty and forgivnes, then to lead a wearisom life of unloving & unquiet conversation with one who neither affects nor is affected, much lesse with one who exercises all bitternes, and would commit adultery too, but for envy lest the persecuted condition should thereby get the benefit of his freedom. 'Tis plain therefore that God enjoyns not this supposed strictnes of not divorcing either to punish us, or to try our patience.

Moreover, if man be the image of God, which consists in holines, and woman ought in the same respect to be the image and companion of man, in such wise to be lov'd, as the Church is belov'd of Christ, and if, as God is the head of Christ, and Christ the head of man, so man is the head of woman; I cannot see by this golden dependance of headship and subjection, but that Piety and Religion is the main tye of Christian Matrimony: So as if there be found between the pair a

---

[9]Eve is made by God on the occasion of Adam's request for a help-meet. Compare Adam's description of Eve as "after made / Occasionally" in *Paradise Lost* 8.555–56.

[10]Eve is the first to eat the fruit.

[11]The Cathars (also known as Albigensians) were an ascetic sect of Christians persecuted by orthodox Roman Catholics especially in France and Spain in the thirteenth century. Somehow, Milton transfers them to India, transforms them into something like Jainists, and gives them vermin that they ignore for religious reasons.

notorious disparity either of wickednes or heresie, the husband by all manner of right is disingag'd from a creature, not made and inflicted on him to the vexation of his righteousnes; the wife also, as her subjection is terminated in the Lord, being her self the redeem'd of Christ, is not still bound to be the vassall of him, who is the bondslave of Satan: she being now neither the image nor the glory of such a person, nor made for him, nor left in bondage to him; but hath recours to the wing of charity, and protection of the Church; unless there be a hope on either side; yet such a hope must be meant, as may be a rationall hope, and not an endles servitude. Of which hereafter.

But usually it is objected, that if it be thus, then there can be no true mariage between misbeleevers and irreligious persons? I might answer, let them see to that who are such; the Church hath no commission to judge those without, 1 *Cor.* 5. But this they will say perhaps, is but penuriously to resolv a doubt I answer therefore, that where they are both irreligious, the mariage may be yet true anough to them in a civill relation. For there are left som remains of Gods image in man, as he is meerly man; which reason God gives against the shedding of mans bloud, *Gen.* 9. as being made in Gods image, without expression whether he were a good man or a bad, to exempt the slayer from punishment. So that in those mariages where the parties are alike void of Religion, the wife owes a civill homage and subjection, the husband owes a civill loyalty. But where the yoke is mis-yok't, heretick with faithfull, godly with ungodly, to the grievance and manifest endangering of a brother or sister, reasons of a higher strain then matrimoniall bear sway; unless the Gospel instead of freeing us, debase it self to make us bondmen, and suffer evill to controule good.

[*Male and female created he them.*] This contains another end of matching man and woman, being the right, and lawfulnes of the marige[12] bed; though much inferior to the former end of her being his image and helpe in religious society. And who of weakest insight may not see that this creating of them male and female, cannot in any order of reason, or Christianity, be of such moment against the better and higher purposes of their creation, as to enthrall husband or wife to duties or to sufferings, unworthy and unbeseeming the image of God in them? Now when as not only men, but good men doe stand upon their right, their estimation, their dignity in all other actions and deportments with warrant anough and good conscience, as having the image of God in them, it will not be difficult to determin what is unworthy and unseemly for a man to do or suffer in wedlock; and the like proportionally may be found for woman: if we love not to stand disputing below the principles of humanity. He that said, *Male and female created he them*, immediatly before that said also in the same verse, *In the Image of God created he him*, and redoubl'd it, that our thoughts might not be so full of dregs as to urge this poor consideration of *male and female*, without remembering the noblenes of that former repetition; lest when God sends a wise eye to examin our triviall glosses, they be found extremly to creep upon the ground: especially since they confesse that what here concerns mariage is but a brief touch, only preparative to the institution which follows more expressly in the next Chapter: and that Christ so took it, as desiring to be briefest with them who came to tempt him, account shall be given in due place.

V. 28. *And God blessed them, and God said unto them, be fruitfull, and multiply, and replenish the earth, &c.*

This declares another end of Matrimony, the propagation of mankind; and is again repeated to *Noah* and his sons. Many things might be noted on this place not ordinary, nor unworth the noting; but I undertook not a generall Comment. Hence therefore we see the desire of children is honest and pious; if we be not lesse zealous in our Christianity, then *Plato* was in his heathenism; who in the sixt *of his laws*, counts off-spring therefore desirable, that we may leav in our stead sons of our sons, continuall servants of God: a religious and prudent desire, if people knew as well what were requir'd to breeding as to begetting; which desire perhaps was a cause why the Jews hardly could endure a barren wedlock: and *Philo*[13] in his book of speciall laws esteems him only worth pardon that sends not barrennes away. *Carvilius* the first recorded in Rome to have sought divorce, had it granted him for the barrennes of his wife, upon his oath that he maried to the end he might have children; as *Dionysius* and *Gellius* are authors.[14] But to dismisse a wife only for barrennes, is hard: and yet in som the desire of children is so great, and so just, yea somtime so necessary, that to condemn such a one to a childles age, the fault apparently not being in him, might seem perhaps more strict then needed. Somtimes inheritances, crowns, and dignities are so interested and annext in their common peace and

---

[12]I will preserve the spelling here, though it probably represents a typographical error for "mariage."

[13]Philo Judaeus, *Special Laws* 3.35.
[14]Dionysius of Halicarnassus, *Roman Antiquities* 2.25; and Aulus Gellius, *Attic Nights* 4.3. Both tell the story of Carvilius, made by the censors to confess that he had married in order to have children.

good to such or such lineall descent, that it may prove a great moment both in the affairs of men and of religion, to consider throughly what might be don heerin, notwithstanding the waywardnes of our School Doctors.

Gen. 2. 18.

And the Lord said, It is not good that man should be alone; I will make him a help meet for him.
V. 23. *And Adam said, &c.* V. 24. *Therefore shall a man leave, &c.*

THis second Chapter is granted to be a Commentary on the first; and these verses granted to be an exposition of that former verse, *Male and female created he them*, and yet when this male and female is by the explicite words of God himselfe heer declar'd to be not meant other then a fit help, and meet society; som who would ingrosse to themselves the whole trade of interpreting, will not suffer the cleer text of God to doe the office of explaining it self.

[*And the Lord God said it is not good.*] A man would think that the consideration of who spake, should raise up the attention of our minds to enquire better, and obey the purpos of so great a Speaker: for as we order the busines of Mariage, that which he heer speaks is all made vain; and in the decision of matrimony, or not matrimony, nothing at all regarded. Our presumption, hath utterly chang'd the state and condition of this ordinance: God ordain'd it in love and helpfulnes to be indissoluble, and we in outward act and formality to be a forc't bondage; so that being subject to a thousand errors in the best men, if it prove a blessing to any, it is of meer accident, as mans law hath handl'd it, and not of institution.

[*It is not good for man to be alone.*] Hitherto all things that have bin nam'd, were approv'd of God to be very good: lonelines is the first thing which Gods eye nam'd not good: whether it be a thing, or the want of somthing, I labour not; let it be their tendance, who have the art to be industriously idle. And heer *alone* is meant alone without woman; otherwise *Adam* had the company of God himself, and Angels to convers with; all creatures to delight him seriously, or to make him sport[15] God could have created him out of the same mould a thousand friends and brother *Adams* to have bin his consorts, yet for all this till *Eve* was giv'n him, God reckn'd him to be alone.

[*It is not good.*] God heer presents himself like to a man deliberating; both to shew us that the matter is of high consequence, and that he intended to found it according to naturall reason, not impulsive command, but that the duty should arise from the reason of it, not the reason be swallow'd up in a reasonlesse duty. *Not good*, was as much to *Adam* before his fall, as not pleasing, not expedient; but since the comming of sin into the world, to him who hath not receiv'd the continence, it is not only not expedient to be alone, but plainly sinfull. And therefore he who wilfully abstains from mariage, not being supernaturally gifted, and he who by making the yoke of mariage unjust and intolerable, causes men to abhorr it, are both in a diabolicall sin, equall to that of Antichrist[16] who forbids to marry. For what difference at all whether he abstain men from marying, or restrain them in a mariage hapning totally discommodious, distastfull, dishonest and pernicious to him without the appearance of his fault? For God does not heer precisely say, I make a female to this male, as he did briefly before, but expounding himselfe heer on purpos, he saith, because it is not good for man to be alone, I make him therefore a meet help. God supplies the privation of not good,[17] with the perfect gift of a reall and positive good; it is mans pervers cooking[18] who hath turn'd this bounty of God into a Scorpion, either by weak and shallow constructions, or by proud arrogance and cruelty to them who neither in their purposes nor in their actions have offended against the due honour of wedlock.

Now whereas the Apostle speaking in the Spirit, 1 *Cor.* 7. pronounces quite contrary to this word of God, *It is good for a man not to touch a woman*, and God cannot contradict himself, it instructs us that his commands and words, especially such as bear the manifest title of som good to man, are not to be so strictly wrung, as to command without regard to the most naturall and miserable necessities of mankind. Therefore the Apostle adds a limitation in the 26 v. of that chap. for the present necessity it is good; which he gives us doubtlesse as a pattern how to reconcile other places by the generall rule of charity.

[*For man to be alone.*] Som would have the sense heerof to be in respect of procreation only: and *Austin* contests that manly friendship in all other regards had bin a more becomming solace for *Adam*, then to spend so many secret years in an empty world with one woman. But our Writers deservedly reject this crabbed

---

[15]In *Paradise Lost*, 4.345–47 one of the animals to be sportive around Adam and Eve is "th' unwieldy Elephant / [who] To make them mirth us'd all his might, and wreathd / His Lithe Proboscis."

[16]In this case, as in most Protestant rhetoric in Milton's England, the Roman Catholic Church, which forbade its clergy to marry.
[17]"God fills the gap of 'not good' [with the creation of the woman]."
[18]The image of cooking might imply alchemical transformation or metamorphosis: it is man's perverse imagination that turns the wife, God's bounty, into a scorpion that stings itself or those around it.

opinion; and defend that there is a peculiar comfort in the maried state besides the genial bed, which no other society affords. No mortall nature can endure either in the actions of Religion, or study of wisdome, without somtime slackning the cords of intense thought and labour: which lest we should think faulty, God himself conceals us not his own recreations before the world was built; *I was*, saith the eternall wisdome, *dayly his delight, playing always before him*. And to him indeed wisdom is as a high towr of pleasure, but to us a steep hill, and we toyling ever about the bottom: he executes with ease the exploits of his omnipotence, as easie as with us it is to will: but no worthy enterprise can be don by us without continuall plodding and wearisomnes to our faint and sensitive abilities. We cannot therefore alwayes be contemplative, or pragmaticall abroad, but have need of som delightfull intermissions, wherin the enlarg'd soul may leav off a while her severe schooling;[19] and like a glad youth in wandring vacancy, may keep her hollidaies to joy and harmles pastime:[20] which as she cannot well doe without company, so in no company so well as where the different sexe in most resembling unlikenes, and most unlike resemblance cannot but please best and be pleas'd in the aptitude of that variety. Wherof lest we should be too timorous, in the aw that our flat sages would form us and dresse us, wisest *Salomon* among his gravest Proverbs countenances a kinde of ravishment and erring fondnes in the entertainment of wedded leisures; and in the Song of Songs, which is generally beleev'd, even in the jolliest expressions to figure the spousals of the Church with Christ, sings of a thousand raptures between those two lovely ones farre on the hither side of carnall enjoyment. By these instances, and more which might be brought, we may imagine how indulgently God provided against mans lonelines; that he approv'd it not, as by himself declar'd not good; that he approv'd the remedy therof, as of his own ordaining, consequently good; and as he ordain'd it, so doubtles proportionably to our fal'n estate he gives it; els were his ordinance at least in vain, and we for all his gift still empty handed. Nay such an unbounteous giver we should make him, as in the fables *Jupiter* was to *Ixion*, giving him *a cloud* instead of *Juno*, giving him a mon-

strous issue by her, the breed of *Centaures* a neglected and unlov'd race, the fruits of a delusive mariage, and lastly giving him her with a damnation to that wheele in hell, from a life thrown into the midst of temptations and disorders. But God is no deceitfull giver, to bestow that on us for a remedy of lonelines, which if it bring not a sociable minde as well as a conjunctive body, leavs us no lesse alone then before; and if it bring a minde perpetually avers and disagreeable, betraies us to a wors condition then the most deserted lonelines. God cannot in the justice of his own promise and institution so unexpectedly mock us by forcing that upon us as the remedy of solitude, which wraps us in a misery worse then any wildernes, as the Spirit of God himself judges, Prov. 19. especially knowing that the best and wisest men amidst the sincere and most cordiall designes of their heart doe dayly erre in choosing. We may conclude therfore seeing orthodoxall Expositers confesse to our hands, that by lonelines is not only meant the want of copulation, and that man is not lesse alone by turning in a body to him, unlesse there be within it a minde answerable, that it is a work more worthy the care and consultation of God to provide for the worthiest part of man which is his minde, and not unnaturally to set it beneath the formalities and respects of the body, to make it a servant of its owne vassall, I say we may conclude that such a mariage, wherin the minde is so disgrac't and vilify'd below the bodies interest, and can have no just or tolerable contentment, is not of Gods institution, and therfore no mariage. Nay in concluding this, I say we conclude no more then what the common Expositers themselves give us, both in that which I have recited and much more hereafter. But the truth is, they give us in such a manner, as they who leav their own mature positions like the eggs of an Ostrich in the dust; I do but lay them in the sun; their own pregnancies hatch the truth; and I am taxt of novelties[21] and strange producements, while they, like that inconsiderat bird, know not that these are their own naturall breed.

[*I will make him a help meet for him.*] Heer the heavnly instituter, as if he labourd, not to be mistak'n by the supercilious hypocrisie of those that love to maister their brethren, and to make us sure that he gave us not now a servil yoke, but an amiable knot; contents not himself to say, I will make him a wife, but resolving to give us first the meaning before the name of a wife, saith graciously, *I will make him a help meet for him.* And heer again, as before, I doe not require more full and fair deductions then the whole consent of our Di-

[19]Milton remained a lifelong advocate of recreation and entertainment, when they are used to break the monotony of hard work, following (he thought) the example of God himself.
[20]According to Edward Phillips, his uncle took his own advice: ". . . once in three Weeks or a Month, he would drop into the Society of some Young Sparks of his Acquaintance, the chief whereof were Mr. *Alphry*, and Mr. *Miller*, two Gentlemen of *Gray*'s-Inn, the *Beau*'s of those Times, but nothing near so bad as those now-a-days; with these Gentlemen he would so far make bold with his Body, as now and then to keep a Gawdy day."

[21]"If I am accused of having newfangled opinions."

vines usually raise from this text, that in matrimony there must be first a mutuall help to piety, next to civill fellowship of love and amity, then to generation, so to houshold affairs, lastly the remedy of incontinence. And commonly they reck'n them in such order, as leavs generation and incontinence[22] to be last consider'd. This I amaze me at, that though all the superior and nobler ends both of mariage and of the maried persons be absolutely frustrat, the matrimony stirs not, looses no hold, remains as rooted as the center: but if the body bring but in a complaint of frigidity, by that cold application only, this adamantine *Alpe* of wedlock has leav to dissolve; which els all the machinations of religious or civill reason at the suit of a distressed mind, either for divine worship or humane conversation violated, cannot unfasten. What courts of concupiscence are these, wherin fleshly appetite is heard before right reason, lust before love or devotion? They may be pious Christians together, they may be loving and friendly, they may be helpfull to each other in the family, but they cannot couple; that shall divorce them though either party would not. They can neither serv God together, nor one be at peace with the other, nor be good in the family one to other, but live as they were dead, or live as they were deadly enemies in a cage together; tis all one, they can couple, they shall not divorce till death, no though this sentence be their death. What is this, besides tyranny, but to turn nature upside down, to make both religion, and the minde of man wait upon the slavish errands of the body, and not the body to follow either the sanctity, or the sovranty of the mind unspeakably wrong'd, and with all equity complaining? what is this but to abuse the sacred and misterious bed of mariage to be the compulsive stie[23] of an ingratefull and malignant lust, stirr'd up only from a carnall acrimony, without either love or peace, or regard to any other thing holy or human. This I admire how possibly it should inhabit thus long in the sense of so many disputing *Theologians*, unless it be the lowest lees of a canonicall infection liver-grown[24] to their sides; which perhaps will never uncling, without the strong abstersive[25] of som heroick magistrat, whose mind equal to his high office dares lead him both to know and to do without their frivolous case-putting. For certain he shall have God and this institution plainly on his side. And if it be true both in

divinity and law, that consent alone, though copulation never follow, makes a mariage, how can they dissolv it for the want of that which made it not, and not dissolv it for that not continuing which made it, and should preserve it in love and reason, and difference it from a brute conjugality.

[*Meet for him.*] The originall heer is more expressive then other languages word for word[26] can render it; but all agree effectuall conformity of disposition and affection to be heerby signify'd; which God as it were not satisfy'd with the naming of a help, goes on describing *another self, a second self, a very self it self.* Yet now there is nothing in the life of man through our misconstruction, made more uncertain, more hazardous and full of chance then this divine blessing with such favorable significance heer conferr'd upon us, which if we do but erre in our choice the most unblamable error that can be, erre but one minute, one moment after those mighty syllables pronounc't which take upon them to joyn heavn and hell together unpardnably till death pardon, this divine blessing that lookt but now with such a human smile upon us, and spoke such gentle reason, strait vanishes like a fair skie and brings on such a scene of cloud and tempest, as turns all to shipwrack without havn or shoar but to a ransomles captivity. And then they tell us it is our sin; but let them be told again, that sin through the mercy of God hath not made such wast upon us, as to make utterly void to our use any temporall benefit, much lesse any so much availing to a peacefull and sanctify'd life, meerly for a most incident[27] error which no warines can certainly shun. And wherfore servs our happy redemption, and the liberty we have in Christ, but to deliver us from calamitous yokes not to be liv'd under without the endangerment of our souls, and to restore us in som competent measure to a right in every good thing both of this life, and the other. Thus we see how treatably and distinctly God hath heer taught us what the prime ends of mariage are, mutuall solace and help. That we are now, upon the most irreprehensible[28] mistake in choosing, defeated and defrauded of all this originall benignity, was begun first through the snare of Antichristian canons long since obtruded upon the Church of Rome, and not yet scour'd off by reformation, out of a lingring vain-glory that abides among us to make fair shews in formall ordinances, and to enjoyn continence & bearing of

---

[22]Sexual promiscuity.
[23]As in "pig-sty," the metaphorically dirty place of copulation without love.
[24]Suffering from an enlarged liver. The image seems to be of a diseased growth on the outside of the body, like the wen of *Of Reformation*. "Lees" are normally the dregs of wine.
[25]Medicine having the power to purge or cleanse.

[26]Milton is considering how the various terms have been translated into the languages of the Bible and into his own English, finding the translations inadequate here. He will often modify the translation presented in the Authorized Version to his own tastes.
[27]Likely to occur.
[28]Irreproachable, blameless.

crosses in such a garb as no Scripture binds us, under the thickest arrows of temptation, where we need not stand. Now we shall see with what acknowledgement and assent *Adam* receiv'd this new associat, which God brought him.

V. 23. *And Adam said this is now bone of my bones, and flesh of my flesh, she shall be called Woman, because she was tak'n out of Man.*

That there was a neerer alliance between *Adam* and *Eve*, then could be ever after between man and wife, is visible to any. For no other woman was ever moulded out of her husbands rib, but of meer strangers for the most part they com to have that consanguinity which they have by wedlock. And if we look neerly upon the matter, though mariage be most agreeable to holines, to purity and justice, yet is it not a naturall, but a civill and ordain'd relation. For if it were in nature, no law or crime could disanull it, to make a wife, or husband, otherwise then still a wife or husband, but only death; as nothing but that can make a father no father, or a son no son. But divorce for adultery or desertion, as all our Churches agree but England, not only separats, but nullifies, and extinguishes the relation it self of matrimony, so that they are no more man and wife; otherwise the innocent party could not marry else-where, without the guilt of adultery; next were it meerly naturall why was it heer ordain'd more then the rest of morall law to man in his originall rectitude, in whose brest all that was naturall or morall was engrav'n without externall constitutions and edicts. *Adam* therfore in these words does not establish an indissoluble bond of mariage in the carnall ligaments of flesh and bones, for if he did, it would belong only to himself in the literall sense; every one of us being neerer in flesh of flesh, and bone of bones to our parents then to a wife; they therfore were not to be left for her in that respect. But *Adam* who had the wisdom giv'n him to know all creatures, and to name them according to their properties, no doubt but had the gift to discern perfectly, that which concern'd him much more; and to apprehend at first sight the true fitnes of that consort which God provided him. And therfore spake in reference to those words which God pronounc' t before; as if he had said, this is she by whose meet help and society I shall no more be alone; this is she who was made my image, ev'n as I the Image of God; not so much in body, as in unity of mind and heart. And he might as easily know what were the words of God, as he knew so readily what had bin don with his rib, while he slept so soundly. He might well know, if God took a rib out of his inside, to form of it a double good to him, he would far sooner dis-joyn it

from his outside, to prevent a treble mischief to him: and far sooner cut it quite off from all relation for his undoubted ease, then nail it into his body again, to stick for ever there a thorn in his heart. When as nature teaches us to divide any limb from the body to the saving of his fellows, though it be the maiming and deformity of the whole; how much more is it her doctrin to sever by incision, not a true limb so much, though that be lawfull, but an adherent, a sore, the gangrene of a limb, to the recovery of a whole man. But if in these words we shall make *Adam* to erect a new establishment of mariage in the meer flesh, which God so lately had instituted, and founded in the sweet and mild familiarity of love and solace and mutuall fitnes, what do we but use the mouth of our generall parent, the first time it opens, to an arrogant opposition, and correcting of Gods wiser ordinance. These words therfore cannot import any thing new in mariage, but either that which belongs to *Adam* only, or to us in reference only to the instituting words of God which made a meet help against lonelines. *Adam* spake like *Adam* the words of flesh and bones, the shell and rinde of matrimony; but God spake like God, of love and solace and meet help, the soul both of *Adams* words and of matrimony.

V. 24. *Therefore shall a man leav his father and his mother, and shall cleav unto his wife; and they shall be one flesh.*

This vers, as our common heed expounds it, is the great knot tier,[29] which hath undon by tying, and by tangling, millions of guiltles consciences: this is that greisly Porter, who having drawn men and wisest men by suttle allurement within the train of an unhappy matrimony, claps the dungeon gate upon them, as irrecoverable as the grave. But if we view him well, and hear him with not too hasty and prejudicant ears, we shall finde no such terror in him. For first, it is not heer said absolutely without all reason he shall cleave to his wife, be it to his weal or to his destruction as it happens, but he shall doe this upon the premises and considerations of that meet help and society before mention'd. *Therefore he shall cleave to his wife*, no otherwise a wife, then a fit help. He is not bid to leave the dear cohabitation of his father, mother, brothers and sisters, to link himself inseparably with the meer carcas of a Mariage, perhaps an enemy. This joyning particle *Therefore* is in all equity, nay in all necessity of construction to comprehend first and most principally what God spake concerning the inward essence of Mariage in his insti-

---

[29]This verse, in other words, ties the knot that knits all together.

tution; that we may learn how far to attend what *Adam* spake of the outward materials therof in his approbation. For if we shall bind these words of *Adam* only to a corporall meaning, and that the force of this injunction upon all us his sons to live individually with any woman which hath befaln us in the most mistak'n wedlock, shall consist not in those morall and relative causes of *Eves* creation, but in the meer anatomy of a rib, and that *Adams* insight concerning wedlock reacht no furder, we shall make him as very[30] an idiot as the Socinians make him; which would not be reverently don of us. Let us be content to allow our great forefather so much wisdom, as to take the instituting words of God along with him into this sentence, which if they be well minded, wil assure us that flesh and ribs are but of a weak and dead efficacy to keep Mariage united where there is no other fitnes. The rib of Mariage, to all since *Adam*, is a relation much rather then a bone; the nerves and sinews therof are love and meet help, they knit not every couple that maries, and where they knit they seldom break, but where they break, which for the most part is where they never truly joyn'd, to such at the same instant both flesh and rib cease to be in common; so that heer they argue nothing to the continuance of a false or violated Mariage, but must be led back to receive their meaning from those institutive words of God which give them all the life and vigor they have.

[*Therefore shall a man leav his father, &c.*] What to a mans thinking more plain by this appointment, that the fatherly power should give place to conjugall prerogative? yet it is generally held by reformed writers against the Papist, that though in persons at discretion the Mariage in it self be never so fit, though it be fully accomplisht with benediction, board and bed, yet the father not consenting, his main will without dispute shall dissolv all. And this they affirm only from collective reason, not any direct law: for that in *Exod.* 22.17. which is most particular, speaks that a father may refuse to marry his daughter to one who hath deflour'd her, not that he may take her away from one who hath soberly married her. Yet because the generall honor due to parents is great, they hold he may, and perhaps hold not amisse. But again when the question is of harsh and rugged parents who deferr to bestow their childern seasonably, they agree joyntly that the Church or Magistrat may bestow them, though without the Fathers consent: and for this they have no express autority in Scripture. So that they may see by thir own handling of this very place, that it is not the stubborn letter must govern us, but the divine and softning breath of charity which turns and windes the dictat of every positive command, and shapes it to the good of mankind. Shall the outward accessory of a Fathers will wanting, rend the fittest and most affectionat mariage in twain, after all nuptial consummations, and shall not the want of love and the privation of all civil and religious concord, which is the inward essence of wedlock, doe as much to part those who were never truly wedded? shall a Father have this power to vindicate his own wilfull honour and autority to the utter breach of a most dearly-united mariage, and shall not a man in his own power have the permission to free his Soul, his life, and all his comfort of life from the disastre of a no-mariage. Shall fatherhood, which is but man, for his own pleasure dissolve matrimony, and shall not matrimony, which is Gods Ordinance, for its own honour and better conservation, dissolv it self, when it is wrong, and not fined to any of the cheif ends which it owes us?

[*And they shall bee one flesh.*] These words also inferre that there ought to be an individualty in Mariage; but without all question presuppose the joyning causes. Not a rule yet that we have met with, so universall in this whole institution, but hath admitted limitations and conditions according to human necessity. The very foundation of matrimony, though God laid it so deliberately, *that it is not good for man to bee alone* holds not always, if the Apostle can cure us. Soon after wee are bid leav Father and Mother, and cleav to a Wife, but must understand the Fathers consent withall, els not. *Cleav to a Wife*, but let her bee a wife, let her be a meet help, a solace, not a nothing, not an adversary, not a desertrice; can any law or command be so unreasonable as to make men cleav to calamity, to ruin, to perdition? In like manner heer, *They shall be one flesh*; but let the causes hold, and be made really good, which only have the possibility to make them one flesh. Wee know that flesh can neither joyn, nor keep together two bodies of it self; what is it then must make them one flesh, but likenes, but fitnes of mind and disposition, which may breed the Spirit of concord, and union between them? If that be not in the nature of either, and that there has bin a remediles mistake, as vain wee goe about to compell them into one flesh, as if wee undertook to weav a garment of drie sand. It were more easy to compell the vegetable and nutritive power of nature to assimilations and mixtures which are not alterable each by other; or force the concoctive stomach to turn that into flesh which is so totally unlike that substance, as not to be wrought on. For as the unity of minde is neerer and greater then the union of bodies, so doubtles, is the

---

[30]Truly, verily.

dissimilitude greater, and more dividuall,[31] as that which makes between bodies all difference and distinction. Especially when as besides the singular and substantial differences of every Soul, there is an intimat quality of good or evil, through the whol progeny of *Adam*, which like a radical heat, or mortal chilnes joyns them, or disjoyns them irresistibly. In whom therefore either the will, or the faculty is found to have never joyn'd, or now not to continue so, 'tis not to say, they shall be one flesh, for they cannot be one flesh. God commands not impossibilities; and all the Ecclesiastical glue, that Liturgy, or Laymen can compound, is not able to soder up two such incongruous natures into the one flesh of a true beseeming Mariage. Why did *Moses* then set down thir uniting into one flesh? And I again ask, why the Gospel so oft repeats the eating of our Saviours flesh, the drinking of his blood? *That wee are one body with him, the members of his body, flesh of his flesh and bone of his bone.* Ephes. 5. Yet lest wee should be Capernaitans,[32] as wee are told there that the flesh profiteth nothing, so wee are told heer, if we be not as deaf as adders, that this union of the flesh proceeds from the union of a fit help and solace. Wee know that there was never a more spiritual mystery then this Gospel taught us under the terms of body and flesh; yet nothing less intended then that wee should stick there. What a stupidnes then is it, that in Mariage, which is the neerest resemblance of our union with Christ, wee should deject our selvs to such a sluggish and underfoot Philosophy, as to esteem the validity of Mariage meerly by the flesh; though never so brokn and disjoynted from love and peace, which only can give a human qualification to that act of the flesh, and distinguish it from bestial. The Text therefore uses this phrase that *they shall bee one flesh*, to justify and make legitimat the rites of Mariage bed; which was not unneedfull, if or all this warrant, they were suspected of pollution by some sects of Philosophy, and Religions of old, and latelier among the Papists, and other heretics elder then they. Som think there is a high mystery in those words, from that which *Paul* saith of them, Ephes. 5. *This is a great mystery, but I speak of Christ and the Church*: and thence they would conclude mariage to be inseparable. For me I dispute not now whether matrimony bee a mystery or no; if it bee of Christ and his Church, certainly it is not meant of every ungodly and miswedded mariage, but then only mysterious, when it is a holy, happy, and peaceful match. But when a Saint is joyn'd with a reprobate, or both alike, wicked with wicked, fool with fool, a hee

drunkard with a she, when the bed hath bin nothing els for twenty yeares or more, but an old haunt of lust and malice mixt together, no love, no goodnes, no loyalty, but counterplotting, and secret wishing one anothers dissolution, this is to me the greatest mystery in the world, if such a mariage as this, can be the mystery of ought, unless it bee the mystery of iniquity: According to that which *Paraeus* cites out of *Chrysostom*, that a bad wife is a help for the devill, and the like may be said of a bad husband. Since therfore none but a fit and pious matrimony can signify the union of Christ and his Church, ther cannot hence be any hindrance of divorce to that Dock wherin ther can be no good mystery. Rather it might to a Christian Conscience bee matter of finding it self so much less satisfy'd then before, in the continuance of an unhappy yoke, wherein there can be no representation either of Christ, or of his Church.

Thus having enquir'd the institution how it was in the beginning, both from the 1 Chap. of *Gen.* where it was only mention'd in part, and from the second, where it was plainly and evidently instituted, and having attended each clause and word necessary, with a diligence not drousy, wee shall now fix with som advantage; and by a short view backward gather up the ground wee have gon; and summ up the strength wee have, into one argumentative head, with that *organic* force that *logic* proffers us. All arts acknowledge that then only we know certainly, when we can define; for definition is that which refines the pure essence of things from the circumstance. If therfore we can attain in this our Controversy to define exactly what mariage is, wee shall soon lern, when there is a nullity thereof, and when a divorce.

The part therfore of this Chapter which hath bin heer treated, doth orderly and readily resolv it self into a definition of mariage, and a consectary[33] from thence. To the definition these words cheifly contribute. *It is not good, &c. I will make, &c.* Where the consectary begins this connexion *Therfore* informs us, *Therfore shall a man, &c.* Definition is decreed by Logicians to consist only of causes constituting the essence of a thing. What is not therfore among the causes constituting mariage, must not stay in the definition. Those causes are concluded to be *matter*, and, as the Artist calls it, *Form*. But inasmuch as the same thing may be a cause more waies then one, and that in relations and institutions which have no corporal subsistence, but only a respective beeing, the *Form* by which the thing is what it is, is oft so slender and undistinguishable, that it would soon confuse, were it not sustain'd by the efficient and final

---

[31]Divided.
[32]Those living in Capernaum, chastised for lack of faith proverbially in Matthew 11.23 and Luke 10.15.

[33]Logical conclusion.

causes, which concurre to make up the form invalid otherwise of it self, it will bee needfull to take in all the fowr causes into the definition. First therfore the material cause of matrimony is man and woman; the Author and efficient, God and their consent, the internal *Form* and soul of this relation, is conjugal love arising from a mutual fitnes to the final causes of wedlock, help and society in Religious Civil and Domestic conversation, which includes as an inferior end the fulfilling of natural desire, and specified increase; these are the final causes both moving the *efficient* and perfeting the *form*. And although copulation be consider'd among the ends of mariage, yet the act therof in a right esteem can no longer be matrimonial, then it is an effect of conjugal love. When love findes it self utterly unmatcht, and justly vanishes, nay rather cannot but vanish, the fleshly act indeed may continue, but not holy, not pure, not beseeming the sacred bond of mariage; beeing at best but an animal excretion, but more truly wors and more ignoble then that mute kindlyness among the heards and flocks: in that proceeding as it ought from intellective principles, it participates of nothing rational, but that which the feild and the fould equalls. For in human actions the soule is the agent, the body in a manner passive. If then the body doe out of sensitive force, what the soul complies not with, how can man, and not rather somthing beneath man be thought the doer.

But to proceed in the persute of an accurat definition, it will avail us somthing, and whet our thoughts, to examin what fabric heerof others have already reard. *Paræus* on *Gen.* defines Mariage to be *an indissoluble conjunction of one man and one woman to an individual and intimat conversation, and mutual benevolence, &c.* Wherin is to be markt his placing of intimat conversation before bodily benevolence; for bodily is meant, though indeed *benevolence* rather sounds will then body. Why then shall divorce be granted for want of bodily performance, and not for want of fitnes to intimat conversation, when as corporal benevolence cannot in any human fashion bee without this? Thus his definition places the ends of Mariage in one order, and esteems them in another. His *Tautology* also of indissoluble and individual is not to be imitated; especially since neither indissoluble, nor individual hath ought to doe in the exact definition, beeing but a consectary flowing from thence, as appears by plain Scripture, *Therfore shall a man leav, &c.* For Mariage is not true mariage by beeing individual, but therfore individual, if it be true Mariage. No argument but causes enter the definition; a Consectary is but the effect of those causes. Besides, that Mariage is indissoluble, is not *Catholickly* true, wee know it dissoluble for Adultery, and for desertion by the verdit

of all Reformed Churches. Dr. *Ames*[34] defines it *an individual conjunction of one man and one woman, to communion of body and mutual society of life*; But this perverts the order of God, who in the institution places meet help and society of life before communion of body. And vulgar estimation undervalues beyond comparison all society of life and communion of minde beneath the communion of body; granting no divorce, but to the want, or miscommunicating of that. *Hemingius*,[35] an approved Author, *Melanchtons* Scholler, and who next to *Bucer* and *Erasmus* writes of divorce most like a Divine, thus comprises, *Mariage is a conjunction of one man and one woman lawfully consenting, into one flesh, for mutual helps sake, ordain'd of God.* And in his explanation stands punctually upon the conditions of consent, that it be not in any main matter deluded, as beeing the life of wedloc, and no true mariage without a true consent. *Into one flesh* he expounds into one minde, as well as one body, and makes it the formal cause: Heerin only missing, while he puts the effect into his definition instead of the cause which the Text affords him. For *one flesh* is not the formal essence of wedloc, but one end, or one effect of *a meet help*; The end oft times beeing the effect and fruit of the form, as Logic teaches: Els many aged and holy matrimonies, and more eminently that of *Joseph* and *Mary*, would bee no true mariage. And that *maxim* generally receiv'd, would be fals, that *consent alone, though copulation never follow, makes the mariage.* Therefore to consent lawfully into one flesh, is not the formal cause of Matrimony, but only one of the effects. The Civil Lawyers, and first *Justinian* or *Tribonian* defines Matrimony *a conjunction of man and woman containing individual accustom of life.* Wherin first, individual is not so bad as indissoluble put in by others: And although much cavil might be made in the distinguishing between indivisible, and individual, yet the one tak'n for possible, the other for actuall, neither the one nor the other can belong to the essence of mariage; especially when a Civilian defines, by which Law mariage is actually divorc't for many causes, and with good leav, by mutual consent. Therfore where *conjunction* is said, they who comment the *Institutes*, agree that conjunction of minde is by the Law meant, not necessarily conjunction of body. That Law then had good reason attending to its own definition, that divorce should be granted for the breaking of that conjunction

---

[34]William Ames (1576–1633; in Latin his name is Amesius). His *Marrow of Sacred Divinity* (*Medulla Theologiae* in Latin, 1630) may be a major source for Milton's *On Christian Doctrine*. The citation here can be found in the *Marrow* (1642) 2: 19; 321.

[35]Nicolaus Hemming or Niels Hemmingsen (1513–1600), *De Conjugio*, in *Opuscula Theologica* (Geneva, 1586) col. 941.

which it holds necessary, sooner then for the want of that conjunction which it holds not necessary. And wheras *Tuningus*[36] a famous Lawyer excuses individual as the purpos of Mariage, not always the success, it suffices not. Purpos is not able to constitute the essence of a thing. Nature her self the universal Mother intends nothing but her own perfection and preservation; yet is not the more indissoluble for that. The *Pandects* out of *Modestinus*, though not define, yet well describe Mariage, *the conjunction of male and female, the society of all life, the communion of divine and human right*: which *Bucer* also imitates on the fifth to the *Ephesians*. But it seems rather to comprehend the several ends of Mariage, then to contain the more constituting cause that makes it what it is.

That I therefore among others (for who sings not *Hylas*) may give as well as take matter to be judg'd on, it will be lookt I should produce another definition then these which have not stood the tryal. Thus then I suppose that Mariage by the natural and plain order of Gods institution in the Text may be more demonstratively and essentially defind. *Mariage is a divine institution joyning man and woman in a love fitly dispos'd to the helps and comforts of domestic life. A divine institution.* This contains the prime efficient cause of Mariage; as for consent of Parents and Guardians, it seems rather a concurrence then a cause; for as many, that marry are in thir own power as not; and where they are not thir own, yet are they not subjected beyond reason. Now though efficient causes are not requisite in a definition, yet divine institution hath such influence upon the *Form*, and is so a conserving cause of it, that without it the *Form* is not sufficient to distinguish matrimony from other conjunctions of male and female, which are not to be counted mariage. *Joyning man and woman in a love, &c.* This brings in the parties consent; until which be, the mariage hath no true beeing. When I say *consent*, I mean not error, for error is not properly consent: And why should not consent be heer understood with equity and good to either part, as in all other freindly covnants, and not be strain'd and cruelly urg'd to the mischeif and destruction of both? Neither doe I mean that singular act of consent which made the contract, for that may remain, and yet the mariage not true nor lawful; and that may cease, and yet the mariage both true and lawful, to their sin that break it. So that either as not efficient at all, or but transitory, it comes not into the definition. That consent I mean which is a love fitly dispos'd to mutual help and comfort of life;

this is that happy *Form* of mariage naturally arising from the very heart of divine institution in the Text, in all the former definitions either obscurely, and under mistak'n terms exprest, or not at all. This gives mariage all her due, all her benefits, all her beeing, all her distinct and proper beeing. This makes a mariage not a bondage, a blessing not a curse, a gift of God not a snare. Unless ther be a love, and that love born of fitnes, how can it last? unless it last how can the best and sweetest purposes of mariage be attain'd, and they not attain'd, which are the cheif ends, and with a lawful love constitute the formal cause it self of mariage, how can the essence thereof subsist, how can it bee indeed what it goes for? Conclude therfore by all the power of reason, that where this essence of mariage is not, there can bee no true mariage; and the parties either one of them, or both are free, and without fault rather by a nullity, then by a divorce may betake them to a second choys; if thir present condition be not tolerable to them. If any shall ask, why *domestic* in the definition? I answer, that because both in the Scriptures, and in the gravest Poets and Philosophers I finde the properties and excellencies of a wife set out only from domestic vertues; if they extend furder, it diffuses them into the notion of som more common duty then matrimonial.

Thus farre of the definition; the *Consectary* which flows from thence, and altogether depends theron, is manifestly brought in by this connexive particle *Therfore*; and branches it self into a double consequence; First individual Society, *therfore shall a man leav father and mother*: Secondly conjugal benevolence, *and they shall bee one flesh*. Which as was shewn, is not without cause heer mention'd, to prevent and to abolish the suspect of pollution in that natural and undefiled act. These consequences therfore cannot either in Religion, Law, or Reason bee bound, and posted upon mankind to his sorrow and misery, but receiv what force they have from the meetnes of help and solace, which is the *formal* cause and end of that definition that sustains them. And although it be not for the Majesty of Scripture to humble her self in artificial *theorems*, and definitions, and *Corollaries*, like a professor in the Schools, but looks to be *analys'd*, and interpreted by the logical industry of her Disciples and followers, and to bee reduc't by them, as oft as need is, into those *Sciential* rules, which are the implements of instruction, yet *Moses*, as if foreseeing the miserable work that mans ignorance and pusillanimity would make in this matrimonious busines, and endevouring his utmost to prevent it, condescends in this place to such a methodical and School-like way of defining, and consequencing, as in no place of the whole Law more.

Thus wee have seen, and if wee be not contentious,

---

[36]Milton seems to be scraping the barrel of citations with Gerardus Tuningus, *In Quatuor Libros Institutionum Juris Cvilis Devi Justiniani Commentarius*, "*De Nuptiis*," (Leyden, 1618): 66.

may know what was Mariage in the beginning, to which in the Gospel wee are referr'd; and what from hence to judge of nullity, or divorce. Heer I esteem the work don; in this field the controversie decided; but because other places of Scripture seem to look aversly upon this our decision, although indeed they keep all harmony with it, and because it is a better work to reconcile the seeming diversities of Scripture, then the reall dissentions of neerest friends, I shall assay in three following Discourses to perform that Office.

Deut. 24. 1,2.

1 *When a man hath taken a Wife, and married her, and it come to pass that she find no favour in his eyes, because he hath found som uncleannes in her, then let him write her a bill of divorcement, and give it in her hand, and send her out of his house.*

2 *And when she is departed out of his house, she may goe and be another mans wife.*

THat which is the only discommodity of speaking in a cleer matter, the abundance of argument that presses to bee utter'd, and the suspence of judgement what to choose, and how in the multitude of reason, to be not tedious, is the greatest difficulty which I expect heer to meet with. Yet much hath bin said formerly concerning this Law in *the Doctrine of divorce*; Wherof I shall repeat no more then what is necessary. Two things are heer doubted: First, and that but of late, whether this bee a Law or no, next what this reason of *uncleannes* might mean for which the Law is granted; That it is a plain Law no man ever question'd, till *Vatablus* within these hunder'd years profess'd Hebrew at *Paris*, a man of no Religion, as *Beza* deciphers him. Yet som there be who follow him, not only against the current of all antiquity, both Jewish and Christian, but the evidence of Scripture also, Malach. 2. 16. *Let him who hateth put away saith the Lord God of Israel.* Although this place also hath bin tamper'd with, as if it were to be thus render'd, *The Lord God saith, that hee hateth putting away.* But this new interpretation rests only in the autority of *Junius*; for neither *Calvin*, nor *Vatablus* himself, nor any other known Divine so interpreted before. And they of best note who have translated the Scripture since, and *Diodati*[37] for one,

---

[37]Jean or Giovanni Diodati, the uncle of Milton's friend Charles Diodati, and a theologian and biblical translator whom Milton visited in Geneva on route to England. Milton consulted Diodati's *Pious Annotations upon the Holy Bible* on more than one occasion.

follow not his reading. And perhaps they might reject it, if for nothing els, for these two reasons: First, it introduces in a new manner the person of God speaking less Majestic then he is ever wont; When God speaks by his Profet, he ever speaks in the first person; thereby signifying his Majesty and omni-presence. Hee would have said, I hate putting away, saith the Lord; and not sent word by *Malachi* in a sudden faln stile, The *Lord God saith that hee hateth putting away:* that were a phrase to shrink the glorious omnipresence of God speaking, into a kind of circumscriptive absence. And were as if a Herald in the *Atcheivment* of a King, should commit the *indecorum* to set his helmet sidewaies and close, not full fac't and open in the posture of direction and command. Wee cannot think therfore that this last Profet would thus in a new fashion absent the person of God from his own words as if he came not along with them. For it would also be wide from the proper scope of this place: hee that reads attentively will soon perceav, that God blames not heer the Jews for putting away thir wives, but for keeping strange Concubines, to the *profaning of Juda's holines*, and the vexation of thir Hebrew wives, v. 11. and 14. *Judah hath maried the daughter of a strange God:* And exhorts them rather to put thir wives away whom they hate, as the Law permitted, then to keep them under such affronts. And it is receiv'd that this Profet livd in those times of *Ezra* and *Nehemiah* (nay by som is thought to bee *Ezra* himself) when the people were forc't by these two Worthies to put thir strange wives away. So that what the story of those times, and the plain context of the 11 verse, from whence this rebuke begins, can give us to conjecture of the obscure and curt *Ebraisms* that follow, this Profet does not forbid putting away, but forbids keeping, and commands putting away according to Gods Law, which is the plainest interpreter both of what God will, and what he can best suffer. Thus much evinces that God there commanded divorce by *Malachi*, and this confirmes that he commands it also heer by *Moses*.

I may the less doubt to mention by the way an Author, though counted Apocryphal, yet of no small account for piety and wisdom, the Author of *Ecclesiasticus*. Which Book begun by the Grand-father of that *Jesus* who is call'd the Son of *Sirach*, might have bin writt'n in part, not much after the time when *Malachi* livd; if wee compute by the Reigne of *Ptolemæus Euergetes*. It professes to explain the Law and the Profets; and yet exhorts us to divorce for incurable causes, and to cut off from the flesh those whom it there describes, *Ecclesiastic.* 25. 26. Which doubtles that wise and ancient Writer would never have advis'd, had either *Malachi* so lately forbidd'n it, or the Law by a full precept not left it lawful; But I urge not this for want of better prooff;

our Saviour himself allows divorce to be a command, *Mark* 10. 3.5. Neither doe they weak'n this assertion, who say it was only a sufferance, as shall be prov'd at large in that place of *Matthew*. But suppose it were not a writt'n Law, they never can deny it was a custom, and so effect nothing. For the same reasons that induce them why it should not bee a law, will strait'n them as hard why it should bee allow'd a custom. All custom is either evil or not evil; if it be evil, this is the very end of Law-giving, to abolish evil customs by wholsom Laws; unless wee imagin *Moses* weaker then every negligent and startling[38] Politician. If it be, as they make this of divorce to be, a custom against nature, against justice, against chastity, how, upon this most impure custom tolerated, could the God of purenes erect a nice and precise Law, that the wife married after divorce could not return to her former husband, as beeing defil'd? What was all this following nicenes worth, built upon the leud foundation of a wicked thing allow'd? In few words then, this custom of divorce either was allowable, or not allowable; if not allowable, how could it be allow'd? if it were allowable, all who understand Law will consent, that a tolerated custom hath the force of a Law, and is indeed no other but an unwritt'n Law, as *Justinian* calls it, and is as prevalent as any writt'n statute. So that thir shift of turning this Law into a custom wheels about, and gives the onset upon thir own flanks; not disproving, but concluding it to be the more firm law, because it was without controversy a granted custom; as cleer in the reason of common life, as those giv'n rules wheron *Euclides* builds his propositions. Thus beeing every way a Law of God, who can without blasphemy doubt it to be a just and pure Law. *Moses* continually disavows the giving them any statute, or judgement, but what hee learnt of God; of whom also in his Song hee saith, Deut. 32. *Hee is the rock, his work is perfet, all his waies are judgement, a God of truth and without iniquity, just and right is hee.* And *David* testifies, the judgements of the Lord *are true and righteous altogether.* Not partly right and partly wrong, much less wrong altogether, as Divines of now adaies dare censure them. *Moses* again of that people to whom hee gave this Law saith, Deut. 14. *Yee are the childern of the Lord your God, the Lord hath chosen thee to bee a peculiar people to himself above all the nations upon the earth, that thou shouldst keep all his Commandements; and be high in praise, in name, and in honour, holy to the Lord, Chap.* 26. And in the fourth, *Behold I have taught you statutes and judgements, eevn as the Lord my God commanded mee, keep therfore and doe them. For this is your wisdom and your understanding in the sight of Nations that shall hear all these Statutes and say, surely this great Nation is a wise and understanding people. For what Nation is ther so great, who hath God so nigh to them? and what Nation that hath Statutes and Judgements so righteous as all this Law which I set before you this day?* Thus whether wee look at the purity and justice of God himself, the jealousy of his honour among other Nations, the holines and moral perfection which hee intended by his Law to teach this people, wee cannot possibly think how he could indure to let them slugg[39] & grow inveteratly wicked, under base allowances, & whole adulterous lives by dispensation. They might not eat, they might not touch an unclean thing; to what hypocrisy then were they train'd up, if by prescription of the same Law, they might be unjust, they might be adulterous for term of life? forbid to soile thir garments with a coy imaginary pollution, but not forbid, but countnanc't and animated by Law to soile thir soules with deepest defilements. What more unlike to God, what more like that God should hate, then that his Law should bee so curious to wash vessels, and vestures, and so careles to leav unwasht, unregarded, so foul a scab of *Egypt* in thir Soules? what would wee more? the Statutes of the Lord are all pure and just: and if all, then this of Divorce.

[*Because hee hath found som uncleannes in her.*] That wee may not esteem this law to bee a meer authorizing of licence, as the Pharises took it, *Moses* adds the reason, for *som uncleannes found.* Som heertofore have bin so ignorant, as to have thought, that this *uncleannes* means adultery. But *Erasmus,* who for having writ an excellent Treatise of Divorce, was wrote against by som burly standard Divine, perhaps of *Cullen,*[40] or of *Lovain,* who calls himself *Phimostomus,* shews learnedly out of the Fathers with other Testimonies and Reasons, that *uncleannes* is not heer so understood; defends his former work, though new to that age, and perhaps counted licentious, and fears not to ingage all his fame on the Argument. Afterward, when Expositers began to understand the Hebrew Text, which they had not done of many ages before, they translated word for word not *uncleannes,* but the *nakednes of any thing;* and considering that nakednes is usually referr'd in Scripture to the minde as well as to the body, they constantly expound it any defect, annoyance, or ill quality in nature, which to bee joyn'd with, makes life tedious, and

---

[38]Probably "upstart," as the Yale editor notes (2: 618 n.15).

[39]Lie around idly, as in the compound "slug-a-bed."

[40]Cologne (Köln), in a standard English mispronunciation, still reported in 1890 in England by the *OED.* Both Cologne, and Louvain, the famous university town in what is now Brussels, were known as bastions of Roman Catholic theological training. "*Phimostomus*" has not yet been identified.

such company wors then solitude. So that heer will be no cause to vary from the generall consent of exposition, which gives us freely that God permitted divorce, for whatever was unalterably distastful, whether in body or mind. But with this admonishment, that if the *Roman* law especially in contracts and dowries left many things to equity with these cautions, *ex fide bonâ, quod æquius melius erit, ut inter bonos bene agier*,[41] wee will not grudge to think that God intended not licence heer to every humor, but to such remediles greevances as might move a good, and honest, and faithfull man then to divorce, when it can no more bee peace or comfort to either of them continuing thus joyn'd. And although it could not be avoided, but that men of hard hearts would abuse this liberty, yet doubtles it was intended as all other privileges in Law are, to good men principally, to bad only by accident. So that the sin was not in the permission, nor simply in the action of divorce (for then the permitting also had bin sin) but only in the abuse. But that this Law should, as it were, bee wrung from God and *Moses*, only to serve the hard heartednes, and the lust of injurious men, how remote it is from all sense, and law, and honesty, and therfore surely from the meaning of Christ, shall abundantly be manifest in & order.

Now although *Moses* needed not to adde other reason of this law then that one there exprest, yet to these ages wherin Canons, and *Scotisms*, and *Lumbard* Laws, have dull'd, and almost obliterated the lively Sculpture of ancient reason, and humanity, it will be requisit to heap reason upon reason, and all little enough to vindicat the whitenes and the innocence of this divine Law, from the calumny it findes at this day, of beeing a dore to licence and confusion. When as indeed there is not a judicial point in all *Moses*, consisting of more true equity, high wisdom, and God-like pitty then this Law; not derogating, but preserving the honour and peace of Mariage, and exactly agreeing with the sense and mind of that institution in *Genesis*.

For first, if Mariage be but an ordain'd relation, as it seems not more, it cannot take place above the prime dictats of nature; and if it bee of natural right, yet it must yeeld to that which is more natural, and before it by eldership and precedence in nature. Now it is not natural that *Hugh* marries *Beatrice*, or *Thomas Rebecca*, beeing only a civill contract, and full of many chances, but that these men seek them meet helps, that only is natural; and that they espouse them such, that only is mariage. But if they find them neither fit helps, nor

tolerable society, what thing more natural, more original and first in nature then to depart from that which is irksom, greevous, actively hateful, and injurious eevn to hostility, especially in a conjugal respect, wherin antipathies are invincible, and wher the forc't abiding of the one, can bee no true good, no real comfort to the other. For if hee find no contentment from the other, how can he return it from himself, or no acceptance, how can hee mutually accept? what more equal, more pious then to untie a civil knot for a natural enmity held by violence from parting, to dissolv an accidental conjunction of this or that man & woman, for the most natural and most necessary disagreement of meet from unmeet, guilty from guiltles, contrary from contrary? It beeing certain that the mystical and blessed unity of mariage can bee no way more unhallow'd and profan'd, then by the forcible uniting of such disunions and separations. Which if wee see oft times they cannot joyn or peece up to a common friendship, or to a willing conversation in the same house, how should they possibly agree to the most familiar and united amity of wedlock? *Abraham* and *Lot*, though dear friends and brethren in a strange Country, chose rather to part asunder, then to infect thir friendship with the strife of thir servants: *Paul* and *Barnabas* joyn'd together by the Holy Ghost to a Spiritual work, thought it better to separate when once they grew at variance. If these great Saints joynd by nature, friendship, religion, high providence, and revelation, could not so govern a casual difference, a sudden passion, but must in wisdom divide from the outward duties of a friendship, or a Collegue-ship in the same family, or in the same journey, lest it should grow to a wors division, can any thing bee more absurd and barbarous then that they whom only error, casualty, art or plot hath joynd, should be compell'd, not against a sudden passion but against the permanent and radical discords of nature, to the most intimat and incorporating duties of love and imbracement, therin only rational and human, as they are free and voluntary; beeing els an abject and servile yoke, scars not brutish. And that there is in man such a peculiar sway of liking, or disliking in the affairs of matrimony is evidently seen before mariage among those who can bee freindly, can respect each other, yet to marry each other would not for any perswasion. If then this unfitnes and disparity bee not till after mariage discover'd, through many causes, and colours, and concealements, that may overshadow; undoubtedly it will produce the same effects and perhaps with more vehemence, that such a mistakn pair, would give the world to be unmarried again. And thir condition *Solomon* to the plain justification of divorce expresses, *Prov.* 30.21.23. Where hee tells us of his own accord, that a *hated*, or a *hatefull* woman, *when shee is married, is a thing for which the earth is disquieted and cannot bear it*; thus giving divine testimony to this divine Law, which bids us nothing more then is the first and most innocent lesson of nature, to turn away peaceably from what afflicts and hazards our destruction; especially when our staying can doe no good, and is expos'd to all evil.

Secondly, It is unjust that any Ordinance ordain'd to the good and comfort of man, where that end is missing, without his fault, should be forc't upon him to an unsufferable misery and discomfort, if not commonly ruin. All Ordinances are establisht in thir end; the end of Law is the vertu, is the righteousnes of Law. And therfore him wee count an ill Expounder who urges Law against the intention therof. The general end of every Ordinance, of every severest, every divinest, eevn of Sabbath is the good of man, yea his temporal good not excluded. But marriage is one of the benignest ordinances of God to man, wherof both the general and particular end is the peace and contentment of mans mind, as the institution declares. Contentment of body they grant, which if it bee defrauded, the plea of frigidity shall divorce: But heer lies the fadomles absurdity, that granting this for bodily defect, they will not grant it for any defect of the mind, any violation of religious or civil society. When as, if the argument of Christ bee firm against the ruler of the Synagogue, Luk. 13. *Thou hypocrite, doth not each of you on the Sabbath day loos'n his Oxe or his Asse from the stall, and lead him to watering, and should not I unbind a daughter of Abraham from this bond of Satan?* it stands as good heer, yee have regard in mariage to the greevance of body; should you not regard more the greevances of the mind, seeing the Soul as much excells the body, as the outward man excells the Ass and more; for that *animal* is yet a living creature, perfet in it self; but the body without the Soul is a meer senseles trunck. No Ordinance therfore givn particularly to the good both spiritual and temporal of man, can bee urg'd upon him to his mischeif, and if they yeeld this to the unworthier part, the body, wherabout are they in thir principles, that they yeeld it not to the more worthy, the mind of a good man?

Thirdly, As no Ordinance, so no Covnant, no not between God and man, much less between man and man, beeing as all are, intended to the good of both parties, can hold to the deluding or making miserable of them both. For equity is understood in every Covnant, eevn between enemies, though the terms bee not exprest. If equity therfore made it, extremity may dissolv it. But Mariage, they use to say, is the Covnant of God. Undoubted: and so is any covnant frequently call'd in Scripture, wherin God is call'd to witness: the covnant of freindship between *David* and *Jonathan*, is call'd *the Covnant of the*

Lord, 1 Sam. 20. The covnant of *Zedechiah* with the King of *Babel*, a Covnant to bee doubted whether lawfull or no, yet in respect of God invok't thereto, is call'd *the Oath, and the Covnant of God*, Ezech. 17. Mariage also is call'd the *Covnant of God*, Prov. 2.17. Why, but as before, because God is the witnes therof, Malach. 2.14. So that this denomination adds nothing to the Covnant of Mariage, above any other civil and solemn contract: nor is it more indissoluble for this reason then any other against the end of its own ordination, nor is any vow or Oath to God exacted with such a rigor, where superstition reignes not. For look how much divine the Covnant is, so much the more equal; So much the more to bee expected that every article therof should bee fairly made good, no fals dealing, or unperforming should be thrust upon men without redress, if the covnant bee so divine. But faith they say must be kept in Covnant, though to our dammage. I answer, that only holds true, where the other side performs, which failing, hee is no longer bound. Again, this is true, when the keeping of faith can bee of any use, or benefit to the other. But in Mariage a league of love and willingnes, if faith bee not willingly kept, it scars is worth the keeping; nor can bee any delight to a generous minde, with whom it is forcibly kept: and the question still supposes the one brought to an impossibility of keeping it as hee ought, by the others default, and to keep it formally, not only with a thousand shifts and dissimulations, but with open anguish, perpetual sadnes and disturbance, no willingnes, no cheerfulnes, no contentment, cannot bee any good to a minde not basely poor and shallow, with whom the contract of love is so kept. A Covnant therfore brought to that passe, is on the unfaulty side without injury dissolv'd.

Fourthly, The Law is not to neglect men under greatest sufferances, but to see Covnants of greatest moment faithfullest perform'd. And what injury comparable to that sustain'd in a frustrat and fals dealing Mariage, to loose, for anothers fault against him, the best portion of his temporal comforts, and of his spiritual too, as it may fall out. It was the Law, that for mans good and quiet, reduc't things to propriety, which were at first in common; how much more Law-like were it to assist nature in disappropriating that evil which by continuing proper becomes destructive. But hee might have bewar'd. So hee might in any other covnant, wherin the Law does not constrain error to so dear a forfeit. And yet in these matters wherin the wisest are apt to erre, all the warines that can bee, oft times nothing avails. But the Law can compell the offending party to bee more duteous. Yes, if all these kind of offences were fit in public to bee complain'd on, or beeing compell'd were any satisfaction to a mate not sottish,[42] or malicious. And these injuries work so vehemently, that if the Law remedy them not, by separating the cause when no way els will pacify, the person not releev'd betakes him either to such disorderly courses, or to such a dull dejection, as renders him either infamous, or useles to the service of God and his Country. Which the Law ought to prevent as a thing pernicious to the Common wealth; and what better prevention then this which *Moses* us'd?

Fiftly, The Law is to tender the liberty and the human dignity of them that live under the Law, whether it bee the mans right above the woman, or the womans just appeal against wrong, and servitude. But the duties of mariage contain in them a duty of benevolence, which to doe by compulsion against the Soul, where ther can bee neither peace, nor joy, nor love, but an enthrallment to one who either cannot, or will not bee mutual in the godliest and the civilest ends of that society, is the ignoblest, and the lowest slavery that a human shape[43] can bee put to. This Law therfore justly and piously provides against such an unmanly task of bondage as this. The civil Law, though it favour'd the setting free of a slave, yet if hee prov'd ungratefull to his Patron, reduc't him to a servil condition. If that Law did well to reduce from liberty to bondage for an ingratitude not the greatest, much more became it the Law of God to enact the restorement of a free born man from an unpurpos'd, and unworthy bondage to a rightfull liberty for the most unnatural fraud and ingratitude that can be committed against him. And if that Civilian Emperour in his title of *Donations*, permit the giver to recall his guift from him who proves unthankful towards him, yea, though hee had subscrib'd and sign'd in the deed of his guift, not to recall it though for this very cause of ingratitude, with much more equity doth *Moses* heer the giver to recall no petty guift, but the guift of himself from one who most injuriously & deceitfully uses him against the main ends and conditions of his giving himself, exprest in Gods institution.

Sixthly, Although ther bee nothing in the plain words of this Law, that seems to regard the afflictions of a wife, how great so ever, yet Expositers determin, and doubtles determin rightly, that God was not uncompassionat of them also in the framing of this Law. For should the rescript of *Antoninus* in the Civil Law give release to servants flying for refuge to the Emperours statue, by giving leav to change thir cruel Maisters, and should God who in his Law also is good to injur'd servants, by granting them thir freedom in divers cases, not

consider the wrongs and miseries of a wife which is no servant. Though heerin the counter sense of our Divines, to me, I must confesse seems admirable; who teach that God gave this as a mercifull Law, not for man whom he heer names, and to whom by name hee gives this power, but for the wife whom hee names not, and to whom by name hee gives no power at all. For certainly if man be liable to injuries in mariage, as well as woman, and man be the worthier person, it were a preposterous law to respect only the less worthy; her whom God made for mariage, and not him at all for whom mariage was made.

Seventhly, The Law of mariage gives place to the power of Parents: for wee hold that consent of Parents not had may break the wedlock, though els accomplisht. It gives place to maisterly power, for the Maister might take away from an Hebrew servant the wife which hee gave him, *Exod.* 21. If it be answer'd that the mariage of servants is no matrimony: tis reply'd, that this in the ancient *Roman* Law is true, not in the *Mosaic*. If it bee added, she was a stranger not an Hebrew, therfore easily divorc't, it will be answerd that strangers not beeing *Canaanites*, and they also beeing Converts might bee lawfully maryed, as *Rahab* was. And her conversion is heer suppos'd; for an Hebrew[44] maister could not lawfully give a heathen wife to an Hebrew servant. However, the divorcing of an Israelitish woman was as easy by the Law, as the divorcing of a stranger, and almost in the same words permitted, *Deut.* 24. and *Deut.* 21. Lastly, it gives place to the right of warr, for a captiv woman lawfully maryed, and aferward not belov'd, might bee dismist, only without ransom, *Deut.* 21. If mariage may bee dissolv'd by so many exterior powers, not superior, as wee think, why may not the power of mariage it self for its own peace and honour dissolv it self, wher the persons wedded be free persons, why may not a greater and more natural power complaining dissolv mariage? for the ends why matrimony was ordain'd, are certainly and by all Logic above the Ordinance it self, why may not that dissolv mariage without which that institution hath no force at all? for the prime ends of mariage, are the whole strength and validity therof, without which matrimony is like an Idol, nothing in the world. But those former allowances were all for hardnes of heart. Be that granted, untill we come to where to understand it better: if the Law suffer thus farr the obstinacy of a bad man, is it not more righteous heer, to doe willingly what is but equal, to remove in season the extremities of a good man?

---

[42]Stupid (probably not "drunken," though that sense was also current).
[43]Probably "human being."

[44]Notice the article "an" with "Hebrew," indicating that it should be pronounced "Ebrew," as Milton often spelled it, in contrast to "a heathen."

Eightly, If a man had deflowr'd a Virgin, or brought an ill-name on his wife that shee came not a Virgin to him, hee was amerc't[45] in certain shekles of Silver, and bound never to divorce her all his daies, *Deut.* 22. which shews that the Law gave no liberty to divorce, wher the injury was palpable; and that the absolute forbidding to divorce, was in part the punishment of a deflowrer, and a defamer. Yet not so but that the wife questionles might depart when shee pleas'd. Otherwise this cours had not so much righted her, as deliverd her up to more spight and cruel usage. This Law therfore doth justly distinguish the privilege of an honest and blameles man in the matter of divorce from the punishment of a notorious offender.

Ninthly, Suppose it might bee imputed to a man, that hee was too rash in his choyse and why took hee not better heed, let him now smart, and bear his folly as he may; although the Law of God, that terrible law doe not thus upbraid the infirmities and unwilling mistakes of man in his integrity: But suppose these and the like proud aggravations of som stern hypocrite, more merciles in his mercies, then any literall Law in the vigor of severity, must be patiently heard; yet all Law, and Gods Law especially grants every where to error easy remitments, eevn where the utmost penalty exacted were no undoing. With great reason therfore and mercy doth it heer not torment an error, if it be so, with the endurance of a whole life lost to all houshold comfort and society, a punishment of too vast and huge dimension for an error, and the more unreasonable for that the like objection may be oppos'd against the plea of divorcing for adultery; hee might have lookt better before to her breeding under religious Parents: why did hee not then more diligently inquire into her manners, into what company she kept? every glaunce of her eye, every step of her gate would have propheci'd adultery, if the quick sent of these discerners had bin took along; they had the divination to have foretold you all this; as they have now the divinity to punish an error inhumanly. As good reason to be content, and forc't to be content with your adultress, if these objecters might be the judges of human frailtie. But God more mild and good to man, then man to his brother, in all this liberty givn to divorcement, mentions not a word of our past errors and mistakes, if any were, which these men objecting from their own inventions prosecute with all violence and iniquity. For if the one bee to look so narrowly what hee takes, at the peril of ever keeping, why should not the other bee made as wary what is promis'd, by the peril of loosing? for without those promises the treaty

of mariage had not proceeded. Why should his own error bind him, rather then the others fraud acquit him? Let the buyer beware, saith the old Law-beaten termer. Belike then, ther is no more honesty, nor ingenuity in the bargain of a wedloc, then in the buying of a colt: Wee must it seems drive it on as craftily with those whose affinity wee seek, as if they were a pack of sale men and complotters. But the deceiver deceivs himself in the unprosperous mariage, and therin is sufficiently punisht. I answer, that the most of those who deceiv, are such as either understand not, or value not the true purposes of mariage; they have the prey they seek, not the punishment: yet say it prove to them som cross, it is not equal[46] that error and fraud should bee linkt in the same degree of forfeture, but rather that error should be acquitted, and fraud bereav'd his morsel: if the mistake were not on both sides, for then on both sides the acquitment will be reasonable, if the bondage be intolerable; which this Law graciously determins, not unmindful of the wife, as was granted willingly to the common Expositers, though beyond the letter of this law, yet not beyond the spirit of charity.

Tenthly, Mariage is a solemn thing, som say a holy, the resemblance of Christ and his Church; and so indeed it is where the persons are truly religious; and wee know all Sacred things not perform'd sincerely as they ought, are no way acceptable to God in thir outward formality. And that wherin it differs from personal duties, if they be not truly don, the fault is in our selves; but mariage to be a true and pious mariage is not in the single power of any person; the essence whereof, as of all other Covnants is in relation to another, the making and maintaining causes thereof are all mutual, and must be a communion of spiritual and temporal comforts. If then either of them cannot, or obstinatly will not be answerable in these duties, so as that the other can have no peaceful living, or enduring the want of what he justly seeks, and sees no hope, then strait from that dwelling love, which is the soul of wedloc, takes his flight, leaving only som cold performances of civil and common respects, but the true bond of mariage, if there were ever any there, is already burst like a rott'n thred. Then follows dissimulation, suspicion, fals colours, fals pretences, and wors then these, disturbance, annoyance, vexation, sorrow, temtation eevn in the faultles person, weary of himself, and of all action public or domestic; then comes disorder, neglect, hatred, and perpetual strife, all these the enemies of holines and christianity, and every one of these persisted in, a remediles violation to matrimony. Therfore God who hates all faining and

---

[45]Punished by an arbitrary fine.

[46]Fair or equitable.

formality, wher there should bee all faith and sincerenes, and abhorrs to see inevitable discord, wher there should be greatest concord, when through anothers default, faith and concord cannot bee, counts it neither just to punish the innocent with the transgressor, nor holy, nor honourable for the sanctity of mariage, that should bee the union of peace and love, to be made the commitment, and close fight of enmity and hate. And therfore doth in this Law, what best agrees with his goodnes, loosning a sacred thing to peace and charity, rather then binding it to hatred and contention; loosning only the outward and formal tie of that which is already inwardly, and really brokn, or els was really never joyn'd.

Eleventhly, One of the cheif matrimonial ends is said to seek a holy seed; but where an unfit mariage administers continual cause of hatred and distemper, there, as was heard before, cannot choose but much unholines abide. Nothing more unhallows a man, more unprepares him to the service of God in any duty, then a habit of wrath and perturbation, arising the importunity of troublous causes never absent. And the houshold stands in this plight, what love can ther bee to the unfortunat issue,[47] what care of thir breeding, which is of main conducement to their beeing holy. God therfore knowing how unhappy it would bee for children to bee born in such a family, gives this Law either as a prevention, that beeing an unhappy pair, they should not adde to bee unhappy parents, or els as a remedy that if ther be childern, while they are fewest, they may follow either parent, as shall bee agreed, or judg'd, from the house of hatred and discord, to a place of more holy and peaceable education.

Twelfthly, All Law is available to som good end, but the final prohibition of divorce avails to no good end, causing only the endles aggravation of evil, and therfore this permission of divorce was givn to the Jews by the wisdom and fatherly providence of God; who knew that Law cannot command love, without which, matrimony hath no true beeing, no good, no solace, nothing of Gods instituting, nothing but so sordid and so low, as to bee disdain'd of any generous person. Law cannot inable natural inability either of body, or mind, which gives the greevance; it cannot make equal those inequalities, it cannot make fit those unfitnesses; and where there is malice more then defect of nature, it cannot hinder ten thousand injuries, and bitter actions of despight too suttle and too unapparent for Law to deal with. And while it seeks to remedy more outward wrongs, it exposes the injur'd person to other more inward and more cutting. All these evils unavoidably will redound upon the children, if any be, and the whole family. It degenerates and disorders the best spirits, leavs them to unsettl'd imaginations, and degraded hopes, careles of themselvs, their houshold and their freinds, unactive to all public service, dead to the Common-wealth; wherin they are by one mishapp, and no willing trespas of theirs, outlawd from all the benefits and comforts of married life and posterity. It conferrs as little to the honour and inviolable keeping of Matrimony, but sooner stirrs up temptations, and occasions to secret adulteries, and unchast roaving. But it maintaines public honesty. Public folly rather, who shall judge of public honesty? the Law of God, and of ancientest Christians, and all Civil Nations, or the illegitimat Law of Monks and Canonists, the most malevolent, most unexperienc't, and incompetent judges of Matrimony?

These reasons, and many more that might bee alleg'd, afford us plainly to perceav, both what good cause this Law had to doe for good men in mischances, and what necesity it had to suffer accidentally the hard heartednes of bad men, which it could not certainly discover, or discovering could not subdue, no nor indeavour to restrain without multiplying sorrow to them, for whom all was indeavour'd. The guiltles therfore were not depriv'd thir needful redresses, and the hard hearts of others unchastisable in those judicial Courts, were so remitted there, as bound over to the higher Session of Conscience.

Notwithstanding all this, ther is a loud exception against this Law of God, nor can the holy Author save his Law from this exception, that it opens a dore to all licence and confusion. But this is the rudest, I was almost saying the most graceles objection, and with the least reverence to God and *Moses*, that could bee devis'd: This is to cite God before mans Tribunal, to arrogate a wisdom and holines above him. Did not God then foresee what event of licence or confusion could follow? did not hee know how to ponder these abuses with more prevailing respects, in the most eevn ballance of his justice and purenes, till these correctors came up to shew him better? The Law is, if it stirre up sin any way, to stirre it up by forbidding, as one contrary excites another, *Rom.* 7. but if it once come to provoke sin, by granting licence to sin, according to Laws that have no other honest end, but only to permit the fulfilling of obstinat lust, how is God not made the contradicter of himself? No man denies that best things may bee abus'd: but it is a rule resulting from many pregnant experiences, that what doth most harm in the abusing, us'd rightly doth most good. And such a good to take away from honest men, for beeing abus'd by such as abuse all things, is the greatest abuse of all. That the

---

[47]The issue of the marriage, children.

whole Law is no furder usefull, then as a man uses it lawfully, St. *Paul* teaches, 1 *Tim.* 1. And that Christian liberty may bee us'd for an occasion to the flesh, the same Apostle confesses, *Galat.* 5. yet thinks not of removing it for that, but bidds us rather *Stand fast in the liberty wherwith Christ hath freed us, and not bee held again in the yoke of bondage.* The very permission which Christ gave to divorce for adultery, may bee fouly abus'd, by any whose hardnes of heart can either fain adultery, or dares committ, that hee may divorce. And for this cause the Pope, and hitherto the Church of *England*, forbid all divorce from the bond of mariage, though for openest adultery. If then it bee righteous to hinder for the fear of abuse, that which Gods Law notwithstanding that caution, hath warranted to bee don, doth not our righteousnes come short of Antichrist, or doe we not rather heerin conform our selvs to his unrighteousnes in this undue and unwise fear. For God regards more to releev by this Law the just complaints of good men, then to curb the licence of wicked men, to the crushing withall, and the overwhelming of his afflicted servants. He loves more that his Law should look with pitty upon the difficulties of his own, then with rigor upon the boundlesse riots of them who serv another Maister, and hinder'd heer by strictnes, will break another way to wors enormities. If this Law therfore have many good reasons for which God gave it, and no intention of giving scope to leudnes, but as abuse by accident comes in with every good Law, and every good thing, it cannot be wisdom in us, while we can content us with Gods wisdom, nor can be purity, if his purity will suffice us, to except against this Law, as if it foster'd licence. But if they affirm this Law had no other end, but to permitt obdurat lust, because it would bee obdurat, making the Law of God intentionally to proclame and enact sin lawful, as if the will of God were becom sinfull, or sin stronger then his direct and Law-giving will, the men would bee admonisht to look well to it, that while they are so eager to shut the dore against licence, they doe not open a wors dore to blasphemy. And yet they shall bee heer furder shewn thir iniquity; what more foul and common sin among us then drunkennes, and who can bee ignorant, that if the importation of Wine, and the use of all strong drink were forbid, it would both clean ridde the possibility of committing that odious vice, and men might afterwards live happily and healthfully, without the use of those intoxicating licors. Yet who is ther the severest of them all, that ever propounded to loos his Sack, his Ale, toward the certain abolishing of so great a sin, who is ther of them, the holiest, that less loves his rich Canary at meals, though it bee fetcht from places that hazard the Religion of them who fetch it,

and though it make his neighbour drunk out of the same Tunne? While they forbid not therfore the use of that liquid Marchandise, which forbidd'n would utterly remove a most loathsom sin, and not impair either the health, or the refreshment of mankind, suppli'd many other wayes, why doe they forbid a Law of God, the forbidding wherof brings into an excessive bondage, oft times the best of men, and betters not the wors? Hee to remove a Nationall vice, will not pardon his cupps, nor think it concerns him to forbear the quaffing of that outlandish[48] Grape, in his unnecessary fullnes, though other men abuse it never so much, nor is hee so abstemious as to intercede with the Magistrate that all matter of drunkennes be banisht the Common-wealth, and yet for the fear of a less inconvenience unpardnably requires of his brethren, in thir extreme necessity to debarre themselves the use of Gods permissive Law, though it might bee thir saving, and no mans indangering the more. Thus this peremptory strictnes we may discern of what sort it is, how unequal, and how unjust.

But it will breed confusion. What confusion it would breed, God himself took the care to prevent in the fourth verse of this Chapter, that the divorc't beeing maried to another, might not return to her former Husband. And *Justinians* law counsels the same in his Title of *Nuptials*. And what confusion els can ther bee in separation, to separat, upon extrem urgency, the Religious from the irreligious, the fit from the unfit, the willing from the wilfull, the abus'd from the abuser, such a separation is quite contrary to confusion. But to binde and mixe together holy with Atheist, hevnly with hellish, fitnes with unfitnes, light with darknes, antipathy with antipathy, the injur'd with the injurer, and force them into the most inward neernes of a detested union, this doubtles is the most horrid, the most unnatural mixture, the greatest confusion that can be confus'd?

Thus by this plain and Christian *Talmud* vindicating the Law of God from irreverent and unwary expositions, I trust, wher it shall meet with intelligible perusers, som stay at least of mens thoughts will bee obtain'd, to consider these many prudent and righteous ends of this divorcing permission. That it may have, for the great Authors sake, heerafter som competent allowance to bee counted a little purer then the prerogative of a legal and public ribaldry, granted to that holy seed. So that from hence wee shall hope to finde the way still more open to the reconciling of those places which treat this matter in the Gospel. And thether now without interruption the cours of method brings us.

---

[48]Foreign (most if not all wines drunk in England were imported, many from Roman Catholic countries).

Selected Personal Letters

Milton had much of his private correspondence, thirty-one letters, published in 1674, the last year of his life, under the title *Joannis Miltonii Angli, Epistolarum Familiarum Liber Unus*. Some of the academic prolusions filled out the little volume. The question for biographers, of course, is why Milton would have published letters to his tutor and his schoolmaster and his best friend, among others. The answer seems to have been to reinforce his own sense of mission, fame, and destiny, what Helgerson has called "self-fashioning" and applied to "self-crowned laureates." It is amazing what Milton saved, and what has survived, of his private as well as public writing, including what are now known as the Trinity Manuscript and the Commonplace Book. He seems to have kept his juvenile poems in Latin, Greek, and English; his notes to himself about what was important in his reading; and even his failed poems in English.

What do the letters tell us? The letters to Diodati record what Milton considers an exceptional friendship, with a man who would die young and be memorialized in Milton's Latin *Epitaphium Damonis*. The letters to the tutor and the schoolmaster, Thomas Young and Alexander Gill, preserve something of Milton's training as a poet under Gill, and as a Protestant and Puritan theologian under Young. These were letters that meant something in the intellectual and artistic development of a poet who knew from an early age that he was exceptional, heading toward immortality. Milton is showing us his relationships with friends, intellectual companions, and former students (Richard Heath must have been something of a pupil—*alumne* in Latin—to Milton).

The letters written to Milton's Italian friend Carlo Dati and to Leonard Philaras tell us of Milton's international stature: he was taken seriously by estimable men in other countries in western Europe. The letters to Philaras also tell us that Milton wished to be in touch with an Athenian Greek because of his love for the classical culture, and that he wished to receive the best medical aid for his blindness that could be found, in Paris, if necessary.

TEXT AND TRANSLATION

I have used the texts and the translations from the Yale *Complete Prose Works* of Milton, with the kind permission of Yale University Press. The texts for the English poetry are trustworthy and the translations, though at times dated, fulfill the goal of the translators that they "will please the modern reader and might not displease Milton" (Yale 1: 308). I have not altered the translations, though there are times when I believe that a detail like the capitalization might be misleading. "Medicine," for instance, was capitalized in the original printed text, but "Fables" was not (in the second letter to Diodati). Translations also have a leveling effect: the original letters to Diodati or Philaras, for instance, may have Greek mixed in with the Latin, but the translation makes it seem as if the original were all one language. The reader should consult at least the texts as preserved in the Columbia edition, to see a closer approximation of what each letter in its original languages looked like.

Works Cited

Helgerson, Richard. *Self-Crowned Laureates: Spenser, Jonson, Milton and the Literary System*. Berkeley: U of California P, 1983.

Miller, Leo. "Identifying More Milton Compositions." *John Milton's Writings in the Anglo-Dutch Negotiations, 1651–1654*. Pittsburgh, PA: Duquesne UP, 1992. 56–76.

Shawcross, John T. *John Milton: The Self and the World*. Lexington: UP of Kentucky, 1993.

[To Thomas Young, his Teacher (Latin, 1627?)][1]

Although I had inwardly resolved, best of Teachers, to send you a certain short Letter in meter,[2] I nevertheless did not think I had done enough until I had written yet another with an unfettered pen; for the expression of that unparalleled gratitude which your merits justly claim from me was not to be risked in that cramped style, straitened by fixed feet and syllables, but in the free language of Prose, nay rather, if possible in an Asiatic exuberance of words[3]—although, in truth, to express sufficiently how much I owe you were a work far greater than my strength, even if I should plunder all the Arguments collected by Aristotle and by that Logician of Paris,[4] even if I should exhaust all the springs of eloquence. You complain (as you justly can) that my letters to you are quite few and very short; but I really do not grieve at failing in so delightful and desirable a duty so much as I rejoice and almost exult at holding that position

---

[1]Thomas Young (1587?–1655) was Milton's tutor, possibly from 1618 to 1620, when Milton is supposed to have entered St. Paul's School. Aubrey records that a Puritan from Essex who taught Milton had his hair cut short: this rumored Puritan might have been the Presbyterian Young. Milton was writing to Young and his family in Hamburg, where, Milton's letter implies, he had been exiled for his religious opinions.
[2]Almost certainly Elegy 4.
[3]Ornate, rather than plain.
[4]Probably Peter Ramus (1515-72), whose system of logic replaced that of the Aristotelians, and who died a Protestant in Paris in the St. Bartholemew's Day massacre.

in your friendship which can require frequent letters. So please do not take it amiss that I have not written to you for more than three years, but in view of your wonderful good nature and sincerity, deign to interpret it leniently. For I call God to witness how much I honor you as a Father, with what singular respect I have always followed you, and how much I have feared to disturb you with my Writings. My primary purpose, no doubt, is that since nothing else recommends my letters, their rarity may. Next, since my overpowering longing for you always makes me think you near, and speak to you and look at you as though you were present, and so soothe my sorrow (as in love) with a certain vain fancy of your presence, I really fear that as soon as I should contemplate a letter to you, it would suddenly occur to me what a long distance you are from me; and so the pain of your absence, now almost lulled, would reawaken and shatter the sweet dream. The Hebrew Bible,[5] your very welcome gift, I have long since received. I have written these lines at London among the petty distractions of the city, not, as usual, surrounded by Books. Therefore if anything in this letter has not measured up to your expectation, it shall be compensated by another more carefully written, as soon as I have returned to the haunts of the Muses.[6]

London, March 26. 1625[?].[7]

[To Alexander Gil (Latin, 1628)]

In my former Letter I did not so much answer you, as avoid the duty of answering; and so I silently promised that another letter would soon follow, in which I should reply at somewhat greater length to your most friendly challenge. But even if I had not promised, it must be confessed that this letter is your most rightful due; for I think that each one of your letters cannot be repaid except by two of mine, or if it be reckoned more accurately, not even by a hundred of mine. Included with this letter, behold that project about which I wrote you somewhat more obscurely, a problem on which, when your Letter reached me, I was laboring with great effort, harried by the shortness of time. For by chance

a certain Fellow of our House,[8] who was going to act as Respondent in the Philosophical Disputation at this Academic Assembly, entrusted to my Puerility the Verses which annual custom requires to be written on the questions, he himself being long past light-minded nonsense of that kind and more intent on serious things. It is these, printed, that I have sent you, since I knew you to be the keenest judge of Poetry in general and the most honest judge of mine. Now if you will deign to send me yours in turn, there will certainly be no one who will enjoy them more, though there will be, I confess, one who will better appraise their merit. Indeed whenever I remember your almost constant conversations with me (which even in Athens itself, nay in the very Academy, I long for and need), I think immediately, not without sorrow, of how much benefit my absence has cheated me—me who never left you without a visible increase and growth of Knowledge, quite as if I had been to some Market of Learning. There is really hardly anyone among us, as far as I know, who, almost completely unskilled and unlearned in Philology and Philosophy alike, does not flutter off to Theology unfledged, quite content to touch that also most lightly, learning barely enough for sticking together a short harangue by any method whatever and patching it with worn-out pieces from various sources—a practice carried far enough to make one fear that the priestly Ignorance of a former age may gradually attack our Clergy. And so, finding almost no intellectual companions here, I should longingly look straight to London, did I not consider retiring into a deeply Literary leisure during this summer vacation and hiding as it were in the Cloisters of the Muses. But since you already do so every day, I think it almost a crime to interrupt you longer with my noise at present. Farewell.

Cambridge, July 2, 1628

[To a Friend (English, 1633)][9]

S[r], besides that in sundry other respects I must acknowledge me to proffit by you when ever wee meet, you are often to me, & were yesterday especially, as a good watch man to admonish that the howres of the night passe on (for so I call my life as yet obscure, & un-

---

[5]The book has not been found, but could have been the "Antwerp Polyglot" printed by Christopher Plantin in 1584 (Sims 5).

[6]Cambridge, which is the seat of the Muses when Milton is pleased with it (see the letter to Gill) or not hospitable to them when he is not (Elegy 1, to Diodati).

[7]The letter was more likely to have been written in 1627, according to William Riley Parker, "Milton and Thomas Young, 1620–28," *Modern Language Notes* 53 (1938): 399–407.

[8]The person is not identified, but the house is certainly Christ's College, Cambridge, and the verses are most probably "Naturam non Pati Senium."

[9]The friend is most likely Thomas Young, and the letter was almost undoubtedly written in 1633; see William Riley Parker, "Some Problems on the Chronology of Milton's Early Poems," *Review of English Studies* 11 (1935): 276–83.

serviceable to mankind) & that the day wth me is at hand wherin Christ commands all to Labour while there is light,[10] wch because I am persuaded you doe to no other purpose then out of a true desire that god[11] should be honourd in every one; I therfore thinke my selfe bound though unask'd, to give you account, as oft as occasion is, of this my tardie moving; according to the præcept of my conscience, wch I firmely trust is not w^thout god. Yet now I will not streine for any set apologie, but only referre my selfe to what my mynd shall have at any tyme to declare her selfe at her best ease. But if you thinke, as you said, that too much love of Learning is in fault, & that I have given up my selfe to dreame away my Yeares in the armes of studious retirement like Endymion wth the Moone as the tale of Latmus of [left blank] goes, yet consider that if it were no more but the meere love of Learning, whether it proceed from a principle bad, good, or naturall it could not have held out thus Long against so strong opposition of the other side of every kind, for if it be bad why should not all the fond hopes that forward Youth & Vanitie are fledge with together wth Gaine, pride, & ambition call me forward more powerfully, then a poore regardlesse & unprofitable sin of curiosity should be able to with hold me, wherby a man cutts himselfe off from all action & becomes the most helplesse, pusilanimous & unweapon'd creature in the word,[12] the most unfit & unable to doe that wch all mortals most aspire to either to defend & be usefull to his freinds, or to offend his enimies. Or if it be thought an naturall pronenesse there is against y^t a much more potent inclination inbred wch about this tyme of a mans life sollicits most, the desire of house & family of his owne to wch nothing is esteemed more helpefull then the early entring into credible employment, & nothing more hindering then this affected solitariness and though this were anough yet there is to this another act if not of pure, yet of refined nature no lesse available to dissuade prolonged obscurity, a desire of honour & repute, & immortall fame seated in the brest of every true scholar wch all make hast to by the readiest ways of publishing & divulging conceived merits as well those that shall as those that never shall obtain it, nature therfore would præsently worke the more prævalent way if there were nothing but ye inferiour bet of her selfe to restraine her. Lastly this Love of Learning as it is ye pursuit of something good, it would sooner follow the more excellent & supreme good knowne & præsented and so be

quickly diverted from the emptie & fantastick chase of shadows & notions to the solid good flowing from due & tymely obedience to that command in the gospell set out by the terrible seasing of him that hid the talent. It is more probably therfore that not the endlesse delight of speculation but this very consideration of that great commandment does not presse forward as soone as may be to underg[o] but keeps off wth a sacred reverence & religious advisement how best to undergoe not taking thought of beeing late so it give advantage to be more fit, for those that were latest lost nothing when the maister of the vinyard came to give each one his hire. & heere I am come to a streame[13] head copious enough to disburden it self like Nilus at seven mouthes into an ocean, but then I should also run into a reciprocall contradiction of ebbing & flowing at once & doe that wch I excuse myselfe for not doing preach & not preach. Yet that you may see that I am something suspicio[us] of my selfe, & doe take notice of a certaine belatedness in me I am the bolder to send you some of my nightward thoughts made some while since (because they com in not altogether unfitly) made up in a Petrarchan stanza. wch I told you of

after ye stanza [Sonnet 7]

by this I beleeve you may well repent of having mention at all of this matter, for if I have not all this while won you to this, I have certainly wearied you to it. This therfor alone may be a sufficient reason for me to keepe me as I am least having thus tired you singly, I should deale worse wth a whole congregation, & spoyle all the patience of a Parish. For I my selfe doe not only see my owne tediousnesse but now grow offended wth it that has hinderd [me] thus long from comming to the last & best period of my letter, & that wch must now cheifely worke by pardon that I am

Yo^r true and unfained freind.

[To Charles Diodati (Latin, 1637)]

Now at last I plainly see that you are trying to outdo me once in obstinate silence. If so, congratulations; have your little glory; see, I write first. Yet certainly, if ever we should debate the reasons why neither has written to the other for so long, do not doubt that I shall be much more excused than you. Obviously so, since I am naturally slow and lazy to write, as you well know; whereas you on the other hand, whether by nature or by habit, can usually be drawn into this sort of correspondence with ease. At the same time it is in my

---

[10]John 9.4; 12.35–36.
[11]The lack of capitalization might be an indication that Milton wished to de-mystify the word.
[12]Almost surely "world" was intended.

---

[13]The source of a stream: a spring.

favor that your habit of studying permits you to pause frequently, visit friends, write much, and sometimes make a journey. But my temperament allows no delay, no rest, no anxiety—or at least thought—about scarcely anything to distract me, until I attain my object and complete some great period, as it were, of my studies. And wholly for this reason, not another please, has it happened that I undertake even courtesies more tardily than you. In returning them however, my Diodati, I am not such a laggard; for I have never committed the crime of letting any Letter of yours go unanswered by another of mine. How is it that you, as I hear, have written Letters to the Bookseller, even oftener to your Brother, either of whom could conveniently enough, because of nearness, have been responsible for passing letters on to me—had there been any? But what I really complain of is that you, although you promised that you would visit us whenever you left the city, did not keep your promises. If you had once actually thought of these neglected promises, you would not have lacked immediate reason for writing. And so I had all these things to declaim against you, with reason I think; you will see to the answers yourself. But meanwhile, pray, how is everything? Are you quite well? Are there in those parts any fairly learned people with whom you can associate pleasantly and with whom you can talk, as we have been used to talking? When do you return? How long do you plan to linger among those Hyperboreans?[14] I should like you to answer these questions one by one. But you must not supposed that it is only now that I have your affairs at heart; for know that at the beginning of autumn I turned aside from a journey to see your brother, with the intention of finding out what you were doing. Again recently, when the news had been brought to me accidentally at London (by I know not whom) that you were in the city, immediately and as if by storm I hurried to your lodging, but "'t'was the vision of a shadow,"[15] for nowhere would you appear. Wherefore, if you conveniently can, fly higher with all speed and settle in some place which may offer brighter hope that somehow we may visit each other at least sometimes. Would that you could be as much my rustic neighbor as you are my urban one, but this as it pleases God. I wish I could say more, both about myself and about my studies, but I should prefer to do it in person. Furthermore, tomorrow we return to that country place of

ours, and the journey presses so close that I have scarcely been able to throw these words hastily on paper. Farewell.

London, Septemb. [November?] 2, 1637.[16]

To the Same (Latin, 1637)

I see now why you wish me so many healths, when my other friends in their Letters usually manage to wish me only one: you evidently want me to know that to those mere wishes which were all that you yourself could formerly and others can still offer, there are just now added to your art as well, and the whole mass as it were of medical power. For you bid me well six hundred times, as well as I wish to be, and so on. Certainly you must have recently been made Health's very steward, you so squander the whole store of salubrity; or rather Health herself must doubtless now be your Parasite, you so act the King and order her to obey. And so I congratulate you and must thank you on two scores, both for your friendship and for your excellent skill. Indeed, since we had agreed upon it, I long expected letters from you; but though I had not yet received any, I did not, believe me, allow my old affection towards you to cool because of such a trifle. On the contrary, I had already suspected that you would use that very same excuse for tardiness which you have used at the beginning of your Letter, and rightly so, considering the intimacy of our friendship. For I do not wish true friendship to be weighed by Letters and Salutations, which may all be false but on either hand to rest and sustain itself upon the deep roots of the soul, and, begun with sincere and blameless motives, even though mutual courtesies cease, to be free for life from suspicion and blame. For fostering such a friendship there is need not so much for writing as for a living remembrance of virtues on both sides. Even if you had not written, that obligation would not necessarily remain unfulfilled. Your worth writes to me instead and inscribes real letters on my inmost consciousness; your candor of character writes, and your love of right; your genius writes too (by no means an ordinary one) and further recommends you to me. Therefore do not try to terrorize me, now that you hold that tyrannical citadel of Medicine, as if you would take

---

[14]Probably just "northerners." We do not know where Diodati was when he received the letter.

[15]Quoted from Pindar, *Pythian Odes* 8.95. As the Yale editors point out, "In Milton's copy of Pindar at Harvard, the passage containing these words (p. 430) is underlined" (Yale 1: 324n).

[16]As the Yale editors point out, Milton, in dating the letter "2 IX 1637," Milton "may have taken the numeral to mean the ninth month New Style, or September, instead of Old Style, or November" (Yale 1: 325n). The same problem with dating applies to the next letter to Diodati as well.

back your six hundred healths, withdrawing them little by little, to the last one, should I by chance desert friendship, which God forbid. And so remove that terrible battery which you seem to have trained on me, forbidding me to be sick without your permission. For lest you threaten too much, know that I cannot help loving people like you. For though I do not know what else God may have decreed for me, this certainly is true: He has instilled into me, if into anyone, a vehement love of the beautiful. Not so diligently is Ceres, according to the Fables, said to have sought her daughter Proserpina, as I see for this idea of the beautiful, as if for some glorious image, throughout all the shapes and forms of things ("for many are the shapes of things divine");[17] day and night I search and follow its lead eagerly as if by certain clear traces. Whence it happens that if I find anywhere one who, despising the warped judgment of the public, dares to feel and speak and be that which the greatest wisdom throughout all ages has taught to be best, I shall cling to him immediately from a kind of necessity. But if I, whether by nature or by my fate, am so equipped that I can by no effort and labor of mine rise to such glory and height of fame, still, I think that neither men nor Gods forbid me to reverence and honor those who have attained that glory or who are successfully aspiring to it. But now I know you wish your curiosity satisfied. You make many anxious inquiries, even about what I am thinking. Listen, Diodati, but in secret, lest I blush; and let me talk to you grandiloquently for a while. You ask what I am thinking of? So help me God, an immortality of fame. What am I doing? Growing my wings and practicing flight. But my Pegasus still raises himself on very slender wings. Let me be wise on my humble level. I shall now tell you seriously what I am planning: to move into some one of the Inns of Court, wherever there is a pleasant and shady walk; for that dwelling will be more satisfactory, both for companionship, if I wish to venture forth. Where I am now, as you know, I live in obscurity and cramped quarters. You shall also hear about my studies. By continued reading I have brought the affairs of the Greeks to the time when they ceased to be Greeks. I have been occupied for a long time by the obscure history of the Italians under the Longobards, Franks, and Germans, to the time when liberty was granted to them by Rudolph, King of Germany. From there it will be better to read separately about what each State did by its own Effort. But what about you? How long will you act the son of the family and devote yourself to domestic matters, forgetting urban

companionships? For unless this stepmotherly warfare be more hazardous than the Dacian or Sarmatian, you must certainly hurry, and at least make your winter quarters with us. Meanwhile, if you conveniently can, please send me Giustiani, Historian of the Veneti.[18] On my word I shall see either that he is well cared for until your arrival, or, if you prefer, that he is returned to you shortly. Farewell.

London, Septemb. [November?] 23. 1637.

To Carlo Dati (Latin, 1647)

How new and great a joy fills me, my Charles, at the unexpected arrival of your letter; since I cannot describe it adequately, I want you to form some idea of it, at least from that attendant pain without which men have scarcely ever known delight. For while running through the first part of your letter, in which elegance vies so beautifully with friendship, I should have called my feeling one of unmixed joy, especially since I see that you take pains to make friendship the victor. But as soon as I reach that passage in which you write that you have already sent me three letters, which I know have been lost, then, first, that sincere joy begins to be tainted, and disturbed by a sad longing; soon an even heavier mood creeps over me, a mood in which I am accustomed often to bewail my lot, to lament that those whom perhaps proximity or some unprofitable tie has bound to me, whether by accident or by law, those, commendable in no other way, daily sit beside me, weary me—even exhaust me, in fact—as often as they please;[19] whereas those whom character, temperament, interests had so finely united are now nearly all grudged me by death, or most hostile distance and are for the most part so quickly torn from my sight that I am forced to live in almost perpetual solitude. I strongly congratulate myself that ever since I left Florence, you have, you say, been concerned about my health and have always kept me in mind; and I congratulate myself that the feeling was equal and mutual which I, perhaps with reason, had thought was mine alone. That

---

[17]The stock phrase to end a play by Euripides.

[18]Bernardo Giustiani (called in Latin Justinianus Bernardus), *De Origine Urbis Venetiarum Rebusque ab Ipsa Gestis Historia* (Venice, 1492). As the Yale editors point out, "An Italian translation appeared in 1545 and again in 1608" (Yale 1: 328n).

[19]In 1646 and 1647, Milton's household was large and in political and personal disarray: Mary Powell Milton's Royalist family had moved in with Milton, despite Richard Powell's refusal to pay his son-in-law's dowry and Mrs. Powell's dislike for her daughter's husband. In January 1647 Richard Powell died; in March Milton's father died; and, soon after that, the remaining members of the Powell family, excepting Mary, of course, found lodging elsewhere.

separation, I may not conceal from you, was also very painful for me; and it fixed those stings in my heart which even now rankle whenever I think that, reluctant and actually torn away, I left so many companions and at the same time such good friends, and such congenial ones in a single city—a city distant indeed but to me most dear. I call to witness the tomb of Damon (which shall always be sacred and solemn to me) that when I was burdened with the task of adorning it with every tribute of grief, when I wanted to turn to what comforts I could and pause for breath, I could think of nothing pleasanter than to recall my dearest memory of you all, of you, Dati, especially. All this you must have read for yourself long since, if indeed that poem reached you, as from you I now first hear it did. I had had it sent purposely, so that it might be, however small a proof of talent, by no means an obscure proof of my love for you, at least in those few little verses inserted—as it were inlaid—there. I thought by this means to entice either you or another to write; for if I wrote first, I had either to write to all, or, by preferring one, to offend, I feared, those of the others who came to know it—since I hope there still survive among you many who could surely claim that attention from me. Now you, first, have freed my long-due correspondence from the reproach of the others, both by this letter's most friendly appeal and by your previous triple repetition of the courtesy. Yet I confess that, since I returned home, there has been an additional reason for silence in the extremely turbulent state of our Britain, which quickly compelled me to turn my mind from my studies to protecting life and property in any way I could. Do you think there can be any safe retreat for literary leisure among so many civil battles, so much slaughter, flight, and pillaging of goods? Nevertheless, since you ask about my studies, know that even among these evils we have given to the light not a few things in our native language, which, were they not in English, I should gladly send all of you, whose opinions I value highly. Yet since you wish it, I shall shortly send you that part of the poems which is in Latin; and I should have sent it of my own accord long since, had I not suspected that they would be rather unpleasing to your ears because of those words spoken rather sharply on some pages against the Roman Pope. Now I beg you to obtain from my other friends (for of you I am certain) that same indulgence to freedom of speech which, as you know, you have been used to granting in the past with singular kindness—I do not mean to your Dante and Petrarch in this case, but to me; I crave it now whenever mention be made of your religion according to our custom. I am reading with pleasure your description of the funeral of King Louis, in which I recognize your Mercury, not that presiding

over the cross-roads and dedicated to merchandise, which you jest that you have been cultivating recently, but that which is eloquent, welcome to the Muses, and protector of Mercurial men. It remains for us to decide upon some means whereby our letters may come and go by a sure route. This does not seem very difficult, since so many of our merchants have both large and numerous business transactions in your city; their letter carriers run back and forth every week, and their ships sail from both sides not much less often. This business I shall entrust, rightly I hope, to James, the bookseller, or to his master, a most familiar acquaintance of mine. Meanwhile, my Charles, farewell and give my best greeting to Coltellini, Francini, Frescobaldi, Malatesta, Chimentelli the younger, and any other of our group whom you know to be especially fond of me—in short to the whole Gaddian Academy. Again farewell.

London, April 21, 1647.

To Leonard Philaras (Latin, June, 1652)

To the most distinguished Leonard Philaras, of Athens, Ambassador from the Duke of Parma to the King of France,

I learned of your goodwill toward me, most honored Leonard Philaras, as well as your high opinion of my *Defense of the English People*, from your letter written partly on this subject to Mr. Augier,[20] a man renowned here for his remarkable fidelity in transacting the diplomatic business of this state. Then I received by the same means your greeting sent with your portrait and with the eulogism full worthy of your merits; then finally your most gracious letter.

And since I am wont to spurn not even the talents of the Germans, not even of the Danes or Swedes, you may be sure that I cannot help valuing very highly the opinion held of me by you, who, both born amid Attic learning, and having successfully completed a liberal education in Italy, have attained public office by distinguished handling of practical affairs. For as Alexander the Great himself, waging war to the ends of the earth, declared that he had carried out such vast campaigns "for the sake of the good opinion of the

---

[20]René Augier, French by birth but a naturalized English citizen and an English agent to Paris from November, 1644, to 1649. At the time of this letter, he was "used in special diplomatic business by the Council of State," according to Parker 418 and he served as translator of official documents (Parker 972n).

Athenians,"[21] why should not I congratulate myself and think myself extraordinarily honored by the praises of that man, in whom alone at this time the renowned arts and abilities of the ancient Athenians seem after so long an interval to revive and rebloom? Since so many of the most eloquent men have come from that city, I gladly confess that whatever literary proficiency I have achieved, I learned chiefly by reading their writings from my youth onwards. But if I had received from them and absorbed such power of persuasion that I could call forth our army and navy to free Greece, land of eloquence, from the Ottoman tyrant[22]—an honorable act for which you seem almost to implore our aid—truly there is nothing which I should rather or sooner do. For what did either the bravest or the most eloquent men of old consider more glorious or more worthy of them than "to make the Greeks free and independent,"[23] either by persuasion or by brave action? But there is another thing to be attempted, in my opinion the most important, that someone should stir and ignite the ancient courage, diligence, and endurance in the souls of the Greeks by singing of that bygone zeal. If anyone could accomplish this—which we should expect from none more than you, because of your eminent patriotism, together with greater prudence and military skill, and finally with a powerful passion for recovering former political liberty—I am confident that neither would the Greeks fail themselves, nor any nation fail the Greeks. Farewell.

London, June, 1652.

[To Richard Heath, Latin (December 13, 1652)][24]

To Richard Heath.

If I have ever been able to give any aid, most respected friend, whether in advancing your studies or in arranging assistance for them, it was really little or nothing; still, I am glad on more than one account that it should have been so lightly and auspiciously bestowed on a fine talent (though recognized somewhat late) and that it should have been already so fruitful that it has

produced an upright pastor of the church and a worthy citizen of his country and even a most welcome friend for myself. This of course I can easily perceive not only from the rest of your life and from the opinion which you clearly hold concerning religion and the state but especially from your singular gratitude, which can be diminished or extinguished by no absence, no encroachment of age. For it is not possible, unless you had made more than mediocre progress in virtue and piety and study of the finest things, that you should be so grateful toward those who have given you even the least aid in acquiring them. Therefore, my foster son, for I gladly use this name for you, if you allow, I want you to think that I love you most dearly, and that I should like nothing better, if your convenience and circumstances permitted, and because I see you wish it, than that you live somewhere near me, so that we might have more frequent and more pleasant intercourse of life and studies. But that as God wills and you find expedient.

Hereafter you may, if you please, write in English (although you have made considerable progress in Latin) lest at any time the labor of writing should render either of us slower to write, and so that our feeling for one another may express itself more freely, unfettered by an alien tongue.

Moreover, you may, I think, safely trust your letters to any one of the servants of the family you have mentioned. Farewell.

Westminster, December 13, 1652.

[To Henry Oldenburg (Latin, July 6, 1654)]

To Henry Oldenburg, agent for Bremen to the English Parliament.

Your former letter,[25] most honored sir, was given to me when your messenger was said to be on the point of returning; thus there was no chance of replying at that time, Unless some unexpected business had prevented my intended prompt reply, I should certainly not have sent my book to you (though fortified by the title of defense) so naked and defenseless. Since then behold your second letter, expressing thanks excessive for the slightness of the gift. It occurred to me more than once to answer your Latin in English, so that you, who have learned, in addition, our speech more accurately and successfully than any other foreigner I know, should lose no opportunity for writing it too, which I believe you can do with equal accuracy. But that as you wish,

---

[21]An inexact quotation from Plutarch, *Alexander* 60.3.
[22]The Ottoman Turks controlled the Peloponnesus and most of the Greek islands, treating the Greeks with noted cruelty. As Milton knew, the Ottoman Empire threatened Venice as well.
[23]Again, no specific source has been found, though the Yale editors record that Milton could have been citing Demosthenes from a variety of orations (Yale 4.2: 853n).
[24]For the sparse information we have about Heath, see Austin Woolrych, "Milton and Richard Heath," *Philological Quarterly* 53 (1974): 132–35, which establishes that Heath was Vicar of St. Alkmund's, Shrewsbury, from 1650 to 1662.

[25]Not yet located.

however henceforth the spirit moves. As to your subject matter, you fully agree with me that this sort of cry to heaven exceeds all human powers of perception, wherefore the more shameless he who claims so boldly to have heard it. However, you scruple his identity, notwithstanding that recently, when we talked about this matter several times shortly after you came here from Holland, you seemed to have no doubt that the author was Morus, since that was certainly the opinion there and since no one else was named, so if you have more certain knowledge of the matter, I beg you to inform me. As to the handling of the argument I certainly wish (for why dissemble) that I did not differ from you; what indeed could more easily persuade me to attempt it than the sincere judgment and praise free from flattery of such wise men as you? To prepare myself for other labors, whether nobler or more useful I do not really know (for what among human endeavors can be nobler or more useful than the protection of liberty), I can be easily persuaded, if illness allow and this blindness, which is more oppressive than the whole of old age, and finally the cries of such brawlers. For an idle leisure has never pleased me, and this unexpected contest with the enemies of liberty snatched me unwilling from studies far different and altogether more delightful. Not that I regret the contest by any means, since it was necessary, for I am far from believing that I have spent my labor on vain things, as you seem to suggest.

But of these matters, another time. That I may detain you no further, most learned sir, farewell; and count me among your friends.

Westminster, July 6, 1654.

[To Leonard Philaras (Latin, September 28, 1654)]

To Leonard Philaras, Athenian,

Since I have been from boyhood a worshiper of all things Greek and of your Athens first and foremost, I have always been most firmly convinced that this city would someday nobly recompense my good will towards her. Nor has the ancient spirit of your noble country belied my prophecy, but has given me you, both an Attic brother and a very loving one: it was you who addressed me most kindly by letter, though far distant and knowing me only by my writings; and afterwards, arriving unexpectedly in London, you continued that kindness by going to see one who could not see, even in that misfortune which has made me more respectable to none, more despicable to many. And so, since you tell me that I should not give up all hope of regaining my sight, that you have a friend and intimate

in the Paris physician Thévenin[26] (especially outstanding as an oculist), whom you will consult about my eyes if only I send you the means by which he can diagnose the causes and symptoms of the disease, I shall do what you urge, that I may not seem to refuse aid whencesoever offered, perhaps divinely.

It is ten years, I think, more or less, since I noticed my sight becoming weak and growing dim, and at the same time my spleen and all my viscera burdened and shaking with flatulence. And even in the morning, if I began as usual to read, I noticed that my eyes felt immediate pain deep within and turned from reading, though later refreshed after moderate bodily exercise; as often as I looked at a lamp, a sort of rainbow seemed to obscure it. Soon a mist appearing in the left part of the left eye (for that eye became clouded some years before the other) removed from my sight everything on that side. Objects further forward too seemed smaller, if I chanced to close my right eye. The other eye also failing slowly and gradually over a period of almost three years, some months before my sight was completely destroyed, everything which I distinguished when I myself was still seemed to swim, now to the right, now to the left. Certain permanent vapors seem to have settled upon my entire forehead and temples, which press and oppress my eyes with a sort of sleepy heaviness, especially from mealtime to evening, so that I often think of the Salmydessian seer Phineus in the *Argonauts*,

All round him then there grew
A purple thickness; and he thought the earth
Whirling beneath his feet, and so he sank,
Speechless at length, into a feeble sleep.[27]

But I must not omit that, while considerable sight still remained, when I would first go to bed and lie on one side or the other, abundant light would dart from my closed eyes; then, as sight daily diminished, colors proportionately darker would burst forth with violence and a sort of crash from within; but now, pure black, marked as if with extinguished or ashy light, and as if interwoven with it, pours forth. Yet the mist which always hovers before my eyes both night and day seems always to be approaching white rather than black; and upon the eyes turning, it admits a minute quantity of light as if through a crack.

---

[26]See James H. Hanford, "John Milton Forswears Physic," *Bulletin of the Medical Library Association* 32 (1944): 22–34, for a discussion of the work of François Thévenin (d. 1656), called "*Tevenotus*" in Milton's Latin and "Thévenot" in the Yale Prose (4.2: 869 and n.).

[27]Masson's translation of Apollonius of Rhodes, *Argonautica* 2.205–08. Milton identifies with the prophet Phineus, to whom a vengeful Jove gave a lingering old age and the affliction of blindness, for his irreverence.

Although some glimmer of hope too may radiate from that physician, I prepare and resign myself as if the case were quite incurable; and I often reflect that since many days of darkness are destined to everyone, as the wise man warns,[28] mine thus far, by the signal kindness of Providence, between leisure and study, and the voices and visits of friends, are much more mild than those lethal ones. But if, as proceedeth out of the mouth of God,[29] why should one not likewise find comfort in believing that he cannot see by the eyes alone, but by the guidance and wisdom of God. Indeed while He himself looks out for me and provides for me, which He does, and takes me as if by the hand and leads me throughout life, surely, since it has pleased Him, I shall be pleased to grant my eyes a holiday.

And you, my Philaras, whatever happens, I bid you farewell with a spirit no less stout and bold than if I were Lynceus.[30]

Westminster, September 28, 1654.

To Peter Heimbach (Latin, August 15, 1666)[31]

If, among so many deaths of my countrymen, and in a year so poisonous and plague-ridden, especially because of some rumor you believed that I too (as you write) had been borne away, it is no wonder; and if (as it seems) that rumor sprang up among your people because they were concerned about my welfare, it is not displeasing to me, for I take that as evidence of their good will towards me. But by the blessing of God, who had prepared a safe place for me in the country,[32] I am both alive and well. Let me not be useless, whatever remains for me in this life. But that thoughts of me should come to your mind after so long a time is pleasant indeed, even though as you embellish the fact with words—*admiring* (as you write) the marriage of so many various virtues, you seem to support some *suspicion*[33] that you have forgotten me instead. I should most certainly dread the multifarious offspring of so many marriages, were it not well-known that virtues grow and flourish most in straitened and difficult circumstances. One of those Virtues has not so pleasantly repaid to me the charity of hospitality, however, for the one you call *Policy* (and which I would prefer to call *Patriotism*), after having allured me by her lovely name, has almost *expatriated* me, as it were. The singing of the others sounds well together, however. One's *Patria* is wherever it is well with him. Let me conclude (if I may first beg this of you), that if you should find here anything badly written or not punctuated, blame it on the boy who wrote this down while utterly ignorant of Latin, for I was forced while dictating—and not without some difficulty—to completely spell out every single letter. In the meantime, I am pleased that your merits as a man (whom I knew as a youth of exceptional promise) have brought you to a place of such honor in the favor of your prince;[34] and I wish and hope for you all good fortune. Farewell.

London, August 15, 1666.

[28]"But if a man live many years, and rejoice in them all; yet let him remember the days of darkness; for they shall be many. All that cometh is vanity" (Ecclesiastes 11.8).

[29]". . . man doth not live by bread only, but by every word that proceedeth out of the mouth of the Lord doth man live" (Deuteronomy 8.3).

[30]The Argonaut most famous for his keen eyesight.

[31]Milton's letter is in response to a letter from Peter Heimbach dated May 27/June 6, 1666. The two letters are the last we have of Milton's correspondence. Heimbach, the son of Weinand von Heimbach, Chancellor of the Duchy of Cleves, had sought Milton's recommendation for the position of secretary to George Downing, minister to The Hague, in 1657 (Yale 8: 1). In 1656, the two had been good enough friends for Milton to ask Heimbach to shop for an atlas for him on the Continent and to inscribe for Heimbach a copy of his 1645 *Poems* (*Chronology* 168; John Shawcross, "A Note on a Copy of Milton's Poems," *Milton Quarterly* 25 (1991): 107–08).

[32]At Chalfont St. Giles, about twenty miles from London and therefore presumed safe from the plague, in the house found for Milton by Thomas Ellwood.

[33]Heimbach's Latin word, "suspicio," meant "look up to" or "respect" in classical Latin, but by Milton's time it included the meaning of "suspect" (see Yale 8.4n). Throughout the letter, Milton makes fun of the inept and sometimes tactless Latin of Heimbach's letter to him, a translation of which is in Yale 8: 2–3.

[34]Heimbach had been appointed state councillor to the Elector of Brandenburg in 1664.

The Tenure of Kings and Magistrates
(1649?)

Written between January 15 and 29, 1649 (Campbell, *Chronology*, 1649), shortly before the public execution of King Charles I on January 30, the tract is a public defense of the judicious murder of a king. When a king no longer serves as a public servant, when he listens to the advice of corrupt priests and flatterers, he is apt to become a tyrant. Then the people have the right, Milton believes, to rise up, put the king on trial for malfeasance of duty, and, if necessary, execute him.

Putting both kings and magistrates in his title, with the "and" to connect them, Milton levels the two ranks and derives their position from the consent of the people they are elected to govern. Both kings and magistrates must deserve their offices, and neither should feel divinely appointed or entitled to unlimited power. Kings are not above the law: "on the autority of Law the autority of a Prince depends, and to the Laws ought submitt." In what appears to be the equivalent of subliminal suggestion, Milton has apparently instructed his printer Matthew Simmons to spell the word "Law" almost always with an initial capital letter, as if burying the message that Law is more important than will, and that "King" is a name only, unless the office is honored by the person who fills it. Milton is working toward a theory of government by the consent of the governed, in which election is always better than hereditary inheritance or privileged appointment: ". . . Justice is the onely true sovran and supreme Majesty upon earth."

OCCASION

Milton's service may or may not have been enlisted or instigated by some individual who was a strong partisan of the Independents (Yale 3: 184) in the turbulent time just before the King's execution. Milton, who had recently been writing on what was to become the *History of Britain*, was well prepared to document his subject. He obviously relished the controversy, and his polemical career attacking the church hierarchy in the early 1640s had sharpened his prose. By March of 1649 the writing of *The Tenure* would pay dividends for him. As Christopher Hill puts it, "There followed recognition at last, in an invitation from the Council of State to accept the post of Secretary for Foreign Tongues" (170).

Milton saw the defense of the King's potential execution in terms of epic or tragic heroism. He could picture Parliament as heroic protagonist fighting the evils of tyranny, according to the rhetoric of the Civil Wars, and thus he could combine poetic imagery with the defense of a political position.

With the aid of his printer, Milton constructed a title page that announced his triumph, loudly, "PROVING, That it is Lawfull, and hath been held so through all Ages, for any, who have the Power to call to account a Tyrant, or wicked KING, and after due conviction, to depose, and put him to death; if the ordinary MAGISTRATE have neglected, or deny'd to doe it." To this was added a kind of "I told you so": "And they, who of late so much blame [d]eposing, are the men that did it themselves."

TEXT

Merritt Hughes documents the various issues of the first and second editions (Yale 3: 184–86). One of Milton's favorite printers, Matthew Simmons, carefully printed the edition preferred by editors, that dated 1649 (n.s. 1650, probably published just before Thomason marked it on February 15 of that year). Hughes's edition in the Yale series is remarkable for its thorough notes. William T. Allison produced the only other annotated edition, for *Yale Studies in English* in 1921. Simmons announced the edition proudly as "Published now the second time with some additions, and many Testimonies also added out of the best & learnedest among Protestant Divines asserting the position of this book" (title page).

THE TENURE OF
KINGS
And MAGISTRATES.

IF men within themselves would be govern'd by reason, and not generally give up thir understanding to a double tyrannie, of Custom from without, and blind affections within, they would discerne better, what it is to favour and uphold the Tyrant of a Nation. But being slaves within doors,[1] no wonder that they strive so much to have the public State conformably govern'd to the inward vitious rule, by which they govern themselves. For indeed none can love freedom heartilie, but good men; the rest love not freedom, but licence; which never hath more scope or more indulgence then under Tyrants. Hence it is that Tyrants are not oft offended, nor stand much in doubt of bad men, as being all naturally servile; but in whom vertue and

---

[1] In their own homes.

true worth most is eminent, them they feare in earnest, as by right thir Maisters, against them lies all thir hatred and suspicion. Consequentlie neither doe bad men hate Tyrants, but have been alwayes readiest with the falsifi'd names of *Loyalty*, and *Obedience*, to colour over thir base compliances. And although somtimes for shame, and when it comes to thir owne grievances, of purse especially, they would seeme good Patriots, and side with the better cause, yet when others for the deliverance of thir Countrie, endu'd with fortitude and Heroick vertue to feare nothing by the curse writt'n against those *That doe the worke of the Lord negligently*,[2] would goe on to remove, not only the calamities and thraldoms of a People, but the roots and causes whence they spring, streight[3] these men, and sure helpers at need, as if they hated only the miseries but not the mischiefs, after they have juggl'd and palter'd[4] with the world, bandied and born armes against thir King, devested him, disannointed him, nay curs'd him all over in thir Pulpits and thir Pamphlets, to the ingaging of sincere and real men, beyond what is possible or honest to retreat from, not only turn revolters from those principles, which only could at first move them, but lay the staine of disloyaltie, and worse, on those proceedings, which are the necessary consequences of thir own former actions; nor dislik'd by themselves, were they manag'd to the intire advantages of thir own Faction; not considering the while that he toward whom they boasted thir new fidelitie, counted them accessory; and by those Statutes and Lawes which they so impotently brandish against others, would have doom'd them to a Traytors death, for what they have don alreadie. 'Tis true, that most men are apt anough to civill Wars and commotions as a noveltie, and for a flash hot and active; but through sloth or inconstancie, and weaknes of spirit either fainting, ere thir own pretences, though never so just, be half attain'd, or through an inbred falshood and wickednes, betray oft times to destruction with themselves, men of noblest temper joyn'd with them for causes, wherof they in their rash undertakings were not capable.

If God and a good cause give them Victory, the prosecution wherof for the most part, inevitably draws after it the alteration of Lawes, change of Goverment, downfal of Princes with thir families; then comes the task to those Worthies which are the soule of that enterprize, to be swett and labour'd out amidst the throng and noises of Vulgar and irrational men. Some contesting for privileges, customs, forms, and that old entanglement of Iniquity, thir gibrish Lawes, though the badge of thir ancient slavery. Others who have beene fiercest against thir Prince, under the notion of a Tyrant, and no mean incendiaries of the Warr against him, when God out of his providence and high disposal hath deliver'd him into the hand of thir brethren, on a suddain and in a new garbe of Allegiance, which thir doings have long since cancell'd; they plead for him, pity him, extoll him, protest against those that talk of bringing him to the tryal of Justice, which is the Sword of God, superior to all mortal things, in whose hand soever by apparent signes his testified will is to put it. But certainly if we consider who and what they are, on a suddain grown so pitifull, wee may conclude, thir pitty can be no true, and Christian commiseration, but either levitie, and shallowness of minde, or else a carnal admiring of that worldly pomp and greatness, from whence they see him fall'n; or rather lastly a dissembl'd and seditious pity, fain'd of industry to begett new discord. As for mercy, if it be to a Tyrant, under which Name they themselves have cited him so oft in the hearing of God, of Angels, and the holy Church assembl'd, and there charg'd him with the spilling of more innocent blood by farr, then ever *Nero* did, undoubtedly the mercy which they pretend, is the mercy of wicked men; and their mercies, wee read[5] are cruelties; hazarding the welfare of a whole Nation, to have sav'd one, whom so oft they have tearm'd *Agag*;[6] and vilifying the blood of many *Jonathans*,[7] that have sav'd *Israel*; insisting with much niceness[8] on the unnecessariest clause of thir Covnant wrested, wherein the feare of change, and the absurd contradiction of a flattering hostilitie had hamperd them, but not scrupling to give away for complements, to an implacable revenge, the heads of many thousands Christians more.

Another sort there is, who comming in the cours of these affaires, to have thir share in great actions, above the form of Law or Custom, at least to give thir voice and approbation, begin to swerve, and almost shiver at the Majesty and grandeur of som noble deed, as if they were newly enter'd into a great sin; disputing presidents, forms, and circumstances, when the Common-wealth nigh perishes for want of deeds in substance, don with

---

[2]A marginal note adds "*Jer.* 48.19." Hughes's note (Yale 3: 191) points out that the reference should be to Jeremiah 48.10, curses aimed at the Moabite enemy.
[3]Straightway; immediately. The men are the Presbyterians.
[4]Deceived and equivocated (conned and lied).

[5]There is a marginal note to "*Prov.* 12.10."
[6]The king of the Amelikites whom Samson cut in pieces "before the Lord" (1 Samuel 15.33).
[7]The son of Saul, Jonathan, caused his father's displeasure in his victory over the Philistines but was saved from his wrath by the Israelites (1 Samuel 14. 1–45).
[8]Hairsplitting; too great precision.

just an faithful expedition. To these I wish better instruction, and vertue equal to thir calling; the former of which, that is to say Instruction, I shall indeavour, as my dutie is, to bestow on them; and exhort them not to startle[9] from the just and pious resolution of adhering with all thir strength & assistance to the present Parlament & Army, in the glorious way wherin Justice and Victory hath set them; the only warrants through all ages, next under immediat Revelation, to exercise supream power, in those proceedings which hitherto appeare equal to what hath been don in any age or Nation heretofore, justly or magnanimouslie. Nor let them be discourag'd or deterr'd by any new Apostate Scarcrowes, who under show of giving counsel, send out their barking monitories and *memento's*, empty of ought else but the spleene of a frustrated Faction. For how can that pretended counsel bee either sound or faithfull, when they that give it, see not for madness and vexation of thir ends lost, that those Statutes and Scriptures which both falsly and scandalously, they wrest against thir Friends and Associates, would by sentence of the common adversarie, fall first and heaviest upon thir own heads. Neither let milde and tender dispositions be foolishly softn'd from thir duty and perseverance, with the unmaskuline Rhetorick of any puling[10] Priest or Chaplain, sent as a friendly Letter of advice, for fashion sake in privat, and forthwith publisht by the Sender himself, that wee may know how much of friend there was in it, to cast an odious envie upon them to whom it was pretended to be sent in charitie. Nor let any man be deluded by either the ignorance or the notorious hypocrisie and self-repugnance of our dancing Divines, who have the conscience and the boldness, to come with Scripture in thir mouthes, gloss'd and fitted for thir turnes with a double contradictory sense, transforming the sacred verity of God, to an Idol with two Faces, looking at once two several ways; and with the same quotations to charge others, which in the same case thy made serve to justifie themselves. For while the hope to bee made Classic and Provincial Lords[11] led them on, while pluralities greas'd them thick and deep, to the shame and scandal of Religion, more then all the Sects and Heresies they exclaim against, then to fight against the Kings person, and no less a Party of his Lords and Commons, or to put force upon both the Houses, was good, was lawfull, was no resisting of Superior powers;

they onely were powers not to be resisted, who countenanc'd the good, and punish't the evil. But now that thir censorious domineering is not suffer'd to be universal, truth and conscience to be freed, Tithes and Pluralities[12] to be no more, though competent allowance provided, and the warme experience of large gifts, and they so good at taking them; yet now to exclude & seize upon impeach't Members, to bring Delinquents without exemption to a faire Tribunal by the common National Law against murder, is now to be no less then *Corah*, *Dathan*, and *Abiram*.[13] He who but erewhile in the Pulpits was a cursed Tyrant, an enemie to God and Saints, lad'n with all the innocent blood spilt in three Kingdoms, and so to be fought against, is now, though nothing penitent or alter'd from his first principles, a lawfull Magistrate, a Sovran Lord, the Lords anointed, not to be touch'd, though by themselves improson'd. As if this onely were obedience, to preserve the meere useless bulke of his person, and that onely in prison, not in the field, and to disobey his commands, deny him his dignity and office, every where to resist his power but where they thinke it onely surviving in thir own faction.

But who in particular is a Tyrant cannot be determin'd in a general discours, otherwise then by supposition; his particular charge, and the sufficient proof of it must determin that: which I leave to Magistrates, at least to the uprighter sort of them, and of the people, though in number less by many, in whom faction least hath prevaild above the Law of nature and right reason, to judge if they find cause. But this I dare owne as part of my faith, that if such a one there be, by whose Commission, whole massachers have been committed on his faithfull Subjects, his Provinces offerd to pawn or alienation, as the hire of those whom he had sollicited to come in and destroy whole Citties and Countries; be he King, or Tyrant, or Emperour, the Sword of Justice is above him; in whose hand soever is found sufficient power to avenge the effusion, and so great a deluge of innocent blood. For if all human power to execute, not accidentally but intendedly, the wrath of God upon evil doers without exception, be of God; then that power, whether ordinary, or if that faile, extraordinary so executing that intent of God, is lawfull, and not to be resisted. But to unfold more at large this whole Question, though with all expedient brevity, I shall here set downe from first beginning, the original of Kings; how and wherfore exalted to that dignitie above thir Breth-

---

[9]To jump quickly out of danger, or, metaphorically, to swerve from a resolution.
[10]Babbling, mumbling.
[11]As Hughes points out, the Westminster Assembly had intended that English Presbyterians should be organized into provinces, and, below that, into classical assemblies or classes (Yale 3: 196n).

[12]Tithes were taxes collected for the support of the clergy, a practice that Milton bitterly opposed as late as *Considerations Touching the Likeliest Means* (1659). Pluralities or multiple church appointments were traditionally given to the nobility by virtue of their education.
[13]Biblical monarchs rightfully executed.

ren; and from thence shall prove, that turning to Tyranny they may bee as lawfuly depos'd and punish'd, as they were at first elected· This I shall doe by autorities and reasons, not learnt in corners among Scisms and Heresies, as our doubling Divines are ready to calumniat, but fetch't out of the midst of choicest and most authentic learning, and no prohibited Authors, nor many Heathen, but Mosaical, Christian, Orthodoxal, and which must needs be more convincing to our Adversaries, Presbyterial.

No man who knows ought, can be so stupid to deny that all men naturally were borne free, being the image and resemblance of God himself, and were by privilege above all the creatures, born to command and not to obey: and that they liv'd so. Till from the root of *Adams* transgression, falling among themselves to doe wrong and violence, and foreseeing that such courses must needs tend to the destruction of them all, they agreed by common league to bind each other from mutual injury, and joyntly to defend themselves against any that gave disturbance or opposition to such agreement. Hence came Citties, Townes and Common-wealths. And because no faith in all was found sufficiently binding, they saw it needfull to ordaine som authoritie, that might restrain by force and punishment what was violated against peace and common right. This autoritie and power of self-defence and preservation being originally and naturally in every one of them, and unitedly in them all, for ease, for order, and least each man should be his own partial Judge, they communicated and deriv'd either to one, whom for the eminence of his wisdom and integritie they chose above the rest, or to more then one whom they thought of equal deserving: the first was call'd a King; the other Magistrates. Not to be thir Lords and Maisters (though afterward those names in som places were giv'n voluntarily to such as had been Authors of inestimable good to the people) but, to be thir Deputies and Commissioners, to execute, by vertue of thir intrusted power, that justice which else every man by the bond of nature and of Cov'nant must have executed for himself, and for one another. And to him that shall consider well why among free Persons, one man by civil right should beare autority and jurisdiction over another, no other end or reason can be imaginable. These for a while govern'd well, and with much equity decided all things at thir own arbitrement: til the temptation of such a power left absolute in thir hands, perverted them at length to injustice and partialitie. Then did they who now by tryal had found the danger and inconveniences of committing arbitrary power to any, invent Laws either fram'd, or consented to by all, that should confine and limit the autority or whom they chose to govern them: that so man, of

whose failing they had proof, might no more rule over them, but law and reason abstracted as much as might be from personal errors and frailties. While as the Magistrate was set above the people, so the Law was set above the Magistrate. When this would not serve, but that the Law was either not executed, or misapply'd, they were constrain'd from that time, the onely remedy left them, to put conditions and take Oaths from all Kings and Magistrates at thir first instalment to doe impartial justice by Law: who upon those termes and no other, receav'd allegeance from the people, that is to say, bond or Covnant to obey them in execution of those Lawes which they the people had themselves made, or assented to. And this ofttimes with express warning, that if the King or Magistrate prov'd unfaithfull to his trust, the people would be disingag'd. They added also Counselors and Parlaments, nor to be onely at his beck, but with him or without him, at set times, or at all times, when any danger threatn'd to have care of the public safety. Therefore saith *Claudius Sesell* a French Statesman, *The Parliament was set as a bridle to the King*;[14] which I instance rather, not because our English Lawyers have not said the same long before, but because that French Monarchy is granted by all to be a farre more absolute then ours. That this and the rest of what hath hitherto been spok'n is most true, might be copiously made appeare throughout all Stories Heathen and Christian; ev'n of those Nations where Kings and Emperours have sought meanes to abolish all ancient memory of the Peoples right by thir encroachments and usurpations. But I spare long insertions, appealing to the known constitutions of both the latest Christian Empires in Europe, the Greek and German, besides the French, Italian, Arragonian, English, and not least the Scottish Histories: not forgetting this onely by the way, that *William* the Norman though a Conqueror, and not unsworn at his Coronation, was compell'd the second time to take oath at S. *Albanes*, ere the people would be brought to yeild obedience.

It being thus manifest that the power of Kings and Magistrates is nothing else, but what is only derivative, transferr'd and committed to them in trust from the People, to the Common good of them all, in whom the power yet remaines fundamentally, and cannot be tak'n from them, without a violation of thir natural birthright, and seeing that from hence *Aristotle*[15] and the best of Political writers have defin'd a King, him who governs to the good and profit of his People, and not for his own ends, it follows from necessary causes, that the

---

[14]Claude de Seissel, *La Grand Monarchie de France* (1519), which Milton quoted from in his *Commonplace Book* (Yale 1: 459).
[15]*Nicomathian Ethics* 8.11.1.

Titles of Sov'ran Lord, natural Lord, and the like, are either arrogancies, or flatteries, not admitted by Emperours and Kings of best note, and dislikt by the Church both of Jews, *Isai*. 26.13. and ancient Christians, as appears by *Tertullian*[16] and others. Although generally the people of Asia, and with them the Jews also, especially since the time they chose a King against the advice and counsel of God, are noted by wise Authors much inclinable to slavery.

Secondly, that to say, as is usual, the King hath as good right to his Crown and dignitie, as any man to his inheritance, is to make the Subject no better then the Kings slave, his chattell, or his possession that may be bought and sould. And doubtless if hereditary title were sufficiently inquir'd, the best foundation of it would be found either but in courtesie or convenience. But suppose it to be of right hereditarie, what can be more just and legal, if a subject for certain crimes be to forfet by Law from himself, and posterity, all his inheritance to the King, then that a King for crimes proportional, should forfet all his title and inheritance to the people: unless the people must be thought created all for him, he not for them, and they all in one body inferior to him single, which were a kinde of treason against the dignitie of mankind to affirm.

Thirdly it follows, that to say Kings are accountable to none but God, is the overturning of all Law and government. For if they may refuse to give account, then all cov'nants made with them at Coronation; all Oathes are in vaine, and meer mockeries, all Lawes which they sweare to keep, made to no purpose; for if the King feare not God, as how many of them doe not? we hold then our lives and estates, by the tenure of his meer grace and mercy, as from a God, not a mortal Magistrate, a position that none but Court Parasites or men besotted would maintain. *Aristotle* therefore, whom we commonly allow for one of the best interpreters of nature and morality, writes in the fourth of his politics chap. 19. that Monarchy unaccountable, is the worst sort of Tyranny; and least of all to be endur'd by free born men. And surely no Christian Prince, not drunk with high mind, and prouder then those Pagan *Cæsars* that deifi'd themselves, would arrogate so unreasonably above human condition, or derogate so basely from a whole Nation of men his Brethren, as if for him only subsisting, and to serve his glory; valuing them in comparison of his owne brute will and pleasure, no more then so many beasts, or vermin under his Feet, not to be reason'd with, but to be trod on; among whom

there might be found so many thousand Men for wisdom, vertue, nobleness of mind, and all other respects, but the fortune of his dignity, farr above him. Yet some would perswade us, that this absurd opinion was King *Davids*; because in the 51 *Psalm* he cries out to God, *Against thee onely have I sinn'd*; as if *David* had imagin'd that to murder *Uriah* and adulterate his Wife, had bin no sinn against his Neighbour, when as that Law of *Moses* was to the King expresly, *Deut.* 17. not to think so highly of himself above his Brethren. *David* therfore by those words could mean no other, then either that the depth of his guiltiness was known to God onely, or to so few as had not the will or power to question him, or that the sin against God was greater beyond compare then against *Uriah*. What ever his meaning were, any wise man will see that the pathetical words of a Psalme can be no certaine decision to a poynt that hath abundantly more certain rules to goe by. How much more rationally spake the Heathen King *Demophoon* in a Tragedy of *Euripides*[17] then these Interpreters would put upon King *David*, *I rule not my people by Tyranny, as if they were Barbarians, but am my self liable, if I doe unjustly, to suffer justly*. Not unlike was the speech of *Trajan* the worthy Emperor, to one whom he made General of his Prætorian Forces. Take this drawn sword, saith he, to use for me, if I reigne well, if not, to use against me. Thus *Dion* relates.[18] And not *Trajan* onely, but *Theodosius* the yonger, a Christian Emperor and one of the best, causd it to be enacted as a rule undeniable and fit to be acknowledg'd by all Kings and Emperors, that a Prince is bound to the Laws; that on the autority of Law the autority of a Prince depends, and to the Laws ought submitt. Which Edict of his remains yet in the *Code* of *Justinian.l.1.tit*.24. as a sacred constitution to all the succeeding Emperors. How then can any King in Europe maintain and write himself accountable to none but God, when Emperors in thir own imperial Statutes have writt'n and decreed themselves accountable to Law. And indeed where such account is not fear'd, he that bids a man reigne over him above Law, may bid as well a savage Beast.

It follows lastly, that since the King or Magistrate holds his autoritie of the people, both originaly and naturally for their good in the first place, and not his own, then may the people as oft as they shall judge it for the best, either choose him or reject him, retaine him or depose him though no Tyrant, meerly by the liberty and right of free born Men, to be govern'd as seems to them best. This, though it cannot but stand with plain

---

[16]The Church Father, writing in the second century AD *On the Crown*, had inveighed against temporal crowns in favor of an eternal crown for the followers of Christ.

[17]From Euripides's *Heraclidae* 418–21. Milton would quote from the play again in *A Defence* (Columbia 11: 311).

[18]Dio Cassius, *Roman History* 68.16.

reason, shall be made good also by Scripture. *Deut*.17.14. *When thou art come into the Land which the Lord thy God giveth thee, and shalt say I will set a King over mee, like as all the Nations about mee.* These words confirme us that the right of choosing, yea of changing thir own Goverment is by the grant of God himself in the People. And therfore when they desir'd a King, though then under another form of goverment, and though thir changing displeas'd him, yet he that was himself thir King, and rejected by them, would not be a hindrance to what they intended, furder then by perswasion, but that they might doe therein as they saw good, 1 *Sam*. 8. onely he reserv'd to himself the nomination of who should reigne over them. Neither did that exempt the King, as if he were to God onely accountable, though by his especial command anointed. Therfore *David first made a Covnant with the Elders of Israel, and so was by them anointed King,* 1 *Sam*.5.3. 1 *Chron*. 11. And *Jehoiada* the Priest making *Jehoash* King, made a Cov'nant between him and the People, 2 *Kings* 11.17. Therfore when *Roboam* at his comming to the Crown, rejected those conditions which the Israelites brought him, heare what they answer him, *What portion have we in David, or Inheritance in the son of Jesse? See to thine own House David.* And for the like conditions not perform'd, all Israel before that time depos'd *Samuel*, not for his own default, but for the misgoverment of his Sons. But som will say to both these examples, it was evilly don. I answer, that not the latter, because it was expressly allow'd them in the Law to set up a King if they pleas'd; and God himself joyn'd with them in the work; though in some sort it was at that time displeasing to him in respect of old *Samuel* who had govern'd them uprightly. As *Livy* praises the Romans who took occasion from *Tarquinius* a wicked Prince to gaine thir libertie, which to have extorted, saith hee, from *Numa*, or any of the good Kings before, had not bin seasonable. Nor was it in the former example don unlawfully; for when *Roboam* had prepar'd a huge Army to reduce the Israelites, he was forbidd'n by the Prophet, 1 *Kings* 12.24. *Thus saith the Lord yee shall not goe up, nor fight against your brethren, for this thing is from me.* He calls them thir Brethren, not Rebels, and forbidds to be proceeded against them owning the thing himself, not by single providence, but by approbation, and that not onely of the act, as in the former example, but of the fit season also; he had not otherwise forbidd to molest them. And those grave and wise Counselors whom *Rehoboam* first advis'd with, spake no such thing, as our old gray headed Flatterers now are wont, stand upon your birth-right, scorn to capitulate, you hold of God, not of them; for they knew no such matter, unless conditionally, but gave him politic counsel, as in a civil transaction. Therfore Kingdom and Magistracy, whether supreme or subordinat, is without difference, call'd *a human ordinance*, 1 *Pet*. 2.13.&c. which we are there taught is the will of God wee should alike submitt to, so farr as for the punishment of evil doers, and the encouragement of them that doe well. *Submitt* saith he, *as free men.* But to any civil power unaccountable, unquestionable, and not to be resisted, no not in wickedness, and violent actions, how can we submitt as free men? *There is no power but of God,* saith *Paul, Rom.* 13. as much to say, God put it into mans heart to find out that way at first for common peace and preservation, approving the exercise therof; els it contradicts *Peter* who calls the same autority an Ordinance of man. It must be also understood of lawfull and just power, els we read of great power in the affaires and Kingdoms of the World permitted to the Devil: for saith he to Christ, *Luke* 4.6. *All this power will I give thee and the glory of them, for it is deliver'd to me, & to whomsoever I will, I give it:* neither did he ly, or Christ gainsay what he affirm'd; for in the thirteenth of the *Revelation* wee read how the Dragon gave to the beast *his power, his seate, and great autority:* which beast so autoriz'd most expound[19] to be the tyrannical powers and Kingdoms of the earth. Therefore Saint *Paul* in the forecited Chapter tells us that such Magistrates he meanes, as are, not a terror to the good but to the evil; such as beare not the sword in vaine, but to punish offenders, and to encourage the good. If such onely be mentiond here as powers to be obeyd, and our submission to them onely requir'd, then doubtless those powers that doe the contrary, are no powers ordain'd of God, and by consequence no obligation laid upon us to obey or not to resist them. And it may bee well observd that both these Apostles, whenever they give this precept, express it in termes not *concrete* but *abstract*, as Logicians are wont to speake, that is, they mention the ordinance, the power, the autoritie before the persons that execute it; and what that power is, least we should be deceav'd, they describe exactly. So that if the powers be not such, or the person execute not such power, neither the one nor the other is of God, but of the Devill, and by consequence to bee resisted. From this exposition *Chrysostome*[20] also on the same place dissents not; explaining that these words were not writt'n in behalf of a tyrant. And this is verify'd by *David*, himself a King, and likeliest to bee Author of the *Psalm* 94.20. which saith *Shall the throne of iniquity have fellowship with thee?* And it were worth the knowing, since Kings in these

---

[19]"Most commentators believe to be."
[20]St John Chrysostom, 23rd Homily, referred to in Romans 13.1–2.

dayes, and that by Scripture, boast the justness of thir title, by holding it immediately of God, yet cannot show the time when God ever set on the throne them or thir forefathers by the same reason, since God ascribes as oft to himself the casting down of Princes from the throne, it should not be thought as lawful, and as much from God, when note are seen to do it but the people, and that for just causes. For if it needs must be a sin in them to depose, it may as likely be a sin to have elected. And contrary if the peoples act in election be pleaded by a King, as the act of God, and the most just title to enthrone him; why may not the peoples act of rejection, bee as well pleaded by the people as the act of God, and the most just reason to depose him? So that we see the title and just right of raigning or deposing, in reference to God, is found in Scripture to be all one; visible onely in the people, and depending meerly upon justice and demerit. Thus farr hath bin considerd briefly the power of Kings and Magistrates; how it was and is originally the peoples, and by them conferr'd in trust onely to be imployd to the common peace and benefit; with liberty therfore and right remaining in them to reassume it to themselves, if by Kings or Magistrates it be abus'd; or to dispose of it by any alteration, as they shall judge most conducing to the public good.

Wee may from hence with more ease, and force of argument determin what a Tyrant is, and what the people may doe against him. A Tyrant whether by wrong or by right comming to the Crown, is he who regarding neither Law nor the common good, reigns onely for himself and his faction: Thus St. *Basil* among others defines him.[21] And because his power is great, his will boundless and exorbitant, the fulfilling whereof is for the most part accompanied with innumerable wrongs and oppressions of the people, murders, massachers, rapes, adulteries, desolation, and subversion of Cities and whole Provinces, look how great a good and happiness a just King is, so great a mischeife is a Tyrant; as hee the public father of his Countrie, so this the common enemie. Against whom what the people lawfully may doe, as against a common pest, and destroyer of mankinde, I suppose no man of cleare judgement need goe furder to be guided then by the very principles of nature in him. But because it is the vulgar folly of men to desert thir own reason, and shutting thir eyes to think they see best with other mens, I shall shew by such examples as ought to have most waight with us, what hath bin don in this case heretofore. The *Greeks* and *Romans*, as thir prime Authors witness, held it not

onely lawfull, but a glorious and Heroic deed, rewarded publicly with Statues and Garlands, to kill an infamous Tyrant at any time without tryal: and but reason, that he who trod down all Law, should not be voutsaf'd the benefit of Law. Insomuch that *Seneca* the Tragedian brings in *Hercules*[22] the grand suppressor of Tyrants, thus speaking,

> ----------------*Victima haud ulla amplior*
> *Potest, magisque opima mactari Jovi*
> *Quam Rex iniquus*------------------------
> --------------------*There can be slaine*
> *No sacrifice to God more acceptable*
> *Then an unjust and wicked King*----------

But of these I name no more, lest it bee objected they were Heathen; and come to produce another sort of men that had the knowledge of true Religion. Among the Jews this custom of tyrant-killing was not unusual. First *Ehud*,[23] a man whom God had raysd to deliver Israel from *Eglon* King of *Moab*, who had conquerd and rul'd over them eighteene years, being sent to him as an Ambassador with a present, slew him in his own house. But hee was a forren Prince, an enemie, and *Ehud* besides had special warrant from God. To the first I answer, it imports not whether forren or native: For no Prince so native but professes to hold by Law; which when he himself overturns, breaking all the Covnants and Oaths that gave him title to his dignity, and were the bond and alliance between him and his people, what differs he from an outlandish King, or from an enemie? For look how much right the King of *Spaine* hath to govern us at all, so much right hath the King of *England* to govern us tyrannically. If he, though not bound to us by any League, comming from *Spain* in person to subdue us or to destroy us, might lawfully by the people of *England* either bee slaine in fight, or put to death in captivity, what hath a native King to plead, bound by so many Covnants, benefits and honours to the welfare of his people, why he through the contempt of all Laws and Parlaments, the onely tie of our obedience to him, for his own wills sake, and a boasted prerogative unaccountable, after sev'n years warring and destroying of his best Subjects, overcom, and yeilded prisoner, should think to scape unquestionable, as a thing divine, in respect of whom so many thousand Christians destroy'd, should lie unaccounted for, polluting with their slaughterd carcasses all the Land over, and crying for vengeance against the living that should have righted them. Who knows not that there is a mutual bond of amity and brother-hood between man and man over all

---

[21]See Milton's *Commonplace Book* (Yale 1: 453) for Basil's definition of a tyrant.

[22]*Hercules Furens* 922–24.
[23]The story of overcoming a Moabite tyrant is told in Judges 3.

the World, neither is it the English Sea that can sever us from that duty and relation: a straiter bond yet there is between fellow-subjects, neighbours, and friends; But when any of these doe one to another so as hostility could doe no worse, what doth the Law decree less against them, then op'n enemies and invaders? or if the Law be not present, or too weake, what doth it warrant us to less then single defence, or civill warr? and from that time forward the Law of civil defensive warr differs nothing[24] from the Law of forren hostility. Nor is it distance of place that makes enmitie, but enmity that makes distance. He therfore that keeps peace with me, neer or remote, of whatsoever Nation, is to mee as farr as all civil and human offices an Englishman and a neighbour: but if an Englishman forgetting all Laws, human, civil and religious, offend against life and liberty, to him offended and to the Law in his behalf, though born in the same womb, he is no better then a Turk, a Sarasin, a Heathen. This is Gospel, and this was ever Law among equals; how much rather then in force against any King whatever, who in respect of the people is confessd inferiour and not equal: to distinguish therfore of a Tyrant by outlandish, or domestic is a weak evasion. To the second that he was an enemie, I answer, what Tyrant is not? yet *Eglon* by the Jewes had bin acknowledgd as thir Sovran; they had serv'd him eighteen yeares, as long almost as we our *William* the Conqueror, in all which time he could not be so unwise a Statesman but to have tak'n of them Oaths of Fealty and Allegeance, by which they made themselves his proper Subjects, as thir homage and present sent by *Ehud* testify'd. To the third, that he had special warrant to kill *Eglon* in that manner, it cannot bee granted, because not expressd; tis plain that he was raysd by God to be a Deliverer, and went on just principles, such as were then and ever held allowable, to deale so by a Tyrant that could no otherwise be dealt with. Neither did *Samuel* though a Profet, with his own hand abstain from *Agag*; a forren enemie no doubt; but mark the reason. *As the sword hath made women childless*; a cause that by the sentence of Law it self nullifies all relations. And as the Law is between Brother and Brother, Father and Son, Maister and Servant, wherfore not between King or rather Tyrant and People? And whereas *Jehu* had special command to slay *Jehoram* a successive and hereditarie Tyrant, it seems not the less imitable for that; for where a thing grounded so much on natural reason hath the addition of a command from God, what does it but establish the lawfulness of such an act. Nor is it likely that God who had so many wayes of punish-

ing the house of *Ahab* would have sent a subject against his Prince, if the fact in it self, as don to a Tyrant, had bin of bad example. And if *David* refus'd to lift his hand against the Lords anointed, the matter between them was not tyranny, but privat enmity, and *David* as a privat person had bin his own revenger, not so much the peoples. But when any tyrant at this day can shew to be the Lords anointed, the onely mention'd reason why *David* withheld his hand, he may then but not till then presume on the same privilege.

Wee may pass therfore hence to Christian times. And first our Saviour himself, how much he favord Tyrants, and how much intended they should be found or honord among Christians, declares his mind not obscurely; accounting thir absolute autority no better then Gentilism, yea though they flourish'd it over with the splendid name of Benefactors; charging those that would be his Disciples to usurp no such dominion; but that they who were to bee of most autoritie among them, should esteem themselves Ministers and Servants to the public. *Matt.* 20.25. *The Princes of the Gentiles excercise Lordship over them*, and *Mark* 10.42. *They that seem to rule*, saith he, either slighting or accounting them no lawful rulers, *but yee shall not be so, but the greatest among you shall be your Servant*. And although hee himself were the meekest, and came on earth to be so, yet to a Tyrant we hear him not voutsafe an humble word: but *Tell that Fox*,[25] *Luc.* 13. So farr we ought to be from thinking that Christ and his Gospel should be made a Sanctuary for Tyrants from justice, to whom his Law before never gave such protection. And wherfore did his Mother the Virgin *Mary* give such praise to God in her profetic song, that he had now by the comming of Christ, *Cut down Dynasta's or proud Monarchs from the throne*,[26] if the Church, when God manifests his power in them to doe so, should rather choose all miserie and vassalage to serve them, and let them stil sit on thir potent seats to bee ador'd for doing mischief. Surely it is not for nothing that tyrants by a kind of natural instinct both hate and feare none more then the true Church and Saints of God, as the most dangerous enemies and subverters of Monarchy, though indeed of tyranny; hath not this bin the perpetual cry of Courtiers, and Court Prelats? wherof no likelier cause can be alleg'd, but that they well discern'd the mind and

---

[24]In no way.

[25]When the Pharisees warn Christ that Herod will kill him, he replies "Go ye, and tell that fox, Behold I cast out devils, and I do cures today and tomorrow, and on the third day I shall be perfected" (13.32). There is no punctuation visible after "*Fox*" and "*Luc*" in Bodleian.

[26]Milton quotes indirectly from the Magnificat, Mary's prophetic song, specifically Luke 1.52, "He hath put down the mighty from their seats, and exalted them of low degree." He alters the text in order to use the Greek and Latin plural, "dynastas," to represent powerful rulers.

principles of most devout and zealous men, and indeed the very disciplin of Church, tending to the dissolution of all tyranny. No marvel then if since the faith of Christ receav'd, in purer or impurer times, to depose a King and put him to death for Tyranny, hath bin accounted so just and requisite, that neighbour Kings have both upheld and tak'n part with subjects in the action. And *Ludovicus Pius*,[27] himself an Emperor, and Son of *Charles* the great, being made Judge, *Du Haillan*[28] is my author, between *Milegast* King of the *Vultzes* and his Subjects who had depos'd him, gave his verdit for the Subjects, and for him they had chos'n in his room. Note here that the right of electing whom they please is by the impartial testimony of an Emperor in the people. For, said he, *A just Prince ought to be prefer'd before an unjust, and the end of goverment before the prerogative.* And *Constantinus Leo*, another Emperor, in the *Byzantine* Laws saith, *that the end of a King is for the general good, which he not performing is but the counterfet of a King.* And to prove that som of our own Monarchs have acknowledg'd that thir high office exempted them not from punishment, they had the Sword of St. *Edward* born before them by an officer who was call'd Earle of the Palace, eev'n at the times of thir highest pomp and solemnities, to mind them, saith *Matthew Paris*, the best of our Historians, that if they errd, the Sword had power to restraine them. And what restraint the Sword comes to at length, having both edge and point, if any *Sceptic* will doubt, let him feel. It is also affirm'd from diligent search made in our ancient books of Law, that the Peers and Barons of England had a legal right to judge the King: which was the cause most likely, for it could be no slight cause, that they were call'd his Peers, or equals. This however may stand immovable, so long as man hath to deale with no better then man; that if our Law Judge all men to the lowest by thir Peers, it should in all equity ascend also, and judge the highest. And so much I find both in our own and forren Storie, that Dukes, Earles, and Marqueses were at first not hereditary, not empty and vain titles, but names of trust and office, and with the office ceasing, as induces me to be of opinion, that every worthy man in Parlament, for the word Baron imports no more, might for the public good be though a fit Peer and judge of the King; without regard had to petty caveats, and circumstances, the chief impediment in high affaires, and ever stood upon most by circumstantial[29] men. Whence doubtless our Ancestors who were not ignorant with what rights

either Nature or ancient Constitution had endowd them, when Oaths both at Coronation, and renewd in Parlament would not serve, thought it no way illegal to depose and put to death thir tyrannous Kings. Insomuch that the Parlament drew up a charge against *Richard the second*,[30] and the Commons requested to have judgement decree'd against him, that the realme might not be endangerd. And *Peter Martyr*[31] a Divine of formost rank, on the third of *Judges* approves thir doings. Sir *Thomas Smith* also a Protestant and a Statesman, in his Common-welth of *England*, putting the question whether it be lawfull to rise against a Tyrant, answers that the vulgar[32] judge of it according to the event, and the lerned according to the purpose of them that do it. But far before these days, *Gildas*[33] the most ancient of all our Historians, speaking of those times wherein the Roman Empire decaying quitted and relinquishd what right they had by Conquest to this Iland, and resign'd it all into the peoples hands, testifies that the people thus re-invested with thir own original right, about the year 446, both elected them Kings, whom they thought best (the first Christian Brittish Kings that ever raign'd heer since the Romans) and by the same right, when they apprehended cause, usually depos'd and put them to death. This is the most fundamental and ancient tenure that any King of *England* can produce or pretend to; in comparison of which, all other titles and pleas are but of yesterday. If any object that *Gildas* condemns the Britans for so doing, the answer is as ready; that he condemns them no more for so doing, then hee did before for choosing such, for saith he, *They anointed them Kings, not of God, but such as were more bloody then the rest.* Next hee condemns them not at all for deposing or putting them to death, but for doing it over hastily, without tryal or well examining the cause; and for electing others wors in thir room. Thus we have heer both domestic and most ancient examples that the people of Britain have depos'd and put to death thir Kings in those primitive Christian times. And to couple reason with example, if the Church in all ages, Primitive, Romish, or Protestant, held it ever no less thir duty then the power of thir Keyes, though without express warrant of Scripture, to bring indifferently both King and Peasant under the utmost rigor of thir Canons and

---

[27]Louis the Pious, Holy Roman emperor (AD 814–840).
[28]Girard du Haillan, *Histoire de France*; see Yale 1: 455 for the entry in Milton's *Commonplace Book*.
[29]Probably men who came to their offices by accident.

[30]Probably following the account in Holinshed's *Chronicles of England* (1587), without any reference to Shakespeare's play *Richard II*.
[31]Peter Martyr (1500–1562). His commentary on the Book of Judges is cited in the *Commonplace Book* (Yale 1: 455–56).
[32]The people at large (never a good judge, for Milton).
[33]Milton's choice as the most authoritative and accurate of the early chroniclers of England, Gildas (516?–570) wrote the *Liber Querulus de Excidio Britanniae, the Book of Critical Inquiry into the Fall of Britain* (see Yale 1: 474).

Censures Ecclesiastical, eev'n to the smiting him with a final excommunion, if he persist impenitent, what hinders but that the temporal Law both may and ought, though without a special Text or precedent, extend with like indifference the civil Sword, to the cutting off without exemption him that capitally offends. Seeing that justice and Religion are from the same God, and works of justice ofttimes more acceptable. Yet because that some lately, with the tongues and arguments of Malignant backsliders, have writt'n that the proceedings now in Parlament against the King, are without precedent from any Protestant State or Kingdon, the examples which follow shall be all Protestant and chiefly Presbyterian.

In the yeare 1546. The *Duke of Saxonie, Lantgrave of Hessen*, and the whole Protestant league raysd op'n Warr against *Charles the fifth* thir Emperor, sent him a defiance, renounc'd all faith and allegeance towards him, and debated long in councel whither they should give him so much as the title of *Cæsar. Sleidan.l.*17. Let all men judge what this wanted of deposing or of killing, but the power to doe it.

In the yeare 1559. The Scotch Protestants claiming promise of thir Queen Regent for libertie of conscience, she answering that promises were not to be claim'd of Princes beyond what was commodious for them to grant, told her to her face in the Parlament then at *Sterling*, that if it were so, they renounc'd thir obedience; and soon after betook them to Armes. *Buchanan*[34] *Hist. l.*16. certainly when allegeance is renounc'd, that very hour the King or Queen is in effect depos'd.

In the yeare 1564. *John Knox*[35] a most famous Divine and reformer of *Scotland* to the Presbyterians discipline, at a general Assembly maintaind op'nly in a dispute against *Lethington* the Secretary of State, that Subjects might & ought execute Gods judgements upon thir King; that the fact of *Jehu* and others against thir King having the ground of Gods ordinary command to put such and such offenders to death was not extraordinary, but to bee imitated of all that preferr'd the honour of God to the affection of flesh and wicked Princes; that Kings, if they offend, have no privilege to be exempted from the punishments of Law more then any other subject; so that if the King be a Murderer, Adulterer, or Idolater, he should suffer, not as a King, but as an offender; and this position he repeates again and again before them. Answerable was the opinion of *John Craig* another learned Divine, and that Lawes made by the

tyranny of Princes, or the negligence of people, thir posterity might abrogate, and reform all things according to the orginal institution of Common-welths. And *Knox* being commanded by the Nobilitie to write to *Calvin* and other lerned men for thir judgement in that question, refus'd; alleging that both himself was fully resolv'd in conscience, and had heard thir judgements, and had the same opinion under handwriting of many the most godly and most lerned that he knew in Europe; that if he should move the question to them againe, what should he doe but shew his own forgetfulness or iconstancy. All this is farr more largely in the Ecclesiastic History of *Scotland l.*4. with many other passages to this effect all the Book over; set out with diligence by Scotchmen of best repute among them at the beginning of these troubles, as if they labourd to inform us what wee were to doe, and what they intended upon the like occasion.

And to let the world know that the whole Church and Protestant State of *Scotland* in those purest times of reformation were of the same beleif, three years after, they met in the feild *Mary* thir lawful and hereditary Queen, took her prisoner yeilding before fight, kept her in prison, and the same yeare depos'd her. *Buchan. Hist.l.*18.

And four years after that, the Scots in justification of thir deposing Queen Mary, sent Ambassadors to Queen *Elizabeth*, and in a writt'n Declaration alleg'd that they had us'd toward her more lenity then shee deserv'd, that thir Ancestors had heretofore punish'd thir Kings by death or banishment; that the Scots were a free Nation, made King whom they freely chose, and with the same freedom unkingd him if they saw cause, by right of ancient laws and Ceremonise yet remaining, and old customs yet among the High-landers in choosing the head of thir Clanns, or Families; all which with many other arguments bore witness that regal power was nothing else but a mutual Covnat of stipulation between King and people. *Buch. Hist,l.*20. These were Scotchmen and Presbyterians but what measure then have they lately offerd, to think such liberty less beseeming us then themselves, presuming to put him upon us for a Maister whom thir law scarce allows to be thir own equal? If now then we heare them in another strain then heretofore in the purest times of thir Church, we may be confident it is the voice of Faction speaking in them, not of truth and Reformation. Which no less in *England* then in *Scotland*, but the mouthes of those faithful witnesses commonly call'd Puritans, and Nonconformists, spake as clearly for the putting down, yea the utmost punishing of Kings, as in thir several Treatises may be read; eev'n from the first raigne of *Elizabeth* to these times. Insomuch that one of them, whose name

---

[34]George Buchanan, *Rerum Scoticarum Historia* (Edinburgh, 1582). The Queen Regent is Mary of Lorraine, mother of Mary Queen of Scots.
[35]John Knox (1505–1572), the founder of Scottish Presbyterianism, had written powerfully from exile in Geneva against Bloody Mary.

was *Gibson*, foretold K. *James*, he should be rooted out, and conclude his race, if he persisted to uphold Bishops. And that very inscription stampt upon the first Coines of his Coronation, a naked Sword in a hand with these words, *Si mereor in me, Against me, if I deserve*, not only manifested the judgement of that State, but seem'd also to presage the sentence of Divine justice in this even upon his Son.

In the yeare 1581. the States of *Holland* in a general Assembly at the *Hague*, abjur'd all obedience and subjection to *Philip*, King of *Spaine*; and in a Declaration justifie thir so doing; for that by his tyrannous goverment against saith so many times giv'n & brok'n he had lost his right to all the Belgic Provinces; that therfore they depos'd him and declar'd it lawful to choose another in his stead. *Thuan.l.74*. From that time to this, no State or Kingdom in the world hath equally prosperd: But let them remember not to look with an evil and prejudicial eye upon thir Neighbours walking by the same rule.

But what need these examples to Presbyterians, I mean to those who now of late would seem so much to abhorr deposing, when as they to all Christendom have giv'n the latest and the liveliest example of doing it themseves. I question not the lawfulness of raising Warr against a Tyrant in defence of Religion, or civil libertie; for no Protestant Church from the first *Waldenses* of *Lyons*, and *Languedoc* to this day but have don it round, and maintain'd it lawful. But this I doubt not to affirme, that the Presbyterians, who now so much condemn deposing, were the men themselves that deposd the King, and cannot with all thir shifting and relapsing, wash off the guiltiness from thir own hands. For them themselves, by these thir late doings have made it guiltiness, and turn'd thir own warrantable actions into Rebellion.

There is nothing that so actually makes a King of *England*, as rightful possession and Supremacy *in all causes both civil and Ecclesiastical:* and nothing that so actually makes a Subject of *England* as those two Oaths of Allegeance and Supremacy observ'd *without equivocating, or any mental reservation*. Out of doubt then when the King shall command things already constituted in Church, or State, obedience is the true essence of a subject, either to doe, if it be lawful, or if he hold the thing unlawful, to submitt to that penaltie which the Law imposes, so long as he intends to remaine a Subject. Therfore when the people or any part of them shall rise against the King and his autority executing the Law in any thing establish'd be unlawful, and that they sought first all due means of redress (and no man is furder bound to Law) but I say it is an absolute renouncing both of Supremacy and Allegeance, which in one word is an actual and total deposing of the King, and the

setting up of another supreme autority over them. And whether the Presbyterians have not don all this and much more, they will not put mee, I suppose, to reck'n up a seven years story fresh in the memory of all men. Have they not utterly broke the Oath of Allegeance, rejecting the Kings command and autority sent them from any part of the Kingdom whether in things lawful or unlawful? Have then not abjur'd the Oath of Supremacy by setting up the Parlament without the King, supreme to all thir obedience, and through this Vow and Covnant bound them in general to the Parlament, yet somtimes adhering to the lesser part of Lords and Commons that remaind faithful, as they terme it, and eev'n of them, one while to the Commons without the Lords, another while to the Lords without the Commons? Have they not still declar'd thir meaning, whatever thir Oath were, to hold them onely for supreme whom they found at any time most yeilding to what they petition'd? Both these Oaths which were the straitest bond of an English subject in reference to the King, being thus broke & made voide, it follows undenyably that the King from that time was by them in fact absolutely depos'd; and they no longer in reality to be thought his subjects, notwithstanding thir fine clause in the Covnant to preserve his person, Crown, and dignity, set there by som dodging Casuist with more craft then sincerity to mitigate the matter in case of ill success and not tak'n I suppose by any honest man, but as a condition subordinat to every the least particle that might more concerne Religion, liberty, or the public peace. To prove it yet more plainly that they are the men who have depos'd the King, I thus argue. We know that King and Subject are relatives, and relatives have no longer being then in the relation; the relation between King and Subject can be no other then regal autority and subjection. Hence I inferr past their defending, that if the Subject who is one relative, take away the relation, of force he takes away also the other relative; but the Presbyterians who were one relative, that is to say Subjects, have for this sev'n years tak'n away the relation, that is to say the Kings autority, and thir subjection to it, therfore the Presbyterians for these sev'n years have remov'd and extinguishd the other relative, that is to say the King, or to speak more in brief have depos'd him; not onely by depriving him the execution of his autoritie, but by conferring it upon others. If then thir Oaths of subjection brok'n, new Supremacy obey'd, new Oaths and Covnants tak'n, notwithstanding frivolous evasions, have in plaine termes unking'd the King, much more then hath thir sev'n years Warr not depos'd him onely, but outlaw'd him, and defi'd him as an alien, a rebell to Law, and enemie to the State. It must needs be clear to any man not avers

and positive contraries; and can no more in one subject stand together in respect of the same King, then one person at the same time can be in two remote places. Against whom therfore the Subject is in act of hostility we may be confident that to him he is in no subjection: and in whom hostility takes place of subjection, for they can by no meanes consist together, to him the King can be not onely no King, but an enemie. So that from hence we shall not need dispute whether they have depos'd him, or what they have defaulted towards him as no King, but shew manifestly how much they have don toward the killing him. Have they not levied all these Warrs against him whether offensive or defensive (for defence in Warr equally offends, and most prudently before hand) and giv'n Commission to slay where they knew his person could not be exempt from danger? And if chance or flight had not sav'd him, how oft'n had they killd him, directing thir Artillery without blame or prohibition to the very place where they saw him stand? Have they not Sequester'd him, judg'd or unjudgd, and converted his revenew to other uses, detaining from him as a grand Delinquent, all meanes of livelyhood, so that for them long since he might have perisht, or have starv'd? Have they not hunted and pursu'd him round about the Kingdom with sword and fire? Have they not formerly deny'd to Treat[36] with him, and thir now recanting Ministers preach'd against him, as a reprobate incurable, an enemy to God and his Church markt for destruction, and therfore not to be treated with? Have they not beseig'd him, & to thir power forbidd him Water and Fire, save what they shot against him to the hazard of his life? Yet while they thus assaulted and endangerd it with hostile deeds, they swore in words to defend it with his Crown and dignity; not in order, as it seems now, to a firm and lasting peace, or to his repentance after all this blood; but simply, without regard, without remorse, or any comparable value of all the miseries and calamities sufferd by the poore people, or to suffer hereafter through his obstinacy or impenitence. No understanding man can bee ignorant that Covnants are ever made according to the present state of persons and of things; and have ever the more general laws of nature and of reason included in them, though not express'd. If I make a voluntary Covnant as with a man, to doe him good, and he prove afterward a monster to me, I should conceave a disobligement. If I covnant, not to hurt an enemie, in favour of him & forbearance, & hope of his amendment, & he, after that, shall doe me ten-fould injury and mischief, to what he had don when I so Covnanted, and

stil be plotting what may tend to my destruction, I question not but that his after actions release me; nor know I Covnant so sacred that withholds me from demanding justice on him. Howbeit, had not thir distrust in a good cause, and the fast and loos of our prevaricating Divines oversway'd it, it had bin doubtless better not to have inserted in a Covnant unnecessary obligations, and words not works of a superogating Allegeance to thir enemy; no way advantageous to themselves, had the King prevail'd, as to thir cost many would have felt; but full of snare and distraction to our friends, usefull onely, as we now find, to our adversaries, who under such a latitude and shelter of ambiguous interpretation have ever since been plotting and contriving new opportunities to trouble all again. How much better had it bin, and more becomming an undaunted vertue, to have declar'd op'nly and boldly whom and what power the people were to hold Supreme; as on the like occasion Protestants have don before, and many conscientious men now in these time have more then once besought the Parlament to doe, that they might goe on upon a sure foundation, and not with a ridling Covnant in thir mouths, seeming to sweare conter almost in the same breath Allegeance and no Allegeance; which doubtless had drawn off all the minds of sincere men from siding with them, had they not discern'd thir actions farr more deposing him then thir words upholding him; which words made now the subject of cavillous interpretations, stood ever in the Covnant, by judgement of the more discerning sort, an evidence of thir feare, not of thir fidelity. What should I return to speak on, of those attempts for which the King himself hath oft'n charg'd the Presbyterians of seeking his life, when as in the due estimation of things, they might without a fallacy be sayd to have don the deed outright. Who knows not that the King is a name of dignity and office, not of person: Who therfore kills a King, must kill him while he is a King. Then they certainly who by deposing him have long since tak'n from him the life of a King, his office and his dignity, they in the truest sence may be said to have killd the King: nor onely by thir deposing and waging Warr against him, which besides the danger to his personal life, sett him in the fardest opposite point from any vital function of a King, but by thir holding him in prison, vanquishd and yeilded into thir absolute and *despotic* power, which brought him to the lowest degradement and incapacity of the regal name. I say not by whose matchless valour next under God, lest the story of thir ingratitude thereupon carry me from the purpose in hand, which is to convince them that they, which I repeat againe, were the men who in the truest sense killd the King, not onely as is prov'd before, but by

---

[36]Make a treaty.

depressing him thir King farr below the rank of a subject to the condition of a Captive, without intention to restore him, as the Chancellour of *Scotland* in a speech told him plainly at *Newcastle*, unless hee granted fully all thir demands, which they knew he never meant. Nor did they Treat or think of Treating with him, till thir hatred to the Army that deliverd them, not thir love or duty to the King, joyn'd them secretly with men sentenc'd so oft for Reprobats in thir own mouthes, by whose suttle inspiring they grew madd upon a most tardy and improper Treaty. Whereas if the whole bent of thir actions had not bin against the King himself, but only against his evil counselers, as they faind, & publishd, wherfore did they not restore him all that while to the true life of a King, his office, Crown, and Dignity, when he was in thir power, & they themselves his neerest counselers. The truth therfore is, both that they would not, and that indeed they could not without thir own certain destruction; having reduc'd him to such a final pass, as was the very death and burial of all in him that was regal, and from whence never King of *England* yet reviv'd, but by the new re-inforcement of his own party, which was a kind of resurrection to him. Thus having quite extinguisht all that could be in him of a King, and from a total privation clad him over, like another specifical thing,[37] with formes and habitudes destructive to the former, they left in his person, dead as to Law, and all the civil right either of King or Subject, the life onely of a Prisner, a Captive and a Malefactor. Whom the equal and impartial hand of justice finding, was no more to spare then another ordnary man; not onely made obnoxious[38] to the doom of Law by a charge more then once drawn up against him, and his own confession to the first Article at *Newport*, but summond and arraign'd in the sight of God and his people, curst & devoted to perdition worse then any *Ahab*, or *Antiochus*, with exhortation to curse all those in the name of God that made not Warr against him, as bitterly as *Meroz* was to be curs'd, that went not out against a Canaanitish King, almost in all the Sermons, Prayers, and Fulminations that have bin utterd this sev'n yeares by those clov'n tongues of falshood and dissention; who now, to the stirring up of new discord, acquitt him' and agains thir own disciplin, which they boast to be the throne and scepter of Christ, absolve him, unconfound him, though unconverted, unrepentant, unsensible of all thir pretious Saints and Martyrs whose blood they have so oft laid upon his head: and now againe with a new sovran anoyntment can wash it

all off, as if it were a vile, and no more to be reckn'd for, then the blood of so many Dogs in a time of Pestilence: giving the most opprobrious lye to all the acted zeale that for these many yeares hath filld thir bellies, and fed them fatt upon the foolish people. Ministers of sedition, not of the Gospel, who while they saw it manifestly tend to civil Warr and blood shed, never ceasd exasperating the people against him; and now that they see it likely to breed new commotion, cease not to incite others against the people that have sav'd them from him, as if sedition were thir onely aime, whether against him or for him. But God, as we have cause to trust, will put other thoughts into the people, and turn them from giving eare or heed to these Mercenary noisemakers, of whose fury, and fals prophecies we have anough experience; and from the murmurs of new discord will incline them to heark'n rather with erected minds to the voice of our Supreme Magistracy, calling us to liberty and the flourishing deeds of a reformed Commonwealth; with this hope that as God was heretofore angry with the Jews who rejected him and his forme of Goverment to choose a King, so that he will bless us, and be propitious to us who reject a King to make him onely our leader and supreme governour in the conformity as neer as may be of his own ancient goverment; if we have at least but so much worth in us to entertaine the sense of our future happiness, and the courage to receave what God voutsafes us: wherein we have the honour to preced other Nations who are now labouring to be our followers. For as to this question in hand what the people by thir just right may doe in change of goverment, or of governour, we see it cleerd sufficiently; besides other ample autority eev'n from the mouths of Princes themselves. And surely they that shall boast, as we doe, to be a free Nation, and not have in themselves the power to remove, or to abolish any governour supreme, or subordinat, with the goverment it self upon urgent causes, may please thir fancy with a ridiculous and painted freedom, fit to coz'n babies; but are indeed under tyranny and servitude; as wanting that power, which is the root and sourse of all liberty, to dispose and *œconomize* in the Land which God hath giv'n them, as Maisters of Family in thir own house and free inheritance. Without which natural and essential power of a free Nation, though bearing high thir heads, they can in due esteem be thought no better then slaves and vassals born, in the tenure and occupation of another inheriting Lord. Whose goverment, though not illegal, or intolerable, hangs over them as a Lordly scourge, not as a free goverment; and therfore to be abrogated. How much more justly then may they fling off tyranny, or tyrants; who being once depos'd can be no more then privat men, as subject to the reach of

---

[37] Another species.
[38] Liable to injury; vulnerable.

Justice and arraignment as any other transgressors. And certainly if men, not to speak of Heathen, both wise and Religious have don justice upon Tyrants what way they could soonest, how much more milde & human then is it, to give them faire and op'n tryal? To teach lawless Kings, and all who so much adore them, that not mortal man, or his imperious will, but Justice is the onely true sovran and supreme Majesty upon earth. Let men cease therfoure out of faction & hypocrisie to make out-cries and horrid things of things so just and honorable. Though perhaps till now no protestant State or kingdom can be alleg'd to have op'nly put to death thir King, which lately some have writt'n, and imputed to thir great glory; much mistaking the matter. It is not, neither ought to be the glory of a Protestant State, never to have put thir King to death; It is the glory of a Protestant King never to have deserv'd death. And if the Parlament and Military Councel doe what they doe without precedent, if it appeare thir duty, it argues the more wisdom, vertue, and magnanimity, that they know themselves able to give a precedent to others. Who perhaps in future ages, if they prove not too degenerat, will look up with honour, and aspire toward these exemplary, and matchless deeds of thir Ancestors, as to the highest top of thir civil glory and emulation. Which heretofore, in the persuance of fame and forren dominion, spent it self vain-gloriously abroad; but henceforth may learn a better fortitude,[39] to dare execute highest Justice on them that shall by force of Armes endeavour the oppressing and bereaving of Religion and thir liberty at home: that no unbridl'd Potentate or Tyrant, but to his sorrow for the future, may presume such high and irresponsible licence over mankinde, to havock and turn upside-down whole Kingdoms of men, as though they were no more in respect of his perverse will then a Nation of Pismires.[40] As for the party calld Presbyterian, of whom I believe very many to be good and faithfull Christians, though misledd by som of turbulent spirit, I wish them earnestly and calmly not to fall off from thir first principles; nor to affect rigor and superiority over men not under them; not to compell unforcible things, in Religion especially, which if not voluntary, becomes a sin; nor to assist the clamor and malicious drifts of men whom they themselves have judg'd to be the worst of men, the obdurat enemies of God and his Church: nor to dart against the actions of thir brethren, for want of other argument, those wrested Lawes and Scriptures thrown by Prelats and Malignants against thir own sides, which though they

hurt not otherwise, yet tak'n up by them to the condemnation of thir own doings, give scandal to all men, and discover in themselves either extreame passion, or apostacy. Let them not oppose thir best friends and associats, who molest them not at all, infringe not the least of thir liberties; unless they call it thir liberty to bind other mens conscience, but are still seeking to live at peace with them and brotherly accord. Let them beware an old and perfet enemy, who though he hope by sowing discord to make them his instruments, yet cannot forbeare a minute the op'n threatning of his destind revenge upon them, when they have servd his purposes. Let them, feare therfore if they be wise, rather what they have don already, then what remaines to doe, and be warn'd in time they put no confidence in princes whom they have provok'd, lest they be added to the exampels of those that miserably have tasted the event. Stories can informe them how *Christiern* the second, King of *Denmark* not much above a hundred yeares past, driv'n out by his Subjects, and receiv'd againe upon new Oaths and conditions, broke through them all to his most bloody revenge; slaying his chief opposers when he saw his time, both them and thir children invited to a feast for that purpose. How *Maximilian* dealt with those of *Bruges*, though by mediation of the *German* Princes reconcil'd to them by solem and public writings drawn and seald. How the massacre at *Paris* was the effect of that credulous peace which the French Protestants made with *Charles* the ninth thir King: and that the main visible cause which to this day hath sav'd the *Netherlands* from utter ruin, was thir final not beleiving the perfidious cruelty which, as a constant maxim of State, hath bin us'd by the Spanish Kings on thir Subjects that have tak'n Armes and after trusted them; as no later age but can testifie, heretofore in *Belgia* it self, and this very yeare in *Naples*. And to conclude with one past exception, though farr more ancient, *David*, whose sanctify'd prudence might be alone sufficient, not to warrant us only, but to instruct us, when once he had tak'n Armes, never after that trusted *Saul*, though with tears and much relenting he twise promis'd not to hurt him. These instances, few of many, might admonish them both English and Scotch not to let thir own ends, and the driving on of a faction betray them blindly into the snare of those enemies whose revenge looks on them as the men who first begun, fomented and carri'd on, beyond the cure of any sound or safe accommodation, all the evil which hath since unavoidably befall'n them and thir King.

I have somthing also to the Divines, though brief to what were needfull; not to be disturbers of the civil affairs, being in hands better able and more belonging to manage them; but to study harder, and to attend the

---

[39]Compare "the better fortitude / Of Patience and Heroic Martyrdom / Unsung" (*Paradise Lost*, 9.31–32).
[40]Irritating ants.

office of good Pastors, knowing that he whose flock is least among them hath a dreadfull charge, not performd by mounting twise into the chair with a formal preachment huddl'd up at the odd hours of a whole lazy week, but by incessant pains and watching *in season and out of season, from house to house* over the soules of whom they have to feed. Which if they ever well considerd, how little leasure would they find to be the most pragmatical Sidesmen of every popular tumult and Sedition? And all this while are to learn what the true end and reason is of the Gospel which they teach; and what a world it differs from the censorious and supercilious lording over conscience. It would be good also they liv'd so as might perswade the people they hated covetousness, which worse then heresie, is idolatry; hated pluralities and all kind of Simony; left rambling from Benifice to Benifice, like rav'nous Wolves seeking where they may devour the biggest. Of which if som, well and warmly seated from the beginning, be not guilty, twere good they held not conversation with such as are: let them be sorry that being call'd to assemble about reforming the Church, they fell to progging[41] and solliciting the Parlament, though they had renounc'd the names of Priests, for a new setling of thir Titles and Oblations; and double lin'd themselves with spiritual places of commoditie beyond the possible discharge of thir duty. Let them assemble in Consistory with thir Elders and Deacons, according to ancient Ecclesiastical rule, to the preserving of Church-discipline, each in his several charge, and not a pack of Clergiemen by themselves to belly-cheare in thir presumptuous Sion, or to promote designes, abuse and gull the simple Laity, and stirr up tumult, as the Prelats did, for the maintenance of thir pride and avarice. These things if they observe, and waite with patience, no doubt but all things will goe well without their importunities or exclamations: and the Printed letters which they send subscrib'd with the ostentation of great Characters and little moment, would be more considerable then now they are. But if they be the ministers of Mammon in stead of Christ, and scandalize his Church with the filthy love of gaine, aspiring also to fit the closest & the heaviest of all Tyrants, upon the conscience, and fall notoriously into the same sinns, wherof so lately and so loud they accus'd the Prelates, as God rooted out those wicked ones immediatly before, so will he root out them thir imitators: and to vindicate his own glory and Religion, will uncover thir hypocrisie to the op'n world; and visit upon thir own heads that *curse ye Meroz*, the very *Motto* of thir Pulpits, wherwith so frequently, not as *Meroz*,

but more like Atheists they have blasphem'd the vengeance of God, and traduc'd the zeale of his people. And that they be not what they goe for, true Ministers of the Protestant doctrine, taught by those abroad, famous and religious men, who first reformd the Church, or by those no less zealous, who withstood corruption and the Bishops heer at home, branded with the name of Puritans and Nonconformists, wee shall abound with testimonies to make appeare: that men may yet more fully know the difference between Protestant Divines, and these Pulpit-firebrands.

Luther.

Lib. contra Rusticos apud Sleidan. l. 5.
Is est hodie rerum status, &c. *Such is the state of things at this day, that men neither can, nor will, nor indeed ought to endure longer the domination of you Princes.*

Neque vero Cæsarem, &c. *Neither is Cæsar to make Warr as head of Chrit'ndom, Protector of the Church, Defender of the Faith; these Titles being fals and Sindie, and most Kings being the greatest enemies to Religion.Lib: De bello contra Turcas. apud Sleid.1.* 14. *What hinders then, but that we may depose or punish them?*

These also are recited by *Cochlæus* in his *Miscellanies* to be the words of *Luther*, or some other eminent Divine, then in *Germany*, when the Protestants there entred into solemn Covnant at *Smalcaldia.* Ut ora iis obturem &c. *That I may stop thir mouthes, the Pope and Emperor are not born but elected, and may also be depos'd as hath bin oft'n don.* If *Luther*, or whoever els thought so, he could not stay there; for the right of birth or succession can be no privilege in nature to let a Tyrant sit irremoveable over a Nation free born, without transforming that Nation from the nature and condition of men born free, into natural, hereditary, and successive slaves. Therfore he saith furder: *To displace and throw down this Exactor, this Phalaris, this Nero, is a work well pleasing to God;* Namely, for being such a one: which is a moral reason. Shall then so slight a consideration as his happ to be not elective simply, but by birth, which was a meer accident, overthrow that which is moral, and make unpleasing to God that which otherwise had so well pleasd him? certainly not: for if the matter be rightly argu'd, Election much rather then chance, bindes a man to content himself with what he suffers by his own bad Election. Though indeed neither the one nor other bindes any man, much less any people to a necessary sufferance of those wrongs and evils, which they have abilitie and strength anough giv'n them to remove.

Zwinglius. tom. 1. articul. 42.
Quando vero perfidè, &c. *When Kings raigne*

---

[41]Nagging.

perfidiously, and against the rule of Christ, they may according to the word of God be depos'd.

Mihi ergo compertum non est, &c. *I know not how it comes to pass that Kings raigne by succession, unless it be with consent of the whole people.* ibid.

Quum vero consensu, &c.: *But when by suffrage and consent of the whole people, or the better part of them, a Tyrant is depos'd or put to death, God is the chief leader in that action.* ibid.

Nunc cum tam tepidi sumus, &c. *Now that we are so luke warm in upholding public office, we indure the vices of Tyrants to raign now a dayes with impunity; justly therfore by them we are trod underfoot, and shall at length with them be punisht. Yet ways are not wanting by which Tyrants may be remoov'd, yet there wants public justic.* ibid.

Cavete vobis ô tyranni. *Beware yee Tyrants for now the Gospell of Jesus Christ spreading farr and wide, will renew the lives of so many to love innocence and justice; which if yee also shall doe, yee shall be honourd. But if yee shall goe on to rage and doe violence, yee shall be trampl'd on by all men.* ibid.

Romanum imperium imò quodq; &c. *When the Roman Empire or any other shall begin to oppress Religion, and wee negligently suffer it, wee are as much guilty of Religion so violated, as the Oppressors themselvs.* Idem Epist. ad Conrad. Somium.

Calvin on Daniel. c. 4. v. 25.

Hodie Monarchæ semper in suis titulis, &c. *Nowadays Monarchs pretend alwayes in thir Titles, to be Kings by the grace of God: but how many of them to this end onely pretend it, that they may raigne without controule; for to what purpose is the grace of God mentiond in the Title of Kings, but that they may acknowledge no Superiour? In the meane while God, whose name they use, to support themselves, they willingly would tread under thir feet. It is therfore a meer cheat when they boast to raigne by the grace of God.*

Abdicant se terreni principes, &c. *Earthly Princes depose themselves while they rise against God, yea they are unworthy to be numberd among men: rather it behooves us to spitt upon thir heads then to obey them.* On Dan: c. 6. v. 22.

Bucer on Matth. c. 5

Si princeps superior, &c. *If a Sovran Prince endeavour by armes to defend transgressors, to subvert those things which are taught in the word of God, they who are in autority under him, ought first to disswade him; if they prevaile not, and that he now beares himself not as a Prince, but as an enemie, and seekes to violate priviledges and rights granted to inferior Magistrates, imploring first the assistance of God, rather to try all ways and means,*

then to betray the flock of Christ, to such an enemie of God: for they also are to this end ordain'd, that they may defend the people of God, and maintain those things which are good and just. For to have supreme power less'ns not the evil committed by that power, but makes it the less tolerable, by how much the more generally hurtful. Then certainly the less tolerable, the more unpardonably to be punish'd.

Of *Peter Martyr* we have spoke before.

Paræus in Rom. 13.

Quorum est constituere Magistratus, &c. *They whose part it is to set up Magistrates, may restrain them also from outragious deeds, or pull them down, but all Magistrates are set up either by Parlament, or by Electors, or by other Magistrates; They therfore who exalted them, may lawfully degrade and punish them.*

Of the Scotch Divines I need not mention others then the famousest among them, *Knox,* & his fellow labourers in the reformation of *Scotland;* whose large Treatises on the subject, defend the same Opinion. To cite them sufficiently, were to insert thir whole Books, writt'n purposely on this argument. *Knox Appeal;* and to the Reader; where he promises in a Postscript that the Book which he intended to set forth, call'd, The second blast of the Trumpet, should maintain more at large, that the same men most justly may depose, and punish him whom unadvisedly they have elected, notwithstanding birth, succession, or any Oath of Allegeance. Among our own Divines, *Cartwright* and *Fenner,* two of the Lernedest, may in reason satisfy us what was held by the rest. *Fenner* in his Book of *Theologie* maintaining, That *they who have power, that is to say a Parlament, may either by faire meanes or by force depose a Tyrant,* whom he defines to be him, that wilfully breakes all, or the principal conditions made between him and the Common-wealth. *Fen. Sac: Theolog. c. 13.* and *Cartwright* in a prefix'd Epistle testifies his approbation of the whole Book.

Gilby de obedientiâ. P. 25. & 105.

Kings have thir autoritie of the people, who may upon occasion reassume it to themselves.

Englands Complaint against the Canons.

The people may kill wicked Princes, as monsters and cruel beasts.

Christopher Goodman of Obedience.

When Kings or Rulers become blasphemers of God, oppressors and murderers of thir Subjects, they ought no more to be accounted Kings or lawfull Magistrates, but as privat men to be examind, accus'd, contemn'd and punisht by the Law of God, and being convicted and punisht by that law, it is not mans but Gods doing. C. 10. p. 139.

By the civil laws a foole or Idiot born, and so prov'd shall loose the lands and inheritance wherto he is born, because he is not able to use them aright. And especially ought in no case be sufferd to have the goverment of a whole Nation; But there is no such evil can come to the Common-wealth by fooles and idiots as doth by the rage and fury of ungodly Rulers; Such therfore being without God ought to have no autority over Gods people, who by his Word requireth the contrary. *C.* 11. *p.* 143, 144.

No person is exempt by any Law of God from this punishment, be he King, Queene, or Emperor, he must dy the death, for God hath not plac'd them above others, to transgress his laws as they list, but to be subject to them as well as others, and if they be subject to his laws, then to the punishment also, so much the more as thir example is more dangerous. *C.* 13. *p.* 184.

When Magistrates cease to doe thir Duty, the people are as it were without Magistrates, yea worse, and then God giveth the sword into the peoples hand, and he himself is become immediatly thir head. *p.* 185.

If Princes doe right and keep promise with you, then doe you owe to them all humble obedience: if not, yee are discharg'd, and your study ought to be in this case how ye may depose and punish according to the Law such Rebels against God and oppressors of thir Country. *p.* 190.

This *Goodman* was a Minister of the *English* Church at *Geneva*, as *Dudley Fenner* was at *Middleburrough*, or some other place in that Country. These were the Pastors of those Saints and Confessors who flying from the bloudy persecution of Queen *Mary*, gather'd up at length thir scatterd members into many Congregations; wherof som in upper, some in lower *Germany*, part of them settl'd at *Geneva*; where this Author having preachd on this subject to the great liking of certain lerned and godly men who heard him, was by them sudry times & with much instance requir'd to write more fully on that point. Who therupon took it in hand, and conferring with the best lerned in those parts (among whom *Calvin* was then living in the same City) with their special approbation he publisht this treatise, aiming principally, as is testify'd by *Whittington* in the Preface, that his Brethren of *England*, the Protestants, might be perswaded in the truth of that Doctrine concerning obedience to Magistrates. *Whittingham in Prefat.*

These were the true Protestant Divines of *England*, our fathers in the faith we hold; this was their sense, who for so many yeares labouring under Prelacy, through all stormes and persecutions kept Religion from extinguishing; and deliverd it pure to us, till there arose a covetous and ambitious generation of Divines (for

Divines they call themselfes) who feining on a sudden to be new converts and proselytes from Episcopacy, under which they had long temporiz'd, op'nd thir mouthes at length, in shew against Pluralities and Prelacy, but with intent to swallow them down both; gorging themselves like Harpy's on thos simonious places and preferments of thir outed predecessors, as the quarry for which they hunted, not to pluralitie only but to multiplicitie: for possessing which they had accusd them thir Brethren, and aspiring under another title to the same authoritie and usurpation over the consciences of all men.

Of this faction diverse reverend and lerned Divines, as they are stil'd in the Phylactery of thir own Title page, pleading the lawfulness of defensive Armes against this King, in a Treatise call'd *Scripture and Reason*, seem in words to disclaime utterly the deposing of a King; but both the Scripture and the reasons which they use, draw consequences after them, which without their bidding, conclude it lawfull. For if by Scripture, and by that especially to the *Romans*, which they most insist upon, Kings doing that which is contrary to Saint *Pauls* definition of a Magistrat, may be resisted, they may altogether with as much force of consequence be depos'd or punishd. And if by reason the unjust autority of Kings *may be forfeted in part, and his power be reassum'd in part, either by the Parlament or People, for the case in hazard and the present necessitie,* as they affirm *p.* 34, there can no Scripture be alleg'd, no imaginable reason giv'n, that necessity continuing, as it may alwayes, and they in all prudence and thir duty may take upon them to foresee it, why in such a case they may not finally amerce[42] him with the loss of his Kingdom, of whose amendment they have no hope. And if one wicked action persisted in against Religion, Laws, and liberties may warrant us to thus much in part, why may not forty times as many tyrannies, by him committed, warrant us to proceed on restraining him, till the restraint become total. For the ways of justice are exactest proportion; if for one trespass of a King it require so much remedie or satisfaction, then for twenty more as hainous crimes, it requires of him twenty-fold; and so proportionably, till it com to what is utmost among men. If in these proceedings against thir King they may not finish by the usual cours of justice what they have begun, they could not lawfully begin at all. For this golden rule of justice and moralitie, as well as of Arithmetic, out of three termes which they admit, will certainly and unavoydably bring out the fourth, as any Probleme that ever *Euclid*, or *Apollonius* made good by demonstration.

---

[42]Fine arbitrarily.

And if the Parlament, being undeposable but by themselves, as is affirm'd, *p.* 37,38, might for his whole life, if they saw cause, take all power, authority, and the sword out of his hand, which in effect is to unmagistrate him, why might they not, being then themselves the sole Magistrates in force, proceed to punish him who being lawfully depriv'd of all things that define a Magistrate, can be now no Magistrate, to be degraded lower, but an offender to be punisht. Lastly, whom they may defie, and meet in battel, why may they not as well prosecute by justice? For lawfull warr is but the execution of justice against them who refuse Law. Among whom if it be lawfull (as they deny not, *p.* 19, 20.) to slay the King himself comming in front at his own peril, wherfore may not justice doe that intendedly, which the chance of a defensive warr might without blame have don casually, nay purposely, if there it finde him among the rest. They aske *p.* 19. *By what rule of Conscience or God, a State is bound to sacrifice Religion, Laws and liberties, rather then a Prince defending such as subvert them, should com in hazard of his life.* And I ask by what conscience, or divinity, or Law, or reason, a State is bound to leave all these sacred concernments under a perpetual hazard and extremity of danger, rather then cutt off a wicked Prince, who sitts plotting day and night to subvert them: They tell us that the Law of nature justifies any man to defend himself, eev'n against the King in Person: let them shew us then why the same Law, may not justifie much more a State or whole people, to doe justice upon him, against whom each privat man may lawfully defend himself; seing all kind of justice don, is a defence to good men, as well as a punishment to bad; and justice don upon a Tyrant is no more but the necessary self-defence of a whole Common wealth. To Warr upon a King, that his instruments may be brought to condigne punishment, and therafter to punish them the instruments, and not to spare onely, but to defend and honour him the Author, is the strangest peece of justice to be call'd Christian, and the strangest peece of reason to be call'd human, that by men of reverence and learning, as thir stile imports them, ever yet was vented. They maintain in the third and fourth Section, that a Judge or inferior Magistrate, is anointed of God, is his Minister, hath the Sword in his hand, is to be obey'd by St. *Peters* rule, as well as the Supreme, and without difference any where exprest: and yet will have us fight against the Supreme till he remove and punish the inferior Magistrate (for such were the greatest Delinquents) when as by Scripture, and by reason, there can no more autority be shown to resist the one then the other; and altogether as much, to punish or depose the Supreme himself, as to make Warr upon him, till he punish or deliver up his inferior Magistrates, whom in the same terms we are commanded to obey, and not to resist. Thus while they, in a cautious line or two here and there stuft in, are onely verbal against the pulling down or punishing of Tyrants, all the Scripture and the reason which they bring, is in every lease direct and rational to inferr it altogether as lawful, as to resist them. And yet in all thir Sermons, as that by others bin well noted, they went much furder. For Divines, if ye observe them, have thir postures, and thir motions no less expertly, and with no less variety then they that practice feats in the Artillery-ground. Sometimes they seem furiously to march on, and presently march counter; by and by they stand, and then retreat; or if need be can face about, or wheele in a whole body, with that cunning and dexterity as is almost unperceavable; to winde themselves by shifting ground into places of more advanage. And Providence onely must be the drumm, Providence the word of command, that calls them from above, but always to som larger Benefice, or acts them into such or such figures, and promotions. At thir turnes and doublings no men readier; to the right, or to the left; for it is thir turnes which they serve cheifly; heerin only singular; that with them there is no certain hand right or left; but as thir own commodity thinks best to call it. But if there come a truth to be defended, which to them, and thir interest of this world seemes not so profitable, strait these nimble motionists can find no eev'n leggs to stand upon: and are no more of use to reformation throughly performd, and not superficially, or to the advancement of Truth (which among mortal men is alwaies in her progress) then if on a sudden they were strook maime, and crippl'd. Which the better to conceale, or the more to countnance by a general confomity to thir own limping, they would have *Scripture*, they would have *reason* also made to halt with them for company; and would putt us off with impotent conclusions, lame and shorter then the premises. In this posture they seem to stand with great zeale and confidence on the wall of *Sion*; but like *Jebusites*, not like *Israelites*, or *Levites*: blinde also as well as lame, they discern not *David* from *Adonibezec*: but cry him up for the Lords anointed, whose thumbs and great toes not long before they had cut off upon thir Pulpit cushions. Therfore he who is our only King, the root of *David*, and whose Kingdom is eternal righeousness, with all those that Warr under him, whose happiness and final hopes are laid up in that only just & rightful kingdom (which we pray incessantly may com soon, and in so praying with hasty ruin and destruction to all Tyrants) eev'n he our immortal King, and all that love him, must of necessity have in abomination these blind and lame Defenders of *Jerusalem*; as the soule of *David* hated them, and forbid them entrance into Gods House, and his own. But as to those before them, which I cited first (and with an easie search, for many more might be added) as they there stand, without more in number, being the best and chief of Protestant Divine, we may follow them for faithful Guides, and without doubting may receive them, as Witnesses abundant of what wee heer affirme concerning Tyrants. And indeed I find it generally the cleere and positive determination of them all, (not prelatical, or of this late faction subprelatical) who have writt'n on this argument; that to doe justice on a lawless King, is to a privat man unlawful, to an inferior Magistrate lawfull: or if they were divided in opinion, yet greater then these here alleg'd, or of more autority in the Church, there can be none produc'd. If any one shall goe about by bringing other testimonies to disable these, or by bringing these against themselves in other cited passages of thir Books, he will not only faile to make good that fals and impudent assertion of those mutinous Ministers, that the deposing and punishing of a King or Tyrant, *is against the constant Judgement of all Protestant Divines*, it being quite the contrary, but will prove rather, what perhaps he intended not, that the judgement of Divines, if it be so various and inconstant to it self, is not considerable, or to be esteem'd at all. Ere

which be yeilded, as I hope it never will, these ignorant assertors in thir own art will have prov'd themselves more and more, not to be Protestant Divines, whose constant judgement in this point they have so audaciously bely'd, but rather to be a pack of hungrie Church-Wolves,[43] who in the steps of *Simon Magus* thir Father, following the hot sent of double Livings and Pluralities, advousons, donatives, inductions, and augmentations, though uncall'd to the Flock of Christ, but by the meer suggestion of thir Bellies, like those Priest of *Bel*, whose pranks *Daniel* found out; have got possession, or rather seis'd upon the Pulpit, as the strong hold and fortress of thir sedition and rebellion against the civil Magistrate. Whose friendly and victorious hand having rescu'd them from the Bishops thir insulting Lords, fed them plenteously, both in public and in privat, rais'd them to be high and rich of poore and base; onely suffer'd not thir covetousness & fierce ambition, which as the pitt that sent out thir fellow locusts, hath bin ever bottomless and boundless, to interpose in all things, and over all persons, thir impetuous ignorance and importunity.

THE END.

---

[43]Compare the image of parish priest wolves preying on innocent parishioners in "Lycidas," 128, and again in Sonnet 16, "hireling wolves whose gospel is their maw," and *Paradise Lost* 4.183, where the image is applied to Satan.

ΈΙΚΟΝΟΚΛΑΈΣΤΗΣ

IN

ANSWER

To a Book intitl'd

ΈΙΚΩ`Ν ΒΑΣΙΛΙΚΗ.

THE
Portrature of his sacred Majesty

in his *Solitudes* and *Sufferings*.

The AUTHOR *J. M.*

PROV. 28.15, 16, 17.

15. *As a roaring Lyon, and a ranging Beare, so is a wicked Ruler over the poor people.*

16. *The Prince that wanteth understanding, is also a great oppressor; but he that hateth covetousness shall prolong his dayes.*

17. *A man that doth violence to the blood of any person, shall fly to the pit, let not man stay him.*

Salust. Conjurat. Catilin.

Regiumimperius, quod initio, conservandæ libertatis, atque augendæ reipub. Causâ
    fuerat, in superbam, dominationemque se convertit.
Regibus boni, quam mali, suspectiores sunt; semperq; his aliena virtus formidolosa est.
Impunè quælibet facere, it est regem esse. Idem Bell. Jugurth.

Publish'd now the second time, and much enlarg'd.

London, Printed by *Thomas Newcomb* in Thamestreet over
against *Baynards-Castle* M DC L.

Eikonoklastes (Selections)
(1650)

By 1649, the year of the execution of Charles I, Milton could not bring himself to believe that any king ruled by divine right: he thought it "most fals, that all Kings are the Lords Anointed." Rather than being anointed by God, the king is "but one kind of Magistrat," who, like other magistrates, serves the people. There was no such thing as divine right, and the King should serve under the law, not be above it.

Milton's position, as ever, is that of a member of the intellectual, if not royalist, elite. The rabble is below him, providing for the King's charlatanism "the worthles approbation of an inconstant, irrational, and Image-doting rabble" (below, 1093). But of course the people had spoken through the Parliament in commanding the execution of the King.

OCCASION

Milton's pamphlet answers the smarmy propaganda that made a martyr of Charles I as a type of Christ (Grossman). Milton attacks the holy image implied in the title *Eikon Basilike*, the subtitle of which made it obvious: "The Portraiture of his sacred Majesty in his *Solitudes* and *Sufferings*." Milton pictures himself as the image-breaker implicit in the title *Eikonoklastes*. He had been ordered by the Council of State to write the defense of regicide, probably not long after he had become Secretary for Foreign Tongues, on March 15, 1649 (Yale 3: 147). In the 230 pages he was allowed to fill, Milton justifies the execution of a king he felt had become a tyrant, and he gleefully proves that the entire document pretended to be by the King—supposedly a deathbed confession of his holiness—is a fraud, with bits stolen from no less than Sir Philip Sidney, the infamous "Pamela prayer," to be passed off as composed by Charles in his grief as his last word before his execution. Milton cannot stand the idea that a King could be so poor of spirit as to steal without acknowledgment the intellectual property of a poet of pagan-sounding romances such as Sir Philip Sidney. Charles also violated his own chosen genre, that of Christian lament, by stealing from a pastoral romance, a genre which Milton considered pagan in spirit.

A false image of a Roman Catholic type of martyr had been constructed by Royalist propagandists of limited imagination using pagan prayers. It is funny and pitiful that a King should stoop to stealing prayers from a poet.

Hughes calls the *Eikon Basilike* "a cleric's forgery of a pseudo-autobiographical apology for the dead king and his living partisans" (Yale 3: 149). Hughes demolishes the myth that Milton caused a publisher of the *Eikon Basilike* to insert the Pamela prayer, a prayer Sidney had written to record the thoughts of a woman unjustly imprisoned, into editions of the *Eikon Basilike*. We know now that the King's book was written in utmost secrecy by the cleric John Gauden, who apparently did work from notes written by the dead King. Gauden would be rewarded for his effort with several bishoprics, including that of Exeter given him by Charles II. Achinstein establishes a context for Milton's readers and the King's.

METHOD

Milton was perhaps forced by his commission from the Council of State to attack the *Eikon Basilike* point by point, so that the form of his own book takes its shape from the book it attacks. If he had been left on his own, he might have attacked the King's book in his own person as a poet and potential dramatist, for representing a pseudo-tragedy, with the King resembling Shakespeare's Richard III, hypocritically spouting piety and self-mortification (Yale 3: 301). As Nigel Smith points out, "Milton's defence of the regicide involved him in a redefinition of the contemporary understanding of tragedy" (16).

The dead King Charles had also been presented visually as a Christian martyr. William Marshall, the same engraver whom Milton had mocked for the inadequate portrait he had drawn for his 1645 *Poems*, had pictured Charles as an obvious type of Christ, with his eyes staring at a divine crown on one side of his head and at a divine cloud on the other, a cloud where apparently God exists while separating the light and the dark (Genesis 1. 14–18). In Charles's hands is the crown of thorns worn by Christ in the Crucifixion.

Milton saw the image in terms of a false drama, "drawn out to the full measure of a Masking Scene, and sett there to catch fools and silly gazers" (below, 1078). This was propaganda first published within a week of Charles's execution (Hill 172), the haste of which should have provided a clue of its nature as propaganda. But it was effective propaganda. Hughes records thirty-five editions in London within the first year of its appearance and another twenty-five in the same period in Ireland and on the continent (Yale 3: 150). Milton had to provide a very heavy hammer to break such a sacred image, presented to the people in such a popular package. He might have seen himself as the "Gideon Iconoclastes" he had considered writing a tragedy about, since Gideon overturned pagan altars and conquered the Midianites; then he refused to rule Israel, turning the responsibility over to God Himself (Judges 6-8; Hill 175).

TEXT

The first edition of Eikonoklastes was published at some time before Thomason wrote the date October 6, 1649, in his copy. The second edition, that of 1650, is augmented by the author and it is carefully printed and printed expensively, as befits an important piece of propaganda for a new government uncertain of itself because of the very act of regicide. Unlike Milton's antiprelatical tracts, *Eikonoklastes* has the authority of the government in power, though that government was rather shakily in command in 1650.

The type face is close to that of modern fourteen point, quite readable even by those with failing eyesight (Milton included). Paragraphing is observed for aesthetic reasons (it breaks up the blocks of type) as well as for the usual rhetorical reasons. The compositor paid close attention to Milton's spelling and apparently to his comma usage. Capitalization is rhetorical rather than random identification of nouns.

Works Cited

Achinstein, Sharon. *Milton and the Revolutionary Reader*. Princeton, NJ: Princeton UP, 1994.

Fallon, Robert Thomas. *Divided Empire: Milton's Political Imagery*. University Park, PA: Penn State Press, 1995.

Grossman, Marshall. "The Dissemination of the King," David L. Smith, Richard Strier, and David Bevington, eds. *The Theatrical City: Culture, Theatre, and Politics in London, 1576–1649*. New York: Cambridge UP, 1995.

Hill, Christopher. *Milton and the English Revolution*. New York: Viking, 1977.

Smith, Nigel. *Literature and Revolution in England, 1640–1660*. New Haven, CT: Yale UP, 1994.

Eikonoklastes

The *PREFACE.*

TO descant on the misfortunes of a person fall'n from so high a dignity, who hath also payd his final debt both to Nature and his Faults, is neither of it self a thing commendable, nor the intention of this discours. Neither was it fond ambition, or the vanity to get a Name, present, or with Posterity, by writing against a King: I never was so thirsty after Fame, nor so destitute of other hopes and means, better and more certaine to attaine it. For Kings have gain'd glorious Titles from thir Favourers by writing against privat men, as *Henry* the 8th did against *Luther*; but no man ever gain'd much honour by writing against a King, as not usually meeting with that force of Argument in such Courtly *Antagonists*,[1] which to convince might add to his reputation. Kings most commonly, though strong in legions, are but weak in Arguments; as they who have ever accustom'd from the Cradle to use thir will onely as thir right hand, thir reason alwayes as thir left. Whence unexpectedly constrain'd to that kind of combat, they prove but weak and puny Adversaries. Nevertheless for their sakes who through custom, simplicitie, or want of better teaching, have not more seriously considerd Kings, then in the gaudy name of Majesty, and admire them and thir doings, as if they breath'd not the same breath with other mortal men, I shall make no scruple to take up (for it seems to be the challenge both of him and his party) to take up this Gauntlet, though a Kings, in the behalf of Libertie, and the Common-wealth.

And furder, since it appears manifestly the cunning drift of a factious and defeated Party, to make the same advantage of his Book, which they did before of his Regal Name and Authority, and intend it not so much the defence of his former actions, as the promoting of thir own future designes, making thereby the Book thir own rather then the Kings, as the benefit now must be thir own more then his, now the third time to corrupt and disorder the mindes of weaker men, by new suggestions and narrations, either falsly or fallaciously representing the state of things, to the dishonour of this present Goverment, and the retarding of a generall peace, so needfull to this afflicted Nation, and so nigh obtain'd, I suppose it no injurie to the dead, but a good deed rather to the living, if by better information given

---

[1]The word is italicized perhaps to indicate its Greek origin and its recent introduction (1599, according to the *OED*) into English, by Ben Jonson.

them, or, which is anough, by onely remembring them[2] the truth of what they themselves know to be heer misaffirmd, they may be kept from entring the third time unadvisedly into Warr and bloodshed. For as to any moment of solidity in the Book it self, save only that a King is said to be the Author, then which there needs no more among the blockish vulgar,[3] to make it wise, and excellent, and admir'd, nay to set it next the Bible, though otherwise containing little els but the common grounds of tyranny and popery, drest up, the better to deceive, in a new Protestant guise, and trimmly garnish'd over, or as to any need of answering, in respect of staid and well-principl'd men, I take it on me as a work assign'd rather, then by me chos'n or affected. Which was the cause both of beginning it so late, and finishing it so leasurely, in the midst of other imployments and diversions. And though well it might have seem'd in vaine to write at all; considering the envy and almost infinite prejudice likely to be stirr'd up among the Common sort, against what ever can be writt'n or gainsaid to the Kings book, so advantageous to a book it is, only to be a Kings, and though it be an irksom labour to write with industrie and judicious paines that which neither waigh'd, nor well read, shall be judg'd without industry or the paines of well judging, by faction and the easy literature of custom and opinion, it shall be ventur'd yet, and the truth not smother'd, but sent abroad, in the native confidence of her single self, to earn, how she can, her entertainment in the world, and to finde out, and to finde out her own readers; few perhaps, but those few, such of value and substantial worth, as truth and wisdom, not respecting numbers and bigg names, have bin ever wont in all ages to be contented with.

And if the late King had thought sufficient those Answers and Defences made for him in his life time, they who on the other side accus'd his evil Goverment, judging that on their behalf anough also hath been reply'd, the heat of this controversie was in lykelyhood drawing to an end; and the furder mention of his deeds, not so much unfortunat as faulty, had in tenderness to his late sufferings, bin willingly forborn; and perhaps for the present age might have slept with him unrepeated; while his adversaries, calm'd and asswag'd with the success of thir cause, had bin the less unfavorable to his memory. But since he himself, making new appeale to Truth and the World, hath left behind him this Book as the best advocat and interpreter of his own actions, and that his Friends by publishing, dispersing, commending, and almost adoring it, seem to place therein the chiefe

strength and nerves[4] of thir cause, it would argue doubtless in the other party great deficience and distrust of themselves, not to meet the force of his reason in any field whatsoever, the force and equipage of whose Armes they have so oft'n met victoriously. And he who at the Barr stood excepting against the form and manner of his Judicature, and complain'd that he was not heard, neither he nor his Friends shall have that cause now to find fault being mett and debated with in this op'n and monumental Court of his own erecting; and not onely heard uttering his whole kind at large, but answer'd. Which to doe effectually, if it be necessary that to his Book nothing the more respect be had for being his, they of his own Party can have no just reason to exclaime. For it were too unreasonable that he, because dead, should have the liberty in his Good to speak all evil of the Parlament; and they, because living, should be expected to have less freedom or any for them, to speak home the plain truth of a full and pertinent reply. As he, to acquitt himself, hath not spar'd his Adversaries, to load them with all sorts of blame and accusation, so to him, as in his Book alive, there will be us'd no more Courtship then he uses; but what is properly his own guilt, not imputed any more to his evil Counsellors, (a Ceremony us'd longer by the Parlament then he himself desir'd) shall be laid heer without circumlocutions at his own dore. That they who from the first beginning, or but now of late, by what unhappines I know not, are so much affatuated,[5] not with his person onely, but with his palpable faults, and dote upon his deformities, may have none to blame but thir own folly, as if they live and dye in such a strook'n blindnes, as next to that of *Sodom*[6] hath not happ'nd to any sort of men more gross, or more misleading. Yet neither let his enemies expect to finde recorded heer all that hath been whisper'd in the Court, or alleg'd op'nly of the Kings bad actions; it being the proper scope of this work in hand, not to ripp up and relate the misdoings of his whole life, but to answer only, and refute the missayings of his book.

First then that some men (whether this were by him intended, or by his Friends) have by policy accomplish'd after death that revenge upon thir Enemies, which in life they were not able, hath been oft related. And among other examples we finde that the last will of *Cæsar* being read to the people, and what bounteous Legacies hee had bequeath'd them, wrought more in

---

2"Reminding them that."
3Block-headed common people.

4Muscles.
5The *OED* assumes that the word meant the same as "infatuated," and that Milton invented it.
6The fate of Sodom and Gomorrah was to be destroyed by a rain of brimstone and fire (Genesis 19.24).

that Vulgar audience to the avenging of his death, then all the art he could ever use, to win thir favor in his life-time.[7] And how much their intent, who publish'd these overlate Apologies and Meditations of the dead King, drives to the same end of stirring up the people to bring him that honour, that affection, and by consequence, the revenge to his dead Corps, which hee himself living could never gain to his Person, it appears both by the conceited portraiture before his Book,[8] drawn out to the full measure of a Masking Scene, and sett there to catch fools and silly gazers, and by those Latin words after the end, *Vota dabunt quæ Bella negarunt*; intimating, That what hee could not compass by Warr, he should atchieve by his Meditations. For in words which admitt of various sense, the libertie is ours to choose that inter-pretation which may best minde[9] us of what our restless enemies endeavor, and what wee are timely to prevent. And heer may be well observ'd the loose and negligent curiosity of those who took upon them to adorn the setting out of this Book: for though the Picture set in Front would Martyr him and Saint him to befool the people, yet the Latin Motto in the end, which they understand not, leaves him, as it were a politic contriver to bring about that interest by faire and plausible words, which the force of Armes deny'd him. But quaint Em-blems and devices begg'd from the old Pageantry of some Twelf-nights entertainment at *Whitehall*,[10] will doe but ill to make a Saint or Martyr: and if the People re-solve to take him Sainted at the rate of such a Canon-izing, I shall suspect thir Calendar more then the *Gregorian*.[11] In one thing I must commend his op'nness who gave the title to this Book, *Εἰκὼν Βασιλικὴ*, that is to say, The Kings Image; and by the Shrine he dresses out for him, certainly would have the people come and worship him. For which reason this answer also is in-titl'd *Iconoclastes*, the famous Surname of many Greek Emperors,[12] who in thir zeal to the command of God, after long tradition of Idolatry in the Church, took

courage, and broke all superstitious Images to peeces. But the People, exorbitant and excessive in all thir mo-tions, are prone ofttimes not to a religious onely, but to a civil kinde of Idolatry in idolizing thir Kings; though never more mistak'n in the object of thir worship; heretofore being wont to repute for Saints, those faith-ful and courageous Barons, who lost thir lives in the Field, making glorious Warr against Tyrants for the common Liberty; as *Simon de Momfort*[13] Earl of *Leicester*, against *Henry* the third; *Thomas Plantagenet* Earl of *Lancaster*, against *Edward* the second.[14] But now, with a besotted and degenerate baseness of spirit, except some few, who yet retain in them the old English fortitude and love of Freedom, and have testifi'd it by thir matchless deeds, the rest, imbastartiz'd from the ancient nobleness of thir Ancestors, are ready to fall flatt and give adoration to the Image and Memory of this Man, who hath offer'd at more cunning fetches[15] to undermine our Liberties, and putt Tyranny into an Art, then any British King before him. Which low dejection and debasement of mind in the people, I must confess I cannot willingly ascribe to the natural disposition of an English-man, but rather to two other causes. First, to the Prelats and thir fellow-teachers, though of another Name and Sect, whose Pulpit stuff, both first and last, hath bin the Doctrin and perpetual infusion of servility and wretchedness to all thir hearers; whose lives the type of worldliness and hypocrisie, without the least true pattern of vertue, righteousness, or self-denial in thir whole practice. I attribute it next to the factious inclination of most men divided from the public by several ends and humors of thir own. At first no man less belov'd, no man more generally condemn'd then was the King; from the time that it became his custom to break Parlaments at home, and either wilfully or weakly to betray Protestants abroad, to the beginning of these Combustions. All men inveigh'd against him; all men, except Court-vassals, oppos'd him and his tyran-nical proceedings; the cry was universal; and this full Parlament was at first unanimous in thir dislike and Protestation against his evil Goverment. But when they who sought themselves and not the Public, began to doubt that all of them could not one by one and the same way attain to thir ambitious purposes, then was the King, or his Name at least, as a fit property, first

---

[7]The scene could be based on Shakespeare's recreation of the reading of the will of Caesar (*Julius Caesar* 3.2.140), or Suetonius's *Life of Caesar* 83.

[8]The portrait of Charles is "conceited" in the sense that it is ornamented heavily with emblems or symbols—rays of divine light, mottoes, kingly crowns and Christ's crown of thorns.

[9]Remind.

[10]Carrying on the image of the King's pretense as being like that of masquers at Whitehall Palace on Twelfth Night, the celebration at the end of the Christmas season after which Shakespeare named his play.

[11]The Julian Calendar, in use as Milton wrote, would not be replaced by the Gregorian Calendar until 1751.

[12]The term does not seem to exist in classical Greek, but, as Hughes points out in the *Complete Poetry and Selected Prose*, the title had been give to the Isaurian emperor Leo III, who began a crusade in AD 726 against the worship of images within the Roman Catholic Church (784n).

[13]Simon de Montfort, whose rebellion against Henry III, culminating with his death in 1264, was viewed either as despicable by Royalist forces or heroic by Parliamentary forces.

[14]As in Marlowe's play *Edward II*, that king and Richard II (as in Shakespeare's play) were both considered worthy to be deposed, again by Parliamentary forces.

[15]Tricks, diversions.

made use of, his doing made the best of, and by degrees justifi'd: Which begott him such a party, as after many wiles and struglings with his inward fears, imbold'n'd him at length to sett up his Standard against the Parlament. Whenas before that time, all his adherents, consisting most of dissolute Sword-men[16] and Suburb-roysters,[17] hardly amounted to the making up of one ragged regiment strong anough to assault the unarmed house of Commons. After which attempt, seconded by a tedious and bloody warr on his subjects, wherein he hath so farr exceeded those his arbitrary violences in time of Peace, they who before hated him for his high misgovernment, nay, fought against him with display'd banners in the field, now applaud him and extoll him for the wisest and most religious Prince that liv'd. By so strange a method amongst the mad multitude is a sudden reputation won, of wisdom by wilfulness and suttle shifts, of goodness by multiplying evil, of piety by endeavouring to root out true religion.

But it is evident that the chief of his adherents never lov'd him, never honour'd either him or his cause, but as they took him to set a face upon thir own malignant designes; nor bemoan his loss at all, but the loss of thir own aspiring hopes: Like those captive women whom the Poet notes in his *Iliad*, to have bewaild the death of *Patroclus* in outward show, but indeed thir own condition.

Πάτροκλον πρόφασιν, σφῶν δ'αὐτῶν κήδε᾽ ἑκάστη.
Hom. Iliad. τ.[18]

And it needs must be ridiculous to any judgement un-inthrall'd, that they who in other matters express so little fear either of God or man, should in this one parti-cular outstripp all precisianism[19] with thir scruples and cases, and fill mens ears continually with the noise of thir conscientious Loyaltie and Allegeance to the King, Rebels in the mean while to God in all thir actions be-side: much less that they whose profess'd Loyalty and Allegeance led them to direct Arms against the Kings Person, and thought him nothing violated by the Sword of Hostility drawn by them against him, should now in

earnest think him violated by the unsparing Sword of Justice, which undoubtedly so much the less in vain she bears among Men, by how much greater and in highest place the offender. Els Justice, whether moral or po-litical, were not Justice, but a fals counterfet of that impartial and Godlike vertue. The onely grief is, that the head was not strook off to the best advantage and commodity of them that held it by the hair; an ingrate-full and pervers generation, who having first cry'd to God to be deliver'd from thir King, now murmur against God that heard thir praiers, and cry as loud for thir King against those that deliver'd them. But as to the Author of these Soliloquies,[20] whether it were un-doubtedly the late King, as is vulgarly beleev'd, or any secret *Coadjutor*, and some stick not to name him, it can add nothing, nor shall take from the weight, if any be, of reason which he brings. But allegations, not reasons are the main contents of this Book; and need no more then other contrary allegations to lay the question be-fore all men in an eev'n ballance; though it were sup-pos'd that the testimony of one man in his own cause affirming, could be of any moment[21] to bring in doubt the autority of a Parlament denying. But if these his fair spok'n words shall be heer fairly confronted and laid parallel to his own farr differing deeds, manifest and vi-sible to the whole Nation, then surely we may look on them who notwithstanding shall persist to give to bare words more credit then to op'n deeds, as men whose judgement was not rationally evinc'd and perswaded, but fatally stupifi'd and bewitch'd, into such a blinde and obstinate beleef. For whose cure it may be doubted, not whether any charm, though never so wisely mur-mur'd, but whether any prayer can be available. This however would be remember'd and wel noted, that while the K.[22] instead of that repentance which was in reason and in conscience to be expected from him, without which we could not lawfully re-admitt him, persists heer to maintain and justifie the most apparent of his evil doings, and washes over with a Court-fucus[23] the worst and foulest of his actions, disables and un-creates the Parlament it self, with all our laws and Native liberties that ask not his leave, dishonours and attaints all Protestant Churches, not Prelaticall, and what they piously reform'd, with the slander of rebel-

---

[16]In the *History of Britain*, an assassin is described as a "Sword-man" (Yale 5: 199).

[17]London suburbs seem to have been associated with dissolute behavior, since a prostitute was labeled a "suburb sinner" (*OED* "suburb" 4b). A roister was a riotous or dissolute man.

[18]From the *Iliad* 19. The Yale editors provide Chapman's translation: "Thus spake she weeping, and with her did th'other ladies moan / Patroclus' fortunes in pretext, but in sad truth their own."

[19]The overscrupulousness for many years ascribed to "puritan" preachers or petty public officials. A "precision" was the same thing as a "puritan."

[20]Any sort of talking to oneself, not necessarily dramatic; in this case, Charles's conversations with himself become a kind of confessional genre. The deceit is even greater, if Charles's private thoughts were actually written by a "*Coadjutor*," a helper or in this case a ghostwriter, with the overtones of someone who takes the place of an enfeebled church official (*OED* 2).

[21]"Could be of any consequence."

[22]Standard abbreviation for the title of the King.

[23]A kind of makeup associated with the court (metaphorical, of course).

lion, sacrilege, and hypocrisie; they who seem'd of late to stand up hottest for the Cov'nant, can now sit mute and much pleas'd to hear all these opprobrious things utter'd against thir faith, thir freedom, and themselves in thir own doings made traitors to boot: The Divines also, thir wizzards,[24] can be so braz'n as to cry *Hosanna* to this his book, which cries louder against them for no disciples of Christ, but of *Iscariot*; and to seem now convinc'd with these wither'd arguments and reasons heer, the same which in som other writings of that party, and in his own former Declarations and expresses, they have so oft'n heertofore endeavour'd to confute and to explode; none appearing all this while to vindicate Church or State from these calumnies and reproaches, but a small handfull of men whom they defame and spit at with all the odious names of Schism and Sectarism. I never knew that time in *England*, when men of truest Religion were not counted Sectaries: but wisdom now, valor, justice, constancy, prudence united and imbodied to defend Religion and our Liberties, both by word and deed against tyranny, is counted Schism and faction. Thus in a graceless age things of highest praise and imitation under a right name, to make them infamous and hatefull to the people, are miscall'd. Certainly, if ignorance and perversness will needs be national and universal, then they who adhere to wisdom and to truth, are not therfore to be blam'd, for beeing so few as to seem a sect or faction. But in my opinion it goes not ill with that people where these vertues grow so numerous and well joyn'd together, as to resist and make head against the rage and torrent of that boistrous folly and superstition that possesses and hurries on the vulgar sort. This therfore we may conclude to be a high honour don us from God, and a speciall mark of his favor, whom he hath selected as the sole remainder, after all these changes and commotions, to stand upright and stedfast in his cause; dignify'd with the defence of truth and public libertie; while others who aspir'd to be the topp of Zelots, and had almost brought Religion to a kind of trading monopoly, have not onely by thir late silence and neutrality bely'd thir profession, but founder'd themselves and thir consciences, to comply with enemies in that wicket cause and interest which they have too oft'n curs'd in others, to prosper now in the same themselves.

Ἐικονοκλάστης.[25]

I. *Upon the Kings calling this last Parlament.*

That which the King layes down heer as his first foundation, and as it were the head stone of his whole Structure, that *He call'd this last Parlament not more by others advice and the necessity of his affaires, then by his own chois and inclination,* is to all knowing men so apparently not true, that a more unlucky and inauspicious sentence, and more betok'ning the downfall of his whole Fabric, hardly could have come into his minde. For who knows not that the inclination of a Prince is best known either by those next about him, and most in favor with him, or by the current of his own actions. Those neerest to this King and most his Favorites, were Courtiers and Prelates; men whose chief study was to find out which way the King inclin'd, and to imitate him exactly. How these men stood affected to Parlaments, cannot be forgott'n. No man but may remember it was thir continuall exercise to dispute and preach against them; and in thir common discours nothing was more frequent, then that *they hoped the King should now have no need of Parlaments any more.* And this was but the copy which his Parasites had industriously tak'n from his own words and action, who never call'd a Parlament but to supply his necessities; and having supply'd those, as suddenly and ignominiously dissolv'd it, without redressing any one greevance of the people. Sometimes choosing rather to miss of his Subsidies, or to raise them by illegal course, then that the people should not miss of thir hopes to be releiv'd by Parlaments.

The first he broke off at his comming to the Crown; for not other cause then to protect the Duke of *Buckingham*[26] against them who had accus'd him, besides other hainous crimes, of no less then poysoning the deceased King his Father; concerning which matter the Declaration of *No more addresses,* hath sufficiently inform'd us. And still the latter breaking was with more affront and indignity put upon the House and her worthiest Members, then the former: Insomuch that in the fifth year of his Raign, in a Proclamation he seems offended at the very rumor of a Parlament divulg'd among the people: as if he had tak'n it for a kind of slander, that men should think him that way exorable, much less inclin'd: and forbidds it as a presumption to prescribe him any

---

[24]Any minister of the Church who sided with the King is smeared with the title of "wizard."

[25]The "τ" was omitted from the word in Bodleian; I have restored it, as did the Yale editors.
[26]George Villiers (1592–1628), favorite of James I, created Duke of Buckingham by James in 1623 and eventually assassinated by one of his own officers.

time for Parlaments, that is to say, either by perswasion or Petition, or so much as the reporting of such a rumor; for other manner of prescribing was at that time not suspected. By which fierce Edict, the people, forbidd'n to complain, as well as forc'd to suffer, began from thenceforth to despaire of Parlaments. Whereupon such illegal actions, and especially to get vast summs of Money, were put in practise by the King and his new Officers, as Monopolies, compulsive Knight-hoods, Cote, Conduct and Ship money, the seizing not of one Naboths Vineyard,[27] but of whole Inheritances under the pretence of Forrest, or Crown-Lands, corruption and Bribery compounded for, with impunities granted for the furure, as gave evident proof that the King never meant, nor could it stand with the reason of his affaires, ever to recall Parlaments; having brought by these irregular courses the peoples interest and his own to so direct an opposition, that he might foresee plainly, if nothing but a Parlament could save the people, it must necessarily be his undoing.

Till eight or nine years after, proceeding with a high hand in these enormities, and having the second time levied an injurious Warr against his native Countrie *Scotland*, and finding all those other shifts of raising Money, which bore out his first expedition, not to faile him, not *of his own chois and inclination*, as any Child may see, but urg'd by strong necessities, and the very pangs of State, which his own violent proceedings had brought him to, hee calls a Parlament; first in *Ireland*, which onely was to give him four Subsidies, and so to expire; then in *England*, where his first demand was but twelve Subsidies, to maintain a Scotch Warr, condemn'd and abominated by the whole Kingdom; promising thir greevances should be consider'd afterward. Which when the Parlament, who judg'd that Warr it self one of thir main greevances, made no hast to grant, not enduring the delays of his impatient will, or els fearing the conditions of thir grant, he breaks off the whole Session, and dismisses them and thir greevances with scorn and frustration.

Much less therfore did hee call this last Parlament by his own chois and inclination; but having first try'd in vaine all undue ways to procure Mony, his Army, of thir own accord, being beat'n in the North, the Lords Petitioning, and the general voice of the people almost hissing him and his ill-acted regality off the Stage,[28] com

pell'd at length both by his wants, and by his feares, upon meer extremity he summon'd this last Parlament. And how is it possible that hee should willingly incline to Parlaments, who never was perceiv'd to call them, but for the greedy hope of a whole National Bribe, his Subsidies, and never lov'd, never fulfill'd, never promoted the true end of Parlaments, the redress of greevances, but still put them off, and prolong'd them, whether gratify'd or[29] not gratify'd; and was indeed the Author of all those greevances; To say therfore that hee call'd this Parlament of his own chois and inclination, argues how little truth wee can expect from the sequel of this Book, which ventures in the very first period[30] to affront more then one Nation with an untruth so remarkable; and presumes a more implicit Faith in the people of *England*, then the Pope ever commanded from the Romish Laitie; or els a natural sottishness fitt to be abus'd and ridd'n.[31] While in the judgement of wise Men, by laying the foundation of his defence on the avouchment of that which is so manifestly untrue, he hath giv'n a worse foile to his own cause, then when his whole Forces were at any time overthrown. They therfore who think such great Service don to the Kings affairs in publishing this Book, will find themselves in the end mistak'n: if sense and right mind, or but any mediocrity of knowledge and remembrance hath not quite forsak'n men.

But to prove his inclination to Parlaments, he affirms heer *To have always thought the right way of them, most safe for his Crown, and best pleasing to his People.* What hee thought we know not; but that hee ever took the contrary way wee saw; and from his own actions we felt long agoe what he thought of Parlaments or of pleasing his People: a surer evidence then what we hear now too late in words.

He alleges, that *the cause of forbearing to convene Parlaments, was the sparkes which some mens distempers there studied to kindle.* They were indeed not temper'd to his temper; for it neither was the Law, nor the rule by which all other tempers were to bee try'd; but they were esteem'd and chos'n for the fittest men in thir several Counties, to allay and quench those distempers which his own inordinate doings had inflam'd. And if that were his refusing to *convene*, till those men had been qualify'd to his temper, that is to say, his will, we may easily conjecture what hope ther was of Parlaments, had not fear and his insatiat poverty in the midst

---

[27] A biblical example of gross injustice, the behavior of Jezebel and Ahab in seizing the vineyard of Naboth (1 Kings 21).

[28] The action here suggests that of Satan also acting (in the dramatic sense) before the fallen angels in Book 10 of *Paradise Lost*, and also being met with "A dismal universal hiss, the sound / Of public scorn" (509–10); the imagery links Satan and Charles I. Charles is acting

throughout in the sense that he is a hypocrite; there may also be the suggestion that his life is a farce.

[29] Bodleian has "ot" for "or." I have corrected the typographical error.

[30] The very first sentence.

[31] Probably "Taken advantage of" (*OED* 3).

of his excessive wealth constrain'd him.

Hee hoped by his freedom, and their moderation to prevent misunderstandings. And wherfore not by their freedom and his moderation? But freedom he thought too high a word for them; and moderation too mean[32] a word for himself: this was not the way to prevent misunderstandings. He still *fear'd passion and prejudice in other men*; not in himself: *and doubted not by the weight of his* own *reason, to counterpoyse any Faction;* it being so easie for him, and so frequent, to call his obstinacy, Reason, and other mens reason, Faction. Wee in the mean while must believe, that wisdom and all reason came to him by Title, with his Crown; Passion, Prejudice, and Faction came to others by being Subjects.

He was sorry to hear with what popular heat Elections were carry'd in many places. Sorry rather that Court Letters and intimations prevail'd no more, to divert or to deterr the people from thir free Election of those men, whom they thought best affected to Religion and thir Countries Libertie, both at that time in danger to be lost. And such men they were, as by the Kingdom were sent to advise him, not sent to be cavi'l'd at, because Elected, or to be entertaind by him with an undervalue and misprision of thir temper, judgment, or affection. In vain was a Parlament thought fittest by the known Laws of our Nation, to advise and regulate unruly Kings, if they, in stead of hearkning to advice, should be permitted to turn it off, and refuse it by vilifying and traducing thir advisers, or by accusing of a popular heat those that lawfully elected them.

His own and his Childrens interest oblig'd him to seek and to preserve the love and welfare of his Subjects. Who doubts it? But the same interest, common to all Kings, was never yet available to make them all seek that, which was indeed best for themselves and thir Posterity. All men by thir own and thir Childrens interest are oblig'd to honestie and justice: but how little that consideration works in privat men, how much less in Kings, thir deeds declare best.

He intended to oblige both Friends and Enemies, and to exceed thir desires, did they but pretend to any modest and sober sense; mistaking the whole business of a Parlament. Which mett not to receive from him obligations, but Justice; nor he to expect from them thir modesty, but thir grave advice, utter'd with freedom in the public cause. His talk of modesty in thir desires of the common welfare, argues him not much to have understood what he had to grant, who misconceav'd so much the nature of what they had to desire. And for *sober sence* the expresion was too mean; and recoiles with as much dis-

honour upon himself, to be a King where sober sense could possibly be so wanting in a Parlament.

The odium and offences which some mens rigour, or remissness in Church and State had contracted upon his Goverment, hee resolved to have expiated with better Laws and regulations. And yet the worst of misdemeanors committed by the worst of all his favorites, in the hight of thir dominion, whether acts of rigor or remissness, he hath from time to time continu'd, own'd, and taken upon himself by public Declarations, as oft'n as the Clergy, or any other of his Instruments felt themselves over burd'n'd with the peoples hatred. And who knows not the superstitious rigor of his Sundays Chappel, and the licentious remissness of his Sundays Theater; accompanied with that reverend Statute for *Domenical Jiggs*[33] and May-poles, publish'd in his own Name,[34] and deriv'd from the example of his father *James.* Which testifies all that rigor in superstition, all that remissness in Religion to have issu'd out originally from his own House, and from his own Autority. Much rather then may those general miscarriages in State, his proper Sphear, be imputed to no other person chiefly then to himself. And which of all those oppressive Acts, or Impositions did he ever disclaim or disavow, till the fatal aw of this Parlament hung ominously over him. Yet heer hee smoothly seeks to wipe off all the envie of his evill Goverment upon his Substitutes, and under-Officers: and promises, though much too late, what wonders he purpos'd to have don in the reforming of Religion; a work wherein all his undertakings heretofore declare him to have had little or no judgement. Neither could his Breeding,[35] or his cours of life acquaint him with a thing so Spiritual. Which may well assure us what kind of Reformation we could expect from him; either som politic form of an impos'd Religion, or els perpetual vexation, and persecution to all those that comply'd not with such a form. The like amendment hee promises in State; not a stepp furder *then his Reason and Conscience told him was fit to be desir'd*; wishing *hee had kept within those bounds, and not suffer'd his own judgement to have bin over-borne in some things,* of which things one was

---

[32]Lowly, in the sense of being a lower social standing.

[33]Dances on Sunday, Milton's wonderful combination of the word jig (derived from the French *gigue* but as common as the term "dancing a jig") and "*Domenical,*" a word made up for the occasion based on the Italian *Domenica,* meaning "Sunday."

[34]For the context of Charles I's *Book of Sports,* in which "Caroline masques wrote Charles I and his policies into the heavens; [and] Milton's Attendant Spirit writes them out," see Leah Marcus, *The Politics of Mirth: Jonson, Herrick, Milton, Marvell, and the Defense of Old Holiday Pastimes* (Chicago: U of Chicago P, 1986): 182.

[35]Normally Milton uses the word in a positive sense, as in "good breeding," but here the King's good breeding has set limits on his education about what might be important to his people.

the Earl of *Staffords* execution.[36] And what signifies all this, but that stil his resolution was the same, to set up an arbitrary Goverment of his own; and that all Britain was to be ty'd and chain'd to the conscience, judgement, and reason of one Man; as if thse gifts had been only his peculiar[37] and Prerogative, intal'd[38] upon him with his fortune to be a King. When as doubtless no man so obstinate, or so much a Tyrant, but professes to be guided by that which he calls his Reason, and his Judgement, though never so corrupted; and pretends also his conscience. In the mean while, for any Parlament or the whole Nation to have either reason, judgement, or conscience, by this rule was altogether in vaine, if it thwarted the Kings will; which was easie for him to call by any other more plausible name. He himself hath many times acknowledg'd to have no right over us but by Law; and by the same Law to govern us: but Law in a Free Nation hath bin ever public reason, the enacted reason of a Parlament; which he denying to enact, denies to govern us by that which ought to be our Law; interposing his own privat reason, which to us is no Law. And thus we find these faire and specious promises, made upon the experience of many hard sufferings, and his most mortifi'd retirements, being throughly[39] sifted, to containe nothing in them much different from his former practices, so cross, and so averse to all his Parlaments, and both the Nations of this Iland. What fruits they could in likelyhood have produc'd in his restorement, is obvious to any prudent foresight.

And this is the substance of his first section, till wee come to the devout of it, model'd in the form of a privat Psalter. Which they who so much admire, either for the matter or the manner, may as well admire the ArchBishops late Breviary,[40] and many other as good *Manuals*, and *Handmaids of Devotion*,[41] the lip-work of every Prelatical Liturgist, clapt together, and quilted out of Scripture phrase, with as much ease, and as little need of Christian diligence, or judgement, as belongs to the compiling of any ord'nary and salable peece of English Divinity, that the Shops value.[42] But he who from such a kind of Psalmistry, or any other verbal Devotion,

without the pledge and earnest of sutable deeds, can be perswaded of a zeale, and true righteousness in the person, hath much yet to learn; and knows not that the deepest policy of a Tyrant hath bin ever to counterfet Religious. And *Aristotle* in his Politics,[43] hath mentiond that special craft among twelve other tyrannical *Sophisms*. Neither want wee examples. *Andronicus Comnenus* the *Byzantine* Emperor, though a most cruel Tyrant, is reported by *Nicetas*[44] to have bin a constant reader of Saint *Pauls* Epistles; and by continual study had so incorporated the phrase & stile of that transcendent Apostle into all his familiar Letters, that the imitation seem'd to vie with the Original. Yet this availd not to deceave the people of that empire; who notwithstanding his Saints vizard,[45] tore him to peeces for his Tyranny. From Stories of this nature both Ancient and Modern which abound, the Poets also, and som English, have bin in the point so mindfull of *Decorum*, as to put never more pious words in the mouth of any person, then of a Tyrant. I shall not instance an abstruse Author, wherein the King might be less conversant, but one whom wee well know was the Closet Companion of these his solitudes, *William Shakespeare*;[46] who introduces the Person of *Richard* the third, speaking in as high a strain of pietie, and mortification, as is utterd in any passage of this Book; and sometimes to the same sense and purpose with some words in this place, *I intended*, saith he, *not onely to oblige my Freinds but mine enemies.* The like saith *Richard, Act.2.Scen.*I,

I doe not know that Englishman alive
With whom my soule is any jott at odds,
More then the Infant that is borned to night;
I thank my God for my humilitie.

Other stuff of this sort may be read, throughout the whole Tragedie, wherein the Poet us'd not much licence in departing from the truth of History, which delivers him a deep dissembler, not of his affections onely, but of Religion.

In praying therfore, and in the outward work of Devotion, this King wee see hath not at all exceeded the worst of Kings before him. But herein the worst of Kings, professing Christianism, having by farr exceeded him. They, for ought we know, have still pray'd thir

---

[36]The subject of the chapter that follows this one (omitted in the present edition).
[37]"Peculiar only to him."
[38]Entailed.
[39]Thoroughly (the two words were the same).
[40]Archbishop Laud's Prayer Book, which Milton and other Puritan apologists smeared with Roman Catholic terms like "breviary" or "massbook."
[41]The King's penitential meditations in *Eikon Basilike* were rendered into poetry to become part of religious liturgies and some were later even set to music, as with the *Psalterium Carolinum* published in 1657 (Yale 3: 360n)..
[42]Bookshops that would profit from the sale of devotional literature.

[43]*Politics* 5.9.15.
[44]Eighth century AD Byzantine Christian commentator.
[45]His mask of sainthood, false saintly aura.
[46]It is difficult to see how Milton is presenting Shakespeare here, but it seems to be as an author whom Charles I read, and one whose works should have been instructional to him as a king. The example, from *Richard III*, shows the king practicing hypocritical piety in order to seduce the people of London.

own, or at least borrow'd from fitt Authors. But this King, not content with that which, although in a thing holy, is no holy theft, to attribute to his own making other mens whole Prayers, hath as it were unhallow'd, and unchrist'nd the very duty of prayer it self, by borrowing to a Christian use Prayers offer'd to a Heathen God. Who would have imagin'd so little feare in him of the true all-seeing Deitie, so little reverence of the Holy Ghost, whose office is to dictat and present our Christian Prayers, so little care of truth in his last words, or honour to himself, or to his Friends, or sense of his afflictions, or of that sad howr which was upon him, as immediately before his death to popp into the hand of that grave Bishop who attended him, for a special Relique of his saintly exercises, a Prayer stol'n word for word from the mouth of Heathen fiction praying to a heathen God; & that in no serious Book, but the vain amatorious Poem[47] of S[r] *Philip Sidneys Arcadia*; a Book in that kind full of worth and witt, but among religious thoughts, and duties not worthy to be nam'd; nor to be read at any time without good caution; much less in time of trouble and affliction to be a Christians Prayer-Book. They who are yet incredulous of what I tell them for a truth, that this Philippic[48] Prayer is no part of the Kings goods, may satisfie thir own eyes at leasure in the 3d. Book of Sir *Philips Arcadia* p. 248.[49] comparing *Pammela's* Prayer with the first Prayer of his Majestie, deliverd to Dr. *Juxton*[50] immediately before his death, and Entitl'd, *A prayer in time of Captivity* Printed in all the best Editions of his Book. And since there by a crew of lurking raylers, who in thir Libels, and thir fitts of rayling up and down, as I hear from others, take it so currishly that I should dare to tell abroad the secrets of thir *Ægyptian Apis*,[51] to gratifie thir gall in som measure yet more, which to them will be a kinde of almes (for it is the weekly vomit of thir gall which to most of them is the sole meanes of thir feeding) that they may not starv for me, I shall gorge them once more with this digression[52] somwhat larger then before: nothing troubl'd or offended at the working upward of

thir Sale-venom[53] thereupon, though it happ'n to asperse me; beeing, it seemes thir best livelyhood and the only use or good digestion that thir sick and perishing mindes can make of truth charitably told them. However, to the benefit of others much more worth the gaining, I shall proceed in my assertion; that if only but to tast wittingly of meat or drink offered to an Idol, be in the doctrin of St. *Paul* judg'd a pollution, much more must be his sin who takes a prayer, so dedicated, into his mouth, and offers it to God. Yet hardly it can be thought upon (though how sad a thing) without som kind of laughter at the manner, and solemn transaction of so gross a cousenage:[54] that he who had trampl'd over us so stately and so tragically should leave the world at last ridiculously in his exit, as to bequeath among his Deifying friends that stood about him such a pretious peece of mockery to be publisht by them, as must needs cover both his and their heads wth shame, if they have any left. Certainly they that will, may now see at length how much they were deceiv'd in him, and were ever like to be hereafter, who car'd not, so neer the minute of his death, to deceive his best and deerest freinds with the trumpery of such a prayer, not more secretly then shamefully purloind; yet giv'n them as the royall issue of his own proper Zeal. And sure it was the hand of God to let them fal & be tak'n in such a foolish trapp, as hath exposd them to all derision; if for nothing els, to throw contempt and disgrace in the sight of all men upon this his Idoliz'd Book, and the whole rosarie of his Prayers; thereby testifying how little he accepted them from those who thought no better of the living God then of a buzzard Idol, fitt to be so servd and worshipt in reversion, with the polluted orts[55] and refuse of *Arcadia's* and *Romances*, without being able to discern the affront rather then the worship of such an ethnic[56] Prayer. But leaving what might justly be offensive to God, it was a trespass also more then usual against human right, which commands that every author should have the property of his own work reservd to him after death as well as living. Many Princes have bin rigorous in laying taxes on thir Subjects by the head, but of any King heertofore that made a levy upon thir witt, and seisd it as his own legitimat, I have not whom beside to instance. True it is I lookt rather to have him found gleaning out of Books writt'n purposely to help Devotion. And if in likelyhood he have borrowd much more out of Prayer-books then out of Pastorals, then are

---

[47]Milton seems to be relegating Sidney's love poetry to the place of Ovid's erotic poetry (and his own, in Latin), where they are all, by virtue of their subject matter, inherently light and not worthy of serious consideration.

[48]In effect, something written by a Phillip (probably not a pun on Philippic, which is a pejorative oration).

[49]Hughes points out the fact that the pagination is accurate for the first (1621) through the thirteenth (1674) edition of the *Arcadia* (Yale 3: 363n).

[50]William Juxon (1582–1663), trusted ally of Charles I, who became Archbishop of Canterbury as his reward after the Restoration.

[51]Compare the rites to Apis, Isis, and Osiris alluded to in the Nativity Ode 213–20.

[52]Spelled "digrsestion" in Bodleian; here corrected, as in Yale.

[53]Apparently the sales potential of inflammatory publications, what might be called "hate literature."

[54]Cozinage, trickery.

[55]Bits of food left over from a meal, garbage.

[56]Heathen, pagan.

these painted Feathers, that set him off so gay[57] among the people, to be thought few or none of them his own. But if from his Divines he have borrow'd nothing, nothing out of all the Magazin,[58] and the rheume[59] of thir Mellifluous prayers and meditations, let them who now mourn for him as for *Tamuz*,[60] them who howle in thir Pulpits, and by thir howling declare themselvs right Wolves, remember and consider in the midst of thir hideous faces, when they doe onely not cutt thir flesh for them like those ruefull Preists whom *Eliah*[61] mock'd; that he who was once thir *Ahab*, now thir *Josiah*, though faining outwardly to reverence Churchmen, yet heer hath so extremely set at nought both them and thir praying faculty, that being at a loss himself what to pray in Captivity, he consulted neither with the liturgie, nor with the Directory, but neglecting the huge fardell[62] of all thir honycomb devotions, went directly where he doubted not to find better praying, to his mind with *Pammela* in the Countesses *Arcadia*. What greater argument of disgrace & ignominy could have bin thrown with cunning upon the whole Clergy, then that the King among all his Preistery, and all those numberles volumes of thir theological distillations, not meeting with one man, or book of that coate that could befreind him with a prayer in Captivity, was forc'd to robb Sr. *Philip* and his Captive Shepherdess of thir Heathen orisons,[63] to supply in any fashion his miserable indigence, not of bread, but of a single prayer to God. I say therfore not of bread, for that want may befall a good man, and yet not make him totally miserable: but he who wants a prayer to beseech God in his necessity, tis unexpressible how poor he is; farr poorer within himself then all his enemies can make him. And the unfitness, the undecency of that pittifull supply which he sought, expresses yet furder the deepness of his poverty.

Thus much be said in generall to his prayers, and in speciall to that *Arcadian* prayer us'd in his Captivity, anough to undeceave us what esteeme wee are to set upon the rest. For he certainly whose mind could serve him to seek a Christian prayer out of a Pagan Legend, and assume it for his own, might gather up the rest God knows from whence: one perhaps out of the French *Astræa*,[64] another out of the Spanish *Diana*; *Amadis* and *Palmerin*[65] could hardly scape him. Such a person we may be sure had it not in him to make a prayer of his own, or at least would excuse himself the paines and cost of his invention, so long as such sweet *rapsodies* of Heathenism and Knighterrantry could yeild him prayers. How dishonourable then, and how unworthy of a Christian King were these ignoble shifts to seem holy and to get a Saintship among the ignorant and wretched people; to draw them by this deception, worse then all his former injuries, to go a whooring after him. And how unhappy, how forsook of grace, and unbelovd of God that people who resolv to know no more of piety or of goodnes, then to account him thir chief Saint and Martyr, whose bankrupt devotion came not honestly by his very prayers; but having sharkd them from the mouth of a Heathen worshipper, detestable to teach him prayers, sould them to those that stood and honourd him next to the Messiah, as his own heav'nly compositions in adversity, for hopes no less vain and presumptuous (and death at that time so imminent upon him) then by these goodly reliques to be held a Saint and Martyr in opinion with the cheated People.

And thus farr in the whole Chapter we have seen and consider'd, and it cannot but be cleer to all men, how, and for what ends, what concernments, and necessities the late King was no way induc'd, but every way constrain'd to call this last Parlament: yet heer in his first prayer he trembles not to avouch as in the eares of God, *That he did it with an upright intention, to his glory, and his peoples good:* Of which dreadfull attestation how sincerely meant, God, to whom it was avow'd, can onely judge; and he hath judg'd already; and hath written his impartial Sentence in Characters legible to all Christ'ndom; and besides hath taught us, that there be som, whom he hath giv'n over to delusion; whose very mind and conscience is defil'd; of whom Saint *Paul* to *Titus* makes mention.[66]

[Chapters II-XV are omitted.]

---

[57]Colorful.

[58]Magazine, storehouse.

[59]Disease causing a bodily fluid to flow.

[60]Ezekiel 8.14 describes women of Israel mourning in secret for the death of the Egyptian god Thammuz, alluded to in the Nativity Ode 204.

[61]1 Kings 18.27.

[62]Burden, heavy weight.

[63]Prayers.

[64]Honoré D'Urfé's sophisticated romance, *Astrée*, was published sequentially from 1610 to 1627. It featured long philosophical dialogues about love.

[65]Two romances of dubious authorship or of origin, the anonymous *Amadis* [of Gaul], originally in Spanish or Portuguese, and *Palmerin of England*, by Francesco Moraes (1500–1572), written in Portuguese by Moraes but translated into Spanish by Luis Hurtado.

[66]Titus 1.15.

XVI. *Upon the Ordinance against the Common-Prayer Book.*

WHAT to think of Liturgies, both the sense of Scripture, and Apostolicall[67] practice would have taught him better, then his human reasonings and conjectures: Nevertheless what weight they have, let us consider. If it be *no newes to have all innovations usherd in with the name of Reformation,* sure it is less news to have all reformation censur'd and oppos'd under the name of innovation; *by those* who beeing exalted in high place above their merit,[68] fear all change through of things *never so* ill or so *unwisely settl'd. So hardly can the* dotage of those that dwell upon Antiquitie *allow* present *times any share of godliness or wisdom.*

The removing of Liturgie he traduces[69] to be don onely as a *thing plausible to the People;* whose rejection of it he lik'ns with small reverence to the *crucifying* of our Saviour; next that it was don *to please those men who gloried in thier extemporary vein,* meaning the Ministers. For whom it will be best to answer, as was answer'd for the man born blind, *They are of age let them speak for themselves;*[70] not how they came blind, but whether it were Liturgie that held them tongue-ti'd.

For the matter contain'd in that Book we need no better witness then King *Edward* the sixth, who to the Cornish Rebels confesses it was no other then the old Mass-Book don into English, all but some few words that were expung'd. And by this argument which King *Edward* so promptly had to use against that irreligious Rabble, we may be assur'd it was the carnal fear of those Divines and Polititians that model'd the Liturgie no furder off from the old Mass, least by too great an alteration they should incense the people, and be destitute of the same shifts to fly to, which they had taught the young King.

For the manner of using sett formes, there is no doubt but that, wholesom matter, and good desires rightly conceav'd in the heart, wholesom words will follow of themselves. Neither can any true Christian find a reason why Liturgie should be at all admitted, a prescription not impos'd or practis'd by those first Founders of the Church, who alone had that autority: Without whose precept or example, how constantly the Priest puts on

his Gown and Surplice, so constantly doth his praier put on a servile yoak of Liturgie. This is evident, that they *who use no set formes of prayer,* have words from thir affections; while others are to seek affections fit and proportionable to a certain doss[71] of prepar'd words; which as they are not rigorously forbidd to any mans privat infirmity, so to imprison and confine by force, into a Pinfold[72] of sett words, those two most unimprisonable things, our Prayers that Divine Spirit of utterance that moves thē, is a tyranny that would have longer hands then those Giants who threaten'd bondage to Heav'n.[73] What *we may doe* in the same forme of words is not so much the question, as whther Liturgie may be forc'd, as he forc'd it. It is true that we *pray to the same God,* must we therfor always use the same words? Let us then use but one word, because we pray to one God. *We profess the same truths,* but the Liturgie comprehends not all truths: *wee read the same Scriptures;* but never read that all those Sacred expressions, all benefit and use of Scripture, as to public prayer, should be deny'd us, except what was barrel'd up in a Commonpraier Book with many mixtures of thir own, and which is worse, without salt.[74] But suppose them savoury words and unmix'd, suppose them *Manna* it self, yet if they shall be hoarded up and enjoynd us, while God every morning raines down new expressions into our hearts, in stead of being fit to use, they will be found like reserv'd[75] *Manna,* rather to *breed wormes and stink.*[76] *Wee have the same duties upon us and feele the same wants;* yet not alwayes the same, nor at all times alike; but with variety of Circumstances, which ask varietie of words. Wherof God hath giv'n us plenty; not to use so copiously upon all other occasions, and so niggardly to him alone in our devotions. As if Christians were now in a wors famin of words fitt for praier, then was of food at the seige of Jerusalem, when perhaps the Priests being to remove the shew bread, as was accustom'd, were compell'd every Sabbath day, for want of other Loaves, to bring again still the same. If *the Lords Prayer* had been the *warrant or the pattern of set Liturgies,* as is heer affirm'd, why was neither that Prayer, nor any other sett forme ever after us'd, or so much as mention'd by the Apostles, much less commended to our use? Why was thir care wanting in

---

[67]Connected with the twelve Apostles themselves and therefore issuing from the most ancient and venerable traditions of the Christian Church.
[68]This sounds quite like Satan, "by merit rais'd / To that bad eminence" (*Paradise Lost* 2.5–6).
[69]"To state or affirm slanderously (something) to be so and so; to calumniously blame for, accuse of, charge with" (*OED* 3.b, citing this instance).
[70]The AV reads ". . . he is of age; ask him: he shall speak for himself," about a child born blind.

[71]Dose.
[72]Tight enclosure for animals like sheep.
[73]As in *Paradise Lost* 1.198.
[74]Meat or other food preserved in barrels would ordinarily use salt for preservation.
[75]Unused.
[76]Exodus 16.11–36 explains how some of the children of Israel did not eat the manna provided by God for them in the wilderness; as a result of being kept too long, the manna "bred worms and stank."

a thing so usefull to the Church? So full of danger and contention to be left undon by them to other mens Penning, of whose autority we could not be so certain? Why was this forgott'n by them who declare that they have reveal'd to us the whole Counsel of God; who as he left our affections to be guided by his sanctifying spirit, so did he likewise our words to be put into us without our premeditation;[77] not onely those cautious words to be us'd before Gentiles and Tyrants, but much more those filial words, of which we have so frequent use in our access with freedom of speech to the Throne of Grace. Which to lay aside for other outward dictates of men, were to injure him and his perfet Gift, who is the spirit, and the giver of our abilitie to pray; as if his ministration were incomplete, and that to whom he gave affections, he did not also afford utterance to make his Gift of prayer a perfet Gift, to them especially whose office in the Church is to pray publicly.

And although the gift were onely natural, yet voluntary prayers *are less subject to formal and superficial tempers then sett formes*: For in those, at least for words & matter, he who prays, must consult first wth his heart; which in likelyhood may stirr up his affections; in these, having both words and matter readie made to his lips, which is anough to make up the outward act of prayer, his affections grow lazy, and com not up easilie at the call of words not thir own; the prayer also having less intercours and sympathy with a heart wherein it was not conceav'd, saves it self the labour of so long a journey downward, and flying up in hast on the specious wings of formalitie, if it fall not back again headlong, in stead of a prayer which was expected, presents God with a sett of stale and empty words.

No doubt but *ostentation and formalitie* may taint the best duties: but we are not therfore to leave duties for no duties, and to turne prayer into a kind of Lurrey.[78] Cannot unpremeditated babling be rebuk'd, and restraind in whom we find they are, but the spirit of God must be forbidd'n in all men? But it is the custom of bad men and Hypocrits to take advantage at the least abuse of good things, that under that covert they may remove the goodness of those things, rather then the abuse. And how unknowingly, how weakly is the using of sett forms attributed here to *constancy*, as if it were constancie in the Cuckoo to be alwaies in the same liturgie.[79]

Much less can it be lawfull that an Englisht Mass-Book, compos'd for ought we know, by men neither *lerned*, nor *godly, should justle out*, or at any time *deprive* us the exercise of that Heav'nly gift, which God by special promise powrs[80] out daily upon his Church, that is to say the spirit of Prayer. Wherof to help those many infirmities, which he reck'ns up, *rudeness, impertinencies, flatness*, and the like, we have a remedy of Gods finding out, which is not Liturgie, but his own free spirit. Though we know not what to pray as we ought, yet he with sighs unutterable by any words, much less by a stinted Liturgie, dwelling in us makes intercession for us, according to the mind and will of God, both in privat, and in the performance of all Ecclesiastical duties. For it is his promise also, that where two or three gather'd together in his name shall agree to ask him any thing, it shall be granted; for he is there in the midst of them.[81] If then ancient Churches to remedie the infirmities of prayer, or rather the infections of Arian and Pelagian Heresies,[82] neglecting that ordain'd and promis'd help of the spirit, betook them, almost four hundred yeares after Christ, to Liturgie thir own invention, we are not to imitate them, nor to distrust God in the removal of that Truant help to our Devotion, which by him never was appointed. And what is said of Liturgie is said also of Directory, if it be impos'd: although to forbidd the Service Book there be much more reason, as being of it self superstitious, offensive, and indeed, though Englisht, yet still the Mass-Book: and public places ought to be provide of such as need the help of Liturgies or Directories continually, but are supported with Ministerial gifts answerable to thir Calling.

Lastly that the Common-Prayer Book was rejected because it *prayd so oft for him*, he had no reason to Object: for what large and laborious Prayers were made for him in the Pulpits, if he never heard, tis doubtful they were never heard in Heav'n. We might now have expected that his own following Prayer should add much credit to sett Forms; but on the contrary we find the same imperfections in it, as in most before, which he lays heer upon Extemporal. Nor doth he ask of God to be directed whether Liturgies be lawful, but presumes, and in a manner would perswade him that they be so; praying *that the Church and he may never want them.* What could be prayd wors extempore? unless he mean by wanting, that they may never need them.

---

[77]Milton supplies an explanation for what he will mean by "unpremeditated Verse" in *Paradise Lost* 9.24.

[78]Ritualized and meaningless chant.

[79]The song of the cuckoo, always just the two notes, illustrates the folly of repeating meaningless ritual phrases.

[80]Pours (not powers).

[81]Matthew 18.19–20.

[82]At one time or another, in the critical debates over Milton's theology, he has been given both labels. See various works by Patrides, Adamson, Kelley, and Hunter.

[Chapters XVII through XXVII are omitted.]

XXVIII. *Intitl'd Meditations upon Death.*

IT might be well thought by him who reads no furder then the Title of this last Essay, that it requir'd no answer. For all other human things are disputed, and will be variously thought of to the Worlds end. But this business of death is a plaine case, and admitts no controversie: In that center all Opinions meet. Nevertheless, since out of those few mortifying howrs that should have bin intirest[83] to themselves, and most at peace from all passion and disquiet, he can afford spare time to enveigh bitterly against that Justice which was don upon him, it will be needfull to say somthing in defence of those proceedings; though breifly, in regard so much on this Subject hath been Writt'n lately.

It happen'd once, as we find in *Esdras* and *Josephus*, Authors not less beleiv'd then any under sacred,[84] to be a great and solemn debate in the Court of *Darius*, what thing was to be counted strongest of all other. He that could resolve this, in reward of his excelling wisdom, should be clad in Purple, drink in Gold, sleep on a Bed of Gold, and sitt next *Darius*. None but they doubtless who were reputed wise, had the Question propounded to them. Who after som respit giv'n them by the King to consider, in full Assembly of all his Lords and gravest Counselors, returnd severally what they thought. The first held that Wine was strongest; another that the King was strongest. But *Zorobabel* Prince of the Captive Jewes, and Heire to the Crown of Judah, being one of them, proov'd Women to be stronger then the King, for that he himself had seen a Concubin take his Crown from off his head to set it upon her own: And others beside him have lately seen the like Feat don, and not in jest. Yet he proov'd on, and it was so yeilded by the King himself, & all his sages, that neither Wine nor Women, nor the King, but Truth, of all other things was the strongest. For me, though neither ask'd, nor in a Nation that gives such rewards to wisdom, I shall pronounce my sentence somwhat different from *Zorobabel*; and shall defend, that either Truth and Justice are all one, for Truth is but Justice in our knowledge, and Justice is but Truth in our practice, and he indeed so explaines himself in saying that with Truth is no accepting

of Persons, which is the property of Justice, or els, if there be any odds, that Justice, though not stronger then truth, yet by her office is to put forth and exhibit more strength in the affaires of mankind. For Truth is properly no more then Contemplation; and her utmost efficiency is but teaching: but Justice in her very essence is all strength and activity; and hath a Sword put into her hand, to use against all violence and oppression on the earth. Shee it is most truely, who accepts no Person, and exempts none from the severity of her stroke. Shee never suffers injury to prevaile, but when falshood first prevailes over Truth; and that also is a kind of Justice don on them who are so deluded. Though wicked Kings and Tyrants counterfet her Sword, as som did that Buckler, fabl'd to fall from Heav'n into the Capitol,[85] yet shee communicates her power to none but such as like her self are just, or at least will do Justice. For it were extreme partialitie and injustice, the flat denyall and overthrow of her self, to put her own authentic Sword into the hand of an unjust and wicked Man, or so farr to accept and exalt one mortal person above his equals, that he alone shall have the punishing of all other men transgressing, and not receive like punishment from men, when he himself shall be found the highest transgressor.

We may conclude therfore that Justice, above all other things, is and ought to be the strongest: Shee is the strength, the Kingdom, the power and majestie of all Ages. Truth her self would subscribe to this, though *Darius* and all the Monarchs of the World should deny.[86] And if by sentence thus writt'n it were my happiness[87] to set free the minds of English men from longing to returne poorly under that Captivity of Kings, from which the strength and supreme Sword of Justice hath deliverd them, I shall have don a work not much inferior to that of *Zorobabel*, who by well praising and extolling the force of Truth, in that contemplative strength conquer'd *Darius*; and freed his Countrey, and the people of God from the Captivity of *Babylon*. Which I shall yet not despaire to doe, if they in this Land whose minds are yet Captive, be but as ingenuous to acknowledge the strength and supremacie of Justice, as that heathen king was, to confess the strength of truth: or let them but as he did, grant that, and they will soon perceave that Truth resignes all her outward strength to Justice: Justice therefore must needs be strongest, both in her own and in the strength of Truth. But if a King may doe among men whatsoever is his will

---

[83]Most entire.

[84]The apocryphal book of Esdras would need to be defended because it was not included among the canonical books of the Bible; Josephus likewise was not a Christian. His *Antiquities of the Jews* 11. 38–56 recounts the story of the Hebrew Zorobabel's demonstration of the strength of Darius's concubine in overcoming the king by wearing his crown. Zorobabel became a type of the truth-teller in the controversies over the nature of kingship (Yale 3: 583n).

[85]The story of the miraculous fall of the buckler from heaven is told by Plutarch in the *Life of Numa*.

[86]1 Esdras 4.41–63.

[87]Good fortune.

and pleasure, and notwithstanding be unaccountable to men, then contrary to this magnified wisdom of *Zorobabel*, neither Truth nor Justice, but the King is strongest of all other things: which that Persian Monarch himself in the midst of all his pride and glory durst not assume.

Let us see therfore what this King hath to affirm, why the sentence of Justice and the weight of that Sword which shee delivers into the hands of men, should be more partial to him offending, then to all others of human race. First he pleads that *No Law of God or man gives to subjects any power of judicature without or against him*. Which assertion shall be prov'd in every part to be most untrue. The first express Law of God giv'n to mankind, was that to *Noah*, as a Law in general to all the Sons of men. And by that most ancient and universal Law, *whosoever sheddeth mans blood, by man shall his blood be shed*; we find heer no exception. If a king therfore doe this, to a King, and that by men also, the same shall be don. This in the Law of *Moses*, which came next, several times is repeated, and in one place remarkably, *Numb.* 35. *Ye shall take no satisfaction for the life of a murderer, but he shall surely be put to death: the Land cannot be cleansed of the blood that is shedd therein*, but by the blood of him that shed it.[88] This is so spok'n, as that which concern'd all *Israel*, not one man alone to see perform'd; and if no satisfaction were to be tak'n, then certainly no exception. Nay the King, when they should set up any, was to observe the whole Law, and not onely to see it don, but to *do it*; *that his heart might not be lifted up above his Brethren*,[89] to dreame of vain and reasonless prerogatives or exemptions, wherby the Law it self must needs be founded in unrighteousness.

And were that true, which is most fals, that all Kings are the Lord Anointed, it were yet absurd to think that the Anointment of God, should be as it were a charme against Law; and give them privilege who punish others, to sin themselves unpunishably. The high Preist was the Lords anointed as well as any King, and with the same consecrated oile: yet *Salomon* had put to death *Abiathar*, had it not bin for other respects then that anointment. If God himself say to Kings, *Touch not mine anointed*, meaning his chos'n people, as is evident in that Psalme, yet no man will argue thence, that he protects them from Civil Laws if they offend, then certainly, though *David* as a privat man, and in his own cause, feard to lift his hand against the Lords Anointed, much less can this forbidd the Law, or disarm justice from having legal power against any King. No other supreme Magistrate in what kind of Goverment soever laies claim to any

such enormous Privilege; wherfore then should any King, who is but one kind of Magistrat, and set over the people for no other end then they?

Next in order of time to the Laws of *Moses*, are those of Christ, who declares professedly his judicature to be spiritual, abstract from Civil managements, and therfore leaves all Nations to thir own particular Lawes, and way of Goverment. Yet because the Church hath a kind of Jurisdiction within her own bounds, and that also, though in process of time much corrupted and plainly turn'd into a corporal judicature, yet much approv'd by this King, it will be firm anough and valid against him, if subjects, by the Laws of Church also, be *invested with a power of judicature* both without and against thir King, though pretending, and by them acknowledg'd *next and immediatly under Christ supreme head and Governour*. *Theodosius* one of the best Christian Emperours having made a slaughter of the *Thessalonians* for sedition, but too cruelly, was excommunicated to his face by Saint *Ambrose*,[90] who was his subject: and excommunion is the utmost of Ecclesiastical Judicature, a spiritual putting to death. But this, yee will say, was onely an example. Read then the Story; and it will appeare, both that *Ambrose* avouch'd it for the Law of God, and *Theodosius* confess'd it of his own accord to be so; *and that the Law of God was not to be made voyd in him, for any reverence to his Imperial power*. From hence, not to be tedious, I shall pass into our own Land of *Britain*; and shew that Subjects heer have exercis'd the utmost of spirituall Judicature and more then spirituall against thir Kings, his *Predecessors*. *Vortiger*[91] for committing incest with his daughter was by *Saint German*, at that time his subject, cursd and condemnd in a Brittish Counsel about the yeare 448; and thereupon soon after was depos'd. *Mauricus*[92] a King in *Wales*, for breach of Oath and the murder of *Cynetus* was excomunicated, and curst with all his offspring, by *Oudoceus* Bishop of *Landaff* in full Synod, about the yeare 560; and not restor'd, till he had repented. *Morcant* another King in *Wales* having slain *Frioc* his Uncle, was faine to come in Person and receave judgement from the same Bishop and his Clergie; who upon his penitence acquitted him, for no other cause then lest the Kingdom should be destitute of a Successour in the Royal Line. These examples are of the Primi-

---

[88]Following Numbers 35.31.
[89]Deuteronomy 17.19-20.

[90]For other thoughts on the excommunication of Theodosius, see Milton's *Commonplace Book* (Yale 1: 432).
[91]Vortigern is the subject of Milton's scrutiny in the *History of Britain* (Yale 5: 141-56).
[92]As Hughes points out, Milton may have derived his information about the history of Wales from an unpublished manuscript placed in the Bodleian Library by John Selden (Yale 3: 588n). The manuscript has been published as the *Book of Llan Dav* (ed. J. G. Evans and John Rhys [Oxford, 1893]).

tive, Brittish, and Episcopal Church; long ere they had any commerce or communion with the Church of *Rome*. What power afterward of deposing Kings, and so consequently of putting them to death, was assum'd and practis'd by the Canon Law, I omitt as a thing generally known. Certainly if whole Councels of the Romish Church have in the midst of their dimness discern'd so much of Truth, as to decree at *Constance*,[93] and at *Basil*, and many of them to avouch at *Trent* also, that a Councel is above the Pope, and may judge him, though by them not deni'd to be the Vicar of Christ, we in our clearer light may be asham'd not to discern furder, that a Parlament is, by all equity, and right, above a King, and may judge him, whose reasons and pretensions to hold of God onely, as his immediat Vicegerent, we know how farr fetch'd they are, and insufficient.

As for the Laws of man, it would ask a Volume to repeat all that might be cited in this point against him from all Antiquity. In Greece, *Orestes*[94] the Son of *Agamemnon*, and by succession King of *Argos*, was in that Countrey judg'd and condemn'd to death for killing his Mother: whence escaping, he was judg'd againe, though a Stranger, before the great Counsel of *Areopagus* in *Athens*. And this memorable act of Judicature, was the first that brought the Justice of that grave Senat into fame and high estimation over all *Greece* for many ages after. And in the same Citty Tyrants were to undergoe Legal sentence by the Laws of *Solon*. The Kings of *Sparta*, though descended lineally from *Hercules* esteem'd a God among them, were oft'n judg'd, and somtimes put to death by the most just and renowned Laws of *Lycurgus*; who, though a King, thought it most unequal to bind his Subjects by any Law, to which he bound not himself. In *Rome* the Laws made by *Valerius Publicola* soon after the expelling of *Tarquin* and his race, expell'd without a writt'n Law, the Law beeing afterward writt'n, and what the Senat decreed against *Nero*, that he should be judg'd and punish'd according to the Laws of thir Ancestors, and what in like manner was decreed against other Emperours, is vulgarly known; as it was known to those heathen, and found just by nature ere any Law mentioned it. And that the Christian Civil Law warrants like power of Judicature to Subjects against Tyrants, is writt'n clearly by the best and famousest Civilians. For if it was decreed by *Theodosius*, and stands yet firme in the Code of *Justinian*, that the Law is above the Emperour, then certainly the Emperour being under Law, the Law may judge him, may punish him, may punish him proving tyran-

nous: how els is the Law above him, or to what purpose. These are necessary deductions; and therafter hath bin don in all Ages and Kingdoms, oftner then to be heer recited.

But what need we any furder search after the Law of other Lands, for that which is so fully and so plainly set down lawfull in our own. Where ancient Books tell us, *Bracton*,[95] *Fleta*,[96] and others, that the King is under Law, and inferiour to his Court of Parlament; that although his place *to doe Justice* be highest, yet that he stands as liable *to receave Justice*, as the meanest of his Kingdom. Nay *Alfred* the most worthy King, and by som accounted first absolute Monarch of the Saxons heer, so ordain'd: as is cited out of an ancient Law Book call'd the *Mirror*; in *Rights of the Kingdom, p.* 31. where it is complain'd on, *As the sovran abuse of all*, that *the King should be deem'd above the Law, whereas he ought be subject to it by his Oath*: Of which Oath anciently it was the last clause, that the King *should be as liable, and obedient to suffer right, as others of his people*. And indeed it were but fond and sensless, that the King should be accountable to every petty suit in lesser Courts, as we all know he was, and not be subject to the Judicature of Parlament in the main matters of our common safety or destruction; that he should be answerable in the ordinary cours of Law for any wrong don to a privat Person, and not answerable in Court of Parlament for destroying the whole Kingdom. By all this, and much more that might be added as in an argument overcopious rather then barren, we see it manifest that all Laws both of God and Man are made without exemption of any person whomsoever; and that if Kings presume to overtopp the Law by which they raigne for the public good, they are by Law to be reduc'd into order: and that can no way be more justly, then by those who exalted them to that high place. For who should better understand thir own Laws, and when they are transgrest, then they who are govern'd by them, and whose consent first made them: and who can have more right to take knowledge of things don within a free Nation, then they within themselves?

Those objected Oaths of Allegiance and Supremacy we swore, not to his Person, but as it was invested with his Autority; and his autority was by the People first giv'n him conditionally, in Law and under Law, and under Oath also for the Kingdoms good, and not otherwise: the Oathes then were interchang'd, and mu-

---

[93]Church Councils occurred at Constance (1414–1418), Basle (1430s), and Trent (1563).
[94]Milton is perhaps alluding to Euripides's *Orestes* 943–49.
[95]Henry of Bracton (d. 1268), who compiled the first collection of English laws. In this primary authority, Milton finds evidence that English kings were considered subject to God, to the laws, and to councils.
[96]The name "Fleta" refers to an anonymous work written by someone confined to the Fleet prison, quoted by John Seldon in *Dissertatio* (1647).

tuall; stood and fell together; he swore fidelity to his trust (not as a deluding ceremony, but as a real condition of thir admitting him for King; and the Conqueror himself swore it ofter then at his Crowning) they swore Homage, and Fealty to his Person in that trust. There was no reason why the Kingdom should be furder bound by Oaths to him, then he by his Coronation Oath to us, which he hath every way brok'n; and having brok'n, the ancient Crown-Oath of *Alfred* above mention'd, conceales not his penalty.

As for the Covnant, if that be meant, certainly no discreet Person can imagin it should bind us to him in any stricter sense then those Oaths formerly. The acts of Hostility which we receav'd from him were no such dear obligements that we should ow him more fealty and defence for being our Enemy, then we could before when we took him onely for a King. They were accus'd by him and his Party to pretend Liberty and Reformation, but to have no other end then to make themselves great, and to destroy the Kings Person and autority. For which reason they added that third Article, testifying to the World, that as they were resolvd to endeavor first a Reformation in the Church, to extirpat Prelacy, to preserve the Rights of Parlament, and the Liberties of the Kingdom, so they intended, so farr as it might consist with the preservation and defence of these, to preserve the Kings Person and Autority; but not otherwise. As farr as this comes to, they Covnant and Swear in the sixth Article to preserve and defend the persons and autority of one another, and all those that enter into that League; so that this Covnant gives no unlimitable exemption to the Kings Person, but gives to all as much defence and preservation as to him, and to him as much as to thir own Persons, and no more; that is to say, in order and subordination to those maine ends for which we live and are a Nation of men joynd in society either Christian or at least human. But if the Covnant were made absolute, to preserve and defend any one whomsoever, without respect had, either to the true Religion, or those other Superiour things to be defended and preserv'd however, it cannot then be doubted, but that the Covnant was rather a most foolish, hasty, and unlawfull Vow, then a deliberate and well-waighd Covnant; swearing us into labyrinths, and repugnances, no way to be solv'd or reconcil'd, and therfore no way to be kept: as first offending against the Law of God, to Vow the absolute preservation, defence, and maintinging of one Man through in his sins and offences never so great and hainous against God or his Neighbour; and to except a Person from Justice, wheras his Law excepts none. Secondly, it offends against the Law of this Nation, wherein, as hath bin prov'd, Kings in receiving Justice, & undergoing due tryal, are not differenc'd from the meanest Subject. Lastly, it contradicts and offends against the Covnant it self, which Vows in the fourth Article to bring to op'n trial and condign punishment all those that shall be found guilty of such crimes and Delinquencies, wherof the King by his own Letters and other undeniable testimonies not brought to light till afterward, was found and convicted to be chief actor, in what they thought him at the time of taking that Covnant, to be overrul'd onely by evil Counselers. And those, or whomsoever they should discover to be principal, they vow'd to try, *either by thir own supreme Judicatories*, for so eev'n then they call'd them, *or by others having power from them to that effect*. So that to have brought the King to condign punishment hath not broke the Covnant to have sav'd him from those Judicatories, which both Nations declar'd in that Covnant to be *Supreme* against any person whatsoever. And besides all this, to sweare in covnant the bringing of his evil counselers and accomplices to condign punishment, and not onely to leave unpunisht and untoucht the grand offender, but to receive him back againe from the accomplishment of so many violences and mischeifs, dipt from head to foot and staind over with the blood of thousands that were his faithfull subjects, forc'd to thir own defence against a civil Warr by him first rais'd upon them and to receive him thus, in this goarie pickle,[97] to all his dignities and honours, covering the ignominious and horrid purple-rove of innocent blood that sate so close about him with the glorious purple of Royaltie and Supreme Rule, the reward of highest excellence and vertue here on earth, were not only to sweare and covnant the performance of an unjust Vow, the strangest and most impious to the face of God, but were the most unwise and unprudential act as to civil goverment. For so long as a King shall find by experience that doe the worst he can, his Subjects, overaw'd by the Religion of thir own Covnant, will only prosecute his evil instruments, not dare to touch his Person, and that whatever hath bin on his part offended or transgress'd, he shall come off at last with the same reverence to his Person, and the same honour as for well doing, he will not faile to finde them worke; seeking farr and neere, and inviting to his Court all the concours of evil counselers or agents that might be found: who tempted with preferments and his promise to uphold them, will hazard easily thir own heads, and the chance of ten to one but they shall prevaile at last, over men so quell'd and fitted to be slaves by the fals conceit of a Religious Covnant? And they in that Superstition neither wholly yeilding,

---

[97]Vivid phrase suggesting that Charles was "in a pickle" in the sense of being in a tight place without being able to escape (*OED* 4a), and that he was pickled in the gore of the destruction of human life he had caused.

nor to the utmost resisting, at the upshot of all thir foolish Warr and expence, will finde to have don no more but fetchd a compass only of thir miseries, ending at the same point of slavery, and in the same distractions wherin they first begun. But when Kings themselves are made as liable to punishment as thir evil counselers, it will be both as dangerous from the King himself as from his Parlament, to those that evil-counsel him, and they who else would be his readiest Agents in evil, will then not feare to disswade or to disobey him, not onely in respect of themselves and thir own lives, which for his sake they would not seem to value but in respect of that danger which the King himself may incurr, whom they would seem to love and serve with greatest fidelitie. On all these grounds therfore of the covnant it self, whether religious or political, it appeares likeliest, that both the English Parlament, and the Scotch Commissioners thus interpreting the Covnant (as indeed at that time they were the best and most authentical intepreters joyn'd together) answerd the King unanimously, in thir Letters dated *Jan.* 13th 1645. that till securitie and satisfaction first giv'n to both Kingdoms for the blood spilt, for the Irish Rebels[98] brought over, and for the Warr in *Ireland* by him fomented, they could in no wise yeild thir consent to his returne. Here was satisfaction, full two yeares and upward after the Covnant tak'n, demanded of the King by both Nations in Parlament, for crimes at least Capital,[99] wherwith they charg'd him. And what satisfaction could be giv'n for so much blood, but Justice upon him that spilt it? Till which don, they neither took themselves bound to grant him the exercise of his regal Office by any meaning of the Covnant which they then declar'd (though other meanings have bin since contriv'd) not so much regarded the safety of his person, as to admitt of his return among them from the midst of those whom they declar'd to be his greatest enemies; nay from himself as from an actual enemy, not as from a king, they demanded security. But if the covnant all this notwithstanding swore otherwise to preserv him then in the preservation of true religion & our liberties, against which he fought, if not in armes, yet in resolution to his dying day, and now after death still fights against in this his book, the covnant was better brok'n, the[100] he sav'd. And god hath testifi'd by all propitious, & the most evident signes, whereby in these latter times

he is wont to testifie what pleases him; that such a solemn, and for many Ages unexampl'd act of due punishment, was no *mockery of Justice*, but a most gratefull and well-pleasing Sacrifice. Neither was it to *cover their perjury* as he accuses, but to uncover his perjury to the Oath of his Coronation.

The rest of his discours quite forgets the Title; and turns his Meditations upon death into obloquie and bitter vehemence against his *Judges and accusers*; imitating therin, not our Saviours, but his Grand-mother *Mary Queen of Scots*, as also in the most of his other scruples, exceptions and evasions: and from whom he seems to have learnt, as it were by heart, or els by kind, that which is thought by his admirers to be the most vertuous, most manly, most Christian, and most Martyrlike both of his words and speeches heer, and of his answers and behaviour at his Tryall.

It is a sad fate, he saith, *to have his Enemies both accusers, Parties, and Judges.* Sad indeed, but no sufficient Plea to acquitt him from being so judg'd. For what Malefactor might not somtimes plead the like? If his own crimes have made all men his Enemies, who els can judge him? They of the Powder-plot against his Father might as well have pleaded the same. Nay at the Resurrection it may as well be pleaded, that the Saints who then shall judge the World, are *both Enemies, Judges, Parties, and Accusers.*

So much he thinks to abound in his own defence, that he undertakes an unmeasurable task; to bespeak *the singular care and protection of God over all Kings,* as *being the greatest Patrons of Law, Justice, Order, and Religion on Earth.* But what Patrons they be, God in the Scripture oft anough hath exprest; and the earth it self hath too long groan'd under the burd'n of thir injustice, disorder, and irreligion. Therfore *To bind thir Kings in Chaines, and thir Nobles with links of Iron,* is an honour belonging to his Saints; not to build *Babel* (which was *Nimrods* work the first King,[101] *and the beginning of his Kingdom was Babel*) but to destroy it, especially that spiritual *Babel:* and first to overcome those European Kings, which receive thir power, not from God, but from the beast; and are counted no better then his ten hornes. *These shall hate the great Whore,* and yet *shall give thir Kingdoms to the Beast that carries her; they shall committ Fornication with her,* and yet *shall lament the fall of Babylon,* where they fornicated with her. *Rev.* 17. & 18. chapt.[102]

---

[98]It might be worth noting that the catchword on p. 225 is "Rebell," the singular rather than the plural.

[99]A pun is buried in the phrase "capital crime," in this case, since Charles did lose his head (Latin *caput*).

[100]Then (not them). The abbreviation might indicate that the compositor is running out of space and is using abbreviations and the ampersand (&) to save space.

---

[101]The first king mentioned in the Bible, Nimrod of Genesis 10.10, was also often considered to be the first tyrant (compare *Paradise Lost* 12.39)

[102]The description of the Whore of Babylon in Revelation 17.3 and elsewhere was usually taken by Protestants to signify the Papacy in Rome.

Thus shall they be too and fro, doubtfull and ambiguous in all thir doings, untill at last, *joyning thir Armies with the Beast*, whose power first rais'd them, they shall perish with him by the *King of Kings* against whom they have rebell'd; and *the Foules shall eat thir flesh*. This is thir doom writt'n, *Rev.* 19. and the utmost that we find concerning them in these latter days; which we have much more cause to beleeve, then his unwarranted revelation here, prophecying what shall follow after his death, with the spirit of Enmity, not of Saint *John*.

He would fain bring us out of conceit with the good *success* which God hath voutsaf'd us. Wee measure not our Cause by our success, but our success by our cause. Yet certainly in a good Cause success is a good confirmation; for God hath promis'd it to good men almost in every lease of Scripture. If it argue not for us, we are sure it argues not against us; but as much or more for us, then ill success argues for them; for to the wicked, God hath denounc'd ill success in all that they take in hand.

He hopes much of those *softer tempers,* as he calls them, and *less advantag'd by his ruin, that thir consciences doe already* gripe them. Tis true, there be a sort of moodie, hot-brain'd, and alwayes unedify'd consciences; apt to engage thir Leaders into great and dangerous affaires past retirement,[103] and then, upon a sudden qualm and swimming of thir conscience, to betray them basely in the midst of what was cheifly undertak'n for their sakes. Let such men never meet with any faithfull Parlament to hazzard for them; never with any noble spirit to conduct and lead them out, but let them live and die in servil condition and thir scrupulous queasiness, if not instruction will confirme them. Others there be in whose consciences the loss of gaine, and those advantages they hop'd for, hath sprung a sudden leake. These are they that cry out the Covnant brok'n, and to keep it better slide back into neutrality, or joyn actually with Incendiaries and Malignants. But God hath eminently begun to punish those, first in *Scotland*, then in *Ulster*, who have provok'd him with the most hatefull kind of mockery, to break his Covnant under pretence of strictest keeping it; and hath subjected them to those Malignants, with whom they scrupl'd not to be associats. In God therfore we shall not feare what their fals fraternity can doe against us.

He seeks againe with cunning words to turn our success into our sin. But might call to mind, that the Scripture speaks of those also, who *when God slew them, then sought him;* yet did but *flatter him with thir mouth, and ly'd to him with thir tongues; for thir heart was not right with him*. And there was one, who in the time of his affliction trespass'd more against God; *This was that King Ahaz.*[104]

He glories much in the forgiveness of his Enemies; so did his Grandmother at her death. Wise men would sooner have beleev'd him had he not so oft'n told us so. But he hopes to erect *the Trophies of his charity over us.* And Trophies of Charity no doubt will be as *glorious* as Trumpets before the almes of Hypocrites; and more especially the Trophies of such an aspiring charitie as offers in his Prayer to share Victory with Gods *compassion,* which is over all his works. Such Prayers as these may happly catch the People, as was intended: but how they please God, is to be much doubted, though pray'd in secret, much less writt'n to be divulg'd. Which perhaps may gaine him after death a short, contemptible, and soon fading reward; not what he aims at, to stirr the constancie and solid firmness of any wise Man, or to unsettle the conscience of any knowing Christian, if he could ever aime at a thing so hopeless, and above the genius of his *Cleric* elocution, but to catch the worthles approbation of an inconstant, irrational, and Image-doting rabble; that like a credulous and hapless herd, begott'n to servility, and inchanted with these popular institutes of Tyranny, subscrib'd with a new device of the Kings Picture at his praiers, hold out both thir eares with such delight and ravishment to be stigmatiz'd and board through[105] in witness of thir own voluntary and beloved baseness. The rest, whom perhaps ignorance without malice, or some error, less then fatal, hath for the time misledd, on this side Sorcery or obduration, may find the grace and good guidance to bethink themselves, and recover.

THE END.

---

[103]Past the point of no return.

[104]The king that trespasses against the Lord in 2 Chronicles 28.22.
[105]Milton makes fun of the Roman Catholic belief in receiving stigmata, the marks of the Crucifixion recurring in the faithful, "bored through" by the nails used to fix Christ to the cross.

From
The Second Defence of the English People (1654)

The *Second Defence* is an extended oration (it seems to begin as a speech like *Areopagitica*, then it turns into something else more difficult to define) attacking the man Milton thought had written a small book called, in its translated title, "The Cry of the Royal Blood to Heaven against the English Parricides." The *Regii Sanguinis Clamor ad Coelum Adversus Parricidas Anglicanos* was issued from the press of Adrian Vlacq at the Hague in August, 1652 (Yale 4.2: 1036). Vlacq was an opportunistic but quite possibly an ethical publisher who realized he could profit from the notoriety of slander by publishing documents on both sides of the controversy. The *Clamor* continued the war of strong opinions about regicide that Milton had been fighting with Claude Saumaise (in Latin, Salmasius). That war over whether or not a people had the right to depose and execute a tyrannical king went on, ironically enough, beyond the death of Salmasius in August of 1653, since Salmasius's *Responsio ad Miltonum* would not be published until 1660, when the Restoration of Charles II had driven Milton and other regicides underground and there was no further need for such propaganda.

Milton attacked the wrong man in the *Second Defence*. His informants in Amsterdam and elsewhere fed the blind Milton scurrilous but accurate information about Alexander Morus, reinforcing Milton's notion that Morus was the author. Morus had written only a dedicatory letter for the *Clamor*, and even that letter had been signed by Adrian Vlacq (for Vlacq's career, see Miller). But Milton continued stinging Morus after he had received the news that Morus was not the author (Shawcross, "The Life" 14). The real author was Peter Du Moulin, an Anglican minister with a reformed background, from Adisham in Kent. By 1670, Du Moulin had admitted he wrote the *Clamor*, but by then Salmasius was dead and Milton had already done the damage to Morus—damage so serious that Morus was rumored to have tried unsuccessfully to buy up all existing copies in Amsterdam (Campbell, *Chronology* 24/3 August, 1654). Morus's legal problems continued as the reports in the *Second Defence* were used against him in court (Sellin). The man was undoubtedly a scoundrel with respect to his relationship to Salmasius (who himself might have had a homosexual attachment to his understudy, as I have learned through e-mail correspondence in 1997 with Sellin), and with respect to his abandon-

ment of a woman he had impregnated and his refusal to support their child.

Milton had also been sorely abused by Du Moulin, in print. According to Du Moulin, Milton was a "foul rascal," "an ignoble, commonplace little fellow," and a "cancerous ulcer" (Yale 4.2: 1078)—those were some of the milder insults. Du Moulin slung mud, and Milton slung it back, mistakenly but with great accuracy, at Alexander Morus.

All the principal documents in this case of international publishing intrigue are obscene and funny. Having been lectured that his blindness was brought about by his own moral turpitude, Milton pulled out all the stops in his satirical attack on Morus's morality. Morus unfortunately had a name which meant "fool" in Greek, and "black" and "mulberry" in Latin. His discarded mistress, on the other hand, had a name, Bontia, that sounded to Milton like Pontia, a word that in Latin has relations with bridges and therefore with the pope, the *Pontifex Maximus*. If Morus is Moorish and a mulberry, Pontia is like a *fica* or fig (slang for vagina) and *Pontia pilata* is "depilitated Pontia"; a sycamore combines the two in its etymology. Unmercifully, Milton ran into the ground every possible pun on the names of his victims. As the translator in the Yale edition, Helen North, puts it,

> the style is particularly complex, mingling as it does question and answer, quotation from the *Clamor* and sardonic comment upon it, apt classical allusions, and tireless invective, enlivened by derogatory epigram, scandalous innuendo, and indefensible but irresistible puns.   (Yale 4.1: 545)

Against the dead Salmasius and the living Alexander Morus, Milton stacks all the cards in his own favor, and he wilfully distorts what he thinks Morus had written or what he knew that Salmasius had written, whenever he has a mind to do so.

About himself and his own career, however, he is scrupulously honest, as if he were writing for future biographers. The tone of the Latin becomes elevated when Milton discusses his own sense of vocation; he becomes detached and awe-inspired, as if at those moments he was having a private discussion with his muse.

His flattery of Christina Queen of Sweden is not quite so blatant as it first might appear to be (North calls it "not only sycophantic, but frigid" [Yale 4.1: 546]). He allows that she is a good woman ruler, possibly because she understood a number of different languages, she bought books, and she had the good taste to recognize Salmasius's errors. Milton had first-hand knowledge of what was happening in Christina's court, and of Christina's high opinion of his own writing, from Milton's associate and friend Bulstrode White-locke (Campbell, *Chronology*, February 13, 1654).

The *Second Defence* represents Milton's successful reentry into European politics after the onset of blindness; it "may well have influenced his superiors to reevaluate their concept of his usefulness to the Republic" and convinced them "that this blind Latin Secretary was an asset despite his affliction" (Fallon 139). Milton's continued activity within the inner circle of the Republic would result in, among other more mundane achievements, the great Piedmont sonnet.

Works Cited

Campbell, Gordon. *A Milton Chronology.* Forthcoming from St. Martin's (U.S.) and Macmillan (U.K.), 1997.

Fallon, Robert Thomas. *Milton in Government.* University Park: The Pennsylvania State UP, 1993.

Miller, Leo. "Milton and Vlacq." *Papers of the Bibliographical Society of America* 73 (1979): 145–207.

Sellin, Paul. "Alexander Morus Before the Hof fan Holland: Some Insight into Seventeenth Century Polemics with John Milton." *Studies in Netherlandic Culture and Literature.* Ed. Martinus A. Bakker and Beverly H. Morrison. *Publications of the American Association of Netherlandic Studies* 7 (1994): 1–11.

Shawcross, John T. "The Life of Milton." *The Cambridge Companion to Milton.* Ed. Dennis Danielson. Cambridge: Cambridge UP, 1989. 1–19.

John Milton
ENGLISHMAN
Second Defence
of
The English People
Against the Base Anonymous Libel, Entitled
The Cry of the Royal Blood to Heaven,
against the English Parricides.
BY JOHN MILTON, ENGLISHMAN

In the whole life and estate of man the first duty is to be grateful to God and mindful of his blessings, and to offer particular and solemn thanks without delay when his benefits have exceeded hope and prayer. Now, on the very threshold of my speech, I see three most weighty reasons for my discharge of this duty. First that I was born at a time in the history of my country when her citizens, with pre-eminent virtue and a nobility and steadfastness surpassing all the glory of their ancestors, invoked the Lord, followed his manifest guidance, and after accomplishing the most heroic and exemplary achievements since the foundation of the world, freed the state from grievous tyranny and the church from unworthy servitude. Secondly, that when a multitude had sprung up which in the wonted manner of a mob venomously attacked these noble achievements, and when one man above all,[1] swollen and complacent with his empty grammarian's conceit and the esteem of his confederates, had in a book of unparalleled baseness attacked us and wickedly assumed the defence of all tyrants, it was I and no other who was deemed equal to a foe of such repute and to the task of speaking on so great a theme, and who received from the very liberators of my country this role, which was offered spontaneously with universal consent, the task of publicly defending (if anyone ever did) the cause of the English people and thus of Liberty herself. Lastly, I thank God that in an affair so arduous and so charged with expectation, I did not disappoint the hope or the judgment of my countrymen about me, nor fail to satisfy a host of foreigners, men of learning and experience, for by God's grace I so routed my audacious foe that he fled, broken in spirit and reputation. For the last three years of his life, he did in his rage utter frequent threats, but gave us no further trouble, save that he sought the secret help of certain rogues and persuaded some bungling and immoderate panegyrists to repair, if they could, his fresh and unlooked-for disgrace. All this will shortly be made clear.

In the belief that such great blessings come from on high and that they should properly be recognized both out of gratitude to God and in order to secure favorable auspices for the work in hand, I held that they should be reverently proclaimed, as they are, at the outset. For who does not consider the glorious achievements of his country as his own? But what can tend more to the honor and glory of any country than the restoration of liberty both to civil life and to divine worship? What nation, what state has displayed superior fortune or stouter courage in securing for itself such liberty in either sphere? In truth, it is not in warfare and arms alone that courage shines forth, but she pours out her dauntless strength against all terrors alike, and thus those illustrious Greeks and Romans whom we particularly admire expelled the tyrants from their cities without other virtues than the zeal for freedom, accompanied by ready weapons and eager hands. All else they easily accomplished amid universal praise, applause, and

---

[1]Claude Saumaise, called Claudius Salmasius (1588–1655). For an account of his career, see Yale 4.1: 961–81.

joyful omens. Nor did they hasten so much towards danger and doubtful issues as towards the fair and glorious trial of virtue, towards distinctions, in short, and garlands, and the sure hope of immortality. For not yet was tyranny a sacred institution. Not yet had tyrants, suddenly become viceroys, indeed, and vicars of Christ, sheltered themselves behind the blind superstition of the mob, when they could not fortify themselves with their good will. Not yet had the common people, maddened by priestly machinations, sunk to a barbarism fouler than that which stains the Indians, themselves the most stupid of mortals.[2] The Indians indeed worship as gods malevolent demons whom they cannot exorcize, but this mob of ours to avoid driving out its tyrants, even when it could, has set up as gods over it the most impotent of mortals and to its own destruction has consecrated the enemies of mankind. And against all this close array of long-held opinions, superstitions, slanders, and fears, more dreadful to other men than the enemy himself, the English people had to contend. Being better instructed and doubtless inspired by heaven, they overcame all these obstacles with such confidence in their cause and such strength of mind and courage that although they were indeed a multitude in numbers, yet the lofty exaltation of their minds kept them from being a mob. Britain herself, which was once called a land teeming with tyrants, shall hereafter deserve the everlasting praise of all the ages as a country where liberators flourish. The English people were not driven to unbridled license by scorn for the laws or desecration of them. They were not inflamed with the empty name of liberty by a false notion of virtue and glory, or senseless emulation of the ancients. It was their purity of life and their blameless character which showed them the one direct road to true liberty, and it was the most righteous defence of law and religion that of necessity gave them arms. And so, trusting completely in God, with honorable weapons, they put slavery to flight.

Although I claim for myself no share in this glory, yet it is easy to defend myself from the charge of timidity or cowardice, should such a charge be leveled. For I did not avoid the toils and dangers of military service[3] without rendering to my fellow citizens another kind of service that was much more useful and no less perilous. In time of trial I was neither cast down in spirit nor un-

duly fearful of envy or death itself. Having from early youth been especially devoted to the liberal arts, with greater strength of mind than of body, I exchanged the toils of war, in which any stout trooper might outdo me, for those labors which I better understood, that with such wisdom as I owned I might add as much weight as possible to the counsels of my country and to this excellent cause, using not my lower but my higher and stronger powers. And so I concluded that if God wished those men to achieve such noble deeds, He also wished that there be other men by whom these deeds, once done, might be worthily praised and extolled, and that truth defended by arms be also defended by reason—the only defence truly appropriate to man. Hence it is that while I admire the heroes victorious in battle, I nevertheless do not complain about my own role. Indeed I congratulate myself and once again offer most fervent thanks to the heavenly bestower of gifts that such a lot has befallen me—a lot that seems much more a source of envy to others than of regret to myself. And yet, to no one, even the humblest, do I willingly compare myself, nor do I say one word about myself in arrogance, but whenever I allow my mind to dwell upon this cause, the noblest and most renowned of all, and upon the glorious task of defending the very defenders, a task assigned me by their own vote and decision, I confess that I can scarcely restrain myself from loftier and bolder flights than are permissible in this exordium, and from the search for a more exalted manner of expression. Indeed, in the degree that the distinguished orators of ancient times undoubtedly surpass me, both in their eloquence and in their style (especially in a foreign tongue, which I must of necessity use, and often to my own dissatisfaction), in that same degree shall I outstrip all the orators of every age in the grandeur of my subject and my theme. This circumstance has aroused so much anticipation and notoriety that I do not now feel that I am surrounded, in the Forum or on the Rostra, by one people alone, whether Roman or Athenian, but that, with virtually all of Europe attentive, in session, and passing judgment, I have in the *First Defence* spoken out and shall in the *Second* speak again to the entire assembly and council of all the most influential men, cities, and nations everywhere.[4] I seem now to have embarked on a journey and to be surveying from on high far-flung regions and territories across the sea, faces numberless and unknown, sentiments in complete agreement with mine. Here the manly strength of

---

[2]Milton had contempt for the American Indians because they worshiped the sun (see *Prolusion 1*), and he saw such worship as constricting their lives and offering no blessing in return (see *Tetrachordon*; Yale 2: 590).
[3]Milton never entered military service directly, that we know of, though he was certainly not a pacifist. See Robert Thomas Fallon, *Captain or Colonel: The Soldier in Milton's Life and Art* (Columbia: U of Missouri P, 1984), for Milton's connections with the military.

---

[4]Compare the sonnet to Cyriack Skinner, "What supports me dost thou ask? / The conscience, Friend, t'have lost them [his eyes] overply'd / In liberties defence, my noble task, / Of which all *Europe* talks from side to side."

the Germans, hostile to slavery, meets my eye; there the lively and generous ardor of the Franks, worthy of their name; here the well-considered courage of the Spaniards; there the serene and self-controlled magnanimity of the Italians. Wherever liberal sentiment, wherever freedom, or wherever magnanimity either prudently conceals or openly proclaims itself, there some in silence approve, others openly cast their votes, some make haste to applaud, others, conquered at last by the truth, acknowledge themselves my captives.

Now, surrounded by such great throngs, from the Pillars of Hercules all the way to the farthest boundaries of Father Liber,[5] I seem to be leading home again everywhere in the world, after a vast space of time, Liberty herself, so long expelled and exiled. And, like Triptolemus of old,[6] I seem to introduce to the nations of the earth a product from my own country, but one far more excellent than that of Ceres. In short, it is the renewed cultivation of freedom and civic life that I disseminate throughout cities, kingdoms, and nations. But not entirely unknown, nor perhaps unwelcome, shall I return if I am he who disposed of the contentious satellite of tyrants, hitherto deemed unconquerable, both in the view of most men and in his own opinion. When he with insults was attacking us and our battle array, and our leaders looked first of all to me, I met him in single combat and plunged into his reviling throat this pen, the weapon of his own choice.[7] And (unless I wish to reject outright and disparage the views and opinions of so many intelligent readers everywhere, in no way bound or indebted to me) I bore off the spoils of honor. That this is actually the truth and no empty boast finds ready proof in the following event—which I believe did not occur without the will of God—namely, that when Salmasius (or Salmasia,[8] for which of the two he was the open domination of his wife, both in public and in private, had made it quite difficult to determine), when Salmasius had been courteously summoned by Her Most Serene Majesty, the Queen of the Swedes (whose devotion to the liberal arts and to men of learning has never been surpassed) and had gone thither, there in the very place where he was living as a highly honored guest, he was over taken by my *Defence,* while he was expecting nothing of the kind. Nearly everyone read it immediately, and the Queen

herself, who had been among the first to do so, having regard only for what was worthy of her, omitted nothing of her earlier kindness and generosity towards her guest. But for the rest, if I may report what is frequently mentioned and is no secret, so great a reversal of opinion suddenly took place that he who the day before yesterday had flourished in the highest favor now all but withered away. When he departed, not much later, with good leave, there was but one doubt in many minds, namely, whether he came more honored or went more despised. Nor in other places, it is certain, did less harm befall his reputation.

Yet I have not referred to all these matters with the intention of ingratiating myself with anyone (for there is no need), but only to show more copiously that which I undertook at the outset, for what reasons—and what weighty ones—I began by offering my most fervent thanks to almighty God. I would show that this proem, in which I offer so many convincing proofs that, although by no means exempt from the disasters common to humanity, I and my interests are nevertheless under the protection of God—this proem, I say, will be a source of honor and credit to me. I would show that with respect to matters of well-nigh primary importance, relating to the immediate needs of my country and destined to be of the greatest service to civil life and religion, when I speak, not on behalf of one people nor yet one defendant, but rather for the entire human race against the foes of human liberty, amid the common and well-frequented assembly (so to speak) of all nations, I have been aided and enriched by the favor and assistance of God. Anything greater or more glorious than this I neither can, nor wish to, claim. Accordingly, I beg the same immortal God that, just as, depending on his familiar help and grace alone, I lately defended deeds of supreme courage and justice, so with the same or greater honesty, industry, fidelity, and even good fortune, I may be able to defend from undeserved insults and slanders both the doers of those deeds and myself, who have been linked with these great men for the purpose of ignominy, rather than honor. And if there is anyone who thinks that these attacks might better have been ignored, I for my part agree, provided that they were circulated among men who had an accurate knowledge of us. But how in the world will everyone else be convinced that the lies our enemy has told are not the truth? Yet when I shall have seen to it (as is proper) that Truth the avenger shall follow wherever calumny has gone before, I believe that men will cease to think wrongly of us, and that that creature will perhaps be ashamed of his lies. If he feel no shame, then at last we may properly ignore him.

Meanwhile I should more quickly have sped him a

---

[5]Bacchus, using the title of "Liber" here to identify him with liberty.
[6]A devotee of Ceres used by the goddess to spread news of agriculture throughout the world (Ovid, *Metamorphoses* 5).
[7]A comparison between Milton and Salmasius and David and Goliath might be implied: instead of using the humble slingshot, Milton uses a pen.
[8]Salmasius was rumored to be a hen-pecked husband (Masson 4: 263, 272, 461–63).

reply in accord with his merits, had he not protected himself up until now with false reports, announcing again and again that Salmasius was sweating at the anvil, forging new charges against us, always on the very point of publishing them. By these tactics he achieved but one result—that of postponing for a little while the payment of the penalty for slander, for I thought it better to wait, so that I might keep my strength intact for the more formidable adversary. But with Salmasius, since he is dead, I think my war is over. How he died, I shall not say, for I shall not impute his death as a crime to him, as he imputed my blindness to me. Yet there are those who even place the responsibility for his death on me and on those barbs of mine, too keenly sharpened. While he fixed them more deeply in himself by his resistance, while he saw that the work which he had in hand was proceeding too slowly, that the time for reply had passed and the welcome accorded his work had died, when he realized that his reputation was gone, along with his good name, and finally that the favor of princes was diminished, so far as he was concerned, because of his poor defence of the royal cause, they say that at last, after a three-year illness, worn away by mental distress rather than by bodily disease, he died. However that may be, if I must wage a posthumous war as well, and with a familiar enemy whose attacks I easily sustained when they were fierce and vigorous, there is no reason for me to fear his efforts when feeble and dying.

But now let us come at last to this creature, whatever he is, who cries out against us: a "Cry" indeed I hear, not "of the Royal Blood," as the title boasts, but of some unknown rascal, for nowhere do I find the crier. You there! Who are you? A man or a nobody? Surely the basest of men—not even slaves—are without a name. Shall I then always contend with those who are nameless?[9] But in truth they are exceedingly anxious to be considered king's men. I wonder whether they have persuaded the kings of this. Followers and friends of kings are not ashamed of kings. How then are such men friends of kings? They give no gifts; nay, far more freely do they receive them. They do not risk their own property, who dare not give even their names to the royal cause. What then do they give? Words! But they are not devoted enough to resolve, nor loyal enough to dare, to write down their names and give even words free of charge to their kings. Well, as for me, ὦ ἄνδρες

ἀνώνυμοι[10] (for give me leave to address in Greek those for whom I can find no name in Latin) as for me, I say, when your friend Claudius had begun to compose a book about royal authority (with a subject popular enough, but still without a name) and I could have followed his example, I was so far from being ashamed either of myself or my cause that I considered it disgraceful to attack so great a theme without openly acknowledging my identity.

Why is it that the attack which I, in a republic, am seen to make openly against kings, you, in a kingdom, and under the patronage of kings, do not dare to make against the republic, except furtively and by stealth? Why do you, cautious in the midst of security, like a creature of darkness in broad daylight, becloud the sovereign power, the sovereign grace, with your patently invidious and suspicious timidity? Do you fear that kings will not be able to protect you? Cloaked and muffled as you are, you seem to have come, I swear, not as defenders to assert the right of kings, but as thieves to plunder the treasury. What I am, I, for my part, openly admit. The right which I deny to kings, I would dare to deny to the end in any legitimate kingdom whatsoever. No monarch could injure me without first condemning himself by the confession that he was a tyrant. If I attack tyrants, what is this to kings, whom I am very far from classing as tyrants?[11] As a good man differs from a bad, so much, I hold, does a king differ from a tyrant. Hence it happens that a tyrant not only is not a king but is always an especially dangerous threat to kings. And surely one who glances at the records of history will find that more kings have been crushed and overthrown by tyrants than by their people. He who asserts, therefore, that tyrants must be abolished asserts, not that kings should be abolished, but the worst enemies of kings, the most dangerous, in fact, of all their foes.

But as for you, the right which you assign to kings, to wit that whatever is their pleasure is right, is not a right, but a wrong, a crime evil itself. With a gift so poisonous, rather than benign, you yourself become the murderer of those whom you proclaim to be above all violence and danger. You identify king with tyrant, if the same right belongs to each. For if the king does not use this right of his (and he will never use it as long as he shall be king, not tyrant), it must be ascribed, not to the king, but to the man. What fancy could be more absurd than such a right of kings? Should anyone use it, as often as he wishes to be king, he would cease, for that length of time, to be a good man, and as often as he prefers to be a good man, so often would he prove himself no king. What greater slander can be uttered against kings? He who teaches this right must himself be most unrighteous, the worst of all men, for how could he become worse than by first taking on the very nature which

---

[9]Milton seems to have prided himself on always signing his own publications with his proper name, despite potential problems with licensers (see his remarks about names on title pages in *Areopagitica*; Yale 2: 569).

[10]"O men without a name."

[11]Milton, in other words, has no argument with the institution of kingship, but just with its abuse in tyranny.

a good man, so often would he prove himself no king. What greater slander can be uttered against kings? He who teaches this right must himself be most unrighteous, the worst of all men, for how could he become worse than by first taking on the very nature which he imposes and stamps on others? But if every good man is a king, as was the glorious teaching of a certain school of ancient philosophers,[12] it follows by the same logic that every bad man is a tyrant, each in his own degree. For a tyrant is not something great (let him not be puffed up by the very name), but something utterly base. And to the degree that he is the greatest of all tyrants, to that same degree is he the meanest of all and most a slave. Other men willingly serve only their own vices; he is forced, even against his will, to be a slave, not only to his own crimes, but also to the most grievous crimes of his servants and attendants, and one must yield a certain share of his despotism to all his most abandoned followers. Tyrants then are the meanest of slaves; they are slaves even to their own slaves.[13] Wherefore this name of tyrant may justly be applied either to the most insignificant bodyguard of tyrants or to this crier himself. Why he cries so loudly in this tyrannous cause will soon be clear enough from what has been said and what will be said, and also why he is anonymous, for either he has been basely hired and, after the fashion of Salmasius, has sold this Cry of his to the royal blood, or, being shamefully aware of his disreputable doctrine, or profligate and dissolute in his life, it is no strange thing that he seeks to hide. Or perhaps he is safeguarding himself so that if he should sniff out a richer prospect of gain anywhere, he may be at liberty to abandon kings and go over to some republic, as yet unborn. Not even then would he lack the example of his great Salmasius, who, lured by the gleam of gold, turned in his old age from the orthodox to the bishops, from the popular to the royalist party. You then, who utter your "Cry" from some hovel, do not deceive us about identity. In vain have you sought those hiding places. You will be dragged forth, believe me, nor will that helmet of Pluto[14] any longer conceal you. You will swear, as long as you live, either that I am not blind, or that at least I do not shut my eyes to you.

Now then, hear, if you have time (it is almost a Milesian or a Baian fable)[15] who he is, what his descent, and by what hope he was led, but what bait and what enticement he was coaxed into adopting the royalist cause. He is a certain More, part Scot, part French (that a single race or country be not saddled with the entire disgrace of the man),[16] a rogue and, according to the general evidence, not only of other men but (what is most damning) of his friends, whom he changed from intimates into bitter enemies, he is faithless, treacherous, ungrateful, foulmouthed, a consistent slanderer of men and of women whose chastity he is wont to spare no more than their good name. To omit the more obscure events of his early life, this fellow first taught Greek at Geneva, but although he often demonstrated to his pupils the meaning of his own name Morus in Greek, he could not unlearn the fool and the knave. Indeed, since he was conscious of the guilt of so many crimes (although not yet perhaps detected), he was all the more driven by such frenzy that he did not shrink from seeking the office of pastor in the church and the defiling it by his vicious ways. But he could not long escape the censure of the Elders. A pursuer of women, a liar, marked by many other offences, condemned for many deviations from the orthodox faith—deviations which he basely recanted and yet impiously retained after recanting—he was at last proved to be an adulterer.

He happened to have conceived a passion for a certain maidservant of his host, and although she not long afterwards married another, he did not cease to pursue her. The neighbors had often noticed that they entered all by themselves a certain summerhouse in that garden. Not quite adultery, you say. He could have done anything else in the world. Certainly. He might have talked to her, no doubt about matters horticultural, or he might have drawn from the subject of gardens (say those of Alcinous or Adonis)[17] certain of his lectures for this woman, who had perhaps a smattering of knowledge and a willing ear. He might now have praised the flower beds, might have wished only for some shade, were it possible merely to graft the mulberry on the fig, whence might come forth, with utmost speed, a grove of sycamores—a very pleasant place to tread. He might then have demonstrated to this woman the method of grafting. These things and much else he could have done; who denies it? But he could not deter the elders from

---

[12]The notion that every man should be a king might be associated with the Stoics, who believed in the universal brotherhood of humankind and the rule of virtue as governing the universe and the fate of humans.

[13]Such a logic might be applied to Satan as tyrant in *Paradise Lost*, as in 4.394.

[14]The cap of Pluto conferred invisibility on Perseus, so that he could not be seen by Medusa.

[15]Licentious stories associated with Miletus (the town and the poet named after it) or Baiae, a seaside resort near Naples famous for its loose living (Martial 11.80).

[16]Alexander More (1616–70) was a Frenchman of Scottish descent, his mother French and his father a Scot.

[17]Pleasure gardens of classical mythology, associated with dalliance and romantic love. More obliged the comparison by conducting his affair partly in a garden house.

branding him with censure as an adulterer and forthwith judging him unworthy of the office of pastor. The records of these and like accusations are still kept in the public library of Geneva. In the meantime, while these charges were not publicly known, he was summoned to Holland by the Gallican church at Middleburg, through the influence of Salmasius, but to the great disgust of Spanheim,[18] a genuinely learned man and a blameless pastor, who had previously known him well at Geneva. More at last and with difficulty obtained letters of recommendation (as they are called) and rather cool ones at that, from the people of Geneva, solely on condition that he take his departure. Some thought it intolerable that a man of such character be honored with the recommendation of the church; others thought anything more tolerable than the man himself.

When More arrived in Holland, he set out to call on Salmasius and at his house he cast lustful eyes on his wife's maid, whose name was Pontia, for this creature's desires always light on servant girls. Thereafter he began with the greatest persistence to cultivate Salmasius, and, as often as he could, Pontia. I do not know whether Salmasius, pleased by the fellow's adulation and courtesy, or More thinking that he had devised a likely means of meeting Pontia more often, first broached the subject of Milton's reply to Salmasius. However it was, More undertook to defend Salmasius, and Salmasius for his part promised More the chair of theology in Middleburg.[19] More promised himself both this and another extra tidbit, a secret liaison with Pontia. For the sake of consulting Salmasius about his undertaking, day and night he frequented his house. And as Pyramus was once changed into a mulberry, so now the mulberry suddenly fancied himself turned into Pyramus, the Genevan into the Babylonian.[20] But, surpassing that young man in good fortune no less than in wickedness, More now addressed his Thisbe when he pleased, having ample opportunity beneath the very same roof. No need to seek a chink in the wall! He promised marriage. With this deluding hope, he ruined her. With this crime (I shrink from saying it, but it must be said) a minister

of the holy gospel defiled even the house of his host. From the union resulted at length a marvelous and unnatural prodigy; not only the female but also the male conceived—Pontia a little More, which for a long time afterward persecuted even that persecutor of Pliny, Salmasius; and More conceived this empty wind-egg, from which burst forth the swollen Cry of the King's Blood. At first the egg was pleasant enough for our hungry royalists in Belgium to suck, but now, with the shell broken, they find it rotten and stinking, and they recoil from it. For More, distended by this same fetus of his, and feeling that he had deserved well of the whole Orange party, had now already, in his wicked hopes, swallowed up fresh professorial chairs, and had basely deserted his Pontia, pregnant though she now was, as being but a poor little servant girl. Complaining that she had been despised and deceived, she begged the support of the synod and the magistrates. Thus at length the affair became public, and long provided mirth and merriment for virtually every social and convivial gathering. Hence someone, witty enough, whoever he was, composed this epigram:

> Who, Pontia, would deny that you, with child by Gallic More
> Are mor-ally pure and More-obliging?

Only Pontia was not amused, but her complaints accomplished nothing, for the Cry of the Royal Blood had easily drowned out the cry of violated honor and the lament of the poor girl who had been seduced. Salmasius too, highly indignant that this insult and disgrace had been offered to him and his entire household, and that he had thus been made game of by his friend and supporter, so that he was once more exposed to the enemy, soon thereafter breathed his last, perhaps because this calamity as well had been added to his earlier failure in the royalist cause. But of this more later.

Meanwhile Salmasius, with a fate like that of Salmacis[21] (for like the name, so too the fable is apt enough), unaware that in More he had associated with himself a hermaphrodite, as fit to give birth as to beget, ignorant too of what More had begotten in his home, fondled what he had brought forth, that book in which he found himself so often called "the great" (in his own

---

[18]Frederick Spanheim (1600–49), German-born professor of theology at Geneva and Leyden, who had maintained a feud with Salmasius and More; his son Ezekiel (1629–1710), an antiquarian and diplomat, provided Milton with scandalous information about More (see Yale 4.1: 716).

[19]According to the Yale editor, "Milton badly muddles the time sequence" (4.1: 568n) and the chair at Middleburg could not have been a reward for helping Salmasius. Milton quite deliberately devalues the scholarship and the academic achievements of More.

[20]Milton spoofs the Pyramus and Thisbe story as it was told in Ovid's *Metamorphoses* 4. There is no wall between the lovers because they are in the same house. The connection once again is in the mulberry tree, which was supposed to memorialize Pyramus and Thisbe.

[21]In *Metamorphoses* 4 Salmacis is a nymph who inspires Hermaphroditus to take on traits of both sexes and become a hermaphrodite. Milton plays on the name Salmasius again, and impugns Salmasius's sexual orientation at the same time, since he is both the father and the mother of books, and is father and mother to More's baby. In a passage cut from Salmasius's reply to the *Second Defence*, Salmasius would insinuate that Milton had "sold his buttocks" while he was in Italy (Campbell *Chronology*, January 21/31 1652).

estimation just praise, perhaps, but foolish and absurd in the opinion of others). And so he made haste to find a printer, and in the vain attempt to hold fast to that fame which for so long a time had been slipping from him, he acted as midwife and assistant in bringing to birth these encomia or rather these rank flatteries of himself, which he had anxiously solicited from More and others. For this purpose a certain Vlacq seemed, of all men, best suited. Salmasius easily persuaded him not only to print the book (an act for which no one would have blamed him), but also to sign his name to, and claim authorship of, a letter ostensibly directed to Charles and crammed with innumerable insults and slanders against me, who did not even know the man. That no one may wonder why he so easily allowed himself to be persuaded to attack me thus boldly and with no provocation, and why he made so light of transferring to himself and accepting responsibility for the follies of another, I shall describe, precisely as I have discovered it, his behavior towards the rest of the world.

Where Vlacq came from I do not know, but he is an itinerant bookseller, a notorious rascal and liar. For a time he carried on a clandestine book trade in London, from which city he fled after countless frauds, deep in debt. In Paris the whole Rue St. Jacques[22] knows him to be devoid of credit and pre-eminent in knavery. A fugitive at one time from Paris as well, he dares not approach within many leagues of that city. Now, if anyone needs a thoroughly wicked and corrupt rascal, Vlacq offers his services at The Hague as a newly re-established printer. So that you may understand this fellow—that he is completely indifferent to what he says or does, that he holds nothing more sacred than cash—even a pittance—and that it was not for any public cause, as one might have supposed, that he made this furious assault on me, I shall produce his own testimony to bear witness against him.

When he had observed that my reply to Salmasius had been a source of gain to some booksellers, he wrote to certain of my friends bidding them urge me to entrust to him anything I had to be printed and promising that he would set it up in far better type than had been used by my earlier printer.[23] I replied through the same friends that at present I had nothing in need of printing. But now, behold! He stands forth, not only as the printer, but also as the author (albeit supposititiously) of a most insulting tract against the very man to whom he

had not long before so officiously offered his services. My friends were indignant. Coolly enough he replied that he marveled at their simplicity and naïveté in demanding or expecting of him any regard for duty or honor, when they knew from what source he made his living. He added that he had received the letter in question with the book from Salmasius himself, who requested that he consent to do as a favor that which he did. Should Milton or another choose to reply, it made no difference to Vlacq, if indeed they wished to use these same services, against Salmasius, that is, or against Charles. For nothing else could be expected in such a controversy. What more need I say? You see what the man is.

Now I proceed to the others, for Vlacq is not the only one concerned in the presentation of the tragedy, as it were, of the King's Cry against us. Observe then, at the beginning, as is customary, the cast of characters: the "Cry," as prologue; Vlacq, the buffoon (or if you prefer, Salmasius disguised in the mask and cloak of Vlacq the buffoon); two poetasters, tipsy with stale beer; More the adulterer and seducer.[24] What splendid actors for a tragedy! A pretty contest has been offered me! But since our cause could scarcely find adversaries of another stamp, let us now attack them one by one, such as they are. With only this for preface: if anyone should find our rebuttal at any point somewhat frivolous, let him consider that we are engaged, not with a serious foe, but with a troupe of actors. So long as the nature of my *Defence* had to be suited to them, I thought that I ought to aim, not always at what would have been more decorous, but at what they deserved.

The Cry of the Kings Blood against the English Parricides.

If you, More, had shown that that blood was unjustly shed, your narrative would have been easier to credit, but just as the monks in the early days of the Reformation, when they grew weaker in rational argument, used to have recourse to all sorts of spectres and imaginary prodigies, so you now, after all else has failed, take refuge in Cries that were nowhere heard and in the outmoded devices of the friars. You are far from believing that anyone of our party hears voices from heaven, yet I would easily believe that you heard voices from hell (as you assert about me). But as for this Cry of

---

[22]A street on the Left Bank in Paris near the Sorbonne and associated with book-selling.

[23]Apparently Vlacq attempted to negotiate with Milton through Samuel Hartlib (French 3: 244–45), so that he could publish rebuttals from both parties.

[24]What Milton describes looks more like the Renaissance version of a Roman comedy than it appears to be a tragedy, since it has a buffoon looking something like a commedia dell'arte Pantalone figure in cloak and mask, and two drunken poetasters, possibly like Trinculo and Stefano in Shakespeare's *The Tempest*.

the Kings Blood, tell me, if you please, who heard it? You say that you heard it. Nonsense! For in the first place, you hear ill. Moreover, a shout that would reach heaven is heard, if by anyone other than God, by the just alone, I believe, and all the most upright, since they are able, being themselves blameless, to call down the wrath of God on the guilty. To what end would you hear it? So that you, a wanton, might compose a satyr play?[25] For you seem to have invented this cry to heaven at the very time when you stealthily indulged your passion for Pontia. Many obstacles stand in your way, More, many noises within and without thunder around you to prevent you from hearing such cries borne up to heaven. And if nothing else, certainly the tremendous cry which goes up to heaven against your own self would be sufficient. Against you cries out (in case you do not know) that harlot of yours in the garden, who complained that she had been led astray chiefly by the example of you, her pastor. Against you cries out the husband whose bed you dishonored. Pontia cries out, whom you promised to marry and betrayed. If anyone cries out, it is the tiny baby whom you begot in shame and then abandoned. If you do not hear the cries of all these to Heaven against you, neither could you hear the Cry of the King's Blood. Meanwhile that book of yours will more properly be entitled, not the *Cry of the Kings Blood to Heaven*, but the *Whinny of the Lustful More after His Pontia*.

The long-winded and thoroughly disgusting "Epistle" that follows is dedicated partly to Charles, partly to Milton, in order to exalt the one, and defame the other. From the very beginning, perceive at once what the author is: "The realms of Charles," says he, "have come into the sacrilegious power of parricides and—since proper words are lacking I apply to my own use an expression of Tertullian—of deicides."[26] Whether this hodgepodge is the work of Salmasius or More or Vlacq, let us pass it by. But what comes next must be a source of amusement to others, of anger to Charles. "There is no one alive," says Vlacq, "more concerned for the welfare of Charles, Is there really no one more concerned for the welfare of Charles than you, who offered to his foes this same assistance in both letter-writing and printing? Wretched indeed do you call a king so destitute of friends that a good-for-nothing printer dares to compare himself to the closest intimates that remain.

Wretched above all the king whose most faithful friends are not superior to the faithless Vlacq in loyalty and devotion. What statement could he make that would be more insolent regarding himself, more contemptuous with respect to the king and the kings friends? Nor is it less ridiculous that an ignorant artisan should be portrayed as philosophizing about the weightiest matters and the virtues of kings, and saying things, such as they are, which neither Salmasius himself nor More could have bettered. Here indeed, as in many other places, I have found clear proof that Salmasius, while a man of wide reading, possessed only immature and untried judgment. He must have read that the chief magistrates in Sparta, a state endowed with an excellent constitution, commanded that any word of wisdom which a bad man happened to utter should be taken from him and assigned by lot to some good and temperate man.[27] But Salmasius was so ignorant of all that is meant by decorum that he on the contrary allowed sentiments which he thought proper to an upright and prudent person to be ascribed to a man who is worthless in the extreme.

Be of good cheer, Charles. The imposter Vlacq, "out of his trust in God," bids you be of good cheer. "Do not waste so many sufferings." Vlacq, the utterly ruined spendthrift, who has wasted all his substance, whatever he had, is your authority that you should not waste your sufferings. "Make use of fortune, although she play the stepmother." Can you avoid using her, especially when you are exhorted by such a one, who for so many years has been wont to use other men's fortunes, right or wrong? "You have drunk deep of wisdom; drink on." Such is the advice, such the counsel of the tutor of kings, Vlacq, that bottomless abyss, who, seizing the wineskin in his inky hands, amid his drunken fellow-laborers, with a huge gulp drinks a health to your wisdom. Such are the noble counsels that your friend Vlacq ventures to give, even signing his name, a thing that Salmasius, More, and all your other champions are either too timid or too proud to do. Doubtless, whenever you have need of advice or defence, they are wise and brave, but always in another's name and at another's peril, not their own. Then let the fellow cease, whoever he is, to make empty boasts about his own vigorous and spirited eloquence, while the "man renowned (please God) for his elegant talent" is afraid to publish his "extremely well-known name." The book in which he says that he avenges the king's blood he did not venture even to dedicate to Charles, except through Vlacq as deputy and proxy,

---

[25]Carrying the image of bad actors in a worthless troupe further, Milton defames More by saying that the only play he might write would be like a classical Greek satyr play, one full of priapic obscene comedy.

[26]Killing kings, in other words, is close to murdering gods. The reference to the Church Father Tertullian has to do with the identity of Christ (is he man or god) in the Crucifixion (*Antenicene Fathers* 3: 626).

[27]Plutarch, *Moralia*, ed. Frank C. Babbitt (Loeb Library: London, 1931): 3: 405.

content basely to indicate in the printer's words that he, without a name, "is going to dedicate the book to your name, if you will permit it, O king."

Having dealt thus with Charles, he swells with threats and readies an attack on me: "After these proems the 'thaumasious'[28] Salmasius will blow on his terrible trumpet." It is good health that you predict and a new kind of musical harmony, for no more fitting accompaniment can be imagined for that "terrible trumpet" when it is blown, than a repeated crepitation.[29] But I advise Salmasius not to puff out his cheeks too far, for the more swollen they are, the more tempting until he make them to buffets, which, as both cheeks resound, will echo in time to the rhythmic noise of the "thaumasious" Salmasius, which gives you so much pleasure.

You proceed with your croaking: "Who has neither peer nor second in the whole world of letters and science." By your faith, men of learning, however many you are! Could you believe that you are all inferior to a lousy grammarian, whose entire substance and hope rest on a glossary?[30] A man whom the devil would rightly take as the hindmost, if he should be compared to real scholars? Such foolish statements could not be uttered except by someone base, and sillier even than Vlacq himself.

"And who has now brought to the cause of Your Majesty his marvelous and boundless learning, united with a divine intelligence." If you remember what I have related above, that Salmasius himself brought this letter, with the book, to be printed, that it was written either by himself or by someone anonymous, that he begged the slavish printer to sign his own name (as the author was unwilling to do), you will at once recognize a man of thoroughly paltry and debased mentality, thus pathetically spreading his sails for his own praises and grasping at boundless laudation from so foolish an admirer.

"While a few vainly revile the immortal work, lawyers cannot sufficiently admire the fact that a Frenchman should so swiftly grasp English affairs, laws, decrees, and instruments, elucidate them, and so on." Rather, how he played the fool in respect to our laws and was a mere parrot, we have ample proof, in the testimony of our lawyers.

"But Salmasius himself will shortly, in the second

attack, which he is preparing against the rebels, stop the mouths of the Theons[31] and at the same time punish Milton for us as he deserves." You then, like the herald fish, precede the whale Salmasius, as he threatens to "attack" these shores. We are sharpening our harpoons, prepared to squeeze out whatever oil or fish-sauce may be found in these "attacks" and "chastisement." Meanwhile we shall marvel at the more than Pythagorean goodness of the great Salmasius, in that he, having compassion even for animals and especially fishes, to whose flesh not even Lent shows mercy, has destined so many volumes to wrap them properly and has bequeathed to so many thousands of poor tunnies, I suppose, or herrings, a paper coat apiece.[32]

Rejoice, O herring, and all briney fish,
Who dwell the winter through in freezing moats,
Goodhearted Knight Salmasius doth wish
To clothe your nakedness in paper coats—
Of foolscap prodigal, which boldly flaunts
The name, device, and glory of Saumaise,
That you, through all the saltfishmongers' haunts,
May vaunt yourselves—and thus perchance win praise—
Sir Salmon's vassals, stacked on shelves in rows,
By them that use their sleeve to wipe their nose.[33]

These lines I had in readiness for the long-awaited edition of the famous book. While Salmasius, as you say, was at work on its production, you, More, defiled his house with the vile seduction of Pontia. Salmasius seems indeed to have brooded long and deeply over the completion of this work, for a few days before he died, when a certain scholar, from whom I had the story,[34] had sent to inquire when Salmasius would publish the second part of his attack on the primacy of the Pope, he replied that he would not return to that task until he had finished the work still in preparation against Milton. Thus am I preferred even to the Pope for refutation, and the primacy which Salmasius has denied to him in the church, he voluntarily concedes to me in his enmity. Thus have I brought deliverance to the papal supremacy, which was on the very verge of destruction. I, though not in a toga, like the Consul Tullius of old (not even in sleep, but while engaged in quite another

---

[28]"Full of miracles."
[29]Salmasius, in other words, makes wind from either end. *Crepitus* in Latin is noisy farting.
[30]Something of an odd accusation for Milton to make, since he was at times a grammarian and a lexicographer. See Leo Miller, "Milton, Salmasius and Hammond: The History of an Insult," *Renaissance & Reformation* 9 (1973): 108–15, which discusses Salmasius's sensitivity to being called "*Grammaticus*."

[31]Theon was a legendary and semimythical satirical poet whose name was applied to describe any writer of harsh, witty, derogatory verses. See Horace, *Epistles* 1.18, 82.
[32]Discarded sheets of paper or pages from books that did not sell were used, then and now, to wrap fish in the market. Milton makes an extended joke, and a very funny poem, out of the images of fish and Salmasius's disregarded books.
[33]Milton included this extended Latin epigram in his 1673 *Poems*.
[34]Not yet identified.

task) have turned away from the walls of Rome this Catiline reborn.[35] Certainly more than a mere cardinal's hat will be due me for this debt. I fear that the Roman pontiff, transferring to me the ancient title of our kings, will dub me Defender of the Faith.[36] You see how artful Salmasius was at stirring up against me. But let him take care, since he, after basely abandoning so noble a task, involved himself in other mens disputes and betook himself from the cause of the church to matters civil and foreign, which were no concern of his. Not only did he make a truce with the pope, but, what is most disgraceful, he returned to favor with the bishops, after open war had been declared.

Let us now come to the charges against me. Is there anything in my life or character which he could criticize? Nothing, certainly. What then? He does what no one but a brute and barbarian would have done—casts up to me my appearance and my blindness.

"A monster, dreadful, ugly, huge, deprived of sight." Never did I think that I should rival the Cyclops in appearance. But at once he corrects himself. "Yet not huge, for there is nothing more feeble, bloodless, and pinched." Although it ill befits a man to speak of his own appearance, yet speak I shall, since here too there is reason for me to thank God and refute liars, lest anyone think me to be perhaps a dogheaded ape or a rhinoceros, as the rabble in Spain, too credulous of their priests, believe to be true of heretics, as they call them. Ugly I have never been thought by anyone, to my knowledge, who has laid eyes on me. Whether I am handsome or not, I am less concerned. I admit that I am not tall, but my stature is closer to the medium than to the small. Yet what if it were small, as is the case with so many men of the greatest worth in both peace and war? (Although why is that stature called small which is great enough for virtue?) But neither am I especially feeble, having indeed such spirit and such strength that when my age and manner of life required it, I was not ignorant of how to handle or unsheathe a sword, nor unpracticed in using it each day. Girded with my sword, as I generally was, I thought myself equal to anyone, though he was far more sturdy, and I was fearless of any injury that one man could inflict on another. Today I possess the same spirit, the same strength, but not the same eyes. And yet they have as much the appearance of

being uninjured, and are as clear and bright, without a cloud, as the eyes of men who see most keenly. In this respect alone, against my will, do I deceive. In my face, than which he says there is "nothing more bloodless," still lingers a color exactly opposite to the bloodless and pale, so that although I am past forty, there is scarcely anyone to whom I do not seem younger by about ten years. Nor is it true that either my body or my skin is shriveled. If I am in any way deceitful in respect to these matters, I should deserve the mockery of many thousands of my fellow-citizens, who know me by sight, and of not a few foreigners as well. But if this fellow is proved such a bold and gratuitous liar in a matter by no means calling for deceit, you will be able to draw the same conclusion as to the rest.[37]

So much have I been forced to say about my appearance. Concerning yours, although I have heard that it is utterly despicable and the living image of the falseness and malice that dwell within you, I do not care to speak nor does anyone care to hear. Would that it were equally possible to refute this brutish adversary on the subject of my blindness, but it is not possible. Let me bear it then. Not blindness but the inability to endure blindness is a source of misery. Why should I not bear that which every man ought to prepare himself to bear with equanimity, if it befall him—that which I know may humanly befall any mortal and has indeed befallen certain men who are the most eminent and virtuous in all history? Or shall I recall those ancient bards and wise men of the most distant past, whose misfortune the gods, it is said, recompensed with far more potent gifts, and whom men treated with such respect that they preferred to blame the very gods than to impute their blindness to them as a crime? The tradition about the seer Tiresias is well known. Concerning Phineus, Apollonius sang as follows in the *Argonautica*:

Nor did he fear Jupiter himself,
Revealing truly to men the divine purpose.
Wherefore he gave him a prolonged old age,
But deprived him of the sweet light of his eyes.[38]

But God himself is truth! The more veracious a man is in teaching truth to men, the more like must he be to

---

[35]An elaborate set of comparisons between Milton as savior of England and the Roman orator Cicero (sometimes known by one of his names as Tullius or Tully) who saved the republic of Rome from the conspiracies of Catiline (Plutarch *Cicero* 15) in 65 and 63 BCE.

[36]The famous title bestowed on Henry VIII while he was yet a defender of the Roman Catholic faith but ironically kept by him after England had seceded from Catholicism.

[37]For Milton's image, and for the memories of others concerning what he looked like, the modern reader can consult the early biographers (they repeat or corroborate what he says here) and the portrait at age 62 which appeared as frontispiece to the *History of Britain* (1671).

[38]In the original, the original Greek is quoted, as well as what we assume is Milton's Latin translation. See Apollonius of Rhodes, *Argonautica* 2.181–84.

God and the more acceptable to him. It is impious to believe that God is grudging of truth or does not wish it to be shared with men as freely as possible. Because of no offence, therefore, does it seem that this man who was godlike and eager to enlighten the human race was deprived of his eyesight, as were a great number of philosophers. Or should I mention those men of old who were renowned for statecraft and military achievements? First, Timoleon of Corinth, who freed his own city and all Sicily, than whom no age has borne a man greater or more venerated in his state.[39] Next, Appius Claudius, whose vote, nobly expressed in the Senate, delivered Italy from Pyrrhus, her mortal enemy, but not himself from blindness.[40] Thirdly, Caecilius Metellus, the Pontifex,[41] who, while he saved from fire not the city alone but also the Palladium, the symbol of its destiny, and it innermost mysteries, lost his own eyes, although on other occasions certainly God has given proof that he favors such remarkable piety, even among the heathen. Therefore what has befallen such a man should scarcely, I think, be regarded as an evil.

Why should I add to the list other men of later times, such as the famous Doge of Venice, Dandolo,[42] by far the most eminent of all, or Sizka,[43] the brave leader of the Bohemians and the bulwark of the othodox faith? Why should I add theologians of the highest repute, Hieronymous Zanchius[44] and some others, when it is established that even Isaac the patriarch himself—and no mortal was ever dearer to God—lived in blindness for many years, as did also (for a few years perhaps) Jacob, his son, who was no less beloved by God.[45] When, finally, it is perfectly certain from the divine testimony of Christ our Savior that the man who was healed by Him had been blind from the very womb, through no sin of his own or his parents.

For my part, I call upon Thee, my God, who knowest my inmost mind and all my thoughts, to witness that (although I have repeatedly examined myself on this point as earnestly as I could, and have searched all the corners of my life) I am conscious of nothing, of no deed, either recent or remote, whose wickedness could justify occasion or invite upon me this supreme misfortune. As for what I have at any time written (since the royalists think I am now undergoing this suffering as a penance, and they accordingly rejoice),[46] I likewise call God to witness that I have written nothing of such kind that I was not then and am not now convinced that it was right and true and pleasing to God. And I swear that my conduct was not influenced by ambition, gain, or glory, but solely by considerations of duty, honor, and devotion to my country. I did my utmost not only to free my country, but also to free the church. Hence, when the business of replying to the royal defense had been officially assigned to me, and at that same time I was afflicted at once by ill health and the virtual loss of my remaining eye, and the doctors were making learned predictions that if I should undertake this task, I would shortly lose both eyes, I was not in the least deterred by the warning. I seemed to hear, not the voice of the doctor (even that of Aesculapius, issuing from the shrine at Epidaurus),[47] but the sound of a certain more divine monitor within. And I thought that two lots had now been set before me by a certain command of fate: the one blindness, the other, duty. Either I must necessarily endure the loss of my eyes, or I must abandon my most solemn duty. And there came into my mind those two fates which, the son of Thetis relates, his mother brought back from Delphi, where she inquired concerning him:

Two destinies lead me to the end, which is death:
If staying here I fight around the city of Troy,
Return is denied me, but immortal will be my fame.
If homeward I return to my dear native land,
Lost is fair fame, but long will be my life.[48]

Then I reflected that many men have bought with greater evil smaller good; with death, glory. To me, on the contrary, was offered a greater good at the price of a smaller evil: that I could at the cost of blindness alone

---

[39]Timoleon, whose life was memorialized by Plutarch, was noted for leading a rebellion against his brother because he had become a tyrant in Corinth; in later life, he became blind.

[40]The Roman censor Appius Claudius Caecus ("Caecus" means "the blind"), architect of the Appian Way, spoke against Pyrrhus in the Roman Senate after he was blind. See Plutarch, *Life of Pyrrhus* 18.

[41]Lucius Caecilius Metellus (third century BCE), died while saving the famous statue of Pallas Athene during a fire in the temple of Vesta in Rome (Cicero, *De Senectute* 9.30).

[42]Enrico Dandolo, nearly blind Doge of Venice, elected to that office in 1193.

[43]John Zizka (c. 1376–1424), Hussite leader in Bohemia, who lost each of his eyes during several battles but continued as an effective military and religious leader even after he became blind.

[44]Jerome or Hieronymus Zanchi or Zanchius (1516–1590), a theologian cited by Milton several times in *On Christian Doctrine*.

[45]Genesis 27.2 describes Isaac as being scarcely able to see in his extreme old age. For Jacob in the same condition, see Genesis 48.10.

[46]There are many references to Milton's blindness (mostly among Royalists) as God's punishment for his participating in the killing of a king (see Campbell, *Chronology* 1662).

[47]Aesculapius was the god of physicians and had a shrine at Epidaurus from which healing prophecy might be invoked.

[48]The passage, quoted and translated from the original Greek, also included, is from the *Iliad* 9.411–16. Milton is clearly comparing himself with Achilles, who was as a young man given the choice between a long, dull life, and a short and glorious life: implied is heroism in Milton's choice to allow himself to become blind in service to his country.

fulfill the most honorable requirement of my duty. As duty is of itself more substantial than glory, so it ought to be for every man more desirable and illustrious. I resolved therefore that I must employ this brief use of my eyes while yet I could for the greatest possible benefit to the state. You see what I chose, what I rejected, and why.

Then let those who slander the judgments of God cease to speak evil and invent empty tales about me. Let them be sure that I feel neither regret nor shame for my lot, that I stand unmoved and steady in my resolution, that I neither discern nor endure the anger of God, that in fact I know and recognize in the most momentous affairs his fatherly mercy and kindness towards me, and especially in this fact, that with his consolation strengthening my spirit I bow to his divine will, dwelling more often on what he has bestowed on me than on what he has denied. Finally, let them rest assured that I would not exchange the consciousness of my achievement for any deed of theirs, be it ever so righteous, nor would I be deprived of the recollection of my deeds, ever a source of gratitude and repose.

Finally, as to my blindness, I would rather have mine, if it be necessary, than either theirs, More, or yours. Your blindness, deeply implanted in the inmost faculties, obscures the mind, so that you may see nothing whole or real. Mine, which you make a reproach, merely deprives things of color and superficial appearance. What is true and essential in them is not lost to my intellectual vision. How many things there are, moreover, which I have no desire to see, how many things that I should be glad not to see, how few remain that I should like to see. Nor do I feel pain at being classed with the blind, the afflicted, the suffering, and the weak (although you hold this to be wretched) since there is hope that in this way I may approach more closely the mercy and protection of the Father Almighty. There is a certain road which leads through weakness, as the apostle teaches, to the greatest strength.[49] May I be entirely helpless, provided that in my weakness there may arise all the more powerfully this immortal and more perfect strength; provided that in my shadows the light of the divine countenance may shine forth all the more clearly. For then I shall be at once the weakest and the strongest, at the same time blind and most keen in vision. By this infirmity may I be perfected by this completed. So in this darkness, may I be clothed in light.

To be sure, we blind men are not the least of God's concerns, for the less able we are to perceive anything other than himself, the more mercifully and graciously does he deign to look upon us. Woe to him who mocks us, woe to him who injures us. He deserves to be cursed with a public malediction. Divine law and divine favor have rendered us not only safe from the injuries of men, but almost sacred, nor do these shadows around us seem to have been created so much by the dullness of our eyes as by the shade of angels' wings. And divine favor not infrequently is wont to lighten these shadows again, once made, by an inner and far more enduring light. To this circumstance I refer the fact that my friends now visit, esteem, and attend me more diligently even than before, and that there are some with whom I might as with true friends exchange the conversation of Pylades [with Orestes] and Theseus [with Heracles]:

Orestes: Go slowly as the rudder of my feet.
Pylades: A precious care is this to me.

And elsewhere:

Theseus: Give your hand to your friend and helper.
    Put your arm around my neck, and I will be your
    guide.[50]

For my friends do not think that by this calamity I have been rendered altogether worthless, nor that whatever is characteristic of an honest and prudent man resides in his eyes. In fact, since the loss of my eyesight has not left me sluggish from inactivity but tireless and ready among the first to risk the greatest dangers for the sake of liberty, the chief men in the state do not desert me either, but, considering within themselves what human life is like, they gladly favor and indulge me, and grant to me rest and leisure, as to one who well deserves it. If I have any distinction, they do not remove it, if any public office, they do not take it away, if any advantage from that office, they do not diminish it, and although I am no longer as useful as I was, they think that they should reward me no less graciously. They pay me the same honor as if, according to the custom of ancient Athens, they had decreed that I take my meals in the Prytaneum.[51]

So long as I find in God and man such consolation for

---

[49]Hebrews 11.34, ending a catalogue of those who "won strength out of weakness." Compare 2 Corinthians 12.9, "My grace is sufficient for thee: for my strength is made perfect in weakness," which Milton in 1651 wrote in a friend's album, as a kind of personal motto (Yale 7: 260n).

[50]The quotations are from Euripides: the first is from *Orestes* 795 and the second from *Hercules Furens* 1398 and 1402.
[51]Dining hall in the Athens of Pericles where distinguished citizens might be invited to dine at the state's expense. The Yale editors cite Plato *Apology* 36, in which Socrates that he be allowed to dine for life at the Prytaneum.

my blindness, let no one mourn for my eyes, which were lost in the cause of honor. Far be it from me either to mourn. Far be it from me to have so little spirit that I cannot easily despise the revilers of my blindness, or so little charity that I cannot even more easily pardon them. To you, whoever you are, I return, who with but little consistency regard me now as a dwarf, now as Antaeus.[52] You have (finally) no more ardent desire "for the United Provinces of Holland than that they should dispose of this war as easily and successfully as Salmasius will dispose of Milton." If I give glad assent to this prayer, I think that I express no bad omen or evil wish against our success and the cause of England.

But listen! Another Cry, something strange and hissing I take it that geese are flying in from somewhere or other. Now I realize what it is. I remember that this is the Tragedy of a Cry. The Chorus appears. Behold, two poetasters—either two or a single one, twofold in appearance and of two colors. Should I call it a sphinx, or that monster which Horace describes in the *Ars Poetica,* with the head of a woman, the neck of an ass, clad in varied plumage, with limbs assembled from every source?[53] Yes, this is that very monster. It must be some rhapsode or other, strewn with centos and patches.[54] Whether it is one or two is uncertain, for it also is anonymous.

Now, poets who deserve the name I love and cherish, and I delight in hearing them frequently. Most of them, I know, are bitterly hostile to tyrants, if I should list them from the first down to our own Buchanan.[55] But these peddlers of effeminate little verses—who would not despise them? Nothing could be more foolish, more idle, more corrupt or more false than such as they. They praise, they censure, without choice, without discrimination, judgment, or measure, now princes, now commoners, the learned as well as the ignorant, whether honest or wicked, it makes no difference, according as they are puffed up and swept away by the bottle, by the hope of a halfpenny, or by that empty frenzy of theirs. From every source they accumulate their absurdities of diction and matter, so many, so inconsistent, so disgusting, that it is far better for the object of their praise to suffer their neglect and live, as the saying is, with a crooked nose, than to receive such praise. But he whom they attack should consider it no small honor that he finds no favor with such absurd and paltry fools.

It is doubtful whether the first (if there really are two of them) should be called a poet or a plasterer, to such a degree does he whitewash the facade of Salmasius, or rather whiten and plaster him entirely, as if he were a wall. He brings on in a "triumphal" chariot, no less, the giant-fighting hero, brandishing his "javelins and boxing gloves" and all manner of trifling weapons, with all the scholars following the chariot on foot, but a tremendous distance to the rear, since he is the one "whom divine providence has raised up in evil times for the salvation of the world. At last, therefore, the time was at hand for kings to be protected by such a shield—the parent [no less] of law and empire." Salmasius must have been mad and in his second childhood not only to have been so hugely gratified by such praises but also to have taken such pains to have them printed with all possible haste. Wretched too and ignorant of propriety was the poet if he thought a mere schoolmaster worthy of such immoderate eulogy, since that breed of men has always been at the service of poets and inferior to them.

The other, however, does not write verses, but simply raves, himself the most insane of all the possessed whom he so rabidly assails. As if he were an executioner for Salmasius, a son of Syrian Dama,[56] he calls for the floggers and Cadmus; then drunk with hellebore, he vomits up out of the index to Plautus[57] all the filthy language of slaves and scoundrels that can be found anywhere. You would suppose that he was speaking Oscan,[58] not Latin, or was croaking like a frog from the hellish swamps in which he swims. Then, to show you how great is his mastery of iambics, he is guilty of two false quantities in a single word, one syllable incorrectly prolonged, the other shortened:[59]

Hi trucidate rege per horrendum nefas.

Take away, you ass, those saddlebags filled with your

---

[52]The giant son of Gaia (the Earth) and Poseidon, who, when wrestled, doubled his strength each time he came in contact with his mother. Hercules defeated him by holding him above the earth until his strength ebbed from him. Here Milton points out the contradiction between describing him as a dwarf and then a giant.

[53]Horace, *Ars Poetica,* first three lines.

[54]Rhapsodes were a class of poets, usually looked down on, who recited poetry laced with centos or patchwork selections borrowed from famous poems. Because the rhapsodes often improvised, their work became known as rhapsodic, highly emotional or ecstatic.

[55]George Buchanan (c. 1506–82), Scottish scholar and historian, was best known in his own time as a Latin poet. Buchanan wrote a Latin tragedy, *Baptistes* (1578), translated as *Tyrannicall-Government Anatomized* (1642)—a translation at times attributed falsely to Milton (Parker 836).

[56]A son of slaves who threatens free-born citizens in Horace *Satires* 1.6.38–39.

[57]Roman comedy writer Titus Maccius Plautus (c. 254–184 BCE), who allowed his slaves and other lower-class characters to speak crudely and naturalistically.

[58]A pre-classical Italian dialect, supposed to be primitive and inelegant as compared with Latin.

[59]The Yale editors comment that the two quantities in the word *trucidate* are forced and "The short *u* is made long, and the long *i* is made short" (7: 594n).

emptinesses, and bring us at last just three words, if you can, like a sane and sober man, provided that that pumpkinhead of yours, that "blockhead," can be sensible even for a second. Meanwhile I hand you over, an Orbilius, to be executed by the "harvest of rods" of your pupils.[60]

Continue to curse me as being "worse than Cromwell" in your estimation—the highest praise you could bestow on me. But should I call you a friend, a fool, or a crafty foe? A friend you surely are not, for your words prove you a foe. Why then have you been so inept in your slander that it occurred to you to exalt me above so great a man? Is it possible that you do not understand, or think that I do not understand, that the greater the hatred you show towards me, the greater is your advertisement of my merits with respect to the Commonwealth, and that your insults amount to so many eulogies of me among my own people? For if you hate me most of all, surely I am the one who has injured you most of all, hurt you most of all, and damaged your cause. If such is the case, I am also the one who has deserved most highly of my fellow-citizens, for the testimony or judgment of an enemy, even if in other circumstances somewhat unreliable, is nevertheless by far the most weighty when it concerns his own suffering. Or do you not remember that when Ajax and Ulysses vied for the weapons of the dead Achilles, the poet chose as judges, on the advice of Nestor, not Greeks, their fellow-countrymen, but Trojans, their enemies?

Therefore let the prudent Trojans decide this quarrel. And a little later:

Who will give just judgment concerning these men
Partial to neither party, since all the Achaens with equal
    bitterness
They hate, mindful of their grievous loss.

These are the words of the poet of Smyrna or Calabria.[61]

Hence it follows that you are a crafty foe and take pains to cast infamy on me, when with malicious intent and the purpose of inflicting still deeper injury you pervert and debase that judgment which is wont in the case of an enemy to be impartial and honest. So

perverted are you not just as a man, but even as an enemy. Yet, my fine fellow, I shall without difficulty circumvent you. For although I should like to be Ulysses—should like, that is, to have deserved as well as possible of my country—yet I do not covet the arms of Achilles. I do not seek to bear before me heaven painted on a shield,[62] for others, not myself to see in battle, while I carry on my shoulders a burden, not painted but real, for myself, and not for others to perceive.

Since I bear no grudge whatever nor harbor private quarrels against any man, nor does any man, so far as I know, bear any grudge against me, I endure with the greater equanimity all the curses that are uttered against me, all the insults that are hurled, so long as they are suffered for the sake of the state, not for myself. Nor do I complain that to me has fallen the tiniest share of the rewards and benefits which thus accrue, but the greatest share of ignominy. I am content to have sought for their own sake alone, and to accomplish without recompense, those deeds which honor bade me do. Let others look to that, and do you rest assured that I have not touched these "abundances" and "riches of which you accuse me, nor have I become a penny richer by reason of that renown with which especially you charge me.

Here More begins again, and his second "Epistle" reports his reasons for writing. To whom? "To the Christian reader," no less, More, the adulterer and seducer, sends greeting. A devout letter indeed you presage. Now begin your reasons. "The minds of the nations of Europe and most of all our French Protestants have been aroused to take notice of the parricide and those who committed it," etc. The French, even the Protestants themselves, have waged wars against kings. What more they would have done, if they had met success equal to ours, cannot be stated with assurance. Certainly their kings, if we are to believe the records of those events, were no less fearful of them than was our king of us. And not without reason, whenever they remembered what those men had repeatedly written and often threatened. Let not the French, therefore, whatever pretext you offer, boast too loudly of themselves, or think too ill of us.

He continues with his "reasons": "Indeed I have enjoyed such familiarity with Englishmen of the better stamp"—Those who are "of the better stamp" to you are, in the opinion of decent men, of the very worst stamp.—"that I would venture to say that I know these human monsters inside and out." I thought that you knew only your mistresses and harlots, but you also

---

[60]Orbilius Pupillus (c. 112–17 BCE) was best known as the schoolmaster of Horace noted in the *Epistles* 2.1.70–71 for being a severe disciplinarian, beating his pupils.

[61]Quintus Calaber (fourth century BCE), follower of Homer who provided a continuation of the *Iliad*. He is also Quintus of Smyrna, because he lived there, and "Calaber" because his manuscript was discovered in Calabria. The lines quoted are from 5.157.162–64, from a work sometimes called *The War at Troy*.

[62]Achilles' famous shield, made for him by Hephaistos at his mother Thetis's command, had scenes of Greek life on its inner side (*Iliad* 18.478–617).

know monsters inside and out. "The English with whom I was on familiar terms readily persuaded me to conceal my name." And they were shrewd, for they hoped that thus they would get the benefit of your impudence in a larger degree, and you would in this way do less harm to their cause by your reputation, which was even then vile. For they know you, know how good a keeper of gardens you once were, and how, although now a priest, shaven and shorn, you could not keep your hands off Pontia, even Pontia Pilata.[63] Nor is this hard to understand, for if an executioner [*carnifex*] is thought to take his name from his dealings in flesh [*a conficienda carne*] why should you not seem with equal plausibility to have risen from priest to pontifex by your dealings in Pontia? Although others were not ignorant of these exploits of yours, although you yourself could not be unaware of them, nevertheless, with an unbelievable and in fact accursed blasphemy you dare openly to proclaim that you "seek and defend only the glory of God." While you yourself seek the vilest ends, you dare at the same time to accuse others of "hiding their crimes beneath a mask of piety," although no one has ever done so more brazenly or wickedly than yourself.

"For the order of events," you say that you "have received great assistance not only from other writers but especially from the *Scrutiny of the Recent Insurrection in England.*"[64] Truly you are a feckless creature, if after making such a commotion you impart no information that is your own. But the only writers you have been able to produce against us are authors belonging to the royalist party and therefore justly suspect. If their authority be removed, you could go no further. We shall therefore refute those writers, if need be, and overcome *Scrutiny* by scrutiny, and we shall reply at the proper time, not to them through you, but to you through them. Meanwhile see to it that you can defend what you have brought forward on your own account. Let all the pious folk now hear what its nature is and from what an impious and indeed godless source it has come, and let them shudder. "The love of God commands, and the keen realization of the injury done to his holy name compels us to lift suppliant hands to

God." Hide, yes, hide those vile hands, which you do not scruple to lift, although you grovel in lust and ambition. Hide them lest you dare to defile heaven itself with those hands, with which you have desecrated by your touch the sacred mysteries of religion. The divine vengeance which you rashly and absurdly invoke on others, you will some day learn that you have called down on your own unclean head.

So far the preface, as it were, of the Cry. Now (for the Cry has the chief and virtually the only role in this drama), with the widest possible opening, the jaws part, that the Cry may ascend to heaven, no doubt. If it ascends thither, it will cry out against no one more bitterly than against the crier himself, More. "Although the majesty of kings has been sacred to all ages," etc. In your vulgarity and malice, you declaim many charges against us, More, which are totally irrelevant, for the murder of a king and the punishment of a tyrant are not the same thing, More, they are not the same. They differ enormously from each other and will differ as long as common sense and reason, law and justice, and the power to distinguish straight from crooked shall belong to man. But on these matters enough has already been said again and again; there has been sufficient defence. I shall not allow you, who can do us no injury by so many empty threats, to slay us at last with your twice-told tales. Next, concerning patience and piety you make some fine points, but speaking of virtue,

You wag your tail. Shall I fear you, More,
While you fawn on me?[65]

You say that all Protestants, especially the Dutch and the French, were shocked by our deed, yet you add immediately afterwards, "It was not possible for good men everywhere to think and speak alike." But it is a tiny matter for you to contradict yourself. The following assertion is far more shocking and blasphemous. In comparison with our crime, you say, "the crime of the Jews who crucified Christ was nothing, whether you compare the purpose of the Jews or the effects of their crime." Madman! Do you, a minister of Christ, make so light of the crime committed against Christ that, whatever the "purpose" or "effect," you dare to say that the murder of any king whatsoever is equally wicked? Certainly the Jews could by means of the clearest proofs have recognized the Son of God. We could in no way perceive that Charles was not a tyrant. Moreover, to mitigate the crime of the Jews you foolishly mention its

---

[63]Part of a complex of off-color puns, here working on a perversion of the name Pontius Pilate with "Pontia Pilata," which suggests that Pontia was depilated, as were ancient prostitutes. Her name is still also related to the Pope as "pontifex maximus." Also, More is "shaven and shorn" as if he were a mock-priest, with a tonsure.
[64]A book called *Review of the Late Troubles in England* in the *Clamor*. As the Yale editor points out, Du Moulin's real source was *Elenchus Motuum Nuperorum in Anglia; Simul ac Juris Regii et Parlamentarii Brevis Enarratio*, by George Bate (Edinburgh, 1650)—Yale 4.1: 598n.

[65]Probably an echo of Juvenal, *Satires* 1.2.20–21, which is concerned with a male homosexual attracting others by suggestive motions.

"effect." But I always notice that the more enthusiastic a royalist a man is, the more he is inclined to bear any offence against Christ more easily than one against the king. Although royalists profess that the king should be obeyed chiefly for the sake of Christ, it is easy to see that they truly love neither Christ nor the king, but, having some other object in view, they make this incredible devotion towards kings and this religion of theirs a cloak either for ambition or for certain other concealed lusts.

"Therefore the great prince of letters, Salmasius, came forward." Enough of this word "great," which you repeat so often, More. If you kept uttering it a thousand times, you would never persuade an intelligent man that Salmasius is great, but only that More is very small, a manikin of no worth, who in his ignorance of what is fitting, so childishly abuses the name of "great." To grammarians and critics, whose chief glory lies either in editing the works of others or in correcting the mistakes of scribes, we gladly concede industry, indeed, and knowledge of letters, even praise for no mean learning, and rewards, but we scarcely bestow on them the name of "great." He alone is to be called great who either performs or teaches or worthily records great things. Moreover, those things alone are great which either render this life of ours happy (or at least comfortable and pleasant, without dishonor) or lead us to the other, happier life. But which of these things has Salmasius done? None of them! Or what great thing has he taught or written, except perhaps his treatises against bishops and the primacy of the Pope, which he himself later recanted and completely reversed, both by his own behavior and by what he subsequently wrote against us in favor of Episcopacy. A "great" writer therefore he does not deserve to be called, who either wrote nothing great or dishonorably retracted the most excellent thing he had written in his lifetime.

"Prince of letters," he may be, for all of me, and prince of the whole alphabet too, but to you he is not only prince of letters, but "patron of kings and patron worthy of such clients." Splendidly indeed have you consulted for kings, so that after notable titles they may be called "clients of Claudius Salmasius. By this pronouncement, O kings (namely that you entrust yourselves to the patronage of the grammarian Salmasius and subject your sceptres to his ferrule) no doubt you are released from all other obligations! "To him will kings, as long as the earth shall endure, owe the vindication of their dignity and safety." Give ear, O princes! He who defended you wretchedly, or rather did not defend you at all, for no one came to the attack, credits himself with your dignity and safety. This, I suppose, is all they have achieved, who called in the haughty grammarian from his forum of moths and bookworms to uphold the right of kings.

"To him the church will be no less in debt than will the cause of royalty." No praise indeed will the church owe him, but a richly deserved black mark for deserting her cause. Now you would pour forth praises on the *Defence of the King*. You marvel at "the genius, the earning, the almost boundless experience in affairs, the intimate knowledge of law, both canon and civil, the vigor of the ardent oratory, the eloquence, the fluency of that golden work." While none of these qualities, I maintain, belonged to this man (for what has Salmasius to do with eloquence?), that the work was golden I nevertheless admit a hundred times over, so many gold pieces did Charles count out, not to mention what the Prince of Orange also expended on the same work.[66]

"Never did the great man rise to greater heights, never was he more truly Salmasius." So much greater did he become, in fact, that he burst himself, for how great he was in that effort we have seen, and if, as is rumored, he left any posthumous work on the same theme we shall perhaps see again. I do not indeed deny that, when the book had been published, Salmasius was on everyone's lips and gave tremendous pleasure to the royalists. "He was entertained, with lavish gifts, by the most august Queen of Sweden." Nay, in that whole debate, everything favored Salmasius, almost everything was against me. First, concerning his erudition, men had a high opinion, which he had been fostering for many years by writing a great many books, and very thick ones, not indeed especially useful, but concerned with most obscure subjects and crammed with quotations from the most important authors. There is nothing calculated more quickly to win the admiration of the reading public. But as for me, almost no one in those parts knew who I was. Salmasius had aroused a great anticipation with respect to himself, devoting more care to the work than was his wont, in view of the importance of the subject. I could excite no interest in myself. In fact, many persons tried to discourage me from undertaking the task, on the ground that I was a tyro about to join battle with a veteran. Some were jealous, lest it might somehow prove glorious for me to have engaged so great a foe, some fearful both for me and for our cause, lest I be conquered and leave the field with serious damage to both. Finally, his showy and plausible case, the deep-rooted prejudice (or rather it should be called superstition) of the mob, and their fondness for the name of "king"—all had given additional strength and

---

[66]The Prince of Orange, William II, might have supported Salmasius and Charles II (Masson 4: 25–27).

encouragement to Salmasius. All these things worked against me, and therefore the eagerness with which my reply was snapped up, as soon as it appeared, by great numbers who were anxious to see who in the world was so bold as to risk combat with Salmasius, is less remarkable than the welcome and approval which it found in many quarters—so warm a welcome, that, when account was taken, not of the author, but of truth itself, Salmasius, who had but recently basked in the warmest favor, now, as if the mask beneath which he had lurked was snatched away, suddenly sank both in reputation and in spirits. And even though he strove with every muscle as long as he lived, he could not afterwards re-establish himself.

As for you, most serene ruler of the Swedes,[67] he could not long deceive you and that keen judgment of yours. You have proved yourself the princess, and I might almost say the heavenly guardian, of that course which prefers truth to the heat of partisans. For although you had loaded with many honors this man whom you had invited to court and who at that time enjoyed a unique celebrity by reason of his reputation for extraordinary learning and his support of the royalist cause, yet when the reply appeared and you had read it with remarkable impartiality, and after you had observed that Salmasius was convicted of vanity and very evident corruption, and had said many things that were trivial, many that were extreme, some that were false, others that told against himself and contradicted his earlier sentiments (for which, when he was, as the story goes, summoned to your presence, he had no good explanation), your attitude was so plainly altered that from that time on everyone understood that you neither honored the fellow as before nor made much of his talent or learning, and that (what was certainly unexpected) you were strongly inclined to favor his opponent. For you denied that my attacks on tyrants in any way applied to you. As a result you obtained within yourself the fruit of an upright conscience, and with others its outward fame. For while your actions declare sufficiently that you are not a tyrant, this open revelation of your sentiments showed even more clearly that you are not in any measure guilty of such conduct.

How much more fortunate am I than I had hoped—for I claim no eloquence except that persuasion

which lies in truth itself. When I had fallen on such a time in my country's history as obliged me to become involved in a cause so difficult and so dangerous that I seemed to attack the whole right of kings, I found such a glorious, such a truly royal defender of my honesty to testify that I had uttered no word against kings, but only against tyrants—the pests and plagues of kings. How magnanimous you are, Augusta, how secure and well fortified on all sides by a well-nigh divine virtue and wisdom. Not only could you read with so calm and serene a spirit, with such incredible objectivity and true composure of countenance a work that might seem to have been written against your own right and dignity, but you could adopt such a judgment against your own defender that you seem to most men even to award the palm to his opponent. With what honor, with what respect, O queen, ought I always to cherish you, whose exalted virtue and magnanimity are a source not alone of glory to you, but also of favor and benefit to me! They have freed me from all suspicion and ill-repute in the minds of other kings and by this glorious and immortal kindness have bound me to you for ever. How well ought foreigners to think of your fairness and justice! How high should always be the opinion and the hopes of your people, who, when your own affairs and even your royal power seemed to be at stake, saw you, in no way disturbed, deliver judgment no less calmly concerning your own rights than is your wont concerning those of your people. It was not for nothing that you collected from every source so many costly books, so many works of literature, not as if they could teach you anything, but so that from them your fellow citizens could learn to know you and contemplate the excellence of your virtue and wisdom. If the very image of the goddess of wisdom had not been present within your own mind, if she had not offered herself to you for your eyes to behold, she could not by any mere reading of books have aroused in you such unbelievable love of herself. All the more do we marvel at that vigorous mind of yours, plainly of heavenly origin, that purest particle of the divine air which has fallen, so it seems, into those remote regions. Your dark and cloudy sky could not quench it or weigh it down with any frosts, nor could that rough and unkind soil, which not infrequently hardens also the minds of its inhabitants, create anything in you that was uneven or harsh. In fact, that very land, so rich in metals, if to others a step-mother, to you certainly seems to have been a kind parent, who strove with all her might to bring you forth all gold. I should say that you are the daughter and the only offspring of Adolphus, the unconquered and glorious king, did you not, Christina, as far outshine him as wisdom excels strength, and the arts of peace the

---

[67]Christina of Sweden (1626–1689), Milton's ideal of a just monarch, as compared with a tyrant. Though Milton apparently endorsed "the Nobles, disdaining Female Government" in the *History of Britain* (Yale 5: 217), Christina's superior education and her love of learning may have especially appealed to him. She was the daughter of Gustavus Adolphus (1594–1632), a warlike defender of Protestantism, but she herself would die a Roman Catholic.

crafts of war. From now on, to be sure, the Queen of the South shall not alone be celebrated. The North has now its Queen as well, and one not only worthy of setting forth to hear the sagacious king of the Jews (or any other like him) but worthy to attract others from every quarter as to the most brilliant exemplar of royal virtues and a heroine to be visited by all. Worthy too of their admission that there is on earth no dignity equal to the praises and merits of one in whom they see that her being a queen, the monarch of so many subjects, is but the least merit. Not the least, however, is the fact that she herself regards this as the least of her glories, and takes thought for something far more august and sublime than to rule. She is, for this very reason, to be preferred to countless kings. And so she can, if such a misfortune awaits the Swedish people, abdicate the throne, but, having proved herself worthy of ruling, not Sweden but the whole earth, she can never lay aside her queenliness.

There is no one, I feel, who—so far from blaming—would not commend me for this digression in well-deserved praise of the Queen. Indeed, I could not omit it—even if others were silent—without incurring the greatest blame for ingratitude, since by some happy chance or by some secret agreement or direction of the stars, or of the spirits, or of events, I have found in far-off lands so great a judge as I had least of all expected, but most of all hoped to find, one so fair and favorable to me. Now I must return to the work from which I digressed, a very different matter. We "became frantic," you say, "at the news of the *Defensio Regia* and therefore" we "hunted out some starveling little schoolmaster, who would consent to lend his corrupt pen to the defence of parricide." This tale you have maliciously invented out of your recollection that the royalists, when they were seeking a herald for their own lies and abuse, approached a grammarian, who was, if not hungry, at least more than a little thirsty for gold—Salmasius. He gladly sold them, not only his services at that time, but also his intellectual powers, if any were his before. The tale springs also from your recollection that Salmasius, his reputation now lost and ruined, when he was casting about for some one who might be able in some way to repair his good name, thus damaged and disgraced, found you, by the just judgment of God, not the minister of Geneva (whence you had been expelled) but the bishop of Lampsacus, that is, a Priapus from the garden,[68] the defiler of his own home. Thereafter, revolted by your insipid praises,

which he had purchased with such dishonor, he was converted from a friend into the bitterest enemy and uttered many curses against you, his eulogist, as he died.

"Only one man was found, most assuredly a great hero, whom they could oppose to Salmasius, a certain John Milton." I did not realize that I was a hero, although you may, so far as I am concerned, be the son, perhaps, of some hero or other, since you are totally noxious.[69] And that I alone was found to defend the cause of the people of England, certainly I regret, if I consider the interests of the Commonwealth, but if I consider the glory involved, I am perfectly content that I have no one with whom to share it. Who I am and whence I come is uncertain, you say; so once it was uncertain who Homer was, and who Demosthenes. But in fact, I had learned to hold my peace, I had mastered the art of not writing, a lesson that Salmasius could never learn. And I carried silently in my breast that which, if I had then wished to publish it, would long since have made me as famous as I am today. But I was not greedy for fame, whose gait is slow, nor did I ever intend to publish even this, unless a fitting opportunity presented itself. It made no difference to me even if others did not realize that I knew whatever I knew, for it was not fame, but the opportune moment for each thing that I awaited. Hence it happened that I was known to a good many, long before Salmasius was known to himself. Now he is better known than the nag Andraemon.[70]

"Is he a man or a worm?" Indeed, I should prefer to be a worm, which even King David confesses that he is, rather than hide in my breast your worm that dieth not.[71] "They say," you continue, "that this fellow, expelled from the University of Cambridge, because of his offences, fled his disgrace and his country and traveled to Italy." Even from this statement one can infer how truthful were your sources of information, for on this point everyone who knows me knows that both you and your informants lie most shamelessly, and I shall at once make this fact clear. If I had actually been expelled from Cambridge,[72] why should I travel to Italy, rather than to France or Holland, where you, enveloped

---

[68]The fertility god Priapus, usually represented by a statue in a garden of a male figure with an erection, was associated with the city Lampsacus in Asia Minor.

[69]The Yale editors quote the Latin proverb "*Heroum filii nexae*," "The sons of heroes are nonentities" (Yale 4: 607n).

[70]An allusion to Martial's Epigram 10.9, in which the satirical poet says he should not be envied if he is better known than a packhorse named Andraemone.

[71]Probably Satan, thought to live in "hell, where their worm does not die" (Mark 9.48). The worm in this case is a serpent.

[72]Milton in fact was rusticated or sent home by his first tutor at Cambridge, William Chappell, after a disagreement, but he was allowed to return and complete his degree. His trip to Italy was, as he says, in no way connected with his college experience.

in so many offenses, a minister of the Gospel, not only live in safety, but preach, and even defile with your unclean hands the sacred offices, to the extreme scandal of your church? But why to Italy, More? Another Saturn, I presume, I fled to Latium[73] that I might find a place to lurk. Yet I knew beforehand that Italy was not, as you think, a refuge or asylum for criminals, but rather the lodging-place of *humanitas* and of all the arts of civilization, and so I found it.

"Returning, he wrote his book on divorce." I wrote nothing different from what Bucer had written before me and copiously—about the kingdom of Christ, nothing different from what Fagius had written on Deuteronomy, Erasmus on the first Epistle to the Corinthians (a commentary intended for the benefit of the English people), nothing different from what many other illustrious men wrote for the common good.[74] No one blamed them for so doing, and I fail to understand why it should be to me above all a source of reproach. One thing only could I wish, that I had not written it in the vernacular for then I would not have met with vernacular readers, who are usually ignorant of their own good, and laugh at the misfortunes of others. But do you, vilest of men, protest about divorce, you who procured the most brutal of all divorces from Pontia, the maidservant engaged to you, after you seduced her under cover of that engagement? Moreover, she was a servant of Salmasius, an English woman it is said, warmly devoted to the royalist cause. It is beyond question that you wickedly courted her as royal property and left her as public property. Take care lest you yourself prove to have been the author of the very conversion which you profess to find so distasteful. Take care, I repeat, lest with the rule of Salmasius utterly overthrown you may yourself have converted Pontia into a "republic." And take care lest in this way, you, though a royalist, may be said to have founded many "republics" in a single city, or as minister of state to have served them after their foundation by other men. These are your divorces, or, if you prefer, diversions, from which you emerge against me as a veritable Curius.[75]

Now you continue with your lies. "When the conspirators were agitating the decapitation of the king, Milton wrote to them, and when they were wavering urged them to the wicked course." But I did not write to them, nor did it rest with me to urge men who had already without me determined on precisely this course. Yet I shall describe hereafter what I did write on this subject, and I shall also speak of *Eikonoklastes.* Now since this fellow (I am uncertain whether to call him a man or the dregs of manhood), progressing from adultery with servant girls to the adulteration of all truth, has tried to render me infamous among foreigners, by piling up a whole series of lies against me, I ask that no one take it amiss or make it a source of reproach, or resent it, if I have said previously and shall say hereafter more about myself than I would wish, so that if I cannot rescue my eyes from blindness or my name from oblivion or slander, I can at least bring my life into the light out of that darkness which accompanies disgrace. And I must do this for more reasons than one. First, in order that the many good and learned men in all the neighboring countries who are now reading my works and thinking rather well of me, may not despise me on account of this man's abuse but may persuade themselves that I am incapable of ever disgracing honorable speech by dishonorable conduct, or free utterances by slavish deeds, and that my life, by the grace of God, has ever been far removed from all vice and crime. Next, in order that those distinguished and praiseworthy men whom I undertake to extol may know that I should consider nothing more shameful than to approach the task of praising them while myself deserving blame and censure. Finally, in order that the English people whose defence their own virtue has impelled me to undertake (whether it be my fate or my duty) may know that if I have always led a pure and honorable life, my *Defence* (whether it will be to their honor or dignity I know not) will certainly never be for them a source of shame or disgrace.

Who I am, then, and whence I come, I shall now disclose. I was born in London, of an honorable family. My father was a man of supreme integrity, my mother a woman of purest reputation, celebrated throughout the neighborhood for her acts of charity.[76] My father destined me in early childhood for the study of literature, for which I had so keen an appetite that from

---

[73]Saturn after being deposed by Jupiter was supposed to have civilized Italy and brought on a period of peace, naming it Latium, "place of refuge" (Yale 4: 609n).

[74]Milton protests, citing his conformity to a tradition of writing about divorce as represented by Martin Bucer, Paulus Fagius, and Erasmus, but he omits the fact that divorce was considered by the great majority of western Europeans as a dangerous violation of the sacrament of marriage; instead he blames the reception of his divorce tracts on the "vernacular readers."

[75]A proverbial model for the uncorrupted public official, Manius Curius Dentatus (third century BCE) refused bribes as a military and civic official in Rome.

[76]Notable as Milton's only comment on the accomplishments of his mother, Sara Milton, who died 3 April 1637.

my twelfth year scarcely ever did I leave my studies for my bed before the hour of midnight. This was the first cause of injury to my eyes, whose natural weakness was augmented by frequent headaches. Since none of these defects slackened my assault upon knowledge, my father took care that I should be instructed daily both in school and under other masters at home. When I had thus become proficient in various languages and had tasted by no means superficially the sweetness of philosophy, he sent me to Cambridge, one of our two universities. There, untouched by any reproach, in the good graces of all upright men, for seven years I devoted myself to the traditional disciplines and liberal arts, until I had attained the degree of Master, as it is called, *cum laude*. Then, far from fleeing to Italy, as that filthy rascal alleges, of my own free will I returned home, to the regret of most of the fellows of the college, who bestowed on me no little honor. At my father's country place, whither he had retired to spend his declining years, I devoted myself entirely to the study of Greek and Latin writers, completely at leisure, not, however, without sometimes exchanging the country for the city, either to purchase books or to become acquainted with some new discovery in mathematics or music, in which I then took the keenest pleasure.

When I had occupied five years in this fashion, I became desirous, my mother having died, of seeing foreign parts, especially Italy, and with my father's consent I set forth, accompanied by a single attendant. On my departure Henry Wotton, a most distinguished gentleman, who had long served as King James ambassador to the Venetians, gave signal proof of his esteem for me, writing a graceful letter which contained good wishes and precepts of no little value to one going abroad. On the recommendation of others I was warmly received in Paris by the noble Thomas Scudamore, Viscount Sligo, legate of King Charles. He on his own initiative introduced me, in company with several of his suite, to Hugo Grotius, a most learned man (then ambassador from the Queen of Sweden to the King of France) whom I ardently desired to meet. When I set out for Italy some days thereafter, Scudamore gave me letters to English merchants along my projected route, that they might assist me as they could. Sailing from Nice, I reached Genoa, then Leghorn and Pisa, and after that Florence. In that city, which I have always admired above all others because of the elegance, not just of its tongue, but also of its wit, I lingered for about two months. There I at once became the friend of many gentlemen eminent in rank and learning, whose private academies I frequented—a Florentine institution which deserves great praise not only for promoting humane studies but also for encouraging friendly intercourse.

Time will never destroy my recollection—ever welcome and delightful—of you, Jacopo Gaddi, Carlo Dati, Frescobaldi, Coltellini, Buonmattei, Chimentelli, Francini and many others.

From Florence I traveled to Siena and thence to Rome. When the antiquity and venerable repute of that city had detained me for almost two months and I had been graciously entertained there by Lukas Holste and other men endowed with both learning and wit, I proceeded to Naples. Here I was introduced by a certain Eremite Friar, with whom I had made the journey from Rome, to Giovanni Battista Manso, Marquis of Villa, a man of high rank and influence, to whom the famous Italian poet, Torquato Tasso, dedicated his work on friendship. As long as I was there I found him a very true friend. He personally conducted me through the various quarters of the city and the Viceregal Court, and more than once came to my lodgings to call. When I was leaving he gravely apologized because even though he had especially wished to show me many more attentions, he could not do so in that city, since I was unwilling to be circumspect in regard to religion. Although I desired also to cross to Sicily and Greece, the sad tidings of civil war from England summoned me back. For I thought it base that I should travel abroad at my ease for the cultivation of my mind, while my fellow-citizens at home were fighting for liberty. As I was on the point of returning to Rome, I was warned by merchants that they had learned through letters of plots laid against me by the English Jesuits, should I return to Rome, because of the freedom with which I had spoken about religion.[77] For I had determined within myself that in those parts I would not indeed begin a conversation about religion, but if questioned about my faith would hide nothing, whatever the consequences. And so, I nonetheless returned to Rome. What I was, if any man inquired, I concealed from no one. For almost two more months, in the very stronghold of the Pope, if anyone attacked the orthodox religion, I openly, as before, defended it. Thus, by the will of God, I returned again in safety to Florence, revisiting friends who were as anxious to see me as if it were my native land to which I had returned. After gladly lingering there for as many months as before (except for an excursion of a few days to Lucca) I crossed the Apennines and hastened to Venice by way of Bologna and Ferrara. When I had spent one month exploring that city and had seen to the shipping of the books which I had acquired throughout Italy, I proceeded to Geneva by way of Verona, Milan,

---

[77]See Leo Miller, "Milton Dines at the Jesuit College: Reconstructing the Evening of October 30, 1638," *Milton Quarterly* 13 (1979): 142–46.

and the Pennine Alps, and then along Lake Leman. Geneva, since it reminds me of the slanderer More, impels me once again to call God to witness that in all these places, where so much licence exists, I lived free and untouched by the slightest sin or reproach, reflecting constantly that although I might hide from the gaze of men, I could not elude the sight of God. In Geneva I conversed daily with John Diodati, the learned professor of theology. Then by the same route as before, through France, I returned home after a year and three months, more or less, at almost the same time as Charles broke the peace and renewed the war with the Scots, which is known as the second Bishops War.

The royalist troops were routed in the first engagement of this war, and Charles, when he perceived that all the English, as well as the Scots, were extremely—and justly—ill-disposed towards him, soon convened Parliament, not of his own free will but compelled by disaster. I myself, seeking a place to become established, could I but find one anywhere in such upset and tumultuous times, rented a house in town, sufficiently commodious for myself and my books, and there, blissfully enough, devoted myself to my interrupted studies, willingly leaving the outcome of these events, first of all to God, and then to those whom the people had entrusted with this office. Meanwhile, as Parliament acted with vigor, the haughtiness of the bishops began to deflate. As soon as freedom of speech (at the very least) became possible, all mouths were opened against them. Some complained of the personal defects of the bishops, others of the defectiveness of the episcopal rank itself. It was wrong, they said, that their church alone should differ from all other reformed churches. It was proper for the church to be governed by the example of the brethren, but first of all by the word of God.

Now, thoroughly aroused to these concerns, I perceived that men were following the true path to liberty and that from these beginnings, these first steps, they were making the most direct progress towards the liberation of all human life from slavery—provided that the discipline arising from religion should overflow into the morals and institutions of the state. Since, moreover, I had so practiced myself from youth that I was above all things unable to disregard the laws of God and man, and since I had asked myself whether I should be of any future use if I now failed my country (or rather the church and so many of my brothers who were exposing themselves to danger for the sake of the Gospel) I decided, although at that time occupied with certain other matters, to devote to this conflict all my talents and all my active powers.

First, therefore, I addressed to a certain friend two books on the reformation of the English church.[78] Then, since two bishops of particularly high repute were asserting their prerogatives against certain eminent ministers, and I concluded that on those subjects which I had mastered solely for love of truth and out of regard for Christian duty, I could express myself at least as well as those who were wrangling for their own profit and unjust authority, I replied to one of the bishops in two books, of which the first was entitled *Of Prelatical Episcopacy* and the second *The Reason of Church-government* while to the other bishop I made reply in certain *Animadversions* and later in an *Apology*. I brought succor to the ministers, who were, as it was said, scarcely able to withstand the eloquence of this bishop, and from that time onward, if the bishops made any response, I took a hand. When they, having become a target for the weapons of all men, had at last fallen and troubled us no more, I directed my attention elsewhere, asking myself whether I could in any way advance the cause of true and substantial liberty, which must be sought, not without, but within, and which is best achieved, not by the sword, but by a life rightly undertaken and rightly conducted. Since, then, I observed that there are, in all, three varieties of liberty without which civilized life is scarcely possible, namely ecclesiastical liberty, domestic or personal liberty, and civil liberty, and since I had already written about the first, while I saw that the magistrates were vigorously attending to the third, I took as my province the remaining one, the second or domestic kind. This too seemed to be concerned with three problems: the nature of marriage itself, the education of the children, and finally the existence of freedom to express oneself. Hence I set forth my views on marriage, not only its proper contraction, but also, if need be, its dissolution. My explanation was in accordance with divine law, which Christ did not revoke; much less did He give approval in civil life to any other law more weighty than the law of Moses. Concerning the view which should be held on the single exception, that of fornication, I also expressed both my own opinion and that of others. Our distinguished countryman Selden still more fully explained this point in his *Hebrew Wife,* published about two years later. For in vain does he prattle about liberty in assembly and market-place who at home endures the slavery most unworthy of man, slavery to an inferior. Concerning this matter then I published several books, at the very time when man and wife were often bitter foes, he dwelling at home with their children, she, the mother of the family, in the

---

[78]The two books of *Of Reformation Touching Church-Discipline in England.*

camp of the enemy, threatening her husband with death and disaster. Next, in one small volume, I discussed the education of children, a brief treatment, to be sure, but sufficient, as I thought, for those who devote to the subject the attention it deserves. For nothing can be more efficacious than education in molding the minds of men to virtue (whence arises true and internal liberty), in governing the state effectively, and preserving it for the longest possible space of time.

Lastly I wrote, on the model of a genuine speech, the *Areopagitica* concerning freedom of the press, that the judgment of truth and falsehood, what should be printed and what suppressed ought not to be in the hands of a few men (and these mostly ignorant and of vulgar discernment) charged with the inspection of books, at whose will or whim virtually everyone is prevented from publishing aught that surpasses the understanding of the mob. Civil liberty, which was the last variety, I had not touched upon, for I saw that it was being adequately dealt with by the magistrates, nor did I write anything about the right of kings, until the king, having been declared an enemy by Parliament and vanquished in the field, was pleading his cause as a prisoner before the judges and was condemned to death. Then at last, when certain Presbyterian ministers, formerly bitter enemies of Charles, but now resentful that the Independent parties were preferred to theirs and carried more weight in Parliament, persisted in attacking the decree which Parliament had passed concerning the king (wroth, not because of the fact, but because their own faction had not performed it) and caused as much tumult as they could, even daring to assert that the doctrines of Protestants and all reformed churches shrank from such an outrageous sentence against kings, I concluded that I must openly oppose so open a lie. Not even then, however, did I write or advise anything concerning Charles, but demonstrated what was in general permissible against tyrants, adducing not a few testimonies from the foremost theologians. And I attacked, almost as if I were haranguing an assembly, the pre-eminent ignorance or insolence of these ministers, who had given promise of better things. This book did not appear until after the death of the king, having been written to reconcile men's minds, rather than to determine anything about Charles (which was not my affair, but that of the magistrates, and which had by then been effected). This service of mine, between private walls, I freely gave, now to the church and now to the state. To me, in return, neither the one nor the other offered more than protection, but the deeds themselves undoubtedly bestowed on me a good conscience, good repute among good men, and this honorable freedom of speech. Other men gained for themselves advantages, other men secured offices at no cost to themselves. As for me, no man has ever seen me seeking office, no man has ever seen me soliciting aught through my friends, clinging with suppliant expression to the doors of Parliament, or loitering in the hallways of the lower assemblies. I kept myself at home for the most part, and from my own revenues, though often they were in large part withheld because of the civil disturbance, I endured the tax—by no means entirely just—that was laid on me and maintained my frugal way of life.

When these works had been completed and I thought that I could look forward to an abundance of leisure, I turned to the task of tracing in unbroken sequence, if I could, the history of my country, from the earliest origins even to the present day. I had already finished four books when the kingdom of Charles was transformed into a republic, and the so-called Council of State, which was then for the first time established by the authority of Parliament, summoned me, though I was expecting no such event, and desired to employ my services, especially in connection with foreign affairs. Not long afterwards there appeared a book attributed to the king, and plainly written with great malice against Parliament. Bidden to reply to this, I opposed to the *Eikon* the *Eikonoklastes,* not, as I am falsely charged, "insulting the departed spirit of the king," but thinking that Queen Truth should be preferred to King Charles. Indeed, since I saw that this slander would be at hand for any calumniator, in the very introduction (and as often as I could elsewhere) I averted this reproach from myself. Then Salmasius appeared. So far were they from spending a long time (as More alleges) seeking one who would reply to him, that all, of their own accord, at once named me, then extent in order to stop your mouth, More, and refute your lies, chiefly for the sake of those good men who otherwise would know me not. Do you then, I bid you, unclean More, be silent. Hold your tongue, I say! For the more you abuse me, the more copiously will you compel me to account for my conduct. From such accounting you can gain nothing save the reproach, already most severe, of telling lies, while for me you open the door to still higher praise of my own integrity.

A
TREATISE
OF
Civil power
IN
Ecclesiastical causes
SHEWING
That it is not lawfull for any
power on earth to compell
in matters of
Religion.

The author J. M.

London, Printed by *Tho. Newcomb*
Anno 1659

A Treatise of Civil Power
(1659)

OCCASION AND RHETORICAL STANCE

As Barbara Lewalski summarizes it, *A Treatise on Civil Power* is "a calm, closely reasoned discourse on religious toleration" (339). Milton's stance in this pamphlet is that of a man who had been listened to by the parliamentary government and is once again addressing it honorably—someone who should be listened to. In fact, even though he had been blind for many years, Milton in 1658 and 1659 had continued to translate important state letters for Oliver Cromwell until Cromwell died on September 3, 1658, and then for Cromwell's successor, his son Richard (facetiously called "Tumble-down Dick"), until he resigned and the Commonwealth was reestablished, temporarily, in May of 1659. Milton registered *A Treatise of Civil Power* with the Stationers' Company on February 16, 1659, intending it to be accompanied by another pamphlet shortly, *Considerations Touching the Likeliest Means to Remove Hirelings out of the Church*, to be published in August of the same year.

Since the revised edition of Milton's *Pro Populo Anglicano Defensio* had been published in October of 1658, he could count on some respect from the reading public, or at least the portion of the public that could easily read Latin.

ARGUMENT AND ORGANIZATION

After spending many years on his program advocating domestic or civil liberty, with the often complicated and wordy divorce tracts and the defenses, Milton claims in *A Treatise of Civil Power* that he is writing simply and plainly, on behalf of the liberty of a general audience, and in a plain style. "I rather chose," he writes near the end of the tract, "the common rule, not to make much ado where less may serve." His plain style anticipates that of well-crafted business correspondence—Corns talks about the style as reflecting "a self-image of the busy man speaking to busy men" (271)—though of course Milton's erudition and his deep knowledge of the Bible shine through in all of the support structure of his arguments. His language may be simple but it is hardly simplistic (Woods 201). Hunter conjectures that the quotations from the Bible, though they accord closely with the Authorized Version, were all produced from his prodigious memory; they were most likely dictated verbatim to Milton's scribe or scribes (Yale 7: 235). Some significant changes in translation occur: as with the change from the King James version's "heart" in 1 John 3.20 to "conscience" in Milton, since "conscience" is one of the most often-used nouns in Milton's work (more than 58 times, when one adds "conscientious").

Cedric Brown sees Milton's late tract on liberty in the context of the much earlier, much more famous, *Areopagitica*: "If *Areopagitica* is well known to students of Milton for its self-displaying humanistic defence of the liberty of the press, *Of Civil Power* should be better known for the clear and uncompromising position of Milton in later life concerning liberty of conscience" (145).

Basically, Milton argues for a position that is now taken for granted in democratic societies—that no magistrate should have the power to compel any individual to make a religious choice against his conscience. Any law that imposes itself thus on the individual is a wrongheaded law: "*any law against conscience is alike in force against any conscience.*" Milton's position is a strong endorsement for the separation of church and state and of "*Christian liberty.*" He also expresses strong faith in the "inward perswasive motions of [a person's] spirit," which is what he seems to mean by conscience, God's inner light shining within each human being (Loewenstein 88).

Milton's organization is on the same format as that of *Tetrachordon*. He supports four major arguments in four long paragraphs by constant reference to passages in scripture. Conscience is superior to any external or imposed tradition; civil authority has no right to judge in religious matters; if civil authority does judge in religious matters, it achieves evil, not good; and civil authority, when it restricts human liberty of conscience, can do no good at all (paraphrasing Hunter 229–30). His thesis is made obvious by the information on the title page, "it is not lawfull for any power on earth to compell in matters of religion"; every word in the duodecimo volume supports that thesis.

TEXT

Although *A Treatise of Civil Power* was published long after Milton had gone blind, the longtime printer of his works, Thomas Newcomb, perhaps from habit, honored a number of Milton's known spelling preferences, as with "bin," "thir," "parlament," "perfet," and "autoritie." Thus Milton exerted some influence over the way his dictated text came into print.

My copy-text is the edition of 1659, the only edition published in Milton's lifetime. I am grateful to have been able to compare the excellent transcription made by Danielle Insalaco of New York University with my own.

Works Cited
Editions marked with an asterisk.

Brown, Cedric. *John Milton: A Literary Life*. New York: St. Martins, 1995.

Corns, Thomas. *Uncloistered Virtue: English Political Literature, 1640–1660*. Oxford: Clarendon, 1992.

*Hughes, Merritt Y., ed. *A Treatise of Civil Power in Ecclesiastical Causes*, in *John Milton: Complete Poems and Selected Prose*. New York: Odyssey, 1957. 839–55.

*Hunter, William B., ed. *A Treatise of Civil Power*, in *Complete Prose Works of John Milton*. Rev. ed. New Haven, CT: Yale UP, 1980. 229–72.

*Lewalski, Barbara Keifer, ed. *Of Civil Power*, in *The Prose of John Milton*, gen. ed. J. Max Patrick. New York: New York UP, 1968. 439–74.

Loewenstein, David. *Milton and the Drama of History: Historical Vision, Iconoclasm, and the Literary Imagination*. Cambridge: Cambridge UP, 1990.

*Patrides, C. A., ed. *A Treatise of Civil Power*, in *John Milton: Selected Prose*. Rev. ed. Columbia: U Missouri P, 1985. 296–326.

Woods, Suzanne. "Elective poetics and Milton's prose: *A Treatise of Civil Power* and *Considerations Touching the Likeliest Means to Remove Hirelings Out of the Church.*" *Politics, poetics, and hermeneutics in Milton's prose*. Ed. David Loewenstein and James Grantham Turner. Cambridge: Cambridge UP, 1990. 193–211.

TO THE

PARLAMENT

OF THE

Commonwealth of *ENGLAND*
with the dominions therof.

I Have prepar'd, supream Councel, against the much expected time of your sitting,[1] this treatise; which, though to all Christian magistrates equally belonging, and therfore to have bin written in the common language of Christendom,[2] natural dutie and affection hath confin'd, and dedicated first to my own nation: and in a season wherin the timely reading therof, to the easier accomplishment of your great work, may save you much labor and interruption: of two parts usually propos'd, civil and eccle-

---

[1] The Parliament of Richard Cromwell met first on January 27, 1659 (see Yale 7: 239n). This Parliament was dissolved by the army generals on April 22, but of course Milton would not have been able to anticipate that event.
[2] Latin, the universal language of the intelligentsia, thus intelligible to all magistrates throughout western Europe.

siastical, *recommending civil only to your proper care, ecclesiastical to them only from whom it takes both that name and nature. Yet not for this cause only do I require or trust to finde acceptance, but in a two-fold respect besides: first as bringing cleer evidence of scripture and protestant maxims to the Parlament of* England, *who in all thir late acts, upon occasion, have professd to assert only the true protestant Christian religion, as it is contain'd in the holy scriptures: next, in regard that your power being but for a time, and having in your selves a Christian libertie of your own, which at one time or other may be oppressd, therof truly sensible, it will concern you while you are in power, so to regard other mens consciences,[3] as you would your own should be regarded in the power of others; and to consider that any law against conscience is alike in force against any conscience, and so may one way or other justly redound upon your selves. One advantage I make no doubt of, that I shall write to many eminent persons of your number, alreadie perfet and resolvd in this important article of Christianitie. Some of whom I remember to have heard often for several years,[4] at a councel next in autoritie to your own, so well joining religion with civil prudence, and[5] yet so well distinguishing the different power of either, and this not only voting, but frequently reasoning why it should be so, that if any there present had bin before of an opinion contrary, he might doubtless have departed thence a convert in that point, and have confessd, that then both commonwealth and religion will at length, if ever, flourish in Christendom, when either they who govern discern between civil and religious, or they only who so discern shall be admitted to govern. Till then nothing but troubles, persecutions, commotions can be expected; the inward decay of true religion among our selves, and the utter overthrow at last by a common enemy. Of civil libertie I have written heretofore by the appointment,[6] and not without the approbation of civil power: of Christian liberty I write now; which others long since having don with all freedom under heathen emperors, I should do wrong to suspect, that I now shall with less under Christian governors, and such especially as profess openly thir defence of Christian libertie; although I write this not otherwise appointed or induc'd then by an inward perswasion of the Christian dutie which I may usefully discharge herin to the common Lord and Master of us all, and the certain hope of his*

approbation, first and chiefest to be sought: In the hand of whose providence I remain, praying all success and good event on your publick councels to the defence of true religion and our civil rights.

JOHN MILTON.

A Treatise of Civil power in Ecclesiastical causes.

TWo things there be which have bin ever found working much mischief to the church of God, and the advancement of truth; force on the one side restraining, and hire on the other side corrupting the teachers thereof. Few ages have bin since the ascension of our Saviour, wherin the one of these two, or both together have not prevaild. It can be at no time therfore unseasonable to speak of these things; since by them the church is either in continual detriment and oppression, or in continual danger. The former shall be at this time my argument;[7] the latter[8] as I shall finde God disposing me, and opportunity inviting. What I argue, shall be drawn from the scripture only; and therin from true fundamental principles of the gospel; to all knowing Christians undeniable. And if the governors of this of this commonwealth since the rooting out of the prelats have made least use of force in religion, and most have favor'd Christian liberty of any in this Iland before them since the first preaching of the gospel, for which we are not to forget our thanks to God, and their due praise, they may, I doubt not, in this treatise finde that which not only will confirm them to defend still the Christian liberty which we enjoy, but will incite them also to enlarge it, if in aught they yet straighten it. To them who perhaps herafter, less experienc'd in religion, may come to govern or give us laws, this or other such, if they please, may be a timely instruction: however to the truth it will be at times no unneedfull testimonie; at least some discharge of that general dutie which no Christian but according to what he hath receivd, knows is requir'd of him if he have aught more conducing to the advancement of

[3]God calls *Conscience* "My Umpire" in the memorable phrase in *Paradise Lost* 3.195.
[4]The first-hand account establishes Milton's authority for writing on the subject of the forcing of conscience. The "*councel*" he refers to is the Council of State, for which he had worked as Secretary for Foreign Tongues between 1649 and 1651.
[5]Correcting an inverted letter in "*aud.*"
[6]Milton had been appointed and commissioned to write the two Latin defenses and probably *Eikonoklastes* (see Yale 7: 240n).

[7]Subject matter, as in the Latin *argumentum*.
[8]*Considerations Touching the Likeliest Means to Remove Hirelings out of the Church*, published later in the year, which itself begins with a reference to *A Treatise of Civil Power* (Yale 7: 277).

religion then what is usually endeavourd, freely to impart it.

It will require no great labor of exposition to unfold what is here meant by matters of religion; being as soon apprehended as defin'd, such things as belong chiefly to the knowledge and service of God: and are either above the reach and light of nature without revelation from above, and therfore liable to be variously understood by humane reason, or such things as are enjoind or forbidden by divine precept, which els by the light of reason would seem indifferent to be don or not don; and so likewise must needs appeer to everie man as the precept is understood. Whence I here mean by conscience or religion, that full perswasion wherby we are assur'd that our beleef and practise, as far as we are able to apprehend and probably make appeer, is according to the will of God & his Holy Spirit within us, which we ought to follow much rather then any law of man, as not only his word every where bids us, but the very dictate of reason tells us. *Act.*4.19. *whether it be right in the sight of God, to hearken to you more then to God, judge ye.* That for beleef or practise in religion according to this conscientious perswasion no man ought be punishd or molested by any outward force on earth whatsoever, I distrust not, through Gods implor'd assistance, to make plane by these following arguments.

First it cannot be deni'd, being the main foundation of our protestant religion, that we of these ages, having no other divine rule or autoritie from without us warrantable to one another[9] as a common ground but the holy scripture, and no other within us but the illumination of the Holy Spirit so interpreting that scripture as warrantable only to our selves and to such whose consciences we can so perswade, can have no other ground in matters of religion but only from the scriptures. And these being not possible to be understood without this divine illumination, which no man can know at all times to be in himself,[10] much less to be at any time for certain in any other, it follows cleerly, that no man or body of men in these times can be the infallible judges or determiners in matters of religion to any other mens consciences but thir own. And therfore those Beroeans[11]

are commended, *Act.* 17.11, who after the preaching even of S. *Paul,* *searchd the scriptures daily, whether those things were so.* Nor did they more then what God himself in many place commands us by the same apostle, to search, to try, to judge of these things our selves: And gives us reason also, *Gal.* 6.4,5. *let every man prove his own work, and then shall he have rejoicing in himself alone, and not in another: for every man shall bear his own burden.* If then we count it so ignorant and irreligious in the papist to think himself dischargd in Gods account, beleeving only as the church beleevs, how much greater condemnation will it be to the protestant his condemner, to think himself justified, beleeving only as the state beleevs? With good cause therfore it is the general consent of all sound protestant writers, that neither traditions, councels nor canons of any visible[12] church, much less edicts of any magistrate or civil session, but the scripture only can be the final judge or rule in matters of religion, and that only in the conscience of every Christian to himself. Which protestation made by the first publick reformers of our religion against the imperial edicts of *Charls* the fifth, imposing church-traditions without scripture, gave first beginning to the name of *Protestant*; and with that name hath ever bin receivd this doctrine, which preferrs the scripture before the church, and acknowledges none but the Scripture sole interpreter of it self to the conscience. For if the church be not sufficient to be implicitly beleevd, as we hold it is not, what can there els be nam'd of more autoritie then the church but the conscience; then which God only is greater, 1 *Joh.* 3.20? But if any man shall pretend, that the scripture judges to his conscience for other men, he makes himself greater not only then the church, but also then the scripture, then the consciences of other men; a presumption too high for any mortal; since every true Christian able to give a reason of his faith, hath the word of God before him, the promisd Holy Spirit, and the minde of Christ within him, 1 *Cor.* 2.16; a much better and safer guide of conscience, which as far as concerns himself he may far more certainly know then any outward rule impos'd upon him by others whom he inwardly neither knows nor can know; at least knows nothing of them more sure then this one thing, that they cannot be his judges in religion. 1 *Cor.* 2.15. *the spiritual man judgeth all things, but he himself is judgd of no man.* Chiefly for this cause do all true protestants[13] account the pope antichrist, for that he assumes to himself this infallibilitie over both the conscience and the

---

[9]The two words are run together as "oneanother" in the 1659 edition.

[10]Compare the narrator's comment in *Paradise Lost* concerning his muse, complaining that his effort in presenting his "higher Argument" may be lost "if all be mine / Not Hers who brings it nightly to my Ear" (9.42, 46–47).

[11]The early Christians of Thessalonica and Berea, both cities in northern Greece, are described in the Geneva Bible marginalia as "Not more excellent of birth, but more prompt, and couragious in receiving the worde of God: for he [St. Paul] compareth them of Berea with them of Tessalonica who presecuted the Apostles in Berea. *Joh. 5.39*" (Acts 17.11 margin; abbreviations expanded).

---

[12]The word has a broken letter, making it appear as "visibie," in the 1659 edition.

[13]In the catchword for the previous page, the word is spelled with a capital letter, "Protestants."

scripture; *sitting*[14] *in the temple of God*, as it were opposite to God, *and exalting himself above all that is called god, or is worshipd*, 2 Thess. 2.4. That is to say not only above all judges and magistrates, who though they be calld gods, are far beneath infallible, but also above God himself, by giving law both to the scripture, to the conscience, and to the spirit it self of God within us. Whenas we finde, *James* 4.12, there is one lawgiver, who is able to save and to destroy: who art thou that judgest another? That Christ is the only lawgiver of his church and that it is here meant in religious matters, no well grounded Christian will deny. Thus also *S. Paul*, Rom. 14.4. *who art thou that judgest the servant of another? to his own Lord he standeth or falleth: but he shall stand; for God is able to make him stand.* As therfore of one beyond expression bold and presumptuous, both these apostles demand, *who art thou* that presum'st to impose other law or judgment in religion then the only lawgiver and judge Christ, who only can save and can destroy, gives to the conscience? And the forecited place to the *Thessalonians* by compar'd effects resolvs us, that be he or they who or wherever they be or can be, they are of far less autoritie then the church, whom in these things as protestants they receive not, and yet no less antichrist in this main point of antichristianism, no less a pope or popedom then he at *Rome*, if not much more; by setting up supream interpreters of scripture either those doctors[15] whom they follow, or, which is far worse, themselves as a civil papacie assuming unaccountable supremacie to themselves not in civil only but ecclesiastical causes. Seeing then that in matters of religion, as hath been prov'd, none can judge or determin here on earth, no not churchgovernors themselves against the consciences of other beleevers, my inference is, or rather not mine but our Saviours own, that in those matters they neither can command nor use constraint; lest they run rashly on a pernicious consequence, forewarnd in that parable *Mat.* 13. from the 26[16] to the 31 verse: *least while ye gather up the tares, ye root up also the wheat with them. Let both grow together until the harvest: and in the time of harvest I will say to the reapers, Gather ye together first the tares &c.* whereby he declares that this work neither his own ministers nor any els can discerningly anough or judgingly perform without his own immediat direction, in his own fit season; and that they ought till then not to attempt it. Which is further confirmd 2 *Cor.* 1.24. *not that we have dominion over your faith, but are helpers of*

your joy. If apostles had no dominion or constraining power over faith or conscience, much less have ordinary ministers. I *Pet.* 5.2, 3. *feed the flock of God not by constraint &c. neither as being lords over Gods heritage.* But some will object, that this overthrows all church-discipline, all censure of errors, if no man can determin. My answer is, that what they hear is plane scripture; which forbids not church-sentence or determining, but as it ends in violence upon the conscience unconvinc'd. Let who so will interpret or determin, so it be according to true church-discipline; which is exercis'd on them only who have willingly joind themselves in that covnant of union, and proceeds only to a separation from the rest, proceeds never to any corporal inforcement or forfeture of monie, which in spiritual[17] things are the two arms of Antichrist, not of the true church; the one being an inquisition, the other no better then a temporal indulgence of sin for monie; whether by the church exacted or by the magistrate; both the one and the other a temporal satisfaction for what Christ hath satisfied eternally; a popish commuting of penaltie, corporal for spiritual; a satisfaction to man especially to the magistrate, for what and to whom we owe none: these and more are the injustices of force and fining in religion, besides what I most insist on, the violation of Gods express commandment in the gospel, as hath bin shewn. Thus then if church-governors cannot use force in religion, though but for this reason, because they cannot infallibly determin to the conscience without convincement, much less have civil magistrates autoritie to use force where they can much less judge; unless they mean only to be the civil executioners of them who have no civil power to give them such commission, no nor yet ecclesiastical to any force or violence in religion. To summe up all in brief, if we must beleeve as the magistrate appoints, why not rather as the church? if not as either without convincement, how can force be lawfull? But some are ready to cry out, what shall then be don to blasphemie?[18] Them I would first exhort not thus to terrifie and pose[19] the people with a Greek word: but to teach them better what it is; being a most usual and common word in that language to signifie any slander, any malitious or evil speaking, whether against God or man or any thing to good belonging: blasphemie or evil speaking against God malitiously, is far from con-

---

[14]I have corrected what I assume is a typographical error rather than a variant spelling, "siting."

[15]Learned men.

[16]Probably an inverted letter, since the number should be 29.

[17]The "t" in the word has ridden up and out of sight in the 1659 edition, leaving "spiri al."

[18]As Hunter points out, Milton uses the word in the *Christian Doctrine* to mean "any kind of evil-speaking, directed at any person" (Yale 6: 699; 7: 246n).

[19]"Pose as in "pose a riddle," here indicating that the people are deliberately confused when they are posed a question including the unfamiliar Greek word.

science in religion; according to that of *Marc.* 9.39. *there is none who doth a powerfull work in my name, and can likely speak evil of me.* If this suffice not, I referre them to that prudent and well deliberated act *August 9.* 1650;[20] where the Parlament defines blasphemie against God, as far as it is a crime belonging to civil judicature, *plenius ac melius Chrysippo & Crantore;*[21] in plane English more warily, more judiciously, more orthodoxally then twice thir number of divines have don in many a prolix volume: although in all likelihood they whose whole studie and profession these things are should be most intelligent and authentic therin, as they are for the most part, yet neither they nor these unnerring[22] always or infallible. But we shall not carrie it thus; another Greek apparition stands in our way, *heresie* and *heretic*; in like manner also rail'd at to the people as in a tongue unknown. They should first interpret to them, that heresie, by what it signifies in that language, is no word of evil note; meaning only the choise or following of any opinion good or bad in religion or any other learning: and thus not only in heathen authors, but in the New testament it self without censure or blame. *Acts* 15.5. *certain of the heresie*[23] *of the Pharises which beleevd.* and 26.5. *after the exactest heresie of our religion I livd a Pharise.* In which sense Presbyterian or Independent may without reproach be calld a heresie. Where is it mentiond with blame, it seems to differ little from schism 1 *Cor.* 11.18,19. *I hear that there be schisms among you* &c. *for there must also heresies be among you* &c; though some who write of heresie after their own heads,[24] would make it far worse then schism; whenas on the contrarie, schism signifies division, and in the worst sense; heresie, choise only of one opinion before another, which may bee without discord. In apostolic times therfore ere the scripture was written, heresie was a doctrin maintaind

against the doctrin by them deliverd: which in these times can be no otherwise defin'd then a doctrin maintaind against the light, which we now only have, of the scripture. Seeing therfore that no man, no synod, no session of men, though calld the church, can judge definitively the sense of scripture to another mans conscience, which is well known to be a general maxim of the Protestant religion, it follows planely, that he who holds in religion that beleef or those opinions which to his conscience and utmost understanding appeer with most evidence or probabilitie in the scripture, though to others he seem erroneous, can no more be justly censur'd for a heretic then his censurers; who do but the same thing themselves while they censure him for so doing. For ask them, or any Protestant, which hath most autoritie, the church or the scripture? they will answer, doubtless, that the scripture: and what hath most autoritie, that no doubt but they will confess is to be followd. He then who to his best apprehension follows the scripture, though against any point of doctrine by the whole church receivd, is not the heretic; but he who follows the church against his conscience and perswasion grounded on the scripture. To make this yet more undeniable, I shall only borrow a plane similie, the same which our own writers, when they would demonstrate planest that we rightly preferre the scripture before the church, use frequently against the Papist in this manner. As the Samaritans beleevd Christ, first for the womans word,[25] but next and much rather for his own, so we the scripture; first on the churches word, but afterwards and much more for its own, as the word of God; yea the church it self we beleeve then for the scripture. The inference of it self follows: if by the Protestant doctrine we beleeve the scripture not for the churches saying,[26] but for its own as the word of God, then ought we to beleeve what in our conscience we apprehend the scripture to say, though the visible church with all her doctors gainsay; and being taught to beleeve them only for the scripture, they who so do are not heretics, but the best protestants: and by their opinions, whatever they be, can hurt no protestant, whose rule is not to receive them but from the scripture: which to interpret convincingly to his own conscience none is able but himself guided by the Holy Spirit; and not so guided, none then he to himself can be a worse deceiver. To protestants therfore whose common rule and touchstone is the scripture, nothing can with more

---

[20]The *Act Against several Atheistical, Blasphemous and Execrable Opinions*, passed on the date Milton cites, attempted to impose six month's imprisonment for several Ranter beliefs, or banishment for repeated offences (Yale 7: 246n).

[21]Horace, *Epistles*, 1.2.1–5, expresses the belief that Homer is a better guide for the conduct of life than the writings of many philosophers such as "*Chrysippo & Crantore,*" now generally known as Chrysippus or Crantor. Milton seems to have echoed the sentiment earlier when he described Spenser as "a better teacher then *Scotus* or *Aquinas*" in *Areopagitica* (Yale 2: 516).

[22]Probably a typographical error for "unerring."

[23]Corrected from what seems to be "*herasie*" in the Huntington Library copy of the 1659 edition.

[24]That is, according to their own inclinations. In the Epistle prefaced to *On Christian Doctrine*, Milton writes "since the compilation of the New Testament, nothing can correctly be called heresy unless it contradicts that" (Yale 6: 123). Here as elsewhere, Milton may be defending his own beliefs, whenever they might verge on what the English church might regard as heresy.

[25]John 4.39–42. The story concerns a Samaritan woman who believes in Christ because he "told [her] all that [she] ever did," leading other Samaritans to come to believe in Christ's prophetic authority because they then came and witnessed it firsthand.

[26]"We believe in the scripture, but not because the church tells us to."

conscience, more equitie, nothing more protestantly can be permitted then a free and lawful debate at all times by writing, conference or disputation of what opinion soever, disputable by scripture: concluding, that no man in religion is properly a heretic at this day, but he who maintains traditions or opinions not probable[27] by scripture; who, for aught I know, is the papist only; he the only heretic, who counts all heretics but himself. Such as these, indeed, were capitally punishd by the law of *Moses*, as the only true heretics, idolaters, plane and open deserters of God and his known law: but in the gospel such are punishd by excommunion only. *Tit.* 3.10. *an heretic, after the first and second admonition, reject.* But they who think not this heavie anough and understand not that dreadfull aw and spiritual efficacie which the apostle hath expressd so highly to be in church-discipline, 2 *Cor.* 10. of which anon, and think weakly that the church of God cannot long subsist but in a bodilie fear, for want of other prooff will needs wrest that place of S. *Paul Rom.* 13. to set up civil inquisition, and give power to the magistrate both of civil judgment and punishment in causes ecclesiastical. But let us see with what strength of argument. *Let every soul be subject to the higher powers.* First, how prove they that the apostle means other powers then such as they to whom he writes were then under; who medld[28] not at all in ecclesiastical causes, unless as tyrants and persecuters; and from them, I hope, they will not derive either the right of magistrates to judge in spiritual things, or the dutie of such our obedience. How prove they next, that he intitles them here to spiritual causes, from whom he witheld, as much as in him lay, the judging of civil; 1 *Cor.* 6.1, &c. If he himself appeald to *Cesar*, it was to judge his innocence, not his religion. *For rulers are not a terror to good works, but to the evil.* then are they not a terror to conscience, which is the rule or judge of good works grounded on the scripture. But heresie, they say, is reck'nd among evil works *Gal.* 5.20: as if all evil works were to be punishd by the magistrate; wherof this place, thir own citation, reck'ns up besides heresie a sufficient number to confute them; *uncleanness, wantonness, enmitie, strife, emulations, animosities, contentions, envyings;*[29] all which are far more *manifest* to be judgd by him then heresie, as they define it; and yet I suppose they will not subject these evil works nor

many more such like to his cognisance and punishment. *Wilt thou then not be affraid of the power? do that which is good and thou shalt have praise of the same.* This shews that religious matters are not here meant; wherin from the power here spoken of they could have no praise. *For he is the minister of God to thee for good.* true; but in that office and to that end and by those means which in this place must be cleerly found, if from this place they intend to argue. And how for thy good by forcing, oppressing and insnaring thy conscience? Many are the ministers of God, and thir offices no less different then many; none more different then state and church-government. Who seeks to govern both must needs be worse then any lord prelat or churchpluralist: for he in his own facultie and profession, the other not in his own and for the most part not throughly understood makes himself supream lord or pope of the church as far as his civil jurisdiction stretches, and all the ministers of God therin, his ministers, or his curates rather in the function onely, not in the government: while he himself assumes to rule by civil power things to be rul'd only by spiritual: when as this very chapter v. 6 appointing him his peculiar office, which requires utmost attendance, forbids him this worse then church plurality from that full and waightie charge, wherin alone he is *the minister of God, attending continually on this very thing.* To little purpose will they here instance *Moses*, who did all by immediate divine direction, no nor yet *Asa, Jehosaphat,* or *Josia,*[30] who both might when they pleasd receive answer from God, and had a commonwealth by him deliverd them, incorporated with a national church exercis'd more in bodily then in spiritual worship, so as that the church might be calld a commonwealth and the whole commonwealth a church: nothing of which can be said of Christianitie, deliverd without the help of magistrates, yea in the midst of thir opposition; how little then with any reference to them or mention of them, save onely of our obedience to thir civil laws, as they countnance good and deterr evil: which is the proper work of the magistrate, following in the same verse, and shews distinctly wherin he is the minister of God, *a revenger to execute wrath on him that doth evil.* But we must first know who it is that doth evil: the heretic they say among the first. Let it be known then certainly who is a heretic: and that he who holds opinions in religion professdly from tradition or his own inventions and not from Scripture[31] but rather against it, is the only heretic; and yet though such, not

---

[27]Provable, verifiable.
[28]Meddled.
[29]Galations 5.19–21 actually names the sins of the flesh as "Adultery, fornication, uncleanness, lasciviousness, Idolatry, witchcraft, hatred, variance, emulations, wrath, strife, seditions, heresies, Envyings, murders, drunkenness, revelings, and such like." Milton, in other words, is editing as he transcribes the list.

---

[30]As Hunter points out, this is a list of "good men who exercised the law of Moses in Old Testament history: II Chronicles 14–16; 20.31–37; 34–35" (Yale 7: 251n).
[31]Corrected from "Scipture" in the 1659 edition.

alwaies punishable by the magistrate, unless he do evil against a a civil Law, properly so calld, hath been already prov'd without need of repetition. *But if thou do that which is evil, be affraid.* To do by scripture and the gospel according to conscience is not to do evil; if we therof ought not to be affraid, he ought not by his judging to give cause. causes therfore of Religion are not here meant. *For he beareth not the sword in vain.* Yes altogether in vain, if it smite he knows not what; if that for heresie which not the church it self, much less he, can determine absolutely to be so; if truth for error, being himself so often fallible, he bears the sword not in vain only, but unjustly and to evil. *Be subject not only for wrath, but for conscience sake*: how for conscience sake against conscience? By all these reasons it appeers planely that the apostle in this place gives no judgment or coercive power to magistrates, neither to those then nor these now in matters of religion; and exhorts us no otherwise then he exhorted those *Romans.* It hath now twice befaln me to assert, through Gods assistance, this most wrested and vexd place of scripture; heretofore against *Salmasius* and regal tyranie over the state; now against *Erastus*[32] and state-tyranie over the church. If from such uncertain or rather such improbable grounds as these they endue magistracie with spiritual judgment, they may as well invest him in the same spiritual kinde with power of utmost punishment, excommunication; and then turn spiritual into corporal, as no worse authors did then *Chrysostom, Jerom* and *Austin,*[33] whom *Erasmus*[34] and others in their notes on the New Testament have cited to interpret that *cutting off* which S. *Paul* wishd to them who had brought back the *Galatians* to circumcision, no less then the amercement of thir whole virilitie; and *Grotius*[35] addes that this con-

cising[36] punishment of circumcisers became a penal law therupon among the *Visigothes*: a dangerous example of beginning in the spirit to end so in the flesh: wheras that cutting off much likelier seems meant a cutting off from the church, not unusually so termd in scripture, and a zealous imprecation, not a command. But I have mentiond this passage to shew how absurd they often prove who have not learnd to distinguish rightly between civil power and ecclesiastical. How many persecutions then, imprisonments, banishments, penalties and stripes;[37] how much bloodshed have the forcers of conscience to answer for, and protestants rather then papists! For the papist, judging by his principles, punishes them who beleeve not as the church beleevs though against the scripture: but the protestant, teaching every one to beleeve the scripture though against the church, counts heretical and persecutes, against his own principles, them who in any particular so beleeve as he in general teaches them; them who most honor and beleeve divine scripture, but not against it any humane interpretation though universal; them who interpret scripture only to themselves, which by his own position none but they to themselves can interpret; them who use the scripture no otherwise by his own doctrine to thir edification, then he himself uses it to thir punishing: and so whom his doctrine acknowledges a true beleever, his discipline persecutes as a heretic. The papist exacts our beleef as to the church due above scripture; and by the church, which is the whole people of God, understands the pope, the general councels prelatical only and the surnam'd fathers: but the forcing protestant though he deny such beleef to any church whatsoever, yet takes it to himself and his teachers, of far less autorite then to be calld the church and above scripture beleevd: which renders his practise both contrarie to his beleef, and far worse then that beleef which he condemns in the papist. By all which well considerd, the more he professes to be a true protestant, the more he hath to answer for his persecuting then a papist. No protestant therfor of what sect soever following scripture only, which is the common sect wherin they all agree, and the granted rule of everie mans conscience to himself, ought, by the common doctrine of protestants, to be forc'd or molested[38] for religion. But as for poperie and idolatrie, why they also may not hence plead to be tolerated, I have much less to say. Their religion the more considerd, the less can be acknowledgd a religion; but a Roman principalitie rather, endevouring to keep up her old universal domin-

[32]Followers of Thomas Erastus (1524–1583), who taught that "where there are Christian magistrates there is not need of any other discipline" (*The Oxford Illustrated History of Christianity,* ed. John McManners [Oxford: Oxford UP, 1990]: 261). Erastianism came to mean that the state, or state law (rather than ecclesiastical law), should take precedence in ecclesiastical cases. Milton's position is consistent with his distrust for prelates who enforced church laws using civil methods (as in forcing people to attend church or fining or jailing them).

[33]Three of the early Church Fathers, "*Austin*" being the English familiar name for St. Augustine.

[34]Desiderius Erasmus's *Annotationes ad Novum Testamentum* (printed after Milton's death in *Opera* [London, 1705] 6: 823) interpreted the passage as indicating castration and excommunication. As Hunter points out, Milton's friend the theologian John Downame is "One of the 'others' who interprets the verse as meaning circumcision" (Yale 7: 253n).

[35]Hugo Grotius, the great Dutch jurist and biblical commentator, whom Milton had met in Paris in 1638, in his *Annotationes in Epistolam ad Galatas,* cites Chrysostom and Jerome in favor of interpreting the passage as indicating real castration, mentioning that the Visigoths practiced amputation on those who had been circumcised (*Opera Theologicorum* [London, 1679]: 2: 2, 877).

[36]Mutilating, as in circumcision.

[37]The marks of whipping, when a prisoner received lashes for punishment.

[38]Harassed, pestered.

ion under a new name and meer shaddow of a catholic religion; being indeed more rightly nam'd a catholic heresie against the scripture; supported mainly by a civil, and, except in *Rome*, by a forein power: justly therfore to be suspected, not tolerated by the magistrate of another countrey. Besides, of an implicit faith, which they profess, the conscience also becoms implicit; and so by voluntarie servitude to mans law, forfets her Christian libertie. Who then can plead for such a conscience, as being implicitly enthrald to man instead of God, almost becoms no conscience, as the will not free, becoms no will. Nevertheless if they ought not to be tolerated, it is for just reason of state more then of religion; which they who force, though professing to be protestants, deserve as little to be tolerated themselves, being no less guiltie of poperie in the most popish point. Lastly, for idolatrie, who knows it not to be evidently against all scripture both of the Old and New Testament, and therfore a true heresie, or rather an impietie; wherin a right conscience can have naught to do; and the works therof so manifest, that a magistrate can hardly err in prohibiting and quite removing at least the publick and scandalous use therof.

From the riddance of these objections I proceed yet to another reason why it is unlawfull for the civil magistrate to use force in matters of religion; which is, because to judge in those things; though we should grant him able, which is prov'd he is not, yet as a civil magistrate he hath no right. Christ hath a government of his own, sufficient of it self to all his ends and purposes in governing his church; but much different from that of the civil magistrate; and the difference in this verie thing principally consists, that it governs not by outward force, and that for two reasons. First because it deals only with the inward man[39] and his actions, which are all spiritual and to outward force not lyable:[40] secondly to shew us the divine excellence of his spiritual kingdom, able without worldly force to subdue all the powers and kingdoms of this world, which are upheld by outward force only. That the inward man is nothing els but the inward part of man, his understanding and his will, and that his actions thence proceeding, yet not simply thence but from the work of divine grace upon them, are the whole matter of religion under the gospel,

will appeer planely by considering what that religion is; whence we shall perceive yet more planely that it cannot be forc'd. What euangelic religion is, is told in two words, faith and charitie; or beleef and practise. That both these flow either the one from the understanding, the other from the will, or both jointly from both, once indeed naturally free, but now only as they are regenerat and wrought on by divine grace, is in part evident to common sense and principles unquestiond, the rest by scripture: concerning our beleef, *Mat.* 16.17. *flesh and blood hath not reveald it unto thee, but my father which is in heaven*: concerning our practise, as it is religious and not meerly civil, *Gal.* 5.22, 23 and other places declare it to be the fruit of the spirit only. Nay our whole practical dutie in religion is contained in charitie, or the love of God and our neighbour, no way to be forc'd, yet the fulfilling of the whole law; that is to say, our whole practise in religion. If then both our beleef and practise, which comprehend our whole religion, flow from faculties of the inward man, free and unconstrainable of themselves by nature, and our practise not only from faculties endu'd with freedom, but from love and charitie besides, incapable of force, and all these things by transgression lost, but renewd and regenerated in us by the power and gift of God alone, how can such religion as this admit of force from man, or force be any way appli'd to such religion, especially under the free offer of grace in the gospel, but it must forthwith frustrate and make of no effect both the religion and the gospel? And that to compell outward profession, which they will say perhaps ought to be compelld though inward religion cannot, is to compell hypocrisie not to advance religion, shall yet, though of it self cleer anough, be ere the conclusion further manifest. The other reason why Christ rejects outward force in the goverment of his church, is, as I said before, to shew us the divine excellence of his spiritual kingdom, able without worldly force to subdue all the powers and kingdoms of this world, which are upheld by outward force only: by which to uphold religion otherwise then to defend the religious from outward violence, is no service to Christ or his kingdom, but rather a disparagement, and degrades it from a divine and spiritual kingdom to a kingdom of this world: which he denies it to be, because it needs not force to confirm it: *Joh.* 18.36. *if my kingdom were of this world, then would my servants fight, that I should not be deliverd to the Jewes.* This proves the kingdom of Christ not governd by outward force; as being none of this world, whose kingdoms are maintaind all by force onely: and yet disproves not that a Christian common-wealth may defend it self against outward force in the cause of religion as well as in any other; though Christ himself,

---

[39]St. Paul mentions the "inward man" in Romans 7.22 and expands on the phrase in "though our outward man perish, yet the inward man is renewed day by day" in 2 Corinthians 4.16. Compare what Milton makes of the second passage in *On Christian Doctrine*: "REGENERATION means that THE OLD MAN IS DESTROYED AND THAT THE INNER MAN IS REGENERATED BY GOD THROUGH THE WORD AND THE SPIRIT . . . " (Yale 6: 461–62).

[40]Liable, in the sense of governable or responsible to human or divine laws.

coming purposely to dye for us, would not be so defended. 1 *Cor.* 1. *God hath chosen the weak things of the world to confound the things which are mighty.* Then surely he hath not chosen the force of this world to subdue conscience and conscientious men, who in this world are counted weakest; but rather conscience, as being weakest, to subdue and regulate force, his adversarie, not his aide or instrument in governing the church. 2 *Cor.* 10.3, 4, 5, 6. *for though we walk in the flesh, we do not warre after the flesh: for the weapons of our warfare are not carnal; but mightie through God to the pulling down of strong holds; casting down imaginations and everie high thing that exalts it self against the know-ledge of God; and bringing into captivitie everie thought to the obedience of Christ: and having in a readiness to aveng all disobedience.* It is evident by the first and second verses of this chapter, that the apostle here speaks of that spiritual power by which Christ governs his church, how allsufficient it is, how powerful to reach the conscience and the inward man with whom it chiefly deals and whom no power els can deal with. In comparison of which as it is here thus magnificently describ'd, how uneffectual and weak is outward force with all her boistrous tooles, to the shame of those Christians and especially those churchmen, who to the exercising of church discipline never cease calling on the civil magistrate to interpose his fleshlie force; an argu-ment that all true ministerial and spiritual power is dead within them: who think the gospel, which both began and spread over the whole world for above three hun-dred years under heathen and persecuting emperors, cannot stand or continue, supported by the same divine presence and protection to the worlds end, much easier under the defensive favor onely of a Christian magis-trate, unless it be enacted and settled, as they call it, by the state, a statute or a state-religion: and understand not that the church it self cannot, much less the state, settle or impose one tittle of religion upon our obedience im-plicit,[41] but can only recommend or propound it to our free and conscientious examination: unless they mean to set the state higher then the church in religion, and with a grosse contradiction give to the state in thir settling petition that command of our implicit beleef, which they deny in thir setled confession both to the state and to the church. Let them cease then to importune and in-terrupt the magistrate from attending to his own charge in civil and moral things, the settling of things just, things honest, the defence of things religious settled by the churches within themselves; and the repressing of thir contraries determinable by the common light of

nature; which is not to constrain or to repress religion, probable by scripture, but the violaters and persecuters therof: of all which things he hath anough and more then anough to do, left yet undon; for which the land groans and justice goes to wrack the while: let him also forbear force where he hath no right to judge; for the conscience is not his province: least a worse *woe* arrive him, for worse offending, then was denounc'd by our Saviour *Matt.* 23.23. against the Pharises: ye have forc'd the conscience, which was not to be forc'd; but judg-ment and mercy ye have not executed: this ye should have don, and the other let alone. And since it is the councel and set purpose of God in the gospel by spiri-tual means which are counted weak, to overcom all power which resists him; let them not go about to do that by worldly strength which he hath decreed to do by those means which the world counts weakness, least they be again obnoxious to that saying which in another place is also written of the Pharises, *Luke* 7.30. *that they frustrated the councel of God.* The main plea is, and urgd with much vehemence to thir imitation, that the kings of *Juda*, as I touchd before, and especially *Josia* both judgd and us'd force in religion. 2 *Chr.* 34.33. *he made all that were present in Israel to serve the Lord thir God*: an argument, if it be well weighed, worse then that us'd by the false prophet *Shemaia* to the high priest, that in imitation of *Jehoiada* he ought to put *Jeremie* in the stocks, *Jer.* 29.24,26, &c.[42] for which he receivd his due denouncement from God. But to this besides I return a three-fold answer: first, that the state of religion under the gospel is far differing from what it was under the law: then was the state of rigor, childhood, bondage and works, to all which force was not unbefitting; now is the state of grace, manhood, freedom and faith; to all which belongs willingness and reason, not force: the law was then written on tables of stone, and to be performd according to the letter, willingly or unwillingly; the gos-pel, our new covnant, upon the heart of every beleever, to be interpreted only by the sense of charitie and inward perswasion: the law had no distinct government or governors of church and commonwealth, but the Priests and Levites judg'd in all causes not ecclesiastical only but civil, *Deut.* 17.8, &c. which under the gospel is forbidden to all church-ministers, as a thing which Christ thir master in his ministerie disclam'd *Luke* 12.14; as a thing beneathe them 1 *Cor.* 6.4; and by many

---

[41]"Our guaranteed obedience."

[42]Shemaiah, a false prophet, instructed the Jerusalem priesthood, once under the control of the leader Jehoiada (see 2 Chronicles 22.11–24), to jail anyone Shemaiah considered to be mad, including Jeremiah. Jeremiah, meanwhile, is told by God himself to expose Shemaiah's treachery, and God punishes Shemaiah "because he hath taught rebellion against the Lord" (Jeremiah 29.32).

of our statutes, as to them who have a peculiar and far differing government of thir own. If not, why different the governors? why not church-ministers in state-affairs, as well as stateministers in church-affairs? If church and state shall be made one flesh again as under the law, let it be withall considerd, that God who then join'd them hath now severd them; that which, he so ordaining, was then a lawfull conjunction, to such on either side as join again what he hath severd, would be nothing now but thir own presumptuous fornication. Secondly, the kings of *Juda* and those magistrates under the law might have recours, as I said before, to divine inspiration; which our magistrates under the gospel have not, more then to the same spirit, which those whom they force have oft times in greater measure then themselves: and so, instead of forcing the Christian, they force the Holy Ghost; and, against that wise forewarning of *Gamaliel*,[43] fight against God. Thirdly, those kings and magistrates us'd force in such things only as were undoubtedly known and forbidden in the law of *Moses*, idolatrie and direct apostacie from that national and strict enjoind worship of God; whereof the corporal punishment was by himself expressly set down: but magistrates under the gospel, our free, elective and rational worship, are most commonly busiest to force those things which in the gospel are either left free, nay somtimes abolishd when by them compelld, or els controverted equally by writers on both sides, and somtimes with odds on that side which is against them. By which means they either punish that which they ought to favor and protect, or that with corporal punishment and of thir own inventing, which not they but the church hath receivd command to chastise with a spiritual rod only. Yet some are so eager in thir zeal of forcing, that they refuse not to descend at length to the utmost shift of that parabolical prooff *Luke* 14.16, &c. *compell them to come in.* therfore magistrates may compell in religion. As if a parable were to be straind through every word or phrase, and not expounded by the general scope therof: which is no other here then the earnest expression of Gods displeasure on those recusant Jewes, and his purpose to preferre the gentiles on any terms before them; expressd here by the word *compell.* But how compells he? doubtless no otherwise then he draws, without which no man can come to him, *Joh.* 6.44: and that is by the inward perswasive motions of his spirit and by his ministers; not by the outward compulsions of a magistrate or his officers. The true people of Christ, as is foretold *Psal.* 110.3, *are a willing people in the day of*

his power. then much more now when he rules all things by outward weakness, that both his inward power and their sinceritie may the more appeer. *God loveth a chearfull giver:*[44] then certainly is not pleasd with an unchearfull worshiper; as the verie words declare of his euangelical invitations. *Esa.* 55.1. *ho, everie one that thirsteth, come. Joh.* 7.37. *if any man thirst. Rev.* 3.18. *I counsel thee.* and 22.17. *whosoever will, let him take the water of life freely.* And in that grand commission of preaching to invite all nations *Marc* 16.16, as the reward of them who come, so the penaltie of them who come not is only spiritual. But they bring now some reason with thir force, which must not pass unanswerd; that the church of *Thyatira* was blam'd *Rev.* 2.20 for suffering the false *prophetess to teach and to seduce.* I answer, that seducement is to be hinderd by fit and proper means ordaind in churchdiscipline; by instant and powerfull demonstration to the contrarie; by opposing truth to error, no unequal match; truth the strong to error the weak though slie and shifting. Force is no honest confutation; but uneffectual, and for the most part unsuccessfull, oft times fatal to them who use it: sound doctrine diligently and duely taught, is of herself both sufficient, and of herself (if some secret judgment of God hinder not) alwaies prevalent against seducers. This the *Thyatirians* had neglected, suffering, against Church-discipline, that woman to teach and seduce among them: civil force they had not then in thir power; being the Christian part only of that citie, and then especially under one of those ten great persecutions, wherof this the second was raisd by *Domitian:*[45] force therfore in these matters could not be requir'd of them, who were then under force themselves.

I have shewn that the civil power hath neither right nor can do right by forcing religious things: I will now shew the wrong it doth: by violating the fundamental privilege of the gospel, the new-birthright of everie true beleever, Christian libertie. 2 *Cor. where the spirit of the Lord is, there is libertie. Gal.* 4.26. *Jerusalem which is above, is free; which is the mother of us all.* and 31. *we are not children of the bondwoman but of the free.* It will be sufficient in this place to say no more of Christian libertie, then that it sets us free not only from the bondage of those ceremonies, but also from the forcible imposition of those circumstances, place and time in the worship of

---

[43]The respected Pharisee Gamaliel warns the Jews to let Peter and his followers alone, because "if ye be of God, ye cannot overthrow it; lest haply ye be found even to fight against God" (Acts 5.38).

[44]2 Corinthians 9.7.

[45]Roman emperor from 81 to 96 BCE, who, according to Eusebius, banished the evangelist John, author of Revelation, to the island of Patmos, "because of his testimony to the word of God" (*The History of the Church from Christ to Constantine*, trans. G. A. Williamson [London: Penguin, 1965]: 81).

God: which though by him commanded in the old law, yet in respect of that veritie and freedom which is euangelical, S. *Paul* comprehends both kindes alike, that is to say, both ceremonie and circumstance, under one and the same contemtuous name of *weak and beggarly rudiments Gal. 4.3.9,10. Col. 2.8.* with 16: conformable to what our Saviour himself taught *John 4.21, 23. neither in this mountain nor yet at Jerusalem. In spirit and in truth: for the father seeketh such to worship him.* that is to say, not only sincere of heart, for such he sought ever, but also, as the words here chiefly import, not compelld to place, and by the same reason, not to any set time; as his apostle by the same spirit hath taught us *Rom.* 14.6, &c. *one man esteemeth one day above another, another &c. Gal. 4.10. Ye observe dayes, and moonths &c. Coloss. 2.16.* These and other such places of scripture the best and learnedest reformed writers have thought evident anough to instruct us in our freedom not only from ceremonies but from those circumstances also, though impos'd with a confident perswasion of moralitie in them, which they hold impossible to be in place or time. By what warrant then our opinions and practises herin are of late turnd quite against all other Protestants, and that which is to them orthodoxal, to us become scandalous and punishable by statute, I wish were once again better considerd; if we mean not to proclame a schism in this point from the best and most reformed churches abroad. They who would seem more knowing, confess that these things are indifferent, but for that very cause by the magistrate may be commanded. As if God of his special grace in the gospel had to this end freed us from his own commandments in these things, that our freedom should subject us to a more greevous yoke, the commandments of men. As well may the magistrate call that common or unclean which God hath cleansd, forbidden to S. *Peter Acts* 10.15; as well may he loos'n that which God hath strait'nd,[46] or strait'n that which God hath loos'nd, as he may injoin those things in religion which God hath left free, and lay on that yoke which God hath taken off. For he hath not only given us this gift as a special privilege and excellence of the free gospel above the servile law, but strictly also hath commanded us to keep it and enjoy it. *Gal.* 5.13. *you are calld to libertie.* 1 *Cor.* 7.23. *be not made the servants of men. Gal.* 5.14.[47] *stand fast therfore in the libertie wherwith Christ hath made us free; and be not intangl'd again with the yoke of bondage.* Neither is this a meer command, but for the most part in these forecited places accompanied with the verie waightiest and inmost rea-

sons of Christian religion:[48] *Rom.* 14.9,10. for to this end Christ both dy'd and rose and reviv'd, that he might be Lord both of the dead and living. But why dost thou judge thy brother? *&c.* how presum'st thou to be his lord, to be whose only Lord, at least in these things, Christ both dy'd and rose and livd again? *We shall all stand before the judgment seat of Christ.* why then dost thou not only judge, but persecute in these things for which we are to be accountable to the tribunal of Christ only, our Lord and law-giver? 1 *Cor.* 7.23. *ye are bought with a price; be not made the servants of men.* some trivial price belike, and for some frivolous pretences paid in their opinion, if bought and by him redeemd who is God from what was once the service of God, we shall be enthrald again and forc'd by men to what now is but the service of men. *Gal.* 4.31, with 5.1 *we are not children of the bondwoman &c. stand fast therfore &c. Col.* 2.8. *beware least any man spoil you, &c. after the rudiments of the world, and not after Christ.* Solid reasons wherof are continu'd through the whole chapter, *v.* 10. *ye are complete in him, which is the head of all principalitie and power.* not completed therfore or made the more religious by those ordinances of civil power, from which Christ thir head hath dischargd us; *blotting out the handwriting of ordinances, that was against us, which was contrarie to us; and took it out of the way, nailing it to his cross, v.* 14: blotting out ordinances written by God himself, much more those so boldly written over again by men, ordinances which were against us, that is, against our frailtie, much more those which are against our conscience. *Let no man therfore judge you in respect of &c. v.* 16. *Gal.* 4.3, &c. *even so we, when we were children, were in bondage under the rudiments of the world: but when the fullness of time was come, God sent forth his son &c. to redeem them that were under the law, that we might receive the adoption of sons &c. Wherfore thou art no more a servant, but a son &c. But now &c.* how turn ye again to the weak and beggarly rudiments, wherunto ye desire again to be in bondage? ye observe dayes &c. Hence it planely appeers, that if we be not free we are not sons, but still servants unadopted; and if we turn again to those weak and beggarly rudiments, we are not free; yea though willingly and with a misguided conscience we desire to be in bondage to them; how much more then if unwillingly and against our conscience? Ill was our condition chang'd from legal to euangelical, and small advantage gotten by the gospel, if for the spirit of adoption to freedom, promisd us, we receive again the spirit

---

[46]Tightened, made more narrow.
[47]Galations 5.1 is correct.

[48]As Hunter cleverly points out, Milton quotes a series of passages from the Bible in order to answer each with ironic commentary (Yale 7: 264n; 234–35). I would add that Milton's rhetorical method seems that of the catechism, a series of questions followed by "correct" answers.

of bondage to fear; if our fear which was then servile towards God only, must be now servile in religion towards men: strange also and preposterous fear, if when and wherin it hath attain by the redemption of our Saviour to be filial only towards God, it must be now servile towards the magistrate. Who by subjecting us to his punishment in these things, brings back into religion that law of terror and satisfaction, belonging now only to civil crimes; and thereby in effect abolishes the gospel by establishing again the law to a far worse yoke of servitude upon us then before. It will therfore not misbecome the meanest[49] Christian to put in minde Christian magistrates, and so much the more freely by how much the more they desire to be thought Christian (for they will be thereby, as they ought to be in these things, the more our brethren and the less our lords) that they meddle not rashly with Christian libertie, the birthright and outward testimonie of our adoption: least while they little think it, nay think they do God service, they themselves like the sons of that bondwoman[50] be found persecuting them who are freeborne of the spirit; and by a sacrilege of not the least aggravation bereaving them of that sacred libertie which our Saviour with his own blood purchas'd for them.

A fourth reason why the magistrate ought not to use force in religion, I bring from the consideration of all those ends which he can likely pretend to the interposing of his force therin: and those hardly can be other then first the glorie of God; next either the spiritual good of them whom he forces, or the temporal punishment of their scandal to others. As for the promoting of Gods glory, none, I think, will say that his glorie ought to be promoted in religious things by unwarrantable means, much less by means contrarie to what he hath commanded. That outward force is such, and that Gods glory in the whole administration of the gospel according to his own will and councel ought to be fulfilld by weakness, at least so refuted, not by force; or if by force, inward and spiritual, not outward and corporeal, is already prov'd at large. That outward force cannot tend to the good of him who is forc'd in religion, is unquestionable. For in religion whatever we do under the gospel, we ought to be therof perswaded without scruple; and are justified by the faith we have, not by the work we do. *Rom.* 14.5. *Let every man be fully perswaded in his own mind.* The other reason which follows necessarily, is

obvious. *Gal.* 2.16, and in many other places of St. *Paul*, as the groundwork and foundation of the whole gospel, that we are *justified by the faith of Christ, and not by the works of the law.* if not by the works of Gods law, how then by the injunctions of mans law? Surely force cannot work perswasion, which is faith; cannot therfore justifie not pacifie the conscience; and that which justifies not in the gospel, condemns; is not only not good, but sinfull to do. *Rom.* 14.23. *Whatsoever is not of faith, is sin.* It concerns the magistrate then to take heed how he forces in religion conscientious men: least by compelling them to do that wherof they cannot be perswaded, that wherin they cannot finde themselves justified, but by thir own consciences condemnd, instead of aiming at thir spiritual good, he force them to do evil; and while he thinks himself *Asa, Josia, Nehemia*, he be found *Jeroboam*,[51] who causd Israel to sin; and thereby draw upon his own head all those sins and shipwracks of implicit faith and conformitie, which he hath forc'd, and all the wounds given to those *little ones*,[52] whom to offend he will find worse one day then that violent drowning mentioned *Matt.* 18.6. Lastly as a preface to force, it is the usual pretence, That although tender consciences shall be tolerated, yet scandals thereby given shall not be unpunishd, prophane and licentious men shall not be encourag'd to neglect the performance of religious and holy duties by color of any law giving libertie to tender consciences. By which contrivance the way lies ready, open to them heerafter who may be so minded, to take away by little and little, that liberty which Christ and his gospel, not any magistrate, hath right to give: though this kinde of his giving be but to give with one hand and take away with the other, which is a deluding not a giving. As for scandals, if any man be offended at the conscientious liberty of another, it is a taken scandal not a given. To heal one conscience we must not wound another: and men must be exhorted to beware of scandals in Christian libertie, not forc'd by the magistrate; least while he goes about to take away the scandal, which is uncertain whether given or taken, he take away our liberty, which is the certain and the sacred gift of God, neither to be touchd by him, nor to be parted with by us. None more cautious of giving scandal then St. *Paul*. Yet while he made himself *servant to all*, that he might gain the more, he made himself so of his own accord, was not made so by outward force, testifying at the same time that he *was free*

---

[49]Lowliest.

[50]Hagar was a slave or bondwoman in Abraham's household who bore him a son, Ishmael. When Ishmael, in Genesis 21.9, mocks Abraham's legitimate son by his wife Sarah, Isaac, Abraham with God's help chooses to banish Hagar and Ishmael. St. Paul uses the incident to construct an allegory of old versus new covenants in Galatians 4.29.

[51]Infamous as a king who endorsed the worship of golden calves, Jeroboam also denied various prophecies and was punished by the death of a son (1 Kings 12.28–30; 14.17).

[52]See Mark 10–14, among other places, for various references by Christ to children as "little ones," i.e., the defenseless who need protection and sympathy.

from all men, 1 *Cor.* 9.19: and therafter exhorts us also *Gal.* 5.13. *ye were calld to libertie &c. but by love serve one another:* then not by force. As for that fear least prophane and licentious men should be encourag'd to omit the performance of religious and holy duties, how can that care belong to the civil magistrate, especially to his force? For if prophane and licentious persons must not neglect the performance of religious and holy duties, it implies, that such duties they can perform; which no Protestant will affirm. They who mean the outward performance, may so explane it; and it will then appeer yet more planely, that such performance of religious and holy duties especialy by prophane and licentious persons, is a dishonoring rather then a worshiping of God; and not only by him nor requir'd but detested: *Prov.* 21.27. *the sacrifice of the wicked is an abomination: how much more when he bringeth it with a wicked minde?* To compell therfore the prophane to things holy in his prophaneness, is all one under the gospel, as to have compelld the unclean to sacrifise in his uncleanness under the law. And I adde withall, that to compell the licentious in his licentiousness, and the conscientious against his conscience, coms all to one; tends not to the honor of God, but to the multiplying and the aggravating of sin to them both. We read not that Christ ever exercis'd force but once; and that was to drive prophane ones out of his temple, not to force them in: and if thir beeing there was an offence, we finde by many other scriptures that thir praying there was an abomination: and yet to the Jewish law that nation, as a servant, was oblig'd; but to the gospel each person is left voluntarie, calld only, as a son, by the preaching of the word; not to be driven in by edicts and force of arms. For if by the apostle, *Rom.* 12.1, we are *beseechd as brethren by the mercies of God to present our bodies a living sacrifice, holy, acceptable to God, which* is our *reasonable service* or worship, then is no man to be forc'd by the compulsive laws of men to present his body a dead sacrifice, and so under the gospel most unholy and unacceptable, because it is his unreasonable service, that is to say, not only unwilling but unconscionable. But if prophane and licentious persons may not omit the performance of holy duties, why may they not partake of holy things? why are they prohibitied the Lords supper; since both the one and the other action may be outward; and outward performance of dutie may attain at least an outward participation of benefit? The church denying them that communion of grace and thanksgiving, as it justly doth, why doth the magistrate compell them to the union of performing that which they neither truly can, being themselves unholy, and to do seemingly is both hatefull to God, and perhaps no less dangerous to perform holie duties irreligiously then to receive holy signes or sacraments unworthily. All prophane and licentious men,

so known, can be considerd but either so without the church as never yet within it, or departed thence of thir own accord, or excommunicate: if never yet within the church, whom the apostle, and so consequently the church have naught to do to judge, as he professes 1 *Cor.* 5.12, then[53] by what autoritie doth the magistrate judge, or, which is worse, compell in relation to the church? if departed of his own accord, like that lost sheep *Luke* 15.4, &c. the true church either with her own or any borrowd force worries him not in again, but rather in all charitable manner sends after him; and if she finde him, layes him gently on her shoulders; bears him, yea bears his burdens; his errors, his infirmities any way tolerable, *so fulfilling the law of Christ, Gal.* 6.2: if excommunicate, whom the church hath bid go out, in whose name doth the magistrate compell to go in? The church indeed hinders none from hearing in her publick congregation, for the doors are open to all: nor excommunicates to destruction, but, as much as in her lies, to a final saving. Her meaning therfore must needs bee, that as her driving out brings on no outward penaltie, so no outward force or penaltie of an improper and only a destructive power should drive in again her infectious sheep; therfore sent out because infectious, and not driven in but with the danger not only of the whole and sound, but also of his own utter perishing. Since force neither instructs in religion nor begets repentance or amendment of life, but, on the contrarie, hardness of heart, formalitie, hypocrisie,[54] and, as I said before, everie way increase of sin; more and more alienates the minde from a violent religion expelling out and compelling in, and reduces it to a condition like that which the Britains complain of in our storie,[55] driven to and fro between the Picts and the sea. If after excommunion he be found intractable, incurable, and will not hear the church, he becoms as one never yet within her pale, *a heathen or a publican, Mat.* 18. 17; not further to be judgd, no not by the magistrate, unless for civil causes; but left to the final sentence of that judge, whose coming shall be in flames of fire; that *Maran athà*, 1 *Cor.* 16.22;[56] then which to him so left nothing can be more dreadful and ofttimes to him particularly nothing more speedie, that is to say, the Lord cometh: In the mean while deliverd up to Satan, 1 *Cor.* 5.5. 1 *Tim.* 1.20. that is, from the fould[57] of Christ and kingdom of grace to the

---

[53]Correcting "them" in the 1659 edition.
[54]All characteristics of evil, and specifially Satan, in *Paradise Lost.*
[55]History, as with Milton's *History of Britain*, where the image of the Picts and Scots forcing the early Britons to the sea can be found (Yale 5: 138).
[56]"If any man love not the Lord Jesus Christ, let him be Anathema Maranatha." An anathema is the worst curse imaginable, occurring at Christ's final judgment of humankind.
[57]Fold; safe enclosure.

world again which is the kingdom of Satan; and as he was receivd *from darkness to light, and from the power of Satan to God, Acts* 26. 18, so now deliverd up again from light to darkness, and from God to the power of Satan; yet so as is in both places manifested, to the intent of saving him, brought sooner to contrition by spiritual then by any corporal severitie. But grant it belonging any way to the magistrate, that prophane and licentious persons omit not the performance of holy duties, which in them were odious to God even under the law, much more now under the gospel, yet ought his care both as a magistrate and a Christian, to be much more that conscience be not inwardly violated, then that licence in these things be made outwardly conformable: since his part is undoubtedly as a Christian, which puts him upon this office much more then as a magistrate, in all respects to have more care of the conscientious then of the prophane; and not for their sakes to take away (while they pretend[58] to give) or to diminish the rightfull libertie of religious consciences.

On these four scriptural reasons as on a firm square[59] this truth, the right of Christian and euangelic liberty, will stand immoveable against all those pretended consequences of license and confusion which for the most part men most licentious and confus'd them-selves, or such as whose severitie would be wiser then divine wisdom, are ever aptest to object against the waies of God: as if God without them when he gave us this libertie, knew not of the worst which these men in thir arrogance pretend will follow: yet knowing all their worst, he gave us this liberty as by him judgd best. As to those magistrates who think it their work to settle religion, and those ministers or others, who so oft call upon them to do so, I trust, that having well considerd what hath bin here argu'd, neither they will continue in that intention, nor these in that expectation from them: when they shall finde that the settlement of religion belongs only to each particular church by perswasive and spiritual means within it self, and that the defence only of the church belongs to the magistrate. Had he once learnt not further to concern himself with church affairs, half his labor might be spar'd, and the commonwealth better tended. To which end, that which I premis'd in the beginning, and in due place treated of more at large, I desire now concluding, that they would consider seriously what religion is: and they will find it to be in summe, both our beleef and our practise depending upon God only. That there can be no place then left for the magistrate or his force in the settlement of religion, by appointing either what we shall beleeve in divine things or practise in religious (neither of which things are in the power of man either to perform himself or to enable others) I perswade me in the Christian ingenuitie of all religious men, the more they examin seriously, the more they will finde cleerly to be true: and finde how false and deceivable that common saying is, which is so much reli'd upon, that the Christian Magistrate is *custos utriusque tabulæ*, keeper of both tables; unless is meant by keeper the defender only: neither can that maxim be maintaind by any prooff or argument which hath not in this discours first or last bin refuted. For the two tables, or ten commandments,[60] teach our dutie to God and our neighbour from the love of both; give magistrates no autoritie to force either: they seek that from the judicial law; though on false grounds, especially in the first table, as I have shewn; and both in first and second execute that autoritie for the most part not according to Gods judicial laws but thir own. As for civil crimes and of the outward man, which all are not, no not of those against the second table, as that of coveting; in them what power they have, they had from the beginning, long before *Moses* or the two tables were in being. And whether they be not now as little in being to be kept by any Christian as they are two legal tables, remanes yet as undecided, as it is sure they never were yet deliverd to the keeping of any Christian magistrate. But of these things perhaps more some other time; what may serve the present hath bin above discourst sufficiently out of the scriptures: and to those produc'd might be added testimonies, examples, experiences of all succeeding ages to these times asserting this doctrine: but having herin the scripture so copious and so plane, we have all that can be properly called true strength and nerve;[61] the rest would be but pomp and incumbrance. Pomp and ostentation of reading is admir'd among the vulgar: but doubtless in matters of religion he is learnedest who is planest. The brevitie I use not exceeding a small manual, will not therfore, I suppose, be thought the less considerable, unless with them perhaps who think that great books only can determin great matters. I rather chose the common rule, not to make much ado where less may serve. Which in controversies and those especially of religion, would make them less tedious, and by consequence read ofter, by many more, and with more benefit.

The end.

---

[58]Correcting "ptetend."

[59]Probably the image is of a carpenter's square, viewed figuratively, as in "A canon, criterion, or standard; a rule or guiding principle; a pattern or example" (*OED* 2).

[60]The two stone tablets containing the Ten Commandments as they were given to Moses (Exodus 34.28).

[61]Muscle.

The readie and easie way
to establish a
free Commonwealth;
and the excellence therof com-
par'd with the inconveniences
and dangers of readmit-
ting Kingship in
this Nation.

The second edition revis'd and
augmented.
The author J.M.

---

                                                              et nes
consilium dedimus Sylvæ, *demus populo nunc.*

LONDON,
Printed for the Author, 1660.

Readie and Easie Way (1660)

Working against historical odds and placing himself, as a vulnerable blind regicide, in some personal danger, Milton quickly wrote the first edition of *The Readie and Easie Way to Establish a Free Commonwealth,* in February 1660. It was printed in March, by Thomas New-comb, to be sold by the bookseller Livewell Chapman. The printing was over-hasty, and an errata list had to be included with an advertisement for the book in the journal *Mercurius politicus,* in its issue of March 1–8, No. 610.

Milton was trying to stop what was fated to happen—the Restoration of Charles II. Restoration of the monarchy was, for Milton, a return to tyranny and legalized fleecing of the people of England (Milton compares them to sheep) by corrupt courtiers and prelates. By the time the second, heavily augmented edition, came out, in early April, Livewell Chapman was being sought by authorities for publishing seditious material, and the printer of the second edition refused to sign his name on the title page, though Milton, with some courage, signed "J. M." He had moved from political respectability under the Protectorate to a position of isolated danger in the monarchy; as Cedric

Brown points out, he progressed "from spokesman of a commonwealth, to admonitory prophet for a commonwealth, one who stood in peril of the new regime" (153).

It is amazing how much the blind Milton knew of what was happening in Parliament, considering his disability. Though Milton at the time lived in the street called Petty France (in Westminster, not far from Parliament), biographers are largely silent about how he kept on top of the news about the chaotic world of English politics in 1660. How much he was involved in affairs of state in 1659 can be seen from his "Letter to a Freind" of October 20, which outlines what he believed to be "remedies [that] may be likelyest to save us from approaching ruine" (Yale 7: 323).

Parker has noted some of the reaction to the first edition. Samuel Butler, in *The Character of the Rump,* published about March 17, wrote that "John Milton . . . had a ram's head and is good only at batteries—an old heretic both in religion and manners, that by his will would shake off his governors as he doth his wives, four in a fortnight" (quoted in Parker 548; for authorship, see von Maltzahn), attacking Milton not only for his anti-monarchical views but for his divorce tracts. Thus Milton was viewed as a loser once again advocating a lost cause—though we can know by hindsight that his advocacy of a more democratic governing council responsible to the people might be closer to England's modern form of constitutional monarchy than it was to any scheme of rule by divine right.

Milton pictures himself in the second edition, inevitably, as the prophet without honor in his own country, warning the people, as did the prophet Jeremiah (Knoppers, *"Readie"* 213–15), against their coming slavery to king Nebuchaddrezzer in Babylon (Jeremiah 25). Milton saw the English in their return to monarchy as a people returning to slavery under a king who would encourage priestly corruption and dissolute living, the sons of Belial or of Bacchus (Knoppers, *Historicizing* 91). Hill sees Milton in the act of writing the pamphlet as displaying "courage in isolation" (*Milton* 124), which is of course the position of Abdiel in *Paradise Lost,* Samson in *Samson Agonistes,* or of Jesus in *Paradise Regain'd.* Loewenstein writes that the tract "reveals Milton vacillating in his own polemical stance between detaching himself from the drama of history and engaging with it actively" (89). Milton was certainly risking his head, as a regicide writing on behalf of republicanism, on the very eve of the Restoration of Charles II.

Milton's scheme for government by a representative council of elite men appointed for life, without a king or a priestly class, clashed with the schemes of the centralized monarchy of Thomas Hobbes's *Leviathan* (1651) and the legislative two-party commonwealth as constructed in James Harrington's *Oceana* (1656) and by Harrington's subsequent pamphlets. The exchanges between Milton and Harrington are itemized, to some extent, in the notes on the two editions in the Yale *Prose Works*, and discussed more recently by Smith (chapters 5 and 6) and by Luc Borot (in forthcoming articles).

On May 25, 1660, King Charles II was to land at Dover. Four days later he entered London in triumph. Milton's lonely battle against monarchy was ended, and he had to begin to worry if he might survive the new king's anger. He was ordered to be arrested on June 16. A few copies of two of his antimonarchical pamphlets were to be burned in August by the public hangman. In the House of Commons, Sir Hineage Finch said Milton deserved hanging, but his friend and fellow poet Andrew Marvell may have intervened on his behalf, and the Act of Oblivion of August 29 did not name him as one of the unforgiven. Though he was arrested and held briefly in October, he was pardoned and released from the Tower of London December 15 (Yale 7: 223). If he had not been pardoned, we would have no *Paradise Lost*, no *Samson Agonistes*, no *Paradise Regain'd*.

TEXT

The blind Milton obviously exerted less control on the printing of what he wrote than the sighted Milton. Though he may have dictated the spelling "Parlament" in the two editions of *Readie and Easie Way*, he could not control the compositor's irregular "Comonwealth" (with one "m" or two) as compared with what seems to have been his preferred "Common-wealth" (printed hyphenated most of the time by his earlier printers). The compositor of the second edition seems to have been instructed to preserve such elements of Milton's spelling as "thir," "covnant," and "Parlament," but the text of the second edition, probably having been dictated to an amanuensis in some haste, is far removed from Milton's practice in its orthography. The book is unimportant-looking, a duodecimo—printed in gatherings of twelve—a size of book easily hidden.

Spelling and punctuation change before our very eyes in this little book: the apostrophe with possessive nouns begins to appear, in the difference between "the kings good will" and "the king's right" on the original page 68; and quotation marks are beginning to take the place of italics formerly used for the same purposes. Orthography may appear to be fixed, on the printed page, but, like glass, it is deceptively fluid.

Questions of emphasis and capitalization can be a subtle part of the argument: in *Readie and Easie Way* the word "king" is rarely capitalized, whereas the word "Commonwealth" (almost invariably) is.

For a print edition devoted to primary texts, I have had to make a choice between the first and second editions, and I have chosen, as with the *Doctrine and Discipline of Divorce*, to reproduce the second, augmented edition, as representing Milton's last-known wishes about the presentation of the text (see Lewalski for the context of changes made). But in the case of the these two versions, each with historical and literary importance, the most complete modern edition might be one which would show the two editions side by side, in columns or as complementary hypertext, each instantly retrievable when needed. The second edition's interpolations are included in brackets in the 1915 edition of Evert Mordecai Clark. The Yale editors (note that I am using the 1980 revised ed.) reprint both editions, which is useful, if sometimes confusing in its distribution of notes. Merritt Hughes's edition (1957) modernizes the text and provides useful and succinct notes. Patrides's 1974 edition reprints the Columbia text and provides a few notes.

Works Cited
Editions are marked with an asterisk.

Brown, Cedric C. *John Milton: A Literary Life*. New York: St. Martin's, 1995.

Hill, Christopher. *Milton and the English Revolution*. New York: Viking P, 1977.

Knoppers, Laura Lunger. *Historicizing Milton: Spectacle, Power and Poetry in Restoration England*. Athens: U of Georgia P, 1994.

———. "Milton's *The Readie and Easie Way* and the English Jeremiad." *Politics, Poetics, and Hermeneutics in Milton's Prose*. Ed. David Loewenstein and James Grantham Turner. Cambridge: Cambridge UP, 1990. 213–25.

Lewalski, Barbara K. "Milton: Political Beliefs and Polemical Methods, 1659–60." *PMLA* 74 (1959): 191–202.

Loewenstein, David. *Milton and the Drama of History: Historical Vision, Iconoclasm, and the Literary Imagination*. Cambridge: Cambridge UP, 1990.

*Milton, John. *The Readie & Easie Way to Establish a Free Commonwealth*. Ed. Robert W. Ayers. *Complete Prose Works of John Milton*, gen. ed. Don Wolfe. Vol. VII (rev. ed.).

*———. *The Readie and Easie Way to Establish a Free Commonwealth (1660)*. *John Milton: Selected Prose*, ed. C.A. Patrides. Harmondsworth, Eng.: Penguin, 1974.

*———. *The Ready and Easy Way to Establish a Free Commonwealth*. Ed., with Introduction, Notes, and Glossary, by Evert Mordecai Clark. New Haven: Yale UP, 1915.

Smith, Nigel. *Literature and Revolution in England, 1640–1660*. New Haven: Yale UP, 1994.

Von Maltzahn, Nicholas. "Samuel Butler's Milton." *Studies in Philology* 92 (1995): 482–95.

Woolrych, Austin. "The Good Old Cause and the Fall of the Protectorate." *Cambridge Historical Journal* 13 (1957): 133–61.

The readie and easie way to establish a free Commonwealth.

Lthough since the writing of this treatise, the face of things hath had som change, writs for new elections have bin recall'd, and the members at first chosen, readmitted from exclusion, yet not a little rejoicing to hear declar'd the resolution of those who are in power, tending to the establishment of a free Commonwealth, and to remove, if it be possible, this noxious humor of returning to bondage, instilld of late by som deceivers, and nourishd from bad principles and fals apprehensions among too many of the people, I thought best not to suppress what I had written, hoping that it may now be of much more use and concernment to be freely publishd, in the midst of our Elections to a free Parlament, or their sitting to consider freely of the Government; whom it behoves to have all things represented to them that may direct thir judgment therin; and I never read of any State, scarce of any tyrant grown so incurable, as to refuse counsel from any in a time of public deliberation; much less to be offended. If thir absolute determination be to enthrall us, before so long a Lent of Servitude, they may permitt us a little Shrovingtime first, wherin to speak freely, and take our leaves of Libertie. And because in the former edition through haste, many faults escap'd, and many books were suddenly dispersd, ere the note to mend them could be sent,[1] I took the opportunitie from this occasion to revise and somwhat to enlarge the whole discourse, especially that part which argues for a perpetual Senat. The treatise thus revis'd and enlarg'd, is as follows.

The Parlament of *England*, assisted by a great number of the people who appeerd and stuck to them faithfullest in defence of religion and thir civil liberties, judging kingship by long experience a government unnecessarie, burdensome and dangerous, justly and magnanimously abolishd it; turning regal bondage into a free Commonwealth, to the admiration and errour of our emulous neighbours. They took themselves not bound by the light of nature or religion, to any former

covnant,[2] from which the King himself by many forfeitures of a latter date or discoverie, and our longer consideration theron had more & more unbound us, both to himself and his posteritie; as hat bin ever the justice and the prudence of all wise nations that have ejected tyrannie. They covnanted *to preserve the Kings person and autoritie in the preservation of the true religion and our liberites*; not in his endeavoring to bring in upon our consciences a Popish religion, upon our liberties thraldom, upon our lives destruction, by his occasioning, if not complotting, as was after discoverd, the *Irish* massacre, his fomenting and arming the rebellion, his covert leaguing with the rebels against us, his refusing more then seaven times, propositions most just and necessarie to the true religion and our liberties, tenderd him by the Parlament both of *England* and *Scotland*. They made not thir covnant concerning him with no difference between a king and a god, or promisd him as *Job* did to the Almightie, *to trust in him, though he slay us:*[3] they understood that the solemn ingagement, wherin we all forswore kingship, was no more a breach of the covnant,[4] then the covnant was of the protestation before, but a faithful and prudent going on both in the words, well weighd, and in the true sense of the covnant, *without respect of persons*, when we could not serve two contrary maisters, God and the king, or the king and that more supreme law, sworn in the first place to maintain, our safetie and our libertie. They know the people of *England* to be a free people, themselves the representers of that freedom & although many were excluded, & as many fled (so they pretended) from the tumults to *Oxford*, yet they were left a sufficient number to act in Parlament; therefor not bound by any statute of preceding Parlaments, but by the law of nature only,[5] which is the only law of laws truly and properly to all mankinde fundamental; the beginning and the end of all Government; to which no Parlament or people that will throughly[6] reforme, but may and must have recourse; as they had and must yet have in church reformation (if they throughly intend it) to evangelic rules; not to ecclesiastical canons, though

---

[1] Errata for the first edition appeared in *Mercurius Politicus*, March 1–8, 1660. That edition, in other words, was put together so quickly that there had been no time to include in it the normal lists of printing errors.

[2] The Solemn League and Covenant with the Scots, endorsed by the House of Commons, September 25, 1643, which attempted to control Scottish religious loyalties and direct them away from Roman Catholicism and prelacy (church rule by bishops).
[3] Job 13.15, "Though he slay me, yet will I trust in him. . . ." Milton quotes indirectly, rather than re-translating.
[4] Correcting the error "covant."
[5] Milton sets up an opposition between a universal law of nature based on human common sense and "positive laws," statutory laws formally laid down by particular peoples. The Yale editors quote from the *Rolls of Parliament* 5: 122.2: "All the Lawes of the world . . . resteth in three: . . . the Lawe of God, Lawe of nature and posityve Lawe" (Yale 7: 413n).
[6] Thoroughly, completely.

never so ancient, so ratifi'd and establishd in the land by Statutes, which for the most part are meer positive laws, neither natural nor moral, & so by any Parlament for just and serious considerations, without scruple to be at any time repeal'd. If others of thir number, in these things were under force, they were not, but under free conscience; if others were excluded by a power which they could not resist, they were not therefore to leave the helm of government in no hands, to discontinue thir care of the public peace and safetie, to desert the people in anarchie and confusion; no more then when so many of thir members left them, as made up in outward formalitie a more legal Parlament of three estates[7] against them. The best affected also and best principl'd of the people, stood not numbring or computing on which side were most voices in Parlament, but on which side appeerd to them most reason, most safetie, when the house divided upon main matters: what was well motiond and advis'd, they examind not whether fear or perswasion carried it in the vote; neither did they measure votes and counsels by the intentions of them that voted; knowing that intentions either are but guessd at, or not soon anough known; and although good, can neither make the deed such, nor prevent the consequence from being bad: suppose bad intentions in things otherwise welldon; what was welldon, was by them who so thought, not the less obey'd or followd in the state; since in the church, who had not rather follow *Iscariot* or *Simon*[8] the magician, though to covetous ends, preaching, then *Saul*, though in the uprightness of his heart persecuting the gospell?[9] Safer they therefor judgd what they thought the better counsels, though carried on by some perhaps to bad ends, then the wors, by others, though endevord with best intentions: and yet they were not to learn that a greater number might be corrupt within the walls of a Parlament as well as of a citie; wherof in matters of neerest concernment all men will be judges; nor easily permitt, that the odds of voices in thir greatest councel, shall more endanger them by corrupt or credulous votes, then the odds of enemies by open assaults; judging that most voices ought not alwaies to prevail where main matters are in question; if others hence will pretend to disturb all

counsels, what is that to them who pretend not, but are in real danger; not they only so judging, but a great though not the greatest, number of thir chosen Patriots, who might be more in waight, then the others in number; there being in number little vertue, but by weight and measure wisdom working all things: and the dangers on either side they seriously thus waighd: from the treatie, short fruits of long labours and seaven years warr; securitie for twenty years, if we can hold it; reformation in the church for three years: then put to shift again with our vanquishd maister. His justice, his honour, his conscience declar'd quite contrarie to ours; which would have furnishd him with many such evasions, as in a book entitl'd *an inquisition for blood*,[10] soon after were not conceald: bishops not totally remov'd, but left as it were in ambush, a reserve, with ordination in thir sole power; thir lands alreadie sold, not to be alienated, but rented, and the sale of them call'd *sacrilege*; delinquents few of many brought to condigne punishment; accessories punishd; the chief author, above pardon, though after utmost resistance, vanquish'd; not to give, but to receive laws; yet besought, treated with, and to be thankd for his gratious concessions, to be honourd, worshipd, glorifi'd. If this we swore to do, with what righteousness in the sight of God, with what assurance that we bring not by such an oath the whole sea of blood-guiltiness upon our own heads? If on the other side we preferr a free government, though for the present not obtain, yet all those suggested fears and difficulties, as the event will prove, easily overcome, we remain finally secure from the exasperated regal power, and out of snares; shall retain the best part of our libertie, which is our religion, and the civil part will be from these who deferr us, much more easily recoverd, being neither so suttle nor so awefull as a King reinthron'd. Nor were thir actions less both at home and abroad then might become the hopes of a glorious rising Commonwealth: nor were the expressions both of armie and people, whether in thir publick declarations or several writings other then such as testifi'd a spirit in this nation no less noble and well fitted to the liberty of a Commonwealth, then in the ancient *Greeks* or *Romans*. Nor was the heroic cause unsuccessfully defended to all Christendom against the tongue of a famous and thought invincible adversarie; nor the constancie and fortitude that so nobly vindicated our liberty, our victory at once against two the most prevailing usurpers over mankinde, superstition and tyrannie unpraisd or uncelebrated in a written

---

[7]The three estates were composed of the King, the House of Lords, and the House of Commons.

[8]Judas Iscariot, who took money to betray Christ (John 12) and Simon Magus (Acts 8.9), who practiced sorcery, offered to bribe the Apostles Peter and John to discover how to communicate with the Holy Ghost, and gave his name to the practice of simony, the selling of indulgences or benefices (jobs within the church).

[9]Saul was the earlier name of St. Paul. As Saul, the Apostle had persecuted Christians in Jerusalem (Acts 26), before Christian truth had been revealed to him.

---

[10]*An Inquisition After Blood* was published in July 1649: it asserted that the King was not bound to any promises made while "the razor was as it were at his throat" (3; see Yale 7: 417n).

monument, likely to outlive detraction, as it hath hitherto convinc'd[11] or silenc'd not a few of our detractors, especially in parts abroad. After our liberty and religion thus prosperously fought for, gaind and many years possessd, except in those unhappie interruptions, which God hath remov'd, now that nothing remains, but in all reason the certain hopes of a speedie and immediat settlement for ever in a firm and free Commonwealth, for this extolld and magnifi'd nation, regardless both of honour wonn or deliverances voutsaf't from heaven, to fall back or rather to creep back so poorly as it seems the multitude would to thir once abjur'd and detested thraldom of Kingship, to be our selves the slanderers of our own just and religious deeds, though don by som to covetous and ambitious ends, yet not therefor to be staind with their infamie, or they to asperse the integritie of others, and yet these now by revolting from the conscience of deeds welldon both in church and state, to throw away and forsake, or rather to betray a just and noble cause for the mixture of bad men who have ill manag'd and abus'd it (which had our fathers don heretofore, and on the same pretence deserted true religion, what had long ere this become of our gospel and all protestant reformation so much intermixt with the avarice and ambition of som reformers?) and by thus relapsing, to verifie all the bitter predictions of our triumphing enemies, who will now think they wisely discernd and justly censur'd both us and all our actions as rash, rebellious, hypocritical and impious, not only argues a strange degenerate contagion suddenly spread among us fitted and prepar'd for new slaverie, but will render us a scorn and derision to all our neighbours. And what will they at best say of us and of the whole *English* name, but scoffingly as of that foolish builder, mentiond by our Saviour, who began to build a tower, and was not able to finish it. Where is this goodly tower of a Commonwealth, which the English boasted they would build to overshaddow kings, and be another *Rome* in the west? The foundation indeed they laid gallantly; but fell into a wors confusion, not of tongues, but of factions, then those at the tower of *Babel*;[12] and have left no memorial of thir work behinde them remaining, but in the common laughter of *Europ*. Which must needs redound the more to our shame, if we but look on our neighbours the United Provinces,[13] to us inferior in all outward advantages; who notwithstanding, in the midst of greater difficulties, couragiously, wisely, constantly went through

with the same work, and are setl'd in all the happie enjoiments of a flourishing Republic to this day.

Besides this, if we returne to Kingship, and soon repent, as undoubtedly we shall, when we begin to finde the old encroachments coming on by little and little upon our consciences, which must necessarily proceed from king and bishop united inseparably in one interest, we may be forc'd perhaps to fight over again all that we have fought, and spend over again all that we have spent, but are never like to attain thus far as we are not advanc'd to the recoverie of our freedom, never to have it in possession as we now have it, never to be voutsaf't heerafter the like mercies and signal assistances from heaven in our cause, if by our ingrateful backsliding we make these fruitless; flying now to regal concessions from his divine condescensions and gratious answers to our once importuning praiers against the tyrannie which we then groand under: making vain and viler then dirt the blood of so many thousand faithfull and valiant *English* men, who left us in this libertie, bought with thir lives; losing by a strange after game of folly, all the battels we have wonn, together with all *Scotland* as to our conquest, hereby lost, which never any of our kings could conquer, all the treasure we have spent, not that corruptible treasure only, but that far more precious of all our late miraculous deliverances; treading back again with lost labour all our happie steps in the progress of reformation; and more pittifully depriving our selves the instant fruition of that free government which we have so dearly purchasd, a free Commonwealth, not only held by wisest men in all ages the noblest, the manliest, the equallest, the justest government, the most agreeable to all due libertie and proportiond equalitie, both human, civil, and Christian, most cherishing to vertue and true religion, but also (I may say it with greatest probabilitie) planely commended, or rather enjoind by our Saviour himself, to all Christians, not without remarkable disallowance, and the brand of *gentilism*[14] upon kingship. God in much displeasure gave a king to the *Israelites*, and imputed it a sin to them that they sought one: but *Christ* apparently forbids his disciples to admitt of any such heathenish government: *the kings of the gentiles*, saith he, *exercise lordship over them; and they that exercise authoritie upon them, are call'd benefactors: but ye shall not be so; but he that is greatest among you, let him be as the younger; and he that is chief, as he that serveth.* The occasion of these his words was the ambitious desire of *Zebede's* two sons, to be exalted above thir brethren in his kingdom,

---

[11]Written as "covinc'd," here corrected.
[12]Genesis 11.4–9 records the building of the Tower of Babel, and God's separation of people into nations based on different languages.
[13]Republics existing in the Netherlands.

---

[14]Gentilism, in the biblical sense, is worship of gods other than Jehovah or the Christian God (see Matthew 10.5 or Galatians 2.15).

which they thought was to be ere long upon earth. That he speaks of civil government, is manifest by the former part of the comparison, which inferrs the other part to be alwaies in the same kinde. And what government coms neerer to this precept of Christ, then a free Commonwealth; wherin they who are greatest, are perpetual servants and drudges to the public at thir own cost and charges, neglect thir own affairs; yet are not elevated above thir brethren; live soberly in thir families, walk the streets as other men, may be spoken to freely, familiarly, friendly, without adoration. Wheras a king must be ador'd like a Demigod,[15] with a dissolute and haughtie court about him, of vast expence and luxurie, masks and revels, to the debaushing of our prime gentry both male and female; not in thir passetimes only, but in earnest, by the loos imploiments of court service, which will be then thought honorable. There will be a queen also of no less charge; in most likelihood outlandish and a Papist;[16] besides a queen mother such alreadie; together with both thir courts and numerous train: then a royal issue, and ere long severally thir sumptuous courts; to the multiplying of a servile crew, not of servants only, but of nobility and gentry, bred up then to the hopes not of public, but of court office; to be stewards, chamberlains, ushers, grooms, even of the close-stool;[17] and the lower thir mindes debas'd with court opinions, contrarie to all vertue and reformation, the haughtier will be thir pride and profuseness: we may well remember this not long since at home; or need but look at present into the *French* court, where enticements and preferments daily draw away and pervert the Protestant Nobilitie. As to the burden of expence, to our cost we shall soon know it; for any good to us, deserving to be termd no better then the vast and lavish price of our subjection and their debausherie; which we are now so greedily cheapning,[18] and would so fair be paying most inconsideratly to a single person; who for any thing wherin the public really needs him, will have little els to do, but to bestow the eating and drinking of excessive dainties,[19] to set a pompous face upon the superficial actings of State, to pageant himself up and down in progress[20] among the perpetual bowings and cringings of an abject people, on either side deifying and adoring him for nothing don that can deserve it. For what can he more then another man?[21] who even in the expression of a late court-poet,[22] sits only like a great cypher set to no purpose before a long row of other significant figures. Nay it is well and happy for the people if thir King be but a cypher, being oft times a mischief, a pest, a scourge of the nation, and which is wors, not to be remov'd, not to be controul'd, much less accus'd or brought to punishment, without the danger of a common ruin, without the shaking and almost subersion of the whole land. Wheras in a free Commonwealth, any governor or chief counselor offending, may be remov'd and punishd without the least commotion. Certainly then that people must needs be madd or strangely infatuated, that build the chief hope of thir common happiness or safetie on a single person: who if he happen to be good, can do no more then another man, if to be bad, hath in his hands to do more evil without check, then millions of other men. The happiness of a nation must needs be firmest and certainest in a full and free Council of thir own electing, where no single person, but reason only swaies. And what madness is it, for them who might manage nobly thir own affairs themselves, sluggishly and weakly to devolve all on a single person; and more like boyes under age then men, to committ all to his patronage and disposal, who neither can performe what he undertakes, and yet for undertaking it, though royally paid, will not be thir servant, but thir lord? how unmanly must it needs be, to count such a one the breath of our nostrils, to hang all our felicity on him, all our safetie, our well-being, for which if we were aught els but sluggards or babies, we need depend on none but God and our own counsels, our own active vertue and industrie; *Go to the Ant, thou sluggard*, saith *Solomon; consider her waies, and be wise; which having no prince, ruler, or lord, provides her meat in the summer, and gathers her food in the harvest.* which evidently[23] shews us, that they who think the nation undon without a king, though they look grave or haughtie, have not so much true spirit and understanding in them as a pismire:[24] neither are these

---

[15]Milton describes the court of Charles I, projecting the image of the father's court of the late 1630s onto the imagined court of Charles II.

[16]Charles I's Queen, Henrietta Maria, was Roman Catholic and noted for her love of formal late-night entertainments such as masques, which were produced at public expense and perceived by the Puritan factions to be decadent. Milton, of course, had written his own masque, but it hardly endorsed debauchery.

[17]Chamber-pot, or bedroom portable toilet. Milton satirizes an actual court-office, a nobleman's position as someone who took care of the king's bathroom accessories, a "groom of the stool" (see *OED* n. "stole" 2).

[18]Reducing in value, by bargaining for it.

[19]Compare the banquet served by Satan for Jesus in *Paradise Regain'd* 2.337–67.

[20]The king's official visits to noblemen's estates, progresses, are ridiculed, as are his pageants, public spectacles, again held at someone else's expense.

[21]"What greater knowledge can he have than that of the common man?"

[22]Probably Sir William Davenant. See Elsie Duncan-Jones, "Milton's Late Court-Poet," *Notes & Queries*, n.s. 1 (1954): 473.

[23]Correcting the misprint "evidenly."

[24]The government of the societies of bees or ants (pismires) was often studied as an example for human political structure.

diligent creatures hence concluded to live in lawless anarchie, or that commended, but are set the examples to imprudent and ungovernd men, of a frugal and self-governing democratie[25] or Commonwealth; safer and more thriving in the joint providence and counsel of many industrious equals, then under the single domination of one imperious Lord. It may be well wonderd that any Nation styling themselves free, can suffer any man to pretend hereditarie right over them as thir lord; when as by acknowledging that right, they conclude themselves his servants and his vassals, and so renounce thir own freedom. Which how a people and thir leaders especially can do, who have fought so gloriously for liberty, how they can change thir noble words and actions, heretofore so becoming the majesty of a free people, into the base necessitie of court flatteries and prostrations, is not only strange and admirable,[26] but lamentable to think on. That a nation should be so valorous and courageous to winn thir liberty in the field, and when they have wonn it, should be so heartless[27] and unwise in thir counsels, as not to know how to use it, value it, what to do with it or with themselves; but after ten or twelve years prosperous warr[28] and contestation with tyrannie, basely and besottedly to run their necks again into the yoke which they have broken, and prostrate all the fruits of thir victorie for naught at the feet of the vanquishd, besides our loss of glorie, and such an example as kings or tyrants never yet had the like to boast of, will be an ignomine[29] if it befall us, that never yet befell any nation possessd of thir libertie; worthie indeed themselves, whatsoever they be, to be for ever slaves: but that part of the nation which consents not with them, as I perswade me of a great number, far worthier then by their means to be brought into the same bondage. Considering these things so plane, so rational, I cannot but yet furder admire on the other side, how any man who hath the true principles of justice and religion in him, can presume or take upon him to be a king and lord over his brethren, whom he cannot but know whether as men or Christians, to be for the most part every way equal or superior to himself: how he can display with such vanitie and ostentation his regal splendor so supereminently above other mortal men; or being a Christian, can assume such extraordinarie honour and worship to himself, while the kingdom of

Christ our common King and Lord, is hid to this world, and such *gentilish* imitation forbid in express words by himself to all his disciples. All Protestants hold that Christ in his church hath left no vicegerent of his power, but himself without deputie, is the only head therof, governing it from heaven: how then can any Christian-man derive his kingship from Christ, but with wors usurpation then the Pope his headship over the church, since Christ not only hath not left the least shaddow of a command for any such vicegerence from him in the State, as the Pope pretends for his in the Church, but hath expressly declar'd, that such regal dominion is from the gentiles, not from him, and hath strictly charg'd us, not to imitate them therin.

I doubt not but all ingenuous and knowing men will easily agree with me, that a free Commonwealth without single person or house of lords, is by far the best government, if it can be had; but we have all this while say they bin expecting it,[30] and cannot yet attain it. Tis true indeed, when monarchie was dissolvd, the form of a Commonwealth should have forthwith bin fram'd; and the practice therof immediatly begun; that the people might have soon bin satisfi'd and delighted with the decent order, ease and benefit therof: we had bin then by this time firmly rooted, past fear of commotions or mutations, & now flourishing: this care of timely setling a new government instead of yᵉ old, too much neglected, hath bin our mischief. Yet the cause therof may be ascrib'd with most reason to the frequent disturbances, interruptions and dissolutions which the Parlament hath had partly from the impatient or disaffected people, partly from som ambitious people, partly from som ambitious leaders in the Armie; much contrarie, I beleeve, to the mind and approbation of the Armie it self and thir other Commanders, once undeceivd, or in thir own power. Now is the opportunitie, now the very season wherein we may obtain a free Commonwealth and establish it for ever in the land, without difficulty or much delay. Writs are sent out for elections, and which is worth observing in the name, not of any king, but of the keepers of our libertie, to summon a free Parlament: which then only will indeed be free, and deserve the true honor of that supreme title, if they preserve us a free people. Which never Parlament was more free to do; being now call'd, not as heretofore, by the summons of a king, but by the voice of libertie: and if the people, laying aside prejudice and impatience, will seriously and calmly now consider

---

[25]Milton's version of the word "democracy," used almost always in preference to the other form throughout his printed works.
[26]Awe-inspiring.
[27]Lacking in courage.
[28]War with a good outcome, in this case a commonwealth government.
[29]Possibly a typographical mistake for "ignominie," though Milton may be suggesting that the word should have three syllables instead of four (compare *Paradise Lost* 1.115).

---

[30]The sentence seems to be garbled because of its lack of punctuation, but Hughes in his modern-spelling version translates the difficult part as "'But we have all this while,' say they, 'been expecting it, and cannot yet attain it'" (887n).

thir own good both religious and civil, thir own libertie and the only means thereof, as shall be heer laid before them, and will elect thir Knights and Burgesses able men, and according to the just and necessarie qualifications (which for aught I hear, remain yet in force unrepeald, as they were formerly decreed in Parlament) men not addicted to a single person or house of lords, the work is don; at least the foundation firmly laid of a free Commonwealth, and good part also erected of the main structure. For the ground and basis of every just and free government (since men have smarted so oft for committing all to one person) is a general councel of ablest men, chosen by the people to consult of public affairs from time to time for the common good. In this Grand Councel must the sovrantie, not transferrd, but delegated only, and as it were deposited, reside; with this caution they must have the forces by sea and land committed to them for preservation of the common peace and libertie; must raise and manage the public revenue, at least with som inspectors deputed for satisfaction of the people, how it is imploid; must make or propose, as more expressly shall be said anon, civil laws; treat of commerce, peace, or warr with forein nations, and for the carrying on som particular affairs with more secrecie and expedition, must elect, as they have alreadie out of thir own number and others, a Councel of State.

And although it may seem strange at first hearing, by reason that mens mindes are prepossessed[31] with the notion of successive Parlaments, I affirme that the Grand or General Councel being well chosen, should be perpetual: for so thir business is or may be, and oft times urgent; the opportunitie of affairs gaind or lost in a moment. The day of counsel cannot be set as the day of a festival; but must be readie alwaies, to prevent or answer all occasions. By this continuance they will become everie way skilfullest, best provided of intelligence from abroad, best acquainted with the people at home, and the people with them. The ship of the Commonwealth is alwaies under sail; they sit at the stern; and if they stear well, what need is ther to change them; it being rather dangerous? Add to this, that the Grand Councel is both foundation and main pillar of the whole State; and to move pillars and foundations, not faultie, cannot be safe for the building. I see not therefor, how we can be advantag'd by successive and transitorie Parlaments; but that they are much likelier continually to unsettle rather then to settle a free government; to breed commotions, changes, novelties and uncertainties; to bring neglect upon present affairs and opportuni-

ties, while all mindes are suspense[32] with expectation of a new assemblie, and the assemblie for a good space taken up with the new setling of it self. After which, if they finde no great work to do, they will make it, by altering or repealing former acts, or making and multiplying new; that they may seem to see what thir predecessors saw not, and not to have assembld for nothing: till all law be lost in the multitude of clashing statutes. But if the ambition of such as think themselves injur'd that they also partake not of the government, and are impatient till they be chosen, cannot brook the perpetuitie of others chosen before them, or if it be feard that long continuance of power may corrupt sincerest men, the known expedient is, and by som lately propounded, that annually (or if the space be longer, so much perhaps the better) the third part of Senators may go out according to the precedence of thir election, and the like number be chosen in thir places, to prevent the setling of too absolute a power, if it should be perpetual: and this they call a *partial rotation*. But I could wish that this wheel or partial wheel in State, if it be possible, might be avoided; as having too much affinitie with the wheel of fortune. For it appeers not how this can be don, without danger and mischance of putting out[33] a great number of the best and ablest: in whose stead new elections may bring in as many raw, unexperienc'd and otherwise affected, to the weakning and much altering for the wors of public transactions. Neither do I think a perpetual Senat, especially chosen and entrusted by the people, much in this land to be feard, where the well-affected either in a standing armie, or in a setled militia have thir arms in thir own hands. Safest therefor to me it seems and of least hazard or interruption to affairs, that none of the Grand Councel be mov'd, unless by death or just conviction of som crime: for what can be expected firm or stedfast from a floating foundation? however, I forejudge not any probably expedient, any temperament that can be found in things of this nature so disreputable on either side. Yet least this which I affirme, be thought my single opinion, I shall add sufficient testimonie. Kingship it self is therefor counted the more safe and durable, because the king and, for the most part, his councel, is not chang'd during life: but a Commonwealth is held immortal; and therin firmest, safest and most above fortune: for the death of a king, causeth ofttimes many dangerous alterations; but the death now and then of a Senator is not felt; the main bodie of them still continuing permanent in greatest and noblest Commonwealths, and as it were

---

[31]Correcting "prepossed" in the original.

[32]In a state of suspense (the adjective form preceded the modern idiom "be full of suspense").

[33]Expelling, tossing out.

eternal. Therefor among the *Jews*, the supreme councel of seaventie, call'd the *Sanhedrim*, founded by *Moses*, in *Athens*, that of the *Areopagus*, in *Sparta*, that of the Ancients, in *Rome*, the Senat, consisted of members chosen for term of life; and by that means remain as it were still the same to generations. In *Venice* they change indeed ofter then every year som particular councels of State, as that of six, or such other;[34] but the true Senat, which upholds and sustains the government, is the whole aristocracie immovable. So in the United Provinces, the States General, which are indeed but a councel of state deputed by the whole union, are not usually the same persons for above three or six years; but the States of every citie, in whom the sovrantie hath bin plac'd time out of minde, are a standing Senat, without succession, and accounted chiefly in that regard the main prop of thir liberty. And why they should be so in every well orderd Commonwealth, they who write of policie, give these reasons; "That[35] to make the Senat successive, not only impairs the dignitie and lustre of the Senat, but weakens the whole Commonwealth, and brings it into manifest danger; while by this means the secrets of State are frequently divulgd, and matters of greatest consequence committed to inexpert and novice counselors, utterly to seek in the full and intimate knowledge of affairs past." I know not therefor what should be peculiar in *England* to make successive Parlaments thought safest, or convenient here more then in other nations, unless it be the fickl'ness which is attributed to us as we are Ilanders:[36] but good education and acquisit[37] wisdom ought to correct the fluxible fault, if any such be, of our watry situation. It will be objected, that in those places where they had perpetual Senats, they had also popular remedies against thir growing too imperious: as in *Athens*, beside *Areopagus*,

another Senat of four or five hundred;[38] in *Sparta*, the *Ephori*;[39] in *Rome*, the Tribunes of the people. But the event tels us, that these remedies either little availd the people, or brought them to such a licentious and unbridl'd democratie,[40] as in fine[41] ruind themselves with thir own excessive power. So that the main reason urg'd why popular assemblies are to be trusted with the peoples libertie, rather then a Senat of principal men, because great men will be still endeavoring to inlarge thir power, but the common sort will be contented to maintain thir own libertie, is by experience found false; none being more immoderat and ambitious to amplifie thir power, then such popularities;[42] which was seen in the people of *Rome*; who at first contented to have thir Tribunes, at length contended with the Senat that one Consul, then both; soon after, that the Censors and Prætors also should be created Plebeian, and the whole empire put into their hands; adoring lastly those, who most were advers to the Senat, till *Marius* by fulfilling thir inordinat desires, quite lost them all the power for which they had so long bin striving, and left them under the tyrannie of *Sylla*:[43] the ballance therefor must be exactly so set, as to preserve and keep up due autoritie on either side, as well in the Senat as in the people. And this annual rotation of a Senat to consist of three hundred, as is lately propounded,[44] requires also another popular assembly upward of a thousand, with an answerable rotation. Which besides that it will be liable to all those inconveniencies found in the foresaid remedies, cannot but be troublesom and chargeable, both in thir motion and thir session,[45] to the whole land; unweildie with thir own bulk, unable in so great a number to mature thir consultations as they ought, if any be

---

[34]Milton's experience with the republic of Venice might have been firsthand, since he did visit there, but he might also have discussed Venice with its English ambassador, Henry Wotton, in the 1630s. See also the letter to a friend dated October 29, 1659, which shows Milton thinking of Venice's system of government (Yale 7: 327).

[35]In the second edition, as well as the first, each line of text is preceded by a quotation mark, as in French printing practice today. So far as I know, this is the first instance of quotation marks in the printing of any of Milton's works, though not in his manuscript material. Milton may have been quoting Jean Bodin, *De Republica* (Frankfurt, 1641). The Yale editors note that the word "Whole" was deleted in the second edition (7: 437n).

[36]The theory, derived ultimately from Plato (*Laws* 4: 704), made people who lived on islands, thus nearer the ocean, less stable, politically, than inhabitants of a continent. Bodin supposes them to be "more subtill, politike, and cunning, than those that lie farr from the sea and traffique" (Jean Bodin, *The Six Books of a Commonweale*, ed. Kenneth Douglas McRae [Cambridge: Cambridge UP, 1962]: 564).

[37]Acquired, not innate.

[38]The Areopagus, a small body of archons, elite ex-magistrates of Athens, had been appointed for life. About 621 BCE, Draco ordained a council of 401 members, chosen by lot from the citizenry of the city state.

[39]Ephors (corporately the Ephorate) comprised a legislative body in Sparta designed to replace a council of elders. It may have originated in the seventh century BCE.

[40]Milton uses "democritie" here to mean something like "mob-rule."

[41]Ultimately.

[42]Popular or democratic governments.

[43]The conflict of wills led Gaius Marius (157–86 BCE), a tribune who rose to military power in Rome, into a major civil war with the forces of Lucius Cornelius Sulla (138–78 BCE); both leaders tyrannically exterminated their enemies. Milton's source is *Plutarch's Lives*, specifically the lives of Lycurgus and Sulla. Milton quotes Juvenal's remark on Sulla on the title page of this second edition, causing the Yale editors to conclude that Milton was comparing General Monck to Sulla, making him out to be more of a tyrant than a believer in a republic (7: 406).

[44]In one or another of the Rota publications of January and February, 1660.

[45]"Inconvenient and expensive, both in their moving (to and from sittings) and their sittings (in session)" (Yale 7: 441n).

allotted them, and that they meet not from so many parts remote to sit a whole year lieger[46] in one place, only now and then to hold up a forrest of fingers, or to convey each man his bean or ballot into the box,[47] without reason shewn or common deliberation; incontinent[48] of secrets, if any be imparted to them, emulous and always jarring with the other Senat. The much better way doubtless will be in this wavering condition of our affairs, to deferr the changing or circumscribing of our Senat, more then may be done with ease, till the Commonwealth be throughly setl'd in peace and safetie, and they themselves give us the occasion. Militarie men hold it dangerous to change the form of battel in view of an enemie: neither did the people of *Rome* bandie with thir Senat while any of the *Tarquins*[49] livd, the enemies of thir libertie, nor sought by creating Tribunes to defend themselves against the fear of thir Patricians, till sixteen years after the expulsion of thir kings, and in full securitie of thir state, they had or thought they had just cause given them by the Senat. Another way will be, to wel-qualifie and refine elections: not committing all to the noise and shouting of a rude multitude, but permitting only those of them who are rightly qualifi'd, to nominat as many as they will; and out of that number others of a better breeding, to chuse a less number more judiciously, till after a third or fourth sifting and refining of exactest choice, they only be left chosen who are the due number, and seem by most voices the worthiest. To make the people fittest to chuse, and the chosen fittest to govern, will be to mend our corrupt and faulty education, to teach the people faith not without vertue, temperance, modestie, sobrietie, parsimonie, justice; not to admire wealth or honour; to hate turbulence and ambition; to place every one his privat welfare and happiness in the public peace, libertie and safetie. They shall not then need to be much mistrustfull of thir chosen Patriots in the Grand Councel; who will be then rightly call'd the true keepers of our libertie, though the most of thir business will be in forein affairs. But to prevent all mistrust, the people then will have thir several ordinarie assemblies (which will henceforth quite annihilate the odious power and name of Committies) in the chief towns of every countie, without the trouble, charge, or time lost of summoning and assembling from far in so great a number, and so long residing

from thir own houses, or removing of thir families, to do as much at home in thir several shires, entire or subdivided, toward the securing of thir libertie, as a numerous assembly of them all formd and conven'd on purpose with the wariest rotation. Wherof I shall speak more ere the end of this discourse: for it may be referrd to time, so we be still going on by degrees to perfection. The people well weighing and performing these things, I suppose would have no cause to fear, though the *Parlament*, abolishing that name, as originally signifying but the *parlie* of our Lords and Commons with thir *Norman* king when he pleasd to call them, should, with certain limitations of thir power, sit perpetual, if thir ends be faithfull and for a free Commonwealth, under the name of a Grand or General Councel. Till this be don, I am in doubt whether our State will be ever certainly and throughly setl'd; never likely till then to see an end of our troubles and continual changes or at least never the true settlement and assurance of our libertie. The Grand Councel being thus firmly constituted to perpetuitie, and still, upon the death or default of any member, suppli'd and kept in full number, ther can be no cause alleag'd why peace, justice, plentifull trade and all prosperitie should not thereupon ensue throughout the whole land; with as much assurance as can be of human things, that they shall so continue (if God favour us, and our wilfull sins provoke him not) even to the coming of our true and rightfull and only to be expected King, only worthie as he is our only Saviour, the Messiah, the Christ, the only heir of his eternal father, the only by him anointed and ordaind since the work of our redemption finishd, Universal Lord of all mankinde. The way propounded is plane, easie and open before us; without intricacies, without the introducement of new or obsolete forms, or terms, or exotic models; idea's that would effect nothing, but with a number of new injunctions to manacle the native liberty of mankind; turning all vertue into prescription, servitude, and necessitie, to the great impairing and frustrating of Christian libertie: I say again, this way lies free and smooth before us; is not tangl'd with inconveniencies; invents no new incumbrances; requires no perilous, no injurious alteration or circumscription of mens lands and proprieties; secure, that in this Commonwealth, temporal and spiritual lords remov'd, no man or number of men can attain to such wealth or vast possession, as will need the hedge of an Agrarian law[50] (never succesful, but the cause rather of sedition,

---

[46]Ledger, account book.

[47]Milton ridicules either the show-of-fingers vote or the silent vote of placing beans into one container or another.

[48]Indiscreet, blabbing.

[49]The family of Tarquins, semi-legendary but said to be living in the fifth century BCE. The famous rape of Lucrece, wife of Tarquinius Collatinus, by Sextus, son of Tarquinius Superbus, resulted in her death and the overthrow of the Tarquin family in 510 BCE by Junius Brutus.

---

[50]In *Oceana*, Harrington proposed a tax base for his utopian government based on an agrarian law whereby landed estates should not be allowed to exceed the given value of £2000 a year (see *Oceana*, in *Compete Political Works of James Harrington* [Cambridge: Cambridge UP, 1977]).

save only where it began seasonable with first possession) to confine them from endangering our public libertie; to conclude, it can have no considerable objection made against it, that it is not practicable: least it be said hereafter, that we gave up our libertie for want of a readie way or distinct form propos'd of a free Commonwealth. And this facility we shall have above our next neighbouring Commonwealth (if we can keep us from the fond conceit of somthing like a duke of *Venice*, put lately into many mens heads, by som one or other sutly driving on under that notion his own ambitious ends to lurch[51] a crown) that our liberty shall not be hamperd or hoverd over by any ingagement to such a potent familie as the house of *Nassaw*[52] of whom to stand in perpetual doubt and suspicion, but we shall live the cleerest and absolutest free nation in the world.

On the contrarie, if ther be a king, which the inconsiderate multitude are now so madd upon, mark how far short we are like to com of all those happinesses, which in a free state we shall immediatly be possessd of. First, the Grand Councel, which, as I shewd before, should sit perpetually (unless thir leisure give them now and then som intermissions or vacations, easilie manageable by the Councel of State left sitting) shall be call'd, by the kings good will and utmost endeavor, as seldom as may be. For it is only the king's right, he will say, to call a parlament; and this he will do most commonly about his own affairs rather then the kingdom's, as will appeer planely so soon as they are call'd. For what will thir business then be and the chief expence of thir time, but an endless tugging between petition of right and royal prerogative,[53] especially about the negative voice, militia, or subsidies, demanded and oft times extorted without reasonable cause appeering to the Commons, who are the only true representatives of the people, and thir libertie, but will be then mingl'd with a court-faction; besides which within thir own walls, the sincere part of them who stand faithfull to the people, will again have to deal with two troublesom counter-working adversaries from without, meer creatures[54] of the king, spiritual, and the greater part, as is likeliest, of temporal lords, nothing concernd with the peoples libertie. If these prevail not in what they please, though never so much against the peoples interest, the Parlament shall be soon dissolvd, or sit and do nothing; not sufferd to

remedie the least greevance, or enact aught advantageous to the people. Next, the Councel of State shall not be chosen by the Parlament, but by the king, still his own creatures, courtiers and favorites; who will be sure in all thir counsels to set thir maister's grandure and absolute power, in what they are able, far above the peoples libertie. I denie not but that ther may be such a king, who may regard the common good before his own, may have no vitious favorite, may hearken only to the wisest and incorruptest of his Parlament: but this rarely happens in a monarchie not elective; and it behoves not a wise nation to commit the summ of thir welbeing, the whole state of thir safetie to fortune. What need they; and how absurd would it be, when as they themselves to whom his chief vertue will be but to hearken, may with much better management and dispatch, with much more commendation of thir own worth and magnanimitie govern without a maister. Can the folly be paralleld, to adore and be the slaves of a single person for doing that which it is ten thousand to one whether he can or will do, and we without him might do more easily, more effectually, more laudably our selves? Shall we never grow old anough to be wise to make seasonable use of gravest autorities, experiences, examples? Is it such an unspeakable joy to serve, such felicitie to wear a yoke? to clink our shackles, lockt on by pretended law of subjection more intolerable and hopeless to be ever shaken off, then those which are knockt on by the illegal injurie and violence? *Aristotle*, our chief instructer at the Universities,[55] least this doctrine be thought *Sectarian*, as the royalist would have it thought, tels us in the third of his Politics, that certain men at first, for the matchless excellence of thir vertue above others, or som great public benifit, were created kings by the people; in small cities and territories, and in the scarcitie of others to be found like them: but when they abus'd thir power and governments grew larger, and the number of prudent men increasd, that then the people soon deposing thir tyrants, betook them, in all civilest places, to the form of a free Commonwealth. And why should we thus disparage and prejudicate[56] our own nation, as to fear a scarcitie of able and worthie men united in counsel to govern us, if we will but use diligence and impartiality to finde them out and chuse them, rather yoking our selves to a single person, the natural adversarie and oppressor of libertie, though good, yet far easier corruptible by the excess of his singular power and exaltation, or at best, not comparably sufficient to bear

---

[51]Probably to snatch it quickly, before someone else has a chance at it, as with grabbing food at a table (*OED* v. 1.3).

[52]William, Prince of Orange and of the house of Nassau, consolidated his power in the late 1500s as Stadtholder in the republic of the Netherlands.

[53]In the Petition of Right (1628), the rights of the king's subjects were listed.

[54]Agents, representatives.

---

[55]Aristotle, *Politics* 3.9.7.

[56]Judge our nation too hastily, in advance.

the weight of government, nor equally dispos'd to make us happie in the enjoyment of our libertie under him.

But admitt, that monarchie of it self may be convenient to som nations; yet to us who have thrown it out, receivd back again, it cannot but prove pernicious. For kings to com, never forgetting thir former ejection, will be sure to fortifie and arm themselves sufficiently for the future against all such attempts hereafter from the people: who shall be then so narrowly watchd and kept so low, that though they would never so fain and at the same rate of thir blood and treasure, they never shall be able to regain what they now have purchasd and may enjoy, or to free themselves from any yoke impos'd upon them: nor will they dare to go about it; utterly disheartn'd for the future, if these thir highest attempts prove unsuccesfull; which will be the triumph of all tyrants heerafter over any people that shall resist oppression; and thir song will then be, to others, how sped the rebellious *English*? to our posteritie, how sped the rebells your fathers? This is not my conjecture, but drawn from God's known denouncement against the gentilizing *Israelites*; who though they were governd in a Commonwealth[57] of God's own ordaining, he only thir king, they his peculiar people, yet affecting rather to resemble heathen, but pretending the misgovernment of *Samuel's* sons, no more a reason to dislike thir Commonwealth, then the violence of E*li's* sons[58] was imputable to that priesthood or religion, clamourd for a king. They had thir longing; but with this testimonie of God's wrath; *ye shall cry out in that day because of your king whom ye shall have chosen, and the Lord will not hear you in that day.* Us if he shall hear now, how much less will he hear when we cry heerafter, who once deliverd by him from a king, and not without wondrous acts of his providence, insensible and unworthie of those high mercies, are returning precipitantly,[59] if he withold us not, back to the captivitie from whence he freed us. Yet neither shall we obtain or buy at an easie rate this new guilded yoke which thus transports us:[60] a new royal-revenue must be found, a new episcopal; for those are individual: both which being wholy dissipated[61] or

bought by privat persons or assign'd for service don, and especially to the Armie, cannot be recoverd without a general detriment and confusion to mens estates, or a heavie imposition on all mens purses; benifit to none, but to the worst and ignoblest sort of men, whose hope is to be either the ministers of court riot and excess, or the gainers by it: But not to speak more of losses and extraordinarie levies on our estates, what will then be the revenges and offences rememberd and returnd, not only by the chief person, but by all his adherents; accounts and reparations that will be requir'd, suites,[62] inditements, inquiries, discoveries, complaints, informations,[63] who knows against whom or how many, though perhaps neuters, if not to utmost infliction, yet to imprisonment, fines, banishment, or molestation; if not these, yet disfavor, discountnance, disregard and contempt on all but the known royalist or whom he favors, will be plenteous: nor let the new royaliz'd presbyterians[64] perswade themselves that thir old doings, though now recanted, will be forgotten; what ever conditions be contriv'd or trusted on. Will they not beleeve this; nor remember the pacification, how it was kept to the *Scots*; how other solemn promises many a time to us? Let them but now read the diabolical forerunning libells, the faces, the gestures that now appeer foremost and briskest in all public places; as the harbingers of those that are in expectation to raign over us; let them but hear the insolencies, the menaces, the insultings of our newly animated common enemies crept lately out of thir holes, thir hell, I might say, by the language of thir infernal pamphlets, the spue of every drunkard, every ribald; nameless, yet not for want of licence, but for very shame of thir own vile persons, not daring to name themselves, while they traduce others by name; and give us to foresee that they intend to second thir wicked words, if ever they have power, with more wicked deeds. Let our zealous backsliders forethink now with themselves, how thir necks yok'd with these tigers of Bacchus,[65] these new fanatics of not the preaching but the sweating-tub,[66] inspir'd with nothing holier then the Venereal pox, can draw one way under monarchie to

---

[57]Corrected from "Commouwealth" (inverted "n").
[58]The same as Milton's Sons of Belial, described in 1 Samuel 2.12–17 as corrupt priests demanding a portion of the people's food as their due. Milton identified the potential clergy or returning bishops of Charles II with the Sons of Belial, somehow combining violence and simony, ribaldry, drunken vomiting, venereal pox, and devils crawling out of hellholes.
[59]Very swiftly, as if in a free fall.
[60]The people seem to be pictured as being made to purchase a golden yoke that then "transports" or imprisons them.
[61]Dispersed (with the possible overtones of being idly thrown away or wasted).

[62]Suits, as in law-suits.
[63]Sometimes used in the plural in the seventeenth and eighteenth centuries, as would "news" be.
[64]Playing on the irony that the very presbyterians who had supported the execution of Charles I were now supporting his son.
[65]Again, Charles II's followers are compared with dissolute drunkards in the form of followers of Bacchus. Tigers or leopards were supposed to pull the chariot of the wine-god, as *various* "ugly-headed monsters" are associated with Milton's Comus.
[66]The sweating tub would be an enclosure where people with venereal pox try to sweat out the fever, whereas non-conformist preachers would be described as using a preaching tub (*OED* 4), probably the way "soap-box orator" has been used in the twentieth century.

the establishing of church discipline with these new-disgorg'd atheismes: yet shall they not have the honor to yoke with these, but shall be yok'd under them; these shall plow on their backs. And do they among them who are so forward to bring in the single person, think to be by him trusted or long regarded? So trusted they shall be and so regarded, as by kings are wont reconcil'd enemies; neglected and soon after discarded, if not prosecuted for old traytors; the first inciters, beginners, and more then to the third part actors of all that followd; it will be found also, that there must be then as necessarily as now (for the contrarie part will be still feard) a standing armie; which for certain shall not be this, but of the fiercest Cavaliers, of no less expence, and perhaps again under *Rupert*:[67] but let this armie be sure they shall be soon disbanded, and likeliest without arrear or pay; and being disbanded, not be sure but they may as soon be question for being in arms against thir king: the same let them fear, who have contributed monie; which will amount to no small number that must then take thir turn to be made delinquents and compounders. They who past reason and recoverie are devoted to kingship, perhaps will answer, that a greater part by far of the Nation will have it so; the rest therefor must yield. Not so much to convince these, which I little hope, as to confirm them who yield not, I reply: that this greatest part have both in reason and the trial of just battel, lost the right of their election what the government shall be: of them who have not lost that right, whether they for kingship be the greater number who can certainly determin? Suppose they be; yet of freedom they partake all alike, one main end of government: which if the greater part value not, but will degenerately forgoe, is it just or reasonable, that most voices against the[68] main end of government should enslave the less number that would be free? More just it is doubtless, if it com to force, that a less number compell a greater to retain, which can be no wrong to them, thir libertie, then that a greater number for the pleasure of thir baseness, compell a less most injuriously to be thir fellow slaves. They who seek nothing but thir own just libertie, have alwaies right to winn it and to keep it, when ever they have power, be the voices never so numerous that oppose it. And how much we above others are concernd to defend it from kingship, and from them who in pursuance therof so perniciously would betray

us and themselves to most certain miserie and thraldom, will be needless to repeat.

Having thus far shewn with what ease we may now obtain a free Commonwealth, and by it with as much ease all the freedom, peace, justice, plentie that we can desire, on the other side the difficulties, troubles, uncertainties, nay rather impossibilities to enjoy these things constantly under a monarch, I will now proceed to shew more particularly wherin our freedom and flourishing condition will be more ample and secure to us under a free Commonwealth then under kingship.

The whole freedom of man consists either in spiritual or civil libertie. As for spiritual, who can be at rest, who can enjoy any thing in this world with contentment, who hath not libertie to serve God and to save his own soul, according to the best light[69] which God hath planted in him to that purpose, by the reading of his reveal'd will and the guidance of his holy spirit? That this is best pleasing to God, and that the whole Protestant Church allows no supream judge or rule in matters of religion, but the scriptures, and these to be interpreted by the[70] scriptures themselves, which necessarily inferrs liberty of conscience, I have heretofore prov'd at large in another treatise, and might yet furder by the public declarations, confessions and admonitions of whole churches and states, obvious in all historie since the Reformation.

This liberty of conscience which above all other things ought to be to all men dearest and most precious, no government more inclinable not to favor only but to protect, then a free Commonwealth; as being most magnanimous, most fearless and confident of its own fair proceedings. Wheras kingship, though looking big, yet indeed most pusillanimous, full of fears, full of jealousies, startl'd at every ombrage, as it hath bin observd of old to have ever suspected most and mistrusted them who were in most esteem for vertue and generositie of minde, so it is now known to have most in doubt and suspicion them who are most reputed to be religious. Queen *Elizabeth* though her self accounted so good a Protestant, so moderate, so confident of her Subjects love would never give way so much as to Presbyterian reformation in this land, though once and again be-

---

[67]Prince Rupert of Bavaria (1619–1682), who had been engaged by his uncle, Charles I, to become a general in charge of cavalry in the King's forces, in 1642. Though he had been allowed to leave England in 1645, the English parliamentary forces would still remember him as a brilliant strategist.

[68]A repeated "the" follows, in the second edition.

[69]The "inner light" that would also allow individuals to interpret the truths of the Bible with direct inspiration from God, or would allow Milton to feel divine inspiration while writing *Paradise Lost.* Compare the phrase "innerman, which may be term'd the spirit of the soul," in *Reason of Church-government* (Yale 1: 837).

[70]Correcting a doubled "the."

sought, as *Camden* relates,[71] but imprisond and persecuted the very proposers therof; alleaging it as her
minde & maxim unalterable, that such reformation
would diminish regal autoritie. What liberty of conscience can we then expect of others, far wors principl'd
from the cradle, traind up and governd by *Popish* and
Spanish counsels, and on such depending hitherto for
subsistence? Especially what can this last Parlament
expect, who having reviv'd lately and publishd the covnant, have reingag'd themselves, never to readmitt Episcopacie; which no son of *Charls* returning, but will most
certainly bring back with him, if he regard the last and
strictest charge of his father, *to persevere in not the doctrin only, but government of the church of* England; *not to
neglect the speedie and effectual suppressing of errors and
schisms*; among which he accounted Presbyterie one of
the chief: or if notwithstanding that charge of his father,
he submitt to the covnant, how will he keep faith to us
with disobedience to him, or regard that faith given,
which must be founded on the breach of that last and
solemnest paternal charge, and the reluctance, I may say
the antipathie which is in all kings against Presbyterian
and Independent discipline? for they hear the gospel
speaking much of libertie; a word which both monarchie and her bishops both fear and hate, but a free Commonwealth both favors and promotes; and not the word
only, but the thing it self. But let our governors beware
in time, least thir hard measure to libertie of conscience
be found the rock wheron they shipwrack themselves as
others have now don before them in the cours wherin
God was directing thir stearage[72] to a free Commonwealth, and the abandoning of all those whom they call
sectaries,[73] for the detected falshood and ambition of
som, be a wilfull rejection of thir own chief strength and
interest in the freedom of all Protestant religion, under
what abusive name soever calumniated.

The other part of our freedom consists in the civil
rights and advancements of every person according to
his merit: the enjoyment of those never more certain,
and the access to these never more open, then in a free
Commonwealth. Both which in my opinion may be

best and soonest obtain, if every countie in the land
were made a kinde of subordinate Commonaltie or
Commonwealth, and one chief town or more, according as the shire is in circuit,[74] made cities, if they be not
so call'd alreadie; where the nobilitie and chief gentry
from a proportionable compas of territorie annexd to
each citie, may build, houses or palaces, befitting thir
qualitie, may bear part in the government, make thir
own judicial laws, or use these that are, and execute
them by thir own elected judicatures and judges without
appeal, in all things of civil government between man
and man. so they shall have justice in thir own hands,
law executed fully and finally in thir own counties and
precincts, long wishd, and spoken of, but never yet
obtain; they shall have none then to blame but
themselves, if it be not well administerd; and fewer laws
to expect or fear from the supreme autoritie; or to those
that shall be made, of any great concernment to public
libertie, they may without much trouble in these
commonalties or in more general assemblies call'd to
their cities from the whole territorie on such occasion,
declare and publish thir assent or dissent by deputies
within a time limited sent to the Grand Councel: yet so
as this thir judgment declar'd shal submitt to the greater
number of other counties or commonalties, and not
avail them to any exemption of themselves, or refusal of
agreement with the rest, as it may in any of the United
Provinces, being sovran within it self, oft times to the
great disadvantage of that union. In these imploiments
they may much better then they do now, exercise and
fit themselves, till thir lot fall to be chosen into the
Grand Councel, according as thir worth and merit shall
be taken notice of by the people. As for controversies
that shall happen between men of several counties, they
may repair as they do now, to the capital citie, or any
other more commodious, indifferent[75] place and equal
judges. And this I finde to have bin practisd in the old
Athenian Commonwealth, reputed the first and ancientest place of civilitie in all *Greece*; that they had in thir
several cities, a peculiar; in *Athens*, a common government; and thir right, as it befell them, to the
administration of both. They should have heer also
schools and academies at thir own choice, wherin thir
children may be bred up in thir own sight to all learning
and noble education not in grammar only, but in all
liberal arts[76] and exercises. This would soon spread
much more knowledge and civilitie, yea religion
through all parts of the land, by communicating the natural heat of government and culture more distributive-

---

[71]Hughes quotes from William Camden, a book Hughes identifies as *The
History of Elizabeth*: "The Reform'd Religion being now Establish'd by
Parliament, the Queen's chief Care and Concern was how to guard and
protect it from the several Attacks and Practices of . . . its profess'd
Enemies . . . . And as she would admit of no innovations herein, so she
studied to square her own Life and Actions by so even a balance, as to
preserve the character of one not given to change" (896n). I find *The
history of the most renowned and victorious princess Elizabeth* listed in
Wing as being published in London, 1675.
[72]The act of steering a ship.
[73]Milton may be alluding to his own remark in *Eikonoklastes*: "I never
knew that time in *England*, when men of truest Religion were not
counted Sectaries" (Yale 3: 348).

---

[74]According to the boundaries of the shire, and how large it is.
[75]Impartial, unbiased.
[76]Correcting "ars" in the original.

ly to all extreme parts, which now lie numm and neglected, would soon make the whole nation more industrious, more ingenuous at home, more potent, more
honorable abroad. To this a free Commonwealth will
easily assent; (nay the Parlament hath had alreadie som
such thing in designe) for all governments a Commonwealth aims most to make the people flourishing,
vertuous, noble and high spirited. Monarchs will never
permitt: whose aim is to make the people, wealthie indeed perhaps and well fleec't, for thir own shearing and
the supplie of regal prodigalitie; but otherwise softest,
basest, vitiousest, servilest, easiest to be kept under; and
not only in fleece, but in minde also sheepishest; and
will have all the benches of judicature annexd to the
throne, as a gift of royal grace that we have justice don
us; whenas nothing can be more essential to the freedom
of a people, then to have the administration of justice
and all public ornaments in thir own election and
within their own bounds, without long travelling or
depending on remote places to obtain thir right or any
civil accomplishment; so it be not supreme, but
subordinate to the general power and union of the
whole Republic. In which happy firmness as in the
particular above mentiond, we shall also far exceed the
United Provinces, by having, not as they (to the retarding and distracting oft times of thir counsels or
urgentest occasions) many Sovranties united in one
Commonwealth, but many Commonwealths under one
united and entrusted Sovrantie. And when we have our
forces by sea and land, either of a faithful Armie or a
setl'd Militia, in our own hands to the firm establishing
of a free Commonwealth, publick accounts under our
own inspection, general laws and taxes with thir causes
in our own domestic suffrages, judicial laws, office and
ornaments at home in our own ordering and administration, all distinction of lords and commoners, that may
any way divide or sever the publick interest, remov'd,
what can a perpetual senat have then wherin to grow
corrupt, wherin to encroach upon us or usurp; or if they
do, wherin to be formidable? Yet if all this avail not to
remove the fear or envie of a perpetual sitting, it may be
easilie provided, to change a third part of them yearly or
every two or three years, as was above mentiond; or
that it be at those times in the peoples choice, whether
they will change them, or renew thir power, as they
shall finde cause.

I have no more to say at present: few words will save
us, well considerd; few and easie things, now seasonably
don. But if the people be so affected, as to prostitute religion and libertie to the vain and groundless apprehension, that nothing but kingship can restore trade, not remembring the frequent plagues and pestilences that then
wasted this citie, such as through God's mercie we never

have felt since, and that trade flourishes no where more
then in the free Commonwealths of *Italie, Germanie,*
and the Low-Countries before thir eyes at this day, yet
if trade be grown so craving and importunate through
the profuse living of tradesmen, that nothing can
support it, but the luxurious expences of a nation upon
trifles or superfluities, so as if the people generally
should betake themselves to frugalitie, it might prove a
dangerous matter, least tradesmen should mutinie for
want of trading, and that therefor we must forgoe & set
to sale religion, libertie, honor, safetie; all concernments
Divine or human to keep us trading, if lastly, after all
this light among us, the same reason shall pass for current to put our necks again under kingship, as was made
use of by the *Jews* to returne back to *Egypt* and to the
worship of thir idol queen, because they falsly imagind
that they then livd in more plentie and prosperitie, our
condition is not sound but rotten, both in religion and
all civil prudence; and will bring us soon, the way we
are marching, to those calamities which attend alwaies
and unavoidably on luxurie, all national judgments
under forein or domestic slaverie: so far we shall be
from mending our condition by monarchizing our government, whatever new conceit now possesses us.
However with all hazard I ventur'd what I thought my
duty to speak in season, and to forewarne my countrey
in time: wherein I doubt not but ther be many wise men
in all places and degrees, but am sorrie the effects of
wisdom are so little seen among us. Many circumstances
and particulars I could have added in those things
wherof I have spoken; but a few main matters now put
speedily in execution, will suffice to recover us, and set
all right: and ther will want at no time who are good at
circumstances; but men who set thir mindes on main
matters and sufficiently urge them, in these most difficult times I finde not many. What I have spoken, is the
language of that which is not call'd amiss *the good Old
Cause*: if it seem strange to any, it will not seem more
strange, I hope, then convincing to backsliders. Thus
much I should perhaps have said though I were sure I
should have spoken only to trees and stones; and had
none to cry to, but with the Prophet, *O earth, earth,
earth!* to tell the very soil it self, what her perverse
inhabitants are deaf to. Nay though what I have spoke,
should happ'n (which Thou suffer not, who didst create
mankind free; nor Thou next, who didst redeem us
from being servants of men!) to be the last words of our
expiring libertie. But I trust I shall have spoken
perswasion to abundance of sensible and ingenuous
men; to som perhaps whom God may raise of these
stones to become children of reviving libertie; and may
reclaim, thought they seem now chusing them to be a
captain back for *Egypt*, to bethink themselves a little and

consider whither[77] they are rushing; to exhort this torrent also of the people, not to be so impetuos, but to keep thir due channell; and at length recovering and uniting thir better resolutions, now that they see alreadie how open and unbounded the insolence and rage is of our common enemies, to stay these ruinous proceedings; justly and timely fearing to what a precipice of destruction the deluge of this epidemic madness would hurrie us through the general defection of a misguided and abus'd multitude.

The end.

---

[77]Printed as "whether" in the second edition, here corrected to "whither."

Of True Religion (1673)

OCCASION

Milton's fifteen-page pamphlet pleading for religious toleration for all except Roman Catholics was written probably in early 1673, certainly before May 6, when it was first advertised. As Milton well knew, the so-called Clarendon Code, named for Charles's minister Edwin Hyde, Earl of Clarendon, had attempted to control puritan radicalism inch by inch. The Clarendon Code "had put fetters on dissenting Protestants, ejecting ministers, banning meetings, stopping academies, and forcing conformity on lay officials as well" (Brown 185). "In sum, a large proportion of Englishmen were restrained from conscientious worship and their leaders were prevented from earning a livelihood" (Yale 7: 409–10). Though Milton's reputation as a regicide worked against his being taken seriously (von Maltzahn), he again showed singular courage in defying the wishes of Charles II and the policies of his administration. Charles wished for toleration for Roman Catholics, as with his Portuguese and Catholic wife. But Milton and other parliamentarians were justly worried that Charles might convert to Catholicism or might allow a Catholic to succeed him. Milton also rails against the decadence of the Restoration in pointed attacks against drunkenness and debauchery. "As in the jeremiads of the 1660s, Milton interprets the plague and fire [visited on the City of London] as divine punishment . . . [and he also] took advantage of popular feeling against popery to attack Stuart absolutism indirectly" (160–61). His pleas for religious tolerance, however, anticipate those of John Locke and Thomas Jefferson, though he may be pleading for his own parish in his desire that various forms of anti-Trinitarianism or the notion that the God the Son should be considered subordinate to God the Father might be tolerated. True religion, as he defines it, is based only on Scripture, not on the schisms created by human intervention in times later than apostolic.

PROSE STYLE

Milton writes for a common audience, not a highly educated or parliamentary one, and he practices the plain-speaking terseness exemplified in the speech of Jesus in *Paradise Regain'd*. My word-processor tells me that the average sentence length in the pamphlet is about twenty-three words, short by Miltonic standards (Corns 118). There are metaphors and similes, but none so resonant or reverberatory as many of the images in Milton's youthful prose, as in the image of England as falcon or eagle in *Areopagitica*. Probably the most exciting images in *Of True Religion* are the satirical cuts at Popery, as with "they adore their God under Bread and Wine" or "easy Confession, easy Absolution, Pardons, Indulgences, Masses for him both quick and dead, *Agnus Dei's*, Reliques, and the like." Milton saves his last bit of prose invective for the English Sons of Belial who freely embrace "Pride, Luxury, Drunkenness, Whoredom, Cursing, Swearing, bold and open Atheism every where abounding." He was always good at nailing his enemies with lists of their fetishes or of their collective vices.

TEXT

Printed well after the onset of Milton's blindness, *Of True Religion* makes no pretense to be close to Milton's known habits of orthography. In the pamphlet, the pronoun is spelled "their," not "thir," and virtually none of Milton's known spelling habits come through in the printed version. Most likely, the copy-text was the product of a manuscript produced by dictation, since Milton himself was by this time capable only of making his signature, not of writing sentences on paper. Also, whoever left the manuscript with the printer did not try to impose a style sheet on the compositor. Capitalization is more at random than in the average book printed for Milton (adjectives, verbs, and gerunds are sometimes capitalized—not just nouns), following late seventeenth-century practice; spelling is likewise standardized, as opposed to being as eccentric as "voutsafe" or "Parlament."

Works Cited

Brown, Cedric C. *John Milton: A Literary Life*. New York: St. Martin's, 1995.

Corns, Thomas N. *Milton's Language*. Oxford: Blackwell, 1990.

Dzelzainis, Martin. "Milton's *Of True Religion* and the Earl of Castlemaine." *The Seventeenth Century* 7 (1992): 55–64.

Knoppers, Laura Lunger. *Historicizing Milton: Spectacle, Power, and Poetry in Restoration England*. Athens: U of Georgia P, 1994.

Milton, John. *Political Writings* [*Tenure of Kings and Magistrates, A Defence of the People of England*]. Ed. Martin Dzelzainis. Cambridge: Cambridge UP, 1991.

von Maltzahn, Nicholas. "The Whig Milton, 1667–1700." *Milton and Republicanism*. Ed. David Armitage, Armand Himy, and Quentin Skinner. Cambridge: Cambridge UP, 1995.

OF
True RELIGION,
HÆRESIE, SCHISM,
and TOLERATION.

IT is unknown to no man, who knows ought of concernment among us, that the increase of Popery is at this day no small trouble and offence to greatest part of the Nation; and the rejoycing of all good men that it is so; the more the more their rejoycing, that God hath giv'n a heart to the people to remember still their great and happy deliverance from Popish Thraldom, and to esteem so highly the precious benefit of his Gospel, so freely and so peaceably injoy'd among them. Since therefore some have already in Publick with many considerable Arguments exhorted the people to beware the growth of this Romish Weed; I thought it no less then a common duty to lend my hand, how unable soever, to so good a Purpose. I will not now enter into the Labyrinth of Councels and Fathers, an intangl'd wood which the Papist loves to fight in, not with hope of Victory, but to obscure the shame of an open overthrow: which yet in that kind of Combate,[1] many heretofore, and one of late, hath eminently giv'n them. And such matter of dispute with them, to Learned Men, is useful and very commendable: But I shall insist now on what is plainer to Common apprehension,[2] and what I have to say, without longer introduction.

True Religion is the true Worship and Service of God, learnt and believed from the Word of God only. No Man or Angel can know how God would be worshipt and serv'd unless God reveal it: He hath Reveal'd and taught it us in the holy Scriptures by inspir'd Ministers, and in the Gospel by his own Son and his Apostles, with the strictest command to reject all other traditions or additions whatsoever. According to that of St. *Paul, Though wee or an Angel from Heaven preach any other Gospel unto you, than that which wee have preacht unto you, let him be Anathema, or accurst.* And *Deut.* 4.2. *Ye shall not add to the word which I command you, neither shall you diminish ought from it.* Rev. 22.18,19. *If any man shall add,* &c. *If any man shall take away from the Words,* &c. With

good and Religious Reason therefore all Protestant Churches with one Consent, and particularly the Church of *England* in Her thirty nine Articles, Artic. *6th, 19th, 20th, 21st,* and elsewhere, maintain these two points, as the main Principles of true Religion: that the Rule of true Religion is the Word of God only: and that their Faith ought not to be an implicit faith, that is, to believe, though as the Church believes, against or without express authority of Scripture. And if all Protestants as universally as they hold these two Principles, so attentively and Religiously[3] would observe them, they would avoid and cut off many Debates and Contentions, Schisms and Persecutions, which too oft have been among them, and more firmly unite against the common adversary. For hence it directly follows, that no true Protestant can persecute, or not tolerate his fellow Protestant, though dissenting from him in som opinions, but he must flatly deny and Renounce these two his own main Principles, whereon true Religion is founded; while he compels his Brother from that which he believes as the manifest word of God, to an implicit faith (which he himself condemns) to the endangering of his Brothers soul, whether by rash belief, or outward Conformity: for *whatsoever is not of Faith, is Sin.*[4]

I will now as briefly show what is false Religion or Heresie, which will be done as easily: for of contraries the definitions must needs by contrary. Heresie therefore is a Religion taken up and believ'd from the traditions of men and additions to the word of God. Whence also it follows clearly, that of all known Sects or pretended Religions at this day in Christendom, Popery is the only or the greatest Heresie: and he who is so forward to brand all others for Hereticks, the obstinate Papist, the only Heretick. Hence one of their own famous Writers found just cause to stile the Romish Church *Mother of Error, School of Heresie.* And whereas the Papist boasts himself to be a Roman Catholick, it is a meer contradiction, one of the Popes Bulls, as if he should say, universal particular a Catholic Schismatic. For Catholic in Greek signifies universal: and the Christian Church was so call'd, as consisting of all Nations to whom the Gospel was to be preach't, in contradistincion to the Jewish Church, which consisted for the most part of Jews only.

Sects may be in a true Church[5] as well as in a false, when men follow the Doctrin too much for the Teachers sake, whom they think almost infallible; and this becomes, through Infirmity, implicit Faith; and the

---

[1] At least since *Areopagitica*, Milton sees the struggle towards religious truth or political freedom as warfare. *Areopagitica*'s picture of the "warfaring Christian" (Yale 2: 415) may be the first time he pictures such a struggle, and the fights of Jesus and Samson embody similar combat with evil or with conscience in *Paradise Regain'd* and *Samson Agonistes*.
[2] He is, in other words, writing to a popular audience, and not to one composed just of "Learned Men." Compare what Milton says about plainness of style and how it can serve to express learned ideas in *A Treatise of Civil Power* (Yale 7: 272).

[3] There was an inverted letter in "Religionsly" which I have corrected.
[4] "And he that doubteth is damned if he eat, because he eateth not of faith: for whatsoever is not of faith is sin" (Romans 14.23).
[5] Corrected from "may be a in true Church."

name Sectary, pertains to such a Disciple.

Schism is a rent or division in the Church, when it comes to the separating of Congregations; and may also happen to a true Church, as well as to a false; yet in the true needs not tend to the breaking of Communion; if they can agree in the right administration of that wherein they Communicate, keeping their other Opinions to themselves, not being destructive[6] to Faith. The Pharisees and Saduces were two Sects, yet both met together in their common worship of God at *Jerusalem*. But here the Papist will angrily demand, what! Are Lutherans, Calvinists, Anabaptists, Socinians, Arminians, no Hereticks? I answer, all these may have some errors, but are no Hereticks. Heresie is in the Will, in misunderstanding the Scripture after all sincere endeavours to understand it rightly: Hence it was said well by one of the Ancients, *Err I may, but a Heretick I will not be.* It is a humane frailty to err, and no man is infallible here on earth. But so long as all these profess to set the Word of God only before them as the Rule of faith and obedience; and use all diligence and sincerity of heart, by reading, by learning, by study, by prayer for Illumination of the holy Spirit, to understand the Rule and obey it, they have done what man can do: God will assuredly pardon them, as he did the friends of *Job*, good and pious men, though much mistaken, as there it appears, in some Points of Doctrin. But some will say, with Christians it is otherwise, whom God hath promis'd by his Spirit to teach all things. True, all things absolutely necessary to salvation: But the hottest disputes among Protestant calmly and charitably enquir'd into, will be found less then such. The Lutheran holds Consubstantiation; an error indeed, but not mortal. The Calvinist is taxt with Predestination, and to make God the Author of sin; not with any dishonourable thought of God, but it may be overzealously asserting his absolute power, not without plea of Scripture. The Anabaptist is accus'd of Denying Infants their right to Baptism; again they say, they deny nothing but what the Scripture denies them. The Arian and Socinian are charg'd to dispute against the Trinity: they affirm to believe the Father, Son, and Holy Ghost, according to Scripture, and the Apostolic Creed; as for terms of Trinity, Triniunity, Coessentiality, Tripersonality, and the like, they reject them as Scholastic Notions, not to be found in Scripture, which by a general Protestant Maxim is plain and perspicuous abundantly to explain its own meaning in the properest words, belonging to so high a Matter and so necessary to be known; a mystery indeed in their Sophistic Subtilties, but in Scripture a plain Doctrin. Their

other Opinions are of less Moment. They dispute the satisfaction of Christ, or rather the word *Satisfaction*, as not Scriptural: but they acknowledge him both God and their Saviour. The Arminian lastly is condemn'd for setting up free will against free grace; but that Imputation he disclaims in all his writings, and grounds himself largly upon Scripture only. It cannot be deny'd that the Authors or late Revivers of all these Sects or Opinions, were Learned, Worthy, Zealous, and Religious Men, as appears by their lives written, and the same of their many Eminent and Learned followers, perfect and powerful in the Scriptures, holy and unblameable in their lives: and it cannot be imagin'd that God would desert such painful and zealous labourers in his Church, and ofttimes great sufferers for their Conscience, to damnable Errors & a Reprobate sense, who had so often implor'd the assistance of his Spirit; but rather, having made no man Infallible, that he hath pardon'd their errors, and accepts their Pious endeavours, sincerely searching all things according to the rule of Scripture, with such guidance and direction as they can obtain of God by Prayer. What Protestant then who himself maintains the same Principles, and disavowes all implicit Faith, would persecute, and not rather charitably tolerate such men as these, unless he mean to abjure the Principles of his own Religion? If it be askt how far they should be tolerated? I answer doubtless equally, as being all Protestants; that is on all occasions to give account of their Faith, either by Arguing, Preaching in their several Assemblies, Public writing, and the freedom of Printing. For if the *French* and *Polonian* Protestants injoy all this liberty among Papists, much more may a Protestant justly expect it among Protestants; and yet some times here among us, the one persecutes the other upon every slight Pretence.

But he is wont to say he enjoyns only things indifferent. Let them be so still; who gave him authority to change their nature by injoyning them? If by his own Principles, as is prov'd, he ought to tolerate controverted points of Doctrine not slightly grounded on Scripture, much more ought he not impose things indifferent without Scripture. In Religion nothing is indifferent, but, if it come once to be Impos'd, is either a command or a Prohibition, and so consequently an addition to the word of God, which he professes to disallow. Besides, how unequal, how uncharitable must it needs be, to Impose that which his conscience cannot urge him to impose, upon him whose conscience forbids him to obey? What can it be but love of contention for things not necessary to be done, to molest the conscience of his Brother, who holds them necessary to be not done? To conclude, let such a one but call to

---

[6]Corrected from "destuctive."

mind[7] his own principles above mention'd, and he must necessarily grant, that neither he can impose, nor the other believe or obey ought in Religion, but from the Word of God only. More amply to understand this, may be read the 14*th*. And 15*th*. Chapters to the Romans, and the Contents of the 14th, set forth no doubt but with full authority of the Church of *England*; the Gloss is this. *Men may not contemn, or condemn one the other for things indifferent.* And in the 6th Article above mentioned, *Whatsoever is not read in Holy Scripture, nor may be proved thereby, is not to be required of any man as an article of Faith, or necessary to salvation.* And certainly what is not so, is not to be required at all; as being an addition to the Word of God, expressly forbidden.

Thus this long and hot Contest, whether Protestants ought to tolerate one another, if men will be but Rational and not Partial, may be ended without need of more words to compose it.

Let us now enquire whether Popery be tolerable or no. Popery is a double thing to deal with, and claims a twofold Power, Ecclesiastical, and Political, both usurpt, and the one supporting the other.

But Ecclesiastical is ever pretended to[8] Political. The Pope by this mixt faculty, pretends right to Kingdoms and States, and especially to this of *England*, Thrones and Unthrones Kings, and absolves the people from their obedience to them; sometimes inderdicts to whole Nations the Publick worship of God, shutting up their Churches: and was wont to dreign away greatest part of the wealth of this then miserable Land, as part of his Patrimony, to maintain the Pride and Luxury of his Court and Prelates: and now since, through the infinite mercy and favour of God, we have shaken off his *Babylonish* Yoke, hath not ceas'd by his Spyes and Agents, Bulls and Emissaries, once to destroy both King and Parliament;[9] perpetually to seduce, corrupt, and pervert as many as they can of the People. Whether therefore it be fit or reasonable, too tolerate men thus principl'd in Religion towards the State, I submit it to the consideration of all Magistrates, who are best able to provide for their own and the publick safety. As for tolerating the exercise of their Religion, supporting their State activities not to be dangerous, I answer, that Toleration is either public or private; and the exercise of

their Religion, as far as it is Idolatrous, can be tolerated neither way: not publicly, without grievous and unsufferable scandal giv'n to all consciencious Beholders; not privately, without great offence to God, declar'd against all kind of Idolatry, though secret. *Ezekiel* 8.7,8. *And he brought me to the door of the Court, and when I looked, behold a hole in the Wall. Then said he unto me, Son of Man, digg now in the wall; and when I had digged, behold a Door, and he said unto me, go in, and behold the wicked Abominations that they do here.* And verse 12. *Then said he unto me, Son of Man, hast thou seen what the Antients of the house of* Israel *do in the dark?* &c. And it appears by the whole Chapter, that God was no less offended with these secret Idolatries, then with those in public; and no less provokt, then to bring on and hasten his Judgements on the whole Land for these also.

Having shown thus, that Popery, as being Idolatrous, is not to be tolerated either in Public or in Private; it must be now thought how to remove it and hinder the growth thereof, I mean in our Natives, and not Forreigners, Privileg'd by the Law of Nations. Are we to punish them by corporal punishment, or fines in their Estates, upon account of their Religion? I suppose it stands not with the Clemency of the Gospel, more then what appertains to the security of the State: But first we must remove their Idolatry, and all the furniture thereof, whether Idols, or the Mass wherein they adore their God under Bread and Wine: for the Commandment forbids to adore, not only *any Graven Image, but the likeness of any thing in Heaven above, or in the Earth beneath, or in the Water under the Earth, thou shouldt not bow down to them nor worship them for I the Lord thy God am a Jealous God.* If they say that by removing their Idols we violate their Consciences, we have not warrant to regard Conscience which is not grounded on Scripture: and they themselves confess in their late defences, that they hold not their Images necessary to salvation, but only as they are enjoyn'd them by tradition.

Shall we condescend to dispute with them? The Scripture is our only Principle in Religion; and by that only they will not be Judg'd, but will add other Principles of their own, which, forbidden by the Word of God, we cannot assent to. And the common Maxim also in *Logic* is, *against them who deny Principles, we are not to dispute.* Let them bound their disputations on the Scripture only, and an ordinary Protestant, well read in the Bible, may turn and wind[10] their Doctors. They will not go about to prove their Idolatries by the Word of God, but run to shifts and evasions, and frivolous distinctions:

---

[7]Correcting "miud" (inverted letter) in the original.

[8]Claimed to be; professed falsely to be (see *OED* 2.c).

[9]In the Gunpowder Plot, a Roman Catholic conspiracy to blow up King James I and the Houses of Parliament on November 5, 1605, a subject about which Milton had written "In Quintum Novembris" and another Latin poem at the age of seventeen. History would repeat itself in the plot of Titus Oates in 1678 to kill Charles II, so that Milton's fears of potential violence had some grounds.

---

[10]Probably to argue against using devious or serpentine arguments.

Idols they say are *Laymens* Books,[11] and a great means to stir up pious thoughts and Devotion in the Learnedst. I say they are no means of Gods appointing, but plainly the contrary: Let them hear the Prophets; *Jerem.* 10.8. *The stock is a Doctrin of Vanities.* Habakkuk 2.18. *What profiteth the graven Image that the maker thereof hath graven it: The Molten Image and a teacher of Lyes?* But they alleadge in their late answers, that the Laws of *Moses* giv'n only to the Jews, concern not us under the Gospel: and remember not that Idolatry is forbidden as expressly, [in several places of the Gospel,][12] But with these wiles and fallacies *compassing Sea and Land, like the Pharisees of old, to make one Proselite,* they lead away privily many simple and ignorant Souls, men or women, *and make them twofold more the Children of Hell then themselves,* Matt. 23.15. But the Apostle hath well warn'd us, I may say, from such Deceivers as these, for their Mystery was then working. *I beseech you Brethren,* saith he, *mark them which cause divisions and offences, contrary to the doctrin which ye have learned, and avoid them; for they that are such serve not our Lord Jesus Christ, but their own belly, and by good words and fair speeches deceive the heart of the simple.* Rom. 16.17,18.

The next means to hinder the growth of Popery will be to read duly and diligently the Holy Scriptures, which as St. *Paul* saith to *Timothy,* who had known them from a child, *are able to make wise unto salvation.* And to the whole Church of *Colossi; Let the word of Christ dwell in you plentifully, with all wisdome,* Coloss. 3.16. The Papal Antichristian Church permits not her Laity to read the Bible in their own tongue: Our Church on the contrary hath proposd it to all men, and to this end translated it into English, with profitable Notes on what is met with[13] obscure, though what is most necessary to be known be still plainest: that all sorts and degrees of men, not understanding the Original, may read it in their Mother Tongue. Neither let the Countryman, the Tradesman, the Lawyer, the Physician, the Statesman, excuse himself by his much business from the studious reading thereof. Our Saviour saith, Luke 10.41,42. *Thou art careful and troubled about many things, but one thing is needful.* If they were ask't, they would be loath[14] to set earthly things, wealth, or honour before the wisdom of salvation. Yet most men

in the course and practice of their lives are found to do so; and through unwillingness to take the pains of understanding their Religion by their own diligent study, would fain be sav'd by a Deputy. Hence comes implicit faith, ever learning and never taught, much hearing and small proficience, till want of Fundamental knowledg easily turns to superstition or Popery: Therefore the Apostle admonishes, Eccles. 4.14. *That we henceforth be no more children tossed to and fro and carried about with every wind of Doctrine, by the sleight of men, and cunning craftiness whereby they lye in wait to deceive.* Every member of the Church, at least of any breeding or capacity, so well ought to be grounded in spiritual knowledg, as, if need be, to examine their Teachers themselves, Act. 17.11. *They searched the Scriptures dayly, whether those things were so.* Rev. 2.2. *Thou hast tryed them which say they are Apostles, and are not.* How should any private Christian try[15] his Teachers unless he be well grounded himself in the Rule of Scripture, by which he is taught. As therefore among Papists, their ignorance in Scripture cheifly upholds Popery; so among Protestant People, the frequent and serious reading thereof will soonest pull Popery down.

Another means to abate Popery arises from the constant reading of Scripture, wherein Believers who agree in the main, are every where exhorted to mutual forbearance and charity one towards the other, though dissenting in some opinions. It is written that the Coat of our Saviour was without seame:[16] whence some would infer that there should be no division in the Church of Christ. It should be so indeed; Yet seams in the same cloth, neigher hurt the garment, nor misbecome it; and not only seams, but Schisms will be while men are fallible: But if they who dissent in matters not essential to belief, while the common adversary is in the field, shall stand jarring and pelting at each other, they will be soon routed and subdued. The Papist with open mouth makes much advantage of our several opinions; not that he is able to confute the worst of them, but that we by our continual jangle among our selves make them worse then they are indeed. To save our selves therefore, and resist the common enemy, it concerns us mainly to agree within our selves, that with joynt forces we may not only hold our own, but get ground; and why should we not? The Gospel commands us to tolerate one another, though of various opinions, and hath promised a good and happy event[17] thereof, *Phil.* 3.15. *Let us therefore as many as be perfect be thus minded; and*

---

[11]The Protestant accusation against Roman Catholicism for creation of idols or images is at stake here. Milton wrote in the *De Doctrina Christiana,* "So the Papists are mistaken when they call idols the layman's books" (Yale 6: 693).

[12]The brackets are in the original. Neither I nor the Yale editors have any explanation for why they might be there, other than the possibility that the compositor had run out of parentheses.

[13]Supply "that is" here.

[14]The "l" in this word is set as a capital "I."

---

[15]Test or question.

[16]Jesus' coat, when it is stripped from him after the Crucifixion, "was without seam, woven from the top throughout" (John 19.23).

[17]Outcome.

if in any thing ye be otherwise minded, God shall reveal even this unto you. And we are bid, 1 *Thess.* 5.21. *Prove all things, hold fast that which is good.* St. *Paul* judg'd that not only to tolerate, but to examine and prove all things, was no danger to our holding fast of that which is good. How shall we prove all things, which includes all[18] opinions at least founded on Scripture, unless we not only tolerate them, but patiently hear them, and seriously read them? If he who thinks himself in the truth professes to have learnt it, not by implicit faith, but by attentive study of the Scriptures & full perswasion of heart, with what equity can he refuse to hear or read him, who demonstrates to have gained his knowledge by the same way? Is it a fair course to assert truth by arrogating to himself the only freedome of speech, and stopping the mouths[19] of others equally gifted? This is the direct way to bring in that Papistical implicit faith which we all disclaim. They pretend it would unsettle the weaker sort: the same groundless fear is pretended by the Romish Clergy in prohibiting the Scripture. At least then let them have leave to write in Latin which the common people understand not; that what they hold may be discust among the Learned only. We suffer the Idolatrous books of Papists, without this fear, to be sold & read as common as our own. Why not much rather of Anabaptists, Arians, Arminians, & Socinians? There is no Learned man but will confess he hath much profited by reading Controversies, his Senses awakt, his Judgement sharpn'd, and the truth which he holds more firmly establish't. If then it be profitable for him to read; why should it not at least be tolerable and free for his Adversary to write? In *Logic* they teach, that contraries laid together more evidently appear: it follows then that all controversies being permitted, falshood will appear more false, and truth the more true: which must needs conduce much, not only to the confounding of Popery, but to the general confirmation of unimplicit truth.

The last means to avoid Popery, is to amend our lives: it is a general complaint that this Nation of late years, is grown more numerously and excessively vitious then heretofore: Pride, Luxury, Drunkenness, Whoredom, Cursing, Swearing, bold and open Atheism every where abounding: Where these grow, no wonder if Popery also grow a pace. There is no man so wicked, but at som-

times[20] his conscience will wring him with thoughts of another world, & the Peril of his soul: the trouble and melancholy which he conceives of true Repentance and amendment he endures not; but enclines rather to some carnal Superstition, which may pacify and lull his Conscience with some more pleasing Doctrin. None more ready and officious to offer her self then the *Romish,* and opens wide her Office, with all her faculties to receive him; easy Confession, easy Absolution, Pardons, Indulgences, Masses for him both quick and dead, *Agnus Dei's,* Reliques, and the like: and he, instead of *Working out his salvation with fear and trembling,*[21] strait thinks in his heart (like another kind of fool then he in the Psalms)[22] to bribe God as a corrupt judge; and by his Proctor, some Priest or Fryer, to buy out his Peace with money, which he cannot with his repentance. For God, when men sin outragiously, and will not be admonisht, gives over chastizing them, perhaps by Pestilence, Fire, Sword, or Famin, which may all turn to their good, and takes up his severest punishments, hardness, besottedness of heart, and Idolatry, to their final perdition. Idolatry brought the Heathen to hainous Transgressions. *Romans 2.d.* And hainous Transgressions oft times bring the slight professors of true Religion, to gross Idolatry: 1 Thess. 2.11,12. *For this cause, God shall send them strong delusion that they should believe a lye, that they all might be damnd who believe not the truth, but had pleasure in unrighteousness.* And Isaiah 44.18. Speaking of Idolaters, *They have not known nor understood, for he hath shut their Eyes that they cannot see, and their hearts that they cannot understand.* Let us therefore using this last means, last here spoken of, but first to be done, amend our lives with all speed; least through impenitency we run into that stupidly, which we now seek all means so warily to avoid, the worst of superstitions, and the heaviest of all Gods Judgements, Popery.

FINIS

---

[18]From this point to the end of p. 15, the font size is reduced, indicating possibly that the compositor was budgeting or making space for the last page.
[19]The catchword at the bottom of p. 15 is spelled "mouthes," the inconsistency again indicating some stress on the compositor.

[20]This phrase probably should be read as "at some times his conscience will wring him." The compositor seems to be squeezing the text.
[21]Philippians 2.12: ". . . work out your own salvation with fear and trembling."
[22] "The fool hath said in his heart, There is no God" (Psalm 14.1).

From *On Christian Doctrine*
(1650s?)

UNCERTAINTY ABOUT AUTHORSHIP

In the Yale *Complete Prose Works of John Milton*, the full text of *On Christian Doctrine*, with introductions, notes, and index, takes up 863 pages. The excerpts I print here will give only a taste of what it is like to read the entire document, or to see it in the context of Protestant theology in the seventeenth century. Because of the uncertain state of the provenance of the treatise—the authority of the text, the authorship, and the translations yet made have all been recently called into question—I am forced to be cautious and to present even John Carey's excellent translation of a text as a work in progress, without apparatus except for the introduction.

The conclusions of the report by Gordon Campbell, Fiona Tweedie, David Holmes, Thomas J. Corns, and John Hale, "The Provenance of Milton's *De Doctrina Christiana*," published in the October 1997, *Milton Quarterly*, makes it clear that fresh work needs to be done on the text and the apparatus.

- Milton's authorship of much of the treatise is in doubt, though he almost undoubtedly composed or dictated at least parts of it himself, with the help of amanuenses. He may well have borrowed large parts of it from another author.
- The discrete segments written down by the many copyists and amanuenses who served the blind author need to be sorted out and something like a hypertext edition of the treatise reconstructed from the manuscript.
- If it is possible, the manuscript needs to be tracked even more carefully from Milton's possession through the various clandestine paths that led to its being preserved in the Public Record Office in London, where it was discovered in 1823 by Robert Lemon, to be translated and published by Bishop Charles Sumner in 1825. The report on the provenance of the treatise introduces new information about the somewhat shady career of Daniel Skinner, who first attempted to publish the work. The research of the team of investigators and that of Paul Sellin in the Netherlands may lead to new discoveries that will change our minds about how to read or understand *On Christian Doctrine*.

Meanwhile, work on reconstructing, editing, and printing an extraordinary manuscript proceeds. William B. Hunter's questions about authorship remain largely unanswered. Once a newly edited Latin text can be pasted together, using the linguistic talents of John Hale, Estelle Haan, and Gordon Campbell, a new translation should be made as well, with an apparatus reflecting recent historical and textual discoveries.

The work of the late Maurice Kelley in editing Volume VI of the Yale Milton was exemplary. Kelley's fine book detailing the relationship between Milton's theology and *Paradise Lost*, *This Great Argument*, will remain unsurpassed as a demonstration of how theology may inform literature. C. A. Patrides's very learned *Milton and the Christian Doctrine* tracks some of the epic's conventional Christian theology as well as some of its beliefs bordering on heresy. The work of Hunter, Adamson, Lewalski, Christopher, Steadman, Danielson, and MacCallum has helped establish Milton's theology in its rightful place. It may fit into a small niche of Reformation theology but *On Christian Doctrine* is also an important commentary on great English poems. Until the provenance of *On Christian Doctrine* is established, however, we will know even less than we thought we knew about what Milton thought about such subjects as the subordination of the Son to the Father or the progress of the soul towards reunion with the body at Judgment Day.

WHAT TO MAKE OF THE BIBLE: CITATION AND THEOLOGY

The present generation of college students is among the first not to "have" the Bible as part of their cultural literacy. When I ask a random English class how many of them have read the Bible through to the end, I may see two or three hands go up, out of thirty or so. Milton's devotion to the Bible as the single book most important to human salvation might strike a modern student as obsessional, dull, methodical, doctrinaire, or just quirky. But the Bible was an exciting book to Milton, his source for information on how to live; it provided words to live by from a holy book (*Biblia Sacra* or Holy Bible is what it was called in editions published in Latin or English). To a pious European Protestant in 1650, every word in the Bible was holy, and words and phrases from Old and New Testaments could be mixed and matched to give moral guidance. Because Milton thought of the Bible this way—that it contained everything necessary for Christian salvation—he preferred to keep his own words at a minimum in *On Christian Doctrine*, to let the Bible speak for itself.

Reading such a document with its tissue of citations is tedious for someone who does not have the Bible more or less by heart, as Milton did, but it can be extremely valuable to a reader of *Paradise Lost*, whenever that reader wants to understand the motivation of Adam and Eve before or after the Fall, or needs to fix the identity of the

Son of God in *Paradise Lost* and *Paradise Regain'd*, or wants to know what the duties of good angels might have been, or understand the disobedience of the evil angels.

Realizing that any group of excerpts from *On Christian Doctrine* cannot fulfill all the needs of all teachers and students of Milton, I have sought the advice of colleagues like Michael Lieb, John King, and Tom Corns for guidance in choosing excerpts to reproduce in this edition. I have chosen the passages below on the grounds of the value of each selection to an understanding of the poetry, especially *Paradise Lost*.

Milton's alleged heresies (the term is still very loosely used, even though Milton tries to protect himself against such catch-all labels in his introduction) can be listed here, but they will do little good except as tags, until one becomes immersed in the theology of Milton's time. He has been supposed to be an Arian, a Pelagian, an anti-Trinitarian, or an Arminian. To oversimplify, each of these has something to do with the revaluing of one or another part of the Trinity, assigning more importance to the Father and less to the Son or assigning no importance at all the Holy Ghost. Milton is supposed to have endorsed Thnetopsychism (an awful word having to do with the sleep of the soul between the individual's death and Judgment Day, very difficult to spell or pronounce), and he was surely in favor of divorce and even polygamy. Selections have been made, again with the help of Tom Corns and the team of researchers, on the basis of their being most assuredly by Milton, as compared with material that may have been cribbed from the work of other theologians published or unpublished. The team has applied stylistic tests on various segments of the treatise, comparing its style with that of other Latin prose selections known to be by Milton, to determine how likely it is that he wrote, or rather dictated, those segments.

TEXT AND TRANSLATION

On Christian Doctrine was most likely to have been dictated, according to Kelley, in the years 1658 through 1660, but we are also certain that Milton had been at work on a theological index and a related system of divinity for many years. What we have in the manuscript is quite possibly an unfinished work (Campbell). Because Milton was a regicide, his works were subject to censorship in England. Thus Daniel Skinner may have carried the dog-eared papers around with him to various countries on the Continent, perhaps looking for the best profit on the sale abroad.

Add to that the fact that, from its translation by Bishop (note his title within the Church of England) Sumner, the alleged heterodoxy of Milton's tract has caused problems for orthodox Anglican readers of his work. Then one has to add the problem of interpreting the Latin words in English, to make them palatable to different generations of readers, or theologically correct for orthodox Anglicans. *On Christian Doctrine* is truly a text in search of an author, and a text that on the one hand may now be treated by some scholars as if it were almost anonymous but has until recently been regarded as the unvarnished Truth.

To compound the difficulty of understanding it, the treatise seems at times very personal and revelatory about Milton, as in the segments on divorce and polygamy and the sections on the "duties to be performed towards men" or "a man's duty towards himself." Even though Kelley's notes show that Milton's conclusions were at times very close to that of his favorite Protestant theologians, William Ames and Johan Wolleb, there is no doubt that his theological positions were often the positions that governed his attitudes toward, say, a tyrannical king, toward a bad marriage, or toward an interpretation of the freedom of the press.

Works Cited

Campbell, Gordon. "*De Doctrina Christiana:* Its Structural Principles and Its Unfinished State." *Milton Studies* 9 (1976): 243–60.

Christopher, Georgia A. *Milton and the Science of the Saints.* Princeton, NJ: Princeton UP, 1982.

Danielson, Dennis. *Milton's Good God: A Study in Literary Theodicy.* Cambridge: Cambridge UP, 1982.

Hunter, William B. "Milton on the Incarnation." *Bright Essence: Studies in Milton's Theology.* Hunter, C. A. Patrides, and J. H. Adamson. Salt Lake City: U of Utah P, 1971.

Kelley, Maurice. *This Great Argument: A Study of Milton's "De Doctrina Christiana" as a Gloss upon "Paradise Lost."* Princeton, NJ: Princeton UP, 1941.

MacCallum, Hugh. *Milton and the Sons of God: The Divine Image in Milton's Epic Poetry.* Toronto: U of Toronto P, 1986.

Patrides, C. A. *Milton and the Christian Tradition.* Oxford: Clarendon P, 1966.

Sellin, Paul. "If Not Milton, Who Did Write the *De Doctrina Christiana*: The Amyraldian Connection." Paper to be read at the 1997 Conference on John Milton, October 23–25, Middle Tennessee State University, Murfreesboro.

Steadman, John M. *Milton's Epic Characters: Image and Idol.* Chapel Hill: U of North Carolina P, 1968.

JOHN MILTON

ENGLISHMAN

To All the Churches of Christ and to All in any part of the world who profess the Christian Faith, Peace, Knowledge of the Truth, and Eternal Salvation in God the Father and in our Lord Jesus Christ.

THE process of restoring religion to something of its pure original state, after it had been defiled with impurities for more than thirteen hundred years, dates from the beginning of the last century. Since that time many theological systems have been propounded, aiming at further purification, and providing sometimes brief, sometimes more lengthy and methodical expositions of almost all the chief points of Christian doctrine. This being so, I think I should explain straight away why, if any work has yet been published on this subject which is as exhaustive as possible, I have been dissatisfied with it, and why, on the other hand, if all previous writers have failed in this attempt, I have not been discouraged from making the same attempt myself.

If I were to say that I had focused my studies principally upon Christian doctrine because nothing else can so effectually wipe away those two repulsive afflictions, tyranny and superstition, from human life and the human mind, I should show that I had been concerned not for religion but for life's well-being.

But in fact I decided not to depend upon the belief or judgment of others in religious questions for this reason: God has revealed the way of eternal salvation only to the individual faith of each man, and demands of us that any man who wishes to be saved should work out his beliefs for himself. So I made up my mind to puzzle out a religious creed for myself by my own exertions, and to acquaint myself with it thoroughly. In this the only authority I accepted was God's self-revelation, and accordingly I read and pondered the Holy Scriptures themselves with all possible diligence, never sparing myself in any way.

I shall mention those methods that proved profitable for me, in case desire for similar profit should, perhaps, lead someone else to start out upon the same path in the future. I began by devoting myself when I was a boy to an earnest study of the Old and New Testaments in their original languages, and then proceeded to go carefully through some of the shorter systems of theologians. I also started, following the example of these writers, to list under general headings all passages from the scriptures which suggested themselves for quotation, so that I might have them ready at hand when necessary. At length, gaining confidence, I transferred my attention to more diffuse volumes of divinity, and to the conflicting arguments in controversies over certain heads of faith. But, to be frank, I was very sorry to find, in these works, that the authors frequently evaded an opponent's point in a thoroughly dishonest way, or countered it, in appearance rather than in reality, by an affected display of logical ingenuity or by constant linguistic quibbles. Such writers, moreover, often defended their prejudices tooth and nail, though with more fervor than force, by misinterpretations of biblical texts or by the false conclusions which they wrung from these. Hence, they sometimes violently attacked the truth as error and heresy, while calling error and heresy truth and upholding them not upon the authority of the Bible but as a result of habit and partisanship.

So I considered that I could not properly entrust either my creed or my hope of salvation to such guides. But I still thought that it was absolutely necessary to possess a systematic exposition of Christian teaching, or at any rate a written investigation of it, which could assist my faith or my memory or both. It seemed, then, safest and most advisable for me to make a fresh start and compile for myself, by my own exertion and long hours of study, some work of this kind which might be always at hand. I should derive this from the word of God and from that alone, and should be scrupulously faithful to the text, for to do otherwise would be merely to cheat myself. After I had painstakingly persevered in this work for several years, I saw that the citadel of reformed religion was adequately fortified against the Papists. Through neglect, however, it was open to attack; in many other places where defences and defenders were alike wanting to make it safe. In religion as in other things, I discerned, God offers all his rewards not to those who are thoughtless and credulous, but to those who labor constantly and seek tirelessly after truth. Thus I concluded that there was more than I realized which still needed to be measured with greater strictness against the yardstick of the Bible, and reformed with greater care. I pursued my studies, and so far satisfied myself that eventually I had no doubt about my ability to distinguish correctly in religion between matters of faith and matters of opinion. It was, furthermore, my greatest comfort that I had constructed, with God's help, a powerful support for my faith, or rather that I had laid up provision for the future in that I should not thenceforth be unprepared or hesitant when I needed to give an account of my beliefs.

God is my witness that it is with feelings of universal brotherhood and good will that I make this account public. By so doing I am sharing, and that most willingly, my dearest and best possession with as many people as possible. I hope, then, that all my readers will be sympathetic, and will avoid prejudice and malice, even though they see at once that many of the views I have published are at odds with certain conventional opinions. I implore all friends of truth not to start shouting that the church is being thrown into confusion by free discussion and inquiry. These are allowed in academic circles, and should certainly be denied to no believer. For we are ordered to find out the truth about all things, and the daily increase of the light of truth fills the church much rather with brightness and strength than with confusion. I do not see how anyone should be able or is able to throw the church into confusion by searching after truth, any more than the heathen were thrown into confusion when the gospel was first preached. For assuredly I do not urge or enforce anything upon my own authority. On the contrary I advise every reader, and set him an example by doing the same myself, to withhold his consent from those opinions about which he does not feel fully convinced, until the evidence of the Bible convinces him and induces his reason to assent and to believe. I do not seek to conceal any part of my meaning. Indeed I address myself with much more confidence to learned than to untutored readers or, if the very learned are not always the best judges and critics of such matters, at any rate to mature, strong-minded men who thoroughly understand the teaching of the gospel. Most authors who have dealt with this subject at the greatest length in the past have been in the habit of filling their pages almost entirely with expositions of their own ideas. They have relegated to the margin, with brief reference to chapter and verse, the scriptural texts upon which all that they teach is utterly dependent. I, on the other hand, have striven to cram my pages even to overflowing, with quotations drawn from all parts of the Bible and to leave as little space as possible for my own words, even when they arise from the putting together of actual scriptural texts.

I intend also to make people understand how much it is in the interests of the Christian religion that men should be free not only to sift and winnow any doctrine, but also openly to give their opinions of it and even to write about it, according to what each believes. This I aim to achieve not only by virtue of the intrinsic soundness and power of the arguments, new or old, which my readers will find me bringing forward, but much more by virtue of the authority of the Bible, upon very frequent citations of which these arguments are based. Without this freedom to which I refer, there is no religion and no gospel. Violence alone prevails; and it is disgraceful and disgusting that the Christian religion should be supported by violence. Without this

freedom, we are still enslaved: not, as once, by the law of God but, what is vilest of all, by human law, or rather, to be more exact, by an inhuman tyranny. There are some irrational bigots who, by a perversion of justice, condemn anything they consider inconsistent with conventional beliefs and give it an invidious title—"heretic" or "heresy"—without consulting the evidence of the Bible upon the point. To their way of thinking, by branding anyone out of hand with this hateful name, they silence him with one word and need take no further trouble. They imagine that they have struck their opponent to the ground, as with a single blow, by the impact of the name heretic alone. I do not expect that my unprejudiced and intelligent readers will behave in this way: such conduct would be utterly unworthy of them. But to these bigots I retort that, in apostolic times, before the New Testament was written, the word heresy, whenever it was used as an accusation, was applied only to something which contradicted the teaching of the apostles as it passed from mouth to mouth. Heretics were then, according to Rom. xvi. 17, 18, only those people who caused *divisions of opinion and offences contrary to the teaching of the apostles: serving not our Lord Jesus Christ but their own belly.* On the same grounds I hold that, since the compilation of the New Testament, nothing can correctly be called heresy unless it contradicts that. For my own part, I devote my attention to the Holy Scriptures alone. I follow no other heresy or sect. I had not even studied any of the so-called heretical writers, when the blunders of those who are styled orthodox, and their unthinking distortions of the sense of scripture, first taught me to agree with their opponents whenever these agreed with the Bible. If this is heresy, I confess, as does Paul in Acts xxiv. 14, that *following the way which is called heresy I worship the God of my fathers, believing all things that are written in the law and the prophets* and, I add, whatever is written in the New Testament as well. In common with the whole Protestant Church I refuse to recognise any other arbiters of or any other supreme authorities for Christian belief, or any faith not independently arrived at but "implicit," as it is termed. For the rest, brethren, cherish the truth with love for your fellow men. Assess this work as God's spirit shall direct you. Do not accept or reject what I say unless you are absolutely convinced by the clear evidence of the Bible. Lastly, live in the spirit of our Lord and Savior Jesus Christ, and so I bid you farewell.

THE ENGLISHMAN

JOHN MILTON'S

TWO BOOKS OF INVESTIGATIONS INTO

Christian Doctrine

DRAWN FROM THE SACRED SCRIPTURES ALONE

BOOK I

Chapter I
WHAT CHRISTIAN DOCTRINE IS, AND HOW MANY ITS PARTS

CHRISTIAN DOCTRINE is the doctrine which, in all ages, CHRIST (though he was not known by that name from the beginning) taught by divine communication, for the glory of God and the salvation of mankind, about God and about worshipping him.

We may rightly insist that Christians should believe in the SCRIPTURES, from which this doctrine is drawn. Scriptural authority, however, will be discussed in its proper place.

CHRIST. Matt. xi. 27: *nor does anyone know the Father except the Son, and anyone to whom the Son wishes to reveal him*; John i. 4: *in him was life, and that life was the light of men*, and i. 9: *that was the true light, which gives light to every man who comes into the world*; I Peter iii. 19: *through whom he came and preached even to the spirits which are in prison.* Understand the name Christ as meaning also Moses, and the prophets who foretold his coming, and the apostles whom he sent. Gal. iii. 24: *the law was our escort to school, that is to Christ, so that we might be justified by faith*; Heb. xiii. 8: *Jesus Christ is the same yesterday, today and forever*; Col. ii. 17: *these are mere images of things to come, but the body is Christ's*; I

Peter i. 10–11: *who prophesied about the grace which would come to you: searching out what time or season that prophetic spirit of Christ within them revealed*; Rom. i. 1: *Paul, a servant of Jesus Christ*—in this way he begins nearly all the rest of his epistles; I Cor. iv. 1: *let a man look upon you as ministers of Christ.*

BY DIVINE COMMUNICATION. Isa. li. 4: *a doctrine shall proceed from me*; Matt. xvi. 17: *flesh and blood did not reveal this to you, but my father who is in heaven*; John vi. 45, 46: *they will be taught by God*, and ix. 29: *we know that God spoke to Moses*; Gal. i. 11, 12: *the gospel is not derived from man, for I did not receive it from man*; I Thess. iv. 9: *you yourselves are taught by divine communication.*

We must, then, look for this doctrine not among philosophizing academics, and not among the laws of men, but in the Holy Scriptures alone and with the Holy Spirit as guide. II Tim. i. 14: *guard that wonderful thing which is entrusted to you by means of the Holy Spirit who lives in us*; Col. ii. 8: *lest anyone rob you by means of philosophy*; Dan. iii. 16: *we are not afraid to answer you on this subject*; Acts iv. 19: *decide for yourselves whether it is right in the sight of God to obey you rather than God.*

I do not teach anything new in this work. I aim only to assist the reader's memory by collecting together, as it were, into a single book texts which are scattered here and there throughout the Bible, and by systematizing them under definite headings, in order to make reference easy. This procedure might well be defended on grounds of Christian prudence, but in fact a more powerful argument in its favor is that apparently it fulfills God's own command: Matt. xiii. 52: *every scribe who has been instructed in the kingdom of heaven, is like a householder who brings you! of his treasure new and old possessions.* So also the apostle says to Timothy, II Tim. i. 13: ὑποτύπωσιν ἔχε, "Hold fast the pattern," which the author of the epistle to the Hebrews seems to have been determined to do, so as to teach the main points of Christian doctrine methodically: Heb. vi. 1–3: *of repentance, faith, the doctrine of Baptisms, and of the laying on of hands, the resurrection of the dead and eternal judgment: and this we will do if God permit.* This was a very convenient way of instructing catechumens when they were making their first profession of faith in the Church. The same method is indicated in Rom. vi. 17: *You have listened from the heart to that pattern of doctrine which you were taught.* In this quotation the Greek word ὑπος like ὑποτύπωσις in II Tim. i. 13, seems to mean either those parts of the gospels that were actually written at the time (as in Rom. ii. 20 the word μόρφωσις, meaning "form" or "semblance", signifies the law itself in the phrase "the *form* of knowledge and of truth in the law"), or else some systematic course of instruction derived from those parts or from the whole doctrine of the gospel. It appears from Acts xx. 27: *I have not avoided making known to you God's whole counsel*, that there is a complete corpus of doctrine, conceived in terms of a definite course of instruction. This was of no great length, however, since the whole course was completed, and perhaps even repeated several times, in about three years, while Paul was at Ephesus.

The PARTS of CHRISTIAN DOCTRINE are two: FAITH, or KNOWLEDGE OF GOD, and LOVE, or THE WORSHIP OF GOD. Gen. xvii. 1: *walk in sight of me and be perfect*; Psal. xxxvii. 3: *have faith in God, and do good*; Luke xi. 28: *blessed are those who hear and obey*; Acts xxiv. 14; *I, as one who believes*, and xxiv. 16: *I train myself*; II Tim.i.13: *hold fast the pattern of words with faith and love, which is in Christ Jesus*; I Tim. i. 19: *keeping faith and a good conscience*; Titus iii. 8: *that those who have believed may be eager*; I John iii. 23: *that we should believe and love*.

Although these two parts are distinguished in kind, and are divided for the purpose of instruction, in practice they are inseparable. Rom. ii. 13: *not hearers but doers*; James i. 22: *be doers not merely hearers*. Besides, obedience and love are always the best guides to knowledge, and often cause it to increase and flourish, though very small at first. Psal. xxv. 14: *the secret of Jehovah is with those who reverence him*; John vii. 17: *if any man wants what he wills, he shall know about the doctrine*, and viii. 31, 32: *if you remain, you will know, and the truth will make you free*; I John ii. 3: *if we keep his commandments we know, by this, that we know him*.

Faith, however, in this section, does not mean the habit of believing, but the things which must habitually be believed. Acts vi. 7: *was obedient to the faith*; Gal. i. 23: *he preaches the faith*.

CHAPTER II
OF GOD

THAT there is a God, many deny: *for the fool says in his heart, There is no God*, Psal. xiv. 1. But he has left so many signs of himself in the human mind, so many traces of his presence through the whole of nature, that no sane person can fail to realise that he exists. Job xii. 9: *who does not know from all these things?*; Psal. xix. 2: *the heavens declare the glory of God*; Acts xiv. 17: *he did not allow himself to exist without evidence*, and xvii. 27, 28: *he is not far from every one of us*; Rom. i. 19, 20: *that which can be known about God is obvious*, and ii. 14, 15: *the Gentiles show the work of the law written in their hearts; their conscience is evidence of the same thing*;

I Cor. i. 21: because, in accordance with God's wisdom, the world failed to know God by its wisdom, it pleased God to save those who believe by the foolishness of preaching. It is indisputable that all the things which exist in the world, created in perfection of beauty and order for some definite purpose, and that a good one, provide proof that a supreme creative being existed before the world, and had a definite purpose of his own in all created things.

There are some who prattle about nature or fate, as if they were to be identified with this supreme being. But nature or *natura* implies by its very name that it was *natam*, born. Strictly speaking it means nothing except the specific character of a thing, or that general law in accordance with which everything comes into existence and behaves. Surely, too, fate or *fatum is* only what is *fatum*, spoken, by some almighty power.

Moreover, those who want to prove that all things are created by nature, have to introduce the concept of chance as well, to share godhead with nature. What, then, do they gain by their theory? In place of one God, whom they find intolerable, they are forced to set up as universal rulers two goddesses who are almost always at odds with each other. In fact, then, many visible proofs, the fulfillment of many prophecies and the narration of many marvels have driven every nation to the belief that either God or some supreme evil power of unknown name presides over the affairs of men. But it is intolerable and incredible that evil should be stronger than good and should prove the true supreme power. Therefore God exists.

Further evidence for the existence of God is provided by the phenomenon of Conscience, or right reason. This cannot be altogether asleep, even in the most evil men. If there were no God, there would be no dividing line between right and wrong. What was to be called virtue, and what vice, would depend upon mere arbitrary opinion. No one would try to be virtuous, no one would refrain from sin because he felt ashamed of it or feared the law, if the voice of Conscience or right reason did not speak from time to time in the heart of every man, reminding him, however unwilling he may be to remember it, that a God does exist, that he rules and governs all things, and that everyone must one day render to him an account of his actions, good and bad alike.

The whole of scripture proves the same point, and it is absolutely requisite that those who wish to learn Christian doctrine should be convinced of this fact from the outset. This is stated in Heb. xi. 6: *he who comes to God must believe that he is God*. The fact that the Jews, an extremely ancient nation, are now dispersed all over the world, demonstrates the same thing. God often warned them that this would be the outcome of their sins. Amidst the constant flux of history they have been preserved in this state, scattered among the other nations, right up to the present day. This has been done not only to make them pay the penalty of their sins but much rather to give the whole world a perpetual, living proof of the existence of God and the truth of the scriptures.

No one, however, can form correct ideas about God guided by nature or reason alone, without the word or message of God: Rom. x. 14: *how shall they believe in him about whom they have not heard?*

We know God, in so far as we are permitted to know him, from either his nature or his efficiency.

When we talk about knowing God, it must be understood in terms of man's limited powers of comprehension. God, as he really is, is far beyond man's imagination, let alone his understanding: I Tim. vi. 16: *dwelling in unapproachable light.* God has revealed only so much of himself as our minds can conceive and the weakness of our nature can bear: Exod. xxxiii. 20, 23: *no one can see me and live: but you will see my back parts;* Isa. vi. 1: *I saw the Lord sitting on a throne which was raised high in the air, and the fringe of his garment spread over the whole of the temple;* John i. 18: *no man has ever seen God,* and vi. *46: not that anyone has seen the Father, except him who is from God; he has seen the Father,* and v. 37: *nor have you heard his voice;* I Cor. xiii. 12: *in a mirror, in a riddle, partially.*

It is safest for us to form an image of God in our minds which corresponds to his representation and description of himself in the sacred writings. Admittedly, God is always described or outlined not as he really is but in such a way as will make him conceivable to us. Nevertheless, we ought to form just such a mental image of him as he, in bringing himself within the limits of our understanding, wishes us to form. Indeed he has brought himself down to our level expressly to prevent our being carried beyond the reach of human comprehension, and outside the written authority of scripture, into vague subtleties of speculation.

In my opinion, then, theologians do not need to employ anthropopathy, or the ascription of human feelings to God. This is a rhetorical device thought up by grammarians to explain the nonsense poets write about Jove. Sufficient care has been taken, without any doubt, to ensure that the holy scriptures contain nothing unfitting to God or unworthy of him. This applies equally to those passages in scripture where God speaks about his own nature. So it is better not to think about God or form an image of him in anthropopathetic terms, for to do so would be to follow the example of men, who are always inventing more and more subtle theories about

him. Rather we should form our ideas with scripture as a model, for that is the way in which he has offered himself to our contemplation. We ought not to imagine that God would have said anything or caused anything to be written about himself unless he intended that it should be a part of our conception of him. On the question of what is or what is not suitable for God, let us ask for no more dependable authority than God himself. If *Jehovah repented that he had created man,* Gen. vi. *6, and repented because of their groanings,* Judges ii. 18, let us believe that he did repent. But let us not imagine that God's repentance arises from lack of foresight, as man's does, for he has warned us not to think about him in this way: Num. xxiii. 19: *God is not a man that he should lie, nor the son of man that he should repent.* The same point is made in I Sam. xv. 29. If *he grieved in his heart* Gen. vi. 6, and if, similarly, *his soul was grieved,* Judges x. 16, let us believe that he did feel grief. For those states of mind which are good in a good man, and count as virtues, are holy in God. If it is said that God, after working for six days, *rested and was refreshed,* Exod. xxxi. 17, and if he *feared his enemy's displeasure,* Deut. xxxii. 27, let us believe that it is not beneath God to feel what grief he does feel, to be refreshed by what refreshes him, and to fear what he does fear. For however you may try to tone down these and similar texts about God by an elaborate show of interpretative glosses, it comes to the same thing in the end. After all, if *God is said to have created man in his own image, after his own likeness,* Gen. i. 26, and not only his mind but also his external appearance (unless the same words mean something different when they are used again in Gen. v. 3: Adam begot his son *after his own likeness, in his own image*), and if God attributes to himself again and again a human shape and form, why should we be afraid of assigning to him something he assigns to himself, provided we believe that what is imperfect and weak in us is, when ascribed to God, utterly perfect and utterly beautiful? We may be certain that God's majesty and glory were so dear to him that he could never say anything about himself which was lower or meaner than his real nature, nor would he ever ascribe to himself any property if he did not wish us to ascribe it to him. Let there be no question about it: they understand best what God is like who adjust their understanding to the word of God, for he has adjusted his word to our understanding, and has shown what kind of an idea of him he wishes us to have. In short, God either is or is not really like he says he is. If he really is like this, why should we think otherwise? If he is not really like this, on what authority do we contradict God? If, at any rate, he wants us to imagine him in this way, why does our imagination go off on some other tack? Why does our imagination shy away from a notion of God which he himself does not hesitate to promulgate in unambiguous terms? For God in his goodness has revealed to us in ample quantity those things which we need to understand about him for our salvation: Deut. xxix. 29: *hidden things are in the power of Jehovah, but the things which are revealed are revealed to us that we may do them.* We do not imply by this argument that God, in all his parts and members, is of human form, but that, so far as it concerns us to know, he has that form which he attributes to himself in Holy Writ. God, then, has disclosed just such an idea of himself to our understanding as he wishes us to possess. If we form some other idea of him, we are not acting according to his will, but are frustrating him of his purpose, as if, indeed, we wished to show that our concept of God was not too debased, but that his concept of us was.

Since it has no causes, we cannot define the "divine nature." However, this is the name given to it in II Pet. i. 4: *that you might be made sharers of the divine nature* (though "nature" here does not mean the essence but the image of God) and in Gal. iv. 8: *which by nature are not Gods,* while Θεότης in Col. ii. 9, Θειότης; in Rom. i. 20, and τὸ Θεῖον in Acts xvii. 29 are all translated "godhead". But though God, by his very nature, transcends everything, including definition, some description of him may be gathered from his names and attributes, as in Isa. xxviii. 29. [The rest of I, II (Yale 6: 138–52) is omitted, as is Chapter III.]

Chapter IV
OF PREDESTINATION

The principal SPECIAL DECREE of God which concerns men is called PREDESTINATION: by which GOD, BEFORE THE FOUNDATIONS OF THE WORLD WERE LAID, HAD MERCY ON THE HUMAN RACE, ALTHOUGH IT WAS GOING TO FALL OF ITS OWN ACCORD, AND, TO SHOW THE GLORY OF HIS MERCY, GRACE AND WISDOM, PREDESTINED TO ETERNAL SALVATION, ACCORDING TO HIS PURPOSE or plan IN CHRIST, THOSE WHO WOULD IN THE FUTURE BELIEVE AND CONTINUE IN THE FAITH.

In academic circles the word "predestination" is habitually used to refer to reprobation as well as to election. For the discussion of such an exacting problem, however, this usage is too slapdash. Whenever the subject is mentioned in scripture, specific reference is made only to election: Rom. viii. 29, 30: *he predestined that they should be shaped to the likeness of his son: and those whom he has predestined he has also called, justified and made glorious;* I Cor. ii. 7: *the wisdom which God predestined, before the creation of the world, to our glory;* Ephes. i. 5: *he has predestined us to adoption,* and i. 11: *in whom, indeed, we have been given our share, as we were predestined according to his purpose;* Acts ii. 23: *when he had been given to you by the deliberate counsel and foreknowledge of God,* compared with iv. 28: *that they might do everything which your power and your counsel predestined would be done*—in order, that is, to procure the salvation of man.

When other terms are used to signify predestination, the reference is always to election alone: Rom. viii. 28: *who are called according to his purpose,* or plan, and ix. 23, 24: *vessels of mercy which he prepared for glory beforehand; even those whom he has called;* Eph. iii. 11: *according to the eternal purpose which he appointed in Jesus Christ;* II Tim. i. 9: *according to his purpose and grace;* I Thess. v. 9: *God has not appointed us to anger, but to obtain salvation through our Lord Jesus Christ.* It does not follow from the negative part of this last quotation that others are appointed to anger. Nor does the clause in Pet ii. 8: *to which they had been appointed,* mean that they were predestined from eternity, but rather from some time after they rebelled, just as the apostles are said to be "elected" in time and "appointed" by Christ to their employment, John xv. 16.

If, in such a controversial question, any importance can be attached to metaphor and allegory, it is worth noting that mention is often made of "enrollment among the living" and of "the book of life," but never of the "book of death": Isa. iv. 3: *enrolled among the living;* Dan. xii. 1: *at that time the people will be set free, each one that will be found written in that book;* Luke x. 20: *rejoice rather, because your names are written in heaven;* Phillip. iv. 3: *whose names are in the book of life.* However, this metaphor from writing does not seem to signify predestination from eternity, which is general, but rather some particular decree made by God within the bounds of time, and referring to certain men, on account of their works. Psal. lxix. 28: *let them be blotted out from the book of life, and not enrolled with the righteous:* it follows they were not enrolled from eternity. Isa. lxv. 6: *behold, it is written in my sight: I will not be at rest unless I recompense;* Rev. xx. 12: *the dead were judged in accordance with the things which had been written in these books, in accordance with the things they had done*—clearly, then, this was not the book of eternal predestination, but of their deeds. Similarly those people were not marked down from eternity who are described in Jude 4 as *marked down for this doom long ago.* Why should we extend the sense of *long ago* so much, and not interpret it rather as "from the time when they became inveterate and hardened sinners"? Why, I repeat, should we extend the meaning of *long ago* so far into the past, either in this quotation or in the passage from which it seems to be taken, II Pet. ii. 3: *the judgment long ago decreed for them has not been idle; destruction waits for them with unsleeping eyes?* Here it clearly means "from the time of their apostasy," however long they concealed it.

Another text which is quoted against me is Prov. xvi. 4: *Jehovah has made all things for himself, even the wicked man for the day of evil.* But God did not make man wicked, much less did he make him so "for himself". What did he do? He threatened the wicked man with the punishment he deserved, as was just, but did not predestine to punishment the man who did not deserve it. The point is clearer in Eccles. vii. 29: *that God has made man upright, but they have thought up numerous devices.* The day of evil follows as certainly from this as if the wicked man had been made for it.

PREDESTINATION, then, must always be taken to refer to election, and seems often to be used instead of that term. What Paul says, Rom. viii. 29: *those whom he foreknew, he also predestined* has the same meaning as I Pet. i. 2: *elect according to foreknowledge;* Rom. ix. 11: *God's purpose with regard to election* and xi. 5: *with regard to election by grace;* Eph. i. 4: *he chose us in him;* Col. iii. 12: *as the elect of God holy and loved;* II Thess. ii. 13: *because God has from the beginning elected you for salvation.* There could, then, be nothing of reprobation in predestination: I Tim. ii. 4: *who wishes that all men should be saved and should come to a knowledge of the truth;* II Pet. iii. 9: *he is patiently disposed towards us, not wishing that any should perish but that all should come to repentance. Towards us,* that is, all men: not only the elect, as some propose, but particularly towards the wicked; thus Rom. ix. 22: *tolerated the vessels of wrath.* If, as some object, Peter would hardly have numbered himself among the unbelievers, then surely neither would he have numbered himself, in the previous quotation, among the elect who had not yet repented. Besides, God does not delay on account of the elect, but hurries rather: Matt. xxiv. 22: *those days shall be shortened.*

I do not understand by the term election that general or, so to speak, national election by which God chose the whole nation of Israel as his own people, Deut. iv. 37: *because he loved your forefathers and elected their seed after them,* and vii. 6–8: *Jehovah selected you to be a people peculiar to him,* and elsewhere, Isa. xlv. 4: *for Israel, my elect.* Nor do I mean the election by which, after rejecting the Jews, God chose the Gentiles to whom he wished the gospel should be preached. This is spoken of particularly in Rom. ix. and xi. Nor do I mean the election by which he chooses an individual for some em-

ployment, I Sam. x. 24: *do you see whom Jehovah has chosen?;* John vi. 70: *have I not chosen you twelve, and one of you is a devil;* whence they are sometimes called elect who are superior to the rest for any reason, as II John 1: *to the elect Lady,* which means, as it were, most excellent, and II John 13: *of your elect sister;* I Pet. ii. 6: *the elect stone, precious;* I Tim. v. 21: *of the elect angels.* I mean, rather, that special election which is almost the same as eternal predestination. Election, then, is not a part of predestination; much less is reprobation. Predestination, strictly speaking, includes a concept of aim, namely the salvation at least of believers, a thing in itself desirable. The aim of reprobation, on the other hand, is the destruction of unbelievers, a thing in itself repulsive and hateful. Clearly, then, God did not predestine reprobation at all, or make it his aim. Ezek. xviii. 32: *I have no pleasure in the death of a man who dies,* and xxiii. 11: *may I not live,* etc. *if I have pleasure in the death of the wicked, but* etc. If God wished neither for sin nor for the death of the sinner, that is neither for the cause nor for the effect of reprobation, then certainly he did not wish for reprobation itself. Reprobation, therefore, is no part of divine predestination.

BY WHICH GOD: meaning, of course, the Father. Luke xii. 32: *it was your father's pleasure;* similarly whenever mention is made of the divine decree or plan: John xvii. 2: *as many as you have given him;* xvii. 6: *those you gave me, chosen from the world;* similarly xi. 24. Eph. i. 4: *he chose us in him,* i. 5: *he has predestined us,* i. 11: *predestined according to his purpose.*

BEFORE THE FOUNDATIONS OF THE WORLD WERE LAID: Eph. i. 4; II Tim. i. 9: *before the world began;* similarly Tit. i. 2.

HAD MERCY ON THE HUMAN RACE, ALTHOUGH IT WAS GOING TO FALL OF ITS OWN ACCORD. The matter or object of predestination was not simply man who was to be created, but man who was going to fall of his own free will. For the demonstration of divine mercy and grace which God purposed as the final end of predestination necessarily presupposes man's sin and misery, originating in man alone. Everyone agrees that man could have avoided falling. But if, because of God's decree, man could not help but fall (and the two contradictory opinions are sometimes voiced by the same people), then God's restoration of fallen man was a matter of justice not grace. For once it is granted that man fell, though not unwillingly, yet by necessity, it will always seem that that necessity either prevailed upon his will by some secret influence, or else guided his will in some way. But if God foresaw that man would fall of his own accord, then there was no need for him to make a decree about the fall, but only about what would become of man who was going to fall. Since, then, God's supreme wisdom foreknew the first man's falling away, but did not decree it, it follows that, before the fall of man, predestination was not absolutely decreed either. Predestination, even after the fall, should always be considered and defined not so much as the result of an actual decree but as arising from the immutable condition of a decree.

PREDESTINED: that is designated, elected. He made the salvation of man the goal and end, as it were, of his purpose. Hence may be refuted those false theories about preterition from eternity and the abandonment of the non-elect. For in opposition to these God has clearly and frequently declared, as I have quoted above, that he desires the salvation of all and the death of none, that he hates nothing he has made, and has omitted nothing which might provide salvation for everyone.

TO SHOW THE GLORY OF HIS MERCY, GRACE AND WISDOM. This is the supreme end of predestination: Rom. ix. 23: *that he might make known the riches of his glory towards the vessels of mercy;* Eph. i. 6: *to the praise of his glorious grace;* I Cor. ii. 7: *we speak God's wisdom, hidden in a mystery, which he predestined before the creation of the world to our glory.*

ACCORDING TO HIS PURPOSE or plan IN CHRIST: Eph. iii. 10, 11: *the wisdom of God in all its forms; according to his eternal purpose, which he appointed in Jesus Christ our Lord;* i. 4: *he chose us in him;* and i. 5: *he has predestined us to adoption through Jesus Christ;* i. 11: *in him, in whom indeed we have been given our share, as we were predestined according to his purpose.* Hence that love of God shown to us in Christ: John iii. 16: *God loved the world so much that he gave his only begotten Son;* Eph. ii. 4, 5: *on account of his great love, you are saved by grace;* I John iv. 9, 10: *by this God's love towards us was made clear, because his own Son,* etc. Except for Christ, then, who was foreknown, no grace was decided upon, no reconciliation between God and man who was going to fall. Since God has so openly declared that predestination is the effect of his mercy, love, grace, and wisdom in Christ, we ought not attribute it, as is usually done, to his absolute and inscrutable will, even in those passages which mention will alone: Exod. xxxiii. 19: *I shall be gracious to him to whom I shall be gracious,* that is, not to elaborate further upon the causes of my graciousness at present. Rom. ix. 18: *he has mercy on whom he will,* that is to say, by the method he determined upon in Christ: and in passages of this kind God is, in fact, usually speaking of his extraordinary grace and mercy, as will be evident when we examine particular texts. Thus Luke xii. 32: *it was your father's pleasure;* Eph. i. 5: *by himself through Jesus Christ, according to the good pleasure of his will,* i. 11: *in him . . . according to the resolution of his will;* James i. 18: *because*

he wished it he has begotten us by the word of truth, that is, through Christ, who is the word and the truth of God.

THOSE WHO WOULD IN THE FUTURE BELIEVE AND CONTINUE IN THE FAITH. This is the immutable condition of his decree. It does not attribute any mutability to God or his decrees. *This, God's solid foundation, stands sure and bears this inscription,* II Tim. ii. 19: *the Lord knows his own,* and these are *all who leave wickedness and name the name of Christ,* that is, all who believe. The mutability is all on the side of those who renounce their faith: thus in II Tim. ii. 13: *if we do not believe, nevertheless, he remains faithful, he cannot deny himself.* It seems, then, that predestination and election are not particular but only general: that is, they belong to all who believe in their hearts and persist in their belief. Peter is not predestined or elected as Peter, or John as John, but each only insofar as he believes and persists in his belief. Thus the general decree of election is individually applicable to each believer, and is firmly established for those who persevere.

The whole of scripture makes this very clear. It offers salvation and eternal life to all equally, on condition of obedience to the Old Testament and faith in the New. Without doubt the decree as it was made public was consistent with the decree itself. Otherwise we should have to pretend that God was insincere, and said one thing but kept another hidden in his heart. This is, indeed, the effect of that academic distinction which ascribes a twofold will to God: the revealed will, by which he instructs us what he wants us to do, and the will of his good pleasure, by which he decrees that we will never do it. As good split the will in two and say: will in God is twofold—a will by which he wishes, and a will by which he contradicts that wish! But, my opponents reply, we find in scripture these two statements about the same matter: God wishes Pharaoh to let the people go, because he orders it: he does not wish it, because he hardens Pharaoh's heart. But, in fact, God wished it only. Pharaoh did not wish it, and to make him more unwilling God hardened his heart. He postponed the accomplishment of his will, which was the opposite of Pharaoh's, so that he might punish the latter all the more severely for his prolonged unwillingness. To order us to do right but decree that we shall do wrong!—this is not the way God dealt with our forefather, Adam, nor is it the way he deals with those he calls and invites to grace. Could anything be imagined more absurd than such a theory? To make it work, you have to invent a necessity which does not necessitate and a will which does not will.

The other point which must be proved is that the decree, as it was made public, is everywhere conditional: Gen. ii 17: *do not eat of this, for on the day you eat it you will die.* This is clearly as if God had said: I do not wish you to eat of this, and therefore I have certainly not decreed that you will eat it; for if you eat it you will die, if you do not you will live. Thus the decree itself was conditional before the fall, and it is evident from numerous other passages that it was conditional after the fall as well: Gen. iv. 7: *surely, if you do well, lenity awaits you? but if you do not do well, sin is at the door*, or rather, *sin's penalty, ever watchful*. Exod. xxxii. 32, 33: *blot me out now from your book which you have written. I shall blot out from my book the man who sins against me.* Here Moses, on account of his love for his people, forgot that the faithful cannot be blotted out so long as they remain faithful: or perhaps his speech should be modified by reference to Rom. ix. i, etc.: *indeed I should wish, if it were possible. . . .* But God's reply, though metaphorical, shows quite clearly that the principle of predestination has a conditional basis: *I shall blot out the man who sins.* This is shown at greater length when the compact of the law is laid down, Deut. vii. 6, 7, 8. Here God declares most particularly that he has chosen and loved his people out of kindness. At vii. 9, where he wishes to be known as *a supremely faithful God, mindful of the compact he has made and of his kindness*, he adds, nevertheless, a condition: *towards those who love* that is *who love him and keep his commandments.* It is plainest of all in vii. 12: *because you listen to these judgments and, in the future, observe and obey them, Jehovah your God will be mindful in his dealings with you of the compact and the kindness which he promised upon oath to your ancestors.* These and similar passages seem chiefly to refer to the election either of a whole nation to the public worship of God or of some individual man or family to a particular employment. Indeed, in the Old Testament, you will scarcely find a single mention or trace of election in the proper sense, that is, election to eternal life. Nevertheless the principle of the divine decree is the same in both cases. Thus it is said of Solomon, as of another Christ: I Chron. xxviii. 6: *I have chosen him to be as a son to me and I shall be as a father to him.* But what are the conditions? *If he will be constant in putting my commandments and judgments into effect, as at this time*, xxviii. 7, 9: *if you diligently seek him, he will be at hand; but if you forsake him, he will cast you off for ever.* The election of Solomon's descendants, also, depended upon the same stipulation, II Chron. vi. 16: *provided that*, or, *only if your sons shall be mindful*, etc., and similarly xxxiii. 8. Also, xv. 1, 2: *if you seek him, he will be at hand, but if you forsake him*, etc., whence Isaiah is not afraid to say, xiv. 1: *he will choose Israel again*, similarly Zech. i. 16. Isaiah also shows who the elect are, lxv. 9, 10: *my elect will possess that inheritance*, etc. *and the region of Sharon . . . for my people who have sought me.* Jer. xxii. 24: *though Coriah were the signet upon my right hand, yet would I pluck you from that place.*

The same thing should be borne in mind in the New Testament, wherever the condition is not added; but it generally is. Mark xvi. 16: *he who believes and has been baptized will be saved; but he who does not believe will be condemned.* Imagine that you hear God voicing his predestination in these terms: by this one sentence you will dispose of countless controversies: or by this, John iii. 16: *God loved the world so much that he gave his only begotten Son, so that everyone who believes in him may not perish*, and xv. 6: *if a man does not abide in me he is cast out of the vineyard*, etc. and xv. 10: *if you keep my commandments you will abide*, etc. *even as I* and xvii. 20: *I pray not only for these but also for those who through their words shall put their faith in me*, that is, such as the Father has predestined. Thus the Pharisees and lawyers, Luke vii. 30: *who were not baptized by him, rejected God's purpose for themselves*: if they had believed, therefore, even they would have been predestined. Who was more certainly elect than Peter? Yet we find a condition imposed, John xiii. 8: *if I do not wash you, you bear no part with me.* What then? Peter willingly complied and bore a part with Christ: had he not complied, he would have borne no part. For Judas bore no part, although it is said not only that he was elected, which may refer to his apostleship, but also that he was given to Christ by the Father: John xvii. 12: *those you gave me I have guarded, and none of them has perished except the son of perdition; that the scripture might be fulfilled.* Thus John i. 11, 12: *he came to his own and his own did not receive him. But to as many as did receive him he gave*, etc. Namely to those who believe in his name. Before they had received him and believed, he gave them nothing, not even those who were called his own. So Paul writes, Eph. i. 13: *after you believed in him you were sealed with that spirit*, etc. Clearly, those he calls holy at the beginning of the epistle were not sealed until after they had believed: they were not individually predestined before that: II Cor. vi. 1: *I beseech you*, says Paul, *not to receive the grace of God in vain*; Rev. iii. 5: *he who conquers shall be clothed*, etc., *and I shall never blot out his name from the book of life*, but xxii. 19: *if anyone takes anything away from the words of the book of this prophecy, God shall take away his share from the book of life.*

Again, if God has predestined us in Christ, as has been proved above, this must mean through faith in Christ: II Thess. ii. 13: *because God has from the beginning elected you for salvation through sanctification of the spirit and belief in the truth*, not, then, if you will not believe. Tit. i. 1: *according to the faith of God's elect and acceptance of the truth, which is in keeping with piety*; Heb. xi. 6: *it is impossible for anyone without faith to please God*, and thus to be elect. Whence I infer that "the elect" are the same as "believers," and that the terms are synonymous. So Matt. xx. 16: *many are called but few elected* is as much as to say "but few are believers." Rom. viii. 33: *who will lay charges against God's elect?*, that is, against believers. Otherwise, by separating election from faith, and therefore from Christ, we become involved in perplexing and, indeed, in repulsive and unreasonable doctrines. So also Rom. xi. 7: *the elect*, that is, believers, *have achieved it;* from xi. 20 we learn that *you* namely, the elect, *stand through faith*, and xi. 22: *if you remain in goodness, otherwise you will be cut off too.* Paul's interpretation, in his own case, is similar: I Cor. ix. 27: *for fear that somehow, after preaching to others, I should find myself rejected;* Philipp. iii. 12: *not that I have yet obtained my goal, or am yet perfect, but I press on to see whether I too may take hold of that for which Jesus Christ took hold of me;* II Tim. ii. 10, 12: *I endure all things for the sake of the elect so that they too may obtain salvation, which is in Christ Jesus*, but, ii. 13: *if we do not believe,* etc.

Two difficult texts remain, which must be explained by reference to many clearer passages which resemble them; for clear things are not elucidated by obscure things, but obscure by clear. The first passage is Acts xiii. 48, the second Rom. viii. 28–30. I shall deal first with the latter as in my opinion it is less difficult. The words are as follows: *but we know that with those who love God all things work together for good; with those who are called according to his purpose. For those whom he foreknew he also predestined that they should be shaped to the likeness of his Son, etc. and those whom he has predestined he has also called; those he has called, he has also justified, and those he has justified he has also made glorious.*

First it must be noticed that, in viii. 28, *those who love God* and *those who are called according to his purpose* are the same, and that they are identical with *those whom he foreknew* and *those whom he has predestined* and *those he has called* in viii. 30. Hence it is evident that the method and order of general election is being outlined here, not of the election of certain individuals in preference to others. It is just as if Paul had said: We know that with those who love God, that is, those who believe (for those who love, believe) all things work together for good: and the order of events is as follows. First, God foreknew those who would believe; that is, he decided or approved that it should be those alone upon whom, through Christ, he would look kindly: in fact, then, that it should be all men, if they believed. He predestined these to salvation, and, in various ways, he called all men to believe, that is, truly to acknowledge God. He justified those who believed in this way, and finally glorified those who persevered in their belief. But to

make it clearer who they are whom God has foreknown, it must be realized that there are three different ways in which God is said to know a person or thing. First, by universal knowledge, as in Acts xv. 8: *all God's works are known to him from the beginning of time.* Secondly, by knowledge which implies approval or grace, which is a Hebraic idiom, and must therefore be explained more fully: Exod. xxxiii. 12: *I know you by name, and also you have found grace in my eyes;* Psal. i. 6: *Jehovah knows the way of the just;* Matt. vii. 23: *I have never known you.* Thirdly, by knowledge which implies displeasure: Deut. xxxi. 21: *I know the product of their imagination* etc.; II Kings xix. 27: *I know your coming in and your rage against me;* Rev. iii. 1: *I know all your works, that you have a name for being alive, but are dead.* It is clear that, in our passage, the knowledge which implies approval can alone be intended. But God foreknew or approved no one except in Christ; no one except a believer in Christ. Those loved ones, then, who were going to love, that is, were going to believe, God foreknew or approved of. That is to say, he approved of all in general, if they would believe. Those he foreknew in this way he predestined, and called on them to believe; those who believed, he justified. But if God justified believers, and believers alone, because only belief justifies, then he foreknew only those who would be believers, for he justified those he foreknew. Therefore those he justified were the same as those he foreknew, namely, those alone who would believe. So in Rom. xi. 2: *God has not abandoned his people, whom he foreknew*, the reference is to believers, as is clear from xi. 20. II Tim. ii. 19: *the Lord knows his own*, namely, *all who leave wickedness and name the name of Christ*, in fact, believers. I Pet. i. 2: *to the elect, according to the foreknowledge of God the Father, through sanctification of the Spirit, to obedience and the sprinkling of Jesus Christ's blood.* What does all this mean, except "to believers"? God elected believers according to his foreknowledge or approval of them, through the sanctification of the Spirit, and through belief, without which the sprinkling of Christ's blood would have been of no profit to them. It seems, therefore, that most commentators are wrong in interpreting the foreknowledge of God in these passages as meaning prescience. For God's prescience seems to have nothing to do with the principle or essence of predestination. God has predestined and elected each person who believes and persists in his belief. What is the point of knowing whether God had prescience about who in the future would believe or not believe? For no man believes because God had prescience about it, but rather God had prescience about it because the man was going to believe. It is hard to see what purpose is served by introducing God's prescience or foreknowledge about particular individuals into the doctrine of predestination, except that of raising useless and utterly unanswerable questions. For why should God foreknow particular individuals? What could he foreknow in them which might induce him to predestine them in particular, rather than all in general, once the general condition of belief had been laid down? Suffice it to know, without investigating the matter any further, that God, out of his supreme mercy and grace in Christ, has predestined to salvation all who shall believe.

Chapter V
PREFACE

I AM now going to talk about the Son of God and the Holy Spirit, and I do not think I should broach such a difficult subject without some fresh preliminary remarks. The Roman Church demands implicit obedience on all points of faith. If I professed myself a member of it, I should be so indoctrinated, or at any rate so besotted by habit, that I should yield to its authority and to its mere decree even if it were to assert that the doctrine of the Trinity, as accepted at present, could not be proved from any passage of scripture. As it happens, however, I am one of those who recognize God's word alone as the rule of faith; so I shall state quite openly what seems to me much more clearly deducible from the text of scripture than the currently accepted doctrine. I do not see how anyone who calls himself a Protestant or a member of the Reformed Church, and who acknowledges the same rule of faith as myself, could be offended with me for this, especially as I am not trying to browbeat anyone, but am merely pointing out what I consider the more credible doctrine. This one thing I beg of my reader: that he will weigh each statement and evaluate it with a mind innocent of prejudice and eager only for the truth. For I take it upon myself to refute, whenever necessary, not scriptural authority, which is inviolable, but human interpretations. That is my right, and indeed my duty as a human being. Of course, if my opponents could show that the doctrine they defend was revealed to them by a voice from heaven, he would be an impious wretch who dared to raise so much as a murmur against it, let alone a sustained protest. But in fact they can lay claim to nothing more than human powers and that spiritual illumination which is common to all men. What is more just, then, than that they should allow someone else to play his part in the business of research and discussion: someone else who is hunting the same truth, following the same track, and using the same methods as they, and who is equally anxious to benefit his fellow men? Now, relying on God's help, let us come to grips with the subject itself.

OF THE SON OF GOD

So far the efficiency of God has been treated as INTERNAL, residing in his decrees.

His EXTERNAL efficiency takes the form of the execution of these decrees. By this he effects outside himself something he has decreed within himself.

EXTERNAL efficiency subdivides into GENERATION, CREATION, and THE GOVERNMENT OF THE UNIVERSE.

By GENERATION God begot his only Son, in accordance with his decree. That is the chief reason why he is called Father.

Generation must be an example of external efficiency, since the Son is a different person from the Father. Theologians themselves admit as much when they say that there is a certain emanation of the Son from the Father. This point will appear more clearly in the discussion of the Holy Spirit, for although they maintain that the Spirit is of the same essence as the Father, they admit that it emanates and issues and proceeds and is breathed from the Father, and all these expressions denote external efficiency. They also hold that the Son is of the same essence as the Father, and generated from all eternity. So this question, which is quite difficult enough in itself, becomes very complicated indeed if you follow the orthodox line. In scripture there are two senses in which the Father is said to have begotten the Son: one literal, with reference to production; the other metaphorical, with reference to exaltation. Many commentators have cited those passages which allude to the exaltation of the Son, and to his function as mediator, as evidence of his generation from eternity. As a matter of fact they have some excuse, if there is any room for excuse at all, because not a scrap of real evidence for the eternal generation of the Son can be found in the whole of scripture. Whatever certain modern scholars may say to the contrary, it is certain that the Son existed in the beginning, under the title of the Word or Logos, that he was the first of created things, and that through him all other things, both in heaven and earth, were afterwards made. John i. 1–3: *in the beginning was the Word, and the Word was with God and the Word was God*, etc., and xvii. 5: *now therefore glorify me, Father, with your own self, with the glory which I had with you before the world was;* Col. i. 15, 18: *the first born of all created things;* Rev. iii. 14; *the beginning of God's creation;* I Cor. viii. 6: *Jesus Christ, through whom all things are;* Eph. iii. 9: *who created all these things through Jesus Christ;* Col. i. 16: *through him all things were created,* etc.; Heb. i. 2: *through whom also he made the world*—hence i. 10: *you have created.* For more on this subject see below, Chapter vii, On the Creation. All these passages prove that the Son existed before the creation of the World, but not that his generation was from eternity. The other texts which are cited indicate only metaphorical generation, that is resurrection from the dead or appointment to the functions of mediator, according to St. Paul's own interpretation of the second Psalm: Psal. ii. 7: *I will declare the decree: Jehovah has said to me, You are my Son, I have begotten you today,* which Paul interprets thus, Acts xiii. 32, 33: *having raised up Jesus, as indeed it is written in the second Psalm, You are my Son, I have begotten you today.* Rom. i. 4: *powerfully defined as the Son of God, according to the Spirit of holiness, by the resurrection from the dead;* hence Col. i. 18; Rev. i. 4: *the firstborn from the dead.* Then, again, we have Heb. i. 5, where it is written of the Son's exaltation above the angels: *for to which of the angels did he ever say, You are my Son, I have begotten you today? And again, I will be to him a Father, and he shall be to me a Son.* And v. 5, 6, with reference to the priesthood of Christ: *so also Christ did not confer upon himself the glory of becoming high priest, but he who said to him, You are my Son, I have begotten you today.* As also in another Psalm he says, *You are a priest for ever,* etc. From the second Psalm it will also be seen that God begot the Son in the sense of making him a king, Psal. ii. 6, 7: *anointing my king, I have set him upon my holy hill of Sion.* Then, in the next verse, having anointed his king, from which process the name "Christ" is derived, he says: *I have begotten you today.* Similarly Heb. i. 4, 5: *made as superior to the angels as the name he has obtained as his lot is more excellent than theirs.* What name, if not "Son"? The next verse drives the point home: *for to which of the angels did he ever say, You are my Son, I have begotten you today?* The Son declares the same of himself, John x. 35, 36: *do you say that I, whom the Father has sanctified and sent into the world, blaspheme, because I have said, I am the Son of God?* By the same figure of speech, though in a much less exalted sense, the saints also are said to have been begotten by God.

When all the above passages, especially the second Psalm, have been compared and digested carefully, it will be apparent that, however the Son was begotten, it did not arise from natural necessity, as is usually maintained, but was just as much a result of the Father's decree and will as the Son's priesthood, kingship, and resurrection from the dead. The fact that he is called "begotten," whatever that means, and God's *own Son,*

Rom. viii. 32, does not stand in the way of this at all. He is called God's own son simply because he had no other Father but God, and this is why he himself said that God was his Father, John v. 18. For to Adam, formed out of the dust, God was creator rather than Father; but he was in a real sense Father of the Son, whom he made of his own substance. It does not follow, however, that the Son is of the same essence as the Father. Indeed, if he were, it would be quite incorrect to call him Son. For a real son is not of the same age as his father, still less of the same numerical essence: otherwise father and son would be one person. This particular Father begot his Son not from any natural necessity but of his own free will: a method more excellent and more in keeping with paternal dignity, especially as this Father is God. For it has already been demonstrated from the text of scripture that God always acts with absolute freedom, working out his own purpose and volition. Therefore he must have begotten his Son with absolute freedom.

God could certainly have refrained from the act of generation and yet remained true to his own essence, for he stands in no need of propagation. So generation has nothing to do with the essence of deity. And if a thing has nothing to do with his essence or nature, he does not do it from natural necessity like a natural agent. Moreover, if natural necessity was the deciding factor, then God violated his own essence by begetting, through the force of nature, an equal. He could no more do this than deny himself. Therefore he could not have begotten the Son except of his own free will and as a result of his own decree.

So God begot the Son as a result of his own decree. Therefore it took place within the bounds of time, for the decree itself must have preceded its execution (the insertion of the word *today* makes this quite clear). As for those who maintain that the Son's generation was from eternity, I cannot discover on what passage in the scriptures they ground their belief. Micah v. 2 refers to his works, not his generation, and states only that these were from the beginning of the world—but more of this later. The Son is also called *only begotten,* John i. 14: *and we saw his glory, a glory indeed as of the only begotten having proceeded from the Father,* and i. 18: *the only begotten Son of God who is in the bosom of the Father;* iii. 16: *that he gave his only begotten Son,* similarly iii. 18. I John iv. 9: *he sent his only begotten Son.* Notice that it is not said that he is of the same essence as the Father but, on the contrary, that he is visible and given by, sent from, and proceeding from the Father. He is called *only begotten* to distinguish him from the numerous other people who are likewise said to be begotten by God, John i. 13: *begotten by God;* I John iii. 9: *whoever is born of God,* etc.; James i. 18: *of his own will he begot us with the word of truth*, etc.; I John v. 1: *whoever believes*, etc. *is begotten by God;* I Pet. i. 3: *who according to his great mercy has begotten us to hope*, etc. But since nowhere in the scriptures is the Son said to be begotten except, as above, in a metaphorical sense, it is probable that he is called *only begotten* chiefly because he is the only mediator between God and man.

Then, again, the Son is called *the first born*, Rom. viii. 29: *that he might be the first born among many brothers;* Col. i. 15: *the first born of all created things;* i. 18: *the first born from the dead;* Heb. i. 6: *when he brings in the first born*. All these passages preclude the possibility of his being co-essential with the Father, and of his generation from eternity. Furthermore, the same thing is said of Israel, Exod. iv. 22: *thus says Jehovah, Israel is my Son, my first born*, and of Ephraim, Jer. xxxi. 9: *he is my first born*, and of all the blessed, Heb. xii. 23: *to the assembly of the first born.*

Up to now all mention of generation has been entirely metaphorical. But if one in fact begets another being, who did not previously exist, one brings him into existence. And if God begets as a result of physical necessity, he can beget only a God equal to himself (though really a God cannot be begotten at all). It would follow from the first hypothesis that there are two infinite Gods, and from the second that a first cause can become an effect, which no sane man will allow. So it is necessary to inquire how and in what sense God the Father begot the Son. Once again, we can quickly find the answer in scripture. When the Son is said to be *the first born of every creature* and, Rev. iii. 14, *the beginning of God's creation*, it is as plain as it could possibly be that God voluntarily created or generated or produced the Son before all things: the Son, who was endowed with divine nature and whom, similarly, when the time was ripe, God miraculously brought forth in his human nature from the Virgin Mary. The generation of the divine nature is by no one more sublimely or more fully explained than by the apostle to the Hebrews, i. 2, 3: *whom he has appointed heir of all things, through whom also he made the world. Who, since he is the brightness of his glory and the image of his substance*, etc. What can this imply but that God imparted to the Son as much as he wished of the divine nature, and indeed of the divine substance also? But do not take *substance* to mean total essence. If it did, it would mean that the Father gave his essence to his Son and at the same time retained it, numerically unaltered, himself. That is not a means of generation but a contradiction of terms. What I have quoted is all that is revealed from heaven about the generation of the Son of God. Anyone who wants to be wiser than this is really not wise at all. Lured on by empty philosophy or sophistry, he becomes hopelessly entangled and loses himself in the dark.

In spite of the fact that we all know there is only one God, Christ in scripture is called not merely *the only begotten Son of God* but also, frequently, *God*. Many people, pretty intelligent people in their own estimation, felt sure that this was inconsistent. So they hit upon the bizarre and senseless idea that the Son, although personally and numerically distinct, was nevertheless essentially one with the Father, and so there was still only one God.

The numerical significance of "one" and of "two" must be unalterable and the same for God as for man. It would have been a waste of time for God to thunder forth so repeatedly that first commandment which said that he was the one and only God, if it could nevertheless be maintained that another God existed as well, who ought himself to be thought of as the only God. Two distinct things cannot be of the same essence. God is one being, not two. One being has one essence, and also one subsistence—by which is meant simply a substantial essence. If you were to ascribe two subsistences or two persons to one essence, it would be a contradiction in terms. You would be saying that the essence was at once one and not one. If one divine essence is common to two components, then that essence or divinity will be in the position of a whole in relation to its parts, or of a genus in relation to its several species, or lastly of a common subject, in relation to its non-essential qualities. If you should grant none of these, there would be no escaping the absurdities which follow, as that one essence can be one third of two or more components of an essence.

If my opponents had paid attention to God's own words when he was addressing kings and magnates, Psal. lxxxii. 6: *I say, you are Gods, and all of you sons of the Most High*, and to the words of Christ, John x. 35: *if he called those to whom the word of God came, Gods; and the scripture cannot be blotted out*, and to the words of Paul, I Cor. viii. 5, 6: *although there are those that are called Gods, both in heaven and earth, (for there are many Gods and many Lords), nevertheless for us there is one God, the Father, from whom all things*, etc., and lastly to the words of Peter II. i. 4: *that through these things you might be made partakers or sharers of the divine nature* (which implies much more than the title *gods* in the sense in which kings are said to be gods, and yet no one would conclude from this text that the saints were of one essence with God)—if, I say, my opponents had paid attention to these words, they would not have found it necessary to fly in the face of reason or, indeed, of so much glaring scriptural evidence.

But let us disregard reason when discussing sacred matters and follow exclusively what the Bible teaches.

Accordingly let no one expect me to preface what I have to say with a long metaphysical introduction, or bring into my argument all that play-acting of the persons of the godhead. For a start, it is absolutely clear from innumerable passages of scripture that there is in reality one true and independent supreme God. Since he is called "one"; since human reason and the conventions of language and God's people, the Jews, have always interpreted the term "only one person" to mean one in number, let us examine the sacred books to discover who this one, true, supreme God is. Let us look first at the gospel. This should provide the clearest evidence, for here we find the plain and exhaustive doctrine of the one God which Christ expounded to his apostles and they to their followers. It is very unlikely that the gospel should be ambiguous or obscure on this point. For it was given not for the purpose of spreading new or incredible ideas about God's nature, ideas that his people had never heard of before, but to announce the salvation of the Gentiles through Messiah, the Son of God, which God had promised to Abraham: *no one has ever seen God: the only begotten Son who is in the bosom of the Father, he has revealed him to us*, John i. 18. So first of all lest us consult the Son on the subject of God.

According to the Son's clearest possible testimony, the Father is that one true God from whom are all things. Mark xii. 28, 29, 32, Christ, asked by the lawyer which was the first commandment of all, replied by quoting Deut. vi. 4: *the first commandment of all is: hear, Israel, the Lord our God is one Lord* or, as it is in the Hebrew, *Jehovah our God is one Jehovah*. The lawyer agreed: *there is one God and there is no other except him*. Christ approved of him for agreeing, Mark xii. 34. Now it is absolutely clear that this lawyer and all the Jews understood that there was one God in the sense that he was one person, as that phrase is commonly understood. That this God was none other than the Father is proved by John viii. 41–54: *we have one Father, God. It is my Father who glorifies me, whom you say is your God*, and iv. 21: *neither on this mountain nor in Jerusalem shall you worship the Father*. Christ therefore agrees with all God's people that the Father is that one and only God. Who can believe that the very first of the commandments was so obscure that it was utterly misunderstood by the Church for so many centuries? Who can believe that these two other persons could have gone without their divine honors and remained wholly unknown to God's people right down to the time of the gospel? Indeed God, teaching his people about their worship under the gospel, warns them that they will have for their God the one Jehovah that they have always had, and David, that is, Christ, for their king and their Lord. Jer. xxx. 9: *they shall serve Jehovah their God and David*

their king, whom I will raise up for them. In this passage Christ, as God wished him to be known and worshipped by his people under the gospel, is firmly distinguished, both by nature and title, from the one God Jehovah. Christ himself, then, the Son of God, teaches us nothing in the gospel about the one God other than what the law had taught us already. He asserts everywhere, quite clearly, that it is the Father. John xvii. 3: *this is eternal life, that they may know you, the only true God, and Jesus Christ whom you have sent*, xx. 17: *I ascend to my Father and your Father, and to my God and your God*. If the Father is Christ's God and our God, and if there is only one God, who can be God except the Father?

Paul, the apostle and interpreter of Christ, makes this same point very clearly and distinctly, almost as if it were the sum of his teaching. So much so, that no instructor in the church could have taught a novice under his care more skillfully or more plainly about the one God—one, that is, in the numerical sense in which human reason always understands it. I Cor. viii. 4–6: *we know that an idol is nothing in the world, and that there is no other God but one: for although there are those that are called Gods both in heaven and earth (for there are many Gods and many Lords), nevertheless for us there is one God, the Father, from whom all things are and in whom we are, and one Lord Jesus Christ, through whom all things are and through whom we are*. Here, *there is no other* or *second* God, *but one*, excludes not only a second essence but any second person whatsoever. For it is expressly stated, viii. 6: *the Father is that one God;* therefore there is no *other* person, but one only. There is no other person, that is, in the sense in which Church divines usually argue that there is when they use John xiv. 16 as proof of the existence of the Holy Spirit as a person. Again, the single *God, the Father, from whom all things are* is numerically opposed to *those that are called Gods both in heaven and earth*, and one is numerically opposed to *many*. Though the Son be another God, here he is called only *Lord*. He *from whom all things are* is clearly distinguished from him *through whom all things are*, and since a difference in method of causation proves a difference in essence, the two are distinguished from the point of view of essence as well. Besides, since a numerical difference is the result of a difference in essence, if two things are two numerically, they must also be two essentially. There is one Lord, namely, he whom God the Father has made, Acts ii. 36. The Father who did the making is therefore much more of a Lord, although he is not actually called "Lord" here. But he who calls the Father *one God* also calls him one supreme Lord, as does Psal. cx. 1: *the Lord said to my Lord*—a passage discussed at greater length below. Paul who speaks of *one Lord Jesus Christ* does not call Christ one God, and for this reason above all: both *Lord* and *Christ* were made by God the Father, Acts ii. 36. Thus Paul elsewhere calls the Father God and Lord of the person whom he here refers to as the one *Lord Jesus Christ*. Eph. i. 17: *the God of our Lord Jesus Christ;* I Cor. xi. 3: *the head of Christ is God*, and xv. 28: *the Son himself will be made subject to him.* If the Father is really *the Father of Christ, the God of Christ, the head of Christ*, and the God to whom Christ the Lord and, indeed, Christ the Son is and will be subject, why should not the Father also be the Lord of the same Lord Christ and the God of the same God Christ? For Christ must be God in the same subordinate way that he is Lord and Son. Finally, it is the Father *by whom* and *from whom* and *through whom* and *in whom all things are*, Rom. xi. 36, Heb. ii. 10. The Son is not he *by whom* but only *through whom* all things are—*all things*, that is *which were made*, John i. 3, but with this exception, *all things except him who subjected all things to him*, I Cor. xv. 27. Evidently, then, *through whom* in *through whom all things are* must be understood to mean "by whose secondary and delegated power." Evidently, also, the preposition *through*, when referring to the Father, indicates the prime cause (as in John vi. 57: *I live through the Father*), and when referring to the Son indicates the secondary and instrumental cause: but this will be explained more clearly below.

Similarly Eph. iv. 4–6: *there is one body and one spirit, just as you are called in one hope of your calling: one Lord, one faith, one baptism; one God and Father of all, who is above all and through all and in you all.* Here there is one Spirit and one Lord, but that one is the Father. Thus he is the one God in the same sense as that in which all the other things mentioned are one, that is, numerically, and therefore also one in person. I Tim. ii. 5: *there is one God, and one mediator between God and men: the man, Jesus Christ.* Here the whole person of the mediator is given the name "man," (a name which really applies only to his inferior nature), rather than that he should be thought equal to the Father, or the same God as the Father, when the reference is carefully and specifically to one God. Besides it is quite inconceivable that anyone could be a mediator to himself or on his own behalf. According to Gal. iii. 20: *a mediator however is not needed for one person acting alone, but God is one.* How, then, could God be God's mediator? How is it that the mediator constantly testified when speaking of himself that he did nothing by himself, John viii. 28, and that he did not come from himself, viii. 42? It must follow that he does not act as mediator to himself, or return as mediator to himself. Rom. v. 10: *we were reconciled to God by the death of his Son.* The God to whom we were reconciled, whoever he is, cannot, if he

is one God, be the same as the God by whom we were reconciled, since that God is another person. If he is the same, then he is his own mediator between himself and us, and reconciles us to himself by himself: a quite inexplicable state of affairs!

All this is so obvious in itself that it really needs no explanation. It is quite clear that the Father alone is a self-existent God: clear, too, that a being who is not self-existent cannot be a God. But it is amazing what nauseating subtlety, not to say trickery, some people have employed in their attempts to evade the plain meaning of these scriptural texts. They have left no stone unturned; they have followed every red herring they could find; they have tried everything. Indeed they have made it apparent that, instead of preaching the plain, straightforward truth of the gospel to poor and simple men, they are engaged in maintaining an extremely absurd paradox with the maximum of obstinacy and argumentativeness. To save this paradox from utter collapse they have availed themselves of the specious assistance of certain strange terms and sophistries borrowed from the stupidity of the schools.

Their excuse, however, is that though these opinions may seem inconsistent with reason they are, on account of some other scriptural passages, to be countenanced; otherwise there will appear to be inconsistencies in scripture. So let us, again, disregard reason and concentrate on the text of scripture.

Only two passages are relevant. The first is John x. 30: *I and the Father are one*, that is, as it is commonly interpreted, one in essence. But for God's sake let us not come to any rash conclusions about God! There is more than one way in which two things can be called one. Scripture says and the Son says *I and the Father are one*. I agree. Someone or other guesses that this means one in essence. I reject it as man's invention. For whoever it was in the Church who first took it upon himself to guess about it, the Son has not left the question of how he is one with the Father to our conjecture. On the contrary, he explains the doctrine very clearly himself, insofar as it concerns us to know it. The Father and the Son are certainly not one in essence, for the Son had himself asserted the contrary in the preceding verse, *my Father, who gave me them, is greater than all*, (indeed, he also says, xiv. 28: *he is greater than I*), and in the following verses he expressly denies that by saying *I and the Father are one* he was setting himself up as God. He claims that what he said was only what follows in the next quotation, which amounts to much less, x. 36: *do you say that I whom the Father has sanctified and sent into the world, blaspheme because I have said, I am the Son of God?* It must be that this is said of two persons, distinct in essence and, moreover, not equal to each other. If the

Son is here teaching about the one divine essence of two persons of the Trinity, why does he not rather talk about the one essence of the three persons? Why does he divide the indivisible Trinity? That which is not a whole is not one. So it follows from the convictions of those very people who affirm the truth of the Trinity that the Son and the Father, without the Spirit, are not one in essence. How, then, are they one? The Son alone can tell us this, and he does. Firstly, they are one in that they speak and act as one. He explains himself to this effect in the same chapter, after the Jews have misunderstood his statement: x. 38: *believe in my works so that you may know and believe that the Father is in me and I in him.* Similarly xiv. 10: *do you not believe that I am in the Father and the Father in me? I myself am not the source of the words which I speak to you; but the Father who dwells in me, he performs the works.* Here it is evident that Christ distinguishes the Father from the whole of his own being. However, he does say that the Father dwells in him, though this does not mean that their essence is one, only that their communion is extremely close. Secondly, he declares that he and the Father are one in the same way as we are one with him: that is, not in essence but in love, in communion, in agreement, in charity, in spirit, and finally in glory. John xiv. 20, 21: *on that day you will know that I am in my Father, and you in me, and I in you. He who has my commandments and keeps them, he it is that loves me; and he that loves me shall be loved by my Father,* and xvii. 21: *that all may be one as you, Father, are in me and I in you; that they too may be one in us* etc., and xvii. 23: *I in them and you in me; that they may be made perfect in one, and that the world may know that you have sent me, and that you love them as you have loved me,* and xvii. 22: *I have given them the glory which you gave me, that they may be one as we are one.* Since the Son plainly teaches that there are so many ways in which the Father and he are one, shall I pay no attention to all these ways of being one? Shall I put my mind to it and think up some other way of being one, namely that of being one in essence? Shall I give preference to this idea when some other mere man has thought it up beforehand? Who will stand surety for me if I do? The Church? The orthodox Church herself teaches me otherwise, and rightly. She tells me that I should listen to Christ before her.

The second passage, and that which is generally thought the clearest of all, upon which the orthodox view of the essential unity of the three persons of the Trinity is based, is I John v. 7: *there are three witnesses in heaven, the Father, the Word and the Holy Spirit, and these three are one.* This verse, however, is not found in the Syriac or the other two Oriental versions, the Arabic and the Ethiopic, nor in the majority of the ancient Greek codices. Moreover, in those manuscripts where it does appear a remarkable variety of readings occurs. Anyway, quite apart from this, the verse does not prove that those who are said to be one in heaven are necessarily one in essence, any more than it proves that about those who, in the next verse, are said to be one on earth. The fact that John is speaking here (if John really wrote the verse) only about unity of consent and testimony, as in the last-quoted passage, was not only realized by Erasmus but even admitted by Beza, though reluctantly. (You can go and look at their works to prove it.) Besides, who are these three witnesses? You will admit that there are not three Gods; therefore the *one* in the passage is not a God but the one testimony of the three witnesses; one witnessing. But he who is not essentially one with God the Father cannot be the Father's equal. This text will be discussed more fully, however, in the next chapter.

But it is maintained that, although scripture does not say in so many words that the Father and the Son are essentially one, the fact can be reasonably deduced from these texts and from others. To begin with, granting this to be the case (and I do not, in fact, grant it at all) when the point to be the case (and I do not, in fact, grant it at all) when the point at issue is so sublime and so far above the reach of our understanding, and involves the very elements and, as it were, the first postulates of our faith, we can really base our belief only on God's word, and God's word at its clearest and most distinct, not on mere reason at all. Anyway, reason is loud in its denunciation of the doctrine in question. I ask you, what can reason do here? Can reason maintain an unreasonable opinion? The product of reason must be reason, not absurd notions which are utterly alien to all human ways of thinking. The conclusion just be, then, that this opinion is consonant neither with reason nor scripture. Of the two alternatives only one can remain: namely, that if God is one God, and the Father, and yet the Son is also called God, then he must have received the divine name and nature from God the Father, in accordance with the Father's decree and will, as I said before. This is in no way opposed to reason, and is supported by innumerable texts from scripture.

But not all those who insist that the Son is one with God the Father rely for proof on the two texts I have quoted above. So although deprived of that evidence, they are still confident that they can prove their point quite clearly if they can show, by frequent scriptural quotation, that the name, attributes and works of God, and the divine office itself, are habitually attributed to the Son. To proceed, therefore, in the same line of argument: I do not ask them to believe that the Father alone, and no one else, is God, unless I demonstrate and prove beyond question the following points. First, that all the above particulars are everywhere expressly attributed, both by the Son himself and by his apostles, only to one God, the Father. Second, that if these particulars are anywhere attributed to the Son, it is in such a way that they are easily understood to be attributable, in their primary and proper sense, to the Father alone, and that the Son admits that he possesses whatever measure of Deity is attributed to him, by virtue of the peculiar gift and kindness of the Father, as the apostles also testify. Third, that the Son himself and his apostles acknowledge in everything they say and write that the Father is greater than the Son in all things.

I know the answer that will be made here by those who, while they believe that there is one God, do not believe that that one God is the Father. So I will meet their objection once and for all at the outset, to stop them being disturbed and thrown into uproar by every single passage in turn. They make, as the saying goes, two primary assumptions, which means that they ask us to cede them two points for nothing. First, that wherever the name of God is attributed to the Father alone, it should be understood οὐσιωδῶς, not ὑποστατικῶς: in other words, that the name of the one Father should be accepted as signifying the three persons or the whole essence of the Trinity, not the single person of the Father. This distinction is, for various reasons, absurd. Moreover, it is invented solely for the purpose of supporting their theory, though in fact it does not support it but is supported by it, so that if you invalidate the theory, which you can do merely by denying it, the worthless distinction vanishes at the same time. Indeed, the distinction is not merely worthless, but no distinction at all. What it is, is a pair of synonymous terms tricked out with Greek adverbs to dazzle the eyes of freshmen. For since the nouns "essence" and "hypostasis" mean the same thing, as I showed in the second chapter, there is certainly no difference between the related adverbs "essentially" and "hypostatically." So if the name God is attributed "essentially" to the Father alone, it is attributed hypostatically to the Father alone as well. For one substantial essence is nothing other than one hypostasis, and *vice versa*. I would therefore ask my opponents whether they wish God the Father to be considered as an entity or not. Certainly, they will reply. He is the entity of entities. I say then, that as he has one hypostasis, so he also has an essence proper to himself, absolutely and utterly incommunicable, and common to no one, that is, to no one else. For he cannot have his own proper hypostasis without having his own proper essence. Similarly it is quite impossible for any entity to share its essence with anything else whatsoever, for it is by virtue of its es-

sence that it is what it is, and is distinguished numerically from everything else. If, therefore, the Son, who has his own proper hypostasis, has not also his own proper essence, but that of the Father, then in fact he becomes, according to my opponents' theory, either no entity at all or the same entity as the Father. This doctrine turns the Christian religion completely upside down. The usual reply is that, while one person can only be of one finite essence, many people can be included in an infinite essence. This is ridiculous. For the very fact that the essence is infinite is an additional reason why it can include only one person. Everyone acknowledges that both the essence and the person of the Father are infinite: therefore the essence of the Father cannot be communicated to another person, otherwise there might be two or, indeed, a million infinite persons.

Chapter VII

OF THE CREATION

THE second kind of external efficiency is commonly called CREATION. Anyone who asks what God did before the creation of the world is a fool; and anyone who answers him is not much wiser. Most people think they have given an account of the matter when they have quoted I Cor. ii. 7: *that he preordained, before the creation of the world, his wisdom, hidden in a mystery*, which they take to mean that he was occupied with election and reprobation, and with deciding other related matters. But it would clearly be disproportionate for God to have been totally occupied from eternity in decreeing things which it was to take him only six days to create: things which were to be governed in various ways for a few thousand years, and then finally either received into an unchanging state with God for ever, or else for ever thrown away.

That the world was created, must be considered an article of faith: Heb. xi. 3: *through faith we understand that the world was made by God's word*

CREATION is the act by which GOD THE FATHER PRODUCED EVERYTHING THAT EXISTS BY HIS WORD AND SPIRIT, that is, BY HIS WILL, IN ORDER TO SHOW THE GLORY OF HIS POWER AND GOODNESS.

BY WHICH GOD THE FATHER: Job ix. 8: *who alone spreads out the heavens*; Isa. xliv. 24: *I, Jehovah, make all things, I alone spread out the heavens, and I stretch forth the earth by myself*, and xlv. 6, 7: *that from* the sun's rising and from its setting the nations may know that there is none beside me, that I am Jehovah, and there is none else: that I form the light and create the darkness. If such things as common sense and accepted idiom exist at all, then these words preclude the possibility not only of there being any other God, but also of there being any person, of any kind whatever, equal to him. Neh. ix. 6: *you alone are that Jehovah, you have made the heavens, the heavens of heavens;* Mal. ii. 10: *have we not all one father? Has not one mighty and unparalleled God created us?* Thus Christ himself says, Matt. xi. 25: *Father, Lord of heaven and earth;* and so do all the apostles: Acts iv. 24, compared with iv. 27: *Lord, you are that God who created the heaven and the earth, the sea and all that is in them . . . against your Son;* Rom. xi. 36: *from him and through him and in him are all things;* I Cor. viii. 6: *one God, the Father, from whom all things are,* and II Cor. iv. 6: *since God it is, who commanded light to shine out of darkness, that has shone in our hearts, to give the light of the knowledge of God's glory in the face of Jesus Christ;* Heb. ii. 10: *him, on account of whom and through whom all these things are,* and iii. 4: *but he who built all these things, is God.*

BY HIS WORD: Gen. i. *passim, he said . . . ;* Psal. xxxiii. 6: *by Jehovah's word,* and xxxiii. 9: *he speaks;* Psal. cxlviii. 5: *he commanded;* II Pet. iii. 5: *through the word of God,* that is, as we learn from other passages, through the Son, who apparently derives from this his title of the Word. John i. 3, 10: *all things were made through him: through him the world was made;* I Cor. viii. 6: *one God, the Father, from whom all things are. And one Lord Jesus Christ, through whom all things are;* Eph. iii. 9: *who created all these things through Jesus Christ;* Col. i. 16: *through him all things were created . . . ;* Heb. i. 2: *through whom also he made the world,* hence i. 10: *you have created.* The preposition *through* sometimes denotes the principal cause, *through whom you are called,* and sometimes the instrumental or less important cause, as in the passages quoted above. It does not denote the principal cause in these passages, because if it did the Father himself, by whom all things are, would not be the principal. Nor does it denote a joint cause, because then it would be said not that the Father created *by* the Word and Spirit but *with* the Word and Spirit, or alternatively that the Father, the Word, and the Spirit created. These formulae are nowhere to be found in scripture. Again, "to be *by* the Father" and "to be *through* the Son" are phrases which do not signify the same kind of efficient cause. If they are not of the same kind, then there can be no question of a joint cause, and if there is no joint cause then "the Father *by* whom all things are" will unquestionably be a more important cause than "the Son *through* whom all things are." For the Father is not only

he *by* whom, but also he *from* whom, *in* whom, *through* whom, and *on account* of whom all things are, as I have shown above, inasmuch as he comprehends within himself all lesser causes. But the Son is only he *through* whom all things are, and is therefore the less principal cause. So we often find it said that the Father created the world through the Son, but nowhere that the Son, in the same sense, created the world through the Father. But some try to prove from Rev. iii. 14 that the Son was the joint cause of the creation with the Father, or even the principal cause. The reference there is to *the beginning of God's creation,* and they interpret the word *beginning* as meaning *beginner,* on the authority of Aristotle. But in the first place, the Hebrew language, from which this expression is taken, never allows this use of the word *beginning,* but rather requires a quite contrary sense, as in Gen. xlix. 3: *Reuben, the beginning of my strength.* Secondly, there are two passages in Paul, referring to Christ himself, which make it absolutely clear that the word *beginning* is here used to mean not an agent but something acted upon: Col. i. 15, 18: *the first born of all created things. The beginning, the first born from the dead.* Here both the Greek accent and the verbal passive πρωτότοκος, show that the Son of God was *the first born of all created things* in the same sense as the Son of man who was the πρωτότοκος or *first born* of Mary, Matt. i. 25. The second passage is Rom. viii. 29: *the first born among many brothers,* where *first born* has, of course, a passive sense. Finally it should be noted that Christ is not called merely the *beginning of creation,* but *the beginning of God's creation,* and that can only mean that he was the first of the things which God created. How, then, can he be God himself? Some of the Fathers have suggested that the reason why he is called *the first born of all created things* in Col. i. 15 is that *through him all things were created,* as it says in the next verse. But this argument cannot be admitted, because if St. Paul had meant this, he would have said "who was before every creature" (which is what these Fathers insist that the words mean, although it is a forced reading), not, *who was the first born of all created things.* The words *first born* here are certainly superlative in sense, but they also, in a way, imply that only part of a collective whole is being spoken of. This last remark is true only because the production of Christ was apparently a kind of "birth" or creation: it is not true where Christ is also called the first born *man.* For he is called *first born* in that phrase not just as a title of dignity, but to distinguish him from other men for the chronological reason that *through him all things which are in the heavens were created,* Col. i. 16.

Prov. viii. 22, 23 is no better as a basis for argument, even if we admit that the chapter as a whole should be interpreted as a reference to Christ: *Jehovah possessed me, the beginning of his way; I was anointed before the world.* A thing which was *possessed* and *anointed* could not itself be the primary cause. Besides, even a creature is called the beginning of the ways of God in Job xl. 19: *he is the beginning of God's ways.* As for the eighth chapter of Proverbs, I should say that the figure introduced as a speaker there is not the Son of God but a poetical personification of Wisdom, as in Job xxviii. 20–27: *From where, then, is that wisdom . . . ? then he saw her. . . .*

Another argument is based on Isa. xlv. 12, 23: *I have made the earth . . . ; shall bow to me.* My opponents say that these words are spoken by Christ, and they quote St. Paul in their support: Rom. xiv. 10, 11: *we shall all stand before the judgment seat of Christ: for it is written, As I live, says the Lord, every knee shall bow to me. . . .* But it is obvious from the parallel passage, Philipp. ii. 9–11, that this is said by God the Father, who gave that judgment seat, and all judgment, to the Son, *that at the name of Jesus every knee shall bow . . . ; to the glory of God the Father,* or in other words, *every tongue shall confess to God.*

AND SPIRIT. Gen. i. 2: *the Spirit of God brooded,* that is to say, God's divine power, not any particular person, as I showed in Chapter VI, Of the Holy Spirit. For if it was a person, why is the Spirit named and nothing said about the Son, by whose labor, as we so often read, the world was made? (Unless, of course, the Spirit referred to was Christ, who, as I have shown, is sometimes called *the Spirit* in the Old Testament.) Anyway, even if we grant that it was a person, it seems only to have been a subordinate, since, after God had created heaven and earth, the Spirit merely brooded upon the face of the waters which had already been created. Similarly Job xxvi. 13: *by his spirit he decked the heavens;* Psal. xxxiii. 6: *the heavens were made by Jehovah's word, and all the host of them by the spirit of his mouth.* The person of the Spirit certainly does not seem to have proceeded more from God's mouth than from Christ's, who *shall consume the antichrist with the spirit of his mouth,* II Thess. ii. 8, compared with Isa. xi. 4: *the rod of his mouth.*

BY HIS WILL, Psal. cxxxv. 6: *whatever pleases you;* Rev. iv. 11: *as a result of your will.*

IN ORDER TO SHOW. Gen. i. 31: *whatever he had done, it was very good,* similarly I Tim. iv. 4; Psal. xix. 2, 3: *the heavens declare the glory of God;* Prov. xvi. 4: *he has created all things for himself;* Acts xiv. 15: *that you may turn from these vanities to the living God, who made heaven and earth and the sea and all things in them,* and xvii. 24: *that God who made the world,* etc.; Rom. i. 20: *for both his eternal power and his eternal godhead are discerned.* So far I have established that God the Father

is the first efficient cause of all things.

There is a good deal of controversy, however, about what the original matter was. On the whole the moderns are of the opinion that everything was formed out of nothing (which is, I fancy, what their own theory is based on!). In the first place it is certain that neither the Hebrew verb בָּרָא, nor the Greek κτίζειν, nor the Latin *creare* means "to make out of nothing." On the contrary, each of them always means "to make out of something." Gen. i. 21, 27: *God created . . . which the waters brought forth abundantly, he created them male and female;* Isa. liv. 16: *I have created the maker, I have created the destroyer.* Anyone who says, then, that "to create" means "to produce out of nothing," is, as logicians say, arguing from an unproved premise. The passages of scripture usually quoted in this context do not at all confirm the received opinion, but tend to imply the contrary, namely that all things were not made out of nothing, II Cor. iv. 6: *God who commanded light to shine out of darkness.* It is clear from Isa. xlv. 7 that this darkness was far from being a mere nothing: *I am Jehovah,* etc. *I form the light and create the darkness.* If the darkness is nothing, then when God created the darkness he created nothing, that is he both created and did not create, which is a contradiction in terms. Again, Heb. xi. 3, all we are required *to understand through faith* about *earthly times,* that is, about the world, is that *the things which are seen were not put together from the things which appear.* Now because things do not appear, they must not be considered synonymous with nothing. For one thing, you cannot have a plural of nothing, and for another, a thing cannot be *put together* from nothing as it can from a number of components. The meaning is, rather, that these things are not as they now appear. I might also mention the apocryphal writers, as closest to the scriptures in authority: Wisdom xi. 17: *who created the world out of formless matter;* II Macc. vii. 28: *out of things that were not.* But it is said of Rachel's children in Matt. ii. 18, *they are not,* and this does not mean *they are nothing* but, as frequently in the Hebrew language, they are not among the living.

It is clear, then, that the world was made out of some sort of matter. For since "action" and "passivity" are relative terms, and since no agent can act externally unless there is something, and something material, which can be acted upon, it is apparent that God could not have created this world out of nothing. *Could not,* that is, not because of any defect of power or omnipotence on his part, but because it was necessary that something should have existed previously, so that it could be acted upon by his supremely powerful active efficacy. Since, then, both the Holy Scriptures and reason itself suggest that all these things were made not out of nothing but out of matter, matter must either have always existed, independently of God, or else originated from God at some point in time. That matter should have always existed independently of God is inconceivable. In the first place, it is only a passive principle, dependent upon God and subservient to him; and, in the second place, there is no inherent force or efficacy in time or eternity, any more than there is in the concept of number. But if matter did not exist from eternity, it is not very easy to see where it originally came from. There remains only this solution, especially if we allow ourselves to be guided by scripture, namely, that all things came from God. Rom. xi. 36: *from him and through him and in him are all things;* I Cor. viii. 6: *one God, the Father, from whom all things are from,* as the Greek reads in both cases. Heb. ii. 11: *for both he who sanctifies and he who is sanctified, are all from one.*

There are, to begin with, as everyone knows, four kinds of causes, efficient, material, formal and final. Since God is the first absolute and sole cause of all things, he unquestionably contains and comprehends within himself all these causes. So the material cause must be either God or nothing. But nothing is no cause at all; (though my opponents want to prove that forms and, what is more, human forms were created from nothing). Now matter and form are, as it were, internal causes. These are the things which go to make up the object itself. So either all objects must have had only two causes, external causes that is, or else God was not the perfect and absolute cause of all things. Secondly, it is a demonstration of supreme power and supreme goodness that such heterogeneous, multiform and inexhaustible virtue should exist in God, and exist substantially (for that virtue cannot be accidental which admits various degrees and is, as it were, susceptible to augmentation and remission, according to his will). It is, I say, a demonstration of God's supreme power and goodness that he should not shut up this heterogeneous and substantial virtue within himself, but should disperse, propagate and extend it as far as, and in whatever way, he wills. For this original matter was not an evil thing, nor to be thought of as worthless: it was good, and it contained the seeds of all subsequent good. It was a substance, and could only have been derived from the source of all substance. It was in a confused and disordered state at first, but afterwards God made it ordered and beautiful.

Those who object to this theory, on the grounds that matter was apparently imperfect, should also object to the theory that God originally produced it out of nothing in an imperfect and formless state. What does it matter whether God produced this imperfect matter out of nothing or out of himself? To argue that there

could have been no imperfection in a substance which God produced out of himself, is only to transfer the imperfection to God's efficiency. For why did he not, starting from nothing, make everything absolutely perfect straight away? But in fact, matter was not, by nature, imperfect. The addition of forms (which, incidentally, are themselves material) did not make it more perfect but only more beautiful. But, you will say, how can something corruptible result from something incorruptible? I might well reply, how can God's virtue and efficiency result from nothing? But in fact matter, like the form and nature of the angels, came from God in an incorruptible state, and even since the fall it is still incorruptible, so far as its essence is concerned.

But the same problem, or an even greater one, still remains. How can anything sinful have come, if I may so speak, from God? My usual reply to this is to ask, how can anything sinful have come from that virtue and efficiency which themselves proceed from God? But really it is not the matter nor the form which sins. When matter or form has gone out from God and become the property of another, what is there to prevent its being infected and polluted, since it is now in a mutable state, by the calculations of the devil or of man, calculations which proceed from these creatures themselves? But, you will say, body cannot emanate from spirit. My reply is, much less can it emanate from nothing. Moreover spirit, being the more excellent substance, virtually, as they say, and eminently contains within itself what is clearly the inferior substance; in the same way as the spiritual and rational faculty contains the corporeal, that is, the sentient and vegetative faculty. For not even God's virtue and efficiency could have produced bodies out of nothing (as it is vulgarly believed he did) unless there had been some bodily force in his own substance, for no one can give something he has not got. And indeed, St. Paul himself did not hesitate to attribute something bodily to God, Col. ii. 9: *the whole fulness of the Godhead dwells in him bodily.* And it is not any more incredible that a bodily force should be able to issue from a spiritual substance, than that something spiritual should be able to arise from a body; and that is what we trust will happen to our own bodies at the resurrection. Lastly, I do not see how God can truthfully be called infinite if there is anything which might be added to him. And if something did exist, in the nature of things, which had not first been from God and in God, then that might be added to him.

It seems to me that, with the guidance of scripture, I have proved that God produced all things not out of nothing but out of himself. Now I think I ought to go on to consider the necessary consequence of this, which is that, since all things come not only from God but out of God, no created thing can be utterly annihilated. To begin with, there is not a word in the Bible about any such annihilation. That is the very best reason for rejecting the concept of annihilation altogether, but I will also suggest some other reasons. First, because it seems to me that God neither wishes to nor, properly speaking, can altogether annihilate anything. He does not wish to, because he makes everything to some definite end, and nothing cannot be the end either of God or of any created thing. It cannot be the end of God, because he is himself his own end; and it cannot be the end of any created thing, because the end of all created things is some kind of good, whereas nothing is neither good nor any kind of thing at all. All entity is good: nonentity, not good. It is not consistent, then, with the goodness and wisdom of God, to make out of entity, which is good, something which is not good, or nothing. Moreover God cannot annihilate anything, because by making nothing he would both make and not make at the same time, which involves a contradiction. But, you will say, God does make something when he annihilates: he makes something which exists, cease to exist. My reply is that any complete action involves two things, motion, and something brought about by the motion. Here the motion is the act of annihilation, but there is not anything brought about by the motion, that is, nothing is brought about, no effect: and if there is no effect there is no efficient.

CHAPTER IX
OF THE SPECIAL GOVERNMENT
OF ANGELS

WE have been discussing GENERAL PROVIDENCE. SPECIAL PROVIDENCE is concerned particularly with angels and men, as they are far superior to all other creatures.

There are, however, both good and evil angels. Luke ix. 26 and vii. 2, for it is well known that a great many of them revolted from God of their own free will before the fall of man: John vii. 44: *he did not stand firm in the truth, for there is no truth in him, he speaks like what he is, the father of lies;* II Pet. ii. 4: *he did not spare the angels who sinned;* Jude 6: *the angels who did not maintain their original position;* I John iii. 8: *the devil sins from the beginning;* Psal. cvi. 37: *they sacrificed to devils.*

It seems to some people that the good angels now maintain their position not so much by their own strength as by the grace of God. I Tim. v. 21: *of the elect*

angels, that is, of those who did not revolt; Eph. i. 10: *that he might collect together all things under a single head in Christ, the things in heaven as well;* Col. i. 20: *that through him he might reconcile all things to him, the things which are in heaven as well;* Job iv. 18: *he ascribed folly to his angels,* similarly xv. 15.

Hence the angels take great pleasure in examining the mystery of man's salvation: I Pet i. 12: *things which the angels desire to look into;* Eph. iii. 10: *that through the church the wisdom of God in all its forms might be known to principalities and powers;* Luke ii. 13, 14: *a multitude of the armies praising God,* that is, on account of the birth of Christ; and xv. 10: *there is joy in the presence of the angels over one man who repents.*

As a result, also, they adore Christ: Heb. i. 6: *let all the angels of God adore him;* Matt. iv. 11: *the angels ministered to him;* Philipp. ii. 10: *that every knee shall bow, among the heavenly creatures . . . ;* II Thess. i. 7: *with his angels;* I Pet. iii. 22: *the angels being made subject to him,* Rev. v. 11, 12: *worthy is the Lamb that was sacrificed. . . .* It seems more reasonable, however, to suppose that the good angels stand by their own strength, no less than man did before his fall, and that they are called "elect" only in the sense that they are beloved or choice: also that they desire to contemplate the mystery of our salvation simply out of love, and not from any interest of their own, that they are not included in any question of reconciliation, and that they are reckoned as being under Christ because he is their head, not their Redeemer.

In addition, they stand around the throne of God as ministers. Deut. xxxiii. 2: *he came with a crowd of myriads of saints;* I Kings xxii. 19: *I saw Jehovah sitting on his throne and the whole host of heaven on his right hand and on his left;* Job i. 6: *when the sons of God came to stand in Jehovah's presence,* similarly ii. 1; Dan. vii. 10: *a thousand thousand waited upon him;* Matt. xviii. 10: *angels for ever behold the face of my Father;* Luke i. 19: *I am Gabriel, who stand in the sight of God.*

Praising God: Job xxxviii. 7: *all the sons of God shouted aloud;* Psal. cxlviii. 2: *praise him all his angels;* Neh. ix. 6: *the host of the heavens bows to you;* Isa. vi. 3: *calling one to another, Holy, Holy, Holy;* similarly Rev. iv. 8, and vii. 11, 12: *they lay on their faces before the throne.*

They are absolutely obedient to God in all things: Gen. xxviii. 12: *behold the angels of God ascending and descending on it;* Psal. ciii. 20: *doing his word;* Zech. i. 10: *these are they whom Jehovah has sent to patrol the earth.*

Their chief ministry concerns believers: Heb. i. 14: *they are all ministering spirits who are sent out to minister for the sake of the heirs of salvation;* Psal. xxxiv. 8: *the angels of Jehovah are encamped around those who fear him,* and xci. 11: *he will give his angels commands concerning you;* Isa. lxiii. 9: *the angel of his appearance will save them;* Matt. xviii. 10: *their angels,* and xiii. 41: *kingdom,* and xxiv. 31: *they will collect together his elect from the four winds;* Acts xii. 15: *it is his angel;* I Cor. xi. 10: *on account of the angels,* that is, as some suppose, the angels who guard over the meetings of the faithful. There are innumerable examples available besides these.

And seven of them particularly patrol the earth: Zech. iv. 10: *these seven are the eyes of Jehovah which go to and fro over the earth,* compared with Rev. v. 6: *who are those seven spirits of God sent forth into the whole earth,* see also i. 4 and iv. 5.

It is probable, too, that angels are put in charge of nations, kingdoms and particular districts: Dan. iv. 13, 17: *this word is from the decree of the watchers,* and xii. 1: *that prince who stands for your fellow-countrymen,* and x. 13: *I was left there with the kings of Persia;* II Pet. ii. 11: *whereas angels bring no judgment based on evil speaking against dignitaries before the Lord;* Gen. iii. 24: *to guard the way to the tree of life.*

Sometimes they are ministers of divine vengeance, sent from heaven to punish mortal sins. They destroy cities and peoples: Gen. xix. 13; II Sam. xxiv. 16; I Chron. xxi. 16: *David saw the angel of Jehovah threatening Jerusalem with a drawn sword.* They strike down whole armies with unexpected calamity: II Kings xix. 35, and similar passages.

As a result they often appeared looking like soldiers: Gen. xxxii. 1, 2: *God's battle-array;* Josh. vi. 2: *leader of Jehovah's soldiery;* II Kings vi. 17: *with horses and chariots of fire;* Psal. lxviii. 18: *they are twenty thousand of God's chariots;* Luke ii. 13: *a multitude of the heavenly armies.*

They are also described in Isa. vi; Hos. i. 7; Matt. xxviii. 2, 3; Rev. x. 1.

There seems to be a leader among the good angels, and he is often called Michael: Josh. vi. 2: *I am the leader of Jehovah's soldiery;* Dan. x. 13: *Michael is the first of the chief princes,* and xii. 1: *the greatest prince;* Rev. xii. 7, 8: *Michael with his angels.*

A lot of people are of the opinion that Michael is Christ. But whereas Christ alone vanquished Satan and trod him underfoot, Michael is introduced as leader of the angels and Ἀντίπαλος (antagonist) of the prince of the devils: their respective forces were drawn up in battle array and separated after a fairly even fight, Rev. xii. 7, 8. And Jude says of Michael *when disputing about Moses' body he did not dare . . . ,* whereas it would be quite improper to say this about Christ, especially if he is God. See also I Thess. iv. 16: *the Lord himself will descend with the voice of an archangel.* Finally, it would be very strange for an apostle of the Gospel to talk in such an obscure way, and to call Christ by another name, when reporting these odd and unheard-of things about

him.

The good angels do not see into all God's thoughts, as the Papists pretend. They know by revelation only those things which God sees fit to show them, and they know other things by virtue of their very high intelligence, but there are many things of which they are ignorant. For we find an angel full of curiosity and asking questions: Dan. viii. 13: *how long is this vision?,* and xii. 6: *how far off is its end?;* Matt. xxiv. 36: *no one knows of that day, not even the angels;* Eph. iii. 10: *that through the church it might be known to powers;* Rev. v. 3: *no one in heaven was able to open the book.*

Bad angels are kept for punishment: Matt. viii. 29: *have you come here to torment us before the appointed time?;* II Pet. ii. 4: *he thrust them down to hell and chained them in dark chains, to be kept for damnation;* Jude 6: *he has kept them in darkness and eternal chains for the judgment of that great day;* I Cor. vi. 3: *do you not know that we shall judge angels?;* Matt. xxv. 41: *into the eternal fire which is prepared for the devil and his angels;* Rev. xx. 10: *they shall be tortured for ever and ever.*

But sometimes they are able to wander all over the earth, the air, and even heaven, to carry out God's judgments: Job i. 7: *from going to and fro on the earth;* I Sam. xvi. 15: *the spirit of Jehovah had left Saul, and an evil spirit from Jehovah troubled him;* I Pet. v. 8: *he walks about like a roaring lion;* John xii. 31: *the prince of this world;* II Cor. iv. 4: *the god of this world;* Matt. xii. 43: *he walks through dry places;* Eph. ii. 2: *the prince who has power over the air,* and vi. 1: *spiritual wickednesses in high places.* They even come into the presence of God: Job i. 6 and ii. 1; I Kings xxii. 21: *a certain spirit came forth;* Zech. iii. 1: *he showed me Joshua standing in the presence of the angel of Jehovah, and Satan standing at his right hand to oppose him;* Luke x. 18: *I saw Satan falling like lightning out of heaven;* Rev. xii. 12: *woe to the inhabitants of the earth, for the devil has come down among you.*

But their proper place is hell, which they cannot leave without permission: Luke viii. 31: *they asked him not to command them to go away to hell;* Matt. xii. 43: *seeking rest through dry places;* Mark v. 10: *he prayed that he would not send them out of that region;* Rev. xx. 3: *he threw him into hell and closed it up.* They cannot do anything unless God commands them: Job i. 12: *look, let them be in your power;* Matt. viii. 31: *allow us to go away into this herd of swine;* Rev. xx. 2: *he seized the dragon and bound him.*

Their knowledge is great, but it is a torment to them rather than a consolation; so that they utterly despair of their salvation: Matt. viii. 29: *what have we to do with you, Jesus? Have you come here to torment us before the appointed time?,* similarly Luke iv. 34; James ii. 19: *the devils believe and are horrified*—because they are kept for punishment, as I said before.

The devils have their prince too: Matt. xii. 24: *Beelzebub prince of devils*, similarly Luke xi. 15; Matt. xxv. 41: *for the devil and his angels*; Rev. xii. 9: *that great dragon and his angels*.

They also keep their ranks: Col. ii. 15: *having plundered principalities and powers*; Eph. vi. 12: *against powers and principalities*.

Their chief is the author of all wickedness and hinders all good: Job i and ii; Zech. iii. 1: *Satan*; John viii. 44: *the father of lies*; I Thess. ii. 18: *Satan hindered us*; Acts v. 3: *Satan has filled your heart*; Rev. xx. 3, 8: *to lead the nations astray*; Eph. ii. 2: *the spirit now working in arrogant men*.

As a result he has been give a number of titles, which suit his actions. He is frequently called *Satan*, that is, enemy or adversary, Job i. 6, I Chron. xxi. 1: also *the great dragon, the old serpent, the devil*, that is, the calumniator, Rev. xii. 9: also κατήγορος των αδελφων [*the accuser of the brothers*], xii. 10; and *the unclean spirit*, Matt. xii. 43; and *the tempter*, Matt. iv. 3; and *Abaddon, Apollyon*, that is, destroyer, Rev. ix. 11; and *a great red dragon*, xii. 3.

CHAPTER X
OF THE SPECIAL GOVERNMENT OF MAN BEFORE THE FALL: DEALING ALSO WITH THE SABBATH AND MARRIAGE

THE providence of God which governs man relates either to man's prelapsarian or to his fallen state.

The providence which relates to his prelapsarian state is that by which God placed man in the garden of Eden and supplied him with every good thing necessary for a happy life. And, so that there might be some way for man to show his obedience, God ordered him to abstain only from the tree of the knowledge of good and evil, and threatened him with death if he disobeyed: Gen. i. 28: *subdue the earth and have dominion*, and ii. 15, 16, 17: *he placed him in the garden. You may eat freely the fruit of every tree. On the day you eat the fruit of the tree of the knowledge of good and evil, you will die.*

Some people call this "the covenant of works," though it does not appear from any passage of scripture to have been either a covenant or of works. Adam was not required to perform any works; he was merely forbidden to do one thing. It was necessary that one thing at least should be either forbidden or commanded, and above all something which was in itself neither good nor evil, so that man's obedience might in this way be made evident. For man was by nature good and holy, and was naturally disposed to do right, so it was certainly not necessary to bind him by the requirements of any covenant to something which he would do of his own accord. And he would not have shown obedience at all by performing good works, since he was in fact drawn to these by his own natural impulses, without being commanded. Besides a command, whether it comes from God or from a magistrate, should not be called a covenant just because rewards and punishments are attached: it is rather a declaration of power.

The tree of the knowledge of good and evil was not a sacrament, as is commonly thought, for sacraments are meant to be used, not abstained from; but it was a kind of pledge or memorial of obedience.

It was called the tree of knowledge of good and evil because of what happened afterwards: for since it was tasted, not only do we know evil, but also we do not even know good except through evil. For where does virtue shine, where is it usually exercised, if not in evil?

I do not know whether the tree of life ought to be called a sacrament, rather than a symbol of eternal life or even perhaps the food of eternal life: Gen. iii. 22: *lest he eat and live for ever*; Rev. ii. 7: *to the victor I will give food from the tree of life.*

Man was made in the image of God, and the whole law of nature was so implanted and innate in him that he was in need of no command. It follows, then, that if he received any additional commands, whether about the tree of knowledge or about marriage, these had nothing to do with the law of nature, which is itself sufficient to teach whatever is in accord with right reason (i.e., whatever is intrinsically good). These commands, then, were simply a matter of what is called positive right. Positive right comes into play when God, or anyone else invested with lawful power, commands or forbids things which, if he had not commanded or forbidden them, would in themselves have been neither good nor bad, and would therefore have put no one under any obligation. As for the Sabbath, it is clear that God sanctified it as his own, in memory of the completion of his task, and dedicated it to rest; Gen. ii. 2, 3, compared with Exod. xxxi. 17. But it is not known, because there is nothing about it in scripture, whether this was ever disclosed to Adam or whether any commandment about the observance of the Sabbath existed before the giving of the law on Mount Sinai, let alone before the fall of man. Probably Moses, who seems to have written the book of Genesis long after the giving of the law, inserted this sentence from the fourth commandment in what was, as it were, an opportune place. Thus he seized an opportunity of reminding the people about the reason, which was, so to speak, topical at this point in his narrative, but which God had really given many years later to show why he wanted the Sabbath to be observed by his people, with whom he had at long last made a solemn covenant. For an example of a similar insertion see Exod. xvi. 34, 35: *Moses said to Aaron, take a pot . . . So Aaron set it up . . .* —which, however, happened long afterwards. We read in Exod. xvi that, shortly before the giving of the law, it was commanded that the Sabbath should be observed in the wilderness; for God had said that he would rain manna on every day except the seventh, so that no one should go out to look for it on that day. Judging from a comparison of xvi. 5 with xvi. 22–30, it seems that this command was first given to the Israelites at that time, as a kind of groundwork for the law which was going to be promulgated more clearly a little later on, and that they were previously ignorant about the observation of the Sabbath. For the elders, who ought to have known the commandment about the Sabbath better than anyone else, wondered why the people had gathered twice as much manna on the sixth day, and asked Moses, who told them only then, as if it were something new, that tomorrow would be the Sabbath. So he writes, as if he had just narrated how the Sabbath first came to be observed, *thus the people rested on the seventh day,* xvi. 30.

More than one passage in the prophets seems to confirm that the Israelites had not even heard anything about the Sabbath before that time: Ezek. xx. 10–12: *I led them away into the wilderness; where I gave them my statutes and made my laws known to them. Also I gave them my sabbaths, to be a sign between me and them, hat they might know that I, Jehovah, sanctify them;* Neh. ix. 13, 14: *so you came down on Mount Sinai . . . and gave them judgments . . . and also made known to them your holy sabbath, and prescribed precepts, statutes and a law for them through your servant Moses.* But see Book II Chapter vii for more on the subject of the Sabbath.

Marriage also, if it was not commanded, was at any rate instituted, and consisted in the mutual love, delight, help and society of husband and wife, though with the husband having greater authority: Gen. ii. 18: *it is not good for the man to be alone; I will make him a help before his eyes, as it were;* I Cor. xi. 7–9: *since the man is the image and glory of God, but the woman is the glory of her husband. For the man did not come from the woman, but the woman from the man: so the man was not given for the woman's sake but the woman for the man's.* The husband's authority became still greater after the fall: Gen.

iii. 16: *your desire* or *your obedience will be towards your husband.* So in Hebrew the same word, עַל, means both *husband* and *lord.* Thus Sarah is said, I Pet. iii. 6, to have called her husband Abraham *lord.* I Tim. ii. 12–14: *I do not allow a woman to teach or to usurp authority over a man; she should be silent. For Adam was made first, then Eve; and Adam was not deceived, but the woman was deceived and was the cause of the transgression.*

Marriage, then, is a very intimate relationship between man and woman instituted by God for the procreation of children or the help and solace of life. As a result it is written, Gen. ii. 24: *so a man will leave his father and mother and cling to his wife, and they will be one flesh.* This is neither a law nor a commandment, but an effect or natural consequence of that very intimate relationship which would have existed between Adam and Eve in man's unfallen state. Nothing is being discussed in the passage except the origin of families. In my definition I have not said, as most people do, *between one man and one woman.* I have not done so, in order to avoid accusing the most holy patriarchs and pillars of our faith, Abraham, and others who had more than one wife, of constant fornication and adultery. Otherwise I should be forced to exclude from God's sanctuary as bastards all their most holy offspring, all the children of Israel, in fact, for whom the sanctuary itself was made. For it is written, Deut. xxiii. 2: *a bastard shall not come into the congregation of Jehovah, even to his tenth generation.*

So either polygamy is a true form of marriage, or else all children born in it are bastards: and that means the whole race of Jacob, the twelve holy tribes chosen by God. But it would be absolutely absurd and even downright blasphemous to suggest this. Also it is very unjust, and a very dangerous precedent in religion to consider something a sin when it is not a sin. So I am of the opinion that it is not irrelevant but on the contrary absolutely vital to find out whether polygamy is lawful or not.

Those who deny its lawfulness try to prove their case from Gen. ii. 24: *he will cling to his wife and they will be one flesh,* compared with Matt. xix. 5: *those two will be one flesh. He will cling* they say *to his wife* not *to his wives;* and *those two* not *those several people.* Brilliant! Let me add also Exod. xx. 17: *you shall not covet your neighbor's house nor his manservant nor his maidservant nor his ox nor his ass:* therefore no one has more than one house, manservant, maidservant, ox or ass! How ridiculous it would be to argue like this—it says *house* not *houses, servant* not *servants* and even *neighbor's* not *neighbors'*—and not to realize that in nearly all the commandments the singular of the noun signifies not the number but the species of each thing mentioned. As for the fact that Matt. xix 5 says *those two* and not *those several people*, it must be understood that this passage deals only with one man and with the wife whom he wanted to divorce, and that it is in no way concerned with whether had one wife or several. Then again, it must be understood that marriage is a kind of relationship and that there are only two sides to any one relationship. So that in the same way, if anyone has a number of sons, his paternal relationship towards them all will be various, but towards each one it will be single and complete in itself. Similarly, if anyone has several wives, his relationship towards each one will be no less complete, and the husband will be no less *one flesh* with each one of them, than if he had only one wife. So it is correctly said of Abraham, with Sarah and with Hagar respectively, that *these two were one flesh*. And with good reason, for anyone who associates with prostitutes, however many they may be, is still said to be *one flesh* with each of them. I Cor. vi. 16: *do you not know that he who couples with a prostitute is one body with her? For those two*, he says, *will be one flesh*. So this expression may be used about a husband, even though he has several wives, just as correctly as if he had only one; and may be understood in the same sense as if he had only one. It follows, then, that polygamy is neither forbidden nor opposed by this so-called commandment which, as I have shown above, is not really a commandment at all. Otherwise we must assume either that the Mosaic law contradicts this instruction, or else that though the relevant passage had been frequently studied by innumerable priests, Levites and prophets and by very holy men of all ranks who were most acceptable to God, nevertheless they were so wanting in reason that they were swept by a blind impulse to this passion for constant fornication. This is what we must assume if the effect of the instruction we are considering is to make polygamy an unlawful form of marriage.

The second text quoted to prove polygamy unlawful is Lev. xviii. 18: *you shall not take a woman to her sister, to make enemies of them and to uncover her nakedness, besides the other in her lifetime*. Here Junius translates *a woman to another woman*, instead of *a woman to her sister*, so that with this interpretation, which is plainly forced and inadmissible, he should have some grounds for proving polygamy unlawful. But in drawing up laws, as in writing definitions, it is necessary to use precise words and to interpret them properly, not in any metaphorical way. He claims, however, that these words are found elsewhere in the sense he gives them. I confess that they are, but in a context where there can be no ambiguity, as in Gen. xxvi. 31: *they swore, each man to his brother*, that is, to the other man. For who would think of arguing from this that Isaac was Abime-

lich's brother? And who could fail to conclude that the Leviticus passage was clearly about not taking one sister in marriage after another, especially in a chapter where the verses which immediately precede this deal with the degrees of kinship to which marriage is forbidden? Moreover by taking one sister in marriage after another *nakedness is uncovered*, which is what this passage warns against. If it is another woman who is taken, not the sister of nor related to the first, then there is no need for this caution, because in this case no nakedness would be uncovered. Lastly, why is *in her lifetime* added? Because, though there could not be any doubt that it was permissible, after the death of one wife, to marry another who was not her sister nor related to her, there could be some doubt whether it was permissible to marry the first wife's sister. But, my opponent objects, marriage with a wife's sister is already forbidden by analogy in xviii. 16, so this prohibition is superfluous. I reply, first, that there is no analogy, for by marrying a brother's wife, the brother's nakedness is uncovered, but my marrying a wife's sister it is not a sister's nakedness but only that of a relation by marriage which is uncovered. Secondly, if nothing may be prohibited which has already been prohibited by analogy, why, after marriage with one's father has been forbidden, is marriage with one's mother forbidden as well? Why forbid marriage with one's mother's sister after forbidding it with one's father's sister? If such prohibitions are unnecessary it must be concluded that more than half the laws relating to incest are unnecessary. Moreover if polygamy were really forbidden by this passage, much stronger reasons ought to have been given—reasons affecting the institution itself, as was done in the establishment of the Sabbath—whereas the chief reason suggested here is the prevention of enmity.

The third passage which is adduced, Deut. xvii. 17, does not condemn polygamy either in a king or in anyone else, indeed it expressly allows it, while merely imposing a limit to it in the same way as it imposes a limit to the keeping of horses or the accumulation of wealth. This is clear from the verse cited and the previous one.

Except for the three passages, which are actually irrelevant, no trace of the censure of polygamy can be seen throughout the whole law. Nor, for that matter, can any be found even in all the writings of the prophets, although they interpreted the law very severely, and were constantly censuring the vices of the people. The one exception is a passage in Malachi, the last of the prophets, which some people think utterly destroys the case for polygamy. It would be a real *volte-face* and a long-delayed one at that if a thing which ought to have been prohibited many centuries before was prohibited at long last only after the Babylonian captivity. If it really had been a sin, how could it have escaped the censure of all the prophets who preceded Malachi? What we can be sure of is that if polygamy is not forbidden in the law then it is not forbidden here either, because Malachi did not write a new law. But let us take a look at the words themselves, as Junius translates them, ii. 15: *nonne unum effecit? Quamvis reliqui spiritus ipsi essent: quid autem unum?—[did he not make one? although the remains of the spirit were his: but why one?]*. It would certainly be far too rash and dangerous to make up one's mind on such an important point, and to impose an article of faith upon one's fellow men, on the evidence of such an obscure passage as this: a passage which various interpreters twist and turn in so many different ways. But whatever the words *nonne unum effecit* mean, what do they prove? Does *unum* mean "one woman"; and does the passage therefore establish the fact that a man should marry only one woman? No, because the word is the wrong gender; and as a matter of fact it is the wrong case as well, because nearly all the other translators render the passage: *annon unus fecit? et residuum spiritus ipsi? et quid ille unus?—[did not one make? and is not the rest of the spirit his? and why that one?]* We cannot, then, force a condemnation of polygamy from this very obscure passage, and no such doctrine is mentioned anywhere else, or only in doubtful terms. What we should derive from the passage, rather, is something which we can find all through the scriptures, and which is the chief subject of this very chapter from verse eleven onwards, namely a condemnation of marriage with the daughter of an alien god. As Ezra and Nehemia show it was very common at that time for the Jews to defile themselves by such marriages.

As for the words of Christ, Matt. v. 32 and xix. 5, he repeats the passage from Gen. ii. 24 in order to condemn not polygamy but unlicenced divorce, which is a very different matter; and you have to wrench his words if you want to make them fit polygamy. Some people argue from Matt. v. 32 that if a man who marries another wife after rejecting his first commits adultery, then he does so much more certainly if he marries another and keeps his first wife. But this argument is adulterate itself, and ought itself to be rejected. For in the first place, it is the actual precepts that bind us, not the consequences deduced from them by human reasoning: for what seems to be a reasonable deduction to one person may not seem so to another, though equally intelligent. Secondly, a man who rejects his first wife and marries another, is not said to commit adultery because he marries another, but because when he married the second wife he did not keep the first though he ought to have behaved like a dutiful husband to her

as well. So Mark x. 11 says quite plainly: *he commits adultery against her.* Moreover God himself teaches that it is possible to behave like a dutiful husband towards the first wife, even after marrying a second, Exod. xxi. 10: *if he takes another wife he shall not diminish her food, her clothing or her portion of time*—and God did not make his provisions for adulterers.

It is not correct to argue from I Cor. vii. 2: *let every man have his own wife,* that he should therefore not have more than one. The text says that he should have *his own* wife, meaning that he should keep her for himself, not that she should be the only one. Bishops and priests are explicitly required to have only one wife, I Tim. iii. 2. and Tit. i. 6: *let them be husbands of one wife;* I suppose this was so that they could carry out the ecclesiastical duties which they had undertaken more diligently. And the requirement itself shows plainly enough that polygamy was not forbidden to other people, and that it was common in the church at that time.

Lastly, as for the argument which is based on I Cor. vii. 4: *but in the same way the husband does not have power over his own body, but the wife does,* this is quickly answered by pointing out, as before, that the word *wife* here refers to species not number. Furthermore, the wife's power over her husband's body cannot be different now from what it was under the law, and in Hebrew this power is called עוֹנָה, Exod. xxi. 10, which means *her appointed time.* In the present chapter the same idea is expressed by the phrase *due benevolence,* but the Hebrew word makes it quite clear what *due* means.

On the other hand, the following texts clearly admit polygamy: Exod. xxi. 10: *if he takes another wife he shall not diminish her food, her clothing, or her portion of time;* Deut. xvii. 17: *let him not increase his wives, lest his heart turn from me.* Who would have worded this law so loosely, if it were not meant to grant more than one wife? And who would be so bold as to add to this: therefore let him have only one? The previous verse says *let him not increase his horses,* so shall we add to that: therefore he must have only one horse? We know well enough that the first institution of marriage applied to the king as well as his people: if it allows only one wife, then it does not allow more even to the king. Moreover the reason given for the law is *lest his heart turn from me*—a danger which might arise if he were to marry a great many wives, especially foreign ones, as Solomon afterwards did. But if this law was meant as a renewal of the first institution of marriage, what could have been more appropriate than to have cited that institution here, instead of giving only this other reason?

Let us listen to God himself, the author of the law, and his own best interpreter: II Sam. xii. 8: *I have handed over your master's wives into your breast: and if they were*

not enough I would have added such and such things.
There is no escape here: God gave wives: he gave them
to the man he loved among a number of other great
benefits: he would have given more if these had not
been enough. Besides, the very argument which God
uses against David is more forceful when applied to the
gift of wives than to any other: you should at least have
abstained from another man's wife, not so much because I had given you your master's house or his kingdom, as because I had given you the royal wives. But,
says Beza, therefore David committed incest, with the
wives of his father-in-law. Beza forgets, however, a
point which is made clear by Esther ii. 12, 13, that the
kings had two harems, one for virgins and the other for
concubines, and it is understood that David was given
the former, not the latter. This is evident from I Kings
i. 4 as well: *the king did not know her*; Son of Solomon
vi. 8: *eighty concubines and countless virgins.* Although as
a matter of fact God could be said to have given him his
master's wives if he had given him not necessarily the
same wives, but as many wives as his mater had, and
similar ones. In the same way he did not give him the
actual house and retinue of his master, but a house and
retinue equally royal and magnificent.

The law itself, then, and even the authority of God's
own voice, wholly approve of this practice. So it is not
surprising that the holy prophets should speak of it in
their divine hymns as something absolutely honorable:
Psal. xlv. 10, (which is called "A Son of Sweethearts"):
kings' daughters among your dear ones, and 15, 16: *after
her the virgins, her friends, shall be brought to you.* Indeed
the words of these sweethearts are quoted by the
apostle, Heb. i. 7, etc.: *to the Son, Your throne, O God*, as
the words of God himself to his Son; and no words anywhere in scripture attribute godhead to the Son more
clearly than these words of theirs. Would it have been
proper for God the Father to speak through the mouths
of prostitutes and reveal the godhead of his holy Son to
men through the love-songs of whores? So, too, in the
Song of Solomon, vi. 8, 9, 10, both queens and concubines are clearly given honorable mention, and are all
considered worthy to sing the praises of the bride: *sixty
queens and eighty concubines and countless virgins: the
queens will bless that only one and the concubines will
praise her, saying. . . .* Nor should we forget that passage
in II Chron. xxiv. 2, 3: *and during the whole lifetime of
Jehoiada the priest, Joash did what was right in the sight of
the Jehovah, and Jehoiada took two wives for him.* For
here the two facts, that he did what was right on the
instructions of Jehoiada, and that on Jehoiada's
authority he married two wives, are not stated in
isolation or in opposition to each other, but in
conjunction. In eulogies of kings, if anything which was

less admirable than the rest was added on at the end, it
was usually explicitly excepted from what went before,
contrary to what is done here: thus I Kings xv. 5: *except
in the matter of Uriah*, and 11, 14: *and Asa did what was
right . . . though the high places were not removed;
nevertheless Asa's heart was perfect.* The fact that Joash's
bigamy is mentioned straight after his right conduct,
without any exception being made, indicates, then, that
it was not considered wrong. For the sacred writer
would not have missed such a convenient opportunity
for making an exception in the customary way if there
had been anything less deserving of commendation than
the rest.

Moreover God himself in Ezek. xxiii. 4 says that he
has taken two wives, Aholah and Aholibah. He would
certainly not have spoken about himself like this at such
great length, not even in a parable, nor adopted this
character or likeness at all, if the thing itself had been
intrinsically dishonorable or base.

But how can anything be dishonorable or base when
it is forbidden to no one, even under the gospel (for that
dispensation does not annul any of the merely civil regulations which existed previous to its introduction)? The
only stipulation made is that priests and deacons should
be chosen from among men who had only one wife; see
I Tim. iii and Tit. i. 6, cited above. And this is stipulated
not because it would be a sin to marry more than one
wife, for then it would have been forbidden to everyone
else as well, but so that priests and deacons should be
less involved in household affairs and therefore more at
leisure to attend to the business of the church. Since
then polygamy is forbidden here only to ecclesiastics,
and even then not because it is a sin, and since neither
here nor anywhere else is it forbidden to any other
members of the church, it follows that it was permitted
to all other members of the church, as I said before, and
that it was adopted by many without offence.

Lastly, I argue as follows from Heb. xiii. 4: polygamy
is either marriage or fornication or adultery—for the
apostle admits no halfway state between these. Let no
one dare to say that it is fornication or adultery: the
shame this would bring upon so many patriarchs who
were polygamists will, I hope, prevent anyone from
doing so. For *God will judge fornicators and adulterers*,
whereas he loved the patriarchs above all, and declared
that they were very dear to him. If, then polygamy is
nothing but marriage, it must, in the opinion of the
same apostle, be lawful and honorable as well: *marriage
is honorable for all, and the bed unstained.*

I think I have proved well enough that God's law allows polygamy. But in case this still seems doubtful to
anyone, I will add a large number of examples, all of
them unquestionably holy teachers and lights of our

faith. First, Abraham, father of all the faithful and of the holy seed, Gen. xvi. 1, etc.; Jacob, xxx. Also, if I am not mistaken, Moses Num. xii. 1, for he had married a Cushite. It is incredible that Zipporah, who had been named so often before, should suddenly be given this new title of a Cushite. It is incredible, too, that Aaron and Miriam should now suddenly get angry because, forty years before, Moses had married Zipporah; especially as the whole house of Israel had done her the honor of going out to meet her when she arrived with her father Jethro. If, then, he married a Cushite while Zipporah was still living, it was certainly with God's support, and the severity of Aaron and his sister was punished with exceptional harshness. Next I place Gideon, outstanding for his faith and piety, Judg. viii. 30, 31. Then Elkanah, Samuel's father, a very religious Levite. He was so far from thinking himself less acceptable to God on account of his two wives, that he took them with him every year into God's presence at the sacrifices and annual ceremony. Nor was he reproved for it, but went home with the gift of a fine son, Samuel, I Sam. ii. 10. I will pass over certain other examples, although they are famous men, such as Caleb, I Chron. ii. 46, 48, and *the sons of Issachar*, I Chron. vii. 1, 4, *thirty six thousand men in number, who had many wives and sons*—unlike our modern Europeans, who allow the fields to go to waste instead, in many places, for want of labor; also Manasseh, Joseph's son, I Chron. vii. 14. This brings me to the prophet David, and no mortal was more beloved by God than he. He took two wives besides Michal, and not when he was puffed up by prosperity, but when he was almost beaten down by adversity. He did this at a time when, on the evidence of so many of the Psalms, he was wholly occupied in disclosing God's law and teaching an upright way of life: I Sam. xxv. 42, 43 and afterwards, II Sam. v. 12, 13: *David realized that Jehovah had established him as king over Israel, and that Jehovah was exalting his kingdom for the sake of his people Israel: and David took more concubines and wives.* See what the reason was, what the honorable and holy considerations were which led him to do this: it was the thought of God's kindness towards him for his people's sake. This divine and prophetic man did not see in that primitive institution what we blind moles imagine we see with our keener sight. And he did not hesitate, in the supreme council of his kingdom, to assert his confidence that the children born to him in polygamy were born in a holy and honorable state, when he said I Chron. xxviii. 5: *and from all my sons (for the Lord has given me many sins).* I will omit Solomon, although he was very wise, because he seems to have exceeded the limit: he is not blamed, however, for marrying many wives but for marrying foreign

ones; I Kings xi. 1, etc., and Neh. xiii. 26. Next, his son Rehoboam, not after he had become depraved, but during those three years when he is said still to have been walking in the way of David, II Chron. xi. 17, 21, etc. I have already mentioned King Joash. He had two wives not as a result of kingly lust or corrupt morals, but on the advice and authority of Jehoiada the high priest, a most wise and holy man. Who could believe that so many of the best men sinned throughout so many ages, either through ignorance or because their hearts were hardened? Who could believe that God would have tolerated such a thing in his people? Let that rule so common among theologians hold good here if anywhere: *The practice of the saints interprets the commandments.*

The fruitfulness and prosperity of marriage depends chiefly on God's providence: Prov. xix. 14: *an intelligent wife is Jehovah's gift*, and xviii. 22: *he who finds a wife finds a good thing, and obtains favor from Jehovah.*

If one's parents are alive their consent should be obtained: Exod. xxii. 17: *if the father utterly refuses . . .* ; Deut. vii. 3: *do not give your daughter . . .* ; Jer. xxix. 6: *take wives for your sons.*

But the first and more important point is the mutual consent of the parties concerned, for there can be no love or good will, and therefore no marriage, between those whom mutual consent has not united.

Moreover if the marriage is to be valid this consent must be free from any kind of falsehood, especially on the subject of chastity: Deut. xxii. 20, 21, 23. It will be obvious to anyone with any sense that maturity is necessary as well.

On the question of incest, God's law should be consulted: Lev. xviii; Deut. xxvii, not episcopal regulations or legal precedents. Moreover the text should be given its due weight: no reading should be forced from it. To be wise beyond this point is a sign of superstitious folly or over-fastidiousness.

Religious conviction should also be considered to ensure that husband and wife are of one mind in religious matters. Under the law this was understood to apply to marriages already contracted as well as to those that were planned; Exod. xxxiv. 15, 16; Deut. vii. 3, 4 compared with Ezra x. 11, etc. and Neh. xiii. 23, 30. Under the gospel, marriage between those who differed in their religious opinions was avoided with equal care: I Cor. vii. 39: *she is free to marry whom she likes, as long as it is in the Lord;* II Cor. vi. 14: *not with an unequal match. . . .* But if the marriage is already contracted it should not be dissolved while there is still any hope of winning over the unbeliever: I Cor. vii. 12.

For the rest, there are early examples to show the outcome of such marriages: Gen. vi, Solomon; I Kings

xi. 1, etc., Ahab; xxi. 25, Jehosaphat, who gave his son Jehoram a wife from among the daughters of Ahab, II Kings viii.

The form of marriage consists in the mutual goodwill, love, help and solace of husband and wife, as the institution itself, or its definition, shows.

The end of marriage is almost the same as the form. Its proper fruit is the procreation of children. Since the fall of Adam, the relief of sexual desire has become a kind of secondary end: I Cor. vii. 2.

So not everyone is bound by the command to marry, but only those who cannot live chastely and continently outside marriage: Matt. xix. 11: *not all are able.*

Marriage is intrinsically honorable, and it is not forbidden to any order of men. So the Papists are wrong to prohibit their priests from marrying: it is allowable for anyone to marry: Heb. xiii. 4: *marriage is honorable in all;* Gen. ii. 24; I Cor. ix. 5: *have not we power . . . ;* I Tim. iii. 2: *of one wife . . . ,* and iii. 4: *of his own house. . . .*

Marriage is, by definition, a union of the most intimate kind, but it is not indissoluble or indivisible. Some people argue that it is, on the grounds that in Matt. xix. 5 the words *those two will be one flesh* are added. But these words, rightly considered, do not mean that marriage is absolutely indissoluble, only that it should not be easily dissolved. For this mention of the indissolubility of marriage, whether it is given as a command, or to describe a natural consequence, depends upon what has gone before (i.e., the institution of marriage itself and the due observation of each of its parts). So we find it written: *for this reason he will leave . . . and they will be one flesh*—if, in other words, the wife, according to the institution described in the preceding verses, Gen. ii. 18, 20, is a *fit help* for the husband: that is, if goodwill, love, help, solace and fidelity are firm on both sides, which, as all admit, is the essential form of marriage. But when the form is dissolved it follows that the marriage must really be dissolved as well.

My opponents emphasize above all those words in Matt. xix. 6: *what God has joined together, let no man separate.* The institution of marriage itself shows clearly what it is that God has joined together. He has joined together things compatible, fit, good and honorable: he has not joined chalk and cheese: he has not joined things base, wretched, ill-omened and disastrous. It is violence or rashness or error or some evil genius which joins things like this, not God.

What is there, then, to prevent us from getting rid of an evil so distressing and so deep-seated?

This will not be to separate those whom God has joined together, by his most holy institution, but those whom he has himself separated by his no less holy law:

a law which should carry the same weight now as it did with his people of old. As for my opponents' argument about Christian perfection, perfection is not to be forced upon men by penal laws but only encouraged by Christian admonition. It is certainly only a man who does the separating, when he adds to God's law things which the law does not command, and then under cover of the law separates whom he thinks fit. For it should be remembered that God in his most holy, just and pure law has not only allowed divorce on various grounds, but has even, on some occasions, sanctioned it and on others very firmly insisted upon it: Exod. xxi. 4, 10, 11; Deut. xxi. 14 and xxiv. 1; Ezra x. 3; Neh. xiii. 23, 30.

But, say my opponents, he did this *because of the hardness of their hearts,* Matt. xix. 8. My answer is that Christ is here making a reply appropriate to the occasion. The Pharisees were tempting him, and his intention, as usual, was to deflate their arrogance and avoid their snares. But he had no intention of giving an explanation of the question of divorce in general. He is replying only to those who, on the grounds of Deut. xxiv. 1, taught that it was lawful to divorce a wife for any reason at all, so long as a bill of divorce was given. This is clear from the same chapter, matt. xix. 3: *is it lawful for every cause?*—because a lot of people were giving bills of divorce not for the single reason allowed by Moses (i.e., the discovery of some uncleanness in the woman that might turn love into hatred), but merely on the pretext of uncleanness, without any just cause. Since, however, the law was not able to convict these people, Christ considered that they ought to be tolerated, although they were hard-hearted, rather than that earthly marriages should be indissoluble. For in his opinion marriage was of so much importance in life as a source either of happiness or of misery.

The fact is that if we examine the causes of divorce one by one, we shall find that divorce was always sanctioned for an absolutely just and sufficient reason, and not as a concession to hard-heartedness at all. The first passage is Exod. xxi. 1–4: *these are the judgments which you shall set before them. When you buy a Hebrew slave . . . in the seventh year he shall go free, without paying anything. If he is married, then his wife shall go with him. If his master has given him a wife, and she has borne him sons or daughters, the wife and her children shall be the master's, and the man shall go by himself.* What could be more just? This law certainly did not make allowances for hardness of heart but, on the contrary, opposed it. For it prevented a Hebrew slave, however much he had cost, from being a slave for more than seven years: at the same time it preferred the right of the master to that of the husband. Again, xxi. 10, 11: *if he takes another wife, he shall not diminish her food, her clothing or her portion of time. If he does not maintain these three things, then she shall go free without payment.* Who can fail to appreciate the supreme humanity and justice of this law? The husband is not allowed to divorce his wife merely because of his hard heart; but on the other hand the wife is allowed to leave her husband if he is harsh and inhuman, which is a very just reason indeed. Again (Deut. xxi. 13, 14), it is permissible by the right of war and of property both to marry and to divorce a female captive; but it is not permissible either to sell her after divorcing her, or to keep her for profit, both of which would have been a concession to hard-heartedness. The third passage is Deut. xxiv. 1: *if anyone marries a wife and becomes her husband, and it happens that she does not find favor in his eyes, because he has found some nakedness or shameful thing in her, he shall write her a bill of divorce and give it to her, and send her out of his house.* Here, if the cause is a real one, not a mere fiction, what hardness of heart can there be? For it is clear from the institution of marriage itself that when God originally gave man a wife he intended her to be his help, solace and delight. So if, as often happens, she is found to be a source of grief, shame, deception, ruin and calamity instead, why should be think it displeasing to God if we divorce her? In fact I should be inclined to attribute a thick skin to the man who could keep such a wife, rather than a hard heart to the man who sent her packing. And I am not the only one: Solomon is of the same opinion, or rather the Spirit of God itself is, speaking through the mouth of Solomon, Prov. xxx. 21, 23: *three things shake the earth; or rather there are four things which it cannot bear: an odious woman when she is married. . . .* And on the other hand, Eccles. ix. 12: *enjoy your life under the sun, all the days of your fragile life, with the wife whom you love; indeed God has given this to you:* the wife whom you love, notice, not the wife you hate. Thus Mal. ii. 16: *whoever hates* or *because he hates, let him send her away;* as everyone before Junius through Moses, and repeated it through the mouths of the prophets, not in order to make any concessions to the hard-heartedness of husbands, but to rescue the wretched wives from any hard-heartedness which might occur. For where is the hard-heartedness in sending away honorably and freely a woman who, through her own fault, you cannot love? But that a woman who is not loved but justly neglected, a woman who is loathed and hated, should, in obedience to the harshest of laws, be kept beneath the yoke of a crushing slavery (for that is what marriage is without love), by a man who has no love or liking for her: that is a hardship harder than any divorce. So God gave laws of divorce which, if not abused, are absolutely just, equitable and humane. He even extended these laws to those whom he knew would abuse them, because of their

hard-heartedness. For he considered it preferable to put up with the hard-heartedness of the wicked, rather than fail to help the righteous in their affliction or save the institution of marriage itself from imminent danger. And this danger was that instead of being a God-given benefit marriage should become the bitterest misery of all. The fourth and fifth passages, Ezra x. 3 and Neh. xiii. 23, 30 do not allow divorce, as a concession to hard-heartedness, but rigorously command it for the most sacred religious reasons. But on what authority? These prophets were certainly not bearers of a new law, so what authority could they have except the law of Moses? But the law of Moses nowhere command the dissolution of this kind of marriage. It does, however, forbid its contraction, Exod. xxxiv. 15, 16; Deut. vii. 3, 4. From this they argued that a marriage which should not have been contracted, ought to be dissolved. Hence you can see the falsity of the common saying that "What's done can't be undone."

So marriage gives way to religion, and it gives way, as I showed above, to the right of a master; though it is generally agreed, on the grounds of the scriptural passages cited above, and of numerous provisions in the civil law and the law of nations, that the right of a husband is much the same as the right of a master. Finally, marriage must give way to that natural aversion which anyone may feel for a disgusting object, and also to any really irresistible antipathy. But as for hard-heartedness—if that is really set up as the sole or primary reason for the law's enactment—marriage nowhere gives way to that. Deut. xxii. 19 makes this even clearer: *because he has defamed a virgin of Israel, she shall be his wife: he may not send her away as long as he lives,* and xxii. 29: *she shall be his wife; because he has ravished her, he may not send her away as long as he lives.* Now in this case the Mosaic law does not yield to the hard-heartedness of the ravisher or the defamer if he wishes to send away the ravished virgin or the defamed wife. Why then should it be imagined that it yields only to the hard-heartedness of that man who has formed an aversion because of some uncleanness? In fact, then, Christ was reproving the hard-heartedness of those who abuse this law, that is the Pharisees and those like them, when he said *on account of your hard-heartedness he allowed you to send away your wives.* He did not abrogate the law itself or its legitimate use, for he says that Moses permitted it on account of their hard-heartedness, not that he permitted it wrongly or unjustly. And in this sense almost all the civil law was given on account of their hard-heartedness. This is why Paul rebukes the brethren, I Cor. vi. 6, for using it at all; but no one argues from that that the civil law is or ought to be abrogated. How much less can anyone who understands what the gospel is, believe that it denies to man something which the law allowed, whether it allowed it rightly or through an indulgent attitude towards human weakness?

Christ's words in Matt. xix. 8: *it was not so from the beginning* are only a repetition of what he had said more plainly in xix. 4: *the maker made them from the beginning . . . ;* that is, marriage was first made by God in such a way that it could not be destroyed, even by death. For there was no such thing as death yet, nor was there any sin. But once marriage had been violated by the sin of one of the parties, necessity taught them that death must put an end to it, and reason told them that it must often come to an end, even before death. No age or memorial since the fall of man records any other *beginning* from which *it was not so.* Certainly in the very beginning of our faith Abraham himself, the father of the faithful, sent away his argumentative and quarrelsome wife, Hagar, and had God's authority for it; Gen. xxi. 10, 12, 14.

Moreover Christ himself, Matt. xix. 9, permitted divorce on grounds of fornication. He could not have done this if those whom God had once joined in the bond of matrimony were never afterwards to be separated. Furthermore, as Selden demonstrated particularly well in his *Uxor Hebraea*, with the help of numerous Rabbinical texts, the word *fornication*, if it is considered in the light of the idiom of oriental languages, does not mean only adultery. It can mean also either what is called *some shameful thing* (i.e., the lack of some quality which might reasonably be required in a wife), Deut. xxiv. 1, or it can signify anything which is found to be persistently at variance with love, fidelity, help and society (i.e., with the original institution of marriage). I have proved this elsewhere, basing my argument on several scriptural texts, and Selden has demonstrated the same thing. It would be almost laughable to tell the Pharisees, when they asked whether it was lawful to send away one's wife for every cause, that it was not lawful except in the case of adultery. Because everyone already knew that it was not merely lawful but one's duty to send away an adulteress, and not simply to divorce her but to send her to her death. So the word *fornication* must be interpreted here in a much broader sense than that of adultery. The best text to demonstrate this, and there are many, is Judg. xix. 2: *she fornicated against him.* This was not by committing adultery, because then she would not have dared to run home to her father, but by behaving in an obstinate way towards her husband. To take another example, Paul would not have been able to grant divorce on grounds of desertion by an unbeliever, unless this was a kind of fornication as well. And it is, in fact, irrelevant that an unbeliever was concerned in this case, because anyone who deserts

his family *is worse than an unbeliever*, I Tim. v. 8. For what could be more natural or more in keeping with the original institution of marriage than that a couple whom love, honor and mutual assistance in life have joined together, should be separated if hatred or implacable dislike comes between them, or some dishonorable act for which one of them is responsible? So when human nature was perfect, before the fall, God, in paradise, established marriage as an indissoluble bond. But when man had fallen, he granted by the law of nature and by the Mosaic law, which Christ did not contradict, that it should of necessity be subject to dissolution. In this he intended to prevent the innocent from being exposed to perpetual injury at the hands of the wicked. In the same way practically every treaty and contract is meant to be permanent and indissoluble when it is made, but it is immediately nullified if either party breaks his word. No one has so far been able to produce any good reason why marriage should be an exception to this rule. What is more, the apostle has freed even brothers and sisters from their obligations, not only in cases of desertion, but *in things of that kind*, that is, in any circumstances which result in a shameful subjection: I Cor. vii. 15: *a brother or sister is not bound to subjection in cases of this kind, for God has called us in peace*, or *to peace.* He has not called us, then, so that we should be tormented by continual wrangling and annoyance. We are called to peace and liberty, not to marriage, and certainly not to the perpetual squabbles and the slavish pounding-mill of unhappy marriage which, if the apostle is right, is particularly shameful for a free Christian man. It is quite unthinkable that Christ should have expunged from the Mosaic law any provision which could sanction the extension of charity towards the wretched and the afflicted. It is unthinkable, too, that he should have sanctioned a measure which was far more severe than the civil law. We must conclude that, having reprimanded the abuse of this law, he proceeded to teach what the perfect line of action would be, not by compulsion but, as elsewhere, simply by admonition: for he always utterly renounced the role of a judge. So it is the most flagrant error to twist these injunctions of Christ in the gospels into civil statutes, enforcible by magistrates.

It may be asked why, if Christ was apparently not laying down anything new about divorce, or anything more severe than the existing law, it gave such little satisfaction to the disciples that they said, Matt. xix. 10: *if this is the position of a man with his wife, is it a bad thing to marry?* My reply is that it is not surprising if the disciples, imbued as they were with the doctrines of their time, should have had the same opinions about divorce as the Pharisees. That is why it seemed strange and burdensome to them that it should be unlawful to send away a wife, once she had been given a bill of divorce, for every cause.

Finally, to put the whole thing in a nutshell: everyone admits that marriage may be dissolved if the prime end and form of marriage is violated; and most people say that this is the reason why Christ permitted divorce only on grounds of adultery. But the prime end and form of marriage is not the bed, but conjugal love and mutual assistance in life: nearly everyone admits that this is so. For the prime end and form of marriage can only be what is mentioned in the original institution, and mention is there made of pleasant companionship (a thing which ceases to exist if someone is left by himself), and of the mutual assistance of a married couple (a thing which only thrives where there is love). No mention is made of the bed or of procreation, which can take place even where there is hatred. It follows that wedded love is older and more important than the mere marriage bed, and far more worthy to be considered as the prime end and form of marriage. Who is so base and swinish as to deny that this is so? Violation of the marriage bed is only serious because it violates peace and love. Divorce, then, should rather be granted because love and peace are perpetually being violated by quarrels and arguments, than because of adultery. Christ himself admitted this for, as I have proved above, it is absolutely certain that the word *fornication* means not so much adultery as the wife's constant contrariness, faithlessness and disobedience, which all show that her mind is not her husband's even if her body is. Moreover the common, though mistaken interpretation, which makes an exception only in the case of adultery, although it is meant to protect the law, does, in fact, break it. For the Mosaic law did not sanction the divorce of an adulteress, but her trial and execution.

CHAPTER XI
OF THE FALL OF OUR FIRST PARENTS, AND OF SIN

THE PROVIDENCE of God with regard to the fall of man may be discerned both in man's sin and the misery which followed it, and also in his restoration.

SIN, as defined by the apostle is *ἀνομία* or the breaking of the law, I John iii. 4.

Here the word *law* means primarily that law which is innate and implanted in man's mind; and secondly it means the law which proceeded from the mouth of God; Gen. ii. 17: *do not eat of this*: for the law written down by Moses is of a much later date. So it is written, Rom. ii. 12: *those who have sinned without law will perish without law.*

SIN is either THE SIN COMMON TO ALL MEN or THE SIN OF EACH INDIVIDUAL.

THE SIN COMMON TO ALL MEN IS THAT WHICH OUR FIRST PARENTS, AND IN THEM ALL THEIR POSTERITY COMMITTED WHEN THEY ABANDONED THEIR OBEDIENCE AND TASTED THE FRUIT OF THE FORBIDDEN TREE.

OUR FIRST PARENTS: Gen. iii. 6: *the woman took some of the fruit and ate it, and gave some to her husband, and he ate it.* Hence I Tim. ii. 14: *Adam was not deceived, but the woman was deceived and was the cause of the transgression.* This sin was instigated first by the devil, as is clear from the course of events, Gen. iii and I John iii. 8: *the man who commits sin is of the devil; for the devil sins from the beginning.* Secondly it was instigated by the man's own inconstant nature, which meant that he, like the devil before him *did not stand firm in the truth*, John viii. 44. He did not keep his original state, but left his home, Jude 6. Anyone who examines this sin carefully will admit, and rightly, that it was a most atrocious offence, and that it broke every part of the law. For what fault is there which man did not commit in committing this sin? He was to be condemned both for trusting Satan and for not trusting God; he was faithless, ungrateful, disobedient, greedy, uxorious; she, negligent of her husband's welfare; both of them committed theft, robbery with violence, murder against their children (i.e., the whole human race); each was sacrilegious and deceitful, cunningly aspiring to divinity although thoroughly unworthy of it, proud and arrogant. And so we find in Eccles. vii. 29: *God has made man upright, but they have thought up numerous devices*, and in James ii. 10: *whoever keeps the whole law, and yet offends in one point, is guilty of all.*

AND IN THEM ALL THEIR POSTERITY: for they are judged and condemned in them, although not yet born, Gen. iii. 16, etc., so they must obviously have sinned in them as well. Rom. v. 12: *sin came into the world through one man*, v. 15: *through the offence of that one may many are dead*, and v. 16: *the judgment was one of condemnation from one offence*, and v. 17: *through one offence death reigned through one man*, and v. 18: *through one offence, upon all*, and v. 19: *many sinners, through one man's disobedience*; I Cor. xv. 22: *in Adam all die*: so it is certain that all sinned in Adam.

For Adam, the parent and head of all men, either stood or fell as a representative of the whole human race: this was true both when the covenant was made, that is, when he received God's commands, and also when he sinned. In the same way *Levi also paid tithes in Abraham . . . while he was still in his father's loins*, Heb. vii. 9, 10; *for God has made the whole human race from the blood of one man, Adam*, Acts xvii. 26. If all men did not sin in Adam, why was the condition of all made worse by his fall? Some modern thinkers would say that this deterioration was not moral but physical. But I say that it would be quite as unjust to impair the physical perfection of innocent men, especially as this has so much effect on their morals.

Moreover, it is not only a constant principle of divine justice but also a very ancient law among all races and all religions, that when a man has committed sacrilege (and this tree we ar discussing was sacred), not only he but also the whole of his posterity becomes an anathema and a sin-offering.

This was so in the flood, in the burning of Sodom and in the destruction of Korah, Num. xvi. 27, 32, and in the punishment of Achan, Josh. vii. 24, 25. When Jericho was demolished, the children paid for the sins of their fathers, and even the cattle were given up to slaughter along with their masters, Josh. vi. 21. So, too, with the posterity of Eli, the priest, I Sam. ii. 31, 33, 36; and Saul's sons paid the penalty for his slaughter of the Gibeonites, II Sam. xxi. 1, etc.

God declares that this is his justice, Exod. xx. 5: *punishing the sin of the fathers in the persons of the children, grandchildren and great-grandchildren of those who pursue me with hatred*; Num. xiv. 33: *your sons, feeding their flocks in the wilderness for forty years, will pay the penalty for your fornication*: they were not guiltless themselves, however. God himself explains what the method behind this justice is: Lev. xxvi. 39: *pining away because of their iniquity and also because of the iniquity of their fathers*; II Kings xvii. 14: *they had stiffened their necks as their ancestors stiffened theirs*; and Ezek. xviii. 4: *behold, all souls are mine; just as the soul of the father is mine, so too is the soul of the son: the soul which sins, shall die*. As for infants, the problem is solved by the consideration that all souls are God's, and that though innocent they were the children of sinful parents, and God saw that they would turn out to be like their parents. With everybody else, the explanation is that no one perishes unless he has himself sinned. Thus Agag and his people paid the penalty for the crime of their ancestors four hundred years after the latter had attacked the Israelite fugitives while they were on the march from Egypt, I Sam. xv. 2, 3; true, they were themselves far from guiltless, xv. 33. Then again, Hosea, king of Israel, was better than his ancestors; but when he was guilty of the idolatry of the Gentiles, he paid the penalty for his own sins and the sins of his ancestors as well by the loss of his kingdom, II Kings xvii. 2-4. Similarly Manasseh's sins overflowed onto his children (though they were hardly innocent themselves), xxiii. 26: *because of all the provocations with which Manasseh had provoked him*, compared with Jer. xxv. 3, 4, etc.: *from the thirteenth year of Josiah king of Judah, right up to this day, the word of Jehovah has come to me: and I have spoken it to you incessantly from daybreak onwards, but you have not listened*; and II Kings xxiv. 5: *on account of sins just like those which Manasseh had committed*. So the good king Josiah, and those who were like him, were exempt from the greater part of the punishment. The Pharisees, however, were not exempt, Matt. xxiii. 34, 35: *you shall kill some of them*, etc. *that all righteous blood may come upon you, from the blood of righteous Abel*, etc.

Accordingly penitents are ordered to confess both their own sins and the sins of their fathers: Lev. xxvi. 40: *if they will confess their iniquity and the iniquity of their fathers*, and Neh. ix. 2: *they confessed their sins and the iniquities of their ancestors*: and frequently elsewhere.

So even a whole family may become guilty because of the crime committed by its head: Gen. xii. 14: *Jehovah afflicted Pharaoh and his family with great plagues*, and xx. 7: *if you do not give her back, know that you will certainly die, you and all those who are yours*.

Subjects have to pay the penalty, too, for the sins of their king, as all Egypt did for Pharaoh's sins. Even king David, who thought it unjust that subjects should suffer in this way, also thought it quite equitable that sons should be punished for and with their fathers: II Sam. xxiv. 17: *look, I have sinned and done wrong: but these, these sheep, what have they done? I beg that your hand may be against me and against my father's house*.

Indeed, sometimes a whole nation is punished for the sin of one citizen, Josh. vii, and the offence of a single person is imputed to all, vii. 1, 11.

Furthermore, even the most just men have thought it right that a crime committed against them should be atoned for by the punishment not only of the criminal but also of his children. Thus Noah considered that Ham's offence should be avenged upon Ham's son, Canaan, Gen. ix. 25. [165]

This feature of divine justice, the insistence upon propitiatory sacrifices for sin, was well known among other nations, and never thought to be unfair. So we find in Thucydides I: *For this they and their family are held to be accursed and offenders against the goddess*. And Virgil, *Æneid*, I:

. . . Could angry Pallas, with revengeful spleen,
The Grecian navy burn, and drown the men?
She for the fault of one offending foe . . .

The same fact could easily be demonstrated by a host of other examples and proofs from the pagan writers.

Again, a man convicted of high treason, which is only an offence against another man, forfeits not only his own estate and civil rights but also those of all his family, and lawyers have decided upon the same sentence in other cases of a similar kind. Everyone knows, too, what the right of war is, and that it extends not only to those who are responsible, but to everyone who is in the enemy's power, women, for example, and even children, and people who have done nothing towards the war nor intended to.

THE SIN OF EACH INDIVIDUAL is THE SIN WHICH EACH MAN COMMITS ON HIS OWN ACCOUNT, QUITE APART FROM THAT SIN WHICH IS COMMON TO ALL. All men commit sin of this kind: Job. ix. 20: *if I were to call myself righteous, my own mouth would condemn me . . .*, and x. 15: *even if I am righteous, I cannot lift up my head;* Psal. cxliii. 2: *no living man is righteous in your sight;* Prov. xx. 9: *who can say, I am cleansed from my sin?;* Rom. iii. 23: *everyone has sinned.*

Each type of sin, common and personal, has two subdivisions, whether we call them degrees or parts or modes of sin, or whether they are related to each other as cause and effect. These subdivisions are evil desire, or the will to do evil, and the evil deed itself. James i. 14, 15: *every man is tempted when he is drawn on and enticed by his own lust: then, when lust has conceived, it brings forth sin.* This same point is neatly expressed by the poet:

Mars sees her; seeing desires her; desiring enjoys her.

It was evil desire that our first parents were originally guilty of. Then they implanted it in all their posterity, since their posterity too was guilty of that original sin, in the shape of a certain predisposition towards, or, to use a metaphor, a sort of tinder to kindle sin.

This is called in scripture *the old man* and *the body of sin,* Rom. vi. 6, Eph. iv. 22, Col. iii. 9: or simply *sin,* Rom. vii. 8: *sin seized its opportunity by means of that commandment; sin dwelling in me,* Rom. vii. 17, 20; *evil which is present,* vii. 21; *the law in my members,* vii. 23; *this body of death,* vii. 24; *the law of sin and of death,* viii. 2.

Apparently Augustine, in his writings against Pelagius was the first to call this ORIGINAL SIN. He used the word *original,* I suppose, because in the *origin* or generation of man this sin was transmitted to posterity by our first parents. But if that is what he meant, the term is too narrow, because this evil desire, this law of sin, was not only inbred in us, but also took possession of Adam after his fall, and from his point of

view it could not be called *original.*

The depravity which all human minds have in common, and their propensity to sin, are described in Gen. vi. 5: *that all the thoughts of his heart were always evil and evil alone;* vii. 21: *the devices of a man's heart are evil from childhood;* Jer. xvii. 9: *the heart is deceitful above all things;* Matt. xv. 19: *from the heart come evil thoughts, murders . . . ;* Rom. vii. 14: *the law is spiritual, I am carnal;* and vii. 7: *what the flesh tastes is enmity against God;* Gal. v. 17: *the flesh lusts against the spirit;* Eph. iv. 22: *the old man who is corrupted by deceitful lusts.*

Our first parents implanted it in us: Job. xiv. 4: *who produces purity from impurity?,* and xv. 14: *what is mortal, and pure? what is born of woman, and righteous?;* Psal. li. 7: *I was formed in iniquity and my mother nursed me in sin;* and lviii. 4: *from the womb;* Isa. xlviii. 8: *a sinner from the womb;* John iii. 6: *that which is born from flesh, is flesh;* Eph. ii. 3: *we were by nature children of anger, like the others*—even those who were born of regenerate parents, for although faith removes each man's personal guilt, it does not altogether root out the vice which dwells within us. So it is not man as a regenerate creature, but man as an animal, that begets man: just as the seed, though cleansed from straw and chaff, produces not only the ear or the grain but also the stalk and the husk. Christ alone was free from this contagion, since he was produced by supernatural generation, although descended from Adam: Heb. vii. 26: *holy, spotless.*

Some interpret this term original sin primarily as guiltiness. But guiltiness is not a sin, it is the imputation of sin, called elsewhere *the judgment of God*: Rom. i. 32: *knowing the judgment of God.* As a result of this sinners are held *worthy of death,* and ὑπόδικοι. that is, *liable to condemnation and punishment,* Rom. iii. 19, and *are under sin,* iii. 9. Thus as soon as the fall occurred, our first parents became guilty, though there could have been no original sin in them. Moreover all Adam's descendants were included in the guilt, though original sin had not yet been implanted in them. Finally, guilt is taken away from the regenerate, but they still have original sin.

Others define original sin as the loss of original righteousness and the corruption of the whole mind. But this loss must be attributed to our first parents before it is attributed to us, and they could not have been subject to original sin, as I said before. Their sin was what is called "actual" sin, which these same theologians, as part of their theory, distinguish from original sin. Anyway, their loss was a consequence of sin, rather than a sin itself; or if it was a sin, it was only a sin of ignorance, because they did not expect for a moment that they would lose anything good by eating the fruit, or that they would be worse off in any way at all. So I shall not consider this loss under the heading of sin, but under that of punishment in the next chapter.

The second subdivision of sin, after evil desire, is the evil action or crime itself, which is commonly called "actual" sin. It can be committed not only through actions, as such, but also through words and thoughts and even through the omission of a good action.

It is called "actual" not because sin is really an action, on the contrary it is a deficiency, but because it usually exists in some action. For every action is intrinsically good; it is only its misdirection or deviation from the set course of law which can properly be called evil. So action is not the material out of which sin is made, but only the υποκείμενον, the essence or element in which it exists.

Through words: Matt. xii. 36: *for every idle word they will be called to account,* and xv. 11: *whatever comes out, defiles a man.*

Through thoughts: Exod. xx. 17: *you shall not covet your neighbor's house;* Psal. vii. 14: *see, he will bring forth vanity; as he conceived trouble so he will bring forth lies;* Prov. xxiv. 8: *planning to do evil . . . ;* Jer. xvii. 9: *the heart is deceitful above all things,* etc.; Matt. v. 28: *he has already committed adultery with her in his heart,* and xv. 19: *from the heart . . . evil thoughts;* I John iii. 15: *the man who hates his brother is a murderer.*

Through omission: Matt. xii. 30: *he who is not with me is against me; and he who does not gather with me, scatters,* similarly Luke xi. 23 and vi. 9, where not to save a man is considered the same as destroying him. Matt. xxv. 42: *I was hungry and you did not give;* James iv. 17: *a man who knows how to do right and does not do it, is in the power of sin.*

But all sins are not, as the Stoics maintained, equally great: Ezek. v. 6: *into wickedness more than the nations,* and viii. 15: *abominations greater than these;* John xix. 11: *he has the greater sin.*

This inequality arises from many and various circumstances of person, place, time, and the like: Isa. xxvi. 10: *in the land of righteousness he will deal unjustly.*

A discussion of the difference between mortal and venial sin will fit in better elsewhere. Meanwhile it is indisputable that even the least sin renders a man liable to condemnation: Luke xvi. 10: *he who is unjust in little is also unjust in much.*

Chapter XII
THE PUNISHMENT OF SIN

SO far I have spoken of sin. After sin came death, as its affliction or punishment: Gen. ii. 17: *on the day you eat it, you will die;* Rom. v. 12: *through sin is death,* and vi. 23: *the wages of sin is death,* and vii. 5: *the effects of sin, to bring forth fruit to death.*

But in scripture every evil, and everything which seems to lead to destruction, is indeed under the name of *death.* For physical death, as it is called, did not follow *on the same day as* Adam's sin, as God had threatened.

So four degrees of death may conveniently be distinguished. First, as I said above, come ALL EVILS WHICH TEND TO DEATH AND WHICH, IT IS AGREED, CAME INTO THE WORLD AS SOON AS MAN FELL. I will here set out the most important of these. First: guiltiness, which, although it is a thing imputed to us by God, is nevertheless a sort of partial death or prelude to death in us, by which we are fettered to condemnation and punishment as by some actual bond: Gen. iii. 7: *then both their eyes opened, and they knew that they were naked;* Lev. v. 2, etc.: *although it was hidden from him, nevertheless he is unclean and guilty;* Rom. iii. 19: *the whole world is liable to God's condemnation.* As a result guiltiness is either accompanied or followed by terrors of conscience: Gen. iii. 8: *they heard the voice of God, and Adam hid himself: he said, I was afraid;* Rom. viii. 15: *the spirit of slavery in fear;* Heb. ii. 15: *all those who through fear of death were condemned to slavery all their lives,* and x. 27: *a terrifying expectation of judgment:* also by the loss of divine protection and favor, which results in the lessening of the majesty of the human countenance, and the degradation of the mind: Gen. iii. 7: *they knew that they were naked.* Thus the whole man is defiled: Tit. i. 15: *both their mind and their conscience is defiled.* Hence comes shame: Gen. iii. 7: *they sewed leaves together and made themselves aprons;* Rom. vi. 21: *for which you are now ashamed, for the end of those things is death.*

The second degree of death is called SPIRITUAL DEATH. This is the loss of that divine grace and innate righteousness by which, in the beginning, man lived with God: Eph. ii. 1: *since you were dead in trespasses and sins,* and iv. 18: *alienated from the life of God;* Col. ii. 13: *dead in sins;* Rev. iii. 1: *you have a name for being alive, but are dead.* And this death took place at the same moment as the fall of man, not merely on the same day. Those who are delivered from it are said to be regenerated and born again and created anew. As I will show in my chapter on Regeneration, this is not the work of God alone.

This death consists, first, in the loss or at least the extensive darkening of that right reason, whose function it was to discern the chief good, and which was, as it were, the life of the understanding: Eph. iv. 18: *having a mind obscured by darkness, and alienated from the life of God on account of the ignorance which is in them*, and v. 8: *you were once darkness;* John i. 5: *the darkness did not swallow it up;* Jer. vi. 10: *they cannot pay attention;* John viii. 43: *you cannot . . . ;* I Cor. ii. 14: the natural man cannot receive the things which are of the spirit of God; II Cor. iii. 5: *not that we are fit to think anything out by ourselves*, and iv. 4: *the god of this world has blinded their minds;* Col. i. 13: *he has snatched us from the power of darkness*: secondly, in that extinction of righteousness and of the liberty to do good, and in that slavish subjection to sin and the devil which is, as it were, the death of the will. John viii. 34: *whoever commits sin is the slave of sin.* We have all committed sin in Adam, therefore we are born slaves; Rom. vii. 14: *sold to be subject to sin*, and viii. 3: *since it was devoid of strength in the flesh*, and viii. 7: *it is not subject to the law of God, for indeed it cannot be;* Rom. vi. 16, 17: *you are the slaves of him whom you obey, whether slaves of sin, to death, or . . . ;* Philipp. iii. 19: *whose God is their belly;* Acts xxvi. 18: *from the power of Satan;* II Tim. ii. 26: *out of the snare of the devil, who are made captive by him at his will;* Eph. ii. 2: *the spirit now working in arrogant men.* Lastly sin is its own punishment, and the death of the spiritual life; especially when sins are heaped upon sins: Rom. i. 26: *for this reason he has given them up to filthy desires.* The reason for this is not hard to see. As sins increase so they bind the sinners to death more surely, make them more miserable and constantly more vile, and deprive them more and more of divine help and grace, and of their own former glory. No one should have the least doubt that sin is in itself alone the gravest evil of all, for it is opposed to the chief good, that is, to God. Punishment, on the other hand, seems to be opposed only to the good of the creature, and not always to that.

However, it cannot be denied that some traces of the divine image still remain in us, which are not wholly extinguished by this spiritual death. This is quite clear, not only from the holiness and wisdom in both word and deed of many of the heathens, but also from Gen. ix. 2: *every beast shall have fear of you*, and ix: 6: *who sheds man's blood . . . because God made man in his image.* These traces remain in our intellect, Psal. xix. 2: *the heavens declare . . .* —obviously they do not *declare* it to beings who cannot hear. Rom. i. 19, 20: *that which can be known about God . . . the invisible things are evident from the creation of the world*, and i. 32: *knowing the judgment of God*, and ii. 15: *which show the work of the law written in their hearts;* vii. 23, 24: *I see another law in my members battling against the law of my mind . . . I am a wretched man. Who will rescue me from this body of death?* The freedom of the will is not entirely extinct: first of all, in indifferent matters, whether natural or civil: I Cor. vii. 36, 37, 39: *let him do what he will. He has power over his will. She is free to marry whom she lies.* Secondly, this freedom has clearly not quite disappeared even where good works are concerned, or at least good attempts, at any rate after God has called us and give us grace. But is so weak and of such little moment, that it only takes away any excuse we might have for doing nothing, and does not give us the slightest reason for being proud of ourselves: Deut. xxx. 19: *choose life, that you and your seed may live;* Psal. lxxviii. 8: *a generation which has not set its mind in order;* Jer. viii. 13–16: *because when I speak to you from the dawn onwards, you do not hear, and when I shout at you, you do not answer, therefore . . .* — but why, if he had only been speaking to incapable blockheads? And xxxi. 18: *turn to me and I will be turned;* Zech. i. 3: *turn back to me and I will turn back to you;* Mark ix. 23, 24: *if you can believe this . . . and the boy's father cried out at once and said with tears, Lord, I believe, help my unbelief;* Rom. ii. 14: *when the Gentiles who have not the law do by nature the things contained in the law*, and vi. 16: *do you not know that when you present yourselves as slaves to obey someone, you are the slaves of him whom you obey, whether slaves of sin, to death, or slaves of obedience, to righteousness*, and vii. 18: *I am able to will . . .* , and vii. 21: *to me when I wish to do good.* Paul seems to speak these words in the person of a man not yet fully regenerate who, although called by God and given grace, had not yet been subject to his regenerating influence. This is clear from vii. 14: *I am carnal, sold to be subject to sin.* As for his words in vii. 25: *I thank God through Jesus Christ . . .* , these and similar things could be said and done by a man who had only been called. Rom. ix. 31: *by following the law of righteousness they did not attain the law of righteousness*, and x. 2: *they have zeal for God, but not from knowledge;* I. Cor. ix. 17: *if I do this willingly, I have a reward, but if unwillingly . . . ;* Philipp. iii. 6: *so far as zeal is concerned, persecuting the Church; so far as the righteousness in the law is concerned, blameless;* I. Pet. v. 2: *feed the flock of God . . . not perforce but willingly.* As a result nearly all human beings profess some concern for virtue, and have an abhorrence of some of the more atrocious crimes: I. Cor. v. 1: *fornication of a kind which is not mentioned even among the Gentiles.*

As a vindication of God's justice, especially when he calls man, it is obviously fitting that some measure of free will should be allowed to man, whether this is something left over from his primitive state, or something restored to him as a result of the call of grace. It is also fitting that this will should operate in good works or at least good attempts, rather than in things indifferent. For if God rules all human actions, both natural and civil, by his absolute command, then he is not doing anything more than he is entitled to do, and no one need complain. But if he turns man's will to moral good or evil just as he likes, and then rewards the good and punishes the wicked, it will cause an outcry against divine justice from all sides. It would seem then that God's general government of all things, which is so often referred to, should be understood as operating in natural and civil matters and in things indifferent and in chance happenings—in fact in anything rather than in moral or religious concerns. There are several scriptural texts which corroborate this. II Chron. xv. 12, 14: *they entered into a covenant to seek Jehovah the God of their ancestors with all their heart and with all their soul: and they swore to Jehovah;* Psal. cxix. 106: *I have sworn (and I will perform it), to keep your righteous judgments.* Obviously if religious matters were not under our control, or to some extent within our power and choice, God could not enter into a covenant with us, and we could not keep it, let alone swear to keep it.

BOOK II
OF THE WORSHIP OF GOD

CHAPTER IX
OF THE FIRST KIND OF SPECIAL VIRTUES, CONNECTED WITH A MAN'S DUTY TOWARDS HIMSELF

THE SPECIAL VIRTUES which regulate our appetite for external advantages operate in relation either to the pleasures of the flesh or to the material possessions and distinctions of our life.

The virtue which regulates our appetite for the pleasures of the flesh is called TEMPERANCE. Tit. ii. 11, 12: *for the grace of God which brings salvation to all men has dawned, teaching us that renouncing ungodliness and worldly lusts we should live temperately and justly and piously in this present age;* I Pet. ii. 12: *that as aliens in a foreign land you abstain from fleshly lusts which war* against the soul, and II Pet. ii. 9: *the Lord knows how to .. reserve the wicked under punishment until the day of judgment: but above all those who run after flesh and pollute themselves with lust.*

Temperance includes sobriety and chastity, modesty and decency.

SOBRIETY means forbearance from over-eating and from drinking too much. I Thess. v. 8: *let us, who are of the day, be sober;* I Pet. i. 13: *so gird up the loins of mind, and be sober,* and iv. 7: *the end of all things is upon us, so be temperate and sober, given to prayer,* and v. 8: *be sober, and on the look-out; for your enemy, the devil, like a roaring lion, prowls round looking for someone to devour;* Esth. i. 8: *the drinking was according to the law, no one compelled anyone else to drink, for so the king had laid it down for all the officers of his house to obey, that each guest should do as he wished.*

Opposed to this are drunkenness and gluttony. Noah provides an example, Gen. ix. So does Lot, Gen. xix; Benhadad, I Kings xx. 16; Prov. xx. 1: *wine is a mocker . . . ,* and xxi. 17: *the man who loves wine . . . will not be rich,* and xxiii. 3, etc.: *do not be smitten with desire for his dainty dishes, for they are deceitful food,* and xxiii. 20, 21: *do not be one of those who get drunk on wine or stuff themselves with food . . . ,* and xxiii. 29–32: *Who says, Oh dear? Who says, Alas? Who has quarrels? Who cannot hold his tongue? Who gets hurt and cannot retaliate? Who is red-eyed? Those who sit long over their wine;* Isa. v. 11, 12: *woe to them that get up early in the morning in order to drink themselves drunk . . . : but they do not regard the work of Jehovah,* and v. 22: *woe to mighty wine-drinkers . . . ,* and xxviii. 1, 3, 7, 8: *woe to the crown of pride, to the drunkards of Ephraim . . . ;* Ezek. xvi. 49: *see this was the sin of your sister Sodom, superiority, full stomachs . . . ;* Luke xxi. 34: *keep a watch on yourselves in case your hearts grow heavy with excessive drinking and with drunkenness; so that that day catches you unawares;* Rom. xiii. 13: *let us behave with decency, as befits the day, and not spend our time in revelling and drunkenness;* I Cor. vi. 10: *nor drunkards . . . shall inherit the kingdom of God;* Gal. v. 21: *drinking-bouts, revellings and such like . . . will not inherit the kingdom of God;* Hos. iv. 10: *they shall eat and not be satisfied . . . ,* and vii. 5: *in the day of our king, the princes have made him ill with wine from the bottle . . . ;* Hab. ii. 15, 16: *woe to the man who gives his neighbor drink . . . ;* Eph. v. 18: *do not get drunk on wine, which is the way to debauchery, but . . . ;* I Pet. iv. 3, 4: *it is sufficient for us . . . to have lived in lasciviousness, lust, drunkenness, riot and tippling . . . They are amazed when you do not plunge with them into the same reckless dissipation.*

Allied to sobriety is watchfulness. Matt. xxiv. 42: *watch, for you do not know at what hour your Lord will come;* similarly xxv. 13 and xxvi. 41 and Mark xiii. 35 and 37: *what I say to you, I say to all: Watch;* Luke xii. 37: *blessed are those servants whom the Lord, when he comes, will find watching,* and xxi. 36: *keep watch at all times, praying that you may be held worthy to escape all those things which are going to happen . . . ;* Col. iv. 2: *persist in prayer, keeping watch . . . ;* I Thess. v. 6: *let us not sleep, as others do, but keep watch and be sober;* I Pet. v. 8: *be sober and keep watch;* Rev. iii. 3: *because if you do not keep watch, I shall come upon you like a thief . . . ,* and xvi. 15: *blessed is the man who stays awake and keeps on his clothes, lest he walk naked. . . .* It appears that in most of these passages watchfulness means abstention from mental sluggishness rather than from actual physical sleep.

Opposed to this is sleepiness. Prov. xx. 13: *do not love sleep, lest it impoverish you. . . .*

CHASTITY means forbearance from the unlawful lusts of the flesh; it is also called purity. I Thess. iv. 3: *this is God's will, your purity, your abstention from fornication . . . ;* Rev. xiv. 4: *these are they who were not defiled by contact with women, for they are virgins: they follow the Lamb. . . .*

Opposed to chastity is all impurity: voluptuousness, sodomy, bestiality and so on. To commit any of these sins is to sin against oneself, and to injure oneself primarily, I Cor. vi. 15, 16, 18: *do you not know that your bodies are Christ's limbs? Shall I take . . . Do you not know that he who couples with a prostitute . . . Shun fornication. Every other sin that a man commits is outside the body, but the fornicator sins against his own body;* Prov. vi. 24, etc.; Gen. xxxviii. 9, 10: *but the thing which he did seemed evil in Jehovah's eyes;* Exod. xxii. 19: *anyone who lies with an animal shall be put to death without fail;* Lev. xviii. 22, 23: *you shall not lie with a male . . . ;* Deut. xxiii. 17: *there shall be no prostitute among the daughters of Israel, and no . . . ,* xxvii. 21: *cursed is the man who lies with any kind of animal;* Prov. ii. 16, etc.: *by rescuing you from the foreign woman . . . ,* and v. 3, etc.: *though the lips of the foreign woman drop honey . . . ,* and vi. 24, etc.: *to save you from the wicked woman,* and vi. 32, and vii. 25, etc.: *do not let your heart bend to her ways . . . ,* and ix. 18: *he does not know that the dead are there . . . ,* xxii. 14: *as deep a pit,* and similarly xxiii. 26, 27 and xxx. 20: *this is how the prostitute behaves; she eats and wipes her mouth and says, I have done no wickedness;* I Kings xiv. 24: *also there were sodomites in the land;* Rom. xiii. 13: *not in bed and in lasciviousness . . . ;* I Cor vi. 9, 10: *make no mistake, no fornicators or adulterers, none who are effeminate or homosexual . . . will inherit the kingdom of God . . . ;* and vi. 13 etc.: *the body is not for fornication, but for the Lord, and the Lord for the body . . . ;* Eph. v. 3–5: *fornication and impurity of any kind . . . must not be so much as mentioned among you, as befits those who are*

holy; also obscenity . . . these things are out of place. For you know that no fornicator, and no impure person . . . is an heir to the kingdom of Christ and of God.

MODESTY means abstinence from obscene words and suggestive behavior and, in fact, from anything which fails to conform with the strictest standards of personal or sexual conduct. Deut. xxv. 11, 12: *if men are quarreling . . . ;* Job xxxi. 1: *I had made a covenant with my eyes . . . ;* I Cor. xi. 10: *for this reason a woman should have a sign of authority on her head, on account of the angels;* Heb. xii. 28: *let us worship God with modesty and reverence, so that we may be pleasing to him;* II Kings iv. 15: *when he had called her she stood at her door.* This womanly modesty was found even among the heathen: Homer says of Penelope in *Odyssey* i:

στῆ ῥα παρὰ σταθμὸν τέγεος πύκα ποιητοῖο, etc.

She stood by the threshold, etc.

Opposed to modesty are obscenity in conversation and suggestive or shameless behavior. Isa. iii. 16, etc.: *so Jehovah will make the heads of the daughters of Zion scabby, and will lay bare their private parts . . . ;* Matt. v. 28: *whoever looks at a woman . . . ;* Eph. v. 4: *and obscenity and foolish talk and scurrility, which are not fitting . . . ;* II Pet. ii. 14: *with their eyes full of adultery . . . .*

DECENCY means avoidance of anything shameless or suggestive in one's dress and personal appearance. Exod. xx. 26: *and do not climb up to my altar by steps, in case your private parts should be revealed there;* Deut. xxii. 5: *let no woman wear masculine dress, nor any man put on a woman's clothes, for this is an abomination to Jehovah;* Zeph. i. 8: *it shall come to pass . . . that I will punish all who wear foreign clothes . . . ;* Matt. xi. 8: *see, those who wear luxurious clothes live in kings' palaces;* I Tim. ii. 9: *and similarly that women wear decent clothing, with modesty and propriety, and with nothing abbreviated, and no gold or pearls or costly materials;* I Pet. iii. 3: *and do not let their adornment be outward adornment—curling their hair and putting on gold and gowns . . . ;* II Kings ix. 30: *she painted her face,* etc.

The virtues which limit our material possessions are contentment, frugality, industry and elegance.

CONTENTMENT is the virtue which makes a man feel inward satisfaction, and makes him accept what seems to him to be divine providence. Prov. x. 22: *Jehovah's blessing alone makes a man rich,* and xxx. 8: *give me neither poverty nor riches: feed me with my ration of food;* Eccles. iii. 12, 13: *I know that there is no good in them, unless a man is glad at heart and does good while he lives; yes, it is the gift of God that each man should eat and drink and enjoy the fruit of all his labor,* and v. 18, etc.: *see, this is what I have seen: it is good and beautiful to eat and drink and to enjoy the fruit of all the labor which one performs beneath the sun all the days of one's life, which God himself has given; for this is one's portion. And when God has given any man riches and possessions and the ability to enjoy them and to accept his portion and take pleasure in his labor, this is the gift of God. And if it is not a great gift, he will nevertheless be thankful for the days of his life, because God himself granted them for the delight of his heart,* and vi. 1, 2: *there is an evil which I have seen under the sun, and it is a great evil for men. God has given a man riches, possessions and honor, and he has everything his heart desires; yet God does not give him the ability to enjoy it—a stranger enjoys it,* and ix. 9, 10: *enjoy life with your wife, whom you love . . . ;* Zech. ix. 16, 17: *how great will his prosperity and his beauty be?;* Philipp. iv. 11, 12: *I do not say this because I suffer want, for I have learned to be content with my circumstances, whatever they are. I know what it is to be brought low, and I know what it is to have plenty; I am thoroughly initiated in every sort of condition, in fulness and hunger, in plenty and want;* I Tim. vi. 6, 7: *godliness and a contented mind are great gains: for we brought nothing into this world, and we are able to take nothing out. But if we have food and clothing we shall be satisfied;* Heb. xiii. 5: *be content with what you have.*

Even in poverty. Psal. xxiii. 1, 2: *Jehovah is my shepherd, I cannot want . . . ,* and xxxiv. 9, etc.: *those who fear Jehovah lack nothing. The young lions lack . . . ,* and xxxvii. 16: *the little which a righteous man has is good, rather . . . ,* etc., and 18, 19: *in bad times they will not be shamed, and in time of famine they will have enough,* and xl. 18: *I am poor and needy, but the Lord is mindful of me . . . ,* and lxviii. 11: *of your goodness for the poor and wretched;* Prov. x. 3: *Jehovah does not allow the righteous man's soul to feel hunger.* Poverty, then, should not be thought disgraceful: Prov. xvii. 5: *the man who laughs at the poor is a disgrace to his creator,* and xix. 1: *the poor man who behaves with integrity is better than the rich man who is an evil-speaker,* and xxviii. 6: *the poor man who behaves with integrity is better than the evil man who keeps shifting from this to that, even though the latter be rich,* and xxviii. 11: *the rich man seems wise in his own eyes, but the poor man who is knowing sees through him.* Similarly, we should not put our trust in riches, or pride ourselves upon them. Prov. xi. 28: *he who puts his trust in his riches, shall fall;* Eccles. vi. 11: *since there are many things here, they multiply vanity;* Mark x. 23–25: *with what difficulty will those who have riches enter the kingdom of God? How difficult is it for those who trust in riches to enter the kingdom of God? It is easier for a camel . . . ;* I Tim. vi. 17, 18: *charge those who are rich in this world's goods not to be proud or fix their hopes upon such an uncertain thing as wealth, but upon the living God . . . ;* II

Kings xx. 13, 14: *Hezekiah paid attention to them and showed them his whole treasury. . . .*

Opposed to this is anxiety over food and clothing. Matt. vi. 25, etc.: *do not be anxious about your life, about what you will eat or drink, or about how you will clothe your body . . . ,* and so on, to 33: *seek first the kingdom of God and his righteousness, and all these other things will come to you as well.*

And avarice, Job xx. 15: *he has swallowed down riches, and vomits them up again; God drives them out of his belly;* Josh. vii. 21: *when I saw . . . I coveted them and took them;* Psal. cxix. 36: *and do not allow it to be turned to money-making;* Prov. i. 19: *this is how they behave, all those who devote themselves to making money: money-making destroys those who are devoted to it,* and xv. 27: *the man who is devoted to money-making disturbs his own house,* and xx. 21: *a fortune may be quickly made, but in the end it will not be blessed;* Eccles. ii. 27: *he gives the sinner the job of gathering together and heaping up, so that he may hand it over to the man who seems good in his sight,* and iv. 4: *he is by himself and has no fellow, he has neither son nor brother, yet there is no end to his labor, and his eyes are not sated with riches,* and v. 10: *he who loves money cannot have enough of it;* Isa. lvii. 21: *because of the iniquity of his desire for gain I was angry and struck him . . . ;* Matt. vi. 19: *do not pile up treasures on earth where moth and rust destroy,* and xvii. 5: *but he threw away the pieces of silver . . . ;* Luke xii. 15: *be on your guard and beware of avarice, for a man's life does not depend on the abundance of his possessions;* I Tim. vi. 9, etc.: *those who want to be rich fall into temptations and snares, and many foolish, harmful desires . . . ;* Heb. xiii. 5: *let your behavior be free from avarice.* For avarice is idolatry: Matt. vi. 24: *you cannot serve God and mammon;* Eph. v. 5: *an avaricious man, who is an idolater;* Col. iii. 5: *avarice, which is idolatry.* And the root of all evil is avarice, I Tim. vi. 10: *the root of all evil is the love of money. There are some who covet money, and have thus strayed from the faith.*

Also opposed to this virtue is any grumbling about the way in which God's providence supplies us with the necessaries of life: Jude 16: *they are grumblers, complainers; they follow their own desires. Big words roll from their lips, and they use flattery to gain their ends.*

FRUGALITY or thrift is shown when one spares expense, as much as is decently possible, and when one is careful to preserve anything which may be useful. John vi. 12; *gather up the leftovers.*

It is different from miserliness. I Sam. xxv. 3: *but her husband was tight-fisted . . . ,* and xxv. 11: *shall I take my bread and my water;* Eccles. vi. 2: *God has given a man riches, possessions and honor, and he has everything his heart desires; yet God does not give him the ability to enjoy it—a stranger enjoys it.*

INDUSTRY is the virtue which enables one to make an honest living. Gen. ii. 15: *to cultivate it and look after it,* and iii. 19: *you shall eat your food in the sweat of your face;* Prov. x. 4: *the hands of the diligent make them rich,* and x. 5: *a wise son stores up in summertime,* and xii. 11: *the man who tills his land will have his fill of food,* and xiv. 23: *there is profit in all labor . . . ,* and xxi. 5: *the thoughts of the diligent man make for profit, but all the devices of a rash man lead to poverty,* and xxii. 29: *you have seen a man who is diligent in his work? He will stand firm before kings . . . ;* I Thess. iv. 11, 12: *to work with your own hands, as we ordered you: you will thus behave in a way which will be respected by those outside your own number, and you will not go short of anything;* and II Thess. iii. 12: *we exhort them through our Lord Jesus Christ to work quietly and eat their own bread.*

Laziness in providing for one's needs is the opposite of this virtue. Prov. vi. 6: *go to the ant . . . ,* and x. 5: *a son who sleeps through the harvest is a son to be ashamed of,* and xiii. 4: *the soul of the idler is moved by desire, but he will have nothing,* and xix. 24: *the idler is moved by desire, but he will have nothing,* and xix. 24: *the idler keeps his hand hidden in his sleeve,* and xx. 4: *the idler who will not plough because of the winter weather, will beg in the summer and have nothing,* and xxi. 25, 26: *the idler's desire is the death of him, because his hands refuse to do anything,* and xxii. 13: *the idler says, There is a lion outside . . . ,* and xxiv. 30, etc.: *I went over by the idler's field . . . ,* and xxvi. 14, etc.: *as the door turns . . . ,* and xxviii. 19: *he who follows idle men will have his fill of poverty;* Eccles. iv. 1–2: *the fool folds his arms . . . Better, he says, a handful of quietness than two fistfulls of toil and vexation of spirit;* II Thess. iii. 10: *if anyone will not work, he shall not eat . . .*

ELEGANCE is the discriminating enjoyment of food, clothing and all the civilized refinements of life, purchased with our honest earnings.

Food. Gen xxi. 8: *Abraham gave a great feast . . . ,* Job i. 5: *it happened that when the days of feasting had passed, Job sent and sanctified them . . . ;* Psal. xxiii. 5: *you spread a table before me in the face of my enemies: you anoint my head with oil; my cup runs over,* and civ. 15: *he gladdens the heart of man with wine, and makes his face shine with oil . . . ;* Prov. xxxi. 6: *give strong drink to the man at the point of death . . . ;* Dan. x. 3: *I ate nothing that was at all appetizing . . . ;* Luke v. 29: *Levi gave a big party for him . . . ;* John xii. 2, 3: *they gave a dinner for him . . . Then Mary brought a pound of very costly ointment, liquid nard . . . ;* Acts xiv. 17: *filling our hearts with food and delight.*

Civilized refinements. Gen. xxiv. 22: *and the man took a gold ring and put it on her nose . . . ;* II Sam. i. 24: *who clothed you in purple, with other delights, and put*

golden ornaments on your garments; Prov. xiv. 24: *the crown of the wise is their wealth,* and xxxi. 22, 25: *she makes herself cotton coverlets . . . ;* Eccles. ix. 10: *let your clothes be bright at all times . . . and ointment poured on your head . . .*

Opposed to this is luxury. Prov., xxi. 17: *the pleasure-lover will be a pauper . . . the man who loves wine and ointment will not be rich;* Luke xvi. 19: *there was a certain rich man who wore purple and fine linen and feasted in great magnificence every day.*

Where the distinctions of public life are concerned, the appropriate virtues are humility and high-mindedness.

HUMILITY gives a man a modest opinion of himself and prevents him from blowing his own trumpet, except when it is really called-for. Exod. iii. 11: *who am I, that I should go to Pharaoh?;* Psal. cxxxi. 1: *I was not haughty, my eyes were not elevated; I did not have to do with great or lofty affairs, which are too high for me;* Prov. xi. 2: *wisdom is with the humble;* Prov. xii. 8: *better is the man who knows his own vileness, and has a servant, than him . . . ,* and xv. 33: *before honor, lowliness,* similarly xviii. 12, and xvi. 19: *it is better to be humble in spirit, with the meek, than to divide the spoil with the proud,* and xxix. 23: *honor upholds the man of lowly spirit;* Jer. i. 6, 7: *ah, Lord, I am a child . . . ;* Dan. ii. 30: *not through any wisdom that there is in me . . . ;* Matt. xxiii. 12: *whoever humbles himself will be exalted;* Rom. xii. 10: *giving way to one another with deference;* II Cor. x. 13: *we will not boast of things which are outside our sphere, but according to the limit . . . ,* and x. 15: *and not of things which are outside our sphere . . . ;* Eph. iii. 8: *to me, who am far and away the least of God's people,* and v. 21: *submitting to one another, in the fear of God's people,* and v. 21: *submitting to one another, in the fear of God;* Philipp. ii. 3: *humbly thinking others better than yourselves.*

Blowing his own trumpet, except when it is really called-for etc. Job xii. 1, etc.: *I have a mind as well as you, I am not inferior to you . . . ,* and xiii. 2: *just as you know, so, too, do I . . . ,* and xxix. 8, etc.: *seeing me the boys hid themselves and even the aged got to their feet . . . ;* Judges v. 7: *until I, Deborah, arose; until I arose a mother in Israel;* Eccles. i. 16: *see, I have increased and have amassed more wisdom than all my predecessors . . .*

Opposed to this is arrogance. Prov. xx. 6: *most men proclaim their own goodness;* James iii. 1: *let not many of you be teachers, for you know that we teachers will be judged more severely;* Prov. xxvi. 16: *the idler seems wiser in his own eyes than seven men recalling him to reason.*

And a vain desire for glory. Matt. xxiii. 12: *whoever exalts himself will be humbled;* John v. 41: *I do not strive after glory from men,* and v. 44: *how can you have any faith when you strive to get glory from one another, and*

xii. 42, 43: *they loved the glory of men rather than the glory of God;* Gal. v. 26: *let us not desire empty glory;* I Thess. ii. 6: *not seeking glory from men, from you or from anyone else.*

And boastfulness. Prov. xxv. 14: *like clouds and wind without rain is the man who boasts of a false gift.*

And a crafty or hypocritical playing down of one's own merit, when one is really fishing for compliments.

To pride oneself upon one's crimes and misdeeds is also opposed to this virtue. Psal. lii. 3: *why do you boast of your evil, o mighty man!;* Isa. iii. 10: *they broadcast their sin as Sodom did, instead of hiding it; woe to their souls, they have brought evil upon themselves!*

Allied to humility is the desire for a good reputation and for the approval of good men, along with contempt for that of evil men. Psal. cxix. 22: *remove from me reproach and contempt for I keep your testimonies,* and 39: *turn away my reproach, I dread it . . . ;* Prov. xxii. 1: *reputation is choicer than great wealth, and popularity is better than gold and silver;* Eccles. vii. 1: *a man's reputation is better than the most precious ointment;* I Kings xviii. 12, 13: *surely my lord was informed of what I did when Jezebel killed Jehovah's prophets . . . ?;* Neh. v. 14, 15: *but I did not do so, because of my reverence for God;* Matt. v. 11: *you will be blessed . . . when men tell slanderous lies about you, on my account;* II Cor. vi. 8: *through glory and disgrace, praise and blame; as imposters, yet speaking the truth;* Heb. xi. 24–26: *considering the stigma of Christ greater riches than all the treasures of Egypt . . . ,* and xiii. 13: *let us go to him outside the camp, bearing the stigma that he bore.*

Opposed to this is a shameless neglect of one's good name. Luke xviii. 2: *he did not fear God and cared nothing for any man.*

Also an over-eager pursuit of popularity and of praise, regardless of its source. Prov. xxvii. 2: *let another man's mouth praise you, not your own . . . ;* Matt. xxiii. 5: *they do everything for show;* Luke vi. 26: *alas for you when all men speak well of you . . .*

HIGH-MINDEDNESS is shown when in seeking or not seeking riches, advantages or honors, in avoiding them or accepting them, a man behaves himself as befits his own dignity, rightly understood. Abraham, for example, did not reject the gifts of the king of Egypt, Gen. xii. 13 and xx. 14, though he did those of the king of Sodom, xiv. 22, 23; and he refused to accept Ephron's field when it was offered to him, except at its correct market price, xxiii. 13. So too Job, although restored to his former health and prosperity, did not reject his friends' gifts, xlii. 11. Gideon refused the kingdom, Judges viii. 23. Joseph behaved in accordance with the same principle when his career took him from prison to the highest honors, Gen. xli, and Dan. ii. 48, 49: *then the*

king *made much of Daniel, and gave him many very splendid gifts . . .* Compare v. 17: *he said to the king's face, Keep your gifts to yourself, and pay your fees to someone else . . . ,* as opposed to v. 29: *at Belshazzar's command they clothed Daniel in purple . . .* Daniel behaved in the same way when accepting or refusing honors, vi. 3, etc.: *over these were three Eparchs, of whom Daniel was the first . . . ;* so, too, did Nehemiah, when he made a request, ii. 5: *I said to the king, If it seems good to your majesty, and if your servant has found favor in your eyes, send me into Judah . . . ;* and Samuel, when he resigned his authority, I Sam. x. 1: *then Samuel took an oval bottle of oil and poured it on his head and kissed him and said, Shall I not do this?;* and Elisha, when he refused to take a fee for healing Naaman, II Kings v. 15, 16: *as Jehovah lives, before whom I stand, I will not take . . . ;* and Christ, when he rejected the empire of the world, Matt. iv. 9: *I will give you all these if . . . ,* similarly Luke iv. 6, and John vi. 15: *when he realized that they were going to come to make him king, he went away,* and when he rejected wealth, II Cor. viii. 9: *though he was rich, yet for your sake he became poor . . . ,* and accepted honors, Matt. xxi. 7, etc.: *and they brought the ass . . .* And this is how every true Christian behaves when reckoning his own worth: James i. 9, 10: *let the brother who is in humble circumstances be proud of his elevation, and let the rich brother be proud that he is brought low.*

Allied to this is indignation when praise or honor are given to those unworthy of them, or when such people enjoy prosperity. Prov. xxx. 21, etc.: *three things shake the earth; or rather there are four things which it cannot bear: a servant who is master, a fool who is full of food, an odious woman when she is married, and a maid when she is made heir to her mistress.* To be too indignant, however, is not praiseworthy: Psal. xxxvii. 1: *do not lose your temper over evil-doers,* and xxxvii. 7, 8: *do not lose your temper over a man who is following his own devices and doing well, over a man who is bringing his schemes to success . . . ;* Prov. iii. 31: *do not envy any violent man, or choose to imitate him in any way.* An example of indignant language is Job xxx. 1, etc. Psal. xv. 4: *in his eyes a fraud is despicable, but he honors those that fear Jehovah.* Sometimes, as a result of indignation, such language borders on obscenity; Ezek. xvi. 25, 36.

Opposed to high-mindedness is ambition. Num. xii. 2: *has Jehovah spoken only through Moses? Has he not also spoken through us,* and xvi. 3: *these are all holy, and Jehovah is among them: why, then, do you lift yourselves up above Jehovah's congregation;* Judges ix. 1, 2: *Abimelech went . . . and spoke to them,* etc. *Speak, I pray you, to all the men of Shechem . . . ;* II Sam. xv. 2: *in the morning Absalom got up and stood . . . ,* and xv. 4: *O that they would make me judge in this land . . . ;* Prov. xxv. 27: *to hunt one's own honor is dishonorable.*

And pride, when a man is more puffed up than he ought to be, with no or with insufficient justification, or because of some trifling circumstance. II Sam. xxii. 28: *your eyes frown upon those who are puffed up;* Prov. vi. 16, 17: *Jehovah hates these six things . . . : haughty eyes . . . , and* xv. 25: *Jehovah will tear down the house of the proud, and* xvi. 5: *every haughty person is an abomination to Jehovah, and* xvi. 18: *pride goes before a fall . . . , and* xviii. 12: *man's heart is haughty before a fall, and* xxi. 4: *a haughty look and a swollen head . . . , and* xxix. 23: *a man's haughtiness will be his downfall.*

And faint-heartedness: Saul, when chosen king, exemplifies this, I Sam. x. 21, 22: *when they looked for him he was not to be found . . . . See, he is hiding among the baggage. . . .*

CHAPTER X
OF THE SECOND KIND OF VIRTUES CONNECTED WITH A MAN'S DUTIES TOWARDS HIMSELF

I HAVE spoken of the virtues which regulate our appetite for external advantages. Now I must deal with those which are exhibited in our repulsion or endurance of evils.

These are fortitude and patience.

FORTITUDE is chiefly apparent when we repel evils or stand against them unafraid. Josh. i. 6, 7, 9: *have I not told you? Take heart and be strong: do not be afraid or alarmed;* Heb. xi. 32, etc.: *I shall not have time to tell of Gideon . . . ; who through faith subdued kingdoms;* Psal. iii. 7: *I will not be afraid of the myriads of people who have taken up attacking positions around me;* Psal. xviii. 32, etc. and xxiii. 4: *though I walk through the valley of the shadow of death, I shall fear no evil, because you . . . , and* xxxvii. 12, etc.: *when the wicked man plots against the righteous . . . Their swords will pierce their own hearts . . . , and* xlvi. 2, 3: *God is our refuge and strength . . . So we shall not fear if the earth shift about . . . , and* lvi. 12: *I put my trust in God; I will not fear what man may do to me,* similarly cxviii. 6, and cxii. 7, 8: *he does not fear bad news. . . ;* Prov. iii. 24, 25: *when you lie down you will not be afraid . . . , and* xxiv. 5, 6: *a wise man is strong, and a knowing man adds to his strength . . . , and* xxviii. 1: *the righteous are like a bold young lion;* Isa. xli. 10: *fear not, for I am with you . . . , and* li. 7: *do not fear the reproach*

of men or grow alarmed because of their abuse, and li. 12: *I myself am your comforter: who are you that you should be afraid . . . ;* Dan. iii. 16: *they said to the king, we are not afraid to answer you . . . ;* Matt. x. 28, etc.: *have no fear of those who kill the body . . . .* The greatest example of fortitude is our Savior Jesus Christ. He displayed fortitude throughout the whole of his life and in his death; for instance, in Luke xiii. 31, etc.: *say to that fox, See, today and tomorrow I shall be casting our devils and curing people; and on the third day I shall be perfected;* John xi. 7, 8: *they say to him, Not long ago the Jews tried to stone you, and are you going back there again now?;* II Tim. i. 7: *for God has not given us a spirit of fear, but one of strength, of charity and of soundness of mind;* I John ii. 14: *I have written to you, young men, because you are strong, and the word of God dwells in you, and you have overcome the evil one.*

The opposite of this is timidity. Psal. xxvii. 1: *Jehovah is my light and my salvation, whom shall I fear?, and* Psal. cxii. 7. Prov. x. 24: *what the wicked man fears, shall happen to him, and* xxv. 26: *like a fountain stirred up by feet or a polluted spring, is a righteous man who breaks down before the wicked, and* xxviii. 1: *the wicked run away when no one pursues them, and* xxix. 25: *a timorous man sets a trap for himself;* Isa xli. 13, 14: *Jacob, you worm, do not be afraid . . . ;* Neh. vi. 11: *should a man like me run away . . . ?;* Matt. xxiv. 6: *the time will come when you will hear wars and rumors of wars, see that you are not alarmed;* Rev. xxi. 8: *the cowardly and faithless . . . . a share is assigned to them in the lake . . .*

And also rashness, or the taking of unnecessary risks. Prov. xiv. 16: *the wise man is cautious and withdraws from evil, but the fool exposes himself and is confident.* Amaziah exemplifies this, II Kings xiv. 8; *come, let us look each other in the face;* so does Josiah, II Chron. xxxv. 20–22: *and although he sent ambassadors to him, saying . . . Josiah did not turn his face from him . . .* Christ has taught us to avoid rashness by his own example, John vii. 1: *he would not go to Judea because the Jews were bent on killing him,* and xi. 53, 54: *accordingly Jesus no longer went about publicly among the Jews;* Matt. x. 23: *when they persecute you in one city, run away to another.*

PATIENCE is the endurance of evils and injuries. Psal. lxix. 8: *for your sake I bear reproach, shame covers my face;* Prov. xi. 12: *when the fool contemns his neighbor, the really wise man holds his tongue, and* xvii. 27: *the knowing man keeps his tongue in check, and the intelligent man is cool-tempered, and* xix. 11: *intelligence makes a man longsuffering;* Eccles. vii. 21: *and do not pay attention to every word which is spoken, for you ought not to hear your servant cursing you;* Isa. l. 7, 8: *I set my face like adamant . . . ;* Matt. v. 39: *do not resist a man who wrongs you. If someone slaps you on your right cheek, turn* the other to him; I Cor. vi. 7: *why do you not rather suffer injury . . . ?;* I Thess. v. 14: *be patient towards all.* On the subject of patience towards God, see above. But even holy men sometimes exact compensation for injuries: Acts xvi. 37: *they have flogged us publicly, without a hearing. . . .*

Impatience and softness are both opposed to this virtue. Prov. xxiv. 10: *if you live a soft life you will not have much strength when things get difficult.*

And so is hypocritical patience, which brings unnecessary suffering upon itself, as did the prophets of Baal, I Kings xviii. 28: *they cut themselves . . . ,* and as do our papistical flagellators.

Also the apathy of the Stoics; for sensibility to pain, and complaints or lamentations, are not inconsistent with true patience, as may be seen from the sample of Job and of other holy men in adversity.

CHAPTER XV
OF MAN'S RECIPROCAL DUTIES TOWARDS HIS NEIGHBOR, PARTICULARLY PRIVATE DUTIES

SO far I have spoken of our special virtues or duties towards our neighbor *qua* neighbor. Now I shall deal with our duties TOWARDS OUR NEIGHBOR, WHEN HE IS RELATED TO US IN SOME PARTICULAR WAY.

These are either private or public.

The private duties are either domestic or concern those not of our own household. Gen. xviii. 19: *I know him, and he will teach his children and his household, and they will observe . . . ;* I Tim. v. 8: *if anyone does not make provision for his relations, and especially for members of his own household, he has denied the faith and is worse than an unbeliever.*

Domestic duties are generally reciprocal and include those of husband and wife, parents and children, brothers, kinsfolk, masters and servants.

THE DUTIES OF HUSBAND AND WIFE are either common to both or peculiar to one of them.

Those common to both are outlined in I Cor. vii. 3: *let the husband show due kindness to the wife, and the wife to the husband.*

Duties peculiar to one are peculiar either to husband or to wife.

First, to the husband; Exod. xxi. 10, 11: *he shall not diminish her food, her clothing, or her portion of time. If*

he does not maintain these three things . . . ; Prov. v. 18, 19: *be joyful with the wife of your youth . . . ;* Esther i. 22: *that each man might be ruler in his own house . . . ;* I Cor. xi. 3: *I would have you know that Christ is the head of every man, but woman's head is man;* Eph. v. 25: *husbands, love your wives as Christ loved his church;* Col. iii. 19: *husbands, love your wives and do not be bitter with them;* I Pet. iii. 7: *in the same way, husbands should live with their wives as befits intelligent beings, paying honor to the woman as the weaker vessel. . . .*

Behavior which runs counter to these instructions is deprecated. Mal. ii. 13–15: *Jehovah has been a witness between you and the wife of your youth, towards whom you behave deceitfully . . . ;* Prov. v. 20, 21: *why, my son, do you go astray with a strange woman. . . .*

The wife's duties. Prov. xiv. 1: *every wise woman builds her house,* and xix. 14: *an intelligent wife is Jehovah's gift,* and xxxi. 11, etc.; *her husband's heart trusts in her . . . ;* I Cor. xi. 3, etc.: *a woman is man's glory: for man was not made from woman, but woman from man . . . ;* Eph. v. 22–24: *wives, submit to your own husbands as to the Lord, for the husband is the head of the wife as Christ is the head of the church and it is he that gives salvation to the body: so . . . in everything;* Col. iii. 18: *wives, submit to your husbands, as befits those who are in the Lord;* Tit. ii. 4, 5: *that they may teach the young women to be wise, and to love their husbands and children, and be temperate, chaste, busy at home, good, obedient, to their own husbands. Thus God's word will not be blasphemed;* I Pet. iii. 1, etc.: *let wives subject themselves to their husbands, so that. . . .* The very creation of woman implies that this should be so, Gen. ii. 22: *he made that rib which he had taken from Adam into a woman.* It is wrong for one single part of the body—and not one of the most important parts—to disobey the rest of the body, and even the head. This, at any rate, is the opinion of God: Gen. iii. 16: *he shall rule over you.*

Infringements of these duties are described in Exod. iv. 25: *you are a bloody husband to me;* Job ii. 9: *then his wife said to him . . . ;* II Sam. vi. 20: *Michal, the daughter of Saul, went out to meet David and said . . . ;* Prov. ix. 13: *a foolish woman is noisy . . . ,* and vii. 11: *her feet are not in her house . . . ,* and xiv. 1: *the stupid woman destroys it with her hands,* and xix. 13: *a wife's naggings are like continual drips of water,* similarly xxvii. 15, and xxi. 9: *better live in a garret than . . . ,* and 19: *better live in a desert than . . . ,* similarly xxv. 24; Eccles. vii. 26: *I have found something more bitter than death: a woman whose mind is full of traps and snares, and her hands of bonds. The man who seems good in God's eyes is freed from her, but the sinner is caught.* Above all, adultery. Deut. xxii. 14, 20: *I lay with her but found that she was not a virgin. If these things are true. . . .*

THE DUTIES OF PARENTS are described in Deut. iv. 9: *that you may teach them to your sons and grandsons,* and vi. 6, 7: *these words which I say to you today shall be in your heart, and you shall teach them diligently to your children;* Prov. xiii. 24: *he who spares the rod hates his son, but he who loves him takes care of his education while there is time,* and xix. 18: *chastise your son while there is still hope, and do not let your heart refrain from punishing him, to his destruction,* and xxii. 6: *teach a child in order to keep him on the right path, then he will not leave it even when he is very old,* and xxii. 15: *the rod of correction will drive away from a child the foolishness which is bound in his heart,* and xxiii. 13, 14: *do not withhold chastisement from a child; when you beat him with the rod he will not die: beat him with the rod and rescue his life from the grave,* and xxix. 15, 17: *the rod and reproof give wisdom . . . ;* Lam. iii. 27, 28: *it is good for this man to have borne the yoke in his boyhood . . . ;* Deut. xxi. 18–20: *if anyone has a stubborn and rebellious son who will not heed the voice of his father or mother, though they chastise him . . . ;* Eph. vi. 4: *you fathers, do not make your children angry, bur rear them with the discipline and admonition of the Lord;* Col. iii. 21: *fathers, do not make your children angry, in case they lose heart.*

The opposites are indulgence, exemplified in Eli, the priest, I Sam. ii, and in David's treatment of Absalom and Adonijah, I Kings i. 6: *his father has never troubled him by saying, Why do you do this?;* Gen. xxv. 28: *Isaac loved Esau, because game. . . .*

And too much severity. I Sam. xiv. 45: *you shall certainly die, Jonathan.*

The duties of CHILDREN are laid down in Gen. ix. 23, etc.: *then Shem took his cloak . . . ,* and xxiv. 15, etc.: *with her pitcher on her shoulder,* and xxix. 9: *she came with her father's sheep . . . ;* Exod. ii. 16: *they drew water . . . to water their father's flocks,* and xviii. 7: *Moses went out to meet his father-in-law . . . ,* and xx. 12: *honor your father . . . ;* Lev. xix. 3: *let each of you reverence his mother and father;* I Sam. xx. 32: *Jonathan said to Saul, Why should he be killed? What has he done?;* I Kings ii. 19: *when Bathsheba had come to the king . . . he got up . . . ;* Prov. i. 8: *my son, hear the instruction of your father and do not forsake your mother's teaching,* and vi. 20, 21: *my son, keep your father's commandment . . . ,* and xxiii. 22, 24, 25: *pay heed to your father, who begot you, and do not despise your mother when she grows old . . . ;* Jer. xxxv. 5. 6: *our father forbade us: he said . . . ;* Eph. vi. 1–3: *children, obey your parents in the Lord; for this is right. Honor . . . ;* Col. iii. 20: *children, obey your parents in all things, for this pleases the Lord;* I Tim. v. 4: *if a widow has children or grandchildren let them learn first to show their piety in their own house, and to repay their parents; for this is honorable and pleasing in God's sight.*

Examples of behavior contrary to this are to be found in Gen. ix. 22: *Ham saw his father's nakedness . . . ;* Exod. xxi. 15: *let him who strikes his father or mother be put to death without fail,* and 17: *let him who curses his father or mother be put to death without fail,* similarly Lev. xx. 9; Deut. xxi. 18, etc.: *if anyone has a stubborn and rebellious son . . . ,* and xxvii. 16: *cursed is he who does not value his father or mother;* Prov. x. 1: *a wise son makes his father joyful, but a foolish son . . . ,* and xix. 26: *he lays waste his father . . . ,* and xx. 20: *if any man curses his father or mother, his lantern will be snuffed out on a dark night,* and xxiii. 22: *pay heed to your father, who begot you . . . ,* and xxviii. 24: *he who robs his father or mother . . . ,* and xxx. 17: *the eye which mocks its father and contemns obedience to its mother, will be dug out by the ravens of the valley, or the young eagles will eat it;* Matt. xv. 5: *you say, If a man says to his father . . . and not honor his father or mother,* similarly Mark vii. 11, 12.

Also opposed to this correct behavior is excessive honor for one's parents. Matt. viii. 21, 22: *let me first go and bury my father.*

A certain analogy exists between the parent-child relationship and the relationship of guardian and ward, tutor and pupil, senior and junior, and, indeed, any superior and inferior.

Index

1645 March 4. *Tetrachordon* and *Colasterion* published.

Poems of Mr. John Milton, Both English and Latin . . . 1645 registered for publication.

Makes plans to marry the daughter of a Dr. Davis, "a very Handsome and Witty Gentlewoman," according to Edward Phillips (Darbishire 66). Mary Powell returns.

June 14. Battle of Naseby (end of Charles I's hopes to achieve a military settlement).

1646 The entire Powell family, having been ejected from Oxford as Royalist when the forces of King Charles were no longer in ascendancy there, moves in with Milton.

January 2. *Poems . . . 1645* published.

July 29. Daughter Anne born.

1647 January 1. Father-in-law Richard Powell dies.

March. John Milton Sr. dies, leaving a "moderate Estate" (Darbishire 32) including the Bread Street house.

April 21. Writes to his Italian friend Carlo Dati lamenting that he is surrounded by uncongenial people (Yale 2: 762–63).

The Milton family, after the Powell relatives have returned to Oxford, moves from a larger house in the Barbican to a smaller one in High Holborn, near Lincoln's Inn Fields.

1648 October 25. Daughter Mary born.

1649 January 30. Public execution of King Charles I: "Milton was probably there" (Parker 345).

February 13. *The Tenure of Kings and Magistrates* published.

March. Invited to become Secretary for the Foreign Tongues (a post dealing with diplomatic correspondence, usually in Latin) by the Council of State. Milton was appointed Secretary on March 15, at £288 per year, and ordered to answer *Eikon Basilike*, the book supposedly written by Charles I on the eve of his execution, which depicts the King's image (icon) as that of a martyr.

May 11. Salmasius's *Defensio Regia* ("defense of kingship") appears.

May 16. *Observations on the Articles of Peace* published.

October 6 (?). *Eikonoklastes* ("breaker of icons") published.

November 19. Given lodgings for official work at Scotland Yard.

1650 January 8. Ordered by Council of State to answer Salmasius.

1651 February 24. *Defensio pro populo Anglicano* ("defense of the English people") published, to vindicate the legal English execution of Charles I throughout western Europe.

March 16. Son John born.

Milton family moves to "a pretty Gardenhouse in Petty-France in Westminster" (Darbishire 71).

December 24. John Phillips's *Responsio* published. Milton is reported nearly blind.

1652 February. Becomes completely blind toward the end of the month, most likely as the result of glaucoma.

May 2. Daughter Deborah born.

May 5. Wife Mary dies, probably from complications following childbirth.

June 16 (?). Son John dies under somewhat mysterious circumstances (may have been neglected by a nurse; see Darbishire 71).

August. Pierre du Moulin's *Regii Sanguinis Clamor* ("the outcry of the King's blood") published, in reply to Milton's *Defensio*. Milton is ordered to reply to du Moulin's book by the Council of State.

1653 February 20. Recommends that Andrew Marvell, because of his abilities as translator and scholar, become his assistant.

September 3. Salmasius dies.

1654 May 30. *Defensio Secunda* published.

1655 Allowed to use the services of an amanuensis to take dictation for him in secretaryship; translation duties limited. Resumes private scholarly work, preparing a Latin dictionary and Greek lexicon; possibly he works on *De Doctrina Christiana* ("On Christian Doctrine"), a compendium of theological beliefs; possibly works on *Paradise Lost*. Salary reduced from £288 to £150, but that becomes a pension for life.

August 8. *Defensio Pro Se* ("Defense of Himself") published.

1656 November 12. Marries Katherine Woodcock.

1657 October 19. Daughter Katherine born.

1658 February 3. Katherine Woodcock dies.
March 17. Daughter Katherine dies.
June. Translates Letters of State from Cromwell to Charles X of Sweden, Louis XIV.
September 3. Oliver Cromwell dies.

1659 February 17 (?). *A Treatise of Civil Power* published.
June 16. Parliament looks into the possibility of having Milton arrested.
June 27. The public hangman burns *Defensio pro populo Anglicano* and *Eikonoklastes*.
August. *The Likeliest Means to Remove Hirelings out of the Church* published.
August (?). Takes a house in Holborn, near Red Lion Fields. Soon moves from there to a house in Jewin Street, in September, in fear for his life (Darbishire 74–75).

1660 March 3. *The Readie & Easy Way to Establish a Free Commonwealth* first published.
May (?). Goes into hiding at a friend's house in Bartholomew Close to escape possible retaliation from Charles II's loyalists. He would live there "till the Act of Oblivion [the act pardoning most of those who had abjured Charles I] came forth" (Darbishire 74).
May 30. Restoration of King Charles II.
October (?). Arrested and jailed for a short amount of time (Parker 1087).
December 15. Pardoned and released from custody in the Tower by order of Parliament.
December 17. Andrew Marvell protests Milton's jail fees (£150) in Parliament.

1662 The young Quaker Thomas Ellwood begins reading to Milton from requested Latin works; Ellwood remarks on the composition of *Paradise Lost* and *Paradise Regain'd* in his own autobiography.
September 5 (?). Sonnet to Sir Henry Vane published. Vane had been executed June 14, after defending the sovereignty of Parliament.

1663 February 24. Marries Elizabeth Minshull (she was 24 and he 54). Problems arise in the family before and after the marriage. His daughter Mary is said to have wished him dead rather than married, and his daughters are said to have conspired to sell some of his books "to the dunghill women" (Parker 586). Moves from Jewin Street to "a House in the *Artillery*-walk [near a military marching ground] leading to *Bunhill Fields*." "Here he

finisht his noble Poem, and publisht it in the year 1666" (Darbishire 75).

1665 Thomas Ellwood acts as agent, securing a house for Milton in Chalfont St. Giles, Buckinghamshire, to avoid the plague in London. ("Milton's Cottage," the only residence still standing in which Milton is known to have lived, is now open to the public.)

1666 September. The Bread Street house is among those destroyed in the Great Fire of London, which also burns the old St. Paul's Cathedral.

1667 August 2. *Paradise Lost: A Poem in Ten Books* registered for publication. Milton's agreement with the printer Samuel Simmons, signed on April 27, is the earliest author's contract preserved (Lindenbaum).

1668 *Paradise Lost* reissued twice, with a new title page, arguments, other preliminary matter.

1669 June. *Accedence Commenc't Grammar* published.

1670 Milton's portrait painted in pastels, then engraved, by William Faithorne.
November (?). *History of Britain* published, with the Faithorne engraving as frontispiece.

1671 *Paradise Regain'd* and *Samson Agonistes* published together.

1672 May (?). *The Art of Logic* published.

1673 May (?). *Of True Religion* published.
November (?). *Poems, &c. upon Several Occasions . . . 1673* published.

1674 April 17. Dryden registers *The State of Innocence*, a play based on *Paradise Lost*.
May. *Epistolae Familiares* ("familiar letters" or "letters to friends") and *Prolusiones* ("prolusions," college exercises) registered
July 6 (?). Second edition of *Paradise Lost* published, in twelve books, with commendatory poems by "S. B." and Andrew Marvell.
November 8 (?). Dies "in a fit of the gout, but with so little pain or emotion that the time of his expiring was not perceived by those in the room" (French 5: 96).
November 12. Buried near his father at the altar of the church of St. Giles, Cripplegate.